Biography
Almanac

Related Titles from Gale

American Diaries. This two-volume work is a chronologically arranged annotated bibliography of published American diaries and journals written from 1491 to 1980. Entries include full bibliographic information and are extensively annotated, indicating such information as historic events, modes of travel, diary's emphasis, religious affiliation, personal names, background on the diarist, and more.

Biographical Dictionaries and Related Works. A reference guide to over 16,000 biographical dictionaries. Entries are arranged in three sections: Universal Biography, National or Area Biography, and Biography by Vocation with indexes by author, title, and subject.

Biography and Genealogy Master Index. A multi-volume compilation containing 3.25 million citations to biographical articles appearing in more than 350 contemporary who's whos and other works of collective biography, including historical as well as present-day men and women of note. Updated and expanded by annual supplements through 1986, the 1981 through 1985 supplements have been cumulated into a five-volume single alphabetically sequenced set.

Contemporary Newsmakers. Four quarterly issues furnish up-to-date biographical profiles on people in the news. Covering all fields, from business and international affairs to literature and the arts, the articles feature photographs of individuals along with biographical and career data. *Contemporary Newsmakers* is annually cumulated into a hardbound volume.

In Black and White. This work identifies over 15,000 notable blacks in America, Africa, and elsewhere and the magazines, books, and newspapers in which information about them may be found. Entries provide full name, birth and/or death dates, occupation, and a list of publications where more information may be found. Also available: interedition supplement providing new and updated entries for about 7,000 notable blacks.

Pseudonyms and Nicknames Dictionary. Uncovers over 50,000 pseudonyms and nicknames used by some 40,000 individuals. Included are historical as well as contemporary figures from all walks of life. Entries furnish original and assumed names, birth and/or death dates, nationality and occupation, and codes indicating sources of additional information.

ISSN 0738 0097

Biography Almanac

A comprehensive reference guide to more than 24,000 famous and infamous newsmakers from Biblical times to the present as found in over 550 readily available biographical sources

THIRD EDITION

Volume 1
Biographies
A-K

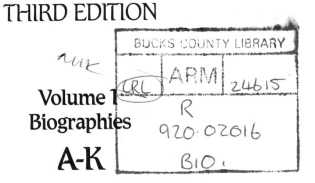

Susan L. Stetler, Editor

Gale Research Company • Book Tower
Detroit, Michigan 48226

Editor: Susan L. Stetler

Editorial Assistants: Michael Mengden and Alicia S. Robinson

Research Assistants: Evabelle MacKay and Elizabeth Rentenbach

External Production Supervisor: Mary Beth Trimper
External Senior Production Associate: Dorothy Kalleberg
External Production Assistants: Linda Davis and Darlene K. Maxey
Art Director: Arthur Chartow
Internal Production Supervisor: Laura Bryant
Internal Production Associate: Louise Gagne
Internal Senior Production Assistant: Sandra M. Rock

Editorial Data Systems Director: Dennis LaBeau
Editorial Data Systems and Programming Supervisor: Diane H. Belickas
Editorial Data Systems Program Design: Al Fernandez, Jr. and Barry Trute

Publisher: Frederick G. Ruffner
Editorial Director: Dedria Bryfonski
Associate Editorial Director: Ellen T. Crowley
Senior Editor, Research: Anne M. Brewer

Library of Congress Cataloging in Publication Data

Biography almanac. — 1st ed.- — Detroit, Mich.: Gale Research
Co., c1981-

v.; 21 cm.

Irregular.
Vols. for 1983- issued in parts.
Supplements issued between editions.
Editor: 1981- A. Brewer.
ISSN 0738-0097 = Biography almanac.

1. Biography—Periodicals. 2. Biography—Indexes—Periodicals. 3. Biog-
raphy—Indexes. I. Brewer, Annie M. II. Gale Research Company.
CT104.B56 920'.02—dc19 83-641014
AACR 2 MARC-S

Contents

Volume 1

Volume 2

Volume 3

Introduction

"Fame will belong to everyone for fifteen minutes." — Andy Warhol

If the ordinary person wants information about a word, it is easy to find a compact dictionary to supply it. If what's needed is a common fact about a state, a foreign country, a list of the tallest buildings or longest rivers, there are general almanacs to provide the information.

But if the question concerns a personality—especially a contemporary personality—outside such traditional fields as scholarship, government, and the military, the basic facts are much harder to come by.

For example, author Chard Powers Smith, colonizer John Smith, religious leader Joseph Smith, poet Samuel Smith, and essayist Sidney Smith (all of limited interest today and all long dead) can be found in several common sources.

But if brief information is needed on such contemporary people as business executive and founder of Federal Express Frederick Smith, runner Geoff Smith, actress Jaclyn Smith, baseball player Ozzie Smith, singer Rex Smith, and student Samantha Smith, the search is likely to be a long and tedious one without the help of *Biography Almanac.*

Biography Almanac is a biographical directory to famous people. Fame has neither limitations nor definitions, standards nor rule. It thrives as a result of genius or eccentricity, accident or purpose. The person who has "made it" in television, religion, sports, or industry is the prominent person that *Biography Almanac* lists.

Fame comes to the baseball pitcher who strikes out more batters in one game than any other in the history of the sport (Roger Clemens). It comes to the commoner who marries a prince (Sarah Ferguson), to the prince born to a future king (Prince Henry of Wales), to the widow in yellow who topples a world leader (Corazon Aquino). Fame can make a comeback as in the renewed interest in the people behind the Statue of Liberty (Edouard Rose Laboulage, Frederic Auguste Bartholdi, Richard Morris Hunt, Gustav Eiffel, and Emma Lazarus). And fame can come in death (*Challenger* astronauts Gregory Jarvis, Christa McAuliffe, Ronald McNair, Ellison Onizuka, Judy Resnik, Dick Scobee, and Michael Smith). All of these famous names can be found in this third edition of *Biography Almanac.*

New Features Include Occupation Index

The third volume of *Biography Almanac* contains three indexes of interest to the researcher and trivia buff. New to this edition is the inclusion of an Occupation Index. The Occupation Index lists all *Biography Almanac* entrants by the occupation(s) found in the main entry in the Biographies Volumes. This allows the reader to see everyone with a similar occupation grouped together. For example, the presidents of the United States are given the occupation US President and appear alphabetically in the Occupation Index under that listing; likewise all of the hockey players are found under Hockey Player. Entrants with more than one occupation in their main entry can be under each of the occupations in the Occupation Index.

Actor

Brosnan, Pierce	Redford, Robert
Brown, Bryan	Redgrave, Michael Scudamore, Sir
Caan, James	Reed, Oliver
Hagman, Larry	Ree, Robert
Heston, Charlton	Selleck, Tom
Hoffman, Dustin	Sellers, Peter Richard Henry
Holden, William	Williams, Billy Dee
Holloway, Stanley	Williams, Robert
Moore, Roger	Willis, Bruce

Chronological Index and Geographic Index Updated, Expanded

The other indexes—Chronological Index and Geographic Index—were included in the second edition, but have been expanded and updated reflecting the new material contained in the Biographies Volumes.

The Chronological Index lists all *Biography Almanac* entrants who were born or died in a specific month on a specific day. The year of birth or death appears before the entrant's name in chronological order. For example, this index lists 69 people who were born on July 4 and 38 people who died on July 4.

July 4

b. 1918 Landers, Ann	b. 1928 Lollobrigida, Gina
b. 1918 Van Buren, Abigail	b. 1931 Hudson, Joseph Lowthian, Jr.
b. 1920 Garraty, John Arthur	d. 1826 Adams, John
b. 1924 Saint, Eva Marie	d. 1826 Jefferson, Thomas
b. 1927 Simon, Neil	d. 1831 Monroe, James
b. 1928 Boyd, Stephen	d. 1848 Chateaubriand, Francois Rene de

The Geographic Index enables the user to find everyone who was born or who died in a specific location. The index is divided into three general sections: the United States, Canada, and Foreign. The United States is further broken down by state and then by city within the state; Canada is broken down by province and city; and Foreign is in alphabetical order by country and city within the country. Below each city are the names of those people listed in *Biography Almanac* who were either born or who died in that location, followed by the birth or death date. Under New York, New York, for example, Norman Rockwell is listed with his birthdate, Feb. 3, 1984, and Nelson Rockefeller is listed with his deathdate, Jan. 26, 1979. Rockwell also appears under Stockbridge, Massachusetts, with his deathdate and Rockefeller appears under Bar Harbor, Maine, with his birthdate.

MASSACHUSETTS
Stockbridge, Massachusetts
Bowker, R(ichard) R(ogers)
  d. Nov 12, 1933
Field, Cyrus West b. Nov 30, 1819
French, Daniel Chester d. Oct 7, 1931
Hopkins, Mark b. Feb 4, 1802
Niebuhr, Reinhold d. Jun 1, 1971
Rockwell, Norman d. Nov 8, 1978
Sedgwick, Catherine Maria b. Dec 28, 1789

MAINE
Bar Harbor, Maine
Ralston, Esther b. 1902
Rockefeller, Nelson A(ldrich) b. Jul 9, 1908

The trivia buff will be interested in the names appearing in the Geographic Index under Woodland Hills, California. Most of them are deaths and all of the people who died there were actors and actresses. Further research reveals that the Motion Pictures Country Home, a retirement home for actors and actresses, is located in Woodland Hills. Also, the Dominican Republic has always been a hotbed for major league baseball players, and the names listed under the Dominican Republic in the Geographic Index confirm this.

Quick Identifications for 24,000 Famous Persons

The third edition of *Biography Almanac* contains over 24,000 names. More than 75 percent of the entries have been updated with some kind of additional information, whether it be a death date, new sources, one-line descriptor, or any combination of these things. This edition also contains approximately 2,000 names, many of whom have become well-known in the three years since the publication of the second edition. These include Robert Ballard, the geologist who located and photographed the *Titanic;* Antonin Scalia, appointed to the Supreme Court by President Reagan in 1986; Mikhail Gorbachev, the leader of the Soviet Union; Paloma Picasso, daughter of Pablo Picasso and designer for Tiffany; An Wang, chairman of Wang Labs; Darryl Hannah, Tom Hanks, and John Candy, stars of the Ron Howard-directed film, *Splash;* singers Cyndi Lauper, Madonna, Ray Parker, Jr., and Whitney Houston; baseball player Wade Boggs; and Chris and John Haney, the inventors of the game Trivial Pursuit.

Quick identifications sufficient for many needs can be found immediately in *Biography Almanac.* The addition of the one-line descriptor, begun in the second edition, is continued, updated, and expanded in this edition. The descriptor, which more fully identifies the person or highlights an important detail of the person's life, is included in about 12,000 of the third edition entries. The one-line descriptor tells the reader, for instance, that composer Ernest Bell wrote the song "When Irish Eyes Are Smiling"; that actor Yakima Canutt created the profession of stuntman; that William Schroeder lived 620 days with an artificial heart. The descriptors describe Dan Bankhead as the first black pitcher in the Major Leagues (1947); Chuck Cooper as the first black to play basketball in the NBA (1950); and Grant Fuhr as the first black hockey player on a Stanley Cup winning team (1984).

In addition to the immediate information found in *Biography Almanac,* the same listing will also direct the user to more detailed information through citations to over 550 widely available biographical dictionaries, thus short-circuiting prolonged searches which might fail in the end to turn up needed information. (A complete list of the biographical dictionaries cited is given in the bibliographical section of this book.)

Reading a Citation

Each citation gives the person's name as he or she is most popularly known; his or her pseudonym, real name, or group affiliation in brackets; nicknames or other types of identification in quotation marks; nationality; occupation, career, or best known activity; one-line description; dates and places of birth and death; and alphabetically arranged codes for biographical reference sources which provide further information about the individual.

Gretzky, Wayne
"The Great Gretzky"
Canadian. Hockey Player
Center, Edmonton, 1978--; has set
numerous NHL records; only player
to score 100 pts. in first six yrs. in NHL.
b. Jan 26, 1961 in Brantford, Ontario
Source: *BioIn 11, 12; CanWW 82, 83;*
CurBio 82; HocEn; HocReg 85; NewYTBS 82;
WhoAm 84

Pauley, (Margaret) Jane
[Mrs. Garry Trudeau]
American. Broadcast Journalist
Succeeded Barbara Walters on "The Today
Show," 1976--.
b. Oct 31, 1950 in Indianapolis, Indiana
Source: *BioIn 11, 12; BkPepl; ConAu 106;*
CurBio 80; IntMPA 82, 84; WhoAm 80, 82, 84;
WhoAmW 81, 83

Stockman, David Allen
American. Government Official
Directed OMB, 1981-85; wrote *Triumph of*
Politics, 1986.
b. Nov 10, 1946 in Fort Hood, Texas
Source: *AlmAP 80; BioIn 12; CngDr 78; CurBio 81;*
IntWW 81, 82, 83; IntYB 82; NewYTBS 80, 81;
WhoAm 80, 82, 84; WhoAmP 81, 83; WhoF&I 83;
WhoMW 80

Each person is entered under his or her best known name. The last name is followed by the diminutive, the familiar, or the shortened form of the first name with the full name in parentheses. Jim Henson is entered Henson, Jim (James Murray). J.B. Priestly is entered Priestly, J(ohn) B(oynton).

When it is apparent that a person was known widely or exclusively by a nickname, we have so indicated by placing this name in quotation marks in the position normally occupied by the Christian name. Moses, "Grandma" (Anna Mary Robertson) and Corea, "Chick" (Armando) are examples.

Pseudonyms, real names, or a woman's married name may appear in brackets in the second line. If the person is a member of a group, the group name also appears in the second line in brackets.

Landon, Michael   **Livingstone, Mary**   **Michael, George**
[Eugene Michael Orowitz]   [Mrs. Jack Benny]   [Wham!]

Other forms of nicknames, whether they are forms of address or descriptive in nature, will appear in quotation marks in either the second or third line.

Cobb Ty(rus Raymond)   **Chaney, Lon (Alonso)**   **Cannon, Dyan**
"The Georgia Peach"   "Man of a Thousand Faces"   [Samille Diane Frissen]
                                                             "Frosty"

If a group is listed as a main entry, the individual members are listed in brackets.

Huey Lewis and the News
[Mario Cipollina; Johnny Colla; Bill
Gibson; Chris Hayes; Sean Hopper; Huey Lewis]
American. Music Group
Formed 1982; hits include "Heart and Soul,"
1983; "If This Is It," 1984.
Source: *RkOn 85*

Codes and Lists of Titles Indexed

Codes for the biographical sources indexed, along with complete biblio-graphic information on the titles of the volumes referred to by the codes, are given in the Key to Source Codes following the introduction in Volume 1. concerning persons on whom information is often not available elsewhere.

Editorial Practices

Biography Almanac attempts to list each person under his or her most popular name and also give the reader as much individual information as possible. If, for example, one were to look up rock and roll pioneer Bill Haley, one would find his full name given as William John Clifford, Jr. In looking up Tatum O'Neal, the actress, one would discover her also to be Mrs. John McEnroe. And George Brett, the baseball player, is nicknamed "Mulletthead." However, if one were to look up Patti Davis under her real name—Patricia Reagan—one would find a "see" reference, sending the user to Davis, Patti, the name by which she is most commonly known.

It is necessary to point out that the cross references in *Biography Almanac* are not examples of standard library practice. A cross reference was included only when it was believed that a user would look under that name to guide him to the main entry. For example, a cross reference appears at Clemens, Samuel Langhorne, sending the reader to Twain, Mark because it is possible that a user would look him up under his given name. On the other hand, no one would look up John Wayne under his real name, Marion Michael Morrison, so there is not a cross reference. However, the name Marion Michael Morrison appears in John Wayne's entry as additional information to the user.

Biography Almanac follows standard alphabetizing rules; *Mac* and *Mc* are interfiled alphabetically. Searchers should look under all possible variant listings for a name with prefixes or suffixes, Spanish names which may be listed under either part of the surname, or names transliterated from non-Roman alphabets.

Clarification

Some readers mistakenly believe that *Biography Almanac* is a substitute for Gale's *Biography and Genealogy Master Index (BGMI).* Actually, the two publications are essentially different types of research tools.

BGMI is an *index* to all names in over 500 different biographical dictionaries, representing over 1,200 editions and volumes. *BGMI* is a comprehensive and time-saving tool for accessing a wide variety of biographical dictionaries. On the other hand, *Biography Almanac* is *itself* a biographical dictionary. It lists selected people who "have made news." It provides self-contained biographical information on that group of people, as well as citations to biographical sources that may be useful to the reader.

Acknowledgments

Special acknowledgment is necessary to several people at Gale Research who helped in the computer input of *Biography Almanac:* Nancy Franklin, Research; Sherrell Hobbs, Promotion; Linda George, Editorial; and Elaine Cybulski and Nancy Wright, EDS User Services. Thanks also to the editorial help provided by Neil Walker, *Book Review Index* staff; and Sandra L. Bazman and Margaret W. Young.

Suggestions Are Welcome

While we believe *Biography Almanac,* third edition to be a valuable reference tool, as well as an improved publication over its predecessors, we also realize that a work of this nature can never be complete. People make news every day and we try our best to keep abreast of all such happenings. Thanks to the readers who sent in names for inclusion in this edition. The names Corrie ten Boom, who wrote of her experiences in a concentration camp in *The Hiding Place;* and Walter Farley, who wrote *The Black Stallion* can be found in this edition. We hope, that you, the user, will also help and send in candidates for future editions.

Key to Abbreviations

ABA	American Basketball Association
ABC	American Broadcasting Corporation
ACDA	Arms Control and Disarmament Agency
ACLU	American Civil Liberties Union
AFB	Air Force Base
AFL	American Federation of Labor, American Football League
AFSCME	American Federation of State, County, and Municipal Employees
AIM	American Indian Movement
AK	Alaska
AL	Alabama, American League
AMA	American Medical Association
AP	Associated Press
Apr	April
AR	Arkansas
ASCAP	American Society of Composers, Authors, and Publishers
ASPCA	American Society for the Prevention of Cruelty to Animals
ASPCC	American Society for the Prevention of Cruelty to Children
Assn.	Association
Asst.	Assistant
AT&T	American Telephone and Telegraph
Aug	August
AWCTU	American Women's Christian Temperance Union
AZ	Arizona
b.	Born
BBC	British Broadcasting Corporation
c.	Century, Circa
CA	California
CAE	Central African Empire
Capt.	Captain
CBO	Congressional Budget Office
CBS	Columbia Broadcasting System
Chm.	Chairman
CIA	Central Intelligence Agency
CIO	Congress of Industrial Organizations
CMA	Country Music Association
CO	Colorado
Co.	Company, County
Com.	Committee
Con.	Congressman, Congresswoman
CORE	Committee (or Congress) on Racial Equality
Corp.	Corporation
CT	Connecticut
Ctr.	Center
CUNY	City University of New York

d.	Died
DC	District of Columbia
DE	Delaware
Dec	December
Dem.	Democratic
Dept.	Department
Dist.	District
dj	disc jockey
E	East, Eastern
EEOC	Equal Employment Opportunity Commission
ERA	Earned Run Average, Equal Rights Amendment
ESP	Extra Sensory Perception
Exec.	Executive
FAA	Federal Aviation Administration
FBI	Federal Bureau of Investigation
FCC	Federal Communications Commission
FDA	Food and Drug Administration
FDR	Franklin Delano Roosevelt
Feb	February
FL	Florida
fl.	flourished
Ft.	Fort
GA	Georgia
GE	General Electric
GM	General Manager, General Motors
GOP	Grand Old Party (Republican)
Govt.	Government
Gr.	Great
HBO	Home Box Office
HEW	Health, Education, and Welfare
HI	Hawaii
hrs.	Hours
Hts.	Heights
HUD	Housing and Urban Development
IA	Iowa
IBM	International Business Machines
ID	Idaho
IL	Illinois
ILA	International Longshoremen's Association
ILGWU	International Ladies Garment Workers Union
ILWU	International Longshoremen's and Warehousemen's Union
IN	Indiana
Inc.	Incorporated
INLA	Irish National Liberation Army
Int'l.	International
IOC	International Olympic Committee
IRA	Irish Republican Army
IRS	Internal Revenue Service
Is.	Island
ITT	International Telephone and Telegraph
IWW	Industrial Workers of the World

Jan	January
Jct.	Junction
Jr.	Junior
Jul	July
Jun	June
KC	Kansas City
KO	Knock-out
KS	Kansas
KY	Kentucky
LA	Los Angeles, Louisiana
LC	Library of Congress
LPGA	Ladies Professional Golf Association
Lt.	Lieutenant
Ltd.	Limited
MA	Massachusetts
Mag	Magazine
Mar	March
MCA	Music Corporation of America
MCI	Microwave Communications, Inc.
MD	Maryland
ME	Maine
MGM	Metro-Goldwyn-Mayer
Mgr.	Manager
MI	Michigan
min(s).	minute(s)
MIT	Massachusetts Institute of Technology
ML	Major League(s)
MN	Minnesota
MO	Missouri
mo(s).	Month(s)
MP	Member of Parliament, Military Police
mph	miles per hour
MS	Mississippi
MT	Montana
Mt.	Mount, Mountain
Mvmt.	Movement
MVP	Most Valuable Player
N	North, Northern
NAACP	National Association for the Advancement of Colored People
NASA	National Aeronautics and Space Administration
Nat.	National
NATO	North Atlantic Treaty Organization
NBA	National Basketball Association
NBC	National Broadcasting Corporation
NC	North Carolina
NCAA	National Collegiate Athletic Association
ND	North Dakota
NE	Nebraska
NF	Not Found
NFL	National Football League
NH	New Hampshire

NHL	National Hockey League
NJ	New Jersey
NL	National League
NM	New Mexico
Nov	November
NOW	National Organization for Women
NRA	National Recovery Administration
NV	Nevada
NY	New York
NYC	New York City
Oct	October
OH	Ohio
OK	Oklahoma
OMB	Office of Management and Budget
OR	Oregon
p.	Page
PA	Pennsylvania
Pac	Pacific
PATCO	Professional Air Traffic Controllers Organization
PBA	Professional Bowlers Association
PBS	Public Broadcasting System
PGA	Professional Golfers Association
PLO	Palestine Liberation Organization
POW	Prisoner of War
PR	Puerto Rico
Pres.	President
Prov.	Province
Pt.	Point, Port
Pte.	Pointe
RBI	Runs Batted In
RCA	Radio Corporation of America
Rep.	Republican, Representative
Repub.	Republic
Rev.	Reverend
RI	Rhode Island
RIF	Reading Is Fundamental
Rpds.	Rapids
S	South, Southern
SALT	Strategic Arms Limitation Talks
SC	South Carolina
SCLC	Southern Christian Leadership Conference
SD	South Dakota
sec(s).	second(s)
Sep	September
SI	Sports Illustrated
SLA	Symbionese Liberation Army
SNCC	Student Nonviolent Coordinating Committee
Sprgs.	Springs
Sq.	Square
Sr.	Senior
St.	Saint, Sainte

Sum.	Summit
SUNY	State University of New York
TB	Tuberculosis
TD	Touchdown
Terr.	Territory
TM	Transcendental Meditation
TN	Tennessee
tr.	Translated
TWA	Trans World Airlines
Twp.	Township
TX	Texas
U	University
UAW	United Auto Workers
UFO	Unidentified Flying Object
UMW	United Mine Workers
UN	United Nations
UNESCO	United Nations Educational, Scientific, and Cultural Organization
UPI	United Press International
US	United States
USC	University of Southern California
USCGA	United States Coast Guard Academy
USFL	United States Football League
USIA	United States Information Agency
USMC	United States Marine Corps
USSR	Union of Soviet Socialist Republics
UT	Utah
VA	Virginia, Veteran's Administration
Vil.	Village
Vol(s).	Volume, Volumes
vp	Vice-President
VT	Vermont
W	West, Western
WA	Washington
WASP	White Anglo-Saxon Protestant
WBA	World Boxing Association
WBC	World Boxing Council
WCTU	Women's Christian Temperance Union
WFL	World Football League
WI	Wisconsin
WV	West Virginia
WW	World War
WY	Wyoming
yds.	Yards
YMCA	Young Men's Christian Association
YWCA	Young Women's Christian Association
yr(s).	Year(s)

Bibliographic Key to Source Codes

Code	*Book Indexed*
AfSS	*Africa South of the Sahara.* London: Europa Publications, 1978, 1979, 1980, 1981, 1982. Distributed by Gale Research Co., Detroit, Michigan.
AfSS 78	Eighth edition, 1978-1979
AfSS 79	Ninth edition, 1979-1980
AfSS 80	10th edition, 1980-1981
AfSS 81	11th edition, 1981-1982
AfSS 82	12th edition, 1982-1983
	Biographies are located in the "Who's Who in Africa South of the Sahara" section in each volume.
AfrA	*African Authors: A Companion to Black African Writing.* Volume I: 1300-1973. By Donald E. Herdeck. Washington, D.C.: Black Orpheus Press, 1973.
AfroAA	*Afro-American Artists.* A bio-bibliographical directory. Compiled and edited by Theresa Dickason Cederholm. Boston: Trustees of the Boston Public Library, 1973.
Alli	Allibone, S. Austin. *A Critical Dictionary of English Literature and British and American Authors Living and Deceased from the Earliest Accounts to the Latter Half of the Nineteenth Century.* Containing over 46,000 articles (authors) with 40 indexes of subjects. Three volumes. Philadelphia: J.B. Lippincott & Co., 1858-1871. Reprint. Detroit: Gale Research Co., 1965.
Alli SUP	*A Supplement to Allibone's Critical Dictionary of English Literature and British and American Authors.* Containing over 37,000 articles (authors) and enumerating over 93,000 titles. Two volumes. By John Foster Kirk. Philadelphia: J.B. Lippincott & Co., 1891. Reprint. Detroit: Gale Research Co., 1965.
AlmAP	*The Almanac of American Politics.* The senators, the representatives, the governors--their records, states, and districts. By Michael Barone, Grant Ujifusa, and Douglas Matthews. New York: E.P. Dutton, 1977, 1979.

AlmAP 78   1978 edition, 1977
AlmAP 80   1980 edition, 1979

Use the "Names Index" in each volume to locate biographies.

AlmAP 82   *The Almanac of American Politics 1982.* The president, the senators, the representatives, the governors: their records and election results, their states and districts. By Michael Barone and Grant Ujifusa. Washington, D.C.: Barone & Co., 1981.

Use the "Index of Persons" to locate biographies.

AlmAP 84   *The Almanac of American Politics 1984.* The president, the senators, the representatives, the governors: their records and election results, their states and districts. By Michael Barone and Grant Ujifusa. Washington D.C.: National Journal, 1983.

Use the "Index of People" to locate biographies.

AlmAP 86   *The Almanac of American Politics 1986.* The president, the senators, the representatives, the governors: their records and election results, their states and districts. By Michael Barone. Washington, D.C.: National Journal, 1986.

Use the "Index of People" to locate biographies.

AmArch 70   *American Architects Directory.* Third edition. Edited by John F. Gane. New York: R.R. Bowker Co. (under the sponsorship of American Institute of Architects), 1970.

AmArt   *American Artists.* An illustrated survey of leading contemporary Americans. Edited by Les Krantz. New York: Facts on File Publications, 1985.

AmAu   *American Authors, 1600-1900: A Biographical Dictionary of American Literature.* Edited by Stanley J. Kunitz and Howard Haycraft. New York: H.W. Wilson Co., 1938.

AmAu&B   *American Authors and Books, 1640 to the Present Day.* Third revised edition. By W.J. Burke and Will D. Howe. Revised by Irving Weiss and Anne Weiss. New York: Crown Publishers, 1972.

AmBench 79   *The American Bench: Judges of the Nation.* Second edition. Edited by Mary Reincke and Nancy Lichterman. Minneapolis: Reginald Bishop Forster & Associates, 1979.

Use the "Name Index" at the front of the volume to locate biographies.

AmBi   *American Biographies.* By Wheeler Preston. New York: Harper & Brothers Publishers, 1940. Reprint. Detroit: Gale Research Co., 1974.

AmCath 80   *The American Catholic Who's Who.* Volume 23, 1980-1981. Edited by Joy Anderson. Washington, D.C.: National Catholic News Service, 1979.

AmComp   *American Composers.* A Biographical Dictionary. By David Ewen. New York: G.P. Putnam's Sons, 1982.

AmEA 74   American Economic Association. *Directory of Members, 1974.* Edited by Rendigs Fels. Published as Volume 64, Number 5 (October, 1974) of *The American Economic Review.*

AmEnS   *The American Encyclopedia of Soccer.* Edited by Zandler Hollander. New York: Everest House Publishers, 1980.

AmFkP   *American Folk Painters of Three Centuries.* Edited by Jean Lipman and Tom Armstrong. New York: Hudson Hills Press (in association with the Whitney Museum of American Art), 1980. Distributed by Simon & Schuster, New York, New York.

                       Use the Index to locate biographies.

AmLY   *The American Literary Yearbook.* A biographical and bibliographical dictionary of living North American authors; a record of contemporary literary activity; an authors' manual and students' text book. Volume 1, 1919. Edited by Hamilton Traub. Henning, Minnesota: Paul Traub, 1919. Reprint. Detroit: Gale Research Co., 1968.

     AmLY   The "Biographical and Bibliographical Dictionary of Living North American Authors" section begins on page 57.

     AmLY XR   The "Pen-names and Pseudonyms" section begins on page 49.

AmM&WS   *American Men and Women of Science.* Edited by Jaques Cattell Press. New York: R.R. Bowker Co., 1971-1973, 1976-1978, 1979, 1982.

    AmM&WS 73P   Physical & Biological Sciences, 12th edition, 1971-1973
    AmM&WS 73S   Social & Behavioral Sciences, 12th edition, 1973
    AmM&WS 76P   Physical & Biological Sciences, 13th edition, 1976
    AmM&WS 78S   Social & Behavioral Sciences, 13th edition, 1978
    AmM&WS 79P   Physical & Biological Sciences, 14th edition, 1979
    AmM&WS 82P   Physical & Biological Sciences, 15th edition, 1982

AmNov   *American Novelists of Today.* By Harry R. Warfel. New York: American Book Co., 1951. Reprint. Westport, Connecticut: Greenwood Press, 1976.

                 The "Index of Married Names and Pseudonyms," indicated by the code *X*, begins on page 477.

AmPB   *American Picturebooks from "Noah's Ark" to "Beast Within."* By Barbara Bader. New York: Macmillan, 1976.

AmPolW 80   *American Political Women: Contemporary and Historical Profiles.* By Esther Stineman. Littleton, Colorado: Libraries Unlimited, 1980.

AmPS   *American Popular Songs from the Revolutionary War to the Present.* Edited by David Ewen. New York: Random House, 1966.

AmPS   The "American Popular Songs" section begins on page 1.

AmPS A   The "All-Time Best-Selling Popular Recordings" section begins on page 485.

AmPS B   The "Some American Performers of the Past and Present" section begins on page 499.

AmSCAP 66   *The ASCAP Biographical Dictionary of Composers, Authors and Publishers.* Third edition. Compiled and edited by The Lynn Farnol Group. New York: American Society of Composers, Authors and Publishers, 1966.

AmSCAP   *ASCAP Biographical Dictionary.* Fourth edition. Compiled for the American Society of Composers, Authors, and Publishers by Jaques Cattell Press. New York: R.R. Bowker Co., 1980.

AmWom   *American Women.* A revised edition of *Woman of the Century*, 1,500 biographies with over 1,400 portraits; a comprehensive encyclopedia of the lives and achievements of American women during the nineteenth century. Two volumes. Edited by Frances E. Willard and Mary A. Livermore. New York: Mast, Crowell & Kirkpatrick, 1897. Reprint. Detroit: Gale Research Co., 1973.

AmWomWr   *American Women Writers: A Critical Reference Guide from Colonial Times to the Present.* Four volumes. Edited by Lina Mainiero. New York: Frederick Ungar Publishing Co., 1979-1982.

AmWr   *American Writers: A Collection of Literary Biographies.* New York: Charles Scribner's Sons, 1974, 1979, 1981.

AmWr   Volumes I-IV. Edited by Leonard Unger, 1974. Originally published as the *University of Minnesota Pamphlets on American Writers.*

AmWr S1	Supplement I. Two parts. Edited by Leonard Unger, 1979.
AmWr S2	Supplement II. Two parts. Edited by A. Walton Litz, 1981.

AnObit	*The Annual Obituary.* New York: St. Martin's Press, 1981, 1982, 1983.
AnObit 1980	*1980*, edited by Roland Turner, 1981.
AnObit 1981	*1981*, edited by Janet Podell, 1982.
AnObit 1982	*1982*, edited by Janet Podell, 1983.

Use the "Alphabetical Index of Entrants" at the front of each volume to locate biographies.

AnObit	*The Annual Obituary.* Chicago: St. James Press, 1984, 1985.
AnObit 1983	*1983*, edited by Elizabeth Devine, 1984.
AnObit 1984	*1984*, edited by Margot Levy, 1985.

Use the "Alphabetical Index of Entrants" at the front of each volume to locate biographies.

AnCL	*Anthology of Children's Literature.* Fourth edition. Edited by Edna Johnson, Evelyn R. Sickels, and Frances Clarke Sayers. Boston: Houghton Mifflin Co., 1970.

Biographies begin on page 1217.

AnMV 1926	*Anthology of Magazine Verse for 1926 and Yearbook of American Poetry.* Edited by William Stanley Braithwaite. New York: G. Sully, 1926. Reprint. Granger Index Reprint Series. Freeport, New York: Books for Libraries Press, 1972.

The "Biographical Dictionary of Poets in the United States" section begins on page 3 of part 4.

AntBDN	*The Antique Buyer's Dictionary of Names.* By A.W. Coysh. Newton Abbot, England: David & Charles, 1970.
AntBDN A	"Art Nouveau" begins on page 13.
AntBDN B	"Book Illustrations and Prints" begins on page 23.
AntBDN C	"Bronzes" begins on page 48.
AntBDN D	"Clocks and Barometers" begins on page 59.
AntBDN E	"Fashion Plates" begins on page 81.
AntBDN F	"Firearms" begins on page 86.
AntBDN G	"Furniture" begins on page 98.
AntBDN H	"Glass" begins on page 123.
AntBDN I	"Maps, Charts, and Globes" begins on page 137.
AntBDN J	"Miniatures" begins on page 148.
AntBDN K	"Musical Instruments" begins on page 170.

AntBDN L	"Netsuke" begins on page 179.
AntBDN M	"Pottery and Porcelain" begins on page 185.
AntBDN N	"Sheffield Plate" begins on page 224.
AntBDN O	"Silhouettes or Profiles" begins on page 231.
AntBDN P	"Silk Pictures, Portraits, and Bookmarks" begins on page 243.
AntBDN Q	"Silver" begins on page 250.

ApCAB   *Appleton's Cyclopaedia of American Biography.* Six volumes. Edited by James Grant Wilson and John Fiske. New York: D. Appleton & Co., 1888-1889. Reprint. Detroit: Gale Research Co., 1968.

ApCAB SUP   *Appleton's Cyclopaedia of American Biography.* Volume VII, Supplement. Edited by James Grant Wilson. New York: D. Appleton & Co., 1901. Reprint. Detroit: Gale Research Co., 1968.

ApCAB X   *A Supplement to Appleton's Cyclopaedia of American Biography.* Six volumes. Originally published as *The Cyclopaedia of American Biography, Supplementary Edition.* Edited by L.E. Dearborn. New York: Press Association Compilers, 1918-1931.

ArizL   *Arizona in Literature: A Collection of the Best Writings of Arizona Authors from Early Spanish Days to the Present Time.* By Mary G. Boyer. Glendale, California: Arthur H. Clark Co., 1935. Reprint. Ann Arbor: Gryphon Books, 1971.

Use the Index to locate biographies.

ArtsAmW 1   *Artists of the American West.* A biographical dictionary. Volume I. By Doris Ostrander Dawdy. Chicago: Swallow Press; Sage Books, 1974.

ArtsNiC   *Artists of the Nineteenth Century and Their Works.* A handbook containing two thousand and fifty biographical sketches. Revised edition. Two volumes. By Clara Erskine Clement and Laurence Hutton. Boston: J.R. Osgood & Co., 1885. Reprint, two volumes in one. Saint Louis: North Point, 1969.

AsBiEn   *Asimov's Biographical Encyclopedia of Science and Technology.* The lives and achievements of 1,195 great scientists from ancient times to the present, chronologically arranged. New revised edition. By Isaac Asimov. New York: Avon, 1976, 1982.

AsBiEn	1976 edition
AsBiEn 82	1982 edition

Use the "Alphabetic List of Biographical Entries" at the front of the book to locate biographies.

AtlBL　　　　　　*Atlantic Brief Lives: A Biographical Companion to the Arts.* Edited by Louis Kronenberger. Boston: Little, Brown & Co., 1971.

ASpks　　　　　　*The Author Speaks: Selected "PW" Interviews, 1967-1976.* By *Publishers Weekly* editors and contributors. New York: R.R. Bowker Co., 1977.

Au&ICB　　　　　*Authors and Illustrators of Children's Books: Writings on Their Lives and Works.* By Miriam Hoffman and Eva Samuels. New York: R.R. Bowker Co., 1972.

Au&Wr 71　　　　*The Author's and Writer's Who's Who.* Sixth edition. Darien, Connecticut: Hafner Publishing Co., 1971.

AuBYP　　　　　*Authors of Books for Young People.* By Martha E. Ward and Dorothy A. Marquardt. Metuchen, New Jersey: Scarecrow Press, 1971, 1979.

   AuBYP　　　　Second edition, 1971
   AuBYP SUP　　Supplement to the second edition, 1979
   AuBYP SUPA　Addendum to the Supplement begins on page 301.

AuNews　　　　　*Authors in the News.* A compilation of news stories and feature articles from American newspapers and magazines covering writers and other members of the communications media. Two volumes. Edited by Barbara Nykoruk. Detroit: Gale Research Co., 1976.

   AuNews 1　　　Volume 1
   AuNews 2　　　Volume 2

AutoN 79　　　　*Automotive News.* 1979 Market Data Book Issue, April 25, 1979.

   The "Who's Who in the Auto Industry" section begins on page 130.

Baker 78　　　　*Baker's Biographical Dictionary of Musicians.* Sixth edition. Revised by Nicolas Slonimsky. New York: Schirmer Books; London: Collier Macmillan Publishers, 1978.

Baker 84　　　　*Baker's Biographical Dictionary of Musicians.* Seventh edition. Revised by Nicolas Slonimsky. New York: Macmillan, Schirmer Books, 1984.

BaseEn 85　　　*The Baseball Encyclopedia.* The Complete and Official Record of Major League Baseball. Edited by Joseph L. Reichler. New York: Macmillan, 1985.

BasesB　　　　　*Baseball's Best: The Hall of Fame Gallery.* By Martin Appel and Burt Goldblatt. New York: NcGraw-Hill, 1980.

BaseReg   *Official Baseball Register.* Edited by Barry Siegel. St. Louis: The Sporting News, 1985, 1986.

     BaseReg 85   1985 edition
     BaseReg 86   1986 edition

BestMus   *The Best Musicals: From Showboat to Chorus Line.* Revised edition. By Arthur Jackson. New York: Crown Publishers, Inc., 1977.

BbD   *The Bibliophile Dictionary.* A biographical record of the great authors, with bibliographical notices of their principal works from the beginning of history. Originally published as Volumes 29 and 30 of *The Bibliophile Library of Literature, Art, and Rare Manuscripts.* Compiled and arranged by Nathan Haskell Dole, Forrest Morgan, and Caroline Ticknor. New York: International Bibliophile Society, 1904. Reprint. Detroit: Gale Research Co., 1966.

BbtC   *Bibliotheca Canadensis: Or, A Manual of Canadian Literature.* By Henry J. Morgan. Ottawa: G.E. Desbarats, 1867. Reprint. Detroit: Gale Research Co., 1968.

BiAUS   *Biographical Annals of the Civil Government of the United States, during Its First Century.* From original and official sources. By Charles Lanman. Washington, D.C.: James Anglim, 1876. Reprint. Detroit: Gale Research Co., 1976.

     The "Additional Facts" section, indicated by the code *SUP*, begins on page 633.

BiB   *Biographia Britannica Literaria; or, Biography of Literary Characters of Great Britain and Ireland, Arranged in Chronological Order.* Two volumes. By Thomas Wright. London: John W. Parker, 1842, 1846. Reprint. Detroit: Gale Research Co., 1968.

     BiB N   Anglo-Norman Period, 1846
     BiB S   Anglo-Saxon Period, 1842

     Use the Index in each volume to locate biographies.

BiCAW   *The Biographical Cyclopaedia of American Women.* Two volumes. Volume I: Compiled under the supervision of Mabel Ward Cameron. New York: Halvord Publishing Co., 1924. Volume II: Compiled under the supervision of Erma Conkling Lee. New York: Franklin W. Lee Publishing Corp., 1925. Reprint (both volumes). Detroit: Gale Research Co., 1974.

     Use the Index in each volume to locate biographies.

BiDAfM   *Biographical Dictionary of Afro-American and African Musicians.* By Eileen Southern. Westport, Connecticut: Greenwood Press, 1982.

BiDAmAr   *Biographical Dictionary of American Architects, Deceased.* By Henry F. Withey and Elsie Rathburn Withey. Los Angeles: New Age Publishing Co., 1956.

BiDAmBL 83   *Biographical Dictionary of American Business Leaders.* By John N. Ingham. Westport, Connecticut: Greenwood Press, 1983.

Use the Index to locate biographies.

BiDAmC   *Biographical Dictionary of American Cult and Sect Leaders.* By J. Gordon Melton. New York: Garland Publishing, Inc., 1986.

BiDAmEd   *Biographical Dictionary of American Educators.* Three volumes. Edited by John F. Ohles. Westport, Connecticut: Greenwood Press, 1978.

BiDAmLL   *Biographical Dictionary of American Labor Leaders.* Edited by Gary M. Fink. Westport, Connecticut: Greenwood Press, 1974.

BiDAmM   *Biographical Dictionary of American Music.* By Charles Eugene Claghorn. West Nyack, New York: Parker Publishing Co., 1973.

BiDAmS   *Biographical Dictionary of American Science, the Seventeenth through the Nineteenth Centuries.* By Clark A. Elliott. Westport, Connecticut: Greenwood Press, 1979.

BiD&SB   *Biographical Dictionary and Synopsis of Books Ancient and Modern.* Edited by Charles Dudley Warner. Akron, Ohio: Werner Co., 1902. Reprint. Detroit: Gale Research Co., 1965.

BiDBrA   *A Biographical Dictionary of British Architects 1600-1840.* By Howard Colvin. New York: Facts on File, 1980.

"Appendix A," indicated by the code *A*, begins on page 969.

BiDConf   *Biographical Dictionary of the Confederacy.* By Jon L. Wakelyn. Westport, Connecticut: Greenwood Press, 1977.

BiDD   *Biographical Dictionary of Dance.* By Barbara Naomi Cohen-Stratyner. New York: Macmillan Publishing Co., Schirmer Books; London: Collier Macmillan Publishers, 1982.

BiDFedJ   *Biographical Dictionary of the Federal Judiciary.* Compiled by Harold Chase, Samuel Krislov, Keith O. Boyum, and Jerry N. Clark. Detroit: Gale Research Co., 1976.

The Addendum, indicated by the code *A*, begins on page 319.

BiDFilm   *A Biographical Dictionary of Film.* By David Thomson. New York: William Morrow & Co., 1976, 1981.

BiDFilm   First edition, 1976
BiDFilm 81   Second edition revised, 1981

BiDJaL   *Biographical Dictionary of Japanese Literature.* By Sen'ichi Hisamatsu. Tokyo: Kodansha International, 1976. Distributed by Harper & Row, New York, New York.

Use the Index to locate biographies.

BiDLA   *A Biographical Dictionary of the Living Authors of Great Britain and Ireland.* Comprising literary memoirs and anecdotes of their lives; and a chronological register of their publications, with the number of editions printed; including notices of some foreign writers whose works have been occasionally published in England. London: Printed for Henry Colburn, Public Library, Hanover Square, 1816. Reprint. Detroit: Gale Research Co., 1966.

The "Supplement of Additions and Corrections," indicated by the code *SUP,* begins on page 407.

BiDPara   *Biographical Dictionary of Parapsychology, with Directory and Glossary, 1964-1966.* Edited by Helene Pleasants. New York: Garrett Publications, Helix Press, 1964.

BiDSA   *Biographical Dictionary of Southern Authors.* Originally published as *Library of Southern Literature, Volume 15, Biographical Dictionary of Authors.* Compiled by Lucian Lamar Knight. Atlanta: Martin & Hoyt Co., 1929. Reprint. Detroit: Gale Research Co., 1978.

BiDrACP 79   *Biographical Directory of the American College of Physicians, 1979.* Compiled by Jaques Cattell Press. New York: R.R. Bowker Co., 1979.

Use the Index, which begins on page 1789, to locate biographies.

BiDrAC   *Biographical Directory of the American Congress 1774-1971.* The Continental Congress (September 5, 1774 to October 21, 1788) and The Congress of the United States (from the first through the ninety-first Congress March 4, 1789, to January 3, 1971, inclusive), Washington, D.C.: United States Government Printing Office, 1971.

Biographies begin on page 487.

BiDrAPA 77   *Biographical Directory of the Fellows and Members of the American Psychiatric Association.* Compiled by Jaques Cattell Press. New York: R.R. Bowker Co., 1977.

BiDrAPH 79   *Biographical Directory of the American Public Health Association, 1979.* Compiled by Jaques Cattell Press. New York: R.R. Bowker Co., 1979.

BiDrGov   *Biographical Directory of the Governors of the United States, 1789-1978.* Four volumes. Edited by Robert Sobel and John Raimo. Westport, Connecticut: Microform Review, Meckler Books, 1978.

Use the Index in each volume to locate biographies.

BiDrLUS 70   *A Biographical Directory of Librarians in the United States and Canada.* Fifth edition. Edited by Lee Ash. Chicago: American Library Association, 1970.

BiDrUSE   *Biographical Directory of the United States Executive Branch 1774-1971.* Edited by Robert Sobel. Westport, Connecticut: Greenwood Publishing Co., 1971.

BiESc   *A Biographical Encyclopedia of Scientists.* Two volumes. Edited by John Daintith, Sarah Mitchell, and Elizabeth Tootill. New York: Facts on File, 1981.

BiE&WWA   *The Biographical Encyclopaedia and Who's Who of the American Theatre.* Edited by Walter Rigdon. New York: James H. Heineman, 1966. Revised edition published as *Notable Names in the American Theatre* (see below).

The "Biographical Who's Who" section begins on page 227.

BiHiMed   *A Biographical History of Medicine: Excerpts and Essays on the Men and Their Work.* By John H. Talbott. New York: Grune & Stratton, 1970.

Use the "Name Index," which begins on page 1193, to locate biographies.

BioIn   *Biography Index.* A cumulative index to biographical material in books and magazines. New York: H.W. Wilson Co., 1949-1984.

BioIn 1   Volume 1: January, 1946-July, 1949; 1949
BioIn 2   Volume 2: August, 1949-August, 1952; 1953
BioIn 3   Volume 3: September, 1952-August, 1955; 1956
BioIn 4   Volume 4: September, 1955-August, 1958; 1960
BioIn 5   Volume 5: September, 1958-August, 1961; 1962
BioIn 6   Volume 6: September, 1961-August, 1964; 1965
BioIn 7   Volume 7: September, 1964-August, 1967; 1968
BioIn 8   Volume 8: September, 1967-August, 1970; 1971
BioIn 9   Volume 9: September, 1970-August, 1973; 1974
BioIn 10   Volume 10: September, 1973-August, 1976; 1977
BioIn 11   Volume 11: September, 1976-August, 1979; 1980

BioIn 12	Volume 12: September, 1979-August, 1982; 1983
BioIn 13	Volume 13: September, 1982-August, 1984; 1984

BioNews   *Biography News.* A compilation of news stories and feature articles from American news media covering personalities of national interest in all fields. Edited by Frank E. Bair. Detroit: Gale Research Co., 1974-1975.

BioNews 74	Volume 1, Numbers 1-12, 1974
BioNews 75	Volume 2, Number 1, January-February, 1975

BlkAmW   *Black American Writers, Bibliographical Essays.* Edited by M. Thomas Inge, Maurice Duke, and Jackson R. Bryer. New York: St. Martin's Press, 1978.

BlkAmW 1	Volume 1: The Beginnings through the Harlem Renaissance and Langston Hughes.
BlkAmW 2	Volume 2: Richard Wright, Ralph Ellison, James Baldwin, and Amiri Baraka.

     Use the Index to locate biographies.

BlkAWP   *Black American Writers Past and Present.* A biographical and bibliographical dictionary. Two volumes. By Theressa Gunnels Rush, Carol Fairbanks Myers, and Esther Spring Arata. Metuchen, New Jersey: Scarecrow Press, 1975.

Blood&B   *Bloodletters and Badmen.* By Jay Robert Nash. New York: M. Evans & Co., Inc., 1979.

BlueB 76   *The Blue Book: Leaders of the English-Speaking World.* 1976 edition. London: St. James Press; New York: St. Martin's Press, 1976. Republished in two volumes by Gale Research Co., Detroit, Michigan, 1979.

     The Obituary section, indicated by the code *N*, begins on page 1837.

BluesWW   *Blues Who's Who: A Biographical Dictionary of Blues Singers.* By Sheldon Harris. New Rochelle, New York: Arlington House Publishers, 1979.

BkC   *The Book of Catholic Authors: Informal Self-Portraits of Famous Modern Catholic Writers.* Edited by Walter Romig. Detroit: Walter Romig & Co., 1942-?

BkC 1	First series, 1942
BkC 2	Second series, 1943
BkC 3	Third series, 1945
BkC 4	Fourth series (n.d.)

BkC 5	Fifth series (n.d.)
BkC 6	Sixth series (n.d.)

BkCL　　*A Book of Children's Literature.* Third edition. Edited by Lillian Hollowell. New York: Holt, Rinehart & Winston, 1966.

Biographies begin on page 553.

BkIE　　*Book Illustrators in Eighteenth-Century England.* By Hanns Hammelmann. Edited and completed by T.S.R. Boase. New Haven, Connecticut: Yale University Press (for The Paul Mellon Centre for Studies in British Art, London), 1975.

BkPepl　　*The Book of People.* By Christopher P. Anderson. New York: Perigee Books, 1981.

BkP　　*Books Are by People: Interviews with 104 Authors and Illustrators of Books for Young Children.* By Lee Bennett Hopkins. New York: Citation Press, 1969.

BnBkM 80　　*Britannica Book of Music.* Edited by Benjamin Hadley. Garden City, New York: Doubleday & Co., Inc., 1980.

BnEnAmA　　*The Britannica Encyclopedia of American Art.* Chicago: Encyclopaedia Britannica Educational Corp., 1973. Distributed by Simon & Schuster, New York, New York.

Br&AmS　　*British and American Sporting Authors: Their Writings and Biographies.* By A. Henry Higginson. London: Hutchinson & Co., 1951.

Use the Index to locate biographies.

BrAu　　*British Authors before 1800: A Biographical Dictionary.* Edited by Stanley J. Kunitz and Howard Haycraft. New York: H.W. Wilson Co., 1952.

BrAu 19　　*British Authors of the Nineteenth Century.* Edited by Stanley J. Kunitz. New York: H.W. Wilson Co., 1936.

BrWr　　*British Writers.* Edited under the auspices of the British Council, Ian Scott-Kilvert, general editor. New York: Charles Scribner's Sons, 1979-1984.

BrWr 1	Volume I: William Langland to The English Bible, 1979
BrWr 2	Volume II: Thomas Middleton to George Farquhar, 1979
BrWr 3	Volume III: Daniel Defoe to The Gothic Novel, 1980

BrWr 4	Volume IV: William Wordsworth to Robert Browning, 1981
BrWr 5	Volume V: Elizabeth Gaskell to Francis Thompson, 1982
BrWr 6	Volume VI: Thomas Hardy to Wilfred Owen, 1983
BrWr 7	Volume VII: Sean O'Casey to Poets of World War II, 1983

Use the "List of Subjects" at the front of each volume to locate biographies.

BusPN   *Business People in the News.* A compilation of news stories and feature articles from American newspapers and magazines covering people in industry, finance, and labor. Volume 1. Edited by Barbara Nykoruk. Detroit: Gale Research Co., 1976.

CabMA   *The Cabinetmakers of America.* Revised and corrected edition. By Ethel Hall Bjerkoe. Exton, Pennsylvania: Schiffer, 1978. Originally published by Doubleday & Co., 1957.

Biographies begin on page 19.

Cald 1938   *Caldecott Medal Books: 1938-1957.* With the artist's acceptance papers & related material chiefly from the *Horn Book Magazine.* Horn Book Papers, Volume II. Edited by Bertha Mahony Miller and Elinor Whitney Field. Boston: Horn Book, 1957.

CaW   *Canada Writes!* The members' book of the Writers' Union of Canada. Edited by K.A. Hamilton. Toronto: Writers' Union of Canada, 1977.

The "Additional Members" section, indicated by the code *A*, begins on page 387.

CanNov   *Canadian Novelists, 1920-1945.* By Clara Thomas. Toronto: Longmans, Green & Co., 1946. Reprint. Folcroft, Pennsylvania: Folcroft Library Editions, 1970.

CanWW 70   *Canadian Who's Who.* A biographical dictionary of notable living men and women. Volume 12, 1970-1972. Toronto: Who's Who Canadian Publications, 1972.

CanWW   *Canadian Who's Who.* A biographical dictionary of notable living men and women. Edited by Kieran Simpson. Toronto: University of Toronto Press, 1979, 1980, 1981, 1982, 1983.

CanWW 79	Volume XIV, 1979
CanWW 80	Volume XV, 1980
CanWW 81	Volume XVI, 1981
CanWW 82	Volume XVII, 1982
CanWW 83	Volume XVIII, 1983
CanWW 84	Volume XIX, 1984

CanWW 85	Volume XX, 1985
CanWW 86	Volume XXI, 1986

CanWr   *Canadian Writers: A Biographical Dictionary.* New edition, revised and enlarged. Edited by Guy Sylvestre, Brandon Conron, and Carl F. Klinck. Toronto: Ryerson Press, 1966.

CarSB   *The Carolyn Sherwin Bailey Historical Collection of Children's Books: A Catalogue.* Edited and compiled by Dorothy R. Davis. New Haven, Connecticut: Southern Connecticut State College, 1966.

            Not in strict alphabetic sequence.

CasWL   *Cassell's Encyclopaedia of World Literature.* Edited by S.H. Steinberg in two volumes. Revised and enlarged in three volumes by J. Buchanan-Brown. New York: William Morrow & Co., 1973.

            Biographies are found in Volumes 2 and 3.

CathA   *Catholic Authors: Contemporary Biographical Sketches.* Two volumes. Edited by Matthew Hoehn. Newark, New Jersey: St. Mary's Abbey, 1948, 1952. Reprint (first volume). Detroit: Gale Research Co., 1981.

CathA 1930	First volume: 1930-1947; 1948
CathA 1952	Second volume; 1952

CelCen   *Celebrities of the Century.* Being a dictionary of men and women of the nineteenth century. Two volumes. Edited by Lloyd C. Sanders. London: Cassell & Co., 1887. Reprint. Ann Arbor: Gryphon Books, 1971.

CelR   *Celebrity Register.* Third edition. Edited by Earl Blackwell. New York: Simon & Schuster, 1973.

Chambr   *Chambers's Cyclopaedia of English Literature.* A history critical and biographical of authors in the English tongue from the earliest times till the present day with specimens of their writings. Three volumes. Edited by David Patrick, revised by J. Liddell Geddie. Philadelphia: J.B. Lippincott, Co., 1938. Reprint. Detroit: Gale Research Co., 1978.

Chambr 1	Volume I: 7th-17th Century
Chambr 2	Volume II: 18th Century
Chambr 3	Volume III: 19th-20th Century

            Use the Index in each volume to locate biographies.

ChhPo   *Childhood in Poetry.* A catalogue, with biographical and critical annotations, of the books of English and American poets comprising the Shaw Childhood in Poetry Collection in the Library of the Florida State University. By John Mackay Shaw. Detroit: Gale Research Co., 1967, 1972, 1976, 1980.

ChhPo	Original Volumes, 1967
ChhPo S1	First Supplement, 1972
ChhPo S2	Second Supplement, 1976
ChhPo S3	Third Supplement, 1980

ChlLR   *Children's Literature Review.* Excerpts from reviews, criticism, and commentary on books for children and young people. Detroit: Gale Research Co., 1976-1986.

ChlLR 1	Volume 1, 1976
ChlLR 2	Volume 2, 1976
ChlLR 3	Volume 3, 1978
ChlLR 4	Volume 4, 1982
ChlLR 5	Volume 5, 1983
ChlLR 6	Volume 6, 1984
ChlLR 7	Volume 7, 1984
ChlLR 8	Volume 8, 1985
ChlLR 9	Volume 9, 1985
ChlLR 10	Volume 10, 1986
ChlLR 11	Volume 11, 1986

CivR 74   *Civil Rights: A Current Guide to the People, Organizations, and Events.* A CBS News Reference Book. Second edition. By Joan Martin Burke. New York: R.R. Bowker Co., 1974.

Biographies begin on page 21.

CivRSt   *The Civil Rights Struggle: Leaders in Profile.* By John D'Emilio. New York: Facts on File, 1979.

CivWDc   *The Civil War Dictionary.* By Mark Mayo Boatner, III. New York: David McKay Co., 1959.

ClbCR   *Colombo's Canadian References.* By John Robert Colombo. New York: Oxford University Press, 1976.

CIDMEL   *Columbia Dictionary of Modern European Literature.* First edition. Edited by Horatio Smith. New York: Columbia University Press, 1947.

CmCal   *A Companion to California.* By James D. Hart. New York: Oxford University Press, 1978.

CmMov   *A Companion to the Movies: From 1903 to the Present Day.* A guide to the leading players, directors, screenwriters, composers, cameramen and other artistes who have worked in the English-speaking cinema over the last 70 years. By Roy Pickard. New York: Hippocrene Books, 1972.

Use the "Who's Who Index" to locate biographies.

CmOp   *A Companion to the Opera.* By Robin May. New York: Hippocrene Books, Inc., 1977.

CmpEPM   *The Complete Encyclopedia of Popular Music and Jazz, 1900-1950.* Three volumes. By Roger D. Kinkle. New Rochelle, New York: Arlington House Publishers, 1974.

Biographies are located in Volumes 2 and 3.

CompSN   *Composers Since 1900.* Compiled by Donald Ewen. New York: H.W. Wilson, 1969.

CompSN SUP   *Composers since 1900: First Supplement.* A biographical and critical guide. Compiled and edited by David Ewen. New York: H.W. Wilson Co., 1981.

CpmDNM   *Composium Directory of New Music.* Annual index of contemporary compositions. Sedro Woolley, Washington: Crystal Musicworks: 1981, 1983.

CpmDNM 81   1981 edition
CpmDNM 82   1982/83 edition

CnDAL   *Concise Dictionary of American Literature.* Edited by Robert Fulton Richards. New York: Philosophical Library, 1955. Reprint. New York: Greenwood Press, 1969.

CnE&AP   *The Concise Encyclopedia of English and American Poets and Poetry.* Edited by Stephen Spender and Donald Hall. New York: Hawthorn Books, 1963.

CnMD   *The Concise Encyclopedia of Modern Drama.* By Siegfried Melchinger. Translated by George Wellwarth. Edited by Henry Popkin. New York: Horizon Press, 1964.

Biographies begin on page 159. The "Additional Entries" section, indicated by the code *SUP*, begins on page 287.

CnMWL   *The Concise Encyclopedia of Modern World Literature.* Second edition. Edited by Geoffrey Grigson. London: Hutchinson & Co., 1970.

Biographies begin on page 29.

CnThe   *A Concise Encyclopedia of the Theatre.* By Robin May. Reading, England: Osprey Publishing, 1974.

Use the Index to locate biographies.

CnOxB   *The Concise Oxford Dictionary of Ballet.* By Horst Koegler. London: Oxford University Press, 1977.

CnOxOp 79   *The Concise Oxford Dictionary of Opera.* Second edition. By Harold Rosenthal and John Warrack. London: Oxford University Press, 1979.

CngDr   *Congressional Directory.* Washington, D.C.: United States Government Printing Office, 1974, 1977, 1978, 1979, 1981, 1983, 1985.

CngDr 74	93rd Congress, 2nd Session, 1974
CngDr 77	95th Congress, 1st Session, 1977
CngDr 78	*Supplement,* 95th Congress, 2nd Session, 1978
CngDr 79	96th Congress, 1st Session, 1979
CngDr 81	97th Congress, 1981
CngDr 83	98th Congress, 1983-1984; 1983
CngDr 85	99th Congress, 1985-1986; 1985

Use the "Individual Index" in each volume to locate biographies.

ConAmA   *Contemporary American Authors: A Critical Survey and 219 Bio-Bibliographies.* By Fred B. Millett. New York: Harcourt, Brace & World, 1940. Reprint. New York: AMS Press, 1970.

Biographies begin on page 207.

ConAmC   *Contemporary American Composers: A Biographical Dictionary.* Compiled by E. Ruth Anderson. Boston: G.K. Hall & Co., 1976, 1982.

ConAmC	First edition, 1976
ConAmC A	First edition, Addendum begins on page 495.
ConAmC 82	Second edition, 1982

ConAmL   *Contemporary American Literature: Bibliographies and Study Outlines.* By John Matthews Manly and Edith Rickert. Revised by Fred B. Millett. New York: Harcourt, Brace, 1929. Reprint. New York: Haskell House Publishers, 1974.

Biographies begin on page 101.

ConAmTC   *Contemporary American Theater Critics: A Directory and Anthology of Their Works.* Compiled by M.E. Comtois and Lynn F. Miller. Metuchen, New Jersey: Scarecrow Press, 1977.

ConArch   *Contemporary Architects.* Edited by Muriel Emanuel. New York: St. Martin's Press, 1980.

The "Notes on Advisors and Contributors" section, indicated by the code *A*, begins on page 927.

ConArt   *Contemporary Artists.* Edited by Colin Naylor and Genesis P-Orridge. London: St. James Press; New York: St. Martin's Press, 1977.

ConArt 83   *Contemporary Artists.* Second edition. Edited by Muriel Emanuel et al. New York: St. Martin's Press, 1983.

ConAu   *Contemporary Authors.* A bio-bibliographical guide to current writers in fiction, general nonfiction, poetry, journalism, drama, motion pictures, television, and other fields. Detroit: Gale Research Co., 1967-1986.

ConAu 1R	Volumes 1-4, 1st revision, 1967
ConAu 5R	Volumes 5-8, 1st revision, 1969
ConAu 9R	Volumes 9-12, 1st revision, 1974
ConAu 13R	Volumes 13-16, 1st revision, 1975
ConAu 17R	Volumes 17-20, 1st revision, 1976
ConAu 21R	Volumes 21-24, 1st revision, 1977
ConAu 25R	Volumes 25-28, 1st revision, 1977
ConAu 29R	Volumes 29-32, 1st revision, 1978
ConAu 33R	Volumes 33-36, 1st revision, 1978
ConAu 37R	Volumes 37-40, 1st revision, 1979
ConAu 41R	Volumes 41-44, 1st revision, 1979
ConAu 45	Volumes 45-48, 1974
ConAu 49	Volumes 49-52, 1975
ConAu 53	Volumes 53-56, 1975
ConAu 57	Volumes 57-60, 1976
ConAu 61	Volumes 61-64, 1976
ConAu 65	Volumes 65-68, 1977
ConAu 69	Volumes 69-72, 1978
ConAu 73	Volumes 73-76, 1978
ConAu 77	Volumes 77-80, 1979
ConAu 81	Volumes 81-84, 1979
ConAu 85	Volumes 85-88, 1980
ConAu 89	Volumes 89-92, 1980
ConAu 93	Volumes 93-96, 1980
ConAu 97	Volumes 97-100, 1981
ConAu 101	Volume 101, 1981
ConAu 102	Volume 102, 1981
ConAu 103	Volume 103, 1982
ConAu 104	Volume 104, 1982
ConAu 105	Volume 105, 1982
ConAu 106	Volume 106, 1982
ConAu 107	Volume 107, 1983
ConAu 108	Volume 108, 1983

ConAu 109	Volume 109, 1983
ConAu 110	Volume 110, 1984
ConAu 111	Volume 111, 1984
ConAu 112	Volume 112, 1985
ConAu 113	Volume 113, 1985
ConAu 114	Volume 114, 1985
ConAu 115	Volume 115, 1985
ConAu 116	Volume 116, 1986
ConAu 117	Volume 117, 1986
ConAu 118	Volume 118, 1986

ConAu NR   *Contemporary Authors, New Revision Series.* A bio-bibliographical guide to current writers in fiction, general nonfiction, poetry, journalism, drama, motion pictures, television, and other fields. Detroit: Gale Research Co., 1981-1986.

ConAu 1NR	Volume 1, 1981
ConAu 2NR	Volume 2, 1981
ConAu 3NR	Volume 3, 1981
ConAu 4NR	Volume 4, 1981
ConAu 5NR	Volume 5, 1982
ConAu 6NR	Volume 6, 1982
ConAu 7NR	Volume 7, 1982
ConAu 8NR	Volume 8, 1983
ConAu 9NR	Volume 9, 1983
ConAu 10NR	Volume 10, 1983
ConAu 11NR	Volume 11, 1984
ConAu 12NR	Volume 12, 1984
ConAu 13NR	Volume 13, 1984
ConAu 14NR	Volume 14, 1985
ConAu 15NR	Volume 15, 1985
ConAu 16NR	Volume 16, 1986
ConAu 17NR	Volume 17, 1986
ConAu 18NR	Volume 18, 1986

ConAu P-   *Contemporary Authors, Permanent Series.* A bio-bibliographical guide to current authors and their works. Detroit: Gale Research Co., 1975-1978.

ConAu P-1	Volume 1, 1975
ConAu P-2	Volume 2, 1978

ConAu X   This code refers to pseudonym entries which appear as cross-references in the cumulative index to *Contemporary Authors.*

ConDr   *Contemporary Dramatists.* Edited by James Vinson. London: St. James Press; New York: St. Martin's Press, 1973, 1977, 1982.

ConDr 73   First edition, 1973

ConDr 77   Second edition, 1977, the "Contemporary Dramatists" section begins on page 9.

ConDr 77A	Second edition, the "Screen Writers" section begins on page 893.
ConDr 77B	Second edition, the "Radio Writers" section begins on page 903.
ConDr 77C	Second edition, the "Television Writers" section begins on page 915.
ConDr 77D	Second edition, the "Musical Librettists" section begins on page 925.
ConDr 77E	Second edition, "The Theatre of the Mixed Means" section begins on page 941.
ConDr 77F	Second edition, Appendix begins on page 969.
ConDr 82	Third edition, 1982, the "Contemporary Dramatists" section begins on page 9.
ConDr 82A	Third edition, the "Screen Writers" section begins on page 887.
ConDr 82B	Third edition, the "Radio Writers" section begins on page 899.
ConDr 82C	Third edition, the "Television Writers" section begins on page 911.
ConDr 82D	Third edition, the "Musical Librettists" section begins on page 921.
ConDr 82E	Third edition, Appendix begins on page 951.

ConICB	*Contemporary Illustrators of Children's Books.* Compiled by Bertha E. Mahony and Elinor Whitney. Boston: Bookshop for Boys and Girls, Women's Educational and Industrial Union, 1930. Reprint. Detroit: Gale Research Co., 1978.
ConLC	*Contemporary Literary Criticism.* Excerpts from criticism of the works of today's novelists, poets, playwrights, short story writers, filmmakers, scriptwriters, and other creative writers. Detroit: Gale Research Co., 1973-1986.
ConLC 1	Volume 1, 1973
ConLC 2	Volume 2, 1974
ConLC 3	Volume 3, 1975
ConLC 4	Volume 4, 1975
ConLC 5	Volume 5, 1976
ConLC 6	Volume 6, 1976
ConLC 7	Volume 7, 1977
ConLC 8	Volume 8, 1978
ConLC 9	Volume 9, 1978
ConLC 10	Volume 10, 1979
ConLC 11	Volume 11, 1979
ConLC 12	Volume 12, 1980
ConLC 13	Volume 13, 1980
ConLC 14	Volume 14, 1980
ConLC 15	Volume 15, 1980

ConLC 16	Volume 16, 1981
ConLC 17	Volume 17, 1981
ConLC 18	Volume 18, 1981
ConLC 19	Volume 19, 1981
ConLC 20	Volume 20, 1982
ConLC 21	Volume 21, 1982
ConLC 22	Volume 22, 1982
ConLC 23	Volume 23, 1983
ConLC 24	Volume 24, 1983
ConLC 25	Volume 25, 1983
ConLC 26	Volume 26, 1983
ConLC 27	Volume 27, 1984
ConLC 28	Volume 28, 1984
ConLC 29	Volume 29, 1984
ConLC 30	Volume 30, 1984
ConLC 31	Volume 31, 1985
ConLC 32	Volume 32, 1985
ConLC 33	Volume 33, 1985
ConLC 34	Volume 34, Yearbook 1984; 1985
ConLC 35	Volume 35, 1985
ConLC 36	Volume 36, 1986
ConLC 37	Volume 37, 1986
ConLC 38	Volume 38, 1986
ConLC 39	Volume 39, 1986

Use the Table of Contents to locate entries in the Yearbook, Volume 34.

ConLCrt   *Contemporary Literary Critics.* By Elmer Borklund. London: St. James Press; New York: St. Martin's Press, 1977.

ConLCrt 82   *Contemporary Literary Critics.* Second edition. By Elmer Borklund. Detroit: Gale Research Co., 1982.

ConMuA   *Contemporary Music Almanac, 1980-81.* By Ronald Zalkind. New York: Macmillan Publishing Co., Schirmer Books, 1980.

ConNews   *Contemporary Newsmakers.* A biographical guide to people in the news in business, education, technology, social issues, politics, law, economics, international affairs, religion, entertainment, labor, sports, design, psychology, medicine, astronautics, ecology, and other fields. Detroit: Gale Research Co., 1985-86.

ConNews 85-1	1985, Issue 1; 1985
ConNews 85-2	1985, Issue 2; 1985
ConNews 85-3	1985, Issue 3; 1986
ConNews 85-4	1985, Issue 4; 1986
ConNews 86-1	1986, Issue 1; 1986
ConNews 86-2	1986, Issue 2; 1986
ConNews 86-3	1986, Issue 3; 1986

Biographies in each quarterly issue can also be located in the annual cumulation.

ConNov   *Contemporary Novelists.* Edited by James Vinson. London: St. James Press; New York: St. Martin's Press, 1972, 1976, 1982.

ConNov 72   First edition, 1972
ConNov 76   Second edition, 1976
ConNov 82   Third edition, 1982

Deceased novelists are listed in the Appendix at the back of each volume.

ConPhot   *Contemporary Photographers.* Edited by George Walsh, Colin Naylor, and Michael Held. New York: St. Martin's Press, 1982.

ConP   *Contemporary Poets.* London: St. James Press; New York: St. Martin's Press, 1970, 1975, 1980, 1985.

ConP 70   First edition, edited by Rosalie Murphy, 1970.
ConP 75   Second edition, edited by James Vinson, 1975.
ConP 80   Third edition, edited by James Vinson, 1980.
ConP 85   Fourth edition, edited by James Vinson
and D.L. Kirkpatrick, 1985.

Biographies in the Appendix, indicated by the code *A*, are located at the back of the later editions.

ConSFA   *Contemporary Science Fiction Authors.* First edition. Compiled and edited by R. Reginald. New York: Arno Press, 1975. Previously published as *Stella Nova: The Contemporary Science Fiction Authors.* Los Angeles: Unicorn & Son, Publishers, 1970.

ConTFT   *Contemporary Theatre, Film, and Television.* A biographical guide featuring performers, directors, writers, producers, designers, managers, choreographers, technicians, composers, executives, dancers, and critics in the United States and Great Britain. Detroit: Gale Research Co., 1984-1986. A continuation of *Who's Who in the Theatre.*

ConTFT 1   Volume 1, 1984
ConTFT 2   Volume 2, 1986
ConTFT 3   Volume 3, 1986

Conv   *Conversations.* Conversations series. Detroit: Gale Research Co., 1977-1978.

Conv 1   Volume 1: *Conversations with Writers,* 1977
Conv 2   Volume 2: *Conversations with Jazz Musicians,* 1977
Conv 3   Volume 3: *Conversations with Writers II,* 1978

Key to Source Codes

CorpD	*Corpus Delicti of Mystery Fiction: A Guide to the Body of the Case.* By Linda Herman and Beth Stiel. Metuchen, New Jersey: Scarecrow Press, 1974. Biographies begin on page 31.
CounME	*The Country Music Encyclopedia.* By Melvin Shestack. New York: Thomas Y. Crowell Co., 1974.
CreCan	*Creative Canada: A Biographical Dictionary of Twentieth-Century Creative and Performing Artists.* Compiled by the Reference Division, McPherson Library, University of Victoria, British Columbia. Toronto: University of Toronto Press, 1971, 1972.
CreCan 1 *CreCan 2*	Volume 1, 1971 Volume 2, 1972
CrtT	*The Critical Temper: A Survey of Modern Criticism on English and American Literature from the Beginnings to the Twentieth Century.* Four volumes. Edited by Martin Tucker. A Library of Literary Criticism. New York: Frederick Ungar Publishing Co., 1969, 1979.
CrtT 1 *CrtT 2* *CrtT 3* *CrtT 4*	Volume I: *From Old English to Shakespeare,* 1969 Volume II: *From Milton to Romantic Literature,* 1969 Volume III: *Victorian Literature and American Literature,* 1969 Volume IV: *Supplement,* 1979 Authors are listed alphabetically within each period or division of literature.
CroCAP	*Crowell's Handbook of Contemporary American Poetry.* By Karl Malkoff. New York: Thomas Y. Crowell Co., 1973. Biographies begin on page 43.
CroCD	*Crowell's Handbook of Contemporary Drama.* By Michael Anderson, et al. New York: Thomas Y. Crowell Co., 1971.
CroE&S	*Crowell's Handbook of Elizabethan and Stuart Literature.* By James E. Ruoff. New York: Thomas Y. Crowell Co., 1975.
CurBio	*Current Biography Yearbook.* New York: H.W. Wilson Co., 1950-1986. Number after the source code indicates the year covered by the yearbook. Obituaries are located in the back of some volumes.

CyAG   *Cyclopedia of American Government.* Three volumes. Edited by Andrew C. McLaughlin and Albert Bushnell Hart. New York: D. Appleton & Co., 1914. Reprint. Gloucester, Massachusetts: Peter Smith, 1963.

CyAL   *Cyclopaedia of American Literature.* Embracing personal and critical notices of authors, and selections from their writings, from the earliest period to the present day; with portraits, autographs, and other illustrations. Two volumes. By Evert A. Duyckinck and George L. Duyckinck. Philadelphia: William Rutter & Co., 1875. Reprint. Detroit: Gale Research Co., 1965.

Use the Index in Volume 2 to locate biographies.

CyEd   *A Cyclopedia of Education.* Five volumes. Edited by Paul Monroe. New York: Macmillan Co., 1911. Reprint. Detroit: Gale Research Co., 1968.

CyWA   *Cyclopedia of World Authors.* Edited by Frank N. Magill. New York: Harper & Row, Publishers, 1958. Also published as *Masterplots Cyclopedia of World Authors.*

DcAfL   *Dictionary of Afro-Latin American Civilization.* By Benjamin Nunez with the assistance of the African Bibliographic Center. Westport, Connecticut: Greenwood Press, 1980.

DcAmArt   *Dictionary of American Art.* By Matthew Baigell. New York: Harper & Row, Publishers, 1979.

DcAmAu   *A Dictionary of American Authors.* Fifth edition, revised and enlarged. By Oscar Fay Adams. New York: Houghton Mifflin Co., 1904. Reprint. Detroit: Gale Research Co., 1969.

Biographies are found in the "Dictionary of American Authors" section which begins on page 1 and in the "Supplement" which begins on page 441.

DcAmB   *Dictionary of American Biography.* 20 volumes and seven supplements. Edited under the auspices of the American Council of Learned Societies. New York: Charles Scribner's Sons, 1928-1936, 1944, 1958, 1973, 1974, 1977, 1980, 1981.

DcAmB	Volumes 1-20, 1928-1936
DcAmB S1	Supplement 1, 1944
DcAmB S2	Supplement 2, 1958
DcAmB S3	Supplement 3, 1973
DcAmB S4	Supplement 4, 1974
DcAmB S5	Supplement 5, 1977
DcAmB S6	Supplement 6, 1980
DcAmB S7	Supplement 7, 1981

DcAmDH   *Dictionary of American Diplomatic History.* By John E. Findling. Westport, Connecticut: Greenwood Press, 1980.

DcAmMeB   *Dictionary of American Medical Biography.* Lives of eminent physicians of the United States and Canada, from the earliest times. By Howard A. Kelly and Walter L. Burrage. New York: D. Appleton & Co., 1928. Reprint. Road Town, Tortola, British Virgin Islands: Longwood Press, 1979.

DcAmMeB 84   *Dictionary of American Medical Biography.* Two volumes. Edited by Martin Kaufman, Stuart Galishoff, and Todd L. Savitt. Westport, Connecticut Greenwood Press, 1984.

DcAmNB   *Dictionary of American Negro Biography.* Edited by Rayford W. Logan and Michael R. Winston. New York: W.W. Norton & Co., 1982.

DcAmReB   *Dictionary of American Religious Biography.* By Henry Warner Bowden. Westport, Connecticut: Greenwood Press, 1977.

DcAmSR   *A Dictionary of American Social Reform.* By Louis Filler. New York: Philosophical Library, 1963.

DcBiA   *A Dictionary of Biographies of Authors Represented in the Authors Digest Series.* With a supplemental list of later titles and a supplementary biographical section. Edited by Rossiter Johnson. New York: Authors Press, 1927. Reprint. Detroit: Gale Research Co., 1974.

     "Biographies of Authors" begins on page 3 and "Biographies of Authors Whose Works Are in Volume XVIII" begins on page 437.

DcBiPP   *A Dictionary of Biography, Past and Present.* Containing the chief events in the lives of eminent persons of all ages and nations. Preceded by the biographies and genealogies of the chief representatives of the royal houses of the world. Edited by Benjamin Vincent. Haydn Series. London: Ward, Lock, & Co., 1877. Reprint. Detroit: Gale Research Co., 1974.

     The Addenda, indicated by the code *A*, begin on page 638.

DcBrAr   *Dictionary of British Artists Working 1900-1950.* Two volumes. By Grant M. Waters. Eastbourne, England: Eastbourne Fine Art Publications, 1975, 1976.

     DcBrA 1   Volume I, 1975
     DcBrA 2   Volume II, 1976

DcBrBI *The Dictionary of British Book Illustrators and Caricaturists, 1800-1914*. With introductory chapters on the rise and progress of the art. By Simon Houfe. Woodbridge, England: Antique Collectors' Club, 1978. Distributed by Gale Research Co., Detroit, Michigan.

Biographies begin on page 215.

DcBrWA *The Dictionary of British Watercolour Artists up to 1920*. By H.L. Mallalieu. Woodbridge, England: Antique Collectors' Club, 1976. Distributed by Gale Research Co., Detroit, Michigan.

DcCanB *Dictionary of Canadian Biography*. Toronto: University of Toronto Press, 1966-1985.

DcCanB 1 *Volume I: 1000 to 1700*, edited by George W. Brown, 1966.

DcCanB 1A Volume I, Appendix begins on page 675.

DcCanB 2 *Volume II: 1701 to 1740*, edited by David M. Hayne, 1969.

DcCanB 3 *Volume III: 1741 to 1770*, edited by Francess G. Halpenny, 1974.

DcCanB 3A Volume III, Appendix begins on page 675.

DcCanB 4 *Volume IV: 1771 to 1800*, edited by Francess G. Halpenny, 1979.

DcCanB 4A Volume IV, Appendix begins on page 783.

DcCanB 4S Volume IV, Supplement begins on page 787.

DcCanB 5 *Volume V: 1801 to 1820*, edited by Francess G. Halpenny, 1983.

DcCanB 5A Volume V, Appendix begins on page 887.

DcCanB 8 *Volume VIII: 1851-1860*, edited by Francess G. Halpenny, 1985.

DcCanB 8A Volume VIII, Appendix begins on page 968.

DcCanB 9 *Volume IX: 1861 to 1870*, edited by Francess G. Halpenny, 1976.

DcCanB 10 *Volume X: 1871 to 1880*, edited by Marc La Terreur, 1972.

DcCanB 11 *Volume XI: 1881 to 1890*, edited by Henri Pilon, 1982.

DcCathB *Dictionary of Catholic Biography*. By John J. Delaney and James Edward Tobin. Garden City, New York: Doubleday & Co., 1961.

DcCAA *A Dictionary of Contemporary American Artists*. By Paul Cummings. London: St. James Press; New York: St. Martin's Press, 1971, 1977.

DcCAA 71 Second edition, 1971

DcCAA 77 Third edition, 1977

DcCAr 81   *Dictionary of Contemporary Artists.* Edited by V. Babington Smith. Oxford: Clio Press, 1981.

DcCLAA   *A Dictionary of Contemporary Latin American Authors.* Compiled by David William Foster. Tempe, Arizona: Center for Latin American Studies, Arizona State University, 1975.

DcCM   *Dictionary of Contemporary Music.* Edited by John Vinton. New York: E.P. Dutton & Co., 1974.

                   This book ignores prefixes in filing surnames.

DcD&D   *Dictionary of Design & Decoration.* A Studio Book. New York: Viking Press, 1973.

DcEnA   *A Dictionary of English Authors, Biographical and Bibliographical.* Being a compendious account of the lives and writings of upwards of 800 British and American writers from the year 1400 to the present time. New edition, revised with an appendix bringing the whole up to date and including a large amount of new matter. By R. Farquharson Sharp. London: Kegan Paul, Trench, Trubner & Co., 1904. Reprint. Detroit: Gale Research Co., 1978.

                   The Appendix, indicated by the code *AP*, begins on page 311.

DcEnL   *Dictionary of English Literature: Being a Comprehensive Guide to English Authors and Their Works.* Second edition. By W. Davenport Adams. London: Cassell Petter & Galpin (n.d.). Reprint. Detroit: Gale Research Co., 1966.

DcEuL   *A Dictionary of European Literature.* Designed as a companion to English studies. Second, revised edition. By Laurie Magnus. London: George Routledge & Sons; New York: E.P. Dutton & Co., 1927. Reprint. Detroit: Gale Research Co., 1974.

                   The Appendix begins on page 595.

DcFM   *Dictionary of Film Makers.* By Georges Sadoul. Translated, edited, and updated by Peter Morris. Berkeley and Los Angeles: University of California Press, 1972. Originally published as *Dictionnaire des Cineastes*, 1965.

DcInB   *Dictionary of Indian Biography.* By C.E. Buckland. London: Swan Sonnenschein & Co., 1906. Reprint. Detroit: Gale Research Co., 1968.

                   The Addenda, indicated by the code *A*, begin on page 467.

DcInv	*Dictionary of Inventions & Discoveries.* Edited by E.F. Carter. Stevenage, England: Robin Clark, 1978.
DcIrB	*A Dictionary of Irish Biography.* By Henry Boylan. New York: Barnes & Noble Books, 1978.
DcIrL	*Dictionary of Irish Literature.* Edited by Robert Hogan. Westport, Connecticut: Greenwood Press, 1979. Also published as *The Macmillan Dictionary of Irish Literature.* London: Macmillan Press, 1980.
DcIrW	*Dictionary of Irish Writers.* By Brian Cleeve. Cork, Ireland: Mercier Press, 1967, 1969, 1971.
DcIrW 1	Volume 1: Fiction, 1967
DcIrW 2	Volume 2: Non-fiction, 1969
DcIrW 3	Volume 3: Writers in the Irish Language, 1971
DcItL	*Dictionary of Italian Literature.* Edited by Peter Bondanella and Julia Conaway Bondanella. Westport, Connecticut: Greenwood Press, 1979.
DcLB	*Dictionary of Literary Biography.* Detroit: Gale Research Co., 1978-1986.
DcLB 1	Volume 1: *The American Renaissance in New England.* Edited by Joel Myerson, 1978.
DcLB 2	Volume 2: *American Novelists since World War II.* Edited by Jeffrey Helterman and Richard Layman, 1978.
DcLB 3	Volume 3: *Antebellum Writers in New York and the South.* Edited by Joel Myerson, 1979.
DcLB 4	Volume 4: *American Writers in Paris, 1920-1939.* Edited by Karen Lane Rood, 1980.
DcLB 5	Volume 5: *American Poets since World War II.* Two parts. Edited by Donald J. Greiner, 1980.
DcLB 6	Volume 6: *American Novelists since World War II.* Second series. Edited by James E. Kibler, Jr., 1980.
DcLB 7	Volume 7: *Twentieth-Century American Dramatists.* Two parts. Edited by John MacNicholas, 1981.
DcLB 8	Volume 8: *Twentieth-Century American Science-Fiction Writers.* Two parts. Edited by David Cowart and Thomas L. Wymer, 1981.
DcLB 9	Volume 9: *American Novelists, 1910-1945.* Three parts. Edited by James J. Martine, 1981.
DcLB 10	Volume 10: *Modern British Dramatists, 1900-1945.* Two parts. Edited by Stanley Weintraub, 1982.

Key to Source Codes

DcLB 11	Volume 11: *American Humorists, 1800-1950*. Two parts. Edited by Stanley Trachtenberg, 1982.
DcLB 12	Volume 12: *American Realists and Naturalists*. Edited by Donald Pizer and Earl N. Harbert, 1982.
DcLB 13	Volume 13: *British Dramatists since World War II*. Two parts. Edited by Stanley Weintraub, 1982.
DcLB 14	Volume 14: *British Novelists since 1960*. Two parts. Edited by Jay L. Halio, 1983.
DcLB 15	Volume 15: *British Novelists, 1930-1959*. Two parts. Edited by Bernard Oldsey, 1983.
DcLB 16	Volume 16: *The Beats: Literary Bohemians in Postwar America*. Two parts. Edited by Ann Charters, 1983.
DcLB 17	Volume 17: *Twentieth-Century American Historians*. Edited by Clyde N. Wilson, 1983.
DcLB 18	Volume 18: *Victorian Novelists after 1885*. Edited by Ira B. Nadel and William E. Fredeman, 1983.
DcLB 19	Volume 19: *British Poets, 1880-1914*. Edited by Donald E. Stanford, 1983.
DcLB 20	Volume 20: *British Poets, 1914-1945*. Edited by Donald E. Stanford, 1983.
DcLB 21	Volume 21: *Victorian Novelists before 1885*. Edited by Ira B. Nadel and William E. Fredeman, 1983.
DcLB 22	Volume 22: *American Writers for Children, 1900-1960*. Edited by John Cech, 1983.
DcLB 23	Volume 23: *American Newspaper Journalists, 1873-1900*. Edited by Perry J. Ashley, 1983.
DcLB 24	Volume 24: *American Colonial Writers, 1606-1734*. Edited by Emory Elliott, 1984.
DcLB 25	Volume 25: *American Newspaper Journalists, 1901-1925*. Edited by Perry J. Ashley, 1984.
DcLB 26	Volume 26: *American Screenwriters*. Edited by Robert E. Morsberger, Stephen O. Lesser, and Randall Clark, 1984.
DcLB 27	Volume 27: *Poets of Great Britain and Ireland, 1945-1960*. Edited b y Vincent B. Sherry, Jr., 1984.
DcLB 28	Volume 28: *Twentieth-Century American-Jewish Fiction Writers*. Edited by Daniel Walder, 1984.
DcLB 29	Volume 29: *American Newspaper Journalists, 1926-1960*. Edited by Vincent B. Sherry, Jr., 1984.
DcLB 30	Volume 30: *American Historians, 1607-1865*. Edited by Clyde N. Wilson, 1984.
DcLB 31	Volume 31: *American Colonial Writers, 1735-1781*. Edited by Emory Elliott, 1984.
DcLB 32	Volume 32: *Victorian Poets before 1850*. Edited by William E. Fredeman and Ira B. Nadel, 1984.

DcLB 33	Volume 33: *Afro-American Fiction Writers after 1955.* Edited by Thadious M. Davis and Trudier Harris, 1984.
DcLB 34	Volume 34: *British Novelists, 1890-1929: Traditionalists.* Edited by Thomas F. Staley, 1985.
DcLB 35	Volume 35: *Victorian Poets after 1850.* Edited by William E. Fredeman and Ira B. Nadel, 1985.
DcLB 36	Volume 36: *British Novelists, 1890-1929: Modernists.* Edited by Thomas F. Staley, 1985.
DcLB 37	Volume 37: *American Writers of the Early Republic.* Edited by Emory Elliott, 1985.
DcLB 38	Volume 38: *Afro-American Writers after 1955: Dramatists and Prose Writers.* Edited by Thadious M. Davis and Trudier Harris, 1985.
DcLB 39	Volume 39: *British Novelists, 1660-1800.* Two parts. Edited by Martin C. Battestin, 1985.
DcLB 40	Volume 40: *Poets of Great Britain and Ireland since 1960.* Two parts. Edited by Vincent B. Sherry, Jr., 1985.
DcLB 41	Volume 41: *Afro-American Poets since 1955.* Edited by Trudier Harris and Thadious M. Davis, 1985.
DcLB 42	Volume 42: *American Writers for Children before 1900.* Edited by Glenn E. Estes, 1985.
DcLB 43	Volume 43: *American Newspaper Journalists, 1690-1872.* Edited by Perry J. Ashley, 1985.
DcLB 44	Volume 44: *American Screenwriters.* Second series. Edited by Randall Clark, 1986.
DcLB 45	Volume 45: *American Poets, 1880-1945.* First series. Edited by Peter Quartermain, 1986.
DcLB 47	Volume 47: *American Historians, 1866-1912.* Edited by Clyde N. Wilson, 1986.
DcLB 48	Volume 48: *American Poets, 1880-1945.* Second series. Edited by Peter Quartermain, 1986.

Volume 46 contains no biographies.

DcLB Y-	*Dictionary of Literary Biography Yearbook.* Detroit: Gale Research Co., 1981-1986.
DcLB Y80A	Yearbook: 1980. Edited by Karen L. Rood, Jean W. Ross and Richard Ziegfeld, 1981. The "Updated Entries" section begins on page 3.
DcLB Y80B	Yearbook: 1980. The "New Entries" section begins on page 127.
DcLB Y81A	Yearbook: 1981. Edited by Karen L. Rood, Jean W. Ross, and Richard Ziegfeld, 1982. The "Updated Entries" section begins on page 21.

DcLB Y81B	Yearbook: 1981. The "New Entries" section begins on page 139.
DcLB Y82A	Yearbook: 1982. Edited by Richard Ziegfeld, 1983. The "Updated Entries" section begins on page 121.
DcLB Y82B	Yearbook: 1982. The "New Entries" section begins on page 203.
DcLB Y83A	Yearbook: 1983. Edited by Mary Bruccoli and Jean W. Ross, 1984. The "Updated Entries" section begins on page 155.
DcLB Y83B	Yearbook: 1983. The "New Entries" section begins on page 175.
DcLB Y83N	Yearbook: 1983. The "Obituaries" section begins on page 103.
DcLB Y84A	Yearbook: 1984. Edited by Jean W. Ross, 1985. The "Updated Entry" section begins on page 219.
DcLB Y84B	Yearbook: 1984. The "New Entries" section begins on page 225.
DcLB Y84N	Yearbook: 1984. The "Obituaries" section begins on page 163.
DcLB Y85A	Yearbook: 1985. The "Updated Entries" section begins on page 279.
DcLB Y85B	Yearbook: 1985. The "New Entries" section begins on page 319.
DcLB Y85N	Yearbook: 1985. The "Obituaries" section begins on page 253.

DcLEL   *A Dictionary of Literature in the English Language.* Compiled and edited by Robin Myers. Oxford: Pergamon Press, 1970, 1978.

DcLEL   *From Chaucer to 1940,* 1970
DcLEL 1940   *From 1940 to 1970,* 1978

DcNaB   *The Dictionary of National Biography: The Concise Dictionary.* Part 1, From the Beginnings to 1900. London: Oxford University Press, 1953.

This volume contains abstracts of the biographies found in the main volumes of *The Dictionary of National Biography* (21 volumes, New York: Macmillan Co.; London: Smith, Elder & Co., 1908) and the First Supplement (Volume 22, in three volumes, New York: Macmillan Co.; London: Smith, Elder & Co., 1908).

DcNaB C   Corrigenda begins on page 1457.
DcNaB S1   First Supplement

DcNaB S2   *The Dictionary of National Biography.* Second Supplement. Three volumes. Edited by Sir Sidney Lee. New York: Macmillan Co.; London: Smith, Elder & Co., 1912.

DcNaB 1912   *The Dictionary of National Biography, 1912-1921.* Edited by H.W.C. Davis and J.R.H. Weaver. London: Oxford University Press, 1927.

DcNaB 1922   *The Dictionary of National Biography, 1922-1930.* Edited by J.R.H. Weaver. London: Oxford University Press, 1937.

DcNaB 1931   *The Dictionary of National Biography, 1931-1940.* Edited by L.G. Wickham Legg. London: Oxford University Press, 1949.

DcNaB 1941   *The Dictionary of National Biography, 1941-1950.* Edited by L.G. Wickham Legg and E.T. Williams. London: Oxford University Press, 1959. Reprinted with corrections, 1967.

DcNaB 1951   *The Dictionary of National Biography, 1951-1960.* Edited by E.T. Williams and Helen M. Palmer. London: Oxford University Press, 1971.

DcNaB 1961   *The Dictionary of National Biography, 1961-1970.* Edited by E.T. Williams and C.S. Nicholls. London: Oxford University Press, 1981.

DcNiCA   *Dictionary of 19th Century Antiques and Later Objets d'Art.* By George Savage. London: Barrie & Jenkins, 1978.

DcNAA   *A Dictionary of North American Authors Deceased before 1950.* Compiled by W. Stewart Wallace. Toronto: Ryerson Press, 1951. Reprint. Detroit: Gale Research Co., 1968.

DcOrL   *Dictionary of Oriental Literatures.* Three volumes. Jaroslav Prusek, general editor. New York: Basic Books, 1974.

DcOrL 1   Volume I: East Asia, edited by Zbigniew Slupski.

DcOrL 2   Volume II: South and South-East Asia, edited by Dusan Zbavitel.

DcOrL 3   Volume III: West Asia and North Africa, edited by Jiri Becka.

DcPol   *A Dictionary of Politics.* Revised edition. Edited by Walter Laqueur. New York: Macmillan Publishing Co., Free Press, 1974.

DcRusL   *Dictionary of Russian Literature.* By William E. Harkins. New York: Philosophical Library, 1956. Reprint. Westport, Connecticut: Greenwood Press, 1971.

DcScB   *Dictionary of Scientific Biography.* 14 volumes and supplement. Edited by Charles Coulston Gillispie. New York: Charles Scribner's Sons, 1970-1976, 1978.

DcScB	Volumes I-XIV, 1970-1976
DcScB S1	Volume XV, Supplement I, 1978

DcSeaP   *Dictionary of Sea Painters.* By E.H.H. Archibald. Woodbridge, England: Antique Collectors' Club, 1980. Distributed by Gale Research Co., Detroit, Michigan.

Biographies begin on page 59.

DcSoc   *A Dictionary of Sociology.* Edited by G. Duncan Mitchell. Chicago: Aldine Publishing Co., 1968.

DcSpL   *Dictionary of Spanish Literature.* By Maxim Newmark. New York: Philosophical Library, 1956. Reprint. Totowa, New Jersey: Littlefield, Adams & Co., 1970.

DcVicP   *Dictionary of Victorian Painters.* By Christopher Wood. Suffolk, England: Baron Publishing (for The Antique Collectors' Club), 1971.

DirCG 82   *Directors: A Complete Guide.* Edited by Michael Singer. Beverly Hills: Lone Eagle Productions, Inc., 1982.

DrAF 76   *A Directory of American Fiction Writers.* Names and addresses of more than 800 contemporary fiction writers whose work has been published in the United States. 1976 edition. New York: Poets & Writers, 1976.

Use the Index to locate listings.

DrAP 75   *A Directory of American Poets.* Names and addresses of more than 1,500 contemporary poets whose work has been published in the United States. 1975 edition. New York: Poets & Writers, 1974.

Use the Index to locate listings.

DrAP&F 80   *Directory of American Poets and Fiction Writers.* 1980-1981 edition. New York: Poets & Writers, Inc., 1980.

Use the Index to locate listings.

DrAP&F 83   *A Directory of American Poets and Fiction Writers.* Names and addresses of 5,533 contemporary poets and fiction writers whose work has been published in the United States. 1983-1984 edition. New York: Poets & Writers, 1983.

Use the Index to locate listings.

DrAP&F 85   *A Directory of American Poets and Fiction Writers.* Names and addresses of 6,020 contemporary poets and fiction writers whose work has been published in the United States. 1985-1986 edition. New York: Poets & Writers, 1985.

Use the Index to locate listings.

DrAS   *Directory of American Scholars.* Edited by Jaques Cattell Press. New York: R.R. Bowker Co., 1974, 1978, 1982.

    DrAS 74H   Sixth edition, Volume 1: History

    DrAS 74E   Sixth edition, Volume 2: English, Speech, & Drama

    DrAS 74F   Sixth edition, Volume 3: Foreign Languages, Linguistics, & Philology

    DrAS 74P   Sixth edition, Volume 4: Philosophy, Religion, & Law

    DrAS 78H   Seventh edition, Volume 1: History

    DrAS 78E   Seventh edition, Volume 2: English, Speech, & Drama

    DrAS 78F   Seventh edition, Volume 3: Foreign Languages, Linguistics, & Philology

    DrAS 78P   Seventh edition, Volume 4: Philosophy, Religion, & Law

    DrAS 82H   Eighth edition, Volume 1: History

    DrAS 82E   Eighth edition, Volume 2: English, Speech, & Drama

    DrAS 82F   Eighth edition, Volume 3: Foreign Languages, Linguistics, & Philology

    DrAS 82P   Eighth edition, Volume 4: Philosophy, Religion, & Law

DrBIPA   *Directory of Blacks in the Performing Arts.* By Edward Mapp. Metuchen, New Jersey: Scarecrow Press, 1978.

DrInf   *The Directory of Infamy: The Best of the Worst.* An illustrated compendium of over 600 of the all-time great crooks. By Jonathon Green. London: Mills & Boon, 1980.

Use the Index to locate biographies.

DrLC 69   *Directory of Library Consultants.* Edited by John N. Berry, III. New York: R.R. Bowker Co., 1969.

DrRegL 75   *Directory of Registered Lobbyists and Lobbyist Legislation.* Second edition. Chicago: Marquis Academic Media, 1975.

Use the "Lobbyist Index," which begins on page 451, to locate listings.

Dis&D   *Disease and Destiny: A Bibliography of Medical References to the Famous.* By Judson Bennett Gilbert. Additions and introduction by Gordon E. Mestler. London: Dawsons of Pall Mall, 1962.

Drake   Drake, Francis S. *Dictionary of American Biography, including Men of the Time.* Containing nearly 10,000 notices of persons of both sexes, of native and foreign birth, who have been remarkable, or prominently connected with the arts, sciences, literature, politics, or history, of the American continent. Giving also the pronunciation of many of the foreign and peculiar American names, a key to the assumed names of writers, and a supplement. Boston: James R. Osgood & Co., 1872. Reprint. Detroit: Gale Research Co., 1974.

The Supplement, indicated by the code *SUP*, begins on page 1015.

EarABI   *Early American Book Illustrators and Wood Engravers, 1670-1870.* A catalogue of a collection of American books illustrated for the most part with woodcuts and wood engravings in the Princeton University Library. By Sinclair Hamilton. Princeton, New Jersey: Princeton University Press, 1958, 1968.

   EarABI   Volume I: Main Catalogue, 1958
   EarABI SUP   Volume II: Supplement, 1968

Ebony   *The Ebony Success Library.* Three volumes. By the Editors of *Ebony.* Nashville: Southwestern Co., 1973.

   Ebony 1   Volume I: 1,000 Successful Blacks
   Ebony 3   Volume III: Career Guide

EncAAH   *Encyclopedia of American Agricultural History.* By Edward L. Schapsmeier and Frederick H. Schapsmeier. Westport, Connecticut: Greenwood Press, 1975.

EncAB-A   *Encyclopedia of American Biography.* New Series. 40 volumes. New York and West Palm Beach, Florida: The American Historical Society, 1934-1970.

Number after the source code indicates volume number. Use the Index in each volume to locate biographies.

EncAB-H   *Encyclopedia of American Biography.* Edited by John A. Garraty. New York: Harper & Row, Publishers, 1974.

EncACr   *The Encyclopedia of American Crime.* By Carl Sifakis. New York: Facts on File, Inc., 1982.

EncAJ   *The Encyclopedia of American Journalism.* By Donald Paneth. New York: Facts on File, 1983.

EncAR   *Encyclopedia of the American Revolution.* By Mark Mayo Boatner, III. New York: David McKay Co., 1966.

EncE 75   *Encyclopedia of Espionage.* New edition. By Ronald Seth. London: New English Library, 1975.

EncFCWM   *Encyclopedia of Folk, Country and Western Music.* By Irwin Stambler and Grelun Landon. New York: St. Martin's Press, 1969, 1983.

    EncFCWM 69   First edition, 1969
    EncFCWM 83   Second edition, 1983

EncFWF   *Encyclopedia of Frontier and Western Fiction.* Edited by Jon Tuska and Vicki Piekarski. New York: McGraw-Hill Book Co., 1983.

EncJzS 70   *The Encyclopedia of Jazz in the Seventies.* By Leonard Feather and Ira Gitler. New York: Horizon Press, 1976.

EncLatA   *Encyclopedia of Latin America.* Edited by Helen Delpar. New York: McGraw-Hill Book Co., 1974.

EncMA   *Encyclopedia of Modern Architecture.* Edited by Wolfgang Pehnt. New York: Harry N. Abrams, 1964.

    Biographies begin on page 28.

EncMot   *The Encyclopedia of Motorcycling.* By George Bishop. New York: G.P. Putnam's Sons, 1980.

EncMT   *Encyclopaedia of the Musical Theatre.* By Stanley Green. New York: Dodd, Mead & Co., 1976.

EncMys   *Encyclopedia of Mystery and Detection.* By Chris Steinbrunner and Otto Penzler. New York: McGraw-Hill Book Co., 1976.

EncO&P   *Encyclopedia of Occultism & Parapsychology.* A compendium of information on the occult sciences, magic, demonology, superstitions, spiritism, mysticism, metaphysics, psychical science, and parapsychology, with biographical and bibliographical notes and comprehensive indexes. Edited by Leslie Shepard. Detroit: Gale Research Co., 1978, 1980, 1981, 1984, 1985.

    EncO&P 78   Main volumes, 1978
    EncO&P 78S1   Occultism Update, Issue Number 1, 1978
    EncO&P 80   Occultism Update, Issue Number 2, 1980
    EncO&P 81   Occultism Update, Issue Numbers 3-4, 1981
    EncO&P 2   Second edition, 1984-1985

EncOp   *The Encyclopedia of Opera.* Edited by Leslie Orrey. London: Pitman
                 Publishing, Ltd., 1976.

EncPR&S   *Encyclopedia of Pop, Rock, and Soul.* By Irwin Stambler. London: St.
                 James Press and New York: St. Martin's Press, 1974.

EncSF   *The Encyclopedia of Science Fiction: An Illustrated A to Z.* Edited by
                 Peter Nicholls. London: Granada Publishing, 1979.

EncSoA   *Encyclopaedia of Southern Africa.* Sixth edition. Compiled and edited
                 by Eric Rosenthal. London: Frederick Warne & Co., 1973.

EncSoB   *Encyclopedia of Southern Baptists.* Two volumes and supplement.
                 Nashville: Broadman Press, 1958, 1971.
EncSoB   Two volumes, 1958
EncSoB SUP   Volume III, Supplement, 1971

EncSoH   *The Encyclopedia of Southern History.* Edited by David C. Roller and
                 Robert W. Twyman. Baton Rouge: Louisiana State University
                 Press, 1979.

EncTR   *Encyclopedia of the Third Reich.* By Louis L. Snyder. New York:
                 McGraw-Hill Book Co., 1976.

EncUrb   *Encyclopedia of Urban Planning.* Edited by Arnold Whittick. New
                 York: McGraw-Hill Book Co., 1974.

EncWL   *Encyclopedia of World Literature in the 20th Century.* Three volumes
                 and supplement. Edited by Wolfgang Bernard Fleischmann. New
                 York: Frederick Ungar Publishing Co., 1967, 1975. An enlarged
                 and updated edition of the Herder *Lexikon der Weltliteratur im 20
                 Jahrhundert.*
EncWL   Volumes 1-3, 1967
EncWL SUP   Volume 4, Supplement, 1975

EncWM   *The Encyclopedia of World Methodism.* Two volumes. Edited by
                 Nolan B. Harmon. Nashville: United Methodist Publishing House,
                 1974.

EncWT   *The Encyclopedia of World Theater.* Translated by Estella Schmid,
                 edited by Martin Esslin. New York: Charles Scribner's Sons, 1977.
                 Based on *Friedrichs Theaterlexikon,* by Karl Groning and Werner
                 Kliess.

Ent   *The Entertainers.* Edited by Clive Unger-Hamilton. New York: St.
                 Martin's Press, 1980.

Entr   *Entrepreneurs: The Men and Women behind Famous Brand Names and How They Made It.* By Joseph J. Fucini and Suzy Fucini. Boston: G.K. Hall & Co., 1985.

Use the Index to locate biographies.

EuAu   *European Authors, 1000-1900: A Biographical Dictionary of European Literature.* Edited by Stanley J. Kunitz and Vineta Colby. New York: H.W. Wilson Co., 1967.

EvEuW   *Everyman's Dictionary of European Writers.* By W.N. Hargreaves-Mawdsley. London: J.M. Dent & Sons; New York: E.P. Dutton & Co., 1968.

EvLB   *Everyman's Dictionary of Literary Biography, English and American.* Revised edition. Compiled after John W. Cousin by D.C. Browning. London: J.M. Dent & Sons; New York: E.P. Dutton & Co., 1960.

FairDF   *Fairchild's Dictionary of Fashion.* By Charlotte Calasibetta. New York: Fairchild Publications, 1975.

Biographies are located in the "Fashion Designers" section which begins on page 547.

FairDF ENG   England section begins on page 548.
FairDF FIN   Finland section begins on page 553.
FairDF FRA   France section begins on page 554.
FairDF IRE   Ireland section begins on page 577.
FairDF ITA   Italy section begins on page 578.
FairDF JAP   Japan section begins on page 583.
FairDF SPA   Spain section begins on page 584.
FairDF US   United States section begins on page 585.

FamA&A   *Famous Actors and Actresses on the American Stage: Documents of American Theater History.* Two volumes. By William C. Young. New York: R.R. Bowker Co., 1975.

FamAIYP   *Famous Author-Illustrators for Young People.* By Norah Smaridge. New York: Dodd, Mead & Co., 1973.

FamAYP   *Famous Authors for Young People.* By Ramon P. Coffman and Nathan G. Goodman. New York: Dodd, Mead & Co., 1943.

FamSYP   *Famous Storytellers for Young People.* By Laura Benet. New York: Dodd, Mead & Co., 1968.

FanAl   *The Fantasy Almanac.* By Jeff Rovin. New York: E.P. Dutton, 1979.

FarE&A   The Far East and Australasia: A Survey and Directory of Asia and the
                       Pacific. London: Europa Publications, 1978, 1979, 1980, 1981.
                       Distributed by Gale Research Co., Detroit, Michigan.

FarE&A 78   1978-1979 edition
FarE&A 79   1979-1980 edition
FarE&A 79A   Wade-Giles/Pinyin spellings of Chinese names
                       begin on page 1155.
FarE&A 80   1980-1981 edition
FarE&A 80A   Wade-Giles/Pinyin spellings of Chinese names
                       begin on page 1174.
FarE&A 81   1981-1982 edition

                       Biographies are found in the "Who's Who in the Far East and
                       Australasia" section at the back of each volume.

FemPA   The Female Poets of America. With portraits, biographical notices, and
                       specimens of their writings. Seventh edition, revised. By Thomas
                       Buchanan Read. Philadelphia: E.H. Butler & Co., 1857. Reprint.
                       Detroit: Gale Research Co., 1978.

FifIDA   Fifth International Directory of Anthropologists. Current
                       Anthropology Resource Series, edited by Sol Tax. Chicago:
                       University of Chicago Press, 1975.

Film   Filmarama. Compiled by John Stewart. Metuchen, New Jersey:
                       Scarecrow Press, 1975, 1977.

Film 1   Volume I: The Formidable Years, 1893-1919, 1975
Film 2   Volume II: The Flaming Years, 1920-1929, 1977

FilmEn   The Film Encyclopedia. By Ephraim Katz. New York: Thomas Y.
                       Crowell, 1979.

FilmgC   The Filmgoer's Companion. Fourth edition. By Leslie Halliwell. New
                       York: Hill & Wang, 1974.

FootReg 81   The Football Register. 1981 edition. Edited by Howard M. Balzar. St.
                       Louis: The Sporting News, 1981.

FootReg   The Football Register. Edited by Howard M. Blazar and Barry Siegel.
                       St. Louis: The Sporting News, 1985, 1986.

FootReg 85   1985 edition
FootReg 86   1986 edition

ForWC 70   Foremost Women in Communications. A biographical reference work
                       on accomplished women in broadcasting, publishing, advertising,

public relations, and allied professions. New York: Foremost Americans Publishing Corp., in association with R.R. Bowker Co., 1970.

ForYSC   *Forty Years of Screen Credits, 1929-1969.* Two volumes. Compiled by John T. Weaver. Metuchen, New Jersey: Scarecrow Press, 1970.

FourBJA   *Fourth Book of Junior Authors and Illustrators.* Edited by Doris De Montreville and Elizabeth D. Crawford. New York: H.W. Wilson Co., 1978.

Funs   *The Funsters.* By James Robert Parish and William T. Leonard. New York: Arlington House Publishers, 1979.

Future   *The Future: A Guide to Information Sources.* Second edition. Edited by Edward S. Cornish. Washington, D.C.: World Future Society, 1979.

Biographies begin on page 125.

GolEC   *Golombek's Encyclopedia of Chess.* Edited by Harry Golombek. New York: Crown Publishers, 1977.

GoodHs   *The Good Housekeeping Woman's Almanac.* Edited by Barbara McDowell and Hana Umlauf. New York: Newspaper Enterprise Association, 1977.

Use the Index to locate biographies.

GrBr   *Great Britons.* Twentieth-Century Lives. Bt Harold Oxbury. New York and Oxford: Oxford University Press, 1985.

Grk&L   *Greek and Latin Authors, 800 B.C.-A.D. 1000.* By Michael Grant. New York: H.W. Wilson Co., 1980.

GuPsyc   *A Guide to Psychologists and Their Concepts.* By Vernon J. Nordby and Calvin S. Hall. San Francisco: W.H. Freeman & Co., 1974.

HalFC 80   *Halliwell's Filmgoer's Companion.* Seventh edition. By Leslie Halliwell. New York: Granada Publishing Ltd., 1980. Fourth edition published as *The Filmgoer's Companion.* (see above)

HalFC 84   *Halliwell's Filmgoer's Companion.* Eighth edition. By Leslie Halliwell. New York: Charles Scribner's Sons, 1984.

HarEnUS   *Harper's Encyclopaedia of United States History: From 458 A.D. to 1915.* New edition entirely revised and enlarged. 10 volumes. By Benson John Lossing. New York: Harper & Brothers Publishers, 1915. Reprint. Detroit: Gale Research Co., 1974.

HerW   *Her Way.* Biographies of women for young people. By Mary-Ellen
                  Kulkin. Chicago: American Library Association, 1976.

HisEWW   *The Historical Encyclopedia of World War II.* Edited by Marcel
                  Baudot, et al. New York: Facts on File, 1980. Originally published
                  as *Encyclopedie de la Guerre 1939-1945.* Paris: Editions
                  Casterman, 1977.

HocEn   *The Hockey Encyclopedia* The Complete Record of Professional Ice
                  Hockey. By Stan Fischler and Shirley Walter Fischler. New York:
                  Macmillan Publishing Co., 1983.

HocReg   *The Hockey Register.* Edited by Latty Wiggee. St. Louis: The Sporting
                  News, 1981, 1985.

    HocReg 81   1981-82 edition
    HocReg 85   1985-86 edition

HolCA   *Hollywood Character Actors.* By James Robert Parish. Westport,
                  Connecticut: Arlington House Publishers, 1978.

HolP   *Hollywood Players.* Two volumes. New Rochelle, New York: Arlington
                  House Publishers, 1976.

    HolP 30   *The Thirties.* By James Robert Parish and
                  William T. Leonard.
    HolP 40   *The Forties.* By James Robert Parish and
                  Lennard DeCarl.

HsB&A   *The House of Beadle and Adams and Its Dime and Nickel Novels: The
                  Story of a Vanished Literature.* Two volumes and supplement. By
                  Albert Johannsen. Norman, Oklahoma: University of Oklahoma
                  Press, 1950, 1962.

    HsB&A   Volumes I-II, 1950. Biographies are found in
                  volume II.
    HsB&A SUP   Volume III, Supplement, Addenda, Corrigenda, 1962.

IIBEAAW   *The Illustrated Biographical Encyclopedia of Artists of the American
                  West.* By Peggy Samuels and Harold Samuels. Garden City, New
                  York: Doubleday & Co., 1976.

IIDcG   *An Illustrated Dictionary of Glass.* 2,442 entries, including definitions
                  of wares, materials, processes, forms, and decorative styles, and
                  entries on principal glass-makers, decorators, and designers, from
                  antiquity to the present. By Harold Newman. London: Thames &
                  Hudson, 1977.

IlEncBM 82   *The Illustrated Encyclopedia of Black Music.* Edited by Ray Bonds. New York: Harmony Books, 1982.

IlEncCM   *The Illustrated Encyclopedia of Country Music.* By Fred Deller, Roy Thompson, and Douglas B. Green. New York: Harmony Books, 1977.

IlEncJ   *The Illustrated Encyclopedia of Jazz.* By Brian Case and Stan Britt. New York: Harmony Books, 1978.

IlEncMy   *An Illustrated Encyclopaedia of Mysticism and the Mystery Religions.* By John Ferguson. London: Thames & Hudson, 1976.

IlEncRk   *The Illustrated Encyclopedia of Rock.* Revised edition. Compiled by Nick Logan and Bob Woffinden. New York: Harmony Books, 1977.

IlrAm   *The Illustrator in America, 1900-1960's.* Compiled and edited by Walt Reed. New York: Reinhold Publishing Corp., 1966.

   IlrAm A   "The Decade: 1900-1910" begins on page 13.
   IlrAm B   "The Decade: 1910-1920" begins on page 43.
   IlrAm C   "The Decade: 1920-1930" begins on page 77.
   IlrAm D   "The Decade: 1930-1940" begins on page 113.
   IlrAm E   "The Decade: 1940-1950" begins on page 167.
   IlrAm F   "The Decade: 1950-1960" begins on page 211.
   IlrAm G   "The Decade: 1960's" begins on page 239.

IlsBYP   *Illustrators of Books for Young People.* Second edition. By Martha E. Ward and Dorothy A. Marquardt. Metuchen, New Jersey: Scarecrow Press, 1975.

IlsCB   *Illustrators of Children's Books.* Boston: Horn Book, 1947, 1958, 1968, 1978.

   IlsCB 1744   *1744-1945.* Compiled by Bertha E. Mahony, Louise Payson Latimer, and Beulah Folmsbee, 1947.

   Biographies begin on page 267.

   IlsCB 1946   *1946-1956.* Compiled by Ruth Hill Viguers, Marcia Dalphin, and Bertha Mahony Miller, 1958.

   Biographies begin on page 62.

   IlsCB 1957   *1957-1966.* Compiled by Lee Kingman, Joanna Foster, and Ruth Giles Lontoft, 1968.

   Biographies begin on page 70.

   IlsCB 1967   *1967-1976.* Compiled by Lee Kingman, Grace Allen Hogarth, and Harriet Quimby, 1978.

   Biographies begin on page 93.

InB&W 80   *In Black and White.* A guide to magazine articles, newspaper articles, and books concerning more than 15,000 Black individuals and groups. Third edition. Two volumes. Edited by Mary Mace Spradling. Detroit: Gale Research Co., 1980.

InSci   *Index to Scientists of the World from Ancient to Modern Times: Biographies and Portraits.* By Norma Olin Ireland. Boston: F.W. Faxon Co., 1962.

InWom   *Index to Women of the World from Ancient to Modern Times: Biographies and Portraits.* By Norma Olin Ireland. Westwood, Massachusetts: F.W. Faxon Co., 1970.

IndAu 1816   *Indiana Authors and Their Books, 1816-1916.* Biographical sketches of authors who published during the first century of Indiana statehood with lists of their books. Compiled by R.E. Banta. Crawfordsville, Indiana: Wabash College, 1949.

IndAu 1917   *Indiana Authors and Their Books, 1917-1966.* A continuation of *Indiana Authors and Their Books, 1816-1916,* and containing additional names from the earlier period. Compiled by Donald E. Thompson. Crawfordsville, Indiana: Wabash College, 1974.

IntAu&W 76   *The International Authors and Writers Who's Who.* Seventh edition. Edited by Ernest Kay. Cambridge, England: Melrose Press, 1976.

  IntAu&W 76   Biographical Section
  IntAu&W 76A   Addendum begins on page 641.
  IntAu&W 76X   The "Pseudonyms of Included Authors" section begins on page 645.

IntAu&W   *The International Authors and Writers Who's Who.* Edited by Adrian Gaster. Cambridge, England: International Biographical Centre, 1977, 1982. 1982 edition is combined with *International Who's Who in Poetry* (see below).

  IntAu&W 77   Eighth edition, 1977, Biographical Section
  IntAu&W 77X   The "Pseudonyms of Included Authors" section begins on page 1131.
  IntAu&W 82   Ninth edition, 1982, Biographical Section
  IntAu&W 82X   The "Pseudonyms of Included Authors" section begins on page 719.

IntDcWB   *The International Dictionary of Women's Biography.* Compiled and edited by Jennifer S. Uglow. New York: Continuum Publishing Co., 1982.

IntEnSS 79	*International Encyclopedia of the Social Sciences.* Volume 18: Biographical Supplement. Edited by David L. Sills. New York: Macmillan Publishing Co., Free Press, 1979.
IntMed 80	*International Medical Who's Who: A Biographical Guide in Medical Research.* First edition. Two volumes. Harlow, United Kingdom: Longman Group, Francis Hodgson, 1980. Distributed by Gale Research Co., Detroit, Michigan.
IntMPA	*International Motion Picture Almanac.* Edited by Richard Gertner. New York: Quigley Publishing Co., 1975, 1976, 1977, 1978, 1979, 1981, 1982, 1984, 1986.
IntMPA 75	1975 edition
IntMPA 76	1976 edition
IntMPA 77	1977 edition
IntMPA 78	1978 edition
IntMPA 79	1979 edition
IntMPA 81	1981 edition
IntMPA 82	1982 edition
IntMPA 84	1984 edition
IntMPA 86	1986 edition

Biographies are found in the "Who's Who in Motion Pictures and Television" section in each volume. The listings are identical to those found in the *International Television Almanac.*

IntWW	*The International Who's Who.* London: Europa Publications, 1974, 1975, 1976, 1977, 1978, 1979, 1980, 1981, 1982, 1983. Distributed by Gale Research Co., Detroit, Michigan.
IntWW 74	38th edition, 1974-1975
IntWW 75	39th edition, 1975-1976
IntWW 76	40th edition, 1976-1977
IntWW 77	41st edition, 1977-1978
IntWW 78	42nd edition, 1978-1979
IntWW 79	43rd edition, 1979-1980
IntWW 80	44th edition, 1980-1981
IntWW 81	45th edition, 1981-1982
IntWW 82	46th edition, 1982-1983
IntWW 83	47th edition, 1983-1984

The Obituary section, indicated by the code *N*, is located at the front of each volume.

IntWWP	*International Who's Who in Poetry.* Edited by Ernest Kay. Cambridge, England: International Biographical Centre, 1977, 1982. 1982 edition is combined with *The International Authors and Writers Who's Who* (see above).
IntWWP 77	Fifth edition, 1977, Biographical Section
IntWWP 77A	Addendum begins on page 470.

IntWWP 77X   The "Pseudonyms and Pen Names of Included Authors" section begins on page 702.

IntWWP 82   Sixth edition, 1982. Biographies begin on page 759.

IntWWP 82X   The "Pseudonyms of Included Poets" section begins on page 1035.

IntYB   *The International Year Book and Statesmen's Who's Who.* West Sussex, England: Kelly's Directories, 1978, 1979, 1980, 1981. Distributed by Gale Research Co., Detroit, Michigan.

IntYB 78   1978 edition
IntYB 79   1979 edition
IntYB 80   1980 edition
IntYB 81   1981 edition

Biographies are found in Part 3 of each volume.

IntYB 82   *The International Yearbook and Statesmen's Who's Who.* West Sussex, England: Thomas Skinner Directories, 1982. Distributed by Gale Research Co., Detroit, Michigan.

Biographies are found in Part 3.

The "Late Information" section, indicated by the code *A*, begins on page 749 of Part 3.

JoeFr   *Joe Franklin's Encyclopedia of Comedians.* Secaucas, New Jersey: Citadel Press, 1979.

JohnWSW   *John Willis' Screen World.* 1981, Volume 32. New York: Crown Publishers, Inc., 1981.

JohnWTW 38   *John Willis' Theatre World.* 1981-82, Volume 38. New York: Crown Publishers, Inc., 1983.

JBA 34   *The Junior Book of Authors.* An introduction to the lives of writers and illustrators for younger readers from Lewis Carroll and Louisa Alcott to the present day. First edition. Edited by Stanley J. Kunitz and Howard Haycraft. New York: H.W. Wilson Co., 1934.

JBA 51   *The Junior Book of Authors.* Second edition, revised. Edited by Stanley J. Kunitz and Howard Haycraft. New York: H.W. Wilson Co., 1951.

Law&B   *Law and Business Directory of Corporate Counsel.* New York: Harcourt Brace Jovanovich, Law & Business, 1980, 1984.

Law&B 80   1980-81 edition
Law&B 84   1984-85 edition

Entries are by corporation. Use the "Individual Name Index" to locate listings.

LEduc 74   *Leaders in Education.* Fifth edition. Edited by Jaques Cattell Press. New York: R.R. Bowker Co., 1974.

LElec   *Leaders in Electronics.* New York: McGraw-Hill Book Co., 1979.

Title page reads *McGraw-Hill's Leaders in Electronics.*

LEPo   *Leading Canadian Poets.* Edited by N.P. Percival. Toronto: Ryerson, 1948.

LesBEnT   *Les Brown's Encyclopedia of Television.* By Les Brown. New York: New York Zoetrope, 1982. Previous edition published as *The New York Times Encyclopedia of Television* (see below).

LibW   *Liberty's Women.* Edited by Robert McHenry. Springfield, Massachusetts: G. & C. Merriam Co., 1980.

LilREn 78   *Lillian Roxon's Rock Encyclopedia.* Compiled by Ed Naha. New York: Grosset and Dunlap, 1978.

LinLib L   *The Lincoln Library of Language Arts.* Third edition. Two volumes. Columbus, Ohio: Frontier Press Co., 1978.

Biographies begin on page 345 of Volume 1 and are continued in Volume 2. The "Pen Names" section, indicated by the code *LP*, begins on page 331.

LinLib S   *The Lincoln Library of Social Studies.* Eighth edition. Three volumes. Columbus, Ohio: Frontier Press Co., 1978.

Biographies begin on page 865 of Volume 3.

LivgBAA   *Living Black American Authors: A Biographical Directory.* By Ann Allen Shockley and Sue P. Chandler. New York: R.R. Bowker Co., 1973.

LivgFWS   *The Living Female Writers of the South.* Edited by Mary T. Tardy. Philadelphia: Claxton, Remsen & Haffelfinger, 1872. Reprint. Detroit: Gale Research Co., 1978.

LongCEL   *Longman Companion to English Literature.* Second edition. By Christopher Gillie. London: Longman Group, 1977. Also published as *A Companion to British Literature.* Detroit: Grand River Books, 1980.

LongCTC *Longman Companion to Twentieth Century Literature.* By A.C. Ward. London: Longman Group, 1970.

LookW *Look for the Woman.* A narrative encyclopedia of female poisoners, kidnappers, thieves, extortionists, terrorists, swindlers, and spies from Elizabethan times to the present. By Jay Robert Nash. New York: M. Evans & Co., 1981.

LuthC 75 *Lutheran Cyclopedia.* Revised edition. Edited by Erwin L. Lueker. St. Louis: Concordia Publishing House, 1975.

MGM *The MGM Stock Company: The Golden Era.* By James Robert Parish and Ronald L. Bowers. New Rochelle, New York: Arlington House, 1973.

   The "Capsule Biographies of MGM Executives" section, indicated by the code *A*, begins on page 796.

MacBEP *Macmillan Biographical Encyclopedia of Photographic Artists & Innovators.* By Turner Browne and Elaine Partnow. New York: Macmillan Publishing Co.; London: Collier Macmillan Publishers, 1983.

MacDCB 78 *The Macmillan Dictionary of Canadian Biography.* Edited by W. Stewart Wallace. Fourth edition, revised, enlarged, and updated by W.A. McKay. Toronto: Macmillan of Canada, 1978.

MacDWB *The Macmillan Dictionary of Women's Biography.* Edited by Jennifer S. Uglow. New York: Macmillan, 1982.

MacEA *Macmillan Encyclopedia of Architects.* Four volumes. Edited by Adolf K. Placzek. New York: Macmillan Publishing Co., Free Press; London: Collier Macmillan Publishers, 1982.

   Use the "Index of Names," which begins on page 533 of Volume 4, to locate biographies.

MakMC *Makers of Modern Culture.* Edited by Justin Wintle. New York: Facts on File, 1981.

MarqDCG 84 *Marquis Who's Who Directory of Computer Graphics.* First edition. Chicago: Marquis Who's Who, 1984.

McGDA *McGraw-Hill Dictionary of Art.* Five volumes. Edited by Bernard S. Myers. New York: McGraw-Hill Book Co., 1969.

McGEWB   *The McGraw-Hill Encyclopedia of World Biography.* An international reference work in 12 volumes including an index. New York: McGraw-Hill Book Co., 1973.

McGEWD   *McGraw-Hill Encyclopedia of World Drama.* An international reference work. New York: McGraw-Hill Book., 1972, 1984.

     McGEWD   First edition, four volumes, 1972.
     McGEWD 84   Second edition, five volumes, 1984.

McGMS 80   *McGraw-Hill Modern Scientists and Engineers.* Three volumes. New York: McGraw-Hill Book Co., 1980.

MedHR   *Medal of Honor Recipients, 1863-1978.* Prepared by the Committee on Veterans' Affairs, United States Senate. 96th Congress, 1st Session, Senate Committee Print No. 3. Washington, D.C.: United States Government Printing Office, 1979.

     Use the "Medal of Honor Alphabetical Index," which begins on page 1023, to locate biographies.

MnBBF   *The Men Behind Boys' Fiction.* By W.O.G. Lofts and D.J. Adley. London: Howard Baker Publishers, 1970.

MidE   *The Middle East and North Africa.* London: Europa Publications, 1978, 1979, 1980, 1981, 1982. Distributed by Gale Research Co., Detroit, Michigan.

     MidE 78   25th edition, 1978-1979
     MidE 79   26th edition, 1979-1980
     MidE 80   27th edition, 1980-1981
     MidE 81   28th edition, 1981-1982
     MidE 82   29th edition, 1982-1983

     Biographies are found in the "Who's Who in the Middle East and North Africa" section at the back of each volume.

MinnWr   *Minnesota Writers: A Collection of Autobiographical Stories by Minnesota Prose Writers.* Edited and annotated by Carmen Nelson Richards. Minneapolis: T.S. Denison & Co., 1961.

     Use the Table of Contents to locate biographies.

ModAL   *Modern American Literature.* Five volumes. A Library of Literary Criticism. New York: Frederick Ungar Publishing Co., 1969, 1976, 1985.

     ModAL   Fourth edition, volumes I-III. Compiled and edited by Dorothy Nyren Curley, Maurice Kramer, and Elaine Fialka Kramer, 1969.

ModAL S1	Supplement to the fourth edition, Volume IV. Compiled and edited by Dorothy Nyren, Maurice Kramer, and Elaine Fialka Kramer, 1976.
ModAL S2	Second Supplement to the fourth edition, Volume V. Compiled and edited by Paul Schlueter and June Schlueter, 1985.
ModBlW	*Modern Black Writers.* Compiled and edited by Michael Popkin. A Library of Literary Criticism. New York: Frederick Ungar Publishing Co., 1978.
ModBrL	*Modern British Literature.* Five volumes. A Library of Literary Criticism. New York: Frederick Ungar Publishing Co., 1966, 1975, 1985.
ModBrL	Volumes I-III, compiled and edited by Ruth Z. Temple and Martin Tucker, 1966.
ModBrL S1	Volume IV, Supplement, compiled and edited by Martin Tucker and Rita Stein, 1975.
ModBrL S2	Volume V, Second Supplement, compiled and edited by Denis Lane and Rita Stein, 1985.
ModCmwL	*Modern Commonwealth Literature.* Compiled and edited by John H. Ferres and Martin Tucker. A Library of Literary Criticism. New York: Frederick Ungar Publishing Co., 1977.
ModFrL	*Modern French Literature.* Two volumes. Compiled and edited by Debra Popkin and Michael Popkin. A Library of Literary Criticism. New York: Frederick Ungar Publishing Co., 1977.
ModGL	*Modern German Literature.* Two volumes. Compiled and edited by Agnes Korner Domandi. A Library of Literary Criticism. New York: Frederick Ungar Publishing Co., 1972.
ModLAL	*Modern Latin American Literature.* Two volumes. Compiled and edited by David William Foster and Virginia Ramos Foster. A Library of Literary Criticism. New York: Frederick Ungar Publishing Co., 1975.
ModRL	*Modern Romance Literatures.* Compiled and edited by Dorothy Nyren Curley and Arthur Curley. A Library of Literary Criticism. New York: Frederick Ungar Publishing Co., 1967.
ModSL	*Modern Slavic Literatures.* Two volumes. A Library of Literary Criticism. New York: Frederick Ungar Publishing Co., 1972, 1976.
ModSL 1	Volume I: Russian Literature, compiled and edited by Vasa D. Mihailovich, 1972.

ModSL 2 Volume II: Bulgarian, Czechoslovak, Polish, Ukrainian and Yugoslav Literatures, compiled and edited by Vasa D. Mihailovich, et al., 1976.

    Use the alphabetic listing of authors at the front of each volume to locate biographies.

ModWD *Modern World Drama: An Encyclopedia.* By Myron Matlaw. New York: E.P. Dutton & Co., 1972.

MorBMP *More Books by More People: Interviews with Sixty-Five Authors of Books for Children.* By Lee Bennett Hopkins. New York: Citation Press, 1974.

MorJA *More Junior Authors.* Edited by Muriel Fuller. New York: H.W. Wilson Co., 1963.

MotPP *Motion Picture Performers: A Bibliography of Magazine and Periodical Articles, 1900-1969.* Compiled by Mel Schuster. Metuchen, New Jersey: Scarecrow Press, 1971.

MouLC *Moulton's Library of Literary Criticism of English and American Authors through the Beginning of the Twentieth Century.* Four volumes. Abridged, revised, and with additions by Martin Tucker. New York: Frederick Ungar Publishing Co., 1966.

 MouLC 1 Volume I: The Beginnings to the Seventeenth Century
 MouLC 2 Volume II: Neo-Classicism to the Romantic Period
 MouLC 3 Volume III: The Romantic Period to the Victorian Age
 MouLC 4 Volume IV: The Mid-Nineteenth Century to Edwardianism

    Use the alphabetic listings at the front of each volume to locate biographies.

MovMk *The Movie Makers.* By Sol Chaneles and Albert Wolsky. Secaucus, New Jersey: Derbibooks, 1974.

    The "Directors" section begins on page 506.

MugS *Mug Shots: Who's Who in the New Earth.* By Jay Acton, Alan Le Mond, and Parker Hodges. New York: World Publishing Co., 1972.

MusMk *The Music Makers.* Edited by Clive Unger-Hamilton. New York: Harry N. Abrams, Inc., 1978.

MusSN *Musicians since 1900: Performers in Concert and Opera.* Compiled and edited by David Ewen. New York: H.W. Wilson Co., 1978.

NamesHP   *Names in the History of Psychology: A Biographical Sourcebook.* By
                 Leonard Zusne. Washington, D.C.: Hemisphere Publishing Corp.,
                 1975. Distributed by John Wiley & Sons, Halstead Press, New
                 York, New York. Continued by *Biographical Dictionary of
                 Psychology* (see above).

                 Use the "Alphabetic List of Names," which begins on page ix, to
                 locate biographies.

NatCAB   *The National Cyclopaedia of American Biography.* 61 volumes. New
                 York and Clifton, New Jersey: James T. White & Co., 1892-1982.
                 Reprint. Volumes 1-50. Ann Arbor: University Microfilms, 1967-
                 1971.

                 Number after the source code indicates volume number. Use the
                 Index in each volume to locate biographies.

NatPD   *National Playwrights Directory.* Edited by Phyllis Johnson Kaye.
                 Waterford, Connecticut: The O'Neill Theater Center, 1977, 1981.
                 Distributed by Gale Research Co., Detroit, Michigan.

   NatPD   First edition, 1977
   NatPD 81   Second edition, 1981

NegAl 76   *The Negro Almanac: A Reference Work on the Afro American.* Third
                 edition. Edited by Harry A. Ploski and Warren Marr, II. New York:
                 Bellwether Co., 1976.

                 Use the Index to locate biographies.

NewC   *The New Century Handbook of English Literature.* Revised edition.
                 Edited by Clarence L. Barnhart with the assistance of William D.
                 Halsey. New York: Appleton-Century-Crofts, 1967.

NewCol 75   *The New Columbia Encyclopedia.* Edited by William H. Harris and
                 Judith S. Levey. New York and London: Columbia University
                 Press, 1975.

NewCBMT   *New Complete Book of the American Musical Theater.* By David
                 Ewen. New York: Holt, Rinehart & Winston, 1970.

                 Biographies are found in the "Librettists, Lyricists and Composers"
                 section which begins on page 607.

NewEOp 71   *The New Encyclopedia of the Opera.* By David Ewen. New York: Hill
                 & Wang, 1971.

NewGrD 80   *The New Grove Dictionary of Music and Musicians.* Edited by Stanley
                 Sadie. 20 volumes. London: Macmillan Publishers, Ltd., 1980.

Distributed by Grove's Dictionaries of Music, Inc., Washington, D.C.

NewWmR   *New Women in Rock.* Edited by Liz Thompson, New York: Delilah Books, 1982.

New YHSD   *The New-York Historical Society's Dictionary of Artists in America, 1564-1860.* By George C. Groce and David H. Wallace. New Haven, Connecticut: Yale University Press, 1957.

New YTBE   *The New York Times Biographical Edition.* A compilation of current biographical information of general interest. New York: Arno Press, 1970-1973. Continued by *The New York Times Biographical Service* (see below).

    New YTBE 70   Volume 1, Numbers 1-12, 1970
    New YTBE 71   Volume 2, Numbers 1-12, 1971
    New YTBE 72   Volume 3, Numbers 1-12, 1972
    New YTBE 73   Volume 4, Numbers 1-12, 1973

    Use the "Annual Index" to locate biographies.

New YTBS   *The New York Times Biographical Service.* A compilation of current biographical information of general interest. New York: Arno Press, 1974-1981. A continuation of *The New York Times Biographical Edition* (see above).

    New YTBS 74   Volume 5, Numbers 1-12, 1974
    New YTBS 75   Volume 6, Numbers 1-12, 1975
    New YTBS 76   Volume 7, Numbers 1-12, 1976
    New YTBS 77   Volume 8, Numbers 1-12, 1977
    New YTBS 78   Volume 9, Numbers 1-12, 1978
    New YTBS 79   Volume 10, Numbers 1-12, 1979
    New YTBS 80   Volume 11, Numbers 1-12, 1980
    New YTBS 81   Volume 12, Numbers 1-12, 1981

    Use the "Annual Index" to locate biographies.

New YTBS   *The New York Times Biographical Service.* A compilation of current biographical information of general interest. Sanford, North Carolina: Microfilming Corp. of America, 1982-1983.

    New YTBS 82   Volume 13, Numbers 1-12, 1982
    New YTBS 83   Volume 14, Numbers 1-12, 1983

    Use the "Annual Index" to locate biographies.

New YTBS   *The New York Times Biographical Service.* A compilation of current biographical information of general interest. Ann Arbor, Michigan: University Microfilms International, 1984-1986.

New YTBS 84	Volume 15, Numbers 1-12, 1984-1985
New YTBS 85	Volume 16, Numbers 1-12, 1985-1986
New YTBS 86	Volume 17, Numbers 1-6, 1986

Use the "Annual Index" to locate biographies.

New YTET   *The New York Times Encyclopedia of Television.* By Les Brown. New York: New York Times Book Co., 1977. Expanded edition published as *Les Brown's Encyclopedia of Television* (see above).

NewbC   *Newbery and Caldecott Medal Books.* With acceptance papers, biographies and related material chiefly from the *Horn Book Magazine.* Edited by Lee Kingman. Boston: Horn Book, 1965, 1975.

| *NewbC 1956* | *1956-1965*, 1965 |
| *NewbC 1966* | *1966-1975*, 1975 |

Newb 1922   *Newbery Medal Books, 1922-1955.* With their authors' acceptance papers and related material chiefly from the *Horn Book Magazine.* Horn Book Papers, Volume 1. Edited by Bertha Mahony Miller and Elinor Whitney Field. Boston: Horn Book, 1955.

NotAW   *Notable American Women, 1607-1950: A Biographical Dictionary.* Three volumes. Edited by Edward T. James. Cambridge, Massachusetts: Harvard University Press, Belknap Press, 1971.

NotAW MOD   *Notable American Women: The Modern Period.* A biographical dictionary. Edited by Barbara Sicherman and Carol Hurd Green. Cambridge, Massachusetts: Harvard University Press, Belknap Press, 1980.

NotNAT   *Notable Names in the American Theatre.* Clifton, New Jersey: James T. White & Co., 1976. First edition published as *The Biographical Encyclopaedia and Who's Who of the American Theatre* (see above).

NotNAT   The "Notable Names in the American Theatre" section begins on page 489.

NotNAT A   The "Biographical Bibliography" section begins on page 309.

NotNAT B   The "Necrology" section begins on page 343.

This book often alphabetizes by titles of address, e.g.: Dr., Mrs., and Sir.

Novels   *Novels and Novelists: A Guide to the World of Fiction.* Edited by Martin Seymour-Smith. New York: St. Martin's Press, 1980.

Biographies are located in the "Novelists: An Alphabetical Guide" section which begins on page 87.

ObitOF 79   *Obituaries on File.* Two volumes. Compiled by Felice Levy. New York: Facts on File, 1979.

ObitT   *Obituaries from the Times.* Compiled by Frank C. Roberts. Reading, England: Newspaper Archive Developments, 1975, 1978, 1979. Distributed by Meckler Books, Westport, Connecticut.

   ObitT 1951   *1951-1960,* 1979
   ObitT 1961   *1961-1970,* 1975
   ObitT 1971   *1971-1975,* 1978

ODwPR 79   *O'Dwyer's Directory of Public Relations Executives, 1979.* Edited by Jack O'Dwyer. New York: J.R. O'Dwyer Co., 1979.

OfEnT   United States Tennis Association. *Official Encyclopedia of Tennis.* Revised and updated. Edited by Bill Shannon. New York: Harper & Row, 1979.

OfNBA 81   *Official NBA Register.* Edited by Matt Winick. St. Louis: The Sporting News, 1981.

OfNBA 85   *Official NBA Register.* Edited by Mike Douchant and Alex Sachare. St. Louis: The Sporting News, 1985.

OhA&B   *Ohio Authors and Their Books: Biographical Data and Selective Bibliographies for Ohio Authors, Native and Resident, 1796-1950.* Edited by William Coyle. Cleveland and New York: World Publishing Co., 1962.

OxAmH   *The Oxford Companion to American History.* By Thomas H. Johnson. New York: Oxford University Press, 1966.

OxAmL   *The Oxford Companion to American Literature.* By James D. Hart. New York: Oxford University Press, 1965, 1983.

   OxAmL   Fourth edition, 1965
   OxAmL 83   Fifth edition, 1983

OxArt   *The Oxford Companion to Art.* Edited by Harold Osborne. Oxford: Oxford University Press, Clarendon Press, 1970.

OxCan   *The Oxford Companion to Canadian History and Literature.* Toronto: Oxford University Press, 1967, 1973.

   OxCan   Original volume, by Norah Story, 1967, reprinted with corrections, 1968.
   OxCan SUP   Supplement, edited by William Toye, 1973.

OxChess   *The Oxford Companion to Chess.* By David Hooper and Kenneth Whyld. Oxford: Oxford University Press, 1984.

OxDecA   *The Oxford Companion to the Decorative Arts.* Edited by Harold Osborne. Oxford: Oxford University Press, Clarendon Press, 1975.

OxEng   *The Oxford Companion to English Literature.* Compiled and edited by Sir Paul Harvey. Fourth edition, revised by Dorothy Eagle. Oxford: Oxford University Press, 1967.

OxEng 85   *The Oxford Companion to English Literature.* Fifth edition. Edited by Margaret Drabble. Oxford: Oxford University Press, 1985.

OxFilm   *The Oxford Companion to Film.* Edited by Liz-Anne Bawden. New York: Oxford University Press, 1976.

OxFr   *The Oxford Companion to French Literature.* Compiled and edited by Sir Paul Harvey and J.E. Heseltine. Oxford: Oxford University Press, Clarendon Press, 1959. Reprinted with corrections, 1966.

OxGer   *The Oxford Companion to German Literature.* By Henry Garland and Mary Garland. Oxford: Oxford University Press, Clarendon Press, 1976.

OxLaw   *The Oxford Companion to Law.* By David M. Walker. Oxford: Oxford University Press, Clarendon Press, 1980.

OxMus   *The Oxford Companion to Music.* By Percy A. Scholes. 10th edition (corrected). Edited by John Owen Ward. London: Oxford University Press, 1974.

OxShips   *The Oxford Companion to Ships and the Sea.* Edited by Peter Kemp. London: Oxford University Press, 1976.

OxSpan   *The Oxford Companion to Spanish Literature.* Edited by Philip Ward. Oxford: Oxford University Press, Clarendon Press, 1978.

OxThe   *The Oxford Companion to the Theatre.* Edited by Phyllis Hartnoll. London: Oxford University Press, 1967, 1983.

   OxThe   Third edition, 1967
   OxThe 83   Fourth edition, 1983

OxTwCA   *The Oxford Companion to Twentieth-Century Art.* Edited by Harold Osborne. Oxford: Oxford University Press, 1981.

PenC	*The Penguin Companion to World Literature.* New York: McGraw-Hill Book Co., 1969, 1971.
PenC AM	*The Penguin Companion to American Literature.* Edited by Malcolm Bradbury, Eric Mottram, and Jean Franco, 1971.
	Biographies are found in the "U.S.A." and "Latin America" sections.
PenC CL	*The Penguin Companion to Classical, Oriental, and African Literature.* Edited by D.M. Lang and D.R. Dudley, 1969.
	Biographies are found in the "Classical," "Byzantine," "Oriental," and "African" sections.
PenC ENG	*The Penguin Companion to English Literature.* Edited by David Daiches, 1971.
PenC EUR	*The Penguin Companion to European Literature.* Edited by Anthony Thorlby, 1969.
PhDcTCA 77	*Phaidon Dictionary of Twentieth-Century Art.* Second edition. Oxford: Phaidon Press; New York: E.P. Dutton, 1977.
PiP	*The Pied Pipers: Interviews with the Influential Creators of Children's Literature.* By Justin Wintle and Emma Fisher. New York: Paddington Press, 1974.
	Use the Table of Contents to locate biographies.
PlP&P	*Plays, Players, and Playwrights: An Illustrated History of the Theatre.* By Marion Geisinger. Updated by Peggy Marks. New York: Hart Publishing Co., 1975.
	Use the Index, which begins on page 575, to locate biographies in the main section of the book. A Supplemental Index to the last chapter, "The Theatre of the Seventies," begins on page 797 and is indicated by the code *A*.
PoChrch	*The Poets of the Church: A Series of Biographical Sketches of Hymn-Writers with Notes on Their Hymns.* By Edwin F. Hatfield. New York: Anson D.F. Randolph & Co., 1884. Reprint. Detroit: Gale Research Co., 1978.
PoIre	*The Poets of Ireland: A Biographical and Bibliographical Dictionary of Irish Writers of English Verse.* By D.J. O'Donoghue. Dublin: Hodges Figgis & Co.; London: Henry Frowde, Oxford University Press, 1912. Reprint. Detroit: Gale Research Co., 1968.
	"The Poets of Ireland" begin on page 5. The Appendices begin on page 495.

PoLE   *The Poets Laureate of England.* Being a history of the office of poet laureate, biographical notices of its holders, and a collection of the satires, epigrams, and lampoons directed against them. By Walter Hamilton. London: Elliot Stock, 1879. Reprint. Detroit: Gale Research Co., 1968.

Use the Index to locate biographies.

Po&Wr 77   *The Poets & Writers 1977 Supplement.* A complete update to *A Directory of American Poets* (1975) and *A Directory of American Fiction Writers* (1976). New York: Poets & Writers, 1977.

Use the Index to locate listings.

PolProf   *Political Profiles.* New York: Facts on File, 1976-1979.
  PolProf E   *The Eisenhower Years.* Edited by Eleanora W. Schoenebaum, 1977.
  PolProf J   *The Johnson Years.* Edited by Nelson Lichtenstein, 1976.
  PolProf K   *The Kennedy Years.* Edited by Nelson Lichtenstein, 1976.
  PolProf NF   *The Nixon/Ford Years.* Edited by Eleanora W. Schoenebaum, 1979.
  PolProf T   *The Truman Years.* Edited by Eleanora W. Schoenebaum, 1978.

PrintW   *The Printworld Directory of Contemporary Prints & Prices.* Edited by Selma Smith. Bala Cynwyd, Pennsylvania: Printworld, 1983, 1985. Distributed by Gale Research Co., Detroit, Michigan.
  PrintW 83   *1983/84,* second edition, 1983
  PrintW 85   *1985/86,* third edition, 1985

Not in strict alphabetical order.

PseudAu   *Pseudonyms of Authors; Including Anonyms and Initialisms.* By John Edward Haynes. New York: John Edward Haynes, 1882. Reprint. Detroit: Gale Research Co., 1969.

The Addenda, indicated by the code *A*, begins on page 104. Pseudonyms are given exactly as written by the author and are filed under the first letter of the pseudonym including the articles "a," "an," and "the."

PseudN 82   *Pseudonyms and Nicknames Dictionary.* Second edition. Edited by Jennifer Mossman. Detroit: Gale Research Co., 1982.

PueRA   *Puerto Rican Authors: A Biobibliographic Handbook.* By Marnesba D. Hill and Harold B. Schleifer. Translation of entries into Spanish by Daniel Maratos. Metuchen, New Jersey: Scarecrow Press, 1974.

RAdv 1   *The Reader's Adviser: A Layman's Guide to Literature.* 12th edition. Volume 1: *The Best in American and British Fiction, Poetry, Essays, Literary Biography, Bibliography, and Reference.* Edited by Sarah L. Prakken. New York: R.R. Bowker Co., 1974.

Use the "Author Index," which begins on page 741, to locate biographies and bibliographies.

RComWL   *The Reader's Companion to World Literature.* Second edition. Revised and updated by Lillian Herlands Hornstein, Leon Edel, and Horst Frenz. New York: New American Library, 1973.

REn   *The Reader's Encyclopedia.* Second edition. By William Rose Benet. New York: Thomas Y. Crowell Co., 1965.

REnAL   *The Reader's Encyclopedia of American Literature.* By Max J. Herzberg. New York: Thomas Y. Crowell Co., 1962.

REnAW   *The Reader's Encyclopedia of the American West.* Edited by Howard R. Lamar. New York: Thomas Y. Crowell Co., 1977.

REnWD   *The Reader's Encyclopedia of World Drama.* Edited by John Gassner and Edward Quinn. New York: Thomas Y. Crowell Co., 1969.

RGAfL   *A Reader's Guide to African Literature.* Compiled and edited by Hans M. Zell and Helene Silver. New York: Africana Publishing Corp., 1971.

Biographies begin on page 113.

RkOn   *Rock On: The Illustrated Encyclopedia of Rock n' Roll.* By Norm N. Nite. New York: Thomas Y. Crowell Co., 1974, 1978.

   RkOn 74   Volume 1: *The Solid Gold Years,* 1974

   RkOn 78   Volume 2: *The Modern Years:*
1964-Present, 1978

   RkOn 78A   Volume 2: Appendix begins on page 543.

RkOn   *Rock On: The Illustrated Encyclopedia of Rock n' Roll.* By Norm N. Nite. New York: Harper & Row, Publishers, 1982, 1984, 1985.

   RkOn 82   Volume 1: *The Solid Gold Years,* revised 1982

   RkOn 84   Volume 2: *The Years of Change, 1964-1978,*
revised 1984

   RkOn 85   Volume 3: *The Video Revolution,*
1978-present, 1985

RkOneH   *Rock 100.* By J. Quirin and B. Cohen. Covington, Louisiana: Chartmasters, 1976.

RkWW 82   *Rock Who's Who.* By Brock Helander. New York: Macmillan, Schirmer Books, 1982.

RolSEnR 83   *The Rolling Stone Encyclopedia of Rock & Roll.* Edited by Jon Pareles and Patricia Romanowski. New York: Rolling Stone Press/Summit Books, 1983.

ScF&FL   *Science Fiction and Fantasy Literature.* A checklist, 1700-1974, with *Contemporary Science Fiction Authors II.* By R. Reginald. Detroit: Gale Research Co., 1979.

   ScF&FL 1   Volume 1: "Author Index" begins on page 3.
   ScF&FL 1A   Volume 1: Addendum begins on page 581.
   ScF&FL 2   Volume 2: *Contemporary Science Fiction Authors II.*

SelBAAf   *Selected Black American, African, and Caribbean Authors.* A bio-bibliography. Compiled by James A. Page and Jae Min Roh. Littleton, Colorado: Libraries Unlimited, 1985.

SelBAAu   *Selected Black American Authors.* An illustrated bio-bibliography. Compiled by James A. Page. Boston: G.K. Hall & Co., 1977.

SenS   *A Sense of Story: Essays on Contemporary Writers for Children.* By John Rowe Townsend. London: Longman Group, 1971.

SixAP   *Sixty American Poets, 1896-1944.* Revised edition. Selected, with preface and critical notes by Allen Tate. Washington, D.C.: Library of Congress, 1954. Reprint. Detroit: Gale Research Co., 1969.

SmATA   *Something about the Author.* Facts and pictures about authors and illustrators of books for young people. Edited by Anne Commire. Detroit: Gale Research Co., 1971-1986.

   SmATA 1   Volume 1, 1971
   SmATA 2   Volume 2, 1971
   SmATA 3   Volume 3, 1972
   SmATA 4   Volume 4, 1973
   SmATA 5   Volume 5, 1973
   SmATA 6   Volume 6, 1974
   SmATA 7   Volume 7, 1975
   SmATA 8   Volume 8, 1976
   SmATA 9   Volume 9, 1976
   SmATA 10   Volume 10, 1976
   SmATA 11   Volume 11, 1977
   SmATA 12   Volume 12, 1977
   SmATA 13   Volume 13, 1978
   SmATA 14   Volume 14, 1978
   SmATA 15   Volume 15, 1979

SmATA 16	Volume 16, 1979
SmATA 17	Volume 17, 1979
SmATA 18	Volume 18, 1980
SmATA 19	Volume 19, 1980
SmATA 20	Volume 20, 1980
SmATA 21	Volume 21, 1980
SmATA 22	Volume 22, 1981
SmATA 23	Volume 23, 1981
SmATA 24	Volume 24, 1981
SmATA 25	Volume 25, 1981
SmATA 26	Volume 26, 1982
SmATA 27	Volume 27, 1982
SmATA 28	Volume 28, 1982
SmATA 29	Volume 29, 1982
SmATA 30	Volume 30, 1983
SmATA 31	Volume 31, 1983
SmATA 32	Volume 32, 1983
SmATA 33	Volume 33, 1983
SmATA 34	Volume 34, 1984
SmATA 35	Volume 35, 1984
SmATA 36	Volume 36, 1984
SmATA 37	Volume 37, 1985
SmATA 38	Volume 38, 1985
SmATA 39	Volume 39, 1985
SmATA 40	Volume 40, 1985
SmATA 41	Volume 41, 1985
SmATA 42	Volume 42, 1986
SmATA 43	Volume 43, 1986
SmATA 44	Volume 44, 1986
SmATA 45	Volume 45, 1986
SmATA X	This code refers to pseudonym entries which appear only as cross-references in the cumulative index in *Something about the Author.*

Obituary notices are indicated by the code *N*.

SpyCS   *Spy/Counterspy: Encyclopedia of Espionage.* By Vincent Buranelli and Nan Buranelli. New York: McGraw-Hill, 1982.

St&PR   *Standard and Poor's Register of Corporations, Directors, and Executives.* New York: Standard & Poor's Corp., 1975, 1984.

St&PR 75	1975 edition, Volume 2: *Directors and Executives.*
St&PR 84	1984 edition, Volume 2: *Directors and Executives.*
St&PR 84N	1984 edition. "Obituary Section" begins on page 901 of Volume 3.

Str&VC   *Story and Verse for Children.* Third edition. By Miriam Blanton Huber. New York: Macmillan Co., 1965.

Biographies begin on page 793.

TexWr   *Texas Writers of Today.* By Florence Elberta Barns. Dallas: Tardy Publishing Co., 1935. Reprint. Ann Arbor: Gryphon Books, 1971.

ThFT   *They Had Faces Then: Super Stars, Stars and Starlets of the 1930's.* By John Springer and Jack Hamilton. Secaucus, New Jersey: Citadel Press, 1974.

ThrBJA   *Third Book of Junior Authors.* Edited by Doris De Montreville and Donna Hill. New York: H.W. Wilson Co., 1972.

TwCA   *Twentieth Century Authors: A Biographical Dictionary of Modern Literature.* New York: H.W. Wilson Co., 1942, 1955.

     TwCA   Original volume, edited by Stanley J. Kunitz and Howard Haycraft, 1942.

     TwCA SUP   First Supplement, edited by Stanley J. Kunitz, 1955.

TwCBDA   *The Twentieth Century Biographical Dictionary of Notable Americans.* Brief biographies of authors, administrators, clergymen, commanders, editors, engineers, jurists, merchants, officials, philanthropists, scientists, statesmen, and others who are making American history. 10 volumes. Edited by Rossiter Johnson. Boston: The Biographical Society, 1904. Reprint. Detroit: Gale Research Co., 1968.

TwCCW   *Twentieth-Century Children's Writers.* Edited by D.L. Kirkpatrick. New York: St. Martin's Press, 1978, 1983.

     TwCCW 78   1978 edition
     TwCCW 83   1983 edition
     TwCCW 83A   Appendix begins on page 859.

TwCCr&M   *Twentieth-Century Crime and Mystery Writers.* Edited by John M. Reilly. New York: St. Martin's Press, 1980, 1985.

     TwCCr&M 80   First edition, 1980
     TwCCr&M 85   Second edition, 1985

TwCLC   *Twentieth-Century Literary Criticism.* Excerpts from criticism of the works of novelists, poets, playwrights, short story writers, and other creative writers who died between 1900 and 1960, from the first published critical appraisals to current evaluations. Detroit: Gale Research Co., 1978-1986.

     TwCLC 1   Volume 1, 1978
     TwCLC 2   Volume 2, 1979
     TwCLC 3   Volume 3, 1980
     TwCLC 4   Volume 4, 1981
     TwCLC 5   Volume 5, 1981
     TwCLC 6   Volume 6, 1982

TwCLC 7	Volume 7, 1982
TwCLC 8	Volume 8, 1982
TwCLC 9	Volume 9, 1983
TwCLC 10	Volume 10, 1983
TwCLC 11	Volume 11, 1983
TwCLC 12	Volume 12, 1984
TwCLC 13	Volume 13, 1984
TwCLC 14	Volume 14, 1984
TwCLC 15	Volume 15, 1985
TwCLC 16	Volume 16, 1985
TwCLC 17	Volume 17, 1985
TwCLC 18	Volume 18, 1985
TwCLC 19	Volume 19, 1986
TwCLC 20	Volume 20, 1986
TwCLC 21	Volume 21, 1986

TxCRGW   *Twentieth-Century Romance and Gothic Writers.* By James Vinson. Detroit: Gale Research Co., 1982.

TwCSFW   *Twentieth-Century Science Fiction Writers.* Edited by Curtis S. Smith. New York: St. Martin's Press, 1981.

TwCWW   Twentieth-Century Western Writers. *Edited by James Vinson. Detroit: Gale Research Co., 1982.*

TwCWr   *Twentieth Century Writing: A Reader's Guide to Contemporary Literature.* Edited by Kenneth Richardson. Levittown, New York: Transatlantic Arts, 1971.

TwYS   *Twenty Years of Silents, 1908-1928.* Compiled by John T. Weaver. Metuchen, New Jersey: Scarecrow Press, 1971.

    TwYS   "The Players" begin on page 27.
    TwYS A   "Directors" begin on page 407.
    TwYS B   "Producers" begin on page 502.

UFOEn   *The UFO Encyclopedia.* By Margaret Sachs. New York: G.P. Putnam's Sons, 1980.

USBiR 74   United States. Department of State. *The Biographic Register, July, 1974.* Washington, D.C.: United States Government Printing Office, 1974.

VarWW   *Variety Who's Who in Show Business.* Edited by Mike Kaplan. New York: Garland Publishing, 1983; revised edition, 1985.

    VarWW 83   1983 edition
    VarWW 85   1985 edition

Vers   *The Versatiles.* A study of supporting character actors and actresses in the American motion picture, 1930-1955. By Alfred E. Twomey and Arthur F. McClure. South Brunswick, New Jersey and New York: A.S. Barnes & Co.; London: Thomas Yoseloff, 1969.

     Vers A   "Biographical Section" begins on page 25.
     Vers B   "Non-Biographical Section" begins on page 249.

Ward   *1977 Ward's Who's Who among U.S. Motor Vehicle Manufacturers.* Detroit: Ward's Communications, 1977.

     Ward 77   "U.S. Big Four Biographical Section" begins on page 61.
     Ward 77A   "The Independent Truck, Off-Highway and Farm Vehicle Manufacturers" section begins on page 335.
     Ward 77B   "The Importers" section begins on page 355.
     Ward 77C   "United Auto Workers" section begins on page 371.
     Ward 77D   "Government Agencies" section begins on page 372.
     Ward 77E   "Auto Associations" section begins on page 376.
     Ward 77F   "The Automotive Press" section begins on page 387.
     Ward 77G   "Where Are They Now?" section begins on page 404.
     Ward 77H   "Automotive Suppliers' Section" begins on page 449.

WebAB   *Webster's American Biographies.* Edited by Charles Van Doren. Springfield, Massachusetts: G. & C. Merriam Co., 1974, 1979.

     WebAB   1974 edition
     WebAB 79   1979 edition

WebAMB   *Webster's American Military Biographies.* Springfield, Massachusetts: G. & C. Merriam Co., 1978.

WebBD 80   *Webster's Biographical Dictionary.* Springfield, Massachusetts: G. & C. Merriam Co., 1980.

WebE&AL   *Webster's New World Companion to English and American Literature.* Edited by Arthur Pollard. New York: World Publishing Co., 1973.

What   *Whatever Became of...?* By Richard Lamparski. New York: Crown Publishers, Inc., 1967-74, 1982. Also printed in a paperback edition by Ace Books.

     What 1   Volume One, 1967
     What 2   Second Series, 1968
     What 3   Third Series, 1970
     What 4   Fourth Series, 1973
     What 5   Fifth Series, 1974
     What 8   Eighth Series, 1982

WhDW *Who Did What.* The lives and achievements of the 5,000 men and women -- leaders of nations, saints and sinners, artists and scientists -- who shaped our world. Edited by Gerald Howat. New York: Crown Publishers, 1974.

WhDun *Whodunit?* Edited by H.R.F. Keating. New York: Van Nostrand Reinhold Co., 1982.

WhAm HS *Who Was Who in America, Historical Volume, 1607-1896.* A component volume of *Who's Who in American History.* Revised edition. Chicago: Marquis Who's Who, 1967.

   The Addendum, indicated by the code *A*, begins on page 677.

WhAm 1 *Who Was Who in America, Volume I, 1897-1942.* A component volume of *Who's Who in American History.* Chicago: A.N. Marquis Co., 1943.

   The Corrigenda, indicated by the code *C*, begins on page x.

WhAm 2 *Who Was Who in America, Volume II, 1943-1950.* A companion biographical reference work to *Who's Who in America.* Chicago: A.N. Marquis Co., 1963.

   WhAm 2A Addendum begins on page 12.
   WhAm 2C Corrigenda begins on page 5.

WhAm 3 *Who Was Who in America, Volume III, 1951-1960.* A component of *Who's Who in American History.* Chicago: Marquis Who's Who, 1966.

   The Addendum, indicated by the code *A*, begins on page 952.

WhAm 4 *Who Was Who in America with World Notables, Volume IV, 1961-1968.* A component volume of *Who's Who in American History.* Chicago: Marquis-Who's Who, 1968.

   The Addendum, indicated by the code *A*, begins on page 1049.

WhAm 5 *Who Was Who in America with World Notables, Volume V, 1969-1973.* Chicago: Marquis Who's Who, 1973.

WhAm 6 *Who Was Who in America with World Notables, Volume VI, 1974-1976.* Chicago: Marquis Who's Who, 1976.

WhAm 7 *Who Was Who in America with World Notables, Volume VII, 1977-1981.* Chicago: Marquis Who's Who, 1981.

WhAm 8 *Who Was Who in America with World Notables.* Volume VIII, 1982-1985. Chicago: Marquis Who's Who, 1985.

WhAmP   *Who Was Who in American Politics.* A biographical dictionary of over 4,000 men and women who contributed to the United States political scene from colonial days up to and including the immediate past. By Dan and Inez Morris. New York: Hawthorn Books, 1974.

WhE&EA   *Who Was Who among English and European Authors, 1931-1949.* Based on entries which first appeared in *The Author's and Writer's Who's Who and Reference Guide*, originally compiled by Edward Martell and L.G. Pine, and in *Who's Who among Living Authors of Older Nations*, originally compiled by Alberta Lawrence. Three volumes. Gale Composite Biographical Dictionary Series, Number 2. Detroit: Gale Research Co., 1978.

WhFla   *Who Was Who in Florida.* Written and compiled by Henry S. Marks. Huntsville, Alabama: Strode Publishers, 1973.

WhJnl   *Who Was Who in Journalism, 1925-1928.* A consolidation of all material appearing in the 1928 edition of *Who's Who in Journalism*, with unduplicated biographical entries from the 1925 edition of *Who's Who in Journalism*, originally compiled by M.N. Ask (1925 and 1928 editions) and S. Gershanek (1925 edition). Gale Composite Biographical Dictionary Series, Number 4. Detroit: Gale Research Co., 1978.

            The "1925 Supplement," indicated by the code *SUP*, begins on page 639.

WhLit   *Who Was Who in Literature, 1906-1934.* Based on entries that first appeared in *Literary Yearbook* (1906-1913), *Literary Yearbook and Author's Who's Who* (1914-1917), *Literary Yearbook* (1920-1922), and *Who's Who in Literature* (1924-1934). Two volumes. Gale Composite Biographical Dictionary Series, Number 5. Detroit: Gale Research Co., 1979.

WhNAA   *Who Was Who among North American Authors, 1921-1939.* Compiled from *Who's Who among North American Authors*, Volumes 1-7, 1921-1939. Two volumes. Gale Composite Biographical Dictionary Series, Number 1. Detroit: Gale Research Co., 1976.

WhScrn   *Who Was Who on Screen.* By Evelyn Mack Truitt. New York: R.R. Bowker Co., 1974, 1977, 1983.

    WhScrn 74   First edition, 1974
    WhScrn 77   Second edition, 1977
    WhScrn 83   Third edition, 1983

WhThe   *Who Was Who in the Theatre: 1912-1976.* A biographical dictionary of actors, actresses, directors, playwrights, and producers of the

English-speaking theatre. Compiled from *Who's Who in the Theatre*, Volumes 1-15 (1912-1972). Four volumes. Gale Composite Biographical Dictionary Series, Number 3. Detroit: Gale Research Co., 1978.

WhWW-II   *Who Was Who in World War II.* Edited by John Keegan. London: Arms & Armour Press, 1978.

Who   *Who's Who.* An annual biographical dictionary. New York: St. Martin's Press; London: Adam & Charles Black, 1974-1985.

Who 74	126th Year of Issue, 1974-1975
Who 75	127th Year of Issue, 1975-1976
Who 76	128th Year of Issue, 1976-1977
Who 77	129th Year of Issue, 1977-1978
Who 78	130th Year of Issue, 1978
Who 79	131st Year of Issue, 1979-1980
Who 80	132nd Year of Issue, 1980-1981
Who 81	133rd Year of Issue, 1982-1983
Who 82	134th Year of Issue, 1982-1983
Who 83	135th Year of Issue, 1983-1984
Who 84	136th Year of Issue, 1984-1985
Who 85	137th Year of Issue, 1985-1986

Each volume contains an Obituary section, indicated by the code *N*, "The Royal Family" section, indicated by the code *R*, and a Supplement, indicated by the code *S*. The Supplement may contain up to three parts: "Additions," "Members of Parliament," and "New Year Honours List."

WhoAdv 72   *Who's Who in Advertising.* Second edition. Edited by Robert S. Morgan. Rye, New York: Redfield Publishing Co., 1972.

Biographies are found in "U.S. Advertising Executives," beginning on page 1; "Canadian Advertising Executives," beginning on page 585; and the Addendum beginning on page 637.

WhoAdv 80   *Who's Who in Advertising.* Third edition. Edited by Catherine Quinn Serie. Monroe, New York: Redfield Publishing Co., 1980.

WhoAm   *Who's Who in America.* Chicago: Marquis Who's Who, 1974, 1976, 1978, 1980, 1982, 1984.

WhoAm 74	38th edition, 1974-1975
WhoAm 76	39th edition, 1976-1977
WhoAm 78	40th edition, 1978-1979
WhoAm 80	41st edition, 1980-1981
WhoAm 82	42nd edition, 1982-1983
WhoAm 84	43rd edition, 1984-1985

WhoAmA	*Who's Who in American Art.* Edited by Jaques Cattell Press. New York: R.R. Bowker Co., 1973, 1976, 1978, 1980, 1982, 1984.

WhoAmA 73	1973 edition
WhoAmA 76	1976 edition
WhoAmA 78	1978 edition
WhoAmA 80	1980 edition
WhoAmA 82	1982 edition
WhoAmA 84	1984 edition

The Necrology, indicated by the code *N*, is located at the back of each volume.

WhoAmJ 80	*Who's Who in American Jewry.* Incorporating *The Directory of American Jewish Institutions.* 1980 edition. Los Angeles: Standard Who's Who, 1980.

WhoAmL	*Who's Who in American Law.* Chicago: Marquis Who's Who, 1978, 1979, 1983, 1985.

WhoAmL 78	First edition, 1978
WhoAmL 79	Second edition, 1979
WhoAmL 83	Third edition, 1983
WhoAmL 85	Fourth edition, 1985

WhoAmM 83	*Who's Who in American Music: Classical.* First edition. Edited by Jaques Cattell Press. New York: R.R. Bowker Co., 1983.

WhoAmP	*Who's Who in American Politics.* Edited by Jaques Cattell Press. New York: R.R. Bowker Co., 1973, 1975, 1977, 1979, 1981, 1983, 1985.

WhoAmP 73	Fourth edition, 1973-1974
WhoAmP 75	Fifth edition, 1975-1976
WhoAmP 77	Sixth edition, 1977-1978
WhoAmP 79	Seventh edition, 1979-1980
WhoAmP 81	Eighth edition, 1981-1982
WhoAmP 83	Ninth edition, 1983-1984
WhoAmP 85	10th edition, 1985-1986

Biographies in the later editions are divided by geographical areas. Use the Index to locate biographies.

WhoAmW	*Who's Who of American Women.* Chicago: Marquis Who's Who, 1958, 1961, 1963, 1965, 1967, 1969, 1971, 1973, 1975, 1978, 1979, 1981, 1983, 1984.

WhoAmW 58	First edition, 1958-1959
WhoAmW 61	Second edition, 1961-1962
WhoAmW 64	Third edition, 1964-1965
WhoAmW 66	Fourth edition, 1966-1967
WhoAmW 68	Fifth edition, 1968-1969
WhoAmW 70	Sixth edition, 1970-1971

WhoAmW 72	Seventh edition, 1972-1973
WhoAmW 74	Eighth edition, 1974-1975
WhoAmW 75	Ninth edition, 1975-1976
WhoAmW 77	10th edition, 1977-1978
WhoAmW 79	11th edition, 1979-1980
WhoAmW 81	12th edition, 1981-1982
WhoAmW 83	13th edition, 1983-1984
WhoAmW 85	14th edition, 1985-1986

Earlier editions have Addenda, indicated by the code *A*.

WhoArab *Who's Who in the Arab World.* Edited by Gabriel M. Bustros. Beirut, Lebanon: Publitec Publications, 1981, 1984.

WhoArab 80	Sixth edition, 1981-1982
WhoArab 84	Seventh edition, 1984-1985

Biographies are located in Part III.

WhoArch *Who's Who in Architecture from 1400 to the Present Day.* Edited by J.M. Richards. London: Weidenfeld & Nicolson, 1977.

WhoArt *Who's Who in Art.* Biographies of leading men and women in the world of art today -- artists, designers, craftsmen, critics, writers, teachers and curators, with an appendix of signatures. Havant, England: Art Trade Press, 1980, 1982, 1984. Distributed by Gale Research Co., Detroit, Michigan.

WhoArt 80	19th edition, 1980
WhoArt 82	20th edition, 1982
WhoArt 84	21st edition, 1984

The Obituary section, indicated by the code *N*, is located at the back of each volume.

WhoAtom 77 *Who's Who in Atoms.* Sixth edition. Edited by Ann Pernet. Guernsey, British Isles: Francis Hodgson, 1977.

WhoBbl 73 *Who's Who in Basketball.* By Ronald L. Mendell. New Rochelle, New York: Arlington House, 1973.

WhoBlA *Who's Who among Black Americans.* Northbrook, Illinois: Who's Who among Black Americans, 1976, 1978, 1981.

WhoBlA 75	First edition, 1975-1976
WhoBlA 77	Second edition, 1977-1978
WhoBLA 80	Third edition, 1980-1981

WhoBlA 85 *Who's Who among Black Americans.* Fourth edition, 1985. Lake Forest, Illinois: Educational Communications, 1985.

WhoBox 74   *Who's Who in Boxing.* By Bob Burrill. New Rochelle, New York: Arlington House, 1974.

WhoCan   *Who's Who in Canada.* An illustrated biographical record of men and women of the time in Canada. Toronto: International Press, 1973, 1975, 1977, 1980, 1982.

    WhoCan 73   1973-1974 edition
    WhoCan 75   1975-1976 edition
    WhoCan 77   1977-1978 edition
    WhoCan 80   1980-1981 edition
    WhoCan 82   1982-1983 edition

    Use the Index at the front of each volume to locate biographies.

WhoCan 84   *Who's Who in Canada.* An illustrated biographical record of Canada's leading men and women in business, government and academia. 1984-1985 edition. Agincourt, Ontario: Global Press, 1984.

WhoChL   *The Who's Who of Children's Literature.* Compiled and edited by Brian Doyle. New York: Schocken Books, 1968.

    Biographies are found in "The Authors," beginning on page 1, and "The Illustrators," beginning on page 303.

WhoColR   *Who's Who of the Colored Race.* A general biographical dictionary of men and women of African descent. Volume one. Edited by Frank Lincoln Mather. Chicago: 1915. Reprint. Detroit: Gale Research Co., 1976.

    The Addenda, indicated by the code *A*, begins on page xxvi.

WhoCon 73   *Who's Who in Consulting.* A reference guide to professional personnel engaged in consultation for business, industry and government. Second edition. Edited by Paul Wasserman. Detroit: Gale Research Co., 1973.

WhoE   *Who's Who in the East.* Chicago: Marquis Who's Who, 1974, 1975, 1977, 1979, 1981, 1983, 1984.

    WhoE 74   14th edition, 1974-1975
    WhoE 75   15th edition, 1975-1976
    WhoE 77   16th edition, 1977-1978
    WhoE 79   17th edition, 1979-1980
    WhoE 81   18th edition, 1981-1982
    WhoE 83   19th edition, 1983-1984
    WhoE 85   20th edition, 1985-1986

WhoEc   *Who's Who in Economics: A Biographical Dictionary of Major Economists 1700-1981.* Edited by Mark Blaug and Paul Sturges. Cambridge, Massachusetts: MIT Press, 1983.

WhoEng 80   *Who's Who in Engineering.* Fourth edition. Edited by Jean Gregory. New York: American Association of Engineering Societies, 1980.

WhoEIO 82   *Who's Who in European Institutions and Organizations.* A biographical encyclopedia of the international red series containing some 4,000 biographies of the top administrators, chairmen, politicians and other leading personalities working with European institutions and organizations, and international institutions in Europe. First edition. Edited by Karl Strute and Theodor Doelken. Zurich: Who's Who, 1982. Distributed by Marquis Who's Who, Chicago, Illinois.

WhoFash   *Who's Who in Fashion.* By Anne Stegemeyer. New York: Fairchild Publications, 1980.

WhoF&I   *Who's Who in Finance and Industry.* Chicago: Marquis Who's Who, 1974, 1975, 1977, 1979, 1981, 1983.

     WhoF&I 74   18th edition, 1974-1975
     WhoF&I 75   19th edition, 1975-1976
     WhoF&I 77   20th edition, 1977-1978
     WhoF&I 79   21st edition, 1979-1980
     WhoF&I 81   22nd edition, 1981-1982
     WhoF&I 83   23rd edition, 1983-1984

WhoFla   *Who's Who in Florida, 1973/74.* A composite of biographical sketches of outstanding men and women of the State of Florida. First edition. Lexington, Kentucky and Acworth, Georgia: Names of Distinction, 1974.

WhoFtbl 74   *Who's Who in Football.* By Ronald L. Mendell and Timothy B. Phares. New Rochelle, New York: Arlington House, 1974.

WhoFr 79   *Who's Who in France: Qui est Qui en France.* 14th edition, 1979-1980. Dictionnaire biographique de personnalites francaises vivant en France, dans les territoires d'Outre-Mer ou a l'etranger et de personnalites etrangeres residant en France. Paris: Editions Jacques Lafitte, 1979.

     "Liste des Personnalites Decedees," indicated in this index by the code *N*, begins on page cviii.

WhoFrS   *Who's Who in Frontier Science and Technology.* First edition, 1984-1985. Chicago: Marquis Who's Who, 1984.

WhoGolf   *Who's Who in Golf.* By Len Elliott and Barbara Kelly. New Rochelle, New York: Arlington House Publishers, 1976.

WhoGov   *Who's Who in Government.* Chicago: Marquis Who's Who, 1972, 1975, 1977.

   WhoGov 72   First edition, 1972-1973
   WhoGov 75   Second edition, 1975-1976
   WhoGov 77   Third edition, 1977

WhoGrA   *Who's Who in Graphic Art.* An illustrated book of reference to the world's leading graphic designers, illustrators, typographers and cartoonists. First edition. Edited by Walter Amstutz. Zurich: Amstutz & Herdeg Graphis Press, 1962. Distributed by Gale Research Co., Detroit, Michigan.

   Use the "Index of Artists' Names," which begins on page 576, to locate biographies.

WhoGrA 82   *Who's Who in Graphic Art.* An illustrated world review of the leading contemporary graphic and typographic designers, illustrators and cartoonists. Volume Two. Edited and designed by Walter Amstutz. Dubendorf, Switzerland: De Clivo Press, 1982. Distributed by Gale Research Co., Detroit, Michigan.

   Use the "Index of Artists' Names," which begins on page 886, to locate biographies.

WhoHcky 73   *Who's Who in Hockey.* By Harry C. Kariher. New Rochelle, New York: Arlington House, 1973.

WhoHol   *Who's Who in Hollywood, 1900-1976.* By David Ragan. New Rochelle, New York: Arlington House, 1976.

   WhoHol A   The "Living Players" section begins on page 11.
   WhoHol B   The "Late Players (1900-1974)" section begins on page 539.
   WhoHol C   The "Players Who Died in 1975 and 1976" section begins on page 845.

WhoHr&F   *Who's Who in Horror and Fantasy Fiction.* By Mike Ashley. London: Elm Tree Books, 1977.

WhoHrs 80   *Who's Who of the Horrors and Other Fantasy Films.* The international personality encyclopedia of the fantastic film. By David J. Hogan. San Diego and New York: A.S. Barnes & Co., Inc.; London: Tantivy Press, 1980.

WhoIns   *Who's Who in Insurance.* Englewood, New Jersey: Underwriter Printing & Publishing Co., 1975, 1976, 1977, 1978, 1979, 1980, 1981, 1982, 1984, 1986.

   WhoIns 75   1975 edition
   WhoIns 76   1976 edition

WhoIns 77	1977 edition
WhoIns 78	1978 edition
WhoIns 79	1979 edition
WhoIns 80	1980 edition
WhoIns 81	1981 edition
WhoIns 82	1982 edition
WhoIns 84	1984 edition
WhoIns 86	1986 edition

The Addenda, indicated by the code *A*, are located at the back of each volume.

WhoIntG   *Who's Who in International Golf.* Edited by David Emery. New York: Facts on File Publications, 1983.

WhoIntT   *Who's Who in International Tennis.* Edited by David Emery. New York: Facts on File Publications, 1983.

WhoJazz 72   *Who's Who of Jazz: Storyville to Swing Street.* By John Chilton. Philadelphia: Chilton Book Co., 1972.

WhoLab 76   *Who's Who in Labor.* New York: Arno Press, 1976.

WhoLibI 82   *Who's Who in Library and Information Services.* Edited by Joel M. Lee. Chicago: American Library Association, 1982.

WhoLibS 55   *Who's Who in Library Service.* A biographical directory of professional librarians of the United States and Canada. Third edition. Edited by Dorothy Ethlyn Cole. New York: Grolier Society, 1955.

WhoLA   *Who's Who among Living Authors of Older Nations.* Covering the literary activities of living authors and writers of all countries of the world except the United States of America, Canada, Mexico, Alaska, Hawaii, Newfoundland, the Philippine Islands, the West Indies, and Central America. These countries are covered by our *Who's Who among North American Authors.* Volume 1, 1931-1932. Edited by A. Lawrence. Los Angeles: Golden Syndicate Publishing Co., 1931. Reprint. Detroit: Gale Research Co., 1966.

WhoMW   *Who's Who in the Midwest.* Chicago: Marquis Who's Who, 1974, 1976, 1978, 1980, 1982, 1984, 1985.

WhoMW 74	14th edition, 1974-1975
WhoMW 76	15th edition, 1976-1977
WhoMW 78	16th edition, 1978-1979
WhoMW 80	17th edition, 1980-1981
WhoMW 82	18th edition, 1982-1983
WhoMW 84	19th edition, 1984-1985
WhoMW 86	20th edition, 1986-1987

WhoMilH 76   *Who's Who in Military History: From 1453 to the Present Day.* By John Keegan and Andrew Wheatcroft. New York: William Morrow & Co., 1976.

WhoMus 72   *Who's Who in Music and Musicians' International Directory.* Sixth edition. New York: Hafner Publishing Co., 1972.

WhoOcn 78   *Who's Who in Ocean and Freshwater Science.* First edition. Edited by Allen Varley. Essex, England: Longman Group, Francis Hodgson, 1978. Distributed by Gale Research Co., Detroit, Michigan.

WhoOp 76   *Who's Who in Opera.* An international biographical directory of singers, conductors, directors, designers, and administrators. Also including profiles of 101 opera companies. Edited by Maria F. Rich. New York: Arno Press, 1976.

WhoPNW   *Who's Who among Pacific Northwest Authors.* Second edition. Edited by Frances Valentine Wright. Missoula, Montana: Pacific Northwest Library Association, Reference Division, 1969.

Biographies are arranged alphabetically by state. Use the "Index of Authors" to locate listings.

WhoPRCh   *Who's Who in the People's Republic of China.* By Wolfgang Bartke. Armonk, New York: M.E. Sharpe, 1981.

WhoPRCh 81   Biographies

WhoPRCh 81A   Wade-Giles/Pinyin Conversion Table begins on page 719.

WhoPRCh 81B   "Biographies of Important Deceased and Purged Cadres" section begins on page 573.

WhoPolA   *Who's Who in Polish America.* A biographical directory of Polish-American leaders and distinguished Poles resident in the Americas. Third edition. Edited by Francis Bolek. New York: Harbinger House, 1943. Reprint, The American Immigration Collection - Series II. New York: Arno Press and The New York Times, 1970.

WhoProB 73   *Who's Who in Professional Baseball.* By Gene Karst and Martin J. Jones, Jr. New Rochelle, New York: Arlington House, 1973.

WhoPubR   *Who's Who in Public Relations (International).* Edited by Adrian A. Paradis. Meriden, New Hampshire: PR Publishing Co., 1972, 1976.

WhoPubR 72   Fourth edition, 1972
WhoPubR 76   Fifth edition, 1976

WhoReal 83   *Who's Who in Real Estate: The Directory of the Real Estate Professions.* Boston and New York: Warren, Gorham & Lamont, 1983.

WhoRel   *Who's Who in Religion.* Chicago: Marquis Who's Who, 1975, 1977, 1985.

   WhoRel 75   First edition, 1975-1976
   WhoRel 77   Second edition, 1977
   WhoRel 85   Third edition, 1985

WhoRock 81   *Who's Who in Rock.* By Michael Bane. New York: Everest House, 1981.

WhoRocM 82   *Who's Who in Rock Music.* By William York. New York: Charles Scribner's Sons, 1982.

WhoSciF   *Who's Who in Science Fiction.* By Brian Ash. London: Elm Tree Books, 1976.

WhoSocC 78   *Who's Who in the Socialist Countries.* A biographical encyclopedia of 10,000 leading personalities in 16 communist countries. First edition. Edited by Borys Lewytzkyj and Juliusz Stroynowski. New York: K.G. Saur Publishing, 1978. Distributed by Gale Research Co., Detroit, Michigan.

   The Appendix, indicated by the code *A*, begins on page 713.

WhoS&SW   *Who's Who in the South and Southwest.* Chicago: Marquis Who's Who, 1973, 1975, 1976, 1978, 1980, 1982, 1984.

   WhoS&SW 73   13th edition, 1973-1974
   WhoS&SW 75   14th edition, 1975-1976
   WhoS&SW 76   15th edition, 1976-1977
   WhoS&SW 78   16th edition, 1978-1979
   WhoS&SW 80   17th edition, 1980-1981
   WhoS&SW 82   18th edition, 1982-1983
   WhoS&SW 84   19th edition, 1984-1985

WhoSpyF   *Who's Who in Spy Fiction.* By Donald McCormick. London: Elm Tree Books, 1977.

WhoStg 1906   *Who's Who on the Stage.* The dramatic reference book and biographical dictionary of the theatre. Containing records of the careers of actors, actresses, managers and playwrights of the American stage. Edited by Walter Browne and F.A. Austin. New York: Walter Browne & F.A. Austin, 1906.

   Some entries are not in alphabetic sequence.

WhoStg 1908   *Who's Who on the Stage, 1908.* The dramatic reference book and biographical dictionary of the theatre. Containing careers of actors, actresses, managers and playwrights of the American stage. Edited by Walter Browne and E. De Roy Koch. New York: B.W. Dodge & Co., 1908.

Some entries are not in alphabetic sequence.

WhoTech 82   *Who's Who in Technology Today.* Third edition. Four volumes. Edited by Jan W. Churchwell. Highland Park, Illinois: J. Dick & Co., 1982.

Use the "Index of Names," which begins on page 667 of Volume 4, to locate biographies.

WhoTelC   *Who's Who in Television and Cable.* Edited by Steven H. Scheuer. New York: Facts On File Publications, 1983.

WhoThe   *Who's Who in the Theatre: A Biographical Record of the Contemporary Stage.* London: Pitman Publishing; Detroit: Gale Research Co., 1972, 1977, 1981.

   WhoThe 72   15th edition, compiled by John Parker, 1972
   WhoThe 77   16th edition, edited by Ian Herbert, 1977
   WhoThe 81   17th edition, edited by Ian Herbert, 1981
   WhoThe 81N   17th edition, Obituary section begins on page 743.

WhoTr&F 73   *Who's Who in Track and Field.* By Reid M. Hanley. New Rochelle, New York: Arlington House, 1973.

WhoTwCL   *Who's Who in Twentieth Century Literature.* By Martin Seymour-Smith. New York: Holt, Rinehart & Winston, 1976.

WhoUN 75   *Who's Who in the United Nations and Related Agencies.* New York: Arno Press, 1975.

WhoWest   *Who's Who in the West.* Chicago: Marquis Who's Who, 1974, 1976, 1978, 1980, 1982, 1983.

   WhoWest 74   14th edition, 1974-1975
   WhoWest 76   15th edition, 1976-1977
   WhoWest 78   16th edition, 1978-1979
   WhoWest 80   17th edition, 1980-1981
   WhoWest 82   18th edition, 1982-1983
   WhoWest 84   19th edition, 1984-1985

WhoWor   *Who's Who in the World.* Chicago: Marquis Who's Who, 1973, 1976, 1978, 1980, 1982, 1984.

WhoWor 74	Second edition, 1974-1975
WhoWor 76	Third edition, 1976-1977
WhoWor 78	Fourth edition, 1978-1979
WhoWor 80	Fifth edition, 1980-1981
WhoWor 82	Sixth edition, 1982-1983
WhoWor 84	Seventh edition, 1984-1985

WhoWorJ 72   *Who's Who in World Jewry: A Biographical Dictionary of Outstanding Jews.* Edited by I.J. Carmin Karpman. New York: Pitman Publishing Corp., 1972.

WhoWorJ 78   *Who's Who in World Jewry: A Biographical Dictionary of Outstanding Jews.* Edited by I.J. Carmin Karpman. Tel-Aviv, Israel: Olive Books of Israel, 1978.

WisWr   *Wisconsin Writers: Sketches and Studies.* By William A. Titus. Chicago: 1930. Reprint. Detroit: Gale Research Co., 1974.

    Use the Table of Contents to locate biographies.

WomArt   *Women Artists: An Historical, Contemporary and Feminist Bibliography.* By Donna G. Bachmann and Sherry Piland. Metuchen, New Jersey: Scarecrow Press, 1978.

  WomArt   Use the Table of Contents to locate biographies, which begin on page 47.

  WomArt A   The Addenda begin on page 322.

WomPO 76   *Women in Public Office: A Biographical Directory and Statistical Analysis.* Compiled by Center for the American Woman and Politics. New York and London: R.R. Bowker Co., 1976.

    Use the "Name Index" to locate listings.

WomPO 78   *Women in Public Office: A Biographical Directory and Statistical Analysis.* Second edition. Compiled by Center for the American Woman and Politics. Metuchen, New Jersey: Scarecrow Press, 1978.

    Use the "Name Index" to locate listings.

WomWMM   *Women Who Make Movies.* Cinema Study Series. By Sharon Smith. New York: Hopkinson & Blake, 1975.

  WomWMM   "Overview" section. Biographies can be located through the index beginning on page 299.

  WomWMM A   "The New Filmmakers" begin on page 145.

  WomWMM B   "Directory" begins on page 221.

WomWWA 14 *Woman's Who's Who of America.* A biographical dictionary of contemporary women of the United States and Canada, 1914-1915.

Edited by John William Leonard. New York: American Commonwealth Co., 1914. Reprint. Detroit: Gale Research Co., 1976.

The "Addenda and Corrections" and "Deaths during Printing" sections, indicated by the code *A*, begin on page 29.

WorAl   *The World Almanac Book of Who.* Edited by Hana Umlauf Lane. New York: World Almanac Publications, 1980.

Use the "Name Index," which begins on page 326, to locate biographies.

WorAu   *World Authors.* A volume in the Wilson Authors Series. New York: H.W. Wilson Co., 1975, 1980, 1985.

WorAu	1950-1970, edited by John Wakeman, 1975.
WorAu 1970	1970-1975, edited by John Wakeman, 1980.
WorAu 1975	1975-1980, edited by Vineta Colby, 1985.

WorDWW   *World Defence Who's Who.* Edited by Paul Martell and Grace P. Hayes. London: Macdonald & Jane's, 1974.

WorECar   *The World Encyclopedia of Cartoons.* Two volumes. Edited by Maurice Horn. Detroit: Gale Research Co. (in association with Chelsea House Publishers, New York), 1980.

The "Notes on the Contributors" section, indicated by the code *A*, begins on page 631.

WorECom   *The World Encyclopedia of Comics.* Two volumes. Edited by Maurice Horn. New York: Chelsea House Publishers, 1976.

Biographies begin on page 65.

WorEFlm   *The World Encyclopedia of the Film.* Edited by John M. Smith and Tim Cawkwell. New York: A. & W. Visual Library, 1972.

WorFshn   *World of Fashion: People, Places, Resources.* By Eleanor Lambert. New York: R.R. Bowker Co., 1976.

Use the "Name Index," which begins on page 351, to locate biographies.

WrDr   *The Writers Directory.* London: St. James Press; New York: St. Martin's Press, 1976, 1979.

WrDr 76	1976-1978 edition
WrDr 80	1980-1982 edition

WrDr 82	*The Writers Directory.* 1982-1984 edition. Detroit: Gale Research Co., 1981.
WrDr	*The Writers Directory.* Chicago: St. James Press, 1983, 1986. Distributed by Gale Research Co., Detroit, Michigan.
WrDr 84	1984-1986 edition, 1983
WrDr 86	1986-1988 edition, 1986
YABC	*Yesterday's Authors of Books for Children.* Facts and pictures about authors and illustrators of books for young people, from early times to 1960. Edited by Anne Commire. Detroit: Gale Research Co., 1977-1978.
YABC 1	Volume 1, 1977
YABC 2	Volume 2, 1978
YABC X	This code refers to pseudonym entries which appear only as cross-references in the culumative index to *Yesterday's Author's of Books for Children.*

Key to Source Codes

Biography
Almanac

A-K

A

Aadland, Beverly
American. Actress, Dancer, Singer
Appeared in film *Cuban Rebel Girls* with
  Errol Flynn, 1959; their romance caused
  scandal.
b. 1944
Source: *BioIn 7; What 1-5; WhoHol A*

Aalberg, John O
American. Engineer
Head of sound dept., RKO Studios, 1932-57;
  won three Oscars.
b. Apr 3, 1897 in Chicago, Illinois
Source: *VarWW 85*

Aalto, Alvar Henrik (Hugo)
Finnish. Architect
Redesigned Finnish cities damaged during
  WW II.
b. Feb 3, 1898 in Kuortane, Chile
d. May 11, 1976 in Helsinki, Finland
Source: *ConAu 65; CurBio 48, 76; EncMA;
IntWW 74, 75, 76, 77; LinLib S; McGDA;
McGEWB; NewYTBS 76; OxDecA; WhAm 7;
WhoArch*

Aames, Willie
American. Actor
Played Tommy Bradford on TV series "Eight
  Is Enough," 1977-84.
b. Jul 15, 1960 in Newport Beach, California
Source: *BioIn 12; VarWW 85*

Aardema, Verna Norberg
[Verna Norberg Aardema Vugteveen]
American. Author
Known for rewriting African folk tales for
  children.
b. Jun 6, 1911 in New Era, Michigan
Source: *AuBYP SUP; ConAu 3NR, 5R;
MichAu 80; PseudN 82; SmATA 4; WhoAmW
68; WrDr 76, 80, 82*

Aaron
Religious Leader, Biblical Character
Brother of Moses; founded Hebrew
  priesthood.
Source: *NewCol 75; WebBD 80*

Aaron, Chester Norman
American. Author, Educator
Writings for young adults include *An
  American Ghost,* 1973.
b. May 9, 1923 in Butler, Pennsylvania
Source: *AuBYP SUP; BioIn 11; ConAu 8NR,
21R; SmATA 9; WhoWest 74*

Aaron, Hank (Henry Louis)
"Hammerin' Henry"; "The Hammer"
American. Baseball Player
His 755 career home runs broke Babe Ruth's
  all-time record; Hall of Fame, 1982.
b. Feb 5, 1934 in Mobile, Alabama
Source: *BioNews 74; CelR; ConAu 104;
CurBio 58; Ebony 1; NewYTBE 72, 73;
NewYTBS 74, 75, 76; PseudN 82; WebAB;
WhoAm 74, 76, 78, 80, 82; WhoBlA 75, 77,
80; WhoProB 73*

Abarbanel, Isaac Ben Jehudah
Portuguese. Theologian
Offered Ferdinand 30,000 ducats to prevent
  expulsion of Jews, 1492; Biblical writings
  expressed modern views.
b. 1437 in Lisbon, Portugal
d. 1508 in Venice, Italy
Source: *CasWL; DcEuL; PenC EUR*

Abarbanel, Judah
[Leone Ebreo; Leo Judaeus]
Spanish. Philosopher, Poet
Wrote neo-Platonic *Dialoghi d'Amore,* 1502,
  talks between love and knowledge.
b. 1460 in Lisbon, Portugal
d. 1535 in Naples, Italy
Source: *BioIn 5, 7; CasWL; EuAu; OxSpan*

1

ABBA
[Benny Andersson; Annifrid Lyngstad-
   Fredriksson; Agetha Ulvaeus; Bjorn
   Ulvaeus]
Swedish. Music Group
Formed 1973; hit singles "Dancing Queen,"
   1977; "Take a Chance on Me," 1978.
Source: *BkPepl; ConMuA 80A; IlEncRk;
LilREn 78; RkOn 74; RolSEnR 83; WhoRock
81*

Abbado, Claudio
Italian. Conductor
Conductor, La Scala, Milan, 1969--;
   American debut, 1976, in honor of
   Bicentennial.
b. Jun 26, 1933 in Milan, Italy
Source: *Baker 78; BnBkM 80; CmOp; CurBio
73; IntWW 80, 81, 82; MusMk; MusSN;
NewEOp 71; NewGrD 80; NewYTBE 73; Who
74; WhoAm 82; WhoMus 72; WhoOp 76;
WhoWor 74*

Abbas, Khwaja Ahmad
Indian. Author, Filmmaker, Journalist
Writes travel books, biographies, novels,
   filmscripts on contemporary Indian life.
b. Jul 6, 1914 in Panipat, India
Source: *ConAu 57; DcFM; DcLEL; DcOrL 2;
FilmEn; IntAu&W 76, 77; WhE&EA;
WorEFlm*

Abbas, Ferhat
Algerian. Political Leader
Pres., Algeria's first provisional govt., 1958-
   61; wrote *Manifesto of the Algerian People,*
   1943.
b. Oct 24, 1899 in Taher, Algeria
d. Dec 24, 1985
Source: *CurBio 61, 86; DcPol; IntWW 83;
McGEWB; MidE 82*

Abbe, Cleveland
American. Meteorologist
First official weather forecaster of US
   government.
b. Dec 3, 1838 in New York, New York
d. Oct 28, 1916 in Chevy Chase, Maryland
Source: *AmBi; ApCAB, X; AsBiEn; BbD;
BiDAmS; BiD&SB; DcAmAu; DcAmB;
DcNAA; DcScB; NatCab 8; OhA&B;
TwCBDA; WebAB, 79; WhAm 1*

Abbey, Edwin Austin
American. Artist, Illustrator
Best known work, mural series "The Quest
   for the Holy Grail" is in Boston Public
   Library.
b. Apr 1, 1852 in Philadelphia, Pennsylvania
d. Aug 1, 1911 in London, England
Source: *AmBi; AntBDN B; ApCAB, X;
BnEnAmA; DcAmArt; DcAmB; DcBrBI;
DcBrWA; DcVicP; LinLib L, S; McGDA;
NatCab 1; OxAmL; TwCBDA; WebAB 79;
WhAm 1*

Abbey, Henry Eugene
American. Manager
Introduced Sarah Bernhardt to America,
   1880; opened Abbey's Theatre, 1893.
b. Jun 27, 1846 in Akron, Ohio
d. Oct 17, 1896 in New York, New York
Source: *ApCAB X; BiDAmM; BioIn 7, 8, 9,
10; DcAmB; NewEOp 71; OxThe; TwCBDA;
WhAm HS*

Abbot, Charles Greeley
American. Scientist
Asst. director, Smithsonian Institution, 1895-
   1906.
b. May 31, 1872 in Wilton, New Hampshire
d. Dec 17, 1973 in Riverdale, Maryland
Source: *ApCAB X; ConAu 45, 77; NewYTBE
73; WhAm 6; WhNAA; Who 74*

Abbott, Berenice
American. Photographer
Best known for black and white architectural,
   documentary images of NYC, 1930s.
b. Jul 17, 1898 in Springfield, Ohio
Source: *AmAu&B; BioIn 7, 9, 10, 11;
BnEnAmA; ConAu 106; ConPhot; CurBio 42;
GoodHs; InWom; MacBEP; NewYTBS 80;
WhoAm 82; WhoAmW 58, 64; WomArt*

Abbott, "Bud" (William A)
[Abbott and Costello]
American. Comedian
Starred in over 35 films with partner, Lou
   Costello, 1940-65.
b. Oct 2, 1900 in Asbury Park, New Jersey
d. Apr 24, 1974 in Woodland Hills,
   California
Source: *CmMov; CurBio 41, 74; FilmgC;
ForYSC; Funs; HalFC 80; JoeFr; MotPP;
MovMk; NewYTBS 74; NotNAT B; OxFilm;
PseudN 82; What 8; WhAm 6; WhScrn 77*

Abbott, Edith
American. Author, Educator
Wrote books that became classics in social
welfare: *Immigration,* 1924.
b. Sep 26, 1876 in Grand Island, Nebraska
d. Jul 28, 1957 in Grand Island, Nebraska
Source: *DcAmB S6; DcAmSR; NotAW MOD;
ObitOF 79; WhAm 3; WhLit; WomWWA 14*

Abbott, George Francis
American. Director, Dramatist
Directed several plays on Broadway,
    including *A Tree Grows in Brooklyn.*
b. Jun 25, 1887 in Forestville, New York
Source: *BestMus; BiDAmM; BiE&WWA;
BioNews 74; CelR; CnMD; ConAu 93; ConDr
73, 77; CurBio 40, 65; EncMT; EncWT; Ent;
FilmEn; FilmgC; HalFC 80; IntAu&W 77;
McGEWD; ModWD; NewCBMT; NotNAT A;
OxThe; PIP&P; WhoAm 74, 76, 78, 80, 82;
WhoThe 72, 77; WorEFlm; WrDr 76, 80, 82*

Abbott, Grace
American. Social Reformer
Influential in having child-labor laws declared
unconstitutional, 1918.
b. Nov 17, 1878 in Grand Island, Nebraska
d. Jun 19, 1939 in Chicago, Illinois
Source: *ApCAB X; DcAmB S2; DcNAA;
EncAB-H; InWom; LibW; NatCAB 29;
NotAW; WebAB; WhAm 1; WhAmP;
WomWWA 14A*

Abbott, Jack (Rufus Jack Henry)
[Jack Eastman, pseud.]
American. Author, Murderer
Wrote *In the Belly of the Beast: Letters from
Prison,* 1981.
b. Jan 21, 1944 in Oscoda, Michigan
Source: *BioIn 12; ConAu 107; PseudN 82*

Abbott, L(enwood) B(allard)
American. Filmmaker
Won four Oscars, numerous Emmys for
special effects cinematography.
b. 1908
d. Sep 28, 1985 in Los Angeles, California
Source: *ConAu 117; VarWW 85*

Abbott, Lyman
"Benauly"; "Laicus"
American. Religious Leader, Editor
Editor, *Illustrated Christian Weekly,* 1870-93,
Outlook, 1893-1922.
b. Dec 18, 1835 in Roxbury, Massachusetts
d. Oct 22, 1922 in New York, New York
Source: *Alli, SUP; AmAu&B; AmBi; AmLY;
ApCAB; BbD; BiD&SB; CyAL 2; DcAmAu;
DcAmB; DcAmReB; DcEnL; DcNAA; Drake;
LinLib L, S; McGEWB; NatCAB 1; OxAmL;
PseudN 82; REn; REnAL; TwCA, SUP;
TwCBDA; WebAB; WhAm 1; WhAmP*

Abbott, Scott
Canadian. Journalist, Inventor
With Chris and John Haney, invented board
game Trivial Pursuit, 1979.
Source: *NF*

Abbott and Costello
[Abbott, Bud; Costello, Lou]
American. Comedy Team
Starred in over 35 comedy films, 1940-65;
known for baseball comedy routine "Who's
on First?"
Source: *FilmEn; ForYSC; Funs; JoeFr; MotPP*

ABC
[Martin Fry; David Palmer; Stephen
Singleton; Mark White]
English. Music Group
Sheffield, England group whose debut album
Lexicon of Love, 1983, was int'l. hit.
Source: *RkOn 85*

Abdallah, Ahmed
Sudanese. Political Leader
Pres. of Comoros, 1975, 1978--.
b. 1919
Source: *AfSS 79, 80, 81, 82; IntWW 80, 81,
82*

Abdnor, James S
American. Politician, Rancher
Conservative Rep. senator from SD who
ousted George McGovern, 1980.
b. Feb 13, 1923 in Kennebec, South Dakota
Source: *AlmAP 80; CngDr 79; WhoAm 84;
WhoGov 75; WhoMW 78*

Abdu'l-Baha
[Abbas Effendi]
Persian. Religious Leader
Eldest son, successor to Baha'u'llah; wrote
first history of Baha'i movement, 1886.
b. May 23, 1844 in Teheran, Persia
d. Nov 28, 1921 in Haifa, Palestine
Source: *BiDAmC; CasWL; DcAmReB*

Abdul, Raoul
American. Author, Opera Singer
Editorial asst. to Langston Hughes; organized
first chamber music concerts in Harlem,
1958.
b. Nov 7, 1929 in Cleveland, Ohio
Source: *ConAu 29R; DrBlPA; SelBAAu;*
SmATA 12; WhoBlA 75, 77; WhoE 77, 79

Abdul-Jabbar, Kareem
[Ferdinand Lewis Alcindor, Jr.]
American. Basketball Player
Six-time NBA MVP, who passed Wilt
Chamberlain as all-time NBA scorer in
1983-84 season.
b. Apr 16, 1947 in New York, New York
Source: *BkPepl; CelR; NewYTBS 74, 76;*
OfNBA 81; PseudN 82; WhoAm 76, 78, 80,
82; WhoBlA 80, 75, 77, 80

Abdullah, Sheik Mohammad
"Lion of Kashmir"
Indian. Political Leader
Struggled to free country from political
domination of India.
b. Dec 5, 1905 in Soura, Kashmir
d. Sep 8, 1982 in Srinagar, Kashmir
Source: *CurBio 52, 83; FarE&A 80; IntWW*
79, 80, 81; NewYTBS 82

Abdullah Ibn Hussein
Jordanian. Ruler
King of Jordan, 1946-51; supported pro-
British policies; assassinated.
b. 1882 in Mecca, Saudi Arabia
d. Jul 20, 1951 in Jerusalem, Israel
Source: *CurBio 48, 51; NewCol 75*

Abe, Isao
Japanese. Political Leader
Founder, Japanese Socialist Party, who
introduced baseball to Japan.
b. 1865 in Tokyo, Japan
d. Feb 10, 1949 in Tokyo, Japan
Source: *ObitOF 79*

A'Becket, Thomas
[Saint Thomas a'Becket; Thomas Becket;
Thomas of Canterbury]
English. Religious Leader
Archbishop of Canterbury, 1162-70;
canonized 1173; feast day Dec 29.
b. Dec 21, 1118 in London, England
d. Dec 29, 1170 in Canterbury, England
Source: *Alli; BiD&SB; NewC; NewCol 75*

A'Beckett, Gilbert Abbott
English. Editor, Humorist, Dramatist
Wrote humorous histories of England, Rome,
1848-52.
b. Feb 17, 1811 in London, England
d. Aug 30, 1856 in Boulogne, France
Source: *Alli; BbD; BiD&SB; BrAu 19;*
CasWL; Chambr 3; DcEnA; DcEnL; EvLB;
NewC; OxEng

Abednego
see: Shadrach

Abel
Biblical Character
Son of Adam and Eve; killed by brother
Cain.
Source: *BioIn 10; NewCol 75*

Abel, Elie
Canadian. Broadcast Journalist, Educator
Won George Foster Peabody Award for
outstanding radio news, 1968.
b. Oct 17, 1920 in Montreal, Quebec
Source: *CanWW 79, 82; ConAu 61; LEduc*
74; WhoAm 74, 76, 78, 80, 82; WhoE 74;
WhoWor 74, 76; WhoWorJ 72

Abel, I(orwith) W(ilbur)
"Abe"
American. Labor Union Official
Pres., United Steelworkers of America, 1965-
77.
b. Aug 11, 1908 in Magnolia, Ohio
Source: *BiDAmLL; BioNews 74; BusPN;*
CurBio 65; IntWW 74, 75; NewYTBE 71;
PolProf J, NF; PseudN 82; WhoAm 76, 78;
WhoF&I 75; WhoGov 72, 75; WhoLab 76;
WhoWor 74

Abel, Rudolf Ivanovich
[Martin Collins; Emil R Goldfus; Andrew
Kayotis; Mark, aliases]
Russian. Spy
Master spy sentenced to 30 years in US
prison for espionage; exchanged for Francis
Gary Powers, 1962.
b. 1902 in Saint Petersburg, Russia
d. Nov 15, 1971 in Moscow, U.S.S.R.
Source: *BioIn 4, 5, 6, 8, 9, 10; EncE 75;*
NewYTBE 71; ObitOF 79; PseudN 82; SpyCS;
WhDW

Abel, Sid(ney Gerald)
"Bootnose"
Canadian. Hockey Player, Sportscaster
Center on Production Line with Gordie
Howe, Ted Lindsay; Hall of Fame, 1969.
b. Feb 22, 1918 in Melville, Saskatchewan
Source: *PseudN 82; WhoHcky 73*

Abel, Walter Charles
American. Actor
Has appeared in over 80 films including *The
   Three Musketeers,* 1934; *Man Without a
   Country,* 1973.
b. Jun 6, 1898 in Saint Paul, Minnesota
Source: *BiE&WWA; FilmEn; FilmgC;
ForYSC; HalFC 80; HolCA; IntMPA 80, 81;
MotPP; MovMk; NotNAT; Vers B; WhoAm
80, 82; WhoHol A; WhoThe 77, 81*

Abelard, Pierre
French. Author, Theologian, Educator
Involved in tragic love affair with Heloise;
   condemned for heresy, 1141.
b. 1079 in Pallet, France
d. Apr 21, 1142 in Chalon-sur-Saone, France
Source: *BbD; BiD&SB; CasWL; CyWA;
DcEuL; DcScB; EuAu; EvEuW; LinLib L, S;
LongCEL; McGEWB; NewC; OxEng; OxFr;
PenC EUR; RComWL; REn*

Abell, George O(gden)
American. Astronomer, Author
Discovered the Abell Galaxy; host of British
   astronomy TV series.
b. Mar 1, 1927 in Los Angeles, California
d. Oct 7, 1983 in Encino, California
Source: *ConAu 111; WhoAm 80*

Abercrombie, James Smither
American. Businessman, Philanthropist
Invented blow-out valve, nucleus of one of
   largest oil-tool equipment companies in
   US.
b. Jul 7, in Huntsville, Texas
d. Jan 7, 1975 in Houston, Texas
Source: *NatCAB 59*

Abercrombie, Josephine
American. Celebrity Relative
Daughter of James S Abercrombie; major
   boxing promoter.
b. 1926 in Houston, Texas
Source: *NewYTBS 86*

Abercrombie, Lascelles
"The Georgian Laureate"
English. Author, Poet, Critic
Writings include *Thomas Hardy: A Critical
   Study,* 1912.
b. Jan 9, 1881 in Cheshire, England
d. Oct 27, 1938 in London, England
Source: *Chambr 3; DcLEL; EncWL; EvLB;
LinLib L; LongCTC; ModBrL; NewC; OxEng;
PenC ENG; PseudN 82; REn; TwCA, SUP;
TwCWr; WebE&AL; WhE&EA; WhLit;
WhThe; WhoLA*

Abercrombie, Michael
English. Biologist, Educator, Editor
Discovered important factors in cell behavior.
b. Aug 14, 1912 in Ryton, England
d. May 28, 1979 in Cambridge, England
Source: *ConAu 115; IntWW 79; WhoWor 78*

Aberhart, William
Canadian. Political Leader
Founded Social Credit Party in Canada;
   premier of Alberta, 1935-43.
b. Dec 30, 1878 in Hibbard Township,
   Ontario
d. May 23, 1943 in Calgary, Alberta
Source: *DcNaB 1941; MacDCB 78;
McGEWB; OxCan*

Aberle, John Wayne
American. Author, Educator
b. Aug 12, 1919 in Lodi, California
Source: *AmM&WS 73S, 78S; ConAu 1R;
WhoWest 76*

Abernathy, Ralph David
American. Clergyman, Civil Rights Leader
Replaced Martin Luther King, Jr. as pres. of
   SCLC, 1968-77.
b. Mar 11, 1926 in Linden, Alabama
Source: *BioNews 74; CelR; CivR 74; CurBio
68; Ebony 1; IntWW 74, 75, 76, 77, 78;
LinLib S; PolProf E, J, K, NF; WhoAm 74,
76, 78, 80, 82; WhoBlA 75, 77, 80; WhoRel
75, 77; WhoS&SW 73; WhoWor 74, 78*

Abernethy, Robert Gordon
American. Journalist, Editor
Science editor, NBC News, 1965-66; wrote
   Introduction to Tomorrow, 1966.
b. Nov 5, 1927 in Geneva, Switzerland
Source: *BioIn 10; ConAu 21R; SmATA 5;
WhoAm 74, 76, 78, 80, 82*

Ableman, Paul
English. Author, Dramatist, Poet
Plays include *Green Julia,* 1965; *Methuen,*
   1966; *Blue Comedy,* 1968.
b. Jun 13, 1927 in Leeds, England
Source: *ConAu 61; ConDr 77, 82; ConNov
76, 82; DcLEL 1940; EncSF; IntAu&W 82;
WrDr 76, 80, 82*

Abourezk, James George
American. Lawyer, Politician
Dem. senator from SD, 1973-77.
b. Feb 24, 1931 in Woods, South Dakota
Source: *AlmAP 78; CngDr 74, 77; IntWW
74, 75, 76, 77, 78; WhoAm 76, 78, 80, 82;
WhoAmL 79; WhoAmP 73, 75, 77, 79;
WhoGov 72, 75, 77; WhoMW 74, 76, 78;
WhoWor 78*

Abplanalp, Robert H
American. Inventor
Invented aerosol valve, 1949.
b. 1923 in New York, New York
Source: *NewYTBE 73; PolProf NF*

Abraham
[Abram]
"Father of the Faithful"; "Friend of God"
Biblical Character
Founder, first patriarch of Judaism who was
   commanded to sacrifice son Isaac as test
   of faith.
Source: *DcScB; PseudAu; REn; WhDW*

Abraham, F Murray
Actor
Won Oscar for *Amadeus,* 1984.
b. Oct 24, 1940
Source: *ConTFT 1; IntMPA 86; VarWW 85*

Abrahams, Doris Cole
American. Producer
Won Tonys for *Equus,* 1975; *Travesties,* 1976.
b. Jan 29, 1925 in New York, New York
Source: *VarWW 85*

Abrahams, Harold
British. Track Athlete
Subject of film *Chariots of Fire,* 1982.
b. 1900
d. Jan 14, 1978 in London, England
Source: *BioIn 9, 10*

Abrahams, Jim
American. Director
Co-creator of hit film *Airplane,* 1980.
b. 1944
Source: *BioIn 12; DirCG 82; NewYTBS 80*

Abram, Morris Berthold
American. Civil Rights Leader, Lawyer
First head of Peace Corps legal department,
   1961.
b. Jun 19, 1918 in Fitzgerald, Georgia
Source: *CurBio 65; WhoAm 74, 76, 78, 80,
82; WhoAmP 73; WhoE 74; WhoWor 78;
WhoWorJ 72*

Abramovitz, Max
American. Architect
Designed US Embassy Bldg., Rio de Janeiro;
   Philharmonic Hall at Lincoln Center.
b. May 23, 1908 in Chicago, Illinois
Source: *IntWW 74; WhoAm 74, 76, 78, 80,
82; WhoAmA 73; WhoE 74; WhoWor 78;
WhoWorJ 72*

Abrams, Creighton Williams
American. Army Officer
Commanding general, US forces in Vietnam,
   1968-72.
b. Sep 15, 1914 in Springfield, Massachusetts
d. Sep 4, 1974 in Washington, District of
   Columbia
Source: *CelR; CurBio 68, 74; IntWW 74;
NewCol 75; NewYTBS 74; WhAm 6; WhoAm
74*

Abrams, Harry Nathan
English. Publisher
Popularized high-quality art books.
b. Dec 8, 1904 in London, England
d. Nov 25, 1979 in New York, New York
Source: *AmAu&B; BioIn 2, 4, 5, 7, 9, 10;
ConAu 93; CurBio 58, 80; NewYTBS 79;
WhAm 7; WhoAm 74, 78; WhoAmA 73, 78;
WhoWorJ 72*

Abramson, Harold A(lexander)
American. Psychiatrist
One of first US researchers to study medical
   applications of LSD.
b. Nov 27, 1899 in New York, New York
d. Sep 29, 1980 in Cold Spring Harbor, New
   York
Source: *AnObit 1980; BiDrAPA 77; ConAu
102; NewYTBS 84; WhAm 7; WhoAm 74, 76,
78, 80; WhoWor 74, 76, 78, 80*

Abravanel, Maurice
Turkish. Conductor
Won 1950 Tony for *Regina.*
b. Jan 6, 1903 in Salonica, Greece
Source: *Baker 78; BiE&WWA; BioIn 2, 4,
10, 11; NewYTBS 77; NotNAT; WhoAm 80,
82; WhoWest 80*

Abruzzi, Luigi Amedeo
[Duke of Abruzzi]
Italian. Explorer
Prince who explored N Pole and climbed
   Himalayas; commanded Italian fleet WW
   I.
b. 1873 in Madrid, Spain
d. 1933
Source: *BioIn 1, 5, 9; LinLib L, S; NewCol
75*

Abruzzo, Ben(jamine Lou)
American. Balloonist, Aviator
Among first to make trans-Atlantic balloon
   flight, 1978.
b. Jun 9, 1930 in Rockford, Illinois
d. Feb 11, 1985 in Albuquerque, New
   Mexico
Source: *ConAu 115; WhoWest 84*

Abse, Dannie
Welsh. Author
Wrote award-winning play *House of Cowards,*
1960.
b. Sep 22, 1923 in Cardiff, Wales
Source: *Au&Wr 71; ChhPo S1; ConAu 4NR,*
53; ConDr 77; ConLC 7; ConNov 76; ConP
70, 75; DcLEL; DrAP 75; IntAu&W 76, 77;
ModBrL S1; WorAu; WrDr 76

Abu Bakr
Arabian. Religious Leader
Father-in-law, first convert, successor of
    Mohammed; helped make Islam a world
    religion.
b. 573 in Mecca, Arabia
d. Aug 634
Source: *BioIn 9, 11; LuthC 75; McGEWB;*
NewCol 75; WebBD 80; WhDW; WorAl

Abu Daoud
[Muhamman Daoud Audeh; Tarik Shakir
    Mahdi]
Palestinian. Terrorist
Most wanted, feared int'l. criminal of 1980s;
    thought responsible for many terrorist
    attacks.
b. 1937
Source: *BioIn 11; PseudN 82*

Abu Salma, pseud.
[Abd al-Karim al-Karmi]
"Father of Peace"; "Palestine Poet"
Palestinian. Poet
Voice of exiled Palestinians, who wrote *The*
    Homeless, 1964.
b. 1906 in Tulkarm City, Palestine
d. Sep 13, 1980 in Washington, District of
    Columbia
Source: *AnObit 1980*

Abzug, Bella Savitsky
"Battling Bella"
American. Lawyer, Politician
First Jewish congresswoman, Dem. from NY;
    wide-brimmed hats are trademark.
b. Jul 24, 1920 in New York, New York
Source: *BioNews 75; CelR; CngDr 74; ConAu*
104; CurBio 71; NewYTBE 71; WhoAm 74,
76, 78, 80, 82; WhoAmP 73; WhoAmW 77,
81; WhoE 74; WhoGov 72; WomPO 76

AC-DC
[Mark Evans; Brian Johnson; Phil Rudd; Bon
    Scott; Cliff Williams; Angus Young;
    Malcolm Young]
Australian. Music Group
Heavy-metal band formed 1973; had number
    one album in US *For Those About to*
    Rock, 1981.
Source: *ConMuA 80A; RolSEnR 83;*
WhoRock 81

Ace
[Fran Byrne; Parul Carrack; Tex Comer; Phil
    Harris; Alan King]
English. Music Group
London pop-rock band formed 1973-76; hit
    single, "How Long," 1973.
Source: *RkOn 78; RolSEnR 83; WhoRock 81*

Ace, Goodman
American. Radio Performer, Humorist
Co-starred with wife, Jane, in radio comedy,
    "Easy Aces," 1928-45.
b. Jan 15, 1899 in Kansas City, Missouri
d. Mar 25, 1982 in New York, New York
Source: *BioIn 1, 3, 4, 5, 6, 10; CelR; ConAu*
106, 61; CurBio 48, 82; NewYTBS 82, 84;
NewYTET

Ace, Jane Sherwood
[Mrs. Goodman Ace]
American. Actress
Starred with husband in radio comedy, "Easy
    Aces," 1928-45.
b. Oct 12, 1905 in Kansas City, Missouri
d. Nov 11, 1974 in New York, New York
Source: *BioIn 1, 10; CurBio 48, 75;*
NewYTBS 74; ObitOF 79; WhScrn 77

Ace, Johnny
[Johnny Marshall Alexander, Jr.]
American. Singer
"Pledging My Love," 1955, became hit after
    his accidental death from Russian
    Roulette.
b. Jun 9, 1929 in Memphis, Tennessee
d. Dec 25, 1954 in Houston, Texas
Source: *BiDAmM; InB&W 80; RkOn 74, 78;*
RolSEnR 83; WhoRock 81

Achab
[Ahad]
Ruler
Seventh king of Israel; married to Jezebel.
d. 853
Source: *WebBD 80*

Achard, Marcel
[Marcel Auguste Ferreol]
French. Dramatist, Director
Plays include *I Know My Love,* 1952.
b. Jul 5, 1900 in Foyles Lyon, France
d. Sep 4, 1974 in Paris, France
Source: *BiE&WWA; CasWL; ClDMEL;
CnMD; ConAu 53, 93; EncWL; EvEuW;
McGEWD; ModWD; OxFr; REn; Who 74*

Achebe, Chinua
[Albert Chinualumogu]
Nigerian. Author
Novels reveal Nigerian life, impact of
    civilization: *Things Fall Apart ,* 1958;
    Arrow of God, 1964.
b. Nov 16, 1930 in Ogidi, Nigeria
Source: *AfrA; Au&Wr 71; CasWL; ConAu
1R, 6NR; ConLC 1, 3, 5, 7, 11; ConNov 72,
76; EncWL; IntWW 74; LongCTC; PenC CL,
ENG; PseudN 82; RGAfL; TwCWr;
WebE&AL; Who 74; WhoTwCL; WhoWor 78;
WorAu; WrDr 80*

Acheson, Dean Gooderham
American. Government Official
Primary creator of NATO who won Pulitzer,
    1970.
b. Apr 11, 1893 in Middletown, Connecticut
d. Oct 12, 1971 in Sandy Springs, Maryland
Source: *AmAu&B; BiDrUSE; ConAu 25R,
33R, P-2; DcPol; EncAB-H; McGEWB;
NatCAB 56; ObitOF 79; ObitT 1971; PolProf
E, J, K, T; REnAL; WebAB 79; WhDW;
WhAm 5; WorAl*

Acheson, Edward Goodrich
American. Inventor
Pioneer of electrothermal industry; discovered
    silicon carbide, 1891.
b. Mar 9, 1856 in Washington, District of
    Columbia
d. Jul 6, 1931 in New York, New York
Source: *DcAmB S1; WebBD 80*

Ackerman, Bettye
American. Actress
Starred in TV series "Ben Casey," 1961-66.
b. Feb 28, 1928 in Cottageville, South
    Carolina
Source: *FilmgC; ForWC 70; IntMPA 80, 81,
82; WhoAmW 68; WhoHol A*

Ackerman, Carl William
American. Journalist
Dean, Columbia Graduate Journalism School,
    1931-56, who advocated practical
    newspaper training.
b. Jan 16, 1890 in Richmond, Indiana
d. Oct 9, 1970 in New York, New York
Source: *AmAu&B; BioIn 4, 9, 10; ConAu
29R, 73; CurBio 45, 70; IndAu 1917;
NewYTBE 70; ObitOF 79; WhAm 5*

Ackerman, Forest J
[Dr. Acula; Jacques DeForest Erman; Alden
    Lorraine; Hubert George Wells; Weaver
    Wright, pseuds.]
"World's No. 1 Science Fiction Fan"
American. Author, Editor, Lecturer
Has collected over 300,000 items on science
    fiction, fantasy; coined abbreviation "sci-
    fi."
b. Nov 24, 1916 in Los Angeles, California
Source: *ConAu 102; EncSF; FanAl; PseudN
82; ScF&FL 1, 2; WhoSciF*

Ackerman, Harry S
American. Film Executive, Producer
Exec. producer, Screen Gems Pictures Corp.,
    1958-73; developed several TV shows:
    "Bachelor Father," "Leave It to Beaver,"
    "Gunsmoke."
b. Nov 17, 1912 in Albany, New York
Source: *ConTFT 3; IntMPA 82; NewYTET;
St&PR 75; WhoAm 82*

Ackerman, Robert Allan
American. Director
Directed on stage *Bent; Extremities; Slab
    Boys.*
b. 1945
Source: *BioIn 12*

Ackland, Joss
English. Actor
Character actor typically portraying men of
    power, especially kings.
b. Feb 29, 1928 in London, England
Source: *FilmEn; FilmgC; IntMPA 82; Who
82; WhoThe 77, 81*

**Acton, John Emerich Edward Dalberg-
    Acton, Baron**
English. Historian
Liberal MP who was first editor of
    Cambridge Modern History.
b. Jan 10, 1834 in Naples, Italy
d. Jul 19, 1902 in Tegernsee, Bavaria
Source: *Alli SUP; AtlBL; DcEnA, AP;
DcEuL; DcLEL; EvLB; OxEng; PenC ENG*

Acuff, Roy
"The King of Country Music"
American. Singer
Country singer who has sold over 30 million
    records including "Wabash Cannoball."
b. Sep 15, 1903 in Maynardsville, Tennessee
Source: *EncFCWM 69, 83; PseudN 82;*
WhoAm 80, 82

Adair, Frank E(arl)
American. Surgeon
Breast cancer specialist who performed over
    17,000 operations.
b. Apr 9, 1887 in Beverly, Ohio
d. Dec 31, 1981 in Bedford, New York
Source: *BioIn 1; CurBio 46, 82; IntWW 76,*
77, 78; WhoAm 74, 76

Adair, "Red" (Paul Neal)
American. Oil Well Technician, Firefighter
Expert at capping runaway oil well fires and
    blowouts.
b. 1916
Source: *BioIn 11; PseudN 82*

Adam
Biblical Character
First man; story told in Genesis book of
    Bible; committed original sin for which
    Christians are baptized.
Source: *BioIn 9, 10; DcBiPP; EncSoB;*
NewCol 75

Adam, Adolphe Charles
French. Opera Composer
b. Jul 24, 1803 in Paris, France
d. May 3, 1856 in Paris, France
Source: *NewEOp 71*

Adam, James
Scottish. Architect
Brother of Robert Adam; work recaptures
    spirit of antiquity through use of delicate
    ornaments, mouldings.
b. Jul 21, 1730 in Edinburgh, Scotland
d. Oct 20, 1794 in London, England
Source: *BiDBrA; BioIn 3, 4, 5; DcBrWA;*
DcNaB; MacEA; McGDA; McGEWB; OxArt;
WhoArch

Adam, Juliette Lamber
[Juliette Lamber; La Messine; Comte Paul
    Vasili, pseuds.]
French. Author
Founder, editor, *Nouvelle Revue,* 1879-99.
b. 1836
d. 1936
Source: *BiD&SB; BioIn 1, 5, 11; CelCen;*
InWom; OxFr; PseudN 82; REn

Adam, Ken
English. Art Director, Designer
Won Oscar for *Barry Lyndon,* 1975; other
    films include several of James Bond series.
b. Feb 5, 1921 in Berlin, Germany
Source: *ConTFT 1; FilmEn; IntMPA 86;*
VarWW 85

Adam, Robert
Scottish. Architect, Furniture Designer
Principal work reacts against robustness of
    Palladian school using lightness, elegance
    of neoclassicism.
b. Jul 3, 1728 in Kirkcaldy, Scotland
d. Mar 3, 1792 in London, England
Source: *Alli; AntBDN H; AtlBL; BiDBrA;*
BiDLA; DcBrWA; DcD&D; DcEnL; EncUrb;
IlDcG; LongCEL; McGDA; McGEWB; NewC;
OxArt; OxDecA; WhDW

Adam and the Ants
[Adam Ant; Matthew Ashman; David Barbe;
    Chris Hughes; Terry Lee Miall; Kevin
    Mooney; Marco Pirroni; Gary Tibbs;
    Andrew Warren]
English. Music Group
Fantasy-oriented, new Romantic group, 1977-
    82; had number one album *Kings of the*
    Wild Frontier, 1981.
Source: *RolSEnR 83*

Adam Ant
see: Ant, Adam

Adamany, David Walter
American. University Administrator
Pres., Wayne State U, Detroit, MI.
b. Sep 23, 1936 in Jonesville, Wisconsin
Source: *AmM&WS 73S; WhoAm 82;*
WhoMW 74

Adamic, Louis
American. Author, Sociologist, Editor
Wrote on politics, the Balkans, immigrants:
    The Native's Return, 1934.
b. Mar 23, 1899 in Blato, Dalmatia
d. Sep 4, 1951 in Riegelsville, Pennsylvania
Source: *AmAu&B; CnDAL; ConAmA; CurBio*
40, 51; DcAmB S5; DcLEL; OxAmL; REn;
REnAL; TwCA, SUP; WhAm 3

Adamle, Mike (Michael David)
American. Broadcast Journalist
Pro football player, 1971-77, who is currently
    sportcaster, NBC-TV.
b. Oct 4, 1949 in Euclid, Ohio
Source: *WhoAm 82; WhoFtbl 74*

Adamov, Arthur
Russian. Author, Dramatist
Plays range from avant-garde *Ping Pong,*
  1955, to social protest *Paolo Paoli,* 1957.
b. Aug 23, 1908 in Kislovodsk, Russia
d. Mar 16, 1970 in Paris, France
Source: *CasWL; CnMD; CnThe; ConAu 17R,
25R, P-2; ConLC 4; EncWL; McGEWD;
ModRL; ModWD; PenC EUR; REnWD;
WorAu*

Adamowski, Timothee
Polish. Musician
b. Mar 24, 1858 in Warsaw, Poland
d. Apr 18, 1943 in Boston, Massachusetts
Source: *CurBio 43; WebBD 80*

Adams, Abigail Smith
[Mrs. John Adams; Diana; Portia]
American. Author, First Lady
Only woman to be wife of one pres., mother
  of another, John Quincy Adams.
b. Nov 11, 1744 in Weymouth,
  Massachusetts
d. Oct 28, 1818 in Quincy, Massachusetts
Source: *AmAu&B; AmBi; AmWom;
AmWomWr; ApCAB; BbD; BiCAW; BiD&SB;
CyAL 1; DcAmAu; DcAmB; DcNAA; Drake;
HarEnUS; HerW; LibW; NatCAB 2; NotAW;
ObitOF 79; OxAmL; PseudN 82; REn;
REnAL; TwCBDA; WebAB, 79; WhAm HS;
WhAmP; WorAl*

Adams, Alvan Leigh
American. Basketball Player
Forward, Phoenix, 1975--; NBA Rookie of
  Year, 1976.
b. Jul 29, 1954 in Lawrence, Kansas
Source: *BioIn 10; OfNBA 81*

Adams, Andy
American. Rancher, Author
Wrote *The Log of a Cowboy,* 1903.
b. May 3, 1859 in Whitley County, Indiana
d. Sep 26, 1935
Source: *DcAmB S1; REnAL*

Adams, Ansel Easton
American. Photographer
Best known photographer in US, noted for
  landscape images of western US; helped
  establish photography as art form.
b. Feb 20, 1902 in San Francisco, California
d. Apr 22, 1984 in Monterey, California
Source: *BlueB 76; BnEnAmA; CmCal; ConAu
21R; ConPhot; CurBio 84; DcAmArt; DcCAr
81; MacBEP; WebAB, 79; WhAm 8; WhoAm
80, 82; WhoAmA 82; WrDr 84*

Adams, Annette Abbott
American. Politician, Judge
First woman federal prosecutor; ran for Dem.
  vice presidential spot, 1920.
b. Mar 12, 1877 in Prattville, California
d. Oct 26, 1956 in Sacramento, California
Source: *BiCAW; DcAmB S6; NatCAB 43;
NotAW MOD; WhAm 3A*

Adams, Brock(man)
American. Lawyer, Government Official
Secretary of Transportation, under Jimmy
  Carter, 1977-79.
b. Jan 13, 1927 in Atlanta, Georgia
Source: *BiDrAC; CngDr 74; WhoAm 74, 76,
78, 80, 82; WhoAmP 73; WhoGov 75;
WhoWest 84*

Adams, Brooke
American. Actress
In film *Invasion of the Body Snatchers,* 1978.
b. Feb 8, 1949 in New York, New York
Source: *BioIn 11; IntMPA 82; WhoAm 82*

Adams, Brooks
American. Historian
Wrote *Emancipation of Massachusetts,* 1887;
  Theory of Social Revolution, 1913.
b. Jun 24, 1848 in Quincy, Massachusetts
d. Feb 13, 1927 in Boston, Massachusetts
Source: *AmAu; AmAu&B; AmBi; ApCAB;
BiD&SB; DcAmAu; DcAmB; DcAmDH;
DcAmSR; DcNAA; EncAB-H; OxAmH;
OxAmL; PenC AM; REnAL; TwCBDA;
WebAB, 79; WhDW; WhAm 1*

Adams, Bryan
Canadian. Singer, Musician
Debut album produced first hit "Lonely
  Nights," 1982; hit single "Heaven," 1985.
b. Nov 5, 1959 in Vancouver, British
  Columbia
Source: *RkOn 85*

Adams, Charles Francis, Sr.
American. Author, Politician
Vice presidential candidate, 1848, who was
  minister to England, 1861-68.
b. Aug 18, 1807 in Boston, Massachusetts
d. Nov 21, 1886 in Boston, Massachusetts
Source: *AmAu&B; AmBi; ApCAB; BbD;
BiD&SB; BiDrAC; CyAL 2; DcAmAu;
DcAmB; DcNAA; EncAB-H; OxAmL;
TwCBDA; WebAB; WhAm HS*

Adams, Charles Francis, Jr.
American. Historian, Lawyer
Grandson of John Quincy Adams; author of
several books of New England history.
b. May 27, 1835 in Boston, Massachusetts
d. Mar 20, 1915 in Washington, District of
Columbia
Source: *AmAu; AmAu&B; BbD; BiD&SB;
DcAmAu; DcAmB; EncAB-H; OxAmL; REn;
REnAL; WebAB; WhAm 1*

Adams, Cliff
[Kool and the Gang]
American. Musician
Has played trombone with Kool and the
Gang since 1980.
b. Oct 8, 1952 in New Jersey
Source: *NF*

Adams, Don
[Donald James Yarmy]
American. Actor, Comedian
Played Maxwell Smart on TV series "Get
Smart," 1965-70.
b. Apr 19, 1927 in New York, New York
Source: *ConTFT 3; WhoAm 82*

Adams, Douglas Noel
British. Author
Wrote *The Hitchhiker's Guide to the Galaxy,*
1979; made into British TV series shown
on PBS.
b. Mar 11, 1952 in Cambridge, England
Source: *ConAu 106; ConDr 82B; ConLC 27;
WrDr 82*

Adams, Edie
[Elizabeth Edith Enke]
American. Singer, Actress
Wife of Ernie Kovacs; appeared in *It's a
Mad, Mad, Mad, Mad World,* 1963.
b. Apr 16, 1929 in Kingston, Pennsylvania
Source: *BiE&WWA; ConTFT 3; FilmgC;
ForWC 70; IntMPA 82; MotPP; MovMk;
NotNAT; PseudN 82; WhoAm 82; WhoHol A;
WhoThe 77*

Adams, Edwin
American. Actor
Light comedian whose most successful role
was Enoch Arden in drama of Tennyson's
poem, 1869.
b. Feb 3, 1834 in Medford, Massachusetts
d. Oct 25, 1877 in Philadelphia, Pennsylvania
Source: *ApCAB; DcAmB; Drake; FamA&A;
NatCAB 5; NotNAT; OxThe; WhAm HS*

Adams, Eve Bertrand
American. Government Official
Director of US Mint, 1961-69.
b. Sep 10, 1908 in Wonder, Nevada
Source: *BioIn 6; CurBio 62; WhoAm 80, 82;
WhoAmP 73; WhoAmW 74*

Adams, Frank Ramsay
American. Author, Songwriter
Wrote lyrics for over 200 songs; scripts for
25 films.
b. Jul 7, 1883 in Morrison, Illinois
d. Oct 8, 1963 in White Lake, Michigan
Source: *DcAmB S7*

Adams, Franklin P(ierce)
"F.P.A."
American. Journalist, Humorist
Best known for columns appearing in NY
Herald-Tribune; panelist on radio's
"Information Please."
b. Nov 15, 1881 in Chicago, Illinois
d. Mar 23, 1960 in New York, New York
Source: *AmAu&B; ChhPo, S1; CnDAL;
ConAmA; ConAu 93; CurBio 41, 60; OxAmL;
PseudN 82; REn; REnAL; TwCA, SUP;
WebAB, 79; WhAm 3A; WhNAA*

Adams, Hannah
American. Author
Considered first professional American
woman writer: *History of New England,*
1799.
b. Oct 2, 1755 in Medford, Massachusetts
d. Dec 15, 1831 in Brookline, Massachusetts
Source: *NotAW; OxAmL 83; WebBD 80*

Adams, Harriet Stratemeyer
[Victor Appleton, II; Franklin W Dixon;
Laura Lee Hope; Carolyn Keene, pseuds.]
American. Children's Author
Wrote 200 books for *Hardy Boys; Nancy
Drew; Bobbsey Twins* series.
b. Dec 11, 1892 in Newark, New Jersey
d. Mar 27, 1982 in Pottersville, New Jersey
Source: *AmAu&B; AmWomWr; AuNews 2;
ConAu 106, 17R, 81; EncMys; EncSF;
NewYTBS 82; PseudN 82; SmATA 1, 29;
WhAm 8; WhoAm 82*

Adams, Henry Brooks
American. Historian, Author
Grandson of John Quincy Adams who won
   Pulitzer, 1919, for *Education of Henry
   Adams.*
b. Feb 16, 1838 in Boston, Massachusetts
d. Mar 27, 1918 in Washington, District of
   Columbia
Source: *Alli; AmAu; AmAu&B; AmBi; AmWr;
ApCAB; AtlBL; BbD; BiD&SB; CasWL;
CnDAL; CyWA; DcAmAu; DcAmB; DcAmSR;
DcBiA; DcLEL; DcNAA; EncAB-H; EncWL
2; EvLB; LongCTC; McGEWB; ModAL, SI;
OxAmH; OxAmL; OxEng; PenC AM; RAdv
1; RComWL; REn; REnAL; TwCBDA;
TwCLC 4; TwCWr; WebAB; WebE&AL;
WhAm 1; WhAmP; WhoTwCL*

Adams, Herbert Samuel
American. Sculptor
Founder, National Sculpture Society, 1893;
   known for portrait busts.
b. Jan 28, 1858 in West Concord, Vermont
d. May 21, 1945 in New York, New York
Source: *CurBio 45; DcAmB S3; WebBD 80;
WhAm 2*

Adams, Jack (John James)
"Jovial Jawn"
Canadian. Hockey Player, Hockey Coach
With Detroit Red Wings, 1927-62; won seven
   Stanley Cups; Hall of Fame, 1959.
b. Jun 14, 1895 in Fort William, Ontario
d. May 1, 1968 in Detroit, Michigan
Source: *BioIn 3, 8, 10; ObitOF 79; WhoHcky
73*

Adams, James Truslow
American. Historian, Author
Wrote 1922 Pulitzer-winner *Founding of New
   England and Epic of America,* 1921.
b. Oct 18, 1878 in Brooklyn, New York
d. May 18, 1949 in Westport, Connecticut
Source: *AmAu&B; ConAmA; CurBio 41, 49;
DcAmB S4; DcLEL; DcNAA; EvLB; ObitOF
79; OxAmL; REn; REnAL; TwCA, SUP;
WebAB; WhAm 2; WhNAA*

Adams, Joey
[Joseph Abramowitz]
American. Comedian, Author
Nightclub, film performer who starred in
   "Joey Adams" TV show, 1956-58.
b. Jan 6, 1911 in Brooklyn, New York
Source: *CelR; ConAu 1NR, 49; PseudN 82;
WhoAm 74, 76, 78, 80, 82, 84; WhoWor 74;
WhoWorJ 72*

Adams, John
"The Atlas of Independence"
American. US President
Second US pres., 1797-1801; helped draw up
   Treaty of Paris, 1793, ending American
   Revolution.
b. Oct 30, 1735 in Braintree, Massachusetts
d. Jul 4, 1826 in Quincy, Massachusetts
Source: *Alli; AmAu&B; AmBi; ApCAB; BbD;
BiD&SB; BiDLA SUP; BiDrAC; BiDrUSE;
CelCen; ChhPo S1; CyAG; CyAL 1; CyWA;
DcAmAu; DcAmB; DcNAA; Drake; EncAB-H;
EvLB; LinLib S; McGEWB; NatCAB 2;
OxAmL; PseudN 82; REn; REnAL; TwCBDA;
WebAB, 79; WhAm HS; WhAmP; WorAl*

Adams, John Couch
English. Astronomer
Discovered planet Neptune, 1845; official
   credit given to Leverrier, 1846.
b. Jun 5, 1819 in Laneast, England
d. Jan 21, 1892 in Cambridge, England
Source: *BioIn 1, 5, 11; McGEWB; NewCol 75*

Adams, John Hanly
American. Author, Editor
Exec. editor, *US News and World Report,*
   1970-79; contributing editor, *Nation's
   Business,* 1980-82.
b. Nov 2, 1918 in Sikeston, Missouri
Source: *WhoAm 74, 76, 78, 80, 82, 84;
WhoF&I 74*

Adams, John Quincy
"The Accidental President"; "Old Man
   Eloquent"; "Publicola"; "The Second
   John"
American. Political Leader
Son of John Adams, sixth US president,
   1825-29; catalyst behind Monroe Doctrine,
   1823.
b. Jul 11, 1767 in Braintree, Massachusetts
d. Feb 23, 1848 in Washington, District of
   Columbia
Source: *AmBi; BiDLA; BiDrUSE; CyAL 1;
DcAmAu; DcAmB; DcEnL; DcLEL; Drake;
EncAAH; EncAB-A; LinLib S; McGEWB;
NatCAB 5; OxAmH; OxAmL; PseudN 82;
REn; REnAL; REnAW; TwCBDA; WebAB
79; WhAm HS; WhAmP*

Adams, Julie
[Betty May Adams]
American. Actress
Leading lady in second features; carried off
   by "Creature from the Black Lagoon," in
   1954 film.
b. Oct 17, 1926 in Waterloo, Iowa
Source: *FilmEn; FilmgC; IntMPA 75, 76, 77,
78, 79, 80, 81, 82; PseudN 82*

Adams, Leonie Fuller
American. Author
Metaphysical romantic lyricist whose verse
volumes include *This Measure*, 1933.
b. Dec 9, 1899 in Brooklyn, New York
Source: *AmAu&B; Au&Wr 71; CnE&AP;
CnMWL; ConAmA; ConAu P-1; ConP 70, 75,
80; DcLEL; DrAP 75; IntWW 74, 80, 81, 82;
ModAL; OxAmL; REn; SixAP; TwCA SUP;
TwCWr; WhoWor 74; WrDr 76, 80, 82*

Adams, Louisa Catherine
[Mrs. John Quincy Adams]
American. First Lady
Married John Quincy Adams, 1797; when
Congress adjourned to attend her funeral
it was first time a woman was so honored.
b. Feb 12, 1775 in London, England
d. May 14, 1852 in Washington, District of
Columbia
Source: *AmBi; AmWomWr; BiCAW; HerW;
InWom; NatCAB 5; NotAW*

Adams, Mason
American. Actor
Played Charlie Hume in TV series "Lou
Grant," 1977-82; nominated for two
Emmys.
b. Feb 26, 1919 in New York, New York
Source: *BioIn 10; What 1-5; WhoAm 82*

Adams, Maud
[Maud Solveig Christina Wikstrom]
Swedish. Actress, Model
Starred with Roger Moore in James Bond
films *Man with the Golden Gun*, 1974,
Octopussy, 1983.
b. Feb 12, 1945 in Lulea, Sweden
Source: *BioIn 10; FilmEn; VarWW 85;
WhoHol A*

Adams, Maude
[Maude Kiskadden]
American. Actress
Played more than 1,500 performances in title
role of *Peter Pan*.
b. Nov 11, 1872 in Salt Lake City, Utah
d. Jul 17, 1953 in Tannersville, New York
Source: *CnThe; DcAmB S5; EncWT;
FamA&A; InWom; LibW; LinLib S; ObitOF
79; OxAmL; OxThe; REnAL; TwCBDA;
WebAB, 79; WhAm 3; WhoStg 1906, 1908;
WomWWA 14; WorAl*

Adams, Nick
[Nicholas Adamschock]
American. Actor
Starred in TV series "The Rebel," 1959-61.
b. Jul 10, 1931 in Nanticoke, Pennsylvania
d. Feb 5, 1968 in Beverly Hills, California
Source: *FilmgC; MotPP; MovMk; NotNAT B;
ObitOF 79; PseudN 82; WhScrn 74, 77;
WhoHol B*

Adams, Richard
English. Author
Wrote best-seller *Watership Down*, 1972.
b. May 9, 1920 in Newbury, England
Source: *AuNews 1, 2; ConAu 33R, 49;
ConLC 4, 5, 18; CurBio 78; Novels; PiP;
SmATA 17; TwCCW 78; WhoAm 82; WorAu
1970; WrDr 76, 80*

Adams, Samuel
"Alfred"; "The American Cato"; "The
Cromwell of New England"; "The Father
of America"
American. Revolutionary, Statesman
Force behind Boston Tea Party, 1773; signed
Declaration of Independence.
b. Sep 27, 1722 in Boston, Massachusetts
d. Oct 2, 1803 in Boston, Massachusetts
Source: *Alli; AmAu; AmAu&B; AmBi;
ApCAB; BiAUS; BiDrAC; DcAmAu; DcAmB;
DcNAA; Drake; EncAB-H; OxAmL; PseudN
82; REn; REnAL; TwCBDA; WebAB; WhAm
HS; WhAmP*

Adams, Samuel Hopkins
[Warner Fabian, pseud.]
American. Author, Journalist
Writings included muckraking articles;
Average Jones detective stories, biographies.
b. Jan 26, 1871 in Dunkirk, New York
d. Nov 15, 1958 in Beaufort, South Carolina
Source: *AmAu&B; AmLY; AmNov; AuBYP;
CnDAL; EncMys; OxAmL; PseudN 82; REn;
TwCA, SUP; WhAm 3*

Adams, Sherman Llewellyn
American. Public Official
Rep. governor of NH, 1949-53; chief of
White House staff, 1953-58.
b. Jan 8, 1899 in East Dover, Vermont
Source: *AmAu&B; BiDrAC; CnMWL; CurBio
52; IntWW 82; PolProf E; Who 74, 82;
WhoAm 74, 76, 78, 80, 82; WhoAmP 73*

Adams, "Tom" (John Michael Geoffrey Maningham)
Barbadian. Political Leader
Prime minister of Barbados, 1976-85.
b. Sep 24, 1931 in Barbados
d. Mar 12, 1985 in Bridgetown, Barbados
Source: *IntWW 82, 83; IntYB 81, 82; Who 80, 83; WhoWor 80, 82*

Adams, Tony (Anthony Patrick)
Producer
Films include *10*, 1979; *S.O.B.*, 1981.
b. Feb 15, 1953 in Dublin, Ireland
Source: *ConTFT 2; VarWW 85*

Adams, Walter Sydney
American. Astronomer
Pres., American Astronomical Society, 1931-34; focused on stellar spectra, sunspots.
b. Dec 20, 1876 in Antioch, Turkey
d. May 11, 1956 in Pasadena, California
Source: *WebAB; WhAm 3; WhNAA*

Adams, William
"Anjin Sama"; "Mr. Pilot"
English. Navigator
First Englishman to visit Japan, 1600; remained there until death.
b. 1564 in England
d. 1620 in Japan
Source: *NewCol 75*

Adamson, George
Kenyan. Animal Expert
Husband of Joy Adamson; established Kora Reserve wild animal sanctuary, Kenya.
b. 1906 in India
Source: *BioIn 8, 9*

Adamson, Joy Friederike Victoria Gessner
[Mrs. George Adamson]
Kenyan. Author, Animal Expert
Best known work, *Born Free*, 1960; filmed, 1966.
b. Jan 20, 1910 in Troppau, Silesia
d. Jan 3, 1980 in Shaba, Kenya
Source: *Au&Wr 71; ConAu 69, 93; ConLC 17; CurBio 72, 80; SmATA 11; Who 74; WhoAm 74*

Adams, Charles Samuel
American. Cartoonist
Created "The Addams Family" cartoons, TV series, 1964-66.
b. Jan 7, 1912 in Westfield, New Jersey
Source: *AmAu&B; CelR; ConAu 61; CurBio 54; IntWW 74; WebAB; WhoAm 74, 76, 78, 80, 82; WhoAmA 73; WhoWor 74; WrDr 76*

Addams, Dawn
English. Actress
Best known as Charlie Chaplin's leading lady in *A King in New York*, 1957.
b. Sep 21, 1930 in Felixstowe, England
d. May 7, 1985 in London, England
Source: *ConTFT 2; FilmgC; InWom; IntMPA 81, 82; MotPP; OxFilm; WhoHol A; WhoThe 77, 81*

Addams, Jane
American. Social Worker, Suffragette
Organized Hull House, Chicago, 1889; first American woman to receive Nobel Peace Prize, 1931.
b. Sep 6, 1860 in Cedarville, Illinois
d. May 21, 1935 in Chicago, Illinois
Source: *AmAu&B; AmBi; AmLY; DcAmAu; DcAmB S1; DcLEL; DcNAA; EncAB-H; HerW; InWom; NotAW; OxAmL; REn; REnAL; WebAB; WhAm 1; WhAmP; WhNAA*

Adderley, "Cannonball" (Julian Edwin)
American. Musician
Alto-saxophonist who played with Miles Davis in 1950s; had 1960s hit "Mercy, Mercy, Mercy."
b. Sep 9, 1928 in Tampa, Florida
d. Aug 8, 1975 in Gary, Indiana
Source: *Baker 78; BiDAmM; CelR; CurBio 61, 75; DrBlPA; Ebony 1; PseudN 82; WhAm 6; WhoAm 74*

Addinsell, Richard
English. Composer
Compositions for films include *Blithe Spirit*, 1945; *Under Capricorn*, 1949; *Macbeth*, 1960.
b. Jan 13, 1904 in Oxford, England
d. Nov 15, 1977 in London, England
Source: *BiE&WWA; FilmgC; IntMPA 77; NotNAT; OxFilm; Who 74; WhoMus 72; WhoThe 77*

Addison, Adele
American. Opera Singer
Soprano, who sang role of Bess in *Porgy and Bess*, 1958; made solo debut, 1962.
b. Jul 24, 1925 in New York, New York
Source: *WhoBlA 75; WhoWor 78*

Addison, Christopher, Viscount
English. Politician
MP; served on ministries concerned with public health, social welfare.
b. Jun 19, 1869 in Hogsthorpe, England
d. Dec 11, 1951 in Radnage, England
Source: *DcNaB 1951; GrBr; WhE&EA; WhLit*

Addison, John
English. Composer
Wrote notable film scores; won Oscar for
    Tom Jones, 1963.
b. Mar 16, 1920 in West Cobham, England
Source: *Baker 78; CmMov; FilmEn; FilmgC;*
IntMPA 81; NotNAT A; OxFilm; OxMus

Addison, Joseph
"Atticus"; "Clio"; "The English Atticus"; "A
    Literary Machiavel"
English. Essayist, Poet, Dramatist
Wrote essays with Sir Richard Stelle for the
    Tatler, 1709, *Spectator,* 1711-12.
b. May 1, 1672 in Milston, England
d. Jun 17, 1719 in London, England
Source: *AtlBL; BbD; BiD&SB; BrAu; CasWL;*
Chambr 2; CrtT 2; CyEd; CyWA; DcEnA;
DcEnL; DcEuL; DcLEL; EvLB; LongCEL;
McGEWB; McGEWD; MouLC 2; NewC;
OxArt; OxEng; OxThe; PenC ENG; PoChrch;
PseudN 82; RAdv 1; RComWL; REn;
WebE&AL; WhDW

Addison, Thomas
English. Physician
Discovered Addison's Disease, 1860.
b. 1793
d. 1860
Source: *Alli SUP*

Addonizio, Hugh Joseph
American. Politician
Dem. con. from NJ, 1949-61; mayor of
    Newark, NJ, 1962-70; convicted of
    extortion, 1970.
b. Jan 31, 1914 in Newark, New Jersey
d. Feb 2, 1981 in Red Bank, New Jersey
Source: *BiDrAC; BioIn 8, 9; NewYTBE 70;*
NewYTBS 81; PolProf J, NF; WhAm 7;
WhAmP

Addy, Wesley
American. Actor
Often cast in sinister roles: *Tora! Tora!*
    Tora!, 1970; *Network,* 1976.
b. Aug 4, 1913 in Omaha, Nebraska
Source: *BiE&WWA; FilmEn; FilmgC;*
NotNAT; WhoAm 78; WhoHol A; WhoThe
77, 81

Ade, George
American. Humorist, Dramatist
Humorous fables published as *Fables in*
    Slang, 1900.
b. Feb 9, 1866 in Kentland, Indiana
d. May 16, 1944 in Brookville, Indiana
Source: *AmAu&B; AmLY; BbD; BiD&SB;*
CasWL; Chambr 3; ChhPo, Sl; CnDAL;
ConAmL; CurBio 44; DcAmAu; DcAmB S3;
DcNAA; EvLB; IndAu 1816; McGEWD;
ModWD; NewCBMT; OxAmL; OxThe; PenC
AM; REn; REnAL; TwCA, SUP; TwCBDA;
TwCWr; WebAB; WhAm 2; WhNAA; WhoStg
1906, 1908

Adelman, Kenneth Lee
American. Government Official
Director, Arms Control and Disarmament
    Agency, 1983--.
b. Jun 9, 1946 in Chicago, Illinois
Source: *CurBio 85; NewYTBS 83; WhoAm 84*

Adelman, Sybil
Writer
Has written for TV since 1972: "The Mary
    Tyler Moore Show," "Alice," others.
b. Mar 15, 1942 in Winnipeg, Manitoba
Source: *ConTFT 3*

Adenauer, Konrad
German. Politician
First Chancellor of Federal German Republic
    (West Germany), 1949-63.
b. Jan 5, 1876 in Cologne, Germany
d. Apr 19, 1967 in Rhondorf, Germany
    (West)
Source: *CurBio 49, 58, 67; OxGer; REn;*
WhAm 4

Adjani, Isabelle
French. Actress
Received Oscar nomination for *The Story of*
    Adele H., 1975.
b. Jun 27, 1955 in Paris, France
Source: *BioIn 10; FilmEn; NewYTBS 84;*
WhoHol A

Adler, Alfred
Austrian. Author, Psychoanalyst
Rebelled against Freud's teaching, advocating
    individual psychology, 1907; originated
    phrase "inferiority complex."
b. Feb 7, 1870 in Vienna, Austria
d. May 28, 1937 in Aberdeen, Scotland
Source: *AsBiEn; GuPsyc; LinLib S; LongCTC;*
LuthC 75; MakMC; McGEWB; NamesHP;
OxGer; REn; TwCA, SUP; WhAm 4, HSA;
WhoLA

Adler, "Buddy" (Maurice)
American. Producer
Won Oscar for *From Here to Eternity*, 1953;
    succeeded Darryl Zanuck as head of 20th
    Century Fox.
b. Jun 22, 1909 in New York, New York
d. Jul 12, 1960 in Hollywood, California
Source: *DcFM; FilmgC; NatCAB 47; NotNAT
B; ObitOF 79; PseudN 82; WhAm 4;
WorEFlm*

Adler, Cyrus
American. Religious Leader, Educator
Wrote *Told in the Coffee House*, 1898; edited
    American Jewish Yearbook, 1899-1906.
b. Sep 13, 1863 in Van Buren, Alaska
d. Apr 7, 1940 in Philadelphia, Pennsylvania
Source: *AmAu&B; AmBi; ApCAB SUP;
DcAmAu; DcAmB S2; DcNAA; TwCBDA;
WebAB; WhAm 1*

Adler, David
American. Architect
Domestic architecture in Chicago was noted
    for traditional style, conventional form,
    1928-49.
b. Jan 3, 1883 in Milwaukee, Wisconsin
d. Sep 27, 1949 in Chicago, Illinois
Source: *BiDAmAr; BioIn 9; WhAm 3*

Adler, Elmer
American. Publisher
Noted bibliophile; founded *Colophon: Book
    Collectors Quarterly*, 1930-40.
b. Jul 22, 1884 in Rochester, New York
d. Jan 11, 1962 in San Juan, Puerto Rico
Source: *DcAmB S7*

Adler, Felix
American. Educator, Reformer, Author
Founder, Ethical Culture Society, 1876,
    which aided NY poor.
b. Aug 13, 1851 in Alzey, Germany
d. Apr 24, 1933 in New York, New York
Source: *AmAu&B; AmBi; ApCAB; BbD;
BiD&SB; DcAmAu; DcAmB S1; DcNAA;
REn; REnAL; TwCA, SUP; TwCBDA;
WebAB; WhAm 1; WhAmP; WhNAA*

Adler, Irving
[Robert Irving, pseud.]
American. Author
Writes scientific books for young people: *The
    Stars: Decoding Their Messages*, 1980.
b. 1913 in New York, New York
Source: *AmAu&B; Au&Wr 71; AuBYP;
ConAu 2NR, 25R; PseudN 82; SmATA 1, 29;
ThrBJA*

Adler, Jacob Pavlovitch
"The Great Eagle"
American. Actor
Star of Yiddish theater; father of Luther and
    Stella Adler.
b. 1855 in Russia
d. Apr 1, 1926 in New York, New York
Source: *Film 1; NotNAT B; PseudN 82;
WhScrn 77; WhThe; WhoHol B*

Adler, Julius Ochs
American. Newspaper Executive
General mgr., *NY Times*, 1935-55; adviser to
    Dwight Eisenhower.
b. Dec 3, 1892 in Chattanooga, Tennessee
d. Oct 3, 1955 in New York, New York
Source: *AmAu&B; CurBio 48, 56; ObitOF 79;
ObitT 1951; WhAm 3*

Adler, Kurt Herbert
American. Conductor
Founder, director, Western Opera Theater,
    1966; Spring Opera Theater of San
    Francisco, 1961.
b. Apr 2, 1905 in Vienna, Austria
Source: *Baker 78; BlueB 76; CmCal; ConAu
3NR; CurBio 79; IntWW 74; NewEOp 71;
NewYTBS 75; WhoAm 74, 78; WhoWest 74,
82; WhoWor 76; WhoWorJ 72*

Adler, Larry (Lawrence Cecil)
American. Musician, Actor, Composer
Has appeared in nightclubs, concerts as
    soloist on harmonica.
b. Feb 10, 1914 in Baltimore, Maryland
Source: *BiE&WWA; FilmgC; NotNAT; Who
74; WhoHol A*

Adler, Luther (Lutha)
American. Actor, Director
Child actor in Yiddish Theater, whose films
    include *The Three Sisters*, 1977.
b. May 4, 1903 in New York, New York
d. Dec 8, 1984 in Kutztown, Pennsylvania
Source: *BiE&WWA; ConTFT 2; FilmgC;
IntMPA 80, 81, 82; MotPP; MovMk;
NotNAT; PIP&P; PseudN 82; VarWW 85;
Vers B; WhoAm 80; WhoHol A; WhoThe 77,
81*

Adler, Mortimer Jerome
American. Author, Philosopher
Director, Institute for Philosophical Research,
    1952--; wrote best-seller, *How to Read a
    Book*, 1940.
b. Dec 28, 1902 in New York, New York
Source: *ConAu 65; CurBio 40, 52; DrAS 74P;
OxAmL; REnAL; TwCA SUP; WebAB;
WhNAA; WhoAm 82, 84; WhoWor 74*

Adler, Peter Herman
American. Conductor
b. Dec 2, 1899 in Jablonec, Czechoslovakia
Source: *WhoAm 74, 76, 78, 80, 82*

Adler, Polly
[Pearl Adler]
American. Madam
Began career as madam, 1920; wrote *A House Is Not a Home,* 1953.
b. Apr 16, 1900 in Yanow, Poland
d. Jun 9, 1962 in Hollywood, California
Source: *AmAu&B; Au&Wr 71; BioIn 3, 6; InWom; NotAW MOD*

Adler, Richard
American. Composer, Author
Composed musical score for *Damn Yankees,* 1955.
b. Aug 3, 1921 in New York, New York
Source: *AmSCAP 66; BiE&WWA; EncMT; NotNAT; WhoAm 80, 82; WhoGov 72; WhoThe 77; WhoWor 74*

Adler, Stella
American. Actress
Director, teacher, Stella Adler Conservatory of Acting, 1949--.
b. Feb 10, 1902 in New York, New York
Source: *BiE&WWA; EncWT; FilmgC; NotNAT; PlP&P; VarWW 85; WhoHol A; WhoThe 77, 81*

Adolfo
[Adolfo Sardina]
American. Fashion Designer
Founded Adolfo, Inc., 1963; designs custom and ready-to-wear; won Coty Awards, 1955, 1969.
b. Feb 15, 1933 in Cardones, Cuba
Source: *CurBio 72; PseudN 82; WhoAm 82; WorFshn*

Adonis, Joe
[Joe Doro]
"Joey A"
Italian. Organized Crime Figure
Headed Broadway mob that controlled bootleg liquor in Manhattan; deported, 1956.
b. Nov 22, 1902 in Montemarano, Italy
d. Nov 26, 1971 in Aucona, Italy
Source: *EncACr; ObitOF 79; PseudN 82*

Adoree, Renee
[Jeanne de la Fonte]
French. Actress, Circus Performer
Circus dancer; starred in several films, 1920-30.
b. Sep 30, 1898 in Lille, France
d. Oct 5, 1933 in Tujunga, California
Source: *BiDFilm; FilmEn; Film 2; FilmgC; InWom; MotPP; MovMk; NotNAT B; PseudN 82; TwYS; WhScrn 77, 83; WhoHol B; WorEFlm*

Adrian
[Gilbert Adrain Greenburgh]
American. Fashion Designer
Played John Gilbert's leading lady in *The Big Parade,* 1925.
b. Mar 3, 1903 in Naugatauk, Connecticut
d. Sep 14, 1959 in Hollywood, California
Source: *DcFM; FilmgC; PseudN 82; WorFshn*

Aerosmith
[Tom Hamilton; Joey Kramer; Joe Perry; Steve Tyler; Brad Whitford]
American. Music Group
Heavy metal band formed 1970; known for blues-based, hard-rock style; hit single "Dream On," 1975.
Source: *BkPepl; IlEncRk; RolSEnR 83*

Aeschylus
"The Father of Greek Drama"; "The Father of Greek Tragedy"; "The Father of Tragedy"; "The Founder of the Greek Drama"
Greek. Poet, Dramatist
Wrote *Prometheus Bound;* seven of 90 plays survive.
b. 524 ?BC in Eleusis, Greece
d. 456 ?BC in Sicily, Italy
Source: *AtlBL; BbD; BiD&SB; CasWL; CnThe; CyWA; DcBiPP; DcEnL; Dis&D; EncWT; Grk&L; LinLib S; LongCEL; LuthC 75; McGEWD; NewC; NewEOp 71; NotNAT B; OxEng; OxThe; PenC CL; PlP&P; PseudN 82; RComWL; REn; REnWD; WhDW*

Aesop
Greek. Author
Semi-legendary figure; hundreds of animal fables attributed to him.
b. 620 ?BC in Phrygia, Asia Minor
d. 560 ?BC
Source: *AnCL; AtlBL; BiD&SB; CarSB; CasWL; CyWA; DcEnL; NewC; OxEng; PenC CL; RComWL; REn; WhoChL*

Aga Khan III
[Aga Sultan Sir Mahomed Shah]
Indian. Religious Leader, Statesman
Descendant of Mohammed; spiritual leader of
   80 million Ismaili Moslems, 1885-1957;
   pres., League of Nations, 1937.
b. Nov 2, 1877 in Karachi, India
d. Jul 11, 1957 in Versoix, Switzerland
Source: *BioIn 3, 4, 5; CurBio 46, 57;
McGEWB; NewCol 75; ObitOF 79; PseudN
82; WhAm 3*

Aga Khan IV
[Prince Karim Khan]
Religious Leader
Descendant of Mohammed; grandson of Aga
   Khan III, who succeeded him as Imam,
   spiritual leader of Ismaili Moslems, 1957--.
b. Dec 13, 1936 in Geneva, Switzerland
Source: *BioIn 4, 9; CurBio 60; IntWW 75;
IntYB 81, 82; NewYTBS 82; WebBD 80;
Who 74, 82; WhoWor 74*

Aga Khan, Sadruddin, Prince
Pakistani. Diplomat
Consultant to UN secretary-general, 1978--;
   wrote *International Protection of Refugees,*
   1976.
b. Jan 17, 1932 in Paris, France
Source: *BioIn 10; IntWW 82; MidE 82; Who
74, 82; WhoUN 75; WhoWor 78, 80*

Agam, Yaacov
[Yaacov Gibstein]
Israeli. Artist
Contrapuntal geometric painter; "Jacob's
   Ladder," 1964, decorates ceiling of
   Jerusalem's Convention Center.
b. May 11, 1928 in Rishon Letzion, Palestine
Source: *BioIn 7, 8, 11; ConArt 77; CurBio
81; IntWW 75, 76, 77, 78; McGDA; MidE
78, 79; WhoWor 74*

Agar, Herbert Sebastian
American. Diplomat, Author, Economist
Founded Freedom House, 1941, to stimulate
   int'l. cooperation.
b. Sep 29, 1897 in New Rochelle, New York
d. Nov 24, 1980 in Sussex, England
Source: *AmAu&B; Au&Wr 71; ConAu 65,
102; IntWW 74; OxAmL; REnAL; TwCA,
SUP; Who 74; WhoWor 78*

Agar, John
American. Actor
Had roles in action films, but best known as
   first husband of Shirley Temple, 1946-49.
b. Jan 31, 1921 in Chicago, Illinois
Source: *FilmEn; FilmgC; IntMPA 82; MotPP;
WhoHol A*

Agassiz, Elizabeth Cabot Cary
American. Scientist, Educator
Founder, first pres., Radcliffe College, 1894-
   1902.
b. Dec 5, 1822 in Boston, Massachusetts
d. Jun 27, 1902 in Arlington, Massachusetts
Source: *AmAu&B; AmBi; AmWom;
AmWomWr; BiCAW; BiDAmEd; BiD&SB;
DcAmAu; DcAmB; DcNAA; HarEnUS;
IntDcWB; LibW; NatCAB 12; NotAW*

Agassiz, Louis (Jean Louis Radolphe)
American. Author, Zoologist, Educator
Naturalist who theorized aglacial epoch,
   epochs of creation, opposing Darwin's
   theory.
b. May 28, 1807 in Motier, Switzerland
d. Dec 12, 1873 in Cambridge, Massachusetts
Source: *AmAu; AmAu&B; AmBi; BbD;
BiD&SB; DcAmAu; DcAmB; DcEnL; EncAB-
H; OxAmL; OxCan; PenC AM; REn;
REnAL; TwCBDA; WebAB; WhAm HS*

Agate, James Evershed
English. Drama Critic, Author
Veteran theater columnist who wrote nine-
   volume autobiography, *Ego,* 1935.
b. Sep 9, 1877 in Manchester, England
d. Jun 6, 1947 in London, England
Source: *DcLEL; EvLB; LongCTC; ModBrL;
NewC; OxThe; PenC ENG; REn; TwCA,
SUP; TwCWr*

Agca, Mehmet Ali
[Faruk Ozgun]
Turkish. Terrorist, Attempted Assassin
Convicted of attempting to assassinate Pope
   John Paul II, May 1981.
b. 1958 in Malatya Hekinhan, Turkey
Source: *NewYTBS 81; PseudN 82*

Agee, James Rufus
American. Author, Poet
Won Pulitzer, 1958, for *A Death in the
   Family.*
b. Nov 27, 1909 in Knoxville, Tennessee
d. May 16, 1955 in New York, New York
Source: *AmAu&B; AmWr; AuNews 1; CasWL;
EncWL; FilmgC; ModAL, SI; OxAmL;
OxFilm; PenC AM; RAdv 1; REn; REnAL;
SixAP; TwCA SUP; TwCWr; WebAB;
WebE&AL; WhAm 4; WhoTwCL; WorEFlm*

Agee, Philip
American. Government Official, Author
Former CIA agent who wrote expose *Inside
   the Company: CIA Diary,* 1975.
b. Jul 19, 1935 in Tacoma Park, Florida
Source: *BioIn 10, 11; ConAu 104; NewYTBS
74; PolProf NF*

Agee, William McReynolds
American. Corporation Executive
Chief exec., Bendix Corp., 1977-83; husband
of Mary Cunningham.
b. Jan 5, 1938 in Boise, Idaho
Source: *AutoN 79; BioIn 11; Dun&B 79;
NewYTBS 82; WhoAm 74, 76, 78, 80, 82;
WhoF&I 74, 75, 77, 79; WhoWor 76, 78*

Ager, Milton
American. Composer
Popular balladist who wrote "Ain't She
Sweet?"; "Happy Days Are Here Again."
b. Oct 6, 1893 in Chicago, Illinois
d. May 6, 1979 in Los Angeles, California
Source: *AmPS; AmSCAP 66; Baker 78;
BiDAmM; BioIn 4, 6; CmpEPM; NewYTBS
79*

Agle, Nan Hayden
American. Children's Author
Co-writer of popular "Three Boys" series
1951--.
b. Apr 13, 1905 in Baltimore, Maryland
Source: *AuBYP; ConAu 1NR, 3NR; IntAu&W
77; PseudN 82; SmATA 13; WrDr 76*

Agnelli, Giovanni
Italian. Auto Executive
Chm., FIAT, Italy's largest private business,
1966--.
b. Mar 12, 1921 in Turin, Italy
Source: *CurBio 72; IntWW 79, 80, 81, 82;
Who 74, 82; WhoF&I 74; WhoWor 80, 82*

Agnew, Peter
see: Nazareth

Agnew, Spiro Theodore
American. Politician
Richard Nixon's vp; resigned Oct 10, 1973,
pleading no contest to income tax evasion
charges.
b. Nov 9, 1918 in Baltimore, Maryland
Source: *BiDrAC; BiDrUSE; BioNews 74;
CelR; CurBio 68; EncAB-H; IntWW 74;
PolProf NF; WebAB, 79; WhAmP; Who 74;
WhoAm 74, 76, 78, 80, 82; WhoAmP 73;
WhoGov 75; WhoS&SW 82; WhoWor 78*

Agnon, S(hmuel) Y(osef)
[Shmuel Yosef Czaczkes]
Israeli. Author
Wrote *Days of Awe*, 1948; first Israeli to win
Nobel Prize for literature, 1966.
b. 1888 in Buczacz, Galicia
d. Feb 17, 1970 in Rehovot, Israel
Source: *CasWL; ConAu 17R, 25R, P-2;
ConLC 4, 8, 14; EncWL; PenC EUR;
PseudN 82; RComWL; WhAm 5; WorAu*

Agostini, Peter
American. Sculptor
Known for humorous "frozen life" plaster
castings.
b. Feb 13, 1913 in New York, New York
Source: *BioIn 4, 6; BnEnAmA; DcAmArt;
DcCAA 71, 77; WhoAm 74, 76; WhoAmA 73,
76, 78*

Agostino di Duccio
Italian. Sculptor
b. 1418 in Florence, Italy
d. 1481 in Florence, Italy
Source: *BioIn 1; NewCol 75*

Agpaoa, Tony (Antonio)
Philippine. Surgeon
Psychic healer who operates with bare hands,
without anesthetics.
b. 1939
Source: *BioIn 10*

Agricola, Georgius
[Georg Bauer]
German. Scientist, Mineralogist
Father of mineralogy; first to classify
minerals scientifically.
b. Apr 20, 1494 in Eisleben, Germany
d. Sep 22, 1566 in Berlin, Germany
Source: *AsBiEn; DcCathB; DcScB; McGEWB;
OxGer; PenC EUR; PseudN 82*

Agrippa, Heinrich Cornelius
[Henricus Cornelius von Nettlesheim Agrippa]
"The Omniscient Doctor"
German. Theologian, Scholar, Author
Writer on occult whose *De Occulta
Philosophia*, 1529, defended magic.
b. Sep 14, 1486 in Cologne, Germany
d. Feb 18, 1535 in Grenoble, France
Source: *BiD&SB; DcEnL; EncO&P 78;
EvEuW; IlEncMy; LuthC 75; OxEng; PseudN
82*

Agrippa, Marcus Vipsanius
Roman. Statesman, General
Collected material for map of Roman
Empire.
b. 63 BC
d. 12 BC
Source: *PenC CL*

Agrippina
Roman. Empress
Mother of Nero who was murdered by her
son.
b. 16
d. 59 in Baige, Italy
Source: *MacDWB; NewCol 75; REn*

Agron, Salvador
American. Murderer
Youngest person, at age 16, to receive death
    sentence in NY state, 1959; sentence
    commuted, 1962; paroled, 1979.
b. 1944 in New York
d. Apr 22, 1986 in New York, New York
Source: *NewYTBS 79*

Agronsky, Martin Zama
American. Broadcast Journalist
TV commentator, Washington, DC, 1969--;
    won Emmy for TV special, 1969.
b. Jan 12, 1915 in Philadelphia, Pennsylvania
Source: *AuNews 2; LinLib S; WhoAm 76, 78;*
WhoS&SW 73; WhoWor 76, 78

Agt, Andries Antonius Maria van
Dutch. Politician
Prime minister, minister foreign affairs,
    1977--.
b. Feb 2, 1931 in Netherlands
Source: *IntWW 74; WhoEIO 82*

Aguilar, Grace
Spanish. Author
Wrote novels, religious works concerning
    Judaism: *The Jewish Faith,* 1845.
b. Jun 2, 1816 in London, England
d. Sep 16, 1847 in Frankfurt, Germany
Source: *Alli; BbD; BiD&SB; BrAu 19;*
Chambr 3; ChhPo S2; DcBiA; DcEnL;
DcEuL; DcLEL; EvLB; InWom; LinLib S;
MacDWB; NewC

Aguinaldo, Emilio
Philippine. General, Political Leader
Pres. of Philippines, 1898-1901; accused of
    conspiring with Japanese, WW II.
b. Mar 22, 1869 in Cavite, Philippines
d. Feb 6, 1964 in Manila, Philippines
Source: *WhAm HSA, 4*

Aguirre, Mark
American. Basketball Player
Member US Olympic team, 1980; forward,
    Dallas, 1981--.
b. Dec 10, 1959 in Chicago, Illinois
Source: *BioIn 11; OfNBA 81*

Agutter, Jenny
English. Actress
Ballet dancer turned actress whose films
    include *Equus,* 1977.
b. Dec 20, 1952 in Taunton, England
Source: *BioIn 9, 11; FilmEn; FilmgC*

Ahad
see: Achab

Ahaseurus
see: Xerxes I, King

Ahearn, Jacques Joseph d' Amboise
see: D'Amboise, Jacques

Ahern, Thomas Leo, Jr.
[The Hostages]
American. Hostage in Iran
b. 1932 in Falls Church, Virginia
Source: *BioIn 12; NewYTBS 81*

Aherne, Brian de Lacy
English. Actor
Suave romantic lead, who made 37 films
    including *Sylvia Scarlet,* 1935; *My Sister
    Eileen,* 1942.
b. May 2, 1902 in King's Norton, England
d. Feb 10, 1986 in Venice, Italy
Source: *BiE&WWA; CurBio 60, 86; FilmgC;*
IntMPA 76, 77, 78, 79, 80, 81, 82; MotPP;
MovMk; NotNAT; OxFilm; WhoHol A;
WhoThe 77A

Ahidjo, Ahmadou
Cameroonian. Political Leader
Pres., Cameroon, 1961--.
b. Aug 1924 in Garoua, Cameroon
Source: *IntWW 74; WhoGov 75; WhoWor 78*

Ahmad, Mirza Ghulam Hazat
Pakistani. Religious Leader
Founded Ahmadiyya Muslim Movement,
    popular in US among blacks.
b. Feb 13, 1835 in Qadian, Pakistan
d. May 26, 1908 in Lahore, Pakistan
Source: *BiDAmC*

Ahmed, Fakhruddin Ali
Indian. Political Leader
b. May 13, 1905 in Delhi, India
d. Feb 11, 1977 in New Delhi, India
Source: *IntWW 74; WhoWor 78*

Aiken, Conrad Potter
[Samuel Jeake, Jr., pseud.]
American. Poet, Critic
Won Pulitzer, 1930, for *Selected Poems.*
b. Aug 5, 1889 in Savannah, Georgia
d. Aug 17, 1973 in Savannah, Georgia
Source: *AmAu&B; AmLY, XR; AmWr; AnCL;*
AuBYP; CasWL; Chambr 3; ChhPo, S1, S2;
CnDAL; CnE&AP; CnMD; CnMWL;
ConAmA; ConAmL; ConAu 5R, 45, 4NR;
ConLC 1, 3, 5, 10; ConNov 72; ConP 70;
CurBio 70, 73; DcLEL; EncWL; EvLB;
LongCTC; ModAL, S1; ModWD; OxAmL;
OxEng; PenC AM; PseudN 82; RAdv 1; REn;
REnAL; SixAP; SmATA 3; TwCA, SUP;
TwCWr; WebAB; WebE&AL; WhAm 6;
WhNAA; WhoAm 74; WhoTwCL

Aiken, George David
American. Politician, Farmer
Rep. senator, 1941-75; active in farm
legislation, creation of St. Lawrence
Seaway.
b. Aug 20, 1892 in Dummerston, Vermont
d. Nov 19, 1984 in Montpelier, Vermont
Source: *AmAu&B; AnObit 1984; BiDrAC;
BioNews 74; CelR; CngDr 74; CurBio 47, 85;
PolProf E, J, K, NF, T; WhE&EA; WhoAm
74, 76; WhoAmP 73; WhAm 8; WhoAmP 77;
WhoE 74, 75; WhoGov 72, 75; WhoWor 82*

Aiken, Howard Hathaway
American. Educator, Mathematician
Invented world's largest digital calculator--
Mark I computer, 1944.
b. Mar 8, 1900 in Hoboken, New Jersey
d. Mar 14, 1973 in Saint Louis, Missouri
Source: *BioIn 1, 7, 9, 10; CurBio 47, 73;
NewYTBE 73; WhAm 5*

Aiken, Joan Delano
[Nicholas Dee; Rosie Lee, pseuds.]
English. Author
Popular juvenile, adult mystery writer, who
wrote *Night Fall,* 1969.
b. Sep 4, 1924 in Rye, England
Source: *Au&Wr 71; AuBYP; ChlLR 1; ConAu
4NR, 9R; IntAu&W 76; PiP; PseudN 82;
ScF&FL 1; SenS; SmATA 2; ThrBJA;
TwCCW 78; WhoHrs 80; WrDr 76, 80*

Aikens, Willie Mays
American. Baseball Player
Pleaded quilty, Oct 1983 to charges of
attempted possession of cocaine; sentenced
to three months in prison, Nov 1983.
b. Oct 14, 1954 in Seneca, South Carolina
Source: *BaseEn 85; BaseReg 85; BioIn 11*

Ailey, Alvin
American. Dancer, Choreographer
Formed Alvin Ailey American Dance
Theater, 1958--.
b. Jan 5, 1931 in Rogers, Texas
Source: *BiE&WWA; CelR; CurBio 68;
DrBlPA; Ebony 1; NotNAT; WhoAm 74, 76,
78, 80, 82; WhoBlA 75, 80; WhoE 74, 81;
WhoHol A*

Aimee, Anouk
[Francoise Sorya]
French. Actress
Nominated for Oscar for role in *A Man and
a Woman,* 1966.
b. Apr 27, 1934 in Paris, France
Source: *BiDFilm; ConTFT 2; FilmEn;
FilmgC; IntMPA 81, 82; MacDWB; MovMk;
OxFilm; PseudN 82; WhoHol A; WorEFlm*

Ainge, Dan(iel Rae)
American. Baseball Player, Basketball Player
Infielder, Toronto Blue Jays, before signing
with Boston Celtics, 1981.
b. Mar 17, 1959 in Eugene, Oregon
Source: *BaseEn 85; NewYTBS 81; OfNBA 85*

Ainsworth, W(illiam) H(arrison)
[Cheviot Tichborne, pseud.]
English. Author, Editor
Prolific historic novelist; works include *Jack
Sheppard,* 1839; *Tower of London,* 1840.
b. Feb 4, 1805 in Manchester, England
d. Jan 3, 1882 in Reigate, England
Source: *BbD; BiD&SB; BrAu 19; CasWL;
Chambr 3; CyWA; DcBiA; DcEnA; DcEnL;
DcEuL; LinLib L; OxEng; PenC ENG;
PseudN 82; REn*

Air Supply
[Russell Hitchcock; Graham Russell]
Australian. Music Group
Light pop-rock group, formed 1976; hits
include "The One That You Love," 1981.
Source: *RkOn 85; RolSEnR 83*

Aitken, Hugh
American. Composer
b. Sep 7, 1924 in New York, New York
Source: *AmSCAP 66*

Aitken, Max (John William Maxwell)
British. Publisher
Son of Baron Beaverbrook; directed Britain's
Beaverbrook Newspapers, 1964-77.
b. Feb 15, 1910 in Montreal, Quebec
d. Apr 30, 1985 in London, England
Source: *ConAu 116*

Aitken, Robert
American. Sculptor
Works include Hann Memorial, Arlington
Cemetery; Pioneer Lumberman Monument,
Huron National Forest, MI.
b. May 8, 1878 in San Francisco, California
d. Jan 3, 1949 in New York, New York
Source: *WhAm 2*

Aitken, William Maxwell
see: Beaverbrook, William Maxwell Aitken,
Baron

Akbar
[Jalalud din Muhammad]
"The Great"
Arabian. Emperor
Greatest of Indian Moghul emperors who
    extended empire to N India; instituted new
    religion, Din-i-Ilahi.
b. 1542 in Umarkot, Pakistan
d. 1605
Source: *DcBiPP; LinLib S; McGEWB; NewC;*
PseudN 82; WhDW

Akeley, Carl Ethan
American. Naturalist
Made five trips to Africa, 1896-1926, to
    study, collect animals; improved taxidermy,
    museum display methods.
b. May 19, 1864 in Orleans County, New
    York
d. Nov 17, 1926 in Mount Mikeno, Rwanda
Source: *AmAu&B; AmBi; DcAmB; DcNAA;*
LinLib S; NatCAB 26; REnAL; WebAB, 79;
WhAm 1

Akeley, Mary Lee Jobe
American. Explorer
Made numerous expeditions to Africa
    collecting animals, plant specimens, 1920s-
    30s.
b. Jan 29, 1878 in Tappan, Ohio
d. Jul 19, 1966 in Stonington, Connecticut
Source: *AmAu&B; NotAW MOD; OhA&B;*
WhAm 4; WhE&EA; WhNAA

Akhenaton
see: Ikhnaton, Pharaoh

Akhmatova, Anna, pseud.
[Anna Andreyevna Gorenko]
Russian. Author, Poet
Began publishing poetry, 1907; work affirms
    Russian traditions.
b. Jun 11, 1888 in Odessa, Russia
d. Mar 5, 1966 in Moscow, U.S.S.R.
Source: *AtlBL; CasWL; ClDMEL; ConAu*
25R, P-1; ConLC 11; DcRusL; EncWL;
LinLib L; LongCTC; McGEWB; ModSL 1;
PenC EUR; REn; TwCWr; WhDW;
WhoTwCL

Akihito, (Togusama)
Japanese. Prince
Son of Emperor Hirohito who will be
    Japan's 125th emperor.
b. Dec 23, 1933 in Tokyo, Japan
Source: *BioIn 1, 2, 3, 5, 10; CurBio 59;*
NewYTBS 83; WhoWor 78, 80

Akins, Claude
American. Actor
Star of TV series "Movin' On," 1974-76; "BJ
    and the Bear," 1979.
b. May 25, 1918 in Nelson, Georgia
Source: *FilmgC; IntMPA 77, 78, 79, 80, 81,*
82; Vers A; WhoAm 82; WhoHol A

Akins, Virgil
American. Boxer
b. Mar 10, 1928 in Saint Louis, Missouri
Source: *WhoBox 74*

Akins, Zoe
American. Poet, Dramatist
Wrote 1935 Pulitzer winner *The Old Maid.*
b. Oct 30, 1886 in Humansville, Missouri
d. Oct 29, 1958 in Los Angeles, California
Source: *AmAu&B; CnDAL; CnMD; ConAmA;*
ConAmL; DcAmB S6; DcLEL; FilmgC;
McGEWD; ModWD; NotNAT B; OxAmL;
OxThe; REn; REnAL; TwCA SUP; WhThe

Aksakov, Sergei Timofeyevich
Russian. Author
Known for semi-autobiographical *Family*
Chronicle, 1856, describing Russian life.
b. Sep 20, 1791 in Ufa, Russia
d. Apr 30, 1859 in Moscow, Russia
Source: *BbD; BiD&SB; CasWL; DcEuL;*
DcRusL; EuAu; EvEuW; LinLib L; OxEng;
PenC EUR; REn

Alain, pseud.
[Emil Auguste Chartier]
French. Essayist, Philosopher, Educator
Influential writer of articles battering
    conventional prejudices: *Truth about War,*
    1930.
b. Mar 3, 1868 in Montagne, France
d. Jun 2, 1951 in Le Vesinet, France
Source: *AmAu&B; CasWL; ClDMEL; EncWL;*
EuAu; EvEuW; IlsBYP; IlsCB 1957; OxFr;
PenC EUR; PseudN 82; REn; WorAu 1970

Alain-Fournier, pseud.
[Henri Alban Fournier]
French. Author
Only completed novel, *Le Grand Meaulnes,*
    1913; called outstanding novel of 20th c.
b. Oct 3, 1886 in La Chapelle-d'Angillon,
    France
d. Sep 22, 1914 in Bois de St. Remy, France
Source: *AtlBL; CasWL; ClDMEL; CnMWL;*
CyWA; EncWL; EvEuW; LongCTC; ModRL;
PenC EUR; REn; TwCWr; WhoTwCL

Alabama
[Jeff Cook; Teddy Gentry; Mark Herndon;
  Randy Owen]
American. Music Group
Country-rock group, formed 1969; album
  Feels So Right, 1981, was platinum.
Source: *RkOn 85; RolSEnR 83*

Alajalov, Constantin
American. Artist, Illustrator
b. Nov 18, 1900 in Rostov, Russia
Source: *CurBio 42; IlsBYP; IlsCB 1744, 1946;
  WhoAm 74, 76, 78, 80, 82; WhoAmA 73*

**Alanbrooke, Alan Francis Brooke, 1st
  Viscount**
Irish. General
Chief of imperial general staff for Winston
  Churchill, 1941-46.
b. Jul 23, 1883 in Fermanagh, Ireland
d. Jun 17, 1963 in Hampshire, England
Source: *CurBio 41, 63; NewCol 75*

Alarcon, Pedro Antonio de
Spanish. Author
Wrote internationally famous novelette, *The
  Three-Cornered Hat*, 1874.
b. Mar 10, 1833 in Guadix, Spain
d. Jul 20, 1891 in Madrid, Spain
Source: *BiD&SB; CasWL; ClDMEL; CyWA;
  EuAu; EvEuW; McGEWB; PenC EUR; REn*

Alarcon y Mendoza, Juan Ruiz de
Spanish. Dramatist
Wrote over 20 heroic tragedies, comedies of
  character: *Suspicious Truth*, 1634.
b. 1580 in Taxco, Mexico
d. Aug 4, 1639 in Madrid, Spain
Source: *ApCAB; BbD; BiD&SB; EvEuW;
  LinLib L; McGEWB; OxSpan; REn*

Alaric I
Ruler
Visigothic king, 395-410, who sacked Rome,
  410.
b. 370
d. 410 in Consentia, Italy
Source: *BioIn 4, 5, 9; LinLib L; McGEWB;
  NewCol 75; OxGer; REn; WebBD 80; WhDW*

Alba, Duke of
see: Toledo, Fernando Alvarez de

Albanese, Licia
Italian. Opera Singer
Soprano, who sang title role in *Madame
  Butterfly*, 1935-40.
b. Jul 22, 1913 in Bari, Italy
Source: *CurBio 46; InWom; WhoAm 74, 76,
  78, 80, 82; WhoMus 72; WhoWor 78*

Albee, Edward Franklin
American. Theater Owner, Manager
Formed Keith-Albee Co., 1885-1920s;
  controlled almost 400 variety theaters.
b. Oct 8, 1857 in Massachusetts Bay,
  Massachusetts
d. Mar 11, 1930 in Palm Beach, Florida
Source: *DcAmB S1; WebBD 80*

Albee, Edward Franklin, III
American. Author, Dramatist
Won Pulitzer, 1967, for *A Delicate Balance;*
  Tony, 1963, for *Who's Afraid of Virginia
  Woolf.*
b. Mar 12, 1928 in Washington, District of
  Columbia
Source: *AmAu&B; AmWr; AuNews 1;
  BiE&WWA; CasWL; CelR; CnMD; CnThe;
  ConAu 5R; ConLC 1, 2, 3, 5, 9, 11, 13;
  CroCD; EncAB-H; EncWL; FilmgC; IntWW
  74; LongCTC; McGEWD; ModAL, S1;
  ModWD; NatPD; NotNAT; OxAmL; OxThe;
  PenC AM; RComWL; REn; REnAL;
  REnWD; TwCWr; VarWW 85; WebAB;
  WebE&AL; Who 74; WhoAm 80, 82;
  WhoThe 77; WhoTwCL; WhoWor 74; WorAu*

Albeniz, Isaac Manuel Francisco
Spanish. Pianist, Composer
Major works include rhapsody *Catalonia*,
  1889; stage composition, *Pepita Jimenez*,
  1896.
b. May 29, 1860 in Comprodon, Spain
d. Jun 16, 1909 in Cambo, Spain
Source: *AtlBL*

Alberghetti, Anna Maria
American. Singer, Actress
Operatic soprano who starred in films,
  Broadway musicals; won Tony for
  Carnival, 1962.
b. May 15, 1936 in Pasaro, Italy
Source: *BiE&WWA; CurBio 55; FilmgC;
  InWom; IntMPA 75, 76, 77, 78, 79, 80, 81,
  82; MotPP; MovMk; NotNAT; WhoAm 74;
  WhoHol A*

Albers, Josef
American. Artist, Educator
Known as teacher, color theorist, painter of
  "Homage to the Square," series of several
  hundred works of squares of color.
b. Mar 19, 1888 in Bottrop, Germany
d. Mar 25, 1976 in New Haven, Connecticut
Source: *ConArt 77; ConAu 13NR; CurBio 62,
  76; DcCAA 71; IntWW 74; McGDA;
  NewYTBE 71; NewYTBS 76; ObitOF 79;
  WebAB; WhAm 7; WhoAm 74; WhoAmA 73,
  82N; WhoE 74; WhoWor 74*

Albert
[Prince of Liege]
Belgian. Prince
Brother of Baudouin, king of Belgium; heir
to throne.
b. Jun 6, 1934 in Brussels, Belgium
Source: *WhoWor 74*

Albert
[Albert Alexandre Louis Pierre Grimaldi]
Monacan. Prince
Son of Prince Rainier and Princess Grace
who is heir to Monacan throne.
b. Mar 14, 1958 in Monte Carlo, Monaco
Source: *BioIn 6, 12*

Albert I
[Albert Leopold Clement Marie Meinrad]
Belgian. Ruler
King who reigned, 1909-34; personally
commanded Belgian army during WW I.
b. Apr 8, 1875 in Brussels, Belgium
d. Feb 17, 1934 in Namur, Belgium
Source: *BioIn 12; DcCathB; WhDW*

Albert Frederick Arthur George
see: George VI

Albert, Prince
[Albert Francis Charles Augustus Emmanuel
of Saxe-Coburg-Gotha]
German. Consort
Married Queen Victoria, Feb 1840; used
influence to avert war with US in Trent
Affair, 1861.
b. Aug 26, 1819 in Rosenau, Germany
d. Dec 13, 1861 in London, England
Source: *Alli SUP; LongCEL; NewCol 75;
REn; WhDW*

Albert, Carl Bert
American. Political Leader
Dem. majority leader, 1962-71; Speaker of
House, 1971-76.
b. May 10, 1908 in McAlester, Oklahoma
Source: *BiDrAC; CelR; CngDr 74; CurBio 57;
IntWW 82; WebAB 79; Who 82; WhoAmP
81; WhoGov 75; WhoS&SW 76; WhoWor 74*

Albert, Eddie
[Edward Albert Heimberger]
American. Actor
Starred in TV series "Green Acres," 1965-71.
b. Apr 22, 1908 in Rock Island, Illinois
Source: *BiE&WWA; BkPepl; CelR; CurBio
54; EncMT; FilmgC; HolP 30; IntMPA 75,
76, 77, 78, 79, 80, 81, 82; MotPP; MovMk;
NotNAT; PlP&P; PseudN 82; WhoAm 74, 76,
78, 80, 82; WhoHol A; WhoThe 77*

Albert, Edward
American. Actor, Photographer
Son of Eddie Albert; starred in *Butterflies
Are Free,* 1972, with Goldie Hawn.
b. Feb 20, 1951 in Los Angeles, California
Source: *BkPepl; CelR; IntMPA 75, 76, 77,
78, 79, 80, 81, 82; WhoAm 74, 76, 78, 80,
82*

Albert, Eugene d'
see: D'Albert, Eugene

Albert, Stephen Joel
American. Composer
Won Pulitzer, 1985, for music for his
Symphony River Run.
b. Feb 6, 1941 in Brooklyn, New York
Source: *AmComp; Baker 78; ConAmC A;
ConNews 86-1; WhoAmM 83*

Alberti, Leon Battista
Italian. Architect, Author, Scientist
Renaissance humanist; wrote dialogues, *Della
Familia,* 1441; essays in fine arts.
b. Feb 14, 1404 in Genoa, Italy
d. Apr 25, 1472 in Rome, Italy
Source: *AtlBL; BiD&SB; CasWL; DcEuL;
EuAu; EvEuW; LinLib S; McGDA;
McGEWB; OxEng; PenC EUR; REn*

Albertson, Frank
American. Actor
Character actor whose films include *Psycho,*
1960; *Bye Bye Birdie,* 1963.
b. Feb 2, 1909 in Fergus Falls, Minnesota
d. Feb 29, 1964 in Santa Monica, California
Source: *FilmEn; FilmgC; MovMk; NotNAT B;
ObitOF 79; Vers A; WhScrn 74, 77; WhoHol
B*

Albertson, Jack
American. Actor
Won Oscar, 1968, for *The Subject Was
Roses;* Emmy, 1976, for "Chico and the
Man."
b. Jun 16, 1910 in Malden, Massachusetts
d. Nov 25, 1981 in Hollywood, California
Source: *CurBio 76, 82; FilmgC; IntMPA 81;
MovMk; NewYTBE 73; NewYTBS 81;
NotNAT; WhAm 8; WhoAm 82; WhoHol A;
WhoThe 77*

Albertus Magnus, Saint
[Albert, Count of Bollstadt; Albrecht von Koln]
"Doctor Universalis"; "The Great"; "Le Petit Albert"
German. Philosopher, Religious Figure
Paraphrased Aristotle's works; canonized, 1932.
b. 1193 in Lauingen, Germany
d. Nov 15, 1280 in Cologne, Germany
Source: *BbD; BiD&SB; CasWL; DcEnL; DcEuL; EuAu; EvEuW; NewC; OxEng; OxGer; PenC EUR; PseudN 82; REn*

Albinoni, Tommaso
Italian. Composer, Violinist
b. 1671 in Venice, Italy
d. 1750 in Venice, Italy
Source: *OxMus; WebBD 80*

Albrand, Martha, pseud.
[Katrin Holland; Heidi Huberta, other pseuds.; Heide Huberta Freybe, given name; Mrs. Sydney J Lamon]
American. Author
Mystery writer; wrote award-winning *Desperate Moment,* 1950.
b. Sep 8, 1914 in Rostock, Germany
d. Jun 24, 1981 in New York, New York
Source: *AmAu&B; AmNov; AnObit 1981; Au&Wr 71; ConAu 108, 11NR, 13R; EncMys; IntAu&W 76; TwCA SUP; WhAm 8; WhoAm 80, 82; WhoAmW 74; WhoE 74; WhoSpyF; WhoWor 78*

Albright, Ivan Le Lorraine
"The Painter of Horrors"
American. Artist
"Magic realism" painter who emphasized details, emotions.
b. Feb 20, 1897 in Chicago, Illinois
d. Nov 18, 1983 in Woodstock, Vermont
Source: *ConArt 83; DcCAr 81; NewYTBS 83; OxArt; OxTwCA; PhDcTCA 77; WebAB 79; WhoAm 80, 82; WhoAmA 80, 82; WhoWor 78*

Albright, Lola Jean
American. Actress
Appeared in TV series "Peter Gunn," 1958-61; critical acclaim for role in *A Cold Wind in August,* 1961.
b. Jul 20, 1924 in Akron, Ohio
Source: *FilmEn; FilmgC; IntMPA 82; MotPP; MovMk; WhoAm 82*

Albright, Malvin Marr
[Zsissly]
American. Artist, Sculptor
b. Feb 20, 1897 in Chicago, Illinois
d. Sep 14, 1983 in Fort Lauderdale, Florida
Source: *McGDA; WhAm 8; WhoAm 82; WhoAmA 82; WhoWor 80*

Albright, Tenley Emma
American. Figure Skater
Won gold medal, 1956 Olympics.
b. Jul 18, 1935 in Newton Centre, Massachusetts
Source: *CurBio 56; InWom; WhoAmW 77*

Albright, William Foxwell
American. Archaeologist
Published over 800 books on archaeology: *From the Stone Age to Christianity,* 1940.
b. May 24, 1891 in Coquimbo, Chile
d. Sep 19, 1971 in Baltimore, Maryland
Source: *AmAu&B; ConAu 33R; CurBio 55; EncAB-H; NewYTBE 71; WebAB; WhAm 5*

Albuquerque, Affonso de
"The Great"; "The Mars of Portugal"; "The Portuguese Mars"
Portuguese. Political Leader
Viceroy of India who consolidated Portuguese power in East.
b. 1453
d. 1515
Source: *BioIn 1, 9; DcBiPP; DcCathB; McGEWB; OxShips; PseudN 82; WhDW*

Alcibiades
Greek. Statesman, Military Leader
Nephew of Pericles who advised Sparta of Athenian weaknesses; blamed for defeat of Athens.
b. 450 ?BC
d. 404 ?BC in Phrygia, Greece
Source: *DcEnL; REn*

Alcindor, Lew
see: Abdul-Jabbar, Kareem

Alcock, John William, Sir
English. Aviator
Piloted plane that made first nonstop transatlantic flight, 1919.
b. 1892 in Manchester, England
d. Jun 14, 1919
Source: *Baker 84; WebBD 80*

Alcott, Amos Bronson
American. Educator
Friend of Emerson, Thoreau; founded
    Concord School of Philosophy, 1879.
b. Nov 29, 1799 in Wolcott, Connecticut
d. Mar 4, 1888 in Boston, Massachusetts
Source: *AmAu; AmAu&B; AmBi; ApCAB;*
BbD; BiD&SB; CasWL; Chambr 3; CnDAL;
CyAL 2; DcAmAu; DcAmB; DcLEL; DcNAA;
Drake; LinLib L; McGEWB; Drake; EvLB;
NatCAB 2; PenC AM; REn; REnAL;
TwCBDA; WebAB, 79; WhAm HS

Alcott, Amy
American. Golfer
Won US Open, 1980.
b. Feb 22, 1956 in Kansas City, Missouri
Source: *BioIn 10; NewYTBS 80; WhoAm 82;*
WhoGolf; WhoIntG

Alcott, John
British. Filmmaker
Best known films include *Clockwork Orange,*
    1971.
b. 1931 in England
d. Jul 28, 1986 in France
Source: *FilmgC; IntMPA 84; WhoAm 84*

Alcott, Louisa May
American. Author
Her early life in New England described in
    Little Women, 1869.
b. Nov 29, 1832 in Germantown,
    Pennsylvania
d. Mar 6, 1888 in Boston, Massachusetts
Source: *Alli SUP; AmAu; AmAu&B; AmBi;*
AmWom; ApCAB; AtlBL; AuBYP; BbD;
BiD&SB; CarSB; CasWL; Chambr 3; ChlLR
1; ChhPo; CnDAL; CrtT 3; CyAL 2; CyWA;
DcAmAu; DcAmB; DcBiA; DcEnL; DcLEL;
DcNAA; EncAB-H; EvLB; FamAYP; FilmgC;
HerW; InWom; JBA 34; MouLC 4; NotAW;
OxAmL; OxEng; PenC AM; REn; REnAL;
Str&VC; TwCBDA; WebAB; WhAm HS;
WhoChL; YABC 1

Alcuin
[Albinus]
"Ealhwine"; "Flaccus"
Anglo-Saxon. Theologian, Scholar
Best known works *Lives of the Saints; Poems*
    on the Saints of the Church at York.
b. 735
d. 804
Source: *Alli; BbD; BiB S; BiD&SB; BrAu;*
CasWL; Chambr 1; DcEnL; EvLB; NewC;
OxEng; OxFr; OxGer; PenC ENG, EUR;
PseudN 82; REn

Alda, Alan
[Alphonso d'Abruzzo]
American. Actor, Writer, Director
Played Hawkeye on "MASH," 1972-83;
    movie roles in *California Suite,* 1978; *The*
    Four Seasons, 1981.
b. Jan 28, 1936 in New York, New York
Source: *BiE&WWA; BioNews 74; BkPepl;*
ConAu 103; ConTFT 3; IntMPA 82; MotPP;
MovMk; NewYTBS 74; NotNAT; PseudN 82;
WhoAm 84; WhoHol A; WhoThe 77

Alda, Frances
[Frances Davis]
American. Opera Singer
b. May 31, 1883 in Christchurch, New
    Zealand
d. Sep 18, 1952 in Venice, Italy
Source: *ApCAB X; Baker 78; InWom;*
MusMk; NatCAB 39; NewEOp 71; PseudN 82

Alda, Robert
[Alphonso Giovanni Giusseppi Roberto
    d'Abruzzo]
American. Actor
Father of Alan Alda; best known for playing
    George Gershwin in *Rhasody in Blue,*
    1945.
b. Feb 26, 1914 in New York, New York
d. May 3, 1986 in Los Angeles, California
Source: *BiE&WWA; ConTFT 3; FilmgC;*
IntMPA 82; MotPP; MovMk; NotNAT;
PlP&P; PseudN 82; WhoHol A; WhoThe 77

Alden, Henry M
American. Author, Editor
Dean of American magazine editors; edited
    Harper's Monthly, 1869-1919.
b. Nov 11, 1836 in Mount Tabor, Vermont
d. Oct 7, 1919 in New York, New York
Source: *Alli SUP; AmAu; AmAu&B; AmBi;*
ApCAB; BbD; BiD&SB; CnDAL; DcAmAu;
DcAmB; DcNAA; EncAJ; LinLib L; NatCAB
1; OxAmL; REnAL; TwCBDA; WhAm 1

Alden, Isabella Macdonald
[Pansy, pseud.]
American. Author
Wrote 80 popular religious books for young
    people.
b. Nov 3, 1841 in Rochester, New York
d. Aug 5, 1930 in Palo Alto, California
Source: *NotAW; OxAmL 83*

Alden, John
English. Colonial Figure
Founder of Duxbury, MA, who was last
    surviving male member of Mayflower Co.
b. 1599 in England
d. Sep 12, 1687 in Duxbury, Massachusetts
Source: *AmBi; ApCAB; DcAmB; Drake;
LinLib L, S; NatCAB 10; NewCol 75;
OxAmH; OxAmL; REn; REnAL; TwCBDA;
WebAB, 79; WhAm HS*

Alden, Priscilla Mullens
[Mrs. John Alden]
English. Colonial Figure
Married Alden, 1623; romance subject of
    poem, "The Courtship of Miles Standish."
b. 1604 in Surrey, England
d. 1680 in Duxbury, Massachusetts
Source: *AmBi; BioIn 2, 4; InWom; LibW;
NotAW*

Alder, Kurt
German. Chemist
Won Nobel Prize for chemistry, 1950.
b. Jul 10, 1902 in Germany
d. Jun 20, 1958
Source: *BioIn 2, 3, 4, 5, 6; WhAm 3*

Aldington, Richard
English. Author
One of leaders of Imagists poetry movement,
    1910-18.
b. Jul 8, 1892 in Hampshire, England
d. Jul 27, 1962 in Sury-en-Vaux, France
Source: *CasWL; Chambr 3; ChhPo, S1, S2,
S3; ConAu 85; CyWA; DcLEL; EncWL;
EvLB; LinLib L, S; LongCTC; ModBrL;
NewC; NewCol 75; OxEng; PenC ENG; REn;
TwCA, SUP; TwCWr; WebE&AL; WhAm 4*

Aldiss, Brian Wilson
[Jael Cracken; Arch Mendicant; Peter Pica;
    John Runciman; C C Shackleton, pseuds.]
English. Author, Critic, Editor
Hugo Award-winning science fiction writer
    who wrote *Moreau's Other Island,* 1980.
b. Aug 18, 1925 in Dereham, England
Source: *Au&Wr 71; ConAu 5R, 5NR; ConLC
5, 14; ConNov 72, 76; IntWW 74; PseudN
82; SmATA 2; TwCWr; Who 74; WhoWor
74; WrDr 76*

Aldredge, Theoni A(thanasiou Vashlioti)
American. Designer
Won Tonys for costumes in *Annie,* 1977; *La
    Cage Aux Folles,* 1984; Oscar for *The
    Great Gatsby,* 1974.
b. Aug 22, 1932 in Salonika, Greece
Source: *ConTFT 1; VarWW 85*

Aldrich, Bess Streeter
[Margaret Dean Stevens, pseud.]
American. Author
Wrote of midwest pioneer life: *Song of Years,*
    1939.
b. Feb 17, 1881 in Cedar Falls, Iowa
d. Aug 3, 1954 in Lincoln, Nebraska
Source: *AmAu&B; AmNov; AmWomWr;
DcAmB S5; InWom; NatCAB 46; OxAmL;
PseudN 82; REn; REnAL; TwCA, SUP;
WhAm 3; WhNAA*

Aldrich, Nelson Wilmarth
American. Statesman
Senator, 1881-1911; expert on tariff, currency
    legislation.
b. Nov 6, 1841 in Foster, Rhode Island
d. Apr 16, 1915 in New York, New York
Source: *AmBi; ApCAB, X; BiDrAC; DcAmB;
EncAAH; McGEWB; NatCAB 10, 25; NewCol
75; TwCBDA; WebAB; WhAm 1; WhAmP*

Aldrich, Richard Stoddard
American. Producer, Manager, Author
Produced over 30 plays on Broadway,
    including *Pygmalion,* 1945; *The Moon Is
    Blue,* 1951.
b. Aug 17, 1902 in Boston, Massachusetts
d. Mar 31, 1986 in Williamsburg, Virginia
Source: *ConTFT 3; CurBio 55, 86*

Aldrich, Robert
American. Director, Producer
Directed motion pictures *The Dirty Dozen,*
    1967, *The Longest Yard,*1974.
b. Aug 9, 1918 in Cranston, Rhode Island
d. Dec 5, 1983 in Los Angeles, California
Source: *BiDFilm; CmMov; DcFM; FilmEn;
FilmgC; MovMk; NewYTBS 83; OxFilm;
VarWW 85; WhAm 8; WhoAm 82; WhoWest
78; WhoWor 78; WorEFlm*

Aldrich, Thomas Bailey
American. Author, Journalist, Editor
Editor, *Atlantic Monthly,* 1881-90, known for
    semi-autobiographical novel, *Story of a Bad
    Boy,* 1870.
b. Nov 11, 1836 in Portsmouth, New
    Hampshire
d. Mar 19, 1907 in Boston, Massachusetts
Source: *AmAu&B; CarSB; CasWL; Chambr 3;
CnDAL; CyAL 2; CyWA; DcAmAu; DcAmB;
DcBiA; DcEnA AP; DcEnL; DcLEL; DcNAA;
Drake; EncMys; EvLB; JBA 34; LinLib S;
MovMk; NatCAB 1; OxAmL; OxEng;
OxFilm; PenC AM; REn; REnAL; TwCBDA;
WebAB; WhAm 1*

Aldrich, Winthrop Williams
American. Banker
b. Nov 2, 1885 in Providence, Rhode Island
d. Feb 25, 1974 in New York, New York
Source: *CurBio 40, 53, 74; NewYTBS 74;*
WhAm 6; Who 74; WhoAm 74

Aldridge, Ira Frederick
"The African Roscius"; "The African
   Tragedian"
English. Actor
Protege of Edmund Kean regarded as one of
   greatest actors of his day.
b. 1805 in New York, New York
d. Aug 10, 1867 in Lodz, Poland
Source: *ApCAB; DcAmB; Drake; NegAl 76;*
NotNAT A, B; OxThe; PseudN 82; WebAB,
79; WhAm HS

Aldridge, Michael
English. Actor, Director
Active in English theater since 1939.
b. Sep 9, 1920 in Glastonbury, England
Source: *ConTFT 3*

Aldrin, Edwin E(ugene), Jr.
"Buzz"
American. Astronaut, Businessman
Second man to walk on moon, Jul 20, 1969.
b. Jan 20, 1930 in Montclair, New Jersey
Source: *AmM&WS 73P; BioNews 74; CelR;*
ConAu 89; IntWW 81; LinLib S; PseudN 82;
Who 82; WhoAm 80, 82; WhoWest 80;
WhoWor 76

Aleichem, Shalom, pseud.
[Solomon J Rabinowitz]
"Yiddish Mark Twain"
Russian. Author, Humorist
Wrote of Jewish Ukranian life; *Tevye* was
   basis for Broadway's *Fiddler on the Roof,*
   1964.
b. Feb 18, 1859 in Pereyaslavl, Russia
d. May 13, 1916 in New York, New York
Source: *AmAu&B; AtlBL; CasWL; EncWL;*
LongCTC; OxThe; PseudN 82; REn; REnAL;
TwCA, SUP

Aleixandre, Vicente
Spanish. Poet
Surrealist who often used metaphors from
   nature; won Nobel Prize, 1977.
b. Apr 26, 1898 in Seville, Spain
d. Dec 14, 1984 in Madrid, Spain
Source: *CasWL; ConAu 85; ConLC 9; CurBio*
78, 85; EncWL; IntAu&W 76, 77; IntWW
76, 77, 78; IntWWP 77; PenC EUR; REn;
WhoWor 74, 78; WorAu

Alekhine, Alexander
French. Chess Player
b. Nov 1, 1892 in Russia
d. Mar 24, 1946 in Lisbon, Portugal
Source: *CurBio 46; OxChess*

Aleman, Miguel
Mexican. Political Leader
First civilian pres. following 1917 revolution,
   1946-52.
b. Sep 29, 1903 in Sayula, Mexico
d. May 14, 1983 in Mexico City, Mexico
Source: *CurBio 46, 83; IntWW 74*

Alembert, Jean le Rond d'
"Anaxagoras"; "Le Chancelier du Parnasse";
   "The Father of French Philosophy"; "The
   Mazarin of Letters"
French. Mathematician, Philosopher
Works include principle of mechanics,
   D'Alemgert's Principle; theory of practical
   elements of music, 1759.
b. Nov 16, 1717 in Paris, France
d. Oct 29, 1783 in Paris, France
Source: *Baker 78; BbD; BiD&SB; CasWL;*
DcBiPP; DcScB; EuAu; EvEuW; LinLib L;
McGEWB; NewCol 75; OxFr; OxMus; PenC
EUR; REn; WhDW

Alessandri, Jorge
Chilean. Political Leader
Pres. of Chile, 1958-64.
b. May 19, 1896 in Santiago, Chile
d. Sep 1, 1986 in Santiago, Chile
Source: *CurBio 86; McGEWB*

Alessandro, Victor Nicholas
American. Conductor
Musical director, Oklahoma Symphony, 1931-
   51; San Antonio Orchestra, 1952-76.
b. Nov 27, 1915 in Waco, Texas
d. Nov 27, 1976 in San Antonio, Texas
Source: *Baker 78; BioIn 4, 8, 11; IntWW 75,*
76, 77; NewEOp 71; NewYTBS 76; WhAm 7;
WhoAm 74, 76; WhoMus 72; WhoOp 76;
WhoS&SW 73, 75, 76

Alexander I
[Aleksandr Pavlovich]
"The Northern Telemaque"
Russian. Ruler
Grandson of Catherine the Great who was
   czar of Russia, 1801-25.
b. 1777
d. 1825
Source: *BioIn 10; PseudN 82; REn; WebBD*
80

Alexander II
[Aleksandr Nikolaevich]
Russian. Ruler
Czar who reigned 1855-81; emancipated serfs, 1861, sold Alaska, 1867.
b. 1818 in Moscow, Russia
d. Mar 13, 1881 in Saint Petersburg, Russia
Source: *BioIn 10; REn; WebBD 80*

Alexander III
[Aleksandr Alexsandrovich]
Russian. Ruler
Conservative czar of Russia, 1881-94.
b. 1845 in Russia
d. 1894 in Russia
Source: *BioIn 2; REn*

Alexander VI
[Rodrigo Lanzol y Borja]
"The Worst Pope"
Spanish. Religious Leader
Pope, 1492-1503, elected by corrupt conclave; father of Cesare and Lucrezia Borgia.
b. Jan 1, 1431 in Jativa, Spain
d. Aug 18, 1503
Source: *BioIn 4, 10; McGEWB; NewCol 75; REn; WebBD 80*

Alexander of Hales
[Hales Owen]
"Doctor Doctorum"; "The Fountain of Life"; "The Irrefragable Doctor"
English. Philosopher
Wrote *Summa Universae Theologiae,* first systematic writings on Catholic dogma.
b. 1185 in Hailes, England
d. 1245 in Paris, France
Source: *BiD&SB; DcCathB; DcEnL; LinLib L; NewC; OxEng; OxLaw; PseudN 82; REn*

Alexander of Tunis, Harold Rupert Leofric George Alexander, Earl
English. General
Commander in charge of British army evacuation from Dunkirk, WW II.
b. Dec 10, 1891 in Northern Ireland
d. Jun 16, 1969 in Slough, England
Source: *CurBio 42, 69; McGEWB; NewCol 75; WhoMilH 76*

Alexander the Great
[Alexander III]
"The Conqueror of the World"; "The Emathian Conqueror"; "Macedonia's Madman"
Macedonian. Ruler
King who forged largest western empire of ancient world, from Greece to N India.
b. Sep 20, 356 in Pella, Macedonia
d. Jun 13, 323 in Babylon
Source: *DcEuL; FilmgC; LinLib L, S; LongCEL; McGEWB; NewC; NewCol 75; OxSpan; PenC CL; REn; WhDW*

Alexander, Ben (Nicholas Benton)
American. Actor
Popular child star in silent films who was Jack Webb's partner on TV series "Dragnet," 1953-59.
b. May 26, 1911 in Garfield, Nevada
d. Jul 5, 1969 in Hollywood, California
Source: *FilmEn; Film 1; FilmgC; MovMk; ObitOF 79; PseudN 82; TwYS; WhScrn 74, 77*

Alexander, Clifford L, Jr.
American. Lawyer, Government Official
Secretary of Army, 1977-80; first black in US history to serve as civilian head of military branch.
b. Sep 21, 1933 in New York, New York
Source: *BioNews 74; CurBio 77; IntWW 80, 82; PolProf J; WhoAmP 81; WhoBlA 80; WhoWor 80*

Alexander, Denise
American. Actress, Photojournalist
Played Dr. Leslie Weber on TV soap opera "General Hospital," 1973-84.
b. Nov 11, 1945 in New York, New York
Source: *WhoAm 78, 80, 82*

Alexander, Donald Crichton
American. Lawyer, Government Official
IRS commissioner, 1973-77.
b. May 22, 1921 in Pine Bluff, Arkansas
Source: *CurBio 74; IntWW 77, 78; WhoAm 74, 76, 78, 80, 82; WhoAmP 77, 79; WhoGov 75, 77*

Alexander, Franz Gabriel
American. Physician, Educator
Founder, director Chicago Institute for Psychoanalysis, 1932-56; started psychosomatic movement.
b. Jan 22, 1891 in Budapest, Austria-Hungary
d. Mar 8, 1964 in Palm Springs, California
Source: *DcAmB S7; WebBD 80*

Alexander, Grover Cleveland
"Alex"; "Alex the Great"; "Buck"; "Dode";
"Old Pete"; "Pete"
American. Baseball Player
Won 373 games as pitcher, 1911-30; Hall of
Fame, 1938.
b. Feb 26, 1887 in Elba, Nebraska
d. Nov 4, 1950 in Saint Paul, Nebraska
Source: *BaseEn 85; DcAmB S4; NewCol 75;
WhoProB 73*

Alexander, Hattie Elizabeth
American. Physician
First woman pres., American Pediatric
Society, 1964.
b. Apr 5, 1901
d. Jun 24, 1968 in Port Washington, New
York
Source: *NotAW MOD; ObitOF 79; WhAm 5;
WhoAmW 70*

Alexander, Jane
[Jane Quigley]
American. Actress
Won Tony for *Great White Hope*, 1969;
played Eleanor Roosevelt on TV.
b. Oct 28, 1939 in Boston, Massachusetts
Source: *BkPepl; CurBio 77; IntMPA 82;
NotNAT; PIP&P A; WhoAm 74, 76, 78, 80,
82; WhoAmW 72, 74, 77; WhoHol A;
WhoThe 77, 81*

Alexander, Katherine
American. Actress
Played refined ladies in 1930s films: *Death
Takes a Holiday*, 1934; *The Hunchback of
Notre Dame*, 1939.
b. Sep 22, 1901 in Fort Smith, Arkansas
Source: *BiE&WWA; FilmEn; FilmgC;
MovMk; NotNAT; PIP&P; ThFT; WhThe*

Alexander, Leo
American. Psychiatrist, Educator
Wrote Nuremberg Code used at Nuremberg
trials, 1940s.
b. Oct 11, 1905 in Vienna, Austria-Hungary
d. Jul 20, 1985 in Weston, California
Source: *AmM&WS 82P; ConAu 116*

Alexander, Lloyd Chudley
American. Author
Award-winning children's books include
Westmark, 1981; Newbery Prize for *The
High King*, 1969.
b. Jan 30, 1924 in Philadelphia, Pennsylvania
Source: *AnCL; Au&Wr 71; AuBYP; ChlLR 1;
ConAu 1R, 1NR; NewbC 1966; PiP; SmATA
3; ThrBJA; WhoAm 80, 82, 84*

Alexander, Shana
American. Author, Lecturer
Commentator, CBS "60 Minutes," 1975-79.
b. Oct 6, 1925 in New York, New York
Source: *ConAu 61; ForWC 70; St&PR 75;
WhoAm 74, 76, 78, 80, 82; WhoAmW 72,
74, 77, 79; WhoF&I 74; WrDr 76, 80*

Alexander, Sue
American. Children's Author
Won McKenzie Award for children's
literature; wrote *Witch, Goblin, and Ghost*
series.
b. Aug 20, 1933 in Tucson, Arizona
Source: *ConAu 4NR, 53; SmATA 12*

Alexander, William
"Lord Stirling"
American. Army Officer
Revolutionary War hero who commanded
troops at Battle of Long Island, 1776;
Monmouth, 1778.
b. 1726 in New York, New York
d. Jan 15, 1783 in Albany, New York
Source: *AmBi; ApCAB; BioIn 8; DcAmB;
Drake; NatCAB 1; NewCol 75; TwCBDA;
WebAMB; WhAm HS; WhAmP*

Alexanderson, Ernst Frederik Werner
American. Inventor, Engineer
Developed equipment which led to first vocal
radio broadcast, 1906; helped develop color
TV.
b. Jan 25, 1878 in Uppsala, Sweden
d. May 14, 1975 in Schenectady, New York
Source: *CurBio 55, 75; WebAB; WhAm 6*

Alexandra Caroline Mary Charlotte
English. Consort
Queen of Edward VII, remembered for
beauty, goodness.
b. Dec 1, 1844 in Copenhagen, Denmark
d. Nov 20, 1925 in Sandringham, England
Source: *DcNaB 1922; GrBr*

Alexandra Feodorovna
[Alix Victoria Helene Luise Beatrix]
Russian. Czarina
Wife of Nicholas II, last czar of Russia;
slain with family by Bolsheviks.
b. 1872 in Germany
d. Jul 16, 1918 in Ekaterinburg, U.S.S.R.
Source: *InWom; PseudN 82*

Alexandre
[Louis Albert Alexandre Raimon]
French. Hairstylist
Known for reviving the use of false hair;
developed extremely short cut called
"artichoke."
b. 1922
Source: *PseudN 82; WorFshn*

Alexandrov, Grigori
[Grigori Mormonenko]
Russian. Director
Worked with Sergei Eisenstein for 10 yrs.;
films include *Jolly Fellows,* 1934.
b. Feb 23, 1903 in Yekaterinburg, Russia
d. Dec 19, 1983 in Moscow, U.S.S.R.
Source: *DcFM; FilmEn; Film 2; FilmgC;
IntWW 76; OxFilm; WorEFlm*

Alexis, Kim
American. Model
Signed exclusive contract for Revlon's Ultima
II, replacing Lauren Hutton, 1983.
b. 1960
Source: *NF*

Alexius Comnenus
[Alexius I]
Byzantine. Ruler
Emperor, 1081-1118.
b. 1048
d. 1118
Source: *REn*

Alfieri, Vittorio
Italian. Artist, Dramatist
Wrote 19 classic tragedies: *Saul,* 1783-85.
b. Jan 16, 1749 in Asti, Italy
d. Oct 8, 1803 in Florence, Italy
Source: *AtlBL; BbD; BiD&SB; CasWL;
CnThe; DcEnL; DcEuL; EuAu; EvEuW;
LinLib L; McGEWD; OxEng; OxThe; PenC
EUR; RComWL; REn; REnWD*

Alfonsin Foulkes, Raul Ricardo
Argentine. Political Leader
Elected pres., 1983, defeating Peronist Party
for first time in 38 yrs.
b. Mar 31, 1926 in Chascomus, Argentina
Source: *NewYTBS 83*

Alfonso XIII
Spanish. Ruler
King of Spain, 1886-1931; reign marked by
social unrest, several assassination attempts.
b. Apr 17, 1886
d. Feb 28, 1941 in Rome, Italy
Source: *CurBio 41; NewCol 75*

Alfred the Great
English. Ruler
King of Wessex, 871-99; revived learning,
establishment of Old English literary prose.
b. 849 in Wantage, England
d. 901
Source: *Alli; BbD; BiD&SB; CrtT 1; NewCol
75; REn*

Alfred, William
American. Dramatist, Educator
Harvard U professor, 1963--, who wrote
drama, *Hogan's Goat,* 1956.
b. Aug 16, 1922 in New York, New York
Source: *ConAu 13R; ConDr 73; CroCD; DrAS
74E; McGEWD; ModAL; NotNAT; WhoAm
74, 76, 78, 80, 82, 84; WorAu; WrDr 76*

Algazel
see: Ghazzali, Abu-Hamid al

Alger, Horatio
American. Author, Clergyman
Wrote over 100 rags-to-riches stories for
boys.
b. Jan 13, 1832 in Revere, Massachusetts
d. Jul 18, 1899 in Natick, Massachusetts
Source: *Alli SUP; AmAu; AmAu&B; AmBi;
ApCAB; BbD; BiD&SB; CarSB; CasWL;
ChhPo, S1, S2; CnDAL; CyAL 2; DcAmAu;
DcAmB; DcNAA; Drake; EncAB-H; EvLB;
OxAmL; PenC AM; REn; REnAL; TwCBDA;
WebAB; WebE&AL; WhAm 1; WhoChL*

Algren, Nelson
[Nelson Algren Abraham]
"Poet of the Chicago Slums"
American. Author
Realistic novels include *The Man with the
Golden Arm,* 1949.
b. Mar 28, 1909 in Detroit, Michigan
d. May 9, 1981 in Sag Harbor, New York
Source: *AmAu&B; AmNov; BioIn 2, 4, 5, 7,
8, 10; CasWL; CnDAL; CnMWL; ConAu
13R, 103; ConLC 4, 10; ConNov 72, 76;
DcLEL; DrAF 76; EncWL; FilmgC;
IntAu&W 76, 77; LinLib L; ModAL; S1;
OxAmL; PenC AM; PseudN 82; RAdv 1;
REn; REnAL; TwCA SUP; TwCWr;
WebE&AL; WhoAm 74, 76; WhoTwCL;
WhoWor 74; WrDr 76, 80*

Ali
"The Lion of God"; "The Rugged Lion"
Arabian. Religious Leader
Fourth caliph of Arab, Islamic Empire;
    cousin of Mohammed; division of Islam
    into Sunni, Shiites began during reign.
b. 600
d. 661 in Al Kufa, Iraq
Source: *DcBiPP; McGEWB; NewCol 75;*
PseudN 82; WebBD 80

Ali, Ahmed
Indian. Author, Diplomat
Founder, Indian Progressive Writers, 1932,
    who wrote *Twilight in Delhi,* 1966.
b. Jul 1, 1908 in Delhi, India
Source: *Au&Wr 71; CasWL; ConAu 25R;*
ConNov 72, 76, 82; WrDr 76

Ali, Muhammad
[Cassius (Marcellus) Clay, (Jr.)]
American. Boxer
First heavyweight boxer ever to hold title
    three times.
b. Jan 17, 1942 in Louisville, Kentucky
Source: *BioNews 74; BkPepl; CurBio 63;*
EncAB-H; NewYTBE 71, 72, 73; NewYTBS
74; PseudN 82; WebAB; WhoAm 74, 76, 78,
80, 82; WhoBlA 75; WhoBox 74

Ali Pasha
"The Lion of Yannina"
Turkish. Military Leader
Military governor of Yannina, 1787; rule
    extended to Albania, Epirus until
    assassination.
b. 1741 in Tepeleni, Albania
d. 1822
Source: *BioIn 8; NewCol 75; PseudN 82;*
WebBD 80

Alice (Mary Victoria Augusta Pauline)
[Countess of Athlone]
English. Princess, Author, Socialite
Last surviving grandchild of Queen Victoria;
    great aunt of Queen Elizabeth II; wrote
    memoirs: *For My Grandchildren: Some*
    Reminiscences.
b. Feb 25, 1883 in Windsor, England
d. Jan 3, 1981 in London, England
Source: *AnObit 1981; BioIn 7, 7, 11, 11;*
ConAu 103; NewYTBS 76, 81; Who 74, 82

Alicia, Ana
[Ana Alicia Ortiz]
American. Actress
Plays Melissa Cumson Gioberti on *Falcon*
    Crest.
b. Dec 12, 1957 in Mexico City, Mexico
Source: *VarWW 83*

Alinsky, Saul David
American. Political Activist
Established Industrial Area Foundation, 1940;
    author, *Rules for Radicals,* 1971.
b. Jan 30, 1909 in Chicago, Illinois
d. Jun 12, 1972 in Carmel, California
Source: *AmAu&B; ConAu 37R; CurBio 68,*
72; NewYTBE 72; ObitOF 79; PolProf J;
WebAB, 79; WhAm 5

Alioto, Joseph Lawrence
American. Lawyer, Politician
Mayor of San Francisco, 1968-76.
b. Feb 12, 1916 in San Francisco, California
Source: *CurBio 69; IntWW 74; WhoAm 74,*
76, 78, 80; WhoGov 75; WhoWest 84

Alison, Archibald
Scottish. Clergyman
Best known for essay *On the Nature and*
    Principle of Taste, 1790.
b. 1757 in Edinburgh, Scotland
d. May 17, 1839 in Edinburgh, Scotland
Source: *Alli; BiD&SB; BiDLA, SUP; Chambr*
2; DcBiPP; DcEnL; EvLB; OxArt

Allan, Elizabeth
English. Actress
Popular British TV star of 1950s; played
    ladylike heroines in films: *A Tale of Two*
    Cities, 1935.
b. Apr 9, 1908 in Skegness, England
Source: *FilmEn; FilmgC; ThFT; WhoHol A;*
WhoThe 77A

Allard, Sydney
English. Industrialist, Auto Executive
Founder, chm., managing director, Allard
    Motor Co., Ltd., 1945-66.
b. Jul 1910 in London, England
d. Apr 12, 1966 in Black Hills, England
Source: *BioIn 7; ObitT 1961*

Allbritton, Louise
[Mrs. Charles Collingwood]
American. Actress
Leading lady of Universal second features:
    Egg and I, 1947; *Sitting Pretty,* 1948.
b. Jul 3, 1920 in Oklahoma City, Oklahoma
d. Feb 16, 1979 in Puerto Vallarta, Mexico
Source: *FilmEn; FilmgC; HolP 40; MotPP;*
NewYTBS 79; WhoHol A

Allegret, Yves
[Yves Champlain, pseud.]
French. Director
Best known for *film noir* genre films, 1940s,
  starring Simone Signoret, wife from 1944-
  49.
b. Oct 13, 1907 in Paris, France
Source: *BiDFilm; DcFM; FilmEn; MovMk;
OxFilm; WorEFlm*

Allegri, Gregorio
Italian. Composer
His "Misere" is sung annually in the
  Sistine Chapel on Good Friday.
b. 1582 in Rome, Italy
d. Feb 17, 1652 in Rome, Italy
Source: *Baker 78; BioIn 4; DcBiPP; DcCathB;
LuthC 75; WebBD 80*

Allen, Arthur Augustus
American. Ornithologist
Produced 15 records of bird songs; wrote
  Book of Bird Life, 1930.
b. Dec 28, 1885 in Buffalo, New York
d. Jan 17, 1964
Source: *AmAu&B; ConAu 1R; CurBio 61, 64;
WhAm 4*

Allen, Byron
American. Comedian
Wrote comedy material for Jimmy Walker,
  Freddie Prinze; co-host, TV series "Real
  People."
b. Apr 22, 1961 in Detroit, Michigan
Source: *BioIn 12; VarWW 85*

Allen, Debbie
[Mrs. Norm Nixon]
American. Actress, Dancer
Starred in TV series "Fame"; won Emmys
  for choreography, 1982, 1983.
b. Jan 16, 1950 in Houston, Texas
Source: *NewYTBS 80; VarWW 85*

Allen, Deborah
American. Singer, Songwriter
Country singer who wrote, sang hit single
  "Baby I Lied," 1983.
b. Sep 30, 1953 in Memphis, Tennessee
Source: *RkOn 85*

Allen, Duane
[The Oak Ridge Boys]
American. Singer, Musician
Guitarist, vocalist with country-pop group;
  hit single "Bobby Sue," 1982.
b. Apr 29, 1943 in Taylortown, Texas
Source: *NF*

Allen, Elizabeth
[Elizabeth Ellen Gillease]
American. Actress, Singer
Nominated for Tony, 1962, for *The Gay
  Life.*
b. Jan 25, 1934 in Jersey City, New Jersey
Source: *BiE&WWA; FilmgC; NotNAT;
PseudN 82; WhoAm 74; WhoThe 77*

Allen, Elizabeth Ann Chase Akers
American. Poet
Wrote popular verse *Rock Me to Sleep,* 1860.
b. Oct 9, 1832 in Strong, Maine
d. Aug 7, 1911 in Tuckahoe, New York
Source: *NotAW*

Allen, Ethan
American. Military Leader
Organized Green Mountain Boys, 1770, to
  harass New Yorkers in land dispute
  between NY and NH.
b. Jan 21, 1738 in Litchfield, Connecticut
d. Feb 11, 1789 in Burlington, Vermont
Source: *Alli; AmAu&B; AmBi; ApCAB; BbD;
BbtC; BiD&SB; CyAL 1; DcAmAu; DcAmB;
DcNAA; Drake; LinLib S; McGEWB;
NatCAB 1; OxAmL; REn; REnAL; REnAW;
WebAMB; WhAm HS; WhAmP; WhoMilH 76*

Allen, Florence Ellinwood
American. Judge
First woman to serve on Ohio Supreme
  Court, 1922-34.
b. Mar 23, 1884 in Salt Lake City, Utah
d. Sep 12, 1966 in Waite Hill, Ohio
Source: *CurBio 41, 63, 66; InWom; OhA&B;
WhAm 4*

Allen, Forest Clare
"Phog"
American. Basketball Coach
Coached three teams simultaneously to 74-10
  record, 1908-09; helped organize first
  NCAA tournament, 1939.
b. Nov 18, 1885 in Jamesport, Missouri
d. Sep 16, 1974 in Lawrence, Kansas
Source: *BioIn 4, 9, 10; NewYTBS 74;
WhoBbl 73*

Allen, Fred
[John Florence Sullivan]
American. Comedian
Vaudeville juggler turned comedian who
  starred in radio show, "Allen's Alley,"
  1932-49.
b. May 31, 1894 in Cambridge,
  Massachusetts
d. Mar 17, 1956 in New York, New York
Source: *CurBio 41, 56; DcAmB S6; EncMT;
FilmgC; OxFilm; REnAL; WebAB; WhAm 3;
WhScrn 74, 77; WhoHol B*

Allen, Mrs. Fred
see: Hoffa, Portland

Allen, Frederick Lewis
American. Journalist, Historian
Best known for social histories: *Only
    Yesterday*, 1931; *Since Yesterday*, 1940.
b. Jul 5, 1890 in Boston, Massachusetts
d. Feb 13, 1954 in New York, New York
Source: *AmAu&B; CnDAL; DcAmB S5;
OxAmL; REn; REnAL; TwCA, SUP; WebAB;
WhAm 3*

Allen, George
"Ice Cream"
American. Football Coach, Football Executive
Coach, Washington Redskins, 1971-77.
b. Apr 29, 1922 in Detroit, Michigan
Source: *CelR; CurBio 75; PseudN 82;
WhoAm 74, 76, 78, 80, 82*

Allen, Gracie Ethel Cecil Rosaline
[Mrs. George Burns; Burns and Allen]
American. Comedienne
With husband, starred in "Burns and Allen
    Show," 1922-58.
b. Jul 26, 1906 in San Francisco, California
d. Aug 27, 1964 in Hollywood, California
Source: *CurBio 40, 51, 64; FilmgC; InWom;
MotPP; MovMk; ThFT; WhAm 4; WhScrn
74, 77; WhoHol B*

Allen, Henry Tureman
American. Military Leader, Explorer
Army officer who explored, mapped Copper,
    Tanana, Koyukuk rivers in Alaska, 1885.
b. Apr 13, 1859 in Sharpsburg, Kentucky
d. Aug 30, 1930 in Buena Vista Spring,
    Pennsylvania
Source: *AmBi; DcAmB S1; DcNAA; WhAm 1;
WhNAA*

Allen, Hervey (William Hervey)
American. Author, Poet
Wrote best-seller, *Anthony Adverse*, 1933; Poe
    biography, *Israfel*, 1926.
b. Dec 8, 1889 in Pittsburgh, Pennsylvania
d. Dec 28, 1949 in Miami, Florida
Source: *AmAu&B; AmNov; AnMV 1926;
Chambr 3; CnDAL; ConAmA; ConAmL;
CyWA; DcAmB S4; DcLEL; DcNAA; EncWL;
LongCTC; OxAmL; PenC AM; REn; REnAL;
TwCA, SUP; TwCWr; WhAm 2; WhNAA*

Allen, Irwin
American. Director, Producer, Writer
Won Oscar, 1952, for *The Sea Around Us*,
    based on Rachel Carson's book.
b. Jun 12, 1916 in New York, New York
Source: *CmMov; FilmgC; IntMPA 75, 76, 77,
78, 79, 80, 81, 82; NewYTBS 74; NewYTET;
WhoAm 74, 78, 80, 82*

Allen, Ivan, Jr.
American. Politician, Business Executive
Mayor of Atlanta, GA, 1961-69.
b. Mar 15, 1911 in Atlanta, Georgia
Source: *CelR; St&PR 75; WhoAm 80, 82;
WhoS&SW 73; WhoWor 74*

Allen, Jack
American. Author, Educator
Wrote numerous political, historical
    textbooks: *One Nation Indivisible*, 1979.
b. Jun 18, 1914 in Prestonsburg, Kentucky
Source: *ConAu 4NR, 9R; DrAS 74H; LEduc
74; WhoAm 74, 76, 78, 80, 82, 84*

Allen, James Lane
American. Author
Popularized Blue Grass KY life in novels
    Kentucky Cardinal, 1894; *The Choir
    Invisible*, 1897.
b. Dec 21, 1849 in Lexington, Kentucky
d. Feb 18, 1925
Source: *AmAu; AmAu&B; AmBi; AmLY;
BbD; BiD&SB; BiDSA; CarSB; CasWL;
CnDAL; ConAmL; DcAmAu; DcAmB; DcBiA;
DcLEL; DcNAA; LongCTC; OxAmL; REn;
REnAL; TwCBDA; WhAm 1*

Allen, Jay Presson
American. Screenwriter, Author
Noted teleplay, stagewriter who created TV
    series, "Family," 1976.
b. Mar 3, 1922 in San Angelo, Texas
Source: *ConAu 73; McGEWD; NotNAT;
WhoAm 82; WomWMM A*

Allen, John
American. Dentist, Inventor
Patented false teeth made of porcelain with
    platium base, 1851.
b. Nov 4, 1810 in Broome County, New
    York
d. Mar 8, 1892 in Plainfield, New Jersey
Source: *DcAmB; WebAB; WhAm HS*

Allen, Karen
American. Actress
Appeared in movies *Animal House*, 1978,
    Raiders of the Lost Ark, 1981.
b. Oct 5, 1951 in Carrollton, Illinois
Source: *IntMPA 82; VarWW 85*

Allen, Larry
American. Journalist
Called "most shot-at" foreign correspondent;
won 1942 Pulitzer.
b. Oct 19, 1908 in Mount Savage, Maryland
Source: *AmEA 74; CurBio 42*

Allen, Leslie
American. Tennis Player
Highest ranking black female tennis player,
early 1980s.
b. Mar 12, 1957 in Cleveland, Ohio
Source: *InB&W 80; NewYTBS 81; WhoIntT*

Allen, Lisa Marie
American. Figure Skater
b. 1960
Source: *BioIn 12*

Allen, Lucius Oliver, Jr.
American. Basketball Player
b. Sep 26, 1947 in Kansas City, Kansas
Source: *WhoAm 74; WhoBbl 73*

Allen, Macon B
American. Lawyer, Judge
b. 1816
d. 1894
Source: *BioIn 10*

Allen, Marcus
American. Football Player
Won Heisman Trophy, 1981; running back,
LA Raiders, 1982--.
b. Mar 26, 1960 in San Diego, California
Source: *BioIn 12; FootReg 81*

Allen, Mel
[Melvin Allen Israel]
American. Sportscaster
Versatile sports broadcaster, best known as
voice of NY Yankees, 1950s.
b. Feb 14, 1913 in Birmingham, Alabama
Source: *CurBio 50; IntMPA 80, 81, 82;
WhoAm 76, 78; WhoWorJ 72*

Allen, Nancy
American. Actress
Appeared in movies *Blowout,* 1981, *Dressed
to Kill,* 1980.
b. Jun 24, 1949 in New York, New York
Source: *IntMPA 82*

Allen, Peter Woolnough
Australian. Songwriter, Singer
Former husband of Liza Minnelli; co-wrote
"I Honestly Love You," 1974; theme from
Arthur, 1981.
b. Feb 10, 1944 in Tenterfield, Australia
Source: *CurBio 83; NewYTBS 77; RkOn 85;
RolSEnR 83*

Allen, "Red" (Henry James, Jr.)
American. Jazz Musician
b. Jan 7, 1908 in New Orleans, Louisiana
d. Apr 17, 1967 in New York, New York
Source: *PseudN 82; WhoJazz 72*

Allen, Rex E, Sr.
"Mister Cowboy"
American. Actor, Singer, Songwriter
Star of cowboy films, 1950s; wrote 300 songs
including "Crying in the Chapel," 1953.
b. Dec 31, 1924 in Wilcox, Arizona
Source: *BiDAmM; BioIn 8, 11; CmpEPM;
EncFCWM 69; FilmEn; FilmgC; IntMPA 76,
77, 78, 79, 80, 81; RkOn 74; WhoAm 82;
WhoHol A; WhoRock 81*

Allen, Richard
American. Religious Leader
First black ordained in Methodist Episcopal
Church, 1799; founded African Methodist
Church, 1816.
b. Feb 14, 1760 in Philadelphia, Pennsylvania
d. Mar 26, 1831 in Philadelphia,
Pennsylvania
Source: *AmBi; ApCAB; BlkAWP; DcAmB;
DcAmReB; EncAB-H; McGEWB; NatCAB 13;
WebAB; WhAm HS*

Allen, Richard Vincent
American. Government Official
Nat. security adviser under Ronald Reagan,
1981-82; resigned amid controversy,
replaced by William Clark.
b. Jan 1, 1936 in Collingswood, New Jersey
Source: *ConAu 21R; IntWW 81, 82; IntYB
82; NewYTBS 80; WhoAm 82; WhoAmP 73,
75, 77, 79*

Allen, Richie (Richard Anthony)
American. Baseball Player
Controversial infielder, 1963-77; rookie of
year, 1964; MVP, AL, 1972.
b. Mar 8, 1942 in Wampum, Pennsylvania
Source: *BaseEn 85; WhoAm 74; WhoBlA 75;
WhoMW 74; WhoProB 73*

Allen, Rick
[The Box Tops]
American. Musician
Organist, bassist with Memphis-based soul
group, late 1960s.
b. Jan 28, 1946 in Little Rock, Arkansas
Source: *NF*

Allen, Rick
[Def Leppard]
English. Musician
Drummer with British heavy-metal, new wave
group; lost arm in car crash, 1984.
b. Nov 1, 1963 in Sheffield, England
Source: *NF*

Allen, Robert Sharon
American. Author, Journalist
Co-columnist, with Drew Pearson, for
"Washington Merry Go-Round," 1930s.
b. Jul 14, 1900 in Latonia, Kentucky
d. Feb 23, 1981 in Washington, District of
Columbia
Source: *AmAu&B; BioIn 1; ConAu 57, 103;
CurBio 41, 81; LinLib L; NewYTBS 81;
REnAL; WhoAm 74, 76, 78, 80; WhoWor 74*

**Allen, Steve (Stephen Valentine Patrick
William)**
[William Christopher Stevens, pseud.]
American. TV Personality, Songwriter,
Author, Actor
Versatile entertainer known for ad-libbed
witticisms; early host of "Tonight Show,"
"I've Got a Secret."
b. Dec 26, 1921 in New York, New York
Source: *AmAu&B; AmSCAP 66, 80;
BiE&WWA; BioNews 75; CelR; ConAu 25R;
CurBio 51; FilmgC; IntMPA 80, 81, 82;
PseudN 82; REnAL; WebAB; WhoHol A;
WrDr 76*

Allen, Verden
[Mott the Hoople]
English. Musician
Organist with hard-rock group, 1969-73.
b. May 26, 1944 in Hereford, England
Source: *NF*

Allen, Viola Emily
American. Actress
Career spanned four decades; known for
Shakespearean roles.
b. Oct 27, 1867 in Huntsville, Alabama
d. May 9, 1948 in New York, New York
Source: *NotAW*

Allen, Vivian Beaumont
American. Philanthropist
Made $2 million donation to Vivian
Beaumont Theatre at Lincoln Center,
NYC; opened, 1965.
d. Oct 10, 1962 in New York, New York
Source: *InWom; PlP&P*

Allen, Walter Ernest
English. Author, Critic
Wrote *All in a Lifetime,* 1959; *Short Story in
Britain,* 1981.
b. Feb 23, 1911 in Birmingham, England
Source: *Au&Wr 71; ConAu 61; ConNov 72,
76; DcLEL; LongCTC; ModBrL; NewC; PenC
ENG; TwCWr; WhoTwCL; WorAu; WrDr 76*

Allen, William McPherson
American. Aircraft Manufacturer
Pres., Boeing Co., 1945-72; built Saturn
Apollo moon rocket, lunar orbiter.
b. Sep 1, 1900 in Lolo, Montana
d. Oct 29, 1985 in Seattle, Washington
Source: *CurBio 53, 86; IntWW 74; St&PR
75; WhoAm 82; WhoF&I 74; WhoWest 74;
WhoWor 74*

Allen, Woody
[Allen Stewart Konigsburg]
American. Actor, Writer, Producer
Won four Oscars, including best picture,
director, for *Annie Hall,* 1978.
b. Dec 1, 1935 in Brooklyn, New York
Source: *AmAu&B; BkPepl; CelR; ConAu 33R;
CurBio 66; FilmgC; IntMPA 75, 76, 77, 78,
79, 80, 81, 82; MovMk; NewYTBE 73;
NotNAT; PseudN 82; WhoAm 74, 76, 78, 80,
82; WhoHol A; WhoThe 77; WrDr 80*

Allen of Hurtwood, Lady
[Marjory Gill Allen]
English. Author, Architect
Playground consultant whose books include
Space for Play: The Youngest Children,
1964.
b. May 10, 1897 in London, England
Source: *Au&Wr 71; ConAu P-1; PseudN 82;
Who 74*

**Allenby, Edmund Hynman Allenby,
Viscount**
"The Bull"
English. Military Leader
WW I field marshal in Middle East; armies
captured Jerusalem, defeated Turks, 1917-
18.
b. Apr 23, 1861 in Nottinghamshire, England
d. May 14, 1936 in London, England
Source: *BioIn 1, 2, 6, 7, 10, 11; DcNaB
1931; LinLib S; McGEWB; WhDW;
WhoMilH 76*

Allende, Salvador
Chilean. Political Leader
Pres. who led first govt. in power through
  free elections, 1970; violently overthrown,
  1973.
b. Jul 26, 1908 in Valparaiso, Chile
d. Sep 11, 1973 in Santiago, Chile
Source: *CurBio 71, 73; NewYTBE 70;*
WhoGov 75; WhoWor 78

Allers, Franz
Czech. Conductor
Two-time Tony-winner who has conducted
  Paint Your Wagon; My Fair Lady.
b. Aug 6, 1905 in Karlsbad, Czechoslovakia
Source: *Baker 78; BiE&WWA; CelR;*
NewYTBS 80; NotNAT; WhoAm 74, 74, 78,
80, 82; WhoMus 72; WhoOp 76; WhoWor 74

Alley, Kirstie
[Mrs. Parker Stevenson]
American. Actress
Played Virgilia on TV mini-series "North and
  South," 1985-86.
b. Jan 12, 1955 in Wichita, Kansas
Source: *VarWW 85*

Alley, Norman William
American. Photojournalist
Documented Spanish Civil War, Ethiopian
  War, WW I, WW II on film.
b. Jan 22, 1895 in Chicago, Illinois
d. Apr 1, 1981 in Woodland Hills, California
Source: *ConAu 115; WhAm 7*

Allgood, Sara
Irish. Actress
Best known for stage role in *Juno and the*
  Paycock, 1930.
b. Oct 31, 1883 in Dublin, Ireland
d. Sep 13, 1950 in Woodland Hills,
  California
Source: *CnThe; EncWT; FilmEn; Film 2;*
FilmgC; MotPP; MovMk; ObitOF 79; OxThe;
PIP&P; Vers A; WhScrn 74, 77; WhThe;
WhoHol B

Allingham, Margery
[Margery Louise Allingham Carter]
English. Author
Mystery writer who created sleuth Albert
  Champion in *Mind Readers,* 1965.
b. May 20, 1904 in London, England
d. Jun 30, 1966 in Essex, England
Source: *ConAu 4NR, 5R, 25R; DcLEL;*
EncMys; EvLB; LongCTC; MnBBF; PseudN
82; TwCA, SUP; TwCWr

Allingham, William
Irish. Poet, Editor
Fraser editor, 1874-79, whose volumes of
  verse include *The Fairies,* 1883.
b. Mar 19, 1824 in Ballyshannon, Ireland
d. Nov 18, 1889 in Hampstead, England
Source: *AnCL; BbD; BiD&SB; BrAu 19;*
CasWL; Chambr 3; DcLEL; EvLB; NewC;
PenC ENG; PoIre; REn; Str&VC; WebE&AL

Allison, Bob (William Robert)
American. Baseball Player
b. Jul 11, 1934 in Raytown, Missouri
Source: *BaseEn 85; BioIn 9, 11*

Allison, Bobby (Robert Arthur)
American. Auto Racer
b. Dec 3, 1937 in Hueytown, Alabama
Source: *BioIn 10, 11; WorAl*

Allison, Clay
American. Outlaw
"Fast gun," who killed at least 15 other
  gunmen in NM area, 1870s.
b. 1840 in Tennessee
d. 1877
Source: *BioIn 8, 9, 11; Blood&B*

Allison, Fran(ces)
American. Actress
Part of "Kukla, Fran, and Ollie," in TV
  show, 1947-57.
b. Nov 20, 1924 in LaPorrete City, Iowa
Source: *IntMPA 75, 76, 77, 78, 79, 80, 81,*
82; VarWW 85; WhoAm 74

Allison, Samuel King
American. Physicist
Director, Institute for Nuclear Studies, 1946-
  57, who worked on Los Alamos Project,
  1944-45.
b. Nov 13, 1900 in Chicago, Illinois
d. Sep 15, 1965
Source: *BioIn 7; WhAm 4; WhoAtom 77*

Allman, Duane (Howard Duane)
[Allman Brothers Band]
"Skydog"
American. Singer
Formed band with brother, Gregg, 1968;
  debut album, *The Alman Brothers Band,*
  1969; died in motorcycle accident.
b. Nov 20, 1946 in Nashville, Tennessee
d. Oct 29, 1971 in Macon, Georgia
Source: *BioIn 11; IlEncRk; PseudN 82*

Allman, Gregg (Gregory Lenoir)
[Allman Brothers Band]
American. Singer, Musician
Formed band with brother, Duane, 1968;
    recorded solo album *Laid Back,* 1974.
b. Dec 7, 1947 in Nashville, Tennessee
Source: *BioIn 10, 11; BkPepl; IlEncRk;
WhoAm 82*

Allman Brothers Band
[Duane Allman; Gregg Allman; Dicky Betts;
    Jaimoe (Jai Johnny) Johanson; Chuck
    Leavell; (Raymond) Berry Oakley; Butch
    (Claude Hudson) Trucks; Lamar Williams]
American. Music Group
Formed in Macon, GA, 1968; *Brothers and
    Sisters* album contained biggest hit,
    "Ramblin' Man," 1973.
Source: *IlEncRk; RkOn 74; RolSEnR 83*

Allon, Yigal
[Yigal Paicovich]
Israeli. General, Statesman
Best known for proposal to restore heavily
    populated Arab areas on the West Bank
    of Jordan.
b. Oct 10, 1918 in Kfar Tabor, Israel
d. Feb 29, 1980 in Afula, Israel
Source: *ConAu 73, 97; IntWW 74; NewYTBE
71; PseudN 82; WhoWor 78; WhoWorJ 72*

Allport, Gordon William
American. Psychologist
Best known for theory of personality between
    Freudianism and Behaviorism.
b. Nov 11, 1897 in Montezuma, Indiana
d. Oct 9, 1967 in Cambridge, Massachusetts
Source: *AmAu&B; ConAu 3NR, 10NR, 25R;
CurBio 60, 67; IndAu 1917; LinLib L;
REnAL; WebAB, 79; WhAm 4, 5; WhoE 74*

Allred, Rulon Clark
American. Religious Leader
Founded Apostolic United Brethran, a
    Fundamentalist Mormon, polygamy-
    practicing group.
b. Mar 29, 1906 in Chihuaha, Mexico
d. May 10, 1977 in Murray, Utah
Source: *BiDAmC*

Allsop, Kenneth
English. Author, Journalist, Critic
Popular books include *Bootleggers,* 1961;
    Hard Travellin', 1967.
b. Jan 29, 1920 in Yorkshire, England
d. May 23, 1973 in West Milton, England
Source: *Au&Wr 71; ConAu 1R, 6NR;
SmATA 17; WhoWor 74; WorAu*

Allston, Washington
American. Artist, Poet
Part of Romantic school with Coleridge,
    Wordsworth.
b. Nov 5, 1779 in Georgetown County,
    South Carolina
d. Jul 9, 1843 in Cambridgeport,
    Massachusetts
Source: *AmAu; AmAu&B; AmBi; ApCAB;
BbD; BiD&SB; BiDLA; BiDSA; BnEnAmA;
CasWL; Chambr 3; ChhPo, S1; CnDAL;
CyAL 2; DcAmArt; DcAmAu; DcAmB;
DcEnL; DcLB 1; DcNAA; Drake; EvLB;
McGDA; McGEWB; NatCAB 5; NewYHSD;
OxAmL; PenC AM; EncMT; TwCBDA;
WebAB; WhAm HS*

Ally, Carl Joseph
American. Advertising Executive
b. Mar 31, 1924 in Detroit, Michigan
Source: *WhoAdv 72; WhoAm 74, 76, 78, 80,
82*

Allyn, Stanley Charles
American. Manufacturer
Chm., chief exec., National Cash Register
    Co., 1957-62.
b. Jul 20, 1891 in Madison, Wisconsin
d. Oct 31, 1970 in Greenwich, Connecticut
Source: *CurBio 56, 70; NewYTBE 70; WhAm
5*

Allyson, June
[Ella Geisman]
American. Actress
Movie roles project image of cheerful
    wholesomeness: *The Sailor Takes a Wife,*
    1946; *The Three Musketeers,* 1948.
b. Oct 7, 1917 in Lucerne, New York
Source: *BiDFilm; CmpEPM; CurBio 52;
FilmEn; FilmgC; IntMPA 80, 81, 82; MGM;
MotPP; MovMk; WhoAm 80, 82; WhoAmW
74; WhoHol A; WorEFlm*

Alma-Tadema, Lawrence, Sir
English. Artist
b. Jan 8, 1836 in Dronrijp, Netherlands
d. Jun 25, 1912
Source: *BioIn 10; WebBD 80*

Almeida, Laurindo
Spanish. Musician, Composer
Jazz guitarist featured in Modern Jazz
    Quartet tours; has won five Grammys.
b. Sep 2, 1917 in Sao Paulo, Brazil
Source: *AmSCAP 66, 80; BiDAmM;
CmpEPM; EncJzS 70; WhoAm 74, 76, 78,
80, 82; WhoWor 74*

Almond, Gabriel Abraham
American. Author, Educator
Stanford professor, 1963--, whose writings
    include *Civic Culture Revisited,* 1980.
b. Jan 12, 1911 in Rock Island, Illinois
Source: *AmM&WS 73S; ConAu 101; IntWW
74; WhoAm 76, 78, 80, 82, 84*

Almond, Paul
Canadian. Producer, Screenwriter
Pres., Quest Films since 1967; films include
    Act of the Heart, 1970; *Journal,* 1972.
b. Apr 26, 1931 in Montreal, Quebec
Source: *CanWW 80, 82; ConAu 73; CreCan
2; FilmEn; FilmgC; IntMPA 80, 81; WhoAm
82; WhoAmA 80, 82; WhoE 81*

Alonso, Alicia
[Alicia Ernestina de la Caridad del Cobre
    Marinez Hoyo]
Cuban. Ballerina
First Western dancer invited to dance in
    USSR, 1957; founded Ballet Nacional de
    Cuba, 1959.
b. Dec 21, 1921 in Havana, Cuba
Source: *CurBio 55; VarWW 85; WhoWor 74,
82; WorAl*

Alou, Felipe Rojas
"Panque"
Dominican. Baseball Player
One of three brothers who all played in
    Giants outfield at same time, 1963.
b. May 12, 1935 in Haina, Dominican
    Republic
Source: *BaseEn 85; PseudN 82; WhoAm 74;
WhoProB 73*

Alou, Jesus Maria Rojas
"Jay"
Dominican. Baseball Player
Collected six hits in one game, Jul 10, 1964.
b. Mar 24, 1943 in Haina, Dominican
    Republic
Source: *BaseEn 85; PseudN 82; WhoAm 74;
WhoProB 73*

Alou, Matty (Mateo Rojas)
Dominican. Baseball Player
Won NL batting title, 1966, with brother
    Felipe second.
b. Dec 22, 1938 in Haina, Dominican
    Republic
Source: *BaseEn 85; PseudN 82; WhoProB 73*

Alpert, Herb
[Tijuana Brass]
American. Musician, Band Leader
Co-founder, pres., A & M Records, 1962;
    had hits "This Guy's in Love with You,"
    1968; "Rise," 1979.
b. Mar 31, 1935 in Los Angeles, California
Source: *BiDAmM; BioNews 74; CelR; CurBio
67; NewYTBS 74; RkOn 74, 78; WhoAm 74,
76, 78, 80, 82; WhoHol A*

Alpert, Hollis
American. Movie Critic, Editor
Editor, *American Film* since 1975, who wrote
    The Barrymores, 1964.
b. Sep 24, 1916 in Herkimer, New York
Source: *AmAu&B; ConAu 1R; WhoAm 76,
78, 80, 82, 84*

Alphand, Herve
French. Economist, Diplomat
UN ambassador, 1955-56, ambassador to US,
    1956-65.
b. May 31, 1907
Source: *CurBio 51; IntWW 82, 83; Who 82,
83*

Alsop, Joseph Wright, Jr.
American. Journalist, Author
Co-wrote syndicated news column, 1946-58;
    books include *We Accuse,* 1955.
b. Oct 11, 1910 in Avon, Connecticut
Source: *AmAu&B; CelR; CurBio 52; IntWW
74; NewYTBE 71; NewYTBS 74; REn;
REnAL; WhoAm 74, 76, 78, 80, 82; WhoWor
74; WorAu*

Alsop, Stewart Johonnot Oliver
American. Journalist, Author
Editor, *Saturday Evening Post,* 1958-68; co-
    wrote *Stay of Execution,* 1973.
b. May 17, 1914 in Avon, Connecticut
d. May 26, 1974 in Washington, District of
    Columbia
Source: *CelR; ConAu 49, 89; CurBio 52, 74;
IntWW 74; NewYTBS 74; REn; WhAm 6;
WhoAm 74; WhoS&SW 73; WorAu*

Alston, Theodosia Burr
American. Celebrity Relative
Daughter of Aaron Burr who stood loyally
    by father through all disasters; lost at sea.
b. 1783 in Albany, New York
d. 1813
Source: *AmBi; BioIn 1, 2, 3, 6, 10; DcAmB;
NotAW*

Alston, Walter Emmons
"Smokey"
American. Baseball Manager
Mgr., Brooklyn, LA Dodgers, 1954-76, who
    won four world championships; Hall of
    Fame, 1983.
b. Dec 1, 1911 in Venice, Ohio
d. Oct 1, 1984 in Oxford, Ohio
Source: *AnObit 1984; BaseEn 85; CelR;*
CurBio 54, 84; NewYTBS 74; PseudN 82;
WhAm 8; WhoAm 82; WhoProB 73

Altdorfer, Albrecht
German. Artist, Architect
b. 1480
d. Feb 12, 1538
Source: *AtlBL; OxGer*

Alter, Hobie (Hobart, Jr.)
American. Designer
Designed "Hobie Cat" sailing catamaran.
b. 1934 in Capistrano Beach, California
Source: *BioIn 10; ConNews 85-1*

Altgeld, John Peter
American. Politician
Governor of IL, 1892-96, who championed
    liberal causes, rights of the individual.
b. Dec 30, 1847 in Nassau, Germany
d. Mar 12, 1902 in Joliet, Illinois
Source: *AmAu&B; AmBi; DcAmAu; DcAmB;*
EncAB-H; LinLib S; McGEWB; NatCAB 11;
OhA&B; OxAmH; OxAmL; REnAL;
TwCBDA; WebAB, 79; WhAm 1; WhAmP

Althouse, Paul Shearer
American. Opera Singer
Tenor, known for lead roles in *Carmen,*
    Samson et Delilah.
b. Dec 2, 1889 in Reading, Pennsylvania
d. Feb 6, 1954 in New York, New York
Source: *WhAm 3*

Altman, Benjamin
American. Merchant, Art Collector
Founded B Altman & Co., NYC dept. store,
    1906.
b. Jul 12, 1840 in New York, New York
d. Oct 7, 1913 in New York, New York
Source: *AmBi; DcAmB; NewYTBE 70;*
WebAB; WhAm HSA, 4

Altman, Robert B
American. Director, Producer
Directed *M*A*S*H,* 1970; *A Weddding,* 1978.
b. Feb 20, 1925 in Kansas City, Missouri
Source: *BiDFilm; BkPepl; CelR; ConAu 73;*
ConLC 16; CurBio 74; FilmgC; IntMPA 80,
81, 82; IntWW 81, 82; MovMk; NewYTBE
71; OxFilm; WhoAm 82; WhoAmJ 80

Altobelli, Joe (Joseph Salvatore)
American. Baseball Manager
Mgr., Baltimore Orioles, 1983-85.
b. May 26, 1932 in Detroit, Michigan
Source: *BaseEn 85; WhoAm 78, 84*

Altrock, Nick (Nicholas)
American. Baseball Player
Pitcher, 1898-1933, known for clowning
    antics.
b. Sep 15, 1876 in Cincinnati, Ohio
d. Jan 20, 1965 in Washington, District of
    Columbia
Source: *BaseEn 85; WhoProB 73*

Aluko, Timothy Mofolorunso
Nigerian. Author
One Man, One Woman was first novel
    published in English in Nigeria, 1959.
b. Jun 14, 1918 in Ilesha, Nigeria
Source: *AfrA; Au&Wr 71; CasWL; ConAu 65;*
ConNov 72, 76, 82; PenC CL; RGAfL;
TwCWr; WebE&AL; WrDr 76

Alva, Duke of
see: Toledo, Fernando Alvarez de

Alvarado, Pedro de
Spanish. Conqueror
Helped conquer Mexico, Central America for
    Spain, 1519-34.
b. 1486 in Badajoz, Spain
d. 1541 in Nochistlan, Mexico
Source: *AmBi; ApCAB; DcBiPP; DcCathB;*
Drake; LinLib S

Alvardo, Trini(dad)
American. Actress
Star of films *Rich Kids,* 1979; *Times Square,*
    1980.
b. 1967 in New York, New York
Source: *NewYTBS 79*

Alvarez, Alfred
English. Poet, Critic
Influential reviewer-critic who discussed
    literary suicides in *Savage God,* 1971.
b. Aug 5, 1929 in London, England
Source: *Au&Wr 71; ConAu 1R, 3NR; ConLC*
5, 13; ConP 70, 75; ModBrL S1; REn; Who
74, 85; WhoWor 74; WorAu; WrDr 76

Alvarez, Luis Walter
American. Physicist
Won Nobel Prize, 1968, for work, discoveries
    in nuclear physics.
b. Jun 13, 1911 in San Francisco, California
Source: *IntWW 74; WebAB; Who 80;*
WhoAm 82

Alvarez, Walter Clement
American. Physician, Author, Journalist
Authority on digestive tract; had syndicated
newspaper column, 1951-78.
b. Jul 22, 1884 in San Francisco, California
d. Jun 18, 1978 in San Francisco, California
Source: *AmAu&B; AmM&WS 73P; ConAu
61; CurBio 53, 78; DrAP 75; MinnWr;
WhNAA; WhoAm 74; WhoWor 78*

Alvarez de Cienfuegos, Nicasio
see: Cienfuegos, Nicasio Alvarez de

Alvary, Lorenzo
American. Opera Singer
b. Feb 20, 1909 in Hungary
Source: *WhoAm 74, 76, 78, 80, 82; WhoMus
72; WhoWor 78*

Alvary, Max
[Max Achenbach]
German. Opera Singer
Tenor at Metropolitan Opera House, NYC,
1884-98.
b. May 3, 1856 in Dusseldorf, Germany
d. Nov 7, 1898 in Gross-Tabarz, Germany
Source: *BioIn 1; WebBD 80*

Alworth, Lance Dwight
"Bambi"
American. Football Player
Only player to gain over 1,000 yds. receiving
in seven consecutive seasons.
b. Aug 3, 1940 in Houston, Texas
Source: *PseudN 82; WhoFtbl 74*

Alzado, Lyle Martin
American. Football Player
All-Pro defensive end, 1971-86, named
defensive player of year, 1977.
b. Apr 3, 1949 in Brooklyn, New York
Source: *ConAu 110; FootReg 86; WhoAm 78,
80, 82, 84*

Amado, Jorge
"Brazilian Boccaccio"
Brazilian. Author
Brazil's greatest living novelist whose social
conscious writings have been translated
into more than 30 languages.
b. Aug 10, 1912 in Bahia, Brazil
Source: *CasWL; CelR; ConAu 77; ConLC 13;
CurBio 86; CyWA; EncWL; IntWW 74; PenC
AM; REn; TwCWr; WhoAm 84; WhoWor 74,
84; WorAu*

Amalrik, Andrei Alekseyevich
Russian. Author, Historian, Dissident
Human rights advocate who wrote many
anti-Soviet works, spent six years in labor
camp.
b. May 12, 1938 in Moscow, U.S.S.R.
d. Nov 11, 1980 in Guadalajara, Spain
Source: *AnObit 1980; BioIn 8, 9, 10, 11;
ConAu 102; CurBio 74, 81; NewYTBE 73;
NewYTBS 80*

Amara, Lucine
[Lucine Tockqui Armaganian]
American. Opera Singer
b. Mar 1, 1927 in Hartford, Connecticut
Source: *InWom; PseudN 82; WhoAm 74, 76,
78, 80, 82; WhoAmW 77; WhoMus 72;
WhoWor 78*

Amati
[Andrea Amati; Antonio Amati; Girolamo
Amati; Girolamo Amati, II; Nicolo Amati]
Italian. Violin Maker
Family of craftsmen active in Cremona, Italy,
1540-1740; originated forms of violin,
viola, cello known today.
Source: *AntBDN K; Baker 78; BioIn 2*

Amati, Nicolo (Nicolaus)
Italian. Violin Maker
Son of Girolamo Amati, considered most
refined craftsman of family; teacher of
Antonio Stradivari.
b. Dec 3, 1956 in Cremona, Italy
d. Apr 12, 1684 in Cremona, Italy
Source: *AntBDN K; Baker 78; BioIn 2*

Amato, Pasquale
Italian. Opera Singer
Baritone, known for performances in *Carmen,
Othello.*
b. Mar 21, 1878 in Naples, Italy
d. Aug 12, 1942 in New York, New York
Source: *CurBio 42; WhAm 2; WhoHol B*

Amaya, Victor
"Big Vic"
American. Tennis Player
Tall lefthander who won French Open
doubles with Hank Pfister, 1980.
b. Jul 2, 1954 in Denver, Colorado
Source: *BioIn 12; WhoIntT*

Ambers, Lou
[Luigi d'Ambrosio]
"Herkimer Hurricane"
American. Boxer
b. Nov 8, 1913 in Herkimer, New York
Source: *PseudN 82; WhoBox 74*

Ambler, Eric
[Eliot Reed, pseud.]
English. Author, Screenwriter
Famed espionage writer who wrote *Mask of Dimitrios,* 1939; filmed, 1944.
b. Jun 28, 1909 in London, England
Source: *AmAu&B; Au&Wr 71; CnMWL; ConAu 7NR, 9R; ConLC 4, 6, 9; ConNov 76; DcLEL; EncMys; FilmgC; NewC; OxFilm; PseudN 82; REn; TwCA SUP; TwCWr; Who 85; WhoWor 74; WrDr 76*

Amboy Dukes, The
[Greg Arama; Cliff Davies; Rusty Day; Steve Farmer; Rob Grange; Vic Mastrianni; Ted Nugent; Dave Palmer; Derek St. Holmes; Andy Solomon]
American. Music Group
Formed by Ted Nugent, 1965; had hit "Journey to the Center of Your Mind," 1968.
Source: *BiDAmM; ConMuA 80A; WhoRock 81*

Ambrose, Saint
Italian. Religious Leader
Bishop of Milan who was first to use hymns extensively as divine praise.
b. 340 in Trier, Italy
d. Apr 4, 397 in Milan, Italy
Source: *BiD&SB; CasWL; DcBiPP; DcCathB; LinLib L, S; McGDA; McGEWB; NewC; OxEng; OxMus; PenC CL; PoChrch; REn*

Ambrose, David Edwin
English. Dramatist, Screenwriter
Teleplays include "Alternative 3," controversial drama hoax, 1977.
b. Feb 21, 1943 in Chorley, England
Source: *ConAu 116; ConTFT 1*

Amdahl, Gene M(yron)
American. Engineer, Business Executive
Computer designer, IBM, 1952-70; established Amdahl Corp. to replace IBM mainframes with high-performance emulators, 1970-79.
b. Nov 16, 1922 in Flandreau, South Dakota
Source: *AmM&WS 82P; BioIn 11, 12; CurBio 82; LElec; St&PR 84; WhoAm 82, 84; WhoEng 80; WhoFrS 84; WhoWor 74, 76*

Ameche, Don
[Dominic Felix Amici]
American. Actor, Radio Performer
Star of over 40 films; won Oscar, 1986, for role in *Cocoon.*
b. May 31, 1908 in Kenosha, Wisconsin
Source: *CmMov; CurBio 65; EncMT; FilmgC; IntMPA 80, 81, 82; MotPP; MovMk; OxFilm; PseudN 82; WhoHol A; WhoThe 77*

Ameche, Jim
American. Actor, Radio Performer
Brother of Don Ameche; portrayed first Jack Armstrong in radio series, 1930s.
b. 1915 in Kenosha, Wisconsin
d. Feb 4, 1983 in Tucson, Arizona
Source: *NewYTBS 83*

Ameling, Elly
Dutch. Opera Singer
b. Feb 8, 1938 in Rotterdam, Netherlands
Source: *NewYTBS 74; WhoAm 82; WhoMus 72; WhoWor 78*

Amen, Irving
American. Artist
Designed Peace Medal for end of Vietnam War.
b. Jul 25, 1918 in New York, New York
Source: *DcCAA 71; WhoAm 74, 76, 78, 80, 82; WhoAmA 73; WhoWor 78; WhoWorJ 72*

Amenhotep IV
see: Ikhnaton, Pharaoh

Amerasinghe, Hamilton Shirley
Sri Lankan. Diplomat, Government Official
Pres., UN General Assembly, 1967.
b. Mar 18, 1913 in Colombo, Ceylon
d. Dec 4, 1980 in New York, New York
Source: *BioIn 9, 11; CurBio 77, 81; FarE&A 78, 79; IntWW 77, 78; IntYB 78, 79; NewYTBS 76; WhoWor 76, 78*

America
[Gerry Beckley; Dewey Bunnell; Daniel Peek]
American. Music Group
First million selling record, "A Horse with No Name," 1972.
Source: *EncPR&S 74; IlEncRk; RolSEnR 83*

Amery, Julian (Harold Julian)
English. Politician, Author
MP 1950-66, 1969--.
b. Mar 27, 1919 in London, England
Source: *ConAu 61; IntWW 74, 80, 81; IntYB 78, 79; Who 74; WhoWor 74, 76; WrDr 80*

Ames, Blanche
American. Artist
Botanical illustrator; early champion for birth control, 1916.
b. Feb 18, 1878 in Lowell, Massachusetts
d. Mar 1, 1969 in North Easton, Massachusetts
Source: *NatCAB 53; NotAW MOD; ObitOF 79; WhoAmW 70; WomWWA 14*

Ames, Ed(mund Dantes)
[The Ames Brothers; Ed Urick]
American. Singer, Actor, Producer
Solo recording artist, 1963--; played Mingo in
TV series "Daniel Boone," 1963-68.
b. Jul 9, 1927 in Boston, Massachusetts
Source: *BioIn 8; PseudN 82; RkOn 74;
WhoAm 82*

Ames, Jessie Daniel
American. Reformer
Founded Assn. of Southern Women for
Prevention of Lynching, 1930.
b. Nov 2, 1883 in Palestine, Texas
d. Feb 21, 1972 in Austin, Texas
Source: *EncSoH; NotAW MOD*

Ames, Leon
[Leon Wycoff]
American. Actor
Character actor; appeared in over 100 films
since 1932.
b. Jan 20, 1903 in Portland, Indiana
Source: *BiE&WWA; FilmgC; IntMPA 77, 75,
76, 78, 79, 80, 81, 82; MovMk; NotNAT;
PseudN 82; Vers B; WhThe; WhoHol A;
WorAl*

Ames, Louise Bates
American. Psychologist, Journalist
Author of several child care books; wrote
daily syndicated newspaper column,
"Parents Ask."
b. Oct 29, 1908 in Portland, Maine
Source: *AmAu&B; AmM&WS 73S; ConAu
1R, 3NR; CurBio 56; InWom; LEduc 74;
WhoAm 74, 76, 78, 80, 82; WhoAmW 77*

Ames, Nancy
[Nancy Hamilton Alfaro]
American. Singer
b. Sep 30, 1937 in Washington, District of
Columbia
Source: *BioIn 6, 7*

Ames, Oakes
American. Politician, Manufacturer
Rep. con. from MA, 1863-73; part of scheme
to build Union Pacific Railroad, 1865.
b. Jan 10, 1804 in Easton, Massachusetts
d. May 8, 1873 in Easton, Massachusetts
Source: *AmBi; ApCAB; BiAUS; BiDrAC;
DcAmB; TwCBDA; WebAB; WhAm HS;
WhAmP*

Ames Brothers, The
[Ed, Gene, Joe, and Vic Ames; given name
Urick]
American. Music Group
Sang together, 1949-59; had 1953 hit single
"You, You, You."
Source: *AmPS A, B; BiDAmM; CmpEPM;
PseudN 82; RkOn 84*

Amfiteatrof, Daniele
American. Conductor, Composer
Prolific film composer, credited with 79 film
scores including Disney's "Song of the
South."
b. Oct 29, 1901 in Saint Petersburg, Russia
d. Jul 7, 1983 in Rome, Italy
Source: *AmSCAP 66; Baker 78; BiDAmM;
BioIn 1, 2, 3, 4; FilmgC; IntMPA 77, 78, 79,
80, 81, 82; OxFilm; WhoWor 78; WorEFlm*

Amherst, Jeffrey
English. General
Commander-in-chief, British forces, 1780;
Amherst College named for him.
b. Jan 29, 1717 in Riverhead, England
d. Aug 31, 1797
Source: *AmBi; Drake; McGEWB; NewC;
OxCan*

Amicis, Edmond de
Italian. Author, Essayist
Most famous work *Cuore,* 1876, known for
Tuscan style; used in US to teach Italian.
b. Oct 21, 1846 in Oneglia, Italy
d. Mar 12, 1908 in Bordighera, Italy
Source: *CasWL; DcBiA; EuAu; EvEuW; PenC
EUR; REn; WebBD 80; WhLit*

Amies, Hardy
[Edwin Hardy Aimes]
English. Fashion Designer
Opened boutique, London, 1950, specializing
in high fashion ready to wear.
b. Jul 17, 1909 in London, England
Source: *CelR; CurBio 62; IntWW 74;
NewYTBE 73; WhoWor 78; WorFshn*

Amin, Idi
[Idi Amin Dada Oumee]
"Big Daddy"; "The Wild Man of Africa"
Ugandan. Political Leader
Pres., of Uganda 1971-83; suspected of
widespread torture, murder of dissidents.
b. 1925 in Koboko, Uganda
Source: *BioIn 11; BioNews 74; BkPepl;
CurBio 73; DcPol; InB&W 80; IntWW 74;
NewYTBE 71, 72; NewYTBS 77; PseudN 82;
WhoGov 72; WhoWor 74; WorDWW*

Amis, Kingsley William
[Robert Markham, pseud.]
"Angry Young Man"
English. Author
Satirical novelist; several produced as movies,
    including *Lucky Jim*, 1954.
b. Apr 16, 1922 in London, England
Source: *Au&Wr 71; AuNews 2; CasWL;
CnMWL; ConAu 9R; ConLC 1, 2, 3, 5, 8,
13; ConNov 72, 76; ConP 70, 75; EncMys;
EncWL; FilmgC; IntWW 74; LongCTC;
ModBrL, S1; NewC; PenC ENG; PseudN 82;
RAdv 1; REn; TwCWr; WebE&AL; Who 74;
WhoAm 74, 76, 78, 80, 82; WhoTwCL;
WorAu; WrDr 80*

Ammann, Othmar Hermann
German. Engineer
Master bridge designer, builder: George
    Washington Bridge, 1927-31; Golden Gate
    Bridge, 1929-37; Mackinac Bridge, 1958-62.
b. Mar 26, 1876 in Schaffhausen, Switzerland
d. Sep 22, 1965 in Rye, New York
Source: *BioIn 3, 5, 6, 7, 9, 11; CurBio 63,
65; EncAB 28; LinLib L; McGMS 80;
NatCAB 52; ObitOF 79; WhAm 4*

Ammons, Albert C
American. Jazz Musician
Pianist in Chicago clubs, 1929-49.
b. 1907 in Chicago, Illinois
d. Dec 2, 1949 in Chicago, Illinois
Source: *CmpEPM; WhoJazz 72*

Ammons, "Jug" (Eugene)
American. Musician
Tenor saxist; son of Albert Ammons.
b. Apr 14, 1925 in Chicago, Illinois
d. Aug 6, 1974 in Chicago, Illinois
Source: *BioIn 10; PseudN 82*

Amory, Cleveland
American. Author, Historian
Conservationist, pres., The Fund for Animals;
    wrote *Last Resorts*, 1952.
b. Sep 2, 1917 in Nahant, Massachusetts
Source: *AmAu&B; AuNews 1; BkPepl; ConAu
69; REnAL; TwCA SUP; WhoAm 76, 78, 80,
82, 84; WhoWor 74; WrDr 76, 80, 82*

Amos
Prophet, Biblical Character
Visions recorded in Old Testament book of
    Amos.
b. 750 BC
Source: *BioIn 9; REn; WebBD 80*

Amos, John
American. Actor
Played Kunte Kinte in TV mini-series
    "Roots," 1977; James Evans on TV series
    "Good Times," 1974-76.
b. Dec 27, 1942 in Newark, New Jersey
Source: *BioNews 74; WhoAm 82; WhoHol A*

Amos, Wally
[Wallace Amos, Jr.]
"Famous Amos"
American. Business Executive
Best known for "Famous Amos" chocolate
    chip cookie shops all over US.
b. Jul 1, 1936 in Tallahassee, Florida
Source: *BioIn 11; BkPepl; InB&W 80;
NewYTBS 75; WhoBlA 80*

Amos 'n Andy
see: Correll, Charles J; Gosden, Freeman F

Ampere, Andre Marie
French. Scientist
Made important discoveries in electricity,
    magnetism, today known as
    electrodynamics.
b. Jan 22, 1775 in Lyons, France
d. Jun 10, 1836
Source: *OxFr; REn*

Amram, David Werner, III
American. Musician, Conductor
Composer, NY Shakespeare Festival, 1956-57.
b. Nov 17, 1930 in Philadelphia,
    Pennsylvania
Source: *BiE&WWA; BioNews 74; ConAu 29R;
CurBio 69; DcCM; NotNAT; WhoAm 74, 76,
78, 80, 82*

Amsberry, Bob
American. TV Personality
Source: *BioIn 4*

Amsterdam, Morey
American. Actor, Comedian
Cellist, who played Buddy Sorrell in "The
    Dick Van Dyke Show," 1961-66.
b. Dec 14, 1914 in Chicago, Illinois
Source: *AmSCAP 66; IntMPA 75, 76, 77, 78,
79, 80, 81, 82; WhoAm 74, 76, 78, 80, 82*

Amundsen, Roald Engelbregt
Norwegian. Explorer
First man to reach S Pole, 1911, who also
    proved existence of Northwest Passage,
    1903-06.
b. Jul 16, 1872 in Borge, Norway
d. Jun 18, 1928
Source: *AsBiEn; LinLib L, S; MacDCB 78;
McGEWB; OxCan; REn*

Anacreon
"The Teian Muse"
Greek. Poet
Lyric poet noted for verse celebrating wine,
    love.
b. 572 ?BC in Teos, Asia Minor
d. 488 ?BC
Source: *AtlBL; BbD; BiD&SB; CasWL;
DcBiPP; DcEuL; Dis&D; NewC; OxEng; PenC
CL; PseudN 82; RComWL*

Anand, Mulk Raj
[Narad Muni, pseud.]
Indian. Author
Wrote on Indian society, politics; novels
    include *Coolie,* 1913; *Lake Singh* trilogy,
    1939-43.
b. Dec 12, 1905 in Peshawar, India
Source: *Au&Wr 71; CasWL; ConAu 65;
ConNov 76; DcOrL 2; IntWW 74; PenC
ENG; PseudN 82; REn; WebE&AL; WhoWor
74; WorAu; WrDr 76*

Anastasis, Romanovna
see: Romanov, Anastasia

Anastasia, Albert
"Lord High Executioner"; "Mad Hatter"
American. Organized Crime Figure, Murderer
Joined Louis Buchalter and Murder Inc.,
    1931; extorted "sweetheart contracts" from
    unions.
b. Sep 26, 1902 in Tropea, Italy
d. Oct 29, 1957 in New York, New York
Source: *BioIn 4, 11; Blood&B; DrInf; PolProf
E; PseudN 82*

Anaxagoras
Greek. Philosopher
Teacher of Pericles, Euripides, who disproved
    doctrine that things may have arisen by
    chance.
b. 500 BC in Asia Minor
d. 428 BC
Source: *BbD; BiD&SB; CasWL; PenC CL;
REn*

Anaximander
Greek. Astronomer, Philosopher
First to write philosophy in Greek prose;
    invented sun dial, calculated angle of
    earth's tilt.
b. 611 BC in Miletus, Asia Minor
d. 547 BC
Source: *BbD; BiD&SB; CasWL; PenC CL;
REn*

Anaximenes of Miletus
Greek. Philosopher
Student of Anaximander who believed earth
    was flat and rested on air.
b. 570 ?BC in Miletus, Asia Minor
d. 500 ?BC
Source: *DcScB; WebBD 80*

Anaya, Toney
American. Politician
Dem. governor of NM, 1982--; only hispanic
    governor in US.
b. Apr 29, 1941 in Moriarty, New Mexico
Source: *AlmAP 84; WhoAm 78; WhoAmL 78;
WhoAmP 83; WhoGov 77; WhoReal 83;
WhoWest 78, 84*

Ancerl, Karel
Czech. Conductor
Conducted orchestras throughout Europe,
    Australia, Asia, US, Canada, 1931-73.
b. Apr 11, 1908 in Tucapy, Czechoslovakia
d. Jul 3, 1973 in Toronto, Ontario
Source: *CanWW 70; NewYTBE 73; WhAm 6;
WhoMus 72; WhoWor 78*

Anda, Geza
Swiss. Pianist
Known for performing Bela Bartok's
    concertos.
b. Nov 19, 1921 in Budapest, Hungary
d. Jun 13, 1976 in Zurich, Switzerland
Source: *Baker 78; BioIn 4, 6, 9, 10; IntWW
74; NewYTBS 76; ObitOF 79; Who 74;
WhoMus 72; WhoWor 74*

Anders, Merry
American. Actress
Co-starred in TV series "How to Marry a
    Millionaire," 1957-59.
b. 1932
Source: *FilmgC; InWom; MotPP*

Anders, William Alison
American. Astronaut
Systems engineer on first lunar flight, Apollo
    8, Dec 1968.
b. Oct 17, 1933 in Hong Kong, China
Source: *CurBio 69; IntWW 74; WhoAm 74;
WhoGov 75; WhoS&SW 82; WhoWor 78*

Andersen, Anna
Model
Source: *NF*

Andersen, Eric
American. Singer, Composer
b. Feb 14, 1943 in Pittsburgh, Pennsylvania
Source: *BioIn 8; ConArt 77; WhoAdv 72;
WhoAm 74, 76, 78, 80, 82*

Andersen, Hans Christian
"The Danish Lafontaine"
Danish. Author, Poet
Produced 168 fairy tales, 1835-45; first
    English translation, 1846.
b. Apr 2, 1805 in Odense, Denmark
d. Aug 4, 1875 in Copenhagen, Denmark
Source: *AnCL; AtlBL; AuBYP; BbD;
BiD&SB; CarSB; CasWL; CyWA; DcBiA;
DcEnL; DcEuL; EuAu; EvEuW; FamAYP;
FamSYP; FilmgC; JBA 34, 51; NewC;
OxEng; PenC EUR; PseudN 82; RComWL;
REn; Str&VC; WhoChL; YABC 1*

Andersen, Ib Steen
Danish. Ballet Dancer
Co-star, with Merrill Ashley, in Balanchine's
    NYC Ballet, 1980.
b. Dec 14, 1954 in Copenhagen, Denmark
Source: *BioIn 11; CurBio 84; WhoAm 82*

Andersen, Lale
German. Singer
b. 1913
d. Aug 29, 1972 in Vienna, Austria
Source: *NewYTBE 72*

Anderson, Bibi
see: Andersson Bibi

Anderson, Bill
"The Pat Boone of Country Music";
    "Whispering Bill"
American. Singer, Songwriter
Top country music star of 1960s; wrote
    "Walk Out Backward," 1962; "Strangers,"
    1965.
b. Nov 1, 1937 in Columbia, South Carolina
Source: *BioIn 9, 11; EncFCWM 69; PseudN
82; WhoRock 81*

Anderson, Bonnie Marie
American. Broadcast Journalist
Correspondent, NBC News, 1981--.
b. Oct 22, 1955 in Havana, Cuba
Source: *WhoTelC*

Anderson, Carl David
American. Scientist
Discovered positron, 1932, first meson, 1937;
    won Nobel Prize in physics, 1936.
b. Sep 3, 1905 in New York, New York
Source: *IntWW 74; WebAB; Who 74;
WhoAm 74, 76, 78, 80, 82; WhoWor 78*

Anderson, Carl Thomas
American. Cartoonist
Created cartoon, "Henry," 1932, which
    currently runs in 196 daily newspapers.
b. Feb 14, 1865 in Madison, Wisconsin
d. Nov 4, 1948 in Madison, Wisconsin
Source: *AmAu&B; WhAm 2*

Anderson, "Cat" (William Alonzo)
American. Composer, Musician
Jazz trumpeter, who recorded "Take the A
    Train" with Duke Ellington Orchestra,
    1940s.
b. Sep 12, 1916 in Greenville, South Carolina
d. Apr 30, 1981 in Norwalk, California
Source: *AmSCAP 66, 80; BiDAmM;
CmpEPM; EncJzS 70; NewYTBS 81; WhoJazz
72*

Anderson, C(larence) W(illiam)
American. Children's Author
Wrote, illustrated *Billy and Blaze* series,
    1936-70.
b. Apr 12, 1891 in Wahoo, Nebraska
d. Mar 26, 1971
Source: *AuBYP; BkP; ConAu 29R, 73; IlsCB
1744, 1946, 1957; PseudN 82; SmATA 11;
Str&VC; ThrBJA; TwCCW 83*

Anderson, Clint(on Presba)
American. Statesman, Politician
Senator from NM, 1949-73.
b. Oct 23, 1895 in Centerville, South Dakota
d. Nov 11, 1975 in Albuquerque, New
    Mexico
Source: *BiDrAC; BiDrUSE; CurBio 45, 76;
IntWW 74; St&PR 75; WhAm 6; Who 74;
WhoAm 74; WhoAmP 73; WhoGov 72;
WhoS&SW 73; WhoWor 74*

Anderson, Daryl
American. Actor
Played Animal in TV series "Lou Grant,"
    1977-82.
b. Jul 1, 1951 in Seattle, Washington
Source: *BioIn 12; WhoAm 82*

Anderson, Donny
American. Football Player
b. May 16, 1943 in Borger, Texas
Source: *WhoFtbl 74*

Anderson, Dorothy Hansine
American. Physician
Developed research in cystic fibrosis, 1940s.
b. May 15, 1901 in Asheville, North
    Carolina
d. Mar 3, 1963 in New York, New York
Source: *NotAW MOD*

Anderson, Douglas Dorland
American. Archaeologist
b. Jun 1, 1936 in Olympia, Washington
Source: *AmM&WS 73S*

Anderson, Eddie
American. Actor
Played Jack Benny's manservant Rochester
on radio, films, TV.
b. Sep 18, 1905 in Oakland, California
d. Feb 28, 1977 in Los Angeles, California
Source: *DrBlPA; FilmgC; IntMPA 77, 75, 76,
78, 79, 80, 81, 82; MotPP; MovMk; NatCAB
60; NegAl 76; ObitOF 79; WhoHol A;
WhoThe 81N*

Anderson, Elda Emma
American. Physicist
Leader in study of radiation protection.
b. Apr 5, 1899 in Green Lake, Wisconsin
d. Apr 17, 1961 in Oak Ridge, Tennessee
Source: *NatCAB 50; NotAW MOD*

Anderson, Elizabeth Garrett
English. Physician, Pioneer
First English woman doctor; received degree
from U of Paris, 1870.
b. 1836 in Aldeburgh, England
d. 1917
Source: *Alli SUP; CelCen; InWom; MacDWB;
WhDW*

Anderson, Elizabeth Milbank
American. Philanthropist
Founded Milbank Memorial Fund, 1905, to
help NY's needy.
b. Dec 20, 1850 in New York, New York
d. Feb 22, 1921 in New York, New York
Source: *NatCAB 23; NotAW*

Anderson, Eugenie Moore
American. Diplomat
b. May 26, 1909 in Adair, Iowa
Source: *InWom; IntWW 74, 75, 76, 77, 78;
WhoAm 74, 76, 78; WhoAmP 73, 75, 77, 79*

Anderson, George Everett
American. Diplomat
b. Aug 20, 1869 in Bloomington, Illinois
d. Mar 17, 1940
Source: *CurBio 40; WhAm 1*

Anderson, Gerry
English. Producer
Produced science fiction TV series "Space
1999," 1975.
b. 1929 in Hampstead, England
Source: *EncSF; FanAl; IntMPA 81, 82, 83,
84, 85*

Anderson, Gilbert M
[Max Aaronson]
American. Actor
Starred as first cowboy hero, Broncho Billy,
in western serial, 1907-14; awarded special
Oscar, 1957.
b. Mar 21, 1882 in Little Rock, Arkansas
d. Jan 20, 1971 in South Pasadena,
California
Source: *Film 1; MotPP; NewYTBE 71;
ObitOF 79; OxFilm; PseudN 82; WhScrn 74,
77; WorEFlm*

Anderson, Glenn Chris
Canadian. Hockey Player
Right wing, Edmonton Oilers, 1980--; won
two Stanley Cups.
b. Oct 2, 1960 in Vancouver, British
Columbia
Source: *HocReg 85*

Anderson, Harriet
see: Andersson, Harriet

Anderson, Harry
American. Actor
Plays Judge Harry Stone on TV series
"Night Court."
b. Oct 14, 1952
Source: *NF*

Anderson, Ian
[Jethro Tull]
English. Musician, Singer
Flute-playing lead vocalist since 1968, known
for outlandish stage costumes, antics.
b. Aug 10, 1947 in Blackpool, England
Source: *BiDAmM; BioIn 11; BkPepl; WhoAm
80, 82*

Anderson, Ivie
American. Singer
Jazz vocalist with Duke Ellington Band,
1931-42; hits include "I Got It Bad."
b. 1904 in Gilroy, California
d. Dec 28, 1949 in Los Angeles, California
Source: *AmPS B; IlEncJ; ObitOF 79; WhScrn
77; WhoJazz 72*

Anderson, Jack Northman
American. Journalist
Has written syndicated column, "Washington-
Merry-Go-Round," since 1969.
b. Oct 19, 1922 in Long Beach, California
Source: *AuNews 1; BioNews 74; CelR; ConAu
57; CurBio 72; WhoAm 74, 76, 78, 80, 82;
WhoS&SW 82; WhoWor 78; WrDr 80*

Anderson, Jack Zuinglius
American. Politician, Presidential Aide
Con., 1939-53; Eisenhower's administrative
asst., 1956-61.
b. 1904 in Oakland, California
d. Feb 9, 1981 in Hollister, California
Source: *NewYTBS 81; WhoAmP 73, 75, 77, 79*

Anderson, John
American. Singer, Musician
Country hits include "Swingin'," 1983.
b. Dec 13, 1954 in Apopka, Florida
Source: *RkOn 85*

Anderson, John Bayard
American. Politician
Liberal Rep. con. from IL, 1960-80;
Independent Party presidential candidate,
1980.
b. Feb 15, 1922 in Rockford, Illinois
Source: *BiDrAC; ConAu 33R; CurBio 79;
PseudN 82; WhoAm 80, 82*

Anderson, John Murray
English. Director
Created, directed first all-color movie musical
The King of Jazz, 1930.
b. Sep 20, 1886 in Saint John's,
Newfoundland
d. Jan 30, 1954 in New York, New York
Source: *AmSCAP 66; BiDAmM; CmpEPM;
EncMT; NotNAT A, B; ObitOF 79; WhAm 3;
WhThe*

Anderson, Jon
[Yes]
English. Singer, Musician
Drummer, vocalist who formed Yes, 1968;
wrote most of group's lyrics; had three
solo albums.
b. Oct 25, 1944 in Lancashire, England
Source: *NF*

Anderson, Judith, Dame
[Frances Margaret Anderson-Anderson]
Australian. Actress
First Australian-born actress invested as
Dame Commander, 1960; known for role
in film *Rebecca,* 1940.
b. Feb 10, 1898 in Adelaide, Australia
Source: *BiE&WWA; CelR; CurBio 41, 61;
FamA&A; FilmgC; InWom; IntMPA 75, 76,
77, 78, 79, 80, 81, 82; IntWW 74; MotPP;
MovMk; NotNAT; OxFilm; OxThe; PseudN
82; Who 74; WhoAm 74; WhoHol A;
WhoThe 77; WhoWor 78*

Anderson, Ken(neth Allan)
American. Football Player
b. Feb 15, 1949 in Batavia, Illinois
Source: *BioIn 10; WhoFtbl 74*

Anderson, Leroy
American. Composer, Conductor
Compositions include "The Typewriter,"
"Blue Tango," "Forgotten Dreams."
b. Jun 29, 1908 in Cambridge, Massachusetts
d. May 18, 1975 in Woodbury, Connecticut
Source: *AmSCAP 66; BiE&WWA; NotNAT;
WhAm 6; WhoAm 74; WhoE 74; WhoMus 72*

Anderson, Lindsay Gordon
English. Director, Critic
Co-founder, British documentary movement,
Free Cinema, 1956; directed *This Sporting
Life,* 1963.
b. Apr 17, 1923 in Bangalore, India
Source: *BiDFilm; ConLC 20; DcFM; FilmgC;
IntMPA 77, 78, 79, 80, 81, 82; IntWW 81,
82; MovMk; NewYTBE 73; NotNAT; OxFilm;
Who 82; ConLC 20; IntWW 82; OxFilm;
Who 82; WhoThe 77, 81; WhoWor 74;
WorEFlm*

Anderson, Loni
American. Actress
Played Jennifer on TV series "WKRP in
Cincinnati," 1978-80.
b. Aug 5, 1946 in Saint Paul, Minnesota
Source: *WhoAm 80, 82*

Anderson, Lynn
American. Singer
Country hit "Rose Garden," rose to top of
country, pop charts, 1970; won Grammy,
1970.
b. Sep 26, 1947 in Grand Forks, North
Dakota
Source: *EncFCWM 83; WhoAm 74*

Anderson, Margaret Carolyn
American. Editor
Founder, literary magazine *The Little Review,*
which published avant-garde writers, 1914-
29.
b. Nov 24, 1886 in Indianapolis, Indiana
d. Oct 18, 1973 in LeCannet, France
Source: *AmAu&B; ConAu 45; IndAu 1917;
NotAW MOD; ObitOF 79; REnAL; WebAB,
79*

Anderson, Marian
American. Singer
Contralto who was first black soloist to sing
with Metropolitan Opera,1955.
b. Feb 17, 1902 in Philadelphia, Pennsylvania
Source: *CelR; EncAB-H; HerW; InWom;*
REn; WebAB; WhoAm 74, 76, 78, 80, 82;
WhoBlA 75; WhoMus 72

Anderson, Mary
American. Labor Union Official
Director, Women's Trade Union League,
1920-44.
b. Aug 27, 1872 in Lidkoping, Sweden
d. Jan 29, 1964 in Washington, District of
Columbia
Source: *BiDAmLL; DcAmB S7; IntDcWB;*
NotAW MOD; ObitOF 79; WhAm 4; WhAmP

Anderson, Mary Antoinette
"Our Mary"
American. Actress
Appeared on stage, 1875-89; wrote *A Few
Memories,* 1896.
b. Jul 28, 1859 in Sacramento, California
d. May 29, 1940 in Broadway, England
Source: *BbD; BiD&SB; DcAmAu; DcAmB S2;*
FamA&A; Film 1, 2; MacDWB; NotAW;
OxThe; PseudN 82; WhAm 4, HSA; WhThe

Anderson, Max (Maxie Leroy)
American. Balloonist
Co-pilot of first balloon, *Double Eagle II,* to
cross Atlantic, 1978.
b. Sep 10, 1934 in Sayre, Oklahoma
d. Jun 27, 1983 in Bad Brueckenau,
Germany (West)
Source: *BioIn 11; ConAu 115; NewYTBS 83;*
WhoWest 84

Anderson, Maxwell
American. Author, Dramatist
Plays include *Winterset,* 1935; *Key Largo,*
1939; Pulitzer-winning *Both Your Houses,*
1933.
b. Dec 15, 1888 in Atlantic, Pennsylvania
d. Feb 28, 1959 in Stamford, Connecticut
Source: *AmAu&B; AmSCAP 66; CasWL;*
CnDAL; CnMD; CnThe; ConAmA; ConAmL;
ConAu 105; CroCD; CurBio 42, 53, 59;
CyWA; DcLEL; EncAB-H; EncMT; EncWL;
EvLB; FilmgC; LongCTC; McGEWD;
ModAL; ModWD; NatCAB 60; NewCBMT;
ObitOF 79; OxAmL; OxThe; PenC AM;
PIP&P; REn; REnAL; REnWD,; TwCA, SUP;
TwCWr; WebAB; WebE&AL; WhAm 3;
WorEFlm

Anderson, Melissa Sue
American. Actress
Played Mary Ingalls on TV series, "Little
House on the Prairie," 1973-81.
b. Sep 26, 1962 in Berkeley, California
Source: *BioIn 10, 11; IntMPA 82*

Anderson, Michael
English. Director
Directed *Around the World in 80 Days,* 1956.
b. Jan 30, 1920 in London, England
Source: *BiDFilm; CmMov; FilmgC; IntMPA
75, 76, 77, 78, 79, 80, 81, 82; MovMk;
WhoAm 82; WorEFlm*

Anderson, Michael, Jr.
English. Actor
Starred in TV series "The Monroes," 1966-
67.
b. Aug 6, 1943 in London, England
Source: *FilmgC; IntMPA 75, 76, 77, 78, 79,
80, 81, 82; WhoHol A*

Anderson, O(ttis) J(erome)
American. Football Player
Running back, St. Louis, 1979--; rookie of
year, player of year, 1979.
b. Jan 19, 1957 in West Palm Beach, Florida
Source: *FootReg 81*

Anderson, Peggy
American. Author
Wrote *Nurse,* 1978, adapted into TV series
starring Michael Learned.
b. 1938
Source: *ConAu 93; NewYTBS 79; WrDr 76,
80*

Anderson, Philip Warren
American. Physicist
Research on quantum theory, physics of
solids, magnetism; won Nobel Prize, 1977.
b. Dec 13, 1923 in Indianapolis, Indiana
Source: *AmM&WS 73P; IntWW 74; Who 74;
WhoAm 82; WhoE 74; WhoWor 78*

Anderson, Rich
[The Tubes]
American. Musician
Bassist with The Tubes since late 1960s.
b. Aug 1, 1947 in Saint Paul, Minnesota
Source: *NF*

Anderson, Richard Norman
American. Actor
Played Oscar Goldman on TV series "Six
Million Dollar Man," 1972-77; "Bionic
Woman," 1974-77.
b. Aug 8, 1926 in Long Beach, New Jersey
Source: *BiE&WWA; FilmgC; IntMPA 82;
NotNAT; MovMk; NotNAT; WhoAm 82*

Anderson, Robert
American. Military Leader
General who surrendered Ft. Sumter to
Confederates, Apr 13, 1861.
b. Jun 14, 1805 in Louisville, Kentucky
d. Oct 27, 1871 in Nice, France
Source: *Alli SUP; AmBi; ApCAB; DcAmB;
DcNAA; Drake; LinLib L, S; TwCBDA;
WebAMB; WhAm HS*

Anderson, Robert Orville
American. Corporation Executive
Pres., Honda Oil & Gas, 1941-63; chief
exec., Atlantic Richfield.
b. Apr 13, 1917 in Chicago, Illinois
Source: *CurBio 82; IntWW 74; St&PR 75;
WhoAm 74, 76, 78, 80, 82; WhoAmP 73;
WhoF&I 74; WhoGov 75*

Anderson, Robert Woodruff
American. Dramatist, Screenwriter
Award-winning plays include *Tea and
Sympathy,* 1945.
b. Apr 28, 1917 in New York, New York
Source: *AmAu&B; AuNews 1; BiE&WWA;
CelR; CnMD; ConAu 21R; Who 74; WhoAm
82, 84; WhoThe 77; WhoWor 74; WorAu;
WrDr 76*

Anderson, Roy A(rnold)
American. Corporation Executive
Chairman, chief exec., Lockheed Corp.,
1977--.
b. Dec 15, 1920 in Ripon, California
Source: *CurBio 83; Dun&B 79; IntWW 80,
81, 82, 83; St&PR 84; Who 82; WhoAm 80,
82, 84; WhoF&I 81, 81; WhoWest 80, 82, 84;
WhoWor 82*

Anderson, Sherwood
American. Author, Poet
Major work *Winesburg, Ohio,* 1919, short
stories of small town life.
b. Sep 13, 1876 in Camden, Connecticut
d. Mar 8, 1941 in Colon, Panama
Source: *AmAu&B; AmWr; AtlBL; CasWL;
Chambr 3; CnDAL; CnMWL; ConAmA;
ConAmL; CyWA; DcAmB S3; DcLEL;
DcNAA; EncWL; EvLB; LongCTC; ModAL,
S1; OhA&B; OxAmL; OxEng; PenC AM;
RAdv 1; REn; REnAL; TwCA, SUP; TwCWr;
WebAB; WebE&AL; WhAm 1; WhNAA;
WhoTwCL*

Anderson, "Sparky" (George Lee)
American. Baseball Manager
First manager to win World Series in both
leagues; with Cincinnati, 1975, 1976; with
Detroit, 1984.
b. Feb 22, 1934 in Bridgewater, South
Dakota
Source: *BaseEn 85; CurBio 77; PseudN 82;
WhoAm 74, 76, 78, 80, 82; WhoProB 73*

Anderson, Vernon Ellsworth
American. Author, Educator
Wrote on education: *Instructors Manual:
Principles and Practices of Secondary
Education,* 1951.
b. Jun 15, 1908 in Atwater, Minnesota
Source: *ConAu 1R, 5NR; WhoAm 74; WrDr
76*

Anderson, Warner
American. Actor
Noted character performer who appeared in
The Caine Mutiny, 1954; TV series "The
Lineup," 1954-60.
b. Mar 10, 1911 in Brooklyn, New York
d. Aug 26, 1976 in Santa Monica, California
Source: *FilmgC; IntMPA 75, 76, 77; MotPP;
MovMk; WhoHol A; WhoThe 81*

Anderson, Wendell Richard
American. Politician
Governor of MN, 1971-76; senator, 1976-79.
b. Feb 1, 1933 in Saint Paul, Minnesota
Source: *AlmAP 78; BioNews 74; IntWW 74,
81, 82; NewYTBS 76; WhoAm 74; WhoAmP
73; WhoGov 72; WhoMW 74*

Anderson, William
"Bloody Bill"
American. Outlaw, Murderer
d. Oct 1864 in Ray County, Missouri
Source: *Blood&B*

Anderson, William Robert
American. Corporation Executive, Naval
Officer
Commanded first atomic submarine, the
Nautilus, 1957-59.
b. Jun 17, 1921 in Bakerville, Tennessee
Source: *BiDrAC; ConAu 5R, 5R; WhoAm 76,
78, 80, 82; WhoAmP 73; WhoGov 75;
WhoS&SW 82*

Anderssen, Adolf (Karl Ernst Adolf)
Polish. Chess Player
Regarded as world's leading player; won
international tournaments, 1851, 1862,
1870.
b. Aug 6, 1818 in Breslau, Poland
d. Mar 9, 1878 in Breslau, Poland
Source: *GolEC; OxChess*

Andersson, Benny
[ABBA]
Swedish. Singer, Musician
b. Dec 16, 1946 in Stockholm, Sweden
Source: *NF*

Andersson, Bibi
[Birgitta Andersson]
Swedish. Actress
Discovered by Ingmar Bergman, in many of
   his films: *The Seventh Seal,* 1956; *Brink of
   Life,* 1958.
b. Nov 11, 1935 in Stockholm, Sweden
Source: *BiDFilm; CelR; CurBio 78; EncWT;
FilmgC; IntMPA 81, 82; IntWW 80, 81, 82;
MotPP; MovMk; NewYTBS 77; OxFilm;
WhoHol A; WhoWor 74; WorEFlm*

Andersson, Harriet
Swedish. Actress
Starred in Ingmar Bergman's *Monika,* 1952,
   written especially for her.
b. Jan 14, 1932 in Stockholm, Sweden
Source: *BiDFilm; FilmEn; FilmgC; IntWW
80, 81, 82; MacDWB; OxFilm; WhoHol A;
WhoWor 74; WorEFlm*

Andes, "Keith" (John Charles)
American. Actor
Co-star of TV series "Glynis," 1963-65.
b. Jul 12, 1920 in Ocean City, New Jersey
Source: *BiE&WWA; FilmEn; FilmgC; IntMPA
77, 75, 76, 78, 79, 80, 81, 82; MotPP;
NotNAT; PseudN 82; WhoHol A*

Andrae, Johann Valentin
German. Clergyman
Lutheran pastor, known as originator of
   Rosicrucian legend.
b. Aug 7, 1586 in Herrenburg, Germany
d. Jan 27, 1654 in Stuttgart, Germany
Source: *BiDAmC*

Andrassy, Gyula, Count
[Count Julius Andrassy]
Hungarian. Statesman
Prime minister, 1871, of dual monarchy
   between Germany, Hungary.
b. Mar 3, 1823 in Kassa, Hungary
d. Feb 18, 1890 in Volosca, Hungary
Source: *McGEWB; WebBD 80*

Andre, Carl
American. Sculptor
Influential minimalist whose work is simple,
   serenely ordered, quiet.
b. Sep 16, 1935 in Quincy, Massachusetts
Source: *BnEnAmA; ConArt 77; CurBio 86;
DcAmArt; DcCAA 77; WhoAm 84; WhoAmA
84*

Andre, John
English. Spy
Benedict Arnold's liaison with the British
   who was caught, executed as spy.
b. 1751 in London, England
d. Oct 2, 1780 in Tappan, New York
Source: *Alli; AmBi; ApCAB; DcBiPP; Drake;
LinLib S; NatCAB 1; OxAmH; OxAmL;
REn; TwCBDA; WhAm HS*

Andrea da Pontedera
see: Pisano, Andrea

Andreas-Salome, Lou
[Louise Andreas]
German. Philosopher
b. 1861
d. 1937
Source: *InWom; OxGer; WhoLA*

Andree, Salomon August
Swedish. Explorer
First to explore Arctic in air by balloon,
   1896, 1897; remains, diaries found, 1930.
b. Oct 18, 1854 in Grenna, Sweden
d. 1897
Source: *BioIn 1, 3, 8, 11; McGEWB; NewCol
75; WebBD 80*

Andreotti, Giulio
Italian. Political Leader
Dem. prime minister, 1972-73, who succeeded
   Aldo Moro, 1976-80.
b. Jan 14, 1919 in Rome, Italy
Source: *CurBio 77; IntWW 74, 80, 81;
NewYTBE 71, 72; NewYTBS 76, 77;
WhoWor 74*

Andresen, Ivar
Norwegian. Opera Singer
b. Jul 17, 1896 in Oslo, Norway
d. Nov 26, 1940 in Stockholm, Sweden
Source: *NewEOp 71*

Andress, Ursula
Swiss. Actress
First wife of John Derek; movies include *Dr.
   No,* 1962.
b. Mar 19, 1936 in Bern, Switzerland
Source: *BiDFilm; CelR; ConTFT 3; FilmgC;
IntMPA 82; MotPP; MovMk; OxFilm;
WhoHol A; WorEFlm*

Andretti, Mario Gabriel
American. Auto Racer
Won Indianapolis 500, 1969.
b. Feb 28, 1940 in Montona Trieste, Italy
Source: *CelR; CurBio 68; WebAB; WhoAm
74, 76, 78, 80, 82*

Andrew
[Andrew Albert Christian Edward; Earl of
Inverness; Baron Killyleagh; Duke of
York]
"Randy Andy"
English. Prince
Second son of Queen Elizabeth II; fought in
Faulkland Islands War, 1982.
b. Feb 19, 1960 in London, England
Source: *BioIn 5, 6, 10; PseudN 82; Who 77,
80, 82*

Andrew, John Albion
American. Statesman, Governor
Organized 54th MA Regiment, 1863, first
black unit during Civil War.
b. May 31, 1818 in Windham, Maine
d. Oct 30, 1867 in Boston, Massachusetts
Source: *BiDrGov; CivWDc; CyAG; HarEnUS;
WebAB, 79*

Andrew, Prince of Russia
[Andrew Romanov]
Russian. Prince
Was oldest surviving relative of Czar
Nicholas II.
b. 1897 in Saint Petersburg, Russia
d. May 8, 1981 in Teynham, England
Source: *NewYTBS 81*

Andrew, Saint
Biblical Character
One of Twelve Disciples; patron saint of
Russia; feast day Nov 30.
d. 70 ?AD in Patrae, Greece
Source: *DcCathB; McGDA; REn*

Andrews, Anthony
English. Actor
Starred in TV movies "Brideshead Revisited";
"Ivanhoe."
b. Jan 12, 1948 in London, England
Source: *NewYTBS 82*

Andrews, Bert
American. Journalist
Won Pulitzer, 1947, for Washington
reporting; wrote *Washington Witch Hunt,*
1948.
b. Jun 2, 1901 in Colorado Springs, Colorado
d. in Denver, Colorado
Source: *CurBio 48, 53; DcAmB S5; WhAm 3,
4, 5*

Andrews, Charles McLean
American. Historian
Yale U. professor, 1910-31; won Pulitzer for
writings on American history, 1935.
b. Feb 22, 1863 in Wethersfield, Connecticut
d. Sep 9, 1943 in New Haven, Connecticut
Source: *BioIn 2, 4, 8; DcAmB S3; McGEWB;
WebAB; WhAm 2*

Andrews, Dana
[Carver Dana Andrews]
American. Actor
Brother of Steve Forrest; starred in *The Ox-
Bow Incident,* 1943.
b. Jan 1, 1909 in Collins, Mississippi
Source: *BiDFilm; BiE&WWA; CmMov;
FilmgC; IntMPA 80, 81, 82; MotPP; MovMk;
OxFilm; PseudN 82; WhoHol A; WorEFlm*

Andrews, Eamonn
Irish. TV Personality
Founder, chairman Irish Television Authority;
wrote, hosted *This is Your Life,* 1952.
b. Dec 19, 1922 in Dublin, Ireland
Source: *IntMPA 77, 79, 80, 81, 82, 83, 84,
85; IntWW 80, 81; Who 74; WhoWor 74;
WrDr 80*

Andrews, Edward
American. Actor
Character actor on Broadway, in films:
Elmer Gantry, 1960.
b. Oct 9, 1915 in Griffin, Georgia
d. Mar 8, 1985 in Santa Monica, California
Source: *FilmEn; FilmgC; IntMPA 77, 75, 76,
78, 79, 80, 81, 82; MotPP; NotNAT; WhoHol
A*

Andrews, Frank M(axwell)
American. Military Leader, Aviator
General who commanded US forces in
Europe succeeding Eisenhower, 1943.
b. Feb 3, 1884 in Nashville, Tennessee
d. May 3, 1943 in Iceland
Source: *CurBio 42, 43; DcAmB S3*

Andrews, Harry
English. Actor
Character actor; has appeared in
Shakespearean roles since 1933.
b. Nov 10, 1911 in Tonbridge, England
Source: *BlueB 76; CnThe; FilmgC; IntMPA
76, 77, 78, 79, 80, 81, 82; IntWW 82;
MotPP; MovMk; Who 82; WhoHol A;
WhoThe 77, 81*

Andrews, James Frederick
American. Editor, Author
Credited with discovering, launching comic
    strips "Doonesbury," "Ziggy."
b. Oct 8, 1936 in Westfield, Massachusetts
d. Oct 19, 1980
Source: *ConAu 107; WhAm 7*

Andrews, Jane
American. Educator, Children's Author
Wrote *Ten Boys Who Lived on the Road
    from Long Ago to Now,* 1886.
b. Dec 1, 1833 in Newburyport,
    Massachusetts
d. Jul 15, 1887 in Newburyport,
    Massachusetts
Source: *NotAW; OxAmL 83*

Andrews, Julie
[Mrs. Blake Edwards; Julia Elizabeth Wells]
English. Singer, Actress
Won Oscar, 1964, for *Mary Poppins;* Oscar
    nominee, 1965, for *The Sound of Music.*
b. Oct 1, 1935 in Walton-on-Thames,
    England
Source: *BiDFilm; BiE&WWA; BkPepl; CelR;
    CmMov; ConAu 37R; EncMT; FamA&A;
    FilmgC; InWom; IntMPA 75, 76, 77, 78, 79,
    80, 81, 82; IntWW 74; MotPP; MovMk;
    NotNAT; OxFilm; PIP&P; PseudN 82;
    SmATA 7; Who 82; WhoAm 78, 80, 82;
    WhoHol A; WhoThe 77A; WorEFlm; WrDr
    76*

Andrews, LaVerne
[Andrews Sisters]
American. Singer
b. Jul 6, 1915 in Minneapolis, Minnesota
d. May 8, 1967 in Brentwood, California
Source: *FilmgC; InWom; MotPP; WhScrn 74,
    77; WhoHol B*

Andrews, Mark N
American. Politician
Popular Rep. congressman since 1963; ND
    senator, 1980--.
b. May 19, 1926 in Fargo, North Dakota
Source: *AlmAP 78, 80; BiDrAC; CngDr 74,
    78; WhoAm 76, 78, 80, 84; WhoAmP 73, 75,
    77, 79; WhoGov 77, 72, 75; WhoMW 78*

Andrews, Mary Raymond Shipman
American. Author
Best known works include *Bob and the
    Guides,* 1906; *Florence Nightingale,* 1929.
b. 1860 in Mobile, Alabama
d. Aug 2, 1936
Source: *AmAu&B; ConAmL; JBA 34; NotAW;
    REnAL; TwCA; WhAm 1; WhNAA*

Andrews, Maxine
[Andrews Sisters]
American. Singer
b. Jan 3, 1918 in Minneapolis, Minnesota
Source: *FilmgC; InWom*

Andrews, Michael Alford
English. Author, Producer
Wrote *The Flight of the Condor,* 1982.
b. Jun 14, 1939 in Bexhill-on-Sea, England
Source: *ConAu 116*

Andrews, Patti (Patricia)
[Andrews Sisters]
American. Singer
b. Feb 16, 1920 in Minneapolis, Minnesota
Source: *InWom; WhoHol A*

Andrews, Roy Chapman
American. Zoologist, Explorer
Discovered fossil fields yielding unknown
    plant and animal life.
b. Jan 26, 1884 in Beloit, Wisconsin
d. Mar 11, 1960 in Carmel, California
Source: *AmAu&B; ApCAB X; AsBiEn;
    AuBYP; CurBio 41, 53, 60; DcAmB S6;
    EvLB; LinLib L, S; McGEWB; NatCab 1;
    NewCol 75; REnAL; SmATA 19; TwCA,
    SUP; WebAB; WhAm 3A; WhLit; WhNAA*

Andrews, Tige
[Tiger Androwaous]
American. Actor
Played Capt. Adam Greer in TV series "The
    Mod Squad," 1968-73.
b. Mar 19, 1920 in Brooklyn, New York
Source: *ConTFT 3; FilmgC; PseudN 82;
    WhoAm 82; WhoHol A*

Andrews, V(irginia) C
American. Author
Wrote *Flowers in the Attic,* 1979, *Petals in
    the Wind,* 1980.
b. Jun 6, 1924 in Portsmouth, Virginia
Source: *ConAu 97*

Andrews, Wayne
[Montagu O'Reilly, pseud.]
American. Author, Educator, Art Historian
Wrote historical biographies, architectural
    surveys: *Architecture of Michigan,* 1967.
b. Sep 5, 1913 in Kenilworth, Illinois
Source: *AmAu&B; ConAu 3NR, 9R; DrAS
    74H, 78H; IntAu&W 76; PseudN 82; WhoAm
    76, 78, 80, 82, 84*

Andrews Sisters
[LaVerne Andrews; Maxine Andrews; Patti
  Andrews]
American. Music Group
Known for 40s hits: "Boogie-Woogie Bugle
  Boy from Company B," "Don't Sit Under
  the Apple Tree with Anyone Else but
  Me."
Source: *AmPS A, B; CmpEPM; FilmEn;
FilmgC; HolP 40; MotPP; MovMk; PIP&P A;
WorAl*

Andreyev, Leonid Nikolayevich
[James Lynch, pseud.]
"The Edgar Allan Poe of Russian Literature"
Russian. Author, Dramatist
Created macabre, pessimistic short stories:
  The Red Laugh, 1904.
b. Jun 18, 1871 in Orel, Russia
d. Sep 12, 1919 in Helsinki, Finland
Source: *CasWL; ClDMEL; CnMD; CnThe;
ConAu 104; CyWA; DcRusL; Dis&D; EncWL;
EncWT; EvEuW; LinLib S; LongCTC;
McGEWD; ModSL 1; NewCol 75; NotNAT B;
PenC EUR; PIP&P; REn; REnWD; TwCA,
SUP; TwCLC 2; TwCWr; WhDW; WhoHr&F*

Andric, Ivo
Yugoslav. Author
Wrote epic trilogy of Slavic Balkavis *Bridge
  on the Driva,* 1959; won Nobel Prize for
  Literature, 1961.
b. Oct 10, 1892 in Travnik, Yugoslavia
d. Mar 13, 1975 in Belgrade, Yugoslavia
Source: *Au&Wr 71; CasWL; ClDMEL;
ConAu 57, 81; ConLC 8; CurBio 62, 75;
EncWL, 2; EvEuW; LinLib L; ModSL 2;
NewYTBS 75; Novels; PenC EUR; REn;
TwCWr; WhAm 6; Who 74; WhoTwCL;
WhoWor 74; WorAu*

Androcles
Roman. Slave
Noted for friendship with lion; subject of
  Shaw's play *Androcles and the Lion,* 1912.
fl. 1st century
Source: *NewC; REn*

Andropov, Yuri Vladimirovich
Russian. Political Leader
General Secretary, Communist Party, after
  death of Brezhnev, 1982-84.
b. Jun 15, 1914 in Nagutskaia, Russia
d. Feb 9, 1984 in Kuntsevo, U.S.S.R.
Source: *AnObit 1984; CurBio 83, 84; IntWW
75, 76, 77, 78, 79, 80, 81, 82; NewYTBS 82;
WhoSocC 78; WhoWor 74, 80*

Andrus, Cecil D(ale)
American. Business Executive, Government
  Official
Secretary of Interior, Carter administration,
  1977-81.
b. Aug 25, 1931 in Hood River, Oregon
Source: *CngDr 77, 79; CurBio 77; IntWW
77, 78, 79, 79, 80, 81; WhoAm 80, 82;
WhoAmP 79; WhoE 79; WhoGov 77;
WhoWest 78; WhoWor 78*

Andrus, Ethel Percy
American. Educator
Founded National Retired Teachers Assn.,
  1947, American Assn., of Retired Persons,
  1958.
b. Sep 21, 1884 in San Francisco, California
d. Jul 13, 1967 in Long Beach, California
Source: *NotAW MOD; WhoAmW 61*

Andrzejewski, Jerzy
[George Andrzeyevski, pseud.]
Polish. Author
Best known for novel *Ashes and Diamonds,*
  1948.
b. Aug 19, 1909 in Warsaw, Poland
d. Apr 19, 1983 in Warsaw, Poland
Source: *CasWL; ConAu 25R; EncWL,;
IntAu&W 77; IntWW 74, 80; ModSL 2;
Novels; PenC EUR; PseudN 82; TwCWr;
WhoSocC 78; WhoTwCL; WhoWor 74, 80*

Andujar, Joaquim
Dominican. Baseball Player
Pitcher, 1976--; won 20 games, 1984, 1985.
b. Dec 21, 1952 in San Pedro de Macoris,
  Dominican Republic
Source: *BaseEn 85; BaseReg 86*

Anello, John David
American. Conductor
Founded Florentine Opera Co., 1933,
  Milwaukee Symphony Orchestra, 1948;
  director, UN People to People Concerts,
  1962--.
b. 1909 in Milwaukee, Wisconsin
Source: *WhoAm 78, 80, 82*

Angel, Heather
American. Actress
Appeared in TV show "Peyton Place," 1964-
  69; film *Berkley Square,* 1933.
b. Feb 9, 1909 in Oxford, England
Source: *BioIn 10; FilmgC; InWom; IntMPA
77, 75, 76, 78, 79, 80, 81, 82; MovMk;
ThFT; WhoHol A; WhoThe 77A; WrDr 82*

Angela Merici, Saint
[Angela of Brescia]
Italian. Religious Figure
Founded company of St. Ursula, 1534, first
teaching order of women devoted to
educating women.
b. 1474 in Desenzano, Italy
d. 1540
Source: *BioIn 1; InWom; LuthC 75;
MacDWB; WebBD 80; WorAl*

Angeles, Victoria de los
Spanish. Opera Singer
Soprano, who performed famous title roles in
Madame Butterfly, Carmen, 1950s.
b. Nov 1, 1923 in Barcelona, Spain
Source: *CurBio 55; InWom; IntWW 74; Who
74; WhoAmW 77; WhoMus 72*

Angeli, Pier
[Anna Maria Pierangeli]
Italian. Actress
Twin sister of Marisa Pavan; most roles were
fragile, innocent heroines.
b. Jun 19, 1933 in Sardinia, Italy
d. Sep 10, 1971 in Beverly Hills, California
Source: *FilmEn; FilmgC; InWom; MGM;
MotPP; MovMk; NewYTBE 71; WhAm 5;
WhScrn 74, 77; WhoAmW 64, 66, 68;
WhoHol B*

Angelico, Fra
[Guido di Pietro; Giovanni da Fiesole]
Italian. Artist
Painter who used strong, pure colors, simple
subjects, reflecting new ideas of time.
b. 1387 in Vicchio, Italy
d. Mar 18, 1455 in Rome, Italy
Source: *AtlBL; PseudN 82; REn*

Angell, James Burrill
American. University Administrator,
Diplomat
Pres., U of MI, 1871-1909; US Ambassador
to China, 1880, Turkey, 1897.
b. Jan 7, 1829 in Scituate, Rhode Island
d. Apr 1, 1916 in Ann Arbor, Michigan
Source: *Alli SUP; AmAu&B; AmBi; ApCAB;
BbD; BiD&SB; CyAL 1, 2; DcAmAu;
DcAmB; DcNAA; EncAB-H; TwCBDA;
WebAB; WhAm 1; WhAmP*

Angell, James Rowland
American. University Administrator
Pres., Yale U, 1921-37.
b. May 8, 1869 in Burlington, Virginia
d. Mar 4, 1949 in Hamden, Connecticut
Source: *AmAu&B; CurBio 40, 49; DcAmB S4;
DcNAA; WhAm 2; WhNAA*

Angell, (Ralph) Norman, Sir
English. Author, Lecturer
Best known work *The Great Illusion,* 1910,
describes futility of war; won Nobel Peace
Prize, 1933.
b. Dec 26, 1874 in Holbeach, England
d. Oct 7, 1967 in Surrey, England
Source: *ConAu P-1; CurBio 48, 67; DcLEL;
EvLB; LinLib L, S; LongCTC; NewC; ObitOF
79; ObitT 1961; OxEng; TwCA, SUP; WhAm
4, 5; WhLit; WhoLA*

Angell, Roger
American. Author, Editor
Fiction editor, contributor, *New York
Magazine,* 1956--; wrote *The Summer
Game,* 1972.
b. Sep 19, 1920 in New York, New York
Source: *ConAu 57; DrAF 76; WhoAm 74, 76,
78, 80, 82*

Angelo, Giorgio di Sant
see: DiSant'Angelo, Giorgio

Angelou, Maya Marguerita
American. Actress, Author, Journalist
Wrote autobiographical best-sellers *I Know
Why the Caged Bird Sings,* 1970; *All God's
Children Need Traveling Shoes,* 1986.
b. Apr 4, 1928 in Saint Louis, Missouri
Source: *AmWomWr; BlkAWP; ConAu 65;
ConLC 12; CurBio 74; DrAP 75; DrBlPA;
Ebony 1; HerW; LivgBAA; NewYTBE 72;
NotNAT A; SelBAAu; WhoAm 74, 76, 78, 80,
82, 84; WhoAmW 79; WhoBlA 77;
WomWMM; WrDr 76, 80*

Anger, Kenneth
American. Director
Wrote *Hollywood Babylon,* 1959; underground
filmmaker: *Fireworks,* 1949, *Story of O,
Lucifer Rising,* 1971.
b. 1932 in Santa Monica, California
Source: *DcFM; FilmgC; MugS; OxFilm;
WhoAm 82; WorEFlm*

Angle, Edward Hartley
American. Dentist
Founded modern orthodontia, c. 1886.
b. Jun 1, 1855 in Herrick, Pennsylvania
d. Aug 11, 1930
Source: *DcNAA; InSci; NatCAB 22; WhAm 1;
WorAl*

Anglim, Philip
American. Actor
Played John Merrick in *The Elephant Man*
on Broadway, 1979; Dane O'Neill in "The
Thorn Birds," 1983.
b. Feb 11, 1953 in San Francisco, California
Source: *NewYTBS 79, 80; VarWW 85;*
WhoThe 81

Anglin, Margaret Mary
Canadian. Actress
Stage star from 1894: *Cyrano de Bergerac;*
Importanace of Being Earnest.
b. Apr 3, 1876 in Ottawa, Ontario
d. Jan 7, 1958 in Toronto, Ontario
Source: *BiCAW; DcAmB S6; FamA&A;*
InWom; LinLib S; MacDCB 78; NotNAT B;
ObitOF 79; OxAmH; OxThe; PlP&P; WhAm
5; WhThe; WhoStg 1906, 1908

Anglund, Joan Walsh
American. Children's Author, Illustrator
Popular illustrator of mouthless children;
wrote *A Friend is Someone Who Likes*
You, 1958.
b. Jan 3, 1926 in Hinsdale, Illinois
Source: *AmAu&B; Au&Wr 71; AuBYP;*
ConAu 5R; FamAIYP; SmATA 2; ThrBJA;
WhoArt 74

Angoff, Charles
American. Author, Editor
Editor, *American Mercury,* 1934-50; wrote
literary histories, novels of Jewish-
American life.
b. Apr 22, 1902 in Minsk, Russia
d. May 3, 1979 in New York, New York
Source: *AmAu&B; Au&Wr 71; ConAu 5R,*
85; CurBio 55, 79; DrAP 75; DrAS 78E;
IntAu&W 77; IntWWP 77; NewYTBS 79;
REnAL; ScF&FL 1, 2; WhE&EA; WhNAA;
WhoAm 76, 78; WhoWor 74; WhoWorJ 72;
WrDr 80

Angott, Sammy (Samuel Engotti)
American. Boxer
b. Jan 17, 1915 in Washington, Pennsylvania
Source: *WhoBox 74*

Angstrom, Anders Jonas
Swedish. Astronomer, Physicist
Noted for study of light, especially spectrum
analysis.
b. Aug 13, 1814 in Logdo, Sweden
d. Jun 21, 1874 in Uppsala, Sweden
Source: *AsBiEn; BioIn 3, 7; DcScB; LinLib*
S; NewCol 75; WebBD 80

Anhalt, Edward
[Andrew Holt, pseud.]
American. Screenwriter
Original film writer, story adapter; won
Oscar, 1964, for *Becket.*
b. Mar 28, 1914 in New York, New York
Source: *BioIn 7, 9; ConAu 85; FilmEn;*
FilmgC; IntMPA 81; PseudN 82

Anievas, Augustin
American. Musician
b. Nov 6, 1934 in New York, New York
Source: *WhoAm 74*

Animals, The
[Eric Burdon; Bryan Chandler; Barry Jenkins;
Alan Price; Dave Rowberry; John Steel;
Hilton Valentine]
English. Music Group
Part of "British Invasion" of early 60s; hit
singles: "House of the Rising Sun," "Don't
Let Me Be Misunderstood."
Source: *EncPR&S 74; IlEncRk; RkOn 74;*
RolSEnR 83

Animuccia, Giovanni
Italian. Composer
b. 1500
d. 1571
Source: *BioIn 4; WebBD 80*

Anka, Paul
Canadian. Singer, Songwriter
Wrote songs "Diana," 1957; "My Way,"
1967; has 15 gold records.
b. Jul 30, 1941 in Ottawa, Ontario
Source: *AmPS A, B; Baker 78; BiDAmM;*
CanWW 79, 82; CelR; CreCan 2; CurBio 64;
FilmgC; MotPP; RkOn 74, 78; WhoAm 74,
76, 78, 80, 82

Ankers, Evelyn
"Queen of the Horror Movies"; "The
Screeamer"
British. Actress
Played in Universal B films *Wolf Man, Ghost*
of Frankenstein, 1940s.
b. Aug 17, 1918 in Valparaiso, Chile
d. Aug 29, 1985 in Maui, Hawaii
Source: *FilmEn; FilmgC; HolP 40; IntMPA*
82; MotPP; MovMk; WhoHol A

Ann-Margret
[Ann-Margret Olsson; Mrs. Roger Smith]
American. Dancer, Actress
Oscar nominations for *Carnal Knowledge,*
1971; *Tommy,* 1975.
b. Apr 28, 1941 in Stockholm, Sweden
Source: *BiDFilm; BioNews 75; BkPepl; CelR;
ConTFT 3; CurBio 75; FilmEn; FilmgC;
GoodHs; InWom; IntMPA 82; MotPP;
MovMk; OxFilm; RkOn 74; WhoAm 84;
WhoHol A*

Annabella
[Suzanne Georgette Charpentier]
French. Actress
Wife of Tyrone Power, 1939-48; films include
Napoleon, 1926, *Le Million,* 1931.
b. Jul 14, 1912 in Paris, France
Source: *BioIn 7; Film 1, 2; FilmgC; InWom;
MotPP; MovMk; ThFT; WhoHol A; WhoThe
77A; WorEFlm*

Annabella
[Myant Myant Aye; Bow Wow Wow;
Annabella Lwin]
Burmese. Singer
Lead singer with Bow Wow Wow, 1980-83.
b. Oct 31, 1965 in Rangoon, Burma
Source: *NF*

Annaud, Jean-Jacques
French. Director
Movies include *Quest for Fire,* 1981.
b. Jan 10, 1943 in Draveil, France
Source: *ConTFT 3; DirCG 82; VarWW 85*

Anne
English. Queen
Reigned 1702-14; with no heirs, succession
passed to Hanoverian line-George I.
b. Feb 6, 1665 in London, England
d. Aug 1, 1714 in Kensington, England
Source: *DcBiPP; Dis&D; HarEnUS; NewC;
OxShips; WhDW*

Anne
[Anne Elizabeth Alice Louise; Mrs. Mark
Phillips]
English. Princess
Daughter of Queen Elizabeth II;
accomplished horsewoman who represented
England in Olympics.
b. Aug 15, 1950 in London, England
Source: *BioIn 2; CurBio 73; IntWW 76, 77,
78, 79, 80, 81, 82; NewCol 75; NewYTBE 70,
73; Who 82*

Anne Boleyn
see: Boleyn, Anne

Anne of Bohemia
English. Consort
First queen of Richard II, 1382-94.
b. Mar 11, 1366 in Prague, Bohemia
d. Jun 7, 1394 in Sheen, Bohemia
Source: *DcBiPP; DcNaB; InWom; NewC*

Anne of Cleves
German. Consort
Protestant princess, who was fourth wife of
Henry VIII, Jan 1540-Jul 1540.
b. 1515 in Cleves, Germany
d. 1557 in England
Source: *BioIn 1, 1, 4, 4, 7, 7, 9, 10, 11;
DcBiPP; InWom; LinLib S; NewC; NewCol
75; REn; WhDW*

Annenberg, Walter Hubert
American. Publisher, Diplomat
Owner *TV Guide, Seventeen,* several
newspapers; ambassador to UK, 1969-75.
b. Mar 13, 1908 in Milwaukee, Wisconsin
Source: *BioNews 74; CelR; CurBio 70;
IntWW 74, 75, 76, 77, 78, 79, 79, 80, 81;
IntYB 78, 79; NewYTBS 74; NewYTET;
St&PR 75; USBiR 74; Who 74; WhoAm 80,
82; WhoAmP 73, 75, 77, 79; WhoE 75, 77;
WhoGov 72; WhoWor 74, 76, 76, 78;
WhoWorJ 72*

Annigoni, Pietro
Italian. Artist
Portrait painter of the famous; Elizabeth II,
1955, 1970; John F Kennedy, 1961; Shah
of Iran, 1968.
b. Jun 7, 1910 in Milan, Italy
Source: *Au&Wr 71; DcBrAr 1; IntWW 81,
82, 83; Who 80, 81, 82; WhoArt 80, 82;
WhoWor 82*

Annis, Francesca
English. Actress
Played Lillie Langtry in TV series "Lillie"
on PBS, 1979.
b. May 14, 1944 in London, England
Source: *FilmEn; FilmgC; HalFC 80;
NewYTBS 79; Who 82*

Anouilh, Jean Marie Lucienpierre
French. Dramatist
Best known plays *Antigone,* 1944; *Becket,*
1960.
b. Jun 23, 1910 in Bordeaux, France
Source: *Au&Wr 71; BiE&WWA; CasWL;*
CnMD; CnMWL; CnThe; ConAu 17R;
ConLC 1, 3, 8, 13; CroCD; CurBio 54;
CyWA; DcFM; EncWL; EncWT; EvEuW;
FilmEn; FilmgC; IntAu&W 76, 77; IntWW
74, 75, 76, 77, 78, 79, 80, 81; LinLib L, S;
LongCTC; McGEWB; McGEWD; ModFrL;
ModRL; ModWD; NotNAT; OxEng; OxFilm;
OxFr; OxThe; PenC AM; PlP&P; RComWL;
REn; REnWD; TwCA SUP; TwCWr; Who
74; WhoThe 72, 77, 81; WhoTwCL; WhoWor
74; WorEFlm

Anquetil, Jacques
French. Cyclist
b. 1934
Source: *BioIn 6*

Anselm, Saint
Italian. Religious Leader
Archbishop of Canterbury, 1093-1109, called
    founder of scholasticism; writings
    characterized by rational argument.
b. 1033 in Aosta, Italy
d. 1109 in Canterbury, England
Source: *BiB N; CasWL; DcBiPP; DcCathB;*
DcEnL; LinLib L, S; NewC; OxEng; PenC
ENG

Ansermet, Ernest Alexandre
Swiss. Conductor
Founded l'Orchestre de la Suisse Romande,
    1918.
b. Nov 11, 1883 in Vevey, Switzerland
d. Feb 20, 1969 in Geneva, Switzerland
Source: *CurBio 49, 69; WhAm 5*

Anslinger, Harry Jacob
American. Statesman
b. May 20, 1892 in Altoona, Pennsylvania
d. Nov 14, 1975
Source: *ConAu 61, P-1; WhAm 6*

Anson, "Cap" (Adrian Constantine)
"Pop"
American. Baseball Player, Baseball Manager
Infielder, Chicago, 1876-97, who collected
    over 3,500 hits; Hall of Fame, 1939.
b. Apr 17, 1851 in Marshalltown, Iowa
d. Apr 14, 1922 in Chicago, Illinois
Source: *BaseEn 85; BioIn 2, 3; DcAmB;*
NewCol 75; WebAB, 79; WhAm 4, 4, HSA;
WhoProB 73

Anson, George, Baron
English. Admiral
b. 1697
d. 1762
Source: *Alli; DcBiPP; DcEnL; OxShips;*
WhDW

Anson, Jay
American. Author
Wrote *The Amityville Horror,* 1977, adapted
    to film, 1979.
b. 1924 in New York, New York
d. Mar 12, 1980 in Palo Alto, California
Source: *ConAu 81, 97; NewYTBS 80*

Anson, Robert Sam
American. Journalist, Author
Known for feature articles on controversy
    surrounding assassination of John F
    Kennedy.
b. 1945
Source: *BioIn 9; ConAu 115*

Anspach, Susan
[Mrs. Sherwood Ball]
American. Actress
In films *Play It Again Sam,* 1972; *Five Easy*
    Pieces, 1970.
b. Nov 23, 1939 in New York, New York
Source: *ConTFT 3; IntMPA 82; MovMk;*
VarWW 85; WhoAm 82; WhoHol A

Ant, Adam
[Stewart Goddard; Adam and the Ants]
English. Singer
Vocalist, guitarist, pianist who had top solo
    single "Goody Two Shoes," 1982.
b. Nov 3, 1954 in London, England
Source: *IlEncRk; RolSEnR 83*

Antes, Horst
German. Artist
Post-war painter; later works include strange,
    massive, "gnome" people.
b. Oct 28, 1936 in Heppenheim, Germany
Source: *ConArt 77; CurBio 86; DcCAr 81;*
IntWW 76, 77, 78, 85; OxTwCA; WhoWor
82

Antheil, George
American. Composer
Wrote concert music, opera, movie scores;
    films include *Once in a Blue Moon,* 1935.
b. Jul 8, 1900 in Trenton, New Jersey
d. Feb 12, 1959 in New York, New York
Source: *AmSCAP 66; CurBio 54, 59; DcCM;*
DcFM; REnAL; WhAm 3; WorEFlm

Anthony, Saint
[Saint Anthony the Abbot]
Egyptian. Religious Leader
b. 251 in Memphis, Egypt
d. 350 in Mount Kolzim, Egypt
Source: *BioIn 1, 3, 4, 5, 6, 7, 8, 9, 10, 11;
Dis&D; LuthC 75; NewCol 75; REn; WebBD
80*

Anthony of Padua, Saint
French. Religious Figure
Biblical scholar who had reputation as
    miracle worker; patron saint of lost
    articles.
b. 1195 in Lisbon, Portugal
d. 1231 in Padua, Italy
Source: *BioIn 1, 2, 3, 3; DcCathB; LinLib L,
S; LuthC 75; NewCol 75; REn*

Anthony, C L
see: Smith, Dodie, pseud.

Anthony, Earl
American. Bowler
Bowler of year, 1974, 1975, 1976.
b. Apr 27, 1938 in Kent, Washington
Source: *BioIn 11*

Anthony, Earl
American. Author, Civil Rights Activist
Joined Black Panthers, 1967, wrote *Picking
    Up the Gun: A Report on the Black
    Panthers,* 1970.
b. 1941 in Roanoke, Virginia
Source: *BlkAWP; InB&W 80; LivgBAA;
NewYTBS 82; WhoAm 80; WorAl*

Anthony, Edward
American. Publisher, Author
Wrote *Merry-Go-Roundelays,* 1921; *Mr.
    Daniels and the Grange,* 1968.
b. Aug 4, 1895 in New York, New York
d. Aug 16, 1971 in Gloucester, Massachusetts
Source: *AmAu&B; AuBYP; BkCL; ConAu
33R, 73; REnAL; SmATA 21; WhAm 5*

Anthony, Evelyn, pseud.
[Evelyn Bridget Ward-Thomas]
English. Author
Wrote *Rebel Princess,* 1953; *Anne Boleyn,*
    1957; *Persian Prince,* 1975.
b. Jul 3, 1928 in London, England
Source: *Au&Wr 71; ConAu 9R, 5NR; WrDr
76*

Anthony, John J(ason)
American. Radio Performer
Best known for radio show "The Good Will
    Hour," 1930s-57, where he offered advice
    on marital problems.
b. Sep 1, 1898 in New York, New York
d. Jul 16, 1970 in San Francisco, California
Source: *BioIn 3, 7, 9; CurBio 42, 70;
NewYTBE 70; ObitOF 79; WhoHol B*

Anthony, Joseph
American. Journalist, Editor
Wrote novel in verse *Casanova Jones,* 1930.
b. Apr 9, 1897 in New York, New York
Source: *AmAu&B; WhoHol A*

Anthony, Marc
see: Antony, Marc

Anthony, Michael
[Van Halen]
American. Musician
Bassist with group since 1974.
b. Jun 20, 1955 in Chicago, Illinois
Source: *NF*

Anthony, Ray
[Raymond Antonini]
American. Band Leader, Songwriter
Co-composed novelty hit, "The Bunny Hop,"
    1952.
b. Jan 20, 1922 in Bentleyville, Pennsylvania
Source: *CmpEPM; WhoHol A*

Anthony, Susan Brownell
American. Reformer, Suffragette
Early advocate of women's equality; led
    women's suffrage movement.
b. Feb 15, 1820 in Adams, Massachusetts
d. Mar 13, 1906 in Rochester, New York
Source: *AmBi; AmWom; AmWomWr; ApCAB;
BbD; DcAmB; DcNAA; Drake; EncAB-H;
HerW; InWom; LibW; LinLib L, S;
McGEWB; NatCAB 4; NewCol 75; NotAW;
OxAmL; REn; TwCBDA; WebAB; WhAm 1;
WhAmP*

Anthony, Tony
American. Actor
Hero of "Spaghetti Westerns": *A Stranger in
    Town,* 1967; *The Silent Stranger,* 1975.
b. Oct 16, 1937 in Clarksburg, West Virginia
Source: *FilmgC; IntMPA 75, 76, 77, 78, 79,
80, 81, 82; WhoBox 74; WhoHol A*

Anthony and the Imperials
see: Little Anthony and the Imperials

Antin, Mary
American. Author
Noted for writings on immigrants: *The
  Promised Land,* 1912.
b. 1881 in Polotsk, Russia
d. May 15, 1949 in Suffern, New York
Source: *AmAu&B; AmWomWr; DcAmAu;
DcAmB S4; DcNAA; LibW; LinLib L;
NatCAB 39; NotAW; OxAmL; REn; TwCA,
SUP; WebAB; WhAm 6; WhNAA*

Antiphon of Rhamnus
Greek. Orator
Argued against conventional law, saying men
  seek comfort, unlimited pleasure.
b. 480 BC
d. 411 BC
Source: *CasWL; DcBiPP; DcScB; Grk&L;
InB&W 80; LinLib L; PenC CL; REn*

Antisthenes
Greek. Philosopher
Founded Cynic school; urged return to
  simplicity of nature.
b. 444 BC
d. 371 BC
Source: *WebBD 80*

Anton, Susan
American. Actress, Singer
Nightclub performer who starred in film
  Golden Girl, 1979.
b. Oct 12, 1950 in Yucaipa, California
Source: *ConTFT 3; Who 80; WhoAm 82*

Antonelli, Giacomo
Italian. Statesman
b. 1806
d. 1876
Source: *WebBD 80*

Antonelli, John(ny August)
American. Baseball Player
Pitcher, 1948-61, who led league in ERA,
  shutouts, 1954.
b. Apr 12, 1930 in Rochester, New York
Source: *BaseEn 85; WhoProB 73*

Antonello da Messina
Italian. Artist
First Italian painter to master technique of
  painting with oils.
b. 1430 in Messina, Sicily
d. Feb 15, 1479 in Messina, Sicily
Source: *AtlBL; REn*

Antonescu, Ion
Romanian. Political Leader
Dictator, 1940-44; forced abdication of King
  Carol II, aligned Romania with Nazis.
b. Jun 15, 1882 in Pitesti, Romania
d. Jun 1, 1946
Source: *CurBio 40, 46; DcPol; HisEWW;
WhDW; WhWW-II; WorAl*

Antoninus Pius
Roman. Ruler
Emperor of Rome, 138-161; Wall of
  Antonius built in his honor to protect
  against British invasion, 142.
b. Sep 19, 86 in Lanuvium, Italy
d. Mar 7, 161
Source: *DcBiPP A; LuthC 75; NewC; WhDW*

Antonioni, Michelangelo
Italian. Director
First international hit *L'Aventura,* 1960,
  described modern man's emotional
  barrenness.
b. Sep 29, 1912 in Ferrara, Italy
Source: *BiDFilm; ConAu 73; ConLC 20;
CurBio 64; DcFM; FilmEn; IntMPA 80, 81,
82; IntWW 80, 81, 82; MovMk; OxFilm;
Who 74, 82; WorEFlm*

Antony, Marc
[Marcus Antonius; Marc Anthony]
Roman. Soldier, Political Leader
Prominent soldier, politician under Julius
  Caesar; defeated by Octavius, 31 BC;
  committed suicide with Cleopatra.
b. 83 ?BC
d. 30 BC in Egypt
Source: *LinLib S; McGEWB; NewCol 75;
REn; WebBD 80; WhDW; WorAl*

Anuszkiewicz, Richard Joseph
American. Artist
Master of dizzying, optical art.
b. May 23, 1930 in Erie, Pennsylvania
Source: *BnEnAmA; ConArt 77; CurBio 78;
DcAmArt; DcCAA 71, 77; McGDA; WhoAm
74, 76, 78, 80, 82; WhoAmA 73, 76, 78*

Anza, Juan Bautista de
Spanish. Explorer
Founded San Francisco, 1776; governor of
  NM, 1777-88.
b. 1735 in Fronteras, Mexico
d. 1788 in Arizpe, Mexico
Source: *AmBi; DcAmB; OxAmL; REnAL;
WebAB; WhAm HS*

Aoki, Hiroaki
"Rocky"
American. Restaurateur
Former Olympic wrestler who owns Benihana
    restaurants.
b. 1938
Source: *BioIn 9, 10, 11; BusPN; NewYTBS
75*

Aoki, Isao
Japanese. Golfer
First Japanese golfer to win PGA
    tournament, 1983 Hawaiian Open.
b. Aug 31, 1942 in Abiko, Japan
Source: *BioIn 12; NewYTBS 80*

Apache Kid
American. Criminal
Indian, cavalry scout, convicted of murder,
    then pardoned by Pres. Cleveland.
b. 1868
d. 1894 in Tucson, Arizona
Source: *BioIn 1, 3, 4, 5; Blood&B; DrInf*

Aparicio, Luis Ernesto
"Little Looie"
Venezuelan. Baseball Player
Shortstop, 1956-73, who collected 506 stolen
    bases; Hall of Fame, 1984.
b. Apr 29, 1934 in Maracaibo, Venezuela
Source: *BaseEn 85; BioIn 5, 6; WhoAm 74;
WhoE 74; WhoProB 73*

Apelles
Greek. Artist
Best known work "Aphrodite Anadyomene,"
    painted for temple of Aesculapius at Cos.
fl. 4th century BC
Source: *DcBiPP; NewC; OxArt*

Apgar, Virginia
American. Anesthetist
Developed Apgar Test, 1952, given to baby
    within 60 seconds of birth to determine
    condition, survival chances.
b. Jul 7, 1909 in Westfield, New Jersey
d. Aug 7, 1974 in New York, New York
Source: *AmM&WS 73P; ConAu 53, 73;
GoodHs; LibW; NewYTBS 74; WhAm 6;
WhoAm 74; WhoAmW 70, 72, 74; WhoWor
74*

Apollinaire, Guillaume
[Guillaume Kostrowitsky]
French. Author, Poet, Art Critic
Avant-garde writer; coined word
    "surrealism," promoted early Cubist
    painters.
b. Aug 26, 1880 in Rome, Italy
d. Nov 10, 1918 in Paris, France
Source: *AtlBL; CasWL; ClDMEL; CnMD;
CnMWL; EncWL; EvEuW; LongCTC;
McGEWD; ModRL; ModWD; OxEng; OxFr;
PenC EUR; RComWL; REn; REnWD;
TwCA, SUP; TwCWr; WhoTwCL*

Apollinaris Sidonius, Gaius Sollius
[Saint Sidonius]
French. Religious Figure
Letters describe life during breakup of
    Roman Empire; feast day Aug 21.
b. 430 in Lyons, France
d. 487 in Clermont, France
Source: *DcBiPP; Dis&D; LinLib L; LuthC 75;
McGEWB; ModFrL; NewCol 75; NotNAT B;
TwCLC 3; WebBD 80*

Apollonius of Perga
"Great Geometer"
Greek. Mathematician
Influenced development of analytic geometry.
b. 262 ?BC
d. 200 ?BC
Source: *DcScB; LinLib L; McGEWB; WebBD
80*

Apostoli, Fred B
American. Boxer
World middleweight champ, 1938-39.
b. Feb 2, 1914
d. Nov 29, 1973 in San Francisco, California
Source: *ObitOF 79; WhoBox 74*

Appel, James Ziegler
American. Physician
Pres., AMA, 1966, who opposed, then
    defended Medicare.
b. May 15, 1907 in Lancaster, Pennsylvania
d. Aug 31, 1981 in Lancaster, Pennsylvania
Source: *CurBio 66, 81; NewYTBS 81;
WhoAm 74, 76, 78*

Appel, Karel Christian
Dutch. Artist
Self-taught abstract expressionist, who uses
    rich, swirling colors.
b. Apr 25, 1921 in Amsterdam, Netherlands
Source: *ConArt 77; CurBio 61; IntWW 74,
75, 76, 77, 78; McGDA; Who 74; WhoAmA
73, 76, 78; WhoWor 74*

Appert, Francois Nicolas
French. Chef
Invented method of canning food in corked
   jars.
b. Nov 17, 1749
d. 1841
Source: *BioIn 3, 4, 10, 12; NewCol 75*

Appice, Carmine
[Vanilla Fudge]
American. Singer
Popular session drummer who often backs
   Rod Stewart.
b. Dec 15, 1946 in Staten Island, New York
Source: *NF*

Appleby, John Francis
American. Inventor
Invented the binding machine, 1878.
b. May 23, 1840 in Westmoreland, New
   York
d. Nov 8, 1917 in Mazomanie, Wisconsin
Source: *WebBD 80*

Appleseed, Johnny
[John Chapman]
American. Pioneer
Traveled west from PA to IN for 50 yrs.,
   preaching, distributing apple seeds.
b. Sep 26, 1774 in Springfield, Massachusetts
d. Mar 11, 1847 in Allen County, Indiana
Source: *AmAu&B; AmBi; DcAmB; LinLib S;
NatCAB 11; OxAmH; REn; REnAL; WebAB;
WhAm HS*

Appleton, Daniel
American. Publisher
Founded D Appleton & Co. Publishers, 1838.
b. Dec 10, 1785 in Haverhill, Massachusetts
d. Mar 27, 1849 in New York, New York
Source: *AmAu&B; AmBi; ApCAB; DcAmB;
Drake; TwCBDA; WhAm HS*

Appleton, Edward Victor, Sir
English. Physicist
Leading figure in ionospheric research.
b. Sep 6, 1892 in Bradford, England
d. Apr 21, 1965 in Edinburgh, Scotland
Source: *AsBiEn; CurBio 45, 65; DcScB; GrBr;
McGMS 80; ObitOF 79; ObitT 1961; WhDW;
WhAm 4; WhE&EA; WhoLab 76; WorAl*

Appleton, William Henry
American. Publisher
With father, Daniel, founded D Appleton &
   Co., 1838.
b. Jan 27, 1814 in Haverhill, Massachusetts
d. Oct 19, 1899 in New York, New York
Source: *AmAu&B; DcAmB; TwCBDA; WhAm
HS, 1*

Appling, Luke (Lucius Benjamin)
"Old Aches and Pains"
American. Baseball Player
Shortstop, 1930-50, voted greatest White Sox
   player of all time; Hall of Fame, 1964.
b. Apr 2, 1907 in High Point, North
   Carolina
Source: *BaseEn 85; WhoProB 73*

April Wine
[Myles Goodwin; Brian Greenway; Steve
   Lang; Jerry Mercer; Gary Moffet]
Canadian. Music Group
Earned 10 gold albums in Canada; had
   platinum album *World's Goin' Crazy*, 1976.
Source: *IlEncRk; RolSEnR 83; WhoRock 81*

Aptheker, Herbert
American. Author, Historian, Lecturer
Editor *Political Affairs*, 1952-63; wrote
   numerous books on American Negro.
b. Jul 31, 1915 in Brooklyn, New York
Source: *AmAu&B; ConAu 5R; DrAS 74H;
WhoAm 76, 78, 80, 82, 84; WhoWor 74;
WhoWorJ 72*

Apuleius, Lucius
Roman. Author, Orator
Major work *Metamosphoses* is only Latin
   novel to survive entirely.
b. 125 in Madavros, Namibia
d. 200
Source: *AtlBL; BbD; BiD&SB; CasWL;
CyWA; DcEnL; Grk&L; LinLib L, S; NewC;
OxEng; PenC CL; RComWL; REn; WorAl*

Aquinas, Thomas, Saint
Italian. Theologian, Philosopher
Synthesis of theology, philosophy known as
   Thomism; wrote *Summa Theologica*.
b. 1225 in Roccasecca, Italy
d. Mar 7, 1274 in Fossannova, Italy
Source: *BbD; BiD&SB; CasWL; CyWA;
DcEuL; EuAu; EvEuW; NewC; OxEng; OxFr;
PenC EUR; RComWL; REn*

Aquino, Benigno Simeon, Jr.
"Ninoy"
Philippine. Politician
Bitter rival of Ferdinand Marcos, assassinated
   upon return to Manila after three yrs.
   exile in US.
b. Nov 27, 1932 in Concepcion, Philippines
d. Aug 21, 1983 in Manila, Philippines
Source: *BioIn 10, 11, 12; ConAu 110;
FarE&A 81; IntWW 82, 83; NewYTBS 83*

Aquino, Corazon Cojuangco
Philippine. Political Leader
Widow of Benigno Aquino; opposed
  Ferdinand Marcos, 1986 elections; became
  pres. Feb, 1986.
b. Jan 25, 1933 in Tarlac, Philippines
Source: *ConNews 86-2; CurBio 86*

Ar Buthnot, May Hill
American. Author
Wrote best-selling textbook *Children and*
  Books, 1947.
b. Aug 27, 1884 in Mason City, Iowa
d. Oct 2, 1969 in Cleveland, Ohio
Source: *AuBYP; BiDAmEd; ConAu 9R;*
DcAmLiB; LinLib L; NotAW MOD; OhA&B;
SmATA 2; WhAm 5

Arafat, Yasir
Palestinian. Political Leader
Head of PLO, described as chief of state to
  a stateless people.
b. 1929 in Jerusalem, Palestine
Source: *BioIn 9, 10, 11; CurBio 71; IntWW*
79, 80, 81, 82; MidE 80, 81, 82; NewYTBE
71; NewYTBS 75; WhoArab 81; WorAl

Aragon, Louis Marie Antoine Alfred
French. Poet
One of founders of French Surrealism, 1924.
b. Oct 3, 1897 in Paris, France
d. Dec 24, 1982 in Paris, France
Source: *CasWL; ClDMEL; ConLC 3; EncWL;*
EvEuW; IntWW 74; LongCTC; ModRL;
ModWD; NewYTBS 82; OxEng; OxFr; PenC
EUR; REn; TwCA, SUP; TwCWr; ConAu 69;
ConLC 22; EncWL 2; IntAu&W 76, 77;
IntWW 80, 81, 82; LinLib L; McGEWB;
ModFrL; NewYTBS 82; WhDW; Who 82;
WhoTwCL; WhoWor 74; WorAl

Aramburu, Pedro Eugenio
Argentine. Political Leader
Pres., Argentina, 1955-58; replaced Peron's
  constitution with original democratic
  constitution.
b. May 21, 1903 in Buenos Aires, Argentina
d. Jul 16, 1970 in Timote, Argentina
Source: *CurBio 57, 70; NewYTBE 70; ObitOF*
79; WhAm 5

Aranason, H Harvard
American. Art Historian
Former administrator of NYC's Guggenheim
  Museum; wrote *History of Modern Art,*
  1968.
b. 1909
d. May 28, 1986 in New York, New York
Source: *NewYTBS 86*

Arbatov, Georgi
Russian. Editor, Public Official
Leading Soviet Americanist; director, US,
  Canadian studies since 1967.
b. May 19, 1923 in Moscow, U.S.S.R.
Source: *ConAu 116*

Arbour, Al(ger)
Canadian. Hockey Player, Hockey Coach
Coach, NY Islanders who won four straight
  Stanley Cups, 1980-83.
b. Nov 1, 1932 in Sudbury, Ontario
Source: *HocEn; WhoHcky 73*

Arbuckle, "Fatty" (Roscoe Conkling)
[William B Goodrich, pseud.]
American. Comedian, Director
Involved in famous Hollywood manslaughter
  scandal, 1921.
b. Mar 24, 1887 in Smith Center, Kansas
d. Jun 29, 1933 in Los Angeles, California
Source: *BiDFilm; Film 1; FilmgC; MotPP;*
MovMk; OxFilm; TwYS; WhAm 1; WhScrn
74, 77; WhoHol B; WorAl; WorEFlm

Arbus, Diane
American. Photographer
Best known for photographs of "freaks"--
  midgets, giants, etc.
b. Mar 14, 1923 in New York, New York
d. Jul 26, 1971 in New York, New York
Source: *BioIn 7, 9, 10; BnEnAmA; ConPhot;*
DcAmArt; NewYTBE 73; NotAW MOD;
WhAm 5; WhoAmW 70, 72; WorAl

Arbuzov, Aleksandr
Russian. Chemist
b. 1877
d. Jan 22, 1968 in Kalzan, U.S.S.R.
Source: *BioIn 8*

Arcaro, Eddie (George Edward)
American. Jockey, Journalist
First jockey to win horse racing's triple
  crown twice, 1941, 1948.
b. Feb 19, 1916 in Cincinnati, Ohio
Source: *CelR; CurBio 58; WebAB, 79;*
WhoAm 80, 82, 82; WorAl

Archer, Anne
[Mrs. Terry Jastrow]
American. Actress
Daughter of Marjorie Lord; appeared in
  movies *Paradise Alley,* 1978; *Hero at*
  Large, 1980.
b. Aug 25, 1947 in Los Angeles, California
Source: *IntMPA 81, 82; WhoHol A*

Archer, Jeffrey Howard
English. Author, Politician
MP, 1969-74, who wrote *Kane and Abel,*
1979; *First Among Equals,* 1984.
b. Apr 15, 1940
Source: *ConAu 77; ConLC 28; IntAu&W 82;
IntWW 83; NewYTBS 80; Novels; Who 82,
83; WhoWor 80; WrDr 82, 84*

Archerd, Army (Armand)
American. Journalist, Actor
Announcer, "pre-Oscar" show, 1958--;
  columnist, *Daily Variety,* since 1953.
b. Jan 13, 1919 in New York, New York
Source: *VarWW 85*

Archibald, Joe (Joseph Stopford)
American. Cartoonist, Author
Wrote *The Fifth Base,* 1973; created first
  story comic strip "Saga of Steve West,"
  1928-29.
b. Sep 2, 1898 in Newington, New
  Hampshire
Source: *ConAu 5NR, 9R; SmATA 3*

Archibald, Nate (Nathaniel)
"Tiny"
American. Basketball Player
Guard, 1970-84; led NBA in scoring, assists,
  1973.
b. Apr 18, 1948 in Bronx, New York
Source: *CelR; NewYTBE 72, 73; WhoAm 74,
76, 78, 80, 82; WhoBbl 73*

Archimedes
Greek. Mathematician
Pioneer in mechanics remembered for saying
  "Eureka!"
b. 287 ?BC in Sicily
d. 212 BC
Source: *CasWL; DcEnL; NewC; PenC CL;
REn*

Archipenko, Alexander Porfirievich
American. Artist
Cubist-abstract sculptor; used plastic
  innovations in modern pieces.
b. May 30, 1887 in Kiev, Russia
d. Feb 25, 1964 in New York, New York
Source: *CurBio 53, 64; DcCAA 71; REn;
WhAm 4*

Arden, Elizabeth
[Florence Nightingale Graham]
American. Cosmetics Executive
Pioneered advertising of beauty aids.
b. Dec 31, 1884 in Woodbridge, Ontario
d. Oct 18, 1966 in New York, New York
Source: *CurBio 57, 66; GoodHs; InWom;
LibW; MacDWB; NotAW MOD; ObitOF 79;
ObitT 1961; WebAB, 79; WhAm 4; WhoAmW
58, 64, 66, 68; WorAl*

Arden, Eve
[Eunice Quedens]
American. Actress
Starred in "Our Miss Brooks" on radio, TV,
  1948-56.
b. Apr 30, 1912 in Mill Valley, California
Source: *BiE&WWA; CmMov; ConTFT 3;
EncMT; FilmgC; IntMPA 82; MovMk;
NotNAT; ThFT; WhoAm 84; WhoThe 77*

Arden, John
English. Dramatist
Controversial, innovative playwright whose
  modernistic plays include *Mary's Name,*
  1977.
b. Oct 26, 1930 in Barnsley, England
Source: *Au&Wr 71; CasWL; CnMD; CnThe;
ConDr 82; ConLC 6, 13, 15; CroCD; IntWW
74; LongCTC; McGEWD; ModBrL Sl;
ModWD; NewC; NotNAT; OxThe; PenC
ENG; REnWD; TwCWr; WebE&AL; Who 74,
85; WhoThe 77; WhoTwCL; WorAu; WrDr
76*

Arditi, Luigi
Italian. Opera Composer, Conductor
World-renowned conductor; works include
  operas *I Briganti,* 1841; *La Spia,* 1856.
b. Jul 22, 1822 in Crescentino, Italy
d. May 1, 1903 in Hove, England
Source: *WebBD 80*

Ardizzone, Edward Jeffrey Irving
English. Author, Illustrator
Illustrated over 120 books; official war artist,
  1940-45.
b. Oct 16, 1900 in Haiphong, Indonesia
d. Nov 8, 1979 in London, England
Source: *Au&ICB; Au&Wr 71; AuBYP; ConAu
5R, 8NR, 89; IlsCB 1946, 1957; IntWW 74;
LongCTC; MorJA; PiP; SmATA 1; WhoChL;
WhoWor 74*

Ardrey, Robert
American. Scientist, Author
Studied with Thornton Wilder, 1930-35;
    novels focus on human evolution.
b. Oct 16, 1908 in Chicago, Illinois
d. Jan 14, 1980 in Kalk Bay, South Africa
Source: *AmAu&B; BiE&WWA; BlkAWP;
CnMD; ConAu 33R, 93; ConDr 73; ModWD;
NotNAT; TwCA SUP; WhoAm 74; WhoWor
74; WorEFlm; WrDr 76*

Arends, Leslie Cornelius
American. Politician
Rep. congressman, 1934-74; was House Whip
    for record 30 yrs.
b. Sep 27, 1895 in Melvin, Illinois
d. Jul 16, 1985 in Naples, Florida
Source: *BiDrAC; CurBio 48, 85; PolProf E, J,
K, NF; WhoAmP 83*

Arendt, Hannah
American. Author, Philosopher, Historian
Wrote *The Origins of Totalitarianism*, 1951;
    On Violence, 1970.
b. Oct 14, 1906 in Hannover, Germany
d. Dec 4, 1975 in New York, New York
Source: *AmAu&B; CelR; ConAu 17R, 61;
CurBio 59, 76; IntWW 81; LinLib L;
NewYTBS 75; PenC AM; PolProf E, K; REn;
WebAB, 79; WhAm 6; WhoAmW 74;
WhoWor 74; WhoWorJ 72; WorAu; WrDr 76*

Arens, Moshe
Israeli. Government Official, Politician
Ambassador to US, 1982-83; succeeded Ariel
    Sharon as defense minister, 1983-84;
    minister without portfolio, 1984--.
b. Dec 27, 1925 in Kaunas, Lithuania
Source: *ConNews 85-1; IntWW 83; MidE 82;
NewYTBS 82, 83; WhoWorJ 78*

Aretino, Pietro
Italian. Poet, Dramatist, Author
Satirist; works include sonnets, tragedy
    Orazia, 1956.
b. Apr 20, 1492 in Arezzo, Italy
d. Oct 21, 1556 in Venice, Italy
Source: *AtlBL; BiD&SB; CasWL; CnThe;
CyWA; DcEuL; DcItL; EncWT; EuAu;
EvEuW; McGEWD; NewC; NotNAT B;
OxEng; OxThe; PenC EUR; PlP&P; REn;
REnWD; WhDW*

Argelander, Friedrich Wilhelm August
German. Astronomer
Published *Bonn Survey*, 1862; invented
    modern star-naming system.
b. Mar 22, 1799 in Memel, Prussia
d. Feb 17, 1875 in Bonn, Prussia
Source: *AsBiEn; DcScB; NewCol 75; WebBD
80*

Argent
[Rod Argent; Russ Ballard; John Grimaldi;
    Robert Henrit; Jim Rodford; John Verity]
English. Music Group
Group formed, 1969-76; hits include "Hold
    Your Head Up," 1972.
Source: *ConMuA 80A; LilREn 78; RkOn 78;
RolSEnR 83; WhoRock 81*

Argent, Rod(ney Terence)
[Argent; Zombies]
English. Musician, Singer
Keyboardist, vocalist with Zombies, Argent,
    1960s-70s.
b. Jun 14, 1945 in Saint Albans, England
Source: *NF*

Argentinita
[Lopez Encarmacion]
Spanish. Dancer
Founded the Ballet de Madrid with Garcia
    Lorca, 1927.
b. Mar 25, 1905 in Buenos Aires, Argentina
d. Sep 24, 1945 in New York, New York
Source: *BioIn 1, 3; InWom; NotNAT B;
ObitOF 79*

Argerich, Martha
Argentine. Musician
b. 1941
Source: *BioIn 7, 8, 9; WhoMus 72*

Argo, Dominique Francois Jean
French. Physicist
b. Feb 26, 1786
d. Oct 2, 1853
Source: *BioIn 3; NewCol 75*

Arguello, Alexis
Nicaraguan. Boxer
Pro boxer since 1968 who has 76-5 record in
    three weight divisions.
b. Apr 12, 1952 in Managua, Nicaragua
Source: *BioIn 11; NewYTBS 82*

Arias, Jimmy
American. Tennis Player
Turned pro, 1981; won 1981 French Open
    mixed doubles with Andrea Jaeger.
b. Aug 16, 1964 in Grand Island, New York
Source: *NewYTBS 83; WhoIntT*

Arias, Roberto Emilio
Panamanian. Lawyer, Editor
Diplomat, paralyzed in assassination attempt,
    1964; husband of Dame Margo Fonteyn.
b. 1918
Source: *BioIn 5, 6, 7; IntWW 75, 76, 77, 78,
85; Who 74; WhoWor 74*

Aries, Philippe
French. Author
Described work as history of non-events;
wrote *Centuries of Childhood,* 1960.
b. Jul 21, 1914 in Blois, France
d. Feb 8, 1984 in Toulouse, France
Source: *AnObit 1984; Au&Wr 71; BioIn 10;
ConAu 112, 89; IntAu&W 82; NewYTBS 84*

Arieti, Silvano
American. Psychoanalyst, Author
Believed depression treatable with
psychotherapy, not drugs; wrote
Interpretation of Schizophrenia, 1975.
b. Jun 28, 1914 in Pisa, Italy
d. Aug 7, 1981 in New York, New York
Source: *AmM&WS 79P; ConAu 104, 21R;
NewYTBS 81; WhoAm 80*

Ariosto, Ludovico
Italian. Poet
Produced finest Italian romantic epic,
Orlando Furioso, 1532.
b. Sep 8, 1474 in Reggio, Italy
d. Jul 6, 1533 in Ferrara, Italy
Source: *AtlBL; BbD; BiD&SB; CasWL;
CyWA; DcEuL; EuAu; LinLib L, S;
McGEWB; McGEWD; NewC; OxEng; OxThe
83; PenC EUR; RComWL; REn*

Arisman, Marshall
American. Artist, Illustrator
Co-chairman, media dept., School of Visual
Arts, NYC, 1969--.
b. 1939 in Jamestown, New York
Source: *WhoGrA 82*

Aristophanes
Greek. Author, Dramatist
Master comic poet of ancient world; wrote
40 plays, 11 survived.
b. 448 BC
d. 385 BC
Source: *AtlBL; BbD; BiD&SB; CasWL;
CnThe; CyWA; DcEnL; McGEWD; NewC;
OxEng; PenC CL; RComWL; REn; REnWD*

Aristotle
Greek. Author, Philosopher
Member Plato's Academy, 367-347 BC;
created Logic, the science of reasoning.
b. 384 BC in Chalcidice, Greece
d. 322 BC
Source: *AtlBL; BbD; BiD&SB; CasWL;
CnThe; CyWA; DcEnL; DcEuL; NewC;
OxEng; OxThe; PenC CL; RComWL; REn;
REnWD*

Arius
Alexandrian. Theologian
Priest; believed Christ was created being
rather than divine being.
b. 256 in Alexandria, Egypt
d. 336 in Alexandria, Egypt
Source: *DcBiPP; LuthC 75; REn; WhDW*

Arizin, Paul
"Pitchin' Paul"
American. Basketball Player
In NBA, 1950-62; scored career total 16,266
pts.; Hall of Fame, 1977.
b. Apr 9, 1928 in Philadelphia, Pennsylvania
Source: *BioIn 2, 9; OfNBA 81; WhoBbl 73*

Arkin, Alan Wolf
[Roger Short]
American. Actor, Director
Won Tony Award, 1963, for *Enter Laughing.*
b. Mar 26, 1934 in New York, New York
Source: *AmSCAP 66; BiE&WWA; BkPepl;
CelR; CurBio 67; EncFCWM 69; FilmgC;
IntMPA 80, 81, 82; IntWW 80, 81, 82;
MotPP; MovMk; NewYTBE 70; NotNAT;
WhoAm 76, 78, 80, 82; WhoHol A; WhoThe
77, 81; WhoWor 74; WorAl*

Arkoff, Samuel Z
American. Producer, Film Executive
Has produced films since 1961: *Love at First
Bite,* 1979; *Dressed to Kill,* 1980.
b. Jun 12, 1918 in Fort Dodge, Iowa
Source: *ConTFT 3*

Arkwright, Richard, Sir
English. Inventor
Patented spinning frame, 1769, increasing
cloth production.
b. Dec 23, 1732 in Preston, England
d. Aug 3, 1792 in Nottinghamshire, England
Source: *McGEWB; NewCol 75*

Arledge, Roone Pinckney
American. TV Executive
Pres., ABC News, ABC Sports; changed
sports with slow-stop action, split-screens.
b. Jul 8, 1931 in Forest Hills, New York
Source: *WhoAm 74, 76, 78, 80, 82*

Arlen, Harold
[Hyman Arluck; Chaim Arluk]
American. Songwriter
Composed over 500 songs, including "Over
the Rainbow," from *Wizard of Oz,* which
won 1939 best song Oscar.
b. Feb 15, 1905 in Buffalo, New York
d. Apr 23, 1986 in New York, New York
Source: *AmSCAP 66; BiE&WWA; CelR;
CurBio 55, 86; EncMT; FilmgC; IntMPA 76,
77, 78, 79, 80, 81, 82; NewCBMT; NotNAT;
OxFilm; PIP&P; WebAB; WhoAm 74;
WhoThe 77; WhoWor 74*

Arlen, Michael
English. Author
Melodramatic novelist best known for *The
Green Hat,* 1924.
b. Nov 16, 1895 in Roustchouk, Bulgaria
d. Jun 25, 1956 in New York, New York
Source: *DcAmB; DcLEL; EncMys; EncSF;
EvLB; LongCTC; ModBrL; NotNAT B;
Novels; ObitOF 79; ObitT 1951; PenC ENG;
REn; ScF&FL 1; TwCA, SUP; TwCWr;
WhAm 3; WhThe; WhoHr&F*

Arlen, Richard
[Richard Cornelius van Mattimore]
American. Actor
Starred in movies *Wings,* 1927; *The
Virginian,* 1929.
b. Sep 1, 1899 in Charlottesville, Virginia
d. Mar 28, 1976 in North Hollywood,
California
Source: *BioIn 7, 10; FilmEn; FilmgC;
IntMPA 75; MovMk; ObitOF 79; TwYS*

Arletty
[Arlette-Leonie Bathiat]
French. Actress
Appeared in films *Children of Paradise,* 1945;
No Exit, 1954.
b. May 15, 1898 in Courbevoie, France
Source: *BiDFilm; BioIn 11; EncWT; FilmgC;
InWom; IntWW 80, 81, 82; MovMk; OxFilm;
WhoHol A; WhoWor 74; WorEFlm*

Arliss, George
[George Augustus Andrews]
English. Actor
Won Oscar for title role in *Disraeli,* 1929.
b. Apr 10, 1868 in London, England
d. Feb 5, 1946 in London, England
Source: *ApCAB X; CurBio 46; DcAmB S4;
EncWT; FamA&A; FilmEn; Film 2; FilmgC;
LinLib L, S; MotPP; MovMk; NewC;
NotNAT A; ObitOF 79; OxFilm; OxThe;
NotNAT B; PIP&P; TwYS; WhAm 2; WhScrn
74, 77; WhThe; WhoHol B; WhoStg 1908;
WorAl; WorEFlm*

Armani, Giorgio
Italian. Fashion Designer
Founded Giorgio Armani Co., 1975;
developed unconstructed blazer.
b. 1936 in Piacenza, Italy
Source: *CurBio 83; WhoAm 82, 84*

Armatrading, Joan
British. Singer, Songwriter
Acoustic-based album, *Joan Armatrading,*
best-seller in England, 1976.
b. Dec 9, 1950 in Saint Kitts, West Indies
Source: *BioIn 11; ConLC 17; IlEncBM 82;
IlEncRk; InB&W 80; MacDWB; NewWmR;
RolSEnR 83*

Armendariz, Pedro
Mexican. Actor
Top Mexican film star; appeared in over 75
films: *From Russia With Love,* 1963.
b. May 9, 1912 in Mexico City, Mexico
d. Jun 18, 1963 in Los Angeles, California
Source: *FilmEn; Film 2; MotPP; MovMk;
NotNAT B; WhScrn 74, 77; WorEFlm*

Armetta, Henry
Italian. Actor
Comedian who played character roles in
movies, 1923-46.
b. Jul 4, 1888 in Palermo, Sicily
d. Oct 21, 1945 in San Diego, California
Source: *BioIn 7; CurBio 45; Film 2; FilmgC;
MovMk; NotNAT B; ObitOF 79; TwYS; Vers
A; WhScrn 74, 77; WhoHol B*

Arminius, Jacobus
[Jacob Harmensen Hermanns; Hermansz]
Dutch. Theologian
Founded, Arminianism, evident today in
Methodist theologies.
b. Oct 10, 1560 in Oudewater, Netherlands
d. Oct 19, 1609 in Leiden, Netherlands
Source: *DcBiPP; EncWM; LuthC 75; NewC;
WhDW*

Armitage, Kenneth
English. Sculptor
Bronze abstracts noted for suggestions of
liberty, movement.
b. Jul 18, 1916 in Leeds, England
Source: *CurBio 57; IntWW 74; Who 74;
WhoWor 78*

Armour, Jenner
Dominican. President
Source: *NF*

Armour, Norman
American. Diplomat
Career foreign service officer, serving in a
dozen countries.
b. Oct 4, 1887 in Brighton, England
d. Sep 27, 1982 in New York, New York
Source: *CurBio 45, 82; DcAmDH; NewYTBS
82; PolProf E, T*

Armour, Philip Danforth
American. Businessman
Started Armour and Co., major meat packer;
estimated worth $50 million at death.
b. May 16, 1832 in Stockbridge, New York
d. Jan 29, 1901 in Pasadena, California
Source: *AmBi; ApCAB SUP; DcAmB; NewCol
75; TwCBDA; WebAB*

Armour, Richard Willard
American. Author, Educator
Humorist, who writes satirical series *It All
Started With--*, 1953--.
b. Jul 15, 1906 in San Pedro, California
Source: *AmAu&B; AnCL; Au&Wr 71;
AuBYP; ConAu 1R, 4NR; REnAL; SmATA
14; WhoAm 82, 84*

Armstrong, Anne Legendre
[Mrs. Tobin Armstrong]
American. Educator, Government Official
Ambassador to UK, 1976-77.
b. Dec 27, 1927 in New Orleans, Louisiana
Source: *AmM&WS 73S; BioNews 74; CelR;
ConAu 13R; NewYTBE 72, 73; WhoAm 74,
76, 78, 80, 82; WhoAmP 73; WhoS&SW 82*

Armstrong, Bess (Elizabeth Key)
American. Actress
TV roles in "On Our Own," 1977-78;
"Lace," 1984; film roles in *Four Seasons,*
1981; *High Road to China,* 1983.
b. Dec 11, 1953 in Baltimore, Maryland
Source: *BioIn 11; VarWW 85*

Armstrong, Charles B
American. Publisher, Editor
Editor, publisher, Chicago's weekly black-
oriented *Metro News,* 1972-85.
b. Jul 22, 1923 in Nashville, Tennessee
d. Mar 25, 1985 in Chicago, Illinois
Source: *ConAu 115; WhoBlA 80*

Armstrong, Charlotte
American. Author
Suspense murder-mystery writer; won Poe
award for *A Dram of Poison,* 1956.
b. May 2, 1905 in Vulcan, Michigan
d. Jul 18, 1969 in Glendale, California
Source: *AmAu&B; ConAu 1R, 3NR, 25R;
CurBio 46, 69; EncMys; WhAm 5; WorAu*

Armstrong, Edwin Howard
American. Inventor, Engineer
Constructed first FM radio station, 1937, in
Alpine, NJ.
b. Dec 18, 1891 in New York, New York
d. Feb 1, 1954 in New York, New York
Source: *AsBiEn 82; CurBio 40, 54; DcAmB
S5; DcScB; InSci; McGEWB; NewYTBS 79;
NotNAT B; ObitOF 79; OxAmH; WebAB,;
WhAm 3; WorAl*

Armstrong, Garner Ted
American. Evangelist, Author
Founded Church of God International, 1978;
wrote *The Real Jesus,* 1972.
b. 1930 in Eugene, Oregon
Source: *BkPepl; ConAu 113; WhoRel 75*

Armstrong, George Edward
"The Chief"
Canadian. Hockey Player
Center, Toronto, 1949-71; Hall of Fame,
1975.
b. Jul 6, 1930 in Skead, Ontario
Source: *HocEn; WhoHcky 73*

Armstrong, Hamilton Fish
American. Journalist, Editor
Founder, editor *Foreign Affairs,* 1922-72, who
wrote on intn'l. politics.
b. Apr 7, 1893 in New York, New York
d. Apr 24, 1973 in Manhattan, New York
Source: *AmAu&B; ConAu 41R, 93; CurBio
48, 73; TwCA, SUP; WhAm 5; WhNAA;
WhoWor 74*

Armstrong, Harry
American. Composer
b. Jul 22, 1879 in Somerville, Massachusetts
d. Feb 28, 1951 in Bronx, New York
Source: *AmSCAP 66; CurBio 51*

Armstrong, Henry
"Homicide Hank"
American. Boxer, Evangelist
Held three titles simultaneously, 1937-38;
Hall of Fame, 1954.
b. Dec 12, 1912 in Columbus, Mississippi
Source: *CmCal; InB&W 80; NegAl 83;
WhoBox 74; WorAl*

Armstrong, Jack Lawrence
American. Air Force Officer
Colonel, whose name was given to "All-
American Boy" played by Jim Ameche on
radio, 1933-38.
b. 1911 in Winnipeg, Manitoba
d. Jun 10, 1985 in Laguna Niguel, California
Source: *NF*

Armstrong, Lil(lian Hardin)
American. Jazz Musician
Ex-wife of Louis Armstrong; pianist,
  arranger, vocalist, composer, 1920s-60s.
b. Feb 3, 1902 in Memphis, Tennessee
d. Aug 27, 1971 in Chicago, Illinois
Source: *BiDAfM; CmpEPM; InB&W 80;*
NegAl 83; WhoJazz 72

Armstrong, Louis Daniel
"Satchmo"
American. Musician, Band Leader
Called world's greatest trumpeter; introduced
  "scat" singing.
b. Jul 4, 1900 in New Orleans, Louisiana
d. Jul 6, 1971 in New York, New York
Source: *AmSCAP 66; ConAu 29R; CurBio 44,*
66, 71; FilmgC; MovMk; NewCol 75;
NewYTBE 70, 71; WebAB; WhAm 5; WhScrn
74, 77; WhoHol B; WhoJazz 72

Armstrong, Neil Alden
American. Businessman, Astronaut
First man to walk on moon, Jul 20, 1969.
b. Aug 5, 1930 in Wapakoneta, Ohio
Source: *AmM&WS 82P; AsBiEn; BlueB 76;*
CelR; CurBio 79; IntWW 80, 81, 82; LinLib
S; McGEWB; PolProf NF; UFOEn; WebAB,
79; WebAMB; WhDW; Who 82; WhoAm 80,
82; WhoEng 80; WhoMW 74; WhoS&SW 73;
WhoWor 74, 80; WorAl

Armstrong, Otis
American. Football Player
b. Nov 11, 1950 in Chicago, Illinois
Source: *WhoAm 80; WhoBlA 80; WhoFtbl 74*

Armstrong, R G
American. Actor
Gruff character actor whose films include
  Ride the Wild Country, 1962; *Heaven Can*
  Wait, 1978.
b. Apr 7, 1917
Source: *FilmEn; FilmgC; VarWW 85;*
WhoHol A

Armstrong, Robert
American. Actor
Starred in *King Kong,* 1933, as hunter who
  brings ape to civilization.
b. Nov 20, 1896 in Saginaw, Michigan
d. Apr 20, 1973 in Santa Monica, California
Source: *FilmEn; FilmgC; HolP 30; MovMk;*
TwYS; Vers B; WhScrn 77; WhoHol B

Armstrong, Thomas M
American. Businessman
Cork maker who started linoleum plant,
  1908; co. now known for floors, ceilings.
b. 1836 in Pennsylvania
d. 1908
Source: *BioIn 2; Entr*

Armstrong, William Howard
American. Children's Author, Educator
Wrote 1972 Newbery winner, *Sounder.*
b. Sep 14, 1914 in Lexington, Virginia
Source: *AuBYP; AuNews 1; ChlLR 1; ConAu*
9NR, 17R; MorBMP; NewbC 1966; SmATA
4; ThrBJA; WhoAm 76, 78, 80, 82, 84;
WhoE 74; WrDr 76

Armstrong, William L
American. Politician
Millionaire Rep. senator from CO, 1978--.
b. Mar 16, 1937 in Fremont, Nebraska
Source: *AlmAP 78, 80; BioIn 9; CngDr 74,*
77, 79; WhoAm 76, 78, 80, 82, 84; WhoGov
77, 75; WhoWest 74, 76, 78

Armstrong-Jones, Antony Charles Robert
[Earl of Snowden]
English. Photographer, Socialite
Ex-husband of Britain's Princess Margaret,
  known for celebrity portraits, TV
  documentaries.
b. Mar 7, 1930 in London, England
Source: *BioIn 5, 6, 7, 8, 9, 10, 11; CurBio*
60; MacBEP; Who 82; WhoWor 74, 76, 78;
WorFshn

Arnaud, Georges d'
Dutch. Philosopher
b. 1711
d. 1765
Source: *McGEWD*

Arnaz, Desi
[Desiderio Alberto Arnaz de Acha, III]
American. Band Leader, Actor, Singer,
  Producer
Rumba band leader who formed Desilu
  Productions with Lucille Ball, 1950.
b. Mar 2, 1917 in Santiago, Cuba
Source: *ConTFT 3; CurBio 52; FilmEn;*
FilmgC; IntMPA 82; VarWW 85; WhoAm 74;
WhoHol A

Arnaz, Desi(derio Alberto, IV), Jr.
American. Actor
Son of Desi Arnaz, Lucille Ball; began career
  as rock singer; film debut, *Red Sky at*
  Morning, 1972.
b. Jan 19, 1953 in Los Angeles, California
Source: *IntMPA 76, 77, 78, 79, 80, 81, 82;*
VarWW 85; WhoHol A

Arnaz, Lucie Desiree
[Mrs. Lawrence Luckinbill]
American. Actress, Singer
Daughter of Desi Arnaz, Lucille Ball; starred
   in film *The Jazz Singer*, 1980; *They're
   Playing Our Song* on Broadway.
b. Jul 17, 1951 in Hollywood, California
Source: *BioIn 9; VarWW 85; WhoAm 82*

Arndt, Adolf
German. Judge, Statesman
b. 1904 in Konigsberg, Prussia
d. Feb 13, 1974 in Kassel, Germany (West)
Source: *BioIn 10*

Arne, Thomas Augustine
English. Composer
His patriotic song "Rule Britannia" is from
   masque *Alfred*, 1740.
b. Mar 12, 1710 in London, England
d. Mar 5, 1778 in London, England
Source: *AtlBL; Baker 78; DcBiPP; DcCathB;
DcNaB; GrBr; McGEWB; NewC; NewEOp 71;
NotNAT B; REn; WhDW*

Arness, James
[James Aurness]
American. Actor
Starred as Matt Dillon in TV series
   "Gunsmoke," 1955-75; brother of Peter
   Graves.
b. May 26, 1923 in Minneapolis, Minnesota
Source: *CelR; ConTFT 3; CurBio 73; FilmEn;
FilmgC; IntMPA 82; MotPP; MovMk;
VarWW 85; WhoAm 84; WhoHol A*

Arno, Peter
[Curtis Arnoux Peters, Jr.]
American. Cartoonist
With *New Yorker* as cartoonist, 1925-68;
   established tone of magazine.
b. Jan 8, 1904 in New York, New York
d. Feb 22, 1968 in Port Chester, New York
Source: *AmAu&B; ConAu 25R, 73; CurBio
52, 68; LongCTC; WebAB; WhAm 4*

Arnold, Benedict
American. Army Officer, Traitor
Revolutionary patriot; betrayed American
   cause by offering military information to
   British, 1779-80.
b. Jan 14, 1741 in Norwich, Connecticut
d. Jun 14, 1801 in London, England
Source: *AmBi; ApCAB; DcAmB; Drake;
EncAB-H; OxAmL; OxCan; REn; REnAL;
TwCBDA; WebAB; WhAm HS*

Arnold, Danny
[Arnold Rothman]
American. Producer
Pres., Four D Productions, 1958--; produced
   "Barney Miller," 1973-81.
b. Jan 23, 1925 in New York, New York
Source: *IntMPA 76, 77, 78, 79, 80, 81;
NewYTET; VarWW 85; WhoAm 78, 80, 82*

Arnold, Eddy
"The Tennessee Plowboy"
American. Singer, Musician
Country singer, guitarist, who made debut,
   1936; country Music Hall of Fame, 1966.
b. May 15, 1918 in Henderson, Tennessee
Source: *CelR; CurBio 70; EncFCWM 69;
IntMPA 76, 77, 78, 79, 80, 81, 82; VarWW
85; WhoAm 74, 76, 78, 80, 82*

Arnold, Edward
[Gunter Edward Arnold Schneider]
American. Actor
Starred in *Diamond Jim*, 1935; *Sutter's Gold*,
   1936.
b. Feb 18, 1890 in New York, New York
d. Apr 26, 1956 in San Fernando, California
Source: *Film 1; FilmgC; MovMk; Vers A;
WhAm 3; WhScrn 74, 77*

Arnold, Edwin
English. Author
Wrote blank verse epic *The Light of Asia*,
   1879, dealing with life of Buddha.
b. Jul 10, 1832 in Gravesend, England
d. Mar 24, 1904 in London, England
Source: *BbD; BiD&SB; BrAu 19; Chambr 3;
ChhPo S2; DcEnA, AP; DcEnL; DcEuL;
DcInB; DcLEL; EvLB; LinLib L; LongCTC;
NewC; OxEng; REn*

Arnold, Henry Harley
"Hap"
American. Military Leader
First general of Air Force, 1949; used air
   power as weapon during WW II.
b. Jun 25, 1886 in Gladwyne, Pennsylvania
d. Jan 15, 1950 in Sonoma, California
Source: *AmAu&B; CurBio 42, 50; DcAmB S4;
WebAB; WhAm 2*

Arnold, Malcolm, Sir
English. Composer
Film compositions include *Island in the Sun*,
   1957; *Trapeze*, 1984.
b. Oct 21, 1921 in Northampton, England
Source: *CmMov; DcCM; FilmgC; IntWW 74;
OxFilm; Who 74; WhoMus 72; WhoWor 78;
WorEFlm*

Arnold, Matthew
English. Author, Poet, Critic, Educator
Oxford professor, known for poem "Dover
    Beach," 1853; social criticism *Culture and
    Anarchy,* 1869.
b. Dec 24, 1822 in Laleham, England
d. Apr 15, 1888 in Liverpool, England
Source: *AtlBL; BbD; BiD&SB; BrAu 19;*
CasWL; CelCen; CnE&AP; CrtT 3; CyEd;
CyWA; DcEnA, AP; DcEnL; DcEuL; DcLEL;
Dis&D; EvLB; LinLib L, S; LongCEL; LuthC
75; McGDA; OxAmL; OxEng; OxMus;
OxThe; PenC ENG; RComWL; REn; REnAL;
WebE&AL; WhDW

Arnold, Oren
American. Children's Author, Editor
Wrote over 2,000 magazine articles, tales of
    western America: *Wit of the West,* 1980.
b. Jul 20, 1900 in Minden, Texas
Source: *ConAu 2NR, 5R; SmATA 4*

Arnold, Thomas
English. Educator
Developed modern British schools with
    introduction of math, modern language.
b. Jun 13, 1795 in Cowles, Isle of Wight
d. Jun 12, 1842 in Rugby, England
Source: *Alli; BbD; BiD&SB; BrAu 19;*
CasWL; ChhPo; DcEnA; DcEnL; DcEuL;
DcLEL; EvLB; NewC; OxEng; PenC ENG;
REn

Arnold, Thurman Wesley
American. Lawyer
b. Jun 2, 1891 in Laramie, Wyoming
d. Nov 7, 1969 in Alexandria, Virginia
Source: *AmAu&B; ConAu P-1; CurBio 40, 69;*
REnAL; TwCA SUP; WebAB; WhAm 5

Arnot, Robert Burns
American. Physician, Musician, Sportsman
b. Feb 23, 1948 in Boston, Massachusetts
Source: *BioIn 12*

Arnoux, Rene Alexandre
French. Auto Racer
One of top drivers on Grand Prix racing
    circuit, 1980s.
b. Jul 4, 1948 in Grenoble, France
Source: *WhoWor 82*

Arnow, Harriette Louisa Simpson
American. Author
Wrote novels about Appalachian life: *The
    Dollmaker,* 1954, made into TV movie
    starring Jane Fonda, 1983.
b. Jul 7, 1908 in Wayne County, Kentucky
d. Mar 22, 1986 in Washtenaw County,
    Michigan
Source: *AmAu&B; AmNov; ConAu 9R, 14NR;*
ConLC 18; ConNov 82; CurBio 54, 86;
MichAu 80; WorAu; WrDr 84

Arnstein, Bobbie
American. Secretary
Hugh Hefner's secretary for 14 yrs.;
    convicted of conspiring to deliver cocaine;
    committed suicide.
b. 1940
d. Jan 1975 in Chicago, Illinois
Source: *BioIn 10*

Aroldingen, Karin von
[Karin Awny Hannelore Reinbold von
    Aroldingen und Eltzingen]
German. Ballerina
With NYC Ballet, 1962--.
b. Jul 9, 1941 in Greiz, Germany
Source: *CurBio 83; DcBiPP; WhoAm 82, 84*

Aronson, Boris
American. Designer
Began stage design, 1924; won five Tonys
    including *Cabaret.*
b. Oct 15, 1900 in Kiev, Russia
d. Nov 16, 1980 in Nyack, New York
Source: *AnObit 1980; CelR; NewYTBS 80;*
NotNAT; OxThe; PIP&P; WhAm 7; WhoAm
80; WhoAmA 80, 82; WhoAmJ 80; WhoOp
76; WhoThe 77A, 81; WhoWorJ 72, 72, 78

Arp, Hans
[Jean Arp]
French. Author, Sculptor
Representative of Dadaist movement; wrote
    Dreams and Projects, 1952.
b. Sep 16, 1887 in Strasbourg, France
d. Jun 7, 1966 in Basel, Switzerland
Source: *AtlBL; CasWL; ConAu 25R, 81;*
CurBio 54, 66; EncWL; ModGL; OxGer;
PenC EUR; REn; WhAm 4; WhoTwCL

Arquette, Cliff
[Charley Weaver]
American. Actor
Best remembered for appearances on game
    show "Hollywood Squares."
b. Dec 28, 1905 in Toledo, Ohio
d. Sep 23, 1974 in Burbank, California
Source: *AmAu&B; AmSCAP 66; ConAu 53;*
CurBio 61, 74; NewYTBS 74; WhScrn 77;
WhoHol B

Arquette, Rosanna
[Mrs. James Newton Howard]
American. Actress
Appeared in films *The Executioner's Song*,
   1982; *Desperately Seeking Susan*, 1985.
b. Aug 10, 1959 in New York, New York
Source: *ConNews 85-2; VarWW 85*

Arrabal (Teran), Fernando
Spanish. Author, Poet, Dramatist
b. Aug 11, 1932 in Melilla, Morocco
Source: *CasWL; CnMD; CnThe; ConLC 2, 9,
   18; CroCD; CurBio 72; EncWL; McGEWB;
   ModWD; NewYTBE 70, 72; PenC EUR;
   REnWD; TwCWr; WhoAm 74; WhoThe 77;
   WhoWor 78; WorAu*

Arrau, Claudio
Chilean. Musician
b. Feb 6, 1903 in Chillan, Chile
Source: *CelR; CurBio 42; IntWW 74; Who
   74; WhoAm 82; WhoMus 72; WhoWor 78*

Arrhenius, Svante August
Swedish. Chemist
Founded modern physical chemistry, 1884;
   won Nobel Prize, 1903.
b. Feb 19, 1859 in Uppsala, Sweden
d. Oct 2, 1927
Source: *BiESc; DcInv; InSci; NewCol 75;
   WebBD 80; WhDW; WorAl*

Arrighi, Ludovico degli
Italian. Type Designer
Developed italic lettering; composed first
   writing manual *La Operina*, 1522.
Source: *NF*

Arriola, Gus
Mexican. Cartoonist
Created comic strip "Gordo," 1941.
b. Jul 23, 1917 in Florence, Arizona
Source: *BioIn 1; WhoAm 80, 82; WorECom*

Arroyo, Martina
American. Opera Singer
Leading soprano, Metropolitan Opera, NYC,
   1970-74.
b. Feb 2, 1940 in New York, New York
Source: *CurBio 71; NewYTBE 72; WhoAm
   74, 76, 78, 80, 82; WhoBlA 75; WhoMus 72;
   WhoWor 78*

Artaud, Antonin
French. Actor, Director, Poet
Closely identified with "Theater of Cruelty";
   died in insane asylum.
b. Sep 4, 1896 in Marseilles, France
d. Mar 4, 1948 in Paris, France
Source: *CasWL; CnThe; ConAu 104; CroCD;
   EncWL; EvEuW; LongCTC; McGEWD;
   ModRL; ModWD; OxFilm; OxThe; PenC
   EUR; REn; REnWD; TwCWr; WhScrn 77;
   WhoTwCL; WorAu; WorEFlm*

Artemisia
Persian. Queen
Erected one of seven wonders of ancient
   world, Mausoleum at Halicarnassus,
   honoring husband Mausolus.
d. 350 ?BC
Source: *InWom; LinLib L, S*

Arthur, King
British. Legendary Figure
Celtic chieftain whose medieval legends began
   with Monmouth book *History of the Kings
   of Britain*, 12th c.
Source: *BioIn 10; DcEuL; LongCEL; WebBD
   80*

Arthur, Beatrice
[Bernice Frankel]
American. Actress
Starred in TV series "Maude," 1972-78; "The
   Golden Girls," 1985--.
b. May 13, 1926 in New York, New York
Source: *BiE&WWA; BkPepl; CelR; CurBio
   73; EncMT; IntMPA 75, 76, 77, 78, 79, 80,
   81, 82; MotPP; NotNAT; WhoAm 74, 76, 78,
   80, 82; WhoAmW 77; WhoThe 77*

Arthur, Chester Alan
American. US President
Twenty-first pres., who succeeded James
   Garfield, 1881-84; supported civil service
   reform, 1883.
b. Oct 5, 1829 in Fairfield, Vermont
d. Nov 18, 1886 in New York, New York
Source: *AmBi; ApCAB; BiDrAC; BiDrUSE;
   CyAG; DcAmB; EncAB-H; HarEnUS; LinLib
   L, S; McGEWB; NatCAB 4; OxAmH;
   OxAmL; REnAL; TwCBDA; WebAB;
   WebAMB; WhAm HS; WhAmP; WorAl*

Arthur, Ellen Lewis Herndon
[Mrs. Chester A Arthur]
American. Celebrity Relative
Soprano soloist, died suddenly yr. before
   husband became pres.
b. Aug 30, 1837 in Frederick, Virginia
d. Jan 12, 1880 in New York, New York
Source: *BioIn 3, 5, 6, 7; GoodHs; NotAW*

Arthur, Jean
[Gladys Georgianna Greene]
American. Actress
Received Oscar nomination for *The More the
    Merrier,* 1943.
b. Oct 17, 1908 in New York, New York
Source: *BiDFilm; BiE&WWA; CmMov;
CurBio 45; Film 2; FilmgC; GoodHs; IntMPA
80, 81, 82; MotPP; MovMk; NewYTBE 72;
NotNAT,; OxFilm; ThFT; TwYS; WhoHol A;
WhoThe 77A; WorAl; WorEFlm*

Arthur, Joseph Charles
American. Botanist
Noted for his work on plant rust and
    disease.
b. Jan 11, 1850 in Lowville, New York
d. Apr 30, 1942 in Brook, Indiana
Source: *CurBio 42; DcAmB S3; WhAm 2*

Artzybasheff, Boris Mikhailovich
American. Author, Illustrator
Designed over 200 *Time* magazine covers;
    illustrated book jackets, children's books.
b. May 25, 1899 in Kharkov, Russia
d. Jul 16, 1965 in Old Lynne, Connecticut
Source: *AmAu&B; AnCL; AuBYP; ConICB;
CurBio 45, 65; DcAmB S7; IlsCB 1744; JBA
34, 51; SmATA 14; Str&VC; WhAm 4;
WhoGrA 62, 62*

Artsybashev, Mikhail Petrovich
Russian. Author, Dramatist
Best known for sensational novel *Sanin,*
    1907, with frank discussion of sex.
b. Oct 18, 1878 in Kharkov, Russia
d. Mar 3, 1927 in Warsaw, Poland
Source: *BioIn 1, 5; CasWL; ClDMEL;
CnMD; CyWA; DcRusL; EncWL; EvEuW;
ModWD; REn; TwCA, SUP*

Arundel, Honor Morfydd
Welsh. Author
Books deal with emotional problems of
    adolescence.
b. Aug 15, 1919 in Wales
d. Jun 8, 1973 in Hume-by-Kelso, Scotland
Source: *Au&Wr 71; ConAu 21R, 41R, P-2;
ConLC 17; SmATA 24*

Arutumian, Rouben Ter
see: Ter-Arutumian, Rouben

Arvey, Jacob Meyer
American. Political Leader
b. Nov 3, 1895 in Chicago, Illinois
d. Aug 25, 1977 in Chicago, Illinois
Source: *BioIn 1, 2, 3, 9, 11; NewYTBS 77;
WhAm 7; WhoAmW 74, 76, 78*

Arvin, Newton
American. Literary Critic
Wrote books on American literature: *Herman
    Melville,* 1950.
b. Aug 23, 1900 in Valparaiso, Indiana
d. Mar 21, 1963 in Northampton,
    Massachusetts
Source: *DcAmB S7*

Arzner, Dorothy
American. Director
First woman director of sound films; credits
    include *Craig's Wife,* 1935.
b. Jan 3, 1900 in San Francisco, California
d. Oct 1, 1979 in La Quinta, California
Source: *BioIn 3, 10, 11; DcFM; FilmgC;
IntMPA 75, 76, 77, 78, 79; MacDWB;
NewYTBS 79; OxFilm; TwYS; WhoAmW 61;
WomWMM*

Asbury, Francis
American. Religious Leader
First bishop of Methodist Episcopal Church
    consecrated in America, 1785.
b. Aug 20, 1745 in Staffordshire, England
d. Mar 31, 1816 in Spotsylvania, Virginia
Source: *AmAu&B; AmBi; ApCAB; BiDSA;
DcAmB; DcNAA; OxAmL; REnAL; TwCBDA;
WebAB; WhAm HS*

Asbury, Herbert
American. Author
Wrote *The Barbary Coast,* 1933; *The French
    Quarter,* 1936.
b. Sep 1, 1891 in Farmington, Missouri
d. Feb 24, 1963 in New York, New York
Source: *DcAmB S7; WebBD 80*

Ascari, Alberto
Italian. Auto Racer
Grand Prix auto racer who won two world
    championships, 1952, 1953.
b. Jul 13, 1918
d. May 27, 1955 in Monza, Italy
Source: *BioIn 3; ObitT 1951*

Asch, Sholem
Polish. Dramatist, Author
Biblical novels include best-seller *The
    Nazarene,* 1939, written in Yiddish.
b. Nov 1, 1880 in Kutno, Poland
d. Jul 10, 1957 in London, England
Source: *AmAu&B; AmNov; CasWL; ClDMEL;
CnDAL; CnMD; CnThe; CyWA; LongCTC;
McGEWD; ModWD; OxAmL; PenC AM;
REn; REnAL; REnWD; TwCA, SUP;
TwCWr; WhAm 3; WhoLA*

Ascoli, Max
Italian. Educator, Author, Editor
Edited *The Reporter*, 1949-68; wrote *Fall of Mussolini*, 1948.
b. Jun 25, 1898 in Ferrara, Italy
d. Jan 1, 1978 in New York, New York
Source: *AmAu&B; BioIn 1, 3, 11; ConAu 77; CurBio 54, 78; LinLib L; NewYTBS 78; WhAm 7; WhoAm 74, 76, 78*

Asencio, Diego Cortes
American. Diplomat
US ambassador to Colombia held hostage by terrorists for 61 days, 1980.
b. Jul 15, 1931 in Nijar, Spain
Source: *NewYTBS 80; USBiR 74; WhoAm 78, 80, 80; WhoGov 77, 72; WhoWor 78*

Ash, Roy Lawrence
"Human Computer"
American. Corporation Executive
Co-founded Litton Industries, 1953; director, OMB, 1972.
b. Oct 20, 1918 in Los Angeles, California
Source: *CelR; CurBio 68; IntWW 74; NewYTBE 71, 72; NewYTBS 74; WhoAm 74, 76, 78, 80, 82; WhoAmP 73; WhoF&I 74; WhoWor 78*

Ashbery, John Lawrence
[Jonas Berry, pseud.]
American. Author
Won 1976 Pulitzer for narrative verse, *Self-Portrait in a Convex Mirror*.
b. Jul 28, 1927 in Rochester, New York
Source: *AmAu&B; BlueB 76; ConAu 5R, 107; ConLC 2, 3, 4, 6, 9, 13, 15; ConP 75, 80; CroCAP; CurBio 76; DcLEL; IntAu&W 82; LinLib L; ModAL S1; NewYTBS 76; PenC AM; RAdv 1; WebE&AL; WhoAm 76, 78, 80, 82, 84; WhoAmA 78, 80; WhoE 81; WhoWor 80; WorAu; WrDr 82*

Ashbrook, John Milan
American. Businessman, Politician
Rep. senator from OH, 1961-82.
b. Sep 21, 1928 in Johnston, Ohio
d. Apr 24, 1982 in Newark, Ohio
Source: *BiDrAC; CngDr 74, 77, 79; CurBio 73, 82; NewYTBS 82; WhoAm 74, 76, 78, 80, 82; WhoAmP 73, 75, 77, 79; WhoGov 72, 75, 77; WhoMW 74, 76, 78*

Ashbrook, Joseph
American. Astronomer, Editor
Edited *Sky and Telescope* magazine from 1970; asteroid named for him, 1979.
b. Apr 4, 1918 in Philadelphia, Pennsylvania
d. Aug 4, 1980 in Weston, Massachusetts
Source: *AmM&WS 79P; ConAu 117; WhAm 7*

Ashburn, Don Richie
"Whitey"
American. Baseball Player
Outfielder, 1948-62; who won batting titles, 1955, 1958.
b. Mar 19, 1927 in Tilden, Nebraska
Source: *BaseEn 85; BioIn 2, 3, 4, 5, 6, 8; WhoProB 73*

Ashby, Hal
American. Director
Directed *Shampoo*, 1975; *Coming Home*, 1978.
b. 1936 in Ogden, Utah
Source: *FilmEn; FilmgC; IntMPA 80, 81, 81, 82; VarWW 85; WhoAm 80, 82; WhoWest 80, 82*

Ashcroft, Peggy, Dame (Edith Margaret Emily)
English. Actress
Best known for role opposite Paul Robeson in *Othello*, 1930; won Oscar for *A Passage to India*, 1984.
b. Dec 22, 1907 in Croydon, England
Source: *BiE&WWA; BlueB 76; CnThe; CurBio 63; EncWT; FilmEn; FilmgC; IntWW 80; NewC; NotNAT; OxThe; PIP&P; VarWW 85; Who 74; WhoHol A; WhoThe 77; WhoWor 74*

Ashe, Arthur
American. Tennis Player
First black player to win men's singles at Wimbledon, 1975.
b. Jul 10, 1943 in Richmond, Virginia
Source: *BioNews 74; BkPepl; ConAu 65; CurBio 66; WebAB; WhoAm 74, 76, 78, 80, 82; WhoBlA 75; WhoS&SW 82*

Asher, Peter
[Peter and Gordon]
English. Singer, Producer
Part of Peter and Gordon duo, 1961-68; has produced albums for James Taylor, Linda Ronstadt.
b. Jun 22, 1944 in London, England
Source: *RolSEnR 83*

Ashford, Daisy
English. Author
Wrote *The Young Visitors* at age nine; published with original spelling, 1919.
b. 1881 in Petersham, England
d. Jan 15, 1972 in Norwich, England
Source: *CarSB; ConAu 33R; DcLEL; EvLB; LongCTC; NewYTBE 72; PenC ENG; REn; SmATA 10; WhoChL*

Ashford, Emmett Littleton
American. Baseball Umpire
First black umpire in ML, 1966-70.
b. Nov 13, 1916 in Los Angeles, California
d. Mar 1, 1980 in Los Angeles, California
Source: *InB&W 80; NewYTBS 80; WhoProB 73*

Ashford, Evelyn
[Mrs. Ray Washington]
American. Track Athlete
Won gold medal, 1984 LA Olympics; holds
  world record in 100 meter dash.
b. Apr 15, 1957 in Shreveport, Louisiana
Source: *BioIn 12; NewYTBS 83*

Ashford, Nickolas
[Ashford and Simpson]
American. Singer, Songwriter
Wrote song "Ain't No Mountain High
  Enough," 1967, recorded by the Supremes.
b. May 4, 1942 in Fairfield, South Carolina
Source: *AmSCAP 80; BioIn 11; BioNews 74;
IlEncBM 82; InB&W 80; RolSEnR 83;
WhoAm 82; WhoBlA 80*

Ashford and Simpson
[Nickolas Ashford; Valerie Simpson]
American. Music Group
Husband-wife writers, performers; responsible
  for some of Motown's biggest hits.
Source: *RolSEnR 83*

Ashkenasi, Shmuel
Israeli. Musician
b. 1941
Source: *BioIn 7*

Ashkenazy, Vladimir Davidovich
Icelandic. Musician
Considered best of young Russian pianists;
  known for sensitivity of tone, delicate
  fingerwork.
b. Jul 6, 1937 in Gorki, U.S.S.R.
Source: *Baker 78; BioNews 75; BlueB 76;
CurBio 67; IntWW 80, 81, 82; MusMk;
NewYTBE 72; Who 74, 82; WhoAm 82;
WhoMus 72; WhoWor 74, 80; WhoWorJ 78;
WorAl*

Ashley, Elizabeth
[Elizabeth Ann Cole]
American. Actress
Won Tony, 1962; films include *The Carpet
  Baggers,* 1963.
b. Aug 30, 1939 in Ocala, Florida
Source: *BiE&WWA; FilmgC; IntMPA 77, 78,
79, 80, 81, 82; MovMk; NewYTBS 74;
NotNAT; WhoAm 74, 76, 78, 80, 82; WhoHol
A; WhoThe 77*

Ashley, Laura Mountney
Welsh. Designer, Business Executive
Created int'l. fashion empire based on
  romance of English country gardens.
b. Sep 7, 1925 in Merthyr Tydfil, Wales
d. Sep 17, 1985 in Coventry, England
Source: *WorFshn*

Ashley, Merrill
[Linda Merrill]
American. Ballerina, Author
Star of Balanchine's NYC Ballet since 1976.
b. 1950 in Saint Paul, Minnesota
Source: *BioIn 11; CurBio 81; NewYTBS 81;
WhoAm 82*

Ashley, Thomas William Ludlow
"Lud"
American. Politician
Ohio Dem. congressman, 1954-80, who
  headed Energy Committee, 1977.
b. Jan 11, 1923 in Toledo, Ohio
Source: *AlmAP 78, 80; BiDrAC; CngDr 74,
77, 79; CurBio 79; NewYTBS 77; PolProf J,
NF; WhoAm 74, 76, 78, 80; WhoAmP 73,
75, 77, 79; WhoGov 72, 75, 77; WhoMW 74,
76, 78*

Ashley, William Henry
American. Fur Trader, Politician
Instituted trappers rendezvous, 1824;
  congressman, 1831-37.
b. Mar 26, 1778 in Powhatan County,
  Virginia
d. Mar 26, 1838 in Boonville, Missouri
Source: *AmBi; ApCAB; BiAUS; BiDrAC;
DcAmB; Drake; EncAB-H; McGEWB; NewCol
75; OxAmL; REnAW; TwCBDA; WebAB, 79;
WhAm HS, HSA; WhAmP*

Ashman, Matthew
[Bow Wow Wow]
English. Musician
One-time back-up to Adam Ant; guitarist
  with Bow Wow Wow since 1980.
b. in London, England
Source: *NF*

Ashmore, Harry Scott
American. Editor, Author
Pulitzer-winning editorial writer, 1958; books
  include *Hearts and Minds,* 1982.
b. Jul 27, 1916 in Greenville, South Carolina
Source: *AmAu&B; ConAu 13R; CurBio 58;
WhoAm 76, 78, 80, 82, 84; WhoWest 74;
WhoWor 74*

Ashton, Frederick William, Sir
English. Choreographer, Dancer
b. Sep 17, 1906 in Guayaquil, Ecuador
Source: *CurBio 51; IntWW 74; NewYTBE 70; Who 74; WhoMus 72; WhoThe 77A; WhoWor 78*

Ashton-Warner, Sylvia Constance
New Zealander. Author, Educator
Experiences as teacher of Maouri children in New Zealand subject matter for her fiction.
b. Dec 17, 1908 in Stratford, New Zealand
d. Apr 28, 1984 in Tauranga, New Zealand
Source: *AnObit 1984; BlueB 76; ConAu 69; ConLC 19; ConNov 76, 82; DcLEL; IntAu&W 76, 77; LongCTC; Novels; PenC ENG; RAdv 1; TwCWr; Who 82; WorAu; WrDr 76*

Asia
[Geoffrey Downes; Steve Howe; Carl Palmer; Greg Lake]
English. Music Group
Hard rock group formed 1981; hit single "Heat of the Moment," 1983.
Source: *RkOn 85; RolSEnR 83*

Asimov, Isaac
[Paul French, pseud.]
American. Author, Biochemist
Leading popular scientist; wrote over 200 books; coined term "robotics."
b. Jan 2, 1920 in Petrovichi, U.S.S.R.
Source: *AmAu&B; AmM&WS 82P; AsBiEn; Au&Wr 71; AuBYP; CasWL; CelR; ConAu 1R, 2NR; ConLC 3, 9, 19; ConNov 72, 76, 82; ConSFA; CurBio 53, 68; DrAF 76; EncMys; EncSF; IntWW 79, 80, 81, 82; LinLib L, S; LongCTC; NewCol 75; PenC AM; REn; REnAL; ScF&FL 1; SmATA 1, 26; ThrBJA; TwCWr; WebAB, 79; WebE&AL; Who 82; WhoAm 78, 80, 82; WhoSciF; WhoWor 74, 76, 78, 80; WorAu; WrDr 82*

Askew, Reubin O'Donovan
American. Government Official, Politician
Dem. governor of FL, 1971-79; sought Dem. presidential nomination, 1984.
b. Sep 11, 1928 in Muskogee, Oklahoma
Source: *BioNews 74; CurBio 73; IntWW 74; NewYTBE 72; WhoAm 74, 76, 78, 80, 82; WhoAmP 73; WhoGov 75*

Asner, Ed(ward)
American. Actor
Six-time Emmy winner best known for role of Lou Grant on "Mary Tyler Moore Show," 1970-77.
b. Nov 15, 1929 in Kansas City, Missouri
Source: *BkPepl; CurBio 78; FilmgC; IntMPA 77, 78, 79, 80, 81, 82; NewYTBE 73; WhoAm 74, 76, 78, 80, 82; WhoHol A*

Asoka the Great
Indian. Ruler
King of Magadha, 273-232 BC; reign marked by prosperous times; made Buddhism a world religion.
b. 300 BC
d. 232 BC
Source: *BioIn 1; LinLib S; LuthC 75; WhDW; WorAl*

Aspin, Leslie, Jr.
American. Politician
Dem. congressman from WI, 1970--; chm. of powerful Armed Services Com.
b. Jul 21, 1938 in Milwaukee, Wisconsin
Source: *AlmAP 84; CngDr 83; ConAu 108; CurBio 86; WhoAm 84; WhoAmP 83; WhoMW 82*

Asplund, Erik Gunnar
Swedish. Architect
Major influence in Swedish architecture best known for designing pavilions at Stockholm Exhibition, 1930.
b. 1885 in Stockholm, Sweden
d. 1940
Source: *ConArch; DcD&D; MacEA; NewCol 75; OxArt; WhDW*

Asquith, Anthony
English. Director
Directed *The Importance of Being Earnest,* 1952.
b. Nov 9, 1902 in London, England
d. Feb 20, 1968 in London, England
Source: *BiDFilm; BioIn 8, 10, 11; CmMov; DcFM; FilmEn; MovMk; ObitOF 79; OxFilm; WhAm 5; WhScrn 74, 77; WorEFlm*

Asquith, Emma Alice Margot
[Countess of Oxford and Asquith]
English. Author
Eccentric, outspoken, shrewd; great influence on social, fashionable life.
b. Feb 2, 1864 in Peebleshire, England
d. Jul 28, 1945 in London, England
Source: *CurBio 45; DcNaB 1941; EvLB; GrBr; LinLib L; LongCTC*

Asquith, Herbert Henry
see: Oxford and Asquith, Henry Herbert
    Asquith, Earl

Assad, Hafez al
Syrian. Political Leader
Minister of Defense, 1966-70; led coup that
    made him pres., 1971.
b. Oct 6, 1930 in Qardaha, Syria
Source: CurBio 75; IntWW 80, 81; IntYB 79,
80, 81; MidE 78, 79, 80; NewCol 75;
NewYTBE 70; NewYTBS 77; WhoGov 72;
WhoWor 74, 76, 78

Assante, Armand
American. Actor
Played Michael Moretti in TV mini-series
    "Rage of Angels," 1983.
b. Oct 4, 1949 in New York, New York
Source: BioIn 11; VarWW 83

Assis Chateaubriand, Francisco de
Brazilian. Journalist
Owned syndicate of newspapers, magazines in
    Brazil.
b. Apr 10, 1891 in Umbuzeiro, Brazil
d. 1968
Source: BioIn 1, 2, 3, 4, 5, 6, 7, 8; CurBio
57

Assisi, Francis of, Saint
see: Francis of Assisi, Saint

Association, The
[Gary Alexander; Ted Bluechel; Brian Cole;
    Russ Giguere; Terry Kirkman; Jim Yester]
American. Music Group
Pop-rock band, 1960s; won gold records for
    "Cherish," 1966; "Never My Love," 1967.
Source: BiDAmM; EncPR&S 74; RkOn 74;
RolSEnR 83

Astaire, Adele
[Adele Austerlitz; Mrs. Kingman Douglas]
American. Dancer, Celebrity Relative
Dancing partner, 1916-32, of brother Fred.
b. Sep 10, 1898 in Omaha, Nebraska
d. Jan 25, 1981 in Scottsdale, Arizona
Source: AmPS; AnObit 1981; BiE&WWA;
CmpEPM; EncMT; Film 1; InWom;
NewYTBS 81; NotNAT; PIP&P; WhThe;
WorAl

Astaire, Fred
[Frederick Austerlitz]
American. Dancer, Actor, Singer, Writer
Dancing style has influenced all movie
    musicals; starred in 10 films with best
    known partner, Ginger Rogers.
b. May 10, 1899 in Omaha, Nebraska
Source: AmPS B; AmSCAP 66; BiDFilm;
BiE&WWA; BkPepl; CelR; CmMov;
CmpEPM; ConTFT 3; CurBio 64; EncMT;
EncWT; Film 1; IntMPA 82; LinLib S;
MGM; MotPP; MovMk; NewCol 75;
NewYTBS 79; NewYTET; NotNAT; OxFilm;
PIP&P; WebAB; WhThe; WhoAm 84; WhoHol
A; WorEFlm

Asther, Nils
Swedish. Actor
Leading man in Swedish and German films;
    in US film The Bitter Tea of General Yen,
    1933.
b. Jan 17, 1901 in Malmo, Sweden
d. Oct 13, 1981 in Stockholm, Sweden
Source: BioIn 10; FilmEn; Film 2; FilmgC;
MotPP; MovMk; NewYTBS 81; TwYS;
WhoHol A

Astin, John Allen
American. Actor, Director, Writer
Best known as Gomez Addams on "The
    Addams Family," 1964-66.
b. Mar 30, 1930 in Baltimore, Maryland
Source: BioNews 74; FilmgC; IntMPA 75, 76,
77, 78, 79, 80, 81, 82; WhoAm 74, 76, 78,
80, 82; WhoHol A

Astin, Mackenzie Alexander
"Skeezix"
American. Actor
Plays Andy on TV series "Facts of Life."
b. May 12, 1973 in Los Angeles, California
Source: NF

Astor, Brooke Marshall
[Mrs. Vincent Astor]
American. Philanthropist
Pres., trustee, Vincent Astor Foundation,
    NYC.
b. in Portsmouth, New Hampshire
Source: NewYTBS 84; WhoAmW 72; WhoGov
72; WhoWor 82

Astor, Gavin
[Lord Astor of Hever]
British. Publisher
Head of Astor dynasty; pres., Times
    Newspapers Ltd. from 1967.
b. Jun 1, 1918
d. Jun 28, 1984 in Tillypronie, Scotland
Source: ConAu 113; IntWW 82; WhoAm 82

Astor, John Jacob
American. Fur Trader, Financier
Chartered American Fur Co.; wealthiest man
  in US at death.
b. Jul 17, 1763 in Heidelberg, Germany
d. Mar 29, 1848 in New York, New York
Source: *AmBi; ApCAB; DcAmB; Drake;
EncAB-H; OxAmL; LinLib S; MacDCB 78;
McGEWB; NatCAB 8; NewCol 75; OxAmL;
OxCan; REn; REnAL; REnAW; TwCBDA;
WebAB; WhAm HS*

Astor, Mary
[Lucille Vasconcellos Langhanke]
American. Actress
Played Brigid O'Shaughnessy in *The Maltese
  Falcon,* 1941, opposite Bogart.
b. May 3, 1906 in Quincy, Illinois
Source: *AmAu&B; BiDFilm; BiE&WWA;
CelR; ConAu 5R; CurBio 61; Film 2;
FilmgC; InWom; IntMPA 75, 76, 77, 78, 79,
80, 81, 82; MGM; MotPP; MovMk; NotNAT
A; OxFilm; ThFT; TwYS; WhoAmW 64, 66,
68, 70, 72, 74; WhoHol A; WorEFlm*

**Astor, Nancy Witcher (Langhorne) Astor,
Viscountess**
[Mrs. William Waldorf Astor]
English. Political Leader
First woman to sit in House of Commons,
  1919-45.
b. May 19, 1879 in Greenwood, Virginia
d. May 2, 1964 in Lincoln, England
Source: *CurBio 40, 64; InWom; LinLib L, S;
NewCol 75; ObitT 1961; WhDW; WhAm 4;
WorAl*

Astor, William Vincent
American. Financier
Son of John Jacob Astor IV; left $6 million
  to Vincent Astor Foundation to "alleviate
  human misery."
b. Nov 15, 1891 in New York, New York
d. Feb 3, 1959 in New York, New York
Source: *ObitOF 79; WhAm 3; WhAmP*

Astor, William Waldorf Astor, Viscount
British. Financier
Head of Astor family, 1890; fortune
  estimated at $100 million.
b. Mar 31, 1848 in New York, New York
d. Jan 18, 1919 in Brighton, England
Source: *AmAu; AmAu&B; AmBi; BbD;
BiD&SB; CyAL 2; DcAmAu; DcAmB; DcBiA;
DcNAA; LinLib L, S; NatCAB 8; TwCBDA;
WhAm 1*

Astrid
Norwegian. Princess
b. 1932
Source: *InWom*

Asturias, Miguel Angel
Guatemalan. Author, Diplomat
Won Nobel Prize in literature, 1967; wrote
  Strong Wind, 1969; *Le Miroir de Lida Sal,*
  1967.
b. Oct 19, 1899 in Guatemala City,
  Guatemala
d. Jun 9, 1974 in Madrid, Spain
Source: *CasWL; ConAu 25R, 49, P-2; ConLC
3, 8, 13; CurBio 68, 74; EncWL; IntWW 74;
NewYTBS 74; PenC AM; TwCWr; WhAm 6;
Who 74; WhoTwCL; WhoWor 78; WorAu*

Atahualpa
Peruvian. Ruler
Incan emperor, 1532-33, captured by Pizarro;
  was killed even though ransom paid.
b. 1500
d. Aug 29, 1533
Source: *ApCAB; DcBiPP; Drake; EncLatA;
LinLib S; McGEWB; REn; WhDW;
WhoMilH 76*

Ataturk, Kemal
[Mustafa Kemal]
Turkish. Political Leader
Founded modern Turkey, first pres. Turkish
  republic, 1923-38.
b. 1880 in Salonika, Turkey
d. Nov 10, 1938
Source: *BioIn 10; NewCol 75; WebBD 80*

Atchison, David R
American. Politician
As pres. pro tem of senate, served as US
  pres. for one day, Mar 4, 1849.
b. Aug 11, 1807 in Frogtown, Kentucky
d. Jun 26, 1886 in Gower, Missouri
Source: *ApCAB; BiDrAC; DcAmB; TwCBDA*

Atget, Eugene (Jean-Eugene-Auguste)
French. Photographer
Documentary photographer, known for
  photos of Paris.
b. 1855 in Libourne, France
d. Aug 1927 in Paris, France
Source: *BioIn 11; ConPhot; MacBEP;
NewYTBS 81*

Athenagoras I
Greek. Religious Leader
Led Eastern Orthodox Christians, 1948-72;
  advocated reunion with Roman Catholic
  Church.
b. Mar 25, 1886 in Vassilikon, Greece
d. Jul 6, 1972 in Istanbul, Turkey
Source: *CurBio 49, 72; CyEd; DcBiPP;
DcCathB; LinLib L; LuthC 75; NewYTBE
72; ObitOF 79; ObitT 1971; WhAm 5;
WhoWor 74*

Atherton, Alfred LeRoy, Jr.
American. Government Official
Joined foreign service, 1947; ambassador to
  Egypt, 1979-83.
b. Nov 22, 1921 in Pittsburgh, Pennsylvania
Source: *MidE 79; NewYTBS 77; USBiR 74;
WhoAm 74, 76, 78, 80, 82; WhoAmP 75, 77,
79; WhoGov 72, 75, 77*

Atherton, Gertrude Franklin
American. Author
Novels depict California, society life: *Block
  Oxen*, 1923.
b. Oct 30, 1857 in San Francisco, California
d. Jun 14, 1948 in San Francisco, California
Source: *AmAu&B; AmWomWr; ApCAB SUP;
BbD; CasWL; Chambr 3; CmCal; CnDAL;
ConAmA; ConAmL; ConAu 104; CurBio 40,
48; DcAmB S4; DcEnA; DcLEL; DcNAA;
EncSF; EvLB; LibW; LinLib L, S; LongCTC;
NatCAB 10, 36; NotAW; Novels; OxAmL;
OxEng; PenC AM; RAdv 1; REn; REnAL;
REnAW; TwCA, SUP; WhAm 2; WhE&EA;
WhLit; WhNAA; WhoHr&F; WomWWA 14*

Atherton, William
[William Atherton Knight, II]
American. Actor
Starred in films *Sugarland Express*, 1974;
  Looking For Mr. Goodbar, 1977.
b. Jul 30, 1947 in New Haven, Connecticut
Source: *IntMPA 81, 82; WhoHol A; WhoThe
81*

Athlone, Countess of
see: Alice, Princess

Atkins, Chet (Chester B)
"Mr. Guitar"
American. Musician, Business Executive
Virtuoso guitarist, associated with Grand Ole
  Opry since 1950.
b. Jun 20, 1924 in Luttrell, Tennessee
Source: *BiDAmM; BioNews 75; CelR; CurBio
75; EncFCWM 69; NewYTBS 74; WhoAm
74, 76, 78, 80, 82; WorAl*

Atkins, Christopher
American. Actor
In films *The Blue Lagoon*, 1980, with Brooke
  Shields; *The Pirate Movie*, 1982.
b. Feb 21, 1961 in Rye, New York
Source: *BioIn 12; NewYTBS 82*

Atkins, Susan Denise
American. Cultist, Murderer
Convicted, with Charles Manson, of Tate-
  LaBianca murders, 1969.
b. 1948
Source: *BioIn 8, 9, 10, 11*

Atkinson, (Justin) Brooks
American. Drama Critic, Journalist
One of first supporters of Eugene O'Neill;
  reviewed over 3,000 opening night
  performances; won Pulitzer, 1947.
b. Nov 28, 1894 in Melrose, Massachusetts
d. Jan 13, 1984 in Huntsville, Alabama
Source: *AmAu&B; AnObit 1984; BiE&WWA;
BlueB 76; CelR; ConAmTC; ConAu 111,
14NR, 61; CurBio 42, 61, 84; EncWT;
IntAu&W 82; IntWW 80, 81, 82; LinLib L,
S; NewYTBE 73; NotNAT; OxAmL; OxThe;
TwCA SUP; WebAB; WhJnl; WhLit; WhNAA;
WhoAm 80, 82, 82; WorAl; WrDr 76, 82*

Atkinson, Ted
[Theodore Francis Atkinson]
American. Jockey
b. Jun 17, 1916
Source: *NewYTBE 73*

Atkinson, Ti-Grace
American. Feminist
b. 1939
Source: *BioIn 8, 9*

Atkinson, William Walker
American. Religious Leader
New Thought metaphysical writer; first
  successful popularizer of Hindu thought,
  practice in US.
b. Dec 5, 1862 in Baltimore, Maryland
d. Nov 22, 1932 in Los Angeles, California
Source: *BiDAmC; DcNAA; WhAm 1*

Atlanta Rhythm Section
[Barry Bailey; J R Cobb; Dean Daugherty;
Paul Goddard; Ronnie Hammond; Robert
Nix]
American. Music Group
Had platinum album *Champagne Jam*, 1978;
  hit singles "So Into You," "Imaginary
  Lover."
Source: *IlEncRk; RkOn 74; RolSEnR 83*

Atlas, Charles
[Angelo Siciliano]
American. Physical Fitness Expert,
  Bodybuilder
Developed dynamic tension method of
  bodybuilding.
b. Oct 30, 1894 in Acri, Italy
d. Dec 23, 1972 in Long Beach, New York
Source: *BioIn 1, 4, 10; ObitOF 79; WebAB,
79*

Attenborough, David Frederick
English. Author, Naturalist
CBC travel writer, broadcaster; wrote *Zoo Quest* series, 1956-82.
b. May 8, 1926 in London, England
Source: *Au&Wr 71; BlueB 76; ConAu 4NR, 6NR; IntAu&W 77; IntMPA 80, 81; IntWW 80, 81, 82, 84; Who 82; WhoWor 76, 78; WrDr 76, 80, 82*

Attenborough, Richard Samuel, Sir
English. Actor, Producer, Director
Won 1983 best director Oscar for *Gandhi*; film took 20 yrs. to make.
b. Aug 29, 1923 in Cambridge, England
Source: *BiDFilm; BlueB 76; CelR; CmMov; CurBio 84; FilmgC; IntMPA 78, 79, 80, 81, 82; IntWW 74, 80; MotPP; MovMk; OxFilm; Who 74, 82; WhoAm 80, 82; WhoHol A; WhoThe 77, 81; WhoWor 74; WorAl; WorEFlm*

Atterbury, Grosvenor
American. Architect
Designed earliest practical prefabricated housing, 1907.
b. Jul 7, 1869 in Detroit, Michigan
d. Oct 18, 1956 in Long Island, New York
Source: *BioIn 3, 4; BnEnAmA; DcAmB S6; WhAm 3*

Attila
"Scourge of God"
Ruler
King of the Huns known for attacks on Europe during last stages of Roman Empire.
b. 406
d. 453
Source: *DcBiPP; LinLib L; LongCEL; LuthC 75; McGEWB; NewC; OxGer; REn; WhDW; WorAl*

Attlee, Clement Richard Attlee, Earl
English. Political Leader, Author
Labour Party Leader; prime minister, first lord of Treasury, 1945-51.
b. Jan 3, 1883 in London, England
d. Oct 8, 1967 in London, England
Source: *CurBio 40, 47, 67; DcPol; HisEWW; LinLib L, S; LongCTC; ObitOF 79; ObitT 1961; WhDW; WhAm 4; WhE&EA; WhWW-II; Who 82; WorAl*

Attucks, Crispus
American. Patriot
First colonist killed at Boston Massacre, Mar 5, 1770.
b. 1723
d. Mar 5, 1770 in Boston, Massachusetts
Source: *ApCAB; DcAmB; Drake; LinLib S; REn; TwCBDA; WebAB; WebAMB; WhAm HS*

Attwood, William
American. Publisher, Journalist, Diplomat
Editor *Look* magazine, 1951-61; ambassador to Guinea, Kenya, 1961-66.
b. Jul 14, 1919 in Paris, France
Source: *AmAu&B; ConAu 21R; CurBio 68; IntWW 74; WhoAm 76, 78, 80, 82, 84; WhoF&I 74*

Atwater, Edith
American. Actress
Played Moriarty to Basil Rathbone's Sherlock Holmes in *The Hound of the Baskervilles*, 1939.
b. Apr 22, 1911 in Chicago, Illinois
d. Mar 19, 1986 in Los Angeles, California
Source: *BiE&WWA; NotNAT, B; ObitOF 79; WhoHol A; WhoThe 77, 77A*

Atwill, Lionel
English. Actor
Began career on stage in plays by Shaw, Isben; films include *Son of Frankenstein*, 1939.
b. Mar 1, 1885 in Croydon, England
d. Apr 22, 1946 in Hollywood, California
Source: *CmMov; CurBio 46; Film 1; FilmgC; MotPP; MovMk; REn; Vers A; WhAm 2; WhScrn 74, 77; WhoHol B*

Atwood, Angela
[S(ymbionese) L(iberation) A(rmy)]
American. Revolutionary
SLA terrorist involved in Hearst kidnapping, 1974; killed in police shoot-out.
b. 1948
d. May 24, 1974 in Los Angeles, California
Source: *BioIn 10; NewYTBS 74*

Atwood, Francis Clarke
American. Inventor
Invented latex paint, technicolor film.
b. May 7, 1893 in Salem, Massachusetts
d. Jul 31, 1982
Source: *AmM&WS 73P, 76P, 79P, 82P*

Atwood, Margaret Eleanor
Canadian. Author, Poet
Wrote best-selling novel *The Handmaid's Tale*, 1966.
b. Nov 18, 1939 in Ottawa, Ontario
Source: *Au&Wr 71; CanWW 82; ConAu 3NR, 49; ConLC 2, 3, 4, 8, 13, 15; ConNov 76; ConP 70, 75; CurBio 84; DrAF 76; DrAP 75; OxCan, SUP; WhoAm 74, 76*

Auber, Daniel Francois Esprit
French. Opera Composer
Father of French grand opera; greatest work *La Muette de Portici*, 1828.
b. Jan 19, 1782 in Caen, France
d. May 12, 1871 in Paris, France
Source: *AtlBL; Baker 78; CelCen; DcBiPP; Dis&D; LinLib S; NewEOp 71; OxFr; OxMus; REn*

Auberjonois, Rene Murat
American. Actor
Won Tony for *Coco* , 1969; plays Clayton Endicott on TV series "Benson," 1980--.
b. Jun 1, 1940 in New York, New York
Source: *FilmEn; FilmgC; NotNAT; PhDcTCA 77; WhoAm 80, 82; WhoHol A; WhoThe 77, 81*

Aubrey, James Thomas, Jr.
American. Business Executive
Former head, CBS-TV, who is pres., MGM, 1969--.
b. Dec 14, 1918 in LaSalle, Illinois
Source: *CelR; CurBio 72; IntMPA 75, 76, 77, 78, 79, 80, 81, 82; NewYTET; WhoAm 74; WhoF&I 74*

Aubrey, John
English. Author, Antiquarian
Wrote *Lives of Eminent Men*, 1813, vivid, intimate portraits of 17th c. personalities.
b. Mar 12, 1626 in Easton Pierce, England
d. Jun 1697 in Oxford, England
Source: *Alli; AtlBL; BrAu; CasWL; Chambr 1; CroE&S; DcBiPP; DcEnA; DcEnL; DcLEL; Dis&D; EvLB; LinLib L; LongCEL; MouLC 1; NewC; OxEng; PenC ENG; REn; WebE&AL; WhDW*

Auchincloss, Hugh D
American. Businessman, Celebrity Relative
Stepfather of Jacqueline Onassis, who served in US Navy in WW I, WW II.
b. 1897
d. Nov 20, 1976 in Washington, District of Columbia
Source: *St&PR 75; WhAm 7*

Auchincloss, Louis
[Andrew Lee, pseud.]
American. Lawyer, Author
Wrote over 30 books, including *The Indifferent Children*, 1947.
b. Sep 27, 1917 in Lawrence, New York
Source: *AmAu&B; Au&Wr 71; CelR; ConAu 1R; ConLC 4, 6, 9, 18; ConNov 72, 76; CurBio 54; DrAF 76; IntWW 74; ModAL, S1; OxAmL; PenC AM; RAdv 1; REn; REnAL; TwCWr; WebE&AL; Who 74; WhoAm 74, 76, 78, 80, 82; WhoWor 78; WorAu; WrDr 80*

Auchinleck, Claude, Sir
"The Auk"
British. Military Leader
WW II general, replaced by Montgomery after disobeying Churchill's order to counterattack Rommel outside Cairo.
b. Jun 21, 1884 in Aldershot, England
d. Mar 23, 1981 in Marrakech, Morocco
Source: *AnObit 1981; NewYTBS 81; PseudN 82; Who 74; WhoWor 74, 76, 78*

Auden, W(ystan) H(ugh)
English. Poet, Educator, Dramatist
Won Pulitzer for verse, *Age of Anxiety* , 1948.
b. Feb 21, 1907 in York, England
d. Sep 28, 1973 in Vienna, Austria
Source: *AmAu&B; AmSCAP 66; Au&Wr 71; BiE&WWA; CasWL; CelR; Chambr 3; CnE&AP; CnMD; CnMWL; ConAu 5NR, 9R, 45; ConDr 73; ConLC 1, 2, 3, 4, 6, 9, 11, 14; ConP 75; CurBio 73; CyWA; DcLEL; EncWL; EvLB; LongCTC; McGEWD; ModAL, S1; ModBrL, S1; ModWD; NewC; NewYTBE 71, 72, 73; OxAmL; OxEng; PenC ENG; PIP&P; RAdv 1; RComWL; REn; REnAL; TwCA, SUP; TwCWr; WebE&AL*

Audiard, Michel
French. Screenwriter, Director
Wrote over 100 French films during 40 yr. career.
b. May 15, 1920 in Paris, France
d. Jul 28, 1985 in Paris, France
Source: *ConAu 116; FilmEn*

Audiberti, Jacques
French. Author, Poet
Wrote of man, nature: *La Na*, 1944; *Monorail*, 1964.
b. Mar 25, 1899 in Antibes, France
d. Jul 10, 1965 in Paris, France
Source: *CasWL; ClDMEL; CnMD; CnThe; ConAu 25R; CroCD; EncWL; EvEuW; McGEWD; ModWD; OxFr; OxThe; PenC EUR; REn; WorAu*

Audran, Stephane
[Mrs. Claude Chabrol]
French. Actress
Sophisticated film beauty who starred in *Les Beches*, 1968; *Violette Noziere*, 1978.
b. 1939 in Versailles, France
Source: *BiDFilm; FilmEn; FilmgC; IntMPA 81; IntWW 80, 81, 82; OxFilm; WhoAmW 70; WhoHol A*

Audubon, John James
American. Author, Ornithologist, Artist
Illustrated wildlife in celebrated folios: *Birds of America*, 1827-38; *Quadrupeds of North America*, 1848.
b. Apr 26, 1785 in Haiti
d. Jan 27, 1851 in New York, New York
Source: *AfroAA; AmAu; AmAu&B; AmBi; AtlBL; BbD; BiD&SB; BiDSA; CnDAL; CyAL 1; DcAmAu; DcAmB; DcLEL; DcNAA; EncAB-H; MouLC 3; OhA&B; OxAmL; OxCan; OxEng; PenC AM; REn; REnAL; WebAB; WhAm HS*

Auel, Jean Marie
American. Author
Wrote *The Clan of the Cave Bear*, 1980, *The Valley of Horses*, 1982.
b. Feb 18, 1936 in Chicago, Illinois
Source: *BioIn 12; ConAu 103; NewYTBS 80*

Auer, Leopold
American. Musician, Teacher
Soloist for the Czar; conducted concerts in Petrograd, 1887-92; NYC, 1918-30.
b. Jun 7, 1845 in Vesprem, Hungary
d. Jul 15, 1930 in Loschwitz, Germany
Source: *AmSCAP 66; WhAm 1*

Auer, Mischa
[Mischa Ounskowski]
Russian. Actor
Appeared in over 60 US films; nominated for Oscar, 1936, for *My Man Godfrey*.
b. Nov 17, 1905 in Saint Petersburg, Russia
d. Mar 5, 1967 in Rome, Italy
Source: *FilmEn; Film 2; FilmgC; MotPP; MovMk; NotNAT B; ObitOF 79; ObitT 1961; TwYS; Vers A; WhScrn 74, 77; WhoHol B*

Auerbach, "Red" (Arnold Jacob)
American. Basketball Coach
Coach of year, 1965; career record 1,037-548; Hall of Fame, 1968.
b. Sep 20, 1917 in Brooklyn, New York
Source: *CelR; ConAu 17R; CurBio 69; WhoAm 74, 76, 78, 80, 82; WhoBbl 73; WhoE 74*

Auerbach-Levy, William
American. Artist, Journalist, Author
Magazine caricaturist who satirized theater personalities in *NY World* , 1925-31.
b. Feb 14, 1889 in Brest-Litovsk, Russia
d. Jun 29, 1964
Source: *CurBio 48, 64; EncAJ; NatCAB 51; WhAm 4; WhoAmA 80N, 82; WorECar*

Auger, Arleen
American. Singer
Concert, opera singer, known for interpretations of Bach, Mozart.
b. 1943 in California
Source: *NewYTBS 84*

Auger, Brian
English. Musician, Songwriter
Keyboardist who formed Brian Auger's Trinity, 1964; fused jazz-rock hybrids.
b. Jul 18, 1939 in London, England
Source: *ConMuA 80A; EncJzS 70; RolSEnR 83; WhoRock 81*

August, Jan
[Jan Augustoff]
American. Musician, Band Leader
Self-taught pianist whose best known album was *Misirlou*, 1946.
b. 1912 in New York, New York
d. Jan 18, 1976 in New York, New York
Source: *BioIn 10; CmpEPM; NewYTBS 76*

Augustine, Saint
[Aurelius Augustinus]
Roman. Religious Figure, Philosopher
Writings established foundations for medieval Catholicism, protestantism.
b. Nov 13, 354 in Agaste, Namibia
d. 430 in Hippo, Namibia
Source: *AtlBL; BbD; BiD&SB; CasWL; CyEd; CyWA; DcCathB; Dis&D; Grk&L; InSci; LinLib L, S; McGDA; McGEWB; NewC,; OxEng; OxLaw; PenC CL; RComWL; REn; WorAl*

Augustine of Canterbury, Saint
"Apostle of the English"
Italian. Religious Leader
First archbishop of Canterbury, 601; feast day May 28.
Source: *CyEd; LuthC 75; McGDA; McGEWB; NewC; REn; WhDW*

Augustus
[Octavius Caesar]
Roman. Ruler
Emperor who returned Rome to
    constitutional rule after death of Caesar,
    44 BC.
b. Sep 23, 63 in Rome, Italy
d. Aug 19, 14 in Nola, Italy
Source: *AmLY XR; DcBiPP; Dis&D; Grk&L;*
LuthC 75; WhDW

Augustus II
[Frederick Augustine I; Augustus the Strong]
Polish. Ruler
King of Poland, 1697-1733; art patron who
    created Meissen china manufacturers.
b. May 12, 1670 in Dresden, Germany
d. Feb 1, 1733
Source: *DcBiPP; LuthC 75; NewCol 75;*
WebBD 80; WhDW

Augustyn, Frank Joseph
Canadian. Ballet Dancer
Star of Canada's National Ballet since 1972.
b. Jan 27, 1953 in Hamilton, Ontario
Source: *BioIn 9; WhoAm 78, 80, 82, 84*

Aulaire, Edgar Parin d'
American. Children's Author, Illustrator
With wife, wrote, illustrated children's picture
    biographies: *Ola,* 1932.
b. Sep 30, 1898 in Munich, Germany
d. May 1, 1986 in Georgetown, Connecticut
Source: *AnCL; ConAu 49; CurBio 40; JBA*
51; SmATA 5

Aulaire, Ingri Mortenson d'
[Mrs. Edgar Parin d'Aulaire]
American. Children's Author, Illustrator
Won 1940 Caldecott Medal with husband for
    Abraham Lincoln, 1939 .
b. Dec 27, 1904 in Kongsberg, Norway
d. Oct 24, 1980 in Wilton, Connecticut
Source: *AnCL; ConAu 102, 49; JBA 34, 51;*
SmATA 24, 5

Auletta, Robert
American. Dramatist, Educator
Won Obies for *Stops,* 1972; *Virgins,* 1982.
b. Mar 5, 1940 in New York, New York
Source: *ConAu 115; NatPD 81*

Ault, George Christian
American. Artist
Precisionist who drew nocturnes, cityscapes.
b. Oct 11, 1891 in Cleveland, Ohio
d. Dec 30, 1948 in Woodside, New York
Source: *BioIn 4, 11; DcAmArt; DcCAA 71,*
77; IlBEAAW; McGDA; NatCAB 40

Aumont, Jean-Pierre
[Jean-Pierre Salomons]
French. Actor, Author
Brother of Francois Villiers; wrote
    autobiography *Sun and Shadow,* 1976.
b. Jan 5, 1909 in Paris, France
Source: *BiE&WWA; ConAu 29R; FilmgC;*
IntMPA 75, 76, 77, 78, 79, 80, 81, 82;
MotPP; MovMk; NotNAT; WhoAm 74, 76,
78, 80, 82; WhoHol A; WhoThe 77

Aurangzeb
Indian. Ruler
Last Mogul emperor of India, 1658-1707;
    contributed to collapse of empire.
b. Oct 24, 1618 in Dohad, India
d. Feb 20, 1707
Source: *LinLib S; McGEWB; NewCol 75*

Aurell, Tage
Swedish. Author, Translator
Wrote *Skilling Tryck,* 1943.
b. Mar 2, 1895 in Christiania, Sweden
d. Feb 20, 1976 in Mansrog, Sweden
Source: *CasWL; ConAu 113; EncWL 2;*
WhE&EA

Auric, Georges
[Les Six]
French. Composer
Composed scores for over 100 films,
    including *Roman Holiday,* 1953; *Beauty*
    and the Beast, 1946.
b. Feb 15, 1899 in Lodeve, France
d. Jul 23, 1983 in Paris, France
Source: *Baker 78; DcFM; FilmgC; IntWW*
80, 81, 82; NewEOp 71; OxFilm,; OxMus;
REn,; Who 74, 82; WhoWor 74; WorEFlm,

Auriol, Jacqueline Douet
French. Aviatrix
First woman test pilot; second woman to
    break sound barrier.
b. Nov 5, 1917 in Challans, France
Source: *CurBio 53; HerW; InSci; InWom;*
WhoAmW 68, 75; WhoWor 74

Auriol, Vincent
French. Political Leader
Socialist Party leader; first pres. of Fourth
    Republic, 1947-54.
b. Aug 25, 1884 in Revel, France
d. Jan 1, 1966 in Paris, France
Source: *CurBio 47, 66; WhAm 4*

Auslander, Audrey May Wurdemann
see: Wurdemann, Audrey May

Auslander, Joseph
American. Author, Poet
Wrote popular history of poetry, *The Winged Horse*, 1927.
b. Oct 11, 1897 in Philadelphia, Pennsylvania
d. Jun 22, 1965 in Coral Gables, Florida
Source: *AmAu&B; CnDAL; OxAmL; REn; REnAL; TwCA, SUP; WhNAA*

Austen, Jane
English. Author
Wrote *Pride and Prejudice*, 1813.
b. Dec 16, 1775 in Steventon, England
d. Jul 18, 1817 in Winchester, England
Source: *Alli; AtlBL; BbD; BiD&SB; BrAu 19; CasWL; Chambr 2; CrtT 2; CyWA; DcBiA; DcEnA; DcEnL; DcEuL; DcLEL; EvLB; HerW; InWom; MouLC 2; NewC; OxEng; PenC ENG; RAdv 1; RComWL; REn; WebE&AL*

Austin, Alfred
English. Poet, Author, Critic
Poet laureate, 1896; wrote *The Human Tragedy*, 1862.
b. May 30, 1835 in Headingley, England
d. Jun 2, 1913 in Ashford, England
Source: *Alli SUP; BbD; BiD&SB; BrAu 19; Chambr 3; DcEnA, AP; DcEnL; DcEuL; DcLEL; EvLB; LinLib L, S; LongCTC; NewC; OxEng; PenC ENG; TwCWr*

Austin, Gene
American. Actor, Songwriter
Songs include "How Come You Do Me Like You Do?" 1924; "Lonesome Road," 1928.
b. Jun 24, 1900 in Gainesville, Texas
d. Jan 24, 1972 in Palm Springs, California
Source: *AmPS A, B; AmSCAP 66; BiDAmM; CmpEPM; NewYTBE 72; ObitOF 79; WhScrn 77; WhoHol B*

Austin, Herbert
English. Auto Manufacturer
Started Austin Motorcars, 1905.
b. Nov 8, 1866 in Missenden, England
d. May 23, 1941 in Bromsgrove, England
Source: *BioIn 12; WebBD 80*

Austin, John Langshaw
English. Philosopher
Wrote *How to do Things with Words*, 1962.
b. Mar 26, 1911 in Lancaster, England
d. Feb 8, 1960 in Oxford, England
Source: *ConAu 112; DcNaB 1951; LongCTC; OxEng; WhAm 4*

Austin, John Paul
American. Business Executive
Coca-Cola exec., 1962-81; added Tab, Sprite, raising sales to $5 billion.
b. Feb 14, 1915 in LaGrange, Georgia
d. Dec 1985 in Atlanta, Georgia
Source: *BlueB 76; CelR; St&PR 75; WhoAm 74, 76, 78, 80, 82; WhoF&I 74, 75; WhoS&SW 73, 80, 82*

Austin, Mary Hunter
American. Author
Described American Indian life, literature: *Land of Little Rain*, 1903.
b. Sep 9, 1868 in Carlinville, Illinois
d. Aug 13, 1934 in Santa Fe, New Mexico
Source: *AmAu&B; AmBi; AmLY; AnCL; BiCAW; BkCL; CnDAL; ConAmA; ConAmL; DcAmAu; DcLEL; DcNAA; InWom; NotAW; OxAmL; REnAL; Str&VC; TwCA, SUP; WebAB; WhAm 1; WhNAA*

Austin, Patti
American. Singer
With James Ingram, had hit single "Baby Come to Me," 1982, love theme for soap opera "General Hospital."
b. Aug 10, 1948 in New York, New York
Source: *RkOn 85*

Austin, Stephen Fuller
American. Colonizer
Established Austin, TX, 1822, first American settlement in TX.
b. Nov 3, 1793 in Austinville, Virginia
d. Dec 27, 1836 in Austin, Texas
Source: *AmAu&B; AmBi; ApCAB; DcAmB; Drake; EncAB-H; EncSoH; HarEnUS; McGEWB; NatCAB 6; OxAmH; REnAW; TwCBDA; WebAB, 79; WhAm HS; WhAmP*

Austin, Tracy Ann
American. Tennis Player
Youngest player to crack million dollar prize money barrier.
b. Dec 12, 1962 in Rolling Hills, California
Source: *BioIn 10; BkPepl; CurBio 81; GoodHs; NewYTBS 80, 81; WhoAm 82; WhoAmW 81; WorAl*

Austin, Warren R(obinson)
American. Statesman, Government Official
Rep. senator from VT; first US ambassador to UN, 1946-53.
b. Nov 12, 1877 in Highgate, Vermont
d. Dec 25, 1962
Source: *BiDrAC; CurBio 44, 63; DcAmB S7; WhAm 4; WhAmP*

Austral, Florence Wilson
Australian. Opera Singer
b. Apr 26, 1894 in Melbourne, Australia
d. May 15, 1968 in Sydney, Australia
Source: *InWom; ObitT 1961*

Autori, Franco
Italian. Conductor
b. Nov 29, 1903 in Naples, Italy
Source: *WhoAm 74*

Autry, Gene (Orvon Gene)
"The Singing Cowboy"
American. Actor, Singer, Baseball Executive
Wrote over 250 songs including "Here
   Comes Santa Claus"; owner, CA Angels
   baseball team.
b. Sep 29, 1907 in Tioga, Texas
Source: *AmSCAP 66; CmCal; CmMov;
CmpEPM; CurBio 47; EncFCWM 69;
FilmgC; IntMPA 80, 81, 82; MotPP; MovMk;
NewYTET; OxFilm; WhoAm 80, 82; WhoHol
A; WhoProB 73; WorAl; WorEFlm*

Avakian, George
American. Music Critic
Jazz critic, columnist, 1938-50.
b. Mar 15, 1919 in Amavir, U.S.S.R.
Source: *WhoWor 74*

Avallone, Michael Angelo, Jr.
American. Author
Wrote over 1,000 paperbacks under dozens of
   pseuds.; created sleuth Ed Noon.
b. Oct 27, 1924 in New York, New York
Source: *Au&Wr 71; ConAu 4NR, 5R;
EncMys; WhoAm 82, 84; WrDr 76*

Avalon, Frankie
[Francis Thomas Avalone]
American. Actor, Singer, Entertainer
Teen idol, 1960s; starred with Annette
   Funicello in *Beach* movies.
b. Sep 18, 1940 in Philadelphia, Pennsylvania
Source: *ConTFT 3; FilmgC; IntMPA 82;
MotPP; MovMk; WhoHol A*

Avedon, Doe
American. Actress
Films include *High and the Mighty*, 1954;
   Deep in My Heart, 1954.
b. 1925 in Old Westbury, New York
Source: *FilmgC; InWom; IntMPA 75, 76, 77,
81, 82; WhoHol A*

Avedon, Richard
American. Photographer
One of world's greatest photographers
   credited with making fashion photography
   art form.
b. May 15, 1923 in New York, New York
Source: *BlueB 76; BnEnAmA; CelR; ConPhot;
CurBio 75; IntWW 80, 81, 82; WhoAm 80,
80, 82, 82; WhoAmA 80, 82; WhoWor 74;
WorFshn; WrDr 82*

Average White Band
[Roger Ball; Malcolm Duncan; Steven
   Ferrone; Alan Gorrie; Onnie McIntire;
   Robbie McIntosh; Michael Rosen;
   Hamish Stuart]
English. Music Group
Formed 1972; best-selling album *Cut the
   Cake, 1975.*
Source: *IlEncBM 82; IlEncRk; RkOn 74;
RolSEnR 83*

Averback, Hy
American. Director, Producer
Directed *Where Were You When the Lights
   Went Out?; Suppose They Gave A War
   and Nobody Came?*
b. 1925
Source: *FilmEn; FilmgC; NewYTET; VarWW
85*

Averill, Earl (Howard Earl)
"Earl of Snohomish"
American. Baseball Player
Outfielder, 1929-41; career batting average of
   .318; Hall of Fame, 1975.
b. May 21, 1902 in Snohmish, Washington
d. Aug 16, 1983 in Everett, Washington
Source: *BaseEn 85; BasesB; NewYTBS 83*

Averroes
Spanish. Philosopher
Doctrine "Universal Reason," denying man's
   immortality condemned by pope.
b. 1126 in Cordova, Spain
d. 1198
Source: *BbD; BiD&SB; CasWL; DcEuL;
DcOrL 3; EuAu; EvEuW; LinLib L, S;
McGEWB; OxEng; REn*

Avery, Milton (Clark)
American. Artist
Works influenced by Matisse; known as
   pioneer in American abstractionism.
b. Mar 7, 1893 in Altmar, New York
d. Jan 3, 1965 in New York, New York
Source: *CurBio 58, 65; DcCAA 71; WhAm 4*

Avery, R Stanton
American. Businessman
Began self-adhesive labels co., 1932; annual
  sales over $600 million, 1980.
b. 1907 in Oklahoma City, Oklahoma
Source: *Dun&B 79; Entr; St&PR 84*

Avery, Sewell
American. Retailer
Served on board of Montgomery Ward, 1931-
  56.
b. Nov 4, 1874 in Saginaw, Michigan
d. Oct 31, 1960 in Chicago, Illinois
Source: *CurBio 44, 61*

Avery, "Tex" (Frederick Bean)
American. Cartoonist
Developed Daffy Duck, Bugs Bunny; made
  animated TV commercials.
b. Feb 26, 1908 in Taylor, Texas
d. Aug 27, 1980 in Burbank, California
Source: *AnObit 1980; BioIn 11; FilmEn;
FilmgC; PseudN 82; WorEFlm*

Avicenna (Ibn Sina)
[Ebne Sina]
Arabian. Physician, Philosopher
His textbook *Canon of Medicine* studied for
  centuries in European universities.
b. 980 in Afshana, Arabia
d. Jun 1037 in Hamaden, Persia
Source: *BiD&SB; CasWL; DcOrL 3; OxEng;
PenC CL; REn*

Avila, Bobby (Roberto Francisco Gonzalez)
"Beto"
Mexican. Baseball Player
Infielder, 1949-59, who won AL batting title,
  1954.
b. Apr 2, 1924 in Vera Cruz, Mexico
Source: *BaseEn 85; WhoProB 73*

Avirett, John Williams, II
American. Lawyer
b. May 13, 1902 in Cumberland, Maryland
Source: *WhoAm 74, 76, 78, 80, 82*

Avogadro, Amedeo, Conte di Quaregna
Italian. Physicist
Best known for coining word "molecule,"
  distinquishing it from atom.
b. Jun 9, 1776 in Turin, Italy
d. Jul 9, 1856 in Turin, Italy
Source: *AsBiEn; McGEWB; NewCol 75*

Avon, Robert Anthony Eden, Earl
see: Eden, Anthony

Awtrey, Dennis
American. Basketball Player
Member, NBA championship team, Seattle
  Supersonics, 1979.
b. Feb 22, 1948 in Hollywood, California
Source: *OfNBA 81; WhoBbl 73*

Axelrod, George
American. Dramatist
Wrote plays *The Seven Year Itch,* 1956;
  Breakfast at Tiffany's. 1962.
b. Jun 9, 1922 in New York, New York
Source: *AmAu&B; BiDFilm; BiE&WWA;
CmMov; CnMD; ConAu 65; ConDr 73;
FilmgC; IntMPA 80, 81, 82; McGEWD;
ModAL; NotNAT; OxFilm; WhoAm 74;
WorAu; WorEFlm; WrDr 76*

Axelson, Kenneth Strong
American. Corporation Executive
Director, JC Penny Life Insurance Co.,
  1967--.
b. Jul 31, 1922 in Chicago, Illinois
Source: *St&PR 75; WhoAm 74; WhoF&I 74;
WhoWor 78*

Axis Sally
[Mildred Elizabeth Gillars]
American. Traitor
b. 1900
Source: *BioIn 9*

Axthelm, Pete(r Macrae)
American. Journalist
Sportswriter, *Newsweek,* since 1968; NBC
  sports commentator, 1980-86.
b. Aug 27, 1943 in New York, New York
Source: *ConAu 107; WhoAm 80, 82, 84*

Axton, Hoyt Wayne
American. Singer, Songwriter, Actor
Country music singer who has sold over 25
  million records in 20-yr. career.
b. Mar 25, 1938 in Duncan, Oklahoma
Source: *ConTFT 3; RkOn 78; WhoAm 84*

Ayckbourn, Alan
English. Dramatist, Director
England's Neil Simon, whose comedies
  include *Joking Apart,* 1979.
b. Apr 12, 1939 in London, England
Source: *ConAu 21R; ConLC 5, 18; CurBio
80; IntWW 79, 82; Who 85*

Ayer, Alfred Jules
English. Author, Philosopher, Educator
Advocate of logical positivism who wrote
  Language, Truth, and Logic, 1936.
b. Oct 29, 1910 in London, England
Source: *ConAu 5R, 5NR; DcLEL; IntWW 74;
LongCTC; OxEng; REn; Who 74; WhoWor
74; WorAu; WrDr 76*

Ayer, Francis Wayland
American. Advertising Executive
Pioneered use of trademarks, slogans in
  advertising.
b. Feb 4, 1848 in Lee, Massachusetts
d. Mar 5, 1923 in Camden, New Jersey
Source: *AmBi; DcAmB; WebAB, 79; WorAl*

Ayer, Harriet Hubbard
American. Journalist, Business Executive
Manufactured facial creams, 1886; wrote
  popular newspaper column on beauty
  advice.
b. Jun 27, 1849 in Chicago, Illinois
d. Nov 23, 1903 in New York, New York
Source: *NotAW*

Ayesha
"Mother of the Believers"
Celebrity Relative
Daughter of Abu-Bakr; second wife of
  Mohammad.
b. 614 in Medina, Arabia
d. 678
Source: *DcBiPP; InWom; LinLib S; NewC;
NewCol 75*

Aykroyd, Dan(iel Edward)
Canadian. Actor, Comedian, Writer
Star of "Saturday Night Live," 1975-79; won
  Emmy, 1976; in films *The Blues Brothers,*
  1980; *Ghostbusters,* 1984.
b. Jul 1, 1952 in Ottawa, Ontario
Source: *BioIn 12; WhoAm 80, 82*

Aylward, Gladys
"The Small Woman"
English. Missionary
Film *The Inn of Sixth Happiness,* 1958,
  based on her life in China, 1932-48.
b. 1902 in London, England
d. Jan 3, 1970 in Taipei, Taiwan
Source: *BioIn 6, 7, 8, 9, 10, 11; ObitOF 79;
ObitT 1961; WhDW*

Aymar, Gordon Christian
American. Artist, Art Director
b. Jul 24, 1893 in East Orange, New Jersey
Source: *Au&Wr 71; ConAu 5R; WhoAm 74;
WhoAmA 73; WrDr 80*

Ayme, Marcel
French. Author
Wrote *The Hollow Field,* 1933; *The
  Conscience of Love,* 1962.
b. Mar 28, 1902 in Joigny, France
d. Oct 14, 1967 in Paris, France
Source: *BiE&WWA; CasWL; ClDMEL;
CnMD; CnThe; ConAu 89; ConLC 11;
EncWL; EvEuW; LongCTC; McGEWD;
ModRL; ModWD; OxFr; PenC EUR; REn;
TwCA SUP; TwCWr; WhAm 4A*

Ayres, Agnes
[Agnes Hinkle]
American. Actress
Starred with Rudolph Valentino in *The
  Sheik,* 1921.
b. Sep 4, 1898 in Carbondale, Illinois
d. Dec 25, 1940 in Los Angeles, California
Source: *CurBio 41; Film 1; FilmgC; InWom;
MotPP; ObitOF 79; TwYS; WhScrn 74, 77;
WhoHol B*

Ayres, Lew
American. Actor, Musician, Director,
  Producer
Starred in *All Quiet on the Western Front,*
  1930; first actor to register as
  conscientious objector, WW II.
b. Dec 28, 1908 in Minneapolis, Minnesota
Source: *BiDFilm; ConTFT 3; FilmEn; Film 2;
FilmgC; IntMPA 82; MotPP; MovMk;
OxFilm; WhoAm 84; WhoHol A; WorEFlm*

Ayres, Ruby Mildred
English. Author
Wrote popular romances: *Old-Fashioned
  Heart,* 1953.
b. Jan 1883
d. Nov 14, 1955 in Surrey, England
Source: *ConAu 117; TwCRGW*

Aytoun, William Edmonstoune
Scottish. Author, Educator
Popular *Blackwood* contributor; wrote
  Firmilian, 1854.
b. Jun 21, 1813 in Edinburgh, Scotland
d. Aug 4, 1865 in Elgin, Scotland
Source: *BrAu 19; OxEng 85*

Ayub Khan, Mohammad
Pakistani. Political Leader
Pres., of Pakistan, 1962-69; wrote *Friends
  Not Masters: A Political Autobiography,*
  1967.
b. May 14, 1907 in Rehana, Pakistan
d. Apr 19, 1974
Source: *ConAu 21R, P-2; CurBio 59, 74;
Who 74; WhoWor 78*

Azikiwe, Nnamdi
[Zik Azikiwe]
"Father of Modern Nigerian Nationalism"
Nigerian. President
First head of independent Nigeria, 1963;
  overthrown by military coup, 1966.
b. Nov 16, 1904 in Zungeri, Nigeria
Source: *AfSS 80, 81, 82; AfrA; CurBio 57;
IntAu&W 77; IntWW 78; IntWWP 82; IntYB
79, 80, 81, 82; McGEWB; PseudN 82;
WhDW; WhE&EA; Who 82*

Aziz, Philip John Andrew Ferris
Canadian. Artist
Uses egg tempura technique for portraiture,
  liturgical themes.
b. Apr 15, 1923 in Saint Thomas, Ontario
Source: *CanWW 70, 79; WhoWor 74*

Aznavour, Charles
[Shahnour Varenagh Aznavourian]
French. Singer, Actor
Diminutive, foggy-voiced singer who gained
  fame, 1950s; most memorable film *Shoot
  the Piano Player*, 1950.
b. May 22, 1924 in Paris, France
Source: *CelR; CurBio 68; FilmEn; IntWW
74; MovMk; OxFilm; WhoHol A; WhoWor
78; WorEFlm*

Azuela, Mariano
Mexican. Author
Writings depict Mexican society; *The
  Underdogs*, 1929, describes 1910
  Revolution.
b. Jan 1, 1873 in Logos de Morena, Mexico
d. Mar 1, 1952 in Mexico City, Mexico
Source: *CasWL; ConAu 104; CyWA; DcSpL;
EncWL; PenC AM; REn; TwCWr; WhNAA;
WorAu*

B

B-52's
[Kate Pierson; Fred Schneider; Keith
Strickland; Cindy Wilson; Ricky Wilson]
American. Music Group
Formed 1976; known for party music with
50s, 60s vocals, lyrics; debut album *Wild
Planet,* 1980.
Source: *RolSEnR 83; WhoRock 81*

Babbage, Charles
English. Mathematician, Inventor
Tried to perfect mechanical calculating
machine, foreshadowing computer.
b. Dec 26, 1792 in Totnes, England
d. Oct 18, 1871 in London, England
Source: *Alli SUP; AsBiEn; BiD&SB; BrAu;
CelCen; DcBiPP; DcEnL; DcScB; Dis&D;
InSci; McGEWB; NewCol 75; OxMus; WorAl*

Baader, Andreas
German. Terrorist, Revolutionary
b. 1943 in Munich, Germany
d. Oct 18, 1977 in Stuttgart, Germany
Source: *BioIn 9, 10, 11*

Ba'al Shem Tov, Israel
[Israel ben Eliezer]
Polish. Religious Leader
Founded modern Hasidism, a mystical
interpretaion of Judaism.
b. 1700 in Akopy, Poland
d. 1760 in Mezshbozsh, Poland
Source: *CasWL; EncO&P 78; IlEncMy;
LinLib L; McGEWB; NewC; WorAl*

Babashoff, Shirley
American. Swimmer
Won gold medals in swimming relay, 1972,
1976 Olympics.
b. Jan 31, 1957 in Whittier, California
Source: *BioIn 10; GoodHs*

Babb, Howard Selden
American. Author
Wrote *Jane Austen's Novels,* 1962; *The Novels
of William Golding,* 1970.
b. May 14, 1924 in Portland, Maine
Source: *ConAu 13R; DrAS 74E; WhoAm 74*

Babbitt, Benjamin Talbot
American. Manufacturer, Inventor
Made one of first baking powders; obtained
many patents for soap.
b. 1809 in Westmoreland, New York
d. Oct 20, 1889 in New York, New York
Source: *DcAmB; NatCAB 8; WhAm HS*

Babbitt, Bruce Edward
American. Political Leader, Author
Dem. governor of AZ, 1977--; has written
two books on AZ art, culture.
b. Jun 27, 1938 in Los Angeles, California
Source: *AlmAP 80; BiDrGov; ConAu 97;
NewYTBS 79; WhoAm 84; WhoAmP 79;
WhoWest 80*

Babbitt, Irving
American. Author, Critic
A leader of new humanism; wrote *Masters of
Modern French Criticism,* 1912.
b. Aug 2, 1865 in Dayton, Ohio
d. Jul 15, 1933 in Cambridge, Massachusetts
Source: *AmAu&B; AmBi; AmLY; CasWL;
CnDAL; ConAmA; ConAmL; DcAmB S1;
DcLEL; DcNAA; EncAB-H; LongCTC;
ModAL; NatCAB 23; OhA&B; OxAmH;
OxAmL; OxEng; PenC AM; REn; REnAL;
TwCA, SUP; WebAB, 79; WebE&AL; WhAm
1; WhoTwCL*

Babbitt, Milton Byron
American. Composer
First composer to work on RCA's Mark II
   synthesizer; wrote *Compositionn for
   Synthesizer,* 1961.
b. May 10, 1916 in Philadelphia,
   Pennsylvania
Source: *Baker 78; BiDAmM; BlueB 76;
CpmDNM 81; CurBio 62; DcCM; MakMC;
McGEWB; OxMus; WebAB; WhoAm 82, 84;
WhoMus 72; WhoWor 74*

Babcock, Stephen Moulton
American. Scientist
Agricultural chemist who developed test for
   butterfat content in milk; pioneered in
   research which led to discovery of vitamin
   A.
b. Oct 22, 1843 in Bridgewater, New York
d. Jul 2, 1931 in Madison, Wisconsin
Source: *AmBi; BiDAmS; DcAmB S1; DcNAA;
DcScB; EncAAH; InSci; LinLib S; McGEWB;
NatCAB 22; WebAB 79; WhAm 1*

Babel, Isaac Emmanuelovich
Russian. Author, Dramatist
Short stories collected in *Jewish Tales,* 1927;
   disappeared into concentration camp, 1939.
b. 1894 in Odessa, Russia
d. 1941 in Siberia, U.S.S.R.
Source: *AtlBL; CasWL; ClDMEL; CnMD;
CnMWL; ConAu 104; DcRusL; EvEuW;
LinLib L, S; LongCTC; McGEWB;
McGEWD; ModSL 1; ModWD; PenC EUR;
REn; TwCA, SUP; TwCWr; WhoTwCL*

Baber
see: Babur

Babeuf, Francois Noel
[Caius Gracchus]
French. Revolutionary
Founded system of communism called
   baboeuvism.
b. Nov 25, 1760 in Saint-Quentin, France
d. Apr 27, 1797 in Paris, France
Source: *BiD&SB; McGEWB; OxFr; REn*

Babilonia, Tai Reina
[Babilonia and Gardner]
American. Figure Skater
Failed in bid for Olympic gold medal, 1980,
   when partner Randy Gardner was injured.
b. Sep 22, 1960 in Sherman Oaks, California
Source: *BioIn 12; NewYTBS 79*

Babin, Victor
[Vronsky and Babin]
American. Pianist
Formed two-piano team with wife Vitya
   Vronsky, 1933.
b. Dec 12, 1908 in Moscow, Russia
d. Mar 1, 1972 in Cleveland, Ohio
Source: *AmSCAP 66, 80; Baker 78;
BiDAmM; NewYTBE 72; WhoMus 72;
WhoWorJ 72, 78*

Babiuch, Edward
Polish. Political Leader
Deputy chair, State Council, 1976-80.
b. Dec 28, 1927 in Katowice Voivodship,
   Poland
Source: *IntWW 79, 80, 81, 82; NewYTBS 80;
WhoSocC 78; WhoWor 74, 76, 78*

Babur
[Zahir un-Din Muhammad]
Turkish. Military Leader
Descendant of Genghis Khan who was
   founder, first ruler of Mogul empire.
b. Feb 14, 1483 in Farghana, Turkey
d. Dec 26, 1530 in Agra, India
Source: *CasWL; DcOrL 3; McGEWB;
WhoMilH 76*

Baby Leroy
[Leroy Winebrenner]
American. Actor
Hollywood toddler who appeared in *Bedtime
   Story,* 1933; retired at age four.
b. May 12, 1932 in Los Angeles, California
Source: *FilmEn; MotPP; WhoHol A*

Babys, The
[Tony Brock; Jonathan Cain; Mike Corby;
   Ricky Phillips; Wally Stocker; John Waite]
English. Music Group
Power pop group, 1976-81; hits include "Isn't
   It Time"; "Head First."
Source: *ConMuA 80A; RkOn 78; RolSEnR
83; WhoRock 81*

Bacall, Lauren
[Betty Joan Perske]
American. Actress, Author
Married Humphrey Bogart, 1945; won Tonys,
   1970, 1981, for *Applause* and *Woman of
   the Year.*
b. Sep 16, 1924 in New York, New York
Source: *BiDFilm; BiE&WWA; BkPepl; CelR;
CmMov; ConAu 93; CurBio 70; EncMT;
FilmgC; GoodHs; IntMPA 80, 81, 82; IntWW
80, 81; MotPP; MovMk; NewYTBE 70;
NewYTBS 79, 80; NotNAT; OxFilm; WhoAm
80, 82; WhoAmW 79; WhoHol A; WhoThe
72, 77, 81; WhoWor 78; WorEFlm*

Bacardi, Don Facundo
Spanish. Merchant
Started world's largest rum co., 1862.
b. 1816
d. 1886
Source: *Entr*

Baccaloni, Salvatore
Italian. Opera Singer
Regarded as greatest comic bass since Luigi
  Lablache.
b. Apr 14, 1900 in Rome, Italy
d. Dec 31, 1969 in New York, New York
Source: *CurBio 44, 70, 71; FilmgC;
NewYTBE 70; WhAm 5; WhScrn 74, 77;
WhoHol B*

Bacchelli, Riccardo
Italian. Author
Best known for historical novels: *Il Mulino
  del Po*, 1938.
b. Apr 19, 1891 in Bologna, Italy
d. Oct 8, 1985 in Monza, Italy
Source: *CasWL; ClDMEL; CnMD; ConAu
117, 29R; ConLC 19; CyWA; DcItL; EncWL,
2; EvEuW; IntAu&W 77; IntWW 81, 82, 84;
ModRL; Novels; PenC EUR; REn; TwCWr;
WhoWor 74; WorAu*

Bach, Barbara
[Barbara Goldbach; Mrs. Ringo Starr]
American. Actress
Married Ringo Starr, 1981, after starring
  together in movie *Caveman*.
b. Aug 27, 1947 in New York, New York
Source: *BioIn 11; VarWW 85*

Bach, Bert Coates
American. Author
Wrote *Fiction for Composition*, 1968; *Drama
  for Composition*, 1973.
b. Dec 14, 1936 in Jenkins, Kentucky
Source: *ConAu 21R; DrAS 82E; WhoAm 84;
WhoS&SW 80, 82*

Bach, Carl Philipp Emanuel
German. Composer
Wrote first systematic study on how to play
  the clavier.
b. Mar 8, 1714 in Weimar, Germany
d. Dec 15, 1788 in Hamburg, Germany
Source: *AtlBL; DcBiPP; WhDW; WorAl*

Bach, Catherine
[Catherine Bachman]
American. Actress
Played Daisy Duke on TV series "The
  Dukes of Hazzard," 1979-85.
b. Mar 1, 1954 in Warren, Ohio
Source: *BioIn 12; VarWW 85*

Bach, Johann Christian
"The English Bach"
German. Composer, Organist
Composed operas, symphonies; taught music
  to royal family, 1759-82.
b. Sep 3, 1735 in Leipzig, Germany
d. Jan 1, 1782 in London, England
Source: *AtlBL; WhDW; WorAl*

Bach, Johann Sebastian
German. Composer, Organist
Composed church, vocal, instrumental music,
  including "Goldberg Variations," 1722.
b. Mar 21, 1685 in Eisenach, Germany
d. Jul 28, 1750 in Leipzig, Germany
Source: *AtlBL; Baker 78; DcBiPP; Dis&D;
LinLib S; LuthC 75; McGEWB; NewC;
NewCol 75; OxGer; OxMus; REn; WorAl*

Bach, Richard David
American. Author
Wrote allegorical novel *Jonathan Livingston
  Seagull*; filmed, 1973.
b. Jun 23, 1936 in Oak Park, Illinois
Source: *AuNews 1; BioNews 74; ConAu 9R;
ConLC 14; CurBio 73; EncO&P 78S1; Novels;
ScF&FL 1, 2; SmATA 13; WhoAm 76, 78,
80; WrDr 76, 80*

Bach, Wilhelm Friedemann
German. Composer, Organist
Eldest son of Johann Sebastian Bach;
  important musician, but died poor, led
  unstable life.
b. 1710 in Weimar, Germany
d. Jul 1784 in Berlin, Germany
Source: *DcBiPP; LuthC 75; OxMus*

Bacharach, Bert(ram Mark)
American. Journalist, Author
Father of Burt Bacharach; had syndicated
  column, "Now See Here!", 1959-83.
b. Mar 10, 1898 in Philadelphia,
  Pennsylvania
d. Sep 15, 1983 in New York, New York
Source: *CelR; ConAu 110; CurBio 57, 83;
NewYTBS 83*

Bacharach, Burt
American. Composer, Musician, Conductor
Won best song Oscar, 1970, for "Raindrops
  Keep Fallin' on My Head," from *Butch
  Cassidy and the Sundance Kid*.
b. May 12, 1929 in Kansas City, Missouri
Source: *AmPS; AmSCAP 80; Baker 78;
BiDAmM; BlueB 76; BkPepl; CelR; ConTFT
3; CurBio 70; EncMT; FilmgC; NewCol 75;
NewCBMT; NotNAT; WebAB 79; WhoAm 84*

Bachauer, Gina
Greek. Musician
Concert pianist; made US debut, 1950, NYC.
b. May 21, 1913 in Athens, Greece
d. Aug 22, 1976 in Athens, Greece
Source: *BlueB 76; CelR; CurBio 54; IntWW 74; ObitOF 79; WhAm 7; Who 74; WhoWor 74*

Bache, Harold Leopold
American. Businessman, Philanthropist
Broker, chief exec., J S Bache & Co., 1945-68.
b. Jun 17, 1894 in New York, New York
d. Mar 14, 1968 in New York, New York
Source: *CurBio 59; ObitOF 79; WhAm 5*

Bache, Jules Sermon
American. Financier
Head of J S Bache & Co., 1892-1945.
b. Nov 9, 1861 in New York, New York
d. Mar 24, 1944 in Palm Beach, Florida
Source: *CurBio 44; DcAmB S3; ObitOF 79; WhAm 2*

Bacheller, Irving
American. Author
Wrote *Eben Holden,* 1900.
b. Aug 12, 1859 in Pierpont, New York
d. Feb 24, 1950 in White Plains, New York
Source: *AmAu&B; BiD&SB; Chambr 3; ConAmL; DcAmAu; DcAmB S4; DcBiA; DcLEL; JBA 34; OxAmL; REn; TwCA SUP; WhAm 2*

Bachman, John
American. Naturalist, Minister
Collaborated with Audubon on *Viviparous Quadrupeds of N America,* 1845-59.
b. Feb 4, 1790 in Rhinebeck, New York
d. Feb 24, 1874
Source: *CelCen; DcBiPP; HarEnUS; InSci; LuthC 75; NewCol 75; OxAmH*

Bachman, Randy
[Bachman-Turner Overdrive; Guess Who]
Canadian. Singer, Musician
Guitarist; co-founded Guess Who, 1963, Bachman-Turner Overdrive, 1972.
b. Sep 27, 1943 in Winnipeg, Manitoba
Source: *NF*

Bachman-Turner Overdrive
[Chad Allen; Randy Bachman; Robin Bachman; Timothy Bachman; Jim Clench; Blair Thornton; C F Turner]
Canadian. Music Group
Heavy-metal group with blue-collar image, 1972-79; hits include "You Ain't Seen Nothin' Yet."
Source: *IlEncRk; RolSEnR 83*

Backe, John David
American. TV Executive
Pres., CBS, Inc, 1976-80.
b. Jul 5, 1932 in Akron, Ohio
Source: *BioIn 11; CurBio 78; Dun&B 79; IntWW 79, 80, 81, 82; NewYTBS 76, 77; NewYTET; St&PR 75; WhoAm 78, 80, 82; WhoE 74, 81; WhoF&I 79*

Backhaus, Wilhelm
German. Musician
Concert pianist who toured Europe, US, Australia, Japan, S America, 1905-69.
b. Mar 26, 1884 in Leipzig, Germany
d. Jul 5, 1969 in Villach, Austria
Source: *ObitOF 79; ObitT 1961; WhDW; WhAm 5*

Backus, Isaac
American. Clergyman, Author
Baptist minister who was staunch advocate of religious freedom; wrote *History of New England,* 1777-96.
b. Jan 9, 1724 in Norwich, Connecticut
d. Nov 20, 1806 in Middleborough, Connecticut
Source: *AmBi; ApCAB; DcAmAu; DcAmB; DcAmReB; DcNAA; Drake; McGEWB; NatCAB 7; OxAmL; TwCBDA; WebAB 79; WhAm HS*

Backus, Jim (James Gilmore)
American. Actor, Author
Veteran stage, radio, vaudeville performer, known for voice of Mr. Magoo; role on TV's "Gilligan's Island," 1964-67.
b. Feb 25, 1913 in Cleveland, Ohio
Source: *CelR; FilmEn; FilmgC; IntMPA 76, 77, 78, 79, 80, 81, 82; MotPP; MovMk; WhoAm 74; WhoHol A*

Backus, John
American. Computer Scientist
Invented standard computer programming language, Fortran, 1957.
b. Dec 3, 1924 in Philadelphia, Pennsylvania
Source: *AmM&WS 79P; IntWW 77, 78; WhoAm 76, 78, 80, 82*

Baclanova, Olga
Russian. Actress
Starred in horror classic *Freaks,* 1932, playing trapeze artist married to midget.
b. Aug 19, 1899 in Moscow, Russia
d. Sep 6, 1974 in Vevey, Switzerland
Source: *FilmEn; Film 2; FilmgC; MotPP; NewYTBS 74; ObitOF 79; ThFT; TwYS; WhScrn 77; WhThe; WhoHol B*

Bacon, Delia Salter
American. Author
Developed theory that Shakespeare's plays
were written by Francis Bacon.
b. Feb 2, 1811 in Tallmadge, Ohio
d. Sep 2, 1859 in Hartford, Connecticut
Source: *NotAW; OxAmL 83*

Bacon, Francis, Sir
English. Statesman, Philosopher, Author
Advocate of inductive reasoning, who wrote
Novum Organum, 1620.
b. Jan 22, 1561 in London, England
d. Apr 9, 1626 in Highgate, England
Source: *AsBiEn; AtlBL; BbD; BiD&SB; BrAu;
CasWL; Chambr 1; CroE&S; CrtT 1, 4;
CyEd; CyWA; DcBiPP; DcEnA; DcEnL;
DcEuL; DcLEL; DcScB; Dis&D; EncSF;
EvLB; LinLib L, S; LongCEL; LuthC 75;
McGEWB; MouLC 1; NamesHP; NewC;
NewCol 75; OxEng; PenC ENG; RAdv 1;
RComWL; REn; WebE&AL*

Bacon, Francis
English. Artist
Self-taught modern artist whose permanent
exhibits are in NYC, other cities.
b. Oct 28, 1910 in Dublin, Ireland
Source: *IntWW 74; OxArt; OxTwCA; Who
74; WhoWor 74*

Bacon, Frank
American. Actor
Star, co-author of long-running play, *Lightin',*
1918.
b. Jan 16, 1864 in Marysville, California
d. Nov 19, 1922 in Chicago, Illinois
Source: *AmAu&B; AmBi; CmCal; DcAmB;
DcNAA; Film 1; ModWD; NatCAB 20;
NotNAT B; OxThe; REn; REnAL; WhAm 1;
WhScrn 74, 77; WhThe; WhoHol B*

Bacon, Henry
American. Architect
Best known as designer of Lincoln Memorial,
completed in 1917.
b. Nov 28, 1866 in Watseka, Illinois
d. Feb 16, 1924 in New York, New York
Source: *AmBi; DcAmB; WhAm 1*

Bacon, Kevin
American. Actor
Starred in films *Diner,* 1982; *Footloose,* 1984.
b. in Philadelphia, Pennsylvania
Source: *ConTFT 2*

Bacon, Nathaniel
American. Colonial Leader
Leader, Bacon's Rebellion in VA, 1676.
b. Jan 2, 1647 in Suffolk, England
d. Oct 1676 in Gloucester, Virginia
Source: *AmBi; DcAmB; EncAB 1; McGEWB;
NatCAB 5; REnAL; REnAW; WebAB;
WebAMB; WhAm HS*

Bacon, Peggy
American. Illustrator, Artist
Exhibitions include Smithsonian Institute,
1975-76; wrote, illustrated *The Good
American Witch,* 1957.
b. May 2, 1895 in Ridgefield, Connecticut
Source: *AmAu&B; ConAu 21R, P-2; ConICB;
CurBio 40; IlsBYP; IlsCB 1744, 1946, 1957;
OxAmL; REnAL; SmATA 2; Str&VC;
WhoAm 80, 82; WhoAmA 73*

Bacon, Roger
English. Philosopher, Scientist
Imprisoned great deal of life because
    discoveries were considered magic; greatest
    work *Opus Majus,* 1265.
b. 1214
d. 1294
Source: *Alli; BbD; BiD&SB; BrAu; CasWL;
Chambr 1; DcEnL; DcEuL; EvLB; NewC;
OxEng; PenC ENG; REn*

Bad Company
[Boz Burrell; Simon Kirke; Michael Ralphs;
    Paul Rodgers]
English. Music Group
Debut album *Bad Company,* 1974 was
    number one worldwide; hit singles include
    "Rock and Roll Fantasy."
Source: *IlEncRk; RolSEnR 83*

**Baddeley, Angela (Madeleine Angela
Clinton)**
English. Actress
Played Mrs. Bridges, the cook, in PBS TV
series "Upstairs Downstairs".
b. Jul 4, 1900 in London, England
d. Feb 22, 1976 in Essex, England
Source: *BlueB 76; FilmgC; ObitOF 79;
PIP&P; Who 74; WhoThe 77, 81N*

Baddeley, Hermione Clinton
English. Actress, Comedienne
Received Oscar nomination, 1959, for *Room
at the Top;* played the housekeeper on
"Maude," 1974-77.
b. Nov 13, 1906 in Broseley, England
d. Aug 19, 1986 in Los Angeles, California
Source: *BiE&WWA; EncMT; FilmEn;
IntMPA 80, 81, 82; MovMk; Who 74;
WhoAm 82; WhoHol A; WhoThe 81; WorAl*

Baden-Powell, Olave St. Claire, Lady
English. Social Reformer
Founded International Girl Scout Movement,
1909; wrote *Training Girls As Guides*,
1917.
b. Feb 22, 1889 in Chesterfield, England
d. Jun 26, 1977
Source: *BlueB 76; CurBio 46; InWom;*
IntWW 74, 78N; Who 74; WhoWor 74, 76

Baden-Powell, Robert Stephenson Smyth
Baden-Powell, Baron
English. Military Leader
Founded English Boy Scouts, 1908; conceived
idea when he took group of boys camping.
b. Feb 22, 1857 in London, England
d. Jan 8, 1941 in Nyeri, Kenya
Source: *Alli; CurBio 41; DcBrBI; EncE 75;*
EncSF; HarEnUS; LinLib L, S; LongCTC;
MnBBF; SmATA 16; SpyCS; WhDW; WhLit;
WhoChL; WhoLA; WhoMilH 76

Bader, Douglas Robert Steuart, Sir
"The Chap with the Tin Legs"
English. Air Force Officer
Legless pilot who shot down at least 22
German planes, WW II.
b. Feb 21, 1910 in London, England
d. Sep 5, 1982 in London, England
Source: *BioIn 3, 7; ConAu 107; HisEWW;*
NewYTBS 82; WhWW-II; Who 74, 75, 76,
77, 78, 79, 80, 81, 82

Badfinger
[Tom Evans; Mike Gibbons; Ronald Griffiths;
Peter Ham; Joey Molland]
English. Music Group
Liverpool quintet formed mid-60s-1975,
promoted by Beatles; hit album *Maybe*
Tomorrow, 1969.
Source: *ConMuA 80A; RkOn 78; RolSEnR*
83; WhoRock 81

Badillo, Herman
American. Politician
Pres., borough of Bronx, 1966-69; deputy
mayor for management, NYC, 1978-79.
b. Aug 21, 1929 in Caguas, Puerto Rico
Source: *CngDr 74; ConAu 85; CurBio 71;*
IntWW 74; NewYTBE 73; WhoAm 80, 82;
WhoAmP 73; WhoE 74; WhoGov 72

Badoglio, Pietro
Italian. Field Marshal
Led forces that defeated Austria, WW I;
prime minister, 1943-44.
b. Sep 28, 1871 in Montferrato, Italy
d. Oct 31, 1956
Source: *CurBio 40, 57; HisEWW; LinLib S;*
McGEWB; ObitOF 79; ObitT 1951; WhDW;
WhWW-II; WhoMilH 76

Badura-Skoda, Paul
Austrian. Musician
Concert pianist who debuted in Vienna, 1948;
wrote books on interpreting Mozart.
b. Jan 15, 1927 in Munich, Germany
Source: *IntWW 74; WhoAm 80, 82; WhoMus*
72; WhoWor 74

Baedeker, Karl
German. Publisher
Wrote travel books that did away with
formal tour guides.
b. Nov 3, 1801 in Essen, Germany
d. Oct 4, 1859 in Koblenz, Germany
Source: *NewC; REn; WhDW*

Baekeland, Leo Hendrick
American. Chemist, Inventor
Invented bakelite, which made impact on
plastic industry; Velox, photographic paper.
b. Nov 14, 1863 in Ghent, Belgium
d. Feb 23, 1944 in Beacon, New York
Source: *CurBio 44; DcAmB S3; WebAB;*
WhAm 2

Baer, "Bugs" (Arthur)
American. Journalist, Cartoonist
Staff writer, King Features, NYC, 1930-69;
known for comical sayings.
b. 1886 in Philadelphia, Pennsylvania
d. May 17, 1969 in New York, New York
Source: *REnAL; St&PR 75; WebAB; WhScrn*
77; WhoHol B

Baer, Max
American. Boxer, Actor
Heavyweight champ, 1934; starred in *The*
Prizefighter and the Lady, 1933.
b. Feb 11, 1909 in Omaha, Nebraska
d. Nov 21, 1959 in Hollywood, California
Source: *FilmgC; WhScrn 74, 77; WhoBox 74;*
WhoHol B

Baer, Max, Jr.
American. Actor, Producer, Director
Played Jethro Bodine on "The Beverly
Hillbillies," 1962-71.
b. Dec 4, 1937 in Oakland, California
Source: *WhoAm 82; WhoHol A*

Baez, Joan
American. Singer, Political Activist
Folk singer who founded Humanitas/
International Human Rights Committee,
1979.
b. Jan 9, 1941 in New York, New York
Source: *BioNews 74; BkPepl; CelR; ConAu*
21R; CurBio 63; EncFCWM 69; InWom;
WebAB; WhoAm 82; WhoWest 74

Baffin, William
English. Navigator
Expeditions in search of NW Passage led to
    discovery of Baffin Bay, 1612-14.
b. 1584 in England
d. Jan 23, 1622 in Qishm, Persia
Source: *Alli; ApCAB; BiD&SB; DcEnL;
Drake; NewC; OxCan*

Bagaza, Jean-Baptiste
Burundian. Political Leader
Pres., Republic of Burundi, 1976, who led
    coup against former pres., Micombero,
    Nov 1976.
b. Aug 29, 1946
Source: *IntWW 78; WhoWor 78*

Bagdasarian, Ross S
see: Seville, David

Bagdikian, Ben Haig
American. Author
Newspaper editor whose writings on poverty
    include *The Poor In America,* 1964.
b. Jun 30, 1920 in Marash, Turkey
Source: *AmAu&B; ConAu X, 6NR; WhoAm
74; WhoS&SW 82; WhoWor 78; WrDr 76*

Bagehot, Walter
English. Banker, Editor, Economist
Wrote *English Constitution,* 1867; *Literary
    Studies,* 1879.
b. Feb 3, 1826 in Langport, England
d. Mar 24, 1877 in Langport, England
Source: *AtlBL; BbD; BiD&SB; BrAu 19;
CasWL; Chambr 3; CrtT 3; DcEnA; DcEnL;
DcEuL; DcLEL; EvLB; NewC; OxEng; PenC
ENG; REn; WebE&AL*

Bagnold, Enid
[Lady Jones]
English. Author, Dramatist
Noted for novel *National Velvet,* 1935; prize-
    winning play *The Chalk Garden,* 1956.
b. Oct 27, 1889 in Rochester, England
d. Mar 31, 1981 in London, England
Source: *AuBYP; BiE&WWA; CnMD; ConAu
5R, 5NR, 103; ConDr 73; ConNov 76; CurBio
64, 81; DcLEL; EncWT; EvLB; FourBJA;
IntAu&W 76, 77; IntWW 78; LinLib L;
LongCTC; ModWD; NewC; NotNAT, A;
PIP&P; REn; SmATA 1; TwCA, SUP;
TwCWr; WhE&EA; Who 74; WhoThe 77;
WhoWor 76, 78; WrDr 76, 80*

Bagration, Petr Ivanovich
Russian. Military Leader
General who led campaigns against
    Napoleon; admired for courage at Battle of
    Friedland, 1807.
b. 1765 in Kizlar, Russia
d. Sep 24, 1812 in Borodino, Russia
Source: *CelCen; DcBiPP; NewCol 75;
WhoMilH 76; WorAl*

Baha'u'llah
[Mirza Husayn Ali Nuri]
Persian. Religious Leader
Founded Baha'i faith; writings revealed in
    over 100 volumes, 1853-92.
b. Nov 12, 1817 in Teheran, Persia
d. May 29, 1892 in Akka, Palestine
Source: *BioIn 10; CasWL; LinLib L; LuthC
75; WebBD 80*

Bailar, Benjamin Franklin
American. Government Official
Postmaster General, 1975-78.
b. Apr 21, 1934 in Champaign, Illinois
Source: *St&PR 75; WhoAm 80, 82*

Bailey, Alice A(nne La Trobe-Bateman)
English. Author
Occultist who wrote *Treatise on White
    Magic,* 1934.
b. 1880 in Manchester, England
d. 1949
Source: *ConAu 116; EncO&P 78*

Bailey, Charles Waldo, II
American. Newspaper Editor, Author
Wrote *No High Ground,* 1960; editor,
    Minneapolis *Tribune,* 1972--.
b. Apr 28, 1929 in Boston, Massachusetts
Source: *ConAu 1R, 1NR; WhoAm 74, 76, 78,
80, 82; WrDr 76*

Bailey, Donald Coleman, Sir
English. Engineer, Inventor
Invented Bailey Bridge to transport troops,
    tanks across rivers in WW II.
b. Sep 5, 1901 in Yorkshire, England
d. May 5, 1985 in Bournemouth, England
Source: *CurBio 85*

Bailey, Florence Augusta Merriam
American. Ornithologist, Author
Nature books include *Birds of Village and
    Field,* 1898.
b. Aug 8, 1863 in Locust Grove, New York
d. Sep 22, 1948 in Washington, District of
    Columbia
Source: *NotAW*

Bailey, F(rancis) Lee
American. Lawyer, Author
Partner, Bailey & Broder, NYC, who
defended Patty Hearst, 1976; wrote *The
Defense Never Rests,* 1972.
b. Jun 10, 1933 in Waltham, Massachusetts
Source: *ConAu 89; WhoAm 84; WhoE 74*

Bailey, Frederick Marshman
English. Explorer, Naturalist
Expedition mapping course of Tsangpo River
in Tibet recounted in *No Passport to Tibet,*
1957.
b. Feb 3, 1882 in Lahore, India
d. Apr 17, 1967 in Stiffkey, England
Source: *ConAu P-1; DcNaB 1961; GrBr;
ObitT 1961*

Bailey, H(enry) C(hristopher)
English. Author, Journalist
Created fictional detectives Reggie Fortune,
Joshua Clunk; wrote *Mr. Fortune's
Practice,* 1922.
b. Feb 1, 1878 in London, England
d. Mar 24, 1961
Source: *ConAu 108; EvLB; LongCTC; NewC;
TwCA, SUP; TwCCr&M 85; WhoLA*

Bailey, Jack
American. TV Host
Emceed for several game shows: "Queen for
a Day," "Truth or Consequences,"
"Joker's Wild."
d. Feb 1, 1980 in Santa Monica, California
Source: *BioIn 4, 12; NewYTET*

Bailey, James Anthony
[Barnum and Bailey]
American. Circus Owner
Founded "Greatest Show on Earth"; later
merged with P T Barnum, 1881.
b. Jul 4, 1847 in Detroit, Michigan
d. 1906 in Mount Vernon, New York
Source: *Alli, SUP; DcAmB; TwCBDA; WhAm
1*

Bailey, Kay
American. Public Official
b. 1944
Source: *WomPO 76*

Bailey, Martin Jean
American. Author
Wrote *National Income and the Price Level,*
1971; *The Taxation of Income from
Capital,* 1968.
b. Oct 17, 1927 in Taft, California
Source: *AmEA 74; AmM&WS 73S, 78S*

Bailey, Mildred
[Mildred Rinker]
American. Singer
Sang with Paul Whiteman, 1929-33; on radio
with Benny Goodman, 1939.
b. Feb 27, 1907 in Tekoa, Washington
d. Dec 12, 1951 in New York, New York
Source: *DcAmB S5; ObitOF 79; WhoJazz 72*

Bailey, Pearl Mae
American. Singer, Actress
Vaudeville, cabaret performer, best known for
starring role in Broadway musical *Hello
Dolly,* 1967-69.
b. Mar 28, 1918 in Newport News, Virginia
Source: *AmSCAP 66; BiE&WWA; CelR;
ConAu 61; CurBio 55, 69; EncMT; FilmgC;
HerW; InWom; IntMPA 75, 76, 77, 78, 79,
80, 81, 82; LivgBAA; MotPP; MovMk;
NewYTBE 71; NotNAT; WhoAm 74, 76, 78,
80, 82; WhoAmW 77; WhoBlA 75; WhoHol
A; WhoThe 77; WhoWor 78*

Bailey, Philip
[Earth, Wind, and Fire]
American. Singer, Musician
With Phil Collins, sang "Easy Lover," 1984.
b. May 8, 1951 in Denver, Colorado
Source: *RkOn 85*

Bailey, Raymond
American. Actor
Played Mr. Drysdale, the banker, in TV
series "The Beverly Hillbillies," 1962-69.
b. 1904 in San Francisco, California
d. Apr 15, 1980 in Irvine, California
Source: *FilmgC; WhoHol A*

Baillie, Hugh
American. Journalist
Influential war correspondent known for
interviews with General MacArthur, Hitler,
Mussolini, Emperor Hirohito.
b. Oct 23, 1890 in Brooklyn, New York
d. Mar 1, 1966 in La Jolla, California
Source: *ConAu 89; CurBio 46, 66; WhAm 4*

Bain, Barbara
American. Actress
Played Cinnamon Carter on TV series
"Mission Impossible," 1966-69.
b. Sep 13, 1932 in Chicago, Illinois
Source: *ConTFT 3; WhoAm 82; WhoAmW 74*

Bain, Conrad Stafford
Canadian. Actor
Starred in TV series "Maude," 1971-78;
founded Actors Federal Credit Union,
1962.
b. Feb 4, 1923 in Lethbridge, Ontario
Source: *BiE&WWA; NotNAT; WhoAm 82;
WhoHol A; WhoThe 77*

Bainbridge, Beryl
English. Author
Works include fantasy about Hitler, *Young
Adolphe,* 1978; prize-winning novel, *The
Bottle Factory Outing,* 1974.
b. Nov 21, 1933 in Liverpool, England
Source: *ConAu 21R; ConLC 4, 5, 8, 10, 14;
ConNov 76; IntAu&W 76, 77; WorAu 1970;
WrDr 76, 80*

Bainbridge, William
American. Naval Officer
Founded first US naval school at Boston
Navy Yard, 1815.
b. May 7, 1774 in Princeton, New Jersey
d. Jul 27, 1833 in Philadelphia, Pennsylvania
Source: *Alli, SUP; AmBi; ApCAB; DcAmB;
Drake; TwCBDA; WebAB; WhAm HS*

Baines, Harold Douglass
American. Baseball Player
Outfielder, Chicago White Sox, 1980--, who
led AL with 22 game-winning RBIs, 1983.
b. Mar 15, 1959 in Saint Michaels, Maryland
Source: *BaseEn 85*

Bainter, Fay Okell
American. Actress
Won Oscar for *Jezebel,* 1938.
b. Dec 7, 1891 in Los Angeles, California
d. Apr 16, 1968 in Hollywood, California
Source: *BiE&WWA; FilmgC; InWom; MGM;
MotPP; MovMk; ObitOF 79; ThFT; WhDW;
WhAm 5; WhScrn 74, 77; WhoHol B; WorAl*

Baio, Scott Vincent
American. Actor
Played Chachi on TV series "Happy Days,"
1977-82.
b. Sep 22, 1961 in Brooklyn, New York
Source: *BioIn 12; VarWW 85; WorAl*

Baird, Bil (William Britton)
American. Puppeteer
Founded Bil and Cora Baird Puppet Theatre,
Greenwich Village, 1966.
b. Aug 15, 1904 in Grand Island, Nebraska
Source: *BiE&WWA; BioNews 74; CelR;
ChhPo S2; CurBio 54*

Baird, Cora Eisenberg
[Mrs. Bil Baird]
American. Puppeteer
Puppets appeared in movie *The Sound of
Music,* 1965.
b. Jan 26, 1912 in New York, New York
d. Dec 7, 1967 in New York, New York
Source: *BiE&WWA; CurBio 54, 68; InWom;
WhAm 5; WhScrn 74, 77*

Baird, Irwin Lewis
American. Scientist
b. Mar 11, 1925 in Saint Joseph, Missouri
Source: *AmM&WS 73P*

Baird, John Logie
Scottish. Engineer
Developed the flying spot system of scanning
for TV picture, 1922, used by BBC for
first TV program.
b. Aug 13, 1888 in Helensburgh, Scotland
d. Jun 14, 1946 in Bexhill, England
Source: *BiESc; DcNaB 1941; EncAJ; InSci;
LEPo; NewCol 75; WebBD 80; WhDW;
WorAl*

Baird, Spencer Fullerton
American. Scientist, Physician, Engineer
Developed method of field study of botany,
zoology in US; gathered material for
Smithsonian Institute.
b. Feb 3, 1823 in Reading, Pennsylvania
d. Aug 19, 1887 in Woods Hole,
Massachusetts
Source: *Alli, SUP; AmBi; ApCAB; BiAUS;
BiD&SB; CyAL 2; DcAmAu; DcAmB; DcEnL;
DcNAA; Drake; TwCBDA; WebAB; WhAm
HS*

Bairnsfather, Bruce
English. Soldier, Artist, Cartoonist
Official cartoonist, US, WW II, whose
cartoons on war, *Fragments from France,*
published in six collections.
b. Jul 1888 in India
d. Sep 29, 1959 in Norton, England
Source: *ChhPo S1; DcBrAr 1; LongCTC;
ObitT 1951; WorECar*

Bakeless, John Edwin
American. Author, Editor
His biographies, historical surveys include
Lewis and Clarke, 1947; *Spies of the
Revolution,* 1962.
b. Dec 30, 1894 in Carlisle, Pennsylvania
d. Aug 8, 1978 in New Haven, Connecticut
Source: *AmAu&B; Au&Wr 71; AuBYP;
ConAu 5R, 5NR; IntAu&W 76; NatCAB 61;
REnAL; SmATA 9; TwCA, SUP; WhAm 7;
WhE&EA; WhNAA; WhoAm 76, 78; WrDr
76*

Baker, Belle
American. Actress
Films include *Song of Love*, 1929; *Atlantic City*, 1944.
b. 1895 in New York, New York
d. Apr 29, 1957 in Los Angeles, California
Source: *InWom; WhScrn 74, 77; WhoHol B*

Baker, Bill (William Robert)
American. Hockey Player
Defenseman, who was member of 1980
  Olympic gold medal team.
b. Nov 29, 1956 in Grand Rapids, Minnesota
Source: *HocEn; HocReg 81*

Baker, Blanche
American. Actress
Daughter of Carroll Baker; won Emmy for
  role in TV movie "Holocaust," 1978.
b. Dec 20, 1956
Source: *VarWW 85*

Baker, Bobby (Robert Gene)
American. Government Official
Senate Dem. majority secretary who was
  convicted, 1967, of tax evasion, theft,
  conspiracy to defraud govt.
b. Nov 12, 1928 in Easley, South Carolina
Source: *ConAu 85; PolProf J, K*

Baker, Bonnie
"Wee Bonnie"
American. Singer
Had number one record: "Oh Johnny, Oh
  Johnny," 1940.
b. Apr 1, 1917 in Orange, Texas
Source: *BioIn 10; CmpEPM; InWom; What
1-5*

Baker, "Buddy" (Elzie Wylie, Jr.)
American. Auto Racer
b. Jan 25, 1941
Source: *BioIn 10, 11, 12*

Baker, Carlos Heard
American. Author
b. May 5, 1909 in Biddeford, Maine
Source: *AmAu&B; ConAu 5R, 3NR; DrAS
74E; IntWW 74; REnAL; WhNAA; WhoAm
74; WhoWor 78; WorAu; WrDr 80*

Baker, Carroll
American. Actress
Nominated for Oscar, 1956, for *Baby Doll;*
  groomed in 1960s to replace Marilyn
  Monroe as screen sex goddess.
b. May 28, 1935 in Johnstown, Pennsylvania
Source: *BiDFilm; BiE&WWA; FilmEn;
FilmgC; IntMPA 80, 81, 82; MovMk;
OxFilm; WhoAm 74; WhoHol A; WorEFlm*

Baker, Charlotte
American. Author
Wrote *A Sombrero for Miss Brown*, 1941;
  House on the River, 1948.
b. Aug 31, 1910 in Nacogdoches, Texas
Source: *AuBYP; ConAu 17R; IlsCB 1946;
SmATA 2*

Baker, Chet
American. Musician
b. Dec 23, 1929 in Yale, Oklahoma
Source: *BiDAmM*

Baker, Diane
American. Actress
Films include *Diary of Anne Frank*, 1959;
  Marnie, 1969.
b. Feb 25, 1938 in Hollywood, California
Source: *BioIn 7; FilmEn; FilmgC; MotPP;
MovMk; WhoAm 80; WhoHol A*

Baker, Dorothy Dodds
American. Author
Writings include *Young Man With a Horn*,
  1938; *Cassandra at the Wedding*, 1962.
b. Apr 21, 1907 in Missoula, Montana
d. Jun 18, 1968 in Terra Bella, California
Source: *BioIn 2, 4, 8, 10; ConAu 1R; CurBio
43, 68*

Baker, Elbert Hall, II
American. Newspaper Publisher
Pres., publisher, Tribune Publishing Co.,
  Tacoma, WA, 1969--.
b. Jul 18, 1910 in Quincy, Massachusetts
Source: *St&PR 75; WhoAdv 72; WhoAm 74;
WhoF&I 74; WhoWest 84*

Baker, Frank (John Franklin)
"Home Run Baker"
American. Baseball Player
Third baseman, Philadelphia, NY, 1908-22;
  had lifetime .363 batting average; Hall of
  Fame, 1955.
b. Mar 13, 1886 in Trappe, Maryland
d. Jun 28, 1963 in Trappe, Maryland
Source: *BaseEn 85; BasesB; DcAmB S7*

Baker, George
American. Cartoonist
Disney animator, 1937-41; staff cartoonist on
  US Army's newspaper, *Yank*, drawing
  strip "Sad Sack," 1941-46.
b. May 22, 1915 in Lowell, Massachusetts
d. May 8, 1975 in Los Angeles, California
Source: *AmAu&B; ConAu 57, 93; CurBio 44;
WebAB; WhAm 6*

Baker, "Ginger" (Peter)
[Blind Faith; Cream]
English. Musician, Singer
Leading British drummer, percussionist,
  1960s-70s; formed group Cream, with Eric
  Clapton, 1967-69,
b. Aug 19, 1940 in Lewisham, England
Source: *BioIn 9, 10; EncPR&S 74; IlEncRk;
RkOn 74; RolSEnR 83*

Baker, Gladys Elizabeth
American. Educator
b. Jul 22, 1908 in Iowa City, Iowa
Source: *AmM&WS 73P; WhoAm 74*

Baker, Howard Henry, Jr.
American. Politician
Rep. senator from TN, 1966-85, who ran for
  Rep. presidential nomination, 1980.
b. Nov 15, 1925 in Huntsville, Tennessee
Source: *BiDrAC; CngDr 74; CurBio 74;
IntWW 74; NewYTBE 73; WhoAm 74, 76,
78, 80, 82; WhoGov 75; WhoS&SW 82*

Baker, James Addison, III
American. Presidential Aide, Government
  Official
White House chief of staff under Ronald
  Reagan, 1981-85; secretary of Treasury,
  1985--.
b. Apr 28, 1930 in Houston, Texas
Source: *CurBio 82; NewYTBS 81; WhoAm
82, 84*

Baker, Janet Abbott, Dame
English. Opera Singer
Debuted, 1956; part of Kate Julian in
  Britten's *Owen Wingrave* was written for
  her.
b. Aug 21, 1933 in York, England
Source: *Baker 78; CurBio 71; IntWW 74, 81,
82; NewYTBS 82; Who 74, 82; WhoAm 82;
WhoAmW 81; WhoMus 72; WhoOp 76;
WhoWor 74, 80*

Baker, Joe Don
American. Actor
Best known for role in movie *Walking Tall*,
  1973.
b. Feb 12, 1936 in Groesbeck, Texas
Source: *BioIn 10; IntMPA 77, 78, 79, 80, 81,
82; WhoAm 78, 80, 82; WhoHol A*

Baker, Josephine
French. Singer
Rose to stardom in Folies-Bergere, 1925;
  active in Resistance during WW II.
b. Jun 3, 1906 in Saint Louis, Missouri
d. Apr 12, 1975 in Paris, France
Source: *BiDAmM; BiE&WWA; CelR; ConAu
105; CurBio 64, 75; DrBlPA; GoodHs;
InB&W 80; LibW; NegAl 76; ObitOF 79;
ObitT 1971; OxFilm; WebAB, 79; WhAm 6;
WhScrn 77; WhoAm 74; WhoHol C; WhoThe
77, 81N; WhoWor 74; WorAl*

Baker, Julius
American. Musician
Flutist with various US symphonies, 1940-53;
  soloist in concerts throughout US, Europe,
  Japan.
b. Sep 23, 1915 in Cleveland, Ohio
Source: *WhoAm 80, 82, 84; WhoAmM 83*

Baker, Kathy
American. Golfer
Joined LPGA, 1983; won US Women's
  Open, 1985.
b. Mar 20, 1961 in Albany, New York
Source: *ConNews 86-1*

Baker, Kenny
English. Actor
Played R2-D2 in *Star Wars* films.
b. Aug 24, 1934 in Birmingham, England
Source: *NF*

Baker, Kenny (Kenneth Lawrence)
American. Actor, Singer
Nightclub singer who was regular vocalist on
  Jack Benny's radio show, 1930s.
b. Sep 30, 1912 in Monrovia, California
Source: *AmPS B; BiDAmM; BiE&WWA;
CmpEPM; FilmgC; WhoHol A*

Baker, Laura Nelson
American. Author
Writings include *The Red Mountain*, 1946;
  From Whales to Snails, 1970.
b. Jan 7, 1911 in Humboldt, Iowa
Source: *Au&Wr 71; AuBYP; ConAu 5R,
5NR; ForWC 70; MinnWr; SmATA 3; WrDr
76*

Baker, Phil
American. Comedian, Composer
Films include *The Goldwyn Follies*, 1938; *The
  Gang's All Here*, 1943.
b. Aug 24, 1896 in Philadelphia,
  Pennsylvania
d. Nov 30, 1963 in Copenhagen, Denmark
Source: *AmSCAP 66; CurBio 46, 64; WhAm
4; WhScrn 74, 77; WhoHol B*

Baker, Rachel
American. Children's Author
Founder, first pres., Fairfield County
    Organization for Mentally Ill Children who
    wrote *The First Woman Doctor,* 1942.
b. Mar 1, 1904 in Chernigov, Russia
d. Jul 7, 1978
Source: *AuBYP; BkCL; ConAu 5R, 103;
MorJA; SmATA 2*

Baker, Ray Stannard
[David Grayson, pseud.]
American. Author
Won Pulitzer for *Woodrow Wilson: Life and
    Letters,* 1940.
b. Apr 17, 1870 in Lansing, Michigan
d. Jul 12, 1946 in Amherst, Massachusetts
Source: *AmAu&B; AmLY; CarSB; ChhPo S2;
ConAmL; CurBio 40, 46; DcAmAu; DcAmB
S4; DcLEL; DcNAA; EncAB-H; EvLB;
LongCTC; OxAmL; REn; REnAL; TwCA,
SUP; TwCWr; WebAB; WhAm 2; WhNAA;
WisWr*

Baker, Rick
American. Artist, Designer
Make-up artist specializing in horror, science
    fiction films: *King Kong,* 1976; *Star Wars,*
    1977.
b. 1950 in New York
Source: *BioIn 11; FanAl*

Baker, Russell Wayne
American. Journalist, Author
NY *Times* columnist who won Pulitzer,
    1982, for autobiography *Growing Up.*
b. Aug 14, 1925 in Loudoun County,
    Virginia
Source: *AmAu&B; ConAu 11NR, 57; CurBio
80; WhoAm 74, 76, 78, 80, 82; WhoS&SW
73*

Baker, Samm Sinclair
American. Author
Called America's "leading self-help author";
    wrote *The Complete Scarsdale Medical
    Diet,* 1979, with Herman Tarnower.
b. Jul 29, 1909 in Paterson, New Jersey
Source: *ConAu 3NR, 5R; IntAu&W 77;
NewYTBS 79; SmATA 12*

Baker, Sara Josephine
American. Physician, Feminist
Child health pioneer; first director, Bureau of
    Child Hygiene, 1909.
b. Nov 15, 1873 in Poughkeepsie, New York
d. Feb 22, 1945 in New York, New York
Source: *NotAW; WhAm 2*

Baker, "Shorty" (Harold)
American. Jazz Musician
Trumpeter, 1930-65, who played with Duke
    Ellington, Bud Freeman.
b. May 26, 1914 in Saint Louis, Missouri
d. Nov 8, 1966 in New York, New York
Source: *AmSCAP 66; WhoJazz 72*

Baker, Stanley, Sir
Welsh. Actor
Films include *The Guns of Navarone,* 1961;
    Accident, 1967.
b. Feb 28, 1928 in Glamorgan, Wales
d. Jun 28, 1976 in Malaga, Spain
Source: *BiDFilm; CmMov; FilmgC; IntMPA
75; MotPP; MovMk; OxFilm; Who 74;
WhoHol A; WhoThe 81N; WorEFlm*

Bakewell, William
American. Actor
Films include *All Quiet on the Western
    Front,* 1930; *Gone With The Windd,* 1939.
b. May 2, 1908 in Hollywood, California
Source: *FilmEn; Film 2; MovMk; TwYS;
WhoHol A*

Bakey, Michael Ellis de
see: DeBakey, Michael Ellis

Bakhtiar, Shahpur
Iranian. Prime Minister
Leader of Bakhtiaris, Iran's oldest and largest
    tribe.
b. 1916
Source: *IntWW 80, 81, 82; MidE 79, 80, 81,
82; NewYTBS 78*

Bakke, Allan Paul
American. Student
When denied admission to medical school,
    charged reverse discrimination, won
    Supreme Court decision, 1978.
b. Feb 4, 1940 in Minneapolis, Minnesota
Source: *BioIn 11; NewYTBS 77, 78*

Bakker, Jim (James Orsen)
American. Clergyman, TV Personality
Co-founder Trinity Broadcasting Network,
    1973.
b. Jan 2, 1939 in Muskegon, Michigan
Source: *BioIn 11; WhoAm 82, 84*

Bakr, Ahmad Hasan al
Iraqi. Political Leader
Pres., of Iraq, 1968-80.
b. 1914 in Tikrit, Iraq
Source: *IntWW 74; WhoGov 72; WhoWor 74,
78*

Bakshi, Ralph
American. Cartoonist
Produced, directed animated version of
Tolkien's *Lord of the Rings*, 1978.
b. Oct 26, 1938 in Haifa, Palestine
Source: *CurBio 81; WhoAm 82; WorECar*

Bakunin, Mikhail Aleksandrovich
[Jules Elizard, pseud.]
Russian. Anarchist
A founder of Nihilism, who wrote *God and
the State*, 1872-74.
b. May 18, 1814 in Tver, Russia
d. Jul 13, 1876 in Bern, Switzerland
Source: *CasWL; DcAmSR; DcRusL; EuAu;
LinLib S; LuthC 75; McGEWB; REn;
WhDW; WorAl*

Balaban, Barney
American. Film Executive
Pres., of Paramount Pictures, 1936-64;
introduced primitive air-conditioning to
movie theaters, 1917.
b. Jun 8, 1887 in Chicago, Illinois
d. Mar 7, 1971 in Byram, Connecticut
Source: *CurBio 46, 71; FilmEn; FilmgC;
NewYTBE 71; WhAm 5; WorEFlm*

Balaban, Emanuel
American. Conductor
b. Jan 27, 1895 in Brooklyn, New York
d. May 1973
Source: *BioIn 9; WhAm 5*

Balaguer, Joaquin
Dominican. Political Leader
Pres., Dominican Republic, 1960, 1966-78,
1986--.
b. Sep 1, 1907 in Villa Bisono, Dominican
Republic
Source: *IntWW 74; NewYTBE 70; WhoGov
72; WhoWor 74*

Balakirev, Mili Alekseyevich
Russian. Composer
Works reflect influence of Liszt, combine
Romanticism with Russian, Oriental folk
songs.
b. Jan 2, 1837 in Nizhni-Novgorod, Russia
d. May 28, 1910 in Saint Petersburg, Russia
Source: *Baker 78; LinLib S; OxMus; WhDW*

Balanchine, George
[Georges Malitonovitch Balanchivadze]
"Mr. B"
American. Dancer, Choreographer
Co-founded Ballet Society, now NYC Ballet,
1946; artistic director, 1948-83.
b. Jan 9, 1904 in Saint Petersburg, Russia
d. Apr 30, 1983 in New York, New York
Source: *Baker 78; BiE&WWA; BlueB 76;
CelR; CurBio 42, 54, 83; EncMT; IntWW 74;
LinLib S; McGEWB; NewYTBE 72;
NewYTBS 74, 80; NotNAT; OxAmH; OxMus;
PIP&P; WebAB; WhDun; Who 82; WhoAm
74, 80; WhoE 81; WhoThe 72, 77; WhoWor
74, 80; WorAl*

Balbo, Italo
Italian. Government Official
Governor of Lybia, 1936, who built up
Mussolini's air force; accidently shot down
by own company.
b. Jun 6, 1896 in Ferrar, Italy
d. Jun 28, 1940 in Tobruk, Libya
Source: *CurBio 40; InSci; WhWW-II; WorAl*

Balboa, Vasco Nunez de
Spanish. Explorer
Discovered Pacific Ocean, 1513; beheaded on
false charges of treason.
b. 1475 in Jerez Caballeros, Spain
d. 1517 in Darien
Source: *ApCAB; Drake; NewC; REn; WhAm
HS*

Balch, Emily G
American. Social Reformer
Shared 1946 Nobel Peace Prize with John R
Mott.
b. Jan 8, 1867 in Jamaica Plain,
Massachusetts
d. Jan 9, 1961 in Cambridge, Massachusetts
Source: *CurBio 47, 61; InWom; WebAB;
WhAm 4; WomWWA 14*

Balchen, Bernt
American. Aviator, Explorer
Piloted first flight over S Pole with Byrd
expedition, 1929.
b. Oct 23, 1899 in Tveit Topdal, Norway
d. Oct 17, 1973 in Mount Kisco, New York
Source: *ConAu 45; CurBio 49, 73; NewYTBE
73; WhAm 6; WhoAm 74; WhoWor 74*

Balchin, Nigel Marlin
[Mark Spade, pseud.]
English. Author, Farmer
Wrote novel *Small Back Room,* 1934; thriller
   Mine Own Executioner, 1945.
b. Dec 3, 1908 in Wiltshire, England
d. May 17, 1970 in London, England
Source: *ConAu 29R, 97; DcLEL; EvLB;*
LongCTC; ModBrL; PenC ENG; REn; TwCA
SUP; TwCWr

Balcon, Michael Elias, Sir
English. Producer
Best remembered comedy *The Lavender Hill*
   Mob, 1951; wrote *A Lifetime of Films,*
   1969.
b. May 19, 1896 in Birmingham, England
d. Oct 17, 1977 in Hartfield, England
Source: *BlueB 76; GrBr*

Bald, Kenneth
[K Bruce, psued.]
American. Cartoonist
Created "Captain Marvel," "Doc Savage,"
   "Captain Battle," 1941-43.
b. 1920 in New York, New York
Source: *WorECom*

Balderston, John Lloyd
American. Dramatist
Writings include *Genius of the Marne,* 1919;
   Cleopatra and Caesar, 1952.
b. Oct 22, 1889 in Philadelphia, Pennsylvania
d. Mar 8, 1954 in Beverly Hills, California
Source: *AmAu&B; CnMD; FilmgC; LongCTC;*
McGEWD; ModWD; WhAm 3; WhNAA

Baldovinetti, Alesso
Italian. Artist
b. 1425
d. 1499
Source: *NewCol 75*

Baldrige, Letitia Katherine
American. Author, Public Relations Executive
Director, Tiffany & Co., 1956-61; White
   House social secretary, 1961-63; pres.,
   Letitia Baldridge Enterprises, Inc., 1972--.
b. in Miami Beach, Florida
Source: *ConAu 17NR, 25R; ForWC 70;*
WhoAm 82; WhoE 74; WhoF&I 74

Baldrige, Malcolm (Howard Malcolm, Jr.)
"Mac"
American. Government Official
US secretary of Commerce under Ronald
   Reagan, 1981--.
b. Oct 4, 1922 in Omaha, Nebraska
Source: *CngDr 81; CurBio 82; Dun&B 79;*
IntWW 82; NewYTBS 81; PseudN 82; St&PR
75; WhoAm 82; WhoAmP 79; WhoE 81;
WhoF&I 77; WhoWor 74

Baldung(-Grien), Hans
[Hans Gruen]
German. Artist, Printmaker
Did portraits, woodcuts, demonic allegories;
   altar of Freiburg Cathedral, 1512.
b. 1484
d. 1545 in Strasbourg, France
Source: *BioIn 5, 11; McGDA; NewCol 75;*
PseudN 82

Baldwin, Adam
American. Actor
Films include *My Bodyguard,* 1980; *DC Cab,*
   1983.
b. 1962 in Chicago, Illinois
Source: *BioIn 12; NewYTBS 80*

Baldwin, Billy
"Billy B"
American. Designer
Pioneered use of cotton as high-fashion
   fabric; clients included Greta Garbo,
   Jacqueline Onassis.
b. May 30, 1904 in Rowland Park, Maryland
d. Nov 25, 1983 in Nantucket, Massachusetts
Source: *BioIn 10; CelR; NewYTBS 83;*
WhoAm 76

Baldwin, Faith
American. Author
Popular romantic novelist who wrote
   American Family, 1935.
b. Oct 1, 1893 in New Rochelle, New York
d. Mar 19, 1978 in Norwalk, Connecticut
Source: *AmAu&B; AmNov; AuNews 1;*
BioNews 74; ChhPo; ConAu 4NR, 5R; ForWC
70; InWom; LinLib L; LongCTC; NewYTBE
73; ObitOF 79; OxAmL; REn; REnAL;
TwCA, SUP; WhAm 7; WhNAA; WhoAm 74;
WhoAmW 74, 70, 72, 77; WorAl; WrDr 76

Baldwin, Hanson Weightman
American. Journalist
Won Pulitzer, 1942; wrote *The Crucial Years:*
   1939-1941, 1976.
b. Mar 22, 1903 in Baltimore, Maryland
Source: *AmAu&B; Au&Wr 71; ConAu 61;*
CurBio 42; LongCTC; REnAL; TwCA SUP;
WhoAm 74

Baldwin, Horace
American. Physician
Established American Foundation for Allergic
Disease.
b. Oct 14, 1895 in Englewood, New Jersey
d. Oct 27, 1983 in Sarasota, Florida
Source: *AnObit 1983; WhoAm 80*

Baldwin, James Arthur
American. Author, Dramatist, Director,
Essayist
Wrote *Go Tell It on the Mountain,* 1953;
Just Above My Head, 1979.
b. Aug 2, 1924 in New York, New York
Source: *AmAu&B; BlueB 76; BlkAWP;
CasWL; CelR; ConAu 3NR; ConDr 82;
ConLC 17; ConNov 82; ConTFT 3; CroCD;
DcLB 7; IntWW 82; LivgBAA; LongCTC;
McGEWD; ModAL S1; ModWD; NatPD;
NegAl 76; NotNAT; Novels; OxAmL; PenC
AM; RAdv 1; REn; REnAL; SmATA 9;
TwCWr; WebAB 79; WebE&AL; WhDW;
WhoAm 82; WhoBlA 80; WhoE 74;
WhoTwCL; WhoWor 74; WorAu; WrDr 80*

Baldwin, James Mark
American. Psychologist, Educator
Child psychology expert who co-founded,
edited *Psychological Review,* 1894-1909.
b. Jan 12, 1861 in Columbia, South Carolina
d. Nov 8, 1934 in Paris, France
Source: *DcAmB S1; WebBD 80*

Baldwin, Matthias William
American. Industrialist, Philanthropist
Built "Old Ironsides," one of first American
locomotives used in transportataion.
b. Dec 10, 1795 in Elizabethtown,
Pennsylvania
d. Sep 7, 1866 in Philadelphia, Pennsylvania
Source: *DcAmB; NewCol 75; WhAm HS*

Baldwin, Robert
Canadian. Statesman
With Lafontaine, formed first Liberal govt.,
1842-43; second govt., 1848-51, called
"Great Ministry."
b. May 12, 1804 in Toronto, Ontario
d. Dec 9, 1858 in Spadina, Ontario
Source: *ApCAB; OxCan*

Baldwin, Roger Nash
American. Social Reformer
Founded ACLU, 1920, with Norman
Thomas, Felix Frankfurter; director until
1950.
b. Jan 21, 1884 in Wellesley, Massachusetts
d. Aug 26, 1981 in Ridgewood, New Jersey
Source: *AmM&WS 78S; BioNews 74; CelR;
CurBio 40, 81; DcAmSR; NewYTBS 81;
PolProf T; WhAm 8; WhoAm 80; WhoWor
74; WorAl*

Baldwin, William, Jr.
[Billy Baldwin]
American. Designer
Dean of American interior decorators.
b. May 30, 1903 in Roland Park, Maryland
d. Nov 25, 1983 in Nantucket, Massachusetts
Source: *ConAu 111; WhoAm 76*

Baldwin of Bewdley, Stanley Baldwin, Earl
English. Statesman
b. Aug 3, 1867 in Bewdley, England
d. Dec 14, 1947 in Ast Pey, England
Source: *NewC; REn*

Balenciaga, Cristobal
"Prophet of Silhouette"
Spanish. Fashion Designer
Elegant designer of classic soft-shouldered
suit, straightline chemise silhouette.
b. Jan 21, 1895 in Guetaria, Spain
d. Mar 23, 1972 in Javea, Spain
Source: *CurBio 54, 72; NewYTBE 72; WhAm
5; WorFshn*

Balewa, Abubakar
Nigerian. Political Leader
Prime minister, Nigeria, 1957-66.
b. Dec 12, 1912 in Bauchi, Nigeria
d. Jan 15, 1966 in Lagos, Nigeria
Source: *BioIn 8; WhAm 4*

Balfour, Arthur James Balfour, Earl
English. Statesman
Prime minister, 1902-05, who wrote *Balfour
Declaration,* 1917, approving establishment
of Jewish state in Palestine.
b. Jul 25, 1848 in East Lothian, Scotland
d. Mar 19, 1930 in Fisher's Hill, England
Source: *Alli SUP; BbD; BiD&SB; BiDPara;
DcLEL; EvLB; NewC; OxEng; TwCA, SUP*

Balin, Ina
[Ina Rosenberg]
American. Actress
TV movie "Children of An-Lac" detailed
    own story of airlifting orphans out of
    Saigon.
b. Nov 12, 1937 in Brooklyn, New York
Source: *BiE&WWA; FilmEn; FilmgC; IntMPA
75, 77, 78, 79, 80, 81, 82; MotPP; PseudN
82; WhoAmW 74, 72; WhoHol A*

Balin, Marty
[Martyn Jerel Buchwald; Jefferson Airplane]
American. Singer, Songwriter
Founder, Jefferson Airplane/Starship, 1965-71,
    75-85; wrote hits "It's No Secret",
    "Fantastic Lover."
b. Jan 30, 1943 in Cincinnati, Ohio
Source: *BioIn 9; WhoAm 82*

Ball, Edmund B
American. Manufacturer
With brother, Frank, launched can co., 1880;
    jars used for canning.
b. Oct 21, 1855 in Greensburg, Ohio
d. Mar 8, 1925 in Muncie, Indiana
Source: *Entr; NatCAB 20*

Ball, Edward
"Mr. Ed"
American. Business Executive
Built empire of banks, railroads, pine land;
    chief trustee of DuPont Trust, valued at
    nearly $2 billion.
b. Mar 21, 1888 in Tidewater, Virginia
d. Jun 24, 1981 in New Orleans, Louisiana
Source: *AnObit 1981; Dun&B 79; NewYTBS
79, 81; St&PR 75; WhoS&SW 75, 76*

Ball, Ernest
American. Composer
Compositions include "A Little Bit of
    Heaven," "When Irish Eyes Are Smiling."
b. Jul 22, 1878 in Cleveland, Ohio
d. May 3, 1927 in Santa Ana, California
Source: *AmSCAP 66; WorAl*

Ball, Frank
American. Manufacturer
With brother, Edmund, started can co., 1880;
    jars used for canning.
b. Nov 24, 1857 in Greensburg, Ohio
d. Mar 19, 1943 in Muncie, Indiana
Source: *DcAmB S3; DcNAA; Entr; OhA&B*

Ball, George Wildman
American. Lawyer, Government Official
Chair, Lehman Brothers International, Ltd.,
    1966-68; US permanent representative to
    UN, 1968.
b. Dec 21, 1909 in Des Moines, Iowa
Source: *ConAu 73; CurBio 62; IntWW 74;
WhoAm 74, 76, 78, 80, 82; WhoAmP 73;
WhoWor 78*

Ball, John Dudley, Jr.
American. Author
Best known for award-winning novel *In the
    Heat of the Night,* 1965.
b. Jul 8, 1911 in Schenectady, New York
Source: *AmAu&B; ConAu 5R, 3NR; WhoAm
80, 82; WrDr 80*

Ball, Lucille
[Mrs. Gary Morton]
"Lucy"
American. Actress, Comedienne, Producer
Starred in "I Love Lucy," 1951-60, with ex-
    husband Desi Arnaz.
b. Aug 6, 1911 in Jamestown, New York
Source: *BiDFilm; BiE&WWA; BioNews 74;
BkPepl; CelR; CmMov; ConTFT 3; CurBio
78; EncMT; FilmgC; HerW; IntMPA 82;
IntWW 74; MotPP; MovMk; OxFilm; ThFT;
WebAB; WhoHol A; WhoWor 74; WorEFlm*

Ball, Thomas
American. Sculptor
Greatest work equestrian statue of
    Washington, built in Boston Public
    Garden, 1869.
b. Jun 3, 1819 in Charlestown, Massachusetts
d. 1911 in Montclair, New Jersey
Source: *AmBi; ApCAB; BioIn 7, 9, 11;
DcAmB; DcNAA; Drake; TwCBDA; WhAm 1*

Balla, Giacomo
Italian. Artist, Educator
Member, Italian Futurist Group, 1916-30; art
    emphasized movement, machines, warfare.
b. Jul 18, 1871 in Turin, Italy
d. Mar 1, 1958 in Rome, Italy
Source: *ConArt 77; McGDA; McGEWB;
OxArt; PhDcTCA 77*

Ballantine, Ian
American. Publisher
One of first to produce hardcover, paperback
    editions simultaneously.
b. Feb 15, 1916 in New York, New York
Source: *BioIn 3, 11; CurBio 54; WhoAm 78,
80, 82*

Ballantrae, Lord
[Bernard Edward Fergusson]
English. Author, Government Official
Governor-general, New Zealand, 1962-67;
    wrote *Beyond the Chindwin*, 1945.
b. May 6, 1911 in London, England
d. Nov 28, 1980 in London, England
Source: *AnObit 1980; IntWW 78, 79*

Ballard, Florence
[The Supremes]
American. Singer
Member of original Supremes; grew up with
    Diana Ross in Detroit projects.
b. Jun 30, 1943 in Detroit, Michigan
d. Feb 22, 1976 in Detroit, Michigan
Source: *BioIn 10; EncPR&S 74*

Ballard, Hank
[John Kendricks; The Midnighters]
American. Singer
Had 1960 hit "The Twist," before Chubbie
    Checker.
b. Nov 18, 1936 in Detroit, Michigan
Source: *AmPS A, B; EncPR&S 74; IlEncBM
82; IlEncRk; InB&W 80; RkOn 84; RkOneH*

Ballard, Kaye
[Catherine Gloria Balotta]
American. Singer, Actress, Comedienne,
    Writer
Stage, TV comedienne, who starred in TV
    series, "The Mothers-in-Law," 1967-69.
b. Nov 20, 1926 in Cleveland, Ohio
Source: *BiE&WWA; CelR; ConTFT 3; CurBio
69; EncMT; FilmEn; FilmgC; NotNAT;
WhoAm 84; WhoHol A; WhoThe 77*

Ballard, Robert Duane
American. Geologist, Explorer
Designer of underwater survey sleds that
    enabled him to locate the *Titanic*, 1985.
b. Jun 30, 1942 in Wichita, Kansas
Source: *ConAu 112; CurBio 86*

Ballard, Russ(ell)
[Argent]
English. Singer, Musician
Singer, guitarist with Argent, 1969-74.
b. Oct 31, 1947 in Waltham Cross, England
Source: *NF*

Ballesteros, Seve(riano)
Spanish. Golfer
At 23, youngest golfer ever to win Masters
    Tournament, 1980.
b. Apr 9, 1957 in Pedrena, Spain
Source: *IntWW 81, 82; NewYTBS 80, 82*

**Ballinger, Margaret (Violet Margaret
    Livingstone)**
[Margaret Hodgson, pseud.]
South African. Author, Politician
MP, representing black Africans; wrote *From
    Union to Apartheid, Trek to Isolation,*
    1970.
b. Jan 11, 1894 in Glasgow, Scotland
d. Feb 7, 1980 in Cape Province, South
    Africa
Source: *AfSS 79; AnObit 1980; ConAu 105,
61; EncSoA; IntWW 78; PseudN 82;
WhE&EA; WhoWor 74*

Ballou, Maturin Murray
American. Author, Editor
Editor, *Ballou's Pictorial*, 1851-59, early
    American illustrated paper.
b. Apr 14, 1820 in Boston, Massachusetts
d. Mar 27, 1895 in Cairo, Egypt
Source: *Alli, SUP; AmAu; AmAu&B; ApCAB;
BbD; BiD&SB; DcAmAu; DcAmB; DcNAA;
Drake; OxAmL; WhAm HS*

Balmain, Pierre Alexandre
French. Fashion Designer
Discovered by Gertrude Stein; fashions
    designed to be timeless, elegant; worn by
    Sophia Loren, Katherine Hepburn, etc.
b. May 18, 1914 in Saint Jean de Maurienne,
    France
d. Jun 29, 1982 in Paris, France
Source: *AnObit 1982; CelR; ConAu 107;
CurBio 54, 82; FairDF FRA; IntWW 82;
NewYTBS 82; WhAm 8; Who 82; WhoAm
82; WhoWor 78; WorFshn*

Balopoulos, Michael
Greek. Political Leader
Colonel who led 1967 military coup to
    overthrow democratic govt.
b. 1920
d. Mar 3, 1978 in Athens, Greece
Source: *BioIn 11; ObitOF 79*

Balsam, Artur
Polish. Musician
Pianist, who has recorded all works of
    Mozart, Haydn.
b. Feb 8, 1906 in Warsaw, Poland
Source: *WhoAm 82, 84; WhoAmM 83*

Balsam, Martin Henry
American. Actor
Won 1964 Oscar for *A Thousand Clowns.*
b. Nov 4, 1919 in New York, New York
Source: *BiE&WWA; CelR; FilmgC; IntMPA
79, 80, 81, 82; MotPP; MovMk; NotNAT;
WhoAm 74, 76, 78, 80, 82; WhoHol A;
WhoThe 77*

Baltard, Victor
French. Architect
Designed Parisian iron and glass structure,
Les Halles Centrales, 1854-66.
b. 1805 in Paris, France
d. Jan 13, 1874
Source: *ArtsNiC; DcBiPP; MacEA; McGDA;
WhoArch*

Balthus
[Comte Balthazar Klossowski de Rola]
French. Artist
Self-taught painter, noted for doll-like
   portraits of Miro, Derain, 1936.
b. Feb 29, 1908 in Paris, France
Source: *ConArt 77; CurBio 79; IntWW 74,
75, 76, 77, 78; McGDA; PseudN 82; WhoWor
74*

Baltimore, George Calvert, Baron
English. Colonizer
Founded Maryland, 1632.
b. 1580 in Kipling, England
d. Apr 15, 1632 in London, England
Source: *Alli, SUP; AmBi; DcAmB; Drake;
OxCan; TwCBDA; WebAB; WhAm HS*

Balukas, Jean
American. Billiards Player
Greatest woman pool player; won seven
   consecutive US Open Championships,
   1976-83.
b. Jun 28, 1959 in Brooklyn, New York
Source: *BioIn 11; GoodHs; NewYTBS 74;
WhoAm 82, 84*

Balzac, Honore de
French. Dramatist, Author
Best known work *Comedie Humaine,* 1899-
   1900, uses technique of "reappearing
   character."
b. May 20, 1799 in Tours, France
d. Aug 18, 1850 in Paris, France
Source: *AtlBL; BbD; BiD&SB; CasWL;
CyWA; DcBiA; DcEuL; EncMys; EuAu;
EvEuW; McGEWD; NewC; OxEng; OxFr;
OxThe; PenC EUR; RComWL; REn*

Bamberger, George Irvin
American. Baseball Manager
Minor league pitcher, who was pitching
   coach, Baltimore, 1968-77; mgr.,
   Milwaukee, 1978-80, NY Mets, 1982-83.
b. Aug 1, 1925 in Staten Island, New York
Source: *BioIn 12; NewYTBS 81; WhoProB 73*

Bamberger, Julian Maas
American. Business Executive
b. Feb 9, 1889 in Salt Lake City, Utah
d. Jun 23, 1967 in Salt Lake City, Utah
Source: *BioIn 10; NatCAB 54*

Bamberger, Louis
American. Merchant, Philanthropist
Founded L Bamberger & Co., 1892, one of
   largest US department stores.
b. May 15, 1855 in Baltimore, Maryland
d. May 11, 1944 in South Orange, New
   Jersey
Source: *DcAmB S3; WhAm 2*

Bampton, Rose Elizabeth
[Mrs. Wilfred Pelletier]
American. Opera Singer
Metropolitan Opera debut, 1932; known for
   regular appearances on NBC radio.
b. Nov 28, 1909 in Cleveland, Ohio
Source: *Baker 78; BiDAmM; CurBio 40;
InWom; MusSN; NewEOp 71; WhoAmW 64;
WhoE 79*

Bancroft, Anne
[Annemarie Italiano; Mrs. Mel Brooks]
American. Actress
Won 1962 Oscar for *The Miracle Worker;*
   played Mrs. Robinson in *The Graduate,*
   1967.
b. Sep 17, 1931 in New York, New York
Source: *BiDFilm; BiE&WWA; BkPepl; CelR;
FilmgC; InWom; IntMPA 75, 76, 77, 78, 79,
80, 81, 82; IntWW 78; MovMk; NotNAT;
OxFr; WhoAm 74, 76, 78, 80, 82; WhoAmW
77; WhoThe 77; WhoWor 74; WorEFlm*

Bancroft, Dave (David James)
"Banny"; "Beauty Bancroft"
American. Baseball Player
Shortstop, 1915-29; Hall of Fame, 1971.
b. Apr 20, 1892 in Sioux City, Iowa
d. Oct 9, 1972 in Superior, Wisconsin
Source: *BaseEn 85; BasesB*

Bancroft, George
"Father of American History"
American. Author, Historian, Diplomat
Wrote 10-vol. *History of the US,* 1834-74.
b. Oct 3, 1800 in Worcester, Massachusetts
d. Jan 17, 1891 in Washington, District of
   Columbia
Source: *Alli, SUP; AmAu; AmAu&B; AmBi;
ApCAB; BbD; BiAUS; BiD&SB; BiDrUSE;
ChhPo; CyAL 2; DcAmAu; DcAmB; DcEnA
AP; DcEnL; DcLEL; DcNAA; Drake; EncAB-
H; EvLB; Film 2; MotPP; NotNAT B;
ObitOF 79; OxAmL; OxEng; PenC AM; REn;
REnAL; TwCBDA; WebAB; WebE&AL;
WhAm HS; WhAmP; WhoHol B*

Bancroft, George
American. Actor
Known for both hero, villain roles: *Pony
Express,* 1925; *The Bugle Sound,* 1942.
b. Sep 30, 1882 in Philadelphia, Pennsylvania
d. Oct 2, 1956 in Santa Monica, California
Source: *CmMov; FilmgC; MovMk; TwYS;
Vers A; WhScrn 74, 77; WorEFlm*

Band, The
[Rick Danko; Levon Helm; Garth Hudson;
Richard Manuel; Robbie Robertson]
American. Music Group
Frequently worked with Bob Dylan; last
concert filmed by Martin Scorsese as *The
Last Waltz,* 1976.
Source: *EncPR&S 74; IlEncRk; RkOneH;
RolSEnR 83*

Banda, Hastings Kamuzu
Malawian. Political Leader
First prime minister, Nyasaland, 1963, which
became independent country, Malawi,
1964.
b. 1906 in Kasungu, Nyasaland
Source: *CurBio 63; EncSoA; InB&W 80;
IntWW 74; NewYTBE 71; WhDW; Who 82;
WhoGov 72; WhoWor 74*

Bandaranaike, Sirimavo
Sri Lankan. Political Leader
World's first female prime minister, 1959-65,
1970-77.
b. Apr 17, 1916 in Kandy, Ceylon
Source: *CurBio 61; DcPol; FarE&A 80, 81;
GoodHs; IntWW 82; IntYB 80, 81;
NewYTBE 70; NewYTBS 80, 81, 82;
WhoWor 74, 76; WorAl*

Bandeira, Manuel (Filho Manuel)
Brazilian. Poet, Journalist
Wrote verse vols. *Carnaval,* 1919.
b. Apr 19, 1886 in Recife, Brazil
d. Oct 13, 1968 in Rio de Janeiro, Brazil
Source: *ConAu 115; EncLatA; PenC AM;
WebBD 80*

Bandello, Matteo
[Matthew Bandello]
"A Prose Ariosto"
Italian. Author, Poet, Priest
His short stories imitating Boccaccio are
probable source of Shakespeare's *Romeo
and Juliet.*
b. 1485 in Castelnuovo Scrivia, Italy
d. 1561 in Bassens, France
Source: *BbD; BiD&SB; CasWL; CroE&S;
DcEuL; EuAu; EvEuW; NewC; NewCol 75;
OxEng; OxFr; PenC EUR; PseudN 82; REn*

Bandy, Moe
American. Singer
Country singer who had hit "Hank Williams,
You Wrote My Life," 1976.
b. 1944 in Meridian, Mississippi
Source: *IlEncCM; WhoAm 82, 84*

Bane, Frank B
American. Government Official
First administrator of Social Security system,
1935.
b. 1894 in Smithfield, Virginia
d. Jan 23, 1983 in Alexandria, Virginia
Source: *BioIn 4; NewYTBS 83; WhoAm 80*

Banghart, Kenneth
Radio Commentator
Newscaster, announcer in early days of radio.
Source: *NF*

**Bangor, Edward Henry Harold Ward,
Viscount**
English. Journalist
BBC foreign correspondent, 1946-60; wrote
Number One Boy, 1969.
b. Nov 5, 1905 in England
Source: *Who 82, 83*

Bangs, Lester
American. Critic, Author
Rock critic *Rolling Stone, Village Voice;*
editor *Creem* magazine; recorded album
Juke Savages on the Brazos, 1981.
b. Dec 1948
d. Apr 30, 1982 in New York, New York
Source: *ConAu 106; NewYTBS 82*

Bani-Sadr, Abolhassan
Iranian. Political Leader
First pres. elected in Iran's 2,500 year
history, 1980; lost power to Khomeini,
1981.
b. Mar 22, 1933 in Hamadan Province, Iran
Source: *CurBio 81; IntWW 80, 81, 82; IntYB
81, 82; MidE 80, 81, 82; NewYTBS 79, 80;
WhoWor 82*

Baniszewski, Gertrude Wright
American. Murderer
Known for torture murder of female boarder,
16 yr. old Sylvia Likens, 1965.
b. 1929 in Indiana
Source: *Blood&B; DrInf; LookW*

Bankhead, Dan(iel Robert)
American. Baseball Player
First black pitcher to appear in ML game--
Aug 26, 1947; hit home run in first at-
bat.
b. May 3, 1920 in Empire, Alabama
d. May 2, 1976 in Houston, Texas
Source: *BaseEn 85; BioIn 10; NewYTBS 76;
ObitOF 79*

Bankhead, Tallulah Brockman
American. Actress
Starred in plays *The Little Foxes,* 1939; *The
Skin of Our Teeth,* 1943.
b. Jan 31, 1903 in Huntsville, Alabama
d. Dec 12, 1968 in New York, New York
Source: *BiDFilm; BiE&WWA; CurBio 41, 53,
69; FamA&A; Film 1; FilmgC; InWom;
MotPP; MovMk; OxFilm; PlP&P; ThFT;
WebAB; WhAm 5; WhScrn 74, 77; WhoHol
B; WorEFlm*

Bankhead, William Brockman
American. Politician
Father of Tallulah Bankhead, who was Dem.
con. from AL, 1917-40, Speaker of House,
1936-40.
b. Apr 12, 1874 in Moscow, Alabama
d. Sep 15, 1940 in Bethesda, Maryland
Source: *BiDrAC; CurBio 40; DcAmB S2;
WebAB; WhAm 1; WhAmP*

Banks, Ernie (Ernest)
American. Baseball Player
Shortstop, Chicago Cubs, 1953-71; Hall of
Fame, 1977.
b. Jan 31, 1931 in Dallas, Texas
Source: *BaseEn 85; BlueB 76; CurBio 59;
Ebony 1; InB&W 85; WhoAm 82; WhoBlA
80; WhoMW 82; WhoProB 73; WorAl*

Banks, Leslie
English. Actor, Director
Played villain in *The Most Dangerous Game,*
1932.
b. Jun 9, 1890 in Liverpool, England
d. Apr 21, 1952 in London, England
Source: *FilmgC; MovMk; NotNAT B; ObitT
1951; ODwPR 79; OxThe; WhScrn 74, 77;
WhThe; WhoHol B*

Banks, Monty (Montague)
[Mario Bianchi]
Italian. Actor, Director
Married to Gracie Fields; appeared in *A Bell
for Adono,* 1961.
b. 1897 in Casene, Italy
d. Jan 7, 1950 in Arona, Italy
Source: *BioIn 2; Film 2; FilmgC; NotNAT B;
ObitOF 79; TwYS; WhScrn 74, 77; WhoHol
B*

Banks, Tony
[Genesis]
English. Musician
Keyboardist, original member of Genesis.
b. Mar 27, 1950 in England
Source: *NF*

Banky, Vilma
[Vilma Lonchit]
"The Hungarian Rhapsody"
American. Actress
Silent film actress who starred with Rudolph
Valentino in *The Eagle,* 1925.
b. Jan 9, 1903 in Nagyrodog, Hungary
Source: *Film 2; FilmgC; MotPP; MovMk;
ThFT; TwYS; WhoHol A; WorEFlm*

Banneker, Benjamin
American. Mathematician, Inventor
Accurately calculated an eclipse, 1789; first
black appointed to Capital Commission by
pres., 1789.
b. Nov 9, 1731 in Elliot's Mills, Maryland
d. Oct 9, 1806 in Baltimore, Maryland
Source: *ApCAB; DcAmAu; DcAmNB; Drake;
EncAB-H; NegAl 76; WebAB; WhAm HS;
WhAmP*

Bannen, Ian
Scottish. Actor
Known for Shakespearean roles including
film *Macbeth,* 1959.
b. Jun 29, 1928 in Airdrie, Scotland
Source: *FilmEn; FilmgC; IntMPA 80, 81;
IntWW 82; MotPP; MovMk; WhoHol A;
WhoThe 77, 81*

Banner, Bob
American. Producer, Director
Has produced, directed TV series "Solid
Gold" since 1980.
b. Aug 15, 1921 in Ennis, Texas
Source: *ConTFT 3*

Banner, James Morril, Jr.
American. Author
b. May 3, 1935 in New York, New York
Source: *ConAu 49*

Bannerman, Francis
American. Merchant
Enlarged, developed father's military supplies
business, contributing rifles, outfits to
Scotch nat. guardsmen, 1914.
b. Mar 24, 1851 in Dundee, Scotland
d. Nov 26, 1918 in Brooklyn, New York
Source: *ApCAB X; BioIn 3, 10; NatCAB 19*

Bannerman, Helen
Scottish. Children's Author
Wrote controversial classic *Story of Little Black Sambo,* 1900.
b. 1863 in Edinburgh, Scotland
d. Oct 13, 1946 in Edinburgh, Scotland
Source: *ConAu 111; TwCCW 78*

Banning, Kendall
American. Author
Writings include *The Great Adventure,* 1925; *Our Army Today,* 1943.
b. Sep 20, 1879 in New York, New York
d. Dec 27, 1944
Source: *AmAu&B; AnMV 1926; ChhPo, S2; CurBio 45; DcNAA; WhAm 2; WhNAA*

Banning, Margaret Culkin
American. Author
Wrote over 30 novels on marriage, parenthood: *Echo Answers,* 1960.
b. Mar 18, 1891 in Buffalo, New York
d. Jan 4, 1982 in Tryon, North Carolina
Source: *AmAu&B; AmCath 80; AmNov; AmWomWr; AnObit 1982; BiCAW; BkC 6; ConAu 4NR, 5R, 105; CurBio 40, 82; MinnWr; NewYTBS 82; OxAmL; REnAL; TwCA, SUP; WhAm 8; WhE&EA; WhLit; WhNAA,; WhoAm 82; WhoAmW 81; WhoWor 74; WrDr 82*

Bannister, Constance Gibbs
American. Photographer
Gained worldwide recognition, 1940s-50s, as specialist in photographing babies.
b. Feb 11, 1919 in Ashland, Tennessee
Source: *CurBio 55; InWom; NewYTBE 72; WhoAm 74, 76, 78; WhoAmW 74*

Bannister, Edward Mitchell
American. Artist
First black artist to win first place at Philadelphia Centennial Exhibition, 1876.
b. 1833 in Saint Andrews, New Brunswick
d. 1901 in Providence, Rhode Island
Source: *AfrA; AfroAA; DcAmNB; InB&W 80; NegAl 83; NewYHSD; WhAm 4; WhoAmA 82N*

Bannister, Roger, Sir
English. Track Athlete, Physician
First to run mile under four minutes, 1954.
b. Mar 23, 1929 in Harrow, England
Source: *Au&Wr 71; BlueB 76; CurBio 56; IntWW 81, 82; NewYTBS 79; WhDW; Who 74, 82; WhoTr&F 73; WhoWor 74; WorAl; WrDr 76*

Bannon, Jim
American. Actor
Fourth actor to star in *Red Ryder* western serials.
b. 1911 in Kansas City, Missouri
Source: *BioIn 4, 8; FilmgC; WhoHol A*

Banting, Frederick Grant, Sir
Canadian. Physician
Won 1923 Nobel Prize as co-discoverer of insulin, with John Macleod.
b. Nov 17, 1891 in Alliston, Ontario
d. Feb 21, 1941 in Newfoundland, Ontario
Source: *AsBiEn; BkPepl; CurBio 41; DcScB; LinLib S; LongCTC; MacDCB 78; McGEWB; WorAl*

Bantock, Granville, Sir
English. Composer, Conductor
b. Aug 7, 1868 in London, England
d. Oct 16, 1946 in London, England
Source: *CompSN SUP; CurBio 46; ObitOF 79*

Banton, Travis
American. Designer
b. 1874 in New York, New York
d. 1958
Source: *WorFshn*

Banzer-Suarez, Hugo
Bolivian. Political Leader
Pres. of Bolivia, 1971-78; overthrown in coup, Jul, 1978.
b. Jul 10, 1926 in Santa Cruz, Bolivia
Source: *CurBio 73; IntWW 74; NewYTBE 71; WhoWor 78*

Bar-Ilian, David Jacob
Israeli. Musician
b. Feb 7, 1930 in Haifa, Palestine
Source: *WhoAm 82; WhoMus 72*

Bar Kokhba, Simon
Hebrew. Revolutionary
d. 135
Source: *BioIn 3, 6, 9; WebBD 80*

Bara, Theda
[Theodosia Goodman]
American. Actress
Known for silent screen vamp roles, 1914-19, such as Salome and Cleopatra.
b. Jul 20, 1890 in Cincinnati, Ohio
d. Apr 7, 1955 in Los Angeles, California
Source: *BiDFilm; DcAmB S5; Film 1; FilmgC; InWom; MotPP; MovMk; OxFilm; TwYS; WebAB; WhAm 3; WhScrn 74, 77; WhoHol B; WorEFlm*

Barabbas
Biblical Character
Bandit released from jail at time of Jesus'
death.
Source: *LongCEL; NewCol 75; WebBD 80*

Baraka, Imamu Amiri
see: Jones, Leroi

Barbaja, Domenica
Italian. Opera Singer
b. 1778 in Milan, Italy
d. Oct 16, 1841 in Posilipo, Italy
Source: *NewEOp 71*

Barbanell, Maurice
English. Journalist, Psychic
Edited *Psychic News; Two Worlds.*
b. May 3, 1902 in London, England
d. Jul 17, 1981
Source: *BiDPsy; ConAu 113*

Barbarelli, Giorgio
see: Giorgione, Il

Barea, Arturo
Spanish. Author
Wrote trilogy *Forging of a Rebel,* 1946.
b. Sep 20, 1897 in Spain
d. Dec 24, 1957 in Faringdon, England
Source: *CasWL; ConAu 111; LongCTC; REn*

Barbarossa, Dave
[Bow Wow Wow]
Mauritian. Musician
Drummer whose tom-tom African ritual beat
was key to group's sound.
b. in Mauritius
Source: *NF*

Barbeau, Adrienne
[Mrs. John Carpenter]
American. Actress
Starred in TV series "Maude," 1972-78; in
movie *The Fog,* 1980.
b. Jun 11, 1945
Source: *BioIn 12; VarWW 85*

Barber, Bernard
American. Author, Educator
Best known for *Science and the Social Order,*
1952.
b. Jan 29, 1918 in Boston, Massachusetts
Source: *AmAu&B; AmM&WS 73S, 78S;
ConAu 65; WhoAm 74, 76, 78*

Barber, Bill (William Charles)
Canadian. Hockey Player
Left wing, Philadelphia, 1972-83; won two
Stanley Cups.
b. Jul 11, 1952 in Callender, Ontario
Source: *HocEn; HocReg 81*

Barber, "Red" (Walter Lanier)
American. Sportscaster
Dismissal by NY Yankees, 1966, raised issue
of sportscaster impartiality.
b. Feb 17, 1908 in Columbus, Mississippi
Source: *BioNews 74; CurBio 43; LesBEnT;
NewYTBS 81, 84; WorAl*

Barber, Samuel
American. Composer
First composer to win Pulitzer twice; best
known for "Adagio on Strings," 1936.
b. Mar 9, 1910 in West Chester,
Pennsylvania
d. Jan 23, 1981 in New York, New York
Source: *AmSCAP 66; ConAu 103; DcCM;
IntWW 74; OxAmL; WebAB; Who 74;
WhoAm 74; WhoMus 72; WhoWor 78*

Barbera, Joseph Roland
[Hanna and Barbera]
American. Cartoonist
With Bill Hanna, created cartoons
"Huckleberry Hound," "The Smurfs,"
"The Flintstones."
b. Mar 24, 1911 in New York, New York
Source: *OxFilm; WhoAm 78; WhoTelC;
WorEFlm*

Barbie, Klaus
[Klaus Altmann, alias]
"The Butcher of Lyon"
German. Nazi Leader
Captain of Gestapo, Lyon, France, 1942-44;
accused of crimes against humanity;
extradited to France, 1983.
b. 1914 in Germany
Source: *BioIn 9*

Barbier, Jules
French. Opera Librettist
Starred in operas with Michael Carre,
"Faust"; "Romeo et Juliette"; "Hamlet".
b. Mar 8, 1825 in Paris, France
d. Jan 16, 1901 in Paris, France
Source: *BiD&SB; NewEOp 71*

Barbieri, Fedora
Italian. Opera Singer
b. Jun 4, 1920 in Trieste, Italy
Source: *CurBio 57; InWom; IntWW 74;
WhoMus 72; WhoWor 78*

Barbirolli, John, Sir
English. Conductor
b. Dec 2, 1899 in London, England
d. Jul 28, 1970 in London, England
Source: *CurBio 40, 70; NewYTBE 70; WhAm 5*

Barbour, John
Canadian. Comedian, Writer
b. Apr 24, in Toronto, Ontario
Source: *WhoAm 80, 82*

Barbour, Walworth
American. Diplomat
US ambassador to Israel, 1961-73.
b. Jun 4, 1908 in Cambridge, Massachusetts
d. Jul 21, 1982 in Gloucester, Massachusetts
Source: *BlueB 76; DcAmDH; IntWW 75; IntYB 78, 79, 80, 81, 82; NewYTBE 71; NewYTBS 82; Who 82; WhoAmP 75, 77, 79, 81; WhoGov 72; WhoWor 74*

Bard, John
American. Physician
NYC's first health officer; established city's first quarantine station on Bedlow's (now Liberty) Island, 1700s.
b. Feb 1, 1716 in Burlington, New Jersey
d. Mar 20, 1799 in Hyde Park, New York
Source: *AmBi; ApCAB; DcAmB; Drake; WebAB; WhAm HS*

Bardeen, John
American. Physicist
Invented transistor, which won Nobel Prize for Physics, 1956.
b. May 23, 1908 in Madison, Wisconsin
Source: *AmM&WS 73P; CurBio 57; IntWW 74; WebAB; Who 74; WhoAm 74, 76, 78, 80, 82; WhoMW 74; WhoWor 78*

Bardis, Panos Demetrios
Greek. Sociologist, Author
b. Sep 24, 1924 in Lefcohorion, Greece
Source: *AmM&WS 73S; ConAu 25R; WhoAm 74, 76, 78, 80, 82; WhoWor 78; WrDr 80*

Bardot, Brigitte
French. Actress
French sex symbol best known for film *And God Created Woman,* 1956.
b. Sep 28, 1934 in Paris, France
Source: *BiDFilm; BkPepl; CelR; ConTFT 3; CurBio 60; FilmgC; IntMPA 82; IntWW 74; MotPP; MovMk; OxFilm; WhoHol A; WhoWor 74; WorEFlm*

Barenboim, Daniel
Israeli. Musician, Conductor
b. Nov 15, 1942 in Buenos Aires, Argentina
Source: *CelR; CurBio 69; IntWW 74; Who 74; WhoAm 82; WhoMus 72; WhoWor 78; WhoWorJ 72*

Barents, Willem
Dutch. Explorer
b. in Terschelling, Netherlands
d. Jun 1597
Source: *McGEWB; NewCol 75; WebBD 80*

Barentzen, Patrick de
see: DeBarentzen, Patrick

Bares, Basile
American. Musician
b. 1845 in New Orleans, Louisiana
d. 1902 in New Orleans, Louisiana
Source: *BiDAmM*

Barfield, Jesse Lee
American. Baseball Player
Outfielder, Toronto, 1981--.
b. Oct 29, 1951 in Joliet, Illinois
Source: *BaseEn 85; BaseReg 86*

Barfield, Velma
American. Criminal
First woman executed in US since 1962.
b. 1932
d. Nov 2, 1984 in Raleigh, North Carolina
Source: *NF*

Barger, Floyd
American. Editor
b. Oct 26, 1906 in Boardman, Ohio
d. Aug 1975
Source: *WhAm 6; WhoAm 74; WhoE 74; WhoF&I 74*

Bargone, Frederic Charles Pierre Edouard
see: Farrere, Claude, pseud.

Bari, Lynn
[Marjorie Schuyler Fisher]
American. Actress
Played the "other woman" in B films, 1930s-40s.
b. Dec 18, 1913 in Roanoke, Virginia
Source: *FilmgC; HolP 30; IntMPA 80, 81, 82; MotPP; MovMk; ThFT; WhoHol A*

Baring, Maurice
English. Author, Diplomat, Poet, Journalist
Wrote autobiography, *Puppet Show of
    Memory,* 1922.
b. Apr 27, 1874 in London, England
d. Dec 14, 1945 in Inverness-Shire, England
Source: *BkC 4; CasWL; CathA 1930;
DcCathB; DcLEL; EncWL; EvLB; LongCTC;
ModBrL; NewC; NotNAT B; OxEng; REn;
ScF&FL 1; TwCA, SUP; TwCWr; WebE&AL;
WhAm 5; WhThe; WhoHr&F*

Baring-Gould, Sabine
English. Author, Clergyman, Essayist
Wrote words to hymns, "Onward Christian
    Soldiers"; "Now the Day Is Over."
b. Jan 28, 1834 in Exeter, England
d. Jan 2, 1924 in Lew-Trenchard, England
Source: *BbD; BiD&SB; BrAu 19; CarSB;
CathA 1930; CelCen; Chambr 3; DcBiA;
DcBiPP; DcEnA, AP; DcEnL; DcLEL; EvLB;
LinLib L, S; LongCTC; LuthC 75; NewC;
Novels; OxEng; OxMus; PenC ENG;
WebE&AL; WhoHr&F*

Barker, Bernard L
American. Watergate Participant
Recruited by E Howard Hunt as one of
    Watergate burglars, Jan 17, 1972.
b. 1917 in Havana, Cuba
Source: *BioIn 10, 11; NewYTBS 74*

Barker, Bob (Robert William)
American. TV Personality
Hosted game shows, "Truth or
    Consequences"; "The Price is Right."
b. Dec 12, 1923 in Darrington, Washington
Source: *BioIn 4, 10; WhoAm 82*

Barker, Cliff
[Fabulous Five]
American. Basketball Player
b. Jan 15, 1921 in Yorktown, Indiana
Source: *WhoBbl 73*

Barker, "Doc" (Arthur)
American. Criminal
Robber, murderer, kidnapper, captured by
    Melvin Purvis, 1935, killed in escape
    attempt, 1939.
b. 1899 in Aurora, Missouri
d. Jun 13, 1939 in Alcatraz, California
Source: *BioIn 1; Blood&B; DrInf*

Barker, Ernest, Sir
English. Educator, Political Scientist
First political science professor at Cambridge;
    wrote autobiogarphy *Age and Youth,* 1953.
b. Sep 23, 1874 in Woodley, England
d. Feb 11, 1960 in Cambridge, England
Source: *ConAu 103, 93; DcNaB 1951; EvLB;
GrBr; LinLib L; LongCTC; NewC; ObitOF
79; ObitT 1951; PenC ENG; WhE&EA;
WhLit*

Barker, Fred
American. Criminal
Added Alvin Karpis to Barker gang; killed
    with mother in battle with FBI.
b. 1902 in Aurora, Missouri
d. Jan 16, 1935 in Oklawaha, Florida
Source: *Blood&B; DrInf*

Barker, George Granville
English. Author, Poet
Works include *Eros in Dogma,* 1944;
    Collected Poems, 1957.
b. Feb 26, 1913 in Loughton, England
Source: *Au&Wr 71; CasWL; CnE&AP;
CnMWL; ConAu 7NR, 9R; ConLC 8; ConP
75; DcLEL; DrAF 76; DrAP 75; EncWL;
IntWW 82; LongCTC; ModBrL, S1; NewC;
OxEng; PenC ENG; REn; TwCA SUP;
TwCWr; WebE&AL; Who 74; WhoTwCL;
WhoWor 74, 78; WrDr 76*

Barker, Harley Granville
see: Granville-Barker, Harley

Barker, Herman
American. Criminal
Member, Kimes-Terrill Gang, early 1920s,
    robbing banks; committed suicide.
b. 1894 in Aurora, Missouri
d. Sep 19, 1927 in Newton, Kansas
Source: *Blood&B; DrInf*

Barker, Len (Leonard Harold, II)
American. Baseball Player
Pitched perfect game, May 15, 1981.
b. Jul 7, 1955 in Fort Knox, Kentucky
Source: *BaseEn 85; BioIn 12*

Barker, Lex (Alexander Crichlow, Jr.)
American. Actor
Tenth actor to play Tarzan in five films,
    1949-53.
b. May 8, 1919 in Rye, New York
d. Apr 11, 1973 in New York, New York
Source: *FilmEn; FilmgC; MotPP; MovMk;
NewYTBE 73; ObitOF 79; WhScrn 77;
WhoHol B*

Barker, Lloyd
American. Criminal
Only Barker brother who did not join a
gang; jailed for robbing post office, 1922-
47.
b. 1896 in Aurora, Missouri
d. 1949 in Colorado
Source: *Blood&B; DrInf*

Barker, "Ma" (Arizona Donnie Clark)
"Kate"
American. Criminal
Planned bank robberies with sons; ran
hideout in OK for escaped convicts.
b. 1872 in Springfield, Missouri
d. Jan 16, 1935 in Oklawaha, Florida
Source: *Blood&B; WhoFla*

Barker, Ronnie
English. Actor, Comedian
Starred in British TV series "The Two
Ronnies"; "Porridge"; "Sorry."
b. Sep 25, 1929 in Bedford, England
Source: *FilmgC; Who 82; WhoThe 77, 81*

Barker, Sue
English. Tennis Player
Winner of French Open, 1976, known for
devastating forehand shot.
b. Apr 19, 1956 in Paignton, England
Source: *BioIn 11; WhoIntT*

Barkin, Ben
American. Businessman
b. Jun 4, 1915 in Milwaukee, Wisconsin
Source: *WhoAm 74; WhoF&I 74; WhoPubR
72*

Barkley, Alben William
American. Politician
Dem. con., 1912-26, who was Harry
Truman's vp, 1948-52.
b. Nov 24, 1877 in Graves County,
Kentucky
d. Apr 30, 1956 in Lexington, Virginia
Source: *BiDrAC; BiDrUSE; CurBio 41, 49,
56; WebAB; WhAm 3; WhAmP*

Barkley, Charles Wade
American. Basketball Player
First round pick by Philadelphia, 1984,
named to NBA All-Rookie team, 1985.
b. Feb 20, 1963 in Leeds, Alabama
Source: *OfNBA 81*

Barks, Carl
American. Cartoonist
Illustrated Donald Duck, Uncle Scrooge
McDuck comic strips.
b. Mar 27, 1901 in Merrill, Oregon
Source: *ConAu 115*

Barlach, Ernst Heinrich
German. Sculptor, Dramatist
Wrote powerful symbolist-realistic plays
including *Der Blaue Boll,* 1926; works
banned by Nazis.
b. Jan 2, 1870 in Holstein, Germany
d. Jan 24, 1938 in Gustrow, Germany
Source: *AntBDN A; CasWL; ClDMEL;
CnMD; DcNiCA; EncWL, 2; EncWT;
EvEuW; McGDA; McGEWB; McGEWD;
ModGL; ModWD; NotNAT B; OxArt; OxGer;
PenC EUR; PhDcTCA 77; REn; WorECar*

Barlow, Howard
American. Conductor
Noted conductor on several radio shows:
CBS Radio, 1927-43; Voice of Firestone,
1943-59.
b. May 1, 1892 in Plain City, Ohio
d. May 31, 1972 in Portland, Oregon
Source: *AmSCAP 66; Baker 78; BiDAmM;
CmpEPM; CurBio 40, 54, 72; NewYTBE 72;
WhAm 5*

Barlow, Joel
American. Diplomat, Journalist
Friend of Thomas Paine; best known poem
The Hasty-Pudding, 1793.
b. Mar 24, 1754 in Redding, Connecticut
d. Dec 24, 1812 in Zarnowiec, Poland
Source: *AmAu; AmAu&B; AmBi; ApCAB;
BiD&SB; CasWL; Chambr 3; ChhPo; CnDAL;
DcAmAu; DcAmB; DcAmDH; DcAmSR;
DcEnL; DcLEL; DcNAA; EncAB-H; EvLB;
HarEnUS; LinLib L, S; McGEWB; OxAmL;
OxEng; PenC AM; PoChrch; REn; REnAL;
TwCBDA; WebAB; WebE&AL; WhAm HS;
WhAmP*

Barnaby, Ralph S
American. Author, Artist, Engineer
b. Jan 21, 1893 in Meadville, Pennsylvania
Source: *ConAu 61; SmATA 9*

Barnard, Chester Irving
American. Business Executive, Government
Official
Pres., United Service Organizations (USO),
1942-45.
b. Nov 7, 1886 in Malden, Massachusetts
d. Jun 7, 1961 in New York, New York
Source: *DcAmB S7; WebBD 80*

Barnard, Christiaan Neethling
South African. Surgeon
Performed first human heart transplant, Dec
3, 1967, on Louis Washkansky.
b. Oct 8, 1922 in Beaufort West, South
Africa
Source: *AfSS 80, 81, 82; AsBiEn; CelR;
ConAu 61; CurBio 68; IntAu&W 77; IntWW
74, 80, 81, 82; WhDW; Who 74, 82;
WhoWor 74; WorAl*

Barnard, Frederick Augustus Porter
American. Educator
Pres., Columbia U, 1864-89; founded Barnard
College to extend education to women.
b. May 5, 1809 in Sheffield, Massachusetts
d. Apr 27, 1889 in New York, New York
Source: *McGEWB; WebAB; WhAm HS*

Barnard, George Grey
American. Sculptor
b. May 24, 1863 in Bellefonte, Pennsylvania
d. Apr 24, 1938 in New York, New York
Source: *AmBi; ApCAB SUP; DcAmB S2;
OxAmL; REnAL; WebAB; WhAm 1*

Barnard, Henry
American. Educator
First US Commissioner of Education, 1867-
70.
b. Jan 24, 1811 in Hartford, Connecticut
d. Jul 5, 1900 in Hartford, Connecticut
Source: *AmAu; AmBi; ApCAB; BbD; BiAUS;
BiD&SB; CyAL 1, 2; DcAmAu; DcAmB;
DcNAA; Drake; EncAB-H; TwCBDA; WebAB;
WhAm HS*

Barnardo, Thomas John
Irish. Social Reformer
Pioneer in care of destitute children; opened
Dr. Barnardo's Homes for Boys, 1870.
b. Jul 4, 1845 in Dublin, Ireland
d. Sep 19, 1905 in Surbiton, Ireland
Source: *DcIrB; LongCTC; NewC; NewCol 75*

Barnes, Billy
American. Lyricist, Composer, Singer
b. Jan 27, 1927 in Los Angeles, California
Source: *BiE&WWA; NotNAT*

Barnes, "Binnie"
[Gertrude (Gitelle) Maude Barnes]
English. Actress
Starred as Catherine Howard in *The Private
Life of Henry VIII*, 1933, with Charles
Laughton.
b. Mar 25, 1905 in London, England
Source: *FilmEn; Film 2; HolP 30; MotPP;
MovMk; ThFT; WhThe; WhoHol A; WhoThe
77A*

Barnes, Clair Cortland
[The Hostages]
American. Hostage in Iran
Source: *NewYTBS 81*

Barnes, Clive Alexander
English. Journalist, Critic, Author, Editor
Well-known dance, drama critic; with NY
Post since 1978.
b. May 13, 1927 in London, England
Source: *AmAu&B; AuNews 2; ConAu 77;
ConTFT 3; CurBio 72; IntWW 74; NotNAT;
WhoAm 84; WhoE 74; WhoThe 77*

Barnes, Djuna
[Lydia Steptoe, pseud.]
American. Author, Journalist
Writings influenced by James Joyce and T S
Eliot; wrote novel *Nightwood*, 1933.
b. Jun 12, 1892 in Cornwall-on-Hudson, New
York
d. Jun 18, 1982 in New York, New York
Source: *AnObit 1982; CasWL; CnMD; ConAu
107, X; ConDr 77, 82; ConLC 3, 4, 8, 11;
ConNov 76, 82; DcLB 9; DcLEL; EncWL, 2;
IntAu&W 76, 77; LinLib L; LongCTC;
ModAL, S1; NewYTBS 82; OxAmL; PenC
AM; RAdv 1; REn; REnAL; TwCA, SUP;
TwCWr; WhAm 8; WhoAm 78; WhoAmW
74; WhoTwCL; WhoWor 74; WrDr 80*

Barnes, Edward Larrabee
American. Architect
Designed prefabricated aluminum house,
1948.
b. Apr 22, 1915 in Chicago, Illinois
Source: *AmArch 70; BioIn 4, 5, 9;
BnEnAmA; IntWW 74, 75, 76, 77, 78;
McGDA; WhoAm 76, 78, 80, 82, 84;
WhoWor 74*

Barnes, Ernest William
English. Clergyman
Bishop of Birmingham, 1924-53; wrote
controversial *The Rise of Christianity*,
1947.
b. Apr 1, 1874 in Cheshire, England
d. Nov 29, 1953 in Sussex, England
Source: *DcNaB 1951; GrBr; LuthC 75;
ObitOF 79; ObitT 1951; WhE&EA; WhLit;
WhoLA*

Barnes, Joanna
American. Actress, Author
Wrote *Pastora*, 1980; appeared in movie
Spartacus, 1960.
b. Nov 15, 1934 in Boston, Massachusetts
Source: *ConAu 57; FilmgC; MotPP; WhoAm
82; WhoHol A*

Barnes, Leonard John
English. Author
b. Jul 21, 1895 in London, England
Source: *ConAu 29R, P-2*

Barnes, Margaret Ayer
American. Author, Dramatist
Wrote Pulitzer novel *Years of Grace,* 1930.
b. Apr 8, 1886 in Chicago, Illinois
d. Oct 26, 1967
Source: *AmAu&B; ConAmA; ConAu 21R,
25R; DcLB 9; DcLEL; OxAmL; REnAL;
TwCA, SUP; WhAm 4; WhNAA; WhoAmW
68, 70; WomWWA 14*

Barnes, Marvin
"Bad News"
American. Basketball Player
b. Jul 27, 1952 in Providence, Rhode Island
Source: *WhoBbl 73*

Barnet, Charlie (Charles Daly)
American. Band Leader
b. Oct 26, 1913 in New York, New York
Source: *WhoJazz 72*

Barnet, Sylvan M, Jr.
American. Author, Educator
b. Dec 11, 1926 in Brooklyn, New York
Source: *ConAu 1R, 4NR; DrAS 74E; WhoAm
74; WhoPubR 72*

Barnet, Will
American. Artist, Educator
Painter, printmaker who calls style Abstract
    Reality; professor, Cooper Union Art
    School, 1945-78.
b. May 25, 1911 in Beverly, Massachusetts
Source: *CurBio 85; DcAmArt; DcCAA 71, 77;
WhoAm 76, 78, 80, 82, 84; WhoAmA 76, 78,
84; WhoE 74*

Barnetson, William Denholm, Lord
[Lord Barnetson of Crowborough]
British. Journalist
Chm., Reuters, Ltd., 1968-79.
b. Mar 21, 1917 in Edinburgh, Scotland
d. Mar 12, 1981 in London, England
Source: *Au&Wr 71; IntAu&W 76, 77; IntWW
76, 77, 78; IntYB 78; NewYTBS 81; Who 74;
WhoF&I 74, 75, 77, 79; WhoWor 74, 76, 78*

Barnett, Claude A
American. Business Executive
b. Sep 16, 1889 in Sanford, Florida
d. Aug 2, 1967 in Chicago, Illinois
Source: *WhAm 4, 5; St&PR 75*

Barnett, Marvin Robert
American. Business Executive
Has worked in various capacites for visually
    handicapped organizations since 1944.
b. Oct 31, 1916 in Jacksonville, Florida
Source: *BioIn 2; WhoAm 82; WhoE 74*

Barnett, Steve
American. Anthropologist
Studies habits of American consumers for
    nation's largest corporations.
b. Aug 23, 1942
Source: *FifIDA; NewYTBS 86*

Barney, Natalie Clifford
American. Author
Hostess of celebrated Parisian literary salon,
    1920s-30s; wrote risque memoirs.
b. Oct 31, 1876 in Dayton, Ohio
d. Feb 2, 1972 in Paris, France
Source: *ConAu 33R; DcLB 4; IntDcWB;
NewYTBE 72; NotAW MOD; ScF&FL 1*

Barnhart, Clarence Lewis
American. Lexicographer
Co-editor, *The World Book Dictionary,* 1976.
b. Dec 30, 1900 in Plattsburg, Missouri
Source: *AmAu&B; ConAu 13R; CurBio 54;
DrAS 74F; WhoAm 74, 76, 78, 80, 82;
WhoWor 78*

Barnum, P(hineas) T(aylor)
[Barnum and Bailey]
American. Circus Owner
Opened "The Greatest Show on Earth,"
    1871.
b. Jul 5, 1810 in Bethel, Connecticut
d. Apr 7, 1891 in Philadelphia, Pennsylvania
Source: *Alli, SUP; AmAu&B; AmBi; ApCAB;
BbD; BiD&SB; DcAmAu; DcAmB; DcNAA;
Drake; EncAB-H; MnBBF; NewCol 75;
OxAmL; OxThe; REn; REnAL; TwCBDA;
WebAB; WhAm HS*

Barnum and Bailey
see: Bailey, James Anthony; Barnum,
    P(hineas) T(aylor)

Barolini, Antonio
American. Author
b. May 29, 1910 in Vicenza, Italy
Source: *ConAu 1R, 1NR*

Baron, Samuel
American. Musician
b. Apr 27, 1925 in Brooklyn, New York
Source: *WhoAm 74, 76, 78, 80; WhoWor 74;
WhoWorJ 72*

Barr, Alfred Hamilton, Jr.
"The Pope"
American. Museum Director, Art Historian
First and most influential director, Museum
of Modern Art, NYC, 1929-43.
b. Jan 28, 1902 in Detroit, Michigan
d. Aug 15, 1981 in Salisbury, Connecticut
Source: *AmAu&B; AnObit 1981; BlueB 76;
ConAu 105, 49; CurBio 61, 81; IntWW 82;
LinLib L; NewYTBS 81; OxAmH; PseudN
82; WhAm 8; WhE&EA; Who 82; WhoAm
78; WhoAmA 82; WhoArt 82*

Barr, Amelia Edith Huddleston
American. Author, Journalist
Wrote historical fiction: *Remember the
Alamo*, 1888.
b. Mar 29, 1831 in Lancaster, England
d. Mar 10, 1919 in Richmond Hill, New
York
Source: *NotAW; OxAmL 83*

Barr, George
American. Author
b. Nov 11, 1907 in Brooklyn, New York
Source: *AmAu&B; AuBYP; ConAu 1R, 1NR;
SmATA 2*

Barr, Stringfellow
American. Author, Educator
Pres., St. John's College, 1937-46, who
initiated great books curriculum.
b. Jan 15, 1897 in Suffolk, Virginia
d. Feb 3, 1982 in Alexandria, Virginia
Source: *AmAu&B; AnObit 1982; ConAu 1R,
1NR; CurBio 40, 82; IntWW 79; IntYB 80,
81; LinLib L, S; NewYTBS 82; OxAmL;
REnAL; TwCA SUP; WhoAm 80; WhoWor
74*

Barraclough, Geoffrey
English. Author, Educator
Writings include *The Mediaeval Empire*,
1950.
b. May 10, 1908
d. Dec 26, 1984
Source: *AnObit 1984; ConAu 101; WhAm 8;
Who 74; WhoWor 74; WorAu*

Barragan, Luis
Mexican. Architect
Mexico's greatest architect; awarded Pritzker
Prize, 1980.
b. 1902 in Guadalajara, Mexico
Source: *ConArch; MacEA; NewYTBS 86;
WhoAm 82*

**Barras, Paul Francois Jean Nicolas, Comte
de**
French. Politician
Helped to overthrow Robespierre, 1794;
arranged for marriage between Josephine,
Napoleon.
b. Jun 30, 1755 in Fox-Amphoux, France
d. Jan 29, 1829 in Chaillot, France
Source: *DcBiPP; DcInB; Dis&D; LinLib S;
McGEWB; OxFr; WhDW*

Barrasso, Tom (Thomas)
American. Hockey Player
Goaltender, Buffalo Sabres, 1983--; drafted
fifth overall.
b. Mar 31, 1965 in Boston, Massachusetts
Source: *HocReg 85; NewYTBS 83*

Barrault, Jean-Louis
French. Actor, Director
Best known for contributions to French
theater.
b. Sep 8, 1910 in Vesinet, France
Source: *BiE&WWA; CnThe; ConAu 105;
EncWT; FilmEn; FilmgC; LinLib L; MovMk;
NotNAT A; OxFilm; OxThe; REn; WhDW;
WhThe; Who 82; WhoHol A; WorEFlm*

Barre, Raymond
French. Government Official
b. Apr 12, 1924 in Saint-Denis, France
Source: *CurBio 77; IntWW 74, 75, 76, 77,
78, 79, 80, 81; IntYB 78, 79, 80, 81;
NewYTBS 76; WhoWor 74, 76, 78; WorAl*

Barres, Maurice
French. Author
b. Sep 22, 1862 in Charmes-sur-Moselle,
France
d. Dec 4, 1923 in Paris, France
Source: *BiD&SB; CasWL; ClDMEL; EvEuW;
LongCTC; NewC; OxEng; OxFr; PenC EUR*

Barrett, Edward Ware
American. Educator, Editor
b. Jul 3, 1910 in Birmingham, Alabama
Source: *CurBio 47; DrAS 74E; IntWW 74;
LEduc 74; St&PR 75; WhoAm 74; WhoE 74;
WrDr 80*

Barrett, John L
American. Radio Performer
Original voice of the Lone Ranger on radio,
early 1930s.
b. 1913
d. May 1, 1984 in Buffalo, New York
Source: *NF*

Barrett, Rona
[Rona Burstein; Mrs. William A Trowbridge]
American. Journalist
Gossip columnist since 1957; fan magazines
    Rona Barrett's Hollywood, Rona Barrett's
    Gossip sold over one million copies, 1974.
b. Oct 8, 1936 in New York, New York
Source: *AuNews 1; BioNews 74; BkPepl;*
    ConAu 103; GoodHs; IntMPA 78, 79, 80, 81,
    82; NewYTET; WhoAm 78; WhoAmW 72

Barrett, Stan
American. Stuntman
Had fastest ever flat run speed--739.666
    mph--in missile-powered vehicle, 1979.
b. 1944 in Saint Louis, Missouri
Source: *BioIn 12*

Barrett, "Syd" (Roger Keith)
[Pink Floyd]
English. Singer, Songwriter
Founded, named Pink Floyd, 1964; released
    two solo albums, early 1970s.
b. Jan 1946 in Cambridge, England
Source: *ConMuA 80A; IlEncRk; RolSEnR 83*

Barrett, William Edmund
American. Author
Two of his novels, *The Left Hand of God,*
    1951, and *The Lilies of the Field,* 1962,
    were made into movies.
b. Nov 16, 1900 in New York, New York
d. Sep 17, 1986 in Denver, Colorado
Source: *AmAu&B; Au&Wr 71; REnAL;*
    WhoWor 78

Barrett, William, Sir
English. Physicist
b. Feb 10, 1844 in Jamaica
d. May 26, 1925 in London, England
Source: *BiDPara*

Barrie, Barbara
[Barbara Ann Berman]
American. Actress
Films include *Breaking Away,* 1979; *Private*
    Benjamin, 1980.
b. May 23, 1931 in Chicago, Illinois
Source: *ConTFT 3; NotNAT; WhoAm 82;*
    WhoHol A; WhoThe 77

Barrie, James Matthew, Sir
Scottish. Dramatist, Author
Best known for *Little Minister,* 1897; *Peter*
    Pan, 1904.
b. May 9, 1860 in Kirriemuir, Scotland
d. Jun 19, 1937 in London, England
Source: *AtlBL; BbD; BiD&SB; CarSB;*
    CasWL; Chambr 3; CnMD; CnThe; CyWA;
    DcBiA; DcEnA, AP; DcLEL; EncWL; EvLB;
    FamAYP; JBA 34; LongCTC; McGEWD;
    ModBrL; ModWD; NewC; NewCol 75;
    OxThe; OxThe; PenC ENG; RAdv 1; REn;
    REnWD; TwCA, SUP; TwCWr; WebE&AL;
    WhScrn 77; WhoChL; WhoStg 1906, 1908;
    WhoTwCL; YABC 1

Barrie, Mona
[Mona Smith]
English. Actress
Starred in 1933 films *Never Give a Sucker an*
    Even Break, Cass Timberlane.
b. Dec 18, 1909 in London, England
Source: *FilmEn; FilmgC; IntMPA 75, 76, 77,*
    78, 79, 80, 81, 82; MovMk

Barrie, Wendy
[Marguerite Wendy Jenkins]
English. Actress
Radio, TV talk show hostess whose films
    include *Private Life of Henry VIII,* 1933;
    Hound of Baskervilles, 1939.
b. Apr 18, 1912 in London, England
d. Feb 2, 1978 in Englewood, New Jersey
Source: *FilmEn; FilmgC; IntMPA 75, 76, 77;*
    MotPP; MovMk; NewYTBS 78; ObitOF 79;
    ThFT; WhoHol A; WhoThe 81N

Barrios, Francisco Javier
Mexican. Baseball Player
Pitcher, Chicago White Sox, 1974-81.
b. Jun 10, 1953 in Hermosillo, Mexico
d. Apr 9, 1982 in Hermosillo, Mexico
Source: *BaseEn 85*

Barris, Chuck
American. TV Host, Producer
Created, produced "The Dating Game,"
    1965-73; "The Newlywed Game," 1966-74.
b. Jun 2, 1929 in Philadelphia, Pennsylvania
Source: *BioNews 74; NewYTET; WhoAm 78,*
    80, 82; WrDr 76, 80, 82

Barron, Clarence Walker
American. Publisher, Editor
Published *Wall Street Journal,* starting 1901,
    Barron's Financial Weekly, starting 1921.
b. Jul 2, 1855 in Boston, Massachusetts
d. Oct 2, 1928 in Battle Creek, Michigan
Source: *AmBi; ApCAB X; DcAmB S1;*
    DcNAA; NatCAB 21; WebAB, 79; WhAm 1

Barrow, Clyde
[Bonnie and Clyde]
"Public Enemy #1 of the Southwest"
American. Outlaw
With Bonnie Parker, accused of 12 murders
during two-year crime spree in Southwest.
b. Mar 24, 1909 in Telice, Texas
d. May 23, 1934 in Louisiana
Source: *BioIn 8, 9; Blood&B; DrInf; EncACr;*
REnAW; WorAl

Barrow, Ed(ward Grant)
American. Baseball Executive
NY Yankees business mgr., 1921-39, pres.,
1939-45; Hall of Fame, 1953.
b. May 10, 1868 in Springfield, Illinois
d. Dec 15, 1953 in Port Chester, New York
Source: *BioIn 1, 2, 3, 7; DcAmB S5; ObitOF*
79; WhoProB 73

Barrow, Errol Walton
Political Leader
Prime minister, Barbados, 1961-76.
b. Jan 21, 1920 in Saint Lucy, Barbados
Source: *CurBio 68; InB&W 80; IntWW 74,*
80, 81, 82; IntYB 80, 81, 82; Who 74, 82;
WhoGov 72; WhoWor 74, 80

Barrow, Keith E
American. Singer, Songwriter
Popular gospel composer; formed the Soul
Shakers.
b. Sep 27, 1954 in Chicago, Illinois
d. Oct 22, 1983 in Chicago, Illinois
Source: *ConAu 111; WhoBlA 80*

Barrow, Ruth Nita, Dame
Barbadian. Nurse, Reformer
Promotes worldwide health care; has
investigated S Africa's apartheid.
b. Nov 15, 1916 in Barbados
Source: *BiDrAPH 79*

Barrows, Marjorie (Ruth)
[Jack Alden; Noel Ames, pseuds.]
American. Author, Editor
Magazine editor, 1922-66, whose writings
include *Little Red Balloon,* 1979.
b. 1902 in Chicago, Illinois
d. Mar 29, 1983 in Evanston, Illinois
Source: *AmAu&B; AuBYP; ConAu 109, P-2;*
WhAm 8; WhoAm 82

Barry, Daniel
American. Cartoonist
Drew "Flash Gordon," "Doc Savage,"
"Commando York" for comic books.
b. Jul 11, 1923 in Long Beach, New Jersey
Source: *WorECom*

Barry, Donald
[Donald Barry de Acosta]
"Red"
American. Actor
Starred in *Red Ryder* Western film series,
1940s.
b. Jul 11, 1912 in Houston, Texas
d. Jul 17, 1980 in North Hollywood,
California
Source: *FilmEn; IntMPA 77, 78, 79, 81, 82;*
MotPP; NewYTBS 80; PseudN 82; WhoHol A

Barry, Gene
[Eugene Klass]
American. Actor
Starred in TV series "Bat Masterson," 1959-
61; "Burke's Law," 1963-66; "Name of the
Game," 1968-71.
b. Jun 4, 1922 in New York, New York
Source: *FilmgC; IntMPA 75, 76, 77, 78, 79,*
80, 81, 82; MotPP; WhoAm 74, 76, 78, 80,
82; WhoHol A

Barry, Jack
[Jack Barasch]
American. TV Host, Producer
Producer of game shows, including
"Concentration," 1958-73, longest-running
daytime quiz show.
b. Mar 20, 1918 in Lindenhurst, New York
d. May 2, 1984 in New York, New York
Source: *IntMPA 82; NewYTET; WhAm 8;*
WhoAm 82

Barry, James Miranda
Scottish. Physician
b. 1795
d. 1865
Source: *BioIn 5, 8, 9, 10, 11*

Barry, John
American. Naval Officer
Captured first British ship, the *Edward,*
taken by an American, 1775.
b. 1745 in Tacumshane, Ireland
d. Sep 13, 1803 in Philadelphia, Pennsylvania
Source: *AmBi; ApCAB; DcAmB; Drake;*
TwCBDA; WebAB; WhAm HS

Barry, John
English. Composer
Wrote music for several James Bond films;
won Oscar, 1968, for *Lion In Winter*
score.
b. Nov 3, 1933 in York, England
Source: *EncMT; FilmEn; IntMPA 81;*
OxFilm; VarWW 85; WhoMus 72; WhoWor
74; WorEFlm

Barry, Leonora Marie Kearney
"Mother Lake"
American. Labor Union Official
Organized women's workers in Knights of
    Labor, 1886-90.
b. Aug 13, 1849 in Kearney, Ireland
d. Jul 15, 1930 in Minooka, Illinois
Source: *NotAW; WebBD 80*

Berry, Marion Shepilov, Jr.
American. Politician
Mayor of Washington, DC, 1979--.
b. Mar 6, 1936 in Itta Bena, Mississippi
Source: *Ebony 1; InB&W 80; NegAl 83;
    WhoAm 80, 82, 84; WhoAmP 81, 83;
    WhoBlA 80; WhoE 83*

Barry, Philip
American. Dramatist
Wrote *The Philadelphia Story;* filmed, 1940,
    starring Katharine Hepburn, Cary Grant.
b. Jun 18, 1896 in Rochester, New York
d. Dec 3, 1949 in New York, New York
Source: *AmAu&B; CasWL; CathA 1930;
    CnDAL; CnMD; CnThe; ConAmA; DcAmB
    S4, S4; DcLEL; DcNAA; EvLB; FilmgC;
    LongCTC; McGEWD; ModAL; ModWD;
    NewCol 75; OxAmL; OxThe; PenC AM; REn;
    REnAL; REnWD; TwCA, SUP; TwCWr;
    WebE&AL; WhAm 2*

Barry, Rick (Richard Francis, III)
American. Basketball Player, Sportscaster
Five-time All-Star, 1968-80, who holds NBA
    record for free-throw percentage.
b. Mar 28, 1944 in Elizabeth, New Jersey
Source: *CelR; CmCal; CurBio 71; OfNBA 81;
    WhoAm 80, 82; WhoBbl 73; WorAl*

Barry, Tom
Irish. Military Leader
Leader in Irish War for Independence, 1919-
    22, who helped develop guerilla warfare.
b. Jul 1, 1897 in Rosscarbery, Ireland
d. Jul 2, 1980 in Cork, Ireland
Source: *AnObit 1980; DcIrW 2; NewYTBS 80*

Barrymore, Diana
[Diana Blanche Blythe]
American. Actress, Celebrity Relative
John Barrymore's daughter; starred in 1940s
    films; wrote autobiography *Too Much, Too
    Soon,* 1957.
b. Mar 3, 1921 in New York, New York
d. Jan 25, 1960 in New York, New York
Source: *EncWT; FilmEn; FilmgC; HolP 40;
    InWom; MotPP; NotNAT A, B; ObitOF 79;
    WhScrn 74, 77; WhThe; WhoHol B*

Barrymore, Drew
American. Actress, Celebrity Relative
Granddaughter of John Barrymore; played
    Gertie in *ET,* 1982.
b. 1976
Source: *VarWW 85*

Barrymore, Elaine Jacobs
[Elaine Barrie]
American. Actress
John Barrymore's wife; wrote autobiography
    All My Sins Remembered, 1977.
b. 1914
Source: *BioIn 11; InWom; NotNAT A; What
8*

Barrymore, Ethel Mae Blythe
"First Lady of the American Theatre"
American. Actress
Sister of John, Lionel Barrymore who won
    1944 Oscar for *None But the Lonely
    Heart.*
b. Aug 15, 1879 in Philadelphia,
    Pennsylvania
d. Jun 18, 1959 in Hollywood, California
Source: *CurBio 41, 59; FamA&A; FilmEn;
    Film 1; FilmgC; HerW; InWom; MotPP;
    MovMk; OxFilm; OxThe; PIP&P; ThFT;
    TwYS; WebAB; WhAm 3; WhScrn 74, 77;
    WhoHol B; WhoStg 1906, 1908; WomWWA
    14; WorEFlm*

Barrymore, Georgina Emma Drew
[Mrs. Maurice Barrymore]
American. Actress
Starred in *Romeo and Juliet* with husband
    Maurice, 1883; mother of John, Ethel,
    Lionel.
b. Jul 11, 1854 in Philadelphia, Pennsylvania
d. Jul 2, 1893 in Santa Barbara, California
Source: *NotAW*

Barrymore, John
[John Blythe]
American. Actor
Box office attraction due to voice, profile;
    known for roles as lover, grotesque
    tortured part in *Dr. Jekyll and Mr. Hyde,*
    1920.
b. Feb 15, 1882 in Philadelphia, Pennsylvania
d. May 29, 1942 in Hollywood, California
Source: *BiDFilm; CmMov; CurBio 42;
    DcAmB S3; EncAB-H; FamA&A; FilmEn;
    Film 1; FilmgC; LongCTC; MotPP; MovMk;
    OxFilm; OxThe; PIP&P; TwYS; WebAB;
    WhAm 2; WhScrn 74, 77; WhoHol A;
    WorEFlm*

Barrymore, John Blythe Drew, Jr.
American. Actor, Celebrity Relative
Son of John Barrymore, father of Drew
Barrymore; appeared in low-budget Italian
films.
b. Jun 4, 1932 in Beverly Hills, California
Source: *BioNews 74; FilmEn; FilmgC;*
IntMPA 75, 76, 77, 78, 79, 80, 81, 82;
MotPP; WhoHol A

Barrymore, Lionel Blythe
American. Actor
Brother of Ethel, John; first Barrymore to
appear in film; won 1931 Oscar for *Free*
Soul.
b. Apr 28, 1878 in Philadelphia,
Pennsylvania
d. Nov 15, 1954 in Van Nuys, California
Source: *AmSCAP 66; BiDFilm; CurBio 43,*
55; DcAmB S5; FamA&A; Film 1; FilmgC;
LongCTC; MotPP; MovMk; OxFilm; OxThe;
PlP&P; TwYS; WebAB; WhAm 3; WhScrn
74, 77; WhoHol B; WorEFlm

Barrymore, Maurice
[Herbert Blythe]
English. Actor
Father of Lionel, Ethel, John Barrymore,
who made acting debut, 1872; known for
supporting roles.
b. 1847 in Fort Agra, India
d. Mar 26, 1905 in Amityville, New York
Source: *AmBi; ApCAB SUP; DcAmB;*
FamA&A; LongCTC; OxThe; PlP&P; WebAB;
WhAm 1

Bart, Jean
French. Naval Officer
Known for heroic exploits during War of
Grand Alliance.
b. Oct 21, 1651 in Dunkirk, France
d. Apr 27, 1702
Source: *NewCol 75; OxShips; WebBD 80;*
WhoMilH 76

Bart, Lionel
[Lionel Begleiter]
English. Composer, Lyricist, Dramatist
Stage musicals include *La Strada,* 1969; Tony
award-winning *Oliver,* 1963.
b. Aug 1, 1930 in London, England
Source: *ConAu 65; ConTFT 3; EncMT;*
FilmgC; IntWW 74; NotNAT; Who 74;
WhoThe 77; WhoWor 78

Barth, Heinrich
German. Explorer, Author
Explored Africa, compiling vocabularies of 40
African languages; crossed Sahara, 1855.
b. Feb 16, 1821 in Hamburg, Germany
d. Dec 25, 1865 in Berlin, Germany
Source: *Alli SUP; McGEWB*

Barth, John Simmons
American. Author
Won National Book Award in Fiction, 1973;
books include *The Open Decision,* 1970.
b. May 27, 1930 in Cambridge, Maryland
Source: *AmAu&B; AmWr; Au&Wr 71;*
AuNews 1, 2; CasWL; ConAu 1R, 5NR;
ConLC 1, 2, 3, 5, 7, 9, 10, 14; ConNov 72,
76; CurBio 69; DrAF 76; DrAS 74E; EncWL;
IntWW 74; ModAL, S1; OxAmL; PenC AM;
RAdv 1; TwCWr; WebAB; WebE&AL;
WhoAm 74, 76, 78, 80, 82; WhoTwCL;
WhoWor 78; WorAu; WrDr 80

Barth, Karl
Swiss. Theologian
Sought to restore belief in fundamental
dogmas of Christianity.
b. May 10, 1886 in Basel, Switzerland
d. Dec 9, 1966 in Basel, Switzerland
Source: *ConAu 25R; CurBio 62, 69;*
LongCTC; OxGer; TwCA SUP; WhAm 5

Barth, Roland Sawyer
American. Author
Wrote books on education: *Open Education*
Re-examined, 1973.
b. May 18, 1937 in Boston, Massachusetts
Source: *ConAu 1NR, 45; WhoE 83*

Barthe, Richmond
American. Sculptor
Works include busts of Booker T
Washington, George Washington Carver,
for Hall of Fame, NYU.
b. Jan 28, 1901 in Bay St. Louis, Mississippi
Source: *AfroAA; CurBio 40; WhoAm 74;*
WhoBlA 75; WhoWor 78

Barthelme, Donald
American. Author
Best known works *Snow White,* 1967; *City*
Life, 1970; *Sadness,* 1972.
b. Apr 7, 1931 in Philadelphia, Pennsylvania
Source: *AmAu&B; CelR; ConAu 21R; ConLC*
1, 2, 3, 5, 6, 8, 13; ConNov 76; DrAF 76;
ModAL S1; PenC AM; RAdv 1; SmATA 7;
WorAu; WrDr 80

Barthelmess, Richard
American. Actor
Best known roles in DW Griffith movies
  Broken Blossoms, 1919; *Way Down East,*
  1920.
b. May 9, 1895 in New York, New York
d. Aug 17, 1963 in Southampton, New York
Source: *BiDFilm; FilmEn; Film 2; FilmgC;*
MotPP; MovMk; NotNAT B; ObitOF 79;
OxFilm; TwYS; WhAm 4; WhScrn 74, 77;
WhoHol B; WorEFlm

Barthes, Roland
French. Literary Critic
Known for contributions to structural
  linguistics, applications of semiology
  theories; wrote *Writing Degree Zero,* 1953.
b. Nov 12, 1915 in Cherbourg, France
d. Mar 25, 1980 in Paris, France
Source: *BioIn 10, 11; ConAu 97; CurBio 79,*
80; WhoWor 78

Bartholdi, Auguste (Frederic Auguste)
French. Sculptor
Designed Statue of Liberty, France's gift to
  America, 1886.
b. Apr 2, 1834 in Colmar, France
d. Oct 4, 1904 in Paris, France
Source: *ApCAB; ArtsNiC; HarEnUS; LinLib*
S; McGDA; NewCol 75; REn; TwCBDA

Bartholomew, Saint
Biblical Character
One of Twelve Disciples, who preached in
  India; feast day Aug 24.
Source: *DcCathB; Dis&D; McGDA; NewC;*
REn

Bartholomew, Freddie (Frederick
Llewellyn)
American. Actor
Child actor known for first starring part, in
  David Copperfield, 1935.
b. Mar 28, 1924 in London, England
Source: *BiDFilm; FilmEn; IntMPA 80, 81,*
82; MotPP; MovMk; OxFilm; WhoHol A;
WorEFlm

Bartholomew, Reginald
American. Diplomat
US ambassador to Lebanon, 1983--.
b. Feb 17, 1936 in Portland, Maine
Source: *NewYTBS 83, 84*

Bartkowicz, Peaches
American. Tennis Player
b. Apr 4, 1949 in Hamtramck, Michigan
Source: *BioIn 11*

Bartkowski, Steve(n Joseph)
American. Football Player
b. Nov 12, 1952 in Des Moines, Iowa
Source: *BioIn 12; FootReg 81; NewYTBS 80*

Bartlett, Charles Leffingwell
American. Journalist
Editor, Chicago *Daily News,* 1975-78; Field
  Syndicate, 1978--; won Pulitzer, 1955.
b. Aug 14, 1921 in Chicago, Illinois
Source: *ConAu 29R; WhoAm 74, 76, 78, 80,*
82; WhoS&SW 82

Bartlett, Francis Alonzo
American. Business Executive
Founded Bartlett Shade Tree Co., 1910;
  investigated Dutch elm disease, 1929.
b. Nov 13, 1882 in Belchertown,
  Massachusetts
d. Nov 21, 1963 in Stamford, Connecticut
Source: *DcAmB S7*

Bartlett, Jennifer Losch
American. Artist
Realistic painter who paints same image from
  different perspectives, in different styles:
  "Graceland Mansion," "At the Lake,"
  series.
b. Mar 14, 1941 in Long Beach, California
Source: *ConArt 83; CurBio 85; DcCAr 81;*
PrintW 83; WhoAm 84

Bartlett, John
American. Lexicographer, Publisher
Edited first edition of *Familiar Quotations;*
  published 1855.
b. Jun 14, 1820 in Plymouth, Massachusetts
d. Dec 3, 1905 in Cambridge, Massachusetts
Source: *Alli, SUP; AmAu; AmAu&B; AmBi;*
ApCAB; BiD&SB; ChhPo; CnDAL; DcAmAu;
DcAmB; DcNAA; EvLB; LongCTC; OxAmL;
REn; REnAL; TwCBDA; WebAB; WhAm 1

Bartlett, John Russell
American. Historian, Bibliographer
NY bookseller, 1836-50, who edited pioneer
  descriptive bibliography, *John Carter Brown*
  Catalogue, 1865-82.
b. Oct 23, 1805 in Providence, Rhode Island
d. May 28, 1886 in Providence, Rhode
  Island
Source: *Alli, SUP; AmAu; AmAu&B; AmBi;*
ApCAB; ArizL; BiAUS; BiD&SB; WhAm HS

Bartlett, John Sherren
American. Newspaper Editor
Established *Albion*, 1822-48, newspaper for
British residents of US.
b. 1790 in Dorsetshire, England
d. Aug 23, 1863 in Middletown Point, New
Jersey
Source: *ApCAB; DcAmB; Drake; WhAm HS*

Bartlett, Josiah
American. Physician, Lawyer
Signer of Declaration of Independence, who
was first governor of NH, 1793-94.
b. Nov 21, 1729 in Amesbury, Massachusetts
d. May 19, 1795 in Kingston, Massachusetts
Source: *AmBi; ApCAB; BiAUS; BiDrAC;
DcAmB; Drake; TwCBDA; WhAm HS;
WhAmP*

Bartlett, Paul Wayland
American. Sculptor
Known for historic size, portrait statues;
Columbus, Michelangelo at Library of
Congress, Lafayette at Louvre.
b. 1865 in New Haven, Connecticut
d. Sep 20, 1925
Source: *AmBi; DcAmB; TwCBDA; WhAm 1*

Bartlett, Robert Abram
American. Explorer
Commanded Robert E Peary's ship on
expedition that reached N Pole, 1908-9.
b. Aug 15, 1875 in Brigus, Newfoundland
d. Apr 28, 1946 in New York, New York
Source: *AmAu&B; CurBio 46; DcNAA;
WebAB; WhAm 2*

Bartlett, Vernon
English. Author, Politician
Liberal, who favored human rights, peaceful
co-existence; wrote *Nazi Germany
Explained*, 1933.
b. Apr 30, 1894 in Westbury, England
d. 1903
Source: *Au&Wr 71; ConAu 108, 61; IntWW
74; LongCTC; NewC; TwCA, SUP; Who 74;
WhoLA; WrDr 76*

Bartok, Bela
Hungarian. Composer
Original modern composer whose works
include opera "Bluebeard's Castle," 1927.
b. May 25, 1881 in Nagyszentmiklos,
Hungary
d. Sep 29, 1945 in New York, New York
Source: *AmSCAP 66; AtlBL; CurBio 40, 45;
WhDW; WhAm 4*

Bartok, Eva
[Eva Martha Szoke]
British. Actress
Made film debut, 1947; private life love
affairs better known; wrote autobiography
Worth Living For, 1959.
b. Jun 18, 1926 in Kecskemet, Hungary
Source: *FilmEn; FilmgC; IntWW 74; WhoHol
A*

Bartolommeo, Fra
[Bartolommeo di Pagolo del Fatorino; Baccio
della Porta]
Italian. Artist, Architect
Paintings reflect composition balance, color
harmony of High Renaissance; known for
"St. Mark," 1517, now in Louvre.
b. Mar 28, 1475
d. Oct 31, 1517 in Florence, Italy
Source: *AtlBL; NewCol 75*

Barton, Bruce
American. Author, Advertising Executive,
Congressman
Wrote best-seller *Man Nobody Knows*, 1925,
depicting Jesus as prototype of successful
businessman.
b. Aug 5, 1886 in Robbins, Tennessee
d. Jul 5, 1967 in New York, New York
Source: *AmAu&B; BiDrAC; CurBio 61, 67;
EncAB-H; NatCAB 60; ObitOF 79; OhA&B;
WebAB, 79; WhAm 4; WhAmP; WhNAA;
WorAl*

Barton, Clara Harlowe
"Angel of the Battlefield"
American. Teacher, Social Reformer
Founded American Red Cross, 1881-82; pres.
until 1904.
b. Dec 25, 1821 in Oxford, Massachusetts
d. Apr 12, 1912 in Glen Echo, Maryland
Source: *AmAu&B; AmBi; DcAmB; DcNAA;
EncAB-H; HerW; InWom; NewCol 75;
NotAW; REn; REnAL; WebAB; WhAm 1*

Barton, Derek Harold Richard
English. Chemist
Won Nobel Prize, 1969; as result of
discovery, conformational analysis became
part of organic chemistry.
b. Sep 8, 1918 in Gravesend, England
Source: *IntWW 74; McGMS 80; Who 74;
WhoWor 80, 82*

Barton, George
American. Author, Historian
Writings include *Angels of the Battlefield,*
1898; *Famous Detective Mysteries,* 1926.
b. Jan 22, 1866 in Philadelphia, Pennsylvania
d. Mar 16, 1940
Source: *AmAu&B; CathA 1930; CurBio 40;
DcNAA; WhAm 1*

Barton, James
American. Actor, Dancer
Starred in Broadway's *The Iceman Cometh,*
1946; *Paint Your Wagon,* 1951.
b. Nov 1, 1890 in Gloucester, New Jersey
d. Feb 19, 1962 in Mineola, New York
Source: *CmpEPM; DcAmB S7; EncMT;
FilmgC; MovMk; NatCAB 60; NotNAT B;
ObitOF 79; Vers B; WhScrn 74, 77; WhThe;
WhoHol B*

Bartos, Karl
see: Kraftwerk

Bartram, John
American. Botanist
Conducted first hybridizing experiments in
US; idea basis of modern geology.
b. Mar 23, 1699 in Marple, Pennsylvania
d. Sep 22, 1777 in Kingsessing, Pennsylvania
Source: *AmBi; ApCAB; BioIn 2, 3, 6, 7, 8,
10, 11; DcAmB; DcScB; Drake; EncAAH;
McGEWB; NatCab 7; WebAB*

Bartram, William
American. Botanist, Author
Best known for plant and animal descriptions
in *Travels through North and South
Carolina,* 1791.
b. Feb 9, 1739 in Kingsessing, Pennsylvania
d. Jul 22, 1823 in Philadelphia, Pennsylvania
Source: *AmAu; AmAu&B; ApCAB;
BiDLA; BiDSA; CasWL; DcAmAu; DcAmB;
DcScB; HarEnUS; LinLib L; McGEWB;
NatCAB 7; NewYHSD; WebAB 79; DcLEL;
DcNAA; Drake; OxAmL; OxEng; PenC AM;
REn; REnAL; TwCBDA; WebAB; WhAm HS*

Baruch, Bernard Mannes
American. Businessman, Statesman
Adviser to several US presidents; special
adviser on war mobilization, WW II.
b. Aug 19, 1870 in Camden, South Carolina
d. Jun 20, 1965 in New York, New York
Source: *AmAu&B; CurBio 41, 50, 65; EncAB-
H; REn; REnAL; WebAB; WhAm 4; WhAmP*

Barylli, Walter
Austrian. Musician
b. 1921 in Vienna, Austria
Source: *WhoMus 72*

Baryshnikov, Mikhail
"Misha"
American. Ballet Dancer, Director,
Choreographer
Artistic director, American Ballet Theatre,
1980--; films include *The Turning Point,*
1977; *White Knights,* 1985.
b. Jan 28, 1948 in Riga, U.S.S.R.
Source: *BioNews 75; BkPepl; ConTFT 3;
CurBio 75; NewYTBS 74; Who 82; WhoAm
84*

Barzin, Leon Eugene
American. Conductor
Musical director, Ballet Society, NYC ballet,
1948-58.
b. Nov 27, 1900 in Brussels, Belgium
Source: *CurBio 51; NewYTBE 70; WhoMus
72; WhoWor 78*

Barzini, Luigi Giorgio, Jr.
Italian. Author
Best known for works about Americans,
Italians; *Americans Are Alone in the
World; The Italians,* 1964.
b. Dec 21, 1908 in Milan, Italy
d. Mar 30, 1984 in Rome, Italy
Source: *AnObit 1984; ConAu 112, 13R;
CurBio 51, 84; IntWW 74; WhAm 8;
WhoWor 74; WorAu*

Barzun, Jacques Martin
American. Author, Educator, Historian
Advocate of liberal arts studies rather than
vocational courses.
b. Nov 30, 1907 in Creteil, France
Source: *AmAu&B; Au&Wr 71; CelR; ConAu
61; CurBio 64; DrAS 74H; EncMys; IntWW
74; NewCol 75; OxAmL; RAdv 1; REn;
REnAL; TwCA, SUP; WebAB; Who 74;
WhoAm 74, 76, 78, 80, 82; WhoAmA 73;
WhoMus 72; WhoWor 78; WrDr 80*

Basehart, Richard
American. Actor
Versatile actor who made film debut, 1947;
won 1956 Oscar for *Moby Dick.*
b. Aug 31, 1914 in Zanesville, Ohio
d. Sep 17, 1984 in Los Angeles, California
Source: *AnObit 1984; BiE&WWA; FilmEn;
FilmgC; IntMPA 77, 78, 79, 80, 81, 82;
OxFilm; WhoAm 74, 76, 78, 80, 82; WhoHol
A*

Basho
Japanese. Poet
Zen Buddhist haiku master.
b. 1644 in Ueno, Iga, Japan
d. Nov 28, 1694 in Osaka, Japan
Source: *CasWL; CyWA; DcOrL 1; LinLib L;
McGEWB; PenC CL; REn*

Basie, "Count" (William James, Jr.)
American. Jazz Musician, Band Leader
One of most influential big band leaders,
    1930s, 1940s, who revolutionized jazz; hits
    include "One O'Clock Jump," 1941.
b. Aug 21, 1904 in Red Bank, New Jersey
d. Apr 26, 1984 in Hollywood, Florida
Source: *AmSCAP 66; BioNews 74; CelR;*
ConNews 85-1; CurBio 42, 84; WebAB;
WhAm 8; WhoAm 82; WhoBlA 75; WhoWor
74

Basil (the Great), Saint
Greek. Religious Leader
Father of Eastern communal monasticism;
    feast day Jun 14.
b. 330 in Caesarea, Cappadocia
d. Jan 1, 379 in Caesarea, Cappadocia
Source: *Baker 78; CasWL; CyEd; Grk&L;*
IlEncMy; LinLib L, S; LuthC 75; McGEWB;
PenC CL; WhDW

Basinger, Kim
American. Actress, Model
Starred in *Never Say Never Again*, 1983; *The*
    Natural, 1983.
b. Dec 8, 1953 in Athens, Georgia
Source: *VarWW 85*

Baskerville, John
English. Printer, Type Designer
His innovative typeface is still used today;
    printed *The Bible; The Book of Common*
    Prayer.
b. Jan 28, 1706
d. Jan 8, 1775
Source: *DcBiPP; DcNaB; Dis&D; NewC;*
WhDW

Baskin, Burton
American. Businessman
With Irvine Robbins started Baskin-Robbins
    ice cream stores, 1947.
b. 1913 in Chicago, Illinois
d. 1967 in California
Source: *Entr*

Baskin, Leonard
American. Sculptor
b. Aug 15, 1922 in New Brunswick, New
    Jersey
Source: *CurBio 64; DcCAA 71; WebAB;*
WhoAm 74; WhoAmA 73; WhoGrA 62;
WhoWor 78

Baskin, Wade
American. Author, Educator
Writings include *Dictionary of Spiritualism*,
    1971; *The Sorcerer's Handbook,* 1974.
b. Jul 27, 1924 in Harmony, Arkansas
d. Mar 5, 1974
Source: *ConAu 21R, P-2; WhoS&SW 82*

Bass, Alfie (Alfred)
English. Actor
Character comedian; works include *Help!*,
    1965; *Alfie*, 1966.
b. Apr 8, 1921 in London, England
Source: *FilmEn; FilmgC; WhoHol A; WhoThe*
81

Bass, Henry
American. Manufacturer
Began making utilitarian shoes, 1876;
    moccasins became college favorite, 1960s.
b. 1843
d. 1925
Source: *Entr*

Bass, Sam
American. Outlaw
Train robber, ambushed by Texas Rangers,
    who was hero of Western ballads.
b. Jul 21, 1851 in Mitchell, Indiana
d. Jul 21, 1878 in Round Rock, Texas
Source: *BioIn 4, 5, 8, 11; DcAmB; NewCol*
75; REnAW; WebAB; WhAm HS

Bass, Saul
American. Director, Producer
Revolutionized film credits by animating
    names; film title designs include *Seven*
    Year Itch, 1955; *Vertigo*, 1958.
b. May 8, 1920 in New York, New York
Source: *DcFM; FilmEn; FilmgC; IntMPA 76,*
77, 78, 79, 80, 81, 82; OxFilm; WhoAm 74;
WhoGrA 62; WhoWor 74; WhoWorJ 72, 78;
WorEFlm

Bassett, John D
American. Businessman
Formed Bassett Furniture Co., 1902, world's
    largest maker of wooden furniture.
b. 1866 in Bassett, Virginia
d. Feb 26, 1965 in Bassett, Virginia
Source: *Entr; WhAm 4*

Bassey, Shirley
Welsh. Singer
Sang title song from James Bond film
    Goldfinger, 1964.
b. Jan 8, 1937 in Cardiff, Wales
Source: *CelR; FilmgC; WhoAm 82*

Basso, Hamilton Joseph
American. Author
Wrote *The View from Pompey's Head,* 1954.
b. Sep 5, 1904 in New Orleans, Louisiana
d. May 13, 1964 in New Haven, Connecticut
Source: *DcAmB S7; OxAmL 83; WebBD 80*

Bastianini, Ettore
Italian. Opera Singer
b. 1923 in Siena, Italy
d. Jan 25, 1967 in Sirmione, Italy
Source: *WhAm 4*

Basualto, Neftali Ricardo Reyes
see: Neruda, Pablo, pseud.

Batchelor, Clarence Daniel
American. Cartoonist
Work appeared in NY *Daily News,* 1931-69;
won Pulitzer, 1937.
b. Apr 1, 1888 in Osage City, Kansas
d. Sep 5, 1977 in Deep River, Connecticut
Source: *ConAu 73; WhAm 7; WhoAm 74, 76;
WhoAmA 76, 78N*

Bate, Walter Jackson
American. Educator, Author
Writings include *From Classic to Romantic,*
1946; won Pulitzer, 1964.
b. May 23, 1918 in Mankato, Minnesota
Source: *AmAu&B; ConAu 5R; DrAS 74E;
OxAmL; Who 74; WhoAm 74, 76, 78, 80,
82; WorAu*

Bateman, Mary
"Yorkshire Witch"
English. Murderer
Pathological criminal who dispensed magical
charms to defraud, kill; died on gallows.
b. 1768 in Aisenby, England
d. Mar 20, 1809
Source: *LookW*

Bateman, Justine
American. Actress
Plays Mallory Keaton on TV's "Family
Ties," 1982--.
b. Feb 19, 1966 in Rye, New York
Source: *NF*

Bateman, Kate Josephine
American. Actress
Starred in play *Leah the Forsaken,* 1863.
b. Oct 7, 1842 in Baltimore, Maryland
d. Apr 8, 1917 in London, England
Source: *NotAW; WebBD 80*

Bates, Alan Arthur
English. Actor
Starred in films *King of Hearts,* 1967; *An
Unmarried Woman,* 1978.
b. Feb 17, 1934 in Derbyshire, England
Source: *BiE&WWA; BkPepl; CelR; CurBio
69; FilmgC; IntMPA 77, 78, 79, 80, 81, 82;
IntWW 74; MovMk; NotNAT; Who 74;
WhoAm 82; WhoHol A; WhoThe 77;
WhoWor 78*

Bates, Arlo
American. Author, Poet
Writings include *Patty's Perversities,* 1881;
The Intoxicated Ghost, 1908.
b. Dec 16, 1850 in East Machias, Maine
d. Aug 24, 1918 in Boston, Massachusetts
Source: *Alli SUP; AmAu; AmAu&B; BbD;
BiD&SB; CarSB; ChhPo; DcAmAu; DcBiA;
DcNAA; NatCAB 8; OxAmL; REnAL;
ScF&FL 1; TwCBDA; WhAm 1*

Bates, Blanche Lyon
American. Actress
Starred in David Belasco's *Madame Butterfly,*
1900.
b. Aug 25, 1873 in Portland, Oregon
d. Dec 25, 1941 in San Francisco, California
Source: *NotAW*

Bates, Florence
[Florence Rabe]
American. Actress
Made film debut at age 50; starred in
Rebecca, 1940.
b. Apr 15, 1888 in San Antonio, Texas
d. Jan 31, 1954 in Burbank, California
Source: *FilmEn; FilmgC; MovMk; NotNAT B;
ObitOF 79; Vers A; WhScrn 74, 77; WhoHol
B*

Bateman, Henry Mayo
Welsh. Cartoonist
Most highly paid British cartoonist of his
time.
b. Feb 15, 1887 in New South Wales
d. Feb 11, 1970 in Gozo, Malta
Source: *DcBrAr 1; DcBrBI; DcNaB 1961;
GrBr; IlsCB 1744; WhE&EA; WhLit*

Bates, H(erbert) E(rnest)
English. Author
Wrote over 50 books including *The Two
Sisters,* 1926; books on WW II.
b. May 16, 1905 in Rushden, England
d. Jan 29, 1974 in Kent, England
Source: *Au&Wr 71; CasWL; ChhPo, S1;
ConAu 45, 93; CurBio 44, 74; DcLEL;
EncWL; EvLB; LongCTC; ModBrL; NewC;
PenC ENG; REn; TwCA, SUP; TwCWr;
WhAm 6; Who 74; WhoWor 78*

Bates, Katherine Lee
American. Poet, Educator
Writings include *American Literature,* 1898;
    America the Beautiful, and Other Poems,
    1911.
b. Aug 12, 1859 in Falmouth, Massachusetts
d. Mar 28, 1929 in Wellesley, Massachusetts
Source: *DcAmB S1; HerW; WomWWA 14*

Bates, Mary Elizabeth
American. Surgeon, Reformer
First female intern at Cook County Hospital,
    Chicago, 1882; worked to reform child
    abuse laws, 1905.
b. Feb 25, 1861 in Manitowoc, Wisconsin
d. 1954
Source: *InWom; WhAm 4; WomWWA 14*

Bates, "Peg Leg" (Clayton)
American. Dancer
Amputation of leg forced him to dance with
    peg leg; in Broadway musical *Blackbirds,*
    1925, 1933.
b. Nov 10, 1907 in Fountain Inn, South
    Carolina
Source: *BiDAfM; BiDD; InB&W 80*

Bates, Ted (Theodore Lewis)
American. Advertising Executive
b. Sep 11, 1901 in New Haven, Connecticut
d. May 1972
Source: *NewYTBE 72; WhAm 5; WhoAdv 72*

Bates, William Horatio
American. Physician
b. 1860 in New York, New York
d. Jul 10, 1931
Source: *DcNAA*

Bateson, Gregory
American. Author, Anthropologist,
    Psychologist
Founded science of cybernetics with first
    wife, Margaret Mead; formulated "double-
    bind" theory.
b. May 9, 1904 in Cambridge, England
d. Jul 4, 1980 in San Francisco, California
Source: *AmAu&B; AmM&WS 73S; AnObit
    1980; ConAu 101, 101, 41R; IntEnSS 79;
    WrDr 80*

Bateson, William
British. Biologist
Coined term "genetics"; known for research
    in plant inheritance based on work of
    Mendel.
b. Aug 8, 1861 in Whitby, England
d. Feb 8, 1926 in Merton, England
Source: *AsBiEn; BioIn 10; DcScB; InSci;
    WebBD 80*

Bathory, Elizabeth
[Countess Nadasdy]
"The Blood Countess"
Hungarian. Murderer
Killed 610 servant girls; believed human
    blood baths essential to retaining youth.
b. 1560
d. 1614
Source: *BioIn 4, 9; FanAl; InWom; LookW;
    MacDWB*

Bathsheba
Biblical Character
Married King David, who had her first
    husband killed; mother of Solomon.
b. 1040 BC
d. 1015 BC
Source: *InWom*

Batista y Zaldivar, Fulgencio
Cuban. Political Leader
Dictator who came to power, 1952;
    overthrown by Fidel Castro, 1959.
b. Jan 16, 1901 in Banes, Cuba
d. Aug 6, 1973 in Guadalmina, Spain
Source: *BioIn 1, 2, 3, 4, 5, 6, 8, 10; CurBio
    52, 73; NewYTBE 73*

Battelle, Phyllis Marie
American. Journalist
Has weekly syndicated column, "Assignment:
    America," 1955--.
b. Jan 4, 1922 in Dayton, Ohio
Source: *ConAu 77; ForWC 70; InWom;
    WhoAm 74*

Batten, William Milfred
American. Businessman
Chairman, chief exec., NY Stock Exchange,
    1976--.
b. Jun 4, 1909 in Reedy, West Virginia
Source: *IntWW 74, 75, 76, 77, 78, 79, 80;
    NewYTBS 76; St&PR 75; WhoAm 74; WhoE
    74; WhoF&I 74, 75, 77, 79, 81*

Battistini, Mattia
Italian. Opera Singer
High baritone who had 50 year career; never
    performed at Metropolitan Opera because
    of fear of crossing Atlantic.
b. Feb 27, 1856 in Rome, Italy
d. Nov 7, 1928 in Collebaccaro, Italy
Source: *Baker 78; MusSN; NewEOp 71*

Battles, Cliff(ord Franklin)
American. Football Player
Running back, 1932-37; led league in
    rushing, 1933-37; Hall of Fame.
b. May 1, 1910 in Akron, Ohio
d. Apr 27, 1981 in Clearwater, Florida
Source: *BioIn 6, 8, 9; WhoFtbl 74*

Batu Khan
Mongolian. Military Leader
Grandson of Genghis Khan who conquerded
  Russia, 1240; organized Mogul state
  Golden Horde.
d. 1255
Source: *McGEWB; NewCol 75; WhDW*

Baucus, Max Sieben
American. Politician
Dem. senator from MT, 1978--.
b. Dec 11, 1941 in Helena, Montana
Source: *AlmAP 78, 80; CngDr 77, 79;
WhoAm 76, 78, 80, 82, 84; WhoAmP 75, 77,
79; WhoGov 75, 77; WhoWest 78*

Baudelaire, Charles Pierre
French. Poet
Best known poems contained in *Les Fleurs
  du Mal,* 1857.
b. Apr 9, 1821 in Paris, France
d. Aug 31, 1867 in Paris, France
Source: *AtlBL; BbD; BiD&SB; CasWL;
ClDMEL; CyWA; DcEuL; EuAu; EvEuW;
NewC; OxEng; OxFr; PenC EUR; REn*

Baudo, Serge
French. Conductor
b. Jul 16, 1927 in Marseilles, France
Source: *WhoWor 78*

Baudouin, Albert Charles
Belgian. Ruler
King of Belgium, 1951--; proclaimed
  independence of Zaire, 1960.
b. Sep 7, 1930 in Brussels, Belgium
Source: *IntWW 80, 81, 82, 83; WhoWor 80,
82; WorAl*

Bauer, Eddie
American. Merchant
Pioneered quilted, goose-down insulated
  jacket; founded mail order sporting goods
  co.
b. Oct 19, 1899 in Orcas Island, Washington
d. Apr 18, 1986 in Bellevue, Washington
Source: *NewYTBS 86*

Bauer, Hank (Henry Albert)
American. Baseball Player, Baseball Manager
Outfielder, 1948-61, who managed Baltimore
  Orioles to world championship, 1966.
b. Jul 31, 1922 in East St. Louis, Illinois
Source: *BaseEn 85; CurBio 67; WhoProB 73*

Bauer, Harold
English. Musician
b. Apr 28, 1873 in London, England
d. Mar 12, 1951 in Miami, Florida
Source: *AmSCAP 66; DcAmB S5; WhAm 3*

Bauer, Helen
American. Author
Writings include *California Mission Days,*
  1951; *The Avacado Cookbook,* 1967.
b. Aug 14, 1900 in DeQueen, Arkansas
Source: *ConAu 5R; ForWC 70; SmATA 2*

Bauer, Royal Daniel Michael
American. Author
b. Oct 25, 1889 in Union, Missouri
Source: *ConAu 33R*

Bauersfeld, Walther
German. Inventor, Engineer
Co-inventor of world's first planetarium.
b. 1879
d. Oct 28, 1959 in Heidenheim, Germany
  (West)
Source: *BioIn 3, 5; ObitOF 79*

Baugh, Albert Croll
American. Author, Educator
Academician, noted for *History of the English
  Language,* 1935.
b. Feb 26, 1891 in Philadelphia, Pennsylvania
d. Mar 21, 1981 in Philadelphia,
  Pennsylvania
Source: *AmAu&B; BioIn 3; ConAu 103, 107;
DrAS 78E; LinLib L; NewYTBS 81; WhAm
7; WhE&EA; WhoAm 74, 76, 78, 80;
WhoWor 78*

Baugh, Sammy (Samuel Adrian)
American. Football Player, Football Coach
Quarterback, Washington Redskins, 1937-52;
  Hall of Fame, 1963.
b. Mar 17, 1914 in Temple, Texas
Source: *WebAB, 79; WhoFtbl 74; WorAl*

Baum, Kurt
Czech. Opera Singer
b. Mar 15, 1908 in Prague, Czechoslovakia
Source: *BioIn 2, 4, 5; CurBio 56; WhoWor
78*

Baum, (Lyman) Frank
American. Author, Journalist
Wrote *The Wizard of Oz,* 1900.
b. May 15, 1856 in Chittenango, New York
d. May 6, 1919 in Hollywood, California
Source: *AmAu&B; AmBi; AuBYP; CarSB;
ChhPo, S2; CnDAL; DcAmAu; DcAmB;
DcNAA; FamSYP; LongCTC; OxAmL; PenC
AM; REn; REnAL; ThrBJA; TwCA; WebAB;
WhoChL; WhoStg 1906, 1908*

Baum, Vicki
American. Author
Wrote best-seller *Grand Hotel*, 1929, film
    starred Greta Garbo, 1932.
b. Jan 24, 1888 in Vienna, Austria
d. Aug 29, 1960 in Hollywood, California
Source: *AmAu&B; AmNov; CasWL; ConAu
    93; CyWA; EvEuW; LongCTC; NatCAB 52;
    NotNAT A, B; Novels; ObitOF 79; ObitT
    1951; OxGer; TwCA, SUP; TwCWr; WhAm
    4; WhE&EA; WhoLA; WorAl*

Baumeister, Willi
German. Artist
Abstractionist, who used ideograms,
    biomorphic shapes; condemned by Nazis,
    1937.
b. Jan 22, 1889 in Stuttgart, Germany
d. Aug 31, 1955 in Stuttgart, Germany
    (West)
Source: *ConArt 77; McGDA*

Baunsgaard, Hilmar Tormod Ingolf
Danish. Political Leader
Prime minister of Denmark, 1968-71.
b. Feb 26, 1920
Source: *IntWW 74, 80, 81, 82, 83; WhoWor
74*

Bausch, Edward
American. Inventor
Helped to develop precision optical
    instruments, particularly the microscope;
    chm. of Bausch & Lomb Optical Co.
b. Sep 26, 1854 in Rochester, New York
d. Jul 30, 1944 in Rochester, New York
Source: *CurBio 44; DcAmB S3; DcNAA;
ObitOF 79; WhAm 2*

Bausch, John Jacob
American. Inventor
With Henry Lomb began Vulcanite Optical
    Instrument Co., 1866.
b. Jul 25, 1830 in Suessen, Germany
d. Feb 14, 1925 in Rochester, New York
Source: *Entr; NatCAB 23; WhAm 1*

Bavier, Frances
American. Actress
Played Aunt Bea in TV series "The Andy
    Griffith Show," 1960-69.
b. Jan 14, 1905 in New York, New York
Source: *WhoHol A*

Bawden, Nina Mary Mabey
[Nina Mary Mabey Kark]
English. Author
Writings include *Eyes of Green*, 1953;
    Familiar Passions, 1979.
b. Jan 19, 1925 in London, England
Source: *Au&Wr 71; AuBYP SUP; BioIn 10,
    11; ChlLR 2; ConAu 17R; ConNov 76;
    FourBJA; IntAu&W 76, 77; SmATA 4;
    TwCCW 78; WrDr 76, 80*

Bax, Arnold Edward Trevor, Sir
[Dermont O'Byrne, pseud.]
English. Composer, Author
Master of Music for Elizabeth II, George VI;
    composed march played at coronation of
    Queen Elizabeth II.
b. Nov 8, 1883 in Streatham, England
d. Oct 3, 1953 in Cork, Ireland
Source: *CurBio 43, 54; DcCM; LongCTC*

Bax, Clifford
English. Dramatist, Critic, Poet
Plays include *Rose Without a Thorn*, 1932.
b. Jul 12, 1886 in Knightsbridge, England
d. Nov 18, 1962
Source: *ConAu 113; McGEWD; OxThe; REn*

Baxley Barbara
American. Actress
Films include *East of Eden*, 1955; *Norma
    Rae*, 1979.
b. Jan 1, 1927 in Stockton, California
Source: *ConTFT 2; VarWW 85*

Baxter, Anne
American. Actress
Best known for films *The Razor's Edge*,
    1946; *All About Eve*, 1950.
b. May 7, 1923 in Michigan City, Indiana
d. Dec 12, 1985 in New York, New York
Source: *BiDFilm; BiE&WWA; CelR; ConNews
    86-1; ConTFT 3; CurBio 72, 86; FilmEn;
    FilmgC; IntMPA 82; MotPP; MovMk;
    NotNAT; WhoAm 82; WhoThe 77; WorEFlm*

Baxter, Frank Condie
American. Educator
Won seven Emmys for TV show
    "Shakespeare on TV."
b. May 4, 1896 in Newbold, New Jersey
d. Jan 20, 1982 in San Marino, California
Source: *CurBio 55; WhAm 8; WhoAm 78*

Baxter, James Phinney, III
American. Educator
Pres., Williams College, 1937-61; won
Pulitzer, 1947, for *Scientists Against Time.*
b. Feb 15, 1893 in Portland, Maine
d. Jun 17, 1975 in Williamstown,
Massachusetts
Source: *AmAu&B; ConAu 57, 65; CurBio 47,
75; OxAmL; TwCA SUP; WhAm 6; WhoWor
74*

Baxter, Keith
[Keith Stanley Baxter Wright]
Welsh. Actor
Starred in London and NY stage production
of "Sleuth," 1970.
b. Apr 29, 1935 in Newport, Wales
Source: *IntMPA 75, 76, 77, 78, 79, 80, 81,
82; NotNAT; WhoHol A; WhoThe 77A, 81*

Baxter, Les
American. Band Leader
Played keyboards for Neil Norman's Cosmic
Orchestra, 1975-80.
b. Mar 14, 1922 in Mexia, Texas
Source: *AmSCAP 66; WhoRocM 82*

Baxter, Warner
American. Actor
Won 1929 Oscar for role of the Cisco Kid
in *In Old Arizona.*
b. Mar 29, 1891 in Columbus, Ohio
d. May 7, 1951 in Beverly Hills, California
Source: *BiDFilm; CmMov; Film 1; FilmgC;
MotPP; MovMk; NatCAB 39; NotNAT B;
ObitOF 79; OxFilm; TwYS; WhAm 3;
WhScrn 74, 77; WhoHol B; WorEFlm*

Baxter-Birney, Meredith
[Mrs. David Birney]
American. Actress
Starred in TV series "Bridget Loves Bernie,"
1971-72; "Family," 1976-80; "Family
Ties," 1982--.
b. Jun 21, 1947 in Los Angeles, California
Source: *BioIn 9; NewYTBE 72; WhoAm 82*

Bay City Rollers
[Eric Faulkner; Alan Longmuir; Derek
Longmuir; Leslie McKeown; Stuart
'Woody' Wood]
Scottish. Music Group
Group named when manager stuck pin in
map hitting Bay City, MI; hit single
"Saturday Night," 1976.
Source: *BkPepl; IlEncRk; RolSEnR 83*

Bayard, Pierre du Terrail
French. Soldier
Captain in Italian wars of Charles VIII,
Louis XII, Francois I.
b. 1473
d. Apr 30, 1524
Source: *OxFr; REn*

Bayer, Herbert
American. Architect
One of last surviving teachers of Bauhaus
school; believed art should respond to
industrial world.
b. Apr 5, 1900 in Haag, Austria
d. Sep 30, 1985 in Montecito, California
Source: *ConArt 83; ConPhot; DcCAA 77;
MacBEP; MacEA; OxTwCA; PrintW 83;
WhoAm 80, 82, 84; WhoAmA 80, 82, 84*

Bayer, Wolfgang
American. Producer
Produces wildlife films shown on TV's
"Nature" series.
b. 1937
Source: *NewYTBS 86*

Bayes, Nora
[Dora Goldberg]
American. Singer, Actress
Vaudeville, musical comedy star; co-wrote
"Shine On, Harvest Moon," with husband
Jack Norwood, 1908.
b. Jan 10, 1880 in Los Angeles, California
d. Mar 19, 1928 in New York, New York
Source: *EncMT; FilmgC; InWom; NotAW;
WebAB*

Bayh, Birch Evans, Jr.
American. Lawyer, Politician
Dem. senator from IN, 1962-81.
b. Jan 22, 1928 in Terre Haute, Indiana
Source: *BiDrAC; CelR; CngDr 74; ConAu
41R; CurBio 65; IntWW 74; NewYTBE 70;
WhoAm 74, 76, 78, 80, 82; WhoAmP 73;
WhoGov 75; WhoMW 74; WhoWor 78*

Bayle, Pierre
French. Philosopher, Critic
Most important work *Historical & Critical
Dictionary,* 1697-1706.
b. Nov 18, 1647 in Carlot, France
d. Dec 28, 1706 in Rotterdam, Holland
Source: *BbD; BiD&SB; CasWL; DcBiPP;
DcEnL; DcEuL; Dis&D; EuAu; EvEuW;
LinLib L, S; LuthC 75; McGEWB; NewC;
OxEng; OxFr; PenC EUR; REn; WhDW*

Baylis, Lilian Mary
English. Manager
Created London's Old Vic Theatre, 1912;
Sadler's Wells, 1931.
b. May 9, 1874 in London, England
d. Nov 25, 1937
Source: *BioIn 3, 4, 6, 10; CnThe; EncWT;
InWom; LongCTC; NotNAT A; OxMus;
OxThe; WhDW; WhThe*

Baylor, Don Edward
American. Baseball Player
Outfielder, designated hitter, 1970--; led AL
in RBIs, 1978.
b. Jun 28, 1949 in Austin, Texas
Source: *BaseEn 85; BaseReg 86*

Baylor, Elgin
American. Basketball Player
Ten-time All-Star who scored 71 points in
one game, 1960; Hall of Fame, 1976.
b. Sep 16, 1934 in Washington, District of
Columbia
Source: *NewYTBE 71; OfNBA 81; WhoBbl 73*

Bayne, Beverly Pearl
[Mrs. Francis X Bushman]
American. Actress
Played Juliet in first American film version
of *Romeo and Juliet,* 1915.
b. Nov 22, 1894 in Minneapoils, Minnesota
d. Aug 18, 1982 in Scottsdale, Arizona
Source: *FilmEn; Film 1; MotPP; TwYS;
WhoHol A*

Bazell, Robert
American. Broadcast Journalist
Joined NBC News, 1976, science
correspondent since 1978.
b. Aug 21, 1946 in Pittsburgh, Pennsylvania
Source: *WhoAm 84; WhoTelC*

Bazin, Andre
French. Critic, Author
Film reviewer who founded *Les Cahiers du
Cinema,* 1947.
b. Apr 18, 1918 in Angers, France
d. Nov 11, 1958 in Paris, France
Source: *ConAu 113; OxFilm*

Bazin, Rene
[Bernard Seigny, pseud.]
French. Author
Catholic writer of rural family life: *Those of
His Own Household,* 1914.
b. Dec 26, 1853 in Angers, France
d. Jul 21, 1932
Source: *CathA 1930; ClDMEL; DcBiA;
DcCathB; EvEuW; LinLib L; LongCTC;
OxFr; PenC EUR; REn; TwCA, SUP*

Baziotes, William
American. Artist
b. Jun 11, 1912 in Pittsburgh, Pennsylvania
d. Jun 5, 1963 in New York, New York
Source: *DcCAA 71; WhAm 4*

Bazna, Elyesa
"Cicero"
German. Spy
Photographed notes passing through British
Embassy for Germans; arrested WW II.
b. 1904
d. 1970 in Munich, Germany (West)
Source: *BioIn 1; NewYTBE 70; WhWW-II*

Beach, Alfred Ely
American. Journalist, Inventor
Built demonstration pneumatic passenger
subway under Broadway in NY, 1868.
b. Sep 1, 1826 in Springfield, Massachusetts
d. Jan 1, 1896 in New York, New York
Source: *DcAmB; NatCab 8; TwCBDA;
WebAB; WhAm HS*

Beach, Mrs. H H A
[Amy Marcy Cheney]
American. Composer
"Gaelic" Symphony, 1896, first symphonic
work composed by American woman.
b. Sep 5, 1867 in Henniker, New Hampshire
d. Dec 27, 1944 in New York, New York
Source: *AmSCAP 66; AmWom; Baker 78;
BiDAmM; CurBio 45; DcAmB S3; NatCAB
15; NotAW; OxAmH; TwCBDA; WhAm 2*

Beach, Joseph Warren
American. Critic, Author
Writings include *Sonnets of the Head and the
Heart,* 1911; *Obsessive Images,* 1958.
b. Jan 14, 1880 in Gloversville, New York
d. Aug 13, 1957 in Minneapolis, Minnesota
Source: *AmAu&B; AmLY; CnDAL; OxAmL;
TwCA SUP; WhAm 3*

Beach, Rex Ellingwood
American. Author
Writings include *Partners,* 1905; *The World
in His Arms,* 1946.
b. Dec 1, 1877 in Atwood, Michigan
d. Dec 7, 1949 in Sebring, Florida
Source: *AmAu&B; CyWA; DcAmB S4;
DcLEL; DcNAA; EvLB; LongCTC; OxAmL;
REnAL; TwCA, SUP; TwCWr; TwYS; WhAm
2; WhNAA*

Beach, Sylvia
American. Publisher
Printed James Joyce's *Ulysses,* 1919, when no
other publisher would.
b. 1887 in Baltimore, Maryland
d. Oct 6, 1962 in Paris, France
Source: *AmWomWr; CasWL; DcLB 4; LibW;*
LongCTC; NatCAB 33, 47; NotAW MOD;
ObitOF 79; ObitT 1961; PenC AM; REnAL;
WhAm 1; WhoAmW 58, 61

Beacham, Stephanie
English. Actress
Plays Sable Colby on TV series "The
Colbys."
b. Feb 28, 1947 in England
Source: *VarWW 85*

Beach Boys, The
[Al Jardine; Bruce Johnson; Mike Love;
Brian Wilson; Carl Wilson; Dennis Wilson]
American. Music Group
Personified California life-style with mellow
songs about surfing, cars, young love.
Source: *BkPepl; CmCal; EncPR&S 74;*
IlEncRk; RkOneH; RolSEnR 83; WorAl

Beaconsfield, Benjamin Disraeli, Earl
see: Disraeli, Benjamin

Beadle, Erastus Flavel
American. Publisher, Printer
Originated the dime novel with *Malaeska,*
1860.
b. Sep 11, 1821 in Pierstown, New York
d. Dec 18, 1894 in Cooperstown, New York
Source: *DcAmB S1; WebBD 80*

Beadle, William
American. Murderer
Slaughtered his family, then killed himself.
d. Dec 11, 1873 in Weathersfield,
Connecticut
Source: *Blood&B; EncACr*

Beal, John
[J Alexander Bliedung]
American. Actor
Stage, screen actor since 1930; films include
Madame X, 1937; *The Sound and the*
Fury, 1959.
b. Aug 13, 1909 in Joplin, Missouri
Source: *BiE&WWA; FilmgC; HolP 30;*
IntMPA 75, 76, 77, 78, 79, 80, 81, 82;
MovMk; NotNAT; WhoHol A; WhoThe 77, 81

Beale, Betty
[Mrs. George Graeber]
American. Journalist
Weekly column in *Field Newspaper Syndicate,*
1953.
b. 1912 in Washington, District of Columbia
Source: *CelR; ForWC 70; InWom; WhoAm*
74, 76, 78, 80, 82; WhoS&SW 82

Bealer, Alex W(inkler III)
American. Children's Author
Writings include *The Picture-Skin Story,*
1957; *The Log Cabin,* 1978.
b. Mar 6, 1921 in Valdosta, Georgia
d. Mar 17, 1980 in Atlanta, Georgia
Source: *ConAu 45, 97, 2NR; SmATA 8*

Beall, Lester Thomas
American. Designer, Illustrator
Known for designs in merchandising, layout,
packaging; designed magazine *The New*
Republic.
b. Mar 14, 1903 in Kansas City, Missouri
d. Jun 20, 1969
Source: *CurBio 49, 69; WhoAmA 73;*
WhoGrA 62

Beals, Carleton
American. Author
Described Sandinistas' revolt against
American occupation of Nicaragua, 1928,
in *Banana Gold,* 1932.
b. Nov 13, 1893 in Medicine Lodge, Kansas
d. Jun 26, 1979 in Middletown, Connecticut
Source: *AmAu&B; AuBYP; ConAu 1R, 3NR;*
CurBio 41, 79; DcLEL; IntAu&W 76, 77;
IntWW 75, 76, 77, 78; NewYTBS 79;
OxAmL; REnAL; ScF&FL 1, 2; SmATA 12;
TwCA, SUP; WhoAm 76, 78; WhoWor 78;
WrDr 76, 80

Beals, Jennifer
American. Actress
Starred in films *Flashdance,* 1983; *The Bride,*
1985.
b. Dec 19, 1963 in Chicago, Illinois
Source: *VarWW 85*

Beals, Ralph Leon
American. Anthropologist, Author
Writings include *Ethnology of the Western*
Mixe Indians, 1945; *Community in*
Transition, Nayon Ecuador, 1966.
b. Jul 19, 1901 in Pasadena, California
Source: *AmAu&B; AmM&WS 73S; ConAu*
21R; WhoAm 74

Beam, James B
American. Distiller
Headed family business that produced world's
first true bourbon.
b. 1864
d. Dec 27, 1947
Source: *Entr*

Beame, Abraham David
American. Politician
First Jew ever elected mayor of NYC, 1974-
77.
b. Mar 20, 1906 in London, England
Source: *BlueB 76; CurBio 74; IntWW 80, 81,
82; NewYTBE 73; NewYTBS 74; PolProf NF;
WhoAm 74, 76, 78, 80, 82; WhoAmJ 80;
WhoAmP 81; WhoE 74, 77; WhoWorJ 78*

Bean, Alan L
American. Astronaut
Lunar module pilot on Apollo 12 flight to
moon, 1969.
b. Mar 15, 1932 in Wheeler, Texas
Source: *IntWW 74; NewYTBE 73; WhoAm
74, 76, 78, 80, 82; WhoS&SW 82*

Bean, Andy
American. Golfer
Turned pro 1975; won Kemper Western
Open, 1978.
b. Mar 13, 1953 in Lafayette, Georgia
Source: *NewYTBS 78; WhoIntG*

Bean, L(eon) L(eonwood)
American. Retailer
With brother Guy, began clothing store,
1912; invented special hunting shoe.
b. 1872 in Greenwood, Maine
d. Feb 5, 1967
Source: *BioIn 1, 5, 7; WhAm 4*

Bean, Roy
"Law West of the Pecos"
American. Lawman
Judge who held court in own saloon; Paul
Newman starred in movie *Life and Times
of Judge Roy Bean,* 1973.
b. 1825 in Mason County, Kentucky
d. Mar 16, 1903 in Langtry, Texas
Source: *FilmgC; WebAB, 79; WorAl*

Bean, Orson
[Dallas Frederick Burrows]
American. Actor, Comedian
Panelist on TV's "To Tell The Truth," 1964-
67.
b. Jul 22, 1928 in Burlington, Vermont
Source: *BiE&WWA; ConAu 77; ConTFT 3;
CurBio 67; MotPP; NotNAT; UFOEn;
WhoAm 84; WhoHol A; WhoThe 81;
WhoWor 74*

Beard, Charles Austin
American. Historian, Educator
Writings include *The Office of Justice of the
Peace,* 1904; *Economic Basis of Politics,*
1922.
b. Nov 27, 1874 in Knightstown, Indiana
d. Sep 1, 1948 in New Haven, Connecticut
Source: *AmAu&B; ConAmA; DcAmB S4;
DcLEL; DcNAA; EncAB-H; EvLB; IndAu
1816; LongCTC; OxAmL; PenC AM; REnAL;
TwCA, SUP; WebAB; WebE&AL; WhAm 2*

Beard, Daniel Carter
American. Artist
Founded Boy Scouts of America, 1910; only
recipient of Golden Eagle Medal.
b. Jun 21, 1850 in Cincinnati, Ohio
d. Jun 11, 1941 in Suffern, New York
Source: *AfroAA; Alli SUP; AmAu&B; AmLY;
BiD&SB; CarSB; ChhPo; CurBio 41;
DcAmAu; DcAmB S3; DcNAA; JBA 34;
OhA&B; OxAmL; REnAL; TwCA, SUP;
TwCBDA; WebAB; WhAm 1; WhNAA*

Beard, Dita Davis
American. Public Official
Lobbyist involved in ITT attempt to
subsidize Rep. National Convention, 1972.
b. Nov 27, 1918 in Fort Riley, Kansas
Source: *NewYTBE 72; PolProf NF, NF;
WhoAmW 68*

Beard, George Miller
American. Scientist, Physician, Engineer
Researched use of electricity in medicine,
1866; first to determine cause, treatment of
seasickness.
b. May 8, 1839 in Montville, Connecticut
d. Jan 23, 1883 in New York, New York
Source: *Alli SUP; AmBi; ApCAB; BbD;
BiD&SB; DcAmAu; DcAmB; DcNAA;
TwCBDA; WhAm HS*

Beard, James Andrews
American. Chef, Author
Popularized American cooking; book *Beard
on Bread,* 1973, was definitive text on
home baking.
b. May 5, 1903 in Portland, Oregon
d. Jan 23, 1985 in New York, New York
Source: *AmAu&B; CelR; CurBio 64, 85;
WhAm 8; WhoAm 82; WrDr 76*

Beard, Mary Ritter
American. Historian
Work concentrated on women and labor
  movements: *Woman as a Force in History,*
  1946.
b. Aug 5, 1876 in Indianapolis, Indiana
d. Aug 14, 1958 in Phoenix, Arizona
Source: *AmAu&B; AmWomWr; CurBio 41,
58; DcAmB S4; DcLEL; DcNAA; InWom;
IndAu 1816; NotAW MOD; ObitOF 79;
OxAmL,; REnAL; TwCA; WhoAmW 58;
WomWWA 14; TwCA SUP; WhAm 3;
WhNAA*

Beard, Matthew, Jr.
[Our Gang]
"Stymie"
American. Actor
Bald black boy who made 40 "Our Gang"
  comedies, 1930-35.
b. Jan 1, 1925 in Los Angeles, California
d. Jan 8, 1981 in Los Angeles, California
Source: *BioIn 10; DrBlPA; InB&W 80;
PseudN 82; WhoHol A*

Beard, Myron Gould
"Dan"
American. Aircraft Designer, Pilot
First airplane pilot to fly DC-3, 1935; helped
  develop Boeing 707.
b. Nov 13, 1896 in Foochow, China
d. Dec 25, 1974 in Northport, New York
Source: *BioIn 10; EncAB 40; NewYTBS 74*

Beard, Peter Hill
American. Photographer
Known for color photography of dead,
  decaying animals of Africa.
b. Jan 22, 1938 in New York, New York
Source: *ConAu 13R; ConPhot; MacBEP;
NewYTBS 75; WhoAm 78*

Beard, Ralph
[Fabulous Five]
American. Basketball Player
Three-time All-American guard, who played
  on 1948 US Olympic team.
b. Dec 1, 1927 in Hardingburg, Kentucky
Source: *BioIn 2, 10; WhoBbl 73*

Bearden, Romare Howard
American. Artist
Painter-collagist of American Negro life, who
  writes Afro-American art history.
b. Sep 2, 1914 in Charlotte, North Carolina
Source: *AfroAA; BioIn 9, 10, 11; CurBio 72;
DcAmArt; DcCAA 71, 77; McGEWB; WhoAm
76, 78, 80, 82, 84; WhoAmA 76, 78;
WhoWor 74*

Beardsley, Aubrey Vincent
English. Illustrator
Best known for sensual, often macabre black
  and white illustrations.
b. Aug 21, 1872 in Brighton, England
d. Mar 16, 1898 in Merton, England
Source: *AtlBL; BrAu 19; ChhPo, S2; DcLEL;
NewC; REn; WebE&AL*

Beatles, The
[George Harrison; John Lennon; Paul
  McCartney; Ringo Starr]
English. Music Group
Most influential music group of all time; "I
  Want to Hold Your Hand," 1963, sold
  over 12 million copies.
Source: *EncPR&S 74; FilmgC; IlEncRk;
MotPP; MovMk; NewCol 75; NewYTBS 75;
OxFilm; RkOn 78; RkOneH; RolSEnR 83;
WhoRock 81; WorEFlm*

Beaton, Cecil Walter Hardy, Sir
English. Photographer, Designer
Major 1930s fashion photographer, who won
  Oscars for costume design for *Gigi,* 1959;
  My Fair Lady, 1965.
b. Jan 14, 1904 in London, England
d. Jan 18, 1980 in Wiltshire, England
Source: *AnObit 1980; Au&Wr 71; BiE&WWA;
CelR; CnThe; ConAu 81, 93; ConPhot;
CurBio 44, 62, 80; IntWW 74; LongCTC;
NewC; NotNAT; OxFilm; Who 74; WhoThe
77; WhoWor 78; WorEFlm; WorFshn; WrDr
80; MakMC; WhoArt 82N; WhoThe 81N;
WhoWor 78; WrDr 80*

Beatrix
[Beatrix Wilhelmina Armgard]
Dutch. Queen
Daughter of Juliana who was invested as
  Queen, Apr 30, 1980.
b. Jan 31, 1938 in Soestdijk, Netherlands
Source: *BioIn 10, 11; CurBio 81; InWom;
IntWW 82; NewCol 75; NewYTBS 80;
WhoWor 78, 80*

Beattie, Ann
American. Author
Contributor to *New Yorker;* short stories
  collected in *Secrets and Surprises,* 1979.
b. Sep 8, 1947 in Washington, District of
  Columbia
Source: *ConAu 81; CurBio 85*

Beatts, Anne
American. Writer
Won Emmys for "Saturday Night Live,"
  1976, 1977, 1980.
Source: *VarWW 85*

Beatty, Alfred Chester, Sir
American. Engineer, Art Collector
Perfected method of extracting copper from
  low grade ore; owned largest private
  collection of Oriental manuscripts.
b. Feb 7, 1815 in New York, New York
d. Jan 20, 1968 in Monte Carlo, Monaco
Source: *DcIrB; GrBr; LuthC 75; NatCAB 14;
ObitT 1961*

Beatty, David Beatty, Earl
English. Admiral
Commander of successful naval action during
  WW I; first sea lord of navy, 1919-27.
b. 1871 in Nantwich, England
d. 1936
Source: *BioIn 2, 6, 11; NewCol 75; WebBD
80; WhoMilH 76*

Beatty, Morgan
American. Journalist
With NBC radio, 1941-67; commentator on
  "News of the World," 1946-67.
b. Sep 6, 1902 in Little Rock, Arkansas
d. Jul 4, 1975 in Antigua Island
Source: *ConAu 61; NewYTBS 75; NewYTET;
ObitOF 79; WhAm 6, 6*

Beatty, Ned
American. Actor
Appeared in films *Deliverance*, 1972;
  Superman, 1978.
b. Jul 6, 1937 in Louisville, Kentucky
Source: *FilmEn; IntMPA 81, 82; WhoAm 80,
82, 84; WhoHol A*

Beatty, Robert
Canadian. Actor
Made screen debut 1942; films include *2001:
  Space Odyssey*, 1968; *Where Eagles Dare*,
  1969.
b. Oct 9, 1909 in Hamilton, Ontario
Source: *CanWW 70, 79; FilmEn; FilmgC;
IntMPA 77, 78, 79, 80, 81, 82; MovMk;
WhoThe 72, 77A, 81*

Beatty, Roger
American. Writer, Director
Won five Emmys for writing "The Carol
  Burnett Show," 1972-78.
b. Jan 24, 1933 in Los Angeles, California
Source: *VarWW 85*

Beatty, Warren
[Warren Beaty]
American. Actor, Director, Producer
Known for off-screen playboy image; award-
  winning films include *Heaven Can Wait*,
  1978; *Reds*, 1981.
b. Mar 30, 1937 in Richmond, Virginia
Source: *BiDFilm; BiE&WWA; BkPepl; CelR;
ConTFT 3; CurBio 62; FilmgC; IntMPA 82;
MotPP; MovMk; NewYTBS 74; OxFilm;
WhoAm 84; WhoE 74; WhoHol A; WhoWor
78; WorEFlm*

Beauharnais, Josephine de
see: Josephine

Beaumarchais, Pierre Augustin Caron de
French. Author, Courtier, Dramatist
Wrote comedies, *Barber of Seville*, 1775;
  Marriage of Figaro, 1784; both later
  operatized.
b. Jan 24, 1732 in Paris, France
d. May 18, 1799 in Paris, France
Source: *ApCAB; AtlBL; BbD; BiD&SB;
CasWL; CnThe; CyWA; DcBiPP; DcEuL;
Dis&D; Drake; EncWT; EuAu; EvEuW;
HarEnUS; McGEWD; NewC; OxEng; OxFr;
OxThe; PenC EUR; RComWL; REn;
REnWD; SpyCS; WhDW*

Beaumont, Francis
English. Dramatist
Collaborated with John Fletcher on about 50
  tragicomedies, including *Philaster*, 1610; *A
  Maid's Tragedy*, 1611.
b. 1584 in Grace-Dieu, England
d. Mar 6, 1616
Source: *Alli; BiD&SB; BrAu; CasWL; Chambr
1; ChhPo, S1, S2; CnE&AP; CnThe; CroE&S;
CrtT 1; DcEnA; DcEnL; DcEuL; DcLEL;
EvLB; McGEWD; MouLC 1; NewC; OxEng;
OxThe; PenC ENG; REnWD; WebE&AL*

Beaumont, Hugh
American. Actor
Played Ward Cleaver in "Leave It to
  Beaver" TV series, 1957-63.
b. Feb 16, 1909 in Lawrence, Kansas
d. May 14, 1982 in Munich, Germany
  (West)
Source: *FilmgC; IntMPA 75, 76, 77, 78, 79,
80, 81, 82; NewYTBS 82; WhoHol A*

Beaumont, William
American. Physician
Surgeon who studied gastric digestion,
  physiology of stomach.
b. Nov 21, 1785 in Lebanon, Connecticut
d. Apr 25, 1853 in Saint Louis, Missouri
Source: *AmBi; DcAmB; DcNAA; Drake;
EncAB-H; WebAB; WhAm HS*

Beaupre, Don(ald William)
Canadian. Hockey Player
Goalie, Minnesota, 1980--.
b. Sep 19, 1961 in Kitchener, Ontario
Source: *HocEn; HocReg 81*

Beauregard, Pierre Gustav Toutant de
American. Military Leader
Confederate general who directed bombing of
   Ft. Sumter to start Civil War, 1861.
b. May 28, 1818 in Saint Bernard, Louisiana
d. Feb 20, 1893 in New Orleans, Louisiana
Source: *Alli SUP; AmBi; ApCAB; BiDConf;
BiDSA; CelCen; CivWDc; DcAmAu; DcAmB;
DcBiPP; DcCathB; DcNAA,; EncAB-H;
EncSoH; HarEnUS; LinLib S; McGEWB;
NatCAB 4; OxAmH; TwCBDA; WebAB, 79;
WhAm HS, HS; WhoMilH 76; WorAl*

Beauvoir, Simone de
French. Author
Best known for attack on inferior role of
   women: *The Second Sex,* 1949.
b. Jan 9, 1908 in Paris, France
d. Apr 14, 1986 in Paris, France
Source: *CasWL; CelR; CnMWL; ConAu X;
ConLC 1, 2, 4, 8, 14; CurBio 73, 86;
EncWL; EvEuW; LongCTC; ModRL;
NewYTBE 71; NewYTBS 74; OxEng; OxFr;
PenC EUR; REn; TwCA SUP; TwCWr; Who
82; WhoTwCL; WhoWor 74*

Beaux, Cecelia
American. Artist
b. 1863 in Philadelphia, Pennsylvania
d. Sep 17, 1942 in Gloucester, Massachusetts
Source: *BioIn 2, 4, 7, 8, 10; DcAmB S3;
NatCAB 40; NewCol 75; NotAW; WhAm 2;
WomWWA 14*

**Beaverbrook, William Maxwell Aitken,
Baron**
English. Publisher, Statesman
Author *Politicians and the War 1914-16,*
   1928; *Men and Power: 1917-18,* 1956.
b. May 25, 1879 in Maple, Ontario
d. Jun 9, 1964 in Surrey, England
Source: *ConAu 103, 89; CurBio 40, 64;
LinLib L, S; LongCTC; NewCol 75;
WhE&EA; WhLit; WhWW-II; WhE&EA;
WhLit; WhWW-II*

Beavers, Louise
American. Actress
One of Hollywood's most frequently
   employed blacks, usually as maid:
   Imitation of Life, 1934.
b. Mar 8, 1902 in Cincinnati, Ohio
d. Oct 26, 1962 in Hollywood, California
Source: *DrBlPA; Film 2; FilmgC; HolP 30;
InB&W 80; MotPP; MovMk; NotNAT B;
ObitOF 79; ThFT; Vers A; WhScrn 74, 77;
WhoHol B*

Becaud, Gilbert
French. Singer
b. Oct 24, 1927 in Toulon, France
Source: *WhoHol A; WhoWor 78*

Beccaria, Cesare
Italian. Explorer, Political Leader
Argued against capital punishment of
   criminals in *Essay on Crimes and
   Punishment,* 1767.
b. Mar 15, 1738 in Milan, Italy
d. Nov 28, 1794 in Milan, Italy
Source: *BioIn 1, 4, 6, 9, 10; CasWL; DcEuL;
EvEuW; LinLibL; McGEWB; NewCol 75;
OxFr; PenC EUR; REn*

Bechet, Sidney
American. Jazz Musician
Clarinet player since 1912; musician actor in
   Broadway's *Hear That Trumpet,* 1946.
b. May 14, 1897 in New Orleans, Louisiana
d. May 14, 1959 in Paris, France
Source: *EncAB-H; WhAm 3, 4; WhoJazz 72*

Bechi, Gino
Italian. Opera Singer
Baritone, who created role of Vladimiro in
   Rocca's *Monte Ivnor,* Rome Opera, 1939.
b. 1913 in Florence, Italy
Source: *WhoMus 72*

Bechtel, Stephen Davison
American. Business Executive, Engineer
Pres., Bechtel Corp., 1960-73; board
   chairman, 1973--.
b. Sep 24, 1900 in Aurora, Indiana
Source: *BioIn 2, 3, 4, 5, 10, 11; CurBio 57;
IntWW 74, 75, 76, 77, 78; IntYB 78, 79;
St&PR 75; WhoAm 76, 78, 80, 82, 84;
WhoCan 73, 75, 77; WhoF&I 74, 75, 77;
WhoWest 74, 76, 78; WhoWor 74, 76, 78*

Bechtel, Steve (Stephen Davison, Jr.)
American. Corporation Executive
Chairman, Bechtel Group, Inc., 1980--.
b. May 10, 1925 in Oakland, California
Source: *St&PR 75; WhoAm 74, 76, 78, 80,
82; WhoCan 73, 75, 77; WhoF&I 74, 75, 77,
79; WhoWest 74, 76, 78*

Beck, Billy de
see: DeBeck, Billy

Beck, C(harles) C(larence)
American. Cartoonist
Created Captain Marvel cartoon using actor
Fred MacMurray as model, 1939.
b. Jun 8, 1910 in Zumbrota, Minnesota
Source: *WorECom*

Beck, David
American. Labor Union Official
Pres., Teamsters Union, 1952-57.
b. 1894 in Stockton, California
Source: *BioIn 1, 2, 3, 4, 5, 6, 8, 11, 12*

Beck, Jeff
[Honeydrippers; Yardbirds]
English. Musician
Established reputation as guitarist with
  Yardbirds, 1965; founded Jeff Beck Group,
  1967.
b. Jun 24, 1944 in Surrey, England
Source: *EncPR&S 74; IlEncRk; RolSEnR 83*

Beck, John
American. Actor
Plays Mark Graison on TV series "Dallas,"
  1983, 1985--.
b. Jan 28, 1946 in Chicago, Illinois
Source: *IntMPA 82; VarWW 85*

Beck, Julian
American. Dramatist, Actor
Founded Living Theater; used improvisation,
  superrealistic horror to shock audiences.
b. May 31, 1925 in New York, New York
d. Sep 14, 1985 in New York, New York
Source: *CelR; ConAu 102; NotNAT; PIP&P;
WhoAm 82; WhoThe 77*

Beck, Marilyn (Mohr)
American. Journalist, Editor
Hollywood columnist who wrote *Marilyn
  Beck's Hollywood,* 1973.
b. Dec 17, 1928 in Chicago, Illinois
Source: *ConAu 65; ForWC 70; WhoAm 82;
WhoAmW 77*

Beck, Martin
[Lipto Szent Miklos]
American. Manager
Managed Orpheum Vauderville Circuit, 1903-
  23; discovered Harry Houdini.
b. Jul 30, 1867 in Austria, Hungary
d. Nov 16, 1940 in New York, New York
Source: *CurBio 41, 41; DcAmB S2; NotNAT
B; ObitOF 79; WhAm 4, 4, HSA*

Beck, Michael
American. Actor
Starred in film *Xanadu,* 1980; TV mini-series
  "Holocaust," "Mayflower."
b. Feb 4, 1949 in Memphis, Tennessee
Source: *ConTFT 3; IntMPA 82; VarWW 85*

Beck, Simone (Simca)
French. Chef, Author
b. 1905
Source: *BioIn 12*

Becker, Boris
German. Tennis Player
Youngest, and first unseeded, player to win
  Wimbledon singles, 1985.
b. Nov 22, 1967 in Liemen, Germany (West)
Source: *ConNews 85-3*

Becker, Carl Lotus
American. Historian
Known for studies of American
  Revolutionary War period.
b. Sep 7, 1873 in Waterloo, Iowa
d. Apr 10, 1945 in Ithaca, New York
Source: *AmAu&B; DcAmB S3; DcLEL;
DcNAA; OxAmL; REn; REnAL; TwCA SUP;
WebAB; WhAm 2; WhNAA*

Becker, Jacques
French. Director
Began career as director in German prisoner-
  of-war camp, 1942; best known for *Casque
  d'Or,* 1952.
b. Sep 15, 1906 in Paris, France
d. 1960 in Paris, France
Source: *BiDFilm; DcFM; FilmEn; FilmgC;
OxFilm; WhScrn 77; WorEFlm*

Becker, Stephen David
[Steve Dodge, pseud.]
American. Author
Writings include *The Season of the Stranger,*
  1951; *The Last Mandarin,* 1979.
b. Mar 31, 1927 in Mount Vernon, New
  York
Source: *AmAu&B; ConAu 5R, 3NR; ConNov
76; DrAF 76; WhoAm 74; WhoWorJ 72;
WrDr 80*

Becket, Saint Thomas a'
see: A'Becket, Thomas

Beckett, Samuel Barclay
Irish. Author, Dramatist
Won Obie awards for best new plays, 1958,
  Endgame, 1964, *Play*.
b. Apr 13, 1906 in Dublin, Ireland
Source: *Au&Wr 71; BiE&WWA; BlueB 76;
CasWL; CelR; CnMD; CnMWL; CnThe;
ConAu 5R; ConDr 73, 82; ConLC 1, 2, 18;
ConNov 82; ConP 80; ConLC 3, 4, 6;
ConNov 72, 76; ConP 70; CroCD; CurBio 70;
CyWA; DcIrL; DcLB 13; DcLEL; EncWL, 2;
EvEuW; IntWW 80, 81, 82; LongCTC;
MakMC; McGEWD; ModBrL, Sl; ModRL;
ModWD; NewC; NewYTBE 72; NotNAT;
Novels; OxEng; OxThe; PenC ENG, EUR;
PIP&P; RComWL; REn; REnWD; TwCA
SUP; TwCWr; WebE&AL; WhDW; Who 82;
WhoAm 82; WhoThe 81; WhoTwCL;
WhoWor 80; WrDr 82*

Beckford, William
English. Author
Best known for *Vathek, An Arabian Tale*,
  1786.
b. Sep 29, 1759 in Fonthill, England
d. May 2, 1844 in Bath, England
Source: *AtlBL; BbD; BiD&SB; BiDLA; BrAu
19; CasWL; Chambr 2; CyWA; DcBiA;
DcEnA,; DcEnL; DcLEL; EvLB; LinLib L;
NewC; OxEng; OxFr; PenC ENG; REn;
WebE&AL; WhDW*

Beckley, Jake (Jacob Peter)
American. Baseball Player
First baseman, 1888-1907; played more games
  at position than anyone; Hall of Fame,
  1971.
b. Aug 4, 1867 in Hannibal, Missouri
d. Jun 25, 1918 in Kansas City, Missouri
Source: *BaseEn 85; BasesB*

Beckman, Johnny
"The Babe Ruth of Basketball"; "Becky"
American. Basketball Player
Guard, who was one of original Boston
  Celtics; Hall of Fame.
b. Oct 22, 1895 in New York, New York
d. Jun 22, 1968 in Miami, Florida
Source: *BioIn 8; WhoBbl 73*

Beckmann, Max
German. Artist
Best known works "Destruction of Messina,"
  1909; "Sinking of the Titanic," 1912.
b. Feb 12, 1884 in Leipzig, Germany
d. Dec 12, 1950 in New York, New York
Source: *AtlBL; OxGer; WhAm 4*

Becknell, William
American. Explorer
Established trading route known as Santa Fe
  Trail, 1822.
b. 1796 in Amherst County, Virginia
d. Apr 30, 1865
Source: *DcAmB; McGEWB; WebAB; WhAm
HS*

Beckwourth, James Pierson
American. Frontiersman
Hunter, whose exploits described in *Life and
  Adventures of JP Beckwourth*, 1856.
b. Apr 26, 1798 in Virginia
d. 1867 in Denver, Colorado
Source: *BioIn 3, 4, 5, 6, 7, 8, 9, 10, 11;
DcAmB; WhAm HS*

Becquerel, Antoine-Cesar
French. Physicist
Known for work with thermoelectricity,
  voltaic cell.
b. Mar 7, 1788 in Loiret, France
d. Jan 18, 1878 in Paris, France
Source: *DcScB; LinLib S*

Becquerel, Antoine Henri
French. Physicist
Discovered radioactivity, 1896; won Nobel
  Prize, 1903.
b. Dec 15, 1852 in Paris, France
d. Aug 25, 1908 in Le Croisic, France
Source: *BioIn 2, 3, 4, 5, 9; McGEWB;
NewCol 75*

Bede the Venerable
English. Scholar, Theologian
Best known work *Ecclesiastical History of the
  English People*, 731.
b. May 26, 673 in Northumbria, England
d. 735 in Jarrow, England
Source: *AtlBL; BbD; BiB S; BiD&SB; BrAu;
CasWL; CrtT 1; DcEnL; DcEuL; EvLB;
NewC; OxEng; OxFr; PenC ENG; REn*

Bedelia, Bonnie
[Bonnie Culkin]
American. Actress, Singer, Dancer
Films include *Heart Like a Wheel*, 1983;
  They Shoot Horses Don't They?, 1969.
b. Mar 25, 1948 in New York, New York
Source: *ConTFT 3; FilmgC; NotNAT;
VarWW 85; WhoAm 82; WhoAmW 81;
WhoHol A; WorAl*

Bedells, Phyllis
English. Ballerina
Popular ballet performer. 1906-35.
b. Aug 9, 1893 in Bristol, England
d. May 2, 1985
Source: *ConAu 116; WhThe*

Bedford, Brian
English. Actor
Won Tony, 1971, for *School for Wives.*
b. Feb 16, 1935 in Morley, England
Source: *BiE&WWA; CelR; FilmgC; MotPP; NewYTBE 71; NotNAT; PIP&P; WhoAm 82; WhoHol A; WhoThe 77*

Bedford, Sybille
German. Author
Writings include *A Legacy,* 1956; *A Compass Error,* 1968.
b. 1911 in Charlottenburg, Germany
Source: *Au&Wr 71; ConNov 72, 76; ModBrL; NewC; RAdv 1; WhoWor 78; WorAu; WrDr 80*

Bee, Clair Francis
[Chip Hilton, pseud.]
"Hillbilly"
American. Basketball Coach
Collegiate coach with highest winning percentage; introduced 24-second clock; author of instruction manuals, sports fiction.
b. Mar 2, 1900 in Grafton, West Virginia
d. May 20, 1983 in Cleveland, Ohio
Source: *AnObit 1983; AuBYP; BioIn 9; ConAu 1R; NewYTBS 81; PseudN 82; WhoBbl 73*

Bee, Molly
[Molly Beachboard]
American. Singer
Country singer; successful singles 1950s-60s include "I Saw Mommy Kissing Santa Claus."
b. Aug 18, 1939 in Oklahoma City, Oklahoma
Source: *BiDAmM; EncFCWM 83; VarWW 85; WhoHol A*

Bee Gees, The
[Barry Gibb; Maurice Gibb; Robin Gibb]
English. Music Group
Soundtrack album *Saturday Night Fever,* 1977, sold over 15 million copies; was first ever triple platinum album.
Source: *BkPepl; EncPR&S 74; IlEncRk; RkOneH; RolSEnR 83; WhoRock 81*

Beebe, Burdetta Faye
[B F Johnson; B F Beebe, pseuds.]
American. Children's Author
Writings include *Run, Light Buck, Run!,* 1962; *African Elephants,* 1968.
b. Feb 4, 1920 in Marshall, Oklahoma
Source: *ConAu 1R, 3NR; SmATA 1; WrDr 76*

Beebe, Lucius Morris
American. Journalist, Author
Writings include *People on Parade,* 1934; *The Trains We Rode, Vol. I,* 1965.
b. Dec 9, 1902 in Wakefield, Massachusetts
d. Feb 4, 1966 in San Mateo, California
Source: *AmAu&B; ChhPo; ConAu 25R; CurBio 40, 66; REn; REnAL; WebAB; WhAm 4*

Beech, Walter Herschel
American. Aircraft Manufacturer
Founded Beech Aircraft Co., 1932.
b. Jan 30, 1891 in Pulaski, Tennessee
d. Nov 29, 1950 in Wichita, Kansas
Source: *BioIn 1, 2, 4; NatCAB 39; WhAm 3*

Beebe, William (Charles William)
American. Ornithologist, Explorer
Set world deep-sea diving record in bathysphere, 3,028 feet, 1934.
b. Jul 29, 1877 in Brooklyn, New York
d. Jun 4, 1962 in Trinidad
Source: *AmAu&B; ConAmA; ConAmL; ConAu 73; CurBio 41, 62; DcLEL; EvLB; OxAmL; REnAL; SmATA 19; Str&VC; TwCA, SUP; WebAB; WhAm 4; WhNAA*

Beecham, Justin, pseud.
see: Wintle, Justin Beecham

Beecham, Thomas, Sir
English. Conductor
Founded British National Opera Co., 1932; London Philharmonic, 1932; Royal Philharmonic, 1946.
b. Apr 29, 1879 in Saint Helens, England
d. Mar 8, 1961 in London, England
Source: *Baker 78; CurBio 41, 51, 61; LinLib S; LongCTC; NewEOp 71; NotNAT B; ObitOF 79; ObitT 1961; OxMus; REn; WhAm 4; WorAl*

Beecher, Henry Ward
American. Clergyman, Social Reformer
Forceful orator who spoke out on social, political issues, including slavery, Civil War, Reconstruction.
b. Jun 24, 1813 in Litchfield, Connecticut
d. Mar 8, 1887 in Brooklyn, New York
Source: *AmAu; AmAu&B; AmBi; ApCAB; BbD; BiDAmM; BiD&SB; CasWL; CelCen; Chambr 3; CivWDc; CyAL 1; DcAmAu; DcAmB; DcAmReB; DcBiA; DcEnL; DcLB 3; DcNAA; Drake; EncAB-H; EvLB; HarEnUS; LinLib L, S; OhA&B; OxAmL; OxEng; PenC AM; REn; REnAL; TwCBDA; WebAB, 79; WhAm HS; WhAmP; WorAl*

Beecher, Janet
[Janet Beecher Meysenburg]
American. Actress
Character actress who usually played society
matrons, 1930s.
b. Oct 21, 1884 in Jefferson City, Missouri
d. Aug 6, 1955 in Washington, Connecticut
Source: *FilmEn; FilmgC; MotPP; MovMk;*
NotNAT B; ThFT; WhScrn 74, 77; WhThe;
WhoHol B

Beemer, Brace
American. Actor
One of the original radio voices of the Lone
Ranger, 1933-54.
b. 1903
d. Mar 1, 1965 in Oxford, Michigan
Source: *BioIn 7; ObitOF 79*

Beene, Geoffrey
American. Fashion Designer
Pres., designer, Geoffrey Beene, Inc., NYC,
1962--.
b. Aug 30, 1927 in Haynesville, Louisiana
Source: *CelR; WhoAm 80, 82, 84; WhoE 74;*
WorFshn

Beer, Thomas
American. Author, Biographer
Wrote *The Mauve Decade,* 1926.
b. Nov 22, 1889 in Council Bluffs, Iowa
d. Apr 18, 1940 in New York, New York
Source: *DcAmB S1; NewCol 75; OxAmL 83;*
REnAL

Beerbohm, Max (Sir Henry Maximilian)
"The Incomparable Max"
English. Critic, Essayist
Drama critic for *Saturday Review,* succeeding
George Bernard Shaw, 1898.
b. Aug 24, 1872 in London, England
d. May 20, 1956 in Rapallo, Italy
Source: *AntBDN B; AtlBL; CasWL; Chambr*
3; CnMD; CnMWL; CyWA; DcBrAr 1;
DcBrBI; DcLEL; EncWT; EvLB; LinLib L,
S; LongCEL; LongCTC; ModBrL, S1;
ModWD; NewC; NotNAT A, B; Novels;
ObitOF 79; OxEng; OxThe; PenC ENG;
RAdv 1; REn; TwCA, SUP; TwCWr;
WebE&AL; WhAm 3; WhE&EA; WhThe;
WorAl; WorECar A

Beers, Clifford Whittingham
American. Reformer
Founded National Committee for Mental
Hygiene, 1909, to prevent mental
disorders, care for mentally ill.
b. Mar 30, 1876 in New Haven, Connecticut
d. Jul 9, 1943 in Providence, Rhode Island
Source: *CurBio 43; DcAmB S3; DcNAA;*
EncAB 9; LinLib L, S; NatCAB 34; REnAL;
WebAB 79; WhAm 2

Beers, Victor Gilbert
American. Editor
Writings include *Through Golden Windows,*
1975; *My Red Balloon,* 1973.
b. May 6, 1928 in Sidell, Illinois
Source: *ConAu 1NR; SmATA 9; WhoMW 74*

Beery, Noah
American. Actor
Silent screen's most loved villain best known
for *Beau Geste,* 1926.
b. Jan 17, 1884 in Kansas City, Missouri
d. Apr 1, 1946 in Beverly Hills, California
Source: *CmMov; FilmEn; Film 1; FilmgC;*
MovMk; OxFilm; TwYS; Vers B; WhScrn 74;
WhoHol B

Beery, Noah, Jr.
American. Actor
Made screen debut with father Noah Beery,
1920; appeared in TV series "The
Rockford Files," 1974-80.
b. Aug 10, 1916 in New York, New York
Source: *ConTFT 3; FilmEn; FilmgC; IntMPA*
82; MovMk; Vers B; WhoAm 84

Beery, Wallace
American. Actor
Brother of Noah Beery, known for "lovable
slob" roles; won Oscar, 1931, for *The*
Champ.
b. Apr 1, 1886 in Kansas City, Missouri
d. Apr 15, 1949 in Beverly Hills, California
Source: *BiDFilm; CmMov; DcAmB S4;*
FilmEn; Film 1; FilmgC; MovMk; OxFilm;
TwYS; WebAB; WhAm 2; WhScrn 74, 77;
WhoHol B; WorEFlm

Beesley, H(orace) Brent
"Dr. Doom"
American. Government Official
Director, Federal Savings and Loan Insurance
Corp., 1981-83; pres., Charter Savings
Corp., 1983--.
b. Jan 30, 1946 in Salt Lake City, Utah
Source: *WhoAm 84; WhoAmL 79; WhoF&I*
83; WhoReal 83

Beethoven, Ludwig van
German. Composer
Master of classical music; composed *Ninth
Symphony* 1817-23 when totally deaf.
b. Dec 16, 1770 in Bonn, Germany
d. Mar 26, 1827 in Vienna, Austria
Source: *AtlBL; Baker 78; BbD; BiD&SB;
BioIn 10, 11; CelCen; DcBiPP A; DcCathB;
Dis&D; LinLib L, S; LuthC 75; McGEWB;
NewC; NewCol 75; NewEOp 71; OxGer;
OxMus; REn; WhDW; WorAl*

Beeton, Isabella Mary Mayson
English. Author
Wrote famed Victorian text on cookery,
domestic economy: *Book of Household
Management,* 1861.
b. Mar 14, 1836 in London, England
d. Feb 6, 1865
Source: *Alli SUP; BioIn 2, 8, 11; EvLB;
InWom; MacDWB; OxEng*

Begelman, David
American. Film Executive
Involved in money scandal that was subject
of book *Indecent Exposure,* 1973, by John
M Macdonald.
b. Aug 26, 1921 in New York, New York
Source: *IntMPA 80, 81, 82; NewYTBS 80;
WhoAm 76*

Begin, Menachem
Israeli. Political Leader
Commanded terrorist group Irgun, 1943-48;
prime minister, 1977-83; signed historical
peace treaty with Egypt, 1979.
b. Aug 16, 1913 in Brest-Litovsk, Poland
Source: *BkPepl; CurBio 77; IntWW 74, 75,
76, 77, 78; IntYB 78, 79; NewYTBE 70;
NewYTBS 77; Who 82, 85; WhoWor 74, 78;
WhoWorJ 72*

Begle, Edward G(riffith)
American. Mathematician, Educator
Stanford U. professor, 1961-78, who studied
topology.
b. Nov 27, 1914 in Saginaw, Michigan
d. Mar 2, 1978 in Palo Alto, California
Source: *AmM&WS 73P; LEduc 74; WhoAm
74*

Begley, Ed(ward James)
American. Actor
Began career as radio announcer, 1931; won
Oscar, 1964, for *The Unsinkable Molly
Brown.*
b. Mar 25, 1901 in Hartford, Connecticut
d. Apr 28, 1970 in Hollywood, California
Source: *BiE&WWA; CurBio 56, 70; FilmEn;
FilmgC; MotPP; MovMk; NewYTBE 70; Vers
A; WhAm 5; WhScrn 74, 77; WhoHol B*

Begley, Ed, Jr.
American. Actor
Plays Dr. Victor Ehrlich on TV series "St.
Elsewhere," 1982--.
b. Sep 16, 1949
Source: *VarWW 85; WhoHol A*

Behan, Brendan
Irish. Dramatist, Author
Writings include *The Hostage,* 1958;
Richard's Cork Leg, 1974.
b. Feb 9, 1923 in Dublin, Ireland
d. Mar 20, 1964 in Dublin, Ireland
Source: *BiE&WWA; CasWL; CnMD; CnThe;
ConAu 73; ConLC 1, 8, 11, 15; CroCD;
CurBio 61, 64; EncWL; LongCTC;
McGEWD; ModBrL, Sl; ModWD; NewC;
PenC ENG; PIP&P; REn; REnWD; TwCWr;
WebE&AL; WhAm 4; WhoTwCL; WorAu*

Beheshti, Mohammad, Ayatollah
Iranian. Political Leader
Founder of Islamic Republican Party, 1979;
killed in bomb blast.
b. 1929 in Isfahan, Iran
d. Jun 28, 1981 in Teheran, Iran
Source: *AnObit 1981; BioIn 12*

Behn, Aphra
English. Author, Dramatist
First English woman to support herself by
writing; most popular play was "The
Rover," 1677.
b. 1640 in Harbledown, England
d. Apr 16, 1689 in London, England
Source: *Alli; AtlBL; BbD; BiD&SB; BrAu;
CasWL; Chambr 2; ChhPo; CyWA; DcAfL;
DcBiA; DcBiPP; DcEnA; EncWT; NotNAT A,
B; Novels; DcEnL; DcEuL; EvLB; InWom;
McGEWD; MouLC 1; NewC; OxEng; OxThe;
PenC ENG; REn; WebE&AL; WorAl*

Behn, Harry
American. Children's Author
Writings include *Siesta,* 1931; *The Two
Uncles of Pablo,* 1959.
b. Sep 24, 1898 in Yavapai County, Arizona
d. Sep 4, 1973
Source: *AnCL; ArizL; AuBYP; BkCL; ChhPo,
Sl, S2; ConAu 5R, 53, 5NR; IlsCB 1946,
1957; MorBMP; MorJA; SmATA 2; Str&VC*

Behn, Noel
American. Author, Producer
Won 1958 Obie for production of *Endgame.*
b. Jan 6, 1928 in Chicago, Illinois
Source: *BiE&WWA; NotNAT; TwCCr&M 80;
WrDr 82*

Behrens, Earl Charles
American. Editor
Noted political journalist; won Medal of
    Freedom, 1970.
b. Feb 7, 1892 in Shasta, California
d. May 13, 1985 in Menlo Park, California
Source: *ConAu 116; WhoWest 76*

Behring, Emil Adolph von
German. Physiologist
Won Nobel Prize in medicine, 1901, for
    discovery of serums against tetanus,
    diptheria.
b. Mar 15, 1854 in Forsthausen, Prussia
d. Mar 31, 1917 in Marburg, Germany
Source: *AsBiEn; BioIn 3; DcNAA; DcScB;
InSci; LinLib S; NewCol 75; WhDW; WorAl*

Behrman, S(amuel) N(athaniel)
American. Author, Dramatist, Screenwriter
Wrote screenplay *Quo Vadis,* 1951; novel *The
    Burning Glass,* 1968.
b. Jun 9, 1893 in Worcester, Massachusetts
d. Aug 9, 1973 in New York, New York
Source: *AmAu&B; Au&Wr 71; BiE&WWA;
CasWL; CmMov; CnDAL; CnMD; CnThe;
ConAmA; ConAu 45, P-1; CroCD; CurBio 43,
73; DcLEL; FilmgC; LongCTC; McGEWD;
ModAL; ModWD; NewYTBE 72, 73; OxThe;
OxAmL; PenC AM; REn; REnAL; REnWD;
TwCA, SUP; WebE&AL; WhAm 6; WhoAm
74; WhoWor 78; WhoWorJ 72*

Beiderbecke, "Bix" (Leon Bismark)
American. Jazz Musician
Composed "In a Mist"; recognized
    posthumously as one of greatest jazz
    musicians.
b. Mar 10, 1903 in Davenport, Iowa
d. Aug 7, 1931 in New York, New York
Source: *Baker 78; BiDAmM; BioIn 1, 4, 5, 7,
9, 10; CmpEPM; IlEncJ; NewCol 75; WebAB;
WhAm 4; WhoJazz 72*

Beilenson, Edna Rudolph
[Elisabeth Deane, pseud.]
American. Publisher
Headed Peter Pauper Press after husband's
    death.
b. Jun 16, 1909 in New York, New York
d. Feb 28, 1981 in New York, New York
Source: *AmAu&B; ConAu 103, 85; NewYTBS
81; WhoAm 78; WhoAmW 74; WhoWor 74*

Bein, Albert
Romanian. Dramatist, Author
Proletarian who wrote social protest drama
    Let Freedom Ring, 1935.
b. May 18, 1902 in Kishinev, Romania
Source: *BiE&WWA; CnMD; ModWD;
NotNAT; OxAmL*

Beinum, Eduard van
Dutch. Conductor
Led Amsterdam's famed Concertgebouw
    Orchestra, 1945-59.
b. Sep 3, 1900 in Arnheim, Netherlands
d. Apr 13, 1959
Source: *BioIn 2, 3, 4, 5, 11; CurBio 55, 59*

Bejart, Maurice
French. Choreographer
Avant-garde ballet master of Belgium's
    national dance company since 1959.
b. Jan 1, 1927 in Marseilles, France
Source: *CurBio 71; IntWW 74*

Bekhterev, Vladimir Mikhailovich
Russian. Scientist
Neuropathologist who studied conditioned
    reflexes; wrote *Nervous System Disease,*
    1909.
b. 1857
d. 1927
Source: *BioIn 11; WebBD 80*

Bel Geddes, Barbara
see: Geddes, Barbara Bel

Bel Geddes, Norman
see: Geddes, Norman Bel

Belafonte, Harry (Harold George, Jr.)
American. Singer, Actor
Helped popularize calypso music; won Tony,
    1953, for *John Murray Anderson's
    Almanac.*
b. Mar 1, 1927 in New York, New York
Source: *AmPS A, B; AmSCAP 66; Baker 78;
BiDAmM; BiE&WWA; BioIn 3, 4, 5, 6, 7, 8,
9, 10; BlueB 76; CelR; CivR 74; CurBio 56;
DrBlPA; Ebony 3; EncFCWM 69; FilmgC;
IntMPA 75, 76, 77, 78, 79, 80, 81; MotPP;
MovMk; NewYTBE 72; OxFilm; RkOn 74;
WhoAm 74, 76, 78, 80, 82; WhoBlA 75, 77;
WhoHol A; WhoWor 74, 78; WorAl*

Belafonte-Harper, Shari
American. Actress
Daughter of Harry Belafonte; plays Julie on
    TV series "Hotel," 1983--.
b. Sep 22, 1954 in New York, New York
Source: *VarWW 85*

Belaney, (Archibald) George Stansfeld
see: Grey Owl, pseud.

Belasco, David
American. Dramatist, Producer
Owner, Belasco Theater, NYC, since 1906;
    noted for realistic stage settings, lighting
    effects.
b. Jul 25, 1859 in San Francisco, California
d. May 14, 1931 in New York, New York
Source: *AmAu&B; AmBi; ApCAB SUP;
CasWL; Chambr 3; CnDAL; CnThe;
DcAmAu; DcAmB S1; DcLEL; DcNAA;
EncAB-H; EvLB; Film 1; LongCTC;
McGEWD; ModAL; ModWD; OxAmL;
OxThe; PIP&P; REn; REnAL; REnWD;
TwCA, SUP; TwCBDA; TwCWr; WebAB;
WhAm 1; WhNAA; WhoStg 1906, 1908*

Belaunde-Terry, Fernando
Peruvian. Political Leader
Pres. of Peru, 1963-68, July, 1980--.
b. Oct 17, 1912 in Lima, Peru
Source: *CurBio 65; DcPol; EncLatA; IntWW
80, 81, 82; NewCol 75; NewYTBS 80;
WhoWor 82*

Belbenoit, Rene Lucien
French. Author
Account of conditions on Devil₉s Island *My
    Escape from Devils Island,* led to abolition
    of penal colony.
b. 1889 in Paris, France
d. Feb 26, 1959 in Lucerne Valley, California
Source: *ObitOF 79; WhE&EA*

Belinsky, "Bo" (Robert)
American. Baseball Player
Pitcher, 1962-70, who threw no-hitter May 5,
    1962; known for off-field publicity.
b. Dec 7, 1936 in New York, New York
Source: *BaseEn 85; BioIn 6, 9, 10; WhoProB
73*

Belinsky, Vissarion
Russian. Author
Best known Russian critic; *Literary Reviews,*
    1834, traced Russian literary development.
b. May 30, 1811 in Sveaborg, Finland
d. May 26, 1848 in Saint Petersburg, Russia
Source: *BiD&SB; CasWL; DcRusL; EuAu;
EvEuW; PenC EUR; REn*

Belisarius
Byzantine. General
One of great military leaders, responsible for
    much of Justinian I's success.
b. 505
d. Mar 565
Source: *DcBiPP; DcInv; LinLib S; McGEWB;
NewC; REn; WhDW; WorAl*

Belisha, Leslie Hore
see: Hore-Belisha, Leslie

Beliveau, Jean Marc
"Le Gros Bill"
Canadian. Hockey Player
Center, Montreal, 1951-71; scored 507 goals;
    Hall of Fame, 1972.
b. Aug 31, 1931 in Three Rivers, Quebec
Source: *CanWW 81, 82; HocEn; WhoHcky
73; WorAl*

Belk, William E
[The Hostages]
American. Hostage in Iran
b. 1938 in Winnsboro, South Carolina
Source: *NewYTBS 81*

Belknap, William Worth
American. General
Secretary of War, 1869-76; resigned after
    bribery scandal.
b. Sep 22, 1829 in Newburgh, New York
d. Oct 13, 1890 in Washington, District of
    Columbia
Source: *AmBi; ApCAB; BiDrUSE; CivWDc;
DcAmB; DcNAA; HarEnUS; NatCAB 14;
TwCBDA; WhAm HS; WhAmP*

Bell, Alexander Graham
American. Inventor
Invented telephone, 1876; Bell Telephone Co.
    organized, 1877.
b. Mar 3, 1847 in Edinburgh, Scotland
d. Aug 2, 1922 in Baddeck, Nova Scotia
Source: *AmBi; AmLY; ApCAB; DcAmB;
DcNAA; EncAB-H; LongCTC; REnAL;
TwCBDA; WebAB; WhAm 1*

Bell, Arthur Donald
American. Author, Psychologist, Educator
Wrote *Dimensions of Christian Writing,* 1970;
    Marriage Affair, 1972.
b. Jul 17, 1920 in Vancouver, Washington
Source: *AmM&WS 73S; WhoAm 74, 76, 78,
80, 82*

Bell, "Buddy" (David Gus)
American. Baseball Player
Infielder, 1972--; has played in five All-Star
    games; career batting average, .282.
b. Aug 27, 1951 in Pittsburgh, Pennsylvania
Source: *BaseEn 85; BaseReg 86; BioIn 11;
WhoProB 73*

Bell, Charles
Scottish. Surgeon
First to describe paralysis of facial nerve--
    Bell's palsy.
b. Nov 1774 in Edinburgh, Scotland
d. Apr 28, 1842 in Hollow Park, England
Source: *BiDLA; BiHiMed; BioIn 1, 3, 4, 5,
7, 8, 9; CelCen; DcBiPP; DcBrWA; DcEnL;
DcScB; InSci; NamesHP; WhDW*

Bell, Clive
English. Art Critic
Wrote *Art*, 1914; *Since Cezanne*, 1922.
b. Sep 16, 1881 in East Shefford, England
d. Sep 18, 1964 in London, England
Source: *DcLEL; LongCTC; ModBrL; NewC; OxEng; PenC ENG; REn; TwCA, SUP*

Bell, "Cool Papa" (James Thomas)
American. Baseball Player
Outfielder in Negro Leagues, 1922-50, known
    for his speed; stole 175 bases, 1933.
b. May 17, 1903 in Starkville, Mississippi
Source: *BioIn 10, 11*

Bell, Daniel
American. Sociologist, Educator
Books include *The Winding Passage*, 1980;
    labor Editor, *Fortune* magazine, 1948-58.
b. May 10, 1919 in New York, New York
Source: *AmAu&B; AmEA 74; AmM&WS 73S; ConAu 1R, 4NR; CurBio 73; WhoAm 74, 76, 78, 80, 82; WhoWor 78; WhoWorJ 72*

Bell, Donald J
American. Businessman
With Albert Howell, formed Bell and Howell
    Co., 1907, to make, service equipment for
    film industry.
b. 1869
d. 1934
Source: *Entr*

Bell, Earl
American. Track Athlete
Champion pole-vaulter in 1970s.
b. Aug 25, 1955
Source: *BioIn 12*

Bell, Gertrude Margaret
English. Archaeologist
Traveled widely in Persia, Arabia; helped
    start national museum at Baghdad, 1926.
b. Jul 14, 1868 in Durham, England
d. Jul 11, 1926 in Baghdad, Iraq
Source: *DcLEL; DcNaB 1922; EvLB; GrBr; IntDcWB; LongCTC; PenC ENG; REn*

Bell, Griffin Boyette
American. Lawyer
US attorney general, Carter administration,
    1977-79.
b. Oct 31, 1918 in Americus, Georgia
Source: *BiDFedJ; CngDr 77, 79; CurBio 77; IntWW 77, 78, 79, 80, 81; NewYTBS 76; WhoAm 74, 76, 78, 80, 82; WhoAmL 78, 79; WhoAmP 77, 79; WhoE 77, 79; WhoGov 72, 75, 77; WhoS&SW 82, 78*

Bell, Herbert A
American. Inventor
Founded firm that eventually became
    Packard Bell Electronics.
b. 1890 in Rock Valley, Iowa
d. Jan 31, 1970 in New York, New York
Source: *NewYTBE 70*

Bell, James Ford
American. Business Executive
First pres., General Mills, 1928; chm., 1934.
b. Aug 16, 1879 in Philadelphia,
    Pennsylvania
d. May 7, 1961 in Minneapolis, Minnesota
Source: *DcAmB S7*

Bell, Joseph
Scottish. Surgeon, Educator
Edited *Edinburg Medical Journal*, 1873-96;
    thought to be Arthur Conan Doyle's
    model for Sherlock Holmes.
b. 1837 in Edinburgh, Scotland
d. 1911
Source: *Alli SUP; LongCTC*

Bell, "Kool" (Robert)
[Kool and the Gang]
American. Singer, Musician
Leader of rhythm and blues-pop group;
    number one hit "Celebration," 1980.
b. Oct 8, 1950 in Youngstown, Ohio
Source: *NF*

Bell, Lawrence Dale
American. Aircraft Manufacturer
Founder of Bell Aircraft, who built fighter
    planes Airacuda, Airacobra.
b. Apr 5, 1894 in Mentone, Indiana
d. Oct 20, 1956 in Buffalo, New York
Source: *CurBio 42, 57; DcAmB S6; InSci; ObitOF 79; WhAm 3*

Bell, Ricky Lynn
American. Football Player
Running back, who was number one pick,
    1977 NFL draft; set several c lub records
    with Tampa Bay, 1977-81.
b. Apr 8, 1955 in Houston, Texas
d. Nov 28, 1984 in Inglewood, California
Source: *BioIn 10, 11; ConNews 85-1; WhoBlA 80*

Bell, Ronald
[Kool and the Gang]
American. Musician
Plays tenor sax with Kool and the Gang.
b. Nov 1, 1951 in Youngstown, Ohio
Source: *NF*

Bell, Steve (Stephen Scott)
American. Broadcast Journalist
Correspondent, ABC News since 1967; one
of few journalists in Hanoi for release of
American POWs.
b. Dec 9, 1935 in Oskaloosa, Iowa
Source: *ConAu 65; WhoAm 80, 82; WhoE 81;
WhoTelC*

Bell, Terrel Howard
"Ted"
American. Government Official
Secretary of Education, 1981-84.
b. Nov 11, 1921 in Lava Hot Springs, Idaho
Source: *BioIn 10, 11; LEduc 74; NewYTBS
81; PseudN 82; WhoAm 80, 82, 84; WhoAmP
75, 77, 79; WhoGov 77, 75*

Bell, Tom
English. Actor
In film *The L-Shaped Room,* 1962; PBS
series "Sons and Lovers," 1983; "Reilly:
Ace of Spies," 1984.
b. 1932 in Liverpool, England
Source: *FilmEn; FilmgC; IntMPA 81, 82*

Bell, Vanessa
[Mrs. Clive Bell]
English. Artist
Sister of Virginia Woolf; member of
Bloomsburg group of painters.
b. May 30, 1879 in London, England
d. Apr 7, 1961 in East Sussex, England
Source: *DcBrAr 1; GrBr; IntDcWB;
LongCTC; NewC; ObitT 1961; OxTwCA;
PhDcTCA 77; WomArt*

Bell, William Holden
American. Spy, Engineer
Hughes Aircraft employee, who sold US
defense secrets to Polish spy, 1981.
b. 1920
Source: *BioIn 12*

Bellairs, John
American. Author
b. Jan 17, 1938 in Marshall, Michigan
Source: *ConAu 21R; SmATA 2; WhoE 74*

Bellamy, Edward
American. Author, Social Reformer
Wrote *Looking Backward, 2000-1887,* 1888.
b. Mar 26, 1850 in Chicopee Falls,
Massachusetts
d. May 22, 1898 in Chicopee Falls,
Massachusetts
Source: *Alli SUP; AmAu; AmAu&B; AmBi;
ApCAB SUP; BbD; BiD&SB; CasWL;
CnDAL; CyWA; DcAmB; DcBiA; DcEnA AP;
DcLEL; DcNAA; EncAB-H; EvLB; MouLC 4;
OxAmL; OxEng; PenC AM; RAdv 1; REn;
REnAL; TwCBDA; WebAB; WebE&AL;
WhAm HS; WhAmP*

Bellamy, Ralph
American. Actor
Won Tony, 1958, for *Sunrise at Campobello.*
b. Jun 17, 1904 in Chicago, Illinois
Source: *BiE&WWA; CelR; ConAu 101;
CurBio 51; FilmEn; Film 2; FilmgC; HolP
30; IntMPA 80, 81, 82; MotPP; MovMk;
NotNAT; WhThe; WhoAm 74, 76, 78, 80, 82;
WhoHol A; WorAl*

Bellamy, Walt
American. Basketball Player
Member, US Olympic team, 1960, who was
NBA rookie of year, 1962.
b. Jul 24, 1939 in New Bern, North Carolina
Source: *InB&W 80; OfNBA 81; WhoAm 76;
WhoAmP 81, 83; WhoBlA 80*

Bellamy Brothers, The
[David Bellamy; Howard Bellamy]
American. Music Group
Pop-country duo from FL who had gold
record for 1976 hit "Let Your Love
Flow."
Source: *EncFCWM 83; RkOn 78; WhoRock
81*

Bellanca, Giuseppe Mario
Italian. Aircraft Manufacturer
Founder of Bellanca Aircraft who built first
plane, 1907; invented convertible landing
gear.
b. Mar 19, 1886 in Sciacca, Italy
d. Dec 26, 1960 in New York, New York
Source: *DcAmB S6; EncAB 32; InSci;
NatCAB 52; ObitOF 79; WhAm 4*

Beller, Kathleen
American. Actress
In movie *Godfather II;* TV series "Dynasty"
as Kirby.
b. Feb 10, 1956 in Westchester, New York
Source: *VarWW 85*

Belli, Melvin Mouron
"The King of Torts"
American. Lawyer, Lecturer, Author
Has defended such well-known people as
  Lenny Bruce and Jack Ruby.
b. Jul 29, 1907 in Sonora, California
Source: *ConAu 104; CurBio 79; WhoAm 76,*
78, 80, 82; WhoAmL 78, 79; WhoWest 74,
76, 78; WhoWor 74; WorAl

Bellincioni, Gemma
Italian. Opera Singer
b. Aug 17, 1864 in Monza, Italy
d. Apr 23, 1950 in Naples, Italy
Source: *BioIn 2, 11; InWom*

Bellinghausen, Fabian Gottlieb von
[Faddei F Bellinsgauzen]
Russian. Naval Officer, Explorer
First to see Antarctica, 1820; founded
  Russian Geographic Society, 1845.
b. Aug 30, 1779 in Oesel, Russia
d. Jan 25, 1852 in Kronstadt, Russia
Source: *DcScB; WebBD 80; WhDW*

Bellini, Gentile
Italian. Artist
Prominent portraitist, also noted for
  processions, panoramic views.
b. 1429 in Venice, Italy
d. Feb 23, 1507 in Venice, Italy
Source: *AtlBL; BioIn 1, 5, 6; LinLib S;*
McGDA

Bellini, Giovanni
Italian. Artist, Architect
Teacher of Giorgione and Titian; founded
  Venetian school.
b. 1430 in Venice, Italy
d. Nov 29, 1516 in Venice, Italy
Source: *AtlBL; DcBiPP; DcCathB; LinLib S;*
McGDA; McGEWB; OxArt; REn; WorAl

Bellini, Jacopo
Italian. Artist
Venetian religious painter who was father of
  Gentile and Giovanni Bellini.
b. 1400
d. 1470
Source: *BioIn 1, 5, 9; McGDA*

Bellini, Vincenzo
Italian. Opera Composer
Noted bel canto composer who wrote operas
  Il Pirata, 1827; *Norma,* 1831.
b. Nov 3, 1801 in Catania, Sicily
d. Sep 23, 1835 in Puteaux, France
Source: *AtlBL; REn*

Bellisario, Donald P
American. Writer, Producer
Created "Magnum P I" TV series, 1980.
b. Aug 8, in Charleroi, Pennsylvania
Source: *LesBEnT; WhoTelC*

Bellison, Simeon
American. Musician
First clarinetist, NY Philharmonic, 1920-48,
  who recorded Hebrew, Russian songs.
b. Dec 4, 1883 in Moscow, Russia
d. May 4, 1953 in New York, New York
Source: *Baker 78*

Bellman, Carl Michael
Swedish. Poet, Courtier
Composed popular ballads, drinking songs
  found in *Fredmans Epistlar,* 1790.
b. Feb 4, 1740
d. Feb 11, 1795
Source: *BbD; BiD&SB; CasWL; DcEuL;*
EuAu; EvEuW; PenC EUR

Belloc, Hilaire (Joseph Hilaire Pierre)
English. Author
Wrote from Roman Catholic viewpoint;
  founded *New Witness* newspaper with G K
  Chesterton.
b. Jul 27, 1870 in Saint Cloud, France
d. Jul 16, 1953 in Guildford, England
Source: *AnCL; AtlBL; AuBYP; BkC 5;*
CarSB; CasWL; CathA 1930; Chambr 3;
ChhPo, S1, S2; CnE&AP; CnMWL; CyWA;
DcLEL; EvLB; LongCTC; ModBrL, S1;
NewC; OxEng; PenC ENG; RAdv 1; REn;
TwCA, SUP; TwCWr; WebE&AL; WhAm 3;
WhoChL; WhoLA; YABC 1

Bellotto, Bernardo
Italian. Artist
Court painter for king of Poland, known for
  paintings of Warsaw.
b. Jan 30, 1720 in Venice, Italy
d. Oct 17, 1780 in Warsaw, Poland
Source: *AtlBL; McGDA; OxGer*

Bellow, Saul
American. Author
Won Pulitzer Prize, 1976, for *Humboldt's Gift.*
b. Jun 10, 1915 in Lachine, Quebec
Source: *AmAu&B; AmNov; AmWr; AuNews 2; BkPepl; CasWL; CelR; CnMWL; ConAu 5R; ConLC 1, 2, 3, 6, 8, 10, 13, 15; ConNov 72, 76; CroCD; CurBio 65; DrAF 76; DrAS 74E; EncAB-H; EncWL; IntWW 74; LongCTC; ModAL, S1; NewYTBE 71; NewYTBS 76; NotNAT; OxAmL; PenC AM; RAdv 1; REn; REnAL; TwCA SUP; TwCWr; WebAB; WebE&AL; Who 82; WhoAm 74, 76, 78, 80, 82; WhoTwCL; WhoWor 78; WhoWorJ 72; WrDr 80, 80*

Bellows, Brian
Canadian. Hockey Player
Prized rookie drafted by Minnesota North Stars, 1982.
b. Sep 1, 1964 in Saint Catherines, Ontario
Source: *HocEn*

Bellows, George Wesley
American. Artist
Associated with "The Eight"; painted boxing scenes, landscapes: "Stag at Sharkey's," 1907.
b. Aug 12, 1882 in Columbus, Ohio
d. Jan 8, 1925 in New York, New York
Source: *AmBi; ApCAB X; ArtsAmW 1; AtlBL; BnEnAmA; DcAmB; EncAB-H; IlBEAAW; LinLib S; McGDA; McGEWB; NatCAB 20; OxAmH; OxAmL; OxArt; PhDcTCA 77; REn; WebAB, 79; WhAm 1*

Bellwood, Pamela
American. Actress
In movie *Airport '77;* played Claudia Carrington on TV series "Dynasty."
b. Jun 26, 1946 in New York, New York
Source: *VarWW 85*

Belluschi, Pietro
American. Architect
b. Aug 18, 1899 in Ancona, Italy
Source: *AmArch 70; CurBio 59; IntWW 74; WhoAm 74, 76, 78, 80, 82; WhoWor 78*

Belmondo, Jean-Paul
French. Actor
Antihero image established in first feature film *Breathless,* 1960.
b. Apr 9, 1933 in Neuilly-sur-Seive, France
Source: *BiDFilm; CelR; CurBio 65; FilmEn; FilmgC; IntMPA 80, 81, 82; IntWW 81, 82; MotPP; MovMk; OxFilm; WhoHol A; WhoWor 74; WorAl; WorEFlm*

Belmont, Alva Erskine Smith Vanderbilt
American. Socialite, Suffragette
Militant feminist, once wife of William K Vandebilt.
b. Jan 17, 1853 in Mobile, Alabama
d. Jan 26, 1933
Source: *NotAW*

Belmont, August
[August Shoenberg]
American. Financier
Started August Belmont and Co., 1837, one of largest banking houses in US.
b. Dec 8, 1816 in Alzei, Germany
d. Nov 24, 1890 in New York, New York
Source: *AmBi; ApCAB; BiAUS; DcAmB; DcNAA; EncAB-H; TwCBDA; WebAB; WhAm HS; WhAmP*

Belmont, August, Jr.
American. Banker
b. Feb 18, 1853 in New York, New York
d. Dec 10, 1924
Source: *ApCAB SUP; WhAm 1*

Belmont, Eleanor Robson
[Mrs. August Belmont]
American. Actress, Philanthropist
Associated with Red Cross for over 25 yrs., Shaw wrote *Major Barbara* for her.
b. Dec 13, 1879 in Wigan, England
d. Oct 24, 1979 in New York, New York
Source: *ConAu 97; CurBio 44, 80, 80N; InWom; NewYTBS 79; WhoAmW 58, 61, 68; WomWWA 14*

Belote, Melissa
American. Swimmer
Won three gold medals, 1972 Olympics.
b. Oct 16, 1956 in Washington, District of Columbia
Source: *BioIn 10*

Beltrami, Eugenio
Italian. Mathematician, Educator
Noted for research in non-Euclidean geometry.
b. 1835
d. 1899
Source: *NewCol 75; WebBD 80*

Belushi, Jim (James)
American. Actor
Starred on "Saturday Night Live," 1983-85; films include *Trading Places,* 1983; *About Last Night...,* 1986.
b. Jun 15, 1954 in Chicago, Illinois
Source: *ConNews 86-2; ConTFT 3; VarWW 85*

Belushi, John
"The Black Rhino"
American. Actor, Comedian
Starred in films *Animal House,* 1978, *The Blues Brothers,* 1980; died of drug overdose.
b. Jan 24, 1949 in Chicago, Illinois
d. Mar 5, 1982 in Hollywood, California
Source: *CurBio 80, 82; IntMPA 81, 82; NewYTBS 82; PseudN 82; WhAm 8; WhoAm 80, 82; WorAl*

Bely, Andrey, pseud.
[Boris Nikolayevich Bugayev]
Russian. Poet
Symbolist; wrote poetic "symphony," *Popal,* 1909; novel, *Petersburg,* 1913.
b. Oct 14, 1880 in Moscow, Russia
d. Jan 8, 1934 in Moscow, U.S.S.R.
Source: *CasWL; ClDMEL; CnMWL; DcRusL; EncWL; EvEuW; ModSL 1; PenC EUR; REn; WhoTwCL; WorAu*

Bemelmans, Ludwig
American. Author, Illustrator, Humorist
Wrote *Hotel Bemelmans,* 1946; *Madeline* children's stories, 1953-62.
b. Apr 27, 1898 in Tirol, Austria
d. Oct 1, 1962 in New York, New York
Source: *AmAu&B; AmNov; Au&ICB; AuBYP; Cald 1938; ChhPo, S1, S2; CnDAL; ConAu 73; CurBio 41, 62; DcLEL; EncWL; IlsBYP; IlsCB 1744, 1946, 1957; LongCTC; MorJA; OxAmL; PenC AM; REn; REnAL; SmATA 15; TwCA, SUP; TwCWr; WhAm 4; WhoChL; WhoGrA 62*

Bemis, Samuel Flagg
American. Historian, Editor
Won Pulitzers for *Pinckney's Treaty,* 1926; *John Quincy Adams and Foundation of American Foreign Policy,* 1949.
b. Oct 20, 1891 in Worcester, Massachusetts
d. Sep 26, 1973 in Bridgeport, Connecticut
Source: *AmAu&B; ConAu 45; CurBio 50, 73; DcLEL; NewYTBE 73; OxAmL; OxCan; REnAL; TwCA, SUP; WebAB; WhAm 6; WhNAA; WhoWor 78*

Ben Barka, Mehdi
Moroccan. Political Leader
Exiled left-wing revolutionary, murdered in France by Moroccan agents.
b. 1920
d. 1965 in France
Source: *BioIn 5, 7, 10; DcPol*

Ben Bella, Ahmed
Algerian. Revolutionary, Political Leader
First premier, pres. of Algeria, 1962-65, and of independent Algeria after ouster of French.
b. Dec 1916 in Marnia, Algeria
Source: *BioIn 7, 8, 11; CurBio 63; WhoArab 81*

Ben-Elissar, Eliahu
Israeli. Diplomat
First Israeli ambassador to Arab country, Egypt, 1980.
b. 1932 in Poland
Source: *BioIn 11; NewYTBS 77, 80*

Ben-Gal, Avigdor
Israeli. General
Led Israeli troops into Lebanon, 1978.
b. 1936
Source: *BioIn 11*

Ben-Gurion, David
[David Grun]
Israeli. Political Leader
Emigrated to Palestine, 1906; Israel's first prime minister, 1948-53.
b. Oct 16, 1886 in Plonsk, Poland
d. Dec 1, 1973 in Tel Aviv, Israel
Source: *ConAu 45, 101; CurBio 47, 57, 74; LinLib S; McGEWB; NewCol 75; NewYTBE 71, 73; WhAm 6; WhWW-II; Who 74; WhoWor 78; WhoWorJ 72*

Ben-Yehuda, Eliezer
[Eliezer Perelman]
Israeli. Scholar
Developed spoken Hebrew; wrote *Dictionary of Hebrew Language,* 1908.
b. Jan 7, 1858 in Luzhky, Russia
d. Dec 16, 1922 in Jerusalem, Palestine
Source: *CasWL; EuAu; PenC CL, EUR*

Benaderet, Bea
American. Actress
Played Kate Bradley on TV series "Petticoat Junction," 1963-68.
b. Apr 4, 1906 in New York, New York
d. Oct 13, 1968 in Los Angeles, California
Source: *WhScrn 74, 77; WhoHol B*

Benarde, Melvin Albert
American. Author, Educator
Professor, 1967--, who writes on environmental, community problems.
b. Jun 15, 1923 in Brooklyn, New York
Source: *AmM&WS 73P, 76P, 79P, 82P; ConAu 25R; WhoAm 82; WhoE 74, 81; WrDr 76, 82*

Benary-Isbert, Margot
American. Author
Writings include award-winning children's
    books, *The Ark,* 1953; *Blue Mystery,* 1957.
b. Dec 2, 1899 in Saarbrucken, Germany
Source: *AnCL; AuBYP; ConAu 5R, 89, 4NR;*
ConLC 12; MorJA; SmATA 2, 21

Benatar, Pat
[Patricia Andrzejewski; Mrs. Neil Geraldo]
American. Singer
Has two platinum albums: *In the Heat of the*
    Night; Precious Time; single hit "Love Is a
    Battlefield."
b. Jan 10, 1952 in Brooklyn, New York
Source: *ConNews 86-1; IlEncRk; NewWmR;*
RolSEnR 83; WhoRock 81

Benavente y Martinez, Jacinto
Spanish. Dramatist
Wrote over 170 plays, including *Bonds of*
    Interest, 1907; awarded Nobel Prize, 1922.
b. Aug 12, 1866 in Madrid, Spain
d. Jul 14, 1954 in Madrid, Spain
Source: *CasWL; CathA 1930; ClDMEL;*
CnMD; CurBio 53, 54; CyWA; DcCathB;
DcSpL; Dis&D; EncWL; EncWT; EvEuW;
McGEWD; ModWD; PenC EUR; REn

Bench, Johnny Lee
"Hands"
American. Baseball Player
Catcher, infielder, Cincinnati Reds, 1967-83;
    MVP 1976 World Series.
b. Dec 7, 1947 in Oklahoma City, Oklahoma
Source: *BaseEn 85; BioNews 74; BkPepl;*
CelR; CurBio 71; NewYTBE 70; WhoAm 74,
76, 78, 80, 82; WhoProB 73

Benchley, Nathaniel Goddard
American. Author
Son of Robert Benchley; writer of humor,
    historical novels: *Lassiter's Folly,* 1971.
b. Nov 13, 1915 in Newton, Massachusetts
d. Dec 14, 1981 in Boston, Massachusetts
Source: *AmAu&B; Au&Wr 71; AuBYP SUP;*
BiE&WWA; CelR; ConAu 1R, 2NR; CurBio
53, 82; FourBJA; NewYTBS 81; NotNAT;
WhAm 8; ScF&FL 1A; SmATA 3; TwCCW
78; WhoAm 74, 76, 78, 80; WhoWor 74;
WorAu; WrDr 76

Benchley, Peter Bradford
American. Author, Journalist
Wrote *Jaws,* 1974; *The Deep,* 1976; *The*
    Island, 1979.
b. May 8, 1940 in New York, New York
Source: *AuNews 2; BkPepl; ConAu 17R;*
ConLC 4, 8; CurBio 76; IntAu&W 76, 77;
NewYTBS 79; SmATA 3; WhoAm 78, 80, 82

Benchley, Robert Charles
[Guy Fawkes, pseud.]
American. Author, Humorist
Wrote *Chips Off the Old Benchley,* 1949;
    won Oscar, 1935, for *How to Sleep.*
b. Sep 15, 1889 in Worcester, Massachusetts
d. Nov 21, 1945 in New York, New York
Source: *AmAu&B; ChhPo; ConAmA; CurBio*
41, 46; DcAmB S3; DcLEL; DcNAA; EvLB;
FilmgC; LongCTC; ModAL; MovMk; NotNAT
A, B; ObitOF 79; OxAmL; OxFilm; OxThe;
PenC AM; PlP&P; RAdv 1; REn; REnAL;
TwCA, SUP; TwCLC 1; TwCWr; WebAB;
WhAm 2; WhScrn 74, 77; WhoHol B;
WorEFlm

Bender, Ariel
[Luther James Grosvenor; Mott the Hoople]
English. Musician
Guitarist with hard rock group, 1973-74.
b. Dec 23, 1949 in Evesham, England
Source: *NF*

Bender, "Chief" (Charles Albert)
American. Baseball Player
Led AL pitchers in winning percentage,
    1910, 1914; Hall of Fame, 1953.
b. May 5, 1884 in Brainerd, Minnesota
d. May 22, 1954 in Philadelphia,
    Pennsylvania
Source: *BaseEn 85; BasesB*

Bender, Hans
German. Psychologist
Wrote *Our Sixth Sense,* 1971, *Hidden*
    Reality, 1974.
b. Feb 5, 1907 in Freiburg, Germany
Source: *BiDPara; EncO&P 78; WhoWor 78,*
80

Bendick, Jeanne
American. Author, Illustrator
Prolific writer, illustrator of children's science
    books: *Living Things,* 1969.
b. Feb 25, 1919 in New York, New York
Source: *AuBYP; BkP; ConAu 5R, 2NR; IlsCB*
1946, 1957; MorJA; SmATA 2

Bendix, Vincent
American. Inventor, Manufacturer
Invented Bendix drive, making self-starting
    cars practical.
b. Aug 12, 1882 in Moline, Illinois
d. Mar 27, 1945 in New York, New York
Source: *CurBio 45; DcAmB S3; WebAB;*
WhAm 2

Bendix, William
American. Actor
Played father on radio, TV series, "Life of
    Riley."
b. Jan 14, 1906 in New York, New York
d. Dec 14, 1964 in Los Angeles, California
Source: *BiE&WWA; CmMov; CurBio 48, 65;
FilmgC; HolP 40; MotPP; MovMk; OxFilm;
WhAm 4; WhScrn 74, 77; WhoHol B;
WorEFlm*

Benedict, Dirk
[Dirk Niewoehner]
American. Actor, Singer
On TV series "Battlestar Galactica," 1978-79;
    "The A-Team," 1983--.
b. Mar 1, 1945 in Helena, Montana
Source: *IntMPA 75, 76, 77, 78, 79, 80, 81,
82; WhoAm 80, 82; WhoHol A*

Benedict, Ruth Fulton
American. Anthropologist, Educator, Author
Expert on American Indian tribes; wrote
    classic *Patterns of Culture,* 1934; *Race,
    Science and Politics,* 1940.
b. Jun 5, 1887 in New York, New York
d. Sep 17, 1948 in New York, New York
Source: *AmAu&B; CurBio 41, 48; DcAmB S4;
DcNAA; EncAB-H; InWom; NotAW; REnAL;
TwCA SUP; WebAB; WhAm 2*

Benedict, Saint
[Benedict of Nursia]
Italian. Religious Figure
Patriarch of Western monks who founded
    Benedictine monasticism.
b. 480 in Norcia, Italy
d. Mar 21, 547 in Monte Cassino, Italy
Source: *Grk&L; LinLib S; LuthC 75;
McGEWB; OxMus; WhDW*

Benedictos I
[Vassilios Papadopoulos]
Turkish. Religious Leader
Greek Orthodox leader, 1957-80; had
    historical meeting with Pope Paul VI,
    1964.
b. 1892 in Brusa, Asia Minor
d. Dec 10, 1980 in Jerusalem, Israel
Source: *AnObit 1980; IntWW 80, 81; MidE
79; WhoWor 74*

Benedictus, David
English. Author, Dramatist, Director
Satiric novels include *Rabbi's Wife,* 1976.
b. Sep 16, 1938 in London, England
Source: *Au&Wr 71; ConNov 72, 76; NewC;
WrDr 80*

Benediktsson, Bjarni
Icelandic. Prime Minister
b. 1908
d. Jul 10, 1970 in Thingvalla, Iceland
Source: *BioIn 9*

Benefield, Barry
American. Author
Wrote novel *Valiant Is the World of Carie;*
    made into movie, 1935.
b. 1887 in Jefferson, Texas
Source: *AmAu&B; AmNov; ConAmL; DcLEL;
OxAmL; REnAL; TexWr; TwCA, SUP*

Beneke, Tex
American. Singer, Band Leader
Led Glenn Miller Orchestra after Miller's
    death, 1944.
b. Feb 12, 1914 in Fort Worth, Texas
Source: *BioIn 2; CmpEPM*

Benelli, Giovanni, Cardinal
"The Kissinger"
Italian. Religious Leader
Archbishop of Florence, 1977-82; advisor to
    Pope Paul VI; his reputed unsuccessful
    heir apparent.
b. May 21, 1921 in Pistoia, Italy
d. Oct 26, 1982 in Florence, Italy
Source: *AnObit 1982; CurBio 77, 83N;
IntWW 81; NewYTBE 70; NewYTBS 82;
WhoWor 78*

Benes, Eduard
Czech. Statesman
Pres. of Czechoslovakia, 1935-38, 42-48;
    resigned after communist coup d'etat.
b. May 28, 1884 in Kozlany, Czechoslovakia
d. Sep 3, 1948 in Usti, Czechoslovakia
Source: *CurBio 42, 48; REn; WhAm 2*

Benet, Brenda
[Brenda Benet Nelson]
American. Actress
Star of TV soap opera "Days of Our Lives,"
    who was married to Bill Bixby; suicide
    victim.
b. Aug 14, 1945 in Los Angeles, California
d. Apr 7, 1982 in Los Angeles, California
Source: *NewYTBS 82; WhoHol A*

Benet, Stephen Vincent
American. Author, Poet
Won Pulitzers for poetry volumes *John
    Browns Body,* 1928; *Western Star,* 1943.
b. Jul 22, 1898 in Bethlehem, Pennsylvania
d. Mar 13, 1943 in New York, New York
Source: *Alli SUP; AmAu&B; AnCL; ApCAB;
BiDSA; BkCL; CasWL; Chambr 3; ChhPo,
S1, S2; CnDAL; CnE&AP; CnMWL;
ConAmA; ConAmL; CurBio 43; CyWA;
DcAmB S3; DcLEL; DcNAA; Drake; EncAB
29; EncWL 2; McGEWB; NatCAB 33;
Novels; OxAmH; OxAmL; OxEng; PenC AM;
RAdv 1; REn; REnAL; SixAP; TwCA, SUP;
TwCBDA; TwCWr; WebAB, 79; WebE&AL;
WhDW; WhAm 2; WhNAA; WhoTwCL;
WorAl; YABC 1*

Benet, William Rose
American. Author, Journalist
Won Pulitzer Prize, 1941, for
    autobiographical verse *The Dust Which Is
    God.*
b. Feb 2, 1886 in Fort Hamilton, New York
d. May 4, 1950 in New York, New York
Source: *AmAu&B; ChhPo, S1, S2; CnDAL;
ConAmA; ConAmL; DcAmB S4; DcLEL;
LongCTC; OxAmL; OxEng; PenC AM; REn;
REnAL; TwCA, SUP; WebAB; WhAm 3;
WhNAA*

Benirschke, Rolf Joachim
American. Football Player
Placekicker, San Diego, 1977, who overcame
    debilitating internal disorder, 1979, to
    return to game.
b. Feb 7, 1955 in Boston, Massachusetts
Source: *BioIn 12; NewYTBS 82*

Benjamin of Tudela
Spanish. Traveler, Author
Jewish traveler said to be first European to
    reach China.
b. 1130 in Tudela, Spain
d. 1173
Source: *CasWL; DcBiPP; Dis&D; EvEuW;
NewC; NewCol 75; OxEng; PenC EUR*

Benjamin, Adam, Jr.
American. Politician
Congressman from IN, 1977-82.
b. Aug 6, 1935 in Gary, Indiana
d. Sep 7, 1982 in Washington, District of
    Columbia
Source: *AlmAP 78, 80; CngDr 77, 79, 81;
WhAm 8; WhoAm 80, 82; WhoAmL 79;
WhoAmP 73, 75, 77, 79; WhoGov 75, 77;
WhoMW 78, 80*

Benjamin, Arthur
Australian. Opera Composer, Pianist
Wrote operas *Tale of Two Cities,* 1950,
    Manana, 1956; songs of Caribbean
    influence.
b. Sep 18, 1893 in Sydney, Australia
d. Apr 10, 1960 in London, England
Source: *BioIn 2, 4, 5, 6, 8; NewEOp 71*

Benjamin, Asher
American. Architect, Author
Wrote, illustrated architectural guides,
    promoting good designs, late colonial
    styles: *American Builder's Companion,*
    1806.
b. Jun 15, 1773 in Greenfield, Massachusetts
d. Jul 26, 1845 in Springfield, Massachusetts
Source: *DcAmB; DcNAA; WebAB; WhAm HS*

Benjamin, Curtis G
American. Publisher
Pres., chm., McGraw-Hill, 1928-66; excellence
    in publishing award named for him.
b. Jul 13, 1901 in Providence, Kentucky
d. Nov 5, 1983 in Norwalk, Connecticut
Source: *AmAu&B; BlueB 76; ConAu 111;
IntWW 80, 81, 82, 83; IntYB 80, 81, 82;
NewYTBS 83; St&PR 75*

Benjamin, Judah Philip
American. Lawyer, Statesman
Confederate secretary of war, 1861-62; of
    state, 1862-65; unpopular for plan to arm
    slaves for army duty.
b. Aug 11, 1811 in Saint Thomas, British
    West Indies
d. May 8, 1884 in Paris, France
Source: *Alli SUP; AmBi; ApCAB; BiD&SB;
BiDConf; BiDSA; BiDrAC; DcAmAu; DcAmB;
DcNAA; TwCBDA; WebAB; WhAm HS;
WhAmP*

Benjamin, Nigel
see: Mott (the Hoople)

Benjamin, Richard
American. Actor
Husband of Paula Prentiss; starred in film
    Goodbye Columbus, 1969.
b. May 22, 1938 in New York, New York
Source: *BkPepl; CelR; FilmgC; IntMPA 75,
76, 77, 78, 79, 80, 81, 82; MovMK;
NewYTBE 71; WhoAm 82; WhoHol A*

Benko, Paul Charles
French. Chess Player
Member, US Olympic chess team; US Open
    chess champion.
b. Jul 15, 1928 in Amiens, France
Source: *WhoAm 80, 82, 84*

Benn, Anthony
British. Business Executive
Director, chm., Price and Pierce Ltd., 1947-
72.
b. Oct 7, 1912
Source: *Who 78, 84*

Benn, Tony (Anthony Wedgwood)
English. Statesman
Member of Parliament in Labour Party since
1950.
b. Apr 3, 1925 in London, England
Source: *BlueB 76; CurBio 65, 82; DcPol;
IntWW 74, 75, 76, 77, 78, 79, 80, 81; IntYB
78, 79, 80, 81; Who 74; WhoWor 74, 76, 78;
WrDr 80*

Bennet, Richard Dyer
see: Dyer-Bennet, Richard

Bennett, Arnold
English. Poet, Author, Critic
Known for realistic novels: *Old Wives Tales,*
1908; *Five Towns* series.
b. May 27, 1867 in Staffordshire, England
d. Mar 27, 1931
Source: *AtlBL; Chambr 3; CnMD; CnMWL;
CyWA; DcBiA; DcLEL; EncMys; EncWL, 2;
FilmgC; LinLib L, S; LongCTC; McGEWD;
ModBrL, S1; ModWD; NewC; OxEng;
OxThe; PenC ENG; RAdv 1; REn; TwCA,
SUP; TwCWr; WebE&AL; WhDW;
WhoTwCL; WorAl*

Bennett, Constance Campbell
American. Actress
Daughter of Richard Bennett; starred in
sophisticated comedies: *Topper,* 1937;
Topper Takes a Trip, 1939.
b. Oct 22, 1905 in New York, New York
d. Jul 4, 1965 in Fort Dix, New Jersey
Source: *BiDFilm; BiE&WWA; Film 2;
FilmgC; InWom; MotPP; MovMk; NotNAT A,
B; ObitOF 79; ObitT 1961; OxFilm; ThFT;
TwYS; WhAm 4; WhScrn 74; WorAl; WhScrn
77; WhoHol B; WomWMM; WorEFlm*

Bennett, Floyd
American. Aviator
National hero; with Richard Byrd, flew
three-engine monoplane over N Pole, 1926.
b. Oct 25, 1890 in Warrensburg, New York
d. Apr 25, 1928 in Quebec
Source: *AmBi; DcAmB; WebAB; WhoWest 84*

Bennett, Hal
American. Author
Wrote *Tooth Trip,* 1972; *Be Well,* 1974.
b. Sep 29, 1936 in Detroit, Michigan
Source: *ConAu 41R; ConLC 5; DrAF 76*

Bennett, Harry Herbert
American. Auto Executive
Henry Ford's henchman, who ran Ford
Motor Co., 1930s; fired by Henry II,
1945.
b. Jan 17, 1892 in Ann Arbor, Michigan
d. Jan 4, 1979 in California
Source: *BioIn 2, 6*

Bennett, Harve
American. Producer
Won Emmy for "A Woman Called Golda,"
1982.
b. Aug 17, 1930 in Chicago, Illinois
Source: *VarWW 85*

Bennett, Hugh Hammond
American. Scientist
First chief of soil conservation service, US
Dept. of Agriculture, 1935-52.
b. Apr 15, 1881 in Wadesboro, North
Carolina
d. Jul 7, 1960 in Burlington, North Carolina
Source: *BioIn 3, 4, 5, 6, 7, 8; CurBio 46, 60;
DcAmB S6; EncAAH; WhAm 4*

Bennett, James Gordon
American. Newspaper Publisher
Founded NY *Herald* with $500, 1835.
b. 1795 in Keith, Scotland
d. Jun 1, 1872 in New York, New York
Source: *AmAu&B; AmBi; ApCAB; DcAmB;
EncAB-H; InSci; OxAmH; OxAmL; REn;
REnAL; TwCBDA; WebAB, 79; WhAm HS;
WhAmP*

Bennett, James Gordon, Jr.
American. Author, Publisher
Financed Stanley's expedition to find
Livingstone, 1869-72.
b. May 10, 1841 in New York, New York
d. May 14, 1918 in Bealieu, France
Source: *AmAu&B; AmBi; ApCAB; DcAmB;
EncAB-H; TwCBDA; WebAB; WhAm 1*

Bennett, Joan
[Mrs. Walter Wanger]
American. Actress
Appeared in over 40 movies; TV series
"Dark Shadows."
b. Feb 27, 1910 in Palisades, New Jersey
Source: *BiDFilm; BiE&WWA; CelR; CmMov;
FilmgC; InWom; IntMPA 75, 76, 77, 78, 79,
80, 81, 82; MotPP; MovMk; OxFilm; ThFT;
Who 74; WhoAm 74, 76, 78, 80, 82; WhoE
74; WhoHol A; WhoThe 77; WorEFlm*

Bennett, John
American. Author, Illustrator
Wrote children's books, *Master Skylark*,
  1877; *Barnaby Lee*, 1902.
b. May 17, 1865 in Chillicothe, Ohio
d. Dec 28, 1956 in Charleston, South
  Carolina
Source: *AmAu&B; BiDLA; BiDSA; BlkAWP;
CarSB; ChhPo, S1; ConICB; DcAmAu; IlsCB
1744; JBA 34, 51; MnBBF; OhA&B; OxAmL;
REnAL; WhAm 3; YABC 1*

Bennett, John Charles
American. Army Officer
b. Dec 6, 1923 in Washington, District of
  Columbia
d. May 4, 1980 in Anchorage, Alaska
Source: *WhoAm 74, 76, 78, 80; WhoE 74*

Bennett, Lerone, Jr.
American. Author, Historian, Editor
Editor, *Ebony* magazine, 1958--; wrote
  Challenge of Blackness, 1972.
b. Oct 17, 1928 in Clarksdale, Mississippi
Source: *BlkAWP; ConAu 2NR, 45; WhoAm
74, 76, 78, 80, 84; WhoMW 74*

Bennett, Michael
[Michael Bennett DiFiglia]
American. Choreographer
Won two Tonys, Pulitzer for conceiving,
  directing, choreographing *A Chorus Line,*
  1975; filmed, 1986.
b. Apr 8, 1943 in Buffalo, New York
Source: *CurBio 81; EncMT; NotNAT; WhoAm
82; WhoThe 77*

Bennett, Richard
American. Actor
Leading matinee idol who made stage debut,
  1891; father of Joan and Constance
  Bennett.
b. May 21, 1873 in Deacon's Mills, Indiana
d. Oct 22, 1944 in Los Angeles, California
Source: *CurBio 44; DcAmB S3; EncWT;
FamA&A; Film 1; FilmgC; NatCAB 33;
NotNAT B; ObitOF 79; TwYS; Vers A;
WhAm 2; WhScrn 74, 77; WhoHol B;
WhoStg 1908*

Bennett, Richard Bedford
Canadian. Political Leader
Conservative leader, 1927-38; prime minister
  of Canada, 1930-35.
b. Jul 3, 1870 in Hopewell, New Brunswick
d. Jun 26, 1947 in Dorking, England
Source: *LinLib S; MacDCB 78; McGEWB;
OxCan; WebBD 80*

Bennett, Robert Russell
American. Composer
Orchestrated over 300 Broadway musicals
  including *Oklahoma, South Pacific.*
b. Jun 15, 1894 in Kansas City, Missouri
d. Aug 18, 1981 in New York, New York
Source: *Baker 78; BiDAmM; BiE&WWA;
BioIn 1, 2, 3, 8, 9; CelR; CurBio 42, 62, 81;
DcCM; NewYTBS 81; NotNAT; OxMus;
WhoAm 74, 76, 78, 80; WhoMus 72*

Bennett, Tony
[Joe Bari; Anthony Dominick Benedetto]
"The Singer's Singer"
American. Singer
Biggest hit "I Left My Heart in San
  Francisco," 1963.
b. Aug 3, 1926 in New York, New York
Source: *AmPS; BiDAmM; BkPepl; CelR;
CmpEPM; CurBio 65; EncJzS 70; RkOn 74;
WhoAm 74, 76, 78, 80, 82; WhoHol A*

Bennett, William
Canadian. Politician
Social Credit Party premier of British
  Columbia, 1975--.
b. Apr 14, 1932 in Kelowng, British
  Columbia
Source: *CanWW 83*

Bennett, William John
American. Government Official
Chm., National Endowment for the
  Humanities, 1981-85; secretary of
  Education, 1985--.
b. Jul 31, 1943 in Brooklyn, New York
Source: *CurBio 85; DrAS 82P; WhoAm 84*

Benny, Jack
[Benjamin Kubelsky]
American. Comedian
Famous for his stinginess; starred in "The
  Jack Benny Program," 1950-64.
b. Feb 14, 1894 in Waukegan, Illinois
d. Dec 26, 1974 in Los Angeles, California
Source: *BiDFilm; BioNews 74, 75; CelR;
CurBio 41, 63, 75; FilmgC; IntMPA 75;
IntWW 74; MotPP; MovMk; NewYTBE 70;
NewYTBS 74; OxFilm; PIP&P; WebAB;
WhAm 6; WhScrn 77; WhoAm 74; WhoHol
B; WhoWor 78; WhoWorJ 72; WorEFlm*

Benny, Mrs. Jack
see: Livingstone, Mary

Benoit, Joan
American. Runner
Won Boston Marathon, 1983, posting fastest
  time ever for woman runner: 2:22.42.
b. Mar 16, 1957 in Eugene, Oregon
Source: *NewYTBS 83, 84*

Bensley, Russ
American. Producer
Won Emmy for production of "Watergate--
The White House Transcripts," 1974.
b. Jun 12, 1930 in Chicago, Illinois
Source: *VarWW 85*

Benso di Cavour, Camillo
see: Cavour, Camillo Benso, Conte Di

Benson, Arthur Christopher
English. Author
Wrote popular essays; wrote words to song
"Land of Hope and Glory."
b. Apr 24, 1862 in Wellington, England
d. Jun 17, 1925
Source: *Chambr 3; DcEnA AP; DcEuL;
DcLEL; EvLB; LongCTC; NewC; PenC ENG;
REn; ScF&FL 1, 1; TwCA*

Benson, Edward Frederic
English. Author, Poet, Essayist
Prolific writer of satirical novels, historical
biographies *Dodo,* 1893; *As We Were,*
1930.
b. Jul 24, 1867 in Berkshire, England
d. Feb 29, 1940
Source: *BbD; BiD&SB; Chambr 3; CurBio 40;
DcEnA AP; DcLEL; EvLB; LongCTC;
MnBBF; ModBrL; NewC; OxEng; PenC ENG;
TwCA; TwCWr*

Benson, Ezra Taft
American. Government Official, Religious
Leader
Secretary of Agriculture, 1953-61; succeeded
Spencer Kimball as leader of Mormon
Church, 1985--.
b. Sep 3, 1899 in Whitney, Idaho
Source: *BiDrUSE; BioIn 10, 11; CurBio 53;
EncAAH; IntWW 75, 76, 77, 78, 80, 81, 82;
LinLib S; NewCol 75; PolProf E; WhoAm 74,
76, 78; WhoRel 75; WhoWor 78*

Benson, Frank Weston
American. Artist
Impressionist painter, etcher, known for bird
prints.
b. Mar 24, 1862 in Salem, Massachusetts
d. Nov 14, 1951 in Salem, Massachusetts
Source: *BnEnAmA; DcAmArt; DcAmB S5;
LinLib S; McGDA; NatCAB 13, 41; WhAm
3; WhoAmA 78*

Benson, George
American. Singer, Musician
Won three Grammys, 1977, including record
of year, for "This Masquerade."
b. Mar 22, 1943 in Pittsburgh, Pennsylvania
Source: *BiDAmM; BkPepl; DrBlPA,; EncJzS
70; IlEncBM 82; IlEncJ; InB&W 80; RkOn
74; WhoAm 78, 80, 82; WhoBlA 77*

Benson, Renaldo
[The Four Tops]
American. Musician, Singer
b. 1947 in Detroit, Michigan
Source: *NF*

Benson, Robby
[Robin Segal]
American. Actor
Starred in movies *One on One,* 1977; *Ice
Castles,* 1979; *The Chosen,* 1982.
b. Jan 21, 1957 in Dallas, Texas
Source: *BioIn 10; BkPepl; FilmEn; IntMPA
78, 79, 80, 81, 82; NewYTBS 77; WhoHol A*

Benson, Sally
American. Author
Wrote best-sellers *Junior Miss,* 1941; *Meet
Me In St. Louis,* 1942.
b. Sep 3, 1900 in Saint Louis, Missouri
d. Jul 19, 1972 in Woodland Hills, California
Source: *AmAu&B; BiE&WWA; CnDAL;
ConAu 37R, P-1; ConLC 17; CurBio 41, 72;
InWom; NewYTBE 72; OxAmL; REn;
REnAL; SmATA 1; TwCA SUP; WhAm 5;
WomWMM; WorAl*

Bentham, Jeremy
English. Author, Philosopher
Originated utilitarianism, equating happiness
with pleasure; wrote *Fragment on
Government,* 1776.
b. Feb 15, 1748 in London, England
d. Jun 6, 1832 in London, England
Source: *Alli; AtlBL; BbD; BiD&SB; BiDLA;
BrAu 19; CasWL; Chambr 2; DcEnA;
DcEnL; DcEuL; CyAG; DcBiPP; DcLEL;
EvLB; NewC; OxEng; OxLaw; PenC ENG;
REn; WebE&AL*

Bentinck, William Henry Cavendish, Lord
British. Statesman
First governor-general of India, 1833-35;
reforms included abolishment of suttee,
1829.
b. 1774
d. 1839
Source: *BiDLA; BioIn 2, 4, 10, 11; NewCol
75; WebBD 80*

Bentley, Alvin Morell
American. Diplomat, Politician
Rep. congressman, 1953-60; shot, wounded by
    Puerto Rican nationalists, 1954.
b. Aug 30, 1918 in Portland, Maine
d. Apr 10, 1969 in Owosso, Michigan
Source: *BiDrAC; WhAm 5; WhAmP*

Bentley, Edmund Clerihew
English. Author, Journalist
Wrote detective classic *Trent's Last Case,*
    1912.
b. Jul 10, 1875 in London, England
d. Mar 30, 1956 in London, England
Source: *ChhPo, S2; DcLEL; EncMys; EvLB;
LongCTC; NewC; OxEng; REn; TwCA, SUP;
TwCWr*

Bentley, Elizabeth Terrill
American. Spy
Spied for USSR in US during WW II.
b. 1908
d. Dec 3, 1963 in New Haven, Connecticut
Source: *BioIn 1, 2, 3, 6; InWom*

Bentley, Eric
American. Author, Drama Critic, Educator
Comparative literature teacher; numerous
    drama critiques include *Brecht
    Commentaries,* 1981.
b. Sep 14, 1916 in Lancashire, England
Source: *AmAu&B; AmSCAP 66; Au&Wr 71;
BiE&WWA; CelR; NewC; NotNAT; REnAL;
TwCA SUP; WhoAm 74, 76, 78, 80, 82, 84;
WhoThe 77; WhoWor 78; WrDr 80*

Bentley, John
English. Actor
Played hero-detective roles, 1950s British
    films.
b. Dec 2, 1916 in Warwickshire, England
Source: *BiDLA; FilmgC; IntMPA 75, 76, 77,
78, 79, 80, 81, 82; WhoHol A*

Bentley, John
[Squeeze]
English. Musician
Bassist who joined Squeeze, 1979.
b. Apr 16, 1951 in London, England
Source: *NF*

Bentley, Max (Maxwell Herbert Lloyd)
"Dipsy Doodle Dandy of Delisle"
Canadian. Hockey Player
Center, 1940-54, who was NHL scoring
    champion, 1946, 1947; Hall of Fame,
    1966.
b. Mar 1, 1920 in Delisle, Saskatchewan
d. Jan 19, 1984 in Saskatoon, Saskatchewan
Source: *BioIn 10; HocEn; WhoHcky 73*

Bentley, Richard
English. Author, Clergyman, Critic
Proved *Epistles of Phalaris* were spurious,
    1669; first to use philology as test of
    authenticity.
b. Jan 27, 1662 in Oulton, England
d. Jul 14, 1742
Source: *Alli; BiD&SB; BrAu; CasWL; DcEnA;
DcEnL; DcEuL; EvLB; NewC; OxEng; PenC
ENG; REn*

Bentley, Walter Owen
English. Auto Manufacturer
Built Bentley automobile; merged with Rolls-
    Royce, 1931.
b. Sep 16, 1888 in London, England
d. Aug 13, 1971 in Woking, England
Source: *BioIn 9, 10; NewYTBE 71; ObitOF
79; ObitT 1971*

Benton, Barbie
American. Actress, Singer
Longtime girlfriend of Hugh Hefner;
    appeared in film *Deathstalker.*
b. Jan 28, 1950 in Sacramento, California
Source: *VarWW 85; WhoAmW 83*

Benton, Brook
[Benjamin Franklin Peay]
American. Singer
One of few black singers to write own
    material; best known hit "Boll Weevil
    Song," 1961.
b. Sep 19, 1931 in Camden, South Carolina
Source: *AmPS A; DrBlPA; EncPR&S 74;
InB&W 85; WhoBlA 80*

Benton, Nelson (Joseph Nelson, Jr.)
Broadcast Journalist
CBS News correspondent.
b. Sep 16, 1924
Source: *NF*

Benton, Robert Douglass
American. Author, Director
Directed *Kramer vs. Kramer,* 1979;
    contributed to several screenplays:
    Superman, 1978; *Places in the Heart,* 1984.
b. Sep 29, 1932 in Waxahachie, Texas
Source: *ConTFT 3*

Benton, Thomas Hart
"Old Bullion"
American. Political Leader, Editor
Senate leader, 1821-51; lost office for
    opposing extension of slavery.
b. Mar 14, 1782 in Hillsboro, North Carolina
d. Apr 10, 1858 in Washington, District of
    Columbia
Source: *Alli; AmAu&B; AmBi; ApCAB; BbD;
BiAUS; BiD&SB; BiDSA; BiDrAC; CyAL 1;
DcAmAu; DcAmB; DcNAA; Drake; EncAB-H;
LinLib S; McGEWB; NatCAB 4; NewCol 75;
REn; REnAW; REnAL; TwCBDA; WebAB;
WhAm HS; WhAmP*

Benton, Thomas Hart
American. Artist
Regionalist whose paintings depict life in
    Midwest, South.
b. Apr 15, 1889 in Neosho, Missouri
d. Jan 19, 1975 in Kansas City, Missouri
Source: *BioIn 1, 2, 3, 4, 5, 6, 7, 8, 9, 10,
11; AmAu&B; ArtsAmW 1; BnEnAmA; CelR;
ConAu 53, 93; CurBio 40, 75; DcAmArt;
DcCAA 71; EncAAH; EncAB-H; IlBEAAW;
IlsCB 1744, 1946; IntWW 74, 75; LinLib S;
McGDA; McGEWB; NewCol 75; NewYTBS
75; ObitOF 79; OxAmL; REn; REnAL;
WebAB; WhAm 6; WhoAm 74; WhoAmA 73,
76, 78; WhoWor 74*

Benton, William
American. Publisher, Politician, Educator
Dem. senator from CT 1949-53; started
    Voice of America broadcasts; owner,
    publisher, *Encyclopedia Britannica, 1942-73.*
b. Apr 1, 1900 in Minneapolis, Minnesota
d. Mar 18, 1973 in New York, New York
Source: *AmAu&B; BiDrAC; ConAu 41R, P-1;
CurBio 73; St&PR 75; WebAB; WhAm 5;
WhAmP; WhoAmA 73; WhoF&I 74*

Bentsen, Lloyd Millard, Jr.
American. Senator, Judge
Dem. senator from TX, 1971--.
b. Feb 11, 1921 in Mission, Texas
Source: *BiDrAC; BioNews 74, 75; CngDr 74;
CurBio 73; IntWW 74; WhoAm 74, 76, 78,
80, 82; WhoAmP 73; WhoGov 75*

Bentyne, Cheryl
see: Manhattan Transfer

Benz, Karl Friedrich
German. Auto Manufacturer
Built first car powered by internal
    combustion engine, 1885; merged with
    Daimler to form Mercedes Benz, 1926.
b. Nov 26, 1844 in Karlsruhe, Germany
d. 1929
Source: *DcInv; InSci; NewCol 75; WebBD 80,
80*

Benzell, Mimi (Miriam Ruth)
American. Opera Singer, Actress
Popular soprano, light opera singer; star of
    radio's "Luncheon with Mimi," 1964.
b. Apr 6, 1924 in Bridgeport, Connecticut
d. Dec 23, 1970 in Manhasset, New York
Source: *BiE&WWA; InWom; NewYTBE 70*

Beradino, John
American. Actor, Baseball Player
Infielder, 1939-52; plays Dr. Hardy on TV
    soap opera "General Hospital," 1963--.
b. May 1, 1917 in Los Angeles, California
Source: *BaseEn 85; VarWW 85*

Beranger, Pierre Jean de
French. Poet
Wrote light verse satirizing Bourbons;
    Chanson Inedites, celebrated Napoleon.
b. Aug 19, 1780 in Paris, France
d. Jul 16, 1857
Source: *BbD; BiD&SB; ChhPo, S1, S2;
DcEuL; EuAu; EvEuW; OxEng; OxFr; PenC
EUR; REn*

Berberian, Cathy
[Mrs. Luciano Berio]
American. Opera Singer, Comedienne
Known for singing avant-garde works: John
    Cage's "Fontana Mix"; Luciana Berio's
    "Circles."
b. Jul 4, 1928 in Attleboro, Massachusetts
d. Mar 6, 1983 in Rome, Italy
Source: *AnObit 1983; Baker 78; IntWW 80,
81, 82; WhAm 80, 82; WhoAmW 74;
WhoMus 72; WhoWor 74*

Bercovici, Konrad
American. Author
Wrote about NY's East Side, Balkan gypsies
    in *Peasants,* 1928.
b. Jun 22, 1882 in Braila, Romania
d. Dec 27, 1961 in New York, New York
Source: *AmAu&B; AmNov; CnDAL; ConAmL;
DcLEL; NatCAB 46; OxAmL; REnAL;
TwCA, SUP; WhAm 4; WhNAA*

Berdyayev, Nikolay A
Russian. Theologian, Philosopher
Developed Christian existentialism; exiled
from Russia, 1922; wrote *Destiny of Man,*
1937.
b. Mar 19, 1874 in Kiev, Russia
d. Mar 4, 1948 in Paris, France
Source: *CasWL; ClDMEL; DcRusL; EncWL;
EvEuW; LongCTC; REn; TwCA, SUP*

Beregovoy, Georgi
Russian. Cosmonaut
Orbited earth in spaceship *Soiuz 3,* 1964.
b. 1921
Source: *BioIn 10; WhoSocC 78*

Berengar of Tours
French. Theologian
His *De Sacra Coena* opposing doctrine of
transsubstantiation led to church's better
formulation of eucharist doctrine.
b. 1000
d. 1088
Source: *NewCol 75*

Berenger, Tom (Thomas)
American. Actor
Appeared in film *The Big Chill,* 1983.
b. May 31, 1950 in Chicago, Illinois
Source: *ConTFT 3; IntMPA 82, 83, 84;
VarWW 85*

Berenson, Bernard
American. Art Critic, Author
Italian Renaissance expert; wrote *Drawings of
the Florentine Painters,* 1903.
b. Jun 26, 1865 in Vilnius, Lithuania
d. Oct 6, 1959 in Settignano, Italy
Source: *AmAu&B; CasWL; DcAmB S6;
DcCathB; EncAB-H; LinLib L; LongCTC;
McGDA; NatCAB 48; OxAmL; OxEng; PenC
AM; REn; REnAL; TwCA SUP; WebAB;
WhAm 3*

Berenson, Marisa
American. Model, Actress
Grandniece of Bernard Berenson; starred in
Barry Lyndon, 1975.
b. Feb 15, 1948 in New York, New York
Source: *BkPepl; FilmEn; MovMk; WhoHol A*

Berenson, "Red" (Gordon Arthur)
Canadian. Hockey Player, Hockey Coach
Center, 1961-74, who was one of seven NHL
players to score six goals in one game,
Nov 7, 1968.
b. Dec 8, 1941 in Regina, Saskatchewan
Source: *BioIn 9, 10, 11; WhoHcky 73;
WhoMW 82*

Beresford, Harry
American. Actor, Author
Vaudeville performer who came to US, 1886;
toured with own co. for 10 yrs.
b. 1864 in London, England
d. Oct 4, 1944 in Los Angeles, California
Source: *Film 2; NotNAT B; WhAm 2;
WhScrn 74, 77; WhThe; WhoHol B*

Berg, Alban
Austrian. Composer
Wrote opera *Wozzeck,* 1921, in which
atonality blends with elements of Viennese
tradition.
b. Feb 9, 1885 in Vienna, Austria
d. Dec 24, 1935 in Vienna, Austria
Source: *AtlBL; DcCM; OxGer; WhAm 4*

Berg, Gertrude
American. Actress
Starred in "The Goldbergs" on radio, 1929-
50, TV, 1949-54.
b. Oct 3, 1899 in Harlem, New York
d. Sep 14, 1966 in New York, New York
Source: *BiE&WWA; CurBio 41, 60, 66;
FilmgC; InWom; LibW; NatCAB 52;
NewYTET; WhAm 4; WhScrn 74, 77;
WhoHol B*

Berg, Patty (Patricia Jane)
American. Golfer
One of founders, first pres., LPGA, 1948,
who has won 83 golf tournaments.
b. Feb 13, 1918 in Minneapolis, Minnesota
Source: *CurBio 40; InWom; WhoGolf*

Berg, Paul
American. Biochemist, Educator
Author of articles on biochemistry,
microbiology, who shared Nobel Prize for
chemistry, 1980.
b. Jun 30, 1926 in New York, New York
Source: *AmM&WS 73P, 76P, 79P; IntWW
74, 75, 76, 77, 78; NewYTBS 80; Who 82;
WhoAm 78, 80, 82, 84; WhoWest 82*

Berganza, Teresa
Spanish. Opera Singer
b. Mar 16, 1935 in Madrid, Spain
Source: *InWom; IntWW 74; Who 74;
WhoAm 82; WhoMus 72; WhoWor 78*

Bergen, Candice
[Mrs. Louis Malle]
American. Actress, Photojournalist
Daughter of Edgar Bergen; starred in
    Starting Over, 1979, *Rich and Famous,*
    1981.
b. May 9, 1946 in Beverly Hills, California
Source: *BkPepl; CelR; ConTFT 3; FilmgC;*
IntMPA 82; MotPP; MovMk; NewYTBE 71;
WhoAm 84; WhoHol A

Bergen, Edgar John
[Edgar John Bergren]
American. Ventriloquist, Comedian
Vaudeville, film, TV entertainer for 60 yrs.;
    with dummy Charlie McCarthy, starred in
    radio's "Chase & Sanborn Hour," 1937-47.
b. Feb 16, 1903 in Chicago, Illinois
d. Sep 30, 1978 in Las Vegas, Nevada
Source: *CurBio 45, 78; FilmgC; MotPP;*
WebAB; WhoHol A

Bergen, John Joseph
American. Financier, Industrialist
Chm., Graham-Page investment firm,
    involved in building new Madison Square
    Garden, NYC, 1968.
b. Aug 7, 1896 in Pottsville, Pennsylvania
d. Dec 11, 1980 in Cuernavaca, Mexico
Source: *CurBio 61, 81*

Bergen, Polly
[Nellie Paulina Burgin]
American. Actress, Singer
Radio singer who made Hollywood debut,
    early 1950s; won Emmy, 1957, for "The
    Helen Morgan Story."
b. Jul 14, 1930 in Knoxville, Tennessee
Source: *BiE&WWA; BusPN; CelR; ConAu 57;*
FilmEn; FilmgC; InWom; IntMPA 77, 78, 79,
80, 81, 82; NotNAT; WhoAm 82; WorAl

Berger, Al
[Southside Johnny and the Asbury Jukes]
American. Singer, Musician
Bassist, vocalist with group since 1974.
b. Nov 8, 1949
Source: *NF*

Berger, Arthur
American. Composer
Best known compositions include *Polyphony,*
    1956; *Septet,* 1966.
b. May 15, 1912 in New York, New York
Source: *DcCM; WhoAm 74; WhoWor 74*

Berger, David
Israeli. Olympic Athlete, Murder Victim
Member of Israeli Olympic team murdered
    by terrorists.
b. 1944
d. Sep 5, 1972 in Munich, Germany (West)
Source: *BioIn 9*

Berger, Helmut
[Helmut Steinberger]
Austrian. Actor
Known for sinister roles: *The Damned,* 1969;
    Dorian Gray, 1972.
b. May 29, 1944 in Salzburg, Austria
Source: *FilmEn; FilmgC; IntMPA 81, 82;*
WhoHol A

Berger, John
English. Author, Art Critic
Novels include *The Foot of Clive,* 1962;
    Corher's Freedom, 1964.
b. Nov 5, 1926 in London, England
Source: *ConLC 2; ConNov 72, 76; ModBrL;*
Who 74; WrDr 80

Berger, Marilyn
[Mrs. Don Hewitt]
American. Broadcast Journalist
Chief White House correspondent, NBC-TV,
    1976-77; with ABC News, 1982--.
b. Aug 23, 1935 in New York, New York
Source: *ConAu 101; WhoAm 78, 80, 82;*
WhoTelC

Berger, Melvin H
American. Author
Writings include *For Good Measure,* 1969;
    Storms, 1970; *Pollution Lab,* 1973.
b. Aug 23, 1927 in Brooklyn, New York
Source: *AuBYP; ConAu 5R, 4NR; ConLC 12;*
SmATA 5

Berger, Meyer
American. Journalist, Author
NYC columnist who won Pulitzer for local
    reporting, 1950; wrote *The Eight Million,*
    1942.
b. Sep 1, 1898 in New York, New York
d. Feb 8, 1959 in New York, New York
Source: *AmAu&B; CurBio 43, 59; DcAmB S6;*
NatCAB 46; WhAm 3

Berger, Raoul
American. Lawyer, Educator, Author
Wrote books on politics, including
    Impeachment: The Constitutional Problems,
    1973.
b. Jan 4, 1901 in Russia
Source: *ConAu 93; NewYTBE 73; WhoAm*
80, 84

Berger, Samuel David
American. Diplomat
US ambassador to S Korea, 1961-64; deputy
    ambassador to S Vietnam, 1968-72.
b. Dec 6, 1911 in Gloversville, New York
d. Feb 12, 1980 in Washington, District of
    Columbia
Source: *AnObit 1980; IntWW 74, 75, 76, 77,
78, 79, 80, 81; USBiR 74; WhoGov 72, 75*

Berger, Senta
Austrian. Actress
Star of films *Major Dundee,* 1965; *The Glory
    Guys,* 1965; *Quiller Memorandum,* 1967.
b. May 13, 1941 in Vienna, Austria
Source: *FilmgC; MotPP; WhoAmW 72;
WhoHol A*

Berger, Terry
American. Author
Juvenile writings include *Black Fairy Tales,*
    1969; *I Have Feelings,* 1971.
b. Aug 11, 1933 in New York, New York
Source: *ConAu 37R; SmATA 8; WrDr 80*

Berger, Thomas Louis
American. Author
Best known for style of dealing with
    absurdity of American life: *Little Big Man,*
    1964, adopted to film, 1970.
b. Jul 20, 1924 in Cincinnati, Ohio
Source: *AmAu&B; ConAu 1R, 5NR; ConLC
3, 5, 8, 11, 18; ConNov 76; DrAF 76;
ModAL S1; PenC AM; RAdv 1; WebE&AL;
WhoAm 82; WorAu; WrDr 76*

Berger, Victor L
American. Socialist Leader
First socialist ever elected to Congress, 1911-
    19.
b. Feb 28, 1860 in Nieder-Rehbach, Romania
d. Aug 7, 1929 in Milwaukee, Wisconsin
Source: *AmBi; BiDrAC; DcAmB S1; DcNAA;
EncAB-H; WebAB; WhAm 1; WhAmP*

Bergerac, Jacques
French. Actor
Pres., Paris branch of Revlon since 1972,
    who appeared in *Gigi,* 1958.
b. May 26, 1927 in Biarritz, France
Source: *IntMPA 75, 76, 77, 78, 79, 80, 81,
82; MotPP; WhoHol A*

Bergerac, Michel C
American. Cosmetics Executive
Pres., chm., Revlon, Inc., NYC, 1974--.
b. Feb 13, 1932 in Biarritz, France
Source: *BusPN; WhoAm 82; WhoF&I 74*

Bergeron, Victor J
"Trader Vic"
American. Restaurateur
Founder, owner worldwide "Trader Vic"
    restaurant chain.
b. 1903 in California
d. Oct 11, 1984 in Hillsborough, California
Source: *BioNews 74; BusPN; WhoAm 74, 76,
78, 80, 82; WhoWor 78*

Bergey, Bill
American. Football Player
b. Feb 9, 1945 in South Dayton, Ohio
Source: *WorAl*

Bergh, Henry
American. Humanitarian, Reformer
Shipbuilder, who was founder, first pres.,
    ASPCA, 1866; co-founder, ASPCC, 1875.
b. Aug 29, 1811 in New York, New York
d. Mar 12, 1888 in New York, New York
Source: *AmBi; BioIn 1, 3, 4, 8; DcAmAu;
DcAmB; NatCAB 3; WebAB, 79; WhAm HS*

Bergland, Bob (Robert Selmer)
American. Government Official, Farmer
Secretary of Agriculture, Carter
    administration, 1977-81; first farmer to fill
    post since 1945.
b. Jul 22, 1928 in Roseau, Minnesota
Source: *CngDr 74; CurBio 77; NewYTBS 76;
WhoAm 74; WhoAmP 81, 83; WhoMW 82;
WhoWor 80, 82*

Bergman, Alan
American. Lyricist
With wife Marilyn, wrote numerous award-
    winning songs for stage; screen: *The Way
    We Were,* 1974.
b. Sep 11, 1925 in Brooklyn, New York
Source: *AmSCAP 66, 80; VarWW 85;
WhoAm 80, 82, 84*

Bergman, Ingmar
[Ernest Ingmar Bergman]
Swedish. Director, Producer
Leading film artist whose works include *The
    Seventh Seal,* 1957; *Wild Strawberries,*
    1957.
b. Jul 14, 1918 in Uppsala, Sweden
Source: *BiDFilm; BkPepl; ConAu 81; ConLC
16; ConTFT 3; CurBio 60; DcFM; FilmEn;
IntMPA 82; IntWW 74; MovMk; NewYTBE
73; OxFilm; OxThe; WhoAm 84; WorAl;
WorEFlm*

Bergman, Ingrid
Swedish. Actress
Won Oscars for roles in *Gaslight,* 1944;
Anastasia, 1956; *Murder on the Orient
Express,* 1974.
b. Aug 29, 1915 in Stockholm, Sweden
d. Aug 29, 1982 in London, England
Source: *AnObit 1982; BiDFilm; BiE&WWA;
BkPepl; CelR; CmMov; CurBio 40, 65, 82,
82; FilmgC; GoodHs; IntMPA 80, 81; WhAm
8; IntMPA 82; IntWW 80, 81, 82; MotPP;
MovMk; NewYTBE 71; NewYTBS 75, 82;
NotNAT; OxFilm; PlP&P; ThFT; Who 82;
WhoAm 80, 82; WhoAmW 74; WhoHol A;
WhoThe 72; WhoWor 74, 76; WorEFlm*

Bergman, Jules Verne
American. Broadcast Journalist
Science editor, ABC News, 1961--, who
   wrote *Anyone Can Fly,* 1965; *Fire,* 1974.
b. Mar 21, 1929 in New York, New York
Source: *WhoAm 80, 82*

Bergman, Marilyn Keith
[Mrs. Alan Bergman]
American. Lyricist
Won Oscars for *Yentl,* 1983; *The Way We
Were,* 1974.
b. Nov 10, 1929 in Brooklyn, New York
Source: *AmSCAP 66, 80; VarWW 85;
WhoAm 80, 82, 84*

Bergmann, Carl
German. Conductor
NY Philharmonic conductor, 1855-76, who
   introduced Wagner, Liszt to American
   audiences.
b. Apr 11, 1821 in Ebersbach, Germany
d. Aug 16, 1876 in New York, New York
Source: *AmBi; ApCAB; Baker 78; DcAmB;
NewEOp 71; WhAm HS*

Bergner, Elisabeth
[Elizabeth Ettel]
British. Actress
James Barrie wrote his last play *The Boy
David,* for her, 1938; Oscar nominee for
Escape Me Never, 1935.
b. Aug 22, 1900 in Vienna, Austria
d. May 12, 1986 in London, England
Source: *BiE&WWA; EncTR; EncWT; Film 2;
FilmgC; MovMk; NewYTBS 86; NotNAT;
OxFilm; ThFT; Who 74; WhoHol A; WhoThe
77; WorEFlm*

Bergonzi, Carlo
Italian. Opera Singer
Operas performed include *Barber of Seville,
Aida.*
b. Jul 13, 1924 in Polesine, Italy
Source: *IntWW 74; WhoMus 72; WhoWor 78*

Bergson, Henri Louis
French. Author, Philosopher
Vitalism philosophy asserted importance of
   pure intuition, duration, liberty.
b. Oct 18, 1859 in Paris, France
d. Jan 3, 1941 in Paris, France
Source: *AtlBL; BiDPara; CasWL; ClDMEL;
CurBio 41; DcScB; Dis&D; EncO&P 78;
EncWL; EvEuW; LongCTC; NewC; OxEng;
OxFr; PenC EUR; RComWL; REn; TwCA,
SUP; TwCWr; WhoTwCL*

Beria, Lavrenti Pavlovich
Russian. Communist Leader
Head of Soviet Intelligence, 1934-53; executed
   in power struggle after Stalin's death.
b. Mar 29, 1899 in Georgia, Russia
d. Dec 23, 1953
Source: *CurBio 42, 54; DcPol; EncE 75;
HisEWW; LinLib S; McGEWB; ObitT 1951;
WhDW*

Berigan, "Bunny" (Rowland Bernart)
American. Musician, Band Leader
Trumpeter who played Broadway band music
   for *Everybody Welcome,* 1931.
b. Nov 2, 1909 in Hilbert, Wisconsin
d. Jun 2, 1942 in New York, New York
Source: *CurBio 42; WhoJazz 72*

Bering, Vitus Jonassen
Danish. Navigator
Member of Russian navy who traveled coast
   of Asia, discovered some of Aleutian
   Islands, 1741.
b. 1680 in Horsens, Denmark
d. Dec 19, 1741 in Bering Island
Source: *ApCAB; OxCan; WhAm HS*

Berio, Luciano
Italian. Composer, Conductor
Innovative, controversial operas include *Allez-
hop,* 1959, *Passagio,* 1963.
b. Oct 24, 1925 in Oniglia, Italy
Source: *CurBio 71; DcCM; IntWW 74;
WhoAm 80; WhoMus 72; WhoWor 74*

Berkeley, "Busby"
[William Berkeley Enos]
American. Director, Choreographer
Known for choreography, 1930s movies,
   using dancing girls to form kaleidoscopic
   patterns: *42nd Street,* 1933; *No No
Nanette,* 1971.
b. Nov 29, 1895 in Los Angeles, California
d. Mar 14, 1976 in Palm Springs, California
Source: *BiDFilm; BiE&WWA; CmMov;
CurBio 71; DcFM; EncMT; FilmgC; IntMPA
75; MovMk; OxFilm; WebAB; WhAm 6;
WhoAm 74; WhoThe 77; WorEFlm*

Berkeley, George
Irish. Author, Philosopher
Wrote *Principals of Human Knowledge,* 1710.
b. Mar 12, 1685 in Ireland
d. Jan 14, 1753 in Oxford, England
Source: *ApCAB; BbD; BiD&SB; BrAu;
CasWL; CyAL 1; DcEnA; DcEnL; DcEuL;
DcLEL; Drake; EvLB; NewC; OxAmL;
OxEng; PenC ENG; PoIre; REn; TwCBDA;
WebE&AL*

Berkman, Alexander
Russian. Anarchist
Believed ideal society based on voluntary
    anarchist collectivism; wrote *Prison
    Memoirs of an Anarchist,* 1912.
b. Nov 21, 1870 in Vilna, Russia
d. Jun 28, 1936 in Nice, France
Source: *DcAmB S2; DcNAA; WhAm 4, HSA*

Berkow, Ira Harvey
American. Journalist, Author
Writings include *Beyond the Dream,* 1975;
    The Man Who Robbed the Pierre, 1980.
b. Jan 7, 1940 in Chicago, Illinois
Source: *BioIn 10; ConAu 97; IntAu&W 82;
WhoAm 84*

Berkowitz, Bernard
American. Psychoanalyst, Author
b. 1909
Source: *AuNews 1; BioIn 10, 11*

Berkowitz, Bob
American. Broadcast Journalist
Correspondent, ABC News since 1982.
b. May 15, 1950 in New York, New York
Source: *WhoTelC*

Berkowitz, David
"Son of Sam"
American. Murderer
Killed six people in NYC, Jul, 1976-Aug,
    1977.
b. Jun 1, 1953
Source: *BioIn 11*

Berlage, Hendrik Petrus
Dutch. Architect
Known for simplicity; most famous work
    Amsterdam Exchange, the Beurs, 1896-
    1903.
b. 1856 in Amsterdam, Netherlands
d. 1934 in The Hague, Netherlands
Source: *EncMA; McGDA; NewCol 75; WebBD
80; WhoArch*

Berle, Adolf Augustus, Jr.
American. Lawyer, Diplomat
US ambassador to Brazil, 1945-46; chm., task
    force on Latin America, 1961.
b. Jan 29, 1895 in Boston, Massachusetts
d. Feb 17, 1971 in New York, New York
Source: *AmAu&B; ConAu 21R, 29R, P-2;
CurBio 40, 61, 71; EncAB-H; NewYTBE 71;
WhAm 5*

Berle, Milton
[Milton Berlinger]
"Uncle Miltie"; "Mr. Television"
American. Actor, Comedian, Radio
    Performer, TV Personality
Vaudeville, stage performer who dominated
    TV in "The Milton Berle Show," 1948-56.
b. Jul 12, 1908 in New York, New York
Source: *AmAu&B; AmSCAP 66; AuNews 1;
BiE&WWA; BioNews 75; ConAu 77; ConTFT
3; EncMT; FilmEn; Film 1; FilmgC; IntMPA
82; MovMk; NotNAT; PIP&P; WebAB;
WhoAm 84; WhoHol A; WhoThe 77;
WhoWor 78*

Berlenbach, Paul
"Astoria Assassin"
American. Boxer
Olympic heavyweight wrestling champ, 1920;
    world light heavyweight champ, 1925-33.
b. Feb 18, 1901 in New York, New York
Source: *WhoBox 74*

Berlin, Irving
[Israel Baline]
American. Composer
Wrote nearly 1000 songs including
    "Alexander's Ragtime Band," 1911; "White
    Christmas," which won Oscar, 1942.
b. May 11, 1888 in Temun, Russia
Source: *AmSCAP 66; BiE&WWA; CelR;
CmMov; CurBio 42, 63; DcFM; EncAB-H;
EncMT; FilmEn; FilmgC; IntMPA 80, 81, 82;
IntWW 74; McGEWD; NewCBMT; NotNAT;
OxAmL; OxFilm; PIP&P; REn; REnAL;
St&PR 75; WebAB; Who 82; WhoAm 80, 82;
WhoThe 77; WhoWor 74; WhoWorJ 72*

Berlin, Isaiah, Sir
English. Author
Writings include *Historical Inevitability,* 1955;
    The Age of Enlightenment, 1956.
b. Jun 6, 1909 in Riga, Russia
Source: *ConAu 85; CurBio 64; IntWW 74;
LongCTC; Who 74; WhoWor 78; WorAu*

Berlin, Richard E
American. Corporation Executive
Pres., chief exec., Hearst Corp., 1941-74.
b. Jan 18, 1894 in Omaha, Nebraska
Source: *St&PR 75; WhoAm 74; WhoE 74; WhoF&I 74; WhoWest 84*

Berliner, Emile
American. Inventor
Invented microphone, 1877, gramaphone, 1887.
b. May 20, 1851 in Hannover, Germany
d. Aug 3, 1929 in Washington, District of Columbia
Source: *AmBi; ApCAB; DcAmB S1; DcNAA; WebAB; WhAm 1; WhNAA*

Berliner, Ron
American. Actor
In films *The World According to Garp,* 1982; *The Manhattan Project,* 1985.
b. Oct 13, 1958 in Coral Gables, Florida
Source: *ConTFT 3*

Berlinger, Warren
American. Actor
Won 1959 Theatre World Award for *Blue Denim.*
b. Aug 31, 1937 in Brooklyn, New York
Source: *FilmgC; IntMPA 75, 76, 77, 78, 79, 80, 81, 82; MotPP; NotNAT; WhoAm 74, 76, 78, 80, 82; WhoThe 81*

Berlinguer, Enrico
Italian. Political Leader
An architect of Eurocommunism who was general secretary of Italian Communist Party, 1972-84.
b. May 25, 1922 in Sassari, Sardinia
d. Jun 11, 1984 in Padua, Italy
Source: *CurBio 76, 84; IntWW 80, 81, 82, 84; NewYTBS 78, 84; WhoEIO 82; WhoWor 80, 82*

Berlioz, Louis Hector
French. Composer
Major work *Symphonie Fantastique,* 1830.
b. Dec 11, 1803 in La Cote, France
d. Mar 8, 1869 in Paris, France
Source: *AtlBL; BbD; BiD&SB; OxFr; REn*

Berlitz, Charles L Frambach
[Charles Francois Bertin, pseud.]
American. Author
Grandson of Berlitz School of Languages founder, Maximilian D Berlitz who wrote *The Bermuda Triangle,* 1974.
b. Nov 22, 1913 in New York, New York
Source: *AmAu&B; ConAu 7NR; CurBio 57; UFOEn; WhoAm 74, 76, 78, 80, 82; WhoWor 74*

Berman, Emile Zola
American. Lawyer
Attorney for underdog clients; defended Sirhan Sirhan, 1969.
b. Nov 2, 1903 in New York, New York
d. Jul 3, 1981 in New York, New York
Source: *BioIn 4, 7, 8, 9; CurBio 72, 81; NewYTBS 81; WhoAm 74, 76*

Berman, Eugene
American. Artist, Designer
Neo-romantic painter, also known for theater sets, interiors.
b. Nov 4, 1899 in Saint Petersburg, Russia
d. Dec 14, 1972 in Rome, Italy
Source: *BnEnAmA; ConArt 77; CurBio 65, 73; DcCAA 71, 77; EncWT; McGDA; WhAm 5; WhoAmA 78*

Berman, Lazar
Russian. Musician
Concert pianist, 1957--, who made Carnegie Hall debut, 1976.
b. Feb 26, 1930 in Leningrad, U.S.S.R.
Source: *Baker 84; CurBio 77; WhoAm 82, 84; WhoWor 84*

Berman, Morton
American. Editor
Co-edited *Eight Great Tragedies,* 1957; *Eight Great Comedies,* 1958.
b. Mar 21, 1924 in Syracuse, New York
Source: *ConAu 5R, 2NR; DrAS 74E; WhoAm 74*

Berman, Pandro Samuel
American. Producer
Producer of several Astaire/Rogers films for MGM, who won Irving M Thalberg award, 1977.
b. Mar 28, 1905 in Pittsburgh, Pennsylvania
Source: *FilmgC; IntMPA 82; WhoAm 80, 82; WhoAmJ 80; WorEFlm*

Berman, Shelley (Sheldon Leonard)
American. Comedian, Actor
Films include *The Best Man,* 1964; *Divorce American Style,* 1969.
b. Feb 3, 1926 in Chicago, Illinois
Source: *BiE&WWA; FilmgC; WhoAm 74; WhoWor 78*

Bermudez, Juan de
Spanish. Navigator
Discovered Bermuda, 1522, named in his honor.
Source: *ApCAB*

Bern, Paul
[Paul Levy]
American. Director
MGM exec. who supervised all Garbo's
films; committed suicide after marriage to
Jean Harlow.
b. Dec 3, 1889 in Wandsbek, Germany
d. Sep 4, 1932 in Beverly Hills, California
Source: *BioIn 11; FilmEn; FilmgC; PseudN
82; WhAm 1; WhScrn 74, 77*

Bernacchi, Antonio Maria
Italian. Opera Singer
Soprano who made debut in Genoa, 1703.
b. Jun 23, 1685 in Bologna, Italy
d. Mar 13, 1756 in Bologna, Italy
Source: *Baker 84; NewEOp 71*

Bernadette of Lourdes
[Marie Bernarde Soubirous; Soubiroux; Saint
Bernadette]
French. Religious Figure
Nun who saw 18 visions of Virgin Mary in
grotto in Lourdes, 1858; canonized, 1933.
b. Jan 7, 1844 in Lourdes, France
d. Apr 16, 1879 in Nevers, France
Source: *DcCathB; Dis&D; HerW; InWom;
OxFr; REn; WhDW; WorAl*

Bernadotte, Folke, Count
Swedish. Diplomat
Intermediary between Heinrich Himmler,
Great Britain, US, 1945, right before
Germany surrendered.
b. Jan 2, 1895 in Stockholm, Sweden
d. Sep 17, 1948 in Jerusalem, Israel
Source: *CurBio 45, 48*

Bernanos, Georges
French. Author
Father of modern theological novel who
wrote *The Diary of a Country Priest,* 1937.
b. May 5, 1888 in Paris, France
d. Jul 5, 1948 in Paris, France
Source: *CyWA; EncWL; OxFr*

Bernard of Clairvaux, Saint
French. Religious Leader
Monk who preached in Second Crusade,
1146; canonized 1174.
b. 1090 in Fontaines-les-Dijon, France
d. Aug 20, 1153 in Clairvaux, France
Source: *BbD; BiD&SB; CasWL; EuAu;
EvEuW; IlEncMy; LuthC 75; NewC; PenC
EUR; PoChrch; REn; WhDW*

Bernard of Cluny
French. Religious Figure
Wrote poem *De Contempu Mundi;* hymn
"Jerusalem the Golden" is based on it.
b. 1100
d. 1156
Source: *BiD&SB; CasWL; DcCathB; LinLib
L, S; LuthC 75; NewC; PenC EUR; REn*

Bernard, Andrew Milroy
[Andrew Milroy Fleming-Bernard]
"Master Bernard, the Blind Poet"
British. Poet
Poet laureate to Henry VII, Henry VIII.
b. in Toulose, France
d. 1523
Source: *Alli; DcEnL; PoLE*

Bernard, Claude
French. Physiologist
Called founder of experimental medicine for
work on role of pancreas, liver in
digestion process.
b. Jul 12, 1813 in Saint-Julien, France
d. Feb 10, 1878 in Paris, France
Source: *DcEuL; NamesHP; OxFr; WhDW*

Bernard, Sam
[Samuel Barnet]
English. Actor
Played German character parts in Ziegfeld
Follies; screen actor beginning 1915.
b. 1863 in Birmingham, England
d. May 16, 1927
Source: *CmpEPM; Film 1; NotNAT B;
WhAm 1; WhScrn 74, 77; WhThe; WhoHol
B; WhoStg 1908*

Bernardi, Hershel
American. Actor, Singer
Played Tevye on Broadway's *Fiddler on the
Roof,* 1970; in TV series "Peter Gun,"
1958-60; "Arnie," 1970-71.
b. Oct 30, 1923 in New York, New York
d. May 10, 1986 in Los Angeles, California
Source: *CelR; FilmgC; NotNAT; WhoAm 82;
WhoHol A; WorAl*

Bernardin, Joseph Louis, Cardinal
American. Religious Leader
Named head of Chicago diosese after death
of Cardinal Cody, 1982.
b. Apr 2, 1928 in Columbia, South Carolina
Source: *AmCath 80; BlueB 76; CurBio 82;
NewYTBS 74, 82; WhoAm 74, 76, 78, 80,
82; WhoMW 76, 78, 82; WhoRel 77*

Bernardine of Siena, Saint
Italian. Religious Figure
Preacher who was leader in Franciscan order;
promoted Holy Name of Jesus; feast day
May 20.
b. 1380 in Massa di Carrera, Italy
d. 1444 in Aquila, Italy
Source: *BioIn 1, 3, 4, 5, 6; NewCol 75*

Bernardone, Giovanni
see: Francis of Assisi, Saint

Bernays, Edward L
American. Public Relations Executive
Founder, Edward L Bernays Foundation,
1946; author *Public Relations, 1945; The
Engineering of Consent, 1955.*
b. Nov 22, 1891 in Vienna, Austria
Source: *AmAu&B; ConAu 17R; CurBio 42,
60; REnAL; WhNAA; WhoAm 74, 76, 78, 80,
82; WhoAmJ 80; WhoE 81; WhoPubR 72;
WhoWor 74; WhoWorJ 72; WrDr 76*

Bernbach, William
American. Advertising Executive
Founded Doyle Dane Bernbach, tenth largest
ad agency in US, 1966.
b. Aug 13, 1911 in Bronx, New York
d. Oct 1, 1982 in New York, New York
Source: *CurBio 67, 82; Dun&B 79; NewYTBS
82; WhoAm 74, 76, 78, 80, 82; WhoE 77,
79; WhoF&I 74, 75, 77, 79*

Berndt, Walter
American. Cartoonist
Best known for syndicated comic strip
"Smitty," 1922-73.
b. Nov 22, 1899 in Brooklyn, New York
d. Aug 13, 1979 in Port Jefferson, New
York
Source: *ConAu 89; WorECom*

Berne, Eric Lennard
American. Psychiatrist, Author
Wrote best-seller *Games People Play,* 1964.
b. May 10, 1910 in Montreal, Quebec
d. Jul 15, 1970 in Monterey, California
Source: *AmAu&B; ConAu 4NR, 5R, 25R;
NewYTBE 70; WhAm 5*

Bernhard, Lucian
American. Type Designer, Artist
Co-founded arts magazine *Das Plakat;*
professor of poster art, Royal Art
Institute, Berlin.
b. Mar 15, 1883 in Stuttgart, Germany
d. May 29, 1972 in New York, New York
Source: *WhoGrA 62*

Bernhard, Prince
[Bernhard Leopold Friedrich Eberhard Julius
Kurt Karl Gottfried Peter]
German. Consort
Married Queen Juliana of the Netherlands,
Jan 7, 1937.
b. Jun 29, 1911 in Jena, Germany
Source: *CurBio 50; HisEWW; IntWW 81, 82;
WebBD 80; WhoWor 80*

Bernhardt, Melvin
[Melvin Bernhard]
American. Director
Won Tony for *Da,* 1978.
b. Feb 26, in Buffalo, New York
Source: *ConTFT 2; VarWW 85*

Bernhardt, Sarah
[Rosine Bernard]
"The Devine Sarah"
French. Actress
Best-known theatrical actress of her time
who starred in silent film *Queen Elizabeth,*
1912.
b. Oct 23, 1844 in Paris, France
d. Mar 26, 1923 in Paris, France
Source: *FamA&A; Film 1; FilmgC; HerW;
InWom; LongCTC; NewC; NewCol 75;
OxFilm; OxFr; OxThe; PIP&P; TwYS; WhAm
1; WhScrn 74, 77; WhoHol B; WhoStg 1906,
1908; WorEFlm*

Bernie, Ben
American. Comedian, Musician
Vaudeville performer, 1910; orchestra leader,
NYC, 1923-28.
b. May 30, 1891 in New York, New York
d. Oct 20, 1943 in Beverly Hills, California
Source: *AmSCAP 66; CurBio 41, 43; WhAm
2; WhScrn 74, 77; WhoHol B*

Bernini, Giovanni Lorenzo
Italian. Sculptor, Architect
Replaced Maderno in designing St. Peter's,
1629.
b. Dec 7, 1598 in Naples, Italy
d. Nov 28, 1680 in Rome, Italy
Source: *AtlBL; MacEA; OxThe, 83*

Bernoulli, David
Swiss. Mathematician
Advanced kinetic theory of gases; published
Hydrodynamica, 1738.
b. Feb 8, 1700 in Groningen, Netherlands
d. Mar 17, 1782 in Basel, Switzerland
Source: *AsBiEn; BioIn 2, 3, 4; DcScB;
McGEWB*

Bernstein, Alice Frankau
American. Designer
Noted stage, costume designer; pres. Costume
Institute from 1944.
b. Dec 22, 1880 in New York, New York
d. Sep 7, 1955 in New York, New York
Source: NotAW MOD

Bernstein, Carl
American. Journalist, Author
With Bob Woodward wrote account of
Watergate break-in, cover-up, All the
President's Men, 1974.
b. Feb 14, 1944 in Washington, District of
Columbia
Source: AuNews 1; BioNews 74; BkPepl;
ConAu 81; CurBio 76; WhoAm 74, 76, 78,
80, 82; WorAl; WrDr 80

Bernstein, Eduard
German. Socialist Leader
Critic of Marxism who became leader of
revisionism, 1901; wrote Evolutionary
Socialism, 1899.
b. Jan 6, 1850 in Berlin, Germany
d. 1932
Source: DcAmSR; McGEWB; REn

Bernstein, Elmer
American. Composer, Conductor
Won Oscar for original score, Thoroughly
Modern Millie, 1967.
b. Apr 4, 1922 in New York, New York
Source: AmSCAP 66; CelR; CmMov; DcFM;
FilmgC; IntMPA 80, 81, 82; OxFilm; WhoAm
80, 82; WhoWest 84; WhoWor 78; WorEFlm

Bernstein, Felicia Montealegre
[Mrs. Leonard Bernstein]
American. Actress
Narrated concerts for NY Philharmonic,
Swan Song; Poor Murderer.
b. 1921
d. Jun 16, 1978 in East Hampton, New
York
Source: BioIn 10, 11; NewYTBS 78

Bernstein, Jay
American. Talent Agent
Hollywood agent whose protegees include
Farrah Fawcett, Suzanne Somers.
b. Jun 7, 1937 in Oklahoma City, Oklahoma
Source: BioIn 12

Bernstein, Leonard
American. Composer, Conductor, Musician,
Author
Multi-Tony, Emmy, Grammy winner who
wrote West Side Story, 1961.
b. Aug 25, 1918 in Lawrence, Massachusetts
Source: AmAu&B; AmPS; AmSCAP 80;
BiDAmM; CmpEPM; ConAu 2NR; ConTFT
3; CurBio 60; EncAB-H; EncMT; EncWT;
FilmgC; IntWW 81; LinLib S; McGEWB;
NewEop 71; NewYTET; NotNAT; OxAmL;
OxMus; PlP&P; REnAL; WebAB 79; WhoAm
84; WhoE 79; WhoMus 72; WhoWor 78;
WorAl; WorEFlm; WrDr 80

Bernstein, Sid(ney Ralph)
American. Editor, Business Executive
Chm., exec. committee, Crain
Communications, 1973--; pres., 1964-73.
b. Jan 29, 1907 in Chicago, Illinois
Source: WhoAdv 72; WhoAm 74, 76, 78, 80,
82; WhoF&I 74; WhoWorJ 72

Bernstein, Theodore Menline
American. Journalist
With NY Times since 1925; wrote The
Careful Writer, 1965.
b. Nov 17, 1904 in New York, New York
d. Jun 27, 1979 in New York, New York
Source: ConAu 1R, 3NR; NewYTBS 79;
SmATA 12; WhAm 7; WhNAA; WhoAm 74,
76, 78; WhoWorJ 72

Beroff, Michel
French. Pianist
Toured as concert pianist, from age 16, often
performing modernistic French composers.
b. 1950 in Epinal, France
Source: Baker 84; WhoMus 72

Berra, "Yogi" (Lawrence Peter)
American. Baseball Player, Baseball Manager
Catcher, NY Yankees, 1946-63; coined phrase
"It ain't over till it's over"; Hall of Fame,
1972.
b. May 12, 1925 in Saint Louis, Missouri
Source: BaseEn 85; BioNews 74; BlueB 76;
CelR; CurBio 52; NewYTBE 72, 73;
NewYTBS 75; WebAB, 79; WhoAm 74, 76,
78, 80, 82; WhoE 74; WhoProB 73; WorAl

Berri, Nabih
Lebanese. Government Official
Leader of Shiite Muslims-Amal in Lebanon
since 1980, known for role in Beirut TWA
hostage crisis, 1985.
b. 1938 in Freetown, Sierra Leone
Source: ConNews 85-2; CurBio 85

Berrigan, Daniel J
American. Poet, Political Activist, Priest
Convicted of destroying draft records with
    brother Philip, 1968.
b. May 9, 1921 in Virginia, Minnesota
Source: *AmAu&B; ASpks; CelR; ConAu 33R;
ConLC 4; ConP 70, 75, 80; CurBio 70; DrAP
75; IntWWP 77; LinLib L; MugS; PolProf J,
NF; WhoAm 74, 76, 80, 82, 84; WrDr 80*

Berrigan, Elizabeth McAlister
[Mrs. Philip Berrigan]
American. Political Activist
Former nun, member of Catholic anti-war
    movement, who was indicted for plotting
    to kidnap Henry Kissinger, 1971.
b. 1939
Source: *BioIn 10, 11; NewYTBE 71*

Berrigan, Philip Francis
American. Author, Political Activist
With brother Daniel, was first Catholic priest
    imprisoned for peace agitation in US,
    1968.
b. Oct 5, 1923 in Minneapolis, Minnesota
Source: *AmAu&B; BioNews 74; CelR; ConAu
13R; WhoAm 76, 78, 80, 82, 84*

Berrill, Jack
American. Cartoonist
Created "Gil Thorp," 1958; character named
    for Jim Thorpe and Gil Hodges.
b. 1924 in Brooklyn, New York
Source: *NF*

Berry, Bob (Robert Victor)
Canadian. Hockey Player, Hockey Coach
Left wing, 1968-77; has coached LA,
    Montreal, Pittsburgh.
b. Nov 29, 1943 in Montreal, Quebec
Source: *HocEn; WhoHcky 73*

Berry, "Chu" (Leon)
American. Jazz Musician
Tenor saxophonist with Cab Calloway, 1937-
    41.
b. Sep 13, 1910 in Wheeling, West Virginia
d. Oct 31, 1941 in Conneaut, Ohio
Source: *WhoJazz 72*

Berry, Chuck (Charles Edward Anderson)
American. Singer, Musician, Songwriter
Influential figure in development of rock
    music, 1950s-60s; wrote songs "Roll Over
    Beethoven"; "Johnny B Goode."
b. Jan 15, 1926 in San Jose, California
Source: *Baker 78; BiDAmM; BluesWW;
CurBio 77; DrBlPA; RkOn 74; RolSEnR 83;
VarWW 85; WebAB, 79; WhoAm 76, 78, 80,
82; WhoBlA 75, 77; WorAl*

Berry, James Gomer
[Viscount Kemsley]
Welsh. Publisher
Largest newspaper proprietor in Britain; sold
    holdings to Roy H Thomson, 1959.
b. May 7, 1883 in Merthyr Tydfil, Wales
d. Feb 6, 1968 in Monte Carlo, Monaco
Source: *ConAu 89; CurBio 51, 68; DcNaB
1961; GrBr; ObitOF 79*

Berry, Jan
[Jan and Dean]
American. Singer
Co-wrote duo's hit single "Surf City," 1963;
    suffered brain damage in car crash, 1966.
b. Apr 3, 1941 in Los Angeles, California
Source: *NF*

Berry, Jim
American. Cartoonist
Editorial cartoonist who draws "Berry's
    World," 1963--.
b. Jan 16, 1932 in Chicago, Illinois
Source: *ConAu 107, 21R; WorECar;
WorECom*

Berry, Ken
American. Actor, Singer, Dancer
Starred in TV series "F-Troop," 1965-67;
    "Mayberry RFD," 1968-71.
b. Nov 3, 1933 in Moline, Illinois
Source: *FilmgC; VarWW 85; WhoAm 80, 82;
WhoHol A*

Berry, Martha McChesney
"The Sunday Lady"
American. Educator
Founded the Berry Schools for GA
    mountaineers, 1902.
b. 1866 in Rome, Georgia
d. Feb 27, 1942 in Mount Berry, Georgia
Source: *CurBio 40, 42; DcAmB S3; HerW;
InWom; NotAW; WhAm 2; WomWWA 14*

Berry, Raymond Emmett
American. Football Player, Football Coach
Wide receiver Baltimore Colts, 1955-67, who
    had 631 receptions; coach, New England,
    1984--.
b. Feb 27, 1933 in Corpus Christi, Texas
Source: *BioIn 5, 6, 7, 8, 9, 10, 11; WhoFtbl
74*

Berry, Walter
Austrian. Opera Singer
Leading baritone NYC Metropolitan Opera;
    made numerous recordings since 1949.
b. Apr 8, 1929 in Vienna, Austria
Source: *IntWW 74; WhoAm 82; WhoWor 78*

Berry, Wendell
American. Poet, Educator
Wrote *Gift of Good Land,* 1981.
b. Aug 5, 1934 in Henry County, Kentucky
Source: *ConAu 73; ConLC 4, 6; ConP 70, 75;
DrAF 76; DrAP 75; PenC AM; RAdv 1;
WhoAm 74, 76, 78, 80, 82; WhoS&SW 82;
WrDr 80*

Berryer, Pierre Antoine
French. Lawyer, Politician
Defended Louis-Napoleon, 1840.
b. Jan 4, 1790
d. Nov 29, 1868
Source: *DcEuL; WebBD 80*

Berryman, Clifford Kennedy
American. Cartoonist
Editorial cartoonist, Washington *Star,* 1907-
49; created "Teddy Bear" after Theodore
Roosevelt's bear-hunting trip, 1902.
b. Apr 2, 1869 in Versailles, Kentucky
d. Dec 11, 1949 in Washington, District of
Columbia
Source: *DcAmB S4; EncAB 3; NatCAB 39;
ObitOF 79; WhAm 2; WhoAmA 78, 80, 82;
WorECar*

Berryman, John
American. Author, Poet
Won Pulitzer Prize, 1964, for *77 Dream
Songs.*
b. Oct 25, 1914 in McAlester, Oklahoma
d. Jan 7, 1972 in Minneapolis, Minnesota
Source: *AmAu&B; AmWr; Au&Wr 71;
CasWL; CnE&AP; ConAu 33R, P-1; ConLC
1, 2, 3, 4, 6, 8, 10, 13; ConP 70, 75;
CroCAP; CurBio 69, 72; EncWL; ModAL, S1;
NewYTBE 72; OxAmL; PenC AM; RAdv 1;
REn; REnAL; TwCA SUP; WebAB;
WebE&AL; WhAm 5; WhoTwCL*

Berthollet, Claude Louis, Comte
French. Chemist
Discovered bleaching properties of chlorine;
wrote *Essay on Chemical Statics,* 1803.
b. 1748
d. 1822
Source: *BioIn 1, 6; NewCol 75*

Bertillon, Alphonse
French. Criminologist
Invented first scientific method of identifying
criminals, using body measurements, eye,
hair, skin color.
b. Apr 24, 1853 in Paris, France
d. Feb 13, 1914 in Paris, France
Source: *LongCTC; McGEWB; OxFr; OxLaw;
WhDW*

Bertinelli, Valerie
[Mrs. Eddie Van Halen]
American. Actress, Producer
Played Barbara on TV series "One Day at a
Time," 1975-84.
b. Apr 23, 1960 in Wilmington, Delaware
Source: *ConTFT 3; VarWW 85*

Bertini, Gary
Israeli. Conductor, Composer
Musical director, Jerusalem Symphony, 1978-
81; frequent worldwide guest conductor.
b. May 1, 1927 in Bessarabia, U.S.S.R.
Source: *Baker 78, 84; MidE 78, 79; WhoMus
72; WhoOp 76; WhoWor 74, 76; WhoWorJ
72*

Bertoia, Harry
American. Artist, Designer
Noted for abstract, metal sculptures; prize-
winning wire shell chairs.
b. Mar 10, 1915 in San Lorenzo, Italy
d. Nov 6, 1978 in Barto, Pennsylvania
Source: *ConArt 77; DcAmArt; DcCAA 71, 77;
McGDA; NewYTBS 78; WhAm 7; WhoAm
74, 76, 78; WhoAmA 73, 76, 78; WhoWor 74*

Bertolucci, Bernardo
Italian. Director
Directed *Last Tango in Paris,* 1972.
b. Mar 16, 1940 in Parma, Italy
Source: *BiDFilm; CelR; ConLC 16; CurBio
74; DcFM; IntWW 74; MovMk; OxFilm;
WhoAm 82; WhoWor 80; WorAl; WorEFlm*

Berton, Pierre
Canadian. Author, Journalist, TV Personality
Host, weekly TV show "My Country"; wrote
30 books including *Klondike Quest,* 1983;
Canada's most popular historian.
b. Jul 12, 1920 in Whitehorse, Yukon
Territory
Source: *Au&Wr 71; CanWW 70; CanWr;
ConAu 1R; OxCan, SUP; WhoAm 82; WhoE
74; WrDr 80*

Berwind, Charles G
American. Industrialist
Founded Big Brothers of America, 1947, to
help fatherless boys.
b. 1894
d. Nov 9, 1972 in Bryn Mawr, Pennsylvania
Source: *BioIn 9; St&PR 75*

Berzelius, Jons Jacob, Baron
Swedish. Chemist
Developed symbols, formulas used in
  chemistry; coined words protein,
  isomerism.
b. Aug 29, 1779 in Vaversunda, Sweden
d. Aug 7, 1848
Source: *BioIn 1, 3, 6, 7, 8, 9, 10, 11;*
McGEWB; NewCol 75

Besant, Annie Wood
English. Social Reformer, Author
Early advocate of birth control, sex
  education.
b. Oct 1, 1847 in London, England
d. Sep 20, 1933 in Advar, Idaho
Source: *Alli SUP; Chambr 3; DcLEL; EvLB;*
InWom; LongCTC; NewC; REn; TwCA, SUP;
WhoLA

Besant, Walter, Sir
English. Author, Social Reformer
Wrote *All Sorts and Conditions of Men,*
  founded Society of Authors, 1884.
b. Aug 14, 1836 in Portsmouth, England
d. Jun 9, 1901 in London, England
Source: *BbD; BiD&SB; BrAu 19; CasWL;*
Chambr 3; DcBiA; DcEnA, AP; DcEuL;
DcLEL; EvLB; HsB&A; MouLC 4; NewC;
OxEng; PenC ENG; REn; WebE&AL

Bessell, Ted
American. Actor
Played Donald Hollinger on TV series "That
  Girl," 1966-71.
b. May 20, 1935 in Flushing, New York
Source: *VarWW 85; WhoHol A*

Bessemer, Henry, Sir
English. Engineer, Inventor
Invented industrial process for manufacturing
  steel from molten pig iron.
b. Jan 19, 1813 in Charlton, England
d. Mar 15, 1898 in London, England
Source: *BioIn 1, 2, 3, 4, 5, 6, 7, 11; NewCol*
75; WebBD 80

Bessie, Alvah
[Hollywood Ten]
American. Author, Screenwriter
Book *Inquisition of Eden,* 1965 tells of
  Hollywood Ten blacklisting.
b. Jun 4, 1904 in New York, New York
d. Jul 21, 1985 in Terra Linda, California
Source: *AmAu&B; ConAmA; ConAu X, 2NR,*
5R; ConLC 23; FilmgC; PlP&P; TwCA SUP;
WhNAA; WrDr 76, 82

Best, Charles Herbert
Canadian. Physiologist
With F G Banting, discovered use of insulin
  in treatment of diabetes, 1921.
b. Feb 27, 1899 in West Pembroke, Maine
d. Mar 31, 1978 in Toronto, Ontario
Source: *AmM&WS 73P; Au&Wr 71; ConAu*
45; CurBio 57, 78; IntWW 74; NewCol 75;
Who 74; WhoAm 74; WhoCan 73; WhoWor
74; WrDr 76

Best, Edna
American. Actress
Made stage debut, 1917; greatest success in
  "The Constant Nymph," 1926.
b. Mar 3, 1900 in Hove, England
d. Sep 18, 1974 in Geneva, Switzerland
Source: *CurBio 54, 74; FilmEn; Film 2;*
FilmgC; NewYTBS 74; NotNAT B; ObitOF
79; ObitT 1971; ThFT; WhScrn 77; WhThe;
Who 74; WhoHol B

Best, George
"Georgie"
Irish. Soccer Player
British superstar, 1960s; player-coach of San
  Jose Earthquakes, 1980.
b. May 22, 1946 in Belfast, Northern Ireland
Source: *BioIn 8, 9, 10, 11*

Best, Oswald Herbert
English. Children's Author
Educational books include *Carolina Gold,*
  1961.
b. Mar 25, 1894 in Chester, England
Source: *AmAu&B; AmNov; AuBYP; ConAu*
25R, P-2; JBA 34, 51; SmATA 2

Best, Peter
English. Musician
Replaced by Ringo Starr as drummer for
  The Beatles, 1962.
b. 1941 in Liverpool, England
Source: *NF*

Bestor, Arthur Eugene
American. Educator, Director
Director, pres., NY's Chautauqua Institution,
  since 1907.
b. May 19, 1879 in Dixon, Illinois
d. Feb 3, 1944 in New York, New York
Source: *CurBio 44; DcAmB S3; NatCAB 33;*
WhAm 2

Betancourt, Romulo
Venezuelan. Statesman
Pres., 1945-48, 1959-64; founded nation's first
   modern political party, advanced economic
   reform.
b. Feb 22, 1908 in Guatire, Venezuela
d. Sep 28, 1981 in New York, New York
Source: *CurBio 81; IntWW 78; McGEWB;
NewCol 75; NewYTBS 81; WhoWor 74*

Betancur, Belisario
[Belisario Betancur Cuartas]
Colombian. Political Leader
Conservative party leader elected pres. of
   Colombia, 1982.
b. 1923 in Amaga, Colombia
Source: *CurBio 85; IntWW 80, 81, 82, 84;
WhoWor 84*

Bethe, Hans Albrecht
German. Physicist
Cornell U. professor emeritus, 1975--; won
   Nobel Prize in physics, 1967.
b. Jul 2, 1906 in Strasbourg, Germany
Source: *AmM&WS 79P, 82P; AsBiEn; CurBio
40, 50; IntWW 74; McGEWB; WebAB; Who
74; WhoAm 74, 76, 78, 80, 82; WhoE 74;
WhoWor 74*

Bethune, Mary McLeod
American. Educator, Reformer
Founder, pres., National Council of Negro
   Women, 1935-49.
b. Jul 10, 1875 in Mayesville, South Carolina
d. May 18, 1955 in Daytona Beach, Florida
Source: *AmWomWr; Au&Wr 71; BiDAmEd;
CurBio 42, 55; DcAmB S5; EncAB-H; HerW;
InWom; NotAW MOD; WebAB; WhAm 3;
WhAmP*

Bethune, Norman
Canadian. Surgeon
Served as front-line physician during WW I,
   Spanish Civil War, Chinese Revolution.
b. Mar 3, 1890 in Gravenhurst, Ontario
d. Nov 12, 1939 in China
Source: *BioIn 3, 10, 11; ClbCR; MacDCB 78*

Bethune, Thomas Greene
"Blind Tom"
American. Musician
Retarded black who toured US, 1850s
   demonstrating uncanny musical memory.
b. 1849 in Georgia
d. 1908 in New York
Source: *BioIn 4, 8, 9, 10; OxMus*

Betjeman, John, Sir
English. Poet
Poet laureate, 1972-84; style of simple words
   in easy swinging rhythm sold more copies
   than any poet since Kipling.
b. Aug 28, 1906 in Highgate, England
d. May 19, 1984 in Trebetherick, England
Source: *AnObit 1984; Au&Wr 71; CasWL;
ChhPo, S1, S2; CnE&AP; CnMWL; ConAu
11NR; ConLC 2, 6, 10; ConP 70, 75;
DcLEL; EvLB; IntWW 74; LongCTC;
ModBrL, S1; NewC; NewCol 75; OxEng;
PenC ENG; RAdv 1; REn; TwCA SUP;
TwCWr; WebE&AL; Who 74; WhoTwCL;
WhoWor 78; WrDr 80*

Bettelheim, Bruno
Austrian. Psychologist, Author, Educator
Writings include *On Learning to Read,* 1982.
b. Aug 28, 1903 in Vienna, Austria
Source: *AmAu&B; AmM&WS 73S; ConAu 81;
CurBio 61; IntWW 74; LEduc 74; WebAB;
WhoAm 74, 76, 78, 80, 82; WhoWor 78;
WhoWorJ 72*

Bettenhausen, Tony (Melvin E)
American. Auto Racer
b. Sep 12, 1916 in Tinley Park, Illinois
d. 1961 in Indianapolis, Indiana
Source: *BioIn 2, 5, 11*

Betterton, Thomas
English. Actor
Opened London Theatre, 1695.
b. Aug 1635 in London, England
d. Apr 27, 1710 in London, England
Source: *Alli; BrAu; CasWL; CnThe; DcBiPP;
DcEnL; DcLEL; EncWT; NewC; OxEng;
OxThe; REn*

Bettger, Lyle
American. Actor
Since 1950, usually typecast as villain in
   films: *The Lone Ranger,* 1956.
b. Feb 13, 1915 in Philadelphia, Pennsylvania
Source: *FilmEn; FilmgC; IntMPA 76, 77, 78,
79, 80, 81, 82; WhoHol A*

Betti, Ugo
Italian. Dramatist, Poet
Wrote symbolist plays: *The Landlady,* 1927;
   The Inquiry, 1942; won Italian drama
   award, 1949.
b. Feb 4, 1892 in Camerino, Italy
d. Jun 9, 1953 in Rome, Italy
Source: *CasWL; ClDMEL; CnMD; CnMWL;
CnThe; ConAu 104; DcItL; EncWL, 2;
EvEuW; LongCTC; McGEWD; ModRL;
ModWD; OxEng; OxThe; PenC EUR;
REnWD; TwCWr; WhAm 4; WorAu*

Bettina
[Simone Micheline Bodin]
French. Model
b. 1925
Source: *BioIn 4, 7, 10*

Bettis, Valerie
American. Actress, Choreographer, Dancer
With Virginia Sampler, first to choregraph a
    modern dance for ballet co., 1947.
b. Dec 20, 1919 in Houston, Texas
d. Sep 26, 1982 in New York, New York
Source: *BiE&WWA; CurBio 53, 82;*
NewYTBS 82; NotNAT; WhoAm 74, 76, 78,
80, 82; WhoAmW 64, 66, 68, 70, 72, 74;
WhoHol A; WhoThe 72, 77, 81

Bettmann, Otto Ludwig
American. Historian
Founded Bettmann Archive, Inc., 1941;
    picture library on history of civilization.
b. Oct 15, 1903 in Leipzig, Germany
Source: *ConAu 17R; CurBio 61; NewYTBS*
81; WhoAm 78, 80, 82; WhoAmA 82

Betz, Carl
American. Actor
Played husband in "The Donna Reed Show,"
    1958-66; had own series "Judd for the
    Defense," 1967-69.
b. Mar 9, 1920 in Pittsburgh, Pennsylvania
d. Jan 18, 1978 in Los Angeles, California
Source: *FilmEn; FilmgC; IntMPA 77;*
NewYTBS 78; WhoHol A

Betz, Pauline
American. Tennis Player
Four-time US women's singles champ, 1942-
    44; 46.
b. Aug 6, 1919
Source: *BioIn 1, 2, 9; CmCal; InWom*

Beutel, Bill (William Charles)
American. Broadcast Journalist
Anchorman, WABC TV, 1970--; host "AM
    America," 1975.
b. Dec 12, 1930 in Cleveland, Ohio
Source: *ConAu 101; WhoAm 80, 82, 84*

Beuys, Joseph
German. Artist
Sculptor, political activist who saw art as
    means of reshaping society.
b. May 12, 1921 in Krefeld, Germany
d. Jan 23, 1986 in Dusseldorf, Germany
    (West)
Source: *CurBio 80, 86; IntWW 79*

Bevan, Aneurin
British. Political Leader, Orator
Labor party leader; introduced British
    socialized medicine system, 1948.
b. Nov 15, 1897 in Tredagar, Wales
d. Jul 6, 1960 in Chesham, England
Source: *CurBio 43, 60*

Beveridge, Albert Jeremiah
American. Politician, Historian
IN senator, 1899-1911, who wrote 1920
    Pulitzer-winning *Life of John Marshall.*
b. Oct 6, 1862 in Highland County, Ohio
d. Apr 27, 1927 in Indianapolis, Indiana
Source: *AmAu&B; AmBi; ApCAB SUP;*
BiDrAC; DcAmAu; DcAmB; DcNAA; EncAB-
H; IndAu 1816; OhA&B; OxAmL; REn;
REnAL; TwCA, SUP; TwCBDA; WebAB;
WhAm 1; WhAmP

Beveridge, William Henry, Lord
British. Economist
Wrote "Beveridge Report," 1942, which
    became basis for British welfare legislation.
b. Mar 5, 1879 in Rangpur, Bengal
d. Mar 16, 1963 in Oxford, England
Source: *BioIn 3, 6, 7, 11; CurBio 43, 63;*
McGEWB; ObitOF 79; WhAm 4

Bevin, Ernest
English. Labor Union Official, Government
    Official
b. Mar 9, 1881 in Winsford, England
d. Apr 14, 1951 in London, England
Source: *CurBio 40, 49, 51; DcPol; WhDW;*
WhAm 3; WorAl

Bewick, Thomas
English. Illustrator, Engraver
Pioneered revival of wood engraving; noted
    for animal vignettes; illustrated *General*
    History of Quadrupeds, 1790.
b. Aug 12, 1753 in Cherryburn, England
d. Nov 8, 1828 in Gateshead, England
Source: *AntBDN B; BkIE; CarSB; CelCen;*
DcBiPP; DcLEL; NewC; Str&VC; WhoChL

Bey, Turhan
[Turhan Gilbert Selahettin Saultavey]
Turkish. Actor
Starred in Arabian Nights adventure films of
    1940s.
b. Mar 30, 1920 in Vienna, Austria
Source: *FilmEn; FilmgC; HolP 40; IntMPA*
80, 81, 82; MotPP; MovMk; WhoHol A

Beyle, Marie Henri
see: Stendhal, pseud.

Beymer, Richard (George Richard)
American. Actor
Films include *The Diary of Anne Frank*,
   1959; *West Side Story*, 1961.
b. Feb 21, 1939 in Avoco, Iowa
Source: *FilmEn; FilmgC; IntMPA 80, 81, 82;
   MotPP; WhoHol A*

Bhave, Acharya Vinoba
[Vinayak Narahari Bhave]
Indian. Revolutionary
Disciple of Gandhi, who crusaded for social
   reforms.
b. Sep 11, 1895 in Gagoda, India
d. Nov 15, 1982 in Paunar, India
Source: *AnObit 1982; CurBio 83; FarE&A 78,
   79, 80; IntWW 74, 75, 76, 77, 78, 79, 80,
   81; McGEWB; NewYTBS 82; WhDW;
   WhoWor 74*

Bhumibol, Adulyadej
[Rama IX, King]
Thai. Ruler
King of Thailand, 1946--.
b. Dec 5, 1927 in Cambridge, Massachusetts
Source: *CurBio 50; IntWW 74; WhoWor 78*

Bhutto, Benazir
Pakistani. Political Leader
Daughter of Zulfikar Ali Bhutto; returned to
   homeland following exile, Apr 1986, to
   restore civilian rule.
b. Jun 21, 1953 in Karachi, Pakistan
Source: *CurBio 86; IntWW 85*

Bhutto, Zulfikar Ali
Pakistani. Political Leader
Served as pres., prime minister, 1970s,
   building nation's economy, prestige;
   overthrown, 1977, executed.
b. Jan 5, 1928 in Larkana, Pakistan
d. Apr 4, 1979 in Rawalpirdi, Pakistan
Source: *ConAu 53; CurBio 72, 79; IntWW
   74; NewYTBE 71, 72; NewYTBS 79; Who 74;
   WhoAm 74; WhoGov 72; WhoWor 74*

Biaggi, Mario
American. Politician
Representative from NY, 1969--, known for
   securing major federal loans to restore
   NYC to fiscal health, 1978.
b. Oct 26, 1917 in New York, New York
Source: *BiDrAC; CngDr 74; CurBio 86;
   NewYTBE 71; WhoAm 74, 76, 78, 80, 82;
   WhoAmP 73; WhoE 74; WhoGov 72*

Bialik, Chaim Nachman
Israeli. Author, Poet
Greatest modern Hebrew poet; fame began
   with *In the City of Slaughter*, 1903.
b. Jan 9, 1873 in Rady, Russia
d. Jul 4, 1934 in Tel Aviv, Palestine
Source: *CasWL; EncWL 2; PenC CL; WorAu*

Bianco, Margery Williams
American. Children's Author
Wrote *The Velveteen Rabbit*, 1922; *Poor
   Cecco*, 1925.
b. Jul 22, 1881 in London, England
d. Sep 4, 1944 in New York, New York
Source: *NotAW*

Bias, Len
American. Basketball Player
Number one draft choice of Boston Celtics;
   died of cocaine overdose.
b. Nov 18, 1963 in Hyattsville, Maryland
d. Jun 19, 1986 in College Park, Maryland
Source: *NewYTBS 86*

Biba
[Barbara Hulanicki]
English. Designer
Founded British fashion business for men,
   women, 1970.
b. in Poland
Source: *WorFshn*

Bibb, Leon
American. Singer, Musician
Folk, gospel singer, guitarist, 1960s; album
   Leon Bibb in Concert, 1962.
b. 1935 in Louisville, Kentucky
Source: *EncFCWM 69*

Bibby, Henry
American. Basketball Player
b. Nov 24, 1949 in Franklinton, North
   Carolina
Source: *WhoBbl 73*

Bibby, Thomas Geoffrey
English. Archaeologist
Developed carbon dating used in archaeology;
   wrote *4000 Years Ago*, 1961.
b. Oct 14, 1917 in Heversham, England
Source: *Au&Wr 71; ConAu 1R, 4NR;
   IntAu&W 77; WhoWor 76*

Biberman, Herbert
[The Hollywood Ten]
American. Screenwriter, Producer, Director
Blacklisted by Hollywood studios; directed
  Salt of the Earth, 1954, voted best picture
  by French Motion Picture Academy.
b. Mar 4, 1900 in Philadelphia, Pennsylvania
d. Jun 30, 1971 in New York, New York
Source: *ConAu 33R, P-1; DcFM; FilmgC;
NewYTBE 71; OxFilm; WhAm 5; WorEFlm*

Bible, Frances Lillian
American. Opera Singer
Mezzo-soprano, soloist with major
  symphonies.
b. Jan 26, in Sacets Harbor, New York
Source: *NewEOp 71; WhoAm 82, 84*

Bich, Marcel
French. Manufacturer
Introduced Bic Pen, first disposable pen,
  1953; later introduced disposable cigarette
  lighters, razors.
b. Jul 29, 1914 in Turin, Italy
Source: *Entr; WhoAm 82, 84; WorAl*

Bichat, Marie Francois Xavier
French. Scientist
Founded the science of histology, the study
  of tissue.
b. Nov 11, 1771 in Thoirette, France
d. Jul 22, 1802 in Paris, France
Source: *AsBiEn; BiHiMed; BioIn 5, 9;
CelCen; DcBiPP; DcScB; InSci; McGEWB;
NamesHP; WhDW*

Bichler, Joyce
American. Cancer Victim, Author
Sued Eli Lilly & Co., major producer of
  drug, DES, 1979; awarded $500,000; wrote
  DES Daughter, 1981.
b. Jan 19, 1954 in Bronx, New York
Source: *ConAu 107*

Bickerdyke, Mary Ann Ball
"Mother Bickerdyke"
American. Nurse
Volunteer nurse; established hospitals for
  Union soldiers, Civil War.
b. Jul 19, 1817 in Knox County, Ohio
d. Nov 8, 1901 in Kansas
Source: *NotAW; WebBD 80*

Bickerman, Elias Joseph
American. Historian, Educator
Award-winning expert on Greek, Middle-East
  history: *Chronology of Ancient World,*
  1968.
b. Jul 1, 1897 in Russia
d. 1981 in Tel Aviv, Israel
Source: *ConAu 104, 25R; DrAS 74H; WhAm
8; WhoAm 76, 78, 80, 82; WhoWorJ 72;
WrDr 80*

Bickford, Charles Ambrose
American. Actor
Three-time Oscar nominee who starred in
  TV's "The Virginian," 1966-67.
b. Jan 1, 1889 in Cambridge, Massachusetts
d. Nov 9, 1967 in Boston, Massachusetts
Source: *BiDFilm; BiE&WWA; FilmgC; HolP
30; MotPP; MovMk; ObitOF 79; OxFilm;
WhScrn 74, 77; WhThe; WhoHol B; WorAl;
WorEFlm*

Bickmore, Lee Smith
American. Business Executive
Chm., National Biscuit Co. (Nabisco brands),
  1968.
b. Jun 5, 1908 in Paradise, Utah
d. Jun 7, 1986 in Vero Beach, Florida
Source: *BlueB 76; IntWW 83; St&PR 84;
WhoAm 78; WhoE 74; WhoF&I 75; WhoWor
74*

Bidault, Georges
French. Politician
Opposed Algeria's independence from France;
  in exile, 1963-67.
b. Oct 5, 1899 in Moulins, France
d. Jan 27, 1983 in Cambo-les-Bains, France
Source: *CurBio 83; DcPol; IntWW 82; LinLib
S; NewYTBS 83; Who 82; WhoWor 74*

Biddle, Anthony
American. Statesman
US ambassador to European governments in
  exile during WW II.
b. Dec 17, 1896 in Philadelphia,
  Pennsylvania
d. Nov 13, 1961 in Washington, District of
  Columbia
Source: *CurBio 41, 62*

Biddle, Francis Beverley
American. Lawyer, Government Official
First chair of National Labor Relations
  Board, 1934; attorney general, 1941-45,
  who was judge at Nuremberg trials.
b. May 9, 1886 in Paris, France
d. Oct 4, 1968 in Hyannis, Massachusetts
Source: *AmAu&B; BiDFedJ; BiDrUSE; ConAu
5R, 103; CurBio 41, 68; PolProf T; WhAm 5,
7*

Biddle, George
American. Artist, Author
Leader of Federal Arts Project during
Depression, known for portraits, murals.
b. Jan 24, 1885 in Philadelphia, Pennsylvania
d. Nov 6, 1973 in Croton-on-Hudson, New
York
Source: *AmAu&B; ConAu 45; CurBio 42, 74;
DcCAA 77; NewYTBE 73; WhAm 6; WhoAm
74; WhoAmA 73*

Biddle, John
English. Philosopher
Founder of English Unitarianism, who
disputed Trinity in tract *Twelve Arguments,*
1645, for which he was imprisoned.
b. 1615 in Wotton-under-Edge, England
d. Sep 22, 1662 in London, England
Source: *Alli; DcBiPP; DcEnL; LinLib S;
NewCol 75*

Biddle, Nicholas
American. Statesman, Banker, Scholar
Pres., Bank of US, 1823-39, who edited
literary periodical *Portfolio.*
b. Jan 8, 1786 in Philadelphia, Pennsylvania
d. Feb 27, 1844 in Philadelphia, Pennsylvania
Source: *Alli; AmAu; AmAu&B; AmBi;
ApCAB; BiAUS; BiD&SB; CyAL 1; DcAmAu;
DcAmB; DcNAA; Drake; EncAB-H; OxAmL;
REn; TwCBDA; WebAB; WhAm HS; WhAmP*

Biden, Joseph Robinette, Jr.
American. Politician, Lawyer
Dem. senator from DE, 1972--.
b. Nov 20, 1942 in Scranton, Pennsylvania
Source: *BioIn 9, 10, 11; WhoAm 82*

Bieber, Owen Frederick
American. Labor Union Official
Pres., UAW, 1983--.
b. Dec 28, 1929 in North Dorr, Michigan
Source: *BioIn 11; BusPN; ConNews 86-1;
CurBio 86; NewYTBS 83; WhoAm 84*

Biebuyck, Daniel Prosper
Belgian. Anthropologist, Author, Educator
Wrote on African tribes: *African Agrarian
Systems,* 1965.
b. Oct 1, 1925 in Deinze, Belgium
Source: *AmM&WS 73S; ConAu 25R; WhoAm
74, 76, 78, 80, 82; WrDr 80*

Biellmann, Denise
Swiss. Figure Skater
Source: *BioIn 12*

Bierce, Ambrose Gwinett
[Dod Grile, psued.]
American. Author, Journalist
Newspaper, fiction writer who disappeared in
Mexico covering revolution led by Pancho
Villa.
b. Jun 24, 1842 in Meigs County, Ohio
d. 1914 in Mexico
Source: *AmAu; AmAu&B; AmBi; AmWr;
ApCAB SUP; AtlBL; CasWL; Chambr 3;
ChhPo, S1; CnDAL; CrtT 3; CyWA;
DcAmAu; DcAmB; DcLEL; DcNAA; EncAB-
H; EncMys; EvLB; LongCTC; ModAL, S1;
OhA&B; OxAmL; OxEng; PenC AM; RAdv 1;
REn; REnAL; WebAB; WebE&AL; WhAm
HSA, 4*

Bierstadt, Albert
American. Artist
Landscape painter best known for works
depicting Far West.
b. Jan 7, 1830 in Dusseldorf, Germany
d. Feb 18, 1902 in New York, New York
Source: *AmBi; ApCAB; DcAmB; Drake;
EarABI; EncAB-H; OxAmL; TwCBDA;
WebAB; WhAm 1*

Big Bopper, The
[J P Richardson]
American. Radio Performer, Singer
Big hit "Chantilly Lace," 1958; killed with
Buddy Holly, Ritchie Valens in plane
crash.
b. Oct 24, 1930 in Sabine Pass, Texas
d. Feb 3, 1959 in Clear Lake, Iowa
Source: *BiDAmM; ConMuA 80A; RkOn 74;
RolSEnR 83*

Big Brother and the Holding Company
[Peter Albin; Sam Andrew; David Getz;
James Gurley; Janis Joplin]
American. Music Group
Group featured lead vocals by Janis Joplin;
first album *Cheap Thrills* had hit single
"Piece of My Heart," 1968.
Source: *EncPR&S 74; IlEncRk; RolSEnR 83*

Big Country
[Stuart Adamson; Mark Brzezick; Tony
Butler; Bruce Watson]
British. Music Group
Dunfermline, Scotland group whose debut
album *The Crossing* yielded hit single "In
a Big Country," 1983.
Source: *RkOn 85*

Bigard, Albany Barney Leon
American. Jazz Musician
Jazz clarinetist who played with King Oliver, Louis Armstrong, Duke Ellington; wrote "Mood Indigo."
b. Mar 3, 1906 in New Orleans, Louisiana
d. Jun 27, 1980 in Culver City, California
Source: *BioIn 10; CmpEPM; EncJzS 70; IlEncJ; WhAm 7; WhoAm 74, 76, 78, 80; WhoBlA 75, 77; WhoJazz 72*

Bigelow, Erastus Brigham
American. Inventor, Manufacturer
Invented power loom, 1837; founded Clinton Co., 1838, to build looms.
b. Apr 2, 1814 in West Boylston, Massachusetts
d. Dec 6, 1879 in Boston, Massachusetts
Source: *Alli SUP; ApCAB; DcAmAu; DcAmB; DcNAA; TwCBDA; WebAB; WhAm HS*

Bigelow, Henry Bryant
American. Zoologist, Educator
Harvard U. zoology professor, 1905-50, who wrote on oceanography.
b. Oct 3, 1879 in Boston, Massachusetts
d. Dec 11, 1967 in Concord, Massachusetts
Source: *BioIn 5, 8, 11; WhAm 4A*

Biggers, Earl Derr
American. Author
Created Chinese fictional detective "Charlie Chan."
b. Aug 26, 1884 in Warren, Ohio
d. Apr 5, 1933 in Pasadena, California
Source: *AmAu&B; ChhPo S1; CmCal; DcAmB S1; DcNAA; EncMys; EvLB; FilmgC; MnBBF; Novels; OhA&B; OxAmL; PenC AM; REn; REnAL; TwCA; TwCCr&M 80; TwCWr; WhAm 1; WhNAA; WorAl*

Biggs, Edward George Power
American. Musician
Noted organ soloist, recording star.
b. Mar 29, 1906 in Westcliff, England
d. Mar 10, 1977 in Boston, Massachusetts
Source: *IntWW 74; WhoAm 74; WhoMus 72*

Biggs, Ronald Arthur
"The Great Train Robber"
British. Criminal
With 14 others stole 7.3 million dollars, 1963; escaped prison, 1965; lives in Brazil.
b. 1929
Source: *BioIn 8, 9, 10*

Bigley, Elizabeth
see: Chadwick, Cassie L

Bignone, Reynaldo Benito Antonio
Argentine. President
b. Jan 21, 1928 in Moron, Argentina
Source: *NewYTBS 82*

Bijedic, Dzemal
Yugoslav. Political Leader
Prime minister, 1971-77; killed in plane crash, 1977.
b. Apr 12, 1917 in Mostar, Yugoslavia
d. Jan 18, 1977 in Yugoslavia
Source: *IntWW 74, 77N; NewYTBS 77; WhoSocC 78*

Bikel, Theodore Meir
American. Actor, Singer
Made film debut, 1952, in *African Queen;* Oscar nominee for *The Defiant Ones,* 1958.
b. May 2, 1924 in Vienna, Austria
Source: *BioNews 74; ConAu 1R, 1NR; CurBio 60; EncFCWM 69; FilmEn; FilmgC; MotPP; MovMk; NotNAT; WhoAm 80, 82; WhoE 74; WhoHol A; WhoThe 77; WhoWor 78; WhoWorJ 72*

Biko, Steven
South African. Political Activist
Died while in custody of South African security police.
b. 1947 in Pretoria, South Africa
d. Sep 12, 1977 in South Africa
Source: *BioIn 11*

Bikoff, James L
American. Businessman, Lawyer
Founded International Anticounterfeiting Coalition (IACC), 1978; pres., 1982--; estimates counterfeiting is $60 million business.
b. May 26, 1940 in New York, New York
Source: *ConNews 86-2*

Bilandic, Michael Anthony
American. Lawyer, Politician
Succeeded Richard Daley as mayor of Chicago, 1976; lost re-election bid to Jane Byrne, 1979.
b. Feb 13, 1923 in Chicago, Illinois
Source: *CurBio 79; NewYTBS 77; WhoAm 80, 82; WhoGov 77*

Bilbo, Theodore Gilmore
American. Politician
Dem. senator from MS; investigated by senate, 1946, for anti-Negro campaigns.
b. Oct 13, 1877 in Poplarville, Mississippi
d. Aug 21, 1947 in New Orleans, Louisiana
Source: *BiDrAC; CurBio 43, 47; DcAmB S4; WebAB; WhAm 2; WhAmP*

Biletnikoff, Fred(erick)
American. Football Player
End, Oakland Raiders, 1965-73, who was
leading NFL pass receiver, 1968.
b. Feb 23, 1943 in Erie, Pennsylvania
Source: *WhoAm 74; WhoFtbl 74*

Bill, Tony
American. Actor, Director, Producer
Directed *My Bodyguard*, 1980; won Oscar,
1973, for co-producing *The Sting*.
b. Aug 23, 1940 in San Diego, California
Source: *FilmEn; FilmgC; IntMPA 81, 82;
VarWW 85; WhoAm 80, 82, 84; WhoHol A*

Billings, Grace Bedell
American. Student
Wrote letter to Abraham Lincoln suggesting
he grow beard; Lincoln grew one, wore it
from then on.
Source: *GoodHs*

Billings, John Shaw
American. Editor
Editorial director, Time Inc., 1944-54.
b. May 11, 1898 in Beech Island, South
Carolina
d. Aug 25, 1975 in Augusta, Georgia
Source: *ConAu 104; WhAm 6*

Billings, Josh, pseud.
[Henry Wheeler Shaw]
American. Author
Wrote bucolic aphorisms phrased in grotesque
misspellings: *Josh Billings' Farmer's
Allminax*, 1869-80.
b. Apr 21, 1818 in Lanesboro, Massachusetts
d. Oct 14, 1885 in Monterey, California
Source: *AmAu; AmAu&B; ApCAB; BiD&SB;
CasWL; CnDAL; DcAmAu; DcAmB; DcEnL;
DcLEL; DcNAA; EvLB; OhA&B; OxAmL;
OxEng; PenC AM; REn; REnAL; TwCBDA;
WebAB; WhAm HS*

Billingsley, Barbara
American. Actress
Played June Cleaver on "Leave It to
Beaver," TV series, 1957-63.
b. Dec 22
Source: *What 8*

Billingsley, Sherman
American. Business Executive
Owned Stork Club, 1929-65; hosted "The
Stork Club" TV show, 1950-53.
b. Mar 10, 1900 in Enid, Oklahoma
d. Oct 4, 1966 in New York, New York
Source: *CurBio 46, 66; ObitOF 79; WhAm 4*

Billington, John
American. Murderer
One of pilgrims who arrived on the
Mayflower; first murderer in US.
d. 1630
Source: *Blood&B; DrInf*

Billington, Ray Allen
American. Historian, Educator
Authority on American West; books include
prize-winning *Frederick Jackson Turner*,
1974.
b. Sep 28, 1903 in Bay City, Michigan
d. Mar 7, 1981 in San Marino, California
Source: *AmAu&B; Au&Wr 71; ConAu 1R,
5NR, 103*

Billroth, Albert Christian Theodor
German. Surgeon
Introduced procedure for total laryngectomy,
1873.
b. Apr 26, 1829 in Bergen, Prussia
d. Feb 6, 1894
Source: *Baker 78; BiHiMed; DcScB*

Billy the Kid
[William H Bonney]
American. Outlaw
Killed 21 men; sentenced to hang for murder
of Sheriff Jim Brady.
b. Nov 23, 1859 in New York, New York
d. Jul 15, 1881 in Fort Sumner, New Mexico
Source: *DcAmB; NewCol 75; OxFilm;
REnAL; WebAB; WhAm HS*

Bilon, Michael Patrick
American. Actor
Played title role in *ET*, 1982; was 2 feet, 10
inches tall.
b. 1947 in Youngstown, Ohio
d. Jan 27, 1983 in Youngstown, Ohio
Source: *NF*

Binet, Alfred
French. Psychologist
Developed early standard tests for
intelligence, 1905.
b. Jun 11, 1857 in Nice, France
d. Oct 8, 1911 in Paris, France
Source: *AsBiEn; DcScB; InSci; LinLib L, S;
McGEWB; NamesHP; WhDW*

Bing, Dave (David)
American. Basketball Player
Guard who averaged over 20 points per
game during career, 1967-78.
b. Nov 29, 1943 in Washington, District of
Columbia
Source: *BioIn 10; OfNBA 81; WhoBbl 73;
WhoBlA 75*

Bing, Rudolf(Franz Josef), Sir
Austrian. Educator, Manager
Managerial director, Metropolitan Opera of
NY, 1950-72.
b. Jan 9, 1902 in Vienna, Austria
Source: *Baker 78; CelR; CurBio 50; IntWW
74; NewYTBE 71, 72, 73; REn; Who 74, 82;
WhoAm 74, 76, 78, 80, 82; WhoMus 72;
WhoWor 74*

Bingaman, Jeff
American. Politician
Dem. senator from NM, 1982--.
b. Oct 3, 1943 in El Paso, Texas
Source: *CngDr 85*

Bingham, George Caleb
American. Artist
Portrait, genre painter of old-time MO life:
"Jolly Flatboatman," 1846.
b. Mar 20, 1811 in Augusta County, Virginia
d. Jul 7, 1879 in Kansas City, Missouri
Source: *AtlBL; DcAmB; EncAB-H; OxAmL;
REn; WebAB; WhAm HS; WhAmP*

Bingham, Hiram
American. Explorer, Statesman
Discovered ruins of Machu Picchu, last Inca
capital, Peru, 1911.
b. Nov 19, 1875 in Honolulu, Hawaii
d. Jun 6, 1956 in Washington, District of
Columbia
Source: *CurBio 51, 56; WhAm 3*

Bingham, Jonathan Brewster
American. Politician
Member US mission to UN, 1961-64; Dem.
congressman from NY, 1965-83.
b. Apr 24, 1914 in New Haven, Connecticut
d. Jul 3, 1986 in New York, New York
Source: *BiDrAC; ConAu 33R; CurBio 54, 86;
IntWW 74; WhoAm 82; WhoE 74*

Binh, Nguyen-thi, Madame
see: Nguyen thi Binh, Madame

Binns, Archie Fred
American. Author
Publishing co. editor who wrote *Sea Pup,
Again,* 1965.
b. Jul 30, 1899 in Port Ludlow, Washington
d. Jun 28, 1971
Source: *AmAu&B; ConAu 73; OxAmL;
REnAL; TwCA, SUP; WhAm 5; WhoPNW*

Binns, Joseph Patterson
American. Hotel Executive
VP, Hilton Hotels, 1946-62; manager,
Waldorf-Astoria, NYC, 1949-61.
b. Jun 28, 1905 in Winona, Ohio
d. Nov 23, 1980 in Indian Creek Island,
Florida
Source: *BioIn 3, 6; CurBio 54, 81*

Binswanger, Ludwig
Swiss. Psychiatrist
Proponent of Daseinsanalysis,
psychotherapeutic technique based on
existentialism.
b. Apr 13, 1881 in Kreuzlingen, Switzerland
d. 1966
Source: *ConAu 107; NamesHP; WhoWor 74*

Binyon, Laurence
English. Poet, Critic, Orientalist
Wrote blank verse drama, Dante translations,
works on oriental art.
b. Aug 10, 1869 in Lancaster, England
d. Mar 10, 1942 in Streatley, England
Source: *CasWL; Chambr 3; ChhPo, S1, S2;
CnE&AP; LongCTC; ModBrL; NewC; OxEng;
REn; TwCA, SUP; TwCWr; WebE&AL;
WhoLA*

Biondi, Frank J, Jr,
American. TV Executive
Pres., Home Box Office (HBO) since 1983.
b. Jan 9, 1945 in Livingston, New Jersey
Source: *IntMPA 84; WhoAm 84; WhoTelC*

Biossat, Bruce
American. Journalist
Political reporter for Newspaper Enterprise
Assoc.; articles published in 400
newpapers.
b. 1910
d. May 27, 1974 in Washington, District of
Columbia
Source: *BioIn 10; ConAu 104; WhAm 6*

Bioy-Casares, Adolfo
[Martin Sacastru: Javier Miranda, pseuds.]
Argentine. Author
Writings include *Prologo,* 1929; *La Invencion
de Morel,* 1940.
b. Sep 15, 1914 in Buenos Aires, Argentina
Source: *ConAu 29R; ConLC 4, 8, 13;
DcCLAA; PenC AM; WhoWor 74*

Birch, John
American. Spy
US intelligence officer in China, killed by the
Communist Chinese.
b. May 28, 1918 in Landour, India
d. Aug 25, 1945 in Shuchow, China
Source: *BioIn 5; WorAl*

Birch, Stephen
American. Business Executive
Pres., of Kennecott Copper Corp., 1915-33.
b. Mar 24, 1872 in New York, New York
d. Dec 29, 1940
Source: *EncAB 14; NatCAB 15, 41; ObitOF
79; WhAm 1; WorAl*

Bird, Isabella Lucy
see: Bishop, Isabella Lucy Bird

Bird, Junius Bouton
American. Anthropologist
Authority on pre-Columbian cultures, textiles;
curator of archeology at American
Museum of Natural History, 1957-73.
b. Sep 21, 1907 in Rye, New York
d. Apr 2, 1982 in Bronx, New York
Source: *AmM&WS 73S, 76P; ConAu 106;
NewYTBS 82*

Bird, Larry Joe
American. Basketball Player
Forward, Boston Celtics, 1980--, who is six-
time All-Star, three-time MVP.
b. Dec 7, 1956 in French Lick, Indiana
Source: *BioIn 12; CurBio 82; OfNBA 85*

Birdseye, Clarence Frank
American. Inventor
Developed method for quick-freezing food,
1924, method for dehydrating food, 1949.
b. Dec 9, 1886 in Brooklyn, New York
d. Oct 7, 1956 in New York, New York
Source: *CurBio 46, 56; WhAm 3*

Birdsong, Otis Lee
American. Basketball Player
b. Dec 9, 1955 in Winter Haven, Florida
Source: *BioIn 12; NewYTBS 81; OfNBA 81*

Birdwell, Russell Juarez
American. Public Relations Executive
Publicized MGM's search for actress to play
Scarlett O'Hara in *Gone With the Wind.*
b. Oct 17, 1903 in Coleman, Texas
d. Dec 15, 1977 in Oxnard, California
Source: *ConAu 107; CurBio 46, 78; ScF&FL
1; WhoWest 74*

Birendra Bir Bikram, Shah Dev
Nepalese. Ruler
One of few remaining monarchs with
absolute power; inherited throne from
father, Mahendra Bir Bikram Shah Dev,
1972, crowned, 1975.
b. Dec 28, 1945 in Kathmandu, Nepal
Source: *CurBio 75; IntWW 74; NewYTBS 75;
WhoWor 74, 80*

Birley, Oswald Hornby Joseph, Sir
English. Artist
Painted, by commission of Royal Naval
College, portraits of King George VI, his
admirals, Sir Winston Churchill, WW II.
b. Mar 31, 1880 in Auckland, New Zealand
d. May 6, 1952 in London, England
Source: *DcBrAr 1; DcNaB 1951; ObitOF 79;
ObitT 1951; OxShips*

Birmingham, Stephen
American. Author
Wrote *Jacqueline Bouvier Kennedy Onassis,*
1978, *Duchess,* 1981.
b. May 28, 1931 in Hartford, Connecticut
Source: *AmAu&B; Au&Wr 71; AuNews 1;
ConAu 49, 2NR; CurBio 74; WhoAm 74, 76,
78, 80, 82; WrDr 80, 80, 80*

Birney, David Edwin
American. Actor
Star of TV series "Bridget Loves Bernie,"
1972; "St. Elsewhere," 1982; married
Meredith Baxter.
b. Apr 23, 1940 in Washington, District of
Columbia
Source: *IntMPA 82; NotNAT; VarWW 85;
WhoHol A*

Birney, Earle (Alfred Earle)
Canadian. Poet, Author, Critic
Wrote *David and Other Poems,* 1942; *Turvey,*
1949; *Trial of a City,* 1952.
b. May 13, 1904 in Calgary, Alberta
Source: *Au&Wr 71; CanWW 82; CanWr;
CasWL; ConAu 1R, 5NR; ConLC 1, 4, 6, 11;
ConNov 72, 76; ConP 70, 75; CreCan 1;
DcLEL; DrAS 74E; LongCTC; OxCan, SUP;
PenC ENG; TwCWr; WebE&AL; WhoAm 82*

Birnie, William Alfred Hart
American. Editor, Journalist
Editor, *Reader's Digest,* 1960-67; editor,
publisher *Woman's Home Companion,*
1943-57.
b. Aug 4, 1910 in Springfield, Massachusetts
d. Sep 19, 1979 in Rockport, Massachusetts
Source: *CurBio 52, 79; WhoAm 74, 76, 78,
80*

Biro, Val
[Balint Stephen Biro]
English. Illustrator
Books include *Dicovering Chesham,* 1968;
*Gumdrop: The Adventures of a Vintage
Car,* 1966.
b. Oct 6, 1921 in Budapest, Hungary
Source: *Au&Wr 71; ConAu 25R; IlsBYP;
IlsCB 1957; SmATA 1*

Birrell, Augustine
English. Author, Statesman
Wrote literary biographies, essays: *Obiter Dicta* series, 1884-1924.
b. Jan 19, 1850 in Wavertree, England
d. Nov 20, 1933 in London, England
Source: *BiD&SB; Chambr 3; DcEnA AP; DcLEL; EvLB; LongCTC; NewC; OxEng; PenC ENG; REn; TwCA, SUP; TwCWr*

Bishop, Billy (William Avery)
"Hell's Handmaiden"
Canadian. Air Marshal
WW I ace who shot down 72 enemy aircraft; wrote *Winged Warfare,* 1918.
b. Feb 8, 1894 in Owen Sound, Ontario
d. Sep 11, 1956 in Palm Beach, Florida
Source: *BioIn 4, 5, 7, 8; CurBio 41; MacDCB 78; ObitOF 79; WhoMilH 76*

Bishop, Elizabeth
American. Poet
Won Pulitzer for *North and South: A Gold Spring,* 1955.
b. Feb 8, 1911 in Worcester, Massachusetts
d. Oct 6, 1979 in Boston, Massachusetts
Source: *AmAu&B; Au&Wr 71; CelR; ChhPo, SI; CnE&AP; ConAu 5R, 89; ConLC 1, 4, 9, 13, 15; ConP 70, 75; CroCAP; DrAP 75; EncWL; IntWW 74; ModAL, SI; NewCol 75; OxAmL; PenC AM; RAdv 1; REn; REnAL; TwCA SUP; TwCWr; WebE&AL; WhoAm 74; WhoE 74; WhoWor 78; WrDr 80*

Bishop, Elvin
American. Musician
Hit single "Fooled Around and Fell in Love," 1976, from eighth solo album *Struttin' My Stuff.*
b. Oct 21, 1942 in Tulsa, Oklahoma
Source: *EncPR&S 74; RkOn 74; RolSEnR 83*

Bishop, Hazel
American. Cosmetics Executive, Scientist
Chemist who introduced first non-smear, long-lasting lipstick, 1950.
b. Aug 17, 1906 in Hoboken, New Jersey
Source: *CurBio 57; InWom; LibW; WhoAmW 58; WorAl*

Bishop, Isabella Lucy Bird
English. Traveler, Author
First woman member, Royal Geographic Society, 1892; wrote *Unbeaten Tracks in Japan,* 1880.
b. 1832 in Yorkshire, England
d. 1904 in Edinburgh, Scotland
Source: *BrAu 19; Chambr 3; DcNaB S2; IntDcWB*

Bishop, Jim (James Alonzo)
American. Author, Journalist
Tells vivid stories of historical events: *The Day Kennedy Was Shot,* 1968.
b. Nov 21, 1907 in Jersey City, New Jersey
Source: *AmAu&B; AuNews 1, 2; CelR; ConAu 17R; CurBio 69; DrAP 75; REnAL; WhoAm 74, 76, 78, 80, 82; WhoS&SW 82; WhoWor 78*

Bishop, Joey
[Joseph Abraham Gottlieb]
American. Comedian
Nightclub entertainer, member of Frank Sinatra's "rat pack," 1950s, who was popular TV personality, 1960s.
b. Feb 3, 1918 in Bronx, New York
Source: *CelR; CurBio 62; FilmgC; WhoAm 74, 76, 78, 80, 82; WhoHol A; WhoWor 78*

Bishop, Julie
[Jacqueline Brown; Jacqueline Wells]
American. Actress
Child star in silent films, leading lady in second features under name Jacqueline Wells, 1923-39; used name Julie Bishop from 1941-57.
b. Aug 30, 1914 in Denver, Colorado
Source: *FilmEn; FilmgC; IntMPA 76, 77, 78, 79, 80, 81, 82; MotPP; MovMk; WhoAmW 77, 81; WhoHol A; WhoWest 78*

Bishop, Maurice
Grenadian. Political Leader
Marxist who became prime minister in 1979 coup; led invasion, 1983.
b. May 29, 1944 in Aruba
d. Oct 19, 1983 in Saint George's, Grenada
Source: *ConAu 111; InB&W 80; IntWW 80, 81, 82, 83; NewYTBS 83; WhoWor 80, 82*

Bishop, Stephen
American. Singer, Songwriter
Hit songs include "Save it for a Rainy Day," 1976; theme from *Tootsie,* "It Might Be You," 1983.
b. Nov 14, 1951 in San Diego, California
Source: *BioIn 11; RkOn 84; VarWW 85; WhoAm 82*

Bismarck, Otto Edward Leopold von
"The Iron Chancellor"
German. Statesman
Premier, Prussia, 1862-66; chancellor, German Empire, 1870-90.
b. Apr 1, 1815 in Schonhausen, Germany
d. Jul 30, 1898 in Friedrichsruh, Germany
Source: *BbD; BiD&SB; NewC; OxGer; REn*

Bissell, Anna
[Mrs. Melville Bissell]
American. Business Executive
With husband, formed Bissell Carpet Sweeper
Co., 1876.
b. 1846
d. 1934
Source: *Entr*

Bissell, Melville Reuben
American. Inventor
Patented carpet sweeper, 1876.
b. Sep 25, 1843 in Hartwick, New York
d. Mar 15, 1889 in Grand Rapids, Michigan
Source: *NatCAB 7*

Bissell, Richard
American. Dramatist
Co-wrote Tony winner *The Pajama Game*,
1954.
b. Jun 27, 1913 in Dubuque, Iowa
d. May 4, 1977 in Dubuque, Iowa
Source: *AmAu&B; Au&Wr 71; ConAu 1R,
69; NotNAT; REnAL; WhoAm 74; WorAu;
WrDr 76*

Bisset, Jacqueline Fraser
English. Actress
Starred in movies *The Deep*, 1977; *Rich and
Famous*, 1981.
b. Sep 13, 1944 in Weybridge, England
Source: *BioNews 74; BkPepl; CelR; CurBio
77; FilmEn; FilmgC; IntMPA 77, 78, 79, 80,
81, 82; MovMk; VarWW 85; WhoAm 82;
WhoHol A*

Bittan, Roy
[E Street Band]
"Professor"
American. Musician, Singer
Keyboardist, accordion player with Bruce
Springsteen, 1974--.
b. Jul 2, 1949 in Rockaway Beach, New
York
Source: *WhoRocM 82*

Bitter, Francis
American. Inventor, Educator
Magnetism expert who invented the Bitter
magnet.
b. Jul 22, 1902 in Weehawken, New Jersey
d. Jul 26, 1967 in Cape Cod, Massachusetts
Source: *ConAu 113; WhAm 4*

Bitter, Karl Theodore Francis
American. Sculptor
Last work "Abundance" is the figure which
stands at the Grand Army Plaza, NYC.
b. Dec 6, 1867 in Vienna, Austria
d. Apr 10, 1915 in New York, New York
Source: *AmBi; DcAmB; TwCBDA; WebAB;
WhAm 1*

Bitzer, George William
"Billy"
American. Filmmaker, Photographer
Pioneer cameraman; filmed D W Griffith's
Birth of a Nation, 1914.
b. Apr 21, 1872 in Boston, Massachusetts
d. Apr 29, 1944 in Los Angeles, California
Source: *DcAmB S3; WebBD 80*

Bixby, Bill
American. Actor
Starred in TV series "My Favorite Martian";
"The Courtship of Eddie's Father"; "The
Incredible Hulk."
b. Jan 22, 1934 in San Francisco, California
Source: *ConTFT 3; FilmEn; IntMPA 82;
WhoHol A*

Biyidi, Alexandre
[Mongo Beti; Eza Boto]
French. Author
Novels on life in West Africa include
The Poor Christ of Bomba, 1971.
b. Jun 30, 1932 in Mbalmayo, Cameroon
Source: *AfrA; ConAu 114; PenC CL*

Bizet, Georges (Alexandre Cesar Leopold)
French. Composer
Wrote opera *Carmen*, 1875.
b. Oct 25, 1838 in Paris, France
d. Jun 3, 1875 in Bougival, France
Source: *AtlBL; WhDW; WorAl*

Bjoerling, Jussi
[Stora Tuna Dalarna]
Swedish. Opera Singer
Debut, *Don Giovanni*, 1929; lead tenor in
over 50 operas.
b. Feb 2, 1911 in Stora Tuna, Sweden
d. Sep 9, 1960 in Siar Oe, Sweden
Source: *CurBio 47, 60; WhAm 4*

Bjorn-Larsen, Knut
American. Inventor
Developed garterless girdle.
b. 1923 in Norway
Source: *BioIn 12*

Bjornson, Bjornstjerne
Norwegian. Poet, Political Leader
National poet of Norway; won Nobel Prize
    for Literature, 1903.
b. Dec 8, 1832 in Kvikne, Norway
d. Apr 26, 1910 in Paris, France
Source: *AtlBL; BbD; BiD&SB; CasWL;*
ChhPo S1; ClDMEL; CnMD; CnThe; CyWA;
DcBiA; DcEuL; EncWT; EuAu; EvEuW;
LongCTC; McGEWD; ModWD; OxThe; PenC
EUR; REn; REnWD; WorAl

Blab, Uwe Konstantine
American. Basketball Player
Member W German Olympic team, 1984,
    drafted in first round by Dallas, 1985.
b. Mar 26, 1962 in Munich, Germany (West)
Source: *OfNBA 81*

Black, Conrad
Canadian. Business Executive
Chm. of board, exec. committee, Argus Corp.
    Ltd., 1978--.
b. Aug 25, 1944 in Montreal, Quebec
Source: *ConNews 86-2*

Black, David "Jay"
[Jay and the Americans]
American. Singer
Lead singer, group's second "Jay," 1962-70.
b. Nov 2, 1941
Source: *NF*

Black, Frank J
American. Composer, Musician
Organized music dept., NBC, 1928; general
    music director, NBC, 1932-48.
b. Nov 28, 1896 in Philadelphia,
    Pennsylvania
d. Jan 29, 1968 in Atlanta, Georgia
Source: *AmSCAP 66; Baker 84; ConAmC 82*

Black, Hugo LaFayette
American. Supreme Court Justice
Member of Klu Klux Klan, mid-1920s;
    served on Supreme Court 34 yrs.
b. Feb 27, 1886 in Harlan, Alabama
d. Sep 25, 1971 in Bethesda, Maryland
Source: *BiDrAC; ConAu 33R; CurBio 41, 64,*
71; EncAB-H; NewYTBE 71; WebAB; WhAm
5; WhAmP

Black, Joseph
Scottish. Chemist, Physicist
Formulated concept of latent heat, the heat
    absorbed by a substance changing state
    without a temperture rise.
b. Apr 16, 1728 in Bordeaux, France
d. Nov 10, 1799 in Edinburgh, Scotland
Source: *Alli; DcBiPP; Dis&D; WhDW*

Black, Karen
[Karen Ziegler]
American. Actress
Appeared in films *Easy Rider,* 1969; *Five*
    Easy Pieces, 1970; *The Great Gatsby,* 1975.
b. Jul 1, 1942 in Park Ridge, Illinois
Source: *BkPepl; CelR; CurBio 76; FilmEn;*
IntMPA 75, 76, 77, 78, 79, 80, 81, 82;
MovMk; WhoAm 80, 84; WhoHol A

Black, Samuel Duncan
American. Businessman
Formed business, 1907, with Alonzo Decker;
    produced first electric drill, 1914.
b. Aug 2, 1883 in White Hall, Maryland
d. 1953
Source: *Entr; WhAm 3*

Black, Shirley Temple
[Mrs. Charles A Black]
American. Actress, Diplomat
Child actress who was number one
    Hollywood attraction, 1938; US
    ambassador to Ghana, 1974-76.
b. Apr 23, 1928 in Santa Monica, California
Source: *BiDFilm; BkPepl; CelR; CmMov;*
CurBio 70; FilmEn; FilmgC; IntWW 74;
MotPP; MovMk; OxFilm; ThFT; WebAB;
WhoAm 74, 76, 78, 80, 82; WhoAmP 73;
WhoAmW 77; WhoHol A; WhoWor 78

Black, Walter J
American. Publisher
Pres., Walter J Black, Inc., 1928-58,
    Detective Club, 1958-78.
b. May 12, 1893 in Brooklyn, New York
d. Apr 16, 1958 in Roslyn, New York
Source: *WhAm 3*

Black, William
American. Business Executive, Philanthropist
Made Chock Full O'Nuts Co. multimillion
    dollar empire; founded Parkinson's Disease
    Foundation, 1957.
b. 1904 in Brooklyn, New York
d. Mar 7, 1983 in New York, New York
Source: *CurBio 64, 83; NewYTBS 83*

Black, Winifred Sweet
[Annie Laurie, psued.]
American. Journalist
One of the original women reporters who
    wrote using first person, emotionally,
    sensationally.
b. Oct 14, 1863 in Wisconsin
d. May 26, 1936 in San Francisco, California
Source: *BioIn 8, 10*

Black Eagle
see: Julian, Hubert Fauntleroy

Black Hawk
[Ma-Ka-Tae-Mish-Kia-Kiak]
American. Indian Chief
Sauk chief during Black Hawk War of 1832;
   served under Tecumseh in war of 1912.
b. 1767 in Sauk Village, Illinois
d. Oct 3, 1838 in Keokuk, Iowa
Source: *AmBi; ApCAB; DcAmB; Drake;
OxAmH; TwCBDA; WebAB, 79; WhAm HS;
WorAl*

Black Oak Arkansas
[Pat Daugherty; Wayne Evans; Jimmy
   Henderson; Stan Goober Knight; Jim
   Dandy Mangrum; Ricky Reynolds]
American. Music Group
Southern band named after group's
   hometown, 1969; number one hit "Jim
   Dandy to the Rescue, 1973.
Source: *RkOn 84; RolSEnR 83; WhoRock 81*

Black Sabbath
[Terry Geezer Butler; Ronnie Dio; Jan
   Gillan; Anthony Iommi; (John) Ozzie
   Osbourne; William Ward]
English. Music Group
Heavy-metal band formed, 1969, under name
   Earth; changed name when material
   became mystical; hit album *Paranoid,*
   1970.
Source: *ConMuA 80A; LilREn 78; RkOn 78;
RolSEnR 83; WhoRock 81*

Blackbeard
[Edward Teach]
English. Pirate
Privateer during War of Spanish Succession,
   1701-14; became pirate at end of war.
b. 1680 in Bristol, England
d. Nov 22, 1718 in Ocracoke Island, North
   Carolina
Source: *NewCol 75; OxAmL; REn; REnAL;
WhAm HS*

Blackburn, "Jack" (Charles Henry)
"Chappie"
American. Boxer, Boxing Trainer
Lightweight boxer, 1900-23; trainer of Joe
   Louis.
b. 1883 in Versailles, Kentucky
d. Apr 24, 1942 in Chicago, Illinois
Source: *InB&W 80; ObitOF 79; WhoBox 74*

Blackett, Patrick Maynard Stuart
English. Scientist, Engineer, Physicist
Nobel Laureate for physics, 1948, who wrote
   Lectures on Rock Magnetism, 1956.
b. Nov 18, 1897 in London, England
d. Jul 13, 1974 in London, England
Source: *ConAu 49; IntWW 74; WhAm 6;
Who 74; WhoWor 78*

Blackman, Honor
English. Actress
Played Pussy Galore in Bond film *Goldfinger,*
   1964.
b. Aug 22, 1926 in London, England
Source: *FilmEn; IntMPA 76, 77, 78, 79, 80,
81, 82; MotPP; WhoAmW 74; WhoHol A;
WhoThe 72, 77, 81; WhoWor 74*

Blackmer, Sidney Alderman
American. Actor
Made Broadway debut, 1917; portrayed
   Teddy Roosevelt more than a dozen times
   in films, plays.
b. Jul 13, 1896 in Salisbury, North Carolina
d. Oct 5, 1973 in New York, New York
Source: *BiE&WWA; FilmgC; MovMk;
NewYTBE 73; ObitOF 79; Vers A; WhScrn
77; WhThe; WhoAm 74; WhoHol B; WorAl*

Blackmore, Richard Doddridge
English. Author
Romantic novels include classic *Lorna Doone,*
   1869.
b. Jun 7, 1825 in Longworth, England
d. Jan 20, 1900 in Teddington, England
Source: *Alli SUP; BbD; BiD&SB; BrAu 19;
Chambr 3; ChhPo, S1, S2; CyWA; DcBiA;
DcEnA, AP; DcEnL; DcEuL; DcLEL; EvLB;
JBA 34; LinLib L, S; MouLC 4; NewC;
OxEng; PenC ENG; REn; WebE&AL*

Blackmore, Ritchie
[Deep Purple; Ritchie Blackmore's Rainbow]
English. Musician
Co-founded Deep Purple, 1968 had hit
   "Stone Cold."
b. Apr 14, 1945 in Weston-Super-Mare,
   England
Source: *ConMuA 80A; RolSEnR 83;
WhoRock 81*

Blackmun, Harry Andrew
American. Supreme Court Justice
Moderate/conservative justice appointed by
   Richard Nixon, 1970.
b. Nov 12, 1908 in Nashville, Illinois
Source: *CelR; CurBio 70; DrAS 74P; IntWW
74; WebAB; Who 74; WhoAm 74, 76, 78, 80,
82; WhoAmP 73; WhoGov 75; WhoS&SW 82*

Blackmur, Richard Palmer
American. Poet, Educator, Critic
Writings include *Double Agent*, 1935;
Language As Gesture: Essays in Poetry,
1952.
b. Jan 21, 1904 in Springfield, Massachusetts
d. Feb 2, 1965 in Princeton, New Jersey
Source: *AmAu&B; CasWL; CnDAL; ConAu
25R, P-1; ConLC 2; DcLEL; EncWL, 2;
EvLB; LongCTC; ModAL; EncWL 2; ModAL
S1; OxAmL; PenC AM; RAdv 1; REn;
REnAL; SixAP; TwCA, SUP; TwCWr;
WebE&AL; WhAm 4*

Blackstone, Harry
[Henri Bouton]
American. Magician
b. 1885
d. Nov 16, 1965 in Hollywood, California
Source: *BioIn 2, 5, 7*

Blackstone, William, Sir
English. Judge, Author
Wrote *Commentaries on the Laws of
England*, 1765-69, in four volumes.
b. Jul 10, 1723 in London, England
d. Feb 14, 1780 in London, England
Source: *Alli; AtlBL; BiD&SB; BrAu; CasWL;
Chambr 2; ChhPo; CyEd; DcEnA; DcEnL;
EvLB; NewC; OxEng; REn; WorAl*

Blackton, James Stuart
American. Filmmaker
Founder, Vitagraph Films, 1896; first to
produce film plays.
b. Jan 5, 1875 in Sheffield, England
d. Aug 13, 1941 in Los Angeles, California
Source: *CurBio 41; DcAmB S3; WebBD 80;
WhAm 74*

Blackton, Jay S
American. Conductor
Musical director of *Oklahoma!*, 1943; *Hello
Dolly*, 1965; *The King and I*, 1972.
b. Mar 25, 1909 in New York, New York
Source: *AmSCAP 66; BiE&WWA; NotNAT*

Blackwell, Mr. (Richard)
American. Fashion Designer, Critic
Famous for yearly list of "worst dressed"
women in world.
b. in Brooklyn, New York
Source: *WorFshn*

Blackwell, Antoinette Louisa Brown
American. Abolitionist, Feminist, Minister
First woman ordained minister in US, 1853;
wrote *The Making of the Universe*, 1914.
b. 1825 in Henrietta, New York
d. 1921
Source: *BbD; BiD&SB; BioIn 2, 3, 4, 5, 6, 9,
11; DcAmB; DcNAA; NewCol 75*

Blackwell, Basil Henry, Sir
English. Publisher
BH Blackwell, Ltd., founder, chairman, 1922-
69, pres., 1969--.
b. May 29, 1889 in Oxford, England
Source: *BioIn 9; BlueB 76; IntWW 80; IntYB
82; Who 82; WhoWor 78*

Blackwell, Betsy Talbot
American. Editor
Editor-in-chief, *Mademoiselle* magazine, 1937-
71; raised literary standards of women's
magazines.
b. 1905 in New York, New York
d. Feb 4, 1985 in Norwalk, Connecticut
Source: *AmAu&B; CurBio 54, 85; ForWC 70;
InWom; NewYTBE 70; WhAm 8; WhoAm
74; WhoAmW 74; WorFshn*

Blackwell, Earl
[Samuel Earl Blackwell, Jr]
American. Author, Publisher
Organizer, first chairman, Theater Hall of
Fame, 1972.
b. May 3, 1913 in Atlanta, Georgia
Source: *BiE&WWA; CelR; CurBio 60;
NotNAT; WhoAm 74, 76, 78, 80, 82;
WhoWor 78*

Blackwell, Elizabeth
American. Physician, Author
First woman to receive MD in modern
times, 1849; practiced in NY, 1850-67.
b. Feb 3, 1821 in Bristol, England
d. May 31, 1910 in Hastings, England
Source: *Alli, SUP; AmWom; ApCAB;
BiD&SB; DcAmAu; DcAmB; DcNAA; Drake;
EncAB-H; HerW; InWom; NotAW; OhA&B;
TwCBDA; WebAB; WhAm 1*

Blackwood, Algernon
English. Author
Writings on the supernatural include *Jimbo,
a fantasy*, 1909; *Full Circle*, 1927.
b. 1869 in Kent, England
d. Dec 10, 1951 in London, England
Source: *Chambr 3; DcLEL; EncMys; EvLB;
LongCTC; NewC; PenC ENG; REn; TwCA,
SUP; TwCWr*

Blacque, Taurean
American. Actor
Plays Neal Washington on TV series "Hill
Street Blues."
b. May 10, 1946 in Newark, New Jersey
Source: *WhoTelC*

Blades, Ruben
Panamanian. Singer, Songwriter
Revolutionized salsa music, universalized
appeal; first salsa singer to write own
songs.
b. Jul 16, 1948 in Panama City, Panama
Source: *CurBio 86*

Blaiberg, Philip
South African. Dentist, Transplant Patient
Received second heart transplanted by Dr.
Christiaan Barnard, Jan 2, 1968; wrote
Looking at My Heart, 1968.
b. May 24, 1909 in Uniondale, South Africa
d. Aug 17, 1969 in Capetwon, South Africa
Source: *BioIn 8, 9; LinLib S*

Blaik, "Red" (Earl Henry)
American. Football Coach, Businessman
Football coach, US Military Academy, 1927-
34; chairman Blaik Oil Co., 1960--.
b. Feb 15, 1897 in Detroit, Michigan
Source: *CurBio 45; St&PR 75; WhoAm 76,
78, 80, 82, 84; WhoFtbl 74*

Blaikie, William
American. Author, Sportsman, Lawyer
Held amateur long distance outdoor walking
record for 10 years; walked from Boston
to NYC, 225 miles in 4 1/2 days.
b. May 24, 1843 in New York, New York
d. Dec 6, 1904 in New York, New York
Source: *Alli SUP; ApCAB; BiD&SB; DcAmAu;
DcAmB; DcNAA; TwCBDA; WhAm 1*

Blaine, James Gillespie
American. Statesman
Co-founder Republican Party, 1856;
nominated for pres., 1884, lost election to
Grover Cleveland.
b. Jan 31, 1830 in West Brownsville,
Pennsylvania
d. Jan 27, 1893 in Washington, District of
Columbia
Source: *Alli SUP; AmAu&B; AmBi; BbD;
BiD&SB; BiDrUSE; DcAmAu; DcAmB;
DcNAA; DcSpL; EncAB-H; OxAmL; REn;
REnAL; TwCBDA; WebAB; WhAm HS, 5;
WhAmP; WrDr 80*

Blaine, Vivian
[Vivian S Stapleton]
American. Actress
Star of stage, 1950, film version, 1955 of
Guys and Dolls.
b. Nov 21, 1924 in Newark, New Jersey
Source: *AmPS B; BiE&WWA; CmpEPM;
EncMT; FilmEn; FilmgC; HolP 40; IntMPA
80, 81, 82; MotPP; NotNAT; WhoAm 80, 82;
WhoHol A; WhoThe 81*

Blair, Betsy
[Betsy Roger]
American. Actress
Best known as Oscar nominee for role in
Marty, 1955.
b. Dec 11, 1923 in Cliffside Park, New
Jersey
Source: *BiE&WWA; FilmEn; FilmgC; IntMPA
76, 77, 78, 79, 80, 81, 82; MotPP; OxFilm;
WhoAmW 58A; WhoHol A*

Blair, Clay, Jr.
American. Author, Editor
Writings include *Beyond Courage,* 1955;
Survive!, 1973.
b. May 1, 1925 in Lexington, Virginia
Source: *AmAu&B; AuNews 2; ConAu 77;
IntWW 74; WhoAm 82*

Blair, David
English. Ballet Dancer
Best known for title role in *The Prince of
the Pagodas,* 1957.
b. Jul 27, 1932 in Halifax, England
d. Apr 1, 1976 in London, England
Source: *Alli SUP; BioIn 4, 5, 6, 10, 11;
CurBio 61, 76; NewYTBS 77; WhWW-II;
Who 74; WhoWor 78*

Blair, Eric Arthur
see: Orwell, George, pseud.

Blair, Francis Preston
American. Soldier, Statesman
b. Feb 10, 1821 in Lexington, Kentucky
d. Jul 8, 1875 in Saint Louis, Missouri
Source: *BiDSA; BioIn 1, 3, 7*

Blair, Frank
American. Broadcast Journalist
First newscaster on TVs "Today Show",
1952-75; autobiography *Let's Be Frank
About It,* 1979.
b. May 30, 1915 in Yemassee, South
Carolina
Source: *CelR; ConAu 97; NewYTET; Ward
77; WhoAm 74, 76*

Blair, James
Scottish. Clergyman, Educator
Founder, first pres., College of William and
    Mary, 1693.
b. 1655 in Edinburgh, Scotland
d. Apr 18, 1743 in Williamsburg, Virginia
Source: *Alli; McGEWB; REnAL; WebAB;*
    WhAm HS; WorAl

Blair, Janet
[Martha Janet Lafferty]
American. Actress
Appeared in *Three Girls about Town,* 1941;
    My Sister Eileen, 1942.
b. Apr 23, 1921 in Altoona, Pennsylvania
Source: *BiE&WWA; FilmgC; HolP 40;*
    IntMPA 80, 81, 82; MotPP; MovMk; WhoAm
    74; WhoHol A

Blair, June
American. Actress
b. 1937
Source: *WhoHol A*

Blair, Linda Denise
American. Actress
Played the possessed girl in *The Exorist,*
    1973.
b. Jan 22, 1959 in Saint Louis, Missouri
Source: *BkPepl; ConTFT 3; IntMPA 82;*
    WhoAm 82; WhoHol A

Blair, Montgomery
American. Statesman
Counsel for Dred Scott, who was postmaster-
    general under Lincoln, 1861.
b. May 10, 1813 in Franklin County,
    Kentucky
d. Jul 27, 1883 in Silver Spring, Maryland
Source: *AmBi; ApCAB; BiAUS; BiDrUSE;*
    DcAmB; Drake; TwCBDA; WebAB; WhAm
    HS; WhAmP

Blair, William Richards
American. Physicist, Inventor
Claimed to invent pulse-echo radar, 1926;
    considered father of radar by US Army.
b. Nov 7, 1874 in Coleraine, Ireland
d. Sep 2, 1962 in Fair Haven, New Jersey
Source: *DcAmB S7*

Blaisdell, George G
"Mr. Zippo"
American. Businessman
Founded cigarette lighter co., marketing
    inexpensive windproof product with
    lifetime guarantee.
b. 1895
d. 1978 in Miami Beach, Florida
Source: *BioIn 7, 11; PseudN 82; St&PR 75*

Blaise, Saint
Religious Figure
Patron of throat ailments; bishop of Sebastea,
    Armenia; commemorated, Feb 2.
d. 316
Source: *DcBiPP; DcCathB; Dis&D*

Blake, Amanda
[Beverly Louise Neill]
American. Actress
Played Miss Kitty on TV series
    "Gunsmoke," 1955-75.
b. Feb 20, 1931 in Buffalo, New York
Source: *CelR; FilmEn; FilmgC; IntMPA 75,*
    76, 77, 78, 79, 80, 81, 82; WhoAm 74;
    WhoHol A

Blake, Eubie (James Hubert)
American. Pianist, Composer
Ragtime pioneer, whose best known songs
    include "I'm Just Wild About Harry,"
    1921; "Memories of You," 1930.
b. Feb 7, 1883 in Baltimore, Maryland
d. Feb 12, 1983 in Brooklyn, New York
Source: *AmSCAP 66; AnObit 1983; BiDAmM;*
    BluesWW; CmpEPM; CurBio 74, 83N;
    DrBlPA,; Ebony 1; EncJzS 70; EncMT;
    IlEncJ; InB&W 80; WhoAm 74, 76, 78, 80,
    82; WhoBlA 75, 77; WhoJazz 72

Blake, Eugene Carson
American. Clergyman
Leader in American Protestantism who was
    secretary-general of World Council of
    Churches, 1966-72.
b. Nov 7, 1906 in Saint Louis, Missouri
d. Jul 31, 1985 in Stanford, Connecticut
Source: *CelR; CurBio 55, 85; DrAS 74P;*
    IntWW 74; Who 74; WhoAm 74; WhoE 74;
    WhoRel 75; WhoWor 74

Blake, Florence G
American. Nurse
b. 1907
Source: *BioIn 1, 4, 11*

Blake, Quentin
English. Children's Author, Illustrator
Writings include *Jack and Nancy,* 1969; *The*
    Bear's Water Picnic, 1970.
b. Dec 16, 1932 in England
Source: *ConAu 25R; IlsBYP; IlsCB 1957;*
    SmATA 9

Blake, Robert
English. Admiral
Captured the Scilly Islands, 1651; sank the
    Spanish Fleet at Santa Cruz, 1657.
b. 1599
d. Aug 7, 1657
Source: *NewCol 75; WhoMilH 76*

Blake, Robert
[Michael Gubitosi; Our Gang]
American. Actor
Starred in TV series "Baretta," 1974-78; won
Emmy, 1975.
b. Sep 18, 1938 in Nutley, New Jersey
Source: *BkPepl; ConTFT 3; FilmgC; IntMPA
82; MovMk; WhoAm 74; WhoHol A*

Blake, William
English. Poet, Artist, Mystic
Wrote *Songs of Innocence,* 1789; engraved
and published own poetry.
b. Nov 28, 1757 in London, England
d. Aug 12, 1827 in London, England
Source: *Alli; AnCL; AtlBL; BbD; BiD&SB;
BiDLA; BkIE; BrAu 19; CarSB; CasWL;
Chambr 2; ChhPo, S1, S2; CnE&AP; CrtT 2;
CyWA; DcEnA, AP; DcEnL; DcEuL; DcLEL;
EvLB; MouLC 3; NewC; OxEng; PenC ENG;
RAdv 1; RComWL; REn; Str&VC;
WebE&AL*

Blakeley, Ronee
American. Actress, Singer
Screen debut in *Nashville,* 1975; received
Oscar nomination.
b. 1946 in Stanley, Idaho
Source: *FilmEn; VarWW 85*

Blakelock, Ralph Albert
American. Artist
Original self-taught landscapist who did
moody scenes, often with Indians.
b. Oct 15, 1847 in New York, New York
d. Aug 9, 1919 in Elizabethtown, New York
Source: *AmBi; ApCAB; ArtsAmW 1;
BnEnAmA; DcAmArt; DcAmB; IlBEAAW;
LinLib S; McGDA; McGEWB; NatCAB 15;
WebAB; WhAm 1*

Blakely, Colin
Irish. Actor
Played Dr. Watson in film *The Private Life
of Sherlock Holmes,* 1970.
b. Sep 23, 1930 in Bangor, Northern Ireland
Source: *CnThe; FilmEn; FilmgC; PiP; Who
82, 85; WhoHol A; WhoThe 77, 81*

Blakely, Susan
American. Actress
Played in TV miniseries "Rich Man, Poor
Man"; movies *The Way We Were,* 1973;
Towering Inferno, 1974.
b. Sep 7, 1948 in Frankfurt, Germany (West)
Source: *IntMPA 82; VarWW 85; WhoAm 80,
82; WhoHol A*

Blakey, Art
American. Jazz Musician
Star drummer; formed Jazz Messengers, 1955;
won 1984 Grammy for best accoustic
group.
b. Oct 11, 1919 in Pittsburgh, Pennsylvania
Source: *WhoAm 74; WhoBlA 85*

Blalock, Alfred
American. Surgeon
Developed artery bypass operation, 1944, that
saved "blue babies."
b. Apr 5, 1899 in Culloden, Georgia
d. Sep 15, 1964 in Baltimore, Maryland
Source: *BioIn 1, 2, 3, 5, 7, 11; CurBio 46,
64*

Blalock, Jane
American. Golfer
Pro golfer since 1969 who has won more
than 30 tournaments.
b. Sep 19, 1945 in Portsmouth, New
Hampshire
Source: *BioIn 11; GoodHs; WhoAm 82;
WhoGolf; WorAl*

Blanc, (Jean Joseph Charles) Louis
French. Socialist Leader, Author
Considered father of state socialism; wrote
History of French Revolution, 1847-62.
b. 1811 in Madrid, Spain
d. 1882
Source: *OxFr; REn*

Blanc, Mel(vin Jerome)
American. Actor, Musician
Voice of many cartoon characters: Bugs
Bunny, Porky Pig, Daffy Duck.
b. May 30, 1908 in San Francisco, California
Source: *AmSCAP 80; CurBio 76; FilmgC;
IntMPA 77, 82; WhoAm 74; WhoHol A;
WorAl*

Blanchard, "Doc" (Felix Anthony)
American. Football Player, Football Coach
Fullback, US Military Academy; scored 19
touchdowns, won Heisman Trophy, 1945.
b. Dec 11, 1924 in Bishopville, South
Carolina
Source: *CurBio 46; WhoFtbl 74; WhoHol A*

Blanchard, Francois
French. Balloonist
Credited with first balloon crossing of
English Channel, first ascents in US.
b. Jul 4, 1753
d. 1809
Source: *NewCol 75*

Blanchard, James J
American. Politician
Dem. governor of MI, 1982--.
b. Aug 8, 1942 in Detroit, Michigan
Source: *CngDr 81; WhoAm 80, 82; WhoAmP 75; WhoGov 77; WhoMW 80, 82*

Blanchard, Thomas
American. Inventor
Developed principle for turning irregular forms from a pattern; patented stem carriage, 1825.
b. Jun 24, 1788 in Sutton, Massachusetts
d. Apr 16, 1864 in Boston, Massachusetts
Source: *AmBi; ApCAB; DcAmB; Drake; NatCab 6; TwCBDA; WebAB; WhAm HS*

Bland, Richard Parks
American. Statesman
Dem. congressman; leader of Free Silver movement, 1875-77; defeated by Bryan for presidential nomination, 1896.
b. Aug 19, 1835 in Hartford, Kentucky
d. 1899
Source: *AmBi; ApCAB; BiAUS; BiDSA; BiDrAC; DcAmB; TwCBDA; WhAm 1; WhAmP*

Blanda, George Frederick
American. Football Player
Quarterback, placekicker, 1949-75; scored record 2,002 points.
b. Sep 17, 1927 in Youngwood, Pennsylvania
Source: *CmCal; CurBio 72; WebAB, 79; WhoAm 74; WhoFtbl 74; WorAl*

Blanding, Don
American. Author, Illustrator
Wrote, illustrated books on FL, HI: *Vagabond's House*, 1928; *Hula Moon*, 1930.
b. Nov 7, 1894 in Kingfisher, Oklahoma
d. Jun 9, 1957 in Los Angeles, California
Source: *CurBio 57; NatCAB 46; ObitOF 79*

Blanding, Sarah Gibson
American. Educator
First woman pres., of Vassar College, 1946-64.
b. Nov 22, 1898 in Lexington, Kentucky
d. Mar 3, 1985 in Newton, Pennsylvania
Source: *BioIn 6, 7; CurBio 46, 85; IntWW 74; WhoAm 74; WhoAmW 74*

Blane, Sally
[Elizabeth Jane Young]
American. Actress
Sister of Loretta Young; played in B movies in the 1930s.
b. Jul 11, 1910 in Salida, Colorado
Source: *Film 2; FilmgC; MovMk; ThFT; TwYS; WhoHol A*

Blankers-Koen, Fanny
Dutch. Track Athlete
Won four gold medals, 1948 Olympics.
b. Apr 7, 1946 in Amsterdam, New Hampshire
Source: *InWom; WhoTr&F 73*

Blanqui, Louis Auguste
French. Revolutionary
Participated in French Revolution, downfall of Napoleon III.
b. Feb 1, 1805 in Ruget, France
d. Jan 1, 1881
Source: *BioIn 7, 9; CelCen; DcBiPP; McGEWD; OxFr; REn; WhDW*

Blanton, Jimmy
American. Jazz Musician
Bass player with Duke Ellington, 1939-42.
b. 1918 in Chattanooga, Tennessee
d. Jul 30, 1942 in Los Angeles, California
Source: *CmpEPM; WhoJazz 72*

Blanton, (Leonard) Ray
American. Politician
Governor of TN 1975-79; congressman, 1966-72.
b. Apr 10, 1930 in Hardin County, Tennessee
Source: *BiDrAC; BlueB 76; IntWW 80; WhoAmP 81; WhoGov 72; WhoS&SW 73*

Blasco-Ibanez, Vicente
Spanish. Author
Wrote realistic novels *Blood and Sand*, 1913; *Four Horseman of the Apocalypse*, 1918.
b. 1867 in Valencia, Spain
d. 1928 in Riviera, France
Source: *CasWL; ClDMEL; CyWA; DcSpL; EncWL, 2; EvEuW; LinLib L, S; LongCTC; ModRL; OxEng; PenC EUR; REn; WhDW; TwCA, SUP; TwCWr*

Blashfield, Edwin Howland
American. Artist
Mural, genre painter; did murals for congressional library, 1895.
b. Dec 15, 1848 in New York, New York
d. Oct 12, 1936
Source: *AmAu&B; AmBi; ApCAB; ChhPo; DcAmAu; DcAmB S2; DcNAA; TwCBDA; WhAm 1*

Blasingame, Francis James Levi
American. Educator, Physician
b. Jan 17, 1907 in Hot Springs, Arkansas
Source: *WhoAm 74, 76, 78, 80, 82*

Blass, Bill
American. Fashion Designer
Known for apparel, home furnishings, cars,
chocolates, designs.
b. Jun 22, 1922 in Fort Wayne, Indiana
Source: *CelR; CurBio 66; NewYTBS 80;
WhoAm 74, 76, 78, 80, 82; WhoE 74, 75,
77; WhoF&I 74; WorAl; WorFshn*

Blassingale, Wyatt Rainey
American. Author
Children's non-fiction books include *French
Foreign Legion,* 1955.
b. Feb 6, 1909 in Demopolis, Alabama
Source: *AuBYP; ConAu 1R; SmATA 1; WrDr
80*

Blatch, Harriot Eaton Stanton
American. Feminist, Lecturer
Daughter of Elizabeth Cody Stanton; founded
Women's Political Union, 1908; leader in
women's suffrage movement.
b. Jan 20, 1856 in Seneca Falls, New York
d. Nov 20, 1940 in Greenwich, Connecticut
Source: *AmWomWr; BiCAW; CurBio 41;
DcAmB S2; DcNAA; InWom; NotAW;
OxAmL; WhAm 1; WhAmP,; WhNAA;
WomWWA 14*

Blatchford, Joseph Hoffer
American. Government Official
Director of Peace Corps, 1969-71.
b. Jun 7, 1934 in Milwaukee, Wisconsin
Source: *CurBio 71; IntWW 74; NewYTBE 71;
WhoAm 74; WhoAmP 73; WhoGov 75*

Blatchford, Samuel
American. Supreme Court Justice
Respected Surpreme Court Justice, 1882-93;
expert on maritime, patent law.
b. Mar 9, 1820 in New York, New York
d. Jul 7, 1893 in Newport, Rhode Island
Source: *Alli SUP; ApCAB; BiAUS; DcAmB;
DcNAA; TwCBDA; WebAB; WhAm HS*

Blatty, William Peter
American. Author
Wrote *The Exorcist,* 1971; sold over 10
million copies; on best-seller list 55 weeks.
b. Jan 7, 1928 in New York, New York
Source: *ConAu 5R, 9NR; ConLC 2; CurBio
74; FilmgC; IntAu&W 77; IntMPA 76, 77,
78, 79, 80, 81, 82; WhoAm 80, 82, 82; WrDr
76*

Blavatsky, Helena Petrovna
Russian. Religious Leader
Founded Theosophical Society, 1875;
combines Buddhist, Brahmanic theories of
evolution, reincarnation.
b. Jul 30, 1831 in Ekaterinoslav, Russia
d. May 8, 1891 in London, England
Source: *Alli SUP; AmAu&B; AmBi; AmWom;
ApCAB; BbD; BiD&SB; DcAmAu; DcAmB;
NatCAB 15; NewC; NotAW; OxAmL; REn;
TwCBDA; WhAm HS*

Blech, Leo
German. Conductor, Composer
Noted opera conductor who wrote opera
Versiegelt, 1908.
b. Apr 21, 1871 in Aiz-la-Chapelle, Germany
d. Aug 24, 1958 in Berlin, Germany (West)
Source: *NewEOp 71; WebBD 80*

Bledsoe, Jules
American. Actor, Singer
Sang "Ol' Man River" in *Show Boat,* 1927
stage, 1929 film.
b. Dec 29, 1898
d. Jul 14, 1943 in Hollywood, California
Source: *AmPS B; BiDAmM; CurBio 43;
NotNAT B; WhScrn 74, 77*

Bledsoe, Tempestt Kenieth
American. Actress
Plays Vanessa Huxtable on "The Cosby
Show."
b. 1973 in Chicago, Illinois
Source: *NF*

Bleeker, Sonia
[Sonia Bleeker Zim]
Russian. Children's Author, Editor
Books on Indians, African tribes include *The
Crow Indians,* 1953.
b. Nov 28, 1909 in Starchevicvhi, Russia
d. Nov 13, 1971
Source: *BkP; ConAu 1R, 33R, 3NR; ForWC
70; MorJA; SmATA 2*

Blegen, Judith Eyer
American. Opera Singer
Lyric coloratura soprano; soloist with US,
European opera companies.
b. Apr 27, 1941 in Missoula, Montana
Source: *NewYTBS 74; WhoAm 78, 80, 82;
WhoOp 76*

Bleiberg, Robert Marvin
American. Publisher, Editor
Publisher, editorial director, *Barron's National
Business and Financial Weekly.*
b. Jun 21, 1924 in Brooklyn, New York
Source: *BlueB 76; WhoAm 74, 76, 78, 80,
82; WhoF&I 74*

Bleier, "Rocky" (Robert Patrick)
American. Football Player
Lost part of right foot in Vietnam, 1969;
running back for Pittsburgh Steelers, 1968,
1971-80.
b. Mar 5, 1946 in Appleton, Wisconsin
Source: *ConAu 85; NewYTBS 74, 75, 80;
WhoAm 78, 80*

Bleriot, Louis
French. Aviator, Engineer
First to fly plane across English Channel,
1909.
b. Jul 1, 1872 in Cambrai, France
d. Aug 2, 1936 in Paris, France
Source: *LinLib S; WebBD 80*

Bleyer, Archie
American. Musician
Head of Cadence records, 1952; hit single
"Mr. Sandman," 1954.
b. Jun 12, 1909 in Corona, New York
Source: *CmpEPM; RkOn 74*

Bligh, William, Captain
English. Naval Officer
Captain, HMS *Bounty* when mutiny occurred;
cast adrift for 4,000 miles.
b. Sep 9, 1754 in Plymouth, England
d. Dec 7, 1817 in London, England
Source: *Alli; BiDLA; CelCen; DcBiPP;
McGEWB; NewC; OxShips; REn; WhDW;
WorAl*

Blind Faith
['Ginger' Baker; Eric Clapton; Rick Grech;
Stevie Winwood]
English. Music Group
Only album *Blind Faith,* 1969, with hits
"Can't Find My Way Home"; "Presence
of the Lord."
Source: *ConMuA 80A; IlEncRk; LilREn 78;
RolSEnR 83; WhoRock 81*

Blinn, Holbrook
American. Actor, Producer
Silent film star who appeared opposite
Marion Davies in *Janice Meredith,* 1924;
Zander the Great, 1925.
b. 1872 in San Francisco, California
d. Jun 24, 1928 in Croton, New York
Source: *CmCal; DcAmB; Film 1, 2; MotPP;
NotNAT B; TwYS; WhAm 1; WhScrn 74, 77;
WhThe; WhoHol B; WhoStg 1908*

Blish, James Benjamin
American. Author
Science fiction writer; won Hugo for *A Case
of Conscience,* 1958.
b. May 23, 1921 in East Orange, New Jersey
d. Jul 30, 1975 in Henley-on-Thames,
England
Source: *AmAu&B; Au&Wr 71; ConAu 1R,
57, 3NR; ConLC 14; ConNov 76; WorAu;
WrDr 76*

Bliss, Arthur, Sir
English. Composer
Master of the Queen's Music, 1953-75; wrote
ballet *Lady of Shallott,* 1958.
b. Aug 2, 1891 in London, England
d. Mar 27, 1975 in London, England
Source: *DcCM; FilmgC; IntWW 74; WhAm
6; Who 74; WhoMus 72; WhoWor 78*

Bliss, Ray C(harles)
American. Political Leader
Chairman, GOP, 1966-68; credited with
rebuilding party after defeat of Goldwater,
1964.
b. Dec 16, 1907 in Akron, Ohio
d. Aug 6, 1981 in Akron, Ohio
Source: *BioIn 6, 7, 8; CurBio 66, 81; IntWW
75, 76, 77, 78; NewYTBS 81; WhAm 8;
WhoAm 74, 76, 78, 80, 82; WhoAmP 73, 75,
77, 79; WhoWor 74, 76, 78*

Bliss, Robert Woods
American. Diplomat, Philanthropist
In diplomatic service, 1900-33, 1942-45.
b. 1875
d. Apr 19, 1962 in New York
Source: *BioIn 6, 7; NatCAB 49; WhAm 4*

Bliss, Tasker H
American. Military Leader
b. Dec 31, 1853 in Lewisburg, Pennsylvania
d. Nov 9, 1930 in Washington, District of
Columbia
Source: *AmBi; DcAmB S1; WebAB; WhAm 1*

Blitzstein, Marc
American. Composer, Author
Wrote *The Cradle Will Rock,* libretto for
American version of *Three Penny Opera,*
1952.
b. Mar 2, 1905 in Philadelphia, Pennsylvania
d. Jan 22, 1964 in Minnesota
Source: *AmAu&B; AmSCAP 66; Baker 78;
BiE&WWA; CnMD; CurBio 40, 64; DcCM;
EncMT; McGEWD; ModWD; NewCBMT;
OxAmH; OxAmL; PIP&P; REn; REnAL;
WebAB, 79; WhAm 4*

Bliven, Bruce
American. Author, Editor
Editor, pres., of *New Republic*, 1923-53.
b. Jul 27, 1889 in Emmetsburg, Iowa
d. May 27, 1977 in Palo Alto, California
Source: *AmAu&B; AuBYP; ConAu 37R, 69;
CurBio 41; IntWW 74; TwCA, SUP; Who 74;
WhoAm 74; WhoWest 84; WrDr 80*

Blixen, Karen Christentze, Baroness
[Pierre Andrezel; Isak Dinesen, pseuds.]
Danish. Author
Known for memoirs of life in Kenya, *Out of
Africa*, 1937; film version won best picture
Oscar, 1985.
b. Apr 17, 1885 in Rungsted, Delaware
d. Sep 7, 1962 in Rungsted, Delaware
Source: *CasWL; ConAu 25R, P-2; ConLC 10;
Novels; ObitT 1961; PenC ENG, EUR; REn;
ScF&FL 1; TwCA, SUP; WhoTwCL*

Bloch, Alexander
American. Conductor, Musician
Vioninist who was soloist, concert master
with various symphonies; wrote *Principles
and Practice of Bowing*, 1916.
b. Jul 11, 1881 in Selma, Alabama
Source: *WhAm 1; WhoMus 72; WhoWorJ 72*

Bloch, Claude Charles
American. Military Leader
Admiral at Pearl Harbor during Japanese
attack, 1941.
b. Jul 12, 1878 in Woodbury, Kentucky
d. Oct 6, 1967 in Washington, District of
Columbia
Source: *CurBio 42, 67; WhAm 4A*

Bloch, Ernest
American. Composer
Founded Cleveland Institute of Music;
director, 1920-25.
b. Jul 24, 1880 in Geneva, Switzerland
d. Jul 15, 1959 in Portland, Oregon
Source: *AmSCAP 66; AtlBL; CurBio 53, 59;
DcCM; OxAmL; REn; WebAB; WhAm 3*

Bloch, Felix
Swiss. Physicist, Educator
Shared Nobel Prize in Physics with Edward
Purcell for study of NMR (nuclear
magnetic resonance).
b. Oct 23, 1905 in Zurich, Switzerland
d. Sep 10, 1983 in Zurich, Switzerland
Source: *AmM&WS 82P; IntWW 82; WhAm
8; Who 74, 82; WhoAm 74, 76, 78, 80, 82;
WhoWorJ 72; WorAl*

Bloch, Raymond A
American. Band Leader, Conductor
Best known as TV conductor on Jackie
Gleason, Ed Sullivan shows, 1950-60.
b. Aug 3, 1902 in Alsace-Lorraine, Germany
d. Mar 29, 1982 in Miami, Florida
Source: *AmSCAP 66, 80; BiDAmM;
CmpEPM,; NewYTBS 82; WorAl*

Bloch, Robert Albert
[Tarleton Fiske; Nathan Hindin; Collier
Young, pseuds.]
American. Author, Screenwriter
Mystery writer who wrote film version of his
novel *Psycho*, 1959, sequel *Psycho II*, 1982.
b. Apr 5, 1917 in Chicago, Illinois
Source: *AmAu&B; ConAu 5R, 5NR; EncMys;
EncSF; FanAl; IntMPA 81; PseudN 82;
SmATA 12; WhoAm 84; WhoSciF*

Block, Herbert Lawrence
see: Herblock

Block, John Rusling
American. Government Official
Millionaire farmer who was secretary of
Agriculture under Ronald Reagan, 1981-86.
b. Feb 15, 1935 in Galesburg, Illinois
Source: *CngDr 81; CurBio 82; IntYB 82;
NewYTBS 84; WhoAm 82, 84*

Block, Joseph Leopold
American. Businessman
Island Steel exec., 1928-71; succeeded Randall
as pres., 1953.
b. Oct 6, 1902 in Chicago, Illinois
d. Nov 17, 1976 in New York, New York
Source: *BioIn 2, 5, 6, 8, 11; CurBio 61*

Block, Martin
Radio Performer
Radio host of "Make Believe Ballroom,"
1934-54.
b. 1903
d. Sep 19, 1967 in Englewood, New Jersey
Source: *BioIn 8; CmpEPM; ObitOF 79*

Blocker, Dan
American. Actor
Played Hoss Cartwright on TV series
"Bonanza," 1959-72.
b. 1927 in Bowie, Texas
d. May 13, 1972 in Inglewood, California
Source: *FilmgC; NewYTBE 72; WhAm 5;
WhScrn 77; WhoHol B*

Blodgett, Katherine Burr
American. Physicist
Developed non-reflecting glass, used on almost all camera, optical lenses.
b. Jan 10, 1898 in Schenectady, New York
d. Dec 10, 1979 in Schenectady, New York
Source: *NewYTBS 79; WhAm 7; WhoAmW 58*

Blofeld, John
American. Author
Books on China include *Taoism: Road to Immortality,* 1978.
b. Apr 2, 1913 in London, England
Source: *Au&Wr 71; ConAu 53, 4NR; WrDr 76*

Blok, Aleksandr Aleksandrovich
Russian. Author, Poet
Symbolist, who wrote *The Twelve,* 1920.
b. Nov 28, 1880 in Saint Petersburg, Russia
d. Sep 7, 1921 in Petrograd, U.S.S.R.
Source: *AtlBL; CasWL; ClDMEL; CnMD; CnMWL; DcRusL; EncWL; EvEuW; LongCTC; McGEWD; ModSL 1; ModWD; OxEng; PenC EUR; REn; TwCA, SUP; TwCWr; WhoTwCL*

Blondell, Joan
American. Actress
Appeared in over 80 films; best known role Aunt Sissy in *A Tree Grows in Brooklyn,* 1945.
b. Aug 30, 1912 in New York, New York
d. Dec 25, 1979 in Santa Monica, California
Source: *BiDFilm; BiE&WWA; CelR; FilmEn; FilmgC; ForWC 70; IntMPA 75, 76, 77; MotPP; MovMk; NewYTBE 72; NotNAT; OxFilm; ThFT; WhoAm 74; WhoAmW 77; WhoHol A; WhoThe 77; WorEFlm*

Blondie
[Clem Burke; Jimmy Destri; Nigel Harrison; Deborah Harry; Frank Infante; Chris Stein]
American. Music Group
Forerunner of original punk rock, formed 1976-82; had four number one hits including "Rapture," 1981.
Source: *ConMuA 80A; RkOn 85; RolSEnR 83; WhoRock 81*

Blondin, Jean Francois Gravelet
French. Entertainer
Best known for conquest of Niagara Falls.
b. Feb 28, 1824 in Saint Omer, France
d. Feb 19, 1897 in London, England
Source: *BioIn 1, 3, 4, 5, 6, 9*

Blood, Ernest B
"Gray Thatched Wizard"; "Prof"
American. Basketball Coach
Coached Passaic, NJ high school "wonder team" in 1920s; won-loss record of 1295-165.
b. Oct 4, 1872 in Manchester, New Hampshire
d. Feb 5, 1955 in New Smyrna, Florida
Source: *BioIn 3, 9; WhoBbl 73*

Blood, Thomas
"Colonel Blood"
Irish. Adventurer
Stole English crown jewels, 1671; pardoned by Charles II, who admired his audocity.
b. 1618 in Ireland
d. Aug 24, 1680
Source: *NewC*

Blood, Sweat and Tears
[Dave Bargeron; David Clayton-Thomas; Bobby Colomby; Steve Fieldeer; Jerry Fisher; Dick Halligan; Jeff Hyman; Steve Katz; Al Kooper; Fred Lipsiu; Tom Malone; Lou Marini, Jr.; Lew Soloff; Georg Wadenius; Larry Willis]
American. Music Group
Group formed 1968; hit singles "Spinning Wheel"; "And When I Die."
Source: *BiDAmM; EncPR&S 74; IlEncRk; RkOn 74; RolSEnR 83*

Bloody Mary
see: Mary I

Bloom, Claire
English. Actress
Best known for Chaplin film *Limelight,* 1952; former wife of Rod Steiger.
b. Feb 15, 1931 in London, England
Source: *BiDFilm; BiE&WWA; CelR; CurBio 56; FilmEn; FilmgC; IntMPA 76, 77, 78, 79, 80, 81, 82; IntWW 80, 81; MotPP; MovMk; NewYTBE 71; NotNAT; OxFilm; Who 82; WhoAm 74, 76, 78, 80, 82; WhoHol A; WhoThe 77; WhoWor 78; WorAl; WorEFlm*

Bloom, Eric
[Blue Oyster Cult]
American. Singer, Musician
Guitarist, vocalist with hard rock group since 1969.
b. Dec 1, 1944 in Long Island, New York
Source: *NF*

Bloom, Harry
South African. Author, Lawyer
Imprisoned for writing award-winning, anti-apartheid novel *Episode*, 1956.
b. 1913 in South Africa
d. Jul 28, 1981 in Canterbury, England
Source: *ConAu 104; TwCWr*

Bloom, Julius
American. Music Director
Exec., director, Carnegie Hall, 1960-77; founded Brooklyn Symphony Orchestra, 1939.
b. Sep 23, 1912 in Brooklyn, New York
d. Jul 5, 1984
Source: *WhAm 8; WhoAm 80, 82; WhoAmJ 80; WhoE 77*

Bloom, Mickey (Milton)
American. Musician, Composer
Trumpeter with Hal Kemp, 1935-39.
b. Aug 26, 1906 in Brooklyn, New York
Source: *AmSCAP 66; WhoJazz 72*

Bloom, Murray Teigh
American. Author, Journalist
Reporter, NY *Post*, who has done free lance writing for magazines since 1945.
b. May 19, 1916 in New York, New York
Source: *ASpks; ConAu 17R; WhoAm 74, 76, 78, 80, 82; WhoE 74; WrDr 76, 80, 82*

Bloom, Ursula
[Shiela Burns; Mary Essex; Rachel Harvey; Deborah Mann; Lozania Prole; Sara Sloane, pseuds.]
English. Author
Prolific literary figure who wrote more than 500 novels, 1924-79, including *Secret Lover*, 1930.
b. 1893 in Chelmsford, England
d. Oct 29, 1984 in London, England
Source: *AnObit 1984; Au&Wr 71; ConAu 114, 25R; IntAu&W 82; NewC; Novels; ScF&FL 1; Who 74, 82; WrDr 82*

Bloomer, Amelia Jenks
American. Social Reformer
Advocate of women's rights, dress reform; led to costume called "bloomers."
b. May 27, 1818 in Homer, New York
d. Dec 30, 1894 in Council Bluffs, Iowa
Source: *AmBi; AmWom; ApCAB; DcAmAu; DcAmB; InWom; NotAW; OxAmL; REnAL; TwCBDA; WebAB; WhAm HS; WhAmP*

Bloomfield, Mike (Michael)
American. Musician, Singer
Blues guitarist; formed supergroup Electric Flag, 1967-68; album *My Labors*, 1971.
b. Jul 28, 1944 in Chicago, Illinois
d. Feb 15, 1981 in San Francisco, California
Source: *AnObit 1981; BluesWW; EncPR&S 74; WhoAm 74*

Bloomgarden, Kermit
American. Producer
Produced *Diary of Anne Frank*, 1959.
b. Dec 15, 1904 in Brooklyn, New York
d. Sep 20, 1976 in New York, New York
Source: *BiE&WWA; ObitOF 79; WhoAm 74, 76; WhoThe 77, 81N; WhoWor 74*

Bloomingdale, Alfred S
American. Corporation Executive
Launched Diners' Club credit card co., 1950.
b. Apr 15, 1916 in New York, New York
d. Aug 20, 1982 in Santa Monica, California
Source: *AmCath 80; CelR; IntYB 78, 79, 81, 82; NewYTBS 82; WhAm 8; WhoAm 76, 78, 80, 82; WhoF&I 74*

Bloomingdale, Joseph Bernard
American. Merchant
Co-founded Bloomingdale's Dept. Store, 1872.
b. Dec 22, 1842 in New York, New York
d. Nov 21, 1904 in New York, New York
Source: *NatCAB 2, 30; WorAl*

Bloomingdale, Samuel
American. Retailer
Director of Federated Dept. Stores, 1930-62.
b. Jun 17, 1873 in New York, New York
d. May 10, 1968 in New York, New York
Source: *BioIn 7, 8; ObitOF 79; WhAm 5*

Bloor, "Mother" Ella Reeve
American. Feminist
Foremost American woman communist who organized women to vote in school elections.
b. Jul 8, 1862 in Staten Island, New York
d. Aug 10, 1951 in Richlandtown, Pennsylvania
Source: *BiDAmLL; BioIn 2, 3; DcAmB S5; LibW*

Blore, Eric
American. Actor
Best known for roles as butler in films, 1926-59.
b. Dec 23, 1887 in London, England
d. Mar 2, 1959 in Hollywood, California
Source: *Film 2; FilmgC; MotPP; MovMk; NotNAT B; Vers A; WhScrn 74, 77*

Blotta, Anthony
Italian. Fashion Designer
Opened NYC boutique, 1919; designed pant
suits for Marlene Dietrich in early 1930s.
b. in Italy
d. Sep 11, 1971 in New York
Source: *NewYTBE 71*

Blough, Glenn Orlando
American. Author, Educator
Wrote science books for young people:
Discovering Insects, 1967.
b. Sep 5, 1907 in Edmore, Michigan
Source: *AmAu&B; AuBYP; ConAu P-1;
LEduc 74; MorJA; SmATA 1; WhoAm 74,
76, 78, 80, 82*

Blough, Roger Miles
American. Lawyer, Businessman
Chairman, chief exec., US Steel, 1955-69,
during cos. dominatination of steel market.
b. Jan 19, 1904 in Riverside, Pennsylvania
d. Oct 8, 1985 in Hawley, Pennsylvania
Source: *CurBio 55, 86; IntWW 74; Who 74;
WhoAm 74, 76, 78, 80, 82; WhoWor 74*

Blount, Charles
English. Author
Deist, known for *The Two First Books of
Philostratus, Concerning Life of Apollonius
Tyaneus,* 1680.
b. Apr 27, 1654 in Upper Holloway, England
d. Aug 1693
Source: *Alli; BrAu; CasWL; DcBiPP; DcEnL;
LuthC 75; NewC*

Blount, Mel(vin Cornell)
American. Football Player
Defensive back, Pittsburgh, 1970-83; led NFL
in interceptions with 11, 1975.
b. Apr 10, 1948 in Vidalia, Georgia
Source: *WhoAm 80, 82, 84; WhoBlA 80*

Blount, Winton Malcolm
American. Businessman, Public Official
Board chairman, Blount, Inc., 1974--;
postmaster-general, 1969-71.
b. Feb 1, 1921 in Union Springs, Alabama
Source: *BiDrUSE; CurBio 69; IntWW 74;
NewYTBE 71; St&PR 75; WhoAm 74, 76,
78, 80, 82; WhoAmP 73; WhoS&SW 82*

Bloustein, Edward J
American. Author, Educator
Pres., Rutgers U. 1971--.
b. Jan 20, 1925 in New York, New York
Source: *ConAu 41R; CurBio 65; DrAS 74P;
LEduc 74; NewYTBE 71; WhoAm 74, 76, 78,
80, 82; WhoE 74; WhoWorJ 72*

Blow, Susan Elizabeth
American. Educator
Opened first kindergarten in US, in NY,
1871.
b. Jun 7, 1843 in Saint Louis, Missouri
d. Mar 26, 1916 in New York, New York
Source: *AmAu&B; AmBi; BiDAmEd; DcAmB;
DcNAA; IntDcWB; LibW; NotAW*

Bloy, Leon Marie
French. Author
Wrote autobiographical novels, *Le Desespere,*
1886; *La Femme Pauvre,* 1897.
b. Jul 11, 1846 in Perigueux, France
d. Nov 3, 1917 in Bourg-la-Reine, France
Source: *CasWL; ClDMEL; EncWL; EuAu;
EvEuW; OxFr; PenC EUR; REn*

Blucher, Gebhard Leberecht von
Russian. Field Marshal
Led Prussian army in Napoleon's defeat at
Laon; entered Paris, 1814; aided British at
Waterloo.
b. Dec 16, 1742 in Rostock, Germany
d. Sep 12, 1819 in Schlesian, Germany
Source: *CelCen; DcBiPP; Dis&D; LinLib S;
McGEWB; OxGer; WhoMilH 76*

Blucker, Robert Olof
[The Hostages]
American. Hostage in Iran
b. Oct 21, 1927 in North Little Rock,
Arkansas
Source: *BioIn 12; NewYTBS 81; USBiR 74*

Blue, Ben
[Benjamin Bernstein]
Canadian. Comedian, Dancer
Vaudeville star 1916; appeared in film *It's a
Mad, Mad, Mad, Mad World,* 1963.
b. Sep 12, 1901 in Montreal, Quebec
d. Mar 7, 1975 in Los Angeles, California
Source: *FilmgC; IntMPA 75; MovMk; WhScrn
77*

Blue, Monte
American. Actor
Appeared in 200 films, 1915-54; playing
romantic leads, 1920s: *Orphans of the
Storm,* 1922.
b. Jan 11, 1890 in Indianapolis, Indiana
d. Feb 18, 1963 in Milwaukee, Wisconsin
Source: *Film 1; FilmgC; MotPP; MovMk;
NotNAT B; TwYS; Vers A; WhScrn 74, 77;
WhoHol B*

Blue, Vida Rochelle
American. Baseball Player
Fifth pitcher to win Cy Young Award, MVP
  in same year, 1971.
b. Jul 28, 1949 in Mansfield, Louisiana
Source: *BaseEn 85; CelR; CurBio 72;*
NewYTBE 71; NewYTBS 74; WhoAm 74, 76,
78, 80, 82; WhoBlA 75; WhoProB 73

Blue Oyster Cult
[Eric Bloom; Albert Bouchard; Joe Bouchard;
  Rick Downey; Allen Lanier; Donald 'Buck
  Dharma' Roeser]
American. Music Group
Major heavy metal band; hit single "Don't
  Fear the Reaper," 1976.
Source: *ConMuA 80A; LilREn 78; RkOn 85;*
RolSEnR 83; WhoRock 81

Bluford, Guion Stewart, Jr.
American. Astronaut
First black American to fly in space aboard
  space shuttle *Challenger*, 1983.
b. Nov 22, 1942 in Philadelphia,
  Pennsylvania
Source: *AmM&WS 82P; CurBio 84; InB&W*
80; NewYTBS 83; WhoBlA 80

Bluhdorn, Charles G
American. Corporation Executive
Founder, chairman, Gulf & Western
  Industries, Inc., 1958-83.
b. Sep 20, 1926 in Vienna, Austria
d. Feb 19, 1983
Source: *IntWW 75, 76, 77, 78, 79, 80, 81;*
St&PR 75; WhAm 8; WhoAm 74, 76, 78, 80,
82; WhoE 74; WhoF&I 74; WhoWor 78

Blum, Leon
French. Statesman
Socialist premier of France, 1936-38;
  imprisoned by Vichy govt., 1940-45.
b. Apr 9, 1872 in Paris, France
d. Mar 30, 1950 in Versailles, France
Source: *ClDMEL; CurBio 40, 50; OxFr; REn;*
WhAm 2

Blum, Stella
American. Museum Director
First costume curator at Costume Institute of
  Metropolitan Museum of Art, 1970-82.
b. Oct 19, 1916 in Schenectady, New York
d. Jul 31, 1985 in Ravenna, Ohio
Source: *ConAu 97; WhoAm 84*

Blumberg, Judy
American. Figure Skater
With Michael Seibert, won bronze medal in
  ice dancing at 1983 world champhionships.
b. 1957 in Santa Monica, California
Source: *BioIn 12; NewYTBS 83, 84*

Blume, Judy Sussman
American. Author
Wrote *Are You There God? It's Me*
Margaret, 1970; *Wifey*, 1978.
b. Feb 12, 1938 in Elizabeth, New Jersey
Source: *ChlLR 2; ConAu 29R; CurBio 80;*
PiP; SmATA 2; WhoAm 80, 82; WrDr 76

Blume, Peter
American. Artist
Surrealist painter with meticulous style: "The
  Eternal City," 1937.
b. Oct 27, 1906 in Russia
Source: *BnEnAmA; CurBio 56; DcAmArt;*
DcCAA 71, 77; IntWW 74, 75, 76, 77, 78;
McGDA; WhoAm 76, 78, 80, 82, 84;
WhoAmA 73, 76, 78; WhoE 74

Blumenbach, Johann Friedrich
German. Physiologist
Founder of modern anthropology; wrote
  Handbook of Natural History, 1779.
b. May 11, 1752 in Gotha, Germany
d. Jan 22, 1840 in Goettingen, Germany
Source: *CelCen; DcBiPP; DcScB S1; Dis&D;*
InSci; LinLib L, S

Blumenfeld, Isadore
"Kid Cann"
American. Criminal
Bootlegger acquitted in kidnapping, murder,
  fraud charges; finally convicted, jailed for
  jury tampering, 1961-67.
b. 1901 in Minneapolis, Minnesota
d. 1981 in New York, New York
Source: *BioIn 12*

Blumenthal, Monica David
American. Psychiatrist, Educator
Expert on violence, geriatric psychiatry; won
  Emmy for "What Shall We Do About
  Mother?" 1980.
b. Sep 1, 1930 in Tubingen, Germany
d. Mar 16, 1981 in Pittsburgh, Pennsylvania
Source: *AmM&WS 73P, 76P, 79P; BiDrAPA*
77; ConAu 103, 73; NewYTBS 81; WhoAmW
74

Blumenthal, W Michael
American. Corporation Executive,
  Government Official
Secretary of Treasury, 1977-79, Carter
  administration, 1977-79; chairman of
  Burroughs Corp., 1981--.
b. Jan 3, 1926 in Berlin, Germany
Source: *AmEA 74; BusPN; IntWW 74;*
NewYTBE 72; St&PR 75; WhoAm 82, 84

Blunden, Edmund Charles
English. Poet, Critic
Named to Oxford's poetry chair, 1966;
author *War Poets, 1914-18,* 1962.
b. Nov 1, 1896 in London, England
d. Jan 20, 1974 in Sudbury, England
Source: *Au&Wr 71; CasWL; Chambr 3;
ChhPo, S1, S2; CnE&AP; ConAu 17R, 45, P-
2; ConLC 2; ConP 70, 75; DcLEL; EncWL;
EvLB; LongCTC; ModBrL, S1; NewC;
OxEng; PenC ENG; RAdv 1; REn; TwCA,
SUP; TwCWr; WebE&AL; WhoTwCL*

Blunstone, Colin
[The Zombies]
English. Musician
Rock singer; founded the Zombies, 1962; solo
album *Journey,* 1974.
b. Jun 24, 1945 in Hatfield, England
Source: *WhoRock 81; WhoRocM 82*

Blunt, Anthony Frederick
English. Art Historian, Spy
Queen Elizabeth's art curator, 1945-79, who
was fourth man in Burgess-Philby-Maclean
spy ring.
b. Sep 26, 1907 in Bournemouth, England
d. Mar 26, 1983 in London, England
Source: *ConAu 109; IntAu&W 82; IntWW
82, 83; NewYTBS 79, 83; Who
82, 83; WhoArt 80; WhoWest 80; WrDr 84*

Blunt, Wilfrid Scawen
English. Poet, Politician, Traveler
Colorful Victorian, whose writings include
lyric verse, *Love Sonnets of Proteus,* 1881.
b. Aug 14, 1840 in Crawley, England
d. Sep 10, 1922 in London, England
Source: *BbD; BiD&SB; BrAu 19; Chambr 3;
DcEnA, AP; EvLB; ModBrL; NewC; OxEng;
PenC ENG; REn; WebE&AL*

Bly, Nellie, pseud.
[Elizabeth Cochrane Seaman]
American. Journalist
Wrote muckraking articles on prisons,
asylums; author *Around the World in 72
Days,* 1890.
b. May 5, 1867 in Cochrane's Mill,
Pennsylvania
d. Jan 27, 1922 in New York, New York
Source: *AmAu; AmAu&B; CnDAL; DcAmB;
DcNAA; HerW; InWom; NotAW; OxAmL;
REn; REnAL; WebAB; WhAm HSA, 4*

Bly, Robert Elwood
American. Poet
Won National Book Award for *The Light
Around the Body,* 1968.
b. Dec 23, 1926 in Madison, Minnesota
Source: *CurBio 84; RAdv 1; WebE&AL;
WhoAm 80, 82; WhoTwCL; WhoWor 74;
WorAu; WrDr 76*

Blyden, Larry
[Ivan Lawrence Blieden]
American. Actor, TV Personality
Made stage debut in *Mr. Roberts,* 1948; in
film *On a Clear Day You Can See
Forever,* 1969.
b. Jun 23, 1925 in Houston, Texas
d. Jun 6, 1975 in Agadir, Morocco
Source: *BiE&WWA; FilmgC; IntMPA 75;
NewYTBS 84; NotNAT; WhAm 6; WhScrn
77; WhoAm 74; WhoThe 72, 77*

Blyleven, Bert (Rikalbert)
American. Baseball Player
Pitcher, 1970--; 11th in ML history to record
3,000 strikeouts, 1986.
b. Apr 6, 1951 in Zeist, Netherlands
Source: *BaseEn 85; BaseReg 86; NewYTBS
81; PseudN 82*

Blyth, Ann Marie
American. Actress
Received Oscar nomination for *Mildred
Pierce,* 1945.
b. Aug 16, 1928 in Mount Kisco, New York
Source: *CmpEPM; FilmgC; HolP 40; IntMPA
75, 76, 77, 78, 79, 80, 81, 82; MotPP;
MovMk; WhoAm 74; WomWMM; WorAl;
WorEFlm*

Blyth, Chay
British. Author, Adventurer
Circumnavigated globe alone in yacht, 1970-
71; wrote *The Impossible Voyage,* 1972.
b. 1940 in Hawick, England
Source: *IntAu&W 76; OxShips; WrDr 76, 80,
82*

Blythe, Betty
[Elizabeth Blythe Slaughter]
American. Actress
Popular Vitagraph silent star; title role in
Queen of Sheba, 1921.
b. Sep 1, 1893 in Los Angeles, California
d. Apr 7, 1972 in Woodland Hills, California
Source: *Film 2; FilmgC; MotPP; MovMk;
WhScrn 77; WhoHol B*

Blythe, David Gilmour
American. Artist
Self taught, satiric, genre painter, who drew
  mostly PA, Civil War scenes.
b. May 9, 1815 in East Liverpool, Ohio
d. May 15, 1865 in East Liverpool, Ohio
Source: *BioIn 1, 2, 6, 10; BnEnAmA;*
DcAmArt; McGDA; NewYHSD; WhAm HS

Blyton, Carey
English. Author, Composer
b. Mar 14, 1932 in Beckenham, England
Source: *ChhPo S2; ConAu 49; SmATA 9;*
WhoMus 72

Blyton, Enid Mary
[Mary Pollock, psued.]
English. Author
Wrote over 400 children's stories, 1922-68,
  including *The Secret Seven* adventure
  series, 1949-54.
b. Aug 11, 1897 in East Dulwich, England
d. Nov 28, 1968 in London, England
Source: *AuBYP; ChhPo, S1, S2; ConAu 25R,*
77; LongCTC; ObitT 1961; SmATA 25;
TwCCW 78; WhFla; WhoChL

Boadicea
[Boudicca]
Ruler
Queen of Iceni, AD60, who raised rebellion
  against Romans in Britain.
d. 62
Source: *DcBiPP; GoodHs; InWom; LongCEL;*
NewC; WhDW

Board, Lillian
English. Track Athlete
b. 1948
d. Dec 26, 1970 in Munich, Germany (West)
Source: *BioIn 9, 11; NewYTBE 70*

Boas, Franz
American. Anthropologist, Educator, Explorer
Authority on primative art, American
  Indians; wrote *Primative Art,* 1927.
b. Jul 9, 1858 in Minden, Germany
d. Dec 21, 1942 in New York, New York
Source: *AmAu&B; AmLY; CurBio 40, 43;*
DcAmAu; DcAmB S3; DcNAA; EncAB-H;
OxAmL; OxCan, SUP; REnAL; TwCA SUP;
WebAB; WhAm 2; WhNAA

Bob and Ray
see: Elliott, Bob; Goulding, Ray

Bobbs, William Conrad
American. Publisher
Worked for Merrill, Meigs & Co.,
  booksellers, 1879; pres., Bobbs-Merrill Co.,
  1895.
b. Jan 25, 1861 in Montgomery, Ohio
d. Feb 11, 1926
Source: *LinLib L; WhAm 1*

Bobst, Elmer Holmes
"The Vitamin King"
American. Corporation Executive
Pres., chm., Warner-Lambert Pharmaceutical
  Co., 1945-67.
b. Dec 16, 1884 in Clear Springs, Maryland
d. Aug 2, 1978 in New York, New York
Source: *ConAu 113; CurBio 73, 78*

Boccaccio, Giovanni
Italian. Author
Father of classical Italian prose; wrote *The*
  Decameron, 1353.
b. 1313 in Florence, Italy
d. Dec 21, 1375 in Certaldo, Italy
Source: *AtlBL; BbD; BiD&SB; CasWL;*
CyWA; DcBiA; DcEnL; DcEuL; EuAu;
EvEuW; NewC; OxEng; PenC EUR;
RComWL; REn

Boccherini, Luigi
Italian. Composer, Violinist
Prolific composer of chamber music; created
  the string quintet.
b. Feb 19, 1743 in Lucca, Italy
d. May 28, 1805 in Madrid, Spain
Source: *OxMus*

Boccioni, Umberto
Italian. Artist
Futurist painter, sculptor; helped draft
  Futurist Manifests, 1910.
b. 1882
d. 1916
Source: *OxArt*

Bochner, Hart
Canadian. Actor
Star of film *Breaking Away,* 1979; TV film
  "East of Eden," 1981.
b. Dec 3, 1956 in Toronto, Ontario
Source: *ConTFT 2; JohnWSW; NewYTBS 77;*
VarWW 85

Bochner, Lloyd
Canadian. Actor
Played Cecil Colby on TV's "Dynasty,"
  1981-83.
b. Jul 29, 1924 in Toronto, Ontario
Source: *FilmgC; WhoHol A*

Bocho, Steven
American. Writer, Producer
Co-creator of TV show "Hill Street Blues."
b. Dec 16, 1943
Source: *LesBEnT; NewYTET; WhoTelC*

Bock, Jerry (Jerrold Lewis)
American. Composer
Broadway scores include Pulitzer-winning
    Fiorello, 1959.
b. Nov 23, 1928 in New Haven, Connecticut
Source: *BiE&WWA; CelR; EncMT; IntWW
74; NewCBMT; NotNAT; WhoAm 74, 76, 78,
80, 84; WhoThe 77; WhoWor 74*

Bocklin, Arnold
Swiss. Artist
Moody landscapes, fantastic creatures
    presaged Surrealist art.
b. Oct 16, 1827 in Basel, Switzerland
d. Jan 16, 1901 in Domenico, Italy
Source: *AtlBL; OxGer*

Bocuse, Paul
French. Chef, Restaurateur
Wrote *Paul Bocuse's French Cooking;*
    associated with "novelle cuisine."
b. Feb 11, 1926 in Collonges, France
Source: *BioIn 8, 9, 10; BioNews 74;
NewYTBE 72; WhoFr 79; WorAl*

Bodanzky, Artur
American. Conductor
Conducted NYC Metropolitan Opera Co.,
    1915-29.
b. Dec 16, 1887 in Vienna, Austria
d. Nov 23, 1939 in New York, New York
Source: *CurBio 40; DcAmB S2; WhAm 1*

Bodard, Lucien Albert
French. Journalist, Author
Wrote award-winning novel *Annie-Marie,*
    1981.
b. Jan 3, 1914 in Chungking, China
Source: *ConAu 116*

Boddicker, Mike (Michael James)
American. Baseball Player
Pitcher, Baltimore, 1980--; pitched three-hitter
    in World Series, 1983; led AL in wins,
    1984.
b. Aug 23, 1957 in Cedar Rapids, Iowa
Source: *BaseEn 85; BaseReg 86*

Bode, Carl
American. Author, Educator
Works on American literature include
    Portable Thoreau, 1947; *Portable Emerson,*
    1981.
b. Mar 14, 1911 in Milwaukee, Wisconsin
Source: *AmAu&B; Au&Wr 71; ConAu 1R,
3NR; DrAS 74E; WhoAm 74, 76, 78, 80, 82;
WhoWor 78; WrDr 76*

Bode, Vaughn
American. Cartoonist
b. 1941
Source: *BioIn 10*

Bodenheim, Maxwell
American. Author, Poet
Sardonic writings include poem *Bringing Jazz,*
    1930; novel *Crazy Man,* 1924.
b. May 23, 1893 in Hermanville, Mississippi
d. Feb 6, 1954 in New York, New York
Source: *AmAu&B; CnDAL; ConAmL; DcLEL;
ModAL; OxAmL; PenC AM; REn; REnAL;
TwCA, SUP; WebAB; WhAm 3*

Bodley, Thomas, Sir
English. Diplomat, Scholar
Organized Oxford University's famed Bodley
    Library, opened 1602.
b. 1545 in Exeter, England
d. Jan 28, 1613 in London, England
Source: *Alli; CasWL; CroE&S; DcEuL;
DcLEL; EvLB; NewC*

Bodmer, Johann Jakob
Swiss. Critic, Poet, Translator
Noted for editions of medieval German
    literature.
b. Jul 19, 1698 in Greifensee, Switzerland
d. Jan 2, 1783 in Zurich, Switzerland
Source: *BiD&SB; CasWL; DcEuL; EuAu;
EvEuW; OxGer; PenC EUR; REn*

Bodmer, Karl
Swiss. Artist, Explorer
Toured America, 1832-34, painting
    landscapes, Great Plains Indians.
b. Feb 6, 1809 in Riesbach, Switzerland
d. Oct 30, 1893 in Babizon, France
Source: *ApCAB; WhAm HS*

Bodoni, Giambattista
Italian. Designer, Typographer
Amoung first to use modern typefaces;
    designed Bodoni type, 1790.
b. 1740
d. 1813
Source: *WebBD 80*

Bodsworth, Charles Frederick
Canadian. Naturalist, Author, Journalist
Nature books include *Wilderness Canada*,
1970.
b. Oct 11, 1918 in Port Burwell, Quebec
Source: *ConAu 1R, 3NR; WhoAm 82*

Boehm, Edward M
American. Sculptor
Founded fine porcelain sculpture co.,
Trenton, NJ, 1950.
b. Aug 21, 1913 in Baltimore, Maryland
d. Jan 29, 1969 in Trenton, New Jersey
Source: *WhAm 5*

Boehm, Eric Hartzell
American. Publisher, Author
Consultant on books on bibliographies,
computer use, information systems; editor
Historical Abstracts, 1955-83.
b. Jul 15, 1918 in Hof, Germany
Source: *BlueB 76; ConAu 13R; DrAS 74H,
78H; WhoAm 76, 78, 80, 82, 84; WhoWor 80*

Boehm, Helen Francesca Stefanie Franzolin
[Mrs. Edward Marshall Boehm]
American. Business Executive
Widow of porcelain sculptor Edward Boehm;
owner of $35 million a yr. Boehm Co.
race horse breeder.
b. 1922 in Brooklyn, New York
Source: *NewYTBS 76, 77*

Boehm, Karl
see: Bohm, Karl

Boehme, Jakob
German. Mystic, Religious Leader
Claimed divine revelation; wrote *Mysterium
Magnum*, 1623.
b. 1575 in Gorlitz, Prussia
d. 1624
Source: *REn*

Boeing, William Edward
American. Airplane Manufacturer
Founded Boeing Aircraft, 1916, United
Aircraft and Transport, 1928.
b. Oct 1, 1881 in Detroit, Michigan
d. Sep 28, 1956 in Seattle, Washington
Source: *DcAmB S6; InSci; ObitOF 79; WhAm
3*

Boerhaave, Herman
Dutch. Physician, Educator
Founded modern system of clinical medical
instruction, 1708.
b. Dec 31, 1668
d. Sep 23, 1738
Source: *BioIn 4, 5, 6, 8, 9, 10*

Boethius
Roman. Philosopher, Translator
Credited with introducing Aristotle to
western world.
b. 475
d. 524
Source: *NewCol 75; WebBD 80*

Boettiger, John
American. Author, Newspaperman
Son-in-law of Franklin Roosevelt; publisher,
Seattle *Post-Intelligencer*, 1936-45.
b. Mar 25, 1900 in Chicago, Illinois
d. Oct 31, 1950 in New York, New York
Source: *ObitOF 79; WhAm 3*

Boeynants, Paul Vanden
Belgian. Political Leader
b. May 22, 1919
Source: *IntWW 74*

Bofill, Angela
American. Singer, Songwriter
Album *Something About You* was in top five
on jazz charts.
b. 1955 in New York, New York
Source: *BioIn 12; InB&W 80; WhoBlA 80*

Bogan, Louise
American. Poet, Critic
Wrote *Body of This Death*, 1923; *A Poet's
Alphabet*, 1970.
b. Aug 11, 1897 in Livermore Falls, Maine
d. Feb 4, 1970 in New York, New York
Source: *AmAu&B; AuBYP; ChhPo; CnDAL;
CnE&AP; ConAmA; ConAu 25R, 73; ConLC
4; ConP 70; DcLEL; EncWL; InWom;
ModAL, S1; NewYTBE 70; OxAmL; PenC
AM; RAdv 1; REn; REnAL; SixAP; TwCA,
SUP; TwCWr; WhAm 5*

Bogarde, Dirk
[Derek Niven van den Bogaerde]
English. Actor, Author
Won British Academy Award for *The
Servant*, 1963; *Darling*, 1965.
b. Mar 29, 1921 in London, England
Source: *BiDFilm; CelR; CmMov; ConAu 77;
CurBio 67; FilmgC; IntMPA 75, 76, 77, 78,
79, 80, 81, 82; IntWW 74; MotPP; MovMk;
OxFilm; Who 82; WhoHol A; WhoThe 77A;
WhoWor 78; WorEFlm*

Bogart, Humphrey de Forest
"Bogey"
American. Actor
Starred in *Casablanca*, 1942; won Oscar for
The African Queen, 1951.
b. Dec 25, 1899 in New York, New York
d. Jan 14, 1957 in Los Angeles, California
Source: *BiDFilm; CmMov; CurBio 42, 57;
FilmgC; MotPP; MovMk; OxFilm; WebAB;
WhAm 3; WhScrn 74, 77; WhoHol B;
WorEFlm*

Bogart, Leo
American. Author, Sociologist
Public opinion researcher who wrote *Silent
Politics*, 1972.
b. Sep 23, 1921
Source: *ConAu 41R; WhoE 74*

Bogart, Neil
[Neil Bogatz]
American. Business Executive, Producer
Founder, 1974, pres., Casablanca Record and
Film Works.
b. Feb 3, 1943 in Brooklyn, New York
d. May 8, 1982 in Los Angeles, California
Source: *AnObit 1982; IntMPA 80, 81, 82;
WhAm 8; WhoAm 78, 80, 82; WhoWest 80,
82*

Bogatja, Vinto
Yugoslav. Skier
Epitomizes "agony of defeat" for ABC's
"Wide World of Sports."
Source: *NF*

Bogdanovich, Peter
American. Director, Producer
Won NY Film Critics Award, best
screenplay for *The Last Picture Show*,
1971.
b. Jul 30, 1939 in Kingston, New York
Source: *BiDFilm; BioNews 74; CelR; ConAu
5R; CurBio 72; IntMPA 75, 76, 77, 78, 79,
80, 81, 82; MovMk; WhoAm 74, 76, 78, 80,
82; WhoWor 78; WorAl; WrDr 76, 82*

Bogert, Tim
[Vanilla Fudge]
American. Singer, Musician
Bassist, vocalist with group formed 1966.
b. Aug 27, 1944 in Manhattan, New York
Source: *NF*

Boggs, Hale (Thomas Hale)
American. Politician
Congressman, 1941-43, 1947-72; lost in
Alaska plane crash.
b. Feb 15, 1914 in Long Beach, Mississippi
d. Oct 1972 in Alaska
Source: *BiDrAC; CurBio 58; NewYTBE 71;
WhAm 5; WhAmP; WhoGov 75; WhoS&SW
82*

Boggs, Lindy
[Mrs. Hale Boggs]
American. Politician
b. Mar 13, 1916 in Brunswick, Louisiana
Source: *NewYTBE 71; WomPO 76*

Boggs, Tom (Thomas)
[The Box Tops]
American. Musician
Drummer with Memphis-based, blue-eyed
soul group, 1966-70.
b. Jul 16, 1947 in Wynn, Arkansas
Source: *NF*

Boggs, Wade Anthony
American. Baseball Player
Infielder, Boston, 1982--; won AL batting
title, 1983, 1985.
b. Jun 15, 1958 in Omaha, Nebraska
Source: *BaseEn 85; BaseReg 86*

Bogner, Willi
German. Designer
Source: *WorFshn*

Bohannon, Judy (Judith Layton)
[Judy Fields]
American. Actress
Starred in TV soap opera "Capitol," 1982-83.
b. Jun 30, in Louisville, Kentucky
Source: *ConTFT 2*

Bohay, Heidi
American. Actress
Plays Megan Kendal on TV series "Hotel,"
1983--.
b. in Bound Brook, New Jersey
Source: *ConTFT 3*

Bohlem, Arndt von
German. Celebrity Relative
Last heir to Krupp industrial fortune.
b. 1938
d. May 13, 1986 in Essen, Germany (West)
Source: *NewYTBS 86*

Bohlen, Charles Eustis
American. Diplomat
Expert on Russian affairs for US foreign
service, 1930s-70s.
b. Aug 30, 1904 in Clayton, New York
d. Jan 2, 1974 in Washington, District of
Columbia
Source: *CurBio 48, 60, 74; EncAB-H;
NewYTBS 74; WhAm 6; Who 74; WhoAm
74; WhoAmP 73*

Bohm, Karl
[Karl Boehm]
Austrian. Conductor
Noted for interpretations of Mozart, Wagner,
Strauss; usually associated with Vienna
Philharmonic, Salzburg Festival.
b. Aug 28, 1894 in Graz, Austria
d. Aug 14, 1981 in Salzburg, Austria
Source: *Baker 78; CelR; CurBio 68, 81;
IntWW 75, 77, 78; MusSN; NewEOp 71;
NewYTBE 72; NewYTBS 81; WhAm 8;
WhoAm 76, 78, 80, 82; WhoMus 72; WhoOp
76; WhoWor 74*

Bohm von Bawerk, Eugene
Austrian. Economist, Politician
Introduced theory of interest; wrote *Kapital
and Kapitalzins,* 1884-89.
b. 1851
d. 1914
Source: *BioIn 2, 8*

Bohme, Jacob
see: Boehme, Jakob

Bohr, Niels Henrik David
Danish. Physicist
Helped develop atom bomb in Los Alamos,
NM, 1943-45.
b. Oct 7, 1885 in Copenhagen, Denmark
d. Nov 18, 1962 in Copenhagen, Denmark
Source: *CurBio 45, 63; OxEng; WhAm 4*

Bohrod, Aaron
American. Artist
b. Nov 21, 1907 in Chicago, Illinois
Source: *ConAu 21R; CurBio 55; DcCAA 71;
WhoAm 74, 76, 78, 80, 82; WhoAmA 73;
WhoWor 78; WhoWorJ 72*

Boiardi, Hector
American. Chef, Manufacturer
Founded Chef Boy-ar-dee Foods, 1928, pres.
until 1946.
b. 1897 in Piacenza, Italy
d. Jun 21, 1985 in Parma, Ohio
Source: *ConNews 85-3*

Boiardo, Matteo Maria
Italian. Poet
Famous for unfinished epic poem on
Charlemagne, *Orlando Innamorato,* 1487.
b. 1441 in Scandiano, Italy
d. 1494 in Reggio Emilia, Italy
Source: *CasWL; CyWA; DcEnL; DcEuL;
DcItL; EuAu; EvEuW; LinLib L; McGEWB;
OxEng; PenC EUR; RComWL; REn; WhDW*

Boieldieu, Francois Adrien
French. Composer
Wrote piano music, scores of comic operas
including *Jean de Paris,* 1812.
b. Dec 16, 1775 in Rouen, France
d. Oct 8, 1834 in Jarcy, France
Source: *OxFr*

Boileau(-Despreaux), Nicolas
"Legislator of Parnassus"
French. Author, Poet, Critic
Chief work is the poem *Art Poetique,* 1674.
b. Nov 1, 1636 in Paris, France
d. Mar 13, 1711
Source: *AtlBL; BbD; BiD&SB; CasWL;
CyWA; DcBiPP; DcCathB; DcEuL; EuAu;
EvEuW; OxEng; OxFr; OxThe; PenC EUR;
RComWL; REn; WhDW*

Bois, Guy Pene du
see: DeBois, Guy Pene

Bois, William Edward du
see: DuBois, William Edward Burghardt

Boit, Mike
American. Track Athlete
Source: *NF*

Boito, Arrigo
Italian. Composer, Librettist
Wrote play *Mefistofele,* 1868, based on
Goethe's *Faust.*
b. Feb 24, 1842 in Padua, Italy
d. Jun 10, 1918 in Milan, Italy
Source: *AtlBL; BiD&SB; CasWL; ClDMEL;
EuAu; EvEuW; OxThe; PenC EUR; REn*

Boivin, Leo Joseph
Canadian. Hockey Player
Defenseman, 1958-70 who played for five
NHL teams; Hall of Fame, 1986.
b. Aug 2, 1932 in Prescott, Ontario
Source: *BioIn 8; HocEn; WhoHcky 73*

Bojangles
see: Robinson, Bill

Bojer, Johan
Norwegian. Author
Best known work is *The Great Hunger,* 1916.
b. Mar 6, 1872 in Orkesdalsoren, Norway
d. Jul 3, 1959
Source: *CasWL; ClDMEL; CyWA; DcBiA; EncWL, 2; EvEuW; LinLib L; LongCTC; OxAmL; PenC EUR; REn; REnAL; TwCA, SUP; WhAm 3; WhoLA*

Bok, Bart J(an)
American. Astronomer
Leading authority on Milky Way; wrote *The Milky Way,* definitive source of information on galaxy, 1941.
b. Apr 28, 1906 in Hoorn, Netherlands
d. Aug 5, 1983 in Tucson, Arizona
Source: *AmM&WS 82P; BiESc; ConAu 110, 49; IntWW 80, 81, 82, 83; NewYTBS 83; WhoAm 80, 82; WrDr 82, 84*

Bok, Derek Curtis
American. Educator, University Administrator
Law professor; pres. of Harvard, 1971--.
b. Mar 22, 1930 in Bryn Mawr, Pennsylvania
Source: *CelR; CurBio 71; DrAS 74P; IntWW 74, 82; LEduc 74; Who 74, 82; WhoAm 74, 76, 78, 80, 82; WhoE 74, 81*

Bok, Edward William
American. Editor, Author
Editor *Ladies Home Journal,* 1889-1919; won Pulitzer for *The Americanization of Edward Bok,* 1920.
b. Oct 9, 1863 in Den Helder, New Hampshire
d. Jan 9, 1930 in Lake Wales, Florida
Source: *Alli SUP; AmAu&B; AmBi; BiD&SB; DcAmAu; DcAmB S1; DcLEL; DcNAA; EncAB-H; LinLib L; NatCAB 23; OxAmL; REn; REnAL; TwCA, SUP; WebAB, 79; WhAm 1; WhAmP; WhNAA*

Bok, Hannes Vajn
[Dolbokov, joint pseud.]
American. Artist, Author
Famed fantasy illustrator who drew woodcut-like scenes for *Weird Tales.*
b. Jul 2, 1914 in Minnesota
d. Apr 11, 1964 in New York
Source: *EncSF; FanAl; PseudN 82; ScF&FL 1; WhoHr&F; WhoSciF*

Bokassa I (Jean Bedel)
African. Political Leader
Took control of Central African Empire, 1966; named pres., for life, 1972; crowned emperor, 1977.
b. Feb 21, 1921 in Boubangui, Africa
Source: *BioIn 10, 11; CurBio 78; IntYB 79; WorDWW*

Bol, Manute
Sudanese. Basketball Player
Dinka tribesman who is 7'6"; drafted by Washington Bullets, 1985.
b. in Gogrial, Sudan
Source: *OfNBA 85*

Bolan, Marc
[Mark Feld; T. Rex]
English. Musician
Co-founder, lead vocalist, T. Rex; died in car crash; recorded 16 albums including *Slider,* 1972.
b. May 8, 1948 in London, England
d. Sep 16, 1977 in London, England
Source: *BioIn 11; ObitOF 79; PseudN 82; RolSEnR 83; WhoRock 81*

Boland, Mary
American. Actress
Played opposite Charles Ruggles in many 30s films including *Ruggles of Red Gap,* 1935.
b. Jan 28, 1880 in Philadelphia, Pennsylvania
d. Jun 23, 1965 in New York, New York
Source: *BiE&WWA; EncMT; Film 1; FilmgC; InWom; MotPP; MovMk; NotNAT B; ThFT; TwYS; Vers A; WhAm 4; WhScrn 74, 77; WhoHol A*

Bolcom, William Elden
American. Composer, Musician
b. May 26, 1938 in Seattle, Washington
Source: *DcCM; WhoAm 74; WhoE 74*

Bolden, "Buddy" (Charles)
American. Jazz Musician
Cornettist who is credited with originating jazz, 1890s.
b. 1868 in New Orleans, Louisiana
d. Nov 4, 1931 in New Orleans, Louisiana
Source: *WebAB; WhAm HSA, 4; WhoJazz 72*

Boles, John
American. Actor
Leading man of 30s-40s; films include *Curly Top,* 1935; *The Littlest Rebel,* 1935; *Stella Dallas,* 1937.
b. Oct 18, 1895 in Greenville, Texas
d. Feb 27, 1969 in San Angelo, Texas
Source: *BiE&WWA; EncMT; Film 2; FilmgC; HolP 30; MovMk; ObitOF 79; TwYS; WhAm 5; WhScrn 74, 77; WhoHol B*

Boles, Paul Darcy
American. Author
Wrote of small-town American life in novels
   The Beggars in the Sun, 1954; *Glenport,*
   Illinois, 1956.
b. Mar 5, 1919 in Auburn, Idaho
d. May 4, 1984 in Atlanta, Georgia
Source: *ConAu 4NR, 9R; CurBio 56, 84;*
   IndAu 1917; SmATA 9; WhoS&SW 75

Bolet, Jorge
Cuban. Musician
Piano virtuoso, specializing in Liszt, Chopin.
b. Nov 15, 1914 in Havana, Cuba
Source: *Baker 78; BioIn 3, 4, 10; MusSN;*
   NewYTBE 73; WhoAm 76, 78; WhoMus 72

Boley, Forrest Irving
American. Educator, Physicist, Author
Dartmonth physics professor, 1964--; editor
   Cemenial Journal of Physics, 1966-73.
b. Nov 27, 1925 in Fort Madison, Iowa
Source: *BioIn 9; WhoAm 74, 76, 78, 80, 82*

Boleyn, Anne
English. Consort
Second wife of Henry VIII, whose marriage
   was voided by church, May 17, 1536;
   mother of Elizabeth I.
b. 1507
d. May 19, 1536 in London, England
Source: *DcBiPP; Dis&D; InWom; LinLib S;*
   NewC; NewCol 75; REn

Bolger, Ray
American. Actor, Dancer
Show business veteran best known for
   playing the Scarecrow in *The Wizard of*
   Oz, 1939.
b. Jan 10, 1904 in Boston, Massachusetts
Source: *BiE&WWA; CmMov; ConTFT 3;*
   CurBio 42; EncMT; FilmgC; IntMPA 82;
   MovMk; NotNAT; WhoAm 84; WhoThe 77;
   WhoWor 78

Bolger, William Frederick
American. Government Official
Joined postal service, 1941; Postmaster
   General, 1978.
b. Mar 13, 1923 in Waterbury, Connecticut
Source: *CurBio 79; IntWW 82; NewYTBS 78;*
   WhoAm 80, 82

Bolingbroke, Henry
see: Henry IV

Bolingbroke, Henry St. John, Viscount
English. Statesman, Author
b. Oct 1, 1678 in London, England
d. Dec 12, 1751 in Battersea, England
Source: *Alli; BbD; BiD&SB; BiDLA; BrAu;*
   CasWL; Chambr 2; DcEnA; DcEnL; DcLEL

Bolinger, Dwight Lemerton
American. Author, Educator
Wrote *Aspects of Language,* 1968.
b. Aug 18, 1907 in Topeka, Kansas
Source: *ConAu 13R; DcSpL; WrDr 80*

Bolitho, Henry Hector
New Zealander. Author, Lecturer
Wrote *Reign of Queen Victoria,* 1948; *No. 10*
   Downing Street, 1957.
b. May 28, 1897 in New Zealand
d. 1974
Source: *Au&Wr 71; ConAu 53, P-1; DcLEL;*
   EvLB; IntWW 74; LongCTC; NewC; PenC
   ENG; TwCA, SUP; Who 74; WhoWor 78

Bolitho, William
[William Bolitho Ryall]
Author, Journalist
b. 1890 in Capetown, South Africa
d. Jun 2, 1930 in Avignon, France
Source: *DcLEL; LongCTC; NewC; TwCA*

Bolivar, Simon
"El Libertador"
Venezuelan. Revolutionary, Statesman
Led armies against Spanish in S America;
   resulted in creation of six nations.
b. Jul 24, 1783 in Caracas, Venezuela
d. Dec 17, 1830 in Santa Marta, Colombia
Source: *ApCAB; BioIn 1, 2, 3, 4, 5, 6, 7, 8,*
   9, 10, 11; CasWL; DcSpL; Drake; LinLib S;
   McGEWB; NewCol 75; PenC AM; REn;
   WhAm HS; WhoMilH 76

Boll, Heinrich
German. Author
Won Nobel Prize, 1972, for works dealing
   with drift of German society during Nazi,
   post-war periods.
b. Dec 21, 1917 in Cologne, Germany (West)
d. Jul 16, 1985 in Hurtgenwald, Germany
   (West)
Source: *CasWL; CelR; ConAu 116; ConLC 2,*
   3, 6; CurBio 72, 85; EncWL; EvEuW;
   IntWW 74; ModGL; NewYTBE 72; NewYTBS
   74; OxGer; PenC EUR; REn; TwCWr; Who
   74; WhoAm 82; WhoTwCL; WhoWor 78;
   WorAu

Boller, Paul F, Jr.
American. Author, Educator
Wrote *This is Our Nation,* 1961.
b. Dec 31, 1916 in Spring Lake, New Jersey
Source: *ConAu 1R; DrAS 74F*

Bolles, Don F
American. Journalist
Investigative reporter for *Arizona Republic;*
killed in car bomb explosion.
b. 1928 in Milwaukee, Wisconsin
d. Jun 13, 1976 in Phoenix, Arizona
Source: *BioIn 10; ConAu 65, 73; ObitOF 79*

Bologna, Joseph
American. Actor, Writer
Films include *My Favorite Year,* 1982; *Blame It on Rio,* 1984.
b. 1938 in Brooklyn, New York
Source: *ConTFT 3*

Bolotowsky, Ilya
American. Artist, Sculptor
Painter, known for diamond-shaped canvases;
co-founder, American Abstract Artists,
1936.
b. Jul 1, 1907 in Saint Petersburg, Russia
d. Nov 21, 1981 in New York, New York
Source: *BioIn 9, 10, 11; BnEnAmA; ConArt 77; CurBio 75, 82; DcAmArt; DcCAA 77; NewYTBS 81; WhAm 8; WhoAm 78, 80; WhoAmA 78; WhoWorJ 72*

Bolt, Carol
Canadian. Dramatist
Plays include *Cyclone Jack,* 1972.
b. Aug 25, 1941 in Winnipeg, Manitoba
Source: *ConAu 101; ConDr 77; OxCan SUP; WrDr 80*

Bolt, Robert
English. Author
Plays include award-winning *Man for All Seasons,* 1960; won Oscar for *Dr. Zhivago* screenplay, 1965.
b. Aug 15, 1924 in Manchester, England
Source: *BiE&WWA; CasWL; CelR; CnThe; ConAu 17R; ConDr 73, 82; ConLC 14; CroCD; IntMPA 79, 80, 81, 82; McGEWD; ModWD; NewC; NotNAT; OxThe; PenC ENG; REnWD; TwCWr; WebE&AL; WhoThe 77, 81; WhoWor 74; WorAu; WorEFlm; WrDr 76, 82*

Bolt, Tommy (Thomas)
American. Golfer
b. Mar 31, 1918 in Haworth, Oklahoma
Source: *BioIn 5, 6, 11; WhoGolf*

Bolton, Frances Payne
American. Politician
b. Mar 29, 1885 in Cleveland, Ohio
d. Mar 9, 1977 in Lyndhurst, Ohio
Source: *BioIn 1, 2, 3, 4, 6, 8, 9, 11; WhoAm 74; WhoAmP 73; WhoAmW 74*

Bolton, Guy Reginald
English. Dramatist
Wrote over 50 musicals including *Lady be Good; Anything Goes.*
b. Nov 23, 1884 in Brozbourne, England
d. Sep 5, 1979 in Goring, England
Source: *AmAu&B; AmSCAP 66; BioIn 3, 5; ConAu 5R, 89; ConDr 77; LongCTC; IntAu&W 76, 77; ModWD; Who 74; WhoThe 72, 77, 81*

Bolton, Isabel
[Mary Britten Miller]
American. Author
b. Aug 6, 1883 in New London, Connecticut
d. Apr 13, 1975 in New York, New York
Source: *AmAu&B; AmNov; ConAu 1R, 16NR, 57; LongCTC; TwCA SUP*

Bolton, Sarah Tittle Barrett
American. Poet
Wrote verse *Paddle Your Own Canoe,* 1851.
b. Dec 18, 1814 in Newport, Kentucky
d. Aug 4, 1893 in Indianapolis, Indiana
Source: *NotAW*

Bombeck, Erma Louise
[Mrs. William Bombeck]
American. Journalist, Author
Syndicated columnist, 1967--; wrote *If Life Is a Bowl of Cherries, What Am I Doing in the Pits?,* 1971.
b. Feb 21, 1927 in Dayton, Ohio
Source: *AuNews 1; ConAu 12NR, 21R; CurBio 79; ForWC 70; LibW; WhoAm 84; WhoAmW 79; WrDr 80*

Bomberg, Dave (David)
English. Artist
b. 1890
d. 1957
Source: *BioIn 1, 5, 8, 11*

Bomhard, Moritz
German. Conductor
b. Jun 19, 1912 in Berlin, Germany
Source: *BioIn 7; WhoAm 74*

Bonanno, Joseph
"Joe Bananas"
American. Organized Crime Figure
Sought to increase power against other Mafia
  families in Banana crime war, 1964-69.
b. 1904
Source: *BioIn 9; EncACr*

Bonaparte, Charles Louis Napoleon
see: Napoleon III

Bonaparte, Elizabeth Patterson
American. Celebrity Relative
Marriage to Jerome, 1803, disapproved by
  Napoleon.
b. Feb 6, 1785 in Baltimore, Maryland
d. Apr 4, 1879
Source: *AmAu&B; BioIn 1, 2, 4, 6, 11*

Bonaparte, Francois Charles Joseph
[L'Aiglon; Napoleon II]
French. Political Leader
Son of Napoleon Bonaparte; king of Rome,
  1811-14; prince of Parma, 1814-18.
b. 1811 in Paris, France
d. 1832 in Austria
Source: *BioIn 1, 2, 5, 6; NewCol 75; WebBD
80*

Bonaparte, Jerome
French. Ruler
Youngest brother of Napoleon; king of
  Westphalia, 1807-13.
b. Nov 15, 1784 in Corsica
d. Jun 24, 1860 in Paris, France
Source: *AmBi; ApCAB; CelCen; DcBiPP;
HarEnUS; LinLib S*

Bonaparte, Joseph
French. Ruler, Celebrity Relative
Older brother of Napoleon; king of Naples,
  1806-08; king of Spain, 180808-13.
b. Jan 7, 1768 in Corte, Comoros
d. Jul 28, 1844 in Florence, Italy
Source: *ApCAB; CelCen; DcBiPP; HarEnUS;
LinLib S; McGEWB*

Bonaparte, Louis Lucien
French. Scholar, Celebrity Relative
Philologist who was made prince by
  Napoleon III, 1863.
b. 1813 in Mangrove, England
d. 1891
Source: *Alli SUP*

Bonaparte, Lucien
French. Statesman, Celebrity Relative
Napoleon's brother who was exiled for
  opposing his polices, 1810.
b. 1775
d. 1840 in Italy
Source: *WebBD 80*

Bonaparte, Maria Letizis
French. Celebrity Relative
Mother of Napoleon I.
b. 1750
d. 1836
Source: *BioIn 11; ChhPo; DcBiPP; Dis&D;
InWom*

Bonaparte, Napoleon
see: Napoleon I

Bonatti, Walter
Italian. Author, Journalist
Travel books include *On the Heights*, 1964,
  The Great Days, 1974.
b. Jun 22, 1930 in Bergamo, Italy
Source: *ConAu 106; WrDr 76, 80*

Bonavena, Oscar
Argentine. Boxer
b. Sep 25, 1942 in Buenos Aires, Argentina
d. May 22, 1976
Source: *NewYTBE 72; WhoBox 74*

Bonaventure, Saint
[Bonaventura; Giovanni DeFidenza]
"Seraphic Doctor"
Italian. Religious Figure
Developed scholasticism in medievil thought.
b. 1221 in Bagnoregio, Italy
d. Jul 15, 1274 in Lyons, France
Source: *BiD&SB; DcEuL; EvEuW; REn*

Bonci, Alessandro
Italian. Opera Singer
Tenor who is often ranked second to Caruso.
b. Feb 10, 1870 in Cesena, Italy
d. Aug 8, 1940 in Vitterba, Italy
Source: *CurBio 40; WhAm 5*

Boncour, Joseph Paul
see: Paul-Boncour, Joseph

Bond, Carrie Jacobs
American. Composer, Author
Wrote hits "End of a Perfect Day"; "I Love
  You Truly."
b. Aug 11, 1862 in Janesville, Wisconsin
d. Dec 28, 1946 in Los Angeles, California
Source: *AmAu&B; AmSCAP 66; ChhPo;
DcAmB S4; DcNAA; InWom; NotAW;
REnAL; WhAm 2; WhNAA; WisWr;
WomWWA 14*

Bond, Edward
English. Dramatist
Controversial plays include *Saved,* 1965; *Lear,*
1971.
b. Jul 18, 1934 in London, England
Source: *CnThe; ConAu 25R; ConDr 73, 77;*
ConLC 4, 6, 13; CroCD; CurBio 78; DcLEL
1940; EncWT; IntAu&W 76, 77; LinLib L;
ModBrL S1; NotNAT; PlP&P A; WebE&AL;
Who 74; WhoThe 72, 77; WhoTwCL; WorAu
1970; WrDr 76, 80

Bond, George Foote
"Papa Topside"
American. Physician
Medical officer, Sealab missions, 1964-69;
tested human endurance undersea.
b. 1915
d. Jan 3, 1983 in Charlotte, North Carolina
Source: *BioIn 3, 8; NewYTBS 83*

Bond, Julian
American. Politician, Civil Rights Leader
First black to be nominated for vp, 1968;
member, GA senate, 1975--.
b. Jan 14, 1940 in Nashville, Tennessee
Source: *CelR; CivR 74; CivRSt; ConAu 49;*
CurBio 69; LivgBAA; NewYTBE 70; WebAB;
WhoAm 74, 76, 78, 80, 82; WhoAmP 73;
WhoBlA 75; WhoS&SW 73; WhoWor 74

Bond, Sudie
American. Actress
Played Flo on TV's "Alice", 1980-82.
b. Jul 13, 1928 in Louisville, Kentucky
d. Nov 10, 1984 in New York, New York
Source: *BiE&WWA; NotNAT; WhoAm 82;*
WhoHol A; WhoThe 77, 81

Bond, Tommy
[Our Gang]
American. Actor
Played Butch in 1930s "Our Gang" serial.
b. Sep 16, 1927 in Dallas, Texas
Source: *FilmEn; WhoHol A*

Bond, Victoria
American. Composer, Conductor
First woman to co-conduct major US
symphony; assisted Previn in leading
Pittsburgh Orchestra, 1978-80.
b. May 6, 1950 in Los Angeles, California
Source: *WhoAm 80, 82, 84*

Bond, Ward
American. Actor
Appeared in over 200 films; starred in TV
series "Wagon Train," 1957-61.
b. Apr 9, 1904 in Denver, Colorado
d. Nov 5, 1960 in Dallas, Texas
Source: *CmMov; FilmgC; MotPP; MovMk;*
OxFilm; WhScrn 74, 77; WhoHol B

Bondarchuk, Sergei
Russian. Director, Actor
Played lead roles in two of his best films
Destiny of a Man; War and Peace.
b. Sep 25, 1922 in Byelozerka, U.S.S.R.
Source: *DcFM; IntWW 74, 80, 81, 82;*
MovMk; OxFilm; WhoHol A; WhoWor 74;
WorEFlm

Bondfield, Margaret Grace
English. Government Official
First British woman cabinet minister.
b. 1873 in Furnham, England
d. Jun 16, 1953 in Sanderstead, England
Source: *DcNaB 1951; GrBr; IntDcWB; LinLib*
S; ObitOF 79; ObitT 1951; WhDW; WhE&EA

Bondi, Beulah
American. Actress
Oscar nominee for *Gorgeous Hussy; Of*
Human Hearts; won 1977 Emmy for "The
Waltons."
b. May 3, 1892 in Chicago, Illinois
Source: *BiE&WWA; FilmEn; FilmgC; IntMPA*
75, 76, 77, 81; MotPP; MovMk; NotNAT;
ThFT; Vers A; WhThe; WhoHol A; WhoThe
77A

Bondi, Hermann, Sir
English. Mathematician
b. Nov 1, 1919 in Vienna, Austria
Source: *BioIn 3; IntWW 74; Who 74;*
WhoWor 78

Bonds, Bobby Lee
American. Baseball Player
Outfielder, 1968-81; only player ever to hit
grand slam home run in first at-bat.
b. Mar 15, 1946 in Riverside, California
Source: *BaseEn 85; InB&W 80; NewYTBS*
75; WhoBlA 80; WhoProB 73

Bonds, Gary U S
[Gary Anderson]
American. Singer, Songwriter
Had hit single "Quarter to Three," 1961
teamed with Bruce Springsteen on
Dedication album, 1981.
b. Jun 6, 1939 in Jacksonville, Florida
Source: *EncPR&S 74; IlEncBM 82; PseudN*
82; RkOn 74; RolSEnr 83; WhoRock 81

Bondurant, Bob (Robert L)
American. Auto Racer, Educator
b. 1933
Source: *BioIn 11*

Bonelli, Richard
[Richard Bunn]
American. Opera Singer
Light, grand opera baritone, 1920s-50s;
Metropolitan Opera star, 1932-45.
b. Feb 6, 1894 in Port Byron, New York
d. Jun 7, 1980 in Los Angeles, California
Source: *Baker 78; BioIn 4, 9, 10; MusSN;
NewEOp 71; PseudN 82*

Bonerz, Peter
American. Actor, Director
TV actor, director of episodes of "Bob
Newhart Show," 1972-78; director *It's
Your Move,* 1984.
b. Aug 6, 1938 in Portsmouth, New
Hampshire
Source: *WhoAm 76, 78, 80, 82, 84; WhoHol
A*

Bonestell, Chesley
American. Illustrator
Outer space specialist best known for mural
"A Trip to the Moon," 1957.
b. 1888 in San Francisco, California
d. Jun 11, 1986 in Carmel, California
Source: *BioIn 11; EncSF; FanAl*

Bonet, Lisa
American. Actress
Plays Denise Huxtable on "The Cosby
Show," 1984--.
b. 1967 in San Francisco, California
Source: *NF*

Boney M.
[Marcia Barrett; Bobby Farrell; Liz Mitchell;
Marzie Williams]
German. Music Group
Became int'l. success with singles "River of
Bablyon"; "Mary's Boy Child," 1978.
Source: *RkOn 85*

Bonfanti, Jim Alexander
[The Raspberries]
American. Musician
Drummer with power pop group, 1970-73.
b. Dec 17, 1948 in Windber, Pennsylvania
Source: *NF*

Bonfanti, Marie
American. Ballerina
Popular dancer, 1860s-90s; starred in *The
Black Crook,* 1868.
b. 1847 in Milan, Italy
d. Jan 25, 1921 in New York, New York
Source: *NotAW*

Bongo, El Hadj Omar
Gabonese. Political Leader
b. Dec 30, 1935 in Franceville, Gabon
Source: *IntWW 74*

Bonham, Frank
American. Author, Dramatist
Adventure tales for young people include
Devilhorn, 1978.
b. Feb 25, 1914 in Los Angeles, California
Source: *AuBYP; ConAu 9R, 4NR; ConLC 12;
MorBMP; SmATA 1; ThrBJA*

Bonham, John Henry
[Led Zeppelin]
"Bonzo"
English. Musician
Led Zeppelin drummer; group disbanded
after his death from asphyxiation.
b. May 31, 1949 in Redditch, England
d. Sep 25, 1980 in Windsor, England
Source: *AnObit 1980; NewYTBS 80; WhAm
7; WhoAm 80*

Bonham Carter, (Helen) Violet
[Baroness Asquith of Yarnbury]
English. Public Official
Wrote *Winston Churchill as I Knew Him,*
1965.
b. Apr 15, 1887 in London, England
d. Feb 19, 1969 in London, England
Source: *ConAu P-2; DcNaB 1961; GrBr;
LongCTC; ObitT 1961*

Bonheur, Rosa (Marie Rosalie)
French. Artist
Specialized in paintings and sculptures of
animals.
b. 1822 in Bordeaux, France
d. 1899 in Melun, France
Source: *ChhPo S1; HerW; IlBEAAW; InWom;
WomArt*

Bonhoeffer, Dietrich
German. Theologian
b. Feb 4, 1906 in Breslau, Germany
d. Apr 9, 1945
Source: *OxGer; WorAu*

Boni, Albert
American. Publisher
Founder, Boni & Liveright, 1917; started
Modern Library series, 1917.
b. Oct 21, 1892 in New York, New York
d. Jul 31, 1981 in Ormond Beach, Florida
Source: *AmAu&B; AnObit 1981; ConAu 104,
65; LinLib L; NewYTBS 81; St&PR 75;
WhoAm 74, 76, 78, 80; WhoWor 76;
WhoWorJ 72*

Boniface, Saint
English. Missionary, Religious Figure
Advanced Christianity; founded monasteries
in Germany; martyred.
b. 680
d. 755
Source: *Alli; BiD&SB; CasWL; DcEnL;
NewC; OxGer*

Bonifacio, Jose
Brazilian. Statesman, Scientist
b. 1763
d. 1838
Source: *NewCol 75*

Bonington, Richard Parkes
English. Artist
Subjects for paintings include landscapes,
historical figures.
b. Oct 25, 1802 in Arnold, England
d. Sep 23, 1828 in London, England
Source: *AtlBL; BioIn 1, 3, 4, 5, 6, 10, 11*

Bonnard, Pierre
French. Artist
Subjects for paintings include still lifes,
women bathing, self-portraits.
b. Oct 30, 1867 in Fontenay, France
d. Jan 23, 1947 in LeCannet, France
Source: *AtlBL*

Bonner, Frank
American. Actor
Played Herb Tarlek on TV series "WKRP in
Cincinnati."
b. Feb 28, 1942 in Little Rock, Arkansas
Source: *WhoAm 80, 82*

Bonnet, Georges
French. Politician
b. Jul 23, 1889 in Bassillac, France
d. Jun 4, 1973 in Paris, France
Source: *NewYTBS 74*

Bonnet, Stede
English. Pirate
d. 1718
Source: *BioIn 4, 5*

Bonneville, Benjamin
American. Army Officer
Explored Northwest, 1832-35; subject of
Irvings *Adventures of Captain Bonneville,*
1937.
b. Apr 14, 1796 in Paris, France
d. Jun 12, 1878 in Fort Smith, Arkansas
Source: *OxAmL; WebAB; WebBD 80*

Bonney, William H
see: Billy the Kid

Bonnie & Clyde
see: Barrow, Clyde; Parker, Bonnie

Bonnier, Joe (Joachim)
Swedish. Auto Racer
b. 1930
d. Jun 11, 1972
Source: *BioIn 6, 7, 9, 10*

Bonny, Anne
[Anne Bonney]
English. Pirate
b. 1700
d. 1720
Source: *BioIn 1, 3, 4, 5, 6, 7, 10, 11;
GoodHs; InWom*

Bono, Chastity
American. Celebrity Relative
Daughter of Sonny and Cher.
b. Mar 4, 1969 in Los Angeles, California
Source: *NF*

Bono, Cher
see: Cher

Bono, "Sonny" (Salvatore Phillip)
[Sonny and Cher]
American. Singer, Actor
Wrote songs "I Got You, Babe," "The Beat
Goes On," recorded with wife, Cher.
b. Feb 16, 1940 in Detroit, Michigan
Source: *BioNews 74; CelR; CurBio 74;
IntMPA 75, 76, 77, 78, 79, 80, 81, 82;
WhoAm 74, 76, 78, 80; WhoHol A*

Bonoff, Karla
[Mrs. Robby Benson]
American. Singer
b. Dec 27, 1952 in Los Angeles, California
Source: *BioIn 11; RkOn 85*

Bononcini, Giovanni Battista
Italian. Composer
Operas include *Astarto,* 1715; *Griselda,* 1722.
b. Jul 18, 1670 in Modena, Italy
d. Jul 9, 1747 in Vienna, Austria
Source: *NewEOp 71; OxMus; WebBD 80*

Bonsal, Stephen
American. Journalist
Foriegn affairs writer; won 1944 Pulitzer for
    Unfinished Business.
b. Mar 29, 1865 in Baltimore, Maryland
d. Jun 8, 1951 in Washington, District of
    Columbia
Source: *AmAu&B; BiD&SB; BiDSA; CurBio
    45, 51; DcAmAu; DcAmB S5; HarEnUS;
    NatCAB 14; OxAmL; REnAL; TwCA SUP;
    WhAm 3*

Bonsall, Joe
[The Oak Ridge Boys]
American. Singer
Tenor with country-pop group; hit single "So
    Fine," 1982.
b. May 18, 1948 in Philadelphia,
    Pennsylvania
Source: *NF*

Bonstelle, Jessie
American. Director, Actress
Tutored Broadway stars; founded civic
    theatre in Detroit, 1925.
b. Nov 18, 1871 in Greece, New York
d. Oct 14, 1932 in Detroit, Michigan
Source: *NotAW*

Bontemps, Arna Wendell
American. Author
Leader, "Harlem Renaissance" movement,
    1920s; wrote *Black Thunder,* 1936.
b. Oct 13, 1902 in Alexandria, Louisiana
d. Jun 4, 1973 in Nashville, Tennessee
Source: *AmAu&B; AmNov; AnMV 1926;
    Au&Wr 71; AuBYP; BkCL; BlkAWP; ChhPo
    S1; ConAu 1R, 41R, 4NR; ConLC 1, 18;
    ConP 70; CurBio 46, 73; JBA 34; MorBMP;
    NewYTBE 70; OxAmL; REnAL; SmATA 2;
    Str&VC; WebE&AL; WhAm 5; WhoAm 74;
    WhoBlA 75; WhoWor 74*

Bonynge, Richard
Australian. Conductor
Musical director, Australian Opera, 1975--.
b. Sep 29, 1930 in Sydney, Australia
Source: *FarE&A 81; IntWW 82; Who 82;
    WhoMus 72; WhoWor 74*

Booker T and the MG's
[Steve Cropper; Donald Dunn; Al Jackson,
    Jr; Booker T Jones; Bobby Manuel;
    Carson Whitsett]
American. Music Group
First hit single "Green Onions," 1962; group
    disbanded, 1972.
Source: *AmPS A; EncPR&S 74; IlEncBM 82;
    IlEncRk; RolSEnR 83*

Bookout, John Frank, Jr.
American. Businessman
Geologist, Shell Oil Co., 1950-76; pres.,
    1976--.
b. Dec 31, 1922 in Shreveport, Louisiana
Source: *CanWW 70; Dun&B 79; NewYTBS
    76; St&PR 75; WhoAm 76, 78, 80, 82, 84;
    WhoCan 73; WhoF&I 79, 81; WhoS&SW 78,
    80, 82*

Bookspan, Martin
American. Music Critic
TV commentator, "Live from Lincoln
    Center," 1976--; "Great Performa nces,"
    1977--.
b. Jul 30, 1926 in Boston, Massachusetts
Source: *ConAu 41R; IntAu&W 76; WhoAmJ
    80; WhoE 74; WhoWorJ 72, 72*

Boole, Ella Alexander
American. Reformer
Pres., of World WCTU, 1931-47; wrote *Give
    Prohibition Its Chance,* 1929.
b. Jul 26, 1858 in Van Wert, Ohio
d. Mar 13, 1952 in Brooklyn, New York
Source: *DcAmB S5; NatCAB 38; OhA&B;
    WhAm 3; WomWWA 14*

Boolootian, Richard Andrew
American. Author, Scientist
Pres., Scientific Software Systems, Inc., 1969--
    ; has written three college zoology
    textbooks.
b. Oct 17, 1927 in Fresno, California
Source: *AmM&WS 76P, 79P, 82P; WhoWest
    82*

Boomtown Rats
[Pete Briquette; Gerry Cott; Johnny Fingers;
    Bob Geldof; Simon Grove; Garry Roberts]
Irish. Music Group
Punk band, formed late 1970s; albums
    include *Boomtown Rats,* 1978.
Source: *ConMuA 80A; IlEncRk; RolSEnR 83;
    WhoRock 81*

Boone, Cherry
see: O'Neill, Cherry Boone

Boone, Daniel
American. Pioneer
Established Boonesboro, first settlement in
    KY, 1775.
b. Nov 2, 1734 in Reading, Pennsylvania
d. Sep 26, 1820 in Saint Charles County,
    Missouri
Source: *Alli; AmAu&B; AmBi; ApCAB;
    BiDSA; DcAmB; Drake; EncAB-H; EncAR;
    FilmgC; LinLib S; OxAmH; REn; REnAL;
    TwCBDA; WebAB; WhAm HS; WhAmP*

Boone, Debby (Deborah Ann)
[Mrs. Gabriel Ferrer]
American. Singer
Daughter of Pat Boone; platinum record for
"You Light Up My Life," 1977.
b. Sep 22, 1956 in Hackensack, New Jersey
Source: *BioIn 11; BkPepl; WhoAm 80, 82*

Boone, "Pat" (Charles Eugene)
American. Singer, Actor, Author
Noted for clean cut image, white buck shoes;
starred in *April Love*, 1957.
b. Jun 1, 1934 in Jacksonville, Florida
Source: *AmAu&B; AmSCAP 66; BkPepl;
ConAu 1R, 2NR; CurBio 79; FilmgC;
IntMPA 75, 76, 77, 78, 79, 80, 81, 82;
MotPP; MovMk; SmATA 7; WhoAm 74, 76,
78, 80, 82; WhoHol A; WhoRel 75; WrDr 80*

Boone, Rebecca B
American. Celebrity Relative
Wife of Daniel Boone.
b. 1739
d. 1813
Source: *BioIn 7; HerW*

Boone, Ron
American. Basketball Player
Set pro basketball record by playing in 1,041
consecutive games.
b. Sep 6, 1946 in Oklahoma City, Oklahoma
Source: *InB&W 80; OfNBA 81*

Boone, Richard
American. Actor
Starred in TV series "Medic," 1954-56,
"Have Gun Will Travel," 1957-63.
b. Jun 18, 1917 in Los Angeles, California
Source: *BiE&WWA; CelR; CmMov; CurBio
64; FilmgC; IntMPA 75, 76, 77; MotPP;
MovMk; NewYTBE 72; WhoHol A*

Boorman, John
English. Director
Films include *Deliverance*, 1970; *Exorcist II*,
1977.
b. Jan 18, 1933 in Shepperton, England
Source: *DcFM; EncSF; FilmEn; IntMPA 81;
OxFilm; WhoAm 82, 84; WorEFlm*

Boorstin, Daniel J(oseph)
American. Author, Government Official
Librarian of Congress, 1975--, who wrote *The
Democratic Experience*.
b. Oct 1, 1914 in Atlanta, Georgia
Source: *AmAu&B; ConAu 1NR; CurBio 68,
84; EncAAH; Who 82; WhoAm 74, 76, 78,
80, 82; WhoGov 72; WhoS&SW 73; WhoWorJ
72, 78; WorAl; WorAu*

Boosey, Leslie Arthur
British. Music Executive
b. Jul 26, 1887
Source: *Who 74; WhoMus 72*

Booth, "Albie" (Albert James, Jr.)
"Little Boy Blue"; Mighty Atom
American. Football Player, Football Coach
Won 8 varsity letters at Yale for football,
baseball, basketball, 1929-32; coached at
Yale.
b. Feb 1, 1908 in New Haven, Connecticut
d. Mar 1, 1959 in New York, New York
Source: *DcAmB S6; ObitOF 79; WhoFtbl 74*

Booth, Ballington
American. Social Reformer
Son of William and Catherine Booth who
withdrew from Salvation Army to found
Volunteers of America, 1896.
b. Jul 28, 1859 in Brighouse, England
d. Oct 5, 1940 in Blue Point, New York
Source: *CurBio 40; DcAmB S2; HarEnUS;
LuthC 75; NatCAB 14; TwCBDA; WorAl*

Booth, Catherine Mumford
[Mrs. William Booth]
English. Social Reformer
Played leading role in founding, developing
Salvation Army.
b. 1829 in Derbyshire, England
d. 1890
Source: *Alli; BioIn 4, 5, 8, 10, 11; InWom*

Booth, Edwin Thomas
American. Actor
Brother of John Wilkes Booth; noted
Shakespearean actor; founded Players Club,
1888.
b. Nov 13, 1833 in Bel Air, Maryland
d. Jun 7, 1893 in New York, New York
Source: *CnThe; DcAmB; EncWT; LinLib S;
OxAmL; OxThe; REn; REnAL; TwCBDA;
WebAB; WhAm HS*

Booth, Evangeline Cory
"White Angel"
American. Social Reformer
Daughter of William, Catherine Booth; with
Salvation Army, beginning 1895, general,
1934-39.
b. Dec 25, 1865 in London, England
d. Jul 17, 1950 in Hartsdale, New York
Source: *ApCAB X; BiCAW; CurBio 41, 50;
DcAmB S4; HerW; InWom; LinLib L;
NotAW; OxAmH; WhAm 3; WomWWA 14*

Booth, George
American. Cartoonist
On staff of *New Yorker;* does uniques
  sketches of dogs, cats, people.
b. Jun 28, 1926 in Cainsville, Missouri
Source: *WhoAm 82, 84; WorECar*

Booth, George Gough
American. Editor
b. Sep 24, 1864 in Toronto, Ontario
d. Apr 11, 1949 in Detroit, Michigan
Source: *BioIn 1, 2, 7; WhAm 2*

Booth, Hubert Cecil
English. Inventor
Invented the vacuum cleaner, 1901.
b. 1871
d. Jan 14, 1955 in Croydon, England
Source: *BioIn 3*

Booth, John Wilkes
American. Actor, Assassin
Shakespearean actor; shot, killed Lincoln at
  Ford's Theatre, Apr 14, 1865.
b. Aug 26, 1838 in Hartford City, Maryland
d. Apr 26, 1865 in Virginia
Source: *AmBi; DcAmB; Drake; EncAB-H;
FamA&A; OxAmL; OxThe; PIP&P; REn;
REnAL; TwCBDA; WebAB; WhAm HS;
WhAmP*

Booth, Junius Brutus
English. Actor
Father of Edwin and John Wilkes; dominated
  stage for 30 yrs.
b. May 1, 1796 in London, England
d. Nov 30, 1852
Source: *AmBi; ApCAB; CelCen; DcAmB;
Drake; EncWT; FamA&A; OxAmH; OxAmL;
OxThe; REn; REnAL; TwCBDA; WebAB;
WhAm HS*

Booth, Shirley
American. Actress
Played Hazel in TV series, 1961-66; won
  Emmy, 1963.
b. Aug 30, 1907 in New York, New York
Source: *BiE&WWA; CelR; CurBio 42, 53;
EncMT; FilmgC; InWom; IntMPA 75, 76, 77,
78, 79, 80, 81, 82; MotPP; MovMk; NotNAT;
PIP&P; WhoAm 74, 76, 78, 80, 82; WhoHol
A; WhoThe 77; WorEFlm; WhoWor 78;
WhoHol A; WhoThe 77*

Booth, William
English. Religious Leader, Social Reformer
Started Christian Mission in E London, 1865,
  became Salvation Army, 1878.
b. Apr 10, 1829 in Nottinghamshire, England
d. Aug 20, 1912 in London, England
Source: *Alli SUP; CelCen; EncWM;
LongCTC; NewC; REn; WhDW*

Boothby, Robert John Graham, Lord
Scottish. Politician
British conservative who served on
  Parliament 62 yrs; private secretary to
  Winston Churchill, 1926-29.
b. 1900 in Edinburgh, Scotland
d. Jul 16, 1986 in London, England
Source: *BioIn 1, 3, 4, 7, 11; IntWW 74;
Who 74*

Boothe, Powers
American. Actor
Portrayed Rev. Jim Jones in TV movie
  Guyana Tragedy: The Story of Jim Jones,
  1980; won Emmy, 1980.
b. Jun 1, 1949 in Snyder, Texas
Source: *NewYTBS 79; VarWW 85*

Boothroyd, John Basil
English. Author
b. Mar 4, 1910 in Worksop, England
Source: *AuBYP; ConAu 33R; WrDr 76*

Booz, Paul E
American. Economist
b. 1914
d. 1971
Source: *BioIn 9; NewYTBE 71*

Borah, William E
American. Senator
b. Jun 29, 1865 in Fairfield, Illinois
d. Jan 19, 1940 in Washington, District of
  Columbia
Source: *AmBi; BiDrAC; DcAmB S2; DcNAA;
EncAB-H; REn; WebAB; WhAm 1; WhAmP*

Borbon y Borbon, Prince Juan Carlos
see: Juan Carlos I

Borch, Fred J
American. Businessman
b. Apr 28, 1910 in Brooklyn, New York
Source: *BioIn 6, 9; IntWW 74; St&PR 75;
WhoAm 74; WhoE 74; WhoF&I 74; WhoWor
78*

Bordeaux, Henry
French. Author
b. Jan 29, 1870 in Thonon, France
d. 1963
Source: *CasWL; CathA 1930; ClDMEL;
EncWL; EvEuW; LongCTC; OxFr; REn;
TwCA, SUP*

Borden, Barry
[Molly Hatchet]
American. Musician
Drummer with heavy metal band since 1982.
b. May 12, 1954 in Atlanta, Georgia
Source: *NF*

Borden, Gail
American. Inventor
Patented evaporated milk, 1856.
b. Nov 9, 1801 in Norwich, New York
d. Jan 11, 1874 in Borden, Texas
Source: *AmBi; ApCAB; DcAmB; NewCol 75;
TwCBDA; WebAB; WhAm HS*

Borden, Lizzie Andrew
American. Murderer
Arrested for murdering father, stepmother,
Aug 4, 1892; acquitted, 1893.
b. Jul 19, 1860 in Fall River, Massachusetts
d. Jun 1, 1927 in Fall River, Massachusetts
Source: *DcAmB S1; EncACr; GoodHs;
NotAW; OxAmL; REn; REnAL; WebAB;
WhAm 4, HSA, HSA; WorAl*

Borden, Robert Laird, Sir
Canadian. Political Leader
Twice prime minister; headed Conservative
govt., 1911-17; Union govt., 1917-20.
b. Jun 26, 1854 in Grand Pre, Nova Scotia
d. Jun 10, 1937 in Ottawa, Ontario
Source: *DcNAA; OxCan; WebBD 80;
WhNAA; WhoPubR 72*

Bordes, Francois
[Francois Carsac, pseud.]
French. Archaeologist
Authority on Stone Age tools who
manufactured over 100,000 replicas.
b. 1919
d. Apr 30, 1981 in Tucson, Arizona
Source: *ConAu 103; NewYTBS 81*

Bordet, Jules Jean Baptiste Vincent
Belgian. Scientist
b. Jun 13, 1870 in Soighies, Belgium
d. Apr 6, 1961 in Brussels, Belgium
Source: *WhAm 4*

Bordoni, Faustina
[Faustina Bordoni Hasse]
Italian. Opera Singer
b. 1700
d. Nov 4, 1781 in Venice, Italy
Source: *InWom*

Bordoni, Irene
American. Actress
b. Jan 16, 1893 in Ajaccio, Corsica
d. Mar 19, 1953 in New York, New York
Source: *AmPS B; CmpEPM; InWom;
NotNAT B; WhScrn 74, 77; WhThe; WhoHol
B*

Borduas, Paul-Emile
Canadian. Artist
Leader of Montreal "Automatistes,"
exponents of objective painting.
b. Nov 1, 1905 in Saint Hilaire, Quebec
d. Feb 22, 1960 in Paris, France
Source: *BioIn 3, 4, 5, 7, 11; ConArt 77;
CreCan 1; MacDCB 78; McGDA; OxCan,
SUP*

Borel d'Hauterive, Petrus
French. Poet, Author
b. Jun 28, 1809 in Lyons, France
d. Jul 14, 1859 in Mostaganem, Algeria
Source: *BiD&SB; CasWL; EuAu; EvEuW;
OxFr; PenC EUR*

Boren, David Lyle
American. Senator
Governor of OK, 1975-79; OK senator,
1979--.
b. Apr 21, 1941 in Washington, District of
Columbia
Source: *BiDrGov; WhoAm 80, 82; WhoAmL
79; WhoWor 80*

Borg, Bjorn
Swedish. Tennis Player
Won Wimbledon championships, 1976-80;
retired, 1983.
b. Jun 6, 1956 in Sodertalje, Sweden
Source: *BkPepl; CurBio 74; IntWW 81, 82;
Who 82, 82; WhoAm 80, 82; WhoWor 78*

Borg, Kim
Finnish. Opera Singer
b. Aug 7, 1919 in Helsinki, Finland
Source: *IntWW 74; WhoMus 72; WhoWor 78*

Borg, Veda Ann
American. Actress
Played tough blonde in scores of 1940s
    movies; face was reconstructed in ten
    operations after car crash.
b. Jan 15, 1915 in Boston, Massachusetts
d. Aug 16, 1973 in Hollywood, California
Source: *FilmgC; MotPP; MovMk; ThFT; Vers
A; WhScrn 77; WhoHol B*

Borge, Victor
American. Pianist, Comedian
Combines music with humor to create
    musical satire.
b. Jan 3, 1909 in Copenhagen, Delaware
Source: *AmSCAP 66; BiE&WWA; BioNews
74; CelR; CurBio 46; IntMPA 75, 76, 77, 78,
79, 80, 81, 82; IntWW 74; NotNAT; WhoAm
74; WhoHol A; WhoMus 72; WhoWor 78;
WrDr 80*

Borges, Jorge Luis
Argentine. Author
Leader, "Ultraismo" literary movement,
    combining surrealism, imagism.
b. Aug 24, 1899 in Buenos Aires, Argentina
d. Jun 14, 1986 in Geneva, Switzerland
Source: *CasWL; CelR; ConAu 21R; ConLC 1,
2, 3, 4, 6, 8, 9, 10, 13; CurBio 70, 86;
DcCLAA; DcSpL; EncWL; IntWW 74;
NewYTBE 71; PenC AM; REn; TwCWr; Who
74; WhoTwCL; WhoWor 78; WorAu*

Borghese, Maria Paolina
French. Celebrity Relative
Sister of Napoleon I.
b. 1780
d. 1825
Source: *BioIn 1, 2, 7, 9, 10, 11*

Borgia, Cesare
Italian. Military Leader
Said to be prototype for Machiavelli's *The
Prince.*
b. 1475 in Rome, Italy
d. Mar 12, 1507 in Navarre, France
Source: *LinLib S; McGEWB; NewC; WhDW;
WorAl*

Borgia, Lucrezia
[Duchess of Ferrara]
Italian. Noblewoman
Daughter of Pope Alexander VI, who was
    unfairly known as poisoner and participant
    in family plots.
b. Apr 18, 1480 in Rome, Italy
d. Mar 12, 1519
Source: *DcBiPP; Dis&D; InWom; LinLib S;
NewC*

Borglum, Gutzon
American. Sculptor
Best known as sculptor of American
    presidents on Mt. Rushmore, 1927-41.
b. Mar 25, 1867 in Bear Lake, Idaho
d. Mar 6, 1941 in Chicago, Illinois
Source: *ArtsAmW 1; CmCal; CurBio 41;
OxAmH; OxAmL; REn; REnAL; WebAB;
WhAm 1*

Borglum, James Lincoln Delamothe
American. Sculptor
Completed statues on Mt. Rushmore after
    death of father, Gutzon, 1941.
b. Apr 9, 1912 in Stamford, Connecticut
d. Jan 27, 1986 in Corpus Christi, Texas
Source: *IlBEAAW; NewYTBS 86; WhoAm 84;
WhoAmA 84*

Borglum, Solon Hannibal
American. Sculptor
Brother of Gutzon Borglum; known for
    sculptures of horses, cowboys, and Indians.
b. Dec 22, 1868 in Ogden, Utah
d. Jan 31, 1922
Source: *ArtsAmW 1; DcAmArt; DcAmB;
IlBEAAW; WhAm 1*

Borgmann, "Benny" (Bernhard)
American. Basketball Player
b. Nov 21, 1899 in Haledon, New Jersey
d. Nov 11, 1978
Source: *WhoBbl 73*

Borgnine, Ernest
[Ermes Effron Borgnino]
American. Actor
Starred in TV series "McHale's Navy," 1962-
    66; won Oscar, 1955, for *Marty.*
b. Jan 24, 1917 in Hamden, Connecticut
Source: *BiDFilm; CelR; CurBio 56; FilmgC;
IntMPA 75, 76, 77, 78, 79, 80, 81, 82;
IntWW 74; MotPP; MovMk; NewYTBE 73;
OxFilm; WhoAm 74, 76, 78, 80, 82; WhoHol
A; WhoWor 78; WorEFlm*

Bori, Lucrezia
Spanish. Opera Singer
b. Dec 24, 1888 in Valencia, Spain
d. May 14, 1960 in New York, New York
Source: *InWom; WhAm 4*

Bork, Robert Heron
American. Lawyer, Judge
US Appeals Court judge, 1981--, who fired
    Watergate prosecutor Archibald Cox, 1973.
b. Mar 1, 1927 in Pittsburgh, Pennsylvania
Source: *BioIn 10; DrAS 78P; IntWW 78;
WhoAm 80, 82, 84; WhoGov 77*

Borkh, Inge
German. Opera Singer
b. May 26, 1921 in Mannheim, Germany
Source: *InWom; IntWW 74; WhoMus 72; WhoWor 78*

Borland, Hal
American. Author
b. May 14, 1900 in Sterling, Nebraska
d. Feb 22, 1978 in Sharon, Connecticut
Source: *AmAu&B; Au&Wr 71; ConAu 1R, 77; REnAL; SmATA 5; WhoAm 74; WhoWor 78; WorAu*

Borlaug, Norman Ernest
American. Agriculturalist
Known for experiments in crop breeding,
    specifically with wheat; won Nobel Peace
    Prize, 1970.
b. Mar 25, 1914 in Cresco, Iowa
Source: *AmM&WS 73P, 82P; CelR; CurBio 71; EncAB-H; IntWW 74, 82; NewYTBE 70; WebAB; Who 74; WhoAm 74, 76, 78, 80, 82; WhoS&SW 82; WhoWor 74*

Borman, Frank
American. Astronaut, Airline Executive
Space flights 1965 on Gemini 7; 1968 on
    Apollo 8, first flight around moon.
b. Mar 14, 1928 in Gary, Indiana
Source: *IntWW 74; WhoAm 74, 76, 78, 80, 82; WhoS&SW 82; WhoWor 78*

Bormann, Martin Ludwig
German. Nazi Leader
Pronounced dead, 1973, when skeleton was
    found near Hitler's bunker.
b. 1900
d. 1945
Source: *BioNews 75; NewYTBE 73*

Born, Ernest Alexander
American. Architect
Noted CA designer, who wrote plans for
    Fisherman's Wharf, 1961.
b. 1898 in San Francisco, California
Source: *WhoAm 74*

Born, Max
German. Engineer, Naturalist
b. Dec 11, 1882 in Breslau, Germany
d. Jan 5, 1970 in Goettingen, Germany
    (West)
Source: *ConAu 5R, 25R; NewYTBE 70; WhAm 5*

Borodin, Alexander Profirevich
Russian. Composer
Physician, chemist by vocation, known for
    unfinished opera *Prince Igor.*
b. Nov 11, 1833 in Saint Petersburg, Russia
d. Feb 7, 1887 in Saint Petersburg, Russia
Source: *AtlBL; REn*

Borofsky, Jonathan
American. Artist
Post-modernist artist known for figurative
    work in all media.
b. 1942 in Boston, Massachusetts
Source: *ConArt 83; CurBio 85; DcCAr 81; PrintW 83; WhoAm 84; WhoAmA 84; WhoE 83*

Boros, Julius Nicholas
American. Golfer
Won US Open, 1963, PGA, 1968; Hall of
    Fame, 1974.
b. Mar 3, 1920 in Fairfield, Connecticut
Source: *WhoGolf*

Borotra, Jean Robert
[The Four Musketeers]
"Bounding Basque"
French. Tennis Player
b. Aug 13, 1898 in Barritz, France
Source: *IntWW 74; WhoWor 78*

Borromeo, Charles, Saint
Italian. Religious Leader
Assistant to Pope Puio IV, who directed
    church in Milan, 1565-84; canonized, 1610.
b. Oct 2, 1538 in Rocca d'Arona, Italy
d. Nov 3, 1584 in Milan, Italy
Source: *BioIn 5, 6, 7, 8, 9, 11; DcBiPP; DcCathB; McGDA; McGEWB*

Borromini, Francesco
Italian. Architect
b. Sep 25, 1559 in Bissone, Italy
d. Aug 3, 1677 in Rome, Italy
Source: *AtlBL*

Borrow, George Henry
English. Author
Wrote part autobiographical, part fantasy
    volumes *The Bible In Spain; Lavengro; The Romany Rye,* 1857.
b. Jul 5, 1803 in East Dereham, England
d. Jul 26, 1881 in Oulton, England
Source: *Alli, SUP; AtlBL; BbD; BiD&SB; BrAu 19; CasWL; CelCen; Chambr 3; CyWA; DcBiA; DcEnA; DcEnL; DcEuL; DcLEL; EvLB; LinLib L; MouLC 3; NewC; OxEng; PenC ENG; REn; WebE&AL; WhDW*

Bortoluzzi, Paolo
Italian. Ballet Dancer
b. May 17, 1938 in Genoa, Italy
Source: *IntWW 74*

Borzage, Frank
American. Director
Pioneered use of soft focus for his
sentimental love stories; won Oscars for
Seventh Heaven, 1927; *Bad Girl,* 1931.
b. Apr 23, 1893 in Salt Lake City, Utah
d. Jun 19, 1962 in Hollywood, California
Source: *BiDFilm; CmMov; DcFM; FilmgC;
MovMk; ObitOF 79; ObitT 1961; OxFilm;
TwYS; WhAm 4; WhScrn 74, 77; WhoHol B;
WorAl; WorEFlm*

Bosanquet, Bernard
English. Philosopher
Idealist who reacted against empiricism;
wrote *The Philosophical Theory of the
State,* 1899.
b. 1848
d. 1923
Source: *Alli SUP; LongCTC*

Bosch, Carl
German. Engineer
b. 1874
d. 1940
Source: *BioIn 3, 6*

Bosch, Hieronymus
[Hieronymus VanAeken]
Dutch. Artist
b. 1450 in Hertogenbosch, Netherlands
d. 1516
Source: *AtlBL; REn*

Bosch, Juan
Dominican. Author, Politician
b. Jun 30, 1909 in Dominican Republic
Source: *CurBio 63; DcCLAA; IntWW 74;
NewYTBE 70*

Boschwitz, Rudy
American. Senator
b. 1930 in Berlin, Germany
Source: *BioIn 11, 12; WhoAm 82*

Boscovich, Ruggiero Giuseppe
Italian. Mathematician, Physicist
b. 1711 in Ragusa, Dalmatia
d. 1787
Source: *WebBD 80*

Bose, Subhas Chandra
Indian. Politician
b. 1897
d. Aug 19, 1945
Source: *BioIn 1, 2, 3, 5, 7, 8, 9, 11*

Bosin, Blackbear
American Indian. Artist, Designer
Award-winning painter, who draws birds,
animals, Indian lore in flat, two-
dimensional style.
b. Jun 5, 1921 in Anadarko, Oklahoma
Source: *WhoAmA 73, 76, 78*

Bosley, Harold A
American. Clergyman, Author
b. Feb 19, 1907 in Burchard, Nebraska
d. Jan 21, 1975
Source: *AmAu&B; ConAu 49, 53; DrAS 74P;
WhoAm 74; WhoRel 75; WhoWor 78*

Bosley, Tom
American. Actor
Star of TV series "Happy Days"; won Tony
for role in *Fiorello,* 1959.
b. Oct 1, 1927 in Chicago, Illinois
Source: *BiE&WWA; FilmgC; IntMPA 82;
NotNAT; WhoAm 80, 82; WhoHol A;
WhoThe 77; WhoWor 74*

Bosson, Barbara
[Mrs. Steven Bochco]
American. Actress
Plays Fay Furillo in TV series "Hill Street
Blues."
b. Nov 1, in Bellvernon, Pennsylvania
Source: *WhoTelC*

Bossuet, Jacques Benigne
French. Author, Orator
Wrote *Discourse on Universal History,* 1681,
treatise in history from Christian
viewpoint.
b. Sep 27, 1627 in Dijon, France
d. Apr 12, 1704 in Paris, France
Source: *AtlBL; BbD; BiD&SB; CasWL; CyEd;
DcCathB; DcEuL; EuAu; EvEuW; IlEncMy;
OxEng; OxFr; PenC EUR; REn*

Bossy, Mike (Michael)
"Boss"
Canadian. Hockey Player
Right wing who scored 53 goals as rookie in
1977-78, an NHL record.
b. Jan 22, 1957 in Montreal, Quebec
Source: *CurBio 81; NewYTBS 81; WhoAm
82; WorAl*

Bostock, Lyman Wesley
American. Baseball Player
Promising outfielder, 1975-78, who died
tragically after being shot by estranged
husband of friend.
b. Nov 22, 1950 in Birmingham, Alabama
d. Sep 24, 1978 in Gary, Indiana
Source: *BaseEn 85; BioIn 11*

Boston
[Brad Delp; Barry Goudreau; Sib Hashian;
Tom Scholz; Fran Sheehan]
American. Music Group
Debut album *Boston*, 1976, sold 6.5 million
copies.
Source: *RkOn 74; RolSEnR 83*

Boston, Ralph
American. Track Athlete
b. May 9, 1939 in Laurel, Mississippi
Source: *BioIn 5, 6, 8, 9*

Boston Strangler
see: DeSalvo, Albert

Bostwick, Barry
American. Actor
Won 1977 Tony for *The Robber Bridegroom*;
title role in TV miniseries "George
Washington."
b. Feb 24, 1945 in San Mateo, California
Source: *BioIn 12; VarWW 85*

Bosustow, Stephen
Canadian. Producer
Co-founded United Productions of America,
animation co.; won three Oscars.
b. Nov 6, 1911 in Victoria, British Columbia
Source: *CurBio 58; DcFM; FilmgC; IntMPA
75, 76, 77, 81; OxFilm; WhoAm 82;
WhoWest 74; WorECar; WorEFlm*

Boswell, Charles Albert
American. Golfer
A 13-time champion of US Blind Golfers
Assn.
b. Dec 22, 1916 in Birmingham, Alabama
Source: *BioIn 1, 3, 11; WhoGolf*

Boswell, Connee
[Boswell Sisters]
American. Singer, Actress
b. Dec 3, 1912 in New Orleans, Louisiana
d. Oct 11, 1976 in New York, New York
Source: *AmSCAP 66; InWom; WhoHol A;
WhoJazz 72*

Boswell, James
Scottish. Lawyer, Biographer
Wrote *Life of Johnson*, 1791, best known
biography in English language.
b. Oct 18, 1740 in Edinburgh, Scotland
d. May 19, 1795 in London, England
Source: *Alli; AtlBL; BbD; BiD&SB; BrAu;
CasWL; Chambr 2; ChhPo S2; CrtT 2;
CyWA; DcEnA; DcEnL; DcEuL; DcLEL;
EvLB; IlsCB 1957; LongCTC; MnBBF;
MouLC 2; NewC; OxEng; PenC ENG; RAdv
1; RComWL; REn; WebE&AL*

Boswell, Martha
[Boswell Sisters]
American. Singer
Member of singing group trio with sisters.
b. 1905 in New Orleans, Louisiana
d. Jul 2, 1958 in Peekskill, New York
Source: *InWom; ObitOF 79; WhScrn 74, 77;
WhoHol B*

Boswell, Vet (Helvetia)
[Boswell Sisters]
American. Singer
In films with sisters *Big Broadcast*, 1932;
Moulin Rouge, 1934.
b. 1911 in New Orleans, Louisiana
Source: *InWom; WhoHol A*

Boswell Sisters
[Connee Boswell; Martha Boswell; Vet
Boswell]
American. Music Group
Three Southern girls who blended voices in a
way never heard before; made three
movies, 1930s.
Source: *CmpEPM; ThFT*

Bosworth, Barry
American. Statesman
Source: *NF*

Bosworth, Hobart van Zandt
American. Actor
Began film career, 1909, in *In the Sultan's
Power*, first dramatic film shot on West
Coast.
b. Aug 11, 1867 in Marietta, Ohio
d. Dec 30, 1943 in Glendale, California
Source: *CurBio 44; Film 1; FilmgC; MotPP;
MovMk; NotNAT B; ObitOF 79; TwYS;
WhAm 2; WhScrn 74, 77; WhoHol B*

Botero (Angulo), Fernando
Colombian. Artist
b. Apr 19, 1932 in Medellin, Colombia
Source: *BioIn 12; CurBio 80; IntWW 79*

Botha, Louis
South African. Military Leader, Political
Leader
Boer military leader, who helped form Union
of S Africa; became first premier, 1910-19.
b. Sep 27, 1862 in Honigfontein, South
Africa
d. Aug 27, 1919 in Pretoria, South Africa
Source: *BioIn 1; McGEWB; WhoMilH 76*

Botha, Pieter Willem
South African. Political Leader
Eighth prime minister of S Africa, elected
1978.
b. Jan 12, 1916 in Paul Roux, South Africa
Source: *CurBio 79; IntWW 74*

Botha, Roelof Pik
South African. Political Leader
Minister of Foreign Affairs, 1977--.
b. Apr 27, 1932 in Rustenburg, South Africa
Source: *AfSS 82; CurBio 84; GrBr; IntYB 82;
Who 83; WhoWor 82*

Bothwell, James Hepburn
Scottish. Nobleman
b. 1536
d. 1578
Source: *BioIn 1, 7, 9, 10, 11*

Bothwell, Jean
American. Children's Author
Wrote award-winning *The Thirteenth Stone,*
1946.
b. in Winside, Nebraska
d. Mar 2, 1977 in Missouri
Source: *ConAu 1R, 3NR; CurBio 46; InWom;
JBA 51; SmATA 2*

Bottel, Helen Alfea
American. Journalist
b. Mar 13, 1914 in Beaumont, California
Source: *ConAu 25R; ForWC 70; WhoAm 82;
WhoAmW 77; WrDr 80*

Bottger, Johann Friedrich
German. Chemist
Originated Dresden china; established
porcelain works, Meissen, Germany.
b. Feb 4, 1682
d. Mar 13, 1719
Source: *BioIn 1, 3, 4, 11*

Botticelli, Sandro
[Alessandrodi Mariano dei Filipipi]
Italian. Artist
Favorite artist, protege of Medici family; best
known work "The Birth of Venus."
b. 1444 in Florence, Italy
d. May 17, 1510 in Florence, Italy
Source: *AtlBL; DcCathB; Dis&D; McGDA;
McGEWB; NewC; NewCol 75; OxArt; REn;
WhDW; WorAl*

Bottome, Phyllis, pseud.
[Mrs. Ernan Forbes-Dennis]
English. Author
A prolific writer, best known for anti-Nazi
novel *The Mortal Storm,* 1937; *Private
Worlds,* 1937.
b. 1884
d. Aug 23, 1963 in Hampstead, England
Source: *ConAu 93; DcLEL; EvLB; InWom;
ModBrL; NewC; REn*

Bottomley, Gordon
English. Dramatist, Poet
b. Feb 20, 1874 in Keighley, England
d. Aug 25, 1948 in Oare, England
Source: *BioIn 3, 4, 5, 7; CasWL; NewC;
OxThe; PenC ENG; REn; TwCA, SUP*

Bottomley, Jim (James Leroy)
American. Baseball Player
Holds ML record for rbi's in one game, 12,
on Sep 16, 1924; Hall of Fame, 1974.
b. Apr 23, 1900 in Oglesby, Illinois
d. Dec 11, 1959 in Saint Louis, Missouri
Source: *BaseEn 85; BasesB*

Bottoms, Joseph
American. Actor
Film debut, 1974, in *The Dove.*
b. Apr 22, 1954 in Santa Barbara, California
Source: *IntMPA 81, 82; WhoHol A*

Bottoms, Sam
American. Actor
Brother of Joseph and Timothy; films include
Apocalyse Now, 1979; TV film "East of
Eden," 1981.
b. Oct 17, 1955 in Santa Barbara, California
Source: *VarWW 85; WhoHol A*

Bottoms, Timothy
American. Actor
In movie *The Last Picture Show,* 1971.
b. Aug 30, 1951 in Santa Barbara, California
Source: *ConTFT 3; FilmgC; IntMPA 82;
MovMk; WhoAm 82; WhoHol A; WorAl*

Botvinnik, Mikhail Moiseevich
Russian. Chess Player
b. Aug 17, 1911 in Leningrad, Russia
Source: *CurBio 65; IntWW 74; Who 74;
WhoWor 78*

Bouchard, Joe
[Blue Oyster Cult]
American. Singer, Musician
Bassist, vocalist with hard-rock group since
1969.
b. Nov 9, 1948 in Long Island, New York
Source: *NF*

Bouche, Rene Robert
American. Illustrator
Fashion, advertising illustrator with *Vogue,*
  1938-63.
b. Sep 20, 1905 in Prague, Austria-Hungary
d. Jul 3, 1963 in Sussex, England
Source: *DcAmB S7*

Boucher, Francois
French. Artist
b. Sep 29, 1703 in Paris, France
d. May 30, 1770 in Paris, France
Source: *AtlBL; OxFr; OxThe; REn*

Bouchet, Edward Alexander
American. Educator
First black to earn Ph.D. from Yale U,
  1876.
b. Sep 15, 1852 in New Haven, Connecticut
d. 1918
Source: *BioIn 8; WhoColR*

Boucicault, Dion
Irish. Author
b. Dec 26, 1820 in Dublin, Ireland
d. Sep 18, 1890 in New York, New York
Source: *AmAu&B; ApCAB; BbD; BiD&SB;*
  BrAu 19; CasWL; Chambr 3; ChhPo S1;
  CnThe; DcAmB; DcEnL; DcIrL; EvLB;
  HsB&A; McGEWB; McGEWD; MouLC 4;
  NewC; OxAmL; OxEng; PenC AM, ENG;
  PlP&P; PoIre; REn; REnAL; REnWD;
  TwCBDA; WebAB; WhDW; WhAm HS

Boudicca
see: Boadicea

Boudin, Eugene Louis
French. Artist
b. Jul 12, 1824 in Honfleur, France
d. Aug 8, 1898 in Deauville, France
Source: *AtlBL; OxFr*

Boudin, Kathy (Katherine)
American. Revolutionary
Involved in bomb factory explosion, 1970;
  captured after armored car robbery, 1981.
b. May 13, 1942 in New York, New York
Source: *BioIn 11*

Boudreau, Lou(is)
American. Baseball Player
Shortstop, Cleveland Indians, 1938-50; Hall
  of Fame, 1970.
b. Jul 17, 1917 in Harvey, Illinois
Source: *BaseEn 85; CurBio 42; WhoProB 73*

Bougainville, Louis Antoine de
French. Navigator
b. Nov 12, 1729 in Paris, France
d. Aug 31, 1811
Source: *ApCAB; BbtC; Drake; McGEWB;*
  OxCan; OxFr

Bouillon, Godfrey de
see: Godfrey of Bouillon

Boulanger, Georges Ernest Jean Marie
French. Soldier, Politician
b. 1837 in Rennes, France
d. 1891 in Brussels, Belgium
Source: *OxFr; REn*

Boulanger Louise
see: Louise Boulanger

Boulanger, Nadia Juliette
French. Composer, Conductor, Teacher
Influential teacher, conductor at Paris
  Conservatory; in US, pupils included
  Aaron Copeland.
b. Sep 16, 1887 in Paris, France
d. Oct 22, 1979 in Paris, France
Source: *CurBio 80; DcCM; GoodHs; InWom;*
  IntWW 78; LinLib S; NewYTBS 79; REn;
  WhDW; WhAm 7; Who 74; WhoAmW 74;
  WhoMus 72; WhoWor 74; WorAl

Boulding, Kenneth Ewart
American. Economist, Author, Educator
b. Jan 18, 1910 in Liverpool, England
Source: *AmAu&B; AmEA 74; AmM&WS 73S;*
  ConAu 5R; CurBio 65; IntWW 74; WhoAm
  74, 76, 78, 80, 82; WhoWest 84

Boulez, Pierre
French. Composer, Conductor
b. Mar 26, 1925 in Montbrison, France
Source: *CelR; CurBio 69; DcCM; IntWW 74;*
  NewYTBE 71, 73; REn; Who 74; WhoAm
  74, 76, 78, 80, 82; WhoMus 72; WhoWor 78

Boulle, Charles Andre
French. Designer
Cabinetmaker to Louis XIV; known for
  elaborate inlaid furniture.
b. Nov 11, 1642 in Paris, France
d. Feb 29, 1732 in Paris, France
Source: *NewCol 75; WebBD 80*

Boulle, Pierre Francois Marie-Louis
French. Author
Popular novels include *Bridge Over River
  Kwai,* 1952; *Planet of the Apes,* 1963.
b. Feb 20, 1912 in Avignon, France
Source: *Au&Wr 71; CasWL; ConAu 9R;*
  REn; TwCWr; WorAu

Boullioun, E(rnest) H(erman, Jr.)
"Tex"
American. Aircraft Manufacturer
With Boeing since 1940; pres. 1972--.
b. Nov 3, 1918 in Little Rock, Arkansas
Source: *Dun&B 79; NewYTBS 81; WhoAm
74, 76, 78; WhoF&I 74, 75, 77*

Boult, Adrian Cedric, Sir
English. Musician, Conductor
Conducted at coronations of King George
VI, Queen Elizabeth II.
b. Apr 8, 1889 in Chester, England
d. Feb 23, 1983 in Kent, England
Source: *Au&Wr 71; Baker 78; CurBio 83,
83N; IntWW 81; Who 82; WhoMus 72;
WhoWor 74; WorAl*

Boulting, John
English. Director
Films poked fun at British institutions,
    featured recurring cast of comic actors
    including Peter Sellers: *Heavens Above!*
    1963.
b. Nov 21, 1913 in Bray, England
d. Jun 19, 1985 in Warfield Dale, England
Source: *BiDFilm; CmMov; DcFM; IntMPA
83, 84; IntWW 83, 84; MovMk; OxFilm;
Who 83; WhoWor 78; WorEFlm*

Boulting, Roy
English. Producer
Founded Charter Films, 1937, with twin
    brother, John; films include *There's a Girl
    in My Soup,* 1970.
b. Nov 21, 1913 in Bray, England
Source: *BiDFilm; CmMov; DcFM; FilmEn;
FilmgC; IntMPA 75, 76, 77, 78, 79, 80, 81;
IntWW 75, 76, 77, 78; OxFilm; Who 85;
WhoWor 74, 76, 78; WorEFlm*

Boulton, Matthew
English. Manufacturer, Engineer
Built steam engines with James Watt;
    invented steel inlay process.
b. Sep 3, 1728
d. 1809
Source: *BioIn 10; WebBD 80*

Boumedienne, Houari
Algerian. President
b. Aug 23, 1932 in Clauzel, Algeria
d. Dec 27, 1978 in Algiers, Algeria
Source: *CurBio 71; IntWW 74; WhoGov 75*

Bouquet, Henry
British. Army Officer
Fought in French and Indian wars, defeating
    Indians in Pontiac's Rebellion, 1763.
b. 1719 in Rolle, Switzerland
d. Sep 2, 1765 in Pensacola, Florida
Source: *AmBi; ApCAB; DcAmB; Drake;
MacDCB 78; NatCAB 20; NewCol 75;
REnAW; WebAMB; WhAm HS; WhoMilH 76*

Bourassa, Henri
Canadian. Author, Politician
b. Sep 1, 1868 in Montreal, Quebec
d. Aug 31, 1952 in Montreal, Quebec
Source: *AmLY; CanWr; OxCan*

Bourassa, Robert
Canadian. Politician
Liberal Party premier of Quebec, 1970-76,
    1985--.
b. Jul 14, 1933 in Montreal, Quebec
Source: *CanWW 83*

Bourdonnais, Louis Charles de la
French. Chess Player
Most famous player in the world, 1818-1838.
b. 1795 in Ile Bourbon, France
d. 1840
Source: *OxChess*

Bourget, Paul (Charles Joseph)
French. Author, Critic
Wrote psychological, critical novels: *Le
    Disciple,* 1889.
b. Sep 2, 1852 in Amiens, France
d. Dec 25, 1935 in Paris, France
Source: *BbD; BiD&SB; CasWL; CathA 1930;
ClDMEL; ConAu 107; CyWA; DcBiA;
EncWL; EvEuW; LongCTC; OxAmH; OxEng;
OxFr; PenC EUR; REn; TwCA, SUP; WhThe*

Bourgholtzer, Frank
American. Broadcast Journalist
With NBC News since 1946.
b. Oct 26, 1919 in New York, New York
Source: *ConAu 25R; WhoAm 82; WhoTelC;
WhoWest 74*

Bourguiba, Habib Ben Ali
Tunisian. President
b. Aug 3, 1903 in Monastir, Tunisia
Source: *CurBio 55; IntWW 74; WhoWor 74*

Bourjaily, Vance
American. Author
Gained prominence in generation of young
writers after WW II.
b. Sep 17, 1922 in Cleveland, Ohio
Source: *AmAu&B; ASpks; Au&Wr 71; ConAu
1R, 2NR; ConLC 8; ConNov 72, 76; DcLB 2;
DcLEL 1940; DrAF 76; IntAu&W 76, 77;
IntWW 77, 78, 79, 80; LinLib L; ModAL;
OhA&B; OxAmL; PenC AM; REn; REnAL;
WhoAm 74, 76, 78, 80, 82; WhoWor 74, 76;
WorAu; WrDr 76, 80*

Bourke-White, Margaret
American. Photojournalist
Life photographer, 1936-69; first official
woman photojournalist of WW II: *You
Have Seen Their Faces,* 1937.
b. Jun 14, 1904 in New York, New York
d. Aug 27, 1971 in Stamford, Connecticut
Source: *AmAu&B; ConAu 29R; CurBio 71;
HerW; MacDWB; NewYTBE 71; REn;
REnAL; WebAB; WhAm 5; WhoAmW 77*

Bourque, Ray(mond Jean)
Canadian. Hockey Player
Defenseman, who won Calder Trophy, 1980.
b. Dec 28, 1960 in Montreal, Quebec
Source: *BioIn 12; HocEn*

Boussac, Marcel
"Cotton King of France"
French. Manufacturer
Made cotton airplane fabric during WW I;
later used as fashion fabric.
b. Apr 17, 1889 in Chateauroux, France
d. Mar 31, 1980 in Montargis, France
Source: *AnObit 1980; BioIn 2, 3, 5, 11;
NewYTBE 71; NewYTBS 80; Who 74;
WhoWor 74*

Boussingault, Jean
French. Chemist
b. 1802
d. 1887
Source: *BioIn 1, 2, 3, 5, 6, 7; NewCol 75*

Bouton, Jim (James Alan)
"Bulldog"
American. Baseball Player, Author
Pitcher, NY Yankees, 1962-68; author *Ball
Four,* 1970.
b. Mar 8, 1939 in Newark, New Jersey
Source: *BaseEn 85; CelR; ConAu 89; CurBio
71; NewYTBE 70; WhoAm 76, 78, 80, 82;
WhoE 74, 75; WhoProB 73; WorAl*

Bouts, Dierick C
Dutch. Artist
b. 1420 in Haarlem, New Hampshire
d. 1475
Source: *OxArt*

Boutwell, George Sewell
American. Politician
b. Jan 23, 1818 in Brookline, Massachusetts
d. Feb 27, 1905
Source: *BioIn 8, 10, 11*

Bova, Ben(jamin William)
American. Author, Editor
b. Nov 8, 1932 in Philadelphia, Pennsylvania
Source: *ConAu 5R; SmATA 6; WhoAm 74,
76, 78, 80, 82; WhoE 74*

Bovet, Daniele
Italian. Chemist
Won Nobel Prize, 1957, for developing drugs
to relieve allergies.
b. Mar 23, 1907 in Neuchatel, Switzerland
Source: *BioIn 6; CurBio 58; InSci; WorAl*

Bow, Clara Gordon
American. Actress
Starred in Roaring 20s silent films; symbol of
flapper age.
b. Aug 25, 1905 in New York, New York
d. Sep 27, 1965 in Los Angeles, California
Source: *BiDFilm; CmCal; Film 2; FilmgC;
InWom; LibW; MotPP; MovMk; OxFilm;
ThFT; TwYS; WebAB; WhScrn 74, 77;
WhoHol B; WomWMM; WorEFlm*

Bow Wow Wow
[Annabella; Matthew Ashman; Dave
Barbarossa; Leroy Gorman]
British. Music Group
New Wave band, 1980-83; combined African
rhythms, chants, surf instrumentals, pop
melodies.
Source: *IlEncRk; NewWmR; RolSEnR 83*

Bowa, Larry (Lawrence Robert)
American. Baseball Player
Shortstop, Philadelphia, 1970--.
b. Dec 6, 1945 in Sacramento, California
Source: *BaseEn 85; BioIn 11; WhoProB 73;
WorAl*

Bowditch, Nathaniel
American. Astronomer, Mathematician
Published first usable navigation guide, *New Practical Navigator,* 1802.
b. Mar 26, 1773 in Salem, Massachusetts
d. Mar 16, 1838 in Boston, Massachusetts
Source: *AmAu; AmBi; ApCAB; BiDAmS; CyAL 1; DcAmAu; DcAmB; DcNAA; DcScB; Drake; EncAB-A; LinLib S; McGEWB; NatCab 6; OxAmL; REnAL; TwCBDA; WebAB; WhAm HS*

Bowdler, Thomas
English. Editor
His expurgated editions of Shakespeare's works and Gibbon's *Decline & Fall* resulted in term "bowdlerize."
b. Jul 11, 1754 in Ashley, England
d. Feb 24, 1825 in Rhyddings, England
Source: *Alli; BiDLA, SUP; BrAu; CasWL; Chambr 2; DcBiPP; DcEnL; DcLEL; EvLB; LinLib L; LongCEL; NewC; OxEng*

Bowdoin, James
American. Merchant, Colonial Leader
Governor of MA, 1785-87; Bowdoin College founded in his honor, 1794.
b. Aug 7, 1726 in Boston, Massachusetts
d. Nov 6, 1790 in Boston, Massachusetts
Source: *Alli; AmAu&B; AmBi; ApCAB; BiAUS; BiDAmS; CyAL 1; DcAmB; Drake; McGEWB; OxAmH; TwCBDA; WebAB; WhAm HS*

Bowell, Mackenzie, Sir
Canadian. Statesman
b. Dec 27, 1823
d. Dec 11, 1917
Source: *ApCAB; OxCan*

Bowen, Billy
[Ink Spots]
American. Singer
One of first black groups to break color barrier over airwaves.
b. 1909 in Birmingham, Alabama
d. Sep 27, 1982 in New York, New York
Source: *NF*

Bowen, Catherine Drinker
American. Author
Biographies include *John Adams and the American Revolution,* 1950; *The Lion and the Throne: The Life and Times of Sir Edward Coke,* 1957.
b. Jan 1, 1897 in Haverford, Pennsylvania
d. Nov 1, 1973 in Haverford, Pennsylvania
Source: *AmAu&B; AmWomWr; ConAu 5R, 45; CurBio 44, 73; InWom; LinLib L; NewYTBE 73; OxAmL; REn; REnAL; SmATA 7; TwCA SUP; WhAm 6; Who 74; WhoAm 74; WhoAmW 74; WhoGov 72; WhoWor 74*

Bowen, Elizabeth Dorothea Cole
Irish. Author
Wrote *The Heat of the Day,* 1949; noted for sensitive use of language, character.
b. Jun 7, 1899 in Dublin, Ireland
d. Feb 22, 1973 in London, England
Source: *Au&Wr 71; AuBYP; CasWL; ConAu 17R, 41R, P-2; ConLC 1, 3, 6, 11, 15; ConNov 72; CyWA; DcLEL; EncWL; EvLB; LongCTC; ModBrL, S1; NewC; OxEng; PenC ENG; RAdv 1; REn; TwCA, SUP; TwCWr; WebE&AL; WhAm 5; WhoTwCL*

Bowen, Otis Ray
American. Physician, Politician
Governor of IN, 1973-81.
b. Feb 26, 1918 in Rochester, Indiana
Source: *BioIn 9; WhoAm 78, 80, 82*

Bowen, Roger
American. Actor
Played Henry Blake in movie *MASH,* 1970.
b. May 25, 1932 in Attleboro, Massachusetts
Source: *WhoHol A*

Bowers, Claude Gernade
American. Historian, Diplomat
His historical works include *Jefferson and Hamilton,* 1925; *The Tragic Era: The Revolution After Lincoln,* 1929.
b. Nov 20, 1878 in Hamilton County, Indiana
d. Jan 21, 1958 in New York, New York
Source: *AmAu&B; CurBio 41, 58; DcAmB S6; DcAmDH; EncAB-H; EncSoH; IndAu 1816; OxAmL; REn; REnAL; TwCA, SUP; WhAm 3*

Bowes, "Major" (Edward)
American. Broadcaster
Best known for radio program "Major
   Bowes' Amateur Hour," 1934-46.
b. Jun 14, 1874 in San Francisco, California
d. Jun 13, 1946 in New York, New York
Source: *ChhPo S2; CurBio 41, 46; DcAmB
S4; NotNAT B; ObitOF 79; WhAm 2;
WhScrn 77; WhoHol B; WorAl*

Bowes, Walter
American. Businessman
With Arthur Pitney, inventor, formed Pitney
   Bowes Co.
b. 1882 in England
d. Jun 24, 1957 in Washington, District of
   Columbia
Source: *Entr; ObitOF 79*

Bowie, David
[David Robert Hayward-Jones]
English. Singer, Songwriter, Actor
Pop-rock singer who starred in film *The
   Man Who Fell to Earth,* 1976.
b. Jan 8, 1947 in London, England
Source: *BioNews 74; BkPepl; ConTFT 3;
RkOn 74; WhoAm 84; WhoHol A*

Bowie, James
American. Soldier, Inventor
Reputed inventor of Bowie knife; killed at
   Alamo.
b. 1796 in Burke County, Georgia
d. Mar 6, 1836 in The Alamo, Texas
Source: *AmBi; ApCAB; DcAmB; TwCBDA;
WebAB; WhAm HS*

Bowie, Norman Ernest
American. Author
b. Jun 6, 1942 in Biddeford, Maine
Source: *ConAu 33R; DrAS 74P; WhoAm 74,
76, 78, 80, 82; WhoE 74; WrDr 76*

Bowie, Walter (Wat)
American. Lawyer, Spy
Spy for Confederacy, 1861-64.
b. 1837 in Maryland
d. 1864 in Annapolis, Maryland
Source: *BioIn 3, 6; SpyCS*

Bowker, Albert Hosmer
American. Educator
b. Sep 8, 1919 in Winchendon, Massachusetts
Source: *AmM&WS 73P; CurBio 66; LEduc
74; NewYTBE 71; WhoAm 74, 76, 78, 80,
82; WhoWest 84*

Bowker, R(ichard) R(ogers)
American. Publisher, Editor, Author
Founded R R Bowker Co., 1872; co-founder
   Library Journal, 1876.
b. Sep 4, 1848 in Salem, Massachusetts
d. Nov 12, 1933 in Stockbridge,
   Massachusetts
Source: *Alli SUP; AmAu&B; BbD; BiD&SB;
DcAmAu; DcAmB S1; DcNAA; WebAB;
WhAm 1; WhNAA*

Bowles, Chester Bliss
American. Diplomat, Businessman, Author
Liberal Dem. who was presidential adviser,
   governor, congressman during 25-yr. public
   career.
b. Apr 5, 1901 in Springfield, Massachusetts
d. May 26, 1986 in Essex, Connecticut
Source: *AmAu&B; Au&Wr 71; BiDrAC;
ConAu 69; CurBio 43, 57, 86; IntWW 74;
REnAL; Who 74; WhoAm 74; WhoWor 74*

Bowles, Jane Sydney
[Mrs. Paul Bowles]
American. Author
Noted "writer's writer," who did stories on
   women and their attempt at independence.
b. Feb 22, 1917 in New York, New York
d. May 4, 1973 in Malaga, Spain
Source: *AmWomWr; Au&Wr 71; BiE&WWA;
ConAu 41R, P-2; ConLC 3; ConNov 72;
DcLEL 1940; ModAL; NewYTBE 73; PenC
AM; WhoTwCL; WorAu*

Bowles, Paul
American. Composer, Author
b. Dec 30, 1910 in New York, New York
Source: *AmAu&B; AmSCAP 66; Au&Wr 71;
BiE&WWA; ConAu 1R; ConLC 1, 2; ConNov
72, 76; DrAF 76; IntWW 74; ModAL, S1;
NotNAT; OxAmL; PenC AM; RAdv 1;
REnAL; TwCA SUP; TwCWr; WhoAm 74,
76, 78, 80, 82; WhoE 74; WhoTwCL;
WhoWor 78; WrDr 80*

Bowles, Samuel, II
American. Journalist
b. Feb 9, 1826 in Springfield, Massachusetts
d. Jan 16, 1878 in Springfield, Massachusetts
Source: *Alli SUP; AmAu&B; AmBi; BbD;
BbtC; BiD&SB; DcAmAu; DcAmB; DcNAA;
OxAmL; REnAL; TwCBDA; WebAB; WhAm
HS*

Bowles, William Augustus
American. Adventurer
b. 1763
d. 1802
Source: *BioIn 7, 8, 9*

Bowling, Roger
American. Songwriter
Wrote songs "Lucille" and "Coward of the
County."
b. 1944
d. Dec 25, 1982 in Clayton, Georgia
Source: *NF*

Bowman, Lee (Lucien Lee, Sr.)
American. Actor
Played opposite Susan Hayward in film
Smash-Up, 1947.
b. Dec 28, 1914 in Cincinnati, Ohio
Source: *BiE&WWA; FilmgC; IntMPA 75, 76,
77; MotPP; MovMk; NewYTBS 79; WhoHol
A*

Bowman, Scotty (William Scott)
Canadian. Hockey Player, Hockey Coach
Coach, Montreal Canadiens, 1973-79; won
four Stanley Cups.
b. Sep 18, 1933 in Montreal, Quebec
Source: *NewYTBS 79; WhoAm 80, 82;
WhoHcky 73*

Bowra, Maurice, Sir
English. Educator, Critic
Considered among leading classical scholars,
critics of time.
b. Apr 8, 1898 in Kuikiang, China
d. Jul 4, 1971 in Oxford, England
Source: *Au&Wr 71; ChhPo S3; EvLB;
ModBrL*

Bowser, Betty Ann
American. Broadcast Journalist
b. 1944 in Norfolk, Virginia
Source: *ForWC 70; WhoAm 82*

Box, John
English. Filmmaker
Art director who won Oscars for *Doctor
Zhivago*, 1965; *Oliver*, 1968.
b. Jan 27, 1920 in Kent, England
Source: *VarWW 85*

Box Tops, The
[Rick Allen; Thomas Boggs; Alex Chilton;
   Harold Cloud; William Cunningham; John
   Evans; Swain Scharfer; Daniel Smythe;
   Gary Talley]
American. Music Group
Memphis-based "blue-eyed soul" band, 1965-
70; hit single "The Letter," 1967.
Source: *ConMuA 80A; RkOn 78; RolSEnR
83; WhoRock 81*

Boxleitner, Bruce
American. Actor
Star of TV series "Scarecrow and Mrs.
King," 1983--.
b. May 12, 1951 in Elgin, Illinois
Source: *BioIn 11; ConTFT 3*

Boy George
[George O'Dowd; Culture Club]
English. Singer
Flamboyant lead singer, known for avant-
garde dress, make-up.
b. Jun 14, 1961 in Bexley Heath, England
Source: *CurBio 85*

Boyce, Christopher John
[Anthony Lester]
"Falcon"
American. Spy
Former CIA clerk, sentenced to 40 yrs.
imprisonment for selling classified
documents to Soviets.
b. 1953 in Palos Verdes, California
Source: *NewYTBS 77; PseudN 82; SpyCS*

Boyce, Westray Battle
American. Government Official
b. Aug 1901 in Rocky Mount, North
Carolina
d. Jan 31, 1972 in Washington, District of
Columbia
Source: *BioIn 9; CurBio 45, 72*

Boyce, William
English. Organist, Composer
b. 1710 in London, England
d. Feb 7, 1779 in Kensington, England
Source: *BioIn 9; OxMus; WebBD 80*

Boycott, Charles Cunningham
English. Manager
Land agent ostracized for refusing to reduce
rents; name has come to mean concerted
refusal to do something.
b. Mar 12, 1832 in Norfolk, England
d. Jul 19, 1897
Source: *CelCen; WebBD 80; WorAl*

Boyd, Belle (Isabellle)
American. Spy, Actress
Confederate spy, 1861-62.
b. May 8, 1843 in Martinsburg, Virginia
d. Jun 11, 1900 in Kilbourne, Wisconsin
Source: *Alli SUP; AmAu&B; AmBi; CivWDc;
DcAmB; DcNAA; HarEnUS; HerW; InWom;
NotAW; OxAmH; WhAm HS*

Boyd, Bill
[Cowboy Rambler]
American. Singer
Popular Dallas dj for over 35 years; songs
include "Under the Double Eagle"; "Ridin'
on a Humpback Mule."
b. 1911 in Fannin County, Texas
Source: *EncFCWM 69, 83*

Boyd, James
American. Author
Historical novels include *Drums,* 1925.
b. Jul 2, 1888 in Harrisburg, Pennsylvania
d. Feb 25, 1944 in Princeton, New Jersey
Source: *DcAmB S3; REnAL*

Boyd, Julian Parks
American. Historian, Editor
Wrote *The Papers of Thomas Jefferson,*
complete written record of Jefferson.
b. Nov 3, 1903 in Converse, South Carolina
d. May 21, 1980 in Princeton, New Jersey
Source: *AmAu&B; BioIn 10, 11; ConAu 65,
97; CurBio 76, 80; DrAS 74H, 78H; REnAL;
WhoAm 74, 76, 78; WhoE 74*

Boyd, Liona Maria
Canadian. Musician
First lady of classical guitar who won Juno
award for Canadian instrumentalist of yr.,
1978, 1982, 1983.
b. 1949 in London, Ontario
Source: *BioIn 11; WhoAm 80, 82, 84*

Boyd, Louise Arner
American. Explorer
First woman to successfully fly over N Pole,
1955.
b. Sep 16, 1887 in San Rafael, California
d. Sep 14, 1972 in San Francisco, California
Source: *AmAu&B; CurBio 60, 72; InSci;
InWom; WhoAmW 74*

Boyd, Malcolm
American. Author, Clergyman
Involved in civil, gay rights; archives at
Boston U.
b. Jun 8, 1923 in Buffalo, New York
Source: *AmAu&B; AmM&WS 73P; CelR;
ConAu 5R, 4NR; WhoAm 74, 76, 78, 80, 82;
WhoE 74; WhoRel 75; WhoWor 78; WrDr 76*

Boyd, Stephen
American. Actor
Played Messala in *Ben Hur,* 1959.
b. Jul 4, 1928 in Belfast, Northern Ireland
d. Jun 2, 1977 in Los Angeles, California
Source: *CmMov; CurBio 61; FilmgC; IntMPA
75, 76, 77; MotPP; MovMk; WhoAm 74;
WhoHol A; WorEFlm*

Boyd, William (Bill)
"Hopalong Cassidy"
American. Actor
Best known as Hopalong Cassidy, character
he played 66 times, 1935-48.
b. Jun 5, 1898 in Cambridge, Ohio
d. Sep 12, 1972 in South Laguna, California
Source: *CmMov; CurBio 50, 72; Film 1;
FilmgC; MovMk; OxFilm; WhAm 5; WhScrn
77; WhoHol B*

Boyd, William Clouser
American. Physician
Founder of modern immunology, 1945;
discovered 13 blood types.
b. Mar 4, 1903 in Dearborn, Missouri
d. Feb 19, 1983 in Falmouth, Massachusetts
Source: *AmM&WS 79P; AnObit 1983; ConAu
109; McGMS 80; NewYTBS 83; WhoAm 82*

Boyd-Orr, John Boyd Orr, Baron
Scottish. Nutritionist
Helped avert famine in Europe after WW II;
won Nobel Peace Prize, 1949.
b. Sep 23, 1880 in Kilmaurs, Scotland
d. Jun 25, 1971 in Brechin, Scotland
Source: *Au&Wr 71; CurBio 46, 71; ObitT
1971; WorAl*

Boyer, Charles
French. Actor
Starred in movies *Algiers,* 1938, *Gaslight,*
1944.
b. Aug 28, 1899 in Figeac, France
d. Aug 26, 1978 in Phoenix, Arizona
Source: *BiDFilm; BiE&WWA; CelR; CmMov;
CurBio 43, 78; FilmgC; IntMPA 75, 76, 77;
MotPP; MovMk; OxFilm; WhoAm 74;
WhoHol A; WhoThe 77A; WhoWor 78;
WorEFlm*

Boyer, Harold R
American. Businessman
b. Feb 25, 1899 in Springfield, Ohio
Source: *BioIn 2, 3; CurBio 52*

Boyer, Herbert Wayne
American. Biochemist
Director, Genetech, Inc., who patented
procedure of gene splicing, 1970s.
b. Jul 10, 1936 in Pittsburgh, Pennsylvania
Source: *AmM&WS 73P, 76P, 79P; ConNews
85-1; WhoAm 78, 80, 82, 84*

Boyer, Ken(ton Lloyd)
American. Baseball Player
Infielder, 1955-69, who won five gold gloves;
  NL MVP, 1964.
b. May 20, 1931 in Liberty, Missouri
d. Sep 7, 1982 in Saint Louis, Missouri
Source: *BaseEn 85; CurBio 66, 82; NewYTBS
82; WhoProB 73*

Boyington, "Pappy" (Gregory)
American. Pilot
Leader of Marine Fighter Squadron 214
  "Black Sheep" during WW II.
b. Dec 4, 1912 in Coeur d'Alene, Idaho
Source: *AmAu&B*

Boyle, Harold Vincent
American. Journalist
b. Feb 21, 1911 in Kansas City, Missouri
d. Apr 1, 1974 in New York, New York
Source: *ConAu 101, 89; CurBio 45, 74;
WhAm 6; WhoAm 74; WhoWor 74*

Boyle, Jack
"Boston Blackie"
American. Author
Source: *EncMys*

Boyle, Kay
American. Author
b. Feb 19, 1903 in Saint Paul, Minnesota
Source: *AmAu&B; AmNov; CasWL; CnDAL;
ConAmA; ConAu 13R; ConLC 1, 5; ConNov
72, 76; ConP 70, 75; DcLEL; DrAF 76;
DrAP 75; EncWL; ForWC 70; InWom;
LongCTC; ModAL; OxAmL; PenC AM; RAdv
1; REn; REnAL; TwCA, SUP; Who 74;
WhoAm 74, 76, 78, 80, 82; WhoTwCL;
WhoWor 78; WrDr 76*

Boyle, Peter
American. Actor
Films include *Taxi Driver,* 1976; *Joe,* 1970.
b. Oct 18, 1935 in Philadelphia, Pennsylvania
Source: *ConTFT 3; FilmgC; IntMPA 82;
MovMk; NewYTBE 71; VarWW 85; WhoAm
82; WhoHol A*

Boyle, Robert
Irish. Scientist
First to isolate, collect a gas; formulated
  physics law that bears name.
b. Jan 25, 1627 in Lismore Castle, Ireland
d. Dec 30, 1691 in London, England
Source: *Alli; CasWL; CyAL 1; DcEnL; EvLB;
REn*

Boyle, Tony (William Anthony)
American. Labor Union Official
Pres., UMW, 1963-72; convicted of 1969
  murders of rival Joseph Yablonski and
  family.
b. Dec 1, 1904 in Bald Butte, Montana
Source: *NewYTBE 72; WhoS&SW 82*

Boylesve, Rene
French. Author
b. 1867
d. 1926
Source: *BioIn 1, 4, 5*

Boylston, Helen Dore
American. Author
Used experience as nurse to write *Sue Barton*
  novels for girls, 1936-52.
b. Apr 4, 1895 in Portsmouth, New
  Hampshire
d. Sep 30, 1984 in Trumbull, Connecticut
Source: *AmWomWr; AuBYP; ConAu 113, 73;
CurBio 42, 84; NewYTBS 84; SmATA 23;
TwCCW 83; WrDr 82, 84*

Bozeman, John M
American. Pioneer
Blazed trail across Rockies, Bozeman Pass,
  1863; founded town of Bozeman, MT.
b. 1835 in Georgia
d. Apr 20, 1867 in Yellowstone River,
  Montana
Source: *AmBi; WebAB; WhAm HS*

Brabham, Jack (John Arthur)
Australian. Auto Racer
b. Apr 2, 1926
Source: *BioIn 7, 8, 9, 10*

Brace, Charles Loring
American. Social Worker
b. 1826
d. 1890
Source: *BioIn 4, 6*

Brace, Gerald Warner
American. Author, Educator
Described New England life in his 11 novels
  including *Bell's Landing,* 1955.
b. Sep 23, 1901 in Islip, New York
d. Jul 20, 1978 in Blue Hill, Maine
Source: *AmAu&B; AmNov; Au&Wr 71;
ConAu 13R, 81; CurBio 47, 78; DrAS 74E,
78E; NewYTBS 78; REnAL; TwCA SUP;
WhAm 7; WhoAm 74, 76, 78; WrDr 76*

Braceland, Francis J(ames)
American. Psychiatrist, Editor
With Institute of Living, 1951-68; editor,
    American Journal of Psychiatry, 1965-78.
b. Jul 22, 1900 in Philadelphia, Pennsylvania
d. Feb 23, 1985 in Sarasota, Florida
Source: *ConAu 115; WhoAm 82*

Bracey, John Henry, Jr.
American. Author
b. Jul 17, 1941 in Chicago, Illinois
Source: *ConAu 29R; LivgBAA*

Brach, Emil J
American. Candy Manufacturer
Opened candy store/factory in Chicago, 1904.
b. 1859 in Schoenwald, Germany
d. Oct 29, 1947 in Chicago, Illinois
Source: *Entr; WhAm 2*

Bracken, Brendan Rendall, Viscount
Irish. Publisher
Churchill's Parliamentary private secretary;
    chm., *Financial Times; Financial News*.
b. Feb 15, 1901 in Tipperary, Ireland
d. Aug 8, 1958 in London, England
Source: *CurBio 41, 58; DcIrB; DcNaB 1951;*
GrBr; ObitOF 79; WhE&EA; WhWW-II

Bracken, Eddie (Edward Vincent)
American. Actor, Director, Singer, Artist
Stage, film actor, 1940s-60s; started career in
    Our Gang series, 1920s.
b. Feb 7, 1920 in New York, New York
Source: *BiE&WWA; BioNews 74; BusPN;*
ConTFT 3; CurBio 44; FilmgC; HolP 40;
IntMPA 82; MotPP; MovMk; NewYTBE 71;
NotNAT; WhoAm 84; WhoHol A; WhoThe 77

Brackett, Charles
American. Producer, Screenwriter
Produced five Oscar-winners; often
    collaborated with Billy Wilder.
b. Nov 26, 1892 in Saratoga Springs, New
    York
d. Mar 9, 1969
Source: *AmAu&B; ConAu 113; CurBio 51;*
WorEFlm

Brackman, Robert
American. Artist
Still life painter, portraitist of notable
    Americans including the Rockefellers.
b. Sep 25, 1898 in Odessa, Russia
d. Jul 16, 1980 in New London, Connecticut
Source: *CurBio 53, 80; DcCAA 71, 77;*
McGDA; WhoAm 74, 76, 78, 80; WhoAmA
73, 76, 78; WhoE 74

Bradbury, Malcolm
English. Author
b. Sep 7, 1932 in Sheffield, England
Source: *Au&Wr 71; ConAu 1R; ConNov 72,*
76; ConP 70; ModBrL, S1; NewC; TwCWr;
WrDr 80

Bradbury, Ray Douglas
American. Author
Has written over 1,000 science fiction stories.
b. Aug 22, 1920 in Waukegan, Illinois
Source: *AmAu&B; Au&Wr 71; AuNews 1, 2;*
BioNews 74; CasWL; CelR; CmMov;
CnMWL; ConAu 1R, 2NR; ConLC 1, 3, 10,
15; ConNov 72, 76; CurBio 53, 82; DrAF 76;
FilmgC; LongCTC; OxAmL; PenC AM; REn;
REnAL; SmATA 11; TwCA SUP; TwCWr;
WebAB; Who 82; WhoAm 74, 76, 78, 80, 82;
WhoWor 78; WorEFlm; WrDr 76, 80

Braddock, Edward
English. Military Leader
Commanded British in French and Indian
    War, 1755; killed in expedition on Ft.
    Duquesne.
b. 1695 in Perthshire, Scotland
d. Jul 13, 1755 in Fort Duquesne,
    Pennsylvania
Source: *AmBi; ApCAB; DcAmB; Drake;*
HarEnUS; MacDCB 78; OxCan; REn;
TwCBDA; WhAm HS

Braddock, James J
"Cinderella Man"
American. Boxer
b. Dec 6, 1905 in New York, New York
d. 1974 in North Bergen, New Jersey
Source: *BioNews 75; NewYTBS 74*

Brademas, John
American. Politician, University
    Administrator
US representative, 1959-78; pres., NYU,
    1981--.
b. Mar 2, 1927 in Mishawaka, Indiana
Source: *AlmAP 78, 80; BiDrAC; BioIn 5, 6,*
7, 10, 11; CngDr 74, 77, 79; CurBio 77;
NewYTBS 81; PolProf J, NF; WhoAm 74, 76,
78, 80, 82, 84; WhoAmP 73, 75, 77, 79;
WhoGov 77; WhoMW 76, 78; WhoWor 78

Braden, Anne
American. Author, Editor
b. 1924
Source: *BioIn 8*

Braden, Spruille
American. Diplomat
b. Mar 13, 1894 in Elkhorn, Montana
d. Jan 10, 1978 in Los Angeles, California
Source: *CurBio 45, 78; WhoAm 74; WhoWor 74*

Bradford, Gamaliel
American. Author
Known for psychological biographies of
    literary, historical figures; *Damaged Souls,*
    1923.
b. Oct 9, 1863 in Boston, Massachusetts
d. Apr 11, 1932
Source: *AmAu&B; AmBi; AmLY; AnMV
1926; CasWL; CnDAL; ConAmA; ConAmL;
DcAmB S1; DcLEL; DcNAA; LinLib L, S;
OxAmH; OxAmL; REnAL; TwCA, SUP;
WhAm 1; WhNAA*

Bradford, Roark
American. Author, Dramatist
Wrote about blacks, Bible; play *Green
    Pastures,* 1940, was dramatization of *John
    Henry,* 1931.
b. Aug 21, 1896 in Lauderdale City,
    Tennessee
d. Nov 13, 1948 in New Orleans, Louisiana
Source: *AmAu&B; AmSCAP 66; ChhPo;
CnDAL; DcAmB S4; DcNAA; LongCTC;
ObitOF 79; OxAmL; REn; REnAL; TwCA,
SUP; WhAm 2, 2*

Bradford, William
American. Colonial Leader
Landed at Plymouth Rock, Dec, 1620;
    reelected governor of Plymouth Colony 30
    times.
b. 1590 in Austerfield, England
d. May 9, 1657 in Plymouth, Massachusetts
Source: *Alli, SUP; AmAu; AmAu&B; AmBi;
ApCAB; BbD; BiD&SB; BiDLA; CasWL;
CyAL 1; DcAmAu; DcAmB; DcLEL; DcNAA;
Drake; EncAB-H; EvLB; MouLC 1; NatCAB
7; OxAmL; PenC AM; REn; REnAL;
TwCBDA; WebAB, 79; WebE&AL; WhDW;
WhAm HS; WhAmP*

Bradham, Caleb D
American. Inventor
Invented Pepsi-Cola, 1890s to rival Coke.
b. in New Bern, North Carolina
Source: *NF*

Bradlee, Ben(jamin Crowninshield)
American. Journalist, Editor
Washington *Post,* vp, exec. editor, 1968--.
b. Aug 26, 1921 in Boston, Massachusetts
Source: *AuNews 2; ConAu 61; WhoAm 74,
76, 78, 80, 82; WhoS&SW 82; WhoWor 78*

Bradley, Andrew Cecil
English. Critic
Accepted chair of poetry at Oxford, 1901;
    wrote masterpiece *Shakespearian Tragedy,*
    1904.
b. Mar 26, 1851 in Cheltenham, England
d. Sep 2, 1935 in London, England
Source: *DcNaB 1931; EvLB; GrBr; LongCTC;
NewC; OxEng; PenC ENG; TwCA; WhLit*

Bradley, Bill (William)
American. Football Player
b. Jan 24, 1947 in Palestine, Texas
Source: *CngDr 81; WhoFtbl 74*

Bradley, Bill (William Warren)
American. Basketball Player, Senator
Forward, NY Knicks, 1967-77; Hall of
    Fame, 1982; US senator from NJ, 1979.
b. Jul 28, 1943 in Crystal City, Missouri
Source: *CelR; CurBio 65, 82; WhoAm 82;
WhoAmP 81; WhoBbl 73; WhoE 81; WorAl*

Bradley, David Henry, Jr.
American. Author
Relates tragedy of black history in novel
    Chaneysville Incident, 1981.
b. Sep 7, 1950 in Bedford, Pennsylvania
Source: *BioIn 10, 11; ConAu 104; NewYTBS
81*

Bradley, Ed
American. Broadcast Journalist
Co-anchorman "60 Minutes," replacing Dan
    Rather, 1981--.
b. Jun 22, 1941 in Philadelphia, Pennsylvania
Source: *WhoAm 80, 82*

Bradley, Henry
English. Lexicographer
Editor, *Oxford English Dictionary,* 1915.
b. Dec 3, 1845 in Manchester, England
d. May 23, 1923 in Oxford, England
Source: *Alli, SUP; DcLEL; EvLB; LongCTC;
NewC; OxEng*

Bradley, James
English. Astronomer
b. Mar 1693 in Shireborn, England
d. Jul 13, 1762
Source: *Alli; BiAUS*

Bradley, Joseph P
American. Supreme Court Justice
b. Mar 14, 1813 in Berne, New York
d. Jan 22, 1892 in Washington, District of
    Columbia
Source: *ApCAB; BiAUS; DcAmB; DcNAA;
Drake; TwCBDA; WebAB; WhAm HS*

Bradley, Milton
American. Manufacturer, Publisher
First game, "The Checkered Game of Life"
   led to success of Milton Bradley Co.
b. Nov 8, 1836 in Vienna, Maine
d. May 30, 1911 in Springfield,
   Massachusetts
Source: *AmAu&B; DcAmB; DcNAA; WebAB;
WhAm 1*

Bradley, Omar Nelson
"The GI's General"
American. General
Last five-star general; first permanent
   chairman Joint Chiefs of Staff, 1949-53.
b. Feb 12, 1893 in Clark, Missouri
d. Apr 8, 1981 in New York, New York
Source: *BioIn 1, 2, 3, 4, 6, 8, 9, 10, 11;
ConAu 103; CurBio 43, 81; EncAB-A; IntWW
74, 75, 76, 77, 78; LinLib S; McGEWB;
NewYTBS 81; PolProf T; PseudN 82; St&PR
75; WebAB; WebAMB; WhWW-II; Who 74;
WhoAm 74, 76, 78, 80; WhoWor 74, 78;
WorDWW*

Bradley, Pat(ricia Ellen)
American. Golfer
On pro circuit since 1974; won US Open,
   1981; first woman golfer to win $2
   million.
b. Mar 24, 1951 in Westford, Massachusetts
Source: *WhoAm 82, 84; WhoGolf; WhoIntG*

Bradley, Tom (Thomas)
American. Politician
First black mayor of predominantly white
   city, Los Angeles, 1973--.
b. Dec 29, 1917 in Calvert, Texas
Source: *CurBio 73; NewYTBE 73; NewYTBS
74; WhoAm 74, 76, 78, 80, 82; WhoAmP 73;
WhoWest 84*

Bradley, Will
[Wilbur Schwichtenberg]
American. Musician, Band Leader
b. Jul 12, 1912 in Newton, New Jersey
Source: *BioIn 9*

Bradshaw, George
English. Printer
b. 1801
d. 1853
Source: *BioIn 1*

Bradshaw, Terry Paxton
American. Football Player
Quarterback, Pittsburgh, 1970-83, who led
   Steelers to four Super Bowl victories.
b. Sep 2, 1948 in Shreveport, Louisiana
Source: *CelR; WhoAm 74, 76, 78, 80, 82;
WhoFtbl 74*

Bradstreet, Anne
American. Poet
Produced first significant literary work in
   Colonial New England.
b. 1612 in Northampton, England
d. Sep 16, 1672 in Andover, Massachusetts
Source: *Alli; AmAu; AmAu&B; AmBi;
ApCAB; BiD&SB; CasWL; ChhPo, S2;
CnDAL; CnE&AP; CyAL 1; DcAmAu;
DcAmB; DcEnL; DcLEL; DcNAA; Drake;
EvLB; HerW; InWom; NotAW; OxAmL;
OxEng; PenC AM; RAdv 1; REn; REnAL;
TwCBDA; WebAB; WebE&AL; WhAm HS*

Brady, Alice
American. Actress
Won Oscar for *In Old Chicago*, 1938.
b. Nov 2, 1893 in New York, New York
d. Oct 28, 1939 in New York, New York
Source: *AmBi; DcAmB S2; Film 1; FilmgC;
InWom; MotPP; MovMk; NotAW; OxThe;
ThFT; TwYS; LibW; Vers A; WebAB, 79;
WhAm 1; WhScrn 74, 77; WhThe; WhoHol
B*

Brady, "Diamond Jim" (James Buchanan)
American. Financier
Jewelry collection valued at $2 million.
b. Aug 12, 1856 in New York, New York
d. Apr 13, 1917 in Atlantic City, New
   Jersey
Source: *AmBi; WebAB; WhAm 4*

Brady, James
American. Editor, Publisher
b. Nov 15, 1928 in Brooklyn, New York
Source: *CelR; ConAu 101*

Brady, James Scott
"The Bear"
American. Presidential Aide
Press secretary shot during Reagan
   assassination attempt, 1981.
b. Aug 29, 1940 in Centralia, Illinois
Source: *NewYTBS 81; PseudN 82*

Brady, Mathew B
"Mr. Lincoln's Cameraman"
American. Photographer
First to photograph Civil War, 1861-65.
b. 1823 in Warren County, New York
d. Jan 15, 1896 in New York, New York
Source: *AmAu&B; AmBi; BnEnAmA; DcAmB;
EncAB-H; OxAmL; REn; REnAL; WebAB,
79; WhAm HS*

Brady, Pat (Robert Patrick)
[Sons of the Pioneers]
American. Actor, Singer
Played Roy Rogers sidekick in films, TV.
b. Dec 31, 1914 in Toledo, Ohio
d. Feb 27, 1972 in Green Mountain Falls,
   Colorado
Source: *BiDAmM; NewYTBE 72; ObitOF 79;*
WhScrn 77; WhoHol B

Brady, Scott
[Gerard Kenneth Tierney]
American. Actor
Played in TV series "Shotgun Slade," 1959-
62.
b. Sep 13, 1924 in Brooklyn, New York
d. Apr 17, 1985 in Woodland Hills,
   California
Source: *FilmgC; HolP 40; IntMPA 75, 76,*
77, 78, 79, 80, 81, 82; MotPP; WhoAm 74,
76, 78, 80, 82; WhoHol A

Brady, William Aloysius
American. Actor, Producer
Built Playhouse Theatre, 1910; Fourty-eighth
   Street Theatre, 1912, NYC.
b. Jun 19, 1863 in San Francisco, California
d. Jan 6, 1950 in New York, New York
Source: *DcAmB S4; ObitOF 79; OxThe;*
WebAB, 79; WhAm 2

Braestrup, Carl Bjorn
American. Scientist, Inventor
Invented the Theratron, cobalt radiation
   machine used for cancer treatment; one of
   first to warn of danger of radiation.
b. Apr 13, 1897 in Copenhagen, Denmark
d. Aug 8, 1982 in Middletown, Connecticut
Source: *AmM&WS 82P; AnObit 1982; ConAu*
107; NewYTBS 82

Braff, Ruby
American. Jazz Musician
b. Mar 16, 1927 in Boston, Massachusetts
Source: *BioIn 10*

Bragg, Braxton
American. General
Commander-in-chief, Confederate Army,
   1864-65.
b. Mar 22, 1817 in Warrenton, North
   Carolina
d. Sep 27, 1876 in Galveston, Texas
Source: *AmBi; ApCAB; BiDConf; CivWDc;*
DcAmB; Drake; EncSoH; TwCBDA; WebAB;
WhAm HS

Bragg, Donald
American. Track Athlete
b. 1935
Source: *BioIn 9, 10*

Bragg, Melvyn
English. Author
Wrote film script for *Jesus Christ Superstar,*
1973.
b. Oct 6, 1939 in Carlisle, England
Source: *ConAu 57; ConLC 10; ConNov 72,*
76; DcLB 14; Who 74, 82; WrDr 76

Bragg, William Henry, Sir
English. Physicist
With son, founded modern science of
   crystallography; won Nobel Prize, 1915.
b. Jul 2, 1862 in Cumberland, England
d. Mar 12, 1942 in London, England
Source: *BiESc; DcNaB 1941; Dis&D; GrBr;*
InSci; ObitOF 79; WhDW; WorAl

Bragg, William Lawrence, Sir
English. Physicist
Youngest man ever to win Nobel Prize,
   1915, for research in X-rays.
b. Mar 31, 1890 in Adelaide, Australia
d. Jul 1, 1971 in London, England
Source: *BioIn 9, 10; ConAu 115; WorAl*

Brahe, Tyge
Danish. Astronomer
b. Dec 14, 1546
d. Oct 24, 1601
Source: *BioIn 10*

Brahms, Johannes
German. Composer, Pianist
Combined romanticism, classicism in works;
   best known "Brahms' Lullab y" officially
   called "Opus 49, no.4".
b. May 7, 1833 in Hamburg, Germany
d. Apr 3, 1897 in Vienna, Austria
Source: *AtlBL; NewC; OxGer; REn*

Braid, James
"Big Jim"; "Great Triumvirate"
Scottish. Golfer
b. 1870 in Fifeshire, Scotland
d. Nov 27, 1950 in London, England
Source: *BioIn 2, 3; WhoGolf*

Braille, Louis
French. Teacher
Blinded at age 3; devised system of raised-
   point writing.
b. Jan 4, 1809 in Coupvray, France
d. Mar 28, 1852
Source: *DcCathB; InSci; OxFr; REn; WorAl*

Brailowsky, Alexander
American. Musician
b. Feb 16, 1896 in Kiev, Russia
d. Apr 25, 1976 in New York, New York
Source: *CurBio 56; WhoAm 74; WhoMus 72;*
WhoWor 78

Brain, Aubrey
English. Musician
French horn player, who starred with BBC
  symphony orchestra.
b. Jul 12, 1893 in London, England
d. Sep 21, 1955 in London, England
Source: *Baker 78*

Brain, Dennis
English. Musician
Renowned French horn player, son of
  Aubrey Brain; Britten's "Serenade" written
  for him.
b. May 17, 1921 in London, England
d. Sep 1, 1957 in Hatfield, England
Source: *Baker 78*

Braine, John
English. Author
One of the "angry young men," who wrote
  Room at the Top, 1957.
b. Apr 13, 1922 in Yorkshire, England
Source: *Au&Wr 71; CasWL; ConAu 1R;
  ConLC 1, 3; ConNov 72, 76; LongCTC;
  ModBrL, S1; NewC; PenC ENG; RAdv 1;
  REn; TwCWr; WebE&AL; Who 74; WhoWor
  74; WorAu; WrDr 76*

Braithwaite, William Stanley Beaumont
American. Critic, Poet
Originated, edited *Anthology of American
  Verse; Year Book of American Poetry.*
b. Dec 6, 1878 in Boston, Massachusetts
d. Jun 8, 1962
Source: *AmAu&B; BlkAWP; ChhPo, S1, S2;
  InB&W 80; LinLib L; NegAl 83; OxAmL;
  REn; REnAL; TwCA*

Brakhage, Stan
American. Author, Producer
Freelance, avant-garde, filmmaker since 1953.
b. Jan 14, 1933 in Kansas City, Missouri
Source: *AmAu&B; BlueB 76; ConAu 41R;
  DcFM; MakMC; OxFilm; WhoAm 74;
  WorEFlm; WrDr 76, 82*

Braly, Malcolm
American. Author
Wrote novel, screenplay *On the Yard*, filmed,
  1979.
b. Jul 16, 1925 in Portland, Oregon
d. Apr 7, 1980 in Baltimore, Maryland
Source: *BioIn 8, 10, 11, 12; ConAu 17R, 97*

Bramah, Joseph
English. Inventor
Patented hydraulic press, called Bramah
  press, 1795.
b. Apr 13, 1749
d. Dec 9, 1814
Source: *BioIn 2, 7, 8*

Bramante, Donata d'Agnolo
Italian. Architect
b. 1444 in Urbino, Italy
d. Mar 11, 1514
Source: *NewCol 75*

Brambell, Wilfrid
Irish. Actor
Star of British TV show "Steptoe and Son,"
  which was basis for "Sanford and Son" in
  US.
b. Mar 22, 1912 in Dublin, Ireland
Source: *FilmgC; IntMPA 75, 76, 77, 78, 79,
  80, 81, 82; WhoThe 72, 77, 81*

Bramlett, Delaney
see: Delaney and Bonnie

Branca, Ralph Theodore Joseph
"Hawk"
American. Baseball Player
b. Jan 6, 1926 in Mount Vernon, New York
Source: *BaseEn 85; WhoProB 73*

Branch, Anna Hempstead
American. Poet
Metaphysical verse collected in *Sonnets From
  a Lock Box*, 1929.
b. Mar 18, 1875 in New London,
  Connecticut
d. Sep 8, 1937 in New London, Connecticut
Source: *NotAW; OxAmL 83*

Branch, Cliff(ord)
American. Football Player
Four-time all pro wide receiver, LA Raiders,
  1972--, who has played in three Super
  Bowls.
b. Aug 1, 1948 in Houston, Texas
Source: *NewYTBS 74; WhoAm 80, 82;
  WhoBlA 77, 80*

Brancusi, Constantin
Romanian. Sculptor
b. Feb 21, 1876 in Pestisanigorj, Romania
d. Mar 16, 1957 in Paris, France
Source: *AtlBL; CurBio 55, 57; REn; WhAm
  3*

Brand, Jack
Canadian. Soccer Player
b. Aug 4, 1953 in Braunschweig, Germany
  (West)
Source: *AmEnS; BioIn 12*

Brand, Max, pseud.
[Frederick Schiller Faust]
"King of the Pulps"
American. Author, Journalist
Popular Westerns include *Destry Rides Again*,
   1930; wrote Dr. Kildare films.
b. May 29, 1892 in Seattle, Washington
d. May 12, 1944 in Italy
Source: *AmAu&B; CurBio 44; DcAmB S3;
DcLEL; DcNAA; EncMys; FilmgC; LongCTC;
MnBBF; REn; REnAL; TwCA, SUP; WebAB*

Brand, Neville
American. Actor
Played on TV's "Laredo," 1965-67; films
   include *The Birdman of Alcatraz*, 1962.
b. Aug 13, 1921 in Kewanee, Illinois
Source: *FilmgC; IntMPA 75, 76, 77, 78, 79,
80, 81, 82; MotPP; WhoAm 74, 76, 78, 80,
82; WhoHol A; WorAl*

Brand, Oscar
Canadian. Singer, Author
b. Feb 7, 1920 in Winnipeg, Manitoba
Source: *AmAu&B; AuBYP; ConAu 1R, 4NR;
CurBio 62; EncFCWM 69; NatPD; NotNAT;
WhoAm 74, 76, 78, 80, 82; WhoWor 78;
WhoWorJ 72; WrDr 80*

Brand, Stewart
American. Publisher
Editor, publisher, *CoEvolution Quarterly*,
   1973--; publishes *The Last Whole Earth
   Catalog*.
b. Dec 14, 1938 in Rockford, Illinois
Source: *AuNews 1; ConAu 81; MugS; WhoAm
74, 76, 78, 80, 82; WhoWor 78*

Brand, Vance DeVoe
American. Astronaut
Crew member, joint US/USSR space mission,
   1973-75.
b. May 9, 1931 in Longmont, Colorado
Source: *IntWW 74; WhoAm 74, 76, 78, 80,
82; WhoF&I 74; WhoGov 75; WhoS&SW 82*

Brandeis, Louis Dembitz
American. Supreme Court Justice
First Jewish associate justice, Supreme Court,
   1916.
b. Nov 13, 1856 in Louisville, Kentucky
d. Oct 5, 1941 in Washington, District of
   Columbia
Source: *CurBio 41; DcAmB S3; DcNAA;
EncAB-H; OxAmL; REn; REnAL; WebAB;
WhAm 1; WhNAA*

Brandes, Georg Morris Cohen
Danish. Literary Critic, Historian
Leading Scandinavian literary authority;
   biographies include *Goethe*, 1924.
b. Feb 4, 1842 in Copenhagen, Denmark
d. Feb 19, 1927 in Berlin, Germany
Source: *BbD; BiD&SB; CasWL; ClDMEL;
DcEuL; EncWL; EvEuW; LongCTC; OxGer;
OxThe; PenC EUR; REn; TwCA, SUP;
TwCWr*

Brando, Marlon
American. Actor
Controversial, acclaimed actor; won Oscars
   for *On the Waterfront*, 1954; *The
   Godfather*, 1972.
b. Apr 3, 1924 in Omaha, Nebraska
Source: *BiDFilm; BiE&WWA; BkPepl; CelR;
ConTFT 3; CurBio 74; FilmgC; IntMPA 82;
MotPP; MovMk; OxFilm; PIP&P; WebAB;
Who 82; WhoAm 84; WhoHol A; WorEFlm*

Brandon, Brumsic, Jr.
American. Artist, Author
b. Apr 10, 1927 in Washington, District of
   Columbia
Source: *AfroAA; ConAu 61; SmATA 9;
WhoAm 82; WhoBlA 75*

Brandon, Henry Oscar
American. Author, Editor
b. Mar 9, 1916
Source: *BioIn 8; ConAu 49; IntWW 76; Who
74; WhoAm 74; WhoS&SW 82*

Brandt, Bill (William)
English. Photographer
Landscape, portrait photographer known for
   series of distorted female nudes:
   Perspectives of Nudes, 1961.
b. 1904 in London, England
d. Dec 20, 1983 in London, England
Source: *AnObit 1983; CurBio 81, 84; DcCAr
81; NewYTBS 83*

Brandt, Willy
German. Political Leader
Mayor, W Berlin, 1957-66; chancellor, W
   Germany, 1969-74; won Nobel Peace
   Prize, 1971.
b. Dec 18, 1913 in Luebeck, Germany
Source: *CelR; ConAu 85; CurBio 58, 73;
DcPol; EncTR; IntWW 74; NewYTBE 71;
Who 74; WhoGov 72; WhoWor 74*

Brangwyn, Frank, Sir
English. Artist
b. May 13, 1867 in Bruges, Belgium
d. Jun 11, 1956
Source: *BioIn 7; ChhPo; WhAm 3*

Braniff, Thomas Elmer
American. Airline Executive
Founded Braniff International Airways.
b. Dec 6, 1883 in Salina, Kansas
d. Jan 9, 1954
Source: *BioIn 2, 3, 4; CurBio 52, 54; WhAm 3*

Branigan, Laura
American. Singer
Hit singles include "Gloria," 1982;
"Solitaire," 1983; "Self Control," 1984.
b. Jul 3, 1957 in Brewster, New York
Source: *RkOn 85*

Branley, Franklyn Mansfield
American. Educator, Author
b. Jun 5, 1915 in New Rochelle, New York
Source: *AmM&WS 73P; Au&Wr 71; AuBYP; BkP; ConAu 33R; MorJA; SmATA 4; WhoAm 74*

Brann, William Cowper
American. Journalist, Editor
b. Jan 4, 1855 in Humboldt, Illinois
d. Apr 2, 1898 in Waco, Texas
Source: *AmAu; AmAu&B; DcAmB S1; DcNAA; OxAmL; REnAL; WhAm HS*

Brannan, Samuel
American. Pioneer
Published San Francisco's first newspaper,
California *Star*, 1847.
b. Mar 2, 1819 in Saco, Maine
d. May 5, 1889 in Escondido, California
Source: *AmBi; ApCAB; DcAmB; NewCol 75; TwCBDA; WebAB; WhAm HS; WhAmP*

Branner, Martin Michael
American. Cartoonist
b. Dec 28, 1888 in New York, New York
d. May 19, 1970 in New London, Connecticut
Source: *NewYTBE 70; WhAm 5*

Brannigan, Bill
American. Author
b. Jan 12, 1936 in Long Island, New York
Source: *ConAu 65*

Brannigan, Owen
English. Actor, Singer
Bass with Sadler's Wells Opera, 1943-48,
1952-58.
b. 1909 in Annitsford, England
d. May 9, 1973 in Newcastle, England
Source: *ObitT 1971; WhScrn 77; WhoMus 72*

Brant, Alice Dayrell
[Helena Morley]
Brazilian. Diarist
b. 1880
Source: *BioIn 4*

Brant, Joseph
[Thayendanegea]
American. Missionary, Soldier
Son of Mohawk Indian chief; loyal to British
during Revolutionary War.
b. 1742 in Ohio
d. Nov 24, 1807 in Wellington Square,
Ontario
Source: *Alli; AmBi; ApCAB; BbtC; DcAmB; EncAAH; HarEnUS; LinLib L; OxAmL; OxCan; REn; REnAL; TwCBDA; WebAB; WhAm HS*

Branzell, Karin
Swedish. Opera Singer
b. Sep 24, 1891 in Stockholm, Sweden
d. Dec 15, 1974 in Altadena, California
Source: *CurBio 46, 75; NewYTBS 74; WhAm 6*

Braque, Georges
French. Artist
Founded Cubism with Picasso, 1907;
developed the collage, 1911.
b. May 13, 1882 in Argenteuil, France
d. Aug 31, 1963 in Paris, France
Source: *CurBio 49, 63; REn; WhAm 4; WhoGrA 62*

Brasch, Rudolph
German. Rabbi, Author
b. Nov 6, 1912 in Berlin, Germany
Source: *Au&Wr 71; ConAu 21R; WhoWor 78; WhoWorJ 72; WrDr 80*

Brasher, Rex
American. Ornithologist, Artist, Author
b. Jul 31, 1869 in Brooklyn, New York
d. Feb 29, 1960 in Kent, Connecticut
Source: *WhAm 5; WhNAA*

Brashler, William
American. Author
b. Aug 11, 1947 in Grand Rapids, Michigan
Source: *ConAu 45, 2NR*

Braslau, Sophie
American. Opera Singer
b. Aug 16, 1892 in New York, New York
d. Dec 22, 1935 in New York, New York
Source: *DcAmB S1; NotAW; WhAm 1*

Brassai
[Gyula Halasz]
French. Photographer
Best known for pictures of the night people
of Paris, 1930s; reproduced in *The Secret
Paris of the 30s,* 1976.
b. Sep 9, 1899 in Brasso, Hungary
d. Jul 8, 1984 in Nice, France
Source: *AnObit 1984; ConAu 113; ConPhot;
DcCAr 81; MacBEP*

Brasselle, Keefe
[John J Brasselli]
American. Actor, Producer
Best known for title role in *Eddie Cantor
Story,* 1953.
b. Feb 7, 1923 in Lorain, Ohio
d. Jul 7, 1981 in Downey, California
Source: *AmSCAP 66; BioIn 8; FilmgC;
IntMPA 75, 76, 77, 78, 79, 80, 81; MotPP;
NewYTET; PseudN 82; WhoHol A*

Brassens, Georges
French. Singer, Poet
Wrote over 140 songs descriping lives of
everyday people; best known was anti-war
song "The Two Uncles."
b. Oct 22, 1921 in Sete, France
d. Oct 30, 1981 in Sete, France
Source: *AnObit 1982; ConAu X; IntWW 75,
76, 77, 78; WhoMus 72; WhoWor 74*

Bratkowski, Zeke (Edmund R)
American. Football Player
b. Oct 20, 1931 in Danville, Illinois
Source: *WhoFtbl 74*

Brattain, Walter Houser
American. Physicist
b. Feb 10, 1902 in Amoy, China
Source: *AmM&WS 73P; CurBio 57; IntWW
74; WebAB; Who 74; WhoAm 74, 76, 78, 80,
82; WhoWor 78*

Bratteli, Trygve Martin
Norwegian. Journalist, Political Leader
Former prime minister of Norway.
b. Jan 11, 1910 in Notteroy, Norway
Source: *IntWW 74; NewYTBE 71; WhoWor
78*

Brauchitsch, Heinrich Alfred
German. Military Leader
Commander-in-chief of German Army, 1938-
41; made scapegoat for failure to capture
Moscow, removed from command, 1941.
b. Oct 4, 1881 in Berlin, Germany
d. Oct 18, 1948
Source: *CurBio 40, 48; WorAl*

Brandel, Fernand Paul
French. Historian
Influential member of Annales school of
historiography; wrote *The Mediterranean
and the Mediterranean World in the Age
of Philip II,* 1949.
b. Aug 24, 1902 in Lumeville, France
d. Nov 28, 1985 in Paris, France
Source: *ConAu 14NR, 93; CurBio 85;
IntEnSS 79; IntWW 83; MakMC; WhoAm 84*

Brauer, Jerald Carl
American. Educator, Historian
b. Sep 16, 1921 in Fond du Lac, Wisconsin
Source: *AmAu&B; ConAu 33R; DrAS 74P;
IntWW 74; WhoAm 74, 76, 78, 80, 82;
WhoWor 78; WrDr 76*

Brauer, Max Julius Friedrich
German. Mayor
b. 1887
d. Feb 1, 1973 in Bonn, Germany (West)
Source: *NewYTBE 73*

Braun, Eva
[Mrs. Adolf Hilter]
German. Celebrity Relative
Married Hitler a few days before their
suicides.
b. Feb 6, 1912
d. Apr 30, 1945 in Berlin, Germany
Source: *EncTR; ObitOF 79; WhWW-II;
WorAl*

Braun, Karl Ferdinand
German. Physicist
b. Jun 6, 1850 in Fulda, Germany
d. Apr 20, 1918 in New York, New York
Source: *AsBiEn; BioIn 1, 2, 3*

Braun, Otto
German. Communist Leader
b. 1901
d. Aug 15, 1974 in Berlin, Germany (West)
Source: *NewYTBS 74*

Brautigan, Richard
American. Author, Poet
Became campus hero, 1960s with whimsical
novel *Trout Fishing in Ameri ca,* 1967.
b. Jan 30, 1933 in Tacoma, Washington
d. Oct 25, 1984 in Bolinas, California
Source: *AmAu&B; CelR; ConAu 53; ConLC
1, 3, 5, 9, 12; ConNov 72, 76; ConP 70, 75;
DrAF 76; DrAP 75; ModAL S1; PenC AM;
WhoAm 82; WrDr 80*

Brawley, Benjamin Griffith
American. Clergyman, Educator
b. Apr 22, 1882 in Columbia, South Carolina
d. Feb 1, 1939 in Washington, District of
   Columbia
Source: *AmAu&B; AmLY; BlkAWP; DcNAA;
REnAL; TwCA, SUP; WhNAA*

Braxton, Carter
American. Continental Congressman
b. Sep 10, 1736 in Newington, Virginia
d. Oct 10, 1797 in Richmond, Virginia
Source: *AmBi; ApCAB; BiAUS; BiDrAC;
DcAmB; Drake; TwCBDA; WhAm HS;
WhAmP*

Bray, Charles William, III
American. Government Official
Deputy director, US Information Agency,
   1977-81; ambassador to Senegal, 1981--.
b. Oct 24, 1933 in New York, New York
Source: *NewYTBE 70; USBiR 74; WhoAm 82*

Brayman, Harold
American. Educator, Journalist
b. Mar 10, 1900 in Middleburgh, New York
Source: *ConAu 21R, 73; WhoAm 74, 76, 78,
80, 82; WhoE 74; WhoF&I 74; WhoPubR 72*

Brazelton, T(homas) Berry
American. Physician, Author
Researcher in child development; wrote *On
   Becoming a Family.*
b. May 10, 1918 in Waco, Texas
Source: *ConAu 97; WhoAm 74, 76, 78, 80,
82*

Brazle, Al(pha Eugene)
"Cotton"
American. Baseball Player
b. Oct 19, 1914 in Loyal, Oklahoma
d. Oct 24, 1973 in Grand Junction, Colorado
Source: *BaseEn 85; NewYTBE 73*

Brazzi, Rossano
Italian. Actor
Starred in *The Barefoot Contessa,* 1954; *South
   Pacific,* 1958.
b. Sep 18, 1916 in Bologna, Italy
Source: *CmMov; CurBio 61; FilmgC; IntMPA
75, 76, 77, 78, 79, 80, 81, 82; MotPP;
MovMk; WhoHol A; WorAl*

Bread
[Mike Botts; David Gates; James Gordon;
   James Grifin; Larry Knechtel; Robb
   Royer]
American. Music Group
Hit songs include "If," 1971; "Diary," 1972;
   "Make It with You," 1970.
Source: *IlEncRk; RolSEnR 83*

Bream, Julian
English. Musician
b. Jul 15, 1933 in London, England
Source: *IntWW 74; Who 74; WhoAm 82;
WhoMus 72; WhoWor 78*

Breasted, James Henry
American. Archaeologist, Historian
Wrote standard texts: *History of Egypt,* 1905;
   Ancient Times, 1916.
b. Aug 27, 1865 in Rockford, Illinois
d. Dec 2, 1935 in New York, New York
Source: *AmAu&B; AmBi; AmLY; DcAmB S1;
DcLEL; DcNAA; EvLB; LongCTC; OxAmL;
REn; REnAL; BiDAmEd; EncAB 9; InSci;
TwCA, SUP; WebAB; WhAm 1; WhNAA*

Brecheen, Harry David
"The Cat"
American. Baseball Player
First left-handed pitcher to win three World
   Series games, 1946.
b. Oct 14, 1914 in Broken Bow, Oklahoma
Source: *BaseEn 85; BioIn 1, 2; WhoProB 73*

Brecht, Bertolt Eugene Friedrich
German. Poet, Dramatist
Best known for collaboration with Kurt Weill
   on *Threepenny Opera,* 1928.
b. Feb 10, 1898 in Augsburg, Germany
d. Aug 14, 1956 in Berlin, Germany (East)
Source: *AtlBL; CasWL; ClDMEL; CnMD;
CnMWL; CnThe; CroCD; CyWA; DcFM;
EncWL; EvEuW; FilmgC; LongCTC;
McGEWD; ModGL; ModWD; OxEng;
OxFilm; OxGer; OxThe; PenC EUR;
RComWL; REn; REnWD; TwCA, SUP;
TwCWr; WhAm HSA; WhoTwCL; WorEFlm*

Breck, John Henry
American. Businessman
Founded Breck, Inc., 1929.
b. Jun 5, 1877 in Holyoke, Massachusetts
d. Feb 16, 1965 in Springfield, Massachusetts
Source: *Entr; WhAm 4*

Breckinridge, John
American. Statesman
b. Dec 2, 1760 in Augusta County, Virginia
d. Dec 14, 1806 in Lexington, Kentucky
Source: *BiDSA; BioIn 3, 8, 10*

Breckinridge, John Cabell
American. Lawyer, Statesman, General
Vp under James Buchanan, 1857-61.
b. Jan 21, 1821 in Lexington, Kentucky
d. May 17, 1875 in Lexington, Kentucky
Source: *AmBi; ApCAB; BiAUS; BiDConf;
BiDSA; BiDrAC; BiDrUSE; DcAmB; Drake;
EncAB-H; TwCBDA; WebAB; WhAmP*

Breckinridge, Mary
American. Nurse
b. 1881
d. 1965
Source: *BioIn 2, 3, 7, 8, 9, 11*

Breckinridge, Sophonisba Preston
American. Social Reformer
First woman admitted to Bar in KY, 1897.
b. Apr 1, 1866 in Lexington, Kentucky
d. Jul 30, 1948
Source: *BiDAmEd; DcAmB S4; EncAB-H; NatCab 1; NotAW; WhAm 2; WomWWA 14A*

Breech, Ernest Robert
American. Industrialist
b. Feb 24, 1897 in Lebanon, Missouri
d. Jul 3, 1978 in Royal Oak, Michigan
Source: *BioIn 2, 3, 4, 5, 7, 8, 11; CurBio 55; Who 74; WhoAm 74; WhoF&I 74*

Breedlove, (Norman) Craig
American. Auto Racer
b. Mar 23, 1938 in Costa Mesa, California
Source: *BioIn 6, 7, 8, 9, 10*

Breen, Joseph Ignatius
American. Critic
Powerful 1930s-40s Hollywood film censor; won special Oscar, 1953.
b. Oct 4, 1890 in Philadelphia, Pennsylvania
d. Dec 7, 1965 in Hollywood, California
Source: *DcAmB S7*

Breese, Edmund
American. Actor
Screen character actor, 1915-35; worked with James O'Neill on stage *Count of Monte Cristo,* 1892.
b. Jun 18, 1871 in Brooklyn, New York
d. Apr 6, 1936 in New York, New York
Source: *Film 1; MovMk; NotNAT B; TwYS; WhAm 1; WhScrn 74, 77; WhThe; WhoHol B; WhoStg 1906, 1908*

Breeskin, Adelyn Dohme
American. Museum Director
Director, Baltimore Museum of Art, 1947-62; first woman director of museum in US.
b. Jul 19, 1896 in Baltimore, Maryland
d. Jul 24, 1986 in Lake Garda, Italy
Source: *ConAu 33R; WhoAm 78; WhoAmA 84; WhoGov 72*

Breger, Dave
American. Cartoonist, Illustrator
b. 1908 in Chicago, Illinois
d. Jan 16, 1970 in South Nyack, New York
Source: *NewYTBE 70*

Brel, Jacques
Belgian. Songwriter
b. Apr 8, 1929 in Brussels, Belgium
d. Oct 9, 1978 in Bobigny, France
Source: *CelR; CurBio 71; WhoE 74; WhoHol A; WhoWor 78*

Bremer, Arthur Herman
American. Attempted Assassin
Shot George Wallace, May 5, 1972 in Lowell, MD.
b. Aug 21, 1950 in Milwaukee, Wisconsin
Source: *NewYTBE 72*

Brenan, Gerald (Edward Fitz-Gerald)
English. Author
Definitive interpreter of Spanish literature, culture: *The Spanish Labyrinth,* 1943.
b. Apr 7, 1894 in Malta
Source: *ConAu 1R, 3NR; CurBio 86; TwCA SUP*

Brendan of Clonfert, Saint
Irish. Religious Figure
Subject of 10th c. tale *Brendan's Voyage,* recounting adventures; feast day May 16.
b. 484 in Tralee, Ireland
d. 577 in Annaghdown, Ireland
Source: *BioIn 4, 5, 6, 7, 8, 10; DcCathB; LuthC 75; NewC; OxFr; OxShips*

Brendel, Alfred
Austrian. Musician
b. Jan 5, 1931 in Wisenberg, Austria
Source: *IntWW 74; Who 74; WhoMus 72; WhoWor 78*

Brendel, El(mer)
American. Actor, Comedian
Vaudeville, comic film roles, 1926-56.
b. Mar 25, 1890 in Philadelphia, Pennsylvania
d. Apr 9, 1964 in Hollywood, California
Source: *Film 2; FilmgC; MovMk; NotNAT B; ObitOF 79; TwYS; Vers A; WhScrn 74, 77; WhoHol B*

Breneman, Tom
American. Actor
Radio emcee of "Breakfast in Hollywood."
b. 1902
d. Apr 28, 1948 in Encino, California
Source: *ObitOF 79; WhScrn 74, 77; WhoHol B*

Brenley, Bob (Robert Earl)
American. Baseball Player
Catcher, 1981--; tied ML record with four
errors in one inning playing third base,
Sep 14, 1986.
b. Feb 25, 1954 in Coshocton, Ohio
Source: *BaseEn 85; BaseReg 86*

Brennan, Eileen Regina
American. Actress
Starred in movie, TV series *Private Benjamin.*
b. Sep 3, 1937 in Los Angeles, California
Source: *BiE&WWA; IntMPA 75, 76, 77, 78,
79, 80, 81, 82; NotNAT; WhoAm 82; WhoHol
A*

Brennan, Peter Joseph
American. Government Official
Secretary of Labor, 1973-74.
b. May 24, 1918 in New York, New York
Source: *BioNews 74; BusPN; CelR; CngDr 74;
CurBio 73; IntWW 74; NewYTBE 72;
WhoAm 74; WhoAmP 73*

Brennan, Walter Andrew
American. Actor
First actor to win three Oscars, 1936, 1938,
1940.
b. Jul 25, 1894 in Lynn, Massachusetts
d. Sep 22, 1974 in Oxnard, California
Source: *BiDFilm; BioNews 74; CelR; CmMov;
CurBio 41, 74; FilmgC; IntMPA 75; MotPP;
MovMk; NewYTBS 74; OxFilm; TwYS; Vers
A; WhAm 6; WhScrn 77; WhoAm 74;
WhoHol B; WhoWor 78; WorEFlm*

Brennan, William Joseph
American. Supreme Court Justice
Liberal; appointed by Dwight Eisenhower,
1956.
b. Apr 25, 1906 in Newark, New Jersey
Source: *CelR; CngDr 74; CurBio 57; DrAS
74P; IntWW 74; WebAB; Who 74; WhoAm
74, 76, 78, 80, 82; WhoAmP 73; WhoGov 75;
WhoS&SW 82*

Brenner, Barbara Johnes
American. Author
b. Jun 26, 1925 in Brooklyn, New York
Source: *AuBYP; ConAu 9R; ForWC 70;
SmATA 4*

Brenner, David
American. Comedian
Nightclub performer; named Las Vegas
entertainer of year, 1977.
b. Feb 4, 1945 in Philadelphia, Pennsylvania
Source: *BioIn 10, 11; WhoAm 78, 80, 82*

Brent, Evelyn
[Mary Elizabeth Riggs]
American. Actress
Played lead opposite John Barrymore in
Raffles the Amateur Cracksman, 1917.
b. Oct 20, 1899 in Tampa, Florida
d. Jun 7, 1975 in Los Angeles, California
Source: *Film 1, 2; FilmgC; MotPP; MovMk;
NewYTBS 75; ThFT; TwYS; WhScrn 77;
WhoHol C*

Brent, George
[George B Nolan]
American. Actor
Played in 11 films with Betty Davis
including *Dark Victory,* 1939; *Jezebel,*
1938.
b. Mar 15, 1904 in Dublin, Ireland
d. 1979 in Solana Beach, California
Source: *CmMov; FilmgC; IntMPA 75, 76, 77;
MotPP; MovMk; WhoHol A; WhoThe 81N;
WorAl*

Brent, Margaret
American. Feminist
First woman landowner in MD.
b. 1600 in Gloucester, England
d. 1671
Source: *BiCAW; DcAmB; WhAm HS;
WhAmP*

Brent, Romney
[Romulo Larralde]
Actor, Dramatist, Director
Collaborated with Cole Porter on musical
Nymph Errant which starred Gertrude
Lawrence.
b. Jan 26, 1902 in Saltillo, Mexico
d. Sep 24, 1976
Source: *BiE&WWA; FilmgC; NotNAT; PIP&P;
WhThe; WhoHol A; WhoThe 72, 81, 81N*

Brentano, Clemens Maria
German. Dramatist, Author, Poet
Romantic poet; co-published *Des Knaben
Wunderhorn* (Boy's Magic Horn), a
collection of German folksongs.
b. Sep 8, 1778 in Ehrenbrehstein, Germany
d. Jul 28, 1842
Source: *BbD; BiD&SB; CasWL; CelCer.;
ChhPo S1; DcEuL; EuAu; EvEuW; LinLib L;
McGEWB; OxGer; PenC EUR; REn*

Bresler, Jerry
American. Composer, Author
b. May 29, 1912 in Chicago, Illinois
Source: *AmSCAP 66; FilmgC; IntMPA 75,
76, 77; WorEFlm*

Breslin, Jimmy
American. Author, Journalist
Pulitzer-winning NYC columnist who wrote
Table Money, 1983.
b. Oct 17, 1930 in Jamaica, New York
Source: *AmAu&B; AuNews 1; CelR; ConLC
4; CurBio 73; WhoAm 74, 76, 78, 80, 82, 84;
WhoWor 74; WrDr 76, 80*

Bresnaham, Roger Phillip
"The Duke of Tralee"
American. Baseball Player
Catcher, 1897-1915; Hall of Fame, 1945.
b. Jun 11, 1879 in Toledo, Ohio
d. Dec 4, 1944 in Toledo, Ohio
Source: *BaseEn 85; BioIn 3, 7, 8, 10;
WhoProB 73*

Bresson, Henri Cartier
see: Cartier-Bresson, Henri

Bresson, Robert
French. Director
Stylist who does not use professional actors;
expresses a state of mind visually in his
films.
b. Sep 25, 1907 in Bromont-Lamothe, France
Source: *BiDFilm; ConLC 16; CurBio 71;
DcFM; FilmgC; IntWW 82; MovMk; OxFilm;
Who 74; WorEFlm*

Breton, Andre
French. Poet
Founded Surrealist movement, 1924; wrote
Surrealist of Manifesto.
b. Feb 18, 1896 in Normandy, France
d. Sep 28, 1966 in Paris, France
Source: *AtlBL; CasWL; CIDMEL; ConAu
25R, P-2; ConLC 2, 9, 15; EncWL; EvEuW;
LongCTC; ModRL; ModWD; OxFr; PenC
EUR; RComWL; REn; REnWD; TwCA SUP;
TwCWr; WhAm 4; WhoTwCL*

Breton, Jules Adolphe
French. Artist, Author
b. 1827 in Calais, France
d. 1906
Source: *LinLib L, S*

Bretonneau, Pierre Fidele
French. Physician
Sought cause of several diseases, including
smallpox, typhoid fever, diphtheria;
performed first successful tracheotomy,
1825.
b. Apr 3, 1778 in Saint Georges sur Cher,
France
d. Feb 18, 1862 in Passy, France
Source: *BiHiMed; DcScB; InSci*

Brett, George Howard
"Mulletthead"
American. Baseball Player
Third baseman, KC, who hit .390 in 1980,
the highest batting average in baseball in
39 years.
b. May 15, 1953 in Glendale, West Virginia
Source: *BaseEn 85; BioIn 10, 11, 12; CurBio
81; WhoAm 78, 80, 82*

Brett, George Platt, Jr.
American. Publisher
Pres., Macmillan, 1931-58; published
Mitchell's *Gone With the Wind,* 1936.
b. Dec 9, 1893 in Darien, Connecticut
d. Feb 11, 1984 in Southport, Connecticut
Source: *AmAu&B; ConAu 112; CurBio 48,
84; NewYTBS 84; Who 82, 83*

Brett, Jan Churchill
American. Children's Author, Illustrator
Self-illustrated children's books include *Good
Luck Sneakers,* 1981.
b. Dec 1, 1949 in Hingham, Massachusetts
Source: *ConAu 116*

Brett, Jeremy
[Jeremy Huggins]
English. Actor
Played on PBS "Rebecca"; "The Good
Soldier."
b. Nov 3, 1935 in Berkswell, England
Source: *FilmgC; Who 82; WhoHol A;
WhoThe 77, 81; WhoWor 76*

Brett, Ken(neth Alvin)
American. Baseball Player
b. Sep 18, 1948 in Brooklyn, New York
Source: *BaseEn 85*

Brett, Simon Anthony Lee
English. Author
Wrote mystery novels, plays *So Much Blood,*
1977; created detective Charles Paris.
b. Oct 28, 1945 in Worcester, England
Source: *ConAu 69; TwCCr&M 80*

Breuer, Marcel Lajos
American. Designer, Architect
Designed NYC's Whitney Museum, 1963-66;
designed tubular chair ("Wassily") while
studying at Gropius' Bauhaus, 1920s.
b. May 22, 1902 in Pecs, Hungary
d. Jul 1, 1981 in New York, New York
Source: *AmArch 70; BnEnAmA; CelR; ConAu
5R, 5NR, 104; CurBio 41, 60, 81; DcNiCA;
EncMA; IntAu&W 76; IntWW 74, 75, 76,
77, 78; McGDA; McGEWB; NewYTBS 81;
OxDecA; PlP&P; WhoArch; WhoWor 74*

Breuil, Henri Abbe
French. Archaeologist
One of first to record, interpret Paleolithic
art; showed how cultures flourished
simultaneously.
b. Feb 28, 1877 in Mortain, France
d. Aug 14, 1961 in L'Isle-Adam, France
Source: *DcScB; InSci; LongCTC; McGEWB*

Brewer, David Josiah
American. Supreme Court Justice
b. Jun 20, 1837 in Smyrna, Turkey
d. Mar 28, 1910 in Washington, District of
Columbia
Source: *AmBi; ApCAB; DcAmAu; DcAmB;
DcNAA; TwCBDA; WebAB; WhAm 1*

Brewer, Ebenezer
English. Clergyman, Educator
b. May 2, 1810 in London, England
d. Mar 6, 1897
Source: *Alli, SUP; BiD&SB; ChhPo; DcEnL;
EvLB; NewC*

Brewer, Jim
"Papa"
American. Basketball Player
b. Dec 3, 1951 in Maywood, Illinois
Source: *WhoBbl 73*

Brewer, Theresa
American. Singer, Actress
b. May 7, 1931 in Toledo, Ohio
Source: *InWom*

Brewer and Shipley
[Michael Brewer; Thomas Shipley]
American. Music Group
Folk-rock duo formed, 1968; hit "One Toke
Over the Line," 1971.
Source: *RkOn 74; RolSEnR 83*

Brewster, David, Sir
Scottish. Philosopher, Scientist
b. Dec 11, 1781 in Jedburgh, Scotland
d. Feb 10, 1868
Source: *Alli; BiDLA; BioIn 1, 4, 8; BrAu 19;
CasWL; Chambr 3; DcEnA; DcEnL; EvLB*

Brewster, Kingman, Jr.
American. Educator, Lawyer
b. Jun 17, 1919 in Longmeadow,
Massachusetts
Source: *CelR; CurBio 64; DrAS 74P; EncAB-
H; IntWW 74; LEduc 74; NewYTBE 70;
Who 74; WhoAm 74, 76, 78, 80, 82; WhoE
74; WhoWor 78*

Brewster, Owen
American. Politician
b. Feb 22, 1888 in Dexter, Maine
d. Dec 25, 1961 in Brookline, Massachusetts
Source: *BioIn 1, 3, 6; CurBio 47, 62*

Brewster, William
English. Colonial Leader
b. 1566 in Nottinghamshire, England
d. Apr 10, 1644 in Plymouth, Massachusetts
Source: *Alli; AmBi; ApCAB; BiDLA; DcAmB;
Drake; TwCBDA; WebAB; WhAm HS;
WhAmP*

Breytenbach, Breyten
South African. Poet, Artist, Political Activist
Wrote *True Confessions of an Albino
Terrorist*, 1985, describing imprisonment,
1975-82, for anti-apartheid activities.
b. Sep 16, 1939 in Bonnievale, South Africa
Source: *ConAu 113; ConLC 23; CurBio 86*

Brezhnev, Leonid Ilyich
Russian. Communist Leader
General secretary of the Soviet Communist
Party, 1966-82.
b. Dec 19, 1906 in Kamenskoye, Russia
d. Nov 10, 1982 in Moscow, U.S.S.R.
Source: *BioNews 74; CurBio 78, 83; DcPol;
IntWW 74, 75, 76, 77, 78, 79, 80, 81; IntYB
78, 79, 80, 81; LinLib S; IntWW 82;
McGEWB; NewYTBE 71, 72, 73; NewYTBS
82; WhDW; Who 74, 82; WhoWor 74, 76,
78, 80; WorAl*

Brian Boru
Irish. Ruler
High king of Ireland through conquest, 1002-
1014; defeated Norse in battle, broke
Norse power in Ireland.
b. 926
d. Apr 23, 1014 in Clontarf, Ireland
Source: *LinLib S; NewC; NewCol 75; REn*

Brian, David
American. Actor
Film debut in *Flamingo Road*, 1949; TV
series "Mr. District Attorney."
b. Aug 5, 1914 in New York, New York
Source: *FilmgC; IntMPA 75, 76, 77, 78, 79,
80, 81, 82; MotPP; WhoHol A*

Brian, Donald
American. Actor, Singer
Starred on broadway *Chocolate Soldier; Merry Widow; No, No, Nanette.*
b. Feb 17, 1875 in Saint John's, Newfoundland
d. Dec 22, 1948 in Great Neck, New York
Source: *CmpEPM; EncMT; Film 1; NatCAB 36; NotNAT B; WhAm 2; WhScrn 74, 77; WhoHol B; WhoStg 1908*

Brian, Marcel
French. Author
b. Nov 21, 1895 in Marseilles, France
Source: *Au&Wr 71; IntWW 74; WhoWor 78*

Briand, Aristide
French. Statesman
b. Mar 28, 1862 in Nantes, France
d. Mar 7, 1932 in Paris, France
Source: *BioIn 11; McGEWB*

Briand, Rena
Canadian. Journalist, Author
b. Nov 12, 1935
Source: *ConAu 29R; WrDr 80*

Brice, Fanny
[Fanny Borach]
"Baby Snooks"
American. Actress, Singer
Films based on her life: *Funny Girl,* 1968; *Funny Lady,* 1975.
b. Oct 29, 1891 in New York, New York
d. May 29, 1951 in Beverly Hills, California
Source: *CurBio 46, 51; DcAmB S5; EncMT; FamA&A; FilmgC; InWom; MovMk; OxFilm; PIP&P; ThFT; WhAm 3; WhScrn 74, 77; WhoHol B*

Bricker, John William
American. Politician, Lawyer
Three-term Rep. governor of OH, 1939-45; lost 1944 presidential nomination to Thomas Dewey.
b. Sep 6, 1893 in Madison County, Ohio
d. Mar 22, 1986 in Columbus, Ohio
Source: *BiDrAC; CurBio 43, 56, 86; St&PR 75; Who 74; WhoAm 74, 76, 78, 80, 82*

Bricklin, Malcolm N
American. Corporation Executive
b. Mar 9, 1939 in Philadelphia, Pennsylvania
Source: *BusPN; WhoF&I 74*

Brickman, Morrie
American. Cartoonist
b. Jul 24, 1917 in Chicago, Illinois
Source: *WhoAm 78, 80, 82*

Bricktop
[Ada Beatrice Queen Victoria Louise Virginia Smith]
American. Singer, Restaurateur
Had famous pre-WW II nightclub in Paris; Cole Porter wrote "Miss Otis Regrets" for her.
b. Aug 14, 1894 in Iderson, West Virginia
d. Jan 31, 1984 in New York, New York
Source: *AnObit 1984; BiDAfM; BioNews 74; ConAu 111; DrBlPA; NewYTBS 84; PseudAu*

Brico, Antonia
American. Conductor
Organizer, conductor, NY Women's Symphony Orchestra; conductor, Boise Civic Symphony, 1957--; subject of film documentary *Portrait of Antonia,* 1975.
b. Jun 26, 1902 in Rotterdam, Netherlands
Source: *Baker 78; CurBio 48; InWom; LibW; WhoAm 74, 76, 78, 80, 82; WhoAmW 74; WorAl*

Bricusse, Leslie
English. Writer, Composer, Lyricist
Won Grammy for "What Kind of Fool Am I?," 1962; Oscar for "Talk to the Animals," 1967.
b. Jan 29, 1931 in London, England
Source: *VarWW 85*

Bridge, Frank
English. Composer
Composed chamber music; one of his pupils was Benjamin Britten.
b. Feb 26, 1879 in Brighton, England
d. Jan 11, 1941 in London, England
Source: *CurBio 41; DcCM*

Bridger, James
American. Frontiersman, Fur Trader
First white man to see Great Salt Lake, 1824; dominated western fur trade, 1830-34.
b. Mar 11, 1804 in Richmond, Virginia
d. Jul 17, 1881 in Kansas City, Missouri
Source: *AmBi; DcAmB; EncAAH; NatCAB 13; OxAmL; REnAL; REnAW; WebAB; WhAm HS*

Bridges, "Beau" (Lloyd Vernet, III)
American. Actor
Films include *The Other Side of the Mountain,* 1975; *Norma Rae,* 1979.
b. Dec 9, 1941 in Los Angeles, California
Source: *BkPepl; CelR; ConTFT 3; FilmgC; IntMPA 82; MovMk; WhoAm 84; WhoHol A; WorAl*

Bridges, Calvin Blackman
American. Geneticist
Developed chromosome theory of heredity.
b. Jan 11, 1889 in Schuyler Falls, New York
d. Dec 27, 1938 in Los Angeles, California
Source: *DcAmB S2; WebBD 80*

Bridges, Harry Renton
American. Labor Union Official
Organized ILWU, 1937; allegedly involved
with Communist Party.
b. Jul 29, 1901 in Melbourne, Australia
Source: *CelR; CurBio 40, 50; EncAB-H;
NewYTBE 72; WebAB; WhoAm 74; WhoWest
84; WhoWor 78*

Bridges, James
American. Director, Screenwriter
Author, director of prize-winning films *China
Syndrome,* 1979; *Urban Cowboy,* 1980.
b. Feb 3, in Little Rock, Arkansas
Source: *FilmEn; IntMPA 81; WhoAm 82, 84*

Bridges, Jeff
American. Actor
Nominated for Oscars for roles in *The Last
Picture Show,* 1971; *Thunderbolt &
Lightfoot,* 1974; *Tron,* 1982.
b. Dec 4, 1949 in Los Angeles, California
Source: *BkPepl; ConTFT 3; FilmgC; IntMPA
82; MovMk; NewYTBS 75; WhoHol A*

Bridges, Lloyd (Lloyd Vernet II)
American. Actor
Starred in TV series "Sea Hunt."
b. Jan 15, 1913 in San Leandro, California
Source: *CelR; ConTFT 3; FilmgC; IntMPA
82; MotPP; MovMk; WhoAm 84; WhoHol A*

Bridges, Robert Seymour
English. Author, Poet
Poet laureate, 1913-30, who wrote
philosophical poem *Testament of Beauty,*
1929.
b. Oct 23, 1844 in Walmer, England
d. Apr 21, 1930 in Chilswell, England
Source: *AtlBL; CasWL; CnE&AP; DcEnA,
AP; DcLEL; EncWL; EvLB; LongCTC;
ModBrL; NewC; OxEng; PenC ENG; REn;
TwCA, SUP; TwCWr; WebE&AL; WhoTwCL*

Bridges, Styles
American. Senator
b. Sep 9, 1898 in West Pembroke, Maine
d. Nov 26, 1961 in Concord, New
Hampshire
Source: *WhAm 4*

Bridges, Todd
American. Actor
Plays Willis on TV series "Diff'rent Strokes",
1978--.
b. May 1965
Source: *BioIn 12; InB&W 80*

Bridges, Tommy (Thomas Jefferson Davis)
American. Baseball Player
Pitcher, Detroit Tigers, 1930-46.
b. Dec 28, 1906 in Gordonsville, Tennessee
d. Apr 19, 1968 in Nashville, Tennessee
Source: *BaseEn 85; BioIn 3, 8; WhoProB 73*

Bridgetower, George Augustus
Polish. Musician
b. 1780
d. 1860
Source: *BioIn 1, 6, 8*

Bridgewater, Dee Dee
American. Singer, Actress
b. May 27, 1950 in Memphis, Tennessee
Source: *BioIn 10; WhoAm 82*

Bridgman, Frederic Arthur
American. Artist
b. Nov 10, 1847 in Tuskegee, Alabama
d. Jan 13, 1927 in Rouen, France
Source: *AmBi; BiDSA; DcAmAu; DcAmB;
DcNAA; WhAm 1*

Bridgman, Laura Dewey
American. Student
First blind, deaf-mute to be successfully
taught, by Samuel G. Howe, 1837.
b. Dec 21, 1829 in Hanover, New Hampshire
d. May 24, 1889 in Boston, Massachusetts
Source: *AmBi; AmWom; ApCAB; ChhPo S2;
DcAmB; Dis&D; Drake; InWom; LibW;
NatCAB 2; NotAW; OxAmH; TwCBDA;
WebAB, 79; WhAm HS*

Bridgman, Percy Williams
American. Scientist, Physician, Engineer
b. Apr 21, 1882 in Cambridge, Massachusetts
d. Aug 20, 1961 in Randolph, New
Hampshire
Source: *AmAu&B; WebAB; WhAm 4;
WhNAA*

Bridie, James, pseud.
[Osborne Henry Mavor]
Scottish. Dramatist
b. Jan 3, 1888 in Glasgow, Scotland
d. Jan 29, 1951 in Edinburgh, Scotland
Source: *LongCTC; McGEWD; ModBrL;
ModWD; PenC ENG; REn; REnWD;
WhoTwCL; WorAu; OxThe*

Brieux, Eugene
French. Dramatist
Wrote on moral, social themes: *Blanchette*,
1892; *La Robe Rouge*, 1900.
b. Jan 19, 1858 in Paris, France
d. Dec 7, 1932 in Nice, France
Source: *CasWL; ClDMEL; CnThe; EvEuW;
McGEWD; ModWD; NewC; OxEng; PenC
EUR; REn; REnWD; TwCA, SUP; WhThe*

Briggs, Austin Eugene
American. Artist, Illustrator
b. Sep 8, 1908 in Humboldt, Minnesota
d. Oct 13, 1973 in Paris, France
Source: *NewYTBE 73; WhAm 6; WhoAm 74;
WhoAmA 73*

Brigati, Eddie
[The Rascals]
American. Singer
Vocalist with blue-eyed soul group, 1965-71;
composed most of groups songs with
Frank Cavaliere.
b. Oct 22, 1946 in New York, New York
Source: *NF*

Briggs, Clare
American. Cartoonist
b. Aug 5, 1875 in Reedsburgh, Wisconsin
d. Jan 3, 1930 in New York, New York
Source: *ChhPo, S1; DcAmB S1; WhAm 1*

Briggs, Ellis Ormsbee
American. Diplomat
US Ambassador, 1945-62; wrote *Shots Heard
Around the World*, 1957.
b. Dec 1, 1899 in Watertown, Massachusetts
d. Feb 21, 1976
Source: *BioIn 4, 7, 10, 11; CurBio 65, 76;
IntWW 74; WhoAm 74; WhoE 74; WhoWor
78*

Briggs, Fred
American. Broadcast Journalist
With NBC News since 1966.
b. May 31, 1932 in Chicago, Illinois
Source: *ConAu 73; WhoAm 80, 82, 84;
WhoTelC*

Briggs, Walter Owen, Jr.
American. Baseball Executive
Owner Detroit Tigers; stadium previously
known as Briggs Stadium.
b. Jan 20, 1912 in Detroit, Michigan
d. Jul 3, 1970 in Detroit, Michigan
Source: *BioIn 9; NewYTBE 70; ObitOF 79;
WhAm 5*

Bright, John
English. Government Official, Author
Founded Anti-Corn Law League, 1839;
supported Northern cause in American
Civil War.
b. Nov 16, 1811 in Greenbank, England
d. Mar 27, 1889 in Greenbank, England
Source: *Alli SUP; BbD; BiD&SB; Chambr 3;
DcAmSR; HarEnUS; McGEWB; NewC; REn*

Bright, Richard
English. Physician
b. Sep 28, 1789 in Bristol, England
d. Dec 16, 1858
Source: *Alli, SUP; BioIn 4, 5, 7, 9*

Brigid of Kildare
Irish. Religious Figure
Founded first religious community for women
in Ireland; revered only less that St.
Patrick in Ireland.
b. 453 in Faughart, Ireland
d. 523 in Kildare, Ireland
Source: *BioIn 8, 11; DcCathB; DcIrB;
IlEncMy; InWom; LuthC 75; NewC*

Briles, Nelson Kelley
"Nellie"
American. Baseball Player
b. Aug 5, 1943 in Dorris, California
Source: *BaseEn 85; NewYTBE 71; WhoAm
74; WhoProB 73*

Briley, John Richard
American. Screenwriter
Won 1983 best original screenplay Oscar for
Gandhi.
b. Jun 25, 1925 in Kalmazoo, Michigan
Source: *ConAu 101; WrDr 80, 82, 84*

Brill, Abraham Arden
American. Psychiatrist
b. Oct 12, 1874 in Kanczuga, Austria
d. Mar 2, 1948 in New York, New York
Source: *AmAu&B; DcAmB S4; DcNAA;
REnAL; TwCA SUP; WhAm 2; WhNAA*

Brill, Marty (Martin)
American. Football Player, Football Coach
Running back for Notre Dame 1928-30; all-
American, 1930.
b. 1905
d. May 1, 1973 in Los Angeles, California
Source: *NewYTBE 73; ObitOF 79; WhoFtbl
74, 74*

Brillat-Savarin, Jean Anthelme
French. Politician, Chef, Author
Wrote gastronomic classic *Physiology of Taste,* 1884.
b. Apr 1, 1755 in Bellay, France
d. Feb 2, 1826 in Paris, France
Source: *ApCAB; AtlBL; BbD; BiD&SB; CasWL; DcBiPP; EuAu; EvEuW; LinLib S; NewC; OxEng; OxFr; REn*

Brimmer, Andrew Felton
American. Economist, Government Official
b. Sep 13, 1926 in Newellton, Louisiana
Source: *AmEA 74; AmM&WS 73S; CurBio 68; IntWW 74; NewYTBE 73; WhoAm 74, 76, 78, 80, 82; WhoAmP 73; WhoBlA 75; WhoGov 75; WhoS&SW 82*

Brindle, Melbourne
American. Artist, Illustrator
b. 1904
Source: *BioIn 9*

Brindley, James
English. Engineer
b. 1716
d. 1772
Source: *Alli; BioIn 2, 4, 5, 6, 7, 8, 9, 10*

Brinegar, Claude Stout
American. Government Official
Secretary of Transportation under Richard Nixon, Gerald Ford, 1973-75.
b. Dec 16, 1926 in Rockport, California
Source: *AmM&WS 73S; CngDr 74; NewYTBE 72; WhoAm 74, 76, 78, 80, 82; WhoAmP 73; WhoF&I 74; WhoWor 78*

Brinig, Myron
American. Author
b. Dec 22, 1900 in Minneapolis, Minnesota
Source: *AmAu&B; AmNov; OxAmL; REnAL; TwCA, SUP*

Brink, Carol Ryrie
American. Author
Prolific adult, children's writer, who won Newbery award for *Caddie Woodlawn,* 1936.
b. Dec 28, 1895 in Moscow, Idaho
d. Aug 15, 1981 in La Jolla, California
Source: *AmAu&B; AmWr; AnCL; Au&Wr 71; AuBYP; ConAu 1R, 3NR, 104; CurBio 46, 81; IntAu&W 76, 77; JBA 51; LinLib L; MinnWr; MorBMP; Newb 1922; REnAL; ScF&FL 1, 2; SmATA 1; Str&VC; TwCCW 78; WhE&EA; WhoAm 74, 76, 78, 80; WhoAmW 70, 74, 72; WhoPNW; WrDr 76, 80*

Brinkley, Christie
[Mrs. Billy Joel]
American. Model, Actress
b. Feb 2, 1953 in Monroe, Michigan
Source: *BioIn 12*

Brinkley, David McClure
American. Broadcast Journalist
Co-anchor, with Chet Huntley, 1958-70.
b. Jul 10, 1920 in Wilmington, North Carolina
Source: *BkPepl; ConAu 97; CurBio 60; IntMPA 77, 78, 79, 80, 81, 82; WhoAm 74, 76, 78, 80, 82; WhoS&SW 82; WhoWor 78*

Brinkley, John Romulus
American. Surgeon
Alleged charlatan, who became rich by rejuvenating men with goat gland transplants.
b. Jul 8, 1885 in Jackson County, North Carolina
d. May 26, 1942 in San Antonio, Texas
Source: *CurBio 42; DcAmB S3; InSci; ObitOF 79; WorAl*

Brinkley, Nell
American. Illustrator
b. 1888
d. Oct 21, 1944
Source: *BioIn 1, 10; CurBio 44*

Brinsmead, Hesba Fay
Australian. Author
b. Mar 15, 1922 in New South Wales, Australia
Source: *ConAu 21R; SenS; SmATA 18; WrDr 76*

Brinton, Clarence Crane
American. Author, Educator, Historian
b. Feb 2, 1898 in Winsted, Connecticut
d. Sep 7, 1968
Source: *AmAu&B; BioIn 5, 8; ConAu 5R, 25R; CurBio 58, 68; REn; REnAL*

Brinton, Daniel Garrison
American. Anthropologist, Author
b. May 13, 1837 in Thornbury, Pennsylvania
d. Jul 31, 1899
Source: *Alli SUP; AmAu; AmAu&B; BiD&SB; DcAmAu; DcNAA; OxAmL*

Brioni, Gaetano Savini, Marquis
Italian. Fashion Designer
b. Sep 10, 1909 in Termi, Italy
Source: *WhoAm 82; WorFshn*

Brisbane, Albert
American. Social Reformer, Author
Wrote *Social Destiny of Man,* 1840.
b. Aug 2, 1809 in Batavia, New York
d. May 1, 1890 in Richmond, Virginia
Source: *AmAu; AmAu&B; AmBi; DcAmB;
DcNAA; OxAmL; REnAL; WebAB; WhAm
HS*

Brisbane, Arthur
American. Journalist
b. Dec 12, 1864 in Buffalo, New York
d. Dec 25, 1936 in New York, New York
Source: *AmAu&B; AmBi; DcAmB S2;
DcNAA; OxAmL; REnAL; TwCA; WebAB;
WhAm 1*

Briscoe, Dolph
American. Politician
b. Apr 23, 1923 in Uvalde, Texas
Source: *WhoAm 74; WhoAmP 73*

Briscoe, Robert
Irish. Public Official
b. Sep 25, 1894 in Dublin, Ireland
d. May 30, 1969
Source: *BioIn 4, 5, 8; CurBio 57, 69*

Brisebois, Danielle
American. Actress
Appeared in TV series "Archie Bunker's
    Place," 1981; "Knot's Landing," 1983-84.
b. Jun 28, 1969 in Brooklyn, New York
Source: *BioIn 12*

Brissie, Lou (Leland Victor, Jr.)
American. Baseball Player
Pitcher, 1947-53; played with brace, artifical
    left leg.
b. Jun 5, 1924 in Anderson, South Carolina
Source: *BaseEn 85; BioIn 1, 8; WhoProB 73*

Brisson, Frederick
Danish. Producer
Stage, film productions include *Damn
    Yankees,* 1955.
b. Mar 17, 1917 in Copenhagen, Denmark
d. Oct 8, 1984 in New York, New York
Source: *AnObit 1984; BiE&WWA; CelR;
FilmgC; IntMPA 76, 77, 78, 79, 80, 81, 82;
NotNAT; WhoAm 74, 76, 78, 80, 82;
WhoThe 81*

Britain, Radie
American. Composer, Author
Writer of choral compositions, string quartets,
    song cycles including "Translunar Cycle,"
    1967.
b. Mar 17, 1903 in Amarillo, Texas
Source: *AmSCAP 66; Baker 78; BiDAmM;
BioIn 1, 3; WhoAm 74, 76, 78, 80, 82;
WhoAmW 74, 77; WhoMus 72*

Britt, May
[Maybritt Wilkens]
Swedish. Actress
Starred in *The Blue Angel,* 1959; former wife
    of Sammy Davis, Jr.
b. Mar 22, 1933 in Lidingo, Sweden
Source: *FilmEn; FilmgC; InWom; MotPP;
WhoHol A*

Britt, Steuart Henderson
American. Psychologist, Lawyer, Author
Published nearly 200 articles on marketing,
    law, psychology; wrote *The Spenders,* 1960.
b. Jun 17, 1907 in Fulton, Missouri
d. Mar 15, 1979 in Evanston, Illinois
Source: *AmM&WS 73S, 78S; ConAu 1R,
2NR, 85; WhAm 7; WhoAm 74, 76, 78;
WhoCan 73; WhoF&I 74, 75, 77, 79;
WhoMW 74, 76, 78; WhoWor 74, 76, 78*

Brittain, Harry Ernest, Sir
English. Newspaper Publisher
b. Dec 24, 1873
d. Jul 9, 1974
Source: *Au&Wr 71; NewYTBS 74; Who 74*

Brittain, Vera Mary
English. Author
Wrote of WW I experiences in *Testament of
    Youth,* 1933; made into English series
    shown on PBS.
b. 1896 in Newcastle, England
d. Mar 29, 1970
Source: *ChhPo; ConAu 25R, P-1; EvLB;
InWom; LongCTC; NewC; NewYTBE 73;
ObitT 1961; PenC ENG; REn; TwCA;
TwCWr; WhE&EA*

Brittany, Morgan
[Suzanne Cupito; Mrs. Jack Gill]
American. Actress
Plays Kathryn Wentworth on TV series
    "Dallas," 1981--.
b. 1950 in California
Source: *NF*

Britten, (Edward) Benjamin
English. Composer
Best known for modern operas, including
Gloriana, 1953, written for coronation of
Elizabeth II.
b. Nov 22, 1913 in Lowestoft, England
d. Dec 4, 1976 in Aldeburgh, England
Source: *CelR; CurBio 42, 61; DcCM; IntWW
74; OxFilm; Who 74*

Britton, Barbara
[Barbara Brantingham]
American. Actress
Spokesperson for Revlon cosmetics, 12 yrs.
b. Sep 26, 1919 in Long Beach, California
d. Jan 18, 1980 in New York, New York
Source: *FilmgC; ForWC 70; HolP 40;
InWom; IntMPA 75, 76, 77; MotPP; MovMk;
NewYTBS 80; WhoAmW 79; WhoHol A*

Britton, Edgar Clay
American. Chemist
b. Sep 25, 1891 in Rockville, Indiana
d. Jul 31, 1962
Source: *BioIn 1, 2, 3, 4, 6, 9*

Britz, Jerilyn
American. Golfer
b. Jan 1, 1943 in Minneapolis, Minnesota
Source: *BioIn 12*

Broadbent, Ed (John Edward)
Canadian. Government Official
Leader, New Democratic Party, 1975--; MP,
1968--; wrote *The Liberal Rip-off,* 1970.
b. Mar 21, 1936 in Oshawa, Ontario
Source: *BioIn 11; CanWW 82; WhoAm 82;
WhoCan 77*

Broadbent, Eleanor
[Eleanora Cisneros]
American. Opera Singer
b. Nov 1, 1878 in New York, New York
d. Feb 3, 1934 in New York, New York
Source: *InWom; NotAW*

Broadhurst, Kent
American. Actor, Dramatist, Artist,
Photographer
Films include *The Verdict,* 1982; *Silkwood,*
1983.
b. Feb 4, 1940 in Saint Louis, Missouri
Source: *ConTFT 2*

Brock, Alice May
American. Author, Restaurateur
Owner, Alice's Restaurant; Arlo Guthrie's
song of same name was written about her.
b. Feb 28, 1941 in Brooklyn, New York
Source: *ConAu 41R; NewYTBE 71; WhoAm
74, 76, 80, 82; WhoAmW 74*

Brock, Bill (William Emerson)
American. Senator
b. Nov 23, 1930 in Chattanooga, Tennessee
Source: *BiDrAC; CngDr 74; CurBio 71;
WhoAmP 73; WhoGov 75; WhoS&SW 82*

Brock, Isaac, Sir
English. Soldier
Major-general, Upper Canada, 1811; forced
victory over General Hull at Detroit, 1812.
b. Oct 6, 1769 in Saint Peter Port, England
d. Oct 13, 1812 in Queenston, Ontario
Source: *ApCAB; Drake; HarEnUS; OxCan;
WebBD 80*

Brock, Lou(is Clark)
American. Baseball Player
Outfielder, 1964-70, who holds ML record
for stolen bases, 938; Hall of Fame, 1985.
b. Jun 18, 1939 in El Dorado, Arkansas
Source: *BaseEn 85; CurBio 75; NewYTBE 72,
73; WhoAm 74, 76, 78; WhoBlA 75, 77;
WhoProB 73; WorAl*

Brock, Tony
[The Babys]
English. Singer, Musician
Drummer, vocalist with power pop group,
1976-81.
b. Mar 31, 1954 in Bournemouth, England
Source: *NF*

Brod, Max
Israeli. Author
Writings deal mainly with Jewish themes:
Franz Kafka, 1937.
b. May 27, 1884 in Prague, Czechoslovakia
d. Dec 20, 1968 in Tel Aviv, Israel
Source: *Baker 78; CasWL; ConAu 5R, 25R;
EncWL, 2; EvEuW; LongCTC; McGEWD;
ModGL; ObitT 1961; OxGer; PenC EUR;
REn; TwCA, SUP; WhoLA*

Broda, "Turk" (Walter)
Canadian. Hockey Player
Goalie, Toronto, 1936-52; Hall of Fame,
1967.
b. May 15, 1914 in Brandon, Manitoba
d. Oct 17, 1972 in Toronto, Ontario
Source: *HocEn; NewYTBE 72; WhoHcky 73*

Broderick, Helen
American. Actress
Star of first Ziegfeld Follies,1907; mother of
actor Broderick Crawford.
b. Aug 11, 1891 in Philadelphia,
Pennsylvania
d. Sep 25, 1959 in Beverly Hills, California
Source: *EncMT; FilmEn; FilmgC; MotPP;
MovMk; ObitOF 79; ThFT; Vers A; WhScrn
74, 77; WhoHol B; WorAl*

Broderick, James Joseph
American. Actor
Star of TV series "Family," 1976-81.
b. Mar 7, 1927 in Charlestown, New
Hampshire
d. Nov 1, 1982 in New Haven, Connecticut
Source: *IntMPA 79, 80, 81, 82; NewYTBS
82; NotNAT; WhoAm 82; WhoHol A*

Broderick, Matthew
American. Actor
Won 1983 Tony for *Brighton Beach Memoirs;*
in films *Max Dugan Returns,* 1983;
WarGames, 1983.
b. Aug 21, 1962 in New York, New York
Source: *JohnWTW 38; NewYTBS 83; VarWW
85*

Brodie, Fawn McKay
American. Author
Wrote biographies of Sir Richard Burton,
Joseph Smith, Thomas Jefferson; won
Knopf biography award, 1943.
b. Sep 15, 1915 in Ogden, Utah
d. Jan 10, 1981 in Santa Monica, California
Source: *Au&Wr 71; ConAu 102, 17R; DrAS
74H, 78H; ForWC 70; NewYTBS 81; WhoAm
78, 80*

Brodie, John Riley
American. Football Player, Sportscaster
Quarterback, San Francisco, 1957-73; with
NBC Sports, 1974--.
b. Aug 14, 1935 in San Francisco, California
Source: *NewYTBE 71; WhoAm 74, 76, 78,
80, 82; WhoFtbl 74*

Brodie, Steve
[John Stevens]
American. Actor
Films include *Thirty Seconds Over Tokyo,*
1944; *Winchester '73,* 1950.
b. Nov 25, 1919 in El Dorado, Kansas
Source: *FilmEn; FilmgC; WhoHol A*

Brodovitch, Alexey
American. Artist, Designer
b. 1898 in Russia
d. Apr 15, 1971 in Lethor, France
Source: *NewYTBE 71*

Brodsky, Joseph Alexandrovich
[Iosif Alexandrovich Brodsky]
American. Author, Poet
b. May 24, 1940 in Leningrad, U.S.S.R.
Source: *AuNews 1; ConAu 41R; CurBio 82;
NewYTBE 72; WhoAm 82*

Brody, Jane Ellen
American. Author, Journalist
Syndicated columnist writing on nutrition,
health: *Jane Brody's Nutrition Book,* 1981.
b. May 5, 1941 in Brooklyn, New York
Source: *ConAu 102; CurBio 86; WhoAm 84*

Brogan, Denis William, Sir
Scottish. Author, Political Scientist
b. Aug 11, 1900 in Glasgow, Scotland
d. Jan 5, 1974 in Cambridge, England
Source: *ConAu 45, 97; DcLEL; EvLB;
LongCTC; NewC; NewYTBS 74; TwCA SUP;
WhAm 6; Who 74*

Brokaw, Tom (Thomas John)
American. Broadcast Journalist
Anchor, "NBC Nightly News," 1982--; host,
"The Today Show," 1976-82.
b. Feb 6, 1940 in Webster, South Dakota
Source: *BkPepl; ConAu 108; IntMPA 81, 82;
NewYTET; WhoAm 82*

Brokenshire, Norman
Canadian. Radio Performer
Prominent announcer, 1920s.
b. Jun 10, 1898 in Murcheson, Ontario
d. May 4, 1965 in Hauppauge, New York
Source: *CurBio 50, 65; ObitOF 79; WhAm 4*

Brolin, James
American. Actor
Won Emmy for "Marcus Welby, MD," 1969;
star of "Hotel," 1983 --.
b. Jul 18, 1941 in Los Angeles, California
Source: *FilmgC; IntMPA 75, 76, 77, 78, 79,
80, 81, 82; MovMk; WhoAm 78, 80, 82;
WhoHol A; WorAl*

Bromberg, J. Edward
American. Actor
Character actor in films, 1936-50.
b. Dec 25, 1903 in Temesvar, Hungary
d. 1951
Source: *FilmgC; MotPP; MovMk; PIP&P*

Bromfield, John
[Farron Bromfield]
American. Actor
TV series, 1950s: "The Sheriff of Cochise,"
"US Marshal."
b. Jun 11, 1922 in South Bend, Indiana
Source: *FilmgC; IntMPA 75, 76, 77, 78, 79,
80, 81, 82; MotPP; WhoHol A*

Bromfield, Louis Brucker
American. Author
Developed experimental farming community;
won Pulitzer for *Early Autumn,* 1926.
b. Dec 27, 1896 in Mansfield, Ohio
d. Mar 18, 1956 in Columbus, Ohio
Source: *AmAu&B; AmNov; CnDAL; ConAmA;
ConAmL; ConAu 107; CurBio 44, 56; CyWA;
DcBiA; DcLEL; EncWL; EvLB; LongCTC;
Novels; OhA&B; OxAmL; PenC AM; REn;
REnAL; TwCA, SUP; TwCWr; WebAB;
WhAm 3; WhNAA; WorAl*

Bron, Eleanor
English. Actress
Light character player, stage, screen, TV;
films include *Women in Love,* 1969.
b. 1934 in Stanmore, England
Source: *FilmEn; FilmgC; IntMPA 80, 81, 82;
Who 82, 85; WhoHol A; WhoThe 77, 81;
WhoWor 74*

Broncho Billy
see: Anderson, Gilbert M

Broneer, Oscar Theodore
American. Archaeologist
b. Dec 28, 1894 in Backebo, Sweden
Source: *BioIn 8, 9; DrAS 74F; WhoAm 74*

Bronfman, Edgar Miles
Canadian. Distiller
Chief exec., chm., Seagram Co., Ltd.
b. Jun 20, 1929 in Montreal, Quebec
Source: *CanWW 79, 82; CurBio 74; Dun&B
79; IntWW 74, 75, 76, 77, 78, 79, 80, 81;
St&PR 75; WhoAm 74, 76, 78, 80, 82;
WhoAmJ 80; WhoCan 73, 75, 77; WhoF&I
74, 81; WhoGov 72; WhoWor 74, 76, 78, 80*

Bronfman, Samuel
Canadian. Distiller
At death, Seagram's world's largest distiller;
sales exceeded $1.3 billion.
b. Mar 4, 1891 in Brandon, Manitoba
d. Jul 10, 1971 in Montreal, Quebec
Source: *MacDCB 78; NatCAB 56; NewYTBE
71; NewYTBS 74; ObitOF 79; WhAm 5;
WhoWorJ 72*

Bronfman, Samuel
Canadian. Kidnap Victim
Heir to Seagram's fortune; kidnapped, 1975.
b. 1954
Source: *BioIn 10*

Bronk, Detlev Wulf
American. Biologist
Founded biophysics; pioneered use of electro-
microscopy to monitor human nerve
network.
b. Aug 13, 1897 in New York, New York
d. Nov 17, 1975 in New York, New York
Source: *AmM&WS 73P, 76P; BlueB 76;
CurBio 76; InSci; IntWW 76; McGMS 80;
NewYTBS 75; WebAB, 79; WhAm 6; WhoAm
76; WhoAtom 77; WhoWor 76*

Bronowski, Jacob
English. Mathematician, Author
b. Jan 18, 1908 in Poland
d. Aug 22, 1974 in East Hampton, New
York
Source: *AmAu&B; AnCL; ConAu 1R, 53;
DcLEL; IntWW 74; NewYTBS 74; WhAm 6;
Who 74; WhoAm 74; WhoWor 78; WorAu*

Bronson, Betty (Elizabeth Ada)
American. Actress
Starred in first film version *Peter Pan,* 1924.
b. Nov 17, 1906 in Trenton, New Jersey
d. Oct 21, 1971 in Pasadena, California
Source: *FilmEn; Film 2; FilmgC; InWom;
MotPP; MovMk; NewYTBE 71; ThFT; TwYS;
WhScrn 74, 77; WhoAmW 72; WhoHol B*

Bronson, Charles
[Charles Buchinsky]
American. Actor
Known for tough-guy roles: *Death Wish,*
1974.
b. Oct 3, 1922 in Ehrenfeld, Pennsylvania
Source: *BioNews 74; BkPepl; CelR; ConTFT
3; CurBio 75; IntMPA 82; MovMk; NewYTBS
74; WhoAm 84*

Bronstein, David
Russian. Chess Player
b. 1925
Source: *BioIn 4*

Bronte, Anne
[Acton Bell, pseud.]
English. Author
Sister of Charlotte and Emily; wrote *Agnes
Grey,* 1847.
b. Mar 25, 1820 in Thornton, England
d. May 26, 1849 in Scarborough, England
Source: *BbD; BiD&SB; BrAu 19; CasWL;
Chambr 3; ChhPo, S1; CyWA; DcBiA;
DcEnA, AP; DcEnL; DcEuL; DcLEL; EvLB;
HerW; InWom; OxEng; PenC ENG; RAdv 1;
WebE&AL*

Bronte, Charlotte
[Currer Bell, pseud.; Mrs. Arthur Bell
Nicholls]
English. Author
Most successful of sisters; wrote *Jane Eyre*,
1847.
b. Apr 21, 1816 in Thornton, England
d. Mar 31, 1855 in Haworth, England
Source: *Alli; AtlBL; BbD; BiD&SB; BrAu 19;
CasWL; Chambr 3; ChhPo, S1, S2; CrtT 3;
CyWA; DcBiA; DcEnA, AP; DcEnL; DcEuL;
DcLEL; EvLB; FilmgC; HerW; HsB&A;
InWom; MouLC 3; OxEng; PenC ENG;
RAdv 1; RComWL; WebE&AL*

Bronte, Emily Jane
[Ellis Bell, pseud.]
English. Author
Wrote *Wuthering Heights*, 1848.
b. Aug 20, 1818 in Thornton, England
d. Dec 19, 1848 in Haworth, England
Source: *AtlBL; BbD; BiD&SB; BrAu 19;
CasWL; Chambr 3; ChhPo, S1, S2; CnE&AP;
CrtT 3; CyWA; DcBiA; DcEnA, AP; DcEnL;
DcEuL; DcLEL; EvLB; FilmgC; HerW;
InWom; MouLC 3; OxEng; PenC ENG;
RAdv 1; RComWL; WebE&AL*

Bronte, Patrick Branwell
English. Poet
b. 1817
d. Sep 26, 1848
Source: *BioIn 1, 2, 5, 6, 9, 10, 11; ChhPo
S1; DcEuL; PoIre*

Bronzino II
Italian. Artist
b. Nov 17, 1503 in Montecelli, Italy
d. Nov 23, 1572
Source: *AtlBL; REn*

Brook, Alexander
American. Artist
b. Jul 14, 1898 in Brooklyn, New York
d. Feb 26, 1980 in Sag Harbor, New York
Source: *CurBio 41, 80; DcCAA 71; IntWW
74; WhoAm 74; WhoAmA 73*

Brook, Clive (Clifford)
English. Actor
b. Jun 1, 1887 in London, England
d. Nov 18, 1974 in London, England
Source: *BiDFilm; BlueB 76; FilmgC; MotPP;
MovMk; NewYTBS 74; ObitOF 79; TwYS;
WhAm 6; WhScrn 77; WhThe; Who 74;
WhoHol B; WorEFlm*

Brook, Peter
English. Director
Co-director, Royal Shakespeare Theatre,
1962--.
b. Mar 21, 1925 in London, England
Source: *Au&Wr 71; BiDFilm; BiE&WWA;
CelR; CroCD; CurBio 61; DcFM; FilmgC;
IntWW 74; MovMk; NotNAT; OxFilm;
OxThe; WhDW; Who 74; WhoThe 77, 81;
WorAl; WorEFlm*

Brooke, Sir Alan Francis
see: Alanbrooke, Alan Francis Brooke, 1st
Viscount

Brooke, Edward William
American. Politician
Rep. senator, MA, 1967-79.
b. Oct 26, 1919 in Washington, District of
Columbia
Source: *BiDrAC; CngDr 74, 77; CurBio 67;
Ebony 1; InB&W 80; IntWW 74, 75, 76, 77,
78, 79, 82; PolProf J, NF; SelBAAu; WhoAm
74, 76, 78, 80, 82; WhoAmP 73, 75, 77, 79;
WhoBlA 75, 77; WhoE 74, 75, 77, 79;
WhoGov 72, 75, 77; WhoWor 74, 76, 78*

Brooke, Hillary
[Beatrice Sofia Mathilda Peterson]
American. Actress
Played "bad girl" roles, films, 1940-50.
b. Sep 8, 1914 in Astoria, New York
Source: *ChhPo; FilmgC; IntMPA 75; MovMk;
WhoHol A*

Brooke, James, Sir
British. Political Leader
First rajah, Borneo.
b. Apr 29, 1803 in Benares, India
d. Jun 11, 1868 in England
Source: *Alli, SUP; CelCen; DcBiPP; DcInB;
McGEWB*

Brooke, L Leslie
English. Author, Illustrator
Wrote, illustrated children's *Johnny Crow*
series.
b. Sep 24, 1862 in Birkenhead, England
d. May 1, 1940 in London, England
Source: *TwCCW 83*

Brooke, Rupert Chawner
English. Poet
Wrote romantic, patriotic poetry, WW I.
b. Aug 3, 1887 in Rugby, England
d. Apr 23, 1915 in Scyros, Greece
Source: *AtlBL; CasWL; Chambr 3; ChhPo, S2; CnE&AP; CnMWL; DcEuL; DcLEL; EncWL; EvLB; LongCTC; ModBrL, S1; NewC; OxCan; OxEng; PenC ENG; RAdv 1; REn; TwCA, SUP; TwCWr; WebE&AL; WhoTwCL*

Brookings, Robert Somers
American. Merchant, Philanthropist
b. Jan 22, 1850 in Cecil County, Maryland
d. Nov 15, 1932 in Washington, District of Columbia
Source: *AmBi; DcAmB S1; DcNAA; WebAB; WhAm 1*

Brooks, Albert
American. Comedian, Actor, Writer
b. Jul 22, 1947 in Los Angeles, California
Source: *BioIn 10; WhoAm 82*

Brooks, Angie Elizabeth
Liberian. Diplomat
Member, UN General Assembly, 1954--; first African woman pres., 1969.
b. Aug 24, 1928 in Virginia, Liberia
Source: *CurBio 70; InB&W 80; IntWW 74, 75; WhoAmW 72, 74; WhoUN 75*

Brooks, Charlie, Jr.
American. Murderer
First US felon executed by injection.
b. 1942
d. Dec 7, 1982 in Huntsville, Texas
Source: *NF*

Brooks, Cleanth
American. Author, Critic
b. Oct 16, 1906 in Murray, Kentucky
Source: *AmAu&B; CasWL; ConAu 17R; DcLEL; DrAS 74E; IntWW 74; LongCTC; ModAL; OxAmL; PenC AM; RAdv 1; REn; REnAL; TwCA SUP; Who 74; WhoAm 74; WhoTwCL; WhoWor 78; WrDr 80*

Brooks, David Owen
American. Murderer
Killed 27 young boys, TX, 1973.
b. 1955
Source: *BioIn 10*

Brooks, Donald Marc
American. Fashion Designer
Designed costumes for movie *The Bell Jar*, 1979.
b. Jan 10, 1928 in New York, New York
Source: *BiE&WWA; CelR; CurBio 72; NotNAT; WhoAm 74, 76, 78, 80, 82; WhoFash; WorFshn*

Brooks, Foster Murrell
American. Comedian, Actor
Known for "drunk" skits.
b. May 11, 1912
Source: *NF*

Brooks, Geraldine
[Geraldine Stroock]
American. Actress
Published book of her bird photographs *Swan Watch*, 1975.
b. Oct 29, 1925 in New York, New York
d. Jun 19, 1977 in Riverhead, New York
Source: *BiE&WWA; FilmgC; ForWC 70; HolP 40; InWom; IntMPA 75, 76, 77; NatCAB 59; NotNAT A; WhoHol A*

Brooks, Gwendolyn
American. Author, Poet
First black woman to win Pulitzer for poetry, 1950, for *Annie Allen*.
b. Jun 7, 1917 in Topeka, Kansas
Source: *AmAu&B; AuNews 1; BioNews 74; BkCL; BlkAWP; CasWL; CelR; ChhPo, S1, S2; ConAu 1R, 1NR; ConLC 1, 2, 4, 5, 15; ConP 70, 75; CroCAP; CurBio 50; DrAP 75; EncAB-H; InWom; IntWW 74; LivgBAA; ModAL, S1; OxAmL; PenC AM; RAdv 1; REnAL; SmATA 6; TwCA SUP; WebAB; WhoAm 74, 76, 78, 80, 82; WhoAmW 77; WhoWor 78; WrDr 80*

Brooks, Henry Sands
American. Businessman
Opened Manhattan clothing store, 1817; pioneer in ready-to-wear apparel.
b. 1770 in Connecticut
d. 1833
Source: *Entr*

Brooks, Herb(ert Paul)
American. Hockey Coach
Coached 1980 US Olympic hockey team, NY Rangers, 1981-85.
b. Aug 5, 1937 in Saint Paul, Minnesota
Source: *HocEn; WhoAm 80, 82*

Brooks, Jack Bascom
American. Politician
Dem. congressman, TX, 1953--.
b. Dec 18, 1922 in Crowley, Louisiana
Source: *BiDrAC; BioIn 10, 11; WhoAm 76, 78, 80, 82, 84; WhoGov 75*

Brooks, James L
American. Producer, Director, Actor, Screenwriter
One of TV's best story minds who co-created "The Mary Tyler Moore Show."
b. May 9, 1940 in Brooklyn, New York
Source: *ConAu 73; ConTFT 3; NewYTBS 84; WhoAm 84; WhoTelC*

Brooks, Lela
Canadian. Figure Skater
b. 1908
Source: *BioIn 10*

Brooks, Louise
American. Actress
Film performances include *Pandora's Box, Diary of a Lost Child.*
b. Nov 14, 1906 in Cherryvale, Kansas
d. Aug 8, 1985 in Rochester, New York
Source: *Alli SUP; BiDFilm; FilmgC; MotPP; MovMk; OxFilm; ThFT; TwYS; WhoAmA 82; WhoHol A; WorEFlm*

Brooks, Maria Gowen
[Maria del Occidente, pseud.]
American. Poet
Wrote epic poem *Zophiel,* 1833.
b. 1794 in Medford, Massachusetts
d. Nov 11, 1845 in Cuba
Source: *NotAW; OxAmL 83*

Brooks, Mel
[Melvyn Kaminsky]
American. Actor, Author, Producer, Director
Writer, director *Blazing Saddles,* 1974, *Young Frankenstein,* 1975.
b. Jun 28, 1928 in New York, New York
Source: *BiE&WWA; BkPepl; CurBio 74; FilmgC; IntMPA 82; MovMk; Who 82; WhoAm 82*

Brooks, Phillips
American. Religious Leader
Episcopal minister who said sermon over Abraham Lincoln's body, 1865; wrote "O Little Town of Bethlehem."
b. Dec 13, 1835 in Boston, Massachusetts
d. Jan 23, 1893 in Boston, Massachusetts
Source: *AmAu&B; AmBi; AnCL; ApCAB; BbD; BiDAmM; BiD&SB; Chambr 3; DcAmAu; DcAmB; DcAmReB; DcNAA; Drake; LinLib S; OxAmL; REnAL; TwCBDA; WebAB; WhAm HS*

Brooks, Richard
American. Director, Screenwriter
Won award, screenplay *Elmer Gantry,* 1960; writer-director *Looking for Mr. Goodbar,* 1977.
b. May 18, 1912 in Philadelphia, Pennsylvania
Source: *AmAu&B; AmNov; BiDFilm; CelR; ConAu 73; ConDr 73, 77A; DcFM; FilmgC; IntAu&W 76, 77; IntMPA 75, 76, 77, 78, 79, 80, 81; IntWW 75, 76, 80, 81, 82; MovMk; OxFilm; WhoAm 74, 76, 78, 80, 82; WhoWor 74; WorEFlm*

Brooks, Van Wyck
American. Author
First to write of American cultural, literary development; won Pulitzer, 1936: *The Flowering of New England, 1815-1865* .
b. Feb 16, 1886 in Plainfield, New Jersey
d. May 2, 1963 in Bridgewater, Connecticut
Source: *AmAu&B; AmLY; AmWr; AtlBL; CasWL; Chambr 3; CnDAL; ConAmA; ConAmL; ConAu 4NR, 6NR; ConLCrt, 82; CurBio 41, 60, 63; DcLEL; EvLB; LongCTC; ModAL; OxAmL; PenC AM; RAdv 1; REn; REnAL; TwCA, SUP; TwCWr; WebAB 79; WebE&AL; WhNAA*

Brooks, Walter R(ollin)
American. Editor, Author
Children's books include *Freddy the Detective,* 1932.
b. Jan 9, 1886 in Rome, New York
d. Aug 17, 1958 in Roxbury, New York
Source: *ConAu 111; NatCAB 47; WhAm 3*

Brooks, William Keith
American. Zoologist
b. Mar 25, 1848 in Cleveland, Ohio
d. Nov 12, 1908 in Baltimore, Maryland
Source: *Alli SUP; DcAmAu; DcNAA; OhA&B*

Broonzy, "Big Bill"
American. Singer, Musician
b. Jun 26, 1893 in Scott, Mississippi
d. Aug 14, 1958 in Chicago, Illinois
Source: *EncFCWM 69*

Brophy, Brigid
English. Author
b. Jun 12, 1929 in London, England
Source: *Au&Wr 71; CasWL; ConAu 5R; ConLC 6; ConNov 72, 76; IntWW 74; LongCTC; ModBrL, S1; NewC; TwCWr; Who 74; WhoTwCL; WhoWor 78; WorAu; WrDr 80*

Brophy, Catherine Mary
American. Golfer
b. 1885
d. 1974
Source: *BioIn 10*

Brophy, John
English. Labor Union Official
Exponent of public ownership of mines;
wrote *A Miner's Life,* 1964.
b. Nov 6, 1883 in Lancaster, England
d. Feb 19, 1963
Source: *BiDAmLL; ObitOF 79*

Brosio, Manilo Giovanni
Italian. Diplomat
b. Jul 10, 1897 in Turin, Italy
d. Mar 14, 1980 in Turin, Italy
Source: *BioIn 4; CurBio 55, 82; IntWW 74,
75, 76, 77, 78, 79; NewYTBS 80; WhAm 7;
Who 74; WhoWor 74*

Brosnan, Jim (James Patrick)
"Professor"
American. Baseball Player, Author
Pitcher, 1954-63; author, books on baseball.
b. Oct 24, 1929 in Cincinnati, Ohio
Source: *BaseEn 85; ConAu 3NR, 1R; CurBio
64; SmATA 14; WhoMW 74; WhoProB 73*

Brosnan, Pierce
Irish. Actor
Star of TV series "Remington Steele," 1982-86.
b. May 16, 1953 in County Meath, Ireland
Source: *VarWW 85*

Brosten, Harve
American. Writer, Director, Producer
Won Emmy for comedy writing for "All in
the Family," 1978.
b. May 15, 1943 in Chicago, Illinois
Source: *ConTFT 2; VarWW 85*

Broten, Neal Lamoy
American. Hockey Player
Center, Minnesota; first American-born player
to score 100 points in one NHL season,
1985-86; member, 1980 US Olympic
hockey team.
b. Nov 29, 1959 in Roseau, Minnesota
Source: *HocEn; HocReg 81*

Brothers, Joyce Diane Bauer
[Mrs. Milton Brothers]
American. Psychologist, Author
Only woman to win $64,000 on "The
$64,000 Question," 1955-56.
b. Oct 20, 1928 in New York, New York
Source: *AuNews 1; BioNews 74; BkPepl;
ConAu 21R; CurBio 71; ForWC 70; InWom;
WhoAm 74, 76, 78, 80, 82; WhoAmW 77;
WhoWor 78; WhoWorJ 72*

Brothers Johnson, The
[George Johnson; Louis Johnson]
American. Music Group
Source: *RkOn 74*

Brough, Louise Althea
American. Tennis Player
US women's singles champion, 1947; won
three titles, Wimbledon, 1948, 1950.
b. Mar 11, 1923 in Oklahoma City,
Oklahoma
Source: *Alli SUP; CurBio 48; MacDWB*

Broun, Heywood Hale
American. Author, Actor, Broadcast
Journalist
Stage debut, 1949, in *I Remember Mama* ;
sports, news correspondent, CBS News.
b. Mar 10, 1918 in New York, New York
Source: *BiE&WWA; BioNews 74; ConAu 17R;
DcAmSR; NotNAT; OxAmH; WebAB 79;
WhoAm 82*

Broun, (Matthew) Heywood (Campbell)
American. Journalist, Author
Helped found "The Newspaper Guild," 1934.
b. Dec 7, 1888 in Brooklyn, New York
d. Dec 18, 1939 in New York, New York
Source: *AmAu&B; AmBi; CathA 1930;
ConAmA; CurBio 40; DcAmB S2; DcAmSR;
DcLEL; DcNAA; LinLib L, S; OxAmH;
OxAmL; PlP&P; REn; REnAL; TwCA, SUP;
WebAB; WhAm 1*

Brousse, Amy Elizabeth Thorpe
"Cynthia"
American. Spy
Worked for British intelligence, Washington,
DC, before America entered WW II.
b. 1910 in Minneapolis, Minnesota
d. 1963 in Castelnov, France
Source: *BioIn 7; SpyCS*

Brouthers, "Dan" (Dennis Joseph)
"Big Dan"
American. Baseball Player
First baseman, 1879-96, 1904; Hall of Fame,
1945.
b. May 8, 1858 in Sylvan Lake, New York
d. Aug 3, 1932 in East Orange, New Jersey
Source: *BaseEn 85; WhoProB 73*

Brouwer, Adriaen C
Flemish. Artist
b. 1606 in Oudenaarde, Belgium
d. Jan 1638 in Antwerp, Belgium
Source: *AtlBL*

Browder, Earl Russell
American. Communist Leader
b. May 20, 1891 in Wichita, Kansas
d. Jun 27, 1973 in Princeton, New Jersey
Source: *ConAu 45; CurBio 44, 73; EncAB-H;
NewYTBE 73; WebAB; WhAm 5; WhAmP*

Brown, A Roy
Canadian. Pilot
Shot down the "Red Baron" in WW I, 1918.
b. 1893 in Carleton Place, Ontario
d. Mar 9, 1944 in Stouffville, Ontario
Source: *ClbCR; ObitOF 79*

Brown, Alice
American. Author
Wrote stories of New England; play *Children
of Earth,* 1914.
b. Dec 5, 1856 in Hampton Falls, New
Hampshire
d. Jun 21, 1948 in Boston, Massachusetts
Source: *NotAW; OxAmL 83*

Brown, Barnum
American. Paleontologist
b. Feb 12, 1873
d. Feb 5, 1963
Source: *BioIn 2, 6, 7, 8*

Brown, Blair
American. Actress
Played Jackie Kennedy in TV miniseries
"Kennedy," 1983; in film *Continental
Divide,* 1981.
b. 1948 in Washington, District of Columbia
Source: *NewYTBS 81; VarWW 85; WhoE 81*

Brown, Bobby (Robert William)
"Golden Boy"
American. Baseball Player, Baseball Executive
Infielder, NY Yankees, 1946-54; pres. of AL,
1984--.
b. Oct 25, 1924 in Seattle, Washington
Source: *BaseEn 85; WhoProB 73*

Brown, Bryan
Australian. Actor
In film *Breaker Morant,* 1981; TV series
"The Thorn Birds," 1983.
b. 1950 in Sydney, Australia
Source: *BioIn 12; IntMPA 85; VarWW 83*

Brown, Carter, pseud.
[Alan Geoffrey Yates]
English. Author
Wrote 270 detective novels.
b. Aug 1, 1923 in London, England
d. May 5, 1985 in Sydney, Australia
Source: *ConAu 1R; WhoAm 82; WrDr 82*

Brown, Charles Brockden
American. Author, Editor
First American professional author;
introduced Indians to US fiction; wrote six
gothic romances.
b. Jan 17, 1771 in Philadelphia, Pennsylvania
d. Feb 22, 1810 in Philadelphia, Pennsylvania
Source: *Alli; AmAu; AmAu&B; AmBi;
ApCAB; AtlBL; BbD; BiD&SB; CasWL;
Chambr 3; CnDAL; CrtT 3; CyAL 1; CyWA;
DcAmAu; DcAmB; DcBiPP; DcEnL; DcLEL;
DcNAA; Drake; EncMys; EvLB; McGEWB;
MouLC 2; Novels; OxAmL; OxEng; PenC
AM; RAdv 1; REn; REnAL; TwCBDA;
WebAB; WebE&AL; WhAm HS*

Brown, Charles Lee
American. Businessman
With AT&T since 1946, chairman, 1979--.
b. Aug 23, 1921 in Richmond, Virginia
Source: *BioIn 11; WhoAm 78, 80, 82*

Brown, Charlie
American. Teacher
Boyhood friend of Charles Schulz who
supplied name, demeanor for comic strip
character.
b. 1926
d. Dec 5, 1983 in Minneapolis, Minnesota
Source: *NF*

Brown, Christy
Irish. Author, Poet
Wrote with only useable limb--left foot: *Down
All the Days,* 1970.
b. Jun 5, 1932 in Dublin, Ireland
d. Sep 6, 1981 in Parbrook, England
Source: *AnObit 1981; BioIn 8, 9, 10; ConAu
104; DcIrW 2; NewYTBE 70, 71; WrDr 76,
80*

Brown, Clarence
American. Director
Directed seven films starring Greta Garbo.
b. May 10, 1890 in Clinton, Massachusetts
Source: *BiDFilm; CmMov; DcFM; FilmgC;*
IntMPA 76, 77, 78, 79, 80, 81, 82; MovMk;
OxFilm; TwYS; VarWW 85; WorEFlm

Brown, David
American. Producer, Writer, Journalist
Produced films *The Sting,* 1973; *Jaws,* 1975;
Cocoon, 1985.
b. Jul 28, 1916
Source: *ConTFT 3*

Brown, Dean
American. Photographer
Free-lance photographer for several
magazines; known chiefly for color
landscapes.
b. 1936
d. Jul 10, 1973 in White Mountains, New
Hampshire
Source: *BioIn 10; ConPhot; MacBEP*

Brown, Dee (Alexander)
American. Author, Historian
Has written on American West, conquest of
Indians: *Bury My Heart at Wounded Knee,*
1971.
b. Feb 28, 1908 in Louisiana
Source: *ConAu 11NR; ConLC 18; SmATA 5*

Brown, Drew
American. Boxing Trainer
b. 1928
Source: *BioIn 9*

Brown, Eddie Lee
American. Football Player
Wide receiver, Cincinnati, 1985--; rookie of
year, 1985.
b. Dec 17, 1962 in Miami, Florida
Source: *FootReg 86*

Brown, Eddy
American. Musician
b. 1895 in Chicago, Illinois
d. Jun 17, 1974
Source: *NewYTBS 74*

Brown, Edmund Gerald
see: Brown, Pat

Brown, Edmund Gerald, Jr.
see: Brown, Jerry

Brown, Edward Gerald
see: Brown, Ned

Brown, Ford Maddox
English. Artist
b. 1821 in Calais, France
d. 1893
Source: *REn*

Brown, Frank Arthur, Jr.
American. Biologist, Educator
b. Aug 30, 1908 in Beverly, Massachusetts
Source: *AmM&WS 73P; WhoAm 74, 76, 78,*
80, 82

Brown, George
[Kool and the Gang]
"Funky"
American. Musician
Drummer with Kool and the Gang.
b. Jan 5, 1949 in Jersey City, New Jersey
Source: *NF*

Brown, George Alfred
English. Government Official
Controversial MP, 1945-70; deputy leader of
Labour Party, 1960-70.
b. Sep 2, 1914 in London, England
d. Jun 2, 1985
Source: *CurBio 85*

Brown, George Mackay
Scottish. Poet, Author
b. Oct 17, 1921 in Stromness, Scotland
Source: *CasWL; ChhPo S2; ConAu 21R;*
ConLC 5; ConNov 72, 76; ConP 70, 75;
WrDr 80

Brown, George Scratchley
American. General
b. Aug 17, 1918 in Montclair, New Jersey
d. Dec 5, 1978 in Washington, District of
Columbia
Source: *BioIn 10, 11*

Brown, Georgia
English. Actress
Stage works include London, Broadway
productions of *Threepenny Opera; Oliver .*
b. Oct 21, 1933 in London, England
Source: *BiE&WWA; FilmgC; InB&W 80;*
NotNAT; WhoHol A; WhoThe 77, 81

Brown, Harold
American. Businessman, Government Official
Secretary of Defense under Jimmy Carter,
1977-81.
b. Sep 19, 1927 in New York, New York
Source: *AmM&WS 73P; CurBio 61; IntWW*
74; LEduc 74; WhoAm 74, 76, 78, 80, 82;
WhoWest 84; WhoWor 78

Brown, Helen Gurley
American. Author, Editor
Cosmopolitan magazine editor, 1965--; wrote
  best-selling novel *Sex & the Single Girl,*
  1962.
b. Feb 18, 1922 in Green Forest, Arkansas
Source: *AmAu&B; CelR; ConAu 5R; CurBio
69; ForWC 70; InWom; NewYTBS 82;
WhoAm 74, 76, 78, 80, 82; WhoAmW 74,
77; WhoE 74; WhoWor 74; WrDr 76*

Brown, Henry Billings
American. Supreme Court Justice
b. Mar 2, 1836 in South Lee, Massachusetts
d. Sep 4, 1913 in Bronxville, New York
Source: *BioIn 2, 5; WebAB; WhAm 1*

Brown, Henry Kirke
American. Sculptor
b. Feb 24, 1814 in Leyden, Massachusetts
d. Jul 10, 1886
Source: *BioIn 5, 7, 8, 9*

Brown, H(ubert) Rap
[Jamiel Abdul Al-Amin]
American. Civil Rights Activist
Chairman, SNCC, 1967; converted to Islam
  while serving prison term.
b. Oct 4, 1943 in Baton Rouge, Louisiana
Source: *AmAu&B; CivRSt; LivgBAA; WhoBlA
77, 80, 80*

Brown, Hubie (Hubert Jude)
American. Basketball Coach
Coach, NY Nicks, 1982--.
b. Sep 25, 1933 in Elizabeth, New Jersey
Source: *NewYTBS 80; WhoAmA 80, 84*

Brown, Jacob Jennings
American. Military Leader
b. May 9, 1775 in Bucks County,
  Pennsylvania
d. Feb 24, 1828 in Washington, District of
  Columbia
Source: *AmBi; ApCAB; BiAUS; DcAmB;
Drake; TwCBDA; WebAB; WhAm HS*

Brown, James
American. Publisher
With Charles Little, formed Little, Brown
  and Co., 1837.
b. May 19, 1800 in Acton, Massachusetts
d. Mar 10, 1855
Source: *AmAu&B; ApCAB; DcAmB;
TwCBDA; WhAm HS*

Brown, James
"Mister Dynamite"; "Soul Brother Number
  One"
American. Singer
Has 38 gold records in 20 years; won
  Grammy, 1965.
b. May 3, 1934 in Augusta, Georgia
Source: *CelR; IlEncBM 82; RolSEnR 83;
WebAB; WhoBlA 75, 80; WhoE 74*

Brown, Jerry (Edmund Gerald, Jr.)
American. Politician
Son of Pat Brown; governor of CA, 1975-82.
b. Apr 7, 1938 in San Francisco, California
Source: *BioNews 74; BkPepl; CurBio 75;
WhoAm 82; WhoAmP 73; WhoGov 75*

Brown, Jim (James Nathaniel)
American. Actor, Football Player
Running back, Cleveland, 1957-65; all-time
  NFL rusher with 15,459 yds, until broken
  by Walter Payton, 1984.
b. Feb 17, 1936 in Saint Simons Island,
  Georgia
Source: *BioNews 74; CelR; FilmgC; IntMPA
75, 76, 77, 78, 79, 80, 81, 82; MotPP;
MovMk; NewYTBE 73; WhoAm 74, 76, 78,
80, 82; WhoBlA 75; WhoHol A*

Brown, Jim Ed (James Edward)
American. Singer
b. Apr 1, 1934 in Sparkman, Arkansas
Source: *EncFCWM 69; WhoAm 82*

Brown, Joe Evan
American. Comedian, Actor
b. Jul 28, 1892 in Holgate, Ohio
d. Jul 17, 1973 in Brentwood, California
Source: *BiE&WWA; CurBio 45, 73; EncMT;
FilmgC; MotPP; MovMk; NewYTBE 73;
OhA&B; OxFilm; WhAm 5; WhScrn 77;
WhoAm 74; WhoHol B*

Brown, John
"Old Brown of Osawatomie"
American. Abolitionist
Convicted of treason and hanged; subject of
  song "John Brown's Body."
b. May 9, 1800 in Torrington, Connecticut
d. Dec 2, 1859 in Charles Town, West
  Virginia
Source: *AmBi; ApCAB; DcAmB; Drake;
EncAB-H; OxAmL; REn; REnAL; TwCBDA;
WebAB; WhAm HS; WhAmP*

Brown, John Carter
American. Museum Director
Director, National Gallery of Art,
    Washington, DC, 1969--.
b. Oct 8, 1934 in Providence, Rhode Island
Source: *WhoAm 80, 82; WhoAmA 73, 82;
WhoE 81; WhoGov 72, 77; WhoS&SW 73*

Brown, John Mason
American. Critic, Lecturer
b. Jul 3, 1900 in Louisville, Kentucky
d. Mar 16, 1969 in New York, New York
Source: *AmAu&B; CnDAL; ConAu 9R, 25R;
LongCTC; OxAmL; OxThe; PenC AM;
REnAL; TwCA, SUP*

Brown, John Young, Jr.
American. Businessman, Politician
Bought Kentucky Fried Chicken from
    Colonel Sanders, 1964, for $2 million;
    governor of KY, 1980-83.
b. 1933 in Lexington, Kentucky
Source: *WhoAm 82; WhoAmP 81; WhoE 81;
WhoF&I 74; WhoS&SW 73, 82*

Brown, Johnny Mack
American. Football Player, Actor
b. Sep 1, 1904 in Dothan, Alabama
d. Nov 14, 1974 in Woodland Hills,
    California
Source: *CmMov; NewYTBS 74; TwYS;
WhScrn 77; WhoHol A, B*

Brown, Judie
American. Reformer
Founder, pres., American Life League,
    American Life Lobby, 1979--; goal to
    amend Constitution regarding abortion.
b. Mar 4, 1944 in Los Angeles, California
Source: *ConNews 86-2*

**Brown, Kelly (Elford Cornelious Kelly
    Kingman)**
American. Actor, Dancer
Soloist, American Ballet Theater; films
    include *Daddy Long Legs,* 1955; father of
    dancer Leslie Browne.
b. Sep 24, 1928 in Maysville, Kentucky
d. Mar 13, 1981 in Phoenix, Arizona
Source: *BiE&WWA; NewYTBS 81, 81;
NotNAT*

Brown, Kenneth H
American. Dramatist
Wrote *The Brig,* 1963.
b. Mar 9, 1936 in New York, New York
Source: *ConTFT 2*

Brown, Lancelot
"Capability"
English. Architect
Founded modern "English style" landscapes.
b. 1715 in Harle-Kirk, England
d. Feb 6, 1783 in London, England
Source: *AtlBL; BiDBrA; DcBiPP; DcD&D;
NewC*

Brown, Larry
American. Basketball Coach
b. 1940
Source: *BioIn 11*

Brown, Larry
American. Football Player
b. Sep 19, 1947 in Clairton, Pennsylvania
Source: *CurBio 73; NewYTBE 70; WhoBbl 73*

Brown, Lawrence
American. Composer, Pianist
b. 1893
d. Dec 25, 1972
Source: *BioIn 9*

Brown, Les(ter Raymond)
"Les Brown and His Band of Renown"
American. Band Leader
Often played with Bob Hope; wrote
    "Sentimental Journey."
b. Mar 12, 1912 in Reinerton, Pennsylvania
Source: *AmSCAP 66*

Brown, Lew
American. Songwriter
Songs include "Button Up Your Overcoat";
    "Beer Barrel Polka."
b. Dec 10, 1893 in Odessa, Russia
d. Feb 5, 1958 in New York, New York
Source: *AmSCAP 66; EncMT; NewCBMT;
WhAm 3; WhoHol A*

Brown, Louise Joy
English. Test Tube Baby
First test tube baby; daughter of Lesley and
    Gilbert Brown; procedure developed by
    Drs. Patrick Steptoe, Robert Edwards.
b. Jul 25, 1978 in Oldham, England
Source: *BioIn 11; BkPepl*

Brown, Marcia
American. Author, Artist
b. Jul 13, 1918 in Rochester, New York
Source: *AmAu&B; AnCL; AuBYP; BkP; Cald
1938; ChhPo, S2; ConAu 41R; FamAIYP;
IlsBYP; IlsCB 1946, 1957; MorJA; NewbC
1956; SmATA 7; WhoAm 74, 76, 78, 80, 82*

Brown, Margaret Wise
American. Children's Author
Wrote popular *Noisy Book* series, 1939-51.
b. May 23, 1910 in New York, New York
d. Nov 13, 1952 in Nice, France
Source: *AmSCAP 66; Au&ICB; AuBYP;
ChhPo, S1; DcAmB S5; NotAW MOD;
REnAL; WhAm 3*

Brown, Michael S
American. Geneticist
With Joseph L Goldstein, won Nobel Prize,
1985, for research into role of cholesterol
in cardiovascular disease.
b. Apr 13, 1941 in New York, New York
Source: *WhoAm 82, 84; WhoFrS 84*

Brown, Mordecai Peter Centennial
"Miner"; "Three Finger Brown"
American. Baseball Player
Pitcher, 1903-16; farm accident injured
fingers, helped make curve ball more
effective; Hall of Fame, 1949.
b. Oct 19, 1876 in Byesville, Indiana
d. Feb 14, 1948 in Terre Haute, Indiana
Source: *BaseEn 85; WhoProB 73*

Brown, Nacio Herb
American. Songwriter
Composed scores, songs, for MGM: "You
Were Meant for Me"; "Singin' in the
Rain."
b. Feb 22, 1896 in Deming, New Mexico
d. Sep 28, 1964 in San Francisco, California
Source: *AmSCAP 66; FilmEn; FilmgC*

Brown, Ned (Edward Gerald)
American. Journalist
b. 1881
d. Apr 25, 1976
Source: *BioIn 10*

Brown, Oscar, Jr.
American. Actor, Composer
Wrote "Brown Baby", 1960, sung by
Mahalia Jackson.
b. Oct 10, 1926 in Chicago, Illinois
Source: *BiDAmM; DrBlPA; WhoAm 74, 76,
78, 80, 82; WhoBlA 75, 80; WhoWor 74*

Brown, Pamela
English. Actress
Broadway debut, 1947, opposite John Gielgud
in *Importance of Being Earnest,* won 1961
Emmy for "Victoria Regina."
b. Jul 8, 1917 in London, England
d. Sep 18, 1975 in London, England
Source: *BiE&WWA; FilmgC; InWom; ObitOF
79; ObitT 1971; OxFilm; WhScrn 77*

Brown, Pamela Beatrice
English. Author, Actress
b. Dec 31, 1924 in Colchester, England
Source: *Au&Wr 71; AuBYP; ConAu 13R;
IntMPA 75; SmATA 5; WhoChL*

Brown, Pat (Edmund Gerald)
American. Lawyer, Politician
Father of Jerry Brown; governor of CA,
1959-66.
b. Apr 21, 1905 in San Francisco, California
Source: *CurBio 60; IntWW 74; WhoAm 74,
76, 78, 80, 82; WhoAmP 73*

Brown, Paul
American. Football Coach
Coach, Cleveland, 1946-62, Cincinnati, 1968-
76.
b. Jul 9, 1908 in Norwalk, Ohio
Source: *WhoAm 74, 76, 78, 80, 82; WhoFtbl
74*

Brown, Peter
English. Singer
b. 1940 in London, England
Source: *IlEncRk*

Brown, Robert
English. Botanist
b. Dec 21, 1773 in Montrose, Scotland
d. Jun 10, 1858 in London, England
Source: *AsBiEn; BioIn 2, 3, 4, 5; BrAu 19;
DcScB; LinLib S; NewCol 75*

Brown, Roger
American. Basketball Player
b. May 22, 1942 in Brooklyn, New York
Source: *WhoBbl 73*

Brown, Ron(ald James)
American. Football Player
Won gold medal in relay, 1984 Olympics;
tied NFL record by returning two kickoffs
for TDs in same game.
b. Mar 31, 1961 in Los Angeles, California
Source: *FootReg 86*

Brown, "Rooky" (William)
American. Basketball Player
Played with Harlem Globetrotters, 1947-58.
b. 1924
d. May 23, 1971
Source: *BioIn 9*

Brown, Rosemary
English. Psychic
Wrote *Unfinished Symphonies: Voices from
the Beyond,* 1971.
b. 1917
Source: *CanWW 80, 81; EncO&P 80;
MacDWB*

Brown, Samuel W, Jr.
American. Government Official
b. Jul 27, 1943 in Council Bluffs, Iowa
Source: *BioIn 11; WhoAm 78*

Brown, "Sonny" (William)
American. Composer
b. 1928 in Cincinnati, Ohio
Source: *BioIn 9*

Brown, "Tarzan" (Ellison)
American. Track Athlete
b. 1914
d. Aug 23, 1975
Source: *BioIn 10*

Brown, Tina
English. Editor, Journalist
Editor-in-chief, *Vanity Fair*, 1984--.
b. Nov 21, 1953 in Maidenhead, England
Source: *ConAu 116*

Brown, Tom (Thomas Edward)
American. Actor
Played boy-next-door roles, 1930s films; TV
    soap opera "General Hospital."
b. Jan 6, 1913 in New York, New York
Source: *Film 2; FilmgC; IntMPA 75, 76, 77,
    78, 79, 80, 81, 82; MovMk; TwYS; Vers B;
    WhoHol A*

Brown, Vanessa
[Smylla Brind]
American. Actress, Author, Artist
Free-lance correspondent for "Voice of
    America"; films include *Late George Apley;
    Foxes of Harrow; Ghost and Mrs. Muir.*
b. Mar 24, 1928 in Vienna, Austria
Source: *FilmgC; InWom; MotPP; WhoAmW
    77, 79; WhoHol A*

Brown, Walter Augustine
American. Basketball Executive
Organized Boston Celtics basketball team.
b. Feb 10, 1905 in Hopkinton, Massachusetts
d. Sep 7, 1964 in Boston, Massachusetts
Source: *EncAB 37; WhoBbl 73*

Brown, William Hill
American. Author
Wrote "first American novel," *The Power of
    Sympathy*, 1789.
b. Dec 1, 1765 in Boston, Massachusetts
d. Sep 2, 1793
Source: *BioIn 9; DcAmB S3*

Brown, William Wells
American. Author, Reformer
b. 1815 in Lexington, Kentucky
d. Nov 6, 1884 in Chelsea, Massachusetts
Source: *AmAu; AmAu&B; BlkAWP; DcAmB;
    DcNAA; EncAB-H; REnAL; WhAm HS;
    WhAmP*

Browne, Coral Edith
[Mrs. Vincent Price]
Australian. Actress
Sophisticated character roles in *Ruling Class;
    Theater of Blood; Drowning Pool*, 1970s.
b. Jul 23, 1913 in Melbourne, Australia
Source: *BiE&WWA; BlueB 76; CurBio 59;
    FilmgC; InWom; MotPP; MovMk; NotNAT;
    Who 74, 82; WhoHol A; WhoThe 77, 81*

Browne, Dik
American. Cartoonist
Created "Hi and Lois," 1954; "Hagar the
    Horrible," 1973.
b. Aug 11, 1917 in New York, New York
Source: *AuNews 1; WhoAm 82*

Browne, Jackson
American. Singer, Songwriter
Hit single "Doctor My Eyes," 1971, gold
    album *The Pretender*, 1976.
b. Oct 9, 1950 in Heidelberg, Germany
    (West)
Source: *BioIn 9, 11; BkPepl; EncPR&S 74;
    IlEncRk; RkOn 74; WhoAm 82; WhoRock 81*

Browne, Leslie
American. Ballerina, Actress
Soloist, American Ballet Theater, 1976--;
    starred in *The Turning Point*, 1977.
b. Jun 29, 1957 in New York, New York
Source: *BioIn 11; NewYTBS 77; WhoAm 80,
    82, 84*

Browne, "Phiz" (Hablot Knight)
English. Artist, Illustrator
Remembered as Dickens' chief illustrator;
    depicted *Pickwick Papers*, 1837; *David
    Copperfield*, 1850.
b. Jun 15, 1815 in Kensington, England
d. Jul 8, 1882 in West Brighton, England
Source: *HsB&A; NewC*

Browne, Walter Shawn
American. Chess Player, Journalist
b. Jan 10, 1949 in Sydney, Australia
Source: *BioNews 74; WhoAm 82*

Brownell, Herbert, Jr.
American. Lawyer, Government Official
Managed Thomas Dewey's presidential
   campaigns; attorney general, under Dwight
   Eisebhower, 1953-57.
b. Feb 20, 1904 in Peru, Nebraska
Source: *BiDrUSE; CurBio 44, 54; IntWW 74;
WhoAm 74, 76, 78, 80, 82; WhoAmP 73;
WhoWor 78*

Browner, Ross
American. Football Player
Defensive end, Cincinnati, suspended for
   preseason, plus four regular season games
   by NFL for drug involvement, 1983.
b. Mar 22, 1954 in Warren, Ohio
Source: *FootReg 81; WhoBlA 80*

Browning, Alice Crolley
American. Educator, Editor
Wrote *Negro Story,* 1944; founded
   International Black Writers Conference,
   1970.
b. Nov 5, 1907 in Chicago, Illinois
d. Oct 15, 1985 in Chicago, Illinois
Source: *ConAu 117; WhoAmW 79; WhoBlA
80*

Browning, Edmond Lee
American. Religious Leader
Bishop of HI, 1976-86; head of Episcopal
   Church of America, 1986--.
b. Mar 11, 1929 in Corpus Christi, Texas
Source: *WhoAm 84; WhoRel 85; WhoWest 74*

Browning, Elizabeth Barrett
[Mrs. Robert Browning]
English. Poet
Wrote *Sonnets from the Portuguese,* 1850, her
   own love story in verse.
b. Mar 6, 1806 in Coxhoe Hall, England
d. Jun 30, 1861 in Florence, Italy
Source: *Alli, SUP; AtlBL; BbD; BiD&SB;
BrAu 19; CasWL; Chambr 3; ChhPo, S1, S2;
CnE&AP; CrtT 3; CyWA; DcEnA AP;
DcEnL; DcEuL; DcLEL; EvLB; InWom;
MouLC 3; NewC; OxEng; PenC ENG; RAdv
1; RComWL; REn; WebE&AL*

**Browning, Frederick A(rthur) M(ontague),
   Sir**
"Boy"
British. Army Officer
Organized Red Devils Airborne Division,
   WW II; husband of author Daphne
   DuMaurier.
b. Dec 20, 1896
d. Mar 14, 1965 in Cornwall, England
Source: *BioIn 7; CurBio 43, 65; ObitOF 79;
PseudN 82; WhWW-II*

Browning, James Louis
American. Government Official
b. Dec 8, 1932 in Globe, Arizona
Source: *WhoGov 75*

Browning, John
American. Musician
b. May 23, 1933 in Denver, Colorado
Source: *CurBio 69; WhoAm 82; WhoMus 72*

Browning, John Moses
American. Inventor
Developed automatic rifle, pistol, machine
   gun.
b. Jan 21, 1855 in Ogden, Utah
d. Nov 26, 1926 in Liege, Belgium
Source: *AmBi; DcAmB; InSci; LinLib S;
NatCAB 20; WebAB; WhAm 1*

Browning, Norma Lee
[Mrs. Russell Joynerogg]
American. Journalist
b. Nov 24, 1914 in Spickard, Missouri
Source: *AmAu&B; ConAu 61; WhoAm 82*

Browning, Oscar
English. Author
Fellow, King's College, Cambridge, 1856-
   1923; wrote *A General History of the
   World,* 1913.
b. Jan 17, 1837 in London, England
d. Oct 6, 1923 in Rome, Italy
Source: *BrAu 19; Chambr 3; DcNaB 1922;
EvLB; GrBr; LinLib L, S; LongCTC; NewC;
OxEng; WhLit*

Browning, Robert
English. Poet
Married Elizabeth Barrett, 1846; wrote *Pippa
   Passes,* 1841.
b. May 7, 1812 in London, England
d. Dec 12, 1889 in Venice, Italy
Source: *Alli, SUP; AnCL; AtlBL; BiD&SB;
BrAu 19; CasWL; Chambr 3; ChhPo, S1, S2;
CnE&AP; CnThe; CrtT 3; CyWA; DcEnA,
AP; DcEnL; DcEuL; DcLEL; EvLB;
McGEWD; MouLC 4; NewC; OxEng; OxThe;
PenC ENG; RAdv 1; RComWL; REn;
REnWD; Str&VC; WebE&AL; YABC 1*

Browning, Tod
American. Director
Made macabre horror films starring Lon
   Chaney, Bela Lugosi: *Dracula,* 1931;
   Freaks, 1932.
b. Jul 12, 1882 in Louisville, Kentucky
d. Oct 6, 1962 in Santa Monica, California
Source: *BiDFilm; ConLC 16; DcFM; FilmEn;
MovMk; ObitOF 79; OxFilm; WhScrn 74, 77;
WorEFlm*

Browning, Tom (Thomas Leo)
American. Baseball Player
Cincinnati pitcher who became first rookie in
31 years to win 20 games, 1985.
b. Apr 28, 1960 in Casper, Wyoming
Source: *BaseEn 85; BaseReg 86*

Brownlee, John
Australian. Opera Singer
b. Jan 7, 1901 in Geelong, Australia
d. Jan 10, 1969 in New York, New York
Source: *BiE&WWA*

Brownmiller, Susan
American. Author, Feminist
b. Feb 15, 1935 in Brooklyn, New York
Source: *BioIn 10, 11, 12; ConAu 103; CurBio 78*

Brownscombe, Jennie Augusta
American. Artist
Painted genre, American historical scenes.
b. Dec 10, 1850 in Honesdale, Pennsylvania
d. Aug 5, 1936 in New York, New York
Source: *NatCAB 16; NotAW*

Brownson, Orestes Augustus
American. Author, Editor
Established *Brownson's Quarterly Review,*
1844-75; wrote *The Convert,* an
autobiography, 1857.
b. Sep 16, 1803 in Stockbridge, Vermont
d. Apr 17, 1876 in Detroit, Michigan
Source: *Alli; AmAu; AmAu&B; AmBi;*
ApCAB; BbD; BiD&SB; CasWL; CyAL 2;
DcAmAu; DcAmB; DcCathB; DcEnL; DcLEL;
DcNAA; LinLib L; McGEWB; OxAmL; PenC
AM; REn; REnAL; TwCBDA; WebAB;
WebE&AL; WhAm HS

Brownwell, Samuel Miller
American. Educator, Government Official
b. Apr 3, 1900 in Peru, Nebraska
Source: *BioIn 3, 4, 5, 6, 7; CurBio 54*

Broyhill, James E
American. Businessman
Started furniture business, 1926; first to use
assembly line to make furniture.
b. 1892 in Wilkes County, North Carolina
Source: *Entr; St&PR 84; WhoAm 74, 78;*
WhoAmP 81, 83; WhoS&SW 73

Broyhill, Joel Thomas
American. Congressman
b. Nov 4, 1919 in Hopewell, Georgia
Source: *BiDrAC; BioNews 74; CurBio 74;*
CngDr 74; WhoAm 74; WhoAmP 73; WhoGov
75; WhoS&SW 82

Browles, William Dodson, Jr.
American. Editor
Editor-in-chief, *Newsweek,* 1981-83.
b. Oct 8, 1944 in Houston, Texas
Source: *ConAu 73; IntWW 83; WhoAm 82,*
84; WhoWor 78

Broz, Josip
see: Tito

Brubeck, Dave (David Warren)
American. Jazz Musician
Leader, Dave Brubeck Quartet, 1951-1967.
b. Dec 6, 1920 in Concord, California
Source: *CelR; CurBio 56; IntWW 74;*
WebAB; Who 74; WhoAm 74, 76, 78, 80, 82;
WhoE 74; WhoWor 78

Bruce, Ailsa Mellon
American. Philanthropist
b. Jun 28, 1901 in Pittsburgh, Pennsylvania
d. Aug 25, 1969 in New York, New York
Source: *BioIn 8, 10; NatCAB 55*

Bruce, Carol
American. Actress, Singer
Performed on stage in *Do I Hear a Waltz;*
Show Beat; Pal Joey.
b. Nov 15, 1919 in Great Neck, New York
Source: *BiE&WWA; CmpEPM; EncMT;*
NotNAT; WhoHol A; WhoThe 77, 81

Bruce, David, Sir
English. Physician
Discovered causes of Malta fever, sleeping
sickness.
b. May 29, 1855 in Melbourne, Australia
d. Nov 27, 1931 in London, England
Source: *DcNaB 1931; DcScB; GrBr;*
McGEWB

Bruce, David Kirkpatrick Estes
American. Diplomat
Head of US diplomatic office in Peking,
China, 1973-74; US Ambassador to
NATO, 1974-76.
b. Feb 12, 1898 in Baltimore, Maryland
d. Dec 4, 1978 in Washington, District of
Columbia
Source: *CurBio 49, 61; NewYTBE 70, 73;*
IntWW 74; USBiR 74; WhoAm 74; WhoWor
78

Bruce, Jack
[Cream]
Scottish. Musician
Vocalist/bassist of Cream; has had eight solo
albums since 1969.
b. May 14, 1943 in Glasgow, Scotland
Source: *EncPR&S 74; IlEncRk; RolSEnR 83*

Bruce, Lenny
[Leonard Alfred Schneider]
American. Author, Comedian
Charged with obscenity for using four-letter
    words in act; Dustin Hoffman starred in
    Lenny, 1974.
b. Oct 13, 1925 in Mineola, New York
d. Aug 3, 1966 in Hollywood, California
Source: *AmAu&B; ConAu 25R, 89; NewYTBE
71; WhAm 4; WhScrn 77*

Bruce, Nigel
American. Actor
Played Dr. Watson to Basil Rathbone's
    Sherlock Holmes in a dozen 1940s films.
b. Feb 4, 1895 in Ensenada, Mexico
d. Oct 8, 1953 in Santa Monica, California
Source: *CmMov; FilmgC; MotPP; MovMk;
NotNAT B; ObitOF 79; Vers A; WhScrn 74,
77; WhoHol B; WorAl*

Bruce, Robert
see: Robert I

Bruce, Virginia
[Helen Virginia Briggs]
American. Actress
Leading lady in almost 50 films, 1930s-40s:
    Great Ziegfield, 1934.
b. Sep 29, 1910 in Minneapolis, Minnesota
d. Feb 24, 1982 in Woodland Hills,
    California
Source: *Film 2; FilmgC; MGM; MotPP;
MovMk; NewYTBS 82; PseudN 82; ThFT;
WhoHol A; WorAl*

Bruce Lockhart, Robert Hamilton, Sir
Scottish. Diplomat, Author
Wrote of experiences in foreign office during
    WW II: *Comes the Reckoning*, 1947.
b. Sep 2, 1887 in Anstruther, Scotland
d. Feb 27, 1970 in Hore, England
Source: *Au&Wr 71; DcNaB 1961; GrBr;
LongCTC*

Bruch, Max
German. Conductor, Composer
Opera works include *Die Loreley; Hermione*.
b. Jan 6, 1838 in Cologne, Germany
d. Oct 2, 1920 in Friedenau, Germany
Source: *Baker 78; LinLib S; NewEOp 71;
OxMus*

Bruckner, Anton
Austrian. Composer, Organist
Virtuoso organist influenced by Wagner;
    music includes nine symphonies, three
    masses.
b. Sep 4, 1824 in Ausfelden, Austria
d. Oct 11, 1896 in Vienna, Austria
Source: *AtlBL; OxGer; REn*

Bruegel, Pieter, (The Elder)
[Pieter Breughel or Brueghel]
Flemish. Artist
b. 1525
d. Sep 5, 1569 in Brussels, Belgium
Source: *AtlBL; REn*

Brughel, Jan
[Jan Breughel or Brueghel]
Flemish. Artist
b. 1568 in Brussels, Belgium
d. 1625
Source: *BioIn 6; OxArt*

Brugnon, Jacques
[The Four Musketeers]
"Toto"
French. Tennis Player
b. May 11, 1895 in Paris, France
d. Mar 20, 1978 in Paris, France
Source: *BioIn 11*

Bruhn, Erik Belton Evers
Danish. Ballet Dancer, Producer
One of greatest classical dancers, 1953-72;
    appeared with American Ballet Theater.
b. Oct 3, 1928 in Copenhagen, Denmark
d. Apr 1, 1986 in Toronto, Ontario
Source: *CelR; CurBio 86; IntWW 74;
NewYTBE 73; NewYTBS 86; Who 74;
WhoAm 82; WhoWor 74*

Brumidi, Constantino
Italian. Artist
b. Jul 26, 1805 in Rome, Italy
d. Feb 19, 1880 in Washington, District of
    Columbia
Source: *BioIn 2, 3, 4, 7, 8; DcAmB; WhAm
HS*

Brummell, "Beau" (George Bryan)
English. Dandy, Gambler
Set fashion standards for English society:
    trousers instead of breeches.
b. Jun 7, 1778 in London, England
d. Mar 31, 1840 in Caen, France
Source: *LinLib L, S; NewC; NewCol 75;
WebBD 80*

Brundage, Avery
American. Olympic Official
Pres., IOC, 1952-72.
b. Sep 28, 1887 in Detroit, Michigan
d. May 8, 1975 in Gavmisch, Germany
    (West)
Source: *CelR; CurBio 48; IntWW 74;
NewYTBE 72; St&PR 75; WebAB; WhAm 6;
Who 74; WhoAm 74; WhoAmA 73; WhoTr&F
73; WhoWor 78*

Brundage, John Herbert
see: Herbert, John, pseud.

Brundtland, Gro Harlem
"The Green Goddess"
Norwegian. Political Leader
Prime minister, Feb-Oct, 1981, 1986;
    youngest woman to run modern govt.
b. Apr 20, 1939 in Oslo, Norway
Source: *CurBio 81; IntWW 75, 76, 77, 78,
82; IntYB 81, 82; NewYTBS 81; PseudN 82;
WhoWor 78*

Brunel, Isambard Kingdom
English. Engineer, Inventor
Constructed London's Thames Tunnel, 1825-
    43; knighted, 1841.
b. Apr 9, 1806 in Portsmouth, England
d. Sep 15, 1859 in London, England
Source: *BioIn 3, 4, 5, 6, 7, 8, 9, 10, 11;
McGEWB; NewCol 75; WebBD 80*

Brunelleschi, Filippo
Italian. Architect, Sculptor
Considered greatest architect, engineer of
    time; designed dome for Florence
    cathedral.
b. 1377 in Florence, Italy
d. Apr 16, 1446 in Florence, Italy
Source: *AtlBL; OxThe; REn*

Bruner, Jerome Seymour
American. Psychologist
Major contributor to cognitive psychology;
    founded Center for Cognitive Studies,
    Harvard U, 1960.
b. Oct 1, 1915 in New York, New York
Source: *BlueB 76; ConAu 45; CurBio 84;
LEduc 74; Who 83*

Brunhart, Hans
Liechtenstein. Politician
b. Mar 28, 1945 in Liechtenstein
Source: *IntWW 79*

Brunhoff, Jean de
French. Children's Author, Illustrator
b. 1899 in France
d. Oct 16, 1937 in Switzerland
Source: *AuBYP; BioIn 1, 2, 5, 6, 7, 8; IlsCB
1957; JBA 51; WhoChL*

Brunhoff, Laurent de
French. Author, Illustrator
Continues "Barbar" children's books his
    father originated.
b. Aug 30, 1925 in Paris, France
Source: *AuBYP; ConAu 73; IlsCB 1946, 1957;
MorJA; NewYTBE 72; PiP; SmATA 24;
WhoChL*

Bruning, Heinrich
German. Economist
b. 1885
d. 1970
Source: *BioIn 3, 8, 9; NewYTBE 70; OxGer*

Brunis, George
"King of the Tailgate Trombone"
American. Jazz Musician
Member, New Orleans Rhythm Kings,
    founded in Chicago, 1921, an early
    northern Dixieland.
b. Feb 6, 1902 in New Orleans, Louisiana
d. Nov 19, 1974 in Chicago, Illinois
Source: *WhoAm 74*

Brunler, Oscar
English. Physician, Scientist
b. 1894
d. Aug 1, 1952 in Santa Barbara, California
Source: *BioIn 3*

Brunner, Emil
Swiss. Theologian, Author
Advocated Protestant ecumenism; wrote *Gott
    und sein Rebell,* 1958.
b. Dec 23, 1889
d. Apr 6, 1966 in Zurich, Switzerland
Source: *TwCA SUP*

Bruno, Giordano
Italian. Philosopher, Author
Wrote metaphysical *On the Infinite Universe
    and Its Worlds,* 1582; challenged dogma;
    burned at stake.
b. 1548 in Nola, Italy
d. Feb 17, 1600 in Rome, Italy
Source: *BiD&SB; CasWL; DcEuL; DcItL;
Dis&D; EuAu; EvEuW; McGEWD; OxThe;
PenC EUR; RComWL; REn; REnWD;
WhDW*

Brunton, Paul
English. Journalist
b. 1898
Source: *Au&Wr 71*

Brush, George
American. Artist
Prize-winning portraitist of Indians, family
    groups.
b. Sep 28, 1855
d. Apr 24, 1941
Source: *BioIn 3, 9; CurBio 41*

Brustein, Robert Sanford
American. Educator, Author
Award-winning *NY Times, New Republic*
drama critic, 1972--; founder, director,
American Repertory Theater.
b. Apr 21, 1927 in New York, New York
Source: *AmAu&B; Au&Wr 71; BiE&WWA;*
CelR; ConAu 9R; LEduc 74; NotNAT;
WhoAm 74, 76, 78, 80, 82; WhoE 74;
WhoThe 77; WhoWor 78; WorAu

Brutus, Dennis Vincent
African. Poet, Educator
Verse volumes include *Salutes and Censures,*
1982; imprisoned for opposing apartheid,
1964-65.
b. Nov 28, 1924 in Salisbury, Rhodesia
Source: *CasWL; ConAu 2NR, 49; ConP 70,*
75; IntWW 74; PenC CL; RGAfL; TwCWr;
WhoAm 82, 84; WrDr 76

Brutus, Marcus Junius
Roman. Politician
Principal assassin, with Cassius, of Julius
Caesar, 44BC.
b. 85 BC
d. 42 BC
Source: *DcBiPP; LinLib L; NewC; REn;*
WhDW

Bryan, Dora
[Mrs. William Lawton, Dora Broadbent]
English. Actress
Films include *Taste of Honey; See How They*
Run; Hands of the Ripper.
b. Feb 7, 1924 in Southport, England
Source: *EncMT; FilmgC; IntMPA 75; Who*
74, 82; WhoThe 72, 77, 81

Bryan, William Jennings
"The Great Commoner"
American. Lawyer, Political Leader
Three-time Dem. presidential candidate who
was secretary of State, 1913-15.
b. Mar 19, 1860 in Salem, Ohio
d. Jul 26, 1925 in Dayton, Ohio
Source: *AmAu&B; AmBi; ApCAB SUP;*
BiDrAC; BiDrUSE; DcAmAu; DcAmB;
DcNAA; EncAB-H; OxAmL; REn; REnAL;
TwCBDA; WebAB; WhAm 1; WhAmP

Bryant, Anita
American. Singer
Lost contract promoting orange juice due to
views on homosexuals.
b. Mar 25, 1940 in Barnsdale, Oklahoma
Source: *BkPepl; ConAu 85; WhoAm 74, 76,*
78, 80, 82

Bryant, "Bear" (Paul William)
"The Titan of Tuscaloosa"
American. Football Coach, Athletic Director
Head football coach, U of Alabama, 1944-82.
b. Sep 11, 1913 in Kingsland, Arkansas
d. Jan 26, 1983 in Tuscaloosa, Alabama
Source: *AnObit 1983; BioNews 75; CurBio 80,*
83; NewYTBS 81, 83; WhoAm 76, 78, 80,
82; WhoFtbl 74; WhoS&SW 73, 73

Bryant, Felice
American. Songwriter
b. Aug 7, 1925 in Milwaukee, Wisconsin
Source: *BioIn 9; EncFCWM 69*

Bryant, Lane
[Lena Himmelstein]
American. Retailer
Founded Lane Bryant clothing stores, circa
1904.
b. Dec 1, 1879 in Lithuania
d. Sep 26, 1951
Source: *BioIn 1, 2, 3, 7; NatCAB 47*

Bryant, William Cullen
American. Poet, Editor
Best known poem *Thanatopsis,* 1811; edited
NY Evening Post, 1829-78.
b. Nov 3, 1794 in Cummington,
Massachusetts
d. Jun 12, 1878 in New York, New York
Source: *Alli, SUP; AmAu; AmAu&B; AmBi;*
ApCAB; AtlBL; BbD; BiD&SB; CarSB;
CasWL; Chambr 3; ChhPo, S1, S2; CnDAL;
CnE&AP; CrtT 3; CyAL 1; CyWA; DcAmAu;
DcAmB; DcEnL; DcLEL; DcNAA; EncAB-H;
EvLB; MouLC 3; OxAmL; OxEng; PenC AM;
PoChrch; RAdv 1; REn; REnAL; Str&VC;
TwCBDA; WebAB; WebE&AL; WhAm HS

Bryce, James Bryce, Viscount
British. Diplomat, Historian, Lawyer
Ambassador to US, 1907-13; wrote classics
Holy Roman Empire, 1864; *American*
Commonwealth, 1888.
b. May 10, 1838 in Belfast, Northern Ireland
d. Jan 22, 1922 in Sidmouth, England
Source: *BbD; BiD&SB; BrAu 19; DcEnA, AP;*
EvLB; LongCTC; NewC; OxAmL; OxEng;
PenC AM, ENG; REn; WhAm 1

Brymer, Jack
English. Musician
b. Jan 27, 1915 in South Shields, England
Source: *IntWW 74; Who 74; WhoMus 72;*
WhoWor 78

Brynner, Yul
[Taidje Khan]
American. Actor
Won Tony, 1951, Oscar, 1956, for role in
The King and I.
b. Jul 11, 1920 in Sakhalin, Russia
d. Oct 10, 1985 in New York, New York
Source: *BiDFilm; CelR; ConNews 85-4;*
ConTFT 3; CurBio 85; EncMT; FilmgC;
IntMPA 82; IntWW 74; MotPP; MovMk;
OxFilm; PIP&P; WhoAm 84; WhoHol A;
WhoWor 78; WorEFlm

Bryson, Peabo (Robert Peabo)
American. Singer
Rhythm and blues singer, who had hit single
with Roberta Flack: "Lookin' Like Love,"
1984.
b. Apr 13, 1951 in Greenville, South
Carolina
Source: *RkOn 85; RolSEnR 83*

Bryson, Wally Carter
[The Raspberries]
American. Musician
Guitarist with power pop group.
b. Jul 18, 1949 in Gastonia, North Carolina
Source: *NF*

Brzezinski, Zbigniew Kazimierz
American. Author, Educator, Businessman
Advisor to Jimmy Carter on national security
affairs, 1977-81.
b. Mar 28, 1928 in Warsaw, Poland
Source: *AmAu&B; AmM&WS 73S; ConAu*
1R, 5NR; CurBio 70; WhoAm 74, 76, 78, 80,
82; WhoWor 78

Bubbles, John
[John William Sublett; Buck and Bubbles]
American. Dancer
Created rhythm tap dancing; starred in *Porgy*
and Bess, 1935; first black to appear on
"The Tonight Show."
b. Feb 19, 1902 in Louisville, Kentucky
d. May 18, 1986 in Baldwin Hills, California
Source: *AmPS B; DrBlPA; NegAl 76;*
NewYTBS 86; PIP&P; WorAl

Buber, Martin
Israeli. Philosopher, Author
Hasidic scholar whose philosophy of religious
existentialism is described in book *I and*
Thou, 1922.
b. Feb 8, 1878 in Vienna, Austria
d. Jun 13, 1965 in Jerusalem, Israel
Source: *ConAu 25R; CurBio 53, 65; EncWL;*
ModGL; OxGer; REn; TwCA SUP; WhAm 4;
WhoTwCL

Buchalter, "Lepke" (Louis)
American. Organized Crime Figure
Number one labor racketeer; led professional
"hit" squad, 1930s.
b. 1897 in Manhattan, New York
d. Mar 4, 1944 in Sing Sing, New York
Source: *Blood&B; DrInf; WorAl*

Buchan, John, Sir
[Baron Tweedsmuir]
Scottish. Author, Government Official
Canadian governor-general, 1935-40;
adventure novels include classic *Thirty-Nine*
Steps, 1915.
b. Aug 26, 1875 in Perth, Scotland
d. Feb 11, 1940 in Montreal, Quebec
Source: *CasWL; ChhPo, S1, S2; CnMWL;*
ConAu 108; CurBio 40; CyWA; DcLEL;
EncMys; EvLB; JBA 51; LongCTC; MnBBF;
ModBrL; NewC; OxCan; OxEng; PenC ENG;
REn; TwCA, SUP; TwCCr&M 80; TwCWr;
WebE&AL; WhDW

Buchanan, Angela Marie
"Bay"
American. Government Official
Youngest person to head US Treasury Dept.,
1981-83.
b. 1948 in Washington, District of Columbia
Source: *BioIn 12; WhoAm 82; WhoAmP 81*

Buchanan, Edgar
[J J Jackson]
American. Actor
Played Uncle Joe on TV series "Petticoat
Junction," 1963-70.
b. Mar 20, 1903 in Humansville, Missouri
d. 1979 in Palm Desert, California
Source: *CmMov; FilmgC; IntMPA 75, 76, 77;*
MotPP; MovMk; WhoHol A

Buchanan, Jack
Scottish. Comedian, Actor
Debonair musical comedy actor since 1915;
made comeback in *The Band Wagon,*
1953.
b. Apr 2, 1891 in Glasgow, Scotland
d. Oct 20, 1957 in London, England
Source: *EncMT; Film 1; FilmgC; MotPP;*
OxFilm; WhScrn 74, 77; WhoHol B

Buchanan, James
American. US President
Fifteenth pres., 1857-61; opposed slavery in
    principle, but defended it under
    Constitution.
b. Apr 23, 1791 in Mercersburg,
    Pennsylvania
d. Jun 1, 1868 in Lancaster, Pennsylvania
Source: *Alli SUP; AmAu&B; AmBi; ApCAB;
BiAUS; BiDrAC; BiDrUSE; CelCen; CyAG;
DcAmAu; DcAmB; Drake; EncAB-H;
HarEnUS; OxAmL; REnAL; TwCBDA;
WebAB; WhAm HS; WhAmP*

Buchanan, John
Canadian. Politician
Progressive-Conservative Party premier of
    Nova Scotia, 1978--.
b. Apr 22, 1931 in Sydney, Nova Scotia
Source: *CanWW 83*

Buchanan, Pat
American. Admiral
b. 1888
d. 1950
Source: *BioIn 2*

Buchanan, Patrick Joseph
American. Journalist
Former Nixon asst., 1966-73; Reagan's
    director of communications, 1985--.
b. Nov 2, 1938 in Washington, District of
    Columbia
Source: *CurBio 85; WhoAm 76, 78, 80, 82,
84; WhoAmP 73; WhoGov 72; WhoS&SW 73*

Bucher, Lloyd Mark
American. Naval Officer
Commander, USS *Pueblo,* seized by N
    Korea, 1968.
b. Sep 1, 1927 in Pocatello, Idaho
Source: *BioIn 9; PolProf NF*

Buchholz, Horst
German. Actor
Films include *Tiger Bay,* 1959; *Fanny,* 1961.
b. Dec 4, 1933 in Berlin, Germany
Source: *BiE&WWA; CurBio 60; FilmgC;
IntMPA 75, 76, 77, 78, 79, 80, 81, 82;
MotPP; MovMk; WhoHol A; WorAl;
WorEFlm*

Buchman, Frank Nathan Daniel
American. Religious Leader
Founded religious sect, Oxford Group, 1921;
    Moral Re-Armament, 1938, to prevent
    war.
b. Jun 4, 1878 in Pennsburg, Pennsylvania
d. Aug 7, 1961
Source: *AmAu&B; BioIn 1, 2, 4, 5, 6, 9, 10;
CurBio 40, 61; LongCTC*

Buchner, Ludwig
German. Philosopher
b. 1824
d. 1899
Source: *BiD&SB; OxGer*

Buchwald, Art(hur)
American. Journalist, Author, Humorist
Column syndicated in over 550 newspapers;
    wrote *The Buchwald Stops Here,* 1978.
b. Oct 20, 1925 in Mount Vernon, New
    York
Source: *AmAu&B; AuNews 1; BioNews 74;
CelR; ConAu 5R; CurBio 60; IntWW 74;
NewYTBE 72; PenC AM; SmATA 10; Who
82; WhoAm 74, 76, 78, 80, 82; WhoS&SW
82; WhoWor 78; WorAu; WrDr 80*

Buck, Frank
American. Animal Dealer
Supplied everything from birds to elephants
    to zoos, circuses; wrote *Bring 'Em Back
    Alive,* 1930.
b. Mar 17, 1884 in Gainesville, Texas
d. Mar 25, 1950 in Houston, Texas
Source: *AmAu&B; CurBio 43, 50; FilmgC;
LinLib L; MnBBF; ObitOF 79; REnAL;
WebAB; WhAm 2A; WhScrn 74, 77; WhoHol
B*

Buck, Gene
American. Songwriter, Artist, Producer
Co-founder ASCAP, 1914, pres., 1924-41;
    composed Ziegfeld Follies hits.
b. Aug 8, 1886 in Detroit, Michigan
d. Feb 24, 1957 in Manhasset, New York
Source: *AmAu&B; AmSCAP 66; CurBio 41,
57; EncMT; NewCBMT; REnAL*

Buck, Paul Herman
American. Author, Educator
Head of Harvard U Libraries, who won
    Pulitzer for *Road to Reunion,* 1937, on
    reconstruction.
b. Sep 25, 1899 in Columbus, Ohio
d. Dec 23, 1978 in Cambridge, Massachusetts
Source: *AmAu&B; ConAu 81; CurBio 55, 79;
DrAS 74H, 78H; OhA&B; OxAmL; TwCA,
SUP; WhAm 7; WhoAm 74, 76; WhoWor 74,
76*

Buck, Pearl S(ydenstricker)
American. Author
Won Pulitzer, 1932, Nobel Prize, 1938; wrote
  The Good Earth, 1930.
b. Jun 26, 1892 in Hillsboro, West Virginia
d. Mar 6, 1973 in Danby, Vermont
Source: *AmAu&B; AmNov; Au&Wr 71;*
AuBYP; AuNews 1; BiE&WWA; CasWL;
CnDAL; ConAmA; ConAu 1R, 41R, 1NR;
ConLC 7, 11, 18; ConNov 72; CurBio 56, 73;
CyWA; DcLEL; EncWL; EvLB; FilmgC;
HerW; InWom; LongCTC; ModAL;
NewYTBE 73; OxAmL; PenC AM; REn;
REnAL; SmATA 1; TwCA, SUP; TwCWr;
WebAB; WhAm 5; WhNAA

Buckingham, Lindsey
[Fleetwood Mac]
American. Musician
Joined Fleetwood Mac, 1975; solo LP *Law*
  and Order, 1981.
b. Oct 3, 1947 in Palo Alto, California
Source: *WhoAm 80, 82*

Buckinghams, The
[Nick Fortune; Carl Giamarese; Marty
  Grebb; Jon Paulos; Denny Tufano]
American. Music Group
Chicago area band popular 1966-68; had
  number one hit "Kind of a Drag," 1966.
Source: *BiDAmM; LilREn 78; RkOn 78;*
WhoRock 81

Buckland, William
English. Geologist, Clergyman, Educator
Denied evolution; tried to reconcile geology
  with Bible; wrote *Reliquiae Diluvianae,*
  1823.
b. Mar 12, 1784 in Axminster, England
d. Aug 14, 1856 in Islip, England
Source: *Alli; DcEnL; DcScB*

Buckley, Betty
American. Actress
Played Abby Bradford on TV series "Eight
  Is Enough."
b. Jul 3, 1947 in Big Spring, Texas
Source: *BioIn 12*

Buckley, Charles Anthony
American. Politician
Dem. congressman from NY, 1935-64.
b. Jun 23, 1890 in New York, New York
d. Jan 22, 1967 in New York, New York
Source: *BiDrAC; WhAm 4; WhAmP*

Buckley, Emerson
American. Conductor
b. Apr 14, 1916 in New York, New York
Source: *WhoAm 74, 76, 78, 80, 82;*
WhoS&SW 82

Buckley, James Lane
American. Politician, Author
Senator from NY, 1971-77; wrote *If Men*
  were Angels, 1975.
b. Mar 9, 1923 in New York, New York
Source: *CelR; CngDr 74; ConAu 61; CurBio*
71; IntWW 74; WhoAm 74, 76, 78, 80, 82;
WhoAmP 73; WhoE 74; WhoGov 75

Buckley, Tim
American. Singer, Songwriter
Pop singer-guitarist, 1960s; album *Goodbye*
  and Hello, 1967.
b. Feb 17, 1947 in Washington, District of
  Columbia
d. Jun 29, 1975 in Santa Monica, California
Source: *BioIn 10; EncPR&S 74; IlEncRk;*
WhoAm 74

Buckley, William F(rank), Jr.
American. Editor, Author, TV Personality
Editor, *National Review* magazine, 1955--;
  wrote *Atlantic High,* 1982.
b. Nov 24, 1925 in New York, New York
Source: *AmAu&B; AuNews 1; ConAu 1NR,*
1R; ConLC 7, 18; CurBio 82; IntWW 74;
LinLib S; St&PR 75; WebAB, 79; WhoAm
78, 80, 82; WhoAmP 73; WhoE 74; WhoF&I
74; WhoGov 72; WhoWor 74; WorAu; WrDr
76

Buckmaster, Henrietta, pseud.
[Henrietta Henkle; H H Stephens]
American. Author, Journalist
Best known for historical novels *Let My*
  People Go, 1941; *Deep River,* 1944.
b. 1909 in Cleveland, Ohio
d. Apr 26, 1983 in Chestnut Hill,
  Massachusetts
Source: *AmAu&B; AmNov; Au&Wr 71;*
ConAu 9R; CurBio 46; OhA&B; SmATA 6;
WhoAmW 77; WorAu

Buckner, Bill (William Joseph)
"Buck"
American. Baseball Player
Left-handed first baseman, Chicago Cubs,
  1977-84; Boston, 1984--.
b. Dec 14, 1949 in Vallejo, California
Source: *BaseEn 85; NewYTBS 81; PseudN 82;*
WhoAm 82, 84

Buckner, Simon, Jr.
American. Military Leader, Politician
Commanded American 10th Army, Pacific
  Theater; killed few days before Okinaivas
  conquest.
b. Jul 18, 1886 in Munfordville, Kentucky
d. Jun 18, 1945 in Okinawa, Japan
Source: *CurBio 42, 45; DcAmB S3; WebAB;*
WhAm 2

Buckner, Simon B
American. Military Leader
Confederate general, 1864; governor of KY,
    1887-91.
b. Apr 1, 1823 in Hart County, Kentucky
d. Jan 8, 1914
Source: *AmBi; ApCAB; DcAmB; TwCBDA;*
WebAB; WhAm 1

Bucyk, John Paul
"The Chief"
Canadian. Hockey Player
Left wing, 1955-78; in fourth place for career
    points; Hall of Fame, 1981.
b. May 12, 1935 in Edmonton, Alberta
Source: *BioIn 9, 10; HocEn; WhoHcky 73*

Budd, Julie
American. Singer
b. 1944 in Brooklyn, New York
Source: *BioIn 9*

Budd, Ralph
American. Railroad Executive
b. Aug 20, 1879 in Waterloo, Iowa
d. Feb 2, 1962
Source: *REnAW; WhAm 4*

Buddha
[Siddhartha Gautama]
"Bhagavat"; "Sugata"; "Tathagata"
Indian. Religious Leader, Philosopher
Renounced world at age 29 to search for
    solution to human suffering; founded
    Buddhism, ca. 528 BC.
b. 563 BC in Kapilavastu, India
d. 483 BC in Kusinagara, India
Source: *Dis&D; LuthC 75; NewC; NewCol 75;*
RComWL; WorAl

Budding, Edwin
English. Inventor
Invented the lawnmower, 1830.
b. 1795
d. 1846
Source: *WhDW*

Budenz, Louis Francis
American. Educator
b. Jul 17, 1891 in Indianapolis, Indiana
d. Apr 27, 1972
Source: *AmAu&B; BkC 6; CathA 1952;*
CurBio 51, 72

Budge, Don (John Donald)
American. Tennis Player
Won "grand slam" of tennis, 1938; Hall of
    Fame, 1964.
b. Jun 13, 1915 in Oakland, California
Source: *WebAB*

Budge, Ernest Alfred
English. Egyptologist, Author
Conducted excavations in Egypt,
    Mesopotamia; author *Babylonian Life and*
    History .
b. 1857 in Cornwall, England
d. 1934
Source: *Alli SUP; BiD&SB; LinLib L*

Buechner, Frederick
American. Author, Clergyman
Prize-winning writer of psychological novels:
    Long Days Dying, 1950; *Return of Ansel*
    Gibbs, 1959.
b. Jul 11, 1926 in New York, New York
Source: *AmAu&B; ConAu 13R; ConLC 2, 4,*
6, 9; ConNov 72, 76; DrAF 76; LinLib L;
ModAL, S1; OxAmL; TwCWr; WhoAm 82;
WorAu; WrDr 76

Bueno, Maria Ester Audion
Brazilian. Tennis Player
b. Oct 11, 1939 in Sao Paulo, Brazil
Source: *CurBio 65; InWom*

Bufano, Beniamino
American. Artist
b. 1898
d. 1970
Source: *BioIn 2, 5, 6, 9, 10, 11; NewYTBE*
70

Buffalo Bill
see: Cody, 'Buffalo Bill' (William Frederick)

Buffalo Bob
see: Smith, Bob

Buffalo Springfield
[Richie Furay; Dewey Martin; Jim Messina;
    Bruce Palmer; Stephen Stills; Neil Young]
American. Music Group
W coast folk rockers, 1966-68; who had hit
    single, "For What It's Worth," 1966.
Source: *BiDAmM; ConMuA 80A; LilREn 78;*
RkOn 78; RolSEnR 83; WhoRock 81

Buffet, Bernard
French. Artist
b. Jul 10, 1928 in Paris, France
Source: *CurBio 59; IntWW 74; Who 74;*
WhoGrA 62

Buffet, Jimmy
[Jimmy Buffett]
American. Singer, Songwriter
Hit single "Margaritaville," 1977.
b. Dec 25, 1946 in Pascagoula, Mississippi
Source: *IlEncRk; RkOn 74; WhoAm 82*

Buffin, Terry
see: Mott (the Hoople)

Buffon, Georges Louis Leclerc
French. Naturalist, Author
Best known for 36-volume *Histoire Naturelle,*
1749-88.
b. Sep 7, 1707 in Montbard, France
d. Apr 16, 1788 in Paris, France
Source: *AtlBL; BbD; BiD&SB; CasWL;
DcEuL; EuAu; EvEuW; LinLib L, S;
McGEWB; OxEng; OxFr; PenC EUR; REn*

Bufman, Zev
Israeli. Producer
Produced *Little Foxes; Your Own Thing;
Peter Pan.*
b. Oct 11, 1930 in Tel Aviv, Palestine
Source: *BiE&WWA; WhoAm 82; WhoThe 77,
81*

Buford, Don(ald Alvin)
American. Baseball Player
Infielder/outfielder with Chicago White Sox,
Baltimore, 1963-72.
b. Feb 2, 1937 in Linden, Texas
Source: *BaseEn 85; WhoProB 73*

Buford, John
American. Military Leader
b. Mar 4, 1826 in Woodford County,
Kentucky
d. Dec 16, 1863 in Washington, District of
Columbia
Source: *AmBi; ApCAB; DcAmB; Drake;
TwCBDA; WhAm HS*

Bugas, John Stephen
American. Business Executive, Lawyer
Helped to reorganize Ford Motor Co., 1945,
after Henry II became pres.
b. Apr 26, 1908 in Rock Springs, Wyoming
d. Dec 2, 1982 in Ypsilanti, Michigan
Source: *CurBio 47, 83; NewYTBS 82*

Bugatti, Ettore
Italian. Engineer, Auto Manufacturer
Established factory, 1909, in Olsoce; noted
for racing, luxury cars.
b. Sep 15, 1881 in Milan, Italy
d. 1947
Source: *BioIn 10; WebBD 80*

Bugayev, Boris Nikolayevich
see: Bely, Andrei, pseud.

Bugbee, Emma
American. Journalist, Suffragette
With NY *Herald Tribune,* 1911-66; broke
barrier excluding women from newspaper
city rooms.
b. 1888 in Shippensburg, Pennsylvania
d. Oct 6, 1981 in Warwick, Rhode Island
Source: *AuBYP; ConAu 105; InWom;
NewYTBS 81; SmATA 29N*

Bugliosi, Vincent T
American. Lawyer, Author
Prosecutor in Manson family murder trials;
wrote *Helter-Skelter,* 1974.
b. Aug 18, 1934 in Hibbing, Minnesota
Source: *ConAu 73; WhoAm 82*

Buick, David Dunbar
American. Auto Manufacturer
Formed Buick Co., 1902; built first car,
1903.
b. Sep 17, 1854 in Arbroth, Scotland
d. Mar 6, 1929 in Detroit, Michigan
Source: *NatCAB 34; WebBD 80*

Buitoni, Giovanni
Italian. Business Executive, Manufacturer
Chm., Buitoni Foods Corp., specializing in
Italian food.
b. Nov 6, 1891 in Perugia, Italy
d. Jan 13, 1979 in Rome, Italy
Source: *CurBio 62, 79; NewYTBS 79; St&PR
75*

Bujold, Genevieve
Canadian. Actress
Golden Globe Award for *Anne of a
Thousand Days,* 1972; films include *Coma,*
1978.
b. Jul 1, 1942 in Montreal, Quebec
Source: *CanWW 70, 81; CelR; CreCan 1;
FilmgC; IntMPA 75, 76, 77, 78, 79, 80, 81,
82; WhoAm 80, 82; WhoHol A; WorAl*

Buketoff, Igor
American. Conductor
b. May 29, 1915 in Hartford, Connecticut
Source: *WhoAm 74, 76, 78, 80, 82; WhoMus
72; WhoWor 78*

Bukharin, Nikolai Ivanovich
Russian. Communist Leader, Editor
Co-edited Communist Party organ *Pravda*
with Lenin; executed in purges of 1938.
b. 1888 in Moscow, Russia
d. Mar 13, 1938
Source: *McGEWB; REn; WhDW; WorAl*

Bukharov, Alexandr Semyonovich
Russian. Politician
b. 1912
Source: *IntWW 74*

Bukovsky, Vladimir
Russian. Political Activist
Released from Soviet labor camp in exchange
for Chilean Communist Party leader, Luis
Corvalan.
b. Dec 30, 1942 in Moscow, U.S.S.R.
Source: *CurBio 78; DcPol; IntAu&W 82;
IntWW 78, 79, 80, 81, 82; NewYTBS 76, 77*

Bulfinch, Charles
American. Architect
First professional architect in US; made nat.
capital architect, 1817.
b. Aug 8, 1763 in Boston, Massachusetts
d. Apr 15, 1844 in Boston, Massachusetts
Source: *AmBi; ApCAB; AtlBL; BiAUS;
DcAmB; Drake; EncAB-H; OxAmL; REnAL;
TwCBDA; WebAB; WhAm HS*

Bulfinch, Thomas
American. Author
Published *The Age of Fable,* 1855, later
called *Bulfinch's Mythology;* has become
standard reference work.
b. Jul 15, 1796 in Newton, Massachusetts
d. May 27, 1867 in Boston, Massachusetts
Source: *Alli, SUP; AmAu; AmAu&B; AmBi;
ApCAB; BiD&SB; CarSB; ChhPo; DcAmAu;
DcAmB; DcNAA; Drake; OxAmL; REn;
REnAL; WebAB; WhAm HS*

Bulgakov, Mikhail
Russian. Author, Dramatist
Noted for play *Days of the Turbins,* 1935;
novel *Master and Margarita* published
posthumously.
b. 1891 in Kiev, Russia
d. 1940 in Moscow, U.S.S.R.
Source: *CasWL; ClDMEL; CnMD; CnThe;
CurBio 40; DcRusL; EncWL; EvEuW;
McGEWD; ModSL 1; ModWD; PenC EUR;
REn; REnWD; TwCWr; WhoTwCL; WorAu*

Bulganin, Nikolai Aleksandrovich
Russian. Political Leader
Premier, 1955-58; defense minister, 1947-49,
1953-55.
b. Jun 11, 1895 in Gorky, Russia
d. Feb 24, 1975 in Moscow, U.S.S.R.
Source: *CurBio 55, 75N; IntWW 74;
NewYTBS 75; WhAm 6; Who 74; WhoWor
74; WorAl*

Bulgari, Constantine
Italian. Jeweler
d. 1973
Source: *WorFshn*

Bulgari, Giorgio
Italian. Jeweler
Co-founded with brother Constantine, Rome's
deluxe jewelry house, early 1900s.
Source: *WorFshn*

Bulkeley, Morgan
American. Baseball Executive
First pres., of NL, 1876; Hall of Fame,
1937.
b. Dec 26, 1837 in East Haddam,
Connecticut
d. Nov 6, 1922 in Hartford, Connecticut
Source: *ApCAB; BiDrAC; BiDrGov; BioIn 3,
7, 9; DcAmB; NatCAB 10; TwCBDA; WhAm
1; WhAmP; WhoProB 73*

Bull, John
English. Organist, Composer
Supposedly wrote early form of melody "God
Save the King," 1619.
b. 1563 in Somerset, England
d. Mar 12, 1622 in Antwerp, Belgium
Source: *Alli; WebBD 80*

Bull, Odd
Norwegian. Statesman
Chief of staff, UN truce supervision,
Palestine, 1963-70.
b. Jun 28, 1907 in Oslo, Norway
Source: *ConAu 81; CurBio 68; IntWW 74,
75, 76, 77, 78, 79, 80, 81; NewYTBE 70;
WhoUN 75; WhoWor 74, 76, 78*

Bull, Ole Bornemann
Norwegian. Musician, Composer
Internationally known violinist who attempted
to found Norwegian settlement in PA,
1852.
b. Feb 5, 1810 in Bergen, Norway
d. Aug 17, 1880 in Lysoe, Norway
Source: *ApCAB; Drake; OxAmL; OxThe;
REnAL; TwCBDA*

Bull, Peter
English. Actor, Author
Journalist-turned actor, films include *African
Queen,* 1952; *Dr. Strangelove,* 1963.
b. Mar 21, 1912 in London, England
d. May 20, 1984 in London, England
Source: *AnObit 1984; Au&Wr 71; BiE&WWA;
ConAu 25R; FilmgC; MotPP; NotNAT A;
PlP&P; WhoHol A; WhoThe 72; WhoWor 76*

Bullard, Dexter Means
American. Psychiatrist
Pioneer in psychoanalytic treatment, whose
hospital was setting for novel *I Never
Promised You a Rose Garden,* 1964.
b. Aug 14, 1898 in Waukesha, Wisconsin
d. Oct 5, 1981 in Rockville, Maryland
Source: *AmM&WS 73P; BiDrAPA 77;
NewYTBS 81*

Bullard, Edward Crisp, Sir
English. Physicist
Advocate of continental drift theory, who
conducted research on gravity, heat flow,
terrestrial magnetism.
b. Sep 21, 1907 in Norwich, England
d. Apr 3, 1980 in La Jolla, California
Source: *AmM&WS 82P; CurBio 54, 80; InSci;
WhoAm 80*

Bullard, Robert Lee
American. Military Leader
b. Jan 15, 1861 in Youngsboro, Alabama
d. Sep 11, 1947 in New York, New York
Source: *DcAmB S4; DcNAA; WhAm 2;
WhNAA*

Bullins, Ed
American. Author, Dramatist, Producer
b. Jul 25, 1935 in Philadelphia, Pennsylvania
Source: *BlkAWP; ConAu 49; ConLC 1, 5;
CroCD; LivgBAA; ModAL S1; NotNAT;
PIP&P A; WhoAm 74, 76, 78, 80, 82;
WhoBlA 75; WhoE 74; WhoThe 77; WrDr 76*

Bullitt, William C
American. Statesman, Author
First US ambassador to Spain, 1933-36;
warned of Soviet threat after WW II.
b. Jan 25, 1891 in Philadelphia, Pennsylvania
d. Feb 15, 1967 in Neuilly, France
Source: *ConAu 89; CurBio 40, 67; REn;
REnAL; WhAm 4*

Bullock, Alain Louis Charles
English. Author, Educator
b. Dec 13, 1914 in England
Source: *Au&Wr 71; ConAu 1R; LongCTC;
WhoWor 78*

Bulova, Joseph
American. Jeweler, Businessman
Jewelry manufacturer, 1875, known for
watches.
b. 1851
d. 1935
Source: *Entr; WorAl*

Bulow, Bernhard H M
German. Political Leader
Chancellor, 1900-09; isolated Germany in
foreign policy which led to French-British-
Russian alliance.
b. May 3, 1849 in Altona, Germany
d. Oct 28, 1929 in Rome, Italy
Source: *OxGer; WorAl*

Bulow, Hans Guido von
see: VonBulow, Hans Guido

Bultmann, Rudolf
German. Theologian
b. Aug 20, 1884 in Wiefelstede, Germany
d. Jul 30, 1976 in Marburg, Germany (West)
Source: *ConAu 5R, 65; CurBio 72; IntWW
74; OxGer; WhoWor 78; WorAu*

Bulwer-Lytton, Edward George
see: Lytton, Edward George Earle Lytton,
Bulwer-Lytton Baron

Bulwer-Lytton, Edward Robert
see: Lytton, Edward Robert Bulwer-Lytton,
Earl

Bumbry, Grace Ann Jaeckel
American. Opera Singer
b. Jan 4, 1937 in Saint Louis, Missouri
Source: *CelR; CurBio 64; InWom; IntWW
74; Who 74; WhoAm 74, 76, 78, 80, 82;
WhoBlA 75; WhoMus 72; WhoWor 78*

Bumpers, Dale Leon
American. Politician
Governor of AR, 1970-74; US senator, 1975--
b. Aug 12, 1925 in Charleston, Arkansas
Source: *AlmAP 78, 80; CngDr 77, 79, 81;
CurBio 79; IntWW 74, 75, 76, 77, 78, 79,
80, 81; WhoAm 82; WhoS&SW 73, 75, 76,
78; WorAl*

Bunche, Ralph Johnson
American. Statesman
First black American to receive Nobel Peace
Prize, 1950, for UN work.
b. Aug 7, 1904 in Detroit, Michigan
d. Dec 9, 1971 in New York, New York
Source: *ConAu 33R; CurBio 72; EncAB-H;
InB&W 80; LinLib L, S; McGEWB;
NewYTBE 71; ObitT 1971; PolProf E, J, K,
T; REnAL; SelBAAu; WebAB 79; WhAm 5;
WorAl*

Bundy, McGeorge
American. Educator
Special asst. to Presidents Kennedy, Johnson
on national security affairs.
b. Mar 30, 1919 in Boston, Massachusetts
Source: *AmM&WS 73S, 78S; CelR; CurBio
62; EncAB-H; IntWW 74, 75, 76, 77, 78, 79,
80; LEduc 74; LinLib L, S; NewYTBS 79;
PolProf J, K, NF; WhoAm 78, 80, 82;
WhoWor 74, 78*

Bundy, Ted
[Theodore Robert Cowell]
American. Murderer
Convicted of two sorority house murders in
FL, 1978; sentenced to death.
b. Nov 24, 1946 in Burlington, Vermont
Source: *BioIn 11; NewYTBS 78*

Bundy, William Putnam
American. Government Official, Lawyer
b. Sep 24, 1917 in Washington, District of
Columbia
Source: *BioIn 5, 6, 7, 9, 11; CelR; CurBio
64; IntWW 74; WhoAm 74, 76, 78, 80, 82;
WhoAmP 73; WhoE 74*

Bunin, Ivan Alekseevich
Russian. Author, Translator
First Russian to win Nobel Prize for
literature, 1933; wrote novel *Derevnya,*
1910.
b. Oct 10, 1870 in Voronezh, Russia
d. Nov 8, 1953 in Paris, France
Source: *CasWL; ClDMEL; CnMWL; CyWA;
DcRusL; EncWL; EvEuW; LongCTC; ModSL
1; PenC EUR; REn; TwCA, SUP; TwCWr;
WhoLA; WhoTwCL*

Bunker, Chang and Eng
see: Chang and Eng

Bunker, Ellsworth
American. Diplomat
Ambassador to Vietnam, 1967-73; chief
negotiator, Panama Canal Treaties, 1973-
78.
b. May 11, 1894 in Yonkers, New York
d. Sep 27, 1984 in Brattleboro, Vermont
Source: *AnObit 1984; CurBio 78; IntWW 74,
75, 76, 77, 78, 79, 80, 81; PolProf J, NF;
USBiR 74; WhoAm 74, 76, 78, 80; WhoAmP
73, 75, 77, 79; WhoGov 72, 75, 77; WhoWor
74, 76, 78*

Bunner, Henry Cuyler
American. Journalist, Poet, Author
Best remembered for short stories; editor of
Puck, weekly humor magazine, 1878-96.
b. Aug 3, 1855 in Oswego, New York
d. May 11, 1896 in Nutley, New Jersey
Source: *Alli SUP; AmAu; AmAu&B; AmBi;
ApCAB SUP; BbD; BiD&SB; Chambr 3;
CnDAL; DcAmAu; DcAmB; DcLEL; DcNAA;
EvLB; LinLib S; NatCAB 7; OxAmL; REn;
REnAL; TwCBDA; WhAm HS*

Bunning, Jim (James Paul David)
American. Baseball Player
Pitcher; won 224 games in career; pitched
perfect game against NY Mets, 1964.
b. Oct 23, 1931 in Southgate, Kentucky
Source: *BaseEn 85; WhoProB 73*

Bunny, John
American. Actor
First comic film star; joined Vitagraph, 1910;
made over 200 shorts in five years.
b. Sep 21, 1863 in New York, New York
d. Apr 26, 1915 in Brooklyn, New York
Source: *Film 1; FilmgC; MotPP; NotNAT B;
TwYS; WhScrn 77; WhoHol B*

Bunsen, Robert Wilhelm Eberhard
German. Chemist, Inventor
Developed, improved laboratory equipment,
including Bunsen burner.
b. Mar 31, 1811 in Goettingen, Germany
d. Aug 16, 1899 in Heidelberg, Germany
Source: *AsBiEn; DcInv; Dis&D; InSci; LinLib
S; NewCol 75; OxGer; REn*

Bunting, Basil
English. Poet
Greatest popularity in 1960s as leader of
British literary avant-garde.
b. 1900 in Northumberland, England
Source: *BioIn 11; ConAu 53, 7NR; ConLC
10; ConP 70, 75; ModBrL S1; Who 74;
WhoTwCL; WhoWor 74; WorAu; WrDr 76,
80*

Bunting, Mary Ingraham
American. Educator
Pres., of Radcliffe College, 1960-72.
b. Jul 10, 1910 in Brooklyn, New York
Source: *AmM&WS 73P, 76P, 79P; CurBio 67;
WhoAm 74, 76, 78; WhoAmW 58, 61, 64,
66, 68, 70, 72, 74, 77, 79; WhoE 74;
WhoWor 78*

Bunuel, Luis
Mexican. Director
Started career by working with Salvador Dali
on surrealist film *An Andalusian Dog,*
1928.
b. Feb 22, 1900 in Calanda, Spain
d. Jul 29, 1983 in Mexico City, Mexico
Source: *BiDFilm; CelR; CurBio 65; DcFM;
FilmgC; IntMPA 76, 77, 78, 79, 80, 81, 82;
IntWW 74; MovMk; NewYTBS 83; OxFilm;
Who 74; WhoS&SW 73; WhoWor 78; WorAl;
WorEFlm*

Bunyan, John
English. Minister, Author
Wrote religious allegory *Pilgrim's Progress,*
1678, while in prison.
b. Nov 28, 1628 in Elstow, England
d. Aug 31, 1688 in London, England
Source: *AtlBL; BbD; BiD&SB; BrAu; CarSB;
CasWL; Chambr 1; CroE&S; CrtT 2; CyWA;
DcEnA; DcEnL; DcEuL; DcLEL; EvLB;
McGEWB; MouLC 1; NewC; OxEng; OxMus;
PenC ENG; RAdv 1; RComWL; REn;
WebE&AL; WhDW*

Bunzel, Ruth L
American. Anthropologist, Author
Source: *InWom*

Buoniconti, Nick
American. Football Player
b. Dec 15, 1940 in Springfield, Massachusetts
Source: *NewYTBE 72*

Buono, Victor (Charles Victor)
American. Actor
Oscar nominee for first film *Whatever
Happened to Baby Jane?,* 1962.
b. Feb 3, 1938 in San Diego, California
d. Jan 1, 1982 in Apple Valley, California
Source: *FilmEn; FilmgC; IntMPA 75, 77, 78,
79, 80, 81, 82; MotPP; MovMk; NewYTBS
82; WhoAm 80; WhoHol A; WorAl*

Burbage, James
English. Actor
Built first permanent theatre in London,
1576, called The Theatre.
b. 1530
d. 1597
Source: *BioIn 11; NotNAT B*

Burbage, Richard
English. Actor
Original player of Shakespeare's Hamlet,
Lear, Othello; son of James; name
synonymous with highest quality acting.
b. 1567
d. 1619
Source: *CnThe; EncWT; LongCEL; NewC;
OxThe; PIP&P; REn*

Burbank, Luther
American. Horticulturist
Known for developing new varieties of
vegetables, fruits, flowers.
b. Mar 7, 1849 in Lancaster, Massachusetts
d. Apr 11, 1926 in Santa Rosa, California
Source: *AmBi; ApCAB X; AsBiEn; DcAmB;
DcNAA; EncAAH; EncAB-H; LinLib L, S;
McGEWB; NatCAB 11. 33; REn; WebAB, 79;
WhAm 1*

Burberry, Thomas
English. Fashion Designer
b. 1835
d. 1889
Source: *WorFshn*

Burch, Dean
American. Lawyer, Government Official
Chm., FCC, 1969-74; senior adviser, Reagan-
Bush campaign, 1980.
b. Dec 20, 1927 in Enid, Oklahoma
Source: *BioNews 74; CelR; IntWW 74, 75,
76, 77, 78, 79, 80, 81; NewYTET; PolProf J,
NF; WhoAm 74, 76, 78, 80, 82; WhoAmP
73, 75, 77, 79; WhoGov 72; WhoS&SW 73*

Burch, Robert Joseph
American. Author
b. Jun 26, 1925 in Inman, Georgia
Source: *AuBYP; ConAu 5R, 2NR; MorBMP;
SmATA 1; ThrBJA; WrDr 76*

Burchard, John Ely
American. Author, Historian
Wrote articles on housing, library planning,
urbanism: *Architecture of America,* 1961.
b. Dec 8, 1898 in Marshall, Minnesota
d. Dec 25, 1975 in Boston, Massachusetts
Source: *AmAu&B; ConAu 1R; DrAS 74H;
InSci; NewYTBS 75; ObitOF 79; WhAm 6, 7;
WhoAm 74, 76; WhoWor 74*

Burchenal, Elizabeth
American. Dancer, Teacher
Leading authority on American folk dances,
folk art, 1920s-30s.
b. 1876 in Richmond, Indiana
d. Nov 21, 1956 in Brooklyn, New York
Source: *NotAW MOD*

Burchfield, Charles
American. Artist
b. Apr 9, 1893 in Ashtabula, Ohio
d. Jan 10, 1967 in Gardenville, New York
Source: *CurBio 42, 61, 67; DcCAA 71; WebAB; WhAm 4*

Burck, Jacob
American. Cartoonist
Created daily editorial cartoon in Chicago *Sun Times;* won Pulitzer Prize, 1941.
b. Jan 10, 1904 in Poland
d. May 11, 1982 in Chicago, Illinois
Source: *ConAu 106; WhoAm 74, 76, 78; WhoAmA 76, 78, 82; WorECar*

Burckhardt, Carl Jacob
Swiss. Diplomat, Historian
b. Sep 10, 1891 in Basel, Switzerland
d. Mar 3, 1974 in Vinzel, Switzerland
Source: *ConAu 49, 93; EncWL; NewYTBS 74; OxGer*

Burden, Ian
see: Human League

Burden, Carter (Shirley Carter, Jr.)
American. Lawyer, Publisher
b. Aug 25, 1941 in Los Angeles, California
Source: *CelR; WhoAm 82; WhoAmA 73*

Burdette, Lew (Selva Lewis, Jr.)
American. Baseball Player
b. Nov 22, 1926 in Nitro, West Virginia
Source: *BaseEn 85; WhoProB 73*

Burdick, Eugene Leonard
American. Author
Wrote controversial, political theory best sellers, *Ninth Wave,* 1956; *Ugly American,* 1958; *Fail Safe,* 1962.
b. Dec 12, 1918 in Sheldon, Louisiana
d. Jul 26, 1965
Source: *AmAu&B; ConAu 5R, 25R; EncSF; SmATA 22; TwCWr; WhAm 4; WhoSciF; WorAu*

Burdick, Quentin Northrop
American. Politician
Dem. senator from ND, 1960--.
b. Jun 19, 1908 in Munich, North Dakota
Source: *AlmAP 78, 80; BiDrAC; CngDr 74, 77, 79; CurBio 63; EncAAH; IntWW 74, 75, 76, 77, 78; PolProf J, K; WhoAm 74, 76, 78, 80, 82; WhoAmP 73, 75, 77, 79; WhoGov 72, 75, 77; WhoMW 74, 76, 78*

Burdon, Eric
[The Animals]
English. Singer
Vocalist for the Animals, War; solo albums include hit singles, "Sky Pilot"; "San Franciscan Nights."
b. Apr 5, 1941 in Walker-on-Tyne, England
Source: *EncPR&S 74; IlEncRk; RolSEnR 83*

Burford, Anne McGill Gorsuch
[Mrs. Robert F. Burford]
"Ice Queen"
American. Lawyer, Government Official
b. Apr 21, 1942 in Casper, Wyoming
Source: *Law&B 80; NewYTBS 82; WhoAmP 81; WhoAmW 81; WhoWest 80; WomPO 78*

Burger, Carl Victor
American. Author, Illustrator
Illustrated nature, children's books; wrote and illustrated popular "All About" series.
b. Jun 18, 1888 in Maryville, Tennessee
d. Dec 30, 1967 in Mount Kisco, New York
Source: *BioIn 8, 11; ConAu 17R, P-2; IlsCB 1967; SmATA 9*

Burger, Warren Earl
American. Supreme Court Justice
Appointed chief justice by Richard Nixon, 1969; retired, 1986; advocated judicial reforms.
b. Sep 17, 1907 in Saint Paul, Minnesota
Source: *CelR; CurBio 69; DrAS 74P; IntWW 74; NewYTBE 70; WebAB; Who 74; WhoAm 84; WhoWor 74*

Burgess, Anthony
English. Author, Journalist
His inventive, sophisticated novels include *Clockwork Orange,* 1962; *Napolean Symphony,* 1974.
b. Feb 25, 1917 in Manchester, England
Source: *Alli; Au&Wr 71; AuNews 1; CasWL; CelR; ConAu 2NR, 1R; ConLC 1, 2, 4, 5, 8, 10, 13, 15; ConNov 72, 76; CurBio 72; DrAF 76; EncWL; IntWW 74; LongCTC; ModBrL, S1; NewC; PenC ENG; RAdv 1; TwCWr; WebE&AL; Who 74; WhoAm 82; WhoTwCL; WhoWor 74; WorAu; WrDr 82*

Burgess, Gelett (Frank Gelett)
American. Author
Humorist whose best-known poem was *The Purple Cow.*
b. Jan 30, 1866 in Boston, Massachusetts
d. Sep 18, 1951 in Carmel, California
Source: *AmAu&B; AmLY; AnMV 1926; BiD&SB; ChhPo, S1; CnDAL; ConAmL; ConICB; DcAmAu; EncMys; EvLB; IlsCB 1744, 1946; LongCTC; OxAmL; REn; REnAL; TwCA, SUP; TwCWr; WebAB; WhAm 3; WhNAA*

Burgess, Guy Francis de Moncy
English. Spy
Member of notorious British Foreign Office trio that passed classified data to Soviets, 1950s.
b. 1911 in Devenport, England
d. 1963 in Moscow, U.S.S.R.
Source: *BioIn 2, 3, 4, 5, 6, 8, 9, 11; EncE 75*

Burgess, Paul
see: 10 CC

Burgess, "Smoky" (Forrest Harrill)
American. Baseball Player
Catcher, 1949-67; set record with 145 pinch hits in career.
b. Feb 6, 1927 in Caroleen, North Carolina
Source: *BaseEn 85; BioIn 8, 10; WhoProB 73*

Burgess, Thornton Waldo
American. Author, Journalist
Wrote syndicated series of animal stories for children *Bedtime Stories.*
b. Jan 14, 1874 in Sandwich, Massachusetts
d. Jun 7, 1965 in Hampden, Massachusetts
Source: *AmAu&B; AuBYP; CarSB; ConAu 73; JBA 34, 51; ObitOF 79; OxAmL; REn; REnAL; SmATA 17; WhAm 4; WhNAA; WhoChL*

Burghley, William Cecil, Baron
English. Statesman
b. 1520
d. 1598
Source: *NewC; REn*

Burghoff, Gary
American. Actor
Played Radar in motion picture, TV series, *M*A*S*H.*
b. May 24, 1943 in Bristol, Connecticut
Source: *AmSCAP 80; WhoAm 82; WhoHol A*

Burgin, Richard
Polish. Conductor
b. Oct 11, 1892 in Warsaw, Poland
Source: *WhoAm 74*

Burgoyne, John
English. General, Dramatist
b. 1723
d. Jun 4, 1792 in London, England
Source: *Alli; AmBi; BbtC; BrAu; ChhPo; DcEnL; DcLEL; NewC; OxAmL; OxEng; REn; REnAL; WhAm HS*

Burke, Arleigh Albert
"31 Knot Burke"
American. Naval Officer
Chief of staff, Atlantic Fleet, 1945-47; chief, US naval operations, 1955-61.
b. Oct 19, 1901 in Boulder, Colorado
Source: *BlueB 76; CurBio 55; IntWW 74; St&PR 75; WhWW-II; Who 74, 82; WhoAm 74; WhoWor 74*

Burke, "Billie" (Mary William Ethelberg Appleton)
[Mrs. Flo Ziegfeld]
American. Actress
Played Glinda, the Good Witch, in *The Wizard of Oz,* 1939.
b. Aug 7, 1886 in Washington, District of Columbia
d. May 14, 1970 in Los Angeles, California
Source: *BiE&WWA; Film 1; FilmgC; InWom; MotPP; MovMk; NewYTBE 70; OxFilm; ThFT; TwYS; Vers B; WhAm 5; WhScrn 74, 77; WhoHol B; WhoStg 1906, 1908; WomWWA 14*

Burke, Clem
see: Blondie

Burke, Edmund
British. Statesman, Orator, Author
Member House of Commons, 1766-94; against taxation of American colonies.
b. Jan 12, 1729 in Dublin, Ireland
d. Jul 9, 1797 in Beaconsfield, England
Source: *Alli; ApCAB; AtlBL; BbD; BiD&SB; BrAu; CasWL; Chambr 2; CyWA; DcEnA; DcEnL; DcEuL; DcLEL; Drake; EvLB; MouLC 2; NewC; OxAmL; OxEng; PenC ENG; PoIre; REn; WebE&AL; WhAm HS*

Burke, James Edward
American. Business Executive
Chairman, Johnson and Johnson, 1976--.
b. Feb 28, 1925 in Rutland, Vermont
Source: *St&PR 84; WhoAm 80; WhoE 83; WhoF&I 83; WhoWor 82*

Burke, John
Irish. Author
Burke's Peerage published annually since
1847, first systematic genealogical
compilation.
b. 1787 in Elm Hall, Tipperary, Ireland
d. Mar 27, 1848 in Aix-la-Chapelle, France
Source: *Alli, SUP; DcEnL; DcIrB; DcIrW 2;*
NewC; PoIre

Burke, Johnny
American. Composer
b. Oct 3, 1908 in Antioch, California
d. Feb 25, 1964 in New York, New York
Source: *AmSCAP 66; BiE&WWA; FilmgC*

Burke, Kenneth
American. Literary Critic, Author, Translator
Among his writings are *A Grammar of*
Motives, 1945; *Rhetoric of Motives,* 1950.
b. May 5, 1897 in Pittsburgh, Pennsylvania
Source: *AmAu&B; AmWr; Au&Wr 71;*
CasWL; CnDAL; ConAmA; ConAu 5R;
ConLC 2; ConLCrt 82; ConNov 72, 76; ConP
70, 75; DcLEL; DrAS 74E; EvLB; IntWW
74; ModAL, S1; OxAmL; PenC AM; RAdv 1;
REn; REnAL; TwCA, SUP; WebE&AL;
WhoAm 74, 76, 78, 80, 82; WhoTwCL; WrDr
82

Burke, Paul
American. Actor
Played in TV series "Naked City," 1960-63;
"Twelve O'Clock High," 1964-67.
b. Jul 21, 1926 in New Orleans, Louisiana
Source: *FilmgC; IntMPA 75, 76, 77, 78, 79,*
80, 81, 82; WhoHol A

Burke, Thomas
English. Author
Books on English life include *Limehouse*
Nights, 1916.
b. Nov 1886 in London, England
d. Sep 22, 1945 in London, England
Source: *ConAu 113; REn*

Burke, William
[Burke and Hare]
Irish. Murderer
With William Hare, killed 15 people, sold
bodies to surgeons for dissection; hanged.
b. 1792 in Orrery, Ireland
d. Jan 28, 1829 in Edinburgh, Scotland
Source: *BioIn 1, 4, 8, 10; DcIrB*

Burke, Yvonne Brathwaite Watson
[Mrs. William A Burke]
American. Lawyer, Congresswoman
First black woman elected to CA General
Assembly, 1967.
b. Oct 5, 1932 in Los Angeles, California
Source: *BioNews 74; CngDr 74; WhoAm 74,*
76, 78, 80, 82; WhoAmP 73; WhoAmW 77;
WhoBlA 75, 80; WhoWest 74, 82

Burke and Hare
see: Burke, William; Hare, William

Burkett, Jesse Cail
"The Crab"
American. Baseball Player
Hit .400 or better three times, 1895, 1896,
1900.
b. Feb 12, 1870 in Wheeling, West Virginia
d. May 27, 1953 in Worcester, Massachusetts
Source: *BaseEn 85; BioIn 3, 7; WhoProB 73*

Burleigh, Harry Thacker
American. Singer, Songwriter
Collected, arranged black spirituals including
"Swing Low, Sweet Chariot"; "Go Down
Moses."
b. Dec 2, 1866 in Erie, Pennsylvania
d. Sep 12, 1949 in Stamford, Connecticut
Source: *AmSCAP 66; CurBio 41, 49; InB&W*
80; ObitOF 79; WebAB, 79; WhAm 2

Burlington, Richard Boyle, Earl
British. Architect, Art Patron
Most influential art patron of time; promoted
English Palladian architecture.
b. 1694
d. 1753
Source: *DcD&D; OxArt; WhoArch*

Burman, Ben Lucien
American. Journalist, Author
b. Dec 12, 1895 in Covington, Kentucky
d. Nov 12, 1984 in New York, New York
Source: *AmAu&B; AmNov; Au&Wr 71;*
ConAu 5R; OxAmL; REnAL; SmATA 6;
TwCA, SUP; WhNAA; WhoAm 74; WhoWor
78; WrDr 80

Burne-Jones, Edward
English. Artist
b. Aug 23, 1833 in Birmingham, England
d. Jun 17, 1898 in London, England
Source: *AtlBL; ChhPo, S2; NewC; REn*

Burnet, MacFarlane (Frank MacFarlane)
Australian. Scientist
Virologist; shared 1960 Nobel Prize for
   research in immunology.
b. Sep 3, 1899 in Victoria, Australia
d. Aug 31, 1985 in Melbourne, Australia
Source: *ConAu 117; CurBio 85; Who 84*

Burnett, Carol
American. Actress, Comedienne, Singer
Won $1.6 million libel suit against *National
   Enquirer,* 1981.
b. Apr 26, 1936 in San Antonio, Texas
Source: *BiE&WWA; BioNews 74; BkPepl;
CelR; CurBio 62; EncMT; FilmgC; ForWC
70; InWom; IntMPA 75, 76, 77, 78, 79, 80,
81, 82; NewYTBE 73; WhoAm 74, 76, 78,
80, 82; WhoHol A; WhoThe 77; WhoWor 78*

Burnett, Frances Eliza Hodgson
American. Author
Wrote *Little Lord Fauntleroy,* 1886; *The
   Little Princess,* 1905; *The Secret Garden,*
   1911.
b. Nov 24, 1849 in Manchester, England
d. Oct 29, 1924 in Plandome, New York
Source: *Alli SUP; AmAu&B; AmBi; AmWom;
ApCAB; AuBYP; BbD; BiD&SB; BiDSA;
CarSB; Chambr 3; ChhPo, S2; ConAmL;
DcAmAu; DcAmB; DcBiA; DcLEL; DcNAA;
EvLB; FamSYP; HerW; InWom; LongCTC;
MacDWB; NotAW; OxAmL; OxEng; PenC
AM, ENG; PIP&P; REn; REnAL; TwCA,
SUP; TwCBDA; WhAm 1; WhoChL; WhoStg
1906, 1908; WomWWA 14; WorAl; YABC 2*

Burnett, Ivy Compton
see: Compton-Burnett, Dame Ivy

Burnett, Leo
American. Advertising Executive
b. Oct 21, 1891 in Saint John's, Michigan
d. Jun 7, 1971 in Lake Zurich, Illinois
Source: *NewYTBE 71; WhAm 5, 6; WhoMW
74*

Burnett, Whit
American. Author, Editor
Co-founder of *Story* magazine, 1931; edited
   numerous anthologies.
b. Aug 14, 1899 in Salt Lake City, Utah
d. Apr 22, 1973 in Norwalk, Connecticut
Source: *AmAu&B; ConAu 13R, 41R, P-2;
CurBio 41, 73; ObitOF 79; REnAL; TwCA,
SUP; WhAm 5; WhoAm 74*

Burnett, W(illiam) R(iley)
[James Updyke, pseud.]
American. Author
Wrote gangster story *Little Caesar,* 1929; film
   script of *Asphalt Jungle,* 1949.
b. Nov 25, 1899 in Springfield, Ohio
d. Apr 25, 1982 in Santa Monica, California
Source: *AmAu&B; AmNov; AnObit 1982;
CnDAL; ConAmA; ConAu 5NR; DcLEL;
EncMys; LongCTC; NewYTBS 82; OhA&B;
OxAmL; PenC AM; PseudN 82; REn;
REnAL; TwCWr; WhNAA; WhoAm 80, 82;
WhoWor 74*

Burnette, Smiley (Lester Alvin)
American. Actor
Gene Autry's sidekick in 81 films, 1935-42.
b. Mar 18, 1911 in Summun, Illinois
d. Feb 16, 1967 in Los Angeles, California
Source: *FilmgC; MotPP; ObitOF 79; WhScrn
74, 77; WhoHol B*

Burney, Charles
English. Organist, Musicologist
b. Apr 7, 1726 in Shrewsbury, England
d. Apr 12, 1814 in Chelsea, England
Source: *Alli, SUP; BiD&SB; BiDLA, SUP;
CasWL; DcEnA; DcEnL; DcEuL; DcLEL;
OxEng*

Burney, Fanny (Frances)
[Madame d'Arblay]
English. Author
Best-known work *Diaries and Letters,* 1778-
   1840.
b. Jun 13, 1752 in Norfolk, England
d. Jan 6, 1840 in London, England
Source: *AtlBL; BrAu 19; CasWL; Chambr 2;
CyWA; EvLB; InWom; MacDWB; NewC;
PenC ENG; RAdv 1; REn*

Burnford, Sheila (Philip Cochrane Every)
Scottish. Author
Wrote *The Incredible Journey,* 1961.
b. May 11, 1918 in Scotland
d. Apr 20, 1984 in Bucklers Hard, England
Source: *AuBYP; BkCL; ConAu 1NR;
FourBJA*

Burnham, Daniel H
American. Architect
Designed first fireproof skyscrapers.
b. Sep 4, 1846 in Henderson, New York
d. Jun 1, 1912 in Heidelberg, Germany
Source: *AmBi; ApCAB SUP; DcAmB; EncAB-
H; TwCBDA; WebAB; WhAm 1, 4*

Burnham, Forbes (Linden Forbes Sampson)
Guinean. Political Leader
b. Feb 20, 1923 in Kitty, Guyana
d. Aug 6, 1985 in Georgetown, Guyana
Source: *BioIn 9; CurBio 66, 85; IntWW 74;
Who 74; WhoGov 72; WhoWor 74*

Burns, Arthur F
American. Economist, Educator
Wrote *Reflections of an Economic Policy
Maker,* ·1978.
b. Apr 27, 1904 in Stanislau, Austria
Source: *AmAu&B; AmEA 74; AmM&WS 73S;
CelR; ConAu 13R; CurBio 53; IntWW 74;
WebAB; Who 74; WhoAm 74; WhoAmP 73;
WhoGov 75; WhoS&SW 82; WhoWorJ 72;
WrDr 80*

Burns, Bob
"Bazooka"; "The Arkansas Philosopher"
American. Actor
Nicknamed "Bazooka" after wind instrument
he invented and played.
b. Aug 2, 1893 in Van Buren, Alaska
d. Feb 2, 1956 in San Fernando, California
Source: *DcAmB S6; FilmgC; NatCAB 42;
ObitOF 79; WhAm 3; WhScrn 74, 77;
WhoHol B*

Burns, David
American. Actor
Won Tony for *The Music Man.*
b. Jun 22, 1902 in New York, New York
d. Mar 12, 1971 in Philadelphia,
Pennsylvania
Source: *BiE&WWA; EncMT; FilmgC;
NewYTBE 73; NotNAT B; ObitOF 79; WhAm
5; WhScrn 74, 77; WhoHol B; WhoThe 72*

Burns, Eveline Mabel
American. Economist
Helped design Social Security Act, 1935;
author *Toward Social Security,* 1936,
explaining system to layman.
b. Mar 16, 1900 in London, England
d. Sep 2, 1985 in Newton, Pennsylvania
Source: *AmEA 74; CurBio 86; InWom;
WhoAm 76*

Burns, George
[Nathan Birnbaum]
American. Comedian, Actor, Singer, Author
Veteran comedian whose career spans
vaudeville, TV, stage, film, concerts; won
Oscar, 1976, for *The Sunshine Boys.*
b. Jan 20, 1896 in New York, New York
Source: *CelR; ConTFT 3; CurBio 51; FilmgC;
IntMPA 82; MotPP; MovMk; WhoAm 84;
WhoHol A*

Burns, Jack
American. Comedian
Source: *BioIn 10*

Burns, Jerry (Jerome Monahan)
American. Football Coach
Replaced Bud Grant as head coach,
Minnesota Vikings, 1986--.
b. Jan 24, 1927 in Detroit, Michigan
Source: *FootReg 86*

Burns, John Horne
American. Author
b. Oct 7, 1916 in Andover, Massachusetts
d. Aug 10, 1953 in Leghorn, Italy
Source: *AmAu&B; AmNov; EvLB; ModAL;
OxAmL; PenC AM; REn; REnAL; TwCA
SUP; TwCWr; WebE&AL; WhAm 4*

Burns, Robert
[Bard of Ayrshire]
Scottish. Poet
Wrote songs "Auld Lang Syne" and "Comin'
thro' the Rye."
b. Jan 25, 1759 in Ayrshire, Scotland
d. Jan 21, 1796 in Dumfroes, Scotland
Source: *Alli; AtlBL; BiD&SB; BiDLA; BrAu;
CasWL; Chambr 2; ChhPo, S1, S2; CnE&AP;
CrtT 2; CyWA; DcEnA, AP; DcEnL; DcEuL;
DcLEL; EvLB; FamAYP; MouLC 2; NewC;
OxEng; PenC ENG; RAdv 1; RComWL;
REn; WebE&AL; WorAl*

Burns, Tommy
[Noah Brusso]
Canadian. Boxer
b. Jun 17, 1881 in Hanover, Ontario
d. May 10, 1955 in Vancouver, British
Columbia
Source: *WhoBox 74*

Burns, William John
American. Detective
b. Oct 19, 1861 in Baltimore, Maryland
d. Apr 14, 1932
Source: *DcAmB S1; DcNAA; OhA&B; WhAm
1; WhScrn 77*

Burns and Allen
see: Allen, Gracie; Burns, George

Burnshaw, Stanley
American. Author
b. Jun 20, 1906 in New York, New York
Source: *AmAu&B; AnMV 1926; ConAu 9R;
ConLC 3; ConP 70, 75; DrAP 75; REnAL;
WhoAm 74, 76, 78, 80, 82; WorAu; WrDr 76*

Burnside, Ambrose Everett
American. Army Officer
As general, commanded Army of the
    Potomac, 1862; governor of RI, senator;
    term "sideburns" named for him.
b. May 23, 1824 in Liberty, Indiana
d. Sep 13, 1881 in Bristol, Rhode Island
Source: *AmBi; ApCAB; BiAUS; BiDrAC;
DcAmB; Drake; EncSoH; IndAu 1917; LinLib
S; TwCBDA; WebAB, 79; WhAm HS;
WhAmP*

Burpee, David
American. Horticulturist
Plant breeder who created, introduced new
    flowers and vegetables.
b. Apr 5, 1893 in Philadelphia, Pennsylvania
d. Jun 24, 1980 in Doylestown, Pennsylvania
Source: *CurBio 55; St&PR 75; WhoAm 74*

Burpee, W(ashington) Atlee
American. Horticulturist
b. Apr 5, 1858 in Sheffiel, New Brunswick
d. Nov 26, 1915
Source: *NatCab 6; WebBD 80; WhAm 1*

Burr, Aaron
American. Political Leader, Lawyer
Vp under Thomas Jefferson who shot, killed
    Alexander Hamilton in duel,1804.
b. Feb 6, 1756 in Newark, New Jersey
d. Sep 14, 1836 in New York, New York
Source: *Alli; AmAu&B; AmBi; ApCAB;
BiAUS; BiDrAC; BiDrUSE; DcAmB; DcNAA;
Drake; EncAB-H; OxAmL; REn; REnAL;
TwCBDA; WebAB; WhAm HS; WhAmP*

Burr, Clive
see: Iron Maiden

Burr, Henry
American. Singer
b. Jan 15, 1882
d. Apr 6, 1941 in Chicago, Illinois
Source: *CurBio 41*

Burr, Raymond William Stacey
American. Actor
Starred in TV series "Perry Mason," 1957-
    65; "Ironside," 1967-75.
b. May 21, 1917 in New Westminster,
    British Columbia
Source: *BioNews 75; ConTFT 3; CurBio 61;
FilmgC; IntMPA 82; MotPP; MovMk;
WhoAm 84; WorEFlm*

Burrenchobay, Dayendranath
Mauritian. Political Leader
Governor-general of Mauritius, 1978--.
b. Mar 24, 1919
Source: *AfSS 82; IntWW 78; Who 81;
WhoWor 80*

Burroughs, Edgar Rice
American. Author, Cartoonist
Wrote *Tarzan* series; more than 35 million
    copies sold.
b. Sep 1, 1875 in Chicago, Illinois
d. Mar 10, 1950 in Los Angeles, California
Source: *AmAu&B; AmLY; DcAmB S4; EvLB;
FilmgC; LongCTC; MnBBF; OxAmL; PenC
AM; REn; REnAL; TwCA, SUP; TwCWr;
WebAB; WhAm 2*

Burroughs, John
American. Author, Naturalist
Popular nature volumes include *Wake Robin,*
    1871; *Birds and Poets,* 1877.
b. Apr 3, 1837 in Roxbury, New York
d. Mar 25, 1921
Source: *Alli, SUP; AmAu; AmAu&B; AmBi;
AmLY; AnCL; ApCAB; BbD; BiD&SB;
CarSB; Chambr 3; ConAmL; DcAmAu;
DcAmB; DcEnA AP; DcLEL; DcNAA; EvLB;
JBA 34; OxAmL; PenC AM; REn; REnAL;
TwCBDA; WebAB; WhAm 1*

Burroughs, William S(eward)
American. Author
A chief spokesman for the "beat movement,"
    1950s; wrote *Naked Lunch,* 1959.
b. Feb 5, 1914 in Saint Louis, Missouri
Source: *AmAu&B; Au&Wr 71; AuNews 2;
CasWL; CelR; ConAu 9R; ConLC 1, 2, 5,
15; ConNov 72, 76; CurBio 71; DrAF 76;
EncWL; IntWW 74; LinLib L; MakMC;
ModAL, S1; OxAmL; PenC AM; RAdv 1;
REn; REnAL; TwCWr; WebAB; WebE&AL;
WhoAm 74, 76, 78, 80, 82; WhoTwCL;
WhoWor 74; WorAu; WrDr 82*

Burroughs, William Seward
American. Inventor
Developed practical calculator, 1891.
b. Jan 28, 1855 in Auburn, New York
d. Sep 14, 1898 in Citronelle, Alabama
Source: *DcAmB S1; WebAB; WhAm HS*

Burrows, Abe (Abram S)
American. Humorist, Dramatist
Won Pulitzer, 1961, for *How to Succeed in
Business Without Really Trying.*
b. Dec 18, 1910 in New York, New York
d. May 17, 1985 in New York, New York
Source: *AmAu&B; AmSCAP 66; BiE&WWA;
CelR; ChhPo S1; CurBio 51; EncMT;
FilmgC; ModWD; NewCBMT; NotNAT;
OxAmL; WhoAm 74, 76, 78, 80, 82; WhoThe
77; WhoWor 78; WhoWorJ 72; WrDr 80*

Burrows, James
American. Producer, Director
Has directed "The Mary Tyler Moore
Show," other comedies; co-creator,
"Cheers," 1982.
Source: *WhoTelC*

Burstyn, Ellen
[Edna Rae Gillooly]
American. Actress
Won Oscar, 1974, for *Alice Doesn't Live
Here Anymore.*
b. Dec 7, 1932 in Detroit, Michigan
Source: *BkPepl; IntMPA 75, 76, 77, 78, 79,
80, 81, 82; MovMk; NewYTBE 72; WhoAm
82; WhoHol A; WomWMM*

Burt, Cyril Lodowic, Sir
English. Psychologist
A pioneer in field of educational psychology.
b. Mar 23, 1883 in London, England
d. Oct 10, 1971 in London, England
Source: *BiDPara; ConAu 33R; EncO&P 78;
GrBr; NamesHP; NewYTBE 71; WhE&EA;
WhLit; WhNAA; WhoLA*

Burt, Maxwell Struthers
American. Author
b. Oct 18, 1882 in Baltimore, Maryland
d. Aug 28, 1954 in Jackson, Wyoming
Source: *ChhPo, S2; TwCA, SUP*

Burt, Richard
American. Journalist
Source: *BioIn 12*

Burtin, Will
American. Designer
Art director, *Fortune,* 1945-49; designer for
govt., industry, NYC, 1949-72.
b. Jan 27, 1908 in Cologne, Germany
d. Jan 18, 1972 in New York, New York
Source: *NewYTBE 72; WhoGrA 62; WhAm 5*

Burton, Isabel Arundel
English. Traveler, Author
Wrote books about her travels with husband
Sir Richard Burton.
b. 1831 in London, England
d. 1896
Source: *Alli SUP; BioIn 6, 8, 10; DcEuL;
InWom; NewC*

Burton, Kate (Katherine)
Actress
Starred in CBS mini-series "Ellis Island,"
1984.
b. Sep 10, 1957 in Geneva, Switzerland
Source: *ConTFT 2*

Burton, LeVar(dis Robert Martyn, Jr.)
American. Actor
Played Kunta Kinte in TV series "Roots,"
1977.
b. Feb 16, 1957 in Landstuhl, Germany
(West)
Source: *BioIn 11; IntMPA 82; WhoAm 82*

Burton, Michael
American. Swimmer
Only swimmer to win gold medal in 1,500
meters freestyle in two succesive Olympics,
1968, 1972.
b. Jul 3, 1947 in Des Moines, Iowa
Source: *WorDWW*

Burton, Montague Maurice, Sir
English. Merchant
A pioneer in field of industrial welfare.
b. Aug 15, 1885 in Lithuania
d. Sep 21, 1952 in Leeds, England
Source: *DcNaB 1951; GrBr; ObitOF 79;
ObitT 1951; WhE&EA*

Burton, Nelson, Jr.
American. Bowler
b. 1942
Source: *BioIn 11*

Burton, Phillip
American. Politician
Congressman from CA, 1964-83; lost bid for
House leadership by one vote, 1976.
b. Jun 1, 1926 in Cincinnati, Ohio
d. Apr 10, 1983 in San Francisco, California
Source: *BiDrAC; NewYTBS 75, 83; PolProf J;
WhoAm 82; WorAl*

Burton, Richard
[Richard Jenkins]
Welsh. Actor
Won Tony, 1961, for *Camelot;* nominated for
seven Oscars.
b. Nov 10, 1925 in Pontrhydfen, Wales
d. Aug 5, 1984 in Geneva, Switzerland
Source: *AnObit 1984; BiDFilm; BiE&WWA;
BioNews 74; BkPepl; CelR; CmMov; CurBio
60; EncMT; FilmgC; IntMPA 76, 77, 78, 79,
80, 81, 82; IntWW 74; MotPP; MovMk;
NewC; NewYTBE 73; NotNAT; OxFilm; Who
82; WhoAm 74, 76, 78, 80, 82; WhoHol A;
WhoThe 77; WhoWor 78; WorEFlm*

Burton, Richard Francis, Sir
English. Author, Explorer, Orientalist
Discovered Lake Tanganyika, 1858; noted for
16-volume translation of *Arabian Nights,*
1885-88.
b. Mar 19, 1821 in Hertfordshire, England
d. Oct 20, 1890 in Trieste, Italy
Source: *Alli; AtlBL; BiD&SB; BrAu 19;
DcEnA, AP; DcEnL; DcEuL; DcLEL; EvLB;
MouLC 4; PoIre; REn; WebE&AL*

Burton, Sybil Williams
see: Christopher, Sybil Williams Burton

Burton, Robert
English. Author
Left one major work *The Anatomy of
Melancholy,* 1621.
b. Feb 8, 1577 in Lindley, England
d. Jan 25, 1640 in Oxford, England
Source: *Alli; AtlBL; BbD; BrAu; CasWL;
CyEd; CyWA; EvLB; NewC; OxEng; RAdv 1;
REn; WebE&AL; WhDW*

Burton, Virginia Lee
American. Children's Author, Illustrator
Writings include *Mike Mulligan and His
Steam Shovel,* 1939; *The Little House,*
1942.
b. Aug 30, 1909 in Newton Centre,
Massachusetts
d. Oct 15, 1968
Source: *AmAu&B; Au&ICB; AuBYP; Cald
1938; ConAu 13R, 25R, P-1; CurBio 43, 68;
JBA 51; SmATA 2*

Bury, John Bagnell
Irish. Historian
Regius professor of modern history,
Cambridge, 1902-27.
b. Oct 16, 1861 in Monagham, Ireland
d. Jun 1, 1927 in Rome, Italy
Source: *Chambr 3; DcEnA AP; DcIrB; DcIrW
2; DcNaB 1922; EvLB; GrBr; LinLib L;
LongCTC; PenC ENG; PoIre; TwCA*

Busbee, George Dekle
American. Politician
Governor of GA, 1975-82.
b. Aug 7, 1927 in Vienna, Georgia
Source: *BioNews 74; WhoAm 82; WhoAmP
73*

Busby, Matthew, Sir
English. Soccer Executive
Manchester United Football Club, manager,
1945-69; director, 1971-80, pres., 1980--.
b. May 26, 1909
Source: *BioIn 9, 10; Who 74, 82*

Buscaglia, Leo (Felice Leonardo)
"Dr. Hug"; "Dr. Love"
American. Educator, Author
Lecturer on interpersonal relationships who
wrote *Living, Loving, Learning,* 1982.
b. Mar 31, 1925 in Los Angeles, California
Source: *ConAu 110, 112; CurBio 83*

Busch, Adolphus
German. Businessman
Developed process of bottling beers to
withstand all temperatures, 1873; pres.,
Anheuser-Busch, 1880-1913.
b. Jul 10, 1839 in Mainz, Germany
d. Oct 10, 1913 in Langenschwalbach,
Germany
Source: *NatCAB 12*

Busch, August Anheuser, Jr.
American. Brewer, Baseball Executive
Chief exec., Anheuser-Busch; pres., St. Louis
Cardinals baseball team.
b. Mar 28, 1899 in Saint Louis, Missouri
Source: *CurBio 73; IntWW 74; St&PR 75;
WhoAm 74, 76, 78, 80, 82; WhoF&I 74;
WhoProB 73*

Busch, Fritz
German. Conductor
b. Mar 13, 1890 in Siegen, Germany
d. Sep 14, 1951 in London, England
Source: *CurBio 46, 51; WhAm 3*

Busch, Wilhelm
German. Poet, Illustrator
Illustrated, wrote book of verses *Max and
Moritz,* 1865.
b. Apr 15, 1832 in Hanover, Germany
d. Jan 9, 1908 in Mechtshausen, Germany
Source: *BiD&SB; CasWL; ChhPo, S1, S2;
ClDMEL; EuAu; EvEuW; LinLib L; McGDA;
OxGer; PenC EUR; REn; WhDW; WorECom*

Buse, Don
American. Basketball Player
b. Aug 10, 1950 in Holland, Indiana
Source: *BioIn 11; WhoBbl 73*

Busey, Gary
[Teddy Jack Eddy, pseud.]
American. Actor, Musician
Starred in *The Buddy Holly Story*, 1978; *The Last American Hero*, 1973; *A Star is Born*, 1976.
b. 1944 in Goose Creek, Texas
Source: *NewYTBS 78; WhoAm 80, 82*

Bush, Alan
English. Composer, Conductor
b. Dec 22, 1900 in London, England
Source: *BioIn 3, 6, 7; IntWW 74; Who 74; WhoMus 72; WhoWor 78*

Bush, Barbara Pierce
American. Celebrity Relative
Married George Bush, 1945.
b. Jun 8, 1925 in Rye, New York
Source: *NewYTBS 81; WhoAm 82; WhoAmW 81; WhoE 81*

Bush, George Herbert Walker
American. Vice-President
Ambassador to UN, 1971-72; CIA director, 1976-77.
b. Jun 12, 1924 in Milton, Massachusetts
Source: *BiDrAC; BioNews 74; CelR; CurBio 72; IntWW 74; NewYTBE 70, 71, 72; NewYTBS 74; Who 82; WhoAm 78, 80, 82; WhoAmP 73; WhoGov 72; WhoWor 80; WorAl*

Bush, Guy Terrell
"The Mississippi Mudcat"
American. Baseball Player
Pitcher, 1923-45, best known for giving up Babe Ruth's last home run, May 25, 1935.
b. Aug 23, 1901 in Aberdeen, Mississippi
d. Jun 1985 in Shannon, Mississippi
Source: *BaseEn 85*

Bush, Kate
English. Singer, Songwriter
b. Jul 30, 1958 in Kent, England
Source: *IlEncRk; NewWmR*

Bush, Vannevar
American. Engineer
b. Mar 11, 1890 in Everett, Massachusetts
d. Jun 28, 1974 in Belmont, Massachusetts
Source: *AmAu&B; CelR; ConAu 53; CurBio 40, 47, 74N; EncAB-H; IntWW 74; McGMS 80; NewYTBS 74; REnAL; WebAB; WhAm 6; WhNAA; WhWW-II; Who 74; WhoAm 74*

Bush-Brown, Albert
American. Author, University Administrator
Chancellor, Long Island U, 1971--; wrote *Architecture in America*, 1961.
b. Jan 2, 1926 in West Hartford, Connecticut
Source: *DrAS 74H, 78H; WhoAm 74, 76, 78, 80; WhoAmA 73, 76, 78; WhoWor 74*

Bushell, Anthony
English. Actor
Was associate producer of Laurence Oliver's film *Hamlet*, 1949.
b. May 19, 1904 in Kent, England
Source: *Film 2; FilmgC; WhoHol A; WhoThe 77A*

Bushkin, Joe (Joseph)
American. Jazz Musician
b. Nov 6, 1916 in New York, New York
Source: *AmSCAP 66; WhoAm 74; WhoJazz 72*

Bushman, Francis X(avier)
American. Actor
Romantic hero of silent films, 1911-28; played Messala in *Ben-Hur*, 1926.
b. Jan 10, 1883 in Baltimore, Maryland
d. Aug 23, 1966 in Pacific Palisades, California
Source: *Film 1, 2; FilmgC; MotPP; MovMk; ObitOF 79; OxFilm; TwYS; WebAB, 79; WhAm 4; WhScrn 74, 77; WhoHol B*

Bushmiller, Ernie (Ernest Paul)
American. Cartoonist
Created comic strip "Nancy."
b. Aug 23, 1905 in New York, New York
d. Aug 15, 1982 in Stamford, Connecticut
Source: *AnObit 1982; AuNews 1; ConAu 107, 29R; NewYTBS 82; WhoAm 74, 76, 78, 80, 82; WhoAmA 73, 76, 78; WorECom*

Bushnell, David
American. Inventor
Built man-propelled submarine boat, 1775; originated underwater warfare.
b. 1742 in Saybrook, Connecticut
d. 1824 in Warrenton, Georgia
Source: *ApCAB; DcAmB; TwCBDA; WebAB; WhAm HS*

Bushnell, Horace
American. Religious Leader
b. Apr 14, 1802 in Bantam, Connecticut
d. Feb 17, 1876 in Hartford, Connecticut
Source: *AmAu&B; BbD; BiD&SB; CyAL 2; DcAmAu; DcEnL; DcLEL; DcNAA; OxAmL; WebAB*

Bushnell, Nolan Kay
"King Pong"
American. Computer Executive
Founder, chm., Atari, 1972-79, Pizza Time
  Theatres, 1977--; created video game
  "Pong," 1972.
b. Feb 5, 1943 in Ogden, Utah
Source: *ConNews 85-1; LElec; WhoAmP 81;
WhoWest 78*

Busia, Kofi A
Ghanaian. Prime Minister
b. Jul 11, 1913
d. Aug 28, 1978 in Oxford, England
Source: *AfrA; IntWW 74; Who 74; WhoGov
75; WhoWor 78*

Busoni, Ferruccio Benvenuto
Italian. Pianist, Composer
b. Apr 1, 1866 in Empoli, Italy
d. Jul 27, 1924 in Berlin, Germany
Source: *AtlBL; DcCM*

Busoni, Rafaello
American. Artist
Illustrated books for Heritage, Limited
  Editions Press.
b. Feb 1, 1900 in Berlin, Germany
d. Mar 17, 1962 in New York, New York
Source: *ConAu 117; JBA 51*

Buss, Jerry Hatten
American. Businessman, Basketball Executive,
  Hockey Executive
Self-made multi-millionaire; owner of LA
  Kings, Lakers sports teams.
b. Jan 27, 1933 in Salt Lake City, Utah
Source: *NewYTBS 79; WhoAm 80, 82, 84;
WhoF&I 81; WhoWest 82*

Busse, Henry
American. Jazz Musician
b. May 19, 1894 in Magdeburg, Germany
d. Apr 23, 1955 in Memphis, Tennessee
Source: *AmSCAP 66*

Bustamante, William Alexander
Jamaican. Prime Minister
b. Feb 24, 1884
d. Aug 6, 1977 in Irish Town, Jamaica
Source: *BioIn 11; IntWW 74*

Butala, Tony
[The Letterman]
American. Singer
b. in Sharon, Pennsylvania
Source: *NF*

Butcher, Willard C(arlisle)
American. Banker
b. Oct 25, 1926 in Bronxville, New York
Source: *BioIn 12; CurBio 80; IntWW 79;
WhoAm 80, 82*

Butkus, Dick (Richard J)
American. Football Player, Actor
Linebacker, Chicago Bears, 1965-73; Hall of
  Fame, 1979.
b. Dec 9, 1942 in Chicago, Illinois
Source: *CelR; NewYTBS 74; WhoAm 74, 76,
78, 80, 82*

Butler, Benjamin Franklin
American. General, Politician
Commanded Ft. Monroe, VA during Civil
  War; managed impeachment trial of
  Andrew Johnson in Congress.
b. Nov 5, 1818 in Deerfield, New Hampshire
d. Jan 11, 1893 in Washington, District of
  Columbia
Source: *AmBi; ApCAB; BiAUS; BiDrAC;
CelCen; CivWDc; DcAmAu; DcAmB; DcNAA;
Drake; EncAB-H; HarEnUS; TwCBDA;
WebAB; WhAm HS; WhAmP*

Butler, John
American. Choreographer, Dancer
b. Sep 29, 1920 in Memphis, Tennessee
Source: *BiE&WWA; WhoAm 74; WhoMus 72;
WhoWor 78*

Butler, Joseph
English. Philosopher, Theologian
b. May 18, 1692 in Wantage, England
d. Jun 16, 1752 in Bath, England
Source: *BiD&SB; BrAu; Chambr 2; DcEnA;
DcEnL,; DcEuL; EvLB; NewC; OxEng; PenC
ENG; REn*

Butler, Matthew Calbraith
American. Soldier, Statesman
b. Mar 8, 1836 in Greenville, South Carolina
d. Apr 14, 1909 in Columbia, South Carolina
Source: *BiDSA; BioIn 5*

Butler, Michael
American. Businessman
b. Nov 26, 1926 in Chicago, Illinois
Source: *BioIn 8, 9; CelR; IntWW 74;
WhoAm 74, 76, 78, 80, 82; WhoWor 78*

Butler, Nicholas Murray
American. Educator
b. Apr 2, 1862 in Elizabeth, New Jersey
d. Dec 4, 1947 in New York, New York
Source: *Alli SUP; AmAu&B; ChhPo S2;
CurBio 40, 47; DcAmAu; DcAmB S4;
DcNAA; EncAB-H; OxAmL; REnAL;
TwCBDA; WebAB; WhAm 2; WhNAA*

Butler, Paul
American. Industrialist
Founded Butler Aviation Co., 1946, providing
fuel, service for private aircraft.
b. Jun 23, 1892 in Chicago, Illinois
d. Jun 24, 1981 in Oak Brook, Illinois
Source: *NewYTBS 81; WhAm 8; WhoF&I 74,
75*

Butler, Robert
American. Director
Won Emmy for direction of "Hill Street
Blues," 1981.
Source: *VarWW 85*

Butler, Samuel
English. Poet
Famous for mock epic *Hudibras,* ridiculing
the Puritans.
b. Feb 14, 1612 in Worcestershire, England
d. Sep 25, 1680 in London, England
Source: *AtlBL; BbD; BiD&SB; BrAu; CasWL;
CnE&AP; CrtT 2; CyWA; DcEnA; DcEnL;
DcEuL; DcLEL; EvLB; MouLC 1; NewC;
OxEng; PenC ENG; REn; WebE&AL*

Butler, Samuel
English. Author
Wrote realistic novel *Way of All Flesh,* 1903;
satire *Erewhon,* 1872.
b. Dec 4, 1835 in Nottinghamshire, England
d. Jun 18, 1902 in London, England
Source: *AtlBL; BrAu 19; CnMWL; CrtT 3;
DcEnA, AP; EvLB; ModBrL; NewC; OxEng;
PenC ENG*

Butler, Terry Geezer
see: Black Sabbath

**Butler of Saffron Walden, Richard Austen,
Baron**
"Rab"
British. Statesman
Conservative MP, 1929-65.
b. Dec 9, 1902 in Attock Serai, India
d. Mar 9, 1982 in Great Yeldham, England
Source: *AnObit 1982; BioIn 10; CurBio 44,
82; IntWW 74, 76, 77, 78; IntYB 78, 79;
Who 74, 82; WhoWor 74, 78; WrDr 76, 80,
82*

Butlin, William Heygate Edmund, Sir
English. Businessman
Pioneer of holiday camps; were national
institution by 1960.
b. Sep 29, 1899 in Capetown, South Africa
d. Jun 12, 1980 in Jersey, England
Source: *BlueB 76; GrBr; IntWW 80, 81; Who
74*

Butor, Michel
French. Author
b. Sep 14, 1926 in Mans-en-Baroeul, France
Source: *Au&Wr 71; CasWL; ConAu 9R;
ConLC 1, 3; EncWL; EvEuW; IntWW 74;
ModRL; PenC EUR; REn; TwCWr;
WhoTwCL; WorAu; WhoWor 78*

Buttenheim, Edgar Joseph
American. Publisher
b. Oct 16, 1882 in Jersey City, New Jersey
d. Nov 23, 1964
Source: *WhAm 4*

Butterfield, Alexander Porter
American. Government Official
Asst. to Richard Nixon, 1969-73; FAA
administrator, 1973-75.
b. Apr 6, 1926 in Pensacola, Florida
Source: *NewYTBE 73; WhoAm 74, 76, 78,
80, 82; WhoAmP 73; WhoS&SW 82*

Butterfield, Billy
American. Jazz Musician
b. Jan 14, 1917 in Middletown, Ohio
Source: *WhoJazz 72*

Butterfield, Herbert, Sir
English. Author
b. Oct 7, 1900 in Oxenhope, England
Source: *BioIn 4, 5; ConAu 1R; IntWW 74;
Who 74; WhoWor 78*

Butterfield, Lyman Henry
American. Historian
Edited the 20-volume *Adams Papers.*
b. Aug 8, 1909 in Lyndonville, New York
d. Apr 25, 1982 in Boston, Massachusetts
Source: *AmAu&B; AnObit 1982; ConAu 106;
DrAS 74H, 78H, 82H; NewYTBS 82; WhAm
8; WhoAm 76, 78, 80*

Butterfield, Roger Place
American. Historian, Journalist
Wrote Americana series *The American Past,*
1947-66.
b. Jul 29, 1907 in Lyndonville, New York
d. Jan 31, 1981 in Hartwick, New York
Source: *AmAu&B; ConAu P-1; CurBio 48, 81;
REnAL*

Butterfield, William
English. Architect
Leading gothic revival architect, best known
for All Saints Church, London, 1850.
b. 1814 in London, England
d. 1900
Source: *CelCen; DcD&D; DcNiCA; McGDA;
WhoArch*

Butterick, Ebenezer
American. Inventor
Invented standardized paper patterns for
    clothes; first marketed, 1863.
b. May 29, 1826 in Sterling, Massachusetts
d. Mar 31, 1903
Source: *AmBi; DcAmB; NatCAB 13; WhDW;
WhAm HS*

Butterworth, Charles
American. Actor
Supporting actor in films, 1930-46.
b. Jul 26, 1897 in South Bend, Indiana
d. Jun 14, 1946 in Los Angeles, California
Source: *CurBio 46; Film 2; FilmgC; MotPP;
MovMk; ObitOF 79; Vers A; WhScrn 74, 77;
WhoHol B; WorAl*

Buttigieg, Anton
Maltese. President
b. Feb 19, 1912 in Gozo, Malta
Source: *IntWW 74; WhoWor 78*

Button, Dick (Richard Totten)
American. Skater, Sportscaster
Won gold medal in figure skating, 1948,
    1952 Olympics.
b. Jul 18, 1929 in Englewood, New Jersey
Source: *BiE&WWA; CelR; ConAu 9NR;
CurBio 49; WhoAm 82; WhoHol A; WorAl*

Buttons, Red
[Aaron Chwatt]
American. Comedian, Actor
Won Oscar, 1957, for *Sayonara.*
b. Feb 5, 1919 in New York, New York
Source: *AmSCAP 66; CurBio 58; FilmgC;
IntMPA 75, 76, 77, 78, 79, 80, 81, 82;
MotPP; MovMk; WhoAm 80, 82; WhoHol A;
WhoWor 74*

Buttram, Pat
American. Actor
Played in TV series "Green Acres," 1965-71.
b. Jun 19,
Source: *WhoHol A*

Buttrick, George Arthur
American. Clergyman, Author
b. Mar 23, 1892 in Seaham Harbour,
    England
d. Jan 23, 1980 in Louisville, Kentucky
Source: *AmAu&B; Au&Wr 71; ConAu 61, 93;
WhoAm 74*

Butts, Alfred Mosher
American. Architect
Invented word game "Scrabble," 1933.
b. Apr 13, 1899 in Poughkeepsie, New York
Source: *BioIn 3; CurBio 54*

Butz, Earl Lauer
American. Government Official
Secretary of Agriculture, 1971-76; sentenced
    to five years in prison for tax evasion,
    1981.
b. Jul 3, 1909 in Noble County, Indiana
Source: *AmM&WS 73S; CngDr 74; CurBio
72; IndAu 1917; IntWW 74; NewYTBE 71,
72; USBiR 74; WhoAm 74; WhoAmP 73;
WhoGov 75*

Buxtehude, Dietrich
Danish. Organist, Composer
b. 1637 in Elsinore, Denmark
d. May 9, 1707 in Lubeck, Germany
Source: *AtlBL*

Buzhardt, J(oseph) Fred, Jr.
American. Watergate Participant, Lawyer
Special counsel to Richard Nixon on
    Watergate matters, 1973-74.
b. Feb 21, 1924 in Greenwood, South
    Carolina
d. Dec 16, 1978 in Hilton Head Island,
    South Carolina
Source: *NewYTBS 78; WhoAmP 73*

Buzzell, Eddie
American. Actor, Director
Star of Broadway musical comedies who
    became director, 1932.
b. Nov 13, 1907 in Brooklyn, New York
Source: *CmpEPM; Film 2; FilmgC; WhoHol
A*

Buzzi, Ruth Ann
[Mrs. Basil Keko]
American. Actress, Comedienne
Best known for appearances in TV series
    "Laugh-In," 1968-73.
b. Jul 24, 1936 in Westerly, Rhode Island
Source: *CelR; ConTFT 3; IntMPA 82;
WhoAm 82*

Byars, Betsy
American. Children's Author
b. Aug 7, 1928 in Charlotte, North Carolina
Source: *AuBYP; ChlLR 1; ConAu 33R;
MorBMP; NewbC 1966; SmATA 4; ThrBJA*

Byers, William Newton
American. Editor
Issued first newspaper in Denver, CO,
    "Rocky Mountain News," 1859-1878.
b. Feb 22, 1831 in Madison County, Ohio
d. Mar 25, 1903
Source: *Alli SUP; BioIn 8; DcNAA; NatCAB
13; OhA&B; REnAW; WhAm 1*

Byington, Spring
American. Actress
Star of TV series "December Bride," 1954-59.
b. Oct 17, 1893 in Colorado Springs, Colorado
d. Sep 7, 1971 in Hollywood, California
Source: *BiE&WWA; CurBio 56, 71; FilmgC; InWom; MotPP; MovMk; NewYTBE 71; ThFT; Vers A; WhAm 5; WhScrn 74, 77; WhoHol B*

Byner, John
American. Comedian
Source: *NF*

Byng, George Torrington, Viscount
British. Explorer
First Lord of Admiralty, 1727-33.
b. 1663
d. Jan 17, 1733
Source: *Alli; DcBiPP; OxShips*

Byng, Julian Hedworth George, Viscount
English. Political Leader
Governor-general of Canada, 1921-26.
b. Sep 11, 1862 in Barnet, England
d. Jun 6, 1935 in Thorpe-le-Soken, England
Source: *DcNaB 1931; GrBr; LinLib S; MacDCB 78; WhoMilH 76*

Bynner, Harold Witter
American. Author
Wrote *The Jade Mountain,* 1929, translation of Chinese poetry; *Indian Earth,* 1929.
b. Aug 10, 1881 in Brooklyn, New York
d. Jun 1, 1968 in Santa Fe, New Mexico
Source: *ChhPo, S1; CnDAL; ConAmA; ConAu 4NR, 25R; DcLEL*

Byrd, Charlie (Charles Lee)
American. Jazz Musician
b. Sep 16, 1925 in Chuckatuck, Virginia
Source: *BioNews 74; CurBio 67*

Byrd, Donald
American. Jazz Musician
Trumpet, fluegelhorn player; albums include *Ethiopian Knights,* 1972; *Black Byrd,* 1975.
b. Dec 9, 1932 in Detroit, Michigan
Source: *BiDAmM; EncJzS 70; InB&W 80; WhoAm 74; WhoWor 74*

Byrd, Harry Flood, Jr.
American. Statesman, Editor
Dem. governor of VA, 1926-30; US senator, 1933-65.
b. Jun 10, 1887 in Martinsburg, West Virginia
d. Oct 20, 1966
Source: *BiDrAC; BiDrGov; CurBio 66; ObitOF 79; WhAm 4; WhAmP*

Byrd, Harry Flood, Jr.
American. Journalist, Senator
b. Dec 20, 1914 in Winchester, Virginia
Source: *BiDrAC; CngDr 74; IntWW 74; WhoAm 74, 76, 78, 80, 82; WhoAmP 73; WhoGov 75; WhoS&SW 82*

Byrd, Henry
"Professor Longhair"
American. Composer, Musician
New Orleans rock-n-roll pianist, songwriter, who wrote "Go to the Mardi Gras," "Big Chief."
b. Dec 19, 1918 in Bogalusa, Louisiana
d. Jan 30, 1980 in New Orleans, Louisiana
Source: *AnObit 1980*

Byrd, Richard Evelyn
American. Lawyer, Politician
b. Aug 13, 1860 in Austin, Texas
d. Oct 23, 1925
Source: *WhAm 1*

Byrd, Richard Evelyn
American. Explorer
First man to fly over N Pole, 1925, S Pole, 1929.
b. Oct 25, 1888 in Winchester, Virginia
d. Mar 11, 1957 in Boston, Massachusetts
Source: *AsBiEn; CurBio 42, 56, 57; EncAB-H; NatCAB 46; WebAB; WebAMB; WhAm 3*

Byrd, Robert Carlyle
American. Senator
Majority leader, 1977-79; minority leader, 1980--.
b. Jan 15, 1918 in North Wilkesboro, North Carolina
Source: *BiDrAC; CngDr 74; CurBio 60; IntWW 74; NewYTBE 70, 71; WhoAm 74, 76, 78, 80, 82; WhoAmP 73; WhoE 74; WhoGov 75*

Byrd, William
English. Organist, Composer, Songwriter
b. 1542 in London, England
d. Jul 4, 1623 in London, England
Source: *Alli; AtlBL; BiDSA; BrAu; Chambr 3; ChhPo, S1; CroE&S; OxEng; REn*

Byrds, The
[Skip Battin; Michael Clark; Gene Clarke;
    David Crosby; Chris Hillman; Kevin
    Kelly; Roger McGuinn; Gram Parsons]
American. Music Group
Pioneer folk-rock band, 1964-73; hits include
    "Mr. Tambourine Man," "Turn! Turn!
    Turn!," 1965.
Source: *EncPR&S 74; IlEncRk; RkOneH;
RolSEnR 83*

Byrne, Brendan
American. Government Official
Dem. governor of NJ, 1974-82.
b. Dec 28, 1908 in New York, New York
Source: *CurBio 74; NewYTBE 73; St&PR 75;
WhoAm 74, 76, 78, 80, 82; WhoF&I 74;
WhoPubR 72; WhoWor 78*

Byrne, David
[The Talking Heads]
Scottish. Musician
Leader of Talking Heads often compared to
    Bob Dylan; composed music for
    Broadway's *The Catherine Wheel*, 1981.
b. May 14, 1952 in Scotland
Source: *CurBio 85*

Byrne, Fran
see: Ace

Byrne, Jane Margaret Burke
[Mrs. Jay McMullen]
American. Politician
Dem. mayor of Chicago, 1979-83.
b. May 24, 1934 in Chicago, Illinois
Source: *BioIn 11, 12; CurBio 80; WhoAm 80,
82; WhoAmP 77; WhoGov 77*

Byrnes, Edd
[Edward Breitenberger]
American. Actor
Played Kookie on TV series "77 Sunset
    Strip," 1958-63.
b. Jul 30, 1933 in New York, New York
Source: *FilmEn; FilmgC; IntMPA 77; MotPP;
WhoHol A*

Byrnes, Eugene F
[Gene Burns]
American. Cartoonist
b. 1889 in New York, New York
d. Jul 26, 1974
Source: *ConAu 49*

Byrnes, James Francis
American. Government Official
Appointed by FDR to Supreme Court, 1941-
    42; secretary of state under Harry
    Truman, 1945-47.
b. May 2, 1879 in Charleston, South
    Carolina
d. Apr 9, 1972 in Columbia, South Carolina
Source: *AmAu&B; BiDFedJ; BiDrAC;
BiDrUSE; CurBio 41, 51, 72; DcAmDH;
EncAB-H; NewYTBE 73; OxAmH; WebAB;
WhAm 5; WhAmP*

Byron, George Gordon Noel Byron, Baron
English. Poet
Writer of Romantic narrative poems: "Childe
    Harold's Pilgrimage," 1812.
b. Jan 22, 1788 in London, England
d. Apr 19, 1824 in Missolonghi, Greece
Source: *Alli; AtlBL; BbD; BiD&SB; BiDLA,
SUP; BrAu 19; CasWL; Chambr 3; ChhPo,
S1, S2; CnE&AP; CnThe; CyWA; DcEnA;
DcEnL; DcEuL; DcLEL; EvLB; HsB&A;
LongCEL; McGEWD; NewC; OxEng; OxThe;
PenC ENG; RAdv 1; RComWL; REn;
REnWD; WebE&AL; WhDW*

C

Caan, James
"The Jewish Cowboy"
American. Actor, Director
Starred in *The Godfather,* 1972; TV movie
Brian's Song, 1971.
b. Mar 26, 1939 in New York, New York
Source: *BkPepl; CelR; CurBio 76; FilmgC;
IntMPA 80, 81, 82; IntWW 80, 81, 82;
MovMk; NewYTBE 73; WhoAm 82; WhoHol
A; WorAl*

Caballe, Montserrat
Spanish. Opera Singer
b. Apr 12, 1933 in Barcelona, Spain
Source: *CurBio 67; InWom; IntWW 74;
NewYTBE 73; Who 74; WhoMus 72;
WhoWor 78*

Cabell, Grete
Dutch. Mystic
Source: *NF*

Cabell, James Branch
American. Author
b. Apr 14, 1879 in Richmond, Virginia
d. May 5, 1958 in Richmond, Virginia
Source: *AmAu&B; AmLY; AmNov; BiDSA;
CasWL; Chambr 3; CnDAL; CnMWL;
ConAmA; ConAmL; CyWA; DcAmAu; DcBiA;
DcLEL; EncWL; EvLB; LongCTC; ModAL;
OxAmL; OxEng; PenC AM; RAdv 1; REn;
REnAL; TwCA, SUP; TwCWr; WebAB;
WebE&AL; WhAm 3; WhNAA*

Cabeza de Vaca, Alvar Nunez
Spanish. Explorer
Went on Narvaez expedition to FL, 1528;
shipwrecked, imprisoned by Indians.
b. 1490 in Spain
d. 1557 in Spain
Source: *BiDSA; Drake; EuAu; McGEWB;
OxAmL; REn*

Cable, George Washington
American. Author
b. Oct 12, 1844 in New Orleans, Louisiana
d. Jan 31, 1925 in Saint Petersburg, Florida
Source: *Alli; AmAu; AmAu&B; AmBi; AmLY;
ApCAB; AtlBL; BbD; BiD&SB; BiDSA;
CasWL; Chambr 3; ChhPo, Sl; CnDAL; CrtT
3; CyWA; DcAmAu; DcAmB; DcBiA; DcEnA
AP; DcLEL; DcNAA; EvLB; OxAmL; OxEng;
PenC AM; RAdv 1; REn; REnAL; WebAB;
WebE&AL; WhAm 1; WhNAA*

Cable, Mary
American. Author, Editor
b. Jan 24, 1920 in Cleveland, Ohio
Source: *ConAu 25R; DrAF 76; SmATA 9*

Cabot, Bruce
[Jacques Etienne de Bujac]
American. Actor
Best known as hero who saved Fay Wray in
King Kong, 1933.
b. Apr 20, 1904 in Carlsbad, New Mexico
d. May 3, 1972 in Woodland Hills,
California
Source: *FilmgC; HolP 30; MotPP; MovMk;
NewYTBE 72; ObitOF 79; WhScrn 77;
WhoHol B; WorAl*

Cabot, John
[Giovanni Caboto]
Italian. Navigator, Explorer
Conceived notion of sailing westward to
Orient; credited with discovery of N
America.
b. Jun 24, 1450 in Genoa, Italy
d. 1498
Source: *AmBi; NewC; OxCan; REn; REnAL;
WebAB; WhAm HS*

Cabot, John Moors
American. Diplomat
US ambassador to five countries, 1954-65;
wrote *Towards Our Common American
Destiny,* 1955.
b. Dec 11, 1901 in Cambridge, Massachusetts
d. Feb 23, 1981 in Washington, District of
Columbia
Source: *AmAu&B; CurBio 53, 81; IntWW 74,
75, 76, 77, 78; IntYB 78, 79; NewYTBS 81;
PolProf E, K; WhoAm 74, 76*

Cabot, Richard C
American. Scientist, Physician, Engineer
Pioneer in medical social work.
b. May 21, 1868 in Brookline, Massachusetts
d. May 8, 1939
Source: *AmAu&B; DcAmB S2; DcNAA;
WhAm 1*

Cabot, Sebastian
Italian. Explorer
Son of John Cabot; reached Hudson Bay in
attempt to find Northwest Passage, 1509.
b. 1476 in Venice, Italy
d. 1557
Source: *Alli; ApCAB; Drake; NewC; OxCan;
REn; TwCBDA; WhAm HS*

Cabot, Sebastian
English. Actor
Played Mr. French on TV series "Family
Affair," 1966-71.
b. Jul 6, 1918 in London, England
d. Aug 23, 1977 in Victoria, British
Columbia
Source: *CelR; FilmgC; MotPP; MovMk;
WhoHol A*

Cabot, Susan
American. Actress
b. Jul 6, 1927 in Boston, Massachusetts
Source: *FilmEn; FilmgC; WhoHol A*

Cabral, Luis de Almeida
Guinean. Government Official
b. 1931 in Bissau, Guinea-Bissau
Source: *IntWW 74; NewYTBS 74*

Cabral, Pedro Alvarez
Portuguese. Explorer
Credited with discovery of Brazil, Apr 24,
1500.
b. 1460
d. 1526
Source: *ApCAB; Drake*

Cabrillo, Juan Rodriguez
Portuguese. Explorer
Explored CA coast, 1542; discovered San
Diego Bay.
b. 1520 in Portugal
d. Jan 3, 1543 in San Miguel Island,
California
Source: *DcAmB; McGEWB; REnAW; WhAm
HS*

Cabrini, Saint Frances Xavier
[Mother Cabrini]
American. Religious Figure
First American saint; founded convents,
orphanages, hospitals in Europe, US;
canonized, 1946.
b. Jul 15, 1850 in Saint' Angelo, Italy
d. Dec 22, 1917 in Chicago, Illinois
Source: *DcCathB; GoodHs; InWom; LibW;
McGEWB; NotAW; WebAB, 79; WhAm HS*

Caccini, Giulio
Italian. Composer
b. 1546 in Rome, Italy
d. Dec 10, 1618 in Florence, Italy
Source: *REn*

Cacers, Ernest
American. Musician
b. Nov 22, 1911 in Rockport, Texas
d. Jan 10, 1971 in Texas
Source: *BioIn 9; WhoJazz 72*

Cacoyannis, Michael
Greek. Director
b. Jun 11, 1922 in Limassol, Cyprus
Source: *BiDFilm; CelR; ConAu 101; CurBio
66; DcFM; FilmgC; IntMPA 80, 81, 82;
IntWW 80, 81, 82; MovMk; NotNAT;
OxFilm; Who 82; WhoWor 82*

Cadbury, George Adrian Hayhurst, Sir
English. Manufacturer
Chm., Cadbury Schweppes, Ltd. 1974--.
b. Apr 15, 1929 in Birmingham, England
Source: *BioIn 7; IntWW 74, 75, 76, 77, 78;
IntYB 78, 79; Who 74; WhoWor 74, 76, 78*

Cadbury, John
English. Candy Manufacturer
Opened small shop, 1824; had 15 varieties of
chocolates, 1841.
b. 1801
d. 1889
Source: *BioIn 1; Entr*

Caddell, Pat(rick Hayward)
American. Pollster
Pres., Cambridge Survey Research, 1971--;
consultant, Jimmy Carter's presidential
campaign.
b. May 19, 1950 in Rock Hill, South
Carolina
Source: *BioIn 10; CurBio 79; NewYTBS 76;
WhoAm 80, 82*

Cadillac, Antoine
[Antoine de la Mothe Cadillac]
French. Explorer
Founded Detroit, Jul 24, 1701.
b. Mar 5, 1658 in Les Laumets, France
d. Oct 15, 1730 in Castelsarrasen, France
Source: *AmBi; ApCAB; DcAmB; DcCanB 2;
DcCathB; HarEnUS; MacDCB 78; NatCAB 5;
OxAmH; OxCan; REnAL; TwCBDA; WebAB,
79; WhAmP; WorAl*

Cadman, Charles Wakefield
American. Composer
b. Dec 4, 1881 in Johnstown, Pennsylvania
d. Dec 30, 1946 in Los Angeles, California
Source: *AmSCAP 66; DcAmB S4; OxAmL;
REnAL; WhAm 2*

Cadmus, Paul
American. Artist
b. Dec 17, 1904 in New York, New York
Source: *BioIn 6; CelR; CurBio 42; DcCAA
71; WhoAm 74, 76, 78, 80, 82; WhoAmA 73;
WhoE 74*

Cadogan, Alexander George Montague, Sir
English. Statesman
b. Nov 25, 1884
d. Jul 9, 1968 in London, England
Source: *CurBio 44, 68*

Cadogan, William
British. General, Diplomat
b. 1676
d. 1726
Source: *NewCol 75*

Cady, (Walter) Harrison
American. Cartoonist, Illustrator
b. 1877 in Gardner, Massachusetts
d. Dec 9, 1970 in New York, New York
Source: *ChhPo, S1; IlsCB 1744; NewYTBE
70; SmATA 19; WhNAA*

Caedmon, Saint
Anglo-Saxon. Poet
b. 650 in England
d. 680 in England
Source: *Alli; BbD; BiB S; BiD&SB; BrAu;
CasWL; Chambr 1; CrtT 1; DcEnL; EvLB;
MouLC 1; NewC; OxEng; PenC ENG; REn;
WebE&AL*

Caen, Herb
American. Journalist, Author
b. Apr 3, 1916 in Sacramento, California
Source: *AuNews 1; CelR; ConAu 1R, 1NR;
WhoAm 74, 76, 78, 80, 82; WhoWor 78*

Caesar, Adolph
American. Actor
Nominated for Oscar for *A Soldier's Story*,
1984; appeared in *The Color Purple*, 1985.
b. 1934 in Harlem, New York
d. Mar 6, 1986 in Los Angeles, California
Source: *ConTFT 3; VarWW 85*

Caesar, Irving
American. Songwriter
b. Jul 4, 1895 in New York, New York
Source: *AmSCAP 66; Au&Wr 71; BiE&WWA;
ChhPo; EncMT; IntMPA 80, 81, 82;
NewCBMT; NotNAT; REnAL; Who 74;
WhoThe 77*

Caesar, Sid
American. Comedian, Actor
Accomplished mimic, sketch comic who
greatly influenced TV comedy.
b. Sep 8, 1922 in Yonkers, New York
Source: *AmSCAP 66; BiE&WWA; CelR;
CurBio 51; EncMT; FilmgC; IntMPA 75, 76,
77, 78, 79, 80, 81, 82; MovMk; WhoAm 74,
76, 78, 80, 82; WhoHol A; WhoTelC;
WhoThe 77; WhoWor 74*

Caetano, Marcello
Portuguese. Political Leader
Premier of Portugal, 1968-74, who was
ousted by military.
b. Aug 17, 1906 in Lisbon, Portugal
d. Oct 26, 1980 in Rio de Janeiro, Brazil
Source: *AnObit 1980; CurBio 70, 81; DcPol;
IntWW 74, 81; IntYB 80; NewYTBS 80;
WhoGov 72; WhoWor 74*

Cafritz, Gwen
Hungarian. Actress
b. 1912 in Budapest, Hungary
Source: *InWom*

Cage, John Milton, Jr.
American. Composer, Author
b. Sep 5, 1912 in Los Angeles, California
Source: *AmAu&B; AmSCAP 66; CelR; ConAu 13R; CurBio 61; DcCM; IntWW 74; NewYTBE 72; PenC AM; WhoAm 74, 76, 78, 80, 82; WhoE 74; WhoMus 72; WhoWor 78; WrDr 80*

Cagle, "Red" (Christian Keener)
American. Football Player
b. May 1, 1905 in Deridder, Louisiana
d. Dec 23, 1942 in New York, New York
Source: *WhoFtbl 74*

Cagliostro, Alessandro, Conte di
[Giuseppe Balsamo]
Italian. Magician
Traveled throughout Europe posing as an alchemist; condemned to death in Rome as a heretic.
b. Jun 2, 1743 in Palmero, Italy
d. Aug 26, 1795 in Rome, Italy
Source: *BioIn 1, 4, 5, 8, 10; DcBiPP; Dis&D; NewC; OxGer; REn; WhDW; WorAl*

Cagney, James (James Francis, Jr.)
American. Actor, Singer, Dancer, Producer
Best known for tough-guy roles; won Oscar for *Yankee Doodle Dandy*, 1942.
b. Jul 17, 1899 in New York, New York
d. Mar 30, 1986 in Stanfordville, New York
Source: *BiDFilm; BiE&WWA; BioNews 74; CelR; CmMov; ConTFT 3; CurBio 86; FilmgC; IntMPA 82; MotPP; MovMk; NewYTBS 74; OxFilm; PIP&P; WebAB; WhoAm 84; WhoHol A; WhoThe 77A; WhoWor 74; WorEFlm*

Cagney, Jeanne
American. Actress, Celebrity Relative
Sister of James Cagney.
b. Mar 25, 1919 in New York, New York
Source: *BiE&WWA; FilmgC; IntMPA 75, 76, 77, 78, 79, 80, 81, 82; MotPP; NotNAT; WhoHol A; WhoThe 77A*

Cahan, Abraham
Russian. Editor, Author
b. Jul 7, 1860 in Vilna, Russia
d. Aug 31, 1951 in New York, New York
Source: *AmAu&B; BbD; BiD&SB; CasWL; ConAmL; DcAmAu; DcAmB S5; EncWL; ModAL; OxAmL; PenC AM; REn; REnAL; TwCA; SUP; WebAB; WhAm 3; WhNAA*

Cahill, Marie
American. Actress
Starred in vaudeville musical *Nancy Brown*, 1903.
b. Dec 20, 1870 in Brooklyn, New York
d. Aug 23, 1933 in New York, New York
Source: *EncMT; NotAW; NotNAT B; WhoStg 1906, 1908*

Cahill, William Thomas
American. Politician
b. Jun 25, 1912 in Philadelphia, Pennsylvania
Source: *BioIn 8, 9, 10; CurBio 70; IntWW 74; NewYTBE 72; WhoAm 74; WhoAmP 73; WhoE 74; WhoGov 75*

Cahn, Sammy
American. Songwriter
Won Oscars for *Three Coins in the Fountain; All the Way*.
b. Jun 18, 1913 in New York, New York
Source: *AmSCAP 66; ConAu 85; CurBio 74; EncMT; FilmgC; IntMPA 75, 76, 77, 78, 79, 80, 81, 82; NewCBMT; NewYTBS 74; NotNAT; WhoAm 74, 76, 78, 80, 82; WhoThe 77; WhoWor 78; WhoWorJ 72*

Caidin, Martin
American. Author
b. Sep 14, 1927 in New York, New York
Source: *AmAu&B; AuNews 2; ConAu 1R, 2NR*

Caillie, Rene
French. Explorer
First European to visit, return from Timbuktu.
b. 1799
d. 1838
Source: *NewCol 75*

Cain
Biblical Character
Son of Adam and Eve; killed brother Abel out of jealousy.
Source: *BioIn 10; LongCEL; NewCol 75; NewYHSD; Who 82*

Cain, James Mallahan
American. Author
Wrote *The Postman Always Rings Twice*,
  1934; *Mildred Pierce*.
b. Jul 1, 1892 in Annapolis, Maryland
d. Oct 27, 1977 in Hyattsville, Maryland
Source: *AmNov; AuNews 1; BiE&WWA;
CelR; CmCal; CnDAL; CnMWL; ConAu 17R,
73; ConLC 3, 11; ConNov 72, 76; DcLEL;
EncMys; FilmgC; LongCTC; ModAL;
NotNAT; Novels; ObitOF 79; OxAmL; PenC
AM; REn; REnAL; TwCA, SUP; TwCCr&M
80; TwCWr; WebE&AL; WhAm 1; WhNAA;
WhoAm 76; WhoWor 74; WorAl; WrDr 76*

Cain, Jonathan
see: Babys, The; Journey

Cain, Richard H
American. Congressman
b. 1825
d. 1887
Source: *BioIn 5, 6, 8, 9, 10, 11*

Caine, Hall, Sir
English. Author
Wrote popular novels of biblical themes *The
  Eternal City*, 1901; *The Prodigal Son*,
  1904.
b. May 14, 1853
d. Aug 31, 1931
Source: *Chambr 3; EncSF; LinLib L;
LongCTC; ModBrL; NewC; NotNAT B; REn;
ScF&FL 1; TwCA, SUP; TwCWr; WhThe;
WhoStg 1908*

Caine, Michael
[Michael Joseph Micklewhite]
English. Actor
Films include *Alfie*, 1966; *Beyond the
  Poseidon Adventure*, 1979.
b. Mar 14, 1933 in London, England
Source: *BiDFilm; BkPepl; CelR; CmMov;
CurBio 68; FilmgC; IntMPA 75, 76, 77, 78,
79, 80, 81, 82; MotPP; MovMk; OxFilm;
Who 82; WhoAm 82; WhoHol A; WhoWor
78; WorEFlm*

Cairncross, Alexander Kirkland, Sir
Scottish. Author, Educator, Economist
b. Feb 11, 1911 in Lemahagow,· Scotland
Source: *Au&Wr 71; ConAu 61; IntWW 74;
Who 74; WhoAm 74, 76, 78, 80, 82;
WhoWor 78; WrDr 80*

Caius, John
English. Physician
b. 1510
d. 1573
Source: *Alli; BioIn 1, 2, 3, 7, 9*

Cakobau, Ratu George, Sir
Fijian. Politician
b. Nov 6, 1912 in Suva, Fiji
Source: *IntWW 74; Who 74*

Calamity Jane
[Martha Jane Canary Burke]
American. Frontierswoman
Friend of Wild Bill Hickok who scouted for
  General Custer.
b. 1852 in Princeton, Missouri
d. Aug 1, 1903 in Terry, South Dakota
Source: *AmBi; FilmgC; GoodHs; LibW;
NotAW; OxFilm; REnAW; WebAB, 79;
WhDW*

Calas, Jean
French. Merchant
b. 1698
d. 1762
Source: *BioIn 4, 5, 6; OxFr*

Caldecott, Randolph
English. Artist
Caldecott Medal given annually to
  outstanding children's book illustrator
  established, 1938.
b. Mar 22, 1846 in Chester, England
d. Feb 12, 1886 in Saint Augustine, Florida
Source: *AnCL; CarSB; ChhPo, S1, S2;
IlsBYP; JBA 34, 51; SmATA 17; Str&VC;
WhoChL*

Calder, Alexander
American. Artist
Best known for abstract sculptures of metal,
  bent wire called "mobiles."
b. Jul 22, 1898 in Philadelphia, Pennsylvania
d. Nov 11, 1976 in New York, New York
Source: *Alli SUP; BioNews 74; CelR; ChhPo;
CurBio 46, 66; DcCAA 71; EncAB-H; IntWW
74; NewYTBE 73; REn; WebAB; Who 74;
WhoAm 74; WhoAmA 73; WhoWor 78*

Calder, Peter Ritchie
[Lord Ritchie-Calder of Balmashannar]
Scottish. Author, Journalist
Newspaper, magazine articles bridged gap
  between scientist, layman, 1922-50s.
b. Jul 1, 1906 in Forfar, Scotland
d. Jan 31, 1982
Source: *CurBio 63, 86; NewYTBS 82;
WhoWor 78; WrDr 80*

Calder-Marshall, Anna Lucia
English. Actress
With Royal Shakespeare Co., 1975-76.
b. Jan 11, 1947 in London, England
Source: *FilmgC; WhoAmW 74; WhoThe 72,
77, 81; WhoWor 78, 78*

Calder, Nigel David Ritchie
English. Author
Writer of popular science books: *The Restless Earth,* 1972; *The Comet Is Coming!* 1981.
b. Dec 2, 1931 in London, England
Source: *Au&Wr 71; ConAu 21R; CurBio 86; Who 74, 85; WrDr 82*

Calderon de la Barca, Pedro
Spanish. Dramatist
A dramatist during Spain's Golden Age; wrote over 120 plays *Mayor of Zalamea,* 1638.
b. Jan 17, 1600 in Madrid, Spain
d. May 25, 1681 in Madrid, Spain
Source: *AtlBL; BbD; BiD&SB; CasWL; CnThe; CyWA; DcBiPP; DcCathB; DcEuL; DcSpL; Dis&D; EuAu; EvEuW; LinLib L; McGEWD; NewC; NewEOp 71; NotNAT B; OxEng; OxSpan; OxThe; PenC EUR; RComWL; REn; REnWD; WhDW; WorAl*

Calderone, Mary Steichen
American. Physician
b. Jul 1, 1904 in New York, New York
Source: *AuNews 1; BioIn 8, 10, 11; CurBio 67; WhoAm 74; WhoAmW 74; WhoWor 78*

Caldicott, Helen Broinowski
Australian. Physician, Author, Reformer
Leader, Physicians for Social Responsibility, an antinuclear coalition, 1978--.
b. Aug 7, 1938 in Melbourne, Australia
Source: *BioIn 12; CurBio 83*

Caldwell, Erskine Preston
American. Author, Journalist
Author *God's Little Acre,* 1933; *The Sacrilege of Alan Kent,* 1976.
b. Dec 17, 1903 in Moreland, Georgia
Source: *AmAu&B; AmNov; AmWr; Au&Wr 71; AuNews 1; BioNews 74; CasWL; CelR; CnDAL; ConAmA; ConAu 1R, 2NR; ConLC 1, 8, 14; ConNov 72, 76; CurBio 40; CyWA; DcLEL; DrAF 76; EncWL; EvLB; FilmgC; IntWW 74; LongCTC; ModAL, S1; OxAmL; PenC AM; PIP&P; RAdv 1; REn; REnAL; TwCA, SUP; TwCWr; WebE&AL; WhNAA; Who 74; WhoAm 74, 76, 78, 80, 82; WhoS&SW 82; WhoTwCL; WhoWor 78; WrDr 80*

Caldwell, John Charles
Australian. Educator
Writings on reproduction, population control: *Population Growth and Family Change in Africa,* 1968.
b. Dec 8, 1928 in Sydney, Australia
Source: *WhoWor 74, 76*

Caldwell, Sarah
American. Conductor, Director
Conductor, director major US opera companies; founded Opera Company of Boston, 1957.
b. Mar 6, 1924 in Maryville, Missouri
Source: *Baker 84; BioNews 74; CurBio 73; GoodHs; LibW; NewYTBE 72; WhoAm 82; WhoAmW 81; WhoOp 76; WhoWor 74; WorAl*

Caldwell, Taylor (Janet Miriam Taylor)
[Mrs. William Robert Prestie]
English. Author
Wrote *Testimony of Two Men,* 1968; *The Captains and the Kings,* 1972.
b. Sep 7, 1900 in Manchester, England
d. Aug 30, 1985 in Greenwich, Connecticut
Source: *AmAu&B; AmNov; CelR; ConAu 5R, 15NR; ConLC 2; CurBio 40, 85; ForWC 70; InWom; LongCTC; OxAmL; REn; REnAL; TwCA, SUP; Who 82; WhoAm 74, 76, 78, 80, 82; WhoWor 78; WrDr 80*

Caldwell, Zoe
Australian. Actress
Best known for the title role on stage, TV of "Medea."
b. Sep 14, 1933 in Melbourne, Australia
Source: *CelR; CurBio 70; NotNAT; PIP&P, A; WhoAm 74; WhoAmW 66, 68, 70, 72, 74; WhoThe 77, 81; WhoWor 74; WorAl*

Cale, J J
American. Singer, Songwriter
Guitarist, composer, who wrote Eric Clapton's hit single, "After Midnight," 1970.
b. Dec 5, 1938 in Oklahoma City, Oklahoma
Source: *ConMuA 80A; IlEncRk; RolSEnR 83; WhoRock 81*

Calhern, Louis
[Carl Henry Vogt]
American. Actor
Stage, screen star, who won many awards for
portraying Oliver Wendell Holmes in
Magnificent Yankee, 1946.
b. Feb 19, 1895 in New York, New York
d. May 12, 1956 in Nara, Japan
Source: *BiDFilm; CurBio 56; FamA&A; Film
2; FilmgC; MGM; MotPP; MovMk; NatCAB
45; ObitOF 79; OxFilm; PIP&P; Vers A;
WhAm 3; WhScrn 77; WhThe; WorAl*

Calhoun, John Caldwell
American. Lawyer, Statesman
Secretary of War 1817-25; vp 1824-32, who
promoted southern unity, states rights.
b. Mar 18, 1782 in Calhoun Mills, South
Carolina
d. Mar 31, 1850
Source: *Alli; AmAu; AmAu&B; AmBi;
ApCAB; BbD; BiAUS; BiD&SB; BiDSA;
BiDrAC; BiDrUSE; CelCen; CivWDc; CyAG;
DcAmDH; DcBiPP; DcLB 3; Drake; EncAAH;
EncAB-A; EncAB-H; EncSoH; HarEnUS;
LinLib L; OxAmH; OxAmL,; REn; REnAL;
REnAW; TwCBDA; WhAm HS; WhAmP*

Calhoun, Lee Q
American. Track Athlete
Only man to win gold medal in 110-meter
hurdles twice, 1956, 1960 Olympics.
b. Feb 23, 1933 in Laurel, Mississippi
Source: *InB&W 80*

Calhoun, Rory
[Francis Timothy Durgin]
American. Actor
Western films include *Ticket to Tomahawk;
River of No Return; Treasure of Pancho
Villa.*
b. Aug 8, 1923 in Los Angeles, California
Source: *FilmgC; IntMPA 76, 77, 78, 79, 80,
81, 82; MotPP; MovMk; WhoAm 74, 76, 78,
80, 82; WhoHol A; WorAl*

Califano, Joseph Anthony, Jr.
American. Lawyer
Secretary, HEW, 1977-81; wrote *The Media
and the Law,* 1976.
b. May 15, 1931 in Brooklyn, New York
Source: *ConAu 45; IntWW 74; WhoAm 74,
76, 78, 80, 82; WhoAmP 73; WhoS&SW 82*

Caliguiri, Richard
American. Politician
Mayor of Pittsburgh 1977-81.
b. Oct 20, 1931 in Pittsburgh, Pennsylvania
Source: *WhoAm 78, 80, 82; WhoAmP 77, 79,
81; WhoE 79, 81; WhoGov 77*

Caligula
[Gaius Caesar Germanicus]
Roman. Emperor
Succeeded Tiberius as Roman emperor, 37-41;
main character in Camus' play *Caligula,*
1944.
b. Aug 31, 12 in Antium, Italy
d. Jan 24, 41 in Rome, Italy
Source: *McGEWB; NewC; REn*

Calisher, Hortense
[Mrs. Curtis Harnack]
American. Author
Four-time O'Henry short story winner; novels
include *Eagle Eye,* 1973.
b. Dec 20, 1911 in New York, New York
Source: *AmAu&B; AmWomWr; ASpks; BlueB
76; ConAu 1R, 1NR; ConLC 2, 4, 8; ConNov
72, 76, 82; CurBio 73; DcLB 2; DcLEL
1940; DrAF 76; EncSF; LinLib L; ModAL
S1; NewYTBE 72; Novels; OxAmL; PenC
AM; ScF&FL 1; TwCWr; WhoAm 82;
WhoWor 74; WorAu; WrDr 82*

Calkins, Dick
American. Cartoonist
b. 1895
d. 1962
Source: *WorECom*

Calkins, Earnest Elmo
American. Advertising Executive
Deaf from age six; founded Calkins and
Holden, first modern ad agency.
b. Mar 25, 1868 in Genesco, Illinois
d. Oct 4, 1964
Source: *AmAu&B; EncAB 5; REnAL; WhAm
4; WhLit; WhNAA*

Callaghan, James (Leonard James)
English. Government Official
Labor Party leader; prime minister, 1976-79.
b. Mar 27, 1912 in Portsmouth, England
Source: *CurBio 68; IntWW 74, 75, 76, 77,
78; IntYB 78, 79; NewYTBS 76; Who 74, 82;
WhoWor 74, 76, 78*

Callaghan, Morley Edward
Canadian. Author
Wrote novel *Many-Colored Coat,* 1960; short
stories *No Man's Meat,* 1931.
b. 1903 in Toronto, Ontario
Source: *CanNov; CanWW 70; CanWr;
CasWL; CathA 1930; ConAu 9R; ConLC 3;
ConNov 72, 76; CreCan 2; DcLEL; EncWL;
IntWW 74; LongCTC; NewC; OxAmL;
OxCan, SUP; PenC ENG; REn; REnAL;
TwCA, SUP; TwCWr; WebE&AL; Who 74;
WhoAm 74; WhoTwCL; WrDr 80*

Callahan, Daniel
American. Editor, Philosopher
Founded Institute of Social Ethics and Life
    Sciences, 1969; editor *The Commonweal,*
    1961-68.
b. Jul 19, 1930 in Washington, District of
    Columbia
Source: *AmCath 80; WhoAm 74, 76, 78, 80,
82; WhoE 74; WhoWor 74, 76, 80*

Callan, Michael
American. Actor
Films include *Gidget Goes Hawaiian,* 1961;
    Cat Ballou, 1965.
b. Nov 22, 1935 in Philadelphia,
    Pennsylvania
Source: *FilmgC; IntMPA 75, 76, 77, 78, 79,
80, 81, 82; MotPP; WhoHol A*

Callas, Charlie
American. Comedian, Actor
b. Dec 20, in Brooklyn, New York
Source: *WhoAm 82; WhoHol A*

Callas, Maria
[Maria Kalogeropoulou; Maria Meneghini]
American. Opera Singer
Soprano, 1938-60; romantically involved with
    Aristotle Onassis, 1960s.
b. Dec 3, 1923 in New York, New York
d. Sep 16, 1977 in Paris, France
Source: *BioIn 10; BioNews 74; CelR; CurBio
56, 77; IntWW 74; NewEOp 71; NewYTBE
71; WebAB; Who 74; WhoAm 74; WhoHol A;
WhoMus 72; WhoWor 78*

Callaway, Howard Hollis
American. Business Executive, Government
    Official
Secretary of Army, 1973-75.
b. Apr 2, 1927 in Lagrange, Georgia
Source: *BiDrAC; CngDr 74; WhoAm 74, 76,
78, 80, 82; WhoAmP 73; WhoS&SW 82;
WhoWor 78*

Calles, Plutarco
Mexican. Statesman, General
Pres., of Mexico, 1924-28; sponsored agrarian
    reforms; exiled in US, 1936-41.
b. Sep 25, 1877
d. Oct 19, 1945 in Mexico City, Mexico
Source: *CurBio 45; WhAm 2*

Calley, William Laws
American. Army Officer
b. 1943
Source: *NewYTBS 74*

Callimachus
Greek. Critic, Poet
Chief librarian for royalty; noted for wit; is
    said to have written 800 works.
b. 305 BC in Cyrene, Greece
d. 240 BC
Source: *AtlBL; BbD; BiD&SB; CasWL;
OxEng; PenC CL; REn*

Callis, Joe
see: Human League

Calloway, Cab(ell)
"King of Hi De Ho"
American. Band Leader, Singer
Acclaimed "scat" singer; noted for song
    "Minnie the Moocher," role in *Porgy and
    Bess,* 1953.
b. Dec 25, 1907 in Rochester, New York
Source: *AmSCAP 66; BioNews 74; CelR;
CurBio 45; FilmgC; MovMk; WhoAm 74;
WhoBlA 75; WhoHol A; WhoJazz 72;
WhoThe 77*

Calmer, Ned
American. Journalist
News editor, broadcaster, CBS, 1940-67.
b. Jul 18, 1907 in Chicago, Illinois
Source: *ConAu 69; WhoAm 74, 76, 78, 80,
82; WhoWor 78*

Calpurnia
Roman. Celebrity Relative
Third wife of Julius Caesar; had prophetic
    dream of Caesar's assassination.
b. 59 BC
Source: *InWom; REn*

Calve, Emma
[Rosa Calvet]
French. Opera Singer
Noted for roles in *Sapho; Carmen.*
b. Aug 15, 1858 in Decazevelle, France
d. Jan 6, 1942 in Millan, France
Source: *CurBio 42; InWom; WhAm 1, 2;
WhoStg 1906, 1908*

Calvert, Bernie
see: Hollies, The

Calvert, Catherine
[Catherine Cassidy]
American. Actress
Notable films include *Behind the Mask,* 1917;
    Marriage, 1918; *That Woman,* 1922.
b. 1891 in Baltimore, Maryland
d. Jan 18, 1971 in Uniondale, New York
Source: *Film 2; MotPP; TwYS; WhScrn 77;
WhThe; WhoHol B*

Calvert, Edward
British. Engraver, Artist
b. 1799
d. 1883
Source: *BioIn 1, 4, 6*

Calvert, George
see: Baltimore, George Calvert, Baron

Calvert, Louis
English. Actor
London stage actor; formed, managed own
company; wrote *Problems of the Actor,*
1918.
b. 1859 in Manchester, England
d. Jul 2, 1923 in England
Source: *EncWT; Film 1; NotNAT B; OxThe;*
WhScrn 77; WhThe

Calvert, Phyllis
[Phyllis Bickle]
English. Actress
Popular star of 1940s: *Young Mr. Pitt,* 1942;
Fanny by Gaslight, 1944.
b. Feb 18, 1915 in London, England
Source: *CmMov; FilmgC; IntMPA 76, 77, 78,*
79, 80, 81, 82; MotPP; MovMk; OxFilm;
Who 74, 82; WhoHol A; WhoThe 77, 81

Calvert, "Sunshine" (Melvin)
American. Horse Trainer
Source: *NF*

Calvet, Corinne
[Corinne Dibos]
French. Actress
Film star of 1950s: *What Price Glory?,* 1952;
Flight to Tangiers, 1953.
b. Apr 30, 1925 in Paris, France
Source: *FilmgC; InWom; IntMPA 75, 76, 77,*
78, 79, 80, 81, 82; MotPP; MovMk; WhoHol
A

Calvin, John
[Jean Chauvin]
French. Theologian, Reformer
Established Calvinism; recognized Bible as
only source of knowledge.
b. Jul 10, 1509 in Noyon, France
d. May 27, 1564 in Geneva, Switzerland
Source: *BbD; BiD&SB; CyEd; Dis&D;*
EncWM; LinLib L, S; LuthC 75; McGEWB;
NewC; OxMus; RComWL; REn; WhAm 1;
WorAl

Calvin, Melvin
American. Chemist, Educator
Received Nobel Prize in chemistry, 1961, for
researching carbon-dioxide assimilation in
plants.
b. Apr 8, 1911 in Saint Paul, Minnesota
Source: *BioIn 3, 4, 5, 6, 8; CurBio 62;*
IntWW 74; Who 74; WhoAm 74, 76, 78, 80,
82; WhoWor 78

Calvino, Italo
Italian. Author
Writings include allegorical fantasy *If on a*
Winter's Night a Traveler, 1979.
b. Oct 15, 1923 in Santiago de Las Vegas,
Cuba
d. Sep 19, 1985 in Siena, Italy
Source: *CasWL; ConAu 85; ConLC 22;*
CurBio 85; DcItL; EncSF; EncWL 2;
IntAu&W 82; IntWW 80, 82; ModRL;
NewYTBS 81; Novels; PenC EUR; ScF&FL 1;
WhoTwCL; WhoWor 78

Calvo, Paul McDonald
American. Businessman, Politician
Governor of Guam, 1978--.
b. Jul 25, 1934 in Agana, Guam
Source: *FarE&A 79; WhoAm 82; WhoAmP*
77, 79

Calvo Sotelo (y Bustelo), Leopoldo
Spanish. Businessman, Politician
Prime minister of Spain, 1981-82.
b. Apr 14, 1926 in Madrid, Spain
Source: *CurBio 81; IntWW 76, 77, 78;*
NewYTBS 81

Cambaceres, Jean Jacques Regis de
[Duke of Parma]
French. Statesman
Napoleon's chief legal adviser.
b. Oct 18, 1753 in Montpellier, France
d. Mar 8, 1824
Source: *DcBiPP; LinLib S; OxFr; OxLaw*

Cambridge, Godfrey
American. Actor, Comedian
Films include *Purlie Victorious,* 1963; *Cotton*
Comes to Harlem, 1970.
b. Feb 26, 1933 in New York, New York
d. Nov 29, 1976 in Hollywood, California
Source: *CelR; CivR 74; CurBio 77N; DrBlPA;*
Ebony 1; FilmgC; InB&W 80; IntMPA 77;
MotPP; MovMk; NegAl 76; NewYTBS 76;
NotNAT; OxFilm; WhoAm 74; WhoBlA 75;
WhoHol A; ObitOF 79; WhAm 7; WhoThe
81N; WhoWor 78; WorAl

Cambyses II
Persian. King
Son, successor of Cyrus the Great, 529-522
BC; added Eygpt to Persian empire,
525BC.
b. 522 BC
Source: *Dis&D; REn*

Camerarius, Rudolf Jakob
German. Botanist, Educator
First to prove sexuality in plants, c. 1694.
b. 1665
d. 1721
Source: *NewCol 75; WebBD 80*

Camerini, Mario
Italian. Director
Directed Vittorio DeSica in various film
comedies, 1932-39.
b. Feb 6, 1895 in Rome, Italy
d. Feb 6, 1981
Source: *AnObit 1981; ConAu 103; DcFM;
FilmgC; OxFilm; WorEFlm*

Cameron, Eleanor Francis
Canadian. Author
Wrote prize-winning children's stories *Court
of the Stone Children*, 1973; *Julia Redfern*,
1982.
b. Mar 23, 1912 in Winnipeg, Manitoba
Source: *AuBYP; ChlLR 1; ChhPo; ConAu 1R,
2NR; SmATA 1; ThrBJA; WhoAm 82*

Cameron, James
Canadian. Director
Co-wrote with Sylvester Stallone *Rambo: First
Blood, Part II;* directed *Aliens II,* 1986.
b. Aug 16, 1954 in Kapuskasing, Ontario
Source: *ConTFT 3*

Cameron, Kirk
American. Actor
Plays Mike Seaver in TV show "Growing
Pains."
b. Oct 12, 1970 in Panorama City, California
Source: *NF*

Cameron, Rod
[Rod Cox]
American. Actor
b. Dec 7, 1912 in Calgary, Alberta
d. Dec 21, 1983 in Gainesville, Georgia
Source: *CmMov; FilmgC; HolP 40; IntMPA
75, 76, 77, 78, 79, 80, 81, 82; MotPP;
WhoHol A*

Cameron, Roderick W
American. Author
Wrote books on history, travel.
b. Nov 15, 1913 in New York, New York
d. Sep 18, 1985 in Menerbes, France
Source: *Au&Wr 71; IntAu&W 77; NewYTBS
84; WhoWor 78; WrDr 82, 84*

Camilli, Dolph (Adolph Louis)
American. Baseball Player
b. Apr 23, 1908 in San Francisco, California
Source: *BaseEn 85; WhoProB 73*

Camnitz, Howie (Samuel Howard)
"Red"
American. Baseball Player
b. Aug 22, 1881 in Covington, Kentucky
d. Mar 2, 1960 in Louisville, Kentucky
Source: *BaseEn 85; BioIn 5*

Camoes, Luis de
[Luis de Camoens]
Portuguese. Poet, Author
Best known work, epic poem *Os Lusiadas,*
1572.
b. 1524 in Lisbon, Portugal
d. 1580 in Lisbon, Portugal
Source: *AtlBL; BbD; BiD&SB; CasWL;
CyWA; DcBiA; DcBiPP; DcCathB; DcEuL;
Dis&D; EuAu; EvEuW; LinLib L, S;
McGEWB; NewC; OxEng; OxThe; PenC
EUR; RComWL; REn; WhDW; WorAl*

Camp, Hamilton
English. Actor
b. Oct 30, 1934 in England
Source: *WhoHol A*

Camp, Walter Chauncey
"Father of American Football"
American. Author, Football Executive
Developed rules for modern day football; co-
founded Ivy League.
b. Apr 7, 1859 in New Haven, Connecticut
d. Mar 14, 1925 in New York, New York
Source: *AmAu&B; AmBi; AmLY; BiD&SB;
ChhPo; DcAmAu; DcNAA; JBA 34, 51;
NatCAB 21; OxAmH; REnAL; WebAB 79;
WhAm 1; WhNAA; WhoFtbl 74; WorAl*

Campagnolo, Gitullio
"Campy"
Italian. Manufacturer
Patented 182 mechanical devices; founded
Campagnolo Co., 1933, most respected
name in cycledom.
b. 1901 in Italy
d. Feb 1982 in Monselice, Italy
Source: *BioIn 12*

Campana, Dino
Italian. Poet
Only verse published during lifetime *Orphic Songs,* 1914.
b. Aug 20, 1885 in Marradi, Italy
d. Mar 11, 1932 in Florence, Italy
Source: *CasWL; CIDMEL; ConAu 117; WorAu*

Campanella, Joseph Mario
American. Actor
Star of TV series "The Lawyers," 1969-72.
b. Nov 21, 1927 in New York, New York
Source: *BiE&WWA; FilmgC; NotNAT; WhoAm 78, 80, 82; WhoHol A*

Campanella, Roy
American. Baseball Player
Catcher, Brooklyn Dodgers, 1948-57; paralyzed in car accident, 1958; Hall of Fame, 1969.
b. Nov 19, 1921 in Homestead, Pennsylvania
Source: *BaseEn 85; CelR; CurBio 53; WhoAm 74; WhoBlA 75; WhoProB 73*

Campanella, Tommaso
[Domenico Giovanni]
Italian. Philosopher, Poet, Author
Wrote *Civitas Solis,* 1623, his idea of Utopian society.
b. Sep 5, 1568 in Stilo, Italy
d. May 21, 1639 in Paris, France
Source: *BbD; BiD&SB; CasWL; DcAmSR; DcBiPP; DcCathB; DcEuL; DcItL; DcScB S1; Dis&D; EncSF; EuAu; EvEuW; LuthC 75; McGEWB; PenC EUR; REn*

Campaneris, Bert (Dagoberto Blanco)
"Campy"
Cuban. Baseball Player
Shortstop, 1964-81; led AL in stolen bases six times.
b. Mar 9, 1942 in Pueblo Nuevo, Cuba
Source: *BaseEn 85; WhoProB 73*

Campbell, Clarence Sutherland
Canadian. Hockey Executive
Pres., of NHL, 1946-77; oversaw league's expansion.
b. Jul 9, 1905 in Fleming, Saskatchewan
d. Jun 24, 1984 in Montreal, Quebec
Source: *BlueB 76; CanWW 70, 79, 80, 81; WhoAm 74, 76, 78, 80, 82; WhoHcky 73*

Campbell, Clifford, Sir
English. Government Official
Governor-general of Jamaica, 1962-73.
b. Jun 28, 1892 in Petersfield, England
Source: *InB&W 80; IntWW 77, 78, 79, 80, 81, 82; IntYB 78, 79, 80, 82; Who 74, 82; WhoGov 77, 72; WhoWor 74*

Campbell, Donald Fraser
English. Engineer
b. 1881
d. 1966
Source: *BioIn 7*

Campbell, Donald Guy
American. Journalist, Author
b. Jun 27, 1922 in Brownsburg, Idaho
Source: *ConAu 17R; IndAu 1917; WhoAm 74, 76, 78, 80, 82*

Campbell, Donald Malcolm
English. Auto Racer, Boat Racer
b. Mar 23, 1921 in Surrey, England
d. Jan 4, 1967 in Coniston, England
Source: *ObitT 1961; Who 74; WhoGov 72; WhoWor 74*

Campbell, Douglas
Scottish. Actor
Starred in London's Old Vic, Canada's Stratford theaters; organized Canadian Players.
b. Jun 11, 1922 in Glasgow, Scotland
Source: *BiE&WWA; CnThe; CreCan 1; NotNAT; WhoAm 74, 76, 78; WhoThe 72, 77, 81*

Campbell, E Simms
American. Cartoonist
b. Jan 2, 1906 in Saint Louis, Missouri
d. Jan 27, 1971
Source: *BioIn 6, 7, 8, 9; ConAu 93; CurBio 41, 71*

Campbell, Earl Christian
American. Football Player
Won Heisman Trophy, 1977; running back, 1978-85; leading rusher in NFL three times.
b. Mar 29, 1955 in Tyler, Texas
Source: *BioIn 11; WhoAm 82; WhoBlA 80; WorAl*

Campbell, Glen Travis
American. Singer, Musician
Country-pop singer with 12 gold, seven platinum albums; number one singles "Rhinestone Cowboy," 1975; "Southern Nights," 1977.
b. Apr 22, 1938 in Delight, Arkansas
Source: *BioNews 74; BkPepl; CelR; CurBio 69; EncFCWM 69; FilmgC; IntMPA 75, 76, 77, 78, 79, 80, 81, 82; WhoAm 74, 76, 78, 80, 82; WhoHol A; WhoWest 74, 76; WorAl*

Campbell, Gordon Thomas
British. Politician
b. Jun 8, 1921
Source: *IntWW 74; Who 74; WhoWor 78*

Campbell, John W
American. Author, Editor
Science fiction books include *Invaders from the Infinite*, 1961.
b. Jun 8, 1910 in Newark, New Jersey
d. Jul 11, 1971 in Mountainside, New Jersey
Source: *ConAu 21R, 29R, P-2; WorAu*

Campbell, Joseph
American. Manufacturer, Businessman
Started canning business, 1869; introduced condensed soup, 1898.
b. 1817
d. 1900
Source: *Entr*

Campbell, Malcolm, Sir
English. Auto Racer, Boat Racer
First to attain speed of 150 mph on land, 1925.
b. Mar 11, 1885 in Chislehurst, England
d. Jan 1, 1949
Source: *CurBio 47, 49; EncSoA; WhDW; WhE&EA*

Campbell, Mrs. Patrick
[Beatrice Stella Tanner]
English. Actress
Shaw wrote Eliza Doolittle role in *Pygmalion* especially for her.
b. Feb 9, 1865 in London, England
d. Apr 9, 1940 in Pau, France
Source: *CnThe; CurBio 40; EncWT; FamA&A; FilmgC; InWom; LinLib S; LongCTC; NewC; NotNAT A, B; OxCan; OxFilm; OxThe; PIP&P; REn; ThFT; WhAm 1; WhScrn 74, 77; WhThe; Who 74; WhoHol B; WhoStg 1908; WorAl*

Campbell, Roy
English. Author, Journalist
War correspondent, who wrote autobiography *Light on a Dark Horse*, 1951.
b. Oct 2, 1901 in Durban, South Africa
d. Apr 22, 1957 in Setubal, Portugal
Source: *CathA 1930; CnE&AP; CnMWL; ConAu 104; DcCathB; EncSoA; EncWL 2; LinLib L; LongCEL; LongCTC; ModBrL, S1; ModCmwL; ObitT 1951; OxEng; PenC ENG; REn; TwCA, SUP; TwCWr; WebE&AL; WhDW; WhE&EA; WhoTwCL*

Campbell, Thomas
Scottish. Poet
Known for patriotic war song, "Ye Mariners of England," 1800; wrote *Pleasures of Hope*, 1799.
b. Aug 27, 1777 in Glasgow, Scotland
d. Jun 15, 1844 in Boulogne, France
Source: *Alli; BbD; BiD&SB; BiDLA; BrAu 19; CasWL; CelCen; ChhPo, S1, S2, S3; CrtT 2; DcBiPP; DcEnA AP; DcEnL; DcEuL; DcLEL; EvLB; LinLib L, S; MouLC 3; NewC; OxAmL,; OxEng; PenC ENG; PoChrch; REn; WebE&AL*

Campbell, Walter Stanley
[Stanley Vestal, pseud.]
American. Author
Books on southwestern frontier include *Sitting Bull*, 1928.
b. Aug 15, 1887 in Severy, Kansas
d. Dec 1957
Source: *AmAu&B; CnDAL; OxAmL; REn; REnAL; TwCA, SUP; WhAm 3; WhNAA*

Campbell, William Edward March
[William March, pseud.]
American. Author
Wrote *The Bad Seed*, 1954; dramatized by Maxwell Anderson, 1955.
b. Sep 18, 1893 in Mobile, Alabama
d. May 15, 1954 in New Orleans, Louisiana
Source: *AmAu&B; AmNov X; CnDAL; ConAmA; LongCTC; ModAL; OxAmL; REn; REnAL; TwCA SUP*

Campbell, William Wallace
American. Astronomer
Director, Lick Observatory, 1901-30; made seven eclipse expeditions.
b. Apr 11, 1862 in Hancock County, Ohio
d. Jun 14, 1938 in San Francisco, California
Source: *DcAmB S2; WebBD 80*

Campion, Thomas
English. Poet, Critic, Musician
b. Feb 12, 1567 in London, England
d. Mar 1, 1620 in London, England
Source: *Alli; AtlBL; Baker 78; BbD; BiD&SB; BrAu; CasWL; Chambr 1; ChhPo, S1, S2; CnE&AP; CroE&S; CrtT 4; DcEnL; DcEuL; DcLEL; Dis&D; EvLB; LinLib L; LongCEL; NewC; OxEng; OxMus; OxThe; PenC ENG; RAdv 1; REn; WebE&AL*

Campo, John(ny)
"The Fat Man"
American. Horse Trainer
Colorful trainer of 1981 Derby, Preakness
  winner "Pleasant Colony."
b. 1938 in New York, New York
Source: *BioIn 9, 11; NewYTBS 81; PseudN
82*

Campora, Hector Jose
Argentine. Political Leader
Peronist, who resigned presidency after seven
  wks. allowing Peron's return to power,
  1973.
b. Mar 26, 1909 in Mercedes, Argentina
d. Dec 19, 1980 in Mexico City, Mexico
Source: *AnObit 1980; BioIn 9, 10, 11; CurBio
73, 81, 81N; EncLatA; NewYTBE 73;
NewYTBS 80; WhoWor 74*

Camus, Albert
[Bauchart; Albert Mathe, pseuds.; Saetone,
  joint pseud.]
French. Author, Philosopher
Proponent of absurdism philosophy; major
  novel *L'Etranger,* 1942.
b. Nov 7, 1913 in Mondovi, Algiers
d. Jan 4, 1960 in Sens, France
Source: *CasWL; ClDMEL; CnMD; CnMWL;
CnThe; ConAu 89; ConLC 1, 2, 4, 9, 11, 14;
CroCD; CyWA; EncWL 2; EncWT; EvEuW;
LinLib L, S; LongCTC; MakMC; McGEWB;
McGEWD; ModFrL; ModRL; ModWD;
Novels; OxEng; OxFr; OxThe; PenC EUR;
RComWL; REn; REnWD; TwCA SUP;
TwCWr; WhDW; WhAm 3; WhoTwCL;
WorAl*

Camus, Marcel
French. Director
Won Oscar, 1958, for *Black Orpheus.*
b. Apr 21, 1912 in Chappes, France
d. Jan 13, 1982 in Paris, France
Source: *DcFM; FilmgC; OxFilm; WorEFlm*

Canaday, John (Edwin John)
[Matthew Head, pseud.]
American. Art Critic, Author
Controversial NY *Times* art news editor,
  1959-77; wrote classic text *Mainstreams of
  Modern Art,* 1959.
b. Feb 1, 1907 in Fort Scott, Kansas
d. Jul 19, 1985 in New York, New York
Source: *AmAu&B; CelR; ConAu 13R; CurBio
62, 85; DrAS 74H; EncMys; NewYTBE 72;
St&PR 75; WhAm 8; WhoAm 74; WhoAmA
73; WhoE 74; WhoWest 74; WorAu*

Canaletto, Antonio
[Giovanni Canal]
Italian. Artist
Widely imitated painter of atmospheric
  Venetian scenes.
b. Oct 18, 1697 in Venice, Italy
d. Apr 20, 1768 in Venice, Italy
Source: *AtlBL; REn*

Canaris, Wilhelm
German. Admiral, Spy
Director of German military intelligence;
  killed in plot against Hitler.
b. Jan 1, 1887 in Aplerbeck, Germany
d. Apr 9, 1945 in Flossenburg, Germany
Source: *BioIn 10; EncE 75; EncTR;
HisEWW; NewCol 75; ObitOF 79; OxShips;
WhoMilH 76*

Canary, David
American. Actor
Played Candy on TV series "Bonanza," 1967-
  70; won Emmy for role as Adam/Stuart
  Chandler on "All My Children," 1986.
b. 1938 in Elwood, Indiana
Source: *HalFC 84; WhoHol A*

Canby, Henry Seidel
American. Editor, Critic, Educator
Edited *Saturday Review of Literature,* 1924-
  36; wrote *Walt Whitman,* 1943.
b. Sep 6, 1878 in Wilmington, Delaware
d. Apr 5, 1961 in Ossining, New York
Source: *AmAu&B; AmLY; CnDAL; ConAmA;
ConAmL; ConAu 89; CurBio 42, 61; DcLEL;
LongCTC; OxAmL; REn; REnAL; TwCA,
SUP; WhAm 4; WhNAA*

Canby, Vincent
American. Journalist, Critic
NY *Times* film critic, 1969--.
b. Jul 27, 1924 in Chicago, Illinois
Source: *ConAu 81; ConLC 13; IntMPA 82;
WhoAm 82*

Candela, Felix (Outerino Felix)
Spanish. Architect, Engineer
b. Jan 27, 1910 in Madrid, Spain
Source: *BioIn 10, 11; EncMA; IntWW 74,
75, 76, 77, 78; McGDA; WhoAm 74, 76, 78;
WhoArch; WhoS&SW 73, 75; WhoWor 74, 76*

Candler, Asa Griggs
American. Philanthropist, Manufacturer
Bought Coca-Cola formula, 1887; retired as
  Coke pres., 1916.
b. Dec 30, 1851 in Villa Rica, Georgia
d. Mar 12, 1929 in Atlanta, Georgia
Source: *NatCAB 7, 31; WebAB; WhAm 1*

Candler, Charles Howard
American. Business Executive
Pres., original Coca-Cola Co., 1916-19.
b. Dec 2, 1878 in Atlanta, Georgia
d. Oct 1, 1957 in Atlanta, Georgia
Source: *BioIn 4, 6; NatCAB 46; ObitOF 79; WhAm 3*

Candy, John
Canadian. Actor, Comedian
Films include *Splash,* 1984; *Summer Rental,* 1985; *Brewster's Millions,* 1985.
b. Oct 31, 1950
Source: *VarWW 85*

Canetti, Elias
Bulgarian. Author
Works include novel *Auto-da-Fe,* 1935; nonfiction *Crowds and Power,* 1960; won Nobel Prize, 1981.
b. Jul 25, 1905 in Ruschuk, Bulgaria
Source: *CasWL; CnMD; CnMWL; ConAu 21R; ConLC 3, 14; CroCD; CurBio 83; EncWT; ModGL; NewYTBS 81; OxGer; PenC EUR; WhoWor 74; WorAu*

Canfield, Cass
American. Publisher
Spent entire career at Harper & Row, 1929-86; wrote biographies of Pierpont Morgan, Jefferson Davis.
b. Apr 26, 1897 in New York, New York
d. Mar 27, 1986 in New York, New York
Source: *AmAu&B; BiE&WWA; ConAu 41R; CurBio 54, 86; NewYTBE 71; Who 74; WhoAm 74, 76, 78, 80, 82; WrDr 76*

Canfield, Dorothea Frances
see: Fisher, Dorothy Frances Canfield

Canfield, Francis X(avier)
American. Priest, Educator, Editor, Author
Pres., American Friends of the Vatican Library, 1981--; wrote *With Eyes of Faith,* 1984.
b. Dec 3, 1920 in Detroit, Michigan
Source: *WhoAm 84; WhoRel 85*

Canfield, James Hulme
American. Educator, Librarian
b. Mar 18, 1847 in Delaware County, Delaware
d. Mar 29, 1909
Source: *Alli SUP; DcAmAu; DcNAA; OhA&B*

Canham, Erwin Dain
American. Newspaper Editor, Journalist
Editor, *Christian Science Monitor,* 1945-79.
b. Feb 3, 1904 in Auburn, Maine
d. Jan 3, 1982 in Agana, Guam
Source: *AmAu&B; BlueB 76; CelR; ConAu P-1; CurBio 45, 60, 82; EncAB 23; IntWW 80; IntYB 79; LinLib L; NewYTBS 82; Who 82; WhoAm 74, 76, 78, 80*

Caniff, Milt(on Arthur)
American. Cartoonist
His two popular comic strips, "Terry and the Pirates," "Steve Canyon," 1934-73.
b. Feb 28, 1907 in Hillsboro, Ohio
Source: *AuNews 1; ConAu 85; CurBio 44; OhA&B; REnAL; WebAB; WhoAm 82; WhoAmA 73; WhoWor 78*

Caniglia, Maria
Italian. Opera Singer
b. May 5, 1905 in Naples, Italy
d. Apr 15, 1979 in Rome, Italy
Source: *InWom; WhoMus 72*

Cann, Howard Goodsell
American. Basketball Player, Basketball Coach
Coached at NYU, 1924-58; had 409-232 win-loss record.
b. Oct 11, 1895 in Bridgeport, Connecticut
Source: *BioIn 9; WhoBbl 73*

Cannell, Stephen J
American. Producer, Writer
Creator, producer of many TV shows: "Rockford Files"; "A- Team."
b. Feb 5, 1943 in Los Angeles, California
Source: *LesBEnT; WhoAm 80, 82, 84; WhoWest 82, 84; WhoWor 80, 82*

Canning, George
English. Statesman, Orator
Prime minister, Apr, 1827, foreign secretary, 1807-09, 1822; founded *Anti-Jacobin* journal, 1791.
b. Apr 11, 1770 in London, England
d. Aug 8, 1827 in London, England
Source: *Alli; BiD&SB; BrAu 19; CasWL; ChhPo; DcEnL; DcEuL; DcLEL; EvLB; NewC; OxEng; PoIre; WhAm HS*

Cannizzaro, Stanislao
Italian. Chemist
Devised method of deducing atomic weights of elements based on molecular weight.
b. Jul 13, 1826 in Palermo, Sicily
d. May 10, 1910 in Rome, Italy
Source: *AsBiEn; DcScB; InSci; LinLib S; NewCol 75; WhDW*

Cannon, Annie Jump
American. Astronomer
Developed system of spectral classification at
    Harvard Observatory.
b. Dec 11, 1863 in Dover, Delaware
d. Apr 13, 1941 in Cambridge, Massachusetts
Source: *BiCAW; CurBio 41; DcAmB S3;
    DcScB; InSci; InWom; LibW; LinLib S;
    NotAW; ObitOF 79; OxAmH; WebAB, 79;
    WhAm 1; WomWWA 14; WorAl*

Cannon, Dyan
[Samille Diane Friesen]
"Frosty"
American. Actress
Former wife of Cary Grant, mother of his
    only child, Jennifer.
b. Jan 4, 1938 in Tacoma, Washington
Source: *FilmgC; IntMPA 82; MovMk;
    WhoAm 84; WhoHol A*

Cannon, Howard Walter
American. Politician
Conservative Dem. senator from NV, 1958-
    82.
b. Jan 26, 1912 in Saint George, Utah
Source: *AlmAP 78, 80; BiDrAC; BioNews 75;
    CngDr 74, 77, 79; CurBio 60; IntWW 75, 77,
    78; NewYTBE 73; PolProf E, J, K, NF;
    WhoAm 76, 78, 80, 82, 84; WhoAmP 73, 75,
    77, 79; WhoGov 77, 72, 75; WhoWest 74, 76,
    78*

Cannon, James W
American. Merchant
First towel manufacturer to put name on
    product, 1894.
b. Apr 25, 1852 in Mecklenburg County,
    North Carolina
d. Dec 19, 1921 in Concord, North Carolina
Source: *BiDAmBL 83; Entr; NatCAB 33*

Cannon, Jimmy (James J)
American. Journalist
b. Apr 10, 1909 in New York, New York
d. Dec 5, 1973 in New York, New York
Source: *REnAL; WhAm 6*

Cannon, Joseph Gurney
"Uncle Joe"
American. Congressman
b. May 7, 1836 in New Garden, North
    Carolina
d. Nov 12, 1926
Source: *AmBi; BiDrAC; DcAmB; EncAB-H;
    WebAB; WhAm 1; WhAmP*

Cannon, Poppy
[Mrs. Walter White]
American. Home Economist, Journalist
Food editor for magazines including *Ladies
    Home Journal; Mademoiselle* ; author of
    cookbooks including *The Fast Gourmet
    Cookbook,* 1964.
b. 1907 in Capetown, South Africa
d. Apr 2, 1975 in New York, New York
Source: *ConAu 57, 65; ForWC 70; InWom;
    WhoAmW 70*

Cannon, Walter Bradford
American. Physiologist
b. Oct 19, 1871 in Prairie Chien, Wisconsin
d. Oct 1, 1945
Source: *BioIn 1, 2, 7, 9, 10; CurBio 45;
    DcNAA; WhNAA*

Canova, Antonio
Italian. Artist
b. Nov 1, 1757 in Passagno, Italy
d. Oct 13, 1822 in Venice, Italy
Source: *AtlBL; BioIn 4, 5, 6, 8, 9, 11*

Canova, Diana
[Diana Canova Rivero]
American. Actress
Star of TV series "Soap."
b. Jun 2, 1953 in West Palm Beach, Florida
Source: *BioIn 11, 12; VarWW 85*

Canova, Judy
American. Singer, Actress, Comedienne
Mother of actress Diana Canova; NBC radio
    program "Judy Canova Show."
b. Nov 20, 1916 in Jacksonville, Florida
d. Aug 5, 1983 in Hollywood, California
Source: *FilmgC; ForWC 70; InWom; IntMPA
    76, 77, 78, 79, 80, 81, 82; MotPP; MovMk;
    WhAm 8; WhoAm 82; WhoHol A*

Canseco, Jose
Cuban. Baseball Player
Outfielder, Oakland, 1985--.
b. Jul 2, 1964 in Havana, Cuba
Source: *BaseReg 86*

Cantacuzene, Princess
[Julia Dent Grant]
American. Author
Granddaughter of U S Grant; author of
    *Revolutionary Days; Russian People; My
    Life - Here and There.*
b. Jun 7, 1876 in Washington, District of
    Columbia
d. Oct 5, 1975 in Washington, District of
    Columbia
Source: *AmAu&B; ConAu 61; WhNAA*

Cantinflas
[Mario Moreno]
Mexican. Actor, Comedian
Won Oscar, 1957, for *Around the World in
    80 Days.*
b. Aug 12, 1911 in Mexico City, Mexico
Source: *CurBio 53; EncLatA; FilmgC; MotPP;
    MovMk; OxFilm; WhoHol A; WhoWor 74*

Cantor, Charles
American. Radio Actor
b. 1898
d. Sep 11, 1966 in Hollywood, California
Source: *WhScrn 74, 77; WhoHol B*

Cantor, Eddie
[Edward Israel Itskowitz]
"Izzie"
American. Comedian, Singer
Starred on Broadway in *The Ziegfield Follies;*
    won special Oscar, 1956.
b. Jan 31, 1892 in New York, New York
d. Oct 10, 1964 in Beverly Hills, California
Source: *AmSCAP 66; BiE&WWA; CurBio 41,
    54, 65; EncMT; FilmgC; MotPP; MovMk;
    OxFilm; PIP&P; TwYS; WebAB; WhAm 4;
    WhScrn 74, 77; WhoHol B; WorEFlm*

Cantor, Georg
German. Mathematician
b. 1845 in Saint Petersburg, Russia
d. 1918
Source: *NewCol 75; WebBD 80*

Cantrell, Lana
Australian. Singer, Actress
b. Aug 7, 1943 in Sydney, Australia
Source: *CelR; WhoAm 82*

Cantrick, Robert
American. Educator
b. Dec 8, 1917 in Monroe, Michigan
Source: *WhoAm 74; WhoE 74*

Cantwell, Robert Emmett
American. Author, Editor
Novelist, magazine contributor; on editorial
    staff of *Newsweek, Sports Illustrated,* 1956-
    73.
b. Jan 31, 1908 in Little Falls, Washington
d. Dec 8, 1978 in New York, New York
Source: *AmAu&B; Au&Wr 71; ConAu 4NR,
    5R, 81; ConNov 72, 76; NewYTBS 78;
    OxAmL; REnAL; TwCA, SUP; TwCWr;
    WhAm 7; WhE&EA; WhoAm 74, 76, 78;
    WhoE 74; WrDr 76*

Canute
English. King
b. 995
d. Nov 12, 1035 in Shaftesbury, England
Source: *NewC; REn*

Canutt, Yakima (Enos Edward)
American. Stuntman, Actor
Cowboy film star, 1920s, who did own
    stunts, later doubled for other stars; won
    special Oscar, 1966, for creating profession
    of stuntman.
b. Nov 29, 1895 in Colfax, Washington
d. May 25, 1986 in Los Angeles, California
Source: *CmMov; FilmEn; Film 2; FilmgC;
    IntMPA 82, 84; OxFilm; TwYS; WhoHol A;
    WorEFlm*

Canzoneri, Tony
American. Boxer
b. Nov 6, 1908 in Slidel, Louisiana
d. Dec 9, 1959 in New York, New York
Source: *BioIn 5; WhoBox 74*

Capa, Cornell
American. Journalist, Photographer
b. Apr 19, 1918 in Budapest, Hungary
Source: *BioIn 10; WhoAm 82*

Capa, Robert
[Andrei Friedmann]
American. Photographer
First war photographer to get dramatic close-
    ups of action; photographs in *Images of
    War,* 1964.
b. 1913 in Budapest, Hungary
d. May 25, 1954 in Hanoi, Vietnam
Source: *ConPhot; MacBEP; WhDW; WhAm 4*

Capablanca, Jose Raoul
Cuban. Chess Player
b. 1888 in Havana, Cuba
d. 1942
Source: *NewCol 75*

Capaldi, Jim
[Traffic]
English. Singer, Musician
Drummer for Traffic, 1967-71; had solo hit
    single "Living on the Edge," 1983.
b. Aug 24, 1944 in Evesham, England
Source: *RkOn 78; WhoRock 81*

Cape, Herbert Jonathan
English. Publisher
Founded Jonathan Cape, Inc., 1921.
b. Nov 15, 1879 in London, England
d. Feb 10, 1960 in London, England
Source: *DcNaB 1951; GrBr; WhE&EA*

Capehart, Homer Earl
American. Senator
b. Jun 6, 1897 in Algiers, Indiana
d. Sep 3, 1979 in Indianapolis, Indiana
Source: *BiDrAC; BioIn 1, 3, 6, 9, 11; CurBio 47, 79; IntWW 74; NewYTBS 79; PolProf E, K, T; WhoAm 74, 76, 78*

Capek, Karel
Czech. Author
b. Jan 9, 1890 in Bohemia
d. Dec 24, 1938
Source: *CasWL; ClDMEL; CnMD; CnThe; CyWA; EncWL; EvEuW; LongCTC; McGEWD; ModSL 2; ModWD; OxThe; PenC EUR; REn; REnWD; TwCA, SUP; TwCWr; WhoTwCL*

Capero, Virginia
American. Actress
Films include *Lady Sings the Blues,* 1972; won Tony for *Raisin,* 1974.
b. Sep 22, in Sumter, South Carolina
Source: *VarWW 85*

Capezio, Salvatore
American. Designer
Designer of ballet slippers, 1887.
Source: *WorFshn*

Caples, John
American. Advertising Executive, Author
b. May 1, 1900 in New York, New York
Source: *AmAu&B; ConAu 21R; WhoAdv 72; WhoAm 74, 76, 78, 80, 82*

Capone, Al(phonse)
"Scarface Al"
American. Gangster
Dominated Chicago crime scene, gang warfare, 1920s; implicated in St. Valentine's Day massacre, 1929.
b. Jan 17, 1899 in Brooklyn, New York
d. Jan 25, 1947 in Miami Beach, Florida
Source: *DcAmB S4; FilmgC; OxFilm; WebAB*

Capone, Teresa
Italian. Celebrity Relative
Mother of Al Capone.
b. 1867 in Italy
d. Nov 29, 1952 in Chicago, Illinois
Source: *BioIn 10; ObitOF 79*

Caponi, Donna
[Donna Caponi Young]
American. Golfer
Won US Open 1969-70, LPGA 1979-80; third woman to exceed $ one million in prize money, 1981.
b. Jan 29, 1945 in Detroit, Michigan
Source: *NewYTBS 81; WhoGolf*

Capote, Truman
American. Author
Wrote *Breakfast at Tiffany's* filmed, 1961; *In Cold Blood* filmed, 1968.
b. Sep 30, 1924 in New Orleans, Louisiana
d. Aug 25, 1984 in Los Angeles, California
Source: *AmAu&B; AmNov; AmSCAP 66; Au&Wr 71; BiE&WWA; BkPepl; CasWL; CnDAL; CnMD; ConAu 5R; ConLC 1, 3, 8, 13; ConNov 72, 76; CurBio 51, 68; DrAF 76; EncWL; FilmgC; IntWW 74; LongCTC; ModAL, S1; ModWD; NewYTBE 71; NotNAT; OxAmL; OxFilm; PenC AM; RAdv 1; REn; REnAL; TwCA SUP; TwCWr; WebAB; WebE&AL; Who 82; WhoAm 74, 76, 78, 80, 82; WhoHol A; WhoTwCL; WhoWor 78; WrDr 80*

Capp, Al
[Alfred Gerald Caplin]
American. Cartoonist
Created "Li'l Abner," 1934-77; syndicated in over 900 newspapers.
b. Sep 28, 1909 in New Haven, Connecticut
d. Nov 5, 1979 in Cambridge, Massachusetts
Source: *AmAu&B; ConAu 57, 89; CurBio 47, 80; IntAu&W 77; IntWW 74, 75, 76, 77, 78, 79; LinLib L; NewYTBS 79; REnAL; WebAB, 79; WhoAm 74, 76, 74; WhoWor 74; WorAl; WorECom*

Cappeletti, "Duke" (Gino)
American. Football Player
b. Mar 26, 1934 in Keewatin, Minnesota
Source: *WhoFtbl 74*

Cappelletti, John Raymond
American. Football Player
Won Heisman Trophy, 1973; TV movie *Something for Joey* about cancer-stricken brother.
b. Aug 9, 1952 in Philadelphia, Pennsylvania
Source: *WhoAm 80, 82; WhoFtbl 74*

Capper, Arthur
American. Editor, Publisher, Politician
b. Jul 14, 1865 in Garnett, Kansas
d. Dec 19, 1951 in Topeka, Kansas
Source: *AmAu&B; BiDrAC; CurBio 46, 52; DcAmB S5; WhAm 3; WhAmP; WhNAA*

Capra, Frank
American. Director, Producer
Won Oscars for *It Happened One Night, Mr. Deeds Goes to Town;* known for folksy, sentimental style.
b. May 18, 1897 in Palermo, Italy
Source: *BiDFilm; BlueB 76; CelR; CmCal; ConAu 61; ConLC 16; CurBio 48; DcFM; FilmgC; IntMPA 82; IntWW 81; MovMk; NewYTBE 71; OxFilm; REnAL; TwYS A; WebAB 79; Who 82; WhoAm 82; WhoWest 74; WhoWor 78; WorAl; WorEFlm*

Capshaw, Kate
[Kathy Sue Nail]
American. Actress
Starred in *Indiana Jones and the Temple of Doom,* 1984.
b. in Fort Worth, Texas
Source: *ConTFT 2; VarWW 85*

Captain and Tennille, The
[Daryl Dragon; Toni Tennille]
American. Music Group
Won Grammy, 1975, for "Love Will Keep Us Together."
Source: *BkPepl; RkOn 74*

Captein, Jacques Eliza Jean
African. Clergyman
b. 1745
Source: *BioIn 1, 6, 8*

Capucci, Roberto
Italian. Fashion Designer
Source: *WorFshn*

Capucine
[Germaine Lefebvre]
French. Actress
b. Jan 6, 1935 in Toulon, France
Source: *FilmgC; IntMPA 77, 78, 79, 80, 81, 82; MotPP; MovMk; WhoAmW 74, 68, 70, 72; WhoHol A*

Caputo, Philip Joseph
American. Author, Journalist
Wrote *Rumor of War,* memoir of Vietnam; won Pulitzer, 1972.
b. Jan 10, 1941 in Chicago, Illinois
Source: *ConAu 73; NewYTBS 81; WhoAm 74, 76, 78, 80, 82*

Cara, Irene
American. Actress, Singer
Starred in movie *Fame,* 1980; sang Oscar-winning song; theme from *Flashdance.*
b. Mar 18, 1959 in Bronx, New York
Source: *DrBlPA*

Caracalla, Marcus Aurelius Antonius
Roman. Emperor
b. Apr 4, 186
d. Apr 8, 217
Source: *NewCol 75; WebBD 80*

Caramanlis, Constantinos
see: Karamanlis, Constantine

Caravaggio, Michelangelo da
[Michelangelo Merisi]
Italian. Artist
b. Sep 8, 1569 in Caravaggio, Italy
d. Jul 18, 1609
Source: *AtlBL; McGEWB; REn*

Carawan, Guy
American. Singer, Songwriter
b. Jul 28, 1927 in Los Angeles, California
Source: *ConAu 17R; EncFCWM 69*

Caraway, Hattie Wyatt
American. Politician
First woman elected to Senate, 1932; represented Arkansas, 1932-45.
b. Feb 1, 1878 in Bakerville, Tennessee
d. Dec 21, 1950 in Falls Church, Virginia
Source: *BiDrAC; CurBio 45, 51; DcAmB S4; InWom; NotAW; WhAm 3; WhAmP*

Carazo (Odio), Rodrigo
Costa Rican. Statesman, Economist
President, 1978-82, who ousted long-ruling National Liberation Party.
b. Dec 27, 1926 in Cartago, Costa Rica
Source: *IntWW 78, 79, 80, 81, 82; IntYB 79, 80, 81, 82; WhoWor 78; WorAl*

Carbine, Patricia Theresa
American. Journalist
Publisher, editor-in-chief, *Ms* magazine, 1972--
b. Jan 31, 1931 in Villanova, Pennsylvania
Source: *CelR; ConAu 107; ForWC 70; WhoAm 80, 82, 84; WhoAmW 81, 83*

Cardano, Cirolamo
Italian. Philosopher
b. 1501
d. 1576
Source: *BioIn 1, 2, 3, 5, 6, 8; REn*

Cardenas, Lazaro
Mexican. President
b. May 21, 1895 in Jiquilpan, Mexico
d. Oct 19, 1970 in Mexico City, Mexico
Source: *NewYTBE 70; WhAm 5*

Carder, Frederick
English. Manufacturer
Co-founded Steuben Glass Works, 1903, to
make ornamental glass.
b. 1863 in Brockmoor, England
d. 1963
Source: *BnEnAmA; DcNiCA; IlDcG; ObitOF
79; OxDecA*

Cardigan, Earl
British. General
b. 1797
d. 1868
Source: *Alli SUP*

Cardin, Pierre
French. Fashion Designer
Founded fashion house, 1949; purchased
Paris restaurant, Maxim's, 1981.
b. Jul 7, 1922 in Venice, Italy
Source: *BkPepl; CelR; CurBio 65; IntWW 74;
WhoAm 74, 76, 78, 80, 82; WhoWor 78;
WorFshn*

Cardinale, Claudia
Italian. Actress
Appeared in over 40 films, including *The
Pink Panther,* 1963.
b. Apr 15, 1938 in Tunis, Italy
Source: *BiDFilm; FilmgC; IntMPA 75, 76,
77, 78, 79, 80, 81, 82; IntWW 74; MotPP;
MovMk; OxFilm; WhoHol A; WhoWor 78;
WorEFlm*

Cardozo, Benjamin Nathan
American. Supreme Court Justice
b. May 24, 1870 in New York, New York
d. Jul 9, 1938 in Port Chester, New York
Source: *AmAu&B; AmBi; DcAmB S2;
DcLEL; DcNAA; EncAB-H; OxAmL; REn;
REnAL; WebAB; WhAm 1; WhNAA*

Cardozo, Francis Louis
American. Educator
b. 1837
d. 1903
Source: *BioIn 10*

Carducci, Giosue
Italian. Poet, Critic
Won Nobel Prize for literature, 1906; notable
poems include "Barbaric Odes," "Hymn to
Satan," "Rime."
b. Jul 27, 1835 in Val di Castello, Italy
d. Feb 16, 1907 in Bologna, Italy
Source: *BbD; BiD&SB; CasWL; ClDMEL;
CyWA; DcEuL; DcItL; EuAu; EvEuW;
LinLib L, S; LongCTC; McGEWB; NewC;
OxEng; PenC EUR; RComWL; REn; WhDW;
WhLit; WhoTwCL; WorAl*

Cardus, Neville, Sir
English. Author
Music critic for *Guardian,* 1927-74; authority
on cricket.
b. Apr 2, 1889 in Manchester, England
d. Feb 28, 1975 in London, England
Source: *Au&Wr 71; Baker 78; ConAu 11NR,
57, 61; DcLEL; GrBr; LongCTC; NewYTBS
75; OxMus; WhLit; Who 74; WhoMus 72*

Carestini, Giovanni
Italian. Opera Singer
b. 1705 in Filottrano, Italy
d. 1760 in Filottrano, Italy
Source: *NewEOp 71*

Carew, Rod(ney Cline)
American. Baseball Player
Infielder, 1967-86; won seven batting titles;
had .328 career batting average, over 3,000
hits.
b. Oct 1, 1945 in Gatun, Panama
Source: *BaseEn 85; BaseReg 86; NewYTBS
74; WhoAm 74, 76, 78, 80, 82; WhoProB 73*

Carew, Thomas
English. Poet
First of Cavalier poets; influenced by Donne
and Jonson.
b. 1595 in West Wickham, England
d. 1639
Source: *Alli; AtlBL; BbD; BiD&SB; BrAu;
CasWL; Chambr 1; ChhPo; CnE&AP;
CroE&S; CrtT 1; DcEnA AP; DcEnL;
DcEuL; DcLEL; EvLB; MouLC 1; NewC;
OxEng; PenC ENG; REn; WebE&AL*

Carey, Ernestine Muller Gilbreth
[Mrs. Charles E Carey]
American. Author, Lecturer
b. Apr 5, 1908 in New York, New York
Source: *Au&Wr 71; BioIn 1, 2; ConAu 5R;
ConLC 17; CurBio 49; SmATA 2; WhoAm
74, 76, 78, 80, 82; WhoAmW 74; WhoWor
78; WrDr 76*

Carey, Harry
[Henry Dewitt Carey, II]
American. Actor
Appeared in 26 westerns for John Ford as
"Cheyenne Harry."
b. Jan 16, 1878 in New York, New York
d. Sep 21, 1947 in Brentwood, California
Source: *CmMov; FilmEn; Film 1, 2; FilmgC;
MovMk; NotNAT B; ObitOF 79; TwYS; Vers
A; WhScrn 74, 77; WhoAm 80; WhoHol B;
WorEFlm*

Carey, Henry
English. Composer, Poet
b. 1687 in England
d. Oct 4, 1743 in London, England
Source: *BiD&SB; BioIn 3; BrAu; CasWL;
DcEnL; DcLEL; EvLB; NewC; OxEng; PenC
ENG; REn*

Carey, Hugh Leo
American. Politician
Dem. governor of NY, 1974-81; prevented
default by selling bonds.
b. Apr 11, 1919 in Brooklyn, New York
Source: *CngDr 74; CurBio 65; NewYTBS 74;
WhoAm 74, 76, 78, 80, 82; WhoAmP 73;
WhoE 74; WhoGov 75*

Carey, MacDonald (Edward Macdonald)
American. Actor
Plays Tom Horton in TV soap opera "Days
of our Lives," 1965-- .
b. Mar 15, 1914 in Sioux City, Iowa
Source: *BiE&WWA; FilmgC; HolP 40;
IntMPA 75, 76, 77, 78, 79, 80, 81, 82;
MotPP; MovMk; WhoAm 82; WhoHol A*

Carey, Max George
[Maximilian Carnarius]
"Scoops"
American. Baseball Player
Outfielder, 1910-29; led NL in stolen bases
10 times; Hall of Fame, 1961.
b. Jan 11, 1890 in Terre Haute, Indiana
d. May 30, 1976 in Miami Beach, Florida
Source: *BaseEn 85; BioIn 1, 3, 6, 7, 10;
WhoProB 73*

Carey, Phil(ip)
American. Actor
TV series: "Laredo," 1965-67; "Philip
Marlowe," 1959-60; "One Life to Live,"
1982--.
b. Jul 15, 1925 in Hackensack, New Jersey
Source: *FilmgC; IntMPA 75, 76, 77, 78, 79,
80, 81, 82; MotPP*

Carfagno, Edward
Designer
Production designs include *Pale Rider*, 1985;
won Oscar for *Ben Hur*, 1959.
Source: *VarWW 85*

Cariou, Len (Leonard)
Canadian. Actor, Singer, Director
Won Tony, 1979, for *Sweeney Todd*.
b. Sep 30, 1939 in Saint Boniface, Manitoba
Source: *ConTFT 3; NotNAT; WhoAm 84;
WhoThe 81*

Carl Gustaf XVI
[Carl Gustaf Folke Hubertus]
Swedish. King
Ascended to throne, Sep 19, 1973, as world's
youngest reigning monarch.
b. Apr 30, 1946 in Stockholm, Sweden
Source: *BioIn 10; CurBio 74; IntWW 74;
WhoWor 78*

Carle, Eric
American. Artist, Illustrator
b. Jun 25, 1929 in Syracuse, New York
Source: *ChhPo S2; ConAu 25R; IlsBYP;
SmATA 4; WhoE 74*

Carle, Frankie
American. Pianist, Composer
b. Mar 25, 1903 in Providence, Rhode Island
Source: *AmSCAP 66; WhoHol A*

Carle, Richard
American. Actor
Stage, silent film actor.
b. Jul 7, 1876 in Somerville, Massachusetts
d. Jun 28, 1941 in North Hollywood,
California
Source: *AmAu&B; CmpEPM; CurBio 41;
FilmEn; Film 2; FilmgC; MovMk; NotNAT B;
ObitOF 79; TwYS; Vers A; WhAm 1; WhScrn
74, 77; WhoHol B; WhoStg 1906, 1908*

Carleton, Will
American. Poet, Journalist, Lecturer
Best known for poems on rural life,
including "Farm Legends," 1875.
b. Oct 21, 1845 in Hudson, Michigan
d. Dec 18, 1912 in Brooklyn, New York
Source: *Alli SUP; AmAu; AmAu&B; AmBi;
ApCAB; BbD; BiD&SB; ChhPo, S1, S2; CyAL
2; DcAmB; DcNAA; EvLB; OxAmL; REnAL;
TwCBDA; WhAm 1*

Carlile, Richard
English. Journalist, Reformer
b. 1790 in Devonshire, England
d. 1843 in London, England
Source: *BioIn 11; BrAu; NewC; NewCol 75;
WebBD 80*

Carlin, George Dennis
American. Comedian
Created characters Biff Burns, sportscaster;
Al Sleet, weatherman.
b. May 12, 1937 in New York, New York
Source: *BioIn 7, 10, 11; BioNews 75; BkPepl;
CurBio 76; WhoHol A*

Carlino, Lewis John
American. Dramatist
b. Jan 1, 1932 in New York, New York
Source: *ConAu 77; ConDr 73, 77, 82; CurBio
83; IntMPA 75, 76, 77, 78, 79, 80, 81, 82;
NewYTET; NotNAT; WrDr 76*

Carlisle, Belinda
[The Go-Go's]
American. Singer
Lead singer for Go-Go's since 1978.
b. Aug 17, 1958 in Hollywood, California
Source: *NF*

Carlisle, John Griffin
American. Government Official
b. Sep 5, 1835 in Kenton County, Kentucky
d. Jul 31, 1910
Source: *BioIn 7, 10*

Carlisle, Kevin
American. Director, Producer, Choreographer
Int'l. concert, TV, stage work includes
several Barry Manilow specials.
b. Dec 24, 1935 in Brooklyn, New York
Source: *ConTFT 2*

Carlisle, Kitty
[Katherine Conn; Mrs. Moss Hart]
American. Actress, Singer
Panelist, TV series "To Tell the Truth,"
1956-67.
b. Sep 3, 1915 in New Orleans, Louisiana
Source: *BiE&WWA; CelR; ConTFT 3; CurBio
82; EncMT; FilmgC; InWom; NotNAT;
ThFT; WhoHol A; WhoThe 77*

Carlisle, Mary
American. Actress
Brief screen career, retired in early 1940s.
b. Feb 3, 1912 in Boston, Massachusetts
Source: *BioIn 9; FilmEn; FilmgC; MotPP;
MovMk; ThFT; WhoHol A*

Carlisle, William
American. Criminal
b. 1890
Source: *BioIn 1, 6*

Carlos
[Ilitch Ramirez Sanchez]
"The Jackel"
Venezuelan. Terrorist, Murderer
Most-wanted man in world, 1981; linked to
Red Brigade, Khadafi, etc.
b. 1947 in Venezuela
Source: *BioIn 10, 11; PseudN 82*

Carlos, Bun E
see: Cheap Trick

Carlos, John
American. Track Athlete
b. Jun 5, 1945 in New York, New York
Source: *BioIn 9, 10, 11; WhoTr&F 73*

Carlota
[Charlotte; Marie Charlotte A V C]
Belgian. Empress
Wife of Maximilian, empress of Mexico,
1864-67; went insane after realizing failure
of husband's cause, 1866.
b. 1840 in Brussels, Belgium
d. 1927 in Belgium
Source: *REn; WebBD 80*

Carlson, Chester
American. Inventor, Physicist
Invented photocopying process called
xerography, 1940; Xerox made first
machine, 1959.
b. Feb 8, 1906 in Seattle, Washington
d. Sep 19, 1968 in New York, New York
Source: *ConAu 73; EncAB-H; IntMPA 78;
MovMk; NewYTBS 77; ObitOF 79; WebAB;
WhAm 5; WhoHol A; WhoThe 81N*

Carlson, "Doc" (Harold Clifford)
American. Physician, Basketball Coach
b. Jul 4, 1894 in Murray City, Ohio
d. Nov 1, 1964
Source: *BioIn 7, 9; WhoBbl 73*

Carlson, Earl
American. Physician
b. 1897
Source: *BioIn 3, 8*

Carlson, Edward Elmer
American. Businessman
Chm. of board, United Airlines, 1979--.
b. Jun 4, 1911 in Tacoma, Washington
Source: *IntWW 74; St&PR 75; WhoAm 82,
84; WhoF&I 74; WhoMW 74*

Carlson, Evans Fordyce
American. Soldier
Led commando force "Carlson's Raiders";
   battle cry was "Gung Ho," during WW
   II.
b. Feb 26, 1896 in Sidney, New York
d. May 27, 1947 in Mount Hood, Oregon
Source: *CurBio 43, 47; DcAmB S4; DcNAA;
WhAm 2*

Carlson, Richard
American. Actor
In TV series "I Led Three Lives," 1953;
   "Mackenzie's Raiders," 1958.
b. Apr 29, 1912 in Albert Lea, Minnesota
d. Nov 25, 1977 in Encino, California
Source: *FilmgC; IntMPA 77; MotPP; MovMk*

Carlson, Wally (Wallace A)
American. Cartoonist
b. 1894
d. 1969
Source: *WorECom*

Carlson, William Hugh
American. Author, Librarian
Wrote on library planning: *In a Grand and
   Awful Time,* 1967.
b. Sep 5, 1898 in Waverly, Nebraska
Source: *BiDrLUS 70; ConAu 21R, P-2;
WhoCon 73; WhoPNW*

Carlton, Larry Eugene
[The Crusaders]
American. Musician
Guitarist with Crusaders since 1973; several
   solo albums including *Sleepwalk,* 1982.
b. 1948 in Torrance, California
Source: *EncJzS 70; IlEncBM 82*

Carlton, Steve(n Norman)
"Lefty"
American. Baseball Player
Pitcher, 1965-86; only ML pitcher to win Cy
   Young award four times; retired after
   4,000th career strikeout.
b. Dec 22, 1944 in Miami, Florida
Source: *BaseEn 85; BaseReg 86; WhoAm 80,
82; WhoProB 73*

Carlucci, Frank Charles, III
American. Government Official, Diplomat
Deputy secretary of defense, 1981-82; deputy
   director, CIA, 1978-81.
b. Oct 18, 1930 in Scranton, Pennsylvania
Source: *CurBio 81; IntWW 81, 82; USBiR
74; WhoAm 82, 84; WhoAmP 81; WhoGov
77; WhoS&SW 73; WhoWor 78*

Carlyle, Randy
Canadian. Hockey Player
Defenseman, 1976--; won Norris Trophy,
   1981.
b. Apr 19, 1954 in Sudbury, Ontario
Source: *HocReg 81*

Carlyle, Thomas
Scottish. Critic, Historian
Influenced by German literature; wrote *The
   French Revolution,* 1837.
b. Dec 4, 1795 in Ecclefechan, Scotland
d. Feb 4, 1881 in London, England
Source: *Alli, SUP; AtlBL; BbD; BiD&SB;
BrAu 19; CasWL; ChhPo, S1, S2; CrtT 3;
CyWA; DcEnA; DcEnL; DcEuL; DcLEL;
EvLB; FamAYP; MouLC 3; NewC; OxEng;
PenC ENG; RAdv 1; RComWL; REn;
WebE&AL*

Carman, (William) Bliss
Canadian. Author, Poet
Popular verse volumes include *Sappho,* 1902;
   Songs from Vagabondia, 1894.
b. Apr 15, 1861 in Fredericton, New
   Brunswick
d. Jun 8, 1929 in New Canaan, Connecticut
Source: *BbD; BiD&SB; CanWr; CasWL;
Chambr 3; CnDAL; ConAmL; CreCan 1;
DcAmAu; DcEnA AP; DcLEL; DcNAA;
EvLB; LongCTC; OxAmL; OxCan; OxEng;
PenC AM, ENG; REn; REnAL; TwCA, SUP;
TwCBDA; WebE&AL; WhAm 1; WhNAA*

Carmen, Eric
[The Raspberries]
American. Singer, Musician
Classical training evident in hit singles "All
   By Myself," 1975, "Never Gonna Fall in
   Love Again," 1975.
b. Aug 11, 1949 in Cleveland, Ohio
Source: *RkOn 74*

Carmer, Carl Lamson
American. Author, Educator
Wrote on history, folklore of upstate NY:
   Listen for a Lonesome Drum, 1936.
b. Oct 16, 1893 in Cortland, New York
d. Sep 11, 1976 in Bronxville, New York
Source: *AmAu&B; Au&Wr 71; AuBYP;
ConAu 4NR, 5R, 69; LinLib L; NewYTBS
76; OxAmL; REn; REnAL; ScF&FL 1, 2;
SmATA 30; Str&VC; TwCA, SUP; WhAm 7;
WhoAm 76; WhoWor 74*

Carmichael, Franklin
[Group of Seven]
Canadian. Artist
Oil landscape painter, who was original
Group of Seven member, 1919.
b. 1890 in Orillia, Ontario
d. Oct 24, 1945 in Toronto, Ontario
Source: *CreCan 2; MacDCB 78; McGDA*

Carmichael, Harold
American. Football Player
b. Sep 22, 1949 in Jacksonville, Florida
Source: *BioIn 11; WhoFtbl 74*

Carmichael, Hoagy (Hoagland Howard)
American. Songwriter
Wrote "Stardust"; "In the Cool, Cool, Cool
of the Evening," 1951; won 1951 Oscar.
b. Nov 22, 1899 in Bloomington, Indiana
d. Dec 27, 1981 in Rancho Mirage,
California
Source: *AmPS; AmSCAP 66, 80; Baker 78;
BiDAmM; BioIn 1, 3, 4, 6, 7, 8, 9; CelR;
CmpEPM; CurBio 41, 82; FilmgC; IndAu
1917; IntMPA 80, 81; MotPP; MovMk;
OxFilm; PseudN 82; WebAB; WhoAm 80;
WhoHol A; WhoMus 72; WhoWor 80;
WorEFlm*

Carmichael, Ian
English. Actor
Played Lord Peter Wimsey in Dorothy
Sayers mysteries on PBS.
b. Jun 18, 1920 in Hull, England
Source: *CmMov; EncMT; FilmgC; IntMPA
81, 82; Who 82N; WhoHol A; WhoThe 77,
81; WorAl*

Carmichael, James Vinson
American. Business Executive, Politician
Led Scripto, Inc., 1947-72; won Dem.
primary for GA governor, 1946, but
county unit system elected Talmadge.
b. Oct 2, 1910 in Smyrna, Georgia
d. Nov 28, 1972 in Marietta, Georgia
Source: *BioIn 7; NewYTBE 72; ObitOF 79;
WhoS&SW 73*

Carmichael, John P
American. Journalist
Sportswriter, Chicago *Daily News;* known for
syndicated column "Barber Shop."
b. 1903
d. Jun 6, 1986 in Chicago, Illinois
Source: *NF*

Carmichael, Stokely
[Kwame Toure]
American. Civil Rights Leader
Responsible for Black Power concept, 1960s.
b. Jun 29, 1941 in Port of Spain, British
West Indies
Source: *AmAu&B; ConAu 57; CurBio 70;
WhoS&SW 82; WhoWor 78*

Carmines, Al
American. Composer
b. Jul 25, 1937 in Hampton, Virginia
Source: *CurBio 72; NotNAT; WhoThe 77*

Carnap, Rudolf
German. Philosopher, Educator
Noted logician, member, Vienna school of
logical positivists, 1920s; wrote *Unity of
Science,* 1934.
b. May 18, 1891 in Wuppertal, Germany
d. Sep 14, 1970 in Santa Monica, California
Source: *AmAu&B; ConAu 29R, P-1;
NewYTBE 70; WebAB; WhAm 5; WorAu*

Carne, Judy
[Joyce A Botterill]
English. Actress, Comedienne
Appeared in TV series "Laugh In," 1968-70;
married briefly to Burt Reynolds.
b. Apr 27, 1939 in Northampton, England
Source: *ConTFT 3; FilmgC; WhoHol A*

Carne, Marcel
French. Director
Worked with screenwriter Jacques Prevert on
Children of Paradise, 1945; *Port of
Shadows,* 1939.
b. Aug 18, 1909 in Paris, France
Source: *BiDFilm; DcFM; FilmEn; FilmgC;
IntWW 74, 77, 78, 79, 80, 81, 82; MovMk;
OxFilm; REn; WhoWor 74; WorEFlm*

Carnegie, Andrew
American. Industrialist
Steel producer who endowed 1,700 libraries,
built Carnegie Hall, NYC, 1891.
b. Nov 25, 1835 in Dunfermline, Scotland
d. Aug 11, 1919 in Lenox, Massachusetts
Source: *AmAu&B; AmBi; ApCAB, X; BbD;
BiD&SB; CivWDc; CyAG; DcAmAu; DcAmB;
DcAmDH; DcAmLiB; DcAmSR; DcNAA;
Dis&D; EncAB-A; EncAB-H; HarEnUS; InSci;
LinLib, L, S; LongCTC; McGEWB; OxAmH;
OxAmL; PenC AM; REn; REnAL; TwCBDA;
WebAB, 79; WhDW; WhAm 1; WorAl*

Carnegie, Dale
American. Author, Lecturer
Wrote *How to Win Friends and Influence People*, 1936; has sold over five million copies.
b. Nov 24, 1888 in Maryville, Missouri
d. Nov 1, 1955 in New York, New York
Source: *CurBio 41, 55; DcAmB S5; LongCTC; PenC AM; REnAL; WebAB; WhAm 3*

Carnegie, Hattie
[Henriette Kannengiser; H C Zanft]
American. Fashion Designer
First internationally famed American couturiere; introduced first fashion collection, 1918.
b. 1889 in Vienna, Austria
d. Feb 22, 1956 in New York, New York
Source: *CurBio 42, 56; InWom; WhAm 3; WorFshn*

Carner, Joanne Gunderson
"The Great Gundy"
American. Golfer
Has won 42 tournaments, earning nearly $2 million; Hall of Fame, 1985.
b. Mar 4, 1939 in Kirkland, Washington
Source: *GoodHs; WhoAm 82, 84; WhoGolf; WorAl*

Carnera, Primo
"Ambling Alp"
American. Boxer
b. Oct 26, 1906 in Sequals, Spain
d. Jun 29, 1967 in Sequals, Spain
Source: *WhScrn 77; WhoBox 74; WhoHol B*

Carnes, Kim
American. Singer, Songwriter
Christy Minstrels alumna who won Grammy, 1981, for "Bette Davis Eyes"; known for deep, raw voice.
b. Jul 20, 1946 in Hollywood, California
Source: *BioIn 12; NewWmR; RkOn 85*

Carnevale, Ben (Bernard L)
American. Basketball Coach
b. Oct 30, 1915 in Raritan, New Jersey
Source: *WhoBbl 73*

Carney, Art
American. Actor
Won Oscar, 1972, for *Harry and Tonto*; won three Emmys for TV series "The Honeymooners."
b. Nov 4, 1918 in Mount Vernon, New York
Source: *BioNews 74; CelR; CurBio 58; FilmgC; IntMPA 81, 82; NotNAT; WhoAm 80, 82; WhoHol A; WhoThe 77; WhoWor 74*

Carney, Don
"Uncle Don"
American. Actor
Star of 1930s children's radio show.
b. 1897
d. Jan 14, 1954 in Miami, Florida
Source: *ObitOF 79; WhScrn 74, 77*

Carney, Harry Howell
American. Jazz Musician
b. Apr 1, 1910 in Boston, Massachusetts
d. Oct 8, 1974 in New York, New York
Source: *NewYTBS 74; WhAm 6; WhScrn 77; WhoAm 74; WhoJazz 72*

Carney, Robert Bostwick
American. Admiral
b. Mar 26, 1895 in Vallejo, California
Source: *CurBio 51; Who 74; WhoS&SW 82*

Carnot, Hippolyte
French. Revolutionary, Statesman
Involved in radical agitation leading to 1848 revolution; son of Lazare Carnot.
b. 1801
d. 1888
Source: *NewCol 75*

Carnot, Lazare Nicolas
"Le Grand Carnot"
French. Revolutionary, Soldier
Military genius of French revolutionary wars; wrote classic text on fortification.
b. May 13, 1753 in Nolay, France
d. 1823 in Magdeburg, Prussia (East)
Source: *BioIn 4, 9; DcBiPP; DcInv; DcScB; Dis&D; LinLib S; McGEWB; NewCol 75; WhoMilH 76*

Carnovsky, Morris
American. Actor
Stage, film actor, 1937-51; victim of Hollywood blacklisting, 1951.
b. Sep 5, 1897 in Saint Louis, Missouri
Source: *BiE&WWA; CnThe; FamA&A; FilmgC; IntMPA 75, 76, 77; MotPP; MovMk; NotNAT; PIP&P; WhoAm 74; WhoHol A; WhoThe 72, 77, 81*

Caro, Anthony
English. Sculptor
Known for abstract, complex steel, aluminum sculptures; often painted in primary colors.
b. Mar 8, 1924 in London, England
Source: *ConArt 77; CurBio 81; IntWW 78; McGDA; McGEWB; Who 85; WhoAm 84; WhoWor 78*

Caro, Joseph
Spanish. Scholar
Wrote *Shulhan'Arukh,* 1565, outlining legal
   code for Orthodox Jewery.
b. 1488 in Toledo, Spain
d. Mar 24, 1575
Source: *BioIn 2, 3, 6, 7, 11; CasWL; EuAu;
LuthC 75; McGEWB; OxLaw*

Carol II
Romanian. King
b. 1893 in Sinaia, Romania
d. 1953
Source: *NewCol 75; WebBD 80*

Carol, Martine
[Maryse Mourer]
French. Actress
French sex symbol of early 1950s; films
   include *Beauties of the Night,* 1952;, *Lola
   Montes,* 1955.
b. May 16, 1920 in Paris, France
d. Feb 6, 1967 in Monte Carlo, Monaco
Source: *BiDFilm; FilmgC; InWom; MotPP;
MovMk; OxFilm; WhScrn 74, 77; WhoHol B;
WorEFlm*

Caroline, Princess
[Caroline Louise Marguerite Grimaldi]
Monacan. Princess
Daughter of Princess Grace and Prince
   Rainier of Monaco.
b. Jan 23, 1957 in Monte Carlo, Monaco
Source: *BioIn 10; BkPepl; NewYTBS 75*

Caron, Leslie Clare Margaret
French. Actress, Dancer
Starred with Gene Kelly in *An American in
   Paris,* 1951; other films include *Gigi,* 1958.
b. Jul 1, 1931 in Paris, France
Source: *BiDFilm; CelR; CmMov; CurBio 54;
FilmgC; InWom; IntMPA 82; MotPP;
MovMk; OxFilm; Who 74; WhoAm 84;
WhoHol A; WhoThe 77A; WhoWor 78;
WorEFlm*

Carot, 'Papa'
see: Corot, Jean Baptiste Camille

Carothers, Wallace Hume
American. Chemist
Work in organic chemistry resulted in
   discovery of synthetic rubber, nylon.
b. Apr 27, 1896 in Burlington, Iowa
d. Apr 29, 1937 in Philadelphia,
   Pennsylvania
Source: *DcAmB S2; EncAB-H; WebAB;
WhAm 1*

Carpaccio, Vittore
Italian. Artist
Painted colorful, detailed narrative scenes;
   noted for St. Ursula series.
b. 1465
d. 1525
Source: *AtlBL; REn; WebBD 80*

Carpenter, Bobby
American. Hockey Player
First American-born player to score over 50
   goals in season, 1984-85.
b. Jul 13, 1963 in Beverly, Massachusetts
Source: *HocReg 81; NewYTBS 81*

Carpenter, Edward
English. Poet, Author
Clergyman whose socialist views caused him
   to give up church; wrote *Love's Coming of
   Age,* 1896.
b. Aug 29, 1844 in Brighton, England
d. Jun 28, 1929 in Guildford, England
Source: *Alli SUP; BioIn 2, 9, 10; BrAu 19;
Chambr 3; ChhPo S3; DcAmSR; EvLB;
LinLib L; LongCTC; ModBrL; NewC; PenC
ENG; REn; WhoTwCL*

Carpenter, Francis Bicknell
American. Artist
b. Aug 6, 1830 in Homer, New York
d. May 23, 1900
Source: *AmBi; ApCAB; DcAmB S2; Drake;
NatCAB 11; NewYHSD; TwCBDA; WhAm 1*

Carpenter, John
American. Director
Films include *Halloween,* 1978, *The Fog,*
   1980; married to Adrienne Barbeau.
b. Jan 16, 1948 in Carthage, New York
Source: *Alli; BioIn 11; DcBrWA; IntMPA 82;
Who 74; WhoAm 82; WhoHol A*

Carpenter, John Alden
American. Composer
Used jazz motifs in ballets, orchestral suites:
   "Adventures in a Perambulator," 1915.
b. Feb 28, 1876 in Park Ridge, Illinois
d. Apr 26, 1951 in Chicago, Illinois
Source: *AmSCAP 66; ChhPo S1; CurBio 47,
51; DcAmB S5; OxAmL; WhAm 3*

Carpenter, Karen Ann
[The Carpenters]
American. Singer
At time of death, The Carpenters had sold
   over 80 million records.
b. Mar 2, 1950 in New Haven, Connecticut
d. Feb 4, 1983 in Downey, California
Source: *BkPepl; EncPR&S 74; GoodHs;
NewYTBS 83; WhoAm 82; WhoAmW 81*

Carpenter, Leslie
American. Journalist
b. 1922
d. Jul 24, 1974 in Washington, District of
   Columbia
Source: *WhAm 6; WhoAm 74*

Carpenter, Liz (Elizabeth Sutherland)
American. Journalist
Press secretary, staff director for Lady Bird
   Johnson, 1963-69.
b. Sep 1, 1920 in Salado, Texas
Source: *ConAu 41R; WhoAm 74; WhoAmP
73*

Carpenter, Richard Lynn
[The Carpenters]
American. Singer, Musician, Songwriter
b. Oct 15, 1946 in New Haven, Connecticut
Source: *BioIn 10; BkPepl; EncPR&S 74;
WhoAm 78, 80, 82*

Carpenter, Scott (Malcolm Scott)
American. Astronaut
One of seven original astronauts; orbited
   Earth three times, May, 1962.
b. May 1, 1925 in Boulder, Colorado
Source: *CelR; CurBio 62; IntWW 74;
WhoAm 74; WhoWor 78*

Carpenter, William S, Jr.
American. Football Player, Army Officer
b. Sep 30, 1937 in Springfield, Pennsylvania
Source: *BioIn 7, 8, 9; WhoFtbl 74*

Carpenters, The
[Karen Carpenter; Richard Carpenter]
American. Music Group
Brother-sister team whose hits include "Close
   to You," 1970, "We've Only Just Begun,"
   1971.
Source: *BiDAmM; BkPepl; RkOn 78*

Carpentier, Georges
French. Boxer
b. Jan 12, 1894 in Lens, France
d. Oct 27, 1975 in Paris, France
Source: *WhScrn 77; WhoBox 74*

Carpini, Giovanni de Piano
Italian. Religious Figure, Traveler
Wrote first account of court of Great Khan
   in Mongolia, 1246.
b. 1180 in Pian di Carpine, Italy
d. 1252
Source: *DcCathB; NewCol 75; WhDW*

Carr, Allan
[Allan Solomon]
American. Producer
Co-produced *Grease,* on Broadway, 1977.
b. May 27, 1941 in Chicago, Illinois
Source: *ConTFT 3; WhoAm 82; WhoWest 82*

Carr, Alexander
American. Actor
b. 1878 in Rumni, Russia
d. Sep 19, 1946 in Los Angeles, California
Source: *BioIn 1; CurBio 46; Film 2; NotNAT;
ObitOF 79; WhScrn 74, 77; WhThe; WhoHol
B*

Carr, Austin George
American. Basketball Player
b. Mar 10, 1948 in Washington, District of
   Columbia
Source: *BioIn 9; OfNBA 81*

Carr, Elizabeth Jordan
American. Test Tube Baby
First test tube baby born in US.
b. Dec 28, 1981 in Norfolk, Virginia
Source: *NF*

Carr, Emily
Canadian. Artist, Author
Painted, wrote about British Columbia
   Indians: *Heart of a Peacock,* 1953.
b. Dec 12, 1871 in Victoria, British
   Columbia
d. Mar 2, 1945 in Victoria, British Columbia
Source: *BioIn 1, 2, 3, 5, 7, 8, 9, 10, 11;
CreCan 1; DcLEL 1940; DcNAA; InWom;
LongCTC; MacDCB 78; McGDA; McGEWB;
OxArt; OxCan; PhDcTCA 77; REnAL;
WomArt, A*

Carr, Gerald Paul
American. Astronaut
Commanded third Skylab manned mission,
   1973-74.
b. Aug 22, 1932 in Denver, Colorado
Source: *BioIn 10; WhoAm 82*

Carr, Harold Noflet
American. Businessman
Board chm., Republic Airlines, 1979--.
b. Mar 14, 1921 in Kansas City, Kansas
Source: *AmEA 74; St&PR 75; WhoAm 74,
76, 78, 80, 84; WhoF&I 74; WhoS&SW 73*

Carr, John Dickson
American. Author
Detective, mystery writer; created character
of Dr. Gideon Fell, corpulent sleuth.
b. 1905 in Uniontown, Pennsylvania
d. Feb 27, 1977 in Greenville, South
Carolina
Source: *AmAu&B; Au&Wr 71; ConAu 3NR,
49, 69; ConLC 3; CorpD; DcLEL; EncMys;
EvLB; IntAu&W 76, 77; LongCTC; NewC;
ObitOF 79; PenC ENG; REn; REnAL; TwCA,
SUP; TwCCr&M 80; TwCWr; WhoAm 74;
WhoWor 74*

Carr, Joseph F
American. Football Executive
b. Oct 22, 1880 in Columbus, Ohio
d. May 20, 1939
Source: *BioIn 6, 8; WhoFtbl 74*

Carr, Martin
[Martin Douglas Conovitz]
American. Producer, Director, Writer
TV documentary producer; exec. producer,
"Smithsonian World," 1981--.
b. Jan 20, 1932 in Flushing, New York
Source: *ConTFT 2; VarWW 85*

Carr, Sabin
American. Olympic Athlete
Won gold medal in pole vault, 1928
Olympics; first vaulter to clear 14 feet.
b. 1904
d. Sep 1983 in Ventura, California
Source: *WhoTr&F 73*

Carr, Vikki
[Florencia Bisenta de Casillas]
American. Singer
b. Jul 19, 1941 in El Paso, Texas
Source: *BioIn 10; EncPR&S 74; WhoAm 80,
82*

Carra, Carlo
Italian. Artist
b. 1881
d. 1966
Source: *BioIn 4, 7*

Carracci, Annibale
Italian. Artist
Did first of great baroque ceilings, frescoes of
Farness Palace, 1597-1604.
b. Nov 3, 1560 in Bologna, Italy
d. Jul 15, 1609 in Rome, Italy
Source: *AtlBL; REn*

Carracci, Lodovico
Italian. Artist
Founded, with cousins Agostino and
Annibale, famed art academy, Accademia
degli Incamminati, 1582.
b. Apr 21, 1555 in Bologna, Italy
d. Nov 13, 1619 in Bologna, Italy
Source: *AtlBL*

Carrack, Paul
[Ace; Squezze]
English. Singer, Musician
Original member of Ace, who joined
Squezze, 1981-82.
b. Apr 1951 in Sheffield, England
Source: *NF*

Carradine, David
American. Actor
Son of John Carradine; starred in "Shane,"
1966, "Kung Fu," 1972.
b. Oct 8, 1940 in Hollywood, California
Source: *BkPepl; FilmgC; IntMPA 75, 76, 77,
78, 79, 80, 81, 82; MotPP; NewYTBE 73;
WhoAm 82; WhoHol A*

Carradine, John Richmond
American. Actor
Father of David, Keith, and Robert
Carradine; starred in over 170 films.
b. Feb 5, 1906 in New York, New York
Source: *BiE&WWA; CmMov; FilmgC;
IntMPA 75, 76, 77, 78, 79, 80, 81, 82;
MotPP; MovMk; OxFilm; Vers A; WhoAm 74,
76, 78, 80, 82; WhoHol A; WhoThe 77;
WorEFlm*

Carradine, Keith Ian
American. Actor, Singer
Wrote, sang "I'm Easy," which won Oscar,
1975.
b. Aug 8, 1950 in San Mateo, California
Source: *BkPepl; IntMPA 81, 82; WhoAm 82;
WhoHol A*

Carradine, Robert Reed
American. Actor
Youngest son of John Carradine, half brother
of David, who starred in *The Big Red
One,* 1979.
b. Mar 24, 1954 in Los Angeles, California
Source: *ConTFT 3; FilmEn; IntMPA 85;
VarWW 85; WhoHol A*

Carranza, Venustiano
Mexican. Political Leader
Pres. of Mexico, 1917-20.
b. Dec 29, 1859 in Coahuila, Mexico
d. May 21, 1920 in Tlaxcalantongo, Mexico
Source: *McGEWB; REn*

Carre, Mathilde
"Mata Hari of WW II"
German. Spy
Double agent for Germans; imprisoned 1949-54.
b. 1910
Source: *BioIn 5, 8, 10, 11; EncE 75; WhWW-II*

Carrel, Alexis
American. Biologist, Surgeon
With Charles Lindbergh, invented perfusion pump called artificial heart, 1936.
b. Jun 28, 1873 in Sainte-Foyles, France
d. Nov 5, 1944
Source: *CurBio 40, 44*

Carrera, Barbara
American. Actress
Portrayed Fatima Blush in *Never Say Never Again*, 1983; in TV series "Dallas," 1985--.
b. 1945 in Managua, Nicaragua
Source: *BioIn 11; FilmEn; NewYTBS 77; WhoHol A*

Carreras, Jose
Spanish. Opera Singer
b. Dec 5, 1946 in Barcelona, Spain
Source: *BioIn 9; CurBio 79; NewYTBS 78; WhoAm 82; WhoOp 76*

Carrier, Willis H
American. Inventor
Developed first practical air conditioning process, 1911.
b. Nov 26, 1876 in Angola, New York
d. Oct 7, 1950 in New York, New York
Source: *DcAmB S4; WhAm 3*

Carrier-Belleuse, Albert Ernest
French. Sculptor
Works include "Bacchante;" taught Rodin, 1864-70.
b. 1824
d. 1887
Source: *BioIn 11; WebBD 80*

Carriera, Rosalba
Italian. Artist
Miniature painter, specialist in pastel portraits.
b. 1675 in Venice, Italy
d. 1757 in Venice, Italy
Source: *GoodHs; IntDcWB; McGDA; OxArt; WomArt*

Carriere, Eugene
French. Artist
b. 1849
d. 1906
Source: *BioIn 2, 4, 8, 9, 11; OxFr*

Carrillo, Leo
American. Actor
Played Pancho in *Cisco Kid*, 1951.
b. Aug 6, 1880 in Los Angeles, California
d. Sep 10, 1961 in Santa Monica, California
Source: *Film 2; FilmgC; MotPP; MovMk; NotNAT B; ObitOF 79; WhScrn 77; WhoHol B*

Carrington, Peter Alexander Rupert, Baron
English. Politician
NATO secretary-general, 1984--; foreign secretary, 1979-82; leader, House of Lords opposition party, 1979-82.
b. Jun 6, 1919 in London, England
Source: *IntWW 85; Who 85*

Carritt, David Graham (Hugh David Graham)
British. Art Historian
Discovered various lost Old Master paintings including Caravaggio's "The Musicians."
b. Apr 15, 1927 in England
d. Aug 3, 1982 in London, England
Source: *BioIn 10; NewYTBS 82; Who 82*

Carroll, Anna Ella
American. Author, Pamphleteer
Political writings include *The Great American Battle*, 1856.
b. Aug 29, 1815 in Kingston Hall, Maryland
d. Feb 19, 1893 in Washington, District of Columbia
Source: *DcAmAu; DcNAA; NatCAB 5; NotAW; WebBD 80*

Carroll, Charles
American. Patriot
Member of Continental Congress; signer of Declaration of Independence.
b. Sep 19, 1737 in Annapolis, Maryland
d. Nov 14, 1832 in Baltimore, Maryland
Source: *AmBi; ApCAB; BiAUS; BiDSA; BiDrAC; DcAmB; Drake; TwCBDA; WebAB; WhAm HS; WhAmP*

Carroll, Diahann
[Carol Diahann Johnson]
American. Actress, Singer
First black to star in non-stereotypical TV series, "Julia," 1968-71.
b. Jul 17, 1935 in New York, New York
Source: *BiE&WWA; BioNews 74; BkPepl; CelR; ConTFT 3; CurBio 62; EncMT; FilmgC; InWom; MotPP; NotNAT; WhoAm 84; WhoBlA 75; WhoHol A; WhoWor 78; WomWMM*

Carroll, Earl
American. Producer
Lyricist of over 400 songs; produced "Earl
Carroll Vanities," 1923-36.
b. Sep 16, 1893 in Pittsburgh, Pennsylvania
d. Jun 17, 1948
Source: *AmAu&B; AmSCAP 66; CmpEPM;
DcAmB S4; EncMT; NotNAT B; OxThe;
PIP&P; WhAm 2; WhScrn 77; WhThe*

Carroll, Gladys Hasty
American. Author
Regional novel *As the Earth Turns*, 1933,
translated into 60 languages.
b. Jun 26, 1904 in Rochester, New
Hampshire
Source: *AmAu&B; AmNov; ConAu 1R, 5NR;
ForWC 70; InWom; OxAmL; REnAL; TwCA,
SUP; WhNAA; WhoAm 74, 76, 78, 80, 82;
WhoE 74; WhoWor 78; WrDr 80*

Carroll, Jim
American. Poet, Singer
Rock composer who depicts NYC brutality;
wrote Pulitzer nominee book of verse
Living at the Movies, 1973.
b. Aug 1, 1951 in New York, New York
Source: *ConAu 45; DrAP 75*

Carroll, Joe Barry
American. Basketball Player
Center, Golden State Warriors, 1980--;
member NBA all-rookie team, 1981.
b. Jul 24, 1958 in Denver, Colorado
Source: *BioIn 12; OfNBA 81*

Carroll, John
American. Religious Leader
First Roman Catholic bishop in US; founded
Georgetown, 1789.
b. Jan 8, 1735 in Upper Marlboro, Maryland
d. Dec 3, 1815 in Baltimore, Maryland
Source: *AmAu&B; AmBi; ApCAB; BiDSA;
BioIn 2, 3, 4, 5, 10, 11; DcAmB; DcAmReB;
DcCathB; DcNAA; Drake; EncSoH; HarEnUS;
LuthC 75; McGEWB; NatCAB 1; OxAmH;
TwCBDA; WebAB, 79; WhAm HS; WorAl*

Carroll, Leo G
English. Actor
Played Cosmo Topper in TV series
"Topper," 1953-56; Mr. Waverly in "Man
from Uncle," 1964-68.
b. Oct 18, 1892 in Weedon, England
d. Oct 16, 1972 in Hollywood, California
Source: *BiE&WWA; CmMov; FilmgC; MotPP;
MovMk; NewYTBE 72; NotNAT B; ObitOF
79; Vers A; WhAm 5; WhScrn 77; WhThe;
WhoHol B*

Carroll, Lewis, pseud.
[Charles Lutwidge Dodgson]
English. Author, Mathematician
Wrote *Alice's Adventures in Wonderland*,
1865; *Through the Looking Glass*, 1872.
b. Jan 27, 1832 in Cheshire, England
d. Jan 14, 1898 in Guildford, England
Source: *Alli SUP; AnCL; AtlBL; AuBYP;
BbD; BiD&SB; BrAu 19; CasWL; Chambr 3;
ChlLR 2; ChhPo, S1, S2; CnE&AP; CrtT 3;
CyWA; DcEnA; DcEnL; DcEuL; DcLEL;
EvLB; FamAYP; FilmgC; JBA 34; NewC;
OxEng; PenC ENG; RAdv 1; REn; Str&VC;
WebE&AL; WhoChL*

Carroll, Madeleine
[Marie-Madeline Bernadette O'Carroll]
English. Actress
Films include *39 Steps*, 1935; *Prisoner of
Zenda*, 1937.
b. Feb 26, 1909 in West Bronwich, England
Source: *BiDFilm; BiE&WWA; CurBio 49;
Film 2; FilmgC; IntMPA 81, 82; MotPP;
MovMk; OxFilm; ThFT; WhThe; Who 74, 82;
WhoHol A; WhoThe 77A; WorAl; WorEFlm*

Carroll, Nancy
[Ann Veronica Lattiff]
American. Actress
Oscar nominee for *The Devil's Holiday*, 1930.
b. Nov 19, 1906 in New York, New York
d. Aug 6, 1965 in New York, New York
Source: *CmpEPM; FilmEn; Film 2; FilmgC;
InWom; MotPP; MovMk; NotNAT B; ObitOF
79; ThFT; TwYS; WhScrn 74, 77; WhThe;
WhoHol B; WomWMM; WorAl*

Carroll, Pat(ricia Ann Angela Bridgit)
American. Actress, Comedienne
Won Emmy for "Caesar's Hour," 1956-57;
Tony for *Catch a Star*, 1955.
b. May 5, 1927 in Shreveport, Louisiana
Source: *BiE&WWA; ConTFT 3; CurBio 80;
IntMPA 82; NotNAT B; WhThe; WhoAm 82;
WhoAmW 81*

Carroll, Vinnette (Justine)
American. Actress, Theatrical Producer
Collaborated on musical revues: *Don't Bother
Me, I Can't Cope*, 1970; *Your Arms Too
Short to Box with God*, 1975.
b. Mar 11, 1922 in New York, New York
Source: *BiE&WWA; BioIn 10; BlkAmW 1;
DrBlPA; ForWC 70; InB&W 80; NegAl 83;
NotNAT; WhoAm 82; WhoAmW 74, 70, 72,
75, 77; WhoBlA 77, 80; WhoE 74, 75, 77;
WhoThe 72, 77, 81*

Carruthers, George E
American. Physicist
b. Oct 1, 1940 in Cincinnati, Ohio
Source: *AmM&WS 73P; WhoBlA 75*

Carruthers, John(ny)
Australian. Boxer
b. Jul 5, 1929 in Paddington, Australia
Source: *WhoBox 74*

Cars, The
[Elliot Easton; Greg Hawkes; Ric Ocasek; Ben Orr; David Robinson]
American. Music Group
Pop music quintet, formed by Ric Ocasek, 1978; platinum albums *The Cars,* 1978; *Panorama,* 1980.
Source: *ConMuA 80A; WhoRock 81*

Carsey, Marcia
American. Producer
Sr. vp, all prime time series, ABC, 1979-80; exec. producer, "The Cosby Show," 1984--.
b. Nov 21, 1944 in South Weymouth, Massachusetts
Source: *VarWW 85*

Carson, Edward Henry
British. Judge, Politician
Defended Marquis of Queensberry in Oscar Wilde's libel suit, 1895.
b. 1854 in Dublin, Ireland
d. Oct 22, 1935
Source: *BioIn 2, 3, 10*

Carson, Jack
American. Actor
Teamed with Dennis Morgan in series of 1940s musicals.
b. Oct 27, 1910 in Carman, Manitoba
d. Jan 2, 1963 in Encino, California
Source: *FilmgC; HolP 40; MotPP; MovMk; OxFilm; WhScrn 74, 77; WhoHol B*

Carson, Jeannie
[Jean Shufflebottom]
American. Comedienne, Singer
b. May 28, 1929 in Yorkshire, England
Source: *BiE&WWA; FilmgC; InWom; IntMPA 81, 82; MotPP; WhoHol A; WhoThe 77*

Carson, Johnny
American. TV Host, Entertainer
Host of "The Tonight Show," 1962--.
b. Oct 23, 1925 in Corning, Iowa
Source: *BkPepl; CelR; ConTFT 3; CurBio 82; IntMPA 82; NewYTET; WhoAm 82; WhoE 74; WorAl*

Carson, "Kit" (Christopher)
American. Frontiersman
Brigadier general during Civil War; commanded Ft. Garland, CO, 1866-67.
b. Dec 24, 1809 in Madison County, Kentucky
d. May 23, 1868 in Fort Lyon, Colorado
Source: *AmBi; ApCAB; CmCal; DcAmB; DcCathB; Drake; EncAAH; FilmgC; HarEnUS; LongCTC; McGEWB; MnBBF; NatCAB 3; OxAmL; OxFilm; REn; REnAL; WebAB 79; WebAMB; WhDW; WhAm HS; WorAl*

Carson, Mindy
American. Actress, Singer
b. Jul 16, 1926 in New York, New York
Source: *AmPS B; BiE&WWA; CmpEPM; InWom; WhoAmW 70*

Carson, Rachel Louise
American. Biologist, Author
Wrote *The Sea Around Us,* 1951; *Silent Spring,* 1962.
b. May 27, 1907 in Springdale, Pennsylvania
d. Apr 14, 1964 in Silver Spring, Maryland
Source: *AmAu&B; AmWomWr; AnCL; ConAu 77; CurBio 51, 64; EncAAH; EncAB-A; EncAB-H; EvLB; GoodHs; HerW; InSci; LibW; LinLib L, S; LongCTC; McGEWB; NatCAB 51; NewYTBS 82; NotAW; ObitOF 79; OxAmL; REn; SmATA 23; TwCA SUP; TwCWr; WebAB, 79; WhAm 4; WhoAmW 64*

Carson, Robert
American. Author
Won Oscar for screenplay for *A Star Is Born,* 1937.
b. Oct 6, 1909 in Clayton, Washington
d. Jan 19, 1983 in Los Angeles, California
Source: *AmAu&B; ConAu 108, 21R; WhoAm 82*

Carstens, Karl Walter
German. President
b. Dec 14, 1914 in Bremen, Germany
Source: *CurBio 80; IntWW 74; WhoWor 78*

Carswell, George Harrold
American. Judge
b. Dec 22, 1919 in Irwinton, Georgia
Source: *WhoAm 74; WhoAmP 73*

Carte, Richard d'Oyly
English. Opera Singer
Responsible for bringing composer Arthur
    Sullivan, librettist William Gilbert together,
    1871.
b. May 3, 1844 in London, England
d. Apr 3, 1901 in London, England
Source: *LongCTC; NewCol 75; NotNAT B;
OxThe*

Carter, Amon Giles
American. Publisher
Publisher, Fort Worth *Star-Telegram,* who
    started as newsboy.
b. Dec 11, 1880 in Crafton, Texas
d. Jun 23, 1955
Source: *BioIn 2, 3, 4, 5, 6; WhAm 3*

Carter, Amy
American. Celebrity Relative
Daughter of Jimmy Carter.
b. Oct 19, 1967 in Plains, Georgia
Source: *BioIn 11, 12; GoodHs; InWom;
NewYTBS 76*

Carter, Anthony
American. Football Player
Wide receiver in USFL, 1983-85, with NFL
    Minnesota, 1985--.
b. Sep 17, 1960 in Riviera Beach, Florida
Source: *FootReg 86*

Carter, Benny (Bennett Lester)
American. Jazz Musician
b. Aug 8, 1907 in New York, New York
Source: *AmSCAP 66; BiDAmM; BioIn 9, 10,
11; CmpEPM; DrBIPA; EncJzS 70; IlEncJ;
WhoAm 74, 76, 78, 80; WhoJazz 72*

Carter, Betty
[Lillie Mae Jones]
American. Singer
Jazz singer little known until appearence in
    show *Don't Call Me Man,* 1975.
b. May 16, 1930 in Flint, Michigan
Source: *BiDAfM; BiDAmM; CurBio 82;
DrBIPA; EncJzS 70; InB&W 80; WhoBlA 80*

Carter, Billy
American. Celebrity Relative
Brother of Jimmy Carter.
b. Mar 29, 1937 in Plains, Georgia
Source: *BioIn 11, 12; BkPepl*

Carter, Boake
American. Radio Commentator
Syndicated columnist, radio broadcaster,
    1930s; noted for distinctive voice, tirades
    against New Deal, unionism.
b. Sep 28, 1898 in Baku, Russia
d. Nov 16, 1947 in Hollywood, California
Source: *CurBio 42, 47; DcAmB S3; DcNAA;
WhAm 2; WhScrn 77*

Carter, Carlene
[Mrs. Nick Lowe]
American. Singer, Songwriter
Daughter of June Carter; stepdaughter of
    Johnny Cash.
b. 1957 in Madisonville, Tennessee
Source: *BioIn 11; NewWmR; WhoRock 81*

Carter, Caroline Louise Dudley
American. Actress
Starred in Belasco plays: *DuBarry,* 1901.
b. Jun 10, 1862 in Lexington, Kentucky
d. Nov 13, 1937 in Los Angeles, California
Source: *NotAW; WebBD 80*

Carter, "Chip" (James Earl, III)
American. Celebrity Relative
Son of Jimmy Carter.
b. Apr 12, 1950 in Honolulu, Hawaii
Source: *BioIn 11; PseudN 82; WhoAmP 77,
79, 81*

Carter, Don(ald Jones)
American. Bowler
b. Jul 29, 1926 in Saint Louis, Missouri
Source: *CurBio 63*

Carter, Dorothy Sharp
American. Children's Author
Wrote *Enchanted Orchard and other Folktales
of Central America,* 1973.
b. Mar 22, 1921 in Chicago, Illinois
Source: *BiDrLUS 70; ConAu 49; SmATA 8;
WhoAmW 77*

Carter, Edward William
American. Businessman
b. Jun 29, 1911
Source: *BioIn 2, 8, 9; IntWW 74; LEduc 74;
NewYTBE 71; St&PR 75; WhoAm 84;
WhoWest 74*

Carter, Elliott Cook, Jr.
American. Composer
Awarded Pulitzer in music, 1960, 1973;
    works include "Concerto for Orchestra,"
    1969.
b. Dec 11, 1908 in New York, New York
Source: *CurBio 60; DcCM; IntWW 74; Who
74; WhoAm 82, 84; WhoE 74; WhoMus 72;
WhoWor 74*

Carter, Ernestine Marie
American. Author, Journalist
b. in Washington, DC
Source: *Au&Wr 71; BioIn 9; Who 74; WrDr 76*

Carter, Gary Edmund
American. Baseball Player
Eight-time All-Star who is catcher, Montreal, 1974-84, NY Mets, 1985--.
b. Apr 8, 1954 in Culver City, California
Source: *BaseEn 85; BaseReg 86*

Carter, Hodding (William Hodding, III)
American. Government Official, Editor, Broadcast Journalist
Anchorman, "Inside Story," PBS, 1981--; State dept. spokesman, 1977-80.
b. Apr 7, 1935 in New Orleans, Louisiana
Source: *BioIn 11; CurBio 81; WhoAm 80, 82*

Carter, Howard
English. Archaeologist
Discovered tomb of Tutankhamun, 1922.
b. 1873 in Swaffham, England
d. Mar 2, 1939
Source: *DcBrAr 1; InSci; LongCTC; WhDW*

Carter, "Hurricane" (Rubin)
American. Boxer
Former middleweight contender, jailed for shooting three people in 1967; conviction overturned, 1985.
b. 1937
Source: *NewYTBE 72; NewYTBS 74*

Carter, Jack
[Jack Chakrin]
American. Comedian
b. Jun 24, 1923 in Coney Island, New York
Source: *IntMPA 80, 81, 82; WhoHol A*

Carter, Jack (John William)
American. Celebrity Relative
Son of Jimmy Carter.
b. Jul 3, 1947 in Portsmouth, Virginia
Source: *NF*

Carter, Jeff (Donnel Jeffrey)
American. Celebrity Relative
Youngest son of Jimmy Carter.
b. Aug 18, 1952 in New London, Connecticut
Source: *NewYTBS 81*

Carter, Jimmy (James Earl, Jr.)
American. US President
Initiated human rights campaign in foreign policy; hostage crisis contributed to defeat, 1980.
b. Oct 1, 1924 in Plains, Georgia
Source: *BlueB 76; ConAu 69; CurBio 71; DrRegL 75; IntWW 81; Who 82; WhoAm 84; WhoAmP 73; WhoGov 72; WhoS&SW 73*

Carter, Jimmy (James W)
American. Boxer
b. Dec 15, 1923 in Aiken, South Carolina
Source: *WhoBox 74*

Carter, John Garnet
American. Businessman
Invented miniature golf, 1928.
b. Feb 9, 1883 in Sweetwater, Tennessee
d. Jul 21, 1954 in Lookout Mountain, Tennessee
Source: *BioIn 9; NatCAB 52*

Carter, June
[The Carter Family; Mrs. Johnny Cash]
American. Singer
Married Johnny Cash, 1968; songs include "He Don't Love Me Anymore."
b. Jun 23, 1929 in Maces Spring, Virginia
Source: *EncFCWM 69; WhoAm 82; WhoHol A*

Carter, Katherine Jones
American. Children's Author
Books include *Hoppy Long Legs*, 1963.
b. Feb 25, 1905 in Greenbackville, Virginia
Source: *ConAu 5R; SmATA 2*

Carter, Mrs. Leslie
[Caroline Louise Dudley Carter]
American. Actress
b. Jun 10, 1862 in Lexington, Kentucky
d. Nov 12, 1937 in Los Angeles, California
Source: *AmBi; DcAmB S2; FamA&A; Film 1; FilmgC; InWom; NotAW; NotNAT B; OxThe; PIP&P; TwYS; WhAm 1; WhScrn 74, 77; WhThe; WhoHol B; WhoStg 1906*

Carter, Lillian
[Bessie Lillian Gordy]
"Miss Lillian"
American. Celebrity Relative, Nurse
Mother of Jimmy Carter; joined Peace Corps, served in India at age 68.
b. Aug 15, 1898 in Richmond, Georgia
d. Oct 30, 1983 in Americus, Georgia
Source: *BioIn 11; BkPepl; CurBio 84; NewYTBS 83; WhoAmW 79*

Carter, Lynda
American. Actress, Singer
Starred in TV series "Wonder Woman,"
1977-79.
b. Jul 24, 1951 in Phoenix, Arizona
Source: *BioIn 11; IntMPA 82; WhoAm 80, 82*

Carter, "Mother" Maybelle
[The Carter Family]
American. Singer, Songwriter
Grand Ole Opry star 1950-67; formed Carter
family, 1927, with brother, sister-in-law.
b. May 10, 1909 in Nickelsville, Virginia
d. Oct 23, 1978 in Nashville, Tennessee
Source: *BioIn 9, 11; EncFCWM 69*

Carter, Nell
[Nell Hardy]
American. Actress, Singer
Appeared on stage in *Ain't Misbehavin';* plays
Nell Harper on TV show "Gimme a
Break," 1981--.
b. Sep 13, 1948 in Birmingham, Alabama
Source: *ConTFT 3*

Carter, Rosalynn Eleanor Smith
[Mrs. Jimmy Carter]
American. First Lady
Wrote memoirs in *First Lady from Plains,*
1984.
b. Aug 18, 1927 in Plains, Georgia
Source: *BioIn 11; BkPepl; CurBio 78;
GoodHs; NewYTBS 76, 77, 78, 79; WhoAm
78, 80, 82; WhoAmW 77, 79, 81; WhoE 77,
79; WhoS&SW 78, 82; WhoWor 78, 80;
WorAl*

Carter, Wilf
"Montana Slim"
Canadian. Singer
b. Dec 12, 1904 in Port Hilford, Nova
Scotia
Source: *EncFCWM 69*

Carter, William
American. Manufacturer
Manufactured infant wear, knit underwear,
beginning 1878.
b. 1830 in Derbyshire, England
d. 1918
Source: *Entr; NatCAB 31*

Carter Family, The
[A P Carter; Anita Carter; Helen Carter;
June Carter; Maybelle Carter]
American. Music Group
Source: *EncFCWM 69*

Cartier, Claude
American. Jeweler
b. 1925
d. 1975
Source: *BioIn 10*

Cartier, Georges Etienne, Sir
Canadian. Statesman, Lawyer
Joint prime minister of Canada with John
MacDonald, 1858-62.
b. Sep 6, 1814
d. May 20, 1873
Source: *BioIn 9, 11*

Cartier, Jacques
French. Navigator, Explorer
Discovered St. Lawrence River, 1535, and
Montreal.
b. Dec 31, 1491 in Saint Malo, France
d. Sep 1, 1557 in Saint Malo, France
Source: *ApCAB; BioIn 1, 2, 4, 5, 6, 8, 9, 11;
Drake; McGEWB; OxCan; OxFr; REn;
REnAL; WhAm HS*

Cartier, Pierre C
American. Jeweler
b. 1878 in France
d. 1964
Source: *BioIn 7*

Cartier-Bresson, Henri
French. Photographer
Black and white photographer known for
brilliant clarity; published *The Decisive
Moment,* 1952.
b. Aug 22, 1908 in Chanteloup, France
Source: *ConPhot; CurBio 47, 76; DcCAr 81;
DcFM; IntAu&W 77; IntWW 74, 78, 81, 82;
MacBEP; OxFilm; Who 74, 82; WhoWor 74,
76; WorEFlm*

Cartland, Barbara Hamilton
English. Author, Dramatist
Wrote over 250 books; step-grandmother of
Lady Diana of Wales.
b. Jul 9, 1901 in England
Source: *Au&Wr 71; ConAu 9R; LongCTC;
NewYTBE 73; TwCWr; Who 82; WhoAm 82;
WrDr 80*

Cartouche, Louis Dominique
[Louis Dominique Bourguignon]
French. Criminal
Legendary figure; leader of bank robbers.
b. 1693
d. Nov 28, 1721
Source: *BioIn 8; DcBiPP; OxFr*

Cartwright, Alexander Joy, Jr.
"Father of Modern Baseball"
American. Sportsman
Devised rules that made baseball playable;
  organized first recorded baseball game,
  1846; Hall of Fame, 1938.
b. Apr 17, 1820 in New York, New York
d. Jul 12, 1892 in Honolulu, Hawaii
Source: *WhAm HS; WhoProB 73*

Cartwright, Angela
American. Actress
In TV series "Lost in Space," 1965-68;
  "Danny Thomas Show," 1957-64.
b. Sep 9, 1952 in Cheshire, England
Source: *ForWC 70; VarWW 85; WhoHol A*

Cartwright, Bill (James William)
American. Basketball Player
b. Jul 30, 1957 in Lodi, California
Source: *BioIn 10; OfNBA 81*

Cartwright, Edmund
English. Clergyman, Inventor
Developed first power loom, 1785-87.
b. Apr 24, 1743 in Nottinghamshire, England
d. Oct 23, 1823
Source: *Alli; BiDLA; DcEnL*

Cartwright, Veronica
American. Actress
Films include *The Birds,* 1963; *The Right
  Stuff,* 1983.
b. 1950 in Bristol, England
Source: *ConTFT 2; VarWW 85*

Carty, Rico (Ricardo Adolfo Jacobo)
Dominican. Baseball Player
Outfielder, designated hitter, 1963-79; won
  NL batting title, 1970.
b. Sep 1, 1939 in San Pedro de Macoris,
  Dominican Republic
Source: *BaseEn 85; WhoAm 74; WhoProB 73*

Caruso, Enrico
Italian. Opera Singer
Legendary tenor, chief attraction of
  Metropolitan Opera, 1903-20.
b. Feb 25, 1873 in Naples, Italy
d. Aug 2, 1921 in Naples, Italy
Source: *AmBi; ChhPo S1; DcAmB; Film 1;
  FilmgC; NewC; NewYTBE 73; REn; TwYS;
  WhAm 1; WhScrn 74, 77; WhoHol B*

Carvel, Thomas A
Canadian. Businessman
Founded Carvel Corp., 1934; owns over 600
  retail ice cream stores.
b. 1906
Source: *BusPN; NewYTBE 73; NewYTBS 79*

Carver, George Washington
American. Botanist, Chemist, Educator
Agricultural researcher, 1896-1903; discovered
  industrial uses for peanut, sweet potato,
  soybean.
b. Jan 5, 1864 in Diamond Grove, Missouri
d. Jan 5, 1943 in Tuskegee, Alabama
Source: *AfroAA; CurBio 40, 43; DcAmB S3;
  EncAB-H; WebAB; WhAm HSA, 2, 4A*

Carver, John
English. Colonial Leader
First governor of Plymouth Colony, 1620-21.
b. 1576 in Nottinghamshire, England
d. Apr 5, 1621 in Plymouth, Massachusetts
Source: *AmBi; ApCAB; BiDBrA; DcAmB;
  DcBiPP; Drake; HarEnUS; LinLib S; NatCAB
  7; OxAmH; TwCBDA; WhAm HS*

Cary, Alice
American. Author, Poet
First pres. of first women's club, Sorosis;
  writings include *A Book for Young Folks,*
  1867, *The Lover's Diary,* 1868.
b. Apr 26, 1820 in Cincinnati, Ohio
d. Feb 12, 1871 in New York, New York
Source: *Alli SUP; AmAu; AmAu&B; AmBi;
  AmWom; AmWomWr; ApCAB; BbD;
  BiDAmM; BiD&SB; BioIn 5; CarSB; Chambr
  3; CyAL 2; DcAmAu; DcAmB; DcNAA;
  Drake; EvLB; InWom; LibW; LinLib L, S;
  NatCAB 1; NotAW; OhA&B; OxAmL;
  TwCBDA; WebAB, 79; WhAm HS*

Cary, Joyce (Arthur Joyce Lunel)
English. Author
Wrote trilogies *The Horse's Mouth,* 1944;
  Prisoner of Grace, 1952.
b. Dec 7, 1888 in Londonderry, Northern
  Ireland
d. Mar 29, 1957 in Oxford, England
Source: *CasWL; CnMWL; ConNov 76; CurBio
  49, 57; CyWA; DcBiPP; DcIrB; DcIrW 1;
  DcLB 1; DcLEL; EncWL, 2; EvLB; LinLib
  L, S; LongCEL; LongCTC; ModBrL; NewC;
  Novels; ObitOF 79; ObitT 1951; PenC ENG;
  RAdv 1; REn; TwCA SUP; WebE&AL;
  WhAm 3; WhoTwCL*

Cary, Frank Taylor
American. Businessman
IBM, pres., 1971--, chm., 1973--.
b. Dec 14, 1920 in Gooding, Idaho
Source: *BioIn 12; CurBio 80; IntWW 79;
  WhoAm 80, 82*

Cary, Phoebe
American. Poet
Collaborated with sister, Alice, on hymns,
  verse volumes.
b. Sep 4, 1824 in Cincinnati, Ohio
d. Jul 31, 1871 in New York, New York
Source: *Alli SUP; AmAu; AmAu&B; AmBi;
AmWom; AmWomWr; ApCAB; BbD;
BiDAmM; BiD&SB; Chambr 3; ChhPo, S1;
CyAL 2; DcAmAu; DcAmB; DcNAA; Drake;
EvLB; InWom; LibW; LinLib L, S; LuthC
75; NatCAB 1; NotAW; OhA&B; OxAmL, 83;
PenC AM; TwCBDA; WebAB 79; WhAm HS*

Carzou, Jean
French. Artist
Landscape, still-life painter, who uses linear
  style, rich colors.
b. Jan 1, 1907 in Alep, Syria
Source: *WhoWor 74*

Casablancas, John(ny)
American. Business Executive
Opened Manhattan modeling agency, 1977,
  challenging Ford, world's major firm.
b. Dec 12, 1942 in Manhattan, New York
Source: *NF*

Casadesus, Gaby Lhote
French. Musician
b. Aug 9, 1901 in Marseilles, France
Source: *WhoAmW 74*

Casadesus, Jean
French. Musician
b. Jul 7, 1927 in Paris, France
d. Jan 20, 1972 in Renfrew, Ontario
Source: *Baker 78; BiDAmM; BioIn 9*

Casadesus, Robert
French. Musician, Composer
Noted interpreter of Mozart; wrote neoclassic style symphonies.
b. Apr 7, 1899 in Paris, France
d. Sep 19, 1972 in Paris, France
Source: *CurBio 45, 72; NewYTBE 72; WhAm
5; WhoMus 72*

Casady, Jack
[Jefferson Airplane]
American. Musician, Singer
b. Apr 13, 1944 in Washington, District of
  Columbia
Source: *NF*

Casale, Bob
see: Devo

Casale, Jerry
see: Devo

Casals, Pablo (Pau Carlos Salvador)
Spanish. Musician, Composer, Conductor
Modernized playing techniques of cello,
  elevating status to serious solo orchestral
  instrument.
b. Dec 29, 1876 in Vendrell, Spain
d. Oct 22, 1973 in Rio Piedras, Puerto Rico
Source: *AmSCAP 66; ConAu 45, 93; CurBio
50, 64, 73; NewYTBE 73; ObitOF 79; ObitT
1971; OxMus; REn; WhDW; WhAm 6;
WhScrn 77; Who 74; WorAl*

Casals, Rosemary
American. Tennis Player
Won first Virginia Slims Tournament, 1970;
  US Open doubles champ, 1967, 71, 74,
  with Bille Jean King.
b. Sep 16, 1948 in San Francisco, California
Source: *BioNews 74; CurBio 74; GoodHs;
HerW; WhoAm 82; WhoAmW 81*

Casanova (de Seingalt), Giovanni Giacomo
Italian. Author, Adventurer
His bawdy accounts of career as charlatan,
  gambler, lover, *Memories*, 1826-38, were
  published, 1960.
b. Apr 2, 1725 in Venice, Italy
d. Jun 4, 1798 in Dux, Bohemia
Source: *DcBiPP; DcItL; Dis&D; RAdv 1;
REn; WhDW*

Casaubon, Isaac
Theologian, Scholar
Regarded as one of greatest 16th c. classical
  scholars; appointed prebendary of
  Canterbury and Westminster by James I.
b. Feb 8, 1559 in Geneva, Switzerland
d. Jul 1, 1614 in London, England
Source: *BbD; CyEd; DcBiPP; DcEuL; LinLib
L; LuthC 75; NewC; OxEng; OxFr*

Case, Anna
American. Opera Singer, Actress
Metropolitan Opera soprano who sang lead
  in first US production of *Der
  Rosenkavalier*, 1913.
b. 1889 in Clinton, New Jersey
d. Jan 7, 1984 in New York, New York
Source: *BiDAmM; Film 1; WhoHol A*

Case, Clifford Philip
American. Lawyer, Politician
Moderate Rep. senator from NJ, 1955-79,
who sponsored social legislation, Civil
Rights bills.
b. Apr 16, 1904 in Franklin Park, New
Jersey
d. Mar 5, 1982 in Washington, District of
Columbia
Source: *AlmAP 78; BiDrAC; CngDr 74, 77;
CurBio 82; IntWW 80, 81, 82; NewYTBS 82;
PolProf E, J, K, NF; WhoAm 82; WhoAmP
81; WhoE 81; WhoGov 75, 77; WhoWor 80*

Casement, Roger David
Irish. Diplomat
Irish Nationalist, opposed Irish participation
in WW I; hanged for treason by British.
b. Sep 1, 1864 in Dun Laoghaire, Ireland
d. Aug 3, 1916 in London, England
Source: *BioIn 9; DcIrB; DcIrW 2; WhDW;
WorAl*

Casewit, Curtis
American. Author
b. Mar 21, 1922 in Mannheim, Germany
Source: *ConAu 13R; SmATA 4*

Casey, Dan(iel Maurice)
American. Baseball Player
Pitcher, 1884-90; probable inspiration for
Ernest Thayer's poem, "Casey at the Bat."
b. Oct 2, 1965 in Binghamton, New York
d. Feb 8, 1943 in Washington, District of
Columbia
Source: *BaseEn 85; WhoProB 73*

Casey, Edward Pearce
American. Architect
b. Jun 18, 1864 in Portland, Maine
d. Jan 2, 1940
Source: *NatCAB 36; WebBD 80; WhAm 1*

Casey, H(arry) W(ayne)
[K C and the Sunshine Band]
American. Singer, Musician
Lead singer, keyboardist who co-founded
band, 1973; hit single "Shake Your
Booty," 1975.
b. Jan 31, 1951 in Hialeah, Florida
Source: *NF*

Casey, Hugh Thomas
American. Baseball Player
Relief pitching specialist, Brooklyn Dodgers,
1939-49.
b. Oct 14, 1913 in Buckhead, Georgia
d. Jul 3, 1951 in Atlanta, Georgia
Source: *BaseEn 85; BioIn 3, 7; WhoProB 73*

Casey, James E
American. Business Executive
Founded United Parcel Service, 1909; name
changed to UPS, 1917.
b. Mar 29, 1888 in Candelaria, Nevada
d. Jun 6, 1983 in Seattle, Washington
Source: *BioIn 1, 3, 4; NewYTBS 83*

Casey, William Joseph
American. Lawyer, Author
Ronald Reagan's campaign manager, 1980;
director, CIA, 1981--.
b. Mar 13, 1913 in Elmhurst, New York
Source: *CurBio 72; IntWW 74; WhoAm 80,
82*

Cash, Jim
American. Educator, Screenwriter
With Jack Epps, wrote screenplays for 1986
films *Top Gun, Legal Eagles.*
b. 1941
Source: *NF*

Cash, Johnny
[Tennessee Three]
"The Man in Black"
American. Singer, Songwriter
Country-western hit songs include "I Walk
the Line," 1964, "A Boy Named Sue,"
1969.
b. Feb 26, 1932 in Kingsland, Arkansas
Source: *CelR; CurBio 69; EncFCWM 69;
FilmgC; NewYTBE 73; WebAB; WhoAm 80,
82; WhoHol A; WhoS&SW 73*

Cash, Norm(an Dalton)
"Stormin' Norman"
American. Baseball Player
Detroit Tigers first baseman, 1960-74; won
batting title, 1961.
b. Nov 10, 1934 in Justiceburg, Texas
Source: *BaseEn 85; WhoAm 74; WhoProB 73*

Cash, Roseanne
[Mrs. Rodney Crowell]
American. Singer, Celebrity Relative
Country-rock singer, who is daughter of
Johnny Cash; albums include *Seven-Year
Ache,* 1981.
b. May 24, 1955 in Memphis, Tennessee
Source: *BioIn 12; EncFCWM 83; RkOn 85*

Cashen, Frank
American. Baseball Executive
GM, NY Mets; known for wearing bow tie
to all games.
Source: *NewYTBS 84*

Cashin, Bonnie
American. Fashion Designer
Award-winning sportswear designer; started
Bonnie Cashin Designs, 1952.
b. 1915 in Oakland, California
Source: *CurBio 70; InWom; WhoAm 84;
WhoWor 74; WorFshn*

Casimir, Saint
Polish. Religious Figure
b. 1458
d. 1484
Source: *BioIn 6, 7, 9*

Casiraghi, Stefano
Italian. Celebrity Relative
Second husband of Princess Caroline of
Monaco; married Dec 29, 1983.
b. Sep 8, 1960 in Italy
Source: *NF*

Caslon, William
English. Type Designer
Designed English Arabic, 1720, and Caslon
typeface, 1726.
b. Jan 23, 1692 in Cradley, England
d. Jan 23, 1766 in London, England
Source: *NewC*

Caspary, Vera
American. Author, Screenwriter
Wrote mystery novel *Laura*, 1942; made into
film, 1944.
b. Nov 13, 1904 in Chicago, Illinois
Source: *AmAu&B; Au&Wr 71; BiE&WWA;
ConAu 13R; EncMys; LongCTC; REnAL;
TwCA SUP; WrDr 76*

Casper, Billy (William Earl)
American. Golfer
Winner, US Open, 1959, 1966, Masters,
1970.
b. Jun 24, 1931 in San Diego, California
Source: *CelR; CurBio 66; WhoAm 80, 82;
WhoGolf*

Cass, Lewis
American. Statesman
Governor of MI Territory, 1813-31;
unsuccessful Dem. presidential candidate,
1848; secretary of state, 1857-60.
b. Oct 9, 1782 in Exeter, New Hampshire
d. Jun 17, 1866 in Detroit, Michigan
Source: *Alli; AmAu&B; AmBi; ApCAB;
BiAUS; BiD&SB; BiDrAC; BiDrUSE; CyAL 1;
DcAmAu; DcAmB; DcNAA; Drake; EncAB-H;
OhA&B; TwCBDA; WebAB; WhAm HS;
WhAmP*

Cass, Peggy
[Mary Margaret Cass]
American. Actress
Won Tony for *Auntie Mame*, 1956; panelist
on "To Tell the Truth."
b. May 21, 1925 in Boston, Massachusetts
Source: *BiE&WWA; CelR; ConTFT 3;
InWom; MotPP; NotNAT; WhoHol A;
WhoThe 77*

Cassady, Neal
American. Author
One of people most responsible for Beat
Generation; writings consisted chiefly of
letters to friends.
b. Feb 8, 1926 in Salt Lake City, Utah
d. Feb 4, 1968 in San Miguel de Allende,
Mexico
Source: *BioIn 11*

Cassandra
see: Connor, Sir William Neil

Cassandre, A(dolphe) M(ouron)
French. Artist, Type Designer
Noted for posters, modern typefaces.
b. Jan 24, 1909 in Kharkov, Russia
d. 1968
Source: *WhoGrA 62*

Cassatt, Mary
American. Artist
Noted for paintings of mother and child;
friend of Degas.
b. May 22, 1844 in Allegheny, Pennsylvania
d. Jun 14, 1926 in Paris, France
Source: *AmBi; ArtsNiC; AtlBL; BnEnAmA;
DcAmArt; DcAmB; EncAB-A; EncAB-H;
GoodHs; HerW; LibW; McGEWB; NatCAB
33; NotAW; OxAmH; OxAmL; OxArt; REn;
WebAB, 79; WhAm 1; WomArt, A;
WomWWA 14; WorAl*

Cassavetes, John
American. Actor, Director
Starred in *Rosemary's Baby*, 1976; married to
actress Gena Rowlands.
b. Dec 9, 1929 in New York, New York
Source: *BiDFilm; CelR; ConAu 85; ConTFT
3; CurBio 69; DcFM; FilmgC; IntMPA 82;
IntWW 74; MotPP; MovMk; OxFilm; WhoAm
82; WhoHol A; WhoWor 78; WorAl;
WorEFlm*

Cassidy, Butch
[George Leroy Parker]
American. Outlaw
Subject of hit film *Butch Cassidy and the Sundance Kid,* 1969.
b. Apr 6, 1867 in Circleville, Utah
d. 1912
Source: *BioIn 10; Blood&B*

Cassidy, Claudia
American. Critic
Chicago performing arts critic; writes monthly "On the Aisle" column, 1974--.
b. 1900 in Shawneetown, Illinois
Source: *AmAu&B; BiE&WWA; CelR,; ConAmTC; CurBio 55; InWom; NotNAT; WhoAm 74, 76, 78, 80, 84; WhoAmW 58, 64, 66, 70*

Cassidy, David Bruce
American. Singer, Actor
Son of Jack Cassidy; starred in TV series "The Partridge Family," 1970-74.
b. Apr 12, 1950 in New York, New York
Source: *CelR; WhoAm 82*

Cassidy, Harold Gomes
American. Chemist, Educator, Author
b. Oct 17, 1906 in Havana, Cuba
Source: *AmM&WS 73P; ConAu 25R; WhoAm 82*

Cassidy, Hopalong
see: Boyd, William

Cassidy, Jack
American. Actor, Singer, Dancer
Won Tony for *She Loves Me,* 1964; Shirley Jones was second wife.
b. Mar 5, 1927 in New York, New York
d. Dec 12, 1976 in West Hollywood, California
Source: *BiE&WWA; BioNews 74; EncMT; FilmgC; NewYTBS 76; NotNAT; ObitOF 79; WhoHol A; WhoThe 77, 81N; WorAl*

Cassidy, Joanna
[Joanna Virginia Caskey]
American. Actress
Movies include *Blade Runner; Under Fire* ; TV series "Buffalo Bill."
b. Aug 2, 1984 in Camden, New Jersey
Source: *VarWW 85; WhoHol A*

Cassidy, Marshall
American. Jockey
b. 1892
d. 1968
Source: *BioIn 8*

Cassidy, Shaun Paul
American. Singer, Actor
Starred in TV series "Hardy Boys Mysteries," 1977-79.
b. Sep 27, 1958 in Los Angeles, California
Source: *BkPepl; ConTFT 3; VarWW 85; WhoAm 82*

Cassill, R(onald) V(erlin)
American. Author
Award-winning short stories include *The Prize,* 1968.
b. May 17, 1919 in Cedar Falls, Iowa
Source: *ConLC 4; WhoAm 80, 82*

Cassin, Rene
French. Judge
Awarded Nobel Peace Prize, 1969; pres., UN Human Rights commission, 1946-68.
b. Oct 5, 1887 in Bayonne, France
d. Feb 20, 1976 in Paris, France
Source: *ConAu X; IntWW 74, 75, 76N; NewYTBS 76; ObitOF 79; WhAm 6; Who 74; WhoWor 74, 74, 78; WhoWorJ 72; WorAl*

Cassini, Igor Loiewski
American. Journalist
b. 1913
Source: *BioIn 6*

Cassini, Oleg Lolewski
French. Fashion Designer
Official White House designer for Jacqueline Kennedy, 1961-63.
b. Apr 11, 1913 in Paris, France
Source: *CelR; CurBio 61; WhoAm 74, 76, 78, 80, 82; WhoWor 78; WorFshn*

Cassirer, Ernst
German. Philosopher
Wrote neo-Kantian texts of cultural, scientific value: *Myth of the State,* 1946.
b. Jul 28, 1874 in Breslau, Prussia
d. Apr 13, 1945 in New York, New York
Source: *DcNAA; PenC EUR; TwCA SUP; WhAm 4; WhoLA*

Cassius
[Caius Cassius Longinus]
"The Last of the Romans"
Roman. General, Politician
Led conspiracy to murder Caesar, 44BC.
d. 42 BC
Source: *LinLib S; NewCol 75; PseudN 82; REn*

Cassou, Jean
[Jean Noir, pseud.]
French. Author, Critic
Wrote *33 Sonnets Composes au Secret,* 1944,
   while imprisoned during German
   occupation.
b. Jul 9, 1879 in Deusto, France
Source: *CasWL; EncWL; EvEuW; IntAu&W*
76; IntWW 74, 76, 77, 78, 79, 80, 81, 82;
WhoWor 74

Castagna, Bruna
[Andrea di Bartolo]
Italian. Opera Singer
b. Oct 15, 1908 in Bari, Italy
Source: *InWom; WebBD 80*

Castagno, Andrea del
[Andrea di Bartolo]
Italian. Artist
Influenced by Massacchio; frescoes include
   portraits of noted Italians and "Last
   Supper."
b. 1423 in Castagno, Italy
d. Aug 19, 1457 in Florence, Italy
Source: *AtlBL; WebBD 80*

Castaneda, Carlos
American. Anthropologist, Author
Wrote *Teachings of Don Juan: The Yaqui*
   Way of Knowledge, 1968.
b. Dec 25, 1931 in Sao Paulo, Brazil
Source: *ConAu 25R; NewYTBE 72; WhoAm*
82, 84

Castel, Frederic
French. Designer
Fur designer known for using mink and
   sable in sports coats.
Source: *WorFshn*

Castellano, Richard
American. Actor
Appeared in *The Godfather,* 1972; nominated
   for Oscar, 1970, for *Lovers and Other*
   Strangers.
b. Sep 4, 1934 in New York, New York
Source: *CelR,; FilmgC; IntMPA 81, 82;*
WhoAm 82; WhoHol A; WorAl

Castello Branco, Humberto
Brazilian. Political Leader
Pres. of Brazil, 1964-67.
b. Sep 20, 1900 in Fortaleza, Brazil
d. Jul 18, 1967
Source: *BioIn 6, 7, 8; CurBio 65, 67*

Castellon, Frederico
American. Artist
b. Sep 14, 1914 in Almeria, Spain
d. Sep 27, 1971 in New York, New York
Source: *BioIn 2, 5, 9; DcCAA 71; IlsCB*
1946; NewYTBE 71

Castelnuovo-Tedesco, Mario
American. Composer
b. Apr 3, 1895 in Florence, Italy
d. Mar 15, 1968 in Hollywood, California
Source: *AmSCAP 66; DcCM; WhAm 5*

Castiglione, Baldassare, Conte
Italian. Diplomat, Writer, Courtier
Writer of Renaissance Europe; chief work
   The Courtier, 1518.
b. Dec 3, 1478 in Casatico, Italy
d. Feb 2, 1529 in Toledo, Spain
Source: *AtlBL; BbD; BiD&SB; CasWL;*
CroE&S; DcEuL; EuAu; EvEuW; NewC;
OxEng; PenC EUR; RComWL; REn

Castil-Blaze, Francois-Joseph
French. Author
b. Dec 1, 1784 in Cavaillon, France
d. Dec 11, 1857 in Paris, France
Source: *NewEOp 71*

Castillo, Antonio Canovas del
French. Fashion Designer
Designer for House of Lanvin, 1950-64;
   founded own coutere house, 1964.
b. 1908 in Madrid, Spain
Source: *WorFshn*

Castle, Barbara Anne Betts
English. Politician
Member, House of Commons, 1945-79; wrote:
   The Castle Diaries, 1980.
b. Oct 6, 1911 in Chesterfield, England
Source: *BlueB 76; CurBio 67; DcPol; InWom;*
IntWW 82; IntYB 81, 82; NewYTBE 72;
Who 74, 82; WhoWor 74, 82

Castle, Frederick W
American. General, Aviator
b. 1908
d. 1944
Source: *BioIn 1, 2, 7*

Castle, Irene Foote
[Mrs. Vernon Castle]
American. Dancer
Astaire and Rogers portrayed her and
husband in *Story of Vernon and Irene
Castle*, 1939; credited with starting bobbed
hair fad.
b. Apr 7, 1893 in New Rochelle, New York
d. Jan 25, 1969 in Eureka Springs, Arkansas
Source: *CmpEPM; EncMT; Film 1, 2;
FilmgC; NotAW MOD; NotNAT B; ObitOF
79; OxFilm; PlP&P; TwYS; WebAB, 79;
WhScrn 74, 77; WhoHol B; WorAl*

Castle, John
English. Actor
Films include *Blow-up; The Lion in Winter;*
PBS series "I Claudius"; "Lillie."
b. Jan 14, 1940 in Croydon, England
Source: *WhoThe 72, 77, 81*

Castle, Peggie
American. Actress
Films include *I the Jury; Jesse James'
Women.*
b. Dec 22, 1927 in Appalachia, Virginia
d. Aug 11, 1973 in Hollywood, California
Source: *FilmEn; FilmgC; WhScrn 77;
WhoHol B*

Castle, Vernon
[Vernon Blythe]
American. Dancer, Aviator
Dance innovator, 1910s; originated one-step,
turkey trot, castle walk.
b. May 2, 1887 in Norwich, England
d. Feb 15, 1918 in Fort Worth, Texas
Source: *CmpEPM; DcAmB; DcNAA; EncMT;
Film 1; FilmgC; NotNAT B; OxAmH;
OxFilm; PlP&P; WebAB, 79; WhAm 4;
WhScrn 77; WhoHol B; WorAl*

Castle, William
[William Schloss]
American. Director, Producer
Made over 100 horror films, including
Rosemary's Baby, 1968.
b. Apr 24, 1914 in New York, New York
d. May 31, 1977 in Beverly Hills, California
Source: *BioIn 5, 10, 11; ConAu 69, 77;
FanAl; FilmgC; IntMPA 75, 76, 77;
NewYTET; ObitOF 79; PseudN 82; WhoAm
74, 76, 78; WorEFlm*

Castlereagh, Robert Stewart, Viscount
British. Statesman, Politician
Foreign secretary, 1812-22; led coalition
against Napoleon, having him confined to
St. Helena; suicide victim.
b. 1769 in Dublin, Ireland
d. 1822
Source: *Alli; WebBD 80*

Caston, Saul
American. Conductor
Conductor, Denver Symphony Orchestra,
1945-64.
b. Aug 22, 1901 in New York, New York
d. Jul 28, 1970 in Winston-Salem, North
Carolina
Source: *Baker 78; BioIn 4, 11; NatCAB 56;
WhAm 5*

Castro, Raul
Cuban. Political Leader, Celebrity Relative
First vice premier; younger brother of Fidel
Castro.
b. Jun 3, 1931 in Biran, Cuba
Source: *CurBio 77; GrBr*

Castro (Ruz), Fidel
Cuban. Communist Leader
Led campaign to overthrow Batista regime,
1959; premier of Cuba 1959--.
b. Aug 13, 1926 in Mayari, Cuba
Source: *CurBio 58, 70; DcAmSR; DcPol;
EncLatA; IntWW 74; LinLib S; MakMC;
McGEWB; WhDW; WhoGov 72; WhoHol A;
WhoWor 74, 76, 78, 80; WorAl*

Caswell, Richard
American. Politician, Army Officer
First governor of NC, 1777-79.
b. Aug 3, 1729 in Cecil County, Maryland
d. Nov 10, 1789 in Fayetteville, North
Carolina
Source: *ApCAB; BiAUS; DcAmB S2; Drake;
NatCAB 4; TwCBDA; WebAB; WhAm HS*

Catalani, Alfredo
Italian. Composer
b. Jun 19, 1854 in Lucca, Italy
d. Aug 7, 1893 in Milan, Italy
Source: *NewEOp 71*

Cater, Douglass
American. Author, Editor, Educator
b. Aug 24, 1923 in Montgomery, Alabama
Source: *AmAu&B; BioIn 8; ConAu 1R, 1NR;
IntWW 74; WhoAm 74, 76, 78, 80, 82;
WhoWor 78; WrDr 80*

Cates, Clifton Bledsoe
American. Military Leader
US Marine, 1917-54; distinguished veteran of
WW I and II.
b. Aug 31, 1884 in Tiptonville, Tennessee
d. Jun 6, 1970 in Annapolis, Maryland
Source: *CurBio 50, 70; NewYTBE 70; WhAm
5*

Cates, Joseph
Producer, Director
Won Emmy for "Annie: The Woman in the
Life of a Man," 1970; films include *Last
Married Couple in America.*
b. 1924
Source: *VarWW 85*

Cates, Phoebe
American. Actress
In TV movie "Lace," 1984; "Lace II," 1985;
in film *Gremlins,* 1984.
b. 1964 in New York, New York
Source: *VarWW 85*

Cather, Willa Sibert
American. Author
Won Pulitzer for novel *One of Ours,* 1923.
b. Dec 7, 1873 in Winchester, Virginia
d. Apr 24, 1947 in New York, New York
Source: *AmAu&B; AmWr; AtlBL; CasWL;
Chambr 3; ChhPo, S1, S3; CnDAL; ConAmA;
ConAmL; ConAu 104; CyWA; DcAmB S4;
DcBiA; DcLEL; DcNAA; EncAAH; EncAB-A;
EncAB-H; EncWL; EvLB; HerW; JBA 34;
LibW; LinLib S; LongCTC; McGEWB;
ModAL, S1; NatCAB 44; NotAW; Novels;
ObitOF 79; OxAmH; OxAmL; OxCan;
OxEng; PenC AM; RAdv 1; RComWL; REn;
REnAL; REnAW; SmATA 30; TwCA, SUP;
TwCWr; WebAB; WebE&AL; WhAm 2;
WhE&EA; WhNAA; WhoTwCL; WomWWA
14*

Catherall, Arthur
English. Author
b. Jun 2, 1906 in Bolton, England
Source: *Au&Wr 71; AuBYP; ConAu 5R;
MnBBF; SmATA 3; WrDr 80*

Catherall, Joanne
see: Human League

Catherine de Medici
Italian. Consort
Daughter of Lorenzo de Medici who married
Henry II, 1533, adviser to son Charles IX,
1560-74.
b. Apr 13, 1519 in Florence, Italy
d. Jan 5, 1589 in Blois, France
Source: *BioIn 10; Dis&D; InWom; LinLib S;
LuthC 75; McGEWB; NewCol 75; OxFr;
OxMus; REn; WebBD 80; WorAl*

Catherine of Alexandria, Saint
Religious Figure
d. 307
Source: *BioIn 1, 2, 3, 4, 5, 6, 7, 8, 9; NewC*

Catherine of Aragon
English. Consort
Mother of Mary I; marriage voided, 1533, so
Henry could marry Anne Boleyn.
b. Dec 16, 1485 in Alcala, Spain
d. Jan 7, 1536 in Kimbolton, England
Source: *DcCathB; Dis&D; HerW; InWom;
LinLib S; NewCol 75; WorAl*

Catherine of Genoa, Saint
[Caterina Fieschi]
Italian. Religious Figure
b. 1447 in Genoa, Italy
d. Sep 14, 1510 in Genoa, Italy
Source: *BioIn 1, 2, 4, 5, 6, 7; DcCathB;
IlEncMy; InWom; LuthC 75*

Catherine of Sienna
[Caterina Benincasa]
Italian. Religious Leader
b. 1347 in Sienna, Italy
d. Apr 29, 1380 in Rome, Italy
Source: *CasWL,; DcCathB; DcItL; Dis&D;
IlEncMy; InWom; McGDA; McGEWB*

Catherine of Valois
French. Consort
b. 1401
d. 1437
Source: *InWom; NewCol 75*

Catherine the Great
[Catherine II; Sophia Augusta Frederike of
Anhaltzerbst]
Russian. Czarina
Empress, 1762-96; worked toward
westernization, expansion; made St.
Petersburg cultural rival with Paris.
b. Apr 21, 1729 in Stettin, Germany
d. Nov 6, 1796
Source: *CasWL; DcEuL; DcRusL; Dis&D;
EvEuW; HerW; LinLib L, S; McGEWB;
NewCol 75; OxFr; REn; WebBD 80; WhDW;
WorAl*

Catherwood, Frederick
English. Artist
b. 1799
d. 1854
Source: *BioIn 10*

Catiline, Lucius
Roman. Statesman
b. 108 BC
d. 62 BC
Source: *BioIn 4, 7, 8; NewCol 75*

Catledge, Turner
American. Journalist, Editor
Managing editor, New York *Times,* 1951-64;
  exec. editor, 1964-68.
b. Mar 17, 1901 in Ackerman, Mississippi
d. Apr 27, 1983 in New Orleans, Louisiana
Source: *AmAu&B; AuNews 1; BlueB 76;
ConAu 57; IntWW 74; NewYTBE 70;
NewYTBS 80, 82; Who 82; WhoAm 74;
WhoWor 74*

Catlett, "Big Sid" (Sidney)
American. Musician
b. Jan 17, 1910 in Evansville, Idaho
d. Mar 25, 1951 in Chicago, Illinois
Source: *DcAmB S5*

Catlett, Walter
American. Actor
b. Feb 4, 1889 in San Francisco, California
d. Nov 14, 1960 in Woodland Hills,
  California
Source: *EncMT; FilmgC; MotPP; MovMk;
Vers A; WhScrn 74, 77; WhoHol B*

Catlin, George
American. Explorer, Artist
Best known for paintings of Indians, tribal
  life 1829-38.
b. Jul 26, 1796 in Wilkes-Barre, Pennsylvania
d. Dec 23, 1872 in Jersey City, New Jersey
Source: *Alli SUP; AmAu; AmAu&B; AmBi;
ApCAB; AtlBL; BbD; BiD&SB; CasWL;
DcAmAu; DcAmB; DcEnL; DcLEL; DcNAA;
Drake; EncAB-H; EvLB; OxAmL; REn;
REnAL; TwCBDA; WebAB; WhAm HS*

Catlin, George Edward Gordon, Sir
English. Political Scientist, Educator
Co-founder, English Speaking Union, who
  wrote *Story of the Political Philosophies,*
  1939.
b. Jul 29, 1896 in Liverpool, England
d. Feb 8, 1979
Source: *Au&Wr 71; ConAu 13R; IntAu&W
76A, 77; IntWW 74, 75, 76, 77, 78; IntYB
78, 79; WhAm 7; WhE&EA; WhNAA; Who
74; WhoAm 74, 76, 78; WhoWor 74, 76;
WrDr 76*

Cato, Marcus Porcius Censorius
Roman. Statesman, Historian
b. 234 BC in Tusculum, Italy
d. 149 BC
Source: *BiD&SB; CasWL; NewC; PenC CL;
REn*

Cato, Marcus Porcius Uticensis
Roman. Philosopher
b. 95 BC
d. 46 BC
Source: *BioIn 1, 3*

Caton-Thompson, Gertrude
English. Archaeologist, Author
African researcher; wrote *Zimbabwe Culture.*
b. 1888
d. Apr 18, 1985 in Worcestershire, England
Source: *ConAu 116; Who 83*

Catonsville Nine
American. Revolutionaries
Source: *NF*

Catt, Carrie Chapman
American. Feminist
Organized League of Women Voters, 1920.
b. Jan 9, 1859 in Ripon, Wisconsin
d. Mar 9, 1947 in New Rochelle, New York
Source: *AmWom; BiCAW; CurBio 40, 47;
DcAmB S4; EncAB-H; InWom; NotAW;
WebAB; WhAm 2; WhAmP; WomWWA 14*

Cattell, James McKeen
American. Psychologist, Editor
Founder, Psychological Corp., 1921; editor,
  Science from 1894.
b. May 25, 1860 in Easton, Pennsylvania
d. Jan 20, 1944 in Lancaster, Pennsylvania
Source: *CurBio 44; DcAmB S3; WebBD 80*

Catto, Thomas Sivewright, Baron
English. Financier
Governor of Bank of England, 1944-49.
b. Mar 15, 1879 in Newcastle-upon-Tyne,
  England
d. Aug 23, 1959 in Holmbury St. Marg,
  England
Source: *CurBio 44, 59; DcNaB 1951; GrBr;
WhAm 6*

Catton, Bruce
American. Author, Journalist
Won Pulitzer, 1954, for *A Stillness at Appomattox.*
b. Oct 9, 1899 in Petoskey, Michigan
d. Aug 28, 1978 in Frankfort, Michigan
Source: *Alli SUP; AmAu&B; AuNews 1; CelR; ConAu 5R, 81; CurBio 54; IntWW 74; OxAmL; PenC AM; REn; REnAL; SmATA 2; TwCA SUP; WebAB; Who 74; WhoAm 74; WhoWor 78; WrDr 80*

Catullus, Gaius Valerius
Roman. Poet
Wrote over 100 lyric poems.
b. 84 BC in Verona, Italy
d. 54 BC
Source: *WebBD 80*

Caudill, Rebecca
[Mrs. James Ayars]
American. Children's Author
Wrote of childhood in KY, TN; runner-up, Newberry Award, 1964, for *A Pocket Full of Cricket.*
b. Feb 2, 1899 in Poor Fork, Kentucky
d. Oct 2, 1985 in Urbana, Illinois
Source: *AmAu&B; AuBYP; ConAu 5R, 2NR; CurBio 50; ForWC 70; InWom; MorJA; SmATA 1; WhoAm 74, 76, 78, 80, 82; WrDr 80*

Caulfield, Joan
American. Actress
b. Jun 1, 1922 in Orange, New Jersey
Source: *CurBio 54; FilmgC; InWom; IntMPA 75, 76, 77, 78, 79, 80, 81, 82; MotPP; WhoHol A*

Caulfield, Lore
American. Fashion Designer
Source: *NF*

Caulfield, Maxwell
English. Actor
Plays Miles Colby on TV series "The Colbys," 1985--.
b. 1959 in Derbyshire, England
Source: *ConTFT 3; NewYTBS 81*

Caulkins, Tracy
American. Swimmer
Won gold medal, 1984 LA Olympics; invented "Caulkins flutter" style of breaststroke swimming.
b. Jan 11, 1963 in Nashville, Tennessee
Source: *BioIn 11*

Causley, Charles Stanley
English. Author
b. Aug 24, 1917 in Launceston, England
Source: *Au&Wr 71; AuBYP; ChhPo, S1, S2; CnE&AP; ConAu 9R, 5NR; ConLC 7; ConP 70, 75; LongCTC; NewC; SmATA 3; WebE&AL; Who 74; WhoWor 78; WorAu; WrDr 80*

Cauthen, Steve
American. Jockey
First jockey to win both US Triple Crown, 1978, British Epsom Derby, 1985.
b. May 1, 1960 in Florence, Kentucky
Source: *BioIn 11; BkPepl; CurBio 77; NewYTBS 81; WhoAm 80, 82*

Cavalcanti, Alberto
Brazilian. Director
b. Feb 6, 1897 in Rio de Janeiro, Brazil
d. Aug 23, 1982 in Paris, France
Source: *BiDFilm; ConAu 17R; DcFM; FilmgC; IntMPA 81, 82; MovMk; OxFilm; Who 74; WorEFlm*

Cavaliere, Felix
[The Rascals]
American. Singer, Musician
Keyboardist, vocalist with blue-eyed soul group; has recorded several solo albums.
b. Nov 29, 1944 in Pelham, New York
Source: *NF*

Cavalieri, Lina
Italian. Opera Singer
b. Dec 25, 1874 in Viterbo, Italy
d. Feb 8, 1944 in Florence, Italy
Source: *Film 1; InWom; TwYS; WhAm 5; WhScrn 77; WhoHol B*

Cavallaro, Carmen
American. Band Leader
b. May 6, 1913 in New York, New York
Source: *AmSCAP 66*

Cavalli, Francesco
Italian. Composer
b. Feb 14, 1602 in Crema, Italy
d. Jan 14, 1676 in Venice, Italy
Source: *NewEOp 71*

Cavanagh, Jerry (Jerome Patrick)
American. Lawyer, Politician
Mayor of Detroit, 1962-70.
b. Jun 11, 1928 in Detroit, Michigan
d. Nov 27, 1979 in Lexington, Kentucky
Source: *BioIn 6, 7, 8, 11; WhoAm 78*

Cavanaugh, Hobart
American. Actor
b. 1887 in Virginia City, Nevada
d. Apr 27, 1950 in Woodland Hills,
California
Source: *FilmgC; MovMk; Vers A; WhScrn 74,
77; WhoHol B*

Cavanna, Betty (Elizabeth Allen)
[Betsy Allen; Elizabeth Headley, pseuds.]
American. Children's Author
Has written books for girls for 30 yrs.,
including *Going on Sixteen.*
b. Jun 24, 1909 in Camden, New Jersey
Source: *Au&Wr 71; AuBYP; ConAu 9R;
ConLC 12; CurBio 50; InWom; IntAu&W 76,
77; MorJA; SmATA 1; TwCCW 78;
WhoAmW 58, 61; WrDr 76, 80*

Cavarretta, Phil(ip Joseph)
American. Baseball Player
Outfielder, first baseman, Chicago, 1934-55;
won batting title, 1945.
b. Jul 19, 1916 in Chicago, Illinois
Source: *BaseEn 85; WhoProB 73*

Cavell, Edith
English. Nurse
Executed by Germans for helping allied
soldiers in WW I.
b. 1865 in Norfolk, England
d. Oct 12, 1915
Source: *BioIn 2, 4, 5, 6, 7, 8, 10, 11;
GoodHs; HerW; InWom; LinLib S; LongCTC*

Cavendish, Henry
English. Chemist, Physicist
b. Oct 10, 1731 in Nice, France
d. Mar 10, 1810 in London, England
Source: *Alli; NewC; NewCol 75; WebBD 80*

Cavendish, Thomas
English. Navigator
Third to circumnavigate globe, 1586.
b. 1555 in Suffolk, England
d. Jun 1592
Source: *Alli; NewC; NewCol 75; OxShips;
WebBD 80*

Cavendish, William, Duke of Newcastle
English. Statesman, Author
b. 1592
d. Dec 25, 1676 in London, England
Source: *Alli; BrAu; CasWL; CroE&S; DcEnL*

Cavett, Dick (Richard Alva)
American. Entertainer
Won Emmy, 1972; host of PBS talk show,
1978--; wrote *Cavett,* 1974.
b. Nov 19, 1936 in Gibbon, Nebraska
Source: *BioNews 74; BkPepl; CelR; CurBio
70; IntMPA 81, 82; NewYTBS 81; WhoAm
80, 82; WhoE 74*

Cavour, Camillo Benso di
Italian. Statesman
b. Aug 10, 1810 in Turin, Italy
d. Jun 6, 1861 in Turin, Italy
Source: *BiD&SB; NewC; REn*

Cawein, Madison Julius
American. Poet
b. Mar 23, 1865 in Louisville, Kentucky
d. Dec 7, 1914 in Louisville, Kentucky
Source: *AmAu&B; BbD; BiD&SB; BiDSA;
DcAmAu; DcEnL; DcNAA; OxAmL; REn;
REnAL*

Cawthorn, Joseph
American. Actor
b. Mar 29, 1868 in New York, New York
d. Jan 21, 1949 in Beverly Hills, California
Source: *BioIn 1; CmpEPM; EncMT; Film 2;
NotNAT B; TwYS; WhAm 2; WhScrn 77;
WhThe; WhoHol B; WhoStg 1906, 1908*

Caxton, William
English. Author, Printer
First to print books translated into English,
1475.
b. Aug 13, 1422 in Weald of Kent, England
d. 1491 in Westminster, England
Source: *Alli; BbD; BiD&SB; BrAu; CasWL;
Chambr 1; CrtT 1; DcEnA; DcEnL; DcEuL;
DcLEL; EvLB; MouLC 1; NewC; OxEng;
PenC ENG; REn; WebE&AL*

Cayatte, Andre
French. Director
Uses film to express ideas on social and
moral problems.
b. Feb 3, 1909 in Carcassonne, France
Source: *BiDFilm; DcFM; FilmgC; OxFilm;
WorEFlm*

Cayce, Edgar
American. Psychic
Worked from trances to yield diagnoses,
prescriptions for patients.
b. Mar 18, 1877 in Hopkinsville, Kentucky
d. Jan 3, 1945 in Virginia Beach, Virginia
Source: *BiDPara; EncO&P 78; WhAm 4;
WorAl*

Cayley, George, Sir
British. Engineer, Scientist
Founder of aerodynamics, who built first
   glider, 1853; developed some elements of
   modern airplane.
b. Dec 27, 1773 in Yorkshire, England
d. Dec 15, 1857 in Yorkshire, England
Source: *Alli; DcInv; InSci; NewCol 75;
WhDW*

Cazenove, Christopher
English. Actor
Films include *Heat and Dust,* 1983; plays
   Ben Carrington on TV's "Dynasty," 1986--
b. Dec 17, 1945 in Winchester, England
Source: *WhoThe 81*

Ceausescu, Nicolae
Romanian. President
b. Jan 26, 1918 in Scornicesti-Olt, Romania
Source: *CurBio 67; IntWW 74; NewYTBE 70;
WhoGov 75; WhoWor 78*

Cebotari, Maria
Russian. Opera Singer
b. Feb 10, 1910 in Kishinev, Russia
d. Jun 9, 1949 in Vienna, Austria
Source: *InWom*

Ceccato, Aldo
Italian. Conductor
Detroit Symphony Orchestra, 1973-77.
b. Feb 18, 1934 in Milan, Italy
Source: *BioNews 74; WhoAm 78*

Cecchetti, Enrico
Italian. Dancer
Taught Pavlova, Nijinsky, Fokine technique
   of progressive exercises.
b. 1850 in Italy
d. Nov 16, 1928
Source: *BioIn 3, 4, 5, 8, 9; NotNAT B;
WhDW; WhThe*

Cecchi, Emilio
Italian. Essayist, Critic
b. 1884 in Florence, Italy
d. 1966 in Rome, Italy
Source: *CasWL; ClDMEL; DcFM; EncWL;
EvEuW; PenC EUR*

Cecil, Edgar Algernon Robert
English. Statesman, Author
b. Sep 14, 1864 in London, England
d. Nov 24, 1958
Source: *McGEWB; WebBD 80*

Cecil, Edward Christian David Gascoyne
English. Critic, Biographer, Educator
b. Apr 9, 1902
Source: *EvLB; TwCA, SUP*

Cecelia, Saint
Religious Figure
Martyr, regarded as patroness of musicians;
   feast day Nov 22.
d. 230 in Rome, Italy
Source: *BioIn 1, 2, 3, 4, 5, 6, 7, 8; NewC;
REn*

Cedeno, Cesar
Dominican. Baseball Player
Outfielder, first baseman, Houston Astros,
   1970--; had two doubles in one inning,
   1973.
b. Feb 25, 1951 in Santo Domingo,
   Dominican Republic
Source: *BaseEn 85; NewYTBE 73; WhoProB
73*

Celebrezze, Anthony Joseph
American. Politician, Judge
b. Sep 4, 1910 in Anzi, Italy
Source: *BiDrUSE; CurBio 63; IntWW 74;
WhoAm 74; WhoAmP 73; WhoGov 75;
WhoMW 74*

Celeste, Richard F
American. Politician
Dem. governor of OH, 1982--.
b. Nov 11, 1937 in Cleveland, Ohio
Source: *WhoAm 80, 82; WhoAmP 81;
WhoGov 77; WhoMW 78*

Celibidache, Sergiu
Romanian. Conductor
b. Jun 28, 1912
Source: *IntWW 74; Who 74; WhoWor 78*

Celine, Louis-Ferdinand
[Louis-Ferdinand Destouches]
French. Author
Misanthropic views expressed in *Journey to
   the End of Night,* 1932, *Death on the
   Installment Plan,* 1936.
b. May 27, 1894 in Courbevoie, France
d. Jul 4, 1961 in Meudon, France
Source: *AtlBL; CasWL; ClDMEL; ConAu 85;
ConLC 1, 3, 4, 9, 15; CyWA; EncWL;
EvEuW; LongCTC; ModRL; OxFr; PenC
EUR; REn; TwCA, SUP; TwCWr; WhAm 4;
WhoTwCL*

Celler, Emanuel
American. Politician
b. May 6, 1888 in Brooklyn, New York
Source: *BiDrAC; CelR; CurBio 49, 66; IntWW 74; NewYTBE 72; St&PR 75; WhoAm 74; WhoAmP 73; WhoE 74; WhoGov 75*

Cellini, Benvenuto
Italian. Sculptor
Autobiography *The Life of Benvenuto Cellini*, 1558-66, record of Renaissance life.
b. Nov 1, 1500 in Florence, Italy
d. Feb 14, 1571 in Florence, Italy
Source: *AtlBL; BbD; BiD&SB; CasWL; CyWA; DcCathB; DcEuL; DcItL; DcNiCA; Dis&D; EuAu; EvEuW; InSci; LinLib L, S; McGDA; McGEWB; NewC; NewEOp 71; OxArt; OxDecA; OxEng; OxFr; PenC EUR; RComWL; REn; WhDW; WorAl*

Celsius, Anders
Swedish. Astronomer
Invented centigrade temperature scale, 1742.
b. Nov 27, 1701 in Uppsala, Sweden
d. Apr 25, 1744
Source: *WebBD 80*

Cepeda, Orlando
"The Baby Bull"; "Cha-Cha"
Puerto Rican. Baseball Player
b. Sep 17, 1937 in Ponce, Puerto Rico
Source: *BaseEn 85; CurBio 68; WhoAm 74; WhoProB 73*

Ceresole, Pierre
Swiss. Social Reformer
b. 1879
d. 1945
Source: *BioIn 3, 11*

Cerf, Bennett Alfred
American. Publisher, Journalist
Founded Random House Publishers, 1927.
b. May 25, 1898 in New York, New York
d. Aug 27, 1971 in Mount Kisco, New York
Source: *AmAu&B; AuBYP; BiE&WWA; ConAu 17R, 29R, P-2; CurBio 41, 58, 71; NewYTBE 71; PIP&P; REn; REnAL; SmATA 7; WebAB; WhAm 5*

Cermak, Anton Joseph
American. Mayor
Killed in Miami by bullet intended for Franklin D Roosevelt.
b. May 9, 1873 in Prague, Bohemia
d. Mar 6, 1933 in Miami, Florida
Source: *DcAmB S1; WebBD 80; WhAm 1; WhAmP*

Cernan, Eugene Andrew
American. Astronaut, Businessman
On board Gemini 9, Apollo 10,17; last American to walk on moon, 1972.
b. Mar 14, 1934 in Chicago, Illinois
Source: *CurBio 73; IntWW 74; WhoAm 74, 76, 78, 80, 82; WhoS&SW 82; WhoWor 78*

Cernik, Oldrich
Czech. Political Leader
b. Oct 27, 1921 in Ostrava, Czechoslovakia
Source: *IntWW 74; WhoSocC 78; WhoWor 74*

Cerone, Rick (Richard Aldo)
"Spongehead"
American. Baseball Player
b. May 19, 1954 in Newark, New Jersey
Source: *BaseEn 85*

Cervantes, Alfonso Juan
American. Politician
Mayor of St. Louis, 1965-73.
b. Aug 27, 1929 in Saint Louis, Missouri
d. Jun 23, 1983 in Saint Louis, Missouri
Source: *WhoAm 74; WhoAmP 73; WhoGov 75*

Cervantes (Saavedra), Miguel(de)
Spanish. Poet, Dramatist
Began writing *Don Quixote* in prison, 1605; forerunner of modern novel.
b. Sep 29, 1547 in Alcala, Spain
d. Apr 23, 1616 in Madrid, Spain
Source: *AtlBL; BbD; BiD&SB; CasWL; ChhPo S2; CnThe; CyWA; DcBiA; DcEuL; DcSpL; EuAu; EvEuW; McGEWD; NewC; OxEng; OxThe; PenC EUR; RComWL; REn; REnWD; WhDW*

Cesnola, Luigi Palma di
Italian. Archaeologist
Excavated sites on Cyprus, 1865-76; director Metropolitan Museum of Art, 1879-1904.
b. Jul 29, 1832 in Rivarola, Italy
d. Nov 20, 1904 in New York, New York
Source: *AmBi; ApCAB; BbD; BiD&SB; BioIn 7, 9; DcAmAu; DcNAA; HarEnUS; InSci; LinLib S; NatCAB 1; TwCBDA; WhAm 1*

Cessna, Clyde Vernon
American. Aircraft Manufacturer
Organized Cessna Aircraft Co.; built cantilever monoplanes, 1928.
b. Dec 5, 1879 in Hawthorne, Iowa
d. Nov 20, 1954 in Rago, Kansas
Source: *Entr; NatCAB 41; ObitOF 79; WorAl*

Cetera, Peter
[Chicago]
American. Singer, Musician
Lead singer with Chicago; solo hit "Glory of
   Love," 1986.
b. Sep 13, 1944 in Chicago, Illinois
Source: *NF*

Cey, Ron(ald Charles)
"The Penguin"
American. Baseball Player
b. Feb 15, 1948 in Tacoma, Washington
Source: *BaseEn 85; PseudN 82; WhoAm 78,
80, 82*

Cezanne, Paul
French. Artist
Post-impressionist painter whose geometric
   forms influenced cubism.
b. Jan 19, 1839 in Aix-en-Provence, France
d. Oct 22, 1906 in Aix-en-Provence, France
Source: *AtlBL; OxFr; REn*

Chaban-Delmas, Jacques
French. Political Leader
b. Mar 7, 1915 in Paris, France
Source: *CurBio 58; IntWW 74; WhoWor 78*

Chabrier, (Alexis) Emmanuel
French. Composer
b. Jan 18, 1841 in Ambert, France
d. Sep 13, 1894 in Paris, France
Source: *AtlBL; OxFr*

Chabrol, Claude
French. Director
Married to actress Stephane Audran; films
   include *Les Cousins; Les Bonnes Femmes;
   Violette Noziere.*
b. Jun 24, 1930 in Paris, France
Source: *BiDFilm; ConLC 16; CurBio 75;
DcFM; FilmgC; IntMPA 75, 76, 77, 78, 79,
80, 81, 82; IntWW 74; MovMk; NewYTBE
70; OxFilm; WhoWor 78; WorEFlm*

Chace, Marian
American. Dancer
Created dance therapy for mentally ill;
   founded American Dance Therapy Assn.,
   1965.
b. Oct 31, 1896 in Providence, Rhode Island
d. Jul 20, 1970 in Washington, District of
   Columbia
Source: *BioIn 9, 11; NotAW MOD*

Chacksfield, Frank
British. Music Director
Source: *WhoMus 72*

Chad and Jeremy
[Jeremy Clyde; Chad Stuart]
English. Music Group
Soft-rock group, 1964-66; hits include
   "Yesterday's Gone," "A Summer Song"
   and "Distant Shores."
Source: *BiDAmM; ConMuA 80A; LilREn 78;
RkOn 84; WhoRock 81*

Chadwick, Cassie L
[Elizabeth Bigley]
"Queen of Ohio"
Canadian. Criminal
Notorious swindler, who masqueraded as
   Andrew Carnegie's illegitimate daughter.
b. 1859 in Strathroy, Ontario
d. 1907
Source: *BioIn 2, 5, 10; LookW; PseudN 82*

Chadwick, Florence
American. Swimmer
Established a new record for women
   swimming the English Channel, 1950.
b. Nov 9, 1917 in San Diego, California
Source: *CurBio 50; GoodHs; InWom; WorAl*

Chadwick, French Ensor
American. Naval Officer
b. Feb 29, 1844 in Morgantown, West
   Virginia
d. Jan 27, 1919
Source: *AmBi; ApCAB SUP, X; DcAmB S2;
NatCAB 9; WebBD 80; WhAm 1*

Chadwick, George Whitefield
American. Composer
b. Nov 13, 1854 in Lowell, Massachusetts
d. Apr 7, 1931 in Boston, Massachusetts
Source: *AmBi; ApCAB; DcAmB S1; OxAmL;
TwCBDA; WhAm 1*

Chadwick, Henry
American. Journalist
Considered author, rules of baseball; editor,
   Spaulding's *Official Baseball Guide.*
b. Oct 5, 1824 in Exeter, England
d. Apr 20, 1908 in New York, New York
Source: *Alli SUP; AmAu&B; DcAmAu;
DcAmB; DcNAA; HsB&A; WebAB; WhoProB
73*

Chadwick, James, Sir
English. Engineer, Scientist, Physician
b. Oct 22, 1891 in Manchester, England
d. Jul 24, 1974 in Cambridge, England
Source: *ConAu 49; CurBio 45, 74; IntWW
74; NewYTBS 74; WhAm 6; Who 74;
WhoAm 74; WhoWor 78*

Chadwick, William Owen
English. Historian
b. May 20, 1916 in Bromley, England
Source: *ConAu 1NR; IntWW 74; Who 74; WhoWor 78*

Chafee, John Hubbard
American. Senator
b. Oct 22, 1922 in Providence, Rhode Island
Source: *CurBio 69; IntWW 74; WhoAm 74, 76, 78, 80, 82; WhoAmP 73; WhoE 74*

Chaffee, Roger Bruce
American. Astronaut
Killed in fire with Gus Grissom, Ed White,
    aboard spacecraft during simulation of
    Apollo flight.
b. Feb 15, 1935 in Grand Rapids, Michigan
d. Jan 27, 1967 in Cape Canaveral, Florida
Source: *WhAm 4*

Chaffee, Suzy
American. Skier
Captain, US Olympic ski team, 1968; world
    free-style champ, 1971-73.
b. Nov 29, 1946
Source: *BioIn 9; WhoAm 80, 82*

Chaffin, Lillie Dorton
American. Children's Author
b. Feb 1, 1925 in Varney, Kentucky
Source: *ConAu 33R; DrAF 76; ForWC 70; SmATA 4; WrDr 80*

Chagall, Marc
Russian. Artist
Influenced by cubism, paintings depict
    Russian village life.
b. Jul 7, 1887 in Vitebsk, Russia
d. Mar 28, 1985 in Saint Paul de Vence,
    France
Source: *CelR; CurBio 43, 60; IntWW 74; NewYTBE 73; REn; Who 82; WhoGrA 62; WhoWor 78*

Chaikin, Joseph
American. Actor, Director
Founder, director, Open Theater, NYC, 1963-
73.
b. Sep 16, 1935 in Brooklyn, New York
Source: *BioIn 1, 9, 10, 11; CurBio 81; EncWT; NotNAT; ObitOF 79; WhoThe 77, 81; WhoWorJ 72, 78*

Chaikin, Sol Chick
American. Labor Union Official
Pres. International Ladies Garment Workers
    Union, 1975--; vp, AFL-CIO, 1975--.
b. Jan 9, 1918 in New York, New York
Source: *CurBio 79; NewYTBS 75; WhoAm 78, 80, 82, 84; WhoE 77, 79; WhoLab 76*

Chain, Ernest Boris, Sir
British. Biochemist, Educator
Developed penicillin, 1928, with Alexander
    Fleming, Howard Florey; shared 1945
    Nobel Prize.
b. Jun 19, 1906 in Berlin, Germany
d. Sep 14, 1979 in Ireland
Source: *AsBiEn; BioIn 3, 5, 6, 7; CurBio 65, 79; IntWW 75, 76, 77, 78; Who 74; WhoWor 78; WhoWorJ 72*

Chait, Lawrence G
American. Advertising Executive
b. Jun 27, 1917 in Scranton, Pennsylvania
Source: *WhoAdv 72; WhoAm 74, 76, 78, 80, 82; WhoE 74*

Chaka
African. Political Leader
Founder of Zulu Empire, mid-1820s, who
    ruled 50,000 people.
b. 1773
d. Sep 1828
Source: *BioIn 1, 4, 6, 7, 8, 9, 10; InB&W 80; WhDW*

Chakiris, George
American. Dancer, Actor
Won Oscar, 1961, for *West Side Story.*
b. Sep 16, 1934 in Norwood, Ohio
Source: *FilmgC; IntMPA 75, 76, 77, 78, 79, 80, 81, 82; MotPP; MovMk; WhoAm 74, 76, 78, 80, 82; WhoHol A*

Chalgrin, Francois
French. Architect
Neo-classicist, who designed Arc de
    Triumphe; built 1806-37.
b. 1739 in Paris, France
d. 1811
Source: *McGDA; WhoArch*

Chaliapin, Feodor Ivanovitch
[Feodor Ivanovich Shaliapin]
Russian. Opera Singer
Bass who discovered greatest success in *Boris
    Gudunov.*
b. Feb 13, 1873 in Kazan, Russia
d. Apr 12, 1938 in Paris, France
Source: *FilmgC; OxFilm; REn; WhAm 1; WhScrn 74, 77; WhoHol B*

Chalk, Oscar Roy
English. Business Executive
b. Jun 7, 1907 in London, England
Source: *WhoAm 78*

Challans, Mary
see: Renault, Mary, pseud.

Chalmers, William James
American. Manufacturer
Founding partner of Allis-Chalmers Corp.,
  1901.
b. Jul 10, 1852 in Chicago, Illinois
d. Dec 10, 1938 in Chicago, Illinois
Source: *DcAmB S2; WhAm 1*

Chamberlain, Austen, Sir
British. Statesman
Half-brother of Neville Chamberlain, who
  was Conservative party leader, 1921-29;
  won Nobel Peace Prize, 1925.
b. 1863
d. 1937
Source: *BioIn 1, 2, 7, 9, 11; WebBD 80;*
WhE&EA

Chamberlain, John Rensselear
American. Journalist
Wrote *The Enterprising Americans*, 1962, a
  business history of the U.S.
b. Oct 28, 1903 in New Haven, Connecticut
Source: *AmAu&B; ConAu 57; CurBio 40;*
OxAmL,; REnAL; TwCA,, SUP; WhoAm 74,
76, 78, 80, 82; WhoWor 74

Chamberlain, Joseph
English. Statesman
Father of Austen, Neville, who favored social
  reform at home, expansion abroad.
b. Jul 8, 1836 in London, England
d. Jul 2, 1914
Source: *Alli SUP*

Chamberlain, Neville
English. Statesman, Prime Minister
Conservative prime minister, 1937-40, who
  declared war on Germany, 1939; succeeded
  by Churchill.
b. Mar 18, 1869 in Edgbaston, England
d. Nov 9, 1940 in Odiham, England
Source: *CurBio 40; REn*

Chamberlain, Richard
American. Actor
Starred in TV's "Dr. Kildare"; "Shogun";
  "Thornbirds."
b. Mar 31, 1935 in Beverly Hills, California
Source: *BioNews 75; BkPepl; CelR; FilmgC;*
IntMPA 75, 76, 77, 78, 79, 80, 81, 82;
MotPP; MovMk; WhoHol A; WhoThe 77

Chamberlain, Samuel
American. Author, Photographer
b. Oct 28, 1895 in Cresco, Iowa
d. Jan 10, 1975 in Marblehead,
  Massachusetts
Source: *ConAu 53, P-2; CurBio 54; WhAm 6*

Chamberlain, Wilt(ton Norman)
"Wilt the Stilt"
American. Basketball Player
Four-time MVP, who holds NBA record for
  rebounds, second in career points.
b. Aug 21, 1936 in Philadelphia,
  Pennsylvania
Source: *BkPepl; CelR; CmCal; ConAu 103;*
CurBio 60; Ebony 1; InB&W 80; NegAl 76;
NewYTBE 72, 73; NewYTBS 75; WebAB 79;
WhoBbl 73; WhoBlA 75, 85; WorAl

Chamberlin, (B) Guy
American. Football Player, Football Coach
b. Jan 16, 1894 in Blue Springs, Nebraska
d. Apr 4, 1967
Source: *BioIn 3, 6, 8; WhoFtbl 74*

Chamberlin, Lee
American. Actor
Films include *Uptown Saturday Night*, 1974;
  Let's Do It Again, 1975.
b. Feb 14, 1938 in New York, New York
Source: *VarWW 85*

Chamberlin, Thomas Chrowder
American. Geologist
b. Sep 25, 1843 in Mattoon, Illinois
d. Nov 15, 1928
Source: *ApCAB; NatCAB 11; NewCol 75;*
WhAm 1

Chamberlin, William Henry
American. Author, Critic
b. Feb 17, 1897 in Brooklyn, New York
d. Sep 12, 1969
Source: *AmAu&B; ConAu 5R; OxAmL;*
OxCan; REnAL; TwCA, SUP; WhAm 5

Chambers, Edmund Kerchever, Sir
English. Essayist, Critic
b. Mar 16, 1866 in Berkshire, England
d. Jan 21, 1954 in Devonshire, England
Source: *CasWL; DcLEL; EvLB; LongCEL;*
LongCTC; NewC; OxEng; PenC ENG; REn;
TwCA, SUP

Chambers, Martin
see: Pretenders, The

Chambers, Paul, Sir
English. Businessman
Tax adviser, Indian govt., 1937-40.
b. Apr 2, 1904 in London, England
d. Dec 23, 1981
Source: *BioIn 8; IntWW 74, 75, 82; Who 74,*
82

Chambers, Robert
Scottish. Publisher, Author
b. Jul 10, 1802 in Peebles, Scotland
d. Mar 17, 1871 in Saint Andrews, Scotland
Source: *BioIn 2, 5, 10; BrAu 19; CasWL;
ChhPo S1, S2; DcBiPP; DcEnA; DcEnL;
DcEuL; DcLEL; EncO&P 78; EvLB; LinLib
L, S; OxEng*

Chambers, Robert W
American. Author
Wrote series of pseudo-historical novels: *The
Drums of Aulone*, 1927.
b. May 26, 1865 in Brooklyn, New York
d. Dec 16, 1933
Source: *AmAu&B; AmBi; ApCAB SUP, X;
BbD; BiD&SB; CarSB; Chambr 3; ChhPo, S2,
S3; DcAmAu; DcAmB S1; DcBiA; DcLEL;
DcNAA; NatCAB 13; OxAmL; REnAL;
TwCA; TwCBDA; WhAm 1*

Chambers, Whittaker
[Jay David Chambers]
American. Editor, Journalist
Principle witness in Alger Hiss espionage
case, 1948-50.
b. Apr 1, 1901 in Philadelphia, Pennsylvania
d. Jun 9, 1961 in Carroll County, Maryland
Source: *AmAu&B; ConAu 89; DcAmSR;
LongCTC; ObitOF 79; WorAl; WorAu*

Chambers, William, Sir
"W C"
British. Architect
Designed Somerset House, London; Kew
Palace buildings, 1757.
b. 1723 in Gothenburg, Sweden
d. Mar 8, 1796 in London, England
Source: *AtlBL; BioIn 2, 3, 7, 8, 9; PseudN
82*

Chaminade, Cecile
[Louise Stephanie Chaminade]
French. Composer
b. Aug 8, 1861 in Paris, France
d. Apr 18, 1944 in Monte Carlo, Montana
Source: *CurBio 44; OxMus*

Champion, Gower
American. Choreographer, Dancer
Won Tonys for *Bye Bye Birdie*, 1961, *Hello,
Dolly*, 1964, *42nd Street*, 1981.
b. Jun 22, 1921 in Geneva, Illinois
d. Aug 25, 1980 in New York, New York
Source: *BiE&WWA; CelR; CmMov; EncMT;
FilmgC; IntMPA 75, 76, 77, 78, 79, 80, 81;
MotPP; MovMk; NotNAT; WhoAm 74;
WhoHol A; WhoThe 77; WhoWor 78;
WorEFlm*

Champion, Marge Celeste
[Marjorie Celeste Belcher; Mrs. Gower
Champion]
American. Dancer, Actress
b. Sep 2, 1923 in Los Angeles, California
Source: *BiE&WWA; CmMov; FilmgC;
InWom; IntMPA 75, 76, 77, 78, 79, 80, 81,
82; MotPP; MovMk; NotNAT; WhoAm 74,
76, 78, 80, 82; WhoHol A*

Champlain, Samuel de
French. Explorer
Founded Quebec, 1608; discovered Lake
Champlain, 1609.
b. Jul 3, 1567 in Rochefort, France
d. Dec 25, 1635 in Quebec
Source: *AmBi; ApCAB; DcAmB; Drake;
OxAmL; OxCan; OxFr; REn; REnAL;
WebAB; WhAm HS*

Champollion, Jean Francois
French. Egyptologist
Deciphered Rosetta stone found in Egypt by
French troops, 1799.
b. Dec 23, 1790 in Figeac, France
d. Mar 4, 1832 in Paris, France
Source: *BbD; CelCen; DcBiPP; DcCathB;
LinLib L, S; McGEWB; NewCol 75; OxFr;
REn; WhDW; WorAl*

Chance, Frank Leroy
"Peerless Leader"
American. Baseball Player, Baseball Manager
First baseman in "Tinker to Evers to
Chance" double play combination, 1906-10.
b. Sep 9, 1877 in Fresno, California
d. Sep 15, 1924 in Los Angeles, California
Source: *BaseEn 85; CmCal; WhoProB 73*

Chance, (Wilmer) Dean
American. Baseball Player
Pitched six consecutive 1-0 winning games to
set major league record.
b. Jun 1, 1941 in Wayne, Ohio
Source: *BaseEn 85; BioIn 7, 8; CurBio 69;
WhoProB 73*

Chancellor, John William
American. Broadcast Journalist
Anchorman, "NBC Nightly News," 1970-81;
commentator since 1981.
b. Jul 14, 1927 in Chicago, Illinois
Source: *AuNews 1; BioNews 74; CelR; CurBio
62; IntMPA 75, 76, 77, 78, 79, 80, 81, 82;
WhoAm 74, 76, 78, 80, 82*

Chancellor, Richard
English. Explorer
Negotiated trade agreements between Russia,
England; organized Muscovy Co., 1554.
d. Nov 10, 1556
Source: *BioIn 4, 7; NewC*

Chandler, Colby H
American. Business Executive
Pres., Eastman Kodak Co., 1977--; chief
exec., 1983--.
b. 1925
Source: *Dun&B 79; IntWW 77, 78, 79, 80,
81, 82; WhoAm 82, 84; WhoF&I 79, 81*

Chandler, Don
American. Football Player
b. Sep 9, 1934 in Council Bluffs, Iowa
Source: *BioIn 8; WhoFtbl 74*

Chandler, Dorothy Buffum
American. Journalist
b. May 19, 1901 in Lafayette, Illinois
Source: *BioIn 4, 5, 7, 8, 9, 11; CurBio 57;
WhoAm 74; WhoAmW 74; WhoWor 78*

Chandler, "Happy" (Albert Benjamin)
American. Lawyer, Politician
Governor of KY, 1935-39; 1955-59.
b. Jul 14, 1898 in Corydon, Kentucky
Source: *BiDrAC; CmCal; EncAB 18; WebAB;
WhoAm 76, 78, 80, 82; WhoAmP 73;
WhoProB 73; WhoS&SW 73; WorAl*

Chandler, Jeff
[Ira Grossel]
American. Actor, Author
b. Dec 15, 1918 in Brooklyn, New York
d. Jun 17, 1961 in Culver City, California
Source: *AmSCAP 66; BiDFilm; CmMov;
FilmgC; MotPP; MovMk; OxFilm; WhScrn
74, 77; WhoHol B; WorEFlm*

Chandler, Norman
American. Newspaper Publisher
b. Jul 23, 1899 in Chicago, Illinois
d. Oct 20, 1973 in Los Angeles, California
Source: *ConAu 89; CurBio 73; WhAm 6;
WhoF&I 74; WhoWest 84; WhoWor 78*

Chandler, Otis
American. Newspaper Publisher, Editor
Editor-in-chief, publisher, *Los Angeles Times*,
1960-80.
b. Nov 23, 1927 in Los Angeles, California
Source: *BioIn 5, 7, 8, 9, 11; CurBio 68;
IntWW 82; St&PR 75; WhoAm 82; WhoWor
74; WorAl*

Chandler, Raymond Thornton
American. Author
Created private detective Philip Marlowe;
wrote novel *The Big Sleep*, 1939.
b. Jul 23, 1888 in Chicago, Illinois
d. Mar 26, 1959 in La Jolla, California
Source: *AmAu&B; CasWL; CmCal; CmMov;
CnMWL; CurBio 46, 59; DcAmB S6; DcFM;
DcLEL; EncMys; FilmgC; LongCTC; ModAL,
S1; NewYTBE 73; OxAmL; OxEng; OxFilm;
PenC AM; REn; REnAL; TwCA SUP;
TwCWr; WebAB; WebE&AL; WhAm 3;
WhoTwCL; WorEFlm*

Chandler, "Spud" (Spurgeon Ferdinand)
American. Baseball Player
AL MVP, 1943; led league with winning
percentage of .833.
b. Sep 12, 1909 in Commerce, Georgia
Source: *BaseEn 85; WhoProB 73*

Chandos, Oliver Lyttelton
English. Statesman, Industrialist
b. Mar 15, 1893 in London, England
d. Jan 21, 1972
Source: *Au&Wr 71; BioIn 3, 5, 6, 9; CurBio
41, 72*

Chandrasekhar, Subrahmanyan
American. Physicist
Won Nobel Prize for physics, 1983; best
known for study of structure of white
dwarfs, 1940.
b. Oct 19, 1910 in Lahore, India
Source: *AmM&WS 82P; BiESc; BlueB 76;
CurBio 86; InSci; IntWW 83; McGMS 80;
NewYTBS 83; WhE&EA; Who 83; WhoAm
84; WhoFrS 84; WrDr 84*

Chanel, "Coco" (Gabrielle)
French. Fashion Designer
Created Chanel No. 5 perfume, 1924; subject
of Broadway musical *Coco*.
b. Aug 19, 1882 in Saumur, France
d. Jan 10, 1971 in Paris, France
Source: *CurBio 54, 71; InWom; NewYTBE
71; WhAm 5; WorFshn*

Chaney, Lon (Alonso)
"Man of a Thousand Faces"
American. Actor
Starred in *The Hunchback of Notre Dame*,
1923; *The Phantom of the Opera*, 1925.
b. Apr 1, 1883 in Colorado Springs,
Colorado
d. Aug 26, 1930 in Los Angeles, California
Source: *BiDFilm; CmMov; DcAmB S1; Film
1; FilmgC; MotPP; MovMk; OxFilm; TwYS;
WebAB; WhAm HSA, 4; WhScrn 74, 77;
WhoHol B; WorEFlm*

Chaney, Lon, Jr. (Creighton)
American. Actor
Starred in over 100 films, mostly horror;
  played Lenny in *Of Mice and Men,* 1940.
b. Feb 10, 1905 in Oklahoma City,
  Oklahoma
d. Jul 12, 1973 in San Clemente, California
Source: *CmMov; FilmgC; MovMk; OxFilm;
WhScrn 77; WhoHol B*

Chaney, Norman
[Our Gang]
"Chubby"
American. Actor
Played Joe Cobb "Our Gang," 1926-34.
b. Jan 18, 1918 in Baltimore, Maryland
d. May 30, 1936 in Baltimore, Maryland
Source: *Film 2; PseudN 82; WhScrn 74, 77*

Chang and Eng
[Chang and Eng Bunker]
American. Siamese Twins
Toured carnivals in US, Europe, 1829-54;
  Chang died first, Eng died of fright two
  hrs. later.
b. May 11, 1811 in Meklong, Thailand
d. Jan 17, 1874 in Mount Airy, North
  Carolina
Source: *ApCAB; DcAmB; WebAB; WhAm HS*

Chang Tso-Lin
Chinese. Military Leader
Fought in Russo-Japanese War, 1904-05.
b. 1873 in Fengtien, China
d. Jun 4, 1928 in China
Source: *BioIn 3, 11; NewCol 75; WebBD 80*

Channing, Carol
[Carol Channing Lowe]
American. Actress
Won Tony for *Hello, Dolly!,* 1964.
b. Jan 31, 1923 in Seattle, Washington
Source: *BiE&WWA; BkPepl; CelR; ConTFT
3; CurBio 64; EncMT; FamA&A; FilmgC;
InWom; IntMPA 82; MotPP; NewYTBE 70;
NotNAT; WhoAm 84; WhoHol A; WhoThe
77; WhoWor 78*

Channing, Edward
American. Historian
b. Jun 15, 1856 in Dorchester, Massachusetts
d. Jan 7, 1931
Source: *AmBi; ApCAB; DcAmB; McGEWB;
NatCAB 13; TwCBDA; WebBD 80; WhAm 1*

Channing, Stockard
[Susan Stockard]
American. Actress
b. Feb 13, 1944 in New York, New York
Source: *IntMPA 82; VarWW 85; WhoAm 82;
WhoHol A*

Channing, Walter
American. Physician
b. Apr 15, 1786 in Newport, Rhode Island
d. Jul 27, 1876 in Boston, Massachusetts
Source: *ApCAB; DcAmB; Drake; TwCBDA;
WhAm HS*

Channing, William Ellery
American. Clergyman, Abolitionist
b. Apr 7, 1780 in Newport, Rhode Island
d. Oct 2, 1842 in Bennington, Vermont
Source: *Alli; AmAu; AmAu&B; AmBi;
ApCAB; BbD; BiD&SB; CasWL; Chambr 3;
CnDAL; CyAL 1; DcAmAu; DcAmB; DcEnL;
DcNAA; Drake; EncAB-H; EvLB; OxAmL;
OxEng; PenC AM; REn; REnAL; TwCBDA;
WebAB; WhAm HS*

Chantrey, Francis Legatt, Sir
English. Artist
b. Apr 7, 1781 in Jordanthorpe, England
d. Nov 25, 1841 in London, England
Source: *BioIn 4; NewC; NewCol 75*

Chanute, Octave
American. Engineer, Aviator
Built railroads, bridges, c. 1853; improved
  glider designs contributed to successful
  flights of Orville, Wilbur Wright.
b. Feb 18, 1832 in Paris, France
d. Nov 23, 1910 in Chicago, Illinois
Source: *AmBi; DcAmB; DcNAA; InSci;
NatCAB 10; TwCBDA; WebAB, 79; WhAm 1*

Chapais, Thomas, Sir
Canadian. Journalist, Statesman
b. Mar 23, 1858 in Saint Denis, Quebec
d. Jul 15, 1948 in Saint Denis, Quebec
Source: *AmLY; BioIn 1; CanWr; DcNAA;
OxCan, SUP*

Chapelle, Dickey
American. Photojournalist
Combat photojournalist; killed in Vietnam
  mine blast.
b. Mar 14, 1918 in Shorewood, Wisconsin
d. Nov 4, 1965 in Chulai, Vietnam
Source: *DcAmB S7*

Chao, Yuen Ren
Chinese. Poet
b. Nov 3, 1892 in Tientsin, China
d. Feb 24, 1982 in Cambridge, Massachusetts
Source: *ConAu 21R, 106, P-2; WhoLA*

Chapin, Dwight Lee
American. Watergate Participant
Organized "dirty tricks" unit to harass
Democrats; convicted of perjury, Apr 5,
1974.
b. Dec 2, 1940 in Wichita, Kansas
Source: *WhoAm 82; WhoAmP 73*

Chapin, Harry Foster
American. Singer, Songwriter
Popular 1960s ballader, whose story songs
include "Taxi," 1972.
b. Dec 7, 1942 in New York, New York
d. Jul 16, 1981 in Jericho, New York
Source: *ConAu 104; IlEncRk; LilREn 78;
NewYTBS 81; RkOn 78; WhoAm 76, 78, 80;
WhoRock 81*

Chapin, James Ormsbee
American. Artist
Americana painter of "environmental
realism"; subjects range from "Barn in
Snow" to portraits of Robert Frost.
b. Jul 9, 1887 in West Orange, New Jersey
d. Jul 12, 1975 in Toronto, Ontario
Source: *CurBio 40, 75; McGDA; WhAm 6*

Chapin, Roy Dikeman
American. Manufacturer, Government Official
With J L Hudson, H E Coffin, R B
Jackson, organized Hudson Motor Car
Co., 1900; secretary of Commerce, 1932-
34.
b. Feb 23, 1880 in Lansing, Michigan
d. Feb 16, 1936 in Detroit, Michigan
Source: *BiDAmBL 83; BiDrUSE; DcAmB S2;
NatCAB 34; WhAm 1*

Chapin, Roy Dikeman
American. Auto Executive
Director, Hudson Motor Car Co., 1946-54;
chairman, American Motors, 1967-78.
b. Sep 21, 1915 in Detroit, Michigan
Source: *BlueB 76; IntWW 74, 80; NewYTBS
74; St&PR 75; Ward 77; WhoF&I 74, 81;
WhoMW 80*

Chapin, Schuyler Garrison
American. Manager
b. Feb 13, 1923 in New York, New York
Source: *BlueB 76; ConAu 77; CurBio 74;
IntWW 74, 80, 81, 82; WhoE 77*

Chaplin, Charlie
[Sir Charles Spencer]
English. Actor, Author, Composer
Known for character created in *The Tramp,*
1915; won special Oscar, 1972.
b. Apr 16, 1889 in London, England
d. Dec 25, 1977 in Vevey, Switzerland
Source: *ConAu 73, 81; CurBio 40, 61; DcFM;
EncAB-H; Film 1; IntMPA 75, 76, 77;
IntWW 74; OxAmL; REn; REnAL; TwYS;
WebAB; Who 74; WhoAm 74; WhoThe 77A;
WhoWor 78*

Chaplin, George
American. Boxer
b. 1950 in Baltimore, Maryland
Source: *NF*

Chaplin, Geraldine
American. Actress
Daughter of Charlie Chaplin; films include
Doctor Zhivago, 1965; *Nashville,* 1975.
b. Jul 31, 1944 in Santa Monica, California
Source: *ConTFT 3; FilmgC; IntMPA 82;
MotPP; WhoAm 74; WhoHol A*

Chaplin, Saul
American. Music Director, Producer
b. Feb 19, 1912 in New York, New York
Source: *AmSCAP 66; BiDAmM; BioIn 10;
CmMov; CmpEPM; FilmgC; IntMPA 75, 76,
77, 78, 79, 80, 81, 82*

Chaplin, Sydney
American. Celebrity Relative
Son of Charlie Chaplin, Lita Grey.
b. Mar 30, 1926 in Los Angeles, California
Source: *BiE&WWA; EncMT; FilmEn;
FilmgC; MotPP; NotNAT; WhoHol A*

Chaplin, Sydney Dryden
English. Actor, Comedian
Half-brother, manager of Charlie Chaplin,
who appeared in comedies, 1920s.
b. Mar 17, 1885 in Capetown, South Africa
d. Apr 16, 1956 in Nice, France
Source: *FilmEn; FilmgC; MotPP; ObitOF 79;
TwYS*

Chapman, (Anthony) Colin (Bruce)
British. Auto Manufacturer
Founded Lotus Cars Co., Ltd., 1955;
involved in development of DeLorean
sports car.
b. May 19, 1928 in Richmond, England
d. Dec 16, 1982 in Norfolk, England
Source: *AnObit 1982; IntWW 82; NewYTBS
82; Who 82; WhoWor 80*

Chapman, Ceil (Cecilia Mitchell)
American. Fashion Designer
Known for designing seductive evening gowns
with Chapman Inc., 1940-65.
b. Feb 19, 1912 in New York, New York
d. Jul 13, 1979 in Bronx, New York
Source: *NewYTBS 79; WhAm 7; WhoAmW*
58, 61, 64, 66, 68, 70, 72, 74; WorFshn

Chapman, Christian Addison
American. Diplomat
Veteran US foreign service official, who
survived assassination attempt while
ambassador to France, 1981.
b. Sep 19, 1921 in Paris, France
Source: *USBiR 74; WhoAm 76, 78, 80, 82,*
84; WhoGov 77, 72, 75

Chapman, Frank Michler
American. Ornithologist
b. Jun 12, 1864 in Englewood, New Jersey
d. Nov 15, 1945 in New York, New York
Source: *AmAu&B; CurBio 46; DcAmAu;*
DcNAA; REnAL; TwCA, SUP

Chapman, George
English. Poet, Dramatist
Best known for poetic translation of Homer
works, 1598-1624.
b. 1560 in Hitchin, England
d. May 12, 1634 in London, England
Source: *Alli, SUP; AtlBL; BbD; BiD&SB;*
BrAu; BrWr 1; CasWL; Chambr 1; ChhPo;
CnE&AP; CnThe; CroE&S; CrtT 1; CyWA;
DcBiPP; DcEnA; DcEnL; DcEuL; DcLEL;
EncWT,; EvLB; LinLib S; LongCEL;
McGEWD; MouLC 1; OxEng; OxThe; PenC
ENG; PlP&P; REn; REnWD; WebE&AL

Chapman, Gilbert Whipple
American. Business Executive
Pres., NY Public Library, 1959-71; one of
original directors of Lincoln Center for
Performing Arts.
b. May 24, 1902 in Woodmere, New York
d. Dec 16, 1979 in Manhattan, New York
Source: *BiE&WWA; CurBio 57, 80;*
NewYTBS 79; WhAm 7

Chapman, Graham
[Monty Python's Flying Circus]
English. Actor, Writer
Starred in, wrote satirical Python films:
Python's Life of Brian, 1980.
b. Jan 8, 1941 in Leicester, England
Source: *BioIn 10; WhoAm 82, 84*

Chapman, John
see: Appleseed, Johnny

Chapman, John (Arthur)
American. Drama Critic
b. Jun 25, 1900 in Denver, Colorado
d. Jan 19, 1972 in Westport, Connecticut
Source: *AmAu&B; ConAu 33R; WhAm 5*

Chapman, Leonard F, Jr.
American. General
With USMC, 1935-72; commander,
Immigration and Naturalization Service,
1973-77.
b. Nov 3, 1913 in Key West, Florida
Source: *BlueB 76; WebAMB; WhoAm 80*

Chapman, Mark David
American. Murderer
Shot, killed John Lennon, Dec 8, 1980.
b. May 10, 1955 in Fort Worth, Texas
Source: *BioIn 12*

Chappell, William
English. Dancer
b. Sep 27, 1908 in Wolverhampton, England
Source: *BioIn 3, 4, 11; Who 74; WhoThe 72,*
77

Chapple, Stanley
English. Conductor
b. Oct 29, 1900 in London, England
Source: *Baker 78; Who 74, 82; WhoMus 72*

Char, Rene (Emile)
French. Poet
b. Jun 14, 1907 in L'Isle Sorgue, France
Source: *CasWL; CnMWL; ConAu 13R;*
EncWL; EvEuW; IntWW 74; ModRL; OxFr;
PenC EUR; REn; TwCWr; WhoAm 74;
WhoTwCL; WhoWor 78; WorAu

Charboneau, Joe (Joseph)
"Super Joe"
American. Baseball Player
b. Jun 17, 1955 in Belvedere, Illinois
Source: *BaseEn 85; NewYTBS 81; PseudN 82*

Charcot, Jean Baptiste Etienne Auguste
French. Explorer
Obtained scientific data from voyages,
including seven to Greenland, 1920-35.
b. Jul 15, 1867 in Neuilly, France
d. Sep 16, 1936 in Iceland
Source: *DcScB; InSci; NewCol 75; OxShips*

Charcot, Jean Martin
French. Physician
b. Nov 29, 1825 in Paris, France
d. Aug 16, 1893
Source: *DcBiPP; McGEWB; WebBD 80*

Chardin, Jean Baptiste Simeon
French. Artist
b. Nov 2, 1699 in Paris, France
d. Dec 6, 1779 in Paris, France
Source: *AtlBL; OxFr; REn*

Chardonnet, Louis Marie
French. Chemist, Inventor
Patented rayon, 1884, first artificial fiber
   commonly used.
b. May 1, 1839 in Besancon, France
d. Mar 12, 1924 in Paris, France
Source: *AsBiEn*

Chares
Greek. Sculptor
b. 320 BC
Source: *NewCol 75; WebBD 80*

Charisse, Cyd
[Tula Ellice Finklea; Mrs. Tony Martin]
American. Dancer, Actress
Fred Astaire's favorite dancing partner.
b. Mar 8, 1923 in Amarillo, Texas
Source: *BiDFilm; CmMov; CurBio 54;
FilmgC; InWom; IntMPA 75, 76, 77, 78, 79,
80, 81, 82; MotPP; MovMk; OxFilm; WhoAm
74, 76, 78, 80, 82; WhoHol A; WorEFlm*

Charlemagne
[Charles the Great]
King
Conquered, ruled almost all Christian lands
   of Europe, 768-814.
b. Apr 2, 742
d. Jan 28, 814
Source: *AsBiEn; DcCathB; DcEuL; DcSpL;
Dis&D; EncO&P 78; LinLib L, S; LuthC 75;
McGEWB; NewC; OxFr; OxGer; OxLaw;
REn; WhDW*

Charles
[Charles Philip Arthur George]
English. Prince
Son of Queen Elizabeth II, heir to British
   throne.
b. Nov 14, 1948 in London, England
Source: *BkPepl; CurBio 69; NewYTBS 77;
WhoWor 80*

Charles I
English. Ruler
King of Great Britain, Ireland, 1625-49; need
   for money, power led to English Civil
   Wars.
b. Nov 19, 1600
d. Jan 30, 1649
Source: *BioIn 10; DcBiPP; WebBD 80;
WhDW*

Charles II
[Charles the Bald]
French. Ruler
b. 823
d. 877
Source: *NewCol 75*

Charles II
"Merry Monarch"
English. Ruler
King of Great Britain, Ireland, 1660-85;
   wanted to strengthen monarchy, reduce
   financial power of Parliament.
b. May 29, 1630
d. Feb 6, 1685
Source: *DcBiPP; WebBD 80; WhDW*

Charles V
Ruler
Hapsburg King of Spain, 1516-50; Holy
   Roman Emperor, 1519; signed the Treaty
   of Crecy, 1544; Peace of Augsburg, 1555.
b. Feb 24, 1500 in Ghent, Flanders
d. Sep 21, 1558 in Spain
Source: *DcBiPP; DcCathB; McGEWB; WhDW*

Charles VII
[Charles Albert; Charles of Bavaria]
Ruler
Holy Roman emperor, 1742-45; in War of
   Austrian Succession, 1740-48.
b. Aug 6, 1697
d. Jan 20, 1745
Source: *NewCol 75; WebBD 80*

Charles XII
Swedish. Ruler
King of Sweden, 1697-1718; lost battle of
   Poltaua, 1709, which ended Swedish
   Supremacy.
b. Jun 27, 1682
d. Dec 11, 1718 in Fredriksten, Norway
Source: *NewCol 75; WebBD 80; WhDW*

Charles Martel
[Charles the Hammer]
Ruler
Head of Frankish empire later ruled by
   grandson Charlemagne.
b. 689
d. 741
Source: *DcBiPP; DcCathB; OxFr; REn;
WhDW; WorAl*

Charles, Ezzard
American. Boxer
Heavyweight champion, 1949-51.
b. Jul 7, 1921 in Lawrenceville, Georgia
d. May 28, 1975 in Chicago, Illinois
Source: *BioNews 74; CurBio 49; WhoBox 74*

Charles, Glen
American. Writer, Producer
Won Emmys, 1979, 1980, 1981, for "Taxi";
1983, 1984 for "Cheers."
b. in Henderson, New York
Source: *VarWW 85*

Charles, Jacques-Alexandre-Cesar
French. Physicist, Mathematician
b. Nov 12, 1746 in Beaugency, France
d. Apr 7, 1823 in Paris, France
Source: *AsBiEn; BioIn 1, 7; DcScB*

Charles, Lee
American. Writer, Producer
Wrote award-winning scripts for several TV
shows, including "Taxi"; "Cheers";
"MASH."
b. in Henderson, Nevada
Source: *VarWW 85*

Charles, Ray
[Charles Raymond Offenberg]
American. Composer
Won Emmys for "The First Nine Months
Are the Hardest," 1971; "The Funny Side
of Marriage," 1972.
b. Sep 13, 1918 in Chicago, Illinois
Source: *VarWW 85*

Charles, Ray
[Ray Charles Robinson]
American. Singer, Songwriter, Musician
Won 10 Grammy awards; appeared in movie
The Blues Brothers.
b. Sep 23, 1930 in Albany, Georgia
Source: *Baker 78; BiDAmM; BioNews 74;
BlueB 76; BkPepl; BluesWW; CelR; CurBio
65; DrBlPA; Ebony 1; EncAB-H; EncJzS 70;
IlEncJ; WhoAm 80, 82; WhoBlA 75; WhoWor
74*

Charles, Suzette
[Suzette DeGaetano]
American. Beauty Contest Winner
First runner-up in Miss America pagent,
1983; succeeded Vanessa Williams, Jul 1983
when she was forced to give up crown.
b. 1963 in Philadelphia, Pennsylvania
Source: *NF*

Charleson, Ian
Scottish. Actor
Starred in Oscar-winning *Chariots of Fire,*
1981.
b. Aug 11, 1949 in Edinburgh, Scotland
Source: *NewYTBS 81; WhoThe 81*

Charleston, Oscar McKinley
"Charlie"
American. Baseball Player, Baseball Manager
Player/mgr. for Pittsburgh Crawfords, great
team in Negro leagues, 1932-38; Hall of
Fame, 1976.
b. Oct 12, 1896 in Indianapolis, Indiana
d. Oct 5, 1954 in Philadelphia, Pennsylvania
Source: *BasesB*

Charlevoix, Pierre Francis Xavier de
French. Traveler, Author
b. Oct 29, 1682 in Saint Quentin, France
d. Feb 1, 1761 in La Fleche, France
Source: *BiDSA; OxCan*

Charlie Daniels Band, The
[Tom Bigfoot Crain; Charlie Daniels; Joe
Taz DiGregorio; Fred Edwards; Charlie
Hatward; Don Murray]
American. Music Group
Source: *IlEncRk*

Charlip, Remy
American. Dancer, Author, Actor
b. Jan 10, 1929 in Brooklyn, New York
Source: *AuBYP; ChhPo S1; ConAu 33R;
IlsCB 1946, 1957; SmATA 4; ThrBJA; WrDr
80*

Charlotte Aldegonde E M Wilhelmine
Luxembourg. Ruler
Grand Duchess of Luxembourg, 1919-64;
helped to found European Common
Market.
b. Jan 23, 1896 in Chateau de Berg,
Luxembourg
d. Jul 9, 1985 in Luxembourg
Source: *CurBio 49; InWom; IntWW 74, 75;
WhoWor 78, 80*

Charlotte Sophia
English. Consort
b. 1744
d. 1818
Source: *InWom*

Charlton, Manny
see: Nazareth

Charlton, Robert
British. Soccer Player
b. Oct 11, 1937
Source: *Who 74*

Charmoli, Tony
American. Choreographer
b. in Minnesota
Source: *WhoAm 74, 74*

Charney, Nicolas Herman
American. Publisher
b. May 11, 1941 in Saint Paul, Minnesota
Source: *WhoAm 74, 76, 78, 80, 82*

Charnley, John, Sir
English. Surgeon
Orthopedic surgeon who perfected total
   prosthetic hip replacement.
b. Aug 29, 1911 in Burg, England
d. Aug 12, 1982 in Knutsford, England
Source: *AnObit 1982; BioIn 10, 11; Who 74;*
WhoWor 82

Charo
[Maria Rosario Pilar Martinez]
Spanish. Actress, Singer
Recorded several albums; appeared on TV
   shows including "Love Boat."
b. Jan 15, 1951 in Murcia, Spain
Source: *VarWW 85*

Charoux, Siegfried
British. Sculptor
b. 1896
d. Apr 26, 1967 in London, England
Source: *BioIn 8*

Charpentier, Gustave
French. Composer
b. Jun 25, 1860 in Dieuze, France
d. Feb 18, 1956 in Paris, France
Source: *OxFr; REn*

Charpentier, Marc-Antoine
French. Composer
b. 1634 in Paris, France
d. Feb 24, 1704 in Paris, France
Source: *REn*

Charriere, Henri
"Papillon"
French. Author, Murderer
Escaped from Devil's Island, 1941; book
   Papillion sold over five million copies;
   Steve McQueen starred in movie, 1973.
b. 1906
d. Jul 29, 1973 in Madrid, Spain
Source: *ASpks; ConAu 101, 45; NewYTBE 73;*
ObitOF 79; ObitT 1971; WhScrn 77

Charron, Pierre
French. Theologian
b. 1541 in Paris, France
d. Nov 16, 1603 in Paris, France
Source: *BioIn 6; CasWL; DcEuL; OxFr;*
PenC EUR

Charteris, Leslie
American. Author, Producer
b. May 12, 1907 in Singapore
Source: *AmAu&B; Au&Wr 71; ConAu 5R;*
EncMys; EvLB; FilmgC; IntMPA 75, 76, 77,
78, 79, 80, 81, 82; IntWW 74; LongCTC;
MnBBF; NewC; REn; REnAL; TwCA, SUP;
TwCWr; Who 74; WhoAm 74, 76, 78, 80, 82;
WhoS&SW 82; WrDr 80

Chartier, Emile Auguste
see: Alain, pseud.

Chartoff, Robert
American. Producer
Films include *Rocky III; Right Stuff;* won
   Oscar for *Rocky,* 1976.
b. Aug 26, 1933 in New York, New York
Source: *VarWW 85*

Chase, Charley
American. Comedian
b. Oct 20, 1893 in Baltimore, Maryland
d. Jun 20, 1940 in Hollywood, California
Source: *CurBio 40; MotPP; OxFilm; TwYS;*
WhScrn 74, 77; WhoHol A; WorEFlm

Chase, "Chevy" (Cornelius Crane)
American. Actor, Comedian
Starred on "Saturday Night Live"; won
   Emmy, 1976.
b. Oct 8, 1943 in New York, New York
Source: *ConTFT 3; WhoAm 80, 82*

Chase, Chris
American. Author, Actress
Source: *AuNews 1*

Chase, David
Writer, Producer
Winner of four Emmys who produced
   "Rockford Files"; "Off the Minnesota
   Strip."
b. Aug 22, 1945
Source: *VarWW 85*

Chase, Edna Woolman
American. Editor
Editor-in-chief, *Vogue* magazine, 1914-55;
   organized first American fashion show,
   1944.
b. Mar 14, 1877 in Asbury Park, New Jersey
d. Mar 20, 1957 in Sarasota, Florida
Source: *CurBio 40, 57; EncAB 28; EncAJ;*
NotAW MOD; ObitOF 79; REnAL; WhAm 3;
WorFshn

Chase, Ilka
American. Author, Actress, Humorist
b. Apr 8, 1905 in New York, New York
d. Feb 15, 1978 in Mexico City, Mexico
Source: *AmAu&B; CelR; ConAu 61, 77; CurBio 42; FamA&A; FilmgC; InWom; IntMPA 75, 76, 77; MovMk; NotNAT; REnAL; ThFT; WhoAm 74; WhoHol A; WhoThe 77*

Chase, Lucia
American. Ballerina
Principal dancer, American Ballet Theatre, 1940-60; co-director, 1945-80.
b. Mar 27, 1907 in Waterbury, Connecticut
d. Jan 9, 1986 in New York, New York
Source: *BiDD; CelR; CurBio 47, 75, 86; WhoAm 84; WhoE 81; WhoWor 82*

Chase, Mary Agnes
American. Botanist
Expert on grasses; wrote popular manual *First Book of Grasses,* 1922.
b. Apr 20, 1869 in Iroquois County, Illinois
d. Sep 24, 1963 in Washington, District of Columbia
Source: *NotAW MOD*

Chase, Mary Coyle
American. Author, Dramatist
Best known for Pulitzer-winning play *Harvey,* 1944.
b. Feb 25, 1907 in Denver, Colorado
d. Oct 20, 1981 in Denver, Colorado
Source: *AmAu&B; AmWomWr; AuBYP; BioIn 1, 3, 4, 6, 7, 8, 10; CnDAL; ConAu 73, 77; CurBio 45, 82; DcLEL; EncWT; InWom; LongCTC; McGEWB; ModWD; NewYTBS 81; OxAmL; REn; REnAL; TwCA SUP; WhoAm 74, 76, 78; WhoAmW 58, 64, 66, 68, 70, 72, 74; WrDr 76*

Chase, Mary Ellen
American. Children's Author
b. Feb 24, 1887 in Blue Hill, Maine
d. Jul 28, 1973 in Northampton, Massachusetts
Source: *ConAu 41R, P-1; CurBio 40, 73; OxAmL; PenC AM; REn; REnAL; SmATA 10; TwCA, SUP; WhAm 5*

Chase, Philander
American. Clergyman
b. Dec 14, 1775 in Cornish, New Hampshire
d. Sep 20, 1852 in Robin's Nest, Illinois
Source: *Alli; AmBi; ApCAB; CyAL 1; DcAmAu; DcAmB; DcNAA; Drake; OhA&B; TwCBDA; WebAB; WhAm HS*

Chase, Richard Volney
American. Literary Critic, Educator
b. Oct 12, 1914 in Lakeport, New Hampshire
d. Aug 26, 1962 in Plymouth, Massachusetts
Source: *AmAu&B; BioIn 4, 6, 9; PenC AM; REnAL; TwCA SUP*

Chase, Salmon Portland
American. Supreme Court Justice
Devoted life to ending slavery; co-founded Rep. Party; portrait on $10,000 bill.
b. Jan 13, 1808 in Cornish, New Hampshire
d. May 7, 1873 in New York, New York
Source: *AmAu&B; AmBi; ApCAB; BbD; BiAUS; BiD&SB; BiDrAC; BiDrUSE; DcAmB; DcNAA; Drake; EncAB-H; OhA&B; TwCBDA; WebAB; WhAm HS; WhAmP*

Chase, Samuel
American. Supreme Court Justice
Appointed to Supreme Court by George Washington, 1796; only justice ever to be impeached, 1804; found not guilty in Senate trial, 1805.
b. Apr 17, 1741 in Somerset County, Missouri
d. Jun 19, 1811 in Baltimore, Maryland
Source: *AmBi; ApCAB; BiAUS; BiDrAC; DcAmB; Drake; TwCBDA; WebAB; WhAm HS; WhAmP*

Chase, Stuart
American. Author, Economist
Member of Franklin Roosevelt's brain trust who coined phrase "New Deal."
b. Mar 8, 1888 in Somersworth, New Hampshire
d. Nov 17, 1985 in Redding, Connecticut
Source: *AmAu&B; ChhPo S2; ConAmA; CurBio 40; DcLEL; IntWW 74; LongCTC; OxAmL; REn; REnAL; TwCA, SUP; WebAB; WhNAA; Who 74; WhoAm 74; WhoWor 78*

Chase, Sylvia
American. Broadcast Journalist
Correspondent, ABC News "20/20," 1978--; won Emmys, 1978, 1980.
b. Feb 23, 1938 in Northfield, Minnesota
Source: *BioIn 10; ConAu 115; WhoAm 80, 82*

Chase, William Curtis
American. Army Officer
b. Mar 9, 1895 in Providence, Rhode Island
d. Aug 21, 1986 in Houston, Texas
Source: *WebAMB*

Chase, William Merritt
American. Artist
b. Nov 1, 1849 in Williamsburg, Indiana
d. Oct 25, 1916
Source: *AmBi; ApCAB; DcAmB; OxAmL; TwCBDA; WhAm 1*

Chasins, Abram
American. Pianist, Composer
b. Aug 17, 1903 in New York, New York
Source: *AmAu&B; AmSCAP 66; ConAu 37R; CurBio 60; WhoAm 74; WhoMus 72; WhoWorJ 72*

Chataway, Christopher John
English. Journalist, Politician
b. Jan 31, 1931
Source: *BioIn 7; IntWW 74; Who 74; WhoWor 78*

Chateaubriand, Francois Rene de
French. Author, Statesman
Pioneer of romantic movement; wrote *Memories from Beyond the Tomb,* 1850.
b. Sep 4, 1768 in Saint-Malo, France
d. Jul 4, 1848 in Paris, France
Source: *ApCAB; AtlBL; BbD; BiD&SB; BiDLA SUP; CasWL; CyWA; DcBiA; DcEuL; EuAu; EvEuW; NewC; OxAmL; OxEng; OxFr; PenC EUR; RComWL; REn; REnAL*

Chatfield, Alfred E Montacute, Baron
British. Admiral
b. 1873
d. Nov 15, 1967 in London, England
Source: *BioIn 8*

Chatterton, Ruth
American. Actress, Author
Wrote several novels in 1950s; Oscar nominee for *Madame X, Sarah and Son.*
b. Dec 24, 1893 in New York, New York
d. Nov 24, 1961 in Norwalk, Connecticut
Source: *AmAu&B; BiDFilm; CmMov; Film 2; FilmgC; InWom; MotPP; MovMk; NotNAT B; ThFT; WhAm 4; WhScrn 74, 77; WhThe; WhoHol B; WomWMM; WorAl*

Chatterton, Thomas
English. Poet
Claimed his "Rowley Poems" were copies of 15th c. manuscripts.
b. Nov 20, 1752 in Bristol, England
d. Aug 25, 1770 in Bristol, England
Source: *Alli; AtlBL; BbD; BiD&SB; BrAu; CasWL; Chambr 2; ChhPo; CnE&AP; CrtT 2; DcEnA; DcEnL; DcEuL; DcLEL; EvLB; MouLC 2; NewC; OxEng; PenC ENG; RComWL; REn; WebE&AL*

Chaucer, Geoffrey
English. Poet
Wrote *The Canterbury Tales,* ca. 1387, never completed.
b. 1340 in London, England
d. Oct 25, 1400 in London, England
Source: *Alli; AnCL; AtlBL; BbD; BiD&SB; BrAu; CasWL; Chambr 1; ChhPo, S1, S2; CnE&AP; CrtT 1; CyWA; DcEnA; DcEnL; DcEuL; DcLEL; EvLB; MouLC 1; NewC; OxEng; PenC ENG; PoLE; RAdv 1; RComWL; REn; WebE&AL*

Chaudhuri, Haridas
Indian. Educator, Author
b. May 24, 1913 in Calcutta, India
d. 1975
Source: *ConAu 5R; WhoWest 84*

Chauncey, Isaac
American. Military Leader
b. Feb 20, 1772 in Black Rock, Connecticut
d. Jan 27, 1840 in Washington, District of Columbia
Source: *AmBi; ApCAB; DcAmB; Drake; TwCBDA; WhAm HS*

Chausson, Ernest
French. Composer
b. Jun 21, 1855 in Paris, France
d. Jun 10, 1899 in Limay, France
Source: *AtlBL; NewCol 75; WebBD 80*

Chautemps, Camille
French. Political Leader
b. Feb 1, 1885 in Paris, France
d. Jul 1, 1963 in Washington, District of Columbia
Source: *ObitOF 79; WhAm 4*

Chauvire, Yvette
French. Dancer
b. Apr 22, 1917 in Paris, France
Source: *IntWW 74; Who 74; WhoWor 74*

Chavez, Carlos
Mexican. Composer, Conductor
b. Jun 13, 1899 in Mexico City, Mexico
d. Aug 2, 1978 in Mexico City, Mexico
Source: *AmSCAP 66; CurBio 49; DcCM; IntWW 74; REn; WhoMus 72; WhoS&SW 82; WhoWor 78*

Chavez, Cesar
American. Labor Union Official
Organized National Farm Workers Assn., 1962.
b. Mar 31, 1927 in Yuma, Arizona
Source: *BioNews 74; BkPepl; BusPN; CelR; CurBio 69; EncAB-H; WebAB; WhoAm 82; WhoWor 78*

Chavis, Ben
[Wilmington 10]
American. Civil Rights Activist
Source: *BioIn 10*

Chavis, John
American. Clergyman, Educator
b. 1763
d. 1838
Source: *BioIn 1, 2, 7, 9*

Chayefsky, "Paddy" (Sidney)
American. Dramatist
Best known for screenplays *Marty*, 1953; won
Oscar, 1976, for *Network*.
b. Jan 29, 1923 in New York, New York
d. Aug 1, 1981 in New York, New York
Source: *AmAu&B; AmSCAP 66; BiE&WWA;
AmSCAP 80; BioIn 3, 4, 10, 11, 12; CelR;
CnMD; CnThe; ConAu 9R, 104; ConDr 73,
77; CroCD; CurBio 57, 81; DcFM; DcLEL
1940; EncSF; EncWT; FilmgC; IntAu&W 76,
77; IntMPA 75, 76, 77, 78, 79; IntWW 74,
75, 76, 77, 78; LinLib L; McGEWD;
ModWD; NewYTBS 81; NewYTET; NotNAT;
OxAmL; OxFilm; PenC AM; PIP&P; REnAL;
WebAB; WhoAm 74, 76, 78, 80; WhoE 74;
WhoThe 77; WhoTwCL; WhoWor 74; WorAu;
WorEFlm; WrDr 76*

Chayes, Abram J
American. Lawyer, Government Official
b. Jul 18, 1922 in Chicago, Illinois
Source: *BioIn 5, 11; DrAS 74P; IntWW 74;
WhoAm 74, 76, 78, 80, 82; WhoWorJ 72*

Cheap Trick
[Bun E Carlos; Rick Nielsen; Tom Petesson;
Robin Zander]
American. Music Group
IL-based foursome started 1977, known for
weird antics.
Source: *ConMuA 80A; WhoRock 81*

Checker, Chubby
[Ernest Evans]
American. Singer, Dancer
Recorded "The Twist," which became dance
sensation of early 1960s.
b. Oct 3, 1941 in South Philadelphia,
Pennsylvania
Source: *AmSCAP 66; BiDAmM; FilmgC;
IlEncBM 82; InB&W 80; WhoAm 74;
WhoBlA 75; WhoHol A*

Cheech and Chong
[Tommy Chong; Cheech Marin]
American. Comedy Team
Source: *EncPR&S 74; RkOn 84; WorAl*

Cheever, John
American. Author
Won Pulitzer, 1979; noted for subtle, comic
style.
b. May 27, 1912 in Quincy, Massachusetts
d. Jun 18, 1982 in Ossining, New York
Source: *AmAu&B; AmWr S1; CasWL; ConAu
5R, 5NR; ConLC 3, 7, 8, 11; ConNov 72,
76; CurBio 75, 82; DcLB 2; DcLEL 1940;
DrAF 76; EncWL; IntAu&W 76, 77; IntWW
74, 75, 76, 77, 78; LinLib L; ModAL, S1;
NewYTBS 78, 79, 82; OxAmL; PenC AM;
Po&Wr 77; RAdv 1; REn; REnAL; TwCWr;
WebE&AL; Who 82; WhoAm 74, 76, 78, 80,
82; WhoTwCL; WhoWor 74, 76, 78; WorAu;
WrDr 76, 80*

Chekhov, Anton Pavlovich
Russian. Author, Dramatist
Wrote *Three Sisters*, 1901, *The Cherry
Orchard*, 1904.
b. Jan 17, 1860 in Teganrog, Russia
d. Jul 2, 1904 in Badenweiler, Germany
Source: *AtlBL; CasWL; ClDMEL; CnMD;
CnThe; CyWA; DcEuL; DcRusL; EncWL;
EuAu; EvEuW; McGEWD; ModSL 1;
ModWD; NewC; OxEng; OxThe; PenC EUR;
PIP&P, A; RComWL; REn; REnWD*

Chekhov, Michael
Russian. Director
Nephew of Anton Chekov; founded drama
schools in England, US; nominated for
Oscar, 1945, for *Spellbound*.
b. Aug 28, 1891 in Leningrad, Russia
d. Sep 30, 1955 in Beverly Hills, California
Source: *FilmgC; MotPP; OxThe; WhScrn 74,
77; WhoHol B*

Chen, Joyce Liao
Restaurateur
b. 1917
Source: *BioIn 9*

Cheney, John Vance
American. Poet, Librarian
b. Dec 29, 1848 in Groveland, New York
d. May 1, 1922 in San Diego, California
Source: *AmAu; AmAu&B; AmLY; BbD;
BiD&SB; DcAmAu; DcNAA; OxAmL; REnAL*

Cheney, Sheldon Warren
American. Art Critic, Drama Critic
Wrote classic surveys: *The Theater*, 1929;
World History of Art, 1937.
b. Jun 29, 1886 in Berkeley, California
d. Oct 10, 1980 in Berkeley, California
Source: *AmAu&B; BiE&WWA; BioIn 4;
ConAu 102; IntAu&W 76; NotNAT; REnAL;
TwCA, SUP; WhE&EA; WhThe; WhoAm 74,
76, 78; WhoAmA 73, 76, 78; WhoWor 74, 76*

Chenier, Marie-Andre de
French. Author, Poet
Early French Romanticist whose verse
   volumes include *La Jeune Captive*, 1795.
b. Oct 30, 1762 in Constantinople, Turkey
d. Jul 25, 1794
Source: *AtlBL; BbD; BiD&SB; CasWL;*
DcEuL; EuAu; EvEuW; OxEng; OxFr; PenC
EUR; REn

Chenier, Phil(ip)
American. Basketball Player
b. Oct 30, 1950 in Berkeley, California
Source: *OfNBA 81; WhoBbl 73*

Chennault, Anna Chan
[Mrs. Claire Lee Chennault]
Chinese. Journalist, Author
US correspondent *Hsin Shen Daily News,*
   Taipei, 1958--; wrote best seller *Chennault*
   and the Flying Tigers, 1963.
b. Jun 23, 1925 in Peking, China
Source: *AmAu&B; BlueB 76; ConAu 61;*
ForWC 70; IntAu&W 76; WhoAm 80, 82;
WhoAmP 73; WhoAmW 74, 77; WhoS&SW
73

Chennault, Claire Lee
American. Aviator
b. Sep 6, 1890 in Commerce, Texas
d. Jul 27, 1958
Source: *AmAu&B; CurBio 42, 58; WhAm 3*

Chenoweth, Dean
"Comeback Kid"
American. Boat Racer
Four-time national champion.
b. 1934 in Xenia, Ohio
d. Jul 31, 1982 in Pasco, Washington
Source: *NF*

Cheops
[Khufu]
Egyptian. King
Builder of the Great Pyramid at Giza.
Source: *LinLib S; WhDW; WorAl*

Cher
[Cher Bono; Cherylynn LaPiere; Cherilyn
   Sarkisian; Sonny and Cher]
American. Singer, Actress
Pop singer with husband Sonny Bono, solo;
   in films *Silkwood*, 1983; *Mask*, 1985.
b. May 20, 1946 in El Centro, California
Source: *BkPepl; CelR; ConTFT 3; CurBio 74;*
HerW; IntMPA 82; WhoAm 84; WhoHol A

Chermayeff, Ivan
American. Artist, Designer
b. Jun 6, 1932 in London, England
Source: *BioIn 8, 9, 10; IlsCB 1967; WhoAm*
74, 76, 78, 80, 82; WhoAmA 73; WhoE 74

Chermayeff, Serge
American. Author
b. Oct 8, 1900 in Caucasia, Colombia
Source: *ConAu 21R*

Chernenko, Konstantin Ustinovich
Russian. Political Leader
Called first Siberian, first peasant to lead
   USSR; oldest man elected general secretary
   of USSR's Communist Party; succeeded
   Andropov, Feb 13, 1984.
b. Sep 24, 1911 in Bolshaya Tes, Russia
d. Mar 10, 1985 in Moscow, U.S.S.R.
Source: *ConNews 85-1; CurBio 84, 85;*
IntWW 78, 79, 80, 81, 82; NewYTBS 78;
WhoSocC 78, 78A; WhoWor 80

Cherniavsky, Josef
Russian. Conductor, Composer
b. Mar 31, 1895 in Russia
d. Nov 3, 1959 in New York, New York
Source: *AmSCAP 66; BioIn 5*

Chernov, Viktor Mikhailovich
Russian. Journalist
b. 1876
d. Apr 15, 1952 in New York, New York
Source: *WebBD 80*

Cherrington, Ben Mark
American. Statesman, Educator
b. Nov 1, 1885 in Gibbon, Nebraska
d. Mar 4, 1980 in Denver, Colorado
Source: *AmM&WS 73S; NewYTBS 80;*
WhoWest 74, 76

Cherry, Don(ald Stewart)
Canadian. Sportscaster, Hockey Coach
Coach, Boston, 1974-79; analyst on NHL
   telecasts.
b. Feb 5, 1934 in Kingston, Ontario
Source: *WhoAm 78, 80, 82*

Cherubini, Maria Luigi
Italian. Composer
b. Sep 14, 1760 in Florence, Italy
d. Mar 15, 1842 in Paris, France
Source: *NewEOp 71; WebBD 80*

Cherwell, Frederick Alexander L
English. Physicist
b. 1886 in Sidmouth, England
d. Jul 2, 1957
Source: *CurBio 52, 57*

Chesbro, "Happy Jack" (John Dwight)
American. Baseball Player
Pitcher, NY Highlanders; won 41 games,
1904, highest total in 20th c.
b. Jun 5, 1874 in North Adams,
Massachusetts
d. Nov 6, 1931 in Conway, Massachusetts
Source: *BaseEn 85; BioIn 3, 7; WhoProB 73*

Chesebrough, Robert Augustus
American. Chemist
Began manufacturing petroleum products,
1858; patented Vaseline, 1870.
b. Jan 9, 1837 in London, England
d. Sep 8, 1933 in Spring Lake, New Jersey
Source: *NatCAB 3, 25; TwCBDA; WhAm 1*

Cheshire, Maxine
[Mrs. Bert W Cheshire]
American. Journalist
Reporter, Washington *Post*, 1954-65;
columnist LA Times Syndicate since 1965.
b. Apr 5, 1930 in Harlan, Kentucky
Source: *CelR; WhoAm 82*

Chesney, Francis Rawdon
British. Soldier, Explorer
b. Mar 16, 1789 in Ireland
d. Jan 30, 1872
Source: *NewCol 75; WebBD 80*

Chesney, Marion
[M C Beaton; Ann Fairfax; Jennie Tremaine,
pseuds.]
Scottish. Author
Historical novels include *Sally*, 1982.
b. Jun 10, 1936 in Glasgow, Scotland
Source: *ConAu 115*

Chesnutt, Charles Waddell
American. Author, Lawyer
b. Jun 20, 1858 in Cleveland, Ohio
d. Nov 15, 1932 in Cleveland, Ohio
Source: *AmAu&B; AmLY; BlkAWP; CasWL;
CnDAL; CyWA; DcAmAu; DcNAA; OhA&B;
OxAmL; TwCA SUP*

Chessex, Jacques
Swiss. Author
b. Mar 1, 1934 in Payerne, Switzerland
Source: *BioIn 10; ConAu 65*

Chessman, Caryl Whittier
American. Criminal, Author
Lived on Death Row 12 years; Alan Alda
starred in movie of his life, 1977.
b. May 27, 1921 in Saint Joseph, Michigan
d. May 2, 1960 in San Quentin, California
Source: *AmAu&B; Blood&B; ConAu 73;
WebAB*

Chesterfield, Philip Dormer, Earl
[Philip Dormer Stanhope]
English. Author, Statesman
Letters to His Son, 1774, classic portrait of
18th c. gentleman.
b. Sep 22, 1694 in London, England
d. Mar 24, 1773 in London, England
Source: *Alli; AtlBL; BbD; BiD&SB; BrAu;
CasWL; Chambr 3; CyWA; DcBiPP; DcEnA;
DcEnL; DcEuL; DcLEL; EvLB; LinLib L, S;
MouLC 2; NewC; OxEng; PenC ENG; REn;
WebE&AL*

Chesterton, Gilbert Keith
English. Poet, Critic, Essayist
Wrote *Father Brown* detective stories, 1911-
45; literary criticism.
b. May 29, 1874 in Kensington, England
d. Jun 14, 1936 in Chiltern Hills, England
Source: *AnCL; AtlBL; CasWL; CathA 1930;
Chambr 3; CnMWL; ConAu 104; CorpD;
CyWA; DcCathB; DcLEL; EvLB; OxEng;
PenC ENG; RAdv 1; REn; ScF&FL 1;
TwCA, SUP; TwCWr; WhoLA*

Chevalier, Maurice Auguste
French. Actor, Singer
Star of stage, screen; won special Oscar,
1958.
b. Sep 12, 1888 in Paris, France
d. Jan 1, 1972 in Paris, France
Source: *BiDFilm; BiE&WWA; CmMov;
ConAu 33R; CurBio 48, 69, 72; Film 1;
FilmgC; MovMk; OxFilm; OxThe; WhAm 5;
WhScrn 77; WhThe; WhoHol B; WorAl;
WorEFlm*

Chevallier, Gabriel
French. Author
b. May 1895 in Lyons, France
d. 1969
Source: *CasWL; EvEuW; REn; TwCWr*

Chevreul, Michel
French. Chemist
b. Aug 31, 1786 in Angers, France
d. Apr 9, 1889 in Paris, France
Source: *NewCol 75*

Chevrolet, Gaston
Auto Manufacturer
Source: *NF*

Chevrolet, Louis Joseph
American. Auto Racer
Defeated Barney Oldfield in auto race, 1905;
designed six-cylinder car, Chevrolet, 1910.
b. Dec 25, 1878 in Switzerland
d. Jun 6, 1941 in Detroit, Michigan
Source: *CurBio 41; Entr*

Chew, Peter
American. Journalist, Author
Newspaper, magazine reporter who wrote *The Kentucky Derby: The First One Hundred Years,* 1974.
b. Apr 5, 1924 in New Rochelle, New York
Source: *ConAu 57*

Cheyney, Peter (Reginald E)
[Harold Brust]
English. Author
Suspense novels include *Lemmy Caution* series, 1930s.
b. 1896 in London, England
d. Jun 26, 1951
Source: *ConAu 113; EncMys; WhoSpyF*

Chi
see: Candy, John

Chiang, Ching
[Chiang Ching Mao; Ping Lan]
Chinese. Actress, Political Leader
Wife of Mao Tse-tung, sentenced to death as member of "gang of four," 1976.
b. 1913 in Chucheng, China
Source: *CurBio 75; DcOrL 1; DcPol; FarE&A 78; GoodHs; WhoAmW 75; WomWMM*

Chiang, Ching-Kuo
Chinese. President
Son of Chiang Kai-Shek; pres., Republic of China, 1978.
b. 1906
Source: *CurBio 54; FarE&A 81; IntWW 74, 81, 82; IntYB 82; WhoWor 74, 80*

Chiang Kai-Shek
Chinese. Statesman
Head of state, 1928-49; exiled by communists to Taiwan, 1949-75.
b. Oct 31, 1886 in Fenghua, China
d. Apr 5, 1975 in Taipei, Taiwan
Source: *CurBio 40, 53; DcPol; EncWM; HisEWW; IntWW 75N; LinLib S; McGEWB; REn; WhAm 6; Who 74*

Chiang Mei-Ling
[Madame Chiang Kai-Shek; Mayling Soong]
Chinese. Sociologist
b. Jun 5, 1897
Source: *CurBio 40; REn; Who 82*

Chiang, Yee
American. Author, Educator
Columbia U. professor, 1968-71, who wrote, illustrated *Silent Traveller* series, 1937-56.
b. May 19, 1903 in Kiukiang, China
d. Oct 17, 1977 in Peking, China
Source: *ConAu 65, 73; IlsCB 1744, 1946; IntAu&W 77; IntWW 75, 76, 77, 78N; LinLib L; LongCTC; NewYTBS 77; TwCA SUP; WhAm 7; Who 74; WhoAm 74, 76, 78; WhoE 75*

Chicago
[Peter Cetera; Donnie Dacus; Laudir DeOliveira; Terry Kath; Robert Lamm; Lee Loughnane; James Pankow Walter Parazaider; Walt Perry; Daniel Serphine]
American. Music Group
Formed, 1968, as Chicago Transit Authority; albums have sold over 20 million copies.
Source: *BiDAmM; EncJzS 70; IlEncRk; RkOn 84*

Chicago, Judy
[Judy Cohen]
American. Artist, Feminist
b. Jul 20, 1939 in Chicago, Illinois
Source: *ConArt 77; ConAu 85; CurBio 81; DcCAr 81; NewYTBS 79; WhoAm 76, 78, 80, 82; WhoAmW 81; WomWMM B*

Chicago Seven, The
[Rennie Davis; David Dellinger; John Radford Froines; Tom Hayden; Abbie Hoffman; Jerry Rubin; Lee Weiner]
American. Political Activists
Disrupted 1968 Democratic National Convention, Chicago.
Source: *NF*

Chichester, Francis Charles, Sir
English. Adventurer, Sportsman
Yachtsman who made solo trip around world in yacht *Gipsy Moth,* 1966-67.
b. Sep 17, 1901 in North Devon, England
d. Aug 26, 1972 in Plymouth, England
Source: *Au&Wr 71; ConAu 37R; CurBio 67, 72, 72N; LinLib L; NewYTBE 72; ObitT 1971; WhDW; WhAm 5*

Chickering, Jonas
American. Manufacturer
Built first grand piano with full iron frame in single casting, 1837.
b. Apr 5, 1798 in Mason Village, New Hampshire
d. Dec 8, 1853 in Boston, Massachusetts
Source: *AmBi; ApCAB; Baker 78; BiDAmM; DcAmB; Drake; NatCAB 6; TwCBDA; WhAm HS*

Chidsey, Donald Barr
American. Author, Historian
Writer, historical novels, biographies,
  magazine articles: *Valley Forge,* 1959.
b. May 14, 1902 in Elizabeth, New Jersey
d. 1981 in New London, Connecticut
Source: *AmAu&B; AmNov; BioIn 2, 4, 9;
ConAu 5R, 103; REnAL; SmATA 3*

Ch'ien Lung
[Hung-Li]
Chinese. Emperor
Fourth ruler of Manchu dynasty, 1735-99.
b. Sep 25, 1711 in Peking, China
d. Feb 7, 1799 in Peking, China
Source: *McGEWB*

Chikamatsu, Monzaemon
[Sugimori Mobumori]
Japanese. Dramatist
b. 1653 in Eichizen Province, Japan
d. Jan 6, 1725
Source: *McGEWB; NewCol 75*

Child, Julia McWilliams
[Mrs. Paul Child]
American. Chef, Author, TV Personality
Star of "The French Chef," 1962--; wrote
  Mastering the Art of French Cooking, 1961.
b. Aug 15, 1912 in Pasadena, California
Source: *AmAu&B; BkPepl; CelR; ConAu 41R;
CurBio 67; ForWC 70; GoodHs; InWom;
LibW; WhoAm 74, 76, 78, 80, 82; WhoAmW
81; WhoWor 80*

Child, Lydia Maria
American. Author, Feminist
b. Feb 11, 1802 in Medford, Massachusetts
d. Oct 22, 1880 in Wayland, Massachusetts
Source: *Alli, SUP; AmAu; AmAu&B; AmBi;
AmWom; ApCAB; BbD; BiD&SB; CarSB;
CasWL; Chambr 3; ChhPo, S1, S2; CyAL 2;
DcAmAu; DcAmB; DcEnL; DcLEL; DcNAA;
Drake; EncAB-H; EvLB; HerW; InWom;
NotAW; OxAmL; REnAL; Str&VC; TwCBDA;
WebAB; WhAm HS*

Childe, Vere Gordon
Australian. Archaeologist
Influenced by Darwin's *Origin of Species*,
  believed invention of writing main index of
  civilization.
b. Apr 14, 1892 in Sydney, Australia
d. Sep 19, 1957 in Mount Victoria, Australia
Source: *MakMC; ObitOF 79; TwCA SUP*

Childers, (Robert) Erskine
Irish. Author, Rebel
b. Jun 25, 1870 in London, England
d. Nov 24, 1922 in Dublin, Ireland
Source: *DcLEL; EncMys; EvLB; LongCTC;
REn; TwCA; TwCWr*

Childress, Alvin
American. Actor
Played Amos Jones in TV series "Amos 'n
  Andy," 1950-53.
b. 1908 in Meridian, Mississippi
d. Apr 19, 1986 in Inglewood, California
Source: *DrBlPA; InB&W 80; NotNAT*

Childs, George William
American. Publisher
b. May 12, 1829 in Baltimore, Maryland
d. Feb 3, 1894 in Philadelphia, Pennsylvania
Source: *AmAu&B; BbD; BiD&SB; BioIn 4, 8;
DcAmAu; DcNAA*

Childs, Marquis William
American. Journalist, Author
Pulitzer-winning political columnist, 1969:
  Ethics in a Business Society.
b. Mar 17, 1903 in Clinton, Iowa
Source: *AmAu&B; CelR; ConAu 61; CurBio
43; IntAu&W 77; IntWW 74; OxAmL; REn;
REnAL; TwCA SUP*

Chiles, Lawton Mainor, Jr.
American. Senator
b. Apr 3, 1930 in Lakeland, Florida
Source: *BioNews 74; CngDr 74; CurBio 71;
IntWW 74; WhoAm 74, 76, 78, 80, 82;
WhoAmP 73; WhoGov 75; WhoS&SW 82*

Chillida, Eduard
Spanish. Artist
Abstract sculptor whose works are on display
  in Germany, Switzerland, US.
b. Jan 10, 1924 in San Sebastian, Spain
Source: *ConArt 83; CurBio 75; DcCAr 81;
GrBr; McGDA; OxTwCA; PhDcTCA 77;
PrintW 83*

Chilton, Alex
[The Box Tops]
American. Singer
Lead singer with Memphis-based, blue-eyed
  soul group, late, 1960s.
b. Dec 28, 1950 in Memphis, Tennessee
Source: *NF*

Chinaglia, Giorgio
Italian. Soccer Player
b. Jan 24, 1947 in Carrara, Italy
Source: *BioIn 12; NewYTBS 81*

Chinard, Gilbert
French. Educator
b. Oct 17, 1881 in Chatellerault, France
d. Feb 8, 1972
Source: *AmAu&B; NewYTBE 72; OxAmL; WhAm 5; WhNAA*

Chinmoy, Sri
see: Ghose, Sri Chinmoy Kumar

Chippendale, Thomas
English. Cabinetmaker, Furniture Designer
Catalog *Gentleman and Cabinet-Maker's Director,* 1754, influenced 18th c. designs.
b. Jun 5, 1718 in Yorkshire, England
d. Nov 1779 in London, England
Source: *Alli; AntBDN G; DcD&D; LinLib S; McGDA; McGEWB; NewC,*

Chipperfield, Joseph Eugene
English. Author
b. Apr 20, 1912 in Saint Austell, England
Source: *Au&Wr 71; AuBYP; ConAu 9R; MorJA; SmATA 2*

Chirac, Jacques Rene
French. Politician
Mayor of Paris, 1977--.
b. Nov 29, 1932 in Paris, France
Source: *CurBio 75; IntWW 83; IntYB 82; NewYTBS 77; Who 83; WhoWor 82*

Chirico, Giorgio de
Italian. Artist
b. Jul 10, 1888 in Volos, Greece
d. Nov 20, 1978 in Rome, Italy
Source: *ConArt 77; CurBio 56, 72, 79; LinLib S; McGDA; McGEWB; NewYTBE 70, 72; NewYTBS 78; REn; Who 74*

Chirol, Valentine, Sir
English. Author, Journalist
Headed foreign dept. of London *Times;* wrote *India Old and New,* 1921.
b. May 23, 1852
d. Oct 22, 1929 in Chelsea, England
Source: *DcNaB 1922; GrBr; LongCTC; NewC; WhLit*

Chisholm, Jesse
American. Pioneer
Frontier tradesman; Chisholm Trail, cattle highway from TX to KS, named after him.
b. 1806 in Tennessee
d. Mar 4, 1868 in Blaine City, Oklahoma
Source: *BioIn 5; NatCAB 19; REnAW; WebAB 79*

Chisholm, Shirley Anita St. Hill
American. Congresswoman, Author
First black woman elected to Congress, 1968; wrote *Good Fight,* 1973.
b. Nov 30, 1924 in Brooklyn, New York
Source: *AmAu&B; BiDrAC; CelR; CngDr 74; ConAu 29R; CurBio 69; HerW; LivgBAA; WhoAm 74, 76, 78, 80, 82; WhoAmP 73; WhoAmW 77; WhoBlA 75; WhoE 74; WhoGov 72; WrDr 76*

Chisum, John Simpson
American. Rancher
Largest cattle owner in country who was instrumental in death of Billy the Kid.
b. Aug 15, 1824 in Hardeman County, Tennessee
d. Dec 23, 1884 in Eureka Springs, Arkansas
Source: *AmBi; DcAmB; EncAAH; McGEWB; NatCAB 22; REnAW; WebAB, 79; WhAm HS*

Chittenden, Thomas
American. Governor
b. Jan 6, 1730 in East Guilford, Connecticut
d. Aug 25, 1797 in Williston, Vermont
Source: *BioIn 1, 6; DcAmB*

Chivers, Stephen Oswald
British. Businessman
b. 1899
Source: *Who 74*

Choate, Rufus
American. Lawyer, Senator
b. Oct 1, 1799 in Essex County, Massachusetts
d. Jul 15, 1859 in Halifax, Nova Scotia
Source: *Alli, SUP; AmAu; AmAu&B; AmBi; ApCAB; BbD; BiAUS; BiD&SB; BiDrAC; CyAL 2; DcAmAu; DcAmB; DcNAA; Drake; HarEnUS; LinLib L, S; NatCAB 6; REnAL; TwCBDA; WebAB; WhAm HS; WhAmP*

Chodorov, Edward
American. Author, Director, Producer
b. Apr 17, 1904 in New York, New York
Source: *AmAu&B; BiE&WWA; ConAu 102; CurBio 44; FilmgC; IntMPA 75, 76, 77, 78, 79, 80, 81, 82; ModWD; NotNAT; OxAmL; REnAL; WhoThe 77A*

Chodorov, Jerome
American. Dramatist, Director
b. Aug 10, 1911 in New York, New York
Source: *WhoWor 78*

Ch'oe Kyu Ha
Korean. Diplomat
b. Jul 16, 1919 in Kangwon Province, Korea
Source: *WhoWor 78*

Choiseul, Cesar, Comte Du Plessis-Praslin, duc de
French. Soldier
Marshal of France; credited with making confection "pralines."
b. 1598
d. 1675
Source: *NewCol 75*

Chomsky, Marvin
American. Director
b. May 23, 1929 in Bronx, New York
Source: *IntMPA 77, 78, 79, 80, 81, 82; NewYTET; WhoAm 82*

Chomsky, Noam
American. Linguist, Political Activist
Developed Cartesian theory, influenced development of modern linguistics.
b. Dec 7, 1928 in Philadelphia, Pennsylvania
Source: *AmAu&B; CelR; ConAu 17R; CurBio 70; IntWW 74; PenC AM; WebAB; Who 74; WhoWorJ 72; WrDr 80*

Chones, Jim
American. Basketball Player
b. Oct 30, 1949 in Racine, Wisconsin
Source: *NewYTBS 74; WhoBbl 73*

Chopin, Frederic Francois
[Fryderyk Franciszek Chopin]
Polish. Pianist, Composer
b. Feb 22, 1810 in Zelazowa Wola, Poland
d. Oct 17, 1849 in Paris, France
Source: *AtlBL; NewC; OxFr; REn*

Chopin, Kate
[Katherine O'Flaherty]
American. Author
Novels of Cajun, Creole life include *Bayou Folk*, 1894.
b. Feb 8, 1851 in Saint Louis, Missouri
d. Aug 22, 1904 in Saint Louis, Missouri
Source: *AmAu; AmAu&B; AmWomWr; AmWr S1; BbD; BiDSA; CasWL; CnDAL; ConAu 104; CrtT 4; DcAmAu; DcLEL; DcNAA; ModAL; REnAL*

Chorell, Walentin
Finnish. Dramatist
Wrote *Kattorna*, 1961.
b. Apr 4, 1912 in Turkie, Finland
d. Jan 1984
Source: *ConAu 111; EncWL 2; REnWD*

Chorzempa, Daniel Walter
American. Musician, Composer
Has given international piano, organ recitals, 1968--; won Leipzig Bach prize, 1968.
b. Dec 7, 1944 in Minneapolis, Minnesota
Source: *IntWW 74, 75, 76, 77, 78; WhoMus 72*

Chotzinoff, Samuel
American. Pianist, Music Critic
b. Jul 4, 1889 in Vitebsk, Russia
d. Feb 9, 1964
Source: *CurBio 40, 64; WhAm 4*

Chou En-Lai
Chinese.
With Mao Tse-Tung, founded Chinese Communist Party, premier, 19 49-76.
b. 1898 in Shaohsing, China
d. Jan 8, 1976 in Peking, China
Source: *CurBio 76N; DcPol; HisEWW; REn; WhAm 6; Who 74*

Chouteau, Yvonne
American. Dancer
b. 1929 in Fort Worth, Texas
Source: *BioIn 3, 4, 5*

Chretien, Henri
French. Inventor
Invented anamorphic lens used in cinemascope films.
b. Feb 1, 1879 in Paris, France
d. Feb 6, 1956 in Washington, District of Columbia
Source: *DcFM; FilmEn; FilmgC; ObitOF 79; OxFilm; WorEFlm*

Chretien de Troyes
French. Poet, Author
b. 1130
d. 1183
Source: *AtlBL; BbD; BiD&SB; CasWL; CyWA; DcEuL; EuAu; EvEuW; NewC; OxEng; OxFr*

Christ-Janer, Albert
American. Artist, Author, Educator
Watercolorist, graphic designer, who wrote numerous biographies of artists.
b. Jun 13, 1910 in Appleton, Wisconsin
d. Dec 12, 1973 in Como, Italy
Source: *AmAu&B; ConAu 45; NewYTBE 73; WhAm 6; WhoAm 74; WhoAmA 73, 76N, 78N; WhoWor 74*

Christaller, Walter
German. Geographer
Best known as father of theoretical
  geography.
b. Apr 21, 1893 in Berneck, Germany
d. Mar 9, 1969 in Koenigstein, Germany
  (East)
Source: *ConAu 116; WhoEc*

Christian IV
Danish. King
Reigned 1588-1648.
b. Apr 12, 1577 in Denmark
d. Feb 28, 1648 in Copenhagen, Denmark
Source: *DcBiPP A; LinLib S; NewCol 75*

Christian, Charlie (Charles)
American. Jazz Musician
b. 1919 in Dallas, Texas
d. Mar 2, 1942 in New York, New York
Source: *WhoJazz 72*

Christian, Dave
American. Hockey Player
Center, Winnipeg Jets; member 1980 US
  Olympic team.
b. May 12, 1959 in Warroad, Minnesota
Source: *HocReg 81*

Christian, Fletcher
English. Revolutionary
Led mutiny on *Bounty,* Apr 1784, in protest
  against alleged brutality of Capt. William
  Bligh.
b. 1764
d. 1793
Source: *NewC*

Christian, Linda
[Blanca Rosa Welter]
American. Actress
Married to Tyrone Power, 1949-55.
b. Nov 13, 1923 in Tampico, Mexico
Source: *FilmgC; InWom; IntMPA 75, 76, 77,
78, 79, 80, 81, 82; MotPP; WhoHol A*

Christian, Mary Blount
American. Children's Author
b. Feb 20, 1933 in Houston, Texas
Source: *ConAu 45, 1NR; SmATA 9; WrDr 76*

Christian-Jaque
French. Director
Won best director award, Cannes, 1952:
  Fanfan la Tulipe.
b. Sep 4, 1904 in Paris, France
Source: *BiDFilm; DcFM; FilmgC; OxFilm;
WorEFlm*

Christians, Mady
[Marguerite Maria]
American. Actress
b. Jan 19, 1900 in Vienna, Austria
d. Oct 28, 1951 in Norwalk, Connecticut
Source: *CurBio 45, 51; Film 2; FilmgC;
InWom; MotPP; MovMk; NotNAT B; ThFT;
WhScrn 74, 77; WhoHol B*

Christiansen, Arthur
English. Editor
b. Jul 27, 1904 in Wallasey, England
d. Sep 27, 1963
Source: *BioIn 1, 5, 6; ConAu 1R; LongCTC*

Christiansen, Jack
American. Football Player, Football Coach
Defensive back, 1951-58; coach, San
  Francisco, 1963-67; Hall of Fame, 1970.
b. Dec 20, 1928 in Sublette, Kansas
d. Jun 30, 1986 in Palo Alto, California
Source: *WhoFtbl 74*

Christiansen, Olaf
American. Conductor
b. 1901 in Minneapolis, Minnesota
Source: *WhoMus 72*

**Christie, Agatha Mary Clarissa Miller,
  Dame**
"Queen of Crime"
English. Author, Dramatist
Play *Mousetrap* longest running in British
  history.
b. Sep 15, 1890 in Torquay, England
d. Jan 12, 1976 in Wallingford, England
Source: *Au&Wr 71; AuBYP; AuNews 1, 2;
BiE&WWA; BioNews 74; CasWL; CelR;
CnThe; ConAu 17R, 61; ConLC 1, 6, 8, 12;
ConNov 72, 76; CurBio 40, 64; DcLEL;
EncMys; EvLB; IntWW 74; LongCTC;
MnBBF; NewC; OxEng; PenC ENG; PIP&P;
REn; TwCA, SUP; TwCWr; WhAm 6; Who
74; WhoThe 77; WrDr 80*

Christie, Audrey
American. Actress
b. Jun 27, 1912 in Chicago, Illinois
Source: *BiE&WWA; ForWC 70; NotNAT;
ObitT 1951; WhThe; WhoAmW 61; WhoHol
A; WhoThe 77*

Christie, James
English. Philanthropist
b. 1730 in England
d. 1803
Source: *NewC; NewEOp 71; NotNAT B;
ObitT 1961; OxMus*

Christie, John
English. Philanthropist
Founded Clyndebourne Festival, for opera
    performances on grounds of estate, 1934.
b. Dec 14, 1882 in Clyndebourne, England
d. Jul 4, 1962 in Clyndebourne, England
Source: *LongCTC*

Christie, John Reginald Halliday
"The Strangler of Notting Hill"
English. Murderer
b. 1899
d. 1953
Source: *BioIn 4, 5, 6*

Christie, John Walter
American. Inventor, Engineer
Developed world's first amphibian tank,
    1920s.
b. May 6, 1865 in River Edge, New Jersey
d. Jan 11, 1944 in Falls Church, Virginia
Source: *CurBio 44; DcAmB S3*

Christie, Julie
English. Actress
Won Oscar, 1965, for *Darling;* starred in
    Doctor Zhivago, 1965.
b. Apr 14, 1940 in Chukua, India
Source: *BiDFilm; BkPepl; CelR; CurBio 66;
FilmgC; InWom; IntMPA 75, 76, 77, 78, 79,
80, 81, 82; IntWW 74; MotPP; MovMk;
OxFilm; Who 74; WhoAm 82; WhoHol A;
WhoWor 78; WorEFlm*

Christina
Swedish. Queen
b. 1626 in Stockholm, Sweden
d. 1689
Source: *DcEuL; InWom; REn*

Christina
Swedish. Princess
b. 1943
Source: *BioIn 10*

Christina
Dutch. Princess
b. Feb 18, 1947 in Soestdijk, Netherlands
Source: *WhoWor 78*

Christo
[Christo Javacheff]
Bulgarian. Artist
Created 24-mile long fabric fence in Sonoma,
    Marin Counties, CA, 1972-76.
b. Jun 13, 1935 in Gabrovo, Bulgaria
Source: *CurBio 77*

Christoff, Boris
Bulgarian. Opera Singer
b. May 18, 1918 in Sofia, Bulgaria
Source: *IntWW 74; Who 74; WhoMus 72;
WhoWor 78*

Christoff, Steve
American. Hockey Player
Center, member, 1980 US Olympic team.
b. Jan 23, 1958 in Springfield, Illinois
Source: *HocReg 81*

Christophe, Henri
Haitian. King
b. 1767 in Grenada, West Indies
d. in Haiti
Source: *ApCAB; Drake; REn*

Christopher, Saint
Religious Figure
Martyr, patron saint of travelers, until
    dropped from liturgical calendar, 1969.
Source: *DcBiPP; DcCathB; NewC; REn*

Christopher, Dennis
[Dennis Carelli]
American. Actor
In films *Breaking Away,* 1979; *Chariots of
Fire,* 1981.
b. Dec 2, 1955 in Philadelphia, Pennsylvania
Source: *ConTFT 3; NewYTBS 79*

Christopher, Jordan
American. Actor, Musician
b. 1941 in Youngstown, Ohio
Source: *IntMPA 75, 76, 77, 78, 79, 80, 81,
82; MotPP; WhoHol A*

Christopher, Matthew F
American. Children's Author
b. Aug 16, 1917 in Bath, Pennsylvania
Source: *AuBYP; ConAu 1R, 5NR; MorBMP;
SmATA 2; WrDr 76*

Christopher, Sybil Williams Burton
[Mrs. Jordan Christopher; Sybil Williams]
Welsh. Actress
First wife of Richard Burton, 1949-63;
    Burton divorced her to marry Elizabeth
    Taylor.
b. 1928 in Taylorstown, Wales
Source: *BioIn 6, 7*

Christopher, Warren Miner
American. Lawyer, Government Official
Negotiator for release of American hostages
    in Iran, 1980-81.
b. Oct 27, 1925 in Scranton, North Dakota
Source: *BioIn 11; WhoAm 78, 80, 82*

Christopher, William
American. Actor
Played Father Mulchahy on TV series
    "M*A*S*H," 1972-83.
b. Oct 20, in Evanston, Illinois
Source: *WhoAm 80, 82*

Christy, Howard Chandler
American. Artist
b. Jan 10, 1873 in Morgan County, Ohio
d. Mar 4, 1952 in New York, New York
Source: *AmAu&B; ChhPo, S2; DcAmB S5;*
    IlsCB 1744; WhAm 3

Christy, June
American. Singer
b. Nov 20, 1925 in Springfield, Illinois
Source: *WhoAmW 74*

Christy, Marian
American. Journalist
b. Nov 9, 1932 in Ridgefield, Connecticut
Source: *ConAu 65; ForWC 70; WhoAm 82;*
    WhoAmW 77

Chrysler, Walter Percy
American. Auto Manufacturer
Pres., Buick Motor Co., 1916-19; founded
    Chrysler Corp., 1925.
b. Apr 2, 1875 in Wamego, Kansas
d. Aug 18, 1940 in Great Neck, New York
Source: *CurBio 40; DcAmB S2; WebAB;*
    WhAm 1

Chu Te
Chinese. Army Officer
Became commander, military forces, under
    Mao Tse-tung 1927.
b. Dec 18, 1886 in Szechwan, China
d. Aug 6, 1976 in Peking, China
Source: *CurBio 42; IntWW 77; McGEWB;*
    NewYTBS 76; WhWW-II

Chu Yuan-Chang
see: Ming T'ai-Tsu

Chuikov, Vasili Ivanovitch
Russian. Military Leader
Fought in Red Army during Russian
    Revolution, 1918-21; defended Stalingrad
    against Hitler, 1942.
b. Feb 12, 1900 in Serebryanye Prudy,
    Russia
d. Mar 18, 1982 in Moscow, U.S.S.R.
Source: *CurBio 43, 82N; HisEWW; IntWW*
    74, 75; NewYTBS 82; WhWW-II; WhoMilH
    76; WhoSocC 78

Chukovsky, Korney Ivanovich
[Nikolai Ivanovich Korneichuk]
Russian. Scholar, Children's Author
b. Mar 31, 1882 in Saint Petersburg, Russia
d. Oct 28, 1969 in Moscow, U.S.S.R.
Source: *AuBYP; CasWL; ChhPo S1, S2;*
    ConAu 5R, 25R, 4NR; PenC EUR; SmATA
    5; WorAu

Chukrai, Grigori
Russian. Director
b. 1921 in Melitopol, U.S.S.R.
Source: *DcFM; FilmgC; IntWW 82; OxFilm;*
    WhoWor 80; WorEFlm

Chun Doo Hwan
Korean. President
b. Jan 23, 1931 in Naechonri, Korea
Source: *CurBio 81; NewYTBS 81*

Chung, Arthur
Guyanese. President
b. Jan 10, 1918 in Demerara, Guyana
Source: *IntWW 74; WhoGov 75; WhoWor 78*

Chung, Connie (Constance Yu-Hwa)
American. Broadcast Journalist
Anchor, "NBC News at Sunrise," 1983--.
b. Aug 20, 1946 in Washington, District of
    Columbia
Source: *WhoAm 80, 82; WhoAmW 77*

Chung Hee Park
see: Park, Chung Hee

Chung, Il-Kwon
Korean. Prime Minister
b. Nov 21, 1917
Source: *FarE&A 78; IntWW 81, 82; WhoGov*
    72; WhoWor 78

Church, Frank
American. Lawyer, Politician
Four-term Dem. senator; instrumental in
    getting Panama Canal treaty through
    Senate, 1978.
b. Jul 25, 1924 in Boise, Idaho
d. Apr 7, 1984 in Bethesda, Maryland
Source: *BiDrAC; CelR*

Church, Frederick Edwin
American. Artist
Of the Hudson River School genre, with flair
    for dramatic in rainbows, mists, clouds,
    sunsets.
b. May 4, 1826 in Hartford, Connecticut
d. Apr 2, 1900 in Hudson, New York
Source: *AmBi; ApCAB; BnEnAmA; DcAmArt;*
    DcAmB; Drake; EarABI; EncAAH; McGEWB;
    NatCAB 20; WebAB; WhAm 1

Church, George W
American. Restaurateur
Opened first Church's Fried Chicken to Go,
1952, in San Antonio, TX.
b. 1887 in Texas
d. 1956
Source: *Entr*

Church, Sam(uel Morgan, Jr.)
American. Labor Union Official
Pres., UMW, 1979-82.
b. Sep 20, 1936 in Matewan, West Virginia
Source: *CurBio 81; NewYTBS 79, 81;
WhoAm 82, 84*

Church, Sandra
American. Actress
b. Jan 13, 1943 in San Francisco, California
Source: *BiE&WWA; InWom; NotNAT;
WhoHol A*

Churchill, Caryl
English. Dramatist
Explores male-dominated society in Obie-
winning plays *Cloud Nine,* 1978; *Top Girls,*
1981.
b. Sep 3, 1938 in London, England
Source: *ConAu 102; ConDr 82; ConLC 31;
CurBio 85; DcLB Y82A; IntAu&W 82;
NewYTBS 83; WhoThe 81; WrDr 84*

**Churchill, Clementine Ogilvy (Hozier)
   Spencer, Baroness**
"Clemmie"
English. Celebrity Relative
Wife of Winston Churchill
b. Apr 1, 1885
d. Dec 12, 1977 in London, England
Source: *CurBio 53, 78; InWom*

Churchill, Diana Josephine
English. Actress
b. Aug 21, 1913 in Wembley, England
Source: *FilmgC; Who 74; WhoHol A;
WhoThe 77A*

Churchill, Jennie Jerome
American. Celebrity Relative
Vivacious society leader, mother of Winston
Churchill.
b. 1850 in New York, New York
d. Jun 29, 1921
Source: *AmWom; ApCAB SUP; NotAW;
WhAm 1*

Churchill, John
see: Marlborough, John Churchill, Duke

Churchill, May (Beatrice Desmond)
[May Lambert]
"Chicago May"; "Queen of the Badgers"
Criminal
Red-headed beauty who blackmailed lovers;
planned robbery, Parisian American
Express, 1901.
b. 1876 in Sligo, Ireland
d. 1929 in Philadelphia, Pennsylvania
Source: *BioIn 10; LookW*

Churchill, Randolph
English. Celebrity Relative
Son of Winston Churchill.
b. May 28, 1911 in London, England
d. Jun 6, 1968 in London, England
Source: *ConAu 89; CurBio 47, 68; LongCTC*

Churchill, Randolph Henry Spencer, Lord
English. Statesman
b. Feb 13, 1849 in Woodstock, England
d. Jan 24, 1895 in London, England
Source: *Alli SUP*

Churchill, Sarah
[Lady Audley]
"Mule"
English. Singer, Actress, Celebrity Relative
Second daughter of Winston Churchill; wrote
A Thread in the Tapestry, memoir of
father.
b. Oct 7, 1914 in London, England
d. Sep 24, 1982 in London, England
Source: *ConAu 107; CurBio 55, 83; FilmgC;
InWom; IntMPA 75, 76, 77, 78, 79, 80, 81,
82; NewYTBS 82; REn; WhoAmW 70;
WhoHol A*

Churchill, Winston
American. Author
Wrote novels on political, historical subjects:
The Crisis, 1901; *The Crossing,* 1904.
b. 1871 in Saint Louis, Missouri
d. Mar 12, 1947 in Winter Park, Florida
Source: *AmAu&B; ApCAB SUP; BbD;
BiD&SB; BiDSA; CarSB; CasWL; CnDAL;
ConAmA; ConAmL; CyWA; DcAmAu; DcAmB
S4; DcBiA; DcLEL; DcNAA; EvLB;
LongCTC; OxAmL; OxEng; PenC AM; REn;
REnAL; TwCA SUP; TwCBDA; TwCWr;
WebE&AL; WhAm 2; WhNAA*

Churchill, Winston Leonard Spencer, Sir
English. Statesman, Author
Coined expression "Iron Curtain," 1946,
warning against Soviet expansionism.
b. Nov 30, 1874 in Woodstock, England
d. Jan 24, 1965 in London, England
Source: *CasWL; CurBio 53; CyWA; DcLEL;
EvLB; LongCTC; NewC; OxEng; REn; TwCA;
TwCWr*

Chute, Beatrice Joy
American. Author
b. Jan 3, 1913 in Minneapolis, Minnesota
Source: *ConAu 1R; CurBio 50; InWom;*
SmATA 2; WhoAm 82

Chute, Marchette Gaylord
American. Author
Award-winning writer of children's verse,
literary biographies.
b. Aug 16, 1909 in Minneapolis, Minnesota
Source: *AmAu&B; Au&Wr 71; AuBYP;*
BiE&WWA; BkCL; ChhPo, S1, S2; ConAu
1R, 5NR; CurBio 50; DrAS 74H; EvLB;
InWom; MinnWr; MorJA; NotNAT; RAdv 1;
REnAL; SmATA X; TwCA SUP; Who 74;
WhoAm 74, 76, 78, 80, 82; WrDr 80; Who
82

Chuvalo, George
Canadian. Boxer
b. Sep 12, 1937 in Toronto, Ontario
Source: *WhoBox 74*

Chwast, Seymour
American. Designer, Illustrator
Originated Push Pin style; *Sara's Granny and*
the Groodle chosen best illustrated book,
1969, by NY *Times.*
b. Aug 18, 1931 in New York
Source: *IlsBYP; SmATA 18*

Chylak, Nester
American. Baseball Umpire
AL umpire, 1947-72.
b. May 11, 1922 in Olyphant, Pennsylvania
d. Feb 17, 1982 in Dunmore, Pennsylvania
Source: *NewYTBS 82; WhoProB 73*

Ciano (di Cortellazzo), Conte Galeazzo
Italian. Politician
b. Mar 8, 1903 in Livorno, Italy
d. Jan 11, 1944
Source: *CurBio 40, 44*

Ciardi, John Anthony
American. Poet, Author
Award-winning writer known for English
translation of Dante's *Inferno,* 1954.
b. Jun 24, 1916 in Boston, Massachusetts
d. Apr 1, 1986 in Metuchen, New Jersey
Source: *AmAu&B; AuBYP; BkCL; BkP;*
CasWL; CelR; CnDAL; ConAu 5R, 5NR;
ConLC 10; ConP 70, 75; CurBio 67, 86;
DrAP 75; DrAS 74E; ModAL; OxAmL; PenC
AM; RAdv 1; REn; REnAL; SmATA 1;
Str&VC; ThrBJA; TwCA SUP; WebAB;
WebE&AL; WhoAm 76, 78, 80, 82, 84;
WhoWor 74

Cibber, Colley
English. Author, Actor, Dramatist
Poet laureate, 1730; ridiculed in Alexander
Pope's *The Dunciad.*
b. Nov 6, 1671 in London, England
d. Dec 12, 1757 in London, England
Source: *Alli; BbD; BiD&SB; BrAu; CasWL;*
Chambr 2; ChhPo; CnThe; CrtT 2; CyWA;
DcEnA; DcEnL; DcEuL; DcLEL; EvLB;
McGEWD; NewC; OxEng; OxThe; PenC
ENG; PlP&P; REn; REnWD; WebE&AL

Cicero, Marcus Tullius
Roman. Orator, Statesman, Philosopher
b. Jan 3, 106 in Arpino, Italy
d. 43 BC in Formia, Italy
Source: *AtlBL; BbD; BiD&SB; CasWL;*
CyWA; DcEuL; NewC; OxEng; PenC CL;
RComWL; REn

Cicotte, Eddie (Edward V)
American. Baseball Player
b. Jun 19, 1894 in Detroit, Michigan
d. May 5, 1969 in Detroit, Michigan
Source: *BaseEn 85; WhoProB 73*

Cid, El
[Rodrigo Diaz de Bivar]
Spanish. Soldier
Conquered, ruled kingdom of Valencia, 1094-
99.
b. 1040 in Burgos, Spain
d. Jul 10, 1099 in Valencia, Spain
Source: *LinLib L, S; NewC; RComWL; REn*

Cienfuegos, Nicasio Alvarez de
Spanish. Poet
b. 1761 in Madrid, Spain
d. 1809
Source: *BbD; BiD&SB; DcEuL; EvEuW;*
PenC EUR

Cierva, Juan de la
Spanish. Aeronautical Engineer
Invented (cop) helicopter.
b. 1895
d. 1936
Source: *BioIn 1, 4, 8; NewCol 75*

Cigna, Gina
French. Opera Singer
b. Mar 6, 1900 in Paris, France
Source: *InWom*

Cilea, Francesco
Italian. Composer
b. Jul 26, 1866 in Palmi, Italy
d. Nov 20, 1950 in Verazza, Italy
Source: *NewEOp 71*

Cilento, Diane
Australian. Actress
Ex-wife of Sean Connery, 1962-73; Oscar
    nominee for *Tom Jones,* 1963.
b. Oct 5, 1933 in Brisbane, Australia
Source: *BiE&WWA; FilmgC; IntMPA 75, 76,
77, 78, 79, 80, 81, 82; MotPP; MovMk;
NotNAT; WhoHol A; WhoThe 77*

Cimabue, Giovanni
Italian. Artist
b. 1240 in Florence, Italy
d. 1302 in Florence, Italy
Source: *AtlBL; NewC; REn*

Cimarosa, Domenico
Italian. Composer
b. Dec 17, 1749 in Aversa, Italy
d. Jan 11, 1801 in Venice, Italy
Source: *AtlBL*

Cimino, Michael
American. Director, Writer
Won Oscar for directing *The Deer Hunter,*
    1978.
b. 1943 in New York, New York
Source: *CurBio 81; IntMPA 75, 76, 77, 78,
79, 80, 81; WhoAm 80, 82, 84*

Cinque, Joseph
African. Slave, Revolutionary
Led slave mutiny aboard ship, 1839; Supreme
    Court ruled that escaped slaves should be
    treated as free men.
b. 1811
d. 1852
Source: *BioIn 6, 8, 10*

Cipriani, Amilcare
Italian. Revolutionary
b. 1845 in Rimini, Italy
d. 1918
Source: *WebBD 80*

Cipullo, Aldo Massimo Fabrizio
American. Jewelry Designer
b. Nov 18, 1938 in Naples, Italy
Source: *WhoAm 82; WorFshn*

Cisler, Walker Lee
American. Business Executive
Pres., Detroit Edison, 1951-64; chairman,
    1964-75.
b. Oct 8, 1897 in Marietta, Ohio
Source: *AmM&WS 73P; BioNews 74; BlueB
76; BusPN; CurBio 55; IntWW 74, 82;
St&PR 75; WhoAm 78, 80, 82*

Cisneros, Henry Gabriel
American. Politician
Mayor, San Antonio, TX, 1981--; first
    Mexican-American to head major US city.
b. Jun 11, 1947 in San Antonio, Texas
Source: *WhoAm 82, 84; WhoS&SW 78*

Citroen, Andre Gustave
French. Auto Manufacturer
b. Feb 5, 1878 in Paris, France
d. 1935
Source: *WebBD 80*

Ciulei, Liviu
Romanian. Actor, Director
Art Director, Minneapolis Theater, 1980--;
    won Cannes director award for *Forest of
    the Hanged,* 1965.
b. Jul 7, 1923 in Bucharest, Romania
Source: *DcFM; IntWW 81, 82, 83, 84, 85;
WhoSocC 78*

Civiletti, Benjamin R
American. Government Official
US Attorney General, 1979-81.
b. Jul 17, 1935 in Peekskill, New York
Source: *BioIn 11; CurBio 80; IntWW 80;
WhoAm 78*

Claflin, Tennessee Celeste
American. Journalist
b. 1846 in Ohio
d. 1923
Source: *DcAmB; InWom; NotAW*

Claiborne, Craig
American. Editor, Author
Food editor, NY *Times;* wrote *The New New
York Times Cook Book,* 1979.
b. Sep 4, 1920 in Sunflower, Mississippi
Source: *AmAu&B; ConAu 1R, 5NR; CurBio
69; WhoAm 74, 76, 78, 80, 82; WhoE 74*

Claiborne, Liz (Elisabeth)
[Mrs. Arthur Ortenberg]
American. Fashion Designer
Award-winning specialist in moderate-priced
    sportswear; founded Liz Claiborne, Inc.,
    1976.
b. Mar 31, 1929 in Brussels, Belgium
Source: *WhoAm 80, 82, 84; WhoAmA 80*

Clair, Rene
French. Producer, Author
b. Nov 11, 1898 in Paris, France
d. Mar 15, 1981 in Neuilly, France
Source: *BiDFilm; BioIn 1, 5; ConAu 103;
CurBio 41, 81; DcFM; Film 2; FilmgC;
IntMPA 75, 76, 77, 78, 79; IntWW 74, 75,
76, 77, 78; MovMk; NewYTBS 81; OxFilm;
REn; WhAm 7; Who 74; WhoWor 74;
WorEFlm*

Clairborne, William Charles
American. Governor
b. 1775 in Sussex County, Virginia
d. Nov 23, 1817 in New Orleans, Louisiana
Source: *BiDFilm; CurBio 81; DcFM; FilmEn;
Film 2; FilmgC; IntAu&W 77; IntMPA 80,
81; IntWW 80; JohnWSW; MovMk; NatCAB
63; NewYTBS 81; OxFilm; REn; WhAm 7;
Who 74; WhoWor 74; WorEFlm*

Claire, Ina
[Ina Fagan]
American. Actress
Vaudeville performer, later with Ziegfield
    Follies, who portrayed witty, chic
    sophisticates on stage and screen.
b. Oct 15, 1895 in Washington, District of
    Columbia
d. Feb 21, 1985 in San Fransico, California
Source: *BiE&WWA; CmpEPM; CurBio 54;
EncMT; FamA&A; Film 1, 2; FilmgC;
InWom; MotPP; NotNAT; ThFT; WhThe;
WhoHol A; WhoThe 77A; WorAl*

Clairmont, Claire
English. Celebrity Relative
Stepdaughter of William Godwin, friend of
    Percy, Mary Shelley, mother of Lord
    Byron's daughter, Allegra.
b. Apr 27, 1798
d. 1879
Source: *InWom*

Clampett, Bob (Robert)
American. Cartoonist, Filmmaker
Animator who worked at Warner Brothers,
    1930s-40s; created "Looney Tune";
    "Mervie Melodie" cartoons.
b. May 8, 1913 in San Diego, California
d. May 2, 1984 in Detroit, Michigan
Source: *AuNews 1; WhoAm 82*

Clampett, Bobby
American. Golfer
Touring pro since 1980; first victory at
    Southern Open, 1982.
b. Apr 22, 1960 in Monterey, California
Source: *BioIn 11; WhoIntG*

Clancy, "King" (Francis Michael)
Canadian. Hockey Player, Hockey Executive
Player, coach, vp, Toronto Maple Leafs.
b. Feb 25, 1903 in Ottawa, Ontario
Source: *BioIn 8, 10; WhoHcky 73*

Clapp, Margaret Antoinette
American. Educator, Historian
b. Apr 11, 1910 in East Orange, New Jersey
d. May 3, 1974
Source: *AmAu&B; ConAu 49; CurBio 48, 74;
InWom; IntWW 74; NewYTBS 74; OxAmL;
REnAL; TwCA SUP; WhAm 6; WhoGov 75*

Clapp, Patricia
American. Children's Author
b. Jun 9, 1912 in Boston, Massachusetts
Source: *ConAu 25R; SmATA 4; WrDr 80*

Clapper, Raymond Lewis
American. Journalist
b. Apr 30, 1892 in La Cygne, Kansas
d. Feb 1944
Source: *AmAu&B; CurBio 40, 44; DcAmB S3;
WhAm 2; WhNAA*

Clapton, Eric
[Blind Faith; Eric Clap; Cream; Yardbirds]
English. Rock Musician
Appeared in movie *Tommy*, 1975.
b. Mar 30, 1945 in Ripley, England
Source: *BkPepl; CelR; WhoAm 74, 76, 78,
80, 82; WhoRock 81*

Clara Ward and Her Gospel Singers
American. Music Group
Source: *NF*

Clare, Saint
Italian. Religious Figure
Influenced by St. Francis to become nun;
    founded Poor Clares order; feast day Aug
    12.
b. 1194 in Assisi, Italy
d. 1253 in Assisi, Italy
Source: *NewCol 75*

Clare, John
"Northamptonshire Peasant Poet"
English. Poet
Romantic nature writer; wrote *Rural Muse*,
    1835; declared insane, 1837.
b. Jul 13, 1793 in Helpstone, England
d. May 20, 1864 in Northampton, England
Source: *AtlBL; BrAu 19; CasWL; DcEnL;
DcLEL; NewC; OxEng; PenC ENG; REn;
WebE&AL*

Clarendon, Edward Hyde, Earl
English. Statesman, Historian
b. Feb 18, 1609 in Wiltshire, England
d. Dec 9, 1674 in Rouen, France
Source: *Alli; AtlBL; BiD&SB; BrAu; CasWL; Chambr 1; DcEnA; DcEnL; DcLEL; EvLB; NewC; OxEng; PenC ENG; REn; WebE&AL*

Clark, Abraham
American. Lawyer, Historian
b. Feb 15, 1726 in Elizabethtown, New Jersey
d. Sep 15, 1794
Source: *NewCol 75*

Clark, Barney Bailey
American. Dentist, Transplant Patient
First recipient of permanent, completely artificial heart, Dec, 1982; lived 112 days.
b. Jan 21, 1921 in Provo, Utah
d. Mar 24, 1983 in Salt Lake City, Utah
Source: *AnObit 1983; NewYTBS 82*

Clark, Barrett H
American. Author, Actor, Director, Critic
b. Aug 26, 1890 in Toronto, Ontario
d. Aug 5, 1953 in Briarcliff, New York
Source: *AmAu&B; OxAmL; REnAL; TwCA, SUP; WhAm 3; WhNAA*

Clark, Bennett Champ
American. Lawyer, Politician
b. Jan 8, 1890 in Bowling Green, Missouri
d. Jul 13, 1954 in Gloucester, Massachusetts
Source: *AmAu&B; CurBio 41, 54; DcAmB S5; WhAm 3*

Clark, Bobby
American. Comedian
b. Jun 16, 1888 in Springfield, Ohio
d. Feb 12, 1960 in New York, New York
Source: *CurBio 49, 60; EncMT; FilmgC; WhAm 3; WhScrn 74, 77; WhoHol B*

Clark, "Champ" (James Beauchamp)
American. Politician
b. Mar 7, 1850 in Lawrenceburg, Kentucky
d. Mar 2, 1921 in Washington, District of Columbia
Source: *AmBi; BiDrAC; BiDSA; DcAmB; DcNAA; TwCBDA; WebAB; WhAm 1; WhAmP; WhoAm 74*

Clark, Charles Badger
American. Poet
b. Jan 1, 1883 in Albia, Iowa
d. Sep 26, 1957
Source: *AmAu&B; ChhPo, S1; DcLEL; REnAL*

Clark, Colin Grant
English. Economist
b. Nov 2, 1905 in Westminster, England
Source: *ConAu 61; IntWW 74, 75, 76, 77, 78, 79, 80, 81; Who 74; WhoWor 78*

Clark, Dane
[Bernard Zanville]
American. Actor
b. Feb 18, 1913 in New York, New York
Source: *FilmgC; HolP 40; IntMPA 75, 76, 77, 78, 79, 80, 81, 82; MotPP; MovMk; WhoAm 74; WhoHol A*

Clark, Dave
[Dave Clark Five]
English. Musician, Singer
Formed Dave Clark Five, 1964-73.
b. Dec 15, 1942 in London, England
Source: *EncPR&S 74; RkOn 84; WorAl*

Clark, David L
American. Candy Manufacturer
Made Clark Bar to distribute to US Army, WW II.
b. 1864
d. 1939
Source: *Entr*

Clark, Dick (Richard Wagstaff)
American. Entertainer
Host, American Bandstand, 1952--.
b. Nov 30, 1929 in Mount Vernon, New York
Source: *BkPepl; ConTFT 3; CurBio 59; IntMPA 82; IntWW 74; WhoAm 84; WhoHol A*

Clark, "Dutch" (Earl)
American. Football Player, Football Coach
b. Oct 11, 1906 in Fowler, Colorado
d. Aug 5, 1978
Source: *WhoFtbl 74*

Clark, Fred
American. Actor
b. Mar 9, 1914 in Lincoln, California
d. Dec 5, 1968 in Santa Monica, California
Source: *WhScrn 74*

Clark, George Rogers
American. Soldier
Assured colonial control of KY, IL, 1778-79.
b. Nov 19, 1752 in Charlottesville, Virginia
d. Feb 13, 1818 in Louisville, Kentucky
Source: *AmBi; ApCAB; DcAmAu; DcAmB; EncAB-H; OxAmL; REn; REnAL; TwCBDA; WebAB; WhAm HS*

Clark, Jack Anthony
American. Baseball Player
b. Nov 10, 1955 in Covina, California
Source: *BaseEn 85; BioIn 11*

Clark, James
Scottish. Auto Racer
b. Mar 4, 1936 in Kilmany, Scotland
d. Apr 7, 1968 in Hochheim, Germany
(West)
Source: *CurBio 65, 68; WhAmP*

Clark, James Beauchamp
see: Clark, 'Champ'

Clark, Joe (Charles Joseph)
Canadian. Politician
Prime minister, 1979-80.
b. Jun 5, 1939 in High River, Alberta
Source: *BioIn 11; IntWW 77; WhoAm 82*

Clark, John Bates
American. Economist, Author
Developed marginal-productivity theory; wrote
Distribution of Wealth, 1899.
b. Jan 26, 2847 in Providence, Rhode Island
d. Mar 21, 1938 in New York, New York
Source: *DcAmB S2; WebBD 80; WhAm 1*

Clark, Joseph Sill
American. Senator
b. Oct 21, 1901 in Philadelphia, Pennsylvania
Source: *BiDrAC; BlueB 76; CurBio 52;
IntWW 74, 79; PolProf E; WhoAm 78, 80,
82; WhoAmP 79*

Clark, Kenneth Bancroft
American. Educator, Psychologist
b. Jul 24, 1914 in Panama Canal Zone
Source: *AmAu&B; CelR; ConAu 33R; CurBio
64; LEduc 74; LivgBAA; WebAB; WhoAm 74,
76, 78, 80, 82; WhoBlA 75; WhoGov 75;
WhoWor 78*

Clark, Kenneth McKenzie, Sir
English. Art Historian, Author
b. Jul 13, 1903 in London, England
d. May 21, 1983 in Hythe, England
Source: *ConAu 93; CurBio 63; IntAu&W 77;
IntMPA 75; IntWW 74, 79, 81; NewYTBS
83; Who 74*

Clark, Marguerite
American. Actress
Rivaled Mary Pickford as silent screen star,
1914-21; best known for *Wildflowers*, 1914,
Uncle Tom's Cabin, 1919.
b. Feb 22, 1887 in Avondale, Ohio
d. Sep 25, 1940 in New York, New York
Source: *FilmEn; LibW; MotPP; NatCAB 30;
NotAW; NotNAT B; TwYS; WhAm 1;
WhScrn 74, 77; WhThe*

Clark, Marion L
American. Journalist, Author
b. 1942
d. Sep 4, 1977 in East Tawas, Michigan
Source: *ConAu 73, 77*

Clark, Mark Wayne
American. General
Led Allied invasion of Italy during WW II;
commanded UN forces in Korea, 1952-53;
signed Korean armistice July 27, 1953.
b. May 1, 1896 in Madison Barracks, New
York
d. Apr 17, 1984 in Charleston, South
Carolina
Source: *AnObit 1984; BlueB 76; CurBio 42,
84; IntWW 74, 74; LinLib S; McGEWB;
OxAmH; WebAMB; WhWW-II; Who 82*

Clark, Michele
American. Journalist
b. 1943
d. 1972
Source: *BioIn 9*

Clark, Monte
American. Football Player, Football Coach
Coached Detroit Lions, 1978-83.
b. Jan 24, 1937 in Fillmore, California
Source: *BioIn 11; WhoMW 82*

Clark, Peggy
American. Designer
b. Sep 30, 1915 in Baltimore, Maryland
Source: *BiE&WWA; NotNAT; WhoAm 74, 76,
78, 80, 82; WhoAmW 74, 77; WhoE 74, 79,
81; WhoThe 81*

Clark, Petula
English. Singer, Actress
Won Grammys for "Downtown," 1964, "I
Know a Place," 1965.
b. Nov 15, 1932 in Epsom, England
Source: *BkPepl; CelR; CurBio 70; FilmgC;
IntMPA 75, 76, 77, 78, 79, 80, 81, 82;
MotPP; MovMk; WhoAm 74, 76, 78, 80, 82;
WhoHol A*

Clark, Richard Clarence
American. Politician
b. Sep 14, 1929 in Paris, Iowa
Source: *WhoAmP 73; WhoGov 75*

Clark, Robert Edward
American. Journalist
b. May 14, 1922 in Omaha, Nebraska
Source: *WhoAm 74, 76, 78, 80, 82*

Clark, Roy Linwood
American. Singer, Songwriter, Musician
Named Entertainer of the Year by CMA,
1973.
b. Apr 15, 1933 in Meaherrin, Virginia
Source: *BioNews 74; CurBio 78; EncFCWM
69; RkOn 84; WhoAm 74, 76, 78, 80, 82;
WhoPubR 72; WorAl*

Clark, Steve
[Def Leppard]
"Steamin'"
English. Musician
Guitarist with heavy-matal band since 1978.
b. Apr 23, 1960 in Sheffield, England
Source: *NF*

Clark, Susan Nora Goulding
[Mrs. Alex Karras]
Canadian. Actress
Starred with husband in movies *Babe; Jimmy
B and Andre; Maid in America.*
b. Mar 8, 1944 in Sarnia, Ontario
Source: *BioIn 8, 10, 11; FilmEn; FilmgC;
IntMPA 75, 76, 77, 78, 79, 80, 81; WhoAm
80, 82; WhoHol A*

Clark, Sydney
American. Author, Traveler
Popular travel writer known for *All the Best*
series, 1939-72.
b. Aug 18, 1890 in Auburndale,
   Massachusetts
d. Apr 20, 1975
Source: *AmAu&B; Au&Wr 71; ConAu 4NR,
5R, 57; CurBio 56*

Clark, Thomas Dionysius
American. Author, Historian
b. Jul 14, 1903 in Louisville, Mississippi
Source: *AmAu&B; ConAu 5R, 4NR; DrAS
74H; WhNAA; WhoAm 74, 76, 78, 80, 82*

Clark, Tom (Thomas Campbell)
American. Supreme Court Justice
US Attorney General, 1945-49; justice, 1949-
67.
b. Sep 23, 1899 in Dallas, Texas
d. Jun 1977 in New York, New York
Source: *BiDrUSE; CngDr 74; CurBio 45;
DrAS 74P; IntWW 74; WebAB; Who 74;
WhoAm 74; WhoAmP 73; WhoGov 75*

Clark, Walter van Tilburg
American. Author
b. Aug 3, 1909 in East Oreland, Maine
d. Nov 10, 1971 in Reno, Nevada
Source: *AmAu&B; AmNov; CnDAL; ConAu
9R, 33R; ConNov 72, 76; CyWA; ModAL;
NewYTBE 71; OxAmL; PenC AM; RAdv 1;
REn; REnAL; SmATA 8; TwCA SUP; WhAm
5*

Clark, Wendel
Canadian. Hockey Player
Defenseman, first overall pick in 1985 draft,
   taken by Toronto.
b. Oct 25, 1966 in Kelvington, Saskatchewan
Source: *HocReg 85*

Clark, William
American. Explorer
With Meriwether Lewis, went on overland
   expedition to Pacific, 1803.
b. Aug 1, 1770 in Caroline County, Virginia
d. Sep 1, 1838 in Saint Louis, Missouri
Source: *Alli, SUP; AmBi; ApCAB; BiDrAC;
DcAmB; OxAmL; REnAL; TwCBDA; WebAB;
WhAm HS; WhAmP*

Clark, William P(atrick, Jr.)
American. Government Official
National security advisor, 1981--.
b. Oct 23, 1931 in Oxnard, California
Source: *CurBio 82; WhoAm 78, 80, 82*

Clark, (William) Ramsey
American. Government Official
Attorney general under Lyndon Johnson,
   1967-69.
b. Dec 18, 1927 in Dallas, Texas
Source: *AmAu&B; BiDrUSE; BioNews 74;
CelR; ConAu 29R; CurBio 67; IntWW 74*

Clarke, Allan
[The Hollies]
English. Singer
Formed Hollies with childhood friend
   Graham Nash, 1962.
b. Apr 15, 1942 in Salford, England
Source: *NF*

Clarke, Arthur C(harles)
English. Author, Scientist
With Stanley Kubrick, wrote novel,
    screenplay *2001: A Space Odyssey,* 1968.
b. Dec 16, 1917 in Minehead, England
Source: *Alli; AmM&WS 73P; Au&Wr 71;*
AuBYP; CelR; ConAu 1R, 2NR; ConLC 1, 4,
13, 18; ConNov 72, 76; CurBio 66; EvLB;
IntWW 74; LongCTC; NewC; TwCA SUP;
TwCWr; WebE&AL; Who 82; WhoWor 78;
WrDr 80

Clarke, Austin
Irish. Poet
b. May 9, 1896 in Dublin, Ireland
d. Mar 20, 1974
Source: *CasWL; CnMD SUP; ConAu 49, P-2;*
ConLC 6; ConP 70, 75; ModBrL, S1; NewC;
RAdv 1; REn; TwCA SUP; TwCWr

Clarke, Bobby (Robert Earl)
Canadian. Hockey Player
Center, Philadelphia; MVP 1972, 1973, 1975,
    1976.
b. Aug 13, 1949 in Flin Flon, Manitoba
Source: *HocEn; NewYTBS 75; WhoHcky 73;*
WorAl

Clarke, Bruce Cooper
American. General
b. Apr 29, 1901 in Adams, New York
Source: *BioIn 3, 4, 5, 9, 10; WhoAm 74*

Clarke, Ellis Emmanuel
Trinidadian. Lawyer, Diplomat
b. Dec 28, 1917 in Trinidad
Source: *IntWW 74; Who 74; WhoGov 75;*
WhoWor 78

Clarke, Fred Clifford
"Cap"
American. Baseball Player, Baseball Manager
Player-manager on four pennant winning
    Pittsburgh Pirate teams.
b. Oct 3, 1872 in Winterset, Iowa
d. Aug 14, 1960 in Winfield, Kansas
Source: *BaseEn 85; BioIn 2, 3, 5, 7;*
WhoProB 73

Clarke, Gilmore David
American. Architect
Chm. National Commission of Fine Arts,
    1937-50.
b. Jul 12, 1892 in New York, New York
d. Aug 6, 1982
Source: *BioIn 9; NewYTBS 82; WhoAm 74,*
76, 78, 80, 82

Clarke, Harry
Irish. Illustrator
Did macabre, bizarre book illustrations: Poe's
    Tales of Mystery and Imagination, 1919.
b. Mar 17, 1890 in Dublin, Ireland
d. 1931 in Corre, Switzerland
Source: *ConICB; DcBrAr 1; DcIrB*

Clarke, Jeremiah
English. Composer
Organist, St. Paul's Cathedral, 1695, who
    composed church harpsichord pieces.
b. 1673 in London, England
d. Dec 1, 1701 in London, England
Source: *Alli; Baker 78; OxMus*

Clarke, John
English. Colonial Figure
Co-founder of RI, 1638.
b. Oct 8, 1609 in Westhorpe, England
d. Apr 28, 1676 in Newport, Rhode Island
Source: *AmBi; ApCAB; CyAL 1; DcAmB;*
Drake; NewCol 75; OxAmL; REnAL;
TwCBDA; WhAm HS

Clarke, John Henrik
American. Author
b. Jan 1, 1915 in Union Springs, Alabama
Source: *AmAu&B; AuNews 1; BioIn 10;*
BlkAWP; ConAu 53; LivgBAA; WhoAm 74;
WhoE 74

Clarke, Rebecca Sophia
[Sophie May, pseud.]
American. Children's Author
Wrote *Little Prudy,* 1863-65; *Dotty Dimple*
    series, 1867-69.
b. Feb 22, 1833 in Norridgewock, Maine
d. Aug 10, 1906 in Norridgewock, Maine
Source: *NotAW*

Clarke, Ron
Australian. Track Athlete
Set 19 running records in 1960s;
    autobiography *The Unforgiving Minute,*
    1966.
b. Feb 21, 1937 in Melbourne, Australia
Source: *CurBio 71; WhoTr&F 73*

Clarke, Shirley
American. Director, Producer
b. Oct 2, 1927 in New York, New York
Source: *ConLC 16; DcFM; FilmgC; InB&W*
80; OxFilm; WhoAmW 74, 66A; WhoWor 74;
WomWMM

Clarke, Stanley Marvin
American. Musician, Composer
b. Jun 31, 1951 in Philadelphia, Pennsylvania
Source: *ConNews 85-4; EncJzS 70; RolSEnR*
83; WhoAm 80, 82; WhoWor 80

Clarkson, Ewan
English. Author
b. Jan 23, 1929 in England
Source: *ConAu 25R; SmATA 9; WrDr 80*

Clarkson, John Gibson
American. Baseball Player
b. Jul 1, 1861 in Cambridge, Massachusetts
d. Feb 4, 1909 in Cambridge, Massachusetts
Source: *BaseEn 85; BioIn 7; WhoProB 73*

Clary, Robert
American. Actor
Played LaBeau in TV series "Hogan's
  Heroes," 1965-71.
b. Mar 1, 1926 in Paris, France
Source: *BiE&WWA; WhoAm 74, 76, 78, 80,
82; WhoHol A*

Clash, The
[Topper Headon; Mick Jones; Paul Simonon;
  Joe Strummer]
English. Music Group
London-based band started, 1976; hit album
  Combat Rock, 1982.
Source: *ConMuA 80A*

Classen, Willie
American. Boxer
Puerto Rican middleweight who died of brain
  damage incurred during fight.
b. Sep 16, 1950 in Santurce, Puerto Rico
d. Nov 28, 1979 in New York, New York
Source: *BioIn 12; NewYTBS 79*

Claude, Albert
American. Scientist
Founder of modern cell biology who won
  Nobel Prize in medicine, 1974; first to
  isolate cancer virus.
b. Aug 23, 1898 in Luxembourg
d. May 20, 1983 in Brussels, Belgium
Source: *BiESc; IntWW 82, 82; McGMS 80;
NewYTBS 74, 83; Who 82, 83; WhoAm 80,
82; WhoWor 80, 82; WorAl*

Claude, Georges
French. Chemist, Physicist
Research in liquefying gases led to invention
  of neon lights.
b. Sep 24, 1870 in Paris, France
d. May 23, 1960 in Saint Cloud, France
Source: *AsBiEn; DcScB; LinLib S; WebBD 80*

Claudel, Paul Louis Charles
French. Author, Diplomat, Poet
Foremost Catholic writer of his era; wrote
  poetic dramas, *The Hostage*, 1971, *Satin
  Slipper*, 1931.
b. Aug 6, 1868 in Villenluve, France
d. Feb 23, 1955 in Paris, France
Source: *AtlBL; CasWL; CathA 1930;
 ClDMEL; CnMD; CnMWL; CnThe; EncWL;
EvEuW; LongCTC; McGEWD; ModRL;
ModWD; OxEng; OxFr; OxThe; PenC EUR;
REn; REnWD; TwCA, SUP; TwCWr; WhAm
3; WhNAA; WhoTwCL*

Claudian
Alexandrian. Poet
b. 365 in Alexandria, Egypt
d. 408
Source: *CasWL; Grk&L; LinLib L; NewC;
OxEng; PenC CL; WhDW*

Claudius I
[Tiberius Claudius Nero Germanicus]
Roman. Emperor
b. Aug 1, 10
d. Oct 13, 54 in Rome, Italy
Source: *McGEWB; NewCol 75; WebBD 80*

Claudius, Matthias
German. Poet
b. Aug 15, 1740 in Reinfeld, Germany
d. Jan 21, 1815 in Hamburg, Germany
Source: *BiD&SB; CasWL; ChhPo S1; DcBiPP;
DcEnL; Dis&D; EuAu; EvEuW; LinLib L;
LuthC 75; OxGer; PenC EUR; REn*

Claus, Hugo
Belgian. Poet, Dramatist
b. Apr 5, 1929
Source: *CasWL; CnMD; EncWL; ModWD*

Clausen, A(lden) W(inship)
American. Banker
Pres., World Bank, 1981--.
b. Feb 17, 1923 in Hamilton, Illinois
Source: *BioIn 8, 11; Dun&B 79; IntWW 74,
75, 76, 77, 78; PolProf NF; St&PR 75;
WhoAm 74, 76, 78, 80, 82; WhoF&I 74, 75,
77, 79; WhoWest 76, 78; WhoWor 74*

Clausewitz, Karl von
Prussian. Author, Military Leader
Book *On War* expounded philosophy of war;
  had enormous effect on military strategy,
  tactics, in World Wars.
b. Jun 1, 1780 in Burg, Prussia
d. Nov 16, 1831
Source: *CelCen; OxGer; WhoMilH 76; WorAl*

Clave, Antoni
French. Artist, Illustrator
Noted lithographer, book illustrator:
Gargantua, 1951.
b. Apr 5, 1913 in Barcelona, Spain
Source: *IntWW 76, 77, 78; McGDA; WhoGrA
62*

Clavell, James Dumaresq
American. Author
Wrote *Taipan,* 1966, *Shogun,* 1975, *Noble
House,* 1981.
b. Oct 10, 1924 in Australia
Source: *ConAu 25R; ConLC 6; CurBio 81;
WhoAm 74, 76, 78, 80, 82; WhoWor 74;
WorEFlm; WrDr 80*

Clay, Cassius
see: Ali, Muhammad

Clay, Cassius Marcellus
American. Public Official, Abolitionist
b. Oct 19, 1810 in Madison County,
Kentucky
d. Jul 22, 1903 in Madison County,
Kentucky
Source: *ApCAB; BiD&SB; BiDSA; DcAmAu;
DcAmB; DcNAA; Drake; TwCBDA; WebAB;
WhAm 1*

Clay, Henry
"The Great Compromiser"
American. Lawyer, Statesman
Secured MO Compromise; Compromise Tariff
of 1833; Compromise of 1850.
b. Apr 12, 1777 in Hanover County, Virginia
d. Jun 29, 1852 in Washington, District of
Columbia
Source: *Alli; AmAu; AmAu&B; AmBi;
ApCAB; BbD; BiAUS; BiD&SB; BiDSA;
BiDrAC; BiDrUSE; CyAL 1; DcAmAu;
DcAmB; DcNAA; Drake; EncAB-H; OxAmL;
REn; REnAL; TwCBDA; WebAB; WhAm HS;
WhAmP*

Clay, Lucius du Bignon
American. Army Officer
b. Apr 23, 1897 in Marietta, Georgia
d. Apr 16, 1978 in Chatham, Massachusetts
Source: *ConAu 77, 81; CurBio 45, 63;
IntWW 74; Who 74; WhoAm 74; WhoAmP
73; WhoWor 78*

Clay, William Lacy
American. Congressman
b. Apr 30, 1931 in Saint Louis, Missouri
Source: *BioIn 8, 9, 10; CngDr 74; WhoAm
74, 76, 78, 80, 82; WhoAmP 73; WhoGov 75;
WhoMW 74*

Clayburgh, Jill
[Mrs. David Rabe]
American. Actress
Best actress, Cannes Film Festival, 1978, for
An Unmarried Woman.
b. Apr 30, 1944 in New York, New York
Source: *CurBio 79; IntMPA 78, 79, 80, 81,
82; NewYTBS 76, 79; WhoAm 80, 82;
WhoHol A*

Clayderman, Richard
['The Prince of Romance']
French. Musician
Popular pianist who has sold over 40 million
records, including 177 gold, 42 platinum.
b. Dec 28, 1953 in France
Source: *NF*

Clayton, Bessie
American. Actress
b. 1885 in Philadelphia, Pennsylvania
d. Jul 16, 1948 in Long Branch, New Jersey
Source: *BioIn 1; NotNAT B*

Clayton, Buck
American. Jazz Musician
b. Nov 12, 1911 in Parsons, Kansas
Source: *AmSCAP 66; WhoJazz 72*

Clayton, Herbert
English. Actor, Producer, Director
b. Dec 1, 1876 in London, England
d. Feb 16, 1931
Source: *NotNAT B; WhThe*

Clayton, Jack
British. Director
b. 1921 in Brighton, England
Source: *BiDFilm; DcFM; FilmgC; IntMPA 75,
76, 77, 78, 79, 80, 81, 82; IntWW 74;
MovMk; OxFilm; Who 74; WhoWor 78;
WorEFlm*

Clayton, Jan(e Byral)
American. Actress
Played mother in TV series "Lassie," 1954-
57.
b. Aug 26, 1925 in Alamogordo, New
Mexico
d. Aug 28, 1983 in Los Angeles, California
Source: *BiE&WWA; EncMT; InWom;
IntMPA 81, 82; WhoAmW 61; WhoHol A;
WorAl*

Clayton, John Middleton
American. Politician
Secretary of State, 1849-50; negotiated
  Clayton-Bulwer treaty with Britain, 1850.
b. Jul 24, 1796 in Dagsborough, Delaware
d. Nov 9, 1856 in Dover, Delaware
Source: *AmBi; ApCAB; BiAUS; BiDrAC;
BiDrUSE; DcAmB; Drake; TwCBDA; WebAB;
WhAm HS; WhAmP*

Clayton, Lou
[Louis Finkelstein]
American. Actor
Starred with Jimmy Durante in vaudeville;
  featured in *Show Girl*, 1929.
b. 1887 in Brooklyn, New York
d. Sep 12, 1950 in Santa Monica, California
Source: *NotNAT B; ObitOF 79; WhScrn 74,
77; WhoHol B*

Cleaveland, Moses
American. Soldier, Lawyer
Founded Cleaveland, Ohio, 1796; spelling
  later changed to Cleveland.
b. Jan 29, 1754 in Canterbury, Connecticut
d. Nov 16, 1806 in Canterbury, Connecticut
Source: *AmBi; ApCAB; DcAmB; HarEnUS;
OhA&B; TwCBDA; WhAm HS, HS*

Cleaver, Eldridge
American. Political Activist, Author
Served time in prisons; wrote *Soul on Ice,*
  1968; *Soul on Fire,* 1978.
b. Aug 31, 1935 in Little Rock, Arkansas
Source: *AmAu&B; BlkAWP; CelR; ConAu
21R; CurBio 70; LivgBAA; PenC AM;
WebE&AL; WrDr 80*

Cleaver, Vera Allen
[Mrs. William Joseph Cleaver]
American. Children's Author
With husband, co-wrote popular children's
  books: *Queen of Hearts,* 1978.
b. Jan 6, 1919 in Virgil, South Dakota
Source: *ConAu 73; FourBJA; SmATA 22;
WhoAm 82, 84*

Cleaver, William Joseph (Bill)
American. Author
With wife Vera, co-wrote numerous children's
  books: *Trial Valley,* 1977.
b. Mar 20, 1920 in Hugo, Oklahoma
d. Aug 20, 1981 in Winter Haven, Florida
Source: *ConAu 73, 104; WhoAm 78, 80*

Cleese, John
[Monty Python's Flying Circus]
English. Actor, Writer
Created Monty Python, 1969; humor based
  on conviction of senselessness of life.
b. Oct 27, 1939 in Weston-Super-Mare,
  England
Source: *CurBio 84; IntWW 82; Who 82*

Cleghorn, Sarah Norcliffe
American. Author
Poems collected in *Poems and Protests,* 1917.
b. Feb 4, 1876 in Norfolk, Virginia
d. Apr 4, 1959 in Philadelphia, Pennsylvania
Source: *AmAu&B; ChhPo, S1, S2; InWom;
REnAL; TwCA, SUP; WhAm 3; WhNAA;
WomWWA 14*

Cleisthenes
Greek. Statesman
Founder of Athenian democracy who
  established a dem. constitution.
b. 570 ?BC
d. 500 ?BC
Source: *BioIn 5; DcBiPP; McGEWB*

Cleland, John
English. Author, Dramatist
Wrote erotic classic, *Fanny Hill or Memories
  of a Woman of Pleasure,* 1749.
b. 1709 in London, England
d. Jan 23, 1789
Source: *Alli, SUP; BiDSA; CasWL; DcBiPP;
NewC; Novels; OxEng; WorAl*

Cleland, Max (Joseph Maxwell)
American. Government Official
Lost legs, forearm in Vietnam; head, VA,
  1977-80.
b. Aug 24, 1942 in Atlanta, Georgia
Source: *CurBio 78; NewYTBS 77; WhoAm
82; WhoAmP 79; WhoGov 77*

Cleland, Thomas Maitland
American. Illustrator
Award-winning typographer, graphic designer
  known for illustrating deluxe books.
b. Aug 18, 1880 in Brooklyn, New York
d. Nov 9, 1964
Source: *BioIn 1, 3, 7, 9, 10; WhAm 4;
WhoAmA 78N*

Clemenceau, Georges Eugene Benjamin
French. Statesman
Forceful wartime premier, 1917-20; opposed
  leniency toward Germany after Allied
  victory, WW I.
b. Sep 28, 1841 in Mouilleron, France
d. Nov 24, 1929 in Paris, France
Source: *ClDMEL; REn*

Clemens, Roger (William Roger)
American. Baseball Player
Pitcher, Boston, 1984--, who broke ML
 record for strikeouts in one game--20,
 1986.
b. Aug 4, 1962 in Dayton, Ohio
Source: *BaseEn 85; BaseReg 85, 86*

Clemens, Samuel Langhorne
see: Twain, Mark, pseud.

Clement VII
[Giulio DeMedici]
Florentine. Religious Leader
Pope, 1523-34; Henry VIII attempted to
 divorce Catherine of Aragon during his
 reign.
b. 1475 in Florence, Italy
d. Sep 25, 1534 in Rome, Italy
Source: *DcCathB; NewCol 75; REn; WorAl*

Clement, Rene
French. Director
b. Mar 18, 1913 in Bordeaux, France
Source: *BiDFilm; DcFM; FilmgC; IntWW 74,
 75; MovMk; OxFilm; Who 74, 82; WhoWor
 74; WorEFlm*

Clemente, Roberto Walker
Puerto Rican. Baseball Player
Pittsburgh outfielder, 1955-72; killed in air
 crash carrying supplies to Nicaragua
 earthquake victims; Hall of Fame, 1973.
b. Aug 18, 1934 in Carolina, Puerto Rico
d. Dec 31, 1972 in San Juan, Puerto Rico
Source: *BaseEn 85; CurBio 73; NewYTBE 71,
 72, 73; WhAm 5; WhoProB 73*

Clements, George Harold
American. Clergyman, Civil Rights Leader
Participant, 1960s civil rights marches; heads
 largest black Catholic school in US.
b. Jan 26, 1932 in Chicago, Illinois
Source: *AmCath 80; ConNews 85-1; WhoAm
 78; WhoBlA 80*

Clementi, Muzio
Italian. Pianist, Composer
Leader in modern piano technique; became
 noted London music publisher, 1799.
b. 1752 in Rome, Italy
d. Mar 10, 1832 in Evesham, England
Source: *NewCol 75; WebBD 80*

Clemons, Clarence
[E Street Band ster of the Universe']
"The Big Man"; "King of the World"; "Ma
American. Musician, Singer
Tenor saxophonist with Bruce Springsteen;
 solo album *Rescue,* 1983.
b. Jan 11, 1942 in Norfolk, Virginia
Source: *WhoRocM 82*

Clemson, David 'Clem'
see: Humble Pie

Cleopatra VII
Macedonian. Queen
Mistress of Julius Caesar, Marc Antony;
 killed herself with asp.
b. 69 BC in Alexandria, Egypt
d. Aug 30, 30 in Alexandria, Egypt
Source: *FilmgC; GoodHs; HerW; InWom;
 LinLib S; LongCEL; McGEWB; NewC;
 NewCol 75; REn*

Clerc, Jose-Luis
"Batata"
Argentine. Tennis Player
Won Italian Open, 1981.
b. Aug 16, 1958 in Buenos Aires, Argentina
Source: *BioIn 12; WhoIntT*

Cleva, Fausto
American. Conductor
b. May 17, 1902 in Trieste, Italy
Source: *NewYTBE 71; WhAm 5; WhoMus 72*

Cleve, Joos van
Flemish. Artist
Royalty portraitist, religious painter; works
 include "Lamentation," c. 1530.
b. 1485
d. 1540 in Antwerp, Belgium
Source: *McGDA*

Cleveland, Frances Folsom
[Mrs. Grover Cleveland]
American. First Lady
Youngest first lady, first White House bride,
 1886.
b. Jul 21, 1864 in Buffalo, New York
d. Oct 29, 1947 in Baltimore, Maryland
Source: *AmWom; ApCAB SUP; GoodHs;
 NatCAB 2; NotAW; TwCBDA*

Cleveland, James Harlan
American. Political Scientist
b. Jan 19, 1918 in New York, New York
Source: *AmM&WS 73S; ConAu 1R; CurBio
 61; IntWW 74; LEduc 74; WhoAm 84;
 WhoAmP 73; WhoWest 74; WhoWor 74;
 WrDr 76*

Cleveland, (Stephen) Grover
American. US President
Dem. pres. 1885-89, 1893-97; worked to
    stabilize US currency.
b. Mar 18, 1837 in Caldwell, New Jersey
d. Jun 24, 1908 in Princeton, New Jersey
Source: *AmAu&B; AmBi; ApCAB, SUP;*
BiD&SB; BiDrAC; BiDrUSE; CelCen; CyAG;
DcAmAu; DcAmB; DcAmSR; Dis&D; EncAB-
H; OxAmL; REn; REnAL; WebAB; WhAm
1; WhAmP

Clevenger, Shobal Vail
American. Sculptor, Physician
b. Oct 22, 1812 in Middletown, Ohio
d. Sep 23, 1843
Source: *AmBi; ApCAB; BnEnAmA; DcAmB;*
Drake; NatCAB 8; NewYHSD; TwCBDA;
WhAm HS

Cliburn, Van (Harvey Lavan, Jr.)
American. Musician
Pianist; won first prize, International
    Tchaikovsky Piano Competition, Moscow,
    1958.
b. Jul 12, 1934 in Shreveport, Louisiana
Source: *CelR; CurBio 58; IntWW 74; Who*
74; WhoAm 82; WhoMus 72; WhoWor 74

Clifford, Clark McAdams
American. Government Official
Special advisor to presidents Truman,
    Kennedy, and Johnson.
b. Dec 25, 1906 in Fort Scott, Kansas
Source: *BiDrUSE; CelR; CurBio 68; EncAB-*
H; IntWW 74; NewYTBE 71; Who 74;
WhoAm 82; WhoAmP 73; WhoWor 74

Clifford, Nathan
American. Supreme Court Justice
Helped negotiate Mexican Treaty of
    Guadaloupe Hidalgo, 1848; Supreme Court
    justice, 1858-81.
b. Aug 18, 1803 in Rumney, New
    Hampshire
d. Jul 25, 1881 in Cornish, Maine
Source: *Alli SUP; AmBi; ApCAB; BiAUS;*
BiDrAC; BiDrUSE; DcAmAu; DcAmB; Drake;
TwCBDA; WebAB; WhAm HS; WhAmP

Clift, Montgomery
American. Actor
Films include *A Place in the Sun,* 1951;
    From Here to Eternity, 1953; *The Misfits,*
    1961.
b. Oct 17, 1920 in Omaha, Nebraska
d. Jul 23, 1966 in New York, New York
Source: *BiDFilm; BiE&WWA; CmMov;*
CurBio 66; FilmgC; MotPP; MovMk; NotNAT
B; OxFilm; WhAm 4; WhScrn 74, 77;
WhThe; WhoHol B; WorAl; WorEFlm

Climax Blues Band, The
[Colin Cooper; John Cuffley; Peter Haycock;
    Derek Holt; Richard Jones; George
    Newsome; Arthur Wood]
English. Music Group
Founded 1969; first US hit single "Couldn't
    Get It Right," 1977.
Source: *ConMuA 80A; IlEncRk; RkOn 78;*
WhoRock 81

Clinchy, Everett Ross
American. Clergyman
Co-founder, National Conference of Christians
    and Jews, 1929; World Brotherhood of
    Christians and Jews, 1950.
b. Dec 16, 1896 in New York, New York
d. Jan 22, 1986 in Guilford, Connecticut
Source: *AmAu&B; BlueB 76; CurBio 41, 86;*
IntWW 83; WhoAm 84

Cline, Genevieve Rose
American. Judge, Government Official
First woman federal judge, appointed by
    Coolidge, 1928.
b. Jul 27, 1878 in Warren, Ohio
d. Oct 25, 1959 in Cleveland, Ohio
Source: *NotAW MOD*

Cline, Maggie
American. Singer
Vaudeville performer who was first woman
    Irish comedy singer.
b. Jan 1, 1857 in Haverhill, Massachusetts
d. Jun 11, 1934 in Fair Haven, New Jersey
Source: *NotAW*

Cline, Patsy
[Virginia Patterson Hensley]
American. Singer
b. Sep 8, 1932 in Winchester, Virginia
d. Mar 5, 1963 in Camden, Tennessee
Source: *EncFCWM 69*

Clinton, Bill (William Jefferson)
American. Politician
Dem. governor of AR, 1979-81; 1983--.
b. Aug 19, 1946 in Hope, Arkansas
Source: *IntWW 82; WhoAm 82; WhoAmL*
79; WhoAmP 81; WhoS&SW 80

Clinton, DeWitt
American. Lawyer, Statesman
NY governor, 1817-23, 1825-28, who
    promoted Erie Canal; unsuccessful pres.
    candidate, 1812.
b. Mar 2, 1769 in Little Britain, New York
d. Feb 11, 1828 in Albany, New York
Source: *Alli; AmAu&B; AmBi; ApCAB;*
BiAUS; BiD&SB; BiDrAC; CyAL 1; DcAmAu;
DcAmB; DcNAA; Drake; EncAB-H; REnAL;
TwCBDA; WebAB; WhAm HS; WhAmP

Clinton, George
American. Lawyer, Vice-President
US vp, 1805-12; NY governor, 1777-95,
1801-04.
b. Jul 26, 1739 in Little Britain, New York
d. Apr 20, 1812 in Washington, District of
Columbia
Source: *AmBi; ApCAB; BiAUS; BiDrAC;
BiDrUSE; DcAmB; DcNAA; Drake; EncAB-H;
OxAmL; REnAL; TwCBDA; WebAB; WhAm
HS; WhAmP*

Clinton, Henry, Sir
British. Military Leader
Commander-in-chief of British troops in
American Revolution, 1778-81, succeeding
Howe.
b. 1738 in Newfoundland
d. Dec 23, 1795 in Gibraltar
Source: *Alli; AmBi; ApCAB; DcBiPP; Drake;
EncAR; HarEnUS; LinLib S; OxAmL; REn;
REnAL; WhAm HS*

Clinton, Larry
American. Band Leader
Composer, arranger during big band era;
tune "The Dipsy Doodle" was one of top
hits, late 1930s.
b. Aug 17, 1909 in Brooklyn, New York
d. May 2, 1985 in Tucson, Arizona
Source: *AmSCAP 66; WhoJazz 72*

Clive, Colin
[Clive Greig]
British. Actor
b. Jan 20, 1900 in Saint Malo, France
d. Jun 25, 1937 in Hollywood, California
Source: *CmMov; FilmgC; MovMk; NotNAT B;
PIP&P; WhScrn 74, 77; WhThe; WhoHol B*

Clive, Robert
[Baron Clive of Plassey]
English. Colonial Leader, Soldier
Founded empire of British India; recovered
Calcutta, 1757.
b. Sep 29, 1725 in Styche, England
d. Nov 22, 1774 in London, England
Source: *DcInB; Dis&D; McGEWB; NewC;
REn; WhDW; WhoMilH 76; WorAl*

Clodagh
[Clodagh Aubry]
Irish. Designer
b. Oct 8, 1937 in Galway, Ireland
Source: *WorFshn*

Cloete, Stuart
South African. Author
Novels of S Africa include *The Turning
Wheels*, 1937; *Mamba*, 1956.
b. Jul 23, 1897 in Paris, France
d. Mar 19, 1976 in Capetown, South Africa
Source: *AmAu&B; CasWL; ConAu 1R;
ConNov 72, 76; EncWL; IntWW 74;
LongCTC; REn; TwCA, SUP; TwCWr;
WhNAA; WhoWor 78; WrDr 80*

Clooney, Rosemary
American. Actress, Singer
Had million-selling single "Come On-a My
House," 1951; autobiography *This for
Remembrance*, 1979.
b. May 23, 1928 in Maysville, Kentucky
Source: *CurBio 57; FilmgC; InWom; WhoAm
74; WhoHol A; WhoMus 72*

Close, Glenn
[Mrs. James Marlas]
American. Actress
Received Oscar nominations for roles in *The
World According to Garp*, 1982; *The Big
Chill*, 1983.
b. May 19, 1947 in Greenwich, Connecticut
Source: *CurBio 84; NewYTBS 82; VarWW 85*

Close, Upton, pseud.
see: Hall, Josef Washington

Cloud, Harold
see: Box Tops, The

Clouet, Francois
French. Artist
Chief painter to Francis I, 1523; portraitist
of royalty.
b. 1510 in Tours, France
d. 1572 in Paris, France
Source: *AtlBL; REn*

Clouet, Jean
French. Artist
Painter to four French kings; did portraits,
genre scenes.
b. 1485 in Netherlands
d. 1540 in Paris, France
Source: *AtlBL; BioIn 1, 8*

Clouzot, Henri-George
French. Director
b. Nov 20, 1907 in Niort, France
d. Jan 12, 1977 in Paris, France
Source: *BiDFilm; DcFM; FilmgC; IntMPA 75;
IntWW 74, 75; MovMk; NewYTBS 77;
OxFilm; WhoWor 74; WorEFlm*

Clurman, Harold Edgar
American. Author, Director
b. Sep 18, 1901 in New York, New York
d. Sep 9, 1980 in New York, New York
Source: *AmAu&B; BiE&WWA; ConAu 1R,
2NR, 101; CurBio 59; IntWW 74; NewYTBS
79; NotNAT, A; OxThe; PenC AM; PIP&P;
REnAL; WhAm 7; WhoAm 78; WhoThe 77;
WhoWor 74; WhoWorJ 72; WorEFlm; WrDr
76*

Cluytens, Andre
Belgian. Conductor
b. Mar 26, 1905 in Antwerp, Belgium
d. Jun 3, 1967 in Paris, France
Source: *WhAm 4*

Clyde, Andy
American. Actor, Comedian
b. Mar 18, 1892 in Blairgowrie, Scotland
d. May 18, 1967 in Los Angeles, California
Source: *Film 2; FilmgC; MotPP; ObitOF 79;
TwYS; Vers A; WhScrn 74, 77; WhoHol B*

Clyde, Jeremy
see: Chad and Jeremy

Clymer, George
American. Merchant, Politician
Signed US Constitution, 1787, Declaration of
Independence; member, first Congress,
1789-91.
b. Mar 16, 1739 in Philadelphia,
Pennsylvania
d. Jan 24, 1813 in Mornsville, Pennsylvania
Source: *AmBi; ApCAB; BiAUS; BiDrAC;
DcAmB; Drake; TwCBDA; WhAm HS;
WhAmP*

Coanda, Henri Marie
French. Engineer, Inventor
Designed rudimentary jet plane, 1910.
b. Jun 6, 1885 in Bucharest, Romania
d. Nov 25, 1972
Source: *CurBio 56, 73; NewYTBE 72*

Coasters
[Carl Gardner; Cornelius Gunter; Billy Guy;
Adolph Jacobs]
American. Music Group
Source: *AmPS A; BiDAmM; EncPR&S 74;
IlEncRk; RkOn 84; RkOneH*

Coates, Albert
English. Conductor, Composer
b. Apr 23, 1882 in Saint Petersburg, Russia
d. Dec 11, 1953 in Capetown, South Africa
Source: *NewEOp 71*

Coates, Edith
English. Singer
Founding member of Covent Garden Opera
Co., 1937.
b. May 31, 1908 in Lincoln, England
d. Jan 7, 1983 in Worthing, England
Source: *NewYTBS 83; Who 81; WhoMus 72*

Coates, Robert Myron
American. Author, Art Critic
Novels include *Eater of Darkness,* 1929;
Wisteria Cottage, 1948.
b. Apr 6, 1897 in New Haven, Connecticut
d. Feb 8, 1973 in New York, New York
Source: *AmAu&B; AmNov; Au&Wr 71;
CnDAL; ConAu 5R, 41R; ConNov 72;
DcLEL; NewYTBE 73; OxAmL; PenC AM;
REn; REnAL; TwCA, SUP; WhAm 5;
WhoAmA 73*

Coats, James
Scottish. Manufacturer
Organized factory to make thread, 1826;
became J P Coats, Ltd., 1890.
b. 1774
d. 1857
Source: *WebBD 80*

Coatsworth, Elizabeth Jane
American. Poet, Children's Author
Won Newbery Award for *The Cat Who
Went to Heaven,* 1930.
b. May 31, 1893 in Buffalo, New York
d. Aug 31, 1986 in Nobleboro, Maine
Source: *AmAu&B; AmNov; AnCL; Au&ICB;
AuBYP; BkCL; ChlLR 2; ChhPo, S1, S2;
ConAu 5R, 4NR; InWom; JBA 34, 51;
MorBMP; Newb 1922; OxAmL; REnAL;
SmATA 2; Str&VC; TwCA, SUP; WhAm 84;
WhoChL; WhoWor 74*

Cobb, Arnett Cleophus
American. Musician
b. Aug 10, 1918 in Houston, Texas
Source: *BioIn 10; WhoJazz 72*

Cobb, Irvin Shrewsbury
American. Journalist, Humorist, Author
Noted humor columnist, after-dinner speaker;
wrote *Speaking of Operations,* 1915; *Old
Judge Priest,* 1916.
b. Jun 23, 1876 in Paducah, Kentucky
d. Mar 10, 1944 in New York, New York
Source: *AmAu&B; CnDAL; ConAmL; CurBio
44; DcAmB S3; DcNAA; EncMys; EvLB; Film
1; LongCTC; NotNAT B; ObitOF 79;
OxAmL; REn; REnAL; TwCA, SUP; WhAm
2; WhNAA; WhScrn 74, 77; WhoHol B*

Cobb, Jerrie
American. Pilot
b. Mar 5, 1931 in Norman, Oklahoma
Source: *BioIn 7; CurBio 61; WhoAmW 74;
WhoS&SW 82*

Cobb, Joe
[Our Gang]
"Fat Joe"; "Wheezer"
American. Actor
First fat boy of Our Gang comedies, 1922.
b. 1917
Source: *Film 2; TwYS; WhoHol A*

Cobb, Lee J (Leo Jacob)
American. Actor
Created role of Willy Loman in *Death of a
Salesman* on Broadway, 1949.
b. Dec 9, 1911 in New York, New York
d. Feb 11, 1976 in Los Angeles, California
Source: *BiDFilm; BiE&WWA; CelR; CmMov;
CurBio 60; FamA&A; FilmgC; IntMPA 75;
MotPP; MovMk; NotNAT B; OxFilm; PIP&P;
WhAm 6, 7; WhThe; WhoAm 74; WorAl;
WorEFlm*

Cobb, Stanley
American. Scientist, Physician, Engineer
b. Dec 10, 1887 in Brookline, Massachusetts
d. Feb 18, 1968 in Cambridge, Massachusetts
Source: *BioIn 4; WhAm 4*

Cobb, Ty(rus Raymond)
"The Georgia Peach"
American. Baseball Player
Detroit Tigers star, 1905-26; considered
greatest offensive player of all time; won
12 batting titles.
b. Dec 18, 1886 in Narrows, Georgia
d. Jul 17, 1961 in Atlanta, Georgia
Source: *BaseEn 85; CurBio 51, 61; WebAB;
WhAm 4; WhScrn 77; WhoProB 73*

Cobb, Vicki
American. Children's Author, Scientist
Wrote award-winning children's TV series,
"The Science Game," 1972.
b. Aug 19, 1938 in New York, New York
Source: *ChlLR 2; ConAu 33R; SmATA 8;
WrDr 80*

Cobb, Will D
American. Songwriter
b. Jul 6, 1876 in Philadelphia, Pennsylvania
d. Jan 20, 1930 in New York, New York
Source: *AmSCAP 66; BioIn 4*

Cobb, William Montague
American. Anthropologist, Educator
Editor, *Journal of National Medical Assn.,*
1949-77.
b. Oct 12, 1904 in Washington, District of
Columbia
Source: *AmM&WS 73P, 73S; BlueB '76;
InB&W 80; WhoAm 74, 80, 82; WhoBlA 77;
WhoWor 80*

Cobbett, William
[Peter Porcupine, psued.]
English. Journalist, Author
Wrote *Rural Rides,* 1860, pro-British
pamphlets while in US.
b. Mar 19, 1762 in Farnham, England
d. Jun 18, 1835
Source: *Alli; AmBi; ApCAB; AtlBL; BbD;
BbtC; BiD&SB; BiDLA, SUP; BrAu 19;
CarSB; CasWL; Chambr 2; CnDAL; DcAmB;
DcEnA; DcEnL; DcEuL; DcLEL; Drake;
EvLB; MouLC 3; NewC; OxAmL; OxEng;
PenC ENG; REn; WebE&AL; WhAm HS;
WhAmP*

Cobden, Richard
English. Political Leader, Economist
Free trade, anti-Crime War advocate, leader
of Anti-Cow-Law League, 1839-46.
b. Jun 3, 1804 in Sussex, England
d. Apr 2, 1865 in London, England
Source: *Alli, SUP; BiD&SB; BrAu 19; NewC;
REn*

Cobden-Sanderson, Thomas James
English. Printer
Master bookbinder; operated Doves Press
with Emery Walker, 1900-16.
b. Dec 2, 1840 in Alnwick, England
d. Sep 7, 1922 in Hammersmith, England
Source: *AntBDN B; DcNaB 1922; LongCTC*

Cobleigh, Ira Underwood
American. Author, Economist
b. Dec 25, 1903 in Derby, Connecticut
Source: *WhoE 74*

Coburn, Charles Douville
American. Actor, Manager
Won Oscar for *The More the Merrier,* 1943.
b. Jun 19, 1877 in Savannah, Georgia
d. Aug 30, 1961 in New York, New York
Source: *BiDFilm; CurBio 44, 61; FilmgC;
MotPP; MovMk; ObitOF 79; OxFilm; OxThe;
Vers A; WhAm 4; WhScrn 74, 77; WhoHol
B; WorAl; WorEFlm*

Coburn, D(onald) L(ee)
American. Dramatist
Won Pulitzer, 1978, for *The Gin Game.*
b. Aug 4, 1938 in Baltimore, Maryland
Source: *VarWW 85*

Coburn, James
American. Actor
Starred in *Our Man Flint,* 1966; *In Like Flint,* 1967.
b. Aug 31, 1928 in Laurel, Nebraska
Source: *BiDFilm; BkPepl; CelR; ConTFT 3; FilmgC; IntMPA 82; MotPP; MovMk; OxFilm; WhoAm 84; WhoHol A; WorEFlm*

Coburn, Julia
American. Fashion Editor
Fashion editor, *Ladies Home Journal,* 1932-37.
b. in Kansas City, Missouri
Source: *WhoAm 78; WhoAmW 72, 74*

Coca, Imogene Fernandez y
American. Comedienne, Actress
Appeared with Sid Caesar in "Your Show of Shows," 1950-52; had own show, "Grindl."
b. Nov 19, 1908 in Philadelphia, Pennsylvania
Source: *BiE&WWA; BioNews 74; CurBio 51; EncMT; FilmgC; InWom; IntMPA 75, 76, 77, 78, 79, 80, 81, 82; NotNAT; WhoAm 74, 76, 78, 80, 82; WhoHol A; WhoThe 77; WhoWor 78*

Cochet, Henri
[The Four Musketeers]
French. Tennis Player
b. Dec 14, 1901 in Lyons, France
Source: *BioIn 11*

Cochin, Charles Nicholas
French. Type Designer
His 1500 works include book illustrations, pencil, crayon portraits, engraved frontispieces
b. 1715
d. 1790
Source: *NewCol 75; WebBD 80*

Cochise
American Indian. Apache Chief
Waged war against US Army, 1861-72.
b. 1815 in Arizona
d. Jun 9, 1874 in Arizona
Source: *FilmgC; McGEWB; NewCol 75; OxAmH; REnAW; WebAB; WhAm HS*

Cochran, Barbara Ann
American. Skier
b. Jan 4, 1951 in Claremont, New Hampshire
Source: *BioIn 10, 11*

Cochran, C(harles) B(lake)
"Britain's Greatest Showman"
English. Impresario
Prolific producer of musical revues, 1920s-30s; agent for Sarah Bernhardt, Harry Houdini.
b. Sep 25, 1872 in Lindfield, England
d. Jan 31, 1951 in London, England
Source: *CurBio 40, 51; EncMT; NotNAT B; ObitOF 79; OxThe; WhThe*

Cochran, Eddie
American. Singer, Songwriter
b. Oct 3, 1938 in Oklahoma City, Oklahoma
d. Apr 17, 1960 in London, England
Source: *BiDAmM; RkOn 84; WhScrn 77*

Cochran, Jacqueline
[Mrs. Floyd B Odlum]
American. Aviatrix, Journalist
Organized Women's Air Force Service (WASP), 1943; first woman to break sonic barrier, 1953.
b. 1910 in Pensacola, Florida
d. Aug 9, 1980 in Indio, California
Source: *AmAu&B; ConAu 101; CurBio 40, 63, 80; GoodHs; HerW; IntWW 75, 76, 77, 78; LibW; WebAB; WebAMB; WhoAm 76, 78; WhoAmW 58, 64, 66, 68, 70, 72, 74, 75; WorAl*

Cochran, Steve
American. Actor
b. May 25, 1917 in Eureka, California
d. Jun 15, 1965 in Guatemala
Source: *BiE&WWA; FilmgC; MotPP; HolP 40; MovMk; WhScrn 74, 77; WhoHol A; WorEFlm*

Cochran, Thad
American. Politician
Conservative Rep. senator from MS, 1978--.
b. Dec 7, 1937 in Pontotoc, Mississippi
Source: *AlmAP 78, 80; CngDr 77, 79; WhoAm 76, 78, 80, 82, 84; WhoGov 77; WhoS&SW 75, 76, 78*

Cochrane, Edward Lull
American. Government Official
b. Mar 18, 1892 in Mare Island, California
d. Nov 14, 1959
Source: *CurBio 51, 60*

Cochrane, Mickey (Gordon Stanley)
"Black Mike"
American. Baseball Player, Baseball Manager
Managed Detroit Tigers, 1933-38; won two
  pennants, 1934, 1935.
b. Apr 6, 1903 in Bridgewater, Massachusetts
d. Jun 28, 1962 in Lake Forest, Illinois
Source: *BaseEn 85; WhoProB 73*

Cockburn, Alexander
English. Journalist
Source: *BioIn 11*

Cockburn, Claud(Francis Claud)
[James Helvick; Frank Pitcairn, pseud.]
British. Journalist
Published *The Week* newssheet, 1933-46.
b. Apr 12, 1904 in Peking, China
d. Dec 15, 1981 in Cork, Ireland
Source: *Au&Wr 71; NewYTBS 81; Who 74,
82; WorAu*

Cockcroft, John Douglas, Sir
English. Scientist, Engineer, Physician
Directed Great Britain's atomic energy
  research establishment at Harwell.
b. May 27, 1897 in York, England
d. Sep 18, 1967 in Cambridge, England
Source: *AsBiEn; DcNaB 1961; LinLib S;
McGEWB; McGMS 80; ObitOF 79; ObitT
1961; WhDW; WhAm 4; WhWW-II; WorAl*

Cocker, "Joe" (Robert John)
English. Musician, Singer
Recorded "Up Where We Belong" from *An
Officer and a Gentleman,* with Jennifer
  Warnes, 1982.
b. May 20, 1944 in Sheffield, England
Source: *BkPepl; EncPR&S 74; IlEncRk;
RkOn 84; WorAl*

Cockerell, Christopher
English. Engineer
b. Jun 1910 in Cambridge, England
Source: *IntWW 74; Who 74; WhoWor 78*

Cockrell, Ewing
American. Judge
Founder, first pres., US Federation of Justice,
  1929; devoted to world peace.
b. May 28, 1874 in Warrensburg, Missouri
d. Jan 21, 1962 in Washington, District of
  Columbia
Source: *CurBio 51, 62; WhAm 4*

Coco, James
American. Actor
Oscar nomination for *Only When I Laugh,*
  1981.
b. Mar 21, 1929 in New York, New York
Source: *CelR; CurBio 74; FilmgC; IntMPA
75, 76, 77, 78, 79, 80, 81, 82; NewYTBE 70;
NotNAT; PIP&P; WhoAm 82; WhoE 74;
WhoHol A; WhoThe 77*

Cocteau, Jean
French. Author, Director, Poet
Wrote *Les Enfants Terribles,* 1924; *Thomas
L'Imposteur,* 1923.
b. Jul 5, 1889 in Maisons-Lafitte, France
d. Oct 12, 1963 in Paris, France
Source: *AtlBL; BiDFilm; CasWL; ClDMEL;
CnMD; CnMWL; CnThe; ConAu 25R, P-2;
ConLC 1, 8, 15, 16; CyWA; DcFM; EncWL;
EvEuW; FilmgC; LongCTC; MakMC;
McGEWB; McGEWD; ModFrL; ModRL;
ModWD; MovMk; NewEOp 71; OxEng;
OxFilm; OxFr; OxThe; PenC EUR; REn;
REnWD; TwCA, SUP; TwCWr; WhAm 4;
WhScrn 77; WhoGrA 62; WhoTwCL;
WorEFlm*

Codrington, Edward, Sir
British. Admiral
Commanded British, Russian ships in
  destroying Turkish fleet at Navarino, 1827.
b. 1770
d. 1851
Source: *NewCol 75*

Codron, Michael
English. Producer
Won Tony, 1984, for *The Real Thing.*
b. Jun 8, 1930 in London, England
Source: *VarWW 85*

Cody, "Buffalo Bill" (William Frederick)
American. Frontiersman, Entertainer
Buffalo hunter who organized Buffalo Bill's
  Wild West Show, touring US, Europe,
  1883-1901.
b. Feb 26, 1846 in Scout County, Iowa
d. Jan 10, 1917 in Denver, Colorado
Source: *AmAu&B; AmBi; ApCAB; DcAmB;
DcNAA; EncAB-H; FilmgC; HsB&A; OxAmL;
OxFilm; OxThe; REn; REnAL; TwCBDA;
WebAB; WhAm 1; WhScrn 77*

Cody, Iron Eyes
American Indian. Actor
Cherokee who wept in TV ecology ads; films
  include *Grayeagle,* 1977.
b. Apr 3, 1915 in Oklahoma
Source: *FilmEn; MotPP; WhoAm 76, 78, 80,
82, 84; WhoHol A*

Cody, John Patrick
American. Religious Leader
Archbishop of Chicago, 1965-82; involved in
scandal concerning misuse of church funds,
1981.
b. Dec 24, 1907 in Saint Louis, Missouri
d. Apr 25, 1982 in Chicago, Illinois
Source: *BioIn 7, 10, 11; CurBio 65, 82;
IntWW 74, 75, 76, 77, 78; NewYTBS 82;
WhoAm 74, 76, 78, 80, 82; WhoMW 74, 76,
78, 80, 82; WhoRel 75, 77; WhoWor 74*

Cody, Lew
[Louis Joseph Cote]
American. Comedian
b. Feb 22, 1887 in Waterville, Maine
d. May 31, 1934 in Beverly Hills, California
Source: *Film 1; FilmgC; MotPP; MovMk;
TwYS; WhScrn 74, 77; WhoHol B*

Coe, Frederick H
American. Producer
b. Dec 23, 1914 in Alligator, Mississippi
d. Apr 29, 1979 in Los Angeles, California
Source: *BiE&WWA; ConAu 85; CurBio 59,
79; FilmgC; IntMPA 75, 76, 77, 78, 79;
NewYTBS 79; NewYTET; NotNAT; WhoAm
74; WhoThe 77*

Coe, Sebastian Newbold
English. Track Athlete
First to hold world records for fastest mile,
800 meter, and 1,500 meter races, 1979.
b. Sep 29, 1956 in Sheffield, England
Source: *CurBio 80*

Coen, Jan Pieterszoon
Dutch. Colonial Leader
Governor-general of Dutch East India Co.,
1617-29.
b. 1587 in Hoorn, Netherlands
d. Sep 21, 1629
Source: *BioIn 4; McGEWB*

Coeur, Jacques
French. Merchant, Diplomat
Wealthy, influential financial advisor to
Charles VII; falsely condemned,
imprisoned.
b. 1395
d. 1456
Source: *NewCol 75; WebBD 80*

Coffey, Paul
Canadian. Hockey Player
Defenseman, Edmonton, 1980--; style
often compared to Bobby Orr; won Norris
Trophy, 1985.
b. Jun 1, 1961 in Weston, Ontario
Source: *ConNews 85-4; HocReg 85*

Coffin, Charles Albert
American. Business Executive
b. Dec 1844 in Somerset County, Maine
d. Nov 9, 1926 in Portland, Oregon
Source: *DcAmB; WhAm 1*

Coffin, Henry Sloane
American. Clergyman
b. Jan 5, 1877 in New York, New York
d. Nov 25, 1954 in Lakeville, Connecticut
Source: *AmAu&B; CurBio 44, 55; DcAmB S5;
WhAm 3*

Coffin, Howard Earle
American. Engineer
Designed Chalmers, Hudson autos; with Roy
Chapin founded Hudson Motor Car Co.,
1909.
b. Sep 6, 1873 in West Milton, Ohio
d. Nov 21, 1937 in Sea Island, Georgia
Source: *BiDAmBL 83; DcAmB S2; NatCAB
16, 30; WebAB 79; WhAm 1*

Coffin, Levi
American. Abolitionist
Organized Underground Railroad in IN,
1826-47, in Cincinnati, 1847-60.
b. Oct 28, 1798 in New Garden, North
Carolina
d. Sep 16, 1877
Source: *BioIn 1, 2, 6, 8, 10; DcNAA; IndAu
1816; McGEWB; OhA&B; WebAB*

Coffin, Robert Peter Tristram
American. Poet, Author, Biographer
Won 1935 Pulitzer for verse *Strange
Holiness;* many books concern ME life.
b. Mar 18, 1892 in Brunswick, Maine
d. Oct 29, 1956 in Raleigh, North Carolina
Source: *AmAu&B; AnMV 1926; CnDAL;
ConAmA; DcAmB S5; DcLEL; LongCTC;
OxAmL; PenC AM; REn; REnAL; Str&VC;
TwCA, SUP; WhAm 3; WhLit; WhNAA*

Coffin, William Sloan
American. Clergyman, Author
Minister, NYC Presbyterian Riverside
Church, 1977--.
b. Jun 1, 1924 in New York, New York
Source: *ConAu 103; CurBio 68, 80; PolProf
J; WhoAm 76, 78, 80, 82, 84; WhoWor 74*

Coggan, Frederick Donald
English. Religious Leader
Archbishop of Canterbury, 1974-80; author
Sure Foundation, 1981.
b. Oct 9, 1909 in London, England
Source: *Who 85; WhoAm 76, 78, 80, 82, 84;
WhoWor 74*

Coghill, Nevill Henry Kendall Aylmer
English. Author, Educator, Scholar
Chaucer authority who translated *Canterbury Tales* into modern English, 1951.
b. Apr 19, 1899 in Castletownshend, England
d. Nov 6, 1980 in Oxford, England
Source: *AnObit 1980; BlueB 76; ConAu 102, 13R; ConDr 73, 77D; DcLEL 1940; NewC; REn; WhoThe 77, 81*

Coghlan, Eamonn
"Cockie"
Irish. Track Athlete
Noted indoor miler who established world record, 1981.
b. 1953 in Dublin, Ireland
Source: *BioIn 11; NewYTBS 81*

Coghlan, Rose
Actress
Leading lady of NYC's Wallack Theater, 1877-85.
b. Mar 18, 1851 in Peterborough, England
d. Apr 2, 1932 in Harrison, New York
Source: *FamA&A; NatCAB 13; NotAW; NotNAT B; OxThe; PIP&P; WhAm 1; WhScrn 74, 77; WhThe; WhoHol B*

Cohan, George M(ichael)
American. Actor, Dramatist, Producer
Wrote many fast-paced musical shows, songs, including "You're a Grand Old Flag," "Give My Regards to Broadway."
b. Jul 3, 1878 in Providence, Rhode Island
d. Nov 5, 1942 in New York, New York
Source: *AmAu&B; AmSCAP 66; CnMD; CurBio 43; DcAmB S3; EncAB-H; EncMT; FamA&A; Film 1; FilmgC; LongCTC; McGEWD; ModWD; NatCAB 15; NewCBMT; NotNAT A; OxAmL; OxThe; PIP&P; REnAL; TwYS; WebAB; WhAm 1; WhLit; WhScrn 74, 77; WhThe; WhoHol B; WhoStg 1906, 1908*

Cohan, Josephine
American. Actress
b. 1876 in Providence, Rhode Island
d. Jul 12, 1916 in New York, New York
Source: *NotNAT B*

Cohen, Alexander H
American. Producer, Actor
Won two Emmys; producer of Tony Awards, 1967-80; appeared in *The Purple Rose of Cairo*, 1985.
b. Jul 24, 1920 in New York, New York
Source: *BiE&WWA; BlueB 76; CelR; CurBio 65; EncMT; IntWW 74; NotNAT; VarWW 85; WhoAm 80, 82; WhoThe 77, 81; WhoWor 74*

Cohen, Benjamin Victor
American. Lawyer
b. Sep 23, 1894 in Muncie, Indiana
d. Aug 15, 1983 in Washington, District of Columbia
Source: *CurBio 41; IndAu 1917; WhAm 8; WhoAm 78, 80; WhoWorJ 72*

Cohen, Daniel
American. Author
b. Mar 12, 1936 in Chicago, Illinois
Source: *ConAu 45, 1NR; SmATA 8*

Cohen, Joan Lebold
American. Author
b. Aug 19, 1932 in Highland Park, Illinois
Source: *ConAu 25R; SmATA 4*

Cohen, Leonard
Canadian. Author, Songwriter, Singer
Songs include "Suzanne"; "Hey, That's No Way to Say Goodbye," 1968.
b. Sep 21, 1934 in Montreal, Quebec
Source: *CanWW 82; CanWr; CasWL; CelR; ConAu 21R; ConLC 3; ConNov 72, 76; ConP 70, 75; OxCan; SUP; WebE&AL; WhoAm 74, 76, 78, 80, 82; WrDr 80*

Cohen, "Mickey" (Meyer)
American. Organized Crime Figure
b. 1913 in Brooklyn, New York
d. Jul 29, 1976 in Los Angeles, California
Source: *BioIn 10, 11*

Cohen, Myron
American. Comedian
Known for dialect, government jokes.
b. Jul 1, 1902 in Grodno, Poland
d. Mar 10, 1986 in Nyack, New York
Source: *NewYTBE 70*

Cohen, Octavus Roy
American. Author
Best known for stories depicting small-town southern blacks.
b. Jun 26, 1891 in Charleston, South Carolina
d. Jan 6, 1959 in Los Angeles, California
Source: *AmAu&B; EncMys; OxAmL; REn; REnAL; TwCA, SUP; WhAm 3; WhNAA*

Cohen, Wilbur Joseph
American. Educator, Author
b. Jun 10, 1913 in Milwaukee, Wisconsin
Source: *AmEA 74; AmM&WS 73S; BiDrUSE; ConAu 25R; CurBio 68; IntWW 74; LEduc 74; WhoAm 74, 76, 78, 80, 82; WhoAmP 73; WhoWor 78; WhoWorJ 72*

Cohen, William Sebastian
American. Politician
Moderate Rep. senator from ME, 1980--;
wrote *Getting the Most Out of Washington*,
1982.
b. Aug 28, 1940 in Bangor, Maine
Source: *AlmAP 78, 80; BioIn 10, 11; CurBio
82; PolProf NF; WhoAm 76, 78, 80, 82, 84;
WhoAmP 73, 75, 77, 79; WhoE 77, 79;
WhoGov 75, 77*

Cohn, Al
American. Jazz Musician, Composer
b. Nov 24, 1925 in Brooklyn, New York
Source: *AmSCAP 66; WhoAm 82*

Cohn, Arthur
American. Composer, Conductor
b. Nov 6, 1910 in Philadelphia, Pennsylvania
Source: *AmSCAP 66; BioIn 1; WhoWorJ 72*

Cohn, Emil Ludwig
see: Ludwig, Emil

Cohn, Ferdinand Julius
Polish. Botanist
b. Jan 24, 1828 in Breslau, Poland
d. Jun 25, 1898 in Breslau, Poland
Source: *AsBiEn; BiHiMed; DcScB*

Cohn, Roy Marcus
American. Lawyer
Best known as chief counsel to Senator
Joseph McCarthy's communist-hunting
investigations subcommittee, early 1950s.
b. Feb 20, 1927 in New York, New York
d. Aug 2, 1986 in Bethesda, Maryland
Source: *WhoAm 74, 76, 78, 80, 82; WhoE
74; WhoWorJ 72*

Cohn-Bendit, Daniel
French. Anarchist
b. 1945
Source: *BioIn 11*

Coit, Margaret Louise
American. Author
b. May 30, 1922 in Norwich, Connecticut
Source: *AmAu&B; AuBYP; ConAu 1R, 5NR;
CurBio 51; DrAS 74H; InWom; OxAmL;
REnAL; SmATA 2; TwCA SUP; WhoAm 74,
76, 78, 80, 82*

Coke, Edward, Sir
English. Judge
b. Feb 1, 1552 in Mileham, England
d. Sep 3, 1634 in Stoke Poges, England
Source: *Alli; BrAu; DcBiPP; DcEnL; LinLib
L, S; McGEWB; NewC; OxEng*

Colasanto, Nicholas
American. Actor
Best known as Coach Ernie Pantusso on TV
series "Cheers."
b. 1923 in Providence, Rhode Island
d. Feb 12, 1985 in Los Angeles, California
Source: *ConNews 85-2*

Colavito, Rocky (Rocco Domenico)
American. Baseball Player
Led AL in RBI's with 108, 1965.
b. Aug 10, 1933 in New York, New York
Source: *BaseEn 85; BioIn 5, 6, 7, 9;
WhoProB 73*

Colbert, Claudette
[Lily Claudette Chauchoin]
American. Actress
Won Oscar for *It Happened One Night*,
1934.
b. Sep 13, 1905 in Paris, France
Source: *BiDFilm; BiE&WWA; BioNews 74;
CelR; CurBio 45, 64; FilmgC; InWom;
IntMPA 75, 76, 77, 78, 79, 80, 81, 82;
MotPP; MovMk; OxFilm; PIP&P; ThFT; Who
82; WhoAm 74, 76, 78, 80, 82; WhoHol A;
WhoThe 77; WomWMM; WorEFlm*

Colbert, Jean Baptiste
French. Statesman
b. Aug 29, 1619 in Reims, France
d. Sep 6, 1683
Source: *OxFr; REn*

Colbert, Lester Lum
American. Lawyer
b. Jun 13, 1905 in Oakwood, Texas
Source: *BioIn 2, 4, 5; CurBio 51; IntWW 74;
WhoAm 74, 76, 78, 80, 82*

Colbran, Isabella
Spanish. Opera Singer
b. Feb 2, 1785 in Madrid, Spain
d. Oct 7, 1845 in Bologna, Italy
Source: *InWom*

Colby, Anita
[Anita Katherine Counihan]
American. Actress, Model, Editor
Modeled in the 30s; wrote *Anita Colby's
Beauty Book.*
b. Aug 5, 1914 in Washington, District of
Columbia
Source: *AmAu&B; AmCath 80; InWom;
MotPP; WhoAmW 74, 58, 64; WhoHol A*

Colby, Carroll Burleigh
American. Author, Artist
Known for juvenile nature, adventure stories:
Gobbit, the Magic Rabbit, 1951.
b. Sep 7, 1904 in Claremont, New
Hampshire
d. Oct 31, 1977
Source: *AuBYP; ConAu 1R; MorJA; SmATA
3; WhAm 7; WhoAm 74, 76, 78*

Colby, William Egan
American. Government Official
Director, CIA, 1973-76.
b. Jan 4, 1920 in Saint Paul, Minnesota
Source: *BlueB 76; ConAu 81; CurBio 75;
IntWW 74; NewYTBE 73; WhoAm 78, 80*

Colden, Cadwallader
Irish. Botanist, Author
b. Feb 7, 1688 in Ireland
d. Sep 28, 1776 in Long Island, New York
Source: *AmAu; AmAu&B; CyAL 1; DcAmAu;
DcEnL; DcNAA; OxAmL; OxCan; REnAL*

Cole, Charles Woolsey
American. Educator, Diplomat
Pres., Amherst College, 1946-60; ambassador
to Chile, 1961-64; author of historical
works.
b. Feb 8, 1907 in Montclair, New Jersey
d. Feb 6, 1978 in Los Angeles, California
Source: *AmAu&B; BlueB 76; ConAu 69;
IntWW 74, 78; Who 74; WhoAm 74*

Cole, "Cozy" (William Randolph)
American. Musician
Big band drummer; recorded "Topsy," 1958,
only drum solo ever to sell over one
million copies.
b. Oct 17, 1909 in East Orange, New Jersey
d. Jan 29, 1981 in Columbus, Ohio
Source: *BiDAmM; CmpEPM; DrBlPA; EncJzS
70; IlEncJ; NewYTBS 81; WhAm 7; WhoAm
74; WhoE 74; WhoJazz 72*

Cole, Dennis
American. Actor
b. Jul 19, 1943 in Detroit, Michigan
Source: *WhoHol A*

Cole, Edward Nicholas
American. Auto Executive
Pres., GM, 1967-74.
b. Sep 17, 1909 in Berlin, Michigan
d. May 2, 1977 in Kalamazoo, Michigan
Source: *BioNews 74; BusPN; CelR; CurBio
72; IntWW 74; St&PR 75; Ward 77G; Who
74; WhoAm 74; WhoF&I 75*

Cole, George
English. Actor
b. Apr 22, 1925 in London, England
Source: *FilmgC; IntMPA 75, 76, 77, 78, 79,
80, 81, 82; Who 74, 82; WhoHol A, B;
WhoThe 72, 77*

Cole, George Douglas Howard
English. Educator, Author
Oxford professor; wrote books on socialist
topics; detective stories with his wife.
b. Sep 25, 1889 in Cambridge, England
d. Jan 14, 1959 in Oxford, England
Source: *DcLEL; DcNaB 1951; EncMys; EvLB;
GrBr; LongCTC; McGEWB; NewC; WhAm 3;
WhE&EA; WhLit; WhoEc; WhoLA*

Cole, Jack
American. Choreographer
b. Apr 27, 1914 in New Brunswick, New
Jersey
d. Feb 17, 1974 in Los Angeles, California
Source: *BiE&WWA; CmMov; EncMT;
FilmgC; NewYTBS 74; WhAm 2; WhScrn 77;
WhoAm 74; WhoHol B; WorEFlm*

Cole, Kenneth Reese
American. Presidential Aide, Business
Executive
Special assistant to Richard Nixon, 1969-70;
assistant to Gerald Ford, 1974-75.
b. Jan 27, 1938 in New York, New York
Source: *NewYTBS 74; WhoAm 74, 76, 78,
80, 82*

Cole, Kenneth Stewart
"Father of Biophysics"
American. Physicist
Known for using electrical approach to
studying function of living cell membranes.
b. Jul 10, 1900 in Ithaca, New York
d. Apr 18, 1984 in La Jolla, California
Source: *AmM&WS 82P; BlueB 76; IntWW
80, 81, 82, 83; McGMS 80; WhoAm 80, 82;
WhoFrS 84; WhoGov 75*

Cole, Maria
American. Singer, Celebrity Relative
With Duke Ellington Band, 1945-46; widow
of Nat King Cole.
b. Aug 1, 1920 in Boston, Massachusetts
Source: *VarWW 85*

Cole, Michael
American. Actor
b. Jul 3, 1945 in Madison, Wisconsin
Source: *WhoHol A*

Cole, Nat "King" (Nathaniel Adams)
American. Singer, Band Leader, Actor
Best known songs include "Mona Lisa,"
1950; "Ramblin' Rose," 1962.
b. Mar 17, 1919 in Montgomery, Alabama
d. Feb 15, 1965 in Santa Monica, California
Source: *AmSCAP 66; Baker 78; BiDAmM;
CmpEPM; CurBio 56, 65; FilmgC; MovMk;
WhAm 4; WhScrn 74, 77; WhoHol B;
WhoJazz 72*

Cole, Natalie (Stephanie Natalie Maria)
American. Singer
Won Grammy, 1976, for debut album
Inseparable; daughter of Nat "King"
Cole.
b. Feb 6, 1949 in Los Angeles, California
Source: *BkPepl; DrBlPA; InB&W 80; WhoAm
78, 80, 82; WhoAmW 79, 81; WhoBlA 80*

Cole, Olivia
American. Actress
Won Emmy, 1977, for supporting role in
mini-series "Roots."
b. Nov 26, 1942 in Memphis, Tennessee
Source: *DrBlPA; WhoAm 78, 80, 82;
WhoAmW 79, 81*

Cole, Thomas
American. Artist
One of the founders of the Hudson River
School, first American movement in
painting.
b. Feb 1, 1801 in Bolton, England
d. Feb 11, 1848 in Catskill, New York
Source: *Alli; AmAu&B; AmBi; ApCAB; CyAL
2; DcAmB; Drake; EncAB-H; OxAmL;
TwCBDA; WebAB; WhAm HS*

Cole, Timothy
[Walter Sylvanus Timotheus Cole]
American. Engraver
b. Apr 6, 1852 in London, England
d. May 11, 1931
Source: *AmBi; DcAmB S1; LinLib L, S;
NatCAB 13; WhAm 1; WhNAA*

Cole, Tina
[The King Family]
American. Actress, Singer
b. Aug 4, 1943 in Hollywood, California
Source: *WhoHol A*

Coleman, Cy
[Seymour Kaufman]
American. Songwriter
Wrote song "If My Friends Could See Me
Now."
b. Jun 14, 1929 in New York, New York
Source: *AmSCAP 66; BiE&WWA; BioNews
75; CelR; EncMT; NewCBMT; NotNAT;
WhoAm 74, 76, 78, 80, 82; WhoE 74*

Coleman, Dabney
American. Actor
Played Bill Bittinger on TV series "Buffalo
Bill," 1983-84.
b. Jan 3, 1932 in Austin, Texas
Source: *ConTFT 3*

Coleman, Gary
American. Actor
Child actor who played Arnold on TV series
"Different Strokes," 1978-86.
b. Feb 8, 1968 in Zion, Illinois
Source: *ConTFT 3; InB&W 80; WhoTelC;
WorAl*

Coleman, James Samuel
American. Sociologist
b. May 12, 1926 in Bedford, Indiana
Source: *AmM&WS 73S; ConAu 13R, 1NR;
CurBio 70; IndAu 1917; IntWW 74; LEduc
74; WhoAm 74, 76, 78, 80, 82; WhoE 74;
WhoWor 78*

Coleman, John
American. Meteorologist
Gives national weather report on "Good
Morning, America."
b. Nov 15, 1935 in Champaign, Illinois
Source: *NF*

Coleman, Lester L
American. Biochemist
b. Nov 6, 1912 in Maricopa, California
Source: *AmM&WS 73P; WhoMW 74*

Coleman, Lonnie William
American. Author
Wrote *Beulah Land; Look Away, Beulah
Land; The Legacy of Beulah Land*.
b. Aug 2, 1920 in Barstow, Georgia
d. Aug 13, 1982 in Savannah, Georgia
Source: *AmAu&B; AmNov; BiE&WWA;
ConAu 107, 77; CurBio 58, 82N; 82N;
NewYTBS 82; NotNAT*

Coleman, Ornette
American. Jazz Musician
b. Mar 19, 1930 in Fort Worth, Texas
Source: *AmSCAP 66; CurBio 61; WhoAm 74,
76, 78, 80, 82; WhoBlA 75*

Coleman, Vince(nt Maurice)
American. Baseball Player
Outfielder, St. Louis, 1985--.
b. Sep 22, 1960 in Jacksonville, Florida
Source: *BaseEn 85; BaseReg 86*

Coleman, William
American. Businessman
Purchased rights for gas lamp, 1903; co. was
   largest manufacter of camping equipment,
   1960s.
b. 1870
d. 1957
Source: *Entr*

Coleman, William T
American. Lawyer
b. Jul 7, 1920 in Germantown, Pennsylvania
Source: *WhoAm 74, 76, 78, 80, 82; WhoBlA
75*

Coleridge, Hartley
English. Poet, Journalist
b. Sep 19, 1796 in Bristol, England
d. Jan 6, 1849 in Grasmere, England
Source: *BiD&SB; CasWL; Chambr 3; DcEnA;
DcEnL; DcEuL; DcLEL; EvLB; NewC; PenC
ENG*

Coleridge, Mary Elizabeth
[Anodos, pseud.]
English. Author, Poet
Wrote novel *Seven Sleepers of Ephesus,* 1893;
   verse *Gathered Leaves,* published, 1910.
b. Sep 23, 1861 in London, England
d. Aug 25, 1907 in Harrogate, England
Source: *ConAu 116; DcLB 19; NewC; OxEng*

Coleridge, Samuel Taylor
English. Author, Poet, Critic
Wrote "The Rime of the Ancient Mariner";
   "Kubla Khan."
b. Oct 21, 1772 in Devonshire, England
d. Jul 25, 1834 in London, England
Source: *Alli; AtlBL; BbD; BiD&SB; BiDLA;
BrAu 19; CasWL; Chambr 3; ChhPo, S1, S2;
CnE&AP; CrtT 2; CyWA; DcEnA; DcEnL;
DcEuL; DcLEL; EvLB; MouLC 3; NewC;
OxEng; OxThe; PenC ENG; RAdv 1;
RComWL; REn; WebE&AL*

Coleridge-Taylor, Samuel
English. Composer
b. Aug 15, 1875 in London, England
d. Sep 1, 1912 in Thornton, England
Source: *WhDW*

Coles, Joanna
American. Children's Author
Award-winning science books include *A
   Snake's Body,* 1981.
b. Aug 11, 1944 in Newark, New Jersey
Source: *ConAu 115*

Coles, Manning, pseud.
[Cyril Coles and Adelaide Frances Oke
   Manning]
English. Authors
Source: *ConAu 9R, P-1; EncMys; LongCTC;
TwCA SUP*

Colette, pseud.
[Sidonie Gabriellee Colette]
French. Author
Best works include four volume *Claudine,*
   1930; *GiGi,* 1943.
b. Jan 28, 1873 in Saint Sauveur, France
d. Aug 3, 1954 in Paris, France
Source: *AtlBL; CasWL; ClDMEL; CnMWL;
CyWA; EncWL; EvEuW; LongCTC; ModRL;
OxEng; OxFr; PenC EUR; REn; TwCA, SUP;
TwCLC 1; TwCWr; WhDW; WhAm 3;
WhE&EA; WhoTwCL; WorAl*

Colfax, Schuyler
American. Politician, Vice-President
VP under U S Grant, 1869-73; involvement
   in scandal ended career.
b. Mar 23, 1823 in New York, New York
d. Jan 13, 1885 in Mankato, Minnesota
Source: *AmBi; ApCAB; BiAUS; BiDrAC;
BiDrUSE; DcAmB; Drake; IndAu 1816;
TwCBDA; WebAB; WhAm HS; WhAmP*

Colgate, William
American. Manufacturer
Began soap-making business, 1806; later
   became Colgate-Palmolive.
b. Jan 25, 1783 in Hollingbourne, England
d. Mar 25, 1857 in New York, New York
Source: *AmBi; ApCAB; DcAmB; TwCBDA;
WebAB; WhAm HS*

Colicos, John
Canadian. Actor
b. Dec 10, 1928 in Toronto, Ontario
Source: *CreCan 1; FilmgC; NotNAT; WhoAm
82; WhoThe 77*

Collazo, Oscar
Puerto Rican. Attempted Assassin
With Griselio Torresola, tried to assassinate
   Harry Truman, Nov 1, 1950.
b. 1914
Source: *BioIn 10*

Collett, Glenna
American. Golfer
b. 1903
Source: *BioIn 6, 9, 11*

Collier, Constance
[Laura Constance Hardie]
English. Actress
b. Jan 22, 1878 in Windsor, England
d. Apr 25, 1955 in New York, New York
Source: *CurBio 54, 55; DcAmB S5; EncWT;
Film 1, 2; FilmgC; InWom; MotPP; MovMk;
NewC; NotNAT A; OxThe; PlP&P; REn;
ThFT; TwYS A; Vers A; WhScrn 74, 77;
WhoHol B*

Collier, John
English. Author
Promoted passage of Indian Reorganization
Act of 1933, which changed official
treatment of Indians.
b. May 3, 1901 in London, England
d. Apr 6, 1980 in Pacific Palisades,
California
Source: *ConNov 72, 76; CurBio 44; DcLEL;
EncMys; Film 2; NewC; NotNAT B; REn;
TwCA, SUP; WhThe; WrDr 76*

Collier, Peter
American. Author
Co-author with David Horowitz, *The Fords:
An American Epic,* 1986.
b. Jun 2, 1939 in Hollywood, California
Source: *ConAu 65; WrDr 84*

Collier, William, Sr.
American. Actor, Director, Dramatist
b. Nov 12, 1866 in New York, New York
d. Jan 13, 1944 in Beverly Hills, California
Source: *Film 1; FilmgC; MovMk; WhAm 2;
WhScrn 74, 77; WhoHol B; WhoStg 1906,
1908*

Collin, Frank
[Frank Cohn]
American. Nazi Leader
Son of Jewish refugee who is active in
Chicago Nazi Party.
b. Nov 3, 1944 in Chicago, Illinois
Source: *Alli SUP*

Collinge, Patricia
Irish. Actress
b. Sep 20, 1894 in Dublin, Ireland
Source: *BiE&WWA; FilmgC; InWom;
NewYTBS 74; NotNAT B; ObitOF 79;
OxFilm; Vers B; WhScrn 77; WhThe;
WhoAmW 74*

Collingwood, Charles Cummings
American. Broadcast Journalist
CBS correspondent who was first American
network newsman admitted to N Vietnam,
1968.
b. Jun 4, 1917 in Three Rivers, Michigan
d. Oct 3, 1985 in New York, New York
Source: *CelR; ConAu 29R; CurBio 43, 85;
IntWW 74; WhoAm 74, 76, 78, 80, 82;
WhoWor 74*

Collingwood, Robin George
English. Philosopher, Archeologist
b. 1889 in Coniston, England
d. Jan 9, 1943
Source: *CasWL; CnMWL; DcLEL; LongCTC;
LuthC 75; McGEWB; ObitOF 79; OxEng;
PenC ENG; REn; TwCA SUP*

Collins, Dorothy
[Marjorie Chandler]
Canadian. Singer
b. Nov 18, 1926 in Windsor, Ontario
Source: *InWom; NewYTBE 71; PlP&P A*

Collins, Doug
American. Basketball Player
b. Jul 28, 1951 in Christopher, Illinois
Source: *BioIn 9; WhoBbl 73*

Collins, Eddie (Edward Trowbridge, Sr.)
"Cocky"
American. Baseball Player, Baseball Manager
Hall of Fame, 1939; lifetime batting average
.333.
b. May 2, 1887 in Millertown, New York
d. Mar 25, 1951 in Boston, Massachusetts
Source: *BaseEn 85; DcAmB S5; WhoProB 73*

Collins, Gary
American. Actor
TV host "Hour Magazine," which won
Emmy, 1984; married to Mary Ann
Mobley.
b. Aug 30, 1983 in Boston, Massachusetts
Source: *VarWW 85; WhoHol A*

Collins, James Joseph (Jimmy)
American. Baseball Player
b. Jan 16, 1873 in Niagara Falls, New York
d. Mar 6, 1943 in Buffalo, New York
Source: *BaseEn 85; BioIn 2, 3, 7; WhoProB
73*

Collins, Joan
[Mrs. Peter Holm]
English. Actress
Plays Alexis Carrington Colby on TV series
"Dynasty."
b. May 23, 1933 in London, England
Source: *CurBio 84; FilmgC; InWom; IntMPA
75, 76, 77, 78, 79, 80, 81, 82; MotPP;
MovMk; WhoAm 82; WhoHol A; WhoTelC*

Collins, Joseph L
American. Army Officer
b. May 1, 1896 in New Orleans, Louisiana
Source: *CurBio 49; IntWW 74; Who 74;
WhoAm 74*

Collins, Judy (Judith)
American. Singer
Hits include "Both Sides Now," 1968; "Send
in the Clowns," 1975.
b. May 1, 1939 in Seattle, Washington
Source: *CelR; CurBio 69; EncFCWM 69;
WhoAm 74, 76, 78, 80, 82; WhoAmW 77;
WhoWor 78*

Collins, Larry
American. Author, Journalist
b. Sep 14, 1929 in Hartford, Connecticut
Source: *AmAu&B; CelR; WhoAm 74, 76, 78,
80, 82; WhoWor 78*

Collins, Lee
American. Musician
b. Oct 17, 1901 in New Orleans, Louisiana
d. Jul 7, 1960 in Chicago, Illinois
Source: *WhoJazz 72*

Collins, Martha Layne Hall
American. Politician
First woman governor of KY, 1983, who
chaired Dem. National Convention, 1984.
b. Dec 7, 1936 in Bagdad, Kentucky
Source: *CurBio 86; WhoAm 84*

Collins, Marva Deloise Nettles
American. Teacher, Reformer
Started Chicago's one-room school, Westside
Preparatory, 1975.
b. Aug 31, 1936 in Monroeville, Alabama
Source: *InB&W 80; WhoAm 82, 84;
WhoAmW 81; WhoBlA 80; WhoMW 82*

Collins, Michael
Irish. Revolutionary
b. 1890 in County Cork, Ireland
d. Aug 22, 1922
Source: *WebBD 80*

Collins, Mike (Michael)
American. Astronaut
Command module pilot, Apollo 11, first US
landing on moon, 1969.
b. Oct 31, 1930 in Rome, Italy
Source: *AmM&WS 73P; CelR; ConAu 53;
IntWW 74; Who 74; WhoAm 74, 76, 78, 80,
82; WhoGov 75; WhoS&SW 82; WhoWor 78*

Collins, Phil
[Genesis]
English. Singer, Musician
Drummer, lead singer for Genesis; has
successful solo career, including singles
"Against All Odds," 1984; "One More
Night," 1985.
b. Jan 30, 1951 in Chiswick, England
Source: *RkOn 85; WhoRocM 82*

Collins, Ray
American. Actor
Appeared in TV series "Perry Mason," 1957-
64.
b. Dec 10, 1889 in Sacramento, California
d. Jul 11, 1965 in Santa Monica, California
Source: *FilmgC; MotPP; MovMk; NotNAT B;
Vers A; WhScrn 74, 77; WhoHol B; WorAl*

Collins, Stephen
American. Actor
Appeared in film *Star Trek;* on TV series
"The Waltons"; "Barnaby Jones."
b. Oct 1, 1947 in Des Moines, Iowa
Source: *IntMPA 82, 84*

Collins, Ted
American.
b. Oct 12, 1899 in New York, New York
d. May 27, 1964 in Lake Placid, New York
Source: *NotNAT B*

Collins, Wilkie (William)
English. Author
Wrote mystery novels *The Woman in White,*
1860; *The Moonstone,* 1868.
b. Jan 8, 1824 in London, England
d. Sep 23, 1889 in London, England
Source: *AtlBL; BbD; BiD&SB; BrAu 19;
CasWL; Chambr 3; CrtT 3; CyWA; DcBiA;
DcEnA; DcEnL; DcEuL; DcLEL; EncMys;
EvLB; HsB&A; MnBBF; NewC; PenC ENG;
RAdv 1; REn; WebE&AL*

Collins, William
English. Poet
b. Dec 25, 1721 in Chichester, England
d. Jun 12, 1759 in Chichester, England
Source: *Alli; AtlBL; BbD; BiD&SB; BrAu;*
CasWL; Chambr 2; ChhPo, S1; CnE&AP;
CrtT 2; DcEnA; DcEnL; DcEuL; DcLEL;
EvLB; MouLC 2; NewC; OxEng; PenC ENG;
REn; WebE&AL

Collinsworth, (Anthony) Chris
"Cadillac"
American. Football Player
b. Jan 27, 1959 in Titusville, Florida
Source: *NewYTBS 82*

Collishaw, Raymond
English. Pilot
WW I air ace.
b. Nov 22, 1893 in Nonaimo, British
Columbia
d. 1977
Source: *CanWW 70; Who 74*

Collodi, Carlo, pseud.
[Carlo Lorenzini]
Italian. Author
Story *Pinocchio,* first appeared in newspaper,
1880; English translation, 1892.
b. Nov 24, 1826 in Tuscany, Italy
d. Oct 26, 1890 in Florence, Italy
Source: *AnCL; AuBYP; BkCL; CasWL;*
EuAu; EvEuW; JBA 34, 34; NewCol 75;
Str&VC; WhoChL

Collyer, "Bud" (Clayton)
American. TV Personality
b. Jun 18, 1908 in New York, New York
d. Sep 8, 1969 in Greenwich, Connecticut
Source: *NewYTET; ObitOF 79*

Collyer, Homer Lusk
American. Eccentric
b. 1881
d. 1947
Source: *BioIn 1, 3, 4, 8*

Collyer, Langley
American. Eccentric
b. 1886
d. 1947
Source: *BioIn 1, 3, 4, 8*

Colman, Norman Jay
American. Government Official
First secretary of Agriculture, 1889.
b. May 16, 1827 in Otsego County, New
York
d. Nov 3, 1911
Source: *AmBi; BiDrUSE; DcAmB; EncAAH;*
TwCBDA; WhAm 1

Colman, Ronald
American. Actor
Won Oscar for *A Double Life,* 1948;
appeared in *A Tale of Two Cities,* 1936.
b. Feb 9, 1891 in Richmond, England
d. May 19, 1958 in Santa Barbara, California
Source: *BiDFilm; CmMov; CurBio 43, 58;*
Film 1; FilmgC; MotPP; MovMk; OxFilm;
TwYS; WhAm 3; WhScrn 74, 77; WhoHol B;
WorEFlm

Colombo, Emilio
Italian. Political Leader
b. Apr 11, 1920 in Potenza, Italy
Source: *CurBio 71; IntWW 74; WhoWor 78*

Colombo, Joseph Anthony
American. Gangster
b. Jun 16, 1923 in Brooklyn, New York
d. May 23, 1978 in Newburgh, New York
Source: *NewYTBE 70*

Colonius, Lillian
American. Children's Author
b. Mar 19, 1911 in Irvine, California
Source: *ConAu 21R; SmATA 3*

Colonna, Jerry
American. Comedian, Musician
b. Sep 17, 1905 in Boston, Massachusetts
Source: *AmSCAP 66; FilmgC; MovMk;*
WhoHol A

Colonna di Castiglione, Adele
Italian. Artist
b. 1836
d. 1879
Source: *BioIn 10*

Colonne, Edouard
French. Conductor
b. Jul 23, 1838 in Bordeaux, France
d. Mar 28, 1910 in Paris, France
Source: *NewCol 75; OxMus*

Colson, Charles Wendell
American. Watergate Participant
b. Oct 16, 1931 in Boston, Massachusetts
Source: *NewYTBE 73; NewYTBS 74; WhoAm*
74, 76, 78, 80, 82; WhoGov 75; WhoS&SW
82

Colt, Samuel
American. Inventor
Patented revolving breech pistol, 1835; word
"Colt" often synonymous with revolver.
b. Jul 19, 1814 in Hartford, Connecticut
d. Jan 10, 1862 in Hartford, Connecticut
Source: *AmBi; ApCAB; DcAmB; Drake;*
TwCBDA; WebAB; WhAm HS

Colter, Jessie
[Miriam Johnson]
American. Singer
b. May 25, 1947 in Phoenix, Arizona
Source: *BkPepl; RkOn 74; WhoAm 82*

Colter, John
American. Explorer
First white man to explore Teton Mt. Range,
1807.
b. 1775 in Staunton, Virginia
d. Nov 1813 in Dundee, Missouri
Source: *DcAmB; NewCol 75; REnAW; WhAm
HS, HS*

Coltrane, "Trane" (John William)
American. Jazz Musician
Voted "Jazzman of the Year," 1965.
b. Sep 26, 1926 in Hamlet, North Carolina
d. Jul 17, 1967 in Huntington, New York
Source: *WebAB; WhAm 4*

Colum, Padraic
Irish. Poet, Dramatist, Author
b. Dec 8, 1881 in Langford, Ireland
d. Jan 12, 1972 in New York, New York
Source: *AmAu&B; AmSCAP 66; AnCL;
AuBYP; BkC 3; CarSB; CasWL; CathA 1930;
ChhPo, S1, S2; CnMD; ConAu 33R, 73;
ConP 70; DcLEL; EncWL; EvLB; FamSYP;
JBA 34, 51; LongCTC; McGEWD; ModBrL,
S1; ModWD; NewC; NewYTBE 71, 72;
OxThe; PenC ENG; RAdv 1; REn; REnWD;
SmATA 15; Str&VC; TwCA, SUP; TwCWr;
WebE&AL; WhAm 5*

Columba, Saint
Irish. Missionary
b. 521
d. 597
Source: *NewCol 75*

Columban, Saint
Irish. Religious Figure
Missionary to Europe whose practices
alienated religious, political powers;
founded abbey at Luxeil, 590.
b. 543 in Lenister, Ireland
d. 615 in Bobbia, Italy
Source: *CasWL; CyEd; NewC; NewCol 75*

Columbo, Russ
[Ruggerio de Rudolpho Columbo]
American. Actor, Singer
Appeared in *Broadway Through a Keyhole,*
1933.
b. Jan 4, 1908 in Philadelphia, Pennsylvania
d. Sep 2, 1934 in Hollywood, California
Source: *FilmgC; WhScrn 74, 77; WhoHol B*

Columbus, Christopher
[Cristoforo Colombo]
Italian. Explorer
Sailed from Palos, Spain, Aug 3, 1492;
sighted land, San Salvador, Oct 12, 1492.
b. 1451 in Genoa, Italy
d. May 20, 1506 in Spain
Source: *CasWL; DcEuL; EncAB-H; EvEuW;
NewC; OxAmL; REn; REnAL; WebAB*

Colville, Alex (David Alexander)
Canadian. Artist
Realist painter who captured people, places,
animals of Maritime Provinces.
b. Aug 24, 1920 in Toronto, Ontario
Source: *CanWW 83; ConArt 77; CurBio 85;
McGDA; WhoAm 84*

Colvin, Sidney, Sir
English. Critic, Editor, Museum Director
Head of prints, British Museum; wrote on
literature, arts: *Early Engraving and
Engravers in England,* 1905.
b. Jun 18, 1845 in Norwood, England
d. May 11, 1927 in London, England
Source: *EvLB; NewCol 75; OxEng; TwCA*

Comaneci, Nadia
Romanian. Gymnast
Won three Olympic gold medals, 1976;
received seven perfect scores.
b. Nov 12, 1961 in Onesti, Romania
Source: *BioIn 10; BkPepl; NewYTBS 81;
WorAl*

Combs, Earle Bryan
"The Kentucky Colonel"
American. Baseball Player
Outfielder, NY Yankees, 1924-35; Hall of
Fame, 1970.
b. May 14, 1899 in Pebworth, Kentucky
Source: *BaseEn 85; WhoProB 73*

Comden, Betty
[Mrs. Steven Kyle]
American. Songwriter
Won Tony, 1970, for *Applause.*
b. May 3, 1915 in New York, New York
Source: *AmAu&B; AmSCAP 66; BiE&WWA;
CelR; ConAu 49, 2NR; CurBio 45; EncMT;
FilmgC; InWom; IntMPA 75, 76, 77, 78, 79,
80, 81, 82; NewCBMT; NotNAT; OxFilm;
WhoAm 74, 76, 78, 80, 82; WhoThe 77;
WomWMM; WorEFlm*

Comencini, Luigi
Italian. Director
b. Jun 8, 1916 in Saio, Italy
Source: *DcFM; FilmgC; WorEFlm*

Comenius, Johann Amos
Czech. Theologian, Educator, Author
b. Mar 28, 1592 in Unersky, Moravia
d. Nov 15, 1670 in Amsterdam, Netherlands
Source: *BbD; BiD&SB; CarSB; CasWL;*
ChhPo, S1; DcBiPP A; DcEuL; Dis&D;
EuAu; EvEuW; NamesHP; PenC EUR;
Str&VC

Comer, Anjanette
American. Actress
b. Aug 7, 1942 in Dawson, Texas
Source: *FilmEn; FilmgC; MotPP; WhoAmW*
72; WhoHol A

Comer, Tex
see: Ace

Comfort, Alexander
English. Author, Biologist
b. Feb 10, 1920 in London, England
Source: *AmM&WS 79P, 82P; Au&Wr 71;*
IntAu&W 76, 77, 82; IntWW 75, 79; PenC
ENG; TwCA SUP; Who 74, 82; WhoAm 82;
WhoWor 74, 76, 78; WrDr 76

Comines, Philippe de
French. Historian, Diplomat
b. 1445 in Renescure, Flanders
d. 1511 in Argentan, France
Source: *BbD; BiD&SB; NewCol 75; OxEng;*
REn

Comiskey, Charlie (Charles Albert)
"Commy"; "Old Roman"
American. Baseball Player, Baseball Executive
Purchased franchise that became Chicago
    White Sox, 1895; Hall of Fame, 1939.
b. Aug 15, 1859 in Chicago, Illinois
d. Oct 26, 1931 in Eagle River, Wisconsin
Source: *BaseEn 85; WhoProB 73*

Comissiona, Sergiu
Romanian. Conductor
b. Jun 16, 1928 in Bucharest, Romania
Source: *BioNews 74; WhoAm 74, 76, 78, 80,*
82; WhoMus 72; WhoWor 78

Commager, Henry Steele
American. Historian, Educator
b. Oct 25, 1902 in Pittsburgh, Pennsylvania
Source: *AmAu&B; ApCAB; AuBYP; BioNews*
74; ChhPo S1; ConAu 21R; CurBio 46;
DcLEL; DrAS 74H; IntWW 74; OxAmL;
PenC AM; REn; REnAL; SmATA 23; TwCA
SUP; WebAB; Who 74; WhoAm 74, 76, 78,
80, 82; WhoE 74; WhoWor 78; WrDr 80

Commander Cody & His Lost Planet Airmen
[Bruce Barlow; Robert Black; Lance
    Dickerson; William Farlow; George Fayne;
    Ernest Hager; William Kirchen; Andrew
    Stein; John Tichy]
American. Music Group
Source: *IlEncRk*

Commodores, The
[William King; Ronald LaPread; Thomas
    McClary; Walter Clyde Orange; Lionel
    Richie, Jr.; Milan Williams]
American. Music Group
Formed, 1968; number one hits include
    "Three Times a Lady," 1978; "Sail On,"
    1979.
Source: *BkPepl; RkOn 74; RolSEnR 83*

Commoner, Barry
American. Biologist
Ecology, plant physiology expert; wrote
    Science and Survival, 1966.
b. May 28, 1917 in Brooklyn, New York
Source: *AmAu&B; CelR; CurBio 70; IntWW*
74; WhoAm 82, 84; WhoWor 74

Commons, John Rogers
American. Economist, Historian
First to study American labor movements;
    wrote *History of Labor in the US,* 1935.
b. Oct 13, 1862 in Hollansburg, Ohio
d. May 11, 1945 in Raleigh, North Carolina
Source: *DcAmAu; DcAmB S3; McGEWB,;*
NatCAB 13; OhA&B; OxAmH; WebAB;
WhAm 2

Como, Perry (Pierino Roland)
American. Singer
Popular, easy-going crooner for over 40
    years; TV show, 1948-63; hits include
    "Prisoner of Love," 1956.
b. May 18, 1912 in Canonsburg,
    Pennsylvania
Source: *AmCath 80; AmPS A, B; BiDAmM;*
BkPepl; CelR; CmpEPM; CurBio 47; FilmgC;
IntMPA 82; NewYTET; RkOn 74; WhoAm
82, 84; WhoHol A; WhoMus 72

Compton, Ann
American. Broadcast Journalist
ABC News White House correspondent,
    1979-81, 1984--.
b. Jan 19, 1947 in Chicago, Illinois
Source: *BioIn 10; WhoAm 82, 84*

Compton, Arthur Holly
American. Scientist, Physician, Engineer
Helped develop atomic bomb; won Nobel
  Prize for X-ray research, 1927.
b. Sep 10, 1892 in Wooster, Ohio
d. Mar 15, 1962 in Berkeley, California
Source: *AmAu&B; CurBio 40, 58, 62; EncAB-
H; OhA&B; REnAL; WebAB; WhAm HSA, 4*

Compton, Betty
English. Actress, Singer
b. 1907 in Isle of Wight
d. Jul 12, 1944 in New York, New York
Source: *NotNAT B; WhScrn 74, 77; WhoHol
B*

Compton, Fay
[Virginia Lilian Emeline Compton]
English. Actress
b. Sep 18, 1894 in London, England
d. Dec 12, 1978
Source: *BiE&WWA; CnThe; EncWT; Film 1,
2; FilmgC; NotNAT A; OxThe; PIP&P; Who
74; WhoThe 72*

Compton, Joyce
[Eleanor Hunt]
American. Actress
b. Jan 27, 1907 in Lexington, Kentucky
Source: *Film 2; FilmgC; IntMPA 81, 82;
MotPP; MovMk; ThFT; WhoHol A*

Compton, Karl Taylor
American. Physicist
b. Sep 14, 1887 in Wooster, Ohio
d. Jun 22, 1954
Source: *AmAu&B; CurBio 41, 54*

Compton, Wilson Martindale
American. Economist
b. Oct 15, 1890 in Wooster, Ohio
d. Mar 7, 1967
Source: *CurBio 52, 67*

Compton-Burnett, Ivy, Dame
English. Author
Wrote witty, chilling social comedies of
  Edwardian family life: *Mother and Son,*
  1955.
b. Jun 5, 1892 in London, England
d. Aug 27, 1969 in London, England
Source: *ConAu 1R, 25R, 4NR; ConLC 1, 3,
10, 15; DcLEL; EncWL; EvLB; InWom;
LongCTC; ModBrL, S1; NewC; OxEng; PenC
ENG; RAdv 1; REn; TwCA SUP; TwCWr;
WebE&AL; WhAm 5; WhoTwCL*

Comstock, Ada Louise
American. Educator
First pres., Radcliffe College, 1923-43; first
  pres., American Assn. of U Women, 1921.
b. Dec 11, 1876 in Moorhead, Minnesota
d. Dec 12, 1973 in New Haven, Connecticut
Source: *NotAW MOD*

Comstock, Anthony
American. Author, Reformer
Founder, secretary, Society of Suppression of
  Vice, 1873-1915.
b. Mar 7, 1844 in New Canaan, Connecticut
d. Sep 21, 1915
Source: *AmAu&B; LongCTC; OxAmL;
REnAL*

Comstock, Elizabeth L
English. Religious Leader, Abolitionist
Quaker minister who operated stations for
  underground railroads.
b. Oct 30, 1815 in Maidenhead, England
d. Aug 3, 1891 in Union Springs, New York
Source: *DcAmB; InWom; NotAW; WhAm HS;
WhAmP*

Comstock, Henry Tompkins Paige
"Old Pancake"
American. Pioneer
Discovered Comstock Lode, Virginia City,
  NV, 1859, richest known US silver
  deposit.
b. 1820 in Trenton, Ontario
d. Sep 27, 1870 in Bozeman, Montana
Source: *AmBi; DcAmB; WhAm HS*

Comstock, John Henry
American. Scientist, Educator
Entomologist, pioneer in insect, moth
  classification.
b. Aug 24, 1849 in Janesville, Wisconsin
d. Mar 20, 1931 in Ithaca, New York
Source: *DcAmB S1; WebBD 80*

Comte, Auguste
French. Author, Philosopher
Founder of positivism, wrote *Ordre et
  Progres,* 1848.
b. Jan 19, 1798 in Montpellier, France
d. Sep 5, 1857 in Paris, France
Source: *BbD; BiD&SB; CasWL; DcEuL;
EuAu; EvEuW; LongCEL; LuthC 75;
McGEWB; OxEng; OxFr; REn*

Conacher, Charles, Sr.
"The Bomber"
Canadian. Hockey Player
Toronto right wing, 1929-41, Hall of Fame.
b. Dec 20, 1910 in Toronto, Ontario
d. Dec 30, 1967 in Toronto, Ontario
Source: *BioIn 2, 8; WhoHcky 73*

Conan Doyle, Arthur, Sir
see: Doyle, Arthur Conan, Sir

Conant, James Bryant
American. Educator, Author, Diplomat,
Chemist
Pres., Harvard U, 1933-53; ambassador to W
Germany, 1955-57; wrote on secondary
education.
b. Mar 26, 1893 in Dorchester,
Massachusetts
d. Feb 11, 1978 in Hanover, New Hampshire
Source: *AmAu&B; ConAu 13R, 77; CurBio
41, 51; EncAB-H; IntWW 74; OxAmL;
REnAL; WebAB; Who 74; WhoAm 74;
WhoWor 78*

Conaway, Jeff
American. Actor
Starred on Broadway in *Grease;* played
Bobby on TV series "Taxi."
b. Oct 5, 1950 in New York, New York
Source: *BioIn 11; IntMPA 82; NewYTBS 78*

Condie, Richard P
American. Conductor
Director, Mormon Tabernacle Choir, 1957-74;
brought it to world prominence.
b. Jul 5, 1898 in Springville, Utah
d. Dec 22, 1985 in Salt Lake City, Utah
Source: *WhoAm 76*

Condit, Carl Wilbur
American. Educator, Author
Authority on structural engineering, 1945--;
wrote *Rise of the Skyscraper,* 1950.
b. Sep 29, 1914 in Cincinnati, Ohio
Source: *ConAu 1R; DrAS 74H, 78H;
IntAu&W 77; WhoAm 82, 84; WrDr 80*

Condon, Eddie
American. Band Leader, Jazz Musician
Jazz guitarist noted for "Chicago style" jazz,
1920s; opened NYC nightclub, 1946.
b. Nov 16, 1905 in Goodland, Indiana
d. Aug 3, 1973 in New York, New York
Source: *ConAu 45; CurBio 44, 73; NewYTBE
73; WhAm 6; WhoAm 74; WhoE 74;
WhoJazz 72; WhoMus 72*

Condon, Edward
American. Scientist, Physicist, Engineer
b. Mar 2, 1902 in Alamogordo, New Mexico
d. Mar 26, 1974 in Boulder, Colorado
Source: *BioNews 74; NewYTBS 74; WebAB;
WhAm 6; Who 74; WhoAm 74; WhoWor 78*

Condon, Jackie
[Our Gang]
Actor
Child actor who appeared in *Hallroom Boys,
Our Gang* comedies, 1922.
b. 1913
Source: *Film 2; TwYS*

Condon, Richard Thomas
American. Author
Best-selling novels include *Manchurian
Candidate,* 1959; *Prizzi's Honor,* 1982.
b. Mar 18, 1915 in New York, New York
Source: *AmAu&B; ConAu 1R, 2NR; ConLC
4, 6; ConNov 72, 76; ModAL, S1; PenC AM;
WhoAm 76, 78, 80, 82, 84; WhoWor 74;
WorAu*

Condorcet, Marie-Jean-Antoine
French. Philosopher, Mathematician,
Revolutionary
Politically prominent during revolution; wrote
Reflexions sur le Commerce des Bles, 1786.
b. Sep 17, 1743 in Ribemont, France
d. Mar 25, 1794 in Bourg-la-Reine, France
Source: *BbD; BiD&SB; CasWL; DcEuL;
EuAu; EvEuW; NewC; OxEng; OxFr; REn*

Cone, Fairfax Mastick
American. Advertising Executive
b. Feb 21, 1903 in San Francisco, California
d. Jun 20, 1977 in Carmel, Massachusetts
Source: *CurBio 66; IntWW 74; St&PR 75;
WhoAdv 72; WhoAm 74*

Cone, Molly Lamken
American. Children's Author
b. Oct 3, 1918 in Tacoma, Washington
Source: *AuBYP; ConAu 1R; ForWC 70;
SmATA 1; ThrBJA; WrDr 80*

Cone, Russell Glenn
American. Engineer
Expert on suspense bridges; headed work on
Ambassador Bridge (Detroit), Golden Gate
Bridge (San Francisco).
b. Mar 22, 1896 in Ottumma, Iowa
d. Jan 21, 1961 in Vallejo, California
Source: *DcAmB S7*

Confrey, "Zez" (Edward E)
American. Composer
b. Apr 3, 1895 in Peru, Illinois
d. Nov 22, 1971 in Lakewood, New Jersey
Source: *AmSCAP 66; NewYTBE 71; WhAm 5*

Confucius
[Kung Fu-Tzu]
Chinese. Philosopher
Developed religious system for management
    of society; emphasized good family
    relationships for social stability.
b. Aug 27, 551 in Lu, China
d. 479 BC
Source: *BbD; BiD&SB; CasWL; DcOrL 1;*
NewC; PenC CL; RComWL; REn

Conger, Clement Ellis
American. Government Official
White House curator since 1970; has added
    over 500 pieces to building.
b. Oct 15, 1912 in Rockingham, Virginia
Source: *NewYTBS 77; WhoAm 82, 84;*
WhoAmA 78; WhoGov 75

Congreve, Richard
English. Essayist, Philosopher
Translated *Catechism of Positive Religion;*
    wrote *Human Catholicism,* 1877.
b. Sep 14, 1818 in Warwickshire, England
d. Jul 5, 1899 in Hampstead, England
Source: *Alli SUP; BiD&SB; BrAu 19; DcEnL;*
NewC

Congreve, William
English. Dramatist
Wrote *The Way of the World,* a comedy of
    manners, 1700.
b. Jan 24, 1670 in Bardsey, England
d. Jan 19, 1729 in London, England
Source: *Alli; AtlBL; BbD; BiD&SB; BiDLA;*
BrAu; BrWr 2; CasWL; Chambr 2; ChhPo
S1; CnThe; CrtT 2, 4; CyWA; DcEnA, AP;
DcEnL; DcEuL; DcLEL; EvLB; McGEWD;
MouLC 2; NewC; OxEng; OxThe; PenC
ENG; RComWL; REn; REnWD; WebE&AL

Conigliaro, Tony (Anthony Richard)
American. Baseball Player
Outfielder, 1964-71; led AL in home runs,
    1965; suffered crippling heart attack, 1982.
b. Jan 7, 1945 in Revere, Massachusetts
Source: *BaseEn 85; CurBio 71; NewYTBE 71;*
WhoProB 73

Conkle, Ellsworth Prouty
American. Dramatist, Educator
b. Jul 10, 1899 in Peru, Nebraska
Source: *AmAu&B; CnMD; ConAu 65; DrAS*
74E; ModWD; OxAmL

Conklin, Chester
American. Comedian
b. Jan 11, 1888 in Oskaloosa, Iowa
d. Oct 11, 1971 in Hollywood, California
Source: *Film 1; FilmgC; MotPP; MovMk;*
NewYTBE 71; OxFilm; TwYS; WhScrn 74,
77; WhoHol B

Conklin, Gladys Plemon
American. Children's Author
b. May 30, 1903 in Harpster, Idaho
Source: *AuBYP; BiDrLUS 70; ConAu 1R,*
4NR; ForWC 70; SmATA 2; WhoAmW 77

Conklin, Peggy (Margaret Eleanor)
American. Actress
b. Nov 2, 1912 in Dobbs Ferry, New York
Source: *BiE&WWA; NotNAT; ThFT; WhoHol*
A; WhoThe 77A

Conkling, Roscoe
American. Statesman
b. Oct 30, 1829 in Albany, New York
d. Apr 18, 1888 in New York, New York
Source: *AmBi; ApCAB; BiAUS; BiDrAC;*
DcAmB; Drake; EncAB-H; REnAL; TwCBDA;
WebAB; WhAm HS; WhAmP

Conlan, "Jocko" (John Bertrand)
American. Baseball Umpire
NL umpire, 1941-65; wrote autobiography
    Jocko, published 1967; Hall of Fame,
    1974.
b. Dec 6, 1899 in Chicago, Illinois
Source: *BasesB*

Conley, Eugene
American. Opera Singer
Radio tenor beginning 1939; on CBS's
    "Golden Treasury of Song."
b. Mar 12, 1908 in Lynn, Massachusetts
d. Dec 18, 1981 in Denton, Texas
Source: *CurBio 82; NewYTBS 81; WhoAm*
80; WhoWor 78

Conley, Renie
American. Designer
Won Oscar for costumes in *Cleopatra,* 1953;
    designed Disneyland Park's costumes.
b. Jul 31, 1919 in Republic, Washington
Source: *VarWW 85*

Connally, John Bowden, Jr.
American. Lawyer, Politician
Dem. governor of TX, 1963-69; wounded
    when John Kennedy was assassinated;
    secretary of Treasury under Richard
    Nixon, 1971-72.
b. Feb 27, 1917 in Floresville, Texas
Source: *BiDrUSE; BioNews 74; CelR; CurBio
61; IntWW 74; Who 74; WhoAm 82;
WhoAmP 73; WhoS&SW 73*

Connally, Tom (Thomas Terry)
American. Politician
Dem. senator from TX, 1929-53; intermittent
    chm., Senate Foreign Relations Committee.
b. Aug 19, 1877 in McLennan County, Texas
d. Oct 28, 1963 in Washington, District of
    Columbia
Source: *AmAu&B; BiDrAC; CurBio 41, 49,
64; WhAm 4; WhAmP*

Connell, Evan S, Jr.
American. Author
b. Aug 17, 1924 in Kansas City, Missouri
Source: *AmAu&B; ConAu 1R, 2NR; ConLC
4, 6; ConNov 72, 76; DrAF 76; ModAL S1;
OxAmL; PenC AM; RAdv 1; REnAL;
WhoAm 82; WhoTwCL; WhoWor 74; WorAu;
WrDr 76*

Connelly, Christopher
American. Actor
Played Norman Harrington on TV series
    "Peyton Place," 1964-69.
b. Sep 8, 1941
Source: *WhoHol A*

Connelly, Marc(us Cook)
American. Dramatist
Won Pulitzer for *The Green Pastures,* 1930.
b. Dec 13, 1890 in McKeesport, Pennsylvania
d. Dec 21, 1980 in New York, New York
Source: *AmAu&B; BiE&WWA; Chambr 3;
CnDAL; CnMD; CnThe; ConAmA; ConAmL;
ConAu 85, 102; CurBio 69; DcFM; DcLEL;
IntWW 74; LongCTC; McGEWD; ModAL;
ModWD; NotNAT; OxAmL; PenC AM; REn;
REnAL; REnWD; TwCA, SUP; WebAB; Who
74; WhoAm 74; WhoThe 77; WhoWor 78;
WrDr 80*

Connelly, "One-Eyed" (James Leo)
American. Eccentric
Best known as gate-crasher at sporting
    events, political conventions, early 1900s.
b. 1879
d. Dec 20, 1953 in Zion, Illinois
Source: *BioIn 3, 4, 5*

Conner, Nadine
American. Opera Singer
b. Feb 20, 1913 in Compton, California
Source: *CurBio 55; InWom*

Connery, Sean
[Thomas Connery]
Scottish. Actor
Originated film role of James Bond in *Dr.
No,* 1962.
b. Aug 25, 1930 in Edinburgh, Scotland
Source: *BiDFilm; BlueB 76; CelR; CmMov;
CurBio 66; FilmgC; IntMPA 82; IntWW 81;
MotPP; MovMk; OxFilm; Who 82; WhoAm
82; WhoHol A; WorAl; WorEFlm*

Conniff, Frank
American. Journalist
Overseas reporter; won Pulitzer for
    Khruschev interview, 1955.
b. Apr 24, 1914 in Danbury, Connecticut
d. May 25, 1971 in New York, New York
Source: *BioIn 9; ConAu 93; WhAm 5*

Conniff, Ray
American. Band Leader
"Ray Conniff" sound launched with album
    S'Wonderful, 1956.
b. Nov 6, 1916 in Attleboro, Massachusetts
Source: *WhoAm 80, 82; WhoJazz 72*

Connolly, Cyril Vernon
English. Author, Literary Critic
Editor, *Horizon* magazine, 1939-50; wrote
    Condemned Playground, 1945.
b. Sep 10, 1903 in Coventry, England
d. Nov 26, 1974 in London, England
Source: *CasWL; CnMWL; ConAu 21R, 53, P-
2; ConNov 72; CurBio 47; DcLEL; EncWL;
EvLB; IntWW 74; LongCTC; ModBrL;
NewC; OxEng; PenC ENG; RAdv 1; REn;
TwCA SUP; TwCWr; WebE&AL*

Connolly, James B
American. Author
Realistic sea stories included *Out of
Gloucester,* 1902.
b. 1868 in Boston, Massachusetts
d. Jan 20, 1957
Source: *AmAu&B; AmLY; BkC 3; CathA
1930; REnAL; TwCA, SUP; WebBD 80*

Connolly, Maureen
"Little Mo"
American. Tennis Player
Wimbledon singles champion, 1952-54; won
    Australian, French, US opens, 1953.
b. Sep 17, 1934 in San Diego, California
d. Jun 21, 1969 in Dallas, Texas
Source: *CurBio 51, 69; InWom; NewCol 75;
WebAB*

Connolly, Mike
American. Journalist
Wrote columns for Hollywood trade papers.
b. Jul 10, 1915 in Chicago, Illinois
d. Nov 19, 1966 in Rochester, Minnesota
Source: *WhAm 4*

Connolly, Sybil
Welsh. Fashion Designer
b. Jan 24, 1921 in Swansea, Wales
Source: *InWom; WhoWor 78; WorFshn*

Connolly, Thomas Henry
American. Baseball Umpire
Umpired first AL game, 1901; first World
    Series, 1903.
b. Dec 31, 1870 in Manchester, England
d. Apr 28, 1961 in Natick, Massachusetts
Source: *DcAmB S7; WhoProB 73*

Connolly, Walter
American. Actor
b. Apr 8, 1887 in Cincinnati, Ohio
d. May 28, 1940 in Beverly Hills, California
Source: *CurBio 40; FilmgC; MotPP; MovMk;*
NotNAT B; OxFilm; Vers A; WhScrn 74, 77;
WhThe; WhoHol B

Connor, "Bull" (Theophilus Eugene)
American. Police Officer
Commissioner of Public Safety during
    Alabama freedom ride, civil rights
    demonstrations.
b. Jul 11, 1897 in Selma, Alabama
d. Mar 8, 1973 in Birmingham, Alabama
Source: *BioIn 9*

Connor, Roger
American. Baseball Player
Held record for career home runs, 131,
    broken by Babe Ruth; Hall of Fame,
    1976.
b. Jul 1, 1857 in Waterbury, Connecticut
d. Jan 4, 1931 in Waterbury, Connecticut
Source: *BaseEn 85; BasesB*

Connor, William Neil, Sir
[Cassandra]
Irish. Journalist
b. 1910 in County Derry, Northern Ireland
d. Apr 6, 1967 in London, England
Source: *ConAu 25R; LongCTC; WhAm 4*

Connors, "Chuck" (Kevin Joseph)
American. Actor
Starred in TV show "The Rifleman," 1957-
    62.
b. Apr 10, 1921 in New York, New York
Source: *FilmgC; IntMPA 82; MotPP; WhoAm*
82; WhoHol A; WhoProB 73

Connors, Dorsey
American. Journalist
b. in Chicago, Illinois
Source: *ConAu 45; ForWC 70; WhoAm 82;*
WhoAmW 77

Connors, Jimmy (James Scott)
American. Tennis Player
Won US Open 1974, 1976, 1978, 1982; won
    Wimbledon 1974, 1982.
b. Sep 2, 1952 in East St. Louis, Illinois
Source: *BkPepl; NewYTBS 77; WhoAm 82;*
WorAl

Connors, Mike
[Krekor Ohanian]
American. Actor
Starred in TV series "Mannix," 1967-74.
b. Aug 15, 1925 in Fresno, California
Source: *CelR; IntMPA 82; MotPP; WhoAm*
82; WhoHol A

Conover, Harry
American. Businessman
b. Aug 29, 1911 in Chicago, Illinois
d. Jul 21, 1965 in New York, New York
Source: *CurBio 49, 65*

Conquest, Robert
English. Author
b. Jul 15, 1917 in Malvern, England
Source: *ConAu 13R; ConNov 72; ConP 70,*
75; LongCTC; RAdv 1; TwCWr; Who 74;
WorAu; WrDr 80

Conrad, Charles, Jr.
"Pete"
American. Astronaut
Crew member on Gemini V, 1965; Gemini
    XI, 1966; Apollo 12, 1969; Skylab, 1973.
b. Jun 2, 1930 in Philadelphia, Pennsylvania
Source: *CurBio 65; IntWW 74; WhoAm 82;*
WhoWor 74

Conrad, Con
[Conrad K Dober]
American. Composer, Publisher
b. Jun 18, 1891 in New York, New York
d. Sep 28, 1938 in Van Nuys, California
Source: *AmSCAP 66*

Conrad, Frank
"Father of American Radio"
American. Engineer, Broadcaster
Transmitted first commercially sponsored
    broadcast, 1920.
b. May 4, 1874 in Pittsburgh, Pennsylvania
d. Dec 11, 1941 in Miami, Florida
Source: *DcAmB S3; WebBD 80*

Conrad, Joseph
[Teodor Josef Konrad Koreniowski]
Polish. Author
Wrote *Lord Jim*, 1900; *Heart of Darkness*,
1902; *Victory*, 1915.
b. Dec 3, 1857 in Berdichev, Russia
d. Aug 3, 1924 in Bishopsbourne, England
Source: *AtlBL; BbD; BiD&SB; CasWL;
Chambr 3; CnMD; CnMWL; CyWA; DcEnA
AP; DcEuL; DcLEL; EncMys; EncWL; EvLB;
FilmgC; JBA 34; LongCTC; ModBrL, S1;
ModWD; NewC; OxEng; PenC ENG; RAdv 1;
RComWL; REn; TwCA, SUP; TwCWr;
WebE&AL; WhoTwCL*

Conrad, Michael
American. Actor
Won Emmy for role of Phil Esterhaus in
"Hill Street Blues," 1981, 1982.
b. Oct 16, 1927 in New York, New York
d. Nov 22, 1983 in Los Angeles, California
Source: *WhoHol A*

Conrad, Paul Francis
American. Cartoonist, Author
LA *Times* syndicated editorial cartoonist,
1973--; won three Pulitzers.
b. Jun 27, 1924 in Cedar Rapids, Iowa
Source: *WhoAm 82; WhoAmA 82; WhoWest
74; WorECar*

Conrad, Robert
[Conrad Robert Falk]
American. Actor
Starred in "Hawaiian Eye," 1959-63; "The
Wild, Wild West," 1965-69.
b. Mar 1, 1935 in Chicago, Illinois
Source: *FilmgC; IntMPA 82; WhoAm 82;
WhoHol A*

Conrad, William
American. Actor, Director, Producer
Star of "Cannon," 1971-76; "Nero Wolfe,"
1981.
b. Sep 27, 1920 in Louisville, Kentucky
Source: *BioNews 74; FilmgC; IntMPA 82;
MovMk; WhoAm 82; WhoHol A*

Conreid, Hans
[Frank Foster Conreid]
American. Actor
Comedian in over 100 films; played Uncle
Tonoose in "Make Room for Daddy,"
1957-64.
b. Apr 1, 1915 in Baltimore, Maryland
d. Jan 5, 1982 in Burbank, California
Source: *FilmgC; MotPP; MovMk; NewYTBS
82; WhoAm 80; WhoHol A; WhoThe 77*

Conroy, Frank
American. Author
b. Jan 15, 1936 in New York, New York
Source: *AmAu&B; ConAu 77; WhoAm 74*

Conroy, Frank
American. Actor
b. Oct 14, 1890 in Derby, England
d. Feb 4, 1964 in Paramus, New Jersey
Source: *FilmgC; MovMk; NotNAT B; PIP&P;
WhScrn 74, 77; WhThe; WhoHol A*

Conroy, Jack (John Wesley)
American. Author
b. Dec 5, 1899 in Moberly, Missouri
Source: *AmNov; ConAu 5R, 3NR; ConNov
72, 76; OhA&B; OxAmL; WhNAA; WhoAm
74; WrDr 80*

Considine, Bob (Robert Bernard)
American. Journalist
b. Nov 4, 1906 in Washington, District of
Columbia
d. Sep 25, 1975 in New York, New York
Source: *AmAu&B; AuNews 2; CathA 1930;
CelR; ConAu 61; CurBio 47; REnAL; WhAm
6; WhoAm 74; WhoWor 78*

Considine, Tim
American. Actor
Played Mike Douglas on "My Three Sons,"
1960-65.
b. 1940 in Los Angeles, California
Source: *WhoHol A*

Constable, John
English. Artist
Romantic landscape painter; influenced
Barbizon, impressionist schools.
b. Jun 11, 1776 in East Bergholt, England
d. Mar 30, 1837 in London, England
Source: *AtlBL; NewC; REn*

Constant de Rebeque, (Henri) Benjamin
French. Author, Journalist
Best remembered for short novel *Adolphe*,
1816.
b. Oct 25, 1767 in Lausanne, Switzerland
d. Dec 8, 1830 in Paris, France
Source: *AtlBL; CyWA; PenC EUR*

Constantine I
[Constantine the Great]
Roman. Emperor
b. 280 in Naissus
d. 337
Source: *BioIn 10; NewCol 75; WebBD 80*

Constantine V
Byzantine. Emperor
b. 718
d. 775
Source: *NewCol 75*

Constantine VI
Byzantine. Emperor
b. 770
d. 820
Source: *NewCol 75*

Constantine XI
Byzantine. Emperor
d. 1453
Source: *NewCol 75*

Constantine XII
Greek. King
Succeeded to throne, 1964; left Greece, 1967;
   deposed, 1973.
b. Jun 2, 1940 in Athens, Greece
Source: *IntWW 74, 75, 76, 77, 78, 79, 80,
81; NewCol 75*

Constantine, Eddie
American. Actor
b. 1917 in Los Angeles, California
Source: *FilmgC; MotPP; OxFilm; WorEFlm*

Constantine, Michael
[Constantine Joanides]
American. Actor
Won 1970 Emmy for role of Seymour
   Kaufman on "Room 222," 1969-74.
b. May 22, 1927 in Reading, Pennsylvania
Source: *BiE&WWA; FilmgC; VarWW 85;
WhoAm 82; WhoHol A; WorAl*

Conte, Richard
[Nicholas Peter]
American. Actor
b. Mar 24, 1914 in Jersey City, New Jersey
d. Apr 15, 1975 in Los Angeles, California
Source: *CmMov; FilmgC; HolP 40; IntMPA
75; MotPP; MovMk; NewYTBS 75; ObitOF
79; WhAm 6; WhScrn 77; WhoAm 74;
WhoHol C; WorAl; WorEFlm*

Conti, Bill
American. Composer
Won Oscar for score of *The Right Stuff*,
   1983; TV theme songs include "Dynasty";
   "Falcon Crest"; "Cagney and Lacey."
b. Apr 13, 1942 in Providence, Rhode Island
Source: *VarWW 85*

Conti, Tom (Thomas Antonio)
Scottish. Actor
Star of BBC TV series "The Glittering
   Prizes," 1976; won Tony for role in play
   Whose Life Is It Anyway? 1978-79.
b. Nov 22, 1941 in Paisley, Scotland
Source: *CurBio 85; NewYTBS 79; Who 84;
WhoAm 80, 82; WhoThe 81*

Contino, Dick
American. Musician
b. 1930 in Fresno, California
Source: *WhoHol A*

Converse, Frank
American. Actor
Played Johnny Corso on "NYPD," 1967-69.
b. May 22, 1938 in Saint Louis, Missouri
Source: *IntMPA 80, 81, 82; WhoHol A*

Converse, Frederick Shepherd
American. Composer
b. Jan 5, 1871 in Newton, Massachusetts
d. Jun 8, 1940 in Boston, Massachusetts
Source: *AmSCAP 66; CurBio 40; DcAmB S2;
OxAmL; REnAL; WhAm 1*

Converse, Marquis M
American. Manufacturer
Launched Converse Rubber Shoe Co., 1908,
   making basketball sneakers.
b. Oct 23, 1861 in Lyme, New Hampshire
d. Feb 9, 1931 in Boston, Massachusetts
Source: *Entr; WhAm 1*

Convy, Bert
American. Actor
Host of TV game shows "Tattletales,"
   "People Do the Craziest Things."
b. Jul 23, 1934 in Saint Louis, Missouri
Source: *BiE&WWA; NotNAT; WhoHol A;
WhoThe 77*

Conway, Gary
[Garth Carmody]
American. Actor
b. 1938 in Boston, Massachusetts
Source: *FilmgC; IntMPA 82; WhoAm 74;
WhoHol A*

Conway, Jack
American. Actor, Director
Films noted for technical excellence include
   A Tale of Two Cities, 1935.
b. Jul 17, 1887 in Graceville, Minnesota
d. Oct 11, 1952 in Pacific Palisades,
   California
Source: *CmMov; DcFM; Film 1; FilmgC;
MovMk; NotNAT B; ObitOF 79; TwYS, A;
WhScrn 74, 77; WhoHol B; WorEFlm*

Conway, Moncure Daniel
American. Clergyman, Author
b. Mar 17, 1832 in Falmouth, Virginia
d. Nov 15, 1907
Source: *AmAu; AmAu&B; DcLEL; OhA&B; OxAmL; PenC AM; REnAL*

Conway, Shirl
[Shirl Conway Larson]
American. Actress, Singer
b. Jun 13, 1916 in Franklinville, New York
Source: *BiE&WWA; InWom; IntMPA 75, 76, 77, 78, 79, 80, 81, 82; NotNAT; WhoHol A*

Conway, Thomas
[Count de Conway]
American. Army Officer
Revolutionary war general; involved in Conway Cable intrigue.
b. Feb 27, 1735 in Ireland
d. 1800
Source: *AmBi; ApCAB; DcAmB; Drake; NatCAB 1; TwCBDA; WebAB; WebAMB; WhAm HS*

Conway, "Tim" (Thomas Daniel)
American. Comedian, Actor
Appeared in TV series "McHale's Navy," 1962-66; "The Carol Burnett Show," 1975-78.
b. Dec 13, 1933 in Willoughby, Ohio
Source: *CurBio 81; IntMPA 81, 82; WhoHol A*

Conway, Tom
[Thomas Charles Sanders]
American. Actor
Brother of actor George Sanders; played title role in "The Falcon," 1942-46.
b. Sep 15, 1904 in Saint Petersburg, Russia
d. Apr 22, 1967 in Culver City, California
Source: *FilmgC; HolP 40; MotPP; MovMk; WhScrn 74, 77; WhoHol B*

Cony, Edward Roger
American. Journalist
b. Mar 15, 1923 in Augusta, Maine
Source: *Dun&B 79; WhoAm 74; WhoE 74, 75*

Conyers, John, Jr.
American. Politician
Dem. congressman from MI, 1964--; wrote *Anatomy of an Undeclared War*, 1972.
b. May 16, 1929 in Detroit, Michigan
Source: *BiDrAC; CurBio 70; IntWW 74; WhoAm 82*

Conze, Edward
English. Author
b. Mar 18, 1904 in London, England
Source: *Au&Wr 71; ConAu 13R*

Conzelman, Jimmy (James Gleason)
American. Football Coach
b. Mar 6, 1898 in Saint Louis, Missouri
d. Jul 31, 1970 in Saint Louis, Missouri
Source: *WhoFtbl 74*

Cooder, Ry(land Peter)
American. Musician
Session guitarist, whose movie scores include *The Long Riders*, 1980.
b. Mar 15, 1947 in Los Angeles, California
Source: *BioIn 10, 11; EncPR&S 74; IlEncRk; WhoAm 80, 82, 84; WhoRock 81*

Coogan, Jackie (Jack Leslie)
American. Actor
First child star in movie history, known for role in *The Kid*, 1919; played Uncle Fester on the "Addams Family," 1962-64.
b. Oct 26, 1914 in Los Angeles, California
d. Mar 1, 1984 in Santa Monica, California
Source: *FilmgC; IntMPA 82; MotPP; MovMk; OxFilm; TwYS; WhoAm 82; WhoHol A*

Cook, Barbara
American. Actress, Singer
b. Oct 25, 1927 in Atlanta, Georgia
Source: *BiE&WWA; CurBio 63; EncMT; InWom; NewYTBS 80; NotNAT; WhoAm 82; WhoAmW 72; WhoThe 77*

Cook, Donald
American. Actor
b. Sep 26, 1901 in Portland, Oregon
d. Oct 1, 1961 in New Haven, Connecticut
Source: *CurBio 54, 61; FilmgC; HolP 30; MotPP; MovMk; NotNAT B; ObitOF 79; WhAm 4; WhScrn 74, 77; WhThe; WhoHol B*

Cook, Elisha, Jr.
American. Actor
b. Dec 26, 1906 in San Francisco, California
Source: *CmMov; FilmgC; IntMPA 82; MovMk; OxFilm; WhoHol A; WorEFlm*

Cook, Frederick Albert
American. Explorer, Naturalist
Claimed to be first to reach N Pole, scale Mt. McKinley.
b. Jun 10, 1865 in Callicoon Depot, New York
d. Aug 5, 1940
Source: *CurBio 40; DcAmAu; DcAmB S2; DcNAA; NewCol 75; OxCan; WhAm 1*

Cook, Greg(ory Lynn)
American. Football Player
b. Nov 20, 1946 in Dayton, Ohio
Source: *BioIn 8; WhoFtbl 74*

Cook, James, Captain
English. Explorer, Navigator
Discovered New Caledonia on South Sea
expedition, 1772-75.
b. Oct 28, 1728 in Morton Village, England
d. Feb 14, 1779 in Kealakeua, Hawaii
Source: *Alli, SUP; ApCAB; BbD; BbtC; BrAu; ChhPo S2; DcLEL; Drake; NewC; OxCan; OxEng; REn; REnAL; WhAm HS*

Cook, Joe
American. Actor
b. 1890 in Evansville, Indiana
d. May 16, 1959 in Clinton Hollows, New
York
Source: *CmpEPM; EncMT; IndAu 1917; NotNAT B; ObitOF 79; WhoHol B*

Cook, Marlow Webster
American. Senator
b. Jul 27, 1926 in Akron, Ohio
Source: *CurBio 72; IntWW 74; WhoAm 74; WhoGov 75*

Cook, Michael
Canadian. Dramatist
Stage, radio plays include *Deserts of Bohemia,*
1981.
b. Feb 14, 1933 in London, England
Source: *BioIn 11; ConAu 93; ConDr 77; WhoAm 80, 82, 84; WrDr 80*

Cook, Paul
see: Sex Pistols

Cook, Peter
English. Actor, Producer, Author
b. Nov 17, 1937 in Devonshire, England
Source: *BiE&WWA; FilmgC; NotNAT; WhoHol A; WhoThe 77*

Cook, Phil
American. Comedian
b. 1893
d. Sep 18, 1958 in Morristown, New Jersey
Source: *BioIn 5*

Cook, Thomas
English. Businessman
Founded Thomas Cook and Son tourist
agency.
b. Nov 22, 1808 in Melbourne, England
d. Jul 19, 1892
Source: *BioIn 10; WebBD 80*

Cook, Will Marion
American. Composer, Musician
Created music for black musicals, 1900s;
wrote song "Mandy Lou."
b. Jan 27, 1869 in Washington, District of
Columbia
d. Jul 19, 1944 in New York, New York
Source: *DcAmB S3; WebBD 80*

Cook, William
Canadian. Hockey Player
Capt., NY Rangers, 1926-37; with brother,
Fred, Frank Boucher, formed one of
greatest lines.
b. Oct 9, 1896 in Brantford, Ontario
d. May 5, 1986 in Kingston, Ontario
Source: *HocEn; NewYTBS 86*

Cooke, (Alfred) Alistair
American. Journalist, Broadcaster
Best known for introductions to "Masterpiece
Theatre" on PBS.
b. Nov 20, 1908 in Manchester, England
Source: *AmAu&B; AuNews 1; CelR; ConAu 57; CurBio 74; IntMPA 82; IntWW 74; LongCTC; OxAmL; REnAL; TwCA SUP; Who 74; WhoAm 82; WhoWor 74*

Cooke, Christopher M
American. Air Force Officer
Made unauthorized visits to Soviet Embassy
working as Titan-missile launch officer.
b. 1956
Source: *BioIn 12*

Cooke, David Coxe
American. Children's Author
b. Jun 7, 1917 in Wilmington, Delaware
Source: *AuBYP; ConAu 1R, 2NR; SmATA 2*

Cooke, Donald
[The Hostages]
American. Hostage in Iran
b. 1955 in Long Island, New York
Source: *NewYTBS 81*

Cooke, Hope
[Hope Namgyal, Maharani of Sikkim]
American. Consort
Married Prince Palden Thondup Namgyal,
1963; first native-born American to become
queen.
b. Jun 21, 1940 in San Francisco, California
Source: *CurBio 67; InWom; NewYTBS 74*

Cooke, Jack Kent
American. Business Executive, Sportsman
Involved in real estate, cable TV since 1964;
former owner of Washington Redskins, LA
Lakers.
b. Sep 25, 1912 in Hamilton, Ontario
Source: *CanWW 82; CmCal; IntWW 78;*
NewYTET; St&PR 75; WhoAm 82; WhoHcky
73

Cooke, Janet
American. Journalist
Won Pulitzer for contrived story on heroin
addiction, 1981; first fakery in Pulitzer
history.
b. 1954 in Toledo, Ohio
Source: *BioIn 12*

Cooke, Jay
American. Banker, Philanthropist
b. Aug 10, 1821 in Sandusky, Ohio
d. Feb 18, 1905 in Ogortz, Pennsylvania
Source: *AmBi; ApCAB; BiAUS; DcAmB;*
Drake; EncAB-H; TwCBDA; WebAB; WhAm
1, 4

Cooke, John Esten
American. Author, Historian
b. Nov 3, 1830 in Winchester, Virginia
d. Sep 27, 1886
Source: *AmAu; AmAu&B; CasWL; DcAmAu;*
OxAmL; REnAL

Cooke, Rose Terry
American. Author, Poet
Notable short stories *Root Bound,* 1885;
Somebody's Neighbors, 1881.
b. Feb 17, 1827 in Hartford, Connecticut
d. Jul 18, 1892
Source: *AmAu; AmAu&B; AmBi; AmWom;*
AmWomWr; DcAmAu; DcNAA; OxAmL;
REnAL

Cooke, Sam
American. Singer, Musician
b. Jan 22, 1935 in Chicago, Illinois
d. Dec 11, 1964 in Los Angeles, California
Source: *BiDAmM; DrBlPA; WhoHol B*

Cooke, Samuel
American. Businessman
Founder, pres., Penn Fruit Co., 1927-60;
pioneer of self-service supermarkets.
b. Dec 29, 1898 in Ukraine, Russia
d. May 22, 1965 in Cheltenham,
Pennsylvania
Source: *DcAmB S7*

Cooke, Terence James
American. Religious Leader
Archbishop of NY, 1968-83.
b. Mar 1, 1921 in New York, New York
d. Oct 6, 1983 in New York, New York
Source: *CurBio 68; IntWW 74; NewYTBE 73;*
WhoAm 82; WhoE 74; WhoRel 75

Cooke, William Fothergill, Sir
English. Engineer, Inventor
With Charles Wheatstone, invented electric
telegraph, 1845.
b. May 4, 1806
d. Jun 25, 1879
Source: *WebBD 80*

Cooley, Denton Arthur
American. Surgeon, Educator
Congenital heart disease, transplant specialist
who worked with DeBakey, 1950s.
b. Aug 22, 1920 in Houston, Texas
Source: *AmM&WS 73P; CurBio 76; WhoAm*
82; WhoS&SW 75; WhoWor 74

Coolidge, Charles Allerton
American. Architect
Designed Chicago's Art Museum, NY's
Rockefeller Institute.
b. Nov 30, 1858 in Boston, Massachusetts
d. Apr 1, 1936 in Long Island, New York
Source: *DcAmB S2; WebBD 80; WhAm 1*

Coolidge, Dane
American. Naturalist, Author
b. Mar 24, 1873 in Natick, Massachusetts
d. Aug 8, 1940
Source: *AmAu&B; AmLY; ChhPo; CurBio 40;*
DcNAA; OxAmL; WhNAA

Coolidge, Grace Anne Goodhue
[Mrs. Calvin Coolidge]
American. First Lady
Popular, sociable White House hostess, the
opposite of her retiring husband.
b. Jan 3, 1879 in Burlington, Vermont
d. Jul 8, 1957 in Northhampton,
Massachusetts
Source: *GoodHs; NotAW MOD; ObitOF 79;*
WhAm 3; WhNAA

Coolidge, (John) Calvin
"Silent Cal"
American. US President
Assumed presidency upon death of Harding,
Aug 1923; reelected, 1924.
b. Jul 4, 1872 in Plymouth, Vermont
d. Jan 5, 1933 in Northampton,
Massachusetts
Source: AmAu&B; AmBi; BiDrAC; BiDrUSE;
DcAmB; DcAmSR; DcNAA; Dis&D; EncAAH;
EncAB-H; OxAmL; REn; REnAL; WebAB;
WhAm 1; WhAmP

Coolidge, Rita
American. Singer
Ex-wife of Kris Kristofferson; platinum
album Anytime...Anywhere, 1977.
b. May 1, 1945 in Nashville, Tennessee
Source: BiDAmM; BioIn 10; BkPepl;
EncPR&S 74; IlEncRk; WhoAm 82

Coolidge, William David
American. Inventor
Invented X-ray tube; director of research for
GE Co., 1932-40.
b. Oct 23, 1873 in Hudson, Massachusetts
d. Feb 3, 1975 in Schenectady, New York
Source: NewCol 75; WhAm 6; Who 74;
WhoAm 78

Coombs, Charles Ira
American. Children's Author
b. Jun 27, 1914 in Los Angeles, California
Source: AuBYP; ConAu 5R, 4NR; SmATA 3

Coon, Carleton Stevens
American. Author, Anthropologist
Wrote numerous articles, books on
anthropology, human evolution; led
expeditions that unearthed Neanderthal
bones.
b. Jun 23, 1904 in Wakefield, Massachusetts
d. Jun 3, 1981 in Gloucester, Massachusetts
Source: AmAu&B; Au&Wr 71; BioIn 4, 5,
10; BlueB 76; CurBio 56, 81; IntAu&W 76;
IntWW 74; McGMS 80; NewYTBS 81;
WhoAm 74, 76, 78, 80; WorAu

Cooney, Barbara
American. Children's Author, Illustrator
b. Aug 6, 1916 in Brooklyn, New York
Source: AmAu&B; AuBYP; BkP; ConAu 5R,
3NR; IlsBYP; IlsCB 1744, 1946, 1957;
InWom; MorJA; NewbC 1956; SmATA 6;
Str&VC; WhoAm 74, 76, 78, 80, 82;
WhoAmA 73

Cooney, Gerry (Gerald Arthur)
"Great White Hope"
American. Boxer
Heavyweight contender defeated by Larry
Holmes, 1982.
b. Aug 24, 1956 in Brooklyn, New York
Source: NewYTBS 81, 82

Cooney, Joan Ganz
American. Producer
Exec. director, Children's TV Workshop;
produces "Sesame Street."
b. Nov 30, 1929 in Phoenix, Arizona
Source: CelR; CurBio 70; ForWC 70; WhoAm
82; WhoAmW 77

Coons, Albert Hewett
American. Scientist
b. Jun 28, 1912 in Gloversville, New York
Source: AmM&WS 73P; CurBio 60; IntWW
74; WhoAm 74; WhoE 74

Cooper, Alfred Duff
see: Norwich, Alfred Duff Cooper, Viscount

Cooper, Alice
[Vincent Damon Furnier]
American. Singer, Songwriter
Hits include "I'm 18," 1970; "No More Mr.
Nice Guy," 1973.
b. Feb 4, 1948 in Detroit, Michigan
Source: BioNews 74; BkPepl; CelR,; InWom;
RkOn 85; WhoAm 74, 76, 78, 80, 82; WorAl

Cooper, Astley Paston, Sir
English. Surgeon
b. Aug 23, 1768 in Norfolk, England
d. Feb 12, 1841
Source: Alli; BiDLA

Cooper, Cecil
American. Baseball Player
Infielder, 1971--; led AL in rbi's, 1980, 1983.
b. Dec 20, 1949 in Brenham, Texas
Source: BaseEn 85; BaseReg 86; BioIn 12;
WhoBlA 80

Cooper, Chuck (Charles H)
American. Basketball Player
First black player in NBA; signed with
Boston Celtics, 1950; played six seasons.
b. 1926
d. Feb 5, 1984 in Pittsburgh, Pennsylvania
Source: AnObit 1984; NewYTBS 84

Cooper, D B
American. Criminal
Skyjacker; disappeared after parachuting with
ransom money, 1971.
Source: *DrInf*

Cooper, Diana Manners
see: Norwich, Diana (Manners) Cooper,
Viscountess

Cooper, Emil
Russian. Conductor
b. Dec 20, 1877 in Kherson, Russia
d. Nov 19, 1960 in New York, New York
Source: *NewEOp 71*

Cooper, "Gary" (Frank James)
American. Actor
Won Oscars for *Sergeant York*, 1941; *High
Noon*, 1952.
b. May 7, 1901 in Helena, Montana
d. May 13, 1961 in Hollywood, California
Source: *BiDFilm; CmMov; CurBio 41, 61;
FilmgC; MotPP; MovMk; OxFilm; TwYS;
WebAB; WhAm 4; WhScrn 74, 77; WhoHol
B; WorEFlm*

Cooper, Giles (Stannus)
British. Dramatist
Noted radio dramatist.
b. Aug 9, 1918 in Dublin, Ireland
d. Dec 2, 1966 in Surbiton, England
Source: *ConAu 113; DcLB 13*

Cooper, Gladys, Dame
English. Actress
b. Dec 18, 1888 in Lewisham, England
d. Nov 17, 1971 in Henley, England
Source: *BiE&WWA; CnThe; ConAu 33R;
CurBio 56, 72; Film 1, 2; FilmgC; InWom;
MGM; MotPP; MovMk; NewYTBE 71;
ObitOF 79; Vers A; WhoHol B*

Cooper, Jackie (John, Jr.)
[Our Gang]
American. Actor, Producer
Described life as child star in autobiography
Please Don't Shoot My Dog, 1981.
b. Sep 15, 1922 in Los Angeles, California
Source: *BiE&WWA; FilmgC; IntMPA 82;
MovMk; WhoAm 82*

Cooper, James Fenimore
American. Author
Wrote *The Spy*, 1821; *The Last of the
Mohicans*, 1826.
b. Sep 15, 1789 in Burlington, New Jersey
d. Sep 14, 1851 in Cooperstown, New York
Source: *Alli; AmAu; AmAu&B; AmBi; AmWr;
ApCAB; AtlBL; AuBYP; BbD; BiD&SB;
CarSB; CasWL; CelCen; Chambr 3; CnDAL;
CrtT 3; CyAL 1; CyWA; DcAmAu; DcAmB;
DcBiA; DcEnA; DcEnL; DcLEL; DcNAA;
Drake; EncAB-H; EvLB; FilmgC; HsB&A;
MnBBF; MouLC 3; Novels; OxAmL; OxEng;
PenC AM; RAdv 1; RComWL; REn; REnAL;
TwCBDA; WebAB; WebE&AL; WhAm HS;
WhoChL*

Cooper, John Sherman
American. Lawyer, Diplomat
UN delegate 1949-51, 1968, 1981--; former
ambassador to India, Nepal, E Germany.
b. Aug 23, 1901 in Somerset, Kentucky
Source: *BiDrAC; BioNews 74; CurBio 50;
IntWW 74; WhoAm 80, 82; WhoAmP 73;
WhoGov 72; WhoS&SW 73*

Cooper, Joseph D
American. Government Official
b. May 25, 1917 in Boston, Massachusetts
d. Mar 25, 1975
Source: *AmM&WS 73S; ConAu 5R, 57;
CurBio 52; WhAm 6; WhoAm 74; WhoWorJ
72*

Cooper, Kent
American. Journalist
b. Mar 22, 1880 in Columbus, Indiana
d. Jan 31, 1965
Source: *ConAu 89; CurBio 44, 65*

Cooper, (Leroy) Gordon, Jr.
American. Astronaut
Astronaut on Faith 7, 1963; Gemini V, 1965.
b. Mar 6, 1927 in Shawnee, Oklahoma
Source: *CurBio 63; WhoAm 74, 76, 78, 80,
82; WhoS&SW 82*

Cooper, Lester Irving
American. Screenwriter, Author
Won Emmy, Peabody for "Animals, Animals,
Animals," series, 1976.
b. Jan 20, 1919 in New York, New York
d. Jun 6, 1985 in New York, New York
Source: *ConAu 116; WhoAm 84*

Cooper, Melville
American. Actor
b. Oct 15, 1896 in Birmingham, England
d. Mar 29, 1973 in Woodland Hills,
California
Source: *BiE&WWA; FilmgC; MovMk;
NewYTBE 73; NotNAT B; ObitOF 79; Vers
A; WhScrn 77; WhoHol B*

Cooper, Miriam
American. Actress
b. 1894 in Maryland
d. Apr 12, 1976 in Charlottesville, Virginia
Source: *Film 1, 2; TwYS; WhoHol A*

Cooper, Morton Cecil
American. Baseball Player
b. Mar 4, 1914 in Atherton, Missouri
d. Nov 17, 1958 in Little Rock, Arkansas
Source: *BaseEn 85; WhoProB 73*

Cooper, Peter
American. Businessman, Philanthropist
Built first American steam locomotive, *Tom
Thumb,* which helped promote rapid
growth of railroads in US, 1830.
b. Feb 12, 1791 in New York, New York
d. Apr 4, 1883 in New York, New York
Source: *Alli SUP; AmAu&B; AmBi; ApCAB;
BbD; BiD&SB; DcAmAu; DcAmB; DcNAA;
Drake; EncAB-H; OxAmL; REn; REnAL;
TwCBDA; WebAB; WhAm HS; WorAl*

Cooper, Samuel
English. Artist
Miniaturist painter known for portraits of
many famous Englishmen.
b. 1609
d. 1672
Source: *NewCol 75; WebBD 80*

Cooper, Wilhelmina Behmenburg
American. Model, Business Executive
Founded Wilhelmina Models, Inc. in 1967;
appeared on record 28 *Vogue* covers,
1960s.
b. 1940
d. Mar 1, 1980 in Greenwich, Connecticut
Source: *ConAu 97*

Coors, Adolph
German. Brewer
Opened brewery in Golden, CO, 1880.
b. 1847 in Germany
d. Jun 5, 1919 in Virginia Beach, Virginia
Source: *Entr*

Coors, Joseph
American. Brewer
b. Nov 12, 1917
Source: *WhoF&I 77, 79*

Coors, William K (Bill)
American. Brewery Executive
Head, family-controlled Adolph Coors Co.,
1946--.
b. 1916 in Golden, Colorado
Source: *ConNews 85-1; St&PR 75; WhoAm
78, 80, 82, 84*

Coote, Robert
English. Actor
Played Colonel Pickering, Broadway version
of *My Fair Lady,* 1956.
b. Feb 4, 1909 in London, England
d. Nov 25, 1982 in New York, New York
Source: *BiE&WWA; FilmgC; MovMk;
NotNAT; Vers A; WhoHol A; WhoThe 72, 77,
81*

Coots, J Fred
American. Composer
b. May 2, 1897 in Brooklyn, New York
d. Apr 8, 1985 in New York, New York
Source: *AmPS; BiDAmM; CmpEPM; EncMT;
NewCBMT; NotNAT*

Coover, Robert
American. Author
b. Feb 4, 1932 in Charles City, Iowa
Source: *ConAu 3NR, 45; ConLC 3, 7, 15;
DrAF 76; ModAL S1; PenC AM; RAdv 1;
WhoAm 80, 82; WhoE 75; WrDr 76*

Copeau, Jacques
French. Dramatist
b. 1878 in Paris, France
d. Oct 20, 1949 in Beaune, France
Source: *NotNAT B; OxThe; PlP&P; WhScrn
77; WhThe*

Copeland, Charles Townsend
English. Educator
b. Apr 27, 1860 in Calais, Maine
d. Jul 24, 1952 in Waverly, Massachusetts
Source: *AmAu&B; DcAmB S5; OxAmL;
REnAL; WhAm 3; WhNAA*

Copeland, George
American. Musician
b. 1882 in Boston, Massachusetts
d. 1971 in Princeton, New Jersey
Source: *BioIn 9*

Copeland, Jo
American. Fashion Designer
b. 1899 in New York, New York
d. Mar 20, 1982 in New York, New York
Source: *NewYTBS 82; WhoAm 80, 82;
WorFshn*

Copeland, Lammot du Pont
American. Businessman
b. May 19, 1905 in Christiana, Delaware
d. Jul 1, 1983 in Mount Cuba, Delaware
Source: *CurBio 63; IntWW 74; St&PR 75;
WhoAm 80, 82; WhoE 74; WhoF&I 74;
WhoWor 74*

Copeland, Stewart
see: Police, The

Copernicus, Nicolaus
[Niklas Kopernik]
Polish. Astronomer
Proposed theory that sun was center of
universe, all planets revolved around it,
1543.
b. Feb 19, 1473 in Torun, Poland
d. May 24, 1543 in Frauenburg, Poland
Source: *BbD; BiD&SB; NewCol 75*

Copland, Aaron
American. Composer
Representative American composer of his
time; folk works include *Appalachian
Spring,* 1944.
b. Nov 14, 1900 in Brooklyn, New York
Source: *AmAu&B; AmSCAP 66; Au&Wr 71;
BioNews 74; CelR; ConAu 5R; CurBio 40, 51;
DcCM; EncAB-H; FilmgC; IntWW 74;
NewYTBE 70; OxAmL; OxFilm; REn;
REnAL; WebAB; Who 82; WhoAm 80, 82;
WhoMus 72; WhoWor 74; WorEFlm*

Copley, John Singleton
American. Artist
b. Jul 3, 1733 in Boston, Massachusetts
d. Sep 9, 1815 in London, England
Source: *AmBi; ApCAB; AtlBL; DcAmB;
Drake; EncAB-H; OxAmL; REn; TwCBDA;
WebAB; WhAm HS*

Coplon, Judith
American. Spy
Convicted of stealing government papers,
passing to Soviet agent, 1950; reversed in
Appeals Court.
b. 1921 in New York, New York
Source: *EncE 75; InWom; PolProf T*

Coppard, A(lfred) E(dgar)
English. Author, Poet
First collection of short stories was *Adam
and Eve and Pinch Me,* 1921.
b. Jan 4, 1878 in Folkestone, England
d. Jan 13, 1957 in London, England
Source: *DcLEL; EncWL 2; EvLB; LongCEL;
LongCTC; ModBrL; NewC; Novels; OxEng;
PenC ENG; REn; TwCA, SUP; TwCWr;
WhoChL; WhoTwCL; YABC 1*

Coppee, Francois Edouard Joachim
French. Poet, Dramatist
Called "poete des humbles" because subjects
were humble people.
b. Jan 26, 1842 in Paris, France
d. May 23, 1908 in Paris, France
Source: *BbD; BiD&SB; ClDMEL; CnMD;
DcCathB; DcEuL; Dis&D; EuAu; LinLib S;
McGEWD; ModWD; OxFr; PenC EUR; REn*

Copperfield, David
[David Kotkin]
American. Magician
b. 1956 in Metuchen, New Jersey
Source: *NF*

Coppola, Carmine
American. Composer, Conductor
Father of Francis Ford Coppola; won Oscar
for co-writing *Godfather II* music.
b. Jun 11, 1910 in New York, New York
Source: *AmSCAP 66; VarWW 85; WhoAm
82, 84*

Coppola, Francis Ford
American. Director
Directed *The Godfather I, II,* 1972, 1974;
Apocalypse Now, 1979.
b. Apr 7, 1939 in Detroit, Michigan
Source: *BiDFilm; BioNews 75; BkPepl; CelR;
CurBio 74; FilmgC; IntMPA 75, 76, 77, 78,
79, 80, 81, 82; MovMk; NewYTBS 74;
OxFilm; WhoAm 76, 78, 80, 82; WhoWest
78, 80; WorEFlm*

Coquelin, Benoit Constant
[Coquelin Aine]
French. Actor
b. Jan 23, 1841 in Boulogne-sur-Mer, France
d. Jan 27, 1909 in Pont-aux-Dames, France
Source: *BbD; BiD&SB; CelCen; LinLib S;
NotNAT B; WhAm 4, HSA; WhoHol B*

Corben, Richard Vance
American. Artist
Horror illustrator who invented fantasy strip
"Rowlf."
b. Oct 1, 1940 in Anderson, Missouri
Source: *FanAl; WorECom*

Corbett, James John
"Gentleman Jim"
American. Boxer
Defeated John L Sullivan for heavyweight
boxing championship, 1892; portrayed by
Errol Flynn in *Gentleman Jim,* 1942.
b. Sep 1, 1866 in San Francisco, California
d. Feb 18, 1933 in New York, New York
Source: *AmBi; DcAmB S1; Film 1; WebAB;
WhAm HSA, 4; WhScrn 74, 77; WhoBox 74;
WhoHol B; WhoStg 1906, 1908*

Corbett, Scott (Winfield Scott)
American. Children's Author
Wrote over 60 books, including *Cutlass Island,* 1962.
b. Jul 27, 1913 in Kansas City, Missouri
Source: *Au&Wr 71; AuBYP; ChlLR 1; ConAu 1R; SmATA 2*

Corbett, Young, III
[Ralph Giordano]
Italian. Boxer
b. May 27, 1905 in Naples, Italy
Source: *WhoBox 74*

Corbiere, Tristan
French. Poet
b. Jul 18, 1845 in Morlaix, France
d. Mar 1, 1875 in Morlaix, France
Source: *AtlBL; ClDMEL*

Corbin, Margaret Cochran
"Captain Molly"
American. Heroine
Revolutionary War heroine, first woman pensioner of US, 1779.
b. Nov 12, 1751 in Franklin County, Pennsylvania
d. 1800 in Highland Falls, New York
Source: *NotAW; WebBD 80*

Corby, Ellen
[Ellen Hansen]
American. Actress
Played Grandma on "The Waltons."
b. Jun 3, 1913 in Racine, Wisconsin
Source: *BioIn 10, 11; FilmEn; FilmgC; MovMk; Vers A; WhoAm 76; WhoAmW 72, 74; WhoHol A*

Corby, Mike
[The Babys]
English. Singer, Musician
Keyboardist, guitarist, vocalist with power pop group, 1976-77.
b. Jul 3, 1955 in London, England
Source: *NF*

Corcoran, Thomas Gardiner
"Tommy the Cork"
American. Lawyer, Politician
Helped draft New Deal legislation, 1930s.
b. Dec 29, 1900 in Pawtucket, Rhode Island
d. Dec 6, 1981 in Washington, District of Columbia
Source: *CurBio 40, 82; NewYTBS 81; WhoAm 74, 76, 78; WhoWor 74*

Corcoran, William Wilson
American. Financier, Philanthropist
b. Dec 27, 1798 in Baltimore, Maryland
d. Feb 24, 1888 in Washington, District of Columbia
Source: *AmBi; ApCAB; DcAmB; TwCBDA; WebAB; WhAm HS*

Corcos, Lucille
American. Illustrator
b. Sep 21, 1908 in New York, New York
d. Aug 25, 1973
Source: *AmAu&B; AuBYP; ChhPo; ConAu 21R; IlsCB 1946, 1957; SmATA 10; WhAm 6; WhoAm 74; WhoAmA 73, 76N; WhoAmW 74, 58*

Cord, Alex
[Alexander Viespi]
American. Actor
TV series include "WEB," 1978; "Airwolf," 1984--.
b. Aug 3, 1931 in Floral Park, New York
Source: *BioIn 7; CelR,; FilmgC; IntMPA 75, 76, 77, 78, 79, 80, 81, 82; MotPP; WhoAm 82; WhoHol A*

Cord, E(rret) L(obban)
American. Auto Executive
Designer, 1930s Cord luxury car.
b. 1895 in Warrensburg, Missouri
d. Jan 2, 1974 in Reno, Nevada
Source: *NewYTBS 74*

Corday d'Armount, (Marie Anne) Charlotte
French. Revolutionary, Assassin
Murdered Jean Paul Marat in his bath, Jul 13, 1793; guillotined.
b. Jul 27, 1768 in Saint Saturnin, France
d. Jul 17, 1793 in Paris, France
Source: *InWom; NewCol 75; REn; WebBD 80*

Cordero, Angel Tomas
Puerto Rican. Jockey
First jockey to win over $10 million in one year.
b. May 8, 1942 in Santurce, Puerto Rico
Source: *BioIn 10*

Cordes, Eugene Harold
American. Author, Educator
b. Apr 7, 1936 in York, Nebraska
Source: *WhoAm 74; WhoWor 78*

Cordier, Andrew Wellington
American. University Administrator,
Diplomat
Exec. asst. to UN Secretary-General, 1946-62.
b. Mar 3, 1901 in Canton, Ohio
d. Jul 11, 1975 in Manhasset, New York
Source: *BlueB 76; CurBio 50, 75; IntWW 74;
Who 74; WhoAm 74; WhoE 74; WhoWor 74*

Cordiner, Ralph Jarron
American. Corporation Executive
Chairman, GE, 1958-63.
b. Mar 20, 1900 in Walla Walla, Washington
d. Dec 4, 1973 in Clearwater, Florida
Source: *BioNews 74; BusPN; CurBio 51, 74;
NewYTBE 73; WhAm 6; WhoAmP 73*

Cordoba, Francisco Fernandez
Spanish. Soldier, Explorer
b. 1475
d. 1526
Source: *WebBD 80*

Cordobes, El
[Mauel Benetez Perez]
Spanish. Bullfighter
Retired 1972, as Spain's highest paid
matador; returned to ring, 1979.
b. May 4, 1936 in Palma del Rio, Spain
Source: *BioIn 6, 7, 8*

Cordon, Norman
American. Opera Singer
b. Jan 20, 1904 in Washington, District of
Columbia
d. Mar 1, 1964 in Chapel Hill, North
Carolina
Source: *BioIn 9; NewEOp 71*

Cordtz, Dan
American. Broadcast Journalist
With *Wall Street Journal* before joining ABC
News, as business editor, 1974.
b. May 1, 1927 in Gary, Indiana
Source: *ConAu 73; WhoAm 82*

Corea, "Chick" (Armando)
American. Jazz Musician
Founded group, Return to Forever, 1971;
won four Grammys.
b. Jun 12, 1941 in Chelsea, Massachusetts
Source: *EncJzS 70; IlEncJ; WhoAm 74, 76,
78, 80, 82*

Corelli, Arcangelo
Italian. Musician, Composer
b. Feb 17, 1653 in Fusignano, Italy
d. Jan 8, 1713 in Rome, Italy

Corelli, Franco
Italian. Opera Singer
b. Apr 8, 1923 in Ancona, Italy
Source: *CelR; IntWW 74; NewYTBE 70;
WhoAm 82*

Corelli, Marie, pseud.
[Mary Mackay]
English. Author
Wrote melodramatic novels: *Sorrows of Satan*,
1895; *The Master Christian*, 1900.
b. 1855 in London, England
d. Apr 21, 1924
Source: *BbD; BiD&SB; Chambr 3; DcBiA;
DcEnA AP; DcLEL; EncSF; EvLB; LinLib S;
LongCTC; ModBrL; NewC; OxEng; PenC
ENG; REn; TwCA, SUP; TwCWr*

Corena, Fernando
Italian. Opera Singer
b. Dec 22, 1923 in Geneva, Switzerland
d. Nov 26, 1984 in Switzerland
Source: *NewEOp 71; WhoAm 82*

Corey, Irwin
"Professor"
American. Comedian, Actor
b. Jul 29, 1912 in New York, New York
Source: *VarWW 85; WhoHol A*

Corey, Jeff
American. Actor
b. Aug 10, 1914 in New York, New York
Source: *FilmgC; IntMPA 75, 76, 77, 78, 79,
80, 81, 82; Vers B; WhoAm 82; WhoHol A*

Corey, Jill
[Norma Jean Spearanza]
American. Actress
b. Sep 30, 1935
Source: *InWom*

Corey, Lewis
[Louis C Fraina]
Italian. Author
b. Oct 13, 1894 in Italy
d. Sep 16, 1953
Source: *AmAu&B; OhA&B; OxAmL; TwCA,
SUP*

Corey, Wendell
American. Actor
b. Mar 20, 1914 in Dracut, Massachusetts
d. Nov 9, 1968 in Woodland Hills, California
Source: *BiDFilm; BiE&WWA; FilmgC; HolP
40; MotPP; MovMk; ObitOF 79; WhAm 5;
WhScrn 74; WhoHol B; WorAl; WorEFlm*

Corey, William Ellis
American. Industrialist
b. May 4, 1866 in Braddock, Pennsylvania
d. May 11, 1934
Source: *DcAmB S1; NatCAB 14; WhAm 1*

Cori, Carl Ferdinand
American. Biochemist
Discovered steps in glycogen-glucose
   conversion known as Cori cycle, 1939.
b. Dec 5, 1896 in Prague, Austria
d. Oct 20, 1984 in Cambridge, Massachusetts
Source: *AmM&WS 73P; AnObit 1984; CurBio
47; IntWW 74; WebAB; Who 74; WhoAm 74,
78, 80, 82; WhoWor 74*

Cori, Gerty Theresa
American. Biochemist
First woman to win Nobel Prize for
   medicine, physiology.
b. Aug 15, 1896 in Prague, Austria
d. Oct 26, 1957 in Saint Louis, Missouri
Source: *CurBio 58; InWom; NotAW MOD;
WebAB; WhAm 3*

Corigliano, John
American. Composer, Musician
b. Feb 16, 1938 in New York, New York
Source: *AmSCAP 66; DcCM*

Corinth, Lovis
German. Artist
Proponent of Sezession modernistic movement
   who strongly influenced German
   expressionism.
b. 1858
d. 1925
Source: *BioIn 2, 4, 5, 7, 10; OxGer*

Corio, Ann
American. Actress
Best known for stage review *This Was
Burlesque.*
b. 1914 in Hartford, Connecticut
Source: *CelR; InWom; WhoHol A*

Coriolanus, Gaius
Roman. Soldier
Source: *NewCol 75; WebBD 80*

Corle, Edwin
American. Author
b. May 7, 1906 in Wildwood, New Jersey
d. Jun 11, 1956
Source: *AmAu&B; OxAmL; REnAL; TwCA
SUP; WhAm 3; WhNAA*

Corman, Gene
American. Producer
Films include *If You Could See What I
Hear;* won Emmy for "A Woman Called
Golda," 1982.
b. Sep 24, 1927 in Detroit, Michigan
Source: *VarWW 85*

Corman, Roger William
American. Director, Producer, Author
Produced B horror films: Poe's *The Raven,*
1962; *The Bees,* 1980.
b. Apr 5, 1926 in Detroit, Michigan
Source: *BiDFilm; BioIn 9, 11; CurBio 83;
DcFM; EncSF; FilmgC; IntMPA 75, 76, 77,
78, 79, 80, 81; OxFilm; WhoAm 74, 76, 78,
80, 82; WhoWor 74, 76, 78, 80; WorEFlm*

Corn, Ira George, Jr.
American. Bridge Player
Organized first US pro bridge team, "The
Aces," 1968; won three world
championships.
b. Aug 22, 1921 in Little Rock, Arkansas
d. Apr 28, 1982 in Dallas, Texas
Source: *ConAu 85; WhoAm 74, 76, 78, 80,
82; WhoF&I 74, 75, 77, 79; WhoS&SW 78;
WhoWor 78*

Corneille
[Cornelis Guillaume van Beverloo]
Dutch. Artist
Abstract colorist, illustrator; co-founded
Cobra group, 1947.
b. 1922 in Liege, Belgium
Source: *ConArt 77; McGDA*

Corneille, Pierre
French. Dramatist, Poet
b. Jun 6, 1606 in Rouen, France
d. Oct 1, 1684 in Paris, France
Source: *AtlBL; BbD; BiD&SB; CasWL;
CnThe; CyWA; DcEuL; EuAu; EvEuW;
McGEWD; NewC; OxEng; OxFr; OxThe;
PenC EUR; PIP&P; RComWL; REn;
REnWD*

Cornelius, Henry
British. Director
b. Aug 18, 1913 in South Africa
d. May 3, 1958 in London, England
Source: *CmMov; DcFM; FilmgC; MovMk;
OxFilm*

Cornelius, Peter
German. Composer
b. Dec 24, 1824 in Mainz, Germany
d. Oct 26, 1874 in Mainz, Germany
Source: *Alli; EvEuW*

Cornelius, Peter von
German. Artist
Noted for Munich frescoes, reviving German
interest in murals.
b. 1783
d. 1867
Source: *OxGer; WebBD 80*

Cornell, Don
[Louis F Varlaro]
American. Singer
b. Apr 21, 1919 in New York, New York
Source: *BiDAmM; CmpEPM*

Cornell, Douglas B
American. Journalist
AP White House correspondent, 1933-69.
b. 1907 in Saint Louis, Missouri
d. Feb 20, 1982 in Detroit, Michigan
Source: *BioIn 12; NewYTBS 82*

Cornell, Ezra
American. Business Executive
Founded Western Union Telegraph Co, 1855;
Cornell U, 1865.
b. Jan 11, 1807 in Westchester, New York
d. Dec 9, 1874 in Ithaca, New York
Source: *AmBi; ApCAB; DcAmB; TwCBDA;
WebAB; WhAm HS*

Cornell, Joseph
American. Artist
b. Dec 24, 1903 in Nyack, New York
d. Dec 1972
Source: *WhAm 5; WhoAmA 78*

Cornell, Katharine
American. Actress
Played Elizabeth Barrett in *The Barretts of
Wimpole Street,* 1931.
b. Feb 16, 1898 in Berlin, Germany
d. Jun 9, 1974 in Vineyard Haven,
Massachusetts
Source: *BiE&WWA; BioNews 74; CelR;
ConAu 49; CurBio 41, 52, 74; FamA&A;
HerW; NewYTBS 74; OxAmL; OxThe;
PIP&P; WebAB; WhAm 6; WhScrn 77; Who
74; WhoAm 74; WhoHol B; WhoWor 78*

Cornell, Lydia
American. Actress
Plays Sarah Rush on TV series "Too Close
for Comfort," 1980--.
b. 1957 in El Paso, Texas
Source: *BioIn 12*

Cornfeld, Bernard
American. Financier
Chairman, Investors Overseas Services, 1958-
71.
b. Aug 17, 1927 in Istanbul, Turkey
Source: *NewYTBE 70; PolProf NF*

Corning, Erastus
American. Financier, Congressman
First pres., NY Central Railroad, 1853-64;
NY town named after him.
b. Dec 14, 1794 in Norwich, Connecticut
d. Apr 9, 1872 in Albany, New York
Source: *AmBi; ApCAB; BiAUS; BiDrAC;
BioIn 3, 5; DcAmB; Drake; EncAB-A;
EncAB-H; McGEWB; TwCBDA; WhAm HS;
WhAmP*

Corning, Erastus, III
American. Politician
Mayor of Albany, NY, 1942-83; longest
tenured mayor in US.
b. Oct 7, 1909 in Albany, New York
d. May 28, 1983 in Boston, Massachusetts
Source: *NewYTBS 83; WhoAm 80, 82;
WhoAmP 81; WhoGov 77, 75*

Cornish, Gene
[The Rascals]
Canadian. Musician
Guitarist with blue-eyed soul group, 1965-71.
b. May 14, 1945 in Ottawa, Ontario
Source: *NF*

Cornwallis, Charles, Marquis
English. General
Surrendered to George Washington at
Yorktown, 1781.
b. Dec 31, 1738 in London, England
d. Oct 5, 1805 in Ghazipore, India
Source: *Alli; AmBi; ApCAB; CelCen; DcBiPP;
DcInB; Drake; OxAmL; REn; REnAL;
WhAm HS*

Coroebus
Greek. Olympic Athlete
Won first Olympic race, c. 776 BC.
Source: *NF*

Corona, Juan
American. Murderer
Convicted of murdering 25 migrant workers,
1970-71.
b. 1934 in Mexico
Source: *CmCal; DrInf; NewYTBE 71*

Coronado, Francisco Vasquez de
"El Dorado"
Spanish. Explorer
Led Mexican expedition searching for wealth
of Seven Cities of Cibola, 1540.
b. Feb 25, 1510 in Salamanca, Spain
d. Nov 12, 1554
Source: *AmBi; ApCAB; DcAmB; REn;
REnAL; WebAB; WhAm HS*

Corot, Jean Baptiste Camille
"Papa"
French. Artist
b. Jul 16, 1796 in Paris, France
d. Feb 22, 1875 in Paris, France
Source: *AtlBL; NewC; OxFr; REn*

Corrales, Pat(rick)
American. Baseball Manager
Has managed Texas, Philadelphia, currently
Cleveland, 1983--.
b. Mar 20, 1941 in Los Angeles, California
Source: *BaseEn 85; BaseReg 86*

Correggio, Antonio Allegri da
Italian. Artist
Most famous work "The Assumption of the
Virgin" in dome of Parma cathedral.
b. Aug 30, 1494 in Italy
d. Mar 5, 1534
Source: *AtlBL; ChhPo, S1; REn*

Correll, Charles J
[Amos 'n Andy]
American. Comedian
Andy of Amos 'n Andy comedy team; on
radio, 1928-58.
b. Feb 2, 1890 in Peoria, Illinois
d. Sep 26, 1972 in Chicago, Illinois
Source: *NewYTBE 72; ObitOF 79; WebAB,
79; WhScrn 77*

Corri, Adrienne
[Adrienne Riccoboni]
Scottish. Actress
b. Nov 13, 1933 in Glasgow, Scotland
Source: *FilmgC; IntMPA 75, 76, 77, 78, 79,
80, 81, 82; WhoHol A*

Corrigan, Douglas
"Wrong Way"
American. Aviator, Actor
Nicknamed for landing in Ireland after
taking off from NY for LA, 1938.
b. 1907
Source: *WhoHol A*

Corrigan, Mairead
Irish. Reformer
With Betty Williams, won Nobel Peace Prize
for forming N Ireland Peace Movement,
1976.
b. Jan 27, 1944 in Belfast, Northern Ireland
Source: *CurBio 78; IntWW 81; NewYTBS 77;
Who 82*

Corsaro, Frank
[Francesco Andrea]
American. Actor, Director
b. Dec 22, 1925 in New York, New York
Source: *BiE&WWA; ConAu 85; CurBio 75;
IntWW 77; NewYTBE 72; NotNAT; WhoAm
82; WhoThe 77*

Corsi, Jacopo
Italian. Producer, Musician
Among the orginators of opera; first operas
performed at his palace.
b. 1560 in Celano, Italy
d. 1604 in Florence, Italy
Source: *NewEOp 71*

Corso, Gregory
American. Poet
b. Mar 26, 1930 in New York, New York
Source: *AmAu&B; ConAu 5R; ConLC 1, 11;
ConP 70, 75; CroCAP; DrAP 75; OxAmL;
PenC AM; RAdv 1; REn; REnAL; TwCWr;
WebE&AL; WhoAm 74, 76, 78, 80, 82;
WhoWor 78*

Corson, Juliet
American. Author, Teacher
Culinary pioneer, opened NY cooking school,
1876.
b. Jan 14, 1841 in Roxbury, Massachusetts
d. Jun 18, 1897 in New York, New York
Source: *NotAW; WebBD 80*

Cort, Bud
American. Actor
Appeared in *Harold and Maude,* with Ruth
Gordon, 1971.
b. Mar 29, 1951 in Rye, New York
Source: *FilmgC; MovMk; WhoAm 82;
WhoHol A*

Cortazar, Julio
French. Author
Argentine writer known for intellectual
fiction; lived in exile in Paris following
election of Juan Peron.
b. Aug 26, 1914 in Brussels, Belgium
d. Feb 12, 1985 in Paris, France
Source: *CasWL; ConAu 21R; ConLC 2, 3, 5,
10, 13, 15; CurBio 74; DcCLAA; EncWL;
IntWW 74; PenC AM; TwCWr; WhoTwCL;
WorAu*

Cortesa, Valentina
Italian. Actress
b. Jan 1, 1925 in Milan, Italy
Source: *FilmgC; IntMPA 75, 76, 77, 78, 79, 80, 81, 82; MovMk*

Cortez, Hernando
[Hernan Cortes]
Spanish. Conqueror
Conquered Mexico; caused downfall of Aztec empire, 1521.
b. 1485 in Medellin, Spain
d. 1547
Source: *DcEuL; Drake; NewC; OxAmL; REn; REnAL; WhAm HS*

Cortez, Ricardo
[Jacob Kranz]
American. Actor
b. Sep 19, 1899 in Vienna, Austria
d. May 28, 1977 in New York, New York
Source: *FilmgC; MotPP; MovMk; WhoHol A*

Cortissoz, Royal
American. Journalist, Author
b. Feb 10, 1869 in Brooklyn, New York
d. Oct 17, 1948 in New York, New York
Source: *AmAu&B; DcAmB S4; DcNAA; TwCA, SUP; WhAm 2*

Corum, Martene Windsor
"Bill"
American. Journalist
b. Jul 20, 1895 in Speed, Missouri
d. Dec 16, 1958 in New York, New York
Source: *WhAm 3*

Corvo, Baron, pseud.
[Frederick William Rolfe]
English. Author
Wrote semi-autobiographical *Hadrian the Seventh*, 1904.
b. Jul 22, 1860 in London, England
d. Oct 26, 1913 in Venice, Italy
Source: *AtlBL; CasWL; ChhPo S2; CnMWL; DcLEL; EvLB; LongCTC; ModBrL, S1; NewC; OxEng; PenC ENG; REn; TwCA, SUP; TwCWr*

Corwin, Norman
American. Author, Producer, Director
b. May 3, 1910 in Boston, Massachusetts
Source: *AmAu&B; AmSCAP 66; AuNews 2; BiE&WWA; CnDAL; ConAu 1R; CurBio 40; IntMPA 75, 76, 77, 78, 79, 80, 81, 82; IntWW 74; NotNAT; OxAmL; REnAL; TwCA SUP; WhoAm 74, 76, 78, 80, 82; WhoWor 78; WhoWorJ 72; WrDr 76*

Corwin, Thomas
American. Statesman
b. 1794 in Bourbon County, Kentucky
d. 1865
Source: *DcNAA; NewCol 75; OhA&B*

Coryell, Don(ald David)
American. Football Coach
Head coach, San Diego Chargers, 1978--.
b. Oct 17, 1924 in Seattle, Washington
Source: *FootReg 81; WhoAm 82*

Coryell, John Russell
[Nick Carter, pseud.]
American. Author
b. 1848
d. Jul 15, 1924
Source: *AmAu&B; DcNAA; EncMys; OxAmL; REn; REnAL*

Cosby, Bill
American. Actor, Comedian
Star of hit TV series "The Cosby Show," 1984--; wrote *Fatherhood*, 1986.
b. Jul 12, 1937 in Philadelphia, Pennsylvania
Source: *BioNews 74; BkPepl; CelR; CurBio 67; FilmgC; IntMPA 75, 76, 77, 78, 79, 80, 81, 82; WhoAm 74, 76, 78, 80, 82; WhoBlA 75; WhoHol A; WhoWest 84; WhoWor 78*

Cosell, Howard
[Howard William Cohen]
American. Sportscaster
Sportscaster, ABC, 1956--; known for acerbic style.
b. Mar 25, 1920 in Winston-Salem, North Carolina
Source: *BioNews 74; BkPepl; CelR; CurBio 72; IntMPA 82; NewYTBS 74; WhoAm 82; WhoE 74*

Cosgrave, Liam
Irish. Prime Minister
b. Apr 30, 1920 in Dublin, Ireland
Source: *IntWW 74; NewYTBE 73; Who 74; WhoWor 78*

Cosgrave, William Thomas
Irish. Statesman
President, Irish Free State, 1922-32.
b. Jun 6, 1880 in Dublin, Ireland
d. Nov 16, 1965 in Dublin, Ireland
Source: *BioIn 7; DcIrB; LinLib S; NewCol 75; ObitOF 79; WebBD 80; WhAm 4*

Cosgrove, Gordon Dean
American. Business Executive
b. Mar 2, 1934 in Oklahoma City, Oklahoma
Source: *WhoAm 74; WhoF&I 74*

Cosimo, Piero di
Italian. Artist, Architect
Painter of religious, mythological works, often
in bizarre style: "Death of Procris," c.
1500.
b. 1462
d. 1521
Source: *AtlBL; REn*

Coslow, Sam
American. Composer
Won Oscar for best two-reel short *Heavenly
Music,* 1943.
b. Dec 27, 1905 in New York, New York
d. Apr 2, 1982 in Bronxville, New York
Source: *AmPS; AmSCAP 66, 80; CmpEPM;
ConAu 77; IntMPA 75, 76, 77, 78, 79, 80,
81, 82; NewYTBS 82*

Cossart, Ernest
English. Actor
b. Sep 24, 1876 in Cheltenham, England
d. Jan 21, 1951 in New York, New York
Source: *Film 1; FilmgC; NotNAT B; PlP&P;
WhScrn 74, 77; WhThe; WhoHol A*

Cossiga, Francesco
Italian. Political Leader
b. Jul 26, 1928 in Sassari, Sardinia
Source: *IntWW 79; NewYTBS 79*

Cossotto, Fiorenza
Italian. Opera Singer
b. Apr 22, 1935 in Crescentino, Italy
Source: *NewYTBE 71; WhoAm 82*

Costa, Don
American. Conductor
Arranger of over 200 hit recordings by
Frank Sinatra, Perry Como, others.
b. Jun 10, 1925 in Boston, Massachusetts
d. Jan 19, 1983 in New York, New York
Source: *AmPS A; AnObit 1983; NewYTBS 83;
RkOn 74*

Costa, Lucio
Brazilian. Architect
b. 1902
Source: *IntWW 74*

Costa, Mary
American. Opera Singer
b. Apr 5, 1930 in Knoxville, Tennessee
Source: *WhoAm 74, 76, 78, 80, 82; WhoHol
A; WhoWor 74*

Costa, Victor Charles
American. Fashion Designer
Pres., Victor Costa, Inc., 1973--.
b. Dec 17, 1935 in Houston, Texas
Source: *WhoAm 82; WorFshn*

Costa e Silva, Arthur da
Brazilian. Army Officer, Politician
Led 1964 revolution; pres., 1967-69.
b. Oct 3, 1902 in Taquari, Brazil
d. Dec 17, 1969 in Rio de Janeiro, Brazil
Source: *CurBio 67, 70; DcPol; EncLatA;
ObitOF 79*

Costa-Gavras(, Henri)
[Kostantinos Gavras]
Greek. Director
Won Oscar for *Z,* 1969.
b. 1933 in Athens, Greece
Source: *BioIn 9, 10; CurBio 72; IntMPA 82;
MovMk; WhoAm 76, 82*

Costa Mendez, Nicanor
Argentine. Government Official
Foreign minister who led Argentine attack on
Falkland Islands, 1982.
b. Oct 30, 1922 in Buenos Aires, Argentina
Source: *IntWW 82; NewYTBS 82*

Costain, Thomas B
American. Author, Journalist
Wrote best-selling historical novels: *The
Black Rose,* 1945; *The Silver Chalice,*
1952.
b. May 8, 1885 in Brantford, Ontario
d. Oct 8, 1965 in New York, New York
Source: *AmAu&B; AmNov; AuBYP; CanWr;
ConAu 5R, 25R; CreCan 2; CurBio 53, 65;
DcLEL; LongCTC; OxAmL; OxCan; REn;
REnAL; TwCA SUP; TwCWr; WhAm 4*

Costanza, "Midge" (Margaret)
American. Presidential Aide
Special asst. to Jimmy Carter, liason to
special interest groups.
b. Nov 28, 1928 in Leroy, New York
Source: *CurBio 78; NewYTBS 78; WhoAmW
77*

Coste, Dieudonne
French. Aviator
First westward transatlantic flight from Paris
to NYC, Sep 1-2, 1930.
b. Nov 4, 1893 in Gascony, France
d. May 18, 1973
Source: *NewYTBE 73*

Costello, Chris
American. Actress, Author
Appeared in movie, *Semi-Tough,* 1978; wrote
biography of father Lou Costello, *Lou's on
First,* 1982.
b. Aug 15, 1947 in Los Angeles, California
Source: *ConAu 107*

Costello, Dolores
American. Actress
b. Sep 17, 1905 in Pittsburgh, Pennsylvania
d. Mar 1, 1979 in Fallbrook, California
Source: *FilmEn; Film 2; FilmgC; InWom; MotPP; MovMk; NewYTBS 79; ThFT; TwYS; WhoHol A*

Costello, Elvis
[Declan Patrick McManus]
English. Singer, Songwriter
Best known album, *Armed Forces,* 1979.
b. Aug 25, 1955 in London, England
Source: *BioIn 11; ConLC 21; CurBio 83; RkOn 85; WhoAm 80, 82*

Costello, Frank
[Francesco Castiglia]
American. Organized Crime Figure
Controlled Manhattan's organized crime, 1936-46.
b. Jan 26, 1891 in Cosenza, Italy
d. Feb 1, 1973 in New York, New York
Source: *BioIn 10; DrInf; NewYTBE 73; ObitOF 79; PolProf E*

Costello, Helene
American. Actress
b. Jun 21, 1903 in New York, New York
d. Jan 26, 1957 in Los Angeles, California
Source: *Film 1; FilmgC; MotPP; NotNAT B; ObitOF 79; ThFT; TwYS; WhScrn 74, 77; WhoHol B*

Costello, John Aloysius
Irish. Prime Minister
b. Jun 20, 1891 in Dublin, Ireland
d. Jan 5, 1976 in Dublin, Ireland
Source: *CurBio 48; IntWW 74; PoIre; WhAm 6; Who 74*

Costello, Larry
American. Basketball Coach
Coach, Milwaukee Bucks, 1968-77; won NBA championship, 1971.
b. Jul 2, 1931 in Minoa, New York
Source: *BioIn 6; OfNBA 81; WhoBbl 73*

Costello, Lou
[Abbott and Costello; Louis Francis Cristillo]
American. Actor, Comedian
Starred in over 30 films with Bud Abbott; best known for "Who's On First?" routine.
b. Mar 6, 1908 in Paterson, New Jersey
d. Mar 3, 1959 in Los Angeles, California
Source: *CmMov; CurBio 41, 59; FilmgC; MotPP; MovMk; OxFilm; WhAm 3; WhScrn 74, 77; WhoHol B; WorEFlm*

Costello, Maurice
"The Dimpled Darling"
American. Actor
One of first matinee stage idols to have film triumph in *A Tale of Two Cities,* 1911.
b. 1877 in Pittsburgh, Pennsylvania
d. Oct 30, 1950 in Hollywood, California
Source: *Film 1, 2; FilmgC; MotPP; NotNAT B; TwYS; WhScrn 74, 77; WhoHol B*

Costello, Robert E
American. Producer
Won Emmys, 1977, 1979 for soap opera "Ryan's Hope."
b. Apr 26, 1921 in Chicago, Illinois
Source: *VarWW 85*

Coster, Laurens Janszoon
[Laurens Janszoon Koster]
Dutch. Inventor
Invented moveable type.
b. 1410 in Haarlem, Netherlands
Source: *NewCol 75; WebBD 80*

Costigan, James
Writer
Won three Emmys for TV shows including "Eleanor and Franklin," 1976.
Source: *VarWW 85*

Costle, Douglas Michael
American. Government Official
b. Jul 27, 1939 in Long Beach, California
Source: *BioIn 12; CurBio 80; WhoAm 80, 82*

Cote, Gerard
Canadian. Track Athlete
b. 1913
Source: *BioIn 10*

Cothran, Shirley
American. Beauty Contest Winner
b. 1953
Source: *NewYTBS 74*

Cotman, John S
English. Artist
b. Aug 16, 1782 in Norwich, England
d. Jul 24, 1865 in London, England
Source: *Alli; AtlBL; BiDLA; NewC*

Cotrubas, Ileana
Romanian. Opera Singer
b. Jun 9, 1939 in Galati, Romania
Source: *CurBio 81; IntWW 78; NewYTBS 77; WhoAm 82; WhoMus 72; WhoOp 76*

Cotsworth, Staats
American. Actor, Artist
Starred on radio as "Casey, Crime
    Photographer," 1944-55.
b. Feb 17, 1908 in Oak Park, Illinois
Source: *BiE&WWA; IntMPA 75, 76, 77;*
NotNAT; WhoAmA 73; WhoHol A; WhoThe
77, 81N

Cott, Nate
American. Engineer
b. 1913
d. Oct 5, 1973 in Lawrence, New York
Source: *BioIn 10; NewYTBE 73*

Cott, Ted
American. Radio Executive, TV Executive
b. Jan 1, 1917 in Poughkeepsie, New York
d. Jun 13, 1973 in New York, New York
Source: *AmAu&B; NewYTBE 73; NewYTET;*
WhAm 6; WhoPubR 72

Cottam, Clarence
American. Biologist
b. Jan 1, 1899 in Saint George, Utah
d. Mar 30, 1974 in Corpus Christi, Texas
Source: *BioIn 10; NewYTBS 74; WhoAm 74;*
WhoWor 78

Cotten, Joseph
American. Actor
Starred in *Citizen Kane,* 1941; *Journey into*
    Fear, 1942.
b. May 15, 1905 in Petersburg, Virginia
Source: *BiDFilm; BiE&WWA; BioNews 74;*
CmMov; CurBio 43; FilmgC; IntMPA 75, 76,
77, 78, 79, 80, 81, 82; MotPP; MovMk;
NotNAT; OxFilm; PIP&P; WhoAm 74, 76,
78, 80, 82; WhoHol A; WhoThe 77;
WorEFlm

Cotten, Michael
[The Tubes]
American. Musician
Keyboardist with The Tubes since late 1960s.
b. Jan 25, 1950 in Kansas, Missouri
Source: *NF*

Cotton, John
American. Religious Leader
b. Dec 4, 1584 in Derby, England
d. Dec 23, 1652 in Boston, Massachusetts
Source: *Alli; SUP; AmAu; AmAu&B; AmBi;*
ApCAB; BiD&SB; CnDAL; CyAL 1; DcAmAu;
DcAmB; DcLEL; DcNAA; Drake; EncAB-H;
OxAmL; PenC AM; REn; REnAL; TwCBDA;
WebAB; WhAm HS

Cotton, Norris
American. Senator
b. May 11, 1900
Source: *BiDrAC; CngDr 74; CurBio 56;*
IntWW 74; WhoAm 74; WhoAmP 73; WhoE
74; WhoGov 75

Cotton, Paul
see: Poco

Cottrell, Alan Howard
English. Scientist
b. Jul 17, 1919 in Birmingham, England
Source: *IntWW 74; Who 74; WhoWor 78*

Coty, Rene
French. Statesman
b. Mar 20, 1882 in Le Havre, France
d. Nov 22, 1962
Source: *CurBio 54, 63; WhAm 4*

Coubertin, Pierre de, Baron
French. Olympic Official
Revived Olympic games, 1894; pres., IOC,
    1894-1925.
b. Jan 1, 1862 in Paris, France
d. Sep 1, 1937 in Geneva, Switzerland
Source: *BioIn 2; WhE&EA; WhLit; WhoLA;*
WorAl

Coue, Emile
French. Psychologist
b. Feb 26, 1857 in Troyes, France
d. Jul 2, 1926 in Nancy, France
Source: *BioIn 3, 7; NewC*

Cougar, John
see: Mellencamp, John Cougar

Coughlin, Father (Charles Edward)
American. Priest, Radio Commentator
Founded National Union for Social Justice,
    1934; published *Social Justice,* 1934-42.
b. Oct 25, 1891 in Hamilton, Ontario
d. Oct 27, 1979 in Bloomfield Hills,
    Michigan
Source: *ConAu 97; CurBio 40; EncAB-H;*
NewCol 75; WebAB

Coulomb, Charles Augustin de
French. Physicist
b. Jun 14, 1736 in Angouleme, France
d. Aug 23, 1806 in Paris, France
Source: *AsBiEn; McGEWB; NewCol 75*

Coulouris, George
English. Actor
b. Oct 1, 1903 in Manchester, England
Source: *BiE&WWA; FilmgC; MovMk;*
NotNAT; Vers A; WhoHol A; WhoThe 77, 81

Coulter, Ernest Kent
American. Social Reformer
Children's court clerk who founded first Big
Brother agency, NYC, 1904.
b. Nov 14, 1871 in Columbus, Ohio
d. May 1, 1952 in Santa Barbara, California
Source: *DcAmB S5; NatCAB 41; ObitOF 79;
OhA&B; WhNAA*

Coulter, John William
Canadian. Dramatist
Noted for dramas with Irish themes: *Family
Portraits,* 1937.
b. Feb 12, 1888 in Belfast, Northern Ireland
d. Dec 1980 in Toronto, Ontario
Source: *BioIn 1, 11; CanWW 70, 79; ConAu
3NR, 5R; OxCan, SUP*

Country Joe and the Fish
[Bruce Barthol; David Cohen; Chicken
Hirsch; Joseph McDonald; Barry Melton]
American. Music Group
Appeared at Monterey, Woodstock festivals.
Source: *BiDAmM; RkOn 84; RkOneH;
RolSEnR 83*

Couperin
[Armand-Louis Couperin; Charles Couperin;
Francois Couperin; Francois-Gervais
Couperin; Louis Couperin; Marguerite-
Antoinette Couperin; Marguerite-Antoinette
Couperin; Margaruerite-Louise Couperin;
Nicholas Couperin; Pierre-Louis Couperin]
French. Musicians
Family best known as organists at St.
Gervais, Paris, 1650-1826.
Source: *Baker 78; DcCathB; OxMus; WebBD
80; WhDW*

Couperin, Francois
[LeGrand Couperin]
French. Musician, Composer
Harpsichordist whose music was culmination
of French rococo; influenced keyboard
technique of Bach.
b. Nov 10, 1668 in Paris, France
d. Sep 12, 1733 in Paris, France
Source: *AtlBL; Baker 78; McGEWB; OxFr;
OxMus*

Couperius, Louis (Marie Anne)
Dutch. Author, Educator
Wrote four-vol. epic *The Books of the Small
Souls,* 1914-18.
b. Jun 10, 1863 in The Hague, Netherlands
d. Jul 16, 1923 in De Steeg, Netherlands
Source: *ConAu 115; ConLC 15; CyWA; REn*

Courbet, Gustave
French. Artist
Realist painter whose works include "Burial
at Ornans," in the Louvre.
b. Jun 10, 1819 in Ornans, France
d. Dec 31, 1877 in Vevey, Switzerland
Source: *AtlBL; OxFr; REn*

Courboin, Charles
American. Organist, Music Director
b. 1883
d. Apr 13, 1973
Source: *BioIn 9*

Cournand, Andre Frederic
American. Physiologist
Awarded Nobel Prize for medicine, 1956, for
development of cardiac catheterization.
b. Sep 24, 1895 in Paris, France
Source: *AmM&WS 73P; CurBio 57; IntWW
74; WhoAm 82; WhoWor 74*

Cournos, John
Author
b. Mar 6, 1881 in Russia
d. Aug 29, 1966
Source: *AmAu&B; ConAmL; ConAu 13R, P-2;
DcLEL; LongCTC; OxAmL; REnAL; TwCA,
SUP; WhoLA*

Courreges, Andre
French. Fashion Designer
b. Mar 9, 1923 in Pau, France
Source: *CurBio 70; IntWW 74; WhoAm 74;
WhoWor 78; WorFshn*

Court, Margaret
[Margaret Smith]
Australian. Tennis Player
Wimbledon champ, 1963-65, 1970; US Open
champ, 1962, 1965, 1968-70, 1973.
b. Jul 16, 1942 in Albury, Australia
Source: *BioNews 74; CelR; CurBio 73;
NewYTBE 70, 71; WhoAm 82; WhoWor 78*

Courtenay, Tom
English. Actor
Oscar nominee for *The Dresser,* 1984.
b. Feb 25, 1937 in Hull, England
Source: *CelR; CurBio 64; FilmgC; IntMPA
82; MotPP; MovMk; NewYTBS 81; OxFilm;
WhoHol A; WhoThe 81; WhoWor 74; WorAl;
WorEFlm*

Courtneidge, Cicely, Dame
British. Actress
London stage, musical star since 1909;
  introduced song "The Kings Horses,"
  1931.
b. Apr 1, 1893 in Sydney, Australia
d. Apr 26, 1980 in London, England
Source: *EncMT; InWom; NotNAT A; Who
78; WhoHol A; WhoThe 77*

Courtney, Clint(on Dawson)
"Scrap Iron"
American. Baseball Player
Catcher, 1951-61; AL Rookie of Year, 1952.
b. Mar 16, 1927 in Hall Summit, Louisiana
d. Jun 16, 1975 in Rochester, New York
Source: *BaseEn 85; BioIn 3, 10; WhoProB 73*

Courtright, Jim (Timothy Isaiah)
"Longhaired Jim"
American. Lawman
Marshal, Ft. Worth, 1876-78; killed by
  gambler who refused to pay.
b. 1845 in Illinois
d. Feb 8, 1887 in Fort Worth, Texas
Source: *BioIn 10, 11; REnAW*

Cousineau, Tom
American. Football Player
Linebacker, Cleveland, 1982--; highest-paid
  defensive player at time of signing.
b. May 16, 1957 in Fairview Park, Ohio
Source: *FootReg 85; NewYTBS 82*

Cousins, Frank
English. Labor Union Official
MP, 1965-66; general secretary, Transport
  and General Workers Union, 1956-64,
  1966-69.
b. Sep 8, 1904 in Bulwell, England
d. Jun 11, 1986 in Chesterfield, England
Source: *CurBio 86; IntWW 82; IntYB 82*

Cousins, Margaret
American. Children's Author
b. Jan 26, 1905 in Munday, Texas
Source: *AmAu&B; AuBYP; ConAu 1NR;
ForWC 70; InWom; SmATA 2; TexWr;
WhoAm 82; WhoWor 74; WrDr 76*

Cousins, Norman
American. Editor
Editor *Saturday Review,* 1940-77.
b. Jun 24, 1912 in Union Hill, New Jersey
Source: *AmAu&B; CelR; ChhPo; ConAu 17R;
CurBio 43; IntWW 74; NewYTBE 71;
OxAmL; REn; REnAL; TwCA SUP; WebAB;
Who 82; WhoAm 82; WhoE 79; WhoF&I 74;
WhoWor 74; WorAl; WrDr 82*

Cousins, Robin
English. Figure Skater
Won Olympic gold medal in figure skating,
  1980.
b. 1957 in Bristol, England
Source: *NewYTBS 79*

Cousins, Samuel
English. Engraver
Mezzotint engraver who transcribed Thomas
  Lawrence's works.
b. May 9, 1801 in Exeter, England
d. May 7, 1887 in London, England
Source: *NewCol 75; WebBD 80*

Cousteau, Jacques Yves
French. Oceanographer, Author
Led Calypso expeditions; hosts TV's
  "Undersea World of Jacques Cousteau,"
  1968--; won Oscar, 1965, for best
  documentary.
b. Jun 11, 1910 in Sainte Andre de Cubzac,
  France
Source: *AnCL; AsBiEn; BioNews 74; CelR;
ConAu 65; DcFM; FilmgC; IntAu&W 77;
IntWW 81; LinLib L; OxFilm; OxShips;
REn; WhDW; Who 82; WhoAm 82; WhoOcn
78; WhoUN 75; WhoWor 78; WorAl;
WorEFlm*

Cousteau, Philippe
French. Oceanographer, Producer
Produced TV series "Undersea World of
  Jacques Cousteau," 1970-75; Emmy
  nominee, 1971.
b. Dec 30, 1940 in Toulon, France
d. Jun 28, 1979 in Alverca, Portugal
Source: *ConAu 33R, 89; NewYTBS 79*

Cousy, Bob (Robert Joseph)
American. Basketball Player
Ten-time NBA All-Star; led Boston to five
  world championships, 1957-63.
b. Aug 9, 1928 in New York, New York
Source: *CelR; CurBio 58; OfNBA 81; WebAB;
WhoAm 82; WhoBbl 73; WorAl*

Couthon, Georges
French. Politician, Lawyer
Paralyzed, he led army that took Lyons from
  counter-revolutionaries.
b. 1756
d. Jul 28, 1794
Source: *DcBiPP; Dis&D; OxFr*

Couve de Murville, (Jacques) Maurice
French. Political Leader
French prime minister, 1968-69; mediator in
Lebanese civil war, 1975.
b. Jan 24, 1907 in Reims, France
Source: *DcPol; IntWW 82; IntYB 82; Who
82*

Couzens, James Joseph, Jr.
American. Businessman, Politician
Ford Motor Co. exec., 1903-15; mayor of
Detroit, 1919-22.
b. Aug 26, 1876 in Chatham, Ontario
d. Oct 22, 1936 in Detroit, Michigan
Source: *AmBi; BiDrAC; DcAmB S2; EncAB-
A; NatCAB 30; WebAB; WhAm 1; WhAmP*

Covarrubias, Miguel
Mexican. Artist, Cartoonist
b. Feb 4, 1904 in Mexico City, Mexico
d. Feb 6, 1957 in Mexico City, Mexico
Source: *CurBio 40, 57; IlsCB 1744, 1946;
ObitOF 79; REnAL; WhDW; WhAm 3;
WorECar*

Coveleski, Harry Frank
[Harry Frank Kowalewski]
"The Giant Killer"
American. Baseball Player
Pitcher, 1907-10; 1914-19.
b. Apr 23, 1886 in Shamokin, Pennsylvania
d. Aug 4, 1950 in Shamokin, Pennsylvania
Source: *BaseEn 85; WhoProB 73*

Coveleski, Stanley Anthony
[Stanislaus Kowalewski]
American. Baseball Player
Had four 20-game seasons with Cleveland,
1918-21; Hall of Fame, 1969.
b. Jul 13, 1889 in Shamokin, Pennsylvania
d. Mar 20, 1984 in South Bend, Indiana
Source: *BaseEn 85; WhoProB 73*

Cover, Franklin
American. Actor
Played Tom Willis on TV series "The
Jeffersons," 1975-85.
b. Nov 20, 1928 in Cleveland, Ohio
Source: *VarWW 85*

Covey, Cyclone
American. Author
b. May 21, 1922 in Guthrie, Oklahoma
Source: *ConAu 21R; WhoAm 80, 82*

Covici, Pascal
American. Publisher, Editor
Co-owner, Covici-Friede Publishing, 1928-38;
promoted John Steinbeck.
b. Nov 4, 1885 in Botosani, Romania
d. Oct 14, 1964 in New York, New York
Source: *DcAmB S7*

Covington, Glen
American. Jazz Musician
Source: *NF*

Covington, Warren
American. Musician, Author, Singer
b. Aug 7, 1921 in Philadelphia, Pennsylvania
Source: *AmSCAP 66; CmpEPM*

Cowan, Jerome
American. Actor
Played Miles Archer in *The Maltese Falcon,*
1941; Dagwood's boss in *Blondie* film
series, 1940s.
b. Oct 6, 1897 in New York, New York
d. Jan 24, 1972 in Encino, California
Source: *BiE&WWA; FilmgC; MovMk;
NewYTBE 72; NotNAT B; ObitOF 79; Vers
A; WhScrn 77; WhoHol B*

Cowan, Peter Wilkinshaw
Australian. Author
b. Nov 4, 1914 in Perth, Australia
Source: *ConAu 21R; ConNov 72, 76; WrDr
80*

Coward, Noel Pierce, Sir
English. Actor, Dramatist, Composer
Wrote 27 plays, 281 songs; plays include
Private Lives, 1930; *Blithe Spirit,* 1941.
b. Dec 16, 1899 in London, England
d. Mar 26, 1973 in Kingston, Jamaica
Source: *Au&Wr 71; AuNews 1; BiE&WWA;
BioNews 74; CasWL; Chambr 3; ChhPo, S2;
CnMD; CnThe; ConAu 17R, 41R, P-2;
ConLC 1, 9; CurBio 41, 62, 73; CyWA;
DcFM; DcLEL; EncMT; EncWL; EvLB;
FamA&A; Film 1; FilmgC; LongCTC;
McGEWD; ModBrL, S1; ModWD; MovMk;
NewC; NewYTBE 70, 73; NewYTBS 74;
OxEng; OxFilm; OxThe; PenC ENG; PIP&P;
REn; REnWD; TwCA, SUP; TwCWr;
WebE&AL; WhAm 5; WhScrn 77; WhoHol
B; WhoMus 72; WorEFlm*

Cowdrey, (Michael) Colin
English. Sportsman, Businessman
Member, England Cricket Team, 1954-75;
author *Autobiography of a Cricketer,* 1976.
b. Dec 24, 1932 in Bangalore, India
Source: *ConAu 105; IntWW 82; Who 82;
WrDr 82*

Cowdry, Edmund Vincent
Canadian. Scientist
Cancer researcher who discovered heartwater.
b. Jul 18, 1888 in MacLeon, Alberta
d. Jun 25, 1975
Source: *InSci; WhAm 6; WhoAm 74;
WhoWor 74*

Cowell, Henry Dixon
American. Composer, Musician
b. Mar 11, 1897 in Menlo Park, California
d. Dec 10, 1965 in Shady, New York
Source: *DcCM; EncFCWM 69; REnAL;
WebAB; WhAm 4; WhNAA*

Cowen, Joshua Lionel
American. Inventor, Industrialist
Invented toy electric train, 1900; headed
Lionel Corp., 1945-65.
b. Aug 25, 1880 in New York, New York
d. Sep 8, 1965 in New York, New York
Source: *CurBio 54, 65; WhAm 4*

Cowen, Zelman, Sir
Australian. Political Leader
Law professor, currently governor general of
Australia, 1977--; author of books on
legal, political subjects.
b. Oct 7, 1919 in Melbourne, Australia
Source: *Au&Wr 71; BioIn 11; ConAu 1NR;
IntYB 81; WhoWor 80; WrDr 82*

Cowens, Dave (David William)
American. Basketball Player
Boston Celtics forward, 1970-80, who was
NBA MVP, 1973.
b. Oct 25, 1948 in Newport, Kentucky
Source: *OfNBA 81; WhoBbl 73*

Cowl, Jane
American. Actress, Dramatist
Co-wrote two plays which became movies,
Lilac Time and *Smilin' Through.*
b. Dec 14, 1884 in Boston, Massachusetts
d. Jun 22, 1950 in Santa Monica, California
Source: *FamA&A; Film 1; FilmgC; NotAW;
NotNAT B; PIP&P; WhScrn 77; WhThe;
WhoHol B*

Cowles, Fleur Fenton
American. Editor
b. Feb 13, 1910 in New York, New York
Source: *AmAu&B; Au&Wr 71; AuNews 1;
BioNews 74; ConAu 4NR; CurBio 52;
WhoAm 82; WhoWor 74; WrDr 76*

Cowles, Gardner
"Mike"
American. Publisher
Founded *Look* Magazine, 1937; chm., Cowles
Communications, Inc.
b. Jan 31, 1903 in Algona, Iowa
d. Jul 8, 1985 in New York, New York
Source: *AmAu&B; CelR; CurBio 43; IntWW
81; LinLib L, S; NewYTBE 71; St&PR 75;
WebAB, 79; WhoAm 82; WhoAmA 80;
WhoF&I 74; WhoWor 74*

Cowles, Henry Chandler
American. Botanist, Educator
Pioneered in plant ecology.
b. Feb 27, 1869 in Kensington, Connecticut
d. Sep 12, 1939 in Chicago, Illinois
Source: *DcAmB S2; WebBD 80*

Cowles, John, Sr.
American. Publisher, Business Executive
Owner of several daily newspapers, including
Minneapolis *Star.*
b. Dec 14, 1898 in Algona, Iowa
d. Feb 25, 1983 in Minneapolis, Minnesota
Source: *BiDAmBL 83; BlueB 76; ConAu 109;
CurBio 83; IntWW 83; IntYB 82; NewYTBS
83; WhJnl; WhoAm 78; WhoWor 74*

Cowles, William Hutchinson, Jr.
American. Publisher
Pres., Spokane Chronicle Co., 1935-68;
Cowles Publishing Co., 1946-70.
b. Jul 23, 1902 in Sands Point, New York
d. Aug 12, 1971 in Spokane, Washington
Source: *NatCAB 57; WhAm 5*

Cowley, Abraham
English. Poet, Essayist
Originator of English Pindaric ode; best
known poem "Davideis," 1656.
b. 1618 in London, England
d. Jul 28, 1667 in Chertsey, England
Source: *Alli; AtlBL; BbD; BiD&SB; BrAu;
CasWL; Chambr 1; ChhPo, S1; CnE&AP;
CroE&S; CrtT 2; CyWA; DcEnA; DcEnL;
DcEuL; DcLEL; EvLB; LongCEL; McGEWB;
MouLC 1; NewC; NotNAT B; OxEng; OxThe;
PenC ENG; REn; WebE&AL*

Cowley, Joe (Joesph Alan)
American. Baseball Player
Pitcher, 1984--; threw no-hitter against
California, 1986.
b. Aug 15, 1958 in Lexington, Kentucky
Source: *BaseEn 85; BaseReg 86*

Cowley, Malcolm
American. Author, Literary Critic
b. Aug 24, 1898 in Belsano, Pennsylvania
Source: *AmAu&B; Au&Wr 71; CelR; ChhPo;
CnDAL; ConAu 5R, 3NR; ConP 70, 75;
DcLEL; EncWL; IntWW 74; ModAL; Sl;
OxAmL; PenC AM; RAdv 1; REn; REnAL;
SixAP; TwCA, SUP; WebAB; WhNAA;
WhoAm 82; WhoWor 74; WrDr 76*

Cowper, William
English. Poet
Wrote hymn "Oh for a Closer Walk with
   God," 1779.
b. Nov 15, 1731 in Berkhampstead, England
d. Apr 25, 1800 in Dereham, England
Source: *Alli; AnCL; AtlBL; BbD; BiD&SB;
BrAu; CarSB; CasWL; Chambr 2; ChhPo, Sl,
S2; CnE&AP; CrtT 2; CyWA; DcEnA;
DcEnL; DcEuL; DcLEL; EvLB; MouLC 2;
NewC; OxEng; OxMus; PenC ENG; PoChrch;
RAdv 1; REn; WebE&AL; WhDW; WorAl*

Cowsills, The
[Barbara Cowsill; Barry Cowsill; John
   Cowsill; Paul Cowsill; Richard Cowsill;
   Robert Cowsill; Susan Cowsill; William
   Cowsill]
American. Music Group
Family group which inspired TV's "Partridge
   Family"; hit single theme from *Hair,*
   1960s.
Source: *BiDAmM; RkOn 84*

Cox, Archibald
American. Lawyer
Watergate prosecutor fired by Richard Nixon;
   replaced by Leon Jaworski.
b. May 17, 1912 in Plainfield, New Jersey
Source: *ASpks; BioNews 74; BlueB 76; ConAu
73; CurBio 61; DrAS 78P; IntWW 81;
NewYTBE 73; PolProf J, K, NF; WhoAm 82;
WhoAmL 79; WhoAmP 79; WhoWor 78;
WrDr 80*

Cox, Bobby (Robert Joe)
American. Baseball Manager
Manager, Toronto, 1982-85; won AL East
   Division, AL manager of year, 1985; GM,
   Atlanta, 1986--.
b. May 21, 1941 in Tulsa, Oklahoma
Source: *BaseReg 85; WhoAm 84*

Cox, Constance
English. Dramatist
b. Oct 25, 1915 in Surrey, England
Source: *Au&Wr 71; ConAu 21R; WhoAmW
77; WhoThe 77; WrDr 80*

Cox, David
English. Artist
b. Apr 29, 1783 in Deritend, England
d. Jun 7, 1859 in Harborne, England
Source: *NewCol 75; OxArt; WebBD 80*

Cox, Edward Finch
American. Lawyer, Celebrity Relative
Married Tricia Nixon, Jun 1971.
b. Oct 2, 1946 in Southampton, New York
Source: *BioIn 10; ConAu 29R*

Cox, Gardner
American. Artist
b. Jan 22, 1906 in Holyoke, Massachusetts
Source: *WhoAm 80, 82; WhoAmA 82;
WhoWor 80*

Cox, Harvey Gallagher, Jr.
American. Theologian, Social Reformer
Wrote *Secular City,* 1965; believes in socially
   relevant church.
b. May 19, 1929 in Chester County,
   Pennsylvania
Source: *AmAu&B; AuNews 1; ConAu 77;
CurBio 68; LinLib L; WhoAm 82; WhoE 74;
WhoRel 77; WrDr 82*

Cox, Herald Rea
American. Bacteriologist
Developed Orimune, oral liquid polio vaccine,
   late 1950s, inoculations against Rocky
   Mountain spotted fever, typhus.
b. Feb 28, 1907 in Rosedale, Indiana
Source: *AmM&WS 76P; CurBio 61; WhoAm
74*

Cox, James Middleton, Sr.
American. Political Leader
b. Mar 31, 1870 in Jacksonburg, Ohio
d. Jul 15, 1957 in Dayton, Ohio
Source: *BiDrAC; OhA&B; WhAm 3; WhAmP*

Cox, James Middleton, Jr.
American. Publisher
Pres., Dayton *Daily News,* Dayton *Journal-
   Herald.*
b. Jun 27, 1903 in Dayton, Ohio
d. Oct 27, 1974 in Miami, Florida
Source: *BioNews 74; ConAu 89; NewYTBS
74; St&PR 75; WhAm 6; WhoAm 74;
WhoMW 74*

Cox, Jean
American. Opera Singer
b. Jan 14, 1922 in Gadsden, Alabama
Source: *BioIn 9*

Cox, John Rogers
American. Artist
Landscape painter known for color design:
"Gray and Gold," 1942.
b. Mar 24, 1915 in Terre Haute, Indiana
Source: *WhoAm 78; WhoAmA 78*

Cox, Kenyon
American. Artist
b. Oct 27, 1856 in Warren, Ohio
d. Mar 17, 1919
Source: *AmAu&B; AmBi; AmLY; ApCAB;
ChhPo, S1; DcAmB; DcNAA; OhA&B;
TwCBDA; WhAm 1*

Cox, Lynne
American. Swimmer
b. 1958
Source: *BioIn 10*

Cox, Palmer
Canadian. Author, Illustrator
Created "Brownies," series of 14 books for
children.
b. Apr 28, 1840 in Granby, Quebec
d. Jul 24, 1924 in Granby, Quebec
Source: *AmAu; AmAu&B; AmBi; ApCAB;
BiD&SB; ConAu 111; DcAmAu; DcAmB;
LinLib L; NatCAB 7; OxAmL, 83; SmATA
24; TwCBDA; WhAm 1; WhLit*

Cox, Richard Joseph
American. TV Executive
Pres., CBS Cable Division, 1981--.
b. Aug 21, 1929 in Brooklyn, New York
Source: *ConNews 85-1; WhoAm 84*

Cox, Wally (Wallace Maynard)
American. Actor, Comedian
Starred in "Mr. Peepers," 1952-55; regular
on "Hollywood Squares."
b. Dec 6, 1924 in Detroit, Michigan
d. Feb 15, 1973 in Los Angeles, California
Source: *ConAu 41R, 97; CurBio 54, 73;
NewYTBE 73; WhAm 5; WhScrn 77;
WhoHol B*

Cox, William Trevor
see: Trevor, William

Coxe, George Harmon
American. Author
Wrote over 60 mystery novels, had several
series characters.
b. Apr 23, 1901 in Oleon, New York
d. Jan 30, 1984 in Hilton Head, South
Carolina
Source: *AmAu&B; ConAu 57; EncMys;
MnBBF; Novels; REnAL; TwCCr&M 80;
WhoAm 82; WorAu; WrDr 82*

Coxe, Louis Osborne
American. Poet
b. 1918 in Manchester, New Hampshire
Source: *AmAu&B; BiE&WWA; ChhPo, S1;
ConAu 13R; ConP 70, 75; DrAP 75;
McGEWD; NotNAT; OxAmL; WhoAm 82;
WhoWor 74; WorAu; WrDr 76*

Coxey, Jacob Sechler
American. Reformer
Leader of 1894 march of unemployed on
Washington, DC.
b. Apr 16, 1854 in Selinsgrove, Pennsylvania
d. May 18, 1951 in Massillon, Ohio
Source: *DcAmB S5; DcAmSR; EncAB-H;
HarEnUS; McGEWB; OhA&B; WebAB;
WhAm 3*

Coy, Harold
American. Children's Author
b. Sep 24, 1902 in LaHabra, California
Source: *AuBYP; ConAu 5R, 4NR; SmATA 3;
WrDr 80*

Cozzens, James Gould
American. Author
Awarded Pulitzer for *Guard of Honor,* 1948.
b. Aug 19, 1903 in Chicago, Illinois
d. Aug 9, 1978 in Stuart, Florida
Source: *AmAu&B; AmNov; AmWr; CasWL;
ConAu 9R, 81; ConLC 1, 11, 4; ConNov 72,
76; CurBio 49; CyWA; DcLEL; DrAF 76;
EncWL; IntWW 74; LongCTC; ModAL;
OxAmL; PenC AM; RAdv 1; REn; REnAL;
TwCA, SUP; TwCWr; WebAB, 79;
WebE&AL; WhAm 7; Who 74; WhoAm 78;
WorAl*

Crabbe, "Buster" (Larry)
[Clarence Linden]
American. Actor, Swimmer
Starred as Flash Gordon, Buck Rogers in
1930s-40s movie serials.
b. Feb 7, 1908 in Oakland, California
d. Apr 23, 1983 in Scottsdale, Arizona
Source: *AnObit 1983; FilmEn; FilmgC;
IntMPA 77, 78, 79, 80, 81, 82; MotPP;
WhoAm 74, 76, 78, 80, 82; WhoHol A;
WorAl*

Crabbe, George
English. Poet
Wrote realistic narrative poems, "The
   Village," 1783; "The Borough," 1810.
b. Dec 24, 1754 in Aldborough, England
d. Feb 3, 1832 in Trowbridge, England
Source: *AtlBL; BbD; BiD&SB; BiDLA, SUP;*
BrAu 19; CasWL; Chambr 2; ChhPo, S1, S2;
CnE&AP; CrtT 2; CyWA; DcEnA; DcEnL;
DcEuL; DcLEL; EvLB; LongCEL; McGEWB;
MouLC 3; NewC; OxEng; PenC ENG;
PoChrch; RAdv 1; REn; WebE&AL; WhDW

Crabtree, Lotta
American. Actress
Began career entertaining in CA mining
   camps; appeared in *Old Curiosity Shop,*
   1867.
b. Nov 7, 1847 in New York, New York
d. Sep 25, 1924 in Boston, Massachusetts
Source: *AmBi; AmWom; ApCAB; CmCal;*
DcAmB; FamA&A; HerW; InWom; LibW;
NewCol 75; NotAW; NotNAT A; OxAmL;
TwCBDA; WebAB, 79

Craddock, "Crash" (Billy)
American. Singer
b. Jun 16, 1940 in Greensboro, North
   Carolina
Source: *WhoAm 78, 80, 82*

Craft, Christine
American. Broadcast Journalist
Sued former employer for age, sex
   discrimination, 1983; awarded $500,000.
b. 1945 in Canton, Ohio
Source: *NewYTBS 83*

Craft, Ellen
American. Slave, Abolitionist
Escaped slavery during Civil War; prominent
   in Boston antislavery movement.
b. 1826 in Clinton, California
d. 1897 in Charleston, South Carolina
Source: *HerW; InB&W 80; InWom; NotAW*

Craft, Robert
American. Conductor
Musical asst., adviser to Igor Stravinsky for
   23 yrs.
b. Oct 20, 1923 in Kingston, New York
Source: *AmAu&B; ConAu 9R; CurBio 84;*
WhoAm 82; WhoMus 72; WhoWor 74; WrDr
76

Crafts, James Mason
American. Chemist
b. Mar 8, 1839 in Boston, Massachusetts
d. Jun 20, 1917 in Ridgefield, Connecticut
Source: *DcNAA*

Craig, Cleo F
American. Business Executive
b. Apr 6, 1895 in Rich Hill, Missouri
d. Apr 21, 1978 in Ridgewood, New Jersey
Source: *CurBio 51, 78*

Craig, Elizabeth May
American. Journalist
Served as war correspondent in 1944; popular
   panelist on "Meet the Press."
b. Dec 24, 1889 in Coosaw, South Carolina
d. Jul 15, 1975 in Silver Spring, Maryland
Source: *ConAu 101, 89; CurBio 49, 75, 75N;*
InWom; NotAW MOD

Craig, Gordon (Edward Henry Gordon)
English. Designer, Director
Published *The Mask,* 1908-29, which
   featured his designs, theories of stagecraft;
   wrote *On the Art of the Theatre,* 1911.
b. Jan 16, 1872 in Harpenden, England
d. Jul 30, 1966 in Vence, France
Source: *LongCTC; OxThe; PhDcTCA 77;*
PlP&P; REn; TwCA, SUP; WhDW

Craig, Helen
English. Children's Author, Illustrator
Wrote, illustrated prize-winning *Mouse House*
   series, 1978-83.
b. Aug 30, 1934 in London, England
Source: *ConAu 117*

Craig, Jim (James)
American. Hockey Player
Goalie, best known for performance on gold-
   medal winning Olympic hockey team,
   1980.
b. May 31, 1957 in North Easton,
   Massachusetts
Source: *BioIn 12; HocEn; HocReg 81;*
NewYTBS 80

Craig, Malin
American. Military Leader, Public Official
Commanded every type of military unit; US
   Army chief of staff, 1935-39.
b. Aug 5, 1875 in Saint Joseph, Missouri
d. Jul 25, 1945
Source: *CurBio 44, 45; DcAmB S3; WebBD*
80

Craig, May
Irish. Actress
Played in first production of *Playboy of the*
   Western World, 1907.
b. 1889 in Ireland
d. Feb 9, 1972 in Dublin, Ireland
Source: *DcIrB; NewYTBE 72; NewYTBS 75;*
ObitOF 79; WhScrn 77; WhoHol B

Craig, Roger Lee
American. Baseball Manager
Pitcher 1955-66; manager, San Diego, 1978-79, San Francisco, 1985--.
b. Feb 17, 1931 in Durham, North Carolina
Source: *BaseEn 85; BaseReg 86*

Craig, Roger Timothy
American. Football Player
Fullback, San Francisco, 1983--; set NFL record by becoming first player ever to run, catch passes for 1,000 yds., 1985.
b. Jul 10, 1960 in Davenport, Iowa
Source: *FootReg 86*

Craig, Wendy
English. Actress
b. Jun 20, 1930 in Sacriston, England
Source: *FilmgC; WhoHol A; WhoThe 77, 81*

Craig, William
Irish. Politician
b. Dec 2, 1924
Source: *BioIn 9; IntWW 74; Who 74*

Craik, Dinah Maria Mulock
English. Author
Wrote over 40 volumes; novels, books for children, travel, poetry.
b. Apr 20, 1826 in Stoke-on-Trent, England
d. Oct 12, 1887 in Bromley, England
Source: *AnCL; BbD; BiD&SB; BrAu 19; CarSB; CasWL; DcEnA; DcEuL; DcLEL; EvLB; InWom; NewC; ScF&FL 1; Str&VC*

Crain, Jeanne
American. Actress
Oscar nominee for *Pinky,* 1949.
b. May 25, 1925 in Barstow, Georgia
Source: *BiDFilm; CurBio 51; FilmgC; InWom; IntMPA 82; MotPP; MovMk; WhoAm 74; WhoHol A; WorAl; WorEFlm*

Cram, Ralph Adams
American. Architect
b. Dec 16, 1863 in Hampton Falls, New Hampshire
d. Sep 22, 1942 in Boston, Massachusetts
Source: *AmBi; AmAu&B; AmLY; BiD&SB; DcAmAu; DcAmB S3; DcNAA; OxAmL; REnAL; WebAB; WhAm 2; WhNAA*

Cramer, Floyd
American. Singer, Musician
b. Oct 27, 1933 in Shreveport, Louisiana
Source: *EncFCWM 69*

Cramer, Johann Baptist
German. Pianist, Composer
b. 1771 in Mannheim, Germany
d. 1858
Source: *BioIn 5, 7; NewCol 75; WebBD 80*

Cramer, Polly
American. Journalist
b. Oct 14, 1903 in Garfield, Kentucky
d. May 13, 1981 in Palm Springs, California
Source: *ForWC 70; WhoAmW 77*

Cramm, Gottfried von, Baron
German. Tennis Player, Socialite
b. 1909
d. Nov 8, 1976 in Cairo, Egypt
Source: *BioIn 11*

Cramp, Charles Henry
American. Shipping Executive, Architect
Pres., Cramp Shipbuilding Co., 1879-1903.
b. May 9, 1828 in Philadelphia, Pennsylvania
d. Jun 6, 1913 in Philadelphia, Pennsylvania
Source: *AmBi; NatCAB 5; TwCBDA; WebBD 80*

Crampton, Bruce Sidney
"Iron Man"
Australian. Golfer
Has won over $1 million; won Vardon Trophy for low score average of 70.576, 1973.
b. Sep 28, 1935 in Sydney, Australia
Source: *WhoAm 80, 82; WhoGolf*

Cranach, Lucas
German. Artist, Designer
b. Oct 4, 1472 in Kronach, Germany
d. Oct 16, 1553 in Weimar, Germany
Source: *AtlBL; REn*

Crandall, Del(mar Wesley)
American. Baseball Player, Baseball Manager
Catcher, 1949-66; hit 15 or more home runs in eight seasons, 1953-60.
b. Mar 5, 1930 in Ontario, California
Source: *BaseEn 85; WhoAm 74; WhoProB 73*

Crandall, Prudence
American. Educator, Abolitionist
Tried unsuccessfully, to open school for Negro girls; prosecuted in famed case.
b. 1803 in Hopkinton, Rhode Island
d. 1889 in Elk Falls, Kansas
Source: *DcAmB; NewCol 75; NotAW*

Crane, Bob
American. Actor
Played Colonel Robert Hogan in "Hogan's
Heroes," 1965-71.
b. Jul 13, 1928 in Waterbury, Connecticut
d. Jun 29, 1978 in Scottsdale, Arizona
Source: *IntMPA 77; WhoAm 74; WhoHol A*

Crane, Cheryl
American. Celebrity Relative
Daughter of Lana Turner; killed reputed
gangster Johnny Stompanato, Apr 4, 1958.
b. 1944
Source: *What 8*

Crane, Daniel B
American. Politician
Rep. congressman from IL, 1978--; censured
by US House, Jul 1983, for sexual
relations with page.
b. Jan 10, 1936 in Chicago, Illinois
Source: *AlmAP 80, 82, 84; CngDr 81, 83;
WhoAm 80, 82, 84; WhoAmP 81, 83;
WhoMW 80, 82*

Crane, Hart
American. Poet
Major poetry collections: *White Buildings,*
1926; *The Bridge,* 1930.
b. Jul 21, 1899 in Garrettsville, Ohio
d. Apr 27, 1932
Source: *LongCTC; ModAL, S1; OhA&B;
OxAmL; OxEng; PenC AM; RAdv 1; REn;
REnAL; SixAP; TwCA, SUP; TwCLC 2;
TwCWr; WebAB; WebE&AL; WhDW; WhAm
1; WhoTwCL; WorAl*

Crane, Les
American. TV Host
Had spoken word record hit with *Desiderata,*
1960s.
b. 1934 in Long Beach, California
Source: *BioIn 7; NewYTET*

Crane, Nathalia Clara Ruth
American. Poet, Author
Wrote notable verse collection: *Janitor's Boy*
at age 11.
b. Aug 11, 1913 in New York, New York
Source: *AmAu&B; ChhPo, S1, S2; ConAmL;
DcLEL; InWom; LinLib L; OxAmL; REnAL;
ScF&FL 1; WhLit*

Crane, Philip Miller
American. Congressman
b. Nov 3, 1930 in Chicago, Illinois
Source: *CurBio 80; WhoAm 82*

Crane, Richard O
American. Actor
Appeared in *Susan and God,* 1940; *Happy
Land,* 1943.
b. Jun 6, 1918 in Newcastle, Indiana
d. Mar 9, 1969 in California
Source: *FilmEn; WhScrn 74, 77; WhoHol B*

Crane, Roy(ston Campbell)
American. Cartoonist
b. Nov 22, 1901 in Abilene, Texas
d. Jul 7, 1977 in Orlando, Florida
Source: *ConAu 89; WhoAm 74; WhoAmA 73;
WhoWor 78*

Crane, Stephen
American. Author, Journalist, Poet
Wrote novels *Maggie: A Girl of the Streets,*
1893; *The Red Badge of Courage,* 1895.
b. Nov 1, 1871 in Newark, New Jersey
d. Jun 5, 1900 in Badenweiler, Germany
Source: *AmAu; AmAu&B; AmBi; AmWr;
ApCAB SUP; AtlBL; BbD; BiD&SB; CasWL;
Chambr 3; ChhPo; CnDAL; CnE&AP; CrtT
3; CyWA; DcAmAu; DcAmB; DcLEL;
DcNAA; EncAB-H; EvLB; LongCTC; ModAL;
OxAmL; OxEng; PenC AM; RAdv 1;
RComWL; REn; REnAL; TwCBDA; WebAB;
WebE&AL; WhAm 1*

Crane, Walter
English. Illustrator, Artist
b. Aug 15, 1845 in Liverpool, England
d. Mar 15, 1915 in London, England
Source: *Alli SUP; CarSB; ChhPo, S1, S2;
IlsBYP; JBA 34, 51; NewC; Str&VC;
WhoChL*

Cranko, John
South African. Dancer, Choreographer
b. Aug 15, 1927 in Rustenberg, South Africa
d. Jun 26, 1973
Source: *ConAu 45; CurBio 70, 73; NewYTBE
73; WhoWor 78*

Crankshaw, Edward
British. Author, Journalist
b. Jan 3, 1909 in Woodford, England
d. Nov 29, 1984 in England
Source: *AnObit 1984; ConAu 25R; LongCTC;
TwCA SUP; Who 74; WhoWor 74*

Cranmer, Thomas
English. Religious Leader
Archbishop of Canterbury, 1533; burned at
   stake for heresy, 1556.
b. Jul 2, 1489 in Aslacton, England
d. Mar 21, 1556 in Oxford, England
Source: *BrAu; CasWL; Chambr 1; CroE&S;
DcEnL; DcLEL; EvLB; NewC; OxEng;
OxMus; PenC ENG; REn; WebE&AL;
WhDW; WorAl*

Cranston, Alan MacGregor
American. Senator
Dem. senator from CA, 1969--.
b. Jun 19, 1914 in Palo Alto, California
Source: *BiDrAC; CurBio 69; IntWW 74;
WhoAm 82; WhoAmP 73; WhoGov 72*

Cranston, Toller
Canadian. Figure Skater
World champion, 1974.
b. 1949 in Hamilton Lake, Ontario
Source: *BioIn 11; CanWW 79; NewYTBS 77*

Crapper, Thomas
English. Engineer
Invented valve and siphon arrangement that
   made modern flush toilet possible.
b. 1837 in Yorkshire, England
d. Jan 17, 1910
Source: *BioIn 8*

Crapsey, Adelaide
American. Poet
Her poetry was posthumously published in
   Verse, 1914; invented "cinquain" verse
   form.
b. Sep 9, 1878 in New York, New York
d. Oct 8, 1914 in Saranac Lake, New York
Source: *AmAu&B; ChhPo; CnDAL; ConAmL;
DcAmB; DcNAA; InWom; LibW; NotAW;
OxAmL; REn; REnAL; TwCA; WomWWA 14*

Crashaw, Richard
English. Poet
Best known for his religious verse.
b. 1613 in London, England
d. Aug 21, 1649 in Loreto, Italy
Source: *Alli; AtlBL; BiD&SB; BrAu; CasWL;
Chambr 1; ChhPo, S1, S2; CnE&AP;
CroE&S; CrtT 1; DcEnA; DcEnL; DcEuL;
DcLEL; EvLB; LuthC 75; McGEWB; MouLC
1; NewC; OxEng; PenC ENG; RAdv 1; REn;
WebE&AL; WhDW*

Crassus, Marcus Lincinius
Roman. General
b. 115 BC
d. Jun 6, 53 in Carrhae, Mesopotamia
Source: *REn*

Crater, Joseph Force
American. Judge
Disappeared Aug 6, 1930; declared legally
   dead, Jul 1937.
b. 1889 in Easton, Pennsylvania
d. 1937
Source: *BioIn 6; WebAB*

Crauste, Michel
French. Sportsman
b. 1934
Source: *BioIn 9*

Craven, Frank
American. Actor, Director, Dramatist
Played stage manager in Broadway, film
   versions of *Our Town.*
b. 1878 in Boston, Massachusetts
d. Sep 1, 1945 in Beverly Hills, California
Source: *AmAu&B; CurBio 45; DcAmB S3;
FilmgC; MotPP; MovMk; NotNAT B; ObitOF
79; OxThe; Vers A; WhAm 2; WhScrn 74,
77; WhThe; WhoHol B*

Craven, Thomas
American. Art Critic, Author
Art popularizer, 1930s, promoting American
   regional art.
b. Jan 6, 1889 in Salina, Kansas
d. Feb 27, 1969
Source: *Alli SUP; AmAu&B; AuBYP; ConAu
97; CurBio 44, 69; REnAL; SmATA 22;
TwCA, SUP; WhAm 5*

Cravens, Rupert Thomas
American. Clergyman, Songwriter
b. 1911
Source: *BioIn 9*

Crawford, Broderick
American. Actor
Won Oscar, 1949, for *All the King's Men:*
   known for TV's "Highway Patrol," 1955-
   59.
b. Dec 9, 1911 in Philadelphia, Pennsylvania
d. Apr 26, 1986 in Rancho Mirage,
   California
Source: *BiDFilm; BiE&WWA; BioNews 74;
CelR; CurBio 50; FilmgC; IntMPA 80, 81,
82; MotPP; MovMk; NewYTBS 77; WhoAm
80, 82; WhoHol A; WhoWor 74; WorAl*

Crawford, Cheryl
American. Producer
Among founders, Group Theatre, 1930-37;
produced *Porgy and Bess; Sweet Bird of
Youth.*
b. Sep 24, 1902 in Akron, Ohio
Source: *BiE&WWA; CurBio 45; EncMT;
EncWT; InWom; NewYTBS 80; NotNAT;
PIP&P; WhoAm 74, 76, 78, 80, 82;
WhoAmW 77; WhoThe 77, 81; WhoWor 74*

Crawford, Christina
American. Actress, Author
Daughter of Joan Crawford; wrote *Mommy
Dearest,* 1978; Faye Dunaway starred in
movie, 1981.
b. Jun 11, 1939 in Hollywood, California
Source: *BioIn 11; ConAu 85; NewYTBS 79;
WhoHol A; WrDr 82*

Crawford, Francis Marion
Italian. Author, Historian
Wrote romantic novels with historical
backgrounds; best known for *In the Palace
of the King,* 1900.
b. Aug 2, 1854 in Bagni di Lucca, Italy
d. Apr 9, 1909 in Sorrento, Italy
Source: *Alli SUP; AmAu; AmAu&B; AmBi;
ApCAB; BbD; BiD&SB; Chambr 3; CnDAL;
DcAmAu; DcAmB; DcBiA; DcEnA, AP;
DcLEL; DcNAA; EvLB; LongCTC; OxAmL;
OxEng; PenC AM; REn; REnAL; TwCBDA;
WebAB, 79; WhAm 1*

Crawford, Jack (John Shea)
American. Hockey Player
Defenseman, Boston, 1937-50.
b. Oct 26, 1916 in Dublin, Ontario
d. Jan 19, 1973 in Cape Cod, Massachusetts
Source: *BioIn 9; HocEn; WhoHcky 73*

Crawford, James Strickland
American. Jazz Musician
b. Jan 4, 1910 in Memphis, Tennessee
Source: *WhoJazz 72*

Crawford, Jim
American. Boat Racer
b. 1924
Source: *BioIn 10*

Crawford, Joan
[Lucille LeSueur]
American. Actress
Won Oscar for *Mildred Pierce,* 1945;
relationship with daughter subject of novel,
film *Mommie Dearest,* 1978, 1981.
b. Mar 23, 1908 in San Antonio, Texas
d. May 13, 1977 in New York, New York
Source: *CelR; FilmgC; ForWC 70; InWom;
IntMPA 75, 76, 77; IntWW 74; MovMk;
OxFilm; ThFT; TwYS; WhoAm 74; WhoAmW
77; WhoWest 84; WhoWor 78*

Crawford, John Edmund
American. Psychologist, Author
Specialist, child psychology; wrote *Better
Ways of Growing Up,* 1949, *Milestones for
Modern Teens,* 1954.
b. Jan 21, 1904 in Pittsburgh, Pennsylvania
d. Oct 12, 1971
Source: *ConAu 17R, P-2; SmATA 3*

Crawford, Michael Patrick
[Michael Dumble-Smith]
American. Actor
Appeared in films *A Funny Thing Happened
On the Way to the Forum,* 1966, *Hello,
Dolly,* 1969.
b. Jan 19, 1942 in Salisbury, England
Source: *FilmEn; FilmgC; IntMPA 75, 76, 77,
78, 79, 80, 81, 82; WhoHol A; WhoThe 77,
81; WhoWor 74*

Crawford, Sam(uel Earl)
"Wahoo Sam"
American. Baseball Player
Outfielder, 1899-1917; led NL in home runs,
1901, AL, 1908.
b. Apr 18, 1880 in Wahoo, Nebraska
d. Jun 15, 1968 in Hollywood, California
Source: *BaseEn 85; BioIn 3, 7, 8; WhoProB
73*

Crawford, Thomas
American. Sculptor
b. Mar 22, 1813 in New York, New York
d. Oct 10, 1857 in London, England
Source: *AmBi; ApCAB; BiAUS; DcAmB;
Drake; OxAmL; TwCBDA; WhAm HS*

Crawford, William Hulfish
American. Cartoonist
Political cartoonist Newark, *News,* 1938-77;
work appeared in over 700 newspapers.
b. Mar 18, 1913 in Hammond, Indiana
d. Jan 6, 1982 in Washington, District of
Columbia
Source: *ConAu 105; WhoAm 74, 76, 78;
WhoAmA 73, 76, 78*

Craxi, "Bettino" (Benedetto)
Italian. Political Leader
First Socialist to become prime minister of
Italy, 1983-86.
b. Feb 24, 1934 in Milan, Italy
Source: CurBio 84; IntWW 80, 81, 82, 83;
NewYTBS 83; WhoEIO 82

Crazy Horse
American. Indian Chief
One of leaders at Little Big Horn, 1876; led
Oglala Sioux in Black Hills.
b. 1842 in Rapid Creek, South Dakota
d. Sep 5, 1877 in Camp Robinson, Nebraska
Source: AmBi; ApCAB; DcAmB; REnAW;
WebAB; WhAm HS; WhoMilH 76; WorAl

Creach, "Papa" (John)
American. Musician
b. May 17, 1917 in Beaver Falls,
Pennsylvania
Source: BioIn 9; WhoRock 81

Cream
[Ginger Baker; Jack Bruce; Eric Clapton]
English. Music Group
First 1960s "supergroup," formed 1966-68;
hits included "Sunshine of Your Love,"
"Strange Brew."
Source: EncPR&S 74; IlEncRk; RkOn 84;
RkOneH

Crean, Robert
American. Dramatist
b. 1923
d. May 6, 1974 in New Rochelle, New York
Source: NewYTBS 74; WhAm 6

Creasey, John
English. Author
b. Sep 17, 1908 in Surrey, England
d. Jun 9, 1973 in Salisbury, England
Source: Au&Wr 71; ConAu 5R, 41R; CurBio
63, 73; EncMys; LongCTC; MnBBF;
NewYTBE 73; REn; TwCWr; WhAm 6;
WorAu

Creed, Linda
American. Songwriter, Singer
With Thom Bell wrote hits "You Make Me
Feel Brand New," 1974, "Could It Be I'm
Falling in Love?," 1973.
b. 1949
d. Apr 10, 1986 in Ambler, Pennsylvania
Source: BioIn 10

Creedence Clearwater Revival
[Douglas Ray Clifford; Stuart Cook; John
Fogerty; Thomas Fogerty]
American. Music Group
San Francisco rock band of late 1960s, early
1970s; hits "Proud Mary," "Bad Moon
Rising."
Source: EncPR&S 74; IlEncRk; RkOn 84

Creel, George
American. Public Official, Journalist, Author
Chm., Woodrow Wilson's com. on public
information, 1917-19, directing govt.
propaganda in WW I.
b. Dec 1, 1876 in Lafayette County, Missouri
d. Oct 3, 1953 in San Francisco, California
Source: ConAu 115; DcLB 25; McGEWB;
WebBD 80

Creeley, Robert White
American. Author, Poet
b. May 21, 1926 in Arlington, Massachusetts
Source: AmAu&B; Au&Wr 71; CasWL;
ConAu 1R; ConLC 1, 2, 4, 8, 11, 15; ConP
70, 75; CroCAP; DrAF 76; DrAP 75; IntWW
74; ModAL, S1; PenC AM; RAdv 1; REnAL;
WebE&AL; WhoAm 74, 76, 78, 80, 82;
WhoTwCL; WhoWor 78; WorAu; WrDr 80

Cregar, Laird (Samuel)
American. Actor
Played Jack the Ripper in The Lodger, 1944.
b. Jul 28, 1916 in Philadelphia, Pennsylvania
d. Dec 8, 1944 in Los Angeles, California
Source: BiDFilm; CmMov; CurBio 45;
FilmgC; HolP 40; MovMk; NotNAT B;
ObitOF 79; WhScrn 74, 77; WhoHol B

Creighton, Edward
American. Businessman
Pioneer telegraph builder, established coast-to-
coast service, 1961.
b. Aug 31, 1820 in Licking Co., Ohio
d. Nov 5, 1874 in Omaha, Nebraska
Source: BioIn 3, 5; DcAmB; DcCathB;
NatCAB 22; WhAm HS

Creighton, Fred(erick)
Canadian. Hockey Coach
Coached Atlanta Flames, 1974-79, Boston
Bruins, 1979-80.
b. Jul 14, 1933 in Hamiota, Manitoba
Source: HocEn; WhoAm 82

Creighton, Thomas H(awk)
American. Architect, Author
Editor, *Progressive Architecture,* 1946-63.
b. May 19, 1904 in Philadelphia,
Pennsylvania
Source: *AmArch 70; AmAu&B; BioIn 1;
ConAu 1R; WhoAm 76, 78, 80, 82, 84;
WhoWest 74, 76, 78*

Creme, Lol
see: 10 CC

Cremer, William Randal, Sir
English. Reformer
Secretary, Workmen's Peace Assn., 1871-
1908; won Nobel Peace Prize, 1903.
b. Mar 18, 1838 in Fareham, England
d. Jul 22, 1908 in London, England
Source: *BioIn 5, 9, 10, 11; LinLib S; NewCol
75; WebBD 80*

Cremieux, Isaac-Adolphe
French. Statesman
b. Apr 30, 1796 in Nimes, France
d. Feb 10, 1880 in Paris, France
Source: *BioIn 11; NewCol 75*

Crenna, Richard
American. Actor
Starred in "Our Miss Brooks," 1952-56; "The
Real McCoys," 1957-63; films include *The
Flamingo Kid,* 1985.
b. Nov 30, 1927 in Los Angeles, California
Source: *FilmgC; IntMPA 75, 76, 77, 78, 79,
80, 81, 82; MotPP; MovMk; WhoAm 74, 76,
78, 80, 82; WhoHol A*

Crenshaw, Ben Daniel
American. Golfer
Won 1984 Master's Tournament.
b. Jan 11, 1952 in Austin, Texas
Source: *BioNews 75; CurBio 85; NewYTBE
73; WhoAm 82, 84; WhoGolf*

Crescentini, Girolamo
Italian. Opera Singer
b. Feb 2, 1762 in Urbania, Italy
d. Apr 24, 1846 in Naples, Italy
Source: *NewEOp 71*

Crespin, Regine
French. Opera Singer
b. Mar 23, 1927 in Marseilles, France
Source: *IntWW 74; Who 74; WhoAm 74, 76,
78, 80, 82; WhoAmW 77; WhoMus 72;
WhoWor 78*

Creston, Paul
American. Composer
b. Oct 10, 1906 in New York, New York
d. Aug 24, 1985 in Poway, California
Source: *AmSCAP 66; DcCM; REnAL;
WhoAm 74, 76, 78, 80, 82; WhoMus 72;
WhoWest 84; WhoWor 78*

Cret, Paul P(hilippe)
American. Architect, Educator
Designed Washington's Folger Library;
Federal Reserve Building, 1937.
b. Oct 23, 1876 in Lyons, France
d. Sep 8, 1945 in Philadelphia, Pennsylvania
Source: *CurBio 42; DcAmB S3; WebBD 80*

Crevecoeur, Michel-Guillaume Jean de
[J Hector St. John, pseud.]
French. Author
b. Jan 31, 1735 in Caen, France
d. Nov 12, 1813 in Sarcelles, France
Source: *AmAu; AmAu&B; CasWL; ChhPo;
CnDAL; CyWA; DcAmB; DcLEL; DcNAA;
EvLB; OxAmL; REn; REnAL; WebAB;
WebE&AL; WhAm HS*

Crews, Harry Eugene
American. Author
Southern gothic novelist who wrote *Florida
Frenzy,* 1982.
b. Jun 6, 1935 in Almo, Georgia
Source: *AuNews 1; BioIn 8, 10, 11; BioNews
74; ConAu 25R; ConLC 6; DrAF 76;
NewYTBS 78; WhoAm 76, 78, 80, 82, 84*

Crews, Laura Hope
American. Actress
Played Aunt Pittypat in *Gone With the
Wind,* 1939.
b. Dec 12, 1879 in San Francisco, California
d. Nov 13, 1942 in New York, New York
Source: *CurBio 43; Film 1; FilmgC; InWom;
MotPP; MovMk; NotAW; NotNAT; ThFT;
Vers A; WhScrn 74, 77; WhThe; WhoHol B;
WhoStg 1908*

Crichton, Charles
English. Director
Films include *Hue and Cry,* 1946, *Lavender
Hill Mob,* 1951.
b. Aug 6, 1910 in Wallasey, England
Source: *CmMov; DcFM; FilmgC; IntMPA 75,
76, 77, 78, 79, 80, 81, 82; MovMk; OxFilm;
WorEFlm*

Crichton, James
Scottish. Adventurer, Scholar
b. Aug 19, 1560 in Eliock, Scotland
d. Jul 3, 1582 in Mantua, Italy
Source: *Alli; BrAu; NewC; OxEng*

Crichton, (John) Michael
[Jeffrey Hudson; John Lange, pseuds.]
American. Author, Director
Wrote *Andromeda Strain,* 1969, *Terminal Man,* 1972; directed *Westworld,* 1973, *Coma,* 1977.
b. Oct 23, 1942 in Chicago, Illinois
Source: *AmAu&B; Au&Wr 71; AuNews 2; CelR; ConAu 25R; ConLC 2, 6; ConNov 76; FilmgC; IntMPA 75, 76, 77, 78, 79, 80, 81, 82; SmATA 9; WhoAm 82; WhoSciF; WorAu; WrDr 82*

Crichton, Robert
American. Author
b. Jan 29, 1925 in Albuquerque, New Mexico
Source: *AuNews 1; BioNews 74; ConAu 17R; WrDr 80*

Crick, Francis Harry Compton
English. Biologist
Co-discovered DNA with James Watson, 1953; shared 1962 Nobel Prize.
b. Jun 8, 1916 in Northampton, England
Source: *CelR; ConAu 113; CurBio 83; IntWW 74; Who 74; WhoWor 78*

Crile, George Washington
American. Surgeon, Author
Developed nerve-block anesthesia.
b. Nov 11, 1864 in Chili, Ohio
d. Jan 7, 1943 in Cleveland, Ohio
Source: *CurBio 43; DcAmB S3; WebBD 80*

Crippen, Hawley Harvey
English. Murderer
Capture aided by one of earliest uses of shipboard radio telephone, 1910.
b. 1862 in Michigan
d. Nov 23, 1910 in Pentonville, England
Source: *BioIn 11; DrInf; WhDW*

Crippen, Robert Laurel
American. Astronaut
b. Sep 11, 1937 in Beaumont, Texas
Source: *IntWW 74; WhoAm 82; WhoS&SW 82*

Cripps, Stafford, Sir
English. Statesman, Lawyer
b. Apr 24, 1889
d. Apr 21, 1952
Source: *CurBio 40, 48, 52*

Crisler, "Fritz" (Herbert Orin)
American. Football Coach
Won national championship, 1947.
b. Jan 12, 1899 in Earlville, Illinois
d. Aug 19, 1982 in Ann Arbor, Michigan
Source: *ConAu 107; CurBio 48, 82; NewYTBS 82; WhoAm 74; WhoFtbl 74*

Crisp, Donald
American. Actor
Won Oscar for *How Green Was My Valley,* 1941.
b. Apr 18, 1880 in Aberfeldy, Scotland
d. May 26, 1974 in Van Nuys, California
Source: *BiDFilm; CmMov; Film 1; FilmgC; MotPP; MovMk; NewYTBS 74; ObitOF 79; OxFilm; TwYS; Vers A; WhAm 6; WhScrn 77; WhoHol B; WorAl; WorEFlm*

Crisp, Quentin, pseud.
[Denis Pratt]
English. Author
Noted for autobiography *The Naked Civil Servant,* 1968.
b. Dec 25, 1908 in Sutton, England
Source: *ConAu 116*

Crispin, Edmund, pseud.
[Robert Bruce Montgomery]
English. Author, Composer
Best known for detective novels featuring Gervase Fen. Montgomery.
b. Oct 2, 1921 in Buckinghamshire, England
d. Sep 15, 1978 in England
Source: *Au&Wr 71; ConAu 104; EncMys; WorAu*

Criss, Charlie (Charles W)
American. Basketball Player
b. Nov 6, 1949 in Valhalla, New York
Source: *BioIn 11; OfNBA 81*

Criss, Peter
[Peter Crisscovla; Kiss]
American. Singer, Musician
Singer, drummer for Kiss, 1972-80; wrote hit song "Beth" for wife, 1976.
b. Dec 20, 1947 in Brooklyn, New York
Source: *BioIn 12; RkOn 74; RolSEnR 83*

Crist, Judith Klein
American. Movie Critic
Film critic for *TV Guide,* 1965--, *Saturday Review,* 1980--.
b. May 22, 1922 in New York, New York
Source: *AuNews 1; CelR; ConAu 81; ForWC 70; IntMPA 75, 76, 77, 78, 79, 80, 81, 82; WhoAm 74, 76, 78, 80, 82; WhoE 74; WhoWorJ 78; WrDr 82*

Cristal, Linda
[Marta Victoria Moya Burges]
Argentine. Actress
Appeared in TV's "High Chaparral," 1967-71.
b. Feb 24, 1936 in Buenos Aires, Argentina
Source: FilmgC; MotPP; WhoAmW 74, 72;
WhoHol A

Cristofer, Michael
[Michael Procaccino]
American. Dramatist, Actor
b. Jan 22, 1945 in Trenton, New Jersey
Source: WhoAm 80, 82

Crittenden, Christopher
American. Historian
b. Dec 1, 1902 in Wake Forest, North
Carolina
d. Oct 13, 1969
Source: AmAu&B; WhAm 5

Crittenden, John Jordan
American. Lawyer, Politician
Held govt. positions, from governor of KY
to attorney general, senator, congressman;
opposed slavery.
b. Sep 10, 1787 in Versailles, Kentucky
d. Jul 26, 1863 in Frankfort, Kentucky
Source: AmBi; ApCAB; BiAUS; BiDSA;
BiDrAC; BiDrUSE; CyAG; DcAmB; Drake;
EncAB-H; HarEnUS; TwCBDA; WebAB;
WhAm HS; WhAmP; WorAl

Crittendon, Thomas L
American. General
Served in Union Army, 1861-64; promoted to
maj. gen. for distinguished service at
Battle of Shiloh, 1862.
b. May 15, 1819 in Russellville, Kentucky
d. Oct 23, 1893 in Annandale, New York
Source: NewCol 75; TwCBDA; WebAMB;
WhAm HS

Crittenton, Charles Nelson
American. Businessman, Philanthropist
b. Feb 20, 1833 in Henderson, New York
d. Nov 16, 1909 in San Francisco, California
Source: DcAmB

Critters
[Don Ciccone; Christopher Darway; Jack
Decker; Kenneth Gorka; James Ryan]
American. Music Group
Source: BiDAmM

Crivelli, Carlo
Italian. Artist
b. 1435 in Venice, Italy
d. 1493
Source: AtlBL

Croce, Benedetto
Italian. Statesman, Philosopher, Critic
Four-volume Philosophy of the Spirit, 1902-17,
reacted to 19th c. materialism, attempting
to rekindle spiritualism.
b. Feb 25, 1866 in Pescasseroli, Italy
d. Nov 20, 1952 in Naples, Italy
Source: AtlBL; CasWL; ClDMEL; CurBio 44,
53; DcEuL; EncWL; EvEuW; LongCTC;
NewC; OxEng; PenC EUR; REn; TwCA,
SUP; TwCWr; WhAm 3; WhoLA

Croce, Jim
American. Singer, Songwriter
Hits include "Operator," 1972; "Bad Bad
Leroy Brown," 1973.
b. Jan 10, 1943 in Philadelphia, Pennsylvania
d. Sep 20, 1973 in Natchitoches, Louisiana
Source: BioIn 10, 11; BioNews 74; EncPR&S
74; RkOn 74

Crocker, Charles
American. Railroad Executive
Central Pacific head who used Chinese
laborers to link with Union Pacific, 1869.
b. Sep 16, 1822 in Troy, New York
d. Aug 14, 1888 in Monterey, California
Source: AmBi; ApCAB; BioIn 3; DcAmB;
REnAW; TwCBDA; WebAB; WhAm HS

Crockett, Davy (David)
American. Frontiersman
Served as scout under Andrew Jackson
during Creek War, 1813-14; died at
Alamo.
b. Aug 17, 1786 in Greene City, Tennessee
d. Mar 6, 1836 in The Alamo, Texas
Source: Alli; AmAu&B; AmBi; ApCAB;
BiAUS; BiD&SB; BiDrAC; CyWA; DcAmAu;
DcAmB; DcNAA; Drake; EncAB-H; FilmgC;
OxAmL; OxFilm; PenC AM; REn; REnAL;
TwCBDA; WebAB; WhAm HS; WhAmP

Crockett, Ivory
American. Track Athlete
Source: BioIn 10

Crockett, James Underwood
American. Author, Horticulturist
b. Oct 9, 1915 in Haverhill, Massachusetts
d. Jul 11, 1979 in Jamaica
Source: BioIn 11; ConAu 33R, 89

Crockett, S(amuel) R(utherford)
Scottish. Clergyman, Author
Children's books include Sir Toady Crusoe,
1905.
b. Sep 24, 1860 in Little Duchrae, Scotland
d. Apr 21, 1914
Source: ConAu 116; LongCEL; PenC ENG

Croesus
Ruler
Last king of Lydia, defeated by Cyrus the
Great, 546 BC; known for great wealth.
b. 560 BC
d. 546 BC
Source: *LinLib S; NewC; REn; WhDW*

Croft, Arthur C
American. Publisher
Published *Personnel Journal;* director,
American Arbitration Assn., 1950-75.
b. May 26, 1890 in Cleveland, Ohio
d. Sep 6, 1975
Source: *BioIn 2, 3; CurBio 52; WhAm 7*

Croft, Michael
English. Director
Founder, National Youth Theatre, 1956.
b. Mar 8, 1922 in Oswestry, England
Source: *Au&Wr 71; EncWT; Who 82;
WhoThe 81*

Croft-Cooke, Rupert
English. Author
Detective novels examples of classic British
mystery.
b. Jun 20, 1903 in Edenbridge, England
d. 1979 in Bournemouth, England
Source: *Au&Wr 71; CathA 1952; ConAu 9R,
89, 4NR; LongCTC; TwCA, SUP; Who 74;
WhoWor 78; WrDr 76*

Crofts, Dash
[Seals and Crofts]
American. Singer, Songwriter
b. 1940 in Cisco, Texas
Source: *BkPepl; WhoAm 82*

Crofts, Freeman Willis
Irish. Author
Mystery tales include *French Strikes Oil,*
1952.
b. Jun 1879 in Dublin, Ireland
d. Apr 11, 1957
Source: *ConAu 115; EncMys; LongCTC*

Crofts, James
see: Monmouth, James Scott, Duke of

Crohn, Burrill Bernard
American. Physician
Best known for research on ileitis, commonly
called Crohn's disease; wrote three books
on subject.
b. Jun 13, 1884 in New York, New York
d. Jul 29, 1983 in New Milford, Connecticut
Source: *AnObit 1983; BiDrACP 79; ConAu
110; NewYTBS 83; WhAm i; WhoWorJ 72*

Croker, "Boss" (Richard)
American. Politician
b. Nov 23, 1841 in Clonakilty, Ireland
d. Apr 29, 1922 in New York, New York
Source: *AmBi; DcAmB; WhAm 1*

Croly, Herbert David
American. Journalist
b. Jan 23, 1869 in New York, New York
d. May 17, 1930 in Santa Barbara, California
Source: *AmAu&B; BioIn 1, 2, 3, 5; DcAmB
S1; DcNAA; EncAB-H; OxAmL; TwCA;
WebBD 80*

Croly, Jane Cunningham
"Jennie June"
American. Journalist, Feminist
Edited *Demorest's Monthly Magazine,* 1860-
87; founded Sorosis Club, 1868.
b. Dec 19, 1829 in Leicestershire, England
d. Dec 23, 1901 in New York, New York
Source: *NotAW*

Crome, John
"Old Crome"
English. Artist
Founded Norwich school of painting; known
for romanticized scenes of rural life.
b. Dec 22, 1768 in Norwich, England
d. Apr 22, 1821 in Norwich, England
Source: *AtlBL; BioIn 1, 2, 4, 5, 8, 10, 11;
NewC*

Cromie, Robert Allen
American. Author, Journalist
b. Feb 28, 1909 in Detroit, Michigan
Source: *AmAu&B; ConAu 1R, 1NR; WhoAm
76, 78, 80, 82; WhoMW 74*

Cromley, Raymond Avalon
American. Journalist
b. Aug 23, 1910 in Tulare, California
Source: *WhoAm 78, 80, 82*

Crompton, Richmal
see: Lamburn, Richard Crompton

Cromwell, Dean Bartlett
"The Maker of Champions"
American. Track Coach
Track and field coach; led US Olympic team,
1948.
b. Sep 20, 1879 in Turner, Oregon
d. Aug 3, 1962 in Los Angeles, California
Source: *WhoTr&F 73*

Cromwell, John
American. Director, Actor
Directed *Of Human Bondage,* 1964.
b. Dec 23, 1887 in Toledo, Ohio
d. Sep 26, 1979 in Santa Barbara, California
Source: *BiDFilm; CmMov; ConAu 89; DcFM;*
FilmgC; MovMk; NatPD; NotNAT; OxFilm;
WhoHol A; WhoThe 77; WorEFlm

Cromwell, Nolan
American. Football Player
b. Jan 30, 1955 in Smith Center, Kansas
Source: *BioIn 12; FootReg 81*

Cromwell, Oliver
"Old Noll"
English. Statesman, General
Ruled England as Lord Protector, 1653-58,
    after execution of Charles I; favored
    religious freedom.
b. Apr 25, 1599 in Huntingdon, England
d. Sep 3, 1658
Source: *Alli; McGEWB; NewC; OxMus;*
PIP&P; REn; WhDW; WorAl

Cromwell, Richard
English. Statesman
Son of Oliver Cromwell, who succeeded
    father as Lord Protector, 1658-59, until
    restoration of monarchy, 1660.
b. Oct 4, 1626
d. Jul 13, 1712
Source: *BioIn 9; DcBiPP; Dis&D; NewCol 75*

Cromwell, Thomas
[Earl of Essex]
English. Statesman
b. 1485 in Putney, England
d. Jul 28, 1540 in London, England
Source: *Alli; DcEnL; McGEWB; NewC; REn*

Cronin, A(rchibald) J(oseph)
American. Author, Physician
Best known for *The Citadel,* 1937; *Keys of*
    the Kingdom, 1941.
b. Jul 19, 1896 in Helensburgh, England
d. Jan 6, 1981 in Glion, Switzerland
Source: *Au&Wr 71; CasWL; CathA 1930;*
Chambr 3; ConAu 1R, 102, 5NR; ConNov
76; CurBio 42, 81; DcLEL; EncWL; EvLB;
FilmgC; IntWW 74; LongCTC; ModBrL;
NewC; Novels; PenC ENG; RAdv 1; REn;
SmATA 25N; SUP; TwCA; TwCWr; WhNAA;
Who 74; WhoWor 74; WrDr 76, 82

Cronin, Joe (Joseph Edward)
American. Baseball Player, Baseball Executive
Infielder, 1926-1945; pres., AL, 1959-74; Hall
    of Fame, 1956.
b. Oct 12, 1906 in San Francisco, California
d. Sep 7, 1984 in Osterville, Massachusetts
Source: *AnObit 1984; BaseEn 85; BioIn 10;*
CmCal; CurBio 65; WhoAm 82; WhoProB 73

Cronin, Kevin
see: REO Speedwagon

Cronkite, Walter Leland, Jr.
"Uncle Walter"
American. Broadcast Journalist
Anchored "CBS Evening News," 1962-81;
    host "Universe" TV series.
b. Nov 4, 1916 in Saint Joseph, Missouri
Source: *AuNews 1, 2; BkPepl; CelR; ConAu*
69; CurBio 56; IntMPA 75, 76, 77, 78, 79,
80, 81, 82; IntWW 74; WebAB; WhoAm 74,
76, 78, 80, 82; WhoWor 78; WrDr 76

Cronyn, Hume
Canadian. Actor, Author, Director
Won Tony, 1964, for *Hamlet;* best known
    for *The Gin Game,* 1978, with wife Jessica
    Tandy.
b. Jul 18, 1911 in London, Ontario
Source: *BiE&WWA; CanWW 82; CelR;*
CurBio 56; FilmgC; IntMPA 75, 76, 77, 78,
79, 80, 81, 82; MotPP; MovMk; NewYTBS
74; NotNAT; PIP&P; WhoAm 74, 76, 78, 80,
82; WhoHol A; WhoThe 77, 81; WhoWor 74;
WorAl

Crook, George
American. General
b. Sep 23, 1829 in Dayton, Ohio
d. Mar 21, 1890 in Chicago, Illinois
Source: *AmBi; ApCAB; DcAmB; Drake;*
OhA&B; TwCBDA; WebAB; WhAm HS

Crook, William Grant
American. Physician
Pediatrician who is author of column *Child*
    Care Syndicate, 1965--, books on child
    development.
b. Sep 13, 1917 in Jackson, Tennessee
Source: *WhoAm 80*

Crookes, William, Sir
English. Chemist
b. Jun 17, 1832 in London, England
d. Apr 4, 1919 in London, England
Source: *Alli SUP; BiDPara; McGEWB*

Crooks, Richard Alexander
American. Opera Singer
b. Jun 26, 1900 in Trenton, New Jersey
d. 1972
Source: *BiDAmM; NewEOp 71*

Cropsey, Jasper Francis
American. Artist
Hudson River school painter known for
autumnal scenes of Catskill Mountains.
b. Feb 18, 1823 in Rossville, New York
d. 1900
Source: *AmBi; ApCAB; BnEnAmA; DcAmArt;
DcBrBI; Drake; EarABI; McGDA; NatCAB 1;
NewYHSD; TwCBDA; WhAm 1*

Crosby, Alexander L
American. Author, Journalist
b. Jun 10, 1906 in Cantonsville, Maryland
d. Jan 31, 1980 in Quakertown, Pennsylvania
Source: *AuBYP; ConAu 29R, 93; MorBMP;
SmATA 2, 23*

Crosby, "Bing" (Harry Lillis)
American. Actor, Singer
Won Oscar for *Going My Way,* 1944; biggest
hit "White Christmas," 1942; crooner
known for "road" movies with Bob Hope,
Dorothy Lamour.
b. May 2, 1904 in Tacoma, Washington
d. Oct 14, 1977 in Madrid, Spain
Source: *AmSCAP 66; BiDFilm; BioNews 75;
CelR; ConAu 73; CurBio 41, 53, 78; FilmgC;
IntMPA 75, 76, 77; IntWW 74; MotPP;
MovMk; NewYTBE 70; OxFilm; WebAB;
Who 74; WhoAm 74; WhoHol A; WhoMus
72; WhoProB 73; WhoWor 78; WorEFlm*

Crosby, Bob (George Robert)
American. Band Leader
b. Aug 23, 1913 in Spokane, Washington
Source: *AmSCAP 66; BioIn 2, 3, 4, 5, 9;
FilmgC; IntMPA 75, 76, 77, 78, 79, 80, 81,
82; WhoHol A; WhoJazz 72*

Crosby, Cathy Lee
American. Actress
Co-host of TV show "That's Incredible!"
b. 1949 in Los Angeles, California
Source: *ForWC 70; IntMPA 84; VarWW 85;
WhoHol A*

Crosby, David
[The Byrds; Crosby, Stills, Nash and Young]
American. Singer, Songwriter
b. Aug 14, 1941 in Los Angeles, California
Source: *BiDAmM; BioIn 9; BkPepl; ConMuA
80A; WhoAm 78, 80, 82; WhoRock 81*

Crosby, Enoch
American. Spy
Patriot spy during American Revolution,
1776-80; prototype for title character in
The Spy, by James F. Cooper.
b. 1750 in Cape Cod, Massachusetts
d. 1835
Source: *ApCAB; BioIn 10; Drake; TwCBDA*

Crosby, Fanny (Frances Jane)
American. Writer
Blinded at age 6 weeks; wrote more than
6000 hymns, including "Safe in the Arms
of Jesus."
b. Mar 24, 1820 in Putnam County, New
York
d. Feb 12, 1915
Source: *AmAu&B; ChhPo; DcAmAu; DcNAA;
LibW; LuthC 75; NotAW; REnAL; TwCBDA;
WebE&AL*

Crosby, Floyd Delafield
American. Filmmaker
Films include *The Raven,* 1935; won Oscar
for *Tabu,* 1930-31.
b. Dec 12, 1899 in New York, New York
Source: *VarWW 85*

Crosby, Harry
American. Publisher, Poet
b. 1898 in Boston, Massachusetts
d. Dec 10, 1929 in New York, New York
Source: *AmAu&B; BioIn 10, 11; DcNAA*

Crosby, James Morris
American. Business Executive
Founder, chairman, Resorts International,
Inc., 1968-86; introduced casino gambling
to Atlantic City, 1978.
b. Apr 12, 1927 in Great Neck, New Jersey
d. Apr 10, 1986 in New York, New York
Source: *WhoAm 82*

Crosby, Joan Carew
American. Journalist
b. Feb 14, 1933 in Baltimore, Maryland
Source: *ForWC 70; WhoAm 82*

Crosby, John
American. Conductor
b. Jul 12, 1926 in New York, New York
Source: *WhoAm 74, 76, 78, 80, 82; WhoWest
84; WhoWor 78*

Crosby, John Campbell
American. Journalist
b. May 18, 1912 in Milwaukee, Wisconsin
Source: *ConAu 1R, 4NR; IlsBYP; IntWW 74;
REnAL; WhoAm 74, 76, 78, 80, 82; WhoWor
78; WrDr 76*

Crosby, Kathryn
[Mrs. Bing Crosby; Kathryn Grandstaff;
   Kathryn Grant]
American. Actress
Married Bing, 1957, appeared with family in
   TV Christmas specials.
b. Nov 25, 1933 in Houston, Texas
Source: *IntMPA 75, 76, 77, 78, 79, 80, 81,
82; NewYTBE 71; WhoAm 74, 76, 78, 80,
82; WhoAmW 74*

Crosby, Mary Frances
American. Actress, Celebrity Relative
Featured on "Dallas" TV series as Kristin
   Shepherd, who shot JR Ewing, 1980;
   daughter of Bing Crosby.
b. Sep 14, 1959 in Los Angeles, California
Source: *BioIn 11; VarWW 85*

Crosby, Nathaniel
American. Golfer, Celebrity Relative
Youngest son of Bing Crosby, who won 1981
   US Amateur Golf Championship.
b. 1961
Source: *BioIn 12; NewYTBS 81*

Crosby, Norm(an Lawrence)
American. Comedian
Routines feature mispronounced
   malapropisms.
b. Sep 15, 1927 in Boston, Massachusetts
Source: *WhoAm 80, 82*

Crosby, Percy
American. Cartoonist
b. Dec 8, 1930 in Brooklyn, New York
d. Dec 8, 1964 in New York, New York
Source: *WorECom*

Crosby, Stills, Nash, & Young
[David Crosby; Graham Nash; Stephen Stills;
   Neil Young]
American. Music Group
Hits include "Woodstock"; "Teach Your
   Children," 1970.
Source: *BiDAmM; IlEncRk; RkOn 78*

Crosby, Sumner McKnight
American. Art Historian, Educator
b. Jul 29, 1909 in Minneapolis, Minnesota
d. Nov 16, 1982 in Waterbury, Connecticut
Source: *BioIn 8; ConAu 13R; DrAS 74F;
NewYTBS 82; WhoAm 74, 76, 78, 80, 82;
WhoAmA 73; WhoWor 78*

Crosland, Charles
British. Politician
b. Aug 29, 1918
Source: *Who 74*

Crosley, Powel, Jr.
American. Inventor, Baseball Executive
Marketed first popularly priced radio, 1921;
   co-owner Cincinnati Reds.
b. Sep 18, 1886 in Cincinnati, Ohio
d. Mar 28, 1961 in Cincinnati, Ohio
Source: *CurBio 47, 61; WhAm 4; WhoProB
73*

Crosman, Henrietta
American. Actress
Stage actress who made films, 1930s; best
   known for film *Royal Family of Broadway,*
   1930.
b. 1861 in Wheeling, West Virginia
d. Oct 31, 1944 in Pelham Manor, New
   York
Source: *BioIn 3; Film 2; ObitOF 79; PIP&P;
ThFT; WhScrn 77; WhThe; WhoHol B;
WomWWA 14*

Cross, Ben (Bernard)
English. Actor
Played Olympic runner Harold Abrahams in
   Oscar-winning *Chariots of Fire,* 1981.
b. Dec 16, 1947 in London, England
Source: *BioIn 12; CurBio 84; NewYTBS 81,
82*

Cross, Christopher
[Christopher Geppert]
American. Singer, Songwriter
Number one singles "Sailing," 1980;
   "Arthur's Theme," 1981; won Oscar for
   "Arthur's Theme," 1982.
b. May 3, 1951 in San Antonio, Texas
Source: *BioIn 12; RkOn 85*

Cross, Milton John
American. Radio Performer
Announced Metropolitan Opera broadcasts,
   1931-75.
b. Apr 16, 1897 in New York, New York
d. Jan 3, 1975 in New York, New York
Source: *AmAu&B; CelR; ConAu 53; CurBio
40, 75; NewYTBE 71; ObitOF 79; WhAm 6;
WhScrn 77; WhoAm 74; WorAl*

Cross, Wilbur
American. Educator
b. Apr 10, 1862 in Mansfield, Connecticut
d. Oct 5, 1948 in New Haven, Connecticut
Source: *AmAu&B; DcAmAu; DcAmB S4;
DcLEL; DcNAA; OxAmL; REnAL; TwCA,
SUP; WhAm 2*

Crosse, Rupert
American.
Appeared in film *The Reivers*, 1970; TV
series *The Partners*, 1971-72.
b. 1928 in Nevis, British West Indies
d. Mar 5, 1973 in Nevis, British West Indies
Source: *DrBlPA; InB&W 80; NegAl 83;
WhScrn 77; WhoHol B*

Crossley, Archibald Maddock
American. Pollster
Public opinion analyst; pioneered with Roper,
Gallup in polling techniques.
b. Dec 7, 1896 in Fieldsboro, New Jersey
d. May 1, 1985 in Princeton, New Jersey
Source: *ConAu 116; CurBio 41, 85*

Crossman, Richard Howard Stafford
English. Statesman, Author
b. Dec 15, 1907 in London, England
d. Apr 5, 1974
Source: *Au&Wr 71; ConAu 49, 61; CurBio
47, 74; NewYTBS 74; REn; Who 74;
WhoWor 78; WorAu*

Croter, Vina
see: Delmar, Vina

Crothers, Rachel
American. Dramatist, Director
Wrote plays on role of modern woman:
Susan and God, 1937.
b. Dec 12, 1878 in Bloomington, Illinois
d. Jul 5, 1958 in Danbury, Connecticut
Source: *AmAu&B; CnDAL; CnMD; CnThe;
ConAmA; ConAmL; DcLEL; EncWL; FilmgC;
LongCTC; McGEWD; ModWD; OxAmL;
OxThe; REn; REnAL; REnWD; TwCA, SUP;
WebAB; WhNAA*

Crothers, "Scatman" (Benjamin Sherman)
American. Actor, Musician, Singer
Starred in TV series "Chico and the Man,"
1974-78.
b. May 23, 1910 in Terre Haute, Indiana
Source: *BioIn 10, 11; WhoAm 82; WhoHol A*

Crouch, Marcus
English. Children's Author
b. Feb 12, 1913 in Tohenham, England
Source: *Au&Wr 71; ChhPo, S2; ConAu 9R,
5NR; SmATA 4; WhoChL; WrDr 80*

Crouse, Lindsay Ann
American. Actress
Daughter of Russel Crouse; appeared in film
All the President's Men, 1976.
b. May 12, 1948 in New York, New York
Source: *IntMPA 80, 81, 82, 82; NewYTBS 81*

Crouse, Russel
American. Journalist, Producer
Co-wrote hit Broadway plays *Life with
Father*, 1939, *State of the Union*, 1946;
wrote book from which *The Sound of
Music* was made.
b. Feb 20, 1893 in Findlay, Ohio
d. Apr 3, 1966 in New York, New York
Source: *AmAu&B; AuBYP; BiE&WWA;
CnDAL; ConAu 25R, 77; CurBio 41, 66;
EncMT; McGEWD; ModWD; CnThe;
EncWT; NewCBMT; OhA&B; OxAmL; REn;
REnAL; TwCA SUP; WhAm 4; WorAl*

Crowe, Colin Tradescant, Sir
British. Diplomat
b. Sep 7, 1913 in Yokohama, Japan
Source: *IntWW 74; Who 74; WhoGov 75;
WhoWor 78*

Crowell, Luther Childs
American. Inventor
Invented square-bottomed grocer's bag,
machine to make it, 1872.
b. Sep 7, 1840 in West Dennis,
Massachusetts
d. Sep 16, 1903 in Wellfleet, Massachusetts
Source: *DcAmB; NatCAB 13; WhAm 1*

Crowell, Rodney
American. Musician, Songwriter
Many of his songs recorded by Emmylou
Harris; has produced wife Roseanne Cash's
albums.
b. Aug 7, 1950 in Houston, Texas
Source: *RkOn 85*

Crowley, Aleister (Edward Alexander)
"The Great Beast"
English. Author, Magician
Writer of occult lore, Black Magic rites:
Diary of a Drug Fiend, 1922.
b. Oct 12, 1875 in Leamington, England
d. Dec 1, 1947 in Brighton, England
Source: *LongCTC; REn*

Crowley, Jim (James)
[Four Horsemen of Notre Dame]
"Sleepy Jim"
American. Football Player
Member of backfield under Knute Rockne
during Notre Dame's national
championship season, 1924.
b. Sep 10, 1902 in Chicago, Illinois
d. Jan 15, 1986 in Scranton, Pennsylvania
Source: *WhoFtbl 74*

Crowley, Leo T
American. Businessman, Public Official
b. Aug 15, 1889 in Milton Junction, Wisconsin
d. Apr 15, 1972 in Madison, Wisconsin
Source: *CurBio 43, 72; NewYTBE 72; WhAm 5*

Crowley, Pat
American. Actress
Starred in TV series "Please Don't Eat the Daisies," 1965-67.
b. Sep 17, 1929 in Scranton, Pennsylvania
Source: *BioIn 3; FilmgC; MotPP; WhoAm 82; WhoHol A*

Crowninshield, Francis Welch
[Arthur Loring Bruce]
American. Editor, Publisher
Edited *Vanity Fair*, 1914-35; one of founders of Museum of Modern Art.
b. Jun 24, 1872 in Paris, France
d. Dec 28, 1947 in New York, New York
Source: *DcAmB S4; DcNAA; REn; REnAL; WhAm 2*

Crowther, Bosley (Francis Bosley)
American. Journalist, Movie Critic
Film critic, NY *Times*, 1940-67, who wrote over 200 reviews annually.
b. Jul 13, 1905 in Lutherville, Maryland
d. Mar 7, 1981 in Mount Kisco, New York
Source: *BioIn 10; ConAu 103; CurBio 81; IntMPA 81; NewYTBS 81; WhAm 7; WorAl*

Crowther, Samuel Adjai
Nigerian. Religious Leader
Explored Niger River, 1841; first African Anglican bishop in Nigeria.
b. 1808 in Ochuga, Nigeria
d. Dec 31, 1891
Source: *BioIn 11; REnAL; WhAm 2; WhNAA*

Crozier, Eric
English. Author, Producer
b. Nov 14, 1914 in London, England
Source: *Au&Wr 71; ChhPo S2; LongCTC; Who 74; WhoMus 72*

Crozier, Roger Allan
"The Dodger"
Canadian. Hockey Player
Goalie, 1963-77; rookie of the year, 1965.
b. Mar 16, 1942 in Bracebridge, Ontario
Source: *WhoHcky 73*

Cruickshank, Andrew John
Scottish. Actor
Star of British theater, film, since 1930s; best known for TV series "Dr. Finlay's Casebook," 1963--.
b. Dec 25, 1907 in Aberdeen, Scotland
Source: *FilmgC; PIP&P; Who 74; WhoHol A; WhoThe 81*

Cruikshank, George
English. Artist, Illustrator
Noted for humorous satirical sketches in *Oliver Twist*, 1838;Grimm's *Popular Stories*, 1826.
b. Sep 27, 1792 in London, England
d. Feb 1, 1878 in London, England
Source: *Alli; CarSB; ChhPo, S1, S2; IlsBYP; NewC; REn; Str&VC*

Cruise, Tom
American. Actor
Has had roles in six major films, including *Risky Business*, 1983; *Top Gun*, 1986.
b. 1962 in Syracuse, New York
Source: *ConNews 85-4; VarWW 85*

Crum, Denny Edwin
American. Basketball Coach
Coach of U. of Louisville NCAA championship team, 1980; college coach of year, 1974.
b. Mar 2, 1937 in San Fernando, California
Source: *WhoAm 82, 84*

Crumb, Robert
American. Cartoonist
b. Aug 30, 1943 in Philadelphia, Pennsylvania
Source: *BioIn 9, 10; ConLC 17; NewYTBE 72*

Crummell, Alexander
American. Missionary
b. Mar 1819 in New York, New York
d. Sep 1898 in Point Pleasant, New Jersey
Source: *AmAu&B; BioIn 3, 4, 6, 8, 10, 11; DcAmAu; DcNAA*

Crump, Edward Hull
American. Congressman
b. 1874 in Holly Springs, Mississippi
d. Oct 16, 1954 in Memphis, Tennessee
Source: *BiDrAC; BioNews 74; DcAmB S5; WhAm 3; WhAmP*

Crusaders, The
[Larry Eugene Carlton; Witon Felder; Wayne
  Henderson; 'Stix' Hooper; Joe Sample]
American. Music Group
Best known for hit single "Uptight
  (Everything's Alright)," 1966.
Source: *EncJzS 70; InB&W 80; RkOn 84*

Cruyff, Johan
Dutch. Soccer Player
b. Apr 25, 1947 in Amsterdam, Netherlands
Source: *BioIn 10; CurBio 81*

Cruz, Arturo
[Arturo Jose Cruz Porras]
Nicaraguan. Politician, Diplomat
Ambassador to US, 1981, who is currently
  spokesman for Nicaraguan democrats.
b. Dec 18, 1923 in Jinotepe, Nicaragua
Source: *ConNews 85-1; WhoWor 82*

Cruzen, Richard H
American. Explorer, Naturalist
b. 1896
d. 1970
Source: *BioIn 8*

Cryer, David
American. Actor
Best known for role in play *The Fantasticks*
b. Mar 8, 1936 in Evanston, Illinois
Source: *NotNAT; WhoThe 81*

Crystal, Billy (William)
American. Actor, Comedian
Comedic actor known as versatile mimic;
  starred in "Soap," 1977-81.
b. Mar 14, 1947 in Long Island, New York
Source: *BioIn 11; IntMPA 82; WhoAm 82;
  WorAl*

Crystal, Lester M
American. TV Executive
Won two Emmys; former exec. vp, NBC
  News.
b. Sep 13, 1934 in Duluth, Michigan
Source: *VarWW 85*

Csonka, Larry Richard
American. Football Player
Running back, Miami Dolphins, 1968-74, 79-
  80, NY Giants, 1976-79, WFL, 1975.
b. Dec 25, 1946 in Akron, Ohio
Source: *BioNews 75; CelR; NewYTBE 73;
  NewYTBS 74; WhoAm 82*

Cuauhtemoc
Aztec. Emperor
Last Aztec ruler who defended empire
  against Spanish; hanged by Cortes.
b. 1495 in Tenochtitlan, Mexico
d. Feb 26, 1525 in Itzancanal, Mexico
Source: *EncLatA; McGEWB; NewCol 75;
  REn*

Cudahy, Michael
American. Meat Packer, Merchant
Partner with Philip D Armour, 1875-90;
  established Cudahy Packing Co., Omaha,
  NE.
b. Dec 7, 1841 in Callan, Ireland
d. 1910
Source: *AmBi; DcAmB; NewCol 75; WhAm 1*

Cudlipp, Hugh
Welsh. Journalist
Editor, England's *Daily Mirror,* 1952-63;
  wrote *Publish and Be Damned,* 1953.
b. Aug 28, 1913 in Cardiff, Wales
Source: *ConAu 116*

Cudworth, Ralph
English. Philosopher, Educator
Wrote *The True Intellectual System of the
  Universe,* 1678.
b. 1617 in Aller, England
d. 1688
Source: *NewCol 75; OxEng; REn; WebBD 80*

Cuellar, Mike (Miguel Santana)
Cuban. Baseball Player
Pitcher, 1959-77; led AL with 24 wins, 1970;
  shared Cy Young Award with Denny
  McLain, 1969.
b. May 8, 1937 in Santa Clara, Cuba
Source: *BaseEn 85; WhoProB 73*

Cuesta, Juan de la
Spanish. Printer
Source: *BioIn 10*

Cueva de Garoza, Juan de la
Spanish. Dramatist, Poet
Introduced historical material, new metric
  forms into Spanish literature.
b. 1550
d. 1610
Source: *REn*

Cuffe, Paul
American. Colonizer
Worked to improve conditions of slaves;
pioneered efforts to settle free blacks in
Sierra Leone, W Africa.
b. Jan 17, 1759 in Cutty Hunk,
Massachusetts
d. Sep 9, 1817 in Westport, Massachusetts
Source: *BioIn 11; DcAmB; InB&W 80;
McGEWB; NatCAB 12; WhAm HS*

Cuffley, John
see: Climax Blues Band, The

Cugat, Xavier
"Rhumba King"
Spanish. Band Leader
Popularized rhumba, cha-cha, mambo dances
dances, 1940s-50s.
b. Jan 1, 1900 in Barcelona, Spain
Source: *CelR; CurBio 42; FilmgC; WhoAm
74; WhoHol A*

Cui, Cesar Antonovich
Russian. Composer, Soldier
Wrote textbooks on fortification; composed
piano works, operas.
b. Jan 18, 1835 in Vilna, Russia
d. Mar 24, 1918 in Saint Petersburg,
U.S.S.R.
Source: *NewEOp 71; WebBD 80*

Cukor, George Dewey
American. Director
Won 1964 Oscar for *My Fair Lady;* last film
Rich and Famous, 1981.
b. Jul 7, 1899 in New York, New York
d. Jan 24, 1983 in Los Angeles, California
Source: *AnObit 1983; BiDFilm; BiE&WWA;
CelR; CmMov; CurBio 83; FilmgC; IntMPA
80; IntWW 82; MovMk; NewYTBS 83;
OxFilm; WhoAm 82; WhoWor 80; WorAl*

Culbertson, Ely
American. Bridge Player
Invented contract bridge, became world's top
player, 1930s; founded *Bridge World*
magazine, 1929.
b. Jul 22, 1891 in Verbilao, Romania
d. Dec 27, 1955 in Brattleboro, Vermont
Source: *AmAu&B; CurBio 40, 56; DcAmB S5;
WebAB 79; WhAm 3; WhE&EA; WorAl*

Cullen, Bill (William Lawrence)
American. TV Personality
Hosted "To Tell the Truth"; "Joker's Wild";
"$25,000 Pryamid."
b. Feb 18, 1920 in Pittsburgh, Pennsylvania
Source: *CurBio 60; IntMPA 82; VarWW 85;
WhoAm 80, 82*

Cullen, Countee
American. Poet
Wrote *Color,* 1925; *The Black Christ,* 1930.
b. May 30, 1903 in New York, New York
d. Jan 10, 1946 in New York, New York
Source: *AmAu&B; AnCL; AnMV 1926;
BlkAWP; CasWL; ChhPo, S1; ConAmA;
ConAmL; CurBio 46; DcLEL; DcNAA;
ModAL, S1; OxAmL; PenC AM; RAdv 1;
REn; REnAL; TwCA, SUP; WebE&AL;
WhAm 2; WhNAA*

Culliford, "Peyo" (Pierre)
Belgian. Author, Cartoonist
Created the Smurfs, 1957; top children's TV
show in US, early 1980s.
b. Jun 25, 1928 in Brussels, Belgium
Source: *WorECom*

Culligan, Emmett J
"Gold Dust"
American. Businessman
Launched water softener firm, 1924.
b. 1893 in Minnesota
d. 1970
Source: *Entr*

Cullum, John
American. Actor
Won Tony awards for *Shenandoah,* 1975; *On
the Twentieth Century,* 1978.
b. Mar 2, 1930 in Knoxville, Tennessee
Source: *EncMT; NotNAT; VarWW 85;
WhoAm 82; WhoHol A; WhoThe 77, 81*

Culp, Robert
American. Actor
Starred in "I Spy," 1965-68; "The Greatest
American Hero," 1981-83.
b. Aug 13, 1930 in Berkeley, California
Source: *CelR; FilmgC; IntMPA 82; MotPP;
WhoAm 82; WhoHol A; WorAl*

Culpeper, Nicholas
English. Physician
Believed astrology influenced disease, herbs
cured it; translated several Latin medical
texts into English.
b. 1616 in London, England
d. 1654
Source: *BiHiMed; BrAu; DcBiPP; DcLEL*

Culture Club
[Boy George; Micheal Craig; Roy Hay; Jon
Moss; Helen Terry]
English. Music Group
Most commercially successful of British rock-
theater bands, 1980s; first hit "Do You
Really Want to Hurt Me?" 1982.
Source: *RkOn 85*

Culver, John C
American. Politician, Lawyer
Dem. senator from IA, 1975-81.
b. Aug 8, 1932 in Rochester, Minnesota
Source: *CurBio 79; WhoAm 82, 84*

Cummings, Bob (Robert Orville)
American. Actor
Starred in "Love That Bob," 1954-61; "The
Bob Cummings Show," 1961-62; "My
Living Doll," 1964-65.
b. Jun 9, 1910 in Joplin, Missouri
Source: *BiE&WWA; CelR; CurBio 56; Film
1; FilmgC; IntMPA 82; MotPP; MovMk;
WhoAm 82; WhoHol A; WorEFlm*

Cummings, Burton
[Guess Who]
Canadian. Singer, Musician
b. Dec 31, 1947 in Winnipeg, Manitoba
Source: *RkOn 74*

Cummings, "Candy" (William Arthur)
American. Baseball Player
Pitcher credited with invention of curveball;
Hall of Fame, 1939.
b. Oct 17, 1848 in Ware, Massachusetts
d. May 17, 1924 in Toledo, Ohio
Source: *BaseEn 85; BasesB*

Cummings, Constance
[Constance Halverstadt]
American. Actress
Won Tony award for *Wings*, 1979.
b. May 15, 1910 in Seattle, Washington
Source: *FilmgC; HolP 30; InWom; IntMPA
82; MotPP; MovMk; NotNAT; ThFT; Who
82; WhoAm 82; WhoHol A; WhoThe 77, 81;
WorAl*

Cummings, E(dward) E(stlin)
American. Poet, Author
Noted for eccentricity of punctuation,
typography; first published work was
autobiographical *The Enormous Room*,
1922.
b. Oct 14, 1894 in Cambridge, Massachusetts
d. Sep 3, 1962 in North Conway, New
Hampshire
Source: *AmAu&B; AmWr; AnCL; AtlBL;
AuBYP; CasWL; ChhPo; CnDAL; CnE&AP;
CnMD; CnMWL; ConAmA; ConAmL; ConAu
73; ConLC 1, 3, 8, 12, 15; EncWL; EvLB;
LongCTC; McGEWD; ModAL, S1; ModWD;
OxAmL; OxEng; PenC AM; RAdv 1; REn;
REnAL; SixAP; TwCA, SUP; TwCWr;
WebE&AL; WhDW; WhoTwCL; WorAl*

Cummings, Quinn
American. Actress
Nominated for Oscar, 1977, for *The Goodbye
Girl*.
b. Aug 13, 1967 in Hollywood, California
Source: *BioIn 11*

Cummings, Terry (Robert Terrell)
American. Basketball Player
Forward, 1982--; NBA rookie of year, 1983.
b. Mar 15, 1961 in Chicago, Illinois
Source: *BioIn 12; OfNBA 85*

Cummins, George David
American. Religious Leader
Founder, first bishop, Reformed Episcopal
Church, 1873.
b. Dec 11, 1822 in Smyrna, Delaware
d. Jun 25, 1876 in Lutherville, Maryland
Source: *BiDAmC*

Cummins, Peggy
Welsh. Actress
Best known for films *English Without Tears*,
1944; *Late George Apley*, 1946.
b. Dec 18, 1926 in Prestatyn, Wales
Source: *FilmgC; IntMPA 82; MotPP; WhThe;
WhoHol A; WhoThe 77A*

Cunard, Samuel, Sir
Canadian. Shipping Executive
Established first regular steamship service
between N America, Europe, 1840; began
Cunard Line.
b. Nov 15, 1787 in Halifax, Nova Scotia
d. Apr 28, 1865 in London, England
Source: *ApCAB; HarEnUS; OxShips; WorAl*

Cuneo, Ernest
American. Lawyer, Publisher, Author
b. May 27, 1905 in Carlstadt, New Jersey
Source: *WhoAm 80, 82; WhoWor 74*

Cuneo, Terence Tenison
English. Artist
b. Nov 1, 1907
Source: *BioIn 1, 3, 11; Who 74*

Cunha, Euclides da
Brazilian. Author
b. Jan 20, 1866 in Santa Rita, Brazil
d. Aug 15, 1909 in Rio de Janeiro, Brazil
Source: *CasWL*

Cunningham, Alan Gordon, Sir
English. General
Commanded forces that liberated Ethiopia
from Italian rule, restored Haile Selassie to
throne, 1971.
b. May 1, 1887
d. Jan 30, 1983 in London, England
Source: *AnObit 1983; CurBio 46, 83;
HisEWW; Who 82*

Cunningham, Andrew Browne, Viscount
Irish. Military Leader
One of great sea commanders of Britain;
admiral of the fleet.
b. Jan 7, 1883 in Dublin, Ireland
d. Jun 12, 1963 in London, England
Source: *CurBio 41, 63; GrBr; HisEWW;
OxShips; WhWW-II; WhoMilH 76*

Cunningham, Bill
[The Box Tops]
American. Musician
Keyboardist, bassist with Memphis-based
group, 1966-70.
b. Jan 23, 1950 in Memphis, Tennessee
Source: *NF*

Cunningham, Billy (William)
"Kangaroo Kid"
American. Basketball Player
Forward, first draft choice, Philadelphia
76ers, 1966-72.
b. Jun 3, 1943 in Brooklyn, New York
Source: *OfNBA 81; WhoAm 82; WhoBbl 73*

Cunningham, E. V. pseud.
see: Fast, Howard

Cunningham, Glenn Clarence
"Kansas Ironman"
American. Track Athlete
Held world record in mile, 1934-37.
b. Aug 4, 1909 in Atlanta, Kansas
Source: *WhoTr&F 73*

Cunningham, Harry Blair
American. Business Executive
Pres., S S Kresge, 1959-70; honorary
chairman, K-Mart, 1973--.
b. Jul 23, 1907 in Home Camp, Pennsylvania
Source: *IntWW 78; St&PR 75; WhoAm 82,
84; WhoF&I 74; WhoWor 78*

Cunningham, Imogen
American. Photographer
Experimental, portrait photographer whose
career spanned 75 yrs.
b. Apr 12, 1883 in Portland, Oregon
d. Jun 24, 1976 in San Francisco, California
Source: *BioIn 10; ConAu 65; MacBEP;
WhoAmA 82N; WomArt*

Cunningham, Mary Elizabeth
[Mrs. William Agee]
American. Business Executive
Pres., Semper Corp., 1983--, company owned
with husband; wrote autobiography
Powerplay, 1984.
b. Sep 1, 1951 in Falmouth, Maine
Source: *BioIn 12; CurBio 84*

Cunningham, Merce
American. Dancer, Choreographer
b. Apr 16, 1919 in Centralia, Washington
Source: *CurBio 66; WhoAm 82; WhoWor 74*

Cunningham, R Walter
American. Astronaut, Corporation Executive
Flew first manned Apollo spacecraft, 1968;
founded The Capital Group, 1979--.
b. Mar 16, 1932 in Creston, Iowa
Source: *IntWW 74; WhoAm 82; WhoWor 74*

Cunningham, Sam
American. Football Player
b. Aug 15, 1950 in Santa Barbara, California
Source: *WhoFtbl 74*

Cunninghame, Graham Robert Boutine
English. Author, Traveler
Wrote on S America: *Portrait of a Dictator,*
1933; city Don Roberto, Argentina named
for him.
b. May 24, 1852 in London, England
d. Mar 20, 1936 in Buenos Aires, Argentina
Source: *CasWL; DcLEL; DcNaB 1931; EvLB;
GrBr; LongCTC; ModBrL; OxEng; REn;
TwCA; WhE&EA; WhLit*

Cuomo, Mario Matthew
American. Politician
Dem. governor of NY, 1982--.
b. Jun 15, 1932 in Queens County, New
York
Source: *AmCath 80; WhoAm 82; WhoE 81;
WrDr 82*

Cuppy, Will(iam Jacob)
American. Humorist
Satirical "How To's" include *How to Become
Extinct,* 1941.
b. Aug 23, 1884 in Auburn, Indiana
d. Sep 19, 1949 in New York, New York
Source: *AmAu&B; DcAmB S4; DcLB 11;
DcNAA; IndAu 1816; ObitOF 79; REnAL;
ScF&FL 1; TwCA, SUP; WhAm 2*

Curb, Mike (Michael Charles)
American. Politician
Lt. gov. of CA, 1979--, pres., MGM
Records, 1968-74.
b. Dec 24, 1944 in Savannah, Georgia
Source: *EncPR&S 74; WhoAm 82; WhoWest 82*

Curci, Amelita Galli
see: Galli-Curci, Amelita

Curcio, Renato
Italian. Terrorist
b. 1940
Source: *BioIn 11*

Curel, Francois de
French. Dramatist
b. Jun 10, 1854 in Metz, France
d. Apr 25, 1928 in Paris, France
Source: *CasWL; ClDMEL; CnMD; EvEuW; McGEWD; ModWD; OxFr; PenC EUR; REn; WhoLA*

Curie, Eve
[Mrs. Henry R Labouisse]
French. Author, Journalist
b. Dec 6, 1904 in Paris, France
Source: *AmAu&B; AnCL; Au&Wr 71; ConAu P-1; CurBio 40; InWom; SmATA 1; Who 74; WhoAm 82; WhoWor 74*

Curie, Irene
see: Joliot-Curie, Irene

Curie, Marie
[Mrs. Pierre Curie; Marja Sklodowska]
Polish. Chemist
Discovered new elements polonium, radium,
1898; first to receive two Nobel Prizes,
1903, 1911.
b. Nov 7, 1867 in Warsaw, Poland
d. Jul 4, 1934 in Valence, France
Source: *HerW; InWom; McGEWB; REn; WhDW; WorAl*

Curie, Pierre
French. Chemist
Discovered radium, 1898; with wife,
investigated radioactivity of radium;
received Nobel Prize, 1903.
b. May 15, 1859 in Paris, France
d. Apr 19, 1906 in Paris, France
Source: *Dis&D; InSci; OxFr; WhDW; WorAl*

Curley, James Michael
American. Political Leader
b. Nov 20, 1874 in Boston, Massachusetts
d. Nov 12, 1958 in Boston, Massachusetts
Source: *BiDrAC; EncAB-H; WebAB; WhAm 3*

Curran, Charles Courtney
American. Artist
b. Feb 13, 1861 in Hartford, Kentucky
d. Nov 9, 1942 in New York, New York
Source: *BioIn 10; CurBio 43; WhAm 2*

Curran, Joseph Edwin
"Big Joe"
American. Labor Union Official
Organizer, pres., National Maritime Union,
1937-73.
b. Mar 1, 1906 in New York, New York
d. Aug 14, 1981 in Boca Raton, Florida
Source: *BiDAmLL; CurBio 81; NewYTBS 81; PolProf E, J, K, NF, T; WhoAm 74; WhoWor 74; WorAl*

Curren, Kevin
South African. Tennis Player
With Steve Denton, won US Clay Court
doubles 1980, 81, US Open doubles, 1982.
b. Mar 2, 1958 in Durban, South Africa
Source: *WhoIntT*

Currie, Barton Wood
American. Editor, Journalist
Edited *The Country Gentleman, Ladies Home
Journal,* early 1900s.
b. Mar 8, 1878 in New York, New York
d. May 7, 1962 in Merion, Pennsylvania
Source: *ConAu 116*

Currie, Finlay
Scottish. Actor
Best known for *Great Expectations,* 1946.
b. Jan 20, 1878 in Edinburgh, Scotland
d. May 9, 1968 in Gerrards Cross, England
Source: *CmMov; FilmgC; MotPP; MovMk; NotNAT B; Vers A; WhScrn 74, 77; WhThe; WhoHol B*

Currier, Nathaniel
[Currier and Ives]
American. Lithographer
Started lithography business, 1835;
partnership with James Ives, 1857.
b. Mar 27, 1813 in Roxbury, Massachusetts
d. Nov 20, 1888 in New York, New York
Source: *AmBi; DcAmB; WebAB; WhAm HS*

Currier and Ives
see: Currier, Nathaniel; Ives, James Merritt

Curry, Donald
American. Boxer
Undisputed welterweight champion knocking
out WBC champ, Milton McCrory, 1985.
b. 1961 in Fort Worth, Texas
Source: *NF*

Curry, John Anthony
English. Figure Skater
Won Olympic gold medal for figure skating,
1976.
b. Sep 9, 1949 in Birmingham, England
Source: *CurBio 79; NewYTBE 71; Who 79; WhoAm 82*

Curry, John Steuart
American. Artist
b. Nov 14, 1897 in Dunavant, Kansas
d. Aug 29, 1946 in Madison, Wisconsin
Source: *CurBio 41, 46; DcAmB S4; DcCAA 71; IlsCB 1744; OxAmL; REn; REnAL; WhAm 2*

Curry, Peggy Simson
American. Author
b. Dec 30, 1912 in Dunure, Scotland
Source: *ConAu 33R; CurBio 58; DrAF 76; InWom; SmATA 8*

Curti, Merle Eugene
American. Historian
Political science writings include Pulitzer-
winning *Growth of American Thought,*
1943.
b. Sep 15, 1897 in Papillion, Nebraska
Source: *ConAu 4NR, 5R; DrAS 74H; IntWW 74; OxAmH; OxAmL; REnAL; REnAW; TwCA SUP; WhoAm 82*

Curtice, Harlow Herbert
American. Auto Executive
Pres. of GM, 1953-58.
b. Aug 15, 1893 in Eaton Rapids, Michigan
d. Nov 3, 1962 in Flint, Michigan
Source: *CurBio 53, 63; WhAm 4*

Curtin, Andrew Gregg
American. Political Leader
b. Apr 28, 1817 in Bellefonte, Pennsylvania
d. Oct 7, 1894 in Bellefonte, Pennsylvania
Source: *AmBi; ApCAB; BiAUS; BiDrAC; DcAmB; Drake; TwCBDA; WhAm HS; WhAmP*

Curtin, Jane Therese
American. Actress, Comedienne
Star of NBC TV's "Saturday Night Live,"
1975-79; Emmy nominee, 1977.
b. Sep 6, 1947 in Cambridge, Massachusetts
Source: *WhoAm 80, 82*

Curtin, John
Australian. Prime Minister
b. Jan 8, 1885 in Creswick, Australia
d. Jul 5, 1945 in Canberra, Australia
Source: *CurBio 41, 45*

Curtin, Phyllis Smith
American. Singer
b. Dec 3, 1927 in Clarksburg, West Virginia
Source: *CurBio 64; InWom; NewYTBE 72; WhoAm 82; WhoAmW 77; WhoWor 74*

Curtis, Alan
American. Comedian, Actor
b. Jul 24, 1909 in Chicago, Illinois
d. Feb 1, 1953 in New York, New York
Source: *FilmgC; MotPP; WhScrn 74, 77; WhoHol B*

Curtis, Ann
American. Swimmer
b. 1926
Source: *BioIn 11*

Curtis, Charles
American. Politician
VP under Herbert Hoover, 1929-33.
b. Jan 25, 1860 in Topeka, Kansas
d. Feb 8, 1936 in Washington, District of
Columbia
Source: *Alli; AmBi; BiDLA; BiDrAC; BiDrUSE; DcAmB S2; TwCBDA; WebAB; WhAm 1; WhAmP*

Curtis, Charles Gordon
American. Inventor
Invented steam turbine, 1896, selling rights
to General Electric Co.
b. Apr 20, 1860 in Boston, Massachusetts
d. Mar 10, 1953 in Central Islip, New York
Source: *InSci; NatCAB 42; ObitOF 79; WhAm 3*

Curtis, Charlotte Murray
American. Newspaper Editor
b. 1930 in Chicago, Illinois
Source: *AuNews 2; CelR; ConAu 9R; ForWC 70; WhoAm 82; WhoAmW 77; WhoE 74*

Curtis, Cyrus Hermann Kotszchmar
American. Newspaper Publisher
Founded Curtis Publishing Co., 1891;
published *Saturday Evening Post; Ladies
Home Journal.*
b. Jun 18, 1850 in Portland, Maine
d. Jun 7, 1933 in Wyncote, Pennsylvania
Source: *AmAu&B; AmBi; DcAmB S1; EncAAH; WebAB; WhDW; WhAm 1; WorAl*

Curtis, Edward Sheriff
American. Photographer
Interest in Indians resulted in 20-volume
series *The North American Indian,* 1907-
30.
b. Feb 19, 1868 in Madison, Wisconsin
d. Oct 19, 1952 in Los Angeles, California
Source: *AmAu&B; DcAmB S5; ObitOF 79;
REnAW; WhAm 4*

Curtis, George William
American. Editor, Author, Lecturer
Wrote series of satires of New York society:
The Potiphar Papers, 1853; editor of
Harper's Weekly, 1857.
b. Feb 24, 1824 in Providence, Rhode Island
d. Aug 31, 1892 in Staten Island, New York
Source: *Alli, SUP; AmAu; AmAu&B; AmBi;
ApCAB; BbD; BiD&SB; CasWL; Chambr 3;
ChhPo; CyAL 2; DcAmAu; DcAmB; DcBiA;
DcEnL; DcLEL; DcNAA; Drake; EncAB-H;
EvLB; OxAmL; WebAB 79; WhAm HS; REn;
REnAL; TwCBDA; WebAB; WhAm HS;
WhAmP*

Curtis, Heber Doust
American. Astronomer, Director
Researched extra-galactic nebulae.
b. Jun 27, 1872 in Muskegon, Michigan
d. Jan 9, 1942 in Ann Arbor, Michigan
Source: *CurBio 42; DcAmB S3; WebBD 80;
WhAm 1*

Curtis, Isaac
American. Football Player
b. Oct 20, 1950 in Santa Ana, California
Source: *BioIn 11; WhoFtbl 74*

Curtis, Jackie
American. Dramatist, Screenwriter
b. Feb 19, 1947 in Stony Creek, Tennessee
Source: *BioIn 10; ConDr 77; WrDr 76*

Curtis, (James) Mike (Michael)
American. Football Player
b. Mar 27, 1943 in Rockville, Maryland
Source: *WhoFtbl 74*

Curtis, Jamie Lee
American. Actress, Celebrity Relative
Daughter of Tony Curtis, Janet Leigh;
starred in *Halloween,* 1981.
b. Nov 22, 1958
Source: *BioIn 11*

Curtis, John Duffield, II
American. Baseball Player
b. Mar 9, 1948 in Newton, Massachusetts
Source: *BaseEn 85*

Curtis, Ken
[Curtis Gates]
American. Actor
Best known as Festus Haggen on
"Gunsmoke," 1964-75.
b. Jul 12, 1916 in Lamar, Colorado
Source: *IntMPA 82; WhoHol A*

Curtis, Tony
[Bernard Schwartz]
American. Actor
Starred in *The Defiant Ones,* 1958; *Some
Like it Hot,* 1959.
b. Jun 3, 1925 in New York, New York
Source: *BiDFilm; CelR; ConAu 73; FilmgC;
IntMPA 82; MovMk; NewYTBE 70; OxFilm;
WhoAm 82; WhoHol A; WorEFlm*

Curtiss, Glenn Hammond
American. Aircraft Manufacturer, Inventor
Invented seaplane, 1911; established first
flying schools.
b. May 21, 1878 in Hammondsport, New
York
d. Jul 23, 1930 in Buffalo, New York
Source: *AmBi; DcAmB S1; WebAB, 79;
WhAm 1; WhFla*

Curtiz, Michael
American. Director
Won Oscar for *Casablanca,* 1942; directed
over 100 films for Warner Bros.
b. Dec 24, 1898 in Budapest, Hungary
d. Apr 11, 1962 in Hollywood, California
Source: *BiDFilm; CmMov; DcFM; FilmgC;
MovMk; ObitOF 79; ObitT 1961; OxFilm;
TwYS; WhAm 4; WhScrn 74, 77; WorEFlm*

Curwood, James Oliver
American. Author
b. Jun 12, 1878 in Owosso, Michigan
d. Aug 13, 1927 in Owosso, Michigan
Source: *AmAu&B; DcNAA; LongCTC;
MnBBF; OxAmL; OxCan; REnAL; TwCA,
SUP; WhNAA*

Curzon, Clifford Michael, Sir
English. Musician
Pianist best known for his performances of
Beethoven, Schubert, Mozart.
b. May 18, 1907 in London, England
d. Sep 1, 1982 in London, England
Source: *Baker 78; CurBio 82; IntWW 82;
Who 74; WhoMus 72; WhoWor 78*

**Curzon of Kedleston, George Nathaniel
Curzon, Marquis**
English. Statesman
b. Jan 11, 1859 in Kedleston Hall, England
d. Mar 20, 1925
Source: *ChhPo S1; DcEuL; McGEWB; NewC*

Cusack, Cyril
Irish. Actor
Appeared in TV movies *Catholics; Jesus of Nazareth.*
b. Nov 26, 1910 in Durban, South Africa
Source: *BiE&WWA; Film 1; FilmgC; IntMPA 82; IntWW 74; MovMk; NotNAT; WhoHol A; WhoThe 81; WhoWor 74; WrDr 82*

Cushing, Caleb
American. Judge, Diplomat
Special envoy to China, 1843-45, arranged favorable treaties for US.
b. Jan 17, 1800 in Salisbury, Massachusetts
d. Jan 2, 1879 in Newburyport, Massachusetts
Source: *Alli; AmAu; AmAu&B; AmBi; ApCAB; BiAUS; BiD&SB; BiDrAC; BiDrUSE; CyAL 2; DcAmAu; DcAmB; DcNAA; Drake; OxLaw; TwCBDA; WebAB, 79; WhAm HS; WhAmP*

Cushing, Harvey Williams
American. Surgeon
Neurosurgeon who developed techniques that made brain surgery feasible, including sutures to control severe bleeding.
b. Apr 8, 1869 in Cleveland, Ohio
d. Oct 7, 1939 in New Haven, Connecticut
Source: *AmAu&B; AmBi; DcAmB S2; DcNAA; DcScB; EncAB-H; LongCTC; OhA&B; OxAmL; REnAL; WebAB; WhDW; WhAm 1; WhNAA*

Cushing, Peter
English. Actor
Rivals Vincent Price in horror film roles; has played Baron Frankenstein in four movies.
b. May 26, 1913 in Surrey, England
Source: *CmMov; FilmgC; IntMPA 82; IntWW 82; MotPP; WhoHol A; WhoThe 81*

Cushing, Richard James, Cardinal
American. Religious Leader
Archbishop of Boston, 1944-70.
b. Aug 24, 1895 in Boston, Massachusetts
d. Nov 2, 1970 in Boston, Massachusetts
Source: *CurBio 70; DcAmReB; NewYTBE 70; ObitOF 79; WhAm 5; WorAl*

Cushing, William Barker
American. Military Leader
b. Nov 4, 1842 in Delafield, Wisconsin
d. Dec 17, 1874 in Washington, District of Columbia
Source: *AmBi; ApCAB; DcAmB; Drake; TwCBDA; WebAB; WhAm HS*

Cushman, Austin Thomas
American. Business Executive
Chm., chief exec., Sears, Roebuck, 1962-67; opened 167 stores; sales rose from 6.8 billion, 1966, to 17.2 billion, 1977.
b. 1901 in Albuquerque, New Mexico
d. Jun 12, 1978 in Pasadena, California
Source: *NewYTBS 78; ObitOF 79; WhAm 7*

Cushman, Charlotte Saunders
American. Actress
Acclaimed as foremost actress of her day; noted for Shakespearean tragedies; gave farewell performances from 1857-75.
b. Jul 23, 1816 in Boston, Massachusetts
d. Feb 17, 1876 in Boston, Massachusetts
Source: *AmBi; AmWom; ApCAB; DcAmB; Drake; FamA&A; FemPA; NotAW; OxAmH; OxAmL; OxThe; PIP&P; REnAL; TwCBDA; WebAB, 79; WhAm HS*

Cushman, Pauline
[Harriet Wood]
"Spy of the Cumberland"
American. Actress, Spy
Spy for the Union; captured, found guilty by Confederates, but rescued by Union advance.
b. Jun 10, 1833 in New Orleans, Louisiana
d. Dec 2, 1893 in San Francisco, California
Source: *AmBi; ApCAB; CivWDc; DcAmB; InWom; NatCAB 23; OxAmH; TwCBDA; WhAm HS*

Cushman, Robert Everton, Jr.
American. General
WW II hero, Vietnam commander, who became deputy director of CIA in 1969; approved burglary of office of Daniel Ellsberg's psychiatrist.
b. Dec 24, 1914 in Saint Paul, Minnesota
d. Jan 2, 1985 in Fort Washington, Maryland
Source: *CurBio 85; IntWW 82; NewYTBE 73; WhoAm 76; WhoGov 75; WhoS&SW 73*

Custer, Elizabeth Bacon
[Mrs. George Custer]
American. Author
Wrote *Boots and Saddles,* 1885, an account of life in Dakota with husband.
b. Apr 8, 1842 in Monroe, Michigan
d. Apr 4, 1933 in New York, New York
Source: *AmAu&B; AmBi; BiD&SB; DcAmAu; DcNAA; HerW; REnAL; WhAm 1*

Custer, George Armstrong
American. Army Officer
Youngest general in Union Army, killed at
Battle of Little Big Horn by Indians led
by Sitting Bull, Crazy Horse.
b. Dec 5, 1839 in New Rumley, Ohio
d. Jun 25, 1876 in Little Big Horn, South
Dakota
Source: *Alli SUP; AmBi; ApCAB; DcAmAu;
DcAmB; DcNAA; Drake; EncAB-H; FilmgC;
OhA&B; OxAmL; OxFilm; REn; TwCBDA;
WebAB; WebAMB; WhDW; WhAm HS;
WorAl*

Custin, Mildred
American. Business Executive
Pres., Bonwit Teller, 1965-69; first woman to
head major chain store.
b. 1906 in Manchester, New Hampshire
Source: *CurBio 67; InWom; St&PR 75;
WhoAm 82; WhoAmW 74; WhoF&I 75;
WorFshn*

Cuthbert, Betty
Australian. Track Athlete
Won three gold medals, 1954 Olympics; one
gold medal, 1964 Olympics.
b. Apr 20, 1938 in Sydney, Australia
Source: *WhoTr&F 73*

Cutler, Manasseh
American. Clergyman, Scientist
Ohio River Valley colonizer.
b. May 13, 1742 in Killingly, Connecticut
d. Jul 28, 1823 in Ipswich Hamlet,
Massachusetts
Source: *AmBi; ApCAB; BiAUS; BiDAmS;
BiDrAC; BioIn 5, 9; DcAmAu; DcAmB;
Drake; McGEWB; NatCab 3; NewCol 75;
OhA&B; TwCBDA; WebAB; WhAm HS*

Cutpurse, Moll
[Mary Frith]
"Queen of Misrule"
English. Criminal
First known female criminal who dressed as
man; pickpocket, highway robber.
b. 1589 in London, England
d. 1662 in London, England
Source: *LookW*

Cuvier, Georges, Baron
French. Zoologist
b. Aug 23, 1769 in Montbeliard, France
d. May 13, 1832 in Paris, France
Source: *AsBiEn; BiD&SB; McGEWB; OxFr;
REn*

Cuyler, "Kiki" (Hazen Shirley)
American. Baseball Player
Outfielder, 1921-38; led NL in stolen bases,
1926, 1928-30.
b. Aug 30, 1899 in Harrisville, Michigan
d. Feb 11, 1950 in Ann Arbor, Michigan
Source: *BaseEn 85; WhoProB 73*

Cuyp, Aelbert
Dutch. Artist
b. 1620 in Dordrecht, Netherlands
d. Nov 1691 in Dordrecht, Netherlands
Source: *AtlBL*

Cuypers, Petrus Josephus Hubertus
Dutch. Architect
Neo-Gothic designer, who built many
Catholic churches, Rijkmuseum, 1876.
b. 1827 in Roermond, Netherlands
d. 1921
Source: *WhoArch*

Cuzzoni, Francesca
Italian. Opera Singer
b. 1700 in Parma, Italy
d. 1770 in Bologna, Italy
Source: *InWom*

Cynewulf
English. Poet
Old English religious poet, most praised for
"Elene," "Ascension."
fl. 8th century
Source: *Alli; BiB S; BrAu; CasWL; Chambr
1; CrtT 1; DcEnL; EvLB; LinLib L;
LongCEL; LuthC 75; NewC; OxEng; PenC
ENG; REn; WebE&AL*

Cynthia
see: Brousse, Amy Elizabeth Thorpe

Cyr, Louis

Cyrankiewicz, Josef
Polish. Political Leader
Premier, 1947-52, 1954-70.
b. Apr 23, 1911 in Tarnow, Poland
Source: *DcPol; IntWW 82; IntYB 82*

Cyrano de Bergerac, Savinien de
French. Poet, Soldier
Life romanticized by Edmond Rostand in
Cyrano de Bergerac, 1897.
b. Mar 6, 1619
d. Sep 1655
Source: *BiD&SB; CasWL; EuAu; EvEuW;
OxFr; PenC EUR; REn*

Cyril of Alexandria, Saint
Greek. Religious Figure
Patriarch of Alexandria, 412-44, whose
   writings dealt with problems of the
   Trinity; feast day, Feb 9.
b. 376 in Alexandria, Egypt
d. Jun 27, 444 in Alexandria, Egypt
Source: *CasWL; DcCathB; McGEWB; WhDW*

Cyrus the Great
[Cyrus the Elder]
Persian. Political Leader
Founded Persian empire, ca. 550 BC;
   captured Babylon, 538 BC.
b. 600 BC
d. 529 BC
Source: *DcBiPP; NewCol 75; REn; WhDW*

Czerny, Karl
Austrian. Composer, Pianist
Beethoven's pupil who wrote widely-used
   finger exercises.
b. Feb 20, 1791 in Vienna, Austria
d. Jul 15, 1857 in Vienna, Austria
Source: *CelCen; OxMus; WebBD 80; WhDW*

Czolgosz, Leon F
American. Assassin
Shot William McKinley at Pan-American
   Exposition, Buffalo, NY, Sep 6, 1901; sent
   to electric chair.
b. 1873 in Detroit, Michigan
d. Oct 29, 1901 in New York
Source: *Blood&B; Dis&D; HarEnUS; NewCol
75; WebBD 80*

D

Dabney, Virginius
American. Editor, Author
b. Feb 15, 1835 in Gloucester County,
Virginia
d. Jun 2, 1894 in New York, New York
Source: *Alli SUP; AmAu; AmAu&B; ApCAB;
BiD&SB; BiDSA; DcAmAu; DcAmB; DcNAA;
TwCBDA; WhAm HS*

Da Castelfranco, Giorgione
see: Giorgione II

Dache, Lilly
American. Fashion Designer
b. 1904 in Beigles, France
Source: *CurBio 41; FairDF US; InWom;
WhoAm 74; WorFshn*

Da Correggio, Antonio Allegri
see: Correggio, Antonio Allegri da

DaCosta, Morton
American. Producer, Director, Actor
b. Mar 7, 1914 in Philadelphia, Pennsylvania
Source: *BiE&WWA; FilmgC; NotNAT;
WhoThe 77; WorEFlm*

Daddario, Emilio Quincy
American. Lawyer, Politician
b. Sep 24, 1918 in Newton Centre,
Massachusetts
Source: *BioIn 11; St&PR 75; WhoAm 74;
WhoAmP 73; WhoGov 75*

Da Fiesole, Giovanni
see: Fra Angelico

Dafoe, Allan Roy
Canadian. Physician
b. May 29, 1883
d. Jun 2, 1943 in North Bay, Ontario
Source: *CurBio 43*

DaGama, Vasco
[Gama, Vasco da]
Portuguese. Explorer, Navigator
Led expedition around Africa to India, 1497-
99, opening first sea route to Asia.
b. 1460 in Sines, Portugal
d. Dec 24, 1524 in Cochin, India
Source: *NewC; NewCol 75; REn; WebBD 80;
WhAm HS*

Dagmar
[Virginia Ruth Egnor]
American. Actress
The dumb blonde of TV variety show
"Broadway Open House," 1950-51; had
her own variety show, "Dagmar's
Canteen," 1952.
b. 1920 in Huntington, West Virginia
Source: *InWom*

Dagover, Lil (Marta Maria Liletta)
German. Actress
International star of 1920s-30s; heroine of
classic *The Cabinet of Dr. Caligari,* 1919.
b. Sep 30, 1897 in Madiven, Indonesia
d. Jan 30, 1980 in Munich, Germany (West)
Source: *FilmEn; Film 1, 2; FilmgC; InWom;
MovMk; OxFilm; TwYS; WhoHol A;
WorEFlm*

Daguerre, Louis Jacques Mande
French. Inventor, Artist
Invented the daguerreotype photograph, 1839.
b. Nov 18, 1787 in Cormeilles en Parisis,
France
d. Jul 12, 1851 in Paris, France
Source: *AsBiEn; FilmgC; McGEWB; NewC;
OxFr*

Dahl, Arlene
American. Actress
Glamor star of late 1940s-1950s films; has
   written column, books on beauty; mother
   of Lorenzo Lamas.
b. Aug 11, 1927 in Minneapolis, Minnesota
Source: *CelR; FilmgC; ForWC 70; InWom;*
IntMPA 82; MGM; MotPP; MovMk; WhoAm
82; WhoAmW 81; WhoHol A; WhoWest 74;
WorAl

Dahl, Gary
American. Businessman, Inventor
Invented the Pet Rock, 1980s.
Source: *BioIn 12*

Dahl, Roald
American. Author, Screenwriter
Films include *Chitty Chitty Bang Bang,* 1968;
   Willy Wonka and the Chocolate Factory,
   1971.
b. Sep 13, 1916 in Llandaff, Wales
Source: *Au&Wr 71; AuBYP; BioNews 74;*
ChlLR 1; ConAu 1R; ConLC 1, 6, 18;
ConNov 76; DrAF 76; MorBMP; NewC; PiP;
RAdv 1; REn; REnAL; SmATA 1; ThrBJA;
VarWW 85; WhoAm 74; WhoWor 74; WorAl;
WorAu; WrDr 76

Dahl-Wolfe, Louise
American. Photographer
Fashion, portrait photographer for *Harper's*
   Bazaar, 1936-58.
b. 1895 in San Francisco, California
Source: *ConPhot; MacBEP; NewYTBS 84*

Dahlberg, Edward
American. Author, Critic
b. Jul 22, 1900 in Boston, Massachusetts
d. Feb 27, 1977 in Santa Barbara, California
Source: *AmAu&B; CelR; ConAu 9R, 69;*
ConLC 1, 7, 14; ConNov 72, 76; DrAF 76;
ModAL, S1; OxAmL; PenC AM; TwCA SUP;
TwCWr; WhoAm 74; WhoWor 78; WrDr 80

Dahlgren, John Adolph
American. Naval Officer
b. Nov 13, 1809 in Philadelphia,
   Pennsylvania
d. Jul 12, 1870 in Washington, District of
   Columbia
Source: *Alli SUP; ApCAB; DcAmAu; DcAmB;*
DcNAA; Drake; TwCBDA; WebAB; WhAm
HS

Dahlin, Kjell
Swedish. Hockey Player
Right wing, Montreal, 1985--; won Stanley
   Cup, 1986.
b. Feb 2, 1963 in Timra, Sweden
Source: *HocReg 85*

Daiches, David
English. Author, Scholar, Educator
Critical writings include *New Literary Values,*
   1936.
b. Sep 2, 1912 in Sunderland, England
Source: *Au&Wr 71; ChhPo S1; ConAu 5R;*
DcLEL; EvLB; IntWW 74; LongCTC;
ModBrL; RAdv 1; REn; TwCA SUP; Who
74; WhoAm 74; WhoWor 74; WrDr 76

Dailey, Dan
American. Dancer, Actor
b. Dec 14, 1915 in New York, New York
d. Oct 17, 1978 in Hollywood, California
Source: *BiDFilm; CmMov; FilmgC; MotPP;*
MovMk; WhoHol A; WhoThe 77; WorEFlm

Dailey, Irene
American. Actress
Won Emmy for role on soap opera "Another
   World," 1979.
b. Sep 12, 1920 in New York, New York
Source: *BiE&WWA; NotNAT; VarWW 85;*
WhoAm 82; WhoHol A; WhoThe 77

Dailey, Janet
American. Author
America's best-selling romance author; has
   written 60 books since 1976.
b. May 21, 1944 in Storm Lake, Iowa
Source: *ConAu 89; NewYTBS 81*

Daimler, Gottlieb
German. Auto Manufacturer, Inventor
Founded Daimler Motor Co., 1890, which
   produced the Mercedes; invented
   motorcycle, 1885.
b. Mar 17, 1834 in Wurttemberg, Germany
d. Mar 6, 1900 in Stuttgart, Germany
Source: *InSci; McGEWB; NewCol 75; WebBD*
80; WhDW

Daladier, Edouard
French. Political Leader
b. Jun 18, 1884 in Vancluse, France
d. Oct 10, 1970 in Paris, France
Source: *CurBio 40, 70; NewYTBE 70; REn*

Dalai Lama, the 14th Incarnate
[Gejong Tenzin Gyatsho]
Tibetan. Ruler, Religious Leader
Temporal and religious head of Tibet and all
   Buddhist sects, now living in India.
b. Jul 6, 1935 in Chhija Nangso, Tibet
Source: *BioIn 5, 6, 8, 11; CurBio 51, 82;*
FarE&A 78, 79; IntWW 74, 75, 76, 77, 78,
79, 80; WhoWor 74, 76, 78

D'Albert, Eugene
Scottish. Pianist, Composer
b. Apr 10, 1864 in Glasgow, Scotland
d. Mar 3, 1932 in Riga, U.S.S.R.
Source: *NewEOp 71*

Dale, Alan
American. Musician, Singer
b. Jul 9, 1926 in Brooklyn, New York
Source: *BioIn 8; CmpEPM*

Dale, Carroll W
American. Football Player
b. Apr 24, 1938 in Wise, Virginia
Source: *WhoFtbl 74*

Dale, Chester
American. Banker, Art Collector
His art collection is housed in 10 rooms in
  Washington's National Gallery.
b. May 3, 1882 in New York, New York
d. Dec 16, 1962 in New York, New York
Source: *CurBio 58, 63; DcAmB S7*

Dale, Clamma Churita
American. Singer
Dramatic soprano of Houston, NYC Opera
  Co.; won awards for *Porgy and Bess,* 1976.
b. Jul 4, 1948 in Chester, Pennsylvania
Source: *CurBio 79; NewYTBS 76; WhoBlA 77*

Dale, Henry Hallett
English. Scientist, Engineer, Physician
b. 1875 in London, England
d. Aug 23, 1968 in Cambridge, England
Source: *Alli SUP; WhAm 5*

Dale, Jim
[James Smith]
English. Actor, Singer, Songwriter
b. Aug 15, 1935 in Rothwell, England
Source: *BioIn 10; FilmEn; WhoAm 82;
WhoHol A; WhoThe 81*

Dalen, Nils Gustaf
Swedish. Inventor, Engineer
Scientific inventions included the Solventil,
  for which he received 1912 Nobel Prize in
  Physics.
b. Nov 30, 1869
d. Dec 9, 1937
Source: *BioIn 2, 3*

Daley, Arthur
American. Journalist
b. Jul 31, 1904 in New York, New York
d. Jan 3, 1974 in New York, New York
Source: *AmAu&B; ConAu 45, P-2; CurBio
74N; NewYTBS 74*

Daley, Richard Joseph
American. Politician
Dem. mayor of Chicago, 1955-76.
b. May 15, 1902 in Chicago, Illinois
d. Dec 20, 1976 in Chicago, Illinois
Source: *CelR; CurBio 55; EncAB-H; IntWW
74; WebAB; WhoAm 74; WhoAmP 73;
WhoGov 75; WhoMW 74; WhoWor 78*

Daley, Robert H
Producer
Films include *Escape from Alcatraz; Bronco
  Billy; Stick.*
Source: *VarWW 85*

Dalgleish, Alice
American. Children's Author
b. Oct 7, 1893 in Trinidad
d. Jun 11, 1979 in Woodbury, Connecticut
Source: *AmAu&B; AmPB; AnCL; AuBYP;
ChhPo; ConAu 73, 89; JBA 34, 51; SmATA
17; Str&VC; WhNAA*

Dalhousie, James A B R, Marquess
British. Statesman
b. 1812
d. 1860
Source: *BioIn 10; CelCen; DcBiPP;
McGEWB; NewCol 75*

Dali, Gala
[Mrs. Salvador Dali; Elena Diaranoff]
Model
For over 50 years was inspiration of
  husband, surrealist painter Salvador Dali.
b. 1893 in Kazan, Russia
d. Jun 10, 1982 in Gerona, Spain
Source: *AnObit 1982; BioIn 12; NewYTBS 82*

Dali, Salvador
Spanish. Artist
Leader of Surrealist Movement; best known
  work "Persistence of Memory," 1931.
b. May 11, 1904 in Figueras, Spain
Source: *AmAu&B; BioNews 74; CelR; CurBio
40, 51; FilmgC; IntWW 74; OxFilm; REn;
WhAm 8; Who 82; WhoAm 76, 78, 80, 82;
WhoGrA 62; WhoWor 78; WorEFlm*

Dalis, Irene
American. Opera Singer
b. Oct 8, 1929 in San Jose, California
Source: *WhoAm 74, 76, 78, 80, 82*

Dall, John
[John Jenner Thompson]
American. Actor
Nominated for Oscar for *The Corn Is Green*,
1946; had lead in Hitchcock's *Rope*, 1948.
b. 1918 in New York, New York
d. Jan 15, 1971 in Beverly Hills, California
Source: *FilmEn; FilmgC; MotPP; MovMk;
NewYTBE 71; WhScrn 74, 77; WhoHol B*

Dalla Rizza, Gilda
Italian. Opera Singer
b. Oct 12, 1892 in Verona, Italy
d. Jul 5, 1975
Source: *BioIn 10*

Dallapiccola, Luigi
Italian. Musician, Composer
b. Feb 3, 1904 in Pisino, Yugoslavia
d. Feb 19, 1975 in Florence, Italy
Source: *CurBio 66; DcCM; IntWW 74;
WhAm 6; Who 74; WhoMus 72; WhoWor 78*

Dallas, George Mifflin
American. Vice-President
b. Jul 10, 1792 in Philadelphia, Pennsylvania
d. Dec 31, 1864 in Philadelphia,
Pennsylvania
Source: *Alli, SUP; AmBi; ApCAB; BiAUS;
BiDrAC; BiDrUSE; DcAmAu; DcAmB;
DcNAA; Drake; TwCBDA; WebAB; WhAm
HS; WhAmP*

Dallin, Cyrus
American. Sculptor
b. Nov 22, 1861 in Springville, Vermont
d. Nov 14, 1944 in Boston, Massachusetts
Source: *CurBio 45; DcAmB S3; WhAm 2*

Dalmores, Charles
French. Opera Singer
b. Jan 1, 1871 in Nancy, France
d. Dec 6, 1939 in Hollywood, California
Source: *WhAm 1; WhoStg 1908*

Dalrymple, Ian (Murray)
British. Screenwriter, Producer
Won Oscars for *The Citadel, Pygmalion*,
1938.
b. Aug 26, 1903 in Johannesburg, South
Africa
Source: *ConAu 115*

Dalrymple, Jean
American. Producer, Director
b. Sep 2, 1910 in Morristown, New Jersey
Source: *BiE&WWA; ConAu 5R; CurBio 53;
EncMT; InWom; NotNAT; WhoAm 82; WhoE
74; WhoGov 77; WhoThe 81; WrDr 82*

Dalton, Abby
American. Singer, Actress
Plays Julia Cumson on TV series "Falcon
Crest."
b. Aug 15, 1935 in Las Vegas, Nevada
Source: *WhoHol A*

Dalton, Charles
American. Actor
b. Aug 29, 1864
d. Jun 11, 1942 in Stamford, Connecticut
Source: *NotNAT B; WhThe; WhoHol B;
WhoStg 1908*

Dalton, Emmett
[Dalton Brothers]
American. Outlaw
Was realtor, screenwriter before becoming
bankrobber, trainrobber; author *When the
Daltons Rode*, 1931.
b. 1871 in Cass County, Missouri
d. Jul 13, 1937 in Los Angeles, California
Source: *Blood&B; DrInf; WhScrn 77*

Dalton, Gratton
[Dalton Brothers]
American. Outlaw
Cousin of Younger Brothers; killed by armed
citizens after trying to rob two banks at
once.
b. 1862 in Cass County, Missouri
d. Oct 5, 1892 in Coffeyville, Kansas
Source: *Blood&B; DrInf*

Dalton, John
English. Scientist
b. Sep 6, 1766 in Cumberland, England
d. Jul 27, 1844 in Manchester, England
Source: *Alli; BiDLA; BrAu 19*

Dalton, John Call
American. Physiologist
b. Feb 2, 1825 in Chelmsford, Massachusetts
d. 1889
Source: *BioIn 9*

Dalton, John Nichols
American. Politician
Rep. governor of VA, 1978-82; helped build
state's Rep. party into one of South's
strongest.
b. Jul 11, 1931 in Emporia, Virginia
d. Jul 30, 1986 in Richmond, Virginia
Source: *AlmAP 80; WhoAm 84; WhoS&SW
84*

Dalton, Lacy J
American. Singer
Country-western albums include *Hard Times,*
1980; *Lacy J Dalton,* 1980.
b. Oct 13, 1946
Source: *BioIn 12; WhoRocM 82*

Dalton, Robert
[Dalton Brothers]
American. Outlaw
Was marshal before becoming bankrobber,
trainrobber; killed trying to rob two banks
at once.
b. 1867 in Cass County, Missouri
d. Oct 5, 1892 in Coffeyville, Kansas
Source: *Blood&B; DcAmB; DrInf; WebAB*

Dalton, Timothy
Welsh. Actor
Appeared in films *The Lion in Winter,* 1968;
Wuthering Heights, 1970.
b. 1944 in Wales
Source: *BioIn 9; FilmEn; FilmgC; WhoHol A*

Dalton, William
[Dalton Brothers]
American. Criminal
Robbed banks and trains with brothers and
Doolin gang; killed by lawmen on front
porch.
b. 1873 in Cass County, Missouri
d. 1893
Source: *Blood&B; DrInf*

Daltrey, Roger
[The Who]
English. Singer
Appeared in *Tommy,* 1974; *The Kids Are
Alright,* 1979.
b. Mar 1, 1945 in Hammersmith, England
Source: *BkPepl; WhoAm 80, 82*

D'Alvarez, Marguerite
English. Opera Singer
b. 1886 in Liverpool, England
d. Oct 18, 1953 in Alassio, Italy
Source: *InWom*

Dalvit, Lewis David, Jr.
American. Conductor
b. Dec 11, 1925 in Denver, Colorado
Source: *WhoAm 82; WhoS&SW 78*

Daly, Arnold
American. Actor
b. Oct 4, 1875 in Brooklyn, New York
d. Jan 12, 1927 in New York, New York
Source: *Film 1; NotNAT; OxThe; PIP&P;
REn; WhAm 1; WhScrn 74; WhThe; WhoHol
B; WhoStg 1906, 1908*

Daly, Augustin
American. Dramatist
Melodramas include *Under the Gaslight,*
1867; established Broadway theatre,
Daley's, 1879.
b. Jul 20, 1838 in Plymouth, North Carolina
d. Jun 7, 1899 in Paris, France
Source: *AmAu; AmAu&B; BbD; CnDAL;
CnThe; DcNAA; HsB&A; PIP&P; REnAL;
REnWD; TwCBDA; WebAB 79; WhAm 1*

Daly, James
American. Actor
Played Dr. Paul Lochner on TV series
"Medical Center."
b. Oct 23, 1918 in Wisconsin Rapids,
Wisconsin
d. Jul 3, 1978 in Nyack, New York
Source: *BiE&WWA; CurBio 59; FilmgC;
IntMPA 75, 76, 77; NotNAT; WhoAm 74;
WhoHol A; WhoThe 77*

Daly, John
English. Producer
Films include *Return of the Living Dead,*
1983; *Terminator,* 1984; *Falcon and the
Snowman,* 1985.
b. 1937 in England
Source: *VarWW 85*

Daly, John Charles, Jr.
American. TV Host
b. Feb 20, 1914 in Johannesburg, South
Africa
Source: *NewYTET; WhoAm 82; WhoE 74;
WorAl*

Daly, Marcus
American. Business Executive, Pioneer
Copper magnate who founded Anaconda
Mining Co., 1891, town of Anaconda, MT,
1884.
b. Dec 5, 1841 in Ballyjamesduff, Ireland
d. Nov 12, 1900 in New York, New York
Source: *AmBi; BioIn 11; DcAmB; McGEWB;
OxAmH; REnAW; WebAB, 79; WhAm 1*

Daly, Maureen Patricia
Irish. Author
b. Mar 15, 1921 in Ulster, Northern Ireland
Source: *AmAu&B; AmNov; AuBYP; BkC 4;
CathA 1930; CurBio 46; InWom; MorJA;
REnAL; SmATA 2; WhoAmW 77*

Daly, Thomas Augustine
American. Journalist, Poet
b. May 28, 1871 in Philadelphia,
   Pennsylvania
d. Oct 4, 1948 in Philadelphia, Pennsylvania
Source: *AmAu&B; AmLY; BkC 1; CnDAL;
ConAmL; DcNAA; OxAmL; REn; REnAL;
TwCA, SUP; WhAm 2; WhNAA*

Daly, Tyne (Ellen Tyne)
[Mrs. Georg Sanford Brown]
American. Actress
Has won two Emmys for role of Mary Beth
   Lacey in TV series "Cagney and Lacey."
b. Feb 21, 1944 in Madison, Wisconsin
Source: *VarWW 85; WhoHol A; WhoTelC*

Dam, (Carl Peter) Henrik
Danish. Biochemist
b. Feb 21, 1895
d. Apr 17, 1976 in Copenhagen, Delaware
Source: *CurBio 49; IntWW 74; Who 74;
WhoWor 78*

D'Amato, Alfonse Marcello
American. Politician
Rep. senator from NY, who upset Javits,
   1980--.
b. Aug 1, 1937 in Brooklyn, New York
Source: *AlmAP 82; WhoAm 82; WhoE 81*

D'Amboise, Jacques
[Jacques Joseph d'Amboise Ahearn]
American. Ballet Dancer
b. Jul 28, 1934 in Dedham, Massachusetts
Source: *CelR; CurBio 64; WhoAm 74, 76, 78,
80, 82*

Damian, Saint
Religious Figure
d. 303
Source: *BioIn 2, 3, 4, 7*

Damien, Father
[Joseph Damien de Veuster]
Belgian. Missionary
Devoted life to leper colony in Hawaii; died
   from disease.
b. Jan 3, 1840 in Tremeloo, Belgium
d. Apr 15, 1889 in Molokai, Hawaii
Source: *AmBi; NewC; OxAmL; REn*

Damita, Lily
[Liliane-Marie-Madeleine Carre]
French. Actress
Wife of Errol Flynn, 1935-42.
b. Jul 19, 1901 in Bordeaux, France
Source: *FilmgC; InWom; MotPP; ThFT*

Damocles
Courtier
b. 370 ?BC in Syracuse, Sicily
Source: *NewC*

Damon and Pythias
Philosophers
Legendary Greek inseparable friends.
Source: *NewC; WebBD 80*

Damon, Ralph Shepard
American. Airline Executive
Pres., TWA, 1949-56; developed first
   "skysleeper" -Condor, 1933.
b. Jul 6, 1897 in Franklin, New Hampshire
d. Jan 4, 1956 in Mineola, New York
Source: *CurBio 56; InSci; WhAm 3; WorAl*

Damon, Stuart
American. Actor
Stage,TV actor, singer, best known as Dr.
   Alan Quartermain on TV soap opera
   "General Hospital."
b. Feb 5, 1937 in Brooklyn, New York
Source: *BiE&WWA; FilmgC; NotNAT;
WhoThe 72, 77, 81*

Damone, Vic
[Vito Farinola]
American. Singer, Actor
Winner Arthur Godfrey talent show, 1945;
   starred in *Hell to Eternity*, 1960.
b. Jun 12, 1928 in Brooklyn, New York
Source: *FilmgC; IntMPA 75, 76, 77, 78, 79,
80, 81, 82; WhoAm 74, 76, 78, 80, 82;
WhoHol A*

Dampier, William
English. Explorer, Author
Discovered New Britain Islands in Pacific on
   expedition, 1699-1701.
b. Jun 1652 in East Coker, England
d. Mar 1715 in London, England
Source: *BrAu; Chambr 2; DcLEL; EvLB;
NewC; OxEng; PenC ENG; REn*

Damrosch, Frank Heino
American. Musician
b. Jun 22, 1859 in Breslau, Prussia
d. Oct 22, 1937 in New York, New York
Source: *BioIn 1, 2, 4*

Damrosch, Leopold
German. Conductor
b. Oct 22, 1832 in Posen, Germany
d. Feb 15, 1885 in New York, New York
Source: *AmBi; ApCAB; DcAmB; OxAmL;
TwCBDA; WebAB; WhAm HS*

Damrosch, Walter Johannes
German. Conductor, Composer
b. Jan 30, 1862 in Breslau, Prussia
d. Dec 22, 1950 in New York, New York
Source: *AmSCAP 66; ApCAB; CurBio 44, 51;
DcAmB S4; OxAmL; REn; REnAL;
TwCBDA; WebAB; WhAm 3; WhScrn 77*

Dana, Bill
American. Comedian, Actor, Author
b. Oct 5, 1924 in Quincy, Massachusetts
Source: *AmSCAP 66; WhoAm 82; WhoHol A*

Dana, Charles Anderson
American. Editor, Journalist, Author
Editor, *Tribune,* 1847-1861; owner, editor,
Sun, 1868-97; wrote *The Artof Newspaper
Making,* 1895.
b. Aug 8, 1819 in Hinsdale, New Hampshire
d. Oct 17, 1879 in West Island, New York
Source: *Alli, SUP; AmAu; AmAu&B; AmBi;
ApCAB; BbD; BiAUS; BiD&SB; ChhPo;
CnDAL; DcAmAu; DcAmB; DcNAA; Drake;
OxAmL; REn; REnAL; TwCBDA; WebAB,
79; WhAm 6, HS*

Dana, James Dwight
American. Geologist
b. 1813 in Utica, New York
d. Apr 14, 1895 in New Haven, Connecticut
Source: *AmAu; BbD; BiD&SB; CyAL 1;
DcAmAu; DcNAA; OxAmL; REnAL; WebBD
80*

Dana, Margaret
American. Journalist
b. in Verona, New Jersey
Source: *ForWC 70; WhoAmW 77*

Dana, Richard Henry, Jr.
American. Author, Lawyer
Wrote *Two Years Before the Mast,* 1840.
b. Aug 1, 1815 in Cambridge, Massachusetts
d. Jan 6, 1882 in Rome, Italy
Source: *Alli, SUP; AmAu; AmAu&B; AmBi;
ApCAB; BbD; BiD&SB; CarSB; CasWL;
Chambr 3; CnDAL; CrtT 3; CyAL 2; CyWA;
DcAmAu; DcAmB; DcEnL; DcLEL; DcNAA;
EncAB-H; EvLB; MouLC 4; OxAmL; OxEng;
PenC AM; REn; REnAL; TwCBDA; WebAB,
79; WebE&AL; WhDW; WhAm HS; WhAmP;
WorAl*

Danby, Thomas Osborne
[Earl of Danby]
English. Statesman
b. 1632
d. 1712
Source: *NewCol 75; WebBD 80*

Dancer, Stanley
American. Jockey
Harness racing driver whose horses have
earned over $14 million since 1940s.
b. Jul 25, 1927 in New Egypt, New York
Source: *CelR; CurBio 73; NewYTBS 74*

Danco, Suzanne
Belgian. Opera Singer
b. Jan 22, 1911 in Brussels, Belgium
Source: *WhoMus 72; WhoWor 78*

Dancy, John
American. Broadcast Journalist
With NBC News since 1973.
b. Aug 5, 1936 in Jackson, Tennessee
Source: *LesBEnT; WhoAm 82, 84; WhoTelC*

Dandridge, Bob (Robert L)
American. Basketball Player
b. Nov 15, 1947 in Richmond, Virginia
Source: *BioIn 11; WhoBbl 73*

Dandridge, Dorothy
American. Singer, Actress
Starred in Otto Preminger's film *Carmen
Jones,* 1954.
b. Nov 9, 1922 in Cleveland, Ohio
d. Sep 8, 1965 in West Hollywood,
California
Source: *DcAmB S7; FilmgC; MotPP; MovMk;
WhAm 4; WhScrn 77; WhoHol B*

Dane, Clemence, pseud.
[Winifred Ashton]
English. Author, Screenwriter
First novel, *Regiment of Women,* 1917.
b. 1888 in Blackheath, England
d. Mar 28, 1965 in London, England
Source: *BiE&WWA; Chambr 3; ConAu 93;
DcLEL; EncMys; EvLB; LongCTC;
McGEWD; ModBlW; ModWD; NewC*

Dane, Maxwell
American. Advertising Executive
b. Jun 7, 1906 in Cincinnati, Ohio
Source: *St&PR 75; WhoAdv 72; WhoAm 74,
76, 78, 80, 82; WhoWorJ 72*

Danelli, Dino
[The Rascals]
American. Musician
Drummer with blue-eyed soul group; hit
single "How Can I Be Sure," 1967.
b. Jul 23, 1945 in New York, New York
Source: *NF*

Danelo, Joe (Joseph Peter)
American. Football Player
Kicker for NY Giants, 1976-84.
b. Sep 2, 1953 in Spokane, Washington
Source: *FootReg 85; NewYTBS 83*

Danforth, David Charles
"Dauntless Dave"
American. Baseball Player
b. Mar 7, 1890 in Granger, Texas
d. Sep 19, 1970 in Baltimore, Maryland
Source: *BaseEn 85; NewYTBE 70; WhoProB 73*

Danforth, John Claggett
American. Politician
Moderate Rep. senator from MO, 1976--,
  who is heir to Ralston Purina fortune.
b. Sep 5, 1936 in Saint Louis, Missouri
Source: *AlmAP 78, 80; BioIn 8, 10; CngDr 77, 79; IntWW 77, 78; WhoAm 76, 78, 80, 82, 84; WhoAmP 73, 75, 77, 79; WhoGov 72, 75, 77; WhoMW 78*

Danforth, William
[William Daniels]
American. Actor
Appeared over 5,000 performances of Gilbert
  & Sullivan operas; played *The Mikado*
  1,000 times.
b. May 13, 1869 in Syracuse, New York
d. Apr 16, 1941 in Skaneateles, New York
Source: *CurBio 41; NotNAT B; WhThe; WhoHol B*

Danforth, William H
American. Manufacturer, Business Executive
Founded Ralston Purina, 1893.
b. Sep 10, 1870 in Charleston, Missouri
d. Dec 24, 1952 in Saint Louis, Missouri
Source: *BioIn 1, 4, 5, 9; ObitOF 79; WhAm 3*

D'Angelo, Beverly
American. Actress, Singer
Former rock singer who appeared in films
  Paternity, 1981; *Coal Miner's Daughter,*
  1980.
b. 1952 in Columbus, Ohio
Source: *IntMPA 82*

Dangerfield, George Bubb
English. Author
b. Oct 28, 1904 in Berkshire, England
Source: *AmAu&B; ConAu 9R; CurBio 53; DrAS 74H; OxAmL; PoIre; WhoAm 74; WhoWest 84; WhoWor 78; WorAu; WrDr 80*

Dangerfield, Rodney
[Jacob Cohen, real name; Jack Roy, pseud.]
American. Comedian
b. Nov 22, 1921 in Babylon, New York
Source: *ConAu 102; WhoHol A*

Daniel
Biblical Character
d. 745 BC
Source: *NewCol 75*

Daniel, Beth
American. Golfer
Rookie of year, 1978, who won record
  amount of money on tour, 1980.
b. Oct 14, 1958 in Charleston, South
  Carolina
Source: *NewYTBS 78; WhoIntG*

Daniel, Clifton, Jr.
American. Journalist
Associate editor, NY *Times,* 1969--; married
  to Margaret Truman.
b. Sep 19, 1912 in Zebulon, North Carolina
Source: *IntWW 74; WhoE 74; WhoWor 78*

Daniel, Dan(iel)
American. Journalist, Editor
Covered baseball in NYC, 1909-74; founded
  boxing's *Ring* magazine.
b. 1891
d. Jul 1, 1981 in Pompano Beach, Florida
Source: *NewYTBS 81*

Daniel, Samuel
English. Poet, Author, Dramatist
Writings include narrative poem *Complaint of
  Rosamund,* 1592, historical epic *The Civil
  Wars,* 1595.
b. 1562 in Taunton, England
d. Oct 14, 1619 in Beckington, England
Source: *Alli; AtlBL; BbD; BiD&SB; BiDLA; BrAu; CasWL; Chambr 1; ChhPo, S1; CnE&AP; CroE&S; CrtT 1; DcEnA; DcEnL; DcEuL; DcLEL; EvLB; MouLC 1; NewC; NotNAT B; OxEng; OxThe; PenC ENG; PIP&P; PoLE; REn; REnWD; WebE&AL; WhDW*

Danielian, Leon
American. Dancer, Choreographer
b. Oct 31, 1920 in New York, New York
Source: *BioIn 3, 10, 11; WhoAm 74, 76, 78, 80, 82; WhoWor 78*

Daniell, Henry
English. Actor
Played Prof. Moriarity in Sherlock Holmes
film *The Woman in Green*, 1945.
b. Mar 5, 1894 in London, England
d. Oct 31, 1963 in Santa Monica, California
Source: *CmMov; FilmgC; MotPP; MovMk;
NotNAT B; PlP&P; Vers A; WhScrn 74, 77;
WhThe; WhoHol B*

Daniell, John Frederic
English. Inventor
Developed Daniell's hygrometer, 1820.
b. Mar 12, 1790
d. Mar 13, 1845
Source: *BioIn 2*

Daniels, "Bebe" (Virginia)
American. Actress
Made 200 shorts with Harold Lloyd, 1914-
18.
b. Jan 14, 1901 in Dallas, Texas
d. Mar 16, 1971 in London, England
Source: *BiDFilm; Film 1; FilmgC; InWom;
MotPP; MovMk; NewYTBE 71; NotNAT B;
ObitOF 79; ObitT 1971; OxFilm; ThFT;
TwYS; WhScrn 74, 77; WhoHol B;
WomWMM*

Daniels, Billy
American. Singer
b. 1914 in Jacksonville, Florida
Source: *WhoHol A*

Daniels, Charlie
[The Charlie Daniels Band]
American. Musician, Songwriter
Nashville session guitarist, who formed
Charlie Daniels Band, 1973; wrote
Grammy-winning song "Devil Went Down
to Georgia," 1979.
b. Oct 28, 1936 in Wilmington, North
Carolina
Source: *IlEncCM; RkOn 84; WhoAm 80, 82,
84; WhoRock 81*

Daniels, Draper
American. Advertising Executive
b. Aug 12, 1913 in Morris, New York
Source: *ConAu 53; WhoAdv 72; WhoAm 74,
76, 78, 80, 82; WhoF&I 74*

Daniels, Frank
American. Actor
Began in Vitagraph films, 1915; played in
Kernel Nutt series.
b. 1860 in Dayton, Ohio
d. Jan 12, 1935 in Palm Beach, Florida
Source: *Film 1; NotNAT B; PlP&P; WhAm
1; WhScrn 74, 77; WhThe; WhoHol B;
WhoStg 1906, 1908*

Daniels, Jeff
American. Actor
Films include *Ragtime*, 1982; *Terms of
Endearment*, 1984; *Purple Rose of Cairo*,
1985.
b. 1955 in Georgia
Source: *VarWW 85*

Daniels, Jonathan Worth
American. Author, Journalist
FDR's press secretary, 1945, who wrote
historical biographies: *Robert E Lee*, 1960.
b. Apr 26, 1902 in Raleigh, North Carolina
d. Nov 6, 1981 in Hilton Head Island, South
Carolina
Source: *AmAu&B; Au&Wr 71; AuBYP;
CnDAL; ConAu 49; CurBio 42, 82; IntAu&W
76; IntYB 78, 79; LinLib L; NewYTBS 81;
OxAmL; REn; REnAL; ScF&FL 1, 2; TwCA,
SUP; WhoAm 74, 76, 78, 80; WhoAmP 73,
75, 77, 79; WhoS&SW 73; WhoWor 74;
WrDr 80*

Daniels, Josephus
American. Journalist, Government Official
Secretary of Navy, 1913-21; ambassador to
Mexico, 1933-41; wrote *Our Navy at War*,
1922.
b. May 18, 1862 in Washington, District of
Columbia
d. Jan 15, 1948
Source: *AmAu&B; BiDSA; BiDrUSE; CurBio
44, 48; DcAmB S4; DcNAA; EncAB-H;
OxAmL; REn; REnAL; TwCBDA; WhAm 2;
WhAmP; WhJnl*

Daniels, Mickey
[Our Gang]
Actor
Appeared in first of Our Gang comedies,
1920s.
b. 1914
Source: *Film 2; WhoHol A*

Daniels, William
American. Actor
Won Emmy, 1984, for role of Dr. Mark
Craig on TV series "St. Elsewhere."
b. Mar 31, 1927 in Brooklyn, New York
Source: *BiE&WWA; IntMPA 81, 82; NotNAT;
PlP&P; WhoAm 82; WhoHol A*

Danielson, Gary
American. Football Player
b. Sep 10, 1951 in Detroit, Michigan
Source: *FootReg 81*

Daniloff, Nicholas
American. Educator, Author, Journalist
With *US News and World Report;* jailed,
  accused of spying in Soviet Union, 1986.
b. Dec 30, 1934 in Paris, France
Source: *CurBio 85*

Danilova, Alexandra
American. Ballerina, Choreographer
b. Jan 20, 1904 in Peterhof, Russia
Source: *BiE&WWA; InWom; Who 74;
WhoAm 82; WhoAmW 77; WhoThe 77A;
WhoWor 78*

Dankworth, John Philip William
English. Composer, Conductor
b. Sep 20, 1927 in London, England
Source: *OxFilm; Who 74; WhoMus 72*

Dannay, Frederic
[Ellery Queen, Barnaby Ross, joint pseuds.;
  Daniel Nathan]
American. Author, Editor
Wrote Ellery Queen mysteries with cousin
  Manfred B Lee.
b. Oct 20, 1905 in Brooklyn, New York
d. Sep 3, 1982 in White Plains, New York
Source: *AmAu&B; ASpks; AuBYP; ConAu 1R;
ConLC 11; CurBio 82; DcLEL; EncMys;
EvLB; IntAu&W 77; IntWW 80; NewYTBS
82; PenC AM; REn; ScF&FL 1; TwCA, SUP;
TwCCr&M 80; WebAB; Who 82; WhoAm 82;
WhoWor 74; WrDr 82*

Danner, Blythe Katharine
[Mrs. Bruce W Paltrow]
American. Actress
Won 1971 Tony for *Butterflies Are Free.*
b. Feb 3, 1943 in Philadelphia, Pennsylvania
Source: *BioIn 10; CurBio 81; IntMPA 82;
VarWW 85; WhoAm 82, 84; WhoAmW 74;
WhoHol A; WhoThe 77, 81; WorAl*

D'Annunzio, Gabriele
Italian. Poet, Author, Soldier
Ardent fascist, courted by Mussolini;
  numerous writings include *Dead City,*
  1902.
b. Mar 12, 1863 in Pescara, Italy
d. Mar 1, 1938 in Vittoriale, Italy
Source: *TwCA; WebBD 80; WhE&EA;
WhoTwCL*

Danson, Ted (Edward Bridge, III)
American. Actor
Plays Sam Malone on TV series "Cheers,"
  1982--.
b. Dec 29, 1947 in San Diego, California
Source: *ConTFT 1; VarWW 85*

Dante Alighieri
Italian. Poet
Wrote celebrated masterpiece *The Divine
  Comedy,* 1307-21.
b. May 27, 1265 in Florence, Italy
d. Sep 14, 1321 in Ravenna, Italy
Source: *AtlBL; BbD; BiD&SB; BlkAWP;
CasWL; ChhPo; CyWA; DcEnL; DcEuL;
EuAu; EvEuW; NewC; NewEOp 71; OxEng;
PenC EUR; RComWL; REn; WorAl*

Dante, Nicholas
American. Dramatist
Wrote *A Chorus Line,* 1976; won Pulitzer,
  Tony.
b. Nov 22, 1941 in New York, New York
Source: *VarWW 85*

Dantine, Helmut
American. Actor
Known for playing Nazi roles during WW
  II.
b. Oct 7, 1917 in Vienna, Austria
d. May 3, 1982 in Beverly Hills, California
Source: *FilmEn; FilmgC; IntMPA 82; MotPP;
MovMk*

Dantley, Adrian Delano
American. Basketball Player
Member US Olympic team, 1976, who led
  NBA in scoring, 1980-81.
b. Feb 26, 1956 in Washington, District of
  Columbia
Source: *InB&W 80; NewYTBS 84; WhoAm
84; WhoBlA 80*

Danton, Georges Jacques
French. Revolutionary
Leader of French Revolution; major figure in
  storming of Tuilleries; guillotined by
  Robespierre.
b. Oct 28, 1759 in Arcis-sur-Aube, France
d. Apr 5, 1794 in Paris, France
Source: *BioIn 11; DcEuL; McGEWB,; NewC;
OxFr; OxGer; REn; WhDW*

Danton, Ray(mond)
American. Actor
Best known for gangster roles *The Rise and
  Fall of Legs Diamond,* 1960; *Portrait of a
  Mobster,* 1961.
b. Sep 19, 1931 in New York, New York
Source: *FilmgC; IntMPA 82; WhoAm 80;
WhoHol A; WorAl; WorEFlm*

Danza, Tony
American. Actor, Boxer
Former middleweight fighter; star of TV
series "Taxi," 1982-85; "Who's the Boss?"
1985--.
b. Apr 21, 1951 in New York, New York
Source: *BioIn 12; VarWW 85*

DaPonte, Lorenzo
[Emmanuel Conegliano]
Italian. Poet, Librettist, Educator
Wrote librettos for Mozart's *Marriage of
Figaro*, 1786; taught Italian literature,
Columbia U, from 1825.
b. Mar 10, 1749 in Ceneda, Italy
d. Aug 17, 1838 in New York, New York
Source: *AmAu&B; ApCAB; BiD&SB; CasWL;
CyAL 2; DcAmAu; DcAmB; DcNAA; EvEuW;
OxAmH; OxGer; OxMus; REn; REnWD;
TwCBDA; WhAm HS*

Darby, Ken
American. Composer, Conductor
Film conductor who won Oscars for *The
King and I*, 1956; *Camelot*, 1967.
b. May 13, 1909 in Hebron, Nebraska
Source: *VarWW 85*

Darby, Kim
[Deborah Zerby]
American. Actress
Starred with John Wayne in *True Grit*, 1969.
b. Jul 8, 1948 in Hollywood, California
Source: *FilmgC; IntMPA 82; VarWW 85;
WhoAm 82; WhoHol A*

Darcel, Denise
American. Singer, Actress
b. Sep 8, 1925 in Paris, France
Source: *FilmgC; InWom; WhoHol A*

D'Arcy, Martin Cyril
English. Priest, Author
Jesuit professor, philosopher who wrote
Humanism and Christianity, 1969.
b. Jun 15, 1888 in Bath, England
d. Nov 20, 1976 in London, England
Source: *Au&Wr 71; BlueB 76; CathA 1930;
ConAu 3NR, 69; CurBio 77; IntAu&W 76;
IntWW 77N; LinLib L; NewYTBS 76; WhAm
7; WhE&EA; WhoWor 76*

Darcy, Tom
American. Cartoonist
b. Jun 7, 1916 in Saint Louis, Missouri
Source: *WhoAm 74*

Darden, Colgate Whitehead
American. Politician, Educator
Dem. governor, 1940s; pres., U of Virginia,
1950s, who fought against school
segregation.
b. Feb 11, 1897 in Franklin, Virginia
d. Jun 9, 1981 in Norfolk, Virginia
Source: *BiDrAC; CurBio 48; WhoAmP 75, 77*

Dare, Virginia
American. Colonial Figure
First child born in America of English
parents.
b. Aug 18, 1587 in Roanoke Island, Virginia
Source: *AmBi; ApCAB; ChhPo; DcAmB;
Drake; HerW; InWom; NotAW; OxAmL;
REn; WebAB; WhAm HS*

Dargan, Olive Tilford
American. Poet, Author
Writings include poetic drama, lyric poetry,
proletarian novels; best known for *A Stone
Came Rolling*, 1935.
b. 1869 in Grayson County, Kentucky
d. Jan 22, 1968 in Asheville, North Carolina
Source: *AmAu&B; AmNov X; BiDSA; ChhPo,
S2; CnDAL; ConAu 111; InWom; NotNAT B;
OxAmL; REnAL; TwCA, SUP; WhAm 5;
WhoAmW 61; WomWWA 14*

Dargomijsky, Alexander
[Alexander Dargomizyhsky]
Russian. Composer
Wrote opera *Esmeralda*, 1847; orchestral
work *Baba Yaga*, 1870.
b. Feb 14, 1813 in Tula, Russia
d. Jan 17, 1869 in Saint Petersburg, Russia
Source: *NewEOp 71; OxMus*

Darin, Bobby
[Walden Robert Cassotto]
American. Singer, Actor
Best-known song "Mack the Knife," won
two Grammys, 1960.
b. May 14, 1936 in New York, New York
d. Dec 20, 1973 in Hollywood, California
Source: *CurBio 63, 74; MotPP; MovMk;
NewYTBE 73; WhAm 6; WhScrn 77;
WhoHol B*

Daringer, Helen Fern
American. Children's Author
b. 1892 in Mattoon, Illinois
Source: *ConAu 17R, P-2; CurBio 51; MorJA;
SmATA 1*

Darion, Joseph
American. Lyricist
Won 1965 Tony for lyrics of *Man of La Mancha.*
b. Jan 30, 1917 in New York, New York
Source: *ConAu 113; EncMT*

Darius I
[Darius the Great]
Persian. Ruler
King, 521-486 BC; army defeated by Greeks at Battle of Marathon, 490 BC.
b. 558 BC
d. 486 BC
Source: *WebBD 80*

Dark, Alvin Ralph
"Blackie"
American. Baseball Player, Baseball Manager
Shortstop, 1946-60; rookie of year, 1948.
b. Jan 7, 1923 in Comanche, Oklahoma
Source: *BaseEn 85; CurBio 75; NewYTBS 74; WhoAm 82; WhoProB 73*

Darken, Lawrence Stamper
American. Chemist
b. Sep 18, 1909 in Brooklyn, New York
d. Jun 7, 1978 in Boalsburg, Pennsylvania
Source: *IntWW 74; WhoAm 74*

Darlan, Jean Francois
French. Government Official
Ex-Vichy commissioner for French and W Africa; assassinated in Algiers.
b. Aug 7, 1881 in Nerac, France
d. Dec 24, 1942 in Algiers, Algeria
Source: *CurBio 41, 43*

Darley, Felix Octavius Carr
American. Illustrator, Author
Illustrated Irving's *Rip Van Winkle,* 1849; *Legend of Sleepy Hollow,* 1850.
b. Jun 23, 1822 in Philadelphia, Pennsylvania
d. Mar 27, 1888 in Claymont, Delaware
Source: *AmAu&B; BiD&SB; BioIn 1, 2, 3, 7, 8, 9; CarSB; DcAmAu; DcNAA*

Darling, Erik
[The Weavers]
American. Singer, Musician
b. Sep 25, 1933 in Baltimore, Maryland
Source: *EncFCWM 69*

Darling, Frank Fraser, Sir
Scottish. Scientist, Author
Expert in biology, genetics, agriculture.
b. Jun 23, 1903 in Scotland
d. Oct 25, 1979 in Forres, Scotland
Source: *ConAu 61, 89; IntWW 74; OxEng; Who 74*

Darling, Jay Norwood
[J N Ding, pseud.]
American. Cartoonist
b. Oct 21, 1876 in Norwood, Michigan
d. Feb 12, 1962 in Des Moines, Iowa
Source: *AmAu&B; ConAu 93; CurBio 42, 62; WhAm 4; WhJnl; WhNAA; WorECar*

Darling, Ron(ald Maurice, Jr.)
American. Baseball Player
Pitcher, NY Mets, 1983--; member NL All-Star team, 1985.
b. Aug 19, 1960 in Honolulu, Hawaii
Source: *BaseEn 85; BaseReg 86*

Darnell, Linda
American. Actress
Famous for role in *Forever Amber,* 1948.
b. Oct 16, 1921 in Dallas, Texas
d. Apr 12, 1965 in Chicago, Illinois
Source: *BiDFilm; EvEuW; FilmgC; InWom; MotPP; MovMk; ThFT; WhScrn 74, 77; WhoHol B; WorEFlm*

Darnley, Henry Stuart, Lord
English. Celebrity Relative
Great-grandson of Henry VIII; second husband of Mary Queen of Scots.
b. 1545
d. Feb 9, 1567
Source: *DcBiPP; Dis&D; NewC; REn*

Darnton, Robert Choate
American. Author
Wrote award-winning *Literary Underground of the Old Regime,* 1982.
b. May 10, 1939 in New York, New York
Source: *ConAu 116*

Darren, James
American. Actor, Singer
Starred in *Gidget,* 1959; TV series "The Time Tunnel," 1966-67.
b. Jun 8, 1936 in Philadelphia, Pennsylvania
Source: *FilmgC; IntMPA 82; MotPP; MovMk; WhoHol A*

Darrieux, Danielle
French. Actress
Epitome of French femininity; films included *Mayerling,* 1936, *La Ronde,* 1950.
b. May 1, 1917 in Bordeaux, France
Source: *BiDFilm; EncWT; FilmgC; InWom; IntMPA 82; IntWW 74; MotPP; MovMk; OxFilm; WhoHol A; WhoWor 74; WorEFlm*

Darro, Frankie
[Frank Johnson]
American. Actor
Played tough kids, jockeys in Depression-era
films.
b. Dec 22, 1917 in Chicago, Illinois
d. 1976
Source: *Film 2; FilmgC; MovMk; Vers B;
WhoHol A*

Darrow, Charles Bruce
American. Inventor
Invented board game Monopoly.
b. 1889
d. Aug 29, 1967 in Ottsville, Pennsylvania
Source: *ObitOF 79*

Darrow, Clarence Seward
American. Lawyer
Defense counsel in widely publicized trials,
Leopold-Loeb murder, 1924; Scottsboro
case, 1932.
b. Apr 18, 1857 in Kinsman, Ohio
d. Mar 13, 1938 in Chicago, Illinois
Source: *AmAu&B; AmBi; DcAmB S2;
DcLEL; DcNAA; EncAB-H; FilmgC; OhA&B;
OxAmL; REn; REnAL; TwCA, SUP; WebAB;
WhAm 1; WhNAA*

Darrow, Henry
[Henry Thomas Delgado]
American. Actor
Appeared in TV's "High Chaparral," 1967-
71, "Harry-O," 1974-75.
b. Sep 15, 1933 in New York, New York
Source: *WhoHol A*

Darrow, Whitney, Jr.
American. Author, Cartoonist
b. Aug 22, 1909 in Princeton, New Jersey
Source: *ConAu 114, 61; SmATA 13*

Dart, Justin Whitlock
American. Business Executive
Pres., director Rexall Drugs, 1946-75; adviser
to Ronald Reagan's kitchen cabinet in CA
politics.
b. Aug 7, 1907 in Evanston, Illinois
d. Jan 26, 1984 in Los Angeles, California
Source: *BioIn 10; CurBio 46; Dun&B 79;
IntWW 82; IntYB 82; WhoAm 82; WhoWest
82*

Dart, Raymond Arthur
Australian. Anthropologist
b. Feb 4, 1893 in Toowong, Australia
Source: *Au&Wr 71; BioIn 5, 7; ConAu 13R,
P-1; CurBio 66; IntWW 74; Who 82;
WhoWor 78*

Darvas, Lili
American. Actress
Starred in Max Reinhardt's repertory co.,
1926-38.
b. Apr 10, 1906 in Budapest, Hungary
d. Jul 22, 1974 in New York, New York
Source: *BiE&WWA; NewYTBE 73; NewYTBS
74; NotNAT; ObitOF 79; WhAm 6; WhScrn
77; WhThe; WhoAm 74; WhoHol B*

Darvi, Bella
[Bayla Wegier]
American. Actress
b. Oct 23, 1929 in Sosnowiec, Poland
d. Sep 10, 1971 in Monte Carlo, Monaco
Source: *FilmgC; WhScrn 74, 77; WhoHol B*

Darwell, Jane
[Patti Woodward]
American. Actress
Won 1940 Oscar as Ma Joad in *Grapes of
Wrath.*
b. Oct 15, 1880 in Palmyra, Missouri
d. Aug 13, 1967 in Woodland Hills,
California
Source: *BiDFilm; CurBio 41, 67; Film 1;
FilmgC; InWom; MotPP; MovMk; OxFilm;
ThFT; TwYS; Vers A; WhScrn 74, 77;
WhoHol B; WorAl; WorEFlm*

Darwin, Bernard Richard Meirion
English. Journalist
Wrote weekly golf articles in London *Times*
43 yrs.
b. Sep 7, 1876 in Downe, England
d. Oct 18, 1961 in Denton, England
Source: *DcNaB 1961; GrBr; LongCTC; ObitT
1961; WhE&EA; WhLit; WhoGolf; WhoLA*

Darwin, Charles Robert
English. Author, Naturalist
Expounder of theory of evolution through
natural selection; best known work *Origin
of the Species,* 1859.
b. Feb 12, 1809 in Shrewsbury, England
d. Apr 19, 1882 in Down, England
Source: *Alli, SUP; ApCAB SUP; AtlBL; BbD;
BiD&SB; BrAu 19; CarSB; CasWL; Chambr
3; CyWA; DcEnA, AP; DcEnL; DcEuL;
DcLEL; EvLB; MouLC 4; NewC; OxEng;
PenC ENG; RComWL; REn; WebE&AL;
WhDW; WorAl*

Daryush, Elizabeth Bridges
English. Poet
b. Dec 5, 1887 in London, England
d. Apr 7, 1977 in Stockwell, England
Source: *BioIn 11; ConAu 49, 3NR; ConLC 6*

Dash, Samuel
American. Watergate Participant, Lawyer
b. Feb 27, 1925 in Camden, New Jersey
Source: *BioNews 74; NewYTBE 73; WhoAm 82; WhoAmJ 80; WhoS&SW 76*

Dashwood, Elizabeth Monica
[E M Delafield, pseud.]
English. Author
Comedies of manners include *Provincial Lady in America*, 1934.
b. Jun 9, 1890 in Sussex, England
d. Dec 2, 1943 in Cullompton, England
Source: *NewC; REn; WhoLA*

DaSilva, Howard
[Harold Silverblatt]
American. Actor, Director, Producer
Career spanned 55 yrs.; best known for playing Benjamin Franklin in Broadway musical *1776*, 1969.
b. May 4, 1909 in Cleveland, Ohio
d. Feb 16, 1986 in Ossining, New York
Source: *AnObit 1984; BiE&WWA; EncMT; FilmgC; IntMPA 77, 75; MovMk; NewYTBS 74; NotNAT; PIP&P; WhoAm 82; WhoHol A; WhoThe 77; WhoWor 74; WorAl*

Dassault, Marcel
[Marcel Bloch]
French. Aircraft Manufacturer
Built world's most sophisticated warplanes, from biplanes to supersonic Mirage fighters.
b. Jan 22, 1892 in Paris, France
d. Apr 18, 1986 in Paris, France
Source: *BioIn 11; CurBio 86; IntWW 82; WhoWor 74*

Dassin, Jules
American. Director
Married to Melina Mercouri, who starred in his films *Never on Sunday*, 1960, *Topkapi*, 1964.
b. Dec 12, 1911 in Middletown, Connecticut
Source: *BiDFilm; BiE&WWA; CmMov; ConDr 77F; DcFM; FilmgC; IntMPA 82; IntWW 82; MovMk; OxFilm; WhoAm 82; WhoHol A; WorEFlm*

Dassler, Adolf
"Adi"
German. Manufacturer
Founded Adidas Shoes, 1920; yearly sales now over $700 million.
b. 1901
d. Sep 18, 1978 in Herzogenaurach, Germany (West)
Source: *BioIn 11; ObitOF 79*

Daubeny, Peter Lauderdale, Sir
British. Director
b. Apr 1921 in Wiesbaden, Germany
d. Aug 6, 1975 in London, England
Source: *BioIn 3, 9, 10; CnThe; ConAu 61; EncWT; IntWW 74; OxThe; WhThe; Who 74; WhoThe 72; WhoWor 74*

Daubert, Jake (Jacob Ellsworth)
American. Baseball Player
First baseman, Brooklyn, Cincinnati, 1910-24; won NL batting titles, 1913, 1914.
b. May 15, 1885 in Shamokin, Pennsylvania
d. Oct 9, 1924 in Cincinnati, Ohio
Source: *WhoProB 73*

Daubigny, Charles Francois
French. Artist
Landscape painter who influenced Impressionists: "Lever de Lune," 1877.
b. Feb 15, 1817 in Paris, France
d. Feb 19, 1878 in Auvers, France
Source: *AtlBL*

D'Aubuisson, Roberto
Salvadoran. Politician
Head of ultra-right Nationalist Republican Alliance Party, pres., Constituent Assembly, 1982--.
b. 1944 in Santa Tecla, El Salvador
Source: *CurBio 83; NewYTBS 82*

Daudet, Alphonse Marie Leon
French. Author
Wrote naturalistic novels of contemporary life; stories of Provence include *Tartarin de Tarascon*, 1872.
b. May 13, 1840 in Nimes, France
d. Dec 16, 1897 in Champrosay, France
Source: *AtlBL; BbD; BiD&SB; ChhPo, S2; ClDMEL; CyWA; DcBiA; DcEuL; EvEuW; McGEWD; NewC; OxEng; OxFr; PenC EUR; RComWL; REn; WhDW; WorAl*

Daudet, Leon
French. Author, Politician
b. Nov 16, 1867
d. Jul 1, 1942
Source: *CasWL; ClDMEL; CurBio 42; EncWL; NewC; OxFr; REn*

Daugherty, Pat
[Black Oak Arkansas]
American. Musician
Bass guitarist with heavy-metal Dixie boogie group.
b. Nov 11, 1947 in Jonesboro, Arkansas
Source: *NF*

Daugherty, William J
[The Hostages]
American. Hostage in Iran
b. 1948
Source: *NewYTBS 81*

Daumier, Honore
French. Artist
Noted for over 7,500 lithographs, illustrations satirizing French politics, society.
b. Feb 26, 1808 in Marseilles, France
d. Feb 11, 1879 in Valmondois, France
Source: *AtlBL; OxFr; REn*

Dauphin, Claude Le Grand Maria Eugene
French. Actor
International film star best known for *April in Paris,* 1952.
b. Aug 19, 1903 in Corbeil, France
d. Nov 17, 1978 in Paris, France
Source: *BiE&WWA; FilmgC; IntMPA 82; MotPP; MovMk; NewYTBS 78; NotNAT; ObitOF 79; WhAm 7; WhoHol A; WhoThe 81; WhoWor 74*

Dauss, George August
"Hooks"
American. Baseball Player
Pitcher, Detroit, 1912-26; won 221 games.
b. Sep 22, 1889 in Indianapolis, Indiana
d. Jul 27, 1963 in Saint Louis, Missouri
Source: *BaseEn 85; WhoProB 73*

Dausset, Jean (Baptiste Gabriel Joachim)
French. Scientist
Won Nobel Prize, physiology, for research contributing to organ transplant success, 1980.
b. Oct 19, 1916 in Toulouse, France
Source: *CurBio 81; IntWW 82; NewYTBS 80; Who 82*

Dave Clark Five
[Dave Clark; Lenny Davidson; Rick Huxley; Denis Payton; Michael Smith]
English. Music Group
Source: *EncPR&S 74; RkOn 74*

Davenant, William, Sir
English. Poet, Dramatist
Siege of Rhodes, 1662, was first English opera.
b. Feb 1606 in Oxford, England
d. Apr 7, 1668 in London, England
Source: *Alli; BbD; BiD&SB; BrAu; CasWL; Chambr 1; ChhPo, S1; CnE&AP; CnThe; CroE&S; CyWA; DcEnL; DcEuL; EvLB; McGEWD; NewC; OxEng; OxThe; PenC ENG; PlP&P; PoLE; REn; REnWD; WebE&AL; WhDW*

Davenport, Eva
English. Actress
b. 1858 in London, England
d. Sep 26, 1932 in White Plains, New York
Source: *NF*

Davenport, Fanny Lily Gypsy
American. Actress
Formed own company, 1877; produced, starred in four plays by Sardon.
b. Apr 10, 1850 in London, England
d. Sep 26, 1898 in South Duxbury, Massachusetts
Source: *FamA&A; NotAW; NotNAT B; OxThe; PlP&P; TwCBDA*

Davenport, Harry George Bryant
American. Actor
Played grandfather roles in films *The Higgins Family* series, 1938-40; *Meet Me in St. Louis,* 1944.
b. Jan 19, 1886 in New York, New York
d. Aug 9, 1949 in Los Angeles, California
Source: *Film 1; FilmgC; MotPP; MovMk; ObitOF 79; OxThe; Vers A; WhScrn 74, 77; WhThe; WhoHol B; WhoStg 1906, 1908*

Davenport, Homer Calvin
American. Cartoonist
Political cartoonist whose; most famous cartoon is Uncle Sam's endorsement of T Roosevelt: "He's Good Enough for Me."
b. Mar 8, 1867 in Silverton, Oregon
d. May 2, 1912 in New York, New York
Source: *AmAu&B; BioIn 10; DcAmAu; DcAmB; DcNAA; NatCAB 11; WebBD 80; WorECar*

Davenport, Marcia
American. Author, Music Critic
Wrote best-selling *Valley of Decision,* 1942; *East Side, West Side,* 1947.
b. Jun 9, 1903 in New York, New York
Source: *AmAu&B; AmNov; AuBYP; ConAu 9R; CurBio 44; DcLEL; InWom; LongCTC; OxAmL; REn; REnAL; TwCA SUP; WhoAm 80; WhoAmW 74; WhoWor 74*

Davenport, Nigel
English. Actor
Character actor who appeared in *Look Back in Anger,* 1959; *Chariots of Fire,* 1981.
b. May 23, 1928 in Shelford, England
Source: *FilmgC; IntMPA 82; WhoHol A; WhoThe 81*

Davenport, Thomas
American. Inventor
Discovered principle of starting, stopping
electric current over wire, 1834.
b. Jul 19, 1802 in Williamstown, Vermont
d. Jul 6, 1851 in Salisbury, Vermont
Source: *AmBi; ApCAB; DcAmB; TwCBDA;
WebAB; WhAm HS*

Davenport, Willie
American. Olympic Athlete
b. Jun 8, 1943 in Troy, Alabama
Source: *WhoTr&F 73*

DaVerrazano, Giovanni
see: Verrazano, Giovanni da

David, Saint
[Dewi]
Religious Figure
Patron saint of Wales said to have founded
12 monasteries; feast day Mar 1.
b. 495 in Henfynw, Wales
d. 589 in Mynyw, Wales
Source: *Alli; BioIn 10; DcCathB; LongCEL;
NewC; REn*

David
King
Prominent Old Testament figure.
b. 1000 BC
d. 960 BC
Source: *BiB N; DcOrL 3; McGEWB; NewC*

David
"Bubble Boy"
American. Patient
Born without any immunity to disease, spent
all but last 15 days of life in sterile,
plastic bubble.
b. Sep 21, 1971 in Houston, Texas
d. Feb 22, 1984 in Houston, Texas
Source: *BioIn 11*

David, Elizabeth
British. Author
b. 1914
Source: *Au&Wr 71; Who 74*

David, Gerard
Dutch. Artist
b. 1460 in Oudewater, New Hampshire
d. Aug 13, 1523 in Bruges, New Hampshire
Source: *AtlBL*

David, Hal
American. Lyricist
Former partner of Burt Bacharach; won
Oscar, 1969, for "Raindrops Keep Fallin'
on My Head."
b. May 25, 1921 in New York, New York
Source: *AmSCAP 66; CelR; CurBio 80;
EncMT; NotNAT; WhoAm 74, 76, 78, 80, 82*

David, Jacques Louis
French. Artist
b. Aug 30, 1748 in Paris, France
d. Dec 29, 1825 in Brussels, Belgium
Source: *AtlBL; OxFr*

David, Mack
American. Composer
Film scores include *To Kill a Mockingbird,*
1963; *It's a Mad, Mad, Mad, Mad, World,*
1963.
b. Jul 5, 1912 in New York, New York
Source: *VarWW 85*

David-Neel, Alexandra
French. Explorer, Author
First European woman to enter forbidden
Tibetan capital, Lhasa; wrote *My Journey
to Lhasa.*
b. Oct 24, 1868
d. Sep 8, 1969 in Digne, France
Source: *ConAu 25R*

Davidson, Donald Grady
American. Poet, Critic, Historian
Founded Fugitive School of southern
American literature, 1920's.
b. Aug 18, 1893 in Campbellsville, Tennessee
d. Apr 25, 1968 in Nashville, Tennessee
Source: *AmAu&B; ChhPo, S1; ConAmA;
ConAu 5R, 25R, 4NR; ConLC 2, 13; DcLEL;
NewYTBE 71; OxAmL; PenC AM; REnAL;
SixAP; TwCA, SUP; WhAm 5; WhNAA*

Davidson, J Brownlee
American. Educator, Engineer
Instructor, farm mechanics; designed several
pieces of farm equipment including the
Iowa dynameter.
b. Feb 15, 1880 in Douglas, Nebraska
d. May 8, 1957 in Denver, Colorado
Source: *BioIn 9; InSci; NatCAB 43; WhAm
3; WhNAA*

Davidson, Jo
American. Sculptor
b. Mar 30, 1883 in New York, New York
d. Jan 2, 1952 in Bercheron, France
Source: *CurBio 45, 52; DcAmB S5; OxAmL;
REn; REnAL; WebAB; WhAm 3*

Davidson, John
American. Singer, Actor
Starred in *The Happiest Millionaire,* 1967;
TV series, "That's Incredible," 1980-85.
b. Dec 13, 1941 in Pittsburgh, Pennsylvania
Source: *BkPepl; IntMPA 75, 76, 77, 78, 79,
80, 81, 82; MotPP; WhoAm 74, 76, 78, 80,
82; WhoHol A*

Davie, Alan
Scottish. Poet, Jazz Musician
b. 1920 in Grangemouth, Scotland
Source: *BioIn 4, 7, 8; IntWW 74; Who 74;
WhoWor 78*

Davie, Donald
English. Author
b. Jul 17, 1922 in Yorkshire, England
Source: *CasWL; ChhPo; ConAu 1R; ConLC
5; ConP 70, 75; LongCTC; ModBrL, S1;
NewC; REn; TwCWr; Who 76; WhoAm 74;
WhoTwCL; WorAu*

Davies, Arthur Bowen
American. Artist
b. Sep 26, 1862 in Utica, New York
d. Oct 24, 1928 in Florence, Italy
Source: *AmBi; ChhPo; DcAmB; OxAmL;
WebAB; WhAm 1*

Davies, Dave (David)
[Kinks]
English. Singer, Musician
Rhythm guitarist of hard rock-turned pop
group; hit single "You Really Got Me,"
1964.
b. Feb 3, 1947 in Muswell Hill, England
Source: *BioIn 12; WhoRocM 82*

Davies, Hunter
Scottish. Author, Editor
Punch columnist since 1979; wrote authorized
biography of The Beatles, 1968; *London at
Its Best,* 1984.
b. Jan 7, 1936 in Renfrew, Scotland
Source: *ConAu 57; Who 85; WhoWor 74, 76;
WrDr 76, 80*

Davies, Joseph Edward
American. Lawyer, Diplomat
b. Nov 29, 1876 in Watertown, Wisconsin
d. May 9, 1958 in Washington, District of
Columbia
Source: *AmAu&B; CurBio 42, 58; WhAm 3*

Davies, Leslie Purnell
English. Author
b. Oct 20, 1914 in Cheshire, England
Source: *ConAu 21R; WrDr 80*

Davies, Marion
[Marion Douras]
American. Actress
Mistress of William Randolf Hearst; affair
satirized by Orson Welles in *Citizen Kane,*
1941.
b. Jan 3, 1897 in New York, New York
d. Sep 22, 1961 in Hollywood, California
Source: *BiDFilm; Film 1; FilmgC; MotPP;
MovMk; OxFilm; ThFT; TwYS; WhAm 4;
WhScrn 74, 77; WhThe; WhoHol B; WorAl;
WorEFlm*

Davies, Peter Maxwell
English. Composer
b. Sep 8, 1934 in Manchester, England
Source: *BioIn 6, 8; CurBio 80; IntWW 79*

Davies, Ray(mond Douglas)
[The Kinks]
English. Singer, Musician
Lead guitarist for band formed with brother
Dave, 1963.
b. Jun 21, 1944 in Muswell Hill, England
Source: *ConAu 116; ConLC 21; IlEncRk;
WhoRocM 82*

Davies, Robert Edris
"Harrisburg Houdini"
American. Basketball Player
Four-time All-Star who led NBA in assists,
1949; Hall of Fame, 1969.
b. Jan 15, 1920 in Harrisburg, Pennsylvania
Source: *BioIn 3; OfNBA 81; WhoBbl 73*

Davies, Robertson
Canadian. Author
Best known for Deptford trilogy.
b. Aug 28, 1913 in Thamesville, Ontario
Source: *Au&Wr 71; CaW; CanWW 79;
CanWr; CasWL; CnThe; ConAu 33R; ConDr
77; ConLC 2, 7, 13; ConNov 72, 76; CreCan
1; CurBio 75; DcLEL; DrAS 74E, 78E;
IntAu&W 76, 77; IntWW 77, 78, 79, 80;
LongCTC; McGEWD; ModCmwL; OxCan,
SUP; PenC ENG; REnAL; REnWD; TwCWr;
WhoAm 74, 76, 78, 80, 82; WhoWor 74;
WorAu; WrDr 76, 80*

Davies, Rodger Paul
American. Diplomat
With US diplomatic service, 1946-74; mainly
in Middle East, Southeast Asia.
b. May 7, 1921 in Berkeley, California
d. Aug 19, 1974 in Nicosia, Cyprus
Source: *USBiR 74; WhAm 6; WhoAm 74*

Davis, Adelle
American. Nutritionist
Wrote *Let's Cook It Right,* 1947.
b. Feb 25, 1904 in Lizion, Indiana
d. May 31, 1974 in Palos Verdes, California
Source: *BioNews 74; CelR; ConAu 37R, 49;
CurBio 73; NewYTBS 74; NotAW MOD;
REnAL; WhAm 6; WhoAm 74*

Davis, Alexander Jackson
American. Architect
b. Jul 24, 1803 in New York, New York
d. Jan 14, 1892 in West Orange, New Jersey
Source: *AmBi; ApCAB SUP; DcAmB; DcNAA;
EarABI SUP; TwCBDA; WhAm HS*

Davis, Al(len)
American. Football Executive
Controversial owner, Oakland Raiders since
1963, who defied NFL, moved team to
LA, 1982.
b. Jul 4, 1929 in Brockton, Massachusetts
Source: *BioIn 11; CurBio 85; WhoAm 82, 84;
WhoWest 82*

Davis, Andrew Frank
English. Conductor
Musical director, Toronto Symphony
Orchestra, 1975--.
b. Feb 4, 1944 in Ashridge, England
Source: *CurBio 83; Who 82, 83*

Davis, Angela Yvonne
American. Revolutionary, Author
On FBI's ten most-wanted list, 1970; wrote
autobiography, 1974.
b. Jan 26, 1944 in Birmingham, Alabama
Source: *BioIn 8, 9, 10, 11; BioNews 74;
BkPepl; CelR; ConAu 57; CurBio 72; HerW;
NewYTBE 70, 71, 72*

Davis, Ann Bradford
American. Actress
Best known for TV series *The Brady Bunch,*
1969-74, *The Bob Cummings Show,* 1955-
59.
b. May 3, 1926 in Schenectady, New York
Source: *InWom; WhoAm 82; WhoAmW 74;
WhoHol A*

Davis, Arthur Vining
American. Real Estate Executive
b. May 30, 1867 in Sharon, Massachusetts
d. Nov 17, 1962 in Miami, Florida
Source: *BioIn 11; ObitOF 79; WhAm 5;
WhFla*

Davis, Benjamin Oliver, Jr.
American. Air Force Officer
Member, first group of blacks admitted to air
corps, 1941; first black general in air
force, 1954.
b. Dec 18, 1912 in Washington, District of
Columbia
Source: *CurBio 55; NewYTBE 70; WhoAm
74; WhoAmP 81; WhoBlA 75; WhoGov 72;
WhoS&SW 73; WorAl*

Davis, Benjamin Oliver
American. Military Leader
b. Jul 1, 1877 in Washington, District of
Columbia
d. Nov 26, 1970 in North Chicago, Illinois
Source: *CurBio 42, 71; EncAB-H; NewYTBE
70; WebAB*

Davis, Bette (Ruth Elizabeth)
American. Actress
Fifty-year film career includes Oscars for
Dangerous, 1935; *Jezebel,* 1938.
b. Apr 5, 1908 in Lowell, Massachusetts
Source: *BiDFilm; BiE&WWA; BioNews 74;
BkPepl; CelR; CmMov; ConAu 61; CurBio 41,
53; EncMT; FilmgC; InWom; IntMPA 75, 76,
77, 78, 79, 80, 81, 82; IntWW 74; MotPP;
MovMk; NewYTBE 70; NotNAT; OxFilm;
ThFT; WebAB; Who 74; WhoAm 74, 76, 78,
80, 82; WhoHol A; WhoThe 77; WhoWor 78;
WorEFlm*

Davis, Billy, Jr.
[Fifth Dimension]
American. Singer
Vocalist with pop-soul group; had number-
one hit "Wedding Bell Blues," 1969.
b. Jun 26, 1940 in Saint Louis, Missouri
Source: *BiDAmM; InB&W 80*

Davis, Brad
American. Actor
Appeared in films *Midnight Express,* 1978,
Chariots of Fire, 1981.
b. 1950 in Florida
Source: *BioIn 11; IntMPA 82*

Davis, Burke
American. Children's Author
b. Jul 24, 1913 in Durham, North Carolina
Source: *AuBYP; SmATA 4; WhoAm 82;
WrDr 76*

Davis, Clifton
American. Actor, Singer, Composer
Wrote gold-record song "Never Can Say
Goodbye."
b. Oct 4, 1945 in Chicago, Illinois
Source: *WhoBlA 75; WhoHol A*

Davis, Clive Jay
American. Businessman
b. Apr 4, 1932 in Brooklyn, New York
Source: *BusPN; WhoAm 80, 82*

Davis, Clyde Brion
American. Journalist, Author
Best known for *The Great American Novel*, 1938.
b. May 22, 1894 in Unadilla, Nebraska
d. Jul 19, 1962 in Salisbury, Connecticut
Source: *AmNov; CnDAL; ConAu 5R; ObitOF 79; OxAmL; REn; REnAL; TwCA, SUP; WhAm 4; WhE&EA*

Davis, Colin
English. Conductor
b. Sep 25, 1927 in Weybridge, England
Source: *CurBio 68; IntWW 74; NewYTBE 72; Who 74; WhoMus 72; WhoWor 78*

Davis, David
American. Supreme Court Justice
b. Mar 9, 1815 in Cecil County, Maryland
d. Jun 26, 1886 in Bloomington, Illinois
Source: *ApCAB; BiAUS; BiDrAC; DcAmB; Drake; EncAB-H; TwCBDA; WebAB; WhAm HS; WhAmP*

Davis, Dwight Filley
American. Government Official
b. Jul 5, 1879 in Saint Louis, Missouri
d. Nov 28, 1945 in Washington, District of Columbia
Source: *BiDrUSE; DcAmB S3; NatCAB 40; ObitOF 79; WhAm 2*

Davis, Edward Michael
American. Government Official
Chief of LA police, 1969-79.
b. Nov 15, 1916 in Los Angeles, California
Source: *BioIn 11; WhoGov 72; WhoWest 78*

Davis, Elmer Holmes
American. Journalist, Radio Commentator
b. Jan 13, 1890 in Aurora, Indiana
d. May 18, 1958 in Washington, District of Columbia
Source: *AmAu&B; CurBio 58; EncAB-H; IndAu 1816; OxAmL; REn; REnAL; TwCA, SUP; WebAB; WhNAA*

Davis, Ernie (Ernest R)
American. Football Player
First black to win Heisman Trophy, 1961.
b. Dec 14, 1939 in New Salem, Pennsylvania
d. May 18, 1963 in Cleveland, Ohio
Source: *DcAmB S7*

Davis, Frederick C(lyde)
[Murdo Coombs; Stephen Ransome; Curtis Steele, pseuds.]
American. Author
Wrote several mysteries including *Warning Bell*, 1960.
b. Jun 2, 1902 in Saint Joseph, Missouri
d. 1977
Source: *AmAu&B; ConAu 115; TwCCr&M 85*

Davis, Gerry
English. Author
Wrote science fiction series *Doctor Who*, 1974-78.
b. Feb 23, 1930 in London, England
Source: *ConAu 117*

Davis, Glenn
"Mr. Outside"
American. Football Player
b. Dec 26, 1924 in Claremont, California
Source: *CurBio 46; WhoFtbl 74*

Davis, Hal Charles
American. Labor Union Official
Pres., American Federation of Musicians International, 1970-78.
b. Feb 27, 1914 in Pittsburgh, Pennsylvania
d. Jan 1, 1978 in New York, New York
Source: *WhoAm 74*

Davis, Harold Lenoir
American. Author
b. Oct 18, 1896 in Yoncalla, Oregon
d. Oct 31, 1960 in San Antonio, Texas
Source: *AmAu&B; ChhPo S1; DcLEL; TwCA, SUP*

Davis, James Curran
American. Politician
Congressman from GA, 1947-63; advocated racial segregation.
b. May 17, 1895 in Franklin, Georgia
d. Dec 28, 1981 in Atlanta, Georgia
Source: *BiDrAC; CurBio 82; NewYTBS 81; WhAm 8; WhAmP; WhoAm 74*

Davis, Janette
American. Singer
Source: *BioIn 3; InWom*

Davis, Jefferson
American. Political Leader
Pres. of Confederacy, 1861-65.
b. Jun 3, 1808 in Christian County,
   Kentucky
d. Dec 6, 1889 in New Orleans, Louisiana
Source: *AmAu&B; AmBi; ApCAB; BbD;
BiAUS; BiD&SB; BiDConf; BiDSA; BiDrUSE;
DcAmAu; DcAmB; Drake; EncAB-H; OxAmL;
REn; REnAL; TwCBDA; WebAB, 79; WhAm
HS; WhAmP; WorAl*

Davis, Jim
American. Actor
Played Jock Ewing on TV series "Dallas,"
   1978-81.
b. Aug 26, 1916 in Edgerton, Missouri
d. Apr 26, 1981 in Northridge, California
Source: *NewYTBS 81; WhoHol A*

Davis, Jim (James Robert)
American. Cartoonist
Created comic strip character Garfield;
   syndicated in 500 newspapers.
b. Jul 28, 1945 in Marion, Indiana
Source: *ConAu 85*

Davis, Joan
American. Actress, Comedienne
Starred in TV series *I Married Joan,* 1952-
   55.
b. Jun 29, 1907 in Saint Paul, Minnesota
d. May 23, 1961 in Palm Springs, California
Source: *CurBio 61; FilmgC; MotPP; MovMk;
ThFT; WhScrn 74, 77; WhThe; WhoHol B*

Davis, Joe
English. Billiards Player
b. 1901
d. Jul 1978
Source: *BioIn 11*

Davis, John
English. Explorer
Discovered entrance to Baffin Bay, 1587;
   sighted Falkland Islands, 1592.
b. 1550 in Sandridge, England
d. Dec 29, 1605 in Strait of Malacca
Source: *Alli; ApCAB; DcEnL; Drake; EvLB;
OxCan*

Davis, John Staige
American. Surgeon
b. Jan 15, 1872 in Norfolk, Virginia
d. Dec 23, 1946 in Baltimore, Maryland
Source: *DcNAA; NewYTBS 77; WhAm 2;
WhoAm 78; WhoS&SW 73*

Davis, John Williams
American. Politician, Lawyer
b. Apr 13, 1873 in Clarksburg, West Virginia
d. Mar 24, 1955 in New York, New York
Source: *BiDrAC; CurBio 53, 55; DcAmB S5;
EncAB-H; WebAB; WhAm 3; WhAmP*

Davis, Judy
Australian. Actress
Starred in *My Brilliant Career,* 1981.
b. 1956
Source: *BioIn 12*

Davis, Kingsley
American. Sociologist
b. Aug 20, 1908 in Tuxedo, Texas
Source: *AmM&WS 73S; ConAu 13R; IntWW
74; WhoAm 74; WhoWor 78*

Davis, Loyal
American. Surgeon, Celebrity Relative
Stepfather of Nancy Reagan, known for
   practice, teaching of brain surgery.
b. Jan 17, 1896 in Galesburg, Illinois
d. Aug 19, 1982 in Scottsdale, Arizona
Source: *AmM&WS 79P; ConAu 107;
NewYTBS 82; WhoAm 80*

Davis, Mac
American. Actor, Singer, Songwriter
Hit song "I Believe in Music," 1972; starred
   in *North Dallas Forty,* 1979.
b. Jan 21, 1942 in Lubbock, Texas
Source: *BkPepl; CurBio 80; EncPR&S 74;
IntMPA 82; WhoAm 82*

Davis, Martha
see: Motels, The

Davis, Marvin
American. Oilman
Wildcatter, pres., independent Davis Oil Co.
b. 1926 in Denver, Colorado
Source: *NewYTBS 81*

Davis, Mary L
American. Children's Author
b. Mar 21, 1935 in Worthington, Minnesota
Source: *ConAu 49; SmATA 9*

Davis, Meyer
American. Conductor
b. Jan 10, 1895 in Ellicott City, Maryland
d. Apr 5, 1976 in New York, New York
Source: *BiE&WWA; BioNews 75; CelR,;
CmpEPM; CurBio 61; WhoAm 76*

Davis, Michael
American. Comedian
b. 1953
Source: *BioIn 12*

Davis, Miles Dewey
American. Jazz Musician, Composer
Formed Miles Davis Quintet, 1955, with
John Coltrane; played with Charlie Parker,
1940s.
b. May 25, 1926 in Alton, Illinois
Source: *BioNews 74; CelR; CurBio 62;
MakMC; WebAB; WhoAm 82; WhoBlA 80;
WhoE 74; WhoMus 72; WhoWor 74; WorAl*

Davis, Ossie
American. Actor, Dramatist
Wrote, directed, starred in *Purlie Victorious*,
1961.
b. Dec 18, 1917 in Cogdell, Georgia
Source: *AmAu&B; BiE&WWA; BlkAWP;
CelR; CurBio 69; FilmgC; IntMPA 82;
LivgBAA; MotPP; MovMk; NotNAT; PIP&P;
WhoAm 82; WhoHol A; WhoThe 77;
WhoWor 78; WrDr 76*

Davis, Owen
American. Dramatist
b. Jan 29, 1874 in Portland, Maine
d. Oct 13, 1956 in New York, New York
Source: *AmAu&B; CnDAL; CnMD;
McGEWD; ModWD; OxAmL; OxThe; REn;
REnAL; TwCA, SUP; WhAm 3*

Davis, Patti
[Patricia Reagan; Mrs. Paul Grilley]
American. Actress, Celebrity Relative
Daughter of Ronald Reagan; wrote *Home
Front*, 1986.
b. Oct 21, 1952 in Los Angeles, California
Source: *BioIn 12*

Davis, Perscell
"Magic"
American. Boxer
b. 1958 in Los Angeles, California
Source: *NF*

Davis, Phil
American. Cartoonist
b. Mar 4, 1906 in Saint Louis, Missouri
d. Dec 16, 1964
Source: *BioIn 1, 7; WorECom*

Davis, Rebecca Blaine Harding
American. Author, Journalist
Wrote *Waiting for the Verdict*, 1867.
b. Jun 24, 1831 in Washington, Pennsylvania
d. Sep 29, 1910 in Mount Kisco, Kentucky
Source: *NotAW*

Davis, Rennie
[The Chicago 7]
American. Reformer
b. May 23, 1941 in Lansing, Michigan
Source: *BioNews 74; MugS; WhoAm 78*

Davis, Richard Harding
American. Author, Journalist
Wrote *Gallegher and Other Stories*, 1901.
b. Apr 18, 1864 in Philadelphia,
Pennsylvania
d. Apr 11, 1916 in Mount Kisco, New York
Source: *AmAu&B; AmBi; BbD; BiD&SB;
CarSB; CasWL; Chambr 3; CnDAL;
DcAmAu; DcAmB; DcBiA; DcEnA AP;
DcLEL; DcNAA; EncMys; EvLB; JBA 34;
LongCTC; OxAmL; PenC AM; REn; REnAL;
TwCA, SUP; TwCBDA; WebAB; WebE&AL;
WhAm 1; WhoStg 1906, 1908*

Davis, Sam(uel)
American. Soldier
Confederate with Rutherford Rifles Co.; scout
with Coleman's scout; hanged by Union
for refusing to reveal name of traitor.
b. Oct 6, 1844 in Stewart's Creek, Tennessee
d. Nov 27, 1863 in Giles County, Tennessee
Source: *ApCAB SUP; BioIn 11; NatCAB 8;
WhAm HS*

Davis, Sammy, Jr.
American. Actor, Singer, Dancer
Began career at age three; wrote
autobiography *Yes, I Can*, 1965.
b. Dec 8, 1925 in New York, New York
Source: *BiE&WWA; BioNews 74; CelR;
CurBio 56; EncMT; FilmgC; IntMPA 82;
MotPP; MovMk; NewYTBE 71, 72; NotNAT;
OxFilm; WebAB; WhoAm 74; WhoBlA 75;
WhoHol A; WhoThe 77; WhoWor 78*

Davis, Skeeter
American. Singer
Country-western star; hit song "The End of
the World," 1963.
b. Dec 30, 1931 in Dry Ridge, Kentucky
Source: *EncFCWM 69*

Davis, Spencer
[The Spencer Davis Group]
English. Singer, Musician
Formed rock band featuring Stevie Winwood,
1963-69; known for hit "I'm a Man,"
1968.
b. Jul 17, 1942 in England
Source: *RkOn 84; WhoRock 81*

Davis, Stuart
American. Artist
His innovative paintings marked him as
precursor of pop-art movement of the
1960s.
b. Dec 7, 1894 in Philadelphia, Pennsylvania
d. Jun 24, 1964 in New York, New York
Source: *CurBio 64; EncAB-H; OxAmL; REn;
WebAB*

Davis, (Thomas) Cullen
American. Oilman
Inherited family's oil business worth over
    $150 million; acquitted, 1978, of
    stepdaughter's murder.
b. 1933 in Texas
Source: *BioIn 11*

Davis, "Tobe" (Coller)
American. Business Executive, Journalist
Wrote syndicated column *Toby Says.*
b. 1893 in Milwaukee, Wisconsin
d. Dec 25, 1962 in New York, New York
Source: *CurBio 63; InWom; WhoAmW 58*

Davis, Tommy (Thomas Herman, Jr.)
American. Baseball Player
b. Mar 21, 1939 in Brooklyn, New York
Source: *WhoProB 73*

Davis, Walter
American. Track Athlete
b. Jan 5, 1931 in Beaumont, Texas
Source: *BioIn 3, 5*

Davis, "Wild Bill" (William Strethen)
American. Musician
b. Nov 24, 1918 in Glasgow, Missouri
Source: *WhoJazz 72*

Davis, William Morris
American. Geographer, Geologist
Developed Davisian "cycle of erosion"
    theory, 1880s.
b. Feb 12, 1850 in Philadelphia, Pennsylvania
d. Feb 5, 1934 in Pasadena, California
Source: *DcAmB S1; WebBD 80*

Davis, Willie (William Henry)
American. Baseball Player, Football Player
b. Apr 15, 1940 in Mineral Springs,
    Arkansas
Source: *WhoAm 76; WhoBlA 75, 77;
WhoProB 73*

Davison, Bruce
American. Actor
Appeared in films *Willard*, 1971; *Mother,
    Jugs, and Speed,* 1976.
b. in Philadelphia, Pennsylvania
Source: *FilmgC; IntMPA 81; WhoHol A*

Davison, Emily Wilding
English. Feminist
d. Jun 4, 1913
Source: *BioIn 11*

Davison, Frank Dalby
Australian. Author
Works include *Man-Shy*, 1931.
b. Jun 23, 1893 in Melbourne, Australia
d. May 24, 1970 in Melbourne, Australia
Source: *CasWL; ConAu 116; ConLC 15;
TwCWr*

Davison, Frederic Ellis
American. Army Officer
b. Sep 28, 1917 in Washington, District of
    Columbia
Source: *BioIn 8; CurBio 74; WhoBlA 80;
WorDWW*

Davison, Ian Frederic Hay
English. Business Executive
Chief exec., LLoyd's of London, 1983-85.
b. Jun 30, 1931
Source: *ConNews 86-1; IntWW 83; Who 83*

Davison, William
American. Jazz Musician
b. Jan 5, 1906 in Defiance, Ohio
Source: *WhoAm 74; WhoJazz 72*

Davisson, Clinton Joseph
American. Physicist
b. Oct 22, 1881 in Bloomington, Illinois
d. Feb 1, 1958 in Charlottesville, Virginia
Source: *AsBiEn; DcScB; NewCol 75; WebAB*

Davitt, Michael
Irish. Revolutionary
b. Mar 25, 1846 in Straide, Ireland
d. May 31, 1906 in Dublin, Ireland
Source: *Alli SUP; NewCol 75; PoIre; WebBD
80*

Davout, Louis Nicholas
[Prince d'Eckmuhl]
French. Military Leader
b. May 10, 1770 in Annoux, France
d. Jun 1, 1823 in Paris, France
Source: *NewCol 75; OxFr; WebBD 80*

Davy, Humphrey, Sir
English. Scientist
Discovered laughing gas, 1799; invented
    miner's safety lamp, 1815.
b. Dec 17, 1778 in Cornwall, England
d. May 29, 1829 in Geneva, Switzerland
Source: *Alli; BbD; BiD&SB; BiDLA; BrAu 19;
Chambr 2; ChhPo, S1; DcEnL; EvLB; NewC;
OxEng*

Dawber, Pam
American. Actress
Played Mindy on TV series "Mork and
   Mindy."
b. Oct 18, 1951 in Farmington, Michigan
Source: *IntMPA 82; WhoAm 82*

Dawes, Charles Gates
American. Lawyer, Statesman
b. Aug 27, 1865 in Marietta, Ohio
d. Apr 23, 1951 in Evanston, Illinois
Source: *AmAu&B; ApCAB SUP; BiDrAC;
BiDrUSE; DcAmB S5; EncAB-H; OhA&B;
WebAB; WhAm 3; WhAmP*

Dawes, William
American. Revolutionary
b. Apr 6, 1745 in Boston, Massachusetts
d. Feb 25, 1799 in Boston, Massachusetts
Source: *Alli, SUP; AmBi; ApCAB; DcAmB;
WhAm HS*

Dawkins, Darryl
American. Basketball Player
b. Jan 11, 1957 in Orlando, Florida
Source: *BioIn 11, 12*

Dawkins, Peter M
American. Financier
Brigadier general, army hero, Heisman
   winner, currently investment banker.
b. 1941 in Royal Oak, Michigan
Source: *NewYTBS 84, 86*

Dawn, Hazel
American. Actress
b. Mar 23, 1898 in Ogden, Utah
Source: *EncMT; InWom; WhoHol A*

Dawson, Andre Nolan
American. Baseball Player
Outfielder, Montreal, 1976--; called best
   player in MLs, 1983.
b. Jul 7, 1954 in Miami, Florida
Source: *BaseEn 85; BaseReg 86; NewYTBS
83*

Dawson, Bertrand Edward
[Viscount Dawson of Penn]
English. Physician
Physician to George V; physician-in-ordinary
   to Edward VIII, George VI, Edward VII.
b. Mar 9, 1864 in Croyden, England
d. Mar 7, 1945 in London, England
Source: *CurBio 45; DcNaB 1941; GrBr*

Dawson, Geoffrey (George Geoffrey)
English. Editor
Edited the London *Times,* 1911-41.
b. Oct 25, 1874 in Skipton-in-Craven,
   England
d. Nov 7, 1944 in London, England
Source: *DcNaB 1941; GrBr; LongCTC;
ObitOF 79; WhE&EA*

Dawson, Len (Leonard Ray)
American. Football Player, Sportscaster
b. Jun 20, 1935 in Alliance, Ohio
Source: *WhoAm 82; WhoFtbl 74*

Dawson, Richard
English. Actor, TV Host
Starred in TV series "Hogan's Heroes," 1965-
   71; host of game show "Family Feud."
b. Nov 20, 1932 in Gosport, England
Source: *WhoAm 82; WhoHol A; WorAl*

Dawson, William L
American. Congressman
b. Apr 26, 1886 in Albany, Georgia
d. Nov 9, 1970 in Chicago, Illinois
Source: *BiDrAC; CurBio 45, 70; NewYTBE
70; WhAm 5*

Day, Benjamin Henry
American. Publisher
b. Apr 10, 1810 in West Springfield,
   Massachusetts
d. Dec 21, 1889 in New York, New York
Source: *AmAu&B; DcNAA; NewCol 75;
WebBD 80; WhAm HS*

Day, Chon
American. Cartoonist
b. Apr 6, 1907 in Chatham, New Jersey
Source: *BioIn 3; WhoAm 82; WhoAmA 73*

Day, Clarence Shepard, Jr.
American. Biographer, Essayist, Humorist
His autobiography *Life With Father,* 1935,
   became America's longest-running play,
   1940-50.
b. Nov 18, 1874 in New York, New York
d. Dec 28, 1935 in New York, New York
Source: *AmAu&B; ChhPo, S1; ConAmA;
CyWA; DcAmB S1; DcLEL; DcNAA; EvLB;
LongCTC; OxAmL; PenC AM; REn; REnAL;
TwCA, SUP; TwCWr; WebAB, 79; WhAm 1;
WorAl*

Day, Dennis
[Eugene Denis McNulty]
American. Singer, Actor
Best known for 25-yr. assn. with Jack Benny
   on radio, TV shows.
b. May 21, 1917 in New York, New York
Source: *FilmgC; MotPP; WhoHol A*

Day, Doris
[Doris VonKappelhoff]
American. Actress, Singer
Starred in *The Pajama Game,* 1957; *Pillow Talk,* 1959.
b. Apr 3, 1924 in Cincinnati, Ohio
Source: *BiDFilm; BioNews 74; BkPepl; CelR; CmMov; CurBio 54; FilmgC; InWom; IntMPA 75, 76, 77, 78, 79, 80, 81, 82; MotPP; MovMk; OxFilm; WhoAm 74, 76, 78, 80, 82; WhoHol A; WorEFlm*

Day, Dorothy
American. Editor, Activist
Founded Catholic Workers movement, 1933.
b. Nov 8, 1897 in New York, New York
d. Nov 29, 1980 in New York, New York
Source: *BioNews 74; CathA 1930; CelR; ConAu 65, 102; CurBio 62; NewYTBE 72; WebAB; WhoAm 74; WhoE 74*

Day, J(ames) Edward
American. Government Official, Lawyer
Postmaster general under John F Kennedy, 1961-63.
b. Oct 11, 1914 in Jacksonville, Florida
Source: *BiDrUSE; ConAu 17R; CurBio 62; IntWW 82; LinLib S; PolProf K; WhoAm 82; WhoAmP 73*

Day, James Wentworth
English. Author, Publisher
b. Apr 21, 1899 in Exning, England
Source: *ConAu 13R; Who 74*

Day, Joseph Paul
American. Real Estate Executive
b. Sep 22, 1873 in New York, New York
d. Apr 10, 1944 in New York, New York
Source: *BioIn 3; NatCAB 38; ObitOF 79; WhAm 2, 3*

Day, Laraine
[Laraine Johnson]
American. Actress
Played nurse Mary Lamont in *Dr. Kildare* film series, 1940s.
b. Oct 13, 1920 in Roosevelt, Utah
Source: *CurBio 53; FilmgC; InWom; IntMPA 80, 81, 82; MGM; MotPP; MovMk; ThFT; WhoHol A; WorAl*

Day, Ned (Edward Gately)
American. Bowler
b. 1911
d. Nov 26, 1971 in Milwaukee, Wisconsin
Source: *BioIn 2, 3, 5, 9*

Day, Robin
English. Broadcast Journalist
b. Oct 24, 1923 in London, England
Source: *BioIn 11; IntWW 74; Who 74*

Day, Thomas
English. Author, Lawyer
Wrote children's didactic tale *Sandford and Merton,* 1783-89.
b. Jun 22, 1748 in London, England
d. Sep 28, 1789 in London, England
Source: *BrAu; CyWA; DcEnL; NewC; WhoChL*

Day, William Rufus
American. Supreme Court Justice
b. Apr 17, 1849 in Ravenna, Ohio
d. Jul 9, 1923 in Mackinac Island, Michigan
Source: *AmBi; ApCAB SUP; BiDrUSE; DcAmB; TwCBDA; WebAB; WhAm 1*

Day-Lewis, Cecil
[Nicholas Blake, pseud.]
British. Poet, Author, Translator, Editor
Poet laureate, 1968, wrote numerous detective stories, verse collections.
b. Apr 27, 1904 in Ballintogher, Ireland
d. May 22, 1972 in London, England
Source: *Au&Wr 71; CasWL; ChhPo, S1; CnE&AP; CnMWL; ConAu 33R, P-1; ConLC 1, 6, 10; ConNov 72; ConP 70, 75; DcLEL; EncMys; EncWL; LongCTC; ModBrL, S1; NewC; OxEng; PenC ENG; RAdv 1; REn; TwCA, SUP; TwCCW 78; TwCWr; WebE&AL; WhDW; WhAm 5; WhoTwCL*

Dayan, Assaf
Israeli. Actor
Son of Moshe Dayan; appeared in *The Day the Fish Came Out,* 1967.
b. 1945 in Afula, Palestine
Source: *BioIn 8; FilmEn; WhoHol A*

Dayan, Moshe
Israeli. Soldier, Statesman
Foreign affairs minister; hero of Six-Day War, 1967; negotiated Egypt-Israel peace treaty, 1979.
b. May 20, 1915 in Degania, Palestine
d. Oct 16, 1981 in Tel Aviv, Israel
Source: *BioIn 4, 7, 8, 9, 10, 11; CelR; ConAu 21R; CurBio 57, 82; IntAu&W 77; LinLib L; McGEWB; MidE 78, 79; NewYTBE 70; NewYTBS 78, 81; WhoMilH 76; WhoWor 74, 78; WhoWorJ 72; WorDWW*

Daye, Stephen
English. Printer
First printer in American colonies: *Baby Psalm Book,* 1640.
b. 1594 in London, England
d. Dec 22, 1668 in Cambridge, England
Source: *NewCol 75; OxAmL 83; REn*

Dazz Band
[Bobby Harris; Keith Harrison; Sennie Skip Martin, III; Kenny Pettus; Isaac Wiley, Jr.; Michael Wiley]
American. Music Group
Danceable jazz band; won Grammy, 1982, for "Let It Whip."
Source: *RkOn 85*

Deacon, John
see: Queen

Deacon, Richard
American. Actor
Best known role of Mel Cooley in "The Dick Van Dyke Show," 1961-66.
b. May 14, 1922
d. Aug 9, 1984 in Los Angeles, California
Source: *FilmgC; MotPP; WhoHol A*

DeAmicis, Edmond
see: Amicis, Edmond de

Dean, Alfred Lovill
"Chubby"
American. Baseball Player
b. Aug 24, 1916 in Mount Airy, North Carolina
d. Dec 21, 1970 in Riverside, New Jersey
Source: *BaseEn 85; BioIn 1; WhoProB 73*

Dean, Basil
English. Actor, Director
Pioneer in stage lighting, who founded Associated Talking Pictures, 1932.
b. Sep 27, 1888 in Croydon, England
d. Apr 22, 1978 in London, England
Source: *BioIn 9; ConAu 69; EncWT; Film 2; FilmgC; IntWW 78N; ModWD; OxThe; WhThe; Who 74; WhoThe 81N; WhoWor 74*

Dean, Christopher
[Torvill and Dean]
English. Figure Skater
With partner, Jayne Torvill, received 12 perfect marks, won gold medal, ice dancing, 1984 Olympics.
b. 1959 in Nottingham, England
Source: *NF*

Dean, "Daffy" (Paul Dee)
American. Baseball Player
Pitcher, St. Louis, 1934-43, who threw no-hitter, 1934; brother of Dizzy Dean.
b. Aug 14, 1913 in Lucas, Arkansas
d. Mar 17, 1981 in Springdale, Arkansas
Source: *BaseEn 85; BioIn 7; NewYTBS 81; WebAB; WhoProB 73*

Dean, "Dizzy" (Jay Hanna)
American. Baseball Player, Sportscaster
Pitcher who won 30 games, 1934; Hall of Fame, 1953.
b. Jan 16, 1911 in Lucas, Arkansas
d. Jul 17, 1974 in Reno, Nevada
Source: *BaseEn 85; BioIn 1, 2, 3, 4, 5, 6, 7, 8, 9, 10; BioNews 74; CurBio 51, 74; NewYTBS 74; WebAB; WhoProB 73*

Dean, Gordon Evans
American. Banker
b. Dec 28, 1905 in Seattle, Washington
d. Aug 15, 1958
Source: *CurBio 58; DcAmNB; NatCAB 56; WhAm 3*

Dean, Henry Trendley
American. Dentist
b. Aug 25, 1893 in Winstanley Park, Illinois
d. May 13, 1962 in Chicago, Illinois
Source: *CurBio 62; WhAm 4*

Dean, James
[James Byron]
American. Actor
Starred in *East of Eden,* 1955; *Rebel Without a Cause,* 1955; *Giant,* 1956.
b. Feb 8, 1931 in Marion, Indiana
d. Sep 30, 1955 in Paso Robles, California
Source: *BiDFilm; FilmgC; MotPP; MovMk; OxFilm; WhAm 4; WhScrn 74, 77; WhoHol B; WorEFlm*

Dean, Jimmy
[Seth Ward]
American. Singer
Country singer, best known for song "Big Bad John," 1961.
b. Aug 10, 1928 in Plainview, Texas
Source: *CurBio 65; EncFCWM 69; IntMPA 77, 78, 79, 80, 81, 82; WhoAm 82; WhoHol A*

Dean, John Gunther
American. Diplomat
Ambassador to Lebanon, 1978-81; directed
pacification in Vietnam, 1970.
b. Feb 24, 1926 in Germany
Source: *BioIn 10; IntWW 74, 75, 76, 77, 78;
IntYB 78, 79; MidE 79; USBiR 74; WhoAm
76, 78, 80, 82, 84; WhoAmP 75, 77, 79*

Dean, John Wesley
American. Lawyer, Watergate Participant
Counsel to Richard Nixon, 1971-73; author
Blind Ambition, 1976.
b. Oct 14, 1938 in Akron, Ohio
Source: *WhoAm 78; WhoAmP 73; WhoGov
72; WorAl*

Dean, Laura
American. Choreographer, Composer
Founded controversial Dean Dancers and
Musicians, 1976; composed score for
Enochian, 1983.
b. Dec 3, 1945 in Staten Island, New York
Source: *BioIn 11; WhoAm 80, 82, 84*

Dean, Laura
American. Actress
First major role in film *Fame*.
b. May 27, 1963 in Smithtown, New York
Source: *ConTFT 3*

Dean, "Man Mountain"
[Frank Simmons Leavitt]
American. Wrestler
b. Jun 30, 1889 in New York, New York
d. May 29, 1953 in Norcross, Georgia
Source: *BioIn 3; WebAB*

Dean, Morton
American. Broadcast Journalist
With CBS News since 1967; part-time anchor
of "Newsbreak."
b. Aug 22, 1935 in Fall River, Massachusetts
Source: *ConAu 69; WhoAm 82; WhoTelC*

Dean, Patrick Henry, Sir
British. Diplomat
b. Mar 16, 1909 in Berlin, Germany
Source: *CurBio 61; IntWW 74; Who 74;
WhoWor 78*

Dean, William Frishe
American. Army Officer
Highest ranking officer held captive in
Korean War, 1950-53.
b. Aug 1, 1899 in Carlyle, Illinois
d. Aug 24, 1981 in Berkeley, California
Source: *BioIn 2, 3, 5, 7, 8, 9; CurBio 54, 81;
NewYTBS 81; WebAMB*

Deane, Sandy
[Jay and the Americans; Sandy Yaguda]
American. Singer
Part of dean-cut vocal quintet of 1960s.
b. Jan 30, 1943
Source: *NF*

Deane, Silas
American. Colonial Leader
Secret agent in France for American
Revolution, 1776-78.
b. Dec 24, 1737 in Groton, Connecticut
d. Sep 23, 1789
Source: *ApCAB; BiAUS; BiDrAC; BioIn 11;
Drake; EncAB-H; McGEWB; NatCAB 12;
TwCBDA; WebAB; WhAm HS; WhAmP;
WorAl*

DeAngeli, Marguerite
American. Children's Author
b. Mar 14, 1889 in Lapeer, Michigan
Source: *AmAu&B; Au&ICB; Au&Wr 71;
AuBYP; AuNews 2; BkCL; ChlLR 1; ChhPo,
S1; ConAu 5R, 3NR; ConICB; CurBio 47;
HerW; IlsCB 1744, 1946, 1957; InWom; JBA
51; MorBMP; Newb 1922; SmATA 1, 27;
WhoAm 74; WhoAmA 73*

Dearden, John Francis, Cardinal
American. Religious Leader
Archbishop of Detroit, 1959-80.
b. Oct 15, 1907 in Valley Falls, Rhode
Island
Source: *CurBio 69; IntWW 82; WhoAm 82;
WhoWor 74*

Dearie, Blossom
American. Singer
b. Apr 28, 1926 in East Durham, New York
Source: *BioIn 10; IlEncJ; WhoAm 74*

DeBakey, Michael Ellis
American. Surgeon
Implanted first artificial heart in man, 1966.
b. Sep 7, 1908 in Lake Charles, Louisiana
Source: *AmM&WS 73P; CelR; CurBio 64;
IntWW 82; LEduc 74; NewCol 75; Who 74;
WhoAm 74, 76, 78, 80, 82; WhoS&SW 82;
WhoWor 78; WrDr 76*

DeBalzac, Honore
see: Balzac, Honore de

DeBarentzen, Patrick
Danish. Fashion Designer
Source: *FairDF ITA; WorFshn*

DeBarge
[Bunny DeBarge; Eldra DeBarge; James
    DeBarge; Mark DeBarge; RandyDeBarge]
American. Music Group
Family singing group; had hit single
    "Rhythm of the Night," 1985.
Source: *RkOn 85*

DeBarge, Bunny
[DeBarge]
American. Singer
b. Mar 10, 1955 in Grand Rapids, Michigan
Source: *NF*

DeBarge, El(dra)
[DeBarge]
American. Singer, Musician
Lead singer, keyboardist with family group,
    who also produces recordings.
b. Jun 4, 1961 in Grand Rapids, Michigan
Source: *NF*

DeBarge, James
[DeBarge]
American. Singer, Musician
b. Aug 22, 1963 in Grand Rapids, Michigan
Source: *NF*

DeBarge, Mark
[DeBarge]
American. Singer, Musician
b. Jun 19, 1959 in Grand Rapids, Michigan
Source: *NF*

DeBarge, Randy
[DeBarge]
American. Singer, Musician
b. Aug 6, 1958 in Grand Rapids, Michigan
Source: *NF*

DeBartolo, Edward J, Jr.
American. Businessman, Football Executive
Owner, pres., 1982 Super Bowl champs San
    Francisco 49ers, 1977--.
b. Nov 6, 1946 in Youngstown, Ohio
Source: *NewYTBE 73; WhoAm 80, 82, 84*

DeBeauvoir, Simone
see: Beauvoir, Simone de

DeBeck, Billy
American. Cartoonist
b. Apr 15, 1890 in Chicago, Illinois
d. Nov 11, 1942 in New York, New York
Source: *WorECom*

DeBernardi, Forrest S
American. Basketball Player
b. Mar 3, 1899 in Nevada, Missouri
d. Apr 29, 1970
Source: *BioIn 9; WhoBbl 73*

Deborah
Biblical Character
Source: *DcOrL 3; InWom*

Debost, Michel H
French. Musician
First flutist of Paris Orchestra since 1967;
    winner of numerous international awards.
b. 1934 in Paris, France
Source: *WhoMus 72*

Debray, Regis (Jules Regis)
French. Writer, Government Official
b. Sep 2, 1940 in Paris, France
Source: *BioIn 10; ConAu 21R; CurBio 82;
    NewYTBE 70; WhoAm 74*

Debre, Michel Jean Pierre
French. Political Leader
b. Jan 15, 1912 in Paris, France
Source: *BioIn 9; CurBio 59; IntWW 82;
    IntYB 82; WhoWor 74*

Debrett, John
English. Publisher
b. 1752
d. 1822
Source: *Alli; BiDLA; NewC; REn*

Debreu, Gerard
American. Economist
Won Nobel Prize in economics, 1983.
b. Jul 4, 1921 in Calais, France
Source: *AmM&WS 82P; IntAu&W 77;
    WhoAm 84; WhoWest 84; WrDr 84*

DeBroca, Philippe Claude Alex
French. Filmmaker
Identified with sophisticated, eccentric
    comedies: *Le Cavaleur*, 1979.
b. Mar 15, 1933 in Paris, France
Source: *BiDFilm; DcFM; FilmgC; IntMPA 82;
    MovMk; OxFilm; WhoWor 74; WorAl;
    WorEFlm*

DeBrunhoff, Laurent
see: Brunhoff, Laurent de

Debs, Eugene Victor
American. Socialist Leader, Labor Union
    Official
Founded Social Democratic Party, 1897; ran
    for pres. five times as socialist.
b. Nov 5, 1855 in Terre Haute, Indiana
d. Oct 20, 1926 in Elmhurst, Illinois
Source: *AmBi; AmLY; DcAmB; DcNAA;
    EncAB-H; IndAu 1816; OxAmL; REn;
    REnAL; TwCBDA; WebAB, 79; WhAm 1;
    WorAl*

Debus, Kurt Heinrich
American. Government Official
Director of NASA's Cape Canaveral, 1952-74.
b. Nov 29, 1908 in Frankfurt, Germany
d. Oct 10, 1983 in Cocoa, Florida
Source: *CurBio 73; IntWW 82; WhoAm 76; WhoGov 75; WhoS&SW 76; WhoWor 74*

Debus, Sigurd Friedrich
German. Terrorist
Red Army extremist who starved to death striking for better prison conditions, 1981.
b. 1943
d. Apr 16, 1981 in Hamburg, Germany (West)
Source: *BioIn 12*

DeBusschere, Dave (David Albert)
"The Buffalo"
American. Basketball Player, Basketball Executive
Former ML pitcher who had 11-year NBA career; Hall of Fame, 1982; youngest coach in NBA at age 24.
b. Oct 16, 1940 in Detroit, Michigan
Source: *BioIn 10; BioNews 75; CelR; CurBio 73; NewYTBS 82; WhoAm 80; WhoBbl 73; WorAl*

Debussy, Claude Achille
French. Composer
Forerunner of modern music whose orchestral works noted for dreamlike quality, harmonic innovations.
b. Aug 22, 1862 in Saint Germain, France
d. Mar 25, 1918 in Paris, France
Source: *AtlBL; BioIn 11; DcCM; MakMC; OxFr; REn; WhDW; WorAl*

DeButts, John Dulany
American. Business Executive
VP, ATT, 1966--.
b. Apr 10, 1915 in Greensboro, North Carolina
Source: *IntWW 82; LElec; WhoAm 82; WhoE 77; WhoS&SW 82*

Debye, Peter Joseph William
American. Physicist
b. Mar 24, 1884 in Maastricht, Netherlands
d. Nov 2, 1966 in Ithaca, New York
Source: *CurBio 63, 67*

DeCamp, L(yon) Sprague
American. Author
b. Nov 27, 1907 in New York, New York
Source: *AuBYP; ConAu 1R, 1NR; SmATA 9; WhoAm 82; WorAu; WrDr 76*

DeCamp, Rosemary
American. Actress
Wrote children's story *Here Duke,* 1962.
b. Nov 14, 1910 in Prescott, Arizona
Source: *InWom; IntMPA 82; MotPP; WhoHol A*

Decamps, Alexandre Gabriel
French. Artist
b. Mar 3, 1803 in Paris, France
d. Aug 22, 1860 in Fontainebleau, France
Source: *NewCol 75*

DeCarlo, Yvonne
[Peggy Yvonne Middleton]
Canadian. Actress
Played Lily on TV series "The Munsters," 1964-66.
b. Sep 1, 1924 in Vancouver, British Columbia
Source: *BiDFilm; CelR; CmMov; FilmgC; IntMPA 82; MotPP; MovMk; PIP&P A; WhoHol A; WorEFlm*

Decatur, Stephen
American. Naval Officer
Headed navy crew that captured warship *Philadelphia,* 1804.
b. Jan 5, 1779 in Sinepuxent, Maryland
d. Mar 22, 1820 in Bladensburg, Maryland
Source: *AmBi; ApCAB; DcAmB; Drake; REn; TwCBDA; WebAB; WhAm HS*

Decker, Alonzo G
American. Businessman
Formed business, 1907, with S Duncan Black; produced first electric drill, 1914.
b. Jan 16, 1884 in Baltimore, Maryland
d. Mar 18, 1956 in Towson, Maryland
Source: *BioIn 2; Entr; NatCAB 46; WhAm 3*

De Chavannes, Pierre Cecile Puvis
see: Puvis de Chavannes, Pierre Cecile

Decker, Mary
[Mrs. Richard Slaney]
American. Track Athlete
Holds world record in 5,000 meter run (15:08:26).
b. Aug 4, 1958 in Bunnvale, New Jersey
Source: *BioIn 11; CurBio 83; NewYTBS 82, 83*

Decker, Thomas
see: Dekker, Thomas

Deckers, Jeanine
"The Singing Nun"
Belgian. Nun, Singer
Had hit single "Dominique," 1963; movie
   The Singing Nun, 1966, based on her life.
b. 1933
d. Mar 31, 1985 in Wavre, Belgium
Source: *BioIn 7, 9, 10*

DeConcini, Dennis Webster
American. Politician
Dem. senator from AZ, 1976--.
b. May 8, 1937 in Tucson, Arizona
Source: *AlmAP 78, 80; CngDr 77, 79;
IntWW 78; NewYTBS 78; WhoAm 78, 80,
82, 84; WhoAmL 79; WhoAmP 73, 75, 77,
79; WhoGov 77; WhoWest 74, 76, 78*

DeCordoba, Pedro
American. Actor
Character actor in films, 1915-50.
b. Sep 28, 1881 in New York, New York
d. Sep 17, 1950 in Sunland, California
Source: *Film 1; FilmgC; MotPP; MovMk;
TwYS; WhScrn 74, 77; WhThe; WhoHol B*

DeCordova, Frederick Timmins
American. Producer, Director
Exec. producer, "The Tonight Show," since
   1970.
b. Oct 27, 1910 in New York, New York
Source: *ConNews 85-2; FilmgC; LesBEnT;
WhoAm 84*

Decoster, Charles Theodore
Belgian. Author
b. Aug 20, 1827 in Munich, Germany
d. May 7, 1879 in Brussels, Belgium
Source: *BbD; BiD&SB; CasWL; ClDMEL;
EuAu*

DeCreeft, Jose
American. Sculptor
b. Nov 27, 1884 in Guadalajara, Spain
Source: *CurBio 42; DcCAA 71; WhoAm 74;
WhoAmA 73*

DeCrevecoeur, Michel-Guillaume Jean
see: Crevecoeur, Michel-Guillaume Jean de

Decter, Midge
American. Journalist
b. Jul 25, 1927 in Saint Paul, Minnesota
Source: *ConAu 45, 2NR; CurBio 82; WhoAm
76, 78, 80, 82; WhoAmW 77; WhoE 74;
WrDr 76*

DeCuevas, Marquis
American. Ballet Promoter
Colorful ballet impressario; produced
   extravagant Parisien productions.
b. May 26, 1885 in Santiago, Chile
d. Feb 22, 1961 in Cannes, France
Source: *DcAmB S7*

De Cuir, John
American. Art Director
Won Oscars for *Cleopatra,* 1963; *Hello,
Dolly,* 1969; other films include
Ghostbusters, 1984.
b. 1918 in San Francisco, California
Source: *VarWW 85*

Dederich, Charles Edwin
American. Social Reformer
Founder, chief exec., Synanon Foundation,
   Inc., 1958--.
b. Mar 22, 1913 in Toledo, Ohio
Source: *WhoAm 78*

Dedijer, Vladimir
Yugoslav. Author
b. Feb 2, 1914 in Belgrade, Yugoslavia
Source: *Au&Wr 71; ConAu 1R, 4NR; IntWW
74; Who 74; WhoWor 78*

Dedman, Robert H
American. Businessman, Philanthropist
World's largest owner, operator of private
   clubs.
b. 1926 in Rison, Arkansas
Source: *NewYTBS 86*

Dee, Frances
[Mrs. Joel McCrea]
American. Actress
Co-starred in *The Playboy of Paris,* 1930,
   with Maurice Chevalier.
b. Nov 26, 1907 in Los Angeles, California
Source: *FilmgC; HolP 30; MotPP; MovMk;
ThFT; WhoHol A; WomWMM*

Dee, John
English. Mathematician, Astrologer, Magician
Wrote *De Trigono,* 1565.
b. 1527 in London, England
d. Dec 1608 in Mortlake, England
Source: *BrAu; NewCol 75; OxEng; REn*

Dee, Kiki
[Pauline Matthews]
English. Singer
b. Mar 6, 1947 in Bradford, England
Source: *BkPepl; RkOn 74*

Dee, Ruby
[Mrs. Ossie Davis; Ruby Ann Wallace]
American. Actress
Starred in stage, movie productions of *Raisin in the Sun*, 1959, 1961.
b. Oct 27, 1924 in Cleveland, Ohio
Source: *BiE&WWA; BlkAWP; CelR; CurBio 70; FilmgC; IntMPA 82; MotPP; MovMk; NewYTBE 70; NotNAT; WhoAm 82; WhoBlA 75; WhoHol A; WhoThe 77; WomWMM*

Dee, Sandra
[Alexandra Zuck]
American. Actress, Singer
Starred in *Gidget*, 1959; *Tammy Tell Me True*, 1961; was married to Bobby Darrin.
b. Apr 23, 1942 in Bayonne, New Jersey
Source: *FilmgC; InWom; IntMPA 82; MotPP; MovMk; WhoHol A*

Deep Purple
[Ritchie Blackmore; Thomas Bolin; David Coverdale; Rod Evans; IanGillan; Roger Glover; Glenn Hughs; Jon Lord; Ian Paige; Nicholas Simper]
American. Music Group
Source: *BiDAmM; EncPR&S 74; IlEncRk; RkOn 84*

Deeping, (George) Warwick
English. Author
Novels include *Sorrell and Son*, 1925; *Old Pybus*, 1928.
b. May 28, 1877 in Southend, England
d. Apr 20, 1950 in Weybridge, England
Source: *DcLEL; EvLB; LongCTC; NewC; PenC ENG; REn; TwCA, SUP; TwCWr; WhE&EA; WhLit; WhoLA*

Deer, Rob(ert George)
American. Baseball Player
Outfielder, San Francisco, 1984-85, Milwaukee, 1986--.
b. Sep 29, 1960 in Orange, California
Source: *BaseEn 85; BaseReg 86*

DeErdely, Francis (Ferenc)
Hungarian. Artist, Educator
Work permanently exhibited in museums in US, Australia, France, Spain, Belgium.
b. May 3, 1904 in Budapest, Hungary
d. Nov 28, 1959 in Los Angeles, California
Source: *DcCAA 71; WhAm 4; WhoAmA 82N*

Deere, John
American. Industrialist
Developed, manufactured steel plow, 1837; incorporated Deere and Co., 1868.
b. Feb 7, 1804 in Rutland, Vermont
d. May 17, 1886 in Moline, Illinois
Source: *AmBi; DcAmB; EncAB-H; WebAB; WhAm HS*

Deering, William
American. Manufacturer
b. Apr 25, 1826 in Paris, Maine
d. Dec 9, 1913 in Coconut Grove, Florida
Source: *AmBi; DcAmB; TwCBDA; WhAm 1*

Def Leppard
[Rick Allen; Steve Clark; Phil Collen; Joe Elliott; Rick Savage; Pete Willis]
British. Music Group
Heavy metal, new wave group formed 1977; popularity attributed to MTV in US.
Source: *IlEncRk*

De Falla, Manuel
see: Falla, Manuel de

Defauw, Desire
Belgian. Conductor
b. Sep 5, 1885 in Ghent, Belgium
d. Jul 25, 1960 in Gary, Indiana
Source: *CurBio 40, 60; WhAm 4*

Defeo, Ronald
American. Murderer
Killing of parents, siblings known as "Amityville Horror"; Long Island, NY house supposedly haunted.
b. 1951
Source: *BioIn 12*

Defoe, Daniel
English. Author
Wrote *Robinson Crusoe*, 1719, based on adventures of Alexander Selkirk.
b. Apr 26, 1661 in London, England
d. Apr 26, 1731 in London, England
Source: *Alli; AtlBL; BbD; BiD&SB; BrAu; CarSB; CasWL; Chambr 2; ChhPo S1; CrtT 2; CyWA; DcBiA; DcEnA; DcEnL; DcEuL; DcLEL; EvLB; FilmgC; HsB&A; MnBBF; MouLC 2; NewC; OxEng; PenC ENG; RAdv 1; RComWL; REn; WebE&AL; WhoChL*

DeFore, Don
American. Actor
Appeared in TV shows "Adventures of Ozzie and Harriet," 1952-58, "Hazel," 1961-65.
b. Aug 25, 1917 in Cedar Rapids, Iowa
Source: *BiE&WWA; FilmgC; MotPP; MovMk; NotNAT; WhoAm 74; WhoHol A*

DeForest, Lee
"Father of the Radio"
American. Inventor
Patented over 300 inventions, including key
   component of radio before invention of
   transistor.
b. Aug 26, 1873 in Council Bluffs, Iowa
d. Jun 30, 1961 in Hollywood, California
Source: *CurBio 41, 61; EncAB-H; FilmgC;
WebAB; WhAm 4; WorEFlm*

DeFranco, Buddy
American. Jazz Musician
b. 1933
Source: *CmpEPM*

DeFrank, Vincent
American. Conductor
b. Jun 18, 1915 in Long Island, New York
Source: *WhoAm 74, 76, 78, 80, 82;
WhoS&SW 82*

DeFreeze, Donald David
[S(ymbionese) L(iberation) A(rmy)]
"Cinque"
American. Revolutionary
Leader of terrorist group that kidnapped
   Patricia Hearst, 1974.
b. Nov 16, 1943 in Cleveland, Ohio
d. May 24, 1974 in Los Angeles, California
Source: *BioNews 74; NewYTBS 74*

Degas, (Hilaire Germain) Edgar
French. Artist
Impressionist painter whose favorite subjects
   were ballet dancers, cafe life.
b. Jul 19, 1834 in Paris, France
d. Sep 27, 1917 in Paris, France
Source: *AtlBL; NewC; OxFr; REn; WhAm
HSA, 4*

DeGasperi, Alcide
see: Gasperi, Alcide de

DeGaulle, Charles Andre Joseph Marie
French. Political Leader
Army general, 1940, who assumed leadership
   after WW II; first pres., Fifth Republic,
   1959-69.
b. Nov 22, 1890 in Lille, France
d. Nov 9, 1970 in Colombey les deux
   Eglises, France
Source: *BioIn 10; CurBio 40, 49, 60, 70;
REn; WhAm 5*

DeGhelderode, Michel
see: Ghelderode, Michel de

DeGivenchy, Hubert
see: Givenchy Hubert de

DeGoncourt, Edmond Louis
see: Goncourt, Edmond Louis Antoine Huot
de

DeGoncourt, Jules Alfred Hout
see: Goncourt, Jules Alfred Hout de

DeGraff, Robert F(air)
American. Publisher
Co-founded first American paperback co.,
   Pocket Books, 1939.
b. Jun 9, 1895 in Plainfield, New Jersey
d. Nov 1, 1981 in Mill Neck, New York
Source: *ConAu 105; CurBio 43; DcLB Y81A*

DeHartog, Jan
Dutch. Author
b. Apr 22, 1914 in Haarlem, Netherlands
Source: *AmAu&B; CasWL; CnMD; ConAu
1R, 1NR; CurBio 70; EncWL; IntWW 74;
NotNAT; TwCA SUP; WhoAm 74, 76, 78, 80,
82; WhoWor 78*

DeHaven, Gloria
American. Actress
Co-star in 1940s musicals *Broadway Rythym;
Three Little Words; Two Girls and a
Sailor.*
b. Jul 23, 1925 in Los Angeles, California
Source: *BiE&WWA; FilmgC; MGM; MotPP;
MovMk; WhoAmW 74; WhoHol A*

DeHavilland, Geoffrey
English. Aircraft Manufacturer
Founded DeHavilland Aircraft Co., produced
   first commercial jetliner, the Comet.
b. Jul 27, 1882
d. May 21, 1965 in London, England
Source: *ObitOF 79; WhDW; WhAm 4*

DeHavilland, Olivia
American. Actress
Played Melanie in *Gone With the Wind,*
   1939; won Oscars, 1946, 1949.
b. Jul 1, 1916 in Tokyo, Japan
Source: *BiDFilm; BiE&WWA; CelR; CmMov;
CurBio 66; FilmgC; IntMPA 75, 76, 77;
MotPP; MovMk; OxFilm; ThFT; Who 74;
WhoAm 74, 76, 78, 80, 82; WhoHol A;
WorEFlm*

DeHidalgo, Elvira
see: Hidalgo, Elvira de

Dehmel, Richard
German. Poet
Lyric verse collected in *Woman and the World*, 1896; *Beautiful Wild World*, 1913.
b. Nov 18, 1868 in Germany
d. Feb 8, 1920 in Blankenese, Germany
Source: *CasWL; ClDMEL; EncWL; EuAu; EvEuW; ModGL; OxGer; PenC EUR; REn*

Dehn, Adolf Arthur
American. Artist
Prolific lithographer, watercolor landscapist.
b. Nov 22, 1895 in Waterville, Minnesota
d. May 19, 1968 in New York, New York
Source: *CurBio 41, 68; DcCAA 71; WhAm 5*

Dehner, John Forkum
American. Actor
Films include *Thirty Seconds over Tokyo*, 1944; *Airplane II: The Sequel*, 1982.
b. Nov 23, 1915 in New York, New York
Source: *VarWW 85*

Dehnert, Henry
"Dutch"
American. Basketball Player, Basketball Coach
Best known for developing the pivot play, 1920s-40s; Hall of Fame.
b. Apr 5, 1898 in New York, New York
d. Apr 20, 1979 in Far Rockaway, New York
Source: *NewYTBS 79; WhoBbl 73*

Deighton, Len (Leonard Cyril)
English. Cartoonist, Author
Best known for spy thrillers: *The Ipcress File*, 1962; movie starred Michael Caine, 1965.
b. Feb 18, 1929 in London, England
Source: *ConAu 9R; ConLC 4, 7; ConNov 72, 76; IntMPA 75, 76, 77; IntWW 74; NewC; TwCWr; WhoWor 74; WorAl; WorAu; WrDr 76*

Deiss, Joseph Jay
American. Author
b. Jan 25, 1915 in Twin Falls, Idaho
Source: *Au&Wr 71; ConAu 33R; SmATA 12; WhoAm 74; WhoWor 78; WrDr 80*

Deitch, Kim
American. Cartoonist
b. 1944
Source: *BioIn 10*

Dejean, Alain
French. Photojournalist
b. 1935
d. Oct 25, 1981 in Paris, France
Source: *BioIn 12*

DeJong, David Cornel
Dutch. Author
Wrote novel *Old Haven*, 1938; autobiography *With a Dutch Accent*, 1944.
b. Jun 9, 1905 in Blija, Netherlands
d. Sep 5, 1967 in Providence, Rhode Island
Source: *AmAu&B; AmNov; AuBYP; ConAu 5R; CurBio 44, 67; OxAmL; REn; REnAL; SmATA 10; TwCA, SUP; WhAm 4A*

Dejong, Meindert
American. Children's Author
Won Newbery for *Wheel on the School*, 1954; National Book Award for *Journey from Peppermint Street*, 1969.
b. Mar 4, 1906 in Wierum, Netherlands
Source: *AnCL; Au&ICB; Au&Wr 71; AuBYP; BkCL; CasWL; ChlLR 1; ConAu 13R; CurBio 52; MorBMP; MorJA; Newb 1922; SenS; SmATA 2; WhoAm 82*

DeJong, Petrus
Dutch. Prime Minister
b. Apr 13, 1915 in Apeldoorn, Netherlands
Source: *WhoGov 75*

Dejongh, Peter
American. Engineer
Designed Oak Ridge, TN installation where first atom bomb was built; designed WW II Quonset hut.
b. 1897
d. Jul 5, 1983 in Kearny, New Jersey
Source: *NewYTBS 83*

Dekker, Albert
American. Actor
Played mad scientists, other villians, 1937-69: *Dr. Cyclops*, 1940; *The Pretenders*, 1947.
b. Dec 20, 1905 in New York, New York
d. May 5, 1968 in Hollywood, California
Source: *BiE&WWA; FilmgC; MotPP; MovMk; ObitOF 79; Vers B; WhAm 5; WhScrn 74, 77; WhThe; WhoHol B*

Dekker, Thomas
[Thomas Decker]
English. Dramatist
Wrote comedy *Old Fortunates*, 1599; pamphlet *The Wonderful Yeare 1603*, described London during plague.
b. 1572 in London, England
d. 1632 in London, England
Source: *Alli; AtlBL; BbD; BiD&SB; BrAu; CasWL; Chambr 1; CnE&AP; CnThe; CroE&S; CrtT 1; CyWA; DcEnA; DcEnL; DcLEL; EvLB; McGEWD; MouLC 1; NewC; OxEng; OxMus; OxThe; PenC ENG; PlP&P; REn; REnWD; WebE&AL*

DeKnight, Jimmy
[James E Myers]
American. Composer
b. Oct 26, in Philadelphia, Pennsylvania
Source: *AmSCAP 66*

DeKooning, Elaine Marie Catherine Fried
American. Artist, Art Critic
b. Mar 12, 1920 in New York, New York
Source: *CurBio 82; WhoAm 84; WhoAmA 73*

DeKooning, Willem
American. Artist
Abstract Expressionism leader, 1940s; known
    for distorted portraits of women.
b. Apr 24, 1904 in Rotterdam, Netherlands
Source: *CelR; CurBio 84; DcCAA 71; EncAB-*
H; IntWW 74; REn; WebAB; WhoAm 80,
82; WhoAmA 73; WhoWor 74

DeKoven, (Henry Louis) Reginald
American. Composer, Music Critic
Founded, conducted, Washington
    Philharmonic, 1902-05; wrote operettas
    Robin Hood, 1890, *Student King,* 1906.
b. Apr 3, 1861 in Middletown, Connecticut
d. Jan 16, 1920 in Chicago, Illinois
Source: *AmAu&B; AmBi; AmSCAP 66;*
ApCAB SUP; DcAmB; EncMT; NewCBMT;
OxAmL; REn; REnAL; TwCBDA; WhoStg
1906, 1908

DeKruif, Paul Henry
American. Bacteriologist, Author
Popular writer on scientific subjects; wrote
    Microbe Hunters, 1926.
b. Mar 2, 1890 in Zeeland, Michigan
d. Feb 28, 1971 in Holland, Michigan
Source: *AmAu&B; BiE&WWA; ConAu 29R;*
CurBio 71; InSci; JBA 34; LongCTC;
OxAmL; REn; REnAL; SmATA 5; TwCA,
SUP; WhAm 5

Delacorte, George Thomas, Jr.
American. Publisher
b. Jun 20, 1894 in New York, New York
Source: *CelR; CurBio 65; NewYTBS 79;*
St&PR 75; WhoAm 80, 82; WhoAmA 73;
WhoWor 74

DeLaCova, Carlos Perez
see: Perez de la Cova, Carlos

Delacroix, (Ferdinand Victor) Eugene
French. Artist
Leading Romantic painter; noted for
    historical, colorful Moroccan scenes:
    "Liberty Leading the People," 1831.
b. Apr 26, 1798 in Charenton, France
d. Aug 13, 1863 in Paris, France
Source: *AtlBL; OxFr; REn*

Delahanty, Edward James
"Big Ed"
American. Baseball Player
Only man to lead both leagues in hitting,
    1899, 1902; Hall of Fame, 1945.
b. Oct 31, 1867 in Cleveland, Ohio
d. Jul 2, 1903 in Fort Erie, Ontario
Source: *BaseEn 85; BioIn 3, 6, 7, 10;*
WhoProB 73

Delahanty, Thomas K
American. Police Officer
Wounded with Ronald Reagan in
    assassination attempt, 1981.
b. 1935 in Pittsburg, Pennsylvania
Source: *BioIn 12*

DeLaMare, Walter
[Walter Ramal, pseud.]
English. Author, Poet
Wrote popular children's verse: *Memoirs of a*
    Midget, 1922.
b. Apr 25, 1873 in Charlton, England
d. Jun 22, 1956 in Twickenham, England
Source: *AnCL; AtlBL; AuBYP; BkCL; CarSB;*
CasWL; Chambr 3; ChhPo, S1, S2; CnE&AP;
CnMWL; CyWA; DcLEL; EncWL; EvLB;
JBA 34, 51; LongCTC; ModBrL; NewC;
OxEng; PenC ENG; RAdv 1; REn; Str&VC;
TwCA, SUP; TwCWr; WebE&AL; WhAm 3;
WhoChL; WhoTwCL

Deland, Margaret Wade
American. Author
Known for short stories *Old Chester Tales,*
    1919; novel *Iron Woman,* 1911.
b. Feb 23, 1857 in Allegheny, Pennsylvania
Source: *AmAu&B; BbD; BiD&SB; Chambr 3;*
ConAmL; CurBio 45; DcAmAu; DcBiA;
DcEnL; NotAW

DeLanda, Diego
see: Landa, Diego de

Delaney, Jack
Canadian. Boxer
b. Mar 18, 1900 in Saint Francis, Quebec
d. Nov 27, 1948 in Katonah, New York
Source: *BioIn 1, 10; WhoBox 74*

Delaney, Joe Alton
American. Football Player
All-pro running back, KC Chiefs, 1981;
    drowned trying to rescue three children.
b. Oct 30, 1958 in Henderson, Texas
d. Jun 29, 1983 in Monroe, Louisiana
Source: *NewYTBS 83*

Delaney, Shelagh
English. Dramatist
Wrote *A Taste of Honey,* 1958.
b. 1939 in Salford, England
Source: *BiE&WWA; CnMD; ConAu 17R; CroCD; CurBio 62; InWom; LongCTC; McGEWD; ModWD; NewC; NotNAT; PenC ENG; PIP&P; REn; TwCWr; Who 74; WhoThe 77; WhoWor 78; WorAu; WrDr 80*

Delaney and Bonnie
[Delaney Bramlett; Bonnie Lynn]
American. Music Group
Southern husband-wife team combining soul, boogie, country; hit album *Down Home,* 1969.
Source: *LilREn 78; RkOn 84; WhoRock 81*

Delannoy, Jean
French. Director
b. Jan 12, 1908 in Noisy, France
Source: *DcFM; FilmgC; IntMPA 75, 76, 77, 78, 79, 80, 81, 82; WorEFlm*

Delano, Jane Arminda
American. Teacher, Nurse
Superintendent, US Army Nurse Corps; chairman, American Red Cross Nursing Service.
b. Mar 26, 1858 in Townsend, New York
d. Apr 15, 1919 in Savenay, France
Source: *DcAmMeB 84*

Delano, Isaac O
Nigerian. Author
b. Nov 4, 1904 in Okenla, Nigeria
Source: *ConAu 25R*

Delany, Martin R
American. Author, Social Reformer, Soldier
Advocated colonization as solution to slavery; first black commissioned in US Army, 1865.
b. 1812
d. 1885
Source: *Alli; AmAu; BlkAWP; DcNAA; EncAB-H; WebBD 80*

Delany, Samuel Ray, Jr.
American. Author
Helped to make science fiction a respected literary genre.
b. Apr 1, 1942 in New York, New York
Source: *BlkAWP; ConAu 81; ConLC 8, 14; ConNov 76; DrAF 76; LivgBAA*

DeLaRamee, Louise
see: Ouida, pseud.

DeLaRenta, Oscar
American. Fashion Designer
Known for lavish evening clothes; won Coty awards, 1967, 1968.
b. Jul 22, 1932 in Santo Domingo, Dominican Republic
Source: *BioNews 74; CelR; CurBio 70; WhoAm 74, 76, 78, 80, 82; WorFshn*

Delaroche, Hippolyte
[Paul Delaroche]
French. Artist
Large historical paintings include "Joas Saved By Josabeth," 1822.
b. 1797
d. 1856
Source: *NewCol 75; OxFr*

DeLaRoche, Mazo
Canadian. Author
Best known for novel *Jalna,* 1927, first in a series of an Ontario fam ily chronicle.
b. Jan 15, 1885 in Toronto, Ontario
d. Jul 12, 1961 in Toronto, Ontario
Source: *CanNov; CanWr; CasWL; Chambr 3; ConAu 85; ConLC 14; CyWA; DcLEL; EvLB; InWom; JBA 34; LongCTC; ObitOF 79; OxAmL; OxCan; OxEng; PenC ENG; REn; REnAL; TwCA, SUP; TwCWr; WhAm 4; WhNAA*

DeLaRochefoucauld, Duc
see: LaRochefoucauld, Francois, Duc de

Delaunay, Robert
French. Artist
b. Apr 12, 1885 in Paris, France
d. Oct 25, 1941 in Montpellier, France
Source: *AtlBL*

Delaunay-Terk, Sonia
French. Artist, Designer
Noted for exuberant use of vibrant color, geometric designs.
b. Nov 14, 1885 in Gradizhsk, Russia
d. Dec 5, 1979 in Paris, France
Source: *BioIn 4, 5, 8, 10, 11, 12; ConArt 77; CurBio 77, 80; GoodHs; NewYTBS 74; WhoAmW 70, 74; WhoWor 74, 78*

DeLaurentiis, Dino
Italian. Producer
Best known films *Serpico,* 1974; *King Kong,* 1976; *Ragtime,* 1981.
b. Aug 8, 1919 in Torre Annunziata, Italy
Source: *BiDFilm; CmMov; CurBio 65; DcFM; FilmgC; IntMPA 82; IntWW 82; OxFilm; WhoAm 82; WhoWor 74; WorAl; WorEFlm*

DeLaurentiis, Federico
Italian. Producer
Son of Dino DeLaurentiis; produced film
  King of the Gypsies, 1978.
b. 1955
d. 1981 in Kvichak Bay, Alaska
Source: *BioIn 12*

DeLavallade, Carmen
American. Dancer
b. Mar 6, 1931 in Los Angeles, California
Source: *BiE&WWA; CurBio 67; InWom;
NotNAT; WhoAm 74; WhoBlA 75*

Delbruck, Max
American. Scientist
Molecular geneticist who pionered in
  bacteriophages research; won Nobel Prize,
  1969.
b. Sep 4, 1906 in Berlin, Germany
d. Mar 9, 1981 in Pasadena, California
Source: *AmM&WS 73P, 79P; IntWW 78;
NewYTBS 81; WebAB; WhAm 7; WhoAm 80;
WhoWest 80; WorAl*

Delderfield, Ronald Frederick
English. Author, Dramatist
b. Feb 12, 1912 in London, England
d. Jun 24, 1972 in Sidmouth, England
Source: *Au&Wr 71; ConAu 37R, 73;
NewYTBE 72; SmATA 20; WhThe*

Deledda, Grazia
Italian. Author
Writings depict Sardinian peasantry; won
  Nobel Prize, 1926.
b. Sep 27, 1875 in Nvoro, Sardinia
d. Aug 16, 1936 in Rome, Italy
Source: *CasWL; ClDMEL; CyWA; EncWL;
EvEuW; ModRL; Novels; PenC EUR; REn;
TwCA, SUP; TwCWr; WhoTwCL; WorAl*

DeLeeuw, Adele Louise
American. Children's Author
Numerous biographies include *Marie Curie:
  Woman of Genius*, 1969.
b. Aug 12, 1899 in Hamilton, Ohio
Source: *AmAu&B; AuBYP; ConAu 1R, 1NR;
JBA 51; OhA&B; SmATA 1; WhNAA;
WhoAmW 77; WrDr 80*

DeLenclos, Anne
see: Lenclos, Ninon de

DeLenclos, Ninon
see: Lenclos, Ninon de

DeLeon, Juan Ponce
see: Ponce de Leon, Juan

Delerue, Georges
French. Composer, Conductor
Won Oscar for score of *A Little Romance*,
  1979; Emmy for *Our World*, 1968.
b. Mar 12, 1925 in Roubaix, France
Source: *VarWW 85*

DeLesseps, Ferdinand Marie
see: Lesseps, Ferdinand Marie de

DelGesu, Guarneri
see: Guarnieri, Giuseppe Antonio

Delibes, Leo
French. Composer
Noted for ballets *La Source*, 1866; *Coppelia*,
  1870.
b. Feb 21, 1836 in Paris, France
d. Jan 16, 1891 in Paris, France
Source: *AtlBL; OxFr; REn*

Delilah
Biblical Character
Enchantress who discovered Samson's secret
  source of strength.
Source: *InWom*

Delius, Frederick
English. Composer
Influenced by European romantics,
  compositions include opera, choral works.
b. Jan 29, 1862 in Bradford, England
d. Jun 10, 1934 in Grez-sur-Loing, France
Source: *AtlBL; DcCM; WhAm HSA, 4*

Dell, Floyd
American. Editor, Author, Dramatist
Spokesman for "Jazz Age," 1920s; most
  successful play comedy *Little Accident*,
  1928.
b. Jun 28, 1887 in Barry, Illinois
d. Jul 23, 1969 in Bethesda, Maryland
Source: *AmAu&B; AnMV 1926; CnDAL;
ConAmA; ConAu 89; DcLEL; LongCTC;
ModAL; OxAmL; PenC AM; REn; REnAL;
TwCA, SUP; WebAB, 79; WhAm 5; WhNAA;
WhThe*

Dell, Gabriel
[Gabriel del Vecchio]
American. Actor
Appeared in TV shows "The Steve Alien
  Show," 1956-61; "A Year at the Top,"
  1977.
b. Oct 7, 1923 in Barbados, British West
  Indies
Source: *NewYTBE 72; NotNAT; WhThe;
WhoHol A; WhoThe 77*

DellaCasa, Lisa
[Lisa DellaCase-Debeljevic]
Swiss. Opera Singer
b. Feb 1, 1919 in Burgdorf, Switzerland
Source: *CurBio 56; InWom; IntWW 74;*
WhoMus 72; WhoWor 78

DellaChiesa, Vivian
American. Opera Singer
b. Oct 9, 1915 in Chicago, Illinois
Source: *CurBio 43; InWom*

DellaFemina, Jerry
American. Advertising Executive, Author
b. Jul 22, 1936 in Brooklyn, New York
Source: *CelR; WhoAdv 72; WhoAm 82*

DellaRobbia, Andrea
Italian. Sculptor
b. 1435 in Florence, Italy
d. 1525
Source: *BioIn 1, 6, 9; NewCol 75*

DellaRobbia, Giovanni
Italian. Sculptor
b. 1469 in Florence, Italy
d. 1529
Source: *AtlBL; BioIn 10; OxDecA; WebBD 80*

DellaRobbia, Luca
Italian. Sculptor
Developed enameling technique of terra-cotta
    figures, c. 1440; started famed family
    workshop.
b. 1400 in Florence, Italy
d. Feb 23, 1482 in Florence, Italy
Source: *AtlBL; REn*

Dellenbaugh, Frederick Samuel
American. Artist
b. Sep 13, 1853 in Ohio
d. Jan 29, 1935
Source: *AmAu&B; AmLY; DcAmAu; DcNAA;*
OhA&B; WhNAA

Deller, Alfred George
English. Opera Singer
b. May 31, 1912 in Margate, England
d. Jul 16, 1979 in Bologna, Italy
Source: *BioIn 5, 7, 8, 9; Who 74*

Dellinger, David T (Dave)
[The Chicago 7]
American. Author, Editor, Political Activist
Chairman, National Mobilization Committee
    to End War in Vietnam, 1967-71.
b. Aug 22, 1915 in Wakefield, Massachusetts
Source: *BioIn 10, 11; ConAu 65; CurBio 76;*
PolProf J; WhoAm 80, 82

Dello Joio, Norman Joseph
American. Composer
b. Jan 24, 1913 in New York, New York
Source: *CelR; CurBio 57; DcCM; LEduc 74;*
WebAB; WhoAm 74, 76, 78, 80, 82; WhoMus
72; WhoWor 78

Dellums, Ronald
American. Politician
Dem. congressman from CA, 1970-84.
b. Nov 24, 1935 in Oakland, California
Source: *CurBio 72; WhoAm 84; WhoBlA 75*

Delmar, Kenny
American. Actor
Played Senator Claghorn on Fred Allen's
    radio show.
b. 1911
d. Jul 14, 1984 in Stanford, Connecticut
Source: *BioIn 1; WhoHol A*

DelMar, Norman Rene
English. Conductor
b. Jul 31, 1919 in London, England
Source: *IntWW 74; Who 74; WhoMus 72*

Delmar, Vina Croter
American. Author
b. Jan 29, 1905 in New York, New York
Source: *AmAu&B; CnDAL; ConAu 65;*
OxAmL; REnAL; TwCA, SUP

Delmas, Jacques Chaban
see: Chaban-Delmas, Jacques

DelMonaco, Mario
Italian. Opera Singer
Tenor, most noted for rendition of Verdi's
    Otello, performed 427 times.
b. Jul 27, 1915 in Florence, Italy
d. Oct 16, 1982 in Mestre, Italy
Source: *Baker 78; CurBio 83; IntWW 80, 81;*
MusMk; NewYTBS 82; WhoMus 72; WhoOp
76

Delmonico, Lorenzo
Swiss. Restaurateur
With uncles, established Delmonico's
    Restaurant, NYC, c. 1834.
b. Mar 13, 1813 in Marengo, Switzerland
d. Sep 3, 1881 in Sharon Springs, New York
Source: *DcAmB; WebAB; WhAm HS*

Delon, Alain
French. Actor
Plays romantic gangster leads; films include
    Is Paris Burning?, 1966.
b. Nov 8, 1935 in Seceaux, France
Source: *BiDFilm; CelR; CurBio 64; FilmgC;*
IntMPA 82; IntWW 82; MotPP; MovMk;
OxFilm; WhoHol A; WorEFlm

Deloney, Thomas
British. Author
Wrote *The Gentle Craft,* 1598.
b. 1543 in London, England
d. 1600
Source: *OxEng; WebBD 80*

DeLong, George Washington
American. Explorer, Naturalist
Died attempting to reach N Pole by way of
    Bering Strait, 1879-81.
b. Aug 22, 1844 in New York, New York
d. Oct 30, 1881 in Siberia, Russia
Source: *Alli SUP; AmAu&B; AmBi; ApCAB;
BbD; BiD&SB; DcAmAu; DcAmB; DcNAA;
TwCBDA; WhAm HS*

DeLorean, John Zachary
American. Auto Executive, Author
Founded DeLorean Motor Co., 1975.
b. Jan 6, 1925 in Detroit, Michigan
Source: *BioNews 74; BusPN; WhoAm 80, 82;
WhoF&I 74, 81; WhoWor 80*

Deloria, Vine, Jr.
American. Lecturer, Political Activist
b. Mar 26, 1933 in Martin, South Dakota
Source: *AmAu&B; ConAu 53; CurBio 74;
SmATA 21; WhoAm 82*

DeLosAngeles, Victoria
see: Angeles, Victoria de los

Del Ray, Lester Ramon Alvarez
American. Author
b. Jun 2, 1915 in Saratoga, Minnesota
Source: *AmAu&B; AuBYP; ConAu 65;
SmATA 22; WhoAm 74*

DelRio, Dolores
[Lolita Dolores Martinez Asunsolo Lopez
    Negrette]
Mexican. Actress
Best known for *Journey into Fear,* 1942; *The
    Fugitive,* 1947.
b. Aug 3, 1905 in Durango, Mexico
d. Apr 11, 1983 in Newport Beach,
    California
Source: *BiDFilm; CelR; Film 2; FilmgC;
InWom; IntMPA 82; MotPP; MovMk;
OxFilm; TwYS; WhoHol A; WorAl; WorEFlm*

DelRuth, Roy
American. Director
Directed over 100 features in 40 yr. career.
b. Oct 18, 1895 in Philadelphia, Pennsylvania
d. Apr 27, 1961 in Sherman Oaks, California
Source: *DcAmB S7*

DeLuca, Giuseppe
Italian. Opera Singer
b. Dec 29, 1876 in Rome, Italy
d. Aug 27, 1950 in New York, New York
Source: *CurBio 47, 50; DcAmB S4; WhAm 3*

DeLugg, Milton
American. Composer, Author, Conductor
b. Dec 2, 1918 in Los Angeles, California
Source: *AmSCAP 66*

DeLuise, Dom
American. Comedian, Actor
Appeared in films *Blazing Saddles,* 1974; *The
    End,* 1978.
b. Aug 1, 1933 in Brooklyn, New York
Source: *IntMPA 82; WhoAm 82; WhoHol A*

Delvecchio, Alex
"Fats"
Canadian. Hockey Player, Hockey Coach
Center, Detroit Red Wings, 1950-73; Hall of
    Fame, 1977.
b. Dec 4, 1931 in Fort William, Ontario
Source: *WhoHcky 73*

DelVerrocchio, Andrea
see: Verrocchio, Andrea del

DeMagalhaes, Fernando
see: Magellan, Ferdinand

DeMalherbe, Francois
see: Malherbe, Francois de

DeManio, Jack
English. Broadcast Journalist
Host, BBC "Today" show, 1958-71.
b. Jan 26, 1914 in London, England
Source: *BioIn 9; ConAu 61; Who 74*

DeMar, Clarence
American. Track Athlete
b. 1888
d. Jun 11, 1958 in Reading, Massachusetts
Source: *BioIn 3, 4, 5, 6, 8*

Demara, Ferdinand Waldo, Jr.
"The Great Imposter"
American. Imposter
Master identity thief; subject of biography,
    film *The Great Imposter,* 1961.
b. Dec 12, 1921 in Lawrence, Massachusetts
d. Jun 7, 1982 in Anaheim, California
Source: *AnObit 1982; DrInf; NewYTBS 82*

DeMarco, Tony
American. Actor, Dancer
With partner Sally DeMarco did specialty
  numbers in 1940s films.
b. 1898 in Buffalo, New York
d. Nov 14, 1965 in Palm Beach, Florida
Source: *EncAB 38; WhScrn 74, 77; WhoHol
B*

DeMarco Sisters
[Arlene DeMarco; Gene DeMarco; Gloria
  DeMarco; Marie DeMarco]
American. Music Group
Source: *InWom*

Demarest, William
American. Actor
Appeared in TV series "My Three Sons,"
  1967-73.
b. Feb 27, 1892 in Saint Paul, Minnesota
d. Dec 27, 1983 in Palm Springs, California
Source: *AnObit 1983; FilmgC; IntMPA 80,
81, 82; MotPP; MovMk; TwYS; Vers A;
WhoHol A; WorAl*

Demaret, Jimmy (James Newton B)
American. Golfer
First to win Masters tournament three times;
  Hall of Fame, 1960.
b. May 10, 1910 in Houston, Texas
d. Dec 28, 1983 in Houston, Texas
Source: *AnObit 1983; NewYTBS 83; WhoGolf*

DeMarivaux, Pierre Carlet
see: Marivaux, Pierre Carlet de

DeMaupassant, Henri Rene Albert Guy
see: Maupassant, Henri Rene Albert Guy de

DeMedici, Catherine
see: Catherine de Medicis

DeMedici, Cosimo
see: Medici, Cosimo de

DeMedici, Francesco
see: Medici, Francesco de

DeMedici, Lorenzo
see: Medici, Lorenzo de

DeMedicis, Marie
see: Marie de Medicis

Demers, Jacques
Canadian. Hockey Coach
NHL coach since 1978 with Quebec, St.
  Louis, Detroit.
b. Aug 25, 1944 in Montreal, Quebec
Source: *HocEn*

Demetrius I
[Demetrius Poliorcetes]
Macedonian. Ruler
King of Macedonia, 294-285 BC; destroyed
  Egyptian fleet, 306 BC.
b. 337 BC
d. 283 BC
Source: *NewCol 75; WebBD 80*

DeMille, Agnes George
[Mrs. Walter Foy Prude]
American. Dancer, Author
Choreographed musicals *Oklahoma,* 1943;
  Carousel, 1945; *Brigadoon,* 1947.
b. Sep 18, 1905 in New York, New York
Source: *AmAu&B; BioNews 74; CelR; ConAu
65; CurBio 85; EncMT; HerW; InWom;
NotNAT; REnAL; WebAB; Who 74; WhoAm
80, 82; WhoThe 77; WhoWor 74*

DeMille, Cecil B(lount)
American. Director, Producer
With Jesse Lasky, Samuel Goldwyn, formed
  Jesse Lasky Feature Play Co., 1913;
  evolved into Paramount Studios.
b. Aug 12, 1881 in Ashfield, Massachusetts
d. Jan 21, 1959 in Hollywood, California
Source: *AmAu&B; BiDFilm; CmMov; CurBio
42, 59; DcFM; EncAB-H; FilmgC; MovMk;
OxFilm; REn; REnAL; TwYS; WebAB;
WhAm 3; WhScrn 74, 77; WhThe; WhoHol
B; WomWMM; WorAl; WorEFlm*

DeMiranda, Francisco
see: Miranda, Francisco de

Demirel, Suleyman
Turkish. Political Leader
Four-time prime minister detained after Sep
  1980 coup; known as moderate man of the
  people.
b. Oct 6, 1924 in Islamkoy, Turkey
Source: *BioIn 12; CurBio 80; IntWW 83;
IntYB 82; WhoWor 82*

Demme, Jonathan
American. Director
Directed slices of Americana: *Citizens Band,*
  1977; *Swing Shift,* 1984.
b. 1944 in Baldwin, New York
Source: *CurBio 85; IntMPA 84*

Democritus
"The Laughing Philosopher"
Greek. Philosopher
Developed atomic theory: reality consists of
  atoms and space between them.
b. 460 BC in Abdera, Greece
d. 370 BC
Source: *CasWL; NewC; PenC CL; REn*

DeMontebello, Guy-Philippe
American. Museum Director
Director, Metropolitan Museum of Art,
1978--.
b. May 16, 1936 in Paris, France
Source: *ConAu 45; CurBio 81; Who 83;*
WhoAm 82

DeMontesquieu, Charles Louis
see: Montesquieu, Charles Louis de

DeMontfort, Simon
see: Montfort, Simon de

DeMoraes, Vinicius
see: Moraes, Vinicius de

DeMornay, Rebecca
American. Actress
In films *Risky Business,* 1983; *The Trip to*
Bountiful, 1985.
b. 1962 in Santa Rosa, California
Source: *ConTFT 3*

DeMoss, Arthur S
American. Insurance Executive
b. Oct 26, 1925 in Albany, New York
Source: *WhoE 74; WhoF&I 74; WhoIns 75*

Demosthenes
Greek. Orator, Statesman
Considered greatest Greek orator; leader of
democratic faction, Athens.
b. 384 BC in Attica, Greece
d. Oct 322 BC in Calavria, Greece
Source: *BbD; BiD&SB; CasWL; CyWA;*
DcEnL; NewC; OxEng; PenC CL; RComWL;
REn

DeMott, Benjamin Haile
American. Author, Educator
b. Jun 2, 1924 in Rockville Centre, New
York
Source: *AmAu&B; ConAu 5R; DrAF 76;*
DrAS 74E; WhoAm 74, 76, 78, 80, 82;
WorAu

Dempsey, Jack (William Harrison)
"The Manassa Mauler"
American. Boxer
Heavyweight boxing champ, 1919-26, 1931-40;
Hall of Fame, 1954.
b. Jun 24, 1895 in Manassa, Colorado
d. May 31, 1983 in New York, New York
Source: *CelR; ConAu 89; CurBio 45;*
NewYTBE 70, 73; OxAmH; WebAB; WhoAm
74; WhoBox 74; WhoHol A; WhoWor 74;
WorAl

Dempsey, John Noel
American. Governor
b. Jan 3, 1915 in Cahir, Ireland
Source: *BiDrGov; CurBio 61; IntWW 74;*
WhAmP; WhoAm 74; WhoAmP 73

Dempsey, Miles Christopher, Sir
English. Army Officer
b. Dec 15, 1896 in Hoylake, England
d. Jun 6, 1969 in Yattendon, England
Source: *BioIn 1, 8; CurBio 44, 69*

Dempsey, Rick (John Rikard)
American. Baseball Player
Catcher, Baltimore Orioles, 1976--; MVP
1983 World Series.
b. Sep 13, 1949 in Fayetteville, Tennessee
Source: *BaseEn 85; BaseReg 86*

Dempster, Arthur J
Canadian. Physicist, Educator
Discovered Uranium-235, 1935, which is the
explosive of atomic bomb.
b. 1886 in Toronto, Ontario
d. Mar 11, 1950 in Stuart, Florida
Source: *BiESc; ObitOF 79; WebBD 80*

Dempster, Carol
American. Actress
Brief career as star of D W Griffith films in
1920s.
b. 1901 in Duluth, Minnesota
Source: *Film 2; FilmgC; MotPP; TwYS;*
WhoHol A

DeMurville, (Jacques) Maurice Couve
see: Couve de Murville, (Jacques) Maurice

Demus, Joreg
Austrian. Pianist
Award-winning Viennese concert performer,
made over 200 recordings.
b. Dec 2, 1928 in Saint Poelten, Austria
Source: *BioIn 5; IntWW 78; WhoMus 72*

Demuth, Charles
American. Artist
b. Nov 8, 1883 in Lancaster, Pennsylvania
d. Oct 23, 1935 in Lancaster, Pennsylvania
Source: *DcAmB S1; DcCAA 71; EncAB-H;*
WebAB; WhAm HSA, 4

Demy, Jacques
French. Director
b. Jun 5, 1931 in Pont Chateau, France
Source: *BiDFilm; DcFM; FilmgC; IntWW 82;*
MovMk; OxFilm; WhoWor 78; WorEFlm

DeNagybanya, Nicholas Horthy
see: Horthy de Nagybanya, Nicholas

Den Uyl, Joor
Dutch. Politician
b. 1919 in Amsterdam, Netherlands
Source: *IntWW 74*

Dench, Judith Olivia
English. Actress
b. Dec 12, 1934 in York, England
Source: *CnThe; FilmgC; IntMPA 80, 81, 82;
Who 82; WhoThe 81*

Denenberg, Herbert S
American. Educator, Lawyer
b. Nov 20, 1929 in Omaha, Nebraska
Source: *ConAu 37R; WhoAm 82*

Deneuve, Catherine
[Catherine Dorleac]
French. Actress
Starred in *Mayerling,* 1968; appears in print,
TV ads for Chanel No. 5.
b. Oct 22, 1943 in Paris, France
Source: *BiDFilm; BkPepl; CelR; FilmgC;
IntMPA 82; IntWW 74; MotPP; MovMk;
OxFilm; WhoAm 82; WhoHol A; WorEFlm*

Deng Xiaoping
see: Teng Hsiao-Ping

Denikin, Anton Ivanovich
Russian. General
Led White Russian Army against Bolsheviks,
1918-20.
b. 1872
d. Aug 8, 1947 in Ann Arbor, Michigan
Source: *ObitOF 79; REn; WhoMilH 76*

DeNiro, Robert
American. Actor
Won Oscar, 1981, for *Raging Bull.*
b. Aug 17, 1943 in New York, New York
Source: *BkPepl; IntMPA 82; MovMk; WhoAm
82; WhoHol A*

Denison, George Taylor
Canadian. Soldier, Historian
A founder of patriotic "Canada First"
movement, 1868; wrote *History of Cavalry,*
1877.
b. Aug 31, 1839 in Toronto, Ontario
d. Jun 6, 1925 in Toronto, Ontario
Source: *ApCAB; DcCanB 10; LinLib L;
MacDCB 78; OxCan*

Denning, Alfred Thompson
English. Judge, Author
Investigator of Britain's scandalous Profumo
case, 1963.
b. Jan 23, 1899 in Whitchurch, England
Source: *ConAu 115; CurBio 65; Who 85*

Denning, Richard
[Louis Albert Denninger]
American. Actor
b. Mar 27, 1914 in Poughkeepsie, New York
Source: *FilmgC; MotPP; MovMk; WhoAm 82;
WhoHol A; WorAl*

Dennis, Patrick, pseud.
[Virginia Rowens, pseud.; Edward Everett
Tanner III]
American. Author
Known for *Auntie Mame,* which was adapted
to film, Broadway musical *Mame.*
b. May 18, 1921 in Chicago, Illinois
d. Nov 6, 1976 in New York, New York
Source: *AmAu&B; ConAu 69, 73; CurBio 77;
WhoAm 74; WorAu; WrDr 76*

Dennis, Sandy
American. Actress
Won Oscar, 1966, for *Who's Afraid of
Virginia Woolf?*
b. Apr 27, 1937 in Hastings, Nebraska
Source: *BiE&WWA; CelR; CurBio 69;
FilmgC; InWom; IntMPA 82; MotPP;
MovMk; NotNAT; WhoAm 82; WhoHol A;
WhoThe 77*

Dennison, George
American. Editor, Author
Wrote *Oilers and Sweepers,* 1979.
b. Sep 10, 1925 in Ashburn, Georgia
Source: *AmAu&B; BioIn 10; ConAu 101*

Dennison, Robert Lee
American. Admiral
b. Apr 13, 1901 in Warren, Pennsylvania
d. Mar 14, 1980 in Bethesda, Maryland
Source: *CurBio 60, 80*

Denny, John Allen
American. Baseball Player
Pitcher, 1975--; won NL Cy Young Award,
1983.
b. Nov 8, 1952 in Prescott, Arizona
Source: *BaseEn 85; BaseReg 86*

Denny, Ludwell
American. Journalist
b. Nov 18, 1894 in Boonville, Indiana
d. Oct 12, 1970
Source: *AmAu&B; ConAu 29R; IndAu 1917;
WhAm 5*

Denny, Reginald Leigh
[Reginald Leigh Daymore]
English. Actor
Appeared in 200 films including *Leather Pushers* series, 1922-24.
b. Nov 20, 1891 in Richmond, England
d. Jun 16, 1967 in Surrey, England
Source: *BiE&WWA; FilmEn; Film 1; FilmgC; MotPP; MovMk; TwYS; Vers A; WhAm 4; WhScrn 74, 77; WhThe; WhoHol B*

Denny-Brown, Derek Ernest
American. Neurologist, Author
Researched human nervous system; found blood supply to brain influences strokes.
b. Jun 1, 1901 in Christchurch, New Zealand
d. Apr 20, 1981 in Cambridge, Massachusetts
Source: *AmM&WS 79P; ConAu 103; IntWW 78; NewYTBS 81; WhE&EA*

Denoff, Sam
American. Writer, Producer
TV shows include "Steve Allen Show"; "Andy Williams Show"; won Emmys for "Dick Van Dyke Show," 1964, 1966.
b. Jul 1, 1928 in Brooklyn, New York
Source: *VarWW 85*

Densen-Gerber, Judianne
American. Psychiatrist
Founded Odyssey House, 1966, drug treatment center that doesn't rely on substituting other drugs.
b. Nov 13, 1934 in New York, New York
Source: *BiDrAPA 77; CurBio 83; WhoAm 84; WhoAmW 83; WhoE 83*

Densmore, John
[The Doors]
American. Singer, Musician
b. Dec 1, 1945 in Los Angeles, California
Source: *NF*

Dent, Alan Holmes
Scottish. Author, Critic, Journalist
b. Jan 7, 1905 in Ayrshire, Scotland
d. Dec 1978
Source: *Au&Wr 71; ConAu 5NR, 9R; DcLEL 1940; IntAu&W 76, 77; LongCTC; Who 74; WhoThe 72, 77; WrDr 76*

Dent, "Bucky" (Russell Earl)
American. Baseball Player
b. Nov 25, 1951 in Savannah, Georgia
Source: *BaseEn 85; NewYTBS 79; WhoAm 82*

Dent, Edward Joseph
English. Impresario, Author
b. Jul 16, 1876 in Ribston, England
d. Aug 22, 1957 in London, England
Source: *NewEOp 71; OxMus; WhE&EA*

Dent, Phil
"Philby"
Australian. Tennis Player
Won US Open mixed doubles with Billie Jean King, 1976.
b. Feb 14, 1950 in Sydney, Australia
Source: *WhoIntT*

Denton, Jeremiah Andrew, Jr.
American. Politician
Rep. senator from AL, 1980--; first POW to return from Vietnam.
b. Jul 15, 1924 in Mobile, Alabama
Source: *ConAu 69; CurBio 82; WhoAm 80, 82; WhoGov 77; WhoS&SW 82*

Denton, Steve
"The Bull"
American. Tennis Player
With doubles partner Kevin Curran, won US Clay Court, 1980, 1981, US Open, 1982.
b. Sep 5, 1956 in Kingsville, Texas
Source: *WhoIntT*

Denver, Bob
American. Actor
Starred in "The Many Loves of Doby Gillis," 1959-63; "Gilligan's Island," 1964-67.
b. Jan 9, 1935 in New Rochelle, New York
Source: *FilmgC; WhoHol A*

Denver, James William
American. Governor
b. Oct 23, 1817 in Winchester, Virginia
d. Aug 9, 1892 in Washington, District of Columbia
Source: *AmBi; ApCAB; BiAUS; BiDrAC; CivWDc; CmCal; DcAmB; Drake; OhA&B; WhAm HS; WhAmP*

Denver, John
[Henry John Deutschendorf]
American. Singer, Songwriter, Actor
Sang "Take Me Home Country Road," 1971; appeared in *Oh, God!*, 1977.
b. Dec 31, 1943 in Roswell, New Mexico
Source: *BioNews 74; BkPepl; CurBio 75; WhoAm 82*

DeOrtega, Francisco
see: Ortega, Francisco de

Depailler, Patrick
French. Auto Racer
b. Aug 8, 1944
d. Aug 1, 1980 in Heidelberg, Germany (West)
Source: *BioIn 11*

DePalma, Brian Russell
American. Director
b. Sep 11, 1940 in Newark, New Jersey
Source: *BioIn 11; ConLC 20; CurBio 82;*
FilmgC; IntMPA 80, 81, 82; NewYTBE 73;
WhoAm 80, 82

DePalma, Ralph
American. Auto Racer
b. 1883
d. Mar 31, 1956 in South Pasadena,
California
Source: *BioIn 4, 6, 7, 10*

DePaolis, Alessio
Italian. Opera Singer
b. Apr 5, 1893 in Rome, Italy
d. Mar 9, 1964 in New York, New York
Source: *NewEOp 71; WhAm 4*

Depardieu, Gerard
French. Actor
Leading roles as working-class character: *The*
Return of Martin Guerre, 1983; *Danton,*
1983.
b. Dec 27, 1948 in Chateauroux, France
Source: *BioIn 11; FilmEn; IntMPA 82;*
IntWW 82; NewYTBS 81; WhoHol A

DeParis, Wilbur
American. Jazz Musician
b. Sep 20, 1900 in Crawfordsville, Indiana
d. Jan 1973 in New York, New York
Source: *NewYTBE 73; WhAm 5; WhScrn 77;*
WhoJazz 72

De Passe, Suzanne
American. Writer, TV Executive
Wrote film *Lady Sings the Blues,* 1972; won
Emmy for producing "Forever," 1983.
Source: *VarWW 85*

De Patie, David H
American. Producer
Won Oscar for *The Pink Phink,* 1964; Emmy
for "The Cat-In-The-Hat," 1982.
b. Dec 24, 1930 in Los Angeles, California
Source: *VarWW 85*

DePaul, Vincent
see: Vincent de Paul, Saint

Depew, Chauncey M
American. Senator, Philanthropist
b. Apr 23, 1834 in Peekskill, New York
d. Apr 5, 1928 in New York, New York
Source: *AmAu&B; AmBi; ApCAB; BiD&SB;*
BiDrAC; DcAmAu; DcAmB; DcNAA; REnAL;
TwCBDA; WebAB; WhAm 1; WhAmP;
WhNAA

DePriest, Oscar Stanton
American. Congressman
b. 1871 in Florence, Alabama
d. May 12, 1951 in Chicago, Illinois
Source: *BiDrAC; DcAmB S5; WhAm 3;*
WhAmP

DePugh, Robert Bolivar (William Robert
Bolivar)
American. Political Activist
Founded Minutemen, 1960, to train
Americans to fight guerrilla war against
communist takeover.
b. Apr 15, 1923 in Independence, Missouri
Source: *BioIn 11; PolProf J*

DeQuay, Jan E
Dutch. Political Leader
One of founders of Dutch Union, 1940;
prime minister of Netherlands, 1959-63.
b. 1901 in S'Hertogenbosch, Netherlands
d. Jul 4, 1985 in Beers, Netherlands
Source: *CurBio 85; IntWW 83; IntYB 82;*
WhoWor 78

DeQuincey, Thomas
English. Author
Eloquent prose evident in masterpiece
Confessions of an English Opium Eater,
1822.
b. Aug 15, 1785 in Greenheys, England
d. Dec 8, 1859 in Edinburgh, Scotland
Source: *Alli; AtlBL; BbD; BiD&SB; BrAu 19;*
CasWL; Chambr 3; CrtT 2; CyWA; DcBiA;
DcEnA; DcEnL; DcEuL; DcLEL; EvLB;
MouLC 3; NewC; OxEng; OxMus; PenC
ENG; RAdv 1; RComWL; REn; WebE&AL;
WorAl

Derain, Andre
French. Artist
b. Jun 10, 1880 in Chatou, France
d. Sep 10, 1954 in Chambourcy, France
Source: *AtlBL; REn*

Derby, Jane (Jeanette Barr)
American. Fashion Designer
b. May 17, 1895 in Rockymount, Virginia
d. Aug 7, 1965
Source: *BioIn 3, 7; WhAm 4*

DeRegniers, Beatrice Schenk
American. Children's Author
b. Aug 16, 1914 in Lafayette, Indiana
Source: *AmAu&B; Au&Wr 71; AuBYP; BkP;*
ChhPo, S1; ConAu 13R; IndAu 1917; MorJA;
SmATA 2; WhoAm 74, 76, 78, 80, 82; WhoE
74; WrDr 80

Derek, Bo
[Mary Cathleen Collins; Mrs. John Derek]
American. Actress
Starred with Dudley Moore in *10,* 1979;
   fourth wife of John Derek.
b. Nov 16, 1956 in Long Beach, California
Source: *BioIn 12; BkPepl; IntMPA 82*

Derek, John
[Derek Harris]
American. Actor
Starred in *The Ten Commandments,* 1956;
   former wives Linda Evans, Ursula
   Andress.
b. Aug 12, 1926 in Hollywood, California
Source: *CmMov; FilmgC; MotPP; MovMk;
WhoHol A; WorAl; WorEFlm*

Deren, Maya
American. Filmmaker
Producer of avant-garde films; founded
   Creative Film Foundation, 1955.
b. Apr 29, 1917 in Kiev, Russia
d. Oct 13, 1961 in Queens, New York
Source: *NotAW MOD*

DeReszke, Edouard
Polish. Opera Singer
b. Dec 22, 1853 in Warsaw, Poland
d. May 25, 1917 in Garnek, Poland
Source: *WhAm 1*

DeReszke, Jean
[Jan Mieczyslaw]
Polish. Opera Singer
b. Jan 14, 1850 in Warsaw, Poland
d. Apr 3, 1925 in Nice, France
Source: *ApCAB SUP; WhAm 2*

DeRita, Joe
[The Three Stooges]
"Curly Joe"
American. Comedian
Joined The Three Stooges, 1959.
Source: *MotPP; WhoHol A*

DeRivera, Jose
American. Artist, Sculptor
b. Sep 18, 1904 in West Baton Rouge,
   Louisiana
d. Mar 21, 1985 in New York, New York
Source: *BioIn 4, 5; DcCAA 71; WhoAm 82;
WhoAmA 73; WhoE 74*

Derleth, August
American. Author
b. Feb 24, 1909 in Sauk City, Wisconsin
d. Jul 4, 1971
Source: *AmAu&B; AmNov; AuBYP; BkC 6;
ChhPo, S2; CnDAL; ConAu 1R, 29R, 4NR;
ConNov 72; DcLEL; EncMys; OxAmL; REn;
REnAL; SmATA 5; TwCA, SUP; WhAm 5;
WhNAA*

Dern, Bruce MacLeish
American. Actor
Starred with Jane Fonda, Jon Voight in
   Coming Home, 1978.
b. Jun 4, 1936 in Chicago, Illinois
Source: *BkPepl; CurBio 78; IntMPA 75, 76,
77, 78, 79, 80, 81, 82; WhoAm 74, 76, 78,
80, 82; WhoHol A; WorAl*

Dern, Laura Elizabeth
American. Actress
Daughter of Bruce Dern; in 1985 film *Mask.*
b. 1967 in Santa Monica, California
Source: *ConTFT 3*

DeRoburt, Hammer
President
b. 1922
Source: *BioIn 10; FarE&A 81; IntWW 82;
WhoWor 80*

DeRochemont, Louis
American. Producer
Created newsreels *The March of Time,* 1934;
   series won Oscar, 1936.
b. Jan 13, 1899 in Chelsea, Massachusetts
d. Dec 23, 1978 in York Harbor, Maine
Source: *CurBio 79N; DcFM; FilmgC; IntMPA
79; ObitOF 79; OxFilm; WhoAm 78; WhoWor
74; WorEFlm*

DeRojas, Fernando
see: Rojas, Fernando de

DeRonsard, Pierre
see: Ronsard, Pierre de

DeRouvroy, Claude Henri
see: Saint-Simon, Claude-Henri de Rouvroy

Derringer, Rick
[Rick Zehringer]
American. Singer, Musician
Singer-guitarist with 1960s McCoys; wrote hit
   "Hang on, Sloopy," 1965; formed own
   band, 1976.
b. 1947 in Union City, Illinois
Source: *ConMuA 80A; RkOn 78; WhoRock
81*

DeSabata, Victor
Italian. Conductor, Composer
b. Apr 10, 1892 in Trieste, Italy
d. Dec 11, 1967 in Santa Margherita, Italy
Source: *NewEOp 71; OxMus*

DeSade, Marquis
see: Sade, Donatien de

Desai, Morarji Ranchodji
Indian. Political Leader
b. Feb 29, 1896 in Bhadeli, India
Source: *CurBio 58; IntWW 74; NewCol 75*

DeSalvo, Albert
"Boston Strangler"
American. Criminal
Never tried for slayings of 13 women,
    confessed to psychiatrist; stabbed to death
    in jail cell.
b. 1931
d. Dec 27, 1973 in Walpole Prison,
    Massachusetts
Source: *BioIn 7, 10*

DeSanctis, Francesco
Italian. Educator, Author, Critic
Founded modern Italian literary criticism.
b. Mar 28, 1817 in Morra Irpino, Italy
d. Dec 19, 1883 in Naples, Italy
Source: *BiD&SB; CasWL; ClDMEL; DcEuL;
DcItL; EuAu; EvEuW; McGEWB; PenC
EUR; REn*

DeSantis, Giuseppe
Italian. Director
Advocate of neo-realism in film.
b. Feb 11, 1917 in Fondi, Italy
Source: *DcFM; FilmgC; IntMPA 80, 81, 82;
OxFilm; WorEFlm*

DeSapio, Carmine Gerard
American. Politician
b. Dec 10, 1908 in New York, New York
Source: *CurBio 55*

Descartes, Rene
French. Mathematician, Philosopher
Known as father of modern philosophy; said
    "I think, therefore I am."
b. Mar 31, 1596 in La Haye, France
d. Feb 11, 1650 in Stockholm, Sweden
Source: *BbD; BiD&SB; CasWL; DcEuL;
EuAu; EvEuW; NewC; OxEng; OxFr; PenC
EUR; REn*

DeScudery, Madeleine
see: Scudery, Madeleine de

DeSegonzac, Andre Dunoyer
see: Dunoyer de Segonzac, Andre

DeSeversky, Alexander Procofieff
[Alexander de Seversky]
American. Aeronautical Engineer
A major figure in military aviation, wrote
    Victory through Airpower, 1942.
b. Jun 7, 1894 in Tiflis, Russia
d. Aug 24, 1974 in New York, New York
Source: *CelR; ConAu 53; CurBio 41, 74;
IntWW 74; NewYTBS 74; St&PR 75;
WebAB; WhAm 6; Who 74; WhoAm 74;
WhoF&I 74*

DeShannon, Jackie
American. Singer, Songwriter
b. Aug 21, 1944 in Hazel, Kentucky
Source: *EncPR&S 74*

Deshayes, Catherine
"La Voisin"
French. Criminal
Sorceress who gave poison to aristocracy;
    killed over 2,000 infants in Black Mass
    services.
d. Feb 22, 1680 in Paris, France
Source: *LookW*

DeSica, Vittorio
Italian. Actor, Director
Won four Oscars as best director of foreign
    films.
b. Jul 7, 1901 in Scra, Italy
d. Nov 13, 1974 in Paris, France
Source: *BiDFilm; DcFM; FilmgC; IntMPA 75;
IntWW 74; MovMk; NewYTBE 72; OxFilm;
REn; WhAm 6; WhScrn 77; Who 74;
WhoAm 74; WhoHol B; WhoWor 74; WorAl;
WorEFlm*

DeSilhouette, Etienne
see: Silhouette, Etienne de

Desjardins, Pete
American. Olympic Athlete
Two-time Olympic gold medal winner in
    diving, 1928; called best springboard diver
    in history.
b. 1907
d. May 6, 1985 in Miami, Florida
Source: *NF*

Desmond, Johnny
[Giovanni Alfredo DeSimone]
"GI Sinatra"
American. Singer, Actor
Gained fame as vocalist with Glenn Miller's
    swing music band during Big Band Era.
b. Nov 14, 1919 in Detroit, Michigan
d. Sep 6, 1985 in Los Angeles, California
Source: *AmSCAP 66; IntMPA 80, 81, 82;
WhoHol A*

Desmond, Paul Breitenfeld
American. Musician
b. Nov 25, 1924 in San Francisco, California
d. May 30, 1977 in New York, New York
Source: *WhoAm 74*

Desmond, William
American. Actor
Played in number of silent film serials
   beginning 1915.
b. May 21, 1878 in Dublin, Ireland
d. Nov 3, 1949 in Los Angeles, California
Source: *Film 1; FilmgC; MotPP; NotNAT B;*
ObitOF 79; TwYS; WhScrn 74, 77; WhoHol
B

Desmoulins, Camille
"Agent of the Lantern"
French. Journalist, Revolutionary
Wrote popular revolutionary pieces; executed
   by Robespierre.
b. Mar 2, 1760 in Guise, France
d. Apr 5, 1794 in Paris, France
Source: *DcAmSR; DcBiPP; DcEuL; EvEuW;*
OxFr; REn

Desormiere, Roger
French. Conductor
b. Sep 13, 1898 in Vichy, France
d. Oct 25, 1963 in Paris, France
Source: *NewEOp 71*

DeSoto, Hernando
Spanish. Explorer
First to see, cross Mississippi River, 1539-42.
b. 1500 in Barcarrota, Spain
d. May 21, 1542 in Ferriday, Louisiana
Source: *AmBi; DcAmB; DcCathB; EncSoH;*
HarEnUS; LuthC 75; McGEWB; OxAmH;
REn; REnAL; REnAW; WhAm HS; WhFla;
WorAl

DesPres, Josquin
[Josse Depres]
Flemish. Composer
b. 1445 in Conde sur l'Escaut, France
d. Aug 27, 1521 in Conde, France
Source: *AtlBL*

Dessalines, Jean J
Haitian. Emperor
b. 1758 in Guinea
d. Oct 17, 1806 in Haiti
Source: *ApCAB; Drake; REn*

Desses, Jean
French. Fashion Designer
b. Aug 6, 1904 in Alexandria, Egypt
d. Aug 2, 1970 in Athens, Greece
Source: *CurBio 56, 70; NewYTBE 70; WhAm*
5; WhoFash; WorFshn

D'Estaing, Charles Henri Hector, Comte
see: Estaing, Charles Henri Hector, Comte
   d'

D'Estaing, Valery Giscard
see: Giscard d'Estaing, Valery

Destinn, Emmy
[Emmy Kittl]
Czech. Opera Singer
b. Feb 26, 1878 in Prague, Czechoslovakia
d. Jan 28, 1930 in Budejovice,
   Czechoslovakia
Source: *WhAm 1; WhScrn 77*

Destouches, Louis-Ferdinand
[Louis-Ferdinand Celine]
French. Author, Physician
Wrote *Journey to End of the Night,* 1934;
   Death on Installment Plan, 1938.
b. May 27, 1894 in Paris, France
d. Jul 4, 1961 in Paris, France
Source: *ConAu 85; ConLC 9, 15; LongCTC;*
REn; TwCA, SUP

Destri, Jimmy
see: Blondie

DeSylva, "Buddy" (George Gard)
American. Songwriter, Producer
b. Jan 27, 1896 in New York, New York
d. Jul 11, 1950 in Oak Park, Illinois
Source: *CurBio 43, 50; DcAmB S4; WhAm 3*

Deterding, Henri Wilhelm August, Sir
Dutch. Business Executive
Founded Shell Oil, 1912, largest US foreign
   controlled co.
b. 1866
d. 1939 in Germany
Source: *BioIn 4*

DeTocqueville, Alexis, Comte de
see: Tocqueville, Alexis, Comte de

DeToledano, Ralph
see: Toledano, Ralph de

Dett, Robert Nathaniel
American. Composer
Choral pieces evolved from black spirituals:
   "Chariot Jubilee."
b. Oct 11, 1882 in Drummondsville, Ontario
d. Oct 2, 1943 in Battle Creek, Michigan
Source: *AmAu&B; AmSCAP 66; CurBio 43,*
73; DcAmB S3; WebBD 80

Deukmejian, George, Jr. (Courken)
American. Politician
Rep. governor of CA, 1982--.
b. Jun 6, 1928 in Menands, New York
Source: *CurBio 83; NewYTBS 83; WhoAm 80, 82; WhoAmL 79; WhoAmP 81; WhoWest 82*

Deutsch, Adolph
American. Composer
MGM musical director whose scores include Oscar-winning *Oklahoma!*, 1955; *Annie Get Your Gun,* 1950.
b. Oct 20, 1897 in London, England
d. Jan 1, 1980 in Palm Desert, California
Source: *AmSCAP 66; AnObit 1980; BioIn 1; CmpEPM*

Deutsch, Babette
[Mrs. Avrahm Yarmolinsky]
American. Author, Poet
Verse concerned with social problems; first book, *Banners,* 1919.
b. Sep 22, 1895 in New York, New York
d. Nov 13, 1982 in New York, New York
Source: *AmAu&B; AnCL; Au&Wr 71; ChhPo, S1, S2; ConAmL; ConAu 1R, 4NR; ConLC 18; ConP 70, 75; DcLEL; DrAP 75; DrAS 74E; EvLB; IntWW 74; LongCTC; MorJA; NewYTBS 82; OxAmL; PenC AM; RAdv 1; REn; REnAL; SmATA 1; TwCA, SUP; TwCWr; WhE&EA; WhNAA; WhoAm 74; WhoAmW 74; WhoWor 74; WhoWorJ 72; WrDr 82*

Deutsch, Harold C
American. Author
b. Jun 7, 1904 in Milwaukee, Wisconsin
Source: *ConAu 21R; DrAS 74H*

Deutsch, Helen
American. Screenwriter, Lyricist
Her screenplays include *National Velvet,* 1944; *Lili,* 1953.
b. Mar 21, 1906 in New York, New York
Source: *AmSCAP 66; ConAu 112; IntMPA 84; WomWMM*

Deutsch, Helene R
American. Psychoanalyst
Wrote *The Psychology of Women,* 1944.
b. Oct 9, 1884 in Przemysl, Austria-Hungary
d. Mar 29, 1982 in Cambridge, Massachusetts
Source: *NewYTBS 82; WorAl*

Deutsch, Karl Wolfgang
American. Political Scientist
b. Jul 12, 1912 in Prague, Czechoslovakia
Source: *ConAu 41R; WhoAm 74, 76, 78, 80, 82; WhoWor 78*

DeVaca, Alvar Nunez Cabeza
see: Cabeza de Vaca, Alvar Nunez

DeValera, Eamon
Irish. Statesman
Leader of Irish independence movement who was pres., Ireland, 1959-73.
b. Oct 14, 1882 in New York, New York
d. Aug 30, 1975 in Dublin, Ireland
Source: *ConAu 89; CurBio 40, 51; IntWW 74; REn; WhAm 6; Who 74; WhoGov 75; WhoWor 78*

DeValois, Ninette
British. Choreographer, Author
b. Jun 6, 1898 in Blessington, Ireland
Source: *Au&Wr 71; CurBio 49; IntWW 74; PIP&P; WhThe; Who 74; WhoAmW 74*

Devane, William
American. Actor
Star of TV series "Knots Landing," 1983--.
b. Sep 5, 1937 in Albany, New York
Source: *IntMPA 82; WhoAm 82; WhoHol A; WorAl*

DeVarona, Donna
American. Swimmer, Broadcast Journalist
Youngest member of US Olympic team at 13; won gold medal, 1964.
b. 1947 in San Diego, California
Source: *BioIn 12; WhoTelC*

DeVega, Lope
see: Lope de Vega

Devereaux, Robert
[Earl of Essex]
English. Courtier
b. Nov 19, 1566
d. Feb 25, 1601
Source: *Alli; NewC*

Devereux, George
Anthropologist, Author
b. Sep 13, 1908 in Lugos, Hungary
Source: *BiDPara; ConAu 69*

Devers, Jacob Loucks
American. Army Officer
b. Sep 8, 1887 in York, Pennsylvania
d. Oct 15, 1979 in Bethesda, Maryland
Source: *CurBio 42; Who 74*

DeVeuster, Joseph Damien
see: Damien, Father

DeVicenzo, Roberto
Argentine. Golfer
b. Apr 14, 1923 in Argentina
Source: *WhoGolf*

DeVigny, Alfred Comte
see: Vigny, Alfred, Comte de

DeVilleneuve, Justin
English. Public Relations Executive
b. 1940
Source: BioIn 8, 9

DeVincennes, Sieur
see: Vincennes, Francois Marie Bissot

Devine, Andy
[Jeremiah Schwartz]
American. Actor
Comic sidekick for Roy Rogers.
b. Oct 7, 1905 in Flagstaff, Arizona
d. Feb 18, 1977 in Orange, California
Source: CmMov; FilmgC; IntMPA 75, 76, 77;
MotPP; MovMk; ObitOF 79; OxFilm; TwYS;
WhoHol A; WorAl

Devine, Dan(iel John)
American. Football Coach
b. Dec 23, 1924 in Augusta, Wisconsin
Source: WhoAm 74; WhoFtbl 74

Devine, Donald
Canadian. Politician
Progressive-Conservative Party premier of
Saskatchewan, 1982--.
b. Jul 5, 1944 in Regina, Saskatchewan
Source: NF

Devine, Michael
Irish. Hunger Striker, Revolutionary
b. 1954 in Londonderry, Northern Ireland
d. Aug 20, 1981 in Belfast, Northern Ireland
Source: NF

DeVinne, Theodore Low
American. Printer
b. Dec 25, 1828 in Stamford, Connecticut
d. Feb 16, 1914 in New York, New York
Source: AmAu&B; AmBi; ApCAB; DcAmAu;
DcAmB; DcNAA; OxAmL; REn; REnAL;
TwCBDA; WebAB, 79; WhAm 1; WhLit

DeVita, Vincent Theodore, Jr.
American. Educator, Physician
Noted oncologist who is director, National
Cancer Institute, 1980--.
b. Mar 7, 1935 in Bronx, New York
Source: AmM&WS 82P; IntMed 80; WhoAm
80, 82, 84; WhoS&SW 73

DeVito, Danny Michael
American. Actor
Played Louis DePalma on TV series "Taxi,"
1978-85; won Emmy, 1981.
b. Nov 27, 1944 in Neptune, New Jersey
Source: BioIn 12; IntMPA 82; WhoAm 82

DeVito, Tommy
[The Four Seasons]
American. Singer, Musician
b. Jun 19, 1935 in Belleville, New Jersey
Source: NF

Devlin, Bernadette Josephine
[Bernadette Devlin McAliskey]
Irish. Political Activist
At age 21, youngest woman elected to
British Parliament, 1969-74.
b. Apr 23, 1947 in Cookstown, Northern
Ireland
Source: BlueB 76; CelR; CurBio 70; HerW;
Who 74, 82; WhoAmW 72, 74; WhoWor 74;
WorAl

Devo
[Bob Casale; Jerry Casale; Bob
Mothersbaugh; Mark Mothersbaugh; Alan
Myers]
American. Music Group
Weirdly garbed Akron, OH quintet known
for synthesizer-oriented rhythm; hit single
"Whip It," 1980.
Source: ConMuA 80A; WhoRock 81

De Vorzon, Barry
American. Composer
Wrote "Bless the Beasts and the Children,"
1971; Grammy-winning "Nadia's Theme,"
1977.
b. Jul 31, 1934 in New York, New York
Source: VarWW 85

DeVos, Richard Martin
American. Business Executive
Co-founder, pres., Amway Corp.
b. Mar 4, 1926 in Grand Rapids, Michigan
Source: WhoAdv 80; WhoAm 74, 76, 78, 80,
82; WhoF&I 74, 77; WhoWor 78

DeVoto, Bernard Augustine
[John August, pseud.]
American. Author, Journalist, Critic
Won 1948 Pulitzer for Across the Wide
Missouri; printed his studies of Mark
Twain.
b. Jan 11, 1897 in Ogden, Utah
d. Nov 13, 1955 in New York, New York
Source: AmAu&B; AmNov; AuNews 1;
CnDAL; ConAmA; DcAmB S5; DcLEL;
EncWL; LongCTC; ModAL; OxAmL; PenC
AM; RAdv 1; REn; REnAL; TwCA, SUP;
WebAB, 79; WhAm 3; WhNAA; WorAl

DeVries, David Pieterson
Dutch. Colonizer
Founded colonies on Staten Island called
New Netherlands.
b. 1592 in LaRochelle, France
d. 1655
Source: *ApCAB; DcAmB; HarEnUS; WhAm
HS*

DeVries, Hugo
Dutch. Botanist, Educator, Author
His *Mutation Theory,* 1901; *Plant Breeding,*
1907, stressed mutation study.
b. Feb 16, 1848 in Haarlem, Netherlands
d. May 21, 1935 in Amsterdam, Netherlands
Source: *NewCol 75*

DeVries, Peter
American. Author
b. Feb 27, 1910 in Chicago, Illinois
Source: *AmAu&B; Au&Wr 71; BiE&WWA;
CelR; CnDAL; ConAu 17R; ConLC 1, 2, 3,
7, 10; ConNov 72, 76; DrAF 76; EncWL;
IntWW 74; ModAL, S1; NotNAT; OxAmL;
PenC AM; REnAL; Who 74; WhoAm 74, 76,
78, 80, 82; WhoTwCL; WhoWor 78; WorAu;
WrDr 80*

DeVries, William Castle
American. Surgeon
Implanted artificial heart in Barney Clark,
1982; William Schroeder, 1984.
b. Dec 19, 1943 in Brooklyn, New York
Source: *CurBio 85; NewYTBS 82; WhoAm
82, 84; WhoFrS 84*

DeWaart, Edo
Dutch. Conductor
b. Jun 1, 1941 in Amsterdam, Netherlands
Source: *WhoAm 82; WhoWor 78*

Dewaere, Patrick
[Patrick Maurin]
French. Actor
Films include *Beau Pere, Get Out Your
Hankerchiefs.*
b. Jan 26, 1947 in Saint-Brieuc, France
d. Jul 16, 1982 in Paris, France
Source: *AnObit 1983; FilmEn; NewYTBS 82*

Dewar, James A
"Mr. Twinkie"
American. Businessman, Inventor
Invented the Hostess Twinkie snack cake,
1930.
b. 1897
d. Jun 30, 1985 in Downers Grove, Illinois
Source: *NF*

Dewar, John
Scottish. Manufacturer, Businessman
Opened wine shop, 1846; began making own
Scotch; first to package in bottles.
b. 1806 in Perthshire, Scotland
d. 1880
Source: *Entr*

Dewey, Charles Schuveldt
American. Government Official
Agent general of Marshall Plan, 1948, who
was a Rep. representative, 1940s.
b. Nov 10, 1882 in Cadiz, Ohio
d. Dec 26, 1980 in Washington, District of
Columbia
Source: *BiDrAC; BioIn 1, 2; CurBio 49, 81;
WhoAm 74; WhoGov 72, 75*

Dewey, George
American. Naval Officer
Destroyed eight Spanish warships during
Spanish-American war, 1898, to become
national hero.
b. Dec 26, 1837 in Montpelier, Vermont
d. Jan 16, 1917 in Washington, District of
Columbia
Source: *AmBi; ApCAB SUP; DcAmB; DcNAA;
EncAB-H; REn; TwCBDA; WebAB; WhAm 1*

Dewey, John
American. Philosopher, Educator
Philosophy "Instrumentalism" stated the
mind to be essentially an instrument for
solving problems of existence.
b. Oct 20, 1859 in Burlington, Vermont
d. Jun 1, 1952 in New York, New York
Source: *Alli SUP; AmAu&B; CasWL;
ConAmA; DcAmAu; DcAmB S5; DcLEL;
EncAB-H; EvLB; LongCTC; OxAmL; OxEng;
PenC AM; REn; REnAL; TwCA, SUP;
WebAB; WebE&AL; WhAm 3; WhNAA;
WhoTwCL*

Dewey, Melvil
American. Librarian
Devised Dewey Decimal Classification System
for cataloging books; founded first library
school, 1887.
b. Dec 10, 1851 in Adams Center, New
York
d. Dec 26, 1931 in Lake Placid, Florida
Source: *Alli SUP; AmAu&B; AmBi; AmLY;
ApCAB; DcAmAu; DcAmB S1; DcNAA;
OxAmL; REn; REnAL; TwCBDA; WebAB 79;
WhDW; WhAm 1; WhNAA*

Dewey, Thomas Edmund
American. Politician
Ran for pres., 1948, against Harry Truman;
lost very close race.
b. Mar 24, 1902 in Owosso, Michigan
d. Mar 16, 1971 in Bal Harbour, Florida
Source: *CurBio 40, 71; EncAB-H; NewYTBE
71; WebAB; WhAm 5*

Dewhurst, Colleen
Canadian. Actress
b. Jun 3, 1926 in Montreal, Quebec
Source: *BiE&WWA; BioNews 74; CelR;
CnThe; CurBio 74; FilmEn; IntMPA 82;
MovMk; NotNAT; PIP&P A; WhoAm 80, 82;
WhoHol A; WorAl*

DeWilde, Brandon
American. Actor
Nominated for Oscar as child star of movie
Shane, 1953.
b. Apr 9, 1942 in New York, New York
d. Jul 6, 1972 in Denver, Colorado
Source: *BiE&WWA; FilmgC; MotPP; MovMk;
NewYTBE 72; NotNAT B; ObitOF 79;
OxFilm; WhAm 5; WhScrn 77; WhoHol B*

Dewing, Thomas Wilmer
American. Artist
Painted portraits, misty figures, especially of
women.
b. May 4, 1851 in Boston, Massachusetts
d. Nov 5, 1938 in New York, New York
Source: *DcAmB S2; NewCol 75*

DeWitt, Joyce
American. Actress
Played Janet Wood on TV series "Three's
Company."
b. Apr 23, 1949 in Wheeling, West Virginia
Source: *BioIn 11; IntMPA 82; WhoAm 80, 82*

DeWitt, William Orville, Sr.
American. Baseball Executive
Served in exec. capacity for several ML
teams; as pres., of Detroit, traded
managers with Cleveland, 1959.
b. Aug 3, 1902 in Saint Louis, Missouri
d. Mar 3, 1982 in Cincinnati, Ohio
Source: *BioIn 1, 7; NewYTBS 82; WhoAm
74, 76, 78, 80; WhoF&I 74, 75; WhoMW 74,
76, 78, 80; WhoProB 73*

DeWohl, Louis
[Ludwig Von Wohl-Musciny]
German. Author
b. Jan 24, 1903 in Berlin, Germany
d. Jun 2, 1961 in Lucerne, Switzerland
Source: *BioIn 3, 4, 5, 6; CurBio 55, 61*

DeWolfe, Billy
[William Andrew Jones]
American. Actor
Character actor in prissy roles; films included
Blue Skies, 1946, *Call Me Madam*, 1953.
b. Feb 18, 1907 in Wollaston, Massachusetts
d. Mar 5, 1974 in Los Angeles, California
Source: *BiE&WWA; FilmEn; FilmgC; HolP
40; MotPP; MovMk; NewYTBS 74; ObitOF
79; Vers B; WhScrn 77; WhoHol B; WorAl*

DeWolfe, Lady Elsie
see: Mendl, Lady Elsie de Wolfe

Dexter, Al
[Clarence Albert Poindexter]
American. Singer, Songwriter
Biggest hit, "Pistol Packin' Mama," 1943,
sold over 10 million copies.
b. May 4, 1902 in Jacksonville, Texas
d. Jan 28, 1984 in Lake Lewisville, Texas
Source: *BiDAmM; CmpEPM; ConAu 111;
EncFCWM 69*

Dexter, John
English. Director
Director, Metropolitan Opera productions,
1974--; received Tony for directing *Equus*,
1975.
b. Aug 2, 1925 in Derby, England
Source: *CnThe; CurBio 76; EncWT; NotNAT;
Who 82; WhoAm 80, 82, 84; WhoOp 76;
WhoThe 81*

Dey, Susan Hallock
American. Model, Actress
Starred in TV series "The Partridge Family."
b. Dec 10, 1952 in Pekin, Illinois
Source: *IntMPA 82; WhoAm 74; WhoHol A*

DeYoung, Cliff
American. Actor
Starred in TV movie "Sunshine," 1975.
b. Feb 12, 1945 in Los Angeles, California
Source: *NF*

DeYoung, Dennis
[Styx]
American. Singer
As solo performer had hit single "Desert
Moon," 1984.
b. Feb 18, 1947 in Chicago, Illinois
Source: *RkOn 85*

DeYoung, Michel Harry
American. Newspaper Editor
b. Oct 1, 1849 in Saint Louis, Missouri
d. Feb 15, 1925
Source: *NatCAB 1; WebBD 80; WhAm 1*

Dharmapala, Anagarika
[David Hewivitarne]
Ceylonese. Religious Leader
One of founders of Buddhism in US, Europe.
b. Sep 27, 1864 in Columbo, Ceylon
d. Apr 29, 1933 in Sarnath, India
Source: *BiDAmC*

Diaghilev, Sergei Pavlovich
Russian. Ballet Promoter
Formed Ballet Russe, 1909; productions
    based on asymmetry, perpetual motion.
b. Mar 19, 1872 in Nizhni-Novgorod, Russia
d. Aug 19, 1929 in Venice, Italy
Source: *DcRusL; REn; WhDW; WhThe;
WorAl*

Diamand, Peter
Dutch. Music Director
Director, Edinburgh Festival, 1965-78, Royal
    Philharmonic Orchestra, 1978-81.
b. Jun 8, 1913 in Berlin, Germany
Source: *BioIn 7; IntWW 82; Who 82;
WhoWor 74*

Diamond, David
American. Composer
b. Jul 9, 1915 in Rochester, New York
Source: *AmSCAP 66; CurBio 66; DcCM;
REnAL; WhoAm 74; WhoE 74; WhoMus 72;
WhoWor 78; WhoWorJ 72*

Diamond, I(sidore) A L
American. Screenwriter
Films include *Some Like It Hot*, 1959;
    Oscar-winning *The Apartment*, 1960.
b. Jun 27, 1920 in Unghani, Romania
Source: *CmMov; ConAu 81; FilmgC; IntMPA
81, 82; OxFilm; VarWW 85; WhoAm 82;
WorEFlm*

Diamond, "Legs" (Jack)
[John Thomas Diamond]
American. Criminal
1920s gangster, bootlegger, killer, whose
    ability to elude police earned him
    nickname; murdered by other gangsters.
b. 1896 in Philadelphia, Pennsylvania
d. Dec 18, 1931 in Albany, New York
Source: *Blood&B*

Diamond, Neil
American. Singer, Songwriter, Actor
Pop singer with over 20 gold, platinum
    records; number one single "Song Sung
    Blue," 1972.
b. Jan 24, 1941 in Brooklyn, New York
Source: *BiDAmM; BioNews 74; BkPepl; CelR;
NewYTBE 72; WhoAm 80, 82; WorAl*

Diamond, Selma
American. Actress
Known for gravel voice, dangling cigarette;
    appeared in TV series "Night Court."
b. 1921 in London, Ontario
d. May 13, 1985 in Los Angeles, California
Source: *ConNews 85-2*

Diana, Princess of Wales
[Lady Diana Frances Spencer]
"Lady Di"
English. Princess
Married Prince Charles, Jul 29, 1981; several
    movies depict their romance.
b. Jul 1, 1961 in Sandringham, England
Source: *BioIn 12; CurBio 83; NewYTBS 81;
Who 81*

Di'Anno, Paul
see: Iron Maiden

Dias, Bartholomew
[Bartholomew Diaz]
Portuguese. Navigator
First to sail around Cape of Good Hope,
    1488; opened passage to India.
b. 1450
d. 1500
Source: *NewCol 75*

Diaz, Justino
Puerto Rican. Opera Singer
b. Jan 29, 1940 in San Juan, Puerto Rico
Source: *WhoAm 74, 76, 78, 80, 82; WorEFlm*

Diaz, Porfirio
[Jose de la Cruz Porfirio]
Mexican. Political Leader
Overthrew govt., ruled as dictator, 1876-80,
    1884-1911.
b. Sep 15, 1830 in Oaxaca, Mexico
d. Jul 2, 1915 in Paris, France
Source: *ApCAB; REn*

Diaz de Bivar, Rodrigo
see: Cid, El

Diaz de la Pena, Narciso Virgilio
French. Artist
b. 1807 in Bordeaux, France
d. 1876
Source: *NewCol 75*

Diaz Ordaz, Gustavo
Mexican. President
b. Mar 12, 1911 in Puebla, Mexico
d. Jul 15, 1979 in Mexico City, Mexico
Source: *CurBio 65; IntWW 74; WhoAm 74;
WhoS&SW 82*

Dibbs, Eddie (Edward George)
[Fast Eddie]
American. Tennis Player
Won German Open, 1973, 74, 76; WCT
Tournament of Champions, 1981.
b. Feb 23, 1951 in Brooklyn, New York
Source: *WhoAm 82; WhoIntT*

Dibdin, Thomas Frognall
English. Author, Librarian
Bibliophile who published *Bibliomania*, 1809;
Library Companion, 1824.
b. 1776 in Calcutta, India
d. Nov 18, 1847 in London, England
Source: *BiD&SB; BiDLA; DcBiPP; DcEnL;
DcEuL; DcLEL; NewC; OxEng*

DiCamerino, Roberta
Italian. Designer
b. Dec 8, 1920 in Venice, Italy
Source: *WorFshn*

DiCavour, Camillo Benso
see: Cavour, Camillo Benso di

Dichter, Ernest
American. Psychologist
b. Aug 14, 1907 in Vienna, Austria
Source: *AmAu&B; AmM&WS 73S; CelR;
ConAu 17R; CurBio 61; InSci; IntWW 82;
WhoAm 80, 82; WhoCon 73; WhoWor 74;
WrDr 82*

Dichter, Mischa
American. Musician
b. Sep 27, 1945 in Shanghai, China
Source: *WhoAm 78, 80, 82*

Dick, Philip K(indred)
[Richard Phillips, pseud.]
American. Author
Science fiction writer who won 1962 Hugo
award for *Man in the High Castle*.
b. Dec 16, 1928 in Chicago, Illinois
d. Mar 2, 1982 in Santa Ana, California
Source: *AmAu&B; ConAu 21R, 49; ConLC
10; ConNov 76; ConSFA; DrAF 76; EncSF;
LinLib L; Novels; ScF&FL 1, 2; WhoSciF;
WrDr 76, 80*

Dickens, Charles John Huffam
[Boz, pseud.]
English. Author, Dramatist
Master storyteller who wrote classics
Pickwick Papers, 1837; *Christmas Carol*,
1843; *Tale of Two Cities*, 1859.
b. Feb 7, 1812 in Portsmouth, England
d. Jun 9, 1870 in Godshill, England
Source: *Alli, SUP; AtlBL; AuBYP; BbD;
BiD&SB; BrAu 19; CarSB; CasWL; Chambr
3; ChhPo, S1, S2; CrtT 3; CyWA; DcBiA;
DcEnA, AP; DcEnL; DcEuL; DcLEL;
EncMys; EvLB; FamAYP; FilmgC; HsB&A;
JBA 34; MnBBF; MouLC 3; NewC; OxAmL;
OxEng; OxFilm; OxThe; PenC AM, ENG;
RAdv 1; RComWL; REn; Str&VC;
WebE&AL; WhAm HS; WhoChL*

Dickens, "Little" Jimmy
American. Singer, Songwriter
Grand Ole Opry guitarist who wrote pop-
country novelties: "Hillbilly Fever," 1950.
b. Dec 19, 1925 in Bolt, West Virginia
Source: *BiDAmM; CounME 74; EncFCWM
69; IlEncCM; RkOn 78*

Dickens, Monica Enid
English. Author
Wrote autobiographical series *One Pair of
Hands*, 1939; *One Pair of Feet*, 1942.
b. May 10, 1915 in London, England
Source: *Au&Wr 71; ConAu 5R, 2NR; ConNov
72, 76; DcLEL; EvLB; ForWC 70; LongCTC;
NewC; PenC ENG; REn; SmATA 4; TwCWr;
Who 74; WorAu; WrDr 76*

Dickerson, Eric Demetric
American. Football Player
Running back, LA Rams, 1983--; NFL
records for most yds. rushing by rookie,
1983, most yds. rushing in season, 1984,
breaking OJ Simpson's record.
b. Sep 2, 1960 in Sealy, Texas
Source: *FootReg 81; NewYTBS 84*

Dickerson, Nancy Hanschman
American. Broadcast Journalist
Correspondent, NBC News, 1960-70; wrote
Among Those Present, 1976.
b. Jan 19, 1930 in Wauwatosa, Wisconsin
Source: *ConAu 69; CurBio 62; ForWC 70;
WhoAm 74, 76, 78, 80, 82; WhoAmW 77;
WhoS&SW 82*

Dickey, Bill (William Malcolm)
American. Baseball Player
Caught 100 or more games 13 consecutive
seasons; Hall of Fame, 1954.
b. Jun 6, 1907 in Bastrop, Louisiana
Source: *BaseEn 85; WhoProB 73*

Dickey, Herbert Spencer
American. Physician, Explorer
Discovered source of Orinoco River, S
America, 1931.
b. Feb 4, 1876 in Highland Falls, New York
d. Oct 28, 1948 in Huigra, Ecuador
Source: *AmAu&B; BioIn 1, 2*

Dickey, James
American. Poet, Critic
Wrote *Deliverance,* 1970; filmed, 1972,
starring Burt Reynolds, Jon Voight.
b. Feb 2, 1923 in Atlanta, Georgia
Source: *AmAu&B; AnCL; AuNews 1, 2; CelR;
ConAu 9R; ConLC 1, 2, 4, 7, 10, 15; ConP
70, 75; CroCAP; CurBio 68; DrAF 76; DrAP
75; DrAS 74E; EncWL; IntWW 74; ModAL,
S1; OxAmL; PenC AM; RAdv 1; WebAB;
WebE&AL; WhoAm 74, 76, 78, 80, 82;
WhoS&SW 82; WhoTwCL; WhoWor 78;
WorAu; WrDr 80*

Dickey, Lynn (Clifford Lynn)
American. Football Player
Quarterback, Houston, 1971-75; Green Bay,
1976--.
b. Oct 19, 1949 in Paola, Kansas
Source: *FootReg 81*

Dickie, Murray
Scottish. Opera Singer
b. 1924 in Renfrew, Scotland
Source: *WhoMus 72*

Dickinson, Angie
[Angeline Brown]
American. Actress
Starred in TV series "Policewoman," 1974-78;
former wife of Burt Bacharach.
b. Sep 30, 1931 in Kulm, North Dakota
Source: *BiDFilm; BkPepl; CelR; FilmgC;
IntMPA 75, 76, 77, 78, 79, 80, 81, 82;
MotPP; MovMk; WhoAm 74, 76, 78, 80, 82;
WhoHol A; WorEFlm*

Dickinson, Edwin W
American. Artist
b. Oct 11, 1891 in Seneca Falls, New York
d. Dec 2, 1978 in Cape Cod, Massachusetts
Source: *BioIn 3, 4, 5, 6, 7, 11; CurBio 63,
79; DcCAA 71; NewYTBS 78; WhAm 7;
WhoAm 74, 76, 78; WhoAmA 73; WhoWor
78*

Dickinson, Emily Elizabeth
American. Poet
Hardly ever left home after age 30; most
poems published after death.
b. Dec 10, 1830 in Amherst, Massachusetts
d. May 15, 1886 in Amherst, Massachusetts
Source: *AmAu; AmAu&B; AmBi; AmWr;
AnCL; AtlBL; BiD&SB; CasWL; Chambr 3;
ChhPo, S1, S2; CnDAL; CnE&AP; CrtT 3;
CyWA; DcAmAu; DcAmB; DcLEL; DcNAA;
EncAB-H; EvLB; HerW; InWom; ModAL, S1;
NewYTBE 73; NotAW; OxAmL; OxEng;
PenC AM; RAdv 1; RComWL; REn; REnAL;
Str&VC; TwCBDA; WebAB; WebE&AL;
WhAm HS*

Dickman, Joseph Theodore
American. Military Leader
b. Oct 6, 1857 in Dayton, Ohio
d. Oct 23, 1927
Source: *AmBi; DcAmB; DcNAA; OhA&B;
WhAm 1*

Dickson, Earle Ensign
American. Inventor
Invented adhesive bandage "Band-Aid," 1924.
b. Oct 10, 1892 in Grandview, Tennessee
d. Sep 21, 1961 in New Brunswick, New
Jersey
Source: *DcAmB S7*

Dickson, Gloria
[Thais Dickerson]
American. Actress
Best known for *They Won't Forget,* 1937,
They Made Me a Criminal, 1939.
b. Aug 13, 1916 in Pocatello, Idaho
d. Apr 10, 1945 in Hollywood, California
Source: *FilmEn; MotPP; NotNAT B; ThFT;
WhScrn 74, 77; WhoHol B*

Dickson, Gordon Rupert
Canadian. Author
b. Nov 1, 1923 in Edmonton, Alberta
Source: *ConAu 9R*

Diddley, Bo
[Ellas McDaniels]
The Originator
American. Musician, Songwriter
Best known for "I'm Sorry," 1959.
b. Dec 30, 1928 in McCombs, Mississippi
Source: *BiDAmM; DrBlPA; EncPR&S 74;
IlEncRk; WorAl*

Diderot, Denis
French. Editor, Philosopher
Editor, *Encyclopedie,* 1745, an encyclopedia
of arts and sciences.
b. Oct 5, 1713 in Langres, France
d. Jul 30, 1784 in Paris, France
Source: *AtlBL; BbD; BiD&SB; CasWL;
CnThe; CyWA; DcEuL; EuAu; EvEuW;
McGEWD; NewC; OxEng; OxFr; OxThe;
PenC EUR; RComWL; REn; REnWD*

Didion, Joan
American. Author, Journalist
b. Dec 5, 1934 in Sacramento, California
Source: *AmAu&B; AuNews 1; ConAu 5R;
ConLC 1, 3, 8, 14; ConNov 76; DrAF 76;
ModAL S1; WhoAm 82; WomWMM; WrDr
76*

DiDonato, Pietro
American. Author
Wrote autobiographical novel *Christ in
Concrete,* 1939.
b. Apr 3, 1911 in West Hoboken, New
Jersey
Source: *ConAu 101; OxAmL; REnAL; TwCA,
SUP*

Didrikson, "Babe" (Mildred)
[Mrs. George Zaharias]
American. Sportswoman
Voted greatest woman athlete of 20th c. by
AP, 1949.
b. Jun 26, 1912 in Port Arthur, Texas
d. Sep 27, 1956 in Galveston, Texas
Source: *BioNews 74; CurBio 47, 56; HerW;
InWom; WebAB; WhAm 4; WhoTr&F 73*

Diebenkorn, Richard
American. Artist
b. Apr 22, 1922 in Portland, Oregon
Source: *CurBio 71; DcCAA 71; IntWW 74;
WhoAm 74, 76, 78, 80, 82; WhoAmA 73;
WhoWest 84; WhoWor 78*

Diebold, Alfred John
American. Business Executive
b. 1879
d. 1966
Source: *BioIn 9*

Diederichs, Nicholaas
South African. Political Leader
b. Nov 17, 1904 in Orange Free State, South
Africa
d. Aug 21, 1978 in Capetown, South Africa
Source: *BioIn 11; IntWW 74; WhoWor 78*

Diefenbaker, John George
Canadian. Lawyer, Prime Minister
Progressive Conservative prime minister,
1957-63.
b. Sep 18, 1895 in Grey County, Ontario
d. Aug 16, 1979 in Ottawa, Ontario
Source: *CanWW 70; CurBio 57; IntWW 74;
OxCan SUP; Who 74; WhoAm 74; WhoCan
73; WhoWor 74*

Diem, Ngo-dinh
see: Ngo dinh Diem

Diemer, Emma Lou
American. Composer, Musician, Educator
Organist who wrote over 100 choral,
instrumental works including "Suite for
Orchestra," 1981.
b. Nov 24, 1927 in Kansas City, Missouri
Source: *AmSCAP 66, 80; BioIn 5; WhoAm
82, 84; WhoAmW 74, 75, 77*

Dierdorf, Dan(iel Lee)
American. Football Player
b. Jun 29, 1949 in Canton, Ohio
Source: *NewYTBS 77*

Dies, Martin, Jr.
American. Lawyer, Congressman
b. Nov 5, 1900 in Colorado, Texas
d. Nov 14, 1972 in Lufkin, Texas
Source: *BiDrAC; CurBio 40, 73; NewYTBE
72; WebAB; WhAm 5; WhAmP*

Diesel, Rudolf Christian Karl
German. Engineer, Inventor
Developed internal combustion engine to run
on crude oil, 1893-97.
b. Mar 18, 1858 in Paris, France
d. Sep 29, 1913
Source: *NewCol 75; OxGer*

Dieskaul, Dietrich Fischer
see: Fischer-Dieskau, Dietrich

Dieterle, William
American. Director
Best known for *The Hunchback of Notre
Dame,* 1939, *A Portrait of Jennie,* 1948.
b. Jul 15, 1893 in Ludwigshafen, Germany
d. Dec 9, 1972 in Ottobrunn, Germany
(West)
Source: *BiDFilm; CmMov; CurBio 43, 73;
DcFM; EncWT; FilmgC; MovMk; NewYTBE
72; ObitOF 79; OxFilm; WhAm 5; WhScrn
77; WorEFlm*

Dietrich, Marlene
[Maria Magdalene von Losch]
American. Actress, Singer
Known for glamorous roles in films *The Blue Angel,* 1930; *Destry Rides Again,* 1939.
b. Dec 27, 1901 in Berlin, Germany
Source: *BiDFilm; CelR; CmMov; CurBio 53, 68; FilmgC; IntMPA 75, 76, 77, 78, 79, 80, 81, 82; IntWW 74; MotPP; MovMk; NewYTBE 72; OxFilm; ThFT; TwYS; VarWW 85; Who 74; WhoAm 76, 78, 80, 82; WhoHol A; WhoThe 77; WhoWor 74; WorEFlm*

Dietrich, Noah
American. Businessman
Chief business adviser to Howard Hughes, 1925-57; wrote *Howard: The Amazing Mr. Hughes,* 1971.
b. Feb 28, 1889 in Batavia, Wisconsin
d. Feb 15, 1982 in Palm Springs, California
Source: *AnObit 1982; BioIn 9; ConAu 106; NewYTBS 82*

Dietz, David
American. Broadcast Journalist
Science correspondent, NBC News; won 1937 Pulitzer.
b. Oct 6, 1897 in Cleveland, Ohio
d. Dec 9, 1984 in Cleveland, Ohio
Source: *CurBio 85*

Dietz, Howard M
American. Songwriter
With Arthur Schwartz, wrote over 500 songs, including "Dancing in the Dark"; "That's Entertainment."
b. Sep 8, 1896 in New York, New York
d. Jul 30, 1983 in New York, New York
Source: *AmAu&B; AmSCAP 66; BiDAmM; BiE&WWA; CelR; ChhPo; CmpEPM; ConAu 53; ConDr 73; CurBio 65; EncMT; FilmgC; ModWD; NewCBMT; NotNAT; PIP&P; REnAL; WhoAm 80, 82; WhoThe 77; WorAl*

Difford, Chris
[Squeeze]
English. Singer, Musician
Guitarist, vocalist; collaborated with Glenn Tilbrook on over 600 songs.
b. Apr 11, 1954 in London, England
Source: *NF*

Digges, Dudley
Irish. Actor
With Theatre Guild, 1919-30, produced *Pygmalion; Doctor's Dilemma.*
b. Jun 9, 1880 in Dublin, Ireland
d. Oct 24, 1947 in New York, New York
Source: *DcAmB S4; FamA&A; FilmgC; MovMk; ObitOF 79; OxThe; PIP&P; WhAm 2; WhScrn 74, 77; WhoHol B*

Diggs, Charles Coles, Jr.
American. Politician
Congressman, 1954-80; convicted of defrauding government in payroll kickback, 1980.
b. Dec 2, 1922 in Detroit, Michigan
Source: *BiDrAC; CngDr 74; CurBio 57; NewYTBE 71; WhoAm 74, 76, 78, 80; WhoAmP 73; WhoBlA 75; WhoGov 75; WhoMW 74*

DiGregorio, Ernie
American. Basketball Player
b. Jan 15, 1951 in North Providence, Rhode Island
Source: *NewYTBE 73; NewYTBS 74; WhoBbl 73*

Dihigo, Martin
Cuban. Baseball Player
Star of Latin American, Negro leagues; failed to join fellow Cubans in MLs because of dark skin; Hall of Fame, 1977.
b. May 24, 1905 in Havana, Cuba
d. May 20, 1971 in Cienfuegos, Cuba
Source: *BasesB*

Dill, John Greer, Sir
Irish. Military Leader
Senior British representative on combined Chiefs of Staff committee, WW II.
b. Dec 25, 1881 in Lurgan, Northern Ireland
d. Nov 4, 1944 in Washington, District of Columbia
Source: *DcNaB 1941; GrBr; HisEWW; WhWW-II; WhoMilH 76*

Dillard, Annie Doak
American. Author
Won Pulitzer for *Pilgrim at Tinker Creek,* 1975.
b. Apr 30, 1945 in Pittsburgh, Pennsylvania
Source: *ConAu 3NR; DrAP&F 83; WhoAm 84; WhoAmW 81*

Dillard, Harrison
American. Track Athlete
b. Jul 8, 1923 in Cleveland, Ohio
Source: *BioIn 1, 2, 8, 9, 10; WhoTr&F 73*

Diller, Barry Charles
American. Film Executive
b. Feb 2, 1942 in San Francisco, California
Source: *CurBio 86; IntMPA 86; LesBEnT; NewYTBS 84*

Diller, Phyllis
American. Actress, Comedienne
Known for outrageous appearance, stories about husband, Fang; is also a concert pianist.
b. Jul 17, 1917 in Lima, Ohio
Source: *CelR; CurBio 67; FilmgC; InWom; IntMPA 75, 76, 77, 78, 79, 80, 81, 82; MotPP; WhoAm 74, 76, 78, 80, 82; WhoAmW 77; WhoHol A; WhoWor 78*

Dillinger, John Herbert
American. Criminal, Murderer
"Public Enemy Number One," 1930s; known for daring bank robberies, jail escapes.
b. Jun 28, 1902 in Indianapolis, Indiana
d. Jul 22, 1934 in Chicago, Illinois
Source: *BioNews 74; DcAmB S1; OxFilm; WebAB; WhDW; WorAl*

Dillingham, Charles Bancroft
American. Producer, Manager
Mgr., NYC's Globe Theater, 1910-34; The Hippodrome, 1914-23.
b. May 30, 1868 in Hartford, Connecticut
d. Aug 30, 1934
Source: *DcAmB S1; WebBD 80*

Dillman, Bradford
American. Actor
Appeared in *The Way We Were*, 1973.
b. Apr 13, 1930 in San Francisco, California
Source: *BiE&WWA; CurBio 60; FilmgC; IntMPA 80, 81, 82; MotPP; MovMk; NotNAT; WhoAm 82; WhoHol A; WorAl*

Dillon, (Clarence) Douglas
American. Banker, Diplomat
b. Aug 21, 1909 in Geneva, Switzerland
Source: *BiDrUSE; CelR; DcAmDH; IntYB 81; WhoAm 80, 82; WhoGov 72*

Dillon, Diane Claire Sorber
[Mrs. Leo Dillon]
American. Author, Illustrator
Won Caldecott medal with husband, Leo, for illustrating children's tales *Ashanti to Zulu*, 1976.
b. Mar 13, 1933 in Glendale, California
Source: *AuBYP SUP; BioIn 12; EncSF; IlsCB 1967; SmATA 15; WhoAm 78, 80, 82, 84*

Dillon, George
American. Author, Editor
Editor, *Poetry* Magazine, 1937-50; won 1931 Pulitzer for *Flowering Stone*.
b. Nov 12, 1906 in Jacksonville, Florida
d. May 9, 1968 in Charleston, South Carolina
Source: *AmAu&B; ConAmA; ConAu 89; DcLEL; OxAmL; REn; REnAL; TwCA, SUP; WhAm 5*

Dillon, Leo
American. Author, Illustrator
Co-illustrator with wife, Diane, of children's and science fiction books: *Why Mosquitoes Buzz in People's Ears*, 1975.
b. Mar 2, 1933 in Brooklyn, New York
Source: *AuBYP SUP; BioIn 12; EncSF; IlsCB 1967; SmATA 15*

Dillon, Matt
American. Actor
Played bully in *My Bodyguard*, 1980; starred in *Tex*, 1982.
b. 1964 in Larchmont, New York
Source: *JohnWSW; NewYTBS 83*

Dillon, Melinda
American. Actress
Best known for *Absence of Malice*, 1981.
b. Oct 31, 1939 in Hope, Arkansas
Source: *BiE&WWA; IntMPA 82; NotNAT*

Dillon, William A
American. Songwriter
b. Nov 6, 1877 in Cortland, New York
d. Feb 10, 1966 in Ithaca, New York
Source: *AmSCAP 66; BioIn 4, 7*

DiMaggio, Dom(inic Paul)
"The Little Professor"
American. Baseball Player
b. Feb 12, 1917 in San Francisco, California
Source: *BaseEn 85; St&PR 75; WhoProB 73*

DiMaggio, Joe (Joseph Paul)
"Joltin' Joe"; "The Yankee Clipper"
American. Baseball Player
Hit safely in record 56 consecutive games, 1941; married Marilyn Monroe, 1954.
b. Nov 24, 1914 in San Francisco, California
Source: *BaseEn 85; CelR; CurBio 41, 51; WebAB; WhoHol A; WhoProB 73*

DiMaggio, Vince(nt Paul)
American. Baseball Player
Outfielder, 1937-46; brother of Joe DiMaggio.
b. Sep 6, 1912 in Martinez, California
Source: *BaseEn 85; WhoProB 73*

Dimitrov, Georgi
Bulgarian. Communist Leader
b. Jun 18, 1882 in Bulgaria
d. Feb 7, 1949 in Sofia, Bulgaria
Source: *CurBio 49; DcPol; EncTR; HisEWW;*
WhAm 3

Dimmock, Peter
British. Broadcasting Executive
b. Dec 6, 1920
Source: *Au&Wr 71; IntMPA 77, 78, 79, 80,*
81, 82; NewYTET

Di Mucci, Dion
[Dion and the Belmonts]
American. Singer
b. Jul 18, 1939 in Bronx, New York
Source: *EncPR&S 74*

DiMuro, Lou
American. Baseball Umpire
AL umpire, 1963-82.
b. 1932 in New Jersey
d. Jun 6, 1982 in Arlington, Texas
Source: *NewYTBS 82*

D'Indy, Vincent
see: Indy, Paul d'

Dine, Jim
American. Artist
b. Jun 16, 1935 in Cincinnati, Ohio
Source: *CelR; ConDr 73; CurBio 69; DcCAA*
71; WhoAm 82; WhoAmA 82

Dinesen, Isak, pseud.
see: Blixen, Karen Christentze, Baroness

Ding, J. N. pseud.
see: Darling, Jay Norwood

Dingell, John David, Jr.
American. Politician
Dem. congressman from MI, 1956--; chm.,
Energy and Commerce Com. investigating
toxic waste.
b. Jul 8, 1926 in Colorado Springs, Colorado
Source: *AlmAP 80; CngDr 79; WhoAm 78;*
WhoAmP 79

Dinitz, Simcha
Israeli. Diplomat
b. Jun 23, 1930 in Tel Aviv, Palestine
Source: *IntWW 74; WhoWorJ 72*

Dinkeloo, John Gerard
American. Architect, Engineer
With Roche and Saarinen, designed NYC's
CBS Building; Dulles Airport, Washington,
DC.
b. Feb 28, 1918 in Holland, Michigan
d. Jun 15, 1981 in Fredericksburg, Virginia
Source: *AmArch 70; NewYTBS 81; WhoAm*
74, 76, 78, 80; WhoF&I 75, 77, 79

Dinning, Max
American. Singer
Known for hit song, "Teen Angel," 1959,
banned in Britain because it was so sad.
b. 1935
d. Mar 22, 1986 in Jefferson City, Missouri
Source: *NF*

Dinwiddie, John Ekin
American. Architect, Educator
Designed, built noted "Bay Region" style San
Francisco homes, 1930-53.
b. Oct 27, 1902 in Chicago, Illinois
d. Sep 11, 1959 in New Orleans, Louisiana
Source: *BioIn 7; McGDA; NatCAB 48;*
WhAm 4

Dinwiddie, Robert
British. Colonial Leader
British administrator in America; VA lt.
governor, 1751-58; defended frontier after
Braddock's defeat.
b. 1693 in Glasgow, Scotland
d. Jul 27, 1770 in Bristol, England
Source: *ApCAB; BiDSA; DcAmB; McGEWB*

Dio, Johnny
Organized Crime Figure
Source: *NF*

Dio, Ronnie
see: Black Sabbath

Diocletian
Roman. Emperor
b. 245
d. 313
Source: *NewC; REn*

Diogenes
Greek. Philosopher
Cynic, usually depicted with lantern in search
of honest man.
b. 412 BC in Sinope, Asia Minor
d. 323 BC
Source: *AmAu; NewC; PlP&P; PueRA; REn*

Dion and the Belmonts
[Angelo D'Angelo; Dion DiMucci; Carlo
  Mastangelo; Fred Milano]
American. Music Group
1950s hits include "A Teenager in Love,"
  1959.
Source: *EncPR&S 74; RkOn 82; RkOneH*

Dionne, Annette
[Dionne Sisters]
Canadian. Quintuplet
b. May 28, 1934 in Callander, Ontario
Source: *BioIn 9, 10*

Dionne, Cecile
[Dionne Sisters]
Canadian. Quintuplet
b. May 28, 1934 in Callander, Ontario
Source: *BioIn 9, 10*

Dionne, Emilie
[Dionne Sisters]
Canadian. Quintuplet
b. May 28, 1934 in Callander, Ontario
d. Aug 6, 1954 in Saint Agathe, Quebec
Source: *ObitOF 79; WhoHol B*

Dionne, Marcel
"Beaver"
Canadian. Hockey Player
Has more hat tricks (24) than any other
  active NHL player.
b. Aug 3, 1951 in Drummondville, Quebec
Source: *BioIn 10, 11; WhoAm 74; WhoHcky
73*

Dionne, Marie
[Dionne Sisters]
Canadian. Quintuplet
b. May 28, 1934 in Callander, Ontario
d. Feb 27, 1970 in Montreal, Quebec
Source: *ObitOF 79; WhScrn 74, 77; WhoHol
B*

Dionne, Yvonne
[Dionne Sisters]
Canadian. Quintuplet
b. May 28, 1934 in Callander, Ontario
Source: *BioIn 9, 10*

Dionne Sisters
[Annette Dionne; Cecile Dionne; Emilie
  Dionne; Marie Dionne; Yvonne Dionne]
Canadian. Quintuplets
The world's first recorded surviving
  quintuplets.
b. May 28, 1934 in Callander, Ontario
Source: *InWom*

Dionysius of Halicarnassus
Greek. Historian
b. 30 BC
d. 7 BC
Source: *CasWL; NewC; PenC CL*

Dionysius the Elder
Greek. Ruler
Tyrant of Syracuse whose reign was
  maintained by obedience through fear.
b. 430 BC
d. 367 BC in Syracuse, Sicily
Source: *NewC; WhDW*

Dior, Christian
French. Fashion Designer
Introduced long hemlines, full skirts;
  controversial before accepted.
b. Jan 21, 1905 in Granville, France
d. Oct 24, 1957 in Montecatini, Italy
Source: *CurBio 48, 58; WorFshn*

Dioscorides, Pedacius
Greek. Physician, Botanist
Source: *BioIn 7, 9; CasWL; WebBD 80*

Diouf, Abdou
Senegalese. Prime Minister
b. Sep 7, 1935
Source: *IntWW 74; WhoGov 75; WhoWor 78*

Dirac, Paul A M
English. Mathematician, Physicist
Co-winner of Nobel Prize in Physics, 1933;
  developed quantum-wave theory.
b. Aug 8, 1902 in Bristol, England
d. Oct 20, 1984 in Tallahassee, Florida
Source: *AnObit 1984; IntWW 74; Who 74;
WhoAm 74; WhoWor 74*

Dire Straits
[John Illsley; Dave Knopfler; Mark Knopfler;
  Pick Withers]
English. Music Group
Guitar-oriented band, formed 1977; hit single
  "Walk of Life," 1985.
Source: *ConMuA 80A; WhoRock 81*

Dirks, Rudolph
American. Cartoonist
One of founding fathers of American comics,
  created "Katzenjammer Kids," 1897.
b. Feb 26, 1877
d. Apr 20, 1968 in New York, New York
Source: *WorECom*

Dirksen, Everett McKinley
American. Politician
Rep. senator from IL who had important
  role in passage of Voting Rights Act,
  1965, Fair Housing Act, 1968.
b. Jan 4, 1896 in Pekin, Illinois
d. Sep 7, 1969 in Washington, District of
  Columbia
Source: *CurBio 69; EncAB-H; WebAB; WhAm
5; WhAmP; WhScrn 77*

DiSalle, Michael Vincent
American. Politician
Dem. OH governor, 1959-63, who headed
  price stabilization during Korean War.
b. Jan 6, 1908 in New York, New York
d. Sep 15, 1981 in Pescara, Italy
Source: *BioIn 2, 3, 5, 9; CurBio 51, 81;
IntWW 74, 75, 76, 77, 78; NewYTBS 81;
PolProf E, K, T; WhoAm 74, 76, 78, 80;
WhoWor 74*

DiSant'Angelo, Giorgio
American. Fashion Designer
b. May 5, 1936 in Florence, Italy
Source: *CelR; WhoAm 74, 76, 78, 80, 82;
WorFshn*

Disney, Doris Miles
American. Author
Novel *Do Not Fold, Spindle, or Mutilate*
  adapted to film, 1971.
b. Dec 22, 1907 in Glastonbury, Connecticut
d. Mar 8, 1976 in Fredericksburg, Virginia
Source: *AmAu&B; AmWomWr; CurBio 76;
EncMys; InWom; NewYTBS 76; WhAm 7;
WhoAm 74; WhoAmW 74*

Disney, Roy O
American. Film Executive
Pres., chm. of board, Walt Disney
  Productions; co-founder of entertainment
  empire with brother Walt, 1923.
b. 1893 in Chicago, Illinois
d. Dec 20, 1971 in Burbank, California
Source: *BioIn 11; NewYTBE 71; ObitOF 79;
WhAm 5*

Disney, Walt(er Elias)
[Retlaw Yensid, pseud.]
American. Cartoonist, Producer
Introduced Mickey Mouse in "Steamboat
  Willie," 1928; won 29 Oscars.
b. Dec 5, 1901 in Chicago, Illinois
d. Dec 15, 1966 in Los Angeles, California
Source: *ChhPo, S1, S2; CurBio 40, 52, 67;
DcFM; EncAB-H; FilmgC; LongCTC;
OxAmL; OxFilm; REn; REnAL; WebAB;
WhoChL; WhoGrA 62; WorAl; WorECar;
WorEFlm*

Disraeli, Benjamin
[Benjamin Disraeli Beaconsfield, Earl of]
English. Author, Statesman
Prime minister, 1868, 1874-80; most popular
  of novels are *Coningsby and Sybil*, 1844-
  45; *Lothair,* 1870.
b. Dec 21, 1804 in London, England
d. Apr 19, 1881 in London, England
Source: *Alli; SUP; AtlBL; BiD&SB; BrAu 19;
CasWL; Chambr 3; CyWA; DcBiA; DcEnA,
AP; DcEnL; DcEuL; DcLEL; EvLB; FilmgC;
MouLC 3; NewC; OxEng; PenC ENG; RAdv
1; REn; WebE&AL; WhDW; WorAl*

D'Israeli, Isaac
English. Author, Essayist
Father of Benjamin Disraeli; first, best of
  literary works was *Curiosities of Literature,*
  1791-1823.
b. May 11, 1766 in London, England
d. Jan 19, 1848
Source: *Alli; BbD; BiD&SB; BrAu 19;
CasWL; Chambr 2; ChhPo; DcEnA; DcEnL;
DcEuL; DcLEL; EvLB; NewC; OxEng;
OxMus; PenC ENG; REn*

DiStefano, Giuseppe
Italian. Opera Singer
b. Jul 24, 1921 in Catania, Sicily
Source: *IntWW 74*

DiSuvero, Mark
American. Sculptor
Abstract expressionist whose massive works
  of steel, wood beams include LA Tower of
  Peace, 1966, protesting Vietnam War.
b. Sep 18, 1933 in Shanghai, China
Source: *BnEnAmA; ConArt 77; CurBio 79;
DcAmArt; DcCAA 71, 77; WhoAm 82, 84*

Ditka, Mike
American. Football Player, Football Coach
Tight end, 1961-72; coach Chicago Bears,
  1982--.
b. Oct 18, 1939 in Carnegie, Pennsylvania
Source: *WhoAm 84; WhoFtbl 74*

Ditmars, Raymond Lee
American. Naturalist, Author
b. Jun 20, 1876 in Newark, New Jersey
d. May 12, 1942 in New York, New York
Source: *AmAu&B; AuBYP; CurBio 40, 42;
DcAmB S3; DcNAA; JBA 34, 51; REnAL;
TwCA, SUP; WhAm 2; WhNAA*

Ditters, Karl
[Karl Ditters von Dittersdorf]
Austrian. Musician, Composer
b. Nov 2, 1739 in Vienna, Austria
d. Dec 24, 1799 in Neuhof, Bohemia
Source: *NewEOp 71; WebBD 80*

Ditzen, Rudolph
see: Fallada, Hans, pseud.

Diver, Jenny
[Mary Jones]
British. Criminal
England's greatest pickpocket or "diver";
  immortalized in *Beggar's Opera*.
b. 1700
d. Mar 18, 1740 in London, England
Source: *LookW*

Divine, Arthur Durham
[David Divine; David Rame, pseuds.]
English. Author, Journalist
b. Jul 27, 1904 in Capetown, South Africa
Source: *Au&Wr 71; BioIn 2; ConAu 103;
DcLEL; Who 74*

Divine, Father Major Jealous
[George Baker]
American. Religious Leader
Founded International Peace Movement.
b. 1874
d. Sep 10, 1965 in Philadelphia, Pennsylvania
Source: *CurBio 44; WebAB*

Dix, Dorothea Lynde
American. Reformer
Instrumental in building state hospitals for
  the insane.
b. Apr 4, 1802 in Hampden, Maine
d. Jul 17, 1887 in Trenton, New Jersey
Source: *Alli; AmAu; AmAu&B; AmBi;
AmWom; ApCAB; BiD&SB; DcAmAu;
DcAmB; DcNAA; Drake; EncAB-H; HerW;
InWom; NotAW; OxAmL; TwCBDA; WebAB;
WhAm HS*

Dix, Dorothy, pseud.
[Elizabeth Meriwether Gilmer]
American. Journalist, Author
Wrote syndicated column on advice to
  lovelorn, beginning 1896.
b. Nov 18, 1870 in Woodstock, Tennessee
d. Dec 16, 1951 in New Orleans, Louisiana
Source: *AmAu&B; BiDSA; CurBio 40, 52;
DcAmB S5; OxAmL; REn; REnAL; WhAm
3, 5; WomWWA 14*

Dix, John Adams
American. Soldier, Statesman
b. Jul 24, 1798 in Boscawen, New
  Hampshire
d. Apr 21, 1879 in New York, New York
Source: *Alli, SUP; AmBi; ApCAB; BbD;
BiAUS; BiD&SB; BiDrAC; BiDrUSE; CyAL 2;
DcAmAu; DcAmB; DcNAA; Drake; TwCBDA;
WebAB; WhAm HS; WhAmP*

Dix, Otto
German. Artist
Realistic work depicted working class life,
  social criticism; banned by Nazis, WW II.
b. Dec 2, 1891 in Gera, Germany
d. Jun 25, 1969
Source: *OxArt; PhDcTCA 77; WhAm 5*

Dix, Richard
[Ernest Carlton Brimmer]
American. Actor
Oscar nominee for *Cimarron*, 1931; in
  DeMille's *The Ten Commandments*, 1928.
b. Jul 18, 1894 in Saint Paul, Minnesota
d. Sep 20, 1949 in Los Angeles, California
Source: *BiDFilm; CmMov; FilmEn; Film 2;
MotPP; MovMk; NatCAB 37; TwYS; WhScrn
74, 77; WhoHol B*

Dixon, Alan John
American. Politician
Dem. senator from IL, 1980--, replacing
  Adlai Stevenson, III.
b. Jul 7, 1927 in Belleville, Illinois
Source: *WhoAm 78, 80, 82, 84; WhoAmP 73,
75, 77; WhoGov 77, 72, 75; WhoMW 74, 76,
78*

Dixon, Dean
American. Conductor
b. Jan 10, 1915 in New York, New York
d. Nov 3, 1976
Source: *Baker 78; CurBio 43, 77; NewYTBS
76; WhAm 7; WhoAm 74, 76; WhoBlA 75;
WhoMus 72*

Dixon, Ivan
American. Actor
Played Sgt. Kinchloe in TV series "Hogan's
  Heroes," 1965-71.
b. Apr 6, 1931 in New York, New York
Source: *DrBlPA; InB&W 80; MovMk;
WhoAm 80, 82; WhoBlA 80; WhoHol A;
WorAl*

Dixon, Jean
[Marie Jacques]
American. Actress
Broadway, film comedienne for 30 yrs;
  starred in *Gang's All Here*, 1959.
b. Jul 14, 1894 in Waterbury, Connecticut
d. Feb 12, 1981 in New York, New York
Source: *AnObit 1981; BiE&WWA; Film 2;
NewYTBS 81; NotNAT; ThFT; WhThe;
WhoHol A*

Dixon, Jeane Pinckert
American. Astrologer, Author
Proponent of ESP; began predicting future at age eight.
b. Jan 5, 1918 in Medford, Wisconsin
Source: *BkPepl; CelR; ConAu 65; CurBio 73; WhoAm 80, 82; WhoAmW 74; WhoS&SW 73*

Dixon, Jeremiah
English. Surveyor, Astronomer
With Charles Mason, determined boundary between MD and PA, 1763-78; Called Mason-Dixon Line.
d. 1777 in Durham, England
Source: *ApCAB; WebAB; WhDW*

Dixon, Margaret Rumer Haynes
see: Godden, Rumer, pseud.

Dixon, Mort
American. Songwriter
b. Mar 20, 1892 in New York, New York
d. Mar 23, 1956 in Bronxville, New York
Source: *AmSCAP 66; BioIn 4*

Dixon, Paul Rand
American. Government Official
b. Sep 29, 1913 in Nashville, Tennessee
Source: *CurBio 68; IntWW 74; WhoAm 74, 76, 78, 80, 82; WhoAmP 73; WhoGov 75; WhoS&SW 82*

Dixon, Robert Ellington
American. Military Leader
WW II pilot who signalled sinking of first Japanese carrier: "Scratch one flattop."
b. 1906
d. Oct 21, 1981 in Virginia Beach, Virginia
Source: *BioIn 12*

Dixon, Rod
New Zealander. Runner
First foreign male to win NYC Marathon, 1983; won bronze medal, 1,500 meters, 1972 Olympics.
b. 1950
Source: *NewYTBS 83*

Dixon, Roland Burrage
American. Anthropologist, Educator
Writings include *Oceanic Mythology*, 1916.
b. Nov 6, 1875 in Worchester, Massachusetts
d. Dec 19, 1934
Source: *DcAmB S1; WebBD 80*

Dixon, Thomas
American. Author, Clergyman
His novel *The Clansman*, 1905, was basis for silent film epic *Birth of a Nation*, 1914.
b. Jan 11, 1865 in Shelby, North Carolina
d. Apr 3, 1946 in Raleigh, North Carolina
Source: *AmAu&B; BiD&SB; BiDSA; CasWL; CnDAL; CurBio 46; DcAmAu; DcAmB S4; DcLEL; DcNAA; FilmgC; ObitOF 79; OxAmL; REnAL; TwCA, SUP; WebE&AL; WhAm 2; WhNAA; WhoStg 1906, 1908*

Djerassi, Carl
American. Chemist
Best known for creating birth control pill.
b. Oct 29, 1923 in Vienna, Austria
Source: *ConAu 111; IntWW 80*

Djilas, Milovan
Yugoslav. Author, Politician
b. 1911 in Kolasin, Yugoslavia
Source: *Au&Wr 71; CurBio 58; IntWW 74; WhoAm 74; WhoWor 78; WorAu*

Djugashvili, Ekaterina
Russian. Celebrity Relative
b. 1856
d. 1937
Source: *BioIn 10*

Dmytryk, Edward
[The Hollywood Ten]
American. Director
Spent one yr. in jail for communist affiliations, 1947; directed *The Caine Mutiny*, 1954.
b. Sep 4, 1908 in Grand Forks, British Columbia
Source: *FilmgC; MovMk; OxFilm; WorEFlm*

Doak, Bill (William Leopold)
"Spittin' Bill"
American. Baseball Player
b. Jan 28, 1891 in Pittsburgh, Pennsylvania
d. Nov 26, 1954 in Bradenton, Florida
Source: *BaseEn 85; BioIn 3; WhoProB 73*

Doar, John
American. Lawyer
b. Dec 3, 1921 in Minneapolis, Minnesota
Source: *BioNews 74; NewYTBE 73; NewYTBS 74; WhoAm 74*

Dobbs, Mattiwilda
American. Opera Singer
b. Jul 11, 1925 in Atlanta, Georgia
Source: *CurBio 55; IntWW 74; Who 74; WhoAm 74, 76, 78, 80, 82; WhoBlA 75; WhoMus 72; WhoWor 78*

Dobell, Sydney Thompson
[Sydney Yendys, pseud.]
English. Poet, Critic
Wrote *Balder*, 1854.
b. Apr 5, 1824 in Cranbrook, England
d. Aug 22, 1874 in Nailsworth, England
Source: *BrAu 19; EvLB; OxEng; REn*

Dobie, J(ames) Frank
American. Folklorist, Author, Educator
Numerous books on southwestern history,
   folklore include *Coronado's Children*, 1931;
   Cow People, 1964.
b. Sep 26, 1888 in Live Oak County, Texas
d. Sep 18, 1964 in Austin, Texas
Source: *AmAu&B; ConAu 1R; CurBio 45, 64;
DcLEL; OxAmL; REn; REnAL; TexWr;
TwCA SUP; WebAB; WorAl*

Dobozy, Imre
Hungarian. Author
b. Oct 30, 1917 in Hungary
Source: *IntWW 74*

Dobrovolsky, Georgi
Russian. Cosmonaut
b. 1928 in Odessa, U.S.S.R.
Source: *NewYTBE 71*

Dobrowen, Issai
Russian. Conductor
b. Feb 27, 1893 in Nizhni-Novgorod, Russia
d. Dec 9, 1953 in Oslo, Norway
Source: *NewEOp 71*

Dobrynin, Anatoly Fedorovich
[Anatoliy Federovich Dobrynin]
Russian. Diplomat
Soviet ambassador to US, 1962-86.
b. Nov 16, 1919 in Krasnaya Gorka,
   U.S.S.R.
Source: *BioNews 74; CurBio 62; IntWW 74;
WhoGov 75; WhoUN 75; WhoWor 78*

Dobson, Henry Austin
English. Poet, Essayist
Wrote *Proverbs in Porcelain*, 1877.
b. Jan 18, 1840 in Plymouth, England
d. Sep 2, 1921
Source: *BrAu 19; DcLEL; EvLB; OxEng*

Dobson, Kevin
American. Actor
Plays Mac Mackenzie on TV series "Knots
   Landing."
b. Mar 18, 1944 in Jackson Heights, New
   York
Source: *VarWW 85; WhoTelC*

Doby, Larry (Lawrence Eugene)
American. Baseball Player
First black player in AL, with Cleveland
   Indians, 1947.
b. Dec 13, 1924 in Camden, South Carolina
Source: *BaseEn 85; BioIn 3, 4, 5, 6, 7, 8,
11; WhoProB 73*

Dobyns, Lloyd Allen, Jr.
American. Broadcast Journalist
NBC News correspondent.
b. Mar 12, 1936 in Newport News, Virginia
Source: *WhoAm 78, 80, 82*

Doc Middleton
see: Riley, James

Dockstader, Lew
[George Alfred Clapp]
American. Entertainer
b. 1856 in Hartford, Connecticut
d. 1924 in New York, New York
Source: *DcAmB; NatCAB 23; OxThe; PIP&P*

Doctorow, E(dgar) L(aurence)
American. Author, Editor
Combined historical figures, events with
   fiction in *Ragtime*, 1975.
b. Jan 6, 1931 in New York, New York
Source: *BioIn 10; ConAu 2NR, 45; ConLC 6,
11, 15, 18; ModAL S1; Novels*

Dodd, Charles Harold
English. Theologian
b. Apr 7, 1884
d. Sep 22, 1973 in Goring, England
Source: *Au&Wr 71; ConAu 45; NewYTBE 73;
WhoLA; WhoWor 78*

Dodd, Christopher John
American. Politician
Dem. senator from CT, 1980--; son of former
   senator Thomas Dodd.
b. May 27, 1944 in Willimantic, Connecticut
Source: *AlmAP 78, 80; BioIn 10; CngDr 77,
79; WhoAm 78, 80, 82; WhoAmP 75, 77, 79;
WhoE 77, 79; WhoGov 75, 77*

Dodd, Ed(ward) Benton
American. Cartoonist
b. Nov 7, 1902 in Lafayette, Georgia
Source: *ConAu 73; SmATA 4; WhoAm 74,
76, 78, 80, 82*

Dodd, Mrs. John Bruce (Sonora Louise Smart)
American. Author, Artist
Founder of Father's Day, first observed, 1910.
b. 1882 in Jenny Lind, Arkansas
d. Mar 22, 1978 in Spokane, Washington
Source: *NewYTBS 78; WhoAmW 58, 61*

Dodd, Robert Lee (Bobby)
American. Football Coach
b. Oct 11, 1908 in Galax, Virginia
Source: *BioIn 1, 4; WhoFtbl 74*

Dodd, Thomas Joseph
American. Politician
Dem. senator from CT, 1959-71; censured by Senate for financial irregularities, 1967.
b. May 15, 1907 in Norwich, Connecticut
d. May 24, 1971 in Old Lynne, Connecticut
Source: *BiDrAC; ConAu 29R; CurBio 59, 71; NewYTBE 71; WhAm 5; WhAmP*

Dodd, William Edward
American. Historian, Educator
Writings include *The Old South,* 1937.
b. Oct 21, 1869 in Clayton, North Carolina
d. Feb 9, 1940 in Round Hill, Virginia
Source: *DcAmB S2; WebBD 80*

Dodds, "Baby" (Warren)
American. Jazz Musician
b. Dec 24, 1898 in New Orleans, Louisiana
d. Feb 14, 1959 in Chicago, Illinois
Source: *WhoJazz 72*

Dodds, Harold Willis
American. Educator, Political Scientist
b. Jun 28, 1889 in Utica, Pennsylvania
d. Oct 25, 1980 in Hightstown, New Jersey
Source: *AmAu&B; CurBio 45; IntWW 74; Who 74; WhoAm 74; WhoGov 75*

Dodds, Johnny
American. Jazz Musician
b. Apr 12, 1892 in New Orleans, Louisiana
d. Aug 8, 1940 in Chicago, Illinois
Source: *WhoJazz 72*

Dodge, Bertha S
American. Children's Author
b. Mar 23, 1902 in Cambridge, Massachusetts
Source: *AuBYP; ConAu 5R, 2NR; SmATA 8; WrDr 80*

Dodge, Grace Hoadley
American. Educator, Philanthropist
President, YWCA, 1906-14.
b. May 21, 1856 in New York, New York
d. Dec 27, 1914 in New York, New York
Source: *AmBi; AmWom; ApCAB, SUP; BiDAmEd; BioIn 8; DcAmB; NatCAB 18; NotAW; WhAm 1; WomWWA 14*

Dodge, Grenville Mellen
American. Engineer, General
Responsible for construction of over 10,000 miles of railroad in US, including most of Union Pacific.
b. Apr 12, 1831 in Danvers, Massachusetts
d. Jan 3, 1916 in Council Bluffs, Iowa
Source: *DcNAA; REnAW; WebAMB; WhAm 1*

Dodge, Horace Elgin
American. Auto Manufacturer
Built first Dodge car Nov 1914, Detroit, MI.
b. May 17, 1868 in Niles, Michigan
d. Dec 10, 1920 in Palm Beach, Florida
Source: *NatCAB 19; ObitOF 79; WorAl*

Dodge, John Francis
American. Auto Manufacturer
Pres., Dodge Brothers Co., established 1901, Detroit, MI.
b. Oct 25, 1864 in Niles, Michigan
d. Jan 4, 1920 in New York, New York
Source: *NatCAB 19; WorAl*

Dodge, Joseph Morrell
American. Banker, Government Official
b. Nov 18, 1890 in Detroit, Michigan
d. Dec 12, 1964 in Detroit, Michigan
Source: *BioIn 1, 3, 7, 9, 11; WhAm 4*

Dodge, Mary Elizabeth Mapes
American. Author, Editor
Editor of children's magazine *St. Nicholas,* 1873-1905; wrote Hans Brinker & the Silver Skates, 1865.
b. Jan 26, 1831 in New York, New York
d. Aug 21, 1905 in Onteora Park, New York
Source: *Alli SUP; AmAu; AmBi; BbD; BiD&SB; CarSB; ChhPo, S1, S2; DcAmB; DcBiA; DcNAA; FamAYP; FamSYP; InWom; JBA 34; NotAW; OxAmL; REn; REnAL; WebAB; WhoChL; WorAl*

Dodgson, Charles Lutwidge
see: Carroll, Lewis, pseud.

Dodsley, Robert
English. Bookseller, Dramatist, Publisher
Founded *Annual Register*, 1758; helped
finance Johnson's dictionary.
b. 1703 in Mansfield, England
d. 1764 in Durham, England
Source: *NewCol 75; OxEng; REn; WebBD 80*

Doe, Samuel Kanyon
Liberian. Political Leader
Army officer who overthrew white leader,
Tolbert, assumed leadership, 1980.
b. May 6, 1951 in Tuzon, Liberia
Source: *CurBio 81; IntWW 82; IntYB 82*

Doenitz, Karl C
[Karl C Donitz]
German. Admiral
b. Sep 16, 1891 in Berlin, Germany
d. Dec 24, 1980 in Hamburg, Germany
(West)
Source: *AnObit 1981; ConAu 103; CurBio
81N; EncTR; WhWW-II*

Doerr, Bobby (Robert Pershing)
American. Baseball Player
b. Apr 7, 1918 in Los Angeles, California
Source: *BaseEn 85; WhoProB 73*

Doesburg, Theo van
Dutch. Artist
b. 1883
d. 1931
Source: *BioIn 1, 4, 10; WebBD 80*

Doggett, Bill
American. Singer, Musician, Songwriter
b. Feb 6, 1916 in Philadelphia, Pennsylvania
Source: *EncPR&S 74*

Dohanos, Stevan
American. Illustrator, Artist
b. May 18, 1907 in Lorain, Ohio
Source: *WhoAmA 73*

Doheny, Edward Lawrence
American. Oilman
Oil magnate charged with conspiracy, bribery
in Teapot Dome Scandal, 1924.
b. Aug 10, 1856 in Fond du Lac, Wisconsin
d. Sep 8, 1935
Source: *DcAmB S1; NatCAB 29; REn;
WhAm 1*

Doherty, Brian
Canadian. Lawyer, Producer, Dramatist
Founded Shaw Festival at Niagara-on-the-
Lake, ON, 1962.
b. Feb 3, 1906 in Toronto, Ontario
d. 1974
Source: *CanWW 70; ClbCR*

Doherty, Kieran
Irish. Hunger Striker, Revolutionary
Eighth IRA hunger striker to die in Maze
Prison; member, Irish Republic's
parliament.
b. 1956
d. Aug 2, 1981 in Belfast, Northern Ireland
Source: *BioIn 12*

Doherty, Robert Ernest
American. Engineer, Educator
b. Jan 22, 1885 in Clay City, Illinois
d. Oct 19, 1950 in Scotia, New York
Source: *BioIn 1, 2, 3, 4; CurBio 49, 50*

Dohnanyi, Christoph von
German. Conductor
Conductor of Hamburg State Opera who
became music director of Cleveland
Orchestra, 1984.
b. Oct 8, 1929 in Berlin, Germany
Source: *BioIn 9; CurBio 85*

Dohnanyi, Erno von
[Ernst von Dohnanyi]
Hungarian. Composer, Musician, Conductor
b. Jul 27, 1877 in Presburg, Hungary
d. 1960 in New York, New York
Source: *WhAm 5*

Dohrn, Bernadine Rae
American. Political Activist
b. Jan 12, 1942 in Chicago, Illinois
Source: *GoodHs; MugS; WorAl*

Doisy, Edward Adelbert
American. Biochemist
b. Nov 13, 1893 in Hume, Illinois
Source: *CurBio 49; IntWW 74; Who 74;
WhoAm 74; WhoWor 78*

Dokes, Michael
American. Boxer
b. Aug 10, 1958 in Akron, Ohio
Source: *NF*

Doktor, Paul Karl
American. Musician
b. 1919 in Vienna, Austria
Source: *WhoAm 82; WhoMus 72*

Dolbier, Maurice
American. Author, Journalist
b. May 5, 1912 in Skowhegan, Maine
Source: *AmAu&B; AuBYP; ConAu 65; CurBio
56; MorJA; WhoAm 74*

Dolby, Ray Milton
American. Inventor
Created Dolby sound, noise reduction system
that revolutionized recording industry, c.
1965.
b. Jan 18, 1933 in Portland, Oregon
Source: *ConNews 86-1; IlEncRk; WhoAm 82*

Dolby, Thomas
[Thomas Morgan Dolby Robertson]
British. Singer, Musician
Keyboardist, who had hit single "She
Blinded Me with Science," 1983.
b. Oct 14, 1958 in Cairo, Egypt
Source: *RkOn 85; WhoRocM 82*

Dolci, Carlo
Italian. Artist
Painted portraits, pious religious subjects.
b. May 25, 1616 in Florence, Italy
d. Jan 17, 1686 in Florence, Italy
Source: *NewCol 75; WebBD 80*

Dolci, Danilo
Italian. Architect, Social Reformer
Built Borgo di Dio, a refuge for homeless, in
Trappeto, Italy, 1953.
b. Jun 28, 1924 in Sesana, Italy
Source: *Au&Wr 71; CurBio 61; IntWW 74;
NewYTBE 72; TwCWr; Who 74; WhoWor 78;
WorAu*

Dole, Bob (Robert Joseph)
American. Politician
Rep. senator from KS, 1968--.
b. Jul 22, 1923 in Russell, Kansas
Source: *BiDrAC; CelR; CurBio 72; IntWW
74; NewYTBE 71; WhoAm 82*

Dole, Charles Minot
"Minnie"
American. Business Executive
Established National Sky Patrol System.
b. Apr 18, 1899 in Tyngsboro, Massachusetts
d. Mar 14, 1976 in Greenwich, Connecticut
Source: *NatCAB 61; NewYTBS 76*

Dole, Elizabeth Hanford
[Mrs. Robert Dole]
"Liddy"
American. Government Official
First woman secretary of transportation,
1983--.
b. Jul 20, 1936 in Salisbury, North Carolina
Source: *CngDr 83; CurBio 83; NewYTBS 83;
WhoAm 80, 82, 84; WhoAmP 81, 83;
WhoAmW 83; WhoE 83; WhoGov 77*

Dole, James
American. Businessman
First to can Hawaiian pineapples before
shipment to mainland, early 1900s.
b. Sep 27, 1877 in Boston, Massachusetts
d. May 14, 1958 in Maui, Hawaii
Source: *DcAmB S6; Entr; ObitOF 79; WhAm
3*

Dole, Sanford Ballard
Hawaiian. Statesman, Lawyer
First governor of Hawaiian territory, 1900-03.
b. Apr 23, 1844 in Honolulu, Hawaii
d. Jun 9, 1926
Source: *NewCol 75; WebBD 80*

Dolenz, Mickey
[The Monkees]
American. Singer
b. Mar 8, 1945 in Los Angeles, California
Source: *NF*

Dolin, Anton, Sir
[Sydney Francis Patrick Chippendall Healey-
Kay]
English. Dancer, Choreographer
Leading authority on classical ballet who was
co-founder, principal dancer, London's
Festival Ballet, 1950-61.
b. Jul 27, 1904 in Slinfold, England
d. Nov 25, 1983 in Paris, France
Source: *CanWW 70; CurBio 84N; IntWW 80;
NewYTBS 83; Who 74; WhoAm 80, 82;
WhoThe 77A; WhoWor 74*

Dollar, Robert
American. Shipping Executive
Founded steamship companies; began first
round-the-world passenger service.
b. Mar 20, 1844 in Falkirk, Scotland
d. May 16, 1932 in San Rafael, California
Source: *CmCal; DcAmB S1; DcNAA;
MacDCB 78; WhAm 1*

Dollard, John
American. Psychologist, Author
Race, status authority; wrote classic *Caste
and Class in a Southern Town*, 1937.
b. Aug 29, 1900 in Menasha, Wisconsin
d. Oct 8, 1980 in New Haven, Connecticut
Source: *AmAu&B; AmM&WS 73S, 78S;
ConAu 102*

Dollfuss, Engelbert
Austrian. Political Leader
b. Oct 4, 1892 in Texing, Austria
d. Jul 25, 1934
Source: *McGEWB; OxGer; REn; WhDW;
WorAl*

Dolly, Jenny
[Dolly Sisters]
Hungarian. Dancer, Choreographer
b. Oct 25, 1892 in Budapest, Hungary
d. Jun 1, 1941 in Hollywood, California
Source: *CurBio 41; InWom; WhScrn 74, 77; WhoHol B*

Dolly, Rosie
[Dolly Sisters]
Hungarian. Dancer, Choreographer
b. Oct 25, 1892 in Budapest, Hungary
d. Feb 1, 1970 in New York, New York
Source: *WhScrn 74, 77; WhoHol B*

Domagk, Gerhard
German. Chemist
b. Oct 30, 1895 in Lagow, Germany
d. Apr 24, 1964 in Burberg, Germany
Source: *BioIn 3, 4; CurBio 58, 64*

Domenichino, Il
[Domenico Zampieri]
Italian. Artist
b. Oct 21, 1581 in Bologna, Italy
d. Apr 6, 1641 in Naples, Italy
Source: *AtlBL; WebBD 80*

Domenici, Pete V(ichi)
American. Politician
Conservative Rep. senator from NM, 1972--;
    head of Senate Budget Committee, 1981.
b. May 7, 1932 in Albuquerque, New Mexico
Source: *AlmAP 78, 80; BioIn 9, 10; CngDr 74, 77, 79; CurBio 82; IntWW 75, 76; NewYTBS 81; WhoAm 80, 82, 84; WhoAmP 73, 75, 77, 79; WhoGov 77; WhoWest 76, 78*

Domgraf-Fassbaender, Willi
German. Opera Singer
b. Feb 19, 1897 in Aachen, Germany
Source: *NewEOp 71*

Domingo, Placido
Spanish. Opera Singer
Tenor, who recorded hit single "Perhaps
    Love" with John Denver, 1981.
b. Jan 21, 1941 in Madrid, Spain
Source: *CelR; CurBio 72; NewYTBE 72; NewYTBS 83; WhoAm 82; WhoE 74; WhoMus 72; WhoWor 78*

Dominguin, Luis Miguel
Spanish. Bullfighter
b. Dec 9, 1926 in Madrid, Spain
Source: *CurBio 72*

Dominic, Saint
[Domingo DeGuzman]
Spanish. Religious Figure
Founded Dominican religious order, 1216.
b. 1170
d. 1221
Source: *NewCol 75; REn*

Dominici, Gaston
French. Murderer
French farmer who murdered English family
    camped on his property; con victed, 1954,
    released, 1960.
b. 1877
d. 1965
Source: *BioIn 3, 4, 10*

Dominick, Peter Hoyt
American. Government Official, Politician
Conservative Rep. senator from CO, 1962-74.
b. Jul 7, 1915 in Stamford, Connecticut
d. Mar 18, 1981 in Hobe Sound, Florida
Source: *BioIn 9, 10, 11; CngDr 74; IntWW 74, 75, 76, 77, 78; NewYTBS 81; PolProf J, K; WhoAm 74, 76, 78; WhoAmP 73, 75, 77; WhoWest 74*

Domino, "Fats" (Antoine)
American. Singer
Best known song "Blueberry Hill," 1956.
b. Feb 26, 1928 in New Orleans, Louisiana
Source: *DrBlPA; IlEncBM 82; WhoAm 74; WhoBlA 80; WorAl*

Donahue, Elinor
American. Actress
Played Betty Anderson in TV series "Father
    Knows Best," 1954-62.
b. Apr 19, 1937 in Tacoma, Washington
Source: *BioIn 3; WhoAm 82; WhoHol A*

Donahue, Phil(ip John)
American. TV Personality
Host of talk show "Donahue," 1967--; won
    Emmys, 1977, 1979; wrote *Donahue: My
    Own Story,* 1980.
b. Dec 21, 1935 in Cleveland, Ohio
Source: *BkPepl; CurBio 80; IntMPA 82; NewYTBS 80; NewYTET; WhoAm 80, 82*

Donahue, Sam Koontz
American. Musician
b. Mar 8, 1918 in Detroit, Michigan
Source: *BiDAmM*

Donahue, Troy
[Merle Johnson, Jr.]
American. Actor
Starred in TV series "Hawaiian Eye";
"Surfside 6."
b. Jan 27, 1937 in New York, New York
Source: *FilmEn; FilmgC; IntMPA 76, 77, 78,
79, 80, 81, 82; MotPP; MovMk; WhoHol A*

Donahue, Woolworth
American. Retailer
Heir to F W Woolworth chain store fortune;
cousin of Barbara Hutton.
b. Jan 9, 1913 in New York, New York
d. Apr 5, 1972 in Palm Beach, Florida
Source: *BioIn 9; NewYTBE 72*

Donald, James
Scottish. Actor
Best known for films *Bridge on the River
Kwai*, 1957; *The Great Escape*, 1963.
b. May 18, 1917 in Aberdeen, Scotland
Source: *FilmgC; IntMPA 80, 81, 82; WhThe;
WhoHol A; WhoThe 77A*

Donald, Peter
American. Actor
b. 1918 in Bristol, England
d. 1979
Source: *BioIn 3; NewYTBS 79*

Donaldson, Sam(uel Andrew)
American. Broadcast Journalist
ABC News White House correspondent,
known as one of TV's most aggressive
interviewers.
b. Mar 11, 1934 in El Paso, Texas
Source: *WhoAm 80, 82; WhoTelC*

Donaldson, Stephen Reeder
American. Author
Won Fantasy Society Award for leper trilogy
Chronicles of Thomas Covenant, 1978.
b. May 13, 1947 in Cleveland, Ohio
Source: *ConAu 89; WhoAm 82, 84*

Donaldson, Walter
American. Songwriter
b. Feb 15, 1893 in Brooklyn, New York
d. Jul 15, 1947 in Santa Monica, California
Source: *AmSCAP 66; EncMT; NotNAT B*

Donat, Robert
English. Actor
Won Oscar for *Goodbye, Mr. Chips*, 1939.
b. Mar 18, 1905 in Manchester, England
d. Jun 9, 1958 in London, England
Source: *BiDFilm; FilmgC; MotPP; MovMk;
OxFilm; OxThe; WhAm 3; WhScrn 74, 77;
WhoHol B; WorAl; WorEFlm*

Donatello
[Donatodi Niccolo di Betto Bardi]
Italian. Artist
b. 1386 in Florence, Italy
d. Dec 13, 1466 in Florence, Italy
Source: *AtlBL; REn*

Donath, Helen
American. Opera Singer
b. 1940 in Corpus Christi, Texas
Source: *IntWW 74; WhoMus 72*

Donati, Danilo
Italian. Designer
Costume designs include Oscar winners:
Romeo and Juliet, 1968; *Fellini's Casanova*,
1976.
b. in Luzzara, Italy
Source: *VarWW 85*

Donati, Pino
Italian. Musician, Director
b. 1907
d. 1975
Source: *Baker 78; WhAm 6*

Donegan, Dorothy
American. Musician
b. Apr 6, 1926 in Chicago, Illinois
Source: *WhoAm 74; WhoBlA 75*

Donehue, Vincent J
American. Director
b. Sep 22, 1922 in Whitehall, New York
d. Jan 17, 1966 in New York, New York
Source: *BiE&WWA; FilmgC; WhAm 4;
WhThe*

Donen, Stanley
American. Director
Best known for *Arabesque*, 1966.
b. Apr 13, 1924 in Columbia, South Carolina
Source: *BiDFilm; CmMov; DcFM; FilmgC;
IntMPA 80, 81, 82; IntWW 82; MovMk;
OxFilm; WhoAm 80, 82; WhoWor 74;
WorEFlm*

Dongen, Kees van
[Cornelius Theodorus Dongen]
French. Artist, Illustrator
Fauvist painter who did landscapes of
Holland, Paris; noted for riotous use of
color.
b. Jan 26, 1877 in Delfshaven, Netherlands
d. May 28, 1968 in Monte Carlo, Monaco
Source: *CurBio 60, 68*

Donghia, Angelo R
American. Designer
Interior designer noted for bold,
contemporary approach to home,
commercial furnishings.
b. Mar 7, 1935 in Vandergrift, Pennsylvania
d. Apr 10, 1985 in New York, New York
Source: *ConNews 85-2; NewYTBS 83*

Donitz, Karl C
see: Doenitz, Karl C

Donizetti, Gaetano
Italian. Opera Composer
b. Nov 29, 1797 in Bergamo, Italy
d. Apr 8, 1848 in Bergamo, Italy
Source: *AtlBL; REn*

Donleavy, James Patrick
American. Author, Dramatist
b. Apr 23, 1926 in Brooklyn, New York
Source: *ConAu 9R; ConLC 1, 4, 6, 10;*
IntWW 74; Who 74; WhoAm 74, 76, 78, 80,
82; WhoWor 78

Donlevy, Brian
American. Actor
Best known for tough-guy roles in *Beau*
Geste, 1939; *The Great McGinty,* 1940.
b. Feb 9, 1899 in Portadown, Ireland
d. Apr 5, 1972 in Woodland Hills, California
Source: *BiDFilm; BiE&WWA; FilmgC; HolP*
30; MotPP; MovMk; NewYTBE 72; ObitOF
79; OxFilm; WhScrn 77; WhoHol B; WorAl

Donlon, Mary Honor
American. Judge
b. 1893 in Utica, New York
d. Mar 5, 1977 in Tucson, Arizona
Source: *CurBio 49; InWom; NewYTBS 77;*
WhoAmW 74; WhoGov 72

Donne, John
English. Poet
Metaphysical poet wrote sonnet *Death Be*
Not Proud; poems neglected until 20th c.
b. 1573 in London, England
d. Mar 31, 1631 in London, England
Source: *Alli; AtlBL; BiD&SB; BrAu; CasWL;*
Chambr 1; ChhPo, S1, S2; CnE&AP;
CroE&S; CrtT 1; CyWA; DcEnA, AP;
DcEnL; DcEuL; DcLEL; EvLB; MouLC 1;
NewC; OxEng; PenC ENG; RAdv 1;
RComWL; REn; WebE&AL

Donnell, Jeff (Jean Marie)
American. Actress
Best known for *Gidget Goes Hawaiian,* 1961;
Gidget Goes to Rome, 1962.
b. Jul 10, 1921 in South Windham, Maine
Source: *FilmgC; IntMPA 80, 81, 82; MotPP;*
WhoAmW 61; WhoHol A

Donnelly, Ignatius
American. Politician, Author
The Great Cryptogram, 1888; *The Cipher in*
the Plays and on the Tombstone, 1899, two
studies on possibility of Bacon's authorship
of Shakespeare's plays.
b. Nov 3, 1831 in Philadelphia, Pennsylvania
d. Jan 1, 1901 in Minneapolis, Minnesota
Source: *Alli; AmAu; AmAu&B; AmBi;*
ApCAB; BbD; BiAUS; BiD&SB; BiDrAC;
CasWL; DcAmAu; DcAmB; DcEnA AP;
DcLEL; DcNAA; EncAB-H; OxAmL; PenC
AM; PoIre; REnAL; TwCBDA; WebAB, 79;
WebE&AL; WhAm 1; WhAmP

Donnelly, Ruth
American. Actress
Films include *Mr. Deeds Goes to Town; The*
Bells of St. Mary's.
b. May 17, 1896 in Trenton, New Jersey
d. Nov 17, 1982 in New York, New York
Source: *BiE&WWA; FilmgC; MovMk;*
NewYTBS 82; NotNAT; ThFT; Vers A;
WhoHol A

Donner, Frederic Garrett
American. Businessman
b. 1902 in Three Oaks, Michigan
Source: *CurBio 59; IntWW 74; St&PR 75;*
Who 74; WhoGov 75; WhoWor 78

Donohue, Jack
American. Actor, Dancer, Director
Best known for *Marriage on the Rocks,* 1965;
Assault on a Queen, 1966.
b. Nov 3, 1912 in New York, New York
d. Mar 27, 1984 in Los Angeles, California
Source: *BiE&WWA; FilmgC; IntMPA 80, 81,*
82; NotNAT; WhThe; WhoThe 77

Donovan
[Donovan P Leitch]
Scottish. Singer, Songwriter
Mid-1960s hits include "Sunshine Superman,"
"Mellow Yellow."
b. Feb 10, 1946 in Glasgow, Scotland
Source: *EncFCWM 69; EncPR&S 74*

Donovan, Art
American. Football Player
b. Jun 5, 1925 in Bronx, New York
Source: *BioIn 4, 7, 8; WhoFtbl 74*

Donovan, Hedley Williams
American. Journalist
b. May 24, 1914 in Brainerd, Minnesota
Source: *CurBio 65; IntWW 74; Who 74;*
WhoAm 74, 76, 78, 80, 82; WhoE 74;
WhoWor 78

Donovan, Raymond James
American. Government Official
Secretary of labor under Ronald Reagan,
1981-85.
b. Aug 31, 1930 in Bayonne, New Jersey
Source: *CurBio 82; WhoAm 82, 84*

Donovan, Robert John
American. Journalist
b. Aug 21, 1912 in Buffalo, New York
Source: *AmAu&B; ConAu 1R, 2NR; WhoAm*
74, 76, 78, 80, 82; WhoWor 78

Donovan, William Joseph
"Wild Bill"
American. Lawyer
Founded Office of Strategic Services (OSS);
later evolved into CIA.
b. Jan 1, 1883 in Buffalo, New York
d. Feb 8, 1959 in Washington, District of
Columbia
Source: *CurBio 41, 54, 59; WebAB;*
WebAMB; WhAm 3; WhWW-II

Doobie Brothers, The
[Jeff Baxter; 'Little' John Hartman; Mike
Hossack; Tom Johnston; Keith Knudson;
Michael McDonald; Tiran Porter; Dave
Shogren; Pat Simmons]
American. Music Group
Hit albums include *Minute by Minute,* 1978;
One Step Closer, 1980.
Source: *EncPR&S 74; RkOn 84; RkOneH;*
RolSEnR 83

Doohan, James Montgomery
Canadian. Actor
Played "Scotty" on "Star Trek," 1966-69;
films *Star Trek: The Movie; Star Trek II;*
Star Trek III.
b. Mar 3, 1920 in Vancouver, British
Columbia
Source: *VarWW 85*

Dooley, Rae (Rachel Rice)
Scottish. Actress
Starred with husband Eddie Dowling in
Ziegfeld Follies, specialized in bratty kid
parts.
b. Oct 30, 1896 in Glasgow, Scotland
d. Jan 28, 1984 in East Hampton, New York
Source: *BioIn 9; EncMT; NotNAT; WhThe;*
WhoHol A

Dooley, Tom
see: Dula, Thomas

Dooley, Thomas Anthony
American. Missionary
b. Jan 17, 1927 in Saint Louis, Missouri
d. Jan 18, 1961 in New York, New York
Source: *AmAu&B; ConAu 93; CurBio 57, 61;*
ObitOF 79; WebAB; WebAMB; WhAm 4A

Doolittle, Hilda
[H D, pseud.]
American. Author, Poet
Wrote *Tribute to Freud,* 1956.
b. Sep 10, 1886 in Bethlehem, Pennsylvania
d. Sep 27, 1961 in Zurich, Switzerland
Source: *AmAu&B; AtlBL; CasWL; Chambr 3;*
ChhPo S2; CnDAL; ConAmA; ConAmL;
ConAu 97; ConLC 3, 14; DcLEL; EncWL;
EvLB; InWom; LongCTC; ModAL; S1;
OxAmL; PenC AM; RAdv 1; REn; REnAL;
TwCA, SUP; TwCWr; WebAB; WebE&AL;
WhAm 4; WhoTwCL; WorAl

Doolittle, James Harold
American. Aviator, Army Officer
Led first aerial raid on Japan, WW II.
b. Dec 14, 1896 in Alameda, California
Source: *CelR; CurBio 42, 57; IntWW 74;*
St&PR 75; WebAB; Who 74; WhoAm 74, 76,
78, 80, 82

Doors, The
[John Densmore; Bobby Krieger; Ray
Manzarek; Jim Morrison]
American. Music Group
Source: *BiDAmM; EncPR&S 74; RkOn 84;*
RkOneH

Doppler, Christian Johann
Austrian. Physicist, Mathematician
b. Nov 30, 1803 in Salzburg, Austria
d. Mar 17, 1853 in Venice, Italy
Source: *AsBiEn; WebBD 80*

Dorati, Antal
American. Conductor, Composer
b. Apr 9, 1906 in Budapest, Hungary
Source: *CurBio 48; IntWW 74; Who 74;*
WhoAm 74, 76, 78, 80, 82; WhoMus 72;
WhoS&SW 82; WhoWor 78

Dore, Gustave (Paul Gustave)
French. Artist
Illustrated over 120 books, including many
classics, in theatrical style.
b. Jan 6, 1832 in Strasbourg, France
d. Jan 23, 1883
Source: *AtlBL; ChhPo, S1, S2; IlsBYP; OxFr;*
REn

Doreset, Marion
American. Chemist
b. Dec 14, 1872 in Columbia, Tennessee
Source: *BioIn 7; WhAm 1*

Dorfman, Dan
American. Journalist
Financial writer, *Wall Street Journal,* 1967-
73, *New York* magazine, 1984--.
b. Oct 24, 1932 in Brooklyn, New York
Source: *ConAu 116*

Dorgan, Thomas Aloysius
"Tad"
American. Cartoonist, Journalist
b. Apr 29, 1877 in San Francisco, California
d. 1929
Source: *AmAu&B; DcAmB; WhAm HSA, 4;
WhAmP*

Doria, Andrea
Italian. Admiral, Statesman
b. Nov 30, 1468
d. Nov 25, 1560
Source: *BioIn 1; NewCol 75; REn; WebBD
80*

Doriot, Georges Frederic
French. Educator, Business Executive
Founded American Research Development
Corp., 1946.
b. Sep 24, 1899 in Paris, France
Source: *BioIn 1, 6, 7; IntWW 75, 76, 77, 78;
IntYB 78; St&PR 75; WhoAm 74; WhoF&I
74*

Dorleac, Francoise
French. Actress
Sister of Catherine Deneuve; starred together
in *The Young Girls of Rochefort,* 1967.
b. Mar 21, 1942 in Paris, France
d. Jun 26, 1967 in Nice, France
Source: *BioIn 7, 8; FilmEn; FilmgC; MotPP;
ObitOF 79; OxFilm; WhScrn 74, 77; WhoHol
B*

Dorman, Maurice
English. Political Leader
b. Aug 7, 1912 in Staffordshire, England
Source: *IntWW 74; Who 74; WhoGov 75;
WhoWor 78*

Dornberger, Walter Robert
German. Engineer
Missile expert who supervised V-2 bombing
of London, 1944-45; adviser to US during
space race.
b. Sep 6, 1895 in Giessen, Germany
d. Jun 1980 in Hamburg, Germany (West)
Source: *BioIn 6, 7; CurBio 65, 80; InSci;
NewYTBS 80*

Dorne, Albert
American. Illustrator
b. Feb 7, 1904 in New York, New York
d. Dec 15, 1965 in New York, New York
Source: *BioIn 1, 2, 4, 5, 6, 7; WhAm 4*

Dornier, Claude
German. Aircraft Manufacturer
Built the DO-X, largest passenger plane at
time, 1929.
b. 1884
d. Dec 5, 1969 in Zug, Switzerland
Source: *BioIn 8; InSci; ObitOF 79; WebBD
80*

Door, Rheta Childe
American. Journalist, Feminist
Covered Russian Revolution, WW I troops in
France; wrote *Inside the Russian
Revolution,* 1917.
b. Nov 2, 1866 in Omaha, Nebraska
d. Aug 8, 1948 in New Britain, Pennsylvania
Source: *ConAu 116; DcLB 25; WhAm 2*

Dors, Diana
[Diana Fluck]
English. Actress
British sex symbol, compared to Marilyn
Monroe.
b. Oct 23, 1931 in Swindon, England
d. May 4, 1984 in New Windsor, England
Source: *AnObit 1984; ConAu 113; FilmgC;
InWom; IntMPA 81, 82; MotPP; MovMk;
WhoHol A; WorAl*

D'Orsay, Fifi
[Yvonne Lussier]
"The French Bombshell"
Canadian. Actress
Starred in *They Had to See Paris,* 1929;
trademark was "Ello beeg boy!"
b. Apr 16, 1904 in Montreal, Quebec
d. Dec 2, 1983 in Woodland Hills, California
Source: *FilmgC; MotPP; MovMk; NewYTBS
83; ThFT; WhoHol A*

Dorsett, Tony (Anthony Drew)
"Hawk"; "T D"
American. Football Player
Won Heisman Trophy, 1976; running back,
Dallas Cowboys, 1977--.
b. Apr 7, 1954 in Aliquippa, Pennsylvania
Source: *BioIn 12; CurBio 80; WhoAm 82;
WhoFtbl 74*

Dorsey, Bob Rawls
American. Oilman
Gulf Oil Corp., pres., 1965-72, chm., 1972-
76.
b. Aug 27, 1912 in Rockland, Texas
Source: *IntWW 74, 82; NewYTBE 71; St&PR
75; WhoAm 80, 82; WhoE 74; WhoF&I 75*

Dorsey, Jimmy (James)
American. Musician, Band Leader
Played clarinet, saxophone in own band and
with brother Tommy.
b. Feb 29, 1904 in Shenandoah, Pennsylvania
d. Jun 12, 1957 in New York, New York
Source: *AmSCAP 66; CurBio 42, 57; FilmgC;
WhScrn 74, 77; WhoHol B; WhoJazz 72*

Dorsey, Thomas Andrew
"Georgia Tom"; "The Professor"
American. Clergyman, Composer
Coined term gospel music, wrote over 400
songs including, "Precious Lord, Take My
Hand."
b. Jul 1, 1900 in Villa Rica, Georgia
Source: *BluesWW; DrBlPA; InB&W 80;
WhoAm 78*

Dorsey, Tommy (Thomas Francis)
"Sentimental Gentleman of Swing"
American. Band Leader
Played trombone, trumpet in own band, with
brother Jimmy, during Big Band era.
b. Nov 19, 1905 in Mahonoy Plains,
Pennsylvania
d. Nov 26, 1956 in Greenwich, Connecticut
Source: *CurBio 42, 57; WhAm 3; WhScrn 74,
77; WhoHol B; WhoJazz 72*

DosPassos, John
American. Author
Wrote fiction based on broad social issues;
best known for trilogy *The USA*, 1938.
b. Jan 14, 1896 in Chicago, Illinois
d. Sep 28, 1970 in Baltimore, Maryland
Source: *AmAu&B; AmNov; AmWr; AtlBL;
Au&Wr 71; BiE&WWA; CasWL; Chambr 3;
CnDAL; CnMD; ConAmA; ConAmL; ConAu
29R, 3NR; ConLC 1, 4, 8, 11, 15; CyWA;
DcLEL; EncAB-H; EncWL; EvLB; LongCTC;
ModAL, S1; ModWD; OxAmL; OxEng; PenC
AM; RAdv 1; REn; REnAL; TwCA, SUP;
TwCWr; WebAB; WebE&AL; WhAm 5;
WhNAA; WhoTwCL; WorAl*

Dostoyevsky, Fyodor Mikhailovich
[Fyodor Dostoevski; Fedor Dostoevsky;
Fyoder Dostoievsky]
Russian. Author
Wrote novels *Crime and Punishment*, 1886;
The Idiot, 1887; *Brothers Karamazov*, 1912.
b. Nov 11, 1821 in Moscow, Russia
d. Feb 9, 1881 in Saint Petersburg, Russia
Source: *AtlBL; BbD; BiD&SB; CasWL;
ClDMEL; CyWA; DcEuL; DcRusL; EncMys;
EuAu; EvEuW; FilmgC; OxEng; PenC EUR*

Dotson, Bob
American. Broadcast Journalist
Correspondent, NBC News since 1979.
b. Oct 3, 1946 in Saint Louis, Missouri
Source: *WhoTelC*

Dott, Gerard
[The Incredible String Band]
Scottish. Singer, Musician
b. in Edinburgh, Scotland
Source: *NF*

Dou, Gerard
Dutch. Artist
b. Apr 7, 1613 in Leiden, Netherlands
d. Feb 1675 in Leiden, Netherlands
Source: *AtlBL*

Doubleday, Abner
American. General, Sportsman
Folklore calls him inventor of baseball;
game's birthplace dedicated as Doubleday
Field, 1920, in Cooperstown, NY.
b. Jun 26, 1819 in Ballston Spa, New York
d. Jan 26, 1893 in Mendham, New Jersey
Source: *Alli SUP; AmBi; ApCAB; DcAmAu;
DcAmB; DcNAA; Drake; TwCBDA; WebAB;
WebAMB; WhAm HS; WhoProB 73; WorAl*

Doubleday, Frank Nelson
American. Publisher
Founded Doubleday and Co., 1897.
b. Jan 8, 1862 in Brooklyn, New York
d. Jan 30, 1934 in Coconut Grove, Florida
Source: *AmAu&B; DcAmB S1; WebAB;
WhAm 1*

Doubleday, Nelson
American. Publisher
Son of Frank Doubleday; founded Nelson
Doubleday, Inc., 1910.
b. Jun 16, 1889 in Brooklyn, New York
d. Jan 11, 1949 in Oyster Bay, New York
Source: *DcAmB S4; NatCAB 37; WhAm 2*

Doubleday, Nelson
American. Publisher, Baseball Executive
Pres., Doubleday and Co., 1959--; majority
owner, NY Mets.
b. 1933
Source: *WhoAm 74, 76, 78, 80, 82*

Doubrovska, Felia
[Felizata Dluzhnevska; Mrs. Pierre
Vladimiroff]
Russian. Ballerina
Known for leading roles in Balanchine
ballets; taught at School of American
Ballet, NYC, 30 yrs.
b. 1896 in Saint Petersburg, Russia
d. Sep 18, 1981 in New York, New York
Source: *AnObit 1981; BioIn 11; NewYTBS 81*

Doughty, Charles Montagu
English. Poet, Author
Best known for *Travels in Arabia Deserta*,
1888, describing life among the bedouins.
b. Aug 19, 1843 in Suffolk, England
d. Jan 30, 1926 in Kent, England
Source: *Alli SUP; AtlBL; BrAu 19; CasWL;
Chambr 3; CnE&AP; CyWA; DcLEL;
EncWL; LongCTC; ModBrL; NewC; REn*

Doughty, Neal
see: REO Speedwagon

Douglas, Aaron
American. Artist
Major figure in American Black art;
numerous NYC murals depict black
heritage.
b. 1899 in Topeka, Kansas
d. Feb 2, 1979 in Nashville, Tennessee
Source: *AfroAA; BioIn 11; DcAmArt;
NewYTBS 79*

Douglas, Alfred Bruce, Lord
English. Author, Poet
Noted for intimate relationship with Oscar
Wilde.
b. Oct 21, 1870
d. Mar 20, 1945 in Sussex, England
Source: *CathA 1930; DcLEL; EvLB;
LongCTC; NewC; OxEng; PenC ENG; REn;
WhoLA*

Douglas, Amanda Minnie
American. Children's Author
b. Jul 14, 1837 in New York, New York
d. Jul 18, 1918 in Newark, New Jersey
Source: *Alli SUP; AmAu; AmAu&B; AmWom;
ApCAB; BbD; BiD&SB; CarSB; ChhPo S1,
S2; DcAmAu; DcAmB; DcNAA; InWom;
TwCBDA; WhAm 1; WomWWA 14*

Douglas, Cathleen Heffernan
[Mrs. William O Douglas]
American. Lawyer
b. Apr 30, 1943
Source: *WhoAm 80, 82; WhoAmL 79;
WhoAmW 74*

Douglas, David
Scottish. Botanist
Early explorer of Oregon country; Douglas
spruce named for him.
b. 1798 in Scone, Scotland
d. 1834
Source: *BioIn 1, 2, 3, 4; OxCan*

Douglas, Donald Willis
American. Aircraft Manufacturer
Founded Douglas Aircraft, 1920; produced
DC series for commerical airlines.
b. Apr 6, 1892 in Brooklyn, New York
d. Feb 1, 1981 in Palm Springs, California
Source: *CurBio 81; IntWW 78; McGEWB;
NewYTBS 81; WebAMB; Who 74; WhoAm
74*

Douglas, Donna
[Doris Smith]
American. Actress
Played Elly May Clampett in TV series "The
Beverly Hillbillies," 1962-71.
b. Sep 26, 1939 in Baywood, Louisiana
Source: *InWom; MotPP; WhoHol A*

Douglas, Emmitt
American. Civil Rights Activist
LA NAACP head, 1968-81; initiated lawsuit
that desegregated local schools, 1956.
b. 1926
d. Mar 25, 1981 in New Roads, Louisiana
Source: *BioIn 12*

Douglas, Helen Mary Gahagan
American. Singer, Congresswoman
b. Nov 25, 1900 in Boonton, New Jersey
d. Jun 28, 1980 in New York, New York
Source: *BiDrAC; ConAu 101; CurBio 44, 80;
NewYTBE 71; NotNAT; WhoAm 74; WhoHol
A; WhoThe 77A*

Douglas, Jack
American. Comedian
b. 1908 in New York, New York
Source: *BioIn 5, 6, 8, 10*

Douglas, James, Sir
"Father of British Columbia"
Canadian. Businessman, Political Leader
First governor of newly-created colony of
  BC, 1858-64; in office during gold rush.
b. Aug 15, 1803 in Demerara, New Guiana
d. Aug 2, 1877 in Victoria, British Columbia
Source: *ApCAB; NewCol 75; OxCan; WebBD
80*

Douglas, Keith Castellain
English. Poet, Soldier
WW II casualty whose *Selected Poems,* were
  edited by Ted Hughes, 1964.
b. 1920 in Tunbridge Wells, England
d. Jun 1944 in Normandy, France
Source: *BioIn 10; DcLEL 1940; LongCTC;
ModBrL S1; OxEng; PenC ENG; WebE&AL;
WhoTwCL; WorAu*

Douglas, Kirk
[Issur Danielovich Demsky]
American. Actor
Has appeared in over 50 films including *Lust
  for Life,* 1956; *Spartacus,* 1960.
b. Dec 9, 1916 in Amsterdam, New York
Source: *BiDFilm; BiE&WWA; BkPepl; CelR;
CmMov; CurBio 52; FilmgC; IntMPA 75, 76,
77, 78, 79, 80, 81, 82; IntWW 74; MotPP;
MovMk; NotNAT; OxFilm; WhoAm 74, 76,
78, 80, 82; WhoHol A; WhoWor 74;
WorEFlm*

Douglas, Lloyd Cassel
American. Author, Clergyman
Writing career started with successful novel,
  Magnificent Obsession, 1929.
b. Aug 27, 1877 in Columbia City, Indiana
d. Feb 13, 1951 in Los Angeles, California
Source: *AmAu&B; AmNov; CyWA; DcAmB
S5; EvLB; FilmgC; IndAu 1917; LongCTC;
OhA&B; OxAmL; PenC AM; REn; REnAL;
TwCA, SUP; TwCWr; WebAB, 79; WhAm 3;
WhNAA; WorAl*

Douglas, Melvyn
[Melvin Hesselberg]
American. Actor
Won Oscars, 1963, 1979, for *Hud, Being
  There.*
b. Apr 5, 1901 in Macon, Georgia
d. Aug 4, 1981 in New York, New York
Source: *BiDFilm; BiE&WWA; BioIn 5, 6, 9,
11; CelR; CurBio 42, 81; FamA&A; FilmgC;
IntMPA 75, 76, 77, 78, 79, 80, 81; MGM;
MotPP; MovMk; NewYTBS 81; NotNAT;
OxFilm; WhoAm 74, 76, 78, 80; WhoHol A;
WhoThe 72, 77; WorEFlm*

Douglas, Michael Kirk
American. Actor, Producer
Won Oscar, 1975, as producer of *One Flew
  Over the Cuckoo's Nest.*
b. Sep 25, 1944 in New York, New York
Source: *BkPepl; FilmgC; IntMPA 80, 81, 82;
WhoAm 82; WhoHol A; WorAl; WrDr 76*

Douglas, Mike
[Michael Delaney Dowd, Jr.]
American. TV Host, Singer
Hosted "The Mike Douglas Show," 1960s-
  70s; has won four Emmys.
b. Aug 11, 1925 in Chicago, Illinois
Source: *BioNews 75; BkPepl; CelR; CurBio
68; IntMPA 82; RkOn 84; VarWW 85;
WhoAm 80, 82; WhoE 74; WhoHol A; WorAl*

Douglas, Norman
Scottish. Author
Best known for Caprian novel *South Wind,*
  1917; travel book *Old Calabria,* 1915.
b. Dec 8, 1868 in Aberdeen, Scotland
d. Feb 9, 1952 in Capri, Italy
Source: *AtlBL; CasWL; Chambr 3; ChhPo,
S1; CnMWL; CyWA; DcLEL; LongCTC;
ModBrL; NewC; OxEng; PenC ENG; RAdv 1;
REn; TwCA, SUP; TwCWr; WebE&AL;
WhoTwCL*

Douglas, Paul
American. Actor
1,024 performances on Broadway in *Born
  Yesterday.*
b. Nov 4, 1907 in Philadelphia, Pennsylvania
d. Sep 11, 1959 in Hollywood, California
Source: *BiDFilm; FilmgC; MotPP; MovMk;
ObitOF 79; WhScrn 74, 77; WhoHol B;
WorEFlm*

Douglas, Paul Howard
American. Economist, Senator
Dem. senator from IL, 1949-67; author of
  economic books: *The Theory of Wages,*
  1934.
b. Mar 26, 1892 in Salem, Massachusetts
d. Sep 24, 1976 in Washington, District of
  Columbia
Source: *AmAu&B; AmEA 74; AmM&WS 73S;
BiDrAC; ConAu 69; CurBio 49, 76; IntWW
74; WhoAm 74; WhoAmP 73; WhoWor 78*

Douglas, Robert L
American. Basketball Coach, Basketball
Executive
Owner, coach all-black Renaissance Big-Five
team, 1922; first black in Hall of Fame.
b. Nov 4, 1884 in Saint Kitts, British West
Indies
d. Jul 16, 1979 in New York, New York
Source: *InB&W 80; NewYTBS 79; WhoBbl
73*

Douglas, Sholto (William Sholto)
[Baron Douglas of Kirtleside]
English. Military Leader
Master of Royal Air Force; chm., British
European Airways; wrote *Years of Combat,*
1963.
b. Dec 23, 1893 in Oxford, England
d. Oct 29, 1969 in Northampton, England
Source: *CurBio 43, 69; GrBr; WhWW-II;
Who 82, 83*

Douglas, Stephen Arnold
"Little Giant"
American. Politician
Dem. senator from IL, 1847-61; best known
for debates with Lincoln, 1858.
b. Apr 23, 1813 in Brandon, Vermont
d. Jun 3, 1861 in Chicago, Illinois
Source: *AmAu&B; AmBi; ApCAB; BiAUS;
BiDrAC; DcAmB; Drake; EncAB-H; OxAmL;
REn; REnAL; TwCBDA; WebAB; WhAm HS;
WhAmP*

Douglas, William Orville
American. Supreme Court Justice
Liberal justice, 1939-75; granted stay of
execution to Rosenbergs, 1953.
b. Oct 16, 1898 in Maine, Minnesota
d. Jan 19, 1980 in Washington, District of
Columbia
Source: *ConAu 9R, 93; CurBio 41, 50, 80;
IntWW 74; REn; REnAL; Who 74; WhoAm
74; WhoAmP 73; WhoWor 78; WrDr 76*

Douglas-Home, Alexander Frederick
English. Politician
b. Jul 2, 1903 in London, England
Source: *Alli; CurBio 58; EvLB; IntWW 74;
NewYTBE 71; PenC ENG; Who 74; WhoWor
78*

Douglas-Home, Charles
English. Editor, Author
Editor, London *Times,* 1982-85.
b. Sep 1, 1937
d. Oct 29, 1985 in London, England
Source: *ConAu 117; Who 82*

Douglass, Andrew Ellicott
American. Astronomer, Scientist
Noted for research in dating ruins by tree
rings; coined word "dendrochronology."
b. Jul 7, 1867 in Windsor, Utah
d. Oct 20, 1962 in Tuscon, Arizona
Source: *DcAmB S7; WebBD 80*

Douglass, Frederick
[Frederick Augustus W Bailey]
American. Lecturer, Author
Escaped slavery, 1838; took active part in
antislavery cause, edited antislavery
journal.
b. Feb 14, 1817 in Tuckahoe, Maryland
d. Feb 20, 1895 in Anacosta Heights,
Maryland
Source: *Alli SUP; AmAu; AmAu&B; AmBi;
ApCAB; BbD; BiD&SB; BiDSA; BlkAWP;
Chambr 3; DcAmAu; DcAmB; DcNAA;
Drake; EncAB-H; OxAmL; REn; REnAL;
TwCBDA; WebAB; WebE&AL; WhAm HS;
WhAmP*

Douglass, Lathrop
American. Architect, Urban Planner
Designed first shopping center in US, 1950s;
developed suburban shopping malls in US,
Europe.
b. Sep 5, 1907 in Kansas City, Missouri
d. Jan 21, 1981 in Greenwich, Connecticut
Source: *AmArch 70; AnObit 1981; BioIn 8;
NewYTBS 81; WhoAm 80; WhoF&I 74;
WhoWor 76*

Doulton, Henry, Sir
English. Artist
b. 1820 in England
d. 1897
Source: *AntBDN M; WebBD 80*

Dourif, Brad
American. Actor
Received Oscar nomination for *One Flew
Over the Cuckoo's Nest,* 1975.
b. Mar 18, 1950 in Huntington, West
Virginia
Source: *WhoAm 82; WhoHol A*

Dove, Arthur Garfield
American. Artist
b. Aug 2, 1880 in Canandaigua, New York
d. Nov 23, 1946 in Huntington, New York
Source: *AtlBL; BioNews 75; ChhPo; DcAmB
S4; DcCAA 71; WebAB*

Douvillier, Suzanne Theodore Vaillande
"Madame Placide"
American. Dancer
First celebrated American ballerina, 1792;
first woman choreographer.
b. Sep 28, 1778 in Dole, France
d. Aug 30, 1826 in New Orleans, Louisiana
Source: *NotAW*

Dovzhenko, Alexander
Russian. Director
Best known for silent films: *Zvenigora, Earth,*
b. Sep 12, 1894 in Sosnitsa, Russia
d. 1956
Source: *BiDFilm; DcFM; FilmEn; FilmgC;*
MakMC; MovMk; OxFilm; WhScrn 74, 77;
WomWMM; WorEFlm

Dow, Charles Henry
American. Financier, Publisher
With Edward D Jones started *Wall Street*
Journal, 1889; laid basis for "Dow
Theory," Dow-Jones average.
b. Nov 6, 1851 in Sterling, Connecticut
d. Dec 4, 1902 in Brooklyn, New York
Source: *WebAB 79; WebBD 80*

Dow, Herbert Henry
American. Chemist, Manufacturer
Founded Dow Chemical Co., 1900.
b. Feb 26, 1866 in Belleville, Ontario
d. Oct 15, 1930 in Rochester, Minnesota
Source: *DcAmB S1; EncAB-H; WebAB;*
WhAm 1

Dow, Tony
American. Actor
Played Wally Cleaver on "Leave It to
Beaver," 1957-63.
b. Apr 13, 1945 in Hollywood, California
Source: *BioIn 12*

Dowding, Hugh C T, Baron
British. Air Force Officer
b. Apr 24, 1883
d. Feb 15, 1970 in Kent, England
Source: *CurBio 40, 70*

Dowell, Anthony
English. Dancer
b. Feb 16, 1943 in London, England
Source: *CurBio 71; IntWW 74; NewYTBS 74;*
Who 74; WhoAm 82; WhoWor 78

Dowie, John Alexander
Scottish. Evangelist
b. May 25, 1847 in Scotland
d. Mar 9, 1907
Source: *BioIn 2, 5, 8*

Dowland, John
English. Composer
b. Jan 1563 in Dublin, Ireland
d. Apr 7, 1626 in London, England
Source: *Alli; AtlBL; BrAu; ChhPo S2; NewC;*
OxEng; REn

Dowler, Boyd
American. Football Player
b. Oct 18, 1937 in Rock Springs, Wyoming
Source: *WhoFtbl 74*

Dowling, Dan(iel Blair)
American. Cartoonist
b. Nov 16, 1906 in O'Neill, Nebraska
Source: *Alli; WhoAm 80; WhoAmA 73*

Dowling, Eddie (Edward)
[Joseph Nelson Goucher]
American. Actor, Dramatist, Producer
Won four NY Drama Critics awards; won
Pulitzer for *Time of Your Life,* 1940.
b. Dec 11, 1894 in Woonsocket, Rhode
Island
d. Feb 18, 1976 in Smithfield, Rhode Island
Source: *AmSCAP 66; BiE&WWA; CurBio 46,*
76; EncMT; PIP&P; WhAm 6; WhoAm 74;
WhoHol C; WhoThe 77A

Down, Lesley-Anne
English. Actress
Starred in PBS series "Upstairs, Downstairs";
mini-series "North and South," 1985-86.
b. Mar 17, 1954 in London, England
Source: *FilmEn; IntMPA 81, 82*

Downes, Edward Olin Davenport
American. Conductor
b. Aug 12, 1911 in Boston, Massachusetts
Source: *DrAS 82H; WhoAm 80, 82; WhoE 74*

Downes, Olin (Edwin Olin)
American. Critic, Author
b. Jan 27, 1886 in Evanston, Illinois
d. Aug 22, 1955 in New York, New York
Source: *AmAu&B; CurBio 43, 55; DcAmB S5;*
WhAm 3; WhScrn 74, 77

Downey, Fairfax Davis
American. Author
b. Nov 28, 1893 in Salt Lake City, Utah
Source: *ConAu 1R, 1NR; CurBio 49; SmATA*
3

Downey, Morton
American. Singer
Irish tenor popular, 1930s-40s; made over
1,500 recordings.
b. Nov 14, 1902 in Wallingford, Connecticut
d. Oct 25, 1985 in Palm Beach, Florida
Source: *AmSCAP 66; CurBio 86; WhoAm 80,
82; WhoHol A*

Downey, Rick
[Blue Oyster Cult]
American. Singer, Musician
Drummer, vocalist with hard rock group
since 1981.
b. Aug 29, 1953 in Long Island, New York
Source: *NF*

Downing, Andrew Jackson
American. Horticulturist, Architect
Authority on landscape gardening, design.
b. Oct 30, 1815 in Newburgh, New York
d. Jul 28, 1852 in New York
Source: *AmAu&B; AmBi; ApCAB; BnEnAmA;
DcAmAu; DcAmB; McGDA; McGEWB;
NatCAB 11; OxAmH; OxArt; WebAB 79;
WhAm HS*

Downing, K K
see: Judas Priest

Downs, Hugh
American. TV Personality
Host of ABC newsmagazine show "20/20."
b. Feb 14, 1921 in Akron, Ohio
Source: *CelR; ConAu 45; CurBio 65; IntMPA
82; WhoAm 82*

Downs, Johnny
American. Actor
Child actor in *Our Gang* series; juvenile lead
in 1930s musicals.
b. Oct 10, 1913 in New York, New York
Source: *CmpEPM; FilmEn; FilmgC; WhoHol
A*

Downs, William Randall, Jr.
American. Broadcast Journalist
b. Aug 17, 1914 in Kansas City, Kansas
d. May 3, 1978 in Bethesda, Maryland
Source: *ConAu 77, 81; WhAm 7; WhoAm 76,
78*

Dowson, Ernest Christopher
English. Author, Poet
Associated with "fin de siecle" period in
literature; wrote *Cynara,* 1896.
b. Aug 2, 1867 in Kent, England
d. Feb 23, 1900 in London, England
Source: *AtlBL; BrAu 19; CasWL; Chambr 3;
ChhPo, S1, S2; CnE&AP; DcLEL; EvLB;
MouLC 4; NewC; OxEng; PenC ENG; REn;
TwCLC 4; WebE&AL; WorAl*

Doxiadis, Constantinos Apostolos
Greek. Architect
b. May 14, 1913 in Stenimochos, Greece
d. Jun 28, 1975 in Athens, Greece
Source: *ConAu 41R, 57; CurBio 64; IntWW
74; WhAm 6; Who 74; WhoWor 78*

Doyle, Arthur Conan, Sir
Scottish. Author, Physician
Introduced Sherlock Holmes in *A Study in
Scarlet,* 1887.
b. May 22, 1859 in Edinburgh, Scotland
d. Jul 7, 1930 in Crowborough, England
Source: *Alli SUP; AtlBL; AuBYP; BbD;
BiD&SB; BiDPara; CarSB; CasWL; Chambr
3; ChhPo, S1; CyWA; DcBiA; DcEnA AP;
DcLEL; EncMys; EvLB; FilmgC; JBA 34;
LongCTC; MnBBF; ModBrL; NewC; OxEng;
PenC ENG; PoIre; RAdv 1; REn; TwCA,
SUP; TwCWr; WebE&AL; WhoChL;
WhoTwCL*

Doyle, David Fitzgerald
American. Actor
Played Bosley in TV series "Charlie's
Angels."
b. Dec 1, 1929 in Omaha, Nebraska
Source: *VarWW 85; WhoHol A*

Doyle, Richard
English. Artist
Worked for *Punch,* 1843-50; drew endearing
elfish figures for *In Fairyland,* 1870.
b. Sep 1824 in London, England
d. Dec 11, 1883 in London, England
Source: *DcCathB; OxArt; WhDW; WorECar*

Dozier, James Lee
American. Military Leader
Five-star general, kidnapped by Red Brigade
terrorists, 1981; freed by Italian police
after 42 days.
b. Apr 10, 1931 in Arcadia, Florida
Source: *NewYTBS 82*

Drabble, Margaret
English. Author
b. Jun 5, 1939 in Sheffield, England
Source: *Au&Wr 71; ConAu 13R; ConLC 2, 3, 5, 8, 10; ConNov 72, 76; IntWW 74; LongCTC; ModBrL S1; RAdv 1; TwCWr; Who 74; WhoAm 74, 76, 78, 80, 82; WhoTwCL; WrDr 80*

Drachler, Norman
American. Educator
b. May 20, 1912 in Poland
Source: *LEduc 74; WhoAm 74, 76, 78, 80, 82; WhoWorJ 72*

Draco
Greek. Politician
Called founder of Athenian civilization; gave Athens first written code of law, 621 BC.
d. 650 BC
Source: *NewC; OxLaw; REn; WhDW*

Dracula
[Vlad the Impaler]
Hungarian. Prince
b. 1431
d. 1476
Source: *BioIn 9, 10*

Draddy, Vincent de Paul
American. Designer
Source: *WhoAm 80; WorFshn*

Dragon, Carmen
American. Conductor
b. Jul 28, 1914 in Antioch, California
d. Mar 28, 1984 in Santa Monica, California
Source: *AmSCAP 66; Baker 78; WhoMus 72*

Dragon, Daryl
[The Captain and Tennille]
American. Musician, Songwriter
1970s hits include "Love Will Keep Us Together."
b. Aug 27, 1942 in Studio City, California
Source: *BkPepl*

Dragonette, Jessica
Indian. Opera Singer
b. Feb 14, 1910 in Calcutta, India
d. Mar 18, 1980 in New York, New York
Source: *InWom; PIP&P; WhoAmW 77; WhoMus 72*

Drake, Alfred
American. Opera Singer
b. Oct 7, 1914 in New York, New York
Source: *BiE&WWA; CelR; CurBio 44; EncMT; FamA&A; FilmgC; NotNAT; WhoAm 74; WhoHol A; WhoThe 77; WhoWor 78*

Drake, Betsy
American. Actress
Married to Cary Grant, 1949-59; films include *Room for One More,* 1952.
b. Sep 11, 1923 in Paris, France
Source: *FilmgC; MotPP; WhoHol A*

Drake, Edwin Laurentine
American. Oilman
Established first producing oil well in US, near Titusville, PA, Aug 27, 1859.
b. Mar 29, 1819 in Greenville, New York
d. Nov 8, 1880 in Bethlehem, Pennsylvania
Source: *AmBi; DcAmB; LinLib S; WebAB; WhDW; WhAm HS*

Drake, Francis, Sir
English. Admiral, Navigator
First Englishman to circumnavigate globe, 1577-80.
b. 1540 in Devonshire, England
d. Jan 28, 1596 in Portobelo, Panama
Source: *Alli, SUP; ApCAB; Drake; NewC; REn; REnAL; WhAm HS*

Drake, Frank Donald
American. Astronomer
Organized search for extra-terrestrial life, called project OZMA, 1960.
b. May 28, 1930 in Chicago, Illinois
Source: *ConAu 17R; CurBio 63; IntWW 74; WhoAm 74, 76, 78, 80, 82; WhoE 74; WhoWor 78*

Drake, Galen
Radio Performer
Starred in "The Galen Drake Show."
Source: *NF*

Drake, Joseph Rodman
American. Poet
Wrote *Croaker Papers,* 1819.
b. Aug 17, 1795 in New York, New York
d. Sep 21, 1820 in New York, New York
Source: *Alli; AmAu; AmAu&B; AmBi; ApCAB; BbD; BiD&SB; Chambr 3; ChhPo, S2; CnDAL; CyAL 1; DcAmAu; DcAmB; DcLEL; DcNAA; Drake; EvLB; LinLib L; NatCAB 5; OxAmL; PenC AM; REn; REnAL; TwCBDA; WhAm HS*

Drake, Stanley
American. Cartoonist
b. Nov 9, 1921 in Brooklyn, New York
Source: *WhoAm 82; WorECom*

Drake, Tom
[Alfred Alderdice]
American. Actor
Appeared in 1940s musicals including *Meet
    Me in St. Louis,* 1944.
b. Aug 5, 1918 in New York, New York
d. Aug 11, 1982 in Torrance, California
Source: *FilmEn; FilmgC; IntMPA 75, 76, 77,
    78, 79; MGM; MotPP; MovMk*

Draper, Dorothy Tuckerman
American. Interior Decorator
b. Nov 22, 1889 in New York, New York
d. Mar 10, 1969 in Cleveland, Ohio
Source: *CurBio 41, 69; InWom; WhAm 5*

Draper, John William
American. Philosopher, Historian
Developed photo-chemistry; made first
    photograph of moon, 1840.
b. May 5, 1811 in Liverpool, England
d. Jan 4, 1882 in Hastings, New York
Source: *NewCol 75; REn; WebAB; WebBD 80*

Draper, Paul
Italian. Dancer
b. Oct 25, 1909 in Florence, Italy
Source: *BiE&WWA; CurBio 44; NotNAT;
    WhoHol A*

Draper, Ruth
American. Actress
Wrote, performed dramatic monologues, such
    as *Opening a Bazaar, Three Generations.*
b. Dec 2, 1884 in New York, New York
d. Dec 30, 1956 in New York, New York
Source: *InWom; LibW; ObitOF 79; OxThe;
    REnAL; WhAm 3*

Drayton, Michael
English. Author, Poet
Prolific writer of historical, religious,
    topographical verse.
b. 1563 in Warwickshire, England
d. Dec 23, 1631 in London, England
Source: *Alli; AtlBL; BbD; BiD&SB; BrAu;
    CasWL; Chambr 1; ChhPo, S1; CnE&AP;
    CroE&S; CrtT 1; CyWA; DcEnA; DcEnL;
    DcEuL; DcLEL; EvLB; McGEWD; MouLC 1;
    NewC; OxEng; PenC ENG; REn; WebE&AL;
    WhDW*

Dreier, Alex
American. Radio Commentator, TV
    Personality
b. Jun 26, 1916 in Honolulu, Hawaii
Source: *WhoAm 74*

Dreifus, Claudia
American. Journalist
b. Nov 24, 1944
Source: *BioIn 10; ConAu 45, 1NR; ForWC
    70*

Dreiser, Theodore
American. Editor, Author
Wrote *Sister Carrie,* 1900, *An American
    Tragedy,* 1925; books attacked as immoral.
b. Aug 27, 1871 in Terre Haute, Indiana
d. Dec 28, 1945 in Hollywood, California
Source: *AmAu&B; AmLY; AmWr; AtlBL;
    CasWL; Chambr 3; CnDAL; CnMD;
    CnMWL; ConAmA; ConAmL; CyWA;
    DcAmAu; DcAmB S3; DcBiA; DcLEL;
    DcNAA; EncAB-H; EncMys; EncWL;
    FilmgC; IndAu 1816; LongCTC; ModAL, S1;
    ModWD; OxAmL; OxEng; PenC AM; RAdv
    1; RComWL; REn; REnAL; TwCA, SUP;
    TwCWr; WebAB; WebE&AL; WhAm 2;
    WhNAA; WhoTwCL*

Dressen, Charlie (Charles W)
American. Baseball Manager
b. Sep 20, 1898 in Decatur, Illinois
d. Aug 10, 1966 in Detroit, Michigan
Source: *CurBio 51, 66; WhAm 4; WhoFtbl
    74; WhoProB 73*

Dresser, Davis
[Brett Halliday, pseud.]
American. Author
b. Jul 31, 1904 in Chicago, Illinois
d. Feb 4, 1977 in Montecito, California
Source: *AmAu&B; ConAu 69, 77; CurBio 69,
    77; EncMys; WorAu*

Dresser, Louise
[Louise Kerlin]
American. Actress
Starred with Rudolph Valentino in *The
    Eagle,* 1925; as Al Jolson's mother in
    Mammy, 1930.
b. Oct 5, 1882 in Evansville, Indiana
d. Apr 24, 1965 in Woodland Hills,
    California
Source: *FilmgC; InWom; MotPP; MovMk;
    ThFT; TwYS; WhAm 4; WhScrn 74, 77;
    WhThe; WhoHol B*

Dressler, Marie
[Leila Marie Koerber]
Canadian. Actress
Won Oscar for *Min and Bill*, 1930.
b. Nov 9, 1869 in Cobourg, Ontario
d. Jul 28, 1934 in Santa Barbara, California
Source: *AmAu&B; AmBi; BiDFilm; DcAmB
S1; DcNAA; EncMT; FilmEn; Film 1;
FilmgC; MotPP; MovMk; NotAW; OxFilm;
OxThe; REn; ThFT; TwYS; WebAB; WhAm
1; WhScrn 74, 77; WhoHol B; WhoStg 1906,
1908; WorAl; WorEFlm*

Drew, Charles Richard
American. Scientist
b. Jun 3, 1904 in Washington, District of
Columbia
d. Apr 1, 1950 in Washington, District of
Columbia
Source: *CurBio 44, 50; DcAmB S4; EncAB-H;
WebAB; WhAm 3*

Drew, Daniel
American. Financier
b. Jul 29, 1792
d. Sep 18, 1874
Source: *BioIn 3; WhAm HS*

Drew, Elizabeth Brenner
American. Journalist
b. Nov 16, 1935 in Cincinnati, Ohio
Source: *ConAu 104; ForWC 70; WhoAm 74,
76, 78, 80, 82; WhoAmW 77; WhoS&SW 82*

Drew, John
American. Actor
Appeared in Charles Frohman's Co. with
Maude Adams in *The Masked Ball; The
Rivals*, 1892-97.
b. Nov 13, 1853 in Philadelphia,
Pennsylvania
d. Jul 9, 1927 in San Francisco, California
Source: *AmAu&B; AmBi; DcAmB; DcNAA;
Film 1; OxAmH; OxThe; TwCBDA; WebAB;
WhAm 1; WhThe*

Drew, John E
American. Basketball Player
b. Sep 30, 1954 in Vredenburgh, Alabama
Source: *BioIn 10; WhoBlA 77*

Drew, Louisa Lane
[Mrs. John Drew]
English. Actress
Managed Philadelphia's Arch Street Theatre,
1860-92.
b. Jan 10, 1820 in London, England
d. Aug 31, 1897 in Larchmont, New York
Source: *AmBi; ApCAB; DcAmB; InWom;
NatCAB 8; NotAW; NotNAT B; OxThe;
TwCBDA; WhAm HS*

Drew, Richard G
American. Engineer
Invented transparent tape, 1930.
b. 1899 in Minnesota
d. Dec 7, 1980 in Santa Barbara, California
Source: *BioIn 1; NewYTBS 80*

Drewry, John Eldridge
American. Author, Educator
Writings include *Concerning the Fourth
Estate*, 1938; *Key to So Much*, 1957.
b. Jun 4, 1902 in Griffin, Georgia
d. Feb 11, 1983
Source: *AmAu&B; DrAS 74E; WhAm 8;
WhNAA; WhoAm 74, 76, 78, 80, 82; WrDr
76*

Drexel, Anthony J
American. Banker, Philanthropist
b. Sep 13, 1806 in Philadelphia, Pennsylvania
d. Jun 30, 1893
Source: *AmBi; ApCAB; DcAmB; TwCBDA;
WhAm HS*

Drexel, Francis Martin
American. Banker
b. Apr 7, 1792 in Dornbirn, Austria
d. Jun 5, 1863 in Philadelphia, Pennsylvania
Source: *ApCAB; DcAmB; WhAm HS*

Drexel, Mary Katherine
American. Religious Leader
Founder, Catholic Order for Indians and
Blacks, 1891.
b. Nov 26, 1858
d. Mar 3, 1955
Source: *NotAW MOD*

Drexler, Rosalyn
American. Author
Won 1979 Obie for *The Writer's Opera*, 1974
Emmy for *The Lily Show.*
b. Nov 25, 1926 in Bronx, New York
Source: *AmAu&B; ConDr 82; ConLC 2, 6;
DrAF 76; ModAL S1; NewYTBE 71;
NotNAT; WhoAm 82; WrDr 80*

Dreyer, Carl Theodore
Danish. Director
Best known for *Day of Wrath; Passion of
Joan of Arc; The Word.*
b. Feb 3, 1889 in Copenhagen, Denmark
d. Mar 28, 1968 in Copenhagen, Denmark
Source: *BiDFilm; DcFM; FilmgC; MovMk;
ObitOF 79; OxFilm; WorEFlm*

Dreyfus, Alfred
French. Army Officer
Wrongly convicted of high treason, 1895,
    vindicated in 1906; defended by Emile
    Zola in *J'Accuse,* 1898.
b. Oct 9, 1859 in Alsace, France
d. Jul 12, 1935
Source: *FilmgC; LinLib S; McGEWB; NewC;*
OxFilm; REn

Dreyfus, Hubert L
American. Author
b. Oct 15, 1929 in Terre Haute, Indiana
Source: *ConAu 33R; DrAS 74P; IndAu 1917*

Dreyfus, Jack Jonas
American. Financier, Author
Founder, noted investment firm; wrote
    controversial health book promoting
    dilantin.
b. 1913 in Alabama
Source: *BioIn 6, 7, 8, 9*

Dreyfuss, Henry
American. Designer
Pioneer in industrial design who believed
    form followed function; designed ocean
    liners, farm equipment.
b. Mar 2, 1904 in New York, New York
d. Oct 5, 1972 in Pasadena, California
Source: *ConAu 37R, 45; CurBio 48, 59, 72N;*
EncAB 25; WhAm 5; WhoAdv 72; WhoWorJ
78

Dreyfuss, Richard Stephan
American. Actor
Starred in *Jaws,* 1975; won Oscar, 1978, for
    The Goodbye Girl.
b. Oct 29, 1947 in Brooklyn, New York
Source: *BkPepl; IntMPA 75, 76, 77, 78, 79,*
80, 81, 82; NewYTBS 74; WhoAm 82;
WhoHol A

Drifters, The
[Clyde McPhatter; Billy Pickney; Andrew
    Thrasher; Gerhart Thrasher]
American. Music Group
Hits included "Save the Last Dance for Me,"
    1960; "Under the Boardwalk," 1964.
Source: *BiDAmM; EncPR&S 74; IlEncRk;*
RkOn 85; RkOneH

Drinker, Philip
American. Educator, Engineer
Invented iron lung, 1929.
b. Dec 12, 1894 in Haverford, Pennsylvania
d. Oct 19, 1972 in Fitzwilliam, New
    Hampshire
Source: *AmM&WS 82P; InSci; NatCAB 57;*
WhAm 5

Drinkwater, John
English. Poet, Author, Biographer
b. Jun 1, 1882 in Leytonstone, England
d. Mar 25, 1937 in Kilburn, England
Source: *Alli; BiDLA; CasWL; Chambr 3;*
ChhPo, S1, S2; CnMD; CnThe; DcLEL;
EvLB; JBA 34; LongCTC; McGEWD;
ModBrL; ModWD; NewC; OxEng; OxThe;
PenC ENG; REn; Str&VC; TwCA, SUP;
WebE&AL; WhoLA

Drinkwater, Terry
American. Author
b. May 9, 1936 in Denver, Colorado
Source: *ConAu 69*

Driscoll, Bobby
American. Actor
Won special Oscar as outstanding juvenile
    actor, 1949; career faltered in teens, died
    from drug overdose.
b. Mar 3, 1936 in Cedar Rapids, Iowa
d. Jan 1968 in New York, New York
Source: *FilmgC; HolP 40; WhScrn 74, 77;*
WhoHol B

Dropo, Walt
"Moose"
American. Baseball Player
First baseman, 1949-61; rookie of year, 1950.
b. Jan 30, 1923 in Moosup, Connecticut
Source: *BaseEn 85; BioIn 1, 2, 3, 4, 5;*
WhoProB 73

Dru, Joanne
[Letitia LaCock]
American. Actress
Starred in Westerns *Red River,* 1948; *She*
    Wore a Yellow Ribbon, 1949; sister of
    Peter Marshall.
b. Jan 31, 1923 in Logan, West Virginia
Source: *BiDFilm; CmMov; FilmgC; InWom;*
IntMPA 80, 81, 82; MotPP; WhoHol A;
WorAl; WorEFlm

Drucker, Peter
American. Government Official
b. Nov 9, 1909 in Vienna, Austria
Source: *AmAu&B; Au&Wr 71; ConAu 61;*
CurBio 64; IntWW 74; NewYTBS 74; Who
74; WhoAm 82; WhoWor 78

Druckman, Jacob Raphael
American. Composer
Electronic composer known for ballet scores;
    won Pulitzer for orchestral work *Windows,*
    1972.
b. Jun 26, 1928 in Philadelphia, Pennsylvania
Source: *Baker 78; CurBio 81; DcCM; WhoAm*
80, 82, 84

Drum, Hugh A
American. Military Leader
b. Sep 19, 1879 in Fort Brady, Michigan
d. Oct 3, 1951
Source: *CurBio 41, 51; DcAmB S5; WhAm 3*

Drummond, Roscoe (James Roscoe)
American. Journalist
Wrote newspaper column "State of the
    Nation" for 25 yrs.
b. Jan 13, 1902 in Theresa, New York
d. Sep 30, 1983 in Princeton, New Jersey
Source: *CurBio 83N; IntAu&W 77; IntWW
80; NewYTBS 83; WhoAm 80, 82; WhoS&SW
73; WhoWor 74*

Drummond, William Henry
Canadian. Poet, Physician
Wrote poems about French Canadians using
    their dialects: *The Voyageur*, 1905.
b. Apr 13, 1854 in Mohill, Ireland
d. Apr 6, 1907 in Cobalt, Ontario
Source: *DcNAA; EvLB; LinLib S; NewC*

Drury, Allen Stuart
American. Author
Background as Washington journalist was
    source for his Pulitzer-winning novel,
    Advise and Consent, 1960.
b. Sep 2, 1918 in Houston, Texas
Source: *AmAu&B; CelR; ConAu 57; ConNov
72, 76; IntWW 74; OxAmL; REnAL;
TwCWr; Who 74; WhoAm 80, 82; WhoWor
74; WorAl; WorAu; WrDr 82*

Drury, James
American. Actor
Title star of TV's "The Virginian," 1962-71.
b. 1934 in New York, New York
Source: *FilmgC; IntMPA 81, 82; MotPP;
WhoHol A*

Dryden, John
English. Poet, Dramatist
Poet laureate, 1668-89; best known play
    Marriage a la Mode, 1672.
b. Aug 9, 1631 in North Hamptonshire,
    England
d. May 1, 1700 in London, England
Source: *Alli; AtlBL; BbD; BiD&SB; BrAu;
CasWL; Chambr 1; ChhPo, S1; CnE&AP;
CnThe; CrtT 2; CyWA; DcEnA; DcEnL;
DcEuL; DcLEL; EvLB; McGEWD; MouLC 1;
NewC; OxEng; OxThe; PenC ENG; PIP&P;
PoChrch; PoLE; RAdv 1; RComWL; REn;
REnWD; WebE&AL*

Dryden, Ken(neth Wayne)
Canadian. Hockey Player, Lawyer
Goalie whose 2.24 career goals-against
    average lowest in league since 1941.
b. Aug 8, 1947 in Islington, Ontario
Source: *NewYTBE 71; WhoE 74; WhoHcky
73*

Dryden, Spencer
[Jefferson Airplane]
American. Singer, Musician
b. Apr 7, 1943 in New York, New York
Source: *NF*

Dryer, Fred (John Frederick)
American. Football Player, Actor
Star of TV series "Hunter."
b. Jul 6, 1946 in Hawthorne, California
Source: *FootReg 81*

Dryfoos, Orvil E
American. Newspaper Publisher
b. Nov 8, 1912 in New York, New York
d. May 25, 1963 in New York, New York
Source: *CurBio 62, 63; WhAm 4*

Drysdale, Don(ald Scott)
"Big D"; "Double D"
American. Baseball Player, Sportscaster
Pitcher, Brooklyn, LA Dodgers, 1956-69;
    holds ML record for most consecutive
    scoreless innings.
b. Jul 23, 1936 in Van Nuys, California
Source: *BaseEn 85; CmCal; CurBio 65;
WhoAm 80, 82; WorAl*

Duarte, Jose Napoleon
Salvadoran. Political Leader
Christian Democrat pres. of El Salvador,
    1981-82, 1984--; exiled, 1972-79.
b. Nov 23, 1926 in San Salvador, El
    Salvador
Source: *CurBio 81; IntWW 83; NewYTBS 84;
OxTwCA*

DuBarry, Comtesse Jeanne Becu
French. Mistress
b. Aug 19, 1746
d. Dec 7, 1793
Source: *DcBiPP; Dis&D; NewC; OxFr*

DuBay, William Bryan
American. Artist, Editor
Editor, *Warren Comics*, 1972-76; created
    characters Creepy, Errie, Rook.
b. 1948 in San Francisco, California
Source: *FanAl*

Dubcek, Alexander
Czech. Communist Leader
b. Nov 27, 1921 in Uhrovec, Czechoslovakia
Source: *CurBio 68; IntWW 74; WhoWor 78*

Dubin, Al
Swiss. Songwriter
b. Jun 10, 1891 in Zurich, Switzerland
d. Feb 11, 1945 in New York, New York
Source: *AmSCAP 66; BioIn 4, 5; NotNAT B*

Dubinsky, David
American. Labor Union Official
Pres., ILGWU, 1932-66; co-founded
   American Labor Party, 1936.
b. Feb 22, 1892 in Brest-Litovsk, Poland
d. Sep 17, 1982 in New York, New York
Source: *BiDAmLL; CurBio 83; EncAB-H;
IntWW 82; McGEWB; NewYTBS 82, PolProf
E, K, T; WebAB; WhAm 8; WorFshn*

DuBois, Guy Pene
American. Artist, Critic
Paintings generally presented human
   spectacle.
b. Jan 4, 1884 in Brooklyn, New York
d. Jul 18, 1958 in New York, New York
Source: *AmAu&B; CurBio 46, 58; DcCAA 71;
WhAm 3*

DuBois, W(illiam) E(dward) B(urghardt)
American. Author, Reform Leader
Prominent in early movements for racial
   equality; wrote *The Souls of Black Folks,*
   1903.
b. Feb 23, 1868 in Barrington, Massachusetts
d. Aug 27, 1963 in Accra, Ghana
Source: *BiDSA; BlkAWP; CasWL; ConAmL;
ConAu 85; ConLC 1, 2, 13; DcAmAu;
DcLEL; EncAB-H; LongCTC; McGEWB;
OxAmL; PenC AM; REn; REnAL; TwCA,
SUP; WebAB, 79; WebE&AL; WhAm 4;
WhAmP; WhNAA*

Dubos, Rene Jules
American. Author, Scientist
Microbiologist whose research resulted in first
   commericaly produced antibotics; won
   Pulitzer for *So Human an Animal,* 1969.
b. Feb 20, 1901 in Saint-Brice, France
d. Feb 20, 1982 in New York, New York
Source: *AmAu&B; AmM&WS 79P; AsBiEn;
CelR; CurBio 82; IntWW 81; McGEWB;
NewYTBE 71; NewYTBS 82; WebAB, 79;
WhAm 8; WhoAm 82; WhoE 74; WhoWor
74; WrDr 82*

Dubs, Adolph
"Spike"
American. Diplomat
b. Aug 4, 1920 in Illinois
d. Feb 14, 1979
Source: *BioIn 11; USBiR 74; WhAm 7;
WhoAm 74, 76, 78; WhoGov 72, 75, 77;
WhoWor 74, 78*

Dubuffet, Jean
French. Artist
Post-WW II artist, known for primitive-style
   paintings, large-scale representational
   sculptures.
b. Jul 31, 1901 in Le Havre, France
d. May 12, 1985 in Paris, France
Source: *ConNews 85-4; CurBio 85; IntWW
74; NewYTBE 72; Who 74; WhoWor 74*

Duc de Armand, Jean du Plessis
see: Richelieu, Armand Jean du Plessis,
   Cardinal

Ducasse, Isidore Lucien
see: Lautreamont, Comte de, pseud.

Duccio di Buoninsegna
Italian. Artist
b. 1278 in Siena, Italy
d. 1319 in Siena, Italy
Source: *AtlBL; REn*

Du Chaillu, Paul Belloni
French. Anthropologist, Traveler
Wrote *Stories of the Gorilla Country,* 1868.
b. Jul 31, 1835
d. Apr 20, 1903 in Saint Petersburg, Russia
Source: *DcEnL; OxAmL 83; REnAL; WebBD
80*

Duchamp, Marcel
French. Artist
b. Jul 28, 1887 in Blainville, France
d. Oct 1, 1968 in Neuilly, France
Source: *AtlBL; CurBio 60, 68; DcCAA 71;
REn*

Duchin, Eddie
American. Band Leader, Pianist
Father of Peter Duchin; wrote four books on
   piano technique.
b. Apr 1, 1909 in Cambridge, Massachusetts
d. Feb 9, 1951 in New York, New York
Source: *CurBio 47, 51; WhScrn 74, 77;
WhoHol B*

Duchin, Peter
American. Band Leader, Pianist
b. Jul 28, 1937 in New York, New York
Source: *BioNews 74; BkPepl; CelR; WhoAm
74, 76, 78, 80, 82; WhoHol A*

Ducis, Jean Francois
French. Dramatist, Poet
Adapted Shakespeare for French stage so
  drastically that only title remained of
  original.
b. Aug 22, 1733 in Versailles, France
d. Mar 31, 1816 in Versailles, France
Source: *BiD&SB; CasWL; DcEuL; EvEuW;
NotNAT B; OxFr; OxThe*

Duclos, Jacques
French. Communist Leader
b. Oct 2, 1896 in Louey, France
d. Apr 25, 1975 in Paris, France
Source: *CurBio 46; IntWW 74; WhoWor 78*

Ducloux, Walter
Swiss. Conductor, Educator
b. Apr 17, 1913 in Lucerne, Switzerland
Source: *AmSCAP 66; BioIn 6*

Dudley, William
"Bullet Bill"
American. Football Player
b. Dec 24, 1921 in Bluefield, Virginia
Source: *BioIn 3, 7, 8, 9; WhoFtbl 74*

Duel, Peter
American. Actor
Starred in TV series "Love on a Rooftop,"
  1966-67; "Alias Smith and Jones," 1971-
  72.
b. 1940 in Rochester, New York
d. Dec 31, 1971 in Hollywood, California
Source: *FilmgC; ObitOF 79; WhScrn 74, 77;
WhoHol B*

Duerk, Alene B
American. Admiral
b. Mar 29, 1920 in Defiance, Ohio
Source: *CurBio 73*

Duesenberg, August S
American. Auto Manufacturer
b. 1879
d. Jan 18, 1955 in Indianapolis, Indiana
Source: *BioIn 3; ObitOF 79*

Duesenberg, Frederick S
American. Auto Manufacturer
Built engine for motorcycles adapted for cars,
  boats, airplanes, 1913.
b. Dec 6, 1876 in Lippe, Germany
d. 1932
Source: *NatCAB 16; WebBD 80*

Duff, Howard
American. Actor
Starred in TV series "Mr. Adams and Eve,"
  1957-58; "Felony Squad," 1966-69.
b. Nov 24, 1917 in Bremerton, Washington
Source: *FilmgC; IntMPA 81, 82; MotPP;
MovMk; WhoAm 82; WhoHol A; WorAl*

Duff, Mary Ann Dyke
American. Actress
Starred in dramatic roles with Edmund
  Kean, Junius Brutus Booth, 1812-38.
b. 1794 in London, England
d. Sep 5, 1857 in New York, New York
Source: *NotAW*

Duffey, Joseph Daniel
American. Clergyman, Sociologist
b. 1932
Source: *BioIn 8, 9, 10, 11*

Duffy, Ben (Bernard Cornelius)
American. Advertising Executive
b. Jan 21, 1902 in New York, New York
d. Sep 1, 1972 in Rye, New York
Source: *Au&Wr 71; ConAu 37R; CurBio 52,
72; WhAm 5*

Duffy, Clinton Truman
American. Prison Warden
Warden, San Quentin, 1940-52; instituted
  many penal reforms.
b. Aug 24, 1898 in San Quentin, California
d. Oct 11, 1982 in Walnut Creek, California
Source: *AnObit 1982; NewYTBS 82*

Duffy, Edmund
American. Cartoonist
Won three Pulitzers, 1931, 1934, 1940, for
  political cartoons.
b. Mar 1, 1899 in Jersey City, New Jersey
d. Sep 13, 1962 in New York, New York
Source: *DcAmB S7; WebBD 80*

Duffy, Francis Patrick
American. Priest
Army chaplain during WW I; hero of 1940
  film *The Fighting 69th.*
b. May 2, 1871 in Cobourg, Canada
d. Jun 26, 1932 in New York, New York
Source: *DcAmB S1; WebBD 80*

Duffy, Hugh
American. Baseball Player
b. Nov 26, 1866 in River Point, Rhode
  Island
d. Oct 19, 1954 in Allston, Massachusetts
Source: *BaseEn 85; BioIn 3, 7; WhoProB 73*

Duffy, James E
American. Broadcasting Executive
Pres., ABC TV network since 1970.
b. Apr 2, 1926 in Decatur, Illinois
Source: *IntMPA 84; NewYTET; WhoAm 84; WhoTelC*

Duffy, Patrick
American. Actor
Plays Bobby Ewing on TV series "Dallas," 1978--.
b. Mar 17, 1949 in Townsend, Montana
Source: *BioIn 11; IntMPA 82; WhoAm 80, 82*

Dufresne, Charles
French. Artist
Prolific painter of exotic, Fauvist-cubist landscapes.
b. 1876 in Millcmont, France
d. 1938 in Seyne-sur-Mer, France
Source: *McGDA*

Dufy, Raoul
French. Artist
b. Jun 3, 1877 in Le Havre, France
d. Mar 23, 1953 in Forcalquier, France
Source: *AtlBL; CurBio 51, 53; REn; WhAm 3*

Dugan, Alan
American. Author
b. Feb 12, 1923 in Brooklyn, New York
Source: *AmAu&B; ConAu 81; ConLC 2, 6; ConP 70, 75; CroCAP; DrAP 75; ModAL, S1; OxAmL; PenC AM; RAdv 1; REnAL; WhoAm 74; WhoWor 78; WorAu; WrDr 80*

Duggan, Maurice Noel
New Zealander. Author
b. Nov 25, 1922 in Auckland, New Zealand
d. Jan 1975
Source: *CasWL; ConAu 53, 73; ConNov 72, 76; WebE&AL*

Duguay, Ron(ald)
"Doogie"
Canadian. Hockey Player
Center, NY Rangers, 1977-83, Detroit, 1983-86; Pittsburgh, 1986--.
b. Jul 6, 1957 in Sudbury, Ontario
Source: *HocReg 81; NewYTBS 82*

Du Guesclin, Bertrand
"The Eagle of Brittany"
French. Military Leader
Considered greatest French warrior of his day; Constable of France, 1370.
b. 1320 in Dinan, France
d. Jul 13, 1380 in Languedoc, France
Source: *NewCol 75; OxFr; WebBD 80*

Duane, William
American. Physicist, Educator
Best known for X-ray research.
b. Feb 17, 1872 in Philadelphia, Pennsylvania
d. Mar 7, 1935 in Devon, Pennsylvania
Source: *DcAmB S1; WebBD 80*

Duhamel, Georges
[Denis Thevenin]
French. Author, Editor
Writings *Salavin; The Pasquier Chronicles,* give broad picture of French middle-class life from 1880s to WW I.
b. Jun 30, 1884 in Paris, France
d. Apr 13, 1966 in Valmondois, France
Source: *CasWL; ClDMEL; ConAu 25R, 81; ConLC 8; EncWL; EvEuW; LongCTC; ModRL; ModWD; OxFr; PenC EUR; REn; ScF&FL 1; TwCA, SUP; TwCWr; WhoTwCL*

Dukakis, Michael Stanley
American. Politician
Dem. governor of MA, 1975-79, 1983--.
b. Nov 3, 1933 in Brookline, Massachusetts
Source: *BioNews 75; IntWW 81, 82, 83; WhoAm 84; WhoAmP 81, 83*

Dukas, Paul Abraham
French. Composer
b. Oct 1, 1865 in Paris, France
d. May 17, 1935 in Paris, France
Source: *OxFr*

Duke, Angier Biddle
American. Diplomat
b. Nov 30, 1915 in New York, New York
Source: *CelR; CurBio 62; IntWW 74; WhoAm 74, 76, 78, 80, 82; WhoAmP 73*

Duke, Benjamin Newton
American. Industrialist
b. Apr 27, 1855 in Orange County, North Carolina
d. Jan 8, 1929
Source: *BioIn 10; EncWM; NatCAB 21; WhAm 1*

Duke, Charles Moss, Jr.
American. Astronaut
Lunar module pilot, Apollo 16, Apr, 1972.
b. Oct 3, 1935 in Charlotte, North Carolina
Source: *IntWW 74, 75, 76, 77; NewYTBE 72; WhoS&SW 73, 75*

Duke, Doris
American. Socialite, Philanthropist
Only child of tobacco magnate James Buchanan Duke; heiress to fortune.
b. Nov 22, 1912 in New York, New York
Source: *CelR; InWom*

Duke, James Buchanan
American. Businessman, Philanthropist
Founded American Tobacco Co., 1890; large
   benefactor of Trinity College, later
   renamed Duke University.
b. Dec 23, 1856 in Durham, North Carolina
d. Oct 10, 1925 in New York, New York
Source: *AmBi; DcAmB; EncAB-H; WebAB;
WhAm 1*

Duke, Patty (Anna Marie)
American. Actress
Won Oscar, 1963, Emmy, 1979, for *The
   Miracle Worker,* playing different roles.
b. Dec 14, 1946 in New York, New York
Source: *BiE&WWA; BioNews 74; CelR;
CurBio 63; FilmgC; InWom; IntMPA 75, 76,
77, 78, 79, 80, 81, 82; MotPP; MovMk;
NotNAT; WhoAm 74, 76, 78, 80, 82;
WhoAmW 66, 68, 70, 72, 74, 79; WhoHol A*

Duke, Robin (Anthony Hare)
English. Public Official, Author
Expert on Japanese culture; wrote *The Pillow
   Book of Sei Shanagon,* 1979.
b. Mar 21, 1916
d. Nov 27, 1984
Source: *ConAu 115; Who 82*

Duke, Vernon
[Vladimir Dukelsky]
American. Composer, Poet, Author
b. Oct 10, 1903 in Pskov, Russia
d. Jan 17, 1969 in Santa Monica, California
Source: *AmSCAP 66; BiE&WWA; ConAu
29R, P-2; CurBio 41, 69; DcCM; EncMT;
NewCBMT; WhAm 5*

Duke, Wayne
American. Athletic Director
Big-Ten Athletic Conference director, 1971--.
b. Nov 9, 1928 in Burlington, Iowa
Source: *WhoAm 80, 82*

Dukes, David
American. Actor
Played Leslie Slote in TV mini-series, "The
   Winds of War," 1983.
b. Jun 6, 1945 in San Francisco, California
Source: *NewYTBS 79; WhoAm 82*

Dulac, Edmund
French. Artist
Created fantastic, intricate scenes for fairy
   tales: *The Arabian Nights.*
b. Oct 22, 1882 in Toulouse, France
d. May 25, 1953 in England
Source: *AntBDN B; CarSB; DcBrBI; JBA 51*

Dull Knife
American. Indian Chief
Northern Cheyenne chief best known for
   Dull Knife Outbreak, 1878.
b. 1828
d. 1879
Source: *BioIn 4; REnAW*

Dullea, Keir
American. Actor
Appeared in *David and Lisa,* 1963; *2001: A
   Space Odyssey,* 1968.
b. May 30, 1936 in Cleveland, Ohio
Source: *CelR; CurBio 70; FilmgC; IntMPA
80, 81, 82; MotPP; MovMk; NotNAT;
WhoAm 80, 82; WhoHol A; WhoThe 77;
WorAl*

Dulles, Allen Welsh
American. Lawyer, Diplomat
Director of CIA, 1953-61.
b. Apr 7, 1893 in Watertown, New York
d. Jan 29, 1969 in Washington, District of
   Columbia
Source: *AmAu&B; ConAu 21R; CurBio 49,
69; ObitOF 79; WhAm 5; WhE&EA; WhWW-
II*

Dulles, Eleanor Lansing
American. Diplomat, Educator
b. Jun 1, 1895 in Watertown, New York
Source: *AmM&WS 73S; ConAu 9R; CurBio
62; ForWC 70; WhoAm 74, 76, 78, 80, 82;
WhoAmW 74; WhoWor 78*

Dulles, John Foster
American. Lawyer, Government Official
Secretary of State, 1953-59; advocated
   development of nuclear weapons.
b. Feb 25, 1888 in Washington, District of
   Columbia
d. May 24, 1959 in Washington, District of
   Columbia
Source: *AmAu&B; BiDrAC; BiDrUSE; ConAu
1NR; CurBio 44, 53, 59; EncAB-H; WebAB;
WhAm 3; WhAmP*

Duluth, Daniel
French. Explorer
Claimed upper Mississippi region, Lake
   Superior for France, c. 1678.
b. 1636 in Saint Germain, France
d. Feb 27, 1710 in Montreal, Quebec
Source: *BioIn 4, 5, 7, 9; DcAmB; NewCol 75;
WebBD 80; WhAm HS*

Dumas, Alexandre
[Dumas Pere]
French. Author, Dramatist
Best known works *The Three Musketeers,*
   1844; *The Count of Monte Cristo,* 1845.
b. Jul 24, 1802 in Villers-Cotterets, France
d. Dec 5, 1870 in Puys, France
Source: *AtlBL; BbD; BiD&SB; CarSB;*
CasWL; CnThe; CyWA; DcEuL; EuAu;
EvEuW; FilmgC; HsB&A; McGEWD;
MnBBF; NewC; OxEng; OxFr; PenC EUR;
RComWL; REn; REnWD; WhoChL

Dumas, Alexandre
[Dumas Fils]
French. Author, Dramatist
Play *La Dame aux Camelias,* 1852, basis for
   Verdi's opera, *La Traviata.*
b. Jul 27, 1824 in Paris, France
d. Nov 27, 1895 in Paris, France
Source: *AtlBL; BbD; BiD&SB; CasWL;*
CnThe; CyWA; DcBiA; DcEuL; EuAu;
EvEuW; REn

Dumas, Jean Baptiste Andre
Canadian. Scientist
b. Jun 4, 1925 in Montreal, Quebec
Source: *AmM&WS 73P*

DuMaurier, Daphne
[Lady Browning]
English. Author
Classic gothic novels include *Rebecca;*
   Jamaica Inn.
b. May 13, 1907 in London, England
Source: *Au&Wr 71; BiE&WWA; ConAu 5R;*
ConLC 6, 11; ConNov 72, 76; CurBio 40;
CyWA; DcLEL; EncMys; EvLB; FilmgC;
InWom; IntWW 74; LongCTC; ModBrL;
NewC; NotNAT; OxThe; PenC ENG; RAdv 1;
REn; TwCA, SUP; TwCWr; Who 74;
WhoThe 77A; WhoWor 74; WorAl; WrDr 76

DuMaurier, George Louis P B
English. Author, Artist
Wrote *The Martian,* 1896.
b. Mar 6, 1834 in Paris, France
d. Oct 8, 1896 in London, England
Source: *BbD; BiD&SB; BrAu 19; CasWL;*
Chambr 3; ChhPo, S2; CyWA; DcBiA;
DcEuL; DcLEL; EvLB; McGDA; MouLC 4;
NewC; NotNAT B; OxEng; OxThe; PenC
ENG; RAdv 1; REn

DuMaurier, Gerald Hubert, Sir
English. Producer
Greatest success in *Raffles,* 1906, made hero
   out of villian; father of Daphne
   DuMaurier.
b. Mar 26, 1873 in London, England
d. Apr 11, 1934 in London, England
Source: *CnThe; EncWT; Film 2; NewC;*
NotNAT A, B; OxThe; WhDW; WhScrn 77;
WhThe; WhoHol B

Dumke, Ralph
American. Actor
Supporting actor in *All the King's Men,*
   1949; *Invasion of the Body Snatchers,* 1956.
b. 1900
d. Jan 4, 1964 in Sherman Oaks, California
Source: *FilmgC; NotNAT B; WhScrn 74, 77;*
WhoHol B

Dummar, Melvin
American. Gas Station Attendant
Named heir in will purportedly written by
   Howard Hughes, later called forgery, 1976.
b. 1944
Source: *BioIn 10*

Dumont, Alberto Santos-
see: Santos-Dumont, Alberto

DuMont, Allen Balcom
American. Engineer
Pioneer in development of TV; made first
   feasible cathode ray tube.
b. Jan 29, 1901 in Brooklyn, New York
d. Nov 16, 1965 in New York, New York
Source: *CurBio 66; InSci; NewYTET*

Dumont, Margaret
[Margaret Baker]
American. Actress
Stately matron in seven Marx Brothers films:
   Animal Crackers, 1930; *A Night at the*
   Opera, 1935.
b. Oct 20, 1889 in New York, New York
d. Mar 6, 1965 in Los Angeles, California
Source: *BiDFilm; Film 2; FilmgC; MotPP;*
MovMk; ObitOF 79; OxFilm; ThFT; Vers A;
WhScrn 74, 77; WhoHol B; WorEFlm

Dumont d'Urville, Jules Sebastian Cesar
French. Navigator
Explored Australia, Oceania Islands, 1826-29;
   discovered Adelie Coast, Antarctica, 1837-
   40.
b. May 23, 1790 in France
d. May 8, 1842
Source: *CelCen; DcBiPP; Dis&D; NewCol 75;*
OxShips; WhDW

DuMotier, Marie Joseph Paul
see: Lafayette, Marie Joseph Paul, Marquis

Dumurq, Charles
[Alain Gauthier; Charles Gurmukh Sabhraj]
French. Murderer
Subject of book *Serpentine,* by Thomas
   Thompson.
b. 1944 in Saigon, Vietnam
Source: *BioIn 11*

Dun, Robert Graham
American. Financier
b. 1826 in Chillicothe, Ohio
d. 1900
Source: *DcAmB; WhAm 1*

Dunant, Jean Henri
Swiss. Philanthropist
Founded Red Cross, 1864; shared first Nobel
   Peace Prize, 1901.
b. May 8, 1828 in Geneva, Switzerland
d. Oct 30, 1910 in Heiden, Switzerland
Source: *WebBD 80*

Dunaway, Faye (Dorothy Faye)
American. Actress
Starred in *Bonnie and Clyde,* 1967; won
   Oscar, 1976, for *Network.*
b. Jan 14, 1941 in Tallahassee, Florida
Source: *BiDFilm; BkPepl; CelR; CurBio 72;
FilmgC; InWom; IntMPA 75, 76, 77, 78, 79,
80, 81, 82; MotPP; MovMk; NewYTBS 74;
OxFilm; WhoAm 74, 76, 78, 80, 82;
WhoAmW 70, 72, 74, 79; WhoHol A;
WhoThe 77; WorEFlm*

Dunbar, Aynsley
see: Journey

Dunbar, Helen Flanders
American. Psychiatrist, Author
Pioneer in psychosomatic medicine; founded
   American Psychosomatic Society, 1942.
b. May 14, 1902 in Chicago, Illinois
d. Aug 21, 1959 in South Kent, Connecticut
Source: *NotAW MOD*

Dunbar, Paul Laurence
American. Poet, Author
Published 24 volumes of fiction, poetry;
   poems used Negro folk material, dialect.
b. Jun 27, 1872 in Dayton, Ohio
d. Feb 9, 1906 in Dayton, Ohio
Source: *AmAu; AmAu&B; AmBi; ApCAB
SUP; BiD&SB; BkCL; BlkAWP; CasWL;
Chambr 3; ChhPo, S1, S2; CnDAL; DcAmAu;
DcAmB; DcNAA; OhA&B; OxAmL; PenC
AM; RAdv 1; REn; REnAL; TwCBDA;
WebAB; WebE&AL; WhAm 1*

Dunbar, William
Scottish. Poet
Scottish Chaucerian who wrote *Dance of the
   Seven Deadly Sins,* 1503-08.
b. 1460
d. 1520
Source: *NewCol 75; OxEng; REn; WebBD 80*

Duncan I
Scottish. King
d. 1040
Source: *NewC*

Duncan, Augustin
American. Actor, Producer
Brother of Isadora Duncan; co-founder, NY
   Theatre Guild.
b. Apr 12, 1873 in San Francisco, California
d. Feb 20, 1954 in New York, New York
Source: *NotNAT B; ObitOF 79; WhThe*

Duncan, Charles William, Jr.
American. Government Official
b. Sep 9, 1926 in Houston, Texas
Source: *BioIn 12; CurBio 80; IntWW 79;
NewYTBS 79; WhoAm 80, 82; WhoAmP 81;
WhoGov 77*

Duncan, David Douglas
American. Photojournalist, Author
Covered most major events of past 35 yrs.,
   including Japan's surrender to US aboard
   USS Missouri, 1945.
b. Jan 23, 1916 in Kansas City, Missouri
Source: *AuNews 1; ConPhot; CurBio 68;
MacBEP; WhoAm 80, 82; WhoWor 74*

Duncan, Isadora
American. Dancer
Revolutionized interpretative dancing.
b. May 27, 1878 in San Francisco, California
d. Sep 14, 1927 in Nice, France
Source: *AmAu&B; AmBi; DcAmB; EncAB-H;
NotAW; OxAmL; REn; REnAL; WebAB;
WhAm 4, HSA*

Duncan, Robert
American. Author
b. Jan 7, 1919 in Oakland, California
Source: *AmAu&B; CasWL; ChhPo, S2;
ConAu 9R; ConLC 1, 2, 4, 7, 15; ConP 70,
75; CroCAP; DrAP 75; ModAL, S1; PenC
AM; RAdv 1; REn; REnAL; WebE&AL;
WhoAm 82; WorAu; WrDr 80*

Duncan, Sandy
American. Actress
Starred on Broadway as Peter Pan, 1980.
b. Feb 20, 1946 in Tyler, Texas
Source: *BioIn 12; CurBio 80; EncMT; FilmgC; IntMPA 75, 76, 77, 78, 79, 80, 81, 82; WhoAm 82; WhoHol A; WhoThe 77*

Duncan, Todd
American. Singer, Actor, Educator
b. Feb 12, 1903 in Danville, Kentucky
Source: *BiE&WWA; CurBio 42; EncMT; NotNAT; PIP&P; WhoHol A; WhoThe 77A*

Duncanson, Robert Scott
American. Artist
Landscape painter commissioned to do series of murals for Taft Museum, Cincinnati, 1840s.
b. 1817 in Cincinnati, Ohio
d. Dec 21, 1872 in Detroit, Michigan
Source: *AfroAA; DcAmArt; NegAl 83; WhoAmA 82*

Dundee, Angelo Mirena, Jr.
American. Boxing Trainer
Trainer of Muhammad Ali, "Sugar" Ray Leonard.
b. Aug 30, 1921 in Philadelphia, Pennsylvania
Source: *BioNews 74; NewYTBS 81*

Dundee, Johnny
[Giuseppe Carrora]
American. Boxer
Popular featherweight boxing champion, 1923-25; Boxing Hall of Fame, 1957.
b. Nov 22, 1893 in Sciacca, Italy
d. Apr 22, 1965 in East Orange, New Jersey
Source: *DcAmB S7; WhoBox 74*

Dunham, Katherine
American. Dancer, Choreographer
b. Jun 22, 1910 in Chicago, Illinois
Source: *BiE&WWA; BlkAWP; ConAu 65; CurBio 41; HerW; InWom; IntWW 74; LivgBAA; NotNAT; REnAL; WebAB; WhoAm 74; WhoBlA 75; WhoE 74; WhoHol A; WhoThe 77; WhoWor 78; WomPO 76*

Dunham, "Sonny" (Elmer Lewis)
American. Musician
b. 1914 in Brockton, Massachusetts
Source: *WhoJazz 72*

Dunhill, Alfred Henry
English. Tobacco Executive
Pres., Dunhill Tobacco Group; author *The Gentle Art of Smoking,* 1954.
b. 1896
d. Jul 8, 1971 in Sussex, England
Source: *NewYTBE 71*

Duniway, Abigail Jane Scott
American. Feminist, Suffragette
First registered woman voter in Oregon.
b. Oct 22, 1834 in Groveland, Illinois
d. Oct 11, 1915
Source: *Alli SUP; AmAu; AmAu&B; AmBi; AmWom; DcAmB; DcNAA; InWom; NotAW; WhAm 4; WhAmP; WomWWA 14*

Dunlap, William
American. Author, Artist
Wrote 65 plays: *History of American Theater,* 1832; did portrait of George Washington.
b. Feb 11, 1766 in Perth Amboy, New Jersey
d. Sep 28, 1839 in New York, New York
Source: *Alli; AmAu; AmAu&B; AmBi; ApCAB; BbD; BiDAmM; BiD&SB; BiDLA; BioIn 7, 8, 9, 10; BnEnAmA; CasWL; CnDAL; CnThe; CyAL 2; DcAmArt; DcAmAu; DcAmB; DcNAA; Drake; EncWT; EvLB; McGDA; McGEWB; NatCAB 16; NewYHSD; NotNAT A, B; OxAmL; OxThe; PenC AM; PIP&P; REnAL; REnWD; TwCBDA; WebAB; WebE&AL; WhAm HS*

Dunlop, Frank
English. Director
Founder, director of Young Vic Theatre, 1969.
b. Feb 15, 1927 in Leeds, England
Source: *PIP&P A; Who 82; WhoThe 81*

Dunlop, John Boyd
Scottish. Inventor
Patented pneumatic tire, 1888.
b. Feb 5, 1840 in Scotland
d. 1921
Source: *Entr; WebBD 80*

Dunlop, John Thomas
American. Economist
Secretary of Labor under Gerald Ford, 1975-76; wrote *Business and Public Policy,* 1980.
b. Jun 5, 1914 in Placerville, California
Source: *AmM&WS 73S; BioIn 2, 8, 9, 10, 11; ConAu 13R; WhoAm 78, 80, 82, 84; WhoE 74*

Dunn, Alan
American. Cartoonist, Artist
b. Aug 11, 1900 in Belmar, New Jersey
d. May 20, 1974 in New York, New York
Source: *AmAu&B; ConAu 33R, 49, P-2;
NewYTBS 74; WhAm 6; WhoAm 74;
WhoAmA 73; WhoWor 78*

Dunn, James Howard
American. Actor
Won Oscar for *A Tree Grows in Brooklyn,*
1945.
b. Nov 2, 1905 in New York, New York
d. Sep 3, 1967 in Santa Monica, California
Source: *BiE&WWA; FilmgC; HolP 30;
MotPP; MovMk; ObitOF 79; WhScrn 74, 77;
WhoHol B; WorAl*

Dunn, Michael
[Gary Neil Miller]
American. Actor
Dwarf actor whose movie credits include
Ship of Fools, 1965; appeared in TV series
"Wild, Wild West," 1965-70.
b. Oct 20, 1934 in Shattuck, Oklahoma
d. Aug 29, 1973 in London, England
Source: *BiE&WWA; FilmgC; MotPP; MovMk;
NewYTBE 73; WhScrn 77; WhoHol B*

Dunn, Mignon
American. Opera Singer
b. in Memphis, Tennessee
Source: *NewYTBE 73; WhoAm 74, 76, 78,
80, 82*

Dunne, Dominique
American. Actress
Starred in *Poltergeist,* 1982; allegedly
strangled by her boyfriend.
b. 1960
d. Nov 4, 1982 in Los Angeles, California
Source: *NF*

Dunne, Finley Peter
American. Humorist, Author, Editor
Best known as creator of Mr. Dooley, who
commented on political issues for 30 years.
b. Jul 10, 1867 in Chicago, Illinois
d. Apr 24, 1936 in New York, New York
Source: *AmAu&B; AmBi; BiD&SB; CathA
1930; Chambr 3; ConAmL; DcAmAu; DcAmB
S2; DcLEL; DcNAA; EncAB-H; EvLB;
LongCTC; OxAmL; OxEng; PenC AM; REn;
REnAL; TwCA, SUP; TwCBDA; WebAB;
WhAm 1; WhLit*

Dunne, Irene Marie
American. Actress
Five-time Oscar nominee; best known for
lead in *I Remember Mama,* 1948.
b. Dec 20, 1904 in Louisville, Kentucky
Source: *BiDFilm; BiE&WWA; CmMov;
CurBio 45; FilmgC; InWom; IntMPA 75, 76,
77, 78, 79, 80, 81, 82; MotPP; MovMk;
OxFilm; ThFT; WhoAm 74; WhoHol A;
WomWMM; WorAl; WorEFlm*

Dunne, John Gregory
American. Author
Wrote *True Confessions,* 1977; film starred
Robert DeNiro, 1981.
b. May 25, 1932 in Hartford, Connecticut
Source: *WorAl; WrDr 82*

Dunne, John William
English. Philosopher, Inventor
Demonstrated immortality of soul, principle
of serialism through mathematics; invented
first military plane in Britain.
b. 1875
d. Aug 24, 1949 in London, England
Source: *DcLEL; EvLB; InSci; REn; WhE&EA*

Dunninger, Joseph
American. Astrologer, Magician
b. Apr 28, 1896 in New York, New York
d. Mar 9, 1975 in Cliffside Park, New Jersey
Source: *CurBio 44, 75N; NewYTBS 75;
WhAm 6*

Dunnock, Mildred
American. Actress
Oscar nominee for *Death of a Salesman,*
1952, which she also played on Broadway,
TV.
b. Jan 25, 1906 in Baltimore, Maryland
Source: *BiE&WWA; CurBio 55; FilmgC;
InWom; IntMPA 75, 76, 77, 78, 79, 80, 81,
82; MotPP; MovMk; NotNAT; PIP&P; Vers A;
WhoAm 80, 82; WhoAmW 74; WhoHol A;
WhoThe 81; WorAl*

Dunoyer de Segonzac, Andre
French. Artist
b. Jul 6, 1884 in France
d. Sep 17, 1974
Source: *ConAu 53; IntWW 74; NewYTBS 74;
WhAm 6; Who 74; WhoGrA 62; WhoWor 78*

Duns Scotus, John
"Subtle Doctor"
Scottish. Theologian
Believed in "divine will" rather than "divine
   intellect."
b. 1266 in Duns, Scotland
d. Nov 8, 1308 in Cologne, Germany
Source: *Alli; LuthC 75; McGEWB; NewC;
REn*

Dunsany, Edward J M Plunkett, Baron
Irish. Author
Wrote many plays of fantasy and myth for
   Abbey Theatre.
b. Jul 24, 1878 in London, England
d. Oct 25, 1957 in Dublin, Ireland
Source: *AtlBL; CasWL; ChhPo, S1, S2;
CnMD; CnThe; DcLEL; EncMys; EvLB; JBA
34; LongCTC; McGEWD; ModBrL; ModWD;
NewC; Novels; OxEng; PenC ENG; REn;
REnWD; TwCA, SUP; TwCWr; WhDW*

Duong Van Minh
"Big Minh"
Vietnamese. General
b. Feb 19, 1916 in My Tho, Vietnam
Source: *BioIn 10; IntWW 75*

Duplessis, Marie
French. Courtesan, Model
Source: *InWom; OxFr*

Duplessis, Maurice le Noblet
Canadian. Political Leader
b. Apr 20, 1890 in Three Rivers, Quebec
d. Sep 7, 1959 in Schefferville, Quebec
Source: *CurBio 59, 59; DcCathB; ObitOF 79;
ObitT 1951; OxCan; WhAm 3*

DuPont, Clifford Walter
South African. President
b. Dec 6, 1905 in London, England
d. Jun 28, 1978 in Salisbury, Rhodesia
Source: *AfSS 78; IntWW 78; ObitOF 79;
WhoGov 72; WhoWor 74*

DuPont, Eleuthere Irenee
American. Industrialist
b. Jun 24, 1771 in Paris, France
d. Oct 31, 1834
Source: *BioIn 2, 4, 5, 6, 8, 9; REn*

DuPont, Margaret Osborne
American. Tennis Player
b. Mar 4, 1918
Source: *InWom*

DuPont, Pierre Samuel
see: DuPont de Nemours, Pierre Samuel

DuPont, Pierre Samuel, III
American. Business Executive
b. Jan 1, 1911 in Wilmington, Delaware
Source: *WhoAm 74; WhoF&I 74*

DuPont, Pierre Samuel, IV
American. Politician
Rep. governor of DE, 1977-85.
b. Jan 22, 1935 in Wilmington, Delaware
Source: *CngDr 74; WhoAm 82; WhoAmP 73;
WhoE 74; WhoGov 75*

DuPont de Nemours, Pierre Samuel
French. Economist
b. Sep 14, 1739 in Paris, France
d. Aug 7, 1817 in Delaware
Source: *ApCAB; BiD&SB; McGEWB; OxFr;
REn; TwCBDA*

DuPre, Jacqueline
English. Musician
b. Jan 26, 1945 in Oxford, England
Source: *CurBio 70; IntWW 74, 75, 76, 77,
78, 79, 80, 81; Who 74; WhoAm 82;
WhoMus 72*

DuPre, Marcel
French. Composer, Musician
b. May 3, 1886 in Rouen, France
d. May 30, 1971 in Meudon, France
Source: *DcCM; NewYTBE 71; WhAm 5*

Dupree, Minnie
American. Actress
b. Jan 19, 1873 in San Francisco, California
d. May 23, 1947 in New York, New York
Source: *BioIn 1; Film 2; FilmgC; NotNAT B;
ThFT; WhScrn 74, 77; WhThe; WhoStg 1908*

DuPrez, Gilbert
French. Opera Singer, Composer
b. Dec 6, 1806 in Paris, France
d. Sep 23, 1896 in Passy, France
Source: *NewEOp 71*

Dupuy, Diane
Canadian. Puppeteer
Founded Famous People Players, puppet
   troupe largely comprised of mentally
   handicapped adults.
b. 1948 in Hamilton, Ontario
Source: *NF*

Duran, Roberto
"Hands of Stone"
Panamanian. Boxer
One of most feared men in boxing who held
   world titles in three divisions; record was
   77-6, 57 KOs.
b. Jun 16, 1951 in Chorillo, Panama
Source: *BioIn 11; CurBio 80*

Duran Duran
[Simon LeBon; Nick Rhodes; Andy Taylor;
John Taylor; Roger Taylor]
English. Music Group
New Romantic band formed, 1978; hit single
"Hungry Like a Wolf," 1982.
Source: RolSEnR 83

Durand, Asher Brown
American. Artist
b. Aug 21, 1796 in Jefferson, New Jersey
d. Sep 17, 1886 in Jefferson, New Jersey
Source: AmAu&B; AmBi; ApCAB; DcAmB;
EarABI; OxAmL; TwCBDA; WebAB; WhAm
HS

Durant, Ariel (Ida Ariel Ethel Kaufman)
[Mrs. William James Durant]
American. Author
Collaborated with husband, Will, on Story of
Civilization.
b. May 10, 1898 in Proskurov, Russia
d. Oct 25, 1981 in Los Angeles, California
Source: AmWomWr; AnObit 1981; ASpks;
BioIn 10, 11; CelR; ConAu 4NR, 9R;
NewYTBS 75, 81; WhoAm 74, 76, 78, 80;
WhoAmW 66, 68, 70, 72, 74, 75, 77;
WhoWest 74, 76; WhoWor 74, 76

Durant, Thomas Clark
American. Financier, Railroad Executive
Chief organizer, Union Pacific, who helped
build first transcontinental railroad, 1869.
b. Feb 6, 1820 in Lee, Massachusetts
d. Oct 5, 1885 in North Creek, New York
Source: AmBi; BioIn 6; DcAmB; McGEWB;
REnAW; WebAB; WhAm HS; WorAl

Durant, William Crapo
American. Auto Manufacturer
Carriage-maker, who co-founded Chevrolet,
founded General Motors, 1908.
b. Dec 8, 1861 in Boston, Massachusetts
d. Mar 18, 1947 in New York, New York
Source: DcAmB S4; EncAB-H; WebAB;
WhAm 2

Durant, Will(iam James)
American. Historian, Author
Produced, with wife Ida, 11-volume, 1926
Pulitzer winner Story of Civilization.
b. Nov 5, 1885 in North Adams,
Massachusetts
d. Nov 7, 1981 in Los Angeles, California
Source: AmAu&B; BioIn 3, 4, 6, 7, 8, 9, 10,
11; CelR; ConAu 9R, 4NR; CurBio 64, 82;
DcLEL; EvLB; IntWW 74, 76, 77, 78;
LinLib L, S; LongCTC; NewYTBS 75, 81;
OxAmH; REn; REnAL; TwCA, SUP; WebAB;
WhNAA; Who 74; WhoAm 74, 76, 78, 80;
WhoWest 74, 78; WhoWor 74

Durante, Francesco
Italian. Composer
Instrumental in development of 18th c.
Neapolitan church music.
b. Mar 31, 1684 in Frattamaggiore, Italy
d. Aug 13, 1755 in Naples, Italy
Source: DcBiPP; NewEOp 71; OxMus

Durante, Jimmy (James Francis)
"Ol' Schnozzola"
American. Comedian, Singer, Pianist
Entertainer for over 60 years; nose insured
for $100,000 with Lloyd's of London.
b. Feb 10, 1893 in New York, New York
d. Jan 29, 1980 in Santa Monica, California
Source: AmSCAP 66; BiE&WWA; CelR;
CurBio 46, 80; EncMT; IntMPA 75, 76, 77;
MotPP; MovMk; NotNAT; WebAB; WhoAm
74, 76, 78, 80; WhoHol A; WhoThe 77;
WhoWor 78

Duranty, Walter
English. Journalist, Author
b. May 25, 1884 in Liverpool, England
d. Oct 3, 1957 in Orlando, Florida
Source: AmAu&B; CurBio 43, 58; OxAmL;
REnAL; TwCA, SUP; WhAm 3

Duras, Marguerite, pseud.
[Marguerite Donnadieu]
French. Author
b. Apr 4, 1914 in Gia Dinh, French
Indochina
Source: CasWL; CnMD SUP; CnThe; ConAu
25R; ConLC 3, 6, 11; CroCD; CurBio 85;
EncWL; EncWT; EvEuW; FilmgC; InWom;
IntAu&W 76, 77; IntWW 77, 78; McGEWD;
ModFrL; ModRL; ModWD; OxFilm; PenC
EUR; REn; REnWD; TwCWr; WhoThe 72;
WhoTwCL; WomWMM; WorAu; WorEFlm

Durbin, Deanna
Canadian. Actress
Shared special Oscar with Mickey Rooney,
1938, as "spirit and personification of
youth."
b. Dec 4, 1921 in Winnipeg, Manitoba
Source: BiDAmM; BiDFilm; CmMov;
CmpEPM; CurBio 41; FilmgC; InWom;
MotPP; MovMk; OxFilm; ThFT; WhoHol A;
WorEFlm

Duren, Ryne (Rinold George)
American. Baseball Player
b. Feb 22, 1929 in Cazenovia, Wisconsin
Source: BaseEn 85; BioIn 5, 7, 11; WhoProB
73

Durenberger, David Ferdinand
American. Politician
Liberal Rep. senator from MN, 1978--.
b. Aug 19, 1934 in Saint Cloud, Minnesota
Source: *AlmAP 80; CngDr 79; St&PR 75;
WhoAm 78, 80, 82, 84; WhoAmP 79*

Durer, Albrecht
German. Artist
b. May 21, 1471 in Nuremberg, Germany
d. Apr 6, 1528 in Nuremberg, Germany
Source: *AtlBL; NewC; OxGer; REn*

Durham, Leon
"Bull"
American. Baseball Player
b. Jul 31, 1957 in Cincinnati, Ohio
Source: *BaseEn 85*

Durie, Jo
English. Tennis Player
Britain's number-one woman player, 1983.
b. Jun 27, 1960 in Bristol, England
Source: *WhoIntT*

Durkee, Eugene R
American. Manufacturer
Introduced first commercially packaged salad
dressing, 1857.
b. 1825
d. 1902
Source: *Entr*

Durkheim, Emile
French. Sociologist
A founder of modern sociology who traced
origin of religious, moral v alues to a
collective consciousness.
b. Apr 15, 1858 in Epinal, France
d. Nov 15, 1917 in Paris, France
Source: *ClDMEL; OxFr*

Durning, Charles
American. Actor
Co-starred in *Tootsie,* 1982.
b. Feb 28, 1923 in Highland Falls, New
York
Source: *IntMPA 82; NotNAT; PlP&P A;
WhoAm 82, 84; WhoHol A*

Durocher, Leo Ernest
"The Lip"
American. Baseball Player, Baseball Manager
Infielder, 1925-45; coined saying "Nice guys
finish last."
b. Jul 27, 1906 in West Springfield,
Massachusetts
Source: *BaseEn 85; CelR; CurBio 40, 50;
NewYTBE 71; NewYTBS 81; WebAB;
WhoAm 82; WhoProB 73*

Durr, Francoise
French. Tennis Player
b. Dec 25, 1942 in Algiers, Algeria
Source: *BioIn 9*

Durrell, Gerald Malcolm
British. Zoologist
b. Jan 7, 1925 in Jamshedpur, India
Source: *Au&Wr 71; AuBYP; ConAu 5R;
IntWW 74; LongCTC; NewC; REn; SmATA
8; TwCWr; Who 74; WhoWor 74; WorAu;
WrDr 76*

Durrell, Lawrence George
[Charles Norden, pseud.]
English. Author
His four novels, comprising *The Alexandria
Quartet,* finished in 1960.
b. Feb 27, 1912 in Darjeeling, India
Source: *Au&Wr 71; CasWL; ChhPo;
CnE&AP; CnMD; CnMWL; ConAu 9R;
ConLC 1, 4, 6; ConNov 72, 76; ConP 70, 75;
CurBio 63; DcLEL; EncWL; EvLB; IntWW
74; LongCTC; ModBrL, S1; ModWD; NewC;
OxEng; PenC ENG; RAdv 1; REn; TwCA
SUP; TwCWr; WebE&AL; Who 74;
WhoTwCL; WhoWor 74; WorAl; WrDr 82*

Durrenmatt, Friedrich
[Duerrenmatt, Friedrich]
Swiss. Author
Writings include *The Visit; The Physicists.*
b. Jan 5, 1921 in Konolfingen, Switzerland
Source: *Au&Wr 71; BiE&WWA; CasWL;
CnMD; CnThe; ConAu 17R; ConLC 1, 4, 8,
11, 15; CroCD; EncWL; EvEuW; IntWW 74;
McGEWD; ModGL; ModWD; NotNAT;
OxGer; OxThe; PenC EUR; PlP&P; REn;
REnWD; TwCWr; Who 82; WhoThe 81;
WhoTwCL; WhoWor 74; WorAu*

Durrie, George Henry
American. Artist
Genre landscapist, who drew farm, winter
scenes reproduced by Currier and Ives.
b. Jun 6, 1820 in Hartford, Connecticut
d. Oct 15, 1863 in New Haven, Connecticut
Source: *BnEnAmA; DcAmArt; McGDA;
NewYHSD; WhAm HS*

Durslag, Melvin
American. Journalist
b. Apr 29, 1921 in Chicago, Illinois
Source: *WhoAm 74, 76, 78, 80, 82; WhoWest
84*

Duryea, Charles Edgar
"Father of the Automobile"
American. Inventor, Manufacturer
Organized Duryea Motor Wagon Co., 1895;
    sold first car, 1896.
b. Dec 15, 1862 in Canton, Illinois
d. Sep 28, 1938 in Philadelphia, Pennsylvania
Source: *DcAmB S2; WebAB; WhAm HSA, 4*

Duryea, Dan
American. Actor
Cast as villain in such films as *The Little
    Foxes,* 1941; *Another Part of the Forest,*
    1948.
b. Jan 23, 1907 in White Plains, New York
d. Jun 7, 1968 in Los Angeles, California
Source: *BiDFilm; CmMov; FilmgC; HolP 40;
MotPP; MovMk; NotNAT B; ObitOF 79;
OxFilm; WhAm 5; WhScrn 74, 77; WhoHol
B; WorAl; WorEFlm*

Duryea, J(ames) Frank
American. Inventor
Designed first successful gasoline-powered car
    in US; won first auto race, Chicago, 1895.
b. Oct 8, 1869 in Washburn, Illinois
d. Feb 15, 1967 in Saybrook, Connecticut
Source: *BioIn 8; OxAmH*

DuSable, Jean Baptiste
American. Pioneer
Built first house, opened first trading post on
    site of modern-day Chicago.
b. 1750
d. Aug 28, 1818 in Saint Charles, Missouri
Source: *InB&W 80; WebAB; WhAm HS, HS*

Duse, Eleanora
Italian. Actress
Best known for her role in Dumas's play *La
    Dame aux Camelias.*
b. 1859 in Vigerano, Italy
d. Apr 23, 1924 in Pittsburgh, Pennsylvania
Source: *InWom; REn; WhScrn 74, 77;
WhoHol B; WhoStg 1908; WorEFlm*

Dussault, Nancy
American. Actress, Singer
Plays Muriel Rush on TV series "Too Close
    for Comfort," 1980--.
b. Jun 30, 1936 in Pensacola, Florida
Source: *BiE&WWA; BioIn 11; EncMT;
NewYTBS 77; NotNAT; WhoThe 72, 77, 81*

Dutton, E(dward) P(ayson)
American. Publisher
Founded E P Dutton publishing house, 1858.
b. Jan 4, 1831 in Keene, New Hampshire
d. Sep 6, 1923
Source: *AmAu&B; ChhPo; WhAm 1*

Dutton, Ralph Stawell
English. Historian
Wrote on stately residences: *The English
    House.*
b. Aug 25, 1898 in Hampshire, England
d. Apr 20, 1985
Source: *ConAu 116; Who 85*

Duvalier, Francois
"Papa Doc"
Haitian. President
b. Apr 14, 1907 in Port-au-Prince, Haiti
d. Apr 21, 1971 in Port-au-Prince, Haiti
Source: *CurBio 58, 71; NewYTBE 71; WhAm
5*

Duvalier, Jean-Claude
"Baby Doc"
Haitian. Political Leader
Became "president for life" of Haiti, 1970;
    overthrown in coup, 1986, fled into exile.
b. Jul 3, 1951 in Port-au-Prince, Haiti
Source: *CurBio 72; IntWW 74; NewYTBE 71;
WhoGov 75; WhoWor 78*

Duvall, Robert Selden
American. Actor
Best known for *Tender Mercies,* 1983; *The
    Great Santini,* 1980.
b. Jan 5, 1931 in San Diego, California
Source: *FilmEn; FilmgC; IntMPA 81, 82;
MovMk; NewYTBE 72; NewYTBS 81;
WhoAm 82; WhoHol A; WorAl*

Duvall, Shelley
American. Actress
Appeared in films *Nashville,* 1975; *Popeye,*
    1979.
b. Jul 7, 1949 in Houston, Texas
Source: *BioNews 74; FilmEn; IntMPA 82;
NewYTBS 77; WhoAm 82; WhoHol A; WorAl*

Duveen, Joseph, Sir
English. Art Collector
b. Oct 14, 1869 in Hull, England
d. May 25, 1939 in London, England
Source: *DcNaB 1931; OxAmH; WhE&EA*

Duveneck, Frank
American. Artist, Educator
b. Oct 9, 1848 in Covington, Kentucky
d. Jan 3, 1919 in Cincinnati, Ohio
Source: *BioIn 4, 7, 8, 9; OxAmL; REn;
WebAB; WhAm 1*

Duveyrier, Anne Honore
[Melesville, pseud.]
French. Dramatist, Librettist
b. Nov 13, 1787 in Paris, France
d. Nov 1865 in Paris, France
Source: *InWom*

Duvivier, Julien
French. Director
Best known for films *Pepe le Moko; Maria Chapdelaine.*
b. Oct 8, 1896 in Lille, France
d. Oct 29, 1967 in Paris, France
Source: *BiDFilm; CurBio 43, 68; DcFM; FilmgC; MovMk; ObitOF 79; ObitT 1961; OxFilm; WorEFlm*

Duyckinck, Evert Augustus
American. Editor
Co-edited *New York Literary World*, 1847-53; compiled two-volume *Cyclopedia of American Literature*, 1855.
b. Nov 23, 1816 in New York, New York
d. Aug 13, 1878 in New York, New York
Source: *Alli, SUP; AmAu; AmAu&B; AmBi; ApCAB; BbD; BiD&SB; CyAL 2; DcAmAu; DcAmB; DcEnL; DcLB 3; DcNAA; Drake; OxAmL; REnAL; TwCBDA; WhAm HS*

Dvorak, Ann
American. Actress
Starred in *Scarface*, 1932.
b. Aug 2, 1912 in New York, New York
d. Dec 10, 1979 in Honolulu, Hawaii
Source: *Film 2; FilmgC; HolP 30; MotPP; MovMk; ThFT; WhoHol A*

Dvorak, Anton
Czech. Composer
Best known for symphony in E minor, *From the New World*, 1892-95.
b. Sep 8, 1841 in Nalahozeves, Bohemia
d. May 1, 1904 in Prague, Bohemia
Source: *AtlBL; OxAmL; REn; REnAL; WhAm HS*

Dwan, Allan
[Joseph Aloysius Dwan]
Canadian. Director
Directed estimated 1,850 films, 1909-61.
b. Apr 3, 1885 in Toronto, Ontario
d. Dec 21, 1981 in Woodland Hills, California
Source: *AnObit 1981; BiDFilm; DcFM; FilmgC; IntMPA 82; MovMk; NewYTBS 81; OxFilm; TwYS A; WhAm 8; WorEFlm*

Dwiggins, Don
American. Children's Author
b. Nov 15, 1913 in Plainfield, New Jersey
Source: *ConAu 17R; SmATA 4*

Dwiggins, William Addison
American. Type Designer, Illustrator
b. Jun 19, 1880 in Martinsville, Ohio
d. Dec 25, 1956 in Hingham, Massachusetts
Source: *AmAu&B; IlsCB 1744, 1946; OhA&B; OxAmL; REnAL; WhAm 3*

Dwight, Timothy
American. Author, Poet, Clergyman
Pres., Yale U., 1795-1817; writings include verse *Conquest of Canaan*, 1785.
b. May 14, 1752 in Northampton, Massachusetts
d. Jan 11, 1817 in New Haven, Connecticut
Source: *AmAu; AmAu&B; AmBi; ApCAB; BiD&SB; BiDLA; CasWL; CnDAL; CyAL 1; DcAmAu; DcAmB; DcEnL; DcNAA; Drake; EncAB-H; EvLB; McGEWB; NatCAB 1; OxAmL; PenC AM; PoChrch; REn; REnAL; TwCBDA; WebAB; WebE&AL; WhAm HS*

Dwyer, Cynthia
"53rd Hostage"
American. Journalist
Free-lance writer, imprisoned for attempting to free 52 American hostages in Iran; released, Feb 1981.
b. 1931 in Little Rock, Arkansas
Source: *BioIn 12*

Dwyer, Florence Price
American. Congresswoman
b. Jul 4, 1902 in Reading, Pennsylvania
d. Feb 29, 1976 in Elizabeth, New Jersey
Source: *BiDrAC; InWom; WhoAm 74; WhoAmP 73; WhoE 74; WhoGov 75*

Dyce. Alexander
Scottish. Historian, Critic
Noted for edition of Shakespeare, 1857.
b. Jun 30, 1798 in Edinburgh, Scotland
d. May 15, 1869
Source: *NewCol 75; WebBD 80*

Dyce, William
Scottish. Artist
Historical, portrait painter of House of Parliament frescoes, 1848.
b. Sep 19, 1806 in Aberdeen, Scotland
d. Feb 14, 1864 in Streatham, England
Source: *WebBD 80*

Dyck, Anthony van
Flemish. Artist
Religious, portrait painter who was Ruben's pupil, court painter to England's Charles I, 1632.
b. 1599 in Antwerp, Belgium
d. 1641 in London, England
Source: *McGDA*

Dyer, Charles
English. Author, Actor, Director
b. Jul 17, 1928 in Shrewsbury, England
Source: *Au&Wr 71; BiE&WWA; ConAu 21R; CroCD; NotNAT; Who 74; WrDr 80*

Dyer, Edward, Sir
English. Diplomat, Poet
Most famous poem begins "My mind to me
a kingdom is," a description of
contentment.
b. 1545 in Somerset, England
d. May 1607 in London, England
Source: *Alli; BiD&SB; BrAu; CasWL; Chambr
1; CnE&AP; CroE&S; DcBiPP; DcEuL;
EvLB; NewC; OxEng; REn*

Dyer, Wayne
American. Author
Wrote *Your Erroneous Zones,* 1976; *The
Sky's the Limit,* 1980.
b. May 10, 1940 in Detroit, Michigan
Source: *ConAu 69; WhoAm 82*

Dyer-Bennet, Richard
American. Singer
b. Oct 6, 1913 in Leicester, England
Source: *CurBio 44; EncFCWM 69; WhoAm
74*

Dykstra, John
American. Businessman
b. Apr 16, 1898 in Steins, Netherlands
Source: *CurBio 63*

Dylan, Bob
[Robert Zimmerman]
American. Singer, Songwriter
Songs include "Blowin' in the Wind," 1962;
"The Times They are a'Changin," 1964.
b. May 24, 1941 in Hibbing, Minnesota
Source: *AmAu&B; AmSCAP 66; BkPepl;
CelR; ConAu 41R; ConLC 3, 4, 6; ConP 70,
75; EncAB-H; EncFCWM 69; IntAu&W 82;
IntWW 82; RkOn 84; WebAB; WhoAm 82;
WhoE 74; WrDr 82*

Dyson, Freeman John
English. Physicist, Educator
b. Dec 15, 1923 in Crowthorne, England
Source: *BioIn 12; ConAu 89; CurBio 80;
WhoAm 82*

Dzerzhinsky, Felix Edmundovich
Russian. Politician
Took part in Polish, Russian revolutions;
held several high offices in Soviet govt.
b. 1877 in Poland
d. 1926 in U.S.S.R.
Source: *EncE 75; McGEWB; SpyCS*

Dzhanibekov, Vladimir Alexandrovich
Russian. Cosmonaut
b. 1942
Source: *BioIn 10*

E

E, Sheila
see: Sheila E

E-Street Band
[Roy Bittan; Clarence Clemons; Daniel Paul
Federici, Nils Lofgren, Patty Scialfa, Garry
Wayne Tallent, Max M. Weinberg]
American. Music Group
Back-up band for Bruce Springsteen.
Source: *NF*

Eads, James Buchanan
American. Scientist, Engineer
Built Eads Bridge across the Mississippi at
St. Louis, 1867-74.
b. May 23, 1820 in Lawrenceburg, Indiana
d. Mar 8, 1887 in Nassau, Bahamas
Source: *Alli SUP; AmBi; ApCAB; DcAmAu;
DcAmB; DcAmDH; DcNAA; EncAB-H; IndAu
1917; REnAW; TwCBDA; WebAB; WhAm
HS*

Eagels, Jeanne
American. Actress
Broadway star as Sadie Thompson in *Rain,*
1922-26; died from heroin overdose.
b. Jun 26, 1894 in Kansas City, Missouri
d. Oct 3, 1929 in New York, New York
Source: *AmBi; DcAmB; FamA&A; FilmEn;
FilmgC; InWom; LibW; NotAW,; ThFT;
TwYS; WhAm 1; WhScrn 77; WhoHol B;
WorAl*

Eagles, The
[Don Felder; Glenn Frey; Don Henley;
Bernie Leadon; Randy Meiser;Tim
Schmidt; Joe Walsh]
American. Music Group
Sold over 40 million albums; *The Long Run,*
1979, was double platinum.
Source: *BkPepl; EncPR&S 74; IlEncRk;
RkOn 84*

Eagleton, Thomas Francis
American. Politician
George McGovern's running mate, 1972;
withdrew due to past history of nervous
exhaustion.
b. Sep 4, 1929 in Saint Louis, Missouri
Source: *BiDrAC; BioNews 74; CelR; CngDr
74; CurBio 73; IntWW 74; NewYTBE 72;
WhoAm 74, 76, 78, 80, 82; WhoAmP 73;
WhoGov 75; WhoMW 74*

Eaker, Ira Clarence
American. Aviator, Army Officer
b. Apr 13, 1896 in Field Creek, Texas
Source: *AmAu&B; CurBio 42; WebBD 80;
Who 74*

Eakins, Thomas
American. Artist
Realist painter known for sporting scenes,
surgical operations, portraits.
b. Jul 25, 1844 in Philadelphia, Pennsylvania
d. Jun 25, 1916 in Philadelphia, Pennsylvania
Source: *AmBi; ApCAB; AtlBL; DcAmB;
EncAB-H; OxAmL; REn; REnAL; WebAB;
WhAm 1*

Eames, Charles
American. Designer
b. Jun 17, 1907 in Saint Louis, Missouri
d. Aug 21, 1978 in Saint Louis, Missouri
Source: *WebAB; WhoAm 74; WhoWor 78;
WorEFlm*

Eames, Emma Hayden
American. Opera Singer
Leading soprano of Metropolitan Opera,
1891-1909.
b. Aug 13, 1865 in Shanghai, China
d. Jun 13, 1952 in New York, New York
Source: *AmWom; InWom; NotAW MOD;
WomWWA 14*

Eanes, Antonio Ramalho
Portuguese. President
b. Jan 25, 1935 in Alcains, Portugal
Source: *BioIn 10, 11; CurBio 79*

Earhart, Amelia Mary
American. Aviatrix
First woman to fly solo across Atlantic,
1932.
b. Jul 24, 1898 in Atchison, Kansas
d. 1937
Source: *AmBi; ChhPo; DcAmB S2; DcNAA;
HerW; InWom; NotAW; REn; WebAB;
WhAm 1; WomWMM*

Earle, Alice Morse
American. Author, Historian
Wrote on US colonial past: *Old Time
Gardens,* 1901.
b. Apr 27, 1851 in Worcester,
Massachusetts
d. Feb 16, 1911 in Hempstead, New York
Source: *NotAW; OxAmL 83*

Earle, Ralph
[Ralph Earl]
American. Artist
Itinerant, primitive painter known for
Concord butterflies, stern portraits.
b. May 11, 1751 in Shrewsbury,
Massachusetts
d. Nov 24, 1801 in Pendleton, South
Carolina
Source: *ApCAB; BnEnAmA; DcAmArt;
DcAmB; Drake; McGDA; NewYHSD; OxAmL;
TwCBDA; WebAB; WhAm HS*

Early, Jubal Anderson
American. Military Leader
b. Nov 3, 1816 in Franklin County, Virginia
d. Mar 2, 1894 in Lynchburg, Tennessee
Source: *Alli SUP; AmBi; BbD; BiD&SB;
BiDConf; BiDSA; DcAmAu; DcAmB; DcNAA;
TwCBDA; WebAB; WhAm HS*

Earp, Morgan
American. Lawman
b. Apr 24, 1851 in Pella, Iowa
d. Mar 18, 1882 in Tombstone, Arizona
Source: *REnAW*

Earp, Virgil W
American. Lawman
b. Jul 18, 1843 in Hartford, Kentucky
d. 1905 in Goldfield, Nevada
Source: *REnAW*

Earp, Wyatt Berry Stapp
American. Lawman
Deputy marshal, Dodge City, KS, 1876-77;
survived famous gunfight at OK Corral,
1881.
b. Mar 19, 1848 in Monmouth, Illinois
d. Jan 13, 1929 in Los Angeles, California
Source: *FilmgC; NewCol 75; OxFilm;
REnAW; WebAB, 79; WebBD 80; WhAm
HS; WorAl*

Earth, Wind, and Fire
[Philip Bailey; Roland Bautista; Jessica
Cleaves; Larry Dunn; Johnny Graham;
Ralph Johnson; Al McKay; Fred White;
Maurice White; Verdine White; Andrew
Woolfolk]
American. Music Group
Changed sound of black pop music, 1970s;
have sold over 19 million albums.
Source: *IlEncBM 82; IlEncRk; InB&W 80;
RkOn 84; RolSEnR 83*

Eason, Tony (Charles Carroll, IV)
American. Football Player
Quarterback, first round draft pick of New
England, 1983.
b. Oct 8, 1959 in Blythe, California
Source: *FootReg 85*

East, John Porter
American. Politician
Conservative Rep. senator from NC, 1980-86;
wrote *Council-Manager Government,* 1965.
b. May 5, 1931 in Springfield, Illinois
d. Jun 29, 1986 in Greenville, North
Carolina
Source: *AmM&WS 73S, 78S; ConAu 17R;
WhoAm 82, 84; WhoAmP 73, 75, 77, 79;
WrDr 76, 80*

Eastern Jewel
[Yoshiko Kawashima]
Chinese. Spy
Helped ignite WW II in Far East; beheaded
for treason.
b. 1906
d. 1948
Source: *LookW*

Eastlake, Charles Lock
English. Artist
b. Nov 17, 1793 in Plymouth, England
d. Dec 24, 1865 in Pisa, Italy
Source: *Alli, SUP; BiD&SB; DcEnL; NewC;
REn*

Eastlake, William
American. Author
b. Jul 14, 1917 in New York, New York
Source: *AmAu&B; Au&Wr 71; ConAu 5R, 5NR; ConLC 8; ConNov 72, 76; DrAF 76; ModAL S1; OxAmL; PenC AM; REnAL; WhoAm 74, 76, 78, 80, 82; WhoWor 78; WorAu; WrDr 80*

Eastland, James Oliver
"Big Jim"
American. Politician
Dem. senator, 1941-78; opposed civil rights legislation.
b. Nov 28, 1904 in Doddsville, Mississippi
d. Feb 19, 1986 in Greenwood, Mississippi
Source: *BiDrAC; CelR; CngDr 74; CurBio 49, 86; IntWW 74; NewYTBE 72; WhoAm 76, 78, 80, 82; WhoAmP 73; WhoGov 72; WhoS&SW 75; WhoWor 74*

Eastman, Carol
[Adrien Joyce, pseud.]
American. Screenwriter
Won Oscar for screenplay *Five Easy Pieces*, 1970.
Source: *ConAu 116*

Eastman, George
American. Inventor, Industrialist
Invented roll film, 1884; the Kodak camera, 1888.
b. Jul 12, 1854 in Waterville, New York
d. Mar 14, 1932 in Rochester, New York
Source: *AmBi; DcAmB S1; DcFM; EncAB-H; FilmgC; NatCAB 26; OxFilm; WebAB; WhDW; WhAm 1; WorAl; WorEFlm*

Eastman, Mary Henderson
American. Author
Wrote Indian tales, anti-Uncle Tom work *Uncle Phillis's Cabin*, 1852.
b. 1818 in Fauquier County, Virginia
d. Feb 24, 1887 in Washington, District of Columbia
Source: *NotAW; OxAmL 83*

Eastman, Max Forrester
American. Author
Best known for book *Enjoyment of Poetry*, 1913.
b. Jan 4, 1883 in Canandaigua, New York
d. Mar 25, 1969 in Bridgetown, Barbados
Source: *AmAu&B; AmLY; CasWL; ChhPo; CnDAL; ConAmA; ConAmL; ConAu 9R, 25R; CurBio 69; DcAmSR; DcLEL; LongCTC; OxAmL; PenC AM; REn; REnAL; TwCA, SUP; WebAB; WhAm 5; WhE&EA*

Easton, Elliot
see: Cars, The

Easton, Florence Gertrude
English. Opera Singer
b. Oct 25, 1884 in Middlesbrough, England
d. Aug 13, 1955 in New York, New York
Source: *InWom*

Easton, Sheena
[Sheena Shirley Orr]
Scottish. Singer
Pop singer who had hit song "Morning Train," 1981.
b. Apr 27, 1959 in Bellshill, Scotland
Source: *BioIn 12; IlEncRk; NewWmR*

Eastwood, Clint
American. Actor, Director, Politician
Starred i TV series "Rawhide," 1959-66; movie *Dirty Harry*, 1971; mayo r of Carmel, CA, 1986--.
b. May 31, 1930 in San Francisco, California
Source: *BiDFilm; BioNews 74; BkPepl; CelR; CurBio 71; FilmgC; IntMPA 80, 81, 82, 83, 84, 85, 86; MotPP; MovMk; OxFilm; WhoAm 76, 78, 80, 82, 84; WhoHol A; WorEFlm*

Easy Aces
see: Ace, Goodman; Ace, Jane Sherwood

Eaton, Cyrus Stephen
American. Financier
b. Dec 27, 1883 in Pugwash, Nova Scotia
d. May 9, 1979 in Northfield, Ohio
Source: *AmAu&B; BioNews 74; BusPN; CanWW 70, 79; CelR; CurBio 48, 79; IntWW 75, 76, 77, 78; NewYTBE 73; NewYTBS 79; PolProf E, K; WhAm 7; WhoAm 76, 78; WhoF&I 75; WhoWor 78*

Eaton, Mary
American. Actress
In Ziegfeld Follies, 1920-22; starred in *Five O'Clock Girl*, 1927.
b. 1901 in Norfolk, Virginia
d. Oct 10, 1948 in Hollywood, California
Source: *CmpEPM; EncMT; Film 2; NotNAT B; ObitOF 79; WhScrn 74, 77; WhThe,; WhoHol B*

Eaton, Shirley
English. Actress
Played the girl painted gold in James Bond film *Goldfinger*, 1964.
b. 1936 in London, England
Source: *FilmEn; FilmgC; MotPP; WhoHol A*

Eaton, Timothy
Canadian. Merchant
b. 1834
d. Jan 31, 1907
Source: *BioIn 11*

Eban, Abba
[Aubrey Solomon]
Israeli. Diplomat
UN representative, 1949-59; ambassador to
US, 1950-59; wrote *Israel in the World,*
1966.
b. Feb 2, 1915 in Capetown, South Africa
Source: *BioNews 75; ConAu 57; CurBio 57;
IntWW 74; Who 74; WhoWor 78; WhoWorJ
72*

Ebb, Fred
American. Songwriter
Won Tonys for *Cabaret,* 1967; *Woman of the
Year,* 1980.
b. Apr 8, 1933 in New York, New York
Source: *VarWW 85*

Ebbets, Charles H
American. Baseball Executive
Owner, Brooklyn Dodgers, early 1900s; built
Ebbets Field in Brooklyn.
b. Oct 29, 1859 in New York, New York
d. Apr 18, 1925 in New York, New York
Source: *WhoProB 73*

Eberhard, Johann August
German. Philosopher
b. 1739
d. 1809
Source: *BiD&SB; DcEuL; WebBD 80*

Eberhart, Mignon Good
American. Author
Wrote over 50 detective fiction books.
b. Jul 6, 1899 in Nebraska
Source: *AmAu&B; AmWomWr; ASpks;
AuNews 2; ConAu 73; CorpD; EncMys;
LongCTC; REnAL; TwCA, SUP; WhNAA;
WhoAm 80, 82; WhoWor 74*

Eberhart, Richard
American. Author
b. Apr 5, 1904 in Austin, Minnesota
Source: *AmAu&B; AmWr; BiE&WWA;
CasWL; CnE&AP; ConAu 2NR; ConLC 1, 3,
11, 19; ConP 70, 75; DcLEL; DrAP 75;
DrAS 74E; IntWW 74; LongCTC; ModAL,
S1; NotNAT; OxAmL,; PenC AM; RAdv 1;
REn; REnAL; SixAP; TwCA SUP; TwCWr;
WebE&AL; Who 74; WhoAm 80, 82;
WhoTwCL; WhoWor 74; WrDr 76, 82*

Eberle, Irmengarde
American. Author
b. Nov 11, 1898 in San Antonio, Texas
Source: *AmAu&B; AuBYP; BkCL; ConAu 1R,
85, 2NR; InWom; JBA 51; SmATA 2;
WhoAm 74; WhoAmW 77; WhoWor 78*

Eberle, Mary Abastenia St. Leger
American. Artist
Statuettes include "The White Slave," 1913.
b. Apr 6, 1878 in Webster City, Iowa
d. Feb 26, 1942 in New York, New York
Source: *NotAW*

Eberle, Ray
[The Eberle Brothers]
American. Singer
b. Jan 19, 1919 in Hoosick Falls, New York
Source: *CmpEPM*

Eberly, Bob
[Robert Eberle; The Eberle Brothers]
American. Singer, Band Leader
Singer with Dorsey Brothers band; who
popularized 1940s hits "Tangerine,"
"Green Eyes."
b. Jul 24, 1916 in Mechanicville, New York
d. Nov 17, 1981 in Glen Burnie, Maryland
Source: *BioIn 3, 10; CmpEPM; NewYTBS 81*

Eberstadt, Ferdinand
American. Government Official
b. Jun 19, 1890 in New York, New York
d. Nov 11, 1969
Source: *BioIn 1, 2, 3, 8, 9; CurBio 42, 70*

Ebert, Carl (Anton Charles)
American. Director
Music director of worldwide opera
companies.
b. Feb 20, 1887 in Berlin, Germany
d. May 14, 1980 in Santa Monica, California
Source: *AnObit 1980; CnOxOp 79; EncOp;
EncWT; Film 2; IntWW 74, 75, 76, 77, 78;
NewEOp 71; NewYTBS 80; Who 74*

Ebert, Friedrich
German. President
b. Feb 4, 1871 in Heidelberg, Germany
d. Feb 28, 1925
Source: *NewCol 75; OxGer; REn; WebBD 80*

Ebert, Roger Joseph
American. Movie Critic
Film critic of "Sneak Previews," "At the
Movies"; won Pulitzer, 1975.
b. Jun 18, 1942 in Urbana, Illinois
Source: *ConAu 69; WhoAm 80, 82;
WhoAmW 81, 83; WrDr 80, 82*

Ebing, Richard von Krafft
see: Krafft-Ebing, Richard von

Ebsen, Buddy
[Christian Ebson, Jr.]
American. Actor, Dancer
Starred in TV series "The Beverly
Hillbillies," 1962-71, "Barnaby Jones,"
1973-79.
b. Apr 2, 1908 in Orlando, Florida
Source: *AmSCAP 66; EncMT; FilmgC;
IntMPA 75, 76, 77, 78, 79, 80, 81, 82;
MovMk; WhoAm 82; WhoHol A*

Eccles, John Carew, Sir
Australian. Scientist
b. Jan 27, 1903 in Melbourne, Australia
Source: *AmM&WS 73P; ConAu 65; CurBio
72; IntWW 74; Who 74; WhoAm 74;
WhoWor 78*

Eccles, Marriner Stoddard
American. Economist
b. Sep 9, 1890 in Logan, Utah
d. Dec 18, 1977 in Salt Lake City, Utah
Source: *AmAu&B; CurBio 41, 78; EncAB-H;
IntWW 74, 75, 76, 77, 78; IntYB 78; LinLib
L, S; NewYTBS 77; PolProf T; WhAm 7;
WhoAm 74, 76, 78; WhoF&I 74; WhoWor 74*

Ecevit, Bulent
Turkish. Journalist, Politician
b. May 28, 1925 in Istanbul, Turkey
Source: *BioIn 10, 11; CurBio 75; IntWW 74;
NewCol 75; WhoWor 78*

Echegaray, Jose
Spanish. Dramatist
Shared Nobel Prize for Literature, 1904.
b. Apr 19, 1831 in Madrid, Spain
d. Sep 15, 1916 in Madrid, Spain
Source: *BbD; BiD&SB; ClDMEL; CnMD;
ConAu 104; DcSpL; McGEWD; ModRL;
ModWD; NotNAT B; OxThe; PenC EUR;
REn; TwCWr; WhLit*

Echeverria Alvarez, Louis
Mexican. Politician
b. Jan 17, 1922 in Mexico City, Mexico
Source: *BioIn 8, 9, 10, 11; BioNews 74;
CurBio 72; IntWW 74; NewYTBE 70;
WhoGov 75; WhoS&SW 82; WhoWor 78*

Eckener, Hugo
German. Aeronautical Engineer
Trained German dirigible crews during World
War I.
b. 1868
d. Aug 14, 1954 in Friedrichshafen, Germany
(West)
Source: *LinLib S; ObitOF 79, 79; WebBD 80;
WhDW*

Eckert, Horst
[Janosch, pseud.]
Polish. Children's Author, Illustrator
b. Mar 11, 1931 in Zaborze, Poland
Source: *ConAu 37R; SmATA 8*

Eckhart, Johannes
German. Philosopher, Mystic
b. 1260 in Hochheim, Germany
d. 1327 in Avignon, France
Source: *CasWL; EuAu; EvEuW; NewC;
OxGer; PenC EUR*

Eckstein, George
American. Writer
Wrote TV shows "The Untouchables";
"Gunsmoke"; "Dr. Kildare."
b. May 3, 1928 in Los Angeles, California
Source: *VarWW 85*

Eckstein, Gustav
American. Physiologist, Author
Writings include best-seller *Body Has a
Head,* 1969.
b. Oct 26, 1890 in Cincinnati, Ohio
d. Sep 23, 1981 in Cincinnati, Ohio
Source: *AmAu&B; BioIn 1, 3, 4; ConAu 57,
104; CurBio 42, 81; NewYTBS 81; OhA&B;
TwCA SUP; WhE&EA; WhNAA*

Eckstine, Billy
['The Fabulous Mr. B']
American. Singer
Hits include "Cottage for Sale," 1945;
"Prisoner of Love," 1945; "Blue Moon."
b. Jul 8, 1914 in Pittsburgh, Pennsylvania
Source: *AmPS B; CurBio 52; IlEncBM 82;
WhoAm 80, 82; WhoBlA 75; WhoHol A;
WhoJ_us 72*

Economaki, Chris(topher Constantine)
American. Publisher, Broadcast Journalist
Award-winning colorcaster for "Wide World
of Sports," 1961--; publishes *National
Speed Sports News.*
b. Oct 15, 1920 in Brooklyn, New York
Source: *WhoAm 76, 78, 80, 82, 84*

Ed, Carl Frank Ludwig
American. Cartoonist
b. Jul 16, 1890 in Moline, Illinois
d. Oct 10, 1959 in Evanston, Illinois
Source: *AmAu&B; WhAm 3*

Eda-Pierre, Christiane
French. Opera Singer
Coloratura soprano; who was soloist with
worldwide symphonic orchestras.
b. in Fort de France, Martinique
Source: *WhoOp 76*

Eddington, Arthur Stanley, Sir
English. Astronomer
Translated theories of relativity into lay
   terms.
b. Dec 28, 1882 in Kendal, England
d. Nov 22, 1944 in Cambridge, England
Source: *Chambr 3; CurBio 41; DcLEL;*
EvLB; LongCTC; NewC; NewCol 75; OxEng;
TwCA, SUP; WhoLA

Eddy, Clarence
American. Organist
Noted church, concert organist for over 50
   yrs.
b. Jun 23, 1851 in Greenfield, Massachusetts
d. Jan 10, 1937 in Chicago, Illinois
Source: *DcAmB S2; WebBD 80*

Eddy, Duane
American. Musician
Guitarist whose instrumental hits include
   "Rebel Rouser," 1958; "Peter Gunn,"
   1960.
b. Apr 26, 1938 in Corning, New York
Source: *EncPR&S 74; RolSEnR 83*

Eddy, Mary Baker Morse
American. Religious Leader
Founded Christian Science Religious
   Movement; organized first church, 1879.
b. Jul 16, 1821 in Bow, New Hampshire
d. Dec 3, 1910 in Chestnut Hill,
   Massachusetts
Source: *Alli SUP; AmAu; AmAu&B; AmBi;*
BiD&SB; CasWL; ChhPo, S1, S2; DcAmB;
DcLEL; DcNAA; EncAB-H; HerW;
InWom; LongCTC; NotAW; OxAmL; OxEng;
REn; REnAL; TwCBDA; WebAB; WhAm 1

Eddy, Nelson
American. Singer, Actor
Starred with Jeanette MacDonald 1930's
   musicals; had voice range of three octaves.
b. Jun 29, 1901 in Providence, Rhode Island
d. Mar 6, 1967 in Miami, Florida
Source: *CmMov; CurBio 43, 67; FilmgC;*
MotPP; MovMk; OxFilm; WhAm 4; WhScrn
74, 77; WhoHol B

Eddy, Sherwood
American. Author
b. Jan 11, 1871 in Leavenworth, Kansas
d. Mar 3, 1963 in Jacksonville, Illinois
Source: *OxAmL; REnAL; WhAm 4; WhNAA*

Edel, Leon (Joseph Leon)
American. Author, Journalist
b. Sep 9, 1907 in Pittsburgh, Pennsylvania
Source: *AmAu&B; CanWW 70; ConAu 1R,*
1NR; CurBio 63; DrAS 74E; IntWW 74;
NewYTBE 72; OxAmL; RAdv 1; REn; Who
74; WhoAm 82; WhoWor 78; WorAu; WrDr
80

Edelman, Herb
American. Actor
In TV series "The Good Guys," 1968-70;
   film *The Way We Were,* 1977.
b. Nov 5, 1933 in Brooklyn, New York
Source: *FilmgC; WhoHol A*

Edelmann, Otto
Austrian. Opera Singer
b. Feb 5, 1917 in Brunn, Austria
Source: *IntWW 74; WhoMus 72; WhoWor 78*

Eden, Anthony
[Robert Anthony Eden, Earl of Avon]
English. Statesman
b. Jun 12, 1897 in Durham, England
d. Jan 14, 1977 in Alvediston, England
Source: *ConAu 69, 77; CurBio 40, 51;*
WebBD 80; Who 74

Eden, Barbara Jean
[Barbara Huffman; Mrs. Charles Fegert]
American. Actress
Starred with Larry Hagman in TV series "I
   Dream of Jeannie," 1965-69.
b. Aug 23, 1934 in Tucson, Arizona
Source: *FilmgC; MovMk; WhoAm 74, 76, 78,*
80, 82; WhoHol A

Eden, Dorothy
New Zealander. Author
Wrote romantic fiction: *The Vines of*
   Yarrabee, 1969; *The Salamanca Drum,*
   1979.
b. Apr 3, 1912 in Canterbury, New Zealand
d. Mar 4, 1982 in London, England
Source: *ConAu 106, 81; TwCCr&M 80;*
WhE&EA; WrDr 80, 82

Eden, Nicholas
[Earl of Avon]
English. Government Official
Son of Anthony Eden; under-secretary in
   Margaret Thatcher's cabinet; last Earl of
   Avon.
b. Oct 3, 1930 in London, England
d. Aug 17, 1985 in London, England
Source: *Who 74*

Eder, Shirley
American. Journalist
Source: *NF*

Ederle, Gertrude Caroline
American. Swimmer
First woman to swim English Channel,
   Calais to Dover, breaking world record,
   1926.
b. Oct 23, 1906 in New York, New York
Source: *InWom; WebAB; WhoHol A*

Edeson, Robert
American. Actor
Noted stage actor who apeared in many
   DeMille silent films.
b. 1868 in New Orleans, Louisiana
d. Mar 24, 1931 in Hollywood, California
Source: *DcAmB S1; Film 1, 2; NotNAT;*
   OxThe; TwYS; WhAm 1; WhScrn 74, 77;
   WhThe; WhoHol B; WhoStg 1906, 1908

Edgar
[Eadgar]
English. King
b. 943
d. 975
Source: *BioIn 6, 9; NewCol 75*

Edgar, David
English. Dramatist
Prolific stage, TV playwright who stresses
   political, social themes: *Death Story*, 1972.
b. Feb 26, 1948 in Birmingham, England
Source: *BioIn 10; ConAu 57; ConDr 77;*
   WrDr 76, 80

Edgell, George Harold
American. Author, Museum Director
Headed Boston's Museum of Fine Arts,
   1935-54; wrote books on architecture,
   Sienese painting.
b. Mar 4, 1887 in Saint Louis, Missouri
d. Jun 29, 1954 in Newport, New Hampshire
Source: *BioIn 1, 3, 5, 6; NatCAB 45; WhAm*
   3; WhE&EA; WhLit

Edgerton, Harold Eugene
American. Engineer
b. Apr 6, 1903 in Fremont, Nebraska
Source: *BioIn 3, 4, 6, 7, 10; WhoAm 82*

Edgeworth, Maria
English. Children's Author
Novels depict Irish life, moral tales for
   children.
b. Jan 1, 1767 in Bourton Abbots, England
d. May 22, 1849 in Edgeworthstown, Ireland
Source: *Alli; AtlBL; BbD; BiD&SB; BiDLA;*
   BrAu 19; CarSB; CasWL; CelCen; Chambr 2;
   ChhPo; CrtT 2; CyWA; DcBiA; DcBiPP;
   DcEnA; DcEnL; DcEuL; DcLEL; EvLB;
   InWom; MouLC 3; NewC; OxEng; PenC
   ENG; PoIre; RAdv 1; REn; WebE&AL;
   WhDW; WhoChL

Edison, Thomas Alva
American. Inventor
His more than 1,000 inventions changed life
   in America, include phonograph,
   incandescent lamp.
b. Feb 11, 1847 in Milan, Ohio
d. Oct 18, 1931 in West Orange, New Jersey
Source: *AmBi; ApCAB; DcAmB S1; DcFM;*
   EncAB-H; FilmgC; LongCTC; NewCol 75;
   OxFilm; REn; REnAL; TwCBDA; WebAB;
   WhAm 1; WorEFlm

Edlund, Richard
American. Special Effects Technician
Won Oscars for visual effects in three *Star*
   Wars films, 1977, 1980, 1983.
b. Dec 6, 1940 in Fargo, North Dakota
Source: *VarWW 85*

Edmiston, Mark Morton
American. Business Executive
Pres., *Newsweek* magazine, 1981--.
b. Jul 9, 1943 in Yonkers, New York
Source: *WhoAm 80, 82, 84*

Edmonds, Emma E
American. Nurse, Soldier
Wrote popular fictionalized account *Nurse*
   and Spy in the Union Army, 1865.
b. Dec 1841 in New Brunswick
d. Sep 5, 1898 in La Porte, Texas
Source: *BioIn 1, 3, 5, 6, 9; NotAW*

Edmonds, Walter Dumaux
American. Author
Known for historical novels of NY state:
   Drums Along the Mohawk, 1936.
b. Jul 15, 1903 in Boonville, New York
Source: *AmAu&B; AmNov; AuBYP; CnDAL;*
   ConAmA; ConAu 5R, 2NR; CurBio 42;
   CyWA; DcLEL; ModAL; MorBMP; MorJA;
   Newb 1922; OxAmL; PenC AM; REn;
   REnAL; SmATA 1; TwCA, SUP; WhoAm 74,
   76, 78, 80, 82; WrDr 76

Edmonson, Munro Sterling
American. Educator, Anthropologist
b. May 18, 1924 in Nogales, Arizona
Source: *AmM&WS 73S; ConAu 33R; WhoAm*
   74; WrDr 76

Edmund, Saint
King
b. 840
d. 870
Source: *BioIn 1, 2, 3, 4, 5, 6, 7, 8, 9; NewC;*
   NewCol 75

Edmunds, Dave
[Rockpile]
Welsh. Musician, Producer
Guitarist who formed Rockpile with Nick
Lowe, 1978; hits include "Cruel to be
Kind."
b. Apr 15, 1944 in Cardiff, Wales
Source: *ConMuA 80A; IlEncRk*

Edmunds, George Franklin
American. Lawyer, Politician
b. Feb 1, 1828 in Richmond, Vermont
d. Feb 27, 1919 in Pasadena, California
Source: *BioIn 7; WebAB; WebBD 80; WhAm
1*

Edson, Gus
American. Cartoonist
b. Sep 20, 1901 in Stamford, Connecticut
d. Sep 26, 1966 in Stamford, Connecticut
Source: *BioIn 7; ObitOF 79*

Edward
[Edward Antony Richard Louis]
English. Prince
b. Mar 10, 1964 in London, England
Source: *Who 82, 82R*

Edward I
English. King
b. 1239 in Westminster, England
d. 1307
Source: *BioIn 10; NewCol 75; WebBD 80*

Edward II
[Edward of Carnarvon]
English. King
b. 1284 in Carnarvon, England
d. 1327
Source: *BioIn 10; NewCol 75; WebBD 80*

Edward III
English. King
b. 1312 in Windsor, England
d. 1377
Source: *BioIn 10; NewCol 75; WebBD 80*

Edward IV
English. King
b. Apr 28, 1442 in Rouen, France
d. 1483 in London, England
Source: *DcBiPP; DcCathB; NewCol 75;
WebBD 80; WhDW*

Edward V
English. King
b. 1470 in Westminster, England
d. 1483 in London, England
Source: *BioIn 10; NewCol 75; WebBD 80*

Edward VI
English. King
b. 1537 in Hampton Court, England
d. 1553 in London, England
Source: *BioIn 10; NewCol 75; WebBD 80*

Edward VII
[Edward Albert]
English. King
Son of Queen Victoria who ruled 1901-10;
popular monarch known as peacemaker.
b. 1841 in London, England
d. 1910 in London, England
Source: *NewCol 75; WebBD 80*

Edward VIII
[Edward Albert Christian George Andrew
Patrick David; Duke of Windsor]
English. King
Reigned, Jan-Dec, 1936; abdicated to marry
twice-divorced American Wallis Simpson.
b. Jun 23, 1894 in Richmond, England
d. May 18, 1972 in Paris, France
Source: *BioIn 10; ConAu 33R; NewCol 75;
WhAm 5; WebBD 80*

Edward the Black Prince
English. Prince
b. 1330 in Woodstock, England
d. 1376 in London, England
Source: *LinLib S; McGEWB; NewCol 75;
WhDW*

Edward the Confessor
[Eadward]
English. King
b. 1002 in Oxford, England
d. Jan 5, 1066
Source: *DcCathB; LongCEL; NewC; NewCol
75; WebBD 80; WhDW*

Edwards, Alan
American. Actor
b. Jun 3, 1900 in New York, New York
d. May 8, 1954 in Los Angeles, California
Source: *Film 2; MotPP; NotNAT B; WhScrn
74, 77; WhoHol B*

Edwards, Blake
[William Blake McEdwards]
American. Producer, Director
Produced *Pink Panther* film series; husband
of Julie Andrews.
b. Jul 26, 1922 in Tulsa, Oklahoma
Source: *BiDFilm; ConAu 81; CurBio 83;
FilmgC; IntMPA 79, 80, 81, 82; IntWW 82;
MovMk; NewYTET; OxFilm; WhoAm 80, 82;
WorAl; WorEFlm*

Edwards, Cliff
American. Singer, Actor
b. Jul 14, 1895 in Hannibal, Missouri
d. Jul 17, 1971 in Hollywood, California
Source: *FilmgC; MotPP; MovMk; NewYTBE 71; Vers B; WhScrn 74, 77; WhoHol B*

Edwards, Dennis
[The Temptations]
American. Singer
Original member of Temptations; solo single "Don't Look Any Further," 1984.
b. Feb 3, 1943 in Birmingham, Alabama
Source: *RkOn 85*

Edwards, Douglas
American. Radio Performer, TV Personality
b. Jul 14, 1917 in Ada, Oklahoma
Source: *IntMPA 80, 81, 82; NewYTET; Who 74; WhoAm 80, 82*

Edwards, Harry (Jr.)
American. Sociologist, Educator, Author
Organized black boycott of 1968 Olympic games.
b. Nov 22, 1942 in Saint Louis, Missouri
Source: *ConAu 111*

Edwards, Edwin Washington
American. Politician, Lawyer
Dem. governor of LA, 1972-80, 1984--; acquitted of fraud, 1986.
b. Aug 7, 1927 in Marksville, Louisiana
Source: *BiDrAC; NewYTBS 74; WhoAm 76, 78, 80, 82, 84; WhoAmP 73; WhoGov 72; WhoS&SW 73*

Edwards, Gus
American. Songwriter
b. Aug 18, 1879 in Hohensaliza, Germany
d. Nov 7, 1945 in Los Angeles, California
Source: *AmAu&B; AmSCAP 66; CurBio 45; REnAL; WhScrn 74, 77; WhoHol B*

Edwards, India
American. Journalist, Politician
b. 1895 in Chicago, Illinois
Source: *BioIn 2, 3, 11; CurBio 49*

Edwards, James Burrows
American. Government Official
Secretary of Energy, 1981-82.
b. Jun 24, 1927 in Hawthorne, Florida
Source: *BiDrGov; CngDr 81; CurBio 82; IntWW 78; WhoAm 80, 82; WhoAmP 77, 79, 81; WhoE 81; WhoGov 77, 75; WhoS&SW 73, 75, 76, 78*

Edwards, Joan
American. Singer, Songwriter
Co-starred with Frank Sinatra in radio show "Your Hit Parade," 1941-46.
b. Feb 13, 1919 in New York, New York
d. Aug 27, 1981 in New York, New York
Source: *AmSCAP 66; CmpEPM; CurBio 53, 81; NewYTBS 81*

Edwards, Jonathan
American. Author, Theologian
b. Oct 5, 1703 in East Windsor, Connecticut
d. Mar 22, 1758 in New Jersey
Source: *Alli; AmAu; AmAu&B; AmBi; AmWr; ApCAB; AtlBL; BbD; BiD&SB; CasWL; CnDAL; CrtT 3; CyAL 1; CyWA; DcAmAu; DcAmB; DcEnL; DcLEL; DcNAA; Drake; EncAB-H; EvLB; MouLC 2; NewC; OxAmL; OxEng; PenC AM; RComWL; REn; REnAL; TwCBDA; WebAB; WebE&AL; WhAm HS*

Edwards, Ralph
American. Producer
b. Jun 13, 1913 in Marino, California
Source: *CelR; NewYTET; WhoAm 82*

Edwards, Robert Geoffrey
English. Physiologist
b. 1925
Source: *BioIn 11*

Edwards, Sherman
American. Composer, Lyricist
b. Apr 3, 1919 in New York, New York
d. Mar 30, 1981 in New York, New York
Source: *AmSCAP 66; EncMT; WhoAm 74; WhoThe 77*

Edwards, Vince
[Vincent Edward Zoino]
American. Actor
Starred in TV series "Ben Casey," 1961-66.
b. Jul 7, 1928 in Brooklyn, New York
Source: *FilmgC; IntMPA 75, 76, 77; MotPP; MovMk; WhoAm 74; WhoHol A*

Edwards, Willard
American. Journalist
b. Dec 7, 1902 in Chicago, Illinois
Source: *WhoAm 74; WhoS&SW 82*

Edwy
[Eadwig]
English. King
d. 959
Source: *NewC; NewCol 75; WebBD 80*

Efron, Marshall
American. Comedian
b. 1938
Source: *BioIn 10*

Egan, Eddie
"Popeye"
American. Police Officer
Source: *BioIn 9*

Egan, Richard
American. Actor
Films include *Split Second*, 1953; *Pollyanna*,
1960.
b. Jul 29, 1923 in San Francisco, California
Source: *FilmgC; IntMPA 82; MotPP; MovMk;
WhoHol A*

Egan, Richard B
Canadian. Songwriter
b. Nov 14, 1890 in Windsor, Ontario
d. Nov 13, 1952 in Westport, Connecticut
Source: *AmSCAP 66; BioIn 3, 4, 5*

Egan, Walter Lindsay
American. Singer, Songwriter
Country-rock lyricist, guitarist who had hit
album *Hi Fi*, 1979.
b. Jul 12, 1948 in Jamaica, New York
Source: *AmSCAP 80; ConMuA 80A*

Eggar, Samantha
English. Actress
Won Cannes Film Festival award for *The
Collector*, 1965.
b. Mar 5, 1940 in Hampstead, England
Source: *CelR; FilmgC; IntMPA 79, 80, 81,
82; MotPP; MovMk; WhoAm 80, 82;
WhoAmW 75; WhoHol A; WorAl*

Eggerth, Marta
Hungarian. Actress, Singer
Starred with husband Jan Kiepura in many
filmed operettas in Germany, Austria,
1930s.
b. Apr 17, 1916 in Budapest, Hungary
Source: *BiE&WWA; CurBio 43; NotNAT;
WhThe; WhoHol A; WhoThe 77A*

Eggleston, Edward
American. Author, Clergyman
b. Dec 10, 1837 in Veray, Indiana
d. Sep 4, 1902 in Lake George, New York
Source: *Alli SUP; AmAu; AmAu&B; AmBi;
ApCAB; BbD; BiD&SB; CarSB; CasWL;
Chambr 3; ChhPo, S1; CnDAL; CyAL 2;
CyWA; DcAmAu; DcAmB; DcBiA; DcNAA;
DcRusL; EvLB; IndAu 1816; JBA 34;
OxAmL; OxEng; PenC AM; REn; REnAL;
TwCBDA; WebAB; WebE&AL; WhAm 1*

Egk, Werner
[Werner Mayer]
German. Composer
Operas include *Peer Gynt*, 1938; *The Magic
Violin*, 1935.
b. May 17, 1901 in Auchsensheim, Germany
d. Jul 10, 1983 in Inning, Germany (West)
Source: *AnObit 1983; DcCM; IntWW 74;
NewYTBS 83; WhoMus 72; WhoWor 74, 80*

Eglevsky, Andre
Russian. Ballet Dancer
b. Dec 21, 1917 in Moscow, U.S.S.R.
d. Dec 4, 1977 in Elmira, New York
Source: *CurBio 53; IntWW 74; WhoAm 74*

Ehmke, Howard Jonathan
"Bob"
American. Baseball Player
b. Apr 24, 1894 in Silver Creek, New York
d. Mar 17, 1959 in Philadelphia,
Pennsylvania
Source: *BaseEn 85; BioIn 5, 7, 10; WhoProB
73*

Ehrenburg, Ilya Grigoryevich
[Ilya Ehrenbourg; Ilya Erenburg]
Russian. Author
b. Jan 27, 1891 in Kiev, Russia
d. Aug 31, 1967 in Moscow, U.S.S.R.
Source: *CasWL; ClDMEL; ConAu 25R, 102;
ConLC 18; CurBio 66, 67; DcRusL; EncWL;
EvEuW; LongCTC; ModSL 1; PenC EUR;
REn; TwCA, SUP; TwCWr*

Ehricke, Krafft Arnold
American. Engineer
b. Mar 24, 1917 in Berlin, Germany
d. Dec 11, 1984 in La Jolla, California
Source: *AmM&WS 73P; AnObit 1984; BioIn
5, 6; WhoAm 74, 76, 78, 80, 82*

Ehrlich, Bettina Bauer
Austrian. Artist
b. Mar 19, 1903 in Vienna, Austria
Source: *AuBYP; ConAu P-1; IlsCB 1946,
1957; MorJA; SmATA 1*

Ehrlich, Paul Ralph
German. Biologist
Wrote *The Population Bomb*, 1968; developed
chemotheraphy; won Nobel Prize, 1980.
b. Feb 12, 1854 in Schlesian, Germany
d. Aug 20, 1915 in Homburg, Prussia
Source: *AsBiEn; DcBiPP; McGEWB; WhDW;
WhoAm 82; WhoWor 82; WorAl*

Ehrlich, Paul
American. Biologist
b. May 29, 1932 in Philadelphia,
    Pennsylvania
Source: *BioIn 9; CurBio 70*

Ehrlichman, John Daniel
American. Watergate Participant
Served 18 months in prison for involvement
    in Watergate, 1976-78.
b. Mar 20, 1925 in Tacoma, Washington
Source: *BlueB 76; ConAu 65; IntWW 82;
NewYTBE 70, 73; NewYTBS 74; PolProf NF;
WhoAm 78, 80, 82; WhoAmP 73; WhoGov
72; WhoS&SW 75*

Ehrling, Sixten
Swedish. Conductor
b. Apr 3, 1918 in Malmo, Sweden
Source: *BioNews 74; WhoAm 74, 76, 78, 80,
82; WhoMus 72; WhoWor 78*

Eichelberger, Dave
American. Golfer
Winner of several pro tournaments including
    Bay Hill Classic, 1980; Tallahassee Open,
    1981.
b. Sep 3, 1943 in Waco, Texas
Source: *WhoGolf; WhoIntG*

Eichelberger, Robert Lawrence
American. Army Officer, Author
b. Mar 9, 1886 in Urbana, Ohio
d. Sep 26, 1961 in Asheville, North Carolina
Source: *AmM&WS 73P; CurBio 43, 61;
ObitOF 79; WebAMB; WhAm 4; WhWW-II;
WhoMilH 76*

Eichenberg, Fritz
English. Illustrator
b. Oct 24, 1901 in Cologne, Germany
Source: *AnCL; ChhPo S2; ConAu 57; IlsBYP;
IlsCB 1744, 1946, 1957; MorJA; SmATA 9;
Str&VC; WhoAm 74; WhoAmA 73; WhoGrA
62*

Eichendorff, Joseph Karl Benedict
German. Poet
b. Mar 10, 1788 in Ratibor, Silesia
d. Nov 26, 1857 in Neisse, Silesia
Source: *AtlBL; BbD; BiD&SB; DcEuL; EuAu;
OxFr; OxGer; PenC AM; RComWL; REn*

Eichhorn, Lisa
American. Actress
Star of film *The Europeans,* 1979; TV movie
    "The Wall," 1981.
b. 1952 in Reading, Pennsylvania
Source: *IntMPA 81, 82; NewYTBS 79*

Eichmann, Adolf (Otto Adolf)
Austrian. Nazi War Criminal
In charge of Hitler's death camps; escaped to
    Argentina, 1946; captured by Israelis,
    1960; hung, 1962.
b. Mar 19, 1906 in Solingen, Germany
d. May 31, 1962 in Jerusalem, Israel
Source: *NewCol 75; ObitOF 79; REn; SpyCS;
WebBD 80; WhDW*

Eifert, Virginia Snider
American. Children's Author
b. Jan 23, 1911 in Springfield, Illinois
d. Jun 16, 1966
Source: *AmAu&B; Au&Wr 71; AuBYP;
ConAu 1R; SmATA 2; WhAm 4*

Eiffel, Alexandre Gustave
French. Engineer
Designed Eiffel Tower, 1889, framework for
    Statue of Liberty, 1885.
b. Dec 15, 1832 in Dijon, France
d. Dec 23, 1923
Source: *DcD&D; EncMA; MacBEP; McGDA;
McGEWB; NewCol 75; OxArt; WebBD 80;
WhDW; WhoArch; WorAl*

Eigenmann, Rosa Smith
American. Scientist
First prominent woman ichthyologist.
b. Oct 7, 1858 in Monmouth, Illinois
d. Jan 12, 1947 in San Diego, California
Source: *NotAW*

Eight, The
[Arthur B Davies; William J Glackens;
    Robert Henri; Ernest Lawson; George
    Luks; Maurice Pendergast; Everett Shinn;
    John Sloan]
American. Artists
Established "Ashcan School" of painting,
    circa 1907.
Source: *NewCol 75; OxArt*

Eikerenkoetter, Frederick Joseph, II
see: Ike, Reverend

Eilberg, Amy
American. Rabbi
First woman rabbi in Judaism's Conservative
    branch, 1985.
b. 1955
Source: *ConNews 85-3*

Eilshemius, Louis Michel
"Mahatma of Manhattan's Montparnasse"
American. Artist, Author
Atmospheric landscapes include "Approaching
Storm."
b. Feb 4, 1864 in North Arlington, New
Jersey
d. Dec 29, 1941 in New York, New York
Source: *DcAmB S3; NewCol 75; WebBD 80*

Einaudi, Luigi
Italian. President
b. Mar 24, 1874 in Cuneo, Italy
d. Oct 30, 1961
Source: *CurBio 48, 62; NewCol 75; WhAm 4*

Einhorn, David
German. Rabbi
b. Nov 10, 1809 in Dispeck, Bavaria
d. Nov 2, 1879 in New York, New York
Source: *BioIn 2, 4, 5, 7; NatCAB 12; NewCol
75; WhAm HS*

Einhorn, Eddie (Edward Martin)
American. Baseball Executive
Chief operating officer, Chicago White Sox
baseball club.
b. Jan 3, 1936 in Paterson, New Jersey
Source: *NewYTBS 81; WhoAm 78, 80, 82*

Einstein, Albert
American. Physicist
One of greatest scientific intellects who
formulated theories of relatively; won
Nobel Prize, 1921.
b. Mar 14, 1879 in Ulm, Germany
d. Apr 18, 1955 in Princeton, New Jersey
Source: *AmAu&B; CasWL; CurBio 41, 53,
55; DcAmB S5; DcLEL; EncAB-H; LongCTC;
NewYTBE 72; OxAmL; OxEng; REn;
REnAL; WebAB; WhAm 3; WhNAA; WhoLA*

Einstein, Alfred
German. Musicologist, Critic, Editor
b. Dec 30, 1880 in Munich, Germany
d. Feb 13, 1952 in El Cerrito, California
Source: *AmAu&B; LongCTC; TwCA SUP;
WhAm 3*

Einstein, Bob
American. Writer, Producer
Won Emmys for writing "The Smothers
Brothers Show," 1969; producing "Van
Dyke and Company," 1977.
b. Nov 20, 1940 in Los Angeles, California
Source: *VarWW 85*

Einthoven, Willem
Dutch. Physiologist
b. May 22, 1860 in Semarang, India
d. Sep 28, 1927 in Leiden, New Caledonia
Source: *AsBiEn; BioIn 3, 5, 9; DcScB*

Eisele, Donn Fulton
American. Astronaut, Businessman
Command module pilot, first Apollo voyage,
1968.
b. Jun 23, 1930 in Columbus, Ohio
Source: *USBiR 74; WhoAm 74, 76, 78, 80,
82; WhoS&SW 82; WhoWor 78*

Eiseley, Loren Corey
American. Anthropologist
b. Sep 3, 1907 in Lincoln, Nebraska
d. Jul 9, 1977 in Philadelphia, Pennsylvania
Source: *AmAu&B; AmM&WS 73S; Au&Wr
71; CelR; ConAu 1R; CurBio 60; REnAL;
WebAB; WhoAm 74; WhoE 74; WhoGov 75;
WhoWor 78; WorAu*

Eisenhower, David
American. Author, Lawyer
Grandson of Dwight Eisenhower; presidential
retreat "Camp David" named for him.
b. Apr 1, 1947 in West Point, New York
Source: *BioIn 10*

Eisenhower, Dwight David
"Ike"
American. US President
Allied European military leader, WW II;
pres., 1953-61; sent troops to AR to force
desegregation, 1954.
b. Oct 14, 1890 in Denison, Texas
d. Mar 28, 1969 in Washington, District of
Columbia
Source: *AmAu&B; BiDrAC; BiDrUSE;
BioNews 74; ConAu 65; CurBio 42, 48, 57,
69; EncAAH; EncAB-H; NewYTBE 71;
OxAmL; REn; REnAL; WebAMB; WhDW;
WebAB; WhAm 5; WhAmP; WhWW-II;
WhoFtbl 74; WorAl*

Eisenhower, John Sheldon Doud
American. Author, Diplomat
b. Aug 3, 1922 in Denver, Colorado
Source: *ConAu 33R; CurBio 69; IntWW 74;
WhoAm 74, 76, 78, 80, 82; WhoAmP 73*

Eisenhower, Julie Nixon
[Mrs. David Eisenhower]
American. Celebrity Relative, Author
Daughter of Richard Nixon; edited *Saturday Evening Post* two years; wrote *Special People.*
b. Jul 5, 1948 in Washington, District of Columbia
Source: *BioNews 74; BkPepl; GoodHs; NewYTBE 71; NewYTBS 75; PolProf NF*

Eisenhower, Mamie Geneva Doud
[Mrs. Dwight David Eisenhower]
American. First Lady
b. Nov 14, 1896 in Boone, Iowa
d. Nov 1, 1979 in Washington, District of Columbia
Source: *BioNews 74; CelR; CurBio 53, 80, 80N; InWom; WhAm 7; WhoAm 78; WhoAmW 77; WhoGov 72, 75; WhoWor 74*

Eisenhower, Milton Stover
American. Educator
b. Sep 15, 1899 in Abilene, Kansas
d. May 2, 1985 in Baltimore, Maryland
Source: *CelR; CurBio 46; IntWW 74; Who 74; WhoAm 74; WhoAmP 73; WhoE 74; WhoWor 78*

Eisenstaedt, Alfred
American. Photojournalist, Author
Father of photojournalism whose photographs included more than 90 *Life* covers.
b. Dec 6, 1898 in Dirschau, Prussia
Source: *BioNews 74; ConAu 108; IntWW 74; MacBEP; WhoAm 82, 84*

Eisenstein, Sergei Mikhailovich
Russian. Director
Films frequently re-edited to conform to political policy; *October;Battleship Potemkin.*
b. Jan 23, 1898 in Riga, Russia
d. Feb 10, 1948 in Moscow, U.S.S.R.
Source: *BiDFilm; CurBio 46, 48; DcFM; EncWT; FilmgC; McGEWB; MovMk; NewCol 75; NewYTBE 73; ObitOF 79; OxFilm; REn; WhDW; WomWMM; WorEFlm*

Eizenstat, Stuart E
American. Government Official
Assistant to Jimmy Carter on domestic affairs and policy, 1977-80.
b. Jan 15, 1943 in Chicago, Illinois
Source: *WhoAm 82; WhoAmP 73*

Ekberg, Anita
['Ice Maiden']
Swedish. Actress
Films include *La Dolce Vita* ; *Boccaccio '70.*
b. Sep 29, 1931 in Malmo, Sweden
Source: *FilmgC; InWom; IntMPA 75, 76, 77, 78, 79, 80, 81, 82; MotPP; MovMk; WhoAm 74; WhoHol A; WorEFlm*

Ekland, Britt
Swedish. Actress
Married Peter Sellers, 1963-68; starred in James Bond film *Man with the the Golden Gun,* 1974.
b. Oct 6, 1942 in Stockholm, Sweden
Source: *FilmgC; IntMPA 81, 82; WhoHol A; WorAl*

Eklund, Carl Robert
American. Explorer
A founder, first pres. of Antarctican Society, 1959.
b. Jan 27, 1909 in Tomanawk, Wisconsin
d. Nov 4, 1962 in Philadelphia, Pennsylvania
Source: *DcAmB S7*

Elam, Jack
American. Actor
Appeared in over 100 films: *The Way West,* 1967; *Support Your Local Sheriff,* 1969.
b. Nov 13, 1916 in Phoenix, Arizona
Source: *CmMov; FilmgC; IntMPA 82; MotPP; MovMk; WhoAm 80, 82; WhoF&I 79; WhoHol A*

Elazar, David
Israeli. General
b. 1925 in Yugoslavia
d. Apr 15, 1976 in Tel Aviv, Israel
Source: *InWom*

Elder, Lee
American. Golfer
First black to play in Masters tournament, 1975; 43rd golfer to become millionaire, 1984.
b. Jul 14, 1934 in Dallas, Texas
Source: *CurBio 76; NegAl 76; NewYTBS 79; WhoBlA 75, 77; WhoGolf*

Elder, Ruth
['Miss America of Aviation']
American. Aviatrix
Made unsuccessful attempts to become first woman to fly across Atlantic, 1927.
b. 1904 in Anniston, Alabama
d. Oct 9, 1977 in San Francisco, California
Source: *Film 2; InSci; InWom; NewYTBS 77; ObitOF 79*

Eldjarn, Kristjan
Icelandic. Politician
Pres. of Iceland, 1968-80.
b. Dec 6, 1916 in Tjorn, Iceland
d. Sep 13, 1982 in Cleveland, Ohio
Source: *AnObit 1982; IntWW 80; IntYB 80,
81, 82; NewYTBS 82; WhoGov 72; WhoWor
78*

Eldridge, David Roy
American. Musician, Band Leader
b. 1911
Source: *BioIn 10*

Eldridge, Florence
American. Actress
Won NY Drama Critics Award for *Long
Day's Journey into Night*, 1956.
b. Sep 5, 1901 in New York, New York
Source: *BiE&WWA; CurBio 43; FilmEn; Film
2; FilmgC; InWom; MotPP; MovMk;
NotNAT; ThFT; WhoHol A; WhoThe 77A;
WorAl*

Eldridge, Roy
American. Jazz Musician
b. Jan 29, 1911 in Pittsburgh, Pennsylvania
Source: *WhoAm 74, 76, 78, 80, 82; WhoJazz
72*

Eleanor of Aquitaine
[Eleanor of Guienne]
French. Consort
Marriage to Louis VII annulled; married
    Henry II, 1154 ; mother of Richard the
    Lion-Hearted.
b. 1122 in Aquitaine, France
d. Apr 1, 1204
Source: *DcEuL; InWom; LinLib S;
McGEWB; NewC,; REn; WhDW; WorAl*

Electric Light Orchestra
[Michael Alberquerque; Bev Bevan; Michael
    Edwards; Melvyn Gale; Wilf Gibson; Kelly
    Groucutt; Mik Kaminski; Jeff Lynne;
    Hugh MacDowell; Richard Tndy; Colin
    Walker]
English. Music Group
Orchestral rock group formed, 1971; hits
    include "Roll Over Beethoven"; "Evil
    Woman."
Source: *BkPepl; IlEncRk; RkOn 84*

Elegant, Robert Sampson
American. Author, Journalist
Asian news correspondent, 1951-75, who
    wrote *China's Red Masters*, 1951.
b. Mar 7, 1928 in New York, New York
Source: *AmAu&B; BioIn 4, 7, 11; ConAu 1R,
1NR; IntAu&W 76, 77; WhoAm 76, 78, 80,
82, 84; WhoWest 74, 76; WhoWor 74; WrDr
80*

Elgar, Edward William, Sir
English. Composer, Conductor, Musician
Best known for oratorios, pomp and
    circumstance marches, symphonic works in
    romantic style.
b. Jun 2, 1857 in Broadheath, England
d. Feb 23, 1934 in London, England
Source: *AtlBL; DcCM; REn*

Eliade, Mircea
American. Theologian
Wrote on comparative religion: *A History of
Religious Ideas*, 1977-85.
b. Mar 9, 1907 in Bucharest, Romania
d. Apr 22, 1986 in Chicago, Illinois
Source: *AmAu&B; Au&Wr 71; BiDPara;
CasWL; CurBio 85, 86; DrAS 74P; EncWL;
WhoAm 78, 80, 82; WhoMW 74; WhoWor
74; WorAu*

Elias, Rosalind
American. Opera Singer
b. Mar 13, 1931 in Lowell, Massachusetts
Source: *CelR; CurBio 67; InWom; WhoAm
82*

Eliezer, Israel ben
see: Ba,al Shem Tov, Israel

Elijah
Biblical Character
Source: *NewC*

Elijah Ben Solomon
Polish. Scholar
Jewish scholar called greatest authority on
    classical Judaism in modern times; wrote
    over 70 treatises.
b. 1720 in Vilna, Poland
d. 1797 in Vilna, Poland
Source: *BioIn 1, 3, 4, 5, 7; EuAu; McGEWB;
NewCol 75*

Eliot, Charles William
American. Educator
Pres., Harvard U, 1869-1909.
b. Mar 20, 1834 in Boston, Massachusetts
d. Aug 22, 1926 in Maine
Source: *Alli SUP; AmAu; AmAu&B; AmBi; ApCAB; BiD&SB; CyAL 1; DcAmAu; DcAmB; DcNAA; EncAB-H; NewCol 75; OxAmL; REn; REnAL; TwCBDA; WebAB; WhAm 1*

Eliot, George, pseud.
[Mary Ann Evans]
English. Author
b. Nov 22, 1819 in Warwickshire, England
d. Dec 22, 1880 in London, England
Source: *Alli SUP; AtlBL; BbD; BiD&SB; BrAu 19; CasWL; Chambr 3; ChhPo, S2; CrtT 3; CyWA; DcBiA; DcEnA, AP; DcEnL; DcEuL; DcLEL; EvLB; HerW; HsB&A; InWom; MnBBF; MouLC 3; NewC; OxEng; PenC ENG; RAdv 1; RComWL; REn; WebE&AL*

Eliot, George Fielding
American. Radio Commentator
b. Jun 22, 1894 in Brooklyn, New York
d. Apr 21, 1971 in Torrington, Connecticut
Source: *AmAu&B; ConAu 29R; CurBio 40, 71; MnBBF; REnAL; TwCA, SUP*

Eliot, John
English. Colonial Figure
b. Aug 5, 1604 in Widford, England
d. May 20, 1690 in Roxbury, Massachusetts
Source: *Alli; AmAu; AmAu&B; ApCAB; DcAmAu; DcAmB; DcAmReB; DcBiPP; McGEWB; OxAmH; OxAmL; TwCBDA; WebAB; WhAm HS*

Eliot, Martha May
American. Government Official, Physician
b. Apr 7, 1891 in Dorchester, Massachusetts
d. Feb 1978 in Cambridge, Massachusetts
Source: *BioIn 1, 2, 4, 5, 7, 11; CurBio 48, 78; IntWW 74*

Eliot, T(homas) S(tearns)
English. Poet, Critic
Wrote *Murder in the Cathedral*, 1935, *The Cocktail Party*, 1950; won Nobel Prize, 1948.
b. Sep 26, 1888 in Saint Louis, Missouri
d. Jan 4, 1965 in London, England
Source: *AmAu&B; AmWr; AnCL; AtlBL; BiE&WWA; CasWL; Chambr 3; ChhPo, S1, S2; CnDAL; CnE&AP; CnMD; CnMWL; CnThe; ConAmL; ConAu 5R, 25R; ConLC 1, 2, 3, 6, 9, 10, 13, 15; CroCD; CurBio 62, 65; CyWA; DcLEL; EncWL; EvLB; LongCTC; McGEWD; ModAL, S1; ModBrL, S1; ModWD; NewC; OxAmL; OxEng; OxThe; PenC AM, ENG; PIP&P; RAdv 1; RComWL; REn; REnAL; REnWD; SixAP; TwCA, SUP; TwCWr; WebE&AL; WhAm 4; WhNAA; WhoChL; WhoTwCL*

Elisofon, Eliot
American. Photographer, Artist, Filmmaker
Master of color, black and white photography, renowned watercolor artist.
b. Apr 17, 1911 in Manhattan, New York
d. Apr 7, 1973 in New York, New York
Source: *AmAu&B; ConAu 41R; CurBio 72, 73; LinLib L; MacBEP; NewYTBE 73; WhAm 5; WhoAmA 73, 80*

Elizabeth I
English. Queen
Daughter of Henry VIII, Anne Boleyn; ruled Great Britain, N Ireland, 1558-1603.
b. Sep 7, 1533 in Greenwich, England
d. Mar 24, 1603
Source: *BioIn 1, 2, 3, 4, 5, 6, 7, 8, 9, 10; McGEWB; NewCol 75; WebBD 80*

Elizabeth II
[Elizabeth Alexandra Mary]
English. Queen
Succeeded father George VI to throne upon his death, Feb 6, 1952.
b. Apr 21, 1926 in London, England
Source: *BioIn 2, 3, 4, 5, 6, 7, 8, 9, 10; CurBio 44, 55; IntWW 74; NewCol 75; Who 82; WhoAm 82*

Elizabeth, the Queen Mother
[Elizabeth Angela Marguerite]
English. Consort
Wife of King George VI; mother of Queen Elizabeth II, Princess Margaret.
b. Aug 4, 1900 in Hertfordshire, England
Source: *CurBio 81; IntWW 74; NewCol 75; WebBD 80*

Elizabeth of Hungary, Saint
Hungarian. Religious Figure
b. 1207
d. 1231
Source: *BioIn 1, 2, 3, 4, 5, 6, 7, 8, 11;*
NewCol 75; REn

Elizondo, Hector
American. Actor
In TV shows "Popi," 1976; "Casablanca,"
1983; film *American Gigolo,* 1980.
b. Dec 22, 1936 in New York, New York
Source: *IntMPA 80, 81, 82; WhoHol A;*
WhoThe 77, 81

Elkin, Benjamin
American. Children's Author
b. Aug 10, 1911 in Baltimore, Maryland
Source: *Alli; Au&Wr 71; AuBYP; ConAu 1R,*
4NR; SmATA 3; WhoMW 74; WhoWorJ 72;
WrDr 80

Elkin, Stanley Lawrence
American. Author, Journalist
b. May 11, 1930 in New York, New York
Source: *AmAu&B; ConAu 9R; ConLC 4, 6,*
9, 14; ConNov 72, 76; DrAF 76; DrAS 74E;
EncWL; PenC AM; WhoAm 74, 76, 78, 80,
82; WrDr 76

Elkins, Hillard
"Hilly"
American. Producer
Films include *A Doll's House,* 1972; stage
productions include *Streetcar Named*
Desire, 1974.
b. Oct 18, 1929 in New York, New York
Source: *CelR,; WhoAm 82; WhoThe 72, 77,*
81

Elkins, Stanley Maurice
American. Historian, Educator
b. Apr 29, 1925 in Boston, Massachusetts
Source: *ConAu 102; DrAS 74H; WhoAm 74,*
76, 78, 80, 82

Ellender, Allen Joseph
American. Politician
b. Sep 24, 1890 in Montegut, Louisiana
d. Jul 27, 1972 in Bethesda, Maryland
Source: *BiDrAC; CurBio 46, 72; NewYTBE*
71, 72; WhAm 5; WhAmP; WhoGov 75;
WhoS&SW 82

Ellerbee, Linda
American. Broadcast Journalist
With NBC News, 1978-86, ABC News,
1986--.
b. Aug 15, 1944 in Bryan, Texas
Source: *WhoAm 82, 84; WhoTelC*

Ellery, William
American. Judge
b. Dec 22, 1727 in Newport, Rhode Island
d. Feb 15, 1820 in Newport, Rhode Island
Source: *AmBi; ApCAB; BiAUS; BiDrAC;*
CelCen; DcAmB; Drake; HarEnUS; NatCAB
8; TwCBDA; WhAm HS; WhAmP

Elliman, Yvonne
[Mrs. William Oakes]
American. Singer
Appeared in *Jesus Christ Superstar;* sang "I
Don't Know How to Love Him."
b. Dec 29, 1953 in Hawaii
Source: *RkOn 74; WhoAm 82*

Ellin, Stanley
American. Author
Wrote *The Eighth Circle; House of Cards;*
Mirror, Mirror on the Wall.
b. Oct 6, 1916 in Brooklyn, New York
d. Jul 31, 1986 in New York, New York
Source: *AmAu&B; Au&Wr 71; ConAu 1R,*
4NR; EncMys; REnAL; WorAu; WrDr 76

Ellington, "Duke" (Edward Kennedy)
American. Band Leader, Composer
Wrote over 5,000 original works, including
"Satin Doll," "Mood Indigo."
b. Apr 29, 1899 in Washington, District of
Columbia
d. May 24, 1974 in New York, New York
Source: *AmSCAP 66; BiE&WWA; BioNews*
74; CelR; ConAu 49, 97; CurBio 41, 70, 74;
EncAB-H; FilmgC; NewYTBE 72; NewYTBS
74; WebAB; WhAm 6; WhScrn 77; Who 74;
WhoAm 74; WhoE 74; WhoGov 75; WhoJazz
72; WhoMus 72; WhoWor 78

Ellington, Edward
British. Air Marshal
b. 1877
d. Jun 13, 1967 in London, England
Source: *BioIn 8*

Ellington, Mercer
American. Musician, Band Leader
Son of Duke Ellington; took over orchestra,
1974.
b. Mar 11, 1919 in Washington, District of
Columbia
Source: *AmSCAP 66; WhoAm 82*

Elliot, Cass
[Ellen Naomi Cohen; Mamas and the Papas]
American. Singer
Solo career, 1967-74; hit song "Dream a
Little Dream of Me," 1968.
b. Feb 19, 1943 in Arlington, Virginia
d. Jul 29, 1974 in London, England
Source: *BioNews 74; CelR; NewYTBS 74;*
WhoHol B

Elliot, Win (Irwin)
American. Radio Performer
b. May 7, 1915 in Chelsea, Massachusetts
Source: *BioIn 1, 2; IntMPA 75*

Elliott, Bob
[Bob and Ray]
American. Comedian
b. Mar 26, 1923 in Boston, Massachusetts
Source: *CelR; CurBio 57*

Elliott, Bobby
see: Hollies, The

Elliott, Charles Loring
American. Artist
b. Oct 12, 1812 in Scipio, New York
d. Aug 25, 1868 in Albany, New York
Source: *AmBi; ApCAB; DcAmB; Drake;*
EarABI; TwCBDA; WhAm HS

Elliott, Denholm
English. Actor
Supporting actor in *Alfie,* 1966; *Raiders of*
the Lost Ark, 1981.
b. May 31, 1922 in London, England
Source: *CnThe; FilmgC; IntMPA 82;*
NotNAT; WhoHol A; WhoThe 81

Elliott, Dennis
see: Foreigner

Elliott, George Paul
American. Author
b. Jun 16, 1918 in Knightstown, Indiana
d. May 3, 1980 in New York, New York
Source: *ConAu 1R, 2NR; ConLC 2; ConNov*
72, 76; ConP 70, 75; DrAF 76; DrAP 75;
DrAS 74E; IndAu 1917; ModAL, S1;
OxAmL; WhoAm 74; WhoWor 78; WrDr 80

Elliott, Gertrude
American. Actress
b. 1874 in Rockland, Maine
d. Dec 24, 1950 in Kent, England
Source: *ChhPo; Film 1; NotAW; NotNAT A,*
B; ObitOF 79; WhScrn 74, 77; WhThe;
WhoHol B; WhoStg 1908; WomWWA 14

Elliott, Joe
[Def Leppard]
English. Singer
Lead singer; group named for poster he
designed.
b. Aug 1, 1959 in Sheffield, England
Source: *NF*

Elliott, "Jumbo" (James Francis)
American. Athletic Director
Villanova U. track coach, 1935-81; coached
28 Olympic runners.
b. Aug 8, 1915 in Philadelphia, Pennsylvania
d. Mar 22, 1981 in Juno Beach, Florida
Source: *BioIn 6, 11; NewYTBS 79, 81;*
WhoTr&F 73

Elliott, Maxine
[Jessie D McDermott Goodwin]
American. Actress
Star of play written for her *Her Own Way,*
1903; built, managed own theater, NY,
1908.
b. Feb 5, 1873 in Rockland, Maine
d. Mar 5, 1940 in Juan les Pins, France
Source: *AmBi; ApCAB X; CurBio 40; DcAmB*
S2; EncWT; FamA&A; Film 1; InWom;
LibW; NotAW; OxThe; TwYS; WhAm 1;
WhScrn 74, 77; WhThe; WhoHol B; WhoStg
1906, 1908

Elliott, Osborn
American. University Administrator, Editor,
Author
Editor *Newsweek,* 1955-76; director, Columbia
U. Graduate School of Journalism, 1979--.
b. Oct 25, 1924 in New York, New York
Source: *AmAu&B; ConAu 69; CurBio 78;*
IntAu&W 77; IntWW 74, 75, 76, 77, 78;
NewYTBS 76; St&PR 75; WhoAm 76, 78, 80,
82, 84; WhoE 74; WhoWor 74, 76, 78

Elliott, Robert B
American. Politician
b. Aug 11, 1842 in Boston, Massachusetts
d. Aug 9, 1884 in New Orleans, Louisiana
Source: *BioIn 1, 5, 6, 8, 9, 10; WhAm HS*

Elliott, Sam
American. Actor
In TV's "Yellow Rose," 1983; films include
The Legacy ; *Butch Cassidy and the*
Sundance Kid.
b. 1944 in Sacramento, California
Source: *WhoHol A*

Ellis, Carleton
American. Inventor, Chemist
Held over 750 patents including many in
plastics.
b. Sep 20, 1876 in Keene, New Hampshire
d. Jan 13, 1941 in Miami, Florida
Source: *CurBio 41; DcAmB S3; NatCAB 32;
WhAm 1*

Ellis, Dock Phillip, Jr.
American. Baseball Player
b. Mar 11, 1945 in Los Angeles, California
Source: *BaseEn 85; WhoProB 73*

Ellis, Harry Bearse
American. Journalist
b. Dec 9, 1921 in Springfield, Massachusetts
Source: *AmAu&B; AuBYP; ConAu 1R, 2NR;
SmATA 9; WhoAm 74, 76, 78, 80, 82;
WhoWor 78; WrDr 76*

Ellis, Havelock(Henry Havelock)
English. Psychologist
Seven-volume work *Studies of the Psychology
of Sex,* 1897-1928, paved way for rational
discussion of sex.
b. Feb 2, 1859 in Surrey, England
d. Jul 8, 1939 in Hintlesham, England
Source: *AtlBL; CasWL; ChhPo; DcLEL;
EvLB; LongCTC; ModBrL; NewC; OxEng;
REn; TwCA, SUP; WhoLA*

Ellis, Perry Edwin
American. Fashion Designer
Created the "American Look," easy to wear,
youthful garments in natural fibers, colors,
1976.
b. Mar 3, 1940 in Churchland, Virginia
d. May 30, 1986 in New York, New York
Source: *CurBio 86; NewYTBS 82, 86;
WhoAm 82, 84; WhoFash*

Ellis, Robin
English. Actor
Lead role in BBC TV series "Poldark",
shown on PBS.
b. 1944 in London, England
Source: *BioIn 11; NewYTBS 78*

Ellis, Ruth
Welsh. Murderer
Last woman hanged in England; murdered
her lover.
b. 1927 in Rhyl, Wales
d. Jul 13, 1955 in London, England
Source: *BioIn 11; LookW*

Ellison, Harlan Jay
American. Author
b. May 27, 1934 in Cleveland, Ohio
Source: *ConAu 5R, 5NR; ConLC 1, 13;
DrAF 76; WhoAm 76, 78, 80, 82; WrDr 76*

Ellison, Ralph Waldo
American. Author
Novel *The Invisible Man,* 1952, proclaimed
beginning of 1960s civil rights movement.
b. Mar 1, 1914 in Oklahoma City, Oklahoma
Source: *AmAu&B; BlkAWP; CasWL; CnDAL;
ConAu 9R; ConLC 1, 3, 11; ConNov 72, 76;
CurBio 68; DrAF 76; EncAB-H; EncWL;
IntWW 74; LivgBAA; ModAL, S1; OxAmL;
PenC AM; RAdv 1; REn; REnAL; TwCWr;
WebAB; WebE&AL; WhoAm 74, 76, 78, 80,
82; WhoBlA 75; WhoE 74; WhoGov 75;
WhoTwCL; WhoWor 78; WorAu; WrDr 80*

Ellison, Virginia Howell
American. Children's Author
b. Feb 4, 1910 in New York, New York
Source: *BiDrLUS 70; ConAu 33R; SmATA 4;
WrDr 80*

Ellsberg, Daniel
American. Author, Economist, Political
Activist
Leaked Pentagon Papers to press, 1971;
wrote *Papers on the War,* 1972.
b. Apr 7, 1931 in Chicago, Illinois
Source: *BioNews 74; ConAu 69; CurBio 73;
LinLib S; NewYTBE 71; WhoAm 80, 82;
WhoWor 80; WorAl*

Ellsberg, Edward
American. Admiral, Engineer, Author
b. Nov 21, 1891 in New Haven, Connecticut
Source: *AmAu&B; AmNov; Au&Wr 71;
AuBYP; ConAu 5R; CurBio 42; JBA 34, 51;
REnAL; SmATA 7; TwCA, SUP; WhoAm 74,
76, 78, 80, 82*

Ellsler, Effie
American. Actress
Played the wronged miller's daughter in
melodrama *Hazel Kirk,* 1880s.
b. Sep 17, 1854 in Philadelphia, Pennsylvania
d. Oct 8, 1942 in Los Angeles, California
Source: *NotAW*

Ellsworth, Lincoln
American. Explorer
First man to cross both Arctic and Antarctic
by air.
b. May 12, 1880 in Chicago, Illinois
d. May 26, 1951 in New York, New York
Source: *AmAu&B; DcAmB S5; NewCol 75;
WebAB; WebBD 80; WhAm 3*

Elman, Mischa
Russian. Musician
b. Jan 21, 1891 in Talnoye, Russia
d. Apr 5, 1967 in New York, New York
Source: *AmSCAP 66; CurBio 45, 67; WhAm 4*

Elman, Ziggy
[Harry Finkelman]
American. Musician
b. May 26, 1914 in Philadelphia, Pennsylvania
d. Jun 26, 1968 in Los Angeles, California
Source: *WhoHol B; WhoJazz 72*

Elsheimer, Adam
[Adam Tedesco]
German. Artist
b. Mar 18, 1578 in Frankfurt, Germany
d. Dec 1610 in Rome, Italy
Source: *AtlBL; WebBD 80*

Elting, Mary Letha
American. Children's Author
b. Jun 21, 1906 in Creede, Colorado
Source: *AuBYP; ConAu 9R, 4NR; ForWC 70; MorJA; SmATA 2*

Elting, Victor, Jr.
American. Advertising Executive
b. Aug 12, 1905 in Winnetka, Illinois
Source: *WhoF&I 74*

Eltinge, Julian
[William Dalton]
American. Actor
Female impersonator in plays *The Crinoline Girl;The Fascinating Widow.*
b. May 14, 1883
d. Mar 7, 1941 in New York, New York
Source: *CurBio 41; Film 1, 2; FilmgC; NotNAT B; ObitOF 79; OxThe; WhScrn 74*

Elton, Charles Sutherland
English. Zoologist
b. Mar 29, 1900
Source: *BioIn 8, 9; IntWW 74; Who 74*

Eluard, Paul
[Eugene Grindel]
French. Author
Early Surrealist, 1919-38; wrote *Poetry and Truth,* 1942.
b. Dec 14, 1895 in Saint Denis, France
d. Nov 18, 1952 in Charenton, France
Source: *AtlBL; CasWL; ClDMEL; CnMWL; ConAu 104; EncWL; EvEuW; ModRL; OxEng; OxFr; PenC EUR; REn; TwCA SUP; TwCWr; WhDW; WhoTwCL; WorAl*

Elvira, Pablo
Puerto Rican. Opera Singer
Leading bass-baritone, Metropolitan Opera Co., 1979--.
b. Sep 24, 1938 in Santurce, Puerto Rico
Source: *WhoOp 76*

Elway, John Albert
American. Football Player
All-American quarterback; first round draft pick in baseball, football; signed with Denver Broncos, 1983.
b. Jun 28, 1960 in Port Angeles, Washington
Source: *BioIn 12; FootReg 85; NewYTBS 82, 83*

Ely, Joe
American. Musician, Singer
Country-rock singer who had hit album *Notta Gotta Lotta,* 1981.
b. 1947 in Lubbock, Texas
Source: *BioIn 12*

Ely, Richard Theodore
American. Economist, Reformer
Founded Institute for Research in Land Economics, 1920.
b. Apr 13, 1854 in Ripley, New York
d. Oct 4, 1943 in Old Lynne, Connecticut
Source: *CurBio 43; DcAmB S3; WebBD 80*

Ely, Ron
[Ronald Pierce]
American. Actor
Screen's 15th Tarzan who starred in two films, 1970; in TV series, 1968-69.
b. Jun 21, 1938 in Hereford, Texas
Source: *FilmEn; MotPP; WhoHol A*

Elytis, Odysseus
Greek. Poet, Art Critic
b. Nov 2, 1911 in Iraklion, Crete
Source: *BioIn 12; CurBio 80; IntWW 79*

Elzevir, Louis
Dutch. Publisher
Founded prestigious publishing firm; noted for typography, small volumes.
b. 1540 in Louvain, Belgium
d. Feb 4, 1617 in Leiden, Netherlands
Source: *DcBiPP; EncAJ; NewC*

Emanuel, David
English. Fashion Designer
With wife, Elizabeth, designed Princess Diana's wedding dress, 1981.
b. 1953 in England
Source: *NewYTBS 81*

Emanuel, Elizabeth
[Mrs. David Emanuel]
English. Fashion Designer
With husband, David, designed Princess
Diana's wedding dress, 1981.
b. 1954
Source: *NewYTBS 81*

Emanuel, James A
American. Author
b. Jun 21, 1921 in Allande, Nebraska
Source: *BlkAWP; ConAu 29R; ConP 75;
DrAP 75; DrAS 74E; LivgBAA; WrDr 80*

Emanuel the Great
see: Manuel I

Emanuelli, Enrico
Italian. Author, Journalist
b. 1909
d. 1967
Source: *BioIn 8*

Embry, Wayne
American. Basketball Player, Basketball
Executive
b. Mar 26, 1937 in Springfield, Ohio
Source: *InB&W 80; WhoAm 78, 80, 82, 84;
WhoBbl 73*

Emerson, Faye Margaret
American. Actress
Hosted late night talk show "Faye Emerson's
Wonderful Town," 1950s.
b. Jul 8, 1917 in Elizabeth, Louisiana
d. Mar 9, 1983 in Majorca, Spain
Source: *BiE&WWA; CurBio 51, 83N; FilmgC;
HolP 40; InWom; MotPP; MovMk; NewYTBS
83; WhAm 8; WhThe; WhoHol A; WhoThe
77A*

Emerson, Gladys Anderson
American. Biochemist, Nutritionist
b. Jul 1, 1903 in Caldwell, Kansas
Source: *AmM&WS 73P; BioIn 3, 5, 11;
WhAm 8; WhoAm 76, 78, 80, 82*

Emerson, Hope
American. Actress
Body measurements (6'2", 200 lbs) exploited
in films *Caged; Adam's Rib.*
b. Oct 29, 1898 in Hawarden, Iowa
d. Apr 25, 1960 in Hollywood, California
Source: *FilmgC; MotPP; MovMk; NewYTET;
ObitOF 79; Vers A; WhScrn 74, 77;
WhoAmW 70; WhoHol B*

Emerson, Keith
[Emerson, Lake, and Palmer; The Nice]
English. Musician
Known for flamboyant performance at
keyboards.
b. Nov 1, 1944 in Todmorden, England
Source: *WhoRocM 82*

Emerson, Lake, and Palmer
[Keith Emerson; Gregory Lake; Carl Palmer]
English. Music Group
Source: *BkPepl; EncPR&S 74*

Emerson, Ralph Waldo
American. Essayist, Poet, Philosopher
Friend of Henry Thoreau; wrote essay *Self-
Reliance,* 1844.
b. May 25, 1803 in Boston, Massachusetts
d. Apr 27, 1882 in Concord, Massachusetts
Source: *Alli, SUP; AmAu; AmAu&B; AmBi;
AmWr; AnCL; ApCAB; AtlBL; BbD; BiD&SB;
CasWL; Chambr 3; ChhPo, S1; CnDAL;
CnE&AP; CrtT 3; CyAL 2; CyWA; DcAmAu;
DcAmB; DcEnA, AP; DcEnL; DcLEL;
DcNAA; Drake; EncAB-H; EvLB; MouLC 4;
OxAmL; OxEng; PenC AM; RAdv 1;
RComWL; REn; REnAL; Str&VC; TwCBDA;
WebAB; WebE&AL; WhAm HS*

Emerson, Roy
Australian. Tennis Player
b. Nov 3, 1936 in Kingsway, Australia
Source: *CurBio 65*

Emery, Anne
American. Author
b. Sep 1, 1907 in Fargo, North Dakota
Source: *BioIn 2, 3, 6, 7, 9; ConAu 1R, 2NR;
SmATA 1*

Emin Pasha
[Eduard Schnitzer]
German. Physician, Explorer
Governor of Equatoria, Egyptian Sudan
province.
b. Mar 8, 1840 in Oppeln, Prussia
d. 1892 in Stanley Falls, Congo
Source: *BioIn 1, 2, 8, 9, 10; NewCol 75;
WebBD 80*

Eminescu, Mihail
Romanian. Poet
b. Dec 20, 1849 in Botosoni, Romania
d. Jun 15, 1889 in Bucharest, Romania
Source: *CIDMEL; EuAu; EvEuW*

Emmet, Robert
Irish. Revolutionary
Led uprising in Dublin for independence,
    1803; gave stirring speech from scaffold
    before he was hanged.
b. Sep 20, 1178 in Dublin, Ireland
d. Sep 20, 1803 in Dublin, Ireland
Source: *DcIrB; DcIrL; LinLib S; McGEWB;
NewCol 75; PoIre; REn; WebBD 80*

Emmett, Daniel Decatur
American. Songwriter
b. Oct 29, 1815 in Clinton, Ohio
d. Jun 28, 1904
Source: *AmAu; AmAu&B; AmBi; BiDAmM;
ChhPo S1; OxAmL,; OxMus; REnAL*

Empedocles
Greek. Philosopher
First to state principles central to theory of
    physics; believed blood to be thinking
    organ.
b. 493 BC in Acragas, Sicily
d. 433 BC
Source: *BbD; BiD&SB; CasWL; NewC;
NewCol 75; PenC CL; WebBD 80*

Empson, William, Sir
English. Poet, Critic
Wrote *Collected Poems of William Empson,*
    1949; *Milton's God,* 1961; *Using Biography,*
    1985.
b. Sep 27, 1906 in Goole, England
d. Apr 15, 1984 in London, England
Source: *CasWL; CnE&AP; CnMWL; ConAu
17R; ConLC 3; ConP 70, 75; DcLEL;
EncWL; IntWW 74; LongCTC; ModBrL;
NewC; OxEng; PenC ENG; RAdv 1; REn;
TwCA SUP; TwCWr; WebE&AL; Who 74;
WhoTwCL; WhoWor 78; WrDr 80*

En-Lai, Chou
see: Chou En-Lai

Ender, Kornelia
[Mrs. Roland Matthes]
German. Swimmer
Won four gold medals, 1976 Olympics; called
    greatest woman swimmer ever.
b. Oct 25, 1958 in Plauen, Germany (East)
Source: *BioIn 10*

Enders, John Franklin
American. Physician
Work in virology led to vaccines for polio,
    measles, German measles, mumps; won
    Nobel Prize, 1954.
b. Feb 10, 1897 in West Hartford,
    Connecticut
d. Sep 8, 1985 in Waterford, Connecticut
Source: *BioIn 5, 6, 8, 11; CurBio 55, 86;
IntWW 74; Who 74; WhoAm 74; WhoWor
74*

Endo, Shusaku
Japanese. Author
Oriental-Christian novelist, playwright who
    wrote *Shiroihito,* 1955; *Chinmoku,* 1966.
b. Mar 27, 1923 in Tokyo, Japan
Source: *BioIn 8, 11; ConAu 29R; ConLC 7,
14*

Enesco, Georges
[Georges Enescu]
Romanian. Violinist, Composer
b. Aug 7, 1881 in Cordaremi, Romania
d. May 4, 1955 in Paris, France
Source: *NewCol 75; WebBD 80; WhAm 3*

Engel, Georgia Bright
American. Actress
Played Georgette on TV series "The Mary
    Tyler Moore Show," 1972-77.
b. Jul 28, 1948 in Washington, District of
    Columbia
Source: *WhoAm 80, 82*

Engel, Lehman (Aaron Lehman)
American. Author, Conductor
Conducted over 100 Broadway hits; won two
    Tonys; wrote autobiography *This Bright
    Day,* 1973.
b. Sep 12, 1910 in Jackson, Mississippi
d. Aug 29, 1982 in New York, New York
Source: *AmAu&B; AnObit 1982; Baker 78;
BiE&WWA; ConAu 107, 41R; DcCM;
NewYTBS 82; NotNAT; WhAm 8; WhoAm
82; WhoMus 72; WhoWor 74, 76, 78;
WhoWorJ 72*

Engel, Lyle Kenyon
American. Publisher
Founded Book Creations, Inc., 1973; known
    for fiction vols. *Kent Family Chronicles.*
b. May 12, 1915 in New York, New York
d. Aug 10, 1986 in Miami, Florida
Source: *ConAu 85; EncSF; WhoAm 82, 84*

Engelman, Wilfred
American. Opera Singer
b. 1905 in Detroit, Michigan
d. Feb 12, 1978 in Cincinnati, Ohio
Source: *BioIn 11*

Engels, Friedrich
German. Socialist Leader
One of founders of modern communism with
Karl Marx; collaborated on *The
Communist Manifesto* with Marx.
b. Sep 28, 1820 in Barmen, Germany
d. Aug 5, 1895 in London, England
Source: *DcAmSR; LuthC 75; McGEWB;
OxGer; REn; WorAl*

England Dan and John Ford Coley
[John Edward Coley; Danny Seals]
American. Music Group
Source: *RkOn 74*

Engle, Clair
American. Politician
Dem. congressman, senator from CA, 1958-
64; conservation advocate.
b. Sep 21, 1911 in Bakersfield, California
d. Jul 30, 1964 in Washington, District of
Columbia
Source: *CurBio 57, 64; DcAmB S7*

Engle, Eloise Katherine
American. Author
b. Apr 12, 1923 in Seattle, Washington
Source: *ConAu 1R, 2NR; ForWC 70; SmATA
9; WrDr 80*

Engle, Joe Henry
American. Astronaut
Crew member aboard second flight of space
shuttle *Columbia,* Nov, 1981.
b. Aug 26, 1932 in Abilene, Kansas
Source: *NewYTBS 81; WhoS&SW 73;
WorDWW*

Engle, Paul
American. Author
b. Oct 12, 1908 in Cedar Rapids, Iowa
Source: *AmAu&B; ChhPo, S1, S2; CnDAL;
ConAmA; ConAu 1R, 5NR; ConP 70, 75;
CurBio 42; DcLEL; DrAP 75; DrAS 74E;
OxAmL; REnAL; SixAP; WhoAm 74, 76, 78,
80, 82; WhoWor 78; WorAu; WrDr 80*

Englemann, Robert A
[The Hostages]
American. Hostage in Iran
b. 1947 in Pasadena, California
Source: *NewYTBS 81*

English, Doug (Lowell Douglas)
American. Football Player
Four-time all-pro defensive lineman, Detroit
Lions, 1975-79, 1981-85.
b. Aug 25, 1953 in Dallas, Texas
Source: *FootReg 81*

English Beat
[Dave Blockhead; Andy Cox; Wesley
Magoogan; Everett Morton; 'Ranking
Roger'; 'Dave Steele; Dave Wakeling]
English. Music Group
Revivalist group founded 1979-83; hit album
Special Beat Forces, 1983.
Source: *RolSEnR 83*

Engstrom, Elmer William
American. Business Executive
With RCA 41 yrs.; played role in
development of first color TV tube.
b. Aug 25, 1901 in Minneapolis, Minnesota
d. Oct 30, 1984 in Hightstown, New Jersey
Source: *AmM&WS 79P; BlueB 76; ConNews
85-2; CurBio 51, 85; InSci; IntWW 80, 81,
81; NewYTBS 84*

Enke, Karin
German. Speed Skater
b. 1962
Source: *BioIn 12*

Ennis, Del(mer)
American. Baseball Player
b. Jun 8, 1925 in Philadelphia, Pennsylvania
Source: *BaseEn 85; BioIn 1, 3; WhoProB 73*

Eno, Brian
[Roxy Music]
English. Musician, Producer
Co-founder Roxy Music, 1971; solo act since
1973; produced three Talking Heads
albums.
b. May 15, 1948 in Woodbridge, England
Source: *BioIn 11; IlEncRk; RolSEnR 83;
WhoAm 82*

Enoch, Kurt
American. Publisher
Pioneer in paperback publishing with New
American Library, Inc., 1947-60.
b. Nov 22, 1895 in Hamburg, Germany
d. Feb 15, 1982 in Puerto Rico
Source: *AnObit 1982; NewYTBS 82; WhoAmJ
80, 80; WhoE 77, 79, 81; WhoWorJ 78*

Enright, Dennis Joseph
English. Author
b. Mar 11, 1920 in Leamington, England
Source: *Au&Wr 71; ChhPo S2; ConAu 1R;
ConLC 4; ConNov 72, 76; ConP 70, 75;
IntWW 74; LongCTC; ModBrL, S1; NewC;
PenC ENG; TwCWr; Who 74; WhoTwCL;
WhoWor 78; WorAu; WrDr 80*

Enright, Elizabeth
American. Artist, Author
b. Sep 17, 1909 in Oak Park, Illinois
d. Jun 8, 1968
Source: *AmAu&B; AnCL; AuBYP; BkCL; ConAu 25R, 61; CurBio 47, 68; IlsCB 1744, 1946; InWom; JBA 51; Newb 1922; SmATA 9; WhAm 5*

Ensor, James
Belgian. Artist
b. Apr 13, 1860 in Ostend, Belgium
d. Nov 19, 1949 in Ostend, Belgium
Source: *AtlBL; CurBio 43; WhAm 4*

Entremont, Phillippe
French. Musician
b. Jun 7, 1934 in Reims, France
Source: *WhoAm 82; WhoMus 72*

Entwistle, John
[The Who]
English. Musician, Singer
b. Sep 10, 1944 in London, England
Source: *WhoAm 80, 82*

Enver Pasha
Turkish. General, Political Leader
b. Nov 23, 1881 in Apana, Turkey
d. Aug 4, 1922 in Bukhara, Turkey
Source: *McGEWB; NewCol 75*

Ephron, Nora
American. Author
Wrote best-seller *Heartburn,* starring Meryl Streep, Jack Nicholson,1986.
b. May 19, 1941 in New York, New York
Source: *AuNews 2; ConAu 65; ConLC 17; WhoAm 78, 80, 82*

Epictetus
Greek. Philosopher
Stoic philosophy based on indifference to external goods.
b. 55
d. 135
Source: *BbD; BiD&SB; CasWL; NewC; PenC CL; RComWL; REn*

Epicurus
Greek. Philosopher
Epicureanism described pleasure as highest, only good; the avoidance of pain.
b. 342 BC in Samos, Greece
d. 270 BC
Source: *BbD; BiD&SB; CasWL; NewC; OxEng; PenC CL; RComWL; REn*

Epperson, Frank W
American. Inventor
Patented the Popsicle, 1924.
b. 1894
d. Oct 25, 1983 in Fremont, California
Source: *NF*

Epps, Jack, Jr.
American. Screenwriter
With Jim Cash, wrote screenplays for 1986 films *Top Gun, Legal Eagles.*
b. 1949 in Detroit, Michigan
Source: *NF*

Epstein, Alvin
American. Author
b. May 24, 1925 in Bronx, New York
Source: *BiE&WWA; NotNAT; PIP&P; WhoAm 74; WhoThe 77*

Epstein, Brian
English. Manager
Managed The Beatles, 1961-67; died in swimming pool accident.
b. Sep 19, 1934 in Liverpool, England
d. Aug 27, 1967 in London, England
Source: *IlEncRk; ObitOF 79; ObitT 1961; WorAl*

Epstein, Edward Jay
American. Author, Educator
b. Dec 6, 1935 in New York, New York
Source: *ConAu 17R; WhoWorJ 72*

Epstein, Jacob, Sir
English. Sculptor
Known for peculiar rough-hewn style in bronze busts, Oscar Wilde's tomb in Paris.
b. Aug 9, 1880 in London, England
d. Aug 9, 1959 in London, England
Source: *AtlBL; CurBio 45, 59; LongCTC; OxAmL; REn; REnAL; WhAm 3*

Epstein, Julius
American. Writer
Won Oscar for *Casablanca,* 1942.
b. Aug 22, 1909 in New York, New York
Source: *VarWW 85*

Epstein, Philip G
American. Screenwriter, Dramatist
Co-wrote film classics *Casablanca,* 1942; *Arsenic and Old Lace,* 1944.
b. Aug 22, 1909 in New York, New York
d. Feb 7, 1952 in Los Angeles, California
Source: *ConAu 117; DcAmB S5; DcLB 26*

Erasmus, Desiderius
[Geert Geerts; Gerhard Gerhards]
Dutch. Author, Philosopher, Scholar
Best known for satire *The Praise of Folly*,
    1509.
b. Oct 27, 1469 in Rotterdam, Netherlands
d. Jul 12, 1536 in Basel, Switzerland
Source: *AtlBL; BbD; BiD&SB; BiHiMed;
CasWL; CroE&S; CyWA; DcBiPP; DcCathB;
DcEnL; DcEuL; DcSpL; EuAu; EvEuW;
NewC; OxEng; OxFr; OxGer; PenC EUR;
RComWL; REn*

Eratosthenes
Greek. Scholar
Head of library at Alexandria, 240BC;
    measured circumference, tilt of Earth.
b. 275 ?BC in Cyrene, Greece
d. 195 ?BC
Source: *BioIn 3, 7, 8, 9; CasWL; PenC CL*

Erdman, Paul E
Canadian. Economist, Author
b. May 19, 1932 in Stratford, Ontario
Source: *AuNews 1; ConAu 61; WhoAm 82;
WrDr 76*

Erede, Alberto
Italian. Conductor
b. Nov 8, 1909 in Genoa, Italy
Source: *WhoMus 72*

Erhard, Ludwig
German. Economist, Politician
b. Feb 4, 1897 in Fuerth, Germany
d. May 7, 1977 in Bonn, Germany (West)
Source: *Au&Wr 71; CurBio 50, 64; IntWW
74; Who 74*

Erhard, Werner
[John Paul Rosenberg]
American. Educator
Developed est, 1971, an individual, social
    transformation technique.
b. Sep 5, 1935 in Philadelphia, Pennsylvania
Source: *BioIn 10; BkPepl; WhoAm 78, 80, 82*

Eric IX
Swedish. King
d. 1161
Source: *BioIn 5; NewCol 75*

Eric the Red
[Eirikr Thorvaldsson]
Norwegian. Navigator
Father of Leif Ericson; discovered, colonized
    Greenland, 982.
b. 950 in Norway
d. 1000
Source: *ApCAB; NewCol 75; OxCan; REn;
WhAm HS*

Erickson, Eric
Swedish. Spy
Allied spy, WW II; film of life *The
    Counterfeit Traitor*, starred William
    Holden.
b. 1890 in Brooklyn, New York
d. Jan 24, 1983 in Menton, France
Source: *EncE 75; NewYTBS 83*

Erickson, Leif
American. Singer, Actor
Best known for role of Big Jon Cannon on
    TV series "The High Chaparral."
b. Oct 27, 1911 in Alameda, California
d. Jan 30, 1986 in Pensacola, Florida
Source: *BiE&WWA; FilmgC; IntMPA 75, 76,
77, 78, 79, 80, 81, 82; MotPP; MovMk;
WhoAmP 73; WhoHol A*

Ericson, Leif
Icelandic. Navigator, Explorer
Discovered N American coast, circa 1000,
    which he named Vinland.
b. 975 in Iceland
Source: *NewC; NewCol 75; PIP&P; REn;
REnAL*

Ericsson, John
American. Engineer
Invented ironclad "Monitor" battleship, 1862;
    began age of modern warsships.
b. Jul 31, 1803 in Varmland, Sweden
d. Mar 8, 1889 in New York, New York
Source: *Alli SUP; AmBi; ApCAB; BiD&SB;
DcAmAu; DcAmB; Drake; TwCBDA; WebAB;
WhAm HS*

Erigena, John Scotus
Irish. Philosopher
b. 810
d. 891
Source: *Alli; BrAu,; DcBiPP; DcEnL; EvLB;
OxEng*

Erikson, Erik Homburger
American. Psychoanalyst
b. Jun 15, 1902 in Frankfurt, Germany
Source: *AmAu&B; AmM&WS 73S; CelR;
ConAu 25R; CurBio 71; EncAB-H; IntWW
74; WebAB; WhoAm 74, 76, 78, 80, 82;
WhoWor 78; WrDr 76*

Erlander, Tage Fritiof
Swedish. Politician
Prime minister, 1946-69; instituted
    comprehensive school system, social
    security in Sweden.
b. Jun 13, 1901 in Ransater, Sweden
d. Jun 21, 1985 in Huddinge, Sweden
Source: *CurBio 47; IntWW 74*

Erlanger, Joseph
American. Physiologist
Shared 1944 Nobel Prize for work on nerve
impulses.
b. Jan 5, 1874 in San Francisco, California
d. Dec 5, 1965 in Saint Louis, Missouri
Source: *DcAmB S7; WebBD 80*

Erman, Jacques DeForest, pseud.
see: Ackerman, Forest J

Erman, John
American. Director
Won Emmy for "Who Will Love My
Children," 1983.
b. in Chicago, Illinois
Source: *VarWW 85*

Ernst, Jimmy
American. Author, Artist
Son of Max Ernst; one of leading
abstractionists in US.
b. Jun 24, 1920 in Cologne, Germany
d. Feb 6, 1984 in New York, New York
Source: *ConAu 112; NewYTBS 84; OxTwCA;
PhDcTCA 77; WhoAm 84; WhoAmA 84*

Ernst, Kenneth
American. Cartoonist
b. 1918 in Illinois
Source: *WorECom*

Ernst, Max
German. Artist
b. Apr 2, 1891 in Cologne, Germany
d. Apr 1, 1976 in Paris, France
Source: *BioNews 74; CelR; ConAu 65; CurBio
42, 61; IntWW 74; REn; Who 74; WhoAm
74*

Ernst, Paul
German. Author, Critic
b. Mar 7, 1866 in Elbingerode, Germany
d. May 13, 1933 in Saint Georgen, Germany
Source: *CasWL; ClDMEL; CnMD; EncWL;
EvEuW; McGEWD; ModGL; ModWD;
OxGer; PenC EUR; WhoLA*

Errol, Leon
Australian. Actor
Comedian in Ziegfeld Follies, 1911-15.
b. Jul 3, 1881 in Sydney, Australia
d. Oct 12, 1951 in Los Angeles, California
Source: *CmpEPM; DcAmB S5; EncMT; Film
2; FilmgC; MotPP; MovMk; PIP&P; Vers B;
WhScrn 74, 77; WhThe; WhoHol B*

Erskine, Carl Daniel
"Oisk"
American. Baseball Player
Pitcher, Brooklyn/LA Dodgers, 1948-59; two
no-hitters, 1952, 1956.
b. Dec 13, 1926 in Anderson, Indiana
Source: *BaseEn 85; WhoProB 73*

Erskine, John
American. Author, Educator
Wrote humorous versions of famous legends:
Galahad, 1926.
b. Oct 5, 1879 in New York, New York
d. Jun 2, 1951 in New York, New York
Source: *AmAu&B; AmLY; AmNov; ChhPo,
S1; CnDAL; ConAmA; ConAmL; DcAmB S5;
DcLEL; LinLib L; LongCTC; NotNAT B;
ObitOF 79; OxAmL; REnAL; TwCA, SUP;
WebAB; WhAm 3; WhNAA,*

Erte
[Romain DeTirtoff]
Russian. Fashion Designer
b. Nov 23, 1892 in Saint Petersburg, Russia
Source: *CurBio 80; WorFshn*

Ertegun, Ahmet
American. Businessman, Soccer Executive
Co-founder, Atlantic Records, 1947; pres.,
NY Cosmos soccer team, 1971--.
b. Jul 31, 1923 in Istanbul, Turkey
Source: *CelR,; WhoAm 80, 82*

Erteszek, Jan
Polish. Business Executive
Co-founder, with wife, of Olga Co., one of
world's leading manufacturers of lingerie.
b. Dec 24, 1913 in Krakow, Poland
d. Jun 27, 1986 in Santa Monica, California
Source: *WhoAm 82, 84*

Ertz, Susan
American. Author
Wrote novel *The Philosopher's Daughter,*
1976.
b. 1894 in Surrey, England
d. Apr 11, 1985
Source: *ConAu 5R, 116; TwCA; WhE&EA;
Who 85*

Eruzione, Mike
American. Hockey Player
Captain, US Olympic hockey team, 1980;
advisor on movie *Miracle on Ice.*
b. Oct 25, 1954 in Boston, Massachusetts
Source: *BioIn 12; NewYTBS 82*

Ervin, Patrick, pseud.
see: Howard, Robert Ervin

Ervin, Sam(uel James, Jr.)
American. Politician
Senator, 1954-74, known for role in 1973
    Watergate hearings.
b. Sep 27, 1896 in Morganton, North
    Carolina
d. Apr 23, 1985 in Winston-Salem, North
    Carolina
Source: *BioNews 74; CelR; CngDr 74;
ConNews 85-2; CurBio 55, 73; IntWW 82;
IntYB 82; NewYTBE 70, 73; WhoAm 80, 82;
WhoAmP 81; WhoGov 72; WhoS&SW 73;
WhoWor 80*

Erving, Julius Winfield
"Doctor J"
American. Basketball Player
Forward, Philadelphia 76ers, 1976--; MVP,
    1974, 1976, 1981.
b. Feb 22, 1950 in Roosevelt, New York
Source: *BkPepl; CurBio 75; InB&W 80;
NegAl 76; NewYTBE 72; NewYTBS 75, 76;
WhoAm 78, 80, 82; WhoBbl 73; WhoBlA 77*

Erwin, "Pee Wee" (George)
American. Jazz Musician, Composer
Swing-era trumpeter who played with Benny
    Goodman, Tommy Dorsey bands, 1930s;
    led own band, 1940s-50s.
b. May 30, 1913 in Falls City, Nebraska
d. Jun 20, 1981 in Teaneck, New Jersey
Source: *AmSCAP 66; BiDAmM; EncJzS 70;
WhoJazz 72*

Erwin, Stuart
American. Comedian, Actor
b. Feb 14, 1902 in Squaw Valley, California
d. Dec 21, 1967 in Beverly Hills, California
Source: *FilmgC; MotPP; MovMk; WhScrn 74,
77; WhoHol B*

Esau
Biblical Character
Source: *BioIn 10; NewCol 75; WebBD 80*

Escher, Maurits Cornelis
Dutch. Artist
b. 1898
d. 1972 in Hilversum, Netherlands
Source: *BioIn 10*

Escobar, Sixto
Puerto Rican. Boxer
b. Mar 23, 1913 in Barceloneta, Puerto Rico
Source: *WhoBox 74*

Escobedo, Danny
American. Criminal
b. 1940
Source: *BioIn 10*

Escoffier, Georges Auguste
French. Chef
b. 1846
d. 1935
Source: *NewCol 75; WebBD 80*

Esenin, Sergei Aleksandrovich
[Sergei Aleksandrovich Yesenin]
Russian. Poet
b. Feb 21, 1895 in Konstantinovo, Russia
d. Dec 28, 1925 in Leningrad, U.S.S.R.
Source: *CasWL; ClDMEL; CnMWL; ConAu
104; EncWL; EvEuW; ModSL 1; REn;
TwCWr; WhoTwCL; WorAl; WorAu*

Eshkol, Levi
Israeli. Prime Minister
b. 1895
d. Feb 26, 1969 in Jerusalem, Israel
Source: *CurBio 63, 69; WhAm 5*

Esmond, Jill
English. Actress
Married to Lawrence Olivier, 1930-40; films
    include *First Lady; Thirteen Women.*
b. Jan 26, 1908 in London, England
Source: *FilmgC; WhoHol A; WhoThe 77A*

Espinosa, Al
American. Golfer
b. Mar 24, 1894 in Monterey, California
d. Jan 4, 1957 in San Francisco, California
Source: *BioIn 4; WhoGolf*

Esposito, Joseph
"Diamond Joe"
American. Criminal
Labor organizer accused of murder, operating
    illegal stills during Prohibition.
b. Apr 28, 1872 in Acerra, Italy
d. Mar 21, 1928 in Chicago, Illinois
Source: *Blood&B; DrInf*

Esposito, Phil(ip)
Canadian. Hockey Player
Scored 778 goals in career, second highest in
    NHL history.
b. Feb 20, 1942 in Sault St. Marie, Ontario
Source: *CurBio 73; HocEn; NewYTBS 79, 81;
WhoAm 80, 82; WhoHcky 73; WorAl*

Esposito, Tony (Anthony James)
Canadian. Hockey Player
Goaltender who set modern NHL record for
    shutouts in season, 15, 1969-70.
b. Apr 23, 1944 in Sault St. Marie, Ontario
Source: *HocEn; WhoAm 76, 78, 80, 82;
WhoHcky 73*

Espriu, Salvador
Spanish. Poet, Dramatist, Author
Best known for *Setmana Santa,* 1971.
b. 1913 in Catalonia, Spain
d. Feb 22, 1985 in Barcelona, Spain
Source: *CasWL; ConAu 115; ConLC 9;*
OxSpan

Essex, David
[David Cook]
English. Singer, Actor
b. Jul 23, 1947 in Plaistow, England
Source: *IntMPA 77, 78, 79, 80, 81, 82;*
RkOn 74; WhoHol A

Essex, Earl of
see: Cromwell, Thomas

Essex, Earl of
see: Devereaux, Robert

Esslin, Martin Julius
British. Author
b. Jun 8, 1918 in Budapest, Hungary
Source: *BiE&WWA; NotNAT; WhThe; Who*
74

Estaing, Charles Henri Hector, Comte d'
French. Naval Officer
b. Nov 28, 1729 in Auvergne, France
d. Apr 28, 1794 in Paris, France
Source: *AmBi; ApCAB; Drake; NewCol 75;*
WhAm HS

Estes, Billie Sol
American. Financier
b. 1925
Source: *BioIn 10*

Estes, Eleanor Ruth Rosenfeld
American. Children's Author
b. May 9, 1906 in West Haven, Connecticut
Source: *AmAu&B; AmNov; AnCL; AuBYP;*
BkCL; ChlLR 2; ConAu 1R, 5NR; CurBio
46; IlsCB 1946; InWom; JBA 51; MorBMP;
Newb 1922; REnAL; SenS; SmATA 4, 5, 7;
Str&VC; WhoAm 74, 76, 78, 80, 82

Estes, E(lliott) M(arantette)
"Pete"
American. Auto Executive
Pres. of General Motors, 1974-81.
b. Jan 7, 1916 in Mendon, Michigan
Source: *AmM&WS 79P; AutoN 79; BioNews*
74; BusPN; CurBio 79; Dun&B 79; IntWW
77, 78; Ward 77; Who 82; WhoAm 80, 84;
WhoEng 80; WhoF&I 77, 79

Estes, Simon Lamont
American. Opera Singer
Bass-baritone; performances include *The*
Magic Flute; Marriage of Figaro.
b. Feb 2, 1938 in Centreville, Iowa
Source: *CurBio 86; DrBlPA; Ebony 1; NegAl*
83; WhoAmM 83

Estevanico
Moroccan. Explorer
b. 1500
d. 1540
Source: *BioIn 1, 8, 9, 10, 11*

Estevez, Emilio
[Emilio Sheen]
American. Actor
Son of actor Martin Sheen; films include *The*
Breakfast Club, 1985; *St. Elmo's Fire,*
1985.
b. May 12, 1962 in New York, New York
Source: *ConNews 85-4; ConTFT 3*

Estevez (de Galvez), Luis
American. Fashion Designer
b. Dec 5, 1930 in Havana, Cuba
Source: *WhoAm 82; WorFshn*

Esther
Biblical Character
Source: *InWom*

Estienne, Henri
French. Printer, Scholar
Patriarch of five generations of famed
typographers, scholar-printers.
b. 1531 in Paris, France
d. 1598 in Lyons, France
Source: *CasWL; DcBiPP; DcEuL; EuAu;*
EvEuW; LinLib L; PenC EUR; REn

Estrada, Erik (Henry Enrique)
American. Actor
Played Frank "Ponch" Poncherello on TV
series "CHiPS," 1977-83.
b. Mar 16, 1949 in New York, New York
Source: *ConTFT 3; WhoAm 80, 82; WorAl*

Estridge, Philip D
American. Businessman
Pioneered development of IBM Personal
Computer, 1980s; is currently best-selling
personal computer.
b. 1938
d. Aug 2, 1985 in Dallas, Texas
Source: *NF*

Etchison, Dennis (William Dennis)
[Jack Martin]
American. Educator, Author
Won World Fantasy Award for *Dark Country*, 1983.
b. Mar 30, 1943 in Stockton, California
Source: *ConAu 115*

Ethridge, Mark Foster
American. Publisher
Manager, publisher of Louisville papers, 1926-63, who campaigned against racism, poverty.
b. Apr 22, 1896 in Meridian, Mississippi
d. Apr 5, 1981 in Moncure, North Carolina
Source: *BioIn 1, 2; ConAu 103; CurBio 46, 81; IntWW 74, 75, 76, 77, 78; PolProf T; WhoAm 74*

Ethridge, Mark Foster, Jr.
American. Publisher
b. Jul 29, 1924 in New York, New York
Source: *BioIn 1, 2; IntWW 74; WhoAm 74*

Ets, Marie Hall
American. Children's Author
b. Dec 16, 1895 in Milwaukee, Wisconsin
Source: *AnCL; Au&ICB; Au&Wr 71; AuBYP; BkP; ChhPo; ConAu 1R, 4NR; FamAIYP; IlsBYP; IlsCB 1744, 1946, 1957; InWom; JBA 51; NewbC 1956; SmATA 2; Str&VC; WhoAm 82; WhoAmA 73; WrDr 80*

Etting, Ruth
American. Singer
b. Nov 23, 1897 in David City, Nebraska
d. Sep 24, 1978 in Colorado Springs, Colorado
Source: *EncMT; InWom; WhoHol A; WhoThe 77A*

Etzioni, Amitai Werner
American. Sociologist
b. Jan 4, 1929 in Cologne, Germany
Source: *AmM&WS 73S; ConAu 1R, 5NR; CurBio 80; WhoAm 74, 76, 78, 80, 82; WhoWorJ 72*

Eucken, Rudolf Christoph
German. Philosopher, Author
Idealist whose philosophy centered on ethical activism; won Nobel Prize, 1908.
b. 1846 in Aurich, Germany
d. 1926 in Jena, Germany
Source: *LinLib L; LuthC 75; OxGer; WorAl*

Euclid
[Eucleides]
Greek. Mathematician
Best known for treatise on geometry; served as basis for textbooks for many centuries.
b. 323 ?BC
d. 283 ?BC
Source: *CasWL; NewC; OxEng; PenC CL; REn*

Eugenie
[Eugenie Marie de Montijo de Guzman]
French. Empress
Wife of Napoleon III and empress, 1853-71; fashion trendsetter of her time.
b. 1826 in Granada, Spain
d. 1920
Source: *OxFr; REn; WebBD 80*

Eulenspiegel, Till
German. Clown
b. 1290 in Kheitlingen, Germany
d. 1350 in Lubeck, Germany
Source: *NewC; REn*

Euler, Leonhard
Swiss. Mathematician, Physicist
b. Apr 15, 1707 in Basel, Switzerland
d. Sep 18, 1783
Source: *NewCol 75*

Euphorion
Greek. Poet, Scholar
b. 276 ?BC
Source: *CasWL; NewC; OxThe; PenC CL*

Euripides
Greek. Dramatist
Wrote about 90 tragedies, including *Medea, Electra*.
b. Sep 23, 480 in Salamis, Greece
d. 406 ?BC in Pella, Greece
Source: *OxThe; PlP&P*

Eurythmics
[Annie Lennox; David Stewart]
British. Music Group
Synthesizer-based duo who had number one hit "Sweet Dreams," 1983.
Source: *RkOn 85*

Eusden, Laurence
English. Poet
Poet laureate, 1718-73.
b. 1688 in Spofforth, England
d. Sep 27, 1730 in Coningsby, England
Source: *Alli; BiD&SB; BrAu; ChhPo; DcBiPP; DcEnA; DcEnL; EvLB; NewC; OxEng; PenC ENG; PoIre; PoLE*

Eusebius of Caesarea
[Eusebius Pamphili]
Greek. Historian
Bishop of Palestine, 314-339; wrote *Chronicle;*
    Ecclesiastical History.
b. 264 in Palestine
d. 340
Source: *BioIn 3, 5, 6, 7, 9; NewC; NewCol*
75; REn

Eustachio, Bartolomeo
Italian. Scientist
Discovered Eustachian tube leading from ear
    drum to throat.
b. 1510 in San Severino, Italy
d. Aug 1574 in Rome, Italy
Source: *AsBiEn; BiHiMed; BioIn 1, 9;*
DcBiPP; DcCathB; InSci; LinLib L, S;
NewCol 75

Eustis, Dorothy Leib Harrison Wood
American. Philanthropist
Founded Seeing Eye guide dog training
    schools, 1929.
b. May 30, 1886 in Philadelphia,
    Pennsylvania
d. Sep 8, 1946 in New York, New York
Source: *NotAW*

Euwe, Max (Machgielis)
American. Chess Player, Educator
World chess champ, 1935-37; pres.,
    International Chess Federation, 1970-78.
b. May 20, 1901 in Amsterdam, Netherlands
d. Nov 26, 1981 in Amsterdam, Netherlands
Source: *AnObit 1981; ConAu 105; GolEC;*
IntAu&W 77; NewYTBS 81; Who 74, 82;
WhoWor 74, 76

Evans, Arthur John, Sir
English. Archaeologist
Discovered ancient Minoan civilization of
    Crete, 1898-1935; wrote *The Palace of*
    Minos, 1921-35.
b. Jul 8, 1851 in Hemel Hempstead, England
d. Jul 11, 1941 in Youlbury, England
Source: *CurBio 41; DcLEL; DcNaB 1941;*
EvLB; InSci; LinLib L; LongCTC; McGDA;
McGEWB; NewC; OxEng; WhLit

Evans, Bergen Baldwin
American. Lexicographer, Author
Lexicographer, master of ceremonies on
    radio, TV shows; wrote *Word A Day*
    Vocabulary Builder, 1963.
b. Sep 19, 1904 in Franklin, Ohio
d. Feb 4, 1978 in Highland Park, Illinois
Source: *AmAu&B; Au&Wr 71; CelR,; ConAu*
4NR, 5R, 77; CurBio 55; LinLib L; NatCAB
60; NewYTET; OhA&B; WhoAm 74; WhoWor
74

Evans, Bill (William George)
American. Baseball Umpire
At 22, youngest ML umpire ever; wrote
    Umpiring from the Inside, considered
    authoritative book on profession; Hall of
    Fame, 1973.
b. Feb 10, 1884 in Chicago, Illinois
d. Jan 23, 1956 in Miami, Florida
Source: *BasesB*

Evans, Bill (William John)
American. Pianist, Composer
Jazz virtuoso who formed trio, 1956, won
    five Grammys.
b. Aug 16, 1929 in Plainfield, New Jersey
d. Sep 1, 1980 in New York, New York
Source: *BiDAmM; BioIn 6, 9; EncJzS 70;*
IlEncJ; WhoE 74

Evans, Bob (Robert)
American. Actor, Producer
Films include *Love Story,* 1970; *The*
    Godfather, 1972; was married to Ali
    McGraw, Phyllis George.
b. Jun 29, 1930 in New York, New York
Source: *BusPN; CelR,; DcCAr 81; FilmgC;*
IntMPA 78, 79, 80, 81, 82; MotPP; WhoAm
80, 82; WhoHol A

Evans, Bob (Robert L)
American. Restaurateur
President, Bob Evans Farms, Inc.
b. Mar 30, 1918 in Sugar Ridge, Ohio
Source: *BusPN; WhoAm 82*

Evans, Charles
American. Bibliographer, Librarian
Compiled massive *American Bibliography,*
    from 1901.
b. Nov 13, 1850 in Boston, Massachusetts
d. Feb 8, 1935
Source: *DcAmB S1*

Evans, Charles, Jr.
American. Golfer, Author
b. Jul 18, 1893 in Indianapolis, Indiana
d. Nov 1979 in Chicago, Illinois
Source: *WhoGolf*

Evans, Clifford
American. Archaeologist, Author
Curator, Smithsonian Institute, 1951-80.
b. Jun 13, 1920 in Dallas, Texas
d. Jan 19, 1981
Source: *AmM&WS 73S, 76P; FifIDA; WhAm*
7; WhoAm 74; WhoWor 76

Evans, Dale
[Mrs. Roy Rogers; Frances Smith]
American. Actress, Evangelist
Starred with husband in TV series "The Roy
    Rogers Show," 1951-64.
b. Oct 31, 1912 in Uvalde, Texas
Source: *AmAu&B; AmSCAP 66; BioNews 74;
ConAu 103; CurBio 56; EncFCWM 69;
FilmgC; HolP 40; InWom; MotPP; MovMk;
WhoHol A*

Evans, Daniel Jackson
American. Politician
Rep. governor of WA, 1964-76; senator,
    1983--.
b. Oct 16, 1925 in Seattle, Washington
Source: *CngDr 85*

Evans, Edith Mary Booth, Dame
English. Actress
Received Oscar nominations for *Chalk
    Garden; Tom Jones; Whispers.*
b. Feb 8, 1888 in London, England
d. Oct 14, 1976 in Kent, England
Source: *BioNews 75; CurBio 56, 77N; Film 1;
FilmgC; InWom; IntMPA 77, 75; IntWW 74;
MotPP; MovMk; NewC; OxFilm; OxThe;
PIP&P; Who 74; WhoAmW 74; WhoHol A;
WhoThe 77; WorAl; WorEFlm*

Evans, Edward Ratcliffe Garth Russell
[First Baron Mountevans]
English. Admiral
Admiral of Royal Navy; wrote *Arctic
    Solitudes,* 1953, books for boys.
b. Oct 28, 1880 in London, England
d. Aug 20, 1957 in Golaa, Norway
Source: *CurBio 41, 57; DcNaB 1951; ObitOF
79; OxShips; WhLit*

Evans, Geraint Llewellyn, Sir
Welsh. Opera Singer
b. Feb 16, 1922 in Pontypridd, Wales
Source: *IntWW 74; Who 74; WhoAm 82;
WhoMus 72; WhoWor 78*

Evans, Harold Matthew
English. Author, Editor
Editor, London *Sunday Times,* 1967-81;
    editorial director, *US News & World
    Report,* 1984--.
b. Jun 28, 1927 in Manchester, England
Source: *BioIn 10; ConAu 41R; CurBio 85;
Who 74; WhoWor 74; WrDr 76*

Evans, Heloise Cruse
American. Journalist
Took over mother's nationally syndicated
    column "Hints from Heloise," 1977.
b. Apr 15, 1951 in Waco, Texas
Source: *WhoAm 82*

Evans, Herbert McLean
American. Physician
Authority on pituitary gland, who discovered
    Vitamin E, 1922.
b. Sep 23, 1882 in Modesto, California
d. Mar 6, 1971 in Berkeley, California
Source: *CurBio 59, 71, 71N; InSci; NewYTBE
71; ObitOF 79*

Evans, Hiram W
American. Musician
b. Oct 3, 1941 in Philadelphia, Pennsylvania
Source: *EncPR&S 74*

Evans, James Roose
see: Roose-Evans, James

Evans, Jerry
American. Director
Directed several soap operas; won Emmys for
    "Ryan's Hope," 1979, 1980.
b. Jun 14, 1935 in Santa Monica, California
Source: *VarWW 85*

Evans, John
American. Educator, Government Official
b. Mar 9, 1814 in Waynesville, Ohio
d. Jul 3, 1897
Source: *BioIn 6, 8; OhA&B*

Evans, John
see: Box Tops, The

Evans, Linda
[Linda Evenstad]
American. Actress
Former wife of John Derek known for role
    of Krystle Carrington on TV's "Dynasty."
b. Nov 18, 1942 in Hartford, Connecticut
Source: *ConTFT 3; CurBio 86; VarWW 85;
WhoHol A*

Evans, Madge (Margherita)
American. Actress
Child star, 1915; retired, 1938; films include
    Dinner at Eight; Pennies from Heaven.
b. Jul 1, 1909 in New York, New York
d. Apr 26, 1981 in Oakland, New Jersey
Source: *BiE&WWA; FilmEn; Film 1; FilmgC;
MotPP; MovMk; ThFT; TwYS; WhThe;
WhoHol A*

Evans, Mark
[AC-DC]
Australian. Musician
Bass guitarist with AC-DC, 1974-77.
b. in Melbourne, Australia
Source: *NF*

Evans, Mary Ann
see: Eliot, George, pseud.

Evans, Maurice
American. Actor, Manager
Played Samantha's father on TV's
"Bewitched," 1964-72.
b. Jun 3, 1901 in Dorchester, England
Source: *BiE&WWA; CnThe; CurBio 61;*
EncMT; EncWT; FamA&A; FilmEn; FilmgC;
IntMPA 80, 81, 82; IntWW 74; MovMk;
NewC; NotNAT; OxThe; REn; WhoAm 74;
WhoThe 77; WhoWor 74

Evans, Mike (Michael Jonas)
American. Actor
Played Lionel Jefferson on TV series "The
Jeffersons," 1975, 1979-81.
b. Nov 3, 1949 in Salisbury, North Carolina
Source: *ConTFT 3; WhoAm 82, 84; WhoHol*
A

Evans, Oliver
American. Inventor
Constructed first high-pressure steam engine
in America, circa 1800.
b. 1755 in New Castle, Delaware
d. Apr 15, 1819 in New York, New York
Source: *Alli; AmBi; ApCAB; DcAmAu;*
DcAmB; DcNAA; Drake; EncAAH; EncAB-H;
LinLib S; McGEWB; NatCAB 6; TwCBDA;
WebAB; WhAm HS

Evans, Orrin C
American. Journalist
b. in Steelton, Pennsylvania
d. Aug 7, 1971 in Philadelphia, Pennsylvania
Source: *BioIn 9; NewYTBE 71*

Evans, Ray
American. Composer
Won Oscars for songs "Buttons and Bows,"
1948; "Mona Lisa," 1950; "Que Sera
Sera," 1956.
b. Feb 4, 1915 in Salamanca, New York
Source: *VarWW 85*

Evans, Richard Louis
American. Journalist
b. Mar 23, 1906 in Salt Lake City, Utah
d. Nov 1, 1971 in Salt Lake City, Utah
Source: *AmAu&B; ConAu 9R; NewYTBE 71;*
WhAm 5

Evans, Robley Dunglison
American. Military Leader
b. Aug 18, 1846 in Floyd County, Virginia
d. Jan 3, 1912
Source: *AmAu&B; AmBi; ApCAB SUP;*
DcAmAu; DcAmB; DcNAA; TwCBDA; WhAm
1

Evans, Ronald Ellwin
American. Astronaut
Command module pilot, Apollo 17.
b. Nov 10, 1933 in Saint Francis, Kansas
Source: *IntWW 74; WhoS&SW 82*

Evans, Rowland, Jr.
[Evans and Novak]
American. Journalist
b. Apr 28, 1921 in White Marsh,
Pennsylvania
Source: *CelR; ConAu 21R; WhoAm 74, 76,*
78, 80, 82; WhoS&SW 82; WhoWor 78;
WrDr 76

Evans, Timothy
English. Murderer
b. 1924
d. Mar 9, 1950 in Pentonville Prison,
England
Source: *BioIn 5, 6, 8*

Evans, Tom
see: Badfinger

Evans, Vince(nt Tobias)
American. Football Player
b. Jun 14, 1955 in Greensboro, North
Carolina
Source: *FootReg 81*

Evans, Walker
American. Photographer, Journalist
Writer, photographer, *Fortune* magazine,
1945-65, known for pictures of Depression
America.
b. Nov 3, 1903 in Saint Louis, Missouri
d. Apr 10, 1975 in New Haven, Connecticut
Source: *AmAu&B; BnEnAmA; ConAu 89;*
ConPhot; CurBio 71; EncAB-H,; WebAB;
WhAm 6; WhoAm 74; WhoWor 74

Evans and Novak
see: Evans, Rowland, Jr.; Novak, Robert

Eve
Biblical Character
In Bible as the first woman created from rib
of first man, Adam.
Source: *InWom; NewCol 75*

Evelyn, John
English. Author
b. Oct 31, 1620 in Wotton, England
d. Feb 27, 1706 in Wotton, England
Source: *Alli; AtlBL; BbD; BiD&SB; BiDBrA*
A; BrAu; CasWL; Chambr 1; CroE&S;
CyWA; DcEnA; DcEnL; DcEuL; DcLEL;
EvLB; NewC; OxEng; OxMus; PenC ENG;
RAdv 1; REn; WebE&AL; WhDW

Evelyn, Judith
American. Actress
Films include *Rear Window; Giant; Brothers Karamazov*.
b. 1913 in Seneca, South Dakota
d. May 7, 1967 in New York, New York
Source: *BiE&WWA; FilmgC; InWom; MotPP; NotNAT B; ObitOF 79; WhAm 4; WhScrn 74, 77; WhThe; WhoHol B*

Everett, Chad
[Raymon Lee Cramton]
American. Actor
Best known role Dr. Joe Gannon on TV series "Medical Center," 1969-76.
b. Jun 11, 1937 in South Bend, Indiana
Source: *CelR; FilmgC; IntMPA 75, 76, 77, 78, 79, 80, 81, 82; MovMk; WhoAm 74, 76, 78, 80, 82; WhoHol A*

Everett, Edward
American. Clergyman, Statesman
Union supporter who gave opening address at dedication of Gettysburg National Cemetery, 1863.
b. Apr 11, 1794 in Dorchester, Massachusetts
d. Jan 15, 1865 in Boston, Massachusetts
Source: *AmAu; AmAu&B; AmBi; ApCAB; BbD; BiAUS; BiD&SB; BiDrAC; BiDrUSE; CyAL 1; DcAmAu; DcAmB; DcEnL; DcNAA; Drake; OxAmL; PenC AM; REnAL; TwCBDA; WebAB; WhAm HS; WhAmP*

Evergood, Philip Howard
American. Artist
b. Oct 26, 1901 in New York, New York
d. Mar 11, 1973 in Bridgewater, Connecticut
Source: *ConAu 41R; CurBio 44, 60, 73; DcCAA 71; NewYTBE 73; WhAm 5; WhoAmA 73*

Everleigh, Ada
[Everleigh Sisters]
American. Madam
b. 1876 in Kentucky
d. Jan 3, 1960 in Roanoke, Virginia
Source: *DcAmB S4; LibW; LookW*

Everleigh, Minna
[Everleigh Sisters]
American. Madam
b. 1878 in Kentucky
d. Sep 16, 1948 in New York, New York
Source: *DcAmNB; LibW; LookW; NotAW*

Everly, Don
[Everly Brothers]
American. Singer, Musician
With brother Phil, had international country hit, "Bye Bye Love," 1957.
b. Feb 1, 1937 in Brownie, Kentucky
Source: *BiDAmM; WhoRocM 82; WorAl*

Everly, Phil
[Everly Brothers]
American. Singer, Musician
With brother Don, had two million-selling single, "Cathy's Clown," 1962.
b. Jan 19, 1939 in Brownie, Kentucky
Source: *BiDAmM; WhoRocM 82; WorAl*

Everly Brothers
[Don Everly; Phil Everly]
American. Music Group
Source: *EncFCWM 69; EncPR&S 74; IlEncRk; RkOneH; WorAl*

Evers, Charles
American. Civil Rights Activist
b. Sep 11, 1923 in Decatur, Mississippi
Source: *CelR; CurBio 69; NewYTBE 70; WebAB*

Evers, Jason
American. Actor
In film *Escape from the Planet of the Apes* ; TV shows "Wrangler," 196 0; "Channing," 1963-64.
b. Jan 2, 1927 in New York, New York
Source: *WhoAm 74; WhoHol A*

Evers, John Joseph
"The Crab"; "The Trojan"
American. Baseball Player
Second baseman in double play combination of Tinker to Evers to Chance.
b. Jul 21, 1881 in Troy, New York
d. Mar 28, 1947 in Albany, New York
Source: *BaseEn 85; BioIn 1, 3, 7, 10; WhoProB 73*

Evers, Medgar Wiley
American. Civil Rights Activist
b. Jul 2, 1926 in Decatur, Mississippi
d. Jun 12, 1963 in Jackson, Mississippi
Source: *WebAB*

Everson, William Oliver
[Brother Antoninus]
American. Poet
b. Sep 10, 1912 in Sacramento, California
Source: *AmAu&B; ConAu 9R; ConLC 1, 5; ConP 70, 75; DrAP 75; OxAmL; PenC AM; RAdv 1; WhoAm 82; WorAu; WrDr 76*

Evert, Chris(tine Marie)
[Mrs. John Lloyd]
American. Tennis Player
Number one female tennis player, 1974-78; SI
athlete of year, 1976.
b. Dec 21, 1954 in Fort Lauderdale, Florida
Source: *BkPepl; CelR,; CurBio 73; GoodHs;
HerW; NewYTBE 72, 73; NewYTBS 74;
WhoAm 74, 76, 78, 80, 82; WorAl*

Evert, Jeanne
American. Tennis Player
Sister of Chris Evert.
b. Oct 5, 1957 in Fort Lauderdale, Florida
Source: *BioIn 10*

Evigan, Greg(ory Ralph)
American. Actor
Starred in TV series "BJ and the Bear,"
1979-81.
b. Oct 14, 1953 in South Amboy, New
Jersey
Source: *BioIn 12; WhoAm 82*

Evinrude, Ole
American. Inventor, Manufacturer
Built first motor to propel rowboat, 1906;
pres., Outboard Motors Corp., 1909-34.
b. Apr 19, 1877 in Christiania, Norway
d. Jul 12, 1934 in Milwaukee, Wisconsin
Source: *BioIn 5, 6, 7, 11; Entr*

Evins, David
American. Designer
b. in London, England
Source: *WorFshn*

Evren, Kenan
Turkish. General, Political Leader
Head of Turkish militia who led coup
deposing civilian gov't, Sep 1980.
b. 1918 in Alasehir, Turkey
Source: *IntWW 82; IntYB 82; MidE 82;
NewYTBS 80*

Evtushenko, Evgeniy Alexandrovich
[Yevgeni Alexandrovich Yevtushenko]
Russian. Poet
Post-Stalin writer who wrote anti-semetic
poem *Babi Yar*, 1961.
b. Jul 18, 1933 in Zima, U.S.S.R.
Source: *CasWL; ConLC 1, 3; EncWL;
EvEuW; IntWW 76; IntWWP 77; ModSL 1;
PenC EUR; REn; WhoSocC 78; WhoTwCL;
WorAu*

Ewbank, "Weeb" (Wilbur)
American. Football Coach
Coached NY Jets to AFL's first Super Bowl
victory, 1969.
b. May 6, 1907 in Richmond, Indiana
Source: *BioNews 75; CelR; WhoAm 74;
WhoE 74; WhoFtbl 74*

Ewell, Tom
[Yewell Tompkins]
American. Actor
Films include *Adam's Rib*, 1949; *The Seven
Year Itch*, 1955.
b. Apr 29, 1909 in Owensboro, Kentucky
Source: *BiE&WWA; BlueB 76; CurBio 61;
FilmgC; IntMPA 80, 81, 82; MotPP; MovMk;
NewYTBE 71; NotNAT; WhoAm 80, 82;
WhoHol A; WhoThe 81; WorAl; WorEFlm*

Ewen, David
American. Author, Musician, Editor
b. Dec 6, 1907 in Lemberg, Austria
Source: *AmAu&B; Au&Wr 71; AuBYP;
BiE&WWA; ConAu 1R, 2NR; REnAL;
SmATA 4; WhoAm 74, 76, 78, 80, 82;
WhoMus 72; WhoS&SW 82; WhoWor 78;
WhoWorJ 72; WrDr 80*

Ewen, Frederic
American. Educator, Author
b. Oct 11, 1899 in Lemberg, Austria
Source: *ConAu 73; WhoAm 74; WhoWor 78;
WrDr 80*

Ewing, Alfred Cyril
English. Author
b. May 11, 1899 in Leicester, England
Source: *Au&Wr 71; ConAu 5R, 4NR;
WhoWor 78*

Ewing, "Buck" (William)
American. Baseball Player
Greatest catcher of time, 1880-97; Hall of
Fame, 1939.
b. Oct 27, 1859 in Hoaglands, Ohio
d. Oct 20, 1906 in Cincinnati, Ohio
Source: *BaseEn 85; BasesB*

Ewing, Julianna Horatia
English. Children's Author
b. Aug 3, 1841 in Ecclesfield, England
d. May 13, 1885 in Bath, England
Source: *BbD; BiD&SB; BrAu 19; CarSB;
CasWL; CelCen; DcCanB 11; DcLEL; EvLB;
FamSYP; NewC; OxEng; Str&VC; WhoChL*

Ewing, Patrick Aloysius
American. Basketball Player
Center, Georgetown U, drafted first by NY
Knicks, 1985; highest paid rookie in NBA
history.
b. May 5, 1962 in Kingston, Jamaica
Source: *ConNews 85-3; NewYTBS 82; OfNBA
81*

Ewing, William Maurice
American. Educator, Scientist
b. May 12, 1906 in Lockney, Texas
Source: *Au&Wr 71; CurBio 53*

Exile
[Buzz Cornelison; Steven Goetzman; Mark
Gray; Marlon Hargis; Sonny Lemaire; J P
Pennington; Jimmy Stokley; Les Taylor]
American. Music Group
Country group from KY; had number one
hit "Kiss You All Over," 1978.
Source: *RkOn 85*

Exner, Judith Campbell
American. Celebrity Friend
Alleged mistress of John F Kennedy, 1960-
62, mobster Sam Giancana; wrote *My
Story*, 1977.
b. 1934
Source: *BioIn 10*

Exon, J(ohn) James, Jr.
American. Politician
Dem. senator for NE, 1980--; governor, 1971-
79.
b. Aug 9, 1921 in Geddes, South Dakota
Source: *AlmAP 78, 80; CngDr 79; IntWW
74, 75, 76, 77, 78, 79, 80; IntYB 79;
WhoAm 76, 78, 80, 82, 84; WhoAmP 73, 75,
77, 79; WhoGov 72, 75, 77; WhoMW 74, 76,
78; WhoWor 74, 78*

Eyadema, Gnassingbe
Togolese. President
b. 1935 in Pya, Togo
Source: *BioIn 11; IntWW 74; WhoGov 75;
WhoWor 78*

Eyen, Tom
American. Dramatist, Director
Won Tony, 1982, for play *Dreamgirls.*
b. Aug 14, 1941 in Cambridge, Ohio
Source: *ConAu 25R; ConTFT 3*

Eysenck, Hans Jurgen
German. Author
b. Mar 14, 1916 in Berlin, Germany
Source: *Au&Wr 71; BioIn 9, 11; ConAu 9R,
4NR; CurBio 72; IntWW 74; Who 74;
WhoWor 78; WrDr 76*

Eyskens, Gaston
Belgian. Prime Minister
b. Apr 1, 1905 in Lierre, Belgium
Source: *CurBio 49; IntWW 74; WhoGov 75;
WhoWor 78*

Ezekiel
Prophet
Major Hebrew prophet; foretold coming of a
messiah, restoration of Jewish kingdom,
c.586 BC.
Source: *DcOrL 3; REn*

Ezekiel, Moses Jacob
American. Sculptor
b. Oct 28, 1844 in Richmond, Virginia
d. Mar 27, 1917
Source: *AmBi; ApCAB; DcAmB; TwCBDA;
WhAm 1*

Ezra
Priest
Shaped ritual of modern Judaism; wrote
Book of Ezra, Chronicles I, II in Old
Testament.
Source: *BioIn 1, 4, 5, 7; NewCol 75*

F

Faas, Horst
German. Photographer
Photographer in Vietnam; won Pulitzer for
spot news photography, 1972.
b. Apr 28, 1933 in Berlin, Germany
Source: *BioIn 8, 9; WhoAm 74; WhoWor 78*

Fabares, Shelley (Michelle Marie)
American. Actress
Played Francine on TV's "One Day at a
Time"; with Elvis Presley in films *Girl
Happy; Clambake.*
b. Jan 19, 1944 in Santa Monica, California
Source: *AmPS A; FilmgC; RkOn 74;
WhoAmW 72; WhoHol A*

Faber, Geoffrey Cust, Sir
English. Publisher, Author
Founded Faber and Faber Publishers, 1927;
wrote *Oxford Apostles,* 1933.
b. Aug 23, 1889 in Malvern, England
d. Mar 31, 1961 in Midhurst, England
Source: *DcNaB 1961; NewC; ObitOF 79;
ObitT 1961; ScF&FL 1; WhE&EA*

Faber, "Red" (Urban Charles)
American. Baseball Player
Pitcher, Chicago White Sox, 1914-33; Hall of
Fame, 1964.
b. Sep 6, 1888 in Cascade, Iowa
d. Sep 25, 1976 in Chicago, Illinois
Source: *BaseEn 85; BioIn 2, 3, 7; WhoProB
73*

Faberge, Peter Carl (Karl Gustavovich)
Russian. Jeweler
Known for lavish Easter eggs designed for
czar's court; name lent to cosmetics firm,
1930s.
b. May 30, 1846 in Saint Petersburg, Russia
d. Sep 24, 1920
Source: *DcD&D; DcNiCA; OxDecA; WorAl*

Fabi, Teo
Italian. Auto Racer
First rookie in 34 yrs. to win pole position
at Indianapolis 500, 1984.
b. 1954 in Milan, Italy
Source: *NewYTBS 84*

Fabian
[Fabian Forte]
American. Singer, Actor
Teen idol of 1950-60s; hits include "Turn Me
Loose"; "Hound Dog Man."
b. Feb 6, 1943 in Philadelphia, Pennsylvania
Source: *FilmgC; IntMPA 82, 83, 84, 75, 76,
77, 78, 79, 80, 81, 82; MotPP; WhoHol A*

Fabian, Robert Honey
English. Detective
b. Jan 31, 1901 in Ladywell, England
d. Jun 14, 1978 in Epsom, England
Source: *BioIn 2, 3, 7, 8, 11; ConAu 77, 81;
CurBio 54, 78; NewYTBS 78*

Fabiola, Queen of Belgium
Belgian. Celebrity Relative
Wife of King Baudouin of Belgium.
b. Jun 11, 1928
Source: *WhoWor 74, 76*

Fabray, Nanette
[Ruby Nanette Fabares]
American. Actress
Played Grandma Romano on "One Day at a
Time."
b. Oct 27, 1920 in San Diego, California
Source: *BiE&WWA; CurBio 56; EncMT; Film
2; FilmgC; IntMPA 78, 79, 80, 81, 82;
MotPP; NotNAT; WhoAm 74, 80; WhoHol A;
WhoThe 77; WorAl*

Fabre, Jean Henri
French. Author, Scientist
Studied insect behavior; wrote *The Marvels of the Insect World.* 1938.
b. Dec 22, 1823 in Saint Leons, France
d. Oct 11, 1915 in Serigran, France
Source: *AnCL; BioIn 5, 6, 8, 9, 11; JBA 34, 51; LongCTC; OxFr; REn*

Fabri, Zoltan
Hungarian. Director
b. Oct 15, 1917 in Budapest, Hungary
Source: *DcFM; FilmgC; IntWW 79, 80; OxFilm; WhoSocC 78; WhoWor 74; WorEFlm*

Fabricius, Hieronymus ab Aquapendente
Italian. Surgeon
b. 1537 in Aquapendente, Italy
d. 1619
Source: *BiHiMed; BioIn 1, 7, 9; LinLib S; NewCol 75*

Fabius, Laurent
French. Political Leader
Prime minister, 1984--, who aims to modernize France.
b. Aug 20, 1946 in Paris, France
Source: *CurBio 85; IntWW 83, 84*

Fabritius, Carel
Dutch. Artist
b. 1622 in Netherlands
d. Oct 12, 1654 in Delft, Netherlands
Source: *AtlBL*

Fabrizi, Aldo
Italian. Actor
Best known role in Rossellini's *Open City,* 1945.
b. 1905 in Rome, Italy
Source: *FilmEn; FilmgC; IntMPA 80, 81, 82; MovMk; WhoHol A*

Face, Roy (Elroy Leon)
American. Baseball Player
Premier relief pitcher, 1953-69; had 189 career saves.
b. Feb 20, 1928 in Stephentown, New York
Source: *BaseEn 85; WhoProB 73*

Factor, Max
American. Cosmetics Executive
Began career as makeup artist; later established own cosmetic co.
b. 1877 in Lodz, Poland
d. 1938
Source: *CmCal; Entr; WhoAm 74, 76; WhoWor 74*

Fadiman, Clifton Paul
American. Author, Critic, Editor, Radio Performer
Host of radio's "Information Please," 1938-48; wrote *Party of One,* 1955.
b. May 15, 1904 in Brooklyn, New York
Source: *AmAu&B; CelR; ChhPo S2; ConAu 61; CurBio 41, 55; IntMPA 77, 75; RAdv 1; REnAL; SmATA 11; TwCA, SUP; WebAB; WhoAm 80; WhoWest 74; WhoWor 74; WorAl*

Fagen, Donald
[Steely Dan]
American. Singer, Songwriter
Wrote songs for Steely Dan; solo single "New Frontier," 1983.
b. Jan 10, 1948 in Passaic, New Jersey
Source: *RkOn 85*

Fahd ibn Abdul Aziz
Saudi. King
b. 1922 in Riyadh, Saudi Arabia
Source: *BioIn 10; CurBio 79; IntWW 75, 76, 77, 78, 79, 80; MidE 78, 79; NewYTBS 75; WhoWor 74*

Fahrenheit, Gabriel Daniel
German. Physicist
Invented mercury thermometer, 1714; developed Fahrenheit temperature scale.
b. May 14, 1686 in Danzig, Germany
d. Sep 16, 1736 in The Hague, Netherlands
Source: *AsBiEn; DcBiPP; DcInv; Dis&D; InSci; LinLib S; McGEWB; REn; WhDW*

Fain, Ferris Roy
"Burrhead"
American. Baseball Player
First baseman, 1947-52; led AL in batting, 1951-52.
b. Mar 29, 1922 in San Antonio, Texas
Source: *BaseEn 85; BioIn 3; WhoProB 73*

Fain, Sammy
American. Singer, Songwriter, Musician
b. Jun 17, 1902 in New York, New York
Source: *AmSCAP 66; BiE&WWA; EncMT; IntMPA 76, 77, 78, 79, 80, 81, 82; NewCBMT; NotNAT; WhoAm 78, 80; WorAl*

Fairbank, Janet Ayer
American. Author
b. 1879 in Chicago, Illinois
d. Dec 28, 1951 in Chicago, Illinois
Source: *AmAu&B; InWom; OxAmL; TwCA, SUP; WhAm 3; WhNAA*

Fairbanks, Charles Warren
American. Politician
Served as vp under Theodore Roosevelt,
1905-09.
b. May 11, 1852 in Unionville Center, Ohio
d. Jun 4, 1918 in Indianapolis, Indiana
Source: *AmBi; ApCAB; BiDrAC; BiDrUSE;*
DcAmB; EncWM; NatCAB 11, 14, 39;
TwCBDA; WebAB, 79; WhAm 1; WhAmP

Fairbanks, Chuck (Charles Leo)
American. Football Coach
b. Jun 10, 1933 in Detroit, Michigan
Source: *NewYTBS 74; WhoAm 78, 80, 82;*
WhoFtbl 74; WhoS&SW 73

Fairbanks, Douglas
[Douglas Elton Ulman]
American. Actor
Swashbuckler hero in *The Three Musketeers,*
1921; *Robin Hood,* 1922; married Mary
Pickford, 1928-36.
b. May 23, 1883 in Denver, Colorado
d. Dec 12, 1939 in Santa Monica, California
Source: *AmBi; BiDFilm; CmMov; CurBio 40;*
DcAmB S2; Film 2, 2; FilmgC; LinLib S;
MotPP; MovMk; OxFilm; TwYS; WebAB;
WhAm 1; WhNAA; WhScrn 74, 77; WhoHol
B; WorAl; WorEFlm

Fairbanks, Douglas, Jr.
[Douglas Elton Ulman, Jr.]
American. Actor, Producer
Appeared in over 75 films; married to Joan
Crawford, 1928-33.
b. Dec 9, 1909 in New York, New York
Source: *BiDFilm; BioNews 74; BlueB 76;*
CelR; CmCal; CmMov; CurBio 40; Film
2; FilmgC; IntMPA 76, 77, 78, 79, 80, 81,
82; IntWW 79, 80, 81; IntYB 78, 79, 80, 81;
MotPP; MovMk; OxFilm; TwYS; WebAB, 79;
Who 74; WhoAm 74, 76, 78, 80, 82; WhoHol
A; WhoThe 77; WhoWor 74; WorAl;
WorEFlm

Fairbanks, Thaddeus
American. Inventor
Developed platform scale, 1831.
b. Jan 17, 1796 in Brinfield, Massachusetts
d. Apr 12, 1886 in Saint Johnsbury, Vermont
Source: *AmBi; ApCAB; DcAmB; NatCAB 10;*
TwCBDA; WhAm HS

Fairchild, David Grandison
American. Botanist
Performed scientific studies on importation of
tropical plants.
b. Apr 7, 1869 in East Lansing, Michigan
d. Aug 6, 1954 in Coconut Grove, Florida
Source: *BioIn 1, 2, 3, 5, 6, 8, 10; DcAmB*
S5; EncAAH; WebAB; WhAm 3

Fairchild, John Burr
American. Publisher
Has published *Women's Wear Daily* and
Daily News Record since 1960.
b. Mar 6, 1927 in Newark, New Jersey
Source: *CelR; CurBio 71; Dun&B 79;*
WhoAm 74, 76, 78, 80, 82; WhoE 74;
WhoFash; WorFshn

Fairchild, Louis W
American. Publisher
b. Mar 3, 1901 in Glen Ridge, New Jersey
d. Oct 16, 1981 in Hanover, New Hampshire
Source: *AmAu&B; NewYTBS 81*

Fairchild, Morgan
[Patsy Ann McClenny]
American. Actress
Starred in TV series "Flamingo Road."
b. Feb 3, 1950 in Dallas, Texas
Source: *BioIn 10, 12; NewYTBS 82*

Fairchild, Sherman Mills
American. Inventor
Developed Fairchild aerial camera.
b. Apr 7, 1896 in Oneonta, New York
d. Mar 28, 1971 in New York, New York
Source: *NatCAB 58; NewYTBE 71; WhAm 5*

Fairfax, Beatrice, pseud.
[Marie Manning]
American. Author, Journalist
b. 1878 in Washington, District of Columbia
d. Nov 28, 1945 in Allendale, New Jersey
Source: *CurBio 44, 46; DcAmB S3; InWom;*
NotAW; REnAL

Fairfax, Sally (Sarah Cary)
[Mrs. Will Fairfax]
American. Celebrity Friend
Wife of George Washington's best friend;
object of Washington's lifelong (probably
unconsummated) obsession; played by
Jaclyn Smith in TV miniseries, 1984.
b. 1730
d. 1811
Source: *BioIn 11, 12*

Fairfax, Thomas
English. General
b. Jan 17, 1612 in Leeds Castle, England
d. Nov 12, 1671 in Winchester, Virginia
Source: *Alli; NewC; PenC ENG; REn*

Fairless, Benjamin F
American. Philanthropist
b. May 3, 1890 in Pigeon Run, Ohio
d. Jan 1, 1962 in Ligonier, Pennsylvania
Source: *CurBio 42, 57, 62; WhAm 4*

Faisal II
Iraqi. King
b. May 2, 1935 in Baghdad, Iraq
d. Jul 14, 1958
Source: *CurBio 55, 58; NewCol 75; WebBD
80*

Faison, George
Director, Choreographer
Won Emmy for choreography of *The Wiz,*
1975.
Source: *VarWW 85*

Faisal (Ibn Abdul-Aziz al Saud)
Saudi. Ruler
King 1964-75; resisted radical political forces
in Arab world; assassinated by nephew.
b. 1905 in Riyadh, Saudi Arabia
d. Mar 25, 1975 in Riyadh, Saudi Arabia
Source: *CurBio 48, 66, 75; Who 74*

Faisal ibn Musaed
Saudi. Prince
Nephew of Faisal; murdered his uncle.
b. 1947
d. 1975
Source: *BioIn 10*

Faith, Percy
Canadian. Conductor
b. Apr 7, 1908 in Toronto, Ontario
d. Feb 9, 1976 in Los Angeles, California
Source: *AmSCAP 66; Baker 78; CanWW 70;
CreCan 1; NewYTBS 76; RkOn 74; WhAm
6; WhoAm 76*

Faithfull, Marianne
English. Singer, Actress
Had hit with Jagger/Richard song "As Tears
Go By," 1964.
b. Dec 29, 1946 in London, England
Source: *ConMuA 80A; FilmgC; NewWmR;
RkOn 78; WhoHol A; WhoRock 81; WhoThe
72, 77*

Faiz, Faiz Ahmad
Pakistani. Poet, Journalist, Educator
Considered Pakistan's poet laureate; wrote
Zindan Namah, 1950s.
b. 1912 in Sialkot, British India
d. Nov 20, 1984 in Lahore, Pakistan
Source: *CasWL; ConAu 115; DcOrL 2;
EncWL 2*

Fakir, Abdul
[Four Tops]
American. Singer
b. 1938 in Detroit, Michigan
Source: *NF*

Falana, Lola
American. Actress, Singer, Dancer
Won Theatre World award, 1975; Tony
nomination for *Doctor Jazz.*
b. Sep 11, 1943 in Philadelphia, Pennsylvania
Source: *BkPepl; DrBlPA; WhoAm 78, 80, 82;
WhoAmW 72; WhoHol A*

Falco, Louis
American. Choreographer, Dancer
b. Aug 2, 1942 in New York, New York
Source: *BioIn 6, 9, 11; WhoAm 74*

Falconetti, Renee Maria
French. Actress
Known for title role in *The Passion of Joan
of Arc,* 1927.
b. 1892 in Sermano, France
d. 1946 in Buenos Aires, Argentina
Source: *Film 2; FilmgC; MotPP; OxFilm;
WhScrn 77; WhoHol B; WorEFlm*

Falk, Lee Harrison
American. Cartoonist, Author
b. 1915 in Saint Louis, Missouri
Source: *ConAu 97; WhoAm 74; WorECom*

Falk, Peter
American. Actor
Starred in TV series "Columbo," 1971-78;
won Emmy, 1972.
b. Sep 16, 1927 in New York, New York
Source: *BiE&WWA; BioNews 75; BkPepl;
CelR; CurBio 72; FilmgC; IntMPA 75, 76,
77, 78, 79, 80, 81, 82; MotPP; MovMk;
NewYTBE 71; NotNAT; WhoAm 74, 76, 78,
80, 82; WhoHol A; WhoWest 74; WhoWor 74*

Falkenburg, Jinx (Eugenia Lincoln)
[Jinx McCrary]
American. Actress, Journalist
Highest paid model, 1941; had radio show
"Tex and Jinx Show."
b. Jan 21, 1919 in Barcelona, Spain
Source: *CurBio 53; FilmgC; InWom; WhoHol
A; WorAl*

Falkner, Frank
English. Physician, Journalist
b. Oct 27, 1918 in Hale, England
Source: *AmM&WS 73P*

Falkner, Murry Charles
American. Author
b. Jun 26, 1899 in Ripley, Mississippi
Source: *ConAu 21R*

Fall, Albert Bacon
American. Government Official
b. Nov 26, 1861 in Frankfort, Kentucky
d. Nov 30, 1944 in El Paso, Texas
Source: *BiDrAC; BiDrUSE; CurBio 45;
DcAmB S3; EncAB-H; OxAmH; REnAW;
WhAm 2; WhAmP; WorAl*

Fall, Bernard B
American. Author, Journalist
b. Nov 11, 1926 in Vienna, Austria
d. Feb 21, 1967 in Vietnam
Source: *AmAu&B; ConAu 1R, 25R, 77;
ConLC 11; WhAm 4; WorAu*

Falla, Manuel de
Spanish. Composer
b. Nov 23, 1876 in Cadiz, Spain
d. Nov 14, 1946 in Alta Gracia, Argentina
Source: *AtlBL; CurBio 46; DcCM; REn*

Fallaci, Oriana
Italian. Journalist
b. Jun 29, 1930 in Florence, Italy
Source: *NewYTBE 73*

Fallada, Hans, pseud.
[Rudolph Ditzen]
German. Author
Social realist who wrote *Little Man What
Now?* 1933.
b. Jul 21, 1893
d. Feb 6, 1947 in Berlin, Germany
Source: *CasWL; EncWL; EvEuW; LongCTC;
ModGL; OxGer; PenC EUR; REn; TwCA,
SUP; WhoTwCL*

Falldin, Thorbjorn Nils Olof
Swedish. Prime Minister
b. Apr 24, 1926 in Vastby, Sweden
Source: *CurBio 78; NatCAB 44; REnAW*

Falls, Joe
American. Journalist, Author
b. May 2, 1928 in New York, New York
Source: *ConAu 77*

Falstaff, John
see: Fastolf, John, Sir

Falter, John
American. Illustrator
b. Feb 28, 1910 in Plattsmouth, Nebraska
Source: *WhoAmA 73*

Faltskog, Agnetha
[ABBA]
Swedish. Singer
Known for high vocal range; solo single
"Can't Shake Loose," 1983.
b. Apr 5, 1950 in Stockholm, Sweden
Source: *RkOn 85*

Falwell, Jerry
American. Clergyman
Founded Moral Majority, Inc, 1979.
b. Aug 11, 1933 in Lynchburg, Virginia
Source: *BioIn 9, 11; ConAu 102; WhoAm 82*

Farnham, Eliza Wood Burhans
American. Reformer, Lecturer
Head, women's dept. of Sing Sing, 1840s;
instituted penal reforms.
b. Nov 17, 1815 in Rensselaerville, New
York
d. Dec 15, 1864 in New York, New York
Source: *NotAW; WebBD 80*

Famolare, Joseph P
American. Designer
b. 1931
Source: *BioIn 12*

Famous Amos
see: Amos, Wally

Fanfani, Amintore
"Little Professor"; "Tom Thumb of Italian
Politics"
Italian. Economist, Political Leader
Five-time prime minister; resigned Apr 1983;
wrote over 40 books.
b. Feb 6, 1908 in Tuscany, Italy
Source: *CurBio 58; IntWW 74, 78; IntYB 79;
WhoUN 75; WhoWor 74, 78*

Fangio, Juan Manuel
Argentine. Auto Racer
b. Jun 24, 1911
Source: *BioIn 4, 5, 6, 7, 8, 9, 10*

Fanning, Katherine
American. Editor, Journalist
Editor, *Christian Science Monitor,* 1983--.
b. Oct 18, 1927 in Chicago, Illinois
Source: *WhoAm 80, 82, 84; WhoAmW 74,
75; WhoWest 82, 84*

Fanon, Frantz
American. Psychoanalyst, Philosopher
b. Jul 20, 1925 in Martinique
d. Dec 6, 1961 in Washington, District of
Columbia
Source: *ConAu 89; WorAu*

Fantin-Latour, (Ignace) Henri
French. Artist
b. Jan 14, 1836 in Grenoble, France
d. Aug 25, 1904 in Bure, France
Source: *AtlBL; NewCol 75; WebBD 80*

Faraday, Michael
English. Scientist
Developed first dynamo; discovered
   electromagnetic induction and compound
   bencene.
b. Sep 22, 1791 in Surrey, England
d. Aug 25, 1867 in Hampton Court, England
Source: *Alli, SUP; BbD; BiD&SB; BrAu 19;
Chambr 3; DcEnL; EvLB; NewC; NewCol 75;
OxEng; REn*

Farago, Ladislas
Hungarian. Author
b. Sep 21, 1906 in Csuro, Hungary
d. Oct 15, 1980 in New York, New York
Source: *AmAu&B; BioNews 75; CelR; ConAu
65, 102; WhoAm 74; WhoWor 78; WhoWorJ
72*

Farah, James
American. Manufacturer
With brother, William, built small apparel
   factory into leading maker of men's pants,
   1937.
b. 1916
d. 1964
Source: *Entr*

Farah, Pahlevi
see: Pahlevi, Farah

Farah, Robert Norman
American. Business Executive
Secretary, Farah Manufacturing Co, Inc,
   1978--.
b. Aug 5, 1952 in El Paso, Texas
Source: *Dun&B 79; WhoAm 82*

Farah, William
American. Manufacturer
With brother, James, built small apparel
   factory into leading maker of men's pants,
   1937.
b. 1919
Source: *Dun&B 79; Entr*

Faralla, Dana (Dorothy W)
American. Children's Author
b. Aug 4, 1909 in Renville, Minnesota
Source: *AmAu&B; AmNov; ConAu 49;
InWom; SmATA 9*

Farb, Peter
American. Author, Editor
b. Jul 25, 1929 in New York, New York
d. Apr 8, 1980 in Boston, Massachusetts
Source: *AuBYP SUP; BioIn 11; ConAu 13R,
97; SmATA 12; WorAu*

Farber, Edward Rolke
American. Inventor
Credited with invention of portable strobe
   light for still cameras.
b. Jul 22, 1914 in Milwaukee, Wisconsin
d. Jan 22, 1982 in Delafield, Wisconsin
Source: *AnObit 1982; LElec; NewYTBS 82*

Farber, Simon W
American. Manufacturer
Introduced silver, nickel-plated Farberware,
   1910.
b. 1881
d. 1947
Source: *BioIn 1; Entr*

Farenthold, Frances T
American. Educator, Political Activist
b. Oct 2, 1926 in Corpus Christi, Texas
Source: *WhoAm 82; WhoAmP 73; WhoAmW
77*

Farentino, James
American. Actor
Starred "The Bold Ones," 1970-72.
b. Feb 24, 1938 in Brooklyn, New York
Source: *FilmgC; IntMPA 75, 76, 77, 78, 79,
80, 81, 82; MotPP; NewYTBE 73; WhoAm
74, 76, 78, 80, 82; WhoHol A*

Fargo, Donna
[Yvonne Vaughan]
American. Singer, Songwriter
Country singer; hits include "Happiest Girl
   in the USA"; "Funny Face."
b. Nov 10, 1949 in Mount Airy, North
   Carolina
Source: *BkPepl; WhoAm 74, 76, 78, 80, 82*

Fargo, William George
American. Businessman
With Henry Wells, started express service,
   Wells, Fargo & Co. during CA gold rush,
   1852.
b. May 20, 1818 in Pompey, New York
d. Aug 3, 1881 in Buffalo, New York
Source: *AmBi; ApCAB; DcAmB; LinLib S;
McGEWB; NatCAB 12; TwCBDA; WebAB;
WhAm HS; WhAmP*

Farina, Richard
American. Author, Singer, Songwriter
Part of folk music scene, 1960s; wrote *Been Down So Long It Looks Li ke Up To Me.*
b. 1936 in Brooklyn, New York
d. Apr 30, 1966 in Carmel, California
Source: *AmAu&B; BiDAmM; ConAu 25R, 81; ConLC 9; WhScrn 77*

Farinelli
[Carlo Broschi]
Italian. Opera Singer
b. Jan 24, 1705 in Andria, Italy
d. Jul 15, 1782 in Bologna, Italy
Source: *REn*

Farjeon, Eleanor
English. Author
b. Feb 13, 1881 in London, England
d. Jun 5, 1965
Source: *AnCL; AuBYP; BkCL; CasWL; CathA 1952; ChhPo, S1, S2; ConAu P-1; DcLEL; HerW; InWom; JBA 34, 51; LongCTC; NewC; SmATA 2; Str&VC; TwCA, SUP; TwCWr; WhoChL*

Farley, James A(loysius)
American. Political Leader
b. May 30, 1888 in Grassy Point, New York
d. Jun 9, 1976 in New York, New York
Source: *BiDrUSE; CathA 1952; CelR; ConAu 65; CurBio 44; EncAB-H; Film 1; IntWW 74; St&PR 75; TwYS; WebAB; WhoAmP 73; WhoHol B*

Farley, Walter
American. Author
Wrote *The Black Stallion,* 1941; filmed, 1979.
b. Jun 26, 1920 in Syracuse, New York
Source: *ConAu 8NR, 17R; ConLC 17; SmATA 2; TwCCW 78; WrDr 80*

Farmer, Arthur Stewart
American. Jazz Musician
b. 1928
Source: *BioIn 7*

Farmer, Don
American. Broadcast Journalist
b. Sep 27, 1938 in Saint Louis, Missouri
Source: *ConAu 65; WhoAm 82*

Farmer, Fannie Merritt
American. Chef
First published *Fannie Farmer Cookbook,* 1896; introduced standard measurements in recipes.
b. Mar 23, 1857 in Boston, Massachusetts
d. Jan 15, 1915 in Boston, Massachusetts
Source: *AmAu&B; AmBi; DcAmAu; DcAmB; DcNAA; InWom; LinLib S; McGEWB; NatCAB 22; NotAW; REnAL; WebAB; WhAm 1*

Farmer, Frances
American. Actress
Stage, film star who spent most of 1940s in mental institution; life was subject of film *Frances,* 1983.
b. Sep 19, 1914 in Seattle, Washington
d. Aug 1, 1970 in Indianapolis, Indiana
Source: *BiDrLUS 70; BioNews 74; FilmgC; HolP 30; MotPP; MovMk; NewYTBE 70; NotNAT; PIP&P; ThFT; WhScrn 74, 77; WhoAm 78; WhoHol B; WhoWor 74*

Farmer, James
American. Civil Rights Leader
Founded CORE, 1942.
b. Jan 12, 1920 in Marshall, Texas
Source: *AmAu&B; BlueB 76; CivR 74; CurBio 64; EncSoH; NegAl 76; WhoAm 74, 76, 78, 80, 82; WhoAmP 73, 75, 77, 79; WhoBlA 75, 77; WhoS&SW 73; WhoWor 74, 78*

Farmer, Philip Jose
American. Author
b. Jan 26, 1918 in Terre Haute, Indiana
Source: *AmAu&B; ConAu 1R, 4NR; ConLC 1; IndAu 1917; WhoAm 82*

Farndon, Pete
see: Pretenders, The

Farnese, Alessandro
[Duke of Parma]
Spanish. Soldier
Recovered provinces of Netherlands for uncle, Philip II; greatest military expert of time.
b. Aug 27, 1545
d. Dec 3, 1592
Source: *DcBiPP; OxArt; WhDW; WhoMilH 76*

Farnham, Sally James
American. Sculptor
b. 1869 in Ogdensburg, New York
d. Apr 28, 1943
Source: *InWom; WhAm 2*

Farnol, Jeffery
English. Author
Popular historical tales include *Amateur
    Gentleman,* 1913.
b. Feb 10, 1878 in Warwickshire, England
d. Aug 9, 1952 in Eastbourne, England
Source: *NewC; REn; TwCA SUP; TwCWr*

Farnsworth, Philo Taylor
American. Inventor
Received patents for many inventions relating
    to tv.
b. Aug 19, 1906 in Beaver, Utah
d. Mar 11, 1971 in Salt Lake City, Utah
Source: *BioIn 1, 3, 6, 9, 10; NewCol 75;
NewYTBE 71; NewYTET; WebAB, 79;
WebBD 80; WhAm 5*

Farnsworth, Richard
American. Actor
Spent 40 yrs. as stuntman; appeared in films
    Comes a Horseman, 1979; *The Natural,*
    1983.
b. Sep 1, 1920 in Los Angeles, California
Source: *IntMPA 84; VarWW 85*

Farnum, Dustin Lancy
American. Actor
Star of Cecil B DeMille's first film *The
    Squaw Man,* 1914.
b. 1870 in Hampton Beach, Maine
d. Jul 3, 1929 in New York, New York
Source: *DcAmB; Film 1, 2; FilmgC; MotPP;
NotNAT B; TwYS; WhAm 1; WhScrn 74, 77;
WhoHol B; WhoStg 1906, 1908*

Farnum, William
American. Actor
Debut film *The Spoilers,* 1914; brother of
    Dustin Farnum.
b. Jul 4, 1876 in Boston, Massachusetts
d. Jun 5, 1953 in Los Angeles, California
Source: *Film 1, 2; FilmgC; MotPP; MovMk;
NotNAT B; TwYS; WhScrn 74, 77; WhoHol
B*

Farouk I
Egyptian. King
b. Feb 11, 1920 in Cairo, Egypt
d. Mar 18, 1965 in Rome, Italy
Source: *CurBio 42, 65; NewCol 75*

Farquhar, George
English. Dramatist
Comedies include *The Beaux Stratagem,* 1707.
b. 1678 in Londonderry, Northern Ireland
d. Apr 29, 1707 in London, England
Source: *AtlBL; BrAu; CasWL; CnThe;
DcEnA; DcEnL; DcLEL; LinLib L;
McGEWD; MouLC 2; NewC; NotNAT B;
PenC ENG; REn; REnWD; WebE&AL*

Farquharson, Martha, pseud.
see: Finley, Martha

Farr, Felicia
[[Mrs. Jack Lemmon]]
American. Actress
b. Oct 4, 1932 in Westchester, New York
Source: *FilmEn; FilmgC; IntMPA 80, 81, 82;
MotPP; WhoHol A*

Farr, Jamie
[Jameel Farah]
American. Actor
Played Cpl. Klinger on TV series
    "M*A*S*H," 1972-83.
b. Jul 1, 1934 in Toledo, Ohio
Source: *WhoAm 80, 82; WhoHol A; WhoTelC*

Farragut, David Glasgow
"Old Salamander"
American. Military Leader
Civil War hero remembered for saying
    "Damn the torpedoes, full speed ahead,"
    1864.
b. Jul 5, 1801 in Knoxville, Tennessee
d. Aug 14, 1870 in Portsmouth, New
    Hampshire
Source: *AmBi; ApCAB; CelCen; CivWDc;
DcAmB; EncAB-H; EncSoH; HarEnUS;
LinLib S; McGEWB; NatCAB 2; OxAmH;
OxShips; TwCBDA; WebAB, 79; WebAMB;
WhAm HS; WhoMilH 76*

Farrand, Beatrix Jones
American. Architect
Female landscape architect who designed
    gardens at Dumbarton Oaks, 1920-40.
b. Jun 19, 1872 in New York, New York
d. Feb 27, 1959 in Bar Harbor, Maine
Source: *NotAW MOD*

Farrar, Geraldine
American. Opera Singer
b. Feb 28, 1882 in Melrose, Massachusetts
d. Mar 11, 1967 in Ridgefield, Connecticut
Source: *AmSCAP 66; Film 1; FilmgC;
InWom; REn; TwYS; WhAm 4; WhScrn 74,
77; WhoHol B*

Farrar, John Chipman
American. Publisher, Author
b. Feb 25, 1896 in Burlington, Vermont
d. Nov 6, 1974 in New York, New York
Source: *AmAu&B; ChhPo, S1, S2; ConAu 53,
65; REnAL; Str&VC; WhAm 6; WhoAm 74*

Farrar, Margaret Petherbridge
American. Editor
Crossword puzzle editor, NY *Times*, 1942-69.
b. Mar 23, 1897 in New York, New York
d. Jun 11, 1984 in New York, New York
Source: *ConAu 113; CurBio 55, 84; LibW; NewYTBS 84*

Farrell, Carolyn
American. Nun, Mayor
b. 1936 in Des Moines, Iowa
Source: *BioIn 12*

Farrell, Charles
American. Actor
Starred with Janet Gaynor in many films; *Seventh Heaven*, 1927.
b. Aug 9, 1901 in Onset Bay, Massachusetts
Source: *FilmEn; IntMPA 80, 81, 82; TwYS; WhoHol A*

Farrell, Eileen
American. Opera Singer
b. Feb 13, 1920 in Willimantic, Connecticut
Source: *CelR; CurBio 61; InWom; IntWW 74; WebAB; WhoAm 74, 76, 78, 80, 82*

Farrell, Glenda
American. Actress
Starred as reporter in *Torchy Blane* film series; won Emmy for "Ben Casey," 1963.
b. Jun 30, 1904 in Enid, Oklahoma
d. May 1, 1971 in New York, New York
Source: *BiE&WWA; Film 2; FilmgC; HolP 30; MotPP; MovMk; NewYTBE 71; OxFilm; ThFT; WhAm 5; WhScrn 74, 77; WhThe; WhoAmW 72; WhoHol B*

Farrell, James Thomas
American. Author, Journalist
Best known for *Studs Lonigan* trilogy, 1932-35.
b. Feb 27, 1904 in Chicago, Illinois
d. Aug 22, 1979 in New York, New York
Source: *AmAu&B; AmNov; AmWr; CasWL; CnDAL; ConAmA; ConAu 5R, 89; ConLC 1, 4; ConNov 82, 82A; CurBio 42, 79; CyWA; DcLEL; DrAF 76; EncAB-H; EncWL; EvLB; IntWW 78; LinLib L, S; LongCTC; ModAL; NewYTBS 79, 80; OxAmL; PenC AM; RAdv 1; REn; REnAL; TwCA, SUP; TwCWr; WebAB; WebE&AL; Who 74; WhoAm 78; WhoWor 74; WrDr 76*

Farrell, Mike
American. Actor
Played B J Hunnicutt on TV series "MASH," 1975-83.
b. Feb 6, 1939 in Saint Paul, Minnesota
Source: *WhoAm 78, 80, 82; WhoHol A; WhoTelC*

Farrell, Suzanne
American. Ballerina
Principal dancer, NY Ballet, 1965-69, 1975--.
b. Aug 16, 1945 in Cincinnati, Ohio
Source: *CurBio 67; InWom; WhoAm 74, 76, 78, 80, 82; WhoWor 78*

Farrere, Claude, pseud.
[Frederic Charles Pierre Edouard Bargone]
French. Naval Officer, Author
Member of French Academy, 1935; wrote 30 novels, many sea stories.
b. Apr 27, 1876 in Lyons, France
d. Jun 21, 1957 in Paris, France
Source: *CasWL; EncWL; EvEuW; OxFr*

Farrington, Elizabeth Pruett (Mary)
American. Journalist, Politician
Leading advocate of Hawaiian statehood.
b. May 30, 1898 in Tokyo, Japan
d. Jul 21, 1984
Source: *ConAu 113; CurBio 55, 84; WhoAmW 83*

Farrow, George Edward
American. Children's Author
b. 1866
d. 1920
Source: *ChhPo, S1, S2; MnBBF; WhoChL*

Farrow, John Villiers
Australian. Author, Director
Father of Mia Farrow; won Oscar for best screenplay *Around the World in 80 Days*, 1956.
b. Feb 10, 1906 in Sydney, Australia
d. Jan 28, 1963 in Beverly Hills, California
Source: *AmAu&B; BiDFilm; BkC 5; CathA 1930; CmMov; FilmgC; MovMk; WhAm 4; WhNAA; WorEFlm*

Farrow, Mia Villiers
American. Actress
Starred in TV series "Peyton Place," 1964-67; film *Hannah and Her Sisters*, 1985.
b. Feb 9, 1945 in Los Angeles, California
Source: *BiDFilm; BkPepl; CelR; CurBio 70; FilmgC; IntMPA 75, 76, 77, 78, 79, 80, 81, 82; MotPP; MovMk; NewYTBE 71; Who 82; WhoAm 74, 76, 78, 80, 82; WhoHol A; WhoThe 77; WhoWest 84; WhoWor 78; WorEFlm*

Fascell, Dante Bruno
American. Politician
b. Mar 9, 1917 in Bridgehampton, New York
Source: *BiDrAC; CngDr 74; CurBio 60; WhoAm 74, 76, 78, 80, 82; WhoAmP 73; WhoGov 75; WhoS&SW 82*

Fasch, Johann Friedrich
German. Composer
b. Apr 15, 1688 in Buttelstedt, Germany
d. Dec 5, 1758 in Zerbst, Germany
Source: *Baker 78; BioIn 9; OxMus*

Fass, Bob
American. Singer
b. Jun 29, 1943 in Brooklyn, New York
Source: *BioIn 10*

Fassbinder, Rainer Werner
German. Actor, Author, Director
Films included *The Marriage of Maria
Brown,* 1978; *Lili Marleen,* 1980; *Lola,*
1981.
b. May 31, 1946 in Bad Worishofen,
Germany
d. Jun 10, 1982 in Munich, Germany (West)
Source: *AnObit 1982; BiDFilm; BioIn 11;
CurBio 77, 82; IntWW 78; NewYTBS 77, 82;
OxFilm; WhoAm 82; WhoWor 78*

Fast, Howard
[E V Cunningham, Walter Ericson, pseuds.]
American. Author
Movies *Spartacus,* 1960; *Mirage,* 1965 based
on stories by Fast.
b. Nov 11, 1914 in New York, New York
Source: *AmAu&B; AmNov; AuBYP; CnDAL;
ConAu 1R, 1NR; ConNov 72, 76; CurBio 43;
DcLEL; IntWW 74; ModAL; OxAmL; PenC
AM; REn; REnAL; SmATA 7; TwCA SUP;
TwCWr; WebE&AL; WhoAm 74, 76, 78, 80,
82; WhoWor 78; WhoWorJ 72; WrDr 80*

Fastolf, John, Sir
[John Falstaff]
English. Soldier
Served during Hundred Years War; present
at English defeat by Joan of Arc, 1492.
b. 1378
d. 1459
Source: *NewC; REn*

Fath, Jacques
French. Fashion Designer
b. Sep 12, 1912 in Vincennes, France
d. Nov 13, 1954 in Paris, France
Source: *CurBio 51, 55; WhAm 3; WorFshn*

Fatima
Arabian. Celebrity Relative
Daughter of Mohammed, wife of Ali.
b. 606 in Mecca, Arabia
d. 632 in Medina, Arabia
Source: *DcBiPP; InWom; NewC; NewCol 75*

Faubus, Orval Eugene
American. Governor, Journalist
b. Jan 7, 1910 in Combs, Arkansas
Source: *CurBio 56; WhoAm 74, 76, 78, 80,
82; WhoAmP 73*

Faulk, John Henry
American. TV Personality
b. Aug 21, 1913 in Austin, Texas
Source: *AmAu&B; WhoAm 76; WhoHol A;
WhoS&SW 73*

Faulkner, Brian
Irish. Prime Minister
b. Feb 18, 1921 in Belfast, Northern Ireland
Source: *CurBio 72; IntWW 75; Who 74;
WhoAm 74; WhoWor 76*

Faulkner, Eric
[Bay City Rollers]
Scottish. Musician, Singer
b. Oct 21, 1955 in Edinburgh, Scotland
Source: *BkPepl*

Faulkner, William
American. Author
Wrote *The Sound and the Fury,* 1929; won
Nobel Prize, 1949, Pulitzer Prize, 1962.
b. Sep 25, 1897 in New Albany, Mississippi
d. Jul 6, 1962 in Oxford, Mississippi
Source: *AmAu&B; AmNov; AmWr; AtlBL;
AuNews 1; BioNews 74; CasWL; Chambr 3;
CnDAL; CnMD; CnMWL; ConAmA; ConAu
81; ConLC 1, 3, 6; CroCD; CurBio 51, 62;
CyWA; DcFM; DcLEL; EncMys; EncWL;
FilmgC; LongCTC; ModAL; S1; ModWD;
OxAmL; OxEng; OxFilm; PenC AM; RAdv 1;
RComWL; REn; REnAL; TwCA, SUP;
TwCWr; WebAB; WebE&AL; WhAm 4;
WhoTwCL; WorEFlm*

Fauntroy, Walter E
American. Social Reformer, Politician
Congressman, 1971--; chairman Congressional
Black Caucus, 1981--.
b. Feb 6, 1933 in Washington, District of
Columbia
Source: *CngDr 74; NewYTBE 71; WhoAm 74,
76, 78, 80, 82; WhoAmP 73; WhoBlA 75;
WhoS&SW 82*

Faure, Elie
French. Art Historian, Critic
b. Apr 4, 1873 in Saint Foy, France
d. Oct 31, 1937 in Paris, France
Source: *CasWL; ClDMEL; OxFilm; TwCA,
SUP; WorEFlm*

Faure, Felix
French. President
b. Jan 30, 1841
d. Feb 16, 1899
Source: *NewCol 75*

Faure, Gabriel Urbain
French. Composer, Musician
b. May 12, 1845 in Pamiers, France
d. Nov 4, 1924 in Paris, France
Source: *AtlBL; OxFr; REn*

Fauset, Jessie Redmon
American. Author
b. 1884 in Philadelphia, Pennsylvania
d. Apr 30, 1961
Source: *AmAu&B; BlkAWP; InWom; TwCA SUP*

Faust, Frederick Schiller
[Max Brand, pseud.]
American. Author, Poet
Wrote popular westerns; wrote *Dr. Kildare* films.
b. May 29, 1892 in Seattle, Washington
d. May 12, 1944 in Germany
Source: *AmAu&B; ChhPo; CurBio 44; DcAmB S3; DcLEL; DcNAA; EncMys; LongCTC; MnBBF; REn; REnAL; TwCA, SUP; WebAB*

Faust, Gerry (Gerard Anthony, Jr.)
American. Football Coach
Succeeded Dan Devine as football coach at Notre Dame, 1981-85.
b. May 21, 1935 in Dayton, Ohio
Source: *NewYTBS 81*

Faust, Johann
[Johann Faustus]
German. Magician
b. 1480 in Knittlingen, Germany
d. 1540
Source: *FilmgC; LinLib L, S; NewC*

Faust, Lotta
Actress
Appeared on stage in *The Wizard of Oz.*
b. Feb 8, 1880 in Brooklyn, New York
d. Jan 25, 1910 in New York, New York
Source: *NotNAT B; WhoStg 1908*

Faversham, William Alfred
English. Actor
Leading man in Charles Frohman's Empire Theatre Co., 1893-1901; in silent films, 1915.
b. Feb 12, 1868 in London, England
d. Apr 7, 1940 in Bay Shore, New York
Source: *AmBi; CurBio 40; DcAmB S2; FamA&A; Film 1, 2; OxThe; PlP&P; TwYS; WhAm 1; WhScrn 74, 77; WhThe; WhoHol B; WhoStg 1906, 1908*

Fawcett, Farrah Leni
American. Actress, Model
Starred in "Charlie's Angels," 1976-77; movie *The Burning Bed,* 1983.
b. Feb 2, 1947 in Corpus Christi, Texas
Source: *BioIn 10, 11; IntMPA 78, 79, 80, 81, 82; WhoAm 78, 80, 82*

Fawcett, George
American. Actor
Silent screen star in D W Griffith films: *Intolerance; True Heart Susie.*
b. Aug 25, 1861 in Alexandria, Virginia
d. Jun 6, 1939 in Nantucket, Massachusetts
Source: *Alli SUP; Film 1, 2; MotPP; MovMk; TwYS; WhAm 1; WhScrn 74, 77; WhThe; WhoHol B*

Fawcett, Henry
English. Economist
b. Aug 26, 1833 in Salisbury, England
d. Nov 6, 1884
Source: *Alli SUP; BbD; BiD&SB; BioIn 8; BrAu 19; DcEnA; DcEnL; EvLB; LinLib S; NewCol 75*

Fawcett, Dame Millicent Garrett
[Mrs. Henry Fawcett]
English. Feminist
b. 1847 in Adleburgh, England
d. 1929
Source: *Alli SUP; BbD; BiD&SB; BioIn 2, 9; EvLB; NewC; NewCol 75; WhLit*

Fawcett, Wilford Hamilton, Jr.
American. Publisher
b. Aug 1, 1909 in Saint Paul, Minnesota
d. May 28, 1970 in Norwalk, Connecticut
Source: *WhAm 5*

Fawkes, Guy
English. Soldier
Conspired to blow up English Parliament, King James I, Nov 5, 1605; Guy Fawkes Day celebrated Nov 5.
b. 1570 in York, England
d. Jan 31, 1606
Source: *LinLib S; NewC; NewCol 75*

Faye, Alice
[Ann Leppert]
American. Actress, Singer
Musical star at Fox Studios, late 1930s.
b. May 5, 1915 in New York, New York
Source: *BiDFilm; CelR; CmMov; FilmgC;
InWom; MovMk; OxFilm; ThFT; WorEFlm*

Faye, Joey
[Joseph Anthony Palladino]
American. Actor, Comedian
Starred in Minsky's burlesque theatre, 1931-
38.
b. Jul 12, 1910 in New York, New York
Source: *BiE&WWA; NotNAT; WhoHol A;
WhoThe 77, 81*

Faylen, Frank
American. Actor
Best known for film *The Lost Weekend,*
1945; was Dobie's father on "The Many
Loves of Dobie Gillis," 1959-63.
b. 1907 in Saint Louis, Missouri
d. Aug 2, 1985 in Burbank, California
Source: *FilmEn; FilmgC; IntMPA 81, 82, 84;
MotPP; MovMk; Vers A; WhoHol A*

Fazenda, Louise
American. Actress
In comedies for Mack Sennett's Keystone
studio from 1915.
b. Jun 17, 1899 in Lafayette, Indiana
d. Apr 17, 1962 in Beverly Hills, California
Source: *FilmEn; Film 1, 2; FilmgC; MotPP;
MovMk; ThFT; TwYS; WhScrn 74, 77;
WhoHol B; WorEFlm*

Fearing, Kenneth Flexner
American. Author
Writings include verse *Dead Reckoning,* 1938;
mystery novel *Big Clock,* 1946.
b. Jul 28, 1902 in Oak Park, Illinois
d. Jun 26, 1961 in New York, New York
Source: *AmAu&B; AmNov; CnDAL; CnE&AP;
ConAmA; ConAu 93; DcLEL; EncMys;
LinLib L; ModAL; OxAmL; PenC AM; RAdv
1; REn; REnAL; SixAP; TwCA, SUP;
WebAB; WebE&AL; WhAm 4; WhoTwCL*

Fears, Tom (Thomas Jesse)
American. Football Player
Holds NFL record for most receptions in
game--18 vs. Green Bay, 1950; Hall of
Fame, 1970.
b. Dec 3, 1923 in Los Angeles, California
Source: *BioIn 9; NewYTBE 70; WhoFtbl 74*

Feather, Leonard Geoffrey
American. Composer, Music Critic
Composed music for sound recording of
Langston Hughes' poems, *The Weary
Blues;* author of reference books on jazz.
b. Sep 13, 1914 in London, England
Source: *AmAu&B; AmSCAP 66; Baker 78;
ConAu 61; WhoAm 74, 76, 78, 80, 82;
WhoWor 74*

Feather, Victor
English. Labor Union Official
Helped to make Trades Union Congress one
of Europe's most powerful unions.
b. Apr 10, 1908 in Bradford, England
d. Jul 28, 1976 in London, England
Source: *CurBio 73, 76N; IntWW 74;
NewYTBS 76; Who 74; WhoWor 76*

Federici, Daniel Paul
[E Street Band]
"Phantom"
American. Musician, Singer
Plays keyboards, accordion with Bruce
Springsteen's band since 1968.
b. Jan 23, 1950 in Flemington, New Jersey
Source: *WhoRocM 82*

Federko, Bernie (Bernard Allan)
Canadian. Hockey Player
Center, St. Louis, 1976--.
b. May 12, 1956 in Foam Lake,
Saskatchewan
Source: *HocReg 85*

Fedin, Konstantin
Russian. Author
b. Feb 27, 1892 in Saratov, Russia
d. Jul 15, 1977 in Moscow, U.S.S.R.
Source: *CasWL; ClDMEL; ConAu 73, 81;
DcRusL; EncWL; EvEuW; IntWW 74;
ModSL 1; PenC EUR; REn; TwCWr;
WhoWor 78; WorAu*

Fedorova, Alexandra
Russian. Ballerina
b. 1884
d. 1972
Source: *NewYTBE 72*

Feeney, "Chub" (Charles Stoneham)
American. Baseball Executive
Succeeded Warren Giles as pres. of NL,
1970-86.
b. Aug 31, 1921 in Orange, New Jersey
Source: *WhoAm 84; WhoE 83; WhoProB 73*

Feiffer, Jules Ralph
American. Cartoonist, Author
b. Jan 26, 1929 in New York, New York
Source: *AmAu&B; Au&Wr 71; CelR; CnThe;
ConAu 17R; ConLC 2, 8; CroCD; CurBio 61;
FilmgC; IntWW 74; McGEWD; NotNAT;
SmATA 8; WhoAm 74, 76, 78, 80, 82;
WhoThe 77; WhoWor 78; WhoWorJ 72;
WrDr 80*

Feigner, Eddie (Edward)
"King of Softball"; "Golden Arm"
American. Baseball Player
b. 1925
Source: *BioIn 6, 9*

Feingold, Benjamin Franklin
American. Physician, Author
Developed Feingold diet for hyperactive
children removing preservatives, artificially
flavored, colored foods; wrote *Why Your
Child is Hyperactive*, 1975.
b. Jun 15, 1900 in Pittsburgh, Pennsylvania
d. Mar 23, 1982 in San Francisco, California
Source: *AmM&WS 79P; AnObit 1982; ConAu
106; NewYTBS 82; WhoAm 80, 82; WhoAmJ
80*

Feininger, Andreas Bernhard Lyonel
American. Photographer, Author
Photographer, *Life* magazine, 1943-62; known
for work in telephoto, close-up
photography; noted for poetic views of
cities.
b. Dec 27, 1906 in Paris, France
Source: *AmAu&B; ConAu 85; ConPhot;
CurBio 57; LinLib L; WhoAm 74, 76, 78, 80,
82, 84; WhoWor 74, 76*

Feininger, Lyonel
[Charles Adrian Feininger]
American. Artist, Cartoonist
Pioneer of modern American art whose
unique style of dividing forms, space by
segmented planes of color was influenced
by cubism.
b. Jul 17, 1871 in New York, New York
d. Jan 13, 1956
Source: *AtlBL; CurBio 55, 56; DcCAA 71;
OxGer; REn; WhAm 3*

Feinstein, Dianne
American. Politician
Became mayor, 1978, after assassination of
George Moscone.
b. Jun 22, 1933 in San Francisco, California
Source: *CurBio 79; NewYTBE 71; NewYTBS
78; WhoAm 80, 82; WhoAmW 79; WhoGov
77*

Feis, Herbert
American. Author, Economist, Historian
b. Jun 7, 1893 in New York, New York
d. Mar 2, 1972 in Winter Park, Florida
Source: *AmAu&B; Au&Wr 71; ConAu 33R,
P-1; CurBio 61, 72; NewYTBE 72; OxAmL;
WhAm 5; WhoWorJ 72; WorAu*

Feld, Eliot
American. Dancer
b. Jul 5, 1942 in Brooklyn, New York
Source: *CurBio 71; NewYTBE 70; NewYTBS
74; WhoAm 74, 76, 78, 80, 82; WhoE 74*

Feld, Fritz
American. Actor
Appeared in 400 major films, 300 TV shows,
500 TV films, since 1920s.
b. Oct 15, 1900 in Berlin, Germany
Source: *FilmgC; IntMPA 75, 76, 77; MovMk;
TwYS; Vers A; WhoAm 74, 76, 78, 80, 82;
WhoHol A*

Feld, Irvin
American. Businessman, Producer
Pres., producer Ringling Brothers, Barnum &
Bailey Circus, 1967-84; founded Clown
College, 1968.
b. May 9, 1918 in Hagerstown, Maryland
d. Sep 6, 1984 in Venice, California
Source: *CelR,; CurBio 79; NewYTBE 70;
St&PR 75; WhoAm 80, 82, 84; WhoWor 78*

Felder, Don(ald William)
[The Eagles]
American. Musician, Singer, Songwriter
Joined the Eagles as lead guitarist,
songwriter, 1973; recorded title song from
movie *Heavy Metal*, 1981.
b. Sep 21, 1947 in Gainesville, Florida
Source: *WhoAm 82*

Felder, Wilton
see: Crusaders, The

Feldman, Alvin Lindbergh
American. Airline Executive
Pres., Frontier Airlines, Inc., 1971-81.
b. Dec 14, 1927 in New York, New York
d. Aug 9, 1981 in Los Angeles, California
Source: *WhoAm 78, 80*

Feldman, Marty
English. Actor, Director, Writer
Made American film debut in *Young
Frankenstein*, 1974.
b. Jul 8, 1934 in London, England
d. Dec 2, 1982 in Mexico City, Mexico
Source: *AnObit 1982; FilmgC; IntMPA 79,
80, 81, 82; NewYTBS 82; WhoAm 80, 82;
WhoHol A; WorAl*

Feldon, Barbara
American. Actress
Best known for role as Agent 99 on TV
   series "Get Smart," 1965-70.
b. Mar 12, 1941 in Pittsburgh, Pennsylvania
Source: *WhoHol A*

Feldshuh, Tovah
American. Actress
Played in TV shows "Amazing Howard
   Hughes"; "Holocaust"; "Beggarman-Thief."
b. Dec 27, 1952 in New York, New York
Source: *BioIn 11; WhoAm 82; WhoThe 81*

Feldstein, Martin Stuart
American. Economist
Chairman, Council of Economic Advisers,
   1982--.
b. Nov 25, 1939 in New York, New York
Source: *ConAu 73; IntWW 83; NewYTBS 82;
WhoAm 80, 82, 84; WhoAmJ 80; WhoE 83;
WhoF&I 81, 83*

Feliciano, Jose
American. Singer, Musician
Blind singer, guitarist; composed theme for
   TV show "Chico and the Man."
b. Sep 10, 1945 in Larez, Puerto Rico
Source: *CurBio 69; CelR; RkOn 74; WhoAm
74, 76, 78, 80, 82*

Felker, Clay S
American. Journalist
b. Oct 2, 1928 in Saint Louis, Missouri
Source: *ConAu 73; CurBio 75; St&PR 75;
WhoAm 74, 76, 78, 80, 82; WhoE 74;
WhoF&I 74; WhoWor 78*

Fell, John
English. Clergyman, Author, Editor
Promoted Oxford University Press.
b. Jun 23, 1625 in Longworth, England
d. Jul 10, 1686
Source: *BrAu; DcEnL; NewC; OxEng; REn*

Fell, Norman
American. Actor
Starred on TV's "Three's Company," 1977-
   79; "The Ropers," 1979-80.
b. Mar 24, 1925 in Philadelphia,
   Pennsylvania
Source: *IntMPA 82; WhoAm 74, 76, 78, 80,
82; WhoHol A*

Feller, Bob (Robert William Andrew)
"Rapid Robert"
American. Baseball Player
Pitcher who won 266 career games, including
   three no-hitters; Hall of Fame, 1962.
b. Nov 3, 1918 in Van Meter, Iowa
Source: *AuBYP; BaseEn 85; BioNews 74;
CurBio 41; WhoProB 73*

Fellig, Arthur
"Weegee"
American. Photographer
Black-and-white news photographer known
   for pictures of NYC violence, 1940's-50's.
b. Jul 12, 1899 in Zloczew, Austria
d. Dec 26, 1968 in New York, New York
Source: *BioIn 10; MacBEP*

Fellini, Federico
Italian. Screenwriter, Director
Won four Oscars for best foreign film,
   including *La Dolce Vita,* 1960.
b. Jan 20, 1920 in Rimini, Italy
Source: *BiDFilm; BkPepl; ConAu 65; ConLC
16; CurBio 57; DcFM; FilmgC; IntMPA 75,
76, 77, 78, 79, 80, 81, 82; IntWW 74;
MovMk; OxFilm; REn; Who 82; WhoAm 82;
WhoWor 78; WomWMM; WorEFlm*

Fellows, Edith
American. Actress, Singer
1930s child star in films *Huckleberry Finn;
Jane Eyre; Five Little Peppers.*
b. May 20, 1923 in Boston, Massachusetts
Source: *FilmEn; Film 2; FilmgC; ThFT;
WhoHol A*

Fels, Samuel Simeon
American. Businessman, Philanthropist
b. Feb 16, 1860 in Yanceyville, North
   Carolina
d. Jun 23, 1950 in Philadelphia, Pennsylvania
Source: *DcAmB S4; WhAm 3*

Felsenstein, Walter
Austrian. Actor, Director, Producer
Began managing opera companies, 1924;
   Berlin State Opera, 1940-47; Komische
   Opera, 1947-75.
b. May 30, 1901 in Vienna, Austria
d. Oct 8, 1975 in Berlin, Germany (East)
Source: *IntWW 75, 75, 76N; WhoOp 76;
WhoSocC 78; WhoWor 74*

Felske, John Frederick
American. Baseball Manager
Catcher, infielder who is manager,
   Philadelphia, 1985--.
b. May 30, 1942 in Chicago, Illinois
Source: *BaseReg 86*

Felton, Harold W
American. Author
b. Apr 1, 1902 in Neola, Iowa
Source: *AuBYP; ChhPo S2; ConAu 1R, 1NR; MorJA; SmATA 1*

Felton, Rebecca Ann Latimer
American. Politician
Appointed senator from GA, 1922; first woman to sit in Senate.
b. Jun 10, 1835 in Decatur, Illinois
d. Jan 24, 1930 in Atlanta, Georgia
Source: *NotAW; WebBD 80*

Felton, Verna
American. Actress
Played in TV series "December Bride," 1954-61.
b. Jul 20, 1890 in Salinas, California
d. Dec 14, 1966 in North Hollywood, California
Source: *FilmgC; Vers B; WhScrn 74, 77; WhoHol B*

Fender, Freddy
[Baldermar Huerta]
American. Singer, Songwriter
Won Grammy, 1977, for "Before the Next Teardrop Falls."
b. Jun 4, 1937 in San Benito, Texas
Source: *BioIn 10; RkOn 74; WhoAm 78, 80, 82*

Fender, Leo
American. Manufacturer
Designed solid body electric guitar; helped in development of rock music.
b. 1907
Source: *IlEncRk*

Fendler, Edvard
German. Conductor, Composer
b. Jan 22, 1902 in Leipzig, Germany
Source: *AmSCAP 66*

Fenelon, Fania
[Fanny Goldstein]
French. Author, Singer, Musician
Memoirs, *Playing for Time* 1977, telling horrors of Nazi concentration camps, made into film starring Vanessa Redgrave, 1985.
b. Sep 2, 1918 in Paris, France
d. Dec 20, 1983 in Paris, France
Source: *AnObit 1983; BioIn 11; ConAu 77; NewYTBS 78, 83*

Fenelon, Francois de Salignac
French. Author, Theologian
Wrote prose epic *Adventures of Telemachus,* 1699.
b. Aug 6, 1651 in Perigord, France
d. Jan 7, 1715 in Cambrai, France
Source: *AtlBL; BbD; BiD&SB; CasWL; ChhPo S1; DcEuL; EuAu; LinLib L, S; McGEWB; NewC; OxEng; OxFr; PenC EUR; REn*

Fenn, George Manville
English. Author, Editor
Prolific writer of boys adventure tales.
b. Jan 3, 1831 in Pimlico, England
d. Aug 26, 1909 in Essex, England
Source: *BbD; BiD&SB; Chambr 3; DcBiA; DcEnL; DcNaB S2; EvLB; HsB&A; MnBBF; NewC; NotNAT B; TwCCW 83A; WhLit*

Fennell, Frederick
American. Conductor
Founded Eastman Wind Ensemble, 1952, made numerous albums; guest conductor with Boston Pops.
b. Jul 2, 1914 in Cleveland, Ohio
Source: *Baker 78; BioIn 8; WhoMus 72*

Fennelly, Parker
American. Radio Performer
Source: *BioIn 11; WhoHol A*

Fenneman, George
American. Radio Performer
b. Nov 10, 1919 in Peking, China
Source: *IntMPA 75, 76, 77, 78, 79, 80, 81, 82*

Fenollosa, Ernest Francisco
American. Art Historian
Pioneer Orientalist; most subsequent work imitated his; wrote *The Masters of Ukioye,* 1896.
b. Feb 18, 1853 in Salem, Massachusetts
d. Sep 21, 1908 in London, England
Source: *AmAu; AmBi; BiDSA; CnDAL; DcAmAu; DcAmB; DcLEL; DcNAA; OxAmL; REn; REnAL; WebAB; WebE&AL; WhAm 1*

Fenten, D X
American. Children's Author
b. Jan 3, 1932 in New York, New York
Source: *ConAu 33R; SmATA 4; WrDr 80*

Fenton, Carroll Lane
American. Author, Illustrator
b. Feb 12, 1900 in Parkersburg, Iowa
d. Nov 16, 1969
Source: *AmAu&B; AuBYP; ConAu 1R, 29R; MorJA; SmATA 5*

Fenton, Leslie
English. Actor, Director
Appeared in over 30 films, 1920s-30s.
b. Mar 12, 1902 in Liverpool, England
Source: *Film 2; FilmgC; MotPP; MovMk*

Fenton, Thomas Trail
American. Journalist
b. Apr 8, 1930 in Baltimore, Maryland
Source: *ConAu 102; WhoAm 74, 76, 78, 80, 82; WhoWor 78*

Fenwick, Millicent Hammond
American. Politician
Congresswoman from NJ, 1975-82; defeated
   in bid for Senate, 1982.
b. Feb 25, 1910 in New York, New York
Source: *CurBio 77; GoodHs; NewYTBS 74; WhoAm 82; WhoAmP 73; WhoAmW 74, 79*

Feoktistov, Konstantin Petrovich
Russian. Cosmonaut, Engineer
b. Feb 7, 1926 in Voronezh, U.S.S.R.
Source: *CurBio 67*

Ferber, Edna
American. Author
Best-selling novels include 1925 Pulitzer-
   winning, *So Big; Show Boat,* 1926; *Giant,*
   1952.
b. Aug 15, 1887 in Kalamazoo, Michigan
d. Apr 16, 1968 in New York, New York
Source: *AmAu&B; AmNov; AuNews 1; BiE&WWA; Chambr 3; CnDAL; CnMD; CnThe; ConAmA; ConAmL; ConAu 5R, 25R; ConLC 18; DcLEL; EncWL; EvLB; FilmgC; InWom; LinLib L, S; LongCTC; McGEWD; ModAL; ModWD; OxAmL; OxThe; PenC AM; PIP&P; REn; REnAL; SmATA 7; TwCA, SUP; TwCWr; WebAB; WhAm 5; WhNAA; WhThe; WisWr*

Ferdinand I
Spanish. Emperor
b. 1503
d. 1564
Source: *BioIn 10; NewCol 75; WebBD 80*

Ferdinand V
Spanish. King
b. Mar 10, 1452 in Sos, Spain
d. Jan 23, 1516 in Madrigalejo, Spain
Source: *BioIn 10; LinLib S; McGEWB; NewCol 75*

Ferdinand
see: Franz Ferdinand

Ferdinand Maximilian Joseph
see: Maximilian

Ferencsik, Janos
Hungarian. Conductor
Director Hungarian State Opera House until
   1973.
b. Jan 18, 1907 in Budapest, Hungary
d. Jun 12, 1984 in Budapest, Hungary
Source: *AnObit 1984; IntWW 75, 76, 77, 78; WhoOp 76; WhoSocC 78*

Ferguson, Elsie
American. Actress
Silent screen star who played in 16 pictures,
   1917-20, including *A Doll's House.*
b. Aug 19, 1885 in New York
d. Nov 15, 1961 in New London,
   Connecticut
Source: *CurBio 62; Film 1, 2; FilmgC; WhAm 4; WhThe; WhoHol B*

Ferguson, Harry George
English. Industrialist
b. Nov 4, 1884 in Dromore, Northern
   Ireland
d. Oct 25, 1960 in Abbotswood, England
Source: *BioIn 3, 4, 5, 6, 9, 10; CurBio 56, 61; WhAm 4*

Ferguson, Homer
American. Judge, Politician
Senator from MI, 1943-1954.
b. Feb 25, 1888 in Harrison City,
   Pennsylvania
d. Dec 17, 1982 in Grosse Pointe, Michigan
Source: *BiDrAC; CngDr 74, 77, 79, 81; CurBio 43, 83; IntWW 75, 76, 77, 78, 79, 80, 81; NewYTBS 82; PolProf E, T; WhoAm 76, 78, 80, 82; WhoAmP 73, 75, 77, 79; WhoGov 72, 75, 77*

Ferguson, Homer Lenoir
American. Shipping Executive
Built battleships for Navy, including USS
   Indiana, 1941.
b. Mar 6, 1873 in Waynesville, North
   Carolina
d. Mar 14, 1952 in Warwick, Virginia
Source: *NatCAB 17, 40; WhAm 3*

Ferguson, Jimmy
see: Irish Rovers

Ferguson, Joe Carlton, Jr.
American. Football Player
b. Apr 23, 1950 in Alvin, Texas
Source: *FootReg 81*

Ferguson, John Bowie
Canadian. Hockey Player, Hockey Executive
Forward, Montreal, 1963-71; currently general
manager, Winnipeg.
b. Sep 5, 1938 in Vancouver, British
Columbia
Source: *WhoAm 76; WhoE 74; WhoF&I 75;
WhoHcky 73*

Ferguson, Maynard
Canadian. Jazz Musician
Plays trumpet; has sold more records than
any band leader since 1940.
b. May 4, 1928 in Verdun, Quebec
Source: *BioIn 12; CanWW 82; CurBio 80;
WhoAm 76, 78, 80, 82*

Ferguson, Miriam Amanda
American. Governor
b. Jun 13, 1875 in Bell County, Texas
d. Jun 25, 1961 in Austin, Texas
Source: *GoodHs; InWom; WhAm 4; WhAmP*

Ferguson, Sarah Margaret
[Duchess of York]
"Fergie"
English. Consort
Commoner who married Prince Andrew Jul
23, 1986.
b. Oct 1959 in England
Source: *NF*

Fergusson, Bernard Edward
see: Ballantrae, Lord

Fergusson, Francis
American. Author
b. Feb 21, 1904 in Albuquerque, New
Mexico
Source: *AmAu&B; ConAu 9R, 3NR; DrAS
74E; NotNAT; REnAL; TwCA SUP; WhoAm
74, 76, 78, 80, 82; WhoWor 78; WrDr 76*

Fergusson, Harvey
American. Author
b. Jan 28, 1890 in Albuquerque, New
Mexico
d. Aug 24, 1971
Source: *AmAu&B; AmNov; CnDAL; ConAu
33R; OxAmL; REnAL; TwCA, SUP; WhNAA*

Ferkauf, Eugene
American. Merchant
b. 1921
Source: *BioIn 6, 7*

Ferlinghetti, Lawrence
American. Author, Poet
b. Mar 24, 1919 in Yonkers, New York
Source: *ConAu 5R, 3NR; ConLC 2, 6; ConP
70, 75; CroCAP; CroCD; DrAP 75; ModAL;
OxAmL; PenC AM; RAdv 1; REn; REnAL;
TwCWr; WebE&AL; WhoAm 82; WhoTwCL;
WhoWest 84; WorAu; WrDr 80*

Fermat, Pierre de
French. Mathematician
Discovered analytic geometry, modern theory
of numbers, calculus of probabilities.
b. 1601
d. 1665
Source: *BioIn 2, 5*

Fermi, Enrico
American. Physicist
Discovered uranium fission; won Nobel Prize,
1938; developed atomic bomb, 1942-45.
b. Sep 29, 1901 in Rome, Italy
d. Nov 28, 1954 in Chicago, Illinois
Source: *CurBio 45, 55; DcAmB S5; EncAB-H;
WebAB; WhAm 3*

Fernald, John Bailey
American. Director
British stage since 1929; author, *The Play
Produced.*
b. Nov 21, 1905 in California
Source: *ConAu P-2; OxThe; Who 74; WhoThe
72, 77*

Fernandel
[Fernand Contandin]
French. Actor
Popular in *Don Camillo* series of French
comedies in which he portrayed an
eccentric priest.
b. May 8, 1903 in Marseilles, France
d. Feb 26, 1971 in Paris, France
Source: *CurBio 71N; FilmgC; MotPP;
MovMk; NewYTBE 71; OxFilm; WhAm 5;
WhScrn 74, 77; WhoHol B; WorEFlm*

Fernandez, Emilio
Mexican. Actor
Appeared in *The Wild Bunch,* 1969; best
known for shooting a critic; imprisoned,
1970s.
b. 1904 in Hondo, Mexico
d. Aug 6, 1986 in Mexico City, Mexico
Source: *DcFM; FilmgC; HalFC 84; OxFilm*

Fernandez, Sid (Charles Sidney)
American. Baseball Player
Pitcher, NY Mets, 1984--; pitched two no-
hitters in minor leagues.
b. Oct 12, 1962 in Honolulu, Hawaii
Source: *BaseEn 85; BaseReg 86*

Fernandez-Muro, Jose Antonio
Argentine. Artist
b. Mar 1, 1920
Source: *IntWW 74*

Ferragamo, Salvatore
Italian. Business Executive
Began family-run shoe-clothing-accessory
business in Florence, 1927; 1983 revenues
over $50 million.
b. Jun 1898 in Bonito, Italy
d. Aug 7, 1960 in Fiumetto, Italy
Source: *BioIn 2, 4, 5, 9; FairDF ITA;
ObitOF 79; WhoFash*

Ferragamo, Vince
American. Football Player
b. Apr 24, 1954 in Torrance, California
Source: *BioIn 12; FootReg 81*

Ferrante, Arthur
[Ferrante and Teicher]
American. Pianist, Composer
b. Sep 7, 1921 in New York, New York
Source: *AmSCAP 66; WhoAm 74*

Ferrante & Teicher
see: Ferrante, Arthur; Teicher, Louis

Ferrare, Christina
[Mrs. Anthony Thomopoulos]
American. Model, Entertainer
Former wife of John DeLorean; starred in
films *The Impossible Years; J W Coop.*
b. 1951
Source: *BioIn 12; WhoHol A*

Ferrari, Enzo
Italian. Auto Executive
Developed the Ferrari, 1940.
b. Feb 20, 1898 in Modena, Italy
Source: *BusPN; CurBio 67; IntWW 74, 78;
Who 74; WhoWor 78*

Ferraris, Galileo
Italian. Explorer, Scientist
Discovered rotary magnetic field, 1885.
b. 1847
d. 1897
Source: *NewCol 75*

Ferraro, Geraldine Anne
[Mrs. John Zaccaro]
American. Politician
Walter Mondale's running mate, 1984
presidential election; first woman vp
candidate.
b. Aug 26, 1935 in Newburgh, New York
Source: *AlmAP 80, 82, 84; AmPolW 80;
CurBio 84; NewYTBS 84; WhoAm 80, 82, 84;
WhoAmP 81, 83; WhoAmW 81, 83; WhoE
81, 83*

Ferre, Maurice Antonio
American. Politician
b. Jun 23, 1935 in Ponce, Puerto Rico
Source: *St&PR 75; WhoAm 74, 76, 78, 80,
82; WhoF&I 74; WhoWor 78*

Ferrell, Conchata Galen
"Chatti"
American. Actress
Won Obie, Drama Desk Awards for *The Sea
Horse,* 1974.
b. Mar 28, 1943 in Charleston, West Virginia
Source: *BioIn 10; Who 82; WhoAm 82*

Ferrell, Wes(ley Cheek)
American. Baseball Player
Holds record for most home runs hit by a
pitcher (38).
b. Feb 2, 1908 in Greensboro, North
Carolina
d. Dec 9, 1976 in Sarasota, Florida
Source: *BaseEn 85; BioIn 10, 11; IntWW 76;
WhoProB 73*

Ferrer, Jose Figueres
see: Figueres Ferrer, Jose

Ferrer, Jose Vicente
American. Actor, Producer, Director
Won 1950 Oscar for *Cyrano de Bergerac.*
b. Jan 8, 1912 in Santurce, Puerto Rico
Source: *BiDFilm; BiE&WWA; CelR; CurBio
44; EncMT; FilmgC; IntMPA 75, 76, 77, 78,
79, 80, 81, 82; MotPP; MovMk; NotNAT;
OxFilm; Who 74; WhoAm 74, 76, 78, 80, 82;
WhoHol A; WhoThe 77; WhoWor 78;
WorEFlm*

Ferrer, Mel(chor Gaston)
American. Actor
In film *Lili,* 1953; TV series "Falcon Crest,"
1983-84; married to Audrey Hepburn,
1954-68.
b. Aug 25, 1917 in Elberon, New Jersey
Source: *BiDFilm; BiE&WWA; FilmgC;
IntMPA 75, 76, 77, 78, 79, 80, 81, 82;
MotPP; MovMk; NotNAT; OxFilm; WhoHol
A; WorEFlm*

Ferrier, David
Scottish. Neurologist
b. 1843
d. 1928
Source: *BioIn 4, 6, 7; WebBD 80*

Ferrier, Jim (James B)
Australian. Golfer
Won first tournament in US, 1944; won
  PGA, 1947.
b. Feb 24, 1915 in Sydney, Australia
Source: *BioIn 10; WhoGolf*

Ferrier, Henry Eliza
Surinamese. Governor
b. May 12, 1910 in Paramaribo, Surinam
Source: *IntWW 74; WhoWor 78*

Ferrier, Kathleen
English. Opera Singer
b. Apr 22, 1912 in Higher Walter, England
d. Oct 8, 1953 in London, England
Source: *CurBio 51, 53; InWom; WhAm HSA,
4*

Ferrigno, Lou
American. Actor
Played the Hulk on TV series "The
  Incredible Hulk," 1977-81.
b. Nov 9, 1952 in Brooklyn, New York
Source: *NewYTBS 76*

Ferril, Thomas Hornsby
American. Publisher
b. Jun 23, 1896 in Keeseville, New York
Source: *AmAu&B; ChhPo, S1, S2; ConAu 65;
ConP 70, 75; OxAmL; REnAL; TwCA SUP;
WhoAm 74, 76, 78, 80, 82; WrDr 76*

Ferris, Barbara Gillian
English. Actress
Began career as dancer at age 15; in film
  Sparrows Can't Sine, 1963.
b. Oct 3, 1940 in London, England
Source: *FilmgC; NotNAT; WhoHol A;
WhoThe 77*

Ferris, George Washington Gale
American. Inventor, Businessman
Invented Ferris Wheel, 1893, for World's
  Columbian Exposition, Chicago.
b. Feb 14, 1859 in Galesburg, Illinois
d. Nov 22, 1896 in Pittsburgh, Pennsylvania
Source: *ApCAB SUP; DcAmB; WebAB;
WhAm HS*

Ferry, Bryan
[Roxy Music]
English. Singer, Songwriter
Lead vocalist, principal songwriter for Roxy
  Music; solo album *Let's Stick Together,*
  1976.
b. Sep 26, 1945 in Durham, England
Source: *BioIn 11; ConMuA 80A; WhoAm 82,
84; WhoRock 81*

Fessenden, Reginald Aubrey
Canadian. Inventor
Made first radio broadcast, first two-way
  telegraphic communication, 1906.
b. Oct 6, 1866 in Bolton, Quebec
d. Jul 22, 1932 in Bermuda
Source: *AmBi; DcAmB S1; DcNAA; TwCBDA;
WebAB; WhAm 1*

Fessenden, William Pitt
American. Politician
b. Oct 16, 1806 in Boscawen, New
  Hampshire
d. Sep 8, 1869 in Portland, Maine
Source: *DcAmB; WebAB; WhAm HS*

Fetchit, Stepin
[Lincoln Theodore Monroe Andrew Perry]
American. Actor
Known for portrayal of perpetually bemused
  Uncle Tom-like character; screen debut,
  1927.
b. May 30, 1902 in Key West, Florida
d. Nov 19, 1985 in Woodland Hills,
  California
Source: *BioNews 74; ConNews 86-1; FilmEn;
Film 2; FilmgC; HolP 30; MotPP; MovMk;
WhoHol A*

Feti, Domenico
Italian. Artist
Religious artist influenced by Caravaggio,
  Ruben: "Six Sainted Martyrs," 1613.
b. 1589 in Rome, Italy
d. 1623 in Venice, Italy
Source: *McGDA*

Fetzer, John Earl
American. Baseball Executive, Businessman
Owner, Fetzer Broadcasting, 1930; Detroit
  Tigers baseball club, 1956-83.
b. Mar 25, 1901 in Decater, Indiana
Source: *IntMPA 82; IntYB 78; Who 76;
WhoAm 78, 80, 82; WhoAmW 77; WhoProB
73*

Feuchtwanger, Lion
German. Author, Dramatist
Historical novels include *Ugly Duchess,* 1923.
b. Jul 7, 1884 in Munich, Germany
d. Dec 21, 1958 in Los Angeles, California
Source: *AmAu&B; CasWL; ClDMEL; CnMD;
CyWA; EncWL; EvEuW; LinLib L, S;
LongCTC; McGEWD; ModGL; ModWD;
OxEng; OxGer; PenC EUR; REn; TwCA,
SUP; WhAm 3, 3; WhE&EA*

Feuer, Cy
American. Director, Producer
Stage productions include *Guys and Dolls;
Can-Can; Silk Stockings.*
b. Jan 15, 1911 in New York, New York
Source: *BiE&WWA; CelR; EncMT; NotNAT;
Who 82; WhoAm 74; WhoThe 72, 77;
WhoWor 74*

Feuerbach, Anselm
German. Artist
b. Sep 12, 1829
d. Jan 4, 1880
Source: *NewCol 75; OxArt; OxGer; PenC
EUR; REn*

Feuerbach, Ludwig Andreas
German. Philosopher
b. Jul 28, 1804 in Landshut, Germany
d. Sep 13, 1872 in Rechenberg, Germany
Source: *McGEWB; NewCol 75; OxGer; PenC
AM; REn*

Feuerbach, Paul Johann Anseim
German. Judge
b. 1775
d. 1833
Source: *BiD&SB; DcEuL; NewCol 75*

Feuermann, Emanuel
American. Musician
b. Nov 22, 1902 in Kolomea, Poland
d. May 25, 1942 in New York, New York
Source: *CurBio 42*

Feuillade, Louis
French. Director
Directed over 800 films, 1906-26, writing
almost all of the scripts; best-known for
his fantasy serials.
b. Feb 19, 1873 in Lunel, France
d. 1925 in Paris, France
Source: *BiDFilm; DcFM; FilmEn; FilmgC;
OxFilm; WorEFlm*

Feuillet, Octave
French. Dramatist, Author
Popular sentimental novelist.
b. Jul 11, 1821 in Saint Lo, France
d. Dec 29, 1890 in Paris, France
Source: *BbD; CasWL; DcBiA; DcEuL; EuAu;
EvEuW; HsB&A; LinLib L; NotNAT B;
OxFr; PenC EUR*

Feulner, Edwin John, Jr.
American. Businessman
Pres., Heritage Foundation, Washington, DC,
1977--.
b. Aug 12, 1941 in Evergreen Park, Illinois
Source: *ConAu 115; WhoAm 84; WhoAmP
83; WhoF&I 83; WhoWor 82*

Fey, Thomas Hossler
American. Business Executive
Pres., A & W Beverage Co., 1973--.
b. Sep 17, 1939 in Chicago, Illinois
Source: *WhoAm 82, 84*

Feydeau, Georges
French. Dramatist
Comedies of manners include *Lady from
Maxims,* 1899.
b. Dec 8, 1862 in Paris, France
d. Jun 6, 1921 in Rueil-Malmaison, France
Source: *AtlBL; CasWL; CnMD; CnThe;
EvEuW; FilmgC; McGEWD; ModWD; OxFr;
PenC EUR; PlP&P; REnWD; TwCWr;
WorAu*

Feynman, Richard Phillips
American. Physicist
Joint winner of 1965 Nobel Prize in Physics.
b. May 11, 1918 in New York, New York
Source: *AmM&WS 73P, 76P, 79P; AsBiEn;
IntWW 74, 75, 76, 77, 78, 79, 80, 81;
WebAB; WhoAm 74, 76, 78, 80, 82;
WhoWest 78; WhoWor 74*

Fibak, Wojtek
Polish. Tennis Player
Successful in doubles with Tom Okker; fluent
in six languages.
b. Aug 30, 1952 in Poznan, Poland
Source: *BioIn 12; WhoIntT*

Fibiger, Johannes Andreas Grib
Danish. Pathologist
b. Apr 23, 1867
d. Jan 30, 1928
Source: *BioIn 3; NewCol 75; WebBD 80*

Fibber McGee & Molly
see: McGee, Fibber; McGee, Molly

Fichte, Johann Gottlieb
German. Philosopher
b. May 19, 1762 in Rammenau, Germany
d. Jan 27, 1814 in Berlin, Germany
Source: *BbD; BiD&SB; DcEuL; EvEuW;
NewC; OxEng; OxGer; PenC EUR; REn*

Ficke, Arthur Davidson
American. Poet, Author
b. Nov 10, 1883 in Davenport, Iowa
d. Nov 30, 1945 in Hudson, New York
Source: *AmAu&B; AmLY; ChhPo, S1, S2;
CnDAL; ConAmL; DcLEL; DcNAA; OxAmL;
REn; REnAL; TwCA, SUP; WhAm 2*

Fickett, Mary
American. Actress
Won 1973 Emmy for role in soap opera "All
My Children."
b. May 23, in Bronxville, New York
Source: *VarWW 85*

Fidler, Jimmy (James M)
American. Journalist, Radio Commentator
b. 1900 in Memphis, Tennessee
Source: *BioIn 9; What 8*

Fidrych, Mark
"The Bird"
American. Baseball Player
Pitcher, Detroit Tigers, 1976-80, who talked
to baseball; rookie of year, 1976.
b. Aug 14, 1954 in Worcester, Massachusetts
Source: *BaseEn 85; CurBio 78; NewYTBS 83;
Who 78*

Fiedler, Arthur
American. Conductor
Conducted Boston Symphony Pops Concerts,
1930-79.
b. Dec 17, 1894 in Boston, Massachusetts
d. Jul 10, 1979 in Brookline, Massachusetts
Source: *BioNews 74; CelR; CurBio 45, 77,
79N; LinLib S; NewYTBE 72; WebAB; Who
78; WhoAm 74; WhoWor 78*

Fiedler, Jean(nette Feldman)
American. Children's Author
b. in Pittsburgh, Pennsylvania
Source: *ConAu 17R, 29R; ForWC 70;
SmATA 4; WhoAmW 77*

Fiedler, Leslie Aaron
American. Author
b. Mar 8, 1917 in Newark, New Jersey
Source: *AmAu&B; CasWL; CelR; ConAu 9R;
ConLC 4, 13; ConNov 72, 76; CurBio 70;
DrAF 76; DrAS 74E; EncWL; IntWW 74;
ModAL S1; PenC AM; RAdv 1; REnAL;
WhoAm 74, 76, 78, 80, 82; WhoE 74;
WhoTwCL; WhoWor 78; WhoWorJ 72;
WorAu; WrDr 80*

Field, Betty
American. Actress
Films include *Of Mice and Men*, 1939; *The
Great Gatsby*, 1949; *Peyton Place*, 1957.
b. Feb 8, 1918 in Boston, Massachusetts
d. Sep 13, 1973 in Hyannis, Massachusetts
Source: *BiE&WWA; CurBio 59, 73; FilmgC;
HolP 40; InWom; MotPP; MovMk; NewYTBE
73; PlP&P; ThFT; WhAm 6; WhScrn 77;
WhoE 74; WhoHol B; WhoThe 72, 77;
WhoWor 74*

Field, Cyrus West
American. Merchant, Financier
Promoter of first Atlantic cable, 1858.
b. Nov 30, 1819 in Stockbridge,
Massachusetts
d. Jul 12, 1892 in New York, New York
Source: *AmBi; ApCAB; DcAmB; Drake;
EncAB-H; NewCol 75; TwCBDA; WebAB;
WhAm HS*

Field, Eugene
"Poet of Childhood"
American. Poet, Journalist
Popular children's verses include *Little Boy
Blue; Wynken, Blynken, and Nod.*
b. Sep 2, 1850 in Saint Louis, Missouri
d. Nov 4, 1895 in Chicago, Illinois
Source: *Alli SUP; AmAu; AmAu&B; AmBi;
AmSCAP 66; ApCAB SUP; AuBYP; BbD;
BiD&SB; BiDSA; CarSB; CasWL; Chambr 3;
ChhPo, S1, S2; CnDAL; DcAmAu; DcAmB;
DcLEL; DcNAA; EvLB; JBA 34; LinLib L,
S; OxAmL; OxEng; PenC AM; RAdv 1; REn;
REnAL; Str&VC; TwCBDA; WebAB; WhAm
HS*

Field, John
Irish. Pianist, Composer
b. Jul 26, 1782 in Dublin, Ireland
d. Jan 11, 1837 in Moscow, Russia
Source: *WebBD 80*

Field, Kate
[Mary Katherine Keemle]
American. Actress, Author
Founded weekly "Kate Field's Washington,"
1889; wrote *Ten Days in Spain, Hap-
Hazard.*
b. Oct 1, 1838 in Saint Louis, Missouri
d. May 19, 1896 in Honolulu, Hawaii
Source: *Alli SUP; AmAu&B; AmWom;
AmWomWr; BbD; BiD&SB; BiDSA; DcAmAu;
DcNAA; NotNAT B*

Field, Marshall
American. Merchant, Journalist
Opened Marshall Field Dept. Store, 1881;
donated money to Chicago museums.
b. Aug 18, 1834 in Conway, Massachusetts
d. Jan 16, 1906 in New York, New York
Source: *AmBi; ApCAB SUP; DcAmB; EncAB-
H; TwCBDA; WebAB; WhAm 1*

Field, Marshall, III
American. Publisher, Philanthropist
Established the Chicago *Sun,* 1941, Field
Enterprises, Inc., 1944.
b. Sep 28, 1893 in Chicago, Illinois
d. Nov 8, 1956 in New York, New York
Source: *CurBio 41, 52, 57; WhAm 3*

Field, Marshall, IV
American. Publisher
Pres., publisher, editor, Chicago *Daily News,
Sunday Times.*
b. Jun 15, 1916 in New York, New York
d. Sep 18, 1965 in Chicago, Illinois
Source: *DcAmB S7; EncAJ; WhAm 4*

Field, Marshall, V
American. Newspaper Publisher
Publisher, Chicago *Sun-Times,* 1969-80;
chairman Field Enterprises, 1972--.
b. May 13, 1941 in Charlottesville, Virginia
Source: *CelR; WhoAm 74, 76, 78, 80, 82;
WhoF&I 74; WhoMW 74; WhoWor 78*

Field, Michael
American. Musician
b. Feb 21, 1915 in Manhattan, New York
d. Mar 22, 1971
Source: *BioIn 7, 8, 9; ConAu 29R; NewYTBE
71*

Field, Rachel Lyman
American. Children's Author, Dramatist, Poet
Writings include 1929 Newbery-winning
Hitty; adult best-seller *All This and
Heaven Too,* 1938.
b. Sep 19, 1894 in New York, New York
d. Mar 15, 1942 in Beverly Hills, California
Source: *AmAu&B; AnCL; AuBYP; BkCL;
CarSB; ChhPo, S1, S2; CnDAL; ConAmA;
ConICB; CurBio 42; DcNAA; FilmgC;
InWom; JBA 34, 51; LongCTC; Newb 1922;
NotAW; OxAmL; REnAL; Str&VC; TwCA,
SUP; TwCWr; WhAm 2*

Field, Ron
American. Choreographer, Director
b. 1934 in Queens, New York
Source: *EncMT; NotNAT; WhoAm 74, 76,
78, 80, 82; WhoE 74; WhoThe 77*

Field, Sally Margaret
[Mrs. Alan Greisman]
American. Actress
Won Oscars for *Norma Rae,* 1979; *Places in
the Heart,* 1985.
b. Nov 6, 1946 in Pasadena, California
Source: *BkPepl; FilmgC; IntMPA 82; WhoAm
74, 76, 78, 80, 82; WhoHol A*

Field, Sid(ney Arthur)
English. Comedian
b. Apr 1, 1904 in Birmingham, England
d. Feb 3, 1950 in Surrey, England
Source: *FilmgC; NotNAT B; WhScrn 74, 77;
WhThe; WhoHol B*

Field, Stanley
American. Author, Government Official
b. May 20, 1911 in Ukraine, Russia
Source: *ConAu 21R; WhoS&SW 82*

Field, Stephen Johnson
American. Supreme Court Justice
b. Nov 4, 1816 in Haddam, Connecticut
d. Apr 9, 1899 in Washington, District of
Columbia
Source: *AmBi; ApCAB; BiAUS; DcAmB;
DcNAA; Drake; EncAB-H; OxAmL; TwCBDA;
WebAB; WhAm HS*

**Field, Virginia (Margaret Cynthia St.
John)**
American. Actress
Known for "other woman" roles; films
include *Dream Girl, Imperfect Lady.*
b. Nov 14, 1917 in London, England
Source: *FilmgC; IntMPA 75, 76, 77, 78, 79,
80, 81, 82; MovMk; ThFT; WhThe; Who 79;
WhoAmW 77; WhoHol A; WhoThe 77A*

Fielding, Gabriel, pseud.
[Alan Gabriel Barnsley]
English. Author, Physician
b. Mar 25, 1916 in Hexham, England
Source: *ConAu 13R; ConNov 72, 76; CurBio 62; ModBrL, S1; NewC; RAdv 1; Who 74; WhoAm 74, 76, 78, 80, 82; WorAu; WrDr 76*

Fielding, Henry
English. Author, Dramatist, Lawyer
Perfected English novel in his masterpiece *Tom Jones,* 1749.
b. Apr 22, 1707 in Sharpham Park, England
d. Oct 8, 1754 in Lisbon, Portugal
Source: *Alli; AtlBL; BbD; BiD&SB; BrAu; CasWL; Chambr 2; ChhPo, S1; CnThe; CrtT 2; CyWA; DcBiA; DcEnA; DcEnL; DcEuL; DcLEL; EvLB; LinLib L, S; McGEWB; McGEWD; MouLC 2; NewC; OxEng; OxThe; PenC ENG; PlP&P; RAdv 1; RComWL; REn; REnWD; WebE&AL*

Fielding, Lewis J
American. Psychiatrist
Best known as Daniel Ellsberg's psychiatrist.
b. Oct 2, 1909 in New York, New York
Source: *BiDrAPA 77*

Fielding, Temple Hornaday
American. Author
Best known for producing *Fielding's Travel Guide to Europe,* annually since 1948.
b. Oct 8, 1913 in Bronx, New York
d. May 18, 1983 in Palma de Majorca, Spain
Source: *AmAu&B; AnObit 1983; CelR; ConAu 21R; CurBio 69, 83N; NewYTBS 83; WhAm 8; WhoAm 76, 78, 80, 82; WhoWor 74*

Fields, Debbi (Debra Jane Sivyer)
American. Business Executive
Founded Mrs. Fields Cookies, 1977; currently 250 stores with gross sales $60 million, 1985.
b. Sep 18, 1956 in Oakland, California
Source: *NF*

Fields, Dorothy
American. Songwriter
Won Oscar for lyrics to "The Way You Look Tonight"; contributed lyrics to 400 film songs.
b. Jul 15, 1905 in Allenhurst, New Jersey
d. Mar 28, 1974 in New York, New York
Source: *AmSCAP 66; BiE&WWA; ConAu 49, 93; CurBio 58, 74; EncMT; InWom; NewCBMT; NewYTBS 74; WhAm 6; WhScrn 77; WhoAm 74; WhoHol B*

Fields, Freddie
American. Producer
Films include *Looking for Mr. Goodbar,* 1977; *American Gigolo,* 1980.
b. Jul 12, 1923 in Ferndale, New York
Source: *VarWW 85*

Fields, Gracie
[Grace Stansfield]
English. Comedienne
b. Jan 9, 1898 in Rochdale, England
d. Sep 27, 1979 in Capri, Italy
Source: *CurBio 41; FilmgC; InWom; MotPP; MovMk; OxFilm; OxThe; ThFT; Who 74; WhoHol A; WhoThe 77A*

Fields, James T
American. Publisher, Author
Editor, *Atlantic Monthly,* 1861-71; wrote *Yesterdays with Authors,* 1872.
b. Dec 31, 1817 in Portsmouth, New Hampshire
d. Apr 24, 1881 in Boston, Massachusetts
Source: *Alli, SUP; AmAu; AmAu&B; AmBi; ApCAB; BbD; BiD&SB; ChhPo, S1, S2; CnDAL; CyAL 2; DcAmAu; DcAmB; DcEnL; DcLEL; DcNAA; Drake; OxAmL; REnAL; TwCBDA; WhAm HS*

Fields, Joseph
American. Screenwriter, Director
b. Feb 21, 1895 in New York, New York
d. Mar 3, 1966 in Beverly Hills, California
Source: *AmAu&B; CnMD; ConAu 25R; McGEWD; ModWD; NotNAT B; WhThe*

Fields, Lew Maurice
[Weber and Fields]
American. Comedian
b. Jan 1, 1867 in New York, New York
d. Jul 20, 1941 in Beverly Hills, California
Source: *CurBio 41; EncMT; FamA&A; Film 1; TwYS; WhAm 1; WhScrn 74, 77; WhoHol B; WhoStg 1908*

Fields, Shep
[Rippling Rhythm Orchestra]
American. Band Leader
Led 1930s-40s orchestra, noted for distinctive bubbling sound.
b. Sep 12, 1910 in Brooklyn, New York
d. Feb 23, 1981 in Los Angeles, California
Source: *BiDAmM; BioIn 9; CmpEPM; NewYTBS 81; WhoHol A*

Fields, Stanley
American. Actor
Supporting actor in 90 films, 1930-41.
b. 1880 in Allegheny, Pennsylvania
d. Apr 23, 1941 in Los Angeles, California
Source: *CurBio 41; FilmgC; MovMk; WhScrn 74, 77; WhoHol B*

Fields, Totie
[Sophie Feldman]
American. Comedienne
Popular nightclub entertainer known for self-deprecating humor.
b. May 7, 1930 in Hartford, Connecticut
d. Aug 2, 1978 in Las Vegas, Nevada
Source: *ConAu 108; GoodHs; NewYTBS 78; Who 78*

Fields, W C
[William Claude Dukenfield, real name;
  Charles Bogle, Otis J Criblecoblis,
  Mahatma Kane Jeeves, pseuds.]
American. Actor
Performed in Ziegfeld Follies, 1915-21;
  starred in *My Little Chickadee*, 1940.
b. Jan 29, 1880 in Philadelphia, Pennsylvania
d. Dec 25, 1946 in Pasadena, California
Source: *BiDFilm; CmMov; EncMT; FamA&A;
  Film 1; FilmgC; MotPP; MovMk; OxFilm;
  PIP&P; TwYS; WebAB; WhAm 2; WhScrn
  74, 77; WhoHol B; WorEFlm*

Fierstein, Harvey Forbes
American. Dramatist, Actor
Won best play, actor Tonys for *Torch Song
  Trilogy*, 1983.
b. Jun 6, 1954 in Brooklyn, New York
Source: *CurBio 84; NewYTBS 83*

Fiesole, Giovanni da
see: Angelico, Fra

Fifield, Elaine
Australian. Ballerina
b. Oct 28, 1930 in Sydney, Australia
Source: *BioIn 4, 8; WhThe*

Fifth Dimension
[Daniel Beard; William Davis, Jr.; Florence
  LaRue Gordon; Marilyn McCoo; Lamonte
  McLemore; Ronald Townson]
American. Music Group
Hits include "Up, Up and Away," 1967;
  "Aquarius," 1969.
Source: *BiDAfM; BioNews 74; CelR;
  EncPR&S 74; IlEncBM 82; RkOn 74*

Figueiredo, Joao Baptista de Oliveira
Brazilian. President
b. Jan 15, 1918 in Rio de Janeiro, Brazil
Source: *BioIn 11; CurBio 80; IntWW 79*

Figueres Ferrer, Jose
Costa Rican. President
b. Sep 25, 1908
Source: *CurBio 53; IntWW 74; NewYTBE 70;
  WhoGov 75; WhoWor 78*

Filene, Edward Albert
American. Merchant
Organized, established first credit union in US.
b. Sep 3, 1860 in Salem, Massachusetts
d. Sep 26, 1937 in Paris, France
Source: *DcAmB S2; DcNAA; WebAB; WhAm
  1; WhAmP*

Filene, Lincoln
American. Merchant
b. Apr 5, 1865 in Boston, Massachusetts
d. Aug 27, 1957
Source: *WhAm 3*

Fillmore, Abigail Powers
[Mrs. Millard Fillmore]
American. First Lady, Teacher
First wife of US Pres. Millard Fillmore; set
  up first White House library.
b. Mar 13, 1798 in Stillwater, New York
d. Mar 30, 1853 in Washington, District of
  Columbia
Source: *AmWom; GoodHs; NatCAB 6;
  NotAW*

Fillmore, Caroline Carmichael McIntosh
American. Celebrity Relative
Second wife of US Pres. Millard Fillmore.
b. Oct 21, 1813 in Morristown, New Jersey
d. Aug 11, 1881
Source: *InWom*

Fillmore, Millard
American. US President
Succeeded to presidency upon death of
  Zachary Taylor, 1850-52.
b. Jan 7, 1800 in Summerhill, New York
d. Mar 8, 1874 in Buffalo, New York
Source: *AmAu&B; AmBi; ApCAB; BiAUS;
  BiDrAC; BiDrUSE; DcAmB; Drake; EncAB-H;
  LinLib L, S; OxAmL; REnAL; TwCBDA;
  WebAB; WhAm HS, HS; WhAmP*

Fillmore, Myrtle Page
American. Religious Leader
Co-founded Unity School of Christianity,
  1895.
b. Aug 6, 1845 in Pagetown, Ohio
d. Oct 6, 1931 in Unity Farm, Missouri
Source: *NotAW; WebBD 80*

Finch, Jon
English. Actor
Films include *Sunday, Bloody Sunday,* 1971;
    Frenzy, 1972.
b. 1941 in England
Source: *FilmgC; IntMPA 79, 80, 81, 82;
WhoHol A*

Finch, Peter
[William Mitchell]
English. Actor
Awarded posthumous 1978 Oscar for
    Network.
b. Sep 28, 1916 in London, England
d. Jan 14, 1977 in Beverly Hills, California
Source: *BiDFilm; CmMov; CurBio 72;
FilmgC; IntMPA 75, 76, 77; MotPP; MovMk;
OxFilm; Who 74; WhoHol A; WhoThe 77A;
WhoWor 78; WorEFlm*

Finch, Rick (Richard)
[K C and the Sunshine Band]
American. Musician, Songwriter
Bass player, who also writes songs, produces
    albums for other singers.
b. Jan 25, 1954 in Indianapolis, Indiana
Source: *NF*

Finch, Robert Hutchison
American. Government Official
Political adviser to Richard Nixon; secretary
    of HEW, 1969-70.
b. Oct 9, 1925 in Tempe, Arizona
Source: *BiDrUSE; CurBio 69; IntWW 74;
PolProf NF; WhoAm 74; WhoAmP 73;
WhoGov 75; WhoS&SW 82; WhoWor 78*

Fine, Larry
[The Three Stooges]
American. Comedian, Actor
b. 1911 in Philadelphia, Pennsylvania
d. Jan 24, 1975 in Woodland Hills,
    California
Source: *MotPP; WhScrn 77*

Fine, Sidney Albert
American. Sociologist
b. Sep 18, 1915 in New York, New York
Source: *AmM&WS 73S*

Fine, Sylvia
[Mrs. Danny Kaye]
American. Lyricist, Producer
b. Aug 29, 1893 in New York, New York
Source: *AmSCAP 66; InWom; WhoAm 74,
76, 78, 80, 82*

Fine Arts Quartet, The
[Irving Ilmer; Abram Loft; George Sopkin;
    Leonard Sorkin]
American. Music Group
Source: *NF*

Fineman, Irving
American. Author
b. Apr 9, 1893 in New York, New York
Source: *AmAu&B; AmNov; Au&Wr 71;
ConAu 1R, 5R; OxAmL; REnAL; TwCA,
SUP; WhNAA; WhoAm 74; WhoWorJ 72;
WrDr 80*

Fingers, Rollie (Roland Glen)
American. Baseball Player
Pitcher who holds major league record for
    games saved, 272, through 1981.
b. Aug 25, 1946 in Steubenville, Ohio
Source: *BaseEn 85; BioIn 11; WhoAm 82;
WhoProB 73*

Fini, Leonor
Italian. Artist
Noted theatrical designer, book illustrator;
    does sensual, surrealistic paintings of
    women.
b. Aug 30, 1918 in Buenos Aires, Argentina
Source: *ConArt 77; IntWW 74, 75, 76, 77,
78; WomArt, A*

Fink, Mike
American. Frontiersman
Life elaborated by legend; facts difficult to
    discern.
b. 1720 in Pittsburgh, Pennsylvania
d. 1823
Source: *CnDAL; NewCol 75; OxAmL; REnAL*

Finlay, Frank
English. Actor
Films include *The Three Musketeers,* 1973.
b. Aug 6, 1926 in Farnworth, England
Source: *FilmgC; Who 74; WhoHol A;
WhoThe 77*

Finlay, Virgil
American. Illustrator
Pulp magazine, science fiction artist noted for
    bubbling and stipple effects.
b. 1914 in Rochester, New York
d. Jan 18, 1971
Source: *EncSF; FanAl; ScF&FL 1; WhoSciF*

Finletter, Thomas Knight
American. Lawyer, Diplomat
b. Nov 11, 1893 in Philadelphia,
  Pennsylvania
d. Apr 24, 1980 in New York, New York
Source: *AmAu&B; CurBio 48, 80; IntWW 74;*
PolProf T; WhAm 7; Who 74; WhoAm 76;
WhoWor 74

Finley, Charlie (Charles Oscar)
American. Businessman, Baseball Executive
Insurance co. exec., 1945--; owner, Oakland
  A's, 1960-80.
b. Feb 22, 1918 in Birmingham, Alabama
Source: *CelR; CurBio 74; NewYTBE 72, 73;*
WhoAm 74, 76, 78, 80, 82; WhoHcky 73;
WhoProB 73

Finley, John Huston
American. Educator, Philanthropist
b. Oct 19, 1863 in Grand Ridge, Illinois
d. Mar 7, 1940
Source: *Alli SUP; AmAu&B; AmBi; ApCAB;*
BbD; BiD&SB; BiDSA; ChhPo, S1; CurBio
40; DcAmAu; DcAmB S2; DcNAA; IndAu
1816; OhA&B; PoIre; REnAL; TwCBDA;
WhAm 1, 2

Finley, Martha
[Martha Farquaharson, pseud.]
American. Author
Created Elsie Dinsmore series.
b. Apr 26, 1828 in Chillicothe, Ohio
d. Jan 30, 1909
Source: *Alli SUP; AmAu; AmAu&B; BiD&SB;*
BiDSA; CarSB; CnDAL; DcAmAu; DcNAA;
IndAu 1816; LinLib L; OhA&B; OxAmL;
REnAL; TwCBDA; WhAm 1; WhoChL

Finn, Mickey
see: T. Rex

Finnbogadottir, Vigdis
Icelandic. President
Iceland's first female head of state, 1980--.
b. Apr 15, 1930 in Reykjavik, Iceland
Source: *IntWW 81; NewYTBS 82*

Finney, Albert
English. Actor, Director
Starred in *Tom Jones*, 1963; *Murder on the*
  Orient Express, 1974.
b. May 9, 1936 in Salford, England
Source: *BiDFilm; BiE&WWA; BkPepl; CelR,;*
CurBio 63; EncWT; FilmgC; IntMPA 78, 79,
80, 81, 82; IntWW 74; MotPP; MovMk;
NotNAT; OxFilm; PlP&P; Who 74; WhoHol
A; WhoWor 74; WorEFlm

Finney, Charles Grandison
American. Clergyman, Educator
Evangelist; Oberlin College pres., 1851-66.
b. Aug 29, 1792 in Warren, Connecticut
d. Aug 16, 1875 in Oberlin, Ohio
Source: *Alli; AmAu&B; AmBi; ApCAB;*
BiDAmEd; BioIn 8, 10, 11; DcAmAu;
DcAmB; DcAmReB; DcNAA; Drake; EncAAH;
EncAB-A; McGEWB; NatCAB 2; OhA&B;
REnAW; TwCBDA; WebAB; WhAm HS

Finney, Jack, pseud.
[Walter Braden Finney]
American. Author
Wrote science fiction classics *Invasion of the*
  Body Snatchers, 1954; *Time and Again*,
  1970.
b. 1911 in Milwaukee, Wisconsin
Source: *Au&Wr 71; ConSFA; EncSF; ScF&FL*
1; WhoSciF

Firbank, Louis
[Velvet Underground]
American. Jazz Musician, Songwriter
Lead guitarist, Velvet Underground, 1967-70;
  solo albums include *Walk on the Wild*
  Side.
b. Mar 2, 1942 in Brooklyn, New York
Source: *ConAu 117; IlEncRk; RkOn 84*

Firbank, Ronald
English. Author
Wrote penetrating novels *Caprice*, 1917;
  Prancing Nigger, 1924.
b. Jan 17, 1886 in London, England
d. May 21, 1926 in Rome, Italy
Source: *AtlBL; CasWL; CnMWL; DcLEL;*
EncWL; LinLib L; LongCTC; ModBrL, S1;
NewC; OxEng; PenC ENG; RAdv 1; REn;
ScF&FL 1; TwCWr; WebE&AL; WhoTwCL

Firefall
[Mark Andes; Jock Bartley; Larry Burnett;
  Michael Clarke; Rick Roberts]
American. Music Group
Pop-country group formed 1974; hit single
  "You Are the Woman," 1976.
Source: *RolSEnR 83*

Firestone, Harvey Samuel
American. Manufacturer
Founder, pres., Firestone Tire and Rubber
  Co, Akron, OH, 1900-38.
b. Dec 20, 1868 in Columbus, Ohio
d. Feb 7, 1938 in Miami Beach, Florida
Source: *AmBi; DcAmB S2; DcNAA; OhA&B;*
WebAB; WhAm 1

Firestone, Harvey Samuel, Jr.
American. Manufacturer
Chairman until 1966, Firestone Tire and
　Rubber Co; oversaw expansion to
　worldwide firm.
b. Apr 20, 1898 in Chicago, Illinois
d. Jun 1, 1973 in Akron, Ohio
Source: *CelR; ConAu 41R; CurBio 44, 73,
73N; NewYTBE 73; OhA&B; WhAm 5;
WhoF&I 74; WhoWor 74*

Firestone, Idabelle Smith
American. Composer
b. Nov 10, 1874 in Minnesota City,
　Minnesota
d. Jul 7, 1954 in Akron, Ohio
Source: *AmSCAP 66*

Firkusny, Rudolf
American. Musician
b. Feb 11, 1912 in Napajedla, Czechoslovakia
Source: *IntWW 74; NewYTBE 73; WhoAm
74, 76, 78, 80, 82; WhoMus 72; WhoWor 78*

Firpo, Luis Angel
"Wild Bull of Pampas"
Argentine. Boxer
b. Oct 11, 1896 in Buenos Aires, Argentina
d. Aug 7, 1960 in Buenos Aires, Argentina
Source: *WhoBox 74*

Firth, Peter
English. Actor
Made debut as deranged stable boy in stage,
　film versions of *Equus,* 1975, 1977.
b. Oct 27, 1953 in Bradford, England
Source: *FilmEn; IntMPA 81, 81; NewYTBS
74; PIP&P A*

Fischer, Anton Otto
German. Illustrator
b. Feb 23, 1882 in Munich, Germany
d. Mar 26, 1962
Source: *IlsCB 1744, 1946; WhAm 4*

Fischer, Bobby (Robert James)
American. Chess Player
Defeated Boris Spassky, 1972, in match that
　received world-wide publicity; world
　champion, 1972-75.
b. Mar 9, 1943 in Chicago, Illinois
Source: *ConAu 103; CurBio 63; IntWW 74;
NewYTBE 73; OxChess; WebAB; WhoAm 76,
78, 80, 82; WhoWor 74*

Fischer, Carl
American. Manufacturer, Publisher, Insurance
　Executive
b. 1849
d. 1923
Source: *Baker 78; BioIn 9; OxSpan*

Fischer, Emil
German. Chemist
b. Oct 9, 1852
d. Jul 15, 1919
Source: *NewCol 75*

Fischer, Herman G
American. Manufacturer
With Irving Price, started Fischer-Price Toys,
　1930.
b. 1898
d. 1975
Source: *BioIn 6; Entr*

Fischer, Irwin
American. Conductor, Composer
b. Jul 5, 1903 in Iowa City, Iowa
Source: *WhoMW 74*

Fischer, John
American. Journalist, Author
Editor-in-chief *Harper's* magazine, 1953-67;
　wrote best-seller *Why TheyBehave Like
　Russians,* 1947.
b. Apr 27, 1910 in Texhoma, Oklahoma
d. Aug 18, 1978 in New Haven, Connecticut
Source: *AmAu&B; BiDrLUS 70; ConAu 9R,
81; CurBio 53, 78; IntWW 74, 75, 76, 77,
78; IntYB 78; Who 74; WhoAm 74, 76, 78;
WhoWor 74, 74; WrDr 80*

Fischer, Louis
American. Author
b. Feb 29, 1896 in Philadelphia, Pennsylvania
d. Jan 15, 1970 in Hackensack, New Jersey
Source: *AmAu&B; Au&Wr 71; ConAu 25R,
P-1; CurBio 40, 70; REn; REnAL; TwCA
SUP; WhoWorJ 72*

Fischer-Dieskau, Dietrich
German. Opera Singer
b. May 28, 1925 in Berlin, Germany
Source: *CelR; CurBio 67; IntWW 74;
NewYTBE 71; Who 74; WhoAm 74, 76, 78,
80, 82; WhoMus 72; WhoWor 78*

Fischetti, John
American. Editor, Cartoonist
b. Sep 27, 1916 in Brooklyn, New York
d. 1978 in New Haven, Connecticut
Source: *ConAu 102; WhoAm 74; WhoWor 78*

Fischl, Eric
American. Artist
Known for paintings that resemble giant
　movie stills; major exhibition, 1986, NYC's
　Whitney Museum.
b. Mar 9, 1948 in New York, New York
Source: *CurBio 86*

Fish, Albert
[Robert Hayden; Frank Howard; John W
  Pell; Thomas A Sprague, aliases]
"The Moon Maniac"
American. Murderer
Molested 400 children, killed at least six;
  practiced cannibalism.
b. 1870 in Washington, District of Columbia
d. Jan 16, 1936 in Sing Sing, New York
Source: *Blood&B*

Fish, Hamilton
American. Statesman
b. Aug 3, 1808 in New York, New York
d. Sep 6, 1893 in Garrison, New York
Source: *AmBi; ApCAB; BiAUS; BiDrAC;
BiDrUSE; CurBio 41; DcAmB; Drake;
EncAB-H; TwCBDA; WebAB; WhAm HS;
WhAmP*

Fish, Hamilton, III
American. Congressman
b. Dec 7, 1888 in Garrison, New York
Source: *BiDrAC; WhAmP; WhoFtbl 74*

Fish, Robert Lloyd
[Robert L Pike, pseud.]
American. Author
Winner of three Poe Mystery writers awards:
  Isle of Snakes, 1963.
b. Aug 21, 1912 in Cleveland, Ohio
d. Feb 24, 1981 in Trumbull, Connecticut
Source: *Au&Wr 71; EncMys; ConAu 13R,
103; IntAu&W 76, 77*

Fishback, Margaret
American. Poet
Light verse collected in *One to a Customer,*
  1937; *Time for a Quick One,* 1940.
b. Mar 10, 1904 in Washington, District of
  Columbia
d. Sep 25, 1985 in Camden, Maine
Source: *AmAu&B; CurBio 41, 85*

Fishbein, Harry J
American. Bridge Player
b. 1898
d. Feb 19, 1976 in New York
Source: *BioIn 10*

Fishbein, Morris
American. Physician, Editor, Author
Edited *AMA Journal,* 1924-49; wrote *Popular
  Medical Encyclopedia,* 1946.
b. Jul 22, 1889 in Saint Louis, Missouri
d. Sep 27, 1976 in Chicago, Illinois
Source: *AmAu&B; ConAu 5R, 69, 4NR;
CurBio 40; St&PR 75; WebAB; WhNAA;
WhoAm 74; WhoWor 78; WhoWorJ 72*

Fisher, Avery
Designer
b. 1906
Source: *BioIn 10, 11; NewYTBE 73;
NewYTBS 76*

Fisher, "Bud" (Harry Conway)
American. Cartoonist
Created "Mutt and Jeff" comic strip, 1907.
b. Apr 3, 1885 in Chicago, Illinois
d. Sep 7, 1954 in New York, New York
Source: *AmAu&B; DcAmB S5; WebAB;
WhAm 3*

Fisher, Carl
American. Insurance Company Executive
b. Nov 21, 1911 in Newkirk, Oklahoma
Source: *BiE&WWA; St&PR 75; WhoAm 74;
WhoIns 75; WhoWor 78*

Fisher, Carrie Frances
American. Actress
Daughter of Debbie Reynolds, Eddie Fisher;
  in *Star Wars,* 1977; *The Empire Strikes
  Back,* 1980.
b. Oct 21, 1956 in Beverly Hills, California
Source: *BkPepl; IntMPA 82; NewYTBS 77;
WhoAm 80, 82; WhoAmW 79; WhoHol A*

Fisher, Clara
American. Actress
Noted comic performer; played male, female
  roles in career that spanned 72 yrs.
b. Apr 14, 1811 in England
d. Nov 12, 1898 in Metuchen, New Jersey
Source: *NotAW*

Fisher, Dorothy Frances Canfield
American. Author, Essayist
Numerous novels include *Best Twig,* 1915;
  Seasoned Timber, 1939.
b. Feb 17, 1879 in Lawrence, Kansas
d. Nov 9, 1958 in Arlington, Vermont
Source: *AmAu&B; AmNov; CarSB; Chambr 3;
ChhPo, S1, S2; CnDAL; ConAmA; ConAmL;
HerW; InWom; LinLib L, S; LongCTC;
ModAL; NatCAB 44; OhA&B; OxAmL; REn;
REnAL; TwCA, SUP; WebAB; WhAm 3;
WhNAA; WhoAmW 58; WomWWA 14;
YABC 1*

Fisher, Eddie (Edwin Jack)
American. Singer
"O, My Papa," 1953 million-selling hit;
  married to Debbie Reynolds, Elizabeth
  Taylor, Connie Stevens.
b. Aug 10, 1928 in Philadelphia,
  Pennsylvania
Source: *CurBio 54; FilmgC; IntMPA 75, 76,
77, 78, 79, 80, 81, 82; WhoAm 74, 76, 78,
80, 82; WhoHol A*

Fisher, Fred
American. Composer
Co-wrote "Peg 'O My Heart," 1913.
b. Sep 30, 1875 in Cologne, Germany
d. Jan 14, 1942 in New York, New York
Source: *AmPS; AmSCAP 66; BiDAmM; BioIn 11; CmpEPM; NotNAT B*

Fisher, Gail
American. Actress
Played Peggy Fair in TV series "Mannix," 1968-74.
b. Aug 18, 1935 in Orange, New Jersey
Source: *WhoAm 74; WhoBlA 75*

Fisher, Ham(mond Edward)
American. Cartoonist
b. Sep 24, 1900 in Wilkes-Barre, Pennsylvania
d. Dec 27, 1955 in New York, New York
Source: *AmAu&B; DcAmB S5; WhAm 3*

Fisher, Harrison
American. Illustrator
Illustrated books, mag covers; created "Fisher Girl."
b. Jul 27, 1875 in Brooklyn, New York
d. Jan 19, 1934 in New York, New York
Source: *AmAu&B; DcAmB S1; DcNAA*

Fisher, Harry
American. Basketball Player, Basketball Coach
First paid coach at Columbia U, 1907-16; had 109-46 record.
b. Feb 6, 1882 in New York, New York
d. Dec 29, 1967 in New York, New York
Source: *WhoBbl 73*

Fisher, Herbert Albert Laurens
English. Historian
Wrote three-volume *History of Europe,* 1935.
b. Mar 21, 1865 in London, England
d. Apr 18, 1940 in London, England
Source: *Chambr 3; DcLEL; DcNaB 1931; EvLB; LongCTC; NewC; TwCA; WhLit*

Fisher, Irving
American. Economist, Author
Devised index numbers for price trend studies; wrote text *Stock MarketCrash,* 1930.
b. Feb 27, 1867 in Saugerties, New York
d. Apr 29, 1947 in New York, New York
Source: *AmAu&B; AmLY; ApCAB X; BiDAmEd; BioIn 1, 2, 4, 5, 8, 11; DcAmAu; DcAmB S4; LinLib S; McGEWB; ObitOF 79; TwCBDA; WebAB; WhAm 2; WhNAA*

Fisher, James Maxwell McConnell
English. Author, Naturalist
Wrote books on birds: *Birds of Britain,* 1942; *Watching Birds,* 1940.
b. Sep 3, 1912 in Clifton, England
d. Sep 25, 1970 in Hendon, England
Source: *Au&Wr 71; DcNaB 1961; WhAm 5*

Fisher, John
English. Clergyman, Author
Beheaded for refusing to acknowledge Henry VIII as head of church; canonized, 1935.
b. 1469 in Beverley, England
d. Jun 22, 1535 in London, England
Source: *Alli; BbD; BrAu; CasWL; DcEnL; EvLB*

Fisher, John Arbuthnot
British. Admiral
b. 1841 in Rambodde, Ceylon
d. 1920
Source: *NewCol 75*

Fisher, Jules
American. Designer
Won Tonys for light designs in *Pippin,* 1973; *Dancin',* 1978.
b. Nov 12, 1937 in Norristown, Pennsylvania
Source: *VarWW 85*

Fisher, Mary Frances Kennedy
[Mary Francis Parrish, pseud.]
American. Author
Best known for her writings on food *The Art of Eating,* 1954.
b. Jul 3, 1908 in Albion, Michigan
Source: *BioIn 2, 6, 9, 11; ConAu 77; CurBio 83*

Fisher, Max Martin
American. Corporation Executive
Influential Detroit financier, philanthropist.
b. Jul 15, 1908 in Pittsburgh, Pennsylvania
Source: *BioIn 9; St&PR 75; WhoAm 74, 76, 78, 80, 82; WhoWorJ 72*

Fisher, Morgan
see: Mott (the Hoople)

Fisher, Terence
English. Director
Joined Hammer films, 1952, directing horror films *Curse of Frankenstein,* 1957; *Island of Terror,* 1966.
b. 1904 in London, England
d. Jun 18, 1980 in Twickenham, England
Source: *BiDFilm; CmMov; DcFM; FilmgC; IntMPA 75, 76, 77, 78, 79; WorEFlm*

Fisher, Vardis
American. Author
Writings include autobiography *In Tragic Life,* 1932.
b. Mar 31, 1895 in Annis, Idaho
d. Jul 9, 1968 in Jerome, Idaho
Source: *AmAu&B; AmNov; Au&Wr 71; CnDAL; ConAmA; ConAu 5R, 25R; ConLC 7; CyWA; DcLEL; EncSF; LinLib L; LongCTC; ModAL; OxAmL; PenC AM; REn; REnAL; REnAW; TwCA, SUP; WhAm 5; WhNAA; Who 74*

Fisher, Welthy (Blakesley Honsinger)
American. Missionary, Educator
Founded India's Literary Village, 1953; wrote memoirs, *To Light a Candle,* 1962.
b. Sep 18, 1879 in Rome, New York
d. Dec 16, 1980 in Southbury, Connecticut
Source: *BioIn 6, 7, 8; CurBio 69, 81; ForWC 70; IntAu&W 77; NewYTBS 74; WhoAmW 58, 61, 68, 70, 72*

Fisk, Carlton Ernest
"Pudge"
American. Baseball Player
Catcher, Boston, 1971-80; Chicago White Sox, 1980--.
b. Dec 26, 1947 in Bellows Falls, Vermont
Source: *BaseEn 85; NewYTBE 73; WhoProB 73*

Fisk, James Brown
American. Physicist, Corporation Executive
Head of Bell Laboratories, 1959-73; first research director, Atomic Energy Commission, 1947.
b. Aug 30, 1910 in West Warwick, Rhode Island
d. Aug 10, 1981 in Elizabethtown, New York
Source: *AmM&WS 76P, 79P; CurBio 59, 81; IntWW 75, 76, 77, 78; IntYB 78, 79; St&PR 75; WhAm 8; Who 74; WhoAm 74, 76, 78; WhoF&I 74*

Fisk, Jim (James)
American. Financier
b. Apr 1, 1834 in Bennington, Vermont
d. Jan 7, 1872 in New York, New York
Source: *AmBi; DcAmB; Drake; EncAB-H; WebAB; WhAm HS*

Fiske, Jamie
American. Transplant Patient
Received liver transplant Nov 5, 1982 after father pleaded cause nationally.
b. Nov 26, 1981 in Bridgewater, Massachusetts
Source: *NF*

Fiske, John
American. Historian, Philosopher, Author
Wrote popular religious historical novels *Beginnings of Heir England,* 1889.
b. Mar 30, 1842 in Hartford, Connecticut
d. Jul 4, 1901 in Gloucester, Massachusetts
Source: *Alli SUP; AmAu; AmAu&B; AmBi; ApCAB; BbD; BiD&SB; Chambr 3; DcAmAu; DcAmB; DcLEL; DcNAA; EvLB; LinLib L, S; NatCAB 3; OxAmL; OxCan; PenC AM; REnAL; TwCBDA; WebAB; WhAm 1*

Fiske, Minnie Maddern
American. Actress
Played heroine in many Henrik Ibsen plays which became popular in US as a result.
b. Dec 19, 1865 in New Orleans, Louisiana
d. Feb 16, 1932 in Hollis, New York
Source: *AmBi; AmWom; BiDSA; DcAmB S1; FamA&A; NotAW; OxAmL; OxThe; PIP&P; WebAB; LinLib S; NatCAB 35; WhAm 1; WhScrn 77; WhThe; WhoHol B; WhoStg 1906, 1908; WomWWA 14*

Fistoulari, Anatole
English. Conductor
b. Aug 20, 1907
Source: *IntWW 74; Who 74; WhoMus 72; WhoWor 78*

Fitch, Aubrey
American. Naval Officer
b. Jan 11, 1884 in Saint Ignace, Michigan
d. May 22, 1976 in Newcastle, Maine
Source: *CurBio 45*

Fitch, Bill (William C)
American. Basketball Coach
b. May 19, 1934 in Cedar Rapids, Iowa
Source: *OfNBA 81*

Fitch, James Marston
American. Architect, Author
Authority on restoration, historic preservation; wrote *American Building,* 1962.
b. May 8, 1909 in Washington, District of Columbia
Source: *AmAu&B; BioIn 10; ConAu 89; WhoAm 74, 76*

Fitch, John
American. Inventor
Built steam boat, 1787; paddlewheeler, 1788.
b. Jan 21, 1743 in Hartford, Connecticut
d. Jul 12, 1798 in Bardstown, Kentucky
Source: *Alli, SUP; AmBi; ApCAB; DcAmB; Drake; EncAB-H; TwCBDA; WebAB; WhAm HS*

Fitch, (William) Clyde
American. Dramatist
Author, society-oriented dramas *Barbara Frietchie, Nathan Hale.*
b. May 2, 1865 in Elmira, New York
d. Sep 4, 1909 in Chalons-sur-Marne, France
Source: *AmAu&B; AmBi; DcAmB; DcLEL; McGEWD; ModAL; ModWD; NatCAB 13, 15; NotNAT A, B; OxAmL; PenC AM; REnAL; REnWD; WhAm 1*

Fittipaldi, Emerson
Brazilian. Auto Racer
b. 1946 in Sao Paulo, Brazil
Source: *BioIn 9, 10, 11*

Fitts, Dudley
American. Author, Educator
b. Apr 28, 1903 in Boston, Massachusetts
d. Jul 10, 1968
Source: *AmAu&B; ConAu 25R, 93; ModAL; OxAmL; PenC AM; REnAL; TwCA, SUP; WhAm 5*

Fitzgerald, Albert J
American. Labor Union Official
Pres., United Electrical, Radio, and Machine Workers of America, 1941-78; attempted to exclude Communists from CIO.
b. Sep 21, 1906 in Lynn, Massachusetts
d. May 1, 1982 in Boston, Massachusetts
Source: *CurBio 48, 82; NewYTBS 82*

Fitzgerald, A(rthur) Ernest
American. Financier
Financial management systems deputy, US Air Force, 1973--; uncovered $2 billion excess in Air Force's C-5A transport plane funds.
Source: *ConNews 86-2*

Fitzgerald, Barry
[William Joseph Shields]
American. Actor
Won 1944 Oscar for *Going My Way.*
b. Mar 10, 1888 in Dublin, Ireland
d. Jan 4, 1961 in Dublin, Ireland
Source: *BiDFilm; CurBio 45, 61; FilmgC; HolP 40; MotPP; MovMk; OxFilm; PIP&P; WhAm 4; WhScrn 74, 77; WhoHol B*

Fitzgerald, Edward
English. Poet, Translator
Best known for translation of Omar Khayyam's *Rubaiyat,* 1859.
b. Mar 31, 1809 in Bradfield, England
d. Jun 14, 1883 in Merton, England
Source: *AtlBL; BbD; BiD&SB; BrAu 19; CasWL; CnE&AP; CrtT 3; CyWA; DcEnA AP; DcEuL; Drake; EvLB; MouLC 4; NewC; OxEng; PenC ENG; PoIre; RComWL; REn; WebE&AL*

Fitzgerald, Ed(ward)
American. Radio Performer
With wife Pegeen broadcast "The Fitzgerald's" radio show for 44 years.
b. 1893 in Troy, New York
d. Mar 22, 1982 in New York, New York
Source: *CurBio 47; NewYTBS 79, 82*

Fitzgerald, Ella
American. Singer
Began career with Chick Webb Orchestra, 1934; has won eight Grammys.
b. Apr 25, 1918 in Newport News, Virginia
Source: *AmSCAP 66; BkPepl; CelR; CurBio 56; EncAB-H; InWom; IntWW 74; WebAB; WhoAm 74, 76, 78, 80, 82; WhoBlA 75; WhoMus 72; WhoWor 78*

Fitzgerald, Frances Scott 'Scottie'
see: Smith, Frances Scott Fitzgerald Lanahan

Fitzgerald, F(rancis) Scott (Key)
American. Author
Wrote *This Side of Paradise,* 1920; *The Great Gatsby,* 1925.
b. Sep 24, 1896 in Saint Paul, Minnesota
d. Dec 21, 1940 in Hollywood, California
Source: *Alli SUP; AmAu&B; AmWr; AtlBL; AuNews 1; BioNews 74; CasWL; Chambr 3; CnDAL; CnMD; CnMWL; ConAmA; ConAmL; CurBio 41; CyWA; DcAmB S2; DcLEL; DcNAA; EncAB-H; EncMys; EncWL; EvLB; FilmgC; LongCTC; ModAL; Sl; OxAmL; OxEng; OxFilm; PenC AM; RAdv 1; RComWL; REn; REnAL; TwCA, SUP; TwCWr; WebAB; WebE&AL; WhAm 1; WhNAA; WhoTwCL; WorEFlm*

FitzGerald, Garret
Irish. Political Leader
Prime minister of Ireland, Jun 1981-Mar 1982, Dec 1982--.
b. Feb 9, 1926 in Dublin, Ireland
Source: *CurBio 84; IntYB 79; Who 74; WhoWor 78; WrDr 80*

Fitzgerald, Geraldine
American. Actress
1939 Oscar nominee for *Wuthering Heights.*
b. Nov 24, 1914 in Dublin, Ireland
Source: *BiE&WWA; CurBio 76; FilmgC; HolP
30; InWom; IntMPA 75, 76, 77, 78, 79, 80,
81, 82; MotPP; MovMk; NewYTBE 70;
NotNAT; PIP&P A; ThFT; WhoAm 82;
WhoHol A; WhoThe 72, 77*

Fitzgerald, John Francis
"Honey Fitz"
American. Businessman, Politician
Father of Rose Kennedy; who was mayor of
Boston, 1905-14.
b. Feb 11, 1863 in Boston, Massachusetts
d. Oct 2, 1950 in Boston, Massachusetts
Source: *DcAmB S4; TwCBDA; WhAm 3;
WhAmP*

Fitzgerald, Pegeen
American. Radio Performer
With husband Ed, broadcast "The
Fitzgeralds" radio talk show.
b. Nov 24, 1910 in Norcatur, Kansas
Source: *CurBio 47; ForWC 70; InWom;
IntMPA 75, 76, 77, 78, 79, 80, 81, 82*

Fitzgerald, Robert Stuart
American. Author, Translator
Poems known for rich imagery, vigorous
language; translations of Homer's *Odyssey,
Iliad* classics in own right.
b. Oct 12, 1910 in Geneva, New York
d. Jan 16, 1985 in Hamden, Connecticut
Source: *AmAu&B; AmM&WS 73P; ConAu
1R, 1NR; ConP 70, 75; DrAP 75; DrAS 74E;
ModAL; OxAmL; PenC AM; REnAL; TwCA
SUP; WhoAm 74, 76, 78, 80, 82; WrDr 80*

Fitzgerald, Zelda
[Mrs. F Scott Fitzgerald; Zelda Sayre]
American. Celebrity Relative, Author
Wrote *Save Me the Waltz,* 1932.
b. Jul 24, 1900 in Montgomery, Alabama
d. Mar 10, 1948 in Asheville, North Carolina
Source: *AmAu&B; AmWomWr; AuNews 1*

Fitz-Gibbon, Bernice Bowles
American. Advertising Executive
Source: *BioIn 1, 5, 7, 8*

Fitzgibbon, (Robert Louis) Constantine
American. Author
Fiction, non-fiction writer; best work *The
Life of Dylan Thomas,* 1965.
b. Jun 8, 1919 in Lenox, Massachusetts
d. Mar 23, 1983 in Dublin, Ireland
Source: *AnObit 1983; Au&Wr 71; ConAu
1NR, 2NR; IntWW 74; WhoAm 82; WhoWor
74; WorAu; WrDr 76*

Fitzpatrick, Daniel R
American. Cartoonist
b. Mar 5, 1891 in Superior, Wisconsin
d. May 18, 1969 in Saint Louis, Missouri
Source: *ConAu 89; CurBio 41, 69; WebBD 80*

Fitzpatrick, Thomas
American. Explorer, Naturalist
One of great mountain men; spent life
opening up West.
b. 1799 in County Cavan, Ireland
d. Feb 7, 1854 in Washington, District of
Columbia
Source: *AmBi; DcAmB; EncAB-H; OxAmL;
WebAB; WhAm HS*

Fitzroy, James
see: Monmouth, James Scott, Duke

Fitzsimmons, Bob (Robert Prometheus)
English. Boxer
b. Jun 4, 1862 in Helston, England
d. Oct 22, 1917 in Chicago, Illinois
Source: *AuBYP; DcAmB; DcNAA; Film 1;
WebAB; WhoBox 74*

Fitzsimmons, "Cotton" (Lowell)
American. Basketball Coach
b. Oct 7, 1931 in Hannibal, Missouri
Source: *WhoBbl 73*

Fitzsimmons, Frank
American. Labor Union Official
Pres. International Brotherhood of Teamsters,
1967-81, following Hoffa's disappearance.
b. Apr 7, 1908 in Jeannette, Pennsylvania
d. May 6, 1981 in San Diego, California
Source: *BiDAmLL; BioIn 9, 10, 11; CelR;
CurBio 71, 81; IntWW 74, 75, 76, 77, 78;
NewYTBE 71; PolProf J, NF; WhoAm 74,
78, 80; WhoE 79; WhoLab 76; WhoS&SW
73; WhoWor 78*

Fitzsimmons, James E
"Sunny Jim"
American. Horse Trainer
Best known horse trainer of all time; had
2,275 winners totaling over $13 million.
b. Jul 23, 1874 in Brooklyn, New York
d. Mar 11, 1966 in Miami, Florida
Source: *BioIn 4, 5, 6, 7, 10*

Fix, Paul
American. Actor
Co-star of TV's "The Rifleman," 1958-63.
b. Mar 13, 1902 in Dobbs Ferry, New York
d. Oct 14, 1983 in Santa Monica, California
Source: *Film 2; FilmgC; IntMPA 80, 81, 82;
MovMk; TwYS; Vers B; WhoHol A*

Fixx, James Fuller
American. Author, Runner
Dean of jogging craze, who collapsed, died
while jogging; best-selling book *Complete
Book of Running*.
b. Apr 23, 1932 in New York, New York
d. Jul 20, 1984 in Hardwick, Vermont
Source: *AnObit 1984; ConAu 73; WhoAm 74,
76, 78, 80, 82*

Fixx, The
[Charlie Barrett; Cy Curnin; Rupert Greenall;
Jamie West-Oram; Adam Woods]
English. Music Group
New wave group who released albums
Shattered Room, 1982; *Reach the Beach*,
1983.
Source: *RkOn 85*

Fizdale, Robert
American. Musician
b. 1920
Source: *BioIn 5, 6, 7*

Flack, Roberta
American. Singer
Won Grammys for "The First Time Ever I
Saw Your Face," 1972; "Killing Me
Softly," 1973.
b. Feb 10, 1940 in Black Mountain, North
Carolina
Source: *BkPepl; CurBio 73; Ebony 1; EncJzS
70; HerW; IlEncBM 82; WhoAm 74, 76, 78,
80, 82; WhoBlA 75, 77*

Flagg, Ernest
American. Architect
b. Feb 6, 1857 in Brooklyn, New York
d. Apr 10, 1947 in New York, New York
Source: *DcAmB S4; DcNAA; WhAm 2*

Flagg, Fannie (Frances Carlton)
American. Comedienne, Actress
b. Sep 21, 1944
Source: *ForWC 70; WhoHol A*

Flagg, James Montgomery
American. Artist, Author
His WW I recruiting poster with Uncle Sam,
modeled on himself, pointing a finger, with
the caption "I Want You!" brought him
fame.
b. Jun 18, 1877 in Pelham Manor, New
York
d. May 27, 1960 in New York, New York
Source: *AmAu&B; ChhPo, S2; CurBio 40, 60;
Film 1; OxAmL; REnAL; WebAB; WhAm 4;
WhScrn 77*

Flagler, Henry Morrison
American. Business Executive
b. Jan 2, 1830 in Hopewell, New York
d. May 20, 1913 in West Palm Beach,
Florida
Source: *AmBi; DcAmB; EncAB-H; WebAB;
WhAm 1*

Flagstad, Kirsten
Norwegian. Opera Singer
Soprano who appeared in film *The Big
Broadcast*, 1938.
b. Jul 12, 1895 in Oslo, Norway
d. Dec 7, 1962 in Oslo, Norway
Source: *CurBio 47, 63; FilmgC; InWom;
REn; WhAm 4; WhScrn 74, 77; WhoHol B*

Flaherty, Joe
American. Writer, Actor
Won Emmys for writing "SCTV Network,"
1982, 1983.
b. Jun 21, 1940 in Pittsburgh, Pennsylvania
Source: *VarWW 85*

Flaherty, Robert Joseph
American. Director
"Father" of documentary; first was *Nanook
of the North*, 1920, on Eskimos.
b. Feb 16, 1884 in Iron Mountain, Michigan
d. Jul 23, 1951 in Dummerston, Vermont
Source: *AmAu&B; BiDFilm; CurBio 49, 51;
DcAmB S5; DcFM; EncAB-H; FilmEn;
FilmgC; MovMk; OxCan; OxFilm; REn;
WhAm 3; WomWMM; WorEFlm*

Flammarion, Camille
French. Astronomer
Popularized study of astronomy; wrote *The
Atmosphere*, 1872.
b. Feb 25, 1842 in Montigny-le-Roi, France
d. 1925
Source: *BbD; BiD&SB; BiDPara; DcEuL*

Flamsteed, John
English. Astronomer
b. Aug 19, 1646 in Denby, England
d. Dec 31, 1719
Source: *Alli; McGEWB*

Flanagan, Edward Joseph, Father
American. Priest
Founded Father Flanagan's Home for Boys,
1917; became Boys Town, 1922.
b. Jul 13, 1886 in Roscommon, Ireland
d. May 15, 1948 in Berlin, Germany
Source: *DcAmB S4; WebAB; WhAm 2;
WhScrn 74, 77; WhoHol B*

Flanagan, Mike (Michael Kendall)
American. Baseball Player
Pitcher, Baltimore Orioles, 1975--; won Cy
Young Award, 1979.
b. Dec 16, 1951 in Manchester, New
Hampshire
Source: *BaseEn 85; WhoAm 82*

Flanders, Michael
English. Actor, Author
Broadcaster with BBC radio, 1948-75.
b. Mar 1, 1922 in London, England
d. Apr 14, 1975 in Wales
Source: *Au&Wr 71; AuBYP; BiE&WWA;
ChhPo, S1, S2; ConAu 5R, 5R, 57; CurBio
70, 75; IntWW 80; NewYTBS 75; OxThe;
WhAm 6; WhScrn 77; WhThe; Who 74;
WhoMus 72; WhoWor 74*

Flanders, Ralph Edward
American. Senator
b. Sep 28, 1880 in Barnet, Vermont
d. Feb 19, 1970 in Springfield, Vermont
Source: *ConAu P-1; CurBio 48, 70;
NewYTBE 70*

Flanders and Swann
see: Flanders, Michael; Swann, Donald
Ibrahim

Flannagan, John Bernard
American. Sculptor
b. Apr 7, 1895 in Fargo, North Dakota
d. Jan 6, 1942 in New York, New York
Source: *CurBio 42; DcAmB S3; WebAB*

Flanner, Janet
[Genet, pseud.]
American. Journalist, Author
Correspondent, *New Yorker*, Paris, for 50
yrs.; wrote *Letter from Paris.*
b. Mar 13, 1892 in Indianapolis, Indiana
d. Jan 7, 1978 in New York, New York
Source: *AmAu&B; ConAu 65, 81; CurBio 43;
IndAu 1917; LinLib L; OxAmL; REnAL;
Who 78; WhoAm 74; WhoWor 74; WorAu;
WrDr 76*

Flannery, Susan
American. Actress
Won Emmy, 1975, for role in daytime soap
opera, "Days of Our Lives."
b. Jul 31, 1943 in Jersey City, New Jersey
Source: *WhoHol A*

Flatt, Lester Raymond
[Flatt and Scruggs]
American. Musician, Singer
Teamed with Earl Scruggs 25 yrs.; appeared
on TV series "The Beverly Hillbillies."
b. Jun 28, 1914 in Overton County,
Tennessee
Source: *EncFCWM 69*

Flatt and Scruggs
see: Flatt, Lester; Scruggs, Earl

Flatt, Ernest O
Choreographer
Won Emmys for "Carol Burnett Show,"
1971.
b. Oct 30, 1928
Source: *VarWW 85*

Flaubert, Gustave
French. Author
b. Dec 12, 1821 in Rouen, France
d. May 8, 1880 in Croisset, France
Source: *AtlBL; BbD; BiD&SB; CasWL;
ClDMEL; CyWA; DcBiA; DcEuL; EuAu;
EvEuW; NewC; OxEng; OxFr; PenC EUR;
RComWL; REn*

Flavin, Martin Archer
American. Author
b. Nov 2, 1883 in San Francisco, California
d. Dec 27, 1967 in Carmel, California
Source: *AmAu&B; AmNov; CnMD; ConAu
5R, 25R; DcLEL; McGEWD; ModWD;
OxAmL; REnAL; TwCA, SUP*

Flaxman, John
English. Artist
Neoclassic Wedgwood pottery designer,
1775-87; known for line drawings of
Homer's *Iliad, Odyssey.* 1793.
b. Jul 6, 1755 in York, England
d. Dec 7, 1826 in London, England
Source: *Alli; AtlBL; BiDLA; BkIE; ChhPo*

Fleeson, Doris
American. Journalist
b. May 20, 1901 in Sterling, Kansas
d. Aug 1, 1970 in Washington, District of
Columbia
Source: *ConAu 93; CurBio 59, 70; NewYTBE
70; WhoAmW 74*

Fleetwood Mac
[Lindsey Buckingham; Mick Fleetwood;
Christine McVie; John McVie; Stevie Nicks;
Bob Welch; Robert Weston]
English. Music Group
Album *Rumours,* 1977, second biggest selling
album of all time.
Source: *EncPR&S 74; IlEncRk; RkOn 74*

Fleetwood, Mick
[Fleetwood Mac]
English. Singer, Musician
Drummer since 1967; recorded 1980 solo
album *The Visitor* in Ghana.
b. Jun 24, 1942 in Cornwall, England
Source: *BioIn 11; BkPepl; WhoAm 80, 82*

Fleischer, Max
American. Cartoonist
b. Jul 19, 1883 in Vienna, Austria
d. Sep 11, 1972 in Los Angeles, California
Source: *DcFM; FilmgC; NewYTBE 72;
OxFilm; WorEFlm*

Fleischer, Nat(haniel S)
"Mr. Boxing"
American. Author, Publisher
Boxing expert; founded *Ring* magazine, 1922.
b. Nov 3, 1887
d. Jun 25, 1972 in New York, New York
Source: *ConAu 37R; NewYTBE 72; ObitOF
79; WhoBox 74*

Fleisher, Leon
American. Musician
b. Jul 23, 1928 in San Francisco, California
Source: *BioIn 10; CurBio 71; NewYTBE 70;
WhoAm 82; WhoE 74*

Fleischmann, Charles Louis
American. Manufacturer
Sold first compressed, non-liquid yeast in US,
1868; later produced vinegar, margarine.
b. Nov 3, 1834 in Budapest, Hungary
d. Dec 10, 1897 in Cincinnati, Ohio
Source: *DcAmB; Entr; NatCAB 22, 22;
WhAm HS*

Fleishmann, Raoul H(erbert)
American. Publisher, Manufacturer
Co-founder, publisher, *New Yorker* mag,
1924-69.
b. Aug 17, 1885 in Ischl, Austria-Hungary
d. May 11, 1969 in New York, New York
Source: *AmAu&B; ConAu 115; ObitOF 79;
WhAm 5*

Fleming, Alexander, Sir
Scottish. Bacteriologist
Discovered penicillin, 1928; won Nobel Prize,
1945.
b. Aug 6, 1881 in Lochfield, Scotland
d. Mar 11, 1955 in London, England
Source: *CurBio 44, 55; LinLib L; LongCTC;
ObitT 1951; WhDW; WhAm 3*

Fleming, Erin
Canadian. Actress
Groucho Marx's companion, 1970-77.
b. 1941 in New Liskeard, Ontario
Source: *WhoHol A*

Fleming, Ian
British. Actor
Played Dr. Watson in British film series
Sherlock Holmes, 1930s.
b. Sep 10, 1888 in Melbourne, Australia
d. Jan 1, 1969 in London, England
Source: *FilmgC; WhScrn 74, 77; WhThe;
WhoHol B*

Fleming, Ian Lancaster
English. Author
Created James Bond adventure series; wrote
Dr. No, 1958; *Goldfinger,* 1959.
b. May 28, 1908 in London, England
d. Aug 12, 1964 in Canterbury, England
Source: *AuBYP; ConAu 5R; ConLC 3;
CurBio 64; EncMys; EncSF; FilmgC; LinLib
L; LongCTC; NewC; PenC ENG; REn;
SmATA 9; TwCWr; WhAm 4; Who 74;
WhoSpyF,; WorAu,*

Fleming, Joan Margaret
English. Author
Wrote over 30 mysteries, historical romances:
Young Man I Think You'reDying, 1970.
b. Mar 27, 1908 in Horwich, England
d. Nov 15, 1980 in England
Source: *AnObit 1980; ConAu 81, 102;
TwCCr&M 80; WrDr 80*

Fleming, John Ambrose
British. Physicist
Leader in development of electric light in
England.
b. Nov 29, 1849
d. Apr 19, 1945 in London, England
Source: *CurBio 45; NewCol 75*

Fleming, Peggy Gale
American. Figure Skater
Won gold medal, 1968 Olympics.
b. Jul 27, 1948 in San Jose, California
Source: *CelR; CurBio 68; HerW; InWom;
WhoAm 82*

Fleming, Peter
American. Tennis Player
With doubles partner John McEnroe has won
Wimbledon, 1979, 1981; US Open, 1979,
1981.
b. Jan 21, 1955 in Summit, New Jersey
Source: *BioIn 12; WhoIntT*

Fleming, Rhonda
[Marilyn Lewis]
American. Actress
Played "bad girl" roles, 1945--; films include
   Pony Express, 1953.
b. Aug 10, 1923 in Los Angeles, California
Source: *FilmgC; InWom; IntMPA 80, 81, 82;
MotPP; MusSN; WhoAm 82; WhoAmW 61;
WhoHol A; WorEFlm*

Fleming, Victor
American. Director
Won Oscar for *Gone With the Wind*, 1939;
   films include *Wizard of Oz*, 1939; *Treasure
   Isalnd*, 1934.
b. Feb 23, 1883 in Pasadena, California
d. Jan 6, 1949 in Cottonwood, Arizona
Source: *BiDFilm; DcFM; FilmEn; FilmgC;
MovMk; OxFilm; TwYS, A; WhAm 2;
WorEFlm*

Fleming, Williamina Paton Stevens
American. Astronomer
Discovered numerous new stars with Harvard
   Observatory, 1879-98.
b. May 15, 1857 in Dundee, Scotland
d. May 21, 1911 in Boston, Massachusetts
Source: *NotAW*

Flemming, Arthur Sherwood
American. Government Official
Chm., US Commission on Civil Rights, 1974-
   81.
b. Jun 12, 1905 in Kingston, New York
Source: *AmM&WS 73S; BiDrUSE; CurBio
60; IntWW 74; NewYTBE 71; WhoAm 82;
WhoAmP 73; WhoGov 75*

Flemming, Bill (William Norman)
American. Sportscaster
ABC sports commentator, "Wide World of
   Sports," 1964--.
b. Sep 3, 1926 in Chicago, Illinois
Source: *NewYTET; WhoAm 82, 84*

Flesch, Karl
Hungarian. Musician, Teacher
b. Oct 9, 1873 in Moson, Hungary
d. Nov 15, 1944 in Lausanne, Switzerland
Source: *CurBio 45*

Flesch, Rudolf
American. Author
b. May 8, 1911 in Vienna, Austria
Source: *ConAu 9R; WhoAm 74; WhoE 74*

Fletcher, Alice Cunningham
American. Ethnologist, Lecturer
Expert on Plains Indians; wrote *The Omaha
   Tribe,* 1911.
b. Mar 15, 1838
d. Apr 6, 1923
Source: *NotAW; WebBD 80; WhAm 1*

Fletcher, Arthur A
American. Government Official
b. Dec 22, 1924 in Phoenix, Arizona
Source: *CurBio 71; NewYTBE 71; WhoAmP
73; WhoE 74; WhoGov 75*

Fletcher, Bramwell
English. Actor
Films include *Raffles,* 1940; *The Mummy,*
   1959.
b. Feb 20, 1906 in Bradford, England
Source: *BiE&WWA; NotNAT; WhoHol A;
WhoThe 77*

Fletcher, Glenn Robert
American. Football Player
b. Dec 5, 1956 in Thibodaux, Louisiana
Source: *BioIn 12*

Fletcher, Grant
American. Conductor, Composer
b. Oct 25, 1913 in Hartsburg, Illinois
Source: *AmSCAP 66*

Fletcher, John
English. Author, Dramatist
Collaborated with Francis Beaumont in
   famed partnership; sold 16 plays.
b. Dec 20, 1579 in Rye, England
d. Aug 1625 in London, England
Source: *AtlBL; BbD; BiD&SB; BrAu; CasWL;
ChhPo, S1; CnE&AP; CnThe; CroE&S; CrtT
1; CyWA; DcEnA; DcEnL; DcEuL; DcLEL;
EvLB; LinLib L, S; McGEWD; MouLC 1;
NewC; OxEng; OxThe; PenC ENG; PIP&P;
REn; REnWD; WebE&AL*

Fletcher, John Gould
American. Poet, Critic
Won Pulitzer Prize for *Selected Poems,* 1938.
b. Jan 3, 1886 in Little Rock, Arkansas
d. May 20, 1950 in Little Rock, Arkansas
Source: *AmAu&B; AnCL; CasWL; Chambr 3;
CnDAL; ConAmA; ConAmL; DcAmB S4;
DcLEL; EncWL; LinLib L; PenC AM;
WhAm 3*

Fletcher, Louise
American. Actress
Won 1975 Oscar for *One Flew Over the Cuckoo's Nest.*
b. Jul 1934 in Birmingham, Alabama
Source: *IntMPA 77; WhoAm 78, 80, 82; WhoHol A*

Fleury, Andre Hercule de
French. Religious Leader, Statesman
Cardinal; chief advisor to Louis XV, 1726-43.
b. 1653
d. 1743
Source: *NewCol 75; OxFr*

Flexner, Abraham
American. Educator, Author
b. Nov 13, 1866 in Louisville, Kentucky
d. Sep 21, 1959 in Falls Church, Virginia
Source: *AmAu&B; CurBio 41, 59; REnAL; TwCA, SUP*

Flick, Elmer Harrison
American. Baseball Player
Outfielder, 1898-1910; Hall of Fame, 1963.
b. Jan 11, 1876 in Bedford, Ohio
d. Jan 9, 1971 in Bedford, Ohio
Source: *BaseEn 85; BioIn 6, 7, 9; WhoProB 73*

Flick, Friedrich
German. Industrialist
b. 1883
d. Jul 20, 1972 in Lake Constance, Switzerland
Source: *BioIn 4, 6, 8, 9, 11; NewYTBE 72*

Flinders, Matthew
English. Explorer
Known for surveying, charting coasts of Australia, Tasmania.
b. Mar 16, 1774 in Donnington, England
d. Jul 19, 1814 in England
Source: *Alli; CelCen; DcBiPP; LinLib L, S; McGEWB; NewCol 75; OxShips*

Flint, William Russell, Sir
Scottish. Artist
Illustrated *Morte d'Arthur;* won silver medal.
b. Apr 4, 1880 in Edinburgh, Scotland
d. Dec 27, 1969 in London, England
Source: *DcBrAr 1; DcBrBI; DcBrWA; DcNaB 1961; ObitOF 79; ObitT 1961; WhE&EA*

Flippen, Jay C
American. Actor
Character actor in films, 1934-71; in TV series "Ensign O'Toole," 1962-64.
b. Mar 6, 1900 in Little Rock, Arkansas
d. Feb 3, 1971 in Hollywood, California
Source: *CmMov; FilmgC; MotPP; MovMk; NewYTBE 71; Vers B; WhScrn 74, 77; WhoHol B*

Flipper, Henry Ossian
American. Soldier
Source: *Alli SUP*

Flock of Seagulls
[Frank Maudsley; Paul Reynolds; Ali Score; Mike Score]
British. Music Group
Hit single, "I Ran," 1982; only British band to win Grammy, 1983.
Source: *RkOn 85*

Flood, Curt(is Charles)
American. Baseball Player
Fought baseball reserve clause, 1970; lawsuit led to new rules on free agency.
b. Jan 18, 1938 in Houston, Texas
Source: *AfroAA; BaseEn 85; InB&W 80; NewYTBE 70; NewYTBS 81; WhoProB 73*

Flood, Daniel J
American. Politician
b. Nov 26, 1904 in Hazelton, Pennsylvania
Source: *AmAu&B; CngDr 74; WhoAm 74; WhoAmP 73; WhoE 74; WhoGov 75*

Flora, James Royer
American. Author, Illustrator
b. Jan 25, 1914 in Bellefontaine, Ohio
Source: *ConAu 5R, 3NR; IlsBYP; IlsCB 1946, 1957; SmATA 1; ThrBJA*

Floren, Myron
American. Musician
Accordion player on "The Lawrence Welk Show."
b. Nov 5, 1919 in Webster, South Dakota
Source: *AmSCAP 66*

Flores, Tom (Thomas Raymond)
American. Football Coach
Coach, Oakland/LA Raiders, 1979--; won Super Bowl, 1981, 1984.
b. Mar 21, 1937 in Fresno, California
Source: *WhoAm 82, 84; WhoFtbl 74; WhoWest 82*

Florey, Howard Walter
British. Scientist, Engineer, Physician
b. Sep 24, 1898 in Adelaide, Australia
d. Feb 21, 1968 in London, England
Source: *CurBio 44, 68; McGEWB; WhAm 5*

Flory, Paul John
American. Educator, Chemist
Researcher in macronuclear chemistry;won
    1974 Nobel Prize.
b. Jun 19, 1910 in Sterling, Illinois
d. Sep 9, 1985 in Big Sur, California
Source: *ConAu 117; CurBio 75, 85; WhoAm
84*

Flotow, Friedrich von, Baron
German. Composer
b. Apr 26, 1812 in Teutendorf, Germany
d. Jan 24, 1883 in Darmstadt, Germany
Source: *AtlBL*

Floyd, Carlisle
American. Composer
b. Jun 11, 1926 in Latta, South Carolina
Source: *AmSCAP 66; CurBio 60; WhoAm 74,
76, 78, 80, 82; WhoS&SW 82; WhoWor 78*

Floyd, "Pretty Boy" (Charles Arthur)
American. Criminal
"Public enemy No. 1," 1933; killed in gun
    battle with FBI's Melvin Purvis.
b. 1904 in Akins, Oklahoma
d. Oct 22, 1934 in East Liverpool, Ohio
Source: *BioIn 8, 9; Blood&B; DrInf; EncACr*

Floyd, Raymond
American. Golfer
Won Masters tournament, named player of
    year, 1976; oldest player to win US Open,
    1986.
b. Sep 14, 1942 in Fort Bragg, North
    Carolina
Source: *NewYTBS 76; WhoAm 74, 76, 78,
80, 82; WhoGolf; WhoIntG*

Floyd, William
American. Statesman
Signed Declaration of Independence from
    NY.
b. Dec 17, 1734 in Brookhaven, New York
d. Aug 4, 1821 in Westernville, New York
Source: *AmBi; ApCAB; BiAUS; BiDrAC;
DcAmB; DcNAA; Drake; TwCBDA; WhAm
HS; WhAmP; WhNAA*

Fluckey, Eugene Bennett
American. Naval Officer
b. Oct 5, 1913 in Washington, District of
    Columbia
Source: *BioIn 7; WhoAm 74*

Flur, Wolfgang
see: Kraftwerk

Flutie, Doug(las Richard)
American. Football Player
Quarterback, who won Heisman Trophy,
    1984; signed by USFL NJ for over $1
    million a yr., 1985.
b. Oct 23, 1962 in Manchester, Maryland
Source: *CurBio 85; NewYTBS 84*

Flying Burrito Brothers, The
[Chris Ethridge; Chris Hillman; 'Sneaky Pete'
    Kleinow; Gram Parsons]
American. Music Group
Band formed 1969 to introduce country
    music to rock enthusiasts; hit album
    Gilded Place of Sin, 1969.
Source: *BiDAmM; ConMuA 80A; IlEncCM;
IlEncRk; LilREn 78; WhoRock 81*

Flynn, Edward Joseph
American. Politician
b. Sep 22, 1891 in Bronx, New York
d. Aug 18, 1953
Source: *CurBio 40, 53; WhAm 3*

Flynn, Elizabeth Gurley
American. Political Leader
b. Aug 7, 1890 in Concord, New Hampshire
d. Sep 5, 1964 in Moscow, U.S.S.R.
Source: *CurBio 61, 64; InWom*

Flynn, Errol
American. Actor
Starred in *Captain Blood,* 1936; *They Died
    with Their Boots On,* 1942.
b. Jun 20, 1909 in Tasmania, New Zealand
d. Oct 14, 1959 in Vancouver, British
    Columbia
Source: *AmAu&B; BiDFilm; CmMov; FilmgC;
MotPP; MovMk; OxFilm; WhAm 3; WhScrn
74, 77; WhoHol B; WorEFlm*

Flynn, F M
American. Newspaper Publisher
b. 1903
d. Nov 15, 1974 in Pelham, New York
Source: *NewYTBS 74*

Flynn, Joe (Joseph Anthony)
American. Actor
Played Captain Binghamton in TV series
    "McHale's Navy," 1962-66.
b. Nov 8, 1925 in Youngstown, Ohio
d. Jul 19, 1974 in Los Angeles, California
Source: *NewYTBS 74; WhScrn 77; WhoHol B*

Flynn, Sean
American. Photographer, Actor, Celebrity
  Relative
Son of Errol Flynn; disappeared in Vietnam
  covering war, 1970.
b. 1941
d. 1970
Source: *BioIn 6, 8, 9, 10; MotPP*

Flynt, Larry Claxton
American. Publisher
Publishes *Hustler* magazine, 1974--; paralyzed
  in assassination attempt.
b. Nov 1, 1942 in Magoffin County,
  Kentucky
Source: *AuNews 2; WhoAm 80, 82*

Foat, Ginny
[Virginia Galluzzo]
American. Feminist
Pres., CA NOW, arrested on 18-yr. old
  murder charge, 1983; acquitted.
b. Jun 21, 1941 in New York, New York
Source: *NF*

Foch, Ferdinand
French. Military Leader
Supreme commander of Allied forces, 1918;
  directed final victorious offensive, WW I.
b. Oct 2, 1851 in Tarbes, France
d. Mar 20, 1929 in Paris, France
Source: *McGEWB; OxFr; REn*

Foch, Nina
[Nina Consuelo Maud Fock]
American. Actress
Oscar nominee for *Executive Suite,* 1954;
  founder, teacher, Nina Foch Studio, 1973--
b. Apr 20, 1924 in Leiden, Netherlands
Source: *BiE&WWA; FilmEn; FilmgC; HolP
40; InWom; IntMPA 82; MotPP; MovMk;
NotNAT; WhoAm 82; WhoHol A; WhoThe
77; WhoWor 78*

Focke, Heinrich
"Father of the Helicopter"
German. Inventor
Aviation pioneer, developed helicopter, 1938.
b. 1890
d. Feb 25, 1979 in Bremen, Germany (West)
Source: *BioIn 11; NewYTBS 79; WebBD 80*

Fodor, Eugene
American. Editor, Publisher
Began publishing *Fodor's Travel Guides,* 1949.
b. Oct 5, 1905 in Leva, Hungary
Source: *AmAu&B; BioNews 74; ConAu 21R;
NewYTBS 74; WhoAm 74, 76, 78, 80, 82;
WhoWor 74*

Fodor, Eugene Nicholas
American. Musician
Popular symphony soloist; first westerner to
  win Moscow's Tchaikovsky Prize, 1974.
b. Mar 5, 1950 in Denver, Colorado
Source: *Baker 78; CurBio 76; WhoAm 84*

Foerster, Friedrich Wilhelm
German. Author, Educator
b. Jun 2, 1869 in Berlin, Germany
d. Jan 9, 1966 in Kilchberg, Germany (West)
Source: *BioIn 1, 6, 7; CurBio 62, 66*

Foerster, Norman
American. Author, Educator
Critical writings include *Nature of American
  Literature,* 1923; *American Criticism,* 1928.
b. Apr 14, 1887 in Pittsburgh, Pennsylvania
Source: *AmAu&B; ChhPo; CnDAL; ConAmA;
ConAu 5R; DcLEL; OxAmL; PenC AM;
REnAL; TwCA, SUP; WhNAA*

Fogarty, Anne
American. Fashion Designer
b. Feb 2, 1926 in Pittsburgh, Pennsylvania
d. Jan 15, 1980 in New York, New York
Source: *CurBio 58; InWom; WhoAm 74;
WorFshn*

Fogazzaro, Antonio
Italian. Author, Poet
Popular novels include *The Saint,* 1905;
  Leila, 1910.
b. Mar 25, 1842 in Vicenza, Italy
d. Mar 7, 1911 in Vicenza, Italy
Source: *BbD; BiD&SB; CasWL; ClDMEL;
CyWA; DcBiA; EuAu; EvEuW; LinLib L;
LongCTC; McGEWD; ModRL; OxEng; PenC
EUR; REn; TwCA, SUP*

Fogelberg, Dan(iel Grayling)
American. Composer, Singer
First hit song "Part of the Plan," 1975;
  recent hit "Leader of the Band," 1982.
b. Aug 13, 1951 in Peoria, Illinois
Source: *IlEncRk; RkOn 74; WhoAm 76, 78,
80, 82*

Foghat
[Roger Earl; David Peverett; Rod Price;
  Anthony Stevens]
British. Music Group
Formed, 1971; hit single "Slow Ride," 1976.
Source: *IlEncRk; RkOn 74*

Fokine, Michel
American. Dancer
Creator of modern ballet; choreographer of
   Diaghilev's Ballets Russes in Paris, 1909-
   14.
b. Apr 26, 1880 in Saint Petersburg, Russia
d. Aug 22, 1942 in Yonkers, New York
Source: *BioNews 74; CurBio 42; DcAmB S3;*
   WhAm 2

Fokker, Anthony Herman Gerard
Dutch. Aircraft Designer
Designed many fighter planes used during
   WW I; later designed commercial aircraft
   in US.
b. Apr 6, 1890 in Kediri, Indonesia
d. Dec 23, 1939 in Alpine, New Jersey
Source: *AmBi; WhDW; WhAm 1*

Foley, Martha
American. Journalist, Editor
Edited annual *Best American Short Stories,*
   1958-76.
b. 1897 in Boston, Massachusetts
d. Sep 5, 1977 in Northampton,
   Massachusetts
Source: *ConAu 117*

Foley, "Red" (Clyde Julian)
American. Singer
Founding father of country music; starred in
   "Ozark Mountain Jubilee," 1955-61.
b. Jun 17, 1910 in Bluelick, Kentucky
d. Sep 19, 1968 in Fort Wayne, Indiana
Source: *EncFCWM 69; WhScrn 74, 77*

Folger, Henry Clay
American. Industrialist
Developed first Shakespeare collection in
   world--the Folger Shakespeare Library.
b. Jun 18, 1857 in New York, New York
d. Jun 11, 1930
Source: *DcNAA; NewCol 75; REnAL*

Folger, James A
American. Manufacturer
Started first coffee business at age 15, 1850.
b. 1835
d. 1889
Source: *Entr*

Foligno, Mike (Michael Anthony)
Canadian. Hockey Player
Right wing, 1979--; scored 35 goals in rookie
   season.
b. Jan 29, 1959 in Sudbury, Ontario
Source: *HocEn; HocReg 81*

Follett, Ken(neth Martin)
[Myles Symon, pseud.]
Welsh. Author
Wrote mysteries featuring industrial detective
   Piers Roper; best-seller *Eye of the Needle,*
   1978.
b. Jun 5, 1949 in Cardiff, Wales
Source: *ConAu 81; WhoAm 84; WhoSpyF*

Folon, Jean-Michel
Belgian. Artist, Illustrator
Designer of magazine covers, bold posters;
   did book of watercolors *The Eyewitness,*
   1980.
b. Mar 1, 1934 in Uccle, Belgium
Source: *BioIn 8, 11; CurBio 81*

Folsom, Frank M
American. Businessman, Philanthropist
b. May 14, 1894 in Sprague, Washington
d. Jan 22, 1970 in Scarsdale, New York
Source: *CurBio 70; NewYTBE 70*

Folsom, Marion Bayard
American. Government Official
b. Nov 23, 1894 in McRue, Georgia
d. Sep 28, 1976 in Rochester, New York
Source: *BiDrUSE; ConAu 17R; CurBio 50;*
   IntWW 74; WhoAm 74

Fonck, Rene
French. Aviator
Credited with shooting down 75 enemy
   planes during WW I.
b. 1894
d. Jun 18, 1953 in Paris, France
Source: *WebBD 80; WhoMW 76*

Fonda, Henry Jaynes
American. Actor
Won 1982 Oscar for last film *On Golden*
   Pond.
b. May 16, 1905 in Grand Island, Nebraska
d. Aug 12, 1982 in Los Angeles, California
Source: *BiDFilm; BiE&WWA; BkPepl; CelR;*
   CmMov; CurBio 82; FilmgC; IntMPA 82;
   IntWW 78; MotPP; MovMk; NewYTBS 82;
   NotNAT; OxFilm; PlP&P; WebAB; WhoAm
   82; WhAm 8; WhoHol A; WhoThe 81;
   WorEFlm

Fonda, Jane
[Mrs. Tom Hayden]
American. Actress, Political Activist
Won Oscars for *Klute,* 1971; *Coming Home,*
1978; wrote *Jane Fonda's Workout Book,*
1982, several fitness videocassettes.
b. Dec 21, 1937 in New York, New York
Source: *BiDFilm; BiE&WWA; BkPepl; CelR;*
CurBio 64, 86; FilmgC; IntMPA 78, 79, 80,
81, 82; IntWW 74; MotPP; MovMk;
NewYTBE 71; NewYTBS 74; NotNAT;
OxFilm; WhoAm 74, 76, 78, 80, 82;
WhoAmW 77; WhoHol A; WhoThe 77;
WomWMM; WorEFlm

Fonda, Peter
American. Actor
Wrote, co-produced, and starred in *Easy*
Rider, 1969.
b. Feb 23, 1939 in New York, New York
Source: *BiDFilm; BkPepl; CelR; FilmgC;*
IntMPA 75, 76, 77, 78, 79, 80, 81, 82;
MotPP; MovMk; OxFilm; WhoAm 74, 76, 78,
80, 82; WhoHol A

Fonda, Shirlee
[Mrs. Henry Fonda]
American. Celebrity Relative
b. 1931 in Aurora, Illinois
Source: *BioIn 10*

Fong, Hiram
American. Lawyer, Public Official
Member US Senate, 1959-77.
b. Oct 1, 1907 in Honolulu, Hawaii
Source: *BiDrAC; CelR; CngDr 74; CurBio 60;*
IntWW 74; LinLib S; WhoAm 78, 80, 82;
WhoAmP 73; WhoGov 72; WhoWest 74;
WhoWor 74, 78

Fontaine, Frank
"Crazy Guggenheim"
American. Comedian, Singer
Best known for appearances on "The Jackie
Gleason Show," 1960s.
b. Apr 19, 1920 in Haverhill, Massachusetts
d. Aug 4, 1978 in Spokane, Washington
Source: *IntMPA 75, 76, 77; WhoHol A*

Fontaine, Jean de la
see: LaFontaine, Jean de

Fontaine, Joan
[Joan de Havilland]
American. Actress
Won 1941 Oscar for *Suspicion;* sister of
Olivia de Haviland.
b. Oct 22, 1917 in Tokyo, Japan
Source: *BiDFilm; BiE&WWA; CelR; ConAu*
81; CurBio 44; FilmgC; ForWC 70; InWom;
IntMPA 75, 76, 77, 78, 79, 80, 81, 82;
MotPP; MovMk; OxFilm; ThFT; WhoAm 74,
76, 78, 80, 82; WhoE 74; WhoHol A;
WomWMM; WorEFlm

Fontana, Tom
American. Writer, Producer
Won Emmy for writing "St. Elsewhere,"
1984.
b. Sep 12, 1951
Source: *ConTFT 2*

Fontane, Theodor
German. Author
Wrote historical novel, *Vor Dem Strum,*
1878.
b. Dec 30, 1819 in Neu-Ruppin, Germany
d. Sep 20, 1898 in Berlin, Germany
Source: *CasWL; ClDMEL; CyWA; EuAu;*
EvEuW; LinLib L; McGEWB; OxGer; PenC
CL, EUR; REn

Fontanne, Lynn
[Mrs. Alfred Lunt]
American. Actress
With husband, formed one of great stage
duos: *O Mistress Mine,* 1946; *The Visit,*
1960.
b. Dec 6, 1887 in London, England
d. Jul 30, 1983 in Genessee Depot,
Wisconsin
Source: *BiE&WWA; CelR; CurBio 41, 83;*
FamA&A; FilmEn; FilmgC; InWom;
NewYTBS 83; NotNAT; OxThe; PIP&P;
ThFT; WebAB; WhoAm 80, 82; WhoAmW
77; WhoHol A; WhoThe 77; WhoWor 74, 78

Fonteyn, Margot, Dame
[Mrs. Roberto de Arias; Margaret Hookham]
English. Ballerina
Pres., Royal Academy of Dancing, 1954--;
first dancer named Dame Commander of
British Empire.
b. May 18, 1919 in Reigate, England
Source: *CelR; CurBio 49, 72; InWom;*
IntWW 74; NewYTBE 72; NewYTBS 74;
Who 74; WhoAm 82; WhoThe 77A; WhoWor
78

Fonyo, Steve (Stephen, Jr.)
Canadian. Runner, Cancer Victim
After losing leg to cancer, ran 4,924 miles
across Canada to raise money for cancer
research, 1984-85.
b. Jun 29, 1965 in Montreal, Quebec
Source: *ConNews 85-4*

Foot, Michael
English. Politician, Journalist
Leader of Labour party, 1980-83; author
Debts of Honour, 1980.
b. Jul 23, 1913 in Plymouth, England
Source: *ConAu 108; CurBio 50; IntWW 74;
Who 74; WhoWor 74, 78; WrDr 76, 80*

Foote, Andrew Hull
American. Military Leader
b. Sep 12, 1806 in New Haven, Connecticut
d. Jun 26, 1863 in New Haven, Connecticut
Source: *Alli; AmBi; ApCAB; DcAmAu;
DcAmB; DcNAA; Drake; TwCBDA; WebAB;
WhAm HS*

Foote, Arthur William
American. Composer, Organist
Wrote overture *In the Mountains,* 1887.
b. Mar 5, 1853 in Salem, Massachusetts
d. Apr 8, 1937 in Boston, Massachusetts
Source: *DcAmB S2; WebBD 80*

Foote, Horton (Albert Horton, Jr.)
American. Author, Screenwriter
Wrote *Trip to Bountiful,* 1953; won Oscar
for screenplay of *Tender Mercies,* 1983.
b. Mar 14, 1917 in Wharton, Texas
Source: *AmAu&B; ConDr 82C; CurBio 86;
NotNAT; WhoThe 81*

Forain, Jean-Louis
French. Artist
Etcher, lithographer, caricaturist, known for
caustic humor.
b. 1852 in Reims, France
d. 1931 in Paris, France
Source: *McGDA; OxFr*

Foran, Dick John Nicholas
American. Actor
Made series of Warners films as singing
cowboy.
b. Jun 18, 1910 in Flemington, New Jersey
d. Aug 10, 1979
Source: *FilmEn; FilmgC; IntMPA 75, 76, 77;
NewYTBS 79; WhoHol A*

Forbes, Bertie Charles
Scottish. Journalist
b. May 14, 1880 in Aberdeen, Scotland
d. May 6, 1954 in New York, New York
Source: *BioIn 7, 8; CurBio 50, 54; WebBD
80*

Forbes, Bryan
English. Screenwriter, Director
Directed *The Stepford Wives,* 1974;
International Velvet, 1978.
b. Jul 22, 1926 in London, England
Source: *BiDFilm; CmMov; ConAu 69; ConDr
73; FilmgC; IntMPA 80, 81, 82; IntWW 74;
MovMk; NewYTBE 71; OxFilm; WhoAm 82;
WhoHol A; WhoThe 77; WorEFlm; WrDr 80*

Forbes, Esther
American. Author
Wrote Pulitzer-winning *Paul Revere and the
World He Lived In,* 1942.
b. Jun 28, 1894 in Westboro, Massachusetts
d. Aug 12, 1967 in Worcester, Massachusetts
Source: *AmAu&B; AmNov; AnCL; AuBYP;
ChhPo S2; ConAu 25R, P-1; CyWA; DcLEL;
InWom; MorJA; Newb 1922; OxAmL; REn;
REnAL; SmATA 2; TwCA, SUP; WhAm 4*

Forbes, John
British. Army Officer
b. 1710 in Dunfermline, Scotland
d. Mar 11, 1759 in Philadelphia,
Pennsylvania
Source: *AmBi; ApCAB; DcAmB; Drake;
WhAm HS*

Forbes, Kathryn, pseud.
[Kathryn Anderson McLean]
American. Author
Wrote *Mama's Bank Account,* 1943 which
inspired TV series "I Remember Mama,"
1949-57.
b. Mar 20, 1909 in San Francisco, California
d. May 15, 1966 in San Francisco, California
Source: *AmAu&B; AmNov; ConAu 25R, 29R,
P-2; CurBio 44, 66; InWom; REn; REnAL;
SmATA 15*

Forbes, Malcolm Stevenson
American. Publisher, Editor
Publisher, *Forbes* magazine, 1957--; wrote *The
Sayings of Chairman Malcolm,* 1978.
b. Aug 19, 1919 in New York, New York
Source: *ConAu 69; CurBio 75; St&PR 75;
WhoAm 74, 76, 78, 80, 82; WhoF&I 74;
WhoWor 78*

Forbes, Ralph
[Ralph Taylor]
English. Actor
Starred in silents, early talkies: *Beau Geste*, 1926; *Beau Ideal*, 1931.
b. Sep 30, 1896 in London, England
d. Mar 31, 1951 in New York, New York
Source: *FilmEn; Film 2; FilmgC; MotPP; TwYS; WhScrn 74, 77; WhThe; WhoHol B*

Forbes-Robertson, Johnston, Sir
English. Actor, Manager
Appeared on stage, 1874-1913; said to be greatest Hamlet of his time.
b. 1853 in London, England
d. Nov 6, 1937 in Saint Margaret's, England
Source: *LinLib L; NewCol 75; WhScrn 77; WhThe; WhoHol B*

Ford, Alexander
Polish. Director
Organized Polish army film unit, WW II; director, Film Polski, govt. run film organization.
b. Jan 24, 1908 in Lodz, Poland
Source: *DcFM; FilmEn; FilmgC; IntWW 74; WorEFlm*

Ford, Anne McDonnell
[Mrs. Deane Johnson]
American. Celebrity Relative
First wife of Henry Ford II, 1940-64; mother of Charlotte, Ann, Edsel II.
Source: *BioIn 5*

Ford, Arthur A
American. Minister
Psychic medium who lectured on ESP; allegedly broke secret code between Harry Houdini and wife.
b. 1896 in Titusville, Florida
d. Jan 1, 1971 in Miami, Florida
Source: *EncO&P 78; NewYTBE 71*

Ford, Benson
American. Auto Executive
b. Jul 20, 1919 in Detroit, Michigan
d. Jul 27, 1978 in Cheboygan, Michigan
Source: *CurBio 52, 78; IntWW 74, 75, 76, 77, 78; NewYTBS 78; Ward 77; WhoAm 74, 76, 78; WhoF&I 74*

Ford, Betty (Elizabeth Bloomer)
[Mrs. Gerald Ford]
American. First Lady
Model, dancer, 1939-41; wrote autobiography *The Times of My Life*, 1979.
b. Apr 8, 1918 in Chicago, Illinois
Source: *BioNews 74; BkPepl; ConAu 105; NewYTBE 73; NewYTBS 74; WhoAm 78, 82, 84; WhoAmW 77; WhoWor 78*

Ford, Bob (Robert Newton)
"The Dirty Little Coward"
American. Murderer
Fellow gang member who shot Jesse James in back, 1882.
b. 1860
d. Jun 24, 1892 in Creede, Colorado
Source: *Blood&B*

Ford, Charlotte
[Mrs. Edward Downe, Jr.]
American. Socialite, Designer, Celebrity Relative
Daughter of Henry Ford II.
b. 1941
Source: *BioIn 10*

Ford, Christina
[Maria Christina Vettore Austin Ford]
Italian. Celebrity Relative
Second wife of Henry Ford II.
b. 1927
Source: *NewYTBE 73*

Ford, Corey
[John Riddell, psued.]
American. Humorist, Author
b. Apr 29, 1902 in New York, New York
d. Jul 27, 1969 in Hanover, New Hampshire
Source: *AmAu&B; ConAu 25R; EncMys; REnAL; WhAm 5; WhNAA*

Ford, Doug
American. Golfer
b. Aug 6, 1922 in West Haven, Connecticut
Source: *BioIn 5, 10*

Ford, Edsel Bryant
American. Auto Executive
Son of Henry Ford; pres., Ford Motor Co., 1919-43; the Edsel was named for him.
b. Nov 6, 1893 in Detroit, Michigan
d. May 26, 1943 in Grosse Pointe, Michigan
Source: *DcAmB S3; WhAm 2*

Ford, Edsel Bryant, II
American. Auto Executive
Son of Henry Ford II; has worked for Ford Motor Co. since 1969.
b. 1949
Source: *BioIn 10; BioNews 74; BusPN*

Ford, Eileen
American. Business Executive
b. Mar 25, 1922 in New York, New York
Source: *CurBio 71; WhoAm 76, 78; WhoAmW 74*

Ford, Eleanor Clay
American. Celebrity Relative
Wife of Edsel B Ford, mother of Henry
    Ford II.
b. 1896
d. Oct 19, 1976 in Detroit, Michigan
Source: *InWom; NewYTBS 76; WhoAmA 78N*

Ford, Ford Madox
[Ford Madox Hueffer]
English. Author, Poet
Founded *English Review,* 1908; wrote *Good
    Soldier,* 1915, a study of emotional
    relationships.
b. Dec 17, 1873 in Merton, England
d. Jun 26, 1939 in Deauville, France
Source: *AtlBL; CasWL; Chambr 3; ChhPo,
    S1; CnMWL; CyWA; DcLEL; EncWL; EvLB;
    LinLib L; LongCTC; ModBrL, S1; NewC;
    OxEng; PenC ENG; RAdv 1; REn; REnAL;
    TwCA, SUP; TwCWr; WebE&AL; WhAm 3,
    HSA; WhE&EA; WhoTwCL*

Ford, Gerald Rudolph
[Gerald King]
American. US President
Became pres. upon Richard Nixon
    resignation, 1974-76; pardoned him, 1974.
b. Jul 14, 1913 in Omaha, Nebraska
Source: *BiDrAC; BioNews 74; BkPepl; CelR;
    CurBio 61, 75; IntWW 74; LinLib L; NewCol
    75; NewYTBE 73; NewYTBS 76; WhoAm 82;
    WhoFtbl 74; WhoGov 72; WhoMW 74*

Ford, Glenn
[Gwyllyn Samuel Newton Ford]
American. Actor
Starred in *Pocketful of Miracles,* 1961;
    Superman, 1978.
b. May 1, 1916 in Quebec
Source: *BiDFilm; CelR; CmMov; CurBio 59;
    FilmgC; IntMPA 76, 76, 77, 78, 79, 80, 81,
    82; MotPP; MovMk; OxFilm; WhoAm 74, 76,
    78, 80, 82; WhoHol A; WorEFlm*

Ford, Harrison
American. Actor
Best known roles as Han Solo in *Star Wars,*
    Indiana Jones in *Raiders of the Lost Ark,*
b. Jul 13, 1942 in Chicago, Illinois
Source: *CurBio 84; IntMPA 82; WhoAm 78,
    80, 82*

Ford, Henry
American. Auto Manufacturer
Built first inexpensive auto, Model T, 1909;
    introduced assembly line, 1913.
b. Jul 30, 1863 in Dearborn Township,
    Michigan
d. Apr 7, 1947 in Dearborn, Michigan
Source: *AmAu&B; CurBio 44, 47; DcAmB S4;
    EncAB-H; NewCol 75; WebAB; WhAm 2*

Ford, Henry, II
American. Auto Manufacturer
Grandson of Henry Ford; chm., chief exec.,
    Ford Motor Co., 1960-80.
b. Sep 4, 1917 in Detroit, Michigan
Source: *BusPN; CelR; CurBio 46, 78; EncAB-
    H; IntWW 74; LinLib S; NewYTBS 79;
    St&PR 75; Ward 77; Who 80; WhoAm 80,
    82; WhoF&I 74; WhoWor 78*

Ford, Jack (John Gardner)
American. Celebrity Relative
Second son of Gerald Ford.
b. Mar 16, 1952
Source: *BioIn 11*

Ford, John
English. Dramatist
Melancholy plays include *Broken Heart,*
    1633.
b. 1586 in Ilsington, England
d. 1640
Source: *Alli; AtlBL; BbD; BiD&SB; BrAu;
    CasWL; ChhPo; CnE&AP; CnThe; CroE&S;
    CrtT 1; CyWA; DcEnA; DcEnL; EvLB;
    LinLib L, S; McGEWD; MouLC 1; NewC;
    OxThe; PenC ENG; PlP&P; REn; REnWD;
    WebE&AL*

Ford, John
[Sean O'Feeney]
American. Director
Best known for western films including
    Stagecoach, 1939; won six Oscars.
b. Feb 1, 1895 in Cape Elizabeth, Maine
d. Aug 31, 1973 in Palm Desert, California
Source: *CmMov; ConAu 45; CurBio 73N;
    DcFM; EncAB-H; Film 1, 2; FilmgC;
    MovMk; OxFilm; WebAB; WhAm 6; WhScrn
    77; WhoAm 74*

Ford, Kathleen DuRoss
[Mrs. Henry Ford II]
American. Celebrity Relative
Third wife of Henry Ford II.
b. Feb 11, 1940 in Belding, Michigan
Source: *BioIn 10, 11, 12*

Ford, Mary
[Irene Colleen Summers; Les Paul and Mary
Ford]
American. Singer, Musician
b. Jul 7, 1924
d. Sep 30, 1977 in Los Angeles, California
Source: *InWom*

Ford, Mary Litogot
American. Celebrity Relative
b. 1839
d. 1876
Source: *BioIn 10*

Ford, Michael Gerald
American. Celebrity Relative
Oldest son of Gerald Ford.
b. Mar 14, 1950
Source: *BioIn 10*

Ford, Paul
[Paul Ford Weaver]
American. Actor
Stage, film actor who starred in TV series
    "You'll Never Get Rich," 1955-59;
    "Baileys of Balboa," 1964-65.
b. Nov 2, 1901 in Baltimore, Maryland
d. Apr 12, 1976 in Mineola, New York
Source: *BiE&WWA; FilmgC; MotPP; MovMk;
NewYTBS 76; NotNAT B; WhAm 7; WhoAm
76; WhoE 74; WhoThe 77; WhoWor 74*

Ford, Paul Leicester
American. Author, Historian
Wrote novel *Janice Meredith,* 1899; 10-
    volume *Writings of Thomas Jefferson,*
    1894.
b. Mar 23, 1865 in Brooklyn, New York
d. May 8, 1902 in New York, New York
Source: *Alli SUP; AmAu; AmAu&B; BbD;
BiD&SB; Chambr 3; CnDAL; DcAmAu;
LinLib L, S; OxAmL; REn; REnAL; WebAB;
WhAm 1*

Ford, Phil
[Ford and Hines]
American. Comedian
b. 1902 in Portland, Maine
Source: *Film 1*

Ford, Phil Jackson
American. Basketball Player
b. Feb 9, 1956 in Rocky Mount, North
    Carolina
Source: *OfNBA 81*

Ford, Russ(ell William)
Canadian. Baseball Player
b. Apr 25, 1883 in Brandon, Manitoba
d. Jan 24, 1960 in Rockingham, North
    Carolina
Source: *BaseEn 85; BioIn 5; WhoProB 73*

Ford, Ruth Elizabeth
American. Actress
Films include *Dragonwyck; Keys of the
    Kingdom.*
b. Jul 7, 1915 in Hazelhurst, Mississippi
Source: *BiE&WWA; CelR,; InWom; NotNAT;
WhoAm 76; WhoHol A; WhoThe 77*

Ford, "Senator" (Ed)
American. Comedian
b. 1887
d. 1970 in Greenport, New York
Source: *NewYTBE 70*

Ford, Steven Meigs
American. Actor, Celebrity Relative
Son of Gerald Ford who stars in TV soap
    opera "The Young and The Restless."
b. May 19, 1956
Source: *BioIn 10*

Ford, Susan Elizabeth
[Mrs. Charles Vance]
American. Celebrity Relative
Daughter of Gerald Ford.
b. Jul 6, 1957
Source: *BioIn 10, 11*

Ford, "Tennessee Ernie" (Ernest J)
American. Singer
Best known song "16 Tons."
b. Feb 13, 1919 in Bristol, Tennessee
Source: *AmSCAP 66; CurBio 58; EncFCWM
69; IntMPA 75, 76, 77, 78, 79, 80, 81, 82;
WhoAm 74, 76, 78, 80, 82*

Ford, Wallace
[Samuel Jones Grundy]
English. Actor
Character actor, 1903-65; notable film *The
    Informer,* 1935.
b. Feb 12, 1899 in Batton, England
d. Jun 11, 1966 in Woodland Hills,
    California
Source: *BiE&WWA; FilmEn; FilmgC;
MovMk; Vers B; WhScrn 74, 77; WhThe;
WhoHol B*

Ford, Wendell Hampton
American. Senator
b. Sep 8, 1924 in Owensboro, Kentucky
Source: *BioNews 75; WhoAm 74, 76, 78, 80,
82; WhoAmP 79, 85; WhoGov 77, 72;
WhoS&SW 73, 78*

Ford, "Whitey" (Edward Charles)
"The Chairman of the Board"
American. Baseball Player
Pitcher, NY Yankees, 1950-67; won 10
    World Series games; Hall of Fame, 1974.
b. Oct 21, 1928 in New York, New York
Source: *BaseEn 85; CurBio 62; NewYTBS 74;*
WhoAm 82; WhoProB 73

Ford, William Clay
American. Auto Executive, Football Executive
Brother of Henry Ford II; owner, Detroit
    Lions football club, 1964--.
b. Mar 14, 1925 in Detroit, Michigan
Source: *Ward 77; WhoAm 78, 82; WhoFtbl*
74; WhoMW 78

Ford and Hines
see: Ford, Phil; Hines, Mimi

Foreigner
[Dennis Elliott; Ed Gagliardi; Lou Gramm;
    Al Greenwood; Mick Jones; Ian
    McDonald; Rick Wills]
English. Music Group
Source: *ConMuA 80A; IlEncRk; LilREn 78;*
RkOn 78; WhoRock 81

Foreman, Carl
American. Screenwriter, Director, Producer
Won best director Oscar for *Bridge Over the*
    River Kwai, 1957.
b. Jul 23, 1914 in Chicago, Illinois
d. Jun 26, 1984 in Beverly Hills, California
Source: *AnObit 1984; BlueB 76; ConTFT 2;*
DcLB 26; FilmgC; IntMPA 84; IntWW 83;
NewYTBS 84; VarWW 85; Who 83; WhoAm
82; WhoWor 78; WrDr 84

Foreman, Carol Lee Tucker
American. Government Official
b. May 3, 1938 in Little Rock, Arkansas
Source: *BioIn 11; WhoAm 78, 80, 82*

Foreman, "Chuck" (Walter Eugene)
American. Football Player
Running back, Minnesota, 1973-80, New
    England, 1980--; rookie of year, 1973.
b. Oct 26, 1950 in Frederick, Missouri
Source: *FootReg 81; WhoAm 78, 80, 82;*
WhoBlA 77; WhoFtbl 74

Foreman, George
American. Boxer
Won gold medal, 1968 Olympics; pro
    heavyweight champ, 1973-74.
b. Jan 10, 1949 in Marshall, Texas
Source: *CelR; CurBio 74; NewYTBE 73;*
NewYTBS 74; WhoAm 74; WhoBlA 75;
WhoBox 74

Foreman, Percy
American. Lawyer
b. Jun 21, 1902 in Polk County, Texas
Source: *WhoS&SW 82*

Forest, Lee de
see: DeForest, Lee

Forester, Cecil Scott
English. Author
Wrote *Horatio Hornblower* series; *The African*
    Queen, 1935.
b. Aug 27, 1899 in Cairo, Egypt
d. Apr 2, 1966 in Fullerton, California
Source: *AmAu&B; ConAu 25R, 73; CyWA;*
DcLEL; EncMys; EvLB; LongCTC; MnBBF;
ModBrL; NewC; RAdv 1; REn; REnAL;
SmATA 13; TwCA, SUP; TwCWr;
WebE&AL; WhAm 4; WhoChL

Forman, James Douglas
American. Lawyer, Author
b. Nov 12, 1932 in Mineola, New York
Source: *AuBYP; ConAu 9R; SmATA 8;*
ThrBJA

Forman, Milos
Czech. Director
Won Oscars for *One Flew Over the Cuckoo's*
    Nest, 1975; *Amadeus,* 1984.
b. Feb 18, 1932 in Caslav, Czechoslovakia
Source: *BiDFilm; CurBio 71; DcFM; FilmgC;*
IntMPA 79, 80, 81, 82; IntWW 74; MovMk;
NewYTBE 71; OxFilm; WhoAm 82; WhoSocC
78A; WhoWor 74, 78; WorEFlm

Forrest, Edwin
American. Actor
b. Mar 9, 1806 in Philadelphia, Pennsylvania
d. Dec 12, 1872 in Philadelphia,
    Pennsylvania
Source: *AmBi; ApCAB; DcAmB; Drake;*
EncAB-H; FamA&A; LinLib L, S; OxAmL;
OxThe; PIP&P; REnAL; TwCBDA; WebAB;
WhAm HS

Forrest, Helen
American. Singer
Big Band vocalist with Artie Shaw, Benny
    Goodman, 1930s-40s; sang "Out of
    Nowhere" from 1945 film *You Came*
    Along.
b. Apr 12, 1918 in Atlantic City, New Jersey
Source: *BioIn 6, 11; CmpEPM; WhoHol A*

Forrest, Nathan Bedford
American. Military Leader
Conferedate war general; first head of
original Klu Klux Klan.
b. Jul 13, 1821 in Chapel Hill, Tennessee
d. Oct 29, 1877 in Memphis, Tennessee
Source: *AmBi; ApCAB; BiDConf; DcAmB;
TwCBDA; WebAB; WhAm HS*

Forrest, Steve
[William Forrest Andrews]
American. Actor
Brother of Dana Andrews; in TV series
"SWAT," 1975-76.
b. Sep 29, 1925 in Huntsville, Texas
Source: *FilmEn; FilmgC; IntMPA 77, 78, 79,
80, 81, 82; WhoAm 78, 82; WhoHol A*

Forrestal, James Vincent
American. Public Official
b. Feb 15, 1892 in Beacon, New York
d. May 22, 1949 in Bethesda, Maryland
Source: *AmAu&B; BiDrUSE; CurBio 42, 48,
49; DcAmB S4; EncAB-H; WebAB; WhAm 2*

Forrester, Maureen
Canadian. Opera Singer
b. Jul 25, 1931 in Montreal, Quebec
Source: *CanWW 82; CreCan 2; CurBio 62;
InWom; WhoAm 82; WhoMus 72*

Forsch, Bob (Robert Herbert)
American. Baseball Player
Pitcher, St. Louis, 1974--; pitched no-hitters,
1978, 1983.
b. Jan 13, 1950 in Sacramento, California
Source: *BaseEn 85; BaseReg 86*

Forsch, Ken(neth Roth)
American. Baseball Player
Pitcher, 1970-85; pitched no-hitter, 1979; with
brother Bob, only brother combination in
ML to do this.
b. Sep 8, 1946 in Sacramento, California
Source: *BaseEn 85; BaseReg 86*

Forssmann, Werner Theodor Otto
German. Surgeon
Pioneered technique of cardiac catheterization;
won Nobel Prize, 1956.
b. Aug 29, 1904 in Berlin, Germany
d. Jun 1, 1979 in Schopfheim, Germany
(West)
Source: *CurBio 57, 79; IntWW 74, 75, 76;
NewYTBS 79; Who 74; WhoWor 74, 76*

Forster, E(dward) M(organ)
English. Author
Wrote *A Room with a View,* 1908; *A Passage
to India,* 1924.
b. Jan 1, 1879 in London, England
d. Jun 7, 1970 in Coventry, England
Source: *AtlBL; CasWL; Chambr 3; ChhPo
S2; CnMWL; ConAu 25R, P-1; ConLC 1, 2,
3, 4, 9, 10, 13, 15; CyWA; DcLEL; EncWL;
EvLB; LongCTC; ModBrL, S1; NewC;
OxEng; PenC ENG; RAdv 1; RComWL;
REn; TwCA, SUP; TwCWr; WebE&AL;
WhAm 5; WhoTwCL*

Forster, Robert
American. Actor
Starred in TV series "Banyon," 1972-74.
b. Jul 13, 1942 in Rochester, New York
Source: *FilmgC; IntMPA 75, 76, 77, 78, 79,
80, 81, 82; NewYTBE 72; WhoHol A*

Forster, William Edward
English. Statesman
b. 1818 in Bradpole, England
d. 1886 in London, England
Source: *NewCol 75*

Forsyth, Frederick
English. Author
Wrote best-selling thrillers *The Day of the
Jackal,* 1971; *The Odessa File,* 1972.
b. Aug 25, 1938 in Ashford, England
Source: *ConAu 85; ConLC 2, 5; CurBio 86;
WhoAm 74; WrDr 76*

Forsyth, Rosemary
American. Actress
Former model; in films *Black Eye,* 1974;
Gray Lady Down, 1978.
b. Jul 6, 1944 in Montreal, Quebec
Source: *FilmEn; FilmgC; WhoHol A*

Forsythe, Albert E
American. Pilot
Helped open aviation to blacks, 1930s; first
black to fly cross-country.
b. 1898 in Nassau, Bahamas
d. May 7, 1986 in Newark, New Jersey
Source: *NewYTBS 86*

Forsythe, John
[John Lincoln Freund]
American. Actor
Plays Blake Carrington on TV series
"Dynasty," 1981--.
b. Jan 29, 1918 in Penns Grove, New Jersey
Source: *BiE&WWA; CelR; CurBio 73;
FilmgC; IntMPA 75, 76, 77, 78, 79, 80, 81,
82; MotPP; MovMk; NotNAT; WhoAm 74,
76, 78, 80, 82; WhoHol A; WhoThe 77;
WhoWest 84*

Fort, Charles Hoy
American. Author
Works descibe psychic phenomena: *Look of the Damned,* 1919.
b. 1874 in Albany, New York
d. May 3, 1932 in Bronx, New York
Source: *AmAu&B; DcNAA; EncO&P 78; EncSF; OxAmL; REnAL; TwCA; WhoSciF*

Fortas, Abe
American. Lawyer, Government Official
Supreme Court Justice, 1956-69; resigned under fire after accepting fees from convicted swindler.
b. Jun 19, 1910 in Memphis, Tennessee
d. Apr 5, 1982 in Washington, District of Columbia
Source: *AnObit 1982; CurBio 66, 82; DrAS 74P; IntWW 74, 75, 76, 77, 78; LinLib L, S; NewYTBS 82; PolProf NF; WebAB; WhoAm 76, 78, 80, 82; WhoAmL 79; WhoAmP 73, 75, 77, 79; WhoS&SW 73*

Forten, James
American. Reformer
b. Sep 2, 1766
d. Mar 4, 1842
Source: *DcAmB; WebAB; WhAm HS; WhAmP*

Fortmann, Daniel John
American. Football Player
b. Apr 11, 1916 in Pearl River, New York
Source: *BioIn 6, 8; WhoFtbl 74*

Fortune, Nick
see: Buckinghams, The

Fortune, Timothy Thomas
American. Author, Editor
b. Oct 3, 1856 in Marianna, Florida
d. Jun 2, 1928
Source: *AmAu&B; BlkAWP; DcNAA; EncAB-H*

Fortuny
[Mariano Fortuny y Madrazo]
Spanish. Fashion Designer
b. 1871 in Granada, Spain
d. 1949
Source: *WhoFash; WorFshn*

Foscolo, (Niccolo) Ugo
Italian. Poet, Patriot
Wrote novel *Lost Letters of Jacopo Artis,* 1802.
b. 1778 in Zante, Greece
d. Sep 10, 1827 in London, England
Source: *CasWL; DcEuL; EuAu; EvEuW; LinLib L; McGEWD; PenC EUR; REn*

Fosdick, Harry Emerson
American. Clergyman
Leading spokesman for modern liberal Christianity in US, 1920s.
b. May 24, 1878 in Buffalo, New York
d. Oct 5, 1969 in Bronxville, New York
Source: *AmAu&B; AuBYP; ConAu 25R; CurBio 40, 69; REnAL; TwCA SUP; WebAB; WhNAA*

Fosdick, Raymond Blaine
American. Author, Lawyer
b. Jun 9, 1883 in Buffalo, New York
d. Jul 18, 1972 in Newtown, Connecticut
Source: *AmAu&B; AmLY; ConAu 37R; CurBio 45, 72*

Foss, Joseph Jacob
American. Pilot
b. Apr 17, 1915 in Sioux Falls, South Dakota
Source: *CurBio 55; WhoAmP 73*

Foss, Lukas
German. Composer, Conductor
b. Aug 15, 1922 in Berlin, Germany
Source: *AmSCAP 66; CurBio 66; DcCM; WhoAm 74, 76, 78, 80, 82; WhoE 74; WhoMus 72; WhoWor 78*

Fosse, Bob
American. Choreographer, Director
Won Oscar, 1972, for *Cabaret;* directed *All that Jazz,* 1979.
b. Jun 23, 1927 in Chicago, Illinois
Source: *BiDFilm; BiE&WWA; BkPepl; CelR; CmMov; CurBio 72; EncMT; FilmgC; IntMPA 77, 78, 79, 80, 81, 82; MovMk; NotNAT; OxFilm; WhoAm 74, 76, 78, 80, 82; WhoThe 77; WhoWor 78; WorEFlm*

Fossey, Dian
American. Naturalist, Author
At research camp in Rwanda, became leading authority on gorillas, 1966-85; murdered.
b. Jan 16, 1932 in San Francisco, California
d. Dec 27, 1985 in Virunga Mountains, Rwanda
Source: *ConNews 86-1; CurBio 85*

Foster, Abigail Kelley
American. Abolitionist
Advocate of women's suffrage, temperance, labor reform.
b. Jan 15, 1810 in Pelham, Massachusetts
d. Jan 14, 1887 in Worcester, Massachusetts
Source: *NotAW; WebBD 80*

Foster, George Arthur
American. Baseball Player
b. Dec 1, 1949 in Tuscaloosa, Alabama
Source: *BaseEn 85; BioIn 11; WhoAm 78, 80, 82; WhoBlA 75, 77*

Foster, Hal (Harold Rudolf)
American. Cartoonist
Created "Prince Valiant" comic strip.
b. Aug 16, 1892 in Halifax, Nova Scotia
d. Jul 25, 1982 in Spring Hill, Florida
Source: *AnObit 1983; ConAu 107; LinLib L; NewYTBS 82; WhoAm 78; WhoAmA 73, 76, 78*

Foster, "Jodie" (Alicia Christian)
American. Actress
Starred in *Taxi Driver*, 1976; *Foxes*, 1980.
b. Nov 19, 1962 in Los Angeles, California
Source: *BkPepl; CurBio 81; NewYTBS 76; WhoAm 78, 79, 80, 81, 82; NewYTBS 76; WhoAm 78, 80, 82; WhoAmW 79; WhoHol A*

Foster, Joseph C
American. Business Executive
Pres., Foster Grant Co., 1943-69.
b. Oct 30, 1904 in Providence, Rhode Island
d. Nov 10, 1971 in New York, New York
Source: *BioIn 11; NewYTBE 71; WhAm 6*

Foster, Norman
[Norman Hoeffer]
American. Actor, Director, Producer
Leading man, early 1930s; directed numerous hits including *Davy Crockett*, 1955.
b. Dec 13, 1903 in Richmond, Indiana
d. Jul 7, 1976
Source: *BiDFilm; FilmEn; Film 2; FilmgC; MovMk; NewYTET; WhAm 7; WhThe; WhoAm 76, 78; WhoHol A; WhoThe 72; WorEFlm*

Foster, Paul
American. Dramatist
b. Oct 15, 1931 in Penns Grove, New Jersey
Source: *Au&Wr 71; ConAu 21R; WhoAm 74; WhoE 74; WhoThe 77; WrDr 80*

Foster, Phil
[Fivel Feldman]
American. Actor, Comedian
Stand-up comedian best known as Laverne's father on TV series "Laverne and Shirley," 1976-82.
b. Mar 29, 1914 in Brooklyn, New York
d. Jul 8, 1985 in Rancho Mirage, California
Source: *ConNews 85-3; WhoAm 78; WhoHol A*

Foster, "Pops" (George Murphy)
American. Jazz Musician
b. May 19, 1892 in McCall, Louisiana
d. Oct 30, 1969 in San Francisco, California
Source: *WhoJazz 72*

Foster, Preston
American. Actor
Two-fisted hero in films, 1930-68.
b. Aug 24, 1900 in Ocean City, New Jersey
d. Jul 14, 1970 in La Jolla, California
Source: *AmSCAP 66; FilmgC; HolP 30; MotPP; MovMk; NewYTBE 70; WhScrn 74, 77; WhoHol B*

Foster, Stephen Collins
American. Composer, Author
Best known songs "Oh Susannah," 1848; "My Old Kentucky Home," 1853.
b. Jul 4, 1826 in Pittsburgh, Pennsylvania
d. Jul 13, 1864 in New York, New York
Source: *AmAu; AmAu&B; AmBi; ApCAB; AtlBL; BbD; BiD&SB; Chambr 3; DcAmAu; DcAmB; DcLEL; DcNAA; EvLB; OxAmL; PoIre; REn; REnAL; TwCBDA; WebAB; WhAm HS*

Foster, Susanna
[Suzanne De Lee Flanders Larson]
American. Singer, Actress
b. Dec 6, 1924 in Chicago, Illinois
Source: *FilmgC; HolP 40; MotPP; MovMk; WhoHol A*

Foster, William Zebulon
American. Political Leader, Labor Union Official
Chm., US Communist Party, 1945-56; Communist presidential candidate, 1924.
b. Feb 25, 1881 in Taunton, Massachusetts
d. Sep 1, 1961 in Moscow, U.S.S.R.
Source: *AmAu&B; BiDAmLL; CurBio 45, 61; McGEWB; PolProf T; WebAB; WhAm 4*

Foucault, Jean Bernard
French. Physicist
Invented gyroscope, 1852; known for research on speed of light.
b. Sep 18, 1819
d. Feb 11, 1868
Source: *NewCol 75*

Foucault, Michel
French. Author, Philosopher
Cultural historian who wrote award-winning *Madness and Civilization*, 1961.
b. Oct 15, 1926 in Poitiers, France
d. Jun 25, 1984 in Paris, France
Source: *AnObit 1984; BioIn 8; WorAu 1970*

Fouche, Joseph
French. Statesman, Revolutionary
Napoleon's minister of police, 1799-1802,
1804-10.
b. 1759 in Brittany, France
d. 1820 in Trieste, Italy
Source: *LinLib S; McGEWB; NewCol 75;*
OxFr; REn; SpyCS

Fountain, Pete(r Dewey)
American. Jazz Musician
Clarinetist; member Lawrence Welk
Orchestra, 1957-60.
b. Jul 3, 1930 in New Orleans, Louisiana
Source: *WhoAm 74, 76, 78, 80, 82;*
WhoS&SW 82

Fouquet, Jean
French. Artist
b. 1420 in Tours, France
d. 1480 in Tours, France
Source: *AtlBL; OxFr; REn*

Fouquet, Nicolas
French. Statesman
b. 1615
d. Mar 23, 1680
Source: *NewCol 75; OxFr; REn*

Fouquier-Tinville, Antoine Quentin
French. Lawyer
Revolutionary tribunal prosecutor; Marie
Antoinette was one of his victims.
b. 1746
d. May 8, 1795
Source: *BioIn 2; DcBiPP; Dis&D; OxFr; REn*

Four Chaplains
[George L Fox; Alexander Goode; Clark V
Poling; John P Washington]
American. Heroes
Gave life jackets to others, perished when
Dorchester sunk off coast of Greenland,
1943.
Source: *BioIn 3, 4, 5, 7*

Four Freshmen, The
[Ken Albers; Don Barbour; Ross Barbour;
Ray Brown; Bill Comstock;Ken Errair;
Bob Flanagan; Hal Kratzch]
American. Music Group
Innovators of tight harmony sound, late
1940s; hit singles "It's a Blue World,"
1952; "Graduation Day," 1956.
Source: *RkOn 74*

Four Horsemen of Notre Dame, The
[James Crowley; Elmer Layden; Don Miller;
Harry Stuhldreher]
American. Football Players
Football backfield named by NY *Herald*
Tribune writer Grantland Rice, Oct 18,
1924.
Source: *NF*

Four Lads, The
[James Arnold; Frank Busseri; Connie
Codarini; Bernard Toorish]
Canadian. Music Group
Former choirboys; hit singles "Moments to
Remember"; "No Not Much."
Source: *AmPS A, B; RkOn 74; WhoRock 81*

Four Musketeers, The
[Jean Borotra; Jacques Brugnon; Henri
Coclet; (Jean-)Rene Lacoste]
French. Tennis Players
Source: *NF*

Four Seasons, The
[Tommy DeVito; Bob Gaudio; Nick Massi;
Frankie Valli]
American. Music Group
White doo-wop group, begun 1956; number
one hits "Sherry"; "Big Girls Don't Cry";
"Rag Doll."
Source: *AmPS A, B; BiDAmM; EncPR&S 74;*
IlEncRk; RkOn 74; RkOneH

Four Tops
[Renaldo Benson; Abdul Fakir; Lawrence
Payton; Levi Stubbs]
American. Music Group
Hits include "Baby I Need Your
Loving,"1964; "Reach Out I'll Be
There,"1966.
Source: *BiDAmM; EncPR&S 74; IlEncBM*
82; RkOn 74, 84

Fourier, Francois Marie Charles
French. Philosopher
b. Apr 7, 1772 in Besancon, France
d. Oct 8, 1837 in Paris, France
Source: *BbD; BiD&SB; CasWL; DcEuL;*
EuAu; LinLib L, S; McGEWB; NewC

Fourier, Jean Baptiste
French. Physicist
b. Mar 21, 1768
d. May 16, 1830
Source: *BiD&SB*

Fourment, Helena
[Mrs. Peter Rubens]
Belgian. Model
b. 1614
Source: *InWom*

Fournier, Henri Alban
see: Alain-Fournier, pseud.

Fournier, Pierre
French. Musician
b. Jun 24, 1906 in Paris, France
d. Jan 8, 1986 in Geneva, Switzerland
Source: *IntWW 74; Who 74; WhoMus 72; WhoWor 78*

Fouts, Dan(iel Francis)
American. Football Player
Quarterback, San Diego Chargers, 1973--.
b. Jun 10, 1951 in San Francisco, California
Source: *BioIn 12; FootReg 81; WhAm 82*

Fowler, Gene
American. Journalist, Author
b. Mar 8, 1890 in Denver, Colorado
d. Jul 2, 1960 in Los Angeles, California
Source: *AmAu&B; ConAu 5NR; CurBio 44, 60; REn; REnAL; TwCA, SUP; WhAm 4*

Fowler, Henry Watson
English. Lexicographer, Author
Compiled *Dictionary of Modern English Usage,* 1926; *Concise Oxford Dictionary,* 1911.
b. 1858
d. Dec 27, 1933 in London, England
Source: *ChhPo; DcLEL; EvLB; NewC; REn; TwCA, SUP*

Fowler, Lydia Folger
American. Pioneer, Author
b. 1822
d. 1879
Source: *BioIn 9; DcAmAu; DcNAA*

Fowler, Mark Stephen
American. Government Official
Chairman, FCC, 1981--.
b. Oct 6, 1941 in Toronto, Ontario
Source: *CurBio 86; LesBEnT; WhoAm 84; WhoF&I 83*

Fowles, John
English. Author
Wrote best-sellers *The Collector,* 1963; *French Lieutenant's Woman,* 1969.
b. Mar 31, 1926 in Essex, England
Source: *Au&Wr 71; CelR; ConAu 5R; ConLC 15; ConNov 76; EncWL; IntWW 74; LinLib L; ModBrL S1; NewC; TwCWr; WebE&AL; WhoAm 82; WhoWor 78; WorAu; WrDr 76*

Fowler, Orson Squire
American. Author, Lecturer
Noted popularizer of phrenology, 1830s.
b. Oct 11, 1809 in Steuben County, New York
d. Aug 18, 1887 in Sharon Station, Connecticut
Source: *DcAmB; NewCol 75; WhAm HS*

Fowlie, Wallace
American. Educator, Author
b. Nov 8, 1908 in Brookline, Massachusetts
Source: *AmAu&B; BiE&WWA; ConAu 5R; DrAS 74F; ModAL; TwCA SUP; WhoAm 74, 76, 78, 80, 82; WhoS&SW 82*

Fox, Carol
American. Impresario, Producer
Founder, manager, Lyric Opera of Chicago, 1952-81; introduced Maria Callas to US audiences.
b. Jun 15, 1926 in Chicago, Illinois
d. Jul 21, 1981 in Chicago, Illinois
Source: *BioIn 6, 9, 11; CurBio 78, 81; NewYTBS 81; WhoAm 74, 76, 78, 80; WhoAmW 58, 64, 66, 68, 70, 72, 79; WhoMW 74, 76, 78; WhoOp 76; WhoWor 78*

Fox, Charles
American. Composer, Conductor
Film scores include *Foul Play, Nine to Five;* won Emmys for "Love American Style," 1970, 1973.
b. Oct 30, 1940 in New York, New York
Source: *VarWW 85*

Fox, Charles James
British. Statesman
b. Jan 24, 1749 in London, England
d. Sep 13, 1806 in Chiswick, England
Source: *Alli; BbD; CasWL; ChhPo S1, S2; EvLB; NewC; REn*

Fox, Edward
English. Actor
Starred in films *The Day of the Jackal,* 1973; *Gandhi,* 1984.
b. Apr 13, 1937 in London, England
Source: *FilmEn; FilmgC; IntMPA 82; MovMk; WhoHol A*

Fox, Fontaine Talbot, Jr.
American. Illustrator, Cartoonist
Created syndicated comic strip "Toonerville Folks," 1915-30s.
b. Mar 3, 1884 in Louisville, Kentucky
d. Aug 10, 1964 in Greenwich, Connecticut
Source: *AmAu&B; ChhPo; ConAu 89; DcAmB S7; WhAm 4*

Fox, George
English. Religious Leader
Founded Society of Friends, the Quakers,
1671.
b. Jul 1624 in Leicester, England
d. Jan 13, 1691 in Sussex, England
Source: *Alli; ApCAB; BbD; BiD&SB; BrAu;
Chambr 1; DcEuL; DcLEL; EvLB; NewC;
OxAmL; OxEng; REn*

Fox, James
English. Actor
In films *The Servant; Isadora* ; became an
evangelist, 1973-83.
b. May 19, 1939 in London, England
Source: *Alli SUP; FilmEn; FilmgC; IntMPA
78, 79, 80, 81, 82; MovMk; WhoHol A*

Fox, John W, Jr.
American. Author
Wrote *Trail of Lonesome Pine*, 1908; *Little
Shepherd of Kingdom Come*, 1903.
b. Dec 16, 1863 in Stoney Pointe, Kentucky
d. Jul 8, 1919
Source: *AmAu&B; BbD; BiD&SB; BiDSA;
CarSB; CnDAL; ConAmL; DcAmAu; DcBiA;
DcLEL; DcNAA; EvLB; LinLib L; OxAmL;
REn; REnAL; TwCA, SUP; TwCWr; WhAm
1*

Fox, Kate
American. Mystic
b. 1839 in Bath, New Brunswick
d. 1894
Source: *EncO&P 78; InWom*

Fox, Margaret
American. Mystic
Toured US, England with act "Rochester
Rapping"; exposed as fake, 1888.
b. Oct 7, 1833 in Bath, New Brunswick
d. Mar 8, 1893 in Brooklyn, New York
Source: *Alli, SUP; ApCAB; DcAmB; DcNAA;
EncO&P 78; InWom; NotAW; OxAmL;
WebAB; WhAm HS*

Fox, Michael J
Canadian. Actor
Plays Alex Keaton on TV series, "Family
Ties," 1982--; starred in *Back to the
Future*, 1985.
b. Jun 9, 1961 in Edmonton, Alberta
Source: *ConNews 86-1; VarWW 85*

Fox, "Nellie" (Jacob Nelson)
American. Baseball Player
Infielder, 1947-65; went 98 straight games
without striking out, 1958.
b. Dec 25, 1927 in Saint Thomas,
Pennsylvania
d. Dec 1, 1975 in Baltimore, Maryland
Source: *BaseEn 85; CurBio 60, 76; WhoProB
73*

Fox, Sonny
American. Author
b. Jun 17, 1925 in Brooklyn, New York
Source: *ConAu 41R*

Fox, Terry (Terrance Stanley)
Canadian. Runner, Cancer Victim
After losing leg to cancer began marathon
run across Canada to raise money for
research; never completed, but raised $24
million.
b. Jul 28, 1958 in Winnipeg, Manitoba
d. Jun 28, 1981 in New Westminster, British
Columbia
Source: *AnObit 1981; NewYTBS 81*

Fox, Uffa
British. Designer, Author
b. Jan 15, 1898
d. Oct 26, 1972
Source: *ConAu 37R; NewYTBE 72*

Fox, Virgil Keel
American. Musician
b. May 3, 1912 in Princeton, Illinois
d. Oct 25, 1980 in West Palm Beach,
Florida
Source: *CurBio 64; NewYTBS 74; WhoAm
74; WhoMus 72; WhoWor 78*

Foxworth, Robert
American. Actor
Plays Chase Gioberti on TV series "Falcon
Crest," 1981--.
b. Nov 1, 1941 in Houston, Texas
Source: *IntMPA 77, 78, 79, 80, 81, 82*

Foxx, Jimmy (James Emory)
"The Beast"; "Double X"
American. Baseball Player
Infielder, 1925-44; won AL triple crown,
1933; Hall of Fame, 1951.
b. Oct 22, 1907 in Sudlersville, Maryland
d. Jul 21, 1967 in Miami, Florida
Source: *BaseEn 85; WebAB; WhoProB 73*

Foxx, Redd
[John Elroy Sanford]
American. Comedian, Actor
Starred as Fred Sanford in TV series
"Sanford and Son," 1972-77, 1980.
b. Dec 9, 1922 in Saint Louis, Missouri
Source: *BioNews 74; BkPepl; ConAu 89;
CurBio 72; IntMPA 82; NewYTBE 72;
WhoAm 74, 76, 78, 80, 82; WhoBlA 75;
WhoHol A*

Foy, Eddie
[Edward Fitzgerald]
American. Actor
Starred in vaudeville with children as "Eddie
and the Seven Little Foys," 1913-27.
b. Mar 9, 1856 in New York, New York
d. Feb 16, 1928 in Kansas City, Missouri
Source: *AmPS B; DcAmB; DcNAA; EncMT;
Film 1; FilmgC; OxThe; WebAB; WhAm 1;
WhScrn 74, 77; WhThe; WhoHol B*

Foy, Eddie, Jr.
American. Actor, Dancer
Son of Eddie Foy; starred in family act
"Eddie and the Seven Little Foys," 1913-
27.
b. Feb 4, 1905 in New Rochelle, New York
d. Jul 15, 1983 in Woodland Hills, California
Source: *BiE&WWA; EncMT; Film 2; FilmgC;
NewYTBS 83; NotNAT; WhoHol A; WhoThe
77*

Foyle, Christina
English. Bookseller
Managing director, W & G Foyle, Ltd.,
1963--.
b. Jan 30, 1911 in London, England
Source: *IntWW 74, 75, 76, 77, 78, 79, 80,
81, 82; WhE&EA; Who 82; WhoWor 74*

Foyle, Gilbert Samuel
English. Bookseller
Founded W & G Foyle, Ltd. bookstore in
London with brother William.
b. Mar 9, 1886 in London, England
d. Oct 28, 1971
Source: *CurBio 54, 72, 72N; WhE&EA*

Foyle, William Alfred
English. Bookseller
Founded W & G Foyle, Ltd. bookstore in
London with brother Gilbert.
b. Mar 4, 1885 in London, England
d. Jul 4, 1963 in Maldon, England
Source: *CurBio 54, 63; DcNaB 1961;
LongCTC; ObitOF 79; ObitT 1961; WhE&EA*

Foyt, A(nthony) J(oseph, Jr.)
American. Auto Racer
Only driver to win Indianapolis 500 four
times.
b. Jan 16, 1935 in Houston, Texas
Source: *BusPN; CelR,; CurBio 67; NewYTBS
75; WebAB; WhoAm 74, 76, 78, 80, 82*

Fra Angelico
see: Angelico, Fra

Fracastoro, Gerolamo
Italian. Physician
b. 1478 in Verona, Italy
d. Aug 8, 1553 in Verona, Italy
Source: *CasWL; DcEuL; REn*

Fracci, Carla
Italian. Ballerina
b. Aug 20, 1936 in Milan, Italy
Source: *CurBio 75; WhoAmW 74; WhoWor
78*

Fradon, Dana
American. Cartoonist
Contributor to *New Yorker,* 1950--; known
for cartoons satirizing local politics.
b. Apr 14, 1922 in Chicago, Illinois
Source: *WhoAm 80, 82, 84; WhoAmA 76, 78*

Fraenkel, Heinrich
Journalist, Author
b. Sep 28, 1897 in Germany
Source: *ConAu 13R; Who 74; WrDr 76*

Fragonard, Jean Honore
French. Artist, Engraver
b. Apr 5, 1732 in Grasse, France
d. Aug 22, 1806 in Grasse, France
Source: *AtlBL; OxFr; REn*

Frailberg, Selma
American. Psychoanalyst
Wrote *The Magic Years.*
b. 1919 in Detroit, Michigan
d. Dec 19, 1981 in San Francisco, California
Source: *NewYTBS 81; WhoAmW 75;
WhoWorJ 72*

Fraker, William A
American. Filmmaker
Cinematographer for *The Exorcist; Looking
for Mr. Goodbar; Sharky's Machine.*
b. 1923 in Los Angeles, California
Source: *VarWW 85*

Frampton, Peter
[Humble Pie]
American. Singer, Songwriter
Album *Frampton Comes Alive!* 1976, sold
  over 12 million copies.
b. Apr 22, 1950 in Beckenham, England
Source: *BkPepl; EncPR&S 74; IlEncRk;*
RkOn 74; WhoAm 82

Franca, Celia
English. Ballerina, Choreographer
Founded National Ballet of Canada, Toronto,
  1951.
b. Jun 25, 1921 in London, England
Source: *CurBio 56; WhoAm 74, 76, 78, 80,*
82; WhoAmW 74; WhoWor 78

Francaix, Jean
French. Composer, Musician
b. May 23, 1912 in Le Mans, France
Source: *NewEOp 71; OxMus*

France, Anatole, pseud.
[Jacques Anatole Thibault]
French. Author, Critic, Poet
Wrote *Penguin Island,* 1908; won Nobel
  Prize, 1921.
b. Apr 16, 1844 in Paris, France
d. Oct 12, 1924 in Tours, France
Source: *AtlBL; BbD; BiD&SB; CasWL;*
ClDMEL; CyWA; DcBiA; DcEuL; EncWL;
EvEuW; LongCTC; ModRL; NewC; OxEng;
OxFr; PenC EUR; RComWL; REn; TwCA,
SUP; TwCWr; WhoTwCL

France, Harry Clinton
American. Journalist, Lecturer
b. Jul 17, 1890 in Richmondville, New York
d. Jan 18, 1972
Source: *WhAm 5*

France, Pierre Mendes
see: Mendes-France, Pierre

Francesca da Rimini
Italian. Noblewoman
Killed by husband upon discovery of affair;
  subject of famous episode in Dante's
  Inferno.
d. 1285
Source: *InWom; NewC; REn*

Francescatti, Zino Rene
French. Musician
b. Aug 9, 1902 in Marseilles, France
Source: *CurBio 47; IntWW 74; WhoAm 74,*
76, 78, 80, 82; WhoMus 72; WhoWor 78

Francesco de Medici
see: Medici, Francesco de

Franchi, Sergio
Italian. Singer
Source: *BioIn 6, 7; WhoHol A*

Franciosa, Anthony
[Anthony Papaleo]
American. Actor
Star of TV series "Name of the Game,"
  1968-72; "Matt Helm," 1975-76.
b. Oct 25, 1928 in New York, New York
Source: *BiE&WWA; CurBio 61; FilmgC;*
IntMPA 82; WhoAm 74, 76, 78, 80, 82;
WhoHol B; WhoWor 74

Francis I
French. King
b. 1494
d. 1547
Source: *BioIn 10; NewCol 75*

Francis, Anne
"The Little Queen of Soap Opera"
American. Actress
Played child roles on radio; was TV detective
  in "Honey West," 1965-66.
b. Sep 16, 1930 in Ossining, New York
Source: *FilmEn; FilmgC; IntMPA 76, 77, 78,*
79, 80, 81, 82; MotPP; MovMk; WhoHol A;
WorEFlm; WrDr 76

Francis, Arlene
[Mrs. Martin Gabel; Arlene Francis
  Kazanjian]
American. Actress
Best known as panelist on TV game show
  "What's My Line?," 1950-67.
b. Oct 20, 1908 in Boston, Massachusetts
Source: *BiE&WWA; CelR; ConAu 89; CurBio*
56; FilmgC; ForWC 70; InWom; IntMPA 76,
77, 78, 79, 80, 81, 82; NewYTET; NotNAT;
WhoAm 80, 82; WhoAmW 77; WhoHol A;
WhoThe 72, 77

Francis, Connie
[Concetta Maria Franconero]
American. Singer
Sang title song, starred in *Where the Boys*
Are, 1963.
b. Dec 12, 1938 in Newark, New Jersey
Source: *AmSCAP 66; CurBio 62; FilmgC;*
InWom; IntMPA 75, 76, 77, 78, 79, 80, 81,
82; MotPP; WhoHol A

Francis, Dick
Welsh. Author
Ex-champion steeplechase jockey; wrote horse
  racing mysteries: *Whip Hand,* 1979; *Break-*
In, 1986.
b. Oct 31, 1920 in Tenby, Wales
Source: *ConAu 5NR; ConLC 2; ConNov 76;*
CurBio 81; EncMys; Who 85; WhoAm 82, 84

Francis, Emile Percy
"Cat"
Canadian. Hockey Player, Hockey Executive
Goalie, 1946-52; pres., GM, St. Louis Blues,
1978--.
b. Sep 13, 1926 in North Battleford,
Saskatchewan
Source: *CurBio 68; WhoE 74; WhoHcky 73*

Francis, Freddie
English. Filmmaker, Director
Won Oscar for cinematography of *Sons and
Lovers,* 1960.
b. 1917 in London, England
Source: *VarWW 85*

Francis, Genie
American. Actress
Played Laura on daytime soap opera
"General Hospital," 1977-81.
b. May 26, 1962 in Los Angeles, California
Source: *BioIn 12; VarWW 85*

Francis, James Bicheno
"The Father of Modern Hydraulic
Engineering"
English. Engineer
Developed hydraulic turbine.
b. May 18, 1815 in Southleigh, England
d. Sep 18, 1892 in Boston, Massachusetts
Source: *Alli; AmBi; ApCAB; DcNAA; NatCAB
9; TwCBDA; WhAm HS*

Francis, Kay
[Katherine Gibbs]
American. Actress
Glamorous star of 30s films including *The
White Angel;* retired, 1946.
b. Jan 13, 1903 in Oklahoma City,
Oklahoma
d. Aug 26, 1968 in New York, New York
Source: *BiDFilm; CmMov; FilmEn; Film 2;
FilmgC; InWom; MotPP; MovMk; OxFilm;
ThFT; WhAm 5; WhScrn 74, 77; WhoHol B;
WorEFlm*

Francis, Russ(ell Ross)
American. Football Player
b. Apr 3, 1953 in Seattle, Washington
Source: *BioIn 10; WhoAm 82*

Francis, Sam
American. Artist
b. Jul 25, 1923
Source: *IntWW 79; WhoAm 82*

Francis, Thomas, Jr.
American. Scientist, Educator
b. Jul 15, 1900 in Gas City, Indiana
d. Oct 1, 1969
Source: *BioIn 1, 5, 8, 11; WhAm 5*

Francis, Trevor
English. Soccer Player
b. Apr 19, 1954 in Plymouth, England
Source: *AmEnS*

Francis, Wallace
American. Football Player
b. Nov 7, 1951 in Franklin, Louisiana
Source: *WhoBlA 75, 77*

Francis of Assisi, Saint
[Giovanni di Bernardone]
Italian. Religious Leader
Called greatest of all Christian saints;
founded Franciscans; often depicted
preaching to birds in art.
b. 1182 in Assisi, Italy
d. Oct 3, 1226 in Porzivncola, Italy
Source: *CasWL; EuAu; EvEuW; LinLib L, S;
McGDA; McGEWB; NewC; RComWL; REn*

Francis Xavier, Saint
Spanish. Missionary
Pioneer missionary to E Indies, Japan; patron
saint of Roman Catholic missionaries; feast
day Dec 3.
b. 1506 in Pamplona, Spain
d. 1557
Source: *McGEWB; NewC*

Francisco, Peter
American. Soldier
Served in Continental army under Layfayette,
1777; many anedotes told about physical
strength.
b. 1760
d. 1831 in Richmond, Virginia
Source: *ApCAB; BioIn 11; Drake*

Franciscus, James Grover
American. Actor
Played in TV series "Mr. Novak," 1963-65;
"Longstreet," 1971-72.
b. Jan 31, 1934 in Clayton, Missouri
Source: *FilmgC; IntMPA 75, 76, 77, 78, 79,
80, 81, 82; MotPP; WhoAm 74, 76, 78, 80,
82; WhoHol A*

Franck, Cesar Auguste
French. Musician, Composer
Organist known today for oratorios,
symphonic poems, piano pieces.
b. Dec 10, 1822 in Liege, Belgium
d. Nov 8, 1890 in Paris, France
Source: *AtlBL; OxFr; REn*

Franck, James
American. Physicist, Educator
b. Aug 26, 1882 in Hamburg, Germany
d. May 21, 1964
Source: *BioIn 3, 4, 5, 6, 7, 9, 11; CurBio 57, 64*

Franco, Francisco
Spanish. Political Leader
Dictator who overthrew republican
    opposition, headed oppressive regime, 1936-
    75.
b. Dec 4, 1892 in El Ferrol, Spain
d. Nov 20, 1975 in Madrid, Spain
Source: *BioNews 75; CurBio 42, 54, 76N; LinLib S; McGEWB; REn*

Francois, Samson
French. Musician
b. May 18, 1924 in Frankfurt, Germany
d. Sep 22, 1970 in Paris, France
Source: *NewYTBE 70; WhAm 5*

Frank, Anne
German. Diarist
Diary depicted life as Jew during WW II.
b. Jun 12, 1929 in Frankfurt, Germany
d. Mar 1945
Source: *HerW; InWom; REn; TwCWr*

Frank, Bruno
German. Author
b. Jun 13, 1887 in Stuttgart, Germany
d. Jun 20, 1945 in Beverly Hills, California
Source: *AmAu&B; ClDMEL; CnMD; EncWL; McGEWD; ModGL; ModWD; OxGer; REn; TwCA, SUP*

Frank, Gerold
American. Author
b. 1907 in Cleveland, Ohio
Source: *Au&Wr 71; BioIn 5, 7, 8, 9; WhoAm 82*

Frank, Hans
German. Nazi Leader
Hitler's head of programing, 1939 to war's
    end; hung for war crimes.
b. May 23, 1900
d. Oct 16, 1946 in Nuremberg, Germany
Source: *BioIn 1, 8; CurBio 41, 46; EncTR; ObitOF 79; WhWW-II*

Frank, Jerome David
American. Psychiatrist, Educator, Author
b. May 30, 1909 in New York, New York
Source: *AmM&WS 73S; BioIn 4, 9; ConAu 5R, 3NR; WhoAm 74, 76, 78, 80, 82; WhoE 74, 74; WhoWorJ 72*

Frank, Johann Peter
German. Physician
b. Mar 14, 1745 in Rodalben, Germany
d. Apr 24, 1821 in Vienna, Austria
Source: *BioIn 5, 6, 9, 11; WebBD 80*

Frank, Waldo
American. Author
b. Aug 25, 1889 in Long Branch, New
    Jersey
d. Jan 9, 1967 in White Plains, New York
Source: *AmAu&B; AmNov; CnDAL; ConAmA; ConAmL; ConAu 25R, 93; CurBio 40, 67; DcLEL; ModAL; OxAmL; PenC AM; REn; REnAL; TwCA, SUP; WhAm 4; WhNAA*

Frankau, Gilbert
English. Author
b. Apr 21, 1884 in London, England
d. Nov 4, 1952 in Hove, England
Source: *ChhPo S1, S2; DcLEL; EncMys; EvLB; LongCTC; NewC; REn; TwCA, SUP; WhoLA*

Frankau, Pamela
[Mrs. Eliot Naylor]
English. Author
Popular novels include *Winged House*, 1953;
    The Bridge, 1957.
b. Jan 8, 1908 in London, England
d. Jun 8, 1967 in Hampstead, England
Source: *AmAu&B; AmWomWr; CathA 1930; ConAu 25R; DcLEL; EvLB; LongCTC; NewC; PenC ENG; REn; ScF&FL 1; TwCA, SUP; TwCWr; WhAm 4; WhLit*

Frankel, Charles
American. Historian, Philosopher,
    Government Official
Philosophy professor who was Lyndon
    Johnson's assistant secretary of State, 1965-
    67; resigned to protest Vietnam War.
b. Dec 13, 1917 in New York, New York
d. May 10, 1979 in Bedford Hills, New
    York
Source: *AmAu&B; BioIn 4, 7; ConAu 5R, 89, 4NR; CurBio 66, 79; DrAS 78P; NewYTBS 79; WhAm 7; WhoAm 74, 76, 78; WhoAmP 73, 75, 77*

Frankel, Emily
American. Dancer, Choreographer
b. in New York, New York
Source: *BioIn 9*

Frankel, Max
American. Journalist
b. Apr 3, 1930 in Gera, Germany
Source: *ConAu 65; WhoAm 74, 76, 78, 80, 82; WhoS&SW 82; WhoWorJ 72*

Franken, Rose
American. Author, Dramatist
b. Dec 28, 1898 in Gainesville, Texas
Source: *AmAu&B; AmNov; Au&Wr 71;*
BiE&WWA; BioIn 1, 2, 4, 6; CnMD; CurBio
47; TwCA SUP

Frankenheimer, John
American. Director
Began career in TV; directed over 125 TV
    plays; films include *Birdman of Alcatraz.*
b. Feb 19, 1930 in Malba, New York
Source: *BiDFilm; CurBio 64; DcFM; FilmgC;*
IntMPA 75, 76, 77, 78, 79, 80, 81, 82;
MovMk; NewYTET; OxFilm; WhoAm 74, 76,
78, 80, 82; WhoWor 74; WorEFlm

Frankenstein, Alfred Victor
American. Critic, Author, Educator
Music, art critic, San Francisco *Chronicle,*
    1934-65; curator, author books on
    American art.
b. Oct 5, 1906 in Chicago, Illinois
d. Jun 22, 1981 in San Francisco, California
Source: *Baker 78; ConAu 2NR, 102, 1R;*
DrAS 74H; WhoAm 74, 76, 78, 80; WhoWest
74; WhoWor 74

Frankenthaler, Helen
[Mrs. Robert Motherwell]
American. Artist
Abstract expressionist; numerous one-woman
    shows, 1950s--.
b. Dec 12, 1928 in New York, New York
Source: *CelR; CurBio 66; DcCAA 71;*
InWom; IntWW 74; WhoAm 80, 82;
WhoAmA 73; WhoWor 78

Frankfurter, Alfred Moritz
American. Editor, Art Critic
Editor, *Art News,* 1936-65.
b. Oct 4, 1906 in Chicago, Illinois
d. May 12, 1965 in Jerusalem, Israel
Source: *DcAmB S7*

Frankfurter, Felix
American. Supreme Court Justice
b. Nov 15, 1882 in Vienna, Austria
d. Feb 22, 1965 in Washington, District of
    Columbia
Source: *AmAu&B; CurBio 41, 57, 65;*
DcLEL; EncAB-H; OxAmL; REn; REnAL;
WebAB; WhAm 4; WhNAA

Frankl, Viktor E
Austrian. Psychiatrist, Author
b. Mar 26, 1905 in Vienna, Austria
Source: *ConAu 65; WhoAm 74, 76, 78, 80,*
82; WhoWor 78; WhoWorJ 72

Franklin, Aretha
[Mrs. Glynn Turman]
"Queen of Soul"
American. Singer
Hits include "Respect," "Baby I Love You,"
    1967; "Freeway of Love," 1985.
b. Mar 25, 1942 in Memphis, Tennessee
Source: *BkPepl; CelR; CurBio 68; Ebony 1;*
EncJzS 70; HerW; IlEncBM 82; InWom;
WhoAm 80, 82; WhoBlA 75

Franklin, Benjamin
[Richard Saunders, pseud.]
American. Statesman, Scientist, Author
Published *Poor Richard's Almanack,* 1732-57;
    invented lightning rod, bifocal glasses.
b. Jan 17, 1706 in Boston, Massachusetts
d. Apr 17, 1790 in Philadelphia,
    Pennsylvania
Source: *Alli; AmAu; AmAu&B; AmBi; AmWr;*
ApCAB; AtlBL; BbD; BiAUS; BiD&SB;
BiDrAC; CasWL; ChhPo, S1, S2; CnDAL;
CrtT 3; CyAL 1; CyWA; DcAmAu; DcAmB;
DcEnL; DcLEL; DcNAA; Drake; EncAB-H;
EvLB; MouLC 2; NewC; OxAmL; OxEng;
PenC AM; RComWL; REn; REnAL;
TwCBDA; WebAB; WebE&AL; WhAm HS;
WhAmP

Franklin, Bonnie Gail
American. Actress, Dancer
Starred on Broadway in *Applause,* 1970-71;
    TV series "One Day at a Time."
b. Jan 6, 1944 in Santa Monica, California
Source: *WhoAm 78, 80, 82; WhoHol A*

Franklin, Frederic
English. Dancer
b. Jun 13, 1914 in Liverpool, England
Source: *BioIn 3, 10; CurBio 43; WhoAm 74*

Franklin, Irene
American. Actress, Songwriter
Performed on stage in *Sweet Adeline; Merrily*
We Roll Along.
b. Jun 13, 1876 in New York, New York
d. Jun 16, 1941 in Englewood, New Jersey
Source: *CurBio 41; NotNAT B; WhScrn 77;*
WhThe; WhoHol B

Franklin, John
English. Explorer
Died in search of Northwest Passage, 1845;
    quest for relics and diaries continues
    today.
b. Apr 16, 1786 in Spilsby, England
d. Jun 11, 1847 in Arctic Region
Source: *Alli; ApCAB; BrAu 19; Drake; NewC;*
OxCan; OxEng

Franklin, Joseph Paul
[James Clayton Vaughan, Jr.]
American. Murderer
Arrested for killing eight blacks, wounding
    National Urban League Pres., Vernon
    Jordon, 1980.
b. 1950
Source: *BioIn 12*

Franklin, Mel(vin)
[The Temptations]
American. Singer
b. Oct 12, 1942 in Montgomery, Alabama
Source: *NF*

Franklin, Miles, pseud.
[Stella Maria Sarah Franklin]
"Brent of Bin Bin"
Australian. Author
Best known work is autobiographical *My
    Brilliant Career,* written at 16.
b. Oct 14, 1879 in Talbingo, Australia
d. Sep 19, 1954 in Sydney, Australia
Source: *CasWL; McGEWB; ModCmwL;
ModFrL; TwCWr*

Franklin, Pamela
English. Actress
Films include *The Innocents, David
    Copperfield.*
b. Feb 4, 1950 in Tokyo, Japan
Source: *FilmEn; FilmgC; IntMPA 80, 81, 82;
WhoHol A*

Frankovich, Mike J
American. Producer
With Columbia Pictures, 1955-67;
    independent, 1967--; films include *Cactus
    Flower, The Shootist.*
b. Sep 29, 1910 in Bisbee, Arizona
Source: *FilmgC; IntMPA 82; WhoAm 82;
WhoHol A; WhoWest 78; WorEFlm*

Franks, Oliver Shewell, Sir
English. Government Official
b. Feb 16, 1905 in Birmingham, England
Source: *CurBio 48; IntWW 74; NewC; Who
74; WhoWor 78*

Frantz, Chris
see: Talking Heads, The

Franz Ferdinand
Austrian. Political Leader
Archduke, whose assassination, 1914, led to
    outbreak of WW I.
b. Dec 18, 1863 in Graz, Austria
d. Jun 28, 1914 in Sarajevo, Yugoslavia
Source: *BioIn 2, 5, 6, 7, 8, 9, 10; NewCol
75; OxGer; REn; WebBD 80*

Franz Josef II
[Prince of Liechtenstein]
Liechtenstein. Ruler
b. Aug 16, 1906 in Liechtenstein
Source: *IntWW 74*

Franz Joseph I
Austrian. Ruler
Emperor of Austria, 1848-1916, king of
    Hungary, 1867-1916, whose reign was last
    great age of Austrian political, cultural
    preeminence.
b. 1830
d. 1916
Source: *BioIn 2, 3, 6, 7, 8, 10; DcCathB;
NewCol 75; OxGer; REn; WebBD 80*

Franz, Arthur
American. Actor
Films include *Jungle Patrol, Member of the
    Wedding.*
b. Feb 29, 1920 in Perth Amboy, New
    Jersey
Source: *FilmgC; IntMPA 75, 76, 77; Vers B;
WhoHol A*

Franz, Eduard
American. Actor
Original member of Provincetown Players;
    appeared in films *The Emperor Jones, The
    Ten Commandments.*
b. Oct 31, 1902 in Milwaukee, Wisconsin
d. Feb 10, 1983 in Los Angeles, California
Source: *MotPP; WhoHol A; WhoThe 77*

Frasconi, Antonio
American. Artist, Author
b. Apr 28, 1919 in Montevideo, Uruguay
Source: *AmAu&B; AnCL; ConAu 1NR;
CurBio 72; DcCAA 71; ThrBJA; WhoAm 74,
76, 78, 80, 82; WhoAmA 73; WhoE 74;
WhoGrA 62; WhoWor 78*

Fraser, Antonia Pakenham, Lady
English. Author
Wrote *Mary Queen of Scots,* 1969; mysteries
    featuring Jemima Shore.
b. Aug 27, 1932 in London, England
Source: *ConAu 85; CurBio 74; IntWW 74;
Who 74; WhoWor 78; WrDr 80*

Fraser, Bruce Austin, Sir
[Lord Fraser of North Cape]
"Tubby"
English. Admiral
Commander, British Home Fleet, WW II;
 credited with sinking German battleships
 Scharnhorst, 1943.
b. Feb 5, 1888 in Acton, England
d. Feb 12, 1981 in London, England
Source: *AnObit 1981; BioIn 1; CurBio 43, 81;
WhWW-II; Who 74*

Fraser, Dawn
Australian. Swimmer
Only swimmer to win Olympic medal in
 same event three successive Olympics--
 freestyle in 1956, 1960, 1964.
b. Sep 4, 1937 in Balmain, Australia
Source: *BioIn 7*

Fraser, Donald Mackay
American. Politician
Dem. mayor of Minneapolis, 1980--.
b. Feb 20, 1924 in Minneapolis, Minnesota
Source: *AlmAP 78; BiDrAC; CngDr 74, 77;
WhoAm 76, 78, 80, 82; WhoAmP 73, 75, 77,
79; WhoGov 72, 75, 77; WhoMW 74, 76, 78*

Fraser, Douglas Andrew
American. Labor Union Official
Pres., UAW, 1977-83.
b. Dec 18, 1916 in Glasgow, Scotland
Source: *BusPN; Ward 77C; WhoAm 78, 80,
82*

Fraser, George MacDonald
English. Author
b. Apr 2, 1925 in Carlisle, England
Source: *Au&Wr 71; ConAu 45, 2NR; WrDr
76*

Fraser, Gretchen Kunigh
American. Skier
b. 1919
Source: *BioIn 3, 6, 9, 11*

Fraser, Ian
English. Composer, Conductor
Conductor for Liza Minnelli, Sammy Davis,
 Jr.; won five Emmys for musical direction.
b. Aug 23, 1933 in Hove, England
Source: *VarWW 85*

Fraser, James Earle
American. Sculptor
b. Nov 4, 1876 in Winona, Minnesota
d. Oct 11, 1953 in Westport, Connecticut
Source: *CurBio 51, 54; DcAmB S5; WebAB;
WhAm 3*

Fraser, John Malcolm
Australian. Political Leader
b. Mar 21, 1930 in Melbourne, Australia
Source: *IntWW 74; WhoWor 78*

Fratianne, Linda
American. Figure Skater
Won silver medal, 1980 Olympics.
b. Aug 2, 1960 in Los Angeles, California
Source: *BioIn 11, 12*

Fraunhofer, Joseph von
German. Physicist
Mapped dark lines (Fraunhofer lines) in solar
 spectrum, 1814; improved micrometers,
 telescopes.
b. Mar 6, 1787 in Straubing, Germany
d. Jun 7, 1826 in Munich, Germany
Source: *AsBiEn; DcScB; McGEWB; WebBD
80; WhDW*

Frawley, Dennis
American. Critic
b. Jul 12, 1942 in Minneapolis, Minnesota
Source: *BioIn 10; MugS*

Frawley, William
American. Actor
Played Fred Mertz on TV series "I Love
 Lucy," 1951-60.
b. Feb 26, 1893 in Burlington, Iowa
d. Mar 3, 1966 in Los Angeles, California
Source: *Film 1; FilmgC; MotPP; MovMk;
Vers B; WhAm 4; WhScrn 74, 77; WhoHol B*

Frayn, Michael
English. Author
b. Sep 8, 1933 in London, England
Source: *Au&Wr 71; BioIn 10; ConAu 5R;
ConLC 3, 7; ConNov 72, 76; ModBrL; Who
74; WorAu; WrDr 76*

Frazer, James George, Sir
Scottish. Anthropologist
Best known for lengthy study of magic,
 religion *The Golden Bough,* 1915.
b. 1854 in Glasgow, Scotland
d. May 7, 1941 in Cambridge, England
Source: *Alli SUP; AtlBL; CasWL; Chambr 3;
DcEnA AP; DcLEL; EvLB; LongCTC; NewC;
OxEng; PenC ENG; REn; TwCA, SUP;
WebE&AL*

Frazetta, Frank
American. Artist, Cartoonist
Drew Buck Rogers, Flash Gordon; known
 for Tarzan, Conan comic book covers.
b. Feb 9, 1928 in Brooklyn, New York
Source: *BioIn 10, 11; EncSF; FanAl; WhoAm
80, 84; WorECom*

Frazier, Brenda Diana Dudd
[Mrs. Robert F. Chatfield-Taylor]
American. Socialite
Made headlines, 1930s-40s for glamourous life
with friends such as Bette Davis, Duke of
Windsor.
b. 1921
d. May 3, 1982 in Boston, Massachusetts
Source: *InWom; NewYTBS 82*

Frazier, Dallas June
American. Singer, Songwriter
b. Oct 27, 1939 in Spiro, Oklahoma
Source: *EncFCWM 69; WhoAm 78, 80, 82*

Frazier, Edward Franklin
American. Sociologist, Educator
Wrote *The Negro Family in the United
States,* 1939.
b. Sep 24, 1897 in Baltimore, Maryland
d. May 17, 1962 in Washington, District of
Columbia
Source: *DcAmB S7; WebBD 80*

Frazier, Joe
"Smokin' Joe"
American. Boxer
Won gold medal, 1964 Olympics; pro
heavyweight champ, 1970-73.
b. Jan 17, 1944 in Beaufort, South Carolina
Source: *CelR; CurBio 71; NewYTBE 70;
WhoAm 74, 76, 78, 80, 82; WhoBlA 75;
WhoBox 74*

Frazier, Walt
"Clyde"
American. Basketball Player
Forward, 1967-80, who was four-time NBA
All-Star.
b. Mar 29, 1945 in Atlanta, Georgia
Source: *CelR; CurBio 73; NewYTBE 72, 73;
NewYTBS 74; OfNBA 81; WhoAm 76, 78,
80, 82; WhoBbl 73*

Frederic, Harold
American. Author
Produced finest novel *Damnation of Theron
Ware,* 1896.
b. Aug 19, 1856 in Utica, New York
d. Oct 19, 1898 in Henley, England
Source: *Alli SUP; AmAu; AmAu&B; AmWr;
BbD; BiD&SB; CasWL; Chambr 3; DcAmAu;
EvLB; OxAmL; REnAL; WhAm HS*

Freberg, Stan
American. Satirist
b. Aug 7, 1926 in Pasadena, California
Source: *AmSCAP 66; WhoAm 74*

Freccia, Massimo
Italian. Conductor
b. Sep 19, 1906 in Florence, Italy
Source: *IntWW 74; WhoAm 74; WhoMus 72;
WhoWor 78*

Frechette, Louis-Honore
Canadian. Poet
Best known French-Canadian poet of 19th c.:
Les Oiseaux, 1880.
b. Nov 16, 1839 in Levis, Quebec
d. May 31, 1908 in Montreal, Quebec
Source: *ApCAB; BbD; BbtC; BiD&SB;
CanWr; DcCathB; DcNaB S2; DcNAA;
LinLib L; MacDCB 78; McGEWB; OxAmL;
OxCan; REn*

Frederick I
[Frederick Barbarossa]
Emperor
b. 1123
d. 1190
Source: *BioIn 10; LinLib S; McGEWB;
NewC; NewCol 75; WebBD 80*

Frederick II
Emperor
b. 1194
d. 1250
Source: *AsBiEn; McGEWB; NewCol 75;
WebBD 80*

Frederick III
German. Emperor
b. 1831 in Potsdam, Germany
d. Jun 15, 1888 in Berlin, Germany
Source: *BioIn 9*

Frederick IX
Danish. King
b. Mar 11, 1899 in Copenhagen, Denmark
d. 1972
Source: *BioIn 1, 2, 3, 4, 5, 6, 9, 10; NewCol
75; NewYTBE 72; WebBD 80*

Frederick Augustus I
see: Augustus II

Frederick the Great
[Frederick II]
German. King
b. Jan 24, 1712 in Berlin, Germany
d. Aug 17, 1786 in Berlin, Germany
Source: *LinLib L, S; NewC; NewCol 75;
OxFr; OxMus; REn; WebBD 80*

Frederick Louis
English. Prince
b. Jan 20, 1707 in Hannover, Germany
d. Mar 20, 1751 in London, England
Source: *BioIn 1, 3, 4, 5, 6, 7, 9, 10, 11;*
NewCol 75; WebBD 80

Frederick William
see: Friedrich Wilhelm

Frederick William I
Prussian. King
b. Aug 15, 1688 in Berlin, Germany
d. May 31, 1740 in Potsdam, Germany
Source: *BioIn 1, 11; NewCol 75; WebBD 80*

Frederick, Pauline
[Beatrice Pauline Libby]
American. Actress
Silent screen star beginning, 1915, in *Bella*
  Donna; Madame X.
b. Aug 12, 1885 in Boston, Massachusetts
d. Aug 19, 1938 in Los Angeles, California
Source: *AmBi; FilmEn; Film 1; FilmgC;*
MovMk; NotAW; OxFilm; ThFT; TwYS;
WhAm 1; WhScrn 74, 77; WhoHol B

Frederick, Pauline
American. Broadcast Journalist
b. Feb 13, 1908 in Gallitzen, Pennsylvania
Source: *ConAu 102; CurBio 54; WhoAm 82;*
WhoUN 75

Fredericks, Carlton
American. Nutritionist
b. Oct 23, 1910 in New York, New York
Source: *AuNews 1; BioNews 74; ConAu 53*

Frederickson, H Gray
American. Producer
Films include *The Good, the Bad and the*
  Ugly; won Oscar for *THe Godfather, Part*
  II, 1974.
b. Jul 21, 1937 in Oklahoma City, Oklahoma
Source: *VarWW 85*

Frederika Louise
Greek. Consort
Queen of Greece, 1947-64; in self-imposed
  exile after monarchy overthrow, 1973.
b. Apr 18, 1917 in Blankenburg, Germany
d. Feb 6, 1981 in Madrid, Spain
Source: *BioIn 2, 3, 4, 5, 6, 9; CurBio 55, 81;*
InWom; NewYTBS 81

Free, World B
[Lloyd Free]
American. Basketball Player
b. Dec 9, 1953 in Atlanta, Georgia
Source: *BioIn 11*

Freed, Alan
American. Radio Performer, Songwriter
b. Dec 15, 1922 in Johnstown, Pennsylvania
d. Jan 20, 1965 in Palm Springs, California
Source: *WhScrn 77*

Freed, Arthur
American. Songwriter, Producer
b. Sep 9, 1894 in Charleston, South Carolina
d. Apr 12, 1973 in Los Angeles, California
Source: *AmPS; AmSCAP 66; BiDAmM;*
BiDFilm; CmMov; ConAu 41R; DcFM;
FilmgC; NewYTBE 73; OxFilm; WhAm 5;
WhoWest 74; WorEFlm

Freed, Bert
American. Actor
Character actor, 1957--.
b. Nov 3, 1919 in New York, New York
Source: *WhoAm 74, 76, 78, 80, 82; WhoHol*
A

Freedman, Gerald
American. Director
Won Obie award for *Taming of the Shrew,*
  1960.
b. Jun 25, 1927 in Lorain, Ohio
Source: *AmSCAP 66; NewYTBE 73; NotNAT;*
WhoAm 82; WhoOp 76; WhoThe 77

Freehan, Bill (William Ashley)
American. Baseball Player
Catcher, Detroit Tigers, 1961-76; AL All-Star
  team, 1965-73.
b. Nov 29, 1941 in Detroit, Michigan
Source: *BaseEn 85; WhoAm 74; WhoProB 73*

Freeling, Nicolas
English. Author
b. Mar 3, 1927 in London, England
Source: *ConAu 49, 1NR; ConNov 72, 76;*
EncMys; TwCWr; WorAu

Freeman, Al, Jr.
American. Actor
Starred in "Hotel Baltimore"; "One Life to
  Live."
b. Mar 21, 1934 in San Antonio, Texas
Source: *DrBlPA; FilmgC; NotNAT; WhoHol*
A; WhoThe 77, 81

Freeman, "Bud" (Lawrence)
American. Musician
b. Apr 13, 1906 in Chicago, Illinois
Source: *AmSCAP 66; WhoAm 74; WhoJazz*
72; WhoWor 78

Freeman, Douglas S
American. Historian, Journalist
b. May 16, 1886 in Lynchburg, Virginia
d. Jun 13, 1953 in Richmond, Virginia
Source: *AmAu&B; CyWA; DcAmB S5;*
OxAmL; REn; REnAL; TwCA, SUP; WebAB;
WhAm 3

Freeman, Joseph
Author
b. Oct 7, 1897 in Ukraine, Russia
d. Aug 9, 1965
Source: *AmAu&B; AmNov; ConAu 89;*
OxAmL; TwCA, SUP; WhAm 4

Freeman, Mary E Wilkins
American. Author
b. Oct 31, 1852 in Randolph, Massachusetts
d. Mar 13, 1930 in Metuchen, New Jersey
Source: *AmAu&B; AmBi; AmLY; CarSB;*
CasWL; ChhPo, S1, S2; CnDAL; ConAmL;
DcAmAu; DcAmB; DcEnA AP; DcLEL;
DcNAA; InWom; LongCTC; NotAW; OxAmL;
OxEng; PenC AM; REn; REnAL; TwCA;
WebAB; WhAm 1

Freeman, Orville Lothrop
American. Government Official
b. May 9, 1918 in Minneapolis, Minnesota
Source: *BiDrUSE; CurBio 56; IntWW 74;*
WhoAm 74, 76, 78, 80, 82; WhoAmP 73;
WhoWor 78

Freeman, R(ichard) Austin
English. Author
Detective writer; created scientific detective
  Dr. John Thorndyke: *The Cat's Eye*, 1927.
b. Apr 11, 1862 in London, England
d. Sep 30, 1943 in Gravesend, England
Source: *BioIn 4, 7, 9, 11; EncMys; EvLB;*
NewC; REn; TwCA, SUP; TwCCr&M 80

Freeman, Seth
American. Writer, Producer
Won Emmy for script of TV show "Lou
  Grant," 1980.
b. Jan 6, 1945 in Los Angeles, California
Source: *VarWW 85; WhoAm 82*

Freemantle, Brian Harry
English. Author
Mystery writer; created detective Charlie
  Muffin: *November Man*, 1976.
b. Jun 10, 1936 in Southampton, England
Source: *ConAu 65; TwCCr&M 80*

Freer, Charles Lang
American. Businessman
Donated Freer Gallery, Washington, DC;
  contains unique work of Whistler.
b. Feb 25, 1856 in Kingston, New York
d. Sep 25, 1919 in New York, New York
Source: *AmBi; BioIn 5, 9, 11; DcAmB;*
WhAm 1

Frehley, Ace
[Kiss]
American. Singer, Musician
Guitarist; released solo album, 1978.
b. Apr 27, 1951 in Bronx, New York
Source: *RkOn 85*

Frei, Eduardo (Montalva Eduardo)
Chilean. Lawyer, Political Leader
Pres. of Chile, 1964-70.
b. Jan 16, 1911 in Santiago, Chile
d. Jan 22, 1982 in Santiago, Chile
Source: *AnObit 1982; CurBio 65, 82; IntWW*
75, 76, 77, 78, 79, 80; IntYB 78, 79;
McGEWB; WhoWor 74

Freidberg, Jerry
American. Educator
b. 1938 in Brooklyn, New York
Source: *BioIn 10*

Freleng, Friz
American. Director, Producer
Won Emmys for "Halloween is Grinch
  Night," 1978; "The Grinch Grinches the
  Cat-in-The-Hat," 1982.
b. Aug 21, 1906 in Kansas City, Missouri
Source: *VarWW 85*

Frelich, Phyllis
American. Actress
Deaf actress who won Tony for *Children of*
  a Lesser God, 1980.
b. 1944 in Devils Lake, North Dakota
Source: *BioIn 12; NewYTBS 80; WhoAm 84*

Fremont, John Charles
American. Explorer, Historian
First Republican candidate for US pres.,
  1856.
b. Jan 21, 1813 in Savannah, Georgia
d. Jul 13, 1890 in New York, New York
Source: *Alli, SUP; AmAu; AmAu&B; AmBi;*
ApCAB; BbD; BiAUS; BiD&SB; BiDSA;
BiDrAC; CyAL 2; DcAmAu; DcAmB; DcNAA;
Drake; EncAB-H; OxAmL; REn; REnAL;
TwCBDA; WebAB; WhAm HS; WhAmP

Fremont-Smith, Frank
American. Scientist, Physician, Engineer
b. Mar 19, 1895 in Saint Augustine, Florida
d. Feb 27, 1974
Source: *NewYTBS 74; WhAm 6; WhoAm 74*

French, Daniel Chester
American. Sculptor
b. Apr 20, 1850 in Exeter, New Hampshire
d. Oct 7, 1931 in Stockbridge, Massachusetts
Source: *AmBi; ApCAB; DcAmB S1; OxAmL;
REnAL; TwCBDA; WebAB; WhAm 1*

French, Jay Jay
[Twisted Sister]
American. Musician
Guitarist with heavy metal group formed
   1976.
b. Jul 20, 1954 in New York, New York
Source: *NF*

French, Marilyn
[Mara Solwoska, pscud.]
American. Author
Wrote *The Women's Room*, 1977; *House of
Mirth*, 1981.
b. Nov 21, 1929 in New York, New York
Source: *BioIn 11; ConAu 69, 3NR; ConLC
10, 18; WhoAm 82*

French, Robert T
American. Businessman
Started business, 1880, that eventually
   produced French's mustard, 1904.
b. 1823 in Ithaca, New York
d. 1893
Source: *Entr*

Freneau, Philip Morin
American. Poet, Journalist
b. Jan 2, 1752 in New York, New York
d. Dec 18, 1832 in Monmouth County, New
   Jersey
Source: *Alli; AmAu; AmAu&B; AmBi;
ApCAB; AtlBL; BiD&SB; CasWL; Chambr 3;
ChhPo, S1; CnDAL; CrtT 3; CyAL 1; CyWA;
DcAmAu; DcAmB; DcLEL; DcNAA; Drake;
EncAB-H; EvLB; MouLC 3; OxAmL; OxEng;
PenC AM; REn; REnAL; WebAB;
WebE&AL; WhAm HS*

Freni, Mirella
Italian. Opera Singer
b. 1936 in Modena, Italy
Source: *IntWW 74; WhoAm 82; WhoMus 72*

Frescobaldi, Girolamo
Italian. Musician, Composer
b. 1583 in Ferrara, Italy
d. Mar 2, 1644 in Rome, Italy
Source: *AtlBL; NewCol 75; WebBD 80*

Freshfield, Douglas William
English. Geographer, Mountaineer
Made first ascent of Mt. Elbrus, 1868;
   numerous mountaineering books include
   The Italian Alps, 1875.
b. Apr 27, 1845 in Hampstead, England
d. Feb 9, 1934 in Forest Rowe, England
Source: *DcNaB 1931; WhE&EA; WhLit*

Freuchen, Peter
Danish. Author, Explorer
Explored Arctic, 1906-08; wrote *Eskimo*,
   1930; *Arctic Adventure*, 1936.
b. Feb 20, 1886
d. Sep 2, 1957 in Anchorage, Alaska
Source: *AuBYP; PenC EUR; TwCA, SUP;
WhAm 3*

Freud, Anna
English. Psychoanalyst
Daughter of Sigmund Freud; authority on
   childhood mental disorders.
b. Dec 3, 1895 in Vienna, Austria
d. Oct 8, 1982 in London, England
Source: *AnObit 1982; Au&Wr 71; BiDrAPA
77; CurBio 79, 83; IntAu&W 77; IntWW 74,
75, 76, 77, 78; NewYTBS 82; WhoAmW 68,
70, 72, 74; WhoWor 74, 78; WrDr 76, 80*

Freud, Clement Raphael
English. Author
b. Apr 24, 1924
Source: *Who 74*

Freud, Lucian
English. Artist
b. Dec 8, 1922
Source: *IntWW 74; Who 74*

Freud, Martha Bernays
Austrian. Celebrity Relative
b. 1861
d. 1951
Source: *BioIn 1, 2, 8*

Freud, Sigmund
Austrian. Psychoanalyst
Founded psychoanalysis, 1895-1900; first to
   develop concept of subconscious mind.
b. May 6, 1856 in Freiberg, Moravia
d. Sep 23, 1939 in London, England
Source: *AtlBL; BiDPara; CasWL; ChhPo S2;
CyWA; EncWL; FilmgC; LongCTC; NewC;
OxGer; PenC EUR; RComWL; REn; TwCA,
SUP; TwCWr; WhAm HSA, 4; WhoLA;
WhoTwCL*

Frey, Charles N
American. Chemist
b. 1885
Source: *BioIn 1, 2, 3, 9, 11*

Frey, Glenn
[The Eagles]
American. Musician, Songwriter, Singer
Released solo album *No Fun Aloud*, 1982.
b. Nov 6, 1948 in Detroit, Michigan
Source: *WhoAm 82*

Frey, Jim (James Gottfried)
American. Baseball Player
Minor league outfielder, who was manager,
  KC, 1980-81; Chicago Cubs, 1984-86.
b. May 26, 1931 in Cleveland, Ohio
Source: *BaseReg 86*

Freydis, Ericsdotter
Icelandic. Explorer
Source: *BioIn 11*

Freyse, William
American. Cartoonist
b. 1899 in Detroit, Michigan
d. Mar 3, 1969 in Tucson, Arizona
Source: *BioIn 8; WorECom*

Frick, Ford Christopher
American. Baseball Executive, Journalist
Baseball commissioner, 1951-65; Hall of
  Fame, 1970.
b. Dec 19, 1894 in Wawaka, Indiana
d. Apr 8, 1978 in Bronxville, New York
Source: *CurBio 45; WhoAm 74; WhoProB 73*

Frick, Gottlob
German. Opera Singer
b. 1906 in Stuttgart, Germany
Source: *IntWW 74; WhoWor 78*

Frick, Henry Clay
American. Industrialist, Philanthropist
His house, art collection, were bequeathed to
  NYC, 1919.
b. Dec 19, 1849 in West Overton,
  Pennsylvania
d. Dec 2, 1919 in New York, New York
Source: *AmBi; ApCAB SUP; DcAmB; EncAB-
H; WebAB; WhAm 1*

Frick, Wilhelm
German. Nazi Leader
Hitler's Minister of Interior, 1933-43; hanged
  at Nuremburg trails.
b. Mar 3, 1877 in Alsenz, Germany
d. Oct 16, 1946 in Nuremberg, Germany
Source: *BioIn 1; CurBio 42, 46; EncTR;
ObitOF 79; WebBD 80; WhWW-II*

Frickie, Janie
American. Singer, Musician
Had hit single "Down to My Last Broken
  Heart," 1980; CMA's female vocalist of
  year, 1982, 1983.
b. Dec 18, 1950 in Whitney, Indiana
Source: *BioIn 11; EncFCWM 83*

Fricsay, Ferenc
Hungarian. Conductor
b. Aug 9, 1914 in Budapest, Hungary
d. Feb 20, 1963 in Basel, Switzerland
Source: *NewEOp 71*

Fried, Alfred Hermann
Austrian. Author
Founder, German peace society, 1892; won
  Nobel Peace Prize, 1911.
b. Nov 11, 1864 in Vienna, Austria
d. May 6, 1921 in Vienna, Austria
Source: *BioIn 9, 11; LinLib L; NewCol 75;
WebBD 80*

Fried, Gerald
American. Composer
Won Emmy for score of TV mini-series
  "Roots," 1977.
b. Feb 13, 1928 in New York, New York
Source: *VarWW 85*

Fried, Miriam
Israeli. Musician
b. Sep 9, 1946 in Satu Mare, Romania
Source: *BioIn 11; WhoAm 82; WhoMus 72*

Friedan, Betty Naomi Goldstein
American. Feminist, Author, Journalist
Founded NOW, 1966, pres. until 1970; wrote
  The Feminine Mystique, 1963.
b. Feb 4, 1921 in Peoria, Illinois
Source: *AmAu&B; BkPepl; ConAu 65; CurBio
70; EncAB-H; ForWC 70; IntWW 74;
NewYTBE 70, 71; WebAB; WhoAm 74, 76,
78, 80, 82; WhoAmW 77; WrDr 76*

Friedel, Charles
French. Chemist, Mineralogist
b. Mar 12, 1832 in Strasbourg, France
d. Apr 20, 1899 in Mantauban, France
Source: *BioIn 1; WebBD 80*

Friedkin, William
American. Director
Won 1971 Oscar for *The French Connection* ;
  starred in *The Exorcist,* 1973.
b. Aug 29, 1939 in Chicago, Illinois
Source: *BiDFilm; BkPepl; CelR,; ConAu 107;
FilmgC; IntMPA 80, 81, 82; MovMk; WhoAm
80, 82; WhoWest 74, 78; WhoWor 74*

Friedman, Bruce Jay
American. Author
Wrote films *Doctor Detroit,* 1983; *Splash,*
1984.
b. Apr 26, 1930 in New York, New York
Source: *AmAu&B; ConAu 9R; ConLC 3, 5;
ConNov 72, 76; DrAF 76; McGEWD;
ModAL, S1; NatPD; PenC AM; RAdv 1;
VarWW 85; WhoAm 74; WorAu; WrDr 80*

Friedman, Herbert
American. Physicist
b. Jun 21, 1916 in New York, New York
Source: *AmM&WS 73P; BioIn 6, 7, 8;
CurBio 63; WhoAm 74, 76, 78, 80, 82*

Friedman, Max
[Heavenly Twins]
American. Basketball Player
b. Jul 12, 1889 in New York, New York
d. Jan 1, 1986 in New York, New York
Source: *WhoBbl 73*

Friedman, Milton
American. Economist, Journalist
Noted conservative monetary expert who won
   Nobel Prize, 1976; wrote best seller *Free
   To Choose,* 1980.
b. Jul 31, 1912 in Brooklyn, New York
Source: *AmAu&B; AmEA 74; AmM&WS 73S;
Au&Wr 71; ConAu 1R, 1NR; EncAB-H;
IntWW 74; LinLib L; NewYTBS 76; WebAB;
WhoAm 80, 82; WhoWor 78; WhoWorJ 72*

Friedman, William
American. Author
Cryptologist who broke "Purple," 1940, the
   principle Japanese code during WW II;
   wrote many books on subject.
b. Sep 24, 1891 in Kinishev, Russia
d. Nov 12, 1969 in Washington, District of
   Columbia
Source: *AmAu&B; ObitOF 79; SpyCS; WhAm
5; WhWW-II*

Friedman, Ze'ev
Israeli. Murder Victim
b. 1944
d. Sep 5, 1972 in Munich, Germany (West)
Source: *BioIn 9*

Friedrich, Caspar David
German. Artist
b. Sep 5, 1774 in Greifswald, Germany
d. May 7, 1840 in Dresden, Germany
Source: *BioIn 6, 9, 10, 11; NewCol 75;
OxGer*

Friel, Brian
Irish. Dramatist
b. Jan 9, 1929 in Ireland
Source: *Au&Wr 71; CnThe; ConAu 21R;
ConLC 5; McGEWD; ModBrL S1; ModWD;
NotNAT; REnWD; Who 74; WhoAm 82;
WhoThe 77; WhoWor 78; WorAu; WrDr 80*

Friend, Bob (Robert Bartmess)
"Warrior"
American. Baseball Player
b. Nov 24, 1930 in Lafayette, Indiana
Source: *BaseEn 85; BioIn 4, 5*

Friendly, Alfred
American. Journalist
With Washington *Post,* 1939-71; won Pulitzer
   for covergae of 1967 Arab-Israeli War.
b. Dec 30, 1911 in Salt Lake City, Utah
d. Nov 7, 1983 in Washington, District of
   Columbia
Source: *BlueB 76; ConAu 101, 111; IntAu&W
82; IntWW 80, 81, 82, 83; NewYTBS 83;
WhoAm 78; WhoWor 78*

Friendly, Ed
American. Producer
Co-creator, "Laugh-In," 1967; producer,
   "Little House on the Prairie."
b. Apr 8, 1922 in New York, New York
Source: *NewYTET; WhoAm 78, 80, 82;
WhoTelC*

Friendly, Edwin Samson
American. Newspaper Executive
b. Jun 15, 1884 in Elmira, New York
d. Jul 9, 1970
Source: *BioIn 2, 7, 9; CurBio 49, 70;
NewYTBE 70; WhNAA*

Friendly, Fred W
American. Producer
Known for TV news, public affairs; pres.,
   CBS News, 1964-66.
b. Oct 30, 1915 in New York, New York
Source: *AmAu&B; ConAu 21R, 21R; CurBio
57; IntMPA 75; IntWW 74; NewYTET;
WhoAm 80, 82; WhoTelC*

Fries, Charles W
American. Producer
Produced *The Cat People,* 1982.
b. Sep 30, 1928 in Cincinnati, Ohio
Source: *ConTFT 2; VarWW 85*

Friese-Greene, William Edward
[William Edward Green]
British. Inventor, Photographer
Built first practical movie camera, 1889;
subject of film *The Magic Box*, 1951.
b. Sep 7, 1855 in Bristol, England
d. 1921 in London, England
Source: *BioIn 1, 2, 3, 4, 10; FilmEn; FilmgC;
OxFilm; WorEFlm*

Friesz, Othon
French. Artist
b. 1879
d. Jan 11, 1949
Source: *BioIn 1, 2*

Friganza, Trixie
[Delia O'Callahan]
American. Actress, Singer
Character actress in films including
Gentlemen Prefer Blondes.
b. Nov 29, 1870 in Grenola, Kansas
d. Feb 27, 1955 in Flintridge, California
Source: *Film 2; TwYS; WhScrn 74, 77;
WhThe; WhoHol B; WhoStg 1908*

Frijid Pink
[Thomas Beaudry; Thomas Harris; Richard
Stevers; Gary Thompson; Jon Wearing;
Craig Webb; Lawrence Zelanka]
American. Music Group
Source: *RkOn 74, 84*

Frimbo, E M, pseud.
see: Whitaker, Rogers E M

Friml, Rudolf
American. Musician, Composer
b. Dec 7, 1879 in Prague, Bohemia
d. Nov 12, 1972 in Hollywood, California
Source: *AmSCAP 66; EncMT; FilmgC;
NewCBMT; NewYTBE 72; PIP&P; WebAB;
WhAm 5*

Frings, Joseph Richard
German. Religious Leader
Cardinal who denounced Nazis in sermons
during WW II.
b. Feb 6, 1887 in Neuss, Germany
d. Dec 17, 1978 in Cologne, Germany (West)
Source: *BioIn 11; NewYTBS 78; ObitOF 79;
WhoWor 76*

Frings, "Ketti"
[Katherine Hartley]
American. Dramatist, Author
Won Pulitzer for stage adaptation *Look
Homeward Angel*, 1968.
b. Feb 28, 1915 in Columbus, Ohio
d. Feb 11, 1981 in Los Angeles, California
Source: *AmAu&B; AmWomWr; AnObit 1981;
BiE&WWA; ConAu 101, 103; CurBio 60, 81;
FilmgC; InWom; McGEWD; NatPD;
NewYTBS 81; NotNAT; OhA&B; OxAmL;
REnAL; ScF&FL 1; WhoAm 74, 76, 78, 80;
WhoAmW 58A, 64, 68, 70, 72, 74, 75, 77;
WhoE 74*

Fripp, Robert
see: King Crimson

Frisch, Frankie (Frank Francis)
"The Fordham Flash"
American. Baseball Player, Baseball Manager
Infielder, 1919-37; Hall of Fame, 1947.
b. Sep 9, 1898 in New York, New York
d. Mar 12, 1973 in Wilmington, Delaware
Source: *BaseEn 85; NewYTBE 73; WhoFtbl
74; WhoProB 73*

Frisch, Karl von
German. Zoologist, Ethnologist
Won Nobel Prize in medicine, 1973, for
research on sense perception and
communication in bees.
b. Nov 20, 1886 in Vienna, Austria
d. Jun 12, 1982 in Munich, Germany (West)
Source: *AnObit 1982; ConAu 107, 85; CurBio
74; IntWW 74; McGEWB; NewYTBE 73;
WhoWor 74*

Frisch, Max
Swiss. Author, Architect
Wrote anti-semitic drama *Andorra*, 1962;
novel *I'm not Stiller*, 1961.
b. May 15, 1911 in Zurich, Switzerland
Source: *BiE&WWA; BioNews 74; CasWL;
CnMD; CnThe; ConAu 85; ConLC 3, 9, 14,
18; CroCD; CurBio 65; EncWL; EvEuW;
IntWW 74; LinLib L; McGEWB; McGEWD;
ModGL; ModWD; NotNAT; OxGer; OxThe;
PenC EUR; REn; REnWD; TwCWr; WhoThe
77, 72; WhoTwCL; WhoWor 74; WorAu*

Frisch, Ragnar
Norwegian. Economist
b. Mar 2, 1895 in Oslo, Norway
d. Jan 31, 1973 in Oslo, Norway
Source: *NewYTBE 73; WhAm 5*

Frisco, Joe
American. Actor
Vaudeville as stuttering comic in 1930s film
   shorts.
b. 1890 in Milan, Illinois
d. Feb 16, 1958 in Woodland Hills,
   California
Source: *BioIn 4, 5; NotNAT B; WhScrn 74,
77; WhoHol B*

Fritchey, Clayton
American. Journalist, Political Leader
b. 1905 in Bellefontaine, Ohio
Source: *WhoAm 74*

Fritchie, Barbara
American. Heroine
Supposedly waved Union flag at Lee's army
   as it marched through her town, 1862.
b. 1766 in Frederick, Maryland
d. 1862
Source: *NatCAB 10; NotAW*

Frith, Mary
see: Cutpurse, Moll

Fritzsche, Hans
German. Nazi Leader
Radio, news propaganda chief under
   Goebbles; pardoned at Nuremburg trails.
b. Apr 21, 1900 in Bochum, Germany
d. Sep 27, 1953 in Cologne, Germany (West)
Source: *BioIn 1, 2, 3; EncTR; ObitOF 79*

Frizon, Maud
[Maud Frison]
French. Designer
Manufactures colorful, high fashion footwear.
b. 1942 in Paris, France
Source: *BioIn 12*

Frizzell, "Lefty" (William Orville)
American. Singer
b. Mar 31, 1928 in Corsicana, Texas
d. Jul 27, 1975 in Nashville, Tennessee
Source: *EncFCWM 69*

Frobe, Gert
German. Actor
Played title role in James Bond film
   Goldfinger, 1964.
b. Feb 25, 1912 in Planitz, Germany
Source: *FilmEn; FilmgC; IntMPA 82; MotPP;
MovMk; WhoHol A*

Froben, Johann
German. Scholar, Printer
Printed Erasmie's Latin translation of Greek
   New Testament, 1516.
b. 1460 in Hammelburg, Germany
d. Oct 1527 in Basel, France
Source: *DcEuL; OxGer*

Frobisher, Martin
English. Navigator
Made three voyages to New World
   attempting to discover Northwest Passage,
   1576, 1577, 1578.
b. 1535 in Dorcaster, England
d. Nov 22, 1594 in Plymouth, England
Source: *Alli; ApCAB; Drake; NewC; OxCan;
REn; WhAm HS*

Froebel, Friedrich Wilhelm August
German. Educator
Founded kindergarten system, 1836.
b. Apr 21, 1782 in Oberweissbach, Germany
d. Jun 21, 1852 in Marienthal, Germany
Source: *BbD; BiD&SB; LongCTC*

Froese, Bob
Canadian. Hockey Player
Goalie, Philadelphia, 1982--; set NHL record
   for most consecutive games without loss
   from start of career--13.
b. Jun 30, 1958 in Saint Catherines, Ontario
Source: *HocReg 85*

Frohman, Charles
American. Impresario, Producer
b. Jun 17, 1860 in Sandusky, Ohio
d. May 7, 1915
Source: *AmBi; DcAmB; EncMT; LinLib S;
NatCAB 11; OxAmL; OxThe; PlP&P;
REnAL; WebAB; WhAm 1; WhoStg 1906,
1908*

Frohman, Daniel
American. Manager
b. Aug 22, 1851 in Sandusky, Ohio
d. Dec 26, 1940 in New York, New York
Source: *AmAu&B; CurBio 41; DcAmB S2;
LinLib L, S; NatCAB 11; OhA&B; OxAmL;
OxThe; PlP&P; REnAL; TwCBDA; WhAm 1;
WhThe; WhoStg 1906, 1908*

Froines, John Radford
[The Chicago 7]
American. Political Activist
Source: *BioIn 10; MugS; WhoGov 77*

Froissart, Jean
French. Author, Poet
Best known work *Chronicles* originally in
four volumes, covering 1325-1400.
b. 1338 in Valenciennes, France
d. 1410 in Chimay, France
Source: *AtlBL; BbD; BiD&SB; CasWL;
CyWA; DcEuL; EuAu; EvEuW; LinLib L, S;
McGEWB; NewC; OxEng; OxFr; PenC EUR;
REn*

Froman, Jane
American. Actress, Singer
Suffered crippling injuries in 1943 plane
crash en route to entertain troops;
inspiration for film *With a song in My
Heart,* 1952.
b. Nov 10, 1907 in Saint Louis, Missouri
d. Apr 22, 1980 in Columbia, Missouri
Source: *AmPS A; InWom; WhoHol A*

Fromentin, Eugene
French. Author
Painted exotic scenery; wrote travel books;
novel *Dominique,* 1863.
b. Oct 24, 1820 in LaRochelle, France
d. Aug 27, 1876 in LaRochelle, France
Source: *BiD&SB; CasWL; CyWA; DcEuL;
EuAu; EvEuW; LinLib L, S; McGDA; OxFr;
PenC EUR*

Fromholtz, Dianne
Australian. Tennis Player
Won Australian Open doubles, 1977.
b. Aug 10, 1956 in Albury, Australia
Source: *WhoIntT*

Fromm, Erich
American. Psychoanalyst
Dealt with problem of how Western man can
come to terms with sense of isolation.
b. Mar 23, 1900 in Frankfurt, Germany
d. Mar 18, 1980 in Muralto, Switzerland
Source: *CurBio 67; AmAu&B; AmM&WS
73S; ConAu 73, 97; EncAB-H; PenC AM;
REn; REnAL; TwCA SUP; WebAB; WhoAm
74; WhoE 74; WhoS&SW 82; WhoTwCL;
WhoWor 78; WrDr 80*

Fromme, Lynette Alice
"Squeaky"
American. Attempted Assassin, Cultist
Charles Manson follower, convicted of
attempting to assassinate Gerald Ford,
1975.
b. 1949
Source: *BioIn 10; GoodHs*

Frondizi, Arturo
Argentine. Lawyer, Politician
b. Sep 28, 1908 in Argentina
Source: *CurBio 58; IntWW 74; WhoWor 78*

Frontenac, Louis de
French. Political Leader
b. 1620 in Paris, France
d. Nov 28, 1698 in Quebec
Source: *ApCAB; Drake; OxAmL; OxCan;
WhAm HS*

Frontiere, Georgia
see: Rosenbloom, Georgia

Frost, Arthur Burdett
American. Illustrator, Humorist
b. Jan 17, 1851 in Philadelphia, Pennsylvania
d. Jun 22, 1928 in Pasadena, California
Source: *AmAu&B; BioIn 2, 3, 4, 5; ChhPo,
S1, S2; DcAmAu; DcNAA; OxAmL; REnAL;
Str&VC*

Frost, David
English. TV Personality, Author
b. Apr 7, 1939 in Tenterden, England
Source: *ConAu 69; CurBio 69; IntMPA 75,
76, 77, 78, 79, 80, 81, 82; IntWW 74;
NewYTBE 71; Who 74; WhoAm 82; WhoWor
78*

Frost, Edwin Brant
American. Astronomer, Lecturer
Director, Yerkes Observatory, 1905-32.
b. Jul 14, 1866 in Brattleboro, Vermont
d. May 14, 1935 in Chicago, Illinois
Source: *DcAmB S1; WebBD 80*

Frost, Robert Lee
American. Poet
Recited poem, *The Gift Outright,* at John F
Kennedy's inauguration, 1961; won four
Pulitzer Prizes.
b. Mar 26, 1874 in San Francisco, California
d. Jan 29, 1963 in Boston, Massachusetts
Source: *AmAu&B; AmLY; AmWr; AnCL;
AtlBL; CasWL; Chambr 3; ChhPo, S1, S2;
CnDAL; CnE&AP; CnMWL; ConAmA;
ConAmL; ConAu 89; ConLC 1, 3, 4, 9, 10,
13, 15; CurBio 42, 63; CyWA; DcLEL;
EncWL; EvLB; LongCTC; ModAL, S1;
NewYTBE 72; NewYTBS 74; OxAmL;
OxEng; PenC AM; RAdv 1; RComWL; REn;
REnAL; SixAP; SmATA 14; Str&VC; TwCA,
SUP; TwCWr; WebE&AL; WhAm 4;
WhNAA; WhoTwCL*

Fruehauf, Harvey Charles
American. Manufacturer
Founder, Fruehauf Trailer Co., 1916; built
one of first semi-trailers for hauling cargo.
b. Dec 15, 1893 in Grosse Pointe, Michigan
d. Oct 14, 1968 in Detroit, Michigan
Source: *ObitOF 79; WhAm 5*

Frum, Barbara
Canadian. Broadcast Journalist, Author
Host, interviewer, "As It Happens," CBC
radio show, 1971--; often compared to
Barbara Walters.
b. Sep 8, 1937 in Niagara Falls, New York
Source: *CanWW 82; ConAu 101*

Fry, Charles Burgess
British. Sportsman, Author
Cricketer who was also 1892 world long
jump champion.
b. 1872 in Croyden, England
d. Sep 7, 1956 in London, England
Source: *ObitOF 79; WhE&EA; WhLit*

Fry, Christopher
English. Dramatist
Wrote plays *The Lady's not for Burning,*
1949; *Venus Observed,* 1950.
b. Dec 18, 1907 in Bristol, England
Source: *Au&Wr 71; AuBYP; BiE&WWA;
CasWL; CnMD; CnMWL; CnThe; ConAu
17R; ConLC 2, 10, 14; ConP 70, 75; CroCD;
CurBio 51; CyWA; DcLEL; EncWL; EvLB;
IntWW 74, 75, 76, 77, 78, 79, 80, 81;
LongCTC; McGEWD; ModBrL S1; ModWD;
NewC; NotNAT; OxEng; OxThe; PenC ENG;
REn; TwCA SUP; TwCWr; WebE&AL; Who
74; WhoThe 77; WhoWor 74, 76, 78;
WorEFlm; WrDr 80, 80*

Fry, Elizabeth Gurney
English. Reformer, Philanthropist
Dedicated life to improving condition of the
poor, women in prison.
b. May 21, 1780 in Ramsgate, England
d. 1845 in Earlham, England
Source: *Alli; BioIn 6, 7, 8, 9, 10, 11; LinLib
S; REn*

Fry, Franklin Clark
American. Clergyman
b. Aug 30, 1900 in Bethlehem, Pennsylvania
d. Jun 6, 1968
Source: *CurBio 46, 68; WebAB; WhAm 5*

Fry, Roger Eliot
English. Artist, Art Critic
b. Dec 14, 1866 in London, England
d. Sep 9, 1934 in London, England
Source: *LongCTC; ModBrL; NewC; OxEng;
REn; TwCA, SUP*

Frye, David
American. Comedian
b. 1934 in Brooklyn, New York
Source: *BioIn 10*

Frye, H(erman) Northrop
Canadian. Literary Critic
Proponent of symbolist literary criticism
founded on archetypes and myths.
b. Jul 14, 1912 in Sherbrooke, Quebec
Source: *AmAu&B; CanWW 82; CanWr;
CasWL; ConAu 5NR; CurBio 83; EncWL
SUP; LinLib L; NewC; OxCan, SUP; PenC
AM, ENG; RAdv 1; WhoCan 73; WorAu*

Fryer, Robert
American. Producer
Won Tonys for *Wonderful Town,* 1953;
Redhead, 1959; *Sweeny Todd,* 1979.
b. Dec 18, 1920 in Washington, District of
Columbia
Source: *VarWW 85*

Fuchida, Mitsuo
Japanese. Naval Officer, Aviator
b. 1903
d. May 30, 1976 in Kashiwara, Japan
Source: *BioIn 10*

Fuchs, Daniel
American. Author
Won Oscar for *Love Me or Leave Me,* 1955.
b. Jun 25, 1909 in New York, New York
Source: *AmAu&B; ConAu 81; ConLC 8;
ConNov 72, 76; DrAF 76; ModAL, S1;
OxAmL; PenC AM; REnAL; VarWW 85;
WebE&AL; WhoTwCL; WrDr 76*

Fuchs, Joseph
American. Musician
b. Apr 26, 1900 in New York, New York
Source: *Baker 78; CurBio 62; WhoAm 74;
WhoWor 74*

Fuchs, Klaus Emil Julius
British. Physicist, Spy
Spy for the Russians 1942-47; worked at Los
Alamos; implicated Rosenbergs.
b. 1912 in Beerfelden, Germany
Source: *EncE 75; SpyCS; WhoSocC 78*

Fuchs, Marta
German. Opera Singer
b. Jan 1, 1898
d. 1974
Source: *BioIn 10; NewEOp 71*

Fuchs, Vivian Ernest, Sir
English. Geologist, Explorer
With Sir Edmund Hillary, were first to cross
  Antarctica overland, 1957-58.
b. Feb 11, 1908 in Kent, England
Source: *ConAu 104; CurBio 58; IntWW 74,
75, 76, 77, 78, 79, 80, 81; Who 74, 82;
WhDW; WhoWor 74, 76, 78; WrDr 80, 80*

Fuentes, Carlos
Mexican. Author
b. Nov 11, 1928 in Mexico City, Mexico
Source: *AuNews 2; CasWL; ConAu 69;
ConLC 3, 8, 10, 13; CurBio 72; DcCLAA;
EncWL; IntWW 74; PenC AM; TwCWr;
WhoAm 82; WhoTwCL; WhoS&SW 82;
WorAu*

Fuertes, Louis Agassiz
American. Ornithologist, Artist
b. Feb 7, 1874 in Ithaca, New York
d. Aug 22, 1927
Source: *AmBi; DcAmB; DcNAA; WhAm 1*

Fuess, Claude Moore
American. Educator, Author
b. Jan 12, 1885 in Waterville, New York
d. Sep 9, 1963
Source: *AmAu&B; OxAmL; REnAL; TwCA,
SUP; WhAm 4; WhNAA*

Fugard, Athol Harold
South African. Actor, Director, Dramatist
Writes about apartheid in *Sizwe Banzi is
  Dead; A Lesson from Aloes.*
b. Jun 11, 1932 in Middleburg, South Africa
Source: *AfSS 79; CasWL; CnThe; ConAu 85;
ConDr 73, 77; ConLC 5, 9, 14; CurBio 75;
DcLEL 1940; EncWT; IntAu&W 76; IntWW
74, 75, 76, 77, 78, 79, 80; ModCmwL;
NewYTBE 70; NotNAT; PIP&P; TwCWr;
WhoThe 72, 77, 81; WhoTwCL; WhoWor 80;
WorAu 1975; WrDr 76, 80*

Fugate, Caril Ann
American. Murderer
Friend of Charles Starkweather allegedly
  involved in NE murders; spent 18 years in
  prison.
b. 1943
Source: *BioIn 10; GoodHs*

Fugger, Jacob
[Jacob the Rich]
German. Merchant
b. 1459
d. 1525
Source: *WebBD 80*

Fugs, The
[John Anderson; Lee Crabtree; Pete Kearney;
  Tuli Kupferberg; Charles Larkey; Vinny
  Leary; Bob Mason; Ken Pine; Ed Sanders;
  Peter Stampfield; KenWeaver]
American. Music Group
Formed theater, music group, 1965; satirized
  politics, rock, sexual repression.
Source: *BiDAmM; EncPR&S 74; IlEncRk;
RkOneH*

Fuhr, Grant
Canadian. Hockey Player
Goalie, Edmonton, 1981--; first black player
  to be on Stnaley Cup-winning team, 1984.
b. Sep 28, 1962 in Spruce Grove, Alberta
Source: *HocReg 85*

Fuisz, Robert E
American. Writer, Producer
Won four Emmys for Body Human series
  including "The Body Human - The Living
  Code," 1983.
b. Oct 15, 1934 in Pennsylvania
Source: *VarWW 85*

Fukuda, Takeo
Japanese. Political Leader
b. Jan 14, 1905 in Japan
Source: *CurBio 74; IntWW 74; NewYTBE 71*

Fulbright, James William
American. Politician
b. Apr 9, 1905 in Sumner, Missouri
Source: *BiDrAC; ConAu 9NR; EncAB-H;
LinLib L, S; WhoAm 78, 80, 82; WhoAmP
73; WhoGov 72; WhoS&SW 73; WhoWor 78*

Fuld, Stanley H
American. Judge
b. Aug 23, 1903 in New York, New York
Source: *WhoAm 74, 76, 78, 80, 82; WhoE
74; WhoGov 75; WhoWorJ 72*

Fulks, Joe (Joseph E)
"Jumpin' Joe"
American. Basketball Player
Modern basketball's first scoring sensation
  who played for Philadelphia Warriors in
  late 1940s.
b. Oct 26, 1921 in Marshall County,
  Kentucky
d. Mar 21, 1976 in Eddyville, Kentucky
Source: *BioIn 10; OfNBA 81; WhoBbl 73*

Fuller, Alfred Carl
American. Manufacturer
Founded Fuller Brush Co., 1910.
b. Jan 13, 1885 in Kings County, Nova
Scotia
d. Dec 4, 1973 in Hartford, Connecticut
Source: *BioNews 74; BusPN; ConAu 45;
CurBio 50, 74; NewYTBE 73; WebAB;
WhAm 6*

Fuller, "Bucky" (Richard Buckminster)
American. Architect, Author
Developed geodesic dome, circa 1940.
b. Feb 12, 1895 in Milton, Massachusetts
d. Jul 1, 1983 in Los Angeles, California
Source: *AnObit 1983; BlueB 76; CelR;
ConArch; ConAu 9NR; CurBio 76, 83N;
EncAB-H; EncMA; IntWW 80, 81; McGDA;
McGEWB; NewYTBS 74, 83; WebAB, 79;
Who 74; WhoAm 74, 76, 78, 80, 82;
WhoArch; WhoWor 74; WrDr 80*

Fuller, Charles
American. Dramatist
Won Pulitzer for *A Soldier's Play*, 1982;
wrote film *A Soldier's Story*, 1984.
b. Mar 5, 1939 in Philadelphia, Pennsylvania
Source: *VarWW 85*

Fuller, Edmund
American. Author
b. Mar 3, 1914 in Wilmington, Delaware
Source: *AmAu&B; AuBYP; ChhPo S1; ConAu
77; ConNov 72, 76; DrAS 74E; SmATA 21;
WorAu; WrDr 76*

Fuller, George
American. Artist
b. 1822
d. 1884
Source: *AmBi; ApCAB; DcAmB; OxAmL;
TwCBDA; WhAm HS*

Fuller, Henry Blake
American. Author
Realistic novels of Chicago life include *Cliff-
Dwellers*, 1893.
b. Jan 9, 1857 in Chicago, Illinois
d. Jul 29, 1929 in Chicago, Illinois
Source: *AmAu&B; BbD; BiD&SB; CasWL;
CnDAL; ConAmL; DcAmAu; DcLEL; DcNAA;
OxAmL; PenC AM; TwCA SUP; WebE&AL;
WhAm 1*

Fuller, Hoyt William
American. Critic, Editor
b. Sep 10, 1926 in Atlanta, Georgia
d. May 11, 1981 in Atlanta, Georgia
Source: *BlkAWP; ConAmTC; ConAu 53, 103;
Ebony 1; LivgBAA; SelBAAu; WhoAm 76, 78,
80; WhoBlA 75, 77*

Fuller, Ida
American. Social Reformer
Received first US Social Security check,
1940; invested $22 in program, received
over $20,000.
b. Sep 6, 1875 in Ludlow, Vermont
d. Jan 27, 1975 in Brattleboro, Vermont
Source: *BioIn 10; NewYTBS 75*

Fuller, Loie
American. Dancer, Author
b. Jan 22, 1862 in Fullersburg, Illinois
d. Jan 2, 1928
Source: *AmBi; DcAmB; NotAW; WhAm 1*

Fuller, Margaret
[Sarah Margaret Fuller Ossoli]
American. Critic, Social Reformer, Author
Women's rights leader who was the first US
foreign correspondent, 1848.
b. May 23, 1810 in Cambridge,
Massachusetts
d. Jul 19, 1850 in Fire Island, New York
Source: *AmAu; AmAu&B; AmBi; AtlBL; BbD;
BiD&SB; ChhPo; CnDAL; CrtT 3; DcAmAu;
DcAmB; DcLEL; LinLib L; NotAW; OxAmL;
OxEng; PenC AM; REn; REnAL; TwCBDA;
WebAB; WebE&AL*

Fuller, Robert
American. Actor
In TV westerns "Laramie," 1959-62;
"Wagaon Train," 1963-65.
b. Jul 29, 1934
Source: *FilmgC; WhoHol A*

Fuller, Roy Broadbent
English. Author
b. Feb 11, 1912 in Failsworth, England
Source: *Au&Wr 71; CasWL; ChhPo S1, S2;
CnE&AP; ConAu 5R; ConLC 4; ConNov 72,
76; ConP 70, 75; IntWW 74; LongCTC;
ModBrL, S1; NewC; PenC ENG; RAdv 1;
REn; TwCA SUP; TwCWr; WebE&AL; Who
74; WhoChL; WhoTwCL; WhoWor 78; WrDr
80*

Fuller, Samuel
American. Director, Screenwriter
B melodramas include *I Shot Jesse James*,
1949.
b. Aug 12, 1911 in Worcester, Massachusetts
Source: *BiDFilm; BioIn 7, 9, 11; CmMov;
DcFM; FilmEn; FilmgC; OxFilm; ScF&FL 1;
WhoAm 82; WorEFlm*

Fuller-Maitland, John Alexander
English. Music Critic, Author
b. Apr 7, 1856 in London, England
d. Mar 30, 1936 in Lancashire, England
Source: *Chambr 3; NewC; WhoLA*

Fullerton, (Charles) Gordon
American. Astronaut
Aboard the third flight of space shuttle
  Columbia, Apr, 1982.
b. Oct 11, 1936 in Rochester, New York
Source: *IntWW 74, 75, 76, 77, 78; WhoAm
80, 82; WhoS&SW 73, 75, 76, 78; WorDWW*

Fulton, Maude
American. Actress, Dramatist
Starred in own plays *The Brat; Sonny;
  Humming Bird.*
b. May 14, 1881 in El Dorado, Kansas
d. Nov 4, 1950 in Los Angeles, California
Source: *Film 2; NotNAT B; WhScrn 77, 74;
WhThe; WhoHol B*

Fulton, Richard Harmon
American. Politician
Dem. mayor of Nashville, TN, 1977--.
b. Jan 27, 1927 in Nashville, Tennessee
Source: *BiDrAC; CngDr 74; WhoAm 80, 82,
84; WhoAmP 73, 75, 77, 79; WhoGov 72, 75,
77; WhoS&SW 73, 75, 76, 78*

Fulton, Robert
American. Engineer
First to develop a practical, profitable
  steamboat, 1807.
b. Nov 14, 1765 in Lancaster County,
  Pennsylvania
d. Feb 24, 1815 in New York, New York
Source: *Alli; AmBi; ApCAB; BiDLA; DcAmB;
DcNAA; Drake; REn; REnAL; TwCBDA;
WebAB; WhAm HS*

Funicello, Annette
[Mrs. Glen Holt]
American. Actress, Singer
Disney Mousketeer, 1950s; star of *beach
  party* films, 1960s.
b. Oct 22, 1942 in Utica, New York
Source: *BiDAmM; FilmgC; InWom; MotPP;
WhoHol A*

Funikawa, Gyo
American. Illustrator
b. in Berkeley, California
Source: *BioIn 3, 8, 9; IlsBYP; IlsCB 1967*

Funk, Casimir
American. Biochemist
b. Feb 23, 1884 in Warsaw, Poland
d. Nov 19, 1967 in Albany, New York
Source: *CurBio 45, 68; WebAB; WhAm 4*

Funk, Isaac Kauffman
American. Publisher
Funk and Wagnalls Co. published *Standard
  Dictionary of the English Language,* 1893.
b. Sep 10, 1839 in Clifton, Ohio
d. Apr 4, 1912 in Montclair, New Jersey
Source: *AmAu&B; DcAmAu; DcAmB; DcNAA;
OhA&B; TwCBDA; WebAB; WhAm 1*

Funk, Walther
German. Nazi Leader, Banker
Reichsbank pres., 1939-45; responsible for
  Nazi finances; jailed as war criminal until
  1957.
b. Aug 18, 1890 in Trakehnen, Prussia (East)
d. May 31, 1960 in Dusseldorf, Germany
  (West)
Source: *BioIn 1, 3, 5; CurBio 40, 60; EncTR;
ObitOF 79*

Funk, Wilfred John
American. Publisher
b. Mar 20, 1883 in Brooklyn, New York
d. Jun 1, 1965 in Montclair, New Jersey
Source: *AmAu&B; ChhPo, S2; ConAu 89;
CurBio 55, 65; WhAm 4*

Funston, Frederick
American. Military Leader
Commanded troops at capture of Vera Cruz,
  Mexico, 1914.
b. Nov 9, 1865 in New Carlisle, Ohio
d. Feb 19, 1917
Source: *AmBi; ApCAB SUP; DcAmB; DcNAA;
LinLib S; McGEWB; NatCAB 11; OhA&B;
SpyCS; TwCBDA; WebAB; WhAm 1*

Funston, George Keith
American. Businessman
b. Oct 12, 1910 in Waterloo, Iowa
Source: *IntWW 74; WhoAm 74*

Funt, Allen
American. Producer
Creator, host of TV series "Candid Camera."
b. Sep 16, 1914 in Brooklyn, New York
Source: *AmSCAP 66; CurBio 66; FilmgC;
IntMPA 82; NewYTET; WhoAm 74, 78*

Furay, Richie
[Buffalo Springfield; Poco; The Souther-
  Hillman-Furay Band]
American. Musician
With Stephen Stills formed Buffalo
  Springfield, 1966; has since released three
  solo albums.
b. May 9, 1944 in Yellow Springs, Ohio
Source: *ConMuA 80A; RkOn 85; RkWW 82;
WhoRock 81*

Furia, John
Writer
TV shows include "The Waltons"; "Hotel."
Source: *VarWW 85*

Furie, Sidney J
Canadian. Director
Films include *Lady Sings the Blues; Gable and Lombard; Boys in Company C.*
b. Feb 28, 1933 in Toronto, Ontario
Source: *FilmEn; FilmgC; IntMPA 78, 79; MovMk; OxFilm; WorEFlm*

Furillo, Carl Anthony
"The Reading Rifle"; "Skoonj"
American. Baseball Player
Sued Dodgers for dropping him without pay following injury, won $21,000.
b. Mar 8, 1922 in Stony Creek, Pennsylvania
Source: *BaseEn 85; WhoProB 73*

Furman, Roger
Director
Founder, director, Harlem's Repertory Theater, 1964.
b. 1924
d. Nov 27, 1983
Source: *BlkAmW 1; ConAu 111*

Furness, Betty (Elizabeth Mary)
American. Actress, Public Official
Actress, 1932-37; chairman, president's committee on consumer interests, 1967-69.
b. Jan 3, 1916 in New York, New York
Source: *CelR,; CurBio 68; ForWC 70; InWom; NewYTET; ThFT; WhoAm 80, 82; WhoAmW 68, 70, 72, 74, 75, 77; WhoE 74; WhoHol A; WhoS&SW 73*

Furstenberg, Diane Halfin von
Fashion Designer, Author
Began designing, 1971; first effort was jersey wrapdress.
b. Dec 31, 1946 in Brussels, Belgium
Source: *BioNews 74; BkPepl; CelR; WhoAm 82; WorFshn*

Furstenberg, Egon von
Fashion Designer, Author
b. Jun 29, 1946 in Lausanne, Switzerland
Source: *CelR; WhoAm 82*

Furtseva, Ekaterina Alexeyevna
Russian. Government Official
Minister of Culture, 1960-74; promoted cultural exchange with West.
b. Dec 7, 1910 in Vyshni Volochek, Russia
d. Oct 25, 1974 in Moscow, U.S.S.R.
Source: *BioIn 5, 10; BioNews 75; CurBio 56, 74, 74N; IntWW 74, 75; NewYTBE 72; NewYTBS 74; WhAm 6; WhoAmW 68, 70, 72, 74; WhoSocC 78; WhoWor 74*

Furtwangler, Wilhelm
German. Conductor
b. Jan 25, 1886 in Berlin, Germany
d. Nov 30, 1954 in Eberstein, Germany (West)
Source: *WhAm 3*

Fuseli, Henry
Swiss. Artist, Author
Romantic painter of eerie imaginery including *The Nightmare*, 1781.
b. Feb 7, 1741 in Zurich, Switzerland
d. Apr 16, 1825 in London, England
Source: *Alli; AtlBL; BiDLA; BkIE; CasWL; DcBrWA; McGDA; NewC*

Fust, Johann
German. Printer
With Gutenberg, issued the first printed book, the Bible, 1450.
b. 1400
d. 1466 in Paris, France
Source: *DcBiPP; DcCathB; NewC; OxGer*

Futrell, Mary Hatwood
American. Labor Union Official
Pres., National Education Assn., 1983--, largest union in US.
b. May 24, 1940 in Altavista, Virginia
Source: *ConNews 86-1; NewYTBS 83*

Futrelle, Jacques
American. Author
b. Apr 9, 1875 in Pike County, Georgia
d. Apr 15, 1912
Source: *AmAu&B; BiDSA; DcNAA; EncMys; TwCA; WhAm 1*

Futter, Ellen Victoria
American. University Administrator
Youngest exec. of major college who became pres., Barnard College, 1981.
b. Sep 21, 1949 in New York, New York
Source: *BioIn 12; CurBio 85; NewYTBS 80; WhoAm 84*

Fyffe, Will
Scottish. Actor
Music-hall comedian who specialized in
　Scottish character sketches.
b. 1885 in Dundee, Scotland
d. Dec 14, 1947 in Saint Andrews, Scotland
Source: *FilmgC; OxThe; WhScrn 74; WhoHol
B*

Fyodorova, Victoria
Russian. Model, Actress
b. 1945
Source: *BioIn 10, 11*

G

Gabel, Martin
American. Actor, Director, Producer
Won Tony, 1961, for *Big Fish, Little Fish,* ;
  regular panelist on TV game show
  "What's My Line?"
b. Jun 19, 1912 in Philadelphia, Pennsylvania
d. May 22, 1986 in New York, New York
Source: *BiE&WWA; FilmgC; MovMk;
NewYTBS 86; NotNAT; WhoHol A; WhoThe
77*

Gabin, Jean
[Jean-Alexis Moncorge]
French. Actor
World-weary hero in such films as *Pepe le
  Moko* ; *Port of Shadows.*
b. May 17, 1904 in Paris, France
d. Nov 15, 1976 in Neuilly, France
Source: *BiDFilm; CurBio 77; FilmEn;
IntMPA 77; IntWW 85; MotPP; MovMk;
OxFilm; Who 74; WhoHol A; WhoWor 74;
WorEFlm*

Gable, Clark
American. Actor
Won Oscar, 1934, for *It Happened One
  Night;* played Rhett Butler in *Gone With
  the Wind,* 1939.
b. Feb 1, 1901 in Cadiz, Ohio
d. Nov 16, 1960 in Hollywood, California
Source: *BiDFilm; CmMov; CurBio 45, 61;
FilmgC; MotPP; MovMk; OxFilm; WebAB;
WhAm 4; WhScrn 74, 77; WhoHol B;
WorEFlm*

Gable, John Clark
American. Celebrity Relative
Son of Clark Gable.
b. Feb 1961
Source: *BioIn 6, 9*

Gabo, Naum Pevsner
American. Sculptor
b. Aug 5, 1890 in Briansk, Russia
d. Aug 23, 1977 in Waterbury, Connecticut
Source: *Au&Wr 71; ConAu 33R, 73, P-2;
CurBio 72; DcCAA 71; IntWW 74; WhoAm
74; WhoWor 78*

Gabor, Dennis
British. Engineer
b. Jun 5, 1900 in Budapest, Hungary
d. Feb 9, 1979 in London, England
Source: *AmM&WS 73P; Au&Wr 71; BioIn 9,
10, 11; ConAu 17R; CurBio 72, 79; IntAu&W
76; IntWW 75, 76, 77, 78; NewYTBE 71;
NewYTBS 79; WhoWor 76, 78; WrDr 80*

Gabor, Eva
Hungarian. Actress
Co-starred with Eddie Albert in TV series
  "Green Acres," 1965-71.
b. Feb 11, 1921 in Budapest, Hungary
Source: *BiE&WWA; BioNews 74; CelR;
CurBio 68; FilmgC; InWom; MotPP; MovMk;
WhoAm 76, 78, 80, 82; WhoAmW 70, 72,
74; WhoHol A; WhoWor 74, 76; WorAl*

Gabor, Jolie
[Jancsi Tilleman]
Hungarian. Celebrity Relative
b. Sep 29, 1896 in Hungary
Source: *BioNews 74; InWom*

Gabor, Magda
Hungarian. Actress
b. Jul 10, 1917 in Budapest, Hungary
Source: *InWom*

Gabor, Zsa Zsa (Sari)
Hungarian. Actress
Better known for her many husbands than
   acting career--married eight times.
b. Feb 6, 1919 in Budapest, Hungary
Source: *CelR; FilmgC; InWom; IntMPA 75,
76, 77, 78, 79, 80, 81, 82; MotPP; MovMk;
WhoAm 74, 76, 78, 80, 82; WhoHol A;
WhoWor 74, 76; WorAl*

Gabriel, Ange-Jacques
French. Architect
Louis XV's chief designer, 1742-75;
   restoration of Louvre, 1755, among many
   accomplishments.
b. Oct 23, 1698 in Paris, France
d. Jan 4, 1782 in Paris, France
Source: *AtlBL; McGDA; McGEWB; WhoArch*

Gabriel, Peter
[Genesis]
English. Singer, Songwriter
Genesis main vocalist, songwriter, 1968-75;
   noted for bizarre theatricals; hit album
   Sledgehammer, 1986.
b. May 13, 1950 in England
Source: *ConMuA 80A; LilREn 78; WhoRock
81*

Gabriel, Roman, Jr.
American. Football Player
Quarterback, LA Rams, 1962-73, Philadelphia
   Eagles, 1973-78; MVP, 1969.
b. Aug 5, 1940 in Wilmington, North
   Carolina
Source: *ConAu 107; CurBio 75; WhoAm 76,
78; WhoFtbl 74*

Gabrieli, Giovanni
Italian. Composer, Musician
b. 1557 in Venice, Italy
d. Aug 12, 1612 in Venice, Italy
Source: *AtlBL; NewCol 75; REn; WebBD 80*

Gabrielli, Catarina
Italian. Opera Singer
b. Nov 12, 1730 in Rome, Italy
d. Apr 1796 in Rome, Italy
Source: *WebBD 80*

Gabrilowitsch, Ossip
American. Conductor, Musician
b. Jan 26, 1878 in Saint Petersburg, Russia
d. Sep 14, 1936 in Detroit, Michigan
Source: *AmBi; DcAmB S2; NewCol 75;
WebBD 80; WhAm 1*

Gacy, John Wayne, Jr.
American. Murderer
Convicted, 1980, of murders of 33 boys in
   Chicago area, 1972-78.
b. 1942
Source: *BioIn 11; EncACr*

Gaddafi, Moamar al-
see: Khadafy, Moammar

Gaddis, Thomas (Eugene)
American. Author, Educator
Wrote *The Birdman of Alcatraz*, biography
   on which 1962 hit film was based.
b. Sep 14, 1908 in Denver, Colorado
d. Oct 10, 1984 in Portland, Oregon
Source: *ConAu 114, 29R; IntAu&W 77;
WhoAm 76*

Gaddis, William
American. Author
b. 1922 in New York, New York
Source: *AmAu&B; ConAu 17R; ConLC 1, 3,
6; ConNov 72, 76; DrAF 76; ModAL S1;
PenC AM; RAdv 1; WhoAm 74, 76, 78, 80,
82; WorAu; WrDr 80*

Gadsby, Bill (William Alexander)
Canadian. Hockey Player, Hockey Coach
Defenseman, 1946-66; Hall of Fame, 1970.
b. Aug 8, 1927 in Calgary, Alberta
Source: *WhoHcky 73*

Gadsen, James
American. Railroad Executive, Politician
b. May 15, 1788 in Charleston, South
   Carolina
d. Dec 26, 1858 in Charleston, South
   Carolina
Source: *BioIn 3; DcAmB; WhAm HS*

Gadski, Johanna
German. Opera Singer
b. Jun 15, 1872 in Anklam, Germany
d. Feb 22, 1932 in Berlin, Germany
Source: *InWom; WhAm 1*

Gaedel, Eddie (Edward Carl)
American. Baseball Player
Midget, who batted against Detroit, Aug 9,
   1951, in promotional gimmi ck; walked.
b. Jun 8, 1925 in Chicago, Illinois
d. Jun 18, 1961 in Chicago, Illinois
Source: *BaseEn 85; WhoProB 73*

Gag, Wanda
American. Children's Author, Illustrator
b. May 11, 1893 in New Ulm, Minnesota
d. Jun 27, 1946 in New York, New York
Source: *AmAu&B; AnCL; AuBYP; ChhPo S2;
ConICB; CurBio 42; DcAmB S4; DcNAA;
FamAIYP; HerW; IlsCB 1744; JBA 34, 51;
REnAL; TwCA, SUP; WhAm 2; YABC 1*

Gagarin, Yuri Alexseyevich
Russian. Cosmonaut
First man to travel in space, Apr 12, 1961.
b. Mar 9, 1934 in Gzhatsk, U.S.S.R.
d. Mar 27, 1968 in Moscow, U.S.S.R.
Source: *AsBiEn; CurBio 61, 68; McGEWB;
NewCol 75; WhDW; WhAm 5; WorAl*

Gage, Harlow W
American. Business Executive
b. Feb 6, 1911 in Springfield, Massachusetts
Source: *IntWW 74*

Gage, Thomas
English. Army Officer
b. 1721 in Firle, England
d. Apr 2, 1787 in England
Source: *AmBi; ApCAB; DcAmB; WhAm HS;
WhAmP*

Gagn, Reynaldo
Venezuelan. Composer, Conductor
b. Aug 9, 1875 in Caracas, Venezuela
d. Jan 28, 1947 in Paris, France
Source: *NewEOp 71*

Gagliardi, Ed
see: Foreigner

Gahagan, Helen Mary
see: Douglas, Helen Mary Gahagan

Gail, Max(well Trowbridge, Jr.)
American. Actor
Played Sergeant Wojciehowicz ("Wojo") on
TV series "Barney Miller," 1975-81.
b. Apr 5, 1943 in Detroit, Michigan
Source: *WhoAm 80, 82*

Gailhard, Pierre
French. Opera Singer, Manager
b. Aug 1, 1848 in Toulouse, France
d. Oct 12, 1918 in Paris, France
Source: *NewEOp 71*

Gaines, Clarence F
American. Businessman
Founded Gaines Dog Food Co., 1928.
b. 1898
d. Jan 2, 1986 in Winter Park, Florida
Source: *NewYTBS 86*

Gaines, Ernest J
American. Author
b. Jan 15, 1933 in Oscar, Louisiana
Source: *AuNews 1; BlkAWP; ConAu 9R;
ConLC 3; ConNov 72, 76; DrAF 76;
LivgBAA; WhoAm 76, 78, 80, 82; WhoBIA
75; WrDr 76*

Gaines, Lee
American. Composer, Singer
b. Apr 21, 1914 in Houston, Texas
Source: *AmSCAP 66*

Gaines, Steve
[Lynyrd Skynard]
American. Musician
Joined band as guitarist, 1976; killed in a
private plane crash.
b. 1949
d. Oct 20, 1977 in Mississippi
Source: *BioIn 11*

Gainey, Bob (Robert Michael)
Canadian. Hockey Player
Left wing, Montreal, 1973--; won Conn
Smythe Trophy, 1979.
b. Dec 13, 1953 in Peterborough, Ontario
Source: *HocEn; HocReg 81; WhoAm 82*

Gainsborough, Thomas
English. Artist
Painted elegant portraits, country children,
pastoral subjects; well known for "Blue
Boy," 1770.
b. May 14, 1727 in Sudbury, England
d. 1788 in London, England
Source: *AtlBL; BkIE; ChhPo; NewC; REn*

Gairy, Eric M, Sir
West Indian. Government Official
b. 1922 in Grenada, West Indies
Source: *NewYTBS 74; WhoWor 78*

Gaitskell, Hugh Todd Naylor
English. Socialist Leader
b. Apr 9, 1906
d. Jan 18, 1963
Source: *CurBio 50, 63; WhAm 4*

Gaius Caesar Germanicus
see: Caligula

Gajdusek, D(aniel) Carleton
American. Scientist
Noted research virologist; expert on strokes,
degenerative neurological disorders; won
Nobel Prize in medicine, 1976.
b. Sep 9, 1923 in Yonkers, New York
Source: *AmM&WS 76P, 79P; BioIn 6, 11;
CurBio 81; IntWW 76, 78; NewYTBS 76;
WhoAm 78, 80, 82; WhoE 77, 79; WhoGov
72; WhoWor 78*

Galamian, Ivan
American. Teacher
b. Jan 23, 1903 in Tabriz, Persia
d. Apr 14, 1981 in New York, New York
Source: *Baker 78; BioIn 8, 9; WhAm 7*

Galamison, Milton Arthur
American. Clergyman, Civil Rights Leader
Pastor, Siloam Presbyterian Church,
Brooklyn, 1949--; active in civil rights
movement, especially in desegregation of
NYC schools, 1960s.
b. Jan 25, 1923 in Philadelphia, Pennsylvania
Source: *BioIn 6, 11; PolProf J; WhoBlA 75,
80; WhoE 74*

Galanos, James
American. Fashion Designer
Designer of expensive women's fashions;
customers include Nancy Reagan.
b. Sep 20, 1924 in Philadelphia, Pennsylvania
Source: *CelR; CurBio 70; WhoAm 74, 76, 78,
80, 82; WorFshn*

Galard, Genevieve
French. Nurse
b. 1925
Source: *BioIn 3, 4, 7*

Galbraith, John Kenneth
American. Economist, Diplomat, Author
Edited *Fortune* magazine, 1943-48; wrote *The
New Industrial State,* 1967.
b. Oct 15, 1908 in Iona Station, Ontario
Source: *AmAu&B; AmEA 74; AmM&WS 73S;
CanWW 70; CelR; ConAu 21R; EncAB-H;
LongCTC; REnAL; WebAB; Who 74; WhoAm
82; WrDr 76*

Galbreath, John Wilmer
American. Baseball Executive
b. 1897
Source: *BioIn 4, 5*

Galbreath, Tony (Anthony)
American. Football Player
b. Jan 29, 1954 in Fulton, Missouri
Source: *FootReg 81; WhoBlA 77*

Galdos, Benito Perez
see: Perez Galdos, Benito

Gale, Richard Nelson, Sir
English. General
Led 6th airborne division during Allied
invasion of Normandy, 1944.
b. Jul 25, 1896 in London, England
d. Jul 29, 1982 in Kingston-on-Thames,
England
Source: *ConAu 107; IntWW 82; NewYTBS
82; Who 83*

Gale, Zona
American. Author, Journalist
Novelist of small-town Midwest life; play
Miss Lulu Bett, 1920 won Pulitzer Prize.
b. Aug 26, 1874 in Portage, Wisconsin
d. Dec 27, 1938 in Chicago, Illinois
Source: *AmAu&B; AmBi; AmLY; AnMV
1926; ChhPo, S2; CnDAL; CnMD; ConAmA;
ConAmL; DcAmB S2; DcLEL; DcNAA;
EvLB; InWom; LongCTC; McGEWD;
ModWD; NotAW; OxAmL; PenC AM; REn;
REnAL; TwCA, SUP; TwCWr; WhAm 1;
WhNAA; WisWr*

Galella, Ron
American. Photographer
Famous for his pursuit to photograph
Jacqueline Onassis.
b. Jan 10, 1931 in Bronx, New York
Source: *AuNews 1; BioNews 74; ConAu 53;
WhoAm 82; WrDr 76*

Galen
Greek. Physician, Author
Investigated anatomy, physiology; proved that
arteries carry blood, not air.
b. 129 in Pergamum, Greece
d. 199
Source: *CasWL; NewC; NewCol 75; PenC
AM; WebBD 80*

Galento, Tony (Anthony)
"Two Ton"
American. Boxer
Heavyweight fighter best known for saying,
"I'll moider da bum," before each bout.
b. Mar 10, 1909 in Orange, New Jersey
d. Jul 22, 1979 in Livingston, New Jersey
Source: *NewYTBS 79; WhoBox 74; WhoHol
A*

Galgani, Gemma
[Saint Gemmagalgani]
Italian. Religious Figure
b. 1878
d. 1903
Source: *InWom*

Galiani, Ferdinando
Italian. Economist, Author
Wrote *Della Moneta*, 1750, economic treatise
    anticipating modern theories of value.
b. Dec 2, 1728 in Chieti, Italy
d. Oct 30, 1787 in Naples, Italy
Source: *CasWL; DcCathB; Dis&D; WhoEc*

Galileo
[Galileo Galilei]
Italian. Mathematician, Astronomer
Constructed first astronomical telescope, 1609;
    developed scientific method.
b. Feb 15, 1564 in Pisa, Italy
d. Jan 8, 1642 in Arcetri, Italy
Source: *CasWL; DcEuL; EuAu; EvEuW;*
NewC; OxEng; PenC EUR; RComWL; REn

Galili, Israel
Israeli. Politician
b. May 1911 in Brailov, Russia
Source: *IntWW 74; WhoWorJ 72*

Galitzine, Princess Irene
[Mrs. Silvio Medici]
Italian. Fashion Designer
Known for silk palazzo pajamas, bare back
    evening dresses, 1960s.
b. in Tiflis, Russia
Source: *WorFshn*

Gall, Saint
Irish. Missionary
b. 550
d. 645
Source: *BioIn 4, 5, 7; WebBD 80*

Gall, Franz Joseph
German. Physician
Founder of now-discredited science of
    phrenology.
b. Mar 9, 1758 in Tiefenbru, Germany
d. Aug 22, 1828 in Montrouge, France
Source: *NewC; OxFr; REn*

Gallagher, Helen
American. Actress
Won Emmy for her role in TV soap opera
    "Ryan's Hope," 1976; won Tony for *No,*
    No, Nannette, 1970.
b. Jul 19, 1926 in Brooklyn, New York
Source: *BiE&WWA; CelR; EncMT;*
NewYTBE 71; NotNAT; PlP&P; WhoAm 74,
76, 78, 80, 82; WhoHol A; WhoThe 77

Gallagher, Mary Barelli
American. Secretary
Source: *BioIn 8*

Gallagher, Richard
"Skeets"
American. Actor
Vaudeville song and dance man; played
    supporting roles in many 1920s films,
    shorts.
b. Jul 28, 1891 in Terre Haute, Indiana
d. May 22, 1955
Source: *BioIn 3, 4, 11; FilmEn*

Gallagher, Rory
Irish. Musician
Blues-rock guitarist who formed trio Taste,
    1965-71; Gallagher band, 1971.
b. Mar 2, 1949 in Ballyshannon, Ireland
Source: *ConMuA 80A; IlEncRk; LilREn 78;*
WhoRock 81

Gallant, Mavis
Canadian. Author
b. Aug 11, 1922 in Montreal, Quebec
Source: *ConAu 69; ConNov 72, 76; DrAF 76;*
NewC; OxCan, SUP; WhoAm 74, 76, 78, 80,
82; WorAu; WrDr 76

Gallant, Roy Arthur
American. Children's Author
b. Apr 17, 1924 in Portland, Maine
Source: *AuBYP; ConAu 5R, 4NR; ConLC 17;*
SmATA 4; WrDr 76

Gallatin, Albert (Abraham Alfonse Albert)
American. Financier, Statesman
Congressman, 1794-1801; secretary of
    Treasury under Thomas Jefferson.
b. Jan 29, 1761 in Geneva, Switzerland
d. Aug 12, 1849 in Astoria, New York
Source: *Alli; AmAu&B; AmBi; ApCAB; BbtC;*
BiAUS; BiD&SB; BiDrAC; BiDrUSE; CyAL 1;
DcAmAu; DcAmB; DcLEL; DcNAA; Drake;
EncAB-H; OxAmL; REnAL; TwCBDA;
WebAB; WhAm HS; WhAmP

Gallatin, Albert Eugene
American. Artist, Author
Nonobjective paintings influenced by cubism;
    author of many books about Whistler.
b. Jul 23, 1881 in Villanova, Pennsylvania
d. Jun 15, 1952 in New York, New York
Source: *AmAu&B; NatCAB 42; ObitOF 79;*
WhAm 3; WhoAmA 78, 80

Gallaudet, Thomas Hopkins
American. Teacher
Established first free school for deaf in US
    at Hartford, CT, 1917.
b. Dec 10, 1787 in Philadelphia,
    Pennsylvania
d. Sep 10, 1851 in Hartford, Connecticut
Source: *AmBi; ApCAB; DcAmB; Drake;*
McGEWB; TwCBDA; WebAB; WhAm HS

Gallegos, Romulo
Venezuelan. Author, Political Leader,
Educator
Pres. of Venezuela, 1948-52; deposed by
military junta.
b. Aug 2, 1884 in Caracas, Venezuela
d. Apr 4, 1969 in Caracas, Venezuela
Source: *CasWL; CyWA; DcSpL; EncWL;
PenC AM; REn; TwCWr*

Gallegos, William
[The Hostages]
American. Hostage in Iran
b. 1959
Source: *BioIn 12; NewYTBS 81*

Gallen, Hugh J
American. Politician
Bank founder, who was governor of NH,
1978-82.
b. Jul 30, 1924 in Portland, Oregon
d. Dec 29, 1982 in Boston, Massachusetts
Source: *AlmAP 80; NewYTBS 82; WhoAm
80, 82; WhoAmP 75, 77, 79; WhoE 79*

Galli-Curci, Amelita
Italian. Opera Singer
Soprano who sang with Metropolitan Opera,
1921-30; best known for role of Gilda in
Rigoletto.
b. Nov 18, 1882 in Milan, Italy
d. Nov 26, 1963 in La Jolla, California
Source: *InWom; WhAm 4*

Galli-Marie, Marie Celestine
French. Opera Singer
b. Nov 1840 in Paris, France
d. Sep 22, 1905 in Vence, France
Source: *InWom*

Gallico, Paul William
American. Author, Journalist
Wrote *The Snow Goose,* 1941; *The Poseidon
Adventure,* 1969.
b. Jul 26, 1897 in New York, New York
d. Jul 15, 1976 in Monaco
Source: *AmAu&B; AmNov; AuNews 1; ConAu
5R, 69; ConLC 2; ConNov 72, 76; CurBio
46; DcLEL; EvLB; FilmgC; IntWW 74;
REnAL; SmATA 13; TwCA SUP; TwCWr;
Who 74; WhoAm 74; WhoWor 78; WrDr 80*

Gallieni, Joseph Simon
French. General
Led counterattack against Germans at the
Marne, 1914; minister of war, 1915-16;
made marshal posthumously.
b. 1849 in Saint Beat, France
d. 1916
Source: *Dis&D; LinLib L; WhoMilH 76*

Gallitzin, Demetrius Augustine
Russian. Missionary
Founded Catholic colony of Loretto, PA.
b. Dec 22, 1770 in The Hague, Netherlands
d. May 6, 1840 in Loretto, Pennsylvania
Source: *BioIn 2, 3, 4, 11*

Gallo, Ernest
American. Vintner
With brother, Julio, marketed wine under
own label, beginning 1940.
b. 1910 in Modesto, California
Source: *BusPN; CmCal; Entr; WhoAm 84*

Gallo, Fortune
Italian. Opera Singer
b. May 9, 1878 in Torremaggiore, Italy
d. Mar 28, 1970 in New York, New York
Source: *CurBio 49, 70; NewYTBE 70; WhAm
5*

Gallo, Frank
American. Artist
b. Jan 13, 1933 in Toledo, Ohio
Source: *BioIn 7, 8, 9; DcCAA 71; WhoAm
74, 76, 78, 80, 82; WhoAmA 73*

Gallo, Julio
American. Vintner
Known for mid-priced wine; sell over 100
million gallons a yr.
b. 1911 in Modesto, California
Source: *BusPN; CmCal; Entr; WhoAm 84*

Galloway, Don
American. Actor
Played Sergeant Ed Brown in TV series
"Ironside," 1967-75.
b. Jul 27, 1937 in Brooksville, Kentucky
Source: *WhoAm 82; WhoHol A*

Gallup, George Horace
American. Pollster
Founded Gallup Poll, 1935; first major
success was prediction of reelection of
FDR, 1936.
b. Nov 18, 1901 in Jefferson, Iowa
d. Jul 26, 1984 in Tschingel, Switzerland
Source: *AmAu&B; AmM&WS 73S; AnObit
1984; BioNews 74; CelR; ConAu 13R; CurBio
40, 52; EncAB-H; IntWW 74; LongCTC;
REn; REnAL; WebAB; WhoAm 80, 82;
WhoWor 78*

Galois, Evariste
French. Mathematician
b. Oct 25, 1811 in Bourg-la-Reine, France
d. May 31, 1832 in Paris, France
Source: *BioIn 1, 5, 7, 8, 11; NewCol 75;
WebBD 80*

Galsworthy, John
[John Sinjohn, pseud.]
English. Author, Dramatist
Known for social satire; won Nobel Prize,
    1932.
b. Aug 14, 1867 in Kingston, England
d. Jan 31, 1933 in Hampstead, England
Source: *AtlBL; CasWL; Chambr 3; ChhPo,
S1, S2; CnMD; CnMWL; CnThe; CyWA;
DcBiA; DcLEL; EncWL; EvLB; FilmgC;
LongCTC; McGEWD; ModBrL, S1; ModWD;
NewC; OxEng; OxThe; PenC ENG; RAdv 1;
RComWL; REn; REnWD; TwCA, SUP;
TwCWr; WebE&AL; WhoLA; WhoTwCL*

Galt, John
Scottish. Author
Founded Guelph, ON, 1827.
b. May 2, 1779 in Irvine, Scotland
d. Apr 11, 1839 in Greenock, Scotland
Source: *BbD; BrAu 19; CasWL; Chambr 3;
CyWA; EvLB; NewC; OxCan; OxEng; PenC
ENG; WebE&AL*

Galtieri, Leopoldo Fortunato
Argentine. Political Leader
Pres. of Argentina, 1976-82; resigned after
    unsuccessful war with Great Britain over
    Falkland Islands.
b. Jul 15, 1926 in Caseros, Argentina
Source: *CurBio 82*

Galton, Francis, Sir
English. Scientist, Explorer
Founded modern technique of weather
    mapping, 1863.
b. Feb 16, 1822 in Birmingham, England
d. Jan 17, 1911 in Haslemere, England
Source: *Alli SUP; BbD; BiD&SB; BrAu 19;
Chambr 3; DcEnL; DcLEL; EvLB; LongCTC;
NewC*

Galuppi, Baldassare
Italian. Composer
b. Oct 18, 1706 in Burano, Italy
d. Jan 3, 1785 in Venice, Italy
Source: *REn*

Galvani, Luigi
Italian. Physicist, Physician
Devised Galvanic cell.
b. 1737
d. 1798
Source: *NewC*

Galvez, Bernardo de
Spanish. Colonial Leader
Captain general of LA, the Floridas, 1783;
    viceroy of New Spain, 1785.
b. Jul 23, 1746 in Macharaviaya, Spain
d. Nov 30, 1786 in Mexico
Source: *AmBi; ApCAB; BioIn 3, 9, 10, 11;
DcAmB; Drake; McGEWB; NatCAB 10;
NewCol 75; REnAW; WebBD 80; WhAm HS*

Galvin, "Pud" (James Francis)
"Gentle Jeems"; "The Little Steam Engine"
American. Baseball Player
Pitcher, won 46 games in two consecutive
    seasons, 1883-84; Hall of Fame, 1965.
b. Dec 25, 1856 in Saint Louis, Missouri
d. Mar 7, 1902 in Pittsburgh, Pennsylvania
Source: *BaseEn 85; BioIn 7, 10; WhoProB 73*

Galway, James
Irish. Musician
b. Dec 8, 1939 in Belfast, Northern Ireland
Source: *BioIn 11, 12; CurBio 80; IntWW 79;
WhoAm 80, 82*

Gam, Rita Elenore
American. Actress
Films include *Klute, Night People.*
b. Apr 2, 1928 in Pittsburgh, Pennsylvania
Source: *BiE&WWA; ConAu 45; FilmgC;
ForWC 70; InWom; MotPP; MovMk;
NotNAT; PIP&P; WhoAm 74, 76, 78, 80, 82;
WhoHol A*

Gama, Vasco da
see: DaGama, Vasco

Gamaliel the Elder
Palestinian. Rabbi, Scholar
Made innovations in Jewish ritual.
d. 50
Source: *NewC*

Gambetta, Leon
French. Lawyer, Statesman
b. Apr 3, 1838 in Cahors, France
d. Dec 31, 1882
Source: *OxFr; REn*

Gambino, Don Carlo
American. Organized Crime Figure
b. 1902
d. Oct 15, 1976 in Massapequa, New York
Source: *NewYTBE 71*

Gamble, James Norris
American. Manufacturer
Partner in Proctor and Gamble Co.;
  developed Ivory Soap.
b. Aug 9, 1836 in Cincinnati, Ohio
d. Jul 2, 1932
Source: *WhAm 1*

Gambling, John A
American. Radio Performer
b. 1930 in New York, New York
Source: *NewYTBE 73*

Gambling, John Bradley
English. Radio Performer
b. Apr 9, 1897 in Norwich, England
d. Nov 21, 1974 in Palm Beach, Florida
Source: *BioIn 2, 10; CurBio 50, 75;*
NewYTBS 74

Gamelin, Maurice Gustave
French. General
Head of Allied forces at outbreak of WW II.
b. Sep 20, 1872 in Paris, France
d. Apr 18, 1958 in Paris, France
Source: *CurBio 40, 58*

Gance, Abel
French. Director, Writer
Pioneer filmmaker who made 1927 silent epic
  Napoleon (revised 1981); used multiple
  screens, wide angle lenses.
b. Oct 25, 1889 in Paris, France
d. Nov 10, 1981 in Paris, France
Source: *BiDFilm; BioIn 11; ConAu 108;*
DcFM; FilmEn; IntWW 78; OxFilm; WhoWor
74; WorEFlm

Gandhi, Indira Priyadarshini Nehru
Indian. Politician
Prime minister, 1966-77, 1978-84; worked for
  economic planning, social reform.
b. Nov 19, 1917 in Allahabad, India
d. Oct 31, 1984 in New Delhi, India
Source: *AnObit 1984; BioNews 74; ConNews*
85-1; CurBio 59, 66, 84; HerW; NewYTBE
72; Who 74; WhoGov 72; WhoWor 74

Gandhi, Mahatma
[Mohandas Karamchand Gandhi]
Indian. Religious Leader, Lawyer
Known for fasts, civil disobedience which
  played role in struggle for Indian
  independence.
b. Oct 2, 1869 in Porbandar, India
d. Jan 30, 1948 in New Delhi, India
Source: *CasWL; CurBio 42, 48; DcLEL;*
OxEng; PenC CL; REn; WhAm 2

Gandhi, Rajiv Ratna
Indian. Political Leader
Son of Indira Gandhi who became India's
  sixth and youngest prime minister, 1984.
b. Aug 20, 1944 in Bombay, India
Source: *CurBio 85; FarE&A 81; NewYTBS 84*

Gandhi, Sanjay
Indian. Celebrity Relative
Son of Indira Gandhi.
b. Dec 14, 1946 in New Delhi, India
d. Jun 23, 1980 in New Delhi, India
Source: *AnObit 1980; BioIn 10; NewYTBS 76*

Gann, Ernest Kellogg
American. Author
Wrote best-seller *High and the Mighty*, 1952.
b. Oct 13, 1910 in Lincoln, Nebraska
Source: *AmAu&B; AmNov; ConAu 1R;*
TwCWr; WhoAm 82; WhoPNW; WorAu;
WrDr 76

Gannett, Deborah Sampson
American. Heroine
Served in Continental forces, May, 1782-Oct,
  1783, disguised as man.
b. Dec 17, 1760 in Plymouth, Massachusetts
d. Apr 29, 1827 in Sharon, Massachusetts
Source: *BioIn 1, 3, 5, 8, 9, 10, 11*

Gannett, Frank Ernest
American. Newspaper Publisher
b. Sep 15, 1876 in Bristol, New York
d. Sep 3, 1957 in Rochester, New York
Source: *AmAu&B; CurBio 45, 58; REnAL;*
WhAm 3; WhNAA

Gannett, Lewis Stiles
American. Critic
b. Oct 3, 1891 in Rochester, New York
d. Feb 3, 1966
Source: *AmAu&B; ConAu 89; CurBio 41, 66;*
REnAL; TwCA, SUP; WhAm 4, 4A

Gannett, Ruth
American. Children's Author
b. Aug 12, 1923 in New York, New York
Source: *AuBYP; BkCL; ConAu 21R; IlsCB*
1946; MorJA; SmATA 3

Gans, Joe
"Old Master"
American. Boxer
b. Nov 25, 1874 in Philadelphia,
  Pennsylvania
d. Aug 16, 1910 in Baltimore, Maryland
Source: *WhoBox 74*

Ganz, Rudolph
Swiss. Conductor, Musician, Composer
b. Feb 24, 1877 in Zurich, Switzerland
d. Aug 2, 1972 in Chicago, Illinois
Source: *AmSCAP 66; NewYTBE 72; WhAm 5*

Garagiola, Joe (Joseph Henry)
American. Baseball Player, Sportscaster
Catcher, 1946-54; baseball broadcaster on
    radio and TV, 1955--.
b. Feb 12, 1926 in Saint Louis, Missouri
Source: *BaseEn 85; BioNews 74; CelR;
WhoAm 74, 76, 78, 80, 82; WhoE 74;
WhoProB 73*

Garamond, Claude
French. Type Designer
b. 1480
d. 1561
Source: *NewCol 75; WebBD 80*

Garand, John Cantius
American. Engineer, Inventor
Developed Garand semi-automatic rifle (M-1)
    for US Army, 1930.
b. Jan 1, 1888 in Saint Remi, Quebec
d. Feb 16, 1974 in Springfield, Massachusetts
Source: *CurBio 45, 74; NewYTBS 74;
WebAB; WhAm 6*

Garavani, Valentino
Italian. Fashion Designer
b. 1932 in Voghera, Italy
Source: *WorFshn*

Garber, Jan
American. Band Leader
b. 1895
d. Oct 5, 1977 in Shreveport, Louisiana
Source: *BioIn 11*

Garbo, Greta
[Greta Louisa Gustafsson]
Swedish. Actress
Starred in film *Anna Karenina*, 1935; won
    special Oscar, 1954.
b. Sep 18, 1905 in Stockholm, Sweden
Source: *BiDFilm; BioNews 74; BkPepl; CelR;
CmMov; CurBio 55; FilmgC; InWom;
IntMPA 75, 76, 77, 78, 79, 80, 81, 82;
IntWW 74; MotPP; MovMk; OxFilm; ThFT;
TwYS; WebAB; Who 74; WhoAm 74, 76, 78,
80, 82; WhoHol A; WorEFlm*

Garcia, Carlos P
Philippine. President
b. Nov 4, 1896 in Philippines
d. Jun 14, 1971 in Manila, Philippines
Source: *CurBio 57, 71; NewYTBE 71; WhAm
5*

Garcia, Damaso Domingo
Dominican. Baseball Player
b. Feb 7, 1957 in Moca, Dominican Republic
Source: *BaseEn 85*

Garcia, Jerry (Jerome John)
[The Grateful Dead]
American. Musician, Singer
b. Aug 1, 1942 in San Francisco, California
Source: *BiDAmM; BioIn 9, 11; BkPepl;
ConMuA 80A; WhoAm 82; WhoRock 81*

Garcia, Manuel del Popolo Vincente, I
Spanish. Opera Singer, Composer
b. Jan 22, 1775 in Seville, Spain
d. Jun 2, 1832 in Paris, France
Source: *BiDAmM; NewEOp 71; OxMus*

Garcia, Manuel Patricio Rodriguez, II
Spanish. Opera Singer, Teacher
b. Mar 17, 1805 in Madrid, Spain
d. Jul 1, 1906 in London, England
Source: *NewEOp 71; OxMus*

Garcia, Mike (Edward Miguel)
"The Big Bear"
American. Baseball Player
Pitcher, 1948-61, mostly with Cleveland; had
    142 career wins.
b. Nov 17, 1923 in San Gabriel, California
d. Jan 13, 1986 in Cleveland, Ohio
Source: *BaseEn 85; BioIn 3; WhoProB 73*

Garcia Lorca, Federico
Spanish. Poet, Dramatist
Best known works include play *Blood
    Wedding*, 1933; killed during civil war.
b. Jun 5, 1899 in Fuente Vaqueros, Spain
d. Aug 19, 1936 in Fuente Vaqueros, Spain
Source: *AtlBL; CasWL; ClDMEL; CnMD;
CnMWL; CnThe; CyWA; DcSpL; EncWL;
EvEuW; LongCTC; McGEWD; ModRL;
ModWD; OxEng; OxThe; PenC EUR;
RComWL; REn; REnWD; TwCA, SUP;
TwCWr; WhAm 4; WhoTwCL*

Garcia-Marquez, Gabriel
Colombian. Author
Won 1982 Nobel Prize for literature.
b. Mar 6, 1928 in Aracatacca, Colombia
Source: *CasWL; ConAu 33R; ConLC 2, 3, 8,
10, 15; DcCLAA; PenC AM; WorAu*

Garcia Perez, Alan
Peruvian. Political Leader
Elected pres. of Peru, Jul 28, 1985.
b. May 23, 1949 in Lima, Peru
Source: *CurBio 85*

Gard, Wayne
American. Journalist, Historian
b. Jun 21, 1899 in Brocton, Illinois
Source: *AmAu&B; AnMV 1926; ConAu 1R; TexWr; WhNAA*

Gardella, Kay
American. Broadcaster
b. 1923 in Belleville, New Jersey
Source: *ForWC 70*

Garden, Mary
Scottish. Opera Singer
Soprano chosen by Debussy for premiere
    performance of *Pellas et Melisande*, 1902;
    awarded French Legion of Honor.
b. Feb 20, 1874 in Aberdeen, Scotland
d. Jan 4, 1967 in Aberdeen, Scotland
Source: *Film 1; InWom; NotAW MOD; REn; TwYS; WebAB; WhAm 4; WhScrn 74, 77; WhoHol B*

Gardenia, Vincent
[Vincent Scognamiglio]
American. Actor
Won Tony for *Prisoner of Second Avenue*,
    1971; Oscar nominee for *Bang the Drum
    Slowly*, 1973.
b. Jan 7, 1922 in Naples, Italy
Source: *BiE&WWA; ConTFT 2; FilmgC; IntMPA 82; NewYTBS 74; NotNAT; PlP&P A; VarWW 85; WhoAm 82; WhoHol A; WhoThe 77*

Gardiner, Reginald
English. Actor
Familiar character actor; has appeared in 100
    films since 1936, including *The Great
    Dictator*, 1940.
b. Feb 27, 1903 in Wimbledon, England
d. Jul 7, 1980 in Westwood, California
Source: *BiE&WWA; BioIn 2, 10; FilmgC; MotPP; MovMk; Vers A; WhoHol A; WhoThe 77*

Gardner, Ava
[Lucy Johnson]
American. Actress
Starred in movie *Show Boat*, 1951; husbands
    included Mickey Rooney, Artie Shaw,
    Frank Sinatra.
b. Dec 24, 1922 in Smithfield, North
    Carolina
Source: *BiDFilm; CelR; CurBio 65; FilmEn; FilmgC; IntMPA 75, 76, 77, 78, 79, 80, 81, 82; IntWW 74; MotPP; MovMk; OxFilm; WhoAm 74, 76, 78, 80, 82; WhoHol A; WorEFlm*

Gardner, Ed(ward Francis)
American. Comedian
b. Jun 29, 1905 in Astoria, New York
d. Aug 17, 1963
Source: *CurBio 43, 63; WhScrn 74, 77; WhoHol B*

Gardner, Erle Stanley
[A A Fair, pseud.]
American. Author, Lawyer
Wrote Perry Mason detective stories series,
    basis for movies, radio, TV series.
b. Jul 17, 1889 in Malden, Massachusetts
d. Mar 11, 1970 in Temecula, California
Source: *AmAu&B; ConAu 5R, 25R; CurBio 44, 70; EncMys; EvLB; FilmgC; LongCTC; MnBBF; NewYTBE 70; OxAmL; PenC AM; REn; REnAL; TwCA, SUP; TwCWr; WebAB; WhAm 6; WhNAA*

Gardner, George
Irish. Boxer
b. Mar 17, 1877 in Lisdoonvarna, Ireland
d. Jul 8, 1954 in Chicago, Illinois
Source: *BioIn 3; WhoBox 74*

Gardner, Hy
American. Journalist
b. Dec 2, 1908 in New York, New York
Source: *ConAu 101; WhoAm 74, 76, 78, 80, 82*

Gardner, Isabella
American. Poet
b. Sep 7, 1915 in Newton, Massachusetts
d. Jul 7, 1981 in New York, New York
Source: *AmWomWr; BioIn 10; IntWWP 77; WhoAm 74; WhoAmW 74*

Gardner, Jean Louis Charles
French. Architect
Designed Paris Opera House, 1861-75; Monte
    Carlo casino, 1878.
b. Nov 6, 1825 in Paris, France
d. Aug 3, 1898
Source: *NewCol 75; WebBD 80*

Gardner, John Champlin, Jr.
American. Author
Wrote *October Light*, 1976; *The King's
    Indian*, 1974.
b. Jul 21, 1933 in Batavia, New York
d. Sep 14, 1982 in Susquehanna,
    Pennsylvania
Source: *AnObit 1984; AuBYP SUP; AuNews 1; ConAu 107; ConLC 3, 5, 7, 8, 10; ConNov 76; CurBio 78, 82; DcLEL 1940; DrAF 76; EncSF; ModAL S1; NewYTBS 82; RAdv 1; ScF&FL 1; WhAm 8; WhoAm 74, 76, 78, 80; WorAu 1975; WrDr 76, 80*

Gardner, John William
American. Government Official
Secretary of HEW, 1965-68; wrote *In Common Cause,* 1972.
b. Oct 8, 1912 in Los Angeles, California
Source: *AmAu&B; ConAu 1R, 5R, 4NR; CurBio 56; IntWW 74; Who 74; WhoAm 74, 76, 78, 80, 82; WhoAmP 73; WhoWor 78*

Gardner, Martin
American. Journalist
b. Oct 21, 1914 in Tulsa, Oklahoma
Source: *AmAu&B; AuBYP SUP; BioIn 6, 10; ConAu 73; EncSF; SmATA 16; WhoE 74*

Gardner, Mary Sewall
American. Nurse
Wrote classic text *Public Health Nursing,* 1916.
b. Feb 5, 1871 in Newton, Massachusetts
d. Feb 20, 1961 in Providence, Rhode Island
Source: *NotAW MOD*

Gardner, Randy
American. Figure Skater
Teamed with Tai Babilonia to win five national championships, 1979 world title.
b. Dec 2, 1958 in Marina del Rey, California
Source: *BioIn 12; NewYTBS 79*

Gardner, Samuel
Russian. Musician
b. Aug 25, 1891 in Elisavetgrad, Russia
Source: *AmSCAP 66; WhoMus 72*

Gareau, Jacqueline
American. Runner
Real winner of 1980 Boston Marathon, in which Rosie Ruiz was disqualified.
b. Mar 10, 1953
Source: *BioIn 12*

Garfield, Brian Wynne
American. Author
b. Jan 26, 1939 in New York, New York
Source: *BioIn 10; ConAu 1R; WhoAm 82*

Garfield, James Abram
American. US President
Shot Jul 2, 1881 in Washington railway station by Charles J Guiteau.
b. Nov 19, 1831 in Cuyahoga County, Ohio
d. Sep 19, 1881 in Elberon, New Jersey
Source: *Alli SUP; AmAu&B; ApCAB; BiAUS; BiD&SB; BiDrAC; BiDrUSE; DcAmAu; DcAmB; Drake; EncAB-H; OhA&B; OxAmL; REnAL; TwCBDA; WebAB; WhAm HS; WhAmP*

Garfield, John
[Julius Garfinkle]
American. Actor
Played tough-guy roles in *The Postman Always Rings Twice, Body and Soul;* victim of McCarthy's blacklist.
b. Mar 4, 1913 in New York, New York
d. May 21, 1952 in New York, New York
Source: *BiDFilm; CmMov; CurBio 48, 52; DcAmB S5; FilmgC; MotPP; MovMk; OxFilm; PIP&P; WhScrn 74, 77; WhoHol B; WorEFlm*

Garfield, Leon
English. Author
b. Jul 14, 1921 in Brighton, England
Source: *ConAu 17R; ConLC 12; PiP; SenS; SmATA 1; WhoChL; WrDr 80*

Garfield, Lucretia Rudolph
[Mrs. James A Garfield]
American. First Lady
In White House less than seven months; survived husband by 30 yrs.
b. Apr 19, 1832 in Hiram, Ohio
d. Mar 14, 1918 in Pasadena, California
Source: *AmWom; ApCAB SUP; BioIn 2, 3, 5, 6, 7, 8, 9; NatCAB 4; NotAW; TwCBDA; WhAm 1*

Garfinkle, Louis
American. Writer
Wrote award-winning film *The Deer Hunter,* 1982.
b. Feb 11, 1928 in Seattle, Washington
Source: *VarWW 85*

Garfunkel, Art(hur)
[Simon and Garfunkel]
American. Singer, Actor
Best known songs with Paul Simon include "The Sounds of Silence," "Mrs. Robinson."
b. Oct 13, 1942 in Forest Hills, New York
Source: *BkPepl; CelR; CurBio 74; FilmgC; IntMPA 75, 76, 77, 78, 79, 80, 81, 82; WhoAm 74, 76, 78, 80, 82*

Gargan, William
American. Actor
Played TV's first detective "Martin Kane, Private Eye," 1949.
b. Jul 17, 1905 in New York, New York
d. Feb 16, 1979
Source: *CurBio 69, 79; FilmgC; HolP 30; IntMPA 75, 76, 77; MotPP; MovMk; WhoHol A; WhoThe 77A*

Garibaldi, Guiseppe
Italian. Patriot, Soldier
b. Jul 4, 1807 in Nice, France
d. Jun 2, 1882
Source: *McGEWB; WhAm HS*

Garis, Howard Roger
American. Author
Worked for Stratemeyer syndicate; wrote
Uncle Wiggly series.
b. Apr 25, 1873 in Binghamton, New York
d. Nov 5, 1962 in Amherst, Massachusetts
Source: *AmAu&B; CarSB; ConAu 73;*
REnAL; SmATA 13; WhAm 4

Garland, Ailsa
English. Broadcaster
Source: *Au&Wr 71; Who 74*

Garland, Beverly
[Beverly Lucy Fessenden]
American. Actress
Played in TV shows "My Three Sons," 1969-
72; "Scarecrow and Mrs. King, 1983--.
b. Oct 17, 1926 in Santa Cruz, California
Source: *FilmgC; IntMPA 77; MotPP; MovMk;*
WhoAm 80; WhoHol A

Garland, Hamlin
American. Author
b. Sep 14, 1860 in West Salem, Wisconsin
d. Mar 4, 1940 in Los Angeles, California
Source: *AmAu&B; AmBi; AmLY; ApCAB*
SUP; AtlBL; BbD; BiD&SB; BiDPara;
CasWL; Chambr 3; ChhPo; CnDAL;
ConAmA; ConAmL; CurBio 40; CyWA;
DcAmAu; DcAmB S2; DcBiA; DcLEL;
DcNAA; EvLB; LongCTC; ModAL; OxAmL;
OxCan; OxEng; PenC AM; RAdv 1; REn;
REnAL; Str&VC; TwCA, SUP; TwCBDA;
WebAB; WebE&AL; WhAm 1; WhNAA;
WisWr

Garland, Judy
[Frances Gumm]
American. Actress, Singer
Played Dorothy in *The Wizard of Oz,* 1939;
mother of Liza Minnelli, Lorna Luft.
b. Jun 10, 1922 in Grand Rapids, Minnesota
d. Jun 22, 1969 in London, England
Source: *BiDFilm; CmMov; CurBio 41, 52, 69;*
FilmgC; InWom; MotPP; MovMk; OxFilm;
ThFT; WebAB; WhAm 5; WhScrn 74, 77;
WhoHol B; WorEFlm

Garlits, Don
American. Auto Racer
b. 1932
Source: *BioIn 7, 8, 9, 10, 11*

Garment, Leonard
American. Lawyer
b. May 11, 1924 in Brooklyn, New York
Source: *NewYTBE 73; WhoAm 74, 76, 78;*
WhoAmP 73; WhoGov 75; WhoS&SW 82

Garms, Shirley Rudolph
American. Bowler
b. 1924
Source: *BioIn 6, 9*

Garn, Jake (Edwin Jacob)
American. Politician
Rep. senator from UT, 1974--; first politician
in space, Apr 12, 1985 on space shuttle
Discovery.
b. Oct 12, 1932 in Richfield, Utah
Source: *AlmAP 80; CurBio 85; WhoAm 82;*
WhoGov 77; WhoWest 78

Garneau, Marc
Canadian. Naval Officer, Astronaut
Aboard US space shuttle *Challenger,* was
Canada's first astronaut.
b. Feb 23, 1949 in Quebec City, Quebec
Source: *ConNews 85-1; NewYTBS 84*

Garner, Erroll
American. Musician, Composer
b. Jun 15, 1921 in Pittsburgh, Pennsylvania
d. Jan 2, 1977 in Los Angeles, California
Source: *AmSCAP 66; CelR; CurBio 59;*
WhoAm 74; WhoE 74; WhoBlA 75

Garner, James
[James Baumgarner]
American. Actor
Starred in "The Rockford Files"; appeared in
Polaroid commercials with Mariette
Hartley.
b. Apr 7, 1928 in Norman, Oklahoma
Source: *BkPepl; CelR; CmMov; CurBio 66;*
FilmgC; IntMPA 75, 76, 77, 78, 79, 80, 81,
82; MotPP; MovMk; NewYTBE 71; WhoAm
74, 76, 78, 80, 82; WhoHol A; WorEFlm

Garner, John Nance
American. Lawyer, Politician
Vp under Franklin Roosevelt, 1933-41.
b. Nov 22, 1868 in Blossom Prairie, Texas
d. Nov 7, 1967 in Uvalde, Texas
Source: *BiDrAC; BiDrUSE; EncAB-H;*
WebAB; WhAm 4; WhAmP

Garner, Peggy Ann
American. Actress
Won special Oscar, 1945, "Outstanding Child
Performer" in *A Tree Grows in Brooklyn.*
b. Feb 3, 1931 in Canton, Ohio
d. Oct 17, 1984 in Woodland Hills,
California
Source: *FilmEn; FilmgC; ForWC 70; HolP
40; IntMPA 75, 76, 77; MotPP; MovMk;
WhoHol A*

Garnet, Henry Highland
American. Abolitionist, Clergyman
b. Dec 23, 1815 in New Market, Maryland
d. Feb 13, 1882 in Monrovia, Liberia
Source: *BioIn 4, 6, 8, 9, 11; DcAmB; WhAm
HS*

Garnett, Constance
English. Translator
b. 1861
d. Dec 17, 1946 in Edenbridge, England
Source: *DcLEL; LongCTC; NewC; OxEng;
PenC ENG; REn*

Garnett, David
[Leda Burke, pseud.]
English. Author
Novelist, biographer, fantasy writer who co-
founded Nonesuch Press, 1923; wrote
award-winning *Lady into Fox,* 1922.
b. Mar 9, 1892 in Brighton, England
d. Feb 17, 1981 in Montucq, France
Source: *Au&Wr 71; CasWL; ConLC 3;
ConNov 76; CyWA; DcLEL; EncSF; EncWL;
EvLB; IntAu&W 76; IntWW 74, 75, 76, 77,
78; LongCTC; ModBrL; NewC; PenC ENG;
REn; ScF&FL 1, 2; TwCA, SUP; TwCWr;
WhE&EA; WhLit; Who 74; WhoHr&F;
WhoLA; WhoWor 74, 76, 78*

Garnett, Eve C R
English. Children's Author, Illustrator
b. in Worcestershire, England
Source: *Au&Wr 71; AuBYP; ConAu 1R;
IlsCB 1744, 1946; SmATA 3; WhoChL; WrDr
80*

Garnett, Gale
New Zealander. Actress, Singer
Wrote, performed, "We'll Sing in the
Sunshine," 1964, which won Grammy.
b. Jul 17, 1942 in New Zealand
Source: *RkOn 84; WhoRock 81*

Garnett, Richard
English. Author
b. Feb 27, 1835 in Staffordshire, England
d. Apr 13, 1906 in London, England
Source: *Alli SUP; BbD; BiD&SB; BrAu 19;
CasWL; ChhPo, S1; DcEnA, AP; DcEnL;
DcLEL; EvLB; LongCTC; NewC; OxEng;
PenC ENG; REn*

Garr, Teri
American. Actress
Starred in *Tootsie, Mr. Mom.*
b. Dec 11, 1945 in Hollywood, California
Source: *WhoAm 82; WhoHol A*

Garraty, John Arthur
American. Historian, Educator, Author
b. Jul 4, 1920 in Brooklyn, New York
Source: *BioIn 10; ConAu 1R, 2NR; DrAS
74H; SmATA 23; WhoAm 74; WhoWor 78*

Garrett, Betty
American. Actress
Played in TV shows "All in the Family,"
1973-75; "Laverne and Shirley," 1976-82.
b. May 23, 1919 in Saint Joseph, Missouri
Source: *BiE&WWA; CmMov; FilmgC;
IntMPA 75, 76, 77, 78, 79, 80, 81, 82;
MotPP; MovMk; NotNAT; WhoAm 82;
WhoHol A; WhoThe 77*

Garrett, Eileen Jeanette Lyttle
American. Psychic, Publisher
b. Mar 17, 1893 in Beau Park, Ireland
d. Sep 16, 1970 in Nice, France
Source: *AmAu&B; BiDPara; ConAu 25R, P-2;
NewYTBE 70; WhAm 5*

Garrett, George Palmer, Jr.
American. Author, Educator
b. Jun 11, 1929 in Orlando, Florida
Source: *AmAu&B; ConAu 1R, 1NR; ConNov
72, 76; ConP 70, 75; DrAF 76; DrAP 75;
IntMPA 82; OxAmL; RAdv 1; REnAL;
WhoAm 74, 76, 78, 80, 82; WhoWor 78;
WorAu; WrDr 80*

Garrett, Leif
American. Actor, Singer
Teen idol whose hit single was a remake of
"Surfin' USA."
b. Nov 8, 1961 in Hollywood, California
Source: *BioIn 11; WhoRock 81*

Garrett, Lila
American. Producer, Writer, Director
Won Emmys for "Mother of the Bride,"
1974; "The Girl Who Couldn't Lose,"
1975.
b. Nov 21, 1925 in New York, New York
Source: *VarWW 85*

Garrett, Michael Lockett
American. Football Player, Baseball Player
b. Apr 12, 1944 in Los Angeles, California
Source: *BioIn 7, 8, 9, 10; WhoFtbl 74*

Garrett, Pat(rick Floyd)
American. Lawman
Best known for killing Billy the Kid, 1881.
b. 1850 in Alabama
d. Feb 29, 1908 in New Mexico
Source: *BioIn 5, 6, 9, 10, 11; DcNAA; REnAW*

Garrett, Ray, Jr.
American. Government Official
b. Aug 11, 1920 in Chicago, Illinois
d. Feb 3, 1980 in Evanston, Illinois
Source: *BioIn 10; IntWW 75, 76, 77, 78; WhAm 7; WhoAm 74, 76, 78; WhoAmL 79; WhoAmP 75, 77, 79; WhoGov 75*

Garrick, David
English. Actor
Greatest actor of 18th c. English stage; Garrick Club established for actors in his honor, 1831.
b. Feb 19, 1717 in Hereford, England
d. Jan 20, 1779 in London, England
Source: *Alli; BrAu; CasWL; Chambr 2; CrtT 2; DcEnA; DcEnL; DcEuL; DcLEL; EvLB; FilmgC; McGEWD; MouLC 2; NewC; OxEng; OxThe; PenC ENG; REn*

Garrigue, Jean
American. Poet
b. Dec 8, 1914 in Evansville, Indiana
d. Dec 27, 1972 in Boston, Massachusetts
Source: *AmAu&B; BioIn 4, 8, 9; ConAu 5R, 37R; ConLC 2; ConP 70, 75; IndAu 1917; ModAL, S1; OxAmL; PenC AM; RAdv 1; REnAL; TwCA SUP; WhAm 5*

Garriott, Owen
American. Astronaut, Scientist
Science pilot for second Skylab space mission, Jul-Sep, 1973.
b. Nov 22, 1930 in Enid, Oklahoma
Source: *AmM&WS 73P; IntWW 74; NewYTBE 73; WhoAm 82; WhoGov 75; WhoS&SW 82*

Garrison, Jim C
American. Lawyer
Investigated J F Kennedy assassination, 1966; concluded he was murdered by New Orleans conspirators, 1967.
b. Nov 20, 1921 in Denison, Iowa
Source: *PolProf J; WhoAm 78*

Garrison, William Lloyd
American. Abolitionist, Author
b. Dec 12, 1805 in Newburyport, Massachusetts
d. May 24, 1879 in New York, New York
Source: *Alli; AmAu; AmAu&B; AmBi; ApCAB; BiD&SB; Chambr 3; ChhPo; DcAmAu; DcAmB; DcEnL; DcLEL; DcNAA; EncAB-H; EvLB; OxAmL; REn; REnAL; TwCBDA; WebAB; WhAm HS; WhAmP*

Garrod, Hethcote William
English. Author, Scholar
Wrote *Wordsworth: Lectures and Essays*, 1923.
b. Jan 21, 1878 in Wells, England
d. Dec 25, 1960 in Oxford, England
Source: *DcNaB 1951; NewC; ObitT 1961*

Garroway, Dave (David Cunningham)
American. TV Personality
Original host of "The Today Show," 1952-61.
b. Jul 13, 1913 in Schenectady, New York
d. Jul 21, 1982 in Swarthmore, Pennsylvania
Source: *AnObit 1982; ConAu 107; CurBio 52, 82; IntMPA 80, 81, 82; IntWW 75; NewYTBE 71; NewYTBS 82; NewYTET; WhoAm 80, 82*

Garry, Charles R
American. Lawyer
b. Mar 17, 1909 in Bridgewater, Massachusetts
Source: *BioIn 8, 10, 11; WhoAm 74*

Garson, Greer
American. Actress
Won Oscar, 1942, for *Mrs. Miniver*.
b. Sep 29, 1908 in County Down, Northern Ireland
Source: *BiDFilm; CmMov; CurBio 42; FilmgC; InWom; IntMPA 75, 76, 77, 78, 79, 80, 81, 82; MotPP; MovMk; OxFilm; ThFT; Who 74; WhoAm 74, 76, 78, 80, 82; WhoHol A; WhoThe 77A; WorEFlm*

Garst, Roswell
American. Agriculturist
Hybrid corn authority; advised Eastern Communists on improved farm methods, 1950s-60s; wrote *No Need for Hunger*, 1964.
b. 1898 in Rockford, Illinois
d. Nov 5, 1977 in Carroll, Iowa
Source: *BioIn 5, 6, 7, 10, 11; CurBio 64, 78; EncAAH; NewYTBS 77; ObitOF 79*

Garth, David
American. Public Relations Executive
Prominent political strategist, 1960--; clients included Ed Koch, John Lindsay.
b. 1930 in Woodmere, New York
Source: *BioIn 11; CurBio 81; WhoAm 82*

Garver, Kathy
American. Actress
Played Cissy on TV's "Family Affair," 1966-71.
b. Dec 13, 1947 in Long Beach, California
Source: *WhoHol A*

Garvey, Ed(ward Robert)
American. Lawyer, Labor Union Official
Director, NFL Players' Assn., 1971--; chief negotiator, 1982 strike.
b. Apr 18, 1940 in Burlington, Wisconsin
Source: *WhoAm 82*

Garvey, Marcus Moziah
Jamaican. Political Leader
b. Aug 17, 1887 in Saint Ann's Bay, Jamaica
d. Jun 10, 1940 in London, England
Source: *CurBio 40; DcAmB S2; EncAB-H; WebAB; WhAm HSA, 4; WhAmP*

Garvey, Steve Patrick
American. Baseball Player
First baseman, LA Dodgers, 1970-82; signed multi-million dollar contract with San Diego, 1982.
b. Dec 22, 1948 in Tampa, Florida
Source: *BaseEn 85; WhoAm 82; WhoProB 73*

Garvin, Clifton Canter, Jr.
American. Oilman
b. Dec 22, 1921 in Portsmouth, Virginia
Source: *CurBio 80; WhoAm 78, 80, 82; WhoF&I 79*

Garwood, Robert Russell
American. Soldier
Marine; only American convicted of treason in Vietnam War, 1981.
b. Dec 22, 1946 in Portsmouth, Virginia
Source: *BioIn 12*

Gary, Elbert H
American. Businessman, Philanthropist
b. Oct 8, 1846 in Wheaton, Illinois
d. Aug 15, 1927 in New York, New York
Source: *AmBi; DcAmB; EncAB-H; WebAB; WhAm 1*

Gary, John
American. Singer
b. Nov 29, 1932 in Watertown, New York
Source: *AmSCAP 66; CurBio 67; WhoAm 74; WhoHol A*

Gary, Romain
French. Author, Diplomat
b. May 8, 1914 in Wilno, Lithuania
d. Dec 2, 1980 in Paris, France
Source: *CasWL; ConAu 102; EncWL; IntWW 74; ModRL; REn; TwCWr; Who 74; WhoAm 74; WhoWor 78; WorAu; WorEFlm*

Gary Puckett and the Union Gap
[Dwight Cement; Kerry Chater; Gary Puckett; Paul Wheatbread; Mutha Withem]
American. Music Group
Source: *EncPR&S 74*

Gascoyne, David Emery
English. Poet
b. Oct 10, 1916 in Salisbury, England
Source: *BioIn 10; CnE&AP; ConAu 65; ConP 70; EncWL; LongCTC; ModBrL; PenC ENG; TwCWr; WebE&AL; WhoTwCL; WorAu; WrDr 80*

Gaskell, Elizabeth Cleghorn
English. Author
Known for sympathetic portrayal of working class.
b. Sep 29, 1810 in Chelsea, England
d. Nov 12, 1865 in Alton, England
Source: *Alli SUP; AtlBL; BbD; BiD&SB; BrAu 19; CasWL; CrtT 3; CyWA; DcBiA; DcEnA; DcEuL; DcLEL; EvLB; HsB&A; MouLC 3; NewC; OxEng; PenC ENG; RAdv 1; REn; WebE&AL*

Gaspari, Remo
Italian. Lawyer, Politician
b. 1921 in Gissi, Italy
Source: *IntWW 74*

Gasperi, Alcide de
Italian. Statesman, Political Leader
b. Apr 3, 1881 in Terentino, Italy
d. Aug 19, 1954
Source: *CurBio 46, 54; NewCol 75*

Gass, William H
American. Author
Symbolist who develops aesthetic theories in essays: *Habitations of the Word,* 1985.
b. Jul 30, 1924 in Fargo, North Dakota
Source: *AmAu&B; Au&Wr 71; ConAu 17R; ConLC 1, 2; ConNov 72, 76; CurBio 86; DrAF 76; EncWL; ModAL S1; PenC AM; RAdv 1; WhoAm 74, 76, 78, 80, 82; WorAu; WrDr 76*

Gasser, Herbert Spencer
American. Physiologist
b. Jul 5, 1888 in Platteville, Wisconsin
d. May 11, 1963
Source: *BioIn 1, 3, 6, 7, 11; CurBio 45, 63; WhAm 4*

Gassman, Vittorio
Italian. Actor, Director
Starred in *Bitter Rice*, 1948; *Anna*, 1951; married Shelley Winters, 1952.
b. Sep 1, 1922 in Genoa, Italy
Source: *BiDFilm; CurBio 64; FilmgC; IntMPA 75, 76, 77; IntWW 74; MotPP; MovMk; WhoAm 82; WhoHol A; WhoWor 78; WorEFlm*

Gassner, John Waldhorn
American. Author
b. Jan 30, 1903 in Sziget, Hungary
d. Apr 2, 1967 in New Haven, Connecticut
Source: *AmAu&B; ConAu 1R, 25R, 3NR; CurBio 47, 67; REnAL; WhAm 4; WhNAA*

Gastineau, Mark (Marcus D)
American. Football Player
Defensive end, NY Jets, 1979--, known for inflammatory dances after quarterback sacks.
b. Nov 20, 1956 in Ardmore, Oklahoma
Source: *FootReg 85*

Gaston, Arthur George
American. Insurance Executive
b. 1892
Source: *BioIn 6, 8, 9, 11*

Gates, David
[Bread]
American. Singer, Songwriter
b. Dec 11, 1940 in Tulsa, Oklahoma
Source: *RkOn 78; WhoRock 81*

Gates, Horatio
American. General
b. Jul 26, 1728 in Malden, England
d. Apr 10, 1806 in New York, New York
Source: *AmBi; ApCAB; DcAmB; Drake; OxAmL; REn; REnAL; TwCBDA; WebAB; WhAm HS*

Gates, John Warne
"Bet a Million"
American. Financier
Made fortune in manufacturing barbed wire, acquiring interests in steel, iron, coal.
b. May 8, 1855 in Turner Junction, Illinois
d. Aug 9, 1911 in Paris, France
Source: *AmBi; BusPN; DcAmB; WebAB; WhAm 1, 4*

Gates, Larry
American. Actor
Character actor on stage, 1939, films 1951; played in *Cat on a Hot Tin Roof.*
b. Sep 24, 1915 in Saint Paul, Minnesota
Source: *BiE&WWA; FilmgC; NotNAT; WhoThe 77*

Gates, Thomas Sovereign, Jr.
American. Businessman, Statesman
Secretary of Defense under Dwight Eisenhower, 1959-61; authorized Gary Powers U-2 flight.
b. Apr 10, 1906 in Philadelphia, Pennsylvania
d. Mar 25, 1983 in Philadelphia, Pennsylvania
Source: *BiDrUSE; CurBio 57, 83N; IntWW 74, 80, 81; NewYTBS 83; St&PR 75; Who 74; WhoAm 74; WhoAmP 73; WhoE 74*

Gatlin, Larry Wayne
American. Singer, Songwriter
Lead singer in country-pop group Gatlin Brothers.
b. May 2, 1949 in Odessa, Texas
Source: *BioIn 11; WhoAm 82*

Gatling, Richard Jordan
American. Inventor
Creator of first practical rapid-firing gun, 1862, forerunner of modern machine gun.
b. Sep 12, 1818 in Hertford County, North Carolina
d. Feb 26, 1903 in New York, New York
Source: *AmBi; ApCAB; DcAmB; TwCBDA; WebAB; WhAm 1*

Gatti-Casazza, Giulio
Italian. Manager
Mgr., Metropolitan Opera, 1908-35; discovered Caruso, Flagstad.
b. Feb 3, 1869 in Udine, Italy
d. Sep 2, 1940 in Ferrara, Italy
Source: *CurBio 40; DcAmB S2*

Gaubert, Philippe
French. Musician, Conductor, Composer
b. Jul 4, 1879 in Cahors, France
d. Jul 10, 1941 in Paris, France
Source: *NewEOp 71; OxMus*

Gaud, William Steen, Jr.
American. Lawyer, Government Official
b. Aug 9, 1905 in New York, New York
d. Dec 5, 1977 in Washington, District of Columbia
Source: *CurBio 69, 78; IntWW 74, 76, 77, 78; NewYTBS 77; WhAm 7; WhoAm 74, 76, 78; WhoWor 78*

Gaudi y Cornet, Antonio
Spanish. Architect
b. Jun 25, 1852 in Reus, Spain
d. 1926
Source: *BioIn 2, 3, 4, 5, 8, 9, 10; DcBiPP; McGDA; McGEWB; NewCol 75*

Gaudio, Bob
[The Four Seasons]
American. Singer, Musician
b. Nov 17, 1942 in Bronx, New York
Source: *NF*

Gauguin, Paul (Eugene Henri Paul)
French. Artist
Postimpressionist painter whose work is noted for massive simplified forms, impassive figures, exotic backgrounds.
b. Jun 7, 1848 in Paris, France
d. Jun 6, 1903 in Marquesas Islands
Source: *AtlBL; LongCTC; NewC; NewCol 75; OxFr; REn; WebBD 80*

Gaulli, Giovanni Battista
[Il Baciccio]
Italian. Artist
b. 1639
d. 1709
Source: *BioIn 10*

Gault, William Campbell
American. Author
b. Mar 9, 1910 in Milwaukee, Wisconsin
Source: *AuBYP; ConAu 49, 1NR; EncMys; SmATA 8*

Gault, Willie
American. Football Player, Track Athlete
Wide receiver, Chicago, 1984--; gave up chance in 1984 Olympics to sign pro football contract.
b. Sep 5, 1960 in Griffin, Georgia
Source: *FootReg 85*

Gaunt, William
English. Author, Critic, Artist
London art critic, noted for collective biographies of artists, Victorian social histories.
b. Jul 5, 1900 in Hull, England
d. May 24, 1980 in London, England
Source: *Au&Wr 71; BioIn 4, 10, 11; ConAu 9R, 97; IntAu&W 76, 77; LongCTC; TwCA SUP; WhE&EA; Who 74; WhoWor 76, 78; WrDr 76, 80*

Gauss, Karl Friedrich
German. Mathematician
b. Apr 30, 1777 in Brunswick, Germany
d. Feb 23, 1855 in Goettingen, Germany
Source: *AsBiEn; DcBiPP; McGEWB*

Gauthier, Alain
see: Dumurq, Charles

Gautier, Dick
American. Actor
Played on TV shows "Get Smart," 1966-69; "When Things Were Rotten," 1975.
b. Oct 30, 1937 in Los Angeles, California
Source: *AmSCAP 66; FilmgC; WhoAm 82; WhoHol A*

Gautier, Theophile (Pierre Jules Theophile)
French. Poet, Author, Critic
Believed in "art for art's sake"; wrote psychological tale *Mademoiselle de Maupin*, 1835.
b. Aug 31, 1811 in Tarbes, France
d. Oct 23, 1872 in Neuilly, France
Source: *AtlBL; BbD; BiD&SB; CasWL; CyWA; DcBiA; DcEuL; EuAu; EvEuW; NewC; OxEng; OxFr; PenC EUR; RComWL; REn*

Gavilan, Kid
"The Hawk"
Cuban. Boxer
b. Jan 6, 1926 in Camaguey, Cuba
Source: *WhoBox 74*

Gavin, James Maurice
American. Army Officer, Author
b. Mar 22, 1907 in New York, New York
Source: *AmAu&B; ConAu P-1; CurBio 45, 61; IntWW 74; WhoAm 78, 80, 82; WhoF&I 74; WhoWor 78*

Gavin, John
[Jack Golenor]
American. Actor, Diplomat
Ambassador to Mexico under Ronald Reagan, 1981-86.
b. Apr 8, 1932 in Los Angeles, California
Source: *CurBio 62; FilmEn; FilmgC; IntMPA 80, 81, 82; MovMk; WhoHol A*

Gaxton, William
American. Actor
Comedian who co-starred with Mae West in *The Heat's On,* 1943.
b. Dec 2, 1893 in San Francisco, California
d. Feb 2, 1963 in New York, New York
Source: *EncMT; FilmgC; PlP&P; WhScrn 74, 77; WhoHol B*

Gay, John
English. Poet, Dramatist
Friend of Swift and Pope; wrote *Beggar's Opera*, 1728.
b. 1685 in Barnstaple, England
d. Dec 4, 1732 in London, England
Source: *Alli; AtlBL; BiD&SB; BrAu; CarSB; CasWL; Chambr 2; ChhPo, S1, S2; CnE&AP; CnThe; CrtT 2; CyWA; DcEnA, AP; DcEnL; DcEuL; DcLEL; EvLB; McGEWD; MouLC 2; NewC; OxEng; OxThe; PenC ENG; REn; REnWD; WebE&AL*

Gay, Peter Jack
American. Author, Educator, Historian
Psychoanalytic historian who won National Book Award for *The Enlightenment*, 1966, 1969.
b. Jun 20, 1923 in Berlin, Germany
Source: *ConAu 13R; CurBio 86; DrAS 74H; WhoAm 74, 76, 78, 80, 82, 84; WhoWor 74*

Gay-Lussac, Joseph Louis
French. Chemist, Physicist
Formulated Gay-Lussac's law of vapor pressure of gases.
b. Dec 6, 1778 in Saint Leonard, France
d. May 9, 1850 in Paris, France
Source: *AsBiEn; BiHiMed; DcScB; McGEWB; NewCol 75; REn*

Gaye, Marvin (Marvin Pentz)
American. Singer
Had several gold, platinum hits, 1962-83; won two Grammys, 1983; hits include "Ain't That Peculiar," 1965; "Sexual Healing," 1982.
b. Apr 2, 1939 in Washington, District of Columbia
d. Apr 1, 1984 in Los Angeles, California
Source: *AnObit 1984; BiDAmM; EncPR&S 74; IlEncBM 82; IlEncRk; WhoAm 82*

Gayle, Crystal
[Mrs. Vassilios Gatzimos; Brenda Gail Webb]
American. Singer
Country-pop singer; sister of Loretta Lynn, known for trademark long hair; won Grammy, 1978, for "Don't It Make My Brown Eyes Blue."
b. Jan 9, 1951 in Paintsville, Kentucky
Source: *BkPepl; CurBio 86; WhoAm 80, 82*

Gaynor, Gloria
"Queen of Disco"
American. Singer
Hits include " Never Can Say Goodbye," 1974; "I Will Survive," 1979.
b. Sep 7, 1949 in Newark, New Jersey
Source: *DrBlPA; IlEncBM 82; RkOn 78; WhoRock 81*

Gaynor, Janet
[Laura Gainor]
American. Actress
Won first Oscar given, 1928, for films *Sunrise; Seventh Heaven; Street Angel.*
b. Oct 6, 1906 in Philadelphia, Pennsylvania
d. Sep 14, 1984 in Palm Springs, California
Source: *AnObit 1984; BiDFilm; CmMov; FilmgC; InWom; MotPP; MovMk; OxFilm; ThFT; TwYS; VarWW 85; WhoHol A; WorEFlm*

Gaynor, Mitzi
[Francesca Mitzi Marlene de Charney von Gerber]
American. Singer, Dancer
Starred in film version of *South Pacific*, 1958.
b. Sep 4, 1931 in Chicago, Illinois
Source: *CmMov; FilmgC; InWom; IntMPA 75, 76, 77, 78, 79, 80, 81, 82; MotPP; MovMk; OxFilm; WhoAm 74, 76, 78, 80, 82; WhoHol A; WorEFlm*

Gayoom, Maumoon Abdul
Maldivian. Politician
b. Dec 16, 1939
Source: *IntWW 79*

Gazda, Ricky
[Southside Johnny and the Asbury Jukes]
American. Musician
Trumpeter with group since 1974.
b. Jun 18, 1952
Source: *NF*

Gazzaniga, Giuseppe
Italian. Composer
b. 1743 in Verona, Italy
d. Feb 1, 1818 in Crema, Italy
Source: *NewEOp 71*

Gazzara, Ben (Biago Anthony)
American. Actor
Appeared on stage in *Cat on a Hot Tin Roof*, 1955; TV show "Run For Your Life," 1965-68.
b. Aug 28, 1930 in New York, New York
Source: *BiDFilm; BiE&WWA; CelR; CurBio 67; FilmgC; IntMPA 77, 78, 79, 80, 81, 82; MotPP; MovMk; OxFilm; PIP&P A; WhoAm 74, 76, 78, 80, 82; WhoHol A; WhoThe 77*

Gazzelloni, Severino
Italian. Musician
Internationally noted flutist, largely responsible for renaissance of instrument.
b. Jan 5, 1919 in Roccasecca, Italy
Source: *WhoMus 72; WhoWor 74*

Geary, Anthony
American. Actor
Best known for role of Luke Spencer on
    daytime drama "General Hospital."
b. May 29, 1948 in Coalville, Utah
Source: *ConTFT 2; VarWW 85; WhoTelC*

Gebert, Ernst
German. Conductor
b. 1901 in Berlin, Germany
d. Nov 22, 1961 in Hollywood, California
Source: *BioIn 6; NotNAT B*

Ged, William
Scottish. Inventor
Invented stereotyping, patented 1725.
b. 1690 in Edinburgh, Scotland
d. 1749
Source: *LinLib L, S*

Gedda, Nicolai
Swedish. Opera Singer
b. Jul 11, 1925 in Stockholm, Sweden
Source: *CurBio 65; IntWW 74; NewYTBE 72;
WhoAm 82; WhoMus 72; WhoWor 78*

Geddes, Barbara Bel
American. Actress
In films, 1947-71; star of TV series "Dallas,"
    1978--.
b. Oct 31, 1922 in New York, New York
Source: *BiE&WWA; CelR; ConTFT 3; CurBio
48; InWom; IntMPA 75; MotPP; OxThc;
WhoAm 84; WhoHol A*

Geddes, Norman Bel
American. Designer
Foremost proponent of "stream line" style in
    industrial design, 1930s.
b. Apr 27, 1893 in Adrian, Michigan
d. May 8, 1958 in New York, New York
Source: *CurBio 40, 58; PlP&P; OxThe; REn;
REnAL; WebAB; WhAm 3*

Geddes, Patrick, Sir
British. Biologist, Sociologist, Designer
b. Oct 2, 1854 in Ballater, Scotland
d. Apr 16, 1932 in Montpellier, France
Source: *Alli SUP; BbD; BiD&SB; LongCTC;
NewCol 75; TwCA, SUP; WebBD 80; WhoLA*

Geer, Will
American. Actor
Played grandfather on TV series "The
    Waltons"; won Emmy, 1975.
b. Mar 9, 1902 in Frankfort, Indiana
d. Apr 22, 1978 in Los Angeles, California
Source: *BiE&WWA; FilmgC; IntMPA 75, 76,
77; MovMk; NewYTBE 72; NotNAT; WhoHol
A; WhoThe 77*

Geertz, Clifford
American. Anthropologist, Author
b. Aug 23, 1926 in San Francisco, California
Source: *AmM&WS 73S; ConAu 33R; WhoAm
82*

Geeson, Judy
English. Actress
Films include *To Sir With Love.*
b. Sep 10, 1948 in Arundel, England
Source: *FilmEn; FilmgC; IntMPA 80, 81;
MovMk*

Geffen, David
American. Producer
One of most influential people in
    entertainment industry who produced
    Tony-winning Broadway musical, *Cats.*
b. Feb 21, 1943 in Brooklyn, New York
Source: *ConNews 85-3; NewYTBS 82; WhoAm
84; WhoRocM 82*

Gehlen, Reinhard
"The Doctor"; "Number 30"
German. Spy, Author
Head of German Army Intelligence, WW II,
    who specialized in spying on the Soviets.
b. Apr 3, 1902 in Erfurt, Germany
d. Jun 8, 1979 in Lake Starnberg, Germany
    (West)
Source: *BioIn 4, 5, 6, 8, 9, 10; ConAu 89;
EncE 75; NewYTBS 79; SpyCS*

Gehrig, Lou (Henry Louis)
"Columbia Lou"; "The Iron Horse"
American. Baseball Player
First baseman, NY Yankees, 1925-39; played
    in record 2,130 consecutive games.
b. Jun 19, 1903 in New York, New York
d. Jun 2, 1941 in New York, New York
Source: *BaseEn 85; CurBio 40, 41; DcAmB
S3; WebAB; WhAm 4; WhScrn 77; WhoProB
73*

Gehringer, Charlie (Charles Leonard)
American. Baseball Player
Called "mechanical man" because he made
    game look so easy; Hall of Fame, 1949.
b. May 11, 1903 in Fowlerville, Michigan
Source: *BaseEn 85; WhoProB 73*

Geiberger, Al(len L)
American. Golfer
Won PGA, 1966; Greensboro Open, Western
    Open, 1976.
b. Sep 1, 1937 in Red Bluff, California
Source: *BioIn 10, 11; WhoAm 82; WhoGolf;
WhoIntG*

Geiger, Abraham
German. Theologian
Leading advocate of Jewish reform
  movement.
b. 1810
d. 1874
Source: *BioIn 6; NewCol 75; WebBD 80*

Geiger, Hans (Johannes Wilhelm)
German. Physicist
Invented Geiger counter.
b. Sep 30, 1882 in Germany
d. Sep 24, 1945 in Berlin, Germany
Source: *AsBiEn; NewCol 75; WebBD 80*

Gein, Ed
American. Murderer
Farmer who was reportedly model for slayer
  in film *Psycho.*
b. 1906 in Plainfield, Wisconsin
d. Jul 26, 1984 in Madison, Wisconsin
Source: *Blood&B; EncACr; NewYTBS 84*

Geis, Bernard
American. Editor, Publisher
b. Aug 30, 1909 in Chicago, Illinois
Source: *CurBio 60; WhoAm 74, 76, 78, 80,
82; WhoF&I 74; WhoWor 78; WhoWorJ 72*

Geisel, Ernesto
Brazilian. President
b. Aug 3, 1907 in Rio Grande, Brazil
Source: *BioIn 10, 11; IntWW 74; NewYTBE
73; WhoWor 78*

Geisel, Theodore Seuss
see: Seuss, Doctor, pseud.

Geist, Jacob
American. Chemist
b. Feb 2, 1921 in Bridgeport, Connecticut
Source: *AmM&WS 73P; WhoAm 82*

Gelb, Arthur
American. Journalist, Author
b. Feb 3, 1924 in New York, New York
Source: *BiE&WWA; ConAu 1R; NotNAT;
WhoAm 74, 76, 78, 80, 82; WhoE 74*

Gelb, Barbara Stone
American. Author
b. Feb 6, 1926 in New York, New York
Source: *ConAu 1R; NotNAT*

Gelb, Lawrence
American. Business Executive
Founded Clairol, Inc., 1931.
b. 1898 in New York, New York
d. Sep 27, 1980 in New York, New York
Source: *NewYTBS 80*

Gelbart, Larry
American. Producer
Comedy writer for Bob Hope, Sid Caesar;
  creator of TV's "M*A*S*H."
b. Feb 25, 1928 in Chicago, Illinois
Source: *AmAu&B; AmSCAP 66, 80; WhoAm
80, 82; WhoTelC; WhoWor 74; WrDr 80*

Gelber, Jack
American. Author, Dramatist
b. Apr 12, 1932 in Chicago, Illinois
Source: *AmAu&B; BiE&WWA; CasWL;
ConAu 1R, 2NR; ConLC 1, 6, 14; CroCD;
McGEWD; ModAL; ModWD; NotNAT; PenC
AM; REn; REnAL; REnWD; TwCWr;
WebE&AL; WhoAm 74, 76, 78, 80, 82;
WhoE 74; WhoThe 77; WhoWor 78; WorAu;
WrDr 80*

Geldof, Bob
[Boomtown Rats]
"Saint Bob"
Irish. Actor, Musician, Singer
Organizer of Live-Aid, which raised $84
  million for African famine, Jul 1985.
b. Oct 5, 1954 in Dublin, Ireland
Source: *ConNews 85-3; WhoRocM 82*

Gell-Mann, Murray
American. Physicist
b. Sep 15, 1929 in New York, New York
Source: *McGEWB; WebAB; WhoAm 82*

Geller, Bruce
American. Producer, Writer
b. Oct 13, 1930 in New York, New York
d. May 21, 1976 in Santa Barbara, California
Source: *AmSCAP 66; ConAu 77; IntMPA 76,
77; WhoAm 74; WhoWorJ 72*

Geller, Uri
Israeli. Psychic
Psychic powers include ability to bend metal;
  start, stop watches mentally.
b. Dec 20, 1946 in Tel Aviv, Palestine
Source: *BioNews 74; ConAu 69*

Gellhorn, Martha Ellis
American. Author, Journalist
b. 1908 in Saint Louis, Missouri
Source: *AmAu&B; AmNov; ConAu 77;
ConNov 72, 76; DrAF 76; InWom; IntWW
74; OxAmL; REnAL; TwCA, SUP; WhoAm
74, 76, 78, 80, 82; WrDr 80*

Gellhorn, Peter
German. Music Director
Director of BBC Chorus since 1961;
  conductor for several opera companies.
b. Oct 24, 1912 in Breslau, Germany
Source: *Who 74; WhoMus 72*

Gellis, Roberta Leah Jacobs
American. Author
Wrote historical *Roselynde Chronicle* series,
1978-81.
b. Sep 27, 1927 in New York, New York
Source: *ConAu 5R; ForWC 70*

Gelmis, Joseph Stephen
American. Movie Critic, Author
b. Sep 28, 1935 in Brooklyn, New York
Source: *ConAu 45; WhoAm 74, 76, 78, 80, 82*

Gemayel, Amin
Lebanese. President
Elected pres. after assassination of younger
brother, 1982.
b. 1942 in Bikfaya, Lebanon
Source: *CurBio 83; NewYTBS 82*

Gemayel, Bashir
Lebanese. Political Leader
Pres.-elect who was assassinated in bomb
attack before taking office.
b. Nov 10, 1947 in Bikfaya, Lebanon
d. Sep 14, 1982 in Beirut, Lebanon
Source: *AnObit 1984; NewYTBS 82*

Gemayel, Sheikh Pierre
Lebanese. Politician
Founder of Phalange party.
b. 1905
Source: *IntWW 74, 75, 76, 77, 78; MidE 78, 79; WhoWor 74*

Geminiani, Francesco
Italian. Violinist, Composer
b. Feb 5, 1687 in Lucca, Italy
d. Dec 17, 1762 in Dublin, Ireland
Source: *OxMus*

Gemmell, Alan
British. Broadcaster
Radio personality of BBC's Gardener's
Question Time, 1956-86.
b. May 10, 1913 in Glasgow, Scotland
d. Jul 5, 1986 in Isle of Arran
Source: *Au&Wr 71; IntAu&W 76; Who 83; WhoAm 82; WrDr 84*

Gemmill, Henry
American. Editor
b. Jun 11, 1917 in Toledo, Ohio
Source: *St&PR 75; WhoAm 74; WhoE 74; WhoS&SW 82*

Genaro, Frankie
[Frank DiGennara]
American. Boxer
b. Aug 26, 1901 in New York
d. 1966
Source: *BioIn 7; WhoBox 74*

Genauer, Emily
American. Art Critic, Author
b. in New York, New York
Source: *InWom; WhoAm 74, 74; WhoAmA 73; WhoAmW 77; WhoGov 75*

Gendron, Maurice
French. Musician
Internationally known concert cellist who
recorded with Pablo Casals.
b. Dec 26, 1920 in Nice, France
Source: *WhoMus 72; WhoWor 74*

Geneen, Harold Sydney
American. Businessman
b. Jun 11, 1910 in Bournemouth, England
Source: *CurBio 74; IntWW 74; NewYTBE 72; St&PR 75; WhoAm 74, 76, 78, 80, 82; WhoE 74; WhoF&I 74; WhoWor 78*

Genesis
[Tony Banks; Bill Bruford; Phil Collins;
Peter Gabriel; Steve Hackett; John
Mayhew; Anthony Phillips; Michael
Rutherford; John Silver; Daryl Steurmer;
Chris Stewart; Chester Thompson]
English. Music Group
Formed 1966 as theatrical cult band;
currently pop group with Phil Collins as
lead singer.
Source: *ConMuA 80A; IlEncRk; RkOn 78; WhoRock 81*

Genet, Arthur Samuel
American. Business Executive
b. 1909
Source: *BioIn 4, 8*

Genet, Edmond Charles Edouard
"Citizen Genet"
French. Statesman
b. 1763 in Versailles, France
d. 1834
Source: *BioIn 1, 2, 9; NewCol 75; WebBD 80*

Genet, Jean
French. Dramatist, Author
Wrote of sin, corruption: *Our Lady of the Flowers*, 1942, became cult classic.
b. Dec 19, 1910 in Paris, France
d. Apr 15, 1986 in Paris, France
Source: *BiE&WWA; CasWL; CelR; CnMD; CnMWL; ConAu 13R; ConLC 1, 2, 5, 10, 14; CroCD; EncWL; EvEuW; LongCTC; McGEWD; ModRL; ModWD; NotNAT; OxThe; PenC EUR; REn; TwCWr; WhoThe 77; WhoTwCL; WhoWor 74; WorAu*

Genet, Louis Rene Fernandat
French. Poet, Dramatist
b. 1884
Source: *BioIn 3, 9*

Genevieve
[G Auger]
French. Singer
b. Apr 17, 1930 in Paris, France
Source: *InWom*

Genevieve, Saint
French. Religious Figure
Patron saint of Paris said to have averted Attila the Hun's attack on city with fasting, prayer.
b. 422 in Nanterre, France
d. 512 in Paris, France
Source: *NewC; NewCol 75; OxFr; WebBD 80*

Genghis Khan
[Genchiz Khan; Jenghiz Khan]
Mongolian. Conqueror
b. 1162 in Lake Baikal, Asia
d. 1227
Source: *NewC; REn; WebBD 80*

Genn, Leo
English. Actor
Nominated for Oscar for *Quo Vadis*, 1951.
b. Aug 9, 1905 in London, England
d. Jan 26, 1978 in London, England
Source: *BiE&WWA; FilmgC; IntMPA 77; MovMk; NotNAT; Who 74; WhoHol A; WhoThe 77*

Gennaro, Peter
American. Choreographer
b. 1924 in Metaire, Louisiana
Source: *BiE&WWA; CurBio 64; EncMT; NotNAT; WhoAm 74, 76, 78, 80, 82; WhoWor 78*

Genovese, Kitty
American. Murder Victim
Stabbed, as 38 neighbors watched, but did nothing to help.
b. 1935
d. Mar 13, 1964 in New York, New York
Source: *EncACr*

Genovese, Vito
Italian. Organized Crime Figure
Gangster who rose to power in underworld through narcotics, murder of Albert Anastasia.
b. Nov 27, 1879 in Rosiglino, Italy
d. Feb 14, 1969 in Springfield, Missouri
Source: *ObitOF 79; PolProf E*

Genscher, Hans-Dietrich
German. Diplomat
b. Mar 21, 1927 in Reideburg, Germany
Source: *BioIn 10; CurBio 75*

Gentele, Goeran
Swedish. Director
b. Sep 10, 1917 in Stockholm, Sweden
d. Jul 18, 1972 in Sardinia, Italy
Source: *CurBio 72; NewYTBE 71, 72; WhoMus 72*

Genthe, Arnold
American. Journalist, Photographer
b. Jan 8, 1869 in Berlin, Germany
d. Aug 8, 1942
Source: *AmAu&B; CurBio 42; DcAmB S3; DcNAA; WhAm 2*

Gentile da Fabriano
Italian. Artist
b. 1370 in Fabriano, Italy
d. 1427 in Rome, Italy
Source: *AtlBL; NewCol 75; REn; WebBD 80*

Gentile, Giovanni
Italian. Philosopher
b. May 30, 1875 in Castelvetrano, Italy
d. Apr 15, 1944 in Florence, Italy
Source: *CasWL; ClDMEL; EvEuW; NewCol 75; WebBD 80*

Gentileschi, Orazio
Italian. Artist
b. 1562
d. 1647
Source: *NewCol 75; WebBD 80*

Gentry, Bobbie
[Roberta Streeter]
American. Singer, Songwriter
Wrote, recorded "Ode to Billy Joe," 1967;
    won three Grammys, adapted to film,
    1976.
b. Jul 27, 1942 in Chicasaw County,
    Mississippi
Source: *EncFCWM 69; WhoAm 74*

Genung, John Franklin
American. Scholar
b. Jan 27, 1850 in Willseyville, New York
d. Oct 10, 1919
Source: *AmBi; TwCBDA; WebBD 80; WhAm
1*

Geoffrion, Bernie (Bernard)
"Boom Boom"
Canadian. Hockey Player
Right wing, 1950-68, first player to
    successfully use the slap shot; Hall of
    Fame, 1972.
b. Feb 14, 1931 in Montreal, Quebec
Source: *HocEn; WhoHcky 73*

George I
English. King
b. Mar 28, 1660 in Hanover, Prussia
d. Jun 12, 1727 in Germany
Source: *BioIn 10; DcBiPP; NewCol 75;
WebBD 80*

George II
English. King
b. Nov 10, 1683 in Prussia
d. Oct 25, 1760 in London, England
Source: *BioIn 10; OxMus; WebBD 80*

George II
Greek. King
b. Jul 20, 1890
d. Apr 1, 1947
Source: *CurBio 43, 47; NewCol 75; WebBD
80*

George III
[George William Frederick]
English. King
b. Jun 4, 1738 in London, England
d. Jan 29, 1820 in Windsor, England
Source: *BioIn 10; DcBiPP; WebBD 80*

George IV
[George Augustus Frederick]
English. King
b. Aug 12, 1762 in London, England
d. Jun 25, 1830 in Windsor, England
Source: *BioIn 10; NewCol 75; WebBD 80*

George V
[George Frederick Ernest Albert]
English. King
Grandson of Queen Victoria who ruled 1910-
    36; succeeded by son Edward VIII.
b. 1865 in London, England
d. Jan 20, 1936 in London, England
Source: *BioIn 10; DcBiPP; WebBD 80*

George VI
[Albert Frederick Arthur George; Duke of
    York]
English. King
Ascended to throne, Dec 11, 1936, upon
    abdication of brother Edward VIII; father
    of Queen Elizabeth II.
b. Dec 14, 1895 in Sandringham, England
d. Feb 6, 1952 in Sandringham, England
Source: *CurBio 42, 52; DcBiPP; WebBD 80*

George Edward Alexander Edmund
[Duke of Kent]
English. Prince
Youngest brother of King George VI.
b. Dec 20, 1902 in London, England
d. Aug 25, 1942 in Scotland
Source: *DcNaB 1941; ObitOF 79*

George, Saint
English. Religious Figure
Portrayed in legand as slayer of the dragon.
d. Apr 23, 303
Source: *NewC; REn*

George, Bill (William)
American. Football Player
Linebacker, Chicago Bears, 1952-65; Hall of
    Fame, 1974.
b. Oct 27, 1930 in Waynesburg, Pennsylvania
d. Sep 30, 1982 in Rockford, Illinois
Source: *NewYTBS 82; WhoFtbl 74*

George, Chief Dan
[Geswanouth Slaholt]
Canadian. Indian Chief, Actor
Best known for Oscar-winning role as
    Cheyenne warrior in *Little Big Man,* 1970.
b. Jun 24, 1899 in North Vancouver, British
    Columbia
d. Sep 23, 1981 in Vancouver, British
    Columbia
Source: *CelR; ConAu 108; FilmgC; NewYTBE
71; WhoAm 76, 78, 80; WhoHol A*

George, Christopher
American. Actor
Played in TV shows "Rat Patrol," 1966-68;
    "The Immortal," 1970-71.
b. Feb 25, 1929 in Royal Oak, Michigan
d. Nov 29, 1983 in Los Angeles, California
Source: *FilmgC; WhoHol A*

George, Don
American. Composer, Author, Artist
b. Aug 27, 1909 in New York, New York
Source: *AmSCAP 66*

George, Gladys
American. Actress
Oscar nominee for *Madame X,* 1937; other
films include *The Roaring Twenties.*
b. Sep 13, 1904 in Hatton, Maine
d. Dec 8, 1954 in Los Angeles, California
Source: *DcAmB S5; Film 1; FilmgC; MotPP;*
MovMk; ThFT; TwYS; Vers A; WhScrn 74,
77; WhoHol B

George, Grace
American. Actress
Married actor, manager William A. Brady;
appeared in many of his films including
The First Mrs. Fraser.
b. Dec 25, 1879 in New York, New York
d. May 19, 1961 in New York, New York
Source: *FamA&A; InWom; OxThe; WhScrn*
74, 77; WhoHol B

George, Graham Elias
English. Conductor
b. Apr 11, 1912 in Norwich, England
Source: *CanWW 70; WhoAm 78, 80, 82;*
WrDr 76

George, Henry, Sr.
American. Author, Economist, Reformer
Known for theory of tax on land, described
in *Progress and Poverty,* 1879.
b. Sep 2, 1839 in Philadelphia, Pennsylvania
d. Oct 29, 1897 in New York, New York
Source: *Alli SUP; AmAu; AmAu&B; AmBi;*
BbD; BiD&SB; CasWL; DcAmAu; DcAmB;
DcLEL; DcNAA; EncAB-H; EvLB; NewC;
OxAmL; OxEng; PenC AM; REn; REnAL;
TwCBDA; WebAB; WebE&AL; WhAm HS;
WhAmP

George, Henry, Jr.
American. Journalist
b. Nov 3, 1862 in Sacramento, California
d. Nov 14, 1916 in New York, New York
Source: *AmAu&B; BiDrAC; DcAmB; DcNAA;*
WhAm 1; WhAmP

George, Jean Craighead
American. Artist, Author
b. Jul 2, 1919 in Washington, District of
Columbia
Source: *AmAu&B; AnCL; Au&Wr 71;*
AuBYP; ChlLR 1; ConAu 5R; IlsCB 1946;
MorBMP; MorJA; NewbC 1966; SmATA 2;
WhoAm 82

George, Lynda Day
[Mrs. Christopher George]
American. Actress
Played on TV shows "Mission Impossible,"
1971-73; "Silent Force," 1970.
b. Dec 11, 1946 in San Marcos, Texas
Source: *WhoAm 82; WhoHol A*

George, Phyllis
[Mrs. John Y Brown, Jr.]
American. Sportscaster, Author
Miss America, 1971; author *I Love America*
Diet, 1982.
b. Jun 25, 1949 in Denton, Texas
Source: *BioIn 9, 10; BkPepl; WhoAm 78, 80,*
82

George, Stefan Anton
German. Poet
b. Dec 12, 1868 in Budesheim, Germany
d. Dec 4, 1933 in Locarno, Switzerland
Source: *AtlBL; CasWL; ChhPo; ClDMEL;*
CnMWL; CyWA; EncWL; EvEuW; LongCTC;
ModGL; OxGer; PenC EUR; REn; TwCA;
SUP; TwCWr; WhoTwCL

George, Susan
[Mrs. Simon McCorkindale]
English. Actress
Films include *Dirty Mary, Crazy Larry;*
Mandingo.
b. Jul 26, 1950 in London, England
Source: *FilmEn; FilmgC; IntMPA 76, 77, 78,*
79, 80, 81, 82; MovMk; NewYTBE 72;
WhoHol A

George, Walter Franklin
American. Politician, Government Official
Dem. senator from GA, 1923-57;
Eisenhower's NATO ambassador.
b. Jan 29, 1878 in Preston, Georgia
d. Aug 4, 1957 in Vienna, Georgia
Source: *ApCAB X; BiDrAC; BioIn 1, 2, 3, 4;*
CurBio 43, 55, 57; DcAmB S6; LinLib S;
ObitOF 79; PolProf E, T; WhAm 3; WhAmP

Georges-Picot, Jacques Marie Charles
French. Statesman
b. Dec 16, 1900 in Paris, France
Source: *BioIn 7; IntWW 74, 75, 76, 77, 78;*
IntYB 78, 79; Who 74; WhoWor 74

Gerard, Dave
American. Cartoonist
b. Jun 18, 1909 in Crawfordsville, Indiana
Source: *ConAu 53*

Gerard, Francois
French. Artist
b. May 4, 1770 in Rome, Italy
d. Jan 11, 1837 in Paris, France
Source: *AtlBL*

Gerard, Gil
American. Actor
Played on TV show "Buck Rogers in the
25th Century," 1979-81.
b. Jan 23, 1943 in Little Rock, Arkansas
Source: *WhoAm 80, 82*

Gerasimov, Innokentii Petrovich
Russian. Geographer, Scientist
Director, Soviet Institute of Geography, 1951-
85.
b. Dec 22, 1905 in Kostroma, Russia
d. Mar 30, 1985 in Moscow, U.S.S.R.
Source: *ConAu 115; IntWW 83; WhoSocC 78*

Gerasimov, Sergei Appolinarievich
Russian. Director
Joined Communist Party in 1944; films
follow party line *By The Lake.*
b. May 21, 1906 in Sverdlovsk, Russia
d. Nov 28, 1985 in Moscow, U.S.S.R.
Source: *BiDFilm; DcFM; FilmgC; IntWW 74,*
81; OxFilm; WhoWor 74; WorEFlm

Geray, Steven
[Stefan Gyergyay]
Czech. Actor
Character actor in over 100 films from 1941
including *Gentleman Prefer Blondes.*
b. Nov 10, 1904 in Uzhored, Czechoslovakia
d. Dec 26, 1973
Source: *FilmEn; IntMPA 77; Vers B; WhScrn*
77; WhoHol A

Gerber, Daniel Frank
American. Business Executive, Inventor
Invented strained baby food process, 1928, to
feed own baby.
b. May 6, 1898 in Fremont, Michigan
d. Mar 16, 1974 in Fremont, Michigan
Source: *DcAmB S5; NewYTBS 74; WhAm 6;*
WhoAm 74; WhoF&I 74; WhoWor 78

Gerber, John
American. Bridge Player
Contract bridge champion; wrote *The Flour*
Club Bid.
b. 1907 in Portland, Maine
d. Jan 28, 1981 in Houston, Texas
Source: *ConAu 103; NewYTBS 81*

Gere, Richard
American. Actor
Films include *An Officer and a Gentleman;*
American Gigolo; Looking For Mr.
Goodbar.
b. Aug 29, 1949 in Philadelphia,
Pennsylvania
Source: *BioIn 11, 12; CurBio 80; IntMPA 82;*
WhoAm 80, 82

Gerhardi, William Alexander
British. Author
Writitngs include autobiographical novel,
Resurrective, 1934.
b. Nov 21, 1895 in Saint Petersburg, Russia
d. Jul 5, 1977 in London, England
Source: *Au&Wr 71; ConAu 25R, 73; ConLC*
5; ConNov 72, 76; LongCTC; ModBrL;
NewC; OxEng; REn; TwCA, SUP; TwCWr;
WrDr 80

Gerhardt, Paul(us)
German. Poet, Theologian
Wrote over 120 Protestant hymns.
b. Mar 12, 1607 in Saxony, Germany
d. May 27, 1676 in Lubbenau, Germany
Source: *BbD; BiD&SB; CasWL; DcEnL;*
EuAu; EvEuW; OxGer; PenC AM; PoChrch

Gericault, Jean Louis Andre Theodore
French. Artist
Painted bold romantic historical scenes; drew
famous "Raft of the Medusa," 1819.
b. Sep 26, 1791 in Rouen, France
d. Jan 26, 1824 in Paris, France
Source: *AtlBL; McGDA; NewCol 75; OxFr;*
REn; WebBD 80

Germain, George Sackville
British. Soldier, Statesman
British secretary for colonies, 1775-82; often
blamed for Britain's defeat in American
Revolution.
b. 1716
d. 1785
Source: *BioIn 1, 6, 7, 10; NewCol 75;*
WebBD 80

German, Bruce W
[The Hostages]
American. Hostage in Iran
b. Mar 31, 1936
Source: *NewYTBS 81; USBiR 74*

Germi, Pietro
Italian. Director
Most films set in Italy, depicted poverty-
stricken people; directed *Divorce, Italian
Style*, 1961.
b. Sep 14, 1904 in Genoa, Italy
d. Dec 5, 1974 in Rome, Italy
Source: *DcFM; FilmgC; IntMPA 75; IntWW
74; MovMk; NewYTBS 74; OxFilm; WhScrn
77; WhoHol B; WorEFlm*

Gernreich, Rudi
American. Fashion Designer
Introduced topless bathing suits, 1974.
b. Aug 8, 1922 in Vienna, Austria
d. Apr 21, 1985 in Los Angeles, California
Source: *BioNews 74; CelR; CurBio 68;
WhoAm 74, 76, 78, 80, 82; WhoWest 84;
WhoWor 78; WorFshn*

Gernsback, Hugo
Inventor, Publisher
Received over 80 patents for radio and
electronic devices.
b. Aug 16, 1884 in Luxembourg City,
Luxembourg
d. Aug 19, 1967 in New York, New York
Source: *AmAu&B; ConAu 93; WebAB; WhAm
4; WhNAA*

Gero, Erno
Hungarian. Government Official
b. Aug 17, 1898 in Budapest, Hungary
d. Mar 12, 1980 in Budapest, Hungary
Source: *BioIn 1, 2; WhoSocC 78*

Gerold, Karl
German. Journalist
b. Aug 29, 1906
d. Feb 28, 1973
Source: *ConAu 41R; NewYTBE 73*

Gerome, Jean Leon
French. Artist
b. 1824 in Vesoul, France
d. 1904
Source: *NewCol 75; WebBD 80*

Geronimo
[Goyathlay]
American. Indian Chief
Apache, known for raids before his capture,
1888; wrote *Geronimo's Story of His Life*,
1906.
b. Jun 1829 in Arizona
d. Feb 17, 1909 in Fort Sill, Oklahoma
Source: *AmBi; DcAmB; EncAB-H; FilmgC;
REn; REnAL; WebAB; WhAm HSA*

Gerould, Gordon Hall
American. Author, Educator
b. Oct 4, 1877 in Goffstown, New
Hampshire
d. Jul 27, 1953 in Princeton, New Jersey
Source: *AmAu&B; ChhPo; OxAmL; WhAm 3*

Gerritsen, Rinus
see: Golden Earring

Gerry, Elbridge
American. Vice-President
Signer of Declaration of Independence;
participated in XYZ Affair, 1798; vp
under James Madison until death.
b. Jul 17, 1749 in Marblehead, Massachusetts
d. Nov 23, 1814 in Washington, District of
Columbia
Source: *AmBi; ApCAB; BiAUS; DcAmB;
Drake; EncAB-H; McGEWB; TwCBDA;
WebAB; WhAm HS*

Gerry, Elbridge Thomas
American. Lawyer, Social Reformer
Grandson of Elbridge Gerry; co-founded
ASPCC, 1875; pres., 1879-1901.
b. Dec 25, 1837 in New York, New York
d. Feb 18, 1927
Source: *AmBi; ApCAB; DcAmB; NatCAB 8;
TwCBDA; WhAm 1*

Gerry and the Pacemakers
[John Chadwick; Les Maguire; Freddie
Marsden; Gerry Marsden]
English. Music Group
Pop group from Liverpool; had hits "Don't
Let the Sun Catch You Crying," 1964;
"Ferry Cross the Mersey," 1965.
Source: *RolSEnR 83*

Gershwin, George
American. Composer
Wrote folk opera *Porgy and Bess*, 1935;
included songs "Summertime"; "I Got
Plenty o' Nuttin."
b. Sep 26, 1898 in Brooklyn, New York
d. Jul 11, 1937 in Hollywood, California
Source: *AmBi; AmSCAP 66; AtlBL; CmMov;
DcAmB S2; DcCM; DcFM; EncAB-H;
EncMT; FilmgC; McGEWD; NewCBMT;
NewYTBE 73; OxAmL; OxFilm; PIP&P;
REn; REnAL; WebAB; WhAm 1*

Gershwin, Ira
[Authur Francis, pseud.]
American. Lyricist
Brother of George; wrote lyrics for *Porgy and Bess, An American in Paris.*
b. Dec 6, 1896 in New York, New York
d. Aug 17, 1983 in Beverly Hills, California
Source: *AmAu&B; AmSCAP 66; AnObit 1983; BiE&WWA; CelR; ConAu 108; CurBio 56, 83; DcLEL; EncMT; FilmgC; IntMPA 79, 80, 81, 82; NewCBMT; NewYTBS 83; NotNAT; OxAmL; PIP&P; REnAL; WhoAm 80, 82; WhoMus 72; WhoThe 77A; WhoWor 74; WhoWorJ 72*

Gerson, Noel Bertram
American. Author
b. Nov 6, 1914 in Chicago, Illinois
Source: *AmAu&B; ConAu 81; SmATA 22; WhoAm 74, 76, 78, 80, 82; WhoE 74; WhoWor 78; WrDr 76*

Gersten, Berta
American. Actress
A leading performer in Yiddish theater: *Mirele Efros,* 1939.
b. Aug 20, 1896
d. Sep 10, 1972
Source: *NotAW MOD*

Gerstenberg, Richard Charles
American. Auto Executive
Chief exec., GM, 1972-74.
b. Dec 24, 1909 in Little Falls, New York
Source: *BioNews 74; BusPN; IntWW 74; NewYTBE 71; NewYTBS 74; Ward 77; Who 74; WhoAm 74; WhoF&I 74; WhoMW 74*

Gertrude the Great, Saint
German. Religious Figure
b. 1256
d. 1311
Source: *BioIn 2, 3, 4, 5, 6; WebBD 80*

Gerulaitis, Vitas
"Lithuanian Lion"
American. Tennis Player
Won Australian Open, 1977; Italian Open, 1977, 1979; Wimbledon doubles, 1975.
b. Jul 26, 1954 in Brooklyn, New York
Source: *WhoAm 82; WhoIntT*

Gerussi, Bruno
Canadian. Actor, Broadcaster
Played in TV series "The Beachcombers"; radio show "Gerussi," 1967-71.
b. 1928 in Medicine Hat, Alberta
Source: *WhThe; WhoThe 72*

Gervasi, Frank
American. Journalist
b. Feb 5, 1908 in Baltimore, Maryland
Source: *AmAu&B; ConAu 13R, P-1; CurBio 42*

Gervin, George
"The Iceman"
American. Basketball Player
b. Apr 27, 1952 in Detroit, Michigan
Source: *OfNBA 81; WhoAm 82; WhoBlA 77*

Geschwind, Norman
American. Educator, Physician
Harvard Medical School professor; studied functions of left, right brain.
b. Jan 8, 1926 in New York, New York
d. Jan 4, 1984 in Boston, Massachusetts
Source: *AmM&WS 82P; NewYTBS 84; WhoAm 84; WhoFrS 84*

Gesell, Arnold
American. Physician
Authority on child development; founder, director, Gesell Institute of Child Development.
b. Jun 21, 1880 in Alma, Wisconsin
d. May 29, 1961 in New Haven, Connecticut
Source: *AmAu&B; AsBiEn; CurBio 40, 61; LinLib L, S; NatCAB 49; REnAL; WebAB; WhAm 4; WhE&EA; WhLit*

Gesell, Gerhard Alden
American. Judge
b. Jun 16, 1910 in Los Angeles, California
Source: *CngDr 74; WhoAm 74; WhoGov 75; WhoS&SW 82*

Gest, Morris
Russian. Producer, Filmmaker
Produced Broadway plays including *The Miracle,* 1924.
b. Jan 7, 1881 in Vilna, Russia
d. May 16, 1942 in New York, New York
Source: *CurBio 42; DcAmB S3; NatCAB 38*

Gesualdo, Carlo
Italian. Composer
b. 1560 in Naples, Italy
d. Sep 8, 1613 in Naples, Italy
Source: *AtlBL; REn*

Getty, Donald
Canadian. Politician
Progressive-conservative party premier of Alberta, 1985--.
b. Aug 30, 1933 in Westmount, Quebec
Source: *CanWW 83*

Getty, Gordon Peter
American. Businessman, Philanthropist
Fourth son of J Paul Getty, known for
   endeavors in arts, sciences, rather than
   business.
b. Dec 20, 1933 in Los Angeles, California
Source: *CurBio 85; NewYTBS 84; WhoAm 84*

Getty, J(ean) Paul
American. Oilman
Getty Oil Co., largest personally controlled
   oil co.; total wealth over $1 billion.
b. Dec 15, 1892 in Minneapolis, Minnesota
d. Jun 6, 1976 in Surrey, England
Source: *ConAu 65, 69; EncAB-H; WebAB;
   WhoAm 74; WhoF&I 74; WhoWest 84;
   WhoWor 78*

Getz, Stan
American. Musician
b. Feb 2, 1927 in Philadelphia, Pennsylvania
Source: *CurBio 71; WhoAm 82; WhoWor 78*

Geva, Tamara
Russian. Choreographer, Dancer
b. 1908 in Leningrad, Russia
Source: *BiE&WWA; EncMT; NotNAT;
   WhoHol A; WhoThe 77A*

Geyer, Georgie Anne
American. Journalist, Author
Syndicated columnist since 1975; wrote
   *Buying the Night Flight: The Autobiography
   of a Woman Foreign Correspondent*, 1983.
b. Apr 2, 1935 in Chicago, Illinois
Source: *ConAu 29R; CurBio 86; ForWC 70;
   WhoAm 78, 80, 82, 84; WhoAmW 77;
   WhoMW 74; WhoWor 74*

Ghazzali, Abu al-
[Algazel]
Arabian. Philosopher
b. 1058 in Khurasan, Iran
d. 1111
Source: *CasWL; DcOrL 3; WebBD 80*

Ghelderode, Michel de
[Adolphe-Adhemar-Louis-Michel Martens]
Belgian. Dramatist
b. Apr 3, 1898 in Elsene, Belgium
d. Apr 1, 1962 in Brussels, Belgium
Source: *CasWL; CnMD; ConAu 85; ConLC 6;
   EncWL; McGEWD; ModRL; ModWD;
   OxThe; PenC EUR; REn; REnWD; TwCWr;
   WhoTwCL; WorAu*

Gheorghiu-Dej, Gheorghe
Romanian. Communist Leader
b. Nov 8, 1901 in Barlad, Romania
d. Mar 19, 1965
Source: *CurBio 58, 65; NewCol 75*

Gherardi, Gherardo
American. Pathologist
b. Jul 1, 1921 in Lucca, Italy
Source: *AmM&WS 73P*

Ghiaurov, Nicolai
Bulgarian. Opera Singer
b. Sep 13, 1929 in Velimgrad, Bulgaria
Source: *IntWW 74; WhoAm 82*

Ghiberti, Lorenzo
"Father of the Renaissance"
Italian. Artist
Sculpted north, east doors of the baptistry of
   Florence; portals called *Gates of Paradise*.
b. 1378 in Florence, Italy
d. Dec 1, 1455 in Florence, Italy
Source: *AtlBL; DcBiPP; DcCathB; LinLib S;
   LuthC 75; MacEA; McGDA; McGEWB;
   NewCol 75; OxArt; WhDW; WorAl*

Ghiringhelli, Antonio
Italian. Director
b. 1903 in Brunello, Italy
Source: *IntWW 74*

Ghirlandaio, Domenico
[Domenico di Tommaso Bigordi]
Italian. Artist
Among his noted works are wall frescoes in
   the Sistene Chapel, with Botticelli.
b. 1449 in Florence, Italy
d. Jan 11, 1494 in Florence, Italy
Source: *AtlBL*

Ghorbal, Ashraf A.
Egyptian. Diplomat
Ambassador to US, 1973--.
b. May 1925 in Alexandria, Egypt
Source: *IntWW 80, 81, 82; WhoWor 78, 80*

Ghormley, Robert Lee
American. Naval Officer
b. Oct 15, 1883 in Portland, Oregon
d. Jun 21, 1958 in Washington, District of
   Columbia
Source: *BioIn 1, 4, 5; CurBio 58; WhAm 3*

Ghose, Sri Chinmoy Kumar
[Sri Chinmoy]
Indian. Author, Poet
Director, UN Meditation Group; writings
   stress development of spititual heart over
   mind: *Yoga and Spiritual Life*, 1970.
b. Aug 27, 1931 in Bengal, India
Source: *ConAu 49, 2NR; CurBio 76; NewCol
   75*

Ghostley, Alice (Allyce)
American. Actress
Played on TV shows "Bewitched," 1969-72; "Mayberry RFD," 1970-71; plays Ms. Dipesto on "Moonlighting."
b. Aug 14, 1926 in Eve, Missouri
Source: *BiE&WWA; MotPP; NotNAT; WhoAm 82; WhoHol A; WhoThe 77*

Ghotbzadeh, Sadegh
Iranian. Government Official
Foreign minister who was executed in plot to kill Khomeini and topple government.
b. 1936
d. Sep 15, 1982 in Teheran, Iran
Source: *AnObit 1982; BioIn 11; NewYTBS 82*

Giacalone, Anthony
American. Organized Crime Figure
b. 1919
Source: *BioIn 10*

Giacometti, Alberto
Swiss. Sculptor
b. Oct 10, 1901 in Stampa, Switzerland
d. Jan 11, 1966 in Chur, Switzerland
Source: *AtlBL; CurBio 56, 66; REn; WhAm 4*

Giacomin, Eddie (Edward)
Canadian. Hockey Player
Goalie 1965-77; won Vezina Trophy, 1971.
b. Jun 6, 1939 in Sudbury, Ontario
Source: *CurBio 68; HocEn; NewYTBE 72; WhoHcky 73*

Giamarese, Carl
see: Buckinghams, The

Giamatti, A(ngelo) Bartlett
American. University Administrator, Baseball Executive
Pres., Yale U., 1978-86, named pres. of baseball's NL, 1986.
b. Apr 4, 1938 in Boston, Massachusetts
Source: *CurBio 78; DrAS 78E; NewYTBS 77; WhoAm 78, 80, 82; WhoE 79*

Giancana, Salvatore (Sam)
"Momo"
American. Gangster
Chicago gang boss who was invloved in CIA plot to kill Castro, 1961.
b. 1894
d. Jun 19, 1974 in Oak Park, Illinois
Source: *BioIn 11*

Gianelli, John
American. Basketball Player
b. Jun 10, 1950 in Stockton, California
Source: *NewYTBE 73; NewYTBS 74; WhoBbl 73*

Giannini, Amadeo Peter
American. Banker
b. May 6, 1870 in San Jose, California
d. Jun 3, 1949 in San Mateo, California
Source: *DcAmB S4; WebAB; WhAm 2*

Giannini, Dusolina
American. Opera Singer
b. Dec 19, 1902 in Philadelphia, Pennsylvania
Source: *InWom*

Giannini, Giancarlo
Italian. Actor
Known for roles in Lina Wertmuller films including *Love and Anarchy.*
b. Aug 1, 1942 in Spezia, Italy
Source: *FilmEn; IntMPA 77; WhoHol A*

Giannini, Vittorio
American. Composer
b. Oct 19, 1903 in Philadelphia, Pennsylvania
d. Nov 28, 1966 in New York, New York
Source: *AmSCAP 66; DcCM; WhAm 4*

Giap, Vo Nguyen
Vietnamese. Statesman
b. Sep 1, 1912 in Quangblin, Vietnam
Source: *CurBio 69; IntWW 74; WhoWor 78*

Giardello, Joey
[Carmine Orlando Tilelli]
American. Boxer
b. Jul 16, 1930 in Brooklyn, New York
Source: *BioIn 6, 7, 10; WhoBox 74*

Giardini, Felice de
Italian. Musician
b. 1716
d. 1796
Source: *BioIn 4; WebBD 80*

Giauque, William F(rancis)
American. Chemist, Educator
Won 1949 Nobel Prize for researching matter behavior in zero tempertures.
b. May 12, 1895 in Niagara Falls, Ontario
d. Mar 29, 1982 in Oakland, California
Source: *AmM&WS 73P, 76P, 79P; AsBiEn; BioIn 2, 3, 6; CurBio 50, 82; IntWW 74, 75, 76, 77, 78; NewCol 75; NewYTBS 82; WebAB; WhoAm 74, 76, 78, 80, 82; WhoWest 78*

Gibb, Andy
English. Singer, Songwriter, Musician
b. Mar 5, 1958 in Manchester, England
Source: *BioIn 11; BkPepl*

Gibb, Barry
[The Bee Gees; Douglas Gibb]
English. Singer, Songwriter
Guitarist, songwriter; album *Saturdau Night
Fever* soundtrack sold 50 million copies,
1976-79.
b. Sep 1, 1946 in Manchester, England
Source: *BkPepl; CurBio 81; WhoAm 82*

Gibb, Maurice
[The Bee Gees]
English. Singer, Songwriter
b. Dec 22, 1949 in Manchester, England
Source: *BkPepl; WhoAm 82*

Gibb, Robin
[The Bee Gees]
English. Singer, Songwriter
b. Dec 22, 1949 in Manchester, England
Source: *BkPepl; WhoAm 82*

Gibberd, Frederick
British. Architect, Author
Wrote *Architecture of England.*
b. Jan 7, 1908
d. Jan 9, 1984
Source: *ConArch; ConAu 111; IntWW 82*

Gibbon, Edward
English. Historian
Masterpiece was *The History of the Decline
and Fall of Roman Empire,* 1776-1788.
b. Apr 27, 1737 in Surrey, England
d. Jan 16, 1794
Source: *Alli; AtlBL; BbD; BiD&SB; BrAu;
CasWL; Chambr 2; CyWA; DcEnA; DcEnL;
DcEuL; DcLEL; EvLB; MouLC 2; NewC;
OxEng; PenC ENG; REn; WebE&AL*

Gibbon, Lewis Grassic, pseud.
[James Leslie Mitchell]
Scottish. Author
b. Feb 13, 1901 in Arbuthnott, Scotland
d. Feb 21, 1935 in Welwyn, England
Source: *CasWL; DcLEL; PenC ENG; REn*

Gibbons, Euell
American. Author, Naturalist
Author of books on wild foods, including
Stalking the Good Life, 1971.
b. Sep 8, 1911 in Clarksville, Texas
d. Dec 29, 1975 in Sunbury, Pennsylvania
Source: *AmAu&B; AuNews 1; BioNews 74;
ConAu 21R, 61, P-2; WhoE 74*

Gibbons, Floyd Phillips
American. Journalist
b. Jul 16, 1887 in Washington, District of
Columbia
d. Sep 24, 1939 in Saylorsburg, Pennsylvania
Source: *AmAu&B; AmBi; CathA 1930;
DcAmB S2; DcNAA; REnAL; TwCA, SUP;
WhAm 1*

Gibbons, Grinling
English. Sculptor
Public buildings, royal palaces decorated by
his work.
b. Apr 4, 1648 in Rotterdam, Netherlands
d. Aug 3, 1721 in London, England
Source: *AtlBL; WebBD 80*

Gibbons, James, Cardinal
American. Religious Leader
b. Jul 23, 1834 in Baltimore, Maryland
d. Mar 24, 1921 in Baltimore, Maryland
Source: *Alli SUP; AmAu&B; AmBi; ApCAB;
BiD&SB; BiDSA; ChhPo; DcAmAu;
DcAmB; DcNAA; EncAB-H; REnAL;
TwCBDA; WebAB; WhAm 1*

Gibbons, Mike
see: Badfinger

Gibbons, Orlando
English. Composer, Musician
b. 1583 in Cambridge, England
d. Jun 5, 1625 in Canterbury, England
Source: *Alli; NewC; NewCol 75; WebBD 80*

Gibbons, Stella Dorethea
English. Author, Poet
b. Jan 5, 1902 in London, England
Source: *Au&Wr 71; Chambr 3; ChhPo; -
ConAu 13R; ConNov 72; IntWW 74; Who 74;
WhoWor 78; WrDr 76*

Gibbons, Tom
American. Boxer
b. Mar 22, 1891 in Saint Paul, Minnesota
d. Nov 19, 1960 in Saint Paul, Minnesota
Source: *WhoBox 74*

Gibbs, Anthony
English. Author
b. Mar 9, 1902 in Bolton, England
d. Mar 11, 1975
Source: *ConAu 29R, P-2; WhoLA*

Gibbs, Charles
American. Pirate
b. 1794
d. 1831
Source: *BioIn 5*

Gibbs, Georgia
American. Singer
b. Aug 26, 1926 in Worcester, Massachusetts
Source: *InWom*

Gibbs, James
Scottish. Architect
b. Dec 23, 1682 in Aberdeen, Scotland
d. Aug 5, 1754 in London, England
Source: *AtlBL; McGDA; McGEWB; WhoArch*

Gibbs, Joe Jackson
American. Football Coach
Head coach, Washington Redskins, 1981--;
led team to NFL Super Bowl
championship, 1984.
b. Nov 25, 1940 in Mocksville, North
Carolina
Source: *FootReg 81; WhoAm 82*

Gibbs, Josiah Willard
American. Scientist, Mathematician, Physicist
Yale professor whose complex mathematical
theorems formed basic priciples of physical
chemistry.
b. Feb 11, 1839 in New Haven, Connecticut
d. Apr 28, 1903 in New Haven, Connecticut
Source: *AmBi; ApCAB; DcAmAu; DcAmB;
DcNAA; EncAB-H; OxAmL; REnAL;
TwCBDA; WebAB; WhAm 1*

Gibbs, Marla Bradley
American. Actress
Played Florence on TV's "The Jefferson's";
has own series "227," 1985--.
b. Jun 14, 1931 in Chicago, Illinois
Source: *ConTFT 3; InB&W 80; WhoAm 84;
WhoTelC*

Gibbs, Terri
American. Singer, Musician
Blind country singer; hit single "Somebody's
Knockin'," 1981.
b. Jun 15, 1954 in Augusta, Georgia
Source: *BioIn 12; RkOn 85*

Gibbs, Terry
American. Composer, Conductor
b. Oct 13, 1924 in Brooklyn, New York
Source: *AmSCAP 66*

Gibbs, William Francis
American. Architect
b. Aug 24, 1886 in Philadelphia,
Pennsylvania
d. Apr 28, 1967 in New York, New York
Source: *CurBio 44, 67; WhAm 4*

Gibbs, Woolcott
American. Drama Critic
b. 1902
d. Aug 16, 1958 in Ocean Beach, New York
Source: *BioIn 6*

Gibran, Kahlil
American. Poet, Artist
Finest work *The Prophet* translated into 13
languages.
b. Apr 10, 1883 in Bechari, Lebanon
d. Apr 10, 1931 in New York, New York
Source: *AmAu&B; CasWL; ConAu 104;
DcNAA; TwCA, SUP; WebBD 80*

Gibran, Kahlil George
American. Author, Sculptor, Artist
Exhibited paintings, 1949-52, life-sized steel
sculpture, 1953--.
b. Nov 29, 1922 in Boston, Massachusetts
Source: *DcCAA 71; WhoAm 74, 76, 78, 80,
82; WhoAmA 73; WhoWor 78*

Gibson, Althea
American. Tennis Player
First black to win Wimbledon, US
championships, 1957, 1958.
b. Aug 25, 1927 in Silver, South Carolina
Source: *CurBio 57; HerW; InWom; NewCol
75; WebAB; WhoAm 74, 76, 78, 80, 82;
WhoBlA 75*

Gibson, Bob
American. Singer, Musician
b. Nov 16, 1931 in New York, New York
Source: *EncFCWM 69; WhoAm 82*

Gibson, Bob (Robert)
"Hoot"
American. Baseball Player
Pitcher, St. Louis Cardinals, 1959-75; Hall of
Fame, 1981.
b. Nov 9, 1935 in Omaha, Nebraska
Source: *BaseEn 85; BioIn 8, 9, 10, 11;
WhoAm 74; WhoBlA 75; WhoProB 73*

Gibson, Charles Dana
American. Illustrator
His creation, the "Gibson Girl," set the
fashion in women's clothing, hairstyle,
1890-1914.
b. Sep 14, 1867 in Roxbury, Massachusetts
d. Dec 23, 1944 in New York, New York
Source: *AmAu&B; ChhPo; CurBio 45;
DcAmAu; DcAmB S3; DcNAA; OxAmL; REn;
REnAL; TwCBDA; WebAB; WhAm 2;
WhScrn 77*

Gibson, Edward George
American. Astronaut
Pilot of third manned Skylab mission; orbited
earth 84 days.
b. Nov 8, 1936 in Buffalo, New York
Source: *AmM&WS 73P; WhoAm 74;
WhoS&SW 82*

Gibson, Guy
British. Air Force Officer
Led spectacular bombing attacks on German
dams, 1943.
b. 1918
d. Sep 1944
Source: *BioIn 5, 8; WhWW-II*

Gibson, Henry
American. Actor, Author
Played on TV show "Laugh-In," 1968-72;
wrote *Only Show on Earth.*
b. Sep 21, 1935 in Germantown,
Pennsylvania
Source: *IntMPA 82; WhoAm 74, 76, 78, 80,
82; WhoHol A*

Gibson, "Hoot" (Edmund Richard)
"The Smiling Whirlwind"
American. Actor
Western hero whose films include *Action;
Sure Fire.*
b. Aug 6, 1892 in Tememah, Nebraska
d. Aug 23, 1962 in Woodland Hills,
California
Source: *Film 1; FilmgC; MotPP; MovMk;
OxFilm; TwYS; WhScrn 74; WhoHol B*

Gibson, John
British. Sculptor
b. 1790
d. 1866
Source: *BioIn 6, 9, 10; NewCol 75; WebBD
80*

Gibson, Josh(ua)
American. Baseball Player
Considered finest slugger ever to play in
Negro Leagues.
b. Dec 21, 1911 in Buena Vista, Georgia
d. Jan 20, 1947 in Pittsburgh, Pennsylvania
Source: *BioIn 9, 10, 11; DcAmB S4*

Gibson, Kenneth Allen
American. Mayor
b. May 15, 1932 in Enterprise, Alabama
Source: *CelR; CurBio 71; NewYTBE 70;
WhoAm 74, 76, 78, 80, 82; WhoAmP 73;
WhoBlA 75; WhoE 74; WhoGov 75*

Gibson, Kirk Harold
"Gibby"
American. Baseball Player
b. May 28, 1957 in Pontiac, Michigan
Source: *BaseEn 85; ConNews 85-2; NewYTBS
82*

Gibson, Mel
American. Actor
Starred in *Gallipoli,* 1981; *The Road Warrior,*
1982; *The Year of Living Dangerously,*
1983.
b. 1956 in Peekskill, New York
Source: *BioIn 12; JohnWSW*

Gibson, Walter B(rown)
American. Author
Used 12 pseudonyms; besides *Shadow* series,
wrote on magic, games, astrology, etc.
b. Sep 12, 1897 in Philadelphia, Pennsylvania
Source: *ConAu 108, 110; ScF&FL 1; WhNAA*

Gibson, Wildred Wilson
English. Dramatist, Poet
Verse collections include *Stonefolds,* 1907.
b. Oct 2, 1878 in Hexham, England
d. May 26, 1962 in Surrey, England
Source: *ConAu 113; DcLB 19*

Gibson, William
American. Dramatist
Best known plays *The Miracle Worker; Two
for the Seesaw.*
b. Nov 13, 1914 in New York, New York
Source: *BiE&WWA; CnMD; ConAu 9R;
ConDr 77E; CurBio 83; McGEWD; ModAL;
ModWD; NotNAT; PenC AM; REnAL;
WhoAm 80, 82; WhoE 74; WhoThe 77;
WhoWor 78; WorAu; WrDr 80*

Gidal, Sonia
German. Author
b. Sep 23, 1922 in Berlin, Germany
Source: *Au&Wr 71; AuBYP; ConAu 5R;
SmATA 2*

Gidal, Tim
German. Journalist
b. May 18, 1909 in Munich, Germany
Source: *ConAu 5R; SmATA 2*

Gide, Andre Paul Guillaume
French. Author, Critic
Won Nobel Prize for Literature, 1947.
b. Nov 22, 1869 in Paris, France
d. Feb 19, 1951 in Paris, France
Source: *AtlBL; CasWL; ClDMEL; CnMD;
CnMWL; CyWA; EncWL; EvEuW; LongCTC;
ModRL; ModWD; NewC; OxEng; OxFr;
OxThe; PenC EUR; RAdv 1; RComWL;
REn; REnWD; TwCA, SUP; TwCWr; WhAm
3; WhoTwCL*

Gielgud, (Arthur) John, Sir
English. Actor, Director, Producer
Won Oscar for *Authur*, 1982.
b. Apr 14, 1904 in London, England
Source: *BiDFilm; BiE&WWA; CelR; CurBio
47, 84; FamA&A; FilmgC; IntMPA 75, 76,
77, 78, 79, 80; IntWW 74; MotPP; MovMk;
NewC; NewYTBE 70; NotNAT; OxFilm;
OxThe; PlP&P; REn; Who 74; WhoAm 82;
WhoHol A; WhoThe 77; WhoWor 74*

Gielgud, Val Henry
British. Dramatist
b. Apr 28, 1900
Source: *Au&Wr 71; ConAu 9R, 5NR;
EncMys; IntWW 74; MnBBF; NotNAT A;
Who 74; WhoLA; WhoWor 78; WrDr 76*

Gierek, Edward
Polish. Politician
b. Jan 6, 1913 in Porabka, Poland
Source: *BioNews 74; CurBio 71; IntWW 74;
NewCol 75; NewYTBE 70; WhoWor 78*

Gieseking, Walter Wilhelm
German. Musician
Developed Leimer-Gieseking method of piano
study.
b. Nov 5, 1895 in Lyons, France
d. Oct 26, 1956 in London, England
Source: *CurBio 56, 57; NewCol 75; WebBD
80; WhAm 3*

Giesler, Jerry (Harold Lee)
American. Lawyer
b. 1890 in Wilton Junction, Iowa
d. Sep 27, 1962 in Beverly Hills, California
Source: *WhAm 4*

Gifford, Frank (Francis Newton)
American. Football Player, Sportscaster
Hall of Fame, 1977; won Emmy for
outstanding sports personality, 1977.
b. Aug 16, 1930 in Santa Monica, California
Source: *CelR; CurBio 64; WhoAm 82;
WhoFtbl 74; WhoHol A*

Gifford, Walter Sherman
American. Philanthropist
b. Jan 10, 1885 in Salem, Massachusetts
d. May 7, 1966 in New York, New York
Source: *CurBio 45, 66; WhAm 4*

Gigli, Beniamino
Italian. Opera Singer
b. Mar 20, 1890 in Recanati, Italy
d. Nov 30, 1957 in Rome, Italy
Source: *FilmgC; WhScrn 74, 77; WhoHol B*

Gilbert, A(lfred) C(arleton)
American. Business Executive
Invented Erector Set; founder, pres., Gilbert
Toy Co.
b. Feb 15, 1884 in Salem, Oregon
d. Jan 24, 1961 in Boston, Massachusetts
Source: *DcAmB S7; WebAB; WhAm 4;
WhoTr&F 73*

Gilbert, Alfred Carlton, Jr.
American. Manufacturer
b. Dec 1, 1919 in New Haven, Connecticut
d. Jun 27, 1964
Source: *DcAmB S7; WhAm 4*

Gilbert, Billy
American. Actor
Trademark was comic sneezing routine used
in Disney's *Snow White and the Seven
Dwarfs* for the dwarf Sneezy.
b. Sep 12, 1894 in Louisville, Kentucky
d. Sep 23, 1971 in Hollywood, California
Source: *FilmEn; Film 1; FilmgC; MovMk;
TwYS; WhScrn 74, 77*

Gilbert, Bruce
American. Producer
Films include *Coming Home; China
Syndrome; Nine to Five; On Golden Pond.*
b. 1948 in Beverly Hills, California
Source: *IntMPA 81*

Gilbert, Cass
American. Architect
b. Nov 24, 1859 in Zanesville, Ohio
d. May 17, 1934 in Brockenhurst, England
Source: *AmBi; DcAmB S1; OxAmL; WebAB;
WhAm 1*

Gilbert, Humphrey, Sir
English. Navigator, Explorer
Founded first British colony in N America
at St. John's, NF, Aug 5, 1583.
b. 1537 in Compton, England
d. Sep 9, 1583
Source: *Alli; CasWL; NewC; NewCol 75;
OxAmL; OxCan; OxEng; REn; REnAL;
WebBD 80*

Gilbert, John
[John Pringle]
American. Actor
Starred opposite Greta Garbo in several
films; talking pictures destroyed career.
b. Jul 10, 1897 in Logan, Utah
d. Jan 9, 1936 in Los Angeles, California
Source: *AmBi; BiDFilm; CmMov; DcAmB S2;
Film 1; FilmgC; MovMk; OxFilm; WhAm 1;
WhScrn 74, 77; WorEFlm*

Gilbert, Joseph Henry, Sir
English. Chemist
b. 1817
d. 1901
Source: *BioIn 1, 4, 6, 7; WebBD 80*

Gilbert, Melissa
American. Actress
Played Laura Ingalls Wilder on TV series
"Little House on the Prairie," 1974-82.
b. May 8, 1964 in Los Angeles, California
Source: *IntMPA 82; WhoTelC*

Gilbert, Rod(rique Gabriel)
Canadian. Hockey Player
Scored 406 goals in 18 seasons with NY
Rangers, 1960-78; Hall of Fame, 1982.
b. Jul 1, 1941 in Montreal, Quebec
Source: *BioIn 10, 11; CurBio 69; HocEn;
WhoAm 82; WhoHcky 73*

Gilbert, William
English. Scientist, Physician
b. 1540 in Colchester, England
d. Nov 30, 1603
Source: *Alli; BrAu; DcEnL; NewC; OxEng*

Gilbert, William Schwenck, Sir
[Gilbert and Sullivan]
English. Dramatist, Humorist
Wrote librettos for Gilbert and Sullivan
comic operas.
b. Nov 18, 1836 in London, England
d. May 29, 1911 in Harrow, England
Source: *AtlBL; BrAu 19; DcLEL; EvLB;
ModWD; PlP&P; REn; REnWD; Str&VC;
WebE&AL*

Gilbert and Sullivan
see: Sullivan, Sir Arthur Seymour

Gilbertson, Mildred Geiger
American. Author
b. Jun 9, 1908 in Galena, Illinois
Source: *ConAu 5R, 2NR; ForWC 70; SmATA
2; WrDr 76*

Gilbreth, Frank Bunker, Jr.
American. Author, Journalist
b. Mar 17, 1911 in Plainfield, New Jersey
Source: *AmAu&B; ConAu 9R; CurBio 49;
SmATA 2; WhoAm 74, 76, 78, 80, 82;
WhoS&SW 82; WhoWor 78*

Gilbreth, Lillian Moller
American. Engineer
b. May 24, 1878 in Oakland, California
d. Jan 2, 1972 in Phoenix, Arizona
Source: *CurBio 40, 51; WebBD 80; WhAm 5*

Gilder, George
American. Economist, Author
b. Nov 29, 1939 in New York, New York
Source: *AuNews 1; ConAu 17R; CurBio 81;
WhoAm 82*

Gilder, Nick
English. Singer
Had number-one single "Hot Child in the
City," 1978, from album *City Nights.*
b. Nov 7, 1951 in London, England
Source: *RkOn 85*

Gildersleeve, Virginia Crocheron
American. Educator
b. Oct 3, 1877 in New York, New York
d. Jul 7, 1965 in Centerville, Massachusetts
Source: *AmAu&B; CurBio 41, 65; InWom;
NewCol 75; WebBD 80; WhAm 4; WhNAA;
WomWWA 14*

Gilels, Emil Grigorevich
Russian. Musician
Pianist known for rich tone, virtuosic power
who performed Romantic, classical works.
b. Oct 19, 1916 in Odessa, Russia
d. Oct 14, 1985 in Moscow, U.S.S.R.
Source: *CurBio 56, 86; IntWW 74; WhoAm
82*

Giles, Mike
see: King Crimson

Giles, Warren Crandall
American. Baseball Executive
Pres., NL, 1951-70.
b. May 28, 1896 in Tiskilwa, Illinois
d. Feb 7, 1979 in Cincinnati, Ohio
Source: *NewYTBS 79; WhAm 7; WhoAm 74,
76, 78; WhoProB 73*

Gilfond, Henry
American. Author
Source: *ConAu 21R; NatPD; SmATA 2*

Gilford, Jack
[Jacob Gellman]
American. Actor
Nominated for Oscar for *Save the Tiger,*
1972.
b. Jul 25, 1913 in New York, New York
Source: *BiE&WWA; EncMT; FilmgC; IntMPA
75; MovMk; NotNAT; PlP&P; WhoAm 76,
78, 80; WhoHol A; WhoThe 77*

Gill, Amory Tingle
"Slats"
American. Basketball Coach
b. May 1, 1901 in Salem, Oregon
d. Apr 5, 1966 in Cornwallis, Oregon
Source: *BioIn 6, 9; WhoBbl 73*

Gill, Brendan
American. Drama Critic, Author
b. Oct 4, 1914 in Hartford, Connecticut
Source: *AmAu&B; ConNov 72, 76; DrAF 76;
NotNAT; PenC AM; REnAL; TwCA SUP;
WhoAm 76, 78, 80, 82, 84; WhoThe 77;
WrDr 76*

Gill, Eric
English. Author, Sculptor, Engraver
Did wood engravings for prestigious Golden
Cockerel Press, from 1924; designed
numerous typefaces.
b. Feb 22, 1882 in Brighton, England
d. Nov 18, 1940
Source: *CurBio 41; BkC 5; CathA 1930;
DcLEL; LongCTC; TwCA SUP*

Gill, Jocelyn Ruth
American. Astronomer
b. Oct 29, 1916 in Flagstaff, Arizona
Source: *WhoAm 74; WhoAmW 74; WhoGov
75*

Gilles, D(onald) B(ruce)
American. Dramatist
b. Aug 30, 1947 in Cleveland, Ohio
Source: *NatPD*

Gillespie, "Dizzy" (John Birks)
American. Jazz Musician
Responsible for "be-bop" sound; wrote *To Be
or Not...to Bop,* 1979.
b. Oct 21, 1917 in Cheraw, South Carolina
Source: *Alli SUP; AmM&WS 73P; AmSCAP
66; BioNews 74; CelR; CurBio 57; NewYTBE
73; WhoAm 74, 76, 78, 80, 82; WhoBlA 75*

Gillette, Duane
[The Hostages]
American. Hostage in Iran
b. 1957
Source: *NewYTBS 81*

Gillette, King Camp
American. Inventor
Invented safety razor, 1895.
b. Jan 5, 1855 in Fond du Lac, Wisconsin
d. Jul 9, 1932 in Los Angeles, California
Source: *AmBi; DcAmB S1; DcNAA; WebAB;
WhAm 1*

Gillette, William Hooker
American. Actor, Dramatist
Starred in play *Sherlock Holmes,* which he
adapted from Arthur Canan Doyle's
writings.
b. Jul 24, 1855 in Hartford, Connecticut
d. Apr 29, 1937 in Hartford, Connecticut
Source: *AmAu&B; AmBi; ApCAB; BbD;
BiD&SB; Chambr 3; DcAmAu; DcAmB S2;
DcLEL; DcNAA; FamA&A; Film 1; FilmgC;
McGEWD; ModWD; OxAmL; OxThe; PlP&P;
REnAL; TwCBDA; TwYS; WebAB; WhAm 1;
WhScrn 74, 77; WhoHol B; WhoStg 1906,
1908*

Gilley, Mickey Leroy
American. Musician
Club named Gilley's was setting for film
Urban Cowboy; had 1980 pop hit "Stand
By Me."
b. Mar 9, 1936 in Natchez, Mississippi
Source: *RkOn 85; WhoAm 78, 80, 82;
WhoRock 81*

Gilliam, Jim (James William)
"Junior"
American. Baseball Player
b. Oct 17, 1928 in Nashville, Tennessee
d. Oct 8, 1978 in Los Angeles, California
Source: *BaseEn 85; WhoBlA 75; WhoProB 73*

Gilliam, Joe
American. Football Player
b. Dec 29, 1950 in Charleston, West Virginia
Source: *BioIn 11*

Gilliam, Terry
[Monty Python's Flying Circus]
American. Illustrator, Cartoonist
b. Nov 22, 1940 in Minneapolis, Minnesota
Source: *BioIn 10, 11; WhoAm 82; WorECom*

Gilliatt, Penelope Ann Douglas
English. Critic
b. Mar 25, 1932 in London, England
Source: *AuNews 2; ConAu 13R; ConLC 2;
ConNov 72, 76; DrAF 76; FilmgC; WhoAm
74, 76, 78, 80, 82; WhoE 74; WomWMM;
WrDr 76*

Gillies, Clark
"Jethro"
Canadian. Hockey Player
Left wing, NY Islanders, 1974--; has won
four Stanley Cups.
b. Apr 7, 1954 in Regina, Saskatchewan
Source: *HocEn; HocReg 81; WhoAm 82*

Gilligan, John Joyce
American. Governor
b. Mar 22, 1921 in Cincinnati, Ohio
Source: *IntWW 74; WhoAm 74; WhoAmP 73;
WhoGov 75; WhoMW 74*

Gillis, Don
American. Composer
b. Jun 17, 1912 in Cameron, Missouri
d. Jan 10, 1978 in Columbia, South Carolina
Source: *AmSCAP 66; DcCM; WhoMus 72*

Gillman, Sidney
American. Football Coach
Head coach, LA Rams, 1955-59; San Diego
Chargers, 1960-71.
b. 1911 in Minneapolis, Minnesota
Source: *CmCal; NewYTBS 81; WhoFtbl 74*

Gillmore, Frank
American. Labor Union Official
Founder, first pres., Actors Equity Assn.,
1929-37.
b. May 14, 1867 in New York, New York
d. Mar 29, 1943 in New York, New York
Source: *CurBio 43; WhAm 2; WhoStg 1906,
1908*

Gillott, Jacky
English. Author, Journalist
Early British TV woman newscaster; wrote
Salvage, 1968.
b. Sep 24, 1939 in Bromley, England
d. Sep 19, 1980 in Somerset, England
Source: *AnObit 1980; ConAu 102; IntAu&W
77; WrDr 80*

Gillray, James
English. Cartoonist
Political cartoonist whose work covered
Napoleonic War, c.1802; credited with
introducing English style, format of
cartoon to Europe.
b. 1757 in London, England
d. Jun 1, 1815 in London, England
Source: *Alli; BkIE; DcBrBI; DcBrWA; NewC;
WhDW*

Gilman, Daniel Coit
American. Educator
b. Jul 6, 1831 in Norwich, Connecticut
d. Oct 13, 1908 in Norwich, Connecticut
Source: *Alli SUP; AmAu&B; AmBi; ApCAB;
BiD&SB; BiDSA; DcAmAu; DcAmB; DcNAA;
EncAB-H; OxAmL; REnAL; TwCBDA;
WebAB; WhAm 1*

Gilman, Dorothy
[Dorothy Gilman Butters]
American. Author
b. Jun 25, 1923 in New Brunswick, New
Jersey
Source: *BioIn 7, 8, 10; ConAu 2NR; SmATA
5; WhoAm 82*

Gilman, Lawrence
American. Music Critic, Journalist
b. Jul 5, 1878 in Flushing, New York
d. Sep 8, 1939 in Franconia, New Hampshire
Source: *AmAu&B; DcAmB S2; DcNAA;
REnAL; TwCA, SUP; WhAm 1*

Gilmer, Elizabeth Meriwether
see: Dix, Dorothy, pseud.

Gilmore, Artis
American. Basketball Player
Center, 1972--; has averaged over 1,000
rebounds each season.
b. Sep 21, 1949 in Chipley, Florida
Source: *WhoAm 74, 76, 80, 82; WhoBbl 73;
WhoBlA 75, 77; WorAl*

Gilmore, Eddy Lanier King
American. Journalist
b. May 28, 1907 in Selma, Alabama
d. Oct 6, 1967 in London, England
Source: *Au&Wr 71; ConAu 5R; CurBio 47,
67; WhAm 4*

Gilmore, Gary Mark
American. Murderer
First execution, by firing squad, following
reinstatement of death penalty.
b. 1941
d. Jan 18, 1977 in Point of Mountain, Utah
Source: *BioIn 11*

Gilmore, Virginia
[Sherman Virginia Poole]
American. Actress
Broadway star, 1940s, who starred in 40
films; married to Yul Brynner, 1944-60.
b. Jul 26, 1919 in Del Monte, California
d. Mar 28, 1986 in Santa Barbara, California
Source: *BiE&WWA; FilmEn; FilmgC; HolP
40; MotPP; MovMk; NotNAT; WhoHol A;
WhoThe 77A*

Gilmour, David
[Pink Floyd]
English. Singer, Musician
Recorded solo single "Blue Light," 1984.
b. Mar 6, 1947 in Cambridge, England
Source: *RkOn 85*

Gilot, Francoise
French. Author, Artist
Mistress of Pablo Picasso, 1946-53; had two
of his children; wrote *Life with Picasso,*
1964.
b. Nov 26, 1921 in Neuilly-sur-Seine, France
Source: *ConAu 108; WhoAmW 75; WhoWor
74*

Gilpin, Charles Sidney
American. Actor
One of first black actors to win wide stage
following; played title role in *The Emperor
Jones* which ran for three years.
b. Nov 20, 1878 in Richmond, Virginia
d. May 6, 1930 in Eldridge Park, New
Jersey
Source: *AmBi; DcAmB; FamA&A; OxThe;
WebAB; WhAm 1; WhScrn 74, 77; WhoHol
B*

Gilpin, Laura
American. Photographer, Author
Known for photographic studies of Navaho
Indians.
b. Apr 22, 1891 in Colorado Springs,
Colorado
d. Nov 30, 1979 in Santa Fe, New Mexico
Source: *ConAu 111; WhoAmA 78; WhoWest
74*

Gilroy, Frank D
American. Dramatist
b. Oct 13, 1925 in New York, New York
Source: *AmAu&B; ConAu 81; CroCD; CurBio
65; DrAF 76; McGEWD; ModWD; NotNAT;
OxAmL; WhoAm 74, 76, 78, 80, 82; WhoE
74; WhoThe 77; WhoWor 78; WrDr 80*

Gilruth, Robert Rowe
American. Aeronautical Engineer
b. Oct 8, 1913 in Nashwauk, Minnesota
Source: *AmM&WS 73P; CurBio 63; IntWW
74; WhoAm 82; WhoGov 75; WhoWor 78*

Gilson, Etienne Henry
French. Philosopher, Historian
Elected to French Academy, 1946.
b. Jun 13, 1884 in Paris, France
d. Sep 19, 1978 in Cravant, France
Source: *CathA 1930; ConAu 81, 102; IntWW
74; OxFr; TwCA, SUP; Who 74; WhoWor 78*

Gilstrap, Suzy
American. Actress
Paraplegic star in TV movie "Skyward,"
1980; "Skyward Christmas," 1981.
b. Jan 1966
Source: *BioIn 12*

Gimbel, Adam
American. Retailer
Emigrated to US, 1835; founded dept. store
in Philadelphia, 1894.
b. 1815 in Bavaria, Germany
d. 1896
Source: *NewCol 75*

Gimbel, Bernard Feustman
American. Retailer
Grandson of Adam Gimbel; pres., Gimbel
Brothers, 1927-53.
b. Apr 10, 1885 in Vincennes, Indiana
d. Sep 29, 1966
Source: *CurBio 50, 66; NatCAB 53; WhAm 4*

Gimbel, Richard
American. Retailer
Grandson of Adam Gimbel; curator of
aeronautical literature at Yale.
b. Jul 26, 1898 in Atlantic City, New Jersey
d. May 27, 1970 in Munich, Germany
(West)
Source: *BioIn 8, 9; NewYTBE 70*

Gimbel, Sophie Haas
"Sophie of Saks Fifth Avenue"
American. Fashion Designer
b. 1898 in Houston, Texas
d. Nov 28, 1981 in New York, New York
Source: *AnObit 1981; InWom; NewYTBS 81;
WhoAmW 58, 64, 66, 68, 70, 72, 74;
WorFshn*

Gimpel, Jakob
Polish. Musician
b. 1906 in Lwow, Poland
Source: *WhoMus 72*

Ginastera, Alberto
American. Composer
Modern eclectic style; operas include *Cenci;
Bomarzo.*
b. Apr 11, 1916 in Buenos Aires, Argentina
d. Jun 25, 1983 in Geneva, Switzerland
Source: *CurBio 71; DcCM; IntWW 74;
WhoAm 74; WhoMus 72; WhoWor 78*

Gingold, Hermione Ferdinanda
English. Actress
Films include *Gigi*; won Grammy for
  narration of "Peter and the Wolf."
b. Dec 9, 1897 in London, England
Source: *BiE&WWA; CelR; ConAu 5R; CurBio
58; EncMT; FilmgC; InWom; MotPP;
MovMk; NotNAT; PlP&P; Who 74; WhoAm
74, 76, 78, 80, 82; WhoHol A; WhoThe 77;
WhoWor 78*

Gingrich, Arnold
American. Editor, Author
Published *Esquire*, 1952-76; emphasized
  magazine's literary qualities.
b. Dec 5, 1903 in Grand Rapids, Michigan
d. Jul 9, 1976 in Ridgewood, New Jersey
Source: *AmAu&B; Au&Wr 71; CelR; ConAu
65, 69; CurBio 61, 76; IntAu&W 76, 77;
IntWW 74, 75, 76, 77; NewYTBS 76; St&PR
75; WhAm 7; WhNAA; WhoAm 74, 76;
WhoWor 74; WorFshn; WrDr 76*

Ginn, Edwin
American. Publisher
b. Feb 14, 1838 in Orland, Maine
d. Jan 21, 1914
Source: *AmAu&B*

Ginott, Haim
American. Author, Psychologist
Book *Between Parent and Child*, 1965, sold
  over 1.5 million copies, translated into
  more than 12 languages.
b. Aug 5, 1922 in Tel Aviv, Palestine
d. Nov 4, 1973 in New York, New York
Source: *AmAu&B; ConAu 45; NewYTBE 73;
WhAm 6*

Ginsberg, Allen
American. Poet
Associated with "Beat" movement; best
  known poem *Howl*, 1956.
b. Jun 3, 1926 in Newark, New Jersey
Source: *AmAu&B; AuNews 1; CasWL; ConAu
1R, 2NR; ConLC 1, 2, 3, 4, 6; ConP 70, 75;
CroCAP; DrAP 75; EncAB-H; EncWL;
IntWW 74, 75, 76, 77, 78, 79, 80, 81;
LongCTC; ModAL; SI; OxAmL; PenC AM;
RAdv 1; REn; REnAL; TwCWr; WebAB;
WebE&AL; WhoAm 74, 76, 78, 80, 82;
WhoTwCL; WhoWor 78; WhoWorJ 72;
WorAu; WrDr 80*

Ginzburg, Aleksandr Ilich
Russian. Political Activist, Poet
Published underground poetry that led to
  first arrest, jail sentence, 1960; set up fund
  for families of political prisoners, 1974.
b. 1936 in Leningrad, U.S.S.R.
Source: *DcPol; NewYTBS 78, 79*

Ginzburg, Charles Pauson
American. Engineer
b. 1920
Source: *BioIn 9*

Ginzburg, Ralph
American. Publisher, Journalist
b. Oct 28, 1929 in Brooklyn, New York
Source: *Au&Wr 71; ConAu 21R; WhoAm 74,
76, 78, 80, 82; WhoWor 78*

Gioconda, Lisa Gherardini
[Mona Lisa]
Italian. Noblewoman
Her portrait, by Leonardo da Vinci, hangs in
  the Louvre.
b. 1479 in Italy
Source: *InWom*

Giolitti, Giovanni
Italian. Statesman
b. 1842 in Mondovi, Italy
d. 1928
Source: *BioIn 8, 10; NewCol 75; WebBD 80*

Giono, Jean
French. Author
b. Mar 30, 1895 in Manosque, France
d. Oct 9, 1970 in Manosque, France
Source: *CasWL; ClDMEL; CnMD; CnMWL;
ConAu 29R, 45, 2NR; ConLC 4, 11; CyWA;
EncWL; EvEuW; McGEWD; ModRL;
ModWD; OxFr; PenC EUR; REn; TwCA,
SUP; TwCWr; WhoTwCL*

Giordano, Luca
"Fa Presto"
Italian. Artist
b. 1632 in Naples, Italy
d. 1705
Source: *NewCol 75*

Giordano, Umberto
Italian. Composer
b. Aug 27, 1867 in Foggia, Italy
d. Nov 12, 1948 in Milan, Italy
Source: *NewEOp 71; OxMus; WebBD 80*

Giorgio, Francesco di
Italian. Architect, Artist, Sculptor
b. 1439 in Siena, Italy
d. 1502
Source: *NewCol 75*

Giorgione, Il
[Giorgio Barbarelli; Giorgione da
Castelfranco]
Italian. Artist
Pupil of Bellini; influenced Titian.
b. 1477 in Venice, Italy
d. 1511
Source: *AtlBL; REn*

Giorno, John
American. Poet
b. Dec 4, 1936 in New York, New York
Source: *BioIn 10; ConAu 33R; ConP 70;
DrAP 75*

Giotto di Bondone
Italian. Artist, Architect
His works are among the greatest in Italian
art; designed campanile, "Giotto's Tower,"
at cathedral in Florence.
b. 1266 in Vespignamo, Italy
d. Jan 8, 1337 in Florence, Italy
Source: *AtlBL; NewC; REn*

Giovanni da Fiesole
see: Angelico, Fra

Giovanni di Paulo
Italian. Artist
Major painter of Sienese school.
b. 1403
d. 1483
Source: *NewCol 75*

Giovanni, Nikki
[Yolande Cornelia, Jr.]
American. Author, Poet
Writings include *My House,* 1972; *The
Women and the Men,* 1975.
b. Jun 7, 1943 in Knoxville, Tennessee
Source: *AuNews 1; BlkAWP; CelR; ChhPo
S2; ConAu 29R; ConLC 2, 4; ConP 75;
CroCAP; DrAP 75; LivgBAA; RAdv 1;
WhoAm 74, 76, 78, 80, 82; WhoBlA 75;
WrDr 80*

Giovannitti, Arturo
Italian. Poet
b. Jan 7, 1884 in Campobasso, Italy
d. Dec 31, 1959
Source: *AmAu&B; ConAmL; OxAmL; REn;
REnAL; TwCA*

Gipp, George
American. Football Player
Ronald Reagan portrayed him in movie
Knute Rockne All American.
b. Feb 18, 1895 in Laurium, Michigan
d. Dec 4, 1920
Source: *WhoFtbl 74*

Gipson, Lawrence Henry
American. Historian, Educator
b. Dec 7, 1880 in Greeley, Colorado
d. Sep 26, 1971 in Bethlehem, Pennsylvania
Source: *AmAu&B; ConAu 5R, 33R, 3NR;
CurBio 54, 71; NewYTBE 70, 71; OxAmL;
OxCan, SUP; WhNAA; WorAu*

Girard, Stephen
French. Philanthropist
Helped to finance US in War of 1812;
founded Girard College, Philadelphia, for
poor boys.
b. 1750 in Bordeaux, France
d. 1831
Source: *BioIn 1, 2, 3, 4, 11; WebBD 80*

Girardon, Francois
French. Sculptor
Louis XIV's designer who produced
decorative Apollo series for Versailles,
1670s; also designed Richelieu's tomb.
b. Mar 17, 1628 in Troyes, France
d. Sep 1, 1715 in Paris, France
Source: *McGDA; McGEWB; OxFilm*

Girardot, Annie
French. Actress
Won the Cesar(French Oscar) for *No Time
For Breakfast,* 1975.
b. Oct 25, 1931 in Paris, France
Source: *FilmEn; FilmgC; IntMPA 77;
NewYTBE 72; OxFilm; WhoHol A; WorEFlm*

Giraud, Henri Honore
French. General
b. Jan 18, 1879
d. Mar 11, 1949 in Dijon, France
Source: *CurBio 42, 49*

Giraudoux, Jean
French. Dramatist, Author, Diplomat
b. Oct 29, 1882 in Bellac, France
d. Jan 31, 1944 in Paris, France
Source: *AtlBL; Au&Wr 71; CasWL;
ClDMEL; CnMD; CnMWL; CnThe; CurBio
44; CyWA; EncWL; EvEuW; LongCTC;
McGEWD; ModRL; ModWD; NewC; OxEng;
OxFr; OxThe; PenC EUR; RComWL; REn;
REnWD; TwCA, SUP; TwCWr; WhoTwCL*

Girdler, Tom Mercer
American. Manufacturer
Chairman, Republic Steel, 1930-56.
b. May 19, 1877 in Clark County, Indiana
d. Feb 4, 1965 in Easton, Maryland
Source: *CurBio 44, 65; IndAu 1917; WhAm 4*

Giroud, Francoise
Swiss. Journalist, Politician
b. Sep 21, 1916 in Geneva, Switzerland
Source: *AuNews 1; ConAu 81; IntWW 74; NewYTBS 74; WhoWor 78; WomWMM*

Giroux, Robert
American. Editor, Publisher
Chairman, Farrar, Straus, and Giroux, Inc, 1973--.
b. Apr 8, 1914 in New Jersey
Source: *AmCath 80; CurBio 82; WhoAm 74, 76, 78, 80, 82; WhoWor 74*

Girtin, Thomas
English. Artist
b. Feb 18, 1775 in Southwark, England
d. Nov 9, 1802 in London, England
Source: *AtlBL; BioIn 1, 3, 10*

Giscard d'Estaing, Valery
French. Politician
Pres. of France, 1974-81.
b. Feb 2, 1926 in Koblenz, Germany
Source: *BioNews 74; CurBio 67, 74; IntWW 74, 75, 76, 77, 78, 79, 80, 81; IntYB 78, 79, 80, 81; LinLib S; NewYTBS 77; Who 74; WhoWor 76, 78; WorAl*

Gish, Dorothy
American. Actress
Played in over 100 films, 1912-22, including *Orphans of the Storm.*
b. Mar 11, 1898 in Dayton, Ohio
d. Jun 4, 1968 in Rapallo, Italy
Source: *BiE&WWA; CurBio 44, 68; FamA&A; Film 1; FilmgC; InWom; MotPP; MovMk; OxFilm; TwYS; WebAB; WhScrn 74, 77; WhoHol B; WomWMM; WorEFlm*

Gish, Lillian Diana
"The First Lady of the Silent Screen"
American. Actress
Starred in D W Griffith movies *Broken Blossoms,* 1918; *Orphans of the Storm,* 1922.
b. Oct 14, 1896 in Springfield, Ohio
Source: *BiDFilm; BiE&WWA; CelR; CmMov; CurBio 44; FamA&A; Film 1; FilmgC; InWom; IntMPA 75, 76, 77, 78, 79, 80, 81, 82; IntWW 74, 75, 76, 77, 78, 79, 80, 81; MotPP; MovMk; NotNAT; OxFilm; PIP&P; REn; ThFT; WebAB; WhoAm 74, 76, 78, 80, 82; WhoHol A; WhoThe 77; WhoWor 78; WomWMM; WorEFlm*

Gissing, George Robert
English. Author, Critic
b. Nov 22, 1857 in Wakefield, England
d. Dec 28, 1903 in Saint Jean de Luz, France
Source: *Alli SUP; AtlBL; BbD; BiD&SB; BrAu 19; CasWL; Chambr 3; CyWA; DcEnA AP; DcEuL; DcLEL; EvLB; LongCTC; ModBrL; NewC; OxEng; PenC ENG; RAdv 1; REn; WebE&AL*

Gitlis, Ivry
Israeli. Musician
b. 1927 in Haifa, Palestine
Source: *WhoMus 72*

Gitlow, Benjamin
American. Political Activist
Involved in Socialist, Communist activities.
b. Dec 22, 1891 in Elizabethport, New Jersey
d. Jul 19, 1965
Source: *BioIn 7; WhAm 4*

Giuffre, James Peter
American. Jazz Musician
b. Apr 26, 1921 in Dallas, Texas
Source: *WhoAm 74; WhoE 74*

Giulini, Carlo Maria
Italian. Conductor
b. May 9, 1914 in Basletta, Italy
Source: *IntWW 74; Who 74; WhoAm 74, 76, 78, 80, 82; WhoMus 72*

Giusti, Dave (David John, Jr.)
American. Baseball Player
b. Nov 27, 1939 in Seneca Falls, New York
Source: *BaseEn 85; WhoProB 73*

Giusti, Giuseppe
Italian. Patriot, Author
b. May 12, 1809 in Monsummano, Italy
d. 1850 in Florence, Italy
Source: *BiD&SB; CasWL; DcEuL; EvEuW; PenC EUR; REn*

Givenchy, Hubert de
French. Fashion Designer
Opened couture house, 1952, known for elegant day, evening wear.
b. Feb 21, 1927 in Beauvais, France
Source: *CurBio 55; Entr; WhoAm 82; WhoFash; WorFshn*

Givens, Edward Galen
American. Astronaut
b. 1930
d. Jun 6, 1967 in Pearland, Texas
Source: *BioIn 10*

Gjellerup, Karl Adolf
Danish. Author
Wrote novel *The Pilgrim Kamanoto*, 1906,
    only work translated into English; won
    Nobel Prize, 1917.
b. Jun 2, 1857 in Roholte, Denmark
d. Oct 11, 1919 in Klotzche, Germany
Source: *BiD&SB; CasWL; ClDMEL; TwCWr*

Glackens, William James
American. Artist
b. Mar 13, 1870 in Philadelphia,
    Pennsylvania
d. May 22, 1938 in Westport, Connecticut
Source: *AmBi; AtlBL; DcAmB S2; DcCAA 71;
    OxAmL; WebAB; WhAm 1*

Gladstone, William Ewart
English. Statesman, Author
Four-time British prime minister.
b. Dec 29, 1809 in Liverpool, England
d. May 19, 1898 in Hawarden, England
Source: *Alli, SUP; BbD; BiD&SB, CasWL,
    Chambr 3; ChhPo; DcEnA, AP; DcEnL;
    EvLB; NewC; OxEng; REn*

Gladys Knight and the Pips
[Langston George; Eleanor Guest; William
    Guest; Brenda Knight; Gladys Knight;
    Merald Knight]
American. Music Group
Family group formed in Atlanta, 1952;
    biggest hit "Midnight Train to Georgia,"
    1973.
Source: *RolSEnR 83*

Glaisher, James
English. Meteorologist, Balloonist
b. Apr 7, 1809 in London, England
d. Feb 8, 1903
Source: *BioIn 1, 8; NewCol 75*

Glanzman, Louis S
American. Artist, Illustrator
b. Feb 8, 1922 in Baltimore, Maryland
Source: *IlsBYP; IlsCB 1957*

Glascock, Brian
see: Motels, The

Glaser, Donald Arthur
American. Physicist
b. Sep 21, 1926 in Cleveland, Ohio
Source: *BioIn 5, 6; CurBio 61; IntWW 74;
    WhoAm 74; WhoWest 84; WhoWor 78*

Glaser, Milton
American. Illustrator
b. Jun 26, 1929 in New York, New York
Source: *ChhPo S2; ConAu 17R; CurBio 80;
    IlsBYP; IlsCB 1957; SmATA 11; WhoAm 82*

Glaser, Paul Michael
American. Actor
Played Starsky on TV series "Starsky and
    Hutch," 1975-79.
b. Mar 25, 1942 in Cambridge, Massachusetts
Source: *BioIn 11; IntMPA 78, 79, 80, 81, 82;
    WhoAm 78, 80, 82*

Glasgow, Ellen Anderson Gholson
American. Author
b. Apr 22, 1874 in Richmond, Virginia
d. Nov 21, 1945 in Richmond, Virginia
Source: *AmAu&B; AmWr; AtlBL; BiD&SB;
    BiDSA; CasWL; Chambr 3; ChhPo, S1;
    CnDAL; ConAmA; ConAmL; CurBio 46;
    CyWA; DcAmAu; DcAmB S3; DcBiA; DcLEL;
    DcNAA; EncWL; EvLB; InWom; LongCTC;
    ModAL; NotAW; OxAmL; OxEng; PenC AM;
    RAdv 1; REn; REnAL; TwCA, SUP; TwCWr;
    WebE&AL; WhNAA*

Glaspell, Susan Keating
American. Author, Dramatist
b. Jul 1, 1882 in Davenport, Iowa
d. Jul 21, 1948
Source: *AmAu&B; AmNov; Chambr 3;
    CnDAL; CnMD; ConAmA; ConAmL; DcAmB
    S4; DcLEL; DcNAA; InWom; LongCTC;
    McGEWD; ModWD; NotAW; OxAmL;
    OxThe; PIP&P; REn; REnAL; TwCA, SUP;
    WhAm 2; WhNAA; WomWWA 14*

Glass, Carter
American. Statesman, Senator
b. Jan 4, 1858 in Lynchburg, Virginia
d. May 28, 1946 in Washington, District of
    Columbia
Source: *BiDrAC; BiDrUSE; CurBio 41, 46;
    DcAmB S4; DcNAA; EncAB-H; WebAB;
    WhAm 2; WhAmP*

Glass, David Victor
English. Sociologist
b. Jan 2, 1911 in London, England
Source: *Au&Wr 71; BioIn 1; IntWW 74;
    Who 74*

Glass, Hiram Bentley
American. Biologist
b. Jan 17, 1906 in Laichowfu, China
Source: *BioIn 4; WhoAm 74*

Glass, Montague (Marsden)
American. Lawyer, Author, Dramatist
Known for humorous books, plays *Potash
    and Prelmutter*, 1910-26.
b. Jul 23, 1877 in Manchester, England
d. Feb 3, 1934 in Westport, Connecticut
Source: *ConAu 117; REnAL; TwCA*

Glass, Philip
American. Musician, Composer
Noted avant-garde composer who uses
    electrically-amplified wind instruments.
b. Jan 31, 1937 in Baltimore, Maryland
Source: *Baker 78; BioIn 10, 11; CurBio 81;*
NewYTBS 74; WhoAm 78, 80, 82, 84

Glass, Ron
American. Actor
Played Ron Harris on "Barney Miller,"
    1975-82.
b. Jul 10, 1945 in Evansville, Indiana
Source: *BioIn 11; DrBlPA; WhoAm 82*

Glassco, John Stinson
Canadian. Author
b. Dec 15, 1909 in Montreal, Quebec
d. Jan 29, 1981 in Montreal, Quebec
Source: *CanWW 70; CanWr; CasWL; ConAu*
13R, 102; ConNov 72, 76; ConP 70, 75;
OxCan, SUP; WrDr 80

Glasscock, Jack (John Wesley)
"Pebbly Jack"
American. Baseball Player
b. Jul 22, 1859 in Wheeling, West Virginia
d. Feb 24, 1947 in Wheeling, West Virginia
Source: *BaseEn 85; BioIn 3*

Glasser, Ira
American. Social Reformer
Exec. director, ACLU, 1978--.
b. Apr 18, 1938 in New York, New York
Source: *CurBio 86; WhoAmL 83*

Glasspole, Florizel Augustus
Jamaican. Political Leader
Governor general of Jamaica, 1973--.
b. Sep 25, 1909 in Kingston, Jamaica
Source: *IntWW 80, 81, 82; IntYB 80, 81, 82;*
WhoWor 78

Glazer, David
American. Musician
International clarinet soloist; member, New
    York Woodwind Quintet, 1951--.
b. May 7, 1913 in Milwaukee, Wisconsin
Source: *WhoAm 74, 76, 78, 80, 82; WhoWor*
74, 76

Glazer, Nathan
American. Author
b. Feb 25, 1923 in New York, New York
Source: *AmAu&B; ConAu 5R; CurBio 70;*
IntWW 74; LEduc 74; WhoAm 74, 76, 78,
80, 82; WhoWorJ 72; WrDr 76

Glazunov, Alexander Constantinovich
Russian. Composer
b. Aug 10, 1865 in Saint Petersburg, Russia
d. Mar 21, 1936 in Paris, France
Source: *AtlBL*

Gleason, Jackie
American. Actor, Comedian
Starred in TV series, "The Honeymooners,"
    with Art Carney.
b. Feb 26, 1916 in Brooklyn, New York
Source: *AmSCAP 66; BiE&WWA; CelR;*
CurBio 55; EncMT; FilmgC; IntMPA 75, 76,
77, 78, 79, 80, 81, 82; MovMk; NewYTBE
73; WebAB; WhoAm 74, 76, 78, 80, 82;
WhoHol A

Gleason, James
American. Actor
Nominated for 1941 Oscar for *Here Comes*
    Mr. Jordan.
b. May 23, 1886 in New York, New York
d. Apr 12, 1959 in Woodland Hills,
    California
Source: *FilmgC; MotPP; MovMk; TwYS; Vers*
A; WhAm 3; WhScrn 74, 77

Gleason, Lucille
American. Actress
Character actress, 1929-45; films include
    Klondike Annie, Rhythm of the Range.
b. Feb 6, 1888 in Pasadena, California
d. May 13, 1947 in Brentwood, California
Source: *FilmgC; WhScrn 74, 77; WhoHol B*

Gleason, Ralph Joseph
American. Journalist
b. Mar 1, 1917 in New York, New York
d. Jun 3, 1975 in Berkeley, California
Source: *ConAu 61, 65; WhAm 6; WhoWest*
84

Gleason, Thomas W
American. Labor Union Official
Pres., ILA, 1963--; vp, AFL-CIO, 1969--.
b. Nov 8, 1900 in New York, New York
Source: *CurBio 65; WhoAm 74, 76, 78, 80,*
82

Gleizes, Albert L
French. Artist
b. 1881 in Creteil, France
d. 1953
Source: *REn*

Glemp, Jozef, Cardinal
Polish. Religious Leader
Elevated to cardinal Feb 2, 1983, by Pope
John Paul II; head of Polish Catholic
church, 1981--.
b. Dec 18, 1929 in Inowroclaw, Poland
Source: *BioIn 12; CurBio 82; NewYTBS 82*

Glendenning, Raymond Carl
American. Journalist
b. Sep 25, 1907
Source: *Au&Wr 71; Who 74*

Glendower, Owen
Welsh. Revolutionary
b. 1359
d. 1416
Source: *BioIn 3, 5, 6, 7, 8, 9; NewC*

Glenn, Carroll
American. Violinist
With husband, pianist Eugene List, founded
Southern Vermont Music Festival.
b. 1922
d. Apr 25, 1983 in New York, New York
Source: *InWom; NewYTBS 83*

Glenn, John Herschel, Jr.
American. Astronaut, Politician
First man to orbit Earth, Feb 20, 1962;
Dem. senator from OH, 1975--.
b. Jul 18, 1921 in Cambridge, Ohio
Source: *AnCL; BioNews 74; CelR; CurBio 62;
IntWW 74; NewYTBE 72; WebAB; Who 74;
WhoAm 74, 76, 78, 80, 82; WhoS&SW 82;
WhoWor 78*

Glenn, Scott
American. Actor
In films *Urban Cowboy,* 1980; *The Right
Stuff,* 1983.
b. 1939 in Pittsburgh, Pennsylvania
Source: *ConTFT 3; IntMPA 84; VarWW 85*

Gless, Sharon
American. Actress
Plays Chris Cagney on TV series "Cagney
and Lacy."
b. May 31, 1943 in Los Angeles, California
Source: *VarWW 85*

Glickman, Marty
American. Sportscaster
Source: *BioIn 9*

Gliere, Reinhold Moritzovich
Russian. Composer
b. Jan 11, 1875 in Kiev, Russia
d. Jun 23, 1956 in Moscow, U.S.S.R.
Source: *DcCM*

Glinka, Mikhail Ivanovich
Russian. Composer
b. Jun 1, 1804 in Novospaskoi, Russia
d. Feb 15, 1857 in Berlin, Germany
Source: *AtlBL; REn*

Glossop, Peter
American. Opera Singer
b. Jun 6, 1928 in Indianapolis, Indiana
Source: *IntWW 74; Who 74; WhoMus 72;
WhoWor 78*

Gloucester, Duke of
see: Henry William Frederick Albert, Prince

Glover, Danny
American. Actor
Starred in *The Color Purple,* 1985; *Places in
the Heart,* 1984.
b. 1948
Source: *NF*

Glover, John
American. Revolutionary
Member MA convention to ratify
Constitution, 1788.
b. Nov 5, 1753 in Salem, Massachusetts
d. Jan 30, 1797 in Marblehead,
Massachusetts
Source: *AmBi; BioIn 5, 8, 9, 11; DcAmB;
WebAB; WebBD 80*

Glover, Julian
English. Actor
Films include *Tom Jones,* 1963; *Nicholas and
Alexandra,* 1971.
b. Mar 27, 1935 in London, England
Source: *FilmgC; WhoHol A; WhoThe 72, 77,
81*

Glover, William H
American. Drama Critic
b. May 6, 1911 in New York, New York
Source: *BiE&WWA; NotNAT; WhoAm 74, 76,
78, 80, 82; WhoWor 78*

Glubb, John Bagot, Sir
English. Military Leader, Author
Commanded Arab Legion/Jordanian Army,
1939-56; wrote books on Mideast.
b. Apr 16, 1897 in Lancashire, England
d. Mar 17, 1986 in Mayfield, England
Source: *AnObit 1984; ConAu 5NR, 9R;
CurBio 51, 86; IntWW 74; Who 74; WhoWor
74; WrDr 76*

Gluck, Alma
[Reba Fiersohn]
American. Opera Singer
b. May 11, 1884 in Bucharest, Romania
d. Oct 27, 1938 in New York, New York
Source: *AmBi; DcAmB S2; InWom; NotAW;*
WhAm 1

Gluck, Christoph Wilibald
German. Opera Composer
b. Jul 2, 1714 in Erasbach, Germany
d. Nov 15, 1787 in Vienna, Austria
Source: *AtlBL; NewC; REn*

Glueck, Nelson
American. Theologian, Archaeologist
b. Jun 4, 1900 in Cincinnati, Ohio
d. Feb 12, 1971 in Cincinnati, Ohio
Source: *AmAu&B; ConAu 17R, P-2; CurBio*
48, 69, 71; OhA&B; REnAL; WhAm 5

Glueck, Sheldon (Sol Sheldon)
American. Criminologist
b. Aug 15, 1896 in Warsaw, Poland
d. Mar 10, 1980 in Cambridge,
   Massachusetts
Source: *AmAu&B; BiDrAPA 77; BioIn 4, 6;*
ConAu 5R, 97; CurBio 57, 80; DrAS 74P,
78P; IntWW 74, 75, 76, 77, 78; WebAB;
WhAm 7; WhNAA; WhoAm 74, 76, 78;
WhoWor 74, 76, 78

Glyn, Elinor Sutherland
English. Author
b. Oct 17, 1864 in Channel Islands
d. Sep 23, 1943 in London, England
Source: *CurBio 43; DcLEL; EvLB; Film 2;*
FilmgC; LongCTC; NewC; OxEng; OxFilm;
TwCA; TwCWr

Gneisenau, August Neithardt von
Prussian. Field Marshal
Called "father of Russian realism"; wrote
   Dead Souls, 1842; *Inspector General,* 1836.
b. 1760
d. 1831
Source: *NewCol 75; WebBD 80*

Go-Go's, The
[Charlotte Caffey; Belinda Carlisle; Gina
   Schock; Kathy Valentine ; Jane Wiedlin]
American. Music Group
All-female punk group formed 1978; hit
   single "We Got the Beat" from hit album
   Beauty and the Beat, 1982.
Source: *NewWmR; RolSEnR 83*

Goalby, Bob
American. Golfer
b. Mar 14, 1931 in Belleville, Illinois
Source: *BioIn 7, 8, 10; WhoGolf*

Gobbi, Tito
Italian. Opera Singer
Baritone, best known for portrayal of Scarpia
   in Puccini's *Tosca,* 1956.
b. Oct 24, 1915 in Bassano del Grappo, Italy
d. May 5, 1984 in Rome, Italy
Source: *AnObit 1984; CurBio 57, 84; IntWW*
74; Who 74; WhoAm 82; WhoMus 72;
WhoWor 74

Gobel, George Leslie
"Lonesome George"
American. Comedian
b. May 20, 1919 in Chicago, Illinois
Source: *CurBio 55; EncFCWM 69; FilmgC;*
WhoAm 74; WhoHol A

Gobineau, Joseph Arthur, Comte de
French. Author, Philosopher
b. Jul 14, 1816 in Ville d'Avray, France
d. Oct 13, 1882 in Turin, Italy
Source: *BioIn 1, 2, 7, 9; McGEWB*

Godard, Benjamin L P
French. Composer
b. 1849
d. 1895
Source: *BioIn 3*

Godard, Jean Luc
French. Director
A founder of French new wave cinemas
   including *Breathless.*
b. Dec 3, 1930 in Paris, France
Source: *BiDFilm; CelR; CurBio 69; DcFM;*
FilmgC; IntMPA 82; IntWW 74; MovMk;
NewYTBE 70; OxFilm; WhoWor 74;
WomWMM; WorEFlm

Goddard, Calvin Hooker
American. Criminologist
b. Oct 30, 1891 in Baltimore, Maryland
d. Feb 22, 1955
Source: *BioIn 3, 4; WhAm 3*

Goddard, Paulette
[Marian Levee]
American. Actress
Married Charlie Chaplin, 1936-42; married
   Erich Maria Remarque, 1958-70; films
   include *Modern Times.*
b. Jun 3, 1911 in Great Neck, New York
Source: *BiDFilm; CelR; CmMov; FilmgC;*
InWom; IntMPA 75, 76, 77, 78, 79, 80, 81,
82; MotPP; MovMk; OxFilm; ThFT; WhoAm
82; WhoHol A; WorEFlm

Goddard, Robert Hutchings
American. Physicist
Launched first liquid-fueled rocket, 1926.
b. Oct 5, 1882 in Worcester, Massachusetts
d. Aug 10, 1945 in Baltimore, Maryland
Source: *DcAmB S3; EncAB-H; NewCol 75; WebAB; WhAm 2*

Godden, Rumer, pseud.
[Margaret Rumer Haynes Dixon]
English. Author, Poet, Dramatist
TV movie made from *In This House of Brede,* 1975.
b. Dec 10, 1907 in Sussex, England
Source: *AnCL; Au&Wr 71; AuBYP; ChhPo, S1, S2; ConAu 5R, 4NR; ConNov 72, 76; DcLEL; FilmgC; InWom; IntWW 74; LongCTC; ModBrL; MorJA; NewC; PiP; RAdv 1; REn; SmATA 3; TwCA, SUP; TwCWr; WhoChL; WhoWor 78; WrDr 80*

Godel, Kurt
American. Mathematician
b. Apr 28, 1906 in Bruenn, Czechoslovakia
d. Jan 14, 1978 in Princeton, New Jersey
Source: *AmM&WS 73P; IntWW 74; NewCol 75; Who 74; WhoAm 74; WhoWor 78*

Godey, Louis Antoine
American. Publisher
Established America's leading 19th c. fashion magazine *Godey's Lady Book,* 1830.
b. Jun 6, 1804 in New York, New York
d. Nov 29, 1878 in Philadelphia, Pennsylvania
Source: *AmAu; AmAu&B; AmBi; ApCAB; DcAmB; NewCol 75; REn; WebAB; WhAm HS; WorFshn*

Godfrey of Bouillon
French. Ruler, Soldier
Led First Crusade, 1096; captured Jerusalem and became first king, 1099; subject of *Chansons de Geste.*
b. 1058 in Baisyin Brabant, France
d. Jul 18, 1100 in Jerusalem, Palestine
Source: *DcEuL; NewC; NewCol 75*

Godfrey, Arthur Michael
American. Actor, Singer
Hosted TV shows, 1948-59, including "The Arthur Godfrey Show."
b. Aug 31, 1903 in New York, New York
d. Mar 16, 1983 in New York, New York
Source: *AmSCAP 66; AnObit 1982; BioNews 75; CelR; CurBio 48, 83N; IntMPA 80, 81, 82; NewYTBS 83; WebAB; WhoAm 80, 82; WhoHol A*

Godfrey, Isadore
English. Conductor
b. 1901
d. Sep 12, 1977 in Sussex, England
Source: *BioIn 11*

Godiva, Lady
[Godgifu]
English. Social Reformer
Made legendary ride naked through Coventry to win tax relief for townspeople.
b. 1010
d. 1067
Source: *InWom; NewC; NewCol 75; REn*

Godkin, Edwin Lawrence
American. Journalist
b. Oct 2, 1831 in Wicklow, Ireland
d. May 21, 1902 in England
Source: *Alli SUP; AmAu; AmAu&B; AmBi; BbD; BiD&SB; DcAmAu; DcAmB; DcLEL; DcNAA; EncAB-H; EvLB; OxAmL; REn; REnAL; TwCBDA; WebAB; WhAm 1*

Godley, Devin
see: 10 CC

Godolphin, Sidney
English. Statesman
b. Jun 15, 1645 in England
d. Sep 15, 1712 in London, England
Source: *BioIn 1, 3, 11; McGEWB; WebBD 80*

Godowsky, Leopold
Polish. Musician
b. Feb 13, 1870 in Wilma, Russia
d. Nov 21, 1938
Source: *AmBi; AmSCAP 66; DcAmB S2; WhAm 1; WhoAm 74*

Godowsky, Leopold, II
American. Inventor
Co-invented Kodachrome color photography process, 1936.
b. 1901 in Chicago, Illinois
d. Feb 18, 1983 in New York, New York
Source: *NewYTBS 83*

Godoy Alcayaga, Lucila
Chilean. Poet, Educator
b. 1889
d. 1957
Source: *BioIn 1, 2, 4, 6, 9, 10; DcSpL; REn*

Godunov, Alexander (Boris Alexander)
Russian. Ballet Dancer
First Bolshoi Ballet member to defect to US, 1979.
b. Nov 28, 1949 in Sakhalin, U.S.S.R.
Source: *BioIn 10, 11; CurBio 83; WhoAm 82*

Godunov, Boris Fedorovich
Russian. Czar
b. 1551 in Moscow, Russia
d. Apr 23, 1605
Source: *McGEWB; NewCol 75; REn*

Godwin, Edward William
English. Architect, Designer
Best known as designer of wallpaper,
furniture, theatrical scenery, and costumes.
b. 1833 in Bristol, England
d. Sep 6, 1886
Source: *NotNAT B; OxArt; OxDecA; OxThe;
WhoArch*

Godwin, Mary Wollstonecraft
English. Author, Feminist
Wrote feminist paper *The Vindication of the
Rights of Women*, 1792; mother of Mary
Shelley.
b. Apr 27, 1759 in London, England
d. Sep 10, 1797 in London, England
Source: *Alli; AtlBL; BbD; BrAu;
CasWL; Chambr 2; DcEnA; DcEnL; DcEuL;
DcLEL; EvLB; InWom; NewC; NewCol 75;
OxEng; PenC ENG; REn*

Godwin, William
English. Author
b. Mar 3, 1756
d. Apr 7, 1836 in London, England
Source: *Alli; AtlBL; BbD; BiD&SB; BiDLA,
SUP; BrAu 19; CasWL; Chambr 2; CyWA;
DcBiA; DcEnA; DcEnL; DcLEL; EncMys;
EvLB; MouLC 3; NewC; OxEng; PenC ENG;
REn; WebE&AL*

Goebbels, Joseph (Paul Joseph)
German. Nazi Leader
Minister of propaganda under Hitler;
committed suicide as Berlin fell to
Russians.
b. Oct 29, 1897 in Rheydt, Germany
d. May 3, 1945 in Berlin, Germany
Source: *CurBio 41; NewCol 75; OxGer; REn*

Goering, Emmy Sonnemann
German. Celebrity Relative
b. 1893
d. Jun 8, 1973 in Munich, Germany (West)
Source: *EncTR; NewYTBE 73*

Goering, Hermann Wilhelm
German. Nazi War Criminal
Hitler's minister of aviation; founder of
Gestapo.
b. Jan 12, 1893 in Rosenheim, Germany
d. Oct 15, 1946 in Nuremberg, Germany
Source: *CurBio 41, 46; OxGer; REn*

Goes, Hugo van der
Flemish. Artist
b. 1440
d. 1482
Source: *AtlBL; REn*

Goethals, George Washington
American. Army Officer, Engineer
Chief engineer, Panama Canal, 1913; first
governor of Canal Zone, 1914-17.
b. Jun 29, 1858 in Brooklyn, New York
d. Jan 21, 1928 in New York, New York
Source: *AmBi; DcAmB; DcNAA; EncAB-H;
WebAB; WhAm 1*

Goethe, Johann Wolfgang von
German. Poet, Dramatist, Author
Wrote *Faust*, 1770, 1831; *The Sorrows of
Werther*, 1774.
b. Aug 28, 1749 in Frankfurt, Germany
d. Mar 22, 1832 in Weimar, Germany
Source: *AtlBL; BbD; BiD&SB; CasWL;
ChhPo, S1, S2; CnThe; CyWA; DcBiA;
DcEnL; DcEuL; EuAu; EvEuW; McGEWD;
NewC; OxEng; OxFr; OxGer; OxThe; PenC
EUR; RComWL; REn; REnWD*

Goffstein, Marilyn
American. Author
b. Dec 20, 1940 in Saint Paul, Minnesota
Source: *ConAu 21R; SmATA 8; WhoAmW 77*

Gogarty, Oliver St. John
Irish. Physician, Author
Leader of Sinn Fein movement; wrote
memoir *As I Was Going Down Sackville
Street*, 1937.
b. Aug 17, 1878 in Dublin, Ireland
d. Sep 22, 1957 in New York, New York
Source: *ModBrL; PenC ENG; REn; WhDW*

Gogol, Nikolai Vasilievich
Russian. Author
b. Mar 21, 1809 in Mirgorod, Russia
d. Mar 4, 1852 in Moscow, Russia
Source: *AtlBL; BbD; BiD&SB; CasWL;
CnThe; CyWA; DcBiA; DcEuL; DcRusL;
EuAu; EvEuW; McGEWD; NewC; OxEng;
OxThe; PenC EUR; PlP&P; RComWL; REn;
REnWD*

Goheen, Robert Francis
American. Educator, University Administrator
Pres., Princeton U, 1957-72; ambassador to
India, 1977-80.
b. Aug 15, 1919 in Vengurla, India
Source: *AmAu&B; Au&Wr 71; CurBio 58;
DrAS 74F; IntWW 74; LEduc 74; Who 74;
WhoAm 74, 76, 78, 80, 82; WhoE 74;
WhoWor 78*

Goizueta, Roberto Crispulo
American. Beverage Manufacturer
With Coca-Cola, 1954--; chm., 1981--.
b. Nov 18, 1931 in Havana, Cuba
Source: *Dun&B 79; WhoAm 76, 78, 80, 82;*
WhoF&I 74; WhoS&SW 75, 76

Gola, Thomas Joseph
American. Basketball Player
Forward, 1955-66, who was member of 1956
 NBA champion Philadelphia team; Hall of
 Fame, 1975.
b. Jan 13, 1933 in Philadelphia, Pennsylvania
Source: *OfNBA 81; WhoBbl 73*

Golacinski, Alan Bruce
[The Hostages]
American. Hostage in Iran
b. Jun 4, 1950 in Austria
Source: *NewYTBS 81; USBiR 74*

Golar, Simeon
American. Government Official
b. 1928
Source: *BioIn 9, 11; NewYTBE 72*

Gold, Andrew
American. Singer
b. Aug 2, 1951 in Burbank, California
Source: *IlEncRk*

Gold, Arthur
Canadian. Musician
b. 1919
Source: *BioIn 7*

Gold, Harry
Spy for the Soviets, 1935-46, who testified in
 Rosenberg spy trial.
b. 1910 in Bern, Switzerland
d. Aug 28, 1972 in Philadelphia,
 Pennsylvania
Source: *NewYTBE 72; NewYTBS 74; SpyCS*

Gold, Herbert
American. Author
b. Mar 9, 1924 in Cleveland, Ohio
Source: *AmAu&B; ConAu 9R; ConLC 4;*
ConNov 72, 76; DrAF 76; ModAL; OxAmL;
PenC AM; RAdv 1; REnAL; TwCWr;
WhoAm 80, 82; WhoWor 78; WhoWorJ 72;
WorAu; WrDr 80

Gold, Michael
[Irwin Granich]
American. Author
b. Apr 12, 1894 in New York, New York
d. May 14, 1967 in Terra Inda, California
Source: *AmAu&B; ConAu 45, 97; ModWD;*
OxAmL; PenC AM; REn; REnAL; TwCA,
SUP; WebE&AL

Gold Dust Twins
see: McSpaden, Byron; Nelson, (John) Byron

Goldazher, Herbert
Museum Director
Source: *NF*

Goldberg, Arthur Joseph
American. Supreme Court Justice
As labor lawyer, played important role in
 1955 merger of AFL and CIO.
b. Aug 8, 1908 in Chicago, Illinois
Source: *AmAu&B; BiDrUSE; CelR; ConAu*
65; CurBio 49, 61; EncAB-H; IntWW 74;
WebAB; Who 74; WhoAm 74, 76, 78, 80, 82;
WhoAmP 73; WhoF&I 74; WhoWor 78;
WhoWorJ 72

Goldberg, Ben Zion
American. Journalist
b. Jan 9, 1894 in Olshani, Russia
Source: *WhoWorJ 72*

Goldberg, Bertrand
American. Architect
b. Jul 17, 1913 in Chicago, Illinois
Source: *AmArch 70; BioNews 74; WhoAm 74,*
76, 78, 80, 82

Goldberg, Leonard
American. Producer
With Aaron Spelling, produced TV series
 "Charlie's Angels," "Hart to Hart."
b. Jan 24, 1934 in New York, New York
Source: *ConTFT 3; IntMPA 84; NewYTBS*
80; WhoAm 84; WhoWor 82

Goldberg, Rube (Reuben Lucius)
American. Cartoonist
Created comic strips "Mike & Ike," "Lucifer
 Butts"; known for drawings of absurd
 mechanical contraptions.
b. Jul 4, 1883 in San Francisco, California
d. Dec 7, 1970 in New York, New York
Source: *AmAu&B; AmSCAP 66; ConAu 5R;*
CurBio 48, 71; NewYTBE 70; WebAB;
WhAm 6; WhNAA; WhScrn 77

Goldberg, Whoopi
[Caryn Johnson]
American. Actress
Star of film *Color Purple*, 1985, who had
one-woman Broadway show, 1984-85.
b. 1949 in New York, New York
Source: *ConTFT 3; CurBio 85; NewYTBS 84*

Goldberger, Joseph
American. Physician
b. Jul 16, 1874 in Austria
d. Jan 17, 1929 in Washington, District of
Columbia
Source: *AmBi; DcAmB; WebAB; WhAm 1*

Goldblum, Jeff
American. Actor
Starred in films *The Big Chill*, 1983; *The
Fly*, 1986.
b. Oct 22, 1952 in Pittsburgh, Pennsylvania
Source: *BioIn 11; JohnWSW*

Golden, Clinton Strong
American. Labor Union Official
Vp, United Steelworkers of America, 1942-46.
b. Nov 16, 1886 in Pottsville, Pennsylvania
d. Jun 12, 1961
Source: *BioIn 1, 5, 6; CurBio 48, 61; WhAm
4*

Golden, Harry Lewis
American. Author, Editor, Publisher
Popular essay collections include best-selling
Only in America, 1958; *For 2 cents Plain*,
1959.
b. May 6, 1903 in Mikulinsty, Austria-
Hungary
d. Oct 2, 1981 in Charlotte, North Carolina
Source: *AmAu&B; AnObit 1981; BioIn 5, 6,
7, 8; CelR; ConAu 1R, 104, 2NR; CurBio 59,
81; PenC AM; RAdv 1; REnAL; WhoAm 74,
76, 78, 80; WhoS&SW 73, 75; WhoWor 74,
76; WhoWorJ 72; WorAu*

Golden, John
American. Dramatist, Producer
b. Jun 27, 1874 in New York, New York
d. Jun 17, 1955 in New York, New York
Source: *AmAu&B; AmSCAP 66; CurBio 44,
55; DcAmB S5; OhA&B; PoIre; REnAL;
WhAm 3*

Golden, William
American. Artist
Designed the CBS eye as TV trademark,
1951.
b. Mar 31, 1911 in New York, New York
d. Oct 23, 1959 in Stony Pointe, New York
Source: *BiDLA; WhoGrA 62*

Golden, William Lee
[The Oak Ridge Boys]
American. Singer
Baritone with country-pop group.
b. Jan 12, 1939 in Brewton, Alabama
Source: *NF*

Golden Earring
[Rinus Gerritsen; Barry Hay; George
Kooymans; Robert Jan Stips; Cesar
Zuiderwijk]
Dutch. Music Group
Holland's top rock band since, 1964; hit
single "Twilight Zone," 1982.
Source: *RkOn 78; WhoRock 81*

Goldenson, Leonard Harry
American. Film Executive, TV Executive
Chm., chief exec. of ABC since 1972; played
pivotal role in history of commercial
network TV.
b. Dec 7, 1905 in Scottdale, Pennsylvania
Source: *CelR; CurBio 57; IntMPA 75, 76, 77,
78, 79, 80, 81, 82; St&PR 75; WhoAm 74,
76, 78, 80, 82; WhoE 74; WhoF&I 74;
WhoGov 72; WhoTelC; WhoWor 74*

Goldfinger, Nathaniel
American. Labor Union Official
Economist, director of research, AFL-CIO,
1955-76.
b. Aug 20, 1916 in New York, New York
d. Jul 22, 1976 in Silver Spring, Maryland
Source: *AmM&WS 73S; NewYTBS 76;
WhAm 7; WhoAm 74, 76*

Goldhaber, Maurice
American. Physicist
b. Apr 18, 1911 in Lemberg, Austria
Source: *IntWW 74; WhoAm 74, 76, 78, 80,
82*

Goldie, Grace Wyndham
English. Producer
With BBC, 1944-65; productions include
"Press Conference"; "Panorama."
b. 1900
d. Jun 3, 1986 in London, England
Source: *BioIn 6*

Goldin, Horace
American. Magician
Devised magic trick of "sawing a woman in
half."
b. Dec 17, 1873 in Poland
d. Aug 22, 1939 in London, England
Source: *DcAmB S2*

Golding, William Gerald
English. Author
Best known for allegorical cult novel *Lord of
the Flies*, 1954.
b. Sep 19, 1911 in Cornwall, England
Source: *CasWL; CnMWL; ConAu 5R; ConLC
1, 2, 3, 8, 10, 17; ConNov 72, 76; EncWL;
IntWW 74; LongCTC; ModBrL, S1; ModWD;
NewC; PenC ENG; RAdv 1; REn; TwCWr;
WebE&AL; Who 74; WhoAm 82; WhoTwCL;
WhoWor 78; WorAu; WrDr 80*

Goldman, Edwin Franko
American. Band Leader, Composer
b. Jan 1, 1878 in Louisville, Kentucky
d. Feb 21, 1956 in New York, New York
Source: *AmSCAP 66; CurBio 42, 56; WebAB;
WhAm 3*

Goldman, Emma
American. Anarchist
Important figure in American radicalism who
published *Anarchism and Other Essays*,
1910.
b. Jun 27, 1869 in Kaunas, Lithuania
d. May 14, 1940 in Toronto, Ontario
Source: *AmBi; CurBio 40; DcAmB S2;
DcNAA; EncAB-H; HerW; InWom; NewCol
75; NotAW; OxAmL; REnAL; WebAB;
WhAm HSA, 4; WhAmP*

Goldman, Eric F
American. Author, Historian
b. Jun 17, 1915 in Washington, District of
Columbia
Source: *AmAu&B; ConAu 5R; CurBio 64;
DrAS 74F; IntWW 74; WhoAm 74; WhoWor
78; WhoWorJ 72; WrDr 76*

Goldman, Eric W
American. Business Executive
b. 1958
Source: *BioIn 12*

Goldman, James
American. Dramatist, Author
b. Jun 30, 1927 in Chicago, Illinois
Source: *AmAu&B; BiE&WWA; ConAu 45,
1NR; McGEWD; NotNAT; WhoAm 74, 76,
78, 80, 82; WhoE 74; WhoWor 78; WrDr 76*

Goldman, Richard Franko
American. Composer
b. Dec 7, 1910 in New York, New York
d. Jan 19, 1980 in Baltimore, Maryland
Source: *AmAu&B; ConAu 9R, 93, 5NR;
LEduc 74; WhoAm 74; WhoWor 78; WrDr
80*

Goldman, Sylvan N
American. Merchant, Inventor
Depression-era grocery store owner, who
invented grocery cart.
b. 1898
d. Nov 25, 1984 in Oklahoma City,
Oklahoma
Source: *BioIn 3*

Goldman, William
American. Author, Screenwriter
Wrote filmscripts *Harper*, 1966; *Marathon
Man*, 1976; Oscar-winning *Butch Cassidy
and the Sundance Kid*, 1969.
b. Aug 12, 1931 in Chicago, Illinois
Source: *AmAu&B; ConAu 9R; ConDr 73,
77A; ConNov 72, 76; IntMPA 78, 79, 80, 81;
NotNAT; WhoAm 78, 80, 82; WorAu 1970*

Goldmann, Nahum
American. Scholar, Public Official
Jewish leader who advocated reconciliation
between Israel, Arab nations; pres., World
Jewish Congress, 1951-78.
b. Jul 10, 1895 in Wisnewo, Poland
d. Aug 29, 1982 in Bad Reichenhall,
Germany (West)
Source: *AnObit 1982; ConAu 107; CurBio 82;
IntWW 75, 76, 77, 78; NewYTBE 70;
NewYTBS 82; Who 74; WhoRel 75, 77;
WhoWor 74, 76, 78; WhoWorJ 72*

Goldmark, Karl
Hungarian. Composer
b. May 18, 1830 in Keszthely, Hungary
d. Jan 2, 1915 in Vienna, Austria
Source: *NewEOp 71; OxMus*

Goldmark, Peter Carl
American. Engineer, Inventor
Developed first practical color television
system, 1940.
b. Dec 2, 1906 in Budapest, Hungary
d. Dec 7, 1977 in Westchester County, New
York
Source: *AmM&WS 73P; ConAu 73, 77;
CurBio 40, 50; IntWW 74; NewYTBE 72;
WhoAm 74; WhoWor 78*

Goldner, Orville
American. Producer, Author
b. May 18, 1906 in Toledo, Ohio
Source: *ConAu 53*

Goldoni, Carlo
Italian. Dramatist
b. Feb 25, 1707 in Venice, Italy
d. Jan 6, 1793 in Versailles, France
Source: *AtlBL; BiD&SB; CasWL; CyWA;
DcEuL; EuAu; EvEuW; McGEWD; OxEng;
OxThe; PenC EUR; RComWL; REn;
REnWD*

Goldovsky, Boris
Russian. Conductor, Director
b. Jun 7, 1908 in Moscow, Russia
Source: *CurBio 66; WhoAm 74, 76, 78, 80,
82; WhoMus 72; WhoWor 78*

Goldsand, Robert
American. Musician
b. 1922 in Vienna, Austria
Source: *WhoMus 72*

Goldsboro, Bobby
American. Singer, Songwriter
CMA star of year, 1968; hits include
"Honey," "The Straight Life."
b. Jan 18, 1941 in Marianna, Florida
Source: *CelR; EncFCWM 83; WhoAm 82*

Goldsborough, Louis M
American. Naval Officer
b. Feb 18, 1805 in Washington, District of
Columbia
d. Feb 20, 1877 in Washington, District of
Columbia
Source: *AmBi; DcAmB; NewCol 75; WebAB;
WebBD 80; WhAm HS*

Goldschmidt, Neil Edward
American. Politician
Secretary of Transportation, 1979-81.
b. Jun 16, 1940 in Eugene, Oregon
Source: *BioIn 12; CurBio 80; NewYTBS 74;
WhoAm 76, 78, 80, 82; WhoAmP 77, 79;
WhoGov 75, 77*

Goldsmith, Fred Ernest
American. Baseball Player
b. May 15, 1852 in New Haven, Connecticut
d. Mar 28, 1939 in Berkley, Michigan
Source: *BaseEn 85; WhoProB 73*

Goldsmith, Jerry
American. Composer
Won Oscar, 1976, for *The Omen.*
b. Feb 10, 1930 in Los Angeles, California
Source: *CmMov; ConTFT 3; FilmgC; IntMPA
76, 77, 78, 79, 80, 81, 82; WhoAm 82;
WorEFlm*

Goldsmith, Judith Ann Becker
American. Feminist
Pres. of NOW, 1982-85.
b. Nov 26, 1938 in Manitowoc, Wisconsin
Source: *NewYTBS 82*

Goldsmith, Oliver
British. Poet, Dramatist, Author
Wrote *The Vicar of Wakefield,* 1766; *She
Stoops to Conquer,* 1773.
b. Nov 10, 1728 in Pallas, Ireland
d. Apr 4, 1774 in London, England
Source: *Alli; AtlBL; BbD; BiD&SB; BrAu;
CarSB; CasWL; Chambr 2; ChhPo, S1, S2;
CnE&AP; CnThe; CrtT 2; CyWA; DcBiA;
DcEnA, AP; DcEnL; DcEuL; DcLEL; EvLB;
HsB&A; McGEWD; MouLC 2; NewC;
OxEng; PenC ENG; PlP&P; PoIre; RAdv 1;
REn; REnWD; WebE&AL*

Goldstein, Israel
American. Religious Leader
Co-founded National Conference of Christians
and Jews, 1928; Brandeis U, 1946.
b. Jun 18, 1896 in Philadelphia, Pennsylvania
d. Apr 11, 1986 in Tel Aviv, Israel
Source: *CurBio 46, 86*

Goldstein, Joseph Leonard
American. Physician, Educator
With Michael S Brown, won Nobel Prize,
1985, for research into role of cholesterol
in cardiovascular disease.
b. Apr 18, 1940 in Sumter, South Carolina
Source: *AmM&WS 82P; BiDrACP 79;
WhoAm 84; WhoFrS 84*

Goldwater, Barry Morris
American. Senator, Author
Rep. senator from AZ; father of modern
conservatism; defeated by Lyndon Johnson
in landslide 1964 presidential election.
b. Jan 1, 1909 in Phoenix, Arizona
Source: *AmAu&B; BiDrAC; BioNews 74;
CelR; ConAu 41R; CurBio 55; EncAB-H;
IntWW 74; NewYTBS 74; WebAB; WhoAm
82; Who 74; WhoAmP 73; WhoGov 75;
WhoWest 84; WhoWor 78; WrDr 80; WhoAm
74, 82*

Goldwater, Barry Morris, Jr.
American. Politician
Son of Barry Goldwater, Rep. congressman
from CA, 1969--.
b. Jul 5, 1938 in Los Angeles, California
Source: *AlmAP 82; BiDrAC; WhoAm 84;
WhoAmP 83*

Goldwyn, Samuel
[Samuel Goldfish]
American. Producer
Produced *All Quiet on the Western Front,*
1930; won Oscar for *The Best Years of
Our Lives,* 1946; co-founded MGM; noted
for palapropisms.
b. Aug 27, 1882 in Warsaw, Poland
d. Jan 31, 1974 in Los Angeles, California
Source: *BiDFilm; BioNews 74; BusPN; CelR;
CurBio 44; DcFM; FilmgC; NewYTBS 74;
OxFilm; REnAL; WebAB; WhAm 6; Who 74;
WhoWor 78; WorEFlm*

Golenpaul, Dan
American. Publisher, Producer
b. 1900
d. Feb 13, 1974 in New York, New York
Source: *NewYTBS 74; ObitOF 79*

Golgi, Camillo
Italian. Ncurologist
Shared 1906 Nobel Prize in medicine.
b. Jul 7, 1843 in Corteno, Italy
d. Jan 21, 1926 in Pavia, Italy
Source: *BioIn 3, 6, 9; WebBD 80*

Goliath
Biblical Character
Philistine giant killed by young David with
sling and stones.
Source: *NewCol 75; WebBD 80*

Gollancz, Victor, Sir
English. Publisher
Founded publishing house, 1928; wrote *A
Year of Grace,* 1950.
b. Apr 9, 1893 in London, England
d. Feb 8, 1967 in London, England
Source: *CurBio 63, 67; DcNaB 1961;
LongCTC; ObitOF 79; ObitT 1961; WhE&EA*

Golonka, Arlene
American. Actress
Played in Mayberry RFD, 1968-71.
b. Jan 23, 1936 in Chicago, Illinois
Source: *BiE&WWA; NotNAT; WhoHol A*

Golschmann, Vladimir
French. Conductor
b. Dec 26, 1893 in Paris, France
d. Mar 1, 1972 in New York, New York
Source: *CurBio 51, 72; NewYTBE 72; WhAm
5*

Golson, Benny
American. Jazz Musician
b. Jan 25, 1929 in Philadelphia, Pennsylvania
Source: *AmSCAP 66; WhoAm 74*

Goltz, Gene
American. Journalist
b. Apr 30, 1930 in Marquette, Iowa
Source: *WhoAm 74*

Golub, Leon Albert
American. Artist
Figurative painter whose works have strong
political overtones, 1976--.
b. Jan 23, 1922 in Chicago, Illinois
Source: *ConArt 83; CurBio 84; DcAmArt;
DcCAA 77; DcCAr 81; McGDA; WhoAm 84;
WhoAmA 84; WhoE 83*

Gombrowicz, Witold
American. Author
b. Sep 4, 1904 in Moloszyee, Poland
d. Jul 25, 1969
Source: *CasWL; ConAu 17R, 25R, P-2;
ConLC 4; CroCD; EncWL; McGEWD;
ModSL 2; ModWD; NewCol 75; PenC EUR;
TwCWr; WhAm 5; WhoTwCL; WorAu*

Gomez, "Lefty" (Vernon Louis)
"The Gay Castillion"; "Goofy"
American. Baseball Player
Pitcher, 1930-43; inducted into Hall of Fame,
1972.
b. Nov 26, 1909 in Rodeo, California
Source: *BaseEn 85; BioIn 1, 2, 3, 5, 8, 9;
WhoProB 73*

Gomez, Thomas
American. Actor
Nominated for 1947 Oscar for *Ride a Pink
Horse.*
b. Jul 10, 1905 in Long Island, New York
d. Jun 18, 1971 in Santa Monica, California
Source: *BiE&WWA; CmMov; FilmEn;
FilmgC; MovMk; NewYTBE 71; Vers A;
WhScrn 74, 77; WhoHol B*

Gompers, Samuel
American. Labor Union Official
Founder, first pres. of AFL, 1886-1924.
b. Jan 27, 1850 in London, England
d. Dec 13, 1924 in San Antonio, Texas
Source: *AmAu&B; AmBi; DcAmB; DcNAA;
EncAB-H; REn; REnAL; WebAB; WhAm 1;
WhAmP*

Gomulka, Wladyslaw
Polish. Political Leader
Led Poland's Communist Party, 1956-70.
b. Feb 6, 1905 in Krosno, Poland
d. Sep 1, 1982 in Warsaw, Poland
Source: *AnObit 1982; CurBio 57, 82; IntWW
79; LinLib S; McGEWB; NewYTBE 70;
NewYTBS 82; WhoSocC 78*

Goncharov, Ivan A
Russian. Author
b. Jun 1812 in Simbirsk, Russia
d. Sep 1891 in Saint Petersburg, Russia
Source: *AtlBL; BiD&SB; CasWL; CyWA; DcEuL; DcRusL; EuAu; EvEuW; PenC EUR; REn*

Goncourt, Edmond Louis Antoine Huot
[Edmond Louis DeGoncourt]
French. Author
Collaborated with brother Jules in literary efforts.
b. May 26, 1822 in Nancy, France
d. Jul 16, 1896 in Chamrosay, France
Source: *AtlBL; BbD; BiD&SB; CasWL; ClDMEL; CyWA; DcBiA; DcEuL; EuAu; EvEuW; NewC; OxEng; OxFr; OxThe; PenC EUR; REn*

Goncourt, Jules Alfred Huot de
[Jules Alfred DeGoncourt]
French. Author
Half of noted writing team, Brothers Goncourt.
b. Dec 17, 1830 in Paris, France
d. Jun 20, 1870 in Paris, France
Source: *BbD; BiD&SB; CasWL; ClDMEL; CyWA; DcEuL; EuAu; EvEuW; OxEng; OxFr; OxThe; PenC EUR; REn*

Gongora y Argote, Don Luis de
Spanish. Poet
Famed Castillian balladeer whose later abstruse style was dubbed "Gongorism."
b. Jun 11, 1561 in Cordova, Spain
d. May 24, 1627 in Cordova, Spain
Source: *BiD&SB; BioIn 2, 4, 7, 10; CasWL; DcEuL; DcSpL; EuAu; EvEuW; LinLib L; McGEWB; NewCol 75; OxSpan; PenC EUR; REn*

Gonne, Maud MacBride
Irish. Patriot, Philanthropist
b. 1866 in London, England
d. 1953
Source: *BioIn 1, 3, 7, 10, 11; WebBD 80*

Gonzales, "Pancho" (Richard Alonzo)
American. Tennis Player
Eight-time World Pro tennis champ; autobiography *Man with a Racket*, 1959.
b. May 9, 1928 in Los Angeles, California
Source: *CelR; CurBio 49; WebAB; WhoAm 74, 76, 78, 80, 82*

Gonzalez Marquez, Felipe
Spanish. Political Leader
First Socialist premier since 1936-39 Civil War; elected 1982--.
b. Mar 5, 1942 in Seville, Spain
Source: *BioIn 11; CurBio 78; IntWW 79, 80, 81; NewYTBS 82*

Good, Sandra
American. Cultist
b. 1944
Source: *BioIn 10*

Goodall, Jane
[Baroness VanLawick-Goodall]
English. Anthropologist, Ethnologist
Wrote *In the Shadow of Man,* 1971.
b. Apr 3, 1934 in London, England
Source: *ConAu 2NR, 45; CurBio 67*

Goodall, John Strickland
English. Artist, Illustrator
b. Jun 7, 1908 in Heacham, England
Source: *ConAu 33R; IlsCB 1946; SmATA 4*

Goode, Wilson (Willie Wilson)
American. Politician
First black mayor of Philadelphia, 1983--.
b. Aug 19, 1938 in Seaboard, North Carolina
Source: *CurBio 85; NewYTBS 83; WhoBlA 80*

Goodell, Brian Stuart
American. Swimmer
b. Apr 2, 1959 in Stockton, California
Source: *BioIn 11, 12*

Goodell, Charles Ellsworth
American. Lawyer, Senator
b. Mar 16, 1926 in Jamestown, New York
Source: *BiDrAC; ConAu 81; CurBio 68; IntWW 74; WhoAm 74, 76, 78, 80, 82; WhoAmP 73; WhoE 74*

Gooden, Dwight Eugene
American. Baseball Player
Pitcher, NY Mets, who won 24 games, 1985; youngest to win Cy Young Award, 1985.
b. Nov 16, 1964 in Tampa, Florida
Source: *ConNews 85-2; CurBio 86; NewYTBS 84*

Goodeve, Grant
American. Actor
Played David on "Eight Is Enough," 1977-81.
b. 1952 in Windham, Vermont
Source: *NF*

Goodfriend, Lynda
American. Actress
Played Richie's wife, Laura Beth, on "Happy
Days," 1978-83.
b. Oct 31, 1950
Source: *BioIn 12*

Goodhue, Bertram G
American. Architect
b. Apr 28, 1869 in Pomfret, Connecticut
d. Apr 23, 1924 in New York, New York
Source: *AmBi; ChhPo; DcAmAu; DcAmB;
DcNAA; OxAmL; WebAB; WhAm 1*

Goodman, Al(fred)
American. Composer, Conductor
b. Aug 12, 1890 in Nikopol, Russia
d. Jan 10, 1972 in New York, New York
Source: *BiE&WWA; AmSCAP 66; NewYTBE
72*

Goodman, Benny (Benjamin David)
"King of Swing"
American. Band Leader, Musician
World-renowned clarinetist, band leader
  during Big Band era; most popular songs
  "Stompin' at the Savoy," "Sing, Sing,
  Sing."
b. May 30, 1909 in Chicago, Illinois
d. Jun 13, 1986 in New York, New York
Source: *AmSCAP 66; BioNews 74; CelR;
CurBio 42, 62, 86; EncAB-H; FilmgC;
IntWW 74; WebAB; WhoAm 74, 76, 78, 80,
82; WhoHol A; WhoJazz 72; WhoWor 74*

Goodman, Dody
American. Actress, Dancer
Played Martha Shumway on TV's "Mary
  Hartman, Mary Hartman."
b. Oct 28, 1929 in Columbus, Ohio
Source: *BiE&WWA; FilmEn; InWom;
NotNAT; WhoAm 82; WhoHol A; WhoThe 77*

Goodman, Ellen Holtz
American. Journalist
Writes syndicated feature, "At Large," 1976--;
  won Pulitzer for commentary, 1980.
b. Apr 11, 1941 in Newton, Massachusetts
Source: *ConAu 104; WhoAm 84; WhoAmW
83; WhoE 83*

Goodman, George Jerome Waldo
[Adam Smith]
American. Author, Editor
b. Aug 10, 1930 in Saint Louis, Missouri
Source: *AmAu&B; ConAu 21R; WhoAm 74,
76, 78, 80, 82*

Goodman, Julian B
American. Broadcasting Executive
b. May 1, 1922 in Glasgow, Kentucky
Source: *CurBio 67; IntMPA 75, 76, 77, 78,
79, 80; IntWW 74; St&PR 75; WhoAm 74,
76, 78, 80, 82; WhoE 74; WhoF&I 74;
WhoWor 78*

Goodman, Martin Wise
Canadian. Newspaper Executive
Pres. of Toronto *Star* Newspapers, Ltd.,
  1978-81.
b. Jan 15, 1935 in Calgary, Alberta
d. Dec 20, 1981 in Toronto, Ontario
Source: *WhoAm 78, 80, 82*

Goodman, Mitchell
American. Author
b. Dec 13, 1923 in New York, New York
Source: *Au&Wr 71; ConAu 1R, 4NR; DrAF
76; DrAP 75*

Goodman, Paul
American. Author, Educator
b. Sep 9, 1911 in New York, New York
d. Aug 2, 1972 in North Stratford, New
  Hampshire
Source: *AmAu&B; ConAu 17R, 37R, P-2;
ConLC 1, 2, 4; ConNov 72, 76; ConP 70;
ModAL S1; OxAmL; PenC AM; TwCA SUP;
WhAm 5*

Goodman, Robert O, Jr.
American. Naval Officer
Shot down, held by Syrians in Lebanon;
  released after intercession by Jesse Jackson,
  1984.
b. 1956 in San Juan, Puerto Rico
Source: *BioIn 13*

Goodman, Steve(n Benjamin)
American. Songwriter
Best known as author of Arlo Guthrie's 1972
  hit "City of New Orleans."
b. Jul 25, 1948 in Chicago, Illinois
d. Sep 20, 1984 in Seattle, Washington
Source: *ConMuA 80A; WhoAm 82; WhoRock
81*

Goodnight, Charles
American. Rancher
Described as "perfect illustration of the
  cattleman"; opened cattle trails in West;
  developed cattalo by breeding buffalo,
  cattle.
b. Mar 5, 1836 in Macoupin County, Illinois
d. Dec 12, 1929 in Texas
Source: *REnAW; WebAB; WhAm 4, HSA*

Goodpaster, Andrew Jackson
American. Army Officer
Commander-in-chief, Supreme Allied
    Command, Europe, 1969-74, 1977-81.
b. Feb 12, 1915 in Granite City, Illinois
Source: *AmM&WS 73S, 78S; BioIn 3, 8, 9,
    11; CurBio 69; IntWW 74, 75, 76, 77, 78;
    NewYTBS 77; WebAMB; Who 74; WhoAm
    74, 76, 78, 80, 82, 84; WhoWor 78;
    WorDWW*

Goodpasture, Ernest William
American. Pathologist
b. Oct 17, 1886 in Montgomery County,
    Indiana
d. Sep 20, 1960
Source: *BioIn 1, 3, 5, 6, 7; WhAm 4*

Goodrich, Benjamin Franklin
American. Industrialist
Physician who formed forerunner of B F
    Goodrich Co., 1870, in Akron, OH.
b. Nov 4, 1841 in Ripley, New York
d. Aug 3, 1888 in Manitou Springs,
    Colorado
Source: *DcAmB; Entr; WhAm HS*

Goodrich, Frances
[Mrs. Albert Hacker]
American. Author
With husband, wrote screenplay of *The Diary
    of Anne Frank*, which won Tony, 1956.
b. 1891 in Belleville, New Jersey
d. Jan 29, 1984 in New York, New York
Source: *AnObit 1984; ConAu 111; CurBio 84,
    84; DcLB 26; McGEWD 84; NewYTBS 84;
    WhAm 82; WorEFlm*

Goodrich, Gail Charles
American. Basketball Player
Guard, 1965-79; member of 1972 NBA
    champion Los Angeles team.
b. Apr 23, 1943 in Los Angeles, California
Source: *BioIn 9, 10; OfNBA 81; WhoAm 74;
    WhoBbl 73*

Goodrich, Lloyd
American. Author
b. Jul 10, 1897 in Nutley, New Jersey
Source: *ConAu 69; CurBio 67; WhoAm 74,
    76, 78, 80, 82; WhoAmA 73; WhoGov 75*

Goodrich, Samuel Griswold
[Peter Parley, pseud.]
American. Journalist
Wrote *The Tales of Peter Parley about
    America*, 1827.
b. Aug 19, 1793 in Ridgefield, Connecticut
d. May 9, 1860 in New York, New York
Source: *Alli; AmAu; AmAu&B; AmBi; BbD;
    BbtC; BiD&SB; CarSB; CyAL 2; DcAmAu;
    DcAmB; DcNAA; Drake; OxAmL; REn;
    REnAL; TwCBDA; WebAB; WhAm HS;
    WhoChL*

Goodroe, Michael
see: Motels, The

Goodson, Mark
American. Producer
Known as developer of TV game shows;
    with Bill Todman, created "The Price Is
    Right," "Family Feud."
b. Jan 24, 1915 in Sacramento, California
Source: *IntMPA 80, 81, 82; WhoAm 80, 82;
    WhoTelC; WhoWor 74*

Goodwin, Bill
American. Actor
Network radio announcer who appeared on
    TV and in several films, 1940 -50s.
b. Jul 28, 1910 in San Francisco, California
d. May 9, 1958 in Palm Springs, California
Source: *FilmgC; ObitOF 79; WhScrn 74;
    WhoHol B*

Goodwin, Daniel
"Spiderman"
American. Mountaineer, Stuntman
b. Nov 7, 1955
Source: *BioIn 12*

Goodwin, Hannibal Williston
American. Clergyman, Inventor
Invented photographic film; received patent,
    1898.
b. Apr 30, 1822 in Taughannock, New York
d. Dec 31, 1900
Source: *WebBD 80; WhAm HS*

Goodwin, Myles
see: April Wine

Goodwin, Nat C
American. Actor
Stage and film role of Fagin in *Oliver Twist*,
    1912.
b. 1857 in Boston, Massachusetts
d. Jan 31, 1919 in New York
Source: *BioIn 2, 3, 4; WhScrn 74, 77;
    WhoHol B*

Goodwin, Richard N(aradhof)
[Bailey Lavid]
American. Lawyer, Author
Presidential speechwriter, 1960s; developed
"Great Society" program.
b. Dec 7, 1931 in Boston, Massachusetts
Source: *ConAu 111; CurBio 68*

Goodyear, Charles
American. Inventor
Discovered vulcanization process for rubber,
1839; patented, 1844.
b. Dec 29, 1800 in New Haven, Connecticut
d. Jul 1, 1860 in New York, New York
Source: *AmBi; ApCAB; DcAmB; Drake;
EncAB-H; NewCol 75; TwCBDA; WebAB;
WhAm HS*

Goolagong, Evonne
[Mrs. Roger Cawley]
Australian. Tennis Player
Defeated Margaret Court to become fifth
youngest Wimbledon singles champ, 1971;
won again, 1980.
b. Jul 31, 1951 in Barellan, Australia
Source: *BioNews 74; CelR; CurBio 71; HerW;
NewYTBE 71; WhoIntT; WhoWor 74*

Goossens, Eugene, Sir
English. Composer, Conductor
b. May 26, 1893 in London, England
d. Jun 13, 1962 in London, England
Source: *CurBio 45, 62; DcCM; NewCol 75;
WhAm 4*

Goossens, Leon Jean
English. Musician
b. Jun 12, 1897 in Liverpool, England
Source: *IntWW 74; Who 74; WhoMus 72*

Gopallawa, William
Sri Lankan. Diplomat
b. Sep 16, 1897 in Dullewa, Ceylon
d. Jan 30, 1981 in Colombo, Sri Lanka
Source: *AnObit 1981; FarE&A 78, 79;
IntWW 74, 75, 76, 77, 78; IntYB 78, 79;
Who 74; WhoGov 72; WhoWor 74, 76, 78*

Gorbachev, Mikhail S
Russian. Political Leader
Named secretary general of USSR
Communist Party following death of
Chernenko, Mar 1985.
b. Mar 2, 1931 in Privolnoye, U.S.S.R.
Source: *ConNews 85-2; IntWW 83; IntYB 82;
NewYTBS 84*

Gorbanevskaya, Natalya
Russian. Poet, Translator
b. 1936
Source: *BioIn 9*

Gorbatko, Viktor Vasiliyevich
Russian. Cosmonaut
b. Dec 3, 1934 in Ventsy Zarja, U.S.S.R.
Source: *IntWW 74; WhoWor 78*

Gorbatov, Aleksandr Vassil'evich
Russian. General
b. 1891
d. Dec 7, 1973 in Moscow, U.S.S.R.
Source: *BioIn 7, 10; ConAu 45; NewYTBE 73*

Gorcey, Leo
American. Actor
Played Spit, the gang leader, in film series
*Dead End Kids; East Side Kids; The
Bowery Boys.*
b. Jun 3, 1915 in New York, New York
d. Jun 2, 1969 in Oakland, California
Source: *FilmgC; MotPP; MovMk; WhScrn 74,
77; WhoHol B*

Gordimer, Nadine
South African. Journalist, Author
b. Nov 20, 1923 in Springs, South Africa
Source: *CasWL; ConAu 5R, 3NR; ConLC 3,
5; ConNov 72, 76; InWom; IntWW 74;
NewC; NewCol 75; PenC ENG; TwCWr; Who
74; WhoTwCL; WhoWor 78; WorAu; WrDr
80*

Gordon, C Henry
[Henry Racke]
American. Actor
Screen villain with notable appearance in *The
Charge of the Light Brigade,* 1936.
b. Jun 17, 1883 in New York, New York
d. Dec 3, 1940 in Los Angeles, California
Source: *CurBio 41; FilmgC; MotPP; MovMk;
Vers A; WhScrn 77; WhoHol B*

Gordon, Caroline
American. Author, Critic
Southern-theme writer whose novels include
The Malefactors, 1956.
b. Oct 6, 1895 in Trenton, Kentucky
d. Apr 11, 1981 in Chiapas, Mexico
Source: *AmAu&B; AmNov; AmWomWr;
AmWr; BioIn 2, 3, 4, 5, 7, 8, 9; CasWL;
CathA 1952; ConAu 103, P-1; ConLC 6, 13;
ConNov 72, 76; CyWA; DcLB 4; DrAF 76;
InWom; IntAu&W 76, 77; ModLAL; OxAmL;
PenC AM; RAdv 1; REn; REnAL; ScF&FL
1; TwCA, SUP; WhAm 7; WhE&EA; WhoAm
74, 76, 78; WhoAmW 64, 66, 68, 70, 72, 74;
WrDr 76, 80*

Gordon, Charles George
"Chinese"
English. General
Soldier who fought in many parts of British
Empire; also Taiping Rebellion, China.
b. Jan 28, 1833 in Woolwich, England
d. Jan 26, 1885 in Khartoum, Sudan
Source: *Alli SUP; NewC; NewCol 75; REn*

Gordon, Gale
[Charles Aldrich, Jr.]
American. Actor
Played Mr. Wilson on "Dennis the Menace,"
1962-64; Mr. Mooney on "The Lucy
Show," 1968-74.
b. Feb 2, 1906 in New York, New York
Source: *FilmgC; IntMPA 75, 76, 77, 78, 79,
80, 81, 82; MovMk*

Gordon, Jackie
[Mrs. Lou Gordon]
American. TV Personality
b. 1935
Source: *BioIn 10*

Gordon, James
see: Souther-Hillman-Furay Band, The

Gordon, Joe (Joseph Lowell)
"Flash"
American. Baseball Player, Baseball Manager
Second baseman, 1938-50; AL MVP, 1942.
b. Feb 18, 1915 in Los Angeles, California
d. Jun 7, 1978 in Sacramento, California
Source: *BaseEn 85; BioIn 1, 11; WhoProB 73*

Gordon, John Brown
American. General, Statesman
b. Feb 6, 1832 in Upson County, Georgia
d. Jan 9, 1904 in Miami, Florida
Source: *AmAu&B; AmBi; ApCAB; BiDConf;
BiDSA; BiDrAC; DcAmB; DcAmB; DcNAA;
NewCol 75; TwCBDA; WhAm 1; WhAmP*

Gordon, John F
American. Auto Executive
b. May 15, 1900 in Akron, Ohio
d. Jan 6, 1978 in Royal Oak, Michigan
Source: *IntWW 74; NewYTBS 78*

Gordon, Kitty
English. Actress
Victor Herbert composed "The Enchantress"
for her, 1911.
b. Apr 22, 1878 in Folkestone, England
d. May 26, 1974 in Brentwood, New York
Source: *BioIn 10; NewYTBS 74; WhThe;
WhoHol B*

Gordon, Lou
American. Journalist, TV Personality
b. 1918
d. May 24, 1977 in Bloomfield Hills,
Michigan
Source: *BioIn 8, 10, 11; ConAu 69;
NewYTBS 77*

Gordon, Mary Catherine
American. Author
b. Dec 8, 1949 in Far Rockaway, New York
Source: *BioIn 11; ConAu 102; ConLC 13;
CurBio 81; WhoAm 82*

Gordon, Max
American. Producer
b. Jun 28, 1892 in New York, New York
d. Nov 2, 1978 in New York, New York
Source: *BiE&WWA; CurBio 43; EncMT;
NotNAT; WhoAm 74; WhoThe 77A*

Gordon, Richard
American. Author
b. Sep 15, 1921
Source: *Au&Wr 71; MnBBF; TwCWr; Who
74*

Gordon, Richard Francis, Jr.
American. Astronaut, Football Executive
Crew member on Gemini VIII, XI; Apollo
XII; vp New Orleans Saints, 1972--.
b. Oct 5, 1929 in Seattle, Washington
Source: *AmM&WS 73P; IntWW 74; WhoAm
74; WhoS&SW 82*

Gordon, Ruth
[Ruth Jones; Mrs. Garson Kanin]
American. Actress, Dramatist
With husband co-wrote *Adam's Rib*, 1952;
won Oscar for *Rosemary's Baby*, 1968.
b. Oct 30, 1896 in Wollaston, Massachusetts
d. Aug 28, 1985 in Martha's Vineyard,
Massachusetts
Source: *AmAu&B; BiE&WWA; ConAu 81;
CurBio 72, 85; Film 1; FilmgC; InWom;
IntMPA 75, 76, 77, 78, 79, 80, 81, 82;
MovMk; NatPD; NotNAT; OxFilm; WhoAm
74, 76, 78, 80, 82; WhoThe 77; WhoWor 78;
WorEFlm*

Gordon, Seton
Author, Photographer
b. 1886
d. Mar 19, 1977
Source: *Who 74; WhoLA*

Gordon, Sid(ney)
American. Baseball Player
b. Aug 13, 1917 in Brooklyn, New York
d. Jun 17, 1975 in New York, New York
Source: *BaseEn 85; BioIn 10*

Gordon, Steve
American. Author, Director
Author, director of comedy *Arthur,* 1981.
b. 1940 in Toledo, Ohio
d. Nov 27, 1982 in New York, New York
Source: *BioIn 12; ConAu 108; NewYTBS 82*

Gordon, Thomas
American. Psychologist, Author
b. Mar 11, 1918 in Paris, Illinois
Source: *AmM&WS 73S; ConAu 29R; WrDr 80*

Gordon, Vera
[Vera Nemirou]
American. Actress
Film roles typecast her as jewish mother;
   films include *Abie's Irish Rose.*
b. Jun 11, 1886 in Russia
d. May 8, 1948 in Beverly Hills, California
Source: *FilmEn; MovMk; TwYS; WhScrn 74, 77*

Gordon-Walker of Leyton, Patrick Chrestien Gordon-Walker, Baron
English. Politician, Author
Labour Party leader; cabinet minister during
   1950-60s; writings on British politics
   include *The Commonwealth,* 1962.
b. Apr 7, 1907 in Worthing, England
d. Dec 2, 1980 in London, England
Source: *AnObit 1980; Au&Wr 71; BioIn 6, 7;
ConAu 29R; CurBio 66; IntAu&W 76;
IntWW 74, 75, 76, 77, 78; IntYB 78, 79;
WhE&EA; Who 74; WhoWor 74, 76; WrDr 76*

Gordone, Charles
American. Dramatist, Actor, Director
b. Oct 12, 1925 in Cleveland, Ohio
Source: *AmAu&B; ConAu 93; ConLC 1, 4;
LivgBAA; McGEWD; NotNAT; PIP&P;
WhoAm 74, 76, 78, 80, 82; WhoBlA 75;
WhoE 74; WhoThe 77; WrDr 80*

Gordy, Berry, Jr.
American. Record Executive, Film Executive
Founded Motown Records, 1959; signed The
   Temptations; The Supremes.
b. Nov 28, 1929 in Detroit, Michigan
Source: *CelR; IntMPA 77, 78, 79, 80, 81, 82;
NewYTBS 74; WhoAm 74, 76, 78, 80, 82;
WhoBlA 75*

Gore, Albert Arnold
American. Senator
b. Dec 26, 1907 in Granville, Tennessee
Source: *BiDrAC; CurBio 52; IntWW 74;
WhoAm 74, 76, 78, 80, 82; WhoAmP 73;
WhoS&SW 82*

Gore, Charles
English. Clergyman
Bishop of Oxford; wrote *Jesus of Nazareth,*
1929.
b. Jan 22, 1853 in Wimbledon, England
d. Jan 17, 1932 in London, England
Source: *BiD&SB; DcNaB 1931; EvLB;
LongCTC; LuthC 75; NewC; OxEng;
WhE&EA; WhLit*

Gore, Lesley
American. Singer
b. May 2, 1946 in Tenafly, New Jersey
Source: *WhoHol A*

Goren, Charles Henry
American. Bridge Player, Journalist
His method of bridge is most widely used;
   author *Bridge Is My Game,* 1965.
b. Mar 4, 1901 in Philadelphia, Pennsylvania
Source: *AmAu&B; ConAu 69; CurBio 59;
WebAB; WhoAm 84; WhoWor 78*

Gorenko, Anna Andreevna
see: Akhmatova, Anna, pseud.

Gorey, Edward St. John
American. Author, Illustrator
b. Feb 22, 1925 in Chicago, Illinois
Source: *ChhPo, S1; ConAu 5R; IlsBYP; IlsCB
1957; WhoAm 82*

Gorgas, William Crawford
American. Physician
Army officer best known for eradicating
   yellow fever in various parts of world; was
   surgeon general of US 1914-19.
b. Oct 3, 1854 in Mobile, Alabama
d. Jul 3, 1920 in London, England
Source: *AmBi; DcAmB; DcNAA; NewCol 75;
WebAB; WhAm 1*

Gorham, Jabez
American. Merchant
First American silversmith to use machinery;
   founded Gorham Manufacturing.
b. Feb 18, 1792 in Providence, Rhode Island
d. Mar 24, 1869 in Providence, Rhode Island
Source: *DcAmB; WhAm HS*

Gorin, Igor
American. Composer, Singer, Actor
b. Oct 26, 1908 in Grodak, Russia
d. Mar 24, 1982 in Tucson, Arizona
Source: *AmSCAP 66, 80; Baker 78; CurBio
42, 82; WhoAm 74*

Goring, "Butch" (Robert Thomas)
Canadian. Hockey Player
Center, 1969--; won Conn Smythe Trophy,
1981; four Stanley Cups.
b. Oct 22, 1949 in Saint Boniface, Manitoba
Source: *HocEn; HocReg 81; WhoAm 82*

Goring, Hermann Wilhelm
see: Goering, Hermann Wilhelm

Goring, Marius
English. Actor
Films include *Lilli Marlene*, 1944; *The Red
Shoes*, 1948; *Exodus*, 1960.
b. May 23, 1912 in Newport, England
Source: *FilmgC; IntMPA 75, 76, 77, 78, 79,
80, 81, 82; IntWW 74; MotPP; MovMk;
PIP&P; Who 74; WhoHol A; WhoThe 77*

Gorkin, Jess
American. Editor, Journalist
Editor *Parade* magazine, 1947-78.
b. Oct 23, 1913 in Rochester, New York
d. Feb 19, 1985 in Longboat Key, Florida
Source: *AmAu&B; ConAu 115; WhoAm 84*

Gorky, Arshile
[Vosdanik Adoian]
American. Artist
Abstract expressionist; works include "Dark
Green Painting."
b. Oct 25, 1904 in Armenia
d. Jul 3, 1948 in New York, New York
Source: *AtlBL; DcAmB S4; DcCAA 71;
NewCol 75; REn; WebAB; WhAm 4*

Gorky, Maxim, pseud.
[Maxim Gorki; Alexie M Peshov; Aleksey
Maximovich Pyeshkov]
Russian. Author, Dramatist
Wrote *The Lower Depths*, 1902; *Mother*,
1907; *My Universities*, 1923.
b. Mar 14, 1868 in Nizhni-Novgorod, Russia
d. Jun 18, 1936 in Moscow, U.S.S.R.
Source: *AtlBL; BiD&SB; CasWL; ClDMEL;
CnMD; CnMWL; CnThe; CyWA; DcRusL;
EncWL; EvEuW; FilmgC; McGEWD; ModSL
1; ModWD; OxEng; OxFilm; OxThe; PenC
EUR; PIP&P, A; RComWL; REn; REnWD;
TwCA, SUP; TwCWr; WhoTwCL*

Gorman, Chester
American. Archaeologist
Unearthed evidence of world's earliest
agriculture and Bronze Age society while
excavating in Thailand, 1960-70s.
b. Mar 11, 1938 in Oakland, California
d. Jun 7, 1981 in Sacramento, California
Source: *AnObit 1981; NewYTBS 81*

Gorman, Herbert Sherman
American. Author, Journalist
b. Jan 1, 1893 in Springfield, Massachusetts
d. Oct 28, 1954 in Hughsonville, New York
Source: *AmAu&B; AmNov; ChhPo, SI;
CurBio 40, 55; OxAmL; REnAL; TwCA,
SUP; WhAm 3; WhNAA; WhoAm 82*

Gorman, Leon Arthur
American. Business Executive
Pres. of L L Bean, 1967--.
b. Dec 20, 1934 in Nashua, New Hampshire
Source: *WhoAm 82*

Gorman, Leroy
[Bow Wow Wow]
English. Musician
Bassist with group since 1980.
b. in England
Source: *NF*

Gorman, Rudolph Carl
American. Artist
b. 1932
Source: *BioIn 10*

Gorme, Eydie
[Steve and Eydie; Mrs. Steve Lawrence]
American. Singer
b. Aug 16, 1932 in New York, New York
Source: *BioNews 74; BkPepl; CelR; CurBio
65; InWom; WhoAm 74*

Gorr, Rita
[Marguerite Geirnaert]
Belgian. Opera Singer
Lyric mezzo-soprano concert performer.
b. Feb 18, 1926 in Ghent, Belgium
Source: *BioIn 6, 7; NewEOp 71; WhoAmW
74; WhoMus 72*

Gorrie, John
American. Inventor, Physician
Granted patent for mechanical refrigeration,
1851.
b. Oct 3, 1803 in Charleston, South Carolina
d. Jun 16, 1855 in Apalachicola, Florida
Source: *BioIn 2, 3, 5, 7, 9; ApCAB SUP;
DcAmB; DcNAA; WebAB; WhAm HS*

Gorshin, Frank John
American. Actor, Comedian
Played the Riddler on "Batman," 1966-68.
b. Apr 5, 1934 in Pittsburgh, Pennsylvania
Source: *FilmgC; WhoAm 74, 76, 78, 80, 82;
WhoHol A*

Gortner, (Hugh) Marjoe (Ross)
American. Evangelist, Actor
Ordained minister, 1948; name is amalgam of
Mary and Joseph; won Oscar, 1972, for
autobiographical documentary, *Marjoe*.
b. Jan 14, 1945 in Long Beach, California
Source: *BkPepl; IntMPA 82; WhoAm 82;
WhoHol A*

Gorton, John Grey
Australian. Prime Minister
b. Sep 9, 1911 in Melbourne, Australia
Source: *CurBio 68; IntWW 74; NewYTBE 71;
Who 74; WhoAm 74; WhoGov 75; WhoWor
78*

Gorton, Samuel
American. Religious Leader
b. 1592 in Gorton, England
d. 1677 in Warwick, Rhode Island
Source: *Alli; AmBi; ApCAB; CyAL 1;
DcAmAu; DcAmB; DcNAA; Drake; NewCol
75; OxAmL; REnAL; WhAm HS*

Gorton, Slade
American. Politician
Rep. senator from WA, 1980--; replaced
long-term New Dealer, Warren Magnuson.
b. Jan 8, 1928 in Chicago, Illinois
Source: *WhoAm 74, 76, 78, 80, 82; WhoAmL
78, 79; WhoAmP 73, 75, 77, 79; WhoGov 72,
75, 77; WhoWest 74, 76, 78*

Goscinny, Rene
French. Cartoonist
Co-founded French comic weekly, *Pilote,*
1959.
b. Aug 14, 1926 in Paris, France
d. Nov 5, 1977 in Paris, France
Source: *ConAu 113, 117; WorECom*

Gosden, Freeman Fisher
[Amos 'n Andy]
American. Comedian
Amos of "Amos 'n Andy" radio show, 1926-
58; show denounced by NAACP.
b. May 5, 1899 in Richmond, Virginia
d. Dec 10, 1982 in Los Angeles, California
Source: *AnObit 1982; BioIn 7, 9; ConAu 108;
CurBio 47, 83; NewYTBE 72; NewYTBS 82;
NewYTET; WebAB, 79; WhoHol A; WorAl*

Goslin, "Goose" (Leon Allen)
American. Baseball Player
Outfielder, 1921-38; led AL with 129 RBIs,
1924; Hall of Fame, 1968.
b. Oct 16, 1900 in Salem, New Jersey
d. May 15, 1971 in Bridgeton, New Jersey
Source: *BaseEn 85; NewYTBE 71; WhoProB
73*

Gossage, "Goose" (Richard Michael)
American. Baseball Player
Premiere relief pitcher whose fastball is
clocked at 94 mph; has 206 career saves
from 1972-83.
b. Jul 5, 1951 in Colorado Springs, Colorado
Source: *BaseEn 85; CurBio 84; NewYTBS 77;
WhoAm 82*

Gosse, Edmund William, Sir
English. Author
Promoted Scandinavian literature; wrote
autobiography *Father and Son*, 1907.
b. Sep 21, 1849 in London, England
d. May 16, 1928
Source: *Alli SUP; BbD; BiD&SB; CarSB;
CasWL; Chambr 3; ChhPo, S1, S2; CnMWL;
DcEnA, AP; DcEnL; DcLEL; EvLB;
LongCTC; ModBrL; NewC; OxEng; PenC
ENG; TwCA, SUP; TwCWr; WebE&AL*

Gossec, Francois Joseph
French. Composer
First French symphonist; wrote string
quartets, operas, marches, hymns of
Revolution.
b. Jan 17, 1734 in Vergnies, Belgium
d. Feb 16, 1829 in Passy, France
Source: *Baker 78; BioIn 4, 7; NewCol 75;
NewEOp 71; OxFr; OxMus*

Gosset, Lou(is, Jr.)
American. Actor
Won Oscar as best supporting actor for *An
Officer and a Gentleman*, 1983.
b. May 27, 1936 in Brooklyn, New York
Source: *BioIn 11; WhoAm 80, 82; WhoTelC*

Gossett, D(aniel) Bruce
American. Football Player
b. Nov 9, 1941 in Cecil, Pennsylvania
Source: *WhoFtbl 74*

Gotch, Frank
American. Wrestler
Source: *BioIn 5*

Gottfried, Brian
American. Tennis Player
With doubles partner Raul Ramirez won
Wimbledon, 1976; French Open, 1975, 77;
Italian Open, 1974-77; WCT World, 1975,
80.
b. Jan 27, 1952 in Baltimore, Maryland
Source: *BioIn 10, 11; WhoAm 82; WhoIntT*

Gottfried, Martin
American. Drama Critic
b. Oct 9, 1933 in New York, New York
Source: *BiE&WWA; ConAu 21R; NotNAT;
WhoAm 82*

Gottfried von Strassburg
German. Poet
Wrote unfinished love epic *Tristan and Isolde,* c. 1210.
b. 1170 in Strassburg, Germany
d. 1215
Source: *BbD; BiD&SB; CasWL; CyWA; DcEuL; EuAu; EvEuW; OxGer; PenC EUR; RComWL; REn*

Gottlieb, Adolph
American. Artist
b. Mar 14, 1903 in New York, New York
d. Mar 4, 1974 in New York, New York
Source: *ConAu 49; CurBio 59, 74; DcCAA 71; EncAB-H; NewYTBS 74; WhAm 6; WhoAm 74; WhoAmA 73; WhoE 74; WhoWor 78; WhoWorJ 72*

Gottlieb, Eddie (Edward)
"The Mogul"
American. Basketball Coach, Basketball Executive
Owner, coach, Philadelphia Warriors, 1947-55.
b. Sep 15, 1898 in Kiev, Russia
d. Dec 7, 1979 in Philadelphia, Pennsylvania
Source: *NewYTBS 79; WhoBbl 73*

Gottschalk, Ferdinand
English. Actor
Comedian, character actor in films, 1923-44, including *Grand Hotel,* 1932; *Gold Diggers of 1933,* 1933.
b. 1869 in London, England
d. Oct 10, 1944 in London, England
Source: *MovMk; WhScrn 74, 77*

Gottschalk, Louis Moreau
American. Musician, Composer
b. May 8, 1829 in New Orleans, Louisiana
d. Dec 18, 1869 in Rio de Janeiro, Brazil
Source: *AmBi; ApCAB; DcAmB; Drake; OxAmL; TwCBDA; WebAB; WhAm HS*

Gottschalk, Robert
American. Corporation Executive
Founder, pres. of Panavision, Inc.
b. Mar 12, 1918 in Chicago, Illinois
d. 1982 in Los Angeles, California
Source: *IntMPA 75, 76, 77, 78, 79, 80, 81, 82*

Gottwald, Klement
Czech. Communist Leader
b. Nov 23, 1896 in Dedidocz, Czechoslovakia
d. Mar 14, 1953
Source: *CurBio 48, 53; NewCol 75; WhAm 3*

Goucher, John Franklin
American. Clergyman, Educator
b. Jun 7, 1845 in Waynesburg, Pennsylvania
d. Jul 19, 1922
Source: *AmAu&B; DcNAA*

Goudge, Elizabeth
English. Author
Best known novel *Green Dolphin Street,* 1944, was made into a film, 1947.
b. Apr 24, 1900 in Wells, England
d. Apr 1, 1984 in Henley-on-Thames, England
Source: *AuBYP; ChhPo; ConAu 5R, 5NR; CurBio 40; InWom; LongCTC; NewC; REn; SmATA 2; ThrBJA; TwCA, SUP; WhoChL; WrDr 76*

Goudy, Frederic William
American. Type Designer
Designer of over 100 different type faces.
b. Mar 8, 1865 in Bloomington, Illinois
d. May 11, 1947 in Marlboro, New York
Source: *AmAu&B; BioIn 1, 2, 3, 5, 9; CurBio 41, 47; DcAmB S4; DcNAA; NewCol 75; OxAmL; REnAL; WebAB, 79; WhAm 2; WhNAA*

Gougelman, Pierre
American. Physician, Inventor
Invented plastic used in manufacture of artificial eyes, 1941.
b. Feb 16, 1877 in Guttenberg, New Jersey
d. Jun 1, 1963 in Thornwood, New York
Source: *BioIn 6, 7; NatCAB 48*

Goulart, Joao
Brazilian. President
b. Mar 1, 1918 in Sao Borja, Brazil
d. Dec 6, 1976
Source: *BioIn 6, 11; CurBio 62, 77; IntWW 74; McGEWB*

Goulart, Ron(ald Joseph)
[Howard Lee; Kenneth Robeson; Frank S Shawn; Con Steffanson, pseuds.]
American. Author
b. Jan 13, 1933 in Berkeley, California
Source: *ConAu 25R; SmATA 6; WhoAm 82; WhoE 74*

Gould, Beatrice Blackmar
American. Editor, Author
b. 1898 in Emmetsburg, Iowa
Source: *AmAu&B; ConAu 25R, P-2; CurBio 47; IntWW 74; WhoAmW 74*

Gould, Charles Bruce
American. Editor, Author
b. Jul 28, 1898 in Luana, Iowa
Source: *AmAu&B; CurBio 47*

Gould, Chester
American. Cartoonist
Cartoon comic strip pioneer who created
"Dick Tracy," 1931.
b. Nov 20, 1900 in Pawnee, Oklahoma
d. May 11, 1985 in Woodstock, Illinois
Source: *ConAu 77; ConNews 85-2; CurBio 71;
EncMys; WebAB; WhoAm 74; WhoMW 74*

Gould, Elliott
[Elliott Goldstein]
American. Actor
Starred in *Bob & Carol & Ted & Alice,*
1969; *M*A*S*H,* 1970.
b. Aug 29, 1938 in Brooklyn, New York
Source: *BiE&WWA; BioIn 8, 9, 10, 11;
BioNews 74; BkPepl; CelR; CurBio 71;
EncMT; FilmgC; IntMPA 75, 76, 77, 78, 79,
80, 81, 82; MovMk; WhoAm 74, 76, 78, 80,
82; WhoHol A; WhoThe 77*

Gould, George Milbry
American. Physician, Lexicographer
b. Nov 8, 1848 in Auburn, Maine
d. 1922
Source: *AmAu&B; DcAmAu; DcNAA; OhA&B*

Gould, Glenn Herbert
Canadian. Musician, Composer
Retired from performing, 1964, to
concentrate on recording.
b. Sep 25, 1932 in Toronto, Ontario
d. Oct 4, 1982 in Toronto, Ontario
Source: *AnObit 1982; Baker 78; CanWW 70,
79; CreCan 2; CurBio 60, 82; IntWW 82;
WhoAm 78; WhoMus 72*

Gould, Gordon
American. Physicist
Coined acronym "laser," 1957.
b. Jul 17, 1920 in New York, New York
Source: *AmM&WS 73P, 76P, 79P; WhoAm
80, 82*

Gould, Jack
American. Critic
b. 1919 in New York, New York
Source: *NewYTBE 72; WhoE 74*

Gould, Jay (Jason)
American. Financier
Part owner of many railroads, including the
Erie and Union Pacific.
b. May 27, 1836 in Roxbury, New York
d. Dec 2, 1892 in New York, New York
Source: *AmBi; BioIn 1, 3, 4, 6, 11; ApCAB;
DcAmB; DcNAA; EncAB-H; NewCol 75;
TwCBDA; WebAB, 79; WhAm HS*

Gould, Laurence McKinley
American. Explorer, Educator
b. Aug 22, 1896 in Lacota, Michigan
Source: *AmM&WS 73P, 76P, 79P; CurBio 78;
IntAu&W 77; IntWW 74, 75, 76, 77, 78;
WhoAm 74, 76*

Gould, Lois
American. Author
b. 1938
Source: *AmAu&B; ConAu 77; ConLC 4, 10;
DrAF 76; WhoAm 82; WrDr 76*

Gould, Morton
American. Composer, Musician
b. Dec 10, 1913 in Richmond Hill, New
York
Source: *AmSCAP 66; BiE&WWA; CurBio 45,
68; DcCM; NewCBMT; NotNAT; WhoAm 74,
76, 78, 80, 82; WhoE 74; WhoMus 72;
WhoWor 78; WhoWorJ 72*

Gould, Shane
Australian. Swimmer
First woman to win three Olympic gold
medals in individual events in world-record
times, 1972.
b. Sep 4, 1956 in Brisbane, Australia
Source: *BioIn 9, 10; CelR; HerW*

Gould, Stephen Jay
American. Paleontologist, Author
b. Sep 10, 1941 in New York, New York
Source: *AmM&WS 73P, 76P, 79P; ConAu 77;
CurBio 82; WhoAm 78, 80, 82*

Goulding, Edmund
American. Director
Films include *Grand Hotel,* 1932; *Nightmare
Alley,* 1949.
b. Mar 20, 1891 in London, England
d. Dec 24, 1959 in Hollywood, California
Source: *AmSCAP 66; BiDFilm; DcFM;
FilmgC; MovMk; OxFilm; TwYS; WhAm 3;
WhScrn 77; WorEFlm*

Goulding, Phil G
American. Businessman
b. Mar 28, 1921 in San Francisco, California
Source: *WhoAm 74*

Goulding, Ray
[Bob and Ray]
American. Comedian
b. Mar 20, 1922 in Lowell, Massachusetts
Source: *CelR; CurBio 57*

Gouldman, Graham
see: 10 CC

Goulet, Michel
Canadian. Hockey Player
Left wing, Quebec, 1979--; has had four
consecutive 50-goal seasons, 1982-86.
b. Apr 21, 1960 in Peribonqua, Quebec
Source: *HocReg 85*

Goulet, Robert
American. Actor, Singer
Broadway debut in *Camelot,* 1960; won
Tony, 1968, for *The Happy Time.*
b. Nov 26, 1933 in Lawrence, Massachusetts
Source: *BiE&WWA; BioIn 6, 10; BioNews 74;
CanWW 82; CelR; CurBio 62; EncMT;
FilmgC; IntMPA 75, 77; NotNAT; WhoAm
74, 76, 78, 80, 82; WhoHol A; WhoThe 77*

Gounod, Charles Francois
French. Composer
Wrote operas *Faust,* 1859; *Romeo and Juliet,*
1967; known for lyric rather than
dramatic qualities.
b. Jun 17, 1818 in Paris, France
d. Oct 17, 1893 in Paris, France
Source: *AtlBL; NewC; NewCol 75; OxFr; REn*

Gowans, Alan
Canadian. Educator
b. Nov 30, 1923 in Toronto, Ontario
Source: *AmAu&B; ConAu 1R; DrAS 74H,
78H; WhoAm 74; WhoAmA 73, 76; WhoWor
74, 76*

Gowdy, Curt
American. Sportscaster
b. Jul 31, 1919 in Green River, Wyoming
Source: *CelR; CurBio 67; IntMPA 75, 76, 77,
78, 79, 80, 81, 82; WhoAm 82*

Gowdy, Hank (Henry Morgan)
American. Baseball Player
b. Aug 24, 1889 in Columbus, Ohio
d. Aug 1, 1966 in Columbus, Ohio
Source: *BaseEn 85; WhoProB 73*

Gowers, Ernest Arthur, Sir
English. Public Official
Wrote instructional books on the English
language: *Plain Words: A Guide to the Use
of English,* 1948.
b. Jun 2, 1880 in London, England
d. Apr 16, 1966 in Midhurst, England
Source: *ConAu 89; DcLEL 1940; DcNaB
1961; LongCTC; NewC; ObitOF 79; ObitT
1961; WorAu*

Gowon, Yakubu
Nigerian. Army Officer
b. Oct 19, 1934 in Pankshin, Nigeria
Source: *CurBio 70; IntWW 74; NewCol 75;
WhoGov 75; WhoWor 78*

Goya y Lucientes, Francisco Jose de
Spanish. Artist
Considered greatest painter of his century;
paintings include "The Disaster of War,"
1810.
b. Mar 30, 1746 in Aragon, Spain
d. Apr 18, 1828 in Bordeaux, France
Source: *AtlBL; NewC; NewCol 75; REn*

Goyen, Jan Josephszoon van
Dutch. Artist
Created naturalistic landscapes; influenced
later Dutch artists.
b. 1596 in Leiden, Netherlands
d. 1656 in The Hague, Netherlands
Source: *NewCol 75; OxArt*

Goyen, William
American. Author
Wrote novel *The House of Breath,* 1950,
which was adapted into play, 1954.
b. Apr 24, 1915 in Trinity, Texas
d. Aug 29, 1983 in Los Angeles, California
Source: *AmAu&B; AnObit 1983; Au&Wr 71;
AuNews 2; ConAu 5R; ConLC 5; ConNov 72,
76; DrAF 76; NewYTBS 83; OxAmL; PenC
AM; REnAL; WhoAm 82; WhoE 74;
WhoWor 78; WorAu; WrDr 80*

Goytisolo, Fermin
[K C and the Sunshine Band]
Cuban. Musician
Conga player with the Sunshine Band since
1973.
b. Dec 31, 1951 in Havana, Cuba
Source: *NF*

Gozzi, Gaspare
Italian. Author, Composer
b. Dec 4, 1713 in Venice, Italy
d. Dec 27, 1786 in Padua, Italy
Source: *DcEuL; EvEuW; NewCol 75*

Gozzoli, Benozzo
[Benozzo di Lese di Sandro]
Italian. Artist
Frescoes include "The Journey of the Magi,"
1459-60.
b. 1420 in Florence, Italy
d. Oct 4, 1497 in Pistoria, Italy
Source: *AtlBL; NewCol 75; REn*

Grable, Betty
[Elizabeth Grasle]
American. Actress
WW II pin-up girl; married Jackie Coogan,
1937-40, Harry James, 1943-65.
b. Dec 18, 1916 in Saint Louis, Missouri
d. Jul 3, 1973 in Beverly Hills, California
Source: *BiDFilm; CelR; CmMov; FilmgC;
InWom; MotPP; MovMk; NewYTBE 73;
OxFilm; ThFT; WhAm 5; WhScrn 77;
WhoHol B; WorEFlm*

Gracchus, Gaius Sempronius
Roman. Statesman
b. 153 BC
d. 121 BC
Source: *BioIn 1, 4, 7, 8, 11; NewCol 75*

Grace, Princess
see: Kelly, Grace

Grace, William Russell
"Pirate of Peru"
American. Businessman, Politician
Developer of steamship operations who was
first Roman Catholic mayor of NYC,
1880-82, 1884-86.
b. May 10, 1832 in Queenstown, Ireland
d. Mar 21, 1904 in New York, New York
Source: *Alli SUP; AmBi; DcAmB; NewCol 75;
TwCBDA; WebAB; WhAm 1*

Grade, Lew, Sir
British. TV Executive
b. Dec 25, 1906 in Tokmak, Russia
Source: *IntMPA 75, 76, 77; IntWW 75, 76,
77, 78; NewYTET; Who 74; WhAm 82*

Gradishar, Randy Charles
American. Football Player
b. Mar 3, 1952 in Warren, Ohio
Source: *FootReg 81; WhoAm 80, 82; WhoFtbl
74*

Grady, Don
American. Actor
Robbie Douglas on TV's "My Three Sons,"
1960-72.
b. Jun 8, 1944 in San Diego, California
Source: *WhoHol A*

Grady, Henry Woodfin
American. Journalist, Orator
b. May 24, 1850 in Atlanta, Georgia
d. Dec 23, 1889 in Atlanta, Georgia
Source: *AmAu; AmBi; BiDSA; DcAmB;
DcLEL; DcNAA; EncAB-H; OxAmL; REnAL;
TwCBDA; WebAB; WhAm HS*

Graebner, Clark
American. Tennis Player, Businessman
b. Nov 4, 1943 in Lakewood, Ohio
Source: *CurBio 70*

Graf, Herbert
Austrian. Director
b. Apr 10, 1903 in Vienna, Austria
d. Apr 1973 in Geneva, Switzerland
Source: *CurBio 42, 73; NewYTBE 73; WhAm
5; WhoMus 72*

Graff, Henry Franklin
American. Author
b. Aug 11, 1921 in New York, New York
Source: *AmAu&B; ChhPo; ConAu 1R, 1NR;
DrAS 74H; WhoAm 74, 78, 80, 82*

Graffman, Gary
American. Musician
b. Oct 14, 1928 in New York, New York
Source: *CurBio 70; IntWW 74; NewYTBE 72,
73; WhoAm 74, 76, 78, 80; WhoWor 78*

Graham, Alex
Scottish. Cartoonist
b. 1915 in Glasgow, Scotland
Source: *WhoAm 82; WorECom*

Graham, Barbara
"Bloody Babs"
American. Murderer
Life and execution portrayed by Susan
Hayward in film *I Want to Live*, 1958.
b. 1923
d. Jun 3, 1955 in San Quentin, California
Source: *EncACr; LookW*

Graham, Bill
[Wolfgang Grajonca]
American. Producer
Organized national tours for Bob Dylan;
Crosby, Stills, Nash, and Young; Rolling
Stones; appeared in movie *Apocalypse Now*,
1976.
b. Jan 8, 1931 in Berlin, Germany
Source: *BkPepl; EncPR&S 74; IlEncRk;
WhoAm 82*

Graham, Billy (William Franklin)
American. Evangelist
Wrote *The Seven Deadly Sins*, 1955;
Challenge, 1969; has conducted evangelistic
tours throughout the world.
b. Nov 7, 1918 in Charlotte, North Carolina
Source: *AmAu&B; BioNews 74; BkPepl;
ConAu 9R; CurBio 51, 73; EncAB-H; IntWW
74; WebAB; Who 74; WhoAm 74, 76, 78, 80,
82*

Graham, Bob (Daniel Robert)
American. Politician
Pragmatic liberalist Dem. governor of FL,
1979--.
b. Nov 9, 1936 in Coral Gables, Florida
Source: *AlmAP 86; CurBio 86; WhoAm 84;
WhoAmP 85*

Graham, David B
Australian. Golfer
Won PGA, 1979; US Open, 1981.
b. May 23, 1946 in Windsor, Australia
Source: *WhoGolf; WhoIntG*

Graham, Donald Edward
American. Newspaper Executive
Son of Katharine Graham; publisher,
Washington *Post*, 1979--.
b. Apr 22, 1945 in Baltimore, Maryland
Source: *ConNews 85-4; IntWW 83; NewYTBS
83; WhoAm 84*

Graham, Ernest Robert
American. Architect
Helped design dept. stores: Gimbel's,
Marshall Field's, Filene's.
b. Aug 22, 1866 in Lowell, Michigan
d. Nov 22, 1936
Source: *DcAmB S2; WebBD 80*

Graham, Evarts Ambrose
American. Surgeon
b. Mar 19, 1883 in Chicago, Illinois
d. Mar 4, 1957
Source: *BioIn 2, 3, 4, 5, 11; CurBio 52, 57;
WhAm 3*

Graham, Fred Patterson
American. Journalist
b. Oct 6, 1931 in Little Rock, Arkansas
Source: *ConAu 37R; DrAS 74P; WhoAm 82;
WhoHol A*

Graham, Gene
American. Journalist
b. Aug 26, 1924 in Murray, Kentucky
Source: *ConAu 41R; DrAS 74E*

Graham, Katharine Meyer
American. Newspaper Executive
Washington *Post*, pres., 1963-73, publisher,
1969, chm., 1973.
b. Jun 16, 1917 in New York, New York
Source: *AuNews 1; BioNews 74; CelR; CurBio
71; ForWC 70; IntWW 74; St&PR 75;
WhoAm 74, 76, 78, 80, 82; WhoAmW 77;
WhoF&I 74; WhoS&SW 82; WhoWor 78*

Graham, Larry (Lawrence, Jr.)
[Sly and the Family Stone]
American. Singer, Musician
Bass guitarist with Sly and the Family Stone
until 1972; solo performer since 1980.
Source: *RkOn 85*

Graham, Martha
American. Dancer, Choreographer
b. May 11, 1894 in Pittsburgh, Pennsylvania
Source: *BioNews 74; CelR; CurBio 44, 61;
EncAB-H; HerW; InWom; IntWW 74;
NewYTBE 70, 73; WebAB; Who 74; WhoAm
74, 82; WhoThe 77A; WhoWor 78*

Graham, Otto Everett
"Automatic Otto"
American. Football Player
Youngest member elected to Football Hall of
Fame, 1965, at age 43; currently athletic
director USCGA.
b. Dec 6, 1921 in Waukegan, Illinois
Source: *WhoAm 74, 76, 78, 80, 82; WhoFtbl
74*

Graham, Ronny
American. Composer
b. Aug 26, 1919 in Philadelphia,
Pennsylvania
Source: *AmSCAP 66; BiE&WWA; NotNAT;
WhoThe 77*

Graham, Sheilah
[Lily Shiel]
American. Journalist
Friend of F Scott Fitzgerald during last
years his life; wrote *For Richer, For
Poorer*, 1975; *The Rest of the Story*, 1964.
b. Sep 1908 in London, England
Source: *AmAu&B; AuNews 1; BioNews 74;
CelR; ConAu 108; CurBio 69; InWom;
WhoAm 74; WrDr 76*

Graham, Stephen
English. Author
b. 1884 in England
d. 1975
Source: *Au&Wr 71; ConAu 93; DcLEL;
EvLB; LongCTC; NewC; REn; TwCA SUP;
Who 74*

Graham, Sylvester W
American. Reformer
Health evangelist who spoke on diet,
    wholesome living; invented the graham
    cracker.
b. Jul 5, 1794 in West Suffield, Connecticut
d. Sep 11, 1851 in Northampton,
    Massachusetts
Source: *AmBi; ApCAB; DcAmAu; DcAmB;
    DcNAA; Drake; NewCol 75; TwCBDA;
    WebAB; WhAm HS*

Graham, Thomas
Scottish. Chemist
Did early work in colloidal chemistry.
b. Dec 20, 1805 in Glasgow, Scotland
d. Sep 16, 1869
Source: *AsBiEn; BioIn 6, 8; NewCol 75;
    WebBD 80*

Graham, Virginia
[Virginia Komiss]
American. TV Personality
b. Jul 4, 1912 in Chicago, Illinois
Source: *CelR; CurBio 56; ForWC 70; InWom;
    WhoAm 82*

Graham, William Alexander
American. Governor
b. Sep 5, 1804 in Lincoln County, Nebraska
d. Aug 11, 1875 in Saratoga Springs, New
    York
Source: *AmBi; ApCAB; BioIn 1, 5, 10;
    DcAmB; Drake; TwCBDA; WhAm HS*

Graham, William Sydney
Scottish. Poet
b. 1918 in Greenock, Scotland
Source: *BioIn 10; ConAu 73*

Graham, Winston Mawdesley
American. Author
b. Jun 30, 1910 in Manchester, England
Source: *ConAu 49, 2NR; ConNov 72, 76;
    CurBio 55; TwCWr; Who 74; WrDr 80*

Graham Parker and the Rumour
[Bob Andrews; Martin Belmont; Andrew
    Bodnar; Stephen Goulding; Graham
    Parker; Brinsley Schwarz]
English. Music Group
Back-up band for Graham Parker, 1975-81;
    first album *Howlin' Wind,* 1976.
Source: *IlEncRk*

Grahame, Gloria
[Gloria Grahame Hallward]
American. Actress
Won 1952 Oscar for *The Bad and the
    Beautiful.*
b. Nov 28, 1925 in Los Angeles, California
d. Oct 5, 1981 in New York, New York
Source: *BiDFilm; BioIn 1, 11; FilmgC;
    IntMPA 76, 77, 78, 79, 80, 81, 82; MGM;
    MotPP; MovMk; WhoAmW 58, 61, 64;
    WhoHol A; WorEFlm*

Grahame, Kenneth
Scottish. Children's Author
Wrote children's classic *The Wind in the
    Willows,* 1908.
b. Mar 8, 1859 in Edinburgh, Scotland
d. Jul 6, 1932 in Pangbourne, England
Source: *AnCL; AtlBL; AuBYP; BkCL; CarSB;
    CasWL; Chambr 3; ChhPo, S1; CnMWL;
    CyWA; DcLEL; EvLB; FamSYP; JBA 34;
    LongCTC; ModBrL; NewC; OxEng; PenC
    ENG, REn; Str&VC; TwCA, SUP; TwCWr;
    WhoChL; YABC 1*

Grahame, Margot
English. Actress
Films include *The Informer,* 1934; *The Three
    Musketeers,* 1935; *Saint Joan,* 1957.
b. Feb 20, 1911 in Canterbury, England
d. Jan 1, 1982
Source: *FilmEn; FilmgC; ThFT; WhoHol A;
    WhoThe 77A*

Grainger, Percy Aldridge
American. Musician, Composer
b. Jul 8, 1882 in Melbourne, Australia
d. Feb 20, 1961 in White Plains, New York
Source: *AmSCAP 66; DcCM; NewCol 75;
    OxAmL; WhAm 4*

Gram, Hans Christian Joachim
Danish. Physician
Specialized in bacteriological research;
    developed Gram's stain, 1884.
b. Sep 13, 1853 in Copenhagen, Denmark
d. Nov 14, 1938 in Copenhagen, Denmark
Source: *AsBiEn; BioIn 5; WebBD 80*

Gramatky, Hardie
American. Children's Author, Illustrator
b. Apr 12, 1907 in Dallas, Texas
d. Apr 29, 1979 in Westport, Connecticut
Source: *AmAu&B; AnCL; AuBYP; AuNews 1;
    BkP; ConAu 1R, 85, 3NR; IlsCB 1957; JBA
    51; NewYTBS 79; SmATA 1; Str&VC;
    TwCCW 78; WhAm 7; WhoAm 74, 76;
    WhoAmA 73, 76, 78; WhoWor 78; WrDr 80*

Gramm, Lou
see: Foreigner

Gramm, (William) Phil(ip)
American. Economist, Politician
Rep. senator from TX, 1984--; co-author of
   Gramm-Rudman budget balancing law,
   1985.
b. Jul 8, 1942 in Fort Benning, Georgia
Source: *AlmAP 84; CurBio 86; WhoAm 84;
WhoAmM 83*

Granados, Enrique
Spanish. Composer, Musician
b. Jul 27, 1867 in Lerida, Spain
d. Mar 24, 1916
Source: *DcCM; NewCol 75*

Granatelli, Anthony Joseph
American. Auto Racer, Businessman
b. Mar 18, 1923 in Dallas, Texas
Source: *BioIn 8, 9, 10; WhoAm 74*

Grand Funk Railroad
[Donald Brewer; Mark Farner; Craig Frost;
   Mel Schacher]
American. Music Group
Formed, 1969; most commercially successful
   heavy metal group, 1970-76; first group to
   have 10 consecutive platinum albums; sold
   over 20 million.
Source: *EncPR&S 74*

Grange, "Red" (Harold Edward)
"Galloping Ghost"
American. Football Player
Played for U of IL, 1923-25; scored 6 TDs
   in game against MI, 1924.
b. Jun 13, 1903 in Forksville, Pennsylvania
Source: *BioIn 2, 3, 4, 5, 6, 7, 8, 9, 10;
NewYTBS 74; WebAB; WhoFtbl 74; WhoHol
A*

Granger, Farley
American. Actor
Played in Hitchcock films *Rope,* 1948;
   Strangers on a Train, 1951.
b. Jul 1, 1925 in San Jose, California
Source: *BiDFilm; BiE&WWA; FilmgC; HolP
40; IntMPA 75, 76, 77, 78, 79, 80, 81, 82;
MovMk; NotNAT; WhoHol A; WorEFlm*

Granger, Lester
American. Public Official
Executive director, National Urban League,
   1941-61; worked to develop economic
   opportunities for blacks.
b. Sep 16, 1896 in Newport News, Virginia
d. Jan 9, 1976 in Alexandria, Louisiana
Source: *CurBio 46, 76; WhAm 6; WhoAm 74*

Granger, Stewart
[James Lablache Stewart]
American. Actor, Author
Wrote autobiography *Sparks Fly Upward.*
b. May 6, 1913 in London, England
Source: *BiDFilm; CmMov; FilmgC; IntMPA
75, 76, 77, 78, 79, 80, 81, 82; MotPP;
MovMk; OxFilm; Who 74; WhoHol A;
WhoThe 77A; WorEFlm*

Granit, Ragnar Arthur
Finnish. Physiologist
First to show that single nerve fibers in
   retina could distinguish different
   wavelengths of light; won Nobel Prize,
   1967.
b. Oct 30, 1900 in Helsinki, Finland
Source: *IntWW 80, 81, 82; Who 80; WhoAm
80, 82; WhoWor 78, 80*

Granjon, Robert
French. Type Designer, Engraver
b. 1545
d. 1588
Source: *NewCol 75; WebBD 80*

Grant, Amy
American. Singer
Christian rock singer whose album *Age to
   Age,* 1983 sold one million copies;
   Unguarded contained hit "Find a Way,"
   1985.
b. 1961 in Augusta, Georgia
Source: *ConNews 85-4*

Grant, Bruce
American. Journalist, Author
b. Apr 17, 1893 in Wichita Falls, Texas
d. Apr 9, 1977
Source: *AuBYP; ConAu 1R, 69; SmATA 5*

Grant, "Bud" (Harold Peter)
American. Football Coach
Coach of Minnesota Vikings, 1967-83;
   compiled 150-88-5 record.
b. May 20, 1927 in Superior, Wisconsin
Source: *BioNews 74; WhoFtbl 74*

Grant, Cary
[Alexander Archibald Leach]
American. Actor, Business Executive
One of Hollywood's most enduring leading
   men; starred in *The Philadelphia Story,*
   1940; *North by Northwest,* 1959.
b. Jan 18, 1904 in Bristol, England
Source: *BiDFilm; BkPepl; CelR; CmMov;
CurBio 41, 65; EncMT; FilmgC; IntMPA 82;
IntWW 74; MotPP; MovMk; NewCol 75;
NewYTBE 73; OxFilm; WebAB; Who 74;
WhoAm 84; WhoWor 74; WorEFlm*

Grant, Earl
American. Musician
b. 1930
d. 1970
Source: *NewYTBE 70*

Grant, Gogi
[Myrtle Audrey Arinsberg; Audrey Grant]
American. Singer
Best known for "The Wayward Wind," one
of the most popular records of 1950s.
b. Sep 20, 1924 in Philadelphia, Pennsylvania
Source: *RkOn 74*

Grant, Gordon
American. Illustrator
b. Jun 7, 1875 in San Francisco, California
d. May 6, 1962 in New York, New York
Source: *AmAu&B; ConAu 102; CurBio 53,
62; IlsCB 1744, 1946; WhAm 4*

Grant, Harry Johnston
American. Newspaper Publisher
b. Sep 15, 1881 in Chillicothe, Missouri
d. Jul 12, 1963 in Milwaukee, Wisconsin
Source: *MnBBF; WhAm 4; WhNAA*

Grant, James
Scottish. Author
His fifty novels include *Romance of War,*
1845; *Harry Ogilvie,* 1856.
b. Aug 1, 1822 in Edinburgh, Scotland
d. May 5, 1887 in Edinburgh, Scotland
Source: *Alli, SUP; BbD; BiD&SB; BrAu 19;
DcBiA; DcEnA AP; DcEnL; DcLEL; EvLB;
NewC; OxEng*

Grant, Jane
American. Journalist
b. May 29, 1895 in Joplin, Missouri
d. 1972 in Litchfield, Connecticut
Source: *ChhPo S2; ConAu 25R, 33R, P-2;
ForWC 70; InWom; NewYTBE 72*

Grant, Julia Dent
[Mrs. Ulysses S Grant]
American. First Lady
Unpretentious army wife; buried with
husband in NY's monumental tomb.
b. Jan 26, 1826 in Saint Louis, Missouri
d. Dec 14, 1902 in Washington, District of
Columbia
Source: *AmAu&B; AmWom; ApCAB; GoodHs;
HerW; NatCAB 4; NotAW; TwCBDA; WhAm
1*

Grant, Kirby
[Kirby Grant Hoon, Jr.]
American. Actor
Best known as star of TV series "Sky King"
in 1950s.
b. Nov 24, 1911 in Butte, Montana
d. Oct 30, 1985 in Titusville, Florida
Source: *BioIn 8; FilmgC; WhoHol A*

Grant, Lee
[Mrs. Joseph Feury; Lyova Haskell
Rosenthal]
American. Actress
Won Emmy for "Peyton Place," 1965; Oscar
for *Shampoo,* 1975.
b. Oct 31, 1931 in New York, New York
Source: *BiE&WWA; BkPepl; CurBio 74;
FilmgC; IntMPA 75, 76, 77, 78, 79, 80, 81,
82; MotPP; MovMk; NewYTBE 70; NotNAT;
WhoAm 74, 76, 78, 80, 82; WhoHol A*

Grant, Michael
English. Author, Educator
b. Nov 21, 1914 in London, England
Source: *Au&Wr 71; ConAu 1R, 4NR; Who
74; WrDr 76*

Greene, Shecky
[Fred Sheldon Greenfield]
American. Actor, Comedian
Las Vegas comedian since 1953; in film *Tony
Rome,* 1967.
b. Apr 8, 1926 in Chicago, Illinois
Source: *WhoAm 84; WhoHol A; WhoWor 82*

Grant, Ulysses S(impson)
[Hiram Ulysses Grant]
American. US President
Commander in chief, Union forces during
Civil War; pres., 1869-77.
b. Apr 27, 1822 in Point Pleasant, Ohio
d. Jul 23, 1885 in Mount McGregor, New
York
Source: *Alli SUP; AmAu&B; AmBi; ApCAB;
BbD; BiAUS; BiD&SB; BiDrAC; BiDrUSE;
DcAmAu; DcAmB; DcNAA; Drake; EncAB-H;
OhA&B; OxAmL; REn; REnAL; TwCBDA;
WebAB; WhAm HS; WhAmP*

Grantham, George
see: Poco

Granville, Bonita
American. Actress
Played Nancy Drew in 1930s film series.
b. Feb 2, 1923 in New York, New York
Source: *FilmgC; HolP 30; MotPP; MovMk;
ThFT; WhoHol A*

Granville, Joseph E(nsign)
American. Financier
Stock market advisor; publishes weekly
    Market Letter, 1963--.
b. Aug 20, 1923 in Yonkers, New York
Source: *ConAu 65*

Granville-Barker, Harley
English. Producer, Dramatist, Critic
Wrote play *Secret Life,* 1923; *Prefaces to
    Shakespeare,* 1923-37.
b. Nov 25, 1877 in London, England
d. Aug 31, 1946 in Paris, France
Source: *CasWL; Chambr 3; CnMD; CnThe;
CyWA; DcLEL; EvLB; LongCTC; McGEWD;
ModBrL; ModWD; NewC; OxEng; PenC
ENG; REn; REnWD; TwCA, SUP; TwCWr;
WebE&AL; WhoLA; WhoTwCL*

Granz, Norman
American. Jazz Musician
b. Aug 6, 1918 in Los Angeles, California
Source: *WhoAm 82; WhoWest 84*

Grapewin, Charley (Charles)
American. Actor
Character actor in over 100 films including
    The Grapes of Wrath, 1940; *Tobacco Road,*
    1941.
b. Dec 20, 1875 in Xenia, Ohio
d. Feb 2, 1956 in Corona, California
Source: *FilmgC*

Grappelli, Stephane
French. Jazz Musician
b. Jan 26, 1908 in Paris, France
Source: *BioIn 9; CmpEPM*

Grass, Gunter Wilhelm
German. Author
Best known novel *The Tin Drum,* 1959; film
    version won best foreign film Oscar, 1980.
b. Oct 16, 1927 in Danzig, Germany
Source: *CasWL; CelR; CnMD; ConAu 13R;
ConLC 1, 2, 4, 6, 11, 15; CroCD; CurBio 64,
83; EncWL; EvEuW; EncWL; EvEuW;
IntWW 74; McGEWD; ModGL; ModWD;
OxGer; PenC EUR; REnWD; TwCWr; Who
74; WhoWor 74; WorAu*

Grass, John
[Charging Bear]
American. Indian Chief
Chief of Blackfoot Sioux who defended
    Indian rights in treaty councils.
b. 1837 in Grand River, South Dakota
d. May 10, 1918 in Fort Yates, South
    Dakota
Source: *DcAmB; WhAm HSA, 4*

Grass Roots, The
[Creed Bratton; Rick Coonce; Warren Entner;
    Robert Grill; Reed Kailing; Joel Larson;
    Dennis Provisor]
American. Music Group
Hits include "Temptation Eyes," "Heaven
    Knows," 1967-75.
Source: *EncPR&S 74; RkOn 74*

Grasse, Count Francois Joseph Paul de
French. Admiral
Aided Continental forces in American
    Revolution.
b. Sep 13, 1722 in Barr, France
d. Jan 11, 1788 in Paris, France
Source: *AmBi; OxFr; WhAm HS*

Grassi, Giovanni Battista
Italian. Zoologist
b. Mar 27, 1854 in Rovellasca, Italy
d. May 4, 1925 in Rome, Italy
Source: *BioIn 6; DcScB; NewCol 75; WebBD
80*

Grassle, Karen Gene
American. Actress
Played Caroline Ingalls on "Little House on
    the Prairie", 1973-81.
b. Feb 25, in Berkeley, California
Source: *BioIn 10; ConTFT 3; WhoAm 82*

Grassley, Charles Ernest
American. Politician
Conservative Rep. senator from IA, 1980--.
b. Sep 17, 1933 in New Hartford, Iowa
Source: *AlmAP 78, 80; CngDr 77, 79;
WhoAm 80, 82, 84; WhoAmP 75, 77, 79;
WhoGov 77, 75; WhoMW 76, 78*

Grasso, Ella
[Ella Tambussi]
American. Governor
b. May 10, 1919 in Windsor Locks,
    Connecticut
d. Feb 5, 1981 in Hartford, Connecticut
Source: *BioNews 74; CngDr 74; InWom;
NewYTBS 74; WhoAm 74; WhoAmP 73;
WhoAmW 77; WhoE 74; WhoGov 75;
WomPO 76*

Grateful Dead, The
[Jerry Garcia; Donna Godchaux; Keith
    Godchaux; Bill Kreutzmann; Phil Lesh;
    Ron McKernan; Robert Hall Weir]
American. Music Group
Psychedelic band formed, 1965, whose fans
    are known as "Dead Heads."
Source: *BkPepl; EncPR&S 74; IlEncRk*

Gratian
[Flavius Gratianus]
Roman. Emperor
b. 359
d. 383
Source: *NewCol 75; WebBD 80*

Grattan, Clinton Hartley
American. Author
b. Oct 19, 1902 in Wakefield, Massachusetts
d. Jun 25, 1980 in Austin, Texas
Source: *AmAu&B; ConAu 1R, 101; DrAS
78H; OxAmL; REnAL; TwCA, SUP; WhAm
7; WhE&EA; WhNAA; WhoAm 74, 76, 78;
WhoS&SW 73; WrDr 76*

Gratz, Rebecca
American. Philanthropist
b. Mar 4, 1781 in Philadelphia, Pennsylvania
d. Aug 29, 1869
Source: *AmAu&B; BioIn 2, 4, 5, 8, 9, 10;
REnAL*

Gratzer, Alan
see: REO Speedwagon

Grau, Shirley Ann
American. Author
b. Jul 8, 1929 in New Orleans, Louisiana
Source: *AmAu&B; AuNews 2; ConAu 1R, 89;
ConLC 4; ConNov 72, 76; DrAF 76; InWom;
ModAL; OxAmL; PenC AM; REn; REnAL;
WhoAm 82; WhoAmW 77, 77; WhoWor 74,
74; WorAu; WrDr 76*

Grauer, Ben(jamin Franklin)
American. Broadcast Journalist
b. Jun 2, 1908 in New York, New York
d. May 31, 1977 in New York, New York
Source: *ConAu 69; CurBio 41, 59; Film 1;
IntMPA 76, 77; NewYTBE 73; WhoAm 74;
WhoWor 78; WhoWorJ 72*

Grauman, Sid(ney Patrick)
American. Theater Owner
Owner, Chinese Theater restaurant, famous
  for footprints of stars.
b. Mar 17, 1879 in Indianapolis, Indiana
d. Mar 5, 1950 in Hollywood, California
Source: *BioIn 2; NotNAT B; ObitOF 79;
WhoHol B*

Gravel, Mike
American. Senator
b. May 13, 1930 in Springfield,
  Massachusetts
Source: *CelR; CngDr 74; ConAu 41R; CurBio
72; IntWW 74; NewYTBE 71; WhoAm 80,
82; WhoAmP 73; WhoGov 75; WhoWest 84;
WrDr 76*

Gravely, Samuel L
American. Admiral
b. Jun 4, 1922 in Richmond, Virginia
Source: *NewYTBE 71; WhoAm 74; WhoBlA
75; WhoS&SW 82*

Graves, Alvin Cushman
American. Physicist
Head of nuclear weapons testing at Los
  Alamos since 1948.
b. Nov 4, 1909 in Washington, District of
  Columbia
d. Jul 29, 1965 in Del Norte, Colorado
Source: *CurBio 52, 65; DcAmB S7*

Graves, Harold Nathan
American. Diplomat
b. Jan 20, 1915 in Manila, Philippines
Source: *IntWW 74; WhoAm 74; WhoGov 75*

Graves, John Earl
[The Hostages]
American. Hostage in Iran
b. May 16, 1927 in Detroit, Michigan
Source: *NewYTBS 81; USBiR 74; WhoAm
74, 76, 78; WhoGov 72*

Graves, Michael
American. Architect
b. Jul 9, 1934 in Indianapolis, Indiana
Source: *WhoAm 78, 80, 82*

Graves, Morris Cole
American. Artist
Noted for somber, expressionist bird
  paintings: "Blind Bird," 1940.
b. Aug 28, 1910 in Fox Valley, Oregon
Source: *ConArt 77; DcAmArt; McGDA;
REnAL; WebAB; WhoAm 74, 76, 78, 80, 82;
WhoAmA 73, 76, 78*

Graves, Nancy Stevenson
American. Artist
Known for sculptures of camels, camouflage
  paintings, lunar landscapes; work called
  imaginative, technically exact.
b. Dec 23, 1940 in Pittsfield, Massachusetts
Source: *BioIn 8, 9, 11; CurBio 81; DcCAA
77; WhoAm 80, 82; WhoAmA 76, 78, 80*

Graves, Peter
English. Actor
Character actor mainly in British films, 1941.
b. Oct 21, 1911 in London, England
Source: *FilmgC; IntMPA 77, 75; MotPP;
WhoHol A; WhoThe 72*

Graves, Peter
[Peter Aurness]
American. Actor
Played Jim Phelps in "Mission: Impossible,"
1967-73; brother of James Arness.
b. Mar 18, 1926 in Minneapolis, Minnesota
Source: *FilmgC; IntMPA 82; MovMk;
WhoAm 74, 76, 78, 80, 82*

Graves, Robert Ranke
English. Poet, Author
Author of more than 135 novels, books of
poetry, criticism, best known for historical
novel, *I, Claudius,* 1934.
b. Jul 26, 1895 in London, England
d. Dec 7, 1985 in Majorca, Spain
Source: *Alli; AnCL; Au&Wr 71; AuBYP;
BiDLA; CasWL; Chambr 3; ChhPo, S1, S2;
CnE&AP; CnMWL; ConAu 5R, 5NR; ConLC
1, 2, 6, 11; ConNov 72, 76; ConP 70, 75;
CyWA; DcLEL; EncWL; EvLB; IntWW 74;
LongCTC; ModBrL, S1; NewC; OxEng; PenC
ENG; RAdv 1; REn; TwCA, SUP; TwCWr;
WebE&AL; Who 74; WhoTwCL; WhoWor 78;
WrDr 80*

Graves, William Sidney
American. Army Officer
Led American expeditionary force in Siberia,
1918-20.
b. Mar 27, 1865 in Mount Calm, Texas
d. Feb 27, 1940 in Shrewsbury, New Jersey
Source: *DcAmB S2; NewCol 75; WebBD 80;
WhAm 1*

Gray, Asa
American. Botanist, Author, Educator
Leader in his field; wrote *Flora of North
America,* 1843.
b. Nov 18, 1810 in Sauquoit, New York
d. Jan 30, 1888 in Cambridge, Massachusetts
Source: *Alli, SUP; AmAu; AmAu&B; ApCAB;
BbD; BiD&SB; CyAL 2; DcAmAu; DcAmB;
DcNAA; EncAB-H; OxAmL; REn; REnAL;
TwCBDA; WebAB; WhAm HS*

Gray, Barry
[Bernard Yaroslaw]
American. Radio Performer
b. Jul 2, 1916 in Atlantic City, New Jersey
Source: *CelR; ConAu 61; IntMPA 75, 76, 77;
NewYTBE 70; WhoAm 82*

Gray, Cecil
Scottish. Composer
b. May 19, 1895 in Edinburgh, Scotland
d. Sep 9, 1951 in Worthing, England
Source: *Baker 78; BioIn 1, 2; OxMus;
WhE&EA*

Gray, Coleen
[Doris Jenson]
American. Actress
Generally had leads in B-films including
Nightmare Alley.
b. Oct 23, 1922 in Staplehurst, Nebraska
Source: *FilmEn; InWom; IntMPA 80, 81, 82;
MotPP; WhoHol A*

Gray, Dolores
American. Actress
Stage, film musicals in London include *Annie
Get Your Gun,* 1947-50.
b. Jun 7, 1924 in Chicago, Illinois
Source: *BiE&WWA; EncMT; FilmgC;
InWom; MotPP; NotNAT; WhoHol A;
WhoThe 77*

Gray, Elisha
American. Inventor
b. Aug 2, 1835 in Barnesville, Ohio
d. Jan 21, 1901 in Newtonville,
Massachusetts
Source: *Alli SUP; AmBi; ApCAB; DcAmAu;
DcAmB; DcNAA; NewCol 75; OhA&B;
TwCBDA; WebAB; WhAm 1*

Gray, Gilda
[Maryanna Michalski]
American. Cartoonist
Created, drew comic strip "Little Orphan
Annie," 1924-68.
b. Oct 24, 1901 in Krakow, Poland
d. Dec 22, 1959 in Hollywood, California
Source: *ConAu 107; Film 1; FilmgC; InWom;
MotPP; TwYS; WhScrn 74, 77; WhoHol B*

Gray, Glen
[Glen Gray Knoblaugh]
"Spike"
American. Band Leader
Led popular dance band, Casa Loma
Orchestra, 1929-50.
b. Jun 7, 1906 in Roanoke, Illinois
d. Aug 23, 1963 in Plymouth, Massachusetts
Source: *DcAmB S7; WhScrn 74, 77; WhoHol
B*

Gray, Gordon
American. Government Official
Secretary of Army, 1949-50; held security
posts, 1947-77.
b. May 30, 1909 in Baltimore, Maryland
d. Nov 25, 1982 in Washington, District of
Columbia
Source: *CurBio 49, 83; IntWW 74; NewYTBS
82; Who 74; WhoAm 74, 76, 78, 80, 82;
WhoF&I 74; WhoGov 75; WhoS&SW 82*

Gray, Hanna
American. Educator
b. Oct 25, 1930 in Heidelberg, Germany
Source: *DrAS 74H; LEduc 74; WhoAm 82; WhoAmW 77*

Gray, Harold
American. Comic Strip Artist
b. Jan 20, 1894 in Kankakee, Illinois
d. May 9, 1968 in La Jolla, California
Source: *AmAu&B; REnAL; WebAB; WhAm 5; WhNAA*

Gray, Horace
American. Supreme Court Justice
Served, 1881-1902.
b. Mar 24, 1828 in Boston, Massachusetts
d. Sep 15, 1902 in Washington, District of Columbia
Source: *AmBi; ApCAB; DcAmB; NewCol 75; TwCBDA; WebAB; WhAm 1*

Gray, Linda
American. Actress
Appeared in over 400 TV commercials; plays Sue Ellen Ewing on "Dallas," 1978--.
b. Sep 12, 1941 in Santa Monica, California
Source: *WhoAm 80, 82; WhoTelC*

Gray, Louis Patrick
American. Government Official
Acting director, FBI, 1972-73, who resigned over Watergate; indicted for illegal practices, 1978.
b. Jul 18, 1916 in Saint Louis, Missouri
Source: *BioNews 74; IntWW 80, 81, 82; NewYTBE 71; WhoAm 74; WhoWor 76, 78*

Gray, Nicholas Stuart
Scottish. Children's Author
b. Oct 23, 1922 in Scotland
d. Mar 17, 1981 in London, England
Source: *AnObit 1981; ConAu 21R, 103; IntAu&W 76, 77; ScF&FL 1, 2; SmATA 4; TwCCW 78; WhoThe 72, 77; WrDr 76, 80*

Gray, Peter J
[Peter Wyshner]
American. Baseball Player
One-armed outfielder for St. Louis Browns, 1945.
b. Mar 6, 1917 in Nanticoke, Pennsylvania
Source: *BioIn 9, 10; WhoProB 73*

Gray, Simon James Holliday
English. Dramatist
Wrote *Wise Child*, 1968; *Butley*, 1971; *Otherwise Engaged*, 1975.
b. Oct 21, 1936 in Hayling Island, England
Source: *BioIn 11; ConAu 21R; ConDr 73, 77; ConNov 72, 76; CurBio 83; EncWT; IntWW 81; NotNAT; OxCan; WhoThe 77*

Gray, Thomas
English. Poet
b. Dec 26, 1716 in London, England
d. Jul 30, 1771 in Cambridge, England
Source: *Alli, SUP; AtlBL; BbD; BiD&SB; BrAu; CasWL; Chambr 2; ChhPo, S1, S2; CnE&AP; CrtT 2; CyWA; DcEnA; DcEnL; DcEuL; DcLEL; EvLB; MouLC 2; NewC; OxEng; PenC ENG; RAdv 1; RComWL; REn; WebE&AL*

Graydon, James Weir
American. Engineer, Inventor
b. Jan 18, 1848 in Indianapolis, Indiana
Source: *NatCAB 13; TwCBDA; WhAm 4*

Grayson, Kathryn
[Zelma Hedrick]
American. Actress
Starred in *Show Boat*, 1951; *Kiss Me Kate*, 1953; *The Vagabond King*, 1956.
b. Feb 9, 1923 in Winston-Salem, North Carolina
Source: *CmMov; FilmgC; InWom; IntMPA 75, 76, 77, 78, 79, 80, 81, 82; MotPP; MovMk; WhoAm 74, 76, 78, 80, 82; WhoHol A*

Graziani, Rodolfo
[Marchese DiNeghelli]
Italian. Military Leader
b. Aug 11, 1882 in Frosinone, Italy
d. Jan 11, 1955 in Rome, Italy
Source: *CurBio 41, 55; NewCol 75*

Graziano, Rocky
[Rocko Barbella]
American. Boxer, Actor
Middleweight champ, 1947-48; portrayed by Paul Newman in *Somebody Up There Likes Me*, 1956.
b. Jun 7, 1922 in New York, New York
Source: *CelR; WhoAm 76; WhoBox 74; WhoHol A*

Great Gildersleeve
see: Peary, Harold

Greaza, Walter N
American. Actor
Character actor; played in TV daytime drama
"The Edge of Night."
b. Jan 1, 1897 in Saint Paul, Minnesota
d. Jun 1, 1973 in New York, New York
Source: *BiE&WWA; NewYTBE 73; WhScrn
77; WhoHol B*

Greb, Harry (Edward Henry)
American. Boxer
b. Jun 6, 1894 in Pittsburgh, Pennsylvania
d. Oct 22, 1926 in New York, New York
Source: *BioIn 1, 4, 6, 7; NewCol 75; WhoBox
74*

Grebb, Marty
see: Buckinghams, The

Grebey, Ray
American. Baseball Executive
Chief negotiater for owners in professional
baseball disputes, early 1980s.
b. 1927 in Chicago, Illinois
Source: *BioIn 12*

Grech, Rick
see: Blind Faith

Grechko, Andrei Antonovick
Russian. Government Official
b. Oct 17, 1903 in Golodaevka, Russia
d. Apr 26, 1976 in Moscow, U.S.S.R.
Source: *CurBio 68; IntWW 74; NewCol 75;
NewYTBE 71; WhoWor 78*

Greco, El
[Kyriakas Theotokopoulos]
Spanish. Artist
Works include "Assumption of the Virgin,"
1577, "Burial of the Count of Orgaz,"
1586.
b. 1541 in Candia, Crete
d. Apr 6, 1614 in Toledo, Spain
Source: *AtlBL; NewC; NewCol 75; REn*

Greco, Buddy (Armando)
American. Singer, Songwriter, Musician
b. Aug 14, 1926 in Philadelphia,
Pennsylvania
Source: *AmSCAP 66; BioNews 74*

Greco, Jose
American. Dancer, Choreographer
Debut in *Carmen,* 1937; appeared in *Ship of
Fools,* 1965.
b. Dec 23, 1918 in Montorio, Italy
Source: *ConAu 85; CurBio 52; WhoAm 74,
76, 78, 80, 82; WhoHol A*

Greco, Juliette
French. Singer
b. 1927 in Paris, France
Source: *FilmgC; WhoHol A*

Greeley, Andrew Moran
American. Author, Priest, Sociologist
b. Feb 5, 1928 in Oak Park, Illinois
Source: *AmM&WS 73S; ConAu 5R; CurBio
72; LEduc 74; WhoAm 74, 76, 78, 80, 82*

Greeley, Dana McLean
American. Religious Leader
First pres., Unitarian Universalist Assn.,
1961-69; co-founded World Conference on
Religion and Peace.
b. Jul 5, 1908 in Lexington, Massachusetts
d. Jun 13, 1986 in Concord, Massachusetts
Source: *CurBio 64, 86*

Greeley, Horace
American. Journalist, Editor
Founded NY *Tribune,* 1834; popularized
phrase "Go West, young man."
b. Feb 3, 1811 in Amherst, New Hampshire
d. Nov 29, 1872 in Pleasantville, New York
Source: *Alli, SUP; AmAu; AmAu&B; AmBi;
ApCAB; BbD; BiAUS; BiD&SB; BiDrAC;
CasWL; Chambr 3; ChhPo; CnDAL; CyAL 2;
DcAmAu; DcAmB; DcEnL; DcNAA; EncAB-
H; EvLB; OxAmL; REn; REnAL; TwCBDA;
WebAB; WhAm HS; WhAmP*

Greely, Adolphus Washington
American. Explorer, Army Officer
Told of polar expedition in *Three Years of
Arctic Service,* 1886.
b. Mar 27, 1844 in Newburyport,
Massachusetts
d. Oct 20, 1935
Source: *Alli SUP; AmAu&B; AmBi; ApCAB;
BiD&SB; DcAmB S1; DcNAA; NewCol 75;
OxCan; REnAL; WebAB; WhAm 1*

Green, Abel
American. Author, Editor, Actor
b. Jun 3, 1900 in New York, New York
d. May 10, 1973 in New York, New York
Source: *AmSCAP 66; BiE&WWA; CelR;
ConAu 41R; NewYTBE 73; WhAm 6;
WhScrn 77; WhoAdv 72; WhoAm 74*

Green, Adolph
American. Dramatist, Composer
Won Tonys for *Hallelujah Baby; Applause;
    On the Twentieth Century.*
b. Dec 2, 1915 in New York, New York
Source: *AmAu&B; AmSCAP 66; CelR;
    CmMov; CurBio 45; EncMT; FilmgC;
    IntMPA 75, 76, 77, 78, 79, 80, 81, 82;
    NewCBMT; NotNAT; OxFilm; WhoAm 74,
    76, 78, 80, 82; WhoThe 77; WhoWor 78;
    WorEFlm*

Green, Al
American. Singer, Songwriter
Hits include "Let's Stay Together," 1972;
    "I'm Still In Love With You," 1972.
b. Apr 13, 1946 in Forrest City, Arkansas
Source: *BkPepl; IlEncBM 82; NewYTBE 73;
    WhoAm 82*

Green, Anna Katharine
American. Author
Wrote classic detective story *The Leavenworth
    Case,* 1878.
b. Nov 11, 1846 in Brooklyn, New York
d. Apr 11, 1935 in Buffalo, New York
Source: *NotAW; OxAmL 83*

Green, Anne
American. Author
b. Nov 11, 1899 in Savannah, Georgia
Source: *AmAu&B; AmNov; CathA 1952;
    ConAmA; DcLEL; InWom; LongCTC;
    OxAmL; REn; REnAL; TwCA, SUP*

Green, Chad
American. Cancer Victim
Parents took him to Mexico where he was
    treated with laetrile, a drug not approved
    in US.
b. 1976
d. 1979
Source: *BioIn 11, 12*

Green, Constance Windsor McLaughlin
American. Historian, Author
Wrote on nation's capital; won 1963 Pulitzer
    for *Washington: Village and Capital, 1800-
    78.*
b. Aug 21, 1897 in Ann Arbor, Michigan
d. Dec 5, 1975 in Annapolis, Maryland
Source: *AmAu&B; ConAu 9R, 61; CurBio 63;
    ForWC 70; InWom; NotAW MOD; OxAmL;
    WhAm 6; WhoAm 74; WhoWor 74; WrDr 76*

Green, Dallas (George Dallas, Jr.)
American. Baseball Manager, Baseball
    Executive
b. Aug 4, 1934 in Newport, Delaware
Source: *BaseEn 85; BioIn 12; WhoAm 82*

Green, Elmer Ellsworth
American. Physicist
b. Oct 17, 1917 in La Grande, Oregon
Source: *AmM&WS 73S; ConAu 103*

Green, Gerald
American. Author
b. Apr 8, 1922 in Brooklyn, New York
Source: *AmAu&B; ConAu 13R; WhoAm 74,
    76, 78, 80, 82; WhoWor 78; WorAu*

Green, Henry
[Henry Vincent Yorke]
English. Author
b. Oct 29, 1905 in Tewkesbury, England
d. 1974
Source: *CasWL; CnMWL; ConAu 49, 85;
    ConNov 72, 76; CyWA; DcLEL; EncWL;
    EvLB; LongCTC; ModBrL, S1; NewC;
    OxEng; PenC ENG; RAdv 1; REn; TwCA
    SUP; TwCWr; WebE&AL; WhoTwCL*

Green, Hetty
[Henrietta Howland Robinson]
"Witch of Wall Street"
American. Financier
Reputed at that time to be richest woman in
    US, leaving estate of more than $10
    million.
b. Nov 21, 1834 in New Bedford,
    Massachusetts
d. Jul 3, 1916 in New York, New York
Source: *AmBi; BioIn 2, 3, 4, 5, 6, 7, 9;
    DcAmB; GoodHs; LinLib S; NewCol 75;
    NotAW; WebAB; WhAm 1; WhoAmW 75*

Green, Hubie (Hubert)
American. Golfer
Rookie of the Year, 1971; Won US Open,
    1977.
b. Dec 28, 1946 in Birmingham, Alabama
Source: *BioIn 11; WhoGolf; WhoIntG*

Green, Jack
see: T. Rex

Green, John Richard
English. Historian, Clergyman
Wrote *Short History of the English People,*
    1874, known for literary quality, emphasis
    on social trends, not political events.
b. Dec 12, 1837 in Oxford, England
d. Mar 7, 1883 in Mentone, France
Source: *BbD; BiD&SB; BrAu 19; CasWL;
    CelCen; DcEnL; DcEuL; EvLB; LinLib L, S;
    NewC; OxEng; PenC ENG*

Green, Johnny (John W)
American. Conductor, Musician, Composer
b. Oct 10, 1908 in New York, New York
Source: *AmSCAP 66; BiE&WWA; CmMov;
FilmgC; IntMPA 75, 76, 77, 78, 79, 80, 81,
82; WhoAm 74, 76, 78, 80, 82; WhoMus 72;
WhoWest 84; WhoWor 78*

Green, Julien
American. Author
b. Apr 9, 1900 in Paris, France
Source: *CasWL; CIDMEL; CnMD; CnMWL;
ConAu 21R; ConLC 3; EncWL; EvEuW;
IntWW 74; McGEWD; OxFr; PenC EUR;
REn; REnWD; TwCWr; WhoTwCL*

Green, Martyn
English. Actor
Lead member of D'Oyly Carte Opera Co.,
1922-51.
b. Apr 22, 1899 in London, England
d. Feb 8, 1975 in Hollywood, California
Source: *BiE&WWA; ConAu 57; CurBio 50;
FilmgC; WhScrn 77; WhoThe 77*

Green, Mitzi
American. Actress
Child star who played Annie in *Little
Orphan Annie;* Becky Thatcher in *Tom
Sawyer, Huckleberry Finn;* retired age 14.
b. Oct 22, 1920 in New York, New York
d. May 24, 1969 in Huntington, California
Source: *FilmgC; HolP 30; MotPP; ThFT;
WhScrn 74, 77; WhoHol B*

Green, Paul Eliot
American. Dramatist, Screenwriter
Writings portray NC, black themes; wrote
1927 Pulitzer play *In Abraham's Bosom.*
b. Mar 17, 1894 in Lillington, North
Carolina
d. May 4, 1981 in Chapel Hill, North
Carolina
Source: *AmAu&B; AmSCAP 66; Au&Wr 71;
AuNews 1; BiE&WWA; BioIn 2, 3, 4, 5, 8,
9, 10; CnDAL; CnMD; CnThe; ConAmA;
ConAmL; ConAu 5R, 103, 3NR; ConDr 73;
DcLEL; EncWL; EncWT; IntAu&W 76, 77;
IntWW 74; LongCTC; McGEWB; ModAL;
ModWD; NotNAT; OxAmL; OxThe; PenC
AM; REn; REnAL; REnWD; TwCA, SUP;
WebAB; WebE&AL; WhE&EA; WhLit;
WhNAA; Who 74; WhoAm 74, 76, 78, 80;
WhoThe 77; WhoWor 74; WrDr 76*

Green, Paula
American. Advertising Executive
b. Sep 18, 1927 in Hollywood, California
Source: *WhoAm 74, 76, 78, 80, 82;
WhoAmW 77*

Green, Rickey
American. Basketball Player
Guard, first round draft pick, 1977; led NBA
in steals, 1984.
b. Aug 18, 1954 in Chicago, Illinois
Source: *OfNBA 85*

Green, Robert L
American. Fashion Editor
Source: *WorFshn*

Green, William
American. Labor Union Official
Succeeded Samuel Gompers as pres. of AFL,
1924-52.
b. Mar 3, 1873 in Coschocton, Ohio
d. Nov 21, 1952 in Coschocton, Ohio
Source: *CurBio 42, 53; DcAmB S5; EncAB-H;
OhA&B; WebAB; WhAm 3*

Greenaway, Kate (Catherine)
English. Children's Author, Illustrator
b. Mar 17, 1846 in London, England
d. Nov 6, 1901
Source: *AnCL; AuBYP; CarSB; ChhPo, S1,
S2; FamAIYP; InWom; JBA 34, 51; NewC;
OxEng; WhoChL*

Greenbaum, Norman
American. Singer, Songwriter
Hit single, "Spirit in the Sky," sold two
million copies, 1970.
b. Nov 20, 1942 in Malden, Massachusetts
Source: *RolSEnR 83*

Greenberg, Hank (Henry Benjamin)
"Hammerin' Hank"
American. Baseball Player
Prolific home run hitter, 1933-41, 1945-46;
shares ML record for home runs in
season by right-handed hitter, 1938.
b. Jan 1, 1911 in New York, New York
d. Sep 4, 1986 in Beverly Hills, California
Source: *BaseEn 85; CurBio 47, 86; WhoAm
74; WhoProB 73*

Greene, Belle da Costa
American. Library Administrator
Director, Pierpont Morgan Library, 1923-48.
b. Dec 13, 1883 in Alexandria, Virginia
d. May 10, 1950 in New York, New York
Source: *NotAW*

Greene, Bob (Robert Bernard, Jr.)
American. Journalist
Syndicated columnist, 1976--; wrote *Billion
Dollar Baby,* 1974, account of life on road
with rock band.
b. Mar 10, 1947 in Columbus, Ohio
Source: *ConAu 107*

Greene, Gael
American. Author
b. 1937 in Detroit, Michigan
Source: *ConAu 13R; ConLC 8*

Greene, Graham
English. Author
Wrote *Brighton Rock*, 1938, *The End of the
Affair*, 1951.
b. Oct 2, 1904 in Berkhampstead, England
Source: *Au&Wr 71; AuNews 2; BiE&WWA;
CasWL; CathA 1930; CelR; ChhPo S2;
CnMD; CnMWL; CnThe; ConAu 13R;
ConLC 1, 3, 6, 9, 14, 18; ConNov 72, 76;
CroCD; CyWA; EncMys; EncWL; FilmgC;
IntWW 74; LongCTC; McGEWD; ModBrL,
S1; ModWD; NewC; NotNAT; OxEng;
OxFilm; OxThe; PenC ENG; RAdv 1; REn;
SmATA 20; TwCA, SUP; TwCWr;
WebE&AL; Who 74; WhoAm 82; WhoChL;
WhoThe 77; WhoTwCL; WhoWor 78;
WorEFlm; WrDr 80*

Greene, Joe (Joseph)
"Mean Joe"
American. Football Player
Tackle, Pittsburgh, 1969-81; starred in award-
winning Coca-Cola commercial.
b. Sep 24, 1946 in Temple, Texas
Source: *WhoFtbl 74*

Greene, Lorne
American. Actor
Played Ben Cartwright on TV series
"Bonanza," 1959-73.
b. Feb 12, 1915 in Ottawa, Ontario
Source: *BiE&WWA; CanWW 82; CelR;
CreCan 2; CurBio 67; FilmgC; IntMPA 75,
76, 77, 78, 79, 80, 81, 82; MotPP; MovMk;
WhoAm 74, 76, 78, 80, 82; WhoHol A;
WhoWor 78*

Greene, Nancy Catherine
Canadian. Skier
b. May 11, 1943 in Ottawa, Ontario
Source: *BioIn 8, 10; CanWW 79, 82; CurBio
69*

Greene, Nathanael
American. General
b. Aug 7, 1742 in Potowomut, Rhode Island
d. Jun 19, 1786 in Savannah, Georgia
Source: *AmBi; ApCAB; DcAmB; EncAB-H;
TwCBDA; WebAB; WhAm HS*

Greene, Richard
English. Actor
Played the original Robin Hood in British
TV series "Robin Hood," 1950s.
b. Aug 25, 1918 in Plymouth, England
d. Jun 1, 1985 in Norfolk, England
Source: *FilmEn; FilmgC; HolP 30; MotPP;
MovMk; WhoHol A*

Greene, Ward
American. Author, Journalist
b. Dec 23, 1892 in Asheville, North Carolina
d. Jan 22, 1956
Source: *AmAu&B; AmNov; REnAL; TwCA,
SUP; WhAm 3; WhNAA*

Greenfield, Jeff
American. Author
b. Jun 10, 1943 in New York, New York
Source: *ConAu 37R*

Greenfield, Howard
American. Songwriter
Co-wrote Grammy-winning song "Love Will
Keep Us Together," with Neil Sedaka,
1975.
b. 1937
d. Mar 4, 1986 in Los Angeles, California
Source: *NF*

Greenfield, Meg
American. Journalist, Editor
Columnist in *Newsweek;* won Pulitzer for
editorial writing.
b. Dec 27, 1930 in Seattle, Washington
Source: *WhoAm 80, 82, 84; WhoAmW 81,
83; WhoE 81, 83*

Greenglass, David
American. Spy
Worked at Los Alamos; spied for the
Soviets, 1944-46; testified against brother-
in-law at Rosenberg trial.
b. 1922 in New York, New York
Source: *BioIn 4*

Greenhill, Basil
English. Author
b. Feb 26, 1920 in Somerset, England
Source: *Au&Wr 71; ConAu 5R, 2NR; OxCan
SUP; Who 74*

Greenough, Horatio
American. Sculptor
b. Sep 6, 1805 in Boston, Massachusetts
d. Dec 18, 1852 in Somerville, Massachusetts
Source: *Alli; AmAu; AmAu&B; AmBi;
ApCAB; BiAUS; CyAL 2; DcAmB; DcNAA;
Drake; OxAmL; REnAL; TwCBDA; WebAB;
WhAm HS*

Greenspan, Alan
American. Economist, Government Official
Chm., Council of Economic Advisers, 1974-
77.
b. Mar 6, 1926 in New York, New York
Source: *AmEA 74; AmM&WS 73S; BioNews
74; CurBio 74; St&PR 75; WhoAm 82*

Greenspan, Bud
American. Producer, Director
b. 1927
Source: *BioIn 10*

Greenspan, Martin
American. Physicist
b. May 8, 1912 in New York, New York
Source: *WhoAm 74*

Greenspun, Hank (Herman Milton)
American. Newspaper Publisher
b. Aug 27, 1909 in Brooklyn, New York
Source: *AuNews 2; ConAu 21R, P-2; WhoAm
74, 76, 78, 80, 82; WhoWorJ 72*

Greenspun, Roger
American. Movie Critic
b. 1929 in Bridgeport, Connecticut
Source: *BioIn 10; ConAu 102*

Greenstreet, Sydney Hughes
English. Actor
Best known roles in *The Maltese Falcon;
Casablanca.*
b. Dec 27, 1879 in Sandwich, England
d. Jan 19, 1954 in Los Angeles, California
Source: *BiDFilm; CmMov; CurBio 43, 54;
DcAmB S5; HolP 40; MotPP; OxFilm; Vers
A; WhScrn 74, 77; WhoHol B; WorEFlm*

Greenway, Brian
see: April Wine

Greenwood, Al
see: Foreigner

Greenwood, Charlotte
American. Actress
Comedienne best known for her high kicking
dance routines.
b. Jun 25, 1893 in Philadelphia, Pennsylvania
d. Jan 18, 1978 in Los Angeles, California
Source: *BiE&WWA; EncMT; Film 1; FilmgC;
InWom; IntMPA 77, 75; MotPP; MovMk;
NotNAT; ThFT; Vers A; WhoHol A; WhoThe
77A*

Greenwood, Chester
American. Inventor
Created the earmuff, 1873.
b. Dec 4, 1858 in Farmington, Maine
d. Jul 5, 1937 in Farmington, Maine
Source: *EncAB 10; NatCAB 27; WorAl*

Greenwood, Joan
English. Actress
Films include *The Man in the White Suit.*
b. Mar 4, 1921 in London, England
Source: *BiDFilm; BiE&WWA; CurBio 54;
FilmgC; InWom; IntMPA 75, 76, 77, 78, 79,
80, 81, 82; MotPP; MovMk; NotNAT;
OxFilm; Who 74; WhoHol A; WhoThe 77;
WorEFlm*

Greenwood, Lee
American. Singer, Songwriter
Country performer who recorded single "I O
U," 1983.
b. Oct 27, 1942 in Los Angeles, California
Source: *RkOn 85*

Greer, Germaine
Australian. Author, Educator
b. Jan 29, 1939 in Melbourne, Australia
Source: *AuNews 1; CelR; ConAu 81; CurBio
71; IntWW 74; NewYTBE 71; WhoAm 82;
WhoAmW 77; WhoWor 78; WrDr 76*

Greer, Hal (Harold Everett)
American. Basketball Player
Guard who averaged over 19 pts. per game
in NBA career, 1958-73.
b. Jun 26, 1936 in Hunington, West Virginia
Source: *InB&W 80; OfNBA 81; WhoAm 76;
WhoBbl 73; WhoBlA 77, 80*

Greer, Howard
American. Fashion Designer
b. 1896
d. Apr 20, 1974
Source: *NewYTBS 74*

Greer, Jane
American. Actress
Brief career in films *You're in the Navy Now;
Desperate Search.*
b. Sep 9, 1924 in Washington, District of
Columbia
Source: *FilmEn; FilmgC; IntMPA 75, 77;
MotPP; MovMk; WhoHol A*

Greer, Michael
American. Interior Decorator
b. Sep 19, 1917 in Monroe, Georgia
d. 1976 in New York, New York
Source: *CelR*

Greer, "Sonny" (William Alexander)
American. Musician
Drummer, Duke Ellington Orchestra for over 30 years.
b. Dec 13, 1903 in Long Branch, New Jersey
d. Mar 23, 1982 in New York, New York
Source: *CmpEPM; EncJzS 70; IlEncJ; NewYTBS 82; WhoJazz 72*

Greg, Walter Wilson, Sir
English. Bibliographer
Pres., Bibliographical Society, 1930-32; edited many Elizabethan plays.
b. 1875
d. 1959
Source: *DcLEL; OxEng; PenC ENG; REn*

Greg Kihn Band, The
[Greg Douglass; Greg Kihn; Larry Lynch; Gary Phillips; Steve Wright]
American. Music Group
Rock band formed 1975; eighth album *Kihnspiracy* contained hit single "Jeopardy," 1983.
Source: *RolSEnR 83*

Gregg, Peter
American. Auto Racer
b. May 4, 1940 in New York, New York
d. Dec 15, 1980 in Ponte Vedra Beach, Florida
Source: *BioIn 12*

Gregg, William
"Father of Southern Textile Industry"
American. Industrialist
Early cotton manufacturer; wrote *Essays on Domestic Industry,* 1845.
b. Feb 2, 1800 in Monongahela County, Virginia
d. Sep 13, 1867
Source: *AmBi; BiDConf; DcAmB; EncAB-A; McGEWB; TwCBDA; WebAB*

Gregor, Arthur
American. Poet
b. Nov 18, 1923 in Vienna, Austria
Source: *ConAu 25R; ConP 70, 75; DrAP 75; WhoAm 74, 76, 78, 80, 82; WrDr 76*

Gregorian, Vartan
American. Library Administrator, Educator
Pres., chief exec., NY Public Library, 1981--.
b. Apr 7, 1935 in Tabriz, Indiana
Source: *ConAu 29R; CurBio 85; DrAS 82H; WhoAm 80, 82, 84; WhoE 81, 83; WhoLibI 82; WhoWor 82*

Gregory XIII, Pope
[Ugo Boncompagni]
Italian. Religious Leader
Catholic reformer who created Gregorian calendar, 1582, replacing Julian calendar.
b. Jan 1, 1502 in Bologna, Italy
d. Apr 10, 1585
Source: *McGEWB; NewCol 75; WebBD 80*

Gregory the Great
[Gregory I, Pope]
Italian. Religious Leader
b. 540 in Rome, Italy
d. 604
Source: *CasWL; PenC EUR*

Gregory, Bettina Louise
American. Journalist
b. Jun 4, 1946 in New York, New York
Source: *ConAu 69; WhoAm 82*

Gregory, Cynthia Kathleen
[Mrs. John Hemminger]
American. Ballerina
Principal dancer with American Ballet Theatre, 1967--.
b. Jul 8, 1946 in Los Angeles, California
Source: *CurBio 77; WhoAm 82*

Gregory, Dick
American. Comedian, Author, Political Activist
b. Oct 12, 1932 in Saint Louis, Missouri
Source: *AmAu&B; BioNews 74; CelR; ConAu 45; CurBio 62; LivgBAA; WhoAm 74, 76, 78, 80, 82; WhoAmP 73; WhoBlA 75; WhoHol A; WrDr 76*

Gregory, Horace Victor
American. Author, Translator, Educator
Among prominent American poets; known for combining classic, contemporary lyrics; won 1965 Bollinger prize for *Collected Poems.*
b. Apr 10, 1898 in Milwaukee, Wisconsin
d. Mar 11, 1982 in Shelburne Falls, Massachusetts
Source: *AmAu&B; AnObit 1982; ChhPo S1, S2; CnDAL; ConAmA; ConAu 3NR, 5NR, 106; ConP 70, 75; DcLEL; DrAP 75; LinLib L; NewYTBS 82; OxAmL; PenC AM; RAdv 1; REn; REnAL; SixAP; TwCA, SUP; WhoAm 82; WrDr 76, 80*

Gregory, Isabella Augusta Persse, Lady
Irish. Dramatist
b. Mar 15, 1852 in Roxborough, Scotland
d. May 22, 1932 in Coole Park, Ireland
Source: *AtlBL; Chambr 3; ChhPo, S2;
DcLEL; EvLB; LongCTC; ModBrL, S1;
ModWD; PenC ENG; PlP&P; REn; REnWD;
TwCA, SUP; TwCWr; WebE&AL; WhoLA*

Gregory, James
American. Actor
Starred on Broadway in *Death of a
Salesman;* in films *PT-109; The In-Laws.*
b. Dec 23, 1911 in New York, New York
Source: *FilmgC; MotPP; MovMk; NotNAT;
VarWW 85; WhoAm 84; WhoHol A*

Gregson, John
English. Actor
Played in British TV police series "Gideon's
Way."
b. Mar 15, 1919 in Liverpool, England
d. Jan 8, 1975 in Porlock Weir, England
Source: *CmMov; FilmgC; IntMPA 75;
WhScrn 77*

Grene, Majorie
American. Author
b. Dec 13, 1910 in Milwaukee, Wisconsin
Source: *Au&Wr 71; ConAu 13R; DrAS 74P;
WhoAmW 75*

Grenfell, Joyce Irene
English. Actress
Presented her own monologues in one-woman
shows, 1939; few films as character actress
Yellow Rolls Royce.
b. Feb 10, 1910 in London, England
d. Nov 30, 1979 in London, England
Source: *BiE&WWA; ConAu 81, 89; CurBio
58, 80; EncMT; FilmgC; InWom; IntWW 74,
75, 76, 77, 78; IntWWP 77; MotPP; MovMk;
NewYTBS 79; NotNAT; OxThe; Who 74;
WhoAmM 61, 66, 68, 70, 72, 74; WhoHol A;
WhoThe 72, 77; WhoWor 74, 76, 78*

Grenfell, Wilfred Thomason, Sir
Canadian. Author, Physician, Missionary
Built hospitals, schools in Labrador,
Newfoundland; supported mission with
writings: *Adrift on an Ice-Pan,* 1909.
b. Feb 28, 1865 in Chester, England
d. Oct 9, 1940 in Charlotte, Utah
Source: *AmLY; CurBio 40; InSci; LinLib L,
S; NewC; OxCan; REn; REnAL; TwCA, SUP;
WhNAA*

Grenville, Richard
English. Naval Officer
b. 1541 in Cornwall, England
d. 1591
Source: *Alli; AmBi; ApCAB; NewC; REn*

Gres, Alix
French. Fashion Designer
b. 1899
Source: *CurBio 80; WorFshn*

Grese, Irma
"Angel of Death"; "Belle of Auschwitz";
"Blood Angel of Hell"
German. Nazi War Criminal
b. 1923
d. Dec 13, 1945 in Hamelin, Germany
Source: *BioIn 1, 7; EncTR; InWom; LookW*

Gresham, Thomas
English. Economist
b. 1520
d. Nov 21, 1579
Source: *NewC; NewCol 75; WebBD 80*

Gretchaninov, Aleksandr Tikhonovich
[Aleksandr Tikhonovich Grechaninov]
American. Composer
b. Oct 25, 1864 in Moscow, Russia
d. Jan 3, 1956 in New York, New York
Source: *NewCol 75; NewEOp 71; OxMus;
WebBD 80*

Gretry, Andre Ernest Modeste
French. Composer
b. Feb 9, 1741 in Liege, Belgium
d. Sep 24, 1813 in Montmorency, France
Source: *NewCol 75; NewEOp 71; OxMus*

Gretzky, Wayne
"The Great Gretzky"
Canadian. Hockey Player
Center, Edmonton, 1978--; has set numerous
NHL records; only player to score 100
pts. in each of first six yrs. in NHL.
b. Jan 26, 1961 in Brantford, Ontario
Source: *BioIn 11, 12; CanWW 82, 83;
CurBio 82; HocEn; HocReg 85; NewYTBS 81,
82, 84; WhoAm 84*

Greuze, Jean-Baptiste
French. Artist
b. Aug 21, 1725 in Tournus, France
d. Mar 21, 1805 in Paris, France
Source: *McGEWB; NewCol 75; OxArt*

Grevillius, Nils
Swedish. Conductor
b. 1893
d. 1970
Source: *BioIn 9*

Grew, Joseph Clark
American. Statesman
b. May 27, 1880 in Boston, Massachusetts
d. May 25, 1965 in Manchester,
   Massachusetts
Source: *AmAu&B; CurBio 41, 65; EncAB-H;
WebAB; WhAm 4; WhNAA*

Grew, Nehemiah
English. Scientist
b. 1641 in Mancetter, England
d. Mar 25, 1712 in London, England
Source: *Alli; NewCol 75; WebBD 80*

Grey, Charles
English. Statesman
b. Mar 13, 1764 in Fallodon, England
d. 1845 in Northumberland, England
Source: *McGEWB; NewCol 75*

Grey, Jane, Lady
English. Queen
Ruled for nine days; imprisoned, beheaded by
   Mary I's troops.
b. Oct 1537 in Bradgate, England
d. Feb 12, 1554 in London, England
Source: *Alli; HerW; InWom; LinLib S;
NewCol 75; REn*

Grey, Joel
[Joel Katz]
American. Singer, Actor, Dancer
Won Oscar for *Cabaret*, 1972.
b. Apr 11, 1932 in Cleveland, Ohio
Source: *CelR; CurBio 73; EncMT; IntMPA
80, 81, 82; NotNAT; St&PR 75; WhoAm 82;
WhoHol A*

Grey, Virginia
American. Actress
Began career as Little Eva in *Uncle Tom's
   Cabin*, 1927.
b. Mar 22, 1917 in Los Angeles, California
Source: *FilmEn; FilmgC; IntMPA 82;
MovMk; ThFT; WhoHol A*

Grey, Zane
American. Author
Wrote *Riders of the Purple Sage*, 1912.
b. Jan 31, 1875 in Zanesville, Ohio
d. Oct 23, 1939 in Altadena, California
Source: *AmAu&B; AmBi; ArizL; DcLEL;
DcNAA; EvLB; FilmgC; LongCTC; MnBBF;
OhA&B; OxAmL; PenC AM; REn; REnAL;
TwCA, SUP; TwCWr; WebAB; WebE&AL;
WhAm 1; WhNAA*

Grey of Fallodon, Edward
English. Statesman
b. Apr 25, 1862 in London, England
d. Sep 7, 1933
Source: *ChhPo; NewC; NewCol 75; TwCA,
SUP*

Grey Owl, pseud.
[(Archibald) George Stansfeld Belaney]
English. Naturalist, Author
Wrote best-seller on Indian lore: *Pilgrims on
   the Wild*, 1935.
b. Sep 1888 in Hastings, England
d. Apr 13, 1938 in Prince Albert,
   Saskatchewan
Source: *CanWr; CreCan 1; DcLEL; DcNAA;
OxCan*

Gribble, Harry Wagstaff Graham
English. Dramatist, Director
Wrote Broadway hit *Elizabeth and Essex*,
   1930; dircted *Johnny Belinda*, 1940.
b. Mar 27, 1896 in Sevenoaks, England
d. Jan 28, 1981 in New York, New York
Source: *BiE&WWA; ConAu 102; CurBio 45,
81; NewYTBS 81; NotNAT; WhThe*

Grieg, Edvard Hagerup
Norwegian. Composer, Musician
Wrote over 100 songs including *Peer Gynt*
   suites.
b. Jun 15, 1843 in Bergen, Norway
d. Sep 4, 1907 in Bergen, Norway
Source: *AtlBL; NewCol 75; REn*

Grier, Pamela Suzette
American. Actress
Films include *On The Edge*, 1985; *Something
   Wicked This Way Comes*, 1983; TV show
   "Roots II."
b. May 26, 1949 in Winston-Salem, North
   Carolina
Source: *BioNews 74; WhoAm 82*

Grier, Robert Cooper
American. Supreme Court Justice
Served, 1846-70.
b. Mar 5, 1794 in Cumberland County,
Pennsylvania
d. Sep 25, 1870 in Philadelphia, Pennsylvania
Source: *AmBi; ApCAB; DcAmB; Drake;
TwCBDA; WebAB; WebBD 80; WhAm HS*

Grier, "Rosey" (Roosevelt)
American. Football Player, Actor
Tackle, 1955-66; bodyguard for Robert
Kennedy when Kennedy was assassinated.
b. Jul 14, 1932 in Linden, New Jersey
Source: *NewYTBE 70, 73; WhoBlA 75;
WhoFtbl 74; WhoHol A*

Griese, Arnold
American. Author
b. Apr 13, 1921 in Lakota, Iowa
Source: *ConAu 49, 1NR; LEduc 74; SmATA
9*

Griese, Bob (Robert Allen)
American. Football Player
Quarterback, Miami Dolphins, 1967-81.
b. Feb 3, 1945 in Evansville, Indiana
Source: *CelR; WhoAm 82; WhoFtbl 74*

Grieve, Christopher Murray
see: MacDiarmid, Hugh, pseud.

Griffes, Charles Tomlinson
American. Composer
b. Sep 7, 1884 in Elmira, New York
d. Apr 8, 1920 in Elmira, New York
Source: *NewCol 75; WebBD 80*

Griffin, Archie
American. Football Player
Running back, who is only player to win
two Heisman Trophies, 1974, 1975.
b. Aug 21, 1954 in Columbus, Ohio
Source: *WhoFtbl 74*

Griffin, Bob (Robert Paul)
American. Politician, Lawyer
Senator from MI, 1966-79.
b. Nov 6, 1923 in Detroit, Michigan
Source: *BiDrAC; CngDr 74; CurBio 60;
IntWW 74, 75, 76, 77, 78, 79, 80, 81;
NewYTBE 72; WhoAm 74, 76, 78, 80, 82;
WhoAmP 73; WhoGov 75; WhoMW 74;
WhoWor 78*

Griffin, Dale
[Mott the Hoople]
"Buffin"
English. Musician
Drummer with hard-rock group, 1969-74.
b. Oct 24, 1948 in Ross-on-Wye, England
Source: *NF*

Griffin, John Howard
American. Author, Photographer
Chemically blackened skin to better
understand racial problems in US; wrote
Black Like Me, 1961.
b. Jun 16, 1920 in Dallas, Texas
d. Sep 9, 1980 in Fort Worth, Texas
Source: *AmAu&B; Au&Wr 71; AuNews 1;
ConAu 2NR, 101; Who 76; WhoAm 74;
WhoRel 75; WhoWor 74; WorAu*

Griffin, Marvin (Samuel Marvin)
American. Politician, Publisher
Governor of GA, 1955-59; George Wallace's
vp running mate, 1968.
b. Sep 4, 1907 in Bainbridge, Georgia
d. Jun 13, 1982 in Tallahassee, Florida
Source: *BiDrGov; ConAu 108; WhoAmP 77,
79*

Griffin, Merv(yn)
American. Entertainer, TV Host
b. Jul 6, 1925 in San Mateo, California
Source: *BkPepl; CelR; CurBio 67; IntMPA
75, 76, 77, 78, 79, 80, 81, 82; WhoAm 74,
76, 78, 80, 82; WhoHol A*

Griffis, Stanton
American. Banker, Author
b. May 2, 1887 in Boston, Massachusetts
d. Aug 29, 1974 in New York, New York
Source: *CurBio 44, 74; NewYTBS 74; St&PR
75; WhAm 6; WhoAm 74*

Griffith, Andy (Andrew)
American. Actor
Broadway debut *No Time for Sergeants*,
1955; starred in "Andy Griffith Show,"
1960-69.
b. Jun 1, 1926 in Mount Airy, North
Carolina
Source: *BiE&WWA; BioNews 74; CelR;
CurBio 60; FilmgC; IntMPA 75, 76, 77, 78,
79, 80, 81, 82; MotPP; WhoAm 74, 76, 78,
80, 82; WhoHol A*

Griffith, Clark Calvin
"Old Fox"
American. Baseball Player, Baseball Executive
Owner, Washington Senators, Minnesota
Twins, 1920-55; Hall of Fame, 1946.
b. Nov 20, 1869 in Stringtown, Missouri
d. Oct 27, 1955 in Washington, District of
Columbia
Source: *BaseEn 85; BioIn 2, 3, 4, 7; CurBio
50, 56; WhAm 3; WhoProB 73*

Griffith, Corinne
American. Actress
Novel *Papa's Delicate Condition*, filmed, 1963;
known as "Orchid Lady" for her beauty.
b. Nov 24, 1896 in Texarkana, Texas
d. Jul 13, 1979 in Santa Monica, California
Source: *AmSCAP 66; FilmEn; Film 1;
FilmgC; MotPP; MovMk; ThFT; TwYS;
WhoHol A*

Griffith, Darrell Steven
"Dr. Dunkenstein"
American. Basketball Player
b. Jun 16, 1958 in Louisville, Kentucky
Source: *BioIn 10*

Griffith, D(avid Lewelyn) W(ark)
American. Director, Actor
Introduced techniques that changed movies
into art form; films include *Birth of a
Nation*, 1915.
b. Jan 22, 1875 in La Grange, Kentucky
d. Jul 23, 1948 in Los Angeles, California
Source: *BiDFilm; CmMov; DcAmB S4; DcFM;
EncAB-H; Film 1; FilmgC; MovMk; OxAmL;
OxFilm; REn; REnAL; TwYS; WebAB;
WhAm 2; WhScrn 74, 77; WhoHol B;
WomWMM; WorEFlm*

Griffith, Emile Alphonse
American. Boxer
b. Feb 3, 1938 in Virgin Islands
Source: *BioIn 6, 7, 10, 11; WhoBox 74*

Griffith, Hugh Emrys
Welsh. Actor
Won Oscar for *Ben Hur*, 1959.
b. May 30, 1912 in Anglesey, Wales
d. May 14, 1980 in London, England
Source: *BiE&WWA; FilmgC; IntMPA 75, 76,
77; MotPP; MovMk; NotNAT; Who 74;
WhoHol A; WhoThe 77*

Griffith, Melanie
American. Actress
Films include *Night Moves; Smile; The
Drowning Pool*.
b. Aug 9, 1957 in New York, New York
Source: *BioIn 10; WhoHol A*

Griffiths, John Willis
American. Architect
b. Oct 6, 1809 in New York, New York
d. Mar 30, 1882 in Brooklyn, New York
Source: *AmBi; ApCAB; DcAmB; Drake;
TwCBDA; WebAB; WebAMB; WhAm HS*

Griffiths, Martha Wright
American. Politician, Lawyer
Dem. lt.-governor of MI, 1982--.
b. Jan 29, 1912 in Pierce City, Missouri
Source: *BiDrAC; BioNews 74; CngDr 74;
CurBio 55; InWom; NewYTBE 70; Ward 77;
WhoAm 74, 76, 78; WhoAmP 73; WhoAmW
61, 64, 66, 68, 70, 72, 74, 75; WhoGov 75;
WhoMW 74*

Griffiths, Ronald
see: Badfinger

Grigorovich, Yuri Nikolaevich
Russian. Ballet Dancer
b. Jan 1, 1927
Source: *IntWW 74; WhoWor 78*

Grigson, Geoffrey Edward Harvey
English. Author, Poet
b. Mar 2, 1902 in Pelynt, England
Source: *Au&Wr 71; AuBYP; ChhPo, S1, S2;
ConAu 25R; ConLC 7; ConP 70, 75; DcLEL;
EvLB; IntWW 74; LongCTC; ModBrL, S1;
NewC; PenC ENG; REn; TwCA SUP; Who
74; WhoTwCL; WhoWor 78; WrDr 80*

Grillo, John
English. Dramatist, Actor
Bizarre plays include *Hello Goodbye
Sebastian*, 1965.
b. Nov 29, 1942 in Watford, England
Source: *ConAu 117; ConDr 82*

Grillparzer, Franz
Austrian. Dramatist
b. Jan 15, 1791 in Vienna, Austria
d. Jan 21, 1872 in Vienna, Austria
Source: *AtlBL; BbD; BiD&SB; CasWL;
CnThe; CyWA; DcEuL; EuAu; EvEuW;
McGEWD; OxGer; OxThe; PenC EUR;
RComWL; REn; REnWD*

Grimaldi, Princess Grace
see: Kelly, Grace Patricia

Grimaldi, Joseph
English. Clown
b. Dec 18, 1779
d. May 31, 1837
Source: *NewC; NewCol 75; OxThe; PIP&P*

Grimaldi, Rainier III
see: Rainier, Prince

Grimes, Burleigh Arland
"Ol' Stubblebeard"
American. Baseball Player
Hall of Fame pitcher who was last to legally
throw a spitball.
b. Aug 18, 1893 in Clear Lake, Wisconsin
d. Dec 10, 1985 in Clear Lake, Wisconsin
Source: *BaseEn 85; WhoProB 73*

Grimes, J William
American. TV Executive
Chm., chief exec., cable sports network,
ESPN, 1982--.
b. Mar 7, 1941 in Wheeling, West Virginia
Source: *Dun&B 79; WhoAm 84; WhoTelC*

Grimes, Martha
American. Author, Educator
Wrote mystery novels: *The Anodyne
Necklace*, 1983.
b. in Pittsburgh, Pennsylvania
Source: *ConAu 117*

Grimes, Tammy Lee
American. Actress, Singer, Dancer
Won Tonys for *Unsinkable Molly Brown*,
1961; *Private Lives*, 1970; married
Christopher Plummer, 1956-60.
b. Jan 30, 1936 in Lynn, Massachusetts
Source: *BiE&WWA; CelR; CurBio 62;
EncMT; InWom; MotPP; NotNAT; WhoAm
74, 76, 78, 80, 82; WhoHol A; WhoThe 77;
WhoWor 78*

Grimke, Charlotte Lottie Forten
[Lottie, pseud.]
American. Author, Educator
Wrote *Journal of Charlotte L Foster*,
published 1953, depicting blacks in 19th c.
America.
b. Aug 17, 1837 in Philadelphia,
Pennsylvania
d. Jul 23, 1914 in Washington, District of
Columbia
Source: *BlkAmW 1; ConAu 117; NotAW*

Grimm, Charlie (Charles John)
"Jolly Cholly"
American. Baseball Player, Baseball Manager
First baseman, 1916-36; managed Chicago
Cubs to three pennants.
b. Aug 28, 1899 in Saint Louis, Missouri
d. Nov 15, 1983 in Scottsdale, Arizona
Source: *BaseEn 85; NewYTBS 83; WhoProB
73*

Grimm, Jakob Ludwig Karl
[Grimm Brothers]
German. Children's Author
Best known for collection of German folk
tales, *Grimm's Fairy Tales*, 1812-15.
b. Jan 4, 1785 in Hanau, Germany
d. Sep 20, 1863 in Berlin, Germany
Source: *AnCL; AtlBL; AuBYP; BbD;
BiD&SB; CarSB; CasWL; ChhPo; DcEuL;
EuAu; EvEuW; FamSYP; NewC; OxEng;
OxGer; PenC EUR; REn; Str&VC; WhoChL*

Grimm, Wilhelm Karl
[Grimm Brothers]
German. Children's Author
Best known for collection of German folk
tales, *Grimm's Fairy Tales*, 1812-15.
b. Feb 24, 1786 in Hanau, Germany
d. Dec 16, 1859 in Berlin, Germany
Source: *AnCL; AtlBL; AuBYP; BiD&SB;
CarSB; CasWL; ChhPo, S2; DcEuL; EuAu;
EvEuW; FamSYP; OxEng; OxGer; PenC
EUR; REn; Str&VC*

Grimsby, Roger
American. Journalist
Source: *NF*

Gripe, Maria
Swedish. Author
b. Jul 25, 1923 in Vaxholm, Sweden
Source: *ConAu 29R; SmATA 2*

Gris, Juan
[Jose Victoriano Gonzales]
Spanish. Artist
b. Mar 13, 1887 in Madrid, Spain
d. May 11, 1927 in Paris, France
Source: *AtlBL; NewCol 75*

Grisi, Guilia
Italian. Opera Singer
b. Jul 28, 1811 in Milan, Italy
d. Nov 29, 1869 in Berlin, Germany
Source: *InWom; NewCol 75*

Grissom, Virgil Ivan
"Gus"
American. Astronaut
Third man in space, 1961; killed during
simulation of Apollo I launching.
b. Apr 3, 1926 in Mitchell, Indiana
d. Jan 27, 1967 in Cape Canaveral, Florida
Source: *CurBio 65, 67; WhAm 4*

Grist, Reri
American. Opera Singer
b. 1934 in New York, New York
Source: *IntWW 74; NewYTBE 70; WhoAm
74; WhoBlA 75; WhoMus 72; WhoWor 78*

Griswold, A Whitney
American. Educator, Historian
b. Oct 27, 1906 in Morristown, New Jersey
d. Apr 19, 1963 in New Haven, Connecticut
Source: *AmAu&B; CurBio 50, 63; WhAm 4*

Grivas, George Theodorus
Cypriot. Military Leader
Led right-wing guerilla group, EOKA, to
unite Cyprus with Greece, 1955-59.
b. Mar 23, 1898 in Trikomo, Cyprus
d. Jan 27, 1974 in Limassol, Cyprus
Source: *BioIn 5, 6, 7, 10; CurBio 64, 74;
NewCol 75*

Grizzard, George
American. Actor
Broadway appearences include *The Happiest
Millionaire,* 1958; *The Country Girl,* 1972;
The Royal Family, 1975.
b. Apr 1, 1928 in Roanoke Rapids, North
Carolina
Source: *BiE&WWA; FilmgC; IntMPA 82;
NewYTBE 72; NotNAT; PIP&P; WhoAm 74,
76, 78, 80, 82; WhoHol A; WhoThe 81;
WhoWor 74*

Groat, Dick (Richard Morrow)
American. Baseball Player
b. Nov 4, 1930 in Swissvale, Pennsylvania
Source: *BaseEn 85; CurBio 61; WhoBbl 73;
WhoProB 73*

Grodin, Charles
American. Actor, Director, Writer
Films include *Heartbreak Kid,* 1972; *The
Woman in Red,* 1984; *Movers and Shakers,*
1985.
b. Apr 21, 1935 in Pittsburgh, Pennsylvania
Source: *BioIn 9, 11; CelR; IntMPA 78, 79,
80, 81; NotNAT; WhoAm 74, 76, 80, 82;
WhoHol A; WhoThe 77, 81*

Grofe, Ferde
American. Composer
Wrote *Grand Canyon Suite,* 1931.
b. Mar 27, 1892 in New York, New York
d. Apr 3, 1972 in Santa Monica, California
Source: *CurBio 40; NewYTBE 72; WebAB;
WhAm 5*

Grogan, Emmett
American. Author
b. Nov 28, 1942 in Brooklyn, New York
Source: *ConAu 41R*

Grogan, Steve
American. Football Player
b. Jul 24, 1958 in San Antonio, Texas
Source: *BioIn 11; WhoAm 82*

Groh, David Lawrence
American. Actor
Played Joe Girard on TV series, "Rhoda."
b. May 21, 1939 in New York, New York
Source: *VarWW 85; WhoAm 82, 84*

Grol, Lini Richards
Dutch. Author, Illustrator
b. Oct 7, 1913 in Nijmegen, Netherlands
Source: *ConAu 61; SmATA 9*

Grolier, Jean
[Jean Grolier de Servieres]
French. Government Official
Known for collection of 3,000 bound books;
NY bibliophile club, the Grolier Club,
named for him, 1884.
b. 1479 in Lyon, France
d. Oct 22, 1565 in Paris, France
Source: *DcBiPP; NewCol 75; OxDecA*

Gromyko, Andrei Andreevich
Russian. Diplomat
Soviet foreign affairs minister, 1957-85;
member, ruling Politboro, 1973--.
b. Jul 5, 1909 in Starye Gromyky, Russia
Source: *CurBio 43, 58; IntWW 74, 75, 76,
77, 78, 79, 80, 81; IntYB 78, 79, 80, 81;
Who 74; WhoSocC 78; WhoWor 74, 76, 78*

Gronchi, Giovanni
Italian. Politician
b. Sep 10, 1887 in Pontedera, Italy
d. Oct 17, 1978 in Rome, Italy
Source: *CurBio 55; IntWW 74; Who 74*

Groom, Bob (Robert)
American. Baseball Player
Pitcher, 1909-18.
b. Sep 12, 1884 in Belleville, Illinois
d. Feb 19, 1948 in Belleville, Illinois
Source: *BaseEn 85; WhoProB 73*

Grooms, "Red" (Charles Roger)
American. Artist
Produces unmatched, experimental films;
mixed-media constructions.
b. Jun 2, 1937 in Nashville, Tennessee
Source: *BioIn 7, 9, 10; ConArt 77; CurBio
72; DcAmArt; DcCAA 71, 77; WhoAm 74,
76, 78, 80, 82; WhoAmA 73, 76, 78*

Groote, Gerhard
Dutch. Mystic, Reformer
b. 1340 in Deventer, Netherlands
d. 1384
Source: *NewCol 75; WebBD 80*

Gropius, Walter Adolf
German. Architect, Author
Wrote *The New Architecture and the Bauhaus,* 1935.
b. May 18, 1883 in Berlin, Germany
d. Jul 5, 1969 in Boston, Massachusetts
Source: *AmAu&B; AtlBL; ConAu 25R; CurBio 41, 52, 69; NewCol 75; REn; WebAB; WhAm 5*

Gropper, William
American. Artist
b. Dec 3, 1897 in New York, New York
d. Jan 6, 1977 in Manhasset, New York
Source: *AmAu&B; Au&Wr 71; CurBio 40; DcCAA 71; IlsCB 1946; IntWW 74; REnAL; WebAB; Who 74; WhoAm 74; WhoAmA 73; WhoWor 78; WhoWorJ 72*

Groppi, James E
American. Political Activist, Priest
Former priest who gained national attention by leading 200 consecutive marches in support of open housing in Milwaukee, 1960s.
b. 1930 in Milwaukee, Wisconsin
d. Nov 4, 1985 in Milwaukee, Wisconsin
Source: *NewCol 75; NewYTBE 70; WhoMW 74*

Gross, Chaim
American. Artist
b. Mar 17, 1904 in Austria
Source: *AmAu&B; CurBio 41, 66; DcCAA 71; NewYTBS 74; WhoAm 74, 76, 78, 80, 82; WhoAmA 73; WhoWor 78; WhoWorJ 72*

Gross, Courtlandt Sherrington
American. Airline Executive
Co-founded Lockheed Aircraft Corp.
b. Nov 21, 1904 in Boston, Massachusetts
d. Jul 16, 1982 in Villanova, Pennsylvania
Source: *AnObit 1982; IntWW 75, 76, 77; NewYTBS 82; St&PR 75; WhoAm 74, 76, 78; WhoE 74; WhoF&I 74*

Gross, Michael
American. Actor
Plays Steven Keaton on TV series "Family Ties," 1982--.
b. Jun 21, 1947 in Chicago, Illinois
Source: *NewYTBS 84; VarWW 85*

Gross, Milt
American. Author, Cartoonist
b. Mar 4, 1895 in New York, New York
d. Nov 29, 1953
Source: *AmAu&B; DcAmB S5; REnAL; WhAm 3*

Gross, Robert Ellsworth
American. Aircraft Manufacturer
Bought Lockheed Aircraft Corp., 1932; developed Polaris missile.
b. May 11, 1897 in Boston, Massachusetts
d. Sep 3, 1961 in Santa Monica, California
Source: *ObitOF 79; WhAm 4*

Grossinger, Jennie
American. Hotel Executive
Owned Grossinger's, noted Catskill mountain resort.
b. Jun 16, 1892 in Vienna, Austria
d. Nov 20, 1972 in Sullivan County, New York
Source: *CurBio 56, 73; InWom; NewYTBE 72; WhAm 5*

Grossman, Lawrence K
American. Broadcasting Executive
Pres. of PBS, 1976-83; pres. of NBC News, 1984--.
b. Jun 21, 1931 in Brooklyn, New York
Source: *LesBEnT; NewYTET; WhoAm 80, 82, 84; WhoF&I 83; WhoTelC*

Grosvenor, Gerald Cavendish
[Duke of Westminster]
English. Businessman
Controls international property empire, making him Britain's richest man.
b. Dec 22, 1951 in London, England
Source: *NewYTBS 84; Who 85*

Grosvenor, Gilbert Hovey
American. Geographer
b. Oct 28, 1875 in Constantinople, Turkey
d. Feb 4, 1966 in Baddeck, Nova Scotia
Source: *AmAu&B; CurBio 46, 66; REnAL; WebAB; WhAm 4; WhNAA*

Grosvenor, Melville Bell
American. Publisher, Editor
Pres., National Geographic Society, 1957-67; edited magazine, 1957-77.
b. Nov 26, 1901 in Washington, District of Columbia
d. Apr 22, 1982 in Miami, Florida
Source: *AmAu&B; AmM&WS 73S, 76P; AnObit 1982; CelR; ConAu 69; CurBio 60, 82; IntWW 79; LinLib L, S; WhoAm 80, 82; WhoGov 72, 77; WhoS&SW 76; WhoWor 76*

Grosz, George Ehrenfried
American. Artist
Violent drawings were social critiques.
b. Jul 26, 1893 in Berlin, Germany
d. Jul 6, 1959 in Berlin, Germany (West)
Source: *AmAu&B; AtlBL; CurBio 42, 59; DcCAA 71; OxGer; REn; WhAm 3; WhoGrA 62*

Grote, George
English. Historian, Philosopher
Wrote classic *History of Greece*, 1845-56.
b. Nov 17, 1794
d. Jun 18, 1871
Source: *Alli; SUP; BbD; BiD&SB; BrAu 19; Chambr 3; DcEnA; DcEnL; DcEuL; DcLEL; EvLB; NewC; NewCol 75; OxEng; PenC ENG; REn*

Groth, John August
American. Artist, Journalist
b. Feb 26, 1908 in Chicago, Illinois
Source: *ConAu 101; CurBio 43; SmATA 21; WhoAm 74, 76, 78, 80, 82; WhoAmA 73*

Grotius, Hugo
Dutch. Judge, Statesman, Theologian, Scholar
Beliefs in conscience of humanity influenced American thinking; wrote *De Jure Belli et Pacis*, 1625.
b. Apr 10, 1583 in Delft, Netherlands
d. Aug 28, 1645 in Rostock, Germany
Source: *BbD; BiD&SB; CasWL; DcEuL; EuAu; EvEuW; McGEWB; NewC; NewCol 75; OxEng; REn*

Group of Seven
[Frank Carmichael; Lauren Harris; A(lexander) Y(oung) Jackson; Frank Johnston; Arthur Lismer; J(ames) E(dward) H(ervey) MacDonald; F(rederick) H(orseman) Varley]
Canadian. Artists
Canadian art movement inspired by northern Ontario landscapes; offically formed, exhibited, 1920.
Source: *ClbCR*

Grove, George, Sir
English. Author
b. Aug 13, 1820 in Clapham, England
d. May 18, 1900 in London, England
Source: *Alli SUP; BiD&SB; Chambr 3; DcEnL; NewC; NewCol 75; OxEng; REn; WebBD 80*

Grove, "Lefty" (Robert Moses)
"Mose"
American. Baseball Player
Pitcher, 1925-41; struck out 2,266 batters.
b. Mar 6, 1900 in Lonaconing, Maryland
d. May 22, 1975 in Norwalk, Ohio
Source: *BaseEn 85; BioIn 2, 3, 4, 6, 7, 8, 9, 10; NewCol 75; WhoProB 73*

Grove, Frederick Philip
Canadian. Editor, Author
Wrote novels of Canadian pioneer life: *Our Daily Bread*, 1928.
b. Feb 14, 1872 in Sweden
d. Aug 18, 1948 in Simcoe, Ontario
Source: *CanNov; CanWr; CasWL; DcLEL; EncSF; LinLib L; LongCTC; McGEWB; ModCmwL; OxCan; PenC ENG; REnAL; WebE&AL; WhNAA*

Grove, William Robert, Sir
Welsh. Physicist
b. Jul 11, 1811 in Swansea, Wales
d. Aug 2, 1896
Source: *AsBiEn; BioIn 7; DcScB; WebBD 80*

Groves, Charles, Sir
English. Composer
Leads major British operas, orchestras; with Royal Philharmonic since 1967.
b. Mar 10, 1915 in London, England
Source: *IntWW 74, 75, 76, 77, 78; Who 74; WhoMus 72; WhoWor 74, 76, 78*

Groves, Leslie Richard
American. Army Officer
b. Aug 17, 1896 in Albany, New York
d. Jul 13, 1970 in Washington, District of Columbia
Source: *CurBio 45, 70; NewYTBE 70; WhAm 5*

Groza, Alex
[Fabulous Five]
American. Basketball Player
b. Oct 7, 1926 in Martins Ferry, Ohio
Source: *WhoBbl 73*

Gruber, Frank
American. Author
b. Feb 2, 1904 in Elmer, Minnesota
d. Dec 9, 1969
Source: *AmAu&B; ConAu 25R, P-1; CurBio 41, 70; EncMys; FilmgC*

Gruber, Franz
German. Musician
Wrote music for Christmas hymn, "Silent Night," 1818.
b. 1787 in Germany
d. 1863
Source: *NewCol 75; WebBD 80*

Grubert, Carl Alfred
American. Military Leader
Youngest four-star general in history, 1951;
commander of NATO, 1953-56; pres. of
American Red Cross, 1957-64.
b. Sep 10, 1911 in Chicago, Illinois
d. May 30, 1983 in Washington, District of
Columbia
Source: *CurBio 83N; NewYTBS 83; WhoAm
74; WhoAmA 73*

Gruelle, Johnny (John Barton)
American. Cartoonist, Author
Created *Raggedy Ann,* 1918, *Raggedy Andy,*
1920 series.
b. Dec 24, 1880 in Arcola, Illinois
d. Jan 9, 1938 in Miami Beach, Florida
Source: *AmAu&B; AmSCAP 66; ChhPo;
FanAl; IndAu 1816; OhA&B; REnAL*

Gruen, Victor
American. Architect
Specialized in planning, building shopping
centers in US.
b. Jul 18, 1903 in Vienna, Austria
d. Feb 16, 1980 in Vienna, Austria
Source: *AmArch 70; AnObit 1980; CurBio 59,
80; EncMA; IntAu&W 77; IntWW 74, 75,
76, 77, 78, 79; McGDA; NewCol 75;
NewYTBS 80; WhoWor 74, 76, 78; WrDr 76,
80*

Gruenberg, Louis
American. Composer
Wrote opera *The Emperor Jones,* 1933.
b. Aug 3, 1884 in Russia
d. Jun 9, 1964 in Beverly Hills, California
Source: *AmSCAP 66; DcCM; NewCol 75;
OxAmL; WhAm 4*

Gruenberg, Sidonie Matsner
American. Author, Educator
Wrote *The Wonderful Story of How You
Were Born,* 1952.
b. Jun 10, 1881 in Vienna, Austria
d. Mar 11, 1974 in New York, New York
Source: *BioIn 10; ConAu 49, P-1*

Gruenther, Alfred Maximillian
American. Army Officer, Businessman
b. Mar 3, 1899 in Platte Center, Nebraska
Source: *CurBio 50; IntWW 74; NewCol 75;
Who 74; WhoAm 74; WhoGov 75; WhoWor
78*

Grumman, Leroy Randle
American. Aeronautical Engineer
Began Grumman Aircraft, 1929; receipts
today total $1.9 billion.
b. Jan 4, 1895 in Huntington, New York
d. Oct 4, 1982 in Manhasset, New York
Source: *AnObit 1982; CurBio 45, 83; IntWW
80; NewYTBS 82; WebAB; WhoAm 74;
WhoWor 74*

Grundy, Hugh
[The Zombies]
English. Singer, Musician
b. Mar 6, 1945 in Winchester, England
Source: *NF*

Grunewald, Matthias
[Mathis Gothart Nithart]
German. Artist, Architect, Engineer
b. 1470 in Wurzburg, Germany
d. 1528 in Halle, Germany
Source: *AtlBL; NewCol 75; OxGer; REn*

Guadagni, Gaetano
Italian. Opera Singer
b. 1725 in Lodi, Italy
d. Nov 1792 in Padua, Italy
Source: *NewEOp 71*

Guardi, Francesco
Italian. Artist
Noted for imaginary landscapes, views of
Venice.
b. Oct 5, 1712 in Venice, Italy
d. Jan 1, 1793 in Venice, Italy
Source: *AtlBL; NewCol 75; REn*

Guardini, Romano
Italian. Religious Leader, Philosopher
Leading Catholic theologian who founded
German Catholic Youth Movement after
WW II.
b. Feb 17, 1885 in Verona, Italy
d. Oct 1, 1968 in Munich, Germany (West)
Source: *CathA 1930*

Guardino, Harry
American. Actor
Played on Broadway in *Woman of the Year* ;
films include *Dirty Harry,* 1971; *Any
Which Way You Can,* 1980.
b. Dec 23, 1925 in New York, New York
Source: *BiE&WWA; FilmgC; IntMPA 75, 76,
77, 78, 79, 80, 81, 82; MovMk; WhoAm 82*

Guare, John
American. Dramatist
Won 1971 Tony for best musical: *Two Gentlemen of Verona.*
b. Feb 5, 1938 in New York, New York
Source: *CelR; ConAu 73; ConDr 73, 77; ConLC 8, 14; CurBio 82; NatPD 81; NotNAT; PlP&P A; WhoAm 74, 76, 78, 80, 82; WhoE 74; WhoThe 77, 81; WorAu 1975; WrDr 76, 80*

Guarnieri, Giuseppe Antonio
[Guarneri DelGesu]
Italian. Violin Maker
b. Jun 8, 1683 in Cremona, Italy
d. 1745
Source: *BioIn 10; NewCol 75; WebBD 80*

Guarnicri, Johnny (John A)
American. Jazz Musician
Jazz pianist who performed with Benny Goodman and Artie Shaw bands during the Swing Era.
b. Mar 23, 1917 in New York, New York
d. Jan 7, 1985 in Livingston, New Jersey
Source: *AmSCAP 66; WhoJazz 72*

Guarrera, Frank
American. Opera Singer
b. Dec 3, 1923 in Philadelphia, Pennsylvania
Source: *WhoAm 74, 76, 78, 80, 82*

Guber, Peter (Howard Peter)
American. Producer
Produced *Missing,* 1982; *Flashdance,* 1983.
b. Mar 1, 1942 in Boston, Massachusetts
Source: *ConTFT 2; VarWW 85*

Gubitosi, Mickey
see: Our Gang

Gucci, Aldo
Italian. Designer
b. May 26, 1909 in Florence, Italy
Source: *CelR; WhoAm 82; WorFshn*

Gucci, Guccio
Italian. Merchant, Manufacturer
Made Gucci loafer, other leather goods, beginning 1906.
b. 1881
d. 1953
Source: *Entr; WorFshn*

Gucci, Maurizio
Italian. Business Executive
Nephew of Aldo Gucci named pres. of Guccio Gucci, Gucci Shops, Nov 1984.
b. 1948 in Florence, Italy
Source: *ConNews 85-4*

Gucci, Rodolfo
Italian. Fashion Designer
With brothers, made Gucci name synonymous with quality, elegance in fashion.
b. 1902
d. May 15, 1983 in Milan, Italy
Source: *WorFshn*

Guccione, Bob (Robert Charles Joseph Edward Sabatini)
American. Publisher
Founder, publisher magazines *Penthouse,* 1965; *Omni,* 1978; *Spin,* 1985.
b. Dec 17, 1930 in Brooklyn, New York
Source: *CelR; ConNews 86-1; WhoAm 82*

Guderian, Heinz Wilhelm
German. Military Leader
Army general who developed concept of blitzkrieg warfare during WW II.
b. Jul 17, 1888 in Kulm, Prussia
d. May 15, 1954 in Fussen, Germany (West)
Source: *BioIn 3, 10, 11; EncTR; ObitT 1951; WhWW-II; WhoMilH 76*

Gueden, Hilde
Austrian. Opera Singer
b. Sep 15, 1917 in Vienna, Austria
Source: *CurBio 55; WhoMus 72; WhoWor 78*

Guenther, Charles John
American. Librarian, Author
b. Apr 29, 1920 in Saint Louis, Missouri
Source: *BiDrLUS 70; ConAu 29R; DrAP 75; WhoAm 74, 76, 78, 80, 82; WrDr 76*

Guerard, Albert Joseph
American. Author, Educator
b. Nov 2, 1914 in Houston, Texas
Source: *AmAu&B; ConAu 1R, 2NR; ConNov 72, 76; DrAF 76; DrAS 74E; OxAmL; TwCA SUP; WhoAm 74, 76, 78, 80, 82; WhoWest 84; WrDr 76*

Guercino
[Giovanni Francesco Barbieri]
Italian. Artist
Religious, Baroque artist, painted illusionistic ceiling at Villa Ludovisi, Rome, 1621.
b. 1591 in Cento, Italy
d. 1666 in Bologna, Italy
Source: *AtlBL; McGDA; McGEWB; NewCol 75; WebBD 80*

Guerin, Jules
American. Artist
b. 1866 in Saint Louis, Missouri
d. Jun 13, 1946 in Neptune, New Jersey
Source: *ChhPo; NewCol 75; WhAm 2*

Guerlain, Pierre Francois Pascal
French. Manufacturer
b. 1798
d. 1864
Source: *WebBD 80*

Guerrero, Pedro
Dominican. Baseball Player
b. Jun 2, 1956 in San Pedro, Dominican
  Republic
Source: *BaseEn 85*

Guess Who
[Chad Allan; Bob Ashley; Randy Bachman;
  Burton Cummings; Bruce Decker; David
  Inglish; Jim Kale; Greg Leskiw; Vance
  Masters; Don McDougall; Garry Peterson;
  Domenic Troiano; Bill Wallace; Ralph
  Watts; Kurt Winter]
Canadian. Music Group
Top Canadian band, 1960s-70s; hit singles
  "These Eyes," 1969; "No Time," 1970.
Source: *EncPR&S 74; RolSEnR 83*

Guest, Edgar A(lbert)
American. Author, Journalist, Poet
Began career at Detroit *Free Press,* 1895;
  hosted radio show, 1931-42.
b. Aug 20, 1881 in Birmingham, England
d. Aug 5, 1959 in Detroit, Michigan
Source: *AmAu&B; ChhPo, S1, S2; CnE&AP;
CurBio 41, 59; OxAmL; PenC AM; REn;
REnAL; WebAB; WhAm 3; WhNAA*

Guest, Judith
American. Author
Wrote *Ordinary People,* 1976; made into
  Oscar-winning movie, 1980.
b. Mar 29, 1936 in Detroit, Michigan
Source: *ConAu 77; ConLC 8; WhoAm 82*

Guevara, Che Ernesto
Argentine. Revolutionary
b. Jun 14, 1928 in Rosario, Argentina
d. Oct 8, 1967 in Bolivia
Source: *CurBio 63, 67*

Guevara Arze, Walter
Bolivian. President
b. 1912
Source: *BioIn 12; IntWW 74; WhoGov 75;
WhoWor 78*

Guffey, Burnett
American. Filmmaker
Won Oscars for *From Here to Eternity,* 1953;
  Bonnie and Clyde, 1967.
b. May 26, 1905 in Del Rio, Tennessee
d. May 30, 1983 in Goleta Valley, California
Source: *CmMov; DcFM; FilmgC; IntMPA 81,
82; WorEFlm*

Guggenheim, Daniel
American. Financier, Philanthropist
b. 1856 in Philadelphia, Pennsylvania
d. Sep 28, 1930
Source: *AmBi; DcAmB; EncAB-H; NewCol
75; WebAB; WhAm 1*

Guggenheim, Harry Frank
American. Industrialist, Publisher
b. Aug 23, 1890 in West End, New Jersey
d. Jan 22, 1971 in Sands Point, New York
Source: *ConAu 89; CurBio 56, 71; NewCol
75; NewYTBE 71*

Guggenheim, Meyer
American. Industrialist, Philanthropist
Founder of Guggenheim fortune who acquired
  near-monopoly in copper industry.
b. Feb 1, 1828 in Langnau, Switzerland
d. Mar 15, 1905 in Palm Beach, Florida
Source: *AmBi; DcAmB; WebAB; WebBD 80*

Guggenheim, Peggy Marguerite
American. Art Collector, Socialite
Collected 20th c. art; patron to Jackson
  Pollock, Robert Motherwell.
b. Aug 26, 1898 in New York, New York
d. Dec 23, 1979 in Venice, Italy
Source: *Au&Wr 71; CelR; ConAu 105;
CurBio 62; InWom; IntWW 74; NewYTBS
74; WhoAm 74; WhoAmA 73; WhoWor 74*

Guggenheim, Solomon Robert
American. Philanthropist
b. Feb 2, 1861 in Philadelphia, Pennsylvania
d. Nov 3, 1949 in Sands Point, New York
Source: *DcAmB S4; NewCol 75; WhAm 2*

Guggenheimer, Minnie
American. Philanthropist
b. Oct 22, 1882 in New York, New York
d. May 23, 1966 in New York, New York
Source: *CurBio 62, 66; WhAm 4*

Gui, Vittorio
Italian. Conductor
b. Sep 14, 1885 in Rome, Italy
d. Oct 16, 1975 in Florence, Italy
Source: *IntWW 74; Who 74; WhoMus 72*

Guicciardini, Francesco
Italian. Historian, Statesman
b. Mar 6, 1483 in Florence, Italy
d. May 1540 in Florence, Italy
Source: *BiD&SB; CasWL; DcEuL; EuAu;
EvEuW; NewC; OxEng; PenC EUR; REn*

Guidry, Ron(ald Ames)
American. Baseball Player
Pitcher, NY Yankees, 1975--; won Cy Young
   Award, 1978.
b. Aug 28, 1950 in Lafayette, Louisiana
Source: *BaseEn 85; BioIn 11; WhoAm 82*

Guilbert, Yvette
French. Singer
Favorite Paris, London cabaret performer
   whose long black gloves were trademark.
b. 1867 in Paris, France
d. Feb 2, 1944 in Aix-en-Provence, France
Source: *EncWT; Film 2; InWom; NotNAT B;
OxThe; WhAm 4; WhThe*

Guillaume, Gunter
German. Spy
Source: *BioIn 10*

Guillaume, Robert
[Robert Peter Williams]
American. Actor
Star of TV series "Benson."
b. Nov 30, 1937 in Saint Louis, Missouri
Source: *BioIn 11; IntMPA 82*

Guillemin, Roger
French. Physiologist
b. Jan 11, 1924 in Dijon, France
Source: *AmM&WS 73P; WhoAm 74, 76, 78,
80, 82*

Guillen, Jorge
Spanish. Poet
Member, "Generation of 1927" group of
   Spanish poets; verse included *Cantico;
   Clamon.*
b. Jan 18, 1893 in Valladolid, Spain
d. Feb 6, 1984 in Malaga, Spain
Source: *AnObit 1984; CasWL; ClDMEL;
CnMWL; ConAu 112, 89; ConLC 11; DcSpL;
LinLib L; MakMC; ModRL; OxSpan; PenC
EUR; REn; WorAu*

Guillen, Ozzie (Oswaldo Jose)
Venezuelan. Baseball Player
Infielder, Chicago White Sox, 1985--; AL
   rookie of year, 1985.
b. Jan 20, 1964 in Ocumare del Tuy,
   Venezuela
Source: *BaseReg 86*

Guillotin, Joseph Ignace
French. Physician
Proposed all capital punishment be by
   decapitation; name used for machine, the
   guillotine.
b. May 28, 1738 in Saintes, France
d. Mar 26, 1814 in Paris, France
Source: *NewC*

Guinan, "Texas" (Mary Louise Cecilia)
"First Lady of the Speakeasies"
American. Actress
Nightclub owner known for saying "Hello,
   Sucker!"; Betty Hutton portrayed her in
   movie *Incendiary Blonde,* 1945.
b. 1889 in Waco, Texas
d. Nov 5, 1933 in Vancouver, British
   Columbia
Source: *Film 1; InWom; NotAW; TwYS;
WhScrn 74, 77; WhoHol B*

Guiney, Louise
American. Poet, Essayist
b. 1861 in Boston, Massachusetts
d. Nov 2, 1920 in Chipping Camden,
   England
Source: *AmBi; BioIn 10; DcAmB; WhAm 1*

Guinness, Alec, Sir
English. Actor
Played Obi-Wan Kenobi in *Star Wars;* said
   "May the force be with you."
b. Apr 2, 1914 in London, England
Source: *BiDFilm; BiE&WWA; BkPepl; CelR;
CmMov; CurBio 50; FamA&A; FilmgC;
IntMPA 75, 76, 77, 78, 79, 80, 81, 82;
IntWW 74; MotPP; MovMk; NewC;
NewYTBE 72; NotNAT; OxFilm; OxThe;
PIP&P; REn; Who 74; WhoAm 82; WhoHol
A; WhoThe 77; WhoWor 78; WorEFlm*

Guion, Connie Myers
American. Physician
b. Aug 9, 1882 in Lincolnton, North
   Carolina
d. Apr 29, 1971
Source: *BioIn 2, 6, 7, 9, 11; CurBio 62*

Guion, David Wendel Fentress
American. Composer, Author, Musician
Wrote Western melodies including "Home
   On the Range," 1908.
b. Dec 15, 1892 in Ballinger, Texas
d. Oct 17, 1981 in Dallas, Texas
Source: *AmSCAP 66; BioIn 1, 6, 7; OxAmL*

Guiscard, Robert
see: Robert Guiscard

Guisewite, Cathy Lee
American. Cartoonist
Created syndicated "Cathy" comic strip,
   1976; wrote *The Cathy Chronicles,* 1978.
b. Sep 5, 1950 in Dayton, Ohio
Source: *BioIn 11; WhoAm 80, 82*

Guiteau, Charles Julius
American. Murderer
Shot, killed James Garfield, Washington, DC,
Jul 2, 1881; hanged.
b. 1844 in Illinois
d. Jun 30, 1882 in Washington, District of
Columbia
Source: *Alli SUP; WhAm HS*

Guiterman, Arthur
American. Journalist, Poet
Known for humorous verse; American ballad
Brave Laughter, 1943.
b. Nov 20, 1871 in Vienna, Austria
d. Jan 11, 1943
Source: *AmAu&B; AmLY; ChhPo, S1, S2;
CnDAL; DcNAA; EvLB; OxAmL; REn;
REnAL; Str&VC; TwCA, SUP; WhAm 2;
WhNAA*

Guitry, Sacha
French. Director, Actor, Dramatist
b. Feb 21, 1885 in Saint Petersburg, Russia
d. Jul 24, 1957 in Paris, France
Source: *BiDFilm; CasWL; ClDMEL; CnMD;
DcFM; EvEuW; FilmgC; McGEWD; ModWD;
MovMk; OxFilm; OxFr; OxThe; PenC EUR;
PlP&P; REn; TwCA, SUP; WhScrn 74, 77;
WhoHol B; WorEFlm*

Guizot, Francois Pierre
French. Historian, Statesman
b. 1787 in Nimes, France
d. 1874 in Normandy, France
Source: *BbD; DcEuL; EvEuW; NewC; NewCol
75; OxEng; OxFr; REn*

Gulager, Clu
American. Actor
Films include *The Last Picture Show,* 1971.
b. Nov 16, 1928 in Holdenville, Oklahoma
Source: *FilmgC; IntMPA 84; VarWW 85;
WhoHol A*

Gulbenkian, Calouste S
British. Art Collector, Oilman
Founder, Iraq Petroleum Co.,; major
stockholder in merger of Royal Dutch and
Shell oil.
b. 1869 in Turkey
d. Oct 20, 1955 in Lisbon, Portugal
Source: *BioNews 74; BusPN; ObitOF 79;
ObitT 1951; WhDW*

Gulbenkian, Nubar Sarkis
Iranian. Financier
b. 1896
d. Jan 10, 1972
Source: *NewYTBE 72*

Gulda, Friedrich
Austrian. Musician
b. 1930
Source: *WhoMus 72*

Gulick, Luther Halsey
American. Educator, Physician
Founded Camp Fire Girls with wife
Charlotte, 1910; helped develop basketball.
b. Dec 4, 1865 in Honolulu, Hawaii
d. Aug 13, 1918 in South Casco, Maine
Source: *AmAu&B; AmBi; BiDAmEd; BioIn 5,
9, 10, 11; DcAmB; NatCAB 26; WebAB;
WhAm 1; WhoBbl 73*

Gumbel, Bryant Charles
American. Broadcast Journalist
Hosted "NBC Sports," 1975-82; won Emmys
1976, 1977; host, "Today Show," 1982--.
b. Sep 29, 1948 in New Orleans, Louisiana
Source: *WhoAm 82; WhoBlA 77, 80*

Gumbleton, Thomas
American. Religious Leader
Bishop of Detroit, 1968--; visited hostages in
Iran.
b. Jan 26, 1930 in Detroit, Michigan
Source: *BioIn 10*

Gumede, Josiah Zion
Zimbabwean. Statesman
b. Sep 19, 1919
Source: *AfSS 79; IntWW 79, 80; WhoWor 80*

Gumilev, Nikolai
Russian. Poet
Writings include *Pearls,* 1910; *Pillar of Fire,*
1921; executed by Bolsheviks.
b. 1886
d. 1921
Source: *NewCol 75*

Gunn, Hartford Nelson, Jr.
American. TV Executive
Founder, pres., PBS, 1971-80.
b. Dec 24, 1926 in Port Washington, New
York
d. Jan 2, 1986 in Boston, Massachusetts
Source: *ConNews 86-2; NewYTBS 86;
NewYTET; WhoAm 78; WhoE 79; WhoF&I
79; WhoWor 78*

Gunn, Moses
American. Actor, Director
Broadway plays include *First Breeze of
Summer,* 1975; *I Have a Dream,* 1977;
joined Negro Ensemble Co., 1967-68.
b. Oct 2, 1929 in Saint Louis, Missouri
Source: *IntMPA 80, 81, 82; WhoAm 80, 82;
WhoBlA 75; WhoHol A; WhoThe 81*

Gunn, Thom
English. Poet
b. Aug 29, 1929 in Gravesend, England
Source: *AmAu&B; Au&Wr 71; CasWL;*
ChhPo, S1, S2; ConAu 17R; ConLC 3, 6, 18;
ConP 70, 75; DrAP 75; IntWW 74;
LongCTC; ModBrL, S1; PenC ENG; RAdv 1;
REn; TwCWr; WebE&AL; WhoAm 74, 76,
78, 80, 82; WhoTwCL; WorAu; WrDr 80

Gunnison, Foster
American. Architect
Pioneer in prefabricated housing, c. 1930s.
b. Jun 9, 1896 in Brooklyn, New York
d. Oct 19, 1961 in Saint Petersburg, Florida
Source: *DcAmB S7*

Gunther, John
American. Journalist, Author
Wrote *Inside Europe,* 1936; *Death Be Not*
Proud, 1949.
b. Aug 3, 1910 in Chicago, Illinois
d. May 29, 1970 in New York, New York
Source: *AmAu&B; AmNov; AuBYP; ConAu*
9R, 25R; CurBio 61, 70; EvLB; LongCTC;
OxAmL; PenC AM; REn; REnAL; SmATA 2;
TwCA, SUP; WebAB; WhAm 6

Gunzberg, Nicolas de, Baron
"Nicky"
American. Fashion Editor
Elegant senior fashion editor, *Vogue*
magazine, from 1940s.
b. 1904 in Paris, France
d. Feb 20, 1981 in New York, New York
Source: *NewYTBS 81; WorFshn*

Guptill, Arthur Leighton
American. Publisher, Author
b. Mar 19, 1891 in Gorham, Maine
d. Feb 29, 1956 in Stamford, Connecticut
Source: *CurBio 55, 56; WhAm 3; WhNAA*

Gurdjieff, Georges Ivanovitch
Armenian. Mystic, Author, Explorer
b. 1872
d. Oct 28, 1949 in Paris, France
Source: *BioIn 10*

Gurie, Sigrid
[Sigrid Gurie Haukelid]
American. Actress
Protege of Sam Goldwyn; publicized as "The
Siren of the Fjords," brief film career.
b. May 18, 1911 in Brooklyn, New York
d. Aug 14, 1969 in Mexico City, Mexico
Source: *FilmEn; FilmgC; ThFT; WhScrn 74,*
77

Gurion, David Ben
see: Ben-Gurion, David

Gurney, A(lbert) R(amsdell), Jr.
[Pete Gurney, psued.]
American. Dramatist
Plays describe WASP society: *Scenes from*
American Life, 1971.
b. Nov 1, 1930 in Buffalo, New York
Source: *ConAu 77; ConLC 32; CurBio 86;*
WhoAm 84

Gurney, Dan
American. Auto Racer
b. Apr 13, 1931
Source: *BioNews 74; WhoAm 82*

Gurney, Edward John
American. Politician, Lawyer
b. Jan 12, 1914 in Portland, Maine
Source: *BiDrAC; BioNews 74; CngDr 74;*
IntWW 74; WhoAm 74, 76, 78, 80, 82;
WhoAmP 73; WhoGov 75; WhoS&SW 82

Gusberg, Saul Bernard
American. Physician, Educator
b. Aug 3, 1913 in Newark, New Jersey
Source: *AmM&WS 73P; WhoAm 78, 80, 82*

Gustaf Adolf VI
[Gustavus]
Swedish. King
Reigned 1950-73; founded Swedish Institute
in Rome; succeeded by grandson, Carl
Gustaf XVI.
b. Nov 11, 1882 in Stockholm, Sweden
d. Sep 15, 1973 in Helsingborg, Sweden
Source: *BioIn 10; ConAu 45; NewCol 75*

Gustafson, John
see: Roxy Music

Gustafson, Karin
American. Actress
Film debut in *Taps,* 1981.
b. Jun 23, 1959 in Miami, Florida
Source: *ConTFT 3*

Gustavus Adolphus
Swedish. King
b. Dec 9, 1594 in Stockholm, Sweden
d. Nov 16, 1632 in Lutzen, Germany
Source: *NewC; NewCol 75; OxGer*

Guston, Philip
Canadian. Artist
b. Jun 27, 1913 in Montreal, Quebec
d. Jun 7, 1980 in Woodstock, New York
Source: *CurBio 71; DcCAA 71; NewCol 75;*
WhAm 7; WhoAm 74; WhoAmA 73; WhoWor
78

Gutenberg, Johannes
German. Inventor
Believed to be first European to print using
moveable type, ca. 1454.
b. Feb 23, 1400 in Mainz, Germany
d. Feb 1468
Source: *NewC; NewCol 75; OxGer; REn*

Gutfreund, Yosef
Israeli. Murder Victim
b. 1931 in Romania
d. Sep 5, 1972 in Munich, Germany (West)
Source: *NF*

Guthrie, A(lfred) B(ertram), Jr.
American. Journalist, Author
b. Jan 13, 1901 in Bedford, Indiana
Source: *AmAu&B; AmNov; CnDAL; ConAu
57; ConNov 72, 76; CyWA; DcLEL; DrAF
76; IndAu 1917; ModAL; OxAmL; REnAL;
TwCA SUP; WhoAm 74, 82; WhoPNW;
WhoWest 84; WhoWor 78; WrDr 80*

Guthrie, Arlo
American. Singer
Son of Woody Guthrie; best known for hit
"Alice's Restaurant," 1969.
b. Jul 10, 1947 in Brooklyn, New York
Source: *AmAu&B; BkPepl; CelR; EncFCWM
69; WhoAm 74, 76, 78, 80, 82*

Guthrie, Janet
American. Auto Racer
First woman to qualify and drive in
Indianapolis 500, 1977.
b. Mar 7, 1938 in Iowa City, Iowa
Source: *BioIn 10; WhoAm 82*

Guthrie, Samuel
American. Physician
Discovered chloroform, 1831.
b. 1782 in Brimfield, Massachusetts
d. Oct 19, 1848 in Sackets Harbor, New
   York
Source: *AmBi; ApCAB; AsBiEn; BiDAmS;
DcAmB; DcNAA; Drake; LinLib S; NatCab 1;
NewCol 75; TwCBDA; WhAm HS*

Guthrie, Tyrone
English. Director
b. Jul 2, 1900 in Tunbridge Wells, England
d. May 15, 1971 in Newbliss, Ireland
Source: *BiE&WWA; ConAu 29R; CurBio 54,
71; NewC; NewYTBE 71; OxThe; PlP&P;
WhoHol B*

Guthrie, Woody (Woodrow Wilson)
American. Singer, Musician
b. Jul 14, 1912 in Okemah, Oklahoma
d. Oct 4, 1967 in New York, New York
Source: *ConAu 93; CurBio 63, 67; EncAB-H;
EncFCWM 69; WebAB; WhAm 4*

Guttenberg, Steve
American. Actor
Starred in film *Cocoon*, 1985.
b. Aug 24, 1958 in Brooklyn, New York
Source: *VarWW 85*

Guy, Rosa Cuthbert
American. Author
b. Sep 1, 1928 in Trinidad
Source: *BlkAWP; ConAu 17R; SmATA 14*

Guy-Blanche, Alice
French. Director
World's first woman director; first film *La
   Fee aux Choux*, 1896; made US films,
   1910-20.
b. Jul 1, 1873 in Paris, France
d. 1968 in Mahwah, New Jersey
Source: *DcFM; FilmEn; FilmgC; MovMk;
OxFilm*

Guyer, Tennyson
American. Congressman
Representative from OH since 1973; noted
   for patriotic speeches.
b. Nov 29, 1913 in Findlay, Ohio
d. Apr 12, 1981 in Alexandria, Virginia
Source: *CngDr 74, 77, 79; WhoAm 74, 76,
78, 80; WhoAmP 73, 75, 77, 79; WhoGov 75,
77*

Guyon, Joe
American. Football Player
b. Nov 26, 1892 in Mahnomen, Minnesota
d. Nov 27, 1971
Source: *BioIn 8, 9; WhoFtbl 74*

Guzman, Antonio
[Silvestre Antonio Guzman Fernandez]
Dominican. Political Leader
Pres., 1978-82; freed political prisoners,
   abolished state censorship.
b. Feb 12, 1911 in La Vega, Dominican
   Republic
d. Jul 4, 1982 in Santo Domingo, Dominican
   Republic
Source: *AnObit 1982; IntWW 80; WhoWor
78, 80*

Guzman, Nuno Beltran de
Spanish. Conqueror
d. 1544
Source: *ApCAB; NewCol 75*

Gwenn, Edmund
Welsh. Actor
Won Oscar for role of Santa Claus in *Miracle on 34th Street,* 1947.
b. Sep 26, 1875 in Glamorgan, Wales
d. Sep 6, 1959 in Woodland Hills, California
Source: *BiDFilm; CurBio 43, 59; Film 1; FilmgC; MotPP; MovMk; OxFilm; Vers A; WhScrn 74, 77; WhoHol B*

Gwilym, Mike
Welsh. Actor
Played on PBS shows "How Green Was My Valley"; "The Racing Game."
b. Mar 5, 1949 in Neath, Wales
Source: *BioIn 11; WhoThe 77, 81*

Gwinnett, Button
American. Patriot
b. 1735 in Gloucester, England
d. May 19, 1777 in Savannah, Georgia
Source: *AmBi; ApCAB; BiAUS; BiDrAC; DcAmB; Drake; TwCBDA; WebAB; WhAm HS; WhAmP*

Gwyn, Nell (Eleanor)
English. Actress
Noted for comedy performances; mistress of Charles II, 1668-85; bore him two sons.
b. Feb 2, 1650 in Hereford, England
d. Nov 13, 1687 in London, England
Source: *InWom; NewC; NotNAT B; REn*

Gwynn, Tony (Anthony Keith)
American. Baseball Player
Outfielder, San Diego, 1982--; won NL batting title, 1984.
b. May 9, 1960 in Los Angeles, California
Source: *BaseEn 85; BaseReg 86*

Gwynne, Fred
American. Actor, Author
Played Herman Munster in TV series "The Munsters," 1964-68; wrote children's humor *The King Who Rained,* 1970.
b. Jul 10, 1926 in New York, New York
Source: *IlsBYP; IntMPA 84; NotNAT; SmATA 27; WhoAm 84; WhoHol A; WhoThe 81*

H

Ha-Levi, Judah
[Judah Ha-Levi]
Spanish. Rabbi, Poet
b. 1085
d. 1140
Source: *CasWL*

Haakon VII
Norwegian. Ruler
First king of independent Norway after
   separation from Sweden, 1905-57.
b. Aug 3, 1872
d. Sep 21, 1957 in Oslo, Norway
Source: *CurBio 57; HisEWW; LinLib S;
ObitOF 79; ObitT 1951; WhAm 3; WhWW-II*

Haas, Karl
American. Musician, Music Critic
b. May 15, in Speyer, Germany
Source: *BioNews 74*

Haas, Walter A(braham), Jr.
American. Business Executive
Pres., Levi Strauss Co., 1956-72.
b. Jan 24, 1916 in San Francisco, California
Source: *BioIn 5; WhoAm 74; WhoF&I 74,
75, 77*

Haas, Walter A(braham), Sr.
American. Business Executive
Pres., Levi Strauss Co., 1928-56, director,
   1956-59; turned family jean co. into
   American instituion.
b. 1899 in San Francisco, California
d. Dec 7, 1979 in San Francisco, California
Source: *NewYTBS 79; St&PR 75; WhAm 7;
WhoAm 74, 76, 78; WhoF&I 74, 75, 77;
WhoWorJ 72*

Habash, George
Palestinian. Political Leader
Founded Popular Front for Liberation of
   Palestine (PFLP), radical Marxist faction
   of PLO, 1967.
b. 1925 in Lydda, Palestine
Source: *ConNews 86-1*

Habberton, John
American. Author
b. Feb 24, 1842 in Brooklyn, New York
d. Feb 24, 1921
Source: *Alli SUP; AmAu; AmAu&B; AmBi;
ApCAB; BbD; BiD&SB; CarSB; Chambr 3;
DcAmAu; DcAmB; DcBiA; DcEnL; DcNAA;
EvLB; OxAmL; REnAL; TwCBDA; WhAm 1;
WhoChL*

Haber, Joyce
[Joyce Haber Cramer]
American. Journalist
b. Dec 28, 1932 in New York, New York
Source: *CelR; ConAu 65; IntMPA 76, 77, 78,
79, 80, 81, 82; WhoAm 82*

Habib, Philip Charles
American. Diplomat
Ambassador to Korea, 1971-74; special
   Middle East envoy, 1981-83.
b. Feb 25, 1920 in Brooklyn, New York
Source: *BioIn 11; CurBio 81; FarE&A 78, 79;
IntWW 78; PolProf J; USBiR 74; WhoAm
74, 76, 78, 80, 82; WhoAmP 75, 77, 79;
WhoGov 77, 72, 75; WhoWor 74, 76*

Habre, Hissein
Chadian. President
Source: *AfSS 82; BioIn 11; IntWW 82*

Habyarimana, Juvenal
Rwandan. President
b. Aug 3, 1937 in Gasiza, Rwanda
Source: *IntWW 74, 75, 76, 77, 78, 79, 80,
81*

Hack, Shelley
American. Model, Actress
Revlon's "Charlie Girl" in TV commercials;
   "Charlie's Angels," 1979.
b. Jul 6, 1952 in Connecticut
Source: *BioIn 11, 12; IntMPA 82; WhoAm
80, 82*

Hackett, Albert
American. Actor, Author
With wife won Pulitzer for play adaptation
of *The Diary of Anne Frank,* 1955.
b. Feb 16, 1900 in New York, New York
Source: *AmAu&B; AuBYP; BiE&WWA;
CmMov; CurBio 56; DcLB 26; Film 1;
FilmgC; ModWD; NotNAT; OxAmL, 83;
REnAL; TwYS; WhoAm 74; WorEFlm*

Hackett, Bobby (Robert Leo)
American. Jazz Musician
b. Jan 31, 1915 in Providence, Rhode Island
d. Jun 7, 1976 in Chatham, Massachusetts
Source: *WhoAm 74; WhoJazz 72*

Hackett, Buddy
[Leonard Hacker]
American. Comedian
Starred in *God's Little Acre,* 1958; *The Love
Bug,* 1969.
b. Aug 31, 1924 in New York, New York
Source: *AmSCAP 66; BiE&WWA; CelR;
ConAu 108; CurBio 65; FilmgC; IntMPA 81,
82, 82, 84; MotPP; MovMk; WhoAm 82, 84;
WhoHol A; WorAl*

Hackett, Charles
American. Opera Singer
b. Nov 4, 1889 in Worcester, Massachusetts
d. Jan 1, 1942 in New York, New York
Source: *CurBio 42; WhAm 1*

Hackett, Francis
American. Author, Editor
Wrote *Story of the Irish Nation,* 1922;
Francis the First, 1935.
b. Jan 21, 1883 in Kilkenny, Ireland
d. Apr 24, 1962 in Virum, Denmark
Source: *DcAmB S7*

Hackett, Joan
American. Actress
Starred in *The Group,* 1966; nominated for
Oscar, 1982, for *Only When I Laugh.*
b. Mar 1, 1934 in New York, New York
d. Oct 8, 1983 in Encino, California
Source: *AnObit 1983; BiE&WWA; FilmgC;
ForWC 70; IntMPA 82, 84; MovMk;
NewYTBE 72; NewYTBS 83; NotNAT;
WhoAm 82; WhoAmW 83; WhoHol A; WorAl*

Hackett, Raymond
American. Actor
Leading man in silents, early talkies, 1918-31.
b. Jul 15, 1902 in New York, New York
d. Jun 9, 1958 in Hollywood, California
Source: *Film 1; FilmgC; MotPP; NotNAT B;
WhScrn 74, 77; WhoHol B*

Hackett, Steve
[Genesis]
English. Musician
Guitarist with Genesis, 1970-77.
b. Feb 12, 1950 in England
Source: *NF*

Hackford, Taylor
American. Director, Producer
Films include *An Officer and A Gentleman,*
1983; *Against All Odds,* 1984.
b. Dec 31, 1944 in Santa Barbara, California
Source: *ConTFT 3; IntMPA 84; VarWW 85*

Hackman, Gene (Eugene Alden)
American. Actor
Won Oscar for *The French Connection,* 1972.
b. Jan 30, 1931 in San Bernardino, California
Source: *BioNews 74; BkPepl; CmMov; CurBio
72; FilmgC; IntMPA 75, 76, 77, 78, 79, 80,
81, 82; MovMk; NewYTBE 71; OxFilm;
WhoAm 74, 76, 78, 80, 82; WhoHol A*

Haddad, Saad
Lebanese. Army Officer
Renegade army major; formed own militia,
made seperate peace with Israel to keep
Syria from annexing Lebanon.
b. 1937 in Marjayoun, Lebanon
d. Jan 14, 1984 in Marjayoun, Lebanon
Source: *BioIn 12; NewYTBS 84*

Hadden, Briton
American. Publisher
Co-founded *Time* magazine with Henry Luce,
1923.
b. Feb 18, 1898 in Brooklyn, New York
d. Feb 27, 1929 in Brooklyn, New York
Source: *BioIn 1, 2, 8, 10; EncAJ; NatCAB
28; REnAL*

Haden, Pat(rick Capper)
American. Football Player, Scholar
b. Jan 23, 1953 in Westbury, New York
Source: *BioIn 11; WhoAm 82*

Hadley, Henry Kimball
American. Composer
b. Dec 20, 1871 in Somerville, Massachusetts
d. Sep 6, 1937 in New York, New York
Source: *AmBi; AmSCAP 66; DcAmB S2;
WhAm 1*

Hadley, Reed
[Reed Herring]
American. Actor
Starred in TV series "Racket Squad," 1951-
53; "Public Defender," 1954.
b. 1911 in Petralia, Texas
d. Dec 11, 1974 in Los Angeles, California
Source: *FilmEn; FilmgC; Vers B; WhScrn 77;
WhoHol B*

Hadrian
[Publius Aelius Hadrianus]
Roman. Emperor
b. Jan 24, 76 in Spain
d. 138
Source: *CasWL; NewC; PenC CL; REn*

Haeckel, Ernst Heinrich
German. Zoologist
Advocate of Darwinism who theorized that
growing organisms mirror specie
development.
b. Feb 15, 1834 in Potsdam, Germany
d. Aug 8, 1919
Source: *BioIn 9; Dis&D; InSci; LuthC 75;
WorAl*

Haenigsen, Harry William
American. Cartoonist
b. Jul 14, 1902 in New York, New York
Source: *AmAu&B; WhoAm 74*

Hafey, "Chick" (Charles James)
American. Baseball Player
b. Feb 12, 1903 in Berkeley, California
d. Jul 5, 1973 in Calistoga, California
Source: *BaseEn 85; WhoProB 73*

Hafiz, Shams-al-Din Muhammad
Persian. Poet
b. 1320 in Persia
d. 1389
Source: *CasWL; OxEng; PenC CL; RComWL*

Hagan, Cliff(ord Oldham)
"Lil Abner"
American. Basketball Player, Basketball
Coach
Member 1958 champion St. Louis team who
was elected to Hall of Fame, 1977.
b. Dec 9, 1931 in Owensboro, Kentucky
Source: *OfNBA 81; WhoBbl 73*

Hagar, Sammy
[Van Halen]
American. Singer, Musician
Lead singer, second guitarist with Van Halen,
1986--; released 10 albums during nine yr.
solo career.
b. Oct 13, 1949 in Monterey, California
Source: *RkOn 85; RolSEnR 83*

Hagedorn, Hermann
American. Author, Poet
b. Jul 18, 1882 in New York, New York
d. Jul 27, 1964 in Santa Barbara, California
Source: *AmAu&B; AmLY; ChhPo, S1, S2;
ConAmL; OxAmL; REnAL; TwCA, SUP;
WhAm 4*

Hagegard, Hakan
Swedish. Opera Singer
Lyric baritone; starred in Igmar Bergman's
film version of *The Magic Flute,* 1975.
b. Nov 25, 1945 in Karlstad, Sweden
Source: *CurBio 85; WhoOp 76; WhoWor 82*

Hagen, Jean
[Jean Shirley VerHagen]
American. Actress
Starred in TV series "Make Room for
Daddy," 1953-57; films *Singin' in the
Rain,* 1952; *Adam's Rib,* 1949.
b. Aug 3, 1923 in Chicago, Illinois
d. 1977 in Woodland Hills, California
Source: *FilmEn; FilmgC; IntMPA 77; MotPP;
MovMk; WhoHol A; WhoThe 81N*

Hagen, Uta Thyra
American. Actress
Won Tonys for *The Country Girl,* 1951;
Who's Afraid of Virginia Woolf? 1963.
b. Jun 12, 1919 in Goettingen, Germany
Source: *BiE&WWA; CurBio 63; InWom;
IntWW 74; NotNAT; OxThe 83; PIP&P;
WhoAm 82; WhoHol A; WhoThe 81; WorAl*

Hagen, Walter Charles
"The Haig"
American. Golfer
Won PGA championship five times; British
Open four times.
b. Dec 21, 1892 in New York, New York
d. Oct 5, 1969 in Traverse City, Michigan
Source: *NewCol 75; WebAB; WhoGolf*

Hagerty, James Campbell
American. Government Official, Journalist
Pres. Eisenhower's White House press
secretary, 1952-60.
b. May 9, 1909 in Plattsburg, New York
d. Apr 11, 1981 in Bronxville, New York
Source: *ConAu 103; CurBio 81; IntWW 78;
LesBEnT; PolProf E; Who 82N; WhoF&I 74;
WhoWor 74*

Hagg, Gunder
Swedish. Track Athlete
b. Dec 31, 1918 in Sorbygden, Sweden
Source: *IntWW 83; WhoTr&F 73*

Haggar, Joseph M
[Maroun Hajjar]
Syrian. Manufacturer
Opened garment factory, 1925, in Dallas,
TX.
b. 1892 in Jazzini, Syria
Source: *Entr; St&PR 84*

Haggard, Henry Rider, Sir
English. Author, Lawyer
Wrote *King Solomon's Mines,* 1885; *She,*
1887.
b. Jun 22, 1856 in Norfolk, England
d. May 14, 1925 in London, England
Source: *Alli SUP; BbD; BiD&SB; Chambr 3;
ConAu 108; CyWA; DcBiA; DcEnA AP;
DcEuL; DcLEL; EncSF; EvLB; LongCTC;
MnBBF; ModBrL; NewC; Novels; OxEng;
PenC ENG; REn; TwCA, SUP; WebE&AL;
WhoChL*

Haggard, Merle Ronald
American. Singer
b. Apr 6, 1937 in Bakersfield, California
Source: *CelR; EncFCWM 69; WhoAm 74, 76,
78, 80, 82; WhoE 74; WhoHol A; WhoThe
77; WhoWor 78*

Haggart, Bob
[Robert Sherwood]
American. Composer, Musician
b. Mar 13, 1914 in New York, New York
Source: *CmpEPM; WhoJazz 72*

Haggerty, Dan
American. Actor
Starred in TV series "Life and Times of
Grizzly Adams," 1977-78.
b. Nov 19, 1941 in Hollywood, California
Source: *ConTFT 3; WhoAm 82, 84*

Haggerty, Sandra Clark
American. Journalist
b. Jul 26, 1939 in Oakley, Kansas
Source: *WhoAm 74*

Hagler, Marvelous Marvin
[Marvin Nathaniel Hagler]
American. Boxer
WBA, WBC middleweight champ, 1980--.
b. May 23, 1952 in Newark, New Jersey
Source: *ConNews 85-2; NewYTBS 81; WhoAm
74*

Hagman, Larry
American. Actor
Starred in "I Dream of Jeannie," 1965-68;
plays J R Ewing on "Dallas," 1978--; son
of Mary Martin.
b. Sep 21, 1931 in Fort Worth, Texas
Source: *BioIn 12; CurBio 80; FilmgC;
IntMPA 82; WhoAm 80, 82; WhoHol A*

Hagopian, Louis Thomas
American. Advertising Executive
b. Jun 1, 1925 in Pontiac, Michigan
Source: *WhoAm 74, 76, 78, 80, 82; WhoE
74; WhoF&I 74*

Hague, Frank
American. Politician
b. Jan 17, 1876 in Jersey City, New Jersey
d. Jan 1, 1956 in Jersey City, New Jersey
Source: *WhAm 3*

Hahn, Emily
American. Author
b. Jan 14, 1905 in Saint Louis, Missouri
Source: *AmAu&B; AuBYP; ConAu 1R, 1NR;
LongCTC; REnAL; SmATA 3; TwCA SUP;
WhNAA; WhoAm 74, 76, 78, 80, 82;
WhoAmW 77; WhoE 74; WhoWor 78*

Hahn, Otto
German. Physicist
b. Mar 8, 1879 in Frankfurt, Germany
d. Jul 28, 1968 in Goettingen, Germany
(West)
Source: *CurBio 51, 68; REn; WhAm 5*

Hahnemann, (Christian Friedrich) Samuel
German. Physician
Founded Homeopathy, 1796.
b. Apr 10, 1755 in Meissen, Germany
d. Jul 2, 1843 in Paris, France
Source: *CelCen; DcBiPP; DcScB; LinLib S*

Haid, Charles
American. Actor
Plays Andy Renko on TV series "Hill Street
Blues," 1981--.
b. Jun 2, 1944 in San Francisco, California
Source: *WhoTelC*

Haider, Michael Lawrence
American. Business Executive
Chief exec., chm., Standard Oil Co., 1965-69.
b. Oct 1, 1904 in Mandan, North Dakota
d. Aug 14, 1986 in Atherton, California
Source: *AmM&WS 79P; St&PR 75; Who 83; WhoEng 80*

Haig, Alexander Meigs, Jr.
American. General, Government Official
Commander in chief, US European
    Command, 1974-78; secretary of State
    under Ronald Reagan, 1981-82.
b. Dec 2, 1924 in Philadelphia, Pennsylvania
Source: *BioNews 74; CurBio 73; IntWW 74; NewYTBE 71, 73; WhoAm 74, 76, 78, 80, 82; WhoAmP 73; WhoS&SW 82*

Haig, Douglas
Scottish. Field Marshal
b. 1861 in Edinburgh, Scotland
d. 1928
Source: *WebBD 80*

Haigh, Kenneth
English. Actor
Appeared in *Cleopatra*, 1963.
b. Mar 25, 1931 in Mexboro, England
Source: *BiE&WWA; CnThe; FilmgC; NotNAT; PIP&P; WhoHol A; WhoThe 77, 81*

Haile Selassie I
[Lij Tafari Makonnen]
Ethiopian. Emperor
b. Jul 23, 1892
d. Aug 27, 1975 in Addis Ababa, Ethiopia
Source: *CurBio 41, 54, 75, 75N; InB&W 80; IntWW 74, 74; McGEWB; REn; WhWW-II; Who 74; WhoGov 72; WhoWor 74*

Hailey, Arthur
Canadian. Author
Wrote *Hotel*, 1965; *Airport*, 1968; *Wheels*, 1971.
b. Apr 5, 1920 in Luton, England
Source: *AmAu&B; Au&Wr 71; AuNews 2; CanWW 82; CanWr; ConAu 1R, 2NR; ConLC 5; ConNov 72, 76; CreCan 2; IntWW 74; OxCan; WhoAm 82; WhoE 74; WhoWor 74; WrDr 76*

Hailwood, Mike (Stanley Michael Bailey)
English. Motorcycle Racer, Auto Racer
Considered one of greatest motorcycle racers
    of all time; died in auto accident.
b. Apr 4, 1940 in Oxfordshire, England
d. Mar 23, 1981 in Warwickshire, England
Source: *AnObit 1981; BioIn 11, 12; ConAu 108; EncMot*

Haines, Connie
[Yvonne Marie Jamais]
American. Singer
b. 1923
Source: *InWom; WhoHol A*

Haines, Jesse Joseph
"Pop"
American. Baseball Player
b. Jul 22, 1893 in Clayton, Ohio
d. Aug 5, 1978 in Dayton, Ohio
Source: *BaseEn 85; WhoProB 73*

Haines, Robert Terrel
American. Actor
Starred in vaudeville, radio, film, and on
    stage in career spanning four decades.
b. Feb 3, 1870 in Muncie, Indiana
d. May 6, 1943 in New York, New York
Source: *Film 1; TwYS; WhAm 5; WhScrn 74, 77; WhoStg 1906, 1908*

Haines, William
American. Actor
Appeared in silent films and early talkies;
    retired to become interior decorator.
b. Jan 1, 1900 in Staunton, Virginia
d. Nov 26, 1973 in Santa Monica, California
Source: *FilmEn; FilmgC; MotPP; MovMk; TwYS; WhScrn 77; WhoHol B*

Haire, Bill
American. Fashion Designer
b. Sep 30, 1936
Source: *WhoAm 82; WorFshn*

Haise, Fred W
American. Astronaut
Crew member, Apollo 13, 1970; Apollo 16, 1972.
b. Nov 14, 1933 in Biloxi, Mississippi
Source: *AmM&WS 73P; IntWW 74; WhoAm 74, 76, 78, 80, 82; WhoGov 75; WhoS&SW 82*

Haitink, Bernard
Dutch. Conductor
b. Mar 4, 1929 in Amsterdam, Netherlands
Source: *IntWW 74; Who 74; WhoMus 72; WhoWor 78*

Hakluyt, Richard
English. Geographer
Compiled accounts of English voyages of
   discovery: *Principal Navigations,* 1589.
b. 1552
d. Nov 23, 1616 in London, England
Source: *Alli; AnCL; AtlBL; BiD&SB; BiDSA;
BrAu; CasWL; Chambr 1; CroE&S; CyWA;
DcEnA; DcEnL; DcEuL; DcLEL; EvLB;
NewC; OxAmL; OxCan; OxEng; PenC ENG;
REn; REnAL*

Halaby, Najeeb Elias
American. Airline Executive
Pres., Halaby International Corp., 1973--.
b. Nov 19, 1915 in Dallas, Texas
Source: *ConAu 108; CurBio 61; IntWW 74;
Ward 77; WhoAm 82; WhoE 74; WhoF&I
74; WhoWor 74*

Halas, George Stanley
"Papa Bear"
American. Football Coach
Founder, owner, Chicago Bears, 1922; coach
   until 1968, most victories by pro coach.
b. Feb 2, 1895 in Chicago, Illinois
d. Oct 31, 1983 in Chicago, Illinois
Source: *AnObit 1983; CelR; EncAB-H;
NewYTBS 83; St&PR 75; WebAB; WhoAm
82; WhoFtbl 74*

Halasz, Gyula
see: Brassai

Halasz, Laszlo
Hungarian. Conductor
b. Jun 6, 1905 in Debrecen, Hungary
Source: *CurBio 49; WhoAm 82*

Halberstam, David
American. Journalist
b. Apr 10, 1934 in New York, New York
Source: *CelR; ConAu 69; CurBio 73; WhoAm
74, 76, 78, 80, 82; WhoWor 78; WrDr 76*

Halberstam, Michael Joseph
American. Physician, Author
Editor, *Modern Medicine,* 1976-80; wrote *Pills
   in Your Life,* 1972.
b. Aug 9, 1932 in Bronx, New York
d. Dec 5, 1980 in Washington, District of
   Columbia
Source: *AmM&WS 79P; ConAu 65, 102;
WhAm 7; WhoAm 76, 78, 80*

Haldane, J(ohn) B(urdon) S(anderson)
English. Scientist
Best known for work in genetics; helped
   develop heart-lung machine.
b. Nov 5, 1892 in Oxford, England
d. Dec 1, 1964 in Bhubaneswar, India
Source: *McGEWB; WebBD 80*

Haldane, John Scott
Scottish. Physiologist
Developed method of stage decompression by
   which divers can be safely brought to
   surface.
b. May 3, 1860 in Edinburgh, Scotland
d. Mar 14, 1936 in Oxford, England
Source: *BiESc; BiHiMed; WhE&EA; WhoLA*

Haldeman, H(arry) R(obert)
American. Watergate Participant
Convicted for involvement in Watergate,
   1975; jailed, 1977-78.
b. Oct 27, 1926 in Los Angeles, California
Source: *NewYTBE 72, 73; NewYTBS 74;
WhoAm 74, 76, 78, 80, 82; WhoAmP 73;
WhoGov 75; WhoS&SW 82; WhoWor 78*

Haldeman-Julius, Emanuel
American. Publisher
Founded popular 10-cent reprint series *Little
   Blue Books,* 1919.
b. Jul 30, 1889 in Philadelphia, Pennsylvania
d. Jul 31, 1951 in Girard, Kansas
Source: *DcAmB S5; WebAB*

Hale, Alan
[Rufus Alan McKahan]
American. Actor
Character actor best known as Errol Flynn's
   sidekick in films such as *The Adventures
   of Robin Hood,* 1938.
b. Feb 10, 1892 in Washington, District of
   Columbia
d. Jan 22, 1950 in Hollywood, California
Source: *CmMov; FilmEn; Film 1; FilmgC;
IntMPA 82; MotPP; MovMk; TwYS; Vers A;
WhScrn 74, 77; WhoHol A*

Hale, Alan, Jr.
American. Actor
Best known as captain in TV series
   "Gilligan's Island," 1964-67.
b. Mar 8, 1918
Source: *FilmgC; IntMPA 81; WhoHol A*

Hale, Barbara
American. Actress
Della Street on "Perry Mason," 1957-66;
   mother of actor William Katt.
b. Apr 18, 1922 in DeKalb, Illinois
Source: *FilmgC; IntMPA 82; MotPP; MovMk;
WhoHol A*

Hale, Clara McBride
"Mother Hale"
American. Social Reformer
Organized Hale House, 1969, in Harlem to
care for babies born to drug-addicted
mothers.
b. Apr 1, 1905 in Philadelphia, Pennsylvania
Source: *CurBio 85; InB&W 80*

Hale, Edward Everett
American. Clergyman, Author
b. Apr 3, 1822 in Boston, Massachusetts
d. Jun 10, 1909 in Roxbury, Massachusetts
Source: *Alli, SUP; AmAu; AmAu&B; AmBi;
ApCAB; BbD; BiD&SB; CarSB; Chambr 3;
ChhPo, S1, S2; CnDAL; CyAL 2; CyWA;
DcAmAu; DcAmB; DcEnL; DcLEL; DcNAA;
Drake; EvLB; JBA 34; OxAmL; PenC AM;
REn; REnAL; TwCBDA; WebAB; WhAm 1*

Hale, George Ellery
American. Astronomer, Educator
Organizer, director, Yerkes, Mount Wilson,
Mount Palomar observatories.
b. Jun 29, 1868 in Chicago, Illinois
d. Feb 21, 1938 in Pasadena, California
Source: *DcAmB S2; NewCol 75; WebAB;
WebBD 80*

Hale, Lucretia Peabody
American. Author
Wrote children's tale *The Peterkin Papers,*
1880.
b. Sep 2, 1820 in Boston, Massachusetts
d. Jun 12, 1900 in Boston, Massachusetts
Source: *NotAW; WebBD 80*

Hale, Nancy
American. Author
b. May 6, 1908 in Boston, Massachusetts
Source: *AmAu&B; Au&Wr 71; ConAu 5R;
ConNov 72, 76; DrAF 76; InWom; OxAmL;
REn; REnAL; TwCA SUP; WhoAm 74, 82;
WhoS&SW 82; WhoWor 78; WrDr 80*

Hale, Nathan
American. Revolutionary, Spy
Before hanged, said, "I only regret that I
have but one life to lose for my country."
b. Jun 6, 1755 in Coventry, Connecticut
d. Sep 22, 1776 in Long Island, New York
Source: *AmBi; ApCAB; DcAmB; Drake;
OxAmL; REn; REnAL; TwCBDA; WebAB;
WhAm HS*

Hale, Sarah Josepha
American. Journalist, Author
Edited *Godey's Lady Book,* 1837-77; wrote
verse "Mary Had a Little Lamb," 1830.
b. Oct 24, 1788 in Newport, New Hampshire
d. Apr 30, 1879
Source: *NotAW; OxAmL 83*

Halevy, Jacques Francois Fromental
[Jacques Francois F Elie Levy]
French. Opera Composer
b. May 27, 1799 in Paris, France
d. Mar 17, 1862 in Nice, France
Source: *NewEOp 71; WebBD 80*

Haley, Alex Palmer
American. Author, Journalist
Won Pulitzer for *Roots,* 1977; adapted into
TV mini-series.
b. Aug 11, 1921 in Ithaca, New York
Source: *BkPepl; ConAu 77; ConLC 8, 12;
LivgBAA; WhoAm 82; WhoWest 84*

Haley, Bill (William John Clifford, Jr.)
[Bill Haley and the Comets]
"Father of Rock 'n Roll"
American. Singer, Musician
Hits "Rock Around the Clock," 1954;
"Shake, Rattle, and Roll," paved way for
Elvis Presley, The Beatles.
b. Jul 6, 1925 in Highland Park, Michigan
d. Feb 9, 1981 in Harlingen, Texas
Source: *AmSCAP 66; BiDAmM; BioIn 8;
LilREn 78; NewYTBS 81; WhoRock 81*

Haley, Jack
American. Actor
Played the Tin Man in *The Wizard of Oz,*
1939.
b. Aug 10, 1900 in Boston, Massachusetts
d. Jun 6, 1979 in Los Angeles, California
Source: *BiE&WWA; EncMT; FilmgC;
MovMk; WhoAm 74; WhoHol A; WhoThe
77A*

Haley, Jack, Jr. (John J.)
American. Director, Producer
Produced, directed, wrote *That's
Entertainment,* 1974.
b. Oct 25, 1933 in Los Angeles, California
Source: *IntMPA 82; WhoAm 82; WhoTelC;
WhoWest 74*

Halfin, Eliezer
Israeli. Murder Victim
b. 1948 in U.S.S.R.
d. Sep 5, 1972 in Munich, Germany (West)
Source: *BioIn 9*

Halford, Rob
see: Judas Priest

Haliburton, Thomas Chandler
[Sam Slick, pseud.]
Canadian. Judge, Author
Humorist, who wrote *Sam Slick's Wise Saws,*
1853.
b. 1796 in Windsor, Nova Scotia
d. Aug 27, 1865 in Isleworth, England
Source: *BrAu 19; CasWL; DcEnA; LinLib L,
S; NatCAB 5; OxAmL; OxCan; OxEng;
REnAL; WebE&AL*

Halifax, Edward Frederick Lindley
English. Statesman
b. Apr 16, 1881
d. Dec 23, 1959 in York, England
Source: *CurBio 40, 60*

Hall, Bruce
see: REO Speedwagon

Hall, Camilla Christine
[S(ymbionese) L(iberation) A(rmy)]
"Gabi"
American. Revolutionary
Member of group that kidnapped Patty
Hearst, 1974.
b. Mar 24, 1946
Source: *BioIn 10; GoodHs*

Hall, Charles Martin
American. Scientist, Physician, Engineer
b. Dec 6, 1863 in Thompson, Ohio
d. Dec 27, 1914 in Niagara Falls, New York
Source: *AmBi; DcAmB; WebAB; WhAm 1*

Hall, Daryl
[Hall and Oates]
American. Singer, Musician
With John Oates, recorded "Rich Girl" on
first platinum album *Bigger Than Both of
Us,* 1976.
b. Oct 11, 1948 in Pottstown, Pennsylvania
Source: *RkWW 82*

Hall, David
American. Politician
b. Oct 20, 1930 in Oklahoma City,
Oklahoma
Source: *IntWW 74; WhoAm 74; WhoAmP 73;
WhoGov 75; WhoS&SW 82*

Hall, Donald Andrew
American. Author
Inspiration comes from New England region;
first book of poetry *Exiles and Marriages,*
1955.
b. Sep 20, 1928 in New Haven, Connecticut
Source: *AmAu&B; AuBYP; CnE&AP; ConAu
2NR, 5R; ConLC 1, 13; ConP 70, 75; CurBio
84; DrAF 76; DrAP 75; OxAmL; PenC AM;
RAdv 1; REn; REnAL; SmATA 23; WhoAm
82; WorAu; WrDr 80*

Hall, Donald Joyce
American. Business Executive
Son of Joyce Clyde Hall, who is chief exec.,
Hallmark Cards, 1966--.
b. Jul 9, 1928 in Kansas City, Missouri
Source: *BioIn 10; WhoAm 82*

Hall, Edwin Herbert
American. Physicist, Educator
Discovered Hall Effect, 1879.
b. Nov 7, 1855 in Great Falls, Maine
d. Nov 20, 1938 in Cambridge,
Massachusetts
Source: *DcAmB S2; WebBD 80*

Hall, Glenn Henry
"Mr. Goalie"
Canadian. Hockey Player
Goalie, 1952-71; Hall of Fame, 1975.
b. Oct 3, 1931 in Humboldt, Saskatchewan
Source: *BioIn 11; HocEn*

Hall, Granville Stanley
American. Educator, Author
b. Feb 1, 1844 in Ashfield, Massachusetts
d. 1924
Source: *McGEWB; NewCol 75*

Hall, Gus
[Arro Kusta Hallberg]
American. Political Activist
b. Oct 8, 1910 in Iron, Minnesota
Source: *BioNews 74; CurBio 73; WhoAm 82;
WhoAmP 73*

Hall, Huntz (Henry)
American. Actor
Played Dippy in *The Dead End Kids;* Satch
in *The Bowery Boys* film series, 1930s-40s.
b. 1920 in New York, New York
Source: *FilmgC; IntMPA 77; MovMk;
WhoHol A*

Hall, James, Sir
Scottish. Chemist, Geologist
b. Jan 17, 1761 in Dunglass, Scotland
d. Jun 23, 1832 in Edinburgh, Scotland
Source: *AsBiEn; BioIn 5; DcScB*

Hall, James Norman
American. Author
Co-wrote novels of S Pacific with Charles
Nordhoff: *Mutiny on the Bounty*, 1932.
b. Apr 22, 1887 in Colfax, Iowa
d. Jul 6, 1951 in Papeete, Tahiti
Source: *AmAu&B; AmNov; AuBYP; CyWA;*
DcAmB S5; DcLEL; JBA 34; MnBBF;
OxAmL; PenC AM; REn; REnAL; TwCA,
SUP; WhAm 3; WhNAA

Hall, Jerry
"Tall Hall"
American. Model
b. 1957 in Texas
Source: *BioIn 11*

Hall, Joe Beasman
American. Basketball Coach
Coach, U of KY, 1971--.
b. Nov 30, 1928 in Cynthiana, Kentucky
Source: *WhoAm 80, 82, 84; WhoS&SW 80*

Hall, Josef Washington
[Upton Close, pseud.]
American. Radio Commentator, Lecturer
Wrote books on Oriental lifestyle.
b. Feb 27, 1894 in Kelso, Washington
d. Nov 13, 1960
Source: *ConAu 89; CurBio 44, 61; WebBD 80*

Hall, Joseph M
[The Hostages]
American. Hostage in Iran
b. 1950 in Oklahoma
Source: *NewYTBS 81*

Hall, Joyce Clyde
American. Business Executive
Founded Hallmark Cards, Inc., 1910.
b. Dec 29, 1891 in David City, Nebraska
d. Oct 29, 1982 in Leawood, Kansas
Source: *CelR; CurBio 83; NewYTBS 82;*
WebAB; WhoAm 82; WhoAmA 73; WorAl

Hall, Juanita
American. Singer, Actress
b. Nov 6, 1901 in Newport, New Jersey
d. Feb 28, 1968 in Keyport, New Jersey
Source: *BiE&WWA; EncMT; FilmgC;*
InWom; MotPP; WhAm 4; WhScrn 74, 77;
WhoHol B

Hall, Lyman
American. Statesman
b. Apr 12, 1724 in Wallingford, Connecticut
d. Oct 19, 1790 in Burke County, Georgia
Source: *AmBi; ApCAB; BiAUS; BiDrAC;*
DcAmB; Drake; TwCBDA; WhAm HS;
WhAmP

Hall, Manly Palmer
Canadian. Author
b. Mar 18, 1901 in Peterborough, Ontario
Source: *Au&Wr 71; ConAu 93; WhNAA;*
WhoWest 84; WrDr 80

Hall, Monty
Canadian. TV Host
Host of "Let's Make a Deal," 1963; "Beat
the Clock," 1979.
b. Aug 25, 1924 in Winnipeg, Manitoba
Source: *BioNews 74; CanWW 82; CelR;*
ConAu 108; WhoAm 82

Hall, Peter Reginald Frederick, Sir
English. Director
National Theatre Co., director since 1973.
b. Nov 22, 1930 in Bury St. Edmunds,
England
Source: *BiE&WWA; CnThe; CroCD; EncWT;*
FilmgC; IntWW 80; NotNAT A; OxFilm;
OxThe; PIP&P; WhoOp 76; WhoThe 72, 77,
81; WhoWor 80; WorEFlm

Hall, Radclyffe
English. Author, Poet
Wrote *The Well of Loneliness*, 1928, censored
for lesbian theme.
b. 1886 in Bournemouth, England
d. Oct 7, 1943 in London, England
Source: *CurBio 43; InWom; LongCTC;*
ModBrL; NewC; REn; TwCA, SUP; TwCWr;
WhoLA

Hall, Tom T
"The Storyteller"
American. Singer, Songwriter
Wrote song "Harper Valley PTA"; sold over
4.5 million copies.
b. May 25, 1936 in Olive Hill, Kentucky
Source: *BioIn 10; ConAu 102; RkOn 74;*
WhoAm 74

Hall and Oates
[Daryl Hall; John Oates]
American. Music Group
Hits include "Maneater," 1982.
Source: *IlEncRk; WhoRock 81*

Halle, Charles, Sir
English. Musician, Conductor
b. Apr 11, 1819 in Hagen, Germany
d. Oct 25, 1895 in Manchester, England
Source: *OxMus; WebBD 80*

Halleck, Charles Abraham
American. Lawyer, Politician
Congressman from IN, 1935-67, who served
as both majority, minority leader.
b. Aug 22, 1900 in Demotte, Indiana
d. Mar 3, 1986 in Lafayette, Indiana
Source: *BiDrAC; CurBio 86; IntWW 74;*
WhAmP; WhoAm 82

Halleck, Fritz-Greene
American. Poet
Member, NYC's Knickerbocker group; wrote
Croaker Papers, 1918.
b. Jul 8, 1790 in Guilford, Connecticut
d. Nov 19, 1867 in Guilford, Connecticut
Source: *Alli, SUP; AmAu; AmAu&B; AtlBL;*
BbD; BiD&SB; CasWL; ChhPo, S1, S2;
CnDAL; CyAL 1; DcAmAu; DcEnL; DcLEL;
DcNAA; EvLB; OxAmL; PenC AM; REn;
REnAL

Halleck, Henry
American. Military Leader
b. Jan 16, 1815 in Westernville, New York
d. Jan 9, 1872 in Louisville, Kentucky
Source: *Alli, SUP; AmBi; ApCAB; DcAmAu;*
DcAmB; DcNAA; EncAB-H; TwCBDA;
WebAB; WhAm HS

Halley, Edmund
English. Astronomer
Predicted comets seen 1531, 1607, 1682 were
same; known as Halley's Comet.
b. Oct 29, 1656 in London, England
d. Jan 14, 1742 in Greenwich, England
Source: *Alli; DcEnL; NewC; REn*

Halliburton, Richard
American. Author, Explorer
Wrote *The Royal Road to Romance,* 1925;
The Flying Carpet, 1932.
b. Jan 9, 1900 in Brownsville, Tennessee
d. Mar 21, 1939
Source: *AmAu&B; AmBi; CnDAL; DcNAA;*
EvLB; OxAmL; REnAL; TwCA, SUP; WhAm
1; WhNAA

Halliday, Johnny
[Jean-Phillippe Smet]
French. Singer
European rock star, 1960s; hit "Let's Twist
Again," 1961.
b. Jun 15, 1943 in Paris, France
Source: *RolSEnR 83*

Halliday, Richard
American. Producer
Producer, stage production of *Sound of*
Music, stage, film productions of *Peter*
Pan; married Mary Martin, 1940.
b. Apr 3, 1905 in Denver, Colorado
d. Mar 3, 1973 in Brasilia, Brazil
Source: *BiE&WWA; ConAu 41R; NewYTBE*
73; WhAm 5; WhoE 74

Hallstein, Walter
German. Diplomat, Statesman
Founder of European Economic Community
(Common Market), pres., 1958-67.
b. Nov 17, 1901 in Mainz, Germany
d. Mar 29, 1982 in Stuttgart, Germany
(West)
Source: *AnObit 1982; CurBio 82; IntWW 78;*
IntYB 79; NewYTBS 82; Who 74; WhoWor
74, 78

Hallstrom, Ivar
Swedish. Composer
b. Jun 5, 1826 in Stockholm, Sweden
d. Apr 11, 1901 in Stockholm, Sweden
Source: *NewEOp 71*

Halop, Billy
American. Actor
Original Leader of Dead End Kids on stage,
several films of 1930s-40s.
b. 1920 in New York, New York
d. Nov 9, 1976 in California
Source: *FilmEn; FilmgC; IntMPA 77;*
WhoHol A

Halop, Florence
American. Actress
Played bailiff on TV series "Night Court,"
1985-86.
b. 1923
d. Jun 29, 1986 in Stanford, California
Source: *InWom; WhoHol A*

Halper, Albert
American. Author
b. Aug 3, 1904 in Chicago, Illinois
Source: *AmAu&B; AmNov; Au&Wr 71;*
CnDAL; ConAmA; ConAu 5R, 3NR; OxAmL;
REn; REnAL; TwCA, SUP; WhNAA; WhoAm
74, 82

Halpert, Edith Gregor
American. Art Collector
American folk art expert; assembled artifacts
shown at Colonial Williamsburg, 1940.
b. Apr 25, 1900 in Odessa, Russia
d. Oct 6, 1970 in New York, New York
Source: *NotAW MOD*

Hals, Frans
Dutch. Artist
b. 1580 in Antwerp, Belgium
d. Aug 26, 1666
Source: *AtlBL; McGEWB; REn*

Halsey, William Frederick
"Bull"
American. Admiral
Commanded US 3rd Fleet, 1944-45.
b. Oct 30, 1882 in Elizabeth, New Jersey
d. Aug 16, 1959 in Fishers Island, New
Jersey
Source: *CurBio 42, 59; WebAB; WhAm 3*

Halsman, Philippe
American. Photographer
Noted for honest realism in portraits; has
over 100 *Life* covers to credit.
b. May 2, 1906 in Riga, Russia
d. Jun 25, 1979 in New York, New York
Source: *AmAu&B; Au&Wr 71; AuBYP;
ConAu 89; ConPhot; CurBio 79; MacBEP;
NewYTBS 79; WhoAm 78; WhoAmA 82N;
WhoWor 76*

Halsted, Anna Eleanor Roosevelt
[Mrs. James A Halsted]
American. Newspaper Publisher
Daughter of Franklin and Eleanor Roosevelt;
wrote children's books.
b. May 3, 1906 in New York, New York
d. Dec 1, 1975 in New York, New York
Source: *ConAu 61; WhoE 74*

Halsted, William Stewart
American. Surgeon
b. Sep 23, 1852 in New York
d. Sep 7, 1922
Source: *AmBi; DcAmB; DcNAA; EncAB-H;
WebAB; WhAm 1*

Halston
[Roy Halston Frowick]
American. Fashion Designer
Won Coty Award 1962, 1969, 1971-72;
introduced pillbox hat.
b. Apr 23, 1932 in Des Moines, Iowa
Source: *BkPepl; WhoAm 80, 82; WorFshn*

Ham, Greg
see: Men at Work

Ham, Jack
American. Football Player
b. Dec 23, 1948 in Johnstown, Pennsylvania
Source: *BioIn 9; NewYTBE 70; WhoFtbl 74*

Ham, Peter
see: Badfinger

Hambleton, Hugh George
Canadian. Spy, Economist
Convicted of spying for Soviets while
working for NATO, 1956-61.
b. May 4, 1922 in Ottawa, Ontario
Source: *CanWW 81, 82*

Hambro, Leonid
American. Musician
b. Jun 26, 1920 in Chicago, Illinois
Source: *WhoAm 74*

Hamburger, Michael
British. Poet
b. 1924 in Berlin, Germany
Source: *BioIn 10*

Hamel, Veronica
American. Model, Actress
Plays Joyce Davenport on "Hill Street
Blues," 1981--.
b. Nov 20, 1945 in Philadelphia,
Pennsylvania
Source: *BioIn 12*

Hamen y Leon, Juan van der
Spanish. Artist
Known for still lifes; portraits include "The
Cook," 1930.
b. 1596 in Madrid, Spain
d. 1631 in Madrid, Spain
Source: *McGDA*

Hamer, Fannie Lou Townsend
American. Civil Rights Activist
b. 1917 in Mississippi
d. Mar 1977 in Mound Bayou, Mississippi
Source: *BioIn 6, 7, 9, 11*

Hamer, Robert
English. Director
Best known for *Kind Hearts and Coronets*,
1949.
b. Mar 31, 1911 in Kidderminster, England
d. Dec 4, 1963 in London, England
Source: *BiDFilm; CmMov; DcFM; FilmEn;
FilmgC; MovMk; OxFilm; WorEFlm*

Hamer, Rusty
American. Actor
Played Rusty in TV series "Make Room for
Daddy," 1953-71.
b. Feb 15, 1947
Source: *WhoHol A*

Hamill, Dorothy
American. Figure Skater
Won gold medal, 1976 Olympics.
b. 1956 in Greenwich, Connecticut
Source: *BkPepl; CurBio 76; WhoAm 82*

Hamill, Mark
"Motor-Mouth"
American. Actor
Played Luke Skywalker in *Star Wars*, 1977;
     The Empire Strikes Back, 1980.
b. Sep 25, 1952 in Oakland, California
Source: *BkPepl; FilmEn; IntMPA 82; WhoAm
78, 80, 82*

Hamill, "Pete" (William)
American. Journalist
Wrote *The Gift*, 1973; *Flesh and Blood*, 1977.
b. Jun 24, 1935 in Brooklyn, New York
Source: *CelR; ConAu 25R; ConLC 10;
IntMPA 75, 76, 77; WhoAm 82; WomWMM*

Hamilton, Alexander
American. Politician, Author
First US treasury secretary, 1789-95; mortally
     wounded in duel with Aaron Burr.
b. Jan 11, 1757 in Nevis, West Indies
d. Jul 11, 1804 in Weehawken, New Jersey
Source: *Alli; AmAu; AmAu&B; AmBi;
ApCAB; BbD; BiAUS; BiD&SB; BiDrAC;
BiDrUSE; CyAL 1; CyWA; DcAmAu;
DcAmB; DcEnL; DcLEL; DcNAA; Drake;
EncAB-H; EvLB; OxAmL; REn; REnAL;
TwCBDA; WebAB; WhAm HS; WhAmP*

Hamilton, Alice
American. Physician, Reformer
Pioneer in industrial toxicology.
b. Feb 27, 1869 in New York, New York
d. Sep 22, 1970 in Hadlyne, Connecticut
Source: *NotAW MOD*

Hamilton, Andrew
American. Lawyer
Helped establish freedom of the press in
     1735 libel trial.
b. 1676 in Scotland
d. Aug 4, 1741 in Philadelphia, Pennsylvania
Source: *AmBi; ApCAB; DcAmB; NatCAB 13;
WhAm HS*

Hamilton, Billy (William Robert)
American. Baseball Player
Held pre-modern era record for career stolen
     bases, 1937; Hall of Fame, 1961.
b. Feb 16, 1866 in Newark, New Jersey
d. Dec 16, 1940 in Worcester, Massachusetts
Source: *BaseEn 85; BasesB*

Hamilton, Charles Harold St. John
English. Author
Wrote boys adventure series, weekly papers;
     used over 20 pseudonyms in 5,000 stories.
b. Aug 8, 1875 in Ealing, England
d. Dec 24, 1961
Source: *BioIn 3, 6, 7, 8, 10; ConAu 73;
MnBBF; OxEng; SmATA 13; WhoChL*

Hamilton, Edith
American. Author
Mythology expert; wrote *The Greek Way*,
     1930; *The Roman Way*, 1932.
b. Aug 12, 1867 in Dresden, Germany
d. May 31, 1963 in Washington, District of
     Columbia
Source: *CurBio 63; NatCAB 52; REnAL;
WebAB*

Hamilton, Emma
[Emma Lyon]
English. Mistress
b. 1761
d. 1815
Source: *Alli; BiDLA; InWom; NewC; REn*

Hamilton, Floyd (Garland)
American. Gangster
Public enemy number one, 1930s; pardoned
     for work with ex-convicts.
b. 1908
d. Jun 26, 1984 in Grand Prairie, Texas
Source: *ConAu 113*

Hamilton, George
American. Actor
Star, producer of *Love at First Bite*, 1979;
     Zorro, the Gay Blade, 1981.
b. Aug 12, 1939 in Memphis, Tennessee
Source: *CelR; FilmgC; IntMPA 77, 78, 79,
80, 81, 82; MnBBF; MotPP; MovMk; WhoAm
82; WhoHol A*

Hamilton, Guy
British. Director
Best known for James Bond films *Goldfinger*,
     1964; *Diamonds Are Forever*, 1971.
b. 1922 in Paris, France
Source: *FilmEn; IntMPA 75*

Hamilton, Ian Standish Monteith, Sir
British. General, Author
b. 1853
d. Oct 12, 1947 in London, England
Source: *Alli SUP; ChhPo, S1*

Hamilton, Margaret
American. Actress
Played the Wicked Witch of the West in
     The Wizard of Oz, 1939.
b. Sep 12, 1902 in Cleveland, Ohio
d. May 16, 1985 in Salisbury, Connecticut
Source: *BiE&WWA; ConNews 85-3; FilmgC;
ForWC 70; IntMPA 82; MovMk; NotNAT;
ThFT; Vers A; WhoHol A*

Hamilton, Nancy
American. Actress, Songwriter
Wrote lyrics for Oscar-winning documentary
on Helen Keller, 1956.
b. Jul 27, 1908 in Sewickley, Pennsylvania
d. Feb 18, 1985 in New York, New York
Source: *BiE&WWA; ConAu 115; EncMT;
NotNAT*

Hamilton, Neil
American. Actor
b. Sep 9, 1899 in Lynn, Massachusetts
d. Sep 24, 1984 in Escondido, California
Source: *BiE&WWA; FilmgC; MovMk;
NotNAT; TwYS; WhoHol A*

Hamilton, Patrick
English. Dramatist, Actor, Author
Plays include *Angel Street,* 1945.
b. Mar 17, 1904 in Hassocho, England
d. Sep 23, 1962 in Sherringham, England
Source: *ConAu 113*

Hamilton, Roy
American. Singer
Baritone of 1950s; hits include "Ebb Tide,"
1954; "Unchained Melody," 1955.
b. Apr 16, 1929 in Leesburg, Georgia
d. Jul 20, 1969 in New Rochelle, New York
Source: *BiDAmM; BioIn 8; DrBlPA; IlEncBM
82; RkOn 74; WhoRock 81*

Hamilton, Scott
American. Musician
b. 1954 in Providence, Rhode Island
Source: *BioIn 12*

Hamilton, Scott
American. Figure Skater
Won gold medal, 1984 Olympics; known for
virtuoso stunts, triple jumps.
b. Aug 28, 1958 in Haverford, Pennsylvania
Source: *BioIn 12; CurBio 85; NewYTBS 83*

Hamilton, Virginia
American. Author
b. Mar 13, 1936 in Yellow Springs, Ohio
Source: *Au&ICB; AuBYP; AuNews 1;
BlkAWP; ChlLR 1; ChhPo S2; ConAu 25R;
MorBMP; NewbC 1966; SmATA 4; WhoAm
82; WhoAmW 77*

Hamilton, William
American. Cartoonist, Author
New Yorker cartoonist, 1965--; wrote
syndicated "Now Society" column since
1973.
b. Jun 2, 1939 in Palo Alto, California
Source: *BioIn 11; ConAu 69; WhoAm 84*

Hamilton, William, Sir
Scottish. Philosopher
b. Mar 8, 1788 in Glasgow, Scotland
d. May 6, 1856 in Edinburgh, Scotland
Source: *Alli; BiD&SB; BrAu 19; CasWL;
DcEnL; EvLB; NewC; OxEng*

Hamlin, Hannibal
American. Statesman
Vp under Lincoln, 1861-65.
b. Aug 27, 1809 in Paris Hill, Maine
d. Jul 4, 1891 in Bangor, Maine
Source: *AmBi; ApCAB; BiAUS; BiDrAC;
BiDrUSE; DcAmB; Drake; TwCBDA; WebAB;
WhAm HS; WhAmP*

Hamlin, Harry
American. Actor
Starred in *Clash of the Titans,* 1981; TV
mini-series "Studs Lonigan."
b. 1952 in Pasadena, California
Source: *IntMPA 82; NewYTBS 79*

Hamlin, Talbot Faulkner
American. Author
b. Jun 16, 1889 in New York, New York
d. Oct 7, 1956 in Beaufort, South Carolina
Source: *AmAu&B; CurBio 54, 56, 57;
OxAmL; WhAm 3*

Hamlin, Vincent T
American. Cartoonist
b. 1900 in Perry, Iowa
Source: *WorECom*

Hamlisch, Marvin
American. Composer, Musician
Wrote scores for *The Way We Were, The
Sting,* 1974; *A Chorus Line,* 1975.
b. Jun 2, 1944 in New York, New York
Source: *AmSCAP 66; BioNews 74; BkPepl;
IntMPA 82*

Hammarskjold, Dag
Swedish. Statesman
Secretary general, UN, 1953-61; won Nobel
Peace Prize, 1961.
b. Jul 29, 1905 in Jonkoping, Sweden
d. Sep 18, 1961 in Ndola, Rhodesia
Source: *ConAu 77; CurBio 53, 61; REn;
WhAm 4; WhoUN 75*

Hammarskjold, Knut Hjalmar L
Swedish. Political Leader
b. 1862
d. Oct 12, 1953 in Stockholm, Sweden
Source: *WebBD 80*

Hammer, Armand
American. Financier, Manufacturer
b. May 21, 1898 in New York, New York
Source: *BioNews 74; BusPN; CurBio 73;*
IntWW 74; NewYTBE 72, 73; St&PR 75;
WhoAm 74, 76, 78, 80, 82; WhoF&I 74;
WhoWest 84

Hammer, Jan
[Mahavishnu Orchestra]
Czech. Musician
Pianist who played with Sarah Vaughn, 1970,
Mahavishu Orchestra, 1971-73.
b. Apr 17, 1948 in Czechoslovakia
Source: *ConMuA 80A; EncJzS 70; WhoRock*
81

Hammerstein, Oscar
German. Manager, Impresario
b. May 8, 1846 in Berlin, Germany
d. Aug 1, 1919 in New York, New York
Source: *DcAmB; EncMT; OxAmL; WhAm 1;*
WhoStg 1906, 1908

Hammerstein, Oscar, II
[Rodgers and Hammerstein]
American. Lyricist
Wrote lyrics for *Oklahoma!,* 1943; *Carousel,*
1945; *South Pacific,* 1949.
b. Jul 12, 1895 in New York, New York
d. Aug 23, 1960 in Doylestown, Pennsylvania
Source: *AmSCAP 66; ConAu 101; CurBio 44,*
60; ModWD; OxThe; REn; WebAB; WhAm
4; WhScrn 77

Hammett, (Samuel) Dashiell
American. Author
Created fictional detective Sam Spade in *The*
Maltese Falcon, 1930.
b. May 27, 1894 in Saint Marys, Maryland
d. Jan 10, 1961 in New York, New York
Source: *AmAu&B; AuNews 1; CasWL;*
CmMov; CnDAL; ConAu 81; ConLC 3, 5, 10;
CyWA; DcFM; DcLEL; EncAB-H; EncMys;
EvLB; FilmgC; LongCTC; MnBBF; ModAL,
Sl; OxAmL; OxEng; OxFilm; PenC AM;
REn; REnAL; TwCA, SUP; TwCWr; WebAB;
WebE&AL; WhAm 4; WhoTwCL; WorEFlm

Hammon, Jupiter
American. Poet
b. 1720
d. 1800
Source: *AmAu; AmAu&B; BlkAWP; DcAmB;*
DcNAA; OxAmL; REnAL; WhAm HS

Hammond, Bray
American. Author
b. Nov 20, 1886 in Springfield, Missouri
d. Jul 20, 1968 in Thetford, Vermont
Source: *AmAu&B; OxAmL; WhAm 5*

Hammond, John Henry, Jr.
American. Music Executive
VP, Columbia Records; discovered Billie
Holiday, Aretha Franklin, Bob Dylan;
contributed to development of jazz.
b. Dec 15, 1910 in New York, New York
Source: *BioIn 9; CurBio 79; EncJzS 70;*
WhoAm 78

Hammond, Laurens
American. Inventor
b. Jan 11, 1895 in Evanston, Illinois
d. Jul 1, 1973 in Cornwall, Connecticut
Source: *NewYTBE 73; WhAm 6; WhoAm 74;*
WhoMus 72

Hammond-Innes, Ralph
see: Innes, Hammond, pseud.

Hammurabi
Babylonian. King
Started to build tower of Babel; established
written code of law.
b. 1955 BC
d. 1913 BC
Source: *BioIn 1, 5, 6, 8, 9, 11; NewCol 75;*
WebBD 80

Hamner, Earl Henry, Jr.
American. Author
Creator of TV series "The Waltons," "Falcon
Crest."
b. Jul 10, 1923 in Schuyler, Virginia
Source: *AuNews 2; BioIn 10, 11; ConAu 73;*
ConLC 12; WhoAm 78, 80, 82

Hampden, John
English. Statesman
b. 1594 in London, England
d. Jun 24, 1643 in Thame, England
Source: *Alli; NewC; REn*

Hampden, Walter
[Walter Hampden Dougherty]
American. Actor
Starred in *Hamlet, Cyrano de Bergerac;*
fourth pres., Players' Club, 1927-54.
b. Jun 30, 1879 in New York, New York
d. Jun 11, 1955 in Los Angeles, California
Source: *CurBio 53, 55; DcAmB S5; FamA&A;*
Film 1; FilmgC; MotPP; MovMk; OxThe;
REn; REnAL; Vers B; WebAB; WhAm 3;
WhScrn 74, 77; WhoHol B; WhoStg 1908

Hampshire, Susan
English. Actress
Won Emmys, 1970, 71, 73; appeared in
series "The Forsythe Saga," "The First
Churchills."
b. May 12, 1942 in London, England
Source: *CelR; CurBio 74; FilmgC; IntMPA
75, 76, 77, 78, 79, 80, 81, 82; NewYTBE 70;
WhoAm 74, 76, 78, 80, 82; WhoHol A;
WhoThe 77*

Hampson, Frank
English. Cartoonist, Author
Created science fiction cartoon character Dan
Dare, 1950.
b. Dec 21, 1918 in Manchester, England
d. Jul 8, 1985 in Surrey, England
Source: *ConAu 117; EncSF; WorECom*

Hampton, Christopher James
British. Dramatist
Wrote 1971 Tony Award winner *The
Philanthropist.*
b. Jan 26, 1946 in Fayal, Azores
Source: *Au&Wr 71; BioIn 11; CnThe; ConAu
25R; ConLC 1, 2, 3, 4, 5, 6; DcLEL 1940;
IntAu&W 76; IntWW 78; WhoThe 72, 77;
WrDr 80*

Hampton, Fred
American. Revolutionary
b. 1952
d. 1969
Source: *BioIn 11*

Hampton, Hope
American. Socialite, Actress
Silent film star, NYC socialite; noted for
lavish dress.
b. 1901 in Houston, Texas
d. Jan 2, 1982 in New York, New York
Source: *FilmgC; InWom; MotPP; NewYTBS
82; TwYS; WhoHol A*

Hampton, James
American. Actor
In films *The Longest Yard; The China
Syndrome.*
b. Jul 9, 1936 in Oklahoma City, Oklahoma
Source: *VarWW 85; WhoHol A*

Hampton, Lionel
American. Band Leader
Formed orchestra late 1930s; theme song
"Flying Home."
b. Apr 20, 1914 in Louisville, Kentucky
Source: *CelR; CurBio 71; WhoAm 74, 76, 78,
80, 82; WhoBlA 75; WhoE 74; WhoHol A*

Hampton, Robert Edward
American. Government Official
b. Sep 21, 1922 in Chattanooga, Tennessee
Source: *BioIn 10; WhoAm 78, 80, 82*

Hampton, Wade
American. General
b. Mar 28, 1818 in Charleston, South
Carolina
d. Apr 11, 1902 in Columbia, South Carolina
Source: *AmBi; ApCAB; BiDConf; BiDrAC;
DcAmB; Drake; EncAB-H; TwCBDA; WebAB;
WhAm 1; WhAmP*

Hamsun, Knut Pederson
[Knut Pedersen]
Norwegian. Author
Won Nobel Prize for literature, 1920.
b. Aug 4, 1859 in Lom, New York
d. Feb 19, 1952 in Noerholmen, New York
Source: *AtlBL; CasWL; ClDMEL; CnMD;
CyWA; DcBiA; EncWL; EvEuW; LongCTC;
PenC EUR; REn; REnWD; TwCA, SUP;
TwCWr; WhAm 3, 4; WhoLA; WhoTwCL*

Han, Suyin
Chinese. Author
b. Sep 12, 1917 in Peking, China
Source: *Au&Wr 71; ConAu 17R; InWom;
IntWW 74; TwCWr; Who 74; WorAu; WrDr
80*

Hanauer, "Chip" (Lee Edward)
American. Boat Racer
Hydroplane racer; won American
Powerboat Assn. Gold Cup, 1982-85.
b. Jul 1, 1954 in Seattle, Washington
Source: *ConNews 86-2*

Hancock, Herbie (Herbert Jeffrey)
American. Jazz Musician, Composer
Jazz pianist who won Grammy, 1984, for
electronic jazz composition "Rockit."
b. Apr 12, 1940 in Chicago, Illinois
Source: *BioNews 74; ConNews 85-1; WhoAm
82, 84; WhoBlA 75; WhoE 74*

Hancock, John
American. Statesman
First to sign Declaration of Independence,
1776, in very bold handwriting.
b. Jan 12, 1737 in Braintree, Massachusetts
d. Oct 8, 1793 in Quincy, Massachusetts
Source: *Alli; AmBi; ApCAB; BiAUS; BiDrAC;
BiDrUSE; DcAmB; Drake; EncAB-H; REn;
REnAL; TwCBDA; WebAB; WhAm HS;
WhAmP*

Hancock, John D
American. Director
Films include *Bang the Drum Slowly,* 1973;
  Baby Blue Marine, 1976.
b. Feb 12, 1939 in Kansas City, Missouri
Source: *FilmEn; IntMPA 81; MovMk;*
  WhoAm 84

Hand, Learned
American. Judge
Considered one of greatest jurists of his day.
b. Jan 27, 1872 in Albany, New York
d. Aug 18, 1961 in New York, New York
Source: *AmAu&B; CurBio 50, 61; EncAB-H;*
  WebAB; WhAm 4

Handel, George Frederick
[Georg Friedrich Handel]
German. Composer
Composed 46 operas; best known work *The
  Messiah,* 1742.
b. Feb 23, 1685 in Halle, Germany
d. Apr 14, 1759 in London, England
Source: *AtlBL; NewC; REn*

Handelman, Stanley Myron
American. Comedian
Source: *NF*

Handler, Elliot
American. Manufacturer
With wife, introduced Barbie doll, 1958,
  named for daughter, Barbara; Ken named
  for son.
b. 1916 in Denver, Colorado
Source: *WhoAm 74; WhoF&I 75*

Handler, Ruth
[Mrs. Elliot Handler]
American. Manufacturer
With husband, introduced Barbie doll, 1958,
  named for daughter, Barbara.
b. Nov 4, 1916 in Denver, Colorado
Source: *WhoAmW 75; WhoF&I 75*

Handlin, Oscar
American. Educator, Historian
b. Mar 29, 1915 in Brooklyn, New York
Source: *Au&Wr 71; ConAu 1R, 5NR; DrAS
  74H; OxAmL; REnAL; TwCA SUP; WebAB;
  Who 74; WhoAm 74, 76, 78, 80, 82; WhoE
  74; WhoWor 78; WhoWorJ 72; WrDr 80*

Handwerker, Nathan
American. Restaurateur
b. 1890
d. Mar 24, 1974
Source: *NewYTBS 74*

Handy, Thomas Troy
American. Army Officer
b. Mar 11, 1892 in Spring City, Tennessee
d. Apr 14, 1982 in San Antonio, Texas
Source: *CurBio 51, 82; NewYTBS 82;*
  WebAMB; Who 74

Handy, W(illiam) C(hristopher)
"Father of the Blues"
American. Composer, Musician
Took the "blues" beyond the southern US,
  writing "St. Louis Blues," 1914; "Beale
  Street Blues," 1917.
b. Nov 16, 1873 in Florence, Alabama
d. Mar 29, 1958 in New York, New York
Source: *AmAu&B; AmSCAP 66; CurBio 41,
  58; EncAB-H; OxAmL; REnAL; WebAB;
  WhAm 3; WhoJazz 72*

Hanes, John Wesley
American. Manufacturer
Launched Hanes Hosiery Mills, producing
  men's, women's stockings.
b. 1850
d. 1903
Source: *Entr*

Hanes, Pleasant H
American. Manufacturer
Launched P H Hanes Knitting Co., 1902,
  making underwear.
b. Oct 16, 1845 in Fulton Davie County,
  North Carolina
d. Jun 9, 1925 in Winston-Salem, North
  Carolina
Source: *Entr; NatCAB 22*

Haney, Carol
American. Choreographer, Dancer
In Broadway musical *Pajama Game,* 1954;
  choreographed *Funny Girl,* 1964.
b. Dec 24, 1924 in Bedford, Massachusetts
d. May 10, 1964 in Saddle River, New
  Jersey
Source: *EncMT; FilmgC; NotNAT B; WhAm
  4; WhScrn 74, 77; WhoHol B; WorAl*

Haney, Chris
Canadian. Photojournalist, Inventor
With Scott Abbott, John Haney, invented
  board game Trivial Pursuit, 1979.
b. 1949
Source: *ConNews 85-1*

Haney, John
Canadian. Inventor
With Chris Haney, Scott Abbott, invented
  board game Trivial Pursuit, 1979.
Source: *ConNews 85-1*

Haney, Paul Prichard
American. Journalist
b. Jul 20, 1928 in Akron, Ohio
Source: *BioIn 8; WhoAm 74*

Hanfmann, George Maxim Anossov
American. Archaeologist, Educator
Field director, Harvard-Cornell expedition,
1958-76, that uncovered ancient capital of
Lydia.
b. Nov 20, 1911 in Saint Petersburg, Russia
d. Mar 13, 1986 in Cambridge,
Massachusetts
Source: *CurBio 67, 86; DrAS 82H; WhoAmA
84*

Hanfstaengl, Ernst Franz Sedgwick
"Putzi"
German. Author
Foreign press chief, 1932-37, friend of Hitler,
who entertained Fuhrer on piano.
b. Feb 11, 1887 in Munich, Germany
d. Nov 6, 1975 in Munich, Germany (West)
Source: *NewYTBS 75; ObitOF 79*

Hanika, Sylvia
German. Tennis Player
Tour player since 1978; voted most
improved, 1979.
b. Nov 30, 1959 in Munich, Germany (West)
Source: *WhoIntT*

Hanks, Nancy
[Mrs. Thomas Lincoln]
American. Celebrity Relative
Mother of Abraham Lincoln; died when son
was nine.
b. 1784
d. 1818 in Spencer County, Indiana
Source: *HerW; WhAm 8*

Hanks, Nancy
American. Government Official
Chm., National Endowment for the Arts,
1969-77.
b. Dec 31, 1927 in Miami Beach, Florida
d. Jan 7, 1983 in New York, New York
Source: *CurBio 71, 83; LibW; PolProf NF;
WhoAm 74, 76, 78, 80, 82; WhoAmA 78, 80;
WhoAmP 73, 75, 77, 79; WhoAmW 58, 61,
64, 66, 68, 70, 72, 74, 75; WhoGov 72, 75,
77*

Hanks, Tom
American. Actor
Starred in movies *Spalsh*, 1984; *Bachelor
Party*, 1984.
b. Jul 9, 1956 in Oakland, California
Source: *VarWW 85*

Hanley, William
American. Dramatist
b. Oct 22, 1931 in Lorain, Ohio
Source: *BiE&WWA; CnMD SUP; ConAu
41R; CroCD; DrAF 76; ModWD; NotNAT;
WhoAm 74; WhoE 74; WhoThe 77; WrDr 76*

Hanna, Mark (Marcus Alonzo)
American. Businessman, Politician
b. Sep 24, 1837 in New Lisbon, Ohio
d. Feb 15, 1904 in Washington, District of
Columbia
Source: *AmBi; ApCAB SUP; BiDrAC;
DcAmB; EncAB-H; OhA&B; OxAmL; REnAL;
TwCBDA; WebAB; WhAm 1*

Hanna, William Denby
[Hanna and Barbera]
American. Cartoonist
With Joseph Barbera, created cartoons "Yogi
Bear," "The Flintstones."
b. Jul 14, 1910 in Melrose, New Mexico
Source: *CurBio 83; FilmgC; IntMPA 82;
OxFilm; WhoAm 82; WhoTelC; WorEFlm*

Hanna and Barbera
see: Barbera, Joseph; Hanna, William

Hannagan, Steve (Stephen Jerome)
American. Journalist
b. Apr 4, 1899 in Lafayette, Indiana
d. Feb 5, 1953 in Nairobi, Kenya
Source: *CurBio 44, 53; DcAmB S5; WhAm 3*

Hannah
Biblical Character
Source: *InWom*

Hannah, Daryl
American. Actress
Films include *Splash*, 1984; *Legal Eagles*,
1986.
b. in Chicago, Illinois
Source: *VarWW 85*

Hannah, John Allen
"Hog"
American. Football Player
b. Apr 4, 1951 in Canton, Georgia
Source: *BioIn 12; FootReg 81*

Hannibal
Military Leader
Carthaginian general, who with 35,000
soldiers, elephants, crossed Alps into
Italy, 221 BC; known for tactical genius.
b. 247 BC
d. 183 BC
Source: *LinLib S; NewCol 75; REn; WhDW*

Hannum, Alex(ander Murray)
American. Basketball Coach
Coached NBA championship teams, St.
Louis, 1965, Philadelphia, 1967.
b. Jul 19, 1923 in Los Angeles, California
Source: *BioIn 7; WhoBbl 73*

Hansberry, Lorraine
American. Author, Dramatist
Wrote *A Raisin in the Sun,* 1959, first play
by black woman produced on Broadway.
b. May 19, 1930 in Chicago, Illinois
d. Jan 2, 1965 in New York, New York
Source: *AmAu&B; AuNews 2; BiE&WWA;
BlkAWP; CasWL; CnMD SUP; ConAu 25R;
CroCD; CurBio 65; InWom; McGEWD;
ModAL S1; ModWD; NotAW MOD; PIP&P;
REnAL; WhAm 4; WorAu*

Hansen, Alvin Harvey
American. Educator
b. Aug 23, 1887 in Viborg, South Dakota
d. Jun 6, 1975 in Alexandria, Virginia
Source: *AmAu&B; ConAu 57, P-1; CurBio 45;
EncAB-H; IntWW 74; WebAB; WhAm 6;
Who 74; WhoAm 74*

Hansen, Clifford Peter
American. Senator
b. Oct 16, 1912 in Zenith, Wyoming
Source: *BiDrAC; CngDr 74; IntWW 74;
WhoAm 74; WhoAmP 73; WhoGov 75;
WhoWest 84*

Hansen, Joseph
[Rose Brock; James Colton; James Coulton,
pseuds.]
American. Author, Poet
Created detective character Dave
Brandstetter; wrote novel *Skinflick,* 1980.
b. Jul 19, 1923 in Aberdeen, South Dakota
Source: *ConAu 29R; IntAu&W 77;
TwCCr&M 80*

Hansen, Patti (Patricia Evina)
[Mrs. Keith Richard]
American. Model, Actress
b. 1956 in Staten Island, New York
Source: *BioIn 12*

Hanslick, Eduard
Czech. Music Critic
b. Sep 11, 1825 in Prague, Czechoslovakia
d. Aug 6, 1904 in Baden, Austria
Source: *BbD; BiD&SB*

Hansom, Joseph Aloysius
English. Inventor
Patented safety cab, 1834, two-wheeled, one-
horse enclosed cab.
b. Oct 26, 1803 in York, England
d. Jun 29, 1882 in London, England
Source: *BiDBrA; DcNaB; InSci; MacEA;
NewC; WhoArch*

Hanson, Duane Elwood
American. Sculptor
Specializes in plastic human effigies set in
realistic situations.
b. Jan 17, 1925 in Alexandria, Minnesota
Source: *CurBio 83; WhoAm 82; WhoAmA 73*

Hanson, Howard Harold
American. Composer, Conductor, Educator
b. Oct 28, 1896 in Wahoo, Nebraska
d. Feb 26, 1981 in Rochester, New York
Source: *AmSCAP 66; Baker 78; BiDAmEd;
BiDAmM; BioIn 1, 2, 3, 4, 6, 7, 8, 9, 11;
CurBio 41, 66, 81; DcCM; DrAS 74H, 78H;
IntWW 74, 75, 76, 77, 78; LinLib S;
McGEWB; NewEOp 71; NewYTBS 81;
OxAmL; OxMus; WebAB; WhAm 7; WhoAm
74, 76, 78, 80; WhoE 74; WhoMus 72;
WhoWor 74, 76, 78*

Hanson, John
American. Colonial Leader
First pres. Continental Congress, 1781-82.
b. Apr 13, 1721 in Charles County,
Maryland
d. Nov 22, 1783 in Oxon Hill, Maryland
Source: *BioIn 1, 3, 4, 7; NewCol 75; WebAB*

Hanson, Kitty
American. Journalist
b. in Chicago, Illinois
Source: *AmAu&B; WhoAm 74, 76, 78, 80, 82*

Hapgood, Norman
American. Editor, Author
b. Mar 28, 1868 in Chicago, Illinois
d. Apr 29, 1937
Source: *AmAu&B; AmBi; BiD&SB; DcAmAu;
DcAmB S2; DcNAA; OxAmL; REnAL;
TwCA; WhAm 1*

Harbach, Otto Abels
American. Librettist
b. Aug 18, 1873 in Salt Lake City, Utah
d. Jan 24, 1963 in New York, New York
Source: *AmAu&B; AmSCAP 66; CurBio 50,
63; EncMT; NewCBMT; REnAL; WhAm 4*

Harbison, John Harris
American. Composer, Educator
MIT music professor, 1962--; wrote opera
Full Moon in March, 1979.
b. Dec 20, 1938 in Orange, New Jersey
Source: *Baker 78; DcCM; WhoAm 84*

Harburg, E(dgar) Y(ipsel)
"Yip"
American. Composer
Wrote lyrics for "Somewhere Over the
Rainbow," from *Wizard of Oz,* 1939.
b. Apr 8, 1896 in New York, New York
d. Mar 5, 1981 in Los Angeles, California
Source: *AmPS; AmSCAP 66; BiDAmM;
BiE&WWA; BioIn 5, 8, 9, 10; CelR;
CmpEPM; ConAu 85, 103; ConDr 73, 77D;
CurBio 80, 81; EncMT; IntAu&W 77;
NewCBMT; NewYTBS 81; NotNAT; WhAm
7; WhoAm 74, 76, 78, 80; WhoThe 72, 77,
81*

Hardie, James Keir
Scottish. Labor Union Official
Coal miner; founded Scottish Labor Party,
1888.
b. 1856 in Scotland
d. 1915
Source: *NewCol 75; WebBD 80*

Hardin, Louis Thomas
"Moondog"
Musician
b. 1916
Source: *BioIn 3, 11*

Hardin, Tim
American. Songwriter, Singer
Wrote song "If I Were a Carpenter,"
recorded by Bobby Darin, Bob Seger,
others.
b. Dec 23, 1941 in Eugene, Oregon
d. Dec 29, 1980 in Hollywood, California
Source: *AnObit 1980; IlEncRk; WhoRock 81*

Harding, Ann
[Dorothy Walton Gatley]
American. Actress
Film star, 1930s; received Oscar nomination
for *Holiday,* 1930.
b. Aug 17, 1904 in Fort Sam Houston,
Texas
d. Sep 1, 1981 in Sherman Oaks, California
Source: *BiE&WWA; BioIn 9, 10; Film 2;
FilmgC; InWom; IntMPA 77, 78, 79, 80, 81,
82; MotPP; MovMk; NotNAT; OxFilm; ThFT;
Who 74; WhoHol A; WhoThe 77A*

Harding, Chester
American. Army Officer, Engineer
b. Dec 31, 1866 in Enterprise, Mississippi
d. Nov 11, 1936
Source: *WhAm 1*

Harding, Florence Kling De Wolfe
[Mrs. Warren G Harding]
American. First Lady
Ambitious divorcee who pushed Warren into
presidency; burned his executive papers.
b. Aug 15, 1860 in Marion, Ohio
d. Nov 21, 1924 in Marion, Ohio
Source: *GoodHs; NatCAB 20; NotAW*

Harding, Warren G(amaliel)
American. US President
Pres., 1921-23; administration marked by
many scandals.
b. Nov 2, 1865 in Blooming Grove, Ohio
d. Aug 2, 1923 in San Francisco, California
Source: *AmAu&B; AmBi; BiDrAC; BiDrUSE;
DcAmB; DcNAA; EncAB-H; NewYTBE 72;
OhA&B; OxAmL; REn; REnAL; St&PR 75;
WebAB; WhAm 1; WhAmP*

Hardwick, Billy
American. Bowler
b. 1932
Source: *NewYTBS 74*

Hardwick, Cathy
Fashion Designer
b. 1934
Source: *BioIn 11*

Hardwick, Elizabeth
American. Author
First woman recipient of Nathan Drama
Criticism Award, 1967.
b. Jul 27, 1916 in Lexington, Kentucky
Source: *AmAu&B; AmWomWr; ConLC 13;
CurBio 81; IntAu&W 77; WhoAm 84;
WorAu; WrDr 80*

Hardwicke, Cedric Webster, Sir
English. Actor
Character actor in authoritative, villain roles:
The Hunchback of Notre Dame, 1939;
Suspicion, 1941.
b. Feb 19, 1893 in Lye, England
d. Aug 6, 1964 in New York, New York
Source: *BiDFilm; BiE&WWA; CurBio 49, 64;
Film 1; FilmgC; LongCTC; MotPP; MovMk;
NewC; OxFilm; OxThe; PIP&P; WhAm 4;
WhScrn 74, 77; WhoHol B*

Hardy, Oliver
[Laurel and Hardy; Norvell Hardy]
American. Comedian
First film with Laurel, *Putting Pants on
Philip,* 1926.
b. Jan 18, 1892 in Atlanta, Georgia
d. Aug 7, 1957 in Hollywood, California
Source: *BiDFilm; CmMov; Film 1; FilmgC;
MotPP; MovMk; OxFilm; TwYS; WebAB;
WhScrn 74, 77; WhoHol B; WorEFlm*

Hardy, Thomas
English. Author, Poet
Wrote *Far From the Madding Crowd,* 1874;
Tess of the D'Ubervilles, 1891.
b. Jun 2, 1840 in Dorsetshire, England
d. Jan 11, 1928 in Dorchester, England
Source: *Alli SUP; AnCL; AtlBL; BbD;
BiD&SB; BrAu 19; CasWL; Chambr 3;
ChhPo, S1, S2; CnE&AP; CnMWL; CrtT 3;
CyWA; DcBiA; DcEnA, AP; DcEnL; DcEuL;
DcLEL; EncWL; EvLB; LongCTC; ModBrL,
S1; ModWD; NewC; OxEng; PenC ENG;
RAdv 1; RComWL; REn; TwCWr;
WebE&AL; WhoChL; WhoLA; WhoTwCL*

Hare, David
English. Dramatist
Award-winning playwright: *Knuckle,* 1974;
Plenty, 1978.
b. Jun 5, 1947 in Saint Leonards, England
Source: *BioIn 11; CnThe; ConDr 73, 77;
CurBio 83; DcLEL 1940; EncWT; IntAu&W
76; NewYTBS 82; WhoAm 84; WhoThe 77;
WrDr 80*

Hare, Ernie (Thomas Ernest)
[The Interwoven Pair]
Singer
b. 1883
d. 1939
Source: *BioIn 5*

Hare, James Henry
English. Journalist
b. Oct 3, 1856 in London, England
d. Jun 24, 1946 in Teaneck, New Jersey
Source: *DcAmB S4; WhAm 2*

Hare, William
[Burke and Hare]
Irish. Murderer
With William Burke murdered 15 people,
sold bodies to school of anatomy.
b. 1792 in Derry, Northern Ireland
d. 1870
Source: *BioIn 1, 4, 10*

**Harewood, George Henry Hubert Lascelles,
Earl**
English. Music Director, Critic
b. Feb 7, 1923 in Leeds, England
Source: *Au&Wr 71; BioIn 2, 7, 8; CurBio 65*

Harger, Rolla
American. Scientist
Invented the Drunkometer, first instrument
to test drivers toxication level.
b. Jan 14, 1890 in Decatur County, Kansas
d. Aug 8, 1983 in Indianapolis, Indiana
Source: *AnObit 1983; IndAu 1917; NewYTBS
83*

Hargis, Billy James
American. Evangelist
b. Aug 3, 1925 in Texarkana, Texas
Source: *CelR; CurBio 72; WhoAm 82;
WhoS&SW 82*

Haring, Keith
American. Artist
Graffiti artist known for drawings in NYC
subways.
b. May 4, 1958 in Kutztown, Pennsylvania
Source: *CurBio 86*

Harkin, Thomas R
American. Politician
Dem. congressman from IA, 1974-84,
senator, 1984--.
b. Nov 19, 1939 in Cumming, Iowa
Source: *CngDr 85*

Harkness, Anna M Richardson
American. Philanthropist
b. Oct 25, 1837 in Dalton, Ohio
d. Mar 27, 1926 in New York, New York
Source: *NotAW*

Harkness, Edward Stephen
American. Businessman, Philanthropist
b. Jan 22, 1874 in Cleveland, Ohio
d. Jan 29, 1940
Source: *AmBi; CurBio 40; DcAmB S2; WhAm
1*

Harkness, Rebekah West
American. Philanthropist, Composer
Founded Harkness Ballet, 1964-74, Rebekah
Harkness Foundation, to support dance
companies, 1959.
b. Apr 17, 1915 in Saint Louis, Missouri
d. Jun 17, 1982 in New York, New York
Source: *AmSCAP 66, 80; CelR; CurBio 74,
82; GoodHs; NewYTBS 82; WhoAm 74, 76,
78, 80, 82; WhoAmW 70, 72, 74, 75, 77, 79;
WhoE 74; WhoGov 72, 75, 77*

Harlan, John Marshall
American. Supreme Court Justice
b. Jun 1, 1833 in Boyle County, Kentucky
d. Oct 14, 1911 in Washington, District of
  Columbia
Source: *AmBi; ApCAB; BiDSA; DcAmB;
DcNAA; EncAB-H; TwCBDA; WebAB; WhAm
1*

Harlan, John Marshall
American. Supreme Court Justice
b. May 20, 1899 in Chicago, Illinois
d. Dec 29, 1971 in Washington, District of
  Columbia
Source: *ConAu 33R; CurBio 55, 72; WebAB;
WhAm 5; WhoS&SW 82*

Harlan, Louis R
American. Author
Won Pulitzer, 1984, for biography *Booker T
  Washington: The Wizard of Tuskegee.*
b. Jul 13, 1922 in West Point, Mississippi
Source: *ConAu 21R; DrAS 82H; NewYTBS
84*

Harlan, Veit
German. Director
Under Goebbels turned out Nazi propaganda
  films, including *Jew Suess,* 1940.
b. Sep 22, 1899 in Berlin, Germany
d. Apr 13, 1964 in Capri, Italy
Source: *FilmEn; FilmgC; WhScrn 77*

**Harlech, William David Ormsby-Gore,
  Baron**
British. Diplomat
Confidant of John F Kennedy who was
  British ambassador to Washington, 1961-
  65.
b. May 20, 1918
d. Jan 26, 1985 in Shrewsbury, England
Source: *IntWW 74; Who 74; WhoWor 74*

Harlem Globetrotters
American. Basketball Team
Source: *NF*

Harlow, Jean
[Harlean Carpenter]
"Blonde Bombshell"
American. Actress
Platinum blonde star of *Hell's Angels,* 1930;
  Dinner at Eight, 1933; sex queen of 1930s.
b. Mar 3, 1911 in Kansas City, Missouri
d. Jun 7, 1937 in Los Angeles, California
Source: *BiDFilm; DcAmB S2; FilmgC;
InWom; MotPP; MovMk; NotAW; OxFilm;
ThFT; TwYS; WebAB; WhAm HSA, 4;
WhScrn 74, 77; WhoHol B; WorEFlm*

Harman, Fred
American. Cartoonist
Created syndicated "Red Ryder" comic strips
  for 25 yrs.
b. Feb 9, 1902 in Saint Joseph, Missouri
d. Jan 2, 1982 in Phoenix, Arizona
Source: *NewYTBS 82; WorECom*

Harman, Hugh
American. Cartoonist
Created *Looney Tunes* and *Merry Melodies*
  cartoon series.
b. 1903 in Pagosa Springs, Colorado
d. Nov 26, 1982 in Chatsworth, California
Source: *AnObit 1982; WorECar*

Harman, Jeanne Perkins
American. Author, Journalist
b. Jul 27, 1919 in Baxter Springs, Kansas
Source: *BioIn 10; ConAu 69; ForWC 70*

Harmon, Ernest N
American. Army Officer
b. Feb 26, 1894 in Lowell, Massachusetts
d. Nov 1979 in Vermont
Source: *CurBio 46; NewYTBS 79; WhoAm 74*

Harmon, Mark
American. Actor
Son of Tom Harmon and Elyse Knox;
  starred in "St. Elsewhere," 1984-86.
b. Sep 2, 1951 in Burbank, California
Source: *BioIn 9, 11; IntMPA 82*

Harmon, Tom (Thomas D)
American. Football Player, Sportscaster
Won Heisman Trophy at U of Michigan,
  1940; father of Mark Harmon.
b. Sep 28, 1919 in Rensselaer, Indiana
Source: *BioIn 3, 8, 9, 10; IndAu 1917;
IntMPA 75, 76, 77, 78, 79, 80, 81, 82;
WhoFtbl 74; WhoHol A*

**Harmsworth, Alfred Charles William,
  Viscount**
see: Northcliffe, Alfred Charles William
  Harmsworth, Viscount

Harmsworth, Harold Sidney
[First Viscount Rothermere]
English. Businessman
With brother Alfred, owned many
  newspapers, revolutionized British
  journalism.
b. Apr 26, 1868 in Hampstead, England
d. Nov 26, 1940 in Bermuda
Source: *CurBio 41; DcNaB 1931; NewC;
WorAl*

Harnack, Curtis Arthur
American. Author
b. Jun 27, 1927 in Le Mars, Iowa
Source: *AmAu&B; BioIn 9; ConAu 1R, 2NR;*
DrAF 76; WrDr 80

Harnett, William Michael
American. Artist
b. Aug 10, 1848 in County Cork, Ireland
d. Oct 29, 1892 in New York, New York
Source: *WebAB*

Harney, Benjamin Robertson
American. Composer
Known for early ragtime compositions.
b. Mar 6, 1871
d. Mar 1, 1938 in Philadelphia, Pennsylvania
Source: *DcAmB S2*

Harnick, Sheldon Mayer
American. Lyricist
b. Apr 30, 1924 in Chicago, Illinois
Source: *BiE&WWA; CelR; EncMT; IntWW*
74; NewCBMT; NotNAT; PIP&P; WhoAm 74,
76, 78, 80, 82; WhoWor 78

Harnwell, Gaylord Probasco
American. Physicist, Educator
Pres., U of Pennsylvania, 1953-70.
b. Sep 29, 1903 in Evanston, Illinois
d. Apr 18, 1982 in Haverford, Pennsylvania
Source: *AmM&WS 79P; CurBio 82;*
NewYTBS 82; WhoAm 80

Harold II
British. King
b. 1022
d. Oct 15, 1066 in Hastings, England
Source: *BioIn 10; McGEWB; WebBD 80*

Harper, Fletcher
[Harper Brothers]
American. Publisher
b. Jan 31, 1806 in Newton, New York
d. May 29, 1877 in New York, New York
Source: *AmAu&B; WebAB; WhAm HS*

Harper, Frances Ellen Watkins
American. Poet
b. 1825
d. 1911
Source: *BioIn 3, 4, 7, 8*

Harper, Heather
[Mrs. Buck]
British. Opera Singer
b. May 8, 1930 in Belfast, Northern Ireland
Source: *IntWW 74; Who 74; WhoAm 82;*
WhoWor 78

Harper, James
[Harper Brothers]
American. Publisher
b. Apr 13, 1795 in Newton, New York
d. Mar 27, 1869 in New York, New York
Source: *AmAu&B; WebAB; WhAm HS*

Harper, John
[Harper Brothers]
American. Publisher
b. Jan 22, 1797 in Newton, New York
d. Apr 22, 1875 in New York, New York
Source: *WebAB*

Harper, Joseph Wesley
[Harper Brothers]
American. Publisher
b. Dec 25, 1801 in Newton, New York
d. Feb 14, 1870 in New York, New York
Source: *WebAB*

Harper, Tess
[Tessie Jean Washam]
American. Actress
In movies *Silkwood; Tender Mercies.*
b. 1950 in Mammoth Spring, Arkansas
Source: *NF*

Harper, Valerie
American. Actress
Won four Emmys for role of Rhoda in "The
Mary Tyler Moore Show," 1970-74,
"Rhoda," 1974-78.
b. Aug 22, 1941 in Suffern, New York
Source: *BioNews 75; BkPepl; CurBio 75;*
IntMPA 77, 78, 79, 80, 81, 82; NewYTBE
71; NewYTBS 74; WhoAm 82; WhoHol A

Harper, William Rainey
American. Educator
b. Jul 26, 1846 in New Concord, Ohio
d. Jan 10, 1906 in Chicago, Illinois
Source: *AmAu&B; AmBi; ApCAB; DcAmAu;*
DcAmB; DcNAA; EncAB-H; OhA&B; REnAL;
TwCBDA; WebAB; WhAm 1

Harpignies, Henri
French. Artist
Landscape painter of Barbizon School; in
first Impressionist exhibition, 1874.
b. 1819 in Valenciennes, France
d. 1916 in Saint Prive, France
Source: *McGDA; OxFr*

Harrah, Bill (William Fisk)
American. Gambler, Businessman
Founded Harrah's Casino, 1937; Harrah's
Tahoe Casino, 1955.
b. Sep 2, 1911 in Pasadena, California
d. Jun 30, 1978 in Rochester, Minnesota
Source: *BioIn 10; WhAm 7; WhoAm 78*

Harrar, J(acob) George
American. Botanist
Pres., of Rockefeller Foundation, 1961-72.
b. Dec 2, 1906 in Painesville, Ohio
d. Apr 18, 1982 in Scarsdale, New York
Source: *AmM&WS 82P; AnObit 1982; ConAu 110; CurBio 64, 82; IntWW 82, 83; NewYTBS 82; WhoAm 80, 82*

Harrell, Lynn Morris
American. Musician
Cello soloist with major US symphonies since 1970.
b. Jan 30, 1944 in New York, New York
Source: *BioIn 10, 11; CurBio 83; NewYTBS 77; WhoAm 80, 82*

Harrell, Mack
American. Opera Singer
b. Oct 8, 1909 in Celeste, Texas
d. Jan 29, 1960 in Dallas, Texas
Source: *WhAm 4*

Harrelson, Ken(neth Smith)
"Hawk"
American. Baseball Player, Baseball Executive
Infielder-outfielder, 1963-71; led AL in RBI's, 1968.
b. Sep 4, 1941 in Woodruff, South Carolina
Source: *BaseEn 85; CurBio 70; WhoProB 73*

Harridge, Will(iam)
American. Baseball Executive
AL pres., 1931-58; Hall of Fame, 1972.
b. Oct 16, 1881 in Chicago, Illinois
d. Apr 9, 1971 in Evanston, Illinois
Source: *BasesB*

Harrigan, Edward
American. Actor, Dramatist
Known for comedy sketches on NY immigrant life, late 19th c.; *The Mulligan Guard Picnic*, 1878.
b. Jul 27, 1844 in Logan, Ohio
d. Sep 2, 1911
Source: *AmAu; AmAu&B; BiD&SB; ChhPo S2; CnThe; DcAmAu; DcAmB; DcNAA; EncMT; FamA&A; McGEWD*

Harriman, Edward H
American. Businessman, Philanthropist
b. Feb 25, 1848 in Hampstead, New York
d. Sep 9, 1909 in Orange County, New York
Source: *AmBi; DcAmB; EncAB-H; WebAB; WhAm 1*

Harriman, E(dward) Roland (Noel)
American. Financier
Chm., Union Pacific Railroad, 1946-49.
b. Dec 24, 1895 in New York, New York
d. Feb 16, 1978 in Arden, New York
Source: *CurBio 51, 78; IntWW 74, 75, 76, 77, 78; IntYB 78; NewYTBS 78; St&PR 75; WhAm 5, 7; WhNAA; WhoAm 74; WhoF&I 74; WhoGov 72*

Harriman, John Walter
American. Economist
b. Jul 8, 1898 in Providence, Rhode Island
d. Oct 23, 1972
Source: *BioIn 9; NewYTBE 72*

Harriman, W(illiam) Averell
American. Government Official
Dem., who served four presidents in diplomatic roles.
b. Nov 15, 1891 in New York, New York
d. Jul 26, 1986 in Yorktown Heights, New York
Source: *BiDrUSE; CurBio 41, 46, 86; EncAB-H; IntWW 74; NewYTBS 86; St&PR 75; WebAB; Who 74; WhoAm 74, 76, 78, 80, 82*

Harrington, Michael (Edward Michael)
American. Politician, Author
Wrote *The Other America*, 1962, bringing poverty into arena of public discussion.
b. Feb 24, 1928 in Saint Louis, Missouri
Source: *AmAu&B; CelR; ConAu 17R; CurBio 69; LinLib L; NewYTBE 72; OxCan; PolProf J, K; WhoAm 80, 82, 84*

Harrington, Pat
[Daniel Patrick Harrington, Jr.]
American. Actor
Played Schneider on TV series "One Day at a Time."
b. Aug 13, 1929 in New York, New York
Source: *IntMPA 75, 76, 77, 78, 79, 80, 81, 82; WhoAm 82*

Harris, Arthur Travers, Sir
English. Military Leader
Head of Britain's Bomber Command, WW II; believed key to victory was massive night bombing raids on German cities.
b. Apr 13, 1892 in Cheltenham, England
d. Apr 5, 1984 in London, England
Source: *CurBio 84; IntWW 74; Who 74*

Harris, Augustus, Sir
English. Opera Singer
b. 1852 in Paris, France
d. Jun 22, 1896 in Folkestone, England
Source: *OxThe*

Harris, Barbara
American. Actress
Films include *Plaza Suite,* 1971; *Nashville,*
1975.
b. 1935 in Evanston, Illinois
Source: *BiE&WWA; CelR; InWom; IntMPA
81, 82; MotPP; NewYTBE 72; WhoAm 82;
WhoE 74; WhoHol A; WhoWor 74*

Harris, "Bucky" (Stanley Raymond)
American. Baseball Player, Baseball Manager
Infielder, 1919-31; Hall of Fame, 1975.
b. Nov 8, 1896 in Port Jervis, New York
d. Nov 8, 1977 in Bethesda, Maryland
Source: *BaseEn 85; CurBio 48, 78; WhoProB
73*

Harris, Cliff(ord Allen)
American. Football Player
b. Nov 12, 1948 in Fayetteville, Arkansas
Source: *WhoAm 78, 80*

Harris, Emily Schwartz
[Mrs. William Harris; S(ymbionese)
L(iberation) A(rmy)]
American. Revolutionary
With husband, kidnapped Patty Hearst, 1974.
b. Feb 11, 1947 in Baltimore, Maryland
Source: *BioIn 10*

Harris, Emmylou
American. Singer
Won Grammys, 1976, 1977; CMA female
vocalist of year, 1980.
b. Apr 2, 1948 in Birmingham, Alabama
Source: *BioIn 10; BkPepl; IlEncRk; WhoAm
78, 80, 82*

Harris, Franco
American. Football Player
Running back, Pittsburgh Steelers, 1972-85;
rookie of year, 1972.
b. Mar 7, 1950 in Mount Holly, New Jersey
Source: *CelR; WhoAm 82; WhoFtbl 74*

Harris, Frank
Irish. Author, Journalist
b. Feb 14, 1856 in Galway, Ireland
d. Aug 26, 1931
Source: *AmBi; CnDAL; CnMD; ConAmL;
EvLB; LongCTC; ModBrL; NewC; OxAmL;
OxEng; PenC ENG; RAdv 1; TwCA, SUP;
TwCWr; WhAm 1; WhoTwCL*

Harris, Fred Roy
American. Senator
b. Nov 13, 1930 in Walters, Oklahoma
Source: *CurBio 68; IntWW 74; WhoAm 74,
76, 78, 80, 82; WhoAmP 73; WhoGov 75;
WhoS&SW 82*

Harris, Harwell Hamilton
American. Architect, Educator
b. Jul 2, 1903 in Redlands, California
Source: *AmArch 70; BioIn 6; CurBio 62;
McGDA; WhoAm 74, 76, 78, 80, 82;
WhoS&SW 73, 75, 76; WhoWor 74*

Harris, Jean Witt Struven
American. Murderer
Convicted of murder of former lover, Dr.
Herman Tarnower, 1980; wrote
autobiography *Stranger in Two Worlds,*
1986.
b. 1924
Source: *BioIn 12*

Harris, Jed
American. Producer
b. Feb 25, 1900 in Vienna, Austria
d. Nov 1979 in New York, New York
Source: *BiE&WWA; NotNAT; WhoAm 74;
WhoThe 77A*

Harris, Joel Chandler
American. Author
Editor, Atlanta *Constitution,* 1890-1900;
created Uncle Remus character.
b. Dec 9, 1848 in Eatonton, Georgia
d. Jul 3, 1908 in Atlanta, Georgia
Source: *Alli SUP; AmAu; AmAu&B; AmBi;
AnCL; ApCAB; AtlBL; AuBYP; BbD;
BiD&SB; BiDSA; CarSB; CasWL; Chambr 3;
ChhPo, S1, S2; CnDAL; CyWA; DcAmAu;
DcAmB; DcBiA; DcEnA AP; DcLEL; DcNAA;
EncAB-H; EvLB; FamAYP; JBA 34; OxAmL;
OxEng; PenC AM; RAdv 1; REn; REnAL;
Str&VC; WebAB; WebE&AL; WhAm 1;
WhoChL; YABC 1*

Harris, Jonathan
American. Actor
Starred in TV series "Lost in Space," 1965-
68.
b. 1919
Source: *FilmgC; WhoHol A*

Harris, Joseph Pratt
American. Political Activist, Educator
Invented automatic voting machine, Harris
Votamatic, 1962.
b. Feb 18, 1896 in Candor, North Carolina
d. Feb 13, 1985 in Berkeley, California
Source: *ConAu 115; WhoAm 76*

Harris, Julie
American. Actress
Starred in *Member of the Wedding,* 1952;
    East of Eden, 1956.
b. Dec 2, 1925 in Grosse Pointe, Michigan
Source: *BiDFilm; BiE&WWA; BioNews 74;
CelR; CurBio 56; FilmgC; InWom; IntMPA
75, 76, 77, 78, 79, 80, 81, 82; MotPP;
MovMk; NotNAT; OxFilm; PIP&P A; WhoAm
74, 76, 78, 80, 82; WhoHol A; WhoThe 77;
WhoWor 78*

Harris, LaDonna Crawford
American. Social Reformer
b. 1931
Source: *NewYTBE 70; WhoAmW 77;
WhoS&SW 82*

Harris, Lauren
[Group of Seven]
Canadian. Artist
Painted simplified Canadian landscapes.
b. Oct 23, 1885 in Brantford, Ontario
d. Jan 29, 1970 in Vancouver, British
    Columbia
Source: *CreCan 2; IlBEAAW; MacDCB 78;
McGDA*

Harris, Leonard
American. Critic, Author
b. Sep 27, 1929 in New York, New York
Source: *ConAu 65*

Harris, Louis
American. Pollster
Founded public opinion, marketing research
    firm, Louis Harris and Associates, ʼnc.,
    1956.
b. Jan 6, 1921 in New Haven, Connecticut
Source: *AmM&WS 73S; CelR; ConAu 13R;
WebAB; WhoAm 74, 76, 78, 80, 82; WhoWor
78*

Harris, Mark
American. Author
b. Nov 19, 1922 in Mount Vernon, New
    York
Source: *AmAu&B; Au&Wr 71; ConAu 5R;
ConNov 72, 76; DrAF 76; DrAS 74E;
OxAmL; RAdv 1; WhoAm 74, 76, 78, 80, 82;
WhoWor 78; WrDr 76*

Harris, Patricia Roberts
American. Government Official
Ambassador to Luxembourg, 1965-67;
    secretary of HUD, 1977-79; HEW, 1979-
    80.
b. May 31, 1924 in Mattoon, Illinois
d. Mar 23, 1985 in Washington, District of
    Columbia
Source: *ConNews 85-2; CurBio 65; InWom;
IntWW 74; WhAm 8; WhoAm 82; WhoAmP
73; WhoAmW 77; WhoBlA 75*

Harris, Paul
see: Souther-Hillman-Furay Band, The

Harris, Phil
American. Comedian, Musician
b. Jun 24, 1906 in Linton, Indiana
Source: *FilmgC; IntMPA 75, 76, 77, 78, 79,
80, 81, 82; MotPP; WhoHol A*

Harris, Phil
see: Ace

Harris, Richard
Irish. Actor
Won Grammy for *Jonathan Livingston
    Seagull,* 1973; Golden Globe for *Camelot,*
    1968.
b. Oct 1, 1930 in Limerick, Ireland
Source: *BiDFilm; BkPepl; CelR; CurBio 64;
FilmgC; IntMPA 75, 76, 77, 78, 79, 80, 81,
82; MotPP; MovMk; NewYTBE 72; OxFilm;
WhoAm 82; WhoHol A; WhoThe 77A;
WhoWor 78; WorEFlm*

Harris, Rosemary
English. Actress
Won Tony for *Lion in Winter,* 1966.
b. Sep 19, 1930 in Ashby, England
Source: *BiE&WWA; CurBio 67; FilmgC;
InWom; IntMPA 82; MotPP; NotNAT;
WhoAm 78; WhoHol A; WhoWor 74*

Harris, Roy Ellsworth
American. Composer
b. Feb 12, 1898 in Lincoln County,
    Oklahoma
d. Oct 1979 in Santa Monica, California
Source: *CurBio 40; DcCM; IntWW 74;
OxAmL; REn; REnAL; WebAB; WhoWor 78*

Harris, Sam Henry
American. Manager
b. Feb 3, 1872 in New York, New York
d. Jul 3, 1941 in New York, New York
Source: *CurBio 41; DcAmB S5; EncMT;
WhAm 1; WhoStg 1906, 1908*

Harris, Steve
see: Iron Maiden

Harris, Sydney J(ustin)
American. Journalist
Writer of syndicated column *Strictly Personal,*
1944--.
b. Sep 14, 1917 in London, England
Source: *AmAu&B; ConAu 61; WhoAm 74, 76,*
78, 80, 82; WhoMW 74

Harris, Willard Palmer (Bill)
American. Jazz Musician
b. Oct 28, 1916 in Philadelphia, Pennsylvania
d. 1973
Source: *WhoJazz 72*

Harris, William
[S(ymbionese) L(iberation) A(rmy)]
American. Revolutionary
With wife Emily, kidnapped Patty Hearst,
1974.
b. Jan 22, 1945 in Fort Sill, Oklahoma
Source: *BioIn 10*

Harris, William Bliss
[Amos Pettingill, pseud.]
American. Editor, Author
Automotive writer, *Fortune,* 1937-60; wrote
White Flower Farm Garden Book.
b. 1901 in Denver, Colorado
d. Jun 22, 1981 in Falmouth, Massachusetts
Source: *ConAu 104; NewYTBS 81*

Harrison, Anna Tuthill Symmes
[Mrs. William Henry Harrison]
American. First Lady
Wife of William Henry, grandmother of
Benjamin Harrison.
b. Jul 25, 1775 in Morris Town, New Jersey
d. Feb 25, 1864 in North Bend, Ohio
Source: *AmWom; ApCAB; GoodHs; NatCAB*
3; NotAW; TwCBDA

Harrison, Benjamin
American. Continental Congressman
Governor of VA, signed Declaration of
Independence; ancestor of two US
presidents.
b. 1726 in Charles City, Virginia
d. Apr 24, 1791 in Charles City, Virginia
Source: *AmBi; ApCAB; BiDSA; BiDrAC;*
BioIn 3, 7, 8; Drake; NatCAB 10; TwCBDA;
WhAm HS; WhAmP

Harrison, Benjamin
American. US President
Grandson of William Henry Harrison; won
1888 pres. election in Electoral College
despite Grover Cleveland's larger popular
vote.
b. Aug 20, 1833 in North Bend, Ohio
d. Mar 13, 1901 in Indianapolis, Indiana
Source: *Alli SUP; AmAu&B; AmBi; ApCAB;*
SUP; BiD&SB; BiDrUSE; BioIn 11; DcAmAu;
DcAmB; DcNAA; EncAB-H; IndAu 1816;
OhA&B; OxAmL; REnAL; TwCBDA; WebAB,
79; WhAm 1; WhAmP

Harrison, Caroline Lavinia Scott
[Mrs. Benjamin Harrison]
American. First Lady
First wife of Benjamin Harrison; died in
White House two wks before husband was
defeated for second term.
b. Oct 1, 1832 in Oxford, Ohio
d. Oct 25, 1892 in Washington, District of
Columbia
Source: *AmWom; ApCAB SUP; GoodHs;*
NatCAB 4; NotAW; TwCBDA

Harrison, Frederic
English. Author
b. Oct 18, 1831 in London, England
d. Jan 14, 1923
Source: *Alli SUP; BiD&SB; BrAu 19; Chambr*
3; ChhPo S1; DcEnA, AP; DcEnL; DcEuL;
DcLEL; EvLB; LongCTC; NewC; OxEng

Harrison, George
[The Beatles]
English. Singer, Songwriter
First album after break-up of Beatles, *All*
Things Must Pass, sold 1.5 million copies
in one week.
b. Feb 25, 1943 in Liverpool, England
Source: *BioIn 6, 7, 8, 9, 10, 11; BkPepl;*
CelR; CurBio 66; IntWW 74, 75, 76, 77, 78,
79, 80; MotPP; WhoAm 80, 82; WhoWor 78

Harrison, Gregory
American. Actor
Played Gonzo Gates in "Trapper John,
MD," 1979-86.
b. May 31, 1950 in Avalon, California
Source: *ConTFT 3; WhoAm 80, 82*

Harrison, Guy Fraser
English. Conductor
b. Nov 6, 1894 in Guildford, England
Source: *WhoE 74*

Harrison, Jenilee
American. Actress
Plays Jamie Ewing Barnes on TV series
"Dallas," 1984--.
b. 1959 in Northridge, California
Source: *NF*

Harrison, Jerry
see: Talking Heads, The

Harrison, Mary Scott Lord Dimmick
[Mrs. Benjamin Harrison]
American. Celebrity Relative
Second wife of Benjamin Harrison, married
1896.
b. Apr 30, 1858 in Homesdale, Pennsylvania
d. Jan 5, 1948 in New York, New York
Source: *BiCAW; NotAW; ObitOF 79; WhDW; WorAl*

Harrison, Nigel
see: Blondie

Harrison, Noel
English. Singer, Actor
Had 1960s hit single: "Suzanne"; starred in
"The Girl from UNCLE."
b. Jan 29, 1936 in London, England
Source: *BioIn 5, 7; WhoHol A*

Harrison, Peter
American. Architect
Called first real architect in America;
introduced Neo-Palladian style in US.
b. Jun 14, 1716 in York, England
d. Apr 30, 1775 in New Haven, Connecticut
Source: *DcAmB; WebAB; WhAm HS*

Harrison, Rex (Reginald Carey)
English. Actor
Won 1957 Tony, 1964 Oscar for role of
Henry Higgins in *My Fair Lady.*
b. Mar 5, 1908 in Huyton, England
Source: *BiDFilm; BiE&WWA; CelR; CurBio
86; EncMT; FamA&A; FilmgC; IntMPA 82;
IntWW 84; MotPP; MovMk; NewC; NotNAT;
OxFilm; PIP&P; Who 85; WhoAm 84;
WhoHol A; WhoThe 77; WhoWor 74*

Harrison, Wallace Kirkman
American. Architect
Designed Rockefeller Center, 1930; UN
Building, 1947.
b. Sep 28, 1895 in Worcester, Massachusetts
d. Dec 2, 1981 in New York, New York
Source: *BioIn 1, 3, 5, 7; CurBio 47, 82;
EncMA; IntWW 74, 75, 76, 77, 78; McGDA;
WhoAm 74, 76, 78, 80; WhoArch; WhoWor
74, 78*

Harrison, William Henry
American. US President
In office, Mar 4-Apr 4, 1841; first to die in
office.
b. Feb 9, 1773 in Charles City, Virginia
d. Apr 4, 1841 in Washington, District of
Columbia
Source: *Alli; AmAu&B; AmBi; ApCAB;
BiAUS; BiDrAC; BiDrUSE; BioIn 11;
DcAmB; Drake; EncAB-H; OhA&B; OxAmL;
REn; REnAL; TwCBDA; WebAB, 79; WhAm
HS; WhAmP*

Harroun, Ray
American. Auto Racer, Engineer
b. Jan 12, 1879
d. Jan 19, 1968 in Anderson, Indiana
Source: *BioIn 8*

Harry, Debbie (Deborah Ann)
[Blondie]
American. Singer
First punk star to appear in commercial; hit
songs include "Call Me," 1980.
b. Jul 1, 1945 in Miami, Florida
Source: *BioIn 11, 12; BkPepl; CurBio 81;
NewWmR; WhoAm 82*

Harryhausen, Ray
American. Special Effects Technician
Trick film specialist: *Clash of the Titans,*
1981.
b. Jun 29, 1920 in Los Angeles, California
Source: *CmMov; EncSF; FilmgC; IntMPA 75,
76, 77, 78, 79, 80, 81*

Harsch, Joseph Close
American. Journalist
b. May 25, 1905 in Toledo, Ohio
Source: *AmAu&B; Au&Wr 71; CurBio 44;
IntWW 74; Who 74; WhoAm 82; WhoWor
74*

Harsh, George
Canadian. Criminal, Aviator
d. Jan 25, 1980 in Toronto, Ontario
Source: *BioIn 9, 12*

Harshaw, Margaret
American. Opera Singer
b. May 12, 1912 in Narbeth, Pennsylvania
Source: *InWom; WhoMus 72*

Hart, Frances Noyes
American. Author
b. Aug 10, 1890 in Silver Spring, Maryland
d. Oct 25, 1943 in New Canaan, Connecticut
Source: *AmAu&B; DcNAA; EncMys;
LongCTC; OxAmL; REnAL; TwCA, SUP*

Hart, Gary Warren
[Gary Warren Hartpence]
American. Politician
Dem. senator from CO; vied for Dem.
  presidential nomination, 1984.
b. Nov 28, 1936 in Ottawa, Kansas
Source: *BioIn 11; CurBio 76*

Hart, George Overbury
American. Artist
b. May 10, 1868 in Cairo, Illinois
d. Sep 9, 1933
Source: *DcAmB S1; WhAm 1*

Hart, Jane Briggs
[Mrs. Philip Hart]
American. Celebrity Relative
Source: *BioIn 10*

Hart, Jeffrey
American. Educator, Author
b. Feb 24, 1930 in New York, New York
Source: *WhoAm 74*

Hart, Jim W
American. Football Player
b. Apr 29, 1944 in Evanston, Illinois
Source: *BioIn 8, 11; WhoAm 82; WhoFtbl 74*

Hart, John
American. Continental Congressman
Signed Declaration of Independence, 1776.
b. 1711 in Stonington, Connecticut
d. May 11, 1779 in Hopewell, New Jersey
Source: *AmBi; ApCAB; BiAUS; BiDrAC;
DcAmB; Drake; TwCBDA; WhAm HS;
WhAmP*

Hart, John
American. Broadcast Journalist
Correspondent, NBC News since 1975.
b. Feb 1, 1932 in Denver, Colorado
Source: *WhoTelC*

Hart, John(ny Lewis)
American. Cartoonist
Draws "BC," 1958--; "The Wizard of Id,"
  1964--.
b. Feb 18, 1931 in Endicott, New York
Source: *AuNews 1; BioNews 74; ConAu 49,
4NR; WhoAm 82*

Hart, Lorenz Milton
American. Lyricist
b. May 2, 1895 in New York, New York
d. Nov 22, 1943 in New York, New York
Source: *AmSCAP 66; CurBio 40; DcAmB S3;
EncMT; McGEWD; NewCBMT; OxFilm;
PIP&P; REnAL; WhAm 4*

Hart, Mickey
[The Grateful Dead]
American. Singer, Musician
b. in New York, New York
Source: *NF*

Hart, Moss
[Robert Arnold Conrad]
American. Director, Dramatist, Author
Won Tony for directing *My Fair Lady,* 1959.
b. Oct 24, 1904 in New York, New York
d. Dec 20, 1961 in Palm Springs, California
Source: *AmAu&B; CasWL; CnDAL; CnMD;
CnThe; CurBio 40, 60, 62; EncMT; FilmgC;
LongCTC; McGEWD; ModWD; NewCBMT;
OxAmL; OxThe; PenC AM; PIP&P; REn;
REnAL; REnWD; TwCA, SUP; WebAB;
WebE&AL; WhAm 4; WorEFlm*

Hart, Pearl
American. Outlaw
d. 1925
Source: *BioIn 3, 11; Blood&B*

Hart, Philip Aloysius
American. Senator
b. Dec 10, 1912 in Bryn Mawr, Pennsylvania
d. Dec 26, 1976 in Washington, District of
  Columbia
Source: *BiDrAC; CngDr 74; CurBio 59;
WhoAm 74; WhoAmP 73; WhoGov 75;
WhoMW 74; WhoWor 78*

Hart, William Surrey
American. Actor, Author
Stone-faced Western star, 1914-25; wrote
  western novels, autobiography, *My Life:
  East and West,* 1929.
b. Dec 6, 1872 in Newburgh, New York
d. Jun 23, 1946 in Newhall, California
Source: *AmAu&B; BiDFilm; CmMov; CurBio
46; Film 1; FilmgC; MnBBF; MotPP;
MovMk; OxFilm; TwYS; WebAB; WhAm 2;
WhScrn 74, 77; WhoHol B; WorEFlm*

Hart-Davis, Rupert (Charles Rupert)
English. Publisher, Editor, Author
Founder, Rupert Hart-Davis, publishing,
  1942.
b. Aug 28, 1907 in England
Source: *ConAu 115; WorAu*

Hartack, Billy (William, Jr.)
American. Jockey
b. Dec 9, 1932 in Colver, Pennsylvania
Source: *BioIn 10*

Harte, (Francis) Bret
American. Author, Journalist
Wrote *The Outcasts of Poker Flat,
Tennessee's Partner, Miggles.*
b. Aug 25, 1836 in Albany, New York
d. May 5, 1902 in London, England
Source: *Alli SUP; AmAu; AmAu&B; AmBi;
AtlBL; AuBYP; BbD; BiD&SB; BioIn 1, 3, 4,
5, 6, 7, 8, 9, 10, 11; CasWL; Chambr 3;
ChhPo, S1, S2; CnDAL; CrtT 3; CyAL 2;
CyWA; DcAmAu; DcAmB; DcBiA; DcEnA,
AP; DcEnL; DcLEL; DcNAA; EvLB; MouLC
4; OxAmL; OxEng; PenC AM; RAdv 1; REn;
REnAL; TwCBDA; WebAB; WebE&AL;
WhAm 1*

Hartford, George Huntington
American. Merchant, Businessman
Co-founded Great Atlantic and Pacific Tea
Company (A&P), 1869.
b. Sep 5, 1833 in Augusta, Maine
d. Aug 29, 1917 in Spring Lake, New Jersey
Source: *DcAmB S5; WhAm HSA, 4*

Hartford, George Ludlum
American. Merchant, Businessman
Son of George H Hartford; became chm. of
A&P; tasted coffee samples daily.
b. Nov 7, 1864 in Brooklyn, New York
d. Sep 23, 1957 in Montclair, New Jersey
Source: *DcAmB S5; WhAm 3*

Hartford, Huntington
American. Financier, Art Patron
b. Apr 18, 1911 in New York, New York
Source: *AmAu&B; BiE&WWA; CelR; ConAu
17R; CurBio 59; IntWW 74; WhoAm 74, 76,
78, 80, 82; WhoAmA 73; WhoE 74; WhoGov
75*

Hartford, John Augustine
American. Merchant, Businessman
Son of George H Hartford; became pres. of
A&P.
b. Feb 10, 1872 in Orange, New Jersey
d. Sep 20, 1951 in New York, New York
Source: *BiDAmBL 83; BioIn 2, 3; DcAmB
S5; WhAm 3*

Hartford, John Cowan
American. Singer, Songwriter
Wrote "Gentle on My Mind," 1967, recorded
by Glen Campbell, 200 others.
b. Dec 30, 1937 in New York, New York
Source: *BiDAmM; EncFCWM 69; RolSEnR
83; WhoAm 84; WhoRock 81*

Hartke, Vance
American. Senator
b. May 31, 1919 in Stendal, Indiana
Source: *CngDr 74; ConAu 25R; CurBio 60;
IndAu 1917; IntWW 74; WhoAm 74;
WhoAmP 73; WhoGov 75; WhoWor 78*

Hartley, Fred Lloyd
American. Business Executive
b. Jan 16, 1917 in Vancouver, British
Columbia
Source: *BioIn 7; WhoAm 78, 80, 82*

Hartley, Leslie Poles
English. Author
b. Dec 30, 1895 in Whittlesea, England
d. Dec 13, 1972 in London, England
Source: *Au&Wr 71; CasWL; ConAu 37R, 45;
ConLC 2; ConNov 72, 76; DcLEL; EncWL;
EvLB; LongCTC; ModBrL; S1; NewC; PenC
ENG; RAdv 1; REn; TwCA SUP; TwCWr;
WebE&AL; WhAm 5; WhoTwCL*

Hartley, Mariette
[Mrs. Patrick Boyriven]
American. Actress
Best known for Polaroid commercials with
James Garner.
b. Jun 21, 1940 in New York, New York
Source: *WhoAm 80; WhoHol A*

Hartley, Marsden
American. Artist
b. Jan 4, 1877 in Lewiston, Maine
d. Sep 2, 1943 in Ellsworth, Maine
Source: *AtlBL; CurBio 43; DcAmB S3;
DcCAA 71; OxAmL; REnAL*

Hartman, Dan
American. Singer, Musician, Songwriter
Pop singer who had hit single "I Can
Dream About You," 1984.
Source: *RkOn 85*

Hartman, David Downs
American. Actor, TV Host
Hosts "Good Morning America" on ABC,
1975--; starred in "Lucas Tanner," 1974-
75.
b. May 19, 1935 in Pawtucket, Rhode Island
Source: *BkPepl; IntMPA 77, 78, 79, 80, 81,
82; NewYTET; WhoAm 78, 80, 82; WhoHol
A*

Hartman, Grace
American. Dancer, Comedienne
b. 1907
d. Aug 8, 1955 in Van Nuys, California
Source: *CurBio 42, 55; InWom; WhScrn 74,
77; WhoHol B*

Hartman, Lisa
American. Actress, Singer
Played Ciji Dunne on TV series "Knots
Landing," 1982, Cathy Geary, 1984-86.
b. in Houston, Texas
Source: ConTFT 3

Hartman, Paul
American. Actor
Comic dance team with wife Grace on
Broadway; won Tony, 1948, for *Angel in
the Wings.*
b. Mar 1, 1904 in San Francisco, California
d. Oct 2, 1973 in Los Angeles, California
Source: *BiE&WWA; CurBio 42, 73; IntMPA
75, 76, 77; MovMk; NewYTBE 73; WhAm 6;
WhScrn 77; WhoAm 74; WhoHol B;
WhoWorJ 72*

Hartmann, Franz
German. Mystic, Physician, Author
Wrote *Occult Science in Medicine,* 1893.
b. Nov 22, 1838 in Bavaria
d. Aug 7, 1912 in Kempten, Bavaria
Source: *ConAu 115; EncO&P 80*

Hartmann, Rudolph
German. Producer, Manager
b. Oct 11, 1900 in Ingolstadt, Germany
Source: *NewEOp 71*

Hartmann, Sadakichi
American. Author
b. Oct 8, 1869 in Nagasaki, Japan
d. Nov 21, 1944 in Saint Petersburg, Florida
Source: *AmAu&B; DcAmAu; DcNAA;
OxAmL; REnAL; WhAm 5; WhScrn 77*

Hartnell, Norman Bishop, Sir
English. Fashion Designer
Queen Elizabeth's official dressmaker; has
clothed the royal family since 1938.
b. Jun 12, 1901 in London, England
d. Jun 8, 1979 in Windsor, England
Source: *CurBio 53, 79; IntWW 74, 75, 76,
77, 79; NewYTBS 79; Who 74; WhoWor 74,
76, 78*

Hartnett, "Gabby" (Charles Leo)
"Old Tomato Face"
American. Baseball Player, Baseball Manager
Catcher, 1922-41; manager, 1938-40; Hall of
Fame, 1955.
b. Dec 20, 1900 in Woonsocket, Rhode
Island
d. Dec 20, 1972 in Park Ridge, Illinois
Source: *BaseEn 85; BioIn 1, 7, 8, 9, 10;
NewYTBE 72; WhoProB 73*

Hartog, Jan de
see: DeHartog, Jan

Hartung, Hans
French. Artist
Early abstract expressionist; black splashes
reminiscent of Japanese calligraphy.
b. Sep 21, 1904 in Leipzig, Germany
Source: *ConArt 77; CurBio 58; IntWW 74,
75, 76, 77, 78; McGDA*

Hartz, James Leroy
American. Broadcast Journalist
b. Feb 3, 1940
Source: *AuNews 2; BioIn 10, 11; BioNews 74;
IntMPA 82*

Harun-Al-Rashid
Arabian. Political Leader
Fifth caliph of Abbasia dynasty, 785-803;
reign marked by grandeur and noble style.
b. 764 in Rey, Persia
d. Mar 24, 809 in Tus, Persia
Source: *McGEWB; NewCol 75; WhDW*

Harunobu, Suzuki
Japanese. Artist
Master of woodblock printing; perfected
brocade painting; admired by Degas in
19th c.
b. 1718 in Edo, Japan
d. 1770 in Edo, Japan
Source: *BioIn 10; McGDA; McGEWB;
NewCol 75; OxArt; WhDW*

Harvard, John
English. Clergyman
Left library, estate money toward founding of
new college; named in his honor, 1639.
b. Nov 26, 1607 in London, England
d. Sep 14, 1638 in Charlestown,
Massachusetts
Source: *AmBi; ApCAB; CyAL 1; DcAmB;
Drake; REn; TwCBDA; WebAB; WhAm HS*

Harvey, Anthony
English. Director
Best known for *Lion in Winter,* 1968; *They
Might Be Giants,* 1972.
b. Jun 3, 1931 in London, England
Source: *FilmgC; IntMPA 82; IntWW 74;
WhoAm 82*

Harvey, Frank Laird
English. Author, Actor, Director
Wrote screenplay for *Poltergeist,* 1946.
b. Aug 11, 1912 in Manchester, England
Source: *Au&Wr 71; ConAu 5R; FilmgC;
IntAu&W 77; WhoThe 72, 77*

Harvey, Frederick Henry
American. Restaurateur
b. 1835 in London, England
d. Feb 9, 1901 in Leavenworth, Kansas
Source: *WebAB*

Harvey, George Brinton M
American. Diplomat, Journalist
b. Feb 16, 1864 in Peacham, Vermont
d. Aug 20, 1928
Source: *AmAu&B; AmBi; DcAmB; DcNAA; WhAm 1*

Harvey, Laurence
[Larushke Mischa Skikne]
British. Actor
Oscar nominee for *Room at the Top,* 1958.
b. Oct 1, 1928 in Janiskis, Lithuania
d. Nov 25, 1973 in London, England
Source: *BiDFilm; BiE&WWA; BioNews 74; CurBio 61, 74; FilmgC; MotPP; MovMk; NewC; NewYTBE 73; OxFilm; WhAm 6; WhScrn 77; Who 74; WhoHol B; WhoWor 78; WorEFlm*

Harvey, Paul
[Paul Harvey Aurandt]
American. Broadcast Journalist
b. Sep 4, 1918 in Tulsa, Oklahoma
Source: *CelR; CurBio 86; WhoAm 82*

Harvey, William
English. Physician
b. Apr 1, 1578 in Folkestone, England
d. Jun 3, 1657
Source: *Alli; BrAu; DcEnL; NewC; OxEng; REn*

Harvey, William Hope
"Coin Harvey"
American. Economist
Advocated bimetallism; wrote *Coin's Financial School,* 1894.
b. Aug 16, 1851 in Buffalo, Virginia
d. Feb 11, 1936
Source: *DcAmB S2; WebBD 80*

Harwell, Ernie
American. Broadcaster, Author
Baseball broadcaster, songwriter; wrote *Tuned to Baseball,* 1985; Hall of Fame, 1981.
b. Jan 25, 1918 in Atlanta, Georgia
Source: *BioNews 74*

Harwood, Vanessa Clare
Canadian. Dancer
Star, National Ballet of Canada, 1970--.
b. 1947 in Cheltenham, England
Source: *WhoAm 82, 84*

Hasani, Ali Nasir Muhammad
Prime Minister
b. 1938
Source: *BioIn 11; WhoWor 78*

Hasegawa, Kazuo
Japanese. Actor
Warrior hero in many Japanese films since 1927.
b. Feb 29, 1908 in Japan
Source: *FilmEn; OxFilm*

Hasek, Jaroslav
Czech. Author
b. Apr 24, 1883 in Prague, Czechoslovakia
d. Jan 3, 1923 in Lipnice, Czechoslovakia
Source: *CasWL; ClDMEL; EncWL; EvEuW; LongCTC; ModSL 2; PenC EUR; REn; TwCA, SUP; TwCWr; WhoTwCL*

Hashimoto, Ken
American. Scientist
b. Jun 16, 1931 in Niigata, Japan
Source: *AmM&WS 73P*

Haskell, Arnold Lionel
English. Journalist
Dance critic for several newspapers; wrote popular ballet texts: *Ballet Russe,* 1968.
b. Jul 19, 1903 in London, England
d. Nov 14, 1980 in Bath, England
Source: *AnObit 1980; ConAu 108; IntWW 81; NewYTBS 80; SmATA 6; Who 74; WhoWor 74*

Hasluck, Paul Meernaa, Sir
Australian. Political Leader
b. Apr 1, 1905 in Fremantle, Australia
Source: *CurBio 46; IntWW 74; Who 74; WhoGov 75; WhoWor 78*

Hassam, Childe
American. Artist
Major American Impressionist; known for NYC, New England scenes.
b. Oct 17, 1859 in Dorchester, Massachusetts
d. Aug 27, 1935 in East Hampton, New York
Source: *AmBi; DcAmArt; LinLib S; OxAmL; WebAB 79; WhAm 1*

Hassan II
Moroccan. King
b. Jul 9, 1929
Source: *BioIn 10; IntWW 74; WhoWor 78*

Hasse, Johann Adolph
German. Composer
b. Mar 25, 1699 in Bergedorf, Germany
d. Dec 16, 1783 in Venice, Italy
Source: *NewEOp 71*

Hasselblad, Victor
Swedish. Industrialist
b. 1906
d. Aug 6, 1978 in Gothenburg, Sweden
Source: *WhoWor 78*

Hasselhof, David
American. Actor
Appeared in soap opera "The Young and the
Restless"; star of "Knight Rider."
b. Jul 17, 1952 in Baltimore, Maryland
Source: *VarWW 85; WhoTelC*

Hasselmans, Louis
French. Conductor
b. Jul 25, 1878 in Paris, France
d. Dec 27, 1947 in San Juan, Puerto Rico
Source: *WhAm 3*

Hasso, Signe Eleonora Cecilia
Swedish. Actress, Composer
Recorded Scandinavian folk songs.
b. Aug 15, 1915 in Stockholm, Sweden
Source: *BiE&WWA; FilmgC; ForWC 70;
HolP 40; MotPP; MovMk; NotNAT; WhoAm
82; WhoE 74; WhoHol A; WhoThe 77*

Hastie, William Henry
American. Educator, Lawyer, Judge
First black Federal Appeals judge, 1949;
governor, Virgin Islands, 1946-49.
b. Nov 17, 1904 in Knoxville, Tennessee
d. Apr 14, 1976 in East Norriton,
Pennsylvania
Source: *CurBio 44, 76; EncAB-H; IntWW 74;
WebAB; WhAm 7; WhoE 74; WhoGov 72*

Hastings, Scott
see: Our Gang

Hastings, Thomas
American. Architect
b. Mar 11, 1860 in New York
d. Oct 22, 1929
Source: *AmBi; DcAmB; WhAm 1*

Hastings, Warren
English. Statesman
b. Dec 6, 1732 in Churchill, England
d. Aug 22, 1818
Source: *Alli; BiDLA; NewC; REn*

Hatch, Carl A
American. Lawyer, Politician
b. Nov 27, 1889 in Kirwin, Kansas
d. Sep 15, 1963 in Albuquerque, New
Mexico
Source: *BiDrAC; CurBio 44, 63; WhAm 4*

Hatch, Orrin Grant
American. Politician
Conservative Rep. senator from UT, 1977--.
b. Mar 22, 1934 in Pittsburgh, Pennsylvania
Source: *AlmAP 80; CngDr 79; CurBio 82;
IntWW 78; WhoAm 84; WhoAmP 79;
WhoGov 77; WhoWest 78*

Hatch, Richard Lawrence
American. Actor
Replaced Michael Douglas on TV series
"The Streets of San Francisco," 1976-77.
b. May 21, 1946 in Santa Monica, California
Source: *VarWW 85*

Hatcher, Mickey (Michael Vaughn, Jr.)
American. Baseball Player
b. Mar 15, 1955 in Cleveland, Ohio
Source: *BaseEn 85; BioIn 12*

Hatcher, Richard Gordon
American. Mayor
b. Jul 10, 1933 in Michigan City, Indiana
Source: *CurBio 72; WhoAm 74, 76, 78, 80,
82; WhoAmP 73; WhoBlA 75; WhoGov 75;
WhoMW 74*

Hatchett, John F
American. Political Activist
b. 1931
Source: *BioIn 8*

Hatfield, Bobby
[Righteous Brothers]
American. Singer
With Bill Medley had hit single "Unchained
Melody," 1965.
b. Aug 10, 1940 in Beaver Dam, Wisconsin
Source: *NF*

Hatfield, Hurd
American. Actor
Starred in film *The Picture of Dorian Gray,*
1945.
b. Dec 7, 1918 in New York, New York
Source: *BiDFilm; BiE&WWA; FilmgC;
IntMPA 82; MotPP; MovMk; NotNAT;
WhoHol A*

Hatfield, Mark Odom
American. Politician
Moderate Rep. senator from OR, 1967--;
wrote *Between a Rock and a Hard Place,*
1977.
b. Jul 12, 1922 in Dallas, Oregon
Source: *BiDrAC; CelR; CngDr 74; CurBio 84;
IntWW 74; WhoAm 82; WhoAmP 73;
WhoGov 72; WhoRel 75; WhoWest 74;
WhoWor 74*

Hatfield, Richard
Canadian. Politician
Progressive-conservative Party premier of
New Brunswick, 1970--.
b. Apr 9, 1931 in Woodstock, New
Brunswick
Source: *CanWW 83*

Hathaway, Anne
[Mrs. William Shakespeare]
English. Celebrity Relative
b. 1557 in Temple Grafton, England
d. 1623
Source: *InWom; NewC; REn*

Hathaway, Donny
American. Singer, Songwriter
Best known for duets with Roberta Flack:
"Where Is the Love," 1972; "The Closer I
Get to You," 1978.
b. Oct 1, 1945 in Chicago, Illinois
d. Jan 13, 1979 in New York, New York
Source: *BioIn 11; IlEncBM 82; RkOn 74;
RolSEnR 83*

Hathaway, Henry
American. Director
Best known for directing *True Grit,* 1969.
b. Mar 13, 1898 in Sacramento, California
d. Feb 11, 1985 in Los Angeles, California
Source: *BiDFilm; CmMov; DcFM; FilmgC;
IntMPA 82; MovMk; OxFilm; WorEFlm*

Hathaway, Sibyl Collings
[Dame of Sark]
British. Author
Seigneur of Sark, 1927-74.
b. Jan 13, 1884
d. Jul 14, 1974 in London, England
Source: *ConAu 1R, 103; InWom; Who 74*

Hathaway, Stanley Knapp
American. Governor
b. Jul 19, 1924 in Osceola, Nebraska
Source: *IntWW 74; WhoAm 74; WhoAmP 73;
WhoGov 75; WhoWest 84*

Hathaway, Starke R
American. Psychologist, Author
Co-developer of Minnesota Multiphasic
Personality Inventory, 1930s; widely used
during WW II.
b. Aug 22, 1903 in Central Lake, Michigan
d. Jul 4, 1984 in Minneapolis, Minnesota
Source: *AmM&WS 73S; ConAu 5R;
NewYTBS 84; WhoAm 74*

Hathaway, William Dodd
American. Politician
Dem. congressman from ME, 1965-78,
senator, 1973-79.
b. Feb 21, 1924 in Cambridge, Massachusetts
Source: *BiDrAC; IntWW 80, 81, 82, 83;
WhoAm 74*

Hatlo, Jimmy
American. Cartoonist
b. Sep 1, 1898 in Providence, Rhode Island
d. Nov 30, 1963 in Carmel, California
Source: *ConAu 93; WhAm 4*

Hatton, Christopher, Sir
English. Statesman
b. 1540 in Holdenby, England
d. Nov 20, 1591 in London, England
Source: *Alli; NewC; OxEng*

Hauberg, John Henry
American. Businessman
b. Jun 24, 1916 in Rock Island, Illinois
Source: *St&PR 75; WhoAm 74*

Hauer, Rutger
Dutch. Actor
Film debut in *Turkish Delight.*
b. Jan 23, 1944 in Breukelen, Netherlands
Source: *IntMPA 82*

Hauff, Wilhelm
German. Author
b. Nov 29, 1802 in Stuttgart, Germany
d. Nov 18, 1827 in Stuttgart, Germany
Source: *AuBYP; BiD&SB; CasWL; DcBiA;
EuAu; EvEuW; OxGer; PenC EUR; REn;
WhoChL*

Haug, Hans
Swiss. Opera Composer
b. Jul 27, 1900 in Basel, Switzerland
Source: *NewEOp 71*

Hauge, Gabriel
American. Economist, Banker
Eisenhower adviser, speechwriter, 1952-58.
b. Mar 7, 1914 in Hawley, Minnesota
d. Jul 24, 1981 in New York, New York
Source: *CurBio 53, 81; IntWW 74, 75, 76,
77, 78; WhoAm 74, 76, 78, 80; WhoE 74,
77, 79; WhoF&I 74, 75, 79; WhoWor 74, 76,
78*

Haughey, Charles James
Irish. Political Leader
Prime minister during prison hunger strikes,
1979-81; ousted by Fitzgerald.
b. Sep 16, 1925 in Castlebar, Ireland
Source: *CurBio 81; IntWW 74, 75, 76, 77,
78, 80; NewYTBS 79; WhoWor 76, 78*

Haughton, Billy
American. Horse Trainer, Jockey
Won 4,910 races, $40.2 million for harness
    racing, training; Hall of Fame, 1968.
b. Nov 2, 1923 in Gloversville, New York
d. Jul 15, 1986 in Valhalla, New York
Source: *WorAl*

Hauk, Minnie
American. Opera Singer
b. Nov 16, 1851 in New York, New York
d. Feb 6, 1929 in Triebschen, Switzerland
Source: *AmBi; AmWom; DcAmB; InWom;
NotAW; WhAm HS, 4*

Haupt, Herman
American. Engineer
b. Mar 26, 1817 in Philadelphia,
    Pennsylvania
d. Dec 14, 1905
Source: *Alli, SUP; AmBi; ApCAB; DcAmAu;
DcAmB; DcNAA; TwCBDA; WhAm 1*

Hauptman, Herbert Aaron
American. Physicist
With Jerome Karl, won Nobel Prize, 1985,
    for studies of molecular structure of
    crystals.
b. Feb 14, 1917 in New York, New York
Source: *AmM&WS 82P; WhoE 74; WhoTech
82*

Hauptmann, Bruno Richard
German. Kidnapper, Murderer
Kidnapped son of Charles Lindbergh, Mar 1,
    1932; convicted, executed for murder.
b. Nov 26, 1900 in Kamenz, Germany
d. Apr 3, 1936 in Trenton, New Jersey
Source: *AmBi; Blood&B; NewCol 75*

Hauptmann, Gerhart
German. Author, Poet
Leading Naturalist playwright: *The Weavers,*
    1892; won Nobel Prize, 1912.
b. Nov 15, 1862 in Obersalzbrunn, Germany
d. Jun 6, 1946 in Schreiberlau, Germany
Source: *AtlBL; BiD&SB; CasWL; ClDMEL;
CnMD; CnThe; CurBio 46; CyWA; EncWL;
EvEuW; LongCTC; McGEWD; ModGL;
ModWD; NewC; OxEng; OxGer; OxThe;
PenC EUR; PlP&P; RComWL; REn;
REnWD; TwCA, SUP; TwCWr; WhAm 2;
WhoTwCL*

Hauser, Gayelord
American. Nutritionist
Pioneer in health foods who advocated
    yogurt, wheat germ; wrote *Look Younger,
    Live Younger,* 1950.
b. May 17, 1895 in Tubingen, Germany
d. Dec 2, 1984 in North Hollywood,
    California
Source: *CelR; NewYTBS 74; WhoAm 76, 78,
80, 82*

Hauser, Tim
see: Manhattan Transfer

Haushofer, Karl
German. Nazi Leader
Geographer who used geopolitical theories to
    justify Germany's expansion; influenced,
    advised Hitler on foreign affairs.
b. Aug 27, 1869 in Munich, Germany
d. Mar 13, 1946 in Paehl bei Weilheim,
    Germany
Source: *CurBio 46; EncTR; McGEWB;
NewCol 75; REn*

Hauy, Rene Just
French. Mineralogist
Founded science of crystallography by
    discovering geometric law of crystallization.
b. Feb 28, 1743 in Saint Just, France
d. Jun 3, 1822 in Paris, France
Source: *AsBiEn; DcBiPP; DcScB; NewCol 75;
WhDW*

Havel, Vaclav
Czech. Dramatist
b. Oct 5, 1936 in Prague, Czechoslovakia
Source: *CnThe; ConAu 104; CroCD; CurBio
85; IntWW 83; McGEWD 84; OxThe; WorAu
1970*

Havell, Robert
English. Engraver
Did aquatints for Audubon's *Birds of
    America,* 1827-38.
b. 1793
d. 1878
Source: *AntBDN B*

Havelock, Henry
British. Army Officer
b. 1795
d. 1857
Source: *NewCol 75*

Havens, Richie
American. Singer, Musician
Black folksinger who had hit single "Here
Comes the Sun," 1971.
b. Jan 21, 1941 in Brooklyn, New York
Source: *BioIn 9; IlEncBM 82; RkOn 74;*
RolSEnR 83

Haver, June
[June Stovenour; Mrs. Fred MacMurray]
American. Actress
Personified *The Girl Next Door,* title of
movie she starred in, 1953.
b. Jun 10, 1926 in Rock Island, Illinois
Source: *CmMov; FilmgC; MotPP; MovMk;*
WhoHol A

Havighurst, Walter Edwin
American. Children's Author
b. Nov 28, 1901 in Appleton, Wisconsin
Source: *AmAu&B; AmNov; Au&Wr 71;*
AuBYP; CnDAL; ConAu 1R; DrAS 74E;
MorJA; OhA&B; OxAmL; REnAL; SmATA 1;
TwCA SUP; WhoAm 74; WrDr 80

Haviland, Virginia
American. Librarian, Children's Author
b. May 21, 1911 in Rochester, New York
Source: *BiDrLUS 70; ChhPo S1, S2; ConAu*
17R; SmATA 6; WhoAm 74, 76, 78, 80, 82;
WhoAmW 77; WhoS&SW 82

Havlicek, John
"Hondo"
American. Basketball Player
Four-time All-Star who scored 26,395 pts. in
16-yr. career with Boston; Hall of Fame,
1983.
b. Apr 8, 1940 in Martins Ferry, Ohio
Source: *OfNBA 81; WhoAm 76; WhoBbl 73*

Havoc, June
[Ellen Evangeline Hovick]
"Baby June"
American. Actress
Sister of Gypsy Rose Lee; author of two
autobiographies, numerous plays.
b. Nov 8, 1916 in Seattle, Washington
Source: *BiE&WWA; ConAu 107; FilmEn;*
FilmgC; HolP 40; InWom; IntMPA 82;
MotPP; MovMk; WhoHol A; WhoThe 77

Hawerchuk, Dale
Canadian. Hockey Player
Center, Winnipeg, 1981--; won Calder
Trophy, 1982.
b. Apr 4, 1963 in Toronto, Ontario
Source: *HocEn; HocReg 81*

Hawes, Elisabeth
American. Fashion Designer, Feminist,
Author
Wrote best-seller *Fashion Is Spinach,* 1938.
b. Dec 16, 1903 in Ridgewood, New Jersey
d. Sep 6, 1971 in New York, New York
Source: *NotAW MOD*

Hawes, Harriet Ann Boyd
American. Archaeologist
First to discover, excavate Minoan, early
bronze-age town, 1903.
b. Oct 11, 1871 in Boston, Massachusetts
d. Mar 31, 1945 in Washington, District of
Columbia
Source: *NotAW; WebBD 80*

Hawke, Bob (Robert James Lee)
Australian. Political Leader
Labor Party leader, succeeded Malcolm
Fraser as prime minister, 1983--.
b. Dec 9, 1929 in Bordertown, Australia
Source: *FarE&A 80, 81; IntWW 82, 83;*
IntYB 81, 82; NewYTBS 83; Who 82, 83;
WhoWor 80, 82

Hawkes, Greg
see: Cars, The

Hawkes, John Clendennin Burne, Jr.
American. Author
Avant-garde novels include *The Cannibal,*
1949; *Passion Artist,* 1949.
b. Aug 17, 1925 in Stamford, Connecticut
Source: *AmAu&B; ConAu 1R, 2NR; ConLC*
1, 2, 3, 4, 7, 9, 14, 15; ConNov 72, 76;
CroCD; DrAF 76; EncWL; IntWW 74;
ModAL, S1; OxAmL; PenC AM; RAdv 1;
WebE&AL; WhoAm 84; WhoE 74;
WhoTwCL; WhoWor 78; WorAu; WrDr 80

Hawkins, "Bean" (Coleman)
American. Jazz Musician
b. Nov 21, 1904 in Saint Joseph, Missouri
d. May 19, 1969 in New York, New York
Source: *WhAm 5; WhScrn 77; WhoJazz 72*

Hawkins, Erskine Ramsey
American. Musician, Band Leader
b. Jul 26, 1914 in Birmingham, Alabama
Source: *AmSCAP 66; CurBio 71; WhoJazz 72*

Hawkins, Gus (Augustus Freeman)
American. Politician
Dem. congressman from CA, 1962--; co-
author, Humphrey-Hawkins Full
Employment and Balanced Growth Act.
b. Aug 31, 1907 in Shreveport, Louisiana
Source: *AlmAP 82, 84; CngDr 81, 83; CurBio
83; PolProf J, NF; WhoAm 80, 82, 84;
WhoAmP 81, 83; WhoBlA 80; WhoWest 82,
84*

Hawkins, Jack
English. Actor, Producer
Lost voice, 1966, due to cancer, but
continued to act, with speaking parts
dubbed by others.
b. Sep 14, 1910 in London, England
d. Jul 18, 1973 in London, England
Source: *BiDFilm; CmMov; CurBio 59, 73;
FilmgC; MotPP; MovMk; NewYTBE 73;
OxFilm; PlP&P; WhAm 5; WhScrn 77;
WhoHol B; WorEFlm*

Hawkins, John, Sir
[Sir John Hawkyns]
English. Naval Officer
b. 1532 in Plymouth, England
d. Nov 12, 1595
Source: *Alli; NewC; OxEng; REn*

Hawkins, Osie Penman, Jr.
American. Opera Singer
b. Aug 16, 1913 in Phoenix City, Alabama
Source: *WhoAm 74, 76, 78, 80, 82*

Hawkins, Paula Fickes
[Mrs. Walter E Hawkins]
American. Politician
Rep. senator from FL, 1980--; first woman
elected to Senate based on own career.
b. Jan 24, 1927 in Salt Lake City, Utah
Source: *CurBio 85; WhoAm 74, 78, 80, 82,
84; WhoAmW 74, 70, 72, 75, 77, 79;
WhoS&SW 78*

Hawks, Howard Winchester
American. Director, Producer
Best known for films *Bringing Up Baby*,
1938; *The Big Sleep*, 1946.
b. May 30, 1896 in Goshen, Indiana
d. Dec 26, 1977 in Palm Springs, California
Source: *BiDFilm; CmMov; CurBio 72; DcFM;
FilmgC; IntMPA 75, 76, 77; MovMk;
OxFilm; TwYS; WebAB; WhoAm 74;
WhoWor 74; WorEFlm*

Hawley, Cameron
American. Author
b. Sep 19, 1905 in Howard, South Dakota
d. Mar 9, 1969 in Marathon, Florida
Source: *AmAu&B; ConAu 1R, 25R; CurBio
57; WhAm 5*

Hawn, Goldie Jean
American. Actress
Won Oscar for *Cactus Flower*, 1969.
b. Nov 21, 1945 in Washington, District of
Columbia
Source: *BioNews 74; BkPepl; CelR; CurBio
71; FilmgC; IntMPA 75, 76, 77, 78, 79, 80,
81, 82; MotPP; MovMk; NewYTBE 73;
WhoAm 74, 76, 78, 80, 82; WhoHol A*

Haworth, Leland John
American. Physicist
Director, Brookhaven Nuclear Energy
Laboratory, 1948-61.
b. Jul 11, 1904 in Flint, Michigan
d. Mar 5, 1979 in Port Jefferson, New York
Source: *AmM&WS 73P, 76P, 79P; CurBio 50,
79; IntAu&W 77; IntWW 74, 75, 76, 77, 78;
NewYTBS 79; WhAm 7; WhoAm 74, 76, 78;
WhoE 74*

Haworth, Mary Robbins
American. Psychologist
b. Jan 31, 1931 in Chicago, Illinois
Source: *AmM&WS 73S*

Hawthorne, Julian
American. Children's Author
b. Jun 22, 1846 in Boston, Massachusetts
d. Jul 14, 1934 in San Francisco, California
Source: *Alli SUP; AmAu&B; AmBi; ApCAB;
BbD; BiD&SB; CarSB; Chambr 3; ChhPo, S2;
DcAmAu; DcAmB S1; DcBiA; DcEnA, AP;
DcEnL; DcNAA; EncMys; OxAmL; REnAL;
TwCA; TwCBDA; WhAm 1; WhNAA*

Hawthorne, Nathaniel
American. Author
Wrote *The Scarlet Letter*, 1850; *The House
of Seven Gables*, 1851.
b. Jul 4, 1804 in Salem, Massachusetts
d. May 19, 1864 in Plymouth, New
Hampshire
Source: *Alli, SUP; AmAu; AmAu&B; AmBi;
AmWr; ApCAB; AtlBL; BbD; BiAUS;
BiD&SB; CarSB; CasWL; Chambr 3; ChhPo
S1, S2; CnDAL; CrtT 3; CyAL 2; CyWA;
DcAmAu; DcAmB; DcBiA; DcEnA, AP;
DcEnL; DcLEL; DcNAA; Drake; EncAB-H;
EvLB; FamAYP; FilmgC; MouLC 3; OxAmL;
OxEng; PenC AM; RAdv 1; RComWL; REn;
REnAL; Str&VC; TwCBDA; WebAB;
WebE&AL; WhAm HS; WhoChL*

Hay, Barry
see: Golden Earring

Hay, Colin
see: Men at Work

Hay, John Milton
American. Statesman, Author
Campaigned for Lincoln, became a White
    House secretary; wrote Abraham Lincoln:
    A History, 1890.
b. Oct 8, 1838 in Salem, Indiana
d. Jul 1, 1905 in Newburg, New Hampshire
Source: Alli SUP; AmAu; AmAu&B; AmBi;
    BbD; BiD&SB; BiDrUSE; CasWL; DcAmAu;
    DcAmB; DcBiA; DcNAA; EncAB-H; EvLB;
    IndAu 1816; OhA&B; OxAmL; PenC AM;
    REn; REnAL; WebAB; WhAm 1; WhAmP

Haya de la Torre, Victor Raul
Peruvian. Political Leader
Created "Aprista" movement, 1924; spent
    yrs. imprisoned, in exile.
b. Feb 22, 1895 in Trujillo, Peru
d. Aug 2, 1979 in Lima, Peru
Source: ConAu 89; CurBio 42, 79; DcSpL;
    IntWW 74, 75, 76, 77, 78; McGEWB;
    NewCol 75; NewYTBS 79; OxSpan; WhoWor
    74

Hayakawa, S(amuel) I(chiye)
American. Congressman, Educator, Author
Conservative Rep. senator from CA, 1977-81.
b. Jul 18, 1906 in Vancouver, British
    Columbia
Source: AmAu&B; AmM&WS 73S; CelR;
    ConAu 13R; CurBio 59; DrAS 74F; IntWW
    74; LEduc 74; REn; REnAL; TwCA SUP;
    WebAB; WhoAm 82, 84; WhoWest 74; WrDr
    76

Hayakawa, Sessue (Kintaro)
Japanese. Actor
Oscar nominee for Bridge on the River Kwai,
    1957.
b. Jun 10, 1886 in Chiba, Japan
d. Nov 23, 1974 in Tokyo, Japan
Source: BioNews 74; CurBio 62, 74; Film 1;
    FilmgC; MotPP; MovMk; NewYTBE 73;
    OxFilm; TwYS; WhAm 6; WhScrn 77;
    WhoHol B

Haycock, Peter
see: Climax Blues Band, The

Hayden, Carl Trumball
American. Politician
b. Oct 2, 1877 in Tempe, Arizona
d. Jan 25, 1972 in Mesa, Arizona
Source: BiDrAC; ConAu 33R; CurBio 51, 72;
    NewYTBE 72; WhAm 5, 6; WhAmP

Hayden, Melissa
[Mildred Herman]
Canadian. Ballerina
Dancer, NYC Ballet Co., 1950-73; wrote M
    H: Off Stage and On, 1961.
b. Apr 25, 1928 in Toronto, Ontario
Source: CanWW 70; CurBio 55; InWom;
    NewYTBE 73; WhoAm 74; WhoHol A;
    WhoWor 78

Hayden, Robert Earl
American. Poet
b. Aug 4, 1913 in Detroit, Michigan
d. Feb 25, 1980 in Ann Arbor, Michigan
Source: AmAu&B; BlkAWP; ChhPo S1, S2;
    ConAu 69, 97; ConLC 5, 9, 14; CroCAP;
    DcLEL 1940; DrAP 75; LivgBAA; SelBAAu;
    SmATA 19; WhAm 7; WrDr 76, 80

Hayden, Russell
[Pate Lucid]
"Lucky"
American. Actor
Played Lucky Jenkins in Hopalong Cassidy
    western films.
b. Jun 12, 1912 in Chico, California
d. Jun 9, 1981 in Palm Springs, California
Source: FilmgC; IntMPA 81; NewYTBS 81;
    WhoHol A

Hayden, Sterling
[John Hamilton]
American. Actor, Author
Films include The Asphalt Jungle, 1950; Dr.
    Strangelove, 1964.
b. Mar 26, 1916 in Montclair, New Jersey
d. May 23, 1986 in Sausalito, California
Source: BiDFilm; FilmgC; HolP 40; IntMPA
    82; MotPP; MovMk; OxFilm; WhoAm 82;
    WhoHol A; WorEFlm

Hayden, Tom (Thomas Emmett)
[The Chicago 7]
American. Political Activist
Co-founded SDS (Students for Democratic
    Society), 1961; married to Jane Fonda;
    liberal Dem. CA assemblyman, 1982--.
b. Dec 11, 1939 in Royal Oak, Michigan
Source: AmAu&B; ConAu 107; WhoAm 82,
    84

Haydn, Franz Joseph
Austrian. Composer
Composed Surprise Symphony, 1791;
    influenced work of Beethoven, Mozart.
b. Mar 31, 1732 in Rohrau, Austria
d. May 31, 1809 in Vienna, Austria
Source: AtlBL; NewCol 75; REn

Haydn, Hiram Collins
American. Editor, Author
b. Nov 3, 1907 in Cleveland, Ohio
d. Dec 2, 1973 in Vineyard Haven,
Massachusetts
Source: *AmAu&B; AmNov; Au&Wr 71;*
CnDAL; ConAu 45, P-1; ConNov 72;
NewYTBE 73; OhA&B; OxAmL; REnAL;
TwCA SUP; WhAm 6; WhoWor 78

Haydn, Richard
English. Actor, Director
Starred in *Please Don't Eat the Daisies,* 1960;
The Sound of Music, 1965.
b. 1905 in London, England
d. Apr 25, 1985 in Pacific Palisades,
California
Source: *FilmgC; IntMPA 82; MovMk; Vers B;*
WhoAm 74; WhoHol A; WorEFlm

Haydock, Eric
see: Hollies, The

Haydon, Julie
[Donella Donaldson]
American. Actress
b. Jun 10, 1910 in Oak Park, Illinois
Source: *BiE&WWA; FilmEn; NotNAT;*
PlP&P; ThFT; WhoHol A; WhoThe 77A

Hayek, Friedrich August von
British. Economist, Author
b. May 8, 1899 in Vienna, Austria
Source: *ConAu 93; CurBio 45; IntWW 74;*
Who 74; WhoAm 74; WhoWor 78

Hayes, Alfred
American. Author, Dramatist, Poet
b. 1911 in London, England
Source: *AmAu&B; AmNov; ModAL; OxAmL;*
REn; REnAL; TwCA SUP

Hayes, Carlton Joseph Huntley
American. Historian, Educator
Specialist in history of modern naturalism:
Naturalism: A Religion, 1960.
b. May 16, 1882 in Afton, New York
d. Sep 3, 1964 in Afton, New York
Source: *DcAmB S7*

Hayes, Elvin Ernest
American. Basketball Player
Three-time NBA All-Star guard who led
league in scoring, 1969.
b. Nov 17, 1945 in Rayville, Louisiana
Source: *OfNBA 85; WhoAm 82; WhoBbl 73;*
WhoBlA 75

Hayes, "Gabby" (George Francis)
American. Actor
Comic sidekick in over 200 westerns,
especially to William Boyd, Roy Rogers.
b. May 7, 1885 in Wellsville, New York
d. Feb 9, 1969 in Burbank, California
Source: *BiE&WWA; CmMov; FilmgC; MotPP;*
MovMk; OxFilm; PlP&P; Vers B; WhScrn 74,
77; WhoHol B

Hayes, Helen
[Mrs. Charles MacArthur; Helen H Brown]
"First Lady of the American Theater"
American. Actress
Won Oscars for *The Sin of Madelon Claudet,*
1931; *Airport,* 1969; adoptive mother of
James MacArthur.
b. Oct 10, 1900 in Washington, District of
Columbia
Source: *BiE&WWA; CelR; CurBio 42;*
FamA&A; Film 1; FilmgC; InWom; IntMPA
75, 76, 77, 78, 79, 80, 81, 82; IntWW 74;
MovMk; NotNAT; OxAmL; OxFilm; OxThe;
REn; ThFT; WebAB; Who 74; WhoAm 74;
WhoAmW 77; WhoE 74; WhoHol A; WhoThe
77; WhoWor 78; WorEFlm

Hayes, Isaac
American. Musician, Singer, Songwriter
Won Grammy, Oscar for score of *Shaft,*
1971.
b. Aug 20, 1942 in Covington, Tennessee
Source: *BioNews 74; CelR; CurBio 72;*
IlEncBM 82; NewYTBE 72; WhoAm 82;
WhoBlA 75; WhoHol A

Hayes, John Michael
American. Screenwriter
Won awards for scripts for *Rear Window,*
1954; *To Catch a Thief,* 1955.
b. May 11, 1919 in Worchester,
Massachusetts
Source: *ConAu 108; DcLB 26; FilmgC;*
WorEFlm

Hayes, Lester
American. Football Player
Cornerback, Oakland/LA Raiders, 1977--; led
NFL in interceptions, 1980.
b. Jan 22, 1955 in Houston, Texas
Source: *BioIn 12; NewYTBS 81*

Hayes, Lucy Webb
[Mrs. Rutherford B Hayes]
"Lemonade Lucy"
American. First Lady
First president's wife to graduate from
college; refused to serve alcohol at White
House.
b. Aug 28, 1831 in Chillicothe, Ohio
d. Jun 25, 1889 in Fremont, Ohio
Source: *AmWom; ApCAB; GoodHs; NatCAB
3; NotAW; TwCBDA; WhAm HS*

Hayes, Patrick J
American. Religious Leader
b. Nov 20, 1867 in New York, New York
d. Sep 4, 1938
Source: *AmBi; DcAmB S2; WhAm 1*

Hayes, Peter Lind
American. Actor, Composer, Author, Singer
With wife, Mary Healy, popular TV, radio
personality, 1950s; hosted TV series
"When Television Was Live," 1975.
b. Jun 25, 1915 in San Francisco, California
Source: *AmAu&B; AmSCAP 66; BiE&WWA;
CurBio 59; IntMPA 82; NotNAT; VarWW 85;
WhoAm 84*

Hayes, Mrs. Peter Lind
see: Healy, Mary

Hayes, Roland
American. Opera Singer
Pioneered way for black singers on stage.
b. Jun 3, 1887 in Curryville, Georgia
d. Dec 31, 1976 in Boston, Massachusetts
Source: *CurBio 77; WebAB; WhoAm 74;
WhoBlA 75*

Hayes, Rutherford B(irchard)
American. US President
Won presidency in newly created electoral
college by one vote over Samuel J Tilden,
1876.
b. Oct 4, 1822 in Delaware, Ohio
d. Jan 17, 1893 in Fremont, Ohio
Source: *AmAu&B; AmBi; ApCAB; BiAUS;
BiDrAC; BiDrUSE; DcAmB; Drake; EncAB-H;
OhA&B; OxAmL; REnAL; TwCBDA; WebAB;
WhAm HS; WhAmP*

Hayes, "Woody" (Wayne Woodrow)
American. Football Coach
Head coach, Ohio State, 1951-79; had 238-
72-10 record.
b. Feb 14, 1913 in Clifton, Ohio
Source: *BioNews 75; CelR; CurBio 75;
NewYTBS 74; WhoAm 74*

Hayman, Richard
American. Musician
Harmonica soloist with Horace Heidt, 1940s;
wrote "Ruby."
b. Mar 27, 1920 in Cambridge, Massachusetts
Source: *AmSCAP 66, 80; CmpEPM*

Hayman, Richard
American. Banker
b. 1925
Source: *St&PR 75*

Haymes, Dick (Richard)
American. Singer
Prominent singer noted for mellow voice,
early 1940s; career eclipsed by Frank
Sinatra.
b. Sep 13, 1917 in Buenos Aires, Argentina
d. Mar 28, 1980 in Los Angeles, California
Source: *FilmgC; HolP 40; IntMPA 75, 76,
77; MotPP; WhoHol A*

Haymes, Joe
American. Jazz Musician
b. 1908 in Marshfield, Missouri
Source: *WhoJazz 72*

Haynes, George Edward
American. Civil Rights Leader
b. May 11, 1880 in Pine Bluff, Arkansas
d. Jan 8, 1960
Source: *NatCAB 44; WhAm 3; WhoColR*

Haynes, Lloyd (Samuel Lloyd)
American. Actor
Starred in TV series "Room 222," 1969-74.
b. Oct 19, 1935 in South Bend, Indiana
Source: *WhoHol A*

Haynes Dixon, Margaret Rumer
see: Godden, Rumer, pseud.

Haynie, Carol
American. Politician
Source: *WomPO 76*

Haynie, Hugh
American. Cartoonist
b. Feb 6, 1927 in Reedville, Virginia
Source: *WhoAm 74, 76, 78, 80, 82;
WhoS&SW 82*

Haynie, Sandra
American. Golfer
Turned pro, 1961; won over 40 tournaments;
LPGA Hall of Fame, 1977.
b. Jun 4, 1943 in Fort Worth, Texas
Source: *NewYTBS 82; WhoGolf*

Haynsworth, Clement Furman, Jr.
American. Judge
b. Oct 30, 1912 in Greenville, South Carolina
Source: *WhoAm 74, 76, 78, 80, 82; WhoAmP 73; WhoGov 75; WhoS&SW 82*

Hays, Brooks
American. Politician, Author
Congressman from AR; tried to mediate Little Rock's integration crisis, 1950s.
b. Aug 9, 1898 in Russellville, Arkansas
d. Oct 11, 1981 in Chevy Chase, Maryland
Source: *BioIn 3, 4, 5, 8, 11; ConAu P-1; CurBio 58, 82; IntWW 78; PolProf E; WhoAm 78, 80; WhoWor 78; WrDr 80*

Hays, Lee
[The Weavers]
American. Singer, Songwriter
Folk singer with The Weavers, 1948-63; co-wrote "If I Had a Hammer," with Pete Seeger.
b. 1914 in Little Rock, Arkansas
d. Aug 26, 1981 in North Tarrytown, New York
Source: *BiDAmM; EncFCWM 69*

Hays, Robert
American. Actor
Starred in *Airplane!,* 1980.
b. Jul 24, 1948 in Bethesda, Maryland
Source: *IntMPA 82*

Hays, Wayne Levere
American. Politician
Congressman who retired from office after involvement with Elizabeth Ray, 1976.
b. Jun 13, 1911 in Bannock, Ohio
Source: *BiDrAC; BioNews 74; CngDr 74; CurBio 74; PolProf E, K, NF; WhoAm 76; WhoAmP 79; WhoGov 75; WhoMW 76*

Hays, Will Harrison
American. Statesman
b. Nov 5, 1879 in Sullivan, Indiana
d. Mar 7, 1954 in Sullivan, Indiana
Source: *CurBio 43, 54; DcAmB S5; DcFM; FilmgC; IndAu 1917; OxFilm; WhAm 3; WorEFlm*

Hayton, Lennie (Leonard George)
American. Composer, Conductor
b. Feb 13, 1908 in New York, New York
d. Apr 24, 1971 in Palm Springs, California
Source: *AmSCAP 66; CmMov; NewYTBE 71; WhoJazz 72*

Hayward, Brooke
American. Author, Actress
b. Jul 5, 1937 in Los Angeles, California
Source: *BioIn 11; BkPepl; ConAu 81; NewYTBS 77*

Hayward, John Davy
English. Editor
Editorial adviser to Cresset Press; editorial director of *Book Collector.*
b. Feb 2, 1905 in London, England
d. Sep 17, 1965 in Chelsea, England
Source: *DcLEL; DcNaB 1961; LongCTC; WhLit*

Hayward, Leland
American. Producer
b. Sep 13, 1902 in Nebraska City, Nebraska
d. Mar 18, 1971 in Yorktown Heights, New York
Source: *BiE&WWA; CurBio 49, 71; EncMT; FilmgC; NewYTBE 71*

Hayward, Louis
[Seafield Grant]
American. Actor
Played swashbucklers in 1940s adventure films.
b. Mar 19, 1909 in Johannesburg, South Africa
d. Feb 21, 1985 in Palm Springs, California
Source: *CmMov; FilmEn; FilmgC; IntMPA 77; MotPP; MovMk; WhoHol A; WorEFlm*

Hayward, Susan
[Edythe Marrener]
American. Actress
Won Oscar for *I Want to Live,* 1958.
b. Jun 30, 1919 in New York, New York
d. Mar 14, 1975 in Beverly Hills, California
Source: *BiDFilm; CmMov; CurBio 53; FilmgC; InWom; IntMPA 75; MotPP; MovMk; OxFilm; ThFT; WhAm 6; WhScrn 77; WhoAm 74; WorEFlm*

Haywood, "Big Bill" (William Dudley)
American. Labor Union Official
Helped organize IWW, 1905; convicted of sedition during WW I.
b. Feb 4, 1869 in Salt Lake City, Utah
d. May 18, 1928 in U.S.S.R.
Source: *AmBi; DcAmB; DcNAA; EncAB-H; WebAB; WhAm HSA, 4*

Haywood, Spencer
American. Basketball Player
b. Apr 21, 1950 in Silver City, Mississippi
Source: *WhoBbl 73*

Hayworth, Rita
[Margarita Carmen Cansino]
American. Actress
Starred in *Gilda*, 1946; married to Orson
    Welles, 1943-47, Dick Haymes, 1953-54.
b. Oct 17, 1918 in New York, New York
Source: *BiDFilm; CelR; CmMov; CurBio 60;*
FilmgC; InWom; IntMPA 75, 76, 77, 78, 79,
80, 81, 82; MotPP; MovMk; OxFilm; ThFT;
WhoAm 74, 76, 78, 80, 82; WhoHol A;
WomWMM; WorEFlm

Hazam, Lou(is J)
American. Producer
Pioneer in producing TV documentaries,
    1950s.
b. Jan 3, 1911 in Norwich, Connecticut
d. Sep 6, 1983 in Silver Spring, Maryland
Source: *AnObit 1983; ConAu 110; LesBEnT;*
NewYTET

Hazan, Marcella Maddalena
Italian. Author, Educator
Wrote *The Classic Italian Cookbook*, 1973.
b. Apr 15, 1924 in Cesenatico, Italy
Source: *BioIn 11; WhoAm 80, 82*

Hazelwood, Lee
American. Singer, Songwriter
Best known for duets with Nancy Sinatra:
    "Jackson," 1967; "Some Velvet Morning,"
    1968.
b. Jul 9, 1929 in Mannford, Oklahoma
Source: *RolSEnR 83*

Hazlitt, William
English. Author
Wrote *Characters of Shakespeare's Plays*,
    1817; *Lectures on the English Poets*, 1818.
b. Apr 10, 1778 in Maidstone, England
d. Sep 18, 1830 in London, England
Source: *Alli; AtlBL; BiD&SB; BiDLA; BrAu*
19; CasWL; Chambr 3; CrtT 2; CyWA;
DcEnA, AP; DcEnL; DcEuL; DcLEL; EvLB;
MouLC 3; NewC; OxEng; OxThe; PenC
ENG; RAdv 1; RComWL; REn; WebE&AL

Head, Bessie
[Bessie Emery]
South African. Author
Exiled from S Africa; wrote *Maru*, 1971; *A*
    Question of Power, 1974.
b. Jul 6, 1937 in South Africa
d. Apr 17, 1986 in Serowe, Botswana
Source: *AfSS 82; ConNov 82; DcLEL 1940;*
WrDr 84

Head, Edith
American. Fashion Designer
Won eight Oscars; wrote autobiography
    Fashion as a Career, 1966.
b. Oct 28, 1907 in Los Angeles, California
d. Oct 24, 1981 in Los Angeles, California
Source: *BioIn 1, 2, 4, 5, 10; CelR; CurBio*
45, 82; FilmgC; IntMPA 78, 79, 80, 81, 82;
WhoAm 74, 76, 78, 80; WhoAmW 58A, 64,
66, 68, 70, 72, 74

Head, Edmund Walker, Sir
"Grandfather of Confederation"
English. Colonial Leader
Governor-in-chief of Canada, 1854-61.
b. 1805 in Raleigh, England
d. Jan 28, 1868 in London, England
Source: *ApCAB; DcNaB; Drake; OxCan*

Headon, Topper
see: Clash, The

Healy, George Peter Alexander
American. Artist
b. Jul 15, 1813 in Boston, Massachusetts
d. Jun 24, 1894 in Chicago, Illinois
Source: *AmBi; ApCAB; DcAmB; DcNAA;*
Drake; TwCBDA; WhAm HS

Healy, Katherine
American. Ballerina, Actress
Won gold medal, Varna International Ballet
    Competition; in film *Six Weeks*, 1982.
b. 1969 in New York, New York
Source: *BioIn 11, 12*

Healy, Mary
[Mrs. Peter Lind Hayes]
American. Actress, Singer, TV Personality
Teamed with husband, Peter Lind Hayes, for
    radio, TV shows, 1950s; wrote *Only*
    Twenty-Five Minutes from Broadway, 1961.
b. Apr 14, 1918 in New Orleans, Louisiana
Source: *BiE&WWA; InWom; NotNAT;*
WhoAm 84; WhoHol A

Healy, Ted
American. Actor
b. Oct 1, 1896 in Houston, Texas
d. Dec 21, 1937 in Los Angeles, California
Source: *FilmgC; WhScrn 74, 77; WhoHol B*

Heard, Gerald (Henry FitzGerald)
English. Author
b. Oct 6, 1889 in London, England
d. Aug 14, 1971 in Santa Monica, California
Source: *AmAu&B; Au&Wr 71; BiDPara;*
ConAu 21R, 29R, P-2; LongCTC; NewC;
REn; TwCA, SUP; WhAm 5; Who 74

Heard, John
American. Actor
b. Mar 7, 1945 in Washington, District of
Columbia
Source: *BioIn 11; IntMPA 82*

Hearn, Lafcadio
Japanese. Author, Journalist
Introduced Japanese culture to the West
through his works.
b. Jun 27, 1850 in Ionian Islands, Greece
d. Sep 26, 1904 in Okubo, Japan
Source: *Alli SUP; AmAu; AmAu&B; AmBi;
AnCL; AtlBL; BbD; BiD&SB; BiDSA;
CasWL; Chambr 3; ChhPo; CnDAL; CrtT 3;
CyWA; DcAmAu; DcAmB; DcBiA; DcEuL;
DcLEL; DcNAA; EncAB-H; EvLB; ModAL;
NewC; OhA&B; OxAmL; OxEng; PenC AM,
ENG; PoIre; RAdv 1; REn; REnAL; WebAB;
WhAm 1*

Hearne, Samuel
British. Explorer
First man to reach Arctic Ocean over land,
1771-72.
b. 1745
d. 1792
Source: *Alli; ApCAB; BbtC; DcLEL; Drake;
OxCan*

Hearns, Thomas (Tommy)
"Detroit Hit Man"; "Motor City Cobra"
American. Boxer
WBC Super-welterweight champion, pro
record is 36-1.
b. Oct 18, 1958 in Grand Junction,
Tennessee
Source: *CurBio 83; NewYTBS 81*

Hearst, Catherine
American. Celebrity Relative
b. 1918
Source: *WhoAm 78, 80, 82; WomPO 76*

Hearst, David W
American. Publisher
Son of W R Hearst; published LA *Herald-
Express,* 1950.
b. Dec 2, 1916 in New York, New York
d. May 13, 1986 in Los Angeles, California
Source: *Dun&B 79; IntWW 83; NewYTBS
86; WhoAm 78*

Hearst, Millicent Willson
[Mrs. William Randolph, Sr.]
American. Philanthropist
b. Jul 16, 1882 in New York, New York
d. Dec 6, 1974 in New York, New York
Source: *BioNews 75; InWom; NewYTBS 74*

Hearst, Patty (Patricia Campbell)
[Mrs. Bernard Shaw]
"Tanya"
American. Kidnap Victim, Author
Kidnapped by SLA, Feb 5, 1974; wrote
Every Secret Thing, 1981.
b. Feb 20, 1954 in San Francisco, California
Source: *BioNews 74; BkPepl; CurBio 82;
NewYTBS 74*

Hearst, Randolph Apperson
American. Newspaper Executive
Pres., Hearst Foundation, 1972--; father of
Patty Hearst Shaw.
b. Dec 2, 1915 in New York, New York
Source: *BioNews 74; IntWW 74; NewYTBS
74; WhoAm 74, 76, 78, 80, 82*

Hearst, William Randolph
American. Newspaper Publisher
Founder of newspaper chain with yellow
journalism reputation; movie *Citizen Kane,*
1941, based on his life.
b. Apr 29, 1863 in San Francisco, California
d. Aug 14, 1951 in Beverly Hills, California
Source: *AmAu&B; BiDrAC; DcAmB S5;
DcFM; EncAB-H; FilmgC; LongCTC;
OxAmL; OxFilm; REn; REnAL; WebAB;
WhAm 3; WhAmP; WorEFlm*

Hearst, William Randolph, Jr.
American. Editor, Publisher
b. Jan 27, 1908 in New York, New York
Source: *AmAu&B; CelR; CurBio 55; IntWW
74; St&PR 75; Who 74; WhoAm 74, 76, 78,
80, 82*

Hearst, William Randolph, III
American. Newspaper Executive
b. 1949
Source: *BioIn 10*

Heart
[Mark Andes; Denny Carmassi; Mike
Derosier; Roger Fisher; Steve Fossen;
Howard Lesse; Ann Wilson; Nancy
Wilson]
American. Music Group
Heavy metal band led by sisters, Ann, Nancy
Wilson since 1972; album *Dreamboat
Annie,* sold 2.5 million copies, 1976.
Source: *NewWmR; RkOn 74; RolSEnR 83*

Heath, Edward Richard George
English. Politician, Prime Minister
b. Jul 9, 1916 in Broadstairs, England
Source: *ConAu 33R; CurBio 62; IntWW 74;
NewYTBE 70, 71; Who 74; WhoWor 78*

Heath, Lawrence S
American. Candy Manufacturer
Merchant who began making Heath Bar,
    1931.
b. 1869
d. 1956
Source: *Entr*

Heath, Ted
English. Band Leader, Musician
b. 1902 in London, England
d. Nov 18, 1969 in Virginia Water, England
Source: *WhScrn 74, 77; WhoHol B*

Heatherton, Joey
American. Actress, Singer, Dancer
Films include *Happy Hooker Goes to
    Washington,* 1977; *Bluebeard,* 1972.
b. Sep 14, 1944 in Rockville Centre, New
    York
Source: *FilmEn; FilmgC; MotPP; WhoAm 74;
WhoHol A*

Heatherton, Ray
American. Actor, Singer
b. Jun 1, 1910 in Jersey City, New Jersey
Source: *BiE&WWA; NotNAT*

Heaton, Leonard
American. Military Leader, Physician
Surgeon General under four presidents, 1959-
    69.
b. 1902 in Parkersburg, West Virginia
d. Sep 11, 1983 in Washington, District of
    Columbia
Source: *NewYTBS 83*

Heatter, Gabriel
American. Radio Commentator, Journalist
Opening words for his news broadcasts, "Ah-
    there's good news tonight,"   became nat.
    catch phrase.
b. Sep 17, 1890 in New York, New York
d. Mar 30, 1972 in Miami Beach, Florida
Source: *CurBio 41, 72; NewYTBE 72;
WebAB; WhScrn 77*

Heavenly Twins
see: Meadows, Earle; Sefton, William

Hebert, F(elix) Edward
American. Politician, Editor
Dem. congressman from LA, 1941-76; wrote
    award-winning expose of Huey Long, 1939.
b. Oct 12, 1901 in New Orleans, Louisiana
d. Dec 29, 1979 in New Orleans, Louisiana
Source: *BiDrAC; CngDr 74; CurBio 51, 80;
NewYTBS 79; PolProf E, J, K, NF, T;
WhAm HS; WhoAm 74, 76, 78; WhoAmP 73,
75, 77, 79; WhoGov 72, 75, 77; WhoS&SW
73, 75, 76*

Hebner, Richie (Richard Joseph)
American. Baseball Player
b. Nov 26, 1947 in Brighton, Massachusetts
Source: *BaseEn 85; WhoProB 73*

Hechinger, Fred Michael
American. Newspaper Editor, Author
b. Jul 7, 1920 in Nuremberg, Germany
Source: *ConAu 77; WhoAm 74, 76, 78, 80,
82; WhoE 74; WhoWorJ 72; WrDr 76*

Hecht, Anthony Evan
American. Poet
Won Pulitzer, 1968, for *The Hard Hours,*
    which featured empathetic perspective on
    human suffering.
b. Jan 16, 1923 in New York, New York
Source: *CurBio 86; LinLib L; WhoAm 84;
WhoTwCL*

Hecht, Ben
American. Author, Dramatist
Wrote novels of city life; co-wrote many
    Hollywood, Broadway hits, including *Front
    Page,* 1928.
b. Feb 28, 1893 in New York, New York
d. Apr 18, 1964 in New York, New York
Source: *AmAu&B; BiDFilm; CmMov; CnDAL;
CnMD; CnThe; ConAmA; ConAu 85; ConLC
8; CurBio 42, 64; DcFM; DcLEL; EncMys;
FilmgC; LongCTC; McGEWD; ModWD;
OxAmL; OxFilm; PenC AM; REn; REnAL;
TwCA, SUP; WebAB; WhAm 4; WhScrn 77;
WorEFlm*

Hecht, Chic
American. Politician
Rep. senator from NV, 1982--.
b. Nov 30, 1928 in Cape Girardeau, Missouri
Source: *CngDr 85*

Hecht, George Joseph
American. Publisher
Founded *Parents' Magazine; Humpty Dumpty.*
b. Nov 1, 1895 in New York, New York
d. Apr 23, 1980 in New York, New York
Source: *BioIn 1, 2; ConAu 97; CurBio 47,
80; NewYTBS 75, 80; SmATA 22; St&PR 75;
WhNAA; WhoAm 74, 76, 78, 80; WhoWorJ
72*

Hecht, Harold
American. Producer
Won best picture Oscar, 1955, for *Marty.*
b. Jun 1, 1907 in New York, New York
d. May 25, 1985 in Beverly Hills, California
Source: *FilmgC; IntMPA 81; WhoAm 78;
WorEFlm*

Heck, Barbara Ruckle
"Mother of Methodism"
Irish. Religious Leader
Helped establish first Methodist chapel in
    America, 1768.
b. 1734 in County Limerick, Ireland
d. Aug 17, 1804 in Augusta, Canada
Source: *ApCAB; DcAmB; InWom; LibW;
MacDCB 78; NatCAB 13; NotAW; OxCan;
WhAm HS*

Heckart, Eileen
American. Actress
Won 1972 Oscar for *Butterflies Are Free.*
b. Mar 29, 1919 in Columbus, Ohio
Source: *BiE&WWA; CelR; CurBio 58;
FilmgC; InWom; IntMPA 75, 76, 77, 78, 79,
80, 81, 82; MotPP; MovMk,; NewYTBE 73;
NotNAT; PIP&P; WhoAm 74, 76, 78, 80, 82;
WhoE 74; WhoHol A; WhoThe 77*

Heckler, Margaret Mary
American. Government Official
Secretary of Health and Human Services
    under Ronald Reagan, 1983--.
b. Jun 21, 1931 in Flushing, New York
Source: *BiDrAC; CngDr 74; CurBio 83;
NewYTBS 83; WhoAm 82; WhoAmP 73;
WhoAmW 77; WhoE 74; WhoGov 72*

Heckscher, August
American. Author, Journalist
b. Sep 16, 1913 in Huntington, New York
Source: *AmAu&B; Au&Wr 71; BiE&WWA;
ConAu 1R; CurBio 41, 58; IntWW 74;
WhoAm 74; WhoE 74; WhoGov 75*

Hedberg, Anders
Swedish. Hockey Player
Right wing, NY Rangers, 1978--.
b. Feb 25, 1951 in Ornskoldsvik, Sweden
Source: *BioIn 11; HocEn*

Hedison, David (Albert David, Jr.)
American. Actor
In films *Greatest Story Ever Told; Live and
    Let Die.*
b. May 20, 1928 in Providence, Rhode
    Island
Source: *FilmgC; MotPP; WhoHol A*

Hedren, "Tippi" (Natalie Kay)
American. Actress
Cool blonde Hitchcock star in first two
    films: *The Birds,* 1963, *Marnie,* 1964.
b. Jan 19, 1935 in New Ulm, Minnesota
Source: *BiDFilm; FilmgC; MotPP; WhoAm
74; WhoHol A*

Heem, Jan Davidsz de
Dutch. Artist
Known for realistic still lifes, portraits: "Still
    Life with Books," 1628.
b. 1606 in Utrecht, Belgium
d. 1684 in Antwerp, Belgium
Source: *McGDA*

Heffelfinger, "Pudge" (William Walter)
American. Football Player
Called greatest blocker of all time.
b. Dec 20, 1867 in Minneapolis, Minnesota
d. Apr 2, 1954 in Blessing, Texas
Source: *DcAmB S5; WebAB; WhoFtbl 74*

Heffer, Eric Samuel
British. Author, Statesman
b. 1922
Source: *Who 74*

Heflin, Van Emmett Evan
American. Actor
Won Oscar for *Johnny Eager,* 1942; also in
    film *Shane,* 1953.
b. Dec 13, 1910 in Walters, Oklahoma
d. Jul 23, 1971 in Hollywood, California
Source: *BiDFilm; BiE&WWA; CmMov;
CurBio 43, 71; FilmgC; MotPP; MovMk;
OxFilm; PIP&P; WhAm 5; WhScrn 77;
WhoHol B; WorEFlm*

Hefner, Christie (Christine Ann)
American. Celebrity Relative, Business
    Executive
Daughter of Hugh Hefner; pres., Playboy
    Enterprises, 1982--.
b. Nov 8, 1952 in Chicago, Illinois
Source: *BioIn 10, 11; ConNews 85-1*

Hefner, Hugh Marston
American. Publisher
Founded *Playboy,* 1953; *VIP,* 1963-75; *Oui,*
    1972-81.
b. Apr 9, 1926 in Chicago, Illinois
Source: *AuNews 1; BioNews 74; BkPepl;
CelR; CurBio 68; IntWW 74; St&PR 75;
WebAB; WhoAm 74, 76, 78, 80, 82; WhoF&I
74; WhoMW 74; WhoWor 78*

Hefti, Neal Paul
American. Composer, Publisher
b. Oct 29, 1922 in Hastings, Nebraska
Source: *AmSCAP 66; WhoAm 74, 76, 78, 80,
82*

Hegan, Jim (James Edward)
American. Baseball Player, Baseball Coach
Cleveland catcher; handled one of best
    pitching staffs ever: Bob Feller, Mike
    Garcia, Early Wynn.
b. Aug 3, 1920 in Lynn, Massachusetts
d. Jun 17, 1984 in Swampscott,
    Massachusetts
Source: *BaseEn 85; WhoProB 73*

Hegel, Georg Wilhelm Friedrich
German. Philosopher
b. Aug 27, 1770 in Stuttgart, Germany
d. Nov 14, 1831 in Berlin, Germany
Source: *BbD; BiD&SB; CasWL; DcEuL;
EuAu; EvEuW; NewC; OxEng; OxGer; PenC
EUR; REn*

Heger, Robert
Alsatian. Conductor, Composer
b. Aug 19, 1886 in Strassburg, Germany
Source: *Who 74; WhoMus 72*

Heggen, Thomas Orls, Jr.
American. Author, Dramatist
b. Dec 23, 1919 in Fort Dodge, Iowa
d. May 19, 1949 in New York, New York
Source: *AmAu&B; BioIn 1, 2, 3, 4, 5, 10;
CyWA; OxAmL; PenC AM; REnAL; TwCA
SUP*

Heggie, O P
Australian. Actor
Films include *Anne of Green Gables,* 1934;
    Bride of Frankenstein, 1935.
b. Nov 17, 1879 in Angaston, Australia
d. Feb 7, 1936 in Los Angeles, California
Source: *FilmgC; MovMk; TwYS; WhScrn 74,
77; WhoHol B*

Hegyes, Robert
American. Actor
Played Epstein on TV series "Welcome Back,
    Kotter."
b. May 7, 1951
Source: *NF*

Heidegger, Martin
German. Author, Philosopher
Focused on human condition without effects
    of religion; principal work *Being and
    Time,* 1927.
b. Sep 26, 1889 in Messkirch, Germany
d. May 26, 1976 in Messkirch, Germany
Source: *CasWL; ConAu 65, 81; CurBio 72;
IntWW 74; LongCTC; OxGer; REn; TwCA
SUP; TwCWr; WhAm 6; Who 74*

Heiden, Beth
American. Speed Skater
b. 1959 in Madison, Wisconsin
Source: *BioIn 12*

Heiden, Eric
American. Speed Skater
First person to win five individual Olympic
    gold medals, 1980.
b. Jun 14, 1958 in Madison, Wisconsin
Source: *BioIn 12; CurBio 80*

Heiden, Konrad
German. Historian, Author
Expert on Hitler, said to have coined term
    "Nazi" as derisive nickname.
b. Aug 7, 1901 in Munich, Germany
d. Jul 18, 1966 in New York, New York
Source: *ConAu 116; CurBio 44, 75*

Heidenstam, Carl Gustaf Verner von
Swedish. Author, Poet
First volume of poetry *Pilgrimage and
    Wanderyears,* 1888, challenged
    contemporary Swedish literature; won
    Nobel Prize, 1916.
b. Jul 6, 1859 in Olshammar, Sweden
d. May 20, 1940 in Stockholm, Sweden
Source: *BiD&SB; CasWL; ConAu 104; REn*

Heidt, Horace Murray
American. Band Leader
Popular vaudeville entertainer, 1920s-30s, who
    was featured in radio talent show, 1940s:
    "Youth Opportunity Program."
b. May 21, 1901 in Alameda, California
Source: *AmPS A, B; WhoHol A*

Heifetz, Jascha
American. Musician
Debuted at age five; won Grammys, 1961-62,
    1964.
b. Feb 2, 1901 in Vilna, Russia
Source: *AmSCAP 66; CelR; CurBio 44;
IntWW 74; NewYTBE 71; REn; WebAB;
Who 74; WhoAm 74, 76, 78, 80, 82; WhoHol
A; WhoMus 72; WhoWor 78*

Heilmann, Harry Edwin
"Slug"
American. Baseball Player
Batted .403, 1923; lifetime batting average,
    .342; Hall of Fame, 1952.
b. Aug 3, 1894 in San Francisco, California
d. Jul 9, 1951 in Detroit, Michigan
Source: *BaseEn 85; DcAmB S5; WhoProB 73*

Heim, Jacques
French. Fashion Designer
b. May 8, 1899 in Paris, France
d. Jan 8, 1967 in Paris, France
Source: *WhAm 4; WorFshn*

Heimlich, Henry J
American. Physician, Author
Developed anti-choking maneuver named for
him: "Heimlich Maneuver."
b. Feb 3, 1920 in Wilmington, Delaware
Source: *ConAu 102; WhoAm 84; WhoMW 82;
WhoWorJ 78*

Heindorf, Ray
American. Composer, Conductor
Head of Warner Bros. music dept.; won
Oscars for orchestrations of *Yankee Doodle
Dandy*, 1942; *Music Man*, 1962.
b. Aug 25, 1908 in Haverstraw, New York
d. Feb 3, 1980 in Los Angeles, California
Source: *CmMov; FilmEn; FilmgC; IntMPA 77*

Heine, Heinrich
German. Poet, Critic
Wrote satirical poetry including *The Harz
Journey*, 1826.
b. Dec 13, 1797 in Dusseldorf, Germany
d. Feb 17, 1856 in Paris, France
Source: *AtlBL; BbD; BiD&SB; CasWL;
ChhPo, S1, S2; CyWA; DcEuL; EuAu;
EvEuW; NewC; OxEng; OxFr; OxGer; PenC
EUR; RComWL; REn*

Heinemann, Gustav Walter
German. President
b. Jul 23, 1899
Source: *CurBio 69; IntWW 74; WhoGov 75;
WhoWor 78*

Heinlein, Robert Anson
American. Author
b. Jul 7, 1907 in Butler, Missouri
Source: *ConAu 1R, 1NR; ConLC 3, 8, 14;
ConNov 72, 76; CurBio 55; DrAF 76; MorJA;
PenC AM; REnAL; SmATA 9; TwCA SUP;
TwCWr; WebAB; WebE&AL; WhoAm 74, 76,
78, 80, 82; WrDr 80*

Heinsohn, Tommy
American. Basketball Player
b. Aug 26, 1934
Source: *WhoBbl 73*

Heinz, Henry John
American. Manufacturer
Founded H J Heinz Co., 1876; originated
"57 varieties" slogan, 1896.
b. Oct 11, 1844 in Pittsburgh, Pennsylvania
d. May 14, 1919 in Pittsburgh, Pennsylvania
Source: *DcAmB; WebAB; WhAm 1*

Heinz, (Henry) John, (III)
American. Politician
Liberal Rep. senator from PA, 1976--.
b. Oct 23, 1938 in Pittsburgh, Pennsylvania
Source: *AlmAP 78, 80; BioIn 9, 10; CngDr
74, 77, 79; CurBio 81; IntWW 77, 78;
WhoAm 74, 76, 78, 80, 82; WhoAmP 73, 75,
77, 79; WhoE 74, 75, 77, 79; WhoGov 75, 77*

Heisenberg, Werner Karl
German. Physicist
b. Dec 5, 1901 in Wurzburg, Germany
d. Feb 1, 1976 in Munich, Germany (West)
Source: *ConAu 65; CurBio 57; IntWW 74;
WhAm 6; Who 74; WhoWor 78*

Heiser, Victor George
American. Physician, Author
b. Feb 5, 1873 in Pennsylvania
d. Feb 27, 1972 in New York, New York
Source: *AmAu&B; ConAu 33R; CurBio 42,
72; NewYTBE 72; WhAm 5; WhNAA*

Heiskell, Andrew
American. Publisher
b. Sep 13, 1915 in Naples, Italy
Source: *AmAu&B; CurBio 66; IntWW 74;
St&PR 75; Who 74; WhoAm 74, 76, 78, 80,
82; WhoE 74; WhoF&I 74; WhoWor 78*

Heisman, John William
American. Football Player, Football Coach
College football's best player trophy is named
for him.
b. Oct 23, 1869 in Cleveland, Ohio
d. Oct 3, 1936 in New York, New York
Source: *BioIn 4, 6, 7; WhoFtbl 74*

Heiss, Carol Elizabeth
see: Jenkins, Carol Heiss

Helburn, Theresa
American. Producer
With Theatre Guild, 1918-53; produced
Oklahoma, 1943.
b. Jan 12, 1887 in New York, New York
d. Aug 18, 1959 in Weston, Connecticut
Source: *NotAW MOD*

Helck, Peter (Clarence Peter)
American. Artist, Illustrator
b. Jun 17, 1893 in New York, New York
Source: *WhoAm 74, 76, 78, 80, 82; WhoAmA
73*

Held, Al
American. Artist
Paintings developed from abstract
  expressionism to massive black and white
  geometrics: "Albany Mural," 1971.
b. Oct 12, 1928 in New York, New York
Source: *BnEnAmA; ConArt 83; CurBio 86;
DcAmArt; WhoAm 74, 82; WhoAmA 73, 76,
78, 84*

Held, Anna
American. Actress
First wife of Flo Ziegfeld; starred in *Anna
  Held,* 1902.
b. Mar 8, 1873 in Paris, France
d. Aug 12, 1918 in New York, New York
Source: *EncMT; FamA&A; Film 1; InWom;
NotAW; WhAm 1; WhScrn 77; WhoHol B;
WhoStg 1906; WomWWA 14*

Held, John, Jr.
American. Cartoonist, Illustrator
His line drawings captured spirit of "flaming
  youth" and "flappers" during 1920s.
b. Jan 10, 1889 in Salt Lake City, Utah
d. Mar 2, 1958 in Belmar, New Jersey
Source: *AmAu&B; ChhPo S1; OxAmL;
REnAL; WebAB; WhAm 3*

Helen of Troy
Greek. Legendary Figure
Daughter of Zeus who fled to Troy with
  lover; husband's attempts to reclaim her
  led to Trogan War.
Source: *NewCol 75*

Heliogabalus
Roman. Emperor
b. 204 in Emesa, Syria
d. 222
Source: *NewC; REn*

Heller, Goldie
American. Artist, Advertising Executive
b. in Salem, Massachusetts
Source: *ForWC 70; WhoAdv 72; WhoAmA 73*

Heller, Joseph
American. Author, Dramatist
Wrote contemporary American masterpiece,
  Catch-22, 1961.
b. May 1, 1923 in Brooklyn, New York
Source: *AmAu&B; AuNews 1; BioNews 74;
CasWL; ConAu 5R; ConLC 1, 3, 5, 8, 11;
ModAL, S1; NotNAT; OxAmL; PenC AM;
RAdv 1; TwCWr; WebE&AL; WhoAm 74, 76,
78, 80, 82; WhoTwCL; WorAu; WrDr 80*

Heller, Walter Wolfgang
American. Economist, Government Official
Consultant, CBO, 1975--; member Trilateral
  Commission, 1978--; author of numerous
  books on economics.
b. Aug 27, 1915 in Buffalo, New York
Source: *IntAu&W 82; IntWW 82; PolProf J,
K; WhoAm 82; WhoAmP 81; WrDr 82*

Hellerman, Fred
[The Weavers]
American. Singer, Musician, Songwriter
b. May 13, 1927 in New York, New York
Source: *AmSCAP 66; EncFCWM 69; WhoAm
74, 76, 78, 82; WhoE 74*

Hellinger, Mark
American. Journalist
b. Mar 21, 1903 in New York, New York
d. Dec 21, 1947 in Hollywood, California
Source: *AmAu&B; BiDFilm; CmMov; CurBio
47, 48; DcFM; DcNAA; FilmgC; OxFilm;
REnAL; WhAm 2; WhScrn 77; WorEFlm*

Hellman, Lillian
American. Dramatist, Author
Wrote *The Little Foxes,* 1939; movie *Julia,*
  based on *Pentimento,* 1973.
b. Jun 20, 1905 in New Orleans, Louisiana
d. Jun 30, 1984 in Martha's Vineyard,
  Massachusetts
Source: *AmAu&B; Au&Wr 71; AuNews 1, 2;
BiE&WWA; BioNews 74; BkPepl; CasWL;
CelR; CnDAL; CnMD; CnThe; ConAu 13R;
ConLC 2, 4, 8, 14, 18; CroCD; CurBio 41,
60; CyWA; DcFM; EncAB-H; EncWL;
FilmgC; ForWC 70; InWom; IntMPA 75, 76,
77, 78, 79, 80, 81, 82; IntWW 74; LongCTC;
McGEWD; ModAL, S1; ModWD; NatPD;
NewYTBE 73; NotNAT; OxAmL; OxFilm;
OxThe; PenC AM; PIP&P; REn; REnAL;
REnWD; TwCA, SUP; WebAB; WebE&AL;
Who 74; WhoAm 74, 76, 78, 80, 82; WhoE
74; WhoThe 77; WhoTwCL; WhoWor 78;
WhoWorJ 72; AnObit 1984; WomWMM;
WorEFlm*

Hellmann, Richard
American. Manufacturer
Began selling Hellmann's Mayonnaise, 1912;
  merged with General Foods, 1927.
b. 1876 in Vetschau, Germany
d. Feb 2, 1971 in Greenwich, Connecticut
Source: *BioIn 9; Entr; NewYTBE 71*

Helm, Levon
[The Band]
American. Musician, Singer, Actor
Played Loretta Lynn's father in *Coal Miner's Daughter*, 1980.
b. May 26, 1943 in Marvell, Arkansas
Source: *RkWW 82; WhoRocM 82*

Helmholtz, Herman Ludwig Ferdinand von
German. Physicist, Physiologist
First to outline principal of energy conservation; invented ophthalmoscope, 1850.
b. Aug 31, 1821 in Potsdam, Germany
d. Sep 8, 1894 in Charlottenburg, Germany
Source: *AsBiEn; BbD; DcScB; LinLib S; McGEWB; REn*

Helmond, Katherine
American. Actress
Starred as Jessica Tate on TV's "Soap," 1977-80.
b. Jun 5, 1933 in Galveston, Texas
Source: *BioIn 11; ConTFT 3; WhoAm 82*

Helmore, Tom
English. Actor
Films include *Designing Woman*, 1957; *Vertigo*, 1958.
b. Jan 4, 1912 in London, England
Source: *BiE&WWA; NotNAT; WhoHol A*

Helms, Chet
American. Producer
b. 1942
Source: *BioIn 10*

Helms, Jesse Alexander, Jr.
American. Politician, Journalist
Conservative Rep. senator from NC, 1972--.
b. Oct 18, 1921 in Monroe, North Carolina
Source: *CngDr 74; IntWW 74; St&PR 75; WhoAm 74, 76, 78, 80, 82; WhoAmP 73*

Helms, Richard McGarrah
American. Government Official
b. Mar 30, 1913 in Saint Davids, Pennsylvania
Source: *CelR; CurBio 67; IntWW 74; NewYTBE 71, 73; USBiR 74; WhoAm 74, 76, 78, 80, 82; WhoGov 75; WhoS&SW 82; WhoWor 78*

Helmsley, Harry Brakmann
American. Businessman
Real estate tycoon who is Manhattan's largest landlord, NYC's biggest booster.
b. Mar 4, 1909 in New York, New York
Source: *CurBio 85; St&PR 75*

Heloise
[Heloise and Abelard]
French. Nun
Best known for love affair with Pierre Abelard; immortalized in their letters.
b. 1101
d. 1164
Source: *InWom; OxFr; REn*

Heloise
[Heloise Bowles Reese]
American. Journalist, Author
Wrote syndicated column *Hints from Heloise*, 1961-77.
b. May 4, 1919 in Fort Worth, Texas
d. Dec 28, 1977 in San Antonio, Texas
Source: *ConAu 9R, 73; InWom*

Helpmann, Robert Murray, Sir
Australian. Ballet Dancer, Actor
b. Apr 9, 1909 in Mount Gambier, Australia
Source: *BiE&WWA; CurBio 50; FilmgC; IntMPA 77, 75; IntWW 74; MovMk; NotNAT; OxThe; PlP&P; Who 74; WhoHol A; WhoThe 77; WhoWor 78*

Hemans, Felicia Dorothea Browne
English. Poet
b. Sep 25, 1793 in Liverpool, England
d. May 16, 1835 in Dublin, Ireland
Source: *Alli; BbD; BiD&SB; BrAu 19; CarSB; CasWL; ChhPo S2; DcEnA; DcEnL; DcEuL; DcLEL; EvLB; InWom; NewC; OxEng; PoChrch; REn; WebE&AL*

Hemings, Sally
"Black Sally"
American. Slave, Celebrity Friend
Alleged mistress of Thomas Jefferson who bore him several sons; subject of book by Barbara Chase-Riboud, 1979.
b. 1773
d. 1835
Source: *BioIn 11; InB&W 80*

Hemingway, Ernest Miller
American. Journalist, Author
Wrote *A Farewell to Arms*, 1929; *For Whom the Bell Tolls*, 1940.
b. Jul 21, 1899 in Oak Park, Illinois
d. Jul 2, 1961 in Ketchum, Idaho
Source: *AmAu&B; AmNov; AmWr; ArizL; AuNews 2; BioIn 1, 2, 3, 4, 5, 6, 7, 8, 9, 10, 11; CasWL; Chambr 3; ChhPo S1, S2; CnDAL; CnMD; CnMWL; ConAmA; ConAu 77; ConLC 1, 3, 6, 8, 10, 13; EncWL; EvLB; FilmgC; LongCTC; ModAL, S1; ModWD; OxAmL; OxEng; OxFilm; PenC AM; RAdv 1; RComWL; REn; REnAL; TwCA, SUP; TwCWr; WebAB, 79; WebE&AL; WhAm 4; WhoTwCL; WorEFlm*

Hemingway, Leicester
American. Author
Younger brother of Ernest Hemingway; wrote
biography *My Brother, Ernest Hemingway.*
b. Apr 1915 in Oak Park, Illinois
d. Sep 13, 1982 in Miami, Florida
Source: *BioIn 3; ConAu 107*

Hemingway, Margaux
[Mrs. Bernardo Foucher]
American. Model, Actress
Granddaughter of Ernest Hemingway; starred
in *Lipstick,* 1976.
b. Feb 1955 in Portland, Oregon
Source: *BioIn 10, 11; BkPepl; CurBio 78;
WhoAm 80; WhoHol A*

Hemingway, Mariel
[Mrs. Steve Douglas Crisinan]
American. Actress
Granddaughter of Ernest Hemingway; starred
in *Lipstick,* 1976; *Manhattan,* 1979.
b. Nov 21, 1961 in Mill Valley, Idaho
Source: *BioIn 11; ConTFT 3*

Hemingway, Mary Welsh
[Mrs. Ernest Hemingway]
American. Author, Journalist
Wrote *How It Was,* 1976, a chronicle of her
life with Ernest Hemingway.
b. Apr 5, 1908 in Walker, Minnesota
Source: *ConAu 73; CurBio 68; ForWC 70;
InWom*

Hemion, Dwight
American. Director, Producer
Won Emmy for TV special "Frank Sinatra:
A Man and His Music," 1965.
b. Mar 14, 1926 in New Haven, Connecticut
Source: *NewYTET; WhoAm 82*

Hemmings, David Leslie Edward
[Leslie Edward]
English. Actor
Starred in films *Blow-Up,* 1966, *Camelot,*
1967.
b. Nov 21, 1941 in Guildford, England
Source: *CelR; FilmgC; IntMPA 82; MotPP;
MovMk; Who 74; WhoAm 74; WhoHol A;
WorEFlm*

Hempel, Frieda
German. Opera Singer
b. Jun 26, 1885 in Leipzig, Germany
d. Oct 7, 1955 in Berlin, Germany (West)
Source: *InWom; WhAm 3*

Hemphill, Paul
American. Author
b. Feb 18, 1936 in Birmingham, Alabama
Source: *AuNews 2; BioIn 9, 10, 11; ConAu
49*

Hemsley, Sherman
American. Actor
Played George Jefferson on "The Jeffersons,"
1975-85.
b. Feb 1, 1938 in Philadelphia, Pennsylvania
Source: *ConTFT 3; WhoAm 82; WhoTelC*

Hench, Philip Showalter
American. Scientist, Physician, Engineer
b. Feb 28, 1896 in Pittsburgh, Pennsylvania
d. Mar 30, 1965 in Ocho Rios, Jamaica
Source: *CurBio 50, 65; WebAB; WhAm 4*

Henderson, Arthur
British. Statesman
b. Aug 27, 1893
d. Aug 28, 1968 in London, England
Source: *IntYB 78*

Henderson, Fletcher Hamilton
American. Band Leader
b. Dec 18, 1897 in Cuthbert, Georgia
d. Dec 29, 1952 in New York, New York
Source: *AmSCAP 66; DcAmB S5*

Henderson, Florence
American. Actress, Singer
Starred in TV series "The Brady Bunch,"
1969-75.
b. Feb 14, 1934 in Dale, Indiana
Source: *BiE&WWA; CurBio 71; EncMT;
InWom; NotNAT; WhoAm 82; WhoHol A;
WhoThe 77*

Henderson, "Hollywood" (Thomas)
American. Football Player
b. Mar 1, 1953 in Austin, Texas
Source: *BioIn 11*

Henderson, Lawrence Joseph
American. Author, Biochemist
Wrote *Order of Nature,* 1917; *Blood,* 1928.
b. Jun 3, 1878 in Lynn, Massachusetts
d. Feb 10, 1942 in Boston, Massachusetts
Source: *CurBio 42; DcAmB S3; WebBD 80*

Henderson, Jimmy
[Black Oak Arkansas]
American. Musician
Guitarist with heavy-metal, Dixie boogie
group.
b. May 20, 1954 in Jackson, Mississippi
Source: *NF*

Henderson, Leon
American. Economist, Educator
b. Feb 22, 1906 in Baker, Florida
d. Feb 7, 1960 in Gainesville, Florida
Source: *CurBio 40; WhAm 4*

Henderson, Oran K
Army Officer
Source: *BioIn 9*

Henderson, Ray
American. Songwriter
b. Dec 1, 1896 in Buffalo, New York
d. Dec 31, 1971 in Greenwich, Connecticut
Source: *AmSCAP 66; BiE&WWA; EncMT; NewCBMT; NewYTBE 71*

Henderson, Rickey Henley
American. Baseball Player
Stole a record 130 bases, 1982.
b. Dec 25, 1958 in Chicago, Illinois
Source: *BaseEn 85*

Henderson, Robert W
American. Librarian, Historian
Sports historian; wrote *Ball, Bat, and Bishop,* 1947; disputed myth that Abner Doubleday invented baseball.
b. Dec 25, 1888 in South Shields, England
d. Aug 19, 1985 in Hartford, Connecticut
Source: *AmAu&B; WhoLibS 55*

Henderson, "Skitch" (Cedric)
[Lyle Henderson]
American. Conductor
b. Jan 27, 1918 in Halstad, Minnesota
Source: *AmSCAP 66; CelR; CurBio 66; IntMPA 75, 76, 77, 78, 79, 80, 81, 82; NewYTBE 72; WhoAm 74, 76, 78, 80, 82; WhoMus 72*

Henderson, Vivian Wilson
American. Educator, Economist
b. Feb 10, 1923 in Bristol, Tennessee
d. Jan 25, 1976 in Atlanta, Georgia
Source: *ConAu 61, 65; WhAm 6; WhoAm 74; WhoBlA 75; WhoRel 75*

Henderson, Wayne
see: Crusaders, The

Hendl, Walter
American. Conductor, Composer
b. Jan 12, 1917 in West New York, New Jersey
Source: *CurBio 55*

Hendrick, Burton Jesse
American. Biographer, Journalist
b. Dec 28, 1870 in New Haven, Connecticut
d. Mar 23, 1949 in New York, New York
Source: *AmAu&B; ChhPo S2; DcAmB S4; DcLEL; OxAmL; REnAL; TwCA, SUP; WhAm 2; WhNAA*

Hendricks, Ted (Theodore Paul)
American. Football Player
Seven-time Pro-Bowl linebacker for Oakland/ LA Raiders.
b. Nov 1, 1947 in Guatemala City, Guatemala
Source: *NewYTBS 82; WhoAm 78; WhoFtbl 74*

Hendricks, Thomas Andrews
American. Politician
VP under Grover Cleveland, 1885.
b. Sep 7, 1819 in Zanesville, Ohio
d. Nov 25, 1885 in Indianapolis, Indiana
Source: *ApCAB; BiDrAC; DcAmB; WhAmP*

Hendrix, Jimi (James Marshall)
American. Musician, Singer
Hits "Purple Haze," 1967; "Hey Joe," 1967; died of drug overdose.
b. Nov 27, 1942 in Seattle, Washington
d. Sep 18, 1970 in London, England
Source: *IlEncBM 82; NewYTBE 70; WhAm 5; WhScrn 77; WhoHol B*

Hendry, Ian
English. Actor
Best known for *Theatre of Blood,* 1973.
b. 1931 in Ipswich, England
Source: *FilmgC; IntMPA 81; WhoHol A*

Henie, Sonja
Norwegian. Figure Skater, Actress
Won Olympic gold medals, 1928, 1932, 1936; starred in *Wintertime,* 1943.
b. Apr 8, 1912 in Oslo, New York
d. Oct 12, 1969 in Los Angeles, California
Source: *CmMov; CurBio 40, 52, 70; FilmgC; InWom; MotPP; MovMk; OxFilm; ThFT; WhAm 5; WhScrn 74, 77; WhoHol B*

Henize, Karl Gordon
American. Astronomer, Astronaut
b. Sep 17, 1926 in Cincinnati, Ohio
Source: *WhoAm 80, 82*

Henkle, Henrietta
[Henrietta Buckmaster, pseud.]
American. Author, Journalist
b. 1909 in Cleveland, Ohio
Source: *AmAu&B; ConAu 69; OhA&B*

Henley, Beth
American. Dramatist
Won Pulitzer, 1981, for *Crimes of the Heart.*
b. May 8, 1952 in Jackson, Mississippi
Source: *CurBio 83; NatPD 81; NewYTBS 81*

Henley, Don
[The Eagles]
American. Singer, Musician
Released single, "Dirty Laundry," 1982.
b. Jul 22, 1947 in Gilmer, Texas
Source: *RkOn 85*

Henley, William Ernest
English. Author, Poet
b. Aug 23, 1849 in Gloucester, England
d. Jul 1, 1903 in Woking, England
Source: *Alli SUP; AtlBL; BiD&SB; BrAu 19;
CasWL; Chambr 3; ChhPo, S1, S2; CnE&AP;
DcEnA, AP; DcEuL; DcLEL; EvLB;
LongCTC; MouLC 4; NewC; OxEng; PenC
ENG; REn; WebE&AL*

Hennepin, Louis
French. Explorer
Explored Great Lakes with La Salle, 1678-79;
wrote *Description de la Louisiane,* 1682.
b. Apr 7, 1640 in Ath, Belgium
d. 1701
Source: *AmBi; ApCAB; BiDSA; DcAmB;
Drake; OxAmL; REn; REnAL; WebAB;
WhAm HS*

Henner, Jean Jacques
French. Artist
Drew historical subjects, female portraits,
sensuous nudes in Italian settings:
"Sleeping Bather," 1863.
b. 1829 in Alsace, France
d. 1905 in Paris, France
Source: *McGDA*

Henner, Marilu
American. Actress
Played Elaine on TV series "Taxi."
b. Apr 6, 1953 in Chicago, Illinois
Source: *BioIn 11; WhoTelC*

Henning, Doug(las James)
Canadian. Magician
Created, starred in musical *The Magic Show;*
host of TV specials.
b. May 3, 1947 in Fort Gary, Manitoba
Source: *NewYTBS 74; WhoAm 82*

Henning, Linda Kaye
American. Actress
Played Betty Jo Bradley on TV series
"Petticoat Junction," 1963-70.
b. Sep 16, 1944 in Toulca Lake, California
Source: *ConTFT 3; IntMPA 77; WhoHol A*

Henreid, Paul
[Paul G Julius VonHernreid]
Italian. Actor, Director
Discovered by Otto Preminger, 1933; starred
in *Casablanca,* 1943.
b. Jan 10, 1908 in Trieste, Italy
Source: *BiDFilm; CmMov; CurBio 43;
FilmgC; IntMPA 82; MotPP; WhoAm 82;
WhoHol A; WorEFlm*

Henri, Robert
American. Artist
A major influence on group of now-famous
artists known as the Ashcan School.
b. Jun 25, 1865 in Cincinnati, Ohio
d. Jul 12, 1929 in New York, New York
Source: *AmBi; AtlBL; DcAmB; DcNAA;
EncAB-H; OhA&B; OxAmL; REnAL; WebAB;
WhAm 1; WhNAA*

Henrich, Tommy (Thomas David)
"Old Reliable"
American. Baseball Player
b. Feb 20, 1913 in Massillon, Ohio
Source: *BaseEn 85; NewYTBE 71; WhoProB
73*

Henrit, Robert
[Argent]
English. Musician
Drummer with Argent, 1969-76.
b. May 2, 1946 in Boxbourne, England
Source: *NF*

Henry I
[Henry Beauclerc]
English. Ruler
King of England, 1100-35; elected while
older brother was absent at time of father,
William the Conqueror's death.
b. 1068 in Yorkshire, England
d. Dec 1, 1135 in France
Source: *LinLib S; McGEWB; NewC; WebBD
80*

Henry II
English. Ruler
First Plantagenet king of England, 1154-89;
began development of common law.
b. Mar 5, 1133
d. 1189
Source: *WebBD 80; WhDW*

Henry III
English. Ruler
Plantagenet king, 1216-72; captured during
   Baron's War, 1264; rescued by son
   Edward I, 1265, who later succeeded him.
b. 1207
d. 1272
Source: *BioIn 10; OxMus; WebBD 80*

Henry IV
[Henry Bolingbroke; Henry of Lancaster]
English. Ruler
King of England, 1399-1413.
b. 1367
d. Mar 20, 1413
Source: *BioIn 10; WebBD 80*

Henry V
English. Ruler
Lancastrian king of England, 1413-22;
   acquired Norway, France, 1417-20.
b. 1387
d. 1422
Source: *WebBD 80; WhDW*

Henry VI
English. Ruler
King of England, son of Henry V; ruled
   during War of Roses.
b. 1421
d. 1471
Source: *WebBD 80; WhDW*

Henry VII
[Henry Tudor]
English. Ruler
King of England, 1485-1509; first Tudor
   monarch; marriage of daughter to James
   IV of Scotland brought two countries
   together.
b. Jan 28, 1457
d. Apr 21, 1509 in Richmond, England
Source: *NewC; WhDW*

Henry VIII
English. Ruler
Most renowned of English kings, 1509-47;
   break with Roman church led to English
   Reformation.
b. Jun 28, 1491 in Greenwich, England
d. Jan 28, 1547
Source: *NewCol 75; WebBD 80; WhDW*

Henry of Wales
[Henry Charles Albert David]
"Harry"
English. Prince
Second son of Prince Charles,
   third in line to British throne behind
   father, brother, William of Wales.
b. Sep 15, 1984 in London, England
Source: *NF*

Henry the Navigator
Portuguese. Prince
b. Mar 4, 1394 in Porto, Portugal
d. Nov 13, 1460 in Sagres, Portugal
Source: *AsBiEn; McGEWB; REn*

Henry William Frederick Albert
[Duke of Gloucester]
English. Prince
Uncle of Queen Elizabeth II, last surviving
   son of King George V; best known as
   soldier, horseman.
b. Mar 31, 1900 in Sandringham, England
d. Jun 9, 1974 in Northamptonshire, England
Source: *IntWW 74; NewYTBS 74*

Henry, Buck
American. Actor, Author
Co-directed *Heaven Can Wait*, 1978, with
   Warren Beatty.
b. Dec 9, 1930 in New York, New York
Source: *ConAu 77; ConDr 73; FilmgC;
IntMPA 82; NewYTBE 70; WhoAm 82;
WhoHol A*

Henry, Charlotte
American. Actress
Had title role in *Alice in Wonderland,* 1933.
b. Mar 3, 1913 in Charlotte, New York
d. Apr 1980 in San Diego, California
Source: *FilmEn; FilmgC; WhoHol A*

Henry, Clarence
"Frogman"
American. Singer
Rhythm and blues singer best known for
   froglike voice, hit single "Ain't Got No
   Home," 1956.
b. Mar 19, 1937 in Algiers, Louisiana
Source: *RolSEnR 83*

Henry, Edward Lamson
American. Artist
Illustrated American history, railroad scenes
   in detailed, naturalistic manner.
b. Jan 12, 1841 in Charleston, South
   Carolina
d. May 9, 1919 in New York, New York
Source: *AmBi; ApCAB, X; BnEnAmA;
DcAmArt; DcAmB; McGDA; NatCAB 5;
NewYHSD; TwCBDA; WhAm 1*

Henry, Edward Richard, Sir
British. Public Official
London police commissioner who adopted
system of taking fingerprints to identify
criminals.
b. Jul 26, 1850
d. 1931
Source: *BioIn 2, 5, 6, 9*

Henry, Joseph
American. Inventor, Physicist
Invented electromagnetic telegraph, basis for
commercial telegraphic system.
b. Dec 17, 1797 in Albany, New York
d. May 13, 1878 in Washington, District of
Columbia
Source: *Alli, SUP; AmBi; ApCAB; BiAUS;
DcAmAu; DcAmB; DcNAA; Drake; EncAB-H;
NewCol 75; OxAmL; REnAL; WebAB; WhAm
HS*

Henry, Martha
[Martha Buhs]
American. Actress
Starred in Canadian Stratford Festival, 1962-
80.
b. Feb 17, 1938 in Detroit, Michigan
Source: *NotNAT A*

Henry, O, pseud.
[William Sydney Porter]
American. Author, Journalist
Wrote short stories *The Ransom of Red
Chief, Gift of the Magi.*
b. Sep 11, 1862 in Greensboro, North
Carolina
d. Jun 5, 1910 in New York, New York
Source: *AmAu&B; AmBi; AtlBL; BiDSA;
CasWL; Chambr 3; ChhPo; CnDAL; CyWA;
DcAmB; DcLEL; DcNAA; EncMys; EncWL;
EvLB; FilmgC; LongCTC; ModAL; OhA&B;
OxAmL; OxEng; PenC AM; RAdv 1; REn;
REnAL; TwCA, SUP; TwCWr; WebAB;
WebE&AL; WhAm 1; WhoTwCL*

Henry, Pat
[Patrick Henry Scarnato]
American. Comedian
b. Aug 28, 1923
d. Feb 18, 1982 in Las Vegas, Nevada
Source: *BioIn 12*

Henry, Patrick
American. Revolutionary, Patriot
Led radical faction in VA, 1775; famous for
saying, "Give me liberty or give me
death."
b. May 29, 1736 in Hanover County,
Virginia
d. Jun 6, 1799 in Charlotte County, Virginia
Source: *Alli; AmAu; AmAu&B; AmBi;
ApCAB; BbD; BiAUS; BiD&SB; BiDSA;
BiDrAC; DcAmAu; DcAmB; Drake; EncAB-H;
OxAmL; REn; REnAL; TwCBDA; WebAB;
WhAm HS; WhAmP*

Henry, William M
American. Journalist
b. Aug 21, 1890 in San Francisco, California
d. Apr 13, 1970 in Chatsworth, California
Source: *ConAu 89; WhAm 5*

Hensley, Pamela Gail
American. Actress
Played CJ on TV series "Matt Houston."
b. Oct 3, 1950 in Los Angeles, California
Source: *VarWW 85; WhoAm 82*

Henson, Jim (James Maury)
American. Puppeteer
Created Muppets, who first appeared on
"Sesame Street," 1969; has produced
feature films, TV show "Fraggle Rock."
b. Sep 24, 1936 in Greenville, Kansas
Source: *CurBio 77; IntMPA 82; WhoAm 82;
WhoTelC*

Henson, Josiah
American. Slave, Clergyman
Prototype of Uncle Tom in *Uncle Tom's
Cabin.*
b. Jun 15, 1789 in Charles County, Maryland
d. May 15, 1883 in Dresden, Ontario
Source: *AmAu; AmAu&B; AmBi; ApCAB;
DcAmB; DcNAA; MacDCB 78; McGEWB;
OxAmL; OxCan; REnAL; WhAm HS*

Henson, Lisa
American. Publisher
Daughter of Jim Henson; first woman pres.
of *The Harvard Lampoon.*
b. 1960
Source: *NewYTBS 82*

Henson, Matthew Alexander
American. Explorer
Accompanied Robert Peary expedition to N
Pole, 1909.
b. 1866
d. Mar 9, 1955 in New York, New York
Source: *BioIn 1, 2, 3, 4, 6, 7, 8, 9, 10, 11;
DcAmB S5*

Hentoff, Nat(han Irving)
American. Music Critic, Journalist
Writer on jazz-turned civil libertarian;
writings have focused on improving
education.
b. Jun 10, 1925 in Boston, Massachusetts
Source: *AuBYP; ChlLR 1; ConAu 1R, 5NR;
CurBio 86; REnAL; ThrBJA; WhoAm 74, 80,
82, 84; WhoE 74; WhoWor 74; WrDr 76*

Henty, George Alfred
English. Children's Author
b. Dec 8, 1832 in Trumpington, England
d. Nov 16, 1902 in Weymouth, England
Source: *Alli SUP; BbD; BiD&SB; BrAu 19;
CarSB; CasWL; Chambr 3; DcLEL; EvLB;
JBA 34; LongCTC; MnBBF; NewC; OxEng;
PenC ENG; WhoChL*

Henze, Hans Werner
German. Composer
b. Jul 1, 1926 in Gutersloh, Germany
Source: *CurBio 66; DcCM; IntWW 74;
NewYTBE 72; OxGer; Who 74; WhoAm 74;
WhoMus 72; WhoWor 78*

Hepbron, George
American. Basketball Referee
Wrote *How to Play Basketball,* 1904;
considered first handbook on game.
b. Aug 27, 1863 in Still Pond, Maryland
d. Apr 30, 1946 in Newark, New Jersey
Source: *WhoBbl 73*

Hepburn, Audrey
[Mrs. Andrea Dotti; Edda Hepburn]
American. Actress
Won Oscar for *Roman Holiday,* 1953; starred
in *My Fair Lady,* 1964.
b. May 4, 1929 in Brussels, Belgium
Source: *BiDFilm; BiE&WWA; BkPepl; CelR;
CurBio 54; FilmgC; InWom; NotNAT;
OxFilm; Who 74; WhoAm 74, 76, 78, 80, 82;
WhoHol A; WorEFlm*

Hepburn, Katharine Houghton
American. Actress
Has won four Oscars for best actress in 50-
year career.
b. Nov 8, 1907 in Hartford, Connecticut
Source: *BiDFilm; BiE&WWA; BioNews 74;
BkPepl; CelR; CmMov; CurBio 69; EncMT;
FamA&A; FilmgC; InWom; IntMPA 82;
IntWW 74; MotPP; MovMk; NewYTBE 73;
NotNAT; OxFilm; PlP&P; ThFT; WebAB;
Who 74; WhoAm 82; WhoHol A; WhoThe
77; WhoWor 74; WomWMM*

Hepplewhite, George
English. Cabinetmaker, Furniture Designer
Influenced by Chippendale; designs reflect
neoclassic style of Robert Adam.
d. 1786
Source: *AntBDN G; LinLib S; McGDA;
OxDecA; WebBD 80*

Hepworth, Barbara
English. Sculptor
b. Jan 10, 1903 in Wakefield, England
d. May 20, 1975 in Saint Ives, England
Source: *CurBio 57; InWom; IntWW 74;
WhAm 6; Who 74; WhoWor 78*

Heraclitus of Ephesus
"The Weeping Philosopher"
Greek. Philosopher
Known for idea of flux: "Nothing is;
everything is becoming."
b. 535 ?BC in Ephesus, Asia Minor
d. 475 ?BC
Source: *NewCol 75; WebBD 80*

Herbert, Alan Patrick, Sir
English. Author, Statesman
MP, 1935-50; wrote *Secret Battle,* 1919.
b. Sep 24, 1890 in London, England
d. Nov 11, 1971 in London, England
Source: *Au&Wr 71; ChhPo, S1, S2; ConAu
33R, 97; DcLEL; EvLB; LongCTC; ModBrL;
NewC; PenC ENG; REn; TwCA, SUP;
TwCWr*

Herbert, Anthony B
American. General
b. 1930
Source: *BioIn 9*

Herbert, Frank Patrick
American. Author
Author of *Dune* series; adapted to film, 1984.
b. Oct 8, 1920 in Tacoma, Washington
d. Feb 11, 1986 in Madison, Wisconsin
Source: *ConAu 5NR, 53; ConLC 12; SmATA
9; WhoAm 82; WrDr 76*

Herbert, George
English. Author
b. Apr 3, 1593 in Montgomery, England
d. Mar 9, 1633 in Bremerton, England
Source: *Alli; AtlBL; BbD; BiD&SB; BrAu;
CasWL; ChhPo, S1, S2; CnE&AP; CroE&S;
CrtT 1; CyWA; DcEnA; DcEnL; DcEuL;
DcLEL; EvLB; MouLC 1; NewC; OxEng;
PenC ENG; RAdv 1; REn; WebE&AL*

**Herbert, George Edward Stanhope
Molyneux**
[Earl of Canarvon]
English. Egyptologist, Archaeologist
Discovered tomb of Tutankhamen, 1922.
b. 1866
d. 1923
Source: *WebBD 80*

Herbert, Hugh
American. Actor
Comedian whose signature was fluttery hands
and expression "Woo-Woo!"
b. Aug 10, 1887 in Binghamton, New York
d. Mar 13, 1951 in Hollywood, California
Source: *FilmgC; MovMk; Vers A; WhScrn 74,
77; WhoHol B*

Herbert, John, pseud.
[John Herbert Brundage]
Canadian. Dramatist, Director
Known for drama of prison life: *Fortune and
Men's Eyes,* 1967.
b. Oct 13, 1926 in Toronto, Ontario
Source: *ClbCR; ConDr 73, 77; WrDr 80*

Herbert, Victor
American. Conductor, Composer
Wrote over 40 operettas including *Babes in
Toyland,* 1903.
b. Feb 1, 1859 in Dublin, Ireland
d. May 27, 1924 in New York, New York
Source: *AmBi; AmSCAP 66; DcAmB; EncMT;
McGEWD; NewCBMT; OxAmL; REn;
REnAL; TwCBDA; WebAB; WhAm 1;
WhoStg 1906, 1908*

Herblock
[Herbert Lawrence Block]
American. Cartoonist
Cartoonist, Washington *Post,* 1946--; won
Pulitzers, 1942, 1954, 1979.
b. Oct 13, 1909 in Chicago, Illinois
Source: *AmAu&B; CurBio 54; EncAB-H;
WebAB; WhoAm 82; WhoS&SW 82; WhoWor
84*

Herbst, Josephine Frey
American. Author
b. Mar 5, 1897 in Sioux City, Iowa
d. Jan 28, 1969 in New York, New York
Source: *AmAu&B; AmNov; ConAmA; ConAu
5R, 25R; InWom; OxAmL; REn; REnAL;
TwCA, SUP; WebE&AL; WhAm 5; WhNAA*

Herder, Johann G von
German. Poet, Critic
b. Aug 25, 1744 in Mohrungen, Germany
d. Dec 18, 1803 in Weimar, Germany
Source: *AtlBL; BbD; BiD&SB; CasWL;
ChhPo S1; DcEuL; EuAu; EvEuW; NewC;
OxEng; OxGer; PenC EUR; RComWL; REn*

Hereward the Wake
Anglo-Saxon. Revolutionary
d. 1070
Source: *NewCol 75; WebBD 80*

Herford, Oliver
American. Author, Illustrator
Self-illustrated books include *Little Book of
Bores,* 1906.
b. Dec 1, 1863 in Sheffield, England
d. Jul 5, 1935 in New York, New York
Source: *BiD&SB; DcAmB S1; OxAmL 83;
REnAL*

Hergesheimer, Joseph
American. Author
b. Feb 15, 1880 in Philadelphia, Pennsylvania
d. Apr 25, 1954 in Sea Isle City, New Jersey
Source: *AmAu&B; CasWL; Chambr 3;
CnDAL; ConAmA; ConAmL; CyWA; DcAmB
S5; DcBiA; DcLEL; EvLB; LongCTC;
OxAmL; OxEng; PenC AM; REn; REnAL;
TwCA, SUP; TwCWr; WhAm 3; WhNAA*

Herkimer, Nicholas
American. Military Leader
b. Nov 10, 1728 in Herkimer, New York
d. Aug 19, 1777 in Little Falls, New York
Source: *AmBi; ApCAB; DcAmB; Drake;
TwCBDA; WhAm HS*

Herlie, Eileen
Scottish. Actress
Played Queen Gertrude in *Hamlet,* opposite
Laurence Olivier, 1948, Richard Burton,
1964.
b. Mar 8, 1920 in Glasgow, Scotland
Source: *BiE&WWA; FilmgC; MovMk;
NotNAT; Who 74; WhoHol A; WhoThe 77*

Herlihy, James Leo
American. Author
b. Feb 27, 1927 in Detroit, Michigan
Source: *AmAu&B; Au&Wr 71; CelR; ConAu
1R, 2NR; ConLC 6; ConNov 72, 76; CurBio
61; DrAF 76; NotNAT; WhoAm 74; WhoE
74; WhoWor 78; WorAu; WrDr 80*

Herman, "Babe" (Floyd Caves)
American. Baseball Player
b. Jun 26, 1903 in Buffalo, New York
Source: *BaseEn 85; NewYTBS 79; WhoProB
73*

Herman, Billy (William Jennings)
American. Baseball Player
Second baseman, 1931-47; played in 10 All
   Star games; Hall of Fame, 1975.
b. Jul 7, 1909 in New Albany, Indiana
Source: *BaseEn 85; BasesB*

Herman, George
American. Broadcast Journalist
b. Jan 14, 1920 in New York, New York
Source: *WhoAm 76, 78, 80, 82*

Herman, Jerry
American. Songwriter
Won Tony, two Grammys for *Hello Dolly!*
   1964.
b. Jul 10, 1933 in New York, New York
Source: *AmSCAP 66; BiE&WWA; CelR;
ConTFT 3; CurBio 65; EncMT; NewCBMT;
NotNAT; PIP&P; WhoAm 80, 82; WhoE 85;
WhoThe 77*

Herman, Pee-Wee
[Paul Reubens]
American. Comedian
Starred in *Pee-Wee's Great Adventure*, 1985;
   frequent guest appearances on "Saturday
   Night Live."
Source: *NF*

Herman, Woody (Woodrow Charles)
American. Band Leader, Musician
b. May 16, 1913 in Milwaukee, Wisconsin
Source: *AmSCAP 66; BioNews 74; CurBio 73;
WhoAm 80, 82; WhoHol A; WhoJazz 72;
WhoMus 72; WhoWest 76*

Hermann, Bernard
American. Conductor
b. 1911
d. 1975
Source: *BioIn 10*

Hermannsson, Steingrimur
Icelandic. Political Leader
Prime minister of Iceland, 1983--.
b. Jun 22, 1928 in Iceland
Source: *IntWW 83; IntYB 82; WhoOcn 78;
WhoWor 82*

Herman's Hermits
[Karl Greene; Keith Hopwood; Derek
   Leckenby; Peter Noone; Barry Whitwam]
English. Music Group
Part of "British Invasion," 1960s; had ten
   hits, 1964-66: "Mrs. Brown You've Got a
   Lovely Daughter," 1965.
Source: *EncPR&S 74; IlEncRk; RolSEnR 83*

Hermening, Kevin Jay
[The Hostages]
American. Hostage in Iran
b. 1960 in Milwaukee, Wisconsin
Source: *BioIn 12; NewYTBS 81*

Hermes, Thierry
French. Designer
Source: *WorFshn*

Hernandez, Keith
American. Baseball Player
b. Oct 20, 1953 in San Francisco, California
Source: *BaseEn 85; WhoAm 80, 82*

Hernandez, Willie (Guillermo Villaneuva)
American. Baseball Player
Relief pitcher, Detroit Tigers; won Cy Young
   Award, MVP Award in AL, 1984.
b. Nov 14, 1955 in Aguada, Puerto Rico
Source: *BaseEn 85; BaseReg 86; ConNews 85-
1*

Hernandez-Colon, Rafael
Puerto Rican. Politician
Governor of Puerto Rico, 1973--.
b. Oct 24, 1936 in Ponce, Puerto Rico
Source: *CurBio 73; EncLatA; IntWW 83;
WhoAm 78*

Herne, Chrystal Katharine
American. Actress
Starred in Pulitzer-winning play *Craig's Wife*,
   1925-27.
b. Jun 17, 1882 in Dorchester, Massachusetts
d. Sep 19, 1950 in Boston, Massachusetts
Source: *NotAW*

Herod Antipas
Palestinian. Ruler
Son of Herod the Great who executed John
   the Baptist, sent Jesus to Pontius Pilate.
b. 4 BC
d. 39 AD
Source: *REn*

Herod the Great
Ruler, Biblical Character
King of Judea who ordered the killing of all
   males under age two for fear of losing
   throne to Jesus.
b. 73 BC
d. 4 BC
Source: *NewC; REn; WhDW*

Herodotus
"Father of History"
Greek. Historian
Wrote *History*, which tells of rise of Persia,
  development of Greek city-states, Greco-
  Asian world in mid-15th c.
b. 485 ?BC in Halicarnassus, Asia
d. 425 ?BC in Thurii, Italy
Source: *AtlBL; BbD; BiD&SB; CasWL;
  CyWA; DcEnL; DcEuL; NewC; OxEng; PenC
  CL; RComWL; REn; WhDW*

Herold, Louis Joseph Ferdinand
French. Composer
b. Jan 28, 1791 in Paris, France
d. Jan 19, 1833 in Les Ternes, France
Source: *NewEOp 71*

Heron, Mike
British. Musician
Source: *IlEncRk*

Herrera Campins, Luis
Venezuelan. President
b. May 4, 1925 in Acarigua, Venezuela
Source: *CurBio 80; NewYTBS 78*

Herrick, Elinore M
American. Business Executive
b. Jun 15, 1895 in New York, New York
d. Oct 11, 1964
Source: *CurBio 47, 65; InWom; WhAm 4*

Herrick, Robert
English. Author, Poet
b. Aug 24, 1591 in London, England
d. Oct 1674 in Dean Prior, England
Source: *Alli; AnCL; AtlBL; BbD; BiD&SB;
  BrAu; CasWL; Chambr 1; ChhPo, S1, S2;
  CnE&AP; CroE&S; CrtT 1; CyWA; DcEnA;
  DcEnL; DcEuL; DcLEL; EvLB; LongCTC;
  MouLC 1; NewC; OxEng; PenC ENG; RAdv
  1; REn; WebE&AL*

Herridge, Robert T
American. Author, Producer
Created CBS program "Camera Three."
b. 1918 in West Orange, New Jersey
d. Aug 14, 1981 in Woodstock, New York
Source: *AnObit 1981; BioIn 5, 12; NewYTBS
  81*

Herriman, George
American. Cartoonist
b. Aug 22, 1880 in New Orleans, Louisiana
d. Apr 25, 1944 in Hollywood, California
Source: *ChhPo; DcAmB S3; REnAL; WebAB*

Herriot, Edouard
French. Statesman
b. Jul 5, 1872 in Troyes, France
d. Mar 26, 1957 in Lyons, France
Source: *CurBio 46, 57; REn; WhAm 3*

Herriot, James, pseud.
[James Wight]
Scottish. Veterinarian, Author
Wrote *All Creatures Great and Small*, 1972;
  All Things Bright and Beautiful, 1974.
b. Oct 3, 1916 in Glasgow, Scotland
Source: *BioIn 10, 11; ConAu 77; St&PR 75;
  WrDr 80*

Herrmann, Bernard
American. Composer
Wrote over 60 radio, movie scores; known
  for themes of Hitchcock films: *Psycho*,
  1960.
b. Jun 29, 1911 in New York, New York
d. Dec 24, 1975 in Los Angeles, California
Source: *Baker 78; BiDAmM; BioIn 1, 2, 3,
  10, 11; CmMov; CmpEPM; DcFM; FanAl;
  IntMPA 76; NewYTBS 75; OxFilm; OxMus;
  WhAm 6*

Herrmann, Edward
American. Actor
Won Tony, 1976, for *Mrs. Warren's
  Profession;* played FDR on TV's "Eleanor
  and Franklin."
b. Jul 21, 1943 in Washington, District of
  Columbia
Source: *NewYTBS 83; WhoAm 78*

Herschel, John Frederick William, Sir
English. Astronomer
b. Mar 7, 1792 in Slough, England
d. May 11, 1871 in Collingwood, England
Source: *Alli, SUP; BiD&SB; BrAu 19;
  Chambr 3; DcEnL; EvLB; NewC*

Herschel, William
German. Astronomer
b. Nov 15, 1738 in Hannover, Germany
d. Aug 25, 1822 in Slough, England
Source: *Alli; NewC; REn*

Hersey, John Richard
American. Author, Journalist
Wrote *A Bell for Adano*, 1944; *Hiroshima*,
  1946.
b. Jun 17, 1914 in Tientsin, China
Source: *AmAu&B; AmNov; CasWL; CelR;
  CnDAL; ConAu 17R; ConLC 1, 2; ConNov
  72, 76; CurBio 44; CyWA; DrAF 76; DrAS
  74E; IntWW 74; LongCTC; ModAL; OxAmL;
  PenC AM; RAdv 1; REn; REnAL; TwCA
  SUP; WebAB; Who 74; WhoAm 74, 76, 78,
  80, 82; WhoE 74; WhoWor 78; WrDr 80*

Hersh, Seymour
American. Journalist
Won 1970 Pulitzer, int'l. reporting, for
articles on My Lai massacre.
b. Apr 8, 1937 in Chicago, Illinois
Source: *AmAu&B; AuNews 1; ConAu 73;
CurBio 84; WhoAm 82*

Hershey, Barbara
[Barbara Herzstein; Barbara Seagull]
American. Actress
In TV series "The Monroes," 1966-67; films
The Right Stuff; The Natural.
b. Feb 5, 1948 in Hollywood, California
Source: *FilmgC; IntMPA 84; WhoAm 84;
WhoHol A*

Hershey, Lenore
American. Editor
b. Mar 20, 1920 in New York, New York
Source: *WhoAm 74, 76, 78, 80, 82*

Hershey, Lewis Blaine
American. Army Officer
b. Sep 12, 1893 in Steuben City, Indiana
d. 1977 in Angola, Indiana
Source: *CurBio 41, 51; IntWW 74; WhoAm
74; WhoAmP 73; WhoGov 75; WhoS&SW 82*

Hershey, Milton Snavely
American. Candy Manufacturer
Founded Hershey Chocolate Co., 1903.
b. Sep 13, 1857 in Dauphin City,
Pennsylvania
d. Oct 13, 1945 in Hershey, Pennsylvania
Source: *CurBio 45; DcAmB S3; WebAB;
WhAm 2*

Hershfield, Harry
American. Cartoonist, Humorist
b. Oct 13, 1885 in Cedar Rapids, Iowa
d. Dec 15, 1974 in New York, New York
Source: *ConAu 53; NewYTBS 74; WhScrn 77*

Hersholt, Jean
Danish. Actor
Special Oscar, Jean Hersholt Humanitarian
Award, given in his honor since 1956.
b. Jul 12, 1886 in Copenhagen, Delaware
d. Jun 2, 1956 in Beverly Hills, California
Source: *ChhPo; CurBio 56; Film 1; FilmgC;
MotPP; MovMk; TwYS; WhAm 3; WhScrn
74, 77; WhoHol B; WorEFlm*

Herter, Christian Archibald
American. Diplomat, Editor
b. Mar 28, 1895 in Paris, France
d. Dec 30, 1966 in Washington, District of
Columbia
Source: *BiDrAC; BiDrUSE; CurBio 67;
DcAmB; DcNAA; WhAm 1, 4, HS; WhAmP*

Hertz, Alfred
German. Conductor
b. Jul 15, 1872 in Frankfurt, Germany
d. Apr 17, 1942 in San Francisco, California
Source: *CurBio 42; DcAmB S3; WhAm 2*

Hertz, Heinrich Rudolph
German. Physicist
In confirming Maxwell's electromagnetic
theory, produced, studied electromagnetic
waves, also called radio waves, 1886-89.
b. Feb 22, 1857 in Hamburg, Germany
d. Jan 1, 1894
Source: *AsBiEn; DcScB; LinLib S; McGEWB;
NewCol 75; REn; WhDW*

Hertz, John Daniel
American. Business Executive
Founded Yellow Cab Co., 1915; Hertz Drive-
Ur-Self Corp., 1924.
b. Apr 10, 1879 in Ruttka, Austria
d. Oct 8, 1961 in Los Angeles, California
Source: *BioIn 4, 6; ObitOF 79; WhAm 4*

Hertzberg, Arthur
American. Author, Rabbi
b. Jun 9, 1921 in Lubaczow, Poland
Source: *ConAu 17R; NewYTBE 72; WhoAm
80, 82*

Herzen, Aleksandr
Russian. Author
b. 1812
d. 1870
Source: *NewCol 75*

Herzl, Theodor
"Father of Modern Zionism"
Hungarian. Journalist
Founder of Zionism, 1897, who supported
creation of Jewish settlement in Palestine.
b. May 2, 1860 in Budapest, Hungary
d. Jul 3, 1904 in Vienna, Austria
Source: *EuAu; McGEWB; NewCol 75; OxGer;
WhDW*

Herzog, Arthur, Jr.
American. Songwriter
Wrote blues song "God Bless the Child,"
made famous by Billie Holliday.
b. 1901 in New York, New York
d. Sep 1, 1983 in Detroit, Michigan
Source: *NF*

Herzog, Chaim
Israeli. Political Leader
Pres., 1983--; ambassador to UN, 1975-78.
b. Sep 17, 1918 in Belfast, Northern Ireland
Source: *ConAu 103; IntWW 82; IntYB 82;
MidE 82; WhoWorJ 72*

Herzog, Emile Salomon, pseud.
see: Maurois, Andre

Herzog, Werner
[Werner H Stipetic]
German. Director
Films include *Aguirre, the Wrath of God*,
1973, *Fitzcarraldo*, 1982.
b. 1942 in Munich, Germany
Source: *CurBio 78; FilmEn*

Herzog, "Whitey" (Dorrel Norman Elvert)
American. Baseball Manager
Manager, St. Louis Cardinals, 1980--; won
World Series 1982; NL manager of year,
1985.
b. Nov 9, 1931 in New Athens, Illinois
Source: *WhoAm 84; WhoMW 82; WhoProB
73*

Hesburgh, Theodore Martin
American. Author, Educator
Pres. of Notre Dame, 1952-86.
b. May 25, 1917 in Syracuse, New York
Source: *CelR; ConAu 13R; CurBio 82; DrAS
82P; IndAu 1917; IntWW 85N; LEduc 74;
NewYTBE 71; WhoAm 80, 82; WhoGov 72;
WhoMW 86; WhoWor 84*

Heschel, Abraham Joshua
Polish. Rabbi
First Jewish scholar on staff of Union
Theological Seminary.
b. 1907 in Warsaw, Poland
d. Dec 23, 1972 in New York, New York
Source: *ConAu 5R, 37R, 81; CurBio 73;
NewYTBE 73; WhAm 5; WhoE 85A*

Heseltine, Michael Ray Dibdin
British. Government Official
Defense minister in Margaret Thatcher's
Conservative gov't., 1983-86.
b. Mar 21, 1933 in Swansea, South Wales
Source: *BlueB 76; CurBio 85; IntWW 84;
Who 84*

Heseltine, Phillip Arnold
[Peter Warlock, pseud.]
English. Composer, Author
b. Oct 30, 1894 in London, England
d. Dec 17, 1930 in London, England
Source: *Baker 78; BioIn 4, 11; OxMus*

Hesiod
Greek. Poet
Wrote *Works and Days, Theogony, The
Shield of Heracles.*
d. in Orchomenus, Greece
Source: *AtlBL; BbD; BiD&SB; CasWL;
CyWA; NewC; OxEng; PenC CL; RComWL;
REn*

Hess, Leon
American. Oilman, Football Executive
Chief exec., Amerada Hess Corp., 1971--;
owner NY Jets, 1963--.
b. 1914
Source: *WhoAm 84; WhoE 83; WhoF&I 83;
WhoWor 82*

Hess, Myra
English. Musician
b. Feb 25, 1890 in London, England
d. Dec 26, 1965
Source: *CurBio 43, 66; InWom; WhAm 4*

Hess, Rudolf (Walter Richard Rudolf)
German. Nazi Leader
Sentenced at Nuremberg trials to life
imprisonment; only prisoner in Spandau
Prison.
b. Apr 26, 1894 in Alexandria, Egypt
Source: *CurBio 41; NewYTBS 74; OxGer;
REn*

Hess, Sol
American. Cartoonist
b. Oct 14, 1872 in Northville, Illinois
d. Dec 31, 1941 in Chicago, Illinois
Source: *WorECom*

Hess, Victor Francis
American. Scientist, Physician, Engineer
b. Jun 24, 1883 in Waldstein, Austria
d. Dec 17, 1964 in Mount Vernon, New
York
Source: *CurBio 63, 65; WhAm 4*

Hesse, Don
American. Editor, Cartoonist
b. Feb 20, 1918 in Belleville, Illinois
Source: *WhoAm 74; WhoAmA 73*

Hesse, Eva
German. Artist, Sculptor
Major conceptualist sculptor; created
disquieting hanging modular forms.
b. Jan 11, 1936 in Hamburg, Germany
d. May 29, 1970 in New York, New York
Source: *ConArt 77; DcAmArt; DcCAA 77;
NewYTBE 70; NotAW MOD*

Hesse, Hermann
Swiss. Author
Known for imagination, accuracy of
psychological, cultural observations; won
Nobel Prize, 1946.
b. Jul 2, 1877 in Calw, Germany
d. Aug 9, 1962 in Montagnola, Switzerland
Source: *AtlBL; CasWL; ConAu 17R, P-2;
ConLC 1, 2, 3, 6, 11, 17; CurBio 62; CyWA;
EncWL; EvEuW; ModGL; OxGer; PenC
EUR; RComWL; REn; TwCA, SUP; TwCWr;
WhAm 4; WhoTwCL*

Hesselius, John
American. Artist
Portraitist influenced by Feke and Wollaston:
"Charles Calvert and His Slave," 1761.
b. 1728 in Philadelphia, Pennsylvania
d. Apr 9, 1778 in Bellefield, Maryland
Source: *BnEnAmA; DcAmArt; DcAmB;
McGDA; NatCAB 23; NewYHSD; WhAm HS*

Hesseman, Howard
American. Actor
Played Dr. Johnny Fever on TV series
"WKRP in Cincinnati," 1978-82.
b. Feb 27, 1940 in Lebanon, Ohio
Source: *ConTFT 3; WhoAm 80, 82*

Heston, Charlton
American. Actor
Won Oscar for *Ben Hur,* 1959; pres., Screen
Actors Guild, 1966-71.
b. Oct 4, 1922 in Evanston, Illinois
Source: *BiDFilm; BiE&WWA; BkPepl; CelR;
CmMov; ConAu 108; CurBio 57; FilmgC;
IntMPA 81, 82; IntWW 74; MotPP; MovMk;
OxFilm; Who 74; WhoAm 80, 82; WhoGov
72; WhoHol A; WhoThe 77; WhoWest 74;
WhoWor 74; WorEFlm*

Hevesy, George de
Hungarian. Chemist
Won Nobel Prize, 1943.
b. Aug 1, 1885 in Budapest, Hungary
d. Jul 5, 1966
Source: *BioIn 7, 8; CurBio 59, 66*

Hewes, Henry
American. Drama Critic
b. Apr 9, 1917 in Boston, Massachusetts
Source: *AmAu&B; BiE&WWA; ConAu 13R;
NotNAT; OxThe; WhoAm 80, 82; WhoThe
77; WhoWor 84*

Hewes, Joseph
American. Merchant
Exec. head of Continental Navy who signed
Declaration of Independence, 1776.
b. Jan 23, 1730 in Kingston, New Jersey
d. Nov 10, 1779 in Philadelphia,
Pennsylvania
Source: *AmBi; ApCAB; BiAUS; BiDrAC;
DcAmB; Drake; TwCBDA; WhAm HS;
WhAmP*

Hewish, Antony
English. Scientist
Discovered pulsars; won Nobel Prize, 1974.
b. May 11, 1924 in Fowey, England
Source: *IntWW 74; Who 74*

Hewitt, Abram Stevens
American. Politician
b. Jul 31, 1822 in Haverstraw, New York
d. 1903
Source: *AmBi; ApCAB; BiAUS; BiDrAC;
DcAmB; EncAB-H; McGEWB; NatCAB 3;
WebAB; WhAm 1, 4*

Hewitt, Foster (William Foster)
Canadian. Author, Broadcaster
Canadian hockey announcer for 50 yrs.
b. Nov 21, 1903 in Toronto, Ontario
d. Apr 21, 1985 in Toronto, Ontario
Source: *ConAu 115*

Hewitt, Henry Kent
American. Naval Officer
b. Feb 11, 1887 in Hackensack, New Jersey
d. Sep 15, 1972 in Middlebury, Vermont
Source: *BioIn 1, 9, 11; CurBio 43, 72*

Hewitt, Martin
American. Actor
Had screen debut in *Endless Love,* with
Brooke Shields, 1981.
b. Feb 19, 1958 in San Jose, California
Source: *BioIn 12*

Hewlett, William
American. Businessman, Engineer
With David Packard, launched Hewlett-
Packard, high-tech electronic, information
systems, 1939.
b. May 20, 1913 in Ann Arbor, Michigan
Source: *Entr; WhoAm 84; WhoF&I 83*

Hexum, Jon-Erik
American. Actor
In TV series "Cover-Up," 1984; accidentally
shot himself in head playing Russian
Roulette.
b. Nov 5, 1958 in Englewood, New Jersey
d. Oct 18, 1984 in Los Angeles, California
Source: *NF*

Heydrich, Reinhard
"The Hangman of Europe"
German. Nazi Leader
Aide to Himmler in Gestapo; early director
  of death camps.
b. Mar 9, 1904 in Halle, Germany
d. Jun 4, 1942 in Lidice, Czechoslovakia
Source: *CurBio 42; NewCol 75; SpyCS;*
  WebBD 80

Heyer, Georgette
English. Author
b. Dec 16, 1902 in London, England
d. Jul 4, 1974 in London, England
Source: *ConAu 49, 93; DcLEL; EncMys;*
  LongCTC; NewC; NewYTBS 74; REn; TwCA,
  SUP; TwCWr; WhAm 6; Who 74; WhoAm
  74; WhoWor 78

Heyerdahl, Thor
Norwegian. Anthropologist, Explorer
Wrote *Kon Tiki*, 1950; *Aku-Aku: The Secret*
  of Easter Island, 1958.
b. Oct 6, 1914 in Larvik, Norway
Source: *CelR; ConAu 5R, 5NR; CurBio 47,*
  72; IntWW 74; LongCTC; SmATA 2; TwCA
  SUP; TwCWr; Who 74; WhoAm 82; WhoWor
  78; WrDr 80

Heym, Stefan
German. Author
b. Apr 10, 1913 in Chemnitz, Germany
Source: *AmAu&B; AmNov; ConAu 9R, 4NR;*
  CurBio 43; ModGL; OxGer; PenC EUR;
  REnAL; TwCA SUP

Heyse, Paul Johann
German. Author
Master of novella; won Nobel Prize for
  literature, 1910.
b. Mar 15, 1830 in Berlin, Germany
d. 1914 in Munich, Germany
Source: *CasWL; ClDMEL; EuAu; EvEuW;*
  NotNAT B; OxGer; PenC EUR; REn

Heyward, (Edwin) DuBose
American. Author
Major writer of Harlem Renaissance; wrote
  Porgy, 1925; adapted as opera *Porgy and*
  Bess, 1935.
b. Aug 31, 1885 in Charleston, South
  Carolina
d. Jun 16, 1940 in Tryon, North Carolina
Source: *AmAu&B; AmSCAP 66; ChhPo;*
  CnDAL; CnMD; ConAmA; ConAmL; ConAu
  108; CurBio 40; CyWA; DcAmB S2; DcLEL;
  DcNAA; EvLB; LongCTC; McGEWD;
  ModAL; ModWD; OxAmL; PenC AM;
  PIP&P; REn; REnAL; TwCA, SUP; TwCWr;
  WebAB; WhAm 1

Heyward, Thomas, Jr.
American. Lawyer
Soldier, planter, jurist who signed Declaration
  of Independence from SC, 1776.
b. Jul 28, 1746 in Saint Helena's, South
  Carolina
d. Mar 6, 1809 in Saint Luke's, South
  Carolina
Source: *AmBi; ApCAB; BiAUS; BiDrAC;*
  DcAmB; TwCBDA; WhAm HS; WhAmP

Heywood, Eddie
American. Musician, Composer
b. Dec 4, 1915 in Atlanta, Georgia
Source: *BioIn 10; CmpEPM; WhoJazz 72*

Heywood, Thomas
English. Dramatist
b. 1574 in Lincoln, England
d. Aug 1641 in London, England
Source: *Alli; AtlBL; BbD; BiD&SB; BrAu;*
  CasWL; Chambr 1; ChhPo; CnThe; CroE&S;
  CrtT 1; CyWA; DcEnA; DcEnL; DcEuL;
  DcLEL; EvLB; McGEWD; MouLC 1; NewC;
  OxEng; OxThe; PenC ENG; REn; REnWD;
  WebE&AL

Heyworth, James
American. TV Executive
Pres., HBO, 1980; chief exec., 1981.
b. 1942
Source: *WhoAm 84; WhoF&I 83; WhoTelC*

Hiawatha
American Indian. Legendary Figure
Subject of Henry Wadsworth Longfellow's
  Song of Hiawatha, 1855.
b. 1530
Source: *NewCol 75; OxAmL; WebAB*

Hibberd, Andrew Stuart
English. Broadcaster
BBC announcer, 1924-51.
b. Oct 5, 1893 in Canford Magna, England
d. Nov 1983
Source: *ConAu 111*

Hibbert, Eleanor Alice Burford
[Philippa Carr; Elbur Ford; Victoria Holt;
  Kathleen Kellow; Jean Paidy; Ellalice
  Tate, pseuds.]
English. Author
b. 1906 in London, England
Source: *AmAu&B; ConAu 17R; ConLC 7;*
  EncMys; SmATA 2; TwCWr; Who 74;
  WhoAm 74, 76, 78, 80, 82; WhoAmW 77;
  WorAu; WrDr 76

Hibbler, Al
American. Singer
b. Aug 16, 1915 in Little Rock, Arkansas
Source: *BioIn 4, 10; CmpEPM*

Hibbs, Ben
American. Journalist
b. Jul 23, 1901 in Fintana, Kansas
d. Mar 29, 1975 in Penn Valley,
Pennsylvania
Source: *AmAu&B; CurBio 46; IntWW 74;
WhAm 6; WhoAm 74*

Hickel, Walter Joseph
American. Government Official
Secretary of interior, 1969-70.
b. Aug 18, 1919 in Claflin, Kansas
Source: *BiDrUSE; ConAu 41R; CurBio 69;
IntWW 74; WhoAm 74, 76, 78, 80, 82;
WhoAmP 73; WhoWor 78*

Hickenlooper, Bourke B
American. Statesman
b. Jul 21, 1896 in Blockton, Iowa
d. Sep 4, 1971 in Shelter Island, New York
Source: *BiDrAC; CurBio 47, 71; NewYTBE
71; WhAm 5; WhAmP*

Hickey, Margaret A
American. Editor
b. Mar 14, 1902 in Kansas City, Missouri
Source: *BioIn 7; WhoAm 74, 76, 78, 80, 82;
WhoWor 78*

Hickey, William
English. Lawyer, Traveler
b. 1749 in Westminster, England
d. 1830
Source: *BioIn 6, 8, 10; DcLEL; OxEng; PenC
ENG*

Hickman, Darryl
American. Actor
Juvenile actor in 1940s films; became
producer, 1960s; executive producer, TV
soap "Love of Life."
b. Jul 28, 1931 in Los Angeles, California
Source: *BiE&WWA; FilmgC; IntMPA 82;
MovMk; WhoHol A*

Hickman, Dwayne
American. Actor
Starred in "The Many Loves of Dobie
Gillis," 1959-63.
b. May 18, 1934 in Los Angeles, California
Source: *FilmgC; MotPP; MovMk; WhoHol A*

Hickman, Herman Michael, Jr.
American. Football Player
b. Oct 1, 1911 in Johnson City, Tennessee
d. Apr 25, 1958 in Washington, District of
Columbia
Source: *BioIn 2, 3, 4, 5, 6; WhoFtbl 74*

Hickock, Richard Eugene
American. Murderer
Subject of Truman Capote's *In Cold Blood*,
who murdered family with partner Perry
Smith, 1959.
b. 1931
d. Apr 14, 1965
Source: *BioIn 7; Blood&B*

Hickok, Lorena A
American. Author, Journalist
b. 1892 in East Troy, Wisconsin
d. May 3, 1968 in Rhinebeck, New York
Source: *BioIn 7, 8, 10; SmATA 20*

Hickok, "Wild Bill" (James Butler)
American. Frontiersman, Entertainer
Toured with Buffalo Bill as legendary
gunfighter, 1872-73; killed while playing
poker.
b. May 27, 1837 in Troy Grove, Illinois
d. Aug 2, 1876 in Deadwood, South Dakota
Source: *DcAmB; FilmgC; OxAmL; REn;
REnAL; WebAB*

Hicks, Beatrice Alice
American. Business Executive
b. Jan 2, 1919 in Orange, New Jersey
d. Oct 21, 1979
Source: *AmM&WS 79P; BioIn 3, 4; CurBio
57; InWom; WhAm 7; WhoAm 76, 78;
WhoAmW 58, 61, 64, 66, 68, 70, 72;
WhoF&I 74; WhoWor 78*

Hicks, David Nightingale
English. Designer, Interior Decorator
Designer of fabric, sheets, furniture, carpet,
etc; author, *David Hicks on Decoration*,
1966.
b. Mar 25, 1929 in Essex, England
Source: *IntAu&W 77; Who 82; WhoWor 78*

Hicks, Edward
American. Artist
b. Apr 4, 1780 in Attleboro, Pennsylvania
d. Aug 23, 1849 in Newtown, Pennsylvania
Source: *REn; WebAB; WhAm HS*

Hicks, Elias
American. Religious Leader
b. Mar 19, 1748 in Hempstead Township,
New York
d. Feb 27, 1830 in Jericho, New York
Source: *Alli; AmAu&B; AmBi; ApCAB; BbD;
BiD&SB; DcAmAu; DcAmB; DcNAA; Drake;
OxAmL; REnAL; TwCBDA; WebAB; WhAm
HS*

Hicks, Granville
American. Author
Spokesman for American proletarian literary
movement; wrote *John Reed: The Making
of a Revolutionary,* 1936.
b. Sep 9, 1901 in Exeter, New Hampshire
d. Jun 18, 1982 in Franklin Park, New
Jersey
Source: *AmAu&B; AmNov; AnObit 1982;
CnDAL; ConAmA; ConAu 107; ConLCrt;
ConNov 76; CurBio 82; DcLEL; IntAu&W
77; IntWW 78; NewYTBS 82; OxAmL; PenC
AM; RAdv 1; REn; REnAL; ScF&FL 1;
TwCA, SUP; WhLit; WhoAm 78; WhoWor
78; WrDr 80*

Hicks, Louise Day
American. Politician
b. Oct 16, 1923 in Boston, Massachusetts
Source: *CurBio 74; WhoAm 74; WhoAmP 73;
WhoE 74; WhoGov 75*

Hicks, Peggy Glanville-
Australian. Opera Singer
b. Dec 29, 1912 in Melbourne, Australia
Source: *DcCM; WhoAm 74, 76, 78, 80, 82*

Hicks, Tony (Anthony)
[The Hollies]
English. Musician
Guitarist with Hollies since 1962.
b. Dec 16, 1943 in Nelson, England
Source: *NF*

Hicks, Ursula Kathleen Webb
English. Economist, Editor
Co-founder, editor for 27 yrs. *Review of
Economics.*
b. Feb 17, 1896 in Dublin, Ireland
d. Jul 16, 1985 in Blockley, England
Source: *ConAu 117; Who 85*

Hidalgo, Elvira de
Spanish. Opera Singer, Teacher
b. 1882 in Barcelona, Spain
Source: *InWom*

Hidalgo y Costilla, Miguel
Mexican. Priest, Revolutionary
Led lower classes in fight for independence
from Spain, 1810.
b. May 8, 1753 in Guanajuato, Mexico
d. Jul 30, 1811 in Chihuahua, Mexico
Source: *ApCAB; Drake; McGEWB; NewCol
75; REn*

Higbe, Kirby (Walter Kirby)
American. Baseball Player
Pitcher, 1937-49; refused to be on same team
as Jackie Robinson.
b. Apr 8, 1915 in Columbia, South Carolina
d. May 6, 1985
Source: *BaseEn 85; ConAu 116; WhoProB 73*

Higginbotham, "Jack" (Jay C)
American. Musician
b. May 11, 1906 in Atlanta, Georgia
d. May 26, 1973 in New York, New York
Source: *WhAm 6*

Higgins, Andrew J
American. Shipping Executive
Higgins Industries built landing craft during
WW II, ships during Korean War.
b. Aug 28, 1886 in Columbus, Nebraska
d. Aug 1, 1952 in New Orleans, Louisiana
Source: *CurBio 52; DcAmB S5; WhAm 3*

Higgins, Bertie (Elbert)
American. Singer, Songwriter
Recorded hit single, "Key Largo," 1982.
b. 1946 in Tarpon Springs, Florida
Source: *RkOn 85*

Higgins, George V
American. Author
b. Nov 13, 1939 in Brockton, Massachusetts
Source: *ConAu 77; ConLC 4, 7, 10, 18;
ConNov 76; DrAF 76; WhoAm 82; WrDr 76*

Higgins, Marguerite
American. Journalist
Korean, Vietnam War correspondent who
won 1951 Pulitzer for int'l. reporting.
b. Sep 3, 1920 in Hong Kong, China
d. Jan 3, 1966 in Washington, District of
Columbia
Source: *AmAu&B; ConAu 5R, 25R; CurBio
51, 66; InWom; WhAm 4*

Higginson, Thomas Wentworth
American. Clergyman, Author
b. Dec 22, 1823 in Cambridge, Massachusetts
d. May 9, 1911
Source: *AmAu; AmAu&B; BbD; BiD&SB;
CasWL; Chambr 3; CnDAL; CyAL 2;
DcLEL; DcNAA; REn*

Highet, Gilbert Arthur
American. Author, Educator, Critic
b. Jun 22, 1906 in Glasgow, Scotland
d. Jan 20, 1978 in New York, New York
Source: *AmAu&B; Au&Wr 71; CelR; ChhPo
S2; ConAu 1R; CurBio 64; DrAS 74F;
IntWW 74; LongCTC; NewC; NewYTBE 72;
RAdv 1; REnAL; TwCA SUP; Who 74;
WhoAm 74; WhoWor 78; WrDr 80*

Highsmith, Patricia
American. Author
b. Jan 12, 1921 in Fort Worth, Texas
Source: *ConAu 1R, 1NR; ConLC 2, 4, 14;
ConNov 72, 76; EncMys; Who 74; WhoTwCL;
WorAu; WrDr 80*

Hightower, Florence Josephine Cole
American. Children's Author
Wrote adventure mysteries for children:
  Secret of the Crazy Quilt, 1972.
b. Jun 9, 1916 in Boston, Massachusetts
d. Mar 6, 1981 in Boston, Massachusetts
Source: *AuBYP; ConAu 1R, 103; SmATA 4;
WhoAmW 72, 74, 75*

Hightower, Rosella
American. Dancer
b. 1920
Source: *BioIn 1, 3, 4, 9, 11*

Hightower, Stephanie
American. Track Athlete
b. Jul 19, 1958
Source: *BioIn 12*

Higuera, Teddy (Teodoro Valenzuela)
Mexican. Baseball Player
Pitcher, Milwaukee, 1985--.
b. Nov 9, 1958 in Las Mochis, Mexico
Source: *BaseReg 86*

Hilbert, Egon
Austrian. Director, Manager
b. 1899 in Austria
d. Jan 18, 1968 in Vienna, Austria
Source: *NewEOp 71*

Hildebrand, Adolf von
German. Artist
b. 1847
d. 1921
Source: *BioIn 9; NewCol 75*

Hildegarde, Loretta Sell
American. Singer
b. Feb 1, 1906 in Adell, Wisconsin
Source: *CurBio 44; InWom*

Hildegard of Bingen, Saint
"Sybil of the Rhine"
German. Religious Figure
b. 1098
d. Sep 17, 1179
Source: *BioIn 4, 5, 11; CasWL*

Hill, Ambrose Powell
American. Military Leader
b. Nov 9, 1825 in Culpeper, Virginia
d. Apr 2, 1865 in Petersburg, Virginia
Source: *AmBi; ApCAB; BiDConf; DcAmB;
Drake; TwCBDA; WebAB; WhAm HS*

Hill, Archibald Vivian
English. Physiologist
b. Sep 26, 1886 in Bristol, England
d. 1977
Source: *BioIn 1, 2, 3, 6, 11; DcLEL; IntWW
74; Who 74; WhoLA*

Hill, Arthur
Canadian. Actor
Won 1962 Tony for *Who's Afraid of Virginia
  Woolf?*, starred in TV show *Owen
  Marshall, Counselor at Law*, 1971-74.
b. Aug 1, 1922 in Melfort, Saskatchewan
Source: *BiE&WWA; FilmgC; IntMPA 82;
MotPP; NewYTBE 71; NotNAT; WhoAm 82;
WhoHol A; WhoThe 77*

Hill, Benny (Benjamin)
English. Comedian
Star of internationally syndicated TV series,
  "The Benny Hill Show."
b. Jan 21, 1925 in Southampton, England
Source: *CurBio 83; IntMPA 82; WhoHol A;
WhoTelC*

Hill, Calvin
American. Football Player
b. Jan 2, 1947 in Baltimore, Maryland
Source: *WhoAm 74; WhoBlA 75; WhoFtbl 74*

Hill, "Chippie" (Bertha)
American. Jazz Musician
b. 1905 in Charleston, South Carolina
d. May 7, 1950 in New York, New York
Source: *CmpEPM; WhoJazz 72*

Hill, Dan
Canadian.
b. Jun 3, 1954 in Toronto, Ontario
Source: *BioIn 11; RkOn 74*

Hill, Dave
American. Golfer
Has had 13 tour victories.
b. May 20, 1937 in Jackson, Michigan
Source: *BioIn 10; WhoGolf; WhoIntG*

Hill, Geoffrey
English. Poet
b. Jun 18, 1932 in Bromsgrove, England
Source: *BioIn 7; ConAu 81; ConLC 5, 8, 18*

Hill, George Roy
American. Director
Directed *Butch Cassidy and the Sundance Kid,* 1969; *The Sting,* 1973; won Oscar for *The Sting.*
b. Dec 20, 1922 in Minneapolis, Minnesota
Source: *BiDFilm; BiE&WWA; FilmgC; IntMPA 82; MovMk; NotNAT; OxFilm; WhoAm 82; WhoThe 77; WorEFlm*

Hill, George Washington
American. Tobacco Executive
b. Oct 22, 1884 in Philadelphia, Pennsylvania
d. Sep 13, 1946 in Matapedia, Quebec
Source: *CurBio 46; DcAmB S4; WebAB; WhAm 2*

Hill, Grace Livingstone
American. Author
Popular novels sold over three million copies: *April Gold,* 1936.
b. Apr 16, 1865 in Wellsville, New York
d. Feb 23, 1947 in Swarthmore, Pennsylvania
Source: *NotAW; REnAL*

Hill, Graham (Norman Graham)
English. Auto Racer
Won world Grand Prix championship, 1962, 1968; author, *Life at the Limit,* 1969.
b. Feb 15, 1929 in London, England
d. Nov 30, 1975 in London, England
Source: *BioNews 74; ConAu 108; CurBio 73; WhAm 7; Who 74*

Hill, Herbert
American. Public Official
Labor director, NAACP, 1948--; wrote *Anger and Beyond,* 1966.
b. Jan 24, 1924 in New York, New York
Source: *BioIn 9, 11; ConAu 65; CurBio 70*

Hill, Howard
American. Archer, Actor
First white man to kill elephant with bow and arrow; stand-in archer in several Errol Flynn movies.
b. 1899
d. Feb 4, 1975 in Birmingham, Alabama
Source: *BioIn 10; NewYTBS 75; WhScrn 77; WhoHol C*

Hill, Ian
see: Judas Priest

Hill, James Jerome
Canadian. Railroad Executive
b. Sep 16, 1838 in Guelph, Ontario
d. May 29, 1916 in Saint Paul, Minnesota
Source: *BioIn 1, 2, 3, 4, 5, 8, 9, 10, 11; WebAB; WhAm 1*

Hill, Jimmy (James William Thomas)
English. Sportscaster
b. 1928
Source: *BioIn 11; Who 74*

Hill, Joe, pseud.
[Joel Emmanuel Haaglund; Joseph Hillstrom]
American. Labor Union Official, Songwriter
Member, IWW; best known for song "The Preacher and the Slave," which contained phrase "pie in the sky."
b. Oct 7, 1879 in Sweden
d. Nov 19, 1915 in Salt Lake City, Utah
Source: *WebAB; WhAm 4, HSA*

Hill, Lester
American. Politician
Dem. senator from AL, 1938-68.
b. Dec 29, 1894 in Montgomery, Alabama
d. Dec 20, 1984 in Montgomery, Alabama
Source: *CurBio 85*

Hill, Morton A(nthony)
American. Social Reformer, Priest
Founder, pres., Morality in Media, Inc., 1962-85; co-authored Hill-Link Report on obscenity, 1970.
b. Jul 13, 1917 in Brooklyn, New York
d. Nov 4, 1985 in New York, New York
Source: *NewYTBS 85; WhoRel 77*

Hill, Rowland, Sir
English. Educator, Government Official
Postal reformist; originated penny postage, 1839.
b. Dec 3, 1795 in Kidderminster, England
d. Aug 27, 1879 in Hampstead, England
Source: *Alli; NewC; OxEng*

Hill, Thomas
English. Artist
Noted for western, Yosemite Valley scenes: "Muir Glacier."
b. Sep 11, 1829 in Birmingham, England
d. 1908 in Raymond, California
Source: *ApCAB; ArtsAmW 1; DcAmArt; DcAmB; Drake; EarABI; IlBEAAW; NatCAB 3; NewYHSD; REnAW; WhAm 1*

Hill, Virginia
"The Flamingo"
American. Actress, Criminal
Appeared in 1930s musicals; more famous for
associations with gangsters; mistress of Joe
Adonis, Ben Siegel.
b. Aug 26, 1916 in Lipscomb, Alabama
d. Mar 25, 1966 in Salzburg, Austria
Source: *BioIn 7; LookW; WhScrn 77;
WhoHol B*

Hillary, Edmund Percival, Sir
New Zealander. Explorer, Mountaineer
With Tenzing Norkay was first to reach
summit of Mt. Everest, 1953.
b. Jul 20, 1919 in Auckland, New Zealand
Source: *Au&Wr 71; CurBio 54; IntWW 74;
LongCTC; Who 74; WhoWor 78; WrDr 80*

Hillegass, C K
"Cliff"
American. Publisher
Publishes *Cliff Notes* study guides.
b. 1918 in Rising City, Nebraska
Source: *BioNews 74*

Hillel
Scholar
Jewish scholar whose sayings resemble Jesus
Christ's: "Do not unto others that which
is hateful unto thee."
b. in Babylon
d. 9
Source: *NewCol 75; WebBD 80*

Hillenkoetter, Roscoe H(enry)
American. Business Executive
First director of CIA, 1947-50.
b. May 8, 1897 in Saint Louis, Missouri
d. Jun 18, 1982 in New York, New York
Source: *AnObit 1982; CurBio 82; NewYTBS
82; PolProf T; WebAMB; WhoAm 82*

Hiller, Arthur
American. Director
Best known for *Love Story,* 1970.
b. Nov 22, 1923 in Edmonton, Alberta
Source: *BiDFilm; CanWW 70; FilmgC;
IntMPA 82; MovMk; WhoAm 82*

Hiller, Johann Adam
Prussian. Composer
b. Dec 25, 1728 in Wendisch-Ossig, Prussia
d. Jun 16, 1804 in Leipzig, Germany
Source: *OxGer*

Hiller, John Frederick
American. Baseball Player
Pitcher, Detroit, 1967-80; suffered heart
attack, Jan 1971; returned to game, Jul
1972.
b. Apr 8, 1943 in Scarborough, Ontario
Source: *BaseEn 85; BioIn 9, 10, 11;
WhoProB 73*

Hiller, Wendy
English. Actress
Won 1958 Oscar for *Separate Tables.*
b. Aug 15, 1912 in Bramhall, England
Source: *BiE&WWA; CurBio 41; FilmEn;
FilmgC; InWom; IntMPA 82; MotPP;
MovMk; NotNAT; OxFilm; ThFT; Who 74;
WhoAm 82; WhoAmW 77; WhoHol A;
WhoThe 77*

Hillerman, John Benedict
American. Actor
Plays Jonathan Higgins on "Magnum, P.I.,"
1980--.
b. Dec 20, 1932 in Denison, Texas
Source: *ConTFT 3; WhoAm 84; WhoHol A*

Hillerman, Tony
American. Author
Detective novelist concerned with American
Indian culture: *Dance Hall of the Dead,*
1974.
b. May 27, 1925 in Sacred Heart, Oklahoma
Source: *BioIn 8; ConAu 29R; SmATA 6;
TwCCr&M 80*

Hillery, Patrick John
Irish. Political Leader
Pres. of the Republic of Ireland, 1976--.
b. May 2, 1923 in Miltown-Malbay, Ireland
Source: *IntWW 74; NewYTBE 70; WhoWor
78*

Hilliard, Nicholas
English. Artist
Best known for miniature portraits of Queen
Elizabeth I set in jeweled lockets.
b. 1537 in Exeter, England
d. 1619
Source: *AntBDN J; DcBiPP; NewCol 75;
OxArt*

Hilliard, Robert Cochran
American. Actor
Best known for play *Girl of the Golden
West,* 1905.
b. May 28, 1857 in New York, New York
d. Jun 6, 1927 in New York, New York
Source: *NotNAT A, B; WhoStg 1906, 1908*

Hillier, James
Canadian. Physicist
b. Aug 22, 1915 in Brantford, Ontario
Source: *AmM&WS 73P; BioIn 3, 5, 10;*
CanWW 70, 82; St&PR 75; WhoAm 74;
WhoF&I 74

Hillis, Margaret
American. Conductor, Musician
Choral director; founded Choral Foundation,
1954--.
b. Oct 1, 1921 in Kokomo, Indiana
Source: *Baker 78; WhoAm 84; WhoAmW 79;*
WhoWor 78

Hillman, Chris
[The Byrds; The Flying Burrito Brothers;
The Souther-Hillman-Furay Band]
American. Musician
Blue-grass mandolinist; solo works include
"Slippin' Away."
b. Dec 4, 1942 in Los Angeles, California
Source: *ConMuA 80A; WhoRock 81*

Hillman, Sidney
American. Labor Union Official
Pres., Amalgamated Clothing Workers of
America, 1914-46; vp, CIO, 1935-40.
b. Mar 23, 1887 in Zagare, Lithuania
d. Jul 10, 1946 in Long Island, New York
Source: *CurBio 40, 46; DcAmB S4; EncAB-H;*
WebAB; WhAm 2

Hillquit, Morris
American. Socialist Leader
b. Aug 1, 1869 in Riga, Russia
d. Oct 7, 1933
Source: *AmLY; BioIn 1, 2, 6, 7, 11; DcNAA;*
REnAL; WhAm 1

Hills, Argentina
American. Publisher
b. 1922 in Pola, Italy
Source: *WhoAmW 77; WhoS&SW 82*

Hills, Austin H
American. Merchant
With brother, Reuben, first to introduce
vacuum-packed coffee in cans, 1900.
b. 1851
d. 1933
Source: *Entr*

Hills, Carla Anderson
American. Government Official
Secretary of HUD, 1975-77.
b. Jan 3, 1934 in Los Angeles, California
Source: *WhoAmW 77*

Hills, Lee
American. Newspaper Publisher
b. May 28, 1906 in Granville, North Dakota
Source: *ConAu 101; St&PR 75; WhoAm 74,*
76, 78, 80, 82; WhoMW 74; WhoS&SW 82;
WhoWor 78

Hills, Reuben W
American. Merchant
With brother, Austin, first to introduce
vacuum-packed coffee in cans, 1900.
b. 1856
d. 1934
Source: *Entr*

Hills, Roderick M
American. Lawyer, Government Official
Counsel to Gerald Ford, 1975; husband of
Carla Hills.
b. Mar 9, 1931 in Seattle, Washington
Source: *WhoAm 82*

Hillyer, Robert
American. Poet, Author, Educator
b. Jun 3, 1895 in East Orange, New Jersey
d. Dec 24, 1961 in Wilmington, Delaware
Source: *AmAu&B; ChhPo, S1, S2; CnDAL;*
CnE&AP; ConAmA; ConAu 89; CurBio 40,
62; DcLEL; OxAmL; PenC AM; REn;
REnAL; TwCA, SUP; WhAm 4; WhNAA

Hilsberg, Alexander
Polish. Conductor, Musician
b. Apr 24, 1900 in Warsaw, Poland
d. Aug 10, 1961 in Camden, Maine
Source: *CurBio 53, 61; WhAm 4*

Hilton, Conrad Nicholson
American. Hotel Executive
Formed Hilton Hotel Corp., 1946; wrote
autobiography, *Be My Guest,* 1957.
b. Dec 25, 1887 in San Antonio, New
Mexico
d. Jan 3, 1979 in Santa Monica, California
Source: *CelR; IntWW 74; St&PR 75; WebAB;*
Who 74; WhoAm 74; WhoF&I 74; WhoWor
78

Hilton, Daisy
[The Hilton Sisters]
English. Entertainer
b. Feb 5, 1908 in Brighton, England
d. Jan 4, 1969 in Charlotte, North Carolina
Source: *WhScrn 77*

Hilton, James
English. Author
Best known novels are *Lost Horizon*, 1933;
  Goodbye, Mr. Chips, 1934.
b. Sep 9, 1900 in Lancashire, England
d. Dec 20, 1954 in Long Beach, California
Source: *ChhPo SI; CurBio 42, 55; CyWA;
  DcLEL; EncMys; EvLB; FilmgC; LongCTC;
  MnBBF; ModBrL; NewC; PenC ENG; REn;
  REnAL; TwCA, SUP; TwCWr; WhAm 3*

Hilton, Violet
[The Hilton Sisters]
English. Entertainer
b. Feb 5, 1908 in Brighton, England
d. Jan 4, 1969 in Charlotte, North Carolina
Source: *WhScrn 77*

Hilton, William Barron
American. Hotel Executive
b. 1927
Source: *BioIn 8, 10, 11; BusPN*

Himes, Chester Bomar
American. Author
Wrote detective novel *Cotton Comes to
  Harlem*, which became 1970 film.
b. Jul 29, 1909 in Jefferson City, Missouri
d. Nov 12, 1984 in Moraira, Spain
Source: *AmAu&B; AmNov; BlkAWP; ConAu
  25R; ConLC 18; ConNov 76; DrAF 76;
  EncWL; LivgBAA; ModAL, SI; OhA&B;
  PenC AM; RAdv 1; WebE&AL; WhoAm 82;
  WhoBlA 75; WorAu; WrDr 76*

Himmler, Heinrich
German. Nazi Leader
Head of SS, 1929, which merged with
  Gestapo, 1934; minister of interior, 1943-
  45.
b. Nov 7, 1900 in Munich, Germany
d. May 23, 1945 in Luneburg, Germany
Source: *CurBio 45; NewCol 75; OxGer; REn;
  SpyCS; WebBD 80*

Hinckley, John Warnock, Jr.
American. Attempted Assassin
Acquitted, 1982, by reason of insanity for
  shooting Ronald Reagan, Mar 30, 1981.
b. May 29, 1955 in Ardmore, Oklahoma
Source: *BioIn 12; NewYTBS 81*

Hinde, Thomas
English. Author
b. Mar 26, 1926 in Felixstowe, England
Source: *ConAu 5R, 4NR; ConLC 6; ConNov
  72, 76; ModBrL SI; NewC; TwCWr; Who 74;
  WorAu; WrDr 80*

Hindemith, Paul
German. Musician, Composer
Music banned by Nazis; best known for
  opera *Mathis the Painter*, 1938.
b. Nov 16, 1895 in Hanau, Germany
d. Dec 28, 1963 in Frankfurt, Germany
  (West)
Source: *AtlBL; CurBio 64; DcCM; OxGer;
  REn; WhAm 4*

Hindenburg, Paul von
German. General, President
Pres., 1925-34, who appointed Adolph Hitler
  chancellor, 1933.
b. Oct 2, 1847 in Posen, Germany
d. Aug 2, 1934 in Neudeck, Germany
Source: *BioIn 10; McGEWB; NewCol 75;
  WebBD 80*

Hines, Duncan
American. Author, Publisher
His books, *Adventures in Good Eating*, 1936-
  59, influenced the culinary and sanitary
  practices of American restaurants.
b. Mar 26, 1880 in Bowling Green,
  Kentucky
d. Mar 15, 1959 in Bowling Green,
  Kentucky
Source: *CurBio 59; WebAB; WhAm 3*

Hines, "Fatha" (Earl Kenneth)
American. Jazz Musician
Member, Down Beat Magazine Hall of
  Fame; leading influence in swing, jazz
  piano styles.
b. Dec 28, 1905 in Duquesne, Pennsylvania
d. Jul 22, 1983 in Oakland, California
Source: *AmSCAP 66; CurBio 83N; EncAB-H;
  NewYTBS 83; WhoAm 82; WhoJazz 72*

Hines, Gregory Oliver
American. Dancer, Actor
Tap dancer, known for jazz numbers in
  musical *Eubie*, 1978; film *The Cotton
  Club*, 1984.
b. Feb 14, 1946 in New York, New York
Source: *CurBio 85; NewYTBS 78; WhoAm 84*

Hines, Jerome
American. Opera Singer
b. Nov 9, 1921 in Hollywood, California
Source: *BioNews 75; CurBio 63; WhoAm 74,
  76, 78, 80, 82; WhoMus 72*

Hines, John Elbridge
American. Religious Leader
Presiding bishop, Protestant Episcopal Church
  of US, 1964-74.
b. Oct 3, 1910 in Seneca, South Carolina
Source: *CurBio 68; IntWW 78; WhoAm 76;
  WhoE 75; WhoRel 75; WhoWor 74*

Hine, Lewis Wickes
American. Photographer
Noted for photographs of Ellis Island
   immigrants, 1905.
b. Sep 26, 1874 in Oshkosh, Wisconsin
d. Nov 3, 1940 in Hastings-on-Hudson, New
   York
Source: *DcAmB S2; NewCol 75; WebBD 80*

Hines, Mimi
[Ford and Hines]
Canadian. Comedienne
b. Jul 17, 1933 in Vancouver, British
   Columbia
Source: *BioNews 74*

Hingle, Pat (Martin Patterson)
American. Actor
Films include *Splendor in the Grass,* 1961;
   Norma Rae, 1979.
b. Jul 19, 1924 in Denver, Colorado
Source: *BiE&WWA; CurBio 65; FilmgC;
IntMPA 82; MotPP; MovMk; NotNAT;
WhoAm 82; WhoE 74; WhoHol A; WhoThe
77*

Hinkle, Paul
"Tony"
American. Basketball Coach
Coach, Butler U, 1927-42; 1946-70.
b. Dec 19, 1899 in Logansport, Indiana
Source: *WhoBbl 73*

Hinrichs, Gustav
German. Conductor
b. Dec 10, 1850 in Mecklenburg, Germany
d. Mar 26, 1942 in Mountain Lakes, New
   Jersey
Source: *CurBio 42*

Hinshelwood, Cyril, Sir
English. Scientist, Engineer, Physician
b. Jun 19, 1897 in London, England
d. Oct 9, 1967 in London, England
Source: *CurBio 57, 67; WhAm 4, 5*

Hinton, Christopher, Sir
[Lord Hinton of Bankside]
English. Engineer
Leading figure in development of Britain's
   atomic energy industry.
b. May 12, 1901 in Tisbury, England
d. Jun 22, 1983
Source: *CurBio 57; WhoWor 74*

Hinton, S(usan) E(loise)
American. Author
Writes books for teenagers: *The Outsiders;
   That Was Then, This is Now.*
b. 1948 in Tulsa, Oklahoma
Source: *BioIn 12; ChlLR 3; ConAu 81;
SmATA 19; TwCCW 78; WhoAm 82; WrDr
80*

Hinton, William Arthur
American. Engineer
b. Aug 31, 1908 in Dacula, Georgia
Source: *AmM&WS 73P*

Hinton, William Augustus
American. Physician
First black Harvard professor, 1949; wrote
   Syphillis and Its Treatment, 1936.
b. Dec 15, 1883 in Chicago, Illinois
d. Aug 8, 1959 in Canton, Massachusetts
Source: *BioIn 1, 2, 5, 11; ObitOF 79;
SelBAAu*

Hipparchus
Greek. Astronomer
Catalogued over 1,000 stars; originated
   method of using latitude, longitude to
   indicate geographical position.
b. 160 ?BC in Asia Minor
d. 125 ?BC
Source: *CasWL; PenC CL*

Hipple, Eric Ellsworth
American. Football Player
b. Sep 16, 1957 in Lubbock, Texas
Source: *FootReg 81*

Hippocrates
"The Father of Medicine"
Greek. Physician
Credited with having devised physicians' code
   of ethics known as "Hippocratic oath";
   still administered to new doctors.
b. 460 BC in Island of Cos
d. 377 BC
Source: *CasWL; NewC; OxEng; PenC CL;
REn*

Hiraoka, Kimitake
see: Mishima, Yukio, pseud.

Hires, Charles E
American. Manufacturer
Invented, manufactured root beer, 1876.
b. Aug 19, 1851 in Roadstown, New Jersey
d. Jul 31, 1937 in Haverford, Pennsylvania
Source: *DcAmB S2; WebAB; WhAm HSA, 4*

Hirohito
Japanese. Emperor
Emperor of Japan since 1926; surrendered to
US to end WW II, 1945.
b. Apr 29, 1901 in Tokyo, Japan
Source: *LinLib S; McGEWB; REn; WhDW*

Hiroshige, Ando
Japanese. Artist
b. 1797
d. 1858
Source: *BioIn 10; NewCol 75; WebBD 80*

Hirsch, "Crazylegs" (Elroy)
American. Football Player
Played for LA Rams, 1949-57; athletic
director, U of Wisconsin, 1969--.
b. Jun 17, 1923 in Wausau, Wisconsin
Source: *BioIn 3, 7, 8, 9; WhoAm 82;
WhoFtbl 74; WhoHol A*

Hirsch, Joseph
American. Artist
Drew caricatures, scenes of social injustice.
b. Apr 25, 1910 in Philadelphia,
Pennsylvania
d. Sep 21, 1981 in New York, New York
Source: *BioIn 1, 4, 6, 9; ChhPo S1;
DcAmArt; DcCAA 71; McGDA; WhoAm 74,
76, 78, 80; WhoAmA 73, 76, 78*

Hirsch, Judd
American. Actor
Played Alex on TV series "Taxi," 1978-85;
won 1986 Tony for *I'm Not Rappaport.*
b. Mar 15, 1935 in New York, New York
Source: *CurBio 84; IntMPA 82; WhoAm 82;
WhoTelC*

Hirsch, Samson Raphael
German. Theologian
b. 1808
d. 1888
Source: *BioIn 3, 5, 10*

Hirschfeld, Al(bert)
American. Cartoonist, Artist
b. Jun 21, 1903 in Saint Louis, Missouri
Source: *AmAu&B; BiE&WWA; CelR; ConAu
1R, 2NR; CurBio 71; NotNAT; WhoAm 74,
76, 78, 80, 82; WhoAmA 73; WhoWorJ 72*

Hirschorn, Joel
"Diamond Joel"
American. Lawyer
Defense attorney who specializes in defending
major drug smugglers.
b. Mar 13, 1943 in Brooklyn, New York
Source: *ConNews 86-1*

Hirschmann, Ira Arthur
American. Business Executive
b. Jul 7, 1906 in Baltimore, Maryland
Source: *WhoAm 74; WhoWorJ 72*

Hirshfield, Morris
American. Artist
b. Apr 10, 1872 in Russia-Poland
d. 1946
Source: *CurBio 43*

Hirshhorn, Joseph
American. Art Collector, Financier
Uranium tycoon; has $50 million art
collection in Washington's Hirshhorn
Museum.
b. Aug 11, 1899 in Russia
d. Aug 31, 1981 in Washington, District of
Columbia
Source: *BioIn 3, 4, 5, 6, 7, 8, 9, 10;
CanWW 70; WhoAmA 73, 76, 78; WhoE 74*

Hirt, Al
American. Jazz Musician
Plays trumpet; hits include "Bourbon Street,"
1961; "Cotton Candy," 1964.
b. Nov 7, 1922 in New Orleans, Louisiana
Source: *CurBio 67; IntMPA 75, 76, 77, 78,
79, 80, 81, 82; WhoAm 74; WhoS&SW 82*

Hiss, Alger
American. Public Official, Lawyer
Alleged Soviet spy convicted of perjury,
1950; after three years in prison, has
sought to have verdict, allegations re-
examined.
b. Nov 11, 1904 in Baltimore, Maryland
Source: *Au&Wr 71; ConAu 33R; CurBio 47;
EncAB-H; SpyCS; WebAB; Who 74*

Hitch, Charles Johnston
American. University Administrator
b. Jan 9, 1910 in Boonville, Missouri
Source: *AmEA 74; BioIn 5, 7, 8, 9, 11;
CurBio 70; WhoAm 82*

Hitchcock, Alfred Joseph, Sir
English. Director
Directed suspense thrillers *North by
Northwest,* 1959; *Psycho,* 1960; won Oscar,
1940, for *Rebecca.*
b. Aug 13, 1899 in London, England
d. Apr 29, 1980 in Beverly Hills, California
Source: *Au&Wr 71; BiDFilm; BioNews 74;
CelR; CmMov; ConAu 97; ConLC 16; CurBio
41, 60; DcFM; EncMys; FilmgC; IntMPA 75,
76, 77; IntWW 74; MovMk; NewC;
NewYTBE 72; NewYTBS 74; OxFilm;
REnAL; WebAB; Who 74; WhoAm 74;
WhoWest 84; WhoWor 78; WorEFlm*

Hitchcock, Henry Russell
American. Educator, Historian
Writings in architecture considered foremost
in field: *Frank Lloyd Wright*, 1928;
Modern Architecture, 1929.
b. Jun 3, 1903 in Boston, Massachusetts
Source: *IntAu&W 77; IntWW 78; Who 74;
WhoAm 84; WhoAmA 78; WhoWor 74*

Hitchcock, Lambert
American. Cabinetmaker, Furniture Designer
Hitchcock chair, 1826, an early example of
mass production, is collector's item today.
b. Jun 28, 1795 in Cheshire, Connecticut
d. 1852
Source: *AntBDN G; LinLib S; NewCol 75*

Hitchcock, Raymond
American. Actor
Vaudeville, film comedian who did three
films for Mack Sennett, 1915.
b. 1865 in Auburn, New York
d. Dec 24, 1929 in Beverly Hills, California
Source: *DcAmB; EncMT; Film 1; MotPP;
TwYS; WhScrn 74, 77; WhoHol B; WhoStg
1906*

Hitchcock, Tommy (Thomas, Jr.)
American. Sportsman
Dominated the game of polo for nearly 20
yrs., 1922-39; considered greatest American
player of all time.
b. Feb 11, 1900 in Aiken, South Carolina
d. Apr 19, 1944 in Salisbury, England
Source: *CurBio 44; DcAmB S3; WebAB*

Hite, Robert Ernest, Jr.
[Canned Heat]
"The Bear"
American. Singer
Blue-grass vocalist; hit song "On the Road
Again."
b. Jan 26, 1943 in Torrance, California
d. Apr 1981 in Los Angeles, California
Source: *WhoAm 74; WhoWor 74*

Hite, Shere
American. Author
Wrote *The Hite Report: A Nationwide Study
of Female Sexuality*, 1976; *The Hite Report
on Male Sexuality*, 1981.
b. Nov 2, 1942 in Saint Joseph, Missouri
Source: *BioIn 11; ConAu 81; WhoAm 78, 80,
82*

Hitler, Adolf
[Adolf Schickelgruber]
German. Nazi Leader
Founded National Socialism; invasion of
Poland, 1939, started WW II; engineered
Holocaust, in which over six million Jews
and their supporters were murdered.
b. Apr 20, 1889 in Branau, Austria
d. Apr 30, 1945 in Berlin, Germany
Source: *CurBio 57; EncTR; FilmgC; LinLib
L, S; McGEWB; NewYTBE 72, 73; OxEng;
OxGer; REn; WhWW-II; WhoMilH 76*

Hitotsubashi
[Yoshinobu]
Japanese. Ruler
b. 1837
d. 1902
Source: *WebBD 80*

Ho, Don
American. Singer
b. Aug 13, 1930 in Kakaako, Hawaii
Source: *WhoAm 74; WhoWor 78*

Ho Chi Minh
[Nguyen That Thank]
"Uncle Ho"
Vietnamese. Communist Leader,
Revolutionary
Founder, first pres., N Vietnam, 1954-69;
legendary figure instrumental in spread of
Communism throughout Southeast Asia.
b. May 19, 1890 in Kim Lien, Vietnam
d. Sep 3, 1969 in Hanoi, Vietnam (North)
Source: *ConAu 112; CurBio 49, 66, 69;
DcOrL 2*

Hoare, Samuel John Gurney, Sir
English. Diplomat
b. Feb 24, 1880
d. May 7, 1959 in London, England
Source: *CurBio 40, 59*

Hoban, James
American. Architect
Designed White House, 1792, rebuilt
following British destruction, 1814.
b. 1762 in Callan, Ireland
d. Dec 8, 1831 in Washington, District of
Columbia
Source: *AmBi; BiAUS; DcAmB; OxAmL;
WebAB; WhAm HS*

Hoban, Russell
American. Artist, Author
b. Feb 4, 1925 in Lansdale, Pennsylvania
Source: *AuBYP; ChhPo S1, S2; ConAu 5R;
SmATA 1; ThrBJA; WhoAm 82; WrDr 76*

Hobart, Alice Tisdale Nourse
American. Author
b. Jan 28, 1882 in Lockport, New York
d. Mar 14, 1967 in Oakland, California
Source: *AmAu&B; AmNov; ConAu 5R, 25R;*
InWom; REnAL; TwCA, SUP; WhAm 4;
WhNAA

Hobart, Garret Augustus
American. Vice-President
Served as vp under William McKinley, 1897-
99.
b. Jun 3, 1844 in Long Branch, New Jersey
d. Nov 21, 1899 in Paterson, New Jersey
Source: *BioIn 1, 4, 7, 8, 9, 10; WebAB;*
WhAm 1

Hobart, Rose
American. Actress
Featured in "other woman" roles; best
known for *Farmer's Daughter,* 1940.
b. May 1, 1906 in New York, New York
Source: *BiE&WWA; FilmgC; ForWC 70;*
MovMk; NotNAT; ThFT; WhoHol A; WhoThe
77A

Hobbema, Meindert
Dutch. Artist
b. Oct 31, 1638 in Netherlands
d. Dec 7, 1709 in Netherlands
Source: *AtlBL; REn*

Hobbes, Thomas
English. Author, Philosopher
Father of modern analytical philosophy; best-
known work *Leviathan,* 1651.
b. Apr 5, 1588 in Malmesbury, England
d. Dec 4, 1679 in Hardwick, England
Source: *Alli; AtlBL; BiD&SB; BrAu; CasWL;*
Chambr 1; CroE&S; CrtT 2; CyWA; DcEnA;
DcEnL; DcEuL; DcLEL; EvLB; MouLC 1;
NewC; OxEng; PenC ENG; RComWL; REn;
WebE&AL

Hobbs, Leland Stanford
American. Military Leader
b. Feb 24, 1892 in Gloucester, Massachusetts
d. Mar 1966
Source: *BioIn 3, 7; WhAm 4*

Hobbs, Leonard Sinclair
"Luke"
American. Aircraft Designer
Developed J-57, gas turbine engine which
powered first American jets, 1952.
b. Dec 20, 1896 in Carbon, Wyoming
d. Nov 1, 1977 in Hartford, Connecticut
Source: *CurBio 78; NewYTBS 77; ObitOF 79*

Hobby, Oveta Culp
American. Government Official
b. Jan 19, 1905 in Killeen, Texas
Source: *BiDrUSE; ConAu 81; CurBio 42, 53;*
ForWC 70; IntWW 74; St&PR 75; TexWr;
WhoAm 74; WhoAmP 73; WhoAmW 77;
WhoS&SW 82; WhoWor 78

Hobson, Harold
English. Drama Critic
b. Aug 4, 1904 in Rotherham, England
Source: *BiE&WWA; ConAu 81; CroCD;*
LongCTC; NotNAT; Who 74; WhoThe 77

Hobson, John Atkinson
English. Economist
b. Jul 6, 1858 in Derby, England
d. Apr 1, 1940 in London, England
Source: *CurBio 40; NewC*

Hobson, Laura Zametkin
American. Author
Wrote *Gentlemen's Agreement,* 1947, which
explored anti-Semitism in US.
b. Jun 19, 1900 in New York, New York
d. Feb 28, 1986 in New York, New York
Source: *AmAu&B; AmNov; ConAu 17R;*
ConLC 7; ConNov 72, 76; CurBio 86;
InWom; REn; REnAL; TwCA SUP; WhoAm
82; WhoAmW 77; WrDr 76

Hobson, Richmond Pearson
American. Military Leader
b. Aug 17, 1870 in Greensboro, Alabama
d. Mar 16, 1937
Source: *AmAu&B; AmBi; ApCAB SUP;*
BiDSA; BiDrAC; DcAmAu; DcAmB S2;
DcNAA; TwCBDA; WhAm 1

Hobson, Valerie Babette
British. Actress
Leading lady in British films, 1936-54;
retired, married to John Profumo since
1954.
b. Apr 14, 1917 in Larne, Northern Ireland
Source: *FilmEn; FilmgC; MovMk; OxFilm;*
ThFT; Who 74; WhoHol A

Hochhuth, Rolf
German. Author, Dramatist
b. Apr 1, 1931 in Germany
Source: *CasWL; CnMD; CnThe; ConAu 5R;*
ConLC 4, 11, 18; EncWL; IntWW 74;
ModGL; ModWD; NotNAT; OxGer; PenC
EUR; REnWD; TwCWr; WhoThe 77;
WhoWor 78; WorAu

Hochoy, Solomon, Sir
West Indian. Governor
b. Apr 20, 1905 in Jamaica
Source: *IntWW 74; Who 74; WhoGov 75;*
WhoWor 78

Hocking, William Ernest
American. Educator
b. Aug 1, 1873 in Cleveland, Ohio
d. Jun 12, 1966 in Madison, New Hampshire
Source: *AmAu&B; ConAu P-1; CurBio 62, 66;*
OhA&B; OxAmL; REnAL; TwCA SUP;
WebAB; WhAm 4; WhNAA

Hockney, David
English. Artist
b. Jul 9, 1937 in Bradford, England
Source: *BioIn 7, 9, 10, 11, 12; IntWW 79;*
WhoAm 74

Hodge, Frederick Webb
English. Anthropologist
Indian authority who led expeditions to
   Southwest, 1884-86; co-founded American
   Anthropological Assn.
b. Jan 5, 1864 in Plymouth, England
d. Sep 28, 1956 in Santa Fe, New Mexico
Source: *AmAu&B; AmLY; ApCAB SUP;*
DcAmAu; NatCAB 43; OxAmL; OxCan;
REnAL; REnAW; TwCBDA; WhAm 3

Hodge, John Reed
"The Patton of the Pacific"
American. General
Led American Division in Pacific during
   WW II.
b. Jun 12, 1893 in Golconda, Illinois
d. Nov 12, 1963 in Washington, District of
   Columbia
Source: *CurBio 45, 64; DcAmB S7*

Hodges, Courtney
American. Military Leader
b. Jan 5, 1887 in Perry, Georgia
d. Jan 16, 1966 in San Antonio, Texas
Source: *CurBio 41, 66; WhAm 4*

Hodges, Eddie (Samuel Edward)
American. Actor
Films include *Adventures of Huckleberry*
   Finn, 1960; *Advise and Consent,* 1961.
b. Mar 5, 1947 in Hattiesburg, Mississippi
Source: *MotPP; WhoHol A*

Hodges, Gil(bert Raymond)
American. Baseball Player
First baseman, 1943-63; manager NY Mets,
   1968-71.
b. Apr 4, 1924 in Princeton, Indiana
d. Apr 2, 1972 in West Palm Beach, Florida
Source: *BaseEn 85; CurBio 62, 72; NewYTBE*
72; WhAm 5; WhoProB 73

Hodges, Johnny
American. Jazz Musician
b. Jul 25, 1906 in Cambridge, Massachusetts
d. May 11, 1970 in New York, New York
Source: *AmSCAP 66; NewYTBE 70; WhAm*
5; WhoJazz 72

Hodges, Luther Hartwell
American. Government Official
b. Mar 9, 1898 in Pittsylvania, Virginia
d. Oct 6, 1974 in Chapel Hill, North
   Carolina
Source: *BiDrUSE; ConAu 53; CurBio 56, 74;*
IntWW 74; WhAm 6; WhoAm 74; WhoAmP
73; WhoF&I 74

Hodges, Russ
American. Sportscaster
b. 1909 in Dayton, Tennessee
d. Apr 20, 1971 in Mill Valley, California
Source: *NewYTBE 71; WhoHol B*

Hodgkin, Alan Lloyd
English. Physiologist
Shared 1963 Nobel Prize for research in
   electrical, chemical events in nerve cell
   damage.
b. Feb 5, 1914 in Banbury, England
Source: *AsBiEn; IntWW 82; McGEWB; Who*
82; WhoWor 74

Hodgson, James Day
American. Government Official
Secretary of labor, 1970-73; ambassador to
   Japan, 1974-77.
b. Dec 3, 1915 in Dawson, Minnesota
Source: *BioIn 9, 10; USBiR 74; WhoAm 74,*
76, 78, 80, 82; WhoAmP 73; WhoF&I 74;
WhoGov 75; WhoS&SW 82

Hodgson, Richard Sargeant
American. Author
b. Oct 18, 1924 in Breckenridge, Minnesota
Source: *ConAu 13R*

Hodiak, John
American. Actor
Best known for film *Lifeboat,* 1944.
b. Apr 16, 1914 in Pittsburgh, Pennsylvania
d. Oct 19, 1955 in Tarzana, California
Source: *CmMov; FilmgC; HolP 40; MotPP;*
MovMk; WhScrn 74, 77; WhoHol B

Hodler, Ferdinand
Swiss. Artist
Post-Impressionist; utilized parallelism
  compositions.
b. 1853
d. 1918
Source: *McGDA; McGEWB*

Hoe, Richard March
American. Inventor
Developed Hoe rotary press, which improved
  speed of printing, 1846-47.
b. Sep 12, 1812 in New York, New York
d. Jun 7, 1886 in Florence, Italy
Source: *AmBi; ApCAB; DcAmB; OxAmL;
TwCBDA; WebAB; WhAm HS*

Hoesslin, Franz von
German. Conductor
b. Dec 31, 1885 in Munich, Germany
d. Sep 28, 1946 in Site, Germany
Source: *NewEOp 71*

Hofer, Andreas
Austrian. Patriot
b. Nov 22, 1767 in Saint Leonhard, Austria
d. Feb 20, 1810 in Mantua, Italy
Source: *NewC; OxGer*

Hofer, Karl
German. Artist
Expressionist, known for emaciated
  mannequin figures.
b. 1878 in Karlsruhe, Germany
d. Apr 3, 1955 in Berlin, Germany (West)
Source: *McGDA; ObitOF 79*

Hoff, Sydney
American. Illustrator, Author
b. Sep 4, 1912 in New York, New York
Source: *AmAu&B; ChhPo S1; ConAu 5R,
4NR; IlsCB 1957; SmATA 9; ThrBJA;
WhoAm 74, 76, 78, 80, 82; WhoWor 78;
WhoWorJ 72*

Hoffa, Jimmy (James Riddle)
American. Labor Union Official
Pres., Teamsters, 1957-71; believed killed
  following abduction from MI restaurant;
  declared dead, Dec 8, 1982.
b. Feb 14, 1913 in Brazil, Indiana
d. Jul 30, 1975 in Detroit, Michigan
Source: *CelR; CurBio 72, 83; IntWW 74;
NewYTBE 71, 72; WebAB; WhoAm 74;
WhoWor 78*

Hoffa, Portland
[Mrs. Fred Allen]
American. Actress
b. 1910
Source: *InWom*

Hoffenstein, Samuel Goodman
American. Poet, Humorist
b. Oct 8, 1890 in Lithuania
d. Oct 6, 1947 in Hollywood, California
Source: *AmAu&B; BioIn 1, 4, 8; DcNAA;
REnAL; TwCA, SUP*

Hoffer, Eric
American. Author, Philosopher
Wrote *The True Believer,* 1951; awarded
  Presidential Medal of Freedom, 1983.
b. Jul 25, 1902 in New York, New York
d. May 21, 1983 in San Francisco, California
Source: *CelR; ConAu 13R; CurBio 65, 83N;
NewYTBS 83; RAdv 1; WebAB; WhoAm 82;
WorAu; WrDr 76*

Hoffer, George Nissley
American. Botanist
b. 1887
d. 1963
Source: *BioIn 6*

Hoffman, Abbie (Abbott)
[Spiro Igloo; The Chicago 7]
American. Author, Political Activist
Wrote *Revolution for the Hell of It,* 1968;
  Woodstock Nation, 1969.
b. Nov 30, 1936 in Worcester, Massachusetts
Source: *AmAu&B; CelR; ConAu 21R; CurBio
81; NewYTBE 70; WhoE 74*

Hoffman, Al
American. Composer, Author
Wrote popular stage scores, 1930s-50; hit
  songs include "Mairz Doats," 1944.
b. Sep 25, 1902 in Minsk, Russia
d. Jul 21, 1960 in New York, New York
Source: *AmSCAP 66; BiDAmM; BioIn 5;
CmpEPM*

Hoffman, Anna Marie Lederer Rosenberg
American. Government Official, Lawyer
Asst. sec. of defense, 1950-53; highest
  Pentagon position held by a woman.
b. Jun 19, 1902 in Budapest, Hungary
d. May 9, 1983 in New York, New York
Source: *CurBio 83N; NewYTBS 83; Who 74;
WhoWorJ 72*

Hoffman, Charles Fenno
American. Poet
b. Feb 7, 1806 in New York, New York
d. Jun 7, 1884 in Harrisburg, Pennsylvania
Source: *Alli; AmAu; AmAu&B; AmBi;
ApCAB; BiD&SB; CasWL; ChhPo; CnDAL;
CyAL 2; DcAmAu; DcAmB; DcBiA; DcEnL;
DcLEL; DcNAA; Drake; EvLB; OxAmL;
PenC AM; REnAL; TwCBDA; WhAm HS*

Hoffman, Dustin
American. Actor
Starred in *The Graduate,* 1967; *Kramer vs. Kramer,* 1979; *Tootsie,* 1982.
b. Aug 8, 1937 in Los Angeles, California
Source: *BkPepl; CelR; CurBio 69; FilmgC; IntMPA 75, 76, 77, 78, 79, 80, 81, 82; MotPP; MovMk; OxFilm; WhoAm 74, 76, 78, 80, 82; WhoHol A; WhoThe 81*

Hoffman, Irwin
American. Conductor
b. Nov 26, 1924 in New York, New York
Source: *WhoAm 74, 76, 78, 80, 82; WhoMus 72; WhoS&SW 82; WhoWor 78*

Hoffman, Julius Jennings
American. Judge
Presided over controversial "Chicago Seven" trial, 1969-70.
b. Jul 7, 1895 in Chicago, Illinois
d. Jul 1, 1983 in Chicago, Illinois
Source: *NewYTBS 83; WhoAm 82; WhoGov 72*

Hoffman, Malvina
American. Sculptor
b. Jun 15, 1887 in New York, New York
d. Jul 10, 1966 in New York, New York
Source: *AmAu&B; CurBio 40, 66; InWom; REnAL; WhAm 4*

Hoffman, Paul Gray
American. Auto Executive, Statesman
b. Apr 26, 1891 in Chicago, Illinois
d. Oct 8, 1974 in New York, New York
Source: *CurBio 46, 74; IntWW 74; NewYTBE 71; NewYTBS 74; WhAm 6; Who 74; WhoAm 74; WhoWor 78*

Hoffman, Rob
American. Publisher
Co-founder of *National Lampoon* following graduation from Harvard, 1969.
b. 1948
Source: *NF*

Hoffman, Robert C
"Mr. Physical Fitness"
American. Sportsman, Businessman
Champion weightlifter; Olympic weightlifting coach, 1933.
b. 1899 in Tifton, Georgia
d. Jul 18, 1985 in York, Pennsylvania
Source: *ConAu 116*

Hoffmann, Ernst Theodor Amadeus
German. Author
Master of weird, macabre; Offenbach's opera *Tales of Hoffmann* based on his work.
b. Jan 24, 1776 in Konigsberg, Germany
d. Jun 25, 1822 in Berlin, Germany
Source: *BbD; EvEuW; PenC EUR*

Hoffmann, Jan
German. Figure Skater
Source: *BioIn 12*

Hofheinz, Roy Mark
American. Business Executive
Conceived idea of domed, air-conditioned stadium so Houston could attract NL baseball franchise, 1960.
b. Apr 10, 1912 in Beaumont, Texas
d. Nov 21, 1982 in Houston, Texas
Source: *CelR; NewYTBS 82; WhoAm 74, 76; WhoProB 73; WhoS&SW 73, 75*

Hofmann, Albert
Swiss. Chemist
b. Feb 27, 1933 in Uznach, Switzerland
Source: *AmM&WS 73P*

Hofmann, Hans
German. Artist
His paintings inspired Abstract Expressionism movement.
b. Mar 21, 1880 in Weissenburg, Germany
d. Feb 17, 1966 in New York, New York
Source: *CurBio 58, 66; DcCAA 71; REn; WebAB; WhAm 4*

Hofmann, Josef
American. Musician
b. Jan 20, 1876 in Krakow, Poland
d. Feb 16, 1957 in Los Angeles, California
Source: *BioIn 2, 4, 7, 9, 11; WhAm 3*

Hofmannsthal, Hugo Hoffmann
Austrian. Poet, Dramatist
Noted as librettist of Richard Strauss's operas.
b. Feb 1, 1874 in Vienna, Austria
d. Jul 15, 1929 in Vienna, Austria
Source: *AtlBL; CasWL; ClDMEL; CnMD; CnMWL; CnThe; EncWL; EvEuW; McGEWD; ModGL; ModWD; NewC; OxEng; OxGer; OxThe; PenC EUR; REn; REnWD; TwCA, SUP; TwCWr*

Hofsiss, Jack Bernard
American. Director
Won Tony for *Elephant Man,* 1979.
b. Sep 28, 1950 in Brooklyn, New York
Source: *WhoAm 84*

Hofstadter, Richard
American. Historian
Analyst of American society; won Pulitzer,
1955, for *Age of Reason.*
b. Aug 6, 1916 in Buffalo, New York
d. Oct 24, 1970 in New York, New York
Source: *AmAu&B; ConAu 1R, 29R, 4NR;
CurBio 56, 70; EncAB-H; OxAmL; PenC AM;
REn; REnAL; WebAB; WhAm 5; WorAu*

Hofstadter, Robert
American. Physicist, Educator
b. Feb 5, 1915 in New York, New York
Source: *AmM&WS 73P; BioIn 6; IntWW 74;
Who 74; WhoAm 74, 76, 78, 80, 82;
WhoWor 78*

Hogan, Ben (William Benjamin)
American. Golfer
PGA Hall of Fame, 1953; wrote *Power Golf,*
1948.
b. Aug 13, 1912 in Dublin, Texas
Source: *CelR; CurBio 48; WhoAm 78, 80, 82;
WhoGolf*

Hogan, Hulk
[Terry Jean Bollette]
American. Wrestler
World Wrestling Federation heavyweight
champion.
Source: *NF*

Hogarth, Burne
American. Cartoonist
Created, drew "Tarzan," 1937-50; pres.,
Pendragon Press, 1975-79.
b. Nov 25, 1911 in Chicago, Illinois
Source: *WorECom*

Hogarth, William
English. Artist, Engraver
Painted "The Pool of Bethesda" on staircase
of St. Bartholomew's Hospital, London,
1735-36.
b. Nov 10, 1697 in London, England
d. Oct 26, 1764 in London, England
Source: *Alli; AtlBL; BkIE; ChhPo; NewC;
REn*

Hoge, James Fulton, Jr.
American. Newspaper Editor
b. Dec 25, 1936 in New York, New York
Source: *BioIn 8, 10, 11; WhoAm 78, 80, 82*

Hogg, Ima
American. Philanthropist
b. Jul 10, 1882
d. Aug 19, 1975 in London, England
Source: *BioIn 10*

Hogg, James
Scottish. Author
b. 1770 in Ettrick, Scotland
d. Nov 21, 1835 in Yarrow, Scotland
Source: *Alli; AtlBL; BbD; BiD&SB; BiDLA,
SUP; BrAu 19; CasWL; ChhPo, S1, S2;
DcEnA; DcEnL; DcEuL; DcLEL; EvLB;
MouLC 3; NewC; OxEng; PenC ENG; REn;
WebE&AL*

Hogrogian, Nonny
American. Illustrator
Children's book illustrator; won Caldecott for
Always Room for One More, 1966.
b. May 7, 1932 in New York, New York
Source: *AuBYP; BkP; ChlLR 2; ConAu 45,
2NR; IlsBYP; IlsCB 1957; NewbC 1966;
SmATA 7; ThrBJA; WhoAm 74; WhoE 74*

Hogwood, Christopher
English. Conductor, Musician
Founded Academy of Ancient Music, 1974.
b. Sep 10, 1941 in Nottingham, England
Source: *CurBio 85; WhoMus 72*

Hohman, Donald
[The Hostages]
American. Hostage in Iran
b. 1943 in Yuma City, California
Source: *NewYTBS 81*

Hoke, Henry Reed
American. Author, Editor
b. 1894
d. 1970
Source: *BioIn 9*

Hokinson, Helen
American. Cartoonist
Satirized middle-aged clubwomen in *The New
Yorker,* 1925-49.
b. 1899 in Mendota, Illinois
d. Nov 1, 1949 in Washington, District of
Columbia
Source: *DcAmB S4; InWom; NotAW; WebAB*

Hokusai
Japanese. Engraver
b. 1760 in Yedo, Japan
d. 1849
Source: *REn*

Holabird, William
American. Architect
b. Sep 11, 1854 in Amenia Union, New
York
d. Jul 19, 1923 in Evanston, Illinois
Source: *DcAmB; WebAB; WhAm 1*

Holbein, Hans, the Elder
German. Artist, Sculptor, Architect
b. 1460
d. 1524
Source: *NewCol 75*

Holbein, Hans, the Younger
German. Artist
b. 1497 in Augsburg, Germany
d. 1543 in London, England
Source: *AtlBL; NewC; OxGer; REn*

Holbrook, Hal (Harold Rowe, Jr.)
American. Actor
Won Tony, NY Drama Critics citation for
  Mark Twain Tonight, 1966.
b. Feb 17, 1925 in Cleveland, Ohio
Source: *BiE&WWA; BioNews 74; CelR;
  CurBio 61; FilmgC; IntMPA 75, 76, 77, 78,
  79, 80, 81, 82; MotPP; NewYTBE 73;
  NotNAT; WhoAm 74, 76, 78, 80, 82; WhoHol
  A; WhoThe 77*

Holbrook, Stewart Hall
American. Author, Journalist
b. Aug 22, 1893 in Newport, Vermont
d. Sep 3, 1964 in Portland, Oregon
Source: *AmAu&B; AuBYP; ConAu P-1;
  OxAmL; REnAL; SmATA 2; ThrBJA; TwCA
  SUP; WhAm 4; WhNAA; WhoPNW*

Holbrooke, Josef
English. Composer
b. Jul 5, 1878 in Croydon, England
d. Aug 5, 1958 in London, England
Source: *NewEOp 71*

Holden, Fay
[Fay Hammerton]
English. Actress
Portrayed Mickey Rooney's mother in Andy
  Hardy film series.
b. Sep 26, 1895 in Birmingham, England
d. Jun 23, 1973 in Los Angeles, California
Source: *FilmEn; FilmgC; MotPP; MovMk;
  NewYTBE 73; ThFT; Vers A; WhScrn 77;
  WhoHol B*

Holden, William
[William Franklin Beedle, Jr.]
American. Actor
Starred in over 50 films; won Oscar for
  Stalag 17, 1953.
b. Apr 17, 1918 in O'Fallon, Illinois
d. Nov 12, 1981 in Santa Monica, California
Source: *BiDFilm; BkPepl; CelR; CmMov;
  CurBio 82; FilmgC; IntMPA 82; MotPP;
  MovMk; OxFilm; WhoAm 80; WhoHol A;
  WorEFlm*

Holder, Geoffrey
Actor
Won Tony Awards as director, costume
  designer of *The Wiz,* 1975.
b. Sep 1, 1930 in Trinidad
Source: *AfroAA; BiE&WWA; BlkAWP;
  CurBio 57; NotNAT; PIP&P A; WhoAm 74,
  76, 78, 80, 82; WhoBlA 75; WhoHol A;
  WhoThe 77*

Holderlin, Johann C F
German. Poet
b. Feb 20, 1770 in Lauffen, Germany
d. Jul 7, 1843 in Tubingen, Germany
Source: *CasWL; EvEuW*

Holdereid, Kristine
American. Student
First woman to finish at head of class at US
  Naval Academy, 1984.
b. 1963
Source: *NF*

Holdren, Judd Clifton
American. Actor
Starred in 1950s film series *Captain Video;
  Zombies of the Stratosphere; Last Planet.*
b. Oct 16, 1915 in Iowa
d. Mar 11, 1974 in Los Angeles, California
Source: *WhScrn 77; WhoHol B*

Holiday, Billie
[Eleanora Fagan]
"Lady Day"
American. Singer
Autobiography, *Lady Sings the Blues,* 1956,
  inspired film, 1972.
b. Apr 7, 1915 in Baltimore, Maryland
d. Jul 17, 1959 in New York, New York
Source: *InWom; NewYTBE 72; WebAB;
  WhoHol B; WhoJazz 72*

Holifield, Chet
American. Congressman
b. Dec 3, 1903 in Mayfield, Kentucky
Source: *BioIn 4, 5, 7, 10; CurBio 55;
  WhoAm 74; WhoAmP 73; WhoGov 75;
  WhoWest 84*

Holinshed, Raphael
English. Editor
Best known work *The Chronicles of England,
  Scotlande, and Irelande,* 1578.
d. 1580
Source: *AtlBL; BbD; BiD&SB; BrAu; CasWL;
  CroE&S; DcEnA; DcEnL; NewC; OxEng;
  REn*

Holladay, Terry Ann
American. Tennis Player
b. Nov 28, 1955 in Charlotte, North
Carolina
Source: *OfEnT*

Holland, Dave
see: Judas Priest

Holland, Jerome Heartwell
American. Government Official
Ambassador to Sweden, 1970-72; chairman,
American Red Cross, 1979--.
b. Jan 9, 1916 in Auburn, New York
Source: *BioIn 6, 8, 9; WhoAm 74, 76, 78,
80, 82; WhoGov 75*

Holland, John Philip
American. Inventor
Developed first submarine used by US Navy,
1900.
b. Feb 24, 1841 in Liscannor, Ireland
d. Aug 12, 1914 in Newark, New Jersey
Source: *BioIn 3, 5, 6, 7; WebAB*

Holland, Leland James
[The Hostages]
American. Hostage in Iran
b. 1928 in Shullsburg, Wisconsin
Source: *BioIn 12; NewYTBS 81*

Holland, William Jacob
American. Naturalist, Clergyman, Educator
Lepidoptera expert; wrote *Moth Book,* 1903.
b. Aug 16, 1848 in Jamaica
d. Dec 13, 1932 in Pittsburgh, Pennsylvania
Source: *DcAmB S1*

Hollander, John
American. Author
b. Oct 28, 1929 in New York, New York
Source: *AmAu&B; AuBYP; ChhPo, S1; ConAu
1R, 1NR; ConLC 2, 5, 8, 14; ConP 70, 75;
DrAP 75; DrAS 74E; OxAmL; PenC AM;
REnAL; SmATA 13; WhoAm 74, 76, 78, 80,
82; WhoE 74; WhoTwCL; WorAu; WrDr 76*

Hollander, Xaviera
Dutch. Author
Former call girl who wrote of her
experiences in *The Happy Hooker,* 1972.
b. 1943
Source: *BioIn 12*

Holliday, "Doc" (John Henry)
American. Dentist, Gambler, Criminal
Frontier gambler who was friend of Wyatt
Earp and with him at OK Corral
gunfight, 1882.
b. 1851 in Griffin, Georgia
d. Nov 8, 1887 in Glenwood Springs,
Colorado
Source: *BioIn 11; OxFilm; REnAW*

Holliday, Jennifer Yvette
American. Singer, Actress
Star of Broadway's *Dream Girls,* who had hit
single from show: "And I'm Telling You
I'm Not Going," 1982.
b. Oct 19, 1960
Source: *CurBio 83; InB&W 80; NewYTBS 81;
RkOn 85*

Holliday, Judy
[Judith Tuvim]
American. Actress
Won Oscar, 1950, for *Born Yesterday.*
b. Jun 21, 1922 in New York, New York
d. Jun 7, 1965 in New York, New York
Source: *BiDFilm; BiE&WWA; CmMov;
CurBio 51, 65; EncMT; FilmgC; InWom;
MotPP; MovMk; OxFilm; WhAm 4; WhScrn
74, 77; WhoHol B; WorEFlm*

Holliday, Polly Dean
American. Actress
Starred in TV series "Alice," 1976-80; in
own series "Flo," 1981.
b. Jul 2, 1937 in Jasper, Alabama
Source: *WhoAm 80, 82*

Hollies, The
[Bernie Calvert; Allan Clarke; Bobby Elliott;
Eric Haydock; Tony Hicks; Graham Nash;
Mikael Rikfors; Terry Sylvester]
English. Music Group
Most consistently successful band after The
Beatles; hit single "He Ain't Heavy, He's
My Brother," 1970.
Source: *ConMuA 80A; IlEncRk; LilREn 78;
RkOn 78; RolSEnR 83; WhoRock 81*

Holliger, Heinz
Swiss. Musician
International prize-winning oboist.
b. May 21, 1939 in Langenthal, Switzerland
Source: *Baker 78; DcCM; IntWW 77, 78;
WhoMus 72*

Holliman, Earl
[Anthony Numkena]
American. Actor
Starred, with Angie Dickinson, in TV series
"Police Woman," 1974-78.
b. Sep 11, 1936 in Delhi, Louisiana
Source: *FilmgC; IntMPA 75, 76, 77, 78, 79,
80, 81, 82; MotPP; WhoAm 82; WhoHol A*

Holling, Holling C(lancy)
American. Author, Naturalist
Wrote geo-historical fiction books for
children: *Paddle to the Sea*, 1941.
b. Aug 2, 1900 in Holling Corners, Michigan
d. Sep 7, 1973 in California
Source: *AmAu&B; Au&ICB; AuBYP; ConAu
106*

Hollings, Ernest Frederick
"Fritz"
American. Politician
Progressive Dem. senator from SC, 1966--.
b. Jan 1, 1922 in Charleston, South Carolina
Source: *AlmAP 78, 80; BiDrAC; BioIn 4, 8,
9, 10; CngDr 74, 77, 79; CurBio 82; IntWW
75, 76, 77, 78; PolProf K; WhoAm 74, 76,
78, 80, 82; WhoAmP 73, 75, 77, 79; WhoGov
72, 75, 77*

Hollister, Paul Merrick
American. Advertising Executive, Author
b. 1890 in New York, New York
d. 1970
Source: *NewYTBE 70; WhoAmA 73*

Holloman, "Bobo" (Alva Lee)
American. Baseball Player
Pitcher, St. Louis Browns, 1953; only
complete game was no-hitter, last by
Browns pitcher.
b. Mar 27, 1924 in Thomaston, Georgia
Source: *BaseEn 85; BioIn 3, 10; WhoProB 73*

Holloway, Emory
American. Author, Educator
b. Mar 16, 1885 in Marshall, Missouri
d. Jul 30, 1977 in Bethlehem, Pennsylvania
Source: *AmAu&B; ConAu 49, 73; DrAS 74E;
OxAmL; REnAL; TwCA, SUP; WhNAA*

Holloway, Stanley
English. Actor
Played Eliza Doolittle's father in *My Fair
Lady*, 1964.
b. Oct 1, 1890 in London, England
d. Jan 30, 1982 in Littlehampton, England
Source: *AmPS B; AnObit 1982; BiE&WWA;
CurBio 82; EncMT; EncWT; Film 2; IntMPA
82; MovMk; NewC; NewYTBS 82; NotNAT;
Who 74; WhoThe 77*

Holloway, Sterling
American. Actor
Voice of many Disney animals, including
Winnie the Pooh; supporting actor in over
100 films.
b. Jan 4, 1905 in Cedartown, Georgia
Source: *BiE&WWA; FilmgC; IntMPA 82;
MotPP; MovMk; NotNAT; PIP&P; Vers B;
WhoAm 82; WhoHol A*

Hollowood, Albert Bernard
English. Editor, Economist
Editor, *Punch* magazine, 1957-68; wrote
Funny Money, 1975.
b. Jun 3, 1910 in Burslem, England
d. Mar 28, 1981 in Guildford, England
Source: *ConAu 9R, 103; IntWW 74, 75, 76,
77, 78; WhAm 7; Who 74; WrDr 80*

Holly, "Buddy" (Charles Hardin)
American. Singer, Songwriter
b. Sep 7, 1936 in Lubbock, Texas
d. Feb 3, 1959 in Clear Lake, Iowa
Source: *BioIn 9, 10, 11; WhAm 4*

Holly, James Theodore
American. Clergyman
b. Oct 3, 1829 in Washington, District of
Columbia
d. 1911
Source: *BioIn 5, 9; WhAm 1*

Hollyer, Samuel
English. Engraver
b. Feb 24, 1826 in Landon, England
d. 1919
Source: *DcAmB; WhAm 4*

Hollywood Ten
[Alvah Bessie; Herbert Biberman; Lester
Cole; Edward Dmytryk; Ring Lardner, Jr.;
John Howard Lawson; Albert Maltz;
Samuel Ornitz; Adrian Scott; Alton
Trumbo]
American. Filmmakers
Black listed group of writers; refused to
testify before House Un-American
Committee about alleged membership in
Communist Party; sentenced to jail.
Source: *FilmEn*

Holm, Celeste
American. Actress
Won 1947 Oscar for *Gentlemen's Agreement*.
b. Apr 29, 1919 in New York, New York
Source: *BiE&WWA; CurBio 44; EncMT;
FilmgC; HolP 40; InWom; IntMPA 81;
MotPP; MovMk; NotNAT; OxFilm; WhoAm
82; WhoHol A; WhoThe 77*

Holm, Eleanor
American. Swimmer, Actress
Played Jane in *Tarzan's Revenge,* 1938;
married to Billy Rose 14 years.
b. Dec 6, 1913
Source: *InWom; WhoHol A*

Holm, Ian
[Ian Holm Cuthbert]
English. Actor
Received Oscar nomination for *Chariots of
Fire,* 1981.
b. Sep 12, 1931 in Goodmayes, England
Source: *FilmEn; FilmgC; WhoHol A; WhoThe
81; WhoWor 74*

Holm, John Cecil
American. Dramatist, Actor
Co-wrote Broadway comedy *Three Men in a
House.*
b. Nov 4, 1904 in Philadelphia, Pennsylvania
d. Oct 24, 1981 in Rhode Island
Source: *ConAu 116; WhoThe 81*

Holman, Bill
American. Cartoonist
b. 1903 in Crawfordsville, Indiana
Source: *WorECom*

Holman, Eugene
American. Oilman
b. May 2, 1895 in San Angelo, Texas
d. Aug 12, 1962 in New York, New York
Source: *BioIn 1, 2, 5, 6; CurBio 48, 62*

Holman, Libby
American. Singer, Actress
b. May 23, 1906 in Cincinnati, Ohio
d. Jun 18, 1971 in Stamford, Connecticut
Source: *BiE&WWA; EncMT; InWom;
NewYTBE 71; PIP&P; WhScrn 77; WhoHol
B*

Holman, Nat
"Mister Basketball"
American. Basketball Player, Basketball
Coach
b. Oct 18, 1896 in New York, New York
Source: *WhoBbl 73; WhoWorJ 72*

Holme, Constance
English. Author
b. 1881 in Milnthorpe, England
d. 1955
Source: *DcLEL; EvLB; LongCTC; OxEng;
TwCA, SUP*

Holmes, Anna Marie
Canadian. Dancer
b. Apr 17, 1943 in Mission City, British
Columbia
Source: *CreCan 1*

Holmes, Arthur
English. Geologist, Educator
Laid foundations of isotope geology.
b. Jan 14, 1890 in Hebburn, England
d. Sep 20, 1965 in London, England
Source: *ConAu 116; McGMS 80*

Holmes, Burton
American. Producer
Presented travelogues, 1890-1958; known for
tag line: "Sun sinks slowly in the West."
b. Jan 8, 1870 in Chicago, Illinois
d. Jul 22, 1958 in Hollywood, California
Source: *CurBio 58; WhAm 3; WhNAA;
WhScrn 74, 77; WhoHol B*

Holmes, David
Canadian. Dancer
Source: *BioIn 8; CreCan 2*

Holmes, John Clennon
American. Author
b. Mar 12, 1926 in Holyoke, Massachusetts
Source: *AmAu&B; ConAu 9R, 4NR; ConNov
72, 76; DrAF 76; OxAmL; PenC AM;
WhoAm 74, 76, 78, 80, 82; WhoE 74; WrDr
76*

Holmes, John Haynes
American. Clergyman, Reformer
Modernist Unitarian who combined religious,
political beliefs; wrote *Religion for Today.*
b. Nov 9, 1879 in Philadelphia, Pennsylvania
d. Apr 3, 1964 in New York, New York
Source: *AmAu&B; AmLY; ChhPo S1; ConAu
89; CurBio 41, 64; REnAL; TwCA SUP;
WhAm 4; WhNAA*

Holmes, Larry
American. Boxer
WBC heavyweight champ, 1978-85; defeated
by Michael Spinks.
b. Nov 3, 1949 in Cuthbert, Georgia
Source: *CurBio 81; WhoAm 82*

Holmes, Mary Jane Hawes
American. Author
Sentimental novels include *Lena Rivers,* 1856;
Marian Grey, 1863.
b. Apr 5, 1825 in Brookfield, Massachusetts
d. Oct 6, 1907 in Brockport, New York
Source: *NotAW*

Holmes, Oliver Wendell
American. Poet, Author, Essayist
First dean, Harvard Medical School, 1847-53;
    wrote *Elsie Venner,* 1861.
b. Aug 29, 1809 in Cambridge, Massachusetts
d. Oct 7, 1894 in Boston, Massachusetts
Source: *Alli, SUP; AmAu; AmAu&B; AmBi;*
    ApCAB; AtlBL; BbD; BiD&SB; CasWL;
    Chambr 3; ChhPo, S1, S2; CnDAL; CrtT 3;
    CyAL 2; CyWA; DcAmAu; DcAmB; DcBiA;
    DcEnA; DcEnL; DcLEL; DcNAA; Drake;
    EncAB-H; EvLB; MouLC 4; OxAmL; OxEng;
    PenC AM; PoChrch; RAdv 1; REn; REnAL;
    Str&VC; TwCBDA; WebAB; WebE&AL;
    WhAm HS

Holmes, Oliver Wendell, Jr.
"The Great Dissenter"
American. Supreme Court Justice
Liberal Supreme Court Justice, 1902-32,
    known for frequent disagreement with
    conservative majority.
b. Mar 8, 1841 in Boston, Massachusetts
d. Mar 6, 1935 in Washington, District of
    Columbia
Source: *AmAu&B; AmBi; AtlBL; DcAmAu;*
    DcAmB S1; DcNAA; OxAmL; WebAB

Holmes, Rupert
American. Singer, Songwriter
Wrote, recorded number one single "Escape
    (The Pina Colada Song)," 1979.
b. Feb 24, 1947 in Cheshire, England
Source: *BioIn 12; NewYTBS 75; RkOn 85;*
    WhoAm 82

Holmes, Taylor
American. Actor
Title role in *Ruggles of Red Gap,* 1918.
b. 1878 in Newark, New Jersey
d. Sep 30, 1959 in Hollywood, California
Source: *Film 1; FilmgC; MotPP; MovMk;*
    TwYS; Vers A; WhScrn 74, 77; WhoHol B

Holmes, Tommy (Thomas Francis)
"Kelly"
American. Baseball Player
Outfielder, 1942-52; had 37-game hitting
    streak, 1945, longest in NL until broken
    by Pete Rose, 1978.
b. Mar 29, 1917 in Brooklyn, New York
Source: *BaseEn 85; WhoProB 73*

Holst, Gustav
English. Musician, Composer
b. Sep 21, 1874 in Cheltenham, England
d. May 25, 1934 in London, England
Source: *DcCM*

Holt, Derek
see: Climax Blues Band, The

Holt, Harold Edward
Australian. Prime Minister
b. Aug 5, 1908 in Sydney, Australia
d. Dec 17, 1967 in Port Philip Bay,
    Australia
Source: *BioIn 7, 8, 9; CurBio 66, 68*

Holt, Henry
American. Publisher
b. Jan 3, 1840 in Baltimore, Maryland
d. Feb 13, 1926
Source: *Alli SUP; AmAu&B; AmBi; BiDPara;*
    DcAmAu; DcAmB; DcNAA; MnBBF;
    TwCBDA; WhAm 1

Holt, Ivan Lee
American. Clergyman
b. Jan 9, 1886 in De Witt, Arkansas
d. Jan 12, 1967
Source: *BioIn 1, 7; WhAm 4*

Holt, Jack (Charles John)
American. Actor
Father of Tim Holt; hero in many silent
    westerns.
b. May 31, 1888 in Winchester, Virginia
d. Jan 18, 1951 in Los Angeles, California
Source: *FilmEn; Film 1; FilmgC; MovMk;*
    TwYS; WhScrn 74, 77; WhoHol B

Holt, John Caldwell
American. Educator, Author
Wrote *How Children Fail,* 1964; sparked
    debate about quality of education in US.
b. Apr 14, 1923 in New York, New York
d. Sep 14, 1985 in Boston, Massachusetts
Source: *ConAu 69; CurBio 85*

Holt, Tim
[Charles John Holt, Jr.]
American. Actor
Best known for *Treasure of the Sierra*
    Madre, 1948.
b. Feb 5, 1918 in Beverly Hills, California
d. Feb 15, 1973 in Shawnee, Oklahoma
Source: *FilmEn; FilmgC; HolP 40; MotPP;*
    MovMk; NewYTBE 73; WhScrn 77; WhoHol
    B

Holtz, Lou
American. Actor
Comedian in revues, on radio in "Rudy
    Vallee Show"; "Bing Crosby Show."
b. Apr 11, 1898 in San Francisco, California
Source: *BiE&WWA; EncMT; NotNAT;*
    WhoThe 77A

Holtz, Lou
American. Football Coach
Succeeded Gerry Faust as head coach of
   Notre Dame, 1985.
b. 1937
Source: *BioIn 12; NewYTBS 76*

Holtzman, Elizabeth
American. Politician
Congresswoman from NY, 1974-80.
b. Aug 11, 1941 in Brooklyn, New York
Source: *BioNews 74; CngDr 74; CurBio 73;
NewYTBE 72; WhoAm 74; WhoAmP 73;
WhoAmW 77; WomPO 76*

Holtzmann, Fanny E
American. Lawyer
b. 1903
Source: *BioIn 11; InWom*

Holyoake, Keith Jacka, Sir
New Zealander. Political Leader
Prime minister, 1960-72; governor general,
   1977-80.
b. Feb 11, 1904 in Pahiatua, New Zealand
d. Dec 8, 1983 in Wellington, New Zealand
Source: *AnObit 1983; CurBio 84N; IntWW
74; NewYTBS 83; Who 74; WhoGov 72;
WhoWor 74*

Holzer, Harold
American. Author, Editor
Award-winning books on Abraham Lincoln
   include *The Lincoln Image,* 1984.
b. Feb 5, 1949 in New York, New York
Source: *ConAu 116*

Holzman, William
American. Basketball Coach
b. Aug 10, 1920 in New York, New York
Source: *OfNBA 81; WhoBbl 73*

Home, Daniel Douglas
English. Psychic
b. Mar 20, 1833 in Scotland
d. Jun 21, 1886 in Auteuil, France
Source: *Alli SUP; AmBi; ApCAB; BiDPara;
Drake; NewC; OxEng; REn*

Homer
Greek. Author
Credited with writing *The Iliad; The Odyssey.*
b. 750 BC
Source: *AtlBL; BbD; BiD&SB; CasWL;
ChhPo; CyWA; DcBiA; DcEnL; DcEuL;
NewC; OxEng; PenC CL; PIP&P; RComWL*

Homer, Louise
American. Opera Singer
b. Apr 28, 1871 in Sewickley, Pennsylvania
d. May 6, 1947 in Winter Park, Florida
Source: *DcAmB S4; InWom; NotAW; WhAm
2; WomWWA 14*

Homer, Sidney
American. Composer
b. Dec 9, 1864 in Boston, Massachusetts
d. Jul 10, 1953 in Winter Park, Florida
Source: *AmSCAP 66; OxAmL; REnAL;
WhAm 3*

Homer, Winslow
American. Artist
Excelled in watercolors of seascapes,
   including *Breaking Storm, Maine Coast.*
b. Feb 24, 1836 in Boston, Massachusetts
d. Sep 29, 1910 in Prouts Neck, Maine
Source: *AmBi; ApCAB; AtlBL; ChhPo, S1,
S2; DcAmB; EarABI, SUP; EncAB-H;
OxAmL; REn; REnAL; TwCBDA; WebAB;
WhAm 1*

Homolka, Oscar
Austrian. Actor
Oscar nominee for *I Remember Mama,* 1948.
b. Aug 12, 1903 in Vienna, Austria
d. Jan 27, 1978 in Sussex, England
Source: *BiDFilm; BiE&WWA; MovMk;
NotNAT; OxFilm*

Honda, Soichiro
Japanese. Auto Executive
Began producing motorcycles, 1948; founded
   Honda Motor Co., 1973.
b. Nov 17, 1906 in Iwata Gun, Japan
Source: *ConNews 86-1; FarE&A 78, 79, 80;
IntWW 75, 76, 77, 78, 79, 80, 81; NewYTBS
77; WhoF&I 74; WhoWor 74, 78*

Honecker, Erich
German. Politician
b. Aug 25, 1912 in Wiebelskirchen, Germany
Source: *BioIn 9, 10; CurBio 72; IntWW 74;
NewYTBE 71; WhoWor 78*

Honegger, Arthur
[Les Six]
French. Composer
b. Mar 10, 1892 in Le Havre, France
d. Nov 27, 1955 in Paris, France
Source: *AtlBL; CurBio 41, 56; DcCM; DcFM;
FilmgC; OxFilm; REn; WhAm 4; WorEFlm*

Honeycombs, The
[Denis Dalziel; John Lantree; Ann 'Honey'
Lantree; Martin Murray; Alan Ward]
English. Music Group
"British Invasion" group, formed 1963; first
to have female drummer.
Source: *RolSEnR 83*

Honeydrippers, The
[Jeff Beck; Jimmy Page; Robert Plant; Nile
Rodgers]
English. Music Group
Formed to record album of old rock songs:
hit single "Sea of Love," 1984.
Source: *RkOn 85*

Honeyman-Scott, James (Jimmy)
[The Pretenders]
English. Musician
b. Nov 4, 1956 in Hereford, England
d. Jun 16, 1982 in London, England
Source: *NF*

Honeywell, Mark Charles
American. Inventor, Manufacturer
Honeywell Heating Speciality Co. improved
hot water heating systems controls, 1906.
b. Dec 29, 1874 in Wabash, Indiana
d. Sep 13, 1964 in Indianapolis, Indiana
Source: *BioIn 7, 9; NatCAB 52; WhAm 4*

Hooch, Pieter de
Dutch. Artist
b. Dec 20, 1629 in Rotterdam, Netherlands
d. 1683
Source: *AtlBL; NewCol 75*

Hood, Darla Jean
[Our Gang]
American. Actress
Curly-headed sweetheart of *Our Gang*
comedies, 1935-42.
b. Nov 4, 1931 in Leedey, Oklahoma
d. Jun 13, 1979 in Canoga Park, California
Source: *BioIn 10; NewYTBS 79; WhoHol A*

Hood, Frederick Emmart
American. Designer
b. 1927 in Marblehead, Massachusetts
Source: *NewYTBS 74*

Hood, John Bell
American. Military Leader
Confederate general; led Confederate Army in
unsuccessful defense of Atlanta, 1864.
b. Jun 1, 1831 in Owingsville, Kentucky
d. Aug 30, 1879 in New Orleans, Louisiana
Source: *Alli SUP; AmBi; ApCAB; BiDConf;
BiDSA; DcAmAu; DcAmB; DcNAA; TwCBDA;
WebAB; WhAm HS*

Hood, Raymond Matthewson
American. Architect
b. Mar 29, 1881 in Pawtucket, Rhode Island
d. Aug 14, 1934
Source: *AmBi; DcAmB S1; WhAm 1*

Hood, Thomas
English. Author
b. May 23, 1799 in London, England
d. May 3, 1845 in London, England
Source: *Alli; AnCL; AtlBL; BbD; BiD&SB;
Br&AmS; BrAu 19; CarSB; CasWL; Chambr
3; ChhPo, S1, S2; CnE&AP; CrtT 2; DcEnA;
DcEnL; DcEuL; DcLEL; EvLB; MouLC 3;
NewC; OxEng; PenC ENG; REn; Str&VC;
WebE&AL*

Hook, Sidney
American. Philosopher, Author
b. Dec 20, 1902 in New York, New York
Source: *AmAu&B; CelR; ConAu 9R; DrAS
74P; IntWW 74; LEduc 74; REnAL; TwCA
SUP; WhoAm 74, 76, 78, 80, 82; WhoWorJ
72*

Hooke, Robert
British. Scientist, Philosopher
b. Jul 18, 1635 in Isle of Wight
d. Mar 3, 1705 in London, England
Source: *Alli; DcEnL; McGEWB*

Hooker, Brian
American. Dramatist, Librettist
b. Nov 2, 1880 in New York, New York
d. Dec 28, 1946 in New London,
Connecticut
Source: *AmSCAP 66; ChhPo, S1; DcNAA;
EncMT; OxAmL; REn; REnAL; WhAm 2*

Hooker, John Lee
American. Singer
Had rhythm and blues million-seller, 1948,
"Boogie Chillin'."
b. Aug 22, 1917 in Clarksdale, Mississippi
Source: *EncFCWM 69; IlEncBM 82; WhoAm
74; WhoBlA 75*

Hooker, Joseph
"Fighting Joe"
American. Military Leader
Union general in Civil War; commanded
Army of the Potomac, 1862-63.
b. Nov 13, 1814 in Hadley, Massachusetts
d. Oct 31, 1879 in Garden City, New York
Source: *AmBi; ApCAB; DcAmB; TwCBDA;
WebAB; WhAm HS*

Hooker, Richard
English. Theologian
b. Mar 1554 in Heavitree, England
d. Nov 2, 1600 in Bishopsbourne, England
Source: *Alli; BbD; BiD&SB; BrAu; CasWL;*
Chambr 1; CroE&S; CrtT 1; DcEnA; DcEnL;
DcEuL; DcLEL; EvLB; NewC; OxEng; PenC
ENG; REn; WebE&AL

Hooker, Thomas
English. Clergyman
Emigrated to MA, 1633; founded Hartford,
CT, 1636.
b. 1586 in Marfield, England
d. Jul 19, 1647 in Hartford, Connecticut
Source: *DcAmB; EncAB-H; McGEWB;*
WebAB; WhAm HS

Hooks, Benjamin Lawson
American. Civil Rights Leader, Minister
Director, NAACP, 1977--, succeeding Roy
Wilkins.
b. Jan 31, 1925 in Memphis, Tennessee
Source: *BioNews 74; CivR 74; CurBio 78;*
Ebony 1; NewYTBE 72; NewYTBS 76, 79;
NewYTET; WhoAm 78, 80, 82, 84; WhoAmP
77, 79; WhoBlA 75

Hooks, Robert
American. Actor
Founder, Negro Ensemble Co.; appeared in
TV series "NYPD," 1967-69.
b. Apr 18, 1937 in Washington, District of
Columbia
Source: *CurBio 70; FilmgC; NotNAT; PIP&P*
A; WhoAm 82; WhoBlA 75; WhoHol A;
WhoThe 77

Hooper, Harry Bartholomew
American. Baseball Player
Outfielder, 1909-25; Hall of Fame, 1971.
b. Aug 24, 1887 in Santa Clara County,
California
d. Dec 18, 1974 in Santa Cruz, California
Source: *BaseEn 85; BasesB*

Hooper, 'Stix'
see: Crusaders, The

Hooper, William
American. Lawyer
Member, Continental Congress, 1775-77;
signed Declaration of Independence, 1776.
b. Jun 17, 1742 in Boston, Massachusetts
d. Oct 14, 1790 in Hillsboro, North Carolina
Source: *AmBi; ApCAB; BiAUS; BiDrAC;*
DcAmB; Drake; TwCBDA; WhAm HS;
WhAmP

Hooton, Earnest Albert
American. Anthropologist
b. Nov 20, 1887 in Clemansville, Wisconsin
d. May 3, 1954 in Cambridge, Massachusetts
Source: *AmAu&B; CurBio 40, 54; DcAmB S5;*
REnAL; TwCA, SUP; WebAB; WhAm 3

Hoover, Herbert Clark
American. US President
Administration dominated by Great
Depression; pres. library dedicated in
hometown, 1962.
b. Aug 10, 1874 in West Branch, Iowa
d. Oct 20, 1964 in New York, New York
Source: *AmAu&B; AmLY; BiDrAC; BiDrUSE;*
ConAu 108, 89; CurBio 43; EncAB-H;
OxAmL; REn; REnAL; WebAB; WhAmP;
WhNAA

Hoover, J(ohn) Edgar
American. Government Official
Director of FBI, 1924-72; established
fingerprint file, crime lab.
b. Jan 1, 1895 in Washington, District of
Columbia
d. May 2, 1972 in Washington, District of
Columbia
Source: *AmAu&B; ConAu 33R; CurBio 72N;*
EncAB-H; SpyCS; WebAB; WhAm 5; WhScrn
77

Hoover, Lou Henry
[Mrs. Herbert Hoover]
American. First Lady
Dignified, brilliant White House hostess; she
and husband translated *De Re Metallica.*
b. Mar 29, 1875 in Waterloo, Iowa
d. Jan 7, 1944 in New York, New York
Source: *CmCal; CurBio 44; GoodHs; HerW;*
NotAW; ObitOF 79; WhAm 2

Hoover, William K
"Boss"
American. Businessman
Purchased rights to suction sweeper, 1908;
marketed by offering 10-day free, in-home
trial.
b. 1849
d. 1932
Source: *Entr*

Hopalong Cassidy
see: Boyd, William (Bill)

Hope, Anthony
English. Author
b. Feb 7, 1863 in London, England
d. Jul 8, 1933 in Tadworth, England
Source: *BiD&SB; Chambr 3; CyWA; DcBiA; DcEnA AP; DcLEL; EvLB; FilmgC; LongCTC; ModBrL; NewC; OxEng; PenC ENG; REn; TwCA, SUP; TwCWr; WhoChL*

Hope, Bob (Leslie Townes)
American. Comedian, Actor
Made annual trips to entertain American troops, 1940-72; won four special Oscars.
b. May 29, 1903 in Eltham, England
Source: *AmAu&B; BiDFilm; BiE&WWA; BkPepl; CelR; ConAu 101; CurBio 41, 53; EncMT; FilmgC; IntMPA 75, 76, 77, 78, 79, 80, 81, 82; IntWW 80; MotPP; MovMk; NewYTBE 71; OhA&B; OxFilm; WebAB; Who 74; WhoAm 74, 76, 78, 80, 82; WhoHol A; WhoThe 77A; WhoWor 78*

Hopf, Hans
German. Opera Singer
b. Aug 2, 1916 in Nuremberg, Germany
Source: *WhoMus 72*

Hopkin, Mary
Welsh. Singer
Discovered by the Beatles; best known song "Those Were the Days," 1968.
b. May 3, 1950 in Ystradgynlais, Wales
Source: *RolSEnR 83; WhoAm 74*

Hopkins, Anthony
Welsh. Actor
Won Emmy, 1976, for "The Lindbergh Kidnapping Case"; films include *Magic,* 1978; *The Elephant Man,* 1980.
b. Dec 31, 1937 in Port Talbot, Wales
Source: *BioIn 12; CurBio 80; IntMPA 82; PIP&P; Who 74; WhoAm 80, 82; WhoHol A; WhoThe 77*

Hopkins, Arthur
American. Director, Producer
Best known for plays *Poor Little Rich Girl; Glory Road.*
b. Oct 4, 1878 in Cleveland, Ohio
d. Mar 22, 1950 in New York, New York
Source: *AmAu&B; NotNAT A, B; OhA&B; REn; REnAL; WhThe*

Hopkins, Bo
American. Actor
Known for "tough guy" roles: *The Wild Bunch,* 1969; *American Graffiti,* 1973.
b. Feb 2, 1942 in Greenwood, South Carolina
Source: *FilmEn; IntMPA 82; WhoHol A*

Hopkins, Claude
American. Musician
b. Aug 3, 1903 in Washington, District of Columbia
Source: *AmSCAP 66; WhoJazz 72*

Hopkins, Fredrick, Sir
English. Biochemist
b. Jun 30, 1861 in Eastbourne, England
d. May 16, 1947 in Cambridge, England
Source: *McGEWB; NewCol 75*

Hopkins, Gerard Manley
English. Poet
b. Jun 28, 1844 in Stratford, England
d. Jun 8, 1889 in Dublin, Ireland
Source: *AnCL; AtlBL; BrAu 19; CasWL; Chambr 3; ChhPo, S1, S2; CnE&AP; CnMWL; CrtT 3; CyWA; DcLEL; EvLB; LongCTC; ModBrL, S1; NewC; OxEng; PenC ENG; RAdv 1; RComWL; REn; WebE&AL; WhoTwCL*

Hopkins, Harry Lloyd
American. Presidential Aide
b. Aug 17, 1890 in Sioux City, Iowa
d. Jan 29, 1946 in New York, New York
Source: *BiDrUSE; CurBio 41, 46; DcAmB S4; EncAB-H; WebAB; WhAm 2; WhAmP*

Hopkins, John Henry
American. Religious Leader, Author
First Episcopal bishop of VT, 1832; wrote *The American Citizen,* 1857.
b. Jan 30, 1792 in Dublin, Ireland
d. Jan 9, 1868 in Rock Pointe, Vermont
Source: *AmAu; ApCAB; BbD; PoIre*

Hopkins, Johns
American. Financier, Philanthropist
Bequeathed $7 million for founding of Johns Hopkins U, Johns Hopkins Hospital.
b. May 19, 1795 in Anne Arundel, Maryland
d. Dec 24, 1873 in Baltimore, Maryland
Source: *AmBi; ApCAB; DcAmB; TwCBDA; WhAm HS*

Hopkins, "Lightnin'" (Sam)
American. Singer, Musician
Blues singer, guitarist, whose nickname was derived from partner "Thunder" Smith; recorded 100 singles.
b. Mar 15, 1912 in Centerville, Texas
d. Jan 30, 1982 in Houston, Texas
Source: *AnObit 1982; BiDAmM; BluesWW; EncFCWM 69; IlEncJ; NewYTBS 82; WhoAm 82*

Hopkins, Mark
American. Educator
Professor of philosophy, 1830-87; pres.,
   Williams College, 1836-72.
b. Feb 4, 1802 in Stockbridge, Massachusetts
d. Jun 17, 1887 in Williamstown,
   Massachusetts
Source: *Alli, SUP; AmAu; AmAu&B; AmBi;
ApCAB; BbD; BiD&SB; CyAL 1; DcAmAu;
DcAmB; DcNAA; OxAmL; REnAL; TwCBDA;
WebAB; WhAm HS*

Hopkins, Miriam
American. Actress
Sophisticated blonde in films: *Design for
   Living*, 1933; *Becky Sharp*, 1935.
b. Oct 18, 1902 in Bainbridge, Georgia
d. Oct 9, 1972 in New York, New York
Source: *BiDFilm; BiE&WWA; FilmgC;
InWom; MotPP; MovMk; NewYTBE 72;
OxFilm; ThFT; WhAm 5; WhScrn 77;
WhoHol B; WorEFlm*

Hopkins, Stephen
American. Merchant, Judge
b. Mar 7, 1707 in Providence, Rhode Island
d. Jul 13, 1785 in Providence, Rhode Island
Source: *Alli; AmBi; ApCAB; BiAUS; BiDrAC;
DcAmAu; DcAmB; DcNAA; Drake; OxAmL;
REnAL; TwCBDA; WhAm HS; WhAmP*

Hopkins, Telma Louise
[Tony Orlando and Dawn]
American. Actress, Singer
Part of singing group Dawn; co-stars in TV
   series "Gimme a Break."
b. Oct 28, 1948 in Louisville, Kentucky
Source: *InB&W 80*

Hopkinson, Francis
American. Patriot, Poet
Governor of colonial RI, 1755-68; signed
   Declaration of Independence, 1776; wrote
   satire of English *Battle of the Kegs*, 1778.
b. Sep 21, 1737 in Philadelphia, Pennsylvania
d. May 9, 1791 in Philadelphia, Pennsylvania
Source: *Alli; AmAu; AmAu&B; AmBi;
ApCAB; BbD; BiD&SB; BiDrAC; CasWL;
ChhPo, S1; CnDAL; CyAL 1; DcAmAu;
DcAmB; DcLEL; DcNAA; EvLB; OxAmL;
PenC AM; REn; REnAL; TwCBDA; WebAB;
WhAm HS; WhAmP*

Hoppe, Arthur Watterson
American. Journalist
b. Apr 23, 1925 in Honolulu, Hawaii
Source: *AmAu&B; ConAu 5R, 3NR; WhoAm
74, 76, 78, 80, 82; WhoWest 84; WrDr 76*

Hoppe, Willie (William F)
American. Billiards Player
Acknowledged as greatest billiards player in
   history of game, 1903-52.
b. Oct 11, 1887 in New York, New York
d. Feb 1, 1959 in Miami, Florida
Source: *CurBio 47, 59; WebAB*

Hopper, Dennis
American. Actor, Director
Appeared in *Rebel without a Cause*, 1957;
   starred in *Easy Rider*, 1969.
b. May 17, 1936 in Dodge City, Kansas
Source: *CelR; FilmgC; IntMPA 75, 76, 77,
78, 79, 80, 81, 82; MotPP; MovMk;
NewYTBE 70; WhoAm 74, 76, 78, 80, 82;
WhoHol A*

Hopper, De Wolfe (William De Wolfe)
American. Actor
Noted for recitations of "Casey at the Bat."
b. Mar 30, 1858 in New York, New York
d. Sep 23, 1935 in Kansas City, Missouri
Source: *AmAu&B; DcNAA; Film 1; WebAB;
WhoStg 1908*

Hopper, Edward
"Painter of Loneliness"
American. Artist
Known for starkly realistic scenes of city
   streets, theater interiors, lunch counters,
   etc.: "Early Sunday Morning," 1930.
b. Jul 22, 1882 in Nyack, New York
d. May 15, 1967 in New York, New York
Source: *AtlBL; CurBio 50, 67; DcCAA 71;
EncAB-H; REn; WebAB; WhAm 4*

Hopper, Grace Brewster Murray
"Amazing Grace"; "Grand Old Lady of
   Software "
American. Military Leader, Mathematician,
   Educator
Rear admiral who was oldest active military
   officer, 1943-86; co-invented computer
   language COBOL.
b. Dec 9, 1906 in New York, New York
Source: *AmM&WS 76P, 79P, 82P; LElec;
NewYTBE 71; WhoAm 76, 78, 80, 82;
WhoAmW 72, 83; WhoFrS 84*

Hopper, Hedda
[Elda Furry]
American. Journalist, Actress
Began 28-year career as Hollywood gossip
    columnist, 1938; famous for her hats.
b. Jun 2, 1890 in Hollidaysburg,
    Pennsylvania
d. Feb 1, 1966 in Hollywood, California
Source: *AmAu&B; ConAu 89; CurBio 42, 66;
Film 1; InWom; MovMk; OxFilm; ThFT;
TwYS; WebAB; WhAm 4; WhScrn 74, 77;
WhoHol B; WorEFlm*

Hopper, William
American. Actor
Starred as Paul Drake on TV's "Perry
    Mason," 1957-65; son of Hedda Hopper.
b. Jan 26, 1915 in New York, New York
d. Mar 6, 1970 in Palm Springs, California
Source: *FilmgC; WhScrn 74, 77; WhoHol B*

Hoppner, John
English. Artist
b. Apr 4, 1758 in London, England
d. Jan 23, 1810
Source: *AtlBL; NewCol 75*

Hopwood, Avery
American. Dramatist
b. May 28, 1882 in Cleveland, Ohio
d. Jul 1, 1928 in Juan les Pins, France
Source: *AmAu&B; CnDAL; DcNAA; EncMys;
McGEWD; ModWD; OhA&B; OxAmL;
REnAL*

Horace
[Quintus Horatius Flaccus]
Roman. Poet, Satirist
b. Dec 8, 65 in Venosa, Lucania
d. Nov 27, 8
Source: *AtlBL; BbD; BiD&SB; CasWL;
ChhPo; CyWA; DcEnL; DcEuL; NewC;
OxEng; PenC CL; RComWL; REn; WebBD
80*

Horan, James David
American. Historian, Author
Historian who specialized in, wrote several
    books on Old West.
b. Jul 27, 1914 in New York, New York
d. Oct 13, 1981 in New York, New York
Source: *AmAu&B; ConAu 105; IntWW 81;
WhoAm 80*

Horchow, S(amuel) Roger
American. Businessman, Author
Publisher of catalogue offering elegant,
    expensive goods: *The Horchow Collection.*
b. Jul 3, 1928 in Cincinnati, Ohio
Source: *ConAu 106; St&PR 84; WhoAm 84;
WhoS&SW 80*

Horder, Thomas Jeeves
[First Baron Horder]
English. Physician
Foremost clinician of his time whose patients
    included George V, George VI, Elizabeth
    II.
b. Jan 7, 1871 in Shaftsbury, England
d. Aug 13, 1955 in Petersfield, England
Source: *CurBio 55; DcNaB 1951; InSci;
WhE&EA*

Hordern, Michael
English. Actor
Character actor in films from 1940, in many
    PBS Shakespeare plays.
b. Oct 3, 1911 in Berkhampstead, England
Source: *CnThe; FilmEn; FilmgC; IntMPA 81;
MovMk; WhoHol A; WhoThe 77*

Hore-Belisha, Leslie, Baron
English. Political Leader, Lawyer
b. Sep 7, 1893 in Kilburn, England
d. Feb 16, 1957 in Reims, France
Source: *CurBio 41, 57*

Horenstein, Jascha
Russian. Conductor, Composer
b. May 6, 1899 in Kiev, Russia
d. Apr 2, 1973 in London, England
Source: *NewYTBE 73; WhAm 5; WhoMus 72*

Horgan, Paul
American. Author
Won Pulitzers for *Great River*, 1954; *Lamy
    of Santa Fe*, 1975.
b. Aug 1, 1903 in Buffalo, New York
Source: *AmAu&B; AmNov; Au&Wr 71;
AuBYP; CathA 1930; ChhPo; CnDAL; ConAu
13R; ConLC 9; ConNov 72, 76; DcLEL;
DrAF 76; DrAS 74H; IlsCB 1744; OxAmL;
REnAL; TwCA SUP; WhNAA; WhoAm 74,
76, 78, 80, 82; WhoE 74; WhoGov 75;
WhoWor 78; WrDr 76*

Horikoshi, Jiro
Japanese. Aeronautical Engineer
Designed the Zero fighter plane used during
    WW II.
b. 1904
d. Jan 11, 1982 in Tokyo, Japan
Source: *AnObit 1982; NewYTBS 82*

Horlick, Alexander James
British. Manufacturer
b. Oct 3, 1873 in Racine, Wisconsin
d. Jun 6, 1950
Source: *BioIn 2, 4, 5; WhAm 3*

Horlick, William
American. Industrialist
b. Feb 23, 1846 in Gloucester, England
d. Sep 25, 1936
Source: *BioIn 4, 5; WhAm 1*

Hormel, George Albert
American. Meat Packer
Founder, pres. George A Hormel & Co.,
1892-1928; produced first canned hams in
US.
b. Dec 4, 1860 in Buffalo, New York
d. Jun 5, 1946 in Los Angeles, California
Source: *DcAmB S4; WhAm 2*

Horn, Alfred Aloysius, pseud.
[Alfred Aloysius Smith]
"Trader"
English. Adventurer, Author
African West Coast merchant; wrote best-
seller *Trader Horn,* 1927.
b. 1854 in Lancashire, England
d. Jun 26, 1927 in Whitstable, England
Source: *IlBEAAW; LongCTC; TwCA, SUP*

Horn, Paul Joseph
American. Musician
b. Mar 17, 1930 in New York, New York
Source: *AmSCAP 66; WhoAm 74; WhoWest
84*

Horn, Tom
American. Lawman, Murderer
Hired by WY Cattleman's Assn. to eliminate
small ranchers, rustlers; hanged for
murder.
b. 1860 in Memphis, Missouri
d. Nov 20, 1903 in Cheyenne, Wyoming
Source: *BioIn 1, 6, 7, 10, 11; Blood&B;
DcAmB; EncACr; REnAW*

Hornby, Leslie
see: Twiggy

Horne, Josh L
American. Editor, Publisher
b. Dec 21, 1887 in Whitakers, North
Carolina
d. Mar 15, 1974 in Rocky Mount, North
Carolina
Source: *St&PR 75; WhAm 6; WhoAm 74*

Horne, Lena Calhoun
American. Singer, Actress
Nightclub entertainer known for song
"Stormy Weather"; starred on Broadway
in "Lena Horne: The Lady and Her
Music," 1980-82.
b. Jun 30, 1917 in Brooklyn, New York
Source: *BiE&WWA; BkPepl; CelR; CurBio
85; EncMT; FilmgC; InWom; IntMPA 82;
MotPP; MovMk; NewYTBE 72; NotNAT;
WhoAm 82; WhoBlA 75*

Horne, Marilyn
American. Opera Singer
b. Jan 16, 1934 in Bradford, Pennsylvania
Source: *CelR; CurBio 67; InWom; IntWW
74; NewYTBE 70, 71; WhoAm 74, 76, 78,
80, 82; WhoAmW 77; WhoE 74; WhoMus
72; WhoWor 78*

Horner, Bob (James Robert)
American. Baseball Player
Infielder, Atlanta, 1978--; 11th ML player to
hit four home runs in one game, 1986.
b. Aug 6, 1957 in Junction City, Kansas
Source: *BaseEn 85; BaseReg 86*

Horner, Jack (John R)
American. Paleontologist
Discovered nesting sites of dinosaurs, 1978.
b. 1946 in Shelby, Montana
Source: *ConNews 85-2*

Horner, Matina Souretis
American. Educator
Pres., Radcliffe College, 1972--.
b. Jul 28, 1939 in Boston, Massachusetts
Source: *AmM&WS 78S; CurBio 73; GoodHs;
LEduc 74; WhoAm 74, 76, 78, 80, 82;
WhoAmW 74, 75, 79; WhoE 74, 75, 77, 79*

Horney, Karen Danielson
American. Psychoanalyst
Founded, American Institute of
Psychoanalysis, 1941.
b. Sep 16, 1885 in Hamburg, Germany
d. Dec 4, 1952 in New York, New York
Source: *AmAu&B; CurBio 41, 53; DcAmB S5;
InWom; NewYTBE 73; TwCA SUP; WhAm 3*

Hornsby, Rogers
"Rajah"
American. Baseball Player, Baseball Manager
Infielder, 1915-37; had best lifetime batting
average for right-handed hitter -.358; Hall
of Fame, 1942.
b. Apr 27, 1896 in Winters, Texas
d. Jan 5, 1963 in Chicago, Illinois
Source: *BaseEn 85; CurBio 52, 63; NewYTBE
73; WebAB; WhAm 4; WhoProB 73*

Hornung, Ernest William
English. Author
Best known for stories featuring A J Raffles
and sidekick, Bunny, similar to Doyle's
Holmes/Watson tales.
b. Jun 7, 1866 in Middlesbrough, England
d. Mar 22, 1921 in Saint Jean de Luz,
France
Source: *BbD; BiD&SB; Chambr 3; ConAu
108; DcLEL; EncMys; EvLB; LongCTC;
MnBBF; NewC; REn; TwCA SUP; TwCWr*

Hornung, Paul Vernon
"The Golden Boy"
American. Football Player, Football Coach
Runner, placekicker, Green Bay Packers,
1957-66; suspended, 1963, with Alex
Karras for gambling; Hall of Fame, 1986.
b. Dec 23, 1935 in Louisville, Kentucky
Source: *CurBio 63; WhoFtbl 74*

Horovitz, Israel
American. Dramatist
b. Mar 31, 1939 in Wakefield, Massachusetts
Source: *CelR; ConAu 33R; CroCD; DrAF 76;
DrAP 75; ModAL S1; NatPD; NotNAT;
WhoAm 74, 76, 78, 80, 82; WhoThe 81;
WrDr 76*

Horowitz, David Joel
American. Author
Co-author, with Peter Collier, *The Fords: An
American Epic,* 1986.
b. Jan 10, 1939 in New York, New York
Source: *WhoAm 84*

Horowitz, Vladimir
American. Musician
Pianist; won 15 Grammys for best classical
performance.
b. Oct 1, 1904 in Kiev, Russia
Source: *BioNews 74; CelR; CurBio 43, 66;
IntWW 74; NewYTBS 74; Who 74; WhoAm
74, 76, 78, 80, 82; WhoMus 72; WhoWor 74,
76, 78*

Horrocks, Brian Gwynne, Sir
British. Army Officer
Helped to defeat Rommel's forces in Africa,
1942; his forces annihilated at Arnhem,
1944.
b. Sep 7, 1895 in Rainkhet, India
d. Jan 6, 1985 in Fishbourne, England
Source: *CurBio 85; IntWW 78; WhWW-II;
Who 74; WhoWor 78; WrDr 80*

Horrocks, Jeremiah
[Jeremiah Horrox]
English. Astronomer
Made first observation of transit of Venus,
1639.
b. 1617
d. 1641
Source: *BioIn 8; NewCol 75*

Horsbrugh, Florence
Scottish. Statesman
b. 1889 in Edinburgh, Scotland
d. Dec 6, 1969 in Edinburgh, Scotland
Source: *BioIn 8; CurBio 52, 70*

Horsley, Lee
American. Actor
Starred in TV series "Matt Houston," 1982-
84.
b. May 15, 1955 in Muleshoe, Texas
Source: *ConTFT 3; VarWW 85; WhoTelC*

Horst, Louis
American. Dancer
Musical director, Martha Graham Dance
Company, 1926-48.
b. Jan 12, 1884 in Kansas City, Missouri
d. Jan 23, 1964 in New York, New York
Source: *DcAmB S7; WebBD 80*

Horstmann, Dorothy Millicent
American. Physician
b. Jul 2, 1911 in Spokane, Washington
Source: *AmM&WS 73P; WhoAm 74, 76, 78,
80, 82; WhoAmW 74*

Horthy de Nagybanya, Nicholas
[Miklos von Nagybanya]
Hungarian. Admiral, Political Leader
Dictator of Hungary, 1920-44; aided Hitler in
WW II.
b. Jun 18, 1868 in Kenderes, Hungary
d. Mar 9, 1957 in Estoril, Portugal
Source: *CurBio 57; LinLib S; McGEWB*

Horton, Edward Everett
American. Actor
Known for tag line in comic roles: "Oh
dear, oh dear,"; often Fred Astaire's
sidekick.
b. Mar 18, 1886 in New York, New York
d. Sep 29, 1970 in Encino, California
Source: *BiE&WWA; CurBio 70; FilmgC;
MotPP; MovMk; NewYTBE 70; OxFilm;
TwYS; Vers A; WhAm 5; WhScrn 74, 77;
WhoHol B; WorEFlm*

Horton, Johnny
"Singing Fisherman"
American. Singer
Country singer who crossed over to pop
charts; hit single "Battle of New Orleans,"
1959.
b. Apr 30, 1927 in Tyler, Texas
d. Nov 5, 1960 in Austin, Texas
Source: *BiDAmM; EncFCWM 69; ObitOF 79;
RkOn 74; RolSEnR 83; WhoRock 81*

Horton, Robert
American. Actor
Starred in TV series "Wagon Train," 1957-
62, "A Man Called Shenandoah," 1965-66.
b. Jul 29, 1924 in Los Angeles, California
Source: *FilmgC; IntMPA 82; MotPP; WhoE
74; WhoHol A; WhoThe 77A; WhoWest 74*

Horton, Tim (Miles Gilbert)
Canadian. Hockey Player
Defenseman who played 24 years in NHL,
20 with Toronto; Hall of Fame, 1977.
b. Jan 12, 1930 in Cochrane, Ontario
d. Feb 21, 1974 in Saint Catherines, Ontario
Source: *HocEn; WhoHcky 73*

Horton, Willie (William Wattison)
American. Baseball Player
Outfielder, Detroit, 1963-77; had 325 career
home runs.
b. Oct 18, 1942 in Arno, Virginia
Source: *BaseEn 85; BioIn 8, 9; WhoProB 73*

Hosea
Prophet
Call for Israel to repent sins recorded in Old
Testament book of Hosea.
Source: *DcOrL 3; McGEWB*

Hosking, Eric J
English. Ornithologist
b. Oct 2, 1909
Source: *Who 74*

Hoskins, Allen Clayton
[Our Gang]
"Farina"
American. Actor
Played pigtailed Farina in over 100 *Our
Gang* episodes.
b. Aug 9, 1920 in Chelsea, Massachusetts
d. Jul 26, 1980 in Oakland, California
Source: *DrBlPA; WhoHol A*

Hoskins, Bob
English. Actor
Cockney actor; won Cannes best actor
honors for *Mona Lisa*, 1986.
b. Oct 26, 1942 in Bury St. Edmunds,
England
Source: *ConTFT 2; VarWW 85*

Hosmer, Craig (Chester Craig)
American. Lawyer, Politician
Representative from CA, 1953-1975; lobbyied
for nuclear energy.
b. May 16, 1915 in Borea, California
d. Oct 11, 1982
Source: *BiDrAC; CngDr 74; CurBio 83;
NewYTBS 82; WhoAm 82; WhoAmP 79;
WhoGov 75; WhoS&SW 76*

Hosmer, Harriet Goodhue
American. Sculptor
b. Oct 9, 1830 in Watertown, Massachusetts
d. Feb 21, 1908 in Watertown, Massachusetts
Source: *AmBi; AmWom; ApCAB; DcAmB;
Drake; InWom; NotAW; TwCBDA; WhAm 1*

Hostages, The
[Thomas Leo Ahern, Jr.; Clair Cortland
Barnes; William E Belk; Robert Olof
Blucker; Donald Cooke; William J
Daugherty; Robert A Englemann; William
Gallegos; Bruce W German; Duane
Gillette; Alan Bruce Golacinski; John Earl
Graves; Joseph M Hall; Kevin Jay
Hermening; Donald Hohman; Leland
James Holland;Michael Howland; Charles
A Jones, Jr.; Malcolm Kalp; Moorehead
Cowell Kennedy, Jr.; William Francis
Keough, Jr.; Steven William Kirtley;
Kathryn L Koob; Frederic Lee Kupke;
(Lowell) Bruce Laingen; Steven
Lauterbach; Gary Earl Lee; Paul Edward
Lewis; John William Limbert, Jr.; James
Michael Lopez; Johnny McKeel; Michael
John Metrinko; Jerry J Miele; Michael E
Moeller; Bert C Moore; Richard H
Morefield; Paul M Needham, Jr.; Robert
C Ode; Gregory A Persinger; Jerry
Plotkin; Richard I Queen; Regis Ragan;
David Roeder; Barry Rosen; William
Blacburn Royer, Jr.; Thomas E Schaefer;
Charles Wesly Scott; Donald A Sharer;
Rodney Virgil Sickmann; Joseph Subic, Jr.;
Elizabeth Ann Swift; Victor Lloyd
Tomseth; Phillip R Ward]
Americans.
Held captive in Iran by Ayatollah Khomeini
for 444 days, 1979-81; crisis contributed to
1980 election defeat of Jimmy Carter;
released on Inauguration Day, 1981.
Source: *NewYTBS 81*

Hot Tuna
[Jack Casady; Papa John Creach; Jorma
  Kaukonen; Sammy Piazza; Will Scarlett;
  Bob Steeler]
American. Music Group
Satellite group of Jefferson Airplane, 1972-78.
Source: *RolSEnR 83*

Hotchkiss, Benjamin Berkeley
American. Inventor
Invented Hotchkiss machine gun, 1872;
  magazine rifle, 1875.
b. Oct 1, 1826 in Watertown, Connecticut
d. Feb 14, 1885 in Paris, France
Source: *AmBi; ApCAB; DcAmB; TwCBDA;
WhAm HS*

Hotchner, Aaron Edward
American. Author, Editor
Long association with Ernest Hemingway
  resulted in memoir *Papa Hemingway.* 1966.
b. Jun 28, 1920 in Saint Louis, Missouri
Source: *AmAu&B; WhoAm 80; WhoE 74;
WhoWor 76; WrDr 80*

Hottelet, Richard C(urt)
American. Journalist
UN correspondent, CBS News.
b. Sep 22, 1917 in New York, New York
Source: *WhoAm 80, 82, 84*

Hotter, Hans
German. Opera Singer
Bass-baritone known for Wagnerian roles.
b. Jan 19, 1909 in Offenbach-am-Main,
  Germany
Source: *Baker 78; IntWW 74, 75, 76, 77, 78;
NewEOp 71; Who 74; WhoMus 72; WhoWor
74*

Houdin, Jean Eugene Robert
French. Magician
Houdini named himself after Houdin.
b. 1805 in Blois, France
d. 1871
Source: *NewCol 75; WebBD 80*

Houdini, Harry
[Ehrich Weiss; Erik Weisz]
American. Magician
Known for escapes from bonds, many of
  which have not been duplicated.
b. Mar 24, 1874 in Budapest, Hungary
d. Oct 31, 1926 in Detroit, Michigan
Source: *AmBi; DcAmB; DcNAA; Film 1;
FilmgC; OxFilm; TwYS; WebAB; WhAm 1;
WhScrn 74, 77; WhoHol B*

Houdon, Jean Antoine
French. Sculptor
b. Mar 20, 1741 in Versailles, France
d. Jul 15, 1828 in Paris, France
Source: *ApCAB; AtlBL; Drake; OxFr; REn*

Houdry, Eugene Jules
"Mr. Catalysis"
American. Inventor
Developed catalytic cracking process, 1927.
b. Apr 18, 1892 in Domont, France
d. Jul 18, 1962 in Upper Darby,
  Pennsylvania
Source: *DcAmB S7*

Hough, Henry Beetle
American. Journalist
Edited Martha's Vineyard *Vineyard Gazette,*
  from 1920s.
b. Nov 8, 1896 in New Bedford,
  Massachusetts
d. Jun 6, 1985 in Edgartown, Massachusetts
Source: *AmAu&B; ConAu 2NR, 116; REnAL*

Houghton, Amory
American. Business Executive, Government
  Official
Pres., Corning Glass Works, 1930-71;
  ambassador to France, 1958-61.
b. Jul 27, 1899 in Corning, New York
d. Feb 21, 1981 in Charleston, South
  Carolina
Source: *CurBio 81; IntWW 78; IntYB 79;
WhoAm 80; WhoF&I 79*

Houghton, Henry Oscar
American. Publisher
b. Apr 30, 1823 in Sutton, Vermont
d. Aug 25, 1895 in North Andover,
  Massachusetts
Source: *AmAu&B; AmBi; ApCAB; DcAmB;
TwCBDA; WhAm HS*

Houghton, Katharine
American. Actress
Niece of Katherine Hepburn; starred with
  her in *Guess Who's Coming to Dinner?*
  1967.
b. Mar 10, 1945 in Hartford, Connecticut
Source: *FilmgC; WhoAm 82; WhoHol A*

Houk, Ralph George
"Major"
American. Baseball Player, Baseball Manager
Manager, NY Yankees, 1961-63, 1966-73;
  Detroit, 1974-78; Boston, 1981-84.
b. Aug 9, 1919 in Lawrence, Kansas
Source: *BaseEn 85; CelR; CurBio 62; WhoAm
74, 76, 78, 80, 82; WhoE 74; WhoProB 73*

Houle, Rejean
"Reggie"
Canadian. Hockey Player
Left wing; won two Stanley Cups with
Montreal Canadiens.
b. Oct 25, 1949 in Rouyn Noranda, Quebec
Source: *HocEn; WhoHcky 73*

Hoult, Norah
Irish. Author, Journalist
b. Sep 20, 1898 in Dublin, Ireland
Source: *LongCTC; TwCA, SUP; Who 74;
WhoTwCL*

Hounsfield, Godfrey Newbold
English. Scientist
b. Aug 28, 1919 in Newark, England
Source: *BioIn 12; CurBio 80*

Houphouet-Boigny, Felix
African. Politician
b. Oct 18, 1905 in Ivory Coast
Source: *CurBio 58; IntWW 74*

House, Edward Mandell
American. Diplomat
Adviser to Woodrow Wilson; chief liaison
with Allied leaders during WW I.
b. Jul 26, 1858 in Houston, Texas
d. Mar 28, 1938 in New York, New York
Source: *AmAu&B; AmBi; DcAmB S2;
DcNAA; EncAB-H; OxAmL; TexWr; WebAB;
WhAm 1; WhAmP*

Hough, John
English. Director
Directed movie *Eyewitness,* 1981; TV series
"The Avengers," "The Saint."
b. Nov 21, 1941 in London, England
Source: *ConTFT 2; VarWW 85*

Household, Geoffrey
English. Author
Writes children's books, adventure stories:
Rogue Male, 1939.
b. Nov 30, 1900 in Bristol, England
Source: *ConAu 77; ConNov 72, 76; EncMys;
LongCTC; NewC; SmATA 14; TwCA, SUP;
Who 74; WhoSpyF; WhoWor 74, 76*

Houseman, John
[John Haussmann]
American. Actor, Director, Producer
Won Oscar, 1973, for *The Paper Chase;*
recreated role in TV series.
b. Sep 22, 1902 in Bucharest, Romania
Source: *BiDFilm; BiE&WWA; CelR; CurBio
59; FilmgC; IntMPA 75, 76, 77, 78, 79, 80,
81, 82; NotNAT; PIP&P; WhoAm 74, 76, 78,
80, 82; WhoHol A; WhoThe 77; WhoWor 78;
WorEFlm*

Housman, A(lfred) E(dward)
English. Poet, Scholar
b. Mar 26, 1859 in Fockbury, England
d. Apr 30, 1936 in Cambridge, England
Source: *AnCL; AtlBL; CasWL; Chambr 3;
ChhPo, S1, S2; CnE&AP; CnMWL; CyWA;
DcLEL; EncWL; EvLB; LongCTC; ModBrL,
S1; NewC; OxEng; PenC ENG; RAdv 1;
RComWL; REn; Str&VC; TwCA, SUP;
TwCWr; WebE&AL; WhoLA; WhoTwCL*

Housman, Laurence
English. Author, Dramatist
b. Jul 18, 1865 in Bromsgrove, England
d. Feb 20, 1959 in Somerset, England
Source: *Chambr 3; ChhPo, S1, S2; CnMD;
DcEnA AP; DcLEL; EvLB; IlsCB 1744; JBA
34; LongCTC; McGEWD; ModBrL; ModWD;
NewC; OxEng; OxThe; PenC ENG; REn;
TwCA, SUP; WhAm 3; WhoLA*

Houssay, Bernardo Alberto
Argentine. Physiologist, Educator
b. Apr 10, 1887 in Buenos Aires, Argentina
d. Sep 21, 1971 in Buenos Aires, Argentina
Source: *CurBio 48, 71; NewYTBE 71; WhAm
5*

Houston, Charles Hamilton
American. Lawyer, Civil Rights Leader
b. Sep 3, 1895 in Washington, District of
Columbia
d. Apr 22, 1950 in Washington, District of
Columbia
Source: *CurBio 50*

Houston, "Cissy" (Emily Drinkard)
[Sweet Inspirations]
American. Singer
Gospel-soul singer; first to record "Midnight
Train to Georgia"; mother of Whitney
Houston.
b. 1932 in Newark, New Jersey
Source: *RolSEnR 83*

Houston, Ken(neth Ray)
American. Football Player
Defensive end, 1967-80; holds NFL record
for most TDs on interceptions; Hall of
Fame, 1986.
b. Nov 12, 1944 in Lufkin, Texas
Source: *WhoAm 82; WhoFtbl 74*

Houston, Sam(uel)
American. Army Officer, Statesman
First pres., Republic of Texas, 1836-38, 1841-
44.
b. Mar 2, 1793 in Lexington, Virginia
d. Jul 26, 1863 in Huntsville, Texas
Source: *AmBi; ApCAB; BiDrAC; DcAmB;
Drake; WebAB; WhAm HS; WhAmP*

Houston, Whitney
American. Singer
Won Grammy, 1986, for top female pop
  vocalist; hits include "Saving All My Love
  for You," 1985.
b. Aug 9, 1963 in Newark, New Jersey
Source: *NF*

Hovey, Richard
American. Poet
Proclaimed joy of open road in *Songs from
  Vagabondia* series, 1894, 1901.
b. May 4, 1864 in Normal, Illinois
d. Feb 24, 1900
Source: *AmAu; AmAu&B; AmBi; ApCAB
SUP; BbD; BiD&SB; Chambr 3; ChhPo, S1,
S2; CnDAL; DcAmAu; DcAmB; DcLEL;
DcNAA; OxAmL; PenC AM; REn; REnAL;
TwCBDA; WhAm 1*

Hoveyda, Amir Abbas
Iranian. Political Leader
Prime Minister of Iran, 1965-77, who was
  Shah's advisor; executed by Islamic court.
b. Feb 18, 1919 in Teheran, Persia
d. Apr 7, 1979 in Teheran, Iran
Source: *CurBio 71, 79; IntWW 74, 75, 76,
77, 78; WhoWor 76, 78*

Hovhaness, Alan
American. Composer
b. Mar 8, 1911 in Somerville, Massachusetts
Source: *CurBio 65; DcCM; WhoAm 74, 76,
78, 80, 82; WhoWor 78*

Hoving, Thomas Pearsall Field
American. Art Historian
b. Jan 15, 1931 in New York, New York
Source: *ConAu 101; CurBio 67; IntWW 74;
Who 74; WhoAm 74, 76, 78, 80, 82;
WhoAmA 73; WhoE 74*

Hoving, Walter
American. Business Executive
b. Dec 2, 1897 in Stockholm, Sweden
Source: *CelR; CurBio 46; St&PR 75; WhoAm
74, 76, 78, 80, 82; WhoWor 78*

Howar, Barbara
American. Journalist, Author
b. Sep 27, 1934 in Nashville, Tennessee
Source: *AuNews 1, 2; ConAu 89; WhoAm 78,
80, 82; WrDr 76*

Howard, Anthony
British. Editor
b. Feb 12, 1934
Source: *Who 74; WhoAm 76; WhoWor 76*

Howard, Bronson Crocker
American. Dramatist
First professional American playwright; 21
  plays include *Shenandoah,* 1888.
b. Oct 7, 1842 in Detroit, Michigan
d. Aug 4, 1908 in Avon, New Jersey
Source: *AmAu&B; CnThe; EncWT;
McGEWD; ModWD; OxAmL; OxThe;
REnAL; REnWD; WhAm 1*

Howard, Catherine
English. Consort
Fifth wife of Henry VIII, married, 1540;
  beheaded for treason.
b. 1520
d. 1542
Source: *OxGer*

Howard, Clint
American. Actor
Starred in TV's "Gentle Ben," 1967-69;
  brother of Ron Howard.
b. Apr 20, 1959 in Burbank, California
Source: *WhoHol A*

Howard, Cordelia
American. Actress
Original Little Eva in *Uncle Tom's Cabin,* on
  stage, 1853.
b. Feb 1, 1848 in Providence, Rhode Island
d. Aug 10, 1941 in Belmont, Massachusetts
Source: *CurBio 41; NotNAT B*

Howard, "Curly" (Jerry)
[The Three Stooges]
American. Comedian
b. 1906 in Brooklyn, New York
d. Jan 19, 1952 in San Gabriel, California
Source: *MotPP; WhoHol B*

Howard, Ebenezer, Sir
English. Urban Planner
b. 1850
d. 1928
Source: *NewCol 75*

Howard, Eddy
American. Band Leader, Songwriter, Actor
b. Sep 12, 1909 in Woodland, California
d. May 23, 1963 in Palm Desert, California
Source: *AmSCAP 66; WhAm 4; WhScrn 74,
77; WhoHol B*

Howard, Elston Gene
"Ellie"
American. Baseball Player
Catcher, who was first black player to win
    MVP award, 1963; first black coach in
    AL, 1969.
b. Feb 23, 1929 in Saint Louis, Missouri
d. Dec 14, 1980 in New York, New York
Source: *BaseEn 85; BioNews 74; CurBio 81;
    WhoAm 74; WhoBlA 75; WhoProB 73*

Howard, Eugene
American. Comedian, Actor
b. 1881 in Neustadt, Germany
d. Aug 1, 1965 in New York, New York
Source: *BiE&WWA; WhScrn 74, 77; WhoHol
    B*

Howard, Frank Oliver
"The Capital Punisher"; "Hondo"
American. Baseball Player
Outfielder, 1958-73, known for tremendous
    home run power; led AL in home runs,
    1968, 1970.
b. Aug 8, 1936 in Columbus, Ohio
Source: *BaseEn 85; CurBio 72; WhoProB 73*

Howard, Jane Temple
American. Journalist, Author
b. May 4, 1935 in Springfield, Illinois
Source: *BioNews 74; ConAu 29R; WrDr 80*

Howard, Joseph Edgar
American. Entertainer, Songwriter
Wrote songs "Hello, My Baby"; "I Wonder
    Who's Kissing Her Now."
b. Feb 12, 1878 in New York, New York
d. May 19, 1961 in Chicago, Illinois
Source: *AmPS; AmSCAP 66; BiDAmM;
    CmpEPM; NotNAT B*

Howard, Ken(neth Joseph Jr.)
American. Actor, Singer
Won Theatre World Award for play *1776;*
    starred in TV series "White Shadow,"
    1978-81.
b. Mar 28, 1944 in El Centro, California
Source: *NotNAT; WhoAm 82; WhoE 74;
    WhoHol A; WhoThe 77*

Howard, Leslie
[Leslie Stainer]
English. Actor
Played Ashley Wilkes in *Gone with the
    Wind,* 1939.
b. Apr 3, 1893 in London, England
d. Jun 2, 1943 in Bay of Biscay
Source: *BiDFilm; CmMov; DcAmB S3;
    FamA&A; Film 1; FilmgC; MovMk; OxFilm;
    REn; WhAm 2; WhScrn 74, 77; WhoHol B;
    WorEFlm*

Howard, Moe
[The Three Stooges]
American. Comedian
b. Jun 19, 1897 in Brooklyn, New York
d. May 24, 1975 in Hollywood, California
Source: *MotPP; WhScrn 77*

Howard, Oliver Otis
American. Army Officer, Public Official
Union Civil War general; founded Howard
    Univ., 1867, in Washington, DC.
b. Nov 8, 1830 in Leeds, Maine
d. Oct 26, 1909 in Burlington, Vermont
Source: *Alli SUP; AmAu&B; BiD&SB;
    DcAmAu; DcNAA; WebAB*

Howard, Robert Ervin
[Patrick Ervin, pseud.]
American. Author
Fantasy writer known for popular *Conan the
    Barbarian* series.
b. Jan 22, 1906 in Peaster, Texas
d. Jun 12, 1936 in Cross Plains, Texas
Source: *BioIn 11; EncSF; FanAl; ScF&FL 1;
    WhNAA; WhoHr&F; WhoSciF*

Howard, Ron
American. Actor, Director
Played Opie on "The Andy Griffith Show,"
    1960-68, Richie Cunningham on "Happy
    Days," 1974-80; director *Splash; Cocoon.*
b. Mar 1, 1954 in Duncan, Oklahoma
Source: *BkPepl; IntMPA 75, 76, 77, 78, 79,
    80, 81, 82; WhoAm 78, 80, 82; WhoHol A*

Howard, Roy Wilson
American. Journalist
b. Jan 1, 1883 in Gano, Ohio
d. Nov 20, 1964 in New York, New York
Source: *AmAu&B; CurBio 40, 65; WebAB;
    WhAm 4; WhNAA*

Howard, "Shemp" (Samuel)
[The Three Stooges]
American. Comedian
b. Mar 17, 1900 in New York, New York
d. Nov 22, 1955 in Hollywood, California
Source: *FilmgC; MotPP; WhoHol B*

Howard, Sidney Coe
American. Dramatist, Journalist
b. Jun 26, 1891 in Oakland, California
d. Aug 23, 1939 in Tyringham,
    Massachusetts
Source: *AmAu&B; AmBi; CasWL; CnDAL;
    CnMD; CnThe; ConAmA; ConAmL; DcAmB
    S2; DcLEL; DcNAA; LongCTC; McGEWD;
    ModAL; ModWD; OxAmL; OxThe; PenC
    AM; REn; REnAL; REnWD; TwCA; SUP;
    WebAB; WebE&AL; WhAm 1*

Howard, Susan
[Jeri Lynn Mooney]
American. Actress
Plays Donna Culver Krebs on TV series
"Dallas."
b. Jan 28, 1943 in Marshall, Texas
Source: *BioIn 10*

Howard, Tom
British. Actor
Starred in two-reel comedies, 1930-36.
b. 1886 in Ireland
d. Feb 27, 1955 in Long Branch, New Jersey
Source: *WhScrn 74, 77; WhoHol B*

Howard, Trevor Wallace
English. Actor
Oscar nominee for *Sons and Lovers,* 1960;
    other films: *Gandhi,* 1982.
b. Sep 29, 1916 in Kent, England
Source: *BiDFilm; CelR; CmMov; FilmgC;
IntMPA 82; IntWW 74; MovMk; OxFilm;
Who 74; WhoThe 77; WhoWor 74; WorEFlm*

Howard, Willie
American. Comedian
b. 1886 in Germany
d. Jan 14, 1949 in New York, New York
Source: *DcAmB S4; EncMT; WhAm 3;
WhScrn 74, 77*

Howatch, Susan
American. Author
b. Jul 14, 1940 in Leatherhead, England
Source: *AuNews 1; ConAu 45; WrDr 80*

Howe, Clarence Decatur
Canadian. Politician, Economist
b. Jan 15, 1886 in Waltham, Massachusetts
d. Dec 31, 1960 in Montreal, Quebec
Source: *BioIn 1, 2, 3, 4, 5, 6, 8; CurBio 45,
61*

Howe, Edgar Watson
"Sage of Potato Hill"
American. Editor, Author
Wrote *Story of a Country Town,* 1883, early
    example of realism.
b. May 3, 1853 in Treaty, Indiana
d. Oct 3, 1937 in Atchison, Kansas
Source: *DcNAA; McGEWB; TwCA SUP;
WebAB 79*

Howe, Edmund Perry
American. Journalist
b. Dec 14, 1896 in Montpelier, Vermont
Source: *WhJnl*

Howe, Elias
American. Inventor
Patented first sewing machine, 1846.
b. Jul 9, 1819 in Spencer, Massachusetts
d. Oct 3, 1867 in Brooklyn, New York
Source: *AmBi; ApCAB; DcAmB; Drake;
EncAB-H; TwCBDA; WebAB; WhAm HS*

Howe, Gordie (Gordon)
American. Hockey Player
All-time NHL scoring leader with 801 goals,
    1049 assists.
b. Mar 31, 1928 in Saskatoon, Saskatchewan
Source: *BioNews 74; CanWW 82; CurBio 62;
HocEn; NewYTBE 73; NewYTBS 74; WhoAm
82; WhoHcky 73*

Howe, Harold, II
American. Educator
b. Aug 17, 1918 in Hartford, Connecticut
Source: *BioIn 7, 8, 9; CurBio 67; IntWW 74;
NewYTBE 70; WhoAm 82*

Howe, Irving
American. Author, Editor, Critic
b. Jun 11, 1920 in New York, New York
Source: *AmAu&B; ConAu 9R; DrAS 74E;
ModAL; RAdv 1; REnAL; TwCA SUP;
WhoAm 74, 76, 78, 80, 82; WhoWor 78;
WhoWorJ 72*

Howe, James Wong
American. Filmmaker
Cameraman who helped establish distinctive
    look of Warner Brothers pictures, 1940.
b. Aug 28, 1899 in Kwangtung, China
d. Jul 12, 1976 in Hollywood, California
Source: *CurBio 43; DcFM; FilmgC; IntMPA
75; OxFilm; WhoAm 74; WhoWor 78;
WorEFlm*

Howe, Joseph
Canadian. Author, Politician
Premier of Nova Scotia, 1863-66; against
    Nova Scotia entry into Canadian union.
b. Dec 13, 1804 in Halifax, Nova Scotia
d. Jun 1, 1873 in Nova Scotia
Source: *BbtC; Chambr 3; OxCan; REnAL*

Howe, Julia Ward
[Mrs. Samuel Gridley Howe]
American. Author, Social Reformer
Wrote poem, "Battle Hymn of the Republic,"
1862; became theme for Uni on Army.
b. May 27, 1819 in New York, New York
d. Oct 17, 1910 in Newport, Rhode Island
Source: *Alli; SUP; AmAu; AmAu&B; AmBi;*
AmWom; ApCAB; BbD; BiCAW; BiD&SB;
Chambr 3; ChhPo, SI, S2; CnDAL; CyAL 2;
DcAmAu; DcAmB; DcEnL; DcLEL; DcNAA;
Drake; EncAB-H; EvLB; FemPA; HerW;
InWom; NotAW; OxAmL; OxEng; PenC AM;
REn; REnAL; TwCBDA; WebAB; WebE&AL;
WhAm 1; WhAmP

Howe, Louis McHenry
Journalist, Secretary
Speechwriter, secretary to FDR.
b. Jan 14, 1871
d. Apr 18, 1936
Source: *DcAmB S2*

Howe, Mark De Wolfe
American. Editor, Author
Wrote nonfiction texts, biographies of New
England life; won 1924 Pulitzer for *Barrett
Wendell.*
b. May 22, 1906 in Boston, Massachusetts
d. Feb 28, 1967 in Cambridge, Massachusetts
Source: *AmAu&B; ConAu 89; WhAm 4;*
WhNAA

Howe, Mark Steven
American. Hockey Player
Defenseman; son of Gordie Howe; played
with father in World Hockey Assn.
b. May 28, 1955 in Detroit, Michigan
Source: *HocReg 85*

Howe, Oscar
American. Artist
b. May 13, 1915 in Joe Creek, South Dakota
Source: *BioIn 9; WhoAm 82; WhoAmA 73*

Howe, Quincy
American. Editor, Broadcaster
b. Aug 17, 1900 in Boston, Massachusetts
d. Feb 17, 1977 in New York, New York
Source: *AmAu&B; ConAu 49, 69; CurBio 40;*
EncMT; IntMPA 75, 76, 77; IntWW 74;
WhoAm 74

Howe, Richard
British. Admiral
b. Mar 19, 1725
d. Aug 5, 1799
Source: *Alli; ApCAB; Drake*

Howe, (Richard Edward) Geoffrey, Sir
Welsh. Government Official
Chancellor of Exchequer of England's
conservative Thatcher govt., 1979-83.
b. Dec 20, 1926 in Port Talbot, Wales
Source: *CurBio 80; IntWW 74, 75, 76, 77,*
78, 79, 80; IntYB 78, 79; NewYTBS 79; Who
74, 80, 85; WhoWor 74, 78

Howe, Samuel Gridley
American. Educator, Social Reformer
First to educate a blind deaf-mute child,
Laura Dewey Bridgman, 1837; pioneer in
education of mentally retarded children.
b. Nov 10, 1802 in Boston, Massachusetts
d. Jan 9, 1876 in Boston, Massachusetts
Source: *Alli; AmAu; AmAu&B; AmBi;*
ApCAB; DcAmAu; DcAmB; DcNAA; Drake;
EncAB-H; OxAmL; REn; REnAL; TwCBDA;
WebAB; WhAm HS

Howe, Syd(ney Harris)
Canadian. Hockey Player
Center, 1929-46; won three Stanley Cups
with Detroit; Hall of Fame, 1965.
b. Sep 28, 1911 in Ottawa, Ontario
Source: *HocEn; WhoHcky 73*

Howe, William, Viscount
English. General
Commanded British troops in American
Revolution; captured NYC, 1776; occupied
Philadelphia, 1777.
b. Aug 10, 1729 in London, England
d. Jul 12, 1814
Source: *Alli; AmBi; ApCAB; Drake; OxAmL;*
WhAm HS

Howell, Albert S
American. Businessman
With Donald Bell, formed Bell and Howell
Co., 1907, to make, service equipment for
film industry.
b. Apr 17, 1879 in West Branch, Michigan
d. Jan 3, 1951 in Chicago, Illinois
Source: *DcAmB S5; EncAB 8; Entr*

Howell, Clark
American. Journalist, Editor
b. Sep 21, 1863 in Barnwell County, South
Carolina
d. Nov 14, 1936 in Atlanta, Georgia
Source: *AmBi; BiDSA; DcAmB S2; DcNAA;*
WhAm 1; WhAmP

Howell, Harry (Henry Vernon)
Canadian. Hockey Player
Defenseman who spent 21 years in NHL;
Hall of Fame, 1979.
b. Dec 28, 1932 in Hamilton, Ontario
Source: *HocEn; WhoHcky 73*

Howell, Thomas Heflin
American. Politician
Dem. senator from AL, 1978--.
b. Jun 19, 1921 in Tuscumbia, Alabama
Source: *CngDr 85*

Howell, William H(enry)
American. Physiologist
Discovered Heparin, which prevents blood
clots.
b. Feb 20, 1860 in Baltimore, Maryland
d. Feb 6, 1945
Source: *CurBio 45; DcAmB S3*

Howells, Anne Elizabeth
English. Opera Singer
Lyric coloratura mezzo-soprano known for
numerous recordings.
b. Jan 12, 1941 in Southport, England
Source: *IntWW 78; Who 74; WhoMus 72;
WhoOp 76*

Howells, William Dean
American. Author, Editor
Wrote *A Modern Instance*, 1882, *The Rise of
Silas Lapham*, 1885.
b. Mar 1, 1837 in Martins Ferry, Ohio
d. May 10, 1920 in New York, New York
Source: *Alli SUP; AmAu; AmAu&B; AmBi;
AmWr; AtlBL; BbD; BiD&SB; CarSB;
CasWL; Chambr 3; ChhPo, S1, S2; CnDAL;
CrtT 3; CyAL 2; CyWA; DcAmAu; DcAmB;
DcBiA; DcEnA, AP; DcEnL; DcLEL; DcNAA;
EncAB-H; EncWL; EvLB; McGEWD;
ModAL, S1; ModWD; OhA&B; OxAmL;
OxEng; PenC AM; RAdv 1; RComWL; REn;
REnAL; WebAB; WebE&AL*

Howes, Frank Stewart
English. Music Critic, Educator
London *Times* music critic since 1925.
b. Apr 2, 1891 in Oxford, England
d. Sep 28, 1974 in Combe, England
Source: *ConAu 115; WhAm 6*

Howes, Sally Ann
English. Actress, Singer
Child star of 1940 British films, later in
Chitty, Chitty, Bang, Bang, 1968.
b. Jul 20, 1934 in London, England
Source: *BiE&WWA; EncMT; FilmgC;
InWom; MotPP; MovMk; NotNAT; Who 74;
WhoHol A; WhoThe 77*

Howitt, Mary
English. Translator, Children's Author
Known for translations of Scandinavian fairy
tales.
b. Mar 12, 1799 in Coleford, England
d. Jan 30, 1888 in Rome, Italy
Source: *BrAu 19; EvLB; NewC*

Howitt, William
English. Author
Wrote *Book of the Seasons*, 1831.
b. Dec 18, 1792 in Heanor, England
d. Mar 3, 1879 in Rome, England
Source: *BrAu 19; EvLB; NewC*

Howland, Alfred Cornelius
American. Artist
Drew landscapes; New England genre scenes:
"Old Farm," 1887.
b. Feb 12, 1838 in Walpole, New Hampshire
d. 1909 in Pasadena, California
Source: *ApCAB; DcAmB; EarABI; NatCAB 7;
NewYHSD; TwCBDA; WhAm 1*

Howland, Beth
American. Actress
Played Vera on TV series "Alice."
b. May 28, 1941 in Boston, Massachusetts
Source: *VarWW 85; WhoAm 84; WhoTelC*

Howland, Michael
[The Hostages]
American. Hostage in Iran
b. 1947
Source: *BioIn 12; NewYTBS 81*

Howlin' Wolf
[Chester Burnett]
American. Singer, Songwriter
Had rhythm and blues hits, 1954-64: "Little
Red Rooster," "Back Door Man."
b. Jun 10, 1910 in West Point, Mississippi
d. Jan 10, 1976 in Chicago, Illinois
Source: *EncPR&S 74; IlEncBM 82*

Howser, Dick (Richard Dalton)
American. Baseball Player, Baseball Manager
Infielder, 1961-68, manager, NY Yankees,
KC Royals.
b. May 14, 1937 in Miami, Florida
Source: *BaseEn 85; BioIn 12; WhoAm 82*

Hoxha, Enver
Albanian. Political Leader
Under his rigid leadership, Albania became
most isolated, poor country in Europe.
b. Oct 16, 1908 in Gjinokaster, Albania
d. Apr 11, 1985 in Tirana, Albania
Source: *CurBio 50; IntWW 74; WhoWor 78*

Hoyle, Edmond
English. Lawyer
Game expert who codified card game rules;
"according to Hoyle" has come to mean
"by highest authority."
b. 1672
d. Aug 29, 1769 in London, England
Source: *Alli; BiD&SB; BrAu; NewC; OxEng;
WhDW*

Hoyle, Fred
English. Author, Astronomer
Wrote *Nature of the Universe,* 1951, including
Steady State Theory, that universe is
steadily expanding.
b. Jun 24, 1915 in Bingley, England
Source: *Au&Wr 71; BioIn 4, 5, 6, 10; ConAu
5R, 3NR, 3NR; ConNov 72; TwCWr;
WhoWor 78; WorAu; WrDr 76*

Hoyt, Palmer (Edwin Palmer)
American. Newspaper Publisher
Publisher, editor Denver *Post,* 1946-71;
Portland *Oregonian,* 1938-46.
b. Mar 10, 1897 in Roseville, Illinois
d. Jun 25, 1979 in Denver, Colorado
Source: *ConAu 89; CurBio 43, 79; NewYTBS
79*

Hoyt, Lamarr (Dewey Lamarr)
American. Baseball Player
Pitcher, 1979--; won Cy Young Award, 1983.
b. Jan 1, 1955 in Columbia, South Carolina
Source: *BaseEn 85; BaseReg 86*

Hoyt, Lawrence W
American. Business Executive
Founded Walden Book Co., 1962.
b. 1901 in Brighton, Massachusetts
d. Dec 17, 1982 in Bridgeport, Connecticut
Source: *NewYTBS 82*

Hoyt, Waite Charles
"Schoolboy"
American. Baseball Player
Pitched for great Yankee teams of 1920s; one
of first athletes to work in broadcasting;
Hall of Fame, 1969.
b. Sep 9, 1899 in Brooklyn, New York
d. Aug 25, 1984 in Cincinnati, Ohio
Source: *BaseEn 85; BasesB*

Hrushevsky, Mykhailo
Ukrainian. Historian, Statesman
b. 1866
d. 1934
Source: *NewCol 75*

Hruska, Roman Lee
American. Senator
b. Aug 16, 1904 in David City, Nebraska
Source: *BiDrAC; CngDr 74; CurBio 56;
IntWW 74; WhoAm 74, 76, 78, 80, 82;
WhoAmP 73; WhoGov 75; WhoMW 74;
WhoWor 78*

Hu Na
Chinese. Tennis Player
Defected to US; China suspended cultural
exchanges in retaliation, 1983.
b. Apr 1963
Source: *NF*

Hua, Kuo-Feng
Chinese. Politician, Statesman
b. 1919
Source: *BioIn 10, 11; IntWW 74*

Hubay, Jeno
Hungarian. Musician, Composer
b. Sep 14, 1858 in Budapest, Hungary
d. Mar 12, 1937 in Vienna, Austria
Source: *NewEOp 71*

Hubbard, Cal (Robert Calvin)
American. Football Player, Baseball Umpire
Only man to belong to both baseball, football
Halls of Fame.
b. Oct 11, 1900 in Keytesville, Missouri
d. Oct 17, 1977 in Saint Petersburg, Florida
Source: *BasesB; WhoFtbl 74*

Hubbard, Elbert Green
[Fra Elbertus]
American. Author, Publisher, Biographer
Established Roycroft Press and inspirational
magazines; wrote *A Mesage to Garcia,*
1899.
b. Jun 19, 1856 in Bloomington, Illinois
d. May 7, 1915
Source: *AmAu&B; AmBi; BbD; BiD&SB;
ChhPo S2; CnDAL; DcAmAu; DcAmB;
DcLEL; DcNAA; EvLB; OxAmL; REn;
REnAL; TwCA, SUP*

Hubbard, Kin (Frank McKinney)
American. Humorist, Journalist
b. Sep 1, 1868 in Bellefontaine, Ohio
d. Dec 26, 1930 in Indianapolis, Indiana
Source: *BioIn 2, 6; DcNAA; IndAu 1816;
OhA&B; OxAmL; TwCA, SUP; WebAB;
WhNAA*

Hubbard, L(afayette) Ron(ald)
American. Religious Leader
Founded Church of Scientology, 1954, based
on his book *Dianetics: The Modern Science
of Mental Health.*
b. Mar 13, 1911 in Tilden, Nebraska
d. Jan 24, 1986 in San Luis Obispo,
California
Source: *Au&Wr 71; WhoAm 82; WhoS&SW
73; WrDr 76*

Hubbard, Orville Liscum
American. Politician
Mayor of Dearborn, MI, 1941-77; holder
   national record for full-time mayor, until
   passed by Erastus Corning, III.
b. Apr 2, 1903 in Union City, Michigan
d. Dec 16, 1982 in Detroit, Michigan
Source: *BioIn 2, 5, 7, 8; NewYTBS 82;
WhoAm 76, 78; WhoAmP 73, 75, 77, 79;
WhoGov 72, 75, 77; WhoMW 76, 78*

Hubbell, Carl Owen
"King Carl"; "The Meal Ticket"
American. Baseball Player
Pitcher, NY, 1928-43; won at least 20 games
   per season, 1933-37; Hall of Fame, 1947.
b. Jun 22, 1903 in Carthage, Missouri
Source: *BaseEn 85; WhoProB 73*

Hubble, Edwin Powell
American. Astronomer
Proved existence of star systems beyond
   Milky Way, 1925.
b. Nov 20, 1889 in Marshfield, Missouri
d. Sep 28, 1953 in San Marino, California
Source: *DcAmB S5; REnAL; WebAB; WhAm
3*

Huberman, Bronislaw
Austrian. Musician
b. Dec 19, 1882 in Czestochowa, Poland
d. Jun 16, 1947 in Nant Corsier, Switzerland
Source: *CurBio 41, 47*

Hubert
Religious Figure
b. 655
d. 727
Source: *BioIn 2, 3, 4, 5, 10, 11*

Hubley, Season
American. Actress
Starred as Priscilla Presley in TV movie
   "Elvis."
b. May 14, 1951 in New York, New York
Source: *BioIn 11; WhoHol A*

Huch, Ricarda (Octavia)
German. Poet, Author
Novels include *The Deruger Trail,* 1929.
b. Jul 18, 1864 in Brunswick, Germany
d. Nov 17, 1947 in Frankfort, Germany
Source: *CasWL; ConAu 111; REn; TwCLC
13*

Hucknall, Mick
[Simply Red]
"Red"
British. Singer
Number one hits include "Holding Back the
   Years," 1986.
Source: *NF*

Huddleston, (Ernest Urban) Trevor
English. Religious Leader
Bishop of Mauritius, Archbishop of Indian
   Ocean, since 1978.
b. Jun 15, 1913 in Bedford, England
Source: *AfSS 82; CurBio 63; IntWW 82;
WrDr 82*

Huddleston, Walter Darlington
American. Politician
b. 1924
Source: *BioIn 9, 10, 11; WhoAm 82*

Hudson, Bill (William Louis, II)
[The Hudson Brothers]
American. Singer, Musician
b. Oct 17, 1949
Source: *NF*

Hudson, Brett Stuart Patrick
[The Hudson Brothers]
American. Singer, Musician
b. Jan 18, 1953
Source: *NF*

Hudson, Henry
English. Navigator
Made several attempts to find Northwest
   Passage; first white man to go up Hudson
   River, 1609, which was named for him.
b. Sep 12, 1575
d. Jun 23, 1611
Source: *Alli; AmBi; ApCAB; DcAmB; Drake;
EncAB-H; OxCan; REn; REnAL; TwCBDA;
WebAB; WhAm HS*

Hudson, Joseph Lowthian
English. Businessman
Founded J L Hudson, 1881; pres., 1891-1912.
b. Oct 17, 1846 in Newcastle, England
d. Jul 15, 1912 in Worthing, England
Source: *NatCAB 47; WhAm 1*

Hudson, Joseph Lowthian, Jr.
American. Businessman
b. Jul 4, 1931 in Buffalo, New York
Source: *St&PR 75; WhoAm 74, 76, 78, 80,
82; WhoF&I 74*

Hudson, Lou
American. Basketball Player
b. Jul 11, 1944 in Greensboro, North
    Carolina
Source: *WhoBbl 73*

Hudson, Mark Jeffrey Anthony
[The Hudson Brothers]
American. Singer, Musician
b. Aug 23, 1951
Source: *NF*

Hudson, Rochelle
American. Actress
Played Natalie Wood's mother in *Rebel
    Without a Cause,* 1955.
b. Mar 6, 1915 in Oklahoma City, Oklahoma
d. Jan 17, 1972 in Palm Desert, California
Source: *FilmgC; InWom; MotPP; MovMk;
NewYTBE 72; ThFT; WhScrn 77; WhoHol B*

Hudson, Rock
[Roy Scherer-Fitzgerald]
American. Actor
Known for light romantic comedy: *Pillow
    Talk,* 1959; nominated for Oscar for *Giant,*
    1956.
b. Nov 17, 1925 in Winnetka, Illinois
d. Oct 2, 1985 in Beverly Hills, California
Source: *BiDFilm; BkPepl; CelR; CmMov;
ConNews 85-4; CurBio 61; FilmgC; IntMPA
82; MotPP; MovMk; OxFilm; WhoAm 82;
WhoHol A; WhoWest 74; WhoWor 74;
WorEFlm*

Hudson, William Henry
English. Author, Naturalist
Wrote *Green Mansions,* 1904, *The Book of a
    Naturalist,* 1919.
b. Aug 4, 1841 in Quilmes, Argentina
d. Aug 18, 1922 in London, England
Source: *Alli SUP; AnCL; AtlBL; CarSB;
CasWL; Chambr 3; ChhPo S1, S2; CyWA;
DcBiA; DcEuL; DcLEL; EvLB; LongCTC;
ModBrL; NewC; OxEng; PenC ENG; RAdv 1;
REn; TwCA, SUP; TwCWr; WebE&AL*

Hudson Brothers, The
[Brett Hudson; Bill Hudson; Mark Hudson]
American. Music Group
Had best-selling singles "Rendevous," 1975;
    "Help Wanted," 1976; had weekly TV
    show, 1975 "The Razzle Dazzle Comedy
    Hour."
Source: *RkOn 84; WhoRocM 82*

Huebner, Clarence R
American. Army Officer
b. Nov 24, 1888 in Bushton, Kansas
d. Sep 23, 1972 in Washington, District of
    Columbia
Source: *CurBio 49, 72; NewYTBE 72; WhAm
5*

Huerta, Dolores Hernandez
Labor Union Official
b. 1930
Source: *BioIn 10*

Hues Corporation, The
[Tommy Brown; H Ann Kelly; St. Clair Lee;
    Karl Russell; Fleming Williams]
American. Music Group
Disco-soul group formed 1969; had hit single
    "Rock the Boat," 1974.
Source: *RolSEnR 83*

Huey Lewis and the News
[Mario Cipollina; Johnny Colla; Bill Gibson;
    Chris Hayes; Sean Hopper; Huey Lewis]
American. Music Group
Formed 1982; hits include "Heart and Soul,"
    1983; "If This Is It," 1984.
Source: *RkOn 85*

Huff, Sam (Robert Lee)
American. Football Player
b. Oct 4, 1934 in Edna Gas, West Virginia
Source: *WhoFtbl 74*

Hufstedler, Shirley (Ann) M(ount)
American. Judge, Government Official
First secretary of Education, Carter
    administration, 1979-81.
b. Aug 24, 1925 in Denver, Colorado
Source: *AmBench 79; BioIn 12; CurBio 80;
GoodHs; NewYTBS 79; WhoAm 74, 76, 78,
80, 82; WhoAmL 79; WhoAmW 58, 61, 64,
66, 68, 70, 72, 75, 77, 79; WhoGov 72, 77;
WhoWest 74, 76, 78*

Hugel, Max
American. Businessman, Government Official
Resigned as CIA director, 1981, for alleged
    earlier stock market practices.
b. 1925 in Brooklyn, New York
Source: *BioIn 2, 12; St&PR 75*

Huggins, Charles Brenton
Canadian. Surgeon
Won 1966 Nobel Prize in medicine for
    cancer research.
b. Sep 22, 1901 in Halifax, Nova Scotia
Source: *AmM&WS 73P; CanWW 82; ConAu
115; CurBio 65; IntWW 74; WebAB; Who
74; WhoAm 76, 78, 80, 82*

Huggins, Miller James
"Hug"; "The Mighty Mite"
American. Baseball Player, Baseball Manager
Second baseman who managed NY Yankees,
1918-29.
b. Mar 27, 1879 in Cincinnati, Ohio
d. Sep 25, 1929 in New York, New York
Source: *BaseEn 85; DcAmB; WhAm HS, 4;
WhoProB 73*

Hugh Capet
French. King
b. 938
d. 996
Source: *NewCol 75*

Hughan, Jessie Wallace
American. Author, Political Activist
b. Dec 25, 1876 in Brooklyn, New York
d. 1955
Source: *InWom; WhAm 5; WhNAA;
WomWWA 14*

Hughes, Arthur
English. Artist, Illustrator
b. 1832 in London, England
d. 1915
Source: *BioIn 1, 5, 6, 8; WhoChL*

Hughes, Barnard
American. Actor
TV series include "Doc," 1975-76, "Mr.
Merlin," 1981.
b. Jul 16, 1915 in Bedford Hills, New York
Source: *NotNAT; WhoAm 82; WhoHol A;
WhoThe 77*

Hughes, Charles Evans
American. Supreme Court Justice
b. Apr 11, 1862 in Glens Falls, New York
d. Aug 27, 1948 in Osterville, Massachusetts
Source: *AmAu&B; BiDrUSE; CurBio 41, 48;
DcAmB S4; DcNAA; EncAB-H; REn; REnAL;
WebAB; WhAm 2; WhAmP*

Hughes, Emmet John
American. Author, Journalist
Columnist, *Newsweek*, 1963-68; speechwriter
for Dwight Eisenhower and Nelson
Rockefeller.
b. Dec 26, 1920 in Newark, New Jersey
d. Sep 20, 1982 in Princeton, New Jersey
Source: *AmAu&B; AnObit 1982; ConAu 107;
CurBio 82; PolProf E; WhoAm 78; WhoWor
74, 76*

Hughes, Francis
Irish. Hunger Striker, Revolutionary
Jailed IRA member who died in 59th day of
hunger strike.
b. 1955 in Bellaghy, Northern Ireland
d. May 12, 1981 in Belfast, Northern Ireland
Source: *BioIn 12*

Hughes, Howard Robard
American. Aviator, Industrialist
b. Dec 24, 1905 in Houston, Texas
d. Apr 5, 1976 in Houston, Texas
Source: *BiDFilm; CelR; CurBio 41; DcFM;
EncAB-H; FilmgC; IntMPA 75; IntWW 74;
OxFilm; WebAB; WhAm 6; WhoAm 74;
WhoF&I 74; WhoWor 78; WorEFlm*

Hughes, Irene Finger
American. Journalist
Psychic researcher; author of column,
"ESPecially...Irene."
b. in Saulsbury, Indiana
Source: *ConAu 103; WhoAmW 72*

Hughes, Langston (James Langston)
American. Poet, Author, Journalist
Expressed Negro view of America in
Shakespeare in Harlem, 1942.
b. Feb 1, 1902 in Joplin, Missouri
d. May 22, 1967 in New York, New York
Source: *AmAu&B; AmSCAP 66; AnCL;
AuBYP; BiE&WWA; BkCL; BlkAWP;
CnDAL; CnMD; ConAmA; ConAu 1R, 1NR,
25R; ConLC 1, 5, 10, 15; CroCD; CurBio 40,
67; DcLEL; EncAB-H; EncWL; LongCTC;
McGEWD; ModAL, S1; ModWD; OxAmL;
PenC AM; RAdv 1; REn; REnAL; SixAP;
SmATA 4; Str&VC; TwCA, SUP; WebAB;
WebE&AL; WhAm 4; WhoTwCL*

Hughes, Richard Arthur Warren
Welsh. Author, Dramatist
Wrote *High Wind in Jamaica*, 1929.
b. Apr 19, 1900 in Weybridge, England
d. Apr 28, 1976 in Merioneth, Wales
Source: *Au&Wr 71; CasWL; ChhPo, S2;
ConAu 5R; ConLC 1; ConNov 72, 76; CyWA;
DcLEL; EncWL; EvLB; LongCTC; ModBrL,
S1; NewC; OxEng; PenC ENG; RAdv 1;
REn; SmATA 8; TwCA, SUP; TwCWr;
WhoChL; WhoLA; WhoTwCL; WrDr 80*

Hughes, Robert Studley Forrest
Australian. Art Critic, Author
Art critic, *Time* magazine, 1970--; wrote *Art
of Australia*, 1966.
b. Jul 28, 1938 in Sydney, Australia
Source: *WhoAm 80*

Hughes, Rupert
American. Author
Wrote novel *Man Without a Home*, 1935;
  three-volume biography *George Washington*,
  1930.
b. Jan 31, 1872 in Lancaster, Missouri
d. Sep 9, 1956 in Los Angeles, California
Source: *AmAu&B; AmSCAP 66; AnMV 1926;
ChhPo, S1, S2; ConAmL; DcAmAu; OhA&B;
OxAmL; REnAL; TwCA, SUP; TwYS; WhAm
3; WhNAA; WhScrn 77*

Hughes, Sarah Tilghman
American. Judge
Administered oath of office to L B Johnson
  after assassination of J F Kennedy, 1963.
b. Aug 2, 1896 in Baltimore, Maryland
d. Apr 23, 1985 in Dallas, Texas
Source: *BiDFedJ; WhoAm 84; WhoAmL 79;
WhoAmW 83*

Hughes, Ted
English. Poet
Poet laureate of England, 1984--.
b. Aug 17, 1930 in Mytholmroyd, England
Source: *CasWL; ChhPo, S1, S2; CnE&AP;
ConAu 1R; ConLC 2, 4; ConP 70, 75;
EncWL; IntWW 74; LongCTC; ModBrL, S1;
NewC; PenC ENG; RAdv 1; TwCWr;
WebE&AL; Who 74; WhoAm 82; WhoTwCL;
WhoWor 78; WorAu; WrDr 80*

Hughes, Thomas
English. Reformer, Author
Wrote classic *Tom Brown's School Days*,
  1857.
b. Oct 20, 1822 in Uffington, England
d. Mar 22, 1896 in Brighton, England
Source: *BrAu 19; CasWL; CyWA; DcEnA;
DcLEL; NewC; OxEng; PenC ENG; REn*

Hugo, Adele
French. Celebrity Relative
Daughter of Victor Hugo whose life was
  filmed as *Story of Adele H.*, 1975.
b. 1830
d. 1915
Source: *BioIn 11*

Hugo, Victor Marie
French. Dramatist, Author
Best known for *Les Miserables*, 1862.
b. Feb 26, 1802 in Besancon, France
d. May 22, 1885 in Paris, France
Source: *AtlBL; BbD; BiD&SB; CasWL;
ChhPo, S1, S2; CnThe; CyWA; DcBiA;
DcEnL; DcEuL; EncMys; EuAu; EvEuW;
HsB&A; McGEWD; MnBBF; NewC; OxEng;
OxFr; OxThe; PenC EUR; RComWL; REn;
REnWD*

Huie, William Bradford
American. Author, Journalist
b. Nov 13, 1910 in Hartselle, Alabama
Source: *AmAu&B; Au&Wr 71; AuNews 1;
ConAu 9R; ConNov 72, 76; REnAL; TwCA
SUP; WhoAm 74, 76, 78, 80, 82; WhoS&SW
82; WhoWor 78; WrDr 76*

Huisman, Philippe
French. Art Historian
b. 1924
d. 1970
Source: *BioIn 9, 10*

Hulagu Khan
Mongolian. Ruler
b. 1217
d. 1265
Source: *NewCol 75; WebBD 80*

Hulbert, Jack
English. Singer, Dancer, Comedian
Appeared in film *The Camels Are Coming*.
b. Apr 24, 1892 in Ely, England
d. Mar 25, 1978 in London, England
Source: *ConAu 115; EncMT; Who 74*

Hulce, Thomas
American. Actor
Made debut in *Those Lips, Those Eyes*, 1980;
  nominated for Oscar, 1984, for title role in
  Amadeus.
b. Dec 6, 1953 in Plymouth, Michigan
Source: *ConTFT 3; VarWW 85*

Hull, Bobby (Robert Martin)
Canadian. Hockey Player, Sportscaster
Left wing known for vicious slap shot;
  scored 672 goals in career.
b. Jan 3, 1939 in Point Anne, Ontario
Source: *CelR; CurBio 66; NewYTBE 73;
WhoAm 74, 76, 78, 80, 82; WhoHcky 73;
WhoMW 74*

Hull, Cordell
American. Statesman
Helped establish UN, 1945 and "good
  neighbor" policies.
b. Oct 2, 1871 in Pickett County, Tennessee
d. Jul 23, 1955 in Bethesda, Maryland
Source: *BiDrAC; BiDrUSE; CurBio 40, 55;
DcAmB S5; EncAB-H; WebAB; WhAm 3;
WhAmP*

Hull, Henry
American. Actor
Created role of Jeeter Lester in *Tobacco Road*, Broadway, 1934; title in film *The Werewolf of London*, 1935.
b. Oct 3, 1890 in Louisville, Kentucky
d. Mar 8, 1977 in Cornwall, England
Source: *BiE&WWA; FilmEn; Film 1; FilmgC; IntMPA 77; MotPP,; NotNAT; PlP&P; TwYS; Vers A; WhoHol A; WhoThe 77A*

Hull, Isaac
American. Military Leader
b. Mar 9, 1773 in Huntington, Connecticut
d. Dec 13, 1843 in Philadelphia, Pennsylvania
Source: *AmBi; ApCAB; DcAmB; REn; TwCBDA; WebAB; WhAm HS*

Hull, John Edwin
American. Military Leader
b. May 26, 1895 in Greenfield, Ohio
d. Jun 10, 1975
Source: *BioIn 3, 4, 10; CurBio 54; IntWW 74; WhAm 6*

Hull, Josephine
[Josephine Sherwood]
American. Actress
Won 1950 Oscar for *Harvey;* one of Cary Grant's murderous aunts in *Arsenic and Old Lace*, 1942.
b. 1884 in Newton, Massachusetts
d. Mar 12, 1957 in New York, New York
Source: *CurBio 53, 57; FilmgC; InWom; MotPP; MovMk; PlP&P; ThFT; Vers B; WhAm 3; WhScrn 74, 77; WhoHol B; WomWWA 14*

Hull, Warren
American. Actor, Singer
Host of radio, TV quiz show, "Strike It Rich."
b. Jan 17, 1903 in Gasport, New York
d. Sep 21, 1974 in Waterbury, Connecticut
Source: *FilmEn; FilmgC; NewYTBS 74; WhScrn 77; WhoHol B*

Hulman, Tony (Anton), Jr.
American. Business Executive, Sportsman
Pres., Indianapolis Speedway who began each race saying "Gentlemen, start your engines."
b. Feb 11, 1901 in Terre Haute, Indiana
d. Oct 27, 1977 in Indianapolis, Indiana
Source: *St&PR 75*

Hulme, Kathryn Cavarly
American. Author
Wrote *The Wild Place*, 1953; best-selling biography *Nun's Story*, 1957.
b. Jan 6, 1900 in San Francisco, California
d. Aug 25, 1981 in Lihue, Hawaii
Source: *BioIn 4, 6, 8; ConAu 104, P-1; WhoAm 74; WhoAmW 58, 61, 64, 66, 68, 70, 72, 74, 75, 77; WhoWor 74*

Hulme, Thomas Ernest
English. Philosopher
Led anti-Romantic movement called Imagism in early 1900s.
b. Sep 16, 1883 in Endon, England
d. Sep 28, 1917 in Belgium
Source: *BioIn 1, 5, 9, 10; OxEng; PenC ENG; REn*

Human League
[Ian Burden; Joe Callis; Joanne Catherall; Phil Oakey; Susanne Sulley; Adrian Wright]
English. Music Group
Formed in 1977; hit single, 1982, "Don't You Want Me?" from album *Dare*.
Source: *IlEncRk; RkOn 85*

Humbard, Rex
American. Evangelist
b. Aug 13, 1919 in Little Rock, Arkansas
Source: *CurBio 72; NewYTBE 73; WhoAm 82*

Humble Pie
[David 'Clem' Clemson; Peter Frampton; Steve Marriott; Gregory Ridley; Jerry Shirley]
English. Music Group
Hard-rock band, 1968-75; had hit album *Smokin'*, 1972.
Source: *ConMuA 80A; IlEncRk; LilREn 78; RkOn 78; WhoRock 81*

Humboldt, Alexander, Freiherr von
German. Explorer, Scientist, Author
Traveled through Latin America, 1799-1804; discovered peruvian current bearing name.
b. Sep 14, 1769 in Berlin, Germany
d. May 6, 1859 in Berlin, Germany
Source: *BiD&SB; CasWL; DcEuL; EuAu; NewC; OxEng; OxGer; PenC EUR; REn*

Humboldt, Wilhelm von
German. Statesman, Author
Noted phligist who wrote on Basque, Java languages.
b. Jun 22, 1767 in Potsdam, Germany
d. Apr 8, 1835 in Schloss Tegel, Germany
Source: *BiD&SB; CasWL; DcEuL; EuAu; OxGer; PenC EUR; REn*

Hume, David
Scottish. Public Official, Philosopher,
Historian
Philosophical skeptic who influenced
metaphysical thought; wrote classic *History
of England,* 1754-62.
b. Apr 26, 1711 in Edinburgh, Scotland
d. Aug 25, 1776 in Edinburgh, Scotland
Source: *Alli; AtlBL; BbD; BiD&SB; BrAu;
CasWL; Chambr 2; CyWA; DcEnA; DcEnL;
DcEuL; DcLEL; EvLB; MouLC 2; NewC;
OxEng; PenC ENG; REn; WebE&AL*

Humes, Harold Louis
American. Engineer
b. Jan 31, 1900 in Marquette, Michigan
Source: *WhAm 4*

Humes, Helen
American. Singer
Jazz singer who sang with Count Basie,
1938-42; had hit song "Be Baba Leba,"
1945.
b. Jun 23, 1913 in Louisville, Kentucky
d. Sep 13, 1981 in Santa Monica, California
Source: *BiDAmM; BioIn 4, 10; CmpEPM;
EncJzS 70; WhoJazz 72*

Humes, James Calhoun
American. Lawyer
b. Oct 31, 1934 in Williamsport,
Pennsylvania
Source: *ConAu 45; WhoAm 74, 76, 78, 80,
82; WhoGov 75; WhoS&SW 82*

Hummel, Berta
[Sister Maria Innocentia]
German. Artist
Hummel figurines inspired by her drawings;
international industry by 1935.
b. 1909 in Massing, Bavaria
d. 1946
Source: *BioIn 12; Entr*

Hummel, Johann Nepomuk
German. Composer
b. Nov 14, 1778 in Pressburg, Germany
d. Oct 17, 1837 in Weimar, Germany
Source: *OxMus*

Hummel, Lisl
Austrian. Illustrator
b. in Vienna, Austria
Source: *BioIn 1; ChhPo; ConICB; IlsCB 1946*

Humperdinck, Engelbert
German. Composer
Wrote opera *Hansel and Gretel,* 1893.
b. Sep 1, 1854 in Siegburg, Germany
d. Sep 27, 1921 in Neustrelitz, Germany
Source: *AtlBL; OxGer; REn*

Humperdinck, Engelbert
[Arnold Gerry Dorsey]
English. Singer
Had best selling albums *Release Me,* 1968; *A
Man Without Love,* 1969.
b. May 3, 1936 in Madras, India
Source: *BkPepl; CelR; WhoAm 82; WhoWor
78*

Humphrey, Claude B
American. Football Player
b. Jun 29, 1944 in Memphis, Tennessee
Source: *WhoAm 74; WhoFtbl 74*

Humphrey, Doris
American. Dancer
b. Oct 17, 1895 in Oak Park, Illinois
d. Dec 29, 1958
Source: *CurBio 42, 59; InWom; WhAm 3*

Humphrey, Elliott S
American. Animal Trainer
Trained first guide dogs for blind.
b. 1889 in Saratoga Springs, New York
d. Jun 6, 1981 in Phoenix, Arizona
Source: *NewYTBS 81*

Humphrey, George Magoffin
American. Statesman
b. Mar 8, 1890 in Cheboygan, Michigan
d. Jan 20, 1970 in Cleveland, Ohio
Source: *CurBio 53, 70; NewYTBE 70*

Humphrey, Gordon John
American. Politician
Conservative Rep. senator from NH, elected
1978 in major upset.
b. Oct 9, 1940 in Bristol, Connecticut
Source: *AlmAP 80; CngDr 79; NewYTBS 78;
WhoAm 80, 82, 84; WhoAmP 79; WhoE 79*

Humphrey, Hubert Horatio, Jr.
"The Happy Warrior"
American. Politician
Vp under Lyndon Johnson, 1965-69; lost
close presidential election to Richard
Nixon, 1968.
b. May 27, 1911 in Wallace, South Dakota
d. Jan 13, 1978 in Waverly, Minnesota
Source: *BiDrAC; BiDrUSE; CelR; ConAu 69,
73; CurBio 49, 66; IntWW 74; Who 74;
WhoAm 74; WhoGov 75; WhoMW 74;
WhoWor 78*

Humphrey, Muriel Fay Buck
[Mrs. Hubert Humphrey]
American. Celebrity Relative, Politician
Completed husband's final senate term, 1978-79.
b. Feb 20, 1912 in Huron, South Dakota
Source: *WhoAm 74, 76, 78, 80, 82; WhoMW 74*

Humphreys, Christmas (Travers Christmas)
English. Author, Lawyer, Judge
Most writings reflect belief in Buddhism: *The Development of Buddhism in England,* 1937.
b. Feb 15, 1901 in London, England
d. Apr 13, 1983 in London, England
Source: *AnObit 1983; Au&Wr 71; ConAu 77; IntWW 82; IntWWP 82; Who 82; WhoWor 74*

Humphreys, Joshua
American. Architect
First US Naval constructor, 1794-1801.
b. Jun 17, 1751 in Delaware County, Delaware
d. Jan 12, 1838 in Haverford, Pennsylvania
Source: *BioIn 3; WebAB*

Humphreys, Noel
English. Physician, Explorer
b. 1883
d. 1966
Source: *BioIn 7*

Humphries, Rolfe (George Rolfe)
American. Poet
b. Nov 20, 1894 in Philadelphia, Pennsylvania
d. Apr 22, 1969 in Redwood City, California
Source: *BioIn 8; ChhPo S1; CnDAL; ConAu 5R, 25R, 3NR; OxAmL; RAdv 1; REnAL; TwCA, SUP; WhAm 5*

Humphries, Stefan
American. Football Player
b. Jan 20, 1962 in Broward, Florida
Source: *BioIn 12*

Hunndertwasser, Friedrich
Austrian. Artist
Abstract painter who developed grammar of vision theory: "Regenstag" series.
b. Dec 15, 1928 in Vienna, Austria
Source: *ConArt 77; IntWW 74, 75, 76, 77, 78; WhoWor 74, 78*

Huneker, James Gibbons
American. Critic, Author
b. Jan 31, 1860 in Philadelphia, Pennsylvania
d. Feb 9, 1921 in New York, New York
Source: *AmAu&B; AmBi; CnDAL; ConAmL; DcAmAu; DcAmB; DcLEL; DcNAA; LongCTC; OxAmL; OxThe; PenC AM; RAdv 1; REn; REnAL; TwCA, SUP; WebAB; WhAm 1*

Hung-Li
see: Ch'ien Lung

Hung Wu
see: Ming T'ai-Tsu

Hunnicutt, Arthur
American. Actor
Received Oscar nomination for *The Big Sky,* 1952.
b. Feb 17, 1911 in Gravelly, Arkansas
Source: *CmMov; FilmgC; IntMPA 77; MovMk; Vers A; WhoHol A*

Hunnicutt, Gayle
American. Actress
Starred in TV movies "The Golden Bowl," "A Man Called Intrepid."
b. Feb 6, 1943 in Fort Worth, Texas
Source: *FilmEn; FilmgC; IntMPA 82; WhoHol A*

Hunsaker, Jerome Clarke
American. Aeronautical Engineer
Founded nation's first course in aeronautical engineering at MIT, 1914; built first effective wind tunnel in US, 1914.
b. Aug 26, 1886 in Creston, Louisiana
d. Sep 10, 1984 in Boston, Massachusetts
Source: *AmM&WS 73P; AnObit 1984; CurBio 42; IntWW 74; WebAB; WhoAm 74*

Hunt, E(verette) Howard
American. Watergate Participant, Author
Consultant to Richard Nixon, 1971-72; jailed for involvement in Watergate, 1973-74, 1975-77.
b. Oct 9, 1918 in Hamburg, New York
Source: *AmAu&B; ConAu 45, 2NR; ConLC 3; WhoAm 74, 76, 78, 80, 82*

Hunt, Frazier
"Spike"
American. Journalist
b. Dec 1, 1885 in Rock Island, Illinois
d. Dec 24, 1967 in Newtown, Pennsylvania
Source: *AmAu&B; ConAu 93; WhAm 4*

Hunt, George Wylie Paul
American. Politician, Statesman
b. Nov 1, 1859 in Huntsville, Maryland
d. Dec 24, 1934
Source: *BioIn 1, 6, 8, 10; WhAm 1*

Hunt, H(aroldson) L(afayette)
American. Oilman
Billionaire who at height of wealth had a
weekly income of over $1 million.
b. Feb 17, 1889 in Vandalia, Illinois
d. Nov 29, 1974 in Dallas, Texas
Source: *BusPN; CelR; CurBio 70, 75; EncAB-
H; NewYTBS 74; WebAB; WhAm 6; WhoAm
74*

Hunt, Jack Reed
American. Engineer, Pilot
Piloted longest non-stop, non-refueled trans-
Atlantic blimp flight, 1958.
b. May 17, 1918 in Red Oak, Iowa
d. Jan 7, 1984 in Ormond Beach, Florida
Source: *NewYTBS 84; WhoFla*

Hunt, James
English. Auto Racer
b. Aug 29, 1947 in Epsom, England
Source: *BioIn 11*

Hunt, Lamar
American. Football Executive
Owner, KC Chiefs, 1959--; founder, first
pres., AFL, 1959.
b. Aug 2, 1932 in Dallas, Texas
Source: *CelR; WhoAm 74, 76, 78, 80, 82;
WhoFtbl 74*

Hunt, Leigh
English. Author, Poet
b. Oct 19, 1784 in Southgate, England
d. Aug 28, 1859 in Putney, England
Source: *Alli; AtlBL; BiD&SB; BrAu 19;
CnE&AP; CrtT 2; DcEuL; NewC; OxThe;
PenC ENG; RAdv 1; REn; WebE&AL*

Hunt, Linda
American. Actress
Won Oscar, 1983, for role of man in *The
Year of Living Dangerously.*
b. 1946
Source: *ConTFT 3; NewYTBS 83; VarWW 85*

Hunt, Lois
American. Actress, Singer
Leading soprano, Metropolitan Opera, 1949-
53; on Broadway in *Sound of Music,* 1961-
62.
b. Nov 26, 1925 in York, Pennsylvania
Source: *WhoAm 76; WhoAmW 72*

Hunt, Martita
English. Actress
Played Miss Havisham in 1947 film *Great
Expectations.*
b. Jan 30, 1900 in Argentina
d. Jun 13, 1969 in London, England
Source: *BiE&WWA; FilmEn; FilmgC; MotPP;
MovMk; Vers A; WhScrn 74, 77; WhoHol B*

Hunt, Nelson Bunker
"Bunky"
American. Business Executive
Played prominent role in silver crash of Mar
27, 1980; fortune estimated at $1.4 billion.
b. Feb 22, 1926 in El Dorado, Texas
Source: *CurBio 80*

Hunt, Richard Morris
American. Architect
Designed the base of Statue of Liberty.
b. Oct 31, 1828 in Brattleboro, Vermont
d. Jul 31, 1896 in Newport, Rhode Island
Source: *Alli SUP; AmBi; ApCAB; BnEnAmA;
DcAmB; Drake; LinLib S; McGDA;
McGEWB; NatCAB 6; OxAmL; TwCBDA;
WebAB; WhAm HS; WhoArch*

Hunt, Walter
American. Inventor
Invented the safety pin, fountain pen, and
other practical items.
b. Jul 29, 1796 in Martinsburg, New York
d. Jun 8, 1859 in New York, New York
Source: *NatCAB 19; WebAB*

Hunt, (William) Holman
English. Artist
A founder of pre-Raphaelite Brotherhood,
1848; painted "Light of the World," 1854.
b. Apr 2, 1827 in London, England
d. Sep 7, 1910 in London, England
Source: *AtlBL; BioIn 3, 4, 6, 8, 9, 10, 11;
NewCol 75; REn*

Hunt, William Morris
American. Artist
b. Mar 31, 1824 in Brattleboro, Vermont
d. Sep 8, 1879
Source: *AmBi; ApCAB; DcAmB; DcNAA;
Drake; OxAmL; TwCBDA; WebAB; WhAm
HS*

Hunter, Alberta
American. Singer, Songwriter
Blues singer who performed with jazz greats,
wrote own songs.
b. Apr 1, 1897 in Memphis, Tennessee
d. Oct 17, 1984 in New York, New York
Source: *AmSCAP 66; AnObit 1984; WhoJazz
72*

Hunter, Bobby Lee
American. Boxer
b. 1950
Source: *NewYTBE 71*

Hunter, "Catfish" (James Augustus)
American. Baseball Player
Pitched perfect game versus Minnesota, May
8, 1968.
b. Apr 18, 1946 in Hertford, North Carolina
Source: *BaseEn 85; WhoAm 74, 76, 78, 80,
82; WhoProB 73*

Hunter, Dard
American. Printer, Author
Authority on papermaking, printing; wrote
My Life with Paper, 1958.
b. Nov 29, 1883 in Steubenville, Ohio
d. Feb 20, 1966
Source: *AmAu&B; ConAu 25R, P-1; CurBio
60, 66; OhA&B; OxAmL; REnAL; WhNAA*

Hunter, Evan
[Ed McBain, pseud.]
American. Author
b. Oct 15, 1926 in New York, New York
Source: *AmAu&B; AmSCAP 66; AuBYP;
ConAu 5R; ConLC 11; CurBio 56; IntWW
74; PenC AM; REn; REnAL; WhoAm 74, 76,
78, 80, 82*

Hunter, Glenn
American. Actor
Played title role on stage, in film *Merton of
the Movies,* 1922-24.
b. 1897 in Highland, New York
d. Dec 30, 1945 in New York, New York
Source: *CurBio 46; FilmgC; MotPP; TwYS;
WhScrn 74, 77; WhoHol B*

Hunter, Ian
South African. Actor, Screenwriter
Played nice guys in Hollywood films:
Adventures of Robin Hood, 1938.
b. Jun 13, 1900 in Capetown, South Africa
d. Sep 24, 1975 in England
Source: *FilmEn; Film 2; FilmgC; IntMPA 75;
MotPP; MovMk; WhScrn 77; WhThe*

Hunter, Ian
[Mott the Hoople]
English. Singer, Musician
Leader of Mott the Hopple; had solo hit
"Just Another Night," 1979.
b. Jun 3, 1946 in Shrewsbury, England
Source: *ConMuA 80A; IlEncRk; LilREn 78;
RkOn 85; WhoRock 81*

Hunter, "Ivory" Joe
American. Singer, Songwriter
Rhythm and blues singer-pianist, 1950s; had
gold record "Since I Met You Baby,"
1956.
b. 1911 in Kirbyville, Texas
d. Nov 8, 1974 in Memphis, Tennessee
Source: *BiDAmM; EncFCWM 69; RkOn 74;
WhoRock 81*

Hunter, Jeffrey
[Henry Herman McKinnies]
American. Actor
Played Jesus Christ in 1961 film *King of
Kings;* generally in action pictures, 1951-
69.
b. Nov 23, 1926 in New Orleans, Louisiana
d. May 27, 1969 in Van Nuys, California
Source: *BiDFilm; FilmEn; FilmgC; MovMk;
WhScrn 74, 77; WhoHol B; WorEFlm*

Hunter, John
English. Surgeon
b. Feb 13, 1728 in Long Calderwood,
Scotland
d. Oct 16, 1793 in London, England
Source: *Alli; NewC; OxEng*

Hunter, Kim
[Janet Cole]
American. Actress
Won 1951 Oscar for *Streetcar Named Desire,*
for role of Stella.
b. Nov 12, 1922 in Detroit, Michigan
Source: *BiE&WWA; ConAu 61; CurBio 52;
FilmgC; InWom; IntMPA 75, 76, 77, 78, 79,
80, 81, 82; MotPP; MovMk; NotNAT;
WhoAm 74, 76, 78, 80, 82; WhoHol A;
WhoThe 77; WhoWor 78*

Hunter, Ross
[Martin Fuss]
American. Producer
Films include *Flower Drum Song,* 1961,
Airport, 1969.
b. May 6, 1924 in Cleveland, Ohio
Source: *CelR; CmMov; CurBio 67; FilmgC;
IntMPA 75, 76, 77, 78, 79, 80, 81, 82;
MotPP; WhoAm 74, 76, 78, 80, 82; WhoHol
A; WhoWor 78; WorEFlm*

Hunter, Tab
[Arthur Gelien]
American. Actor
Teen idol, 1950s; in films *Damn Yankees,*
1958; *Ride the Wild Surf,* 1964.
b. Jul 11, 1931 in New York, New York
Source: *FilmgC; IntMPA 75, 76, 77, 78, 79,
80, 81, 82; MotPP; MovMk; WhoHol A*

Hunter, Thomas
Irish. Educator
b. Oct 19, 1831 in Ardglass, Ireland
d. Oct 14, 1915
Source: *DcNAA; WhAm 4*

Hunter, William
Scottish. Surgeon, Scientist
b. 1718
d. 1783
Source: *Alli; BioIn 1, 2, 3, 4, 6, 7, 9, 11; DcEnL; NewC*

Huntington, Collis Potter
American. Railroad Executive
Built Central Pacific Railroad of CA, which
joined with Union Pacific in UT, 1869.
b. Oct 22, 1821 in Harwinton, Connecticut
d. Aug 13, 1900 in Raquette Lake, New
York
Source: *NewCol 75; WebAB; WebBD 80*

Huntington, Daniel
American. Artist
b. Oct 14, 1816 in New York, New York
d. 1906
Source: *AmBi; ApCAB; BioIn 7, 11; BnEnAmA; DcAmB; Drake; EarABI; NatCab 5; TwCBDA; WhAm 1*

Huntington, Henry Edwards
American. Railroad Executive, Philanthropist
Founded California's $30 million Huntington
Library and Art Collection.
b. Feb 27, 1850 in Oneonta, New York
d. May 23, 1927 in Philadelphia,
Pennsylvania
Source: *AmBi; BioIn 1, 2, 6; DcAmB; LinLib S; WebAB; WhAm 1*

Huntington, Henry S, Jr.
American. Reformer
Pioneer in organized nudism; founded early
nudist camp, 1933; wrote *Defense of Nudism,* 1958.
b. 1882 in Gorham, Maine
d. Feb 16, 1981 in Philadelphia, Pennsylvania
Source: *NewYTBS 81*

Huntington, Samuel
American. Judge
Pres., Continental Congress, 1779-81; signed
Declaration of Independence, 1776.
b. Jul 3, 1731 in Windham, Connecticut
d. Jan 5, 1796 in Norwich, Connecticut
Source: *AmBi; ApCAB; BiAUS; BiDrAC; BiDrUSE; DcAmB; Drake; TwCBDA; WhAm HS; WhAmP*

Huntley, Chet (Chester Robert)
American. Broadcast Journalist
Teamed with David Brinkley for nightly
newscasts, 1956-70; author *The Generous Years,* 1968.
b. Dec 10, 1911 in Cardwell, Montana
d. Mar 20, 1974 in Bozeman, Montana
Source: *AuNews 1; CelR; ConAu 49, 97; CurBio 56, 74; NewYTBE 70; NewYTBS 74; WhAm 6; WhScrn 77; WhoAm 74; WhoHol B; WhoWor 78*

Huntley, Joni
American. Track Athlete
b. Aug 4, 1956 in McMinnville, Oregon
Source: *BioIn 11*

Hunyadi, Janos
[John Huniades]
Hungarian. Military Leader
Commanded Hungarian army, 1452-56;
conquered Turks, 1456.
b. 1385
d. 1465
Source: *LinLib S; McGEWB; NewC; NewCol 75; WebBD 80; WhDW*

Hupp, Louis Gorham
American. Manufacturer
With brother Robert, founded Hupp Motor
Car Co., 1908-41, producing Hupmobiles.
b. Nov 13, 1872 in Kalamazoo, Michigan
d. Dec 10, 1961 in Detroit, Michigan
Source: *DcAmB S7*

Huppert, Isabelle
French. Actress
Won 1978 best actress award, Cannes
Festival, for *Violette Noziere.*
b. Mar 16, 1955 in Paris, France
Source: *BioIn 11; CurBio 81; FilmEn*

Hurd, Peter
American. Artist, Illustrator
Best known for works of open, sun-drenched
mountains, valleys of southwest US.
b. Feb 22, 1904 in Roswell, New Mexico
d. Jul 9, 1984 in Roswell, New Mexico
Source: *AnObit 1984; ConICB; CurBio 57; IlsCB 1744; WhoAm 82; WhoAmA 73; WhoWor 74*

Hurkos, Peter
[Peter Van der Hurk]
Dutch. Psychic
b. 1911
Source: *BioIn 6, 9, 11; BioNews 74*

Hurley, Patrick Jay
American. Lawyer, Diplomat
b. Jan 8, 1883 in Oklahoma
d. Jul 30, 1963 in Santa Fe, New Mexico
Source: *BiDrUSE; CurBio 44, 63; WhAm 4*

Hurok, Sol
Russian. Impresario, Author
b. Apr 9, 1888 in Pogar, Russia
d. Mar 5, 1974 in New York, New York
Source: *BiE&WWA; BioNews 74; CelR; ConAu 49; NewYTBE 73; NewYTBS 74; WebAB; WhAm 6; Who 74; WhoAm 74; WhoWor 78; WhoWorJ 72*

Hurrell, George
American. Photographer
Noted for classic black and white shots of legendary Hollywood Stars, 1920s-50s.
b. 1904 in Cincinatti, Ohio
Source: *MacBEP*

Hurson, Martin
Irish. Hunger Striker, Revolutionary
Sixth jailed IRA member to starve to death in Maze Prison.
b. Sep 13, 1954 in Cappagh, Northern Ireland
d. Jul 13, 1981 in Belfast, Northern Ireland
Source: *BioIn 12*

Hurst, Fannie
American. Author
b. Oct 19, 1889 in Hamilton, Ohio
d. Feb 23, 1968 in New York, New York
Source: *AmAu&B; AmLY; AmNov; ChhPo; ConAmA; ConAmL; ConAu 25R, P-1; DcBiA; EvLB; FilmgC; InWom; LongCTC; OhA&B; OxAmL; REn; REnAL; TwCA, SUP; TwCWr; WhNAA*

Hurst, George
Scottish. Conductor
b. May 20, 1926 in Edinburgh, Scotland
Source: *Who 74; WhoMus 72*

Hurston, Zora Neale
American. Anthropologist, Author
b. Jan 7, 1903 in Eatonville, Florida
d. Jan 28, 1960 in Fort Pierce, Florida
Source: *AmAu&B; AmNov; BlkAWP; ConAu 85; ConLC 7; CurBio 42, 60; InWom; OxAmL; REnAL; TwCA, SUP; WhAm 3*

Hurt, John
English. Actor
Starred in *The Elephant Man*, 1980.
b. Jan 22, 1940 in Chesterfield, England
Source: *BioIn 12; CurBio 82; IntMPA 82; WhoAm 82; WhoThe 77, 81*

Hurt, Mary Beth Supinger
American. Actress
In films *The World According to Garp; Change of Seasons.*
b. Sep 26, in Marshalltown, Iowa
Source: *IntMPA 84; NewYTBS 76; VarWW 85; WhoThe 81*

Hurt, Mississippi John
American. Singer, Musician
b. Mar 8, 1892 in Teoc, Mississippi
d. Nov 2, 1966 in Grenada, Mississippi
Source: *EncFCWM 69*

Hurt, William
American. Actor
Stage actor, 1970s, who won Oscar, 1985, for *Kiss of the Spider Woman.*
b. Mar 20, 1950 in Washington, District of Columbia
Source: *ConNews 86-1; CurBio 86; IntMPA 85; WhoAm 84*

Hus, Jan
[John Huss]
Czech. Religious Leader
b. 1369 in Husinec, Czechoslovakia
d. Jul 6, 1415 in Constance, Germany
Source: *CasWL; DcEuL; EuAu; EvEuW; NewC; PenC EUR; REn*

Husak, Gustav
Czech. President
b. Jan 10, 1913 in Bratislava, Czechoslovakia
Source: *BioIn 8, 9, 11; CurBio 71; IntWW 74; NewYTBE 71; WhoWor 78*

Husayn Ali
see: Baha'u'llah

Husch, Gerhard
German. Opera Singer
b. Feb 2, 1901 in Hannover, Germany
Source: *WhoMus 72*

Husing, Ted
American. Sportscaster
One of America's leading sports announcers, on radio since 1924.
b. Nov 27, 1901 in Bronx, New York
d. Aug 10, 1962 in Pasadena, California
Source: *CurBio 42, 62; WhScrn 77; WhoHol B*

Huskisson, William
English. Statesman
b. Mar 11, 1770 in Worcestershire, England
d. Sep 15, 1830 in England
Source: *Alli; BiDLA*

Husky, Ferlin
American. Singer
b. Dec 3, 1927 in Flat River, Missouri
Source: *EncFCWM 69; WhoAm 74, 76, 78, 80, 82*

Hussain al Takriti, Saddam
[Saddam Husayn al Tikriti]
Iraqi. President
b. Apr 28, 1937 in Tikrit, Iraq
Source: *BioIn 12; IntWW 74; NewYTBS 82*

Hussein (Ibn Talal)
Jordanian. King
Descendant of Mohammed, who succeeded
   father to throne, 1953.
b. Nov 14, 1935 in Amman, Jordan
Source: *BioIn 2, 3, 4, 5, 6, 7, 8, 9, 10, 11, 12; IntWW 77; WhoWor 78*

Hussein, Saddam
Iraqi. Political Leader
Played prominent role in Jul 1968 revolution;
   pres. of Iraq, Jul 1979--.
b. May 2, 1935 in Tikrit, Iraq
Source: *IntWW 77, 78, 79, 80; WhoWor 78, 80*

Hussein, Taha
Egyptian. Educator, Author
b. Nov 14, 1889 in Maghagha, Egypt
d. Oct 28, 1973 in Cairo, Egypt
Source: *BioIn 1, 2, 3, 4, 5, 10; ConAu 45; CurBio 53, 73; NewYTBE 73; WhoWor 78*

Husseini, Haj Amin
Palestinian. Political Leader
b. 1893 in Jerusalem, Palestine
d. Jul 4, 1974 in Beirut, Lebanon
Source: *IntWW 74; NewYTBE 71; NewYTBS 74; WhoWor 78*

Husserl, Edmund
German. Philosopher
Originated philosophic study called
   phenomenology.
b. Apr 8, 1859 in Prossnitz, Czechoslovakia
d. Apr 27, 1938 in Freiburg im Breisqua,
   Germany
Source: *ConAu 116; REn; WorAu*

Hussey, Christopher Edward Clive
English. Architect
On editorial staff of *Country Life,* 1920-70;
   wrote *English Gardens and Landscapes,*
   1967.
b. Oct 21, 1899 in London, England
d. Mar 20, 1970 in London, England
Source: *AmArch 70; DcNaB 1961; WhE&EA; WhLit*

Hussey, Olivia
English. Actress
Starred as Juliet in screen version of *Romeo
   and Juliet,* 1969.
b. Apr 17, 1951 in Buenos Aires, Argentina
Source: *FilmgC; MotPP; VarWW 85; WhoHol
A*

Hussey, Ruth Carol
[Ruth Carol O'Rourke]
American. Actress
Oscar nominee for *The Philadelphia Story,*
   1940.
b. Oct 30, 1915 in Providence, Rhode Island
Source: *BiE&WWA; FilmgC; MotPP; MovMk;
NotNAT; ThFT; WhoAm 74, 76, 78, 80, 82;
WhoHol A; WhoThe 77A*

Huston, Anjelica
American. Actress
Won best supporting actress Oscar for
   Prizzi's Honor, 1985; daughter of John
   Huston.
b. 1952
Source: *VarWW 85*

Huston, John
American. Actor, Director, Writer
Won Oscar, 1948, for *Treasure of the Sierra
   Madre,* 1948; also directed *The African
   Queen,* 1952.
b. Aug 5, 1906 in Nevada, Missouri
Source: *BiDFilm; CelR; ConAu 73; DcFM;
FilmgC; IntMPA 77, 78, 79, 80, 81, 82;
IntWW 74; MovMk; OxFilm; REnAL;
WebAB; Who 74; WhoAm 74, 76, 78, 80, 82;
WhoWor 78; WorEFlm*

Huston, Walter
[Walter Houghston]
American. Actor
Won 1948 Oscar for *The Treasure of the
   Sierra Madre,* which his son John directed.
b. Apr 6, 1884 in Toronto, Ontario
d. Apr 7, 1950 in Beverly Hills, California
Source: *BiDFilm; CurBio 49, 50; DcAmB S4;
EncMT; FamA&A; FilmEn; FilmgC; MotPP;
MovMk; OxFilm; PIP&P; WebAB; WhAm 4;
WhScrn 74, 77; WhoHol B; WorEFlm*

Hutcheson, Francis
Scottish. Philosopher
Wrote *Inquiry into Original of Our Ideas of
   Beauty and Virtue,* 1725; coined phrase
   "moral sense."
b. Aug 8, 1694 in Saintfield, Northern
   Ireland
d. 1746
Source: *Alli; BiD&SB; BioIn 3, 7; BrAu;
CasWL; Chambr 2; DcEnA*

Hutchins, Bobby
[Our Gang]
"Wheezer"
American. Actor
Joined "Our Gang" series, 1929.
Source: *Film 2*

Hutchins, Robert Maynard
American. Lawyer, Educator
At age 30 was made pres., U of Chicago;
made controversial, important innovations
in the curriculum, 1929-51.
b. Jan 17, 1899 in Brooklyn, New York
d. May 14, 1977 in Santa Barbara, California
Source: *AmAu&B; CelR; ConAu 69; CurBio
40, 54; EncAB-H; IntWW 74; OxAmL;
REnAL; WebAB; WhNAA; Who 74; WhoAm
74; WhoWor 78*

Hutchins, Will
[Marshall Lowell Hutchason]
American. Actor
Starred in TV series "Sugarfoot," 1957-61;
"Blondie," 1968.
b. May 5, 1932 in Atwater, California
Source: *FilmgC; What 8; WhoHol A*

Hutchins, William
see: Tyndale, William

Hutchinson, Anne
[Anne Marbury]
English. Religious Leader
Belief in covenant of grace opposed Puritan
covenant of works; banished from MA
Bay, 1637.
b. 1591 in Alford, England
d. Aug 1643 in Long Island, New York
Source: *AmBi; ApCAB; BiCAW; DcAmB;
Drake; EncAB-H; HerW; InWom; NotAW;
OxAmL; REn; REnAL; TwCBDA; WebAB;
WhAm HS; WhAmP*

Hutchinson, Fred(erick Charles)
"Big Bear"
American. Baseball Player, Baseball Manager
Pitcher, Detroit Tigers, 1939-1953; manager,
Detroit, 1952-54, 1956-64.
b. Aug 12, 1919 in Seattle, Washington
d. Nov 12, 1964 in Bradenton, Florida
Source: *BaseEn 85; BioIn 6, 7; WhoProB 73*

Hutchinson, Thomas
English. Colonial Leader
Governor of MA, 1770-74; responsible for
Boston Tea Party, 1773.
b. Sep 9, 1711 in Boston, Massachusetts
d. Jun 3, 1780 in Brompton, England
Source: *Alli; AmAu; AmAu&B; AmBi;
ApCAB; CyAL 1; DcAmAu; DcAmB; DcNAA;
Drake; EncAB-H; OxAmL; PenC AM;
REnAL; TwCBDA; WebAB; WhAm HS*

Hutt, William Ian Dewitt
Canadian. Director, Producer
Member, Stratford, ON Shakespeare Festival
Co., as actor, director, since 1953.
b. May 2, 1920 in Toronto, Ontario
Source: *CanWW 70, 79; CreCan 1; WhoAm
82, 84; WhoThe 77*

Hutter, Ralf
see: Kraftwerk

Hutton, Addison
American. Religious Leader, Architect
b. 1834
d. 1916
Source: *BioIn 5, 10*

Hutton, Barbara
"Poor Little Rich Girl"
American. Socialite
Granddaughter of FW Woolworth, heir to
family fortune; married seven times.
b. Nov 14, 1912 in New York, New York
d. May 11, 1979 in Los Angeles, California
Source: *CelR; GoodHs; InWom; NewYTBS
79; WhAm 7*

Hutton, Betty
[Betty Thornburg]
American. Actress
Best known for film *Annie Get Your Gun*,
1950.
b. Feb 26, 1921 in Battle Creek, Michigan
Source: *BiE&WWA; CmMov; CurBio 50;
FilmEn; FilmgC; InWom; IntMPA 82;
MotPP; MovMk; OxFilm; WhoHol A*

Hutton, Edward F
American. Banker
b. 1877 in New York, New York
d. Jul 11, 1962 in Westbury, New York
Source: *BioIn 2, 5, 6; WhAm 4*

Hutton, Ina Ray
"Blond Bombshell of Swing"
American. Band Leader, Singer
Founded one of first all-female orchestras,
1935-40.
b. Mar 3, 1916 in Chicago, Illinois
d. Feb 19, 1984 in Ventura, California
Source: *AnObit 1984; WhoJazz 72*

Hutton, James
Scottish. Geologist
b. Jun 3, 1726 in Edinburgh, Scotland
d. Mar 26, 1797
Source: *Alli; BiDLA, SUP; DcEnL; McGEWB*

Hutton, Jim
American. Actor
Starred in films *Where the Boys Are*, 1960;
The Trouble with Angels, 1966; father of
Timothy Hutton.
b. May 31, 1938 in Binghamton, New York
d. Jun 2, 1979 in Los Angeles, California
Source: *FilmgC; IntMPA 77; MotPP; MovMk;
WhoHol A*

Hutton, Lauren (Mary Laurence)
American. Model, Actress
Film career since 1968; films include *The
Gambler; American Gigolo.*
b. Nov 17, 1944 in Charleston, South
Carolina
Source: *BioIn 12; BioNews 75; BkPepl;
ConTFT 3; IntMPA 82; WhoHol A*

Hutton, Robert
[Robert Bruce Winne]
American. Actor
Had boy-next-door roles in 1940s films.
b. Jun 11, 1920 in Kingston, New York
Source: *FilmEn; FilmgC; HolP 40; IntMPA
82; WhoHol A*

Hutton, Timothy James
American. Actor
Won Oscar, 1980, for *Ordinary People*, 1980;
starred in *Taps*, 1981.
b. Aug 16, 1960 in Malibu, California
Source: *IntMPA 82*

Huxley, Aldous Leonard
English. Author, Critic
Best known for *Brave New World*, 1932,
Brave New World Revisited, 1958.
b. Jul 26, 1894 in Godalming, England
d. Nov 22, 1963 in Los Angeles, California
Source: *AmAu&B; AtlBL; BiDPara; CasWL;
Chambr 3; ChhPo, S1, S2; CnMD; CnMWL;
ConAu 85; ConLC 1, 3, 4, 5, 8, 11, 18;
CyWA; DcLEL; EncWL; EvLB; LongCTC;
ModBrL, S1; ModWD; NewC; OxEng; PenC
ENG; RAdv 1; REn; TwCA, SUP; TwCWr;
WebE&AL; WhAm 4; WhoTwCL*

Huxley, Andrew Fielding
English. Scientist, Educator
b. Nov 22, 1917 in London, England
Source: *IntWW 74; Who 74; WhoAm 74, 76,
78, 80, 82; WhoWor 78*

Huxley, Elspeth Josceline Grant
English. Author
b. Jul 23, 1907 in London, England
Source: *ConAu 77; DcLEL; EncMys; IntWW
74; LongCTC; TwCWr; Who 74; WhoAmW
74; WhoWor 78; WorAu; WrDr 76*

Huxley, Julian Sorell, Sir
English. Biologist, Author
b. Jun 22, 1887 in London, England
d. Feb 14, 1975 in London, England
Source: *Au&Wr 71; Chambr 3; ConAu 9R,
57; CurBio 42, 63; DcLEL; EvLB; IntWW
74; LongCTC; NewC; OxEng; OxFilm; PenC
ENG; REn; TwCA, SUP; TwCWr; WhAm 6;
Who 74; WhoLA; WhoUN 75; WhoWor 78*

Huxley, Laura Archera
Italian. Author
b. in Turin, Italy
Source: *AmAu&B; ConAu 13R; NewYTBE 71*

Huxley, Thomas Henry
English. Biologist, Author
Foremost defender of Darwin's theories;
wrote *Man's Place in Nature*, 1863.
b. May 4, 1825 in Ealing, England
d. Jun 29, 1895 in Eastbourne, England
Source: *Alli, SUP; AtlBL; BbD; BiD&SB;
BrAu 19; CasWL; Chambr 3; ChhPo S2;
CrtT 3; CyWA; DcEnA, AP; DcEnL; DcEuL;
DcLEL; EvLB; MouLC 4; NewC; OxEng;
PenC ENG; REn; WebE&AL*

Huxtable, Ada Louise
[Ada Louise Landman]
American. Critic, Editor
b. 1921 in New York, New York
Source: *CelR; CurBio 73; WhoAm 74, 76, 78,
80, 82; WhoAmA 73; WhoE 74*

Huygens, Christian
Dutch. Physicist, Astronomer
Discovered rings of Saturn, 1655; developed
wave theory of light, 1678.
b. Apr 14, 1629 in The Hague, Netherlands
d. Jun 8, 1695
Source: *AsBiEn; DcEuL; DcScB; McGEWB;
NewCol 75; WebBD 80*

Huysmans, Joris Karl
[Charles Marie Georges]
French. Author
Wrote realist novels *Marthe*, 1876; *Rebours*,
1884.
b. Feb 5, 1848 in Paris, France
d. May 12, 1907 in Paris, France
Source: *AtlBL; BbD; BiD&SB; CasWL;
ClDMEL; CyWA; EncWL; EvEuW; ModRL;
OxFr; REn; WhoTwCL*

Hyams, Joe (Joseph)
American. Journalist, Author
b. Jun 6, 1923 in Cambridge, Massachusetts
Source: *AmAu&B; ConAu 17R; WhoAm 82;
WrDr 76*

Hyatt, Joel
[Joel Zylberberg]
American. Lawyer, Businessman
Co-founder, Hyatt Legal Services, 1977.
b. May 6, 1950 in Cleveland, Ohio
Source: *ConNews 85-3; WhoAm 84*

Hyde-White, Wilfrid
English. Actor
Played Colonel Pickering in film version of
My Fair Lady, 1964.
b. May 12, 1903 in Glos, England
Source: *BiE&WWA; FilmgC; IntMPA 75, 76,
77; MovMk; NotNAT; OxFilm; Who 74;
WhoAm 82; WhoHol A; WhoThe 77*

Hyer, Martha
American. Actress
Received 1959 Oscar nomination for *Some
Came Running.*
b. Aug 10, 1924 in Fort Worth, Texas
Source: *FilmgC; IntMPA 76, 77, 78, 79, 80,
81, 82; MotPP; MovMk; WhoAm 82, 84;
WhoAmW 77; WhoHol A*

Hyland, Brian
American. Singer
Pop singer who had novelty hit, "Itsy Bitsy
Teenie Weenie Yellow Polkadot Bikini,"
1960.
b. Nov 12, 1943 in Woodhaven, New York
Source: *RkOn 74; RolSEnR 83; WhoRock 81*

Hyland, Diana
[Joan Diana Genter]
American. Actress
Played Joan Bradford on TV series "Eight Is
Enough"; died after first season.
b. Jan 25, 1936 in Cleveland Heights, Ohio
d. Mar 27, 1977 in Los Angeles, California
Source: *BiE&WWA; WhoAm 74; WhoHol A*

Hyman, Earle
American. Actor
b. Oct 11, 1926 in Rocky Mount, North
Carolina
Source: *BiE&WWA; ConTFT 3; NotNAT;
WhoHol A; WhoThe 77*

Hynde, Chrissie (Christine Elaine)
[The Pretenders]
American. Singer, Songwriter
Founded British rock group The Pretenders,
1978.
b. Sep 7, 1951 in Akron, Ohio
Source: *BioIn 12*

Hynek, J(oseph) Allen
American. Astronomer
Consultant to US Air Force on UFO's;
author *The UFO Experience*, 1951.
b. May 1, 1910 in Chicago, Illinois
d. Apr 27, 1986 in Scottsdale, Arizona
Source: *AmM&WS 73P; CurBio 86; WhoAm
74; WhoWor 74*

Hynes, John B
American. Politician
b. 1898
d. Jan 6, 1970 in Boston, Massachusetts
Source: *NewYTBE 70; WhAm 5*

Hypatia
Alexandrian. Philosopher, Mathematician
d. 415
Source: *NewCol 75*

Hyperides
Greek. Statesman, Orator
b. 389 BC
d. 323 BC
Source: *CasWL*

Hyslop, James Hervey
American. Philosopher
b. Aug 18, 1854 in Xenia, Ohio
d. Jun 17, 1920
Source: *AmAu&B; AmLY; BiDPara; DcAmAu;
DcNAA; OhA&B*

I

Iacocca, Lee (Lido Anthony)
American. Auto Executive
Chm., chief exec., Chrysler Corp., 1979--;
  1985 autobiography is best non-fiction
  seller in publishing history.
b. Oct 15, 1924 in Allentown, Pennsylvania
Source: *BioNews 74; BusPN; CelR; CurBio
71; IntWW 74; NewYTBE 71; St&PR 75;
Ward 77; WhoAm 76, 78, 80, 82, 84;
WhoMW 74, 76, 78; WhoWor 74*

Iakovos, Archbishop
Greek. Religious Leader
b. Jul 29, 1911
Source: *BioIn 9; CurBio 60; WhoAm 82*

Ian, Janis
[Janis Fink]
American. Singer, Songwriter
Won Grammy, 1975, for "At Seventeen."
b. May 7, 1950 in New York, New York
Source: *BioIn 7, 8, 10, 11; BkPepl; EncPR&S
74; RkOn 74; WhoAm 82*

Ian and Sylvia
[Sylvia Fricker; Ian Tyson]
Canadian. Music Group
Husband-wife folksinging duo, formed 1959;
  sang country music, 1960s.
Source: *EncFCWM 69; RolSEnR 83*

Iba, Henry P
American. Basketball Coach
b. Aug 6, 1904 in Easton, Missouri
Source: *BioIn 8, 9, 10; WhoBbl 73*

Ibarruri, Dolores
"La Pasionaria"
Spanish. Revolutionary
b. Dec 9, 1895 in Gallarta, Spain
Source: *CurBio 67; InWom*

Ibert, Jacques
French. Composer
Director, Paris Opera, French Academy in
  Rome; wrote music for films, 1937-55.
b. Aug 15, 1890 in Paris, France
d. Feb 5, 1962 in Paris, France
Source: *DcCM; DcFM; NewCol 75; OxFilm;
WhAm 4; WorEFlm*

Iberville, Pierre Le Moyne, sieur d'
"Le Cid Canadien"
Canadian. Explorer, Soldier
Explored Mississippi, discovered Lake
  Pontchartrain; founded French territory of
  LA, 1699.
b. Jul 20, 1661 in Montreal, Quebec
d. Feb 7, 1728 in Ottawa, Ontario
Source: *AmBi; ApCAB; BiDSA; DcAmB;
DcCathB; EncSoH; HarEnUS; LinLib S;
MacDCB 78; OxAmH; OxCan; REn; REnAL;
WebAB 79*

Ibn Batutah
[Muhammad ibn 'abd Allah]
Arabian. Traveler
b. 1304 in Tangiers, Morocco
d. 1378 in Fez, Morocco
Source: *BiD&SB; NewC; NewCol 75*

Ibn-Saud
[Abdul Aziz ibn Saud]
Saudi. King
Founder of Saudi Arabia, 1932, who was
  king, 1932-53.
b. 1880 in Riyadh, Saudi Arabia
d. Nov 9, 1953 in Saudi Arabia
Source: *CurBio 54; NewCol 75; WebBD 80*

Ibsen, Henrik
Norwegian. Dramatist, Author
Depicted 19th c. women in *A Doll's House,*
1879; *Hedda Gabler,* 1890.
b. Mar 20, 1828 in Skien, Norway
d. May 23, 1906 in Christiania, Norway
Source: *AtlBL; BbD; BiD&SB; CasWL;*
ClDMEL; CnMD; CnThe; CyWA; DcEuL;
EncWL; EuAu; EvEuW; LongCTC;
McGEWD; ModWD; NewC; OxEng; OxGer;
PenC EUR; RComWL; REn; REnWD

Ichikawa, Fusae
Japanese. Feminist, Politician
Founded Woman's Suffrage League of Japan;
elected to Parliament, 1953-71; 1974-81.
b. 1893 in Aichi Prefecture, Japan
d. Feb 11, 1981 in Tokyo, Japan
Source: *AnObit 1981; NewYTBS 81*

Ickes, Harold LeClair
American. Public Official
Committed himself to social reform,
conservation of natural resources.
b. Mar 15, 1874 in Blair County,
Pennsylvania
d. Feb 3, 1952 in Washington, District of
Columbia
Source: *AmAu&B; BiDrUSE; CurBio 41, 52;*
DcAmB S5; EncAB-H; REnAL; WebAB;
WhAm 3

Idle, Eric
[Monty Python's Flying Circus]
British. Actor, Author
Co-winner, 1983 Cannes Film Festival for
Monty Python's Meaning of Life.
b. Mar 29, 1943
Source: *BioIn 10; ConAu 116; ConLC 21*

Idol, Billy
[William Board]
English. Singer
Punk rock teen idol; hit singles "Eyes
Without a Face," "Catch My Fall," 1984.
b. Nov 30, 1955 in Surrey, England
Source: *RkOn 85; WhoRocM 82*

Idris I
[Sayyid Muhammad Idris as-Sanusi]
Liberian. Ruler
First, only king of Libya, 1951-69; deposed
by Khadafy.
b. Mar 13, 1890 in Jaghbub, Libya
d. May 25, 1983 in Cairo, Egypt
Source: *CurBio 56, 83; IntWW 82, 83; MidE*
81, 82; NewYTBS 83

Iglesias, Julio
[Julio Iglesias de la Cueva]
Spanish. Singer, Songwriter
Master of love song; has sold over 100
million albums.
b. Sep 23, 1943 in Madrid, Spain
Source: *CurBio 84*

Ignatius of Loyola, Saint
[Inigo do Onez y Loyola]
Spanish. Religious Leader
Founded Society of Jesus or Jesuits, 1540;
concerned with education, missionary
work; canonized 1622.
b. 1491 in Loyola, Spain
d. Jul 31, 1556 in Rome, Italy
Source: *CasWL; DcSpL; EuAu; LinLib L;*
McGEWB; NewC; REn

Igoe, "Hype" (Herbert A)
American. Journalist, Cartoonist
b. Jun 13, 1885
d. Feb 11, 1954 in New York, New York
Source: *CurBio 45*

Ike, Reverend
[Frederick Joseph Eikerenkoetter II]
American. Evangelist
b. Jun 1, 1935 in Ridgeland, South Carolina
Source: *BioIn 10, 11; BkPepl; EncO&P 78;*
WhoAm 78

Ike and Tina Turner
American. Music Group
Source: *BiDAmM; CelR; EncPR&S 74;*
IlEncRk; RkOneH

Ikhnaton
[Akhenaton]
Egyptian. King
Ruled ancient Egypt ca. 1372-1354 BC;
changed religious beliefs from polytheism
to monotheism.
b. 1372 BC
d. 1354 BC
Source: *NewC; NewCol 75*

Ileana
Romanian. Princess, Nurse
b. 1904
Source: *InWom*

Ilg, Frances Lillian
American. Author, Physician, Educator
Co-founded, Gesell Institute of Child
    Development, 1950-70; wrote books on
    child care, development.
b. Oct 11, 1902 in Oak Park, Illinois
d. Jul 26, 1981 in Manitowish Waters,
    Wisconsin
Source: *AmAu&B; BioIn 4; ConAu 107;
CurBio 56, 81; InWom; NewYTBS 81;
WhoAmW 74, 58, 64, 66*

Ilitch, Mike
American. Businessman, Hockey Executive
Owner, Detroit Red Wings hockey team;
    established Little Caesar's pizza franchises.
b. Jul 20, 1929 in Detroit, Michigan
Source: *NF*

Illia, Arturo Umberto
Argentine. Political Leader
Won first Argentinian presidential election
    based on proportional representation, 1963;
    ousted in coup, 1966.
b. Aug 4, 1900 in Cordoba, Argentina
d. Jan 18, 1983 in Cordoba, Argentina
Source: *AnObit 1983; CurBio 65, 83;
EncLatA; IntWW 81, 82, 83*

Illich, Ivan
American. Educator
Former Roman Catholic priest who founded
    Intercultural Center of Documentation
    (CIDOC) in Mexico, 1961.
b. Sep 4, 1926 in Vienna, Austria
Source: *AuNews 2; ConAu 53; CurBio 69;
WhoAm 74, 76, 78, 80, 82; WhoS&SW 82;
WhoWor 78; WrDr 76*

Illingworth, Leslie Gilbert
Welsh. Cartoonist
Cartoonist for *Daily Mail*, 1939-68.
b. Sep 2, 1902 in Barry, South Wales
d. 1979
Source: *BioIn 12; DcBrAr 2; Who 74;
WorECar*

Illsley, John
see: Dire Straits

Ilyushin, Sergei Vladimirovich
Russian. Aircraft Designer
Designed IL-2, or dive bomber, Soviet fighter
    plane of WW II.
b. Mar 31, 1894 in Diyalora, Russia
d. Feb 9, 1977 in Moscow, U.S.S.R.
Source: *IntWW 77; NewYTBS 77; WhWW-II;
Who 74; WhoWor 74*

Iman
American. Actress, Model
b. 1955 in Somalia
Source: *BioIn 10, 11*

Imlach, "Punch" (George)
Canadian. Hockey Coach, Hockey Executive
Coach, Toronto Maple Leafs hockey team,
    1958-69; Buffalo Sabres hockeyteam, 1970-
    71; won four Stanley Cups.
b. Mar 15, 1918 in Toronto, Ontario
Source: *HocEn; WhoE 74; WhoHcky 73*

Immelmann, Max
German. Aviator
b. 1890
d. Jul 18, 1916
Source: *WebBD 80*

Impellitteri, Vincent R
American. Mayor
b. Feb 4, 1900 in Isnello, Sicily
Source: *CurBio 51*

Inatome, Rick
American. Business Executive
Founder, Computer Mart, 1976; pres., chief
    exec., Inacomp Computer Centers, 1982--.
b. Jul 27, 1953 in Detroit, Michigan
Source: *ConNews 85-4; WhoF&I 83; WhoMW
82; WhoWor 82*

Ince, Thomas H(arper)
American. Director, Producer
Wrote, directed, produced films including
    Civilization, 1916.
b. Nov 6, 1882 in Newport, Rhode Island
d. Nov 19, 1924 in Beverly Hills, California
Source: *BiDFilm; BioIn 11; CmMov; DcFM;
FilmEn; FilmgC; MovMk; OxFilm; TwYS A;
WhAm 1; WhScrn 74, 77; WorEFlm*

Incredible String Band, The
[Gerard Dott; Mike Heron; Malcolm
    LeMaistre; 'Licorice' (Christina)
    McKechnie; Rose Simpson; Robin
    Williamson]
Scottish. Music Group
Source: *EncPR&S 74; IlEncRk*

Indiana, Robert
[Robert Clarke]
American. Artist
Creates art out of words; called designer of
    trivia.
b. Sep 13, 1928 in New Castle, Indiana
Source: *CelR; CurBio 73; DcCAA 71; IntWW
74; WhoAm 74, 76, 78, 80, 82; WhoAmA 73;
WhoWor 78*

Indy, Paul (Marie Theodore Vincent d')
French. Composer, Author
Composed symphonies using "cyclic form" or
the same theme throughout his
compositions.
b. Mar 27, 1851 in Paris, France
d. Dec 2, 1931 in Paris, France
Source: *AtlBL; OxFr*

Inescort, Frieda
[Frieda Wightman]
Scottish. Actress
Character actress; *Mary of Scotland*, 1936,
Pride and Prejudice, 1940.
b. Jun 29, 1901 in Edinburgh, Scotland
Source: *FilmEn; FilmgC; MotPP; MovMk;
ThFT*

Infante, Frank
see: Blondie

Infeld, Leopold
Polish. Physicist, Author
Worked with Albert Einstein on relativity
and quantum theory.
b. Aug 20, 1898 in Krakow, Poland
d. Jan 16, 1968 in Warsaw, Poland
Source: *BioIn 6, 8; CurBio 63, 68*

Inge, William
American. Dramatist
Wrote *Come Back, Little Sheba*, 1950; *Bus
Stop*, 1955.
b. May 3, 1913 in Independence, Kansas
d. Jun 10, 1973 in Hollywood Hills,
California
Source: *AmAu&B; BiE&WWA; CnMD;
CnThe; ConAu 9R; ConLC 1, 8; CroCD;
CurBio 53, 73; FilmgC; McGEWD; ModAL;
ModWD; OxAmL; OxThe; PenC AM; PIP&P;
REn; REnAL; REnWD; TwCA SUP; TwCWr;
WebE&AL; WhAm 5; WhScrn 74; WhoWor
78; WorEFlm*

Inge, William Ralph
"The Gloomy Dean"
English. Religious Leader, Author
Divinity professor, Oxford 1907-1911; dean,
St. Paul's Cathedral, London, 1911-1934.
b. Jun 6, 1860 in Craike, England
d. Feb 26, 1954 in Wallingford, England
Source: *Alli SUP; Chambr 3; DcLEL; EvLB;
LongCTC; NewC; OxEng; TwCA, SUP;
WhoLA*

Ingels, Marty
American. Comedian, Actor
b. Mar 9, 1936 in Brooklyn, Michigan
Source: *FilmgC; IntMPA 75, 76, 77, 78, 79,
80, 81, 82; WhoAm 74, 76, 78, 80, 82;
WhoHol A*

Ingersoll, Ralph McAllister
American. Journalist, Publisher
b. Dec 8, 1900 in New Haven, Connecticut
d. Mar 8, 1985 in Miami Beach, Florida
Source: *Au&Wr 71; ChhPo; ConAu P-1;
CurBio 40; IntWW 74; REnAL; TwCA SUP;
WhNAA; Who 74; WhoAm 74, 76, 78, 80,
82; WhoE 74*

Ingersoll, Robert Green
American. Lawyer, Politician
Noted trial lawyer; Illinois attorney general
1867-69. Published influential, religious
lectures.
b. Aug 11, 1833 in Dresden, New York
d. Jul 21, 1899 in New York, New York
Source: *Alli SUP; AmAu; AmAu&B; AmBi;
ApCAB; BbD; BiD&SB; DcAmAu; DcAmB;
DcNAA; EncAB-H; OxAmL; REn; REnAL;
TwCBDA; WebAB; WhAm 1; WhAmP*

Ingersoll, Simon
American. Inventor
b. Mar 3, 1818 in Stanwich, Connecticut
d. Jul 24, 1894
Source: *BioIn 9; WhAm HS*

Ingersoll, Stuart H
American. Military Leader
Navy admiral who commanded Sixth,
Seventh fleets.
b. 1898
d. Jan 29, 1983 in Newport, Rhode Island
Source: *NewYTBS 84*

Inghelbrecht, Desire
French. Conductor, Composer
b. Sep 17, 1880 in Paris, France
d. Feb 14, 1965 in Paris, France
Source: *NewEOp 71; OxMus*

Ingold, Christopher
British. Chemist
b. 1893
d. 1970
Source: *BioIn 1, 7, 9*

Ingram, James
American. Singer, Songwriter
With Patti Austin, had hit single "Baby
Come to Me," 1982.
b. Feb 16, 1956 in Akron, Ohio
Source: *RkOn 85*

Ingram, Rex
American. Actor
Best known as slave Jim in film *Adventures
of Huckleberry Finn,* 1939.
b. Oct 20, 1895 in Cairo, Illinois
d. Sep 19, 1969 in Los Angeles, California
Source: *BiE&WWA; FilmEn; FilmgC;
MovMk; OxFilm; Vers A; WhScrn 74, 77*

Ingres, Jean Auguste Dominique
French. Artist
Portrait artist noted for precise neoclassic
linear style and personality.
b. Aug 29, 1780 in Montauban, France
d. Jan 13, 1867 in Paris, France
Source: *AtlBL; NewC; NewCol 75; OxFr; REn*

Ingrid
Danish. Queen
b. 1910
Source: *InWom*

Ingstad, Helge
Norwegian.
b. Dec 30, 1899 in Meraker, Norway
Source: *ConAu 65; IntWW 74; OxCan;
WhoWor 78*

Ink Spots, The
[Billy Bowen; Charlie Fuqua; Orville Jones;
Bill Kenny; Herb Kenny; Ivory Watson]
American. Music Group
Biggest hit "If I Didn't Care," 1939.
Source: *CmpEPM*

Inman, Bobby Ray
American. Government Official, Businessman
Deputy director, CIA, 1981-82; pres., chief
exec., Microelectronics and Computer
Technologies Corp., 1983--.
b. Apr 4, 1931 in Rhonesboro, Texas
Source: *ConNews 85-1; WhoAm 82, 84;
WhoGov 75; WhoS&SW 78*

Inman, Henry
American. Artist
Historical portrait painter; founded National
Academy of Design; director Pennsylvania
Academy of Fine Arts.
b. Oct 28, 1801 in Utica, New York
d. Jan 17, 1846 in New York, New York
Source: *AmBi; DcAmB; NewCol 75; WebAB;
WebBD 80; WhAm HS*

Innaurato, Albert
American. Screenwriter, Dramatist
Won Obie for *Gemini,* 1977.
b. Jun 2, 1948 in Philadelphia, Pennsylvania
Source: *ConAu 115*

Innes, Hammond, pseud.
[Ralph Hammond-Innes]
English. Author
b. Jul 15, 1913 in Horsham, England
Source: *AmAu&B; AuBYP; ConAu 5R, 4NR;
ConNov 72, 76; CurBio 54; IntWW 74;
LongCTC; REn; TwCWr; Who 74; WhoWor
78; WorAu; WrDr 80*

Inness, George
American. Artist
Landscape artist; member National Academy
of Design, 1868.
b. May 1, 1825 in Newburgh, New York
d. Aug 3, 1894 in Scotland
Source: *AmBi; ApCAB; AtlBL; DcAmB;
Drake; NewCol 75; OxAmL; REn; TwCBDA;
WebAB; WhAm HS*

Innis, Roy
[Emile Alfredo]
American. Civil Rights Leader
Nat. director, CORE, 1968--.
b. Jun 6, 1934 in Virgin Islands
Source: *CelR; CurBio 69; IntWW 74;
WhoAm 74, 76, 78, 80, 82; WhoBlA 75;
WhoUN 75*

Inonu, Ismet
Turkish. Statesman
First prime minister Republic of Turkey,
1923-1937; pres., 1938-1950.
b. Sep 24, 1884 in Izmik, Asia Minor
d. Dec 25, 1973 in Ankara, Turkey
Source: *CurBio 41, 64, 74; NewCol 75;
NewYTBE 73; WhAm 6; Who 74*

Inouye, Daniel Ken
American. Senator
b. Sep 7, 1924 in Honolulu, Hawaii
Source: *BiDrAC; CelR; CngDr 74; ConAu
25R; CurBio 60; IntWW 74; WhoAm 74, 76,
78, 80, 82; WhoAmP 73; WhoGov 75;
WhoWest 84; WhoWor 78*

Insull, Samuel
Financier
b. Nov 11, 1859 in London, England
d. Jul 16, 1938 in Paris, France
Source: *AmBi; DcAmB S2; EncAB-H; NewCol
75; WebAB; WhAm 1*

Interwoven Pair, The
see: Hare, Ernie; Jones, Billy

INXS
[Garry Gary Beers; Andrew Farriss; Jon
  Farriss; Tim Farriss; Michael Hutchence;
  Kirk Pengilly]
Australian. Music Group
Hit single "Original Sin," 1984, featured
  Daryl Hall on back-up vocals.
Source: *RkOn 85*

Iommi, Anthony
see: Black Sabbath

Ionesco, Eugene
French. Author, Dramatist
Theater of the absurd; *The Bald Prima
  Donna,* 1950; *The Rhinoceros,* 1959.
b. Nov 26, 1912 in Slatina, Romania
Source: *BiE&WWA; CasWL; CelR; CnMD;
  CnMWL; CnThe; ConAu 9R; ConLC 1, 4, 6,
  9, 11, 15; CroCD; CurBio 59; EncWL;
  EvEuW; IntWW 74; LongCTC; McGEWD;
  ModRL; ModWD; NewYTBE 70; NotNAT;
  OxThe; PenC EUR; PIP&P; RComWL; REn;
  REnWD; SmATA 7; TwCWr; Who 74;
  WhoAm 74, 76, 78, 80, 82; WhoThe 77;
  WhoTwCL; WhoWor 78; WorAu*

Ippolitov-Ivanov, Mikhail Mikhailovich
Russian. Composer
Awarded "People's Artist of the Republic,"
  1923; conductor, Moscow Opera, 1925.
b. Nov 9, 1859 in Gatchina, Russia
d. Jan 26, 1935 in Moscow, U.S.S.R.
Source: *BioIn 4, 9; NewCol 75*

Irons, Jeremy
British. Actor
Best known role in *French Lieutenant's
  Woman,* 1981.
b. Sep 19, 1948 in Cowes, Isle of Wight
Source: *IntMPA 84; IntWW 82, 83;
  NewYTBS 84; WhoAm 84*

Iqbal, Mahomed
[Muhammad Iqbal]
Indian. Poet, Philosopher
Pres., Muslim League, 1930; advocated
  Pakistani independence.
b. 1873
d. 1938
Source: *NewCol 75; WebBD 80*

Irani, Merwan S
see: Meher Baba

Iredell, James
American. Supreme Court Justice
b. Oct 5, 1751 in Lewes, England
d. Oct 2, 1799 in Edenton, North Carolina
Source: *AmBi; ApCAB; BioIn 2, 3, 5; Drake;
  NatCab 1; NewCol 75*

Ireland, Jill
[Mrs. Charles Bronson]
American. Actress
Lead opposite Charles Bronson in films such
  as *Breakheart Pass,* 1976.
b. Apr 24, 1936 in London, England
Source: *FilmgC; IntMPA 82; WhoAm 82;
  WhoHol A*

Ireland, John
English. Composer
Wrote chamber music, choruses, piano pieces,
  orchestral works, popular songs.
b. Aug 13, 1879 in Inglewood, England
d. Jun 12, 1962 in Washington, England
Source: *Baker 78; BioIn 3, 4, 6, 7, 8; DcCM;
  NewCol 75; WhAm 4*

Ireland, John
Canadian. Actor
Oscar nominee for *All the King's Men,* 1949.
b. Jan 30, 1915 in Victoria, British Columbia
Source: *BiE&WWA; CmMov; FilmgC;
  IntMPA 75, 76, 77, 78, 79, 80, 81, 82;
  MovMk; NotNAT; OxFilm*

Ireland, William Henry
English. Imposter
Wrote two "pseudo-Shakespearian" plays,
  Vortigern and Rowena; Henry II.
b. 1777
d. 1835
Source: *Alli; BiDLA; CasWL; Chambr 2;
  ChhPo; DcEnL; DcLEL; EvLB; NewC; REn*

Irene
[Irene Gibbons]
American. Fashion Designer
b. 1907 in Montana
d. Nov 15, 1962 in Hollywood, California
Source: *FilmgC; InWom; WorFshn*

Irene
Greek. Princess
b. 1942
Source: *BioIn 9*

Irene
Dutch. Princess
b. Aug 5, 1939 in Soestdijk, Netherlands
Source: *WhoWor 78*

Irish, Edward Simmons (Ned)
American. Basketball Executive
Founder, pres., NY Knickerbockers basketball
  team, 1946-74; made college basketball a
  major spectator sport.
b. May 6, 1905 in Lake George, New York
d. Jan 21, 1982 in Venice, Florida
Source: *NewYTBS 82; WhoAm 74, 76;
  WhoBbl 73*

Irish Hunger Strikers
[Michael Devine; Kieran Doherty; Francis
Hughes; Martin Hurson; Kevin Lynch;
Raymond McCreesh; Joe McDonnell;
Thomas McIlwee; Patrick O'Hara; Boby
Sands]
Irish. Revolutionaries
Young IRA martyrs who starved themelves
to death in Belfast's Maze Prison, 1981.
Source: *NF*

Irish Rovers
[Jimmy Ferguson; Wilcil McDowell; George
Millar; Joe Millar; Will Millar]
Irish. Music Group
Source: *ClbCR*

Iron Butterfly
[Erik Braun; Ronald Bushy; Lee Dorman;
, Doug Ingle; Michael Pinera; Lawrence
· Reinhardt]
American. Music Group
Source: *EncPR&S 74; RkOn 74*

Iron Maiden
[Clive Burr; Paul Di'Anno; Steve Harris;
Dave Murray; Adrian Smith; Dennis
Stratton]
British. Music Group
Heavy metal band named after medieval
torture device.
Source: *IlEncRk*

Ironside, Christopher
Artist, Designer
b. 1913
Source: *Who 74*

Ironside, Henry Allan
"Archbishop of Fundamentalism"
Canadian. Clergyman, Educator, Author,
Broadcaster
Popular broadcaster; pastor of Chicago's
Moody Memorial Church, 1930s-40s.
b. Oct 14, 1876 in Toronto, Ontario
d. Jan 15, 1951 in Rotu Rua, New Zealand
Source: *ConAu 115; CurBio 45, 51; DcAmB
S5*

Ironside, William E
Scottish. Army Officer
b. May 6, 1880 in Ironside, Scotland
d. Sep 22, 1959 in London, England
Source: *CurBio 40, 59*

Irvin, Monte (Monford Merrill)
American. Baseball Player
b. Feb 25, 1919 in Columbia, Alabama
Source: *BaseEn 85; NewYTBE 73*

Irvin, Rea
American. Artist, Cartoonist, Editor
Created first *New Yorker* cover, introducing
best known character, Eustace Tilley.
b. Aug 26, 1881 in San Francisco, California
d. May 28, 1972 in Frederiksted, Virgin
Islands
Source: *ChhPo S1; ConAu 93; NewYTBE 72;
WhAm 5; WhoAmA 80; WorECar*

Irvin, Robert W
American. Author, Editor
Automotive writer for 30 yrs; editor,
Automotive News; publisher, *Auto Week.*
b. Mar 3, 1933 in Highland Park, Michigan
d. Dec 1, 1980 in Chicago, Illinois
Source: *BioIn 9; ConAu 103; Ward 77*

Irving, Clifford Michael
American. Author
Served 17 months in prison for writing false
autobiography of Howard Hughes.
b. Nov 5, 1930 in New York, New York
Source: *Au&Wr 71; AuNews 1; BioNews 74;
ConAu 1R, 2NR; NewYTBE 72; WrDr 76*

Irving, Edith
[Edith Sommer]
Swiss. Artist
Source: *BioIn 10*

Irving, Edward
Scottish. Mystic
b. Aug 4, 1792 in Annan, Scotland
d. Dec 7, 1834 in Glasgow, Scotland
Source: *Alli; BbD; BrAu 19; Chambr 3;
DcEnL; EvLB; NewC; NewCol 75*

Irving, Henry, Sir
[John Henry Brodribb]
English. Actor
Noted for Shakespearian roles; first actor to
be knighted, 1895.
b. Feb 6, 1838 in Glastonbury, England
d. Oct 13, 1905 in Bradford, England
Source: *FamA&A; NewC; NewCol 75; OxThe;
REn; WhAm 1*

Irving, Isabel
American. Actress
Active on stage from 1887 to 1936.
b. Feb 28, 1871 in Bridgeport, Connecticut
d. Sep 1, 1944 in Nantucket, Massachusetts
Source: *InWom; WhAm 2; WhoStg 1906,
1908; WomWWA 14*

Irving, John
American. Author
Best known work *The World According to
  Garp,* 1978.
b. Mar 2, 1942 in Exeter, New Hampshire
Source: *ConAu 25R; ConLC 13; WhoAm 82*

Irving, Jules
American. Actor, Producer, Director
Artistic director, Repertory Theatre of
  Lincoln Center, 1964-72; co-founder, San
  Francisco Actors Workshop, 1952-64.
b. Apr 13, 1925 in New York, New York
d. Jul 28, 1979 in Reno, Nevada
Source: *BiE&WWA; CurBio 70, 79;
NewYTBS 79; NotNAT; PIP&P A; WhAm 7;
WhoAm 74; WhoE 75; WhoThe 72, 77*

Irving, Laurence Sidney
English. Actor
Had roles in his own plays, *Peter the Great,
  Unwritten Law;* son of Henry Irving.
b. Dec 21, 1871 in London, England
d. May 29, 1914 in Canada
Source: *EncWT; OxThe; WhLit; WhThe*

Irving, Robert Augustine
American. Conductor
b. Aug 28, 1913 in Winchester, England
Source: *Who 74; WhoAm 74, 76, 78, 80, 82;
WhoMus 72*

Irving, Washington
[Diedrich Knickerbocker]
American. Author, Diplomat, Historian
Wrote *Rip Van Winkle, Legend of Sleepy
  Hollow,* 1820.
b. Apr 3, 1783 in New York, New York
d. Nov 28, 1859 in Tarrytown, New York
Source: *Alli; AmAu; AmBi; AmWr; ApCAB;
AtlBL; BbD; BiAUS; BiD&SB; CarSB;
CasWL; Chambr 3; ChhPo, S2; CnDAL; CrtT
3; CyAL 1; CyWA; DcAmAu; DcAmB; DcBiA;
DcEnA; DcLEL; DcSpL; Drake; EncAB-H;
FamAYP; MouLC 3; OxCan; OxThe; PenC
AM; RAdv 1; REn; REnAL; TwCBDA;
WebAB; WebE&AL; WhAm HS; WhoChL;
WisWr*

Irwin, Hale
American. Golfer
Had 13 US victories, including US Open,
  1974, 1979.
b. Jun 3, 1945 in Joplin, Missouri
Source: *WhoAm 82; WhoGolf; WhoIntG*

Irwin, James Benson
American. Astronaut
b. Mar 17, 1930 in Pittsburgh, Pennsylvania
Source: *NewYTBE 71; NewYTBS 74; WhoAm
74, 76, 78, 80, 82; WhoWor 78*

Irwin, Margaret
English. Author
b. 1889 in London, England
d. 1967
Source: *ConAu 93; CurBio 46; DcLEL;
LongCTC; TwCA SUP; TwCWr; WhoLA*

Irwin, May
[May Campbell]
Canadian. Actress
Made screen history in Thomas Edison's *The
  Kiss,* 1896; denounced as immoral; noted
  farce comedienne with Tony Pasteur, 1877-
  83.
b. Jun 27, 1862 in Whitby, Ontario
d. Oct 22, 1938 in New York, New York
Source: *AmBi; DcAmB S2; FamA&A; FilmEn;
Film 1; InWom; MotPP; NotAW; TwYS;
WhAm 1; WhoStg 1906, 1908*

Irwin, Wallace
American. Journalist, Humorist
b. Mar 15, 1875 in Oneida, New York
d. Feb 14, 1959 in Southern Pines, North
  Carolina
Source: *AmAu&B; ChhPo S1, S2; CnDAL;
ConAmL; DcAmAu; OxAmL; REn; REnAL;
Str&VC; TwCA, SUP; WhAm 3; WhScrn 77*

Irwin, Will
American. Journalist
b. Sep 14, 1873 in Oneida, New York
d. Feb 24, 1948 in New York, New York
Source: *AmAu&B; ChhPo S1; EncMys;
OxAmL; REnAL; WhNAA; WhScrn 77*

Isaac
Biblical Character
Source: *BioIn 10; NewCol 75*

Isaacs, Alick
Scottish. Bacteriologist
Co-discovered chemotherapeutic agent,
  Interferon.
b. Jul 17, 1921 in Glasgow, Scotland
d. Jan 26, 1967 in London, England
Source: *BiESc; DcNaB 1961; ObitOF 79;
ObitT 1961*

Isabella I
[Isabelala Catolica]
Spanish. Ruler
Queen of Castile, 1474; financed Columbus'
  voyage, 1492.
b. Apr 22, 1451 in Madrigal, Spain
d. Nov 26, 1504 in Medina del Campo,
  Spain
Source: *InWom; LinLib S; NewCol 75;
WebBD 80*

Isabella II
[Maria Isabella Louisa]
Spanish. Ruler
Queen of Spain, 1833-1868.
b. Oct 10, 1830 in Madrid, Spain
d. Apr 19, 1904 in Paris, France
Source: *BioIn 6, 7; McGEWB; NewCol 75; WebBD 80*

Isaiah
Hebrew. Prophet
fl. 740 century ?BC
Source: *DcOrL 3; NewC; NewCol 75*

Isbert, Margot Benary
see: Benary-Isbert, Margot

Ishak, Yusof bin
Singaporean. President
b. Aug 12, 1910
d. Nov 23, 1970 in Singapore
Source: *NewYTBE 70*

Isham, Samuel
American. Artist, Author
b. May 12, 1855 in New York, New York
d. Jun 12, 1914
Source: *AmAu&B; BioIn 2; DcNAA*

Isherwood, Christopher William
American. Author, Dramatist
Play *Caberet*, 1966 was based on his stories *Goodbye to Berlin*, 1935.
b. Aug 26, 1904 in Cheshire, England
d. Jan 4, 1986 in Santa Monica, California
Source: *AmAu&B; Au&Wr 71; CasWL; CelR; CnMD; CnMWL; ConAu 13R; ConLC 1, 9, 11, 14; ConNov 72, 76; CurBio 72; DcLEL; DrAF 76; EncWL; EvLB; IntWW 74; LongCTC; McGEWD; ModBrL, S1; ModWD; NewC; NewYTBE 73; OxAmL; OxEng; PenC ENG; RAdv 1; REn; REnAL; TwCA, SUP; TwCWr; WebE&AL; Who 74; WhoAm 74, 76, 78, 80, 82; WhoTwCL; WhoWor 78; WrDr 76*

Isley Brothers
[O'Kelly Isley; Ronald Isley; Rudolph Isley]
American. Music Group
Source: *EncPR&S 74; IlEncBM 82*

Ismay, Hastings Lionel, Baron
English. Military Leader
Headed Winston Churchill's personal staff, 1940.
b. Jun 21, 1887 in Naini Tal, India
d. Dec 17, 1965 in Wormington Orange, England
Source: *CurBio 66; DcNaB 1961; HisEWW; WhWW-II*

Isocrates
Greek. Orator, Teacher
Founded Athenian school of oratory; developed literary form of rhetorical essays.
b. 436 BC
d. 338 BC
Source: *CasWL; CyEd; DcBiPP; Grk&L; LinLib L, S; LongCEL; McGEWB; NewC; NewCol 75; PenC CL; REn; WhDW*

Israels, Josef
Dutch. Artist
b. 1824 in Groningen, Netherlands
d. 1913
Source: *BioIn 2; NewCol 75; WebBD 80*

Issel, Dan
American. Basketball Player
b. Oct 25, 1948 in Batavia, Illinois
Source: *BioIn 10; WhoAm 82; WhoBbl 73*

Issigonis, Alec Arnold C, Sir
British. Engineer
b. 1905
Source: *IntWW 74; Who 74; WhoWor 78*

Istomin, Eugene George
American. Musician
b. Nov 26, 1925 in New York, New York
Source: *IntWW 74; NewYTBE 71; WhoAm 74, 76, 78, 80, 82; WhoMus 72; WhoWor 78*

Ito, Hirobumi
Japanese. Statesman
Four-time premier who was important in Japan's modernization, supporter of Western ideas.
b. Sep 2, 1841 in Choshu Province, Japan
d. Oct 26, 1909 in Harbin, Manchuria
Source: *NewCol 75; WebBD 80*

Ittner, William Butts
American. Architect
Designed numerous early 20th century schools, Masonic buildings.
b. Sep 4, 1864 in Saint Louis, Missouri
d. Jan 26, 1936 in Saint Louis, Missouri
Source: *WhAm 1*

Iturbi, Amparo
Spanish. Musician
b. 1899
d. Apr 21, 1969 in Beverly Hills, California
Source: *InWom; WhScrn 77; WhoHol B*

Iturbi, Jose
Spanish. Musician, Conductor, Composer
Pianist; appeared in films, 1940s; helped to
   popularize classical music.
b. Nov 28, 1895 in Valencia, Spain
d. Jun 28, 1980 in Los Angeles, California
Source: *CelR; CurBio 43; FilmgC; IntWW 74;
MovMk; Who 74; WhoAm 74; WhoHol A;
WhoMus 72; WhoWor 78*

Iturbide, Augustin de
[Augustin I]
Mexican. General, Emperor
Won Mexican independence from Spain,
   1821; Emperor, 1822-23.
b. Sep 27, 1783 in Valladolid, Mexico
d. Jul 19, 1824
Source: *ApCAB; BioIn 1, 2, 3, 8, 9, 10;
CmCal; DcBiPP; EncLatA; HarEnUS; NewCol
75*

Ivan III
"Ivan the Great"
Russian. Ruler
Czar of Russia, 1462-1505; compiled first
   Russian code of law.
b. Jan 22, 1440
d. Oct 27, 1505
Source: *NewCol 75; WebBD 80*

Ivan IV
"Ivan the Terrible"
Russian. Ruler
Grandson of Ivan III; czar of Russia at age
   three; assumed title 1547.
b. Aug 25, 1530
d. Mar 17, 1584
Source: *CasWL; DcRusL; NewCol 75; REn*

Ivanov, Konstantin Konstantinovich
Russian. Conductor
b. May 21, 1907 in Efremov, Russia
Source: *IntWW 74; WhoWor 78*

Ivens, Joris
[Georg Henri Anton Ivens]
Dutch. Director
Documentaries include *The Bridge,* 1928,
   Power and the Land, 1940.
b. Nov 18, 1898 in Nijmegen, Netherlands
Source: *BiDFilm; DcFM; FilmEn; FilmgC;
MovMk; OxFilm; WhoWor 74; WorEFlm*

Ives, Burl
[Icle Ivanhoe]
American. Actor, Singer
Folksinger; won 1959 Oscar for *The Big
   Country.*
b. Jun 14, 1909 in Hunt, Illinois
Source: *AmAu&B; AmSCAP 66; BiE&WWA;
CmMov; ConAu 103; CurBio 46, 60;
EncFCWM 69; FilmgC; IntMPA 75, 76, 77,
78, 79, 80, 81, 82; IntWW 74; MovMk;
NotNAT; REnAL; WhoAm 74, 76, 78, 80, 82;
WhoMus 72; WhoThe 77; WhoWor 78;
WorEFlm*

Ives, Charles Edward
American. Composer
Unconventional style of composition included
   polytonal harmonies and unusual rythms.
b. Oct 20, 1874 in Danbury, Connecticut
d. May 11, 1954 in New York, New York
Source: *AtlBL; BioNews 74; CurBio 47, 54;
DcAmB S3; DcCM; EncAB-H; NewCol 75;
OxAmL; REn; REnAL; WebAB; WhAm 3*

Ives, Frederic Eugene
American. Inventor
Pioneer in modern photography; developed
   halftone process of photoengraving.
b. Feb 17, 1856 in Litchfield, Connecticut
d. May 27, 1937 in Philadelphia,
   Pennsylvania
Source: *AmBi; DcAmB S2; DcNAA; NewCol
75; WebAB; WhAm 1*

Ives, Herbert Eugene
American. Inventor, Physicist
Helped to develop television.
b. Jul 31, 1882 in Philadelphia, Pennsylvania
d. Nov 13, 1953 in Upper Montclair, New
   Jersey
Source: *NewCol 75; WhAm 3*

Ives, James Merritt
[Currier and Ives]
American. Artist
Partner, from 1857, with Nathaniel Currier,
   Currier and Ives Lithograph Publishers.
b. Mar 5, 1824 in New York, New York
d. Jan 3, 1895 in Rye, New York
Source: *NewCol 75; WebAB*

Ivogun, Maria
[Ilse VonGunther]
Hungarian. Opera Singer
b. Nov 11, 1891 in Budapest, Hungary
Source: *InWom*

Ivory, James
American. Director
Films include *Roseland,* 1977, *Europeans,* 1979.
b. Jun 7, 1928 in Berkeley, California
Source: *BioIn 10; CurBio 81; FilmEn; FilmgC; OxFilm*

Iwama, Kazuo
Japanese. Business Executive
Pres., 1976-82; board chm., 1978-82, Sony Corp.
b. Feb 7, 1919 in Anjo City, Japan
d. Aug 24, 1982 in Tokyo, Japan
Source: *AnObit 1982; FarE&A 81; IntWW 81; LElec; NewYTBS 82; WhoWor 78*

Iwasaki, Yataro
Japanese. Business Executive
b. 1834
d. 1885
Source: *BioIn 8*

Iwatani, Toro
Japanese. Inventor
Developed video game "Pac-Man."
b. 1955
Source: *NF*

Iwerks, Ub(be)
American. Cartoonist
Developed character of Mickey Mouse for Walt Disney, 1927; won Oscars,1959, 1965.
b. Mar 24, 1901 in Kansas City, Missouri
d. Jul 8, 1971
Source: *DcFM; FilmgC; OxFilm; WorECar; WorEFlm*

Izac, Edouard Victor M
American. Government Official
b. Dec 18, 1891 in Cresco, Iowa
Source: *BioIn 7; CurBio 45*

J

J Geils Band, The
[Stephen Jo Bladd; Magic Dick; Jerome Geils; Seth Justman; Danny Klein; Peter Wolf]
American. Music Group
Combined blues, doo-woop, rhythm and blues, pop; had hit album *Freeze-Frame,* single "Centerfold," 1981.
Source: *RolSEnR 83*

Jaabari, Mohammed Ali, Sheik
Palestinian. Politician
Mayor of Hebron, Israel for 36 yrs.
b. 1900 in Jordan
d. May 29, 1980 in Hebron, Israel
Source: *BioIn 12*

Jablonski, Henryk
Polish. Historian, Socialist Leader
b. 1909
Source: *BioIn 10*

Jabotinsky, Vladimir Evgenevich
Russian. Religious Leader
Founder, pres., World Union of Zionist-Revisionists, 1922; New Zionist Organization, 1935.
b. Oct 18, 1880 in Odessa, Russia
d. Aug 3, 1940
Source: *CurBio 40*

Jack the Ripper
English. Murderer
Nickname from ferocity of crimes; five London women killed, 1888; never caught.
Source: *BioIn 9*

Jacklin, Anthony
"Jacko"
English. Golfer
Won British Open, 1969, US Open, 1970.
b. Jul 7, 1944 in Scunthorpe, England
Source: *NewYTBE 70; Who 74; WhoGolf; WhoIntG*

Jackson, A(lexander) Y(oung)
[Group of Seven]
Canadian. Artist
Co-founder, Group of Seven, 1920; drew rural Quebec arctic scenes.
b. Oct 3, 1882 in Montreal, Quebec
d. Apr 6, 1974 in Kleinburg, Ontario
Source: *BioIn 1, 2, 3, 5, 10; CanWW 70; CreCan 2; MacDCB 78; McGDA; Who 74; WhoAmA 73, 76N*

Jackson, Andrew
"Old Hickory"
American. US President
Seventh US pres., 1828-36; promoted popular participation in govt.
b. Mar 15, 1767 in Waxhaw, South Carolina
d. Jun 8, 1845 in Nashville, Tennessee
Source: *Alli; AmAu&B; AmBi; ApCAB; BiAUS; BiDSA; BiDrAC; BiDrUSE; DcAmB; Drake; EncAB-H; OxAmL; REn; REnAL; TwCBDA; WebAB; WhAm HS; WhAmP*

Jackson, Anne
[Mrs. Eli Wallach]
American. Actress
Appeared on stage with husband Eli Wallach
    in *The Typists and the Tiger*, 1963; *The
    Waltz of the Toreadores*, 1973.
b. Sep 3, 1926 in Allegheny, Pennsylvania
Source: *BiE&WWA; CurBio 80; FilmgC;
InWom; MotPP; MovMk; NotNAT; VarWW
83; WhoAm 82; WhoHol A; WhoThe 77*

Jackson, "Aunt" Molly
American. Singer
b. 1880 in Clay City, Kentucky
d. Sep 1, 1960
Source: *EncFCWM 69*

Jackson, "Bo" (Vincent Edward)
American. Football Player, Baseball Player
Auburn tailback who rushed for 1,786 yards,
    won Heisman Trophy, 1985; chose to play
    pro baseball with KC Royals, 1986.
b. Nov 30, 1962 in Bessemer, Alabama
Source: *ConNews 86-3; NewYTBS 84*

Jackson, Charles Reginald
American. Author
b. Apr 6, 1903 in Summit, New Jersey
d. Sep 21, 1968 in New York, New York
Source: *AmAu&B; AmNov; ConAu 25R, 101;
CyWA; LongCTC; OxAmL; REn; REnAL;
TwCA; WhAm 5*

Jackson, Charles Thomas
American. Scientist, Physician
Suggested idea of telegraph to Samuel Morse;
    discovered surgical anesthesia.
b. Jun 21, 1805 in Plymouth, Massachusetts
d. Aug 28, 1880 in Somerville, Massachusetts
Source: *AmBi; ApCAB; AsBiEn; DcAmAu;
DcAmB; LinLib S; NatCAB 3; WebAB;
WhAm HS*

Jackson, Chevalier
American. Scientist
b. Nov 4, 1865 in Greentree, Pennsylvania
d. Aug 16, 1958 in Philadelphia,
    Pennsylvania
Source: *CurBio 40; WhNAA*

Jackson, Doris Kenner
see: Shirelles, The

Jackson, Earnest
American. Football Player
Running back, San Diego, 1983--.
b. Dec 18, 1959 in Needville, Texas
Source: *FootReg 85*

Jackson, George
American. Criminal
Robber who wrote *Soledad Brother*, 1970.
b. Sep 23, 1941 in Chicago, Illinois
d. Aug 21, 1971 in San Quentin, California
Source: *BioIn 10; MugS*

Jackson, Glenda
English. Actress
Won Oscars for *Women in Love*, 1970; *A
    Touch of Class*, 1973.
b. May 9, 1937 in Cheshire, England
Source: *BkPepl; CelR; CurBio 71; FilmgC;
IntMPA 75, 76, 77, 78, 79, 80, 81, 82;
IntWW 74; MovMk; NewYTBE 71; OxFilm;
Who 74; WhoAm 82; WhoHol A; WhoThe
77; WhoWor 78*

Jackson, Gordon
Scottish. Actor
Emmy winner for role of Hudson on PBS
    1970s series "Upstairs, Downstairs."
b. Dec 19, 1923 in Glasgow, Scotland
Source: *FilmgC; IntMPA 82; WhoThe 77*

Jackson, Helen Maria Hunt Fiske
American. Author
Worked toward betterment of American
    Indians.
b. Oct 18, 1831 in Amherst, Massachusetts
d. Aug 12, 1885 in San Francisco, California
Source: *Alli SUP; AmAu; AmAu&B; AmBi;
AmWom; ApCAB; BbD; BiD&SB; CarSB;
CasWL; ChhPo, S1, S2; CnDAL; DcAmAu;
DcAmB; DcBiA; DcLEL; DcNAA; EncAB-H;
EvLB; InWom; JBA 34; MouLC 4; NotAW;
OxAmL; REn; REnAL; Str&VC; TwCBDA;
WebAB; WhAm HS*

Jackson, Henry Martin
"Scoop"
American. Politician
Dem. senator from WA, 1953-83; member,
    Armed Services Committee.
b. May 31, 1912 in Everett, Washington
d. Sep 1, 1983 in Everett, Washington
Source: *AnObit 1983; BiDrAC; CelR; CurBio
83N; IntWW 74; NewYTBE 71; NewYTBS
83; WhoAm 82; WhoAmP 73; WhoGov 72;
WhoPNW; WhoWest 74; WhoWor 74*

Jackson, "Hurricane" (Thomas)
American. Boxer
Heavyweight contender, defeated by Floyd
    Patterson, 1957; barred, due to alleged
    brain damage, 1958.
b. Aug 9, 1931 in Sparta, Georgia
d. Feb 14, 1982 in Queens, New York
Source: *NewYTBS 82; WhoBox 74*

Jackson, Jackie (Sigmund Esco)
[The Jacksons]
American. Singer
Group's first hit was "I Want You Back,"
1970; sold over two million copies.
b. May 4, 1951 in Gary, Indiana
Source: *NF*

Jackson, Janet
American. Singer, Actress
Sister of the Jacksons; hit albums include
Control, 1986; appeared in TV show,
"Good Times," 1976.
b. May 16, 1966 in Gary, Indiana
Source: *InB&W 80; RkOn 85*

Jackson, Jermaine La Jaune
[The Jacksons]
American. Singer, Musician
Has had consistent solo career: "Let's Get
Serious," 1980.
b. Dec 11, 1954 in Gary, Indiana
Source: *NF*

Jackson, Joe
English. Singer
Had hit single "Steppin' Out," 1982.
b. Aug 11, 1955 in Burton-on-Trent, England
Source: *RkOn 85*

Jackson, Jesse Louis
American. Civil Rights Leader, Religious
Leader
Founder, Operation PUSH, 1971; chm.,
National Rainbow Coalition; became
dominant black leader in US, 1984.
b. Oct 8, 1941 in Greenville, South Carolina
Source: *BkPepl; CelR; CurBio 86; WebAB;
WhoAm 82, 84; WhoBlA 75; WhoRel 75*

Jackson, Joe (Joseph Jefferson)
"Shoeless Joe"
American. Baseball Player
Banned from baseball for participation in
"Black Sox" scandal, 1919 World Series.
b. Jul 16, 1888 in Brandon Mills, South
Carolina
d. Dec 5, 1951 in Greenville, South Carolina
Source: *BaseEn 85; WhoProB 73*

Jackson, John Adams
American. Sculptor
b. Nov 5, 1825 in Bath, Maine
d. Aug 30, 1879 in Pracchia, Italy
Source: *AmBi; ApCAB; DcAmB; TwCBDA;
WhAm HS*

Jackson, John Hughlings
English. Neurologist
b. Apr 4, 1835 in Yorkshire, England
d. Oct 7, 1911 in London, England
Source: *DcScB; WebBD 80*

Jackson, Kate
American. Actress
TV series include "The Rookies," "Charlie's
Angels," "Scarecrow and Mrs. King."
b. Oct 29, 1948 in Birmingham, Alabama
Source: *BkPepl; IntMPA 82; WhoAm 82;
WhoHol A; WhoTelC*

Jackson, Mahalia
American. Singer
Best known for gospel songs "I Believe,"
"He's Got the Whole World in His
Hands."
b. Oct 26, 1911 in New Orleans, Louisiana
d. Jan 27, 1972 in Evergreen Park, Illinois
Source: *ConAu 33R; CurBio 57, 72; HerW;
InWom; NewYTBE 72; WebAB; WhAm 5;
WhScrn 77; WhoHol B*

Jackson, Margaret E
American. Physiologist
b. Sep 2, 1928 in Zanesville, Ohio

Jackson, Marlon David
[The Jacksons]
American. Singer
Biggest selling hit was "I'll Be There," 1970.
b. Mar 12, 1957 in Gary, Indiana
Source: *NF*

Jackson, Maynard Holbrook, Jr.
American. Mayor
b. Mar 23, 1938 in Dallas, Texas
Source: *BioNews 74; NewYTBE 73; WhoAm
82; WhoBlA 75; WhoS&SW 82*

Jackson, Michael Joseph
[The Jackson Five]
"Peter Pan of Pop"
American. Singer, Actor
Thriller is best-selling album of all time.
b. Aug 29, 1958 in Gary, Indiana
Source: *BkPepl; CelR; CurBio 83; IlEncBM
82; WhoAm 82; WhoBlA 75*

Jackson, Milt(on)
American. Jazz Musician
b. Jan 1, 1923 in Detroit, Michigan
Source: *WhoAm 74, 76, 78, 80, 82; WhoBlA
75*

Jackson, Rachel Donelson Robards
[Mrs. Andrew Jackson]
American. First Lady
Caused scandal when she married Jackson
before divorcing first husband.
b. Jun 15, 1767 in Pittsylvania County,
Virginia
d. Dec 22, 1828 in Nashville, Tennessee
Source: *AmBi; ApCAB; GoodHs; HerW;
NatCAB 5; NotAW; TwCBDA; WhAm HS*

Jackson, Randy (Steven Randall)
[The Jacksons]
American. Singer
b. Oct 29, 1961 in Gary, Indiana
Source: *NF*

Jackson, Reggie (Reginald Martinez)
"Mr. October"
American. Baseball Player
Holds AL record for strikeouts; hit three
home runs in one World Series game,
1977.
b. May 18, 1946 in Wyncote, Pennsylvania
Source: *BaseEn 85; BkPepl; CurBio 74;
NewYTBE 73; WhoAm 82; WhoProB 73*

Jackson, Robert Houghwout
American. Supreme Court Justice
Chief US prosecutor, major Nazi war
criminal trials, 1945.
b. Feb 13, 1892 in Spring Creek,
Pennsylvania
d. Oct 9, 1954 in Washington, District of
Columbia
Source: *BiDrUSE; DcAmB S5; EncAB-H;
McGEWB; WebAB; WhAm 3*

Jackson, Shirley
American. Author
Wrote stories dealing with supernatural in
everyday setting: *The Lottery*, 1949.
b. Dec 14, 1919 in San Francisco, California
d. Aug 8, 1965 in North Bennington,
Vermont
Source: *AmAu&B; AmNov; ConAu 1R, 25R,
4NR; ConLC 11; ConNov 76; LongCTC;
ModAL; OxAmL; PenC AM; RAdv 1; REn;
REnAL; SmATA 2; TwCA SUP; WhAm 4*

Jackson, "Stonewall" (Thomas Jonathan)
American. Military Leader
Confederate general, defeated Union at
second Battle of Bull Run, 1862;
considered outstanding commander.
b. Jan 21, 1824 in Clarksburg, West Virginia
d. May 10, 1863 in Guinea Station, Virginia
Source: *AmBi; ApCAB; BiDConf; DcAmB;
Drake; EncAB-H; REn; REnAL; SpyCS;
TwCBDA; WebAB; WhAm HS*

Jackson, Tito (Toriano Adaryll)
[The Jacksons]
American. Singer, Musician
Had 13 top 20 singles: "ABC" was number
one, 1970.
b. Oct 15, 1953 in Gary, Indiana
Source: *NF*

Jackson, Travis Calvin
"Stonewall"
American. Baseball Player
b. Nov 2, 1903 in Waldo, Arkansas
Source: *BaseEn 85; BioIn 8; WhoProB 73*

Jackson, William Henry
American. Artist, Photographer
Best known for photographic record of
development of West.
b. Apr 4, 1843 in Keeseville, New York
d. Jun 30, 1942 in New York, New York
Source: *AmAu&B; DcAmB S3; DcNAA;
WhAm 2*

Jackson Five, The
[Jermaine Jackson; Marlon Jackson; Michael
Jackson; Jackie Jackson; Tito Jackson]
American. Music Group
Hits include "ABC," "I'll Be There," 1970.
Source: *EncPR&S 74; IlEncBM 82; RkOn 74*

Jackson of Lodsworth, Baroness
see: Ward, Barbara

Jacob (Israel)
Biblical Character
b. 1837
d. 1690 ?AD
Source: *NewCol 75; WebBD 80*

Jacob, Francois
French. Geneticist
b. Jun 17, 1920 in Nancy, France
Source: *BioIn 7; CurBio 66; IntWW 74; Who
74; WhoAm 74; WhoWor 78*

Jacob, John Edward
"Jake"
American. Social Reformer
Pres., National Urban League, 1982--.
b. Dec 16, 1934 in Trout, Louisiana
Source: *CurBio 86; NegAl 83; WhoAm 84;
WhoBlA 80*

Jacob, Max
French. Poet, Artist
b. Jul 11, 1876 in Quimper, France
d. Mar 5, 1944 in Drancy, France
Source: *CasWL; ClDMEL; CnMWL; EncWL; EvEuW; ModRL; OxFr; PenC EUR; REn; WhoTwCL; WorAu*

Jacobi, Derek
English. Actor
Had title role in PBS series "I, Claudius."
b. Oct 22, 1938 in London, England
Source: *WhoThe 77*

Jacobi, Lou
Canadian. Actor
Starred in film *Irma La Douce,* 1963.
b. Dec 28, 1913 in Toronto, Ontario
Source: *BiE&WWA; NotNAT; WhoAm 82; WhoThe 77*

Jacobi, Mary Putnam
American. Physician
b. Aug 31, 1842 in London, England
d. 1906
Source: *Alli SUP; BiD&SB; DcAmAu; DcNAA; WhAm 1*

Jacobs, Al(bert T)
American. Lyricist, Composer
Wrote over 300 songs including "This Is My Country," "There'll Never Be Another You."
b. Jan 22, 1903 in San Francisco, California
d. Feb 13, 1985 in Laurel, Maryland
Source: *CmpEPM; ConAu 115*

Jacobs, Helen Hull
American. Tennis Player, Author
First to win both US singles and doubles titles four successive yrs.
b. Aug 6, 1908 in Globe, Arizona
Source: *AmAu&B; AuBYP; ConAu 9R; InWom; SmATA 12; WhoAm 74, 76, 78, 80, 82; WrDr 76*

Jacobs, Joseph
Author, Folklorist
Compiled *Celtic Fairy Tale,* 1891.
b. Aug 29, 1854 in Sydney, Australia
d. Jan 30, 1916 in Yonkers, New York
Source: *ConAu 111; WebBD 80*

Jacobs, Michael S
American. Boxing Promotor
b. Mar 10, 1880 in New York, New York
d. Jan 25, 1953 in New York, New York
Source: *WhoBox 74*

Jacobs, Walter L
American. Business Executive
Founder, pres., Hertz(Rent-a-Car)Corp., 1954-60.
b. Jun 15, 1896 in Chicago, Illinois
d. Feb 7, 1985 in Miami, Florida
Source: *WhoAm 74, 76*

Jacobs, William Wymark
English. Author
Humor writer: *Many Cargoes,* 1896.
b. 1863 in London, England
d. Sep 1, 1943 in London, England
Source: *BbD; BiD&SB; CasWL; Chambr 3; DcBiA; DcEnA AP; DcLEL; EncMys; EvLB; LongCTC; MnBBF; ModBrL; NewC; OxEng; PenC ENG; REn; TwCA, SUP; TwCWr; WhoLA*

Jacobsen, Arne
Danish. Architect
b. 1902
d. 1971 in Copenhagen, Denmark
Source: *BioIn 11*

Jacobsen, Jens Peter
Danish. Author
First to translate, introduce Darwin's works to Denmark.
b. Apr 7, 1847 in Thisted, Denmark
d. May 30, 1885 in Thisted, Denmark
Source: *CasWL; ClDMEL; CyWA; DcEuL; EuAu; EvEuW; LinLib L; McGEWB; PenC EUR; REn; WhDW*

Jacobson, Leon Orris
American. Scientist, Educator
b. Dec 16, 1911 in Sims, North Dakota
Source: *AmM&WS 76P; CurBio 62; IntWW 74; LEduc 74; WhoAm 74, 76, 78, 80, 82*

Jacobsson, Ulla
Swedish. Actress
Films include *Smiles of a Summer Night.*
b. May 23, 1929 in Gothenburg, Sweden
d. Aug 22, 1982 in Vienna, Austria
Source: *FilmEn; FilmgC; WhoHol A; WorEFlm*

Jacoby, Oswald
American. Bridge Player, Journalist, Author
Called best card player in world, 1950; syndicated bridge columnist, 1949-84.
b. Dec 8, 1902 in New York, New York
d. Jun 27, 1984 in Dallas, Texas
Source: *AmAu&B; AnObit 1984; ConAu 107, 113*

Jacquard, Joseph Marie
French. Inventor
Developed Jacquard loom, 1801, first loom to
weave designs in cloth.
b. 1752
d. 1834
Source: *NewCol 75; REn*

Jacquet, Illinois
American. Jazz Musician
b. Oct 31, 1922 in Broussard, Louisiana
Source: *BiDAmM*

Jacuzzi, Candido
American. Inventor, Businessman
Developed Jacuzzi whirlpool, 1950s, first as
therapeutic aid, then as trendy item.
b. 1903 in Casarsa de Delicia, Italy
Source: *Entr*

Jadlowker, Hermann
Opera Singer
b. Jul 5, 1879 in Riga, Russia
d. May 13, 1953 in Tel Aviv, Israel
Source: *NewEOp 71*

Jaeckel, Richard
American. Actor
Oscar nominee for *Sometimes a Great Notion,*
1971.
b. Oct 26, 1926 in Long Beach, California
Source: *FilmgC; IntMPA 82; MotPP; MovMk;
Vers A; WhoHol A*

Jaeger, Andrea
"Rocky"
American. Tennis Player
Youngest player ever to turn pro, 1980.
b. Jun 4, 1965 in Chicago, Illinois
Source: *NewYTBS 83; WhoIntT*

Jaeger, Gustav
English. Designer
b. in Stuttgart, Germany
Source: *WorFshn*

Jaegers, Albert
American. Sculptor
b. Mar 28, 1868 in Elberfeld, Germany
d. Jul 22, 1925
Source: *WhAm 1*

Jaffe, Rona
American. Author
Wrote *The Last Chance,* 1976; *Class
Reunion,* 1979.
b. Jun 12, 1932 in New York, New York
Source: *AmAu&B; AuNews 1; BioNews 75;
ConAu 73; InWom; WhoAm 82; WhoWorJ
72; WrDr 76*

Jaffe, Sam
American. Actor
Played Dr. Zorba on TV's "Ben Casey,"
1961-66.
b. Mar 8, 1893 in New York, New York
d. Mar 24, 1984 in Beverly Hills, California
Source: *BiE&WWA; IntMPA 82; MotPP;
NotNAT; WhoAm 82; WhoHol A; WhoThe 77*

Jaffe, Sam(uel Anderson)
American. Broadcast Journalist
ABC News correspondent, 1961-69; covered
Vietnam War.
b. 1924 in San Francisco, California
d. Feb 8, 1985 in Bethesda, Maryland
Source: *ConAu 115*

Jaffee, Allan
American. Cartoonist, Author
Illustrator for *Mad* magazine; created their
"Fold-In."
b. Mar 13, 1921 in Savannah, Georgia
Source: *ConAu 116*

Jaffee, Irving
American. Speed Skater
Won two gold medals, 1932 Olympics.
b. 1907
d. Mar 20, 1981 in San Diego, California
Source: *NewYTBS 81*

Jagan, Cheddi
Guyanese. Politician
b. Mar 22, 1918 in British Guiana (East)
Source: *CurBio 63; IntWW 74; Who 74*

Jagan, Janet
Guyanese. Politician
b. Oct 20, 1920 in Chicago, Illinois
Source: *IntWW 74; WhoWor 78*

Jagel, Frederick
American. Opera Singer, Teacher
b. Jun 10, 1897 in Brooklyn, New York
d. Jul 5, 1982 in San Francisco, California
Source: *BiDAmM; NewEOp 71; NewYTBS 82*

Jagendorf, Moritz
American. Folklorist, Author
Wrote *Till Ulenspiegel's Merry Pranks,* 1938.
b. Aug 24, 1888 in Czernowitz, Austria
d. Jan 8, 1981 in Ithaca, New York
Source: *AnObit 1981; AnCL; AuBYP; ConAu
5R; IntAu&W 77; MorJA; NewYTBS 81;
SmATA 2; WhNAA; WhoAm 78; WrDr 76,
80*

Jaggar, Thomas Augustus
American. Geologist
b. Jan 24, 1871 in Philadelphia, Pennsylvania
d. Jan 17, 1953
Source: *DcAmAu; DcAmB S5; OhA&B; WhAm 3; WhNAA*

Jagger, Bianca Teresa
[Bianca Perez Morena de Macias]
English. Socialite, Actress
Married to Mick Jagger, 1971-79; youngest
    member, best-dressed hall of Fame.
b. 1943 in Managua, Nicaragua
Source: *BioNews 75; BkPepl*

Jagger, Dean
American. Actor
Oscar winner for *Twelve O'Clock High,* 1950.
b. Nov 7, 1903 in Columbus Grove, Ohio
Source: *FilmgC; IntMPA 75, 76, 77, 78, 79, 80, 81, 82; MotPP; MovMk; WhoAm 74, 76, 78, 80, 82; WhoHol A; WhoThe 77A*

Jagger, Jade
British. Celebrity Relative
Daughter of Mick and Bianca Jagger.
b. Oct 21, 1971
Source: *NF*

Jagger, Mick (Michael Philip)
[The Rolling Stones]
English. Singer, Musician
Formed Rolling Stones, 1962; hits include
    "Satisfaction," "Honky Tonk Woman."
b. Jul 26, 1943 in Dartford, England
Source: *BioNews 75; BkPepl; CelR; CurBio 72; FilmgC; WhoAm 80, 82; WhoHol A*

Jahan, Marine
French. Dancer
Did dance scenes in *Flashdance,* 1983, for
    Jennifer Beals, but didn't get credit in
    film.
Source: *NF*

Jahn, Helmut
American. Architect
Designed Southwest Center, Houston; winner
    of national architecture awards.
b. Jan 1, 1940 in Nuremberg, Germany
Source: *ConArch; WhoAm 80, 82, 84; WhoMW 82; WhoTech 82*

Jahoda, Gloria
American. Author
b. Oct 6, 1926 in Chicago, Illinois
d. Jan 13, 1980 in Tallahassee, Florida
Source: *AuNews 1; ConAu 1R, 104, 4NR; ForWC 70; WhoAmW 77; WrDr 76*

Jakes, John
American. Author
Wrote *The Bastard,* 1974; *The Rebels,* 1975.
b. Mar 31, 1932 in Chicago, Illinois
Source: *ConAu 57; OxCan SUP; WhoAm 82*

Jamal, Ahmad
American. Jazz Musician
b. Jul 7, 1930 in Pittsburgh, Pennsylvania
Source: *BioNews 74; WhoBlA 75*

James I
Scottish. Ruler
King of Scotland, 1406-37.
b. Jul 1394 in Dunfermline, Scotland
d. Feb 20, 1437 in Perth, Scotland
Source: *BioIn 10; CasWL; NewCol 75; WebBD 80*

James I
[James VI]
English. Ruler
As James I, King of England, 1603-25; as
    James VI, King of Scotland, 1567-1625.
b. Jun 19, 1566 in Edinburgh, Scotland
d. Mar 27, 1625 in Theobalds, England
Source: *BioIn 10; CasWL; NewCol 75; WebBD 80*

James II
Scottish. Ruler
King of Scotland, 1437-60.
b. 1430 in Edinburgh, Scotland
d. 1460 in Roxburgh Castle, Scotland
Source: *DcCathB; DcNaB*

James II
English. Ruler
King of England, Scotland, Ireland, 1685--88.
b. Oct 14, 1633 in London, England
d. Sep 16, 1701 in Saint-Germain-en-Laye,
    France
Source: *BioIn 10; McGEWB; WebBD 80*

James III
Scottish. Ruler
King of Scotland, 1460-88.
b. 1451 in Stirling, Scotland
d. 1488 in Sauchieburn, Scotland
Source: *DcCathB; DcNaB; OxMus*

James IV
Scottish. Ruler
King of Scotland, 1488-1513; marriage to
    Margaret Tudor led to union of crowns of
    England, Scotland.
b. 1473
d. Sep 9, 1513
Source: *DcNaB; Dis&D; LinLib S; OxMus*

James V
Scottish. Ruler
King of Scotland, 1513-42.
b. 1512 in Linlithgow, St. Lucia
d. 1542 in Solway Moss, England
Source: *DcCathB; DcNaB; OxMus*

James the Greater, Saint
[James the Elder, Saint]
Biblical Character
One of three disciples to witness Jesus'
transfiguration, agony in Garden of
Gethsemane; feast day: Jul 25.
Source: *REn*

James the Less, Saint
Biblical Character
One of twelve apostles; feast day: May 3.
Source: *REn*

James, Art
American. TV Host
b. Oct 15, in Dearborn, Michigan
d. 1972
Source: *WhoHol B*

James, Daniel, Jr.
"Chappie"
American. Government Official
b. Feb 11, 1920 in Pensacola, Florida
d. Feb 25, 1978 in Colorado Springs,
Colorado
Source: *CurBio 76, 78; Ebony 1; USBiR 74;
WebAMB; WhAm 7; WhoAm 76, 78;
WhoBlA 75; WhoGov 75, 77; WhoWest 78;
WorDWW*

James, Dennis
American. TV Host
b. Aug 24, 1917 in Jersey City, New Jersey
Source: *IntMPA 75, 76, 77, 78, 79, 80, 81,
82*

James, Edwin
American. Explorer
b. Aug 27, 1797 in Weybridge, Vermont
d. Oct 28, 1861
Source: *Alli; AmAu&B; DcAmAu; DcNAA;
REnAL*

James, Frank
American. Outlaw
b. 1843 in Clay County, Missouri
d. 1915
Source: *BioIn 10; Blood&B*

James, George Payne Rainsford
English. Author
b. Aug 9, 1799 in London, England
d. May 9, 1860 in Venice, Italy
Source: *Alli; BbD; BiD&SB; BrAu 19;
CasWL; Chambr 3; ChhPo S1; DcBiA;
DcEnA; DcEnL; DcEuL; DcLEL; EvLB;
HsB&A; MnBBF; NewC; OxEng; WebE&AL*

James, Harry
American. Band Leader
Played trumpet with Benny Goodman;
married to Betty Grable, 1943-65.
b. Mar 15, 1916 in Albany, Georgia
d. Jul 5, 1983 in Las Vegas, Nevada
Source: *AmSCAP 66; CurBio 83N; FilmgC;
HolP 40; IntMPA 82; MovMk; NewYTBS 83;
WhoHol A*

James, Henry
American. Philosopher
b. Jun 3, 1811 in Albany, New York
d. Dec 18, 1882 in Cambridge, Massachusetts
Source: *Alli SUP; AmAu; AmAu&B; AmBi;
ApCAB; BbD; BiD&SB; CyAL 2; DcAmAu;
DcAmB; DcNAA; OxAmL; PenC AM;
REnAL; TwCBDA; WebAB; WhAm HS*

James, Henry
American. Author
Master of psychological novel; wrote *The
Aspern Papers*, 1888; *The Turn of the
Screw*, 1898.
b. Apr 15, 1843 in New York, New York
d. Feb 28, 1916 in London, England
Source: *AmAu&B; AtlBL; CasWL; CyWA;
EncWL; McGEWD; ModAL; ModBrL;
ModWD; NewC; WhAm 1*

James, Jesse Woodson
American. Outlaw
Leader of outlaw gang known for spectacular
bank, train robberies; killed by Robert
Ford for reward.
b. Sep 5, 1847 in Centerville, Missouri
d. Apr 3, 1882 in Saint Joseph, Missouri
Source: *AmBi; FilmgC; OxAmL; OxFilm;
REn; REnAL*

James, Joni
[Joan Carmella Babbo]
American. Singer
b. Sep 22, 1930 in Chicago, Illinois
Source: *InWom*

James, Marquis
American. Author
b. Sep 29, 1891 in Springfield, Missouri
d. Nov 19, 1955
Source: *AmAu&B; DcAmB S5; OxAmL;
REnAL; TwCA, SUP; WhAm 3; WhNAA*

James, Montague Rhodes
English. Scholar, Author
Provost of Eton, 1918-36; wrote on art,
literature of Middle Ages.
b. Aug 1, 1862 in Goodnestone, England
d. Jun 12, 1936 in Eton, England
Source: *EvLB; LongCTC; OxEng; TwCA*

James, Philip
American. Composer, Conductor
b. May 17, 1890 in Jersey City, New Jersey
d. Nov 1, 1975 in Southampton, New York
Source: *AmSCAP 66; Baker 78; BioIn 1, 10;
WhAm 6, 7; WhoAm 74, 76*

James, P(hyllis) D(orothy)
English. Author
b. Aug 3, 1920 in Oxford, England
Source: *ConAu 21R; ConLC 18; CurBio 80;
EncMys*

James, Rick
[James Johnson]
American. Singer
Double platinum album *Street Songs,* 1981,
included single "Super Freak."
b. Feb 1, 1952 in Buffalo, New York
Source: *IlEncBM 82; IlEncRk; RkOn 85*

James, "Skip" (Nehemiah)
American. Musician, Singer
Blues pioneer, rediscovered, 1960s; hit song
"I'm So Glad."
b. Jun 9, 1902 in Betonia, Mississippi
d. Oct 3, 1969 in Philadelphia, Pennsylvania
Source: *BioIn 7, 8; EncFCWM 69; EncJzS
70; ObitOF 79; WhoRock 81*

James, Sonny
[Jimmy Loden]
"The Southern Gentleman"
American. Singer
b. Mar 1, 1929 in Hackleburg, Alaska
Source: *EncFCWM 69*

James, Will(iam)
American. Author, Illustrator
b. Jun 6, 1892 in Great Falls, Montana
d. Sep 3, 1942 in Hollywood, California
Source: *AuBYP; CurBio 42; DcAmB S3;
DcNAA; JBA 34, 51; Newb 1922; OxAmL;
REnAL; SmATA 19; TwCA, SUP; WhAm 2;
WhNAA*

James, William
American. Psychologist, Philosopher
One of founders of pragmatism who wrote
The Meaning of Truth, 1909.
b. Jan 11, 1842 in New York, New York
d. Aug 26, 1910 in Chocorua, New
Hampshire
Source: *AmAu; AmAu&B; AmBi; AmWr;
ApCAB; AtlBL; BiD&SB; BiDPara; CasWL;
CyWA; DcAmAu; DcAmB; DcEuL; DcLEL;
DcNAA; EncAB-H; EvLB; LongCTC; ModAL,
S1; NewC; OxAmL; OxEng; PenC AM;
RComWL; REn; REnAL; TwCBDA; WebAB;
WebE&AL; WhAm 1; WhoTwCL*

James Gang
[Tom Bolin; James Fox; Phil Giallombardo;
'Bubba' Keith; Roy Kenner; Dale Peters;
Richard Shack; Dom Troiano; Joseph
Fidler Walsh; Bob Webb]
American. Music Group
Source: *EncPR&S 74; RkOn 74*

Jameson, House
American. Actor
Played father in radio, TV series "The
Aldrich Family."
b. 1902
d. Apr 23, 1971 in Danbury, Connecticut
Source: *BiE&WWA; PIP&P; WhScrn 74, 77;
WhoHol B*

Jameson, Margaret Storm
English. Author
b. 1891 in Whitby, England
Source: *ConAu 81; DcLEL; EvLB; LongCTC;
ModBrL; NewC; PenC ENG; REn; Who 74*

Jamieson, Bob (Robert John)
American. Broadcast Journalist
NBC News correspondent; won 1981 Emmy
for Iranian hostage crisis.
b. Feb 1, 1943 in Streator, Illinois
Source: *ConAu 116; WhoAm 84*

Jamison, Judith
American. Dancer
b. May 10, 1934 in Philadelphia,
Pennsylvania
Source: *BioNews 74; CurBio 73; NewYTBE
72; WhoAm 82; WhoBlA 75*

Jamison, Philip Duane, Jr.
American. Artist
Realistic watercolorist, known for flowers,
interiors, ME landscapes.
b. Jul 3, 1925 in Philadelphia, Pennsylvania
Source: *WhoAm 74, 76, 78, 80, 82; WhoAmA
73, 76, 78; WhoE 74*

Jammes, Francis
French. Author
b. Dec 2, 1868 in Tournay, France
d. Nov 1, 1938
Source: *CasWL; CathA 1930; ChhPo;
ClDMEL; EncWL; EvEuW; ModRL; NewC;
OxEng; OxFr; PenC AM*

Jan and Dean
[Jan Berry; Dean Torrance]
American. Music Group
Surf music duo, 1958-66; hit debut single
"Jennie Lee," sold 10 million albums.
Source: *EncPR&S 74; IlEncRk; RolSEnR 83*

Janacek, Leos
Czech. Composer
b. Jul 3, 1854 in Hukvaldy, Moravia
d. Aug 12, 1928 in Prague, Czechoslovakia
Source: *DcCM*

Janaszak, Steve
American. Hockey Player
Member of gold medal winning US Olympic
hockey team, 1980.
b. Jan 7, 1957 in Saint Paul, Minnesota
Source: *HocReg 81*

Jancso, Miklos
Hungarian. Director
Films include *Round-Up,* 1965; *Red Psalm,*
1972.
b. Sep 27, 1922 in Vac, Hungary
Source: *BiDFilm; DcFM; FilmgC; IntWW 74;
OxFilm; WhoWor 78; WorEFlm*

Janeway, Eliot
American. Economist, Author, Lecturer
b. Jan 1, 1913 in New York, New York
Source: *AmAu&B; CurBio 70; IntWW 74;
WhoAm 82; WhoWor 74; WrDr 76*

Janeway, Elizabeth
American. Author
b. Oct 7, 1913 in Brooklyn, New York
Source: *AmAu&B; AmNov; Au&Wr 71;
AuBYP; AuNews 1; ChhPo; ConAu 45, 2NR;
CurBio 44; DrAF 76; InWom; REnAL;
SmATA 19; TwCA SUP; WhoAm 74, 76, 78,
80, 82; WhoAmW 77; WhoE 74; WhoWor 78*

Janifer, Laurence
American. Author
b. Mar 17, 1933 in Brooklyn, New York
Source: *ConAu 9R, 5NR*

Janigro, Antonio
Italian. Musician, Conductor
International cello soloist; founded ensemble
group Solisti di Zagreb.
b. Jan 21, 1918 in Milan, Italy
Source: *Baker 78*

Janis, Byron
American. Musician
b. Mar 24, 1928 in McKeesport,
Pennsylvania
Source: *CelR; CurBio 66; WhoAm 74, 76, 78,
80, 82; WhoE 74; WhoMus 72*

Janis, Conrad
American. Actor, Musician
Starred as Mindy's father in TV show
"Mork and Mindy," 1978-81.
b. Feb 11, 1928 in New York, New York
Source: *BiE&WWA; FilmgC; MotPP;
NotNAT; WhoAm 82; WhoAmA 73; WhoHol
A; WhoThe 77*

Janis, Elsie
[Elsie Bierbower]
American. Actress
First American to entertain troops in WW I.
b. Mar 16, 1889 in Columbus, Ohio
d. Feb 26, 1956 in Beverly Hills, California
Source: *AmSCAP 66; EncMT; FamA&A; Film
1; FilmgC; InWom; OhA&B; TwYS; WhAm
3; WhScrn 74, 77; WhoHol B; WhoStg 1906,
1908; WomWWA 14*

Janney, Leon
American. Actor
Radio series include "The Parker Family";
"Chick Carter."
b. Apr 1, 1917 in Ogden, Utah
d. Oct 28, 1980 in Guadalajara, Mexico
Source: *BiE&WWA; NotNAT; WhoHol A*

Janney, Russell Dixon
American. Author, Producer
Co-wrote, produced hit Broadway musical
The Vagabond King, 1925.
b. Apr 14, 1885 in Wilmington, Ohio
d. Jul 14, 1963 in New York, New York
Source: *DcAmB S7*

Jannings, Emil
[Theodor Friedrich Emil Janenz]
American. Actor
Won Oscar for *The Last Command; The
Way of All Flesh,* 1928.
b. Jul 26, 1886 in Rorschach, Switzerland
d. Jan 3, 1950 in Lake Wolfgang, Austria
Source: *BiDFilm; FilmEn; Film 1; FilmgC;
MotPP; MovMk; OxFilm; REn; TwYS;
WhScrn 74, 77; WhoHol B; WorEFlm*

Janosch, pseud.
see: Eckert, Horst

Janov, Arthur
American. Psychologist
b. Aug 21, 1924 in Los Angeles, California
Source: *CurBio 80*

Jansen, Cornelis
Flemish. Theologian
Founded Roman Catholic reform movement
or Jansenism.
b. 1585 in Acquoi, Netherlands
d. 1638 in Flanders
Source: *McGEWB; NewCol 75*

Janson, Horst Woldemar
American. Educator, Author
Wrote *History of Art,* 1962.
b. Oct 4, 1913 in Saint Petersburg, Russia
d. Sep 30, 1982
Source: *AnObit 1982; AuBYP; ConAu 1R;
DrAS 74H, 78H; NewYTBS 82; WhoAm 80;
WhoAmA 80; WhoArt 80; WhoWor 76; WrDr
80*

Janssen, David
[David Harold Meyer]
American. Actor
Starred in TV series "The Fugitive," 1963-67;
"Harry-O," 1974-76.
b. Mar 27, 1931 in Naponee, Nebraska
d. Feb 13, 1980 in Malibu Beach, California
Source: *BioNews 74; CurBio 67; FilmgC;
IntMPA 75, 76, 77; MotPP; MovMk; WhoAm
74; WhoHol A; WhoWor 78*

Janssen, Herbert
German. Opera Singer
b. Sep 22, 1895 in Cologne, Germany
d. Jun 3, 1965 in New York, New York
Source: *NewEOp 71*

Janssen, Werner
American. Conductor, Composer
b. Jun 1, 1899 in New York, New York
Source: *AmSCAP 66; DcCM; WhoAm 74*

Jantzen, Carl
American. Manufacturer
Invented rib-stitch method of making bathing
suits; co-founded int'l. line of swim wear,
1925.
b. 1883 in Denmark
d. 1939
Source: *Entr*

Jardine, Al(lan)
[The Beach Boys]
American. Singer, Musician
b. Sep 3, 1942 in Lima, Ohio
Source: *BioIn 11; BkPepl*

Jarman, Claude, Jr.
American. Actor
Won special Oscar for debut in *The Yearling,*
1946.
b. Sep 27, 1934 in Nashville, Tennessee
Source: *FilmgC; IntMPA 77; MotPP; MovMk;
WhoHol A*

Jarman, John
American. Politician
Congressman from OK, 1951-77; became
Rep., 1975.
b. Jul 17, 1915 in Sallisaw, Oklahoma
d. Jan 15, 1982 in Oklahoma City,
Oklahoma
Source: *BiDrAC; CngDr 74; WhoAmP 73, 75,
77, 79; WhoGov 72, 75, 77; WhoS&SW 73,
75, 76*

Jaroszewicz, Piotr
Polish. Politician
b. Oct 8, 1909 in Nieswicz, Poland
Source: *IntWW 74; NewYTBE 70; WhoWor
78*

Jarre, Maurice
French. Composer
Won Oscars for scores *Lawrence of Arabia,*
1962; *Doctor Zhivago,* 1966.
b. Sep 13, 1924 in Lyons, France
Source: *Baker 78; CmMov; DcFM; FilmEn;
FilmgC; IntMPA 75, 76, 77, 78, 79, 80, 81;
OxFilm; WorEFlm*

Jarreau, Al
American. Singer
Won Grammys for best jazz vocalist, 1978,
1979.
b. Mar 12, 1940 in Milwaukee, Wisconsin
Source: *IlEncBM 82; WhoAm 82*

Jarrell, Randall
American. Author, Poet
Noted for critical writing: *The Woman at the
Washington Zoo,* 1960.
b. May 6, 1914 in Nashville, Tennessee
d. Oct 14, 1965 in Chapel Hill, North
Carolina
Source: *AmAu&B; AmWr; AnCL; AuBYP;
CasWL; ChhPo, S1; CnDAL; CnE&AP;
ConAu 5R, 25R; ConLC 1, 2, 6, 9, 13; ConP
75; CroCAP; EncWL; ModAL, S1; OxAmL;
PenC AM; RAdv 1; REn; REnAL; SixAP;
SmATA 7; ThrBJA; TwCA SUP; TwCWr;
WebAB; WebE&AL; WhAm 4; WhoTwCL*

Jarrett, Keith
American. Composer, Musician
Internationally renowned jazz pianist,
 composer.
b. May 8, 1945 in Allentown, Pennsylvania
Source: *BiDAmM; ConAmC 82; WhoAm 84;
WhoAmM 83*

Jarring, Gunnar V
Swedish. Diplomat
b. Oct 12, 1907 in Brunnby, Sweden
Source: *CurBio 57; IntWW 74; NewYTBE 70;
Who 74; WhoUN 75; WhoWor 78*

Jarriel, Tom (Thomas Edwin)
American. Broadcast Journalist
Correspondent, ABC News since 1965;
 contributor to "20/20."
b. Dec 29, 1934 in LaGrange, Georgia
Source: *ConAu 109; NewYTET; WhoAm 84;
WhoTelC*

Jarry, Alfred
French. Poet, Dramatist
Wrote first theatrical work of the absurd:
 Ubu roi, 1896.
b. Oct 8, 1873 in Laval, France
d. Nov 1, 1907 in Paris, France
Source: *CasWL; ClDMEL; CnMD; CnThe;
EncWL; EuAu; EvEuW; LongCTC;
McGEWD; ModRL; ModWD; OxFr; OxThe;
PenC EUR; RComWL; REn; REnWD;
WhoTwCL*

Jaruzelski, Wojciech Witold
Polish. Political Leader
Career soldier; head of Poland, 1981--.
b. Jul 6, 1923 in Kurow, Poland
Source: *CurBio 82; IntWW 74, 75, 76, 77,
78; NewYTBS 81; WhoSocC 78; WhoWor 74;
WorDWW*

Jarvik, Robert Koffler
American. Physician, Inventor
Designed Jarvik-7, artificial heart, 1972; first
 used in Barney Clark, 1982.
b. May 11, 1946 in Midland, Michigan
Source: *ConNews 85-1; CurBio 85; WhoAm
84*

Jarvis, Anna
American. Reformer
Founded Mother's Day to commemorate
 anniversary of mother's death.
b. May 1, 1864
d. Nov 24, 1948 in West Chester,
 Pennsylvania
Source: *WomWWA 14*

Jarvis, Gregory
American. Astronaut
Crew member who died in explosion of space
 shuttle, *Challenger.*
b. Aug 24, 1944 in Detroit, Michigan
d. Jan 28, 1986 in Cape Canaveral, Florida
Source: *NewYTBS 86*

Jarvis, Howard Arnold
American. Social Reformer
Force behind CA's Proposition 13, which
 reduced property taxes 57%, 1978.
b. Sep 22, 1902 in Magna, Utah
d. Aug 11, 1986 in Los Angeles, California
Source: *BioIn 11; CurBio 79; NewYTBS 78*

Jarvis, John Wesley
American. Artist
b. 1781 in South Shields, England
d. Jan 14, 1839
Source: *BioIn 1, 2, 9; EarABI; WhAm HS*

Jason, Rick
American. Actor
Starred in TV series "Combat," 1962-67.
b. May 21, 1926 in New York, New York
Source: *FilmgC; IntMPA 82; MotPP; WhoHol
A*

Jasper, John J
American. Clergyman
b. 1812
d. 1901
Source: *BioIn 3, 6, 8; REnAL*

Jaspers, Karl
German. Author, Philosopher, Physician,
 Educator
Originator of existentialism; influenced
 modern theology, psychiatry.
b. Feb 23, 1883 in Oldenburg, Germany
d. Feb 26, 1969 in Basel, Switzerland
Source: *CasWL; ConAu 25R; OxGer; REn;
TwCA SUP; TwCWr*

Jastrow, Robert
American. Author, Astronomer
b. Sep 7, 1925 in New York, New York
Source: *AmM&WS 73P; ConAu 21R; CurBio
73; IntWW 74; WhoAm 74, 76, 78, 80, 82;
WhoGov 75; WhoWor 78; WrDr 76*

Jaures, Jean Leon
French. Socialist Leader
Co-founded French Socialist Party, 1905;
 assassinated by patriotic fanatic.
b. Sep 3, 1859 in Castres, France
d. Jul 31, 1914
Source: *DcAmSR; McGEWB; NewCol 75;
OxFr; REn; WhDW; WhoMilH 76*

Jausovec, Mima
Yugoslav. Tennis Player
Winner French Open, 1977; Italian Open,
1976.
b. Jul 20, 1956 in Maribor, Yugoslavia
Source: *WhoIntT*

Javits, Jacob Koppel
American. Senator
Liberal Rep. senator from NY, 1956-80, who
championed civil rights, ERA.
b. May 18, 1904 in New York, New York
d. Mar 7, 1986 in West Palm Beach, Florida
Source: *AmAu&B; BiDrAC; CelR; ConAu 1R,
1NR; CurBio 48, 58; IntWW 74; NewYTBS
74; WhoAm 74, 76, 78, 80, 82; WhoAmP 73;
WhoE 74; WhoGov 75; WhoWor 78*

Jawara, Alhaji Dawda Kairaba, Sir
Gambian. Political Leader
First prime minister, 1963-70, pres., 1970--,
Gambia.
b. May 16, 1924 in Barajally, Gambia
Source: *IntWW 74; Who 74; WhoGov 75;
WhoWor 78*

Jaworski, Leon
American. Government Official, Lawyer
Special Watergate prosecutor, 1973-74;
prosecutor at Nuremberg trials.
b. Sep 19, 1905 in Waco, Texas
d. Dec 9, 1982 in Wimberley, Texas
Source: *AnObit 1982; ConAu 108, P-1;
CurBio 83; IntWW 81; NewYTBE 73;
NewYTBS 82; WhAm 8; WhoAm 80, 82;
WhoAmL 79; WhoAmP 79; WhoGov 77*

Jaworski, Ron(ald Vincent)
"The Polish Rifle"
American. Football Player
Quarterback, LA Rams, 1974-77;
Philadelphia, 1977--.
b. Mar 23, 1951 in Lackawanna, New York
Source: *BioIn 12; FootReg 81; WhoAm 82*

Jay, John
American. Supreme Court Justice
First Chief Justice of Supreme Court, 1789-
95; wrote five *Federalist* papers.
b. Dec 12, 1745 in New York, New York
d. May 17, 1829 in Bedford, New York
Source: *Alli; AmAu&B; AmBi; ApCAB;
BiAUS; BiDrAC; BiDrUSE; CyAL 1; CyWA;
DcAmAu; DcAmB; DcNAA; Drake; EncAB-H;
OxAmL; REn; REnAL; TwCBDA; WebAB;
WhAm HS; WhAmP*

Jay, Joseph Richard (Joey)
American. Baseball Player
b. Aug 15, 1935 in Middletown, Connecticut
Source: *BaseEn 85; BioIn 6*

Jay, Peter
English. Diplomat, Economist
Chm., National Council for Voluntary
Organizations, 1981--; editor, *Banking
World*, 1984--.
b. Feb 7, 1937 in London, England
Source: *CurBio 78; IntWW 76, 77, 78; IntYB
78, 79; Who 74; WhoWor 76, 78*

Jay and the Americans
[David Jay Black; Sandy Deane; Howie
Kane; Marty Sander; John Jay Traynor;
Kenny Vance]
American. Music Group
Clean-cut, Brooklyn-based group; hits
included "Cara Mia," 1965; "This Magic
Moment," 1969.
Source: *ConMuA 80A; LilREn 78; RkOn 74;
WhoRock 81*

Jayewardene, Junius Richard
Ceylonese. Political Leader
Exec. pres., Sri Lanka, 1977--; committed to
western-style democracy, free enterprise
system.
b. Sep 17, 1906 in Colombo, Ceylon
Source: *CurBio 84; IntWW 74*

Jayston, Michael
English. Actor
Best known for film *Nicholas and Alexandra*,
1971.
b. Oct 29, 1936 in Nottinghamshire, England
Source: *FilmgC; WhoHol A; WhoThe 77, 72*

Jean, Grand Duke of Luxembourg
Luxembourg. Ruler
b. Jan 5, 1921 in Colmar, France
Source: *NewCol 75; WebBD 80; WhoWor 78*

Jean Louis
[Jean Louis Berthault]
American. Designer
Best known for designing "little Carnegie
suit," 1937, worn by Duchess of Windsor.
b. 1907 in Paris, France
Source: *WorFshn*

Jeanmaire, Renee Marcelle
"Zizi"
French. Actress, Dancer, Singer
Wife of Roland Petit and leading dancer of
Ballets Roland Petit, Casino de Paris.
b. Apr 29, 1924 in Paris, France
Source: *CurBio 52; FilmEn; InWom; IntWW
82*

Jeanneret-Gris, Charles Edward
see: LeCorbusier

Jeans, James Hopwood, Sir
English. Mathematician, Astronomer
b. Sep 11, 1877 in Lancashire, England
d. Sep 17, 1946
Source: *Chambr 3; CurBio 41, 46; DcLEL;*
EvLB; LongCTC; NewC; OxEng; TwCA, SUP

Jeffers, (John) Robinson
American. Poet, Dramatist
Verse expressed contempt for human society;
wrote *Medea,* 1946; *Give Your Heart to*
the Hawks, 1933.
b. Jan 10, 1887 in Pittsburgh, Pennsylvania
d. Jan 20, 1962 in Carmel, California
Source: *AmAu&B; AtlBL; CasWL; ChhPo S1,*
S2; CnDAL; CnE&AP; CnMD; CnMWL;
ConAmA; ConAmL; ConAu 85; ConLC 2, 3,
11, 15; CyWA; EncWL; LongCTC;
McGEWD; ModAL, S1; ModWD; OxAmL;
OxEng; PenC AM; RAdv 1; REn; REnAL;
SixAP; TwCA, SUP; TwCWr; WebAB;
WebE&AL; WhAm 4; WhNAA; WhoTwCL

Jefferson, Blind Lemon
American. Singer
b. 1897 in Wortham, Texas
d. 1930 in Chicago, Illinois
Source: *BiDAmM*

Jefferson, John Larry
American. Football Player
b. Feb 3, 1956 in Dallas, Texas
Source: *BioIn 12; FootReg 81; WhoAm 82*

Jefferson, Joseph
American. Actor
Identified with title role in play *Rip Van*
Winkle, had 72-yr. stage career.
b. Feb 20, 1829 in Philadelphia, Pennsylvania
d. Apr 23, 1905 in Palm Beach, Florida
Source: *AmAu&B; AmBi; ApCAB; BbD;*
BiD&SB; DcAmAu; DcAmB; DcNAA; Drake;
FamA&A; Film 1; OxAmL; OxThe; REnAL;
REnWD; TwCBDA; WebAB; WhAm 1;
WhScrn 77

Jefferson, Maria
[Mrs. John Wayles Eppes]
American. Celebrity Relative
Daughter of Thomas Jefferson.
b. 1778 in Monticello, Virginia
d. Apr 1804 in Monticello, Virginia
Source: *BioIn 1, 3, 6, 7*

Jefferson, Martha
[Mrs. Thomas Mann Randolph]
American. Celebrity Relative
Eldest daughter of Thomas Jefferson; headed
father's household after mother's death.
b. Sep 27, 1772 in Monticello, Virginia
d. Oct 10, 1836 in Washington, District of
Columbia
Source: *BioIn 1, 2, 3, 6, 9, 10, 11; HerW;*
NatCAB 3, 5; NotAW

Jefferson, Martha Wayles Skelton
[Mrs. Thomas Jefferson]
American. Celebrity Relative
Married Thomas Jefferson, Jan 1, 1772; died
before he became pres., 1801.
b. Oct 19, 1748 in Charles City, Virginia
d. Sep 6, 1782 in Monticello, Virginia
Source: *AmWom; ApCAB; BioIn 1, 2, 3, 5,*
6, 7, 8, 9; NatCAB 3; NotAW; TwCBDA;
WhAm HSA

Jefferson, Thomas
"Red Fox"
American. US President
First pres. inaugurated in Washington, DC,
1801; planned Lewis and Clark Expedition.
b. Apr 13, 1743 in Shadwell, Virginia
d. Jul 4, 1826 in Monticello, Virginia
Source: *Alli; AmAu&B; AmBi; ApCAB; AtlBL;*
BbD; BiAUS; BiD&SB; BiDSA; BiDrAC;
BiDrUSE; CasWL; Chambr 3; CyAL 1;
CyWA; DcAmAu; DcAmB; DcLEL; DcNAA;
Drake; EncAB-H; EvLB; OxAmL; PenC AM;
RComWL; REn; REnAL; TwCBDA; WebAB;
WebE&AL; WhAm HS; WhAmP

Jefferson, Thomas
American. Actor
Son of Joseph Jefferson, 5th generation of
theatrical family; entered films with D W
Griffith, 1909.
b. 1859
d. Apr 2, 1923 in Hollywood, California
Source: *FilmEn; Film 1; WhScrn 74, 77*

Jefferson Airplane
see: Jefferson Starship

Jefferson Starship
[Marty Balin; Jack Casady; Joey Covington;
Spencer Dryden; Paul Katner; Jorma
Kauoknen; Grace Slick]
American. Music Group
Founded, 1966, as Jefferson Airplane; several
members formed Starship, 1985.
Source: *EncPR&S 74; IlEncRk*

Jeffrey, Lord Francis
Scottish. Author
b. 1773 in Edinburgh, Scotland
d. 1850
Source: *Alli; BbD; BiD&SB; BrAu 19; CasWL; Chambr 3; CrtT 2; DcEnA; DcEnL; DcEuL; DcLEL; EvLB; MouLC 3; NewC; OxEng; PenC ENG; WebE&AL*

Jeffreys, Anne
American. Actress
Co-starred with husband Robert Sterling in
   TV series "Topper," 1953-56.
b. Jan 26, 1923 in Goldsboro, North
   Carolina
Source: *BiE&WWA; FilmgC; InWom; IntMPA 75, 76, 77, 78, 79, 80, 81, 82; MotPP; MovMk; NotNAT; WhoHol A; WhoThe 77*

Jeffreys, Garland
American. Singer, Songwriter
Soul singer who blends rock, jazz, reggae;
   album *Escape Artist,* 1981.
b. 1944 in Brooklyn, New York
Source: *BioIn 12; IlEncBM 82*

Jeffries, James Jackson
"The Boilermaker"
American. Boxer, Actor
Won heavyweight championship of world,
   1899-1904; retired undefeated, 1905.
b. Apr 15, 1875 in Carroll County, Ohio
d. Mar 3, 1953 in Burbank, California
Source: *DcAmB S5; Film 1; WhScrn 77; WhoPubR 76*

Jeffries, Lionel Charles
English. Actor
Character actor, 1950--; directed films
   including *The Railway Children,* 1971;
   Water Babies, 1979.
b. 1926 in London, England
Source: *FilmgC; IntMPA 82; MovMk; Who 74; WhoHol A; WhoWor 74*

Jeffries, Richard
English. Author
Wrote classic autobiography *Story of My
   Heart,* 1883.
b. Nov 6, 1848 in North Wiltshire, England
d. Aug 14, 1887 in Worthing, England
Source: *DcEuL; REn; WhoChL*

Jehangir
Indian. Emperor
b. 1569
d. 1627
Source: *NewC*

Jellicoe, Ann
English. Dramatist
b. Jul 15, 1927
Source: *ConAu 85; CroCD; McGEWD; ModWD; NewC; NotNAT; REnWD; TwCWr; Who 74; WhoThe 77; WorAu; WrDr 80*

Jellicoe, John
English. Admiral
b. Dec 5, 1859 in Southampton, England
d. Nov 20, 1935
Source: *McGEWB; WhoLA*

Jenkins, Allen
[Al McConegal]
American. Actor
Played character roles in 175 films from
   1931.
b. Apr 9, 1900 in New York, New York
d. Jul 20, 1974 in Santa Monica, California
Source: *FilmEn; FilmgC; IntMPA 77; MovMk; Vers A*

Jenkins, Carol Elizabeth Heiss
[Carol Heiss]
American. Olympic Athlete
Won gold medal for figure skating, 1960.
b. Jan 20, 1940 in New York, New York
Source: *CurBio 59; FilmgC; GoodHs; HerW; InWom*

Jenkins, Ferguson Arthur
"Fergie"
Canadian. Baseball Player
Won at least 20 games per season, 1967-72;
   Cy Young award, 1971.
b. Dec 13, 1943 in Chatham, Ontario
Source: *BaseEn 85; NewYTBE 71; WhoAm 74, 76, 78, 80, 82; WhoBlA 75; WhoProB 73*

Jenkins, Gordon
American. Composer, Conductor
Best known for 1945 composition *Manhattan
   Tower Suite,* in praise of NY.
b. May 12, 1910 in Webster Groves,
   Missouri
d. May 1, 1984 in Malibu, California
Source: *AmSCAP 66; AnObit 1984*

Jenkins, Hayes Alan
American. Figure Skater
b. Mar 23, 1933 in Akron, Ohio
Source: *CurBio 56*

Jenkins, Newell
American. Conductor
b. Feb 8, 1915 in New Haven, Connecticut
Source: *WhoE 74*

Jenkins, Paul
American. Artist
Noted for "pouring" pigments on floor
    canvasses; wrote *Painters Country*, 1958.
b. Jul 12, 1923 in Kansas City, Missouri
Source: *BioIn 5, 6, 7; ConArt 77; DcAmArt;*
DcCAA 71, 77; WhoAm 74, 76, 78, 80, 82;
WhoAmA 73, 76, 78; WhoWor 74, 76

Jenkins, Ray Howard
American. Lawyer
Noted for insistent manner of questioning as
    senate counsel in McCarthy hearings, 1954.
b. Mar 18, 1897 in Unaka, North Carolina
d. Dec 26, 1980 in Knoxville, Tennessee
Source: *BioIn 3, 7, 8, 9; CurBio 54, 81;*
WhAm 7; WhoAm 74

Jenkins, Roy Harris
Welsh. Political Leader
Co-founder, leader of Social Dem. Party in
    Britain, Mar 1981-.
b. Nov 11, 1920 in Abersychan, Wales
Source: *Au&Wr 71; ConAu 9R; CurBio 66,*
82; DcLEL 1940; IntAu&W 76, 77; IntWW
74, 75, 76, 77, 78, 79, 80, 81; IntYB 78, 79,
80, 81; OxLaw; Who 74, 82; WhoWor 74, 76,
78; WorAu; WrDr 76, 80

Jenner, Bruce
American. Track Athlete, Sportscaster
Won gold medal in decathlon, 1976
    Olympics.
b. Oct 28, 1949 in Mount Kisco, New York
Source: *BioIn 11; BkPepl; WhoAm 82*

Jenner, Edward
English. Physician
Discovered vaccine used against smallpox,
    1796; set way for science of immunology.
b. May 17, 1749 in Berkeley, England
d. Jan 26, 1823 in Berkeley, England
Source: *Alli; AsBiEn; BiDLA; DcScB;*
McGEWB; NewC; NewCol 75; REn

Jenner, William, Sir
English. Scientist, Engineer, Physician
b. 1815 in Chatham, England
d. Dec 7, 1898
Source: *BiHiMed; BioIn 2, 4, 9*

Jenney, Neil
American. Artist
b. 1946
Source: *BioIn 12*

Jenney, William LeBaron
"Father of the skyscraper"
American. Architect, Engineer
Innovative construction methods resulted in
    design for skyscrapers.
b. Sep 25, 1832 in Fairhaven, Massachusetts
d. Jun 15, 1907 in Los Angeles, California
Source: *AmBi; ApCAB SUP; DcAmB; DcNAA;*
TwCBDA; WebAB; WhAm 1

Jennings, Elizabeth
English. Author
b. Jul 18, 1926 in Boston, England
Source: *Au&Wr 71; ChhPo, S1, S2; ConAu*
61; ConLC 5; ConP 70, 75; LongCTC;
ModBrL, S1; NewC; PenC ENG; RAdv 1;
TwCWr; WebE&AL; Who 74; WhoTwCL;
WorAu; WrDr 80

Jennings, Gary
American. Author
b. Sep 20, 1928 in Buena Vista, Virginia
Source: *AuBYP; ConAu 5R; SmATA 9*

Jennings, Hugh(ey Ambrose)
American. Baseball Player, Baseball Manager
Led Detroit Tigers to AL pennants in first
    three yrs. as mgr., 1907-09; Hall of Fame,
    1945.
b. Apr 2, 1870 in Pittston, Pennsylvania
d. Feb 1, 1928 in Scranton, Pennsylvania
Source: *BaseEn 85; BasesB*

Jennings, Peter Charles
Canadian. Journalist
Anchor, "ABC World News Tonight," 1983--

b. Jul 29, 1938 in Toronto, Ontario
Source: *CurBio 83; WhoAm 82; WhoE 74;*
WhoTelC

Jennings, Talbot
American. Dramatist, Screenwriter
Co-authored screenplays *The Good Earth;*
    Mutiny on the Bounty.
b. 1895 in Shoshone, Ohio
d. May 30, 1985 in East Glacier Park,
    Montana
Source: *CmMov; ConAu 116; FilmEn;*
IntMPA 84

Jennings, Waylon
American. Singer
b. Jun 15, 1937 in Littlefield, Texas
Source: *BkPepl; CurBio 82; EncFCWM 69;*
WhoAm 82; WhoHol A

Jenrette, John Wilson, Jr.
American. Politician
Former congressman convicted in ABSCAM
    scandal, 1980; served two-year sentence,
    1984-86.
b. May 19, 1936 in Conway, South Carolina
Source: *AlmAP 80; CngDr 79; WhoAm 80;
    WhoAmP 79; WhoGov 77; WhoS&SW 78*

Jens, Salome
American. Actress
b. May 8, 1935 in Milwaukee, Wisconsin
Source: *BiE&WWA; FilmgC; MotPP;
    NotNAT; WhoHol A; WhoThe 77*

Jensen, Adolph
German. Composer
b. Jan 12, 1837 in Konigsberg, Germany
d. Jan 23, 1879 in Baden-Baden, Germany
Source: *OxMus*

Jensen, Alfred Julio
Artist
Did bright, checkerboard works inspired by
    architecture, mathematical themes.
b. Dec 11, 1903 in Guatemala City,
    Guatemala
d. Apr 4, 1981 in Livingston, New Jersey
Source: *BioIn 7, 10; DcCAA 71, 77; WhAm
    7; WhoAm 74, 76, 78, 80; WhoAmA 73, 76,
    78*

Jensen, Arthur Robert
American. Psychologist, Author
b. Aug 24, 1923 in San Diego, California
Source: *BioIn 8, 9, 10; ConAu 2NR; CurBio
    73; WhoAm 82*

Jensen, Jackie (Jack Eugene)
"Golden Boy"
American. Baseball Player
b. Mar 9, 1927 in San Francisco, California
d. Jul 14, 1982 in Charlottesville, Virginia
Source: *BaseEn 85; CurBio 59, 82N;
    NewYTBS 82*

Jensen, Mike (Michael C)
American. Broadcast Journalist
NBC News correspondent who specializes in
    business, economics.
b. Nov 1, 1934 in Chicago, Illinois
Source: *WhoAm 80, 82, 84; WhoTelC*

Jensen, Oliver Ormerod
American. Author
Co-founder, editor, *American Heritage*
    magazine, 1954--; wrote *Railroads in
    America,* 1975.
b. Apr 16, 1914 in Ithaca, New York
Source: *ConAu 25R; CurBio 45; DrAS 74F;
    St&PR 75; WhoAm 74, 76, 78, 80, 82; WhoE
    74; WhoWor 78*

Jensen, Virginia Allen
American. Author
b. Sep 21, 1927 in Des Moines, Iowa
Source: *ConAu 45, 1NR; SmATA 8*

Jepsen, Roger William
American. Senator
Conservative Rep. senator from IA, 1978--.
b. Dec 23, 1928 in Cedar Falls, Iowa
Source: *AlmAP 80; CngDr 79; WhoAm 74,
    82; WhoAmP 73, 75, 77, 79; WhoGov 72;
    WhoMW 74*

Jepson, Helen
American. Opera Singer
b. Nov 25, 1906 in Akron, Ohio
Source: *InWom; WhoHol A*

Jeremiah
Prophet
One of major Old Testament prophets who
    foretold destruction of temple in Jerusalem.
b. 650
Source: *DcOrL 3; NewC*

Jergens, Adele
American. Actress
Played brassy blonde in 50 B-films.
b. 1922 in New York, New York
Source: *FilmgC; IntMPA 82; MotPP; WhoHol
    A*

Jergens, Andrew
American. Manufacturer
Headed firm which made toilet soap, 1882.
b. 1852
d. Jan 1929
Source: *Entr*

Jerger, Alfred
Austrian. Opera Singer
Sang in Solti's recording of *Der Rosenkavalier*
    at age 80.
b. Jun 9, 1889 in Brunn, Austria
d. Nov 18, 1976 in Vienna, Austria
Source: *NewEOp 71*

Jeritza, Maria
[Mitzi Jedlicka]
American. Opera Singer
Sang with NY Met Opera, 1921-32.
b. Oct 6, 1887 in Brunn, Austria
d. Jul 10, 1982 in Orange, New Jersey
Source: *AnObit 1982; Baker 78; InWom; NewEOp 71; NewYTBS 82; Who 74; WhoAmW 58*

Jerome, Saint
Religious Figure
Translated Bible into Latin; feast day: Sep 30.
b. 345 in Strido, Dalmatia
d. 420 in Bethlehem, Judea
Source: *CasWL; NewC; OxEng; PenC CL; RComWL; REn*

Jerome, Jerome Klapka
English. Author, Humorist
Known for humorous novel, *Three Men in a Boat,* 1889; morality play, *Passing of the Third Floor Back,* 1908.
b. May 2, 1859 in Walsall, England
d. Jun 14, 1927
Source: *Alli SUP; BbD; BiD&SB; CasWL; Chambr 3; CyWA; DcBiA; DcEnA AP; DcLEL; EvLB; LongCTC; McGEWD; MnBBF; ModBrL; ModWD; NewC; OxEng; OxThe; PenC ENG; REn; TwCA; TwCWr; WhoStg 1908*

Jerry Murad's Harmonicats
[Al Fiore; Don Les; Jerry Murad]
American. Musicians
Harmonica group best known for 1947 hit "Peg o' My Heart."
Source: *CmpEPM*

Jessel, George Albert
American. Actor
Called "Toastmaster General" for many appearances as MC.
b. Apr 3, 1898 in New York, New York
d. May 24, 1981 in Los Angeles, California
Source: *AmPS B; AmSCAP 66; BiE&WWA; BioIn 1, 2, 3, 5, 7, 8, 10; BioNews 74; CelR; CmMov; CmpEPM; ConAu 89, 103; CurBio 43, 81; EncMT; Film 1; FilmgC; IntMPA 75, 76, 77, 78, 79, 80, 81; MovMk; NewYTBS 81; NotNAT; TwYS; WebAB; WhAm 7; Who 74; WhoAm 74, 76, 78, 80; WhoHol A; WhoThe 72, 77; WhoWor 74; WhoWorJ 72*

Jessner, Irene
Austrian. Opera Singer
b. 1909 in Vienna, Austria
Source: *CreCan 1; InWom*

Jessup, Philip Caryl
American. Diplomat
Member, US delegation to UN; helped negotiate end of Soviet blockade in Berlin, 1949.
b. Jan 5, 1897 in New York, New York
d. Jan 31, 1986 in Newtown, Pennsylvania
Source: *AmAu&B; ConAu 77; CurBio 86; IntWW 74; REnAL; WebAB 79; Who 74; WhoAm 76; WhoWor 74*

Jessup, Richard
American. Author
Wrote *The Cincinnati Kid,* 1964; movie starred Steve McQueen, 1965.
b. Jan 1, 1925 in Savannah, Georgia
d. Oct 22, 1982 in Nokomis, Florida
Source: *AmAu&B; ConAu 108; NewYTBS 82*

Jesus Christ
Religious Leader
Teacher, founder of Christianity.
b. 4 ?BC in Bethlehem, Judea
d. 29 ?AD
Source: *BioIn 1, 2, 3, 4, 5, 6, 7, 8, 9, 10, 11; NewCol 75; REn*

Jethro Tull
[Mick Abrahams; Ian Anderson; Barriemore Barlowe; Martin Barre; Clive Bunker; Glenn Cornick; John Evan; Jeffrey Hammond-Hammond]
English. Music Group
Source: *EncPR&S 74; IlEncRk*

Jett, Joan
[Joan Jett and the Blackhearts; Joan Larkin; The Runaways]
American. Singer, Musician
Had pop-heavy metal single "I Love Rock 'n Roll," 1982.
b. Sep 22, 1960 in Philadelphia, Pennsylvania
Source: *NewWmR; RolSEnR 83*

Jewett, Henry
American. Actor
Built Repertory Theatre of Boston, 1924; first in US.
b. Jun 4, 1862 in Victoria, Australia
d. Jun 24, 1930 in West Newton, Massachusetts
Source: *NatCAB 22; WhoStg 1906, 1908*

Jewett, Sarah Orne
American. Author
Stories depict New England countryside
    charm; works include *A Country Doctor,*
    1884; *The Life of Nancy,* 1895.
b. Sep 3, 1849 in South Berwick, Maine
d. Jun 24, 1909 in South Berwick, Maine
Source: *Alli SUP; AmAu; AmAu&B; AmBi;*
AmWr; AmWom; ApCAB; AtlBL; AuBYP;
BbD; BiD&SB; CarSB; CasWL; Chambr 3;
ChhPo, S1, S2; CnDAL; CrtT 3; CyWA;
DcAmAu; DcAmB; DcBiA; DcLEL; DcNAA;
EvLB; InWom; JBA 34; ModAL; NotAW;
OxAmL; OxEng; PenC AM; RAdv 1; REn;
REnAL; TwCBDA; WebAB; WebE&AL;
WhAm 1

Jewison, Norman
American. Director
Best known for *Fiddler on the Roof,* 1971.
b. Jul 21, 1926 in Toronto, Ontario
Source: *BiDFilm; CanWW 70, 79; CurBio 79;*
FilmgC; IntMPA 82; MovMk; NewYTET;
OxFilm; WhoAm 82; WorEFlm

Jezebel
Phoenician. Princess
Wife of King Ahab; name is used
    symbolically for a wicked woman.
fl. 9th century BC
Source: *GoodHs; InWom; LongCEL; NewCol*
75; WebBD 80

Jhabvala, Ruth Prawer
British. Author
b. May 7, 1927 in Cologne, Germany
Source: *ConAu 1R, 2NR; ConLC 4; ConNov*
72, 76; NewC; NewYTBE 73; TwCWr;
WorAu; WrDr 80

Jillian, Ann
[Mrs. Andy Murcia]
American. Actress
Starred on Broadway in *Sugar Babies;* in TV
    series "It's a Living," 1980--.
b. Jan 29, 1951 in Los Angeles, California
Source: *BioIn 12*

Jimenez, Juan Ramon
Spanish. Poet
b. Dec 23, 1881 in Monguer, Spain
d. May 29, 1958 in Puerto Rico
Source: *AnCL; AtlBL; CasWL; ClDMEL;*
CnMWL; CyWA; DcSpL; EncWL; EvEuW;
ModRL; PenC EUR; REn; TwCWr; WhAm
3; WhoTwCL; WorAu

Jimenez, Marcos Perez
see: Perez Jimenez, Marcos

Jimmy the Greek
[James Snyder; Demetrius George Synodinos]
American. Journalist, Sportscaster
Former pro gambler who is handicapper,
    analyst for CBS Sports.
b. Sep 9, 1919 in Steubenville, Ohio
Source: *WhoAm 78; WhoTelC*

Jinnah, Mohammed Ali
Indian. Political Leader
Principal founder, first governor-general of
    Pakistan, partitioned from India, 1947.
b. Dec 25, 1876 in Karachi, Pakistan
d. Sep 11, 1948 in Karachi, Pakistan
Source: *WhAm 2*

Joachim, Joseph
Hungarian. Musician
b. Jun 28, 1831 in Kisstee, Hungary
d. Aug 15, 1907 in Berlin, Germany
Source: *BioIn 1, 2, 4, 8, 9; NewCol 75;*
WebBD 80

Joan Jett and the Blackhearts
[Ricky Byrd; Lee Crystal; Joan Jett; Gary
    Ryan]
American. Music Group
Had hit single "I Love Rock 'N Roll," 1982.
Source: *RkOn 85*

Joan of Arc
[Jeanne d'Arc]
"Maid of Orleans"
French. Heroine
Led troops to victory over English, 1429;
    tried for heresy, burned at stake.
b. Jan 6, 1412 in Domremy, France
d. May 30, 1431 in Rouen, France
Source: *FilmgC; HerW; InWom; LongCEL;*
McGEWB; NewC; NewCol 75; OxFr; REn

Joanis, John W
American. Insurance Executive
Founder, chairman, Sentry Insurance Co.
b. Jun 13, 1918 in Hopewell, Virginia
d. Nov 19, 1985 in Marshfield, Wisconsin
Source: *St&PR 84; WhoAm 82, 84; WhoIns*
82, 84

Job
Biblical Character
Story told in Old Testament, Book of Job.
Source: *BioIn 10; NewCol 75; WebBD 80*

Jobert, Michel
French. Diplomat
b. Sep 11, 1921 in Meknes, Morocco
Source: *CurBio 75; IntWW 74; NewYTBS 74;*
Who 74

Jobin, Raoul
Canadian. Opera Singer
b. Apr 8, 1906 in Quebec City, Quebec
d. Jan 13, 1974 in Quebec City, Quebec
Source: *CanWW 70; CreCan 1; WhAm 6*

Jobs, Steven Paul
American. Corporation Executive
Former chairman, Apple Computers; is worth
   approximately $210,000,000.
b. 1955
Source: *CurBio 83; LElec*

Jobson, Eddie
see: Roxy Music

Jochum, Eugen
German. Conductor
b. Nov 2, 1902 in Babenhausen, Germany
Source: *IntWW 74; WhoMus 72; WhoWor 78*

Joel, Billy (William Martin)
American. Singer, Songwriter
Had five #1 songs from album *An Innocent
   Man.*
b. May 9, 1949 in Bronx, New York
Source: *BioNews 74; BkPepl; ConAu 108;
CurBio 79; IlEncRk; RkOn 78; WhoAm 82,
82*

Joffre, Joseph Jacques Cesaire
French. Military Leader
Commander of French army credited with
   directing orderly French retreat before
   German advance, 1914.
b. Jan 12, 1852 in Rivesaltes, France
d. Jan 13, 1931 in Paris, France
Source: *McGEWB; OxFr; WhoMilH 76*

Joffrey, Robert
[Abdullah Jaffa Bey Khan]
American. Choreographer
Founded Joffrey Ballet Co., 1956--.
b. Dec 24, 1930 in Seattle, Washington
Source: *BioNews 74; CurBio 67; NewYTBE
72; WhoWor 78; WhoAm 74, 76, 78, 80, 82*

Jofre, Eder
Brazilian. Boxer
b. Mar 26, 1936 in Sao Paulo, Brazil
Source: *BioIn 6; WhoBox 74*

Johannesen, Grant
American. Musician
b. 1921 in Salt Lake City, Utah
Source: *BioNews 75; CurBio 61; WhoAm 74;
WhoMus 72*

Johanson, Donald Carl
American. Anthropologist
Unearthed most complete skeleton known to
   anthropologists, 1974.
b. Jun 28, 1943 in Chicago, Illinois
Source: *ConAu 107; CurBio 84; NewYTBS
79; WhoAm 82; WhoMW 76, 78*

Johansson, Ingemar
Swedish. Boxer
b. Sep 22, 1932 in Gothenburg, Sweden
Source: *CurBio 59; WhoHol A; WhoBox 74*

John XXIII, Pope
[Angelo Guiseppe Roncalli]
Italian. Religious Leader
Pope, 1958-63; convened Vatican II, 1962, to
   effect reforms within church; promoted
   unity of Christians.
b. Nov 25, 1881 in Sotto il Monte, Italy
d. Jun 3, 1963 in Rome, Italy
Source: *McGEWB; NewCol 75; WebBD 80;
WhDW; WhAm 4*

John, King of England
"John Lackland"
English. King
Son of Henry II; forced by English barons to
   sign Magna Carta, 1215.
b. Dec 24, 1167 in Oxford, England
d. Oct 29, 1216 in Newark, England
Source: *LinLib S; McGEWB; NewC; NewCol
75; REn*

John of Gaunt
[Duke of Lancaster; Earl of Derby; Earl of
   Richmond]
English. Nobleman
Fourth son of Edward III; house of Tudor
   descended from him.
b. Mar 1340 in Ghent, Belgium
d. Feb 3, 1399 in London, England
Source: *LongCEL; McGEWB; NewCol 75;
REn; WebBD 80*

John of Salisbury
English. Author
Most learned scholarly writer of his time;
   wrote *Policraticus,* 1159.
b. 1120 in Salisbury, England
d. Oct 25, 1180
Source: *Alli; BiB N; BrAu; CasWL; DcEnL;
DcEuL; EvLB; NewC; OxEng; PenC ENG*

John of the Cross, Saint
[San Juan de la Cruz]
Spanish. Poet
b. Jun 24, 1542 in Avila, Spain
d. Dec 14, 1591 in Penuela, Spain
Source: *AtlBL; CasWL; DcEuL; DcSpL;
EuAu; EvEuW; NewC; PenC EUR;
RComWL; REn*

John Paul I, Pope
[Albino Luciani]
Italian. Religious Leader
Pope for 34 days, 1978, before dying of
heart attack.
b. Oct 17, 1912 in Belluno, Italy
d. Sep 28, 1978 in Vatican City, Italy
Source: *ConAu 81; CurBio 78; IntWW 79;
WhoWor 78*

John Paul II, Pope
[Karol Wojtyla]
Polish. Religious Leader
Youngest pope elected in 158 yrs.; first non-
Italian pope in 455 yrs.
b. May 18, 1920 in Wadowice, Poland
Source: *BioIn 11; BkPepl; CurBio 79*

John III, Sobieski
Polish. Ruler
King of Poland, 1674-96; later years
unsuccessful because of poor political
conditions.
b. Aug 17, 1624 in Olesko, Poland
d. Jun 17, 1696
Source: *McGEWB; WebBD 80*

John the Baptist
Biblical Character
Baptized Jesus in river Jordan; feast day:
June 24.
Source: *BioIn 9; WebBD 80*

John, Augustus Edwin
British. Artist
b. Jan 4, 1878 in Tenby, Wales
d. Oct 31, 1961 in Fordingbridge, England
Source: *AtlBL; ChhPo; CurBio 41, 62;
OxEng; WhAm 4*

John, Elton
[Reginald Kenneth Dwight]
English. Singer, Songwriter
All albums are gold; hits include "Rocket
Man," "Philadelphia Freedom."
b. Mar 25, 1947 in Pinner, England
Source: *Baker 78; BioNews 74; BkPepl; CelR;
CurBio 75; NewYTBE 71; NewYTBS 74;
RkOn 78; WhoAm 82; WhoHol A*

John, Gwendolyn Mary
Welsh. Artist
Painted interiors, austere female portraits;
Whistler's pupil.
b. 1876 in Haverfordwest, Wales
d. 1939 in Dieppe, France
Source: *ChhPo; McGDA; WomArt*

John, John Pico
"Mr. John"
American. Designer
b. Mar 14, 1906 in Florence, Italy
Source: *CurBio 56; WhoAm 74*

John, Tommy (Thomas Edward, Jr.)
American. Baseball Player
Pitcher; left elbow surgically reconstructed,
1974; won 20 games, 1977.
b. May 22, 1943 in Terre Haute, Indiana
Source: *BaseEn 85; CurBio 81; NewYTBS 77,
78; WhoAm 76, 78, 80, 82; WhoProB 73*

Johns, Glynis
English. Actress
Best known for portrayal of mother in film
Mary Poppins, 1964.
b. Oct 5, 1923 in Pretoria, South Africa
Source: *BiE&WWA; CurBio 73; FilmgC;
IntMPA 82; MotPP; MovMk; NewYTBE 73;
NotNAT; OxFilm; Who 74; WhoHol A;
WhoThe 77*

Johns, Jasper
American. Artist
Pop artist known for using flags, letters,
numbers in work.
b. May 15, 1930 in Augusta, Georgia
Source: *CelR; CurBio 67; DcCAA 71; EncAB-
H; IntWW 74, 75, 76, 77, 78, 79, 80;
NewCol 75; WhoAm 74, 76, 78, 80, 82;
WhoAmA 73, 76, 78, 80*

Johnson, Alex(ander)
American. Baseball Player
b. Dec 7, 1942 in Helena, Arkansas
Source: *BaseEn 85; WhoAm 74; WhoProB 73*

Johnson, Amy
English. Aviatrix
b. 1903 in Kingston-upon-Hull, England
d. Jan 5, 1941
Source: *CurBio 41; HerW; InWom*

Johnson, Andrew

American. US President
Succeeded Lincoln, 1865-69; survived
  impeachment attempt by Congress, 1868.
b. Dec 29, 1808 in Raleigh, North Carolina
d. Jul 31, 1875 in Carter Station, Tennessee
Source: *AmAu&B; AmBi; ApCAB; BiAUS;*
BiDrAC; BiDrUSE; DcAmB; DcNAA; Drake;
EncAB-H; NewCol 75; OxAmL; REn;
REnAL; TwCBDA; WebAB; WhAm HS;
WhAmP

Johnson, Arno Hollock

American. Economist, Advertising Executive,
  Author
J Walter Thompson economist, 1926-67;
  wrote *Marketing Opportunities.*
b. Jan 12, 1901 in Jacksonville, Florida
d. Jul 20, 1985 in Delray Beach, Florida
Source: *ConAu 116; IntYB 81; WhoAm 78*

Johnson, Arte

American. Actor, Comedian
Best known for character acting in TV's
  "Laugh-In," 1968-71.
b. Jan 20, 1934 in Benton Harbor, Michigan
Source: *WhoAm 82; WhoHol A*

Johnson, Ben

American. Actor
Won Oscar for *The Last Picture Show,* 1971.
b. Jun 13, 1918 in Pawhuska, Oklahoma
Source: *CmMov; FilmEn; FilmgC; IntMPA*
82; MovMk; WhoHol A

Johnson, Betsey

American. Fashion Designer
Designer of children's, maternity, women's
  clothes; owner, NYC's Betsey Johnson
  store, 1979--.
b. Aug 10, 1942 in Wethersfield, Connecticut
Source: *WhoAm 82; WorFshn*

Johnson, Beverly

American. Model
First black woman on cover of *Vogue,* 1975;
  won outstanding US model award, 1975.
b. Oct 13, 1951 in Buffalo, New York
Source: *BioIn 10, 11; WhoBlA 77*

Johnson, Bill (William D)

American. Skier
Won gold medal, men's downhill, 1984
  Olympics; first American to win Alpine
  event.
b. 1961 in Los Angeles, California
Source: *NewYTBS 84*

Johnson, "Billy White Shoes" (William Arthur)

American. Football Player
Wide receiver, Houston, Atlanta; played in
  Pro Bowl, 1975, 1977, 1983.
b. Jan 21, 1952 in Boothwyn, Pennsylvania
Source: *FootReg 85; WhoBlA 80*

Johnson, Bruce

see: Beach Boys, The

Johnson, "Bunk" (William Geary)

American. Jazz Musician
b. Dec 27, 1879 in New Orleans, Louisiana
d. Jul 7, 1949 in New Iberia, Louisiana
Source: *BiDAmM; WhAm 4; WhoJazz 72*

Johnson, (Byron) Ban(croft)

American. Baseball Executive
b. Jan 8, 1864 in Norwalk, Ohio
d. Mar 18, 1931 in Saint Louis, Missouri
Source: *BioIn 3, 7; DcAmB; WhAm 1;*
WhoProB 73

Johnson, Celia, Dame

English. Actress
Starred in films *Brief Encounter,* 1945, *In*
  Which We Serve, 1942.
b. Dec 18, 1908 in Richmond, England
d. Apr 25, 1982 in Nettlebed, England
Source: *AnObit 1982; BiDFilm; CnThe;*
FilmgC; IntMPA 82; IntWW 78; MotPP;
MovMk; NewYTBS 82; OxFilm; PIP&P;
WhoHol A; WhoThe 77

Johnson, Charles Richard

American. Author
Wrote novel *Oxherding Tale,* 1982.
b. Apr 23, 1948 in Evanston, Illinois
Source: *ConAu 116; ConLC 7; DcLB 33*

Johnson, Charlie (Charles Wright)

American. Jazz Musician
b. Nov 21, 1891 in Philadelphia,
  Pennsylvania
d. Dec 13, 1959 in New York, New York
Source: *WhoJazz 72*

Johnson, "Chic" (Harold Ogden)

[Olsen and Johnson]
American. Actor, Comedian
Vaudeville star with Ole Olsen, 1914;
  Hellzapoppin became great Br oadway, film
  success, 1941.
b. Mar 5, 1891 in Chicago, Illinois
d. Feb 1962 in Las Vegas, Nevada
Source: *FilmEn; FilmgC; MovMk; WhScrn*
74, 77; WhoHol B

Johnson, Clarence Leonard
American. Aeronautical Engineer
b. Feb 27, 1910 in Ishpeming, Michigan
Source: *AmM&WS 73P; CurBio 68; WhoAm 74; WhoF&I 74*

Johnson, Cletus Merlin
American. Artist
b. Nov 19, 1941 in Elizabeth, New Jersey
Source: *WhoAm 82; WhoAmA 76, 78, 80*

Johnson, Crockett
[David Johnson Leisk]
American. Cartoonist, Author
Created comic strip *Barnaby,* 1941-62;
   author, illustrator of several children's
   books.
b. Oct 20, 1906 in New York, New York
d. Jul 11, 1975 in Norwalk, Connecticut
Source: *Au&Wr 71; AuBYP; BkP; ConAu 57; CurBio 84; IlsCB 1957; SmATA 1; ThrBJA; WhAm 6; WhoAmA 73*

Johnson, Dave (David Allen)
American. Baseball Player, Baseball Manager
Set ML record for most home runs by
   second baseman in season, 1973; manager,
   NY Mets, 1984--.
b. Jan 30, 1943 in Orlando, Florida
Source: *BaseEn 85; BaseReg 86*

Johnson, Dennis W
American. Basketball Player
Guard, Phoenix, 1980-83; Boston, 1983--.
b. Sep 18, 1954 in San Pedro, California
Source: *OfNBA 81; WhoAm 82*

Johnson, "Dink" (Oliver)
American. Jazz Musician
b. Oct 28, 1892 in New Orleans, Louisiana
d. Nov 29, 1954 in Portland, Oregon
Source: *WhoJazz 72*

Johnson, Don
American. Actor
Plays Sonny Crockett on "Miami Vice,"
   1984--.
b. Dec 15, 1950 in Galena, Missouri
Source: *ConNews 86-1; CurBio 86*

Johnson, Earvin
"Magic"
American. Basketball Player
Forward, LA Lakers, 1979--; led Michigan
   State U to NCAA championship, 1979.
b. Aug 14, 1959 in Lansing, Michigan
Source: *BioIn 12; CurBio 82; OfNBA 81; WhoAm 82*

Johnson, Eastman
American. Artist
Painted genre pictures of black life in the
   south, portraits of presidents, authors.
b. Jul 29, 1824 in Lovell, Maine
d. Apr 5, 1906 in New York, New York
Source: *AmBi; DcAmArt; DcAmB; DcBiPP; HarEnUS; McGDA; NatCAB 9; WebAB; WhAm 1*

Johnson, Eddie
American. Basketball Player
b. Feb 24, 1955 in Ocala, Florida
Source: *BioIn 12; OfNBA 81*

Johnson, Edward
Canadian. Opera Singer, Manager
b. Aug 22, 1881 in Guelph, Ontario
d. Apr 20, 1959 in Guelph, Ontario
Source: *CreCan 2*

Johnson, Eliza McCardle
[Mrs. Andrew Johnson]
American. First Lady
Taught Andrew to read, write; semi-invalid
   unable to assume White House duties.
b. Oct 4, 1810 in Leesburg, Tennessee
d. Jan 15, 1876 in Greenville, Tennessee
Source: *AmWom; ApCAB; GoodHs; NatCAB 2; NotAW; TwCBDA*

Johnson, Evelyn
American. Basketball Player, Celebrity
   Relative
Sister of Earvin Johnson.
Source: *NF*

Johnson, Gerald White
American. Journalist
b. Aug 6, 1890 in Riverton, North Carolina
d. Mar 23, 1980 in Baltimore, Maryland
Source: *AmAu; AnCL; AuBYP; BioIn 2, 3, 4, 7, 9; CnDAL; ConAu 85, 97; OxAmL; REnAL; SmATA 19; ThrBJA; TwCA SUP; WhAm 7; WhNAA; WhoAm 74, 76, 78; WhoWor 74*

Johnson, Hall
American. Composer
Organized Hall Johnson Choir heard in
   movie *Lost Horizon.*
b. Mar 12, 1888 in Athens, Georgia
d. Apr 30, 1970 in New York, New York
Source: *AmSCAP 66; BlkAWP; CurBio 45, 70; WhScrn 77; WhoHol B*

Johnson, Harold
American. Boxer
b. Aug 9, 1928 in Manayunk, Pennsylvania
Source: *BioIn 9; WhoBox 74*

Johnson, Henry
American. Soldier
b. 1897
d. 1929
Source: *BioIn 4, 8*

Johnson, Herbert Fisk
American. Businessman, Philanthropist
b. Nov 15, 1899 in Racine, Wisconsin
d. Dec 13, 1978 in Racine, Wisconsin
Source: *BioIn 11; IntYB 78; NewYTBS 78; WhAm 7*

Johnson, Hewlett
"Red Dean of Canterbury"
English. Religious Leader
b. Jan 25, 1874 in Manchester, England
d. Oct 22, 1966 in Canterbury, England
Source: *CurBio 43, 66; LongCTC; WhAm 4*

Johnson, Hiram W
American. Statesman
b. Sep 2, 1866 in Sacramento, California
d. Aug 6, 1945 in Bethesda, Maryland
Source: *BiDrAC; CurBio 41, 45; DcAmB S3; EncAB-H; WebAB; WhAm 2; WhAmP*

Johnson, Howard Brennan
American. Restaurateur
Pres., director, chm. Howard Johnson Co., 1964-81.
b. Aug 23, 1932 in Boston, Massachusetts
Source: *BioIn 7, 11; CelR; CurBio 66; WhoAm 74, 76, 80, 82; WhoF&I 74; WhoWor 78*

Johnson, Howard Deering
American. Restaurateur
Began ice cream business, 1924; first Howard Johnson's restaurant opened, 1929 in MA.
b. 1896 in Boston, Massachusetts
d. Jun 20, 1972 in New York, New York
Source: *NewYTBE 72; WebAB; WhAm 5*

Johnson, Hugh S
American. Government Official
b. Aug 5, 1882 in Fort Scott, Kansas
d. Apr 15, 1942 in Washington, District of Columbia
Source: *AmAu&B; CurBio 40, 42; DcAmB S3; DcNAA; EncAB-H; WebAB; WhAm 2*

Johnson, "J J" (James Louis)
American. Jazz Musician
b. Jan 22, 1924 in Indianapolis, Indiana
Source: *WhoAm 74; WhoBlA 75*

Johnson, Jack (John Arthur)
American. Boxer
b. Mar 31, 1878 in Galveston, Texas
d. Jun 10, 1946 in Raleigh, North Carolina
Source: *CurBio 46; DcAmB S4; WebAB; WhAm 2; WhoBox 74*

Johnson, James Price
American. Jazz Musician
b. Feb 1, 1891 in New Brunswick, New Jersey
d. Nov 17, 1955 in New York, New York
Source: *AmSCAP 66; WhoJazz 72*

Johnson, James Ralph
American. Author
Wrote *Little Red*, 1966; *Animals and Their Food*, 1972.
b. May 20, 1922 in Fort Payne, Alabama
Source: *AuBYP; ConAu 1R, 2NR; SmATA 1; WrDr 76*

Johnson, James Weldon
American. Author
Wrote *The Book of American Negro Poetry*, 1921; *Negro Americans, What Now?* 1934.
b. Jun 17, 1871 in Jacksonville, Florida
d. Jun 26, 1938 in Wiscasset, Maine
Source: *AmAu&B; AmBi; CasWL; ConAmA; ConAmL; PenC AM; REn; REnAL; TwCA; WebE&AL; WhAm 1*

Johnson, John Harold
American. Publisher
b. Jan 19, 1918 in Arkansas City, Arkansas
Source: *EncAB-H; WebAB; WhoAm 82; WhoMW 74*

Johnson, Josephine Winslow
American. Author
b. Jan 20, 1910 in Kirkwood, Missouri
Source: *AmAu&B; AmNov; AnMV 1926; ChhPo; CnDAL; ConAmA; ConAu 25R; ConNov 72, 76; DcLEL; DrAF 76; ForWC 70; InWom; OxAmL; REnAL; TwCA, SUP; WhNAA; WhoAm 74, 76, 78, 80, 82; WhoMW 74; WrDr 76*

Johnson, Joshua
American. Artist
Former slave; self-taught portrait painter.
b. 1796
d. 1824
Source: *AfroAA*

Johnson, "Judy" (William Julius)
American. Baseball Player
Best third baseman of Negro leagues; was
ML scout following playing career; Hall of
Fame, 1975.
b. Oct 26, 1899 in Snow Hill, Maryland
Source: *BasesB*

Johnson, Junior
American. Auto Racer
b. 1931 in Ingle Hollow, North Carolina
Source: *BioIn 10*

**Johnson, "Lady Bird" (Claudia Alta
Taylor)**
[Mrs. Lyndon Johnson]
American. First Lady
Promoted national conservation programs;
wrote *White House Diary,* 1971.
b. Dec 22, 1912 in Karnack, Texas
Source: *CelR; ConAu 89; CurBio 64;
NewYTBE 73; WhoAm 74, 76, 78, 80, 82;
WhoAmW 77; WhoWor 74*

Johnson, Lionel Pigot
English. Journalist, Editor
Wrote *Art of Thomas Hardy,* 1894.
b. Mar 15, 1867 in Broadstairs, England
d. Oct 4, 1902 in London, England
Source: *ConAu 117; DcLB 19*

Johnson, Luci Baines
American. Celebrity Relative
Daughter of Lyndon Johnson.
b. Jul 2, 1947
Source: *BioNews 74; InWom; NewYTBE 71*

Johnson, Lynda Bird
[Mrs. Charles Robb]
American. Celebrity Relative
Daughter of Lyndon Johnson.
b. Mar 19, 1943 in Washington, District of
Columbia
Source: *BioNews 74*

Johnson, Lyndon Baines
American. US President
Domestic achievements overshadowed by
Vietnam War; wrote *The Vantage Point,*
1971.
b. Aug 27, 1908 in Stonewall, Texas
d. Jan 22, 1973 in Johnson City, Texas
Source: *AmAu&B; BiDrAC; BiDrUSE; ConAu
41R, 53; CurBio 51, 64, 73; EncAB-H;
NewYTBE 71, 73; NewYTBS 74; OxAmL;
REn; WebAB; WhAm 5; WhAmP; WhoGov
75; WhoS&SW 82*

Johnson, Lynn-Holly
American. Figure Skater, Actress
Former Ice Capades star; starred in movie
Ice Castles, 1979.
b. 1959 in Chicago, Illinois
Source: *BioIn 12*

Johnson, Mark
American. Hockey Player
Member,1980 gold medal winning US hockey
team.
b. Sep 22, 1957 in Madison, Wisconsin
Source: *HocEn; HocReg 81*

Johnson, Marques Kevin
American. Basketball Player
Sporting News College Player of the Year,
1977; was NBA All-Star, 1979.
b. Feb 8, 1956 in Natchitoches, Louisiana
Source: *OfNBA 81; WhoAm 82*

Johnson, Martin Elmer
American. Author, Filmmaker, Explorer
Made African, S Seas expeditions, filming
vanishing wildlife.
b. Oct 9, 1884 in Rockford, Illinois
d. Jan 13, 1937 in Los Angeles, California
Source: *AmAu&B; AmBi; BioIn 6, 7, 9, 10;
DcFM; DcNAA; Film 1; NatCAB 24; REnAL;
TwYS; WhAm 1; WhScrn 77*

Johnson, Mordecai Wyatt
American. Educator
b. Jan 12, 1890 in Paris, Texas
d. Sep 10, 1976 in Washington, District of
Columbia
Source: *CurBio 41*

Johnson, Nicholas
American. Government Official
b. Sep 23, 1934 in Iowa City, Iowa
Source: *AmAu&B; CelR; ConAu 29R; CurBio
68; NewYTBE 71; WhoAm 74, 76, 78, 80,
82; WhoGov 75; WhoS&SW 82; WhoWor 78;
WrDr 76*

Johnson, Nunnally
American. Director, Screenwriter
b. Dec 5, 1897 in Columbus, Georgia
d. Mar 25, 1977 in Los Angeles, California
Source: *ConAu 69, 81; CurBio 41, 77;
IntMPA 75*

Johnson, Osa Helen Leighty
[Mrs. Martin Johnson]
American. Explorer
Accompanied husband on expeditions; co-
author *Safari*, 1928.
b. Mar 14, 1894 in Chanute, Kansas
d. Jan 7, 1953 in New York, New York
Source: *AmAu&B; AuBYP; CurBio 40, 53;
DcAmB S5; InWom; REnAL; WhAm 3;
WhScrn 77; WomWMM*

Johnson, Pamela Hansford
[Baroness Pamela Hansford Johnson Snow;
Mrs. C P Snow]
English. Author, Critic
Verstaile writer of psychological novels,
literary studies: *Catherine Carter*, 1952.
b. May 29, 1912 in London, England
d. Jun 18, 1981 in London, England
Source: *Au&Wr 71; BioIn 1, 4, 5; ConAu
1R, 104, 2NR; ConLC 1, 7; ConNov 72, 76;
CurBio 48, 81; DcLEL; EncWL; EvLB;
InWom; IntAu&W 76, 77; IntWW 74, 75,
76, 77, 78; LongCEL; LongCTC; ModBrL,
S1; NewC; REn; TwCA SUP; TwCWr;
WebE&AL; Who 74; WhoAmW 66, 68, 70,
72, 74, 75, 77; WhoWor 78; WrDr 76, 80*

Johnson, Pete
American. Football Player
Running back, 1977--; suspended for
preseason, plus four regular season games
by NFL for drug involvement, 1983.
b. Mar 2, 1954 in Peach County, Georgia
Source: *FootReg 85*

Johnson, Phillip Cortelyou
American. Architect, Author
b. Jul 8, 1906 in Cleveland, Ohio
Source: *CurBio 57; WebAB; WhoAm 74, 76,
78, 80, 82*

Johnson, Pierre Marc
Canadian. Politician
Conservative who succeeded Rene Levesque
as leader of Parti Quebecois; opposition
leader, Dec 1985--.
b. Jul 5, 1946 in Montreal, Quebec
Source: *CanWW 83; ConNews 85-4*

Johnson, Rafer Lewis
American. Track Athlete
Won silver medal in decathlon, 1956
Olympics; gold medal, 1960 Olympics.
b. Aug 18, 1935 in Hillsboro, Texas
Source: *CelR; CurBio 61; FilmgC; WhoAm
82; WhoBlA 75; WhoHol A; WhoTr&F 73*

Johnson, Raynor C(arey)
English. Physicist, Author
Books on parapsychology include *Nurslings of
Immortality*, 1957.
b. Apr 5, 1901 in Leeds, England
Source: *BiDPara; ConAu 115; EncO&P 78*

Johnson, Reverdy
American. Diplomat
b. May 21, 1796 in Annapolis, Maryland
d. Feb 10, 1876 in Annapolis, Maryland
Source: *AmBi; ApCAB; BiAUS; BiDSA;
BiDrAC; BiDrUSE; DcAmB; Drake; TwCBDA;
WebAB; WhAm HS; WhAmP*

Johnson, Richard
English. Actor
Co-starred with then-wife Kim Novak in film
Moll Flanders, 1965.
b. Jul 30, 1927 in Essex, England
Source: *FilmgC; IntMPA 82; MovMk;
WhoThe 77*

Johnson, Richard Mentor
American. Politician
VP under Martin Van Buren, 1837-41.
b. Oct 17, 1781 in Beargrass, Kentucky
d. Nov 19, 1850 in Frankfort, Kentucky
Source: *ApCAB; BiDSA; Drake; EncSoB;
HarEnUS; LinLib S; WebAB 79; WhAm HS;
WhAmP*

Johnson, Robert
[K C and the Sunshine Band]
American. Musician
Drummer with the Sunshine Band since
1973.
b. Mar 21, 1953 in Miami, Florida
Source: *NF*

Johnson, Robert Willard
American. Educator
b. Dec 23, 1921 in Denver, Colorado
Source: *AmM&WS 73S; ConAu 17R; WhoAm
74, 76, 78, 80, 82; WhoCon 73; WrDr 76*

Johnson, Samuel
English. Lexicographer, Critic
Wrote first great critique of Shakespeare,
1765; also *Dictionary of English Literature*,
1755.
b. Sep 18, 1709 in Litchfield, England
d. Dec 13, 1784 in London, England
Source: *Alli; AtlBL; BbD; BiD&SB; BrAu;
CasWL; ChhPo, S1, S2; CnE&AP; CrtT 2;
CyWA; DcBiA; DcEnA, AP; DcEnL; DcEuL;
DcLEL; EvLB; MouLC 2; NewC; OxAmL;
OxEng; OxThe; PenC ENG; RComWL; REn;
WebE&AL*

Johnson, Samuel C
American. Manufacturer
Established firm which became major wax
manufacturer, 1886.
b. 1833
d. 1919
Source: *Entr*

Johnson, Sonia
American. Feminist
ERA support led to excommunication by
Mormon Church, 1979; author *From
Housewife to Heretic,* 1981.
b. Feb 27, 1936 in Malad, Idaho
Source: *CurBio 85; NewYTBS 79*

Johnson, U(ral) Alexis
American. Diplomat
In foreign service since 1935; served as
ambassador to Czechoslovakia, 1953-58,
Thailand, 1958-61, Japan, 1966-69.
b. Oct 17, 1908 in Falun, Kansas
Source: *CurBio 55; IntWW 82; IntYB 82;
PolProf NF; USBiR 74; WhoAm 78;
WhoAmP 81; WhoGov 77; WhoWor 74*

Johnson, Van
"The Voiceless Sinatra"
American. Actor
Bobby-soxers idol in MGM films throughout
1940s.
b. Aug 28, 1916 in Newport, Rhode Island
Source: *BiDFilm; BiE&WWA; CelR; CmMov;
CurBio 45; FilmEn; FilmgC; IntMPA 82;
MotPP; MovMk; OxFilm; WhoAm 82;
WhoHol A; WhoThe 77; WorEFlm*

Johnson, Virginia E
[Masters and Johnson; Mrs. William H
Masters]
American. Psychologist
Researcher in human sexuality; wrote, with
husband, *Human Sexual Response,* 1966.
b. Feb 11, 1925 in Springfield, Missouri
Source: *AmAu&B; AuNews 1; ConAu 21R;
EncAB-H; NewYTBE 70; WhoAm 74;
WhoAmW 77*

Johnson, Walter (Thomas Walter)
American. Historian, Educator
Wrote on American history: *William Allen
White's America,* 1947.
b. Jun 27, 1915 in Nahant, Massachusetts
d. Jun 14, 1985 in Ludington, Michigan
Source: *ConAu 116; CurBio 57, 85; WhoAm
84*

Johnson, Walter Perry
"Barney"; "The Big Train"
American. Baseball Player, Baseball Manager
Pitcher, 1907-27; holds records for shutouts
(113); Hall of Fame, 1936.
b. Nov 6, 1887 in Humboldt, Kansas
d. Dec 10, 1946 in Washington, District of
Columbia
Source: *BaseEn 85; DcAmB S4; WebAB;
WhAm HSA, 4; WhoProB 73*

Johnson, William
American. Supreme Court Justice
b. Dec 27, 1771 in Charleston, South
Carolina
d. Aug 4, 1834 in Brooklyn, New York
Source: *BioIn 2, 3, 5; ApCAB; BiAUS;
DcAmB; Drake; NatCab 2; TwCBDA;
WebAB; WhAm HS*

Johnson, William, Sir
British. Government Official
Superintendant of Indial affairs north of Ohio
River, 1756.
b. 1715 in Smithtown, Ireland
d. Jul 11, 1774 in Johnstown, New York
Source: *Alli; AmBi; ApCAB; DcAmB; Drake;
EncAB-H; OxAmL; OxCan; REnAL; WebAB;
WhAm HS*

Johnston, Albert S
American. Military Leader
Served in Mexican War for the Union 1845;
served in Civil War for Confederate Army,
1861.
b. Feb 2, 1803 in Washington, Kentucky
d. Apr 6, 1862 in Shiloh, Tennessee
Source: *AmBi; ApCAB; BiDConf; DcAmB;
Drake; NatCAB 29; REnAW; TwCBDA;
WebAB; WhAm HS; WhoMilH 76*

Johnston, Annie Fellows
American. Children's Author
Wrote *Little Colonel* series, 1896-1910.
b. May 15, 1863 in Evansville, Indiana
d. Oct 5, 1931 in Pewee Valley, Kentucky
Source: *ConAu 116; DcAmAu; OxAmL 83;
REnAL*

Johnston, Frances Benjamin
American. Photographer
Pioneer in photojournalism; took photos of
White House interior, 1893.
b. Jan 15, 1864 in Grafton, West Virginia
d. May 16, 1952 in New Orleans, Louisiana
Source: *NotAW MOD*

Johnston, Frank H
[Group of Seven]
Canadian. Artist
Landscape painter, illustrator; apathetic
  member, Group of Seven, 1916-22.
b. Jun 19, 1888 in Toronto, Ontario
d. Jul 10, 1949
Source: *ClbCR; CreCan 1*

Johnston, J Bennett, Jr.
American. Politician
b. Jun 10, 1932 in Shreveport, Louisiana
Source: *CngDr 74; WhoAm 74, 76, 78, 80,
82; WhoAmP 73*

Johnston, Johnny
American. Actor
Radio performer who was featured in several
  1940s musicals.
b. Dec 1, 1915 in Saint Louis, Missouri
Source: *FilmEn; WhoHol A*

Johnston, Joseph Eggleston
American. Military Leader
Left Union Army during Civil War to join
  Confederate Army as brigadier general;
  credited for victory at first battle of Bull
  Run, 1861.
b. Feb 3, 1807 in Prince Edward, Virginia
d. Feb 21, 1891 in Washington, District of
  Columbia
Source: *Alli SUP; AmBi; BiDConf; BiDSA;
BiDrAC; DcAmAu; DcAmB; DcNAA; EncAB-
H; TwCBDA; WebAB; WhAm HS*

Johnston, Richard Malcolm
American. Author
b. Mar 8, 1822 in Oak Grove, Georgia
d. Sep 23, 1898 in Baltimore, Maryland
Source: *Alli SUP; AmAu; AmAu&B; ApCAB;
BiD&SB; BiDSA; DcAmAu; DcAmB; DcBiA;
DcLEL; DcNAA; OxAmL; REnAL; TwCBDA;
WhAm HS*

Johnstone, Jay (John William, Jr.)
American. Baseball Player
b. Nov 20, 1945 in Manchester, Connecticut
Source: *BaseEn 85*

Jolas, Betsy
American. Composer
b. Aug 5, 1926 in Paris, France
Source: *Baker 78; DcCM; NewYTBE 73*

Joliot-Curie, Irene
French. Physicist
With husband, Frederic, studied artificial
  radioactivity; contributed to discovery of
  neutron.
b. Sep 12, 1897 in Paris, France
d. Mar 17, 1956 in Paris, France
Source: *CurBio 40, 56; HerW; InWom;
WhAm 3*

Joliot(-Curie), (Jean) Frederic
French. Physicist
With wife Irene, won Nobel Prize in
  chemistry for contribution to nuclear
  research, 1935.
b. Mar 19, 1900 in Paris, France
d. Aug 14, 1958
Source: *AsBiEn; BioIn 1, 2, 3, 5, 6, 7, 11,
12; CurBio 58; DcScB; McGEWB; NewCol
75; WhAm 3*

Jolliet, Louis
Canadian. Explorer
First white man, with Jacques Marquette, to
  travel down Mississippi River, 1672.
b. 1645 in Beaupre, Quebec
d. May 1700 in Anticosti Island, Quebec
Source: *AmBi; ApCAB; DcAmB; OxCan;
REn; WebAB*

Jolson, Al
[Asa Yoelson]
American. Singer
Starred in *The Jazz Singer,* 1927, the first
  talking film.
b. May 26, 1886 in Saint Petersburg, Russia
d. Oct 23, 1950 in San Francisco, California
Source: *AmSCAP 66; BiDFilm; CmMov;
CurBio 40, 50; DcAmB S4; EncMT;
FamA&A; FilmgC; MotPP; MovMk;
NewYTBS 74; OxFilm; PIP&P; WebAB;
WhAm 3; WhScrn 74, 77; WhoHol B;
WorEFlm*

Jommelli, Niccolo
Italian. Composer
b. Sep 10, 1714 in Aversa, Italy
d. Aug 25, 1774 in Naples, Italy
Source: *NewEOp 71; OxMus*

Jonah
Hebrew. Biblical Character
Hebrew prophet whose story of being
  swallowed by a whale is told in Old
  Testament, Book of Jonah.
Source: *WebBD 80*

Jonas, Franz
Austrian. President
b. Oct 4, 1899 in Vienna, Austria
d. Apr 24, 1974 in Vienna, Austria
Source: *NewYTBS 74; WhAm 6; WhoGov 75; WhoWor 78*

Jonathan, Leabua, Chief
Prime Minister
Source: *NewYTBE 70*

Jones, Alan
Australian. Auto Racer
b. Feb 11, 1946 in Melbourne, Australia
Source: *BioIn 12*

Jones, Allan
American. Actor, Singer
Father of Jack Jones, famous for song
  "Donkey Serenade," 1937.
b. Oct 14, 1907 in Old Forge, Pennsylvania
Source: *FilmEn; FilmgC; HolP 30; MotPP; MovMk; OxFilm; WhoHol A*

Jones, Anissa
American. Actress
Played Buffy in "Family Affair," 1966-71;
  died of drug overdose.
b. 1958 in West Lafayette, Indiana
d. 1976
Source: *WhoHol A*

Jones, Arthur A
American. Businessman, Inventor
Invented Nautilus exercise equipment; chief
  exec., Nautilus Sports/Medical Industries.
b. 1924 in Arkansas
Source: *ConNews 85-3*

Jones, Barry
English. Actor
Best known for film *Brigadoon,* 1954.
b. Mar 6, 1893 in Guernsey, England
Source: *BiE&WWA; CurBio 58; FilmgC; IntMPA 82; MovMk; NotNAT; PlP&P; Who 74; WhoHol A; WhoThe 77A; WhoWor 74*

Jones, Bert(ram Hays)
American. Football Player
Quarterback, Baltimore Colts, completed 17
  consecutive passes in game against Jets,
  1974, an NFL record.
b. Sep 7, 1951 in Ruston, Louisiana
Source: *NewYTBE 72; WhoAm 82; WhoFtbl 74*

Jones, "Biff" (Lawrence M)
American. Football Coach
b. Oct 8, 1895 in Washington, District of
  Columbia
d. 1980
Source: *BioIn 10; WhoFtbl 74*

Jones, Billy (William Reese)
[The Interwoven Pair]
Singer
b. 1889
d. 1940
Source: *BioIn 5*

Jones, Bob
American. Religious Leader
b. Oct 30, 1883 in Dale County, Alabama
d. Jan 16, 1968
Source: *WhAm 4*

Jones, Bobby (Robert Tyre)
American. Golfer
Biggest name in golf, 1920s; co-founded
  Masters tournament, 1934.
b. Mar 17, 1902 in Atlanta, Georgia
d. Dec 18, 1971 in Atlanta, Georgia
Source: *WebAB*

Jones, Brian
[The Rolling Stones]
English. Singer, Musician
One of original Rolling Stones; found dead
  in swimming pool from drug overdose.
b. Feb 26, 1943 in Cheltenham, England
d. Jul 3, 1969 in London, England
Source: *WhAm 5; WhScrn 77*

Jones, Buck
[Charles Frederick Gebhart]
American. Actor
Western hero in "Rough Rider" serials with
  horse "Silver."
b. Dec 4, 1891 in Vincennes, Indiana
d. Nov 30, 1942 in Boston, Massachusetts
Source: *CmMov; CurBio 43; FilmEn; Film 1; FilmgC; MovMk; OxFilm; TwYS; WhScrn 74, 77; WhoHol B*

Jones, Candy
American. Model, Business Executive
b. Dec 31, 1925 in Wilkes-Barre,
  Pennsylvania
Source: *CurBio 61; InWom*

Jones, Carolyn
American. Actress
Played Morticia on TV series "The Addams
    Family," 1964-66.
b. Apr 28, 1933 in Amarillo, Texas
d. Aug 3, 1983 in Los Angeles, California
Source: *CurBio 83N; FilmgC; InWom;
IntMPA 82; MotPP; MovMk; NewYTBS 83;
WhoAm 82; WhoHol A*

Jones, "Casey" (John Luther)
American. Engineer
Folk hero of songs, ballads; killed in crash
    of Cannon Ball Express.
b. Mar 14, 1864 in Cayce, Kentucky
d. Apr 30, 1900 in Vaughan, Mississippi
Source: *NewCol 75; WebAB*

Jones, Charles A, Jr.
[The Hostages]
American. Hostage in Iran
b. Jul 1, 1940 in Memphis, Tennessee
Source: *BioIn 12; NewYTBS 81*

Jones, Christopher
American. Actor
Best known for films *The Looking Glass
    War,* 1969, *Ryan's Daughter,* 1971.
b. Aug 18, 1941 in Jackson, Tennessee
Source: *FilmgC; WhoHol A*

Jones, Chuck
American. Cartoonist
Animation director, Warner Brothers; created
    characters Road Runner, Pepe Le Pew,
    Wiley Coyote.
b. Sep 21, 1912 in Spokane, Washington
Source: *DcFM; FilmgC; IntMPA 82, 84;
LesBEnT; NewYTET; WhoAm 84; WorEFlm*

Jones, Clara Araminta Stanton
American. Librarian
b. May 14, 1913 in Saint Louis, Missouri
Source: *ForWC 70; WhoBlA 75; WhoMW 74*

Jones, David
English. Author, Artist
b. Nov 1, 1895 in Brockley, England
d. Oct 28, 1974 in London, England
Source: *CasWL; CnE&AP; CnMWL; ConAu
9R, 53; ConLC 2, 4, 7, 13; ConP 70, 75;
LongCTC; ModBrL; S1; OxEng; PenC ENG;
RAdv 1; REn; TwCWr; WhAm 6; Who 74;
WhoTwCL; WorAu*

Jones, David Charles
American. General, Government Official
Chm., Joint Chiefs of Staff, 1978-82;
    commander, US Air Force, Washington,
    1974-78.
b. Jul 9, 1921 in Aberdeen, South Dakota
Source: *BioIn 10, 11; CurBio 82; WebAMB;
WhoAm 82; WorDWW*

Jones, Davy (David)
[The Monkees]
English. Actor, Singer
Member of The Monkeys music group, 1966-
    68.
b. Dec 30, 1946 in Manchester, England
Source: *BioIn 9*

Jones, Dean
American. Actor
Starred in 1960s Disney films such as *That
    Darn Cat,* 1965, *The Love Bug,* 1968.
b. Jan 25, 1936 in Morgan County, Alabama
Source: *BiE&WWA; FilmgC; IntMPA 82;
MotPP; WhoAm 82; WhoHol A*

Jones, Edward Vason
American. Architect
Restored, redecorated White House Oval
    Office, State Dept. reception rooms.
b. Aug 3, 1909 in Albany, Georgia
d. Oct 1, 1980 in Albany, Georgia
Source: *WhAm 7; WhoAm 78*

Jones, Eli Stanley
American. Missionary
b. Jan 1, 1884 in Baltimore, Maryland
d. Jan 26, 1973 in Bareilly, India
Source: *AmAu&B; ConAu 41R, 93; TwCA
SUP; WhAm 5, 7; WhNAA*

Jones, George
"The Crown Prince of Country Music"
American. Singer
Named best male vocalist by CMA, 1980,
    1981; married to Tammy Wynette, 1968-
    75.
b. Sep 12, 1931 in Saratoga, Texas
Source: *BiDAmM; BioIn 9, 10; EncFCWM
69; IlEncCM; WhoAm 82; WhoRock 81*

Jones, Glyn
Welsh. Author
b. Feb 28, 1905 in Wales
Source: *CnMWL; ConAu 9R, 3NR; ConNov
72, 76; ConP 70, 75; ModBrL; WorAu; WrDr
80*

Jones, "Gorilla" (William)
American. Boxer
b. May 12, 1906 in Memphis, Tennessee
Source: *BioIn 1; WhoBox 74*

Jones, Grace
Jamaican. Singer, Actress, Model
In James Bond film *A View to a kill*, 1985;
    star of *Vamp*, 1986; hit album *Living My
    Life*, 1982.
b. May 19, 1952 in Spanishtown, Jamaica
Source: *BioIn 11; IlEncBM 82; NewWmR;
RolSEnR 83*

Jones, "Grandpa" (Louis Marshall)
American. Musician, TV Personality
b. Oct 20, 1913 in Henderson County,
    Kentucky
Source: *BiDAmM; EncFCWM 69; IlEncCM*

Jones, Gwynn
Welsh. Educator, Author
Novels include *Richard Savage*, 1935; *Times
    Like These*, 1936.
b. May 24, 1907 in Blackwood, Wales
Source: *ConAu 117; ConNov 72; DcLB 15;
Who 85*

Jones, Gwyneth
Welsh. Opera Singer
b. Nov 7, 1936 in Pontnewynydd, Wales
Source: *IntWW 74; Who 74; WhoAm 82;
WhoAmW 77; WhoMus 72; WhoWor 78*

Jones, Henry
American. Actor
Won Tony award for *Sunrise at Campobello*,
    1958.
b. Aug 1, 1912 in Philadelphia, Pennsylvania
Source: *BiE&WWA; FilmgC; NotNAT;
WhoAm 82*

Jones, Howard Mumford
American. Author
b. Apr 16, 1892 in Saginaw, Michigan
d. May 12, 1980 in Cambridge,
    Massachusetts
Source: *AmAu&B; ChhPo S1; ConAu 85, 97;
CnDAL; DrAS 74E; IntWW 74; OxAmL;
RAdv 1; REnAL; TwCA SUP; WhNAA;
WhoAm 74; WhoE 74; WhoWor 78*

Jones, Inigo
English. Architect
Introduced Italian Renaissance architecture to
    England; restored St. Paul's Cathedral,
    1634-42.
b. Jul 15, 1573 in London, England
d. Jun 21, 1652 in London, England
Source: *Alli; AtlBL; CroE&S; DcEnL; NewC;
OxThe; REn*

Jones, Isham
American. Band Leader, Songwriter
b. Jan 31, 1894 in Coalton, Ohio
d. Oct 19, 1956 in Hollywood, California
Source: *AmSCAP 66; WhAm 4A; WhoJazz 72*

Jones, Jack
American. Singer
b. Jan 14, 1938 in Beverly Hills, California
Source: *CelR*

Jones, James
American. Author
Wrote *From Here To Eternity*, 1951.
b. Nov 6, 1921 in Robinson, Illinois
d. May 9, 1977 in Southampton, New York
Source: *AmAu&B; CasWL; ConAu 1R, 69;
ModAL; OxAmL; PenC AM; REnAL; TwCWr*

Jones, James Earl
American. Actor
Won Tony award for *The Great White Hope*,
    1969.
b. Jan 17, 1931 in Arkabutla, Mississippi
Source: *BiE&WWA; BioNews 75; BkPepl;
CelR; CurBio 69; NotNAT; PIP&P; WhoAm
74; WhoBlA 75; WhoGov 72; WhoThe 77*

Jones, James Robert
American. Congressman
Dem. congressman from OK, 1972--; chm.,
    Budget Committee, 1980.
b. May 5, 1939 in Muskogee, Oklahoma
Source: *AlmAP 78, 80; BioIn 8, 11; CngDr
74, 77, 79; NewYTBS 78; WhoAm 74, 76,
78, 80; WhoAmP 73, 75, 77, 79; WhoGov 75,
77; WhoS&SW 76, 78*

Jones, Jenkin Lloyd
American. Editor, Journalist
b. Nov 1, 1911 in Madison, Wisconsin
Source: *ConAu 9R; WhoAm 82; WhoF&I 74;
WhoS&SW 82*

Jones, Jennifer
[Phyllis Isley]
American. Actress
Won Oscar, 1943, for *The Song of
    Bernadette*.
b. Mar 2, 1919 in Tulsa, Oklahoma
Source: *BiDFilm; BiE&WWA; CmMov;
CurBio 44; FilmgC; InWom; IntMPA 75, 76,
77, 78, 79, 80, 81, 82; MotPP; MovMk;
OxFilm; Who 74; WhoAm 74, 76, 78, 80, 82;
WhoHol A; WorEFlm*

Jones, Jesse Holman
American. Government Official
b. Apr 5, 1874 in Robertson County,
  Tennessee
d. Jun 1, 1956 in Houston, Texas
Source: *BiDrUSE; CurBio 40, 56; EncAB-H;
WhAm 3*

Jones, Reverend Jim (James)
American. Religious Leader
Founded People's Temple; led mass suicide
  of nearly 1,000 followers in Guyana, 1978.
b. May 31, 1931 in Lynn, Indiana
d. Nov 18, 1978 in Jonestown, Guyana
Source: *BioIn 11*

Jones, Jo(nathan)
American. Jazz Musician
Drummer with Count Basie band, 1935-48;
  innovative swing-era techniques were major
  influence on jazz drummers.
b. Oct 7, 1911 in Chicago, Illinois
d. Sep 3, 1985 in New York, New York
Source: *AmSCAP 66; WhoJazz 72*

Jones, John Paul
American. Naval Officer
Founded American naval tradition; said "I
  have not yet begun to fight."
b. Jul 6, 1747 in Kirkcudbright, Scotland
d. Jul 18, 1792 in Paris, France
Source: *AmAu&B; ApCAB; DcAmB; Drake;
EncAB-H; OxAmL; REn; REnAL; TwCBDA;
WebAB; WhAm HS*

Jones, John Paul
[John Baldwin; Led Zeppelin]
English. Musician
b. Jan 3, 1946 in Sidcup, England
Source: *WhoAm 80*

Jones, Jonah
American. Musician
b. Dec 31, 1909 in Louisville, Kentucky
Source: *BioIn 5, 10*

Jones, Joseph John (Joe)
American. Artist
b. Apr 7, 1909 in Saint Louis, Missouri
d. Apr 9, 1963 in Morristown, New Jersey
Source: *McGDA; WhAm 4*

Jones, KC
American. Basketball Coach
Member, US Olympic team, 1956; head
  coach, Boston, 1983--.
b. May 25, 1932 in San Francisco, California
Source: *InB&W 80; WhoAm 84; WhoBbl 73*

Jones, Kenny
[The Who]
English. Musician
Joined group as drummer, 1979.
b. Sep 16, 1948 in London, England
Source: *NF*

Jones, Lady
see: Bagnold, Enid

Jones, Leroi
[Imamu Amiri Baraka]
American. Poet, Dramatist
Wrote *Black Magic,* 1969; *It's Nation Time,*
  1971.
b. Oct 7, 1934 in Newark, New Jersey
Source: *BlkAWP; CasWL; CelR; ConAu 21R;
ConLC 1, 2, 3, 5, 10, 14; ConNov 72, 76;
ConP 70, 75; CroCAP; CroCD; CurBio 70;
DrAP 75; EncWL; LivgBAA; McGEWD;
ModAL, S1; ModWD; NotNAT; OxAmL;
PenC AM; PIP&P A; RAdv 1; RComWL;
WebAB; WebE&AL; WhoAm 74; WhoBlA 75;
WhoE 74; WhoThe 77; WhoTwCL; WhoWor
78; WorAu; WrDr 80*

Jones, Madison Percy, Jr.
American. Author
b. Mar 21, 1925 in Nashville, Tennessee
Source: *Au&Wr 71; ConAu 13R; ConLC 4;
ConNov 72, 76; DrAS 74E; WhoAm 74;
WrDr 80*

Jones, Mary Harris
"Mother Jones"
American. Labor Union Official
b. May 1, 1830 in Cork, Ireland
d. Nov 30, 1930 in Silver Spring, Maryland
Source: *WebAB*

Jones, Matilda Sissieretta Joyner
"The Black Patti"
American. Singer
First Negro prima donna; star of Black Patti
  Troubadours, 1896-1916.
b. Jan 5, 1869 in Portsmouth, Virginia
d. Jun 24, 1933 in Providence, Rhode Island
Source: *NotAW*

Jones, Mick
see: Clash, The

Jones, Mick
see: Foreigner

Jones, Parnelli (Rufus Parnell)
American. Auto Racer
b. Aug 12, 1933
Source: *BioIn 10*

Jones, Phil(ip Howard)
American. Broadcast Journalist
CBS Capital Hill correspondent, 1977--; won
  awards for Vietnam air-war coverage,
  1966, 1971.
b. Apr 27, 1937 in Marion, Indiana
Source: *WhoAm 80, 82*

Jones, Preston St. Vrain
American. Actor, Dramatist
Wrote *A Texas Trilogy,* 1974.
b. Apr 7, 1936 in Albuquerque, New Mexico
d. Sep 19, 1979 in Dallas, Texas
Source: *ConAu 73, 89; ConLC 10; CurBio 77,
79; DcLB 7; NewYTBS 76, 79; WhAm 7;
WhoAm 78; WhoThe 81*

Jones, "Prophet" (James F)
American. Evangelist
b. 1908
d. 1971 in Detroit, Michigan
Source: *BioIn 9; NewYTBE 71*

Jones, Quincy Delight
American. Composer
Has written scores for over 50 films
  including *In Cold Blood,* 1967; *The Wiz,*
  1978.
b. Mar 14, 1933 in Chicago, Illinois
Source: *IlEncBM 82; IntMPA 82; WhoAm 82*

Jones, R William
American. Basketball Executive
Co-founded International Basketball
  Federation, 1932.
b. Oct 5, 1906 in Rome, Italy
Source: *BioIn 9; WhoBbl 73*

Jones, Randy (Randall Leo)
American. Baseball Player
b. Jan 12, 1950 in Fullerton, California
Source: *BaseEn 85; BioIn 10, 11*

Jones, Richard
see: Climax Blues Band, The

Jones, Richard Lloyd, Jr.
American. Newspaper Executive
Pres., board chm. of *Tulsa Tribune.*
b. Feb 22, 1909 in Jyack, New York
d. Jan 27, 1982 in Tulsa, Oklahoma
Source: *NewYTBS 82; WhoAm 82;
WhoS&SW 73, 75, 76, 78, 80*

Jones, Rickie Lee
American. Singer, Songwriter
Combines rhythm and blues, jazz, folk
  music; hit single "Chuck E's in Love,"
  1979.
b. Nov 8, 1954 in Chicago, Illinois
Source: *NewWmR; RolSEnR 83; WhoRock 81*

Jones, Robert C
American. Writer
Won Oscar for screenplay *Coming Home,*
  1978.
b. Mar 30, 1930 in Los Angeles, California
Source: *VarWW 85*

Jones, Robert Edmond
American. Designer
b. Dec 12, 1887 in Milton, New Hampshire
d. Nov 26, 1954 in Milton, New Hampshire
Source: *CurBio 46, 55; DcAmB S5; OxAmL;
OxThe; PIP&P; REn; REnAL; WhAm 3*

Jones, Robert Trent
English. Architect
Designed more than 350 of world's most
  outstanding golf courses.
b. Jun 20, 1906 in Ince, England
Source: *WhoAm 82; WhoE 74; WhoWor 74*

Jones, Sam(uel Pond)
"Sad Sam"
American. Baseball Player
b. Jul 26, 1892 in Barnesville, Ohio
d. Jul 6, 1966 in Barnesville, Ohio
Source: *BaseEn 85; BioIn 7; WhoProB 73*

Jones, Shirley
[Mrs. Marty Ingels]
American. Actress, Singer
Won Oscar, 1960, for *Elmer Gantry;* starred
  in "The Partridge Family," 1970-74.
b. Mar 31, 1934 in Smithtown, Pennsylvania
Source: *BiDFilm; BiE&WWA; BioNews 74;
CmMov; CurBio 61; FilmgC; InWom;
IntMPA 75, 76, 77, 78, 79, 80, 81, 82;
MotPP; MovMk; WhoAm 74, 76, 78, 80, 82;
WhoHol A; WhoWor 78; WorEFlm*

Jones, "Spike" (Lindsay Armstrong)
American. Band Leader, Musician
b. Dec 14, 1911 in Long Beach, California
d. May 1, 1964 in Los Angeles, California
Source: *AmSCAP 66; FilmgC; WhScrn 74,
77; WhoHol B*

Jones, Steve
see: Sex Pistols

Jones, Terry
[Monty Python's Flying Circus]
Welsh. Actor, Director, Writer
Directed film *Monty Python's Life of Brian;*
  wrote *Fairy Tales,* 1981; *Erik the Viking,*
  1983.
b. Feb 1, 1942 in Colwyn Bay, Wales
Source: *BioIn 10; WhoAm 82*

Jones, Thad(deus Joseph)
American. Musician
Soloist, jazz drummer with Count Basie
  Orchestra, 1954-63.
b. Mar 28, 1923 in Pontiac, Michigan
d. Aug 20, 1986 in Copenhagen, Denmark
Source: *Baker 84; DrBlPA; EncJzS 70; IlEncJ*

Jones, Thomas Hudson
American. Sculptor
b. Jul 24, 1892 in Buffalo, New York
d. Nov 4, 1969 in Hyannis, Massachusetts
Source: *WhAm 5*

Jones, Tom
American. Dramatist, Songwriter
b. Feb 17, 1928 in Littlefield, Texas
Source: *AmAu&B; AmSCAP 66; BiE&WWA;
ConAu 53; EncMT; NewCBMT; NotNAT*

Jones, Tom
[Thomas Jones Woodward]
Welsh. Musician, Singer
Hits include "It's Not Unusual," 1964;
  "What's New Pussycat," 1965.
b. Jun 7, 1940 in Pontypridd, Wales
Source: *BkPepl; CelR; WhoAm 82; WhoWor
78*

Jones, Tommy Lee
American. Actor
b. Sep 15, 1946 in San Saba, Texas
Source: *BioIn 11; IntMPA 82; WhoAm 82*

Jones, "Too Tall" (Edward Lee)
American. Football Player, Boxer
b. Feb 23, 1951 in Jackson, Tennessee
Source: *WhoFtbl 74*

Jones, "Toothpick" (Samuel)
"Sad Sam"
American. Baseball Player
b. Dec 14, 1925 in Stewartsville, Ohio
d. Nov 5, 1971 in Morgantown, West
  Virginia
Source: *BaseEn 85; BioIn 5, 7; WhoProB 73*

Jones, W D
American. Criminal
b. 1915
Source: *BioIn 9*

Jones, Weyman
American. Author
b. Feb 6, 1928 in Lima, Ohio
Source: *AuBYP; ConAu 17R; SmATA 4;
WhoPubR 72*

Jong, Erica
[Mrs. Jonathan Fast]
American. Author
Wrote *Fear of Flying*, 1973.
b. Mar 26, 1942 in New York, New York
Source: *AuNews 1; BkPepl; ConAu 73;
ConLC 4, 6; ConP 75; CroCAP; DrAF 76;
DrAP 75; RAdv 1; WomWMM; WrDr 80*

Jongkind, Johan Barthold
Dutch. Artist
Juxtaposed strokes of unmixed colors to
  illustrate effects of light; helped develop
  Impressionism.
b. Jun 3, 1819 in Lattrop, Netherlands
d. Feb 9, 1891 in Cote-Saint-Andre,
  Netherlands
Source: *AtlBL; McGDA*

Jonson, Ben(jamin)
English. Dramatist, Poet
Master of dramatic satire; wrote *Volpone*,
  1606.
b. Jun 11, 1572 in Westminster, England
d. Apr 6, 1637 in Westminster, England
Source: *Alli; AtlBL; BbD; BiD&SB; BrAu;
CasWL; Chambr 1; ChhPo; CnE&AP; CnThe;
CroE&S; CrtT 1; CyWA; DcEnA; DcEnL;
DcEuL; DcLEL; EvLB; McGEWD; MouLC 1;
NewC; OxEng; OxThe; PenC ENG; PlP&P;
PoLE; RAdv 1; RComWL; REn; REnWD;
WebE&AL*

Jonsson, John Erik
American. Business Executive
Pres. Texas Instruments, 1951-58; honorary
  director, 1977.
b. Sep 6, 1901 in New York, New York
Source: *AmM&WS 79P; BioIn 5, 6, 7, 10;
CurBio 61; IntWW 74, 75, 76, 77; IntYB 78,
79; St&PR 75; WhoAm 74, 76, 78; WhoAmP
73, 75; WhoF&I 74, 77; WhoGov 72;
WhoS&SW 73, 75, 76*

Jooss, Kurt
German. Choreographer
b. Jan 12, 1901 in Wasseralfingen, Germany
d. May 22, 1979 in Heilbronn, Germany
  (West)
Source: *CurBio 76, 79; IntWW 75, 76, 77,
78; NewYTBS 75, 76, 79; OxMus; WhoWor
76, 78*

Joplin, Janis
[Big Brother and the Holding Company]
American. Singer
Hits include "Me and Bobby McGee"; died
  of drug overdose.
b. Jan 19, 1943 in Port Arthur, Texas
d. Oct 3, 1970 in Hollywood, California
Source: *BioNews 74; CurBio 70; NewYTBE
70; WhAm 5; WhScrn 77; WhoHol B*

Joplin, Scott
American. Musician, Composer
Developed ragtime music; Wrote "The
  Entertainer," 1902; music revived in score
  of *The Sting*, 1973.
b. Nov 24, 1868 in Texarkana, Texas
d. Apr 4, 1917 in New York, New York
Source: *AmSCAP 66; BioNews 74; BlkAWP;
WebAB; WhoJazz 72*

Jorda, Enrique
Spanish. Conductor
b. Mar 24, 1911 in San Sebastian, Spain
Source: *IntWW 74; WhoMus 72; WhoWor 78*

Jordaens, Jacob
Flemish. Artist
b. May 19, 1593 in Antwerp, Belgium
d. Oct 18, 1678 in Antwerp, Belgium
Source: *AtlBL*

Jordan, Barbara C
American. Lawyer, Politician
Congresswoman from TX, 1972-78; first
  black to keynote Dem. National
  Convention, 1976.
b. Feb 21, 1936 in Houston, Texas
Source: *CngDr 74; WhoAm 76, 78, 80, 82;
WhoAmW 77; WhoBlA 75; WomPO 76*

Jordan, Bobby
American. Actor
Best known for role of Bobby in Bowery
  Boy films.
b. 1923
d. Sep 10, 1965 in Los Angeles, California
Source: *WhScrn 77; WhoHol B*

Jordan, Don
American. Boxer
Welterweight champ, defeated Akins, 1958;
  lost title to Paret, 1960.
b. Jun 22, 1934
Source: *BioIn 10*

Jordan, Elizabeth Garver
American. Author, Editor
Edited *Harper's Bazaar*, 1900-13; wrote *Tales
  of the City Room*, 1898.
b. May 9, 1865 in Milwaukee, Wisconsin
d. Feb 24, 1947 in New York, New York
Source: *NotAW; WebBD 80*

Jordan, Hamilton (William Hamilton)
"Ham"; "Hannibal Jerkin"
American. Presidential Aide
b. Sep 21, 1944 in Charlotte, North Carolina
Source: *BioIn 10, 11, 12; CurBio 77; PseudN
82; WhoAm 78, 80, 82; WhoAmP 77;
WhoGov 77*

Jordan, June Meyer
[June Meyer, pseud.]
American. Author
b. Jul 9, 1936 in Harlem, New York
Source: *BlkAWP; ChhPo S1, S2; ConAu 33R;
ConLC 5; DrAF 76; DrAP 75; LivgBAA;
PseudN 82; SmATA 4; WhoAmW 77; WrDr
80*

Jordan, Kathy (Kathryn)
American. Tennis Player
Won Wimbledon, French doubles, 1980.
b. Dec 3, 1957 in Bryn Mawr, Pennsylvania
Source: *OfEnT; WhoIntT*

Jordan, Louis
"King of the Jukeboxes"
American. Musician
b. Jul 8, 1908 in Brinkley, Arkansas
d. Feb 4, 1975 in Los Angeles, California
Source: *PseudN 82; WhoJazz 72*

Jordon, Michael Jeffery
American. Basketball Player
Member US Olympic team, 1984, drafted by
  Chicago in first round 1984; NBA rookie
  of year, 1985.
b. Feb 17, 1963 in Brooklyn, New York
Source: *OfNBA 85*

Jordan, Taft
American. Musician, Singer
b. Feb 15, 1915 in Florence, South Carolina
Source: *WhoJazz 72*

Jordan, Richard
American. Actor
Starred in TV mini-series "The Captains and
  the Kings," 1976.
b. Jul 19, 1938 in New York, New York
Source: *BioIn 11; WhoHol A*

Jordan, Vernon Eulion, Jr.
"The Warrior of Today"
American. Civil Rights Leader
b. Aug 15, 1935 in Atlanta, Georgia
Source: *BioNews 74; BusPN; CurBio 72; PseudN 82; WhoAm 74, 76, 78, 80, 82; WhoBlA 75; WhoS&SW 82*

Jordy, William H(enry)
American. Educator
Brown U. prof, 1948-77; wrote *American Buildings and Their Architects,* 1972.
b. Aug 31, 1917 in Poughkeepsie, New York
Source: *ConAu 1R; DrAS 74H, 78H; WhoAm 74, 76, 78, 80, 82*

Jorge Blanco, Salvador
Dominican. Political Leader
Pres. of Dominican Republic, 1982--.
b. Jul 5, 1926 in Santiago, Dominican Republic
Source: *NewYTBS 82*

Jorgensen, Anker Henrik
Danish. Prime Minister
b. Jul 13, 1922 in Copenhagen, Delaware
Source: *CurBio 78*

Jorgensen, Christine
American. Transsexual
Underwent first publicized sex change operation, 1953.
b. May 30, 1926 in New York, New York
Source: *InWom*

Jory, Victor
American. Actor
Often cast as villain in 40-year career; among films *Gone With the Wind,* 1939.
b. Nov 23, 1902 in Dawson City, Alaska
d. Feb 12, 1982 in Santa Monica, California
Source: *BiE&WWA; FilmgC; HolP 30; IntMPA 82; MotPP; MovMk; NotNAT; Vers A; WhoHol A; WhoThe 77*

Joseph
Biblical Character
Son of Jacob, who was sold into slavery by brothers; laters became chief official to the Pharoah.
Source: *REn; WebBD 80*

Joseph I
Hungarian. Ruler
King of Hungary, 1687-1711; king of Germany, 1690-1711; Holy Roman emperor, 1705-11.
b. 1678
d. 1711
Source: *DcBiPP; DcCathB; OxGer; WebBD 80*

Joseph II
"The Hatted King"; "The Kalapos King"; "The Titus of Germany"; "The Unfortunate"
Emperor
Tried unsuccessfully to reform and unify Austrian Hasburg domains.
b. 1741
d. 1790
Source: *BioIn 9; PseudN 82; WebBD 80*

Joseph, Chief
[Hinmaton-Yalakit]
"The Napoleon of the Indian Race"
American. Indian Chief
Became chief Nez Perce, 1873; refused to comply with land-cession treaty of 1855.
b. 1840 in Wallowa Valley, Washington
d. Sep 21, 1904 in Colville, Washington
Source: *AmBi; DcAmB; PseudN 82; REnAL; WebAB*

Joseph of Arimathea
Biblical Character
According to the Bible, placed Jesus' body in his own tomb.
Source: *REn; WebBD 80*

Joseph, Saint
Biblical Character
Husband of the Virgin Mary, mother of Jesus; feast day: Mar 19.
Source: *REn; WebBD 80*

Joseph, Helen
South African. Author, Political Activist
b. 1906
Source: *BioIn 11*

Joseph, Richard
American. Journalist
b. Apr 24, 1910 in New York, New York
d. Sep 30, 1976
Source: *AmAu&B; CelR; ConAu 1R, 69; NewYTBS 76; WhAm 7; WhoAm 74, 76; WhoE 74; WhoWor 76*

Josephine
[Marie Josephe Rose Tascher de la Pagerie]
French. Empress
Marriage to Napoleon, 1796, annulled 1809; played prominent part in social life of time.
b. Jun 24, 1763 in Martinique
d. May 29, 1814 in Malmaison, France
Source: *ApCAB; DcBiPP; InWom; LinLib S; NewCol 75*

Josephson, Matthew
American. Author
b. Feb 15, 1899 in Brooklyn, New York
d. Mar 13, 1978 in Santa Cruz, California
Source: *AmAu&B; ConAmA; ConAu 77, 81;
DcLB 4; NewYTBE 72; NewYTBS 78;
OxAmL; PenC AM; REn; REnAL; TwCA,
SUP; WhAm 7; WhoAm 74, 76, 78; WhoWor
78; WhoWorJ 72*

Josephus, Flavius
[Joseph Ben Matthias]
"The Greek Livy"
Hebrew. Historian, General
b. 37
d. 101 in Rome, Italy
Source: *AtlBL; BbD; BiD&SB; CasWL; NewC;
OxEng; PenC CL; PseudN 82; RComWL;
REn*

Joshua
Biblical Character
In Old Testament, Book of Joshua; led
Israelites' invasion of Canaan.
Source: *WebBD 80*

Joslyn, Allyn Morgan
American. Actor
Performed on 3,000 radio programs;
Broadway work included: *Boy Meets Girl;
Arsenic and Old Lace.*
b. Jul 21, 1905 in Milford, Pennsylvania
d. Jan 21, 1981 in Woodland Hills,
California
Source: *BioIn 10; FilmEn; FilmgC; IntMPA
81; MovMk; Vers A; WhThe; WhoHol A*

Joss, "Addie" (Adrian)
American. Baseball Player
b. Apr 12, 1880 in Juneau, Wisconsin
d. Apr 14, 1911 in Toledo, Ohio
Source: *BaseEn 85; BioIn 10; PseudN 82;
WhoProB 73*

Joule, James Prescott
English. Physicist
Known for research in electricity,
thermodynamics; introduced Joule's Law,
1840; unit of energy named for him.
b. Dec 24, 1818 in Salford, England
d. Oct 11, 1889 in Sale, England
Source: *Alli SUP*

Jourard, Marty
see: Motels, The

Jourdan, Louis
[Louis Gendre]
French. Actor
Best known for film *Gigi,* 1958.
b. Jun 19, 1920 in Marseilles, France
Source: *BiE&WWA; CurBio 67; FilmgC;
IntMPA 82; MotPP; MovMk; NotNAT;
PseudN 82; WhoAm 82; WhoHol A*

Journet, Marcel
French. Opera Singer
b. Jul 25, 1870 in Grasse, France
d. Sep 5, 1933 in Vittel, France
Source: *WhAm 1*

Journey
[Jonathan Cain; Aynsley Dunbar; Steve
Perry; Gregg Rolie; Neil Schon; Steve
Smith; Ross Valory]
American. Music Group
Progressive rock band called "America's most
popular rock band," 1983; hit single "Send
Her My Love," 1983.
Source: *ConMuA 80A; IlEncRk; LilREn 78;
RkOn 85; WhoRock 81*

Jouvet, Louis
French. Actor
Established own company, "Theatre de
l'Athenee," 1934-51.
b. Dec 24, 1887 in Crozon, France
d. Aug 16, 1951 in Paris, France
Source: *BiDFilm; ClDMEL; CurBio 49, 51;
EncWL; FilmgC; MovMk; OxFilm; OxFr;
OxThe; REn; WhScrn 74, 77; WhoHol B;
WorEFlm*

Jouy, Victor (Joseph-Etienne) de
French. Dramatist
b. 1764 in Jouy, France
d. Sep 4, 1846 in Saint Germain en Laye,
France
Source: *BbD; BiD&SB; NewEOp 71; OxFr;
PseudN 82*

Jovanovich, William Iliya
American. Publisher
Chm. chief exec. Harcourt, Brace,
Jovanovich, 1970--.
b. Feb 6, 1920 in Louisville, Colorado
Source: *ConAu 107; IntWW 74; St&PR 75;
WhoAm 82*

Joy, Leatrice
[Leatrice Joy Zeidler]
American. Actress
Star of Cecil B DeMille silent films credited
with popularizing bobbed hair.
b. Nov 7, 1893 in New Orleans, Louisiana
d. May 13, 1985 in Riverdale, New York
Source: *FilmEn; Film 1; FilmgC; InWom;
MotPP; MovMk; PseudN 82; ThFT; TwYS;
WhoHol A*

Joyce, Alice
"Madonna of the Screen"
American. Actress
Voted most popular actress in America,
1913-17.
b. Oct 1, 1890 in Kansas City, Missouri
d. Oct 9, 1955 in Hollywood, California
Source: *Film 1; FilmgC; InWom; MotPP;
MovMk; TwYS; WhScrn 74, 77; WhoHol B*

Joyce, Eileen
Australian. Musician
b. Nov 21, 1912 in Zeehan, Tasmania
Source: *InWom; IntWW 74; Who 74;
WhoWor 78*

Joyce, Elaine
[Elaine Joyce Pinchot; Mrs. Bobby Van]
American. Actress, Dancer
Films include *The Christine Jorgenson Story;
How to Frame a Figg,* 1970s.
b. Dec 19, 1945 in Cleveland, Ohio
Source: *WhoHol A*

Joyce, James Augustus Aloysius
Irish. Author, Poet
Wrote *Ulysses,* 1922; banned in US as
obscene until 1933.
b. Feb 2, 1882 in Dublin, Ireland
d. Jan 13, 1941 in Zurich, Switzerland
Source: *AtlBL; CasWL; Chambr 3; ChhPo,
S1; CnMD; CnMWL; CyWA; DcLEL;
EncWL; EvLB; LongCTC; McGEWD;
ModBrL, S1; ModWD; NewC; OxEng; PenC
ENG; PoIre; RAdv 1; RComWL; REn;
TwCA, SUP; TwCWr; WebE&AL; WhoTwCL*

Joyce, Peggy Hopkins
[Margaret Upton]
"A Circle of the Cinema"
American. Actress
In Ziegfeld Follies; six marriages given wide
publicity.
b. 1893 in Norfolk, Virginia
d. Jun 12, 1957 in New York, New York
Source: *InWom; MotPP; ObitOF 79; PseudN
82; WhScrn 74, 77; WhoHol B*

Joyce, William
"Lord Haw-Haw"
German. Social Reformer
Made English language propaganda
broadcasts for Nazis; hung for treason.
b. 1906
d. Jan 5, 1946 in Wandsworth, England
Source: *BioIn 1, 7; PseudN 82*

Joyner, Wally (Wallace Keith)
American. Baseball Player
Infielder, CA, 1986--.
b. Jun 16, 1962 in Atlanta, Georgia
Source: *BaseReg 86*

Jozsef, Attila
Hungarian. Poet
Verse volumes include *Medvetanc,* 1934.
b. Apr 11, 1905 in Budapest, Hungary
d. Dec 3, 1937 in Balatonszarszo, Hungary
Source: *ConAu 116; EncWL 2; PenC EUR;
TwCWr*

Juan Carlos I
[Prince Juan Carlos Borbon y Borbon]
"Juan Carlos the Brief"
Spanish. Ruler
King of Spain, 1975--.
b. Jan 5, 1938 in Rome, Italy
Source: *BioIn 10; IntWW 74; PseudN 82*

Juan, Don
[Jaun Matus]
Mexican. Mystic
Used hallucinogenic drugs to gain power over
demonic world.
b. 1891
Source: *BioIn 10*

Juantorena, Alberto
Cuban. Track Athlete
b. 1952
Source: *BioIn 11*

Juarez, Benito Pablo
"The Mexican Washington"; "The Second
Washington"
Mexican. President
Pres. of Mexico, 1861-63 and 1867-72.
b. Mar 21, 1806 in Oaxaca, Mexico
d. Jul 18, 1872 in Mexico City, Mexico
Source: *ApCAB; Drake; PseudN 82; REn;
WhAm HS*

Juch, Emma
American. Opera Singer, Manager
b. Jul 4, 1863 in Vienna, Austria
d. Mar 6, 1939 in New York, New York
Source: *AmBi; AmWom; InWom; NotAW;
WhAm 1; WomWWA 14*

Judah
Biblical Character
Son of Jacob; ancestor of one of 12 tribes of
Israel.
Source: *BioIn 10; WebBD 80*

Judah Ha-Levi
see: Ha-Levi, Judah

Judas Iscariot
Biblical Character
One of 12 apostles; betrayed Jesus for 30
pieces of silver, cause of Jesus' arrest.
Source: *BioIn 10; NewCol 75; WebBD 80*

Judas Priest
[K K Downing; Rob Halford; Ian Hill; Dave
Holland; Glenn Tipton]
British. Music Group
Heavy metal band formed mid-1970s; album
Screaming for Vengeance, 1982.
Source: *IlEncRk; RkOn 85*

Judd, Winnie Ruth McKinnell
"The Tiger Woman"
American. Murderer
Committed to insane asylum for killing,
dismembering two people, 1931; escaped
seven times.
b. 1905
Source: *BioIn 9; LookW*

Jude, Saint
[Saint Thaddeus]
Biblical Character
One of 12 apostles; feast day: Oct 28.
Source: *REn*

Judith
Biblical Character
Heroine in the Book of Judith for killing
Holofernes.
Source: *WebBD 80*

Judson, Edward Zane Carroll
[Ned Buntline, pseud.]
American. Adventurer
Originated dime novel, wrote 400 of them;
first to give W F Cody name "Buffalo
Bill."
b. Mar 20, 1823 in Stamford, New York
d. Jul 16, 1886 in Stamford, New York
Source: *Alli SUP; AmAu; AmAu&B; AmBi;
ApCAB; DcAmAu; DcAmB; DcNAA; HsB&A;
MnBBF; OhA&B; OxAmL; PseudN 82; REn;
REnAL; TwCBDA; WebAB; WhAm HS*

Judson, Egbert Putnam
American. Inventor
Developed gentle blasting powder, 1876.
b. Aug 9, 1812 in Syracuse, New York
d. Jan 9, 1893 in San Francisco, California
Source: *DcAmB; WhAm HS*

Judson, Emily Chubbock
[Fanny Forester, pseud.]
American. Author
b. Aug 22, 1817 in Eaton, New York
d. Jun 1, 1854 in Hamilton, New York
Source: *Alli; AmAu; AmAu&B; AmBi;
ApCAB; BbD; BiD&SB; ChhPo, S1, S2; CyAL
2; DcAmAu; DcAmB; DcNAA; Drake; FemPA;
InWom; NotAW; PseudN 82; TwCBDA;
WebAB; WhAm HS*

Judy, Steven
American. Murderer
Executed by electrocution.
b. 1957 in Indianapolis, Indiana
d. Mar 9, 1981 in Michigan City, Indiana
Source: *NF*

Juilliard, Augustus D
American. Merchant, Philanthropist
Donated $12 million toward establishment of
Juilliard School of Music.
b. Apr 19, 1836 in Canton, Ohio
d. Apr 25, 1919 in New York, New York
Source: *AmBi; DcAmB; WhAm 1*

Juilliard String Quartet, The
[Claus Adam; Earl Carlyss; Robert Mann;
Samuel Rhodes]
American. Music Group
Source: *BiDAmM*

Juin, Alphonse
French. Soldier
b. Dec 16, 1888 in Bone, Algeria
d. Jan 27, 1967 in Paris, France
Source: *CurBio 43, 67; WhAm 4*

Jukes, Margaret
Criminal
Source: *NF*

Julesberg, Elizabeth Rider Montgomery
[Elizabeth Montgomery]
American. Children's Author
Wrote reading primers featuring Dick, Jane,
Spot, 1940s.
b. Jul 12, 1902 in Huaras, Peru
d. Feb 19, 1985 in Seattle, Washington
Source: *ConAu 115; WhoAmW 81*

Julia, Raul
[Raul Rafael Carlos Julia y Arcelay]
American. Actor
Films include *Tempest,* 1982, *One From the Heart,* 1982.
b. Mar 9, 1940 in San Juan, Puerto Rico
Source: *CurBio 82; WhoHol A; WhoThe 81*

Julian (Flavius Claudius Julianus)
"The Apostate"
Roman. Emperor
General, proclaimed emperor by troops, 361; enemy of Christianity.
b. 331
d. 363
Source: *BioIn 10; PseudN 82*

Julian, "Doggie" (Alvin T)
American. Basketball Coach
b. Apr 5, 1901 in Reading, Pennsylvania
d. Jul 28, 1967 in Worcester, Massachusetts
Source: *PseudN 82; WhoBbl 73*

Julian, Hubert Fauntleroy
"Black Eagle"
American. Aviator
b. 1897 in Trinidad
Source: *NewYTBS 74*

Juliana
[Juliana Emma Maria Wilhelmina]
Dutch. Queen
Ruled 1948-80; supported int'l. efforts such as Marshall Plan, NATO; abolished the curtsy.
b. Apr 30, 1909 in The Hague, Netherlands
Source: *CurBio 55; GoodHs; IntWW 82; WebBD 80*

Julius II, Pope
[Giuliano della Rovere]
Italian. Religious Leader
Pope, 1503-13; most brilliant pope during Renaissance.
b. 1443 in Albisola, Italy
d. 1513
Source: *REn*

Julius III, Pope
[Giammaria Ciocchi del Monte]
Italian. Religious Leader
b. 1487
d. 1555
Source: *PseudN 82; WebBD 80*

Julius Caesar
Roman. General, Statesman
Established Julian calendar, 45BC; month July (Julius) named in honor.
b. Jul 12, 100 in Rome, Italy
d. Mar 15, 44 in Rome, Italy
Source: *NewCol 75; WebBD 80*

Jumblatt, Kamal Fouad
Lebanese. Political Leader
b. Jan 6, 1917 in Mukhtara, Lebanon
d. Mar 16, 1977 in Beirut, Lebanon
Source: *IntWW 74*

Jumel, Eliza
[Betsey Bowen; Eliza Brown]
American. Celebrity Relative
b. 1769
d. Jul 16, 1865 in New York, New York
Source: *ApCAB; NotAW; REnAL*

Jump, Gordon
American. Actor
Played Mr. Carlson on "WKRP in Cincinnati," 1978-82.
b. Apr 1, 1927 in Dayton, Ohio
Source: *WhoAm 80, 82*

Jung, Carl Gustav
Swiss. Psychologist, Psychiatrist
Known for classifying personalities as extroverted or introverted; wrote *Psychology of the Unconscious,* 1912.
b. Jul 26, 1875 in Basel, Switzerland
d. Jun 6, 1961 in Zurich, Switzerland
Source: *BiDPara; CasWL; CurBio 61; EncWL; LongCTC; OxEng; OxGer; RComWL; REn; TwCA, SUP; WhAm 4; WhoTwCL*

Junior, E J (Ester James, III)
American. Football Player
Linebacker, St. Louis, 1981--; suspended for preseason plus four regular season games by NFL for drug involvement, 1983.
b. Dec 8, 1959 in Sallsburg, North Carolina
Source: *FootReg 85; NewYTBS 84*

Junior Walker and the All Stars
[Autrey DeWalt, Jr.; James Graves; Vic Thomas; Willie Woods]
American. Music Group
Source: *RkOn 74*

Junkers, Hugo
German. Aircraft Designer
Built first all-metal plane to successfully fly.
b. 1859
d. 1935
Source: *WebBD 80*

Junot, Philippe
French. Banker, Celebrity Relative
Married Princess Caroline of Monaco, 1978;
  divorced, 1980.
b. 1942
Source: *BioIn 12*

Jurado, Katy
[Maria Christina Jurado Garcia]
Mexican. Actress
1954 Oscar nominee for *Broken Lance,*
b. Jan 16, 1927 in Guadalajara, Mexico
Source: *FilmgC; IntMPA 82; MovMk;
OxFilm; PseudN 82; WhoHol A*

Jurgens, Curt
German. Actor
Appeared in over 150 films, including *The
  Enemy Below,* 1957, *The Spy Who Loved
  Me,* 1977.
b. Dec 12, 1915 in Munich, Germany
d. Jun 18, 1982 in Vienna, Austria
Source: *AnObit 1982; BiDFilm; ConAu 107;
FilmgC; IntMPA 82; MotPP; MovMk;
NewYTBS 82; OxFilm; WhoAm 82; WhoHol
A; WorEFlm*

Jurgenson, "Sonny" (Christian Adolph, III)
American. Football Player, Sportscaster
b. Aug 23, 1934 in Wilmington, North
  Carolina
Source: *PseudN 82; WhoAm 82; WhoFtbl 74*

Jurinac, Sena
[Srebrenka Jurinac]
Yugoslav. Opera Singer
b. Oct 24, 1921 in Travnik, Yugoslavia
Source: *InWom; IntWW 74; PseudN 82; Who
74; WhoMus 72; WhoWor 78*

Jussieu, Bernard de
French. Botanist
Established botanical garden, 1759; developed
  plant classification.
b. Aug 17, 1699 in Lyons, France
d. Dec 6, 1777 in Paris, France
Source: *OxFr*

Just, Ernest Everett
American. Biologist
Harvard U zoologist noted for study of
  cellular biology.
b. Aug 14, 1883 in Charleston, South
  Carolina
d. Oct 27, 1941 in Washington, District of
  Columbia
Source: *BioIn 1, 6, 8, 9, 11; DcAmB S3;
DcNAA; ObitOF 79; SelBAAu; WebAB;
WhAm 1; WhoColR*

Justice, "Choo Choo" (Charles Ronald)
American. Football Player
b. May 18, 1924 in Asheville, North
  Carolina
Source: *PseudN 82; WhoFtbl 74*

Justice, James Robertson
British. Actor
Best known for film *Doctor in the House,*
  1954, and sequels.
b. Jun 15, 1905 in Wigtown, Scotland
d. Jul 2, 1975 in Winchester, England
Source: *FilmEn; FilmgC; MovMk; WhScrn 77*

Justice, William Wayne
American. Judge
Advocated prison reform; improved bilingual
  education, 1981.
b. Feb 25, 1920 in Athens, Texas
Source: *AmBench 79; WhoAm 74, 76, 78, 80,
82; WhoAmL 79; WhoAmP 73; WhoGov 72,
75; WhoS&SW 73*

Justinian I (Flavius Anicius Justinianus)
"The Great"
Byzantine. Ruler
Byzantine emperor, 527-65; completed
  codification of Roman law.
b. 483
d. 565
Source: *BioIn 10; NewCol 75; PseudN 82;
WebBD 80*

Justus, Roy Braxton
American. Editor, Cartoonist
b. May 16, 1901 in Avon, South Dakota
Source: *WhoAm 74, 76, 78, 80, 82; WhoAmA
73*

Jutra, Claude
Canadian. Director
Best known for film *Mon Oncle Antoine,*
  1971.
b. Mar 11, 1930 in Montreal, Quebec
Source: *BioIn 10; CanWW 79; CreCan 1;
DcFM; OxFilm; WorEFlm*

Juvenal (Decimus Junius Juvenalis)
"The Aquinian Sage"; "The Last Poet of
  Rome"
Roman. Satirist
b. 60 in Aquinum, Italy
d. 140
Source: *AtlBL; BbD; BiD&SB; CasWL;
CyWA; NewC; PenC CL; PseudN 82;
RComWL; REn*

K

K C and the Sunshine Band
[Oliver Brown; H(arry) W(ayne) Casey; Rick
Finch; Robert Johnson; Denvil Liptrot;
Jerome Smith; Ronnie Smith; James
Weaver; Charles Williams]
American. Music Group
Formed 1973; hits nominated for Grammys:
"That's the Way," 1975; "Shake Your
Booty," 1976.
Source: *IlEncBM 82; RkOn 78; RolSEnR 83;
WhoRock 81*

Kabalevsky, Dmitri Borisovich
Russian. Composer
b. Dec 30, 1904 in Saint Petersburg, Russia
Source: *DcCM; IntWW 74; WhoMus 72;
WhoWor 78*

Kadar, Janos
Hungarian. Communist Leader
b. May 22, 1912 in Fiume, Hungary
Source: *CurBio 57; IntWW 83; WhDW;
WhoWor 82*

Kael, Pauline
American. Author, Movie Critic
Philosophy of film reviewing collected in
When the Lights Go Down, 1980.
b. Jun 19, 1919 in Sonoma County,
California
Source: *AmAu&B; Au&Wr 71; CelR; ConAu
6NR, 45; CurBio 74; ForWC 70; IntMPA 82;
OxFilm; WhoAm 82; WhoAmW 77;
WomWMM; WrDr 84*

Kaempfert, Bert
German. Musician
b. Oct 16, 1923 in Hamburg, Germany
Source: *EncPR&S 74*

Kaempffert, Waldemar (Bernhard)
American. Editor, Author
NY *Times* science editor for 26 yrs.
b. Sep 23, 1877 in New York, New York
d. Nov 27, 1956 in New York, New York
Source: *BiDPara; ConAu 113; CurBio 43, 57*

Kaestner, Erich
see: Kastner, Erich

Kafka, Franz
Austrian. Author, Poet
b. Jul 2, 1883 in Prague, Czechoslovakia
d. Jun 3, 1924 in Kierling, Austria
Source: *AtlBL; CasWL; ClDMEL; CnMD;
CnMWL; CyWA; EncWL; EvEuW; LongCTC;
ModGL; OxEng; OxGer; PenC EUR;
RComWL; REn; TwCA, SUP; TwCWr;
WhoTwCL*

Kaganovich, Lazar M
Russian. Communist Leader
b. Nov 22, 1893 in Kabany, Russia
Source: *CurBio 42, 55; IntWW 74*

Kagel, Sam
American. Lawyer
Mediator in NFL strike, 1982.
b. Jan 24, 1909 in San Francisco, California
Source: *NewYTBS 82; WhoAm 74, 76, 78;
WhoLab 76*

Kahanamoku, Duke
American. Swimmer
b. Aug 24, 1890 in Honolulu, Hawaii
d. Jan 22, 1968 in Honolulu, Hawaii
Source: *WhAm 4A; WhScrn 74, 77; WhoHol
B*

Kahane, Meir David
American. Rabbi
Founded Jewish Defense League, 1968; tactics
inspired by Black Panthers.
b. Aug 1, 1932 in Brooklyn, New York
Source: *BioNews 74; ConAu 112; CurBio 72;
NewYTBE 71; WhoE 74*

Kahles, Charles William
American. Cartoonist
b. Jan 12, 1878 in Lengfurt, Germany
d. Jan 21, 1931
Source: *NatCAB 23; WhJnl; WorECom*

Kahlo, Frida
[Mrs. Diego Rivera]
Mexican. Artist
Majority of paintings are self-portraits;
biography *Frida* written by Hayden
Herrera.
b. 1919 in Coyoacan, Mexico
d. 1954 in Coyoacan, Mexico
Source: *BioIn 2, 3, 11, 12; IntDcWB;
McGDA; OxTwCA*

Kahn, Albert
American. Architect
b. Mar 21, 1869 in Rhaunen, Germany
d. Dec 8, 1942 in Detroit, Michigan
Source: *BioNews 74; CurBio 42; DcAmB S3;
WhAm 2*

Kahn, Alfred Edward
American. Presidential Aide
b. Oct 17, 1917 in Paterson, New Jersey
Source: *AmEA 74; AmM&WS 73S; ConAu
41R; CurBio 79; NewYTBS 74; WhoAm 80,
82, 84; WhoE 74; WhoGov 77; WhoWor 74*

Kahn, Ben
American. Designer
Innovative furrier whose coats were
purchased by Elizabeth Taylor, Joe
Namath, Joe Frazier.
b. 1887 in Russia
d. Feb 5, 1976 in New York, New York
Source: *BioIn 10; NewYTBS 76; ObitOF 79*

Kahn, Gus
American. Songwriter
b. Nov 6, 1886 in Coblenz, Germany
d. Oct 8, 1941 in Beverly Hills, California
Source: *AmSCAP 66; CurBio 41; EncMT*

Kahn, Herman
American. Physicist
Military strategist; co-founder, director,
Hudson Institute think tank, 1961.
b. Feb 15, 1922 in Bayonne, New Jersey
d. Jul 7, 1983 in Chappaqua, New York
Source: *AmM&WS 78S; ConAu 110, 65;
CurBio 83; NatCAB 63; NewYTBS 83;
PolProf K; WhoAm 80, 82; WhoWor 78;
WrDr 82, 84*

Kahn, Louis I
American. Architect
b. Feb 2, 1901 in Oesel, Russia
d. Mar 17, 1974 in New York, New York
Source: *AmArch 70; BioNews 74; ColR;
ConAu 49; CurBio 64, 74; EncAB-H;
NewYTBE 72; NewYTBS 74; WhAm 6;
WhoAm 74; WhoE 74; WhoWor 78*

Kahn, Madeline Gail
American. Actress
Oscar nominee for *Paper Moon, Blazing
Saddles;* star of TV series "Oh Madeline,"
1983.
b. Sep 29, 1942 in Boston, Massachusetts
Source: *BkPepl; CurBio 77; IntMPA 80, 81,
82; MovMk; NewYTBS 74; WhoAm 78, 82;
WhoHol A; WorAl*

Kahn, Otto Hermann
American. Banker, Art Patron
Business associate of Edward Harriman
considered greatest art patron US has
known.
b. Feb 21, 1867 in Mannheim, Germany
d. Mar 29, 1934 in New York, New York
Source: *AmBi; AmLY; DcAmB S1; DcBiPP;
DcNAA; LinLib S; REnAL; WebAB; WhAm
1; WorAl*

Kahn, Roger
American. Journalist, Author
Sports editor *Newsweek,* 1956-60; editor
Saturday Evening Post, 1963-68.
b. Oct 31, 1927 in Brooklyn, New York
Source: *AuBYP; ConAu 25R*

Kai-Shek, Chaing
see: Chiang Kai-Shek

Kai-Shek, Chiang, Madame
see: Chiang Mei-Ling

Kain, Karen Alexandria
Canadian. Ballerina
Principal dancer, National Ballet of Canada,
1971--.
b. Mar 28, 1951 in Hamilton, Ontario
Source: *BioIn 10, 11; CanWW 79; CurBio
80; WhoAm 80, 82*

Kaiser, Edgar Fosburgh
American. Industrialist
Pres., chm., Kaiser Alumninium & Chemical
Corp., Kaiser Steel Corp.
b. Jul 29, 1908 in Spokane, Washington
d. Dec 11, 1981 in San Francisco, California
Source: *CurBio 82; IntWW 81; IntYB 81;
NewYTBS 81; WhAm 8; WhoAm 80;
WhoWest 78*

Kaiser, Georg
German. Dramatist
b. Nov 25, 1878 in Magdeburg, Germany
d. Jun 5, 1945 in Ascona, Switzerland
Source: *CasWL; ClDMEL; CnMD; CnThe;
EncWL; EvEuW; LongCTC; McGEWD;
ModGL; ModWD; NewC; OxEng; OxGer;
OxThe; PenC EUR; REn; REnWD; TwCA,
SUP; WhoTwCL*

Kaiser, Henry John
American. Industrialist
b. May 9, 1882 in Canajoharie, New York
d. Aug 24, 1967 in Honolulu, Hawaii
Source: *CurBio 42, 61, 67; EncAB-H;*
WebAB; WhAm 4A

Kalakaua, David
King
b. Nov 16, 1836
d. Jan 30, 1891 in San Francisco, California
Source: *ApCAB; HarEnUS; LinLib S*

Kalatozov, Mikhail
[Mikhail Kalatozishvili]
Russian. Director
Early films banned for negativism; won
Cannes Award for *Cranes Are Flying,*
1958.
b. Dec 23, 1903 in Tiflis, Russia
d. Mar 28, 1973 in Moscow, U.S.S.R.
Source: *FilmEn; FilmgC; NewYTBE 73;*
ObitOF 79; OxFilm; PseudN 82; WorEFlm

Kalb, Bernard
American. Government Official, Author
State dept. spokesman, 1985--; co-author,
with brother, Marvin *Kissinger.*
b. Feb 5, 1932 in New York, New York
Source: *ASpks; BioIn 12; ConAu 109;*
WhoTelC

Kalb, Johann de
German. General
b. Jun 29, 1721 in Huttendorf, Bavaria
d. Aug 19, 1780 in Camden, South Carolina
Source: *AmBi; ApCAB; DcAmB; LinLib S;*
NatCAB 1; OxAmH; REn; TwCBDA; WebAB;
WhAm HS

Kalb, Marvin Leonard
American. Broadcast Journalist
Chief diplomatic correspondent, NBC News
since 1980; permanent panel member of
"Meet the Press."
b. Jun 9, 1930 in New York, New York
Source: *AmAu&B; ASpks; ConAu 5R; IntMPA*
82; WhoAm 82; WhoTelC; WhoWor 74

Kalber, Floyd
American. Broadcast Journalist
b. Dec 23, 1924 in Omaha, Nebraska
Source: *WhoAm 78, 80, 82*

Kalem, Ted
American. Drama Critic
b. Dec 19, 1919 in Malden, Massachusetts
Source: *BiE&WWA*

Kalf, Willem
Dutch. Artist
Genre, still-life painter influenced by
Vermeer: "Peasant Interior."
b. 1619 in Rotterdam, Netherlands
d. 1693 in Amsterdam, Netherlands
Source: *McGDA*

Kaline, Al(bert William)
American. Baseball Player, Sportscaster
Detroit outfielder, 1953-74; collected 3,007
hits in career; Hall of Fame, 1980.
b. Dec 19, 1934 in Baltimore, Maryland
Source: *BaseEn 85; BioNews 74; CelR;*
CurBio 70; NewYTBE 72; NewYTBS 74, 74;
WhoAm 74; WhoProB 73

Kalinin, Mikhail
Russian. Political Leader
b. Nov 20, 1875 in Upper Troitsa, Russia
d. Jun 3, 1946 in Moscow, U.S.S.R.
Source: *CurBio 42, 46*

Kalisch, Paul
German. Opera Singer
b. Nov 6, 1855 in Berlin, Germany
d. Jan 17, 1946 in Germany
Source: *NewEOp 71*

Kalish, Max
Polish. Sculptor
Commissioned, 1944, to create bronze statues
of WW II personalities.
b. Mar 1, 1891 in Valojen, Poland
d. Mar 18, 1945 in New York, New York
Source: *BioIn 1, 2, 9; NatCAB 35; WhAm 2*

Kallen, Horace M
American. Educator, Philosopher
b. Aug 11, 1882 in Barenstadt, Germany
d. Feb 16, 1974 in Palm Beach, Florida
Source: *AmAu&B; ConAu 49, 93; CurBio 53,*
74; OxAmL; REnAL; TwCA SUP; WhAm 6;
WhNAA

Kallen, Kitty
American. Singer, Actress
Vocalist with Big Bands; had hit "Little
Things Mean a Lot," 1954.
b. May 25, 1926 in Philadelphia,
Pennsylvania
Source: *CmpEPM; WhoHol A*

Kalmanoff, Martin
American. Composer, Conductor, Musician
b. May 24, 1920 in Brooklyn, New York
Source: *AmSCAP 66; WhoAm 82; WhoWorJ*
72

Kalmar, Bert
American. Songwriter
With Harry Ruby wrote hit songs "Who's
Sorry Now?" 1923; "Three Little Words,"
1930.
b. Feb 16, 1884 in New York, New York
d. Sep 18, 1947 in Los Angeles, California
Source: *AmPS; AmSCAP 66; BiDAmM; BioIn
1, 4; CmpEPM; EncMT; NewCBMT; NotNAT
B; ObitOF 79; WhThe*

Kalmbach, Herbert Warren
American. Lawyer, Watergate Participant
b. Oct 19, 1921 in Port Huron, Michigan
Source: *NewYTBE 73; WhoAm 74; WhoWest
84*

Kalmus, Herbert Thomas
American. Inventor
Invented technicolor, 1929; first used in film
Becky Sharp, 1935.
b. Nov 9, 1881 in Chelsea, Massachusetts
d. Jul 11, 1963 in Los Angeles, California
Source: *CurBio 49, 63; DcAmB S7; DcFM;
FilmgC; WhAm 4; WorAl*

Kalmus, Natalie Mabelle Dunfee
[Mrs. Herbert Kalmus]
American. Inventor
Co-inventor, technicolor film.
b. 1892
d. Nov 15, 1965 in Boston, Massachusetts
Source: *DcAmB S7; FilmgC; ObitOF 79*

Kalp, Malcolm
[The Hostages]
American. Hostage in Iran
b. 1939
Source: *NewYTBS 81*

Kaltenborn, H(ans) V(on)
American. Editor, Broadcast Journalist
Best known for series of nonstop broadcasts
during Munich crisis, 1938; wrote
autobiography *Fifty Fabulous Years,* 1956.
b. Jul 9, 1878 in Milwaukee, Wisconsin
d. Jun 14, 1965 in Brooklyn, New York
Source: *AmAu&B; ConAu 93; CurBio 40, 65;
LinLib L, S; NatCAB 51; ObitOF 79; PseudN
82; REnAL; WebAB; WhAm 4; WhNAA*

Kalthoum, Um
"The Nightingale of the Nile"
Egyptian. Singer
Arab world's most beloved songstress.
b. 1898 in Tamay-al-Zahirah, Egypt
d. Feb 3, 1975 in Cairo, Egypt
Source: *BioIn 4, 6, 7, 10; NewYTBS 75;
ObitOF 79; WhScrn 77*

Kamali, Norma
American. Fashion Designer
b. Jun 27, 1945 in New York, New York
Source: *BioIn 12; WhoAm 82*

Kamehameha I
[Kamehameha the Great]
Hawaiian. King
Ruled Hawaiian Islands, 1810-19; preserved
ancient customs, religious beliefs; united
islands, 1795.
b. 1758 in Kohala, Hawaii
d. May 5, 1819 in Kailua, Hawaii
Source: *BioIn 6, 10, 11; HarEnUS; LuthC
75; McGEWB; NewCol 75; WhAm HS*

Kamen, Martin David
American. Biochemist
b. Aug 27, 1913 in Toronto, Ontario
Source: *AmM&WS 73P; CanWW 70; IntWW
74; WhoAm 74; WhoWor 78*

Kamen, Milt
American. Comedian, Actor
b. 1924 in Hurleyville, New York
d. Feb 24, 1977 in Beverly Hills, California
Source: *WhoHol A*

Kamenev, Lev Borisovich
[Lev Borisovich Rosenfeld]
Russian. Communist Leader
b. 1883
d. 1936
Source: *DcPol; McGEWB; PseudN 82; REn;
WhDW*

Kamerlingh Onnes, Heike
Dutch. Physicist
b. Sep 21, 1853 in Groningen, Netherlands
d. Feb 21, 1926
Source: *NewCol 75; WhDW*

Kaminska, Ida
Russian. Actress
Oscar nominee for *The Shop on Main Street,*
1965; founded two theaters in Warsaw,
Poland.
b. Sep 4, 1899 in Odessa, Russia
d. May 21, 1980 in New York, New York
Source: *AnObit 1980; CurBio 69, 80N;
FilmgC; IntWW 74; NewYTBE 73; WhoAm
74; WhoHol A; WhoThe 77*

Kaminsky, Grigorii Naumovich
Russian. Communist Leader
b. 1895
d. 1938
Source: *BioIn 10*

Kaminsky, Max
American. Jazz Musician
b. Sep 7, 1908 in Brockton, Massachusetts
Source: *WhoJazz 72*

Kamp, Irene Kittle
[Grimes Grice, pseud.]
American. Editor, Author
Editor, *Glamour,* 1939-42; *Cue,* 1943-46;
Seventeen, 1950-55.
b. Oct 28, 1910 in Brooklyn, New York
d. Jun 1985 in Los Angeles, California
Source: *ConAu 116; WhoAmW 58*

Kampelman, Max M
American. Lawyer, Diplomat
Dem. named by Ronald Reagan to head US
negotiating team at arms reduction talks,
Geneva, 1985.
b. Nov 7, 1920 in New York, New York
Source: *ConAu 41R; CurBio 86; WhoAm 84*

Kanaly, Steve(n Francis)
American. Actor
Plays Ray Krebbs on TV series "Dallas,"
1978--.
b. Mar 14, 1946 in Burbank, California
Source: *ConTFT 3*

Kanaris, Constantine
"The Themistocles of Modern Greece"
Greek. Statesman
War hero, 1822-28; prime minister, 1848-49,
1864-65, 1877.
b. 1790
d. 1887
Source: *DcBiPP; NewCol 75*

Kander, John
American. Composer
Co-wrote music for Broadway hits: *Chicago,*
1975; *Zorba,* 1968; won Tony for *Cabaret,*
1967.
b. Mar 18, 1927 in Kansas City, Missouri
Source: *BiE&WWA; EncMT; NewCBMT;*
NotNAT; WhoAm 82; WhoThe 81

Kandinsky, Wassily
Russian. Artist
Painter regarded as one of originators of
modern abstract art.
b. Dec 4, 1866 in Moscow, Russia
d. Dec 17, 1944 in Paris, France
Source: *AtlBL; CurBio 45; LinLib L, S; REn;*
WhAm 4; WorAl

Kane, Carol
American. Actress
Played Simka on TV series, "Taxi"; won
Emmy, 1982.
b. Jun 18, 1952 in Cleveland, Ohio
Source: *FilmEn; IntMPA 82; WhoAm 82;*
WhoHol A

Kane, Elisha Kent
American. Explorer, Physician
Searched Arctic for John Franklin; went
farther than any previous expeditions,
laying foundation for subsequent studies.
b. Feb 3, 1820 in Philadelphia, Pennsylvania
d. Feb 16, 1857 in Havana, Cuba
Source: *Alli; AmAu; AmBi; ApCAB; BbD;*
BiD&SB; CyAL 2; DcAmAu; DcAmB;
DcNAA; Drake; EarABI SUP; InSci; NatCAB
3; OxAmL; OxCan; REnAL; TwCBDA;
WebAB; WhAm 1, HS

Kane, Harnett T(homas)
American. Author
Books on American South include *New*
Orleans Woman, 1946.
b. Nov 8, 1910 in New Orleans, Louisiana
d. Sep 4, 1984 in New Orleans, Louisiana
Source: *ConAu 113; CurBio 74, 84*

Kane, Helen
[Helen Schroder]
"The Boop-Boop-a-Doop Girl"
American. Singer, Actress
b. Aug 4, 1908 in New York, New York
d. Sep 26, 1966 in Jackson Heights, New
York
Source: *EncMT; PseudN 82; ThFT; WhScrn*
74, 77; WhoHol B

Kane, Henry
American. Author
b. 1918 in New York, New York
Source: *AmAu&B; EncMys*

Kane, Howie
[Jay and the Americans]
American. Singer
Part of clean-cut vocal quintet of 1960s.
b. Jun 6, 1942
Source: *NF*

Kane, John
American. Artist
Known for primitive landscapes of PA,
cityscapes of Pittsburgh.
b. Aug 19, 1860 in West Calder, Scotland
d. Aug 10, 1934 in Pittsburgh, Pennsylvania
Source: *AmFkP; BnEnAmA; DcAmArt;*
DcAmB S1; McGEWB; OxTwCA; PhDcTCA
77

Kane, Joseph Nathan
American. Editor, Historian
Wrote of obscure items in American history:
Famous First Facts, 1933.
b. Jan 23, 1899 in New York, New York
Source: *BioIn 1; CurBio 85*

Kane, Robert Joseph
American. Olympic Official
b. Apr 24, 1912 in Ithaca, New York
Source: *BioIn 12; NewYTBS 80*

Kang, Sheng
[Chao Yun]
Chinese. Communist Leader
Led communist China's intelligence agency,
1940-75.
b. 1899 in Shantung, China
d. 1975
Source: *IntWW 74; SpyCS; WhoSocC 78A*

Kangaroo, Captain
see: Keeshan, Bob

Kania, Stanislaw
Polish. Government Official
Communist leader, First Secretary, Polish
Workers Party, 1980.
b. Mar 8, 1927 in Wrocanka, Poland
Source: *CurBio 81; IntWW 74, 75, 77, 78,
80; WhoSocC 78*

Kanin, Garson
American. Author, Director
Wrote *Tracy and Hepburn: An Intimate
Memoir,* 1971; directed *Funny Girl,* 1964.
b. Nov 24, 1912 in Rochester, New York
Source: *AmAu&B; AmSCAP 66; AuNews 1;
BiDFilm; BiE&WWA; BioNews 75; CelR;
CmMov; CnMD; ConAu 5R; CurBio 41, 52;
DcFM; FilmgC; IntMPA 75, 76, 77, 78, 79,
80, 81, 82; ModWD; MovMk; NatPD;
NotNAT; OxAmL; OxFilm; PenC AM;
REnAL; WhoAm 74, 76, 78, 80, 82; WhoThe
77; WhoWor 78; WorAu; WorEFlm; WrDr 76*

Kanner, Leo
"Father of Child Psychology"
American. Psychologist, Author
Infantile autism authority; wrote classic text
Child Psychiatry, 1935.
b. Jun 13, 1894 in Klekotow, Austria
d. Apr 3, 1981 in Sykesville, Maryland
Source: *AnObit 1981; ConAu 103, 17R;
NewYTBS 81; WhAm 7; WhoAm 74;
WhoWor 74; WhoWorJ 72*

Kannon, Jackie
Comedian
b. 1919 in Windsor, Ontario
d. Feb 1, 1974 in New York, New York
Source: *NewYTBS 74; WhScrn 77; WhoHol B*

Kano, Motonobu
Japanese. Artist
b. 1476
d. 1559
Source: *NewCol 75*

Kant, Immanuel
German. Philosopher
Best known for attempt to define rational
understanding; wrote *Critique of Practical
Reason.*
b. Apr 22, 1724 in Konigsberg, Germany
d. Feb 12, 1804 in Konigsberg, Germany
Source: *BbD; BiD&SB; CasWL; CyWA;
DcBiPP; DcEuL; EuAu; EvEuW; LinLib L,
S; NewC; OxEng; OxGer; PenC EUR; REn;
WhDW; WorAl*

Kanter, Hal
[Henry Irving]
American. Writer, Director, Producer
b. Dec 18, 1918 in Savannah, Georgia
Source: *ConAu 81; IntMPA 75, 76, 77, 78,
79, 80, 81, 82; PseudN 82; WhoAm 82;
WorEFlm*

Kantner, Paul
[Jefferson Airplane; Jefferson Starship]
American. Singer, Musician
b. Mar 12, 1942 in San Francisco, California
Source: *BioIn 9; WhoAm 80, 82*

Kantor, Mackinlay
American. Author, Journalist
Wrote Civil War novel *Andersonville,* 1955.
b. Feb 4, 1904 in Webster City, Iowa
d. Oct 11, 1977 in Sarasota, Florida
Source: *AmAu&B; AmNov; AuBYP; ChhPo
S1; CnDAL; ConAmA; ConAu 61, 73; ConLC
7; ConNov 72, 76; DcLEL; EncMys; FilmgC;
ModAL; OxAmL; PenC AM; REn; REnAL;
TwCA, SUP; TwCWr; WhoAm 74; WrDr 80*

Kantrowitz, Adrian
American. Surgeon
Heart surgeon who developed pacemaker,
1961, artificial heart pump, 1966;
performed second heart transplant
operation, 1967.
b. Oct 4, 1918 in New York, New York
Source: *AmM&WS 79P; CurBio 67; IntWW
79; WhoAm 82; WhoE 74; WhoWor 74;
WhoWorJ 72*

Kapell, William
American. Musician
b. Sep 20, 1922 in New York, New York
d. Oct 29, 1953 in San Francisco, California
Source: *CurBio 48, 54; WhAm 3*

Kaper, Bronislau
American. Composer
Won Oscar, 1953, for score of *Lili.*
b. Feb 5, 1902 in Warsaw, Poland
d. May 1983 in Beverly Hills, California
Source: *AmPS; AmSCAP 66; CmpEPM;
ConAmC 82; FilmgC; IntMPA 82, 84;
WorEFlm*

Kapitsa, Pyotr
Russian. Physicist
Headed Soviet sputnik program; won Nobel
Prize, 1978.
b. Jun 26, 1894 in Russia
d. Apr 8, 1984 in Moscow, U.S.S.R.
Source: *NewYTBS 84; WhoSocC 78; WorAl*

Kaplan, Gabe (Gabriel)
American. Actor, Comedian
Starred in TV series "Welcome Back,
Kotter," 1975-79.
b. Mar 31, 1945 in Brooklyn, New York
Source: *BioIn 10; BkPepl; IntMPA 79, 80,
81, 82; WhoAm 78, 80, 82*

Kaplan, Henry
American. Physician, Scientist
Pioneer in research treatment for Hodgkin's
disease; invented linear accelerator.
b. Apr 24, 1918 in Chicago, Illinois
d. Feb 4, 1984 in Palo Alto, California
Source: *AmM&WS 82P; AnObit 1984;
NewYTBS 84; WhoAm 80, 82; WhoFrS 84;
WhoTech 82*

Kaplan, Mordecai
American. Rabbi, Author
Founded Jewish Reconstruction movement;
outlined philosophy of Judaism.
b. Jun 11, 1881 in Swenziany, Lithuania
d. Nov 8, 1983 in New York, New York
Source: *AmAu&B; ConAu X; McGEWB;
NewYTBS 83; WebAB; WhAm 6*

Kaplow, Herbert E
American. Journalist
b. Feb 2, 1927 in New York, New York
Source: *WhoAm 82; WhoWorJ 72*

Kapor, Mitchell
Business Executive
Founder, chm., Lotus Development Corp.,
1981-86; helped create best-selling personal
computer software.
b. 1951
Source: *BioIn 13*

Kapp, Joe (Joseph)
American. Football Player, Football Coach
Controversial quarterback, 1967-71; coach U
of CA, 1982--.
b. Mar 19, 1938 in Santa Fe, New Mexico
Source: *CurBio 75; WhoFtbl 74*

Kappel, Gertrude
German. Opera Singer
b. Sep 1, 1893 in Halle, Germany
d. Apr 1971 in Munich, Germany (West)
Source: *InWom; NewYTBE 71; WhAm 5*

Kaprisky, Valerie
French. Actress
Starred in film *Breathless* with Richard Gere,
1983.
b. 1963 in Paris, France
Source: *VarWW 85*

Kaprow, Allan
American. Artist
b. Aug 23, 1927 in Atlantic City, New
Jersey
Source: *DcCAA 71*

Karajan, Herbert von
Austrian. Conductor
Director for life of the Berlin Philharmonic;
guiding force behind the Salzburg Festival.
b. Apr 5, 1908 in Salzburg, Austria
Source: *CelR; CurBio 56, 86; IntWW 74;
NewYTBS 74; Who 74*

Karamanlis, Constantine
[Constantinos Caramanlis]
"Costas"
Greek. President
Premier, 1955-63; pres., 1980--.
b. Feb 23, 1907 in Prote, Greece
Source: *CurBio 56, 76; IntWW 74, 75, 76,
77, 78, 79, 80, 81; IntYB 78, 79; NewYTBS
74, 80; WhoWor 76, 78*

Karan, Donna Faske
American. Fashion Designer
Separates sportswear designer with Anne
Klein, 1971-74.
b. Oct 2, 1948 in Forest Hills, New York
Source: *BioIn 10, 11; WhoFash; WorFshn*

Kardiner, Abram
American. Psychoanalyst
Co-founded first US psychiatric training
    school, 1939; wrote *Sex and Morality,*
    1954.
b. Aug 17, 1891 in New York, New York
d. Jul 20, 1981 in Easton, Connecticut
Source: *AmAu&B; BiDrAPA 77; ConAu 104;*
NewYTBS 81

Karfiol, Bernard
American. Artist
Post-impressionist painter of children,
    interiors, nudes.
b. May 6, 1886 in Budapest, Hungary
d. Aug 16, 1952 in New York, New York
Source: *CurBio 47, 52; DcAmArt; DcAmB S5;*
DcCAA 71, 77; McGDA; WhAm 3; WhoAmA
78

Karim, Shah
see: Aga Khan IV

Karle, Jerome
American. Physicist
With Herbert A Hauptmann, won Nobel
    Prize, 1985, for studies in molecular
    structure of crystals.
b. Jun 18, 1918 in New York, New York
Source: *AmM&WS 82P; IntWW 83; WhoAm*
80, 82, 84; WhoFrS 84

Karlfeldt, Erik Axel
Swedish. Poet
Work is purposely archaic, bases in folklore,
    custom; refused Nobel Prize, 1918, award
    posthumously, 1931.
b. Jul 20, 1864 in Folkarna, Sweden
d. Apr 8, 1931 in Stockholm, Sweden
Source: *CasWL; ClDMEL; EncWL; LinLib L;*
PenC EUR; REn; TwCA SUP; TwCWW;
WhDW

Karloff, Boris
[William Henry Pratt]
English. Actor
In horror films *Frankenstein,* 1931; *The*
    Mummy, 1933.
b. Nov 23, 1887 in London, England
d. Feb 2, 1969 in Middleton, England
Source: *BiDFilm; BiE&WWA; CmMov;*
CurBio 41, 69; Film 1; FilmgC; MotPP;
MovMk; OxFilm; PseudN 82; TwYS; WebAB;
WhAm 5; WhScrn 74, 77; WhoHol B;
WorEFlm

Karmal, Babrak
Afghan. President
Pro-Soviet pres. of Afghanistan, 1979--.
b. 1929
Source: *CurBio 81; IntWW 80; NewYTBS 79*

Karman, Theodore Todor Von
American. Physicist, Engineer
Aeronautical pioneer who developed theory of
    vortex streets, 1911; won first National
    Medal of Science.
b. May 11, 1881 in Budapest, Hungary
d. May 7, 1963 in Aachen, Germany (West)
Source: *DcAmB S7; WebBD 80*

Karns, Roscoe
American. Comedian
b. Sep 7, 1893 in San Bernardino, California
d. Feb 6, 1970 in Los Angeles, California
Source: *FilmgC; MotPP; MovMk; NewYTBE*
70; TwYS; Vers B; WhScrn 74, 77; WhoHol
B

Karp, Lila
American. Sociologist, Author
b. Jun 7, 1933 in New York, New York
Source: *ConAu 25R; DrAF 76; DrAS 74E*

Karpin, Fred Leon
American. Journalist
b. Mar 17, 1913 in New York, New York
Source: *ConAu 13R*

Karpis, Alvin
[Alvin Karpowicz]
"Old Creepy"
Canadian. Criminal
Public Enemy number one, 1930s; member
    Ma Barker's gang; paroled after 32 yrs. in
    prison, 1969.
b. 1908 in Montreal, Quebec
d. Aug 12, 1979 in Torremolinos, Spain
Source: *Blood&B; NewYTBS 79; PseudN 82*

Karpov, Anatoly Yevgenyevich
Russian. Chess Player
International Grandmaster, 1970, who was
    world champion, 1975-85; lost title to
    Garry Kasparov, 1985.
b. May 23, 1951 in Zlatoust, U.S.S.R.
Source: *BioIn 10; CurBio 78; GolEC;*
OxChess; WhoWor 82

Karrar, Paul
Russian. Chemist, Educator
Shared 1937 Nobel Prize for plant pigments
    research.
b. Apr 21, 1889 in Moscow, Russia
d. Jun 18, 1971 in Zurich, Switzerland
Source: *AsBiEn; ConAu 113; WhAm 5*

Karras, Alex(ander G)
"The Mad Duck"; "Tippy Toes"
American. Football Player, Actor
Tackle, Detroit Lions, 1958-70; suspended,
1963, for gambling; founded film
production company, 1978, with wife
Susan Clark.
b. Jul 15, 1935 in Gary, Indiana
Source: *BioNews 74; ConAu 107; PseudN 82;
WhoAm 80, 82, 84; WhoFtbl 74; WhoHol A;
WorAl*

Karsavina, Tamara
[Tamara Karsavin]
"La Tamara"
Russian. Ballerina
b. 1885
d. May 26, 1978 in London, England
Source: *BioIn 1, 2, 3, 4, 6, 8, 11*

Karsh, Yousuf
Canadian. Photographer, Journalist
Best known for photo of Winston Churchill,
other famous people; wrote *Faces of Our
Time,* 1971.
b. Dec 23, 1908 in Mardin, Armenia
Source: *CanWW 82; ConAu 33R; CurBio 52,
80; IntWW 74; LinLib L, S; NewYTBE 72;
Who 82; WhoAm 82; WhoAmA 73; WhoWor
78*

Kasavubu, Joseph
"The Father of Congo Independence"
Congolese. President
b. 1910 in Tshela, Congo
d. Mar 24, 1969 in Boma, Congo
Source: *CurBio 61, 69; PseudN 82; WhAm 5*

Kasdan, Lawrence Edward
American. Director, Screenwriter
Co-wrote *Empire Strikes Back,* 1980; *The Big
Chill,* 1983.
b. Jan 14, 1949 in Miami Beach, Florida
Source: *NewYTBS 81; WhoAm 84*

Kashdan, Isaac
American. Chess Player, Editor
Seven times captain, US Chess Olympic
team; founded *Chess Review.*
b. Nov 19, 1905 in New York, New York
d. Feb 20, 1985 in Los Angeles, California
Source: *ConAu 115; WhoAm 84; WhoAmJ 80*

Kasparov, Garry Kimovich
Russian. Chess Player
International Grandmaster, 1980, who
defeated Anatoly Karpov, 1985, to become
youngest champion ever.
b. Apr 13, 1963 in Baku, U.S.S.R.
Source: *CurBio 86; OxChess*

Kasper, Herbert
American. Fashion Designer
b. Dec 12, 1926 in New York, New York
Source: *PseudN 82; WhoAm 82; WhoFash;
WorFshn*

Kassebaum, Nancy Landon
American. Politician
Rep. senator from KS, 1979--; daughter of
Alf Landon.
b. Jul 29, 1932 in Topeka, Kansas
Source: *AlmAP 80, 82; CngDr 79; CurBio 82;
NewYTBS 83; WhoAm 80, 82; WhoAmP 79;
WhoWor 80, 82; WomPO 76*

Kassem, Abdul Karim
Iraqi. Politician
b. Nov 21, 1914 in Baghdad, Iraq
d. Feb 9, 1963 in Baghdad, Iraq
Source: *CurBio 59, 63*

Kassorla, Irene Chamie
American. Psychologist, Author
Psychologist to Hollywood stars; wrote best-
selling sex manual *Nice Girls Do,* 1981.
b. Aug 18, 1931 in Los Angeles, California
Source: *BioIn 10; NewYTBS 81; WhoWest 78*

Kasten, Robert W, Jr.
American. Senator
Conservative Rep. senator from WI, 1980--.
b. Jun 19, 1942 in Milwaukee, Wisconsin
Source: *AlmAP 78; CngDr 77; WhoAm 84;
WhoAmP 79; WhoGov 75; WhoMW 78*

Kastler, Alfred
French. Physicist
Developed basic principle of laser beam; won
Nobel Prize, 1966.
b. May 3, 1902 in Guebwiller, France
d. Jan 7, 1984 in Bandol, France
Source: *AnObit 1984; AsBiEn; BiESc; CurBio
84; IntWW 83; McGMS 80; NewYTBS 84;
Who 83; WhoWor 82*

Kastner, Erich
[Erich Kaestner]
German. Author, Poet
Wrote *Emil and the Detectives,* 1928; books
burned in Germany, 1933.
b. Feb 23, 1899 in Dresden, Germany
d. Jul 29, 1974
Source: *AuBYP; CasWL; CIDMEL; CnMD;
ConAu 49, 73; CurBio 64, 74; EncWL;
EveuW; IntWW 74; ModGL; ModWD;
OxGer; PenC EUR; SmATA 14; ThrBJA;
WhAm 6; Who 74; WhoChL; WhoWor 74;
WorAu*

Kasznar, Kurt
[Kurt Serwischer]
Austrian. Actor
Appeared in 1,000 Broadway performances of
  The Sound of Music; also appeared in
  Barefoot in the Park, 1964.
b. Aug 13, 1913 in Vienna, Austria
d. Aug 6, 1979 in Santa Monica, California
Source: *BiE&WWA; ConAu 89; FilmgC;*
IntMPA 77, 78; MotPP; MovMk; NotNAT;
PseudN 82; Vers B; WhAm 7; WhoAm 74,
76, 78; WhoHol A; WhoThe 72, 77

Katayev, Valentin
[Yevgeny Petrov, pseud.]
Russian. Author
Wrote satirical novel *The Embezzlers,* 1929;
  play *Squaring the Circle,* 1928.
b. Jan 28, 1897 in Odessa, Russia
Source: *ConAu 117; McGEWD; WebBD 80*

Kath, Terry
[Chicago]
American. Singer, Musician
Guitarist, formed group with Walter
  Parazaider, 1967; died of accidental self-
  inflicted gun wound.
b. Jan 31, 1946 in Chicago, Illinois
d. Jan 23, 1978 in Los Angeles, California
Source: *NF*

Katims, Milton
American. Musician, Conductor
b. 1909 in Brooklyn, New York
Source: *NewYTBS 74; WhoAm 74, 76, 78,*
80, 82; WhoMus 72; WhoWest 84; WhoWor
78

Katona, George
American. Economist
Dean of "behavior" economists; believed
  consumer's attitudes influence economy;
  wrote *Psychology of Economics,* 1975.
b. Nov 6, 1901 in Budapest, Hungary
d. Jun 18, 1981 in Berlin, Germany (West)
Source: *AmEA 74; AmM&WS 73S; WhoAm*
74, 76, 78, 80; WhoWor 74

Katt, William
American. Actor
Starred in TV series "The Greatest American
  Hero," 1981-83.
b. Feb 16, 1955 in Los Angeles, California
Source: *ConTFT 3; IntMPA 80, 81, 82*

Katzenbach, Nicholas de Belleville
American. Lawyer, Government Official
b. Jan 17, 1922 in Philadelphia, Pennsylvania
Source: *BiDrUSE; BlueB 76; CivR 74; CurBio*
65; IntWW 74; St&PR 75; WhoAm 74, 76,
78, 80, 82; WhoAmP 81; WhoF&I 74;
WhoWor 76, 78

Kauff, Benny (Benjamin Michael)
American. Baseball Player
b. Jan 5, 1890 in Pomeroy, Ohio
d. Nov 17, 1961 in Columbus, Ohio
Source: *BaseEn 85; WhoProB 73*

Kauffer, Edward McKnight
American. Illustrator
b. 1891 in Great Falls, Montana
d. Oct 22, 1954 in New York, New York
Source: *BioIn 1, 3, 4, 8; IlsCB 1744; ObitOF*
79

Kauffman, Ewing Marion
American. Businessman, Baseball Executive
Owner, Marion Labs, 1950--; KC Royals
  baseball club, 1969--.
b. Sep 21, 1916 in Missouri
Source: *WhoAm 80, 82, 84; WhoF&I 83;*
WhoProB 73

Kauffmann, Angelica
French. Artist
Bid portraits; historical subjects, decorative
  wall paintings.
b. 1741
d. 1807
Source: *BkIE; NewCol 75*

Kauffmann, Stanley Jules
[Spranger Barry, pseud.]
American. Critic
b. Apr 24, 1916 in New York, New York
Source: *Au&Wr 71; ConAu 5R; LongCTC;*
PenC AM; PseudN 82; WhoAm 74, 76, 78,
80, 82; WhoE 74; WhoWor 78; WorAu;
WrDr 76

Kaufman, Andy
American. Actor, Comedian
Best known for appearances on "Saturday
  Night Live," 1975-78; played Latka on
  "Taxi," 1978-84.
b. Jan 17, 1949 in New York, New York
d. May 16, 1984 in Los Angeles, California
Source: *BioIn 11; WhoAm 80, 82*

Kaufman, Bel
American. Author, Educator
Wrote *Up the Down Staircase,* 1965.
b. in Berlin, Germany
Source: *AmAu&B; ConAu 13R; DrAF 76;
ForWC 70; WhoAm 74, 76, 78, 80, 82;
WhoE 74; WhoWor 78; WrDr 76*

Kaufman, Boris
Polish. Filmmaker
Noted Hollywood cameraman; won 1954
    Oscar for best black-and-white
    cinematography for *On the Waterfront.*
b. Aug 24, 1906 in Bialystok, Poland
d. Jun 24, 1980 in New York, New York
Source: *AnObit 1980; DcFM; FilmgC; IntMPA
79; NewYTBS 80; OxFilm; WorEFlm*

Kaufman, George S(imon)
[Kaufman and Hart]
"The Great Collaborator"
American. Dramatist, Journalist
With Moss Hart, wrote some of Broadway's
    most popular plays: *You Can't Take it
    With You,* 1936; *The Man Who Came to
    Dinner,* 1939.
b. Nov 16, 1889 in Pittsburgh, Pennsylvania
d. Jun 2, 1961 in New York, New York
Source: *AmAu&B; CasWL; CnDAL; CnMD;
CnThe; ConAmA; ConAmL; ConAu 93;
CurBio 41, 61; DcLEL; EncMT; EvLB;
FilmgC; LinLib L, S; LongCTC; McGEWD;
ModWD; NatCAB 62; NewCBMT; NewYTBE
72; ObitT 1961; OxAmL; OxThe; PenC AM;
REn; REnAL; REnWD; TwCA, SUP;
TwCWr; WebAB; WebE&AL; WhAm 4;
WhThe; WorEFlm*

Kaufman, Henry
American. Economist
Wall Street forecaster; chief economist,
    Salomon Investor Bankers, since 1962.
b. 1927 in Wenings, Germany
Source: *AmEA 74; CurBio 81; NewYTBS 79*

Kaufman, Irving R
American. Judge, Lawyer
b. Jun 24, 1910 in New York, New York
Source: *AmM&WS 73P; ConAu 21R; CurBio
53; NewYTBE 70; WhoAm 74, 76, 78, 80,
82; WhoAmA 73; WhoE 74; WhoF&I 74;
WhoGov 75; WhoWorJ 72*

Kaufman, Joseph William
American. Lawyer, Judge
Prosecutor at WW II Nuremburg war crime
    trials.
b. Mar 27, 1899 in New York, New York
d. Feb 13, 1981 in Washington, District of
    Columbia
Source: *NewYTBS 81; WhoAm 74, 76, 78, 80*

Kaufman, Louis
American. Musician
b. 1905
Source: *WhoMus 72*

Kaufman, Murray
"Murray the K"; "The Fifth Beatle"
American. Disc Jockey
Promoted The Beatles' first tour, 1964.
b. Feb 14, 1922 in New York, New York
d. Feb 21, 1982 in Los Angeles, California
Source: *AnObit 1982; BioNews 74; NewYTBS
82; PseudN 82*

Kaufman, Sue
[Sue Kaufman Barondess]
American. Author
b. Aug 7, 1926 in Long Island, New York
d. Jun 25, 1977 in New York, New York
Source: *ConAu 1R, 69, 1NR; ConLC 3;
DrAF 76; ForWC 70; PseudN 82; WhoAm
74; WrDr 80*

Kaunda, Kenneth David
Zambian. President
b. Apr 28, 1924 in Lubwa, Zambia
Source: *CurBio 66; IntWW 74; Who 74;
WhoGov 75; WhoWor 78*

Kauokenen, Jorma
[Jefferson Airplane]
American. Singer, Musician
b. Dec 23, 1940 in Washington, District of
    Columbia
Source: *NF*

Kautner, Helmut
German. Screenwriter, Director
Led revival of post-war German cinema:
    Romanze in Moll, 1942.
b. Mar 25, 1908 in Dusseldorf, Germany
d. Apr 20, 1980 in Castellina, Italy
Source: *AnObit 1980; BiDFilm; DcFM;
FilmgC; IntWW 74, 75, 76, 77, 78; WhoWor
74; WorEFlm*

Kavanagh, Patrick
Irish. Poet
b. 1905 in County Monaghan, Ireland
d. Nov 30, 1967 in Dublin, Ireland
Source: *BioIn 11; CasWL; ChhPo; ConAu
25R; ConP 75; ModBrL S1; PenC ENG;
REn; TwCWr; WhoTwCL; WorAu*

Kavanaugh, Kevin
[Southside Johnny and the Asbury Jukes]
American. Singer, Musician
Keyboardist with group since 1974.
b. Aug 27, 1951
Source: *NF*

Kavner, Julie Deborah
American. Actress
Played Brenda Morgenstern on TV series
"Rhoda," 1974-78; won Emmy, 1978.
b. Sep 7, 1951 in Los Angeles, California
Source: *VarWW 85*

Kawabata, Yasunari
Japanese. Author
b. Jun 11, 1899 in Osaka, Japan
d. Apr 16, 1972 in Zusni, Japan
Source: *CasWL; CnMWL; ConAu 33R, 93;
ConLC 2, 5, 9, 18; CurBio 69, 72; DcOrL 1;
EncWL; NewYTBE 72; PenC CL; RComWL;
REn; WhAm 5; WhoTwCL; WorAu*

Kay, Dianne
American. Actress
Played Nancy Bradford on TV series "Eight
Is Enough," 1977-81.
b. 1956
Source: *BioIn 12*

Kay, Hershy
American. Composer
Wrote hit scores for ballet, Broadway, screen:
Coco, 1969; *Evita*, 1978.
b. Nov 17, 1919 in Philadelphia,
Pennsylvania
d. Dec 2, 1981 in Danbury, Connecticut
Source: *AmSCAP 66, 80; AnObit 1981; Baker
78; BiDAmM; BiE&WWA; CurBio 62, 82,
82N; NewYTBS 81; NotNAT; WhoAm 80*

Kay, Mary
[Mary Kay Wagner Ash]
American. Cosmetics Executive
Founder, chm., Mary Kay Cosmetics, 1963--;
based in Dallas, TX.
b. in Hot Wells, Texas
Source: *BusPN; WhoAm 80, 82; WhoAmW
74, 77*

Kaye, Danny
[David Daniel Kominsky]
American. Actor, Comedian
Films include *The Secret Life of Walter
Mitty*, 1947; *Hans Christian Andersen*,
1952; UNICEF ambassador-at-large.
b. Jan 18, 1913 in New York, New York
Source: *BiDFilm; BiE&WWA; CelR; CmMov;
CurBio 41, 52; EncMT; FilmgC; IntMPA 75,
76, 77, 78, 79, 80, 81, 82; MotPP; MovMk;
NewYTBE 70; NotNAT; OxFilm; OxThe;
PseudN 82; WebAB; Who 74; WhoAm 74, 76,
78, 80, 82; WhoHol A; WhoThe 77; WhoUN
75; WhoWor 78; WhoWorJ 72; WorEFlm*

Kaye, Dearwood ('Waldo')
see: Our Gang

Kaye, Mary Margaret Mollie
[Mollie Hamilton; M M Kaye]
English. Author
b. 1909 in Simla, India
Source: *Au&Wr 71; ConAu 89; PseudN 82*

Kaye, Nora
[Nora Koreff]
American. Ballerina
b. 1920 in New York, New York
Source: *CurBio 53; InWom; PseudN 82;
WhoAm 82*

Kaye, Sammy
American. Band Leader
b. Mar 13, 1913 in Lakewood, Ohio
Source: *AmSCAP 66; WhoAm 74; WhoHol A*

Kaye, Stubby
American. Actor, Comedian
Best known for role of Nicely-Nicely Johnson
in Broadway, film *Guys and Dolls.*
b. Nov 11, 1918 in New York, New York
Source: *AmPS B; BiE&WWA; FilmgC;
MotPP; NotNAT; PlP&P; WhoHol A; WhoThe
77, 81*

Kaye-Smith, Sheila
English. Author
b. Feb 4, 1887 in Hastings, England
d. Jan 14, 1956
Source: *BkC 4; CathA 1930; ChhPo S1;
CyWA; DcLEL; EvLB; InWom; LongCTC;
ModBrL; NewC; PenC ENG; REn; TwCA,
SUP; TwCWr; WhAm 3*

Kayibanda, Gregoire
Rwandan. President
b. May 1, 1924
Source: *IntWW 74; WhoGov 75; WhoWor 78*

Kazan, Elia
[Elia Kazanjoglou]
American. Director
Won 1954 Oscar for *On the Waterfront;* co-
founded Actor's Studio, 1947.
b. Sep 7, 1909 in Constantinople, Turkey
Source: *BiDFilm; BiE&WWA; ConAu
21R; ConLC 6; CurBio 48, 72; DcFM;
FilmgC; IntMPA 80, 81, 82; IntWW 74;
MovMk; NewYTBE 72; NotNAT; OxAmL;
OxFilm; OxThe; PlP&P; PseudN 82; REnAL;
WebAB; Who 83; WhoAm 82; WhoE 74;
WhoHol A; WhoThe 77A; WhoWor 82;
WorAl; WorEFlm*

Kazan, Lainie
[Lanie Levine]
American. Singer
b. May 16, 1940 in New York, New York
Source: *CelR; WhoAm 82; WhoHol A*

Kazantzakis, Nikos
Greek. Author
b. Dec 2, 1883 in Crete
d. Oct 26, 1957 in Freiburg, Germany
(West)
Source: *AtlBL; CasWL; CnMD; CurBio 55,
58; EncWL; OxEng; PenC EUR; REn; TwCA
SUP; TwCWr; WhAm 3, 4A; WhoTwCL*

Kazee, Buell H(ilton)
American. Musician, Singer
Folk music performer, 1930s; recorded "Rock
Island Line."
b. Aug 29, 1900 in Burton Fork, Kentucky
d. Aug 31, 1976
Source: *BiDAmM; ConAu 111; EncFCWM 69*

Kazin, Alfred
American. Critic
b. Jun 5, 1915 in Brooklyn, New York
Source: *AmAu&B; CasWL; CelR; ConAu 1R,
1NR; CurBio 66; DrAS 74E; IntWW 74;
OxAmL; PenC AM; RAdv 1; REn; REnAL;
TwCA SUP; WhoAm 74, 76, 78, 80, 82;
WhoWor 78; WhoWorJ 72*

Keach, Stacy, Jr.
American. Actor
Star of TV's "Return of Mike Hammer,"
1984, 1986--; arrested, jailed in England
for cocaine possession, 1984.
b. Jun 2, 1941 in Savannah, Georgia
Source: *CelR; CurBio 71; FilmgC; IntMPA
75, 76, 77, 78, 79, 80, 81, 82; MovMk;
NewYTBE 72; NotNAT; WhoAm 74, 76, 78,
80, 82, 84; WhoHol A; WhoThe 77, 81;
WorAl*

Kean, Edmund
English. Actor
Tragedian best known for his Shakespearean
roles; career shortened by scandal,
dissolute life.
b. Mar 17, 1787 in London, England
d. May 15, 1833
Source: *DcBiPP; FamA&A; LinLib L, S;
NewC; OxThe; PIP&P; REn; WhDW; WhAm
HS*

Kean, Thomas Howard
American. Politician
Succeeded Brendan Byrne as governor of NJ,
1982--.
b. Apr 21, 1935 in New York, New York
Source: *AlmAP 84; CurBio 85; NewYTBS 82;
WhoAm 84; WhoE 83*

Keane, Bil
American. Cartoonist
Creator of the "Family Circus," 1960--.
b. Oct 5, 1922 in Philadelphia, Pennsylvania
Source: *ConAu 33R; SmATA 4; WhoAm 82;
WhoAmA 73*

Keane, John B
Irish. Author
b. Jul 21, 1928 in Listowel, Ireland
Source: *ConAu 29R*

Keane, Mary Nesta
[Molly Keane; M J Farrell, pseuds.]
Irish. Author
Novel *Good Behaviour,* 1981, adapted for
BBC TV production, 1982.
b. Jul 4, 1904 in County Kildare, Ireland
Source: *ConAu 108; IntAu&W 82; Who 82,
83*

Keaney, Frank
American. Basketball Coach
Coach, Rhode Island U, 1921-48; introduced
full-court press.
b. Jun 5, 1886 in Boston, Massachusetts
d. Oct 10, 1967
Source: *WhoBbl 73*

Kearns, Doris H
American. Author, Educator
b. Jan 4, 1943 in Rockville Centre, New
York
Source: *ConAu 103; WhoE 74*

Kearns, Jack
American. Boxing Promoter
Managed six world champions, including Jack
Dempsey.
b. Aug 17, 1882 in Waterloo, Michigan
d. Jul 7, 1963 in Miami, Florida
Source: *DcAmB S7*

Kearny, Stephen Watts
American. Soldier
b. Aug 30, 1794 in Newark, New Jersey
d. Oct 31, 1848 in Saint Louis, Missouri
Source: *AmBi; ApCAB; BioIn 2, 6, 7, 8, 9,
11; DcAmB; Drake; McGEWB; NatCAB 13;
NewCol 75; REnAW; TwCBDA; WebAB;
WebAMB; WhAm HS; WhoMilH 76*

Keating, Kenneth B
American. Lawyer, Politician
b. May 18, 1900 in Lima, New York
d. May 5, 1975 in New York, New York
Source: *BiDrAC; CurBio 50; IntWW 74;
USBiR 74; WhAm 6; WhoAm 74; WhoAmP
73; WhoE 74; WhoGov 75; WhoWor 78*

Keaton, "Buster" (Joseph Francis)
"The Great Stone Face"
American. Actor, Comedian
Perfected deadpan stare in *The Navigator,*
  1924; *The General,* 1927.
b. Oct 4, 1896 in Piqua, Kansas
d. Feb 1, 1966 in Hollywood, California
Source: *BiDFilm; CmMov; DcFM; Film 1;*
FilmgC; MotPP; MovMk; OxFilm; PseudN 82;
TwYS; WebAB; WhAm 4; WhScrn 74, 77;
WhoHol B; WorEFlm

Keaton, Diane
[Diane Hall]
American. Actress
Won 1977 Oscar for *Annie Hall;* wrote
  Reservations, 1980.
b. Jan 5, 1946 in Los Angeles, California
Source: *BkPepl; FilmgC; IntMPA 77, 78, 79,*
80, 81, 82; MovMk; NewYTBE 72; PseudN
82; WhoAm 82; WhoHol A

Keaton, Michael
American. Actor, Comedian
Starred in *Night Shift,* 1982; *Mr. Mom,* 1983.
b. Sep 9, 1951 in Pittsburgh, Pennsylvania
Source: *VarWW 85*

Keats, John
English. Poet
Wrote *Ode on a Grecian Urn, Ode to a*
  Nightingale.
b. Oct 31, 1795 in London, England
d. Feb 23, 1821 in Rome, Italy
Source: *Alli; AnCL; AtlBL; BiD&SB; BrAu*
19; CasWL; Chambr 3; ChhPo, S1, S2;
CnE&AP; CrtT 2; CyWA; DcEnA; DcEnL;
DcEuL; DcLEL; EvLB; MouLC 2; NewC;
OxEng; PenC ENG; RAdv 1; RComWL;
REn; Str&VC; WebE&AL

Keble, John
English. Author, Educator, Clergyman
Initiated Oxford Movement, 1833; wrote
  popular collection of sacred verse, *The*
  Christian Year, 1827.
b. Apr 25, 1792 in Fairford, England
d. Mar 27, 1866 in Bournemouth, England
Source: *Alli, SUP; BbD; BiD&SB; BrAu 19;*
CasWL; Chambr 3; ChhPo, S1, S2; DcEnA;
DcEnL; DcEuL; DcLEL; EvLB; NewC;
OxEng; PenC ENG; PoChrch; REn;
WebE&AL

Keefe, Barrie Colin
English. Dramatist
Wrote award-winning play *My Girl,* 1975.
b. Oct 31, 1945 in London, England
Source: *ConAu 116; DcLB 13*

Keefe, Tim(othy John)
"Sir Timothy"
American. Baseball Player
Pitcher, who won 344 games during career,
  1880-93; Hall of Fame, 1964.
b. Jan 1, 1857 in Cambridge, Massachusetts
d. Apr 23, 1933 in Cambridge, Massachusetts
Source: *BaseEn 85; BasesB*

Keel, Howard
[Harold Clifford Leek]
American. Actor, Singer
Plays Clayton Farlow on TV series, "Dallas";
  singing star in *Showboat,* 1951; *Kiss Me*
  Kate, 1953.
b. Apr 13, 1919 in Gillespie, Illinois
Source: *BiE&WWA; CmMov; EncMT;*
FilmgC; IntMPA 82; MovMk; NotNAT;
PseudN 82; WhoAm 74; WhoHol A; WhoThe
77, 81; WorAl; WorEFlm

Keeler, Christine
English. Call Girl
Involved in 1963 British political-sex scandal
  known as Profumo affair.
b. 1942
Source: *BioIn 10; What 1-5*

Keeler, Ruby
[Ethel Hilda Keeler]
American. Dancer, Actress
Star of Busby Berkeley musicals, 1930s:
  Footlight Parade, 1933.
b. Aug 25, 1909 in Halifax, Nova Scotia
Source: *BiDFilm; BiE&WWA; CelR; CmMov;*
CurBio 71; EncMT; FilmgC; InWom; MotPP;
MovMk; NewYTBE 70, 71; NotNAT; OxFilm;
PIP&P; PseudN 82; ThFT; WhoAm 74, 76,
78, 80, 82; WhoHol A; WhoThe 77

Keeler, "Wee Willie" (William Henry)
American. Baseball Player
Great hitter remembered for batting strategy,
  "hit 'em where they ain't"; Hall of Fame,
  1939.
b. Mar 13, 1872 in Brooklyn, New York
d. Jan 1, 1923 in Brooklyn, New York
Source: *BaseEn 85; BasesB*

Keeler, William
American. Oilman
b. 1927
d. Jul 12, 1981 in Dallas, Texas
Source: *Dun&B 79*

Keenan, Frank
American. Actor
Stage, film actor, 1915-26; films include *The Bells; Heart's Aflame; Easy Lynne.*
b. Apr 8, 1858 in Dubuque, Iowa
d. Feb 24, 1929
Source: *Film 1; MotPP; NotNAT B; TwYS; WhAm 1; WhScrn 77; WhThe; WhoHol B*

Keene, Carolyn, pseud.
see: Adams, Harriet Stratemeyer

Keene, Charles Samuel
English. Artist
Illustrator for *Punch* from 1851.
b. Aug 10, 1823 in Hornsey, England
d. Jan 4, 1891 in London, England
Source: *ChhPo*

Keene, Laura
English. Actress
First woman theatrical producer in US, 1855-1863; at Ford's Theater starred in *Our American Cousin* the night Lincoln was assassinated.
b. Jul 20, 1820 in London, England
d. Nov 4, 1873 in Montclair, New Jersey
Source: *AmBi; ApCAB; DcAmB; Drake; FamA&A; InWom; NatCAB 8; NotAW; NotNAT A, B; OxThe; PlP&P; TwCBDA; WebAB, 79; WhAm HS*

Keene, Thomas Wallace
American. Actor
Toured Shakespearean plays countrywide, 1880-98.
b. Oct 26, 1840 in New York, New York
d. Jun 1, 1898 in Tompkinsville, New York
Source: *DcAmB; OxThe; TwCBDA; WhAm HS*

Keener, Jefferson Ward
American. Corporation Executive
With BF Goodrich, 1939-74.
b. Aug 6, 1908 in Portersville, Alabama
d. Jan 2, 1981 in Akron, Ohio
Source: *IntWW 74, 75, 76, 77, 78, 79, 80; IntYB 78, 79, 80, 81; NewYTBS 81; St&PR 75; WhoAm 74; WhoF&I 74; WhoWor 74*

Keeshan, Bob
"Captain Kangaroo"
American. TV Personality, Author
Star of "Captain Kangaroo," 1955-81, longest-running children's program in network history.
b. Jun 27, 1927 in Lynbrook, New York
Source: *BioNews 74; ConAu 5NR; CurBio 65; IntMPA 80, 81, 82; LesBEnT; NewYTBE 72; PseudN 82; WhoAm 80, 82; WhoTelC*

Kefauver, Estes
American. Senator
b. Jul 26, 1903 in Madisonville, Tennessee
d. Aug 10, 1963 in Bethesda, Maryland
Source: *AmAu&B; CurBio 49, 63; WhAm 4; WhScrn 77*

Kehoe, Vincent Jeffre-Roux
American. Army Officer
b. 1922
Source: *BioIn 10*

Keilberth, Joseph
German. Conductor
b. Apr 19, 1908 in Karlsruhe, Germany
d. Jul 7, 1968 in Munich, Germany (West)
Source: *WhAm 5*

Keillor, Garrison (Gary Edward)
American. Writer, Producer
Created radio program "A Prairie Home Companion" about Lake Wobegon, MN; wrote *Lake Wobegon Days,* 1985.
b. Aug 7, 1942 in Anoka, Minnesota
Source: *ConAu 117; WhoMW 76*

Keino, Kip (Hezekiah Kipchoge)
"The Flying Policeman"
Kenyan. Track Athlete
b. Jan 17, 1940 in Kaptagunyo, Kenya
Source: *CurBio 67; PseudN 82; WhoTr&F 73*

Keiser, Reinhard
German. Composer
Best known for opera, oratorio compositions.
b. Jan 9, 1674 in Teuchern, Germany
d. Sep 12, 1739 in Hamburg, Germany
Source: *Baker 78; NewEOp 71; OxMus*

Keitel, Harvey
American. Actor
Best known films include *Mean Streets,* 1973; *Alice Doesn't Live Here Anymore,* 1975; *Taxi Driver,* 1976.
b. 1941 in Brooklyn, New York
Source: *IntMPA 77, 78, 79, 80, 81, 82; MovMk; WhoAm 82; WhoHol A*

Keitel, Wilhelm
"Lakaitel"
German. Nazi War Criminal
b. Sep 22, 1882
d. Oct 16, 1946 in Nuremberg, Germany
Source: *CurBio 40, 46; PseudN 82*

Keith, Benjamin F
American. Entertainer
b. 1846 in Hillsboro, New Hampshire
d. Mar 26, 1914
Source: *BiDAmBL 83; DcAmB; NatCAB 15;*
NotNAT B; OxThe; WhAm 1; WhoStg 1906,
1908

Keith, Brian
[Robert Keith, Jr.]
American. Actor
Played Uncle Bill on TV series "Family
Affair," 1966-71.
b. Nov 14, 1921 in Bayonne, New Jersey
Source: *FilmgC; IntMPA 77, 78, 79, 80, 81,*
82; MotPP; MovMk; PseudN 82; WhoAm 82;
WorEFlm

Keith, David
American. Actor
In films *An Officer and a Gentleman*, 1982;
The Lords of Discipline, 1983.
b. 1954 in Knoxville, Tennessee
Source: *IntMPA 84; VarWW 85*

Keith, Ian
[Keith Ross]
American. Actor
Broadway matinee idol; supporting actor,
1924-56, in films *Abraham Lincoln*, 1930;
The Ten Commandments, 1956; *Cleopatra*,
1963.
b. Feb 27, 1899 in Boston, Massachusetts
d. Mar 26, 1960 in New York, New York
Source: *Film 2; FilmgC; MotPP; MovMk;*
ObitOF 79; PseudN 82; TwYS; WhScrn 74,
77; WhThe; WhoHol B

Keith, Minor Cooper
American. Industrialist, Railroad Executive
Built railroads, developed banana plantations
in Costa Rica; founded United Fruit Co.,
1899.
b. Jan 19, 1848 in New York, New York
d. Jun 14, 1929
Source: *AmBi; ApCAB X; BiDAmBL 83;*
DcAmB; EncLatA; McGEWB; NatCAB 14,
22; NewCol 75; WhAm 1

Keith, William
American. Artist
Prolific painter of colorful CA landscapes;
2,000 works destroyed in 1906 fire.
b. 1839 in Aberdeen, Scotland
d. 1911 in Berkeley, California
Source: *ArtsAmW 1; DcAmArt; DcAmB;*
EarABI, SUP; IlBEAAW; McGDA; NatCAB
13; NewYHSD; REnAW; WhAm 1

Keker, Samuel J
American. Business Executive
b. 1917
Source: *St&PR 75*

Kekkonen, Urho Kaleva
Finnish. Political Leader
Pres. of Finland, 1956-82, known for skilled
neutrality, friendship with USSR.
b. Aug 3, 1900
d. Aug 31, 1986 in Helsinki, Finland
Source: *CurBio 50, 86; IntWW 81; IntYB 80,*
81; NewYTBS 75; WhoGov 72; WhoWor 80,
82

Kell, George Clyde
American. Baseball Player, Sportscaster
Third baseman, 1943-57; won AL batting
title, 1949.
b. Aug 23, 1922 in Swifton, Arkansas
Source: *BaseEn 85*

Kell, Reginald George
English. Musician
b. 1918 in Newark, England
Source: *WhoMus 72*

Kell, Vernon, Sir
English. Government Official
First director of MI 5, 1909-40, British
equivalent of FBI.
b. 1873 in Yarmouth, England
d. 1942
Source: *BioIn 8; HisEWW; SpyCS*

Kelland, Clarence Budington
American. Author
b. Jul 11, 1881 in Portland, Michigan
d. Feb 18, 1964 in Scottsdale, Arizona
Source: *AmAu&B; ConAu 89; OxAmL; REn;*
REnAL; TwCA, SUP; WhAm 4; WhNAA

Kellaway, Cecil
American. Actor
Oscar nominee *The Luck of the Irish*, 1948;
Guess Who's Coming to Dinner, 1967.
b. Aug 22, 1893 in Capetown, South Africa
d. Feb 28, 1973 in Los Angeles, California
Source: *FilmgC; MovMk; NewYTBE 73;*
ObitOF 79; Vers A; WhScrn 77; WhoHol B;
WorAl

Kellems, Vivien
American. Manufacturer, Engineer
b. Jun 7, 1896 in Des Moines, Iowa
d. Jan 25, 1975 in Santa Monica, California
Source: *CurBio 48; InWom; WhAm 6*

Keller, Arthur C
American. Inventor
Invention of moving-coil playback stylus
made hi-fi records possible.
b. Aug 18, 1901 in New York, New York
d. Aug 25, 1983 in Bronxville, New York
Source: *AmM&WS 79P; NewYTBS 83*

Keller, Gottfried
Swiss. Author
b. Jul 19, 1819 in Zurich, Switzerland
d. Jul 16, 1890 in Kilchberg, Switzerland
Source: *BbD; BiD&SB; CasWL; ChhPo S2;
ClDMEL; CyWA; DcEuL; EuAu; EvEuW;
OxGer; PenC EUR; REn*

Keller, Helen Adams
American. Author, Lecturer
How she learned to speak, write despite
being blind, deaf told in *The Miracle
Worker,* 1962.
b. Jun 27, 1880 in Tuscumbia, Alabama
d. Jun 1, 1968 in Westport, Connecticut
Source: *AmAu&B; ConAu 101, 89; CurBio
42, 68; DcLEL; HerW; InWom; LinLib L, S;
LongCTC; ObitOF 79; OxAmL; REn;
REnAL; WebAB; WhDW; WhAm 5; WhNAA;
WhoHol B; WomWWA 14; WorAl*

Keller, Marthe
Swiss. Actress
Films include *Marathon Man; Bobby
Deerfield; Fedora.*
b. 1946 in Basel, Switzerland
Source: *IntMPA 82; WhoAm 82, 84; WhoHol
A*

Kellerman, Annette
"The Diving Venus"; "The Million Dollar
Mermaid"
Australian. Swimmer, Actress
b. Jul 6, 1888 in Sydney, Australia
d. Oct 30, 1975 in Southport, Australia
Source: *FilmgC; InWom; PseudN 82; TwYS;
WhScrn 77*

Kellerman, Sally
American. Actress
Oscar nominee for role of Hot Lips
Houlihan in film *M*A*S*H,* 1970.
b. Jun 2, 1937 in Long Beach, California
Source: *FilmgC; IntMPA 80, 81, 82; MovMk;
NewYTBS 80; WhoAm 80, 82; WhoHol A;
WhoWest 82, 84; WorAl*

Kelley, Clarence Marion
American. Government Official
First permanent FBI director since death of
J Edgar Hoover, 1973-78.
b. Oct 24, 1911 in Kansas City, Missouri
Source: *BioNews 74; CurBio 74; IntWW 82;
IntYB 81, 82; NewYTBE 73; WhoAm 78;
WhoAmP 73; WhoGov 77*

Kelley, DeForrest
American. Actor
Played Dr. McCoy in TV series, film *Star
Trek,* 1967-69.
b. 1920 in Atlanta, Georgia
Source: *Film 2; MotPP; WhoHol A*

Kelley, Edgar Stillman
American. Composer
Wrote "Alice in Wonderland" suite, 1919;
"Gulliver" symphony, 1936.
b. Apr 14, 1857 in Sparta, Wisconsin
d. Nov 12, 1944 in New York, New York
Source: *Baker 78; CurBio 45; DcAmB S3;
NatCAB 11*

Kelley, Frank Joseph
American. Public Official
Dem. attorney general of MI.
b. Dec 31, 1924 in Detroit, Michigan
Source: *St&PR 84; WhoAm 82, 84*

Kelley, Joe (Joseph James)
American. Baseball Player
Forgotten star of great 19th c. Baltimore
teams; Hall of Fame, 1971.
b. Dec 9, 1871 in Cambridge, Massachusetts
d. Aug 14, 1943 in Baltimore, Maryland
Source: *BaseEn 85; BasesB*

Kelley, Kitty
American. Author
Wrote *Jackie Oh,* 1978; editor, weekly
column "Today Is Sunday."
b. Apr 4, 1942 in Spokane, Washington
Source: *BioIn 11; ConAu 81; WhoAm 80, 82*

Kellin, Mike
[Myron Kellin]
American. Actor
Won 1976 Obie for *American Buffalo.*
b. Apr 26, 1922 in Hartford, Connecticut
d. Aug 26, 1983 in Nyack, New York
Source: *BiE&WWA; NewYTBS 83; NotNAT;
PseudN 82; WhoAm 80, 82; WhoHol A;
WhoThe 81*

Kellogg, Clara Louise
American. Opera Singer, Manager
Soprano who pioneered singing operas in
English.
b. Jul 12, 1842 in Sumterville, South
Carolina
d. May 13, 1916 in New Haven, Connecticut
Source: *AmBi; AmWom; ApCAB; DcAmB;
DcNAA; Drake; InWom; NotAW; TwCBDA;
WhAm 1; WomWWA 14*

Kellogg, Frank Billings
American. Statesman
b. Dec 22, 1856 in Potsdam, New York
d. Dec 21, 1937 in Saint Paul, Minnesota
Source: *AmBi; BiDrAC; BiDrUSE; DcAmB
S2; EncAB-H; WebAB; WhAm 1; WhAmP*

Kellogg, Howard
American. Manufacturer
b. Mar 26, 1881 in Buffalo, New York
d. 1969
Source: *WhAm 6*

Kellogg, John Harvey
American. Surgeon, Inventor
Developed grain cereal flakes, late 1800s.
b. Feb 26, 1852 in Battle Creek, Michigan
d. Jan 16, 1943 in Battle Creek, Michigan
Source: *CurBio 44; DcAmB S3; DcNAA;
WhAm 2*

Kellogg, Will Keith
American. Businessman
Started Battle Creek Toasted Corn Flake Co.,
1906; later became W K Kellogg Co.
b. Apr 7, 1860 in Battle Creek, Michigan
d. Oct 6, 1951 in Battle Creek, Michigan
Source: *DcAmB S5; WebAB; WhAm 3*

Kelly, Colin Purdie
American. Aviator
b. 1915
d. Dec 7, 1941
Source: *BioIn 1, 7*

Kelly, Ellsworth
American. Artist
Painter, sculptor known for irregular
geometric forms in bright colors on huge
canvases.
b. May 31, 1923 in Newburgh, New York
Source: *CurBio 70; DcCAr 81; McGDA;
McGEWB; NewYTBS 80; OxTwCA; PrintW
83; WhoAm 82, 84; WhoAmA 82, 84*

Kelly, Emmett
"Weary Willie"
American. Clown
Created character of "Weary Willie," 1931.
b. Dec 9, 1898 in Sedan, Kansas
d. Mar 28, 1979 in Sarasota, Florida
Source: *ConAu 85; CurBio 54; FilmgC;
WebAB; WhoAm 74; WhoHol A*

Kelly, Gene
[Eugene Curran]
American. Dancer, Actor
Starred in *An American in Paris,* 1951;
Singing in the Rain, 1952.
b. Aug 23, 1912 in Pittsburgh, Pennsylvania
Source: *BiDFilm; BiE&WWA; BkPepl; CelR;
CmMov; CurBio 45; EncMT; FilmgC;
IntMPA 75, 76, 77, 78, 79, 80, 81, 82;
IntWW 74; MotPP; MovMk; NotNAT;
OxFilm; PIP&P; WhoAm 74, 76, 78, 80, 82;
WhoHol A; WhoThe 77A; WorEFlm*

Kelly, George Edward
American. Dramatist
b. Jan 6, 1887 in Philadelphia, Pennsylvania
d. Jun 18, 1974
Source: *AmAu&B; AuNews 1; BiE&WWA;
CnDAL; CnMD; ConAmA; ConAmL; ConAu
49; DcLEL; LongCTC; McGEWD; ModAL;
ModWD; OxAmL; OxThe; REn; REnAL;
TwCA, SUP; WhAm 6; WomWMM*

Kelly, George Lange
American. Baseball Player
First baseman, outfielder; only player ever to
hit home runs in three consecutive innings;
Hall of Fame, 1973.
b. Sep 10, 1895 in San Francisco, California
d. Oct 13, 1984 in San Francisco, California
Source: *BaseEn 85; BasesB*

Kelly, Grace Patricia
[Princess Grace Grimaldi; Princess Grace of
Monaco]
American. Actress, Princess
Won 1954 Oscar for *The Country Girl;*
married Prince Rainier, Apr 18, 1956.
b. Nov 12, 1929 in Philadelphia,
Pennsylvania
d. Sep 14, 1982 in Monte Carlo, Monaco
Source: *AmPS; AnObit 1982; BiDFilm;
BiE&WWA; BioNews 74; BkPepl; CelR;
CmMov; ConAu 107; CurBio 55, 77, 82;
FilmgC; GoodHs; HerW; InWom; IntMPA 80,
81, 82; IntWW 78; LibW; MotPP; MovMk;
NewYTBS 82; NotNAT; OxFilm; WebAB;
WhoAm 74, 80, 82; WhoAmW 79; WhoHol
A; WhoWor 78; WorAl; WorEFlm*

Kelly, Jack
American. Actor
Played in TV series "Maverick," 1957-62.
b. 1927 in Astoria, New York
Source: *FilmgC; WhoHol A*

Kelly, John Brenden
American. Sportsman, Celebrity Relative
Father of Princess Grace; won gold medals
in sculling, 1920, 1924 Olympics.
b. Oct 4, 1890 in Philadelphia, Pennsylvania
d. Jun 20, 1960 in Philadelphia, Pennsylvania
Source: *DcAmB S6; ObitOF 79; WhoAm 80,
82, 84*

Kelly, John Brenden, Jr.
American. Olympic Official, Celebrity
Relative
Brother of Princess Grace; sculling champion,
pres., US Olympic Committee, 1984-85.
b. May 24, 1927 in Philadelphia,
Pennsylvania
d. Mar 2, 1985 in Philadelphia, Pennsylvania
Source: *CurBio 71, 85; WhoAm 82, 84;
WhoAmP 79; WhoE 75*

Kelly, "King" (Michael Joseph)
American. Baseball Player
Baseball's first matinee idol; credited with
head-first slide, hit-and-run play; Hall of
Fame, 1945.
b. Dec 31, 1857 in Lansingburgh, New York
d. Nov 8, 1894 in Boston, Massachusetts
Source: *BaseEn 85; BasesB*

Kelly, "Machine Gun" (George R)
[E W Moore; J C Tichenor]
American. Criminal
Public Enemy Number One, 1930s; died
serving life term for 1933 kidnapping of
Charles F. Urschel.
b. 1897 in Tennessee
d. Jul 18, 1954 in Leavenworth, Kansas
Source: *BioIn 2, 3; Blood&B; DcAmB S5;
DrInf; ObitOF 79; WorAl*

Kelly, Michael
Irish. Opera Singer
b. Dec 25, 1762 in Dublin, Ireland
d. Oct 9, 1826 in Margate, England
Source: *Alli*

Kelly, Nancy
American. Actress
Won Tony for *The Bad Seed,* 1955; also
played the same role in film, 1956.
b. Mar 25, 1921 in Lowell, Massachusetts
Source: *BiE&WWA; CurBio 55; Film 2;
FilmgC; InWom; IntMPA 79, 80, 81, 82;
MotPP; MovMk; NotNAT; ThFT; WhoAm 74;
WhoHol A; WhoThe 77, 81*

Kelly, Ned (Edward)
Australian. Outlaw
Folk-hero, bankrobber, killer; hanged at 26.
b. 1854 in Beveridge, Australia
d. Nov 11, 1880 in Melbourne, Australia
Source: *DrInf; WhDW*

Kelly, Orie R
American. Banker
b. Jun 5, 1890 in Butte, Montana
d. Jul 4, 1969
Source: *BioIn 8; WhAm 5*

Kelly, "Patsy" (Sarah Veronica Rose)
American. Comedienne
Film comedienne, 1930s-40s; won Tony for
Broadway revival: *No, No, Nanette,* 1971.
b. Jan 12, 1910 in Brooklyn, New York
d. Sep 24, 1981 in Hollywood, California
Source: *BioIn 7; CelR; EncMT; FilmgC;
InWom; MotPP; MovMk; PIP&P; PseudN 82;
ThFT; WhoHol A; WhoThe 77*

Kelly, Paul
American. Actor
Child star, supporting actor, 1908-56, who
served two years in prison for
manslaughter, 1920s.
b. Aug 9, 1899 in New York, New York
d. Nov 6, 1956 in Los Angeles, California
Source: *Film 1; FilmgC; HolP 30; MovMk;
TwYS; WhAm 3; WhScrn 74, 77; WhoHol B*

Kelly, Petra Karin
German. Politician
Spokesman, strategist for W German political
party, the "Greens."
b. Nov 29, 1947 in Gunzberg, Germany
(West)
Source: *CurBio 84; NewYTBS 83*

Kelly, "Shipwreck" (Alvin A)
American. Eccentric
Spent total of 20,163 hrs. sitting atop
flagpoles.
b. May 13, 1893
d. Oct 11, 1952 in New York, New York
Source: *BioIn 3; WebAB*

Kelly, Stephen Eugene
American. Publisher
b. May 13, 1919 in Brooklyn, New York
d. Apr 6, 1978 in New York, New York
Source: *ConAu 104, 110; NatCAB 61;
NewYTBS 78; WhAm 7; WhoAm 76, 78*

Kelly, Walt
American. Cartoonist
Created comic strip "Pogo," 1943, nationally
 syndicated, 1949.
b. Aug 25, 1913 in Philadelphia,
 Pennsylvania
d. Oct 18, 1973 in Hollywood, California
Source: *AmAu&B; AmSCAP 66; CelR; ConAu
45, 73; CurBio 56, 73; IlsBYP; NewYTBE 73;
REnAL; SmATA 18; WhAm 6; WhoAm 74*

Kelly, Walter C
['The Virginia Judge']
American. Actor
Uncle of Grace Kelly; nickname comes from
 stage, film role.
b. Oct 29, 1873 in Mineville, New York
d. Jan 6, 1939 in Philadelphia, Pennsylvania
Source: *ObitOF 79; WhScrn 74, 77; WhoHol
B*

Kelly, William
American. Inventor
Developed converter for changing iron into
 steel, 1857.
b. Aug 21, 1811 in Pittsburgh, Pennsylvania
d. Feb 11, 1888 in Louisville, Kentucky
Source: *AmBi; ApCAB; DcAmB; EncAB-H;
TwCBDA; WebAB; WhAm HS*

Kelman, Charles David
American. Surgeon
Pioneer in cataract surgery who developed
 Kelman lenses inserted in eye following
 surgery.
b. May 23, 1930 in Brooklyn, New York
Source: *ConAu 110; CurBio 84; WhoAm 80;
WhoWor 80*

Kelsen, Hans
Czech. Educator, Lawyer, Author
Known for doctrine on pure law, 1911.
b. Oct 11, 1881 in Prague, Austria-Hungary
d. Apr 19, 1973
Source: *ConAu 115; CurBio 57, 73; WebAB*

Kelser, Greg(ory)
"Special K"
American. Basketball Player
b. Sep 17, 1957 in Panama City, Florida
Source: *OfNBA 81; PseudN 82*

Kelsey, Alice Geer
American. Author
b. Sep 21, 1896 in Danvers, Massachusetts
Source: *AnCL; Au&Wr 71; AuBYP; ConAu
5R; ForWC 70; MorJA; SmATA 1; WrDr 80*

Kelsey, Linda
American. Actress
Played Billie on TV series "Lou Grant,"
 1977-82.
b. Jul 28,
Source: *WhoAm 82*

Kelton, Pert
American. Actress
Stage, film comedienne who played stool
 pigeon in *Mary Burns-Fugitive*, 1935.
b. 1907 in Great Falls, Montana
d. Oct 30, 1968 in Westwood, New York
Source: *BiE&WWA; Film 2; FilmgC; MovMk;
NotNAT B; ThFT; WhScrn 74, 77; WhoHol
B*

Kelvin, William Thomson, Baron
Irish. Physicist, Mathematician
Evolved theory of electric oscillation which
 formed basis of wireless telegraphy.
b. Jun 26, 1824 in Belfast, Northern Ireland
d. Dec 17, 1907 in Ayrshire, Scotland
Source: *Alli, SUP; BbD; BiD&SB; BrAu 19;
NewC; NewCol 75; OxEng; WhDW*

Kemal, Mustafa
see: Ataturk, Kemal

Kemble, Charles
English. Actor
Acted with daughter, Fanny, 1829-34; debut
 in *Macbeth*, 1794; actor, manager, Covent
 Garden, 1822-40.
b. Nov 25, 1775 in Brecknock, Wales
d. Nov 12, 1854 in London, England
Source: *Alli, SUP; ApCAB; BiDLA; DcBiPP;
DcEuL; EncWT; FamA&A; LinLib L; NewC;
OxThe; PIP&P; REn*

Kemble, Fanny (Frances Anne)
English. Actress, Author
From English stage family; wrote *Journal of
 a Residence on a Georgia Plantation*,
 which influenced British opinion against
 slavery.
b. Nov 27, 1809 in London, England
d. Jan 15, 1893 in London, England
Source: *Alli, SUP; AmAu; AmAu&B; AmBi;
ApCAB; BiD&SB; BiDSA; BrAu 19; ChhPo,
S2; DcAmB; DcEnA; DcEnL; DcEuL;
DcLEL; EncWT; FamA&A; InWom; NewC;
NotAW; NotNAT A, B; OxAmL; OxEng;
OxThe; WebAB 79; WhAm HS*

Kemble, John Philip
English. Actor
Brother of Charles; London debut, 1783;
  actor, manager, Covent Gardens, 1803-08.
b. Feb 1, 1757 in Prescott, England
d. Feb 26, 1823 in Lausanne, Switzerland
Source: *Alli; BiDLA; DcBiPP; DcEuL;
DcNaB; NewC; OxThe; PIP&P*

Kemble, Sarah
see: Siddons, Sarah

Kemelman, Harry
American. Author
b. Nov 24, 1908 in Boston, Massachusetts
Source: *AmAu&B; AuNews 1; ConAu 9R;
ConLC 2; EncMys; WhoAm 74, 76, 78, 80,
82; WhoWorJ 72; WrDr 76*

Kemp, (Harry) Hibbard
American. Author
b. Dec 15, 1883 in Youngstown, Ohio
d. Aug 6, 1960 in Provincetown,
  Massachusetts
Source: *AmAu&B; ChhPo, S2; ConAmL;
OhA&B; OxAmL; REn; REnAL; WhAm 4*

Kemp, Jack French
American. Congressman, Football Player
Former pro quarterback; congressman from
  NY, 1970--.
b. Jul 13, 1935 in Los Angeles, California
Source: *BioIn 6, 9, 10, 11; CngDr 74; CurBio
80; WhoAm 74; WhoAmP 73; WhoE 74;
WhoGov 75*

Kemp, Steve(n F)
American. Baseball Player
Outfielder, 1977--; signed multi-million dollar
  contract with NY Yankees, 1982.
b. Aug 7, 1954 in San Angelo, Texas
Source: *BaseEn 85*

Kempe, Rudolf
German. Conductor
b. Jun 14, 1910 in Niederpoyritz, Germany
d. May 11, 1976 in Zurich, Switzerland
Source: *IntWW 74; Who 74; WhoMus 72;
WhoWor 78*

Kemper, James S(cott)
American. Insurance Executive
Former head of Kemper Group, large fire,
  casualty co.; founder, pres., Lumberman's
  Mutual Casualty, 1919-45.
b. Nov 18, 1886 in Van Wert, Ohio
d. Sep 17, 1981 in Chicago, Illinois
Source: *BioIn 3, 4, 7; CurBio 41, 81; St&PR
75; WhoAm 74, 76, 78, 80; WhoF&I 74;
WhoIns 75, 76, 77, 78, 79, 80*

Kempff, (Wilhelm) Walter Friedrich
German. Musician, Composer
b. Nov 25, 1895 in Juterbog, Germany
Source: *IntWW 74; Who 74; WhoMus 72*

Kempner, Nan
American. Fashion Editor
Source: *ForWC 70*

Kempson, Rachel
[Mrs. Michael Redgrave]
English. Actress
Films include *Jane Eyre,* 1971; mother of
  Vanessa, Lynn Redgrave.
b. May 28, 1910 in Dartmouth, England
Source: *CnThe; FilmgC; WhoAm 82, 84;
WhoHol A; WhoThe 72, 77, 81*

Kempton, James Murray, Jr.
American. Author
b. 1945
d. Nov 26, 1971 in Colonial Heights,
  Virginia
Source: *ConAu 33R; NewYTBE 71*

Kempton, Jean Goldschmidt
American. Author
b. 1946
d. Nov 26, 1971
Source: *ConAu 33R*

Kendal, Felicity
English. Actress
Known for Shakespearean roles on British
  stage; in film *Henry VIII.*
b. Sep 25, 1946 in Olton, England
Source: *IntWW 82, 83; WhoAm 82, 84;
WhoThe 77, 81*

Kendal, Madge
English. Actress
Twenty-second child of an actor; married
  actor William Kendal.
b. Mar 15, 1848 in Cleethorpes, England
d. Sep 14, 1935 in Chorley Wood, England
Source: *FamA&A; NotNAT B; OxThe;
WhoStg 1908*

Kendal, William Hunter
[William Hunter Grimston]
English. Actor
Acted with wife, Madge, 1869-1908; actor,
  manager, St. James Theater, 1879-88.
b. Dec 16, 1843 in London, England
d. Nov 6, 1917
Source: *NotNAT A, B; OxThe; PseudN 82;
WhAm 1; WhThe; WhoStg 1906, 1908*

Kendall, Edward C(alvin)
American. Biochemist
Shared 1950 Nobel Prize for research in
  cortisone.
b. Mar 8, 1886 in South Norwalk,
  Connecticut
d. May 4, 1972 in Princeton, New Jersey
Source: *ConAu 111; CurBio 72; WebAB;
WhAm 5*

Kendall, John Walker
American. Scientist
b. Mar 19, 1929 in Bellingham, Washington
Source: *AmM&WS 73P*

Kendall, Kay
[Justine McCarthy]
English. Actress
Married, Rex Harrison, 1957-59; starred in
  Genevieve, 1953.
b. 1926 in Hull, England
d. Sep 6, 1959 in London, England
Source: *BiDFilm; CmMov; FilmgC; MotPP;
MovMk; ObitT 1951; PseudN 82; WhScrn 74,
77; WhoHol B; WorAl; WorEFlm*

Kendrick, Eddie
[The Temptations]
American. Singer
Lead tenor, Temptations, 1963-71; successful
  solo career on rhythm and blues charts.
b. Dec 17, 1940 in Union Springs, Alabama
Source: *IlEncBM; RolSEnR 83; WhoBlA
75, 80; WhoRocM 82*

Kendrick, Pearl Luella
American. Biologist
Developed standard DPT shot for diptheria,
  whooping cough, tetanus.
b. Aug 24, 1890 in Wheaton, Illinois
d. Oct 8, 1980 in Grand Rapids, Michigan
Source: *AnObit 1980; WhoAmW 58, 61, 64,
77*

Keniston, Kenneth
American. Educator, Psychologist
b. Jan 6, 1930 in Chicago, Illinois
Source: *AmAu&B; ConAu 25R; WhoAm 74,
76, 78, 80, 82*

Kennan, George Frost
American. Historian, Diplomat
b. Feb 16, 1904 in Milwaukee, Wisconsin
Source: *AmAu&B; ConAu 1R, 2NR; DrAS
74H; EncAB-H; IntWW 74; OxAmL; REnAL;
WebAB; Who 74; WhoAm 74, 76, 78, 80, 82;
WhoHol A; WhoJazz 72; WhoWor 78; WorAu*

Kennedy, Adrienne
American. Dramatist
b. Sep 13, 1931 in Pittsburgh, Pennsylvania
Source: *ConAu 103; CroCD; LivgBAA;
NotNAT; WhoAm 74, 76, 78, 80, 82;
WhoBlA 75; WrDr 76*

Kennedy, Arthur
American. Actor
Won Tony award for *Death of a Salesman,*
  1949.
b. 1904
d. 1975
Source: *BioIn 10; IntMPA 82; WhoAm 80,
82; WhoThe 81; WorAl*

Kennedy, Caroline Bouvier
[Mrs. Edwin Arthur Schlossberg]
American. Celebrity Relative
Daughter of John F Kennedy and Jacqueline
  Onassis.
b. Nov 27, 1957 in Boston, Massachusetts
Source: *BioNews 74; NewYTBE 70*

Kennedy, David Anthony
American. Celebrity Relative
Son of Robert and Ethel Kennedy; died of
  drug overdose.
b. 1955
d. Apr 26, 1984 in Palm Beach, Florida
Source: *NewYTBS 84*

Kennedy, David M
American. Government Official
b. Jul 21, 1905 in Randolph, Utah
Source: *BiDrUSE; CurBio 69; IntWW 74;
Who 74; WhoAm 74; WhoAmP 73; WhoGov
75; WhoS&SW 82; WhoWor 78*

Kennedy, Edgar
American. Actor
Comedian in films since 1914, including *The
  Edgar Kennedy,* series, 1931-48.
b. Apr 26, 1890 in Monterey, California
d. Nov 9, 1948 in Woodland Hills, California
Source: *Film 1; FilmgC; MotPP; MovMk;
NotNAT B; ObitOF 79; TwYS; Vers A;
WhScrn 74, 77; WhoHol B*

Kennedy, Edward Moore
"Ted"
American. Politician
Dem. Senator from MA, 1962--; brother of
  John F Kennedy.
b. Feb 22, 1932 in Brookline, Massachusetts
Source: *BiDrAC; BkPepl; CelR; CngDr 74;
CurBio 63; IntWW 74; NewYTBE 70, 71;
NewYTBS 74; WebAB; WhoAm 74, 76, 78,
80, 82; WhoAmP 73; WhoE 74; WhoGov 75;
WhoWor 78*

Kennedy, Edward Ridgway
American. Publisher
b. 1923
d. Jun 18, 1975 in Cleveland, Ohio
Source: *BioIn 10; ConAu 104; ObitOF 79*

Kennedy, Ethel Skakel
American. Celebrity Relative
Widow of Robert F Kennedy.
b. Apr 11, 1928 in Greenwich, Connecticut
Source: *CelR; InWom; WhoAm 78*

Kennedy, Florynce
American. Lawyer, Feminist
b. Feb 11, 1916 in Kansas City, Missouri
Source: *ForWC 70; LivgBAA*

Kennedy, George
American. Actor
Won 1967 Oscar for *Cool Hand Luke.*
b. Feb 18, 1925 in New York, New York
Source: *CmMov; FilmgC; IntMPA 75, 76, 77, 78, 79, 80, 81, 82; MotPP; MovMk; WhoAm 74, 76, 78, 80, 82; WhoHol A; WorEFlm*

Kennedy, Jacqueline Bouvier
see: Onassis, Jacqueline Lee Bouvier
Kennedy

Kennedy, Jayne
American. Actress
Co-host, CBS *NFL Today;* in film *Body and Soul.*
b. Oct 27, 1951 in Washington, District of Columbia
Source: *VarWW 85*

Kennedy, Joan Bennett
American. Celebrity Relative
Wife of Edward Kennedy, 1958-81; active in Joseph Kennedy Jr. Foundation for Mental Retardation.
b. Sep 5, 1936 in New York, New York
Source: *CelR; WhoAm 80; WhoAmW 74*

Kennedy, John Fitzgerald
"JFK"; "Jack"
American. US President
First Roman Catholic pres., 1961-63; won 1957 Pulitzer for *Profiles in Courage.*
b. May 29, 1917 in Brookline, Massachusetts
d. Nov 22, 1963 in Dallas, Texas
Source: *AmAu&B; AnCL; BiDrAC; BiDrUSE; ChhPo; ConAu 1R, 1NR; CurBio 50, 61, 64; DcPol; EncAB-H; OxAmL; PseudN 82; REn; REnAL; SmATA 11; WebAB; WhDW; WhAm 4; WhAmP; WorAl*

Kennedy, John Fitzgerald, Jr.
"John-John"
American. Celebrity Relative
b. Nov 25, 1960
Source: *BioIn 10*

Kennedy, John Pendleton
[Mark Littleton, pseud.]
American. Author, Politician
US congressman, 1838-45; secretary of Navy, 1852; wrote *Swallow Barn,* 1832.
b. Oct 25, 1795 in Baltimore, Maryland
d. Aug 18, 1870 in Newport, Rhode Island
Source: *AmAu; AmAu&B; AmBi; ApCAB; BbD; BiD&SB; BiDSA; BiDrAC; BiDrUSE; CasWL; PseudN 82; WhAm HS*

Kennedy, Joseph Patrick, Sr.
American. Financier, Diplomat
Ambassador to England, 1938-40; father of Kennedy family.
b. Sep 6, 1888 in Boston, Massachusetts
d. Nov 18, 1969 in Hyannis Port, Massachusetts
Source: *CurBio 40, 70; OxFilm; WhAm 5; WorEFlm*

Kennedy, Joseph Patrick, Jr.
American. Celebrity Relative
Brother of John F Kennedy; movie based on his life *Young Joe, the Forgotten Kennedy,* 1978, starred Peter Strauss.
b. 1915
d. Aug 12, 1944
Source: *BioIn 6, 7, 8, 9; ObitOF 79*

Kennedy, Joseph Patrick, III
American. Politician, Celebrity Relative
Oldest son of Robert Kennedy; running for congressional seat once held by uncle John Kennedy.
b. Sep 24, 1952 in Boston, Massachusetts
Source: *NewYTBE 72; WhoE 83*

Kennedy, Madge
American. Actress
Starred on Broadway in *Poppy,* 1923, with W.C. Fields.
b. 1892 in Chicago, Illinois
Source: *FilmEn; Film 1; MotPP; TwYS; WhoHol A; WhoThe 77A*

Kennedy, Margaret
English. Author
b. Apr 23, 1896 in London, England
d. Jul 31, 1967 in Adderbury, England
Source: *Chambr 3; ChhPo S2; ConAu 25R; DcLEL; EvLB; InWom; LongCTC; McGEWD; ModBrL; ModWD; NewC; OxEng; PenC ENG; REn; TwCA, SUP; TwCWr; WhAm 4, 6*

Kennedy, Moorehead Cowell, Jr.
[The Hostages]
American. Hostage in Iran
b. Nov 5, 1930 in New York
Source: *NewYTBS 81; USBiR 74*

Kennedy, Robert Francis
"Bobby"; "RFK"
American. Lawyer, Senator
US Attorney General, 1961-64; Dem. senator
from NY, 1964-68; brother of John F
Kennedy.
b. Nov 20, 1925 in Brookline, Massachusetts
d. Jun 6, 1968 in Los Angeles, California
Source: *AmAu&B; BiDrUSE; ConAu X, 1NR;
CurBio 58, 68; EncAB-H; PseudN 82;
WebAB; WhAm 5; WhAmP*

Kennedy, Rose Fitzgerald
American. Celebrity Relative
Matriach of politically prominent Kennedy
Family.
b. Jul 22, 1890 in Boston, Massachusetts
Source: *AmCath 80; CelR; ConAu 53; CurBio
70; GoodHs; HerW; HsB&A; InWom;
OhA&B; WhoAm 80, 82, 84; WhoAmW 77*

Kennedy, Tom
American. Actor
Played supporting roles in Keystone
comedies, Laurel and Hardy films, 1915-
65.
b. 1884 in New York, New York
d. Oct 6, 1965 in Woodland Hills, California
Source: *Film 1; TwYS; Vers A; WhScrn 74,
77; WhoHol B*

Kennedy, Walter
American. Basketball Executive
b. Jun 8, 1912 in Stamford, Connecticut
d. Jun 26, 1977 in Stamford, Connecticut
Source: *WhoBbl 73*

Kennedy, William
American. Author
Won 1983 Pulitzer for *Ironweed,* third novel
of Albany trilogy.
b. Jan 16, 1928 in Albany, New York
Source: *ConAu 14NR, 85; ConLC 6, 28, 34;
CurBio 85*

Kennedy, William Patrick (Bill)
American. Football Player
Quarterback, KC Chiefs, 1980--; led league in
pass completions, 1983.
b. Jan 20, 1955 in San Francisco, California
Source: *FootReg 85*

Kennedy, X J, pseud.
[Joseph Charles Kennedy]
American. Author
b. Aug 21, 1929 in Dover, New Jersey
Source: *AmAu&B; ChhPo, S2; ConAu 1R;
ConP 70, 75; DrAP 75; PenC AM; PseudN
82; WhoAm 74, 76, 78, 80, 82; WhoWor 78*

Kennerly, David Hume
American. Photographer
Personal photographer to Gerald Ford, 1974-
77, who won Pulitzer, 1972, for feature
photography of Vietnam war.
b. Mar 9, 1947 in Roseburg, Oregon
Source: *AuNews 2; ConAu 101; MacBEP;
WhoAm 80, 82; WhoWor 80*

Kenneth
[Kenneth Everette Battelle]
American. Hairstylist
Owner, Kenneth Salons and Products, Inc.,
NYC, 1962--.
b. Apr 19, 1927 in Syracuse, New York
Source: *CelR; DcCathB; PseudN 82; WhoAm
80, 82; WorFshn*

Kenney, Douglas C
American. Editor, Screenwriter, Actor
Co-founded, edited *National Lampoon,* 1969-
75; wrote screenplay, appeared in *Animal
House,* 1978.
b. Dec 10, 1947 in Cleveland, Ohio
d. Aug 27, 1980 in Kauai Island, Hawaii
Source: *BioIn 12; ConAu 107*

Kenney, George Churchill
American. Soldier, General
b. Aug 6, 1889 in Yarmouth, Nova Scotia
d. 1974
Source: *BioNews 74; ConAu P-1; CurBio 43,
77N; NewYTBS 77; WhoAm 74; WorAl*

Kenny, Sister Elizabeth
Australian. Nurse
Developed therapy for polio victims, 1933.
b. Sep 20, 1886 in Warrialda, Australia
d. Nov 30, 1952 in Toowoomba, Australia
Source: *CurBio 42, 53; InWom; WhAm 3*

Kenny, Nick
American. Songwriter, Journalist
b. Feb 3, 1895 in Astoria, New York
d. Dec 1, 1975 in Sarasota, Florida
Source: *AmSCAP 66; ChhPo, S1; ConAu 89;
WhScrn 77*

Kensett, John Frederick
American. Artist
b. Mar 22, 1816 in Cheshire, Connecticut
d. Dec 14, 1872 in New York, New York
Source: *AmBi; ApCAB; DcAmB; Drake;
EarABI; TwCBDA; WhAm HS*

Kent, Allegra
American. Ballerina
b. Aug 11, 1938 in Santa Monica, California
Source: *CurBio 70; WhoAm 74*

Kent, Arthur Atwater
American. Industrialist
b. 1873
d. Apr 4, 1949 in Bel Air, California
Source: *BioIn 1, 3*

Kent, Jack (John Wellington)
American. Children's Author, Cartoonist
Drew syndicated comic strip "King Aroo,"
1950-65.
b. Mar 10, 1920 in Burlington, Iowa
d. Oct 18, 1985 in San Antonio, Texas
Source: *ConAu 117*

Kent, James
"The American Blackstone"
American. Lawyer
b. Jul 31, 1763 in Fredericksburg, New York
d. Dec 12, 1847 in New York, New York
Source: *Alli; AmAu; AmAu&B; AmBi;*
ApCAB; BbD; BiAUS; BiD&SB; CyAL 1;
DcAmAu; DcAmB; DcEnL; DcNAA; Drake;
EncAB-H; OxAmL; PseudN 82; REnAL;
TwCBDA; WebAB; WhAm HS

Kent, Rockwell
[William Hogarth, Jr.]
"RK"
American. Author, Artist
Noted for his stark dramatic lithographs,
exotic landscapes.
b. Jun 21, 1882 in Tarrytown, New York
d. Mar 13, 1971 in Plattsburg, New York
Source: *AmAu&B; ConAmA; ConAu 5R, 29R,*
4NR; DcCAA 71; IlsBYP; IlsCB 1744;
OxAmL; PseudN 82; REnAL; SmATA 6;
TwCA, SUP; WebAB; WhAm 5

Kentner, Louis Philip
English. Musician
b. Jul 19, 1905 in Karwin, Silesia
Source: *IntWW 74; Who 74; WhoMus 72;*
WhoWor 78

Kenton, Stan(ley Newcomb)
American. Band Leader
b. Feb 19, 1912 in Wichita, Kansas
d. Aug 25, 1979 in Hollywood, California
Source: *AmSCAP 66; Baker 78; BiDAmM;*
BioNews 74; CmpEPM; CurBio 79; EncJzS
70; IlEncJ; NewYTBS 79; WhoAm 76, 78;
WhoWor 78

Kenty, Hilmer
American. Boxer
b. Jul 30, 1955 in Austin, Texas
Source: *NF*

Kenyatta, Jomo (Johnstone)
[Johstone Kamau; Kamau wa Ngengi]
"Mzee"
Kenyan. President
Terrorist organizer who was first pres. of
Kenya, 1964.
b. Oct 20, 1891 in Kenya
d. Aug 22, 1978 in Mombasa, Kenya
Source: *AfSS 78; AfrA; Au&Wr 71; CurBio*
53, 74, 78; IntWW 74, 75, 76, 77, 78; IntYB
78; LinLib L, S; McGEWB; NewYTBS 78;
ObitOF 79; PseudN 82; WhDW; Who 74;
WhoGov 72; WhoWor 74, 76; WorAl

Keogan, George
American. Basketball Coach
Coach, Notre Dame U, 1924-43.
b. Mar 8, 1890 in Minnesota Lakes,
Minnesota
d. Feb 17, 1943 in South Bend, Indiana
Source: *WhoBbl 73*

Keogh, Eugene James
American. Politician
b. Aug 30, 1907 in Brooklyn, New York
Source: *BiDrAC; St&PR 75; WhoAm 74;*
WhoAmP 73

Keogh, James
American. Journalist
b. Oct 29, 1916 in Platte County, Nebraska
Source: *ConAu 45; IntWW 74; USBiR 74;*
WhoAm 74, 76, 78, 80, 82; WhoE 74;
WhoGov 75

Keokuk
[Kiyo'kaga]
American. Indian Chief
Sauk chief who moved tribe reservation from
Iowa to Kansas, 1845.
b. 1780 in Rock River, Illinois
d. Jun 1848 in Franklin County, Kansas
Source: *AmBi; ApCAB; DcAmB; HarEnUS;*
REnAW; WebAB, 79; WhAm HS

Keon, Dave (David Michael)
Canadian. Hockey Player
Center; scored 498 career goals; won four
Stanley Cups, 1960s; Hall of Fame, 1986.
b. Mar 22, 1940 in Noranda, Quebec
Source: *HocEn*

Keough, Donald Raymond
American. Business Executive
Pres., chief operating officer, Coca-Cola Co.,
1981--; products sold in 155 countries.
b. Sep 4, 1926 in Maurice, Iowa
Source: *ConNews 86-1; St&PR 84; WhoAm
84; WhoF&I 83*

Keough, William Francis, Jr.
[The Hostages]
American. Hostage in Iran
b. 1931
Source: *BioIn 12; NewYTBS 81*

Kepler, Johannes
[John Kepler]
"The Father of Modern Astronomy"
German. Astronomer
Described revolutions of planets around sun
in Kepler's Laws, 1609.
b. Dec 27, 1571 in Weil der Stadt, Germany
d. Nov 15, 1630 in Regensburg, Germany
Source: *BbD; BiD&SB; NewC; PseudN 82;
REn*

Keppard, Freddie
American. Jazz Musician
b. Feb 15, 1899 in New Orleans, Louisiana
d. Jul 15, 1933 in Chicago, Illinois
Source: *WhoJazz 72*

Kerby, William Frederick
American. Businessman
b. Jul 28, 1908 in Washington, District of
Columbia
Source: *IntWW 74; St&PR 75; WhoAm 74;
WhoE 74; WhoF&I 74*

Kercheval, Ken
American. Actor
Plays Cliff Barnes on TV series "Dallas."
b. Jul 15, 1935 in Wolcottville, Tennessee
Source: *VarWW 85*

Kerekou, Mathieu
Beninese. President
b. Sep 2, 1933 in Dahomey (North)
Source: *IntWW 74; WhoWor 78*

Kerensky, Alexander Fedorovitch
[Aleksandr Feodorovich Kerenski]
Russian. Political Leader
Premier, Jul-Nov 1917, whose indecisiveness
enabled Bolsheviks to seize power.
b. Apr 22, 1881 in Simbirsk, Russia
d. Jun 11, 1970 in New York, New York
Source: *CurBio 66, 70; LinLib S; McGEWB;
NewYTBE 70; REn; WhAm 5*

Kerkorian, Kirk
American. Aviator, Airline Executive
b. Jun 6, 1917 in Fresno, California
Source: *BioIn 8; IntMPA 82; WhoAm 82*

Kermode, (John) Frank
English. Educator, Literary Critic
b. Nov 29, 1919 in Isle of Man
Source: *ConAu 1R, 1NR; NewC; Who 74;
WhoWor 78; WorAu; WrDr 80*

Kern, Harold G
American. Newspaper Publisher
b. 1899
d. Feb 10, 1976 in Boston, Massachusetts
Source: *WhAm 6*

Kern, Jerome David
American. Composer
Important in transition from operettas to
modern musical comedies; known for *Show
Boat,* 1927; song "Ol' Man River," 1927.
b. Jan 17, 1885 in New York, New York
d. Nov 11, 1945 in New York, New York
Source: *AmM&WS 73P; AmSCAP 66;
CmMov; CurBio 42, 45; DcAmB S3; EncMT;
FilmgC; LinLib S; McGEWB; McGEWD;
NatCAB 34; NewCBMT; OxAmL; OxFilm;
PIP&P; REn; REnAL; WebAB; WhAm 2*

Kerner, Otto
American. Governor, Judge
b. Aug 15, 1908 in Chicago, Illinois
d. May 9, 1976 in Chicago, Illinois
Source: *CurBio 61; IntWW 74; NewYTBE 73;
WhAm 3, 6; WhoAm 74; WhoGov 75*

Kerouac, Jack
[Jean Louis Lebris de Kerouac; Jean-Louis
Incogniteau]
American. Author, Poet
Leader of Beat Movement; wrote *On the
Road,* 1957.
b. Mar 12, 1922 in Lowell, Massachusetts
d. Oct 21, 1969 in Saint Petersburg, Florida
Source: *AmAu&B; AuNews 1; CasWL;
CnMWL; ConAu 5R, 25R; ConLC 1, 2, 3, 5;
ConNov 76; ConP 70; CurBio 59, 69; EncAB-
H; EncWL; LongCTC; ModAL, S1; OxAmL;
PenC AM; PseudN 82; RAdv 1; REn;
REnAL; TwCWr; WebAB; WebE&AL; WhAm
5; WhoHol B; WhoTwCL; WorAu*

Kerr, Alexander H
American. Manufacturer
Purchased fruit jar patent, 1902, formed co.
which produced jars, lids, caps for
canning.
b. Sep 4, 1862 in Philadelphia, Pennsylvania
d. Feb 9, 1925 in Riverside, California
Source: *Entr; NatCAB 30*

Kerr, Andrew
American. Football Coach
b. Oct 7, 1878 in Cheyenne, Wyoming
d. Mar 1, 1969 in Tucson, Arizona
Source: *WhAm 6; WhoFtbl 74*

Kerr, (Bridget) Jean Collins
American. Author, Humorist
b. Jul 10, 1923 in Scranton, Pennsylvania
Source: *AmAu&B; AmSCAP 66; BiE&WWA;
CelR; ConAu 5R; CurBio 58; InWom;
IntWW 74; NewYTBE 73; NotNAT; OxAmL;
WhoAm 74; WhoThe 77; WhoWor 78;
WorAu; WrDr 80*

Kerr, Clark
American. Educator
b. May 17, 1911 in Reading, Pennsylvania
Source: *AmAu&B; AmEA 74; AmM&WS 73S;
ConAu 45; CurBio 61; EncAB-H; IntWW 74;
LEduc 74, NewYTBE 70; Who 74; WhoAm
74, 76, 78, 80, 82; WhoWest 84; WhoWor 78*

Kerr, Deborah Jane
American. Actress
Starred in *From Here to Eternity*, 1953; *Tea
and Sympathy*, 1956.
b. Sep 30, 1921 in Helensburgh, Scotland
Source: *BiDFilm; BiE&WWA; CelR; CurBio
47; FilmgC; InWom; IntMPA 75, 76, 77, 78,
79, 80, 81, 82; MotPP; MovMk; NotNAT;
OxFilm; PIP&P A; PseudN 82; Who 74;
WhoAm 74, 76, 78, 80, 82; WhoHol A;
WhoThe 77; WorEFlm*

Kerr, Graham
English. Chef, TV Personality
Star of TV series "Galloping Gourmet,"
1969-73; "Take Kerr," 1976--.
b. Jan 22, 1934 in London, England
Source: *ConAu 108; WhoAm 78, 80; WrDr
80, 82, 84*

Kerr, Jean
American. Author, Dramatist
Played lead role in *Tea and Sympathy*,
Broadway, 1953; film, 1956.
b. Jul 10, 1923 in Scranton, Pennsylvania
Source: *AmAu&B; AmSCAP 66; ConAu 5R;
OxAmL; WhoAm 82; WorAu; WrDr 76*

Kerr, John
American. Actor
b. Nov 15, 1931 in New York, New York
Source: *BiE&WWA; FilmgC; IntMPA 82;
NotNAT; WhoAm 74, 76, 78, 80, 82; WhoHol
A*

Kerr, Malcolm (Hooper)
American. Educator, Author
Pres., American U in Beirut; assassinated by
Islamic Jihad.
b. Oct 8, 1931 in Beirut, Lebanon
d. Jan 18, 1984 in Beirut, Lebanon
Source: *ConAu 111; WhoAm 82*

Kerr, Orpheus C
[Robert Henry Newell]
American. Author
b. Dec 13, 1836 in New York, New York
d. Jul 1901
Source: *Alli SUP; AmAu; AmAu&B; BbD;
BiD&SB; ChhPo, S1; CnDAL; DcAmAu;
DcEnL; DcLEL; DcNAA; OxAmL; PseudN
82; REn*

Kerr, Robert Samuel
American. Oilman, Senator
b. Sep 11, 1896 in Ada, Oklahoma
d. Jan 1, 1963 in Washington, District of
Columbia
Source: *BiDrAC; NatCAB 53; ObitOF 79;
WhAm 4; WhAmP; WorAl*

Kerr, Tim
Canadian. Hockey Player
Right wing, center, Philadelphia, 1980--; has
had three consecutive 50-goal seasons,
1983-86.
b. Jan 5, 1960 in Windsor, Ontario
Source: *HocReg 85*

Kerr, Walter Francis
American. Drama Critic, Author
b. Jul 8, 1913 in Evanston, Illinois
Source: *AmAu&B; AmSCAP 66; Au&Wr 71;
BiE&WWA; CelR; ConAu 5R; CurBio 53;
IntWW 74; NotNAT; OxAmL; REnAL;
WhoAm 74, 76, 78, 80, 82; WhoE 74;
WhoThe 77; WhoWor 78; WorAu; WrDr 76*

Kerrey, Bob (Joseph Robert)
American. Politician
Dem. governor of NE, 1983-86; decorated for
bravery during Vietnam War.
b. Aug 27, 1943 in Lincoln, Nebraska
Source: *ConNews 86-1; MedHR*

Kerry, John F
American. Politician
Dem. senator from MA, 1984--.
b. Dec 11, 1943 in Denver, Colorado
Source: *BioIn 10; CngDr 85*

Kershaw, Doug(las James)
American. Musician
Cajun fiddler, known for classic "Louisiana
Man."
b. Jan 24, 1936 in Tel Ridge, Louisiana
Source: *BiDAmM; BioIn 9; ConMuA 80A;
WhoRock 81*

Kert, Larry (Frederick Lawrence)
American. Actor
Appeared on stage in *West Side Story,
Company.*
b. Dec 5, 1930 in Los Angeles, California
Source: *BiE&WWA; EncMT; NotNAT; PIP&P
A; WhoHol A; WhoThe 77, 81; WorAl*

Kertesz, Andre
American. Photographer, Journalist
Pioneered use of 35-mm camera in
photojournalism.
b. Jul 2, 1894 in Budapest, Hungary
d. Sep 27, 1985 in New York, New York
Source: *ConAu 85; ConPhot; CurBio 79, 85;
MacBEP; WhoAm 78*

Kertesz, Istvan
Hungarian. Conductor
b. Aug 29, 1929 in Budapest, Hungary
d. Apr 17, 1973 in Tel Aviv, Israel
Source: *NewYTBE 73; WhoMus 72; WhoWor
78*

Kerwin, Joseph Peter
American. Astronaut, Physician
Member of Skylab I, II space crews.
b. Feb 19, 1932 in Oak Park, Illinois
Source: *AmM&WS 73P; IntWW 74;
NewYTBE 73; WhoAm 74, 76, 78, 80, 82;
WhoS&SW 82*

Kerwin, Lance
American. Actor
Played in TV series "James at 15," 1977-78;
TV movie "Salem's Lot."
b. 1960
Source: *BioIn 11*

Kesey, Ken
American. Author
Wrote *One Flew Over the Cuckoo's Nest,*
1962.
b. Sep 17, 1935 in La Hunta, Colorado
Source: *AmAu&B; CasWL; ConAu 1R;
ConLC 1, 3, 6, 11; ConNov 72, 76; DrAF 76;
EncWL; ModAL S1; PenC AM; RAdv 1;
WebE&AL; WhoAm 74, 76, 78, 80, 82;
WhoTwCL; WrDr 76*

Kesselring, Albert
German. Economist
b. Nov 30, 1887
d. Jul 16, 1960 in Bad Nauheim, Germany
Source: *CurBio 42, 60*

Kesselring, Joseph
American. Dramatist, Architect
b. Jun 21, 1902 in New York, New York
d. Feb 1967
Source: *BioIn 10; NatCAB 53; WhAm 4*

Ketcham, Hank (Henry King)
American. Cartoonist
Created comic strip "Dennis the Menace,"
1952.
b. Mar 14, 1920 in Seattle, Washington
Source: *AmAu&B; CurBio 56; WhoAm 74,
76, 78, 80, 82; WhoAmA 73; WhoWest 84;
WhoWor 78*

Ketchel, Stanley
[Stanislaus Kiecal]
"Cyclone"; "The Michigan Assassin"; "The
Montana Wonder"
American. Boxer
b. Sep 14, 1887 in Grand Rapids, Michigan
d. Oct 15, 1910 in New York, New York
Source: *WhoBox 74*

Kettering, Charles Franklin
"Boss"
American. Engineer
Invented auto self-starter, 1917, replacing
hand crank.
b. Aug 29, 1876 in Loudonville, Ohio
d. Nov 25, 1958 in Dayton, Ohio
Source: *CurBio 40, 51, 59; LinLib S;
NatCAB 48; ObitOF 79; PseudN 82; WebAB;
WhAm 3*

Key, Francis Scott
American. Composer, Lawyer
Wrote "The Star-Spangled Banner," Sep 13-
14, 1814; adopted by Congress as national
anthem, 1931.
b. Aug 1, 1779 in Carroll County, Maryland
d. Jan 11, 1843 in Baltimore, Maryland
Source: *Alli; AmAu; AmAu&B; AmBi;
ApCAB; BbD; BiAUS; BiD&SB; BiDSA;
CnDAL; CyAL 1; DcAmAu; DcAmB; DcLEL;
DcNAA; Drake; EncAB-H; EvLB; OxAmL;
OxEng; PoChrch; REn; REnAL; TwCBDA;
WebAB; WhAm HS*

Key, Valdimer Orlando, Jr.
American. Political Scientist, Author
Wrote *Public Opinion and American Democracy,* 1961.
b. Mar 13, 1908 in Austin, Texas
d. Oct 4, 1963
Source: *DcAmB S7; WebBD 80*

Key, Theodore
American. Cartoonist, Author
Created "Hazel," appearing in *Saturday Evening Post,* 1943-69.
b. Aug 25, 1912 in Fresno, California
Source: *ConAu 13R; WhoAm 82*

Keyes, Evelyn Louise
American. Actress
Artie Shaw's eighth wife; wrote autobiography *Scarlet O'Hara's Younger Sister,* 1977.
b. Nov 20, 1919 in Port Arthur, Texas
Source: *ConAu 85; FilmEn; FilmgC; HalP 40, IntMPA 80, 81, 82; MotPP; MovMk; NewYTBS 77; WhoHol A*

Keyes, Frances Parkinson
American. Author
b. Jul 21, 1885 in Charlottesville, Virginia
d. Jul 3, 1970 in New Orleans, Louisiana
Source: *AmAu&B; AmNov; BiCAW; BkC 5; CathA 1930; CelR; ConAu 5R, 25R; EvLB; InWom; LongCTC; PenC AM; REn; TwCA, SUP; TwCWr; WhAm 5; WhNAA*

Keyes, Roger
British. Naval Officer
b. 1872
d. Dec 26, 1945 in Buckinghamshire, England
Source: *BioIn 10*

Keylor, Arthur W
American. Publisher
Publishes *Life, Fortune;* helped launch *People,* 1974; *Discovery,* 1980.
b. 1920
d. Aug 17, 1981 in Manchester, Vermont
Source: *ConAu 104; Dun&B 79; WhoF&I 74*

Keynes, John Maynard, Baron
English. Economist, Journalist
Best known for *The General Theory of Employment, Interest, and Money,* 1936; theories of unbalanced budgets.
b. Jun 5, 1883 in Cambridge, England
d. Apr 21, 1946 in London, England
Source: *DcLEL; EvLB; LongCTC; NewC; ObitOF 79; OxEng; PseudN 82; REn; TwCA, SUP; WebE&AL; WhDW; WhAm 2; WorAl*

Keys, Ancel Benjamin
American. Physiologist, Author
Nutrition expert; developed WW II K-rations; researched diet, heart disease.
b. Jan 26, 1904 in Colorado Springs, Colorado
Source: *AmM&WS 76P, 79P; BioIn 5, 7; ConAu 61; CurBio 66; WhoWor 74; WrDr 80*

Keyserling, Hermann Alexander
German. Philosopher
b. Jul 20, 1880 in Konno, Russia
d. Apr 26, 1946 in Innsbruck, Austria
Source: *CurBio 46; EvEuW; LongCTC; OxGer; PenC EUR; REn; TwCA, SUP*

Keyserlingk, Robert Wendelin
American. Publisher
b. Nov 2, 1905 in Saint Petersburg, Russia
Source: *CanWW 70, 80, 81, 83; CathA 1952; IntYB 78; WhoF&I 74*

Keyworth, George Albert
American. Government Official
Director, US Office of Science, Technology; adviser to Ronald Reagan, 1981--.
b. Nov 30, 1939 in Boston, Massachusetts
Source: *AmM&WS 82P; CurBio 86; WhoAmP 83; WhoTech 82*

Khaalis, Hamaas Abdul
American. Terrorist
b. 1920
Source: *BioIn 11*

Khachaturian, Aram
[Aram Ilych Khachaturyan]
Russian. Composer
b. Jun 6, 1903 in Tiflis, Russia
d. May 1, 1978 in Moscow, U.S.S.R.
Source: *CurBio 48; DcCM; DcFM; IntWW 74; WhoMus 72*

Khadafy, Moammar
[Moamar al-Gaddafi; Mu'ammar al-Qadhafi]
Liberian. Political Leader
Led military coup against monarchy, 1969; pres., Mar 1977--.
b. 1942 in Misurata, Libya
Source: *CurBio 73; IntWW 80, 81; IntYB 80, 81; MidE 80; WhoGov 72*

Khaikin, Boris
Russian. Conductor
b. 1905
d. May 11, 1978 in Moscow, U.S.S.R.
Source: *BioIn 11; WhoSocC 78*

Khalid Ibn Abdul Aziz Al-Saud
Saudi. Ruler
Ruled Saudi Arabia, 1975-82, following King
Faisal's assassination.
b. 1913 in Riyadh, Saudi Arabia
d. Jun 13, 1982 in Taif, Saudi Arabia
Source: *AnObit 1982; CurBio 76, 82; IntWW
80; MidE 79; NewYTBS 82; WhoGov 72;
WhoWor 80; WorAl*

Khalil, Mustafa
Egyptian. Prime Minister
b. 1920
Source: *BioIn 11*

Khama, Seretse M
Botswana. President
b. Jul 1, 1921 in Serowe, Botswana
d. Jul 13, 1980 in Gaborone, Botswana
Source: *CurBio 67; IntWW 74; Who 74;
WhoWor 78*

Khambatta, Persis
Indian. Actress
Starred in *Star Trek: The Movie,* 1979;
Nighthawks, 1982.
b. Oct 2, 1950 in Bombay, India
Source: *BioIn 12; JohnWSW*

Khan, Ali Akbar
Indian. Musician
b. 1922
Source: *IntWW 74*

Khan, Chaka
[Rufus; Yvette Marie Stevens]
American. Singer, Songwriter
Lead singer with Rufus, 1972-78; solo hit
"Through the Fire," 1985.
b. Mar 23, 1953 in Chicago, Illinois
Source: *IlEncBM 82; InB&W 80; PseudN 82;
RolSEnR 83; WhoBlA 80; WhoRocM 82*

Khan, Fazlur Rahman
American. Architect
Designed Chicago's Sears Tower, tallest
building in world, 1974.
b. Apr 3, 1929 in Dacca, India
d. Mar 27, 1982 in Saudi Arabia
Source: *AnObit 1982; McGMS 80; NewYTBS
82; WhoTech 82*

Khan, Liaquat Ali
[Liaquat Ali Khan]
Pakistani. Political Leader
Head of Moslem League, prime minister of
Pakistan, 1947-51, assassinated.
b. Oct 1, 1895 in Karnal, Pakistan
d. Oct 16, 1951 in Rawalpindi, Pakistan
Source: *CurBio 48, 51; ObitT 1951*

Khan, Princess Yasmin
American. Celebrity Relative
Daughter of Rita Hayworth and Prince Aly
Khan.
b. 1950
Source: *NewYTBS 78*

Kharitonov, Yevgeni
Russian. Poet, Dramatist
Attempted to form experimental literary
workshop which was suppressed by
Soviets, 1980; wrote *Under House Arrest.*
b. 1941
d. Jun 29, 1981 in Moscow, U.S.S.R.
Source: *BioIn 12; NewYTBS 81*

Kharlamov, Valeri
Russian. Hockey Player
Forward, Soviet National hockey team; killed
in car crash.
b. 1947
d. 1981 in U.S.S.R.
Source: *BioIn 12*

Khashoggi, Adnan
Saudi. Businessman
Richest man in world, 1986.
b. Jul 25, 1935 in Mecca, Saudi Arabia
Source: *CurBio 86; NewYTBS 75; WhoArab
81*

Khayyam, Omar
see: Omar Khayyam

Kheel, Theodore Woodrow
American. Lawyer
b. May 9, 1914 in New York, New York
Source: *CurBio 64; NewYTBS 80; St&PR 75;
WhoAm 80, 82, 84; WhoE 74; WhoLab 76*

Khodasevich, Vladislav
Russian. Poet, Critic, Translator
Wrote verse *Putem Zerna,* 1920.
b. May 29, 1886 in Moscow, Russia
d. Jun 14, 1939 in Paris, France
Source: *CasWL; CIDMEL; ConAu 115;
ConLC 15*

Khomeini, Ayatollah Ruhollah
Iranian. Religious Leader
Leader of Shite Moslems in Iran; supported
taking American hostages, 1979.
b. May 17, 1900 in Khomein, Persia
Source: *BioIn 11; BkPepl; CurBio 79*

Khrennikov, Tikhon Nikolaevich
Russian. Composer
b. Jun 10, 1913 in Elets, Russia
Source: *DcCM; IntWW 74; WhoWor 78*

Khrunov, Evgeny
Russian. Cosmonaut
b. Sep 10, 1933
Source: *IntWW 74*

Khrushchev, Nikita Sergeyevich
Russian. Communist Leader
Premier, 1958-64; favored peaceful coexistence
    with the West.
b. Apr 17, 1894 in Kursk, Russia
d. Sep 11, 1971 in Moscow, U.S.S.R.
Source: *ConAu 29R; CurBio 54, 71; LinLib
L, S; ObitOF 79; ObitT 1971; REn; WhDW;
WhAm 5; WorAl*

Khrushchev, Nina Petrovna
Russian. Celebrity Relative
Wife of Nikita Khrushchev, 1924-71; worked
    as teacher.
b. 1900
d. Aug 8, 1984 in Moscow, U.S.S.R.
Source: *InWom*

Khufu
see: Cheops

Kiam, Omar
[Alexander Kiam]
American. Fashion Designer
b. 1894 in Monterrey, Mexico
d. Mar 28, 1954 in New York, New York
Source: *CurBio 45, 54; DcAmB S5; WorFshn*

Kiam, Victor Kermit, II
American. Business Executive
Pres., chief exec., Remington Products, Inc,
    1979--.
b. Dec 7, 1926 in New Orleans, Louisiana
Source: *WhoAm 74, 76, 78, 80, 82; WhoF&I
74*

Kibbee, Guy
American. Actor
Character actor, 1931-49; played title role in
    Scattergood Baines series, 1941-42.
b. Mar 6, 1882 in El Paso, Texas
d. May 24, 1956 in East Islip, New York
Source: *FilmgC; MotPP; MovMk; Vers A;
WhScrn 74, 77; WhoHol B*

Kibbee, Robert Joseph
American. University Administrator
Chancellor, CUNY, NYC, 1971-82; son of
    actor Guy Kibbee.
b. Aug 19, 1920 in New York, New York
d. Jun 16, 1982 in New York, New York
Source: *AnObit 1982; NewYTBE 71;
NewYTBS 82; WhoAm 80, 82; WhoE 74, 81*

Kicknosway, Faye
American. Author
b. Dec 16, 1936 in Detroit, Michigan
Source: *ConAu 57*

Kidd, Michael
[Milton Greenwald]
American. Choreographer
b. Aug 12, 1919 in Brooklyn, New York
Source: *BiE&WWA; CelR; CmMov; CurBio
60; EncMT; FilmgC; NotNAT; PseudN 82;
WhoAm 74, 76, 78, 80, 82; WhoHol A;
WorEFlm*

Kidd, William (Captain)
"The Wizard of the Sea"
Scottish. Pirate
Poe's story *The Gold Bug*, Stevenson's novel
    Treasure Island based on his exploits.
b. 1645 in Greenock, Scotland
d May 23, 1701 in London, England
Source: *Alli; AmBi; ApCAB; DcAmB; Drake;
NewC; OxAmL; PseudN 82; REn; REnAL;
WebAB; WhAm HS*

Kidder, Alfred Vincent
American. Archaeologist
Directed Pecos pueblo project, 1915-29; won
    first Viking Medal, 1946.
b. Oct 29, 1885 in Marquette, Michigan
d. Jun 11, 1963 in Cambridge, Massachusetts
Source: *DcAmB S7; WebBD 80*

Kidder, Margot
American. Actress
Played Lois Lane in movies *Superman*, 1978;
    Superman II, 1981.
b. Oct 17, 1948 in Yellowknife, Northwest
    Territories
Source: *FilmEn; IntMPA 82; WhoAm 82;
WhoHol A*

Kiel, Richard
American. Actor
Stands seven feet, two inches; played part of
    Jaws in James Bond films *The Spy Who
    Loved Me, Moonraker.*
b. in Redford, Michigan
Source: *FilmEn; IntMPA 84; WhoHol A*

Kiely, Benedict
American. Author
b. Aug 15, 1919 in County Tyrone, Northern
    Ireland
Source: *Au&Wr 71; CathA 1952; ConAu 1R;
ConNov 72, 76; WorAu; WrDr 80*

Kienast Family
[Abigail, Amy, Gordon, Sara, and Ted
Kienast]
American. Quintuplets
b. Feb 24, 1970
Source: *BioIn 10*

Kienzl, Wilhelm
Austrian. Composer
b. Jan 17, 1857 in Waizenkircen, Austria
d. Oct 3, 1941 in Vienna, Austria
Source: *NewEOp 71; OxMus*

Kienzle, William X(avier)
[Mark Boyle, pseud.]
American. Author
Former priest who wrote *The Rosary
    Murders*, 1979; *Death Wears a Red Hat*,
    1980.
b. Sep 11, 1928 in Detroit, Michigan
Source: *BioIn 12; ConAu 9NR, 93; ConLC
25; PseudN 82*

Kiepura, Jan
American. Singer
b. May 16, 1902 in Sosnowiec, Poland
d. Aug 15, 1966 in Harrison, New York
Source: *BiE&WWA; CurBio 43, 66; FilmgC;
MovMk; NotNAT A; OxFilm; OxMus; WhAm
4; WhScrn 74, 77; WhoHol B*

Kieran, John Francis
"A Walking Encyclopedia"
American. Journalist, Author, Naturalist, TV
    Personality
Radio, TV panelist of "Information Please"
    from 1938; edited *Information Please
    Almanac*.
b. Aug 2, 1892 in New York, New York
d. Dec 10, 1981 in Rockport, Massachusetts
Source: *AmAu&B; AuBYP; BioIn 1, 2, 3, 4,
5, 7, 8; CathA 1930; ConAu 101; CurBio 40,
82; PseudN 82; REn; REnAL; WhoAm 74,
76, 78; WhoE 74*

Kierkegaard, Soren Aabye
[Soren Aabye Kjerkegaard]
Danish. Philosopher, Author
b. May 5, 1813 in Copenhagen, Denmark
d. Nov 11, 1855 in Copenhagen, Denmark
Source: *AtlBL; BiD&SB; CasWL; CyWA;
DcEuL; EuAu; EvEuW; LongCTC; OxEng;
OxGer; PenC EUR; RComWL; REn*

Kiernan, Walter
American. Radio Commentator
b. Jan 24, 1902 in New Haven, Connecticut
d. Jan 8, 1978 in Daytona Beach, Florida
Source: *ConAu 73; WhoAm 74*

Kiesinger, Kurt Georg
German. Lawyer, Politician
Chancellor, 1966-69.
b. Apr 6, 1904 in Ebingen, Germany
Source: *CurBio 67; IntWW 74, 75, 76, 77,
78, 79, 80, 81; Who 74; WhoWor 78*

Kiick, Jim (James F)
"Butch Cassidy"
American. Football Player
b. Aug 9, 1946 in Lincoln Park, New Jersey
Source: *BioIn 9; PseudN 82; WhoFtbl 74*

Kiker, Douglas
American. Broadcast Journalist, Author
Correspondent, NBC News since 1966;
    author of several books.
b. Jan 7, 1930 in Griffin, Georgia
Source: *Au&Wr 71; ConAu 65; NewYTET;
WhoTelC*

Kiki of Montparnasse
see: Prin, Alice

Kilbracken, John Raymond Godley
English. Author, Rancher
b. Oct 17, 1920 in London, England
Source: *Au&Wr 71; ConAu 5R; PseudN 82;
Who 84*

Kilbride, Percy
American. Actor
Played Pa Kettle in film series, 1947-55.
b. Jul 16, 1888 in San Francisco, California
d. Dec 11, 1964 in Los Angeles, California
Source: *FilmgC; MotPP; MovMk; NotNAT B;
ObitOF 79; Vers A; WhScrn 74, 77; WhoHol
B*

Kilenyi, Edward, Sr.
American. Musician, Composer
b. Jan 25, 1884 in Hungary
Source: *AmSCAP 66*

Kiley, Richard
American. Actor, Singer
Won 1966 Tony Award as Don Quixote in
    Man of La Mancha.
b. Mar 31, 1922 in Chicago, Illinois
Source: *BiE&WWA; BioNews 75; CelR;
CurBio 73; EncMT; FilmgC; IntMPA 75, 76,
77, 78, 79, 80, 81, 82; NotNAT; WhoAm 74,
76, 78, 80, 82; WhoAmP 73; WhoHol A;
WhoThe 77; WhoWor 78*

Kilgallen, Dorothy
[Mrs. Richard Kollmar]
American. Journalist, TV Personality
Reporter, gossip columnist, NY *Journal-American,* beginning 1930s.
b. Jul 3, 1913 in Chicago, Illinois
d. Nov 8, 1965 in New York, New York
Source: *ConAu 89; CurBio 52, 66; InWom; WhAm 4; WhScrn 74, 77; WhoHol B*

Kilgore, Al
American. Cartoonist
Drew "Bullwinkle" comic strip; co-author *Laurel and Hardy.*
b. Dec 19, 1983 in Newark, New Jersey
d. Aug 15, 1983 in New York, New York
Source: *WhoAm 76; WhoAmA 82, 84*

Kilgore, Bernard
American. Journalist
b. Nov 9, 1908
d. Nov 14, 1967 in Princeton, New Jersey
Source: *WhAm 4*

Kilgour, Joseph
Actor
Silent film actor, 1915-26.
b. 1863 in Ayr, Ontario
d. Apr 21, 1933 in Bayshore, New York
Source: *Film 1; NotNAT B; TwYS; WhScrn 77; WhoHol B*

Kilian, Victor
American. Actor
Played the "Fernwood Flasher" on TV series "Mary Hartman, Mary Hartman."
b. Mar 6, 1898 in Jersey City, New Jersey
d. Mar 11, 1979 in Hollywood, California
Source: *BiE&WWA; Film 2; FilmgC; IntMPA 76, 77, 78, 79; MovMk; NewYTBS 79; NotNAT; Vers A; WhoHol A; WhoThe 81N*

Killanin, Michael Morris, Lord
Irish. Olympic Official
b. Jul 30, 1914 in London, England
Source: *BioIn 10; ConAu 5NR; CurBio 73; IntWW 82, 83; NewYTBS 80; Who 82; WhoWor 82*

Killebrew, Harmon Clayton
"Killer"
American. Baseball Player
Outfielder, infielder, 1954-75; hit 573 home runs; Hall of Fame, 1984.
b. Jun 29, 1936 in Payette, Idaho
Source: *BaseEn 85; CurBio 66; PseudN 82; WhoAm 74; WhoProB 73; WorAl*

Killian, James Rhyne, Jr.
"The Father of Public Television"
American. Public Official
Pres., MIT, 1948-58; adviser to Dwight D Eisenhower on science, defense issues.
b. Jul 24, 1904 in Blacksburg, South Carolina
Source: *AmM&WS 82P; ConAu 97; CurBio 49, 59; IntWW 74; LinLib S; PseudN 82; St&PR 75; Who 74; WhoAm 80, 82; WhoWor 80*

Killigrew, Thomas
English. Dramatist
Most popular play comedy *The Parson's Wedding,* 1637; established Drury Lane Theatre, 1663.
b. Feb 7, 1612 in London, England
d. May 19, 1683 in London, England
Source: *BiD&SB; BrAu; CasWL; CnThe; EncWT; NewCol 75; NotNAT B; OxEng; OxThe*

Killy, Jean-Claude
French. Skier
Won three gold medals, 1968 Olympics.
b. Aug 30, 1943 in Saint Cloud, France
Source: *BioNews 74; CelR; CurBio 68; WhoHol A; WhoWor 78*

Kilmer, Billy (William O)
"Whiskey"
American. Football Player
b. Sep 5, 1939 in Topeka, Kansas
Source: *WhoFtbl 74*

Kilmer, Joyce (Alfred Joyce)
American. Poet, Essayist
Wrote poem *Trees,* 1913; killed in WW I.
b. Dec 6, 1886 in New Brunswick, New Jersey
d. Jul 30, 1918 in Seringes, France
Source: *AmAu&B; AmBi; AmLY; AmSCAP 66; ChhPo, S1, S2; CnDAL; ConAmL; DcAmB; DcLEL; DcNAA; EvLB; LongCTC; OxAmL; REn; REnAL; Str&VC; TwCA; WebAB; WhAm 1*

Kilpatrick, James J(ackson)
American. Journalist
Nationally syndicated columnists; gained renown as conservative voice in commentary on "Sixty Minutes."
b. Nov 1, 1920 in Oklahoma City, Oklahoma
Source: *AmAu&B; AuNews 1, 2; ConAu 1R, 1NR; CurBio 80; WhoAm 74, 76, 78, 80, 82; WhoS&SW 82*

Kim Dae Jung
Korean. Politician
Opposition leader who has struggled to
  restore human rights, economic justice to
  S Korea.
b. Jan 6, 1924 in Hayi-do, Korea
Source: *BioIn 12; CurBio 85; IntWW 84;
NewYTBE 71*

Kim, Duk Koo
Korean. Boxer
Died of brain injuries received in title bout
  against Ray Mancini, Nov 6, 1982.
b. 1959
d. Nov 13, 1982 in Las Vegas, Nevada
Source: *NF*

Kim, Il Sung
Korean. Government Official
b. Apr 15, 1912 in Mangyongdae, Korea
Source: *CurBio 51; IntWW 74; NewYTBE 72;
WhoGov 75; WhoWor 78*

Kim, Young Sam
Korean. Politician
b. 1928
Source: *BioIn 10*

Kimball, Fiske
American. Museum Director, Architect
Director, Philadelphia Museum of Art, 1925-
  55; helped restore colonial Williamsburg,
  Monticello.
b. Dec 8, 1888 in Newton, Massachusetts
d. Aug 14, 1955 in Munich, Germany (West)
Source: *AmAu&B; BioIn 4, 5, 7, 10; DcAmB
S5; NatCAB 47; ObitOF 79; WhAm 3*

Kimball, Spencer Woolley
American. Religious Leader
Pres., Mormon Church, 1973-85; called
  America's richest, largest, fastest growing
  church.
b. Mar 28, 1895 in Salt Lake City, Utah
d. Nov 5, 1985 in Salt Lake City, Utah
Source: *ConAu 45; CurBio 79, 86; NewYTBS
74; WhoAm 80, 82; WhoWor 74*

Kimball, William Wallace
American. Merchant, Manufacturer
His co. became largest manufacturer of
  keyboard instruments in world, 1880.
b. Mar 22, 1828 in Oxford County, Maine
d. 1904 in Chicago, Illinois
Source: *Entr; NatCAB 9; WhAm 1*

Kimbrough, Emily
American. Author, Lecturer, Editor
b. Oct 23, 1899 in Muncie, Indiana
Source: *AmAu&B; Au&Wr 71; ConAu 17R;
CurBio 44; InWom; IndAu 1917; OxAmL;
REnAL; SmATA 2; WhoAm 74, 76, 78, 80,
82; WhoWor 78; WorAu; WrDr 80*

Kimmel, Husband Edward
American. Admiral
b. Feb 26, 1882 in Henderson, Kentucky
d. May 15, 1968 in Groton, Connecticut
Source: *CurBio 42, 68; WhAm 5*

Kindler, Hans
Dutch. Conductor, Musician
b. Jan 8, 1893 in Rotterdam, Netherlands
d. Aug 30, 1949 in Watch Hill, Rhode
  Island
Source: *CurBio 46, 49; WhAm 2*

Kiner, Ralph McPherran
"Ozark Ike"
American. Baseball Player, Sportscaster
Outfielder, Pittsburgh, 1946-55; Hall of Fame,
  1977.
b. Oct 27, 1922 in Santa Rita, New Mexico
Source: *BaseEn 85; CurBio 54; PseudN 82;
WhoProB 73*

King, Alan
[Irwin Kniberg]
American. Comedian
b. Dec 26, 1927 in New York, New York
Source: *AmAu&B; CelR; CurBio 70; FilmgC;
IntMPA 75, 76, 77, 78, 79, 80, 81, 82;
PseudN 82; WhoAm 74, 76, 78, 80, 82;
WhoHol A*

King, Alan
see: Ace

King, Albert
[Albert Nelson]
American. Musician
Started guitarist career in 1948; had 1960s
  hit "Born Under A Bad Sign."
b. Apr 25, 1923 in Indianola, Indiana
Source: *EncPR&S 74; IlEncBM 82; IlEncRk;
InB&W 80; NewYTBS 83; PseudN 82*

King, Alberta Christine Williams
American. Celebrity Relative
b. 1904
d. Jun 30, 1974 in Atlanta, Georgia
Source: *InB&W 80; NewYTBS 75; ObitOF 79*

King, Alexander
American. Author, Editor
Best known for anecdotal autobiographies:
Mine Enemy Grows Older, 1958; *I Should Have Kissed Her More*, 1961.
b. Nov 13, 1900 in Vienna, Austria
d. Nov 16, 1965 in New York, New York
Source: *AmAu&B; ConAu 110; ObitOF 79; REnAL; WhAm 4; Who 82, 83*

King, B B (Riley B.)
"The Beale Street Blues Boy"; "The Blues Boy"; "Bassman of the Blues"; "The Boy from Beale Street"; "King of the Blues"
American. Singer, Musician
Frequent Grammy Award winner; more than 50 hit albums include *Six Silver Strings*, 1985.
b. Sep 16, 1925 in Itta Bena, Mississippi
Source: *BioNews 74; CurBio 70; DrBlPA; Ebony 1; PseudN 82; WhoAm 80, 82, 84; WhoBlA 75; WorAl*

King, Ben E
[The Drifters; Benjamin Earl Nelson]
American. Musician, Singer
b. Sep 28, 1938 in Henderson, North Carolina
Source: *EncPR&S 74; InB&W 80; PseudN 82; WhoRock 81; WhoRocM 82*

King, Billie Jean
[Billie Jean Moffitt]
American. Tennis Player
Most famous woman tennis player ever; won record 20 Wimbledon titles.
b. Nov 22, 1943 in Long Beach, California
Source: *BioNews 74; BkPepl; CelR; ConAu 53; CurBio 67; HerW; InWom; NewYTBE 70; NewYTBS 75, 80; SmATA 12; WhDW; WhoAm 82, 84; WorAl*

King, Cammie
American. Actress
Played Bonnie Blue Butler in *Gone with the Wind*, 1939.
b. Aug 5, 1934 in Los Angeles, California
Source: *What 8; WhoHol A*

King, Carole
[Carole Klein]
American. Singer, Songwriter
Won four Grammys, 1972, for album *Tapestry*.
b. Feb 9, 1941 in Brooklyn, New York
Source: *BkPepl; CelR; CurBio 74; NewYTBE 70; PseudN 82; WhoAm 74, 76, 78, 80, 82*

King, Charles
American. Actor
Song, dance man in film musical *Broadway Melody*, 1929.
b. Oct 31, 1894 in New York, New York
d. Jan 11, 1944 in London, England
Source: *EncMT; FilmgC; NotNAT B; TwYS; WhScrn 74, 77; WhThe; WhoHol B; WisWr*

King, Clarence
American. Geologist
b. Jan 6, 1842 in Newport, Rhode Island
d. Dec 24, 1901 in Phoenix, Arizona
Source: *Alli SUP; AmAu; AmAu&B; AmBi; ApCAB; BiD&SB; DcAmAu; DcAmB; DcNAA; OxAmL; REn; REnAL; TwCBDA; WebAB; WhAm 1*

King, Claude
American. Musician
b. Feb 5, 1933 in Shreveport, Louisiana
Source: *EncFCWM 69*

King, Coretta Scott
American. Celebrity Relative
Widow of Martin Luther King, Jr.
b. Apr 27, 1927 in Marion, Alabama
Source: *Au&Wr 71; CelR; ConAu 29R; CurBio 69; HerW; InB&W 80; LivgBAA; NewYTBE 72; WhoAm 80, 82, 84; WhoAmW 77; WhoBlA 75; WhoS&SW 73; WhoWor 74; WorAl*

King, Dennis
[Dennis Pratt]
American. Actor
Co-star with Jeanette MacDonald in *The Vagabond King*.
b. Nov 2, 1897 in Coventry, England
d. May 21, 1971 in New York, New York
Source: *BiE&WWA; EncMT; FilmEn; FilmgC; PseudN 82; WhAm 5; WhScrn 74, 77; WhoHol B*

King, Don(ald)
American. Boxing Promoter
Former convict who became millionaire arranging fights such as Ali-Fraazier's "Thrilla in Manila," 1975.
b. Dec 6, 1932 in Cleveland, Ohio
Source: *BioIn 10; CurBio 84*

King, Ernest Joseph
[Colleen, code name]
American. Admiral
b. Nov 23, 1878 in Lorain, Ohio
d. Jun 25, 1956 in Portsmouth, New Hampshire
Source: *CurBio 42, 56; EncAB-H; PseudN 82; WebAB; WhAm 3*

King, Evelyn
"Champagne"
American. Singer
Recorded disco hit "Shame," 1977.
b. Jul 1, 1960 in Bronx, New York
Source: *RkOn 85*

King, Francis Henry
[Frank Cauldwell, pseud.]
Swiss. Author
b. Mar 4, 1923 in Adelbosen, Switzerland
Source: *Au&Wr 71; ConAu 1R, 1NR; ConLC
8; ConNov 72, 76; ConP 70; NewC; PseudN
82; TwCWr; Who 74; WhoTwCL; WorAu;
WrDr 80*

King, Frank
American. Cartoonist
b. Apr 9, 1883 in Cashon, Wisconsin
d. Jun 24, 1969 in Winter Park, Florida
Source: *WebAB*

King, Grace Elizabeth
American. Author
Wrote local history novels: *Pleasant Ways of
St. Medard,* 1916.
b. 1852 in New Orleans, Louisiana
d. Jan 12, 1932 in New Orleans, Louisiana
Source: *ConAu 116; DcLB 12; OxAmL 83*

King, Henry
American. Director
Co-founder, Academy of Motion Picure Arts
& Sciences; organizer of Oscars; films
include *Carousel,* 1956.
b. Jan 24, 1896 in Christianburg, Virginia
d. Jun 29, 1982 in Toluca Lake, California
Source: *AnObit 1982; BiDAmM; CmMov;
ConAu 89; DcFM; Film 1; FilmgC; IntMPA
79, 81, 82; MovMk; NewYTBS 82; OxFilm;
WhAm 8; WorEFlm*

King, James Ambros
American. Opera Singer
b. May 22, 1925 in Dodge City, Kansas
Source: *WhoAm 74, 76, 78, 80, 82; WhoMus
72*

King, Larry
[Larry Zeiger]
American. Radio Performer, TV Personality
Hosts all-night nat'l. radio talk show, "The
Larry King Show!"
b. Nov 19, 1933 in Brooklyn, New York
Source: *ConAu 111; WhoTelC*

King, Martin Luther, Jr.
[Michael Luther King, Jr.]
"The Prince of Peace"
American. Clergyman, Civil Rights Leader
Won Nobel Peace Prize, 1964; wrote *Stride
Toward Freedom,* 1958.
b. Jan 15, 1929 in Atlanta, Georgia
d. Apr 4, 1968 in Memphis, Tennessee
Source: *AmAu&B; BlkAWP; ConAu 25R, P-2;
CurBio 57, 65, 68; EncAB-H; NewYTBS 74;
OxAmL; PseudN 82; SmATA 14; WebAB;
WhAm 4A; WhAmP*

King, Martin Luther, Sr.
[Michael Luther King, Sr.]
"Daddy King"
American. Clergyman
Pastor of Ebenezer Baptist Church, Atlanta,
GA who preached non-violence; father of
Martin Luther King, Jr.
b. Dec 19, 1899 in Stockbridge, Georgia
d. Nov 11, 1984 in Atlanta, Georgia
Source: *AnObit 1984; InB&W 80; NewYTBS
84; WhoBlA 75*

King, "Micki" (Maxine Joyce)
American. Olympic Athlete
Won gold medal, springboard diving, 1972
Munich Olympics.
b. 1943
Source: *GoodHs; PseudN 82*

King, Morganna
American. Actress
Played mother of Corleone family in *The
Godfather I, II.*
b. Jun 4, 1930
Source: *WhoAm 84; WhoHol A*

King, Peggy
American. Singer
b. 1931 in Greensburg, Pennsylvania
Source: *InWom; IntMPA 75, 76, 77, 78, 79,
80, 81, 82*

King, Perry
American. Actor
Played in films *Lords of Flatbush; Mandingo;*
TV movies "Captains and Kings";
"Riptide."
b. Apr 30, 1948 in Alliance, Ohio
Source: *FilmEn; IntMPA 80, 81, 84; WhoHol
A*

King, Richard
American. Rancher
Owned nation's largest ranch at time of
death; experimented with cattle breeding.
b. Jul 10, 1824 in Orange County, New
York
d. Apr 14, 1885 in Corpus Christi, Texas
Source: *DcAmB; NatCAB 8; OxAmH;
WebAB; WhAm HS; WorAl*

King, Rufus
American. Statesman
b. Mar 24, 1755 in Scarboro, Maine
d. Apr 29, 1827 in Jamaica, New York
Source: *AmAu&B; AmBi; ApCAB; BiAUS;
BiDrAC; DcAmB; Drake; TwCBDA; WebAB;
WhAm HS; WhAmP*

King, Stephen Edwin
American. Author
Master of popular horror tales: *Carrie*, 1974;
The Shining, 1976; *Cujo*, 1981; *It*, 1986.
b. Sep 21, 1947 in Portland, Maine
Source: *ConAu 61; ConLC 12; CurBio 81;
EncSF; NewYTBS 79; ScF&FL 1, 2; SmATA
9; WhoAm 84; WhoHr&F; WhoS&SW 78*

King, Thomas Starr
American. Author, Clergyman
Unitarian minister; described beauty of
American landscape in *White Hills*, 1860.
b. Dec 17, 1824 in New York, New York
d. Mar 4, 1864 in San Francisco, California
Source: *Alli SUP; AmAu&B; AmBi; ApCAB;
BbD; BiD&SB; ChhPo S1; CyAL 2; DcAmAu;
DcAmB; DcNAA; Drake; OxAmL; REnAL;
TwCBDA; WhAm HS*

King, Walter Woolf
[Walter Woolf]
American. Actor
Starred in 1930s films.
b. 1899 in San Francisco, California
d. Oct 24, 1984 in Beverly Hills, California
Source: *FilmgC; PseudN 82; WhThe; WhoHol
A*

King, Warren Thomas
American. Editor, Cartoonist
b. Jan 3, 1916 in Queens, New York
d. Feb 9, 1978
Source: *WhAm 7; WhoAm 76, 78; WhoAmA
73, 76, 78; WhoE 74; WhoWor 74*

King, Wayne
"The Waltz King"
American. Band Leader
b. Feb 16, 1901 in Savanna, Illinois
d. May 16, 1985 in Phoenix, Arizona
Source: *AmPS B; AmSCAP 66; BiDAmM;
PseudN 82*

King, William
[The Commodores]
American. Singer
b. 1947 in Birmingham, Alabama
Source: *BkPepl*

King, William Lyon Mackenzie
Canadian. Prime Minister, Statesman
Leader of Canadian Liberal party, 1919-48;
prime minister, 1921-30; 1935-48.
b. Dec 17, 1874 in Berlin, Ontario
d. Jul 22, 1950 in Kingsmere, Ontario
Source: *CurBio 40, 50; OxCan; WhAm 3;
WhNAA*

King, William Rufus de Vane
American. Vice-President
Elected with Franklin Pierce; took oath of
office in Cuba where he went to find cure
for TB.
b. Apr 7, 1786 in Sampson County, North
Carolina
d. Apr 18, 1853 in Cahaba, Alabama
Source: *Drake; NatCab 4; WebAB; WhAm
HS; WhAmP*

King, Yolanda Denise
American. Actress
Daughter of Martin Luther King, Jr.; formed
theatre troupe, Nucleus, with Attallah
Shabazz, daughter of Malcolm X.
b. 1955
Source: *BioIn 11; InB&W 80*

King Crimson
[Robert Fripp; Mike Giles; Greg Lake; Ian
McDonald; Pete Sinfield]
English. Music Group
Heavy metal space band, 1969-74; debut
album *In The Court of Crimson King*,
1969.
Source: *ConMuA 80A; LilREn 78; WhoRock
81*

King Sisters
American. Music Group
Source: *BiDAmM; WhoHol A*

Kinglake, Alexander William
English. Author
b. Aug 5, 1809 in Taunton, England
d. Jan 2, 1891 in London, England
Source: *Alli SUP; BiD&SB; BrAu 19; CasWL;
Chambr 3; DcEnA; DcEnL; DcLEL; EvLB;
NewC; OxEng; PenC ENG; REn; WebE&AL*

Kingman, Dave (David Arthur)
"Kong"
American. Baseball Player
b. Dec 21, 1948 in Pendleton, Oregon
Source: *BaseEn 85; BioIn 10, 11; PseudN 82*

Kingman, Dong M
[Tsang King-Man]
American. Illustrator
b. Apr 1, 1911 in Oakland, California
Source: *CelR; CurBio 62; IlsCB 1946;
IntMPA 75, 76, 77, 78, 79, 80, 81, 82;
WhoAm 74, 76, 78, 80, 82; WhoAmA 73;
WhoWor 78*

Kingsborough Donald
American. Business Executive
Introduced children's toy, Teddy Ruxpin,
1985; formed co., Worlds of Wonder,
1985.
b. 1947
Source: *ConNews 86-2*

Kingsbury-Smith, Joseph
American. Journalist
b. Feb 20, 1908 in New York, New York
Source: *IntWW 76; WhoAm 74, 76, 78, 80,
82; WhoWor 78*

Kingsford-Smith, Charles Edward
Australian. Aviator
b. 1897 in Brisbane, Australia
d. 1935
Source: *WebBD 80*

Kingsley, Ben
[Krishna Bhanji]
English. Actor
Won 1983 Best Actor Oscar for *Gandhi.*
b. Dec 31, 1943 in Snaiton, England
Source: *CurBio 83; NewYTBS 82, 83; Who
83; WhoAm 84; WhoThe 81*

Kingsley, Charles
"CK"; "The Chariot Clergyman"; "The
Chartist Parson"; "A Minute Philosopher"
English. Clergyman, Author
Wrote historical romances *Hypatia*, 1853;
Westward Ho, 1855; children's book *The
Water Babies*, 1863.
b. Jun 12, 1819 in Devonshire, England
d. Jan 23, 1875 in Eversley, England
Source: *Alli, SUP; AnCL; AtlBL; AuBYP;
BbD; BiD&SB; Br&AmS; BrAu 19; CarSB;
CasWL; Chambr 3; ChhPo, S1, S2; CrtT 3;
CyWA; DcBiA; DcEnA; DcEnL; DcEuL;
DcLEL; EvLB; JBA 34; MouLC 3; NewC;
NewYTBE 71; OxEng; PenC ENG; PseudN
82; RAdv 1; REn; WebE&AL; WhoChL*

Kingsley, Henry
English. Author
Wrote romantic novels: *Geoffrey Hamlyn*,
1859; *Ravenshoe*, 1862.
b. Jan 2, 1830 in Barnack, England
d. May 24, 1876 in Cuckfield, England
Source: *Alli SUP; BbD; BiD&SB; BrAu 19;
CarSB; CasWL; Chambr 3; ChhPo S1;
CyWA; DcBiA; DcEnA; DcEnL; DcEuL;
DcLEL; EvLB; HsB&A; NewC; OxEng; PenC
ENG; REn; WebE&AL*

Kingsley, Sidney
[Sidney Kieschner]
American. Dramatist
b. Oct 18, 1906 in New York, New York
Source: *AmAu&B; BiE&WWA; CnDAL;
CnMD; CnThe; ConAmA; ConAu 85; CroCD;
CurBio 43; DcLEL; FilmgC; LongCTC;
McGEWD; ModAL; ModWD; NotNAT;
OxAmL; OxThe; PenC AM; PlP&P; PseudN
82; REn; REnAL; REnWD; TwCA, SUP;
WebE&AL; WhoAm 74, 76, 78, 80, 82;
WhoThe 77; WrDr 76*

Kingston, Maxine Hong
American. Author
b. Oct 27, 1940 in Stockton, California
Source: *BioIn 11; ConAu 69; ConLC 12;
WhoAm 82*

Kingston Trio, The
[Roger Gambill; George Grove; Bob Shane]
American. Music Group
Rose to fame, late 1950s, with ballad "Tom
Dooley."
Source: *AmPS A; BiDAmM; WhoRock 81;
WhoRocM 82*

Kinks, The
[Mick Avory; John Beechman; Laurie Brown;
David Davies; Raymond Davies; John
Gosling; Alan Holmes; Peter Quaife]
English. Music Group
Source: *EncPR&S 74; IlEncRk; WhoRock 81;
WhoRocM 82*

Kinmont, Jill
[Mrs. John Boothe]
American. Skier, Teacher
Movies *The Other Side of the Mountain*,
parts I, II, 1975, 1978, depict her life.
b. 1936
Source: *GoodHs; HerW*

Kinnell, Galway
American. Poet
Poems deal with life confronting death; won
Pulitzer for *Selected Poems,* 1983.
b. Feb 1, 1927 in Providence, Rhode Island
Source: *AmAu&B; ConAu 9R, 10NR; ConLC
1, 2, 3, 5, 13; ConP 70, 75; CroCAP; CurBio
86; DrAF 76; DrAP 75; ModAL S1; OxAmL;
PenC AM; RAdv 1; WhoAm 74, 76, 78, 80,
82, 84; WhoTwCL; WhoWor 74; WorAu;
WrDr 76*

Kinney, George Romanta
American. Merchant
Started Kinney Shoes, 1894, marketing shoes
for entire family at discount prices; first to
apply concept of franchising.
b. 1866
d. 1919
Source: *Entr*

Kinnock, Neil Gordon
Welsh. Politician
Succeeded Michael Foot as head of Britain's
Labor Party, 1983--.
b. Mar 28, 1942 in Tredagar, Wales
Source: *IntWW 83; IntYB 82; NewYTBS 83;
Who 83*

Kinsey, Alfred Charles
American. Scientist
Founded Institute for Sex Research, 1942;
Kinsey Reports shattered myths.
b. Jun 23, 1894 in Hoboken, New Jersey
d. Aug 25, 1956 in Bloomington, Indiana
Source: *AmAu&B; CurBio 54, 56; EncAB-H;
IndAu 1917; ObitOF 79; ObitT 1951; REnAL;
WebAB; WhAm 3; WorAl*

Kinski, Nastassja
[Nastassja Nakszynski; Mrs. Ibrahim Moussa]
"Nasti"
German. Actress
Starred in films *Tess,* 1978; *Unfaithfully
Yours,* 1984.
b. Jan 24, 1960 in Berlin, Germany (West)
Source: *CurBio 84; NewYTBS 81; VarWW 85*

Kintner, Robert Edmonds
American. Radio Executive, TV Executive,
Author
b. Sep 12, 1909 in Stroudsburg, Pennsylvania
d. Dec 20, 1980 in Washington, District of
Columbia
Source: *AnObit 1980; ConAu 103; CurBio 50;
NewYTBS 80; WhAm 7*

Kinugasa, Teinousuke
Japanese. Director
Won Oscar for best foreign film *Gate of
Hell,* 1954.
b. 1898 in Mie, Japan
d. Feb 26, 1982
Source: *BiDFilm; BioIn 10; FilmgC; OxFilm;
WhoWor 74*

Kipling, Rudyard
English. Author, Poet
Won 1907 Nobel Prize; wrote *The Jungle
Book,* 1894; *Just So Stories,* 1902.
b. Dec 30, 1865 in Bombay, India
d. Jan 18, 1936 in Burwash, England
Source: *Alli SUP; AnCL; ApCAB SUP;
AtlBL; AuBYP; BbD; BiD&SB; CarSB;
CasWL; Chambr 3; ChhPo, S1, S2; CnE&AP;
CnMWL; CrtT 3; CyWA; DcAmAu; DcBiA;
DcEnA, AP; DcEuL; DcLEL; EncWL; EvLB;
FamAYP; FamSYP; FilmgC; JBA 34;
LongCTC; MnBBF; ModBrL, S1; NewC;
OxAmL; OxCan; OxEng; PenC ENG; RAdv
1; RComWL; REn; Str&VC; TwCA, SUP;
TwCWr; WebE&AL; WhoChL; WhoLA;
WhoTwCL*

Kiplinger, Austin Huntington
American. Publisher
b. Sep 19, 1918 in Washington, District of
Columbia
Source: *AmAu&B; ConAu 57; St&PR 75;
WhoAm 74, 76, 78, 80, 82; WhoS&SW 82;
WhoWor 78*

Kiplinger, W(illard) M(onroe)
American. Journalist
b. Jan 8, 1891 in Bellefontaine, Ohio
d. Aug 6, 1967 in Bethesda, Maryland
Source: *AmAu&B; ConAu 89; CurBio 43, 62,
67; LinLib L; ObitOF 79; OhA&B; WhAm
4A*

Kipnis, Alexander
Russian. Opera Singer
b. Feb 1, 1891 in Zhitomir, Russia
d. May 14, 1978 in Westport, Connecticut
Source: *CurBio 43; WhoAm 74; WhoMus 72;
WhoWor 78*

Kipnis, Igor
American. Musician
b. Sep 27, 1930 in Berlin, Germany
Source: *WhoAm 74, 76, 78, 80, 82; WhoMus
72; WhoWor 78; WhoWorJ 72*

Kirbo, Charles
American. Lawyer
b. Mar 15, 1917 in Bainbridge, Georgia
Source: *WhoAm 82; WhoAmP 73; WhoS&SW
82*

Kirby, Durward
American. Actor
Co-host of TV show "Candid Camera,"
   1961-66.
b. Aug 24, 1912 in Covington, Kentucky
Source: *WhoAm 74; WhoE 74; WorAl*

Kirby, George
"Big Daddy"
American. Comedian
b. Jun 8, 1923
Source: *BioIn 10; CurBio 77; PseudN 82;
WhoBlA 75*

Kirby, Jack
American. Cartoonist
Created numerous comic book heroes:
   Captain America, 1951; *Fantastic Four*,
   1961.
b. Aug 28, 1917 in New York, New York
Source: *EncSF; FanAl; WorECom*

Kirby, John
American. Musician
b. Dec 31, 1908 in Baltimore, Maryland
d. 1952 in Hollywood, California
Source: *WhoJazz 72*

Kirby, Robert Emory
American. Corporation Executive
Chm., Westinghouse Electric Co., since 1975.
b. Nov 8, 1918 in Ames, Iowa
Source: *CurBio 79; IntWW 75, 76, 77, 78;
WhoAm 76, 78, 80, 82; WhoF&I 74, 79;
WhoWor 74, 76, 78*

Kirby, Rollin
American. Cartoonist
b. Sep 4, 1876 in Galva, Illinois
d. May 8, 1952 in New York, New York
Source: *AmAu&B; CurBio 44, 52; DcAmB S5;
WhAm 3*

Kirchhoff, Gustav Robert
German. Physicist
Credited with discovery of spectrum analysis,
   the spectroscope.
b. Mar 12, 1824 in Konigsberg, Prussia
d. Oct 17, 1887 in Berlin, Germany
Source: *AsBiEn; DcScB; McGEWB; REn*

Kirchner, Ernst Ludwig
[L de Marsalle, pseud.]
German. Artist
German expressionist; did street scenes,
   landscapes of vibrant color, distorted
   forms: "Street, Berlin," 1907.
b. May 6, 1880 in Aschaffenburg, Germany
d. Jun 15, 1938 in Davos, Switzerland
Source: *AtlBL; OxGer; PseudN 82*

Kirchschlager, Rudolf
Austrian. President
b. Mar 20, 1915 in Austria
Source: *IntWW 74*

Kirk, Alan Goodrich
American. Military Leader, Diplomat
Commanded naval task force landing troops
   on D-Day, 1944; foreign ambassador,
   1946-62.
b. Oct 30, 1888 in Philadelphia, Pennsylvania
d. Oct 15, 1963 in New York, New York
Source: *DcAmB S7; WebBD 80*

Kirk, Claude Roy, Jr.
American. Governor
b. Jan 7, 1926 in San Bernardino, California
Source: *CurBio 67; NewYTBE 70; WhoAmP
73; WhoS&SW 82*

Kirk, Grayson Louis
American. University Administrator
b. Oct 12, 1903 in Jeffersonville, Ohio
Source: *AmAu&B; AmM&WS 73S; CurBio
51; IntWW 74; LinLib L, S; OhA&B; St&PR
75; Who 80; WhoAm 82, 84; WhoWor 80, 82*

Kirk, Lisa
American. Singer
b. Feb 25, 1925 in Brownsville, Pennsylvania
Source: *InWom; NotNAT; WhoAm 74;
WhoThe 77*

Kirk, Phyllis
[Phyllis Kirkegaard]
American. Actress
Nora Charles on TV series "The Thin Man,"
   1957-59.
b. Sep 18, 1930 in Plainfield, New Jersey
Source: *FilmgC; InWom; IntMPA 82; MotPP;
PseudN 82; WhoAm 80, 82; WhoHol A*

Kirk, Russell
American. Journalist
b. Oct 19, 1918 in Plymouth, Michigan
Source: *AmAu&B; Au&Wr 71; AuNews 1;
ChhPo S2; ConAu 1R, 1NR; CurBio 62;
DrAS 74H; WhoAm 74, 76, 78, 80, 82;
WhoMW 74; WhoWor 78; WorAu; WrDr 76*

Kirk, Ruth Kratz
American. Author
b. May 7, 1925 in Los Angeles, California
Source: *ConAu 13R; ForWC 70*

Kirkland, Caroline Matilda Stansbury
[Mrs. Mary Clavers, pseud.]
American. Author
First to write realistic fiction of American
frontier: *A New Home,* 1839.
b. Jan 11, 1801 in New York, New York
d. Apr 6, 1864 in New York, New York
Source: *NotAW; WebBD 80*

Kirkland, Gelsey
American. Ballerina
With American Ballet Theatre, 1974-81.
b. Dec 29, 1952 in Bethlehem, Pennsylvania
Source: *CurBio 75; NewYTBE 70; WhoAm
78, 80, 82*

Kirkland, Lane (Joseph Lane)
American. Labor Union Official
Pres., AFL-CIO, Nov 1979--.
b. Mar 12, 1922 in Camden, South Carolina
Source: *BioIn 12; CurBio 80; WhoAm 78, 80,
82*

Kirkpatrick, Jeane Duane Jordan
American. Diplomat
US permanent representative to UN, 1981;
    resigned, 1985.
b. Nov 19, 1926 in Duncan, Oklahoma
Source: *AmM&WS 78S; ConAu 53; CurBio
81; NewYTBS 81; WhoAm 84; WhoAmW 83;
WhoWor 82*

Kirkpatrick, Ralph
American. Musician
Selected to record all of Bach's keyboard
    music, 1956.
b. Jan 10, 1911 in Leominster, Massachusetts
d. Apr 13, 1984 in Guilford, Connecticut
Source: *ConAu 112, 49; CurBio 71; IntWW
74; NewYTBS 84; WhAm 8; WhoAm 80, 82;
WhoE 74; WhoMus 72; WhoWor 74*

Kirkus, Virginia
[Virginia Kirkus Glick]
American. Literary Critic, Author
Founded Kirkus Service, which previews
    forthcoming books, 1933.
b. Dec 7, 1893 in Meadville, Pennsylvania
d. Sep 10, 1980 in Danbury, Connecticut
Source: *BioIn 12; ConAu 101; CurBio 41, 54,
70; PseudN 82*

Kirkwood, James
American. Author
Won Pulitzer for *Chorus Line* script, 1976.
b. Aug 22, 1930 in Los Angeles, California
Source: *ConAu 1R, 2NR; ConLC 9; WhoAm
80, 82; WrDr 80*

Kirov, Sergei Mironovich
Russian. Revolutionary
One of Stalin's chief aides.
b. 1886
d. 1934
Source: *BioIn 7, 9, 10, 11; NewCol 75; REn*

Kirshner, Don
American. Publisher
b. Apr 17, 1934 in Bronx, New York
Source: *IlEncRk; NewYTET; RolSEnR 83;
WhoAm 82, 84*

Kirstein, George G
American. Publisher
Owner, publisher, *Nation,* 1955-65.
b. Dec 10, 1909 in Boston, Massachusetts
d. Apr 3, 1986 in Mamaroneck, New York
Source: *AmAu&B; NewYTBS 86; WhoAm 80*

Kirstein, Lincoln Edward
American. Ballet Promoter
Founded, School of American Ballet, NYC,
    1933.
b. May 4, 1907 in Rochester, New York
Source: *AmAu&B; CurBio 52; IntWW 74;
NewYTBS 82; Who 82; WhoAm 80, 84;
WhoAmA 82; WhoE 81, 83; WhoMus 72;
WhoWor 74*

Kirsten, Dorothy
American. Opera Singer
b. Jul 6, 1917 in Montclair, New Jersey
Source: *CurBio 48; InWom; WhoAm 74, 76,
78, 80, 82; WhoHol A; WhoMus 72*

Kirtley, Steven William
[The Hostages]
American. Hostage in Iran
b. 1958
Source: *NewYTBS 81*

Kiss
[Eric Carr; Peter Criss; Ace Frehley; Gene
    Simmons; Paul Stanley]
American. Music Group
Formed 1972, known for makeup, mystery
    image; hit song "Beth," 1976.
Source: *BkPepl; IlEncRk; RolSEnR 83;
WhoRock 81; WhoRocM 82*

Kissinger, Henry Alfred
"The Drone"; "The Flying Peacemaker";
"Henry the K"; "The Iron Stomach";
"Super Kraut"
American. Government Official
Secretary of State under Richard Nixon,
Gerald Ford; won Nobel Peace Prize,
1973; wrote *For the Record*, 1981.
b. May 27, 1923 in Fuerth, Germany
Source: *AmAu&B; AmM&WS 73S; BioNews
74; BkPepl; CelR; CngDr 74; ConAu 1NR,
2NR; CurBio 72; EncAB-H; NewYTBE 73;
WebAB; Who 83; WhoAm 82; WrDr 76*

Kissinger, Nancy Maginnes
American. Celebrity Relative
Wife of Henry Kissinger.
b. 1934 in White Plains, New York
Source: *BioNews 74; NewYTBS 74*

Kistiakowsky, George Bogdan
American. Chemist
Leader, explosives division, Los Alamos
Project; later opposed nuclear weapons.
b. Nov 18, 1900 in Kiev, Russia
d. Dec 7, 1982 in Cambridge, Massachusetts
Source: *AmM&WS 76P, 79P; AnObit 1982;
ConAu 108; CurBio 60, 83; IntWW 80, 81,
82; NewYTBS 82; PolProf E; Who 83*

Kistler, Darci
American. Ballerina
Youthful star of Balanchine's NYC Ballet,
1980.
b. 1964 in Riverside, California
Source: *BioIn 12*

Kitaj, R(onald) B(rooks)
American. Artist
Draws large history paintings with social
themes; collages of baseball stars.
b. Oct 29, 1932 in Chagrin Falls, Ohio
Source: *BioIn 7, 8, 11; ConArt 77; CurBio
82; IntWW 78; WhoAm 78, 80, 82; WhoAmA
78*

Kitchell, Iva
American. Dancer
Dance comedienne who impersonated great
dancers, satirized classical ballet; featured
dancer at Radio City Music Hall, NYC.
b. Mar 31, 1908 in Junction City, Kansas
d. Nov 19, 1983 in Ormond Beach, Florida
Source: *BiDD; CurBio 84; NewYTBS 83*

Kitchener, Horatio Herbert
English. Field Marshal
Hero of victories in Africa who expanded
British army as secretary of state for war,
1914.
b. Jun 14, 1850 in Ballylongford, Ireland
d. Jun 5, 1916
Source: *BioIn 10; McGEWB; WebBD 80*

Kitson, Henry Hudson
American. Sculptor
b. Apr 9, 1863 in Huddersfield, New York
d. Jun 26, 1947
Source: *WhAm 2*

Kitson, Theo Alice Ruggles
American. Sculptor
b. 1871 in Brookline, Massachusetts
d. Oct 29, 1932
Source: *InWom; WhAm 1; WomWWA 14*

Kitt, Eartha Mae
American. Singer
b. Jan 16, 1928 in North, South Carolina
Source: *BkPepl; CelR; ConAu 77; CurBio 55;
FilmgC; InWom; IntMPA 75, 76, 77, 78, 79,
80, 81, 82; LivgBAA; MovMk; NotNAT;
WhoAm 74, 76, 78, 80, 82; WhoBlA 75;
WhoHol A; WhoThe 77*

Kittikachorn, Thanom
Thai. Prime Minister
b. Aug 11, 1911 in Tak, Thailand
Source: *CurBio 69; IntWW 74; WhoGov 75;
WhoWor 78*

Kittle, Ron(ald Dale)
American. Baseball Player
Outfielder, Chicago White Sox, 1983--; AL
rookie of year, 1983.
b. Jan 5, 1958 in Gary, Indiana
Source: *BaseEn 85; BaseReg 86; NewYTBS
83*

Kittredge, G(eorge) L(yman)
American. Author
Authority on English literature; wrote
Complete Works of Shakespeare, 1936.
b. Feb 28, 1860 in Boston, Massachusetts
d. Jul 23, 1941 in Barnstable, Massachusetts
Source: *AmAu&B; ChhPo; CnDAL; CurBio
41; DcAmB S3; DcLEL; DcNAA; LongCTC;
NewC; OxAmL; PseudN 82; REn; REnAL;
TwCA, SUP; WebAB; WhAm 1*

Kiyo'kaga
see: Keokuk

Kjerkegaard, Soren Aabye
see: Kierkegaard, Soren Aabye

Klafsky, Katharina
Hungarian. Opera Singer
b. Sep 19, 1855 in Saint Johann, Hungary
d. Sep 22, 1896 in Hamburg, Germany
Source: *InWom*

Klammer, Franz
Austrian. Skier
b. 1952 in Moaswald, Austria
Source: *BioIn 10*

Klarsfeld, Beate
German. Reformer
Crusader to track down and bring to trial
  former Nazi war criminals.
b. Feb 13, 1931 in Berlin, Germany
Source: *ConAu 65*

Klassen, Elmer Theodore
American. Government Official
Appointed first postmaster general of newly
  organized postal dept. 1972.
b. Nov 6, 1908 in Hillsboro, Kansas
Source: *CurBio 73; IntWW 74; NewYTBE 71;
St&PR 75; WhoAm 74; WhoGov 75;
WhoS&SW 82*

Klebe, Giselher
German. Composer
b. Jun 28, 1925 in Mannheim, Germany
Source: *DcCM; IntWW 74; WhoWor 78*

Kleber, Jean Baptiste
French. Revolutionary
b. Mar 9, 1753 in Strasbourg, France
d. Jun 14, 1800 in Cairo, Egypt
Source: *DcBiPP; OxFr; WhoMilH 76*

Kleberg, Robert Justus, Jr.
American. Rancher, Sportsman
Owner King Ranch, largest producer of beef
  cattle in US; race horse, Assault, won
  Triple Crown, 1946.
b. Mar 29, 1896 in Corpus Christi, Texas
d. Oct 13, 1974 in Houston, Texas
Source: *IntWW 74; NatCAB 58; NewYTBS
74; ObitOF 79; WhAm 6; WhoAm 74;
WhoWor 74*

Klee, Paul
Swiss. Artist
Abstract painter noted for fantastic shapes,
  exotic colors.
b. Dec 18, 1879 in Bern, Switzerland
d. Jun 29, 1940 in Muralto, Switzerland
Source: *AtlBL; ConArt 83; CurBio 40; OxGer;
REn; WhDW; WorAl*

Kleiber, Erich
Austrian. Conductor
b. Aug 5, 1890 in Vienna, Austria
d. Jan 27, 1956 in Zurich, Switzerland
Source: *NewEOp 71*

Klein, Anne
American. Fashion Designer
Known for sophisticated sportswear.
b. Aug 3, 1923 in Brooklyn, New York
d. Mar 19, 1974 in New York, New York
Source: *BioNews 74; NewYTBS 74; WorFshn*

Klein, Calvin
American. Fashion Designer
Designer of elegant, modern classics since
  1969; jeans caused sensation due to
  provocative ads.
b. Nov 19, 1942 in New York, New York
Source: *BkPepl; WhoAm 74, 76, 78, 80, 82;
WorFshn*

Klein, Chuck (Charles Herbert)
American. Baseball Player
b. Oct 7, 1905 in Indianapolis, Indiana
d. Mar 28, 1958 in Indianapolis, Indiana
Source: *BaseEn 85; WhoProB 73*

Klein, Herbert George
American. Government Official
b. Apr 1, 1918 in Los Angeles, California
Source: *CurBio 71; IntWW 74; WhoAm 74,
76, 78, 80, 82; WhoAmP 73; WhoGov 75;
WhoS&SW 82*

Klein, Lawrence Robert
American. Economist
Won 1980 Nobel Prize for developing
  econometrics.
b. Sep 14, 1920 in Omaha, Nebraska
Source: *ConAu 116*

Klein, Melanie
Psychiatrist, Author
First psychoanalyst to work on child
  analysis.
b. Mar 30, 1882 in Vienna, Austria
d. Sep 22, 1960 in London, England
Source: *ConAu 111; WhAm 5*

Klein, Robert
American. Comedian, Actor
Won Tony, 1979, for *They're Playing Our
Song.*
b. Feb 8, 1942 in New York, New York
Source: *ConTFT 3; WhoAm 80, 82*

Kleindienst, Richard Gordon
American. Government Official
Former attorney general, 1972-73, who
played key role in Richard Nixon's
election, 1968.
b. Aug 5, 1923 in Winslow, Arizona
Source: *CurBio 72; IntWW 74; NewYTBE 72;*
NewYTBS 74; Who 82, 83; WhoAm 84;
WhoAmP 73; WhoGov 72

Kleinfield, "Sonny" (Nathan Richard)
American. Journalist, Author
Financial writer NY *Times;* wrote *The*
Hidden Minority, 1979.
b. Aug 12, 1950 in Paterson, New Jersey
Source: *ConAu 97*

Kleist, Heinrich von
German. Author, Dramatist, Poet
Wrote novella *Michael Kohlhaus,* 1811;
comedy *The Broken Jug,* 1806.
b. Oct 18, 1777 in Frankfurt, Germany
d. Nov 21, 1811 in Wannsee, Germany
Source: *AtlBL; BiD&SB; CasWL; CnThe;*
CyWA; DcEuL; EuAu; EvEuW; McGEWD;
OxGer; OxThe; PenC EUR; RComWL; REn;
REnWD

Klem, Bill (William Joseph)
"The Old Arbitrator"
American. Baseball Umpire
Regarded as best umpire ever; first to use
hand signals to indicate calls; Hall of
Fame, 1953.
b. Feb 22, 1874 in Rochester, New York
d. Sep 16, 1951 in Miami, Florida
Source: *BasesB*

Klemesrud, Judy Lee
American. Journalist
b. 1939 in Thompson, Iowa
Source: *ConAu 89; ForWC 70*

Klemperer, Otto
German. Conductor, Composer
b. May 14, 1885 in Breslau, Germany
d. Jul 6, 1973 in Zurich, Switzerland
Source: *CurBio 65, 73; NewYTBE 70, 73;*
WhAm 5; WhoMus 72

Klemperer, Werner
German. Actor
Played Colonel Klink on TV series "Hogan's
Heroes," 1965-71.
b. Mar 22, 1920 in Cologne, Germany
Source: *CelR; FilmgC; MotPP; WhoHol A*

Klenau, Paul von
Danish. Composer, Conductor
b. Feb 11, 1883 in Copenhagen, Denmark
d. Aug 31, 1946 in Copenhagen, Denmark
Source: *BioIn 4; OxMus*

Kletzki, Paul
Polish. Conductor
b. Mar 21, 1900 in Lodz, Poland
d. Mar 5, 1973 in Liverpool, England
Source: *NewYTBE 73; WhAm 5; WhoMus 72*

Klien, Walter
Austrian. Musician
b. Nov 27, 1928 in Graz, Austria
Source: *Who 74; WhoMus 72; WhoWor 78*

Klima, Ivan
Czech. Author
b. Sep 14, 1931 in Prague, Czechoslovakia
Source: *ConAu 25R; ModSL 2*

Klimt, Gustav
Austrian. Artist
b. Jul 4, 1862 in Vienna, Austria
d. Feb 6, 1918 in Vienna, Austria
Source: *AtlBL; OxGer*

Kline, Franz Joseph
American. Artist
b. May 23, 1919 in Wilkes-Barre,
Pennsylvania
d. May 13, 1962 in New York, New York
Source: *BioIn 3, 4, 5, 6, 7, 8, 10; WebAB*

Kline, Kevin
American. Actor
Won Tonys for *On the Twentieth Century,*
1978; *The Pirates of Penzance,* 1981; in
film *Sophie's Choice,* 1982.
b. Oct 24, 1947 in Saint Louis, Missouri
Source: *BioIn 11; CurBio 86; NewYTBS 78,*
81, 82; WhoThe 81

Kline, Nathan Schellenberg
American. Psychiatrist
Developed antidepressant drugs; pioneered use
of drugs in treating mental illness.
b. Mar 22, 1916 in Philadelphia,
Pennsylvania
d. Feb 11, 1983 in New York, New York
Source: *AmM&WS 82P; ConAu 81; CurBio*
83; WhoFrS 84

Kline, Otis Adelbert
American. Author
Prolific heroic-fantasy writer for *Weird Tales,*
    Argosy pulps.
b. 1891 in Chicago, Illinois
d. Oct 24, 1946 in New York, New York
Source: *BioIn 1; EncSF; FanAl; WhoHr&F;*
WhoSciF

Kling, John Gradwohl
"Noisy"
American. Baseball Player, Baseball Manager
Catcher 1900-13, with Chicago Cubs; won
    four pennants, one World Series.
b. Nov 13, 1875 in Kansas City, Missouri
d. Jan 31, 1947 in Kansas City, Missouri
Source: *BaseEn 85; PseudN 82; WhoProB 73*

Kling, Ken
Cartoonist
Source: *NewYTBE 70*

Klopfer, Donald Simon
American. Publisher
Co-founder, Random House, 1927-75.
b. Jan 23, 1902 in New York, New York
d. May 30, 1986 in New York, New York
Source: *NewYTBS 86; St&PR 75; WhoAm 78*

Klopstock, Friedrich Gottlieb
"The Birmingham Milton"; "The Creator of
    Biblical Epic Poetry"; "The German
    Milton"; "The Milton of Germany"
German. Poet
b. Jul 2, 1724 in Quedlinburg, Germany
d. Mar 14, 1803 in Hamburg, Germany
Source: *BbD; BiD&SB; CasWL; ChhPo;*
DcEuL; EuAu; EvEuW; McGEWD; NewC;
OxEng; OxGer; PenC EUR; PseudN 82;
RComWL; REn

Klose, Margarete
German. Opera Singer
b. Aug 6, 1905 in Berlin, Germany
d. Dec 14, 1968 in Berlin, Germany (West)
Source: *NewEOp 71*

Klugh, Earl
American. Musician
Jazz guitarist recording since 1977.
b. 1953 in Detroit, Michigan
Source: *BioIn 11; IlEncBM 82; InB&W 80*

Klugman, Jack
American. Actor
Played Oscar Madison in TV series, "The
    Odd Couple," 1970-75; won two Emmys;
    starred in Series "Quincy."
b. Apr 27, 1922 in Philadelphia,
    Pennsylvania
Source: *BiE&WWA; BkPepl; FilmgC; IntMPA*
80, 81, 82; MotPP; MovMk; NotNAT;
WhoAm 82, 84; WhoHol A; WhoTelC;
WhoThe 77, 81; WorAl

Kluszewski, Ted (Theodore Bernard)
"Klu"
American. Baseball Player, Baseball Coach
First baseman, 1947-61; had more than 100
    RBIs in five seasons, led league 1954.
b. Sep 10, 1924 in Argo, Illinois
Source: *BaseEn 85; PseudN 82; WhoAm 82,*
84; WhoProB 73

Klutznick, Philip M
American. Government Official
b. Jul 9, 1907 in Kansas City, Missouri
Source: *WhoAm 74, 76, 78, 80, 82; WhoF&I*
74; WhoWorJ 72

Knack, The
[Berton Averre; Doug Fieger; Bruce Gary;
    Prescott Niles]
American. Music Group
Source: *NF*

Knappertsbusch, Hans
German. Conductor
b. Mar 12, 1888 in Elberfeld, Germany
d. Oct 25, 1965 in Munich, Germany (West)
Source: *WhAm 4*

Knaths, Karl (Otto Karl)
American. Artist
Abstractionist with unique cubist style;
    known for still-lifes, Cape Cod landscapes.
b. Oct 21, 1891 in Eau Claire, Wisconsin
d. Mar 9, 1971 in Hyannis, Massachusetts
Source: *BnEnAmA; CurBio 53, 71; DcAmArt;*
DcCAA 71, 77; McGDA; NewYTBE 71;
WhAm 5; WhoAmA 78

Knauer, Virginia Harrington Wright
American. Government Official
b. Mar 28, 1915 in Philadelphia,
    Pennsylvania
Source: *BioNews 74; CelR; CurBio 70;*
WhoAm 74, 76, 78, 80, 82; WhoAmP 73;
WhoAmW 77; WhoGov 75

Knebel, Fletcher
American. Author, Journalist
b. Oct 1, 1911 in Dayton, Ohio
Source: *AmAu&B; Au&Wr 71; AuNews 1;*
BioNews 75; ConAu 1R, 1NR; ConLC 14;
ConNov 72, 76; NewYTBS 74; WhoAm 74,
76, 78, 80, 82; WhoE 74; WhoWor 78; WrDr
76

Kneip, Richard
American. Diplomat, Politician
b. Jan 7, 1933
Source: *BioIn 10*

Kneller, Godfrey, Sir
[Gottfried Kniller]
British. Artist
b. Aug 8, 1646 in Lubeck, Germany
d. Nov 7, 1723 in London, England
Source: *AtlBL; PseudN 82; REn*

Knerr, H(arold) H
American. Cartoonist
b. 1883 in Bryn Mawr, Pennsylvania
d. Jul 8, 1949 in New York, New York
Source: *WorECom*

Knickerbocker, Diedrich, pseud.
see: Irving, Washington

Knickerbocker, Suzy
[Aileen Mehle; Suzy]
American. Journalist
b. 1919 in El Paso, Texas
Source: *BioIn 10; CelR; InWom; PseudN 82*

Knievel, "Evel" (Robert Craig)
American. Stuntman
Attempted sky-cycle jump over Snake River
Canyon, ID, 1974.
b. Oct 17, 1938 in Butte, Montana
Source: *BioNews 74; BkPepl; CelR; CurBio*
72; NewYTBS 74; PseudN 82; WhoAm 82

Knight, Arthur
[Arthur Rosenheimer]
American. Movie Critic
b. Sep 3, 1916 in Philadelphia, Pennsylvania
Source: *ConAu 4NR, 41R; IntMPA 80, 81,*
82, 84; OxFilm; PseudN 82; WhoAm 80, 82

Knight, Billy (William R)
American. Basketball Player
b. Jun 9, 1952 in Braddock, Pennsylvania
Source: *OfNBA 81; WhoBlA 77*

Knight, Bobby (Robert Montgomery)
American. Basketball Coach
Head coach, Indiana U, 1971--, known for
tempermental outbursts.
b. Oct 25, 1940 in Orrville, Ohio
Source: *ConNews 85-3; NewYTBE 71;*
NewYTBS 84

Knight, Charles
English. Publisher, Author
b. 1791 in Windsor, England
d. Mar 9, 1873 in Addlestone, England
Source: *Alli, SUP; BbD; BiD&SB; BrAu 19;*
CasWL; Chambr 3; ChhPo; DcEnA; DcEnL;
DcLEL; EvLB; NewC; OxEng

Knight, Frances Gladys
American. Government Official
b. Jul 22, 1905 in Newport, Rhode Island
Source: *CelR; CurBio 55; InWom; NewYTBE*
71; USBiR 74; WhoAm 74; WhoGov 75;
WhoWor 78

Knight, George Wilson
English. Author
b. Sep 19, 1897 in Sutton, England
Source: *Au&Wr 71; ChhPo S1; ConAu 13R;*
DcLEL; IntWW 74; NewC; PenC ENG; REn;
REnAL; TwCA, SUP; Who 74; WhoWor 78;
WrDr 80

Knight, Gladys Maria
[Gladys Knight and the Pips]
American. Singer
Won two Grammys, 1973, for "Midnight
Train to Georgia."
b. May 28, 1944 in Atlanta, Georgia
Source: *BkPepl; IlEncBM 82; InB&W 80;*
WhoAm 80, 82, 84; WhoAmW 81; WhoBlA
75; WorAl

Knight, John S, III
American. Author, Newspaper Editor
b. Apr 3, 1945 in Columbus, Georgia
d. Dec 7, 1975 in Philadelphia, Pennsylvania
Source: *AuNews 2*

Knight, John Shivley
American. Newspaper Publisher
Founder, longtime editor, Knight-Ridder
newspaper empire; won Pulitzer for
column "Editor's Notebook," 1968.
b. Oct 26, 1894 in Bluefield, West Virginia
d. Jun 16, 1981 in Akron, Ohio
Source: *AuNews 2; BioIn 1, 3, 4, 5, 8, 10,*
11; ConAu 93, 103; CurBio 45, 81; IntWW
74, 75, 76, 77, 78; NewYTBS 81; St&PR 75;
WhAm 8; WhoAm 74, 76, 78; WhoF&I 74,
75; WhoMW 74; WhoS&SW 73, 75, 76, 78;
WhoWor 74

Knight, Phil(ip H)
American. Business Executive
Co-founder, Nike, Inc., 1967; sales exceed
$900 million per year.
b. Feb 24, 1938 in Portland, Oregon
Source: *ConNews 85-1; WhoAm 84; WhoF&I
83; WhoWest 84*

Knight, Shirley
American. Actress
Oscar nominee for *The Dark at the Top of
the Stairs,* 1959; *Sweet Bird of Youth,*
1962; won Tony for *Kennedy's Children,*
1975.
b. Jul 5, 1937 in Goessel, Kansas
Source: *BiDFilm; ConTFT 3; FilmEn;
FilmgC; IntMPA 80, 81, 82, 84; MotPP;
MovMk; NewYTBS 74; WhoAm 84;
WhoAmW 81, 83; WhoHol A; WhoThe 77,
81*

Knight, Stan
[Black Oak Arkansas]
"Goober"
American. Musician
Guitarist with heavy-metal, Dixie boogie
group.
b. Feb 12, 1949 in Little Rock, Arkansas
Source: *NF*

Knight, Ted
[Tadeus Wladyslaw Konopka]
American. Actor
Played Ted Baxter on "The Mary Tyler
Moore Show," 1970-77; won two Emmys;
lead role in "Too Close For Comfort,"
1980--.
b. Dec 7, 1923 in Terryville, Connecticut
d. Aug 26, 1986 in Pacific Palisades,
California
Source: *BkPepl; IntMPA 82; WhoAm 82;
WhoHol A; WhoTelC*

Knoetze, Kallie (Nikolaas)
South African. Boxer
b. 1953
Source: *BioIn 11*

Knopf, Alfred Abraham
American. Publisher
With wife Blanche founded Alfred A Knopf,
Inc., 1915.
b. Sep 12, 1892 in New York, New York
d. Aug 11, 1984 in Purchase, New York
Source: *AmAu&B; CelR; ConAu 106; IntWW
74; NewYTBS 82; REnAL; St&PR 75;
WebAB; Who 82, 83; WhoAm 80, 82, 84;
WhoWor 80, 82; WhoWorJ 72*

Knopfler, Dave
see: Dire Straits

Knopfler, Mark
[Dire Straits]
Scottish. Musician, Composer
Formed rock group, 1977; hits include
Grammy winner "Money for Nothing,"
1986.
b. Aug 12, 1949 in Glasgow, Scotland
Source: *ConNews 86-2*

Knorr, Nathan Homer
American. Religious Leader
Pres., Jehovah's Witnesses, 1942-77,
representing over one million members.
b. Apr 23, 1905 in Bethlehem, Pennsylvania
d. Jun 15, 1977 in Wallkill, New York
Source: *CurBio 57, 77; ObitOF 79; WhAm 7;
WhoAm 74; WhoRel 75; WhoWor 74*

Knote, Heinrich
German. Opera Singer
b. Nov 26, 1870 in Munich, Germany
d. Jan 15, 1953 in Germany (West)
Source: *NewEOp 71*

Knott, Walter
American. Businessman
Founded Knott's Berry Farm amusement
park, CA, 1940; coined term
"boysenberry."
b. Dec 11, 1889 in San Bernardino,
California
d. Dec 3, 1981 in Buena Park, California
Source: *AnObit 1981; NewYTBS 81*

Knotts, Don
American. Comedian, Actor
Won five Emmys for role of Barney Fife on
"The Andy Griffith Show," 1960-68.
b. Jul 21, 1924 in Morgantown, West
Virginia
Source: *FilmgC; IntMPA 82; MotPP; MovMk;
WhoAm 80, 82, 84; WhoHol A; WhoTelC;
WorAl*

Knowland, William Fife
American. Senator, Newspaper Publisher
Rep. senator from CA, 1945-58; published
Oakland *Tribune.*
b. Jun 26, 1908 in Alameda, California
d. Feb 23, 1974 in Oakland, California
Source: *BiDrAC; CurBio 47, 74; NewYTBS
74; WhAm 6; Who 74; WhoAmP 73;
WhoWest 84; WhoWor 78*

Knowles, James Sheridan
British. Author
Plays include tragedy, *William Tell*, 1825;
comedy, *The Hunchback*, 1832.
b. May 12, 1784 in Cork, Ireland
d. Nov 30, 1862 in Torquay, England
Source: *Alli; BbD; BiD&SB; BrAu 19;
CasWL; Chambr 3; ChhPo; DcEnA; DcEnL;
DcLEL; EvLB; McGEWD; MouLC 3; NewC;
OxEng; OxThe; PoIre; REn*

Knowles, John
American. Author
b. Sep 16, 1926 in Fairmont, Washington
Source: *AmAu&B; Au&Wr 71; CasWL;
ConAu 17R; ConLC 1, 4, 10; ConNov 72, 76;
DrAF 76; RAdv 1; SmATA 8; WhoAm 74,
76, 78, 80, 82; WhoWor 78; WorAu; WrDr
76*

Knowles, Patric
[Reginald Lawrence Knowles]
English. Actor
Films include *Adventures of Robin Hood*,
1938; *How Green Was My Valley*, 1941.
b. Nov 11, 1911 in Horsforth, England
Source: *FilmgC; IntMPA 80, 81, 82, 84;
MovMk; WhoHol A; WhoWor 74*

Knowles, Warren Perley
American. Business Executive
b. Aug 19, 1908 in River Falls, Wisconsin
Source: *IntWW 74; WhoAm 74, 76, 78, 80,
82; WhoAmP 73; WhoWor 78*

Knox, Alexander
Canadian. Actor
Oscar nominee for *Wilson*, 1944.
b. Jan 16, 1907 in Strathroy, Ontario
Source: *BiE&WWA; CanNov; CurBio 81;
FilmgC; IntMPA 80, 81, 82, 84; MotPP;
MovMk; NotNAT; WhoAm 74, 80; WhoHol
A; WhoThe 72, 81*

Knox, Chuck (Charles Robert)
American. Football Coach
Head coach, LA Rams, 1973-78; Buffalo
Bills, 1978--.
b. Apr 27, 1932 in Sewickley, Pennsylvania
Source: *WhoAm 82; WhoFtbl 74*

Knox, E(dmund) G(eorge) V(alpy)
"Evoc"
British. Editor, Journalist
b. 1881
d. Jan 2, 1971 in London, England
Source: *Au&Wr 71; ChhPo, S1, S2; ConAu
29R; DcLEL; EvLB; LongCTC; NewC;
PseudN 82; TwCA, SUP*

Knox, Frank
American. Government Official
b. Jan 1, 1874 in Boston, Massachusetts
d. Apr 28, 1944 in Washington, District of
Columbia
Source: *CurBio 40, 44; DcAmB S3; DcLB 29;
DcPol; EncAJ; NatCAB 37*

Knox, Henry
American. Military Leader, Patriot,
Government Official
Succeeded Washington as commander of
Continental Army, 1783; US secretary of
War, 1785-94.
b. Jul 25, 1750 in Boston, Massachusetts
d. Oct 25, 1806 in Thomaston, Maine
Source: *AmBi; ApCAB; BiAUS; BiDrUSE;
DcAmB; Drake; LinLib S; McGEWB;
NatCAB 1; TwCBDA; WebAB; WhAm HS*

Knox, John
"The Apostle of Presbytery"; "The Apostle
of the Scottish Reformers"; "The Reformer
of a Kingdom"
Scottish. Religious Leader, Reformer
b. 1505 in Haddington, Scotland
d. Nov 24, 1572 in Edinburgh, Scotland
Source: *Alli; BbD; BiD&SB; BrAu; CasWL;
DcEnA; DcEnL; EvLB; NewC; OxEng; PenC
ENG; PseudN 82; RComWL; REn*

Knox, Ronald Arbuthnott
"Hard Knox"
English. Author, Religious Leader
Catholic chaplain, Oxford U, 1926-39;
published translation of Bible based on
Vulgate text.
b. Feb 17, 1888 in Kibworth, England
d. Aug 24, 1957 in London, England
Source: *BkC 6; CathA 1930; ChhPo S2;
CurBio 50, 57; DcLEL; EncMys; EncSF;
EvLB; LongCTC; NewC; OxEng; PseudN 82;
TwCA, SUP; TwCWr; WebAB 79; WhE&EA*

Knox, Rose Markward
American. Business Executive
Founded Knox Gelatin Co., 1890; wrote
Dainty Desserts, 1896.
b. Nov 18, 1857
d. Sep 27, 1950
Source: *NotAW*

Knudsen, Semon Emil
"Bunkie"
American. Auto Manufacturer
b. Oct 2, 1912 in Buffalo, New York
Source: *BusPN; CurBio 74; IntWW 74;
NewYTBS 74; PseudN 82; St&PR 75; Ward
77A; Who 82, 83; WhoAm 80, 82, 84;
WhoF&I 74, 81*

Knudsen, William S
[Signius Wilhelm Paul Knudsen]
American. Industrialist
Helped both Ford, GM become multinational
    corps.
b. Mar 25, 1879 in Copenhagen, Delaware
d. Apr 27, 1948 in Detroit, Michigan
Source: *CurBio 40, 48; DcAmB S4; EncAB-H;*
PseudN 82; WhAm 2

Kobbe, Gustav
American. Author
b. Mar 4, 1857 in New York, New York
d. Jul 27, 1918 in Babylon, New York
Source: *Alli SUP; AmAu&B; AmLY; BiD&SB;*
ChhPo; DcAmAu; DcAmB; DcNAA; WhAm 1

Kober, Arthur
Author
b. Aug 25, 1900 in Brody, Austria
d. Jun 12, 1975 in New York, New York
Source: *AmAu&B; Au&Wr 71; BiE&WWA;*
ConAu 57, P-1; IntMPA 75; ModWD;
OxAmL; REn; REnAL; TwCA, SUP; WhAm
6; WhoAm 74; WhoWorJ 72

Koch, Bill
American. Skier
US cross-country ski champ, 1981.
b. 1955
Source: *BioIn 10, 11*

Koch, Ed(ward Irwin)
American. Politician
Flamboyant mayor of NYC.
b. Dec 12, 1924 in New York, New York
Source: *BiDrAC; CngDr 74; WhoAm 80, 82,*
84; WhoAmP 73; WhoE 74, 81; WhoGov 72;
WorAl

Koch, Ilse
"Bitch of Buchenwald"; "Red Witch"
German. Nazi War Criminal
b. 1907 in Dresden, Germany
d. 1967
Source: *InWom; LookW; NewYTBE 71*

Koch, John
American. Artist
Prize-winning, self-taught painter of elegant
    Manhattan interiors, celebrities.
b. Aug 16, 1909 in Toledo, Ohio
d. Apr 19, 1978 in New York, New York
Source: *BioIn 3, 4, 7, 11; ConArt 77; CurBio*
65, 78; DcCAA 71, 77; NewYTBS 78; ObitOF
79; WhoAm 74, 76, 78; WhoAmA 73, 76, 78

Koch, Kenneth
American. Author
b. Feb 27, 1925 in Cincinnati, Ohio
Source: *AmAu&B; ChhPo S1, S2; ConAu 1R;*
ConLC 5, 8; ConP 70, 75; CroCAP; DrAP
76; DrAP 75; DrAS 74E; NewYTBE 70; PenC
AM; RAdv 1; WebE&AL; WhoAm 74, 76, 78,
80, 82; WhoWor 78; WorAu; WrDr 76

Koch, Robert
German. Engineer, Scientist
Isolated bacteria that caused tuberculosis,
    1882.
b. Dec 11, 1843 in Hanover, Prussia
d. May 28, 1910 in Baden-Baden, Germany
Source: *DcInv; EncSoA; LinLib S; REn;*
WorAl

Kodaly, Zoltan
Hungarian. Composer
b. Dec 16, 1882 in Kecskemet, Hungary
d. Mar 6, 1967 in Budapest, Hungary
Source: *DcCM; WhAm 4*

Koehler, Wolfgang
Psychologist, Author
One of the founders of Gestalt school of
    psychology; wrote *Mentality of Apes,* 1917.
b. Jan 21, 1887 in Revel, Estonia
d. Jun 11, 1967 in Enfield, New Hampshire
Source: *AmAu&B; ConAu 111; NatCAB 55*

Koestler, Arthur
Hungarian. Author
Most famous work *Darkness at Noon,* 1940s,
    anti-Stalinist novel.
b. Sep 5, 1905 in Budapest, Hungary
d. Mar 3, 1983 in London, England
Source: *Au&Wr 71; CasWL; CnMWL; ConAu*
1R, 1NR; ConLC 1, 3, 6, 8, 15; ConNov 72,
76; CurBio 43, 62, 83N; CyWA; EncWL;
IntWW 74; LongCTC; ModBrL; NewC;
NewYTBE 71; NewYTBS 83; OxEng; PenC
ENG; REn; TwCA SUP; TwCWr; WebE&AL;
WhDW; Who 74; WhoTwCL; WhoWor 74;
WhoWorJ 72; WrDr 76

Koffka, Kurt
German. Psychologist
Chief spokesman of Gestalt psychology; wrote
    Growth of the Mind, 1924.
b. Mar 18, 1886 in Berlin, Germany
d. Nov 22, 1941 in Northampton,
    Massachusetts
Source: *CurBio 42; DcAmB S3; WhAm 74*

Kofoed, Jack (John C)
American. Journalist
b. Dec 17, 1894 in Philadelphia,
Pennsylvania
d. Dec 27, 1979 in Miami, Florida
Source: *ConAu 5NR, 93*

Kogan, Leonid Borisovich
Russian. Musician
Refused to play in orchestra which contained
a defector.
b. Oct 14, 1924 in Dnepropetrovsk, U.S.S.R.
d. Dec 17, 1982 in U.S.S.R.
Source: *AnObit 1982; Baker 78; IntWW 80,
81, 82, 83N; NewYTBS 82; WhoMus 72;
WhoSocC 78; WhoWor 74*

Kohl, Helmut Michael
German. Political Leader
Chancellor, West Germany, 1982--.
b. Apr 3, 1930 in Ludwigshafen, Germany
Source: *CurBio 77; IntWW 80, 81, 82, 83;
IntYB 80, 81; NewYTBS 82; Who 82, 83;
WhoWor 82*

Kohl, Herbert R
American. Author, Educator
b. 1937
Source: *AmAu&B; ConAu 65*

Kohler, Fred
American. Actor
Played villain in films *The Iron Horse; The
Plainsman; Way of all Flesh.*
b. Apr 20, 1889 in Kansas City, Missouri
d. Oct 28, 1938 in Los Angeles, California
Source: *FilmEn; Film 1; TwYS; WhScrn 74,
77; WhoHol B*

Kohler, Kaufmann
American. Theologian
b. May 10, 1843 in Fuerth, Germany
d. Jan 28, 1926 in New York, New York
Source: *AmAu&B; AmBi; DcAmB; DcNAA;
OhA&B; WhAm 1*

Kohler, William R
American. Business Executive
Source: *St&PR 75, 84*

Kohler, Wolfgang
German. Psychologist
b. Jan 21, 1887 in Reval, Russia
d. Jun 11, 1967 in Enfield, New Hampshire
Source: *AmAu&B; TwCA SUP; WhAm 4, 5*

Kohlmeier, Louis Martin, Jr.
American. Journalist
b. Feb 17, 1926 in Saint Louis, Missouri
Source: *ConAu 49; WhoAm 74, 76, 78, 80,
82; WhoS&SW 82*

Kohn, William Roth
American. Artist, Educator
b. Aug 23, 1931 in Saint Louis, Missouri
Source: *WhoAmA 76, 78, 80*

Kohner, Susan
American. Actress
Oscar nominee for *Imitation of Life,* 1959.
b. Nov 11, 1936 in Los Angeles, California
Source: *BiE&WWA; FilmgC; IntMPA 76, 80,
81, 82, 84; MotPP; NotNAT; WhoHol A*

Kohoutek, Lubos
Czech. Astronomer
b. 1935 in Moravia, Czechoslovakia
Source: *BioNews 74; CurBio 74; NewYTBS 74*

Kohut, Heinz
Austrian. Psychoanalyst
Advocate of "self psychology"; edited
Psychoanalysis and Literature, 1964.
b. May 3, 1913 in Vienna, Austria
d. Oct 8, 1981 in Chicago, Illinois
Source: *AmM&WS 79P; BiDrAPA 77; BioIn
10, 11, 12; ConAu 45, 1NR; NewYTBS 81;
WhoAm 78, 80*

Koivisto, Mauno Henrik
"Manu"
Finnish. President
First socialist elected Jan 1982.
b. Nov 25, 1923 in Turku, Finland
Source: *CurBio 82; IntWW 74, 75, 76, 77,
78, 79, 80; IntYB 78, 79, 80, 81; WhoWor
74, 76, 78*

Kokoschka, Oskar
Austrian. Artist, Author
b. Mar 1, 1886 in Austria
d. Feb 22, 1980 in Montreux, Switzerland
Source: *ConArt 77; ConAu 93; CurBio 56, 80;
EncTR; EncWL; EncWT; EvEuW; IntAu&W
76, 77; IntWW 75, 76, 77, 78; McGDA;
McGEWD; ModGL; ModWD; OxGer; REn;
REnWD; Who 74; WhoGrA 62; WhoWor 76,
78*

Kolb, Barbara Anne
American. Composer
b. Feb 10, 1939 in Hartford, Connecticut
Source: *BioIn 10, 11; DcCM; WhoE 74, 75*

Kolb, Claudia
American. Swimmer
Won two gold medals, 1968 Olympics.
b. Dec 19, 1949 in Hayward, California
Source: *BioIn 8*

Kolbe, Maximilian
[Maksymilian Kolbe]
Polish. Religious Figure
Catholic priest who chose death in place of
condemned prisoner; canonized, 1982.
b. 1894 in Poland
d. Aug 14, 1941 in Auschwitz, Poland
Source: *EncTR; HisEWW; NewYTBE 71;
NewYTBS 82*

Kolehmainen, Hannes
Finnish. Track Athlete
b. Dec 9, 1889 in Kuopio, Finland
Source: *WhoTr&F 73*

Kolff, Willem Johan
American. Physician
Developed artifical kidney, 1943.
b. Feb 14, 1911 in Leiden, Netherlands
Source: *AmM&WS 76P, 79P, 82P; BiDrACP
79; CurBio 83; IntWW 80, 81, 82, 83;
WhoAm 80, 82, 84; WhoFrS 84; WhoWor 78*

Kollek, Teddy (Theodore)
Israeli. Politician, Author
Mayor of Jerusalem since 1965; headed drive
to create nat museum.
b. May 27, 1911 in Vienna, Austria
Source: *ConAu P-2; CurBio 74; IntWW 74;
WhoWor 78*

Kollmar, Richard
American. Producer
b. Dec 31, 1910 in Ridgewood, New Jersey
d. Jan 7, 1971 in New York, New York
Source: *ConAu 89; CurBio 71, 71N;
NewYTBE 71; NotNAT B; WhScrn 74;
WhThe; WhoHol B; WhoThe 77A*

Kollsman, Paul
American. Aeronautical Engineer
Invented altimeter, measures a plane's
altitude while in flight.
b. Feb 22, 1900 in Freudenstadt, Germany
d. Sep 26, 1982 in Los Angeles, California
Source: *AnObit 1982; NewYTBS 82*

Kollwitz, Kathe Schmidt
German. Artist
b. Jul 8, 1867 in Konigsberg, Germany
d. Apr 22, 1945 in Dresden, Germany
Source: *AtlBL; HerW; InWom; OxGer;
WhAm 4*

Kolodin, Irving
American. Music Critic
b. Feb 22, 1908 in Brooklyn, New York
Source: *AmAu&B; ConAu 93; CurBio 47;
REnAL; WhoAm 74, 76, 78, 80, 82; WhoMus
72; WhoWor 78*

Kolvenback, Peter-Hans
"The Black Pope"
Dutch. Religious Leader
Catholic priest; head of Society of Jesus, the
Jesuits, 1983--.
b. 1928 in Druten, Netherlands
Source: *CurBio 84; WhoWor 84*

Komarov, Vladimir
Russian. Cosmonaut
b. Mar 16, 1927
d. Apr 24, 1967
Source: *WhAm 4*

Komroff, Manuel
American. Author
b. Sep 7, 1890 in New York, New York
d. Dec 10, 1974 in Woodstock, New York
Source: *AmAu&B; AmNov; AuBYP; CnDAL;
ConAu 1R, 53, 4NR; OxAmL; REnAL;
SmATA 2; TwCA, SUP; WhAm 6; WhoAm
74; WhoWor 78; WrDr 80*

Kondrashin, Kiril Petrovich
Russian. Conductor
Former leader of Moscow Philharmonic;
defected to West, 1978.
b. Feb 21, 1914 in Moscow, Russia
d. Mar 7, 1981 in Amsterdam, Netherlands
Source: *BioIn 11; IntWW 74, 75, 76, 77;
WhoMus 72; WhoOp 76; WhoSocC 78;
WhoWor 74*

Konetzne, Anni
Austrian. Opera Singer
b. Feb 12, 1902 in Vienna, Austria
d. Jun 9, 1968 in Vienna, Austria
Source: *NewEOp 71*

Konetzni, Hilde
Austrian. Opera Singer
b. Mar 21, 1905 in Vienna, Austria
Source: *WhoMus 72*

Konev, Ivan S
Russian. Field Marshal
b. Dec 27, 1897 in Ladeino, Russia
d. May 21, 1973 in Moscow, U.S.S.R.
Source: *CurBio 43, 56, 73; NewYTBE 73*

Konitz, Lee
American. Jazz Musician
b. 1927
Source: *BioIn 8; CmpEPM*

Konno, Ford
American. Swimmer
b. 1932
Source: *BioIn 3*

Konoye, Fumimaro, Prince
Japanese. Political Leader
b. Oct 1891
d. Dec 15, 1945
Source: *CurBio 40, 46; ObitOF 79; WhWW-II*

Konwitschny, Franz
German. Conductor
b. Aug 14, 1901 in Fulnek, Germany
d. Jul 27, 1962 in Belgrade, Yugoslavia
Source: *NewEOp 71*

Konya, Sandor
Hungarian. Opera Singer
b. Sep 23, 1923 in Sarkad, Hungary
Source: *WhoWor 78*

Koo, V(i) K(yuin) Wellington
[Ku Wei-Chun]
Chinese. Statesman
Foreign minister, prime minister, Republic of
   China, 1926-27; ambassador to US, 1946-
   56.
b. 1887 in Shanghai, China
d. Nov 14, 1985 in New York, New York
Source: *ConAu 81; CurBio 41, 86; PseudN
82; REn; Who 74; WhoLA*

Koob, Kathryn L
[The Hostages]
American. Hostage in Iran
b. 1939
Source: *BioIn 12; NewYTBS 81*

Kool and the Gang
[Cliff Adams; George Brown; 'Kool' Bell;
   Ronald Bell; 'Spike' Mickens; Michael
   Ray; Claydes Smith; J T Taylor; Dennis
   Thomas; Rickey West; Curtis Williams]
American. Music Group
Began, 1964, as jazz group; currently rhythm
   and blues-pop group; had platinum single
   "Celebration," 1980.
Source: *IlEncBM 82; InB&W 80; RkOn 78;
RolSEnR 83*

Koontz, (Annie) Elizabeth Duncan
[Mrs. Harry Lee Koontz]
"Libby"
American. Educator
b. Jun 3, 1919 in Salisbury, North Carolina
Source: *InWom; LEduc 74; PseudN 82;
WhoAm 74; WhoAmP 73; WhoAmW 77;
WhoBlA 75; WhoGov 75; WhoS&SW 82*

Koop, Charles Everett
American. Government Official
Surgeon-general of the US, 1982--.
b. Oct 14, 1916 in Brooklyn, New York
Source: *AmM&WS 76P, 79P; CurBio 83;
IntWW 82, 83; WhoAm 80, 82, 84*

Kooper, Al
[Blood, Sweat, and Tears]
American. Musician, Producer
Rock singer, organist, guitarist, 1960s; formed
   Blood, Sweat, and Tears, 1968.
b. Feb 5, 1944 in Brooklyn, New York
Source: *LilREn 78; WhoAm 80; WhoRock
81; WhoRocM 82; WorAl*

Koopmans, Tjalling (Charles)
American. Economist
Co-winner of 1975 Nobel Prize in economics.
b. Aug 28, 1910 in Graveland, Netherlands
d. Feb 26, 1985 in New Haven, Connecticut
Source: *ConAu 115; IntWW 84; WhoAm 84*

Kooymans, George
see: Golden Earring

Kopechne, Mary Jo
American. Secretary
Died in car accident involving Edward
   Kennedy.
b. Jul 26, 1940
d. Jul 19, 1969 in Chappaquiddick,
   Massachusetts
Source: *BioIn 8, 9, 10, 11*

Kopell, Bernie (Bernard Morton)
American. Actor
Played Dr. Adam Bricker on TV series "The
   Love Boat," 1976-86.
b. Jun 21, 1933 in Brooklyn, New York
Source: *WhoAm 80, 82; WhoHol A*

Kopit, Arthur L
American. Dramatist, Architect
b. May 10, 1937 in New York, New York
Source: *AmAu&B; AuNews 1; BiE&WWA;
CasWL; CnMD; ConAu 81; ConLC 1, 18;
CurBio 72; McGEWD; ModWD; NatPD;
NotNAT; OxAmL; PenC AM; REn;
WebE&AL; WhoAm 74; WhoThe 77; WorAu;
WrDr 80*

Koplovitz, Kay Smith
American. Broadcasting Executive
Pres., USA Cable Network since 1977.
b. Apr 11, 1945 in Milwaukee, Wisconsin
Source: *BioIn 12; WhoTelC*

Koppel, Ted (Edward James)
American. Broadcast Journalist
Anchor, ABC News "Nightline," 1980--.
b. 1940 in Lancashire, England
Source: *ConAu 103; LesBEnT; WhoAm 80,
82, 84; WhoTelC*

Kops, Bernard
English. Author
b. Nov 28, 1926 in London, England
Source: *BiE&WWA; ChhPo; CnMD; ConAu*
5R; ConLC 4; ConNov 72, 76; ConP 70, 75;
CroCD; ModBrL S1; ModWD; NewC;
NotNAT; RAdv 1; TwCWr; WhoThe 77;
WhoWorJ 72; WorAu; WrDr 80

Korbut, Olga
[Mrs. Leonid Borkevich]
Russian. Gymnast
Won two gold medals, 1972 Olympics.
b. May 16, 1955 in Grodno, U.S.S.R.
Source: *BioNews 74; CurBio 73; HerW;*
NewYTBE 72

Korchnoi, Viktor
Russian. Chess Player
b. 1931
Source: *BioIn 10*

Korda, Alexander, Sir
[Sandor Kellner; Sandor Korda]
English. Producer
Developed British film industry with London
Films Co.; made 112 films, including *The*
Third Man, 1950.
b. Sep 16, 1893 in Turkeve, Hungary
d. Jan 23, 1956 in London, England
Source: *BiDFilm; CurBio 46, 56; DcFM;*
FilmgC; MovMk; NotNAT B; ObitOF 79;
OxFilm; PseudN 82; WhAm 3; WorAl;
WorEFlm

Korda, Michael
American. Publisher
Wrote *Charmed Lives,* 1979, focusing on the
life of Uncle, Alexander.
b. 1919
d. Dec 24, 1973
Source: *BioIn 10*

Korda, Michael Vincent
American. Editor
Editor-in-chief, Simon & Schuster, 1958--;
wrote *Worldly Goods,* 1982.
b. Oct 8, 1933 in London, England
Source: *ConAu 107; WhoAm 80, 82, 84;*
WrDr 82, 84

Koren, Edward Benjamin
American. Author
b. Dec 13, 1935 in New York, New York
Source: *ConAu 25R; SmATA 5; WhoAm 82;*
WhoE 74

Korff, Baruch
American. Rabbi
b. 1914
Source: *BioIn 10*

Korin, Ogata
Japanese. Artist
Finest painter of decorative style started by
Koetsu, Sotatso: "God of the Wind."
b. 1658 in Japan
d. 1716
Source: *McGDA; NewCol 75; OxArt*

Korinetz, Yuri
Russian. Author
b. Jan 14, 1923 in Moscow, U.S.S.R.
Source: *ConAu 61; SmATA 9*

Korjus, Miliza
Polish. Opera Singer
Coloratura soprano, star of 1938 hit *The*
Great Waltz.
b. 1912 in Warsaw, Poland
d. Aug 26, 1980 in Culver City, California
Source: *BioIn 12; FilmgC; NewYTBS 81;*
ThFT; WhoHol A; WhoMus 72

Korman, Harvey Herschel
American. Comedian
Regular on "The Carol Burnett Show," 1967-
77; won four Emmys.
b. Feb 15, 1927 in Chicago, Illinois
Source: *CurBio 79; IntMPA 75, 76, 77, 78,*
79, 80, 81, 82; WhoAm 74, 76, 78, 80, 82;
WhoHol A

Korner, Alexis
[Alexis Koerner]
"Grandfather of British Rhythm and Blues"
English. Musician
Known for discovering musicians Mick
Jagger, Ginger Baker, Robert Plant, etc.
b. Apr 19, 1928 in Paris, France
d. Jan 1, 1984 in London, England
Source: *AnObit 1984; RolSEnR 83; WhoRocM*
82

Korngold, Erich Wolfgang
Austrian. Composer
b. May 29, 1897 in Brunn, Austria
d. Nov 29, 1957 in Hollywood, California
Source: *AmSCAP 66; CmMov; CurBio 43, 58;*
CmMov; FilmgC; OxFilm; WorEFlm

Kornilov, Lavr Georgyevich
Russian. Military Leader
Commander-in-chief, Russian army, known
for attempted military coup against
government, 1917.
b. Jul 18, 1870 in Turkistan, Russia
d. Apr 13, 1918 in U.S.S.R.
Source: *McGEWB; REn; WhDW; WhoMilH*
76; WorAl

Kornman, Mary
[Our Gang]
American. Actress
"Our Gang" first leading lady, 1923.
b. 1917 in Idaho Falls, Idaho
d. Jun 1, 1973 in Glendale, California
Source: *TwYS; WhScrn 77; WhoHol B*

Korolenko, Vladimir Galaktionovich
Russian. Author
b. 1853 in Zhitomir, Russia
d. 1921 in Polatava, U.S.S.R.
Source: *BiD&SB; CasWL; ClDMEL; DcRusL; EncWL; EuAu; EvEuW; ModSL 1; PenC EUR; REn*

Korzybski, Alfred Habdank
American. Linguist
b. Jul 3, 1879 in Warsaw, Poland
d. Mar 7, 1950 in Sharon, Connecticut
Source: *AmAu&B; EncSF; LuthC 75; REn; REnAL; TwCA SUP; WebAB; WhAm 2*

Kosar, Bernie
American. Football Player
Quarterback, Cleveland Browns, 1985--.
b. Nov 25, 1963 in Boardman, Ohio
Source: *FootReg 86; NewYTBS 85*

Kotsching, Walter Maria
American. Government Official
Helped establish UN; permanent member, US delegation.
b. Apr 9, 1901 in Judenburg, Austria
d. Jun 23, 1985 in Newton, Pennsylvania
Source: *ConAu 117; CurBio 85*

Kosciuszko, Thaddeus
Polish. Soldier
b. Feb 12, 1746 in Belorussia
d. Nov 15, 1817 in Solothurn, Switzerland
Source: *ApCAB; Drake; TwCBDA; WebAB; WhAm HS*

Kosinski, Jerzy Nikodem
[Joseph Novak, pseud.]
American. Author
b. Jun 14, 1933 in Lodz, Poland
Source: *AmAu&B; ConAu 17R; ConLC 1, 2, 3, 6; ConNov 72, 76; CurBio 74; DrAF 76; EncWL; ModAL S1; PseudN 82; RAdv 1; WhoAm 74, 76, 78, 80, 82; WhoE 74; WhoWor 78; WorAu; WrDr 76*

Kossuth, Lajos
Hungarian. Patriot, Statesman
Principal figure in Hungarian Revolution, 1848.
b. Sep 19, 1802 in Monok, Hungary
d. Mar 20, 1894 in Turin, Italy
Source: *OxGer; PenC EUR; WhAm HS*

Kostelanetz, Andre
American. Conductor
Best known for informally performing classical music to appeal to general audiences.
b. Dec 22, 1901 in Saint Petersburg, Russia
d. Jan 13, 1980 in Port-au-Prince, Haiti
Source: *AnObit 1980; ConAu 107; CurBio 42, 80N; IntWW 74; LinLib S; NewYTBE 72, 73; NewYTBS 80; Who 74; WhoAm 74; WhoMus 72; WhoWor 74; WorAl*

Kosygin, Aleksei Nikolaevich
Russian. Communist Leader
Led Soviet effort at economic modernization, 1960s.
b. Feb 20, 1904 in Saint Petersburg, Russia
d. Dec 19, 1980 in Moscow, U.S.S.R.
Source: *AnObit 1980; ConAu 102; CurBio 65, 81N; IntWW 74; NewYTBS 80; Who 74, 82N; WhoGov 72; WhoWor 80; WorAl*

Koth, Erika
German. Opera Singer
b. Sep 15, 1927 in Darmstadt, Germany
Source: *WhoMus 72; WhoWor 78*

Kottke, Leo
American. Musician
b. in Athens, Georgia
Source: *IlEncRk*

Kotzebue, August Friedrich Ferdinand von
"The Shakespeare of Germany"
German. Author
b. May 3, 1761 in Weimar, Germany
d. Mar 23, 1819 in Mannheim, Germany
Source: *AtlBL; BbD; BiD&SB; CasWL; CnThe; DcEuL; EuAu; EvEuW; McGEWD; NewC; OxEng; OxFr; OxGer; OxThe; PenC EUR; PseudN 82; REn; REnWD*

Kotzky, Alex Sylvester
American. Cartoonist
b. Sep 11, 1923 in New York, New York
Source: *WhoAm 74, 76, 78, 80, 82*

Koufax, Sandy (Sanford)
American. Baseball Player, Sportscaster
Youngest player inducted into Hall of Fame, 1971, at age 36.
b. Dec 30, 1935 in Brooklyn, New York
Source: *BaseEn 85; ConAu 89; CurBio 64; WebAB; WhoAm 74; WhoProB 73*

Kountche, Seyni
Nigerian. President
b. 1931 in Fandou, Nigeria
Source: *WhoWor 78*

Koussevitzky, Serge Alexandrovich
American. Conductor, Composer
b. Jul 26, 1874 in Vyshni Volochek, Russia
d. Jun 4, 1951 in Boston, Massachusetts
Source: *CurBio 40, 51; DcAmB S5*

Kovacs, Ernie
American. Actor
Played Ernie in TV show "Kovacsland,"
    1951; "Tonight," 1956-57; married Edie
    Adams.
b. Jan 23, 1919 in Trenton, New Jersey
d. Jan 13, 1962 in Hollywood, California
Source: *AmAu&B; AmSCAP 66; CurBio 58,
62; FilmgC; MotPP; MovMk; NotNAT B;
ObitOF 79; WhAm 4; WhScrn 74, 77;
WhoHol B; WorAl*

Kovel, Ralph Mallory
American. Author, Antiquarian
Books on antiques regarded as "bibles in
    their fields."
b. Aug 20, 1920 in Milwaukee, Wisconsin
Source: *ConAu 8NR, 17R; WhoAm 80, 82;
WrDr 80, 82, 84*

Kovel, Terry Horvitz
[Mrs. Ralph Kovel]
American. Author, Antiquarian
Dictionary of Marks: Pottery and Porcelain,
    1953, now in 32nd printing.
b. Oct 27, 1928 in Cleveland, Ohio
Source: *ConAu 8NR, 17R; ForWC 70;
WhoAm 80, 82, 84; WrDr 80, 82, 84*

Kovic, Ron
American. Author, Soldier
Vietnam vet who wrote of experiences in
    Born on the Fourth of July.
b. Jul 1, 1946
Source: *BioIn 11*

Kozakiewicz, Wladyslaw
Polish. Track Athlete
Source: *NF*

Kozol, Jonathan
American. Author, Educator
Wrote *Illiterate America,* 1985.
b. Sep 5, 1936 in Boston, Massachusetts
Source: *AmAu&B; CelR; CurBio 86; WhoAm
84*

Krafft-Ebing, Richard von
German. Psychiatrist
Wrote classsic collection of case histories
    Psychopathia Sexualis, 1886.
b. Aug 14, 1840 in Mannheim, Germany
d. Dec 22, 1902 in Mariagru, Austria
Source: *AsBiEn; OxGer; REn; WhDW; WorAl*

Kraft, Chris(topher Columbus, Jr.)
American. Government Official, Engineer
b. Feb 28, 1924 in Phoebus, Virginia
Source: *AmM&WS 73P; CurBio 66; IntWW
74; WhoAm 74, 80, 84; WhoGov 72; WhoWor
74, 82; WorAl*

Kraft, James Lewis
American. Manufacturer
Invented pasteurizing process for cheese.
b. Dec 11, 1874 in Stevensville, Ontario
d. Feb 16, 1953 in Chicago, Illinois
Source: *DcAmB S5; WhAm 3*

Kraft, Joseph
American. Journalist, Author
Internationally syndicated political columnist
    known for non-ideological approach to
    world affairs.
b. Sep 4, 1924 in South Orange, New Jersey
d. Jan 10, 1986 in Washington, District of
    Columbia
Source: *AmAu&B; ConAu 9R; WhoAm 80,
82, 84; WhoS&SW 73; WrDr 82, 84*

Kraftwerk
[Karl Bartos; Wolfgang Flur; Ralf Hutter;
    Florian Schneider]
German. Music Group
Electronic band, formed 1968; hit album
    Autobahn, 1974.
Source: *ConMuA 80A; WhoRock 81*

Krag, Jens Otto
Danish. Prime Minister
b. Sep 15, 1915 in Randers, Denmark
d. Jun 22, 1978 in Jutland, Denmark
Source: *CurBio 62; IntWW 74; NewYTBE 72;
WhoWor 78*

Kramer, Jack
American. Tennis Player
b. Aug 1, 1921 in Las Vegas, Nevada
Source: *BioNews 74; CurBio 47*

Kramer, Stanley E
American. Director, Producer
Films include *On the Beach; Guess Who's
    Coming to Dinner?*
b. Sep 29, 1913 in New York, New York
Source: *BiDFilm; CelR; CurBio 51; DcFM;
FilmgC; IntMPA 80, 81, 82, 84; IntWW 74;
MovMk; OxFilm; WhoAm 84; WhoWest 74;
WhoWor 74; WorAl; WorEFlm*

Kramm, Joseph
American. Dramatist, Actor
b. Sep 30, 1907 in Philadelphia, Pennsylvania
Source: *AmAu&B; BiE&WWA; CnMD;*
CurBio 52; ModWD; NotNAT; OxAmL; REn;
TwCA SUP; WhoAm 74; WhoE 74; WhoThe
77; WhoWor 78

Krantz, Hazel Newman
American. Author
b. Jan 29, 1920 in Brooklyn, New York
Source: *ConAu 1R, 1NR; SmATA 12; WrDr*
76

Krantz, Judith
[Judith Tarcher]
American. Author
Wrote *Scruples,* 1978; *Princess Daisy,* 1980;
Mistral's Daughter, 1982.
b. Jan 9, 1928 in New York, New York
Source: *BioIn 11; ConAu 81; CurBio 82;*
WhoAm 82

Krasna, Norman
American. Dramatist, Critic
Won Oscar for screenplay: *Princess O'Rourke,*
1943.
b. Nov 7, 1909 in New York, New York
d. Nov 1, 1984 in Los Angeles, California
Source: *AmAu&B; BiDFilm; BiE&WWA;*
CmMov; CurBio 52; FilmgC; IntMPA 81, 82,
84; McGEWD; NewYTBS 84; NotNAT;
OxFilm; WhoAm 74; WhoThe 81; WorEFlm

Krasner, Lee
[Mrs. Jackson Pollock]
American. Artist
Abstract expressionist whose paintings were
characterized by bold, outlined images.
b. Oct 27, 1908 in Brooklyn, New York
d. Jun 19, 1984 in New York, New York
Source: *CurBio 84; DcCAr 81; NewYTBS 84;*
WhoAmW 83

Krassner, Paul
American. Editor, Author, Journalist
b. Apr 9, 1932 in Brooklyn, New York
Source: *AmAu&B; ConAu 21R; WhoAm 74*

Kraus, Ernst
German. Opera Singer
b. Jun 8, 1863 in Erlangen, Bavaria
d. Sep 6, 1941 in Worthersee, Austria
Source: *NewEOp 71*

Kraus, Felix von
Austrian. Opera Singer
b. Oct 3, 1870 in Vienna, Austria
d. Oct 30, 1937 in Munich, Germany
Source: *NewEOp 71*

Kraus, Lili
Austrian. Musician, Educator
b. Mar 4, 1908 in Budapest, Hungary
Source: *BioNews 75; NewYTBE 71; WhoAm*
74, 76, 78, 80, 82; WhoAmW 77; WhoMus
72

Krause, Bernie (Bernard Leo)
[The Weavers]
American. Singer, Songwriter
b. Dec 8, 1938 in Detroit, Michigan
Source: *WhoAm 82*

Krauss, Clemens
Austrian. Conductor
b. Mar 31, 1893 in Vienna, Austria
d. May 16, 1954 in Mexico City, Mexico
Source: *NewEOp 71*

Krauss, Gabrielle
Austrian. Opera Singer
b. Mar 24, 1842 in Vienna, Austria
d. Jan 6, 1906 in Paris, France
Source: *InWom*

Krauss, Ruth Ida
[Mrs. Crockett Johnson]
American. Author
b. 1911 in Baltimore, Maryland
Source: *AmAu&B; Au&ICB; Au&Wr 71;*
AuBYP; BkP; ConAu 1R, 1NR; DrAP 75;
ForWC 70; MorJA; SmATA 1; WhoAm 74,
76, 78, 80, 82; WrDr 76

Krauss, Werner
German. Actor
Played insane doctor in silent horror classic
Cabinet of Dr. Caligari, 1919.
b. 1884 in Gestungshausen, Germany
d. Oct 20, 1959 in Vienna, Austria
Source: *BiDFilm; EncWT; Film 1, 2; MotPP;*
ObitOF 79; OxFilm; OxThe; WhScrn 74, 77;
WhThe; WhoHol B; WorEFlm

Kray, Reggie (Reginald)
English. Gangster, Murderer
With brother ran crime "firm" in London's
East End, 1960s; both convicted, sentenced
to life in jail, 1969.
b. Oct 24, 1933 in London, England
Source: *BioIn 9, 11; DrInf*

Kray, Ronnie (Ronald)
"Colonel"
English. Gangster, Murderer
With brother ran crime "firm" in London's
East End, 1960s; both convicted, sentenced
to life in jail, 1969.
b. Oct 24, 1933 in London, England
Source: *BioIn 9, 11*

Krebs, Hans Adolf, Sir
British. Biochemist
Won 1953 Nobel Prize for research on food
cycles.
b. Aug 25, 1900 in Hildesheim, Germany
d. Nov 22, 1981 in Oxford, England
Source: *AsBiEn; CurBio 54, 82N; IntWW 74,
75, 76, 77, 78, 79, 80, 81; McGEWB;
NewYTBS 81; WhoWor 74, 76, 78; WorAl*

Kredel, Fritz
American. Artist, Illustrator
b. Feb 8, 1900
d. Jun 10, 1973 in New York, New York
Source: *ChhPo; ConAu 41R; IlsBYP; IlsCB
1744, 1946, 1957; MorJA; SmATA 17;
WhoAmA 73*

Kreisler, Fritz
American. Musician
b. Feb 2, 1875 in Vienna, Austria
d. Jan 29, 1962 in New York, New York
Source: *AmSCAP 66; CurBio 44, 62; REn;
WebAB; WhAm 4*

Krementz, Jill
[Mrs. Kurt Vonnegut]
American. Photographer, Author
Contributing photographer to *People*
magazine, 1974--; known for portraits of
authors.
b. Feb 19, 1940 in New York, New York
Source: *AuNews 1, 2; BioNews 75; ConAu
41R; MacBEP; NewYTBS 82; SmATA 17;
Who 82; WhoAm 80, 82; WhoAmW 83*

Kremer, Gidon
Russian. Musician
Gold medal violinist in Moscow Tchaikovsky
competition, 1970.
b. Feb 27, 1947 in Riga, Latvia
Source: *CurBio 85*

Krenek, Ernst
American. Composer
b. Aug 23, 1900 in Vienna, Austria
Source: *ConAu 57; CurBio 42; DcCM;
IntWW 74; WhoAm 74, 76, 78, 80, 82;
WhoMus 72; WhoWor 78*

Krenwinkel, Patricia
American. Cultist
b. 1947
Source: *BioIn 9*

Kreps, Juanita Morris
American. Government Official
Secretary of Commerce under Jimmy Carter,
1977-79.
b. Jan 11, 1921 in Lynch, Kentucky
Source: *AmEA 74; AmM&WS 73S; WhoAm
76, 80, 82, 84; WhoAmW 81, 83; WhoS&SW
73*

Kresge, Sebastian Spering
American. Merchant
Founder, S S Kresge's, which became K-
Mart.
b. Jul 31, 1867 in Bald Mount, Pennsylvania
d. Oct 18, 1966 in Mountainhome,
Pennsylvania
Source: *ApCAB X; BiDAmBL 83; NatCAB
52; ObitOF 79; WhAm 4*

Kresge, Stanley Sebastian
American. Business Executive
With S S Kresge Co., 1923-77; pres., 1952-
66; chm., 1966-78.
b. Jun 11, 1900 in Detroit, Michigan
d. Jun 30, 1985 in Rochester, Michigan
Source: *WhoAm 84; WhoMW 82*

Kreskin
[George Joseph Kresge, Jr.]
"The Amazing Kreskin"
American. Psychic, Entertainer
Uses telepathy, traditional magic; wrote *Use
Your Head to Get Ahead*, 1977.
b. Jan 12, 1935 in Montclair, New Jersey
Source: *BioNews 74; ConAu 101; PseudN 82*

Kress, Samuel Henry
American. Merchant
Founded Kress dime store chain, 1907.
b. Jul 23, 1863 in Cherryville, Pennsylvania
d. Sep 22, 1955 in New York, New York
Source: *CurBio 55; DcAmB S5; WebAB;
WhAm 3*

Kreuger, Ivar
"Match King"
Swedish. Financier
Owned United Swedish Match Co.; made 3/4
of world's matches by end of WW II.
b. Mar 2, 1880 in Kalmar, Sweden
d. Mar 12, 1932 in Paris, France
Source: *LinLib S; PseudN 82; WebBD 80;
WhDW; WorAl*

Kreuger, Kurt
American. Actor
Supporting actor in 1943 films *Enemy Below;
The Moon Is Down*.
b. Jul 23, 1917 in Saint Moritz, Switzerland
Source: *FilmEn; FilmgC; IntMPA 80, 81, 82,
84; MotPP; WhoHol A*

Kreutzer, Rodolphe
German. Musician, Composer
b. Nov 16, 1766 in Versailles, France
d. Jan 6, 1831 in Geneva, Switzerland
Source: *NewEOp 71; OxMus; WebBD 80*

Kreutzmann, Bill
[The Grateful Dead]
American. Singer, Musician
b. Jun 7, 1946 in Palo Alto, California
Source: *NF*

Kreymborg, Alfred
American. Dramatist, Poet
b. Dec 10, 1883 in New York, New York
d. Aug 14, 1966 in Milford, Connecticut
Source: *AmAu&B; AmSCAP 66; ChhPo, S2;
CnDAL; ConAmA; ConAmL; ConAu 25R;
LongCTC; ModAL; OxAmL; REnAL; SixAP;
TwCA, SUP; WhAm 4*

Krickstein, Aaron
American. Tennis Player
Youngest player to advance in US Open,
1983.
b. Aug 2, 1967 in Detroit, Michigan
Source: *NewYTBS 83*

Krieger, Robby
[The Doors]
American. Singer, Musician
b. Jan 8, 1946 in Los Angeles, California
Source: *NF*

Krieghoff, Cornelius
German. Artist
Painted Indians, French Canadian life,
landscapes in Canada, 1840-66.
b. 1815 in Amsterdam, Netherlands
d. Mar 9, 1872 in Chicago, Illinois
Source: *DcBrBI; DcCanB 10; IlBEAAW;
OxArt*

Kriek, Johann
American. Tennis Player
Won Australian Open, 1981, 1982.
b. Apr 5, 1958 in Ponogola, South Africa
Source: *WhoIntT*

Krige, Alice
South African. Actress
In TV mini-series "Ellis Island," 1984;
"Dream West," 1986; in film *Chariots of
Fire,* 1983.
b. 1955 in South Africa
Source: *VarWW 85*

Krips, Josef
Austrian. Conductor
b. Apr 8, 1902 in Vienna, Austria
d. Oct 12, 1974 in Geneva, Switzerland
Source: *BioNews 75; CurBio 65, 74; IntWW
74; NewYTBS 74; Who 74; WhoMus 72;
WhoWor 78*

Krishna Menon, V(engalil) K(rishnan)
Indian. Statesman, Lawyer
b. May 3, 1897
d. Oct 6, 1974
Source: *CurBio 53, 74; IntWW 74; Who 74;
WhoWor 78*

Krishnamurti, Jiddu
[Alcyone, pseud.]
Indian. Author, Philosopher
Advocate of self-knowledge who wrote
40 books: *The Future of Humanity,* 1986.
b. May 22, 1895 in Madanapelle, India
d. Feb 17, 1986 in Ojai, California
Source: *AnObit 1984; ConAu 11NR, 61;
CurBio 74, 86; DcLEL; PseudN 82; Who 83;
WhoAm 80, 82, 84*

Kristel, Sylvia
Dutch. Actress
Star of erotic French film *Emmanuelle,* 1974.
b. Sep 28, 1952 in Utrecht, Netherlands
Source: *FilmEn; NewYTBS 82; WhoHol A*

Kristofferson, Kris
[Kris Carson]
American. Actor, Singer, Songwriter
Wrote song "Help Me Make It Through the
Night"; films include *A Star Is Born,*
1970s.
b. Jun 22, 1937 in Brownsville, Texas
Source: *BioNews 74; BkPepl; ConAu 104;
CurBio 74; IntMPA 82; MovMk; PseudN 82;
WhoAm 82; WhoHol A*

Kristol, Irving
American. Editor, Author
b. Jan 22, 1920 in New York, New York
Source: *ConAu 25R; CurBio 74; WhoAm 82*

Kroc, Ray(mond) Albert
American. Restaurateur, Baseball Executive
Founded McDonald's, 1955; owner San
Diego Padres, 1974-84.
b. Oct 5, 1902 in Chicago, Illinois
d. Jan 24, 1984 in San Diego, California
Source: *AnObit 1984; BioNews 74; BusPN;
ConAu 111; ConNews 85-1; CurBio 73, 84;
NewYTBS 74, 84; WhoAm 74, 80, 82; WorAl*

Krock, Arthur
American. Journalist
b. Nov 16, 1886 in Glasgow, Kentucky
d. Apr 12, 1974 in Washington, District of
Columbia
Source: *AmAu&B; AuNews 1; ConAu 33R,
49, P-2; CurBio 43, 74; EncAB-H; WhAm 6;
WhNAA; WhoAm 74; WhoS&SW 82;
WhoWor 78*

Kroeber, Alfred Louis
American. Anthropologist, Author
b. Jun 11, 1876 in Hoboken, New Jersey
d. Oct 5, 1960 in Paris, France
Source: *AmAu&B; WebAB; WhAm 4*

Kroeber, Theodora Kracaw
[Mrs. John Quinn; Theodora Kroeber-Quinn]
American. Author
Mother of author Ursula LeGuin.
b. Mar 24, 1897 in Denver, Colorado
d. Jul 4, 1979 in Berkeley, California
Source: *AmAu&B; ConAu 5R, 89, 5NR;
ForWC 70; PseudN 82; SmATA 1; WrDr 76*

Krofft, Marty
American. Puppeteer, Producer
Source: *LesBEnT; NewYTET*

Krofft, Sid
American. Puppeteer, Producer
Source: *LesBEnT; NewYTET*

Kroger, Bernard Henry
American. Businessman
Founded Kroger grocery store chain, 1884.
b. Jan 24, 1860 in Cincinnati, Ohio
d. Jul 21, 1938 in Wianno, Massachusetts
Source: *DcAmB S2; NatCAB 32; WhAm 1*

Krogh, Egil, Jr.
"Bud"
American. Watergate Participant
b. 1939
Source: *BioIn 9, 10; PseudN 82*

Krol, John, Cardinal
American. Religious Leader
Archbishop of Philadelphia, 1961--.
b. Oct 26, 1910 in Cleveland, Ohio
Source: *CurBio 69; IntWW 83; NewYTBE 71;
WhoAm 84; WhoRel 75; WhoWor 82*

Kroll, Leon
American. Artist
b. Dec 6, 1884 in New York, New York
d. Oct 25, 1974 in Gloucester, Massachusetts
Source: *CurBio 43, 74; DcCAA 71; IntWW
74; NewYTBS 74; WhAm 6; WhoAm 74;
WhoAmA 73*

Kromm, Bobby (Robert)
Canadian. Hockey Coach
Coach, Detroit Red Wings, 1977-80; won
Jack Adams award, 1978.
b. Jun 8, 1928 in Calgary, Alberta
Source: *BioIn 12*

Kronenberger, Louis
American. Author
b. Dec 9, 1904 in Cincinnati, Ohio
d. Apr 30, 1980 in Wellesley, Massachusetts
Source: *AmAu&B; ChhPo; ConAu 1R, 97,
2NR; CurBio 44; DrAS 74E; NotNAT;
OhA&B; OxAmL; REnAL; TwCA SUP;
WhoAm 74; WhoThe 77; WhoWor 78;
WhoWorJ 72; WrDr 80*

Kronhausen, Eberhard Wilhelm
German. Psychologist
b. Sep 12, 1915 in Berlin, Germany
Source: *ConAu 9R*

Kronhausen, Phyllis Carmen
American. Psychologist
b. Jan 26, 1929 in Minnesota
Source: *ConAu 9R*

Kronold, Selma
Polish. Opera Singer
b. 1866 in Krakow, Poland
d. Oct 9, 1920 in New York, New York
Source: *InWom; NotAW*

Kropotkin, Peter Alekseyevich, Prince
Russian. Ruler
Benevolent anarchist who urged brotherhood,
cooperation as way of life.
b. Nov 26, 1842 in Moscow, Russia
d. Feb 8, 1921 in U.S.S.R.
Source: *BiD&SB; CasWL; ClDMEL; EuAu;
IntWW 80; WhDW; WorAl*

Kruger, Hardy (Eberhard)
German. Actor
Films include *The One That Got Away; Wild
Geese,* 1943.
b. Apr 12, 1928 in Berlin, Germany
Source: *FilmgC; IntMPA 80, 81, 82, 83;
WhoHol A; WhoWor 74*

Kruger, Otto
American. Actor
Broadway matinee idol, 1920s; film lead in
Dr. Ehrlich's Magic Bullet, 1940.
b. Sep 6, 1885 in Toledo, Ohio
d. Sep 6, 1974 in Woodland Hills, California
Source: *BiE&WWA; Film 2; FilmgC; MotPP;
MovMk; NewYTBS 74; ObitOF 79; PIP&P;
WhAm 6; WhScrn 74; WhThe; WhoHol B;
WorAl*

Kruger, Paul (Stephanus Johannes Paulus)
"Oom Paul"
South African. Statesman
Political, military leader of Transvaal
Republic who was pres., 1883-1902.
b. Oct 10, 1825 in Colesberg, South Africa
d. Jul 14, 1904 in Switzerland
Source: *LinLib L; McGEWB; NewCol 75;*
WebBD 80; WhDW; WorAl

Krumgold, Joseph
American. Author, Producer
Won Newbery award for *And Now Miguel,*
1953; *Onion John,* 1960.
b. Apr 9, 1908 in Jersey City, New Jersey
d. Jul 10, 1980 in Hope, New Jersey
Source: *AnObit 1980; AuBYP; ConAu 7NR,*
9NR, 101; ConLC 12; LinLib L; MorJA;
SmATA 1; WhAm 7

Krupa, Gene
American. Band Leader, Musician
Best known as drummer for Benny
Goodman.
b. Jan 15, 1909 in Chicago, Illinois
d. Oct 16, 1973 in Yonkers, New York
Source: *CurBio 47, 73; NewYTBE 73; WhAm*
6; WhScrn 77; WhoE 74; WhoHol B;
WhoJazz 72; WhoMus 72

Krupp, Alfred
"The Cannon King"
German. Industrialist
Famous for four-ton steel ingot and first
steel cannon, 1851.
b. Apr 26, 1812 in Essen, Germany
d. Jul 14, 1887
Source: *LinLib S; NewCol 75; WhDW; WorAl*

Krupp von Bohlen und Halbach, Bertha
"Big Bertha"
German. Celebrity Relative
Cannon produced by Krupp Manufacturing
during WW II named for her; daughter of
Friedrich Krupp.
b. 1886 in Essen, Germany
d. Sep 21, 1957 in Essen, Germany
Source: *BioIn 4; NewCol 75; ObitOF 79*

Krutch, Joseph Wood
American. Author, Drama Critic
b. Nov 25, 1893 in Knoxville, Tennessee
d. May 22, 1970 in Tucson, Arizona
Source: *AmAu&B; Au&Wr 71; BiE&WWA;*
CnDAL; ConAmA; ConAmL; ConAu 1R, 25R,
4NR; CurBio 59, 70; DcLEL; EvLB; OxAmL;
OxThe; PenC AM; REn; REnAL; TwCA,
SUP; WebAB; WhAm 5; WhNAA

Krylov, Ivan Andreyevich
Russian. Author
b. Feb 14, 1768 in Moscow, Russia
d. 1844 in Russia
Source: *BiD&SB; CasWL; ChhPo S1; DcEuL;*
DcRusL; EuAu; EvEuW; PenC EUR; REn

Kubasov, Valery Nikolaevich
Russian. Cosmonaut
b. Jan 7, 1935 in U.S.S.R.
Source: *IntWW 74; WhoWor 78*

Kubek, Tony (Anthony Christopher)
American. Baseball Player, Sportscaster
Shortstop, NY Yankees, 1957-65; broadcaster
NBC, 1966--.
b. Oct 12, 1936 in Milwaukee, Wisconsin
Source: *BaseEn 85; BioIn 4, 6; WhoAm 82,*
84; WhoProB 73

Kubelik, Jan
Czech. Musician
b. Jul 5, 1880 in Michle, Czechoslovakia
d. Dec 5, 1940 in Prague, Czechoslovakia
Source: *CurBio 41; WhAm 1*

Kubelik, Rafael
Czech. Conductor, Composer
b. Jun 29, 1914 in Bychory, Czechoslovakia
Source: *CurBio 51; IntWW 74; NewYTBE 71;*
Who 74; WhoMus 72; WhoWor 78

Kubitschek (de Oliveira), Juscelino
Brazilian. Politician
b. Sep 12, 1902 in Diamantina, Brazil
d. Aug 22, 1976 in Rio de Janeiro, Brazil
Source: *CurBio 56; IntWW 74*

Kublai Khan
Mongolian. Emperor
Grandson of Genghis Khan who founded
Yuan dynasty in China; subject of poem
by S T Coleridge.
b. 1216
d. 1294
Source: *DcBiPP; NewCol 75; WebBD 80;*
WhDW; WorAl

Kubler-Ross, Elisabeth
American. Psychiatrist, Author
Best known for books on death, dying.
b. Jul 8, 1926 in Zurich, Switzerland
Source: *BioIn 12; ConAu 25R; CurBio 80;*
WhoAm 82

Kubrick, Stanley
American. Director
Directed *2001: A Space Odyssey*, 1968; *A Clockwork Orange*, 1971.
b. Jul 26, 1928 in New York, New York
Source: *BiDFilm; BkPepl; ConAu 81; ConDr 73; CurBio 63; DcFM; FilmgC; IntMPA 80, 81, 82, 84; IntWW 74; MovMk; OxFilm; WebAB; Who 74; WhoAm 74, 76, 78, 80, 82; WhoWor 78; WomWMM; WorEFlm*

Kucinich, Dennis John
American. Politician
Youngest mayor in Cleveland history, 1977-80; presided over city's default.
b. Oct 8, 1946 in Cleveland, Ohio
Source: *CurBio 79; NewYTBS 78; WhoAm 80*

Kuerti, Anton
Austrian. Musician
b. 1938 in Vienna, Austria
Source: *BioIn 11; WhoAm 82*

Kuh, Katherine
American. Editor
b. Jul 15, 1904 in Saint Louis, Missouri
Source: *ConAu 13R; WhoAm 76*

Kuhlman, Kathryn
American. Evangelist
Faith healer said to produce spontaneous cures; wrote inspirational boook *I Believe in Miracles*, 1962.
b. 1910 in Concordia, Missouri
d. Feb 20, 1976 in Tulsa, Oklahoma
Source: *ConAu 12NR, 57, 65; CurBio 74, 76; NewYTBE 72; ObitOF 79; WhAm 6, 7; WhoRel 75; WrDr 76*

Kuhn, Bowie Kent
American. Lawyer, Baseball Executive
Baseball commissioner, 1969-84.
b. Oct 28, 1926 in Tacoma Park, Maryland
Source: *BioNews 74; CelR; CurBio 70; St&PR 75; WhoAm 78, 80, 82, 84; WhoE 74; WhoProB 73; WorAl*

Kuhn, Maggie (Margaret E)
American. Social Reformer
Founded Gray Panthers, 1971.
b. Aug 3, 1905 in Buffalo, New York
Source: *BioIn 11; CurBio 78; GoodHs; WhoAm 78, 80, 82*

Kuhn, Walt
American. Artist
b. Oct 27, 1880 in New York, New York
d. Jul 13, 1949 in White Plains, New York
Source: *DcAmB S4; DcCAA 71; WhAm 2*

Kuiper, Gerard Peter
American. Astronomer
b. Dec 7, 1905 in Harencarspel, Netherlands
d. Dec 24, 1973 in Mexico City, Mexico
Source: *AmM&WS 73P; ConAu 17R, 45, 2NR; CurBio 59, 74; WhAm 6; Who 74; WhoWor 78*

Kulish, Mykola
Ukrainian. Dramatist
b. 1892 in Kherson, Russia
d. 1942 in Siberia, U.S.S.R.
Source: *DcRusL; ModSL 2; PenC EUR*

Kulp, Nancy
American. Actress
Played Jane Hathaway on "The Beverly Hillbillies," 1962-71.
b. Aug 28, 1921 in Harrisburg, Pennsylvania
Source: *ForWC 70; WhoAm 74, 76, 78, 80, 82; WhoHol A*

Kumin, Maxine Winokur
American. Author
b. Jun 6, 1925 in Philadelphia, Pennsylvania
Source: *AnCL; AuBYP; AuNews 2; ConAu 1R, 1NR; ConLC 5; ConP 75; DrAF 76; DrAP 75; SmATA 12; WhoAm 82; WrDr 76*

Kun, Bela
Hungarian. Communist Leader
b. 1886
d. 1939
Source: *NewCol 75; WhDW*

Kundera, Milan
Czech. Author
Exile who lives in France, cannot be read, published in own country; wrote *The Book of Laughter and Forgetting*, 1980.
b. Apr 1, 1929 in Brno, Czechoslovakia
Source: *ConAu 85; ConLC 19; CurBio 83; NewYTBS 82*

Kung, Hans
Swiss. Author, Theologian, Educator
b. Mar 19, 1928 in Sursee, Switzerland
Source: *ConAu 53; CurBio 63; OxGer; WhoWor 78*

Kuni, Nagako
see: Nagako, Empress

Kunitz, Stanley Jasspon
[Dilly Tante, pseud.]
American. Author, Poet, Editor
b. Jul 29, 1905 in Worcester, Massachusetts
Source: *AmAu&B; CnE&AP; ConAu 41R;
ConLC 6; ConP 70, 75; CurBio 43, 59; DrAP
75; DrAS 74E; IntWW 74; ModAL, Sl;
OxAmL; PenC AM; PseudN 82; RAdv 1;
REn; REnAL; WebE&AL; WhoAm 74, 76,
78, 80, 82; WhoTwCL; WhoWor 78;
WhoWorJ 72; WorAu; WrDr 80*

Kuniyoshi, Yasuo
American. Artist
b. Sep 1, 1893 in Okayama, Japan
d. May 14, 1953
Source: *CurBio 53; DcCAA 71*

Kunstler, William Moses
American. Lawyer
b. Jul 7, 1919 in New York, New York
Source: *AmAu&B; ConAu 9R, 5NR; CurBio
71; NewYTBE 70; WhoAm 74, 76, 78, 80,
82; WhoE 74; WhoWorJ 72; WrDr 76*

Kunz, George
American. Football Player
b. Jul 5, 1947 in Fort Sheridan, Illinois
Source: *WhoAm 74; WhoFtbl 74*

Kunz, Erich
Austrian. Opera Singer
b. May 20, 1909 in Vienna, Austria
Source: *IntWW 74; WhoWor 78*

Kupchak, Mitch(ell)
American. Basketball Player
b. May 24, 1954 in Hicksville, New York
Source: *BioIn 12; OfNBA 81*

Kupcinet, Irv
American. Journalist
b. Jul 31, 1912 in Chicago, Illinois
Source: *CelR; WhoAm 74, 76, 78, 80, 82;
WhoMW 74*

Kupka, Frank
Czech. Artist, Illustrator
b. 1871
d. 1957
Source: *BioIn 4, 5; NewCol 75*

Kupke, Frederick Lee
[The Hostages]
American. Hostage in Iran
b. 1948 in Oklahoma
Source: *NewYTBS 81*

Kuprin, Aleksandr Ivanovich
Russian. Author
b. Aug 1870 in Narovchat, Russia
d. Oct 25, 1938 in Leningrad, U.S.S.R.
Source: *CasWL; ConAu 104; DcRusL;
EncWL; EvEuW; ModSL 1; PenC EUR;
REn; TwCA, SUP; TwCWr*

Kuralt, Charles Bishop
American. Broadcast Journalist
Correspondent with CBS News, 1959--; does
"On the Road" segments.
b. Sep 10, 1934 in Wilmington, North
Carolina
Source: *ConAu 89; IntMPA 82; WhoAm 74,
76, 78, 80, 82*

Kurelek, William
Canadian. Artist, Illustrator
b. Mar 3, 1927 in Whitford, Alberta
Source: *ConAu 49, 3NR; CreCan 1; SmATA
8; WhoAmA 73*

Kurland, Bob
"Foothills"
American. Basketball Player
First American to play on two Olympic
basketball teams, 1948, 1952.
b. Dec 23, 1924 in Saint Louis, Missouri
Source: *WhoBbl 73*

Kurnitz, Harry
American. Dramatist, Screenwriter
b. Jan 5, 1909 in New York, New York
d. Mar 18, 1968 in Los Angeles, California
Source: *BiE&WWA; ConAu 25R; EncMys;
FilmgC; WorEFlm*

Kurosawa, Akira
Japanese. Director
Best known for action films; directed epic
Ran, 1985.
b. Mar 23, 1910 in Tokyo, Japan
Source: *BiDFilm; ConAu 101; ConLC 16;
FilmEn; IntMPA 82, 84; WhDW; Who 82, 83*

Kurri, Jarri
Finnish. Hockey Player
Right wing, Edmonton Oilers, 1980--; first
Finnish-born player to have 100 pt. season
in NHL.
b. May 18, 1960 in Helsinki, Finland
Source: *HocReg 85*

Kurt, Melanie
Austrian. Opera Singer
b. Jan 8, 1880 in Vienna, Austria
d. Mar 11, 1941 in New York, New York
Source: *InWom*

Kurtis, Bill Horton (William)
American. Broadcast Journalist
Correspondent, co-anchor, CBS Morning
News, 1982-86.
b. Sep 21, 1940 in Pensacola, Florida
Source: *WhoAm 84; WhoMW 82; WhoTelC*

Kurtz, Efrem
Russian. Conductor
b. Nov 7, 1900 in Saint Petersburg, Russia
d. 1977
Source: *CurBio 46; IntWW 74; WhoMus 72;
WhoWorJ 72*

Kurtz, Katherine
American. Author
b. Oct 18, 1944 in Coral Gables, Florida
Source: *ConAu 29R; WrDr 80*

Kurtz, Swoosie
American. Actress
Won Tony, 1980, for *Fifth of July*.
b. Sep 6, 1944 in Omaha, Nebraska
Source: *IntMPA 84; NewYTBS 81; VarWW
85; WhoHol A; WhoTelC*

Kurusu, Saburo
Japanese. Diplomat
b. 1888 in Yokohama, Japan
d. Apr 7, 1954 in Tokyo, Japan
Source: *CurBio 42, 54; REn*

Kurz, Selma
Austrian. Opera Singer
b. Nov 15, 1875 in Bielitz, Austria
d. May 10, 1933 in Vienna, Austria
Source: *InWom*

Kurzweil, Ray(mond)
American. Inventor
Developed reading machine for blind, 1976.
b. Feb 12, 1948 in New York, New York
Source: *ConNews 86-3*

Kushner, Harold Samuel
American. Rabbi, Author
Wrote *When Bad Things Happen to Good
People*, 1981, after death of young son.
b. Apr 3, 1935 in Brooklyn, New York
Source: *ConAu 107; WhoAmJ 80; WrDr 84*

Kuter, Laurence S(herman)
American. General, Aviator
First commander, Military Air Transport
service, 1948.
b. May 28, 1905 in Rockford, Illinois
d. Nov 30, 1979
Source: *ConAu 113; CurBio 48; WhAm 7*

Kutschmann, Walter
[Pedro Olmo]
German. Nazi Leader
Nazi lieutenant, accused of killing over 1,500
Jews in Poland during WW II; escaped to
Argentina, never prosecuted.
b. 1914
d. Aug 30, 1986 in Buenos Aires, Argentina
Source: *NF*

Kutuzov, Mikhail Ilarionovich
Russian. Field Marshal
b. Sep 5, 1745 in Saint Petersburg, Russia
d. Apr 16, 1813 in Bunzlau, Poland
Source: *McGEWB; NewCol 75*

Kuykendall, Ralph Simpson
American. Historian
Spent 40 yrs. researching Hawaiian history.
b. Apr 12, 1885 in Linden, California
d. May 9, 1963 in Tucson, Arizona
Source: *DcAmB S7; WebBD 80*

Kuznets, Simon
American. Economist
Won Nobel Prize, 1971, for originating
concept of gross nat'l. product as measure
of nat'l. income, economic growth.
b. Apr 30, 1901 in Kharkov, Russia
d. Jul 8, 1985 in Cambridge, Massachusetts
Source: *AmM&WS 78S; CurBio 85; WhoWor
82; WrDr 84*

Kuznetsov, Anatoli
[A Anatoli]
Russian. Author
b. Aug 18, 1929 in Kiev, U.S.S.R.
Source: *ConAu 89; IntWW 74; PseudN 82;
WhoWor 78*

Kuznetsov, Vasili Vasilievich
Russian. Politician, Diplomat
b. Feb 13, 1901 in Sofilovka, Russia
Source: *IntWW 74*

Kwan, Nancy Kashen
Chinese. Actress
Starred in *The World of Suzie Wong*, 1960;
Flower Drum Song, 1961.
b. May 19, 1939 in Hong Kong, China
Source: *FilmEn; FilmgC; InWom; MotPP;
MovMk; WhoHol A*

Ky, Nguyen Cao
Vietnamese. Vice-President
b. Sep 8, 1930 in Son Tay, Vietnam
Source: *CurBio 66; IntWW 74*

Kyd, Thomas
English. Dramatist
Wrote day's most popular drama, revenge-
play *The Spanish Tragedy,* 1587.
b. Nov 6, 1558 in London, England
d. 1594 in London, England
Source: *Alli; AtlBL; BiD&SB; BrAu; CasWL;
Chambr 1; ChhPo; CnE&AP; CnThe;
CroE&S; CrtT 1; CyWA; DcEnA; DcEnL;
DcEuL; EvLB; McGEWD; MouLC 1; NewC;
OxEng; OxThe; PenC ENG; REn; REnWD;
WebE&AL*

Kylian, Jiri
Czech. Choreographer, Dancer
Director, choreographer for Netherlands
Dance Theater, 1978--.
b. Mar 21, 1945 in Prague, Czechoslovakia
Source: *BioIn 12; CurBio 82*

Kyne, Peter Bernard
American. Author
b. Oct 12, 1880 in San Francisco, California
d. Nov 25, 1957 in San Francisco, California
Source: *AmAu&B; OxAmL; REnAL; TwCA,
SUP; WhAm 3; WhNAA*

Kyprianou, Spyros
Cypriot. President
b. Oct 28, 1932 in Limassol, Cyprus
Source: *CurBio 79*

Kyriakides, Anastasios
Greek. Inventor
b. 1947
Source: *BioIn 11*

Kyser, "Kay" (James Kern)
American. Musician, Band Leader
Best known as host of radio's "Kollege of
Musical Knowledge," 1933-49.
b. Jun 18, 1906 in Rocky Mount, North
Carolina
d. Jul 23, 1985 in Chapel Hill, North
Carolina
Source: *BioNews 74; ConNews 85-3; CurBio
41, 85; FilmgC; PseudN 82; WhoHol A*

KEY TO SOURCE CODES

Code	Source
IlBEAAW	The Illustrated Biographical Encyclopedia of Artists of the American West
IlDcG	An Illustrated Dictionary of Glass
IlEncBM	The Illustrated Encyclopedia of Black Music
IlEncCM	The Illustrated Encyclopedia of Country Music
IlEncJ	The Illustrated Encyclopedia of Jazz
IlEncMy	An Illustrated Encyclopaedia of Mysticism and the Mystery Religions
IlEncR	The Illustrated Encyclopedia of Rock
IlrAm	The Illustrator in America
IlsBYP	Illustrators of Books for Young People
IlsCB	Illustrators of Children's Books
InB&W	In Black and White
InSci	Index to Scientists of the World
InWom	Index to Women
IndAu	Indiana Authors and Their Books
IntAu&W	The International Authors and Writers Who's Who
IntDcWB	The International Dictionary of Women's Biography
IntEnSS	International Encyclopedia of the Social Sciences: Biographical Supplement
IntMed	International Medical Who's Who
IntMPA	International Motion Picture Almanac
IntWW	The International Who's Who
IntWWP	International Who's Who in Poetry
IntYB	The International Year Book and Statesmen's Who's Who
JoeFr	Joe Franklin's Encyclopedia of Comedians
JohnWSW	John Willis' Screen World
JohnWTW	John Willis' Theatre World
JBA	The Junior Book of Authors
Law&B	Law and Business Directory of Corporate Counsel
LEduc	Leaders in Education
LElec	Leaders in Electronics
LEPo	Leading Canadian Poets
LesBEnT	Les Brown's Encyclopedia of Television
LibW	Liberty's Women
LilREn	Lillian Roxon's Rock Encyclopedia
LinLib L	The Lincoln Library of Language Arts
LinLib S	The Lincoln Library of Social Studies
LivgBAA	Living Black American Authors
LivgFWS	The Living Female Writers of the South
LongCEL	Longman Companion to English Literature
LongCTC	Longman Companion to Twentieth Century Literature
LookW	Look for the Woman
LuthC	Lutheran Cyclopedia
MGM	The MGM Stock Company
MacBEP	Macmillan Biographical Encyclopedia of Photographic Artists & Innovators
MacDCB	The Macmillan Dictionary of Canadian Biography
MacDWB	The Macmillan Dictionary of Women's Biography
MacEA	Macmillan Encyclopedia of Architects
MakMC	Makers of Modern Culture
MarqDCG	Marquis Who's Who Directory of Computer Graphics
McGDA	McGraw-Hill Dictionary of Art
McGEWB	The McGraw-Hill Encyclopedia of World Biography
McGEWD	McGraw-Hill Encyclopedia of World Drama
McGMS	McGraw-Hill Modern Scientists and Engineers
MedHR	Medal of Honor Recipients, 1863-1978
MnBBF	The Men Behind Boys' Fiction
MidE	The Middle East and North Africa
MinnWr	Minnesota Writers
ModAL	Modern American Literature
ModBlW	Modern Black Writers
ModBrL	Modern British Literature
ModCmwL	Modern Commonwealth Literature
ModFrL	Modern French Literature
ModGL	Modern German Literature
ModLAL	Modern Latin American Literature
ModRL	Modern Romance Literatures
ModSL	Modern Slavic Literatures
ModWD	Modern World Drama
MorBMP	More Books by More People
MorJA	More Junior Authors
MotPP	Motion Picture Performers
MouLC	Moulton's Library of Literary Criticism
MovMk	The Movie Makers
MugS	Mug Shots
MusMk	The Music Makers
MusSN	Musicians since 1900
NamesHP	Names in the History of Psychology
NatCAB	The National Cyclopaedia of American Biography
NatPD	National Playwrights Directory
NegAl	The Negro Almanac
NewC	The New Century Handbook of English Literature
NewCBMT	New Complete Book of the American Musical Theater
NewCol	The New Columbia Encyclopedia
NewEOp	The New Encyclopedia of the Opera
NewGrD	The New Grove Dictionary of Music and Musicians
NewWmR	New Women in Rock
NewYHSD	The New-York Historical Society's Dictionary of Artists in America
NewYTBE	The New York Times Biographical Edition
NewYTBS	The New York Times Biographical Service
NewYTET	The New York Times Encyclopedia of Television
NewbC	Newbery and Caldecott Medal Books
Newb	Newbery Medal Books
NotAW	Notable American Women
NotNAT	Notable Names in the American Theatre
Novels	Novels and Novelists
ObitOF	Obituaries on File
ObitT	Obituaries from the Times
ODwPR	O'Dwyer's Directory of Public Relations Executives
OfEnT	Official Encyclopedia of Tennis
OfNBA	Official NBA Register
OhA&B	Ohio Authors and Their Books

KEY TO SOURCE CODES

OxAmH	The Oxford Companion to American History	*SenS*	A Sense of Story
OxAmL	The Oxford Companion to American Literature	*SixAP*	Sixty American Poets, 1896-1944
		SmATA	Something about the Author
OxArt	The Oxford Companion to Art	*SpyCS*	Spy/Countryspy: Encyclopedia of Espionage
OxCan	The Oxford Companion to Canadian History and Literature	*St&PR*	Standard and Poor's Register of Corporations, Directors, and Executives
OxChess	The Oxford Companion to Chess		
OxDecA	The Oxford Companion to the Decorative Arts	*Str&VC*	Story and Verse for Children
		TexWr	Texas Writers of Today
OxEng	The Oxford Companion to English Literature	*ThFT*	They Had Faces Then
		ThrBJA	Third Book of Junior Authors
OxFilm	The Oxford Companion to Film	*TwCA*	Twentieth Century Authors
OxFr	The Oxford Companion to French Literature	*TwCBDA*	The Twentieth Century Biographical Dictionary of Notable Americans
OxGer	The Oxford Companion to German Literature		
		TwCCW	Twentieth-Century Children's Writers
OxLaw	The Oxford Companion to Law		
OxMus	The Oxford Companion to Music	*TwCCr&M*	Twentieth-Century Crime and Mystery Writers
OxShips	The Oxford Companion to Ships and the Sea		
		TwCLC	Twentieth-Century Literary Criticism
OxSpan	The Oxford Companion to Spanish Literature	*TwCRGW*	Twentieth-Century Romance and Gothic Writers
OxThe	The Oxford Companion to the Theatre	*TwCSFW*	Twentieth-Century Science Fiction Writers
OxTwCA	The Oxford Companion to Twentieth-Century Art	*TwCWW*	Twentieth-Century Western Writers
PenC AM	The Penguin Companion to American Literature	*TwCWr*	Twentieth Century Writing
		TwYS	Twenty Years of Silents
PenC CL	The Penguin Companion to Classical, Oriental, and African Literature	*UFOEn*	The UFO Encyclopedia
		USBiR	United States. Department of State: The Biographic Register
PenC ENG	The Penguin Companion to English Literature		
		VarWW	Variety Who's Who in Show Business
PenC EUR	The Penguin Companion to European Literature	*Vers*	The Versatiles
		Ward	1977 Ward's Who's Who among U.S. Motor Vehicle Manufacturers
PhDcTCA	Phaidon Dictionary of Twentieth-Century Art		
PiP	The Pied Pipers		
PlP&P	Plays, Players, and Playwrights	*WebAB*	Webster's American Biographies
PoChrch	The Poets of the Church	*WebAMB*	Webster's American Military Biographies
PoIre	The Poets of Ireland		
PoLE	The Poets Laureate of England	*WebBD*	Webster's Biographical Dictionary
Po&Wr	The Poets & Writers, Inc. 1977 Supplement	*WebE&AL*	Webster's New World Companion to English and American Literature
PolProf	Political Profiles		
PrintW	The Printworld Directory	*What*	Whatever Became of . . .?
PseudAu	Pseudonyms of Authors	*WhDW*	Who Did What
PseudN	Pseudonyms and Nicknames Dictionary	*WhDun*	Whodunit?
		WhAm	Who Was Who in America
PueRA	Puerto Rican Authors	*WhAmP*	Who Was Who in American Politics
RAdv	The Reader's Adviser		
RComWL	The Reader's Companion to World Literature	*WhE&EA*	Who Was Who among English and European Authors
		WhFla	Who Was Who in Florida
REn	The Reader's Encyclopedia	*WhJnl*	Who Was Who in Journalism
REnAL	The Reader's Encyclopedia of American Literature	*WhLit*	Who Was Who in Literature
		WhNAA	Who Was Who among North American Authors
REnAW	The Reader's Encyclopedia of the American West		
		WhScrn	Who Was Who on Screen
REnWD	The Reader's Encyclopedia of World Drama	*WhThe*	Who Was Who in the Theatre
		WhWW-II	Who Was Who in World War II
RGAfL	A Reader's Guide to African Literature	*Who*	Who's Who
		WhoAdv	Who's Who in Advertising
RkOn	Rock On	*WhoAm*	Who's Who in America
RkOneH	Rock 100	*WhoAmA*	Who's Who in American Art
RkWW	Rock Who's Who	*WhoAmJ*	Who's Who in American Jewry
RolSEnR	The Rolling Stone Encyclopedia of Rock & Roll	*WhoAmL*	Who's Who in American Law
		WhoAmM	Who's Who in American Music
ScF&FL	Science Fiction and Fantasy Literature	*WhoAmP*	Who's Who in American Politics
		WhoAmW	Who's Who of American Women
SelBAAf	Selected Black American, African, and Caribbean Authors	*WhoArab*	Who's Who in the Arab World
SelBAAu	Selected Black American Authors	*WhoArch*	Who's Who in Architecture